Encyclopedia of

INTERIOR DESIGN

Volume 1

Encyclopedia of

INTERIOR DESIGN

Volume 1
A–L

Editor
JOANNA BANHAM

Picture Editor
LEANDA SHRIMPTON

FITZROY DEARBORN PUBLISHERS
LONDON AND CHICAGO

FITZROY DEARBORN PUBLISHERS
70 East Walton Street
Chicago, Illinois 60611
USA

or

11 Rathbone Place
London W1P 1DE
England

British Library Cataloging in Publication Data
Encyclopedia of interior design
1. Interior decoration – Encyclopedias 2. Interior decoration – History – Encyclopedias
I. Banham, Joanna
747'.03

ISBN 1–884964–19–2

Library of Congress Cataloging in Publication Data is available.

First published in the USA and UK 1997

Typeset by Lorraine Hodghton, Radlett, Herts, UK
Printed in Great Britain by the Bath Press.

Cover Illustrations:
vol. 1: entrance hall, Syon House, Middlesex, by Robert Adam, 1760s. Photograph by A.F. Kersting.
vol. 2: entrance hall, Hill House, Helensburgh, by Charles Rennie Mackintosh, 1902. Photograph courtesy of Royal Commission on the Ancient and Historical Monuments of Scotland.

CONTENTS

EDITOR'S NOTE

The overall aim of the *Encyclopedia of Interior Design* is to provide description and analysis of a range of subjects and individuals related to the history of interiors. The entries are arranged in alphabetical order and fall into two broad categories: those on individuals, encompassing architects, critics, designers, makers and patrons; and those dealing with topics such as room types, decoration and particular items of furniture. There are also several longer survey articles relating to individual countries, periods and styles. Given the enormity of the project it was felt that to include a discussion of ecclesiastical interiors would necessitate the publication of one additional volume, if not several. For this reason a decision was taken at the outset to confine the scope of the *Encyclopedia* to the study of secular interiors.

The study of interior design is a task fraught with difficulties, not least because of the amorphous nature of the subject and its comparatively recent emergence as a professional discipline. Much of this complexity is due to the fact that interiors encompass a huge variety of constituents ranging from fixed elements such as room-plans and architectural fittings, to more interchangeable items such as furnishings, to the most ephemeral features such as paint colours, wallcoverings and textiles. The individuals involved in shaping the appearance of an interior have been similarly varied, and prior to the late 19th and early 20th centuries, when an interest in decoration and furnishing was first formalized under the heading interior design, these might have included the patron or client, an architect or designer, as well as myriad craftsmen, suppliers and manufacturers. And finally numerous other factors, including social class, income, gender, convention, new technology and fashion, have exercised important influences on the design and decoration of public and domestic spaces.

But notwithstanding the dangers attendant on embarking on a project of this kind, the need for an *Encyclopedia of Interior Design* was clearly evident. The existing literature consists of dictionaries of individuals, for example architects and designers; dictionaries of objects, defined principally under the heading of the Decorative Arts; and technical manuals. These two volumes represent the first attempt to bring together all the disparate elements and to focus the discussion on interior design within specific entries on individuals and objects. It is hoped that a particular strength of the project is the inclusion of articles on the history and function of common room types such as bedrooms and drawing rooms and generic items of furniture such as tables and chairs that are rarely discussed elsewhere.

The final selection of entries for the *Encyclopedia* was the result of a long process of refining an original much longer list of suggestions on the basis of views and ideas put forward by the project's advisers (listed in the Acknowledgments and on page ix), as well as those of the contributing essayists, and other scholars and commentators. The principal criteria employed in the selection of articles on individuals were, first, that they had been consistently involved in the design of interiors during their careers, and/or second, that their work had had an especially strong or lasting impact on an aspect of interior design. Even so, it has obviously not been possible to include every architect or designer of note, and the *Encyclopedia* does not claim to do so. But where well-known individuals do not appear in separate entries, for example Michelangelo, who worked primarily on ecclesiastical commissions and so does not qualify for inclusion here, they are generally discussed within one of the survey essays (see Renaissance and Italy). A full alphabetical list of subjects and individuals mentioned within the *Encyclopedia* appears in the index at the end of the second volume.

A perhaps inevitable bias of the *Encyclopedia* is towards upper-middle-class and aristocratic interiors. This is partly because these tend to represent the most well-documented and best-preserved examples, and are often where changes in style, new fashions or technology are most clearly reflected. But it is hoped that to some extent this emphasis is offset by the broader focus within many of the topic entries, such as the articles on Coffee Tables and Three-Piece Suites, which discuss objects used in more middle-income rooms. Another bias is the space devoted to individuals and examples dating from the 19th and 20th centuries. Again, this is largely due to the comparative wealth of documentation and scholarship existing on these periods; considerably more research needs to be carried out on the earlier centuries before this imbalance can be adequately redressed. And finally, the content of the *Encyclopedia* is undeniably Eurocentric and North American in its focus. Practical limitations did not allow for much detail on the other parts of the world, but such survey entries as those on Middle Eastern interiors, Japan, China, and Australia are intended as starting points for further study.

The entries themselves consist of a signed critical essay, a summary biography and list of principal works where appropriate, and a list of further reading. The essays provide a broad historical overview of the subject; more detailed study can be pursued through the works cited in the accompanying bibliographies. Once again, the bibliographies (arranged alphabetically by author) are not exhaustive but have been selected to represent a range of available material and include at least one or two in-depth studies containing their own detailed reading lists. The amount and quality of information given in the list of principal works can vary from entry to entry, depending on the quantity and calibre of research available in recent secondary sources. But each item should indicate the date and location of the work and the nature of the individual's involvement; patrons or clients are also often cited here, as well as being mentioned in the essays.

This project has been completed over a two-and-a-half-year period, which still seems like a staggeringly short period of time. At its inception it was intended that all the information should be compressed into a single volume. But like so many interiors of the past, as the ambitions of all those involved have grown, its contents have multiplied and it has expanded to fill two large books. Even so, there is still much more that could and should be written on interior design, and it is hoped that this *Encyclopedia* will be a useful resource for future work.

Acknowledgments

A huge number of people have provided help, advice and support throughout the production of this book. Chief among them are the panel of Advisers — Megan Aldrich, Yvonne Brunhammer, Stephen Calloway, John R. Clarke, Frances Collard, David Crowley, Penelope Eames, Charlotte Gere, Wendy Kaplan, Anne Massey, Sarah Medlam, Sarah Nichols, Steven Parissien, Charles Saumarez Smith, Mary Schoeser, and Gerald W.R. Ward — who grappled with the daunting task of helping to shape the final list of entries and who drew my attention to several important omissions. No less deserving are all the scholars and specialists who have written for the book, several at short notice, and many of whom were unstintingly generous with their time and expertise in answering queries. Special thanks are due to Luciana Arbace, Jody Clowes, Elaine Denby, Clive Edwards, Curtis Evarts, Helen Grainger, Lesley Jackson, Derek Linstrum, John Pile, Katie Scott, Helen Searing, Clive Wainwright, John Wilton-Ely, and Jonathan Woodham. Antonia Boström provided invaluable help with additional research for selected biographies and bibliographies and Jacqueline Griffin proved an enormously skilled and conscientious sub-editor. Many thanks too must go to Leanda Shrimpton and Maja Mihajlovic, who worked on the pictures and who came up with numerous imaginative and useful suggestions. I should also like to thank the staff of the National Art Library and the British Library. But I owe a special debt of gratitude to all my colleagues at Fitzroy Dearborn: Philippe Barbour, Kate Berney, Delia Gaze, Mark Hawkins-Dady, and Lesley Henderson. And above all to Daniel Kirkpatrick, whose unshakable faith in the project and whose scrupulous attention to detail at every stage in its production have contributed more than anything else to ensuring its completion.

JOANNA BANHAM

ADVISERS

Megan Aldrich
Yvonne Brunhammer
Stephen Calloway
John R. Clarke
Frances Collard
David Crowley
Penelope Eames
Charlotte Gere
Wendy Kaplan
Anne Massey
Sarah Medlam
Sarah Nichols
Steven Parissien
Charles Saumarez Smith
Mary Schoeser
Gerald W.R.Ward

CONTRIBUTORS

Annmarie Adams
Megan Aldrich
Craig Allen
Luciana Arbace
Judith Attfield
Nerida C.A. Aylott
Joanna Banham
Paula A. Baxter
Luke Beckerdite
Stella Beddoe
Reed Benhamou
Amanda Birch
Philippa Bishop
Ann L. Black
Jonathan Blackwood
Brian J.R. Blench
Christine Boydell
David Brett
Claire Brisby
Victoria Broakes
Chantal Brotherton-Ratcliffe
Sarah Brown
Catherine Buckner
Paul Caffrey
Douglas G. Campbell
David Cast
Jon Catleugh
Anne Ceresole
Dorian Church
John R. Clarke
Jody Clowes
Marlene Cohen
Linda Coleing
Barbara Corr
Meli Costopoulos
Howard Coutts
J. Ian Cox
Robert M. Craig
David Crellin
David Crowley
Kathryn M. Cureton
Anna T. D'Ambrosio
Darron Dean
Elaine Evans Dee
Elaine Denby
Bridie Dorning
Ed Polk Douglas
Harriet Dover
Philip Drew
Ian Dungavell
Penelope Eames
Pat Earnshaw
Clive D. Edwards
Madeline Siefke Estill

Curtis Evarts
Constance A. Fairchild
Elizabeth A. Fleming
Rainald Franz
Rachel E. French
Catherine L. Futter
David Gebhard
Charlotte Gere
Paul Glassman
Hilary J. Grainger
Jacqueline Griffin
Håkan Groth
Denise Hagströmer
Diana Hale
Widar Halén
Paul Hardy
Frederica Todd Harlow
Jennifer Harris
Emma Hart
Malcolm Haslam
Beverly F. Heisner
Mimi Hellman
Julian Holder
Lesley Hoskins
Katherine S. Howe
Susan Hoyal
Anthony Hoyte
Lesley Jackson
Dawn Jacobson
Bernard Jacqué
Susan Jenkins
Robin D. Jones
Yvonne Jones
Bettina Jost
Jon Kear
Rachel Kennedy
Juliet Kinchin
Brenda King
Boris Kirikov
Marcus Köhler
Eloy Koldeweij
Jennifer A. Komar
Sally Korman
Ute Krebs
Jarl Kremeier
Marijke Kuper
Grace Lees
Hans van Lemmen
P. Leser
Sally L. Levine
Martin P. Levy
Margaret W. Lichter
Stefanie Lieb
Jane Lindsey
Derek Linstrum
Peter Lizon
James Lomax
Meher Shona McArthur
Thomas J. McCormick
Catherine E. McDermott
Otakar Máčel
John McKean
Graham McLaren
Maria L. Makogonova
Joanna Marschner
Anne Massey
Linda Merrill
Lesley Ellis Miller
William C. Miller
Pia Maria Montonen
Christine Morley
Catherine Murray
Jeremy Musson
Nicholas Nuttall
Amy F. Ogata
Ronald J. Onorato
Geoffrey Opie
Scott Oram
Mitchell Owens
Mariella Palazzolo
Steven Parissien
John F. Pile
Mark Pinney
Margaret Ponsonby
M.H. Port
Julia Porter
Christine Riding
Jacqueline Riding
Christopher Riopelle
Daniel Robbins
Gaye Blake Roberts
Sofía Rodríguez Bernis
Treve Rosoman
Kathleen Russo
Jennifer M. Scarce
Mary Schoeser
Katie Scott
William Seale
Helen Searing
Eduard F. Sekler
Jessie Serle
Nicholas Shaddick
Pamela H. Simpson
Lars Sjöberg
Ursula Sjöberg
Astrid Skjerven
C. Murray Smart, Jr.
Mary Peskett Smith
Geraldine Smith-Parr
Patrick A. Snadon
David M. Sokol
Mareike von Spreckelsen
Susan R. Stein
Paul Stirton
Dominic R. Stone
John Sweetman
Clare Taylor
Dorcas Taylor
Christina Thon
Kevin W. Tucker

Mark Turner
John C. Turpin
Danilo Udovicki-Selb
Margaret Birney Vickery
Tatiana Volobaeva
Catherine Hoover Voorsanger
Claire Walsh
Gerald W.R. Ward
Ben Weaver
Christopher Webster
Gabriel P. Weisberg
Janice West
Annabel Westman
Stephen Wildman
Matthew Williams
John Wilton-Ely
Alan Windsor
John Winter
Jane Withers
Jonathan M. Woodham
Christine Woods
Jenny Silverthorne Wright
Olga Zoller

LIST OF ENTRIES

A

Aalto, Alvar 1898–1976

Finnish architect and designer

Alvar Aalto's lyrical, sensuous design drawings poignantly record his process of generating form. These painterly lines, made with soft pencil on tracing paper, expressively describe the emergent, sinuously shaped spaces and forms of his buildings and interior spaces. While capturing the essence of Aalto's architectural production, his sketches also represent the design of an interior space, a piece of furniture, a light fixture, or a glass vase. Aalto's furnishings, paintings, and applied designs exhibit an uncanny resemblance to the formal and spatial configurations of his buildings and spaces. The design and crafting of a chair, a light fixture, or a glass bowl, was as much an architectural proposition as the making of a building or interior space. Engaging in furniture and applied design provided Aalto with the opportunity to examine design issues at a variety of scales and in different media, and this directly influenced his conception of architectural space and form.

As with most internationally respected architects, categorizing their oeuvre into discrete parts is often an artificial proposition. This is true for Aalto, for his intention was to design complete environments in which the unique building is complemented by equally unique interiors, and with furniture and other accessories designed for each particular environment. This intention plays an important role even in his earliest work.

Opening his first office in Jyväskylä in 1923, Aalto worked in a style termed Nordic Classicism, in which a catholic relationship existed between his architecture, interiors, and applied designs. Aalto's furniture and interior decoration in this period were designed to be stylistically compatible with specific spaces and settings. Interiors were often decorated with painted scenic wallpaper of classically inspired motifs, abstracted images of masonry rustication, austere picture mouldings and door and window frames, and stenciled friezes. Interior designs and furnishings for the Kouvola Garrison canteen (1923), the Seurahuone Café in Jyväskylä (1924), and the Hämäläis-Osakunta students' club in Helsinki (1924), are examples of work from this period. In each case, specialty furnishing and applied designs were developed. Exaggeration often played an important role in the furniture design: legs which were thinner or more boldly profiled than normal, balusters which whimsically modified the conventions of the "split spindle" motif, oddly proportioned knobs and turned pieces, and the addition of idiosyncratic decoration are common in the work of this period.

In 1924 Aalto married the architect Aino Marsio (1894–1949), who was an equal partner in their work until her death. Aino's influence informed building design as well as the creation of furniture and applied art objects, and together husband and wife formed a symbiotic unit, complementing and contrasting one another. The situation was, to a similar extent, the same when Aalto married his second wife, the architect Elissa Makiniemi in 1952. She was also active in their practice until Aalto's death in 1976.

When he moved his office from Jyväskylä to Turku in 1927, Aalto enjoyed a modest national reputation; by the time he relocated to Helsinki in 1933, he had achieved international recognition. His international status resulted from four buildings – the Standard Block of Flats (1927–29) and the Turun Sanomat Newspaper Building (1928–29) in Turku, the Paimio Sanatorium (1929–32), and the Viipuri Library (1927–35) – and, significantly, from his furniture and applied designs. Aalto's conversion to Functionalism, as Modernism was termed in Finland, coincided with the move to Turku. His buildings, competition entries, and furniture designs appeared immediately to embrace Functionalism's focus on rational technique, serial production, and machine aesthetics. What Turku provided, along with an active architectural community, was connection to Stockholm and the continent. The significance of this rests in the contacts Aalto made as a result of his travels, for he associated with the European avant-garde and directly experienced the canonical works of the Modern Movement, thus keeping abreast of continental developments.

The Paimio Sanatorium, a potent symbol of the healthy new world Modernism promoted, demonstrates Aalto's mastery of Functionalist ideas. Conceptually, it is a clearly articulated set of discrete "functional" elements, expressed, in turn, in the machine aesthetic of concrete, steel, and glass. The interiors of the Sanatorium assumed the same machine-like quality, exemplifying the health-giving properties provided by sun, light, and fresh air. The manipulation of natural light became an important element in Aalto's interiors at this time, and continued as an important thematic issue permeating his architecture. The transformation seen in Aalto's architecture is also witnessed in his furniture designs.

Aalto: lecture room with undulating wooden ceiling, Municipal Library, Viipuri, 1933–35

Beginning in the late 1920s, Aalto became interested in creating serially manufactured wooden furniture for everyday use. This represented a desire to combine Finland's traditional wood-working industry with modern industrial production technology. During this period, through the development of numerous design prototypes and wood experiments in lamination and continuous moulding, Aalto explored the possibilities for mass-produced furniture. This culminated in the *Paimio* chair (1932) – consisting of laminated birch sides bent into a closed curve combined with a continuously moulded plywood seat back – specifically created for the Sanatorium along with five other pieces of furniture. While Aalto continued to develop furniture pieces throughout his career, his designs produced during this period provided the foundation for later works.

Hoping for increased commissions, Aalto moved to Helsinki in 1933. Though the next several years were a low point in his architectural productivity, it proved the opposite for furniture and applied designs. His mass-produced furniture, originally intended for use in a specific building, was made available to the general public by the firm of ARTEK, founded in 1933, which assumed the responsibility for the production and marketing of all of Aalto's subsequent furniture and fabric designs. The Aalto name became associated with glassware in 1932 through two entries in a competition sponsored by Iittala and Karhula, and culminated in the sinuous, curved forms of the famous *Savoy* vases designed in 1937.

With the Viipuri Library, completed in 1935, Aalto's Functionalism began to wane, and was replaced by a more sinuous, tactile material vocabulary and expressive formal and spatial composition. Complementing the curved, undulating pine ceiling in the Viipuri lecture room, Aalto introduced a ceiling of conical skylights in the library reading room that was the precursor for the numerous interior spaces that followed. In his three most important commissions of the late 1930s – the Finnish Pavilion for the 1937 Paris World's Fair, the Villa Mairea (1938–39), and the Finnish Pavilion for the 1939 New York World's Fair – there is increased sinuosity in spatial organization, a more expressive play between natural and human-made materials, incorporation of natural light through skylights in major spaces, and a picturesqueness in building form. Sinuosity, tactility, light: these qualities dominated Aalto's work, at all levels, from the late 1930s on.

Between 1945 and the early 1960s, Aalto enjoyed an incredibly productive period – one lauded as being uniquely Finnish in feeling. Characterized by the use of red brick, copper and wood, exemplary interior spaces in the major building projects of the period include: the council chamber and entry staircase in the Saynatsalo Town Hall (1950–52), the entry foyer and staircase in the Jyväskylä Teachers' College (1953–56), and the lecture halls in the Technical Institute in Otaniemi (1956–64); and in Helsinki, the interviewing area and restaurant of the National Pensions Institute (1953–57), and the atrium space of the Rautatalo Building (1953–57). The picturesque massing of these buildings, the rich mixture of materials and textural effects, the dynamic manipulation of natural light, and the quality of interior development, especially in the public areas, demonstrate Aalto's mature style. Many of these, as well as later works incorporate a multilevel skylighted atria that is accented by planting and staircases. These spaces often incorporate Aalto-designed wall tiles, fabrics, and lighting fixtures.

The last twenty years of Aalto's practice, beginning with the Vuoksenniska Church (1956–58), produced a more complex, expressive architecture, contrasting with the "bronze" imagery of the 1940s and 1950s. There is continuity with his earlier work – light, sinuosity, tactility, and integrated interiors still figure importantly in the designs – yet more explicit references to classical and romantic ordering qualities emerged at this time. The public interiors in the Seinäjoki Civic Complex (1958–65), the Wolfsburg Cultural Complex (1958–63), Finlandia Hall (1962–75), the Rovaniemi Library (1968), and the Riola Church (1966–78), along with Vuoksenniska, continue the interior qualities seen in Aalto's earlier work and represent the best of this late period. Of particular interest are the Kauffmann Rooms at the Institute of International Education in New York City (1963–65).

During his 50-year career, Aalto developed a rich and complex architectural language that explored the full range of expressive means available to the architect. The unique variety of architectural responses he created resulted from the belief that architecture is an affirmative act and the architect's role is to design and build. Aalto's was an architecture that was extremely humane, yet profoundly tangible.

WILLIAM C. MILLER

See also Modernism; Scandinavian Modern

Biography

Hugo Alvar Henrik Aalto. Born in Kuortane, near Jyväskylä, Finland, 3 February 1898. Married 1) the architect and designer Aino Marsio, 1924 (died 1949): two children; 2) Elissa Mäkiniemi, 1952. Studied architecture at Helsinki Polytechnic, 1916–21. Worked as an exhibition designer in Göteborg, Sweden, then Tampere and Turku, Finland, 1921–22; in private architectural practice, Jyväskylä, Finland, 1923–27; Turku, 1927–33; Helsinki, 1933–76. Worked in partnership with Aino Aalto, 1924–49; in partnership with Elissa Aalto 1952–76. Designed furniture from c.1920; lighting from mid-1920s; textiles and glass from 1930s; founded ARTEK to mass-produce furniture and textile designs, 1933. Professor, College of Architecture, Massachusetts Institute of Technology, Cambridge, 1946–47. Member, Academy of Finland, 1955; honorary member, Akademie der Künste, Berlin; honorary fellow, American Institute of Architects; Gold Medal, Royal Institute of British Architects, 1957. Died in Helsinki, 11 May 1976.

Selected Works

A vast collection of original drawings, designs, correspondence, cuttings and models is contained in the Alvar Aalto Archive, Alvar Aalto Foundation, which is housed in Aalto's house at Munkkiniemi, near Helsinki. Additional designs and collections of furniture, textiles, glass, etc., are in the Alvar Aalto Museum, Jyväskylä, and the Finnish Museum of Architecture, and Finnish Museum of Applied Arts, Helsinki. For a guide to other collections see Weston 1995. A complete catalogue of Aalto's architectural and design work appears in Schildt 1994.

Interiors

1923	Garrison, Kouvola (canteen interiors and furnishings)
1924	Hämäläis-Osakunta Students' Club, Helsinki (interiors and furniture)
1924	Suerahuone Café, Jyväskylä (entrance and interiors, including furniture for the fireplace room, ladies' room, and dining room)
1929	700th Anniversary Fair, Turku (exhibition design and layout; with Erik Bryggman)
1929–32	Sanatorium, Paimio (building, interiors and furnishings)
1933–35	Municipal Library, Viipuri (building and furnishings)
1934–36	Alvar Aalto House, Munkkiniemi, near Helsinki (building, interiors and furnishings)
1937	Finnish Pavilion, Exposition Internationale des Arts et Techniques Appliqués à la Vie Moderne, Paris (building, interiors and displays)
1938–39	Villa Mairea, Noormarkku, near Pori (building, interiors and furnishings): Marie and Harry Gullichsen
1938–40	Finnish Pavilion, World's Fair, New York (building and interiors)
1950–52	Town Hall, Saynatsalo (council chamber and entry staircase)
1953–56	Teachers' College, Jyväskylä (entry foyer and staircase)
1953–57	National Pensions Institute, Helsinki (restaurant and interviewing area)
1956–64	Technical Institute, Otaniemi (lecture halls)
1957–59	Villa, Bazoches sur Guyonne, France (building, interiors and furnishings): Louis Carré
1962–75	Finlandia Hall Concert and Convention Center, Helsinki (buildings and interiors)
1963–65	Institute of International Education, New York (interiors and furnishings for the Kauffmann Rooms): Edgar Kauffmann, Jr.
1963–68	Library, Rovaniemi (building and interiors)

Aalto designed furniture, much of it plywood, from c.1930; his most celebrated works included the *Paimio* chair (1932), subsequently manufactured by ARTEK, and his bentwood series developed in collaboration with Otto Korhonen, from 1933. Aalto's designs for glassware date from 1932 and include the *Savoy* vases (1937).

Publications

An Experimental Town, 1940
"The Humanizing of Architecture" in *Technology Review*, November 1940
Post-War Reconstruction: Rehousing Research in Finland, 1941
Synopsis: Painting, Architecture, Sculpture, edited by Bernhard Hoesli and Basel Birkhäuser, 1970, 2nd edition, 1980
Sketches, edited by Göran Schildt, 1978

Further Reading

The principal monographs on Aalto are Fleig 1963–78 and Schildt 1984–91 and 1994 all of which represent comprehensive and scholarly accounts of his life and work and include long bibliographies. Schildt 1994 also includes a full list of Aalto's writings and an annotated guide to the most useful published secondary sources. For important works on Aalto's furnishings see the exhibition catalogues, Helsinki 1984 and Johnson 1984.

Alvar Aalto, London: Academy, 1978; New York: Rizzoli, 1979
Alvar Aalto Furniture (exhib. cat.), Helsinki: Museum of Finnish Architecture, 1984; Cambridge: Massachusetts Institute of Technology Press, 1985

"Alvar Aalto: His Life, Work and Philosophy" in special issue of *L'Architecture d'Aujourd'hui*, June 1977
Blaser, Werner, *Alvar Aalto als Designer*, Stuttgart: Deutsche Verlagsanstalt, 1982
Fleig, Karl (editor), *Alvar Aalto 1922–1978*, 3 vols., Zürich, London, and New York, 1963–78
Johnson, J. Stewart, *Alvar Aalto: Furniture and Glass* (exhib. cat.), New York: Museum of Modern Art, 1984
Mendini, Alessandro, "L'Opera di Alvar Aalto" in *Casabella*, November 1965
Miller, William C., *Alvar Aalto: An Annotated Bibliography*, New York: Garland, 1984
Pearson, Paul David, *Alvar Aalto and the International Style*, New York: Whitney Library of Design, 1978; London: Mitchell, 1989
Quantrill, Malcolm, *Alvar Aalto: A Critical Study*, London: Secker and Warburg, 1983
Ruusuvuori, Aarno (editor), *Alvar Aalto, 1898–1976* (exhib. cat.), Helsinki: Museum of Finnish Architecture, 1978
Schildt, Göran, *Alvar Aalto: The Early Years*, New York: Rizzoli, 1984
Schildt, Göran, *Alvar Aalto: The Decisive Years*, New York: Rizzoli, 1986
Schildt, Göran, *Aalto Interiors, 1923–1970*, Jyväskylä: Aalto Museo, 1986
Schildt, Göran, *Alvar Aalto: The Mature Years*, New York: Rizzoli, 1991
Schildt, Göran, *Alvar Aalto: The Complete Catalogue of Architecture, Design and Art*, New York: Rizzoli, and London: Academy, 1994
Shand, P. Morton "Viipuri Library, Finland" in *Architectural Review*, 79, 1936, pp.107–14
Viiva / The Line: Original Drawings from the Alvar Aalto Archives (exhib. cat.), Helsinki: Museum of Finnish Architecture, 1993
Weston, Richard, *Alvar Aalto*, London: Phaidon, 1995

Abildgaard, Nicolai Abraham 1743–1809

Danish artist, decorative painter and designer

Born the son of a draughtsman in Copenhagen in 1743, Nicolai Abraham Abildgaard was Denmark's foremost exponent of Neo-Classicism. He was primarily a painter but he also worked as an architect and as a designer of furniture, interiors and medals. From the mid-1790s he designed furniture and interiors for the Danish court and, as Director of the Academy (1789–91 and from 1801), he exercised a wide influence on the next generation of artists and designers, most notably his assistant, the sculptor Thorvaldsen.

Abildgaard was apprenticed as a decorative painter under J. E. Mandelberg and also studied at the Academy of Art in Copenhagen from 1764. A talented student, he won several medals between 1764 and 1767 and in 1771 he was awarded a scholarship that enabled him to study abroad. He left immediately for Italy where he remained – mainly in Rome – until 1777. Much of his time was spent studying the art and architecture of antiquity but he was also impressed by the work of Renaissance artists such as Annibale Carracci, Michelangelo and Raphael and established friendships with J. H. Füssli and the Swedish Neo-Classical sculptor, Johan Tobias Sergel whose work influenced his style. In 1776 he travelled to Naples to examine the new discoveries at Herculaneum and Pompeii. He returned to Denmark, stopping for a short stay in Paris, the following year.

In 1778, Abildgaard was made a member of the Copenhagen Academy, and shortly afterwards he was entrusted with the decoration of the hall in the Schloss Christiansborg. This project involved a large series of 22 allegorical paintings glorifying the history of Denmark and occupied Abildgaard from 1780 to 1791. Sadly, all his work was destroyed by fire in 1794 – an event that prompted Abildgaard to declare "There burns my name" – and all that remains are a few sketches. After the fire the royal family moved to the Amalienborg Palace where Abildgaard was commissioned to decorate the State Apartments. He designed every aspect of these interiors including paintings, furniture and draperies and, given a free hand in the choice of style, he reverted to Antique models. For political reasons he rejected the fashionable Empire style popularised by Percier and Fontaine in favour of a purer brand of classicism that was more akin to the geometric simplicity characteristic of early Neo-Classicism. Once again, however, his interiors did not last long. In 1810 the new king ordered the rebuilding of the Palace and Abildgaard's paintings were put into store where they remained for over a century. Fortunately, much of the furniture has survived.

Abildgaard's designs for furniture date from the last decade of the 18th and the first decade of the 19th century. They represent a highly personal interpretation of the Neo-Classical style and were strongly influenced by Antique fragments and decoration that he saw in Rome, Herculaneum and Pompeii. The furniture itself divides into two categories: that which was made for the future Christian VIII for the Amalienborg Palace, and that which he designed for his own rooms in the Christiansborg.

The oldest of the royal pieces is a throne ordered in 1806 for the Crown prince. Made of mahogany inlaid with lime-tree dolphin emblems and other decoration, and upholstered in shining silk, it was almost certainly executed by the royal cabinet-maker, Gottfried Abe. The rest of the furniture – a sofa, a writing cabinet and six stools – was also made of mahogany with lime-tree inlay and a few gilt bronze mounts. While the elements of all the designs derive from classical architecture, in each piece these are combined in a unique and unusual way. The wide sofa, for example, with its strong, outwardly curving side-arms and its absence of backrail, resembles a banquette more than a sofa. And its feet, with their turned balls, seem quite Baroque although the painted decoration and the lionhead mounts are clearly Neo-Classical. The lions are repeated in the X-shaped stools which derive from both ancient Roman models and French Baroque tabourets.

The furniture that Abildgaard designed for his own apartment, which included a commode, a writing cabinet and some chairs, is even more interesting. The most noteworthy are his Greek *klismos* chairs. Like Abildgaard's X-shaped stools, these chairs were extremely fashionable and coincided with the revival of ancient forms in furniture throughout Europe. A slightly earlier example of a *klismos* chair appears, for example, in a painting by Jacques-Louis David of 1789. Although Abildgaard knew and admired David's work, he is more likely to have been inspired by Scandinavian precedents. Through Sergel, he had connections with Sweden where Louis Masreliez had designed similar, severely Neo-Classical chairs for Gustaf III's Haga Pavilion in 1792. Abildgaard must also have become familiar with the *klismos* chairs depicted in

Antique reliefs during his stay in Rome. He designed two versions, the lighter of which closely follows antique models with pronounced outwardly curving legs and backrail. It is gilded and the backrail is decorated with palmettes in marquetry. The larger chair is Abildgaard's most eccentric piece of furniture. Made of beech veneered with mahogany, it has a relatively wide backrail that is decorated with scenes freely adapted from Passerio's *Picturae Etruscorum* (1767), a copy of which was in Abildgaard's extensive library. Somewhat awkwardly proportioned, it is meant to be seen from the front to allow a full view of the pictorial Etruscan scenes. Both chairs are now upholstered but originally they were designed to have only a loose, red cushion. Abildgaard's preoccupation with the *klismos* form is also demonstrated in two sketches for the paintings for Christiansborg where it is represented as a seat for the king.

Abildgaard's art was both scholarly and versatile, and whether in paintings or in designs, his motifs and models were selected from antiquity and books rather than from life. He exercised a significant influence on the next generation of artists and designers and also encouraged the future Christian VIII to become an important collector and patron of the arts.

PIA MARIA MONTONEN

Biography

Born in Copenhagen in 1743, the son of the painter Sören Abildgaard (1718–c.1800). Trained as a decorative painter under J. E. Mandelberg; enrolled at the Academy of Art, Copenhagen, from 1764. Won several medals between 1764 and 1767; awarded a travel scholarship, 1771; studied in Rome where he met the painter J. H. Füssli and the sculptor J. T. Sergel, 1772–77; visited Naples and Pompeii, 1776. Returned to Copenhagen via Paris, 1777. Active as a painter and made a Member of the Academy, Copenhagen, 1778: Director, 1789–91 and 1801–09. Commissioned to decorate Schloss Christiansborg, 1780–91; involved in the design of interiors, furniture and architecture from the 1790s. Died in Copenhagen, 1809.

Selected Works

Drawings for the decoration of the Royal Palace, Amalienborg, are in the Statens Museum for Kunst, Copenhagen. Examples of the chairs that Abildgaard designed for his own use are in the Museum of Decorative Arts, Copenhagen.

Interiors

1780–91	Schloss Christiansborg, Copenhagen (allegorical paintings and decoration for the Hall): Christian VIII of Denmark
c.1795–1809	Royal Palace, Amalienborg (interiors and furnishings for the State Rooms): Christian VIII
c.1800	Abildgaard Apartment, Christiansborg (interiors and furnishings)

Further Reading

Andersen, Jörgen, *De År I Rom: Abildgaard*, Sergel, Füssli, Copenhagen: Ejler, 1989

Clemmensen, Tove, *Skabener og Interiorer*, Copenhagen: Nationalmuseet, 1984

Gere, Charlotte, *Nineteenth-Century Decoration: The Art of the Interior*, London: Weidenfeld and Nicolson, and New York: Abrams, 1989

Groth, Håkan, *Neoclassicism in the North: Swedish Furniture and Interiors, 1770–1850*, London: Thames and Hudson, and New York: Rizzoli, 1990

Kierkegaard, Bo, "Abildgaard's Genopdagede Rumundsmykning: Restaurering af Salen i Ejendommen Nytorv 5" in *Architectura*, 1991, pp.7–41

Lassen, Erik, *Danske Möbler: Den Klassiske Periode*, Copenhagen: Gyldendal, 1958

Monrad, K., "Abildgaard and the Copenhagen Art Academy at the end of the 18th Century" in *Leids Kunsthistorisch Jaarboek*, 1986–87, pp.549–59

Nannestad, Kirsten, *Nicolai Abildgaard, 1743–1809* (exhib. cat.), Frederiksborg: Nationalhistoriske Museum, 1979

Poulsen, Vagn and others, *Dansk Kunsthistorie*, vol.3: *Akademiet og guldalderen, 1750–1850*, Copenhagen: Politiken, 1972

Swane, Leo, *Abildgaard: Arkitektur og Dekoration*, Copenhagen: Kunstakademiets Arkitekturskole, 1926

Von Abildgaard bis Marstrand: Meisterzeichnungen der Kopenhagener Schule aus dem Besitz der Königlichen Kupferstichsammlung Kopenhagen (exhib. cat.), Munich: Staatliche Graphische Sammlung, 1985

Wanscher, Ole, *Möbelkunsten*, Copenhagen: Thaning & Appels, 1955

Ackermann, Rudolph 1764–1834

British publisher and bookseller

Born in Stolberg, Saxony, Rudolph Ackermann was trained as a coachmaker and worked in Switzerland, France and Belgium before moving to London in 1783. Despite a moderate success in this early career, it is as a publisher of topographical books and the celebrated *Repository of Arts* (1809–28), that he is now primarily remembered. The *Repository*, in particular, played a leading role in the dissemination of fashionable taste in the first quarter of the 19th century. Generously illustrated with coloured lithographs, it represents an important record of Regency colour schemes and designs for furnishings, upholstery and interiors.

The "Repository of Arts" was the name first given to a shop selling prints, books and fancy articles that Ackermann opened in 1795 (Ackermann's continued to operate as successful art dealers until the firm was sold in 1992). According to the *Dictionary of National Biography*, this business was one of the first to be lit by gas, and Ackermann's strong interest in the innovative as well as the fashionable is similarly reflected in his championing of new print techniques such as lithography, and his publishing of scientific books such as Frederick Accum's *Practical Treatise on Gas-Light* (1815).

Ackermann's career as a publisher was well established by the early 1800s and some of his most popular and successful projects were topographical publications such as the *Microcosm of London* and *Ackermann's Cambridge*. These have also proved of great value to architectural and design historians as many of the buildings and interiors illustrated have since been altered or destroyed. For example, plates in the *Microcosm of London* include views of the interiors of James Wyatt's Pantheon (demolished 1937), the Foundling Hospital (demolished 1926) and the old House of Commons (destroyed 1834). However, the plates are of interest as much for Thomas Rowlandson's witty delineations of the Georgian society that inhabited these interiors, as for the interiors themselves. Not surprisingly, the *Microcosm* inspired an early Victorian imitation entitled *London Interiors*.

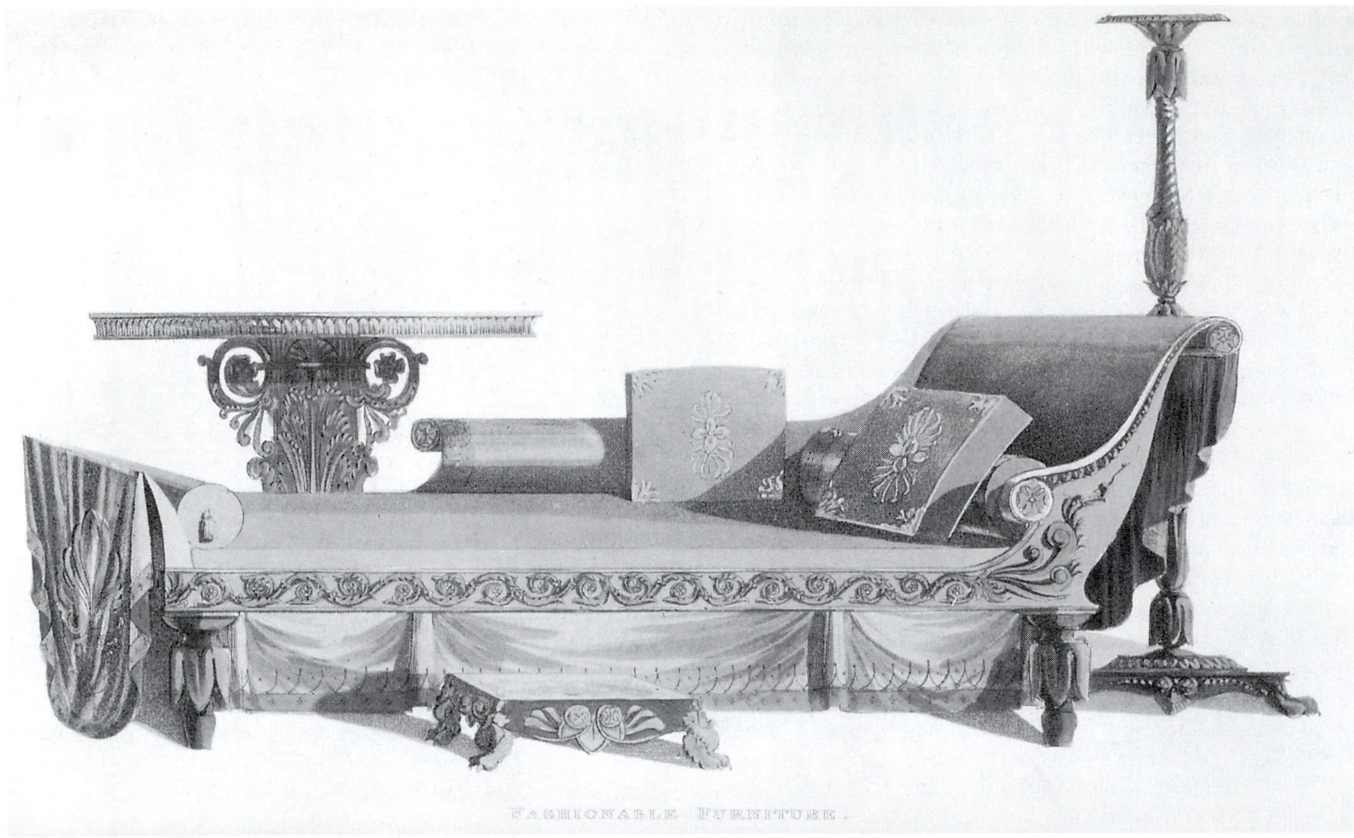

Ackermann: "Fashionable Furniture" from *The Repository of Arts*, vol. 13, plate 9, c.1809

The *Repository of Arts, Literature, Commerce, Manufacture, Fashions and Politics* was published monthly from 1809 and, as its somewhat cumbersome title suggests, it was initially intended to reflect very diverse interests. Similar magazines were already in circulation, particularly in Germany, and it is likely that Ackermann's publication was inspired, if not directly modelled upon, the *Journal des Luxus under der Moden* with whose editor Ackermann had corresponded between 1775 and 1803. It was an immediate success and attracted 3000 subscribers in the first year. The historian Peter Thornton has described the *Repository* as the "principal organ for bringing news of fresh fashion in interior decoration (among much else) to Regency England" and it included illustrations of almost every conceivable type of furnishing and numerous examples of drapery treatments and upholstery. It also included various novelties such as Atkinson's Hair Curling Fluid which was said to "impart a reviving odiferous perfume and keeps it in curl during the dance", and inventions like "Merlin's Mechanical Chair" for invalids and the "Metamorphic library chair", both of which were illustrated in 1811. The readership was drawn from most sections of fashionable society but from around 1816 the magazine was directed more specifically at a female audience and an increasing emphasis upon fiction and the arts replaced material relating to politics, science and medicine. This move perhaps reflects Ackermann's awareness of the growing importance of women as both arbiters of taste and consumers of home furnishings.

The *Repository*'s dominant style was English Grecian with contributions from major champions such as the architect John Buonarotti Papworth, the furniture designer George Smith, and the upholsterer John Stafford of Bath. In 1809 the magazine accompanied designs for a Grecian chaise longue and window seat with the following musings: "We observe with pleasure a more tasteful arrangement daily taking place; the gaudy colours of the chintz and calico furniture have given place to a more chaste style". These comments reveal the editor's sympathy with the new fashion and the view that the Greek style was synonymous with "taste". Papworth's contributions were reprinted as *Select London Views* (1816), *Rural Residences* (1818) and *Hints on Ornamental Gardening* (1823), the latter two representing important contributions to the Picturesque. In turn *Fashionable Furniture* (1823) was an anthology of designs whose principle source was the 1822 *Repository*. Ackermann's periodical was also responsible for bringing to a wider audience design books such as John Stafford's *A Series of Designs for Interior Decorations, comprehending Draperies and Elegancies for the Drawing Room* of 1814 which was reprinted in an abridged form in the *Repository* between 1819 and 1820.

Although dominant, the Grecian style was not promoted to the exclusion of all others. Egyptian ornament (which had enjoyed particular vogue following Nelson's victory at the Battle of the Nile in 1798) was praised for its decorative features, despite reservations in 1809 as to its inherent "barbarity". The *Repository* also reflected the continuing popularity in England for French design with the inclusion of furnishings in the Empire style. The Prince Regent's enthusiastic advocacy of French fashion and the subsequent popularity of Percier and Fontaine's *Recueil de décorations intérieures*, available in book form from 1812, meant that despite Ackermann's active dislike of the French Imperial regime, as a businessman and arbiter of fashion he could not ignore the demand for current French styles.

From 1825, the *Repository* became the vehicle for early Gothic designs by A.C. Pugin. Pugin had earlier been responsible for many of the engravings in Ackermann's topographical publications and his designs for the *Repository* were possibly produced with the assistance of A.W.N. Pugin, his precociously talented son. The 27 plates published between 1825 and 1827 were reissued by Pugin senior as *Pugin's Gothic Furniture* (1827). The *Repository* deemed Gothic a style particularly suitable for the Library as it "possesses a sedate and grave character, that encites the mind to study and reflection", and "the rays passing through its variegated casements cast a religious light upon the venerable tomes". The promotion of Gothic also extended beyond the *Repository* itself to include the publication of separate works by A.W.N. Pugin, such as his *Gothic Furniture in the Style of the 15th Century*, which was published by Ackermann and Co. in 1835 after Ackermann's death. This book was significant in the history of the Gothic Revival not only as Pugin's first independent published work but also for the scholarly nature of the designs. Other Pugin publications produced by Ackermann and Co. include the *Designs for Iron and Brass Work in the Style of the XV and XVI Centuries and Designs for Gold and Silversmiths*, both published in 1836.

JACQUELINE RIDING

See also Regency Style

Biography

Born in Stolberg, Saxony, 20 April 1764, the son of a coachmaker. Moved to Schneeberg, 1775. Trained under his father, and practised as coachmaker in Switzerland, France and Belgium. Settled in London, c.1783. Active as coachmaker until c.1793. Married an English woman, c.1793–95. Opened shop, The Repository of Arts, at the first of several addresses in the Strand, 1795. Patented waterproofing method; built factory in Chelsea, 1801. Opened drawing school, 1806. Published *Microcosm of London*, 1808–10. Published monthly magazine on art, science and fashion, *The Repository of Arts*, 1809–28, including the work of contemporary furniture designers. Set up lithographic press at his shop, 1817, donating one to Society of Arts, 1819. Visited Aloys Senefelder in Germany, 1818; translated Senefelder's *A Complete Course of Lithography*, 1819. Patented moveable carriage axles, 1820. Involved in anti-Napoleonic propaganda, 1807, and in charitable work in Germany from c.1813. Gained Order of Merit from king of Saxony, 1827. Married second time, 1830. Suffered a stroke, 1830. Died in Finchley, 20 March 1834. Eldest son Rudolph (d. 1868) continued business.

Publications

The British Library, London, and National Art Library at the Victoria and Albert Museum, London, hold complete runs of *The Repository of Arts*. For a discussion of the series' influence and a detailed commentary on selected plates see Agius 1984.

Six Lessons for Beginners in the Fine Art, 1796
The Microcosm of London, or London in Miniature, 1808–10
Dr Syntax's Tour in Search of the Picturesque, 1809–12
The Repository of Arts, 84 vols., 1809–28
The History of the Colleges of Winchester, Eton, illustrations by W. Westall, F. Mackenzie, Pugin and T. Uwins, 12 parts, 1816–17
Selection of Ornaments ... for the use of Sculptors, Painters, Carvers, Modellers, Chasers, Embossers, 1817–19
Fashionable Furniture, 1823 (later reprinted as *Modern Furniture*)

Further Reading

Agius, Pauline (editor), *Ackermann's Regency Furniture and Interiors*, Marlborough, Wiltshire: Crowood Press, 1984
Burke, W. J., *Rudolph Ackermann: Promoter of the Arts and Sciences*, New York, 1935 (reprint of the *Bulletin of the New York Public Library*, 1934)
Collard, Frances, *Regency Furniture*, Woodbridge, Suffolk: Antique Collectors' Club, 1985
Ford, John, *Ackermann, 1783–1983: The Business of Art*, London: Ackermann, 1983
Fox, Celina (editor), *London: World City, 1800–1840* (exhib. cat.: Essen), New Haven and London: Yale University Press, 1992
Hill, Rosemary, "Bankers, Bawds and Beau Monde" in *Country Life*, 3 November 1994, pp.64–67
Morley, John, *Regency Design, 1790–1840: Gardens, Buildings, Interiors, Furniture*, London: Zwemmer, and New York: Abrams, 1993
Parissien, Steven, *Regency Style*, London: Phaidon, and Washington, DC: Preservation Press, 1992

Adam, Robert 1728–1792

Scottish architect and designer

The style consciously perfected by Robert Adam and his brothers was to prove among the most popular and widely influential in British interior design. Largely derived from an unprecedented range of classical sources, it provided a system of ornamental design and varied decorative vocabulary readily applicable to virtually every aspect of the decorative arts, particularly within the integrated interior. Moreover, this fashionable style was generated by means of a large number of commissions, using a highly organised office and disseminated through a carefully devised publicity campaign, as epitomised by the publication *Works in Architecture of Robert and James Adam*. While the style dominated British design from the early 1760s to the 1780s, it was to be superseded by the more severely restrained and archaeologically-based Neo-Classicism of Henry Holland, Charles Heathcote Tatham and other designers of the Regency.

Robert was trained by his father, William Adam, then the leading architect in Scotland, along with his brothers John (1721–92) and James (1732–94) – a much younger brother William (1738–1822) was to support the family business later as their contractor – in a vigorous style which blended the fashionable Palladian manner with considerable elements of Vanbrugh's Baroque. Robert's early decorative work, exemplified by interiors carried out at Hopetoun House, near Edinburgh (c.1754), after his father's death, is in a conventional Rococo idiom, and accompanied by contemporary projects for Gothic landscape structures in the manner of Batty Langley. All this was to be dramatically transformed by a period of intense study in Italy (1754–58). During this time he was swift to assimilate an exceptionally wide range of architectural and ornamental forms which ranged from ancient

Adam: anteroom, Syon House, Middlesex, c.1761–69

Rome (including certain debts to the new discoveries at Herculaneum) to the Mannerist vocabulary of the *Cinquecento*, particulary the grotesques in stucco and paint of Raphael's Villa Madama and the Vatican *loggie*, as well as the dynamic spatial language of the Baroque. While Robert was tutored in the latest fashions of draughtsmanship and ornamental composition by the French architect C-L. Clérisseau, it was undoubtedly the Venetian designer G.B. Piranesi's liberating system of composition through architectural fantasy which showed him the means of creating a new and eclectic contemporary style. After a brief study of potential material among the remains of Diocletian's Palace at Spalato (the modern Split), later published in a sumptuous folio in 1764, he returned to Britain in 1758 to open an office in London and James took his turn in Italy. In their developing partnership, Robert was to prove the creative force while James acted in a subordinate role, drafting their aesthetic "credo" in the *Works*, and their elder brother John provided essential capital from the family estate at Blair Adam, near Edinburgh.

Throughout the 1760s Robert Adam, given the lack of totally new commissions, reconstructed a number of interiors in an impressive group of country houses, including Hatchlands, Shardeloes, Croome Court, Bowood, and Harewood. Above all, it was to be at Kedleston Hall (1760–c.70) and Syon House (1761–69) that he produced a sequence of monumental interiors that remain his masterpieces in recreating the patrician architecture of Antiquity, allied to a keen understanding of contemporary needs. These qualities are exemplified at Kedleston by the spatial transition from the top-lit columnar hall (atrium) to the circular domed saloon (vestibulum), and at Syon by the equally scenic progression from entrance hall, via the sumptuous anteroom, dining room, and red drawing room to the cleverly adapted long gallery. This formal language, which is also brilliantly handled at Osterley Park (1762–72), if on a comparatively less grandiose scale, involves a sequence of skilfully modulated spaces, changes of level, tone, lighting and texture which express the dynamic property of Adam's key concept of "movement". Meanwhile, his handling of ceiling as well as chimneypiece design gradually developed away from a bold expression in form and ornament to a far more refined treatment in accord with his continuing study of antique sources, particularly taking into account publications of the emerging Greek Revival as well as discoveries in remote sites such as Palmyra and Baalbek. Similarly, with the design of furniture in keeping with these classicising interiors, Adam's designs for tables, seat furniture and mirrors show an increasing capacity for invention and the ingenious application of motifs which reflect wall and ceiling ornaments within the same space.

While he owed much to pioneers of the integrated interior *al antica*, such as William Kent and Adam's contemporary and rival, James Stuart, never before had walls, ceilings, chimneypieces, floor surfaces and carpets, as well as door-furniture and light fittings, been orchestrated with such a cumulative effect, particularly using a highly original range of colour schemes (an extremely controversial issue in modern restorations). Major examples of this skilful integration of a variety of decorative arts can be seen in the music room at Harewood and the drawing room at Osterley. In achieving such coordination Adam was to rely on an exceptional team of artists and craftsmen including the plasterer Joseph Rose the Younger, decorative painters such as Cipriani, Pergolesi, Biagio Rebecca and Antonio Zucchi, sculptors such as Spang and Wilton, cabinet-makers such as the Linnells, Ince and Mayhew (and, less so, Chippendale), manufacturers in metal such as Matthew Boulton, carpet-makers such as Thomas Moore and, on rare occasions, Josiah Wedgwood, to mention but a few. Equally essential, if intentionally concealed by the brothers, was the team of draughtsmen responsible for producing the formidable quantity of detailed drawings, a large proportion of them in colour (some 9,000 survive in Sir John Soane's Museum), which included George Richardson, Agostino Brunias, Joseph Bonomi and Giuseppe Manocchi.

By the late 1760s, in addition to the other major country houses remodelled, such as Kenwood (with its lavishly monumental library), Saltram, Nostell Priory and Newby (including a pioneering sculpture gallery), the established Adam family firm now embarked upon an ambitious programme of town houses in London, of which the two best surviving are Wynn House, 20 St James's Square (c.1772–74) and Home House, 20 Portman Square (1775–77). In these commissions Robert succeeded in enhancing the narrow confines of the standard Georgian terrace house by means of a sequence of lavish rooms of parade in which he improved on traditional room shapes with the help of apses and screens of columns, segmental ceilings, and an extensive use of mirrored surfaces. The principal floors were connected by means of highly scenic staircases, owing much to Kent's magnificent precedent at 44 Berkeley Square and produced in conscious rivalry to William Chambers's ambitious staircase at Melbourne House (1771–74). By now, the sheer delicacy and increasingly shallow relief of the Adams' geometrically-devised plaster ceilings began to attract as much criticism as their external use of stucco ornament on otherwise unrelieved brickwork. Equally remarkable were a series of chimneypieces, owing much to Piranesi's own eccentric designs for such features, recently published in his influential *Diverse maniere d'adornare i cammini* of 1769. The use of cast-iron balustrades among the fittings within these houses reveals the growing exploitation of industrial mass-production by the Adams, paralleled by the extensive use of artificial materials, such as *scagliola*, and, externally, the use of Coade stone and Liardet cement. The ultimate expression of this entrepreneurial principal of standardization within the Adam style can be seen in the ill-fated speculative housing venture of the Adelphi (1756–72). This luxury housing overlooking the Thames near Charing Cross, despite its grave financial problems, was to set important patterns for the expansion of 19th-century London. When this exceptional development was largely demolished in 1936, a ceiling and chimneypiece from Garrick's rooms in 5 Adelphi Terrace survived to be recreated in the Victoria and Albert Museum.

The Adam achievement by the mid-1770s was to be summed up and expounded by means of the plates and accompanying texts of the exceptional publication – *Works of Architecture of Robert and James Adam*. In this work, which initially appeared in instalments and was later reissued in the form of three lavishly illustrated folio volumes, the authors claimed "to have brought about … a kind of revolution in the whole system of English architecture" and "to have been able to seize ... the beautiful spirit of antiquity, and to transfuse it with novelty and variety". The ingenious use of detailed as well as general plates advertising the Adams' novel decorative vocabulary, was, in itself, to promote a host of imitations in designs of all kinds.

Meanwhile, a serious threat to the brothers was now offered by the young James Wyatt. In response, the mid-1770s involved a new phase of stylistic experiments as exemplified by the suite of new state rooms at Osterley, added by Robert Adam between 1772 and 1780. These included an anteroom incorporating a specially-ordered set of Gobelins tapestries (other such tapestry rooms were created for Croome Court, Moor Park and one, still *in situ*, at Newby), a particularly ingenious state bedchamber, and, most remarkable of all, a painted dressing room in the Etruscan Style (at least a further eight such rooms were produced, the only one of which to survive in part is at Home House), combining inspiration from Piranesi, Wedgwood and Pompeian wall decorations. Other equally idiosyncratic designs included the Glass Drawing Room at Northumberland House, London, of 1770–75 (also partly reassembled in the Victoria and Albert Museum after the main building was demolished in 1874) which had green-painted glass for pilasters, frieze, and dado, with the main glass walls coloured red to simulate porphyry.

The last ten years of Robert's career were largely confined to Scotland where he continued a number of long-awaited official commissions, such as the Register House, Edinburgh, begun in 1774 and incomplete at his death (this retains one of his rare public interiors). On the domestic front, he contributed to the development of the New Town (a well-preserved example of a typical Adam interior, created in 1791, can be visited at 7 Charlotte Square). At the same time he continued to innovate with designs for an exceptional variety of castle-style mansions, only a few of which were executed. He had already tried his hand at the Gothic Revival with a surviving interior for Horace Walpole at Strawberry Hill, Twickenham (c.1766), and later work at Alnwick Castle (c.1770–78, since demolished). However, the interiors of these mock-medieval castles, in marked contrast to the powerfully austere abstraction of their exteriors, as notably seen at Culzean Castle on the Ayrshire coast (c.1778–90), continued to be fashioned in the delicately restrained classical style of the previous decade.

JOHN WILTON-ELY

See also Etruscan Style; Neo-Classicism; Rebecca; Rose Family

Biography

Born in Kirkaldy, Fife, 3 July 1728, son of the architect William Adam (1689–1748); his brothers included the architects John (1721–92) and James (1732–94), and the building contractor William (1738–1822). Educated at Edinburgh High School, 1743; apprenticed to his father 1746–48; in partnership with John and James from 1748. Travelled in Italy, 1754–58; studied drawing with Charles-Louis Clérisseau (1721–1820); travelled with him to Rome and met G.B. Piranesi (1720–78); visited Naples and Herculaneum, and Venice, and studied the ruins of Diocletian's Palace at Spalato (Split), 1757. Returned to England and established an office of the Adam firm in London, 1758; served as architect of the King's Works, 1761–69; surveyor of Chelsea Hospital, London, 1765. Active also as a designer of painted decoration and plasterwork, furniture, carpets, and metalwork from the 1760s. Fellow: Society of Arts, 1758; Society of Antiquaries, 1761; Royal Society, 1761. Elected Member of Parliament for Kinross, 1769. Died in London, 3 March 1792.

Selected Works

Approximately 9,000 drawings by Adam and his staff, including many sketches relating to the decorative projects, are in Sir John Soane's Museum, London. Smaller numbers of drawings are in the Drawings Collection, Royal Institute of British Architects and the Victoria and Albert Museum, London, and in the Metropolitan Museum, New York. The Metropolitan Museum also houses the dining room from Shelburne (later Lansdowne) House and the tapestry room from Croome Court, Hereford; the drawing room from Shelburne House is now in the Philadelphia Museum of Art. Documents and additional drawings can be found in the archives of several Adam houses including Kedleston Hall, Nostell Priory, Osterley Park and Saltram. An important collection of Adam furniture is in the Victoria and Albert Museum.

Interiors

1750–57 Hopetoun House, Newton, Lothian (alterations and interiors including the hall, dining room, drawing room and State bedroom): 2nd Earl of Hopetoun

1760–c.70 Kedleston Hall, Derbyshire (remodelling and interiors including the hall, saloon, dining room, music room, drawing room and library): 1st Lord Scarsdale

c.1761–69 Syon House, Brentford, Middlesex (remodelling, furnishings and interiors including the hall, anteroom, dining room, red drawing room, gallery, closet and green dining room): 1st Duke of Northumberland

c.1761–80 Osterley Park, Middlesex (alterations, portico, and decoration and furnishing of most of the main rooms including the hall, staircase, eating room, library, drawing room, tapestry room, state bedroom and Etruscan dressing room): Francis and Robert Child

c.1762–67 Shelburne (later Lansdowne) House, Berkeley Square, London (building and interiors including the hall, staircase, drawing room and dining room): 3rd Earl of Bute and 1st Marquess of Lansdowne

1764–79 Kenwood House, Hampstead, London (remodelling, additions, furniture and interiors including the hall, staircase, anteroom and "great room" or library): 1st Earl of Mansfield

1765–72 Harewood House, West Yorkshire (decoration of the ground floor rooms including the hall, saloon, library, state bedroom and dressing room, gallery, drawing room, dining room and music room): Edwin Lascelles, 1st Lord Harewood

1766–80 Nostell Priory, West Yorkshire (furniture and interiors including the upper hall, library, tapestry room and saloon): Sir Rowland Winn

1766–81 Alnwick Castle, Northumberland (decoration including the saloon, drawing room, dining room, banqueting room and library): 1st Duke of Northumberland

1767–76 Newby Hall, Ripon, North Yorkshire (furnishings and decoration including the hall, study, tapestry room, dining room and sculpture gallery): William Weddell

1768–69 Saltram House, Devon (furnishings and decoration including the great drawing room and library): John Parker, 1st Lord Bovingdon

c.1770–78 Mellerstain, Gordon, Scotland (additions and interiors including the library, dining room, drawing room, bedroom and hall): Hon. George Baillie

c.1772–74 20 St. James's Square, London (building and interiors including hall, dining room, music room, staircase well, anteroom, back drawing room and dressing room): Sir Watkin Williams-Wynn

1775–77 Home House, 20 Portman Square, London (building and interiors including the library, back and front parlours,

Etruscan bedroom, drawing room and music room): Countess of Home

c.1778–90 Culzean Castle, Maybole, Strathclyde (building and interiors including the armoury, dining rooms, staircase, saloon, drawing rooms, picture room and best bedrooms)

Publications

Ruins of the Palace of the Emperor Diocletian at Spalatro in Dalmatia, 1764

Works in Architecture of Robert and James Adam, London, 1773–79, modern edition edited by Robert Oreskó, 1975

Further Reading

The literature on Adam is substantial and recent studies include Bryant 1992, and Parissien 1992 which also provides a discussion of the influence of Adam's work in America. A useful survey of his architectural and decorative work appears in King 1991, including a gazetteer of houses open to the public and a full bibliography. More detailed studies of Adam's decorative work and furniture appear in Harris 1973 and Stillman 1973 respectively. Many of the Adam brothers' commissions, including some unexecuted schemes, are illustrated in the *Works* 1975.

Beard, Geoffrey, "New Light on Adam's Craftsmen" in *Country Life*, 131, 1962, pp.1098–1100

Beard, Geoffrey, *The Work of Robert Adam*, Edinburgh: Bartholomew, and New York: Arco, 1978

Beard, Geoffrey, *Craftsmen and Interior Decoration in England, 1660–1820*, Edinburgh: Bartholomew, and New York: Holmes and Meier, 1981

Bolton, A.T., *The Architecture of Robert and James Adam*, 1922; reissued Woodbridge, Suffolk: Antique Collectors' Club, 1984

Boyd, Sterling, *The Adam Style in America, 1770–1820*, New York: Garland, 1985

Bryant, Julius, *The Iveagh Bequest: Kenwood*, London: Historic House Museums Trust, 1990

Bryant, Julius, *Robert Adam, Architect of Genius*, London: English Heritage, 1992

Croft-Murray, Edward, *Decorative Painting in England, 1537–1837*, 2 vols., London: Country Life, 1962–70

The Drawings of Robert and James Adam in Sir John Soane's Museum (microfilm), Cambridge: Chadwyck-Healey, and Teaneck, NJ: Somerset House, 1979

Fleming, John, *Robert Adam and His Circle in Edinburgh and Rome*, London: Murray, and Cambridge, MA: Harvard University Press, 1962

Hardy, John, "The Building and Decoration of Apsley House" in *Apollo*, 98, September 1973, pp.12–21

Hardy, John and Maurice Tomlin, *Osterley Park House*, London: Victoria and Albert Museum, 1985

Harris, Eileen, "Robert Adam and the Gobelins" in *Apollo*, 76, April 1962, pp.100–06

Harris, Eileen, *The Furniture of Robert Adam*, London: Academy, and New York: St. Martin's Press, 1973

Harris, Eileen, "Robert Adam on Park Avenue: The Interiors for Bolton House" in *Burlington Magazine*, 187, February 1995, pp.68–76

Harris, Leslie and Gervase Jackson-Stops, *Robert Adam and Kedleston: The Making of a Neo-Classical Masterpiece* (exhib. cat.), London: National Trust, 1987

King, David N., *The Complete Works of Robert and James Adam*, Oxford: Butterworth, 1991

Lees-Milne, James, *The Age of Adam*, London: Batsford, 1947

Musgrave, Clifford, *Adam and Hepplewhite and Other Neo-Classical Furniture*, London: Faber, and New York: Taplinger, 1966

Owsley, D. and W. Rieder, *The Glass Drawing Room from Northumberland House*, London: Victoria and Albert Museum, 1974

Parissien, Steven, *Adam Style*, London: Phaidon, and Washington, DC: Preservation Press, 1992

Rowan, Alistair J., "The Building of Hopetoun" in *Architectural History*, 27, 1984, pp.183–209

Rowan, Alistair J., *Catalogue of Architectural Drawings in the Victoria and Albert Museum: Robert Adam*, London: Victoria and Albert Museum, 1988

Rykwert, Joseph and Anne, *The Brothers Adam: The Men and the Style*, London: Collins, 1985

Stillman, Damie, *The Decorative Work of Robert Adam*, London: Academy, and New York: St. Martin's Press, 1973

Tait, A.A., *Robert Adam: Drawings and Imagination*, Cambridge and New York: Cambridge University Press, 1993

Tomlin, Maurice, *Catalogue of Adam Period Furniture*, London: Victoria and Albert Museum, 1972

Whinney, Margaret, *Home House, No.20 Portman Square*, London: Country Life, 1969

Wilton-Ely, John, "An Electric Revolution in Art: The Adam Achievement Reassessed" in *Journal of the Royal Society of Arts*, CXL, June 1992, pp.452–63

Wilton-Ely, John, *Piranesi as Architect and Designer*, New Haven and London: Yale University Press, 1993

Yarwood, Doreen, *Robert Adam*, London: Dent, and New York: Scribner, 1970

Aesthetic Movement

The Aesthetic Movement of the 1870s and 1880s was a cult of beauty. Not so much a style as a philosophy, the movement defined beauty as an independent vital force that transcended religious, historical and geographic boundaries. Aestheticism emphasized the need for beauty in everyday life, and sought to introduce art to every home. It advocated the cultivation of good taste, and the creation and informed enjoyment of artfully embellished domestic goods. These goods were often known as "Art Furnishings", and Aestheticism and Art Furnishings were closely allied.

Aestheticism had a tremendous impact on British and American interior design of the late 19th century, and exerted influence on virtually all levels of society. Aesthetes argued that beauty uplifted the spirit and mind. In *The Book of American Interiors* (1876), Boston tastemaker Charles Wyllys Elliot foresaw a halcyon day when "in every house, the Beautiful married to the Useful shall make life truer, finer, happier". Women were urged to create homes that were places of spiritual renewal and refuges for their menfolk from the materialistic world of business. Furthermore, a tastefully decorated home would refine the minds of children, enhance the work of servants, and, as a microcosm of society at large, elevate the national culture. Such theories placed tremendous pressure on home decorators, assigning almost overwhelming importance to the choices they made. The Household Art Movement counterbalanced that pressure by disseminating the principles of Aestheticism, and helping consumers to create artful interiors of their own; scores of advice books and art journals were published. Charles Locke Eastlake's *Hints on Household Taste* (1868) was perhaps the most influential of these manuals, soon to be joined by many others, such as the *Art at Home* series edited by W.J. Loftie (1876), and *The House Beautiful* (1878) by Clarence Cook.

Aestheticism evolved from emerging liberal philosophy, as

Aesthetic Movement: bedroom, Château-sur-Mer, Newport, Rhode Island, designed by Seth Bradford, 1851–52 and remodeled by Richard Morris Hunt, 1871–78, for George Peabody Wetmore

well as from the campaign to reform British design. As a reaction against prevailing Victorian bourgeois values, the Aesthetic Movement offered art as an antidote to vulgar materialism. It urged that the pursuit of beauty be given equal, if not greater, importance than the philistine pursuit of wealth. Art was lauded as the highest form of action, complete unto itself, existing for its own sake. Indeed, in his preface to *Mademoiselle Maupin* (1835), the poet Théophile Gautier argued that if art is created to serve any extrinsic ends, then its aesthetic value is diminished. This doctrine stood in stark contrast to traditional criticism that focused on the moral, narrative, and didactic qualities in works of art. James McNeill Whistler's 1878 libel suit against critic John Ruskin dramatized this clash of aesthetics. Ruskin had been outraged by Whistler's painting *The Falling Rocket*, and condemned it as an act of conceit, akin to "flinging a pot of paint in the public's face" (*Fors Clavigera*, July 1877). Whistler, a flamboyant, articulate polemicist for Aestheticism and an acquaintance of Gautier's, countered with the argument that paintings are independent visual sensations in which subject matter is irrelevant. The case was followed exhaustively in the press, and popularized the tenet of "art for art's sake", as well as the wit and extravagance of its leading proponents.

Calls for the reform of British design dated to the 1840s. They became more strident following the Great Exhibition of 1851, when the design failings of contemporary British manufactured goods were displayed for all to see. Overblown and ponderous, overwhelmed with ornamentation, the exhibited goods prompted the establishment of the South Kensington Museum and Design School. Led by Henry Cole, the museum's mission was to expose British designers to the history of art and instil in them principles of proportion and color harmony. On its faculty were Owen Jones and Christopher Dresser, who championed of the use of two-dimensional patterns for the decoration of flat surfaces like carpets and wallpapers; they believed realistic ornamentation in such cases was dishonest. Jones was a student of decorative patterning. His *The Grammar of Ornament* (1856) illustrated stylized interpretations of various historical and national decorative styles, and outlined general rules for ornamentation. He argued that elements of decoration from different styles could be brought together according to these "grammatical" rules, so as to create new ornamental languages. In the process, decorative motifs were divorced from prior symbolism or historical association. This free appropriation and mixing of styles was to be a hallmark of aesthetic interior design.

Design reform was also applied to furniture. Critics valued the honest expression of both construction and materials, qualities they saw inherent in objects from the middle ages. The Modern Gothic style of the 1860s–mid 1870s reinterpreted medieval design, creating rectilinear, relatively simple, pieces of furniture, often decorated with incised, stylized ornamentation. This style was popularized by Bruce Talbert's *Gothic Forms Applied to Furniture, Metal Work and Decoration for Domestic Purposes* (1868). In turn, Talbert's work inspired the Art Furniture created by Americans Frank Furness and Daniel Pabst of Philadelphia, as well as Kimbel and Cabus of New York. Charles Eastlake's *Hints* also was extremely influential; indeed, the Modern Gothic style in America came to be called the Eastlake style.

Some critics believed that both contemporary designs and contemporary means of manufacture needed reform. Leaders of the Arts and Crafts Movement, such as William Morris, sought a revival of hand craftsmanship; they rejected mass-production and suggested a return to the medieval system of guilds. Morris's hand printed wallpaper and textile patterns proved tremendously popular in Aesthetic circles. Their stylized natural forms, sense of organic, rhythmic growth, and use of natural dyes were much in demand to decorate artful interiors on both sides of the Atlantic.

Morris drew on the talents of his friends in producing designs for his firm and, also, in designing the interior of his home, the Red House at Bexleyheath, built in 1859; painters Edward Burne-Jones and Dante Gabriel Rossetti, and architect Philip Webb all worked on the Bexley Heath project. They painted murals on otherwise plain walls, and created ingenious built-in furniture, including a combination cupboard, settle, and minstrels' gallery. Later in the 19th century, built-in furniture found favor among homeowners with Aesthetic pretensions; inglenooks and window-seats were popular, while arch-aesthete Oscar Wilde's London dining room of 1885 featured a sideboard built-in around much of the room.

That painters used their skills in the production of decorative arts had much to do with the influence of John Ruskin. In *The Seven Lamps of Architecture* (1849) Ruskin extolled the virtues of surface ornamentation, describing it as a force for good. He believed that the decorative arts should be given a status equal to the fine arts. Designers and architects began to see themselves as artists, and aesthetic considerations became central to their creations. Painters, poets, and designers mixed socially, and Art Furnishings benefited from their collaborations. In New York City, social clubs like the Century, Lotus, and Grolier brought artists, authors, and patrons together, while the Tile Club was founded by painters like Winslow Homer, who experimented in decorating ceramics.

Perhaps the most famous painter-decorator was Whistler. In 1876 he was commissioned to decorate the London hall and stairway of shipping magnate Frederick Leyland. He embellished those interiors in brown and gold, before reworking the dining room, where his painting *La Princesse du Pays de la Porcelaine* was displayed. The dining room had just been completed by noted designer Thomas Jeckyll, yet Whistler's decorative scheme was largely unrelated to his work. He painted over the antique Spanish leather wall-coverings, in a composition he described as *Harmony in Blue and Gold*. Using colors derived from a peacock's plumage, he also created a mural of peacocks, arranged in the manner of a Japanese screen. Gilded ribs and shelves divided the walls, evoking a Japanese shrine, while allowing the display of the Leyland collection of Oriental porcelain. Whistler conceived of the room as a single, harmonious composition in which his painting was an important, yet not predominant, part. Characteristic of interiors with Aesthetic ambiance was the refined arrangement of each element in a room so that none detracted from the cultivated vision of the whole.

Japanese art and design were instrumental in the evolution of the Aesthetic Movement; their influence extended from the composition of paintings to the arrangement and design of furniture. The first comprehensive public display of Japanese goods in the West was part of the 1862 International

Aesthetic Movement: sideboard by E.W. Godwin in ebonised wood with embossed papier-mâché panels and silverplated fittings, c.1867

Exhibition held in London. Textiles, ceramics, lacquer-ware, prints and furniture crowded the exhibition. Critics lauded the simplicity and refined beauty of the everyday objects; they praised their asymmetry, precision, and delicacy of color. They perceived in Japanese goods the very qualities they appreciated in medieval design: stylized surface ornamentation, rectilinearity, and handcraftsmanship.

Following the Exhibition many of the goods from the Japanese display were offered for sale; Farmer and Rogers Oriental Warehouse sold a large selection. Whistler, Rossetti, Burne-Jones, and E.W. Godwin are all thought to have bought Japanese objects at that time. Similarly, a number of Japanese curio stores opened in Paris. One shop, owned by Mme. Desoye, became a meeting place for young artists, including Whistler, James Tissot, and Baudelaire.

Designers soon incorporated elements of Japanese art into their work. The term "Anglo-Japanese" describes English designs distinguished by Japanese-inspired asymmetry, delicate line, light construction, attenuation, and interplay of solids and voids. The style was developed by E.W. Godwin. Characterized by essayist Max Beerbohm as "the greatest aesthete of them all", Godwin decorated his Bristol townhouse in 1862 with Japanese prints, Persian rugs on bare floors, and a few thoughtfully arranged pieces of 18th-century furniture. Later, Godwin moved to London, where he enlarged the Japanese effect of his decor by using straw-colored matting on his drawing room floor and dado. Wicker chairs with Japanese-patterned cushions provided seating. Art Designers occasionally made furniture from wicker, cane, and bamboo, materials which carried undertones of the exotic East. Lightweight and easy to move, such furniture was well-suited to the freer room arrangements of the 1870s and 1880s.

Godwin also designed furniture for himself. For reasons of economy this was constructed in deal which was then ebonised to suggest the appearance of lacquer. His sideboard of c.1867 is one of the earliest and most extreme examples of Anglo-Japanese furniture. Inspired by the wooden fitments illustrated in Japanese prints, its form is taughtly rectilinear and its beauty rests in the simplicity of its shape and the careful juxtaposition of solids and voids. This and numerous other pieces were sold by William Watt and were illustrated in his catalogue *Art Furniture from Designs by E.W. Godwin ... and Others* (1877).

Many other designers were also drawn to the geometry and abstraction of Japanese goods. Christopher Dresser, for example, produced wallpapers, textiles and furniture in the Anglo-Japanese style. Unlike most of his contemporaries, Dresser's appreciation of Japanese art was informed by a close understanding and thorough knowledge of the culture of Japan. In 1876 he travelled to Japan, where he studied the indigenous art and architecture, and collected a group of objects for the design study collection at Tiffany and Company in New York. Tiffany subsequently sold the items that did not fit into their collection to the public.

The art of Ancient Greece and Egypt were also important influences on Aestheticism, particularly in the later 1870s and 1880s. The impact of late 19th-century classicism was especially strong in the fine arts where classical and mythological subjects were popularized by painters such as Frederic Leighton and Albert Moore, but it also influenced the design of furniture, decoration and even Aesthetic dress. Godwin, for example, designed a range of Greek furniture, illustrated in the *Building News* of 1885, whose bulbous turned legs and incised gilt decoration precisely match museum notes in his sketchbooks, and another of his Greek chairs made by Watt in plain oak was advertised in 1884 as a "Cheap Chair". Similarly, an ebonized armchair illustrated in Dresser's *Principles of Decorative Design* (1873) is described as being "in the Greek style", and much of the incised ornament in other examples of his furniture is clearly indebted to antique precedents. The work of Dresser and Godwin also reveals an interest in Egyptian styles, as did that of several other artists and designers. Ford Madox Brown had designed an "Egyptian" chair for William Holman Hunt in 1857 which was the antecedent of a varied line of Thebes stools patented by Liberty's in 1884 and which were still being produced well into the 1920s. Liberty's also sold a range of Egyptian accessories in its Arab Tea Rooms and specialized in "Moorish" furniture incorporating panels of imported *musharabeyeh* latticework. Items such as small tables and screens provided an exotic note which proved increasingly popular in Aesthetic homes.

American decorators embraced Japonisme in the 1870s. Of particular note is the work of Herter Brothers of New York, who imported Japanese objects, and created beautifully crafted marquetry furniture in the Anglo-Japanese style. Herter Brothers' most spectacular Japanese-inspired commission was the parlor they created for William H. Vanderbilt's New York house in 1882. The parlor evoked Whistler's *Peacock Room* in its elaborate series of light display shelves, and also featured red-lacquered beams, a gilded bamboo frieze, and a chimneypiece that suggested the entrance to a Japanese temple.

In America, the Philadelphia Centennial Exposition of 1876 catalyzed the spread of Aestheticism. Over ten million people streamed through the exhibition, where they were exposed to a vast array of art objects from around the world. The Japanese section both displayed and sold Japanese goods, while the British display featured room settings decorated in a variety of styles, including the Jacobean and the newly popular Queen Anne. A cast- and wrought-iron pagoda designed by Thomas Jeckyll was also part of the British exhibition. Jeckyll surrounded this structure with a railing composed of stylized iron sunflowers. The sunflower was a virtual icon of the Aesthetic Movement and a favorite motif of Jeckyll's. It appeared on sets of andirons he designed, one of which decorated Leyland's Peacock Room.

Aestheticism was popularized further in America by Art Furnishings retailers and by the occasional appearance of figures from the British Aesthetic Movement. In 1873 the London merchant Daniel Cottier opened a New York branch of his firm, specializing in furniture and stained glass by designers such as Godwin and Morris. Christopher Dresser gave a series of art lectures in the United States, while Oscar Wilde was notorious for his posturing eccentricities when he toured the country and described his vision of the House Beautiful in 1882–83.

Few critics or homeowners shared the same vision of domestic beauty. Aestheticism emphasized the free expression of refined taste, and individuals used widely different criteria in selecting decoration for their homes. Interiors that reflected the pure principles of Japanese simplicity and restraint were rare, existing more in theory than in practice; Godwin's design of his own rooms came perhaps closest to the Aesthetic ideal. Other decorators were less extreme, and created rooms that were more artful than purely Aesthetic. While there was no unity of style, the iconography of the Aesthetic Movement was standard: the lily, poppy, sunflower, feather, fan, peacock, Sussex chair, and blue and white china were all hallmarks of Aestheticism. In addition, very broad trends in decorating emerged. An eclectic taste for works of art from all times and places, a use of flat, stylized patterns divided by borders, an enthusiasm for collecting and display, a *horror vacui*, and a complex layering of patterns, textures, and art objects characterized artful decorating. Tertiary, subtle colors were used in many Aesthetic interiors; Oscar Wilde described such colors as "a reaction against the crude primaries of a doubtless more respectable but certainly less cultivated age" (letter to the *Daily Chronicle*, 30 June, 1890). Household Art literature advocated the creation of a series of cosy seating areas, which were seemingly casual, yet carefully planned; screens, parasols, inglenooks, and bay windows were suggested tools for defining separate conversation areas. Aesthetes fashioned art corners, where harmoniously grouped, diverse objects of beauty pleased the cultivated eye and enhanced the composition of the room at large. Eastlake called for shelves to be built above the fireplace, so that a "mantle museum" of collectibles was formed.

Inevitably, decorators reacted against the visual complexity of such interiors. Color schemes lightened and brightened, and eclecticism diminished. In both England and America, designers of the 1880s revived the styles of the 18th century; these developments followed the rediscovery of 17th and 18th century domestic vernacular architecture, notably by Richard Norman Shaw and William Eden Nesfield. Manufacturers made reproduction Queen Anne and Colonial Revival furniture, and antiques were in great demand. The owner of antiques was assigned qualities such as a refined taste and informed discrimination, as well as good breeding and wealth.

Rapacious collectors, foppish Aesthetes and intense connoisseurs all were widely parodied in satirical journals like *Punch*. George du Maurier caricatured both Whistler and Wilde in a series of cartoons featuring the long-haired painter Jellaby Postlethwaite and the poet Maudle, endowing them with posturing affectations and an insatiable passion for Aesthetic icons such as lilies and blue and white china. Wilde's favored attire, knee britches and floppy ties with large flowers at his lapel, was also lampooned. Gilbert and Sullivan's opera *Patience* (1881) brought further attention to the eccentricities of the Aesthetic Movement. Their protagonist Reginald Bunthorne, a poet and posing aesthete, describes himself as "a Japanese young man, a blue and white young man, a greenery-yallery, Grosvenor-Gallery foot-in-the-grave young man". Wilde took such satire in good part, and welcomed the notoriety it gave him. Indeed, his American lecture tour was organized by Richard D'Oyly Carte, the producer of *Patience*, to coincide with the New York opening of the opera.

Aestheticism attracted condemnation as well as satire. The Aesthetes' philosophy that art is the goal of life was denounced as pagan and amoral. Their flamboyant lives were dismissed as decadent self-indulgence. Perhaps the most scathing criticism of the Aesthetic Movement appeared in Henry James's *The Portrait of a Lady* (1881). James describes the Aesthete Gilbert Osmond as an avid collector with a passion for Japanese porcelain, yet a genius only for upholstery. Osmond's attempts to make his own life a work of art expose him as trivial and self-absorbed.

MADELINE SIEFKE ESTILL

See also Aitchison; Art Furnishings; Dresser; Godwin; Herter Brothers; Kimbel and Cabus; J.M. Whistler

Selected Collections

Notable examples of Aesthetic interiors in England survive at Cragside, Northumberland, and in the Refreshment Room in the Victoria and Albert Museum, Leighton House, and Linley Sambourne House, London. Examples of Aesthetic interiors in America can be seen in the Mark Twain House, Hartford, Connecticut; Olana, Hudson, New York; Château-sur-Mer, Rhode Island; and the Peacock Room in the Freer Art Gallery, Washington, DC. Numerous items of American Aesthetic style furnishings are in the American Wing, Metropolitan Museum of Art, New York.

Further Reading

A classic study of the Aesthetic Movement in England is Aslin 1969, with a more recent survey by Lambourne 1996. The influence of Aestheticism in France is covered in *Le Japonisme* 1988. For a detailed and scholarly account of the Aesthetic Movement in America see Burke 1986 which also includes biographies of all the main English and American protagonists and an extensive bibliography of primary and secondary sources.

The Aesthetic Movement and the Cult of Japan (exhib. cat.), London: Fine Art Society, 1972

Aslin, Elizabeth, *The Aesthetic Movement: Prelude to Art Nouveau*, London: Elek, and New York: Praeger, 1969

Aslin, Elizabeth, *E.W. Godwin: Furniture and Interior Decoration* (exhib. cat.), London: Murray, 1986

Burke, Doreen Bolger and others, *In Pursuit of Beauty: Americans and the Aesthetic Movement* (exhib. cat.: Metropolitan Museum, New York), New York: Rizzoli, 1986

Cooper, Jeremy, *Victorian and Edwardian Furniture and Interiors*, London: Thames and Hudson, 1987

Freylinghuysen, Alice Cooney, "Christian Herter's Decoration of the William H. Vanderbilt House in New York City" in *Magazine Antiques*, March 1995, pp.408–17

Freylinghuysen, Alice Cooney, "The Aesthetic Movement in Newport" in *Magazine Antiques*, CXLVII, April 1995, pp.570–77

Gaunt, William, *The Aesthetic Adventure*, revised edition London: Cape, 1975

Gere, Charlotte, *Nineteenth-Century Decoration: The Art of the Interior*, London: Weidenfeld and Nicolson, and New York: Abrams, 1989

Girouard, Mark, *Sweetness and Light: The Queen Anne Movement, 1860–1900*, Oxford: Clarendon Press, 1977; New Haven: Yale University Press, 1984

Habron, Dudley, "Queen Anne Taste and Aestheticism" in *Architectural Review*, 95, July 1943, pp.15–18

Halén, Widar, *Christopher Dresser*, Oxford: Phaidon, 1990

Haweis, Mary Eliza, *Beautiful Houses*, London: Sampson Low, 1882

Le Japonisme (exhib. cat.), Paris: Galeries Nationales du Grand Palais, 1988

Lambourne, Lionel, *The Aesthetic Movement*, London: Phaidon, 1996

Lancaster, Clay, *The Japanese Influence in America*, New York: Rawls, 1963

McClaugherty, Martha Crabill, "Household Art: Creating the Artistic Home, 1868–1893" in *Winterthur Portfolio*, 18, Spring 1983, pp.1–26

Sato, Tomoko and Toshio Watanabe, *Japan and Britain: An Aesthetic Dialogue, 1850–1930* (exhib. cat.), London: Lund Humphries, 1991

Spencer, Robin, *The Aesthetic Movement: Theory and Practice*, London: Studio Vista, and New York: Dutton, 1972

Victorian and Edwardian Decorative Art: The Handley-Read Collection (exhib. cat.), London: Royal Academy, 1972

Watanabe, Toshio, *High Victorian Japonisme*, Frankfurt: Lang, 1991

Weisberg, Gabriel P. and Yvonne M.L. Weisberg, *Japonisme: An Annotated Bibliography*, New York: Garland, 1990

Wichmann, Siegfried, *Japonisme: The Japanese Influence on Western Art in the 19th and 20th Centuries*, New York: Harmony, 1981

Aitchison, George 1825–1910

British architect and designer of furniture and interiors

Born into a family of successful City architects, George Aitchison rose to the very top of the architectural profession. A highly respected scholar and authority on historic ornament,

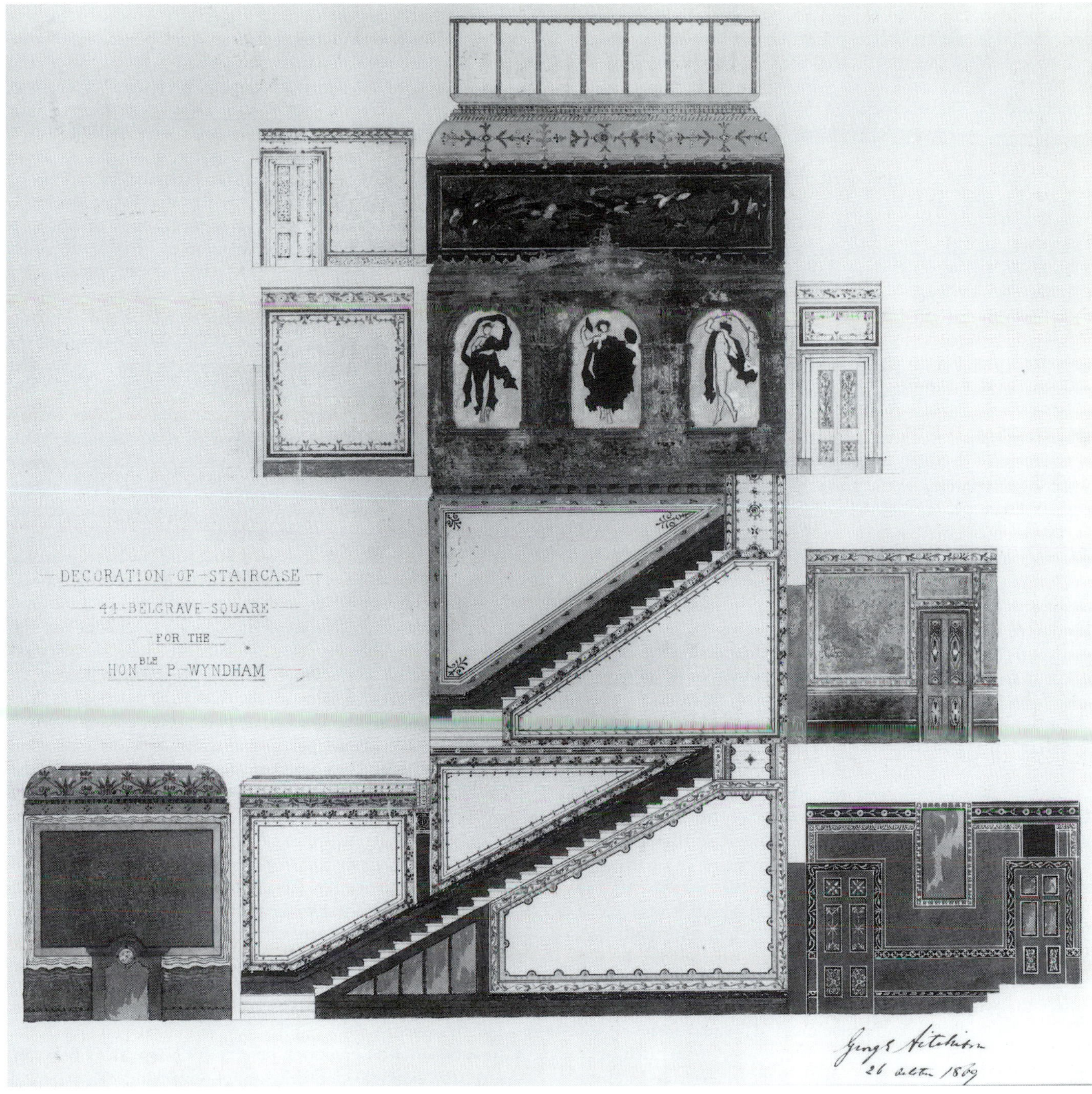

Aitchison: drawing of staircase hall, 44 Belgrave Square, London, 1869

he was made President of the Royal Institute of British Architects in 1896 and by his death he was internationally renowned as one of the foremost members of the architectural establishment. Yet Aitchison's architectural output was actually quite small and his reputation rested far more upon his achievements as an interior decorator than as a designer of buildings. In this capacity he worked for a small but influential group of wealthy, artistically-conscious clients for whom he created customised interiors that featured striking combinations of strong colours, gilding and decorative ornament. Always closely in touch with fashionable and progressive tastes, his work represents Victorian Aestheticism at its most opulent and epitomises the most splendid examples of the late 19th century "House Beautiful".

Aitchison's training in the offices of the St. Katherine's Dock Company provided a solid grounding in the skills of engineering and surveying, and an early commission, for 59–61 Mark Lane, London (1864), indicates a precocious and, at the time, radical interest in the structural possibilities of cast- and wrought-iron. But of much greater significance, certainly as far as his interiors were concerned, was the long tour of Italy that he made between 1853 and 1855 where his eyes were opened to the potential of decorative polychromy through his study of early Renaissance architecture and the work of Italian fresco painters such as Cimabue and Giotto. In Italy he also met a group of architects and artists with whom he formed lifelong friendships. These included William Burges, Alfred Waterhouse, and Edward Poynter, and, most importantly of all, the painter Frederic Leighton whom he met in Rome in 1853, and who commissioned his most celebrated work, Leighton House, in 1864.

Situated in Holland Park Road, Kensington, Leighton House was the first of many large detached studio houses that were erected in the last quarter of the 19th century and whose size and magnificence were designed to underline the artistic prowess and professional status of their successful Royal Academician owners. Leighton House was to become the most well-known and admired of these Palaces of Art but the exterior was, initially at least, fairly restrained. Built of red Suffolk brick with mouldings of light Caen stone, its design echoed that of an Italian Renaissance villa and, with the exception of some classical detailing on the mouldings and the large studio window that dominates the north, garden front, there were few embellishments to attract the eye.

The interiors, by contrast, were far more imposing and on entering the building the visitor was immediately struck by the profusion of boldly contrasting colours and the richness of the decorative materials employed. Iridescent turquoise blue tiles, produced by William De Morgan in 1879–81, covered the walls of the staircase and hall, and the dining room and drawing room were decorated in striking shades of Indian red and tobacco brown. The woodwork in these rooms and throughout the rest of the house was ebonised, and classicizing details, such as rosettes and linear arabesque ornament, on the cornices and door-frames were incised and picked out in gold, forming a dramatic contrast with the gleaming black ground. Upstairs, the studio was painted a deep terracotta, Leighton's preferred colour for the display of paintings. At the east end a large galleried screen containing a number of compartments and cupboards designed to accommodate the artist's easels and brushes, was painted peacock blue and an apsed semi-dome at the opposite end of the room was decorated with gold leaf. Many of these features, like the use of dark wood and the rich colour schemes, were repeated in other commissions and reflect the widespread preoccupations of Aesthetic taste. But certain of the details, in particular the etiolated forms of the staircase balusters, the marble fireplaces ornamented with stencilled decoration or inlaid with serpentine scrolls, and the decoration of the mouldings, were both highly personal and unusual.

Originally, the accommodation consisted of three ground floor rooms and a studio and bedroom on the first floor – Leighton, a bachelor, did not want to encourage overnight guests. However, both the client and architect had always intended to extend and in 1870 Aitchison enlarged the studio incorporating two Arab-style stained glass windows. In 1877 he was called in again to add a library and the Arab Hall.

The Arab Hall is arguably Aitchison's masterpiece. Designed as a showcase for Leighton's priceless collection of 16th- and 17th-century Syrian and Isnik tiles, the room was modelled on a reception hall in the 12th-century Moslem palace of La Zisa, near Palermo, Sicily, that Aitchison had visited with Burges in 1854. Its typically Moorish features include the arched window recesses, squinches and the large pendentive dome. Carved lattice wood screens cover the windows and an 18th-century *zenana*, or harem-screen, was placed above the entrance to the hall. The tiles themselves were set into the walls. The antique elements were skilfully fitted into the architectural shell and contemporary artists were engaged to design new work. Aitchison designed the capitals of the marble columns – carved by the sculptor Edgar Boehm – the mosaic floor, the vertiginous copper and wrought-iron chandelier, and the central pool. William de Morgan designed the new tilework, Walter Crane the mosaic frieze, and Randolph Caldecott the gilt capitals of the alabaster pillars. The result was a harmonious yet highly romantic and dramatic expression of exotic taste; to contemporaries it "conjured up recollections of the finest scenes and grandest palaces described in the Arabian Nights".

Many details of the interior of Leighton House were clearly determined by its owner – it was Leighton, for example, who designed the stencilled decoration on the marble chimneypiece in the drawing room – and the extent to which the building should be viewed as a collaboration between architect and client is still not clear. Nevertheless, the commission as a whole, and in particular the Arab Hall, did much to enhance Aitchison's reputation as a master of decoration and ornament. Moreover, his friendship with Leighton brought him into contact with a new circle of rich, fashionable clients and the two worked together on several subsequent interior schemes. These included a commission for the Eustace Smiths at 52 Princes Gate where Aitchison decorated the boudoir in rose and ivory, and the dining room in pale green, adding a heavy Renaissance-style chimneypiece and overmantle incorporating a Leighton frieze. They collaborated again in 1869 on the decoration of the interior of 44 Belgrave Square, owned by Percy Wyndham, one of the fashionable "Souls" group, who later engaged Philip Webb to build his country house Clouds. The staircase and inner hall of Belgrave Square were decorated in blue and Pompeian red stencilling, and a group of dancing classical figures (painted by Leighton) and a frieze of painted cormorants, storks and other flying birds was placed high up on the stairs.

This collaboration with artists established a pattern that Aitchison was to repeat in later commissions, several of which include friezes or panels painted by prominent painters of the Aesthetic school. In Frederick Lehmann's house at 15 Berkeley Square, for example, the drawing room included a panelled ceiling decorated with gold patterns on the beams, and pale pink walls that appeared below a frieze of peacocks executed by Albert Moore; in Miss Lehmann's dressing room Henry Smallfield painted groups of birds in flight on the doors. Again, when Aitchison took over the decoration of 1 South Audley Street from Frederick Pepys Cockerell in 1882, Walter Crane was called in to design the plaster reliefs on the stairs and the mosaic panels in the upstairs reception room, while the adjoining anteroom was decorated with a frieze of stylised plants and birds painted by W.E.F. Britten.

Unfortunately few of Aitchison's interiors survive, but much of the detail, as well as the overall design of his decorations, is illustrated in the collection of watercolour plans and elevations now housed in the Royal Institute of British Architects. These watercolours show rooms suffused in colours that reflect the delicate palette of the Aesthetic Movement, walls covered in intricately patterned foliate ornament, architectural features picked out in black and gold, and pictorial panels depicting animals, putti or birds. On several occasions Aitchison also designed furniture. Old photographs of Leighton House show a pair of dark wood pedimented bookcases in the studio and a massive angular ebonised fitted sideboard in the dining room, and records in the Gillows Archive indicate that several of Aitchison's designs were made up by this firm. As in every other area of his work, the dominant features of his furniture were sumptuousness and complexity, qualities that are admirably borne out in the comments contained in a lecture of 1895 when he declared: "The ground of the cornices will shine with eternal colours, the piers will be enriched with sparkling panels, and friezes of gold will run the length of our buildings ... This will not be false and paltry luxury; it will be opulence, it will be sincerity" (Richardson, 1980).

JOANNA BANHAM

Biography

Born in London, 7 November 1825, the son of George Aitchison (1792–1861), City architect. Articled to his father; trained at the Royal Academy Schools, London, 1847; graduated from the University of London, 1851; travelled in France and Italy, 1853–55. In partnership with his father from 1859; succeeded him as architect to St. Katherine's Dock Co., 1862; in private practice from 1864. Fellow of the Royal Institute of British Architects, 1862; Vice-President, 1889–93; President, 1896–99; Royal Gold Medalist, 1898. Associate of the Royal Academy, 1881; Professor of Architecture, 1887–1905; Member, 1898. A member of many foreign academies, he also wrote and lectured on architecture and decoration. Died in London, 16 May 1910.

Selected Works

A full list of Aitchison's architectural works appears in his obituary in *The Builder*, 21 May 1910, p.592. An important collection of his designs for decorations and furniture is in the Drawings Collection, Royal Institute of British Architects; additional drawings are in the Victoria and Albert Museum, London.

Interiors

1866–95 Leighton House, Holland Park Road, London (building, interiors and some furniture; Arab Hall, 1877–79): Frederic Leighton P.R.A.

1869 44 Belgrave Square, London (interiors, including the staircase and inner hall): Hon. Percy Wyndham

1872–75 15 Berkeley Square, London (interiors, including the green drawing room, drawing room, boudoir, dressing room, and furniture for the dining room): Frederick Lehmann M.P.

c.1882 1 South Audley Street, London (interiors, including the staircase, drawing room and anteroom): J. Stewart Hodgson

c.1886–95 29 Chesham Place, London (interiors, including the drawing room, music room and conservatory): Sir Sydney Waterlow

Publications

The Principles of Ornament, by James Ward, edited and enlarged by Aitchison, 1896

Further Reading

There is no published monograph on Aitchison but a useful survey of his career appears in Richardson 1980. For additional information on individual commissions, including references to primary sources, see RIBA catalogue 1969.

Calloway, Stephen, "The Eclectic Aesthetes" in *House and Garden* (US), February 1992, pp.100–05

Catalogue of the Drawings Collection of the Royal Institute of British Architects A–G, London: Gregg, 1969

Gere, Charlotte, *Nineteenth-Century Decoration: The Art of the Interior*, London: Weidenfeld and Nicolson, and New York: Abrams, 1989

Hall, Michael, "1 South Audley St., Mayfair" in *Country Life*, 5 November 1992

Jones, Stephen, "Lord Leighton's Palace of Art" in *Antiques*, June 1989, pp.1466–75

Lever, Jill, *Architects' Designs for Furniture*, London: Trefoil, and New York: Rizzoli, 1982

Ormond, Leonee and Richard, *Lord Leighton*, New Haven and London: Yale University Press, 1975

Richardson, Margaret, "George Aitchison: Lord Leighton's Architect" in *Journal of the Royal Institute of British Architects*, 1980, pp.37–40

Simon, Robin (editor), "Lord Leighton 1830–1896 and Leighton House: A Centenary Celebration" special issue of *Apollo*, 1996

Smith, Helen, *Decorative Painting in the Domestic Interior in England and Wales, c.1850–1890*, New York: Garland, 1984

Albertolli, Giocondo 1742–1839

Italian architect and designer of furniture

Giocondo Albertolli played an important role in the success of Neo-Classicism in Lombardy through his activities both as an architect and as a teacher. Etchings of his drawings were published during his lifetime and were dispersed all over Italy.

He was born at Bedano in Ticino. From 1753 he trained at the Accademia in Parma, and came under the influence of the ducal architect, the Frenchman E. A. Petitot. Subsequently he worked at the Villa Poggio Imperiale in Florence, in 1770, and after a second stay in Parma, lived in Rome and Naples, where he studied the antique. He worked at the Royal Palace in Milan in 1774. From 1774–75 he returned to Florence, where he worked on plaster ceilings for the Uffizi and the Pitti Palace.

He settled in Milan in 1775, where as professor of ornament until 1812 he had a close association with the newly established Milan Academy of Fine Arts at the Brera. He also practised as an architect and interior designer; his commissions including the interiors of the Royal Palace, where he began an important collaboration with Piermarini, one of the most influential contemporary architects. With the help of 30 assistants, he was engaged for over two years on his first commission at the palace, the magnificent interior of the central saloon, the Sala dei Cariatidi (1776). He also worked on other interiors in the palace and at the royal villa at Monza (1777–80).

Albertolli managed to combine a refined decorative vocabulary, derived from Antiquity and Renaissance classicism, with contemporary trends in European decorative arts. His decorative schemes are richly embellished with antique leaves, vine-tendrils, volutes, roundels, lozenges, candelabra, sphinxes, eagles and trophies, without a hint of the bizarre or the capricious. His ability to modulate rigorous symmetries enabled him to use refined stucco arabesques of great elegance and grace. These were highlighted with contrasting colours, such as delicate white on pale greens and gold and ivory on light blue, and in order not to compete with the architectural structure, their relief was barely perceptible.

Most of his work has been damaged or destroyed, either through bombing or demolition. However, his ideas on decoration can be studied through his many publications. These include imposing and refined Neo-Classical designs for furniture, metalwork and interior decoration. In his introduction to *Alcune decorazioni di nobili sale ed altri ornamenti* (1787), Albertolli declared the educational aims of his books, stating his hope that young students would not merely copy what they saw on the walls of the antique Roman baths, or at Herculaneum, for they may also have been painted by "second-rate painters", but that their source of inspiration should be great Roman architecture ("Roman architecture should be looked at, not painting"). These ideas closely linked Albertolli with G.B. Piranesi, though he made Piranesi's grandeur and emphasis more accessible by designing furniture which could blend with contemporary life and tastes. His furniture designs also differed from contemporary European fashions, and through their "severe, but graceful archaeological taste" they anticipate the developments in European furniture whose style emphasised the philological approach towards archaeological correctness (Gonzáles-Palacios, 1986).

Among the most interesting plates in *Alcune decorazioni* is number VI, which depicts a stool shaped as a tripod, inspired by antique prototypes. The supports are not as naturalistic as their Roman model, for acanthus leaves are placed on the "knees" of the legs, which end in hoofed feet, but the new element in Albertolli's design is the garland of oak leaves binding them together. The design was copied in carved wood, gilded to resemble gilt-bronze. It represents one of his few surviving documented pieces of furniture and, though restored, the stool is preserved in the Galleria d'Arte Moderna in Milan. Another surviving piece is the *faldistorium* / throne for Archbishop Filippo Maria Visconti. On the same plate in the *Alcune decorazioni* is a design for a sofa that resembles some of the prop-furniture used by Jacques-Louis David in his studio and which can be seen in his paintings.

Although the actual designer of the set of furniture decorating the salons at the Royal Palace in Milan is as yet unidentified, the furniture itself clearly reflects the influence of Albertolli's style. The sofa and chairs are decorated with carved and gilded rosettes, and this type of delicate, yet crisp low-relief carving, which is gilded against a light ground, is originally French. Though common in Piedmont it is seldom found in Lombardy, and Albertolli was the one of the few designers who used it in his furniture. Neo-Classical furniture in Lombardy more commonly included inlay / intarsia, a craft revived by Maggiolini. Albertolli and other designers, including Appiani and Levati, supplied designs for Maggiolini's marquetry panels, and Albertolli's complex compositions often included architecture, figures and delicate landscapes.

From 1808 to 1815 Albertolli designed the Villa Melzi, which is considered "one of the most significant [examples] of neo-classical architecture" (Ottino della Chiesa, 1959). He also designed its interior decoration and furniture, and in one of the villa's rooms is a *trompe-l'oeil* decoration simulating stucco reliefs of Roman trophies and armour and helmets which is closely connected to the decoration of the Royal Palace in Milan and relates to plate XIV of *Ornamenti diversi* (1782).

Albertolli's designs were both highly inventive and extremely influential. They suggested a new direction for interior schemes, and together with the wealth of ornamental motifs illustrated in his published works, they provided a rich source of inspiration for other architects and designers. And perhaps most importantly he represents an influential precursor of later Italian Neo-Classical designers such as Pelagio Palagi.

MARIELLA PALAZZOLO

Biography

Born in Bedano in Ticino, 24 July 1742, the son of Francesco Saverio. Moved to Aosta, 1752, then to Parma to study with his uncle, a sculptor, and at the Academy, under Giuseppe Peroni, 1753. Came into contact with E.-A. Petitot, the ducal architect, with whom he collaborated on a triumphal arch. Began working independently, 1765. Won prizes at the Academy, 1766 and 1768. Married in 1768. Worked in Milan on ecclesiastical and domestic decoration, together with Gerli, and got to know Piermarini, 1769; worked at Poggio Imperiale, Florence, 1770 and on church decoration in Parma, 1772. Visited Rome and Naples, where he worked with Carlo Vanvitelli on church of SS. Annunziata, 1772; in Florence, 1774–75. Professor of ornament at Milan Academy of Fine Arts, 1776–1812. Worked on the royal palaces in Milan, Monza, and Mantua, 1774–80, and on many private Milanese palaces and villas, 1808–15. Designed a monument to Napoleon, 1808–09. Published several books of ornament, 1782–1805. Died 15 November 1839.

Selected Works

The Archivio di Stato, Milan contains much documentary material relating to Albertolli.

Interiors

1769–70	Palazzo Grillo, Milan (building and interiors)
1770	Poggio Imperiale, Florence (stucco ceiling decoration): Leopold I of Lorraine
1774	Royal Palace, Milan (decorations in the Salone)
1774–75	Uffizi, Florence (ceilings of Sala della Niobe): Leopold I of Lorraine
1774–75	Pitti Palace, Florence (ceilings in Sala degli Stucchi, Appartamento della Meridiana): Leopold I of Lorraine
1775–79	Royal Villa, Monza (Throne Room)
1776	Royal Palace, Milan (Sala dei Cariatidi)
1808–15	Villa Melzi, Bellagio (building and interiors): Melzi family
c.1833	Villa Andreani, Moncucco (building and remodelling of chapel): Andreani family

Publications

Ornamenti diversi inventati, disegnati ed eseguiti, 1782
Alcune decorazioni di nobili sale, 1787
Miscellanea pei giovani studiosi del disegno, 1796, 2nd edition 1843
Corso elementare d'ornamenti architettonici, 1805
Cenni storici sovra una cappella antica, ricostruita in oratorio a Moncucco nella provincia di Milano, 1833

Further Reading

The standard monograph on Albertolli is Kauffmann 1911. Mezzanotte 1960 has a useful biography and bibliography.

Da Prato, Cesare, *Real Villa del Poggio Imperiale*, Florence: Seeber, 1895

González-Palacios, Alvar, *Il Tempio del Gusto: Le arti decorative in Italia fra classicismi e barocco*, part 2: *Granducato di Toscana e gli stati settentrionali*, 2 vols., Milan: Longanesi, 1986
Kauffmann, Arthur, *Giocondo Albertolli: Der Ornamentiker des italienischen Klassizismus*, Strassburg: Heitz, 1911
Laraguino, Emilio, *L'arte moderna dai neoclassici ai contemporanei*, revised edition Turin: Unione Torino, 1961
Martinola, G., "Notizie sull'architetto G. Albertolli", in *Archivio Storico Lombardo*, X, 1945–47, pp.1–4
Mezzanotte, P., "Albertolli, Giocondo" in *Dizionario Biografico Italiano*, Rome: Giovanni Treccani, 1963, pp.759–60
Ottino della Chiesa, Angela, *L'età neoclassica in Lombardia* (exhib. cat.), Como, 1959

Albini, Franco 1905–1977

Italian architect and designer

Franco Albini was an Italian architect, active before and after World War II, as much recognised for his work on interior displays and museum installations as for his buildings. He was born in 1905 in the countryside north of Milan into a well-to-do family and educated at the Politecnico in Milan where he graduated in 1929, serving his apprenticeship with Gio Ponti and Emilia Lancia, while at the same time making contacts with artisans and cabinet-makers which impressed upon him the importance of the crafts and the ways in which they could be used. It was also during this period that he discovered Modernism. In 1930 he established his own architectural practice, his first important building being that for the Istituto Nazionale delle Assicurazioni in Milan in 1935. This building embodied a form of design that was to remain with him all his working life. It incorporated something of the language of Mies van der Rohe and the Bauhaus, but tempered by the idea of an Italian tradition of design which encouraged him to move beyond the stricter limits favored by the Rationalist movement in Italy.

Albini's work was noted in the Milan Triennales of 1933 and 1936, and it was in 1936 that he designed the Appartamenti Minetti, Milan, and, with Renato Camus and Giancarlo Palanti, the much praised Fabio Filzi Workers Housing Estate in the Viale Argonne, Milan. The Fabio Filzi project won the Silver Medal in the Paris International Exhibition of 1937. It revealed his style to be in direct opposition to that enunciated in the journal *Architettura*, the magazine of the Fascist Syndicate of Architects and the Neo-Classical architect Marcello Piacentini, which controlled and dominated Italian architecture during the pre-war years.

The war led to a decline in Albini's commissions, but by the early 1950s he was once again fully employed, most notably in the Albergo Pirovano, Cervinia (1949–50) which looked back to Gropius and the Sommerfeld House, and the building for the Istituto Nazionale delle Assicurazioni, Parma (1950), recognised immediately to be one of the first significant post-war buildings in Italy. It was at this time also that Albini produced one of his most important interior designs, for the Municipal Galleries at the Palazzo Bianco, Genoa (1950–51). Here, he introduced to museum design the idea of simple walls and a kind of rationality which, according to the curator of the museum, would allow the works presented to be seen aesthetically and without what was termed sentimentality, that is to say false historical detailing; all the fittings were designed to take up the least space. In some ways this approach to the design of interior spaces looked back to a plan that Albini had envisaged for a design at the Brera in 1941. But at Genoa he established a model that all later museum designers in Italy, such as Carlo Scarpa, BPR, and others, would follow.

Albini worked on the restoration of the Palazzo Rosso, Genoa (1952–61) with his partner, Franca Helg, who joined him in 1952, and it was with Helg that he designed his most famous building, the Rinascente Department Store, Rome (1957–61). The design for this commission went through many stages, but in its final form the plan of the building was determined by a simple steel frame, the elements of this frame being emphasised, as critics noted, so that they look almost like the timbers of an old Japanese temple. Around and amidst this structure are set exposed, pre-cast, mostly windowless walls, that carried within them the service elements – air-conditioning and the like – all ending at the appropriate floors and defining from the inside out the size of each external unit. The result was a pattern of forms that enlivens the otherwise simple, even dull profile, the variations being accentuated further by the shadows of the spandrels above, and by the thin horizontal white bands placed at head height on each floor. As Helg declared, La Rinascente was an investigation into new construction techniques; it was also, according to the critic Paolo Portoghesi, a powerful argument against vulgarity and approximation that all designers should follow.

Albini continued to work on the problems of interior design, most notably in the designs executed in 1962–63 for the Milan metro system, and in the remodelling of the Civic Museum of Padua (1969–89), and Museo Sant'Agostino, Genoa (1963–69 and 1977–86). He was also responsible for a range of interesting and influential furniture designs. These began in 1932 with some lacquered wood furniture designed for the Dassi Company that were exhibited at the Milan Trade Fair. Far more radical, however, were the suspension bookshelves shown at the Milan Triennale in 1940. The structure of these shelves, employing carefully shaped, complex members of wood and brass, and steel cables both for suspending the shelves and acting as stays to the wooden members, recalled not only the structure of suspension bridges but also of ship architecture. They were quite unlike the usual kind of book storage and served as both shelves and room-dividers, a design feature that became increasingly popular in interiors of the 1950s and 1960s. Albini's designs for wicker chairs of the 1950s, and his *Tre Pezzi* tubular steel chair, show him to have also been working in popular contemporary materials. In the 1960s he branched out into lighting design executing a series of innovative designs for the Italian firms Arteluce (1960–62) and Sirrah (1968–71). His last major design commission, never realised, was for an Urban Design Center Kasar-El Hokm, Riyadh, Saudi Arabia (1976) which drew on ideas of civic planning which he had been concerned with from the 1930s.

Albini did not propose or refine a particular architectural theory, but he influenced a large number of Italian designers and architects through his practice and his teaching. From 1945 to 1948 he edited the journal *Casabella*, newly revived after the demise of Fascism; from 1949 to 1964 he was Professor of Architecture in Venice, and from 1964 to 1977 he

Albini: living room of Albini apartment, Milan, 1938–40

was Professor of Architectural Design at his old school, the Politecnico, Milan. From 1968 to 1969 he was also a member of the progressive Congrès Internationaux d'Architecture Moderne (CIAM).

His concern with accommodating the best of the long architectural traditions of Italy with the present social and political realities attracted a significant following and he was always able to gather around him a group of designers sympathetic to his way of working. In formal terms, perhaps, there is no distinctive Albini style, and his designs vary from one to another. But in all his work he tried to emphasise an idea of rationality, marked always with what has been termed the phenomenology of materials. Albini was much influenced in this by Adolf Loos; younger Italian designers like Gino Serfatti and Paolo Rizzatto have willingly acknowledged Albini's influence on them.

DAVID CAST

Biography

Born in Robbiate, near Como, 17 October 1905. Studied architecture at the Politecnico, Milan, and graduated, 1929. Married: son, architect Marco Albini (b.1940). Apprenticed in the studio of Gio Ponti (1891–1979). In private practice as an architect and designer in Milan from 1930; in partnership with Franca Helg (b.1920) from 1952; Antonio Piva from 1962; Marco Albini from 1965. Designs for furniture and exhibition layouts from late 1930s; museum conversions and interiors from 1950s. Editor of *Casabella*, 1945–48. Taught at University Institute of Architecture, Venice, 1949–64; Professor of Architectural Design and Architectural Interiors from 1952. Lecturer, American-Italian Commission of Cultural Exchanges, Rome, 1954–63; Professor of Architectural Composition, Politecnico, Milan, 1964–77. Received numerous awards including Compasso d'Oro Award, Milan, 1955, 1958, 1964; Olivetti National Architecture Medal, Milan, 1957; Biscione d'Oro Award, Milan, 1971. Honorary Royal Designer for Industry, Royal Society of Arts, London, 1971; Honorary Fellow, American Institute of Architects; Member, Scientific Institute of the Italian National Research Centre of Museography. Died in Milan, 1 November 1977.

Selected Works

For a full list of Albini's architectural projects see Leet 1990.

Interiors

1935	Istituto Nazionale delle Assicurazioni, Milan (building and interiors)
1936	Fabio Filzi Workers Housing Estate, Viale Argonne, Milan (buildings and interiors; with Renato Camus and Giancarlo Palanti)
1936	*Dwelling Exhibition*, Milan Triennale ("Room for a Man" and "Apartment for Four" exhibition layouts)
1937–38	Villa Pestarini, Piazza Tripoli, Milan (building and interiors)
1938–40	Albini Apartment, Milan (interiors and furnishings)
1940	*Criteria for the Modern Home*, Milan Triennale ("Living Room for a Villa" exhibition layouts)
1950	Istituto Nazionale delle Assicurazioni, Parma (building and interiors)
1950–51	Palazzo Bianco, Genoa (renovation and remodelling of the interiors)
1952–56	Museum of the Treasury of San Lorenzo, Genoa (building and interiors)
1952–61	Palazzo Rosso, Genoa (museum conversion, with Franca Helg)
1953	*Italian Contemporary Art, Design and Architecture*, Stockholm and Helsinki (exhibition layouts)
1954	Palazzo Rosso, Genoa (Marcenaro apartment conversion and interiors)
1957–61	La Rinascente department store, Rome (building and interiors)
1962–63	Metro stations, Milan (interiors with Franca Helg, Antonio Piva and Bob Noorda)
1963–69 & 1977–86	Sant' Agostino Museum, Genoa (restoration, additions and interiors, with Marco Albini, Franca Helg and Antonio Piva)
1969–89	Civic Museum, Padua (restoration and reorganization of Cloisters and New Painting Gallery; with Marco Albini, Franca Helg and Antonio Piva)

Albini designed numerous items of furniture from the 1930s. Notable examples include the *Tensistructure* suspension bookcases (1940), the *Margherita* and *Gala* wicker chairs (1950), the *Luisa* armchair (1954–55), and the *Tre Pezzi* tubular steel chair (1959). Albini's clients included La Rinascente, Carlo Poggi, Knoll International, Cassina, Arflex, Siemens, Fontana Arte and San Lorenzo. He also designed lighting for Sirrah from the late 1960s.

Further Reading

Argan, Giulio Carlo, *Franco Albini*, Milan, 1962

Branzi, Andrea and Michele De Lucchi, *Design Italiano degli Anni '50*, Milan: Domus, 1980

Campbell-Cole, Barbie and Tim Benton (editors), *Tubular Steel Furniture*, London: Art Book Company, 1979

Carloni, Livia, Enrico Valeriani and Benedetta Montevecchi, *Franco Albini: Architettura per un museo* (exhib.cat.), Rome: De Luca, 1980

De Seta, Cesare, *La Cultura Architettonica in Italia tra le due guerre*, 2nd edition Bari: Laterza, 1983
Fiell, Charlotte and Peter, *Modern Furniture Classics since 1945*, Washington, DC: American Institute of Architects Press, and London: Thames and Hudson, 1991
Franco Albini: Architettura e design, 1930–1970 (exhib. cat.), Florence: Centro Di, 1979; London: Academy, and New York: Rizzoli, 1981
Gregotti, Vittorio, *New Directions in Italian Architecture*, New York: Braziller, and London: Studio Vista, 1968
Leet, Stephen (editor), *Franco Albini: Architecture and Design, 1934–1977*, New York: Princeton Architectural Press, 1990
Louis de Malava, Florita Z., *Franco Albini* (bibliography), Monticello, IL: Vance, 1984
Samanà, Giuseppe, "Franco Albini e la Cultura Architettonica in Italia" in *Zodiac*, 1988, pp.83–115
Sparke, Penny, *Italian Design, 1870 to the Present*, London: Thames and Hudson, 1988; as *Design in Italy, 1870 to the Present*, New York: Abbeville, 1988

Allori, Alessandro 1535–1607

Italian painter and tapestry designer

Alessandro Allori was one of the most prolific and versatile Florentine artists of the second half of the 16th century. He was not only a successful painter of religious art and portraits, but also designed stage costumes, architectural decorations for baptisms, marriages and funerals, and cartoons for tapestries and embroidery. In addition he studied anatomy and wrote prose and poetry. As official artist to the Medici court, his work was both highly visible and extremely influential, and fusing Italian and Northern traditions, he played an important role in the dissemination of Mannerism in Italy.

After his father's death in 1540, Allori was brought up by the painter Agnolo Bronzino (1503–72), who also trained him. Allori designed many of the borders for the twenty tapestries depicting the *Stories of Joseph* made for the Sala dei Dugento in the Palazzo Vecchio in Florence (1549–53) while he was working in Bronzino's workshop. His skill in representing nature and in the use of an ornamental vocabulary which included masks and term-figures is already apparent in these designs.

Another important element in Allori's work derived from his interest in Flemish art which was nurtured by the presence at the Medici court of Northern artists, including Jan van der Straet (Joannes Stradanus) (1523–1605). The influence of Northern painting is found not only in the use of naturalistic elements, such as aquatic fauna and the presence of landscapes in his work, but also in Allori's approach to subject matter. Like many Netherlandish painters, he often included anecdotal and genre details illustrating characters or objects from everyday life; these encouraged the spectator to identify with the scene depicted.

Allori's stay in Rome from 1554 to 1559 completed his artistic education and, together with his Florentine training, it encouraged his reliance on drawing and anatomy. This is revealed in many of his tapestries on sacred and mythological themes where the influence of Northern art is combined with an elegant and refined treatment of figures which appear to be inspired directly by the Florentine nobility.

In 1565 Allori became a member of the Florentine Accademia del Disegno, and around the same date began an enormously prolific career – mainly in the service of the Medici court – which included grotesque painted decoration and designs for tapestries. In the same year he completed one of his most important early commissions, that for 132 costume designs for characters in the *Genealogy of the Gods*, performed on the occasion of the marriage of Francesco I de' Medici and Johanna of Austria. These designs became the source for all his future work. The design for *Truth*, for instance, recalls the "terms" which Allori designed for the borders of the *Story of Joseph* tapestries and for some of his frescoes. Many of his figures resemble those designed by Vasari but they have an added liveliness and are clothed in charming, if somewhat bizarre, highly decorated and detailed costumes. Versions of these figures can be seen in Allori's frescoes for the Medici villa at Poggio a Caiano (1576); a Roman consul and the vivacious Ambassador seated before him are closely connected with a series of his mythological drawings.

Allori also designed a set of tapestries on the theme of the *Hunting of Aquatic Birds* (1576), another important commission for the Poggio a Caiano villa. The set was woven by Benedetto Squilli by 1578. These tapestries have often been unfavourably compared with those by Stradano, but in Allori's work the realism and action of Stradano's designs have been transformed into subtle and refined stories in which noblemen and their entourages are depicted in romantic landscapes brought vividly to life by a profusion of plants and animals. One interesting topical detail is the reference to an exotic landscape suggested by the depiction of figures wearing loincloths made of fig-leaves, working in a pumpkin field. This landscape was inspired by accounts of the West Indies by Gonzalo Fernandez de Oviedo which were well known at the Medici court.

From 1578 Allori was engaged in the design of tapestries depicting Ovid's *Metamorphoses*. The design of these tapestries echoed that of historical frescoes; the main characters were placed in the centre of the composition with the lesser players arranged on either side. The figures themselves have a strong sculptural quality which is combined with graceful garments that are enriched with gold embroidery and diamond buckles. In the *Payment of the Soldiers* Allori sets the characters on different levels parallel to the picture plane. The composition is harmoniously built up using *figures repoussoires* (proscenium figures), and armour is scattered about on the ground like trophies to form a decorative pattern linking the centre to the borders. Allori's designs also took into account demands of weaving; these, and the religious tapestries of the same period, show a remarkable maturity and skill.

In addition to his tapestry designs, Allori executed painted grotesque work at the Uffizi in 1581, and was also active in the service of other Florentine patrons. He designed grotesques and frescoes for a new suite of rooms and for the chapel in Jacopo Salviati's Florentine palace between 1575 and 1580. But it is as a tapestry designer that he is now known. He never abandoned the Florentine tradition of drawing, derived especially from the Mannerist style of Vasari, even though this did not always suit the decorative function and style of the tapestry. And he was at his most successful when he was able to combine his own Italian cultural legacy with the love of detail and the decorative elements he drew from Northern art.

MARIELLA PALAZZOLO

Biography

Born in Florence, 1535. First apprenticed to the painter Agnolo Bronzino (1503–72). In Rome, 1554–59. Met Jan van der Straet (Giovanni Stradano, 1523–1605), a Flemish artist in Medici service, forming a long association in the provision of designs for tapestries. Member, Accademia del Disegno, 1565, and collaborated on the decorations for the marriage of Francesco I de' Medici and Johanna of Austria, 1565. Active in service of Medici family from c.1576–98, as designer and painter. Also worked for other Florentine noble families, and as portraitist and religious painter. Died in Florence, 1607.

Selected Works

Many of Allori's designs and drawings are held in the Uffizi Gallery, Florence. Most of his tapestries are held in deposit at the Palazzo Vecchio, Florence.

1549–53 Border designs for tapestries for Sala dei Dugento, Palazzo Vecchio, Florence: Grand Duke Cosimo I de' Medici
1564 Designs for the catafalque for Michelangelo's funeral in Florence: Medici family
1575–80 Palazzo Salviati, Florence (grotesques and frescoes for suite of rooms and chapel): Jacopo Salviati
1576 Villa Medici, Poggio a Caiano (suite of tapestries): Grand Duke Francesco de' Medici
1581 Uffizi, Florence (grotesque decorations for interiors): Grand Duke Francesco I de' Medici
1583–1607 Cartoons for four tapestries on bull fighting: Grand Duke Francesco I de' Medici
1594 Salone del Cinquecento in Palazzo Vecchio (tapestries): Grand Duke Ferdinando I de' Medici
1613–17 Tapestries with pastoral scenes woven after his designs: Medici family

Further Reading

There is little literature in English. The most comprehensive recent monograph and catalogue raisonné is Lecchini Giovannoni 1991. For Allori's tapestries see Adelson 1980 and 1991, and for his drawings Lecchini Giovannoni 1970.

Adelson, Candace, "Arazzi" in *Palazzo Vecchio: Committenza e collezionismo medicei* (exhib. cat.) Florence: Palazzo Vecchio, 1980, pp.43–116

Adelson, Candace, *The Tapestry Patronage of Cosimo I de' Medici, 1545–1553* (PhD. thesis, New York University, 1990), Ann Arbor, MI: University Microfilms, 1991

Becherucci, Luisa, "Alessandro Allori", in *Dizionario biografico degli italiani*, I, Rome: Istituto della Enciclopedia Italiana, 1960, pp.506–08

Cecchi, A., "A Design for Tapestry by Alessandro Allori", *Master Drawings*, XXV, 2, 1987, pp.146–49

Heikamp, Detlef, "Arazzi a soggetto profano su cartoni di Alessandro Allori", in *Rivista d'arte*, XXXI, 1956, pp.105–55

Heikamp, Detlef, "La manufacture de tapisseries des Médicis", in *L'Oeil*, 1968

Heikamp, Detlef, "Die Arazzeria Medicea im 16. Jahrhundert: Neue Studien", in *Münchener Jahrbuch der bildenden Kunst*, 1969, pp.33–74

Lecchini Giovannoni, Simona, *Mostra di disegni di Alessandro Allori (Firenze 1535–1607)* (exhib. cat.), Florence: Uffizi (Gabinetto Disegni e Stampe), 1970

Lecchini Giovannoni, Simona, *Alessandro Allori*, Turin: Allemandi, 1991

Pampaloni, Guido (editor), *Il Palazzo Portinari-Salviati oggi proprietà della Banca Toscana*, Florence: Banca Toscana, 1960

Rigoni, Cesare, *Catalogo della R. Galleria degli Uffizi*, Florence, 1891

Viale Ferrero, Mercedes, *Arazzi italiani del Cinquecento*, 2nd edition Milan: Vallardi, 1963

Amsterdam School

The name "Amsterdam School" is used in architectural history to denote Dutch Expressionist architecture between 1920 and 1930. This architecture is characterised by a very individual search for form, an intuitive, non-theoretical approach to the design brief and an expressive architectural vocabulary.

The Amsterdam School label, first launched by Jan Gratama in an exhibition catalogue in 1915, is not entirely accurate. The movement centred on Amsterdam, but there was no question of a school in a literal sense. The common bond was mutual friendship and artistic affinity. Most of the leading architects in the movement worked in the Amsterdam office of Eduard Cuypers (1859–1927) at the outset of their careers and knew each other from there. J. van der Mey, P.L. Kramer, Michel de Klerk, G.F. de la Croix and a number of others began there as draughtsmen. Cuypers's practice was international in outlook and allowed its staff considerable freedom. This enabled the up-and-coming architects in the office to familiarise themselves with "English free architecture" and with developments in Darmstadt, Munich and Vienna. Interest in the folk and other art of the Dutch East Indies was also encouraged by Cuypers, partly through his commissions there.

This training at the turn of the century was of great importance to the architects of the Amsterdam School. Not only did they have free access to developments abroad, but they also became acquainted with the broad spectrum of design: architecture, furniture, stained glass and even metalworking. This craft-based introduction to the profession and the synthesising of various sources of inspiration ultimately led them to a plastic and decorative approach in their architecture and applied art. In contrast to Hendrik Berlage's logical rationalism, the Amsterdam School designers stressed the primacy of the notion of form, which subsequently determined the choice of construction and material. The artist's intuition and concept of form were decisive for the end result.

The architecture, interiors and applied art of these architects were part of an all-embracing concept. On the one hand the plastic form of house fronts, the abstract brick ornamentation, the sculpture (reliefs) and the use of wrought iron emphasised the individuality of the building, while on the other hand giving form and definition to the urban space. This latter concern also manifests itself in a similar interest in the design of urban furniture in Amsterdam, including public toilets, transformer stations and tram shelters, municipal giro postboxes, and the detailing on bridges.

The expressive exterior was continued into the interior, with the decorative doors and windows, sometimes featuring stained glass, as the linking elements. The interior pendant to the plasticity of the house front is the panelling, which sometimes extends up from the walls to cover the ceiling, thus creating a spatial unity. Apart from its practical function the furniture serves the same role in spatial terms – each item has a clear plastic volume and presence. The parallel to the brick ornamentation and the reliefs of the exterior can be found in the detailing of the panelling and the furniture, in the use of various types of wood, veneer and fabric. Wrought metal also returns in the interior, no longer as neutral abstract decoration, but in the shape of hanging lamps and cupboard fittings. The formal elements used (trapezoids and parabolas) and the ornamentation are therefore generally co-ordinated and are repeated in various interior components.

At that time the main emphasis in interior design was on intimate domesticity. The windows must not be too big, and the curtains, and sometimes stained glass, subdued the light. If one was to achieve pleasing spatial proportions, the ceiling must not be too high – in older houses people were advised to lower the ceiling. The panelling and the spatially assertive furniture, together with the dark colour of the floor and wallpaper, resulted in a subdued atmosphere.

These characteristics of Amsterdam School interiors apply mostly to those designed as ensembles, as in the Scheepvaarthuis in Amsterdam (de Klerk, Kramer and others, 1913–16) or the Tuschinsky theatre there (Jaap Gidding, 1918–21). In the case of residential housing the nature of the design depended on the financial resources of the client. In the social housing projects in Amsterdam, for which the Amsterdam School has become best known, the window and door shapes were dispensed with, and there was scarcely any unity of interior and exterior. The furniture was far too expensive for working people, and, apart from that, too large for these homes. The leading designers had little or no interest in mass production. Commercial designs were produced in small runs of hand-made, labour-intensive and hence expensive furniture. The all-embracing concept of architecture and interiors was obviously incompatible with mass production and the freedom of choice it offered in constructing interiors.

Of the group of designers in the Amsterdam School, the architects de Klerk and Kramer were regarded as leading figures from an early date. Michel de Klerk (1884–1923), the most talented architect in the group, made his first sketches of furniture in 1910–11 during his travels through Scandinavia. The furniture designs from his first period (1910–14) are eclectic in nature – the inspiration of robust rustic furniture from the Skansen open-air museum in Stockholm combines with elements of Neo-Classical Biedermeier and motifs from the work of Mackintosh. The interior for J.H. Polenaar in The Hague (1913–14) or the boardroom of the Royal Netherlands Packetboat Company in the Scheepvaarthuis in Amsterdam (1912–14) can serve as examples.

The most characteristic furniture and interior designs by de Klerk were produced between 1915 and 1920, mainly in association with the interior design company 't Woonhuys in Amsterdam. De Klerk designed some 75 models, 50 of them in limited editions. These include several ensembles, such as bedroom designs or study suites. All the individual items of furniture, with their extravagant forms, make an emphatic statement in the interior: for example, the seats of the chairs are never square, but semi-circular, oval, triangular or polygonal. Their backs sometimes have the form of an exaggeratedly elongated triangle or oval and in the detailing they are reminiscent of a backbone, like some of Mackintosh's chairs. The stress-carrying function of the chair legs is disguised by all kinds of combinations of horizontal cross members and sledge-shaped feet. The cupboards and beds are massive, often parabolic or trapezoid, with rounded corners. These pieces of furniture were unusual not only in their basic shape, but also in the detailing, with additions such as claws, teeth or serrated points, which sometimes gave them an aggressive quality. The furniture was mostly made of pine covered with plywood and tropical veneers. The furniture designs from 1920 and after are somewhat more restrained in their form, with fewer decorative embellishments.

The furniture and interior designs of Pieter Lodewijk Kramer (1881–1961) were more plastic and compact in form than de Klerk's, and created with a greater eye for proportion. The detailing derives from the basic shape and is not added on. Kramer designed furniture from 1914 onwards, mostly for private clients, in association with various companies, the most important of which was the firm of Nussink en Zoon. Kramer's furniture designs were awarded a Grand Prix at the 1925 Exposition des Arts Décoratifs in Paris, which is an indication of the affinity between the later designs of the Amsterdam School and Art Deco. Kramer's most famous interior, which was unfortunately subsequently remodelled, is the Bijenkorf department store in The Hague (1924–26).

The interior work of the sculptor Hildebrand Lucien Krop (1884–1970) is scarcely distinguishable from that of Kramer. Krop too was aiming for plasticity in his furniture designs, and his training as a sculptor played a prominent part. This is mainly noticeable in the detailing: Krop himself carved the plastic ornaments. Krop also worked in association with the firm of Nussink en Zoon. He is best known for his sculptural embellishment of the Amsterdam bridges designed by Kramer.

The work of other designers of the Amsterdam School moved between linear decoration and a more plastic style, like that of Dirk Greiner (1891–1932) or Piet Vorking (1878–1960). The influence of de Klerk was sometimes visible, for example in the work of Jan A. Snellebrand (1891–1963) and Adolf Ebbink (1893–1975). The Tuschinsky cinema in Amsterdam (1918–21) by Jaap Gidding (1887–1960) represents a mixture of the Expressionism of the Amsterdam School and Art Deco. After 1925 the flow of new ideas from the Amsterdam School dried up and gave way to a more functional view of interior design.

OTAKAR MÁČEL
translated by Paul Vincent

Selected Collections

Examples of furniture by designers associated with the Amsterdam School are in the Rijksmuseum, and the Stedelijk Museums, Amsterdam; the Museum Boymans-Van Beuningen, Rotterdam; and the Gemeentemuseum, The Hague. A large collection of drawings by de Klerk is in the Netherlands Institute of Architecture, Rotterdam.

Further Reading

Adriaansz, E., "Fragmenten uit een Kleurrijk Oeuvre: Drie Bioscopen van Jaap Gidding" in *Jong Holland*, XI, no.2, 1995, pp.6–21

Burkom, Frans van, "Kunstvorming in Nederland" in *Nederlandse Architectuur, 1910–1930: Amsterdamse School* (exhib. cat.), Amsterdam: Stedelijk Museum, 1974, pp.71–102

Burkom, Frans van, *Michel de Klerk: Bouw- en Meubelkunstenaar (1884–1923)*, Rotterdam, 1990

Casciato, Maristella, *La Scuola di Amsterdam*, Bologna: Zanichelli, 1987

Fanelli, Giovanni and Ezio Godoli (editors), *Wendingen, 1918–1931* (exhib. cat.: Palazzo Medici-Riccardi, Florence), Florence: Centro Di, 1982

Frank, Suzanne, *Michel de Klerk 1884–1923, Architect of the Amsterdam School*, Ann Arbor: UMI Research Press, 1984

Kohlenbach, Bernard, *Pieter Lodewijk Kramer 1881–1961: Architect van de Amsterdamse School*, Naarden: V+K, 1994

Lagerweij-Polak, E.J., *Hildo Krop beeldhouwer*, The Hague: SDU, 1992

Mattie, Erik, *Amsterdam School*, Amsterdam: Architectura & Natura, 1991

Timmer, P., "The Amsterdam School and Interior Design: Architects and Craftsmen Against the Rationalists" in Wim de Wit (editor), *The Amsterdam School: Dutch Expressionist Architecture, 1915–1930* (exhib. cat.: Cooper-Hewitt Museum, New York), Cambridge: Massachusetts Institute of Technology Press, 1983, pp.121–143

Vriend, J.J., *The Amsterdam School*, Amsterdam: Meulenhoff, 1970

Antiquarianism

Antiquarianism is the study of antiquities. In the context of interior design, it refers to the collection and display of ancient objects, assembled from different periods, countries, and stylistic traditions and generally valued by the collector, or antiquary, more for age and historical significance than for aesthetic merit. The interior effect is an eclectic mix of objects and histories which exalt the past. The compelling stylistic impression of such an interior, which can indeed vary from room to room in an antiquarian house, might be of Britain in the Middle Ages, or of France at the time of Louis XIV, or of the Islamic Middle East, or even of ancient Greece or Asia. The distinguishing characteristics of an Antiquarian interior are: first, the use of ancient objects; second, the representation of a gamut of periods and styles; and third, the antiquary's individual intentions. Antiquarianism is characterized partly by objects amassed, and partly by the motives of those creating the interiors.

As vehicles of historical and personal reminiscence and monuments of idiosyncratic individuals, Antiquarian interiors remain outside the classification system for interior styles. Born as a reaction against the uniformity of contemporary interior styles, such as the despotic Rococo and Neo-Classical movements which were fully realized in France, Antiquarianism represented a search for a more personal, informal living experience. It developed concurrently with the Picturesque movement which admired the irregularity, drama, and variety of nature. The focus was pictorial and associational, as opposed to structural and archaeologically-correct as became the emphasis of the mature Gothic Revival of A.W.N. Pugin and the Ecclesiologists.

Antiquarianism was essentially the secularization of the great medieval church treasuries on the Continent, such as that of the Abbey of St. Denis, which remained intact until the 18th century. A more immediate precedent was the meticulously-catalogued secular collections, inclusive of man-made and natural items, of the 17th century. These included the Duke of Brandenberg's collection in Berlin, the Tradescant collection and the Earl of Arundel's specialized collection of classical and Renaissance antiquities in Britain, and museums on the Continent such as that of Dane Ole Worm and Italian museums – Ferrante Imperato, Museum Calceolarianum, and Museum Cospiano. Despite the continental precedents, Antiquarianism, like the Gothic Revival, evolved later on the Continent than in Britain. This is partly because of political and social unrest in France, specifically the French Revolution and the Napoleonic Wars.

The central figure in the creation of Antiquarian interiors during the 18th and 19th centuries was the patron – the antiquary. Since the 17th century, the terms *antiquary* and *antiquarian* had been associated with medieval objects and eccentric tastes, whereas *virtuoso* and *connoisseur* referred to genteel collectors of classical antiquities. The antiquary's work was time-consuming, dependent upon the slow assemblage of objects and decorative elements and the extended employment of numerous architects, upholsterers, designers, and antique brokers. Although each Antiquarian interior reflected the particular taste of its patron, there were furnishings common to all. Ancient carved woodwork and stone fragments, retrieved from demolished cathedrals, castles, and monasteries, were used in the creation of rooms and furniture. Windows featured stained glass, either antique plundered from medieval manors and churches or modern with heraldic references and an ancient appearance. A collection of armour was essential to any antiquarian house, as was medieval or Renaissance seating furniture. Most popular were triangular and ebony turned chairs, which, like the stained glass, could be rare antiques or modern renditions.

One of the first and greatest Antiquarian interiors of the 18th century was Horace Walpole's Strawberry Hill (1747–96). Every room was stuffed with objects: some of great historical interest such as Cardinal Wolsey's hat, a silver-gilt clock that was given to Anne Boleyn by Henry VIII, and an ancient oak chair from Glastonbury Abbey; some of aesthetic significance such as a French Limoges enamel casket, c.1540, and a Neo-Classical cabinet for miniatures; and some of innovative contemporary design like chairs designed by Walpole and Richard Bentley that introduced Gothic window tracery as a design source. The effect was a haunting Gothic-inspired work of architecture filled with educational relics. Strawberry Hill drew many visitors and in 1784 Walpole published an illustrated guide, *A Description of the Villa of Mr Horace Walpole Youngest son of Sir Robert Walpole Earl of Orford at Strawberry Hill near Twickenham Middlesex with an inventory of Furniture, Pictures, Curiosities &c* .

Exceptional Antiquarian interiors were beginning to appear in France during the last decades of the 18th century. Alexandre Lenoir opened his Musée des Monuments Français to the public in 1791. Alexandre Du Sommerard (1779–1842), one of the premier French collectors of medieval antiquities, created a series of Antiquarian interiors with a mystique rivaling Walpole's. Initially established in the rue de Menars, Sommerard moved to the rambling medieval Hôtel de Cluny in 1832. Here he opened his ever-expanding collection to the public, and for the next ten years it was one of Paris's great attractions and a focus for Romantic artists and antiquarians.

Antiquarianism: Alexandre Du Sommerard in his study, from *Les Arts du Moyen Age*, 1838–46

Celebrated antiquarians who assembled inspirational Antiquarian interiors in the 19th century include: rapacious collector and creator of Fonthill Abbey William Beckford (1760–1844); Romantic novelist and poet Sir Walter Scott (1771–1832); and arms and armour expert Sir Samuel Rush Meyrick (1783–1848). Publications, fiction and nonfiction, from Sir Walter Scott's *The Antiquary* (1816) to Henry Shaw's *Specimens of Ancient Furniture* (1836) and J.N.L. Durand's *Recueil et parallèle des Edifices de tout genre, anciens et modernes, remarquables par leur beauté, par leur grandeur ou par leur singularité, et dessinés sur une même échelle* (1800), coupled with increased nationalism across Europe, fueled a more universal interest in Antiquarian interiors and ancient regional styles.

The work of both Henry Shaw (1800–1873) and Thomas Willement (1786–1871) profoundly affected the movement's development during the early 19th century. In publishing *Specimens*, Shaw made available for the first time accurate graphic representations of still-existent ancient furniture pieces. In the late 1830s, Willement pioneered both the design of Gothic-inspired heraldic stained glass and encaustic tiles, and that of Elizabethan-styled wallpapers, best exemplified in his work to rehabilitate Charlecote Park (1830–39). The effect was ancient in mood and inspiration, but modern and convenient in living.

More than simple imitation of historical styles or the superficial incorporation of ornament, antiquaries sought to establish a sense of history. However, by the mid-19th century Antiquarian interiors lost many of their erudite associations and became more popularized. A bustling antiques trade flooded the market with objects of dubious provenance and age while an ever-increasing number of cabinet-makers specialized in modern versions of antique styles. Increasingly, Antiquarian interiors came to resemble "Old Curiosity Shops," as opposed to dens of historical instruction and ancient mood. And while the collections amassed by patrons such as Beckford and Walpole had prefigured a more widespread romantic interest in the Middle Ages, the archaeologically-correct approach of medieval scholars such as Pugin sounded its death-knell.

The legacy of Antiquarianism rests on the one hand with the practice, that continues today, of furnishing a home with antiques and bric-a-brac. On the other hand, Antiquarianism foreshadowed elements of the Arts and Crafts Movement: William Morris, for example, shared antiquarians' passion for history and objects with tangible signs of age, albeit to a more rustic end. Finally, Antiquarianism of the 18th and 19th centuries also served as a precedent and foundation for many of today's major museums. Sir Samuel Rush Meyrick's Goodrich Court (1829–35), representing interior styles from the Middle Ages to contemporary France, is the forebear of museums containing period rooms.

ELIZABETH A. FLEMING

See also Beckford; Gothic Revival

Further Reading

The key text for an understanding of Antiquarianism in general, and for a detailed and scholarly discussion of its manifestations in England, is Wainwright 1989 which also includes numerous references to primary sources.

Banham, Joanna, Sally MacDonald and Julia Porter, *Victorian Interior Design*, London: Cassell, 1991; as *Victorian Interior Style*, London: Studio, 1995

Bridgens, Richard, *Furniture, with Candelabra and Interior Decoration*, 1825–26

Gere, Charlotte, *Nineteenth-Century Decoration: The Art of the Interior*, London: Weidenfeld and Nicolson, and New York: Abrams, 1989

Jervis, Simon, "The Pryor's Bank, Fulham" in *Furniture History*, X, 1974, pp.87–98

Jervis, Simon, *Browsholme Hall, near Clitheroe, Lancashire: The Historic Home of the Parker Family*, Derby: English Life, 1980

Joy, Edward, "Elizabethan Furniture of the Early 19th Century" in *Antique Dealer and Collector's Guide*, May 1979, pp.74–77

Mowl, Timothy, *Elizabethan and Jacobean Style*, London: Phaidon, 1993

Shaw, Henry, *Specimens of Ancient Furniture*, 1836

Thornton, Peter, *Authentic Decor: The Domestic Interior, 1620–1920*, London: Weidenfeld and Nicolson, and New York: Viking, 1984

Wainwright, Clive, "Specimens of Ancient Furniture" in *Connoisseur*, 184, October 1973, pp.105–113

Wainwright, Clive, "Walter Scott and the Furnishings of Abbotsford; or, The Gabions of Jonathan Oldbuck, Esq." in *Connoisseur*, June 1974

Wainwright, Clive, "Charlecote Park, Warwickshire" in *Country Life*, CLXXVII, 1985, pp.446–50 and 506–10

Wainwright, Clive, *The Romantic Interior: The British Collector at Home, 1750–1850*, New Haven and London: Yale University Press, 1989

Antiques Movement

Before the middle of the 19th century, collecting was practised mainly by wealthy antiquarians and connoisseurs and was restricted to the rare and ancient. Men such as Horace Walpole at Strawberry Hill and Sir Walter Scott at Abbotsford purchased antiquities and architectural fragments from shops and auctions throughout Europe, or acquired them as presents from friends on their travels. Provenance was of great importance to these collectors who preferred to buy directly from private sources rather than from dealers whose practice it was to "improve" old furniture. Brokers in curiosities, or "nicknacktarians" as they were also known, provided another source of exotic artefacts for the romantic interior.

By the 1870s there was a new emphasis on the amateur collector and collecting was extended to more commonplace objects, "those excellent ordinary works of art" as Mrs. Orrinsmith described them in her popular publication, *The Drawing Room* (1877). The influence of the Queen Anne style, with its stress on informality, irregularity and asymmetrical arrangements, stimulated the demand for antiques. Faded fabrics and patina blended with muted colour schemes that were then in vogue. Collecting became a pleasurable pastime and the arrangement of pieces a creative activity, especially for women. The countless publications on the subject of home decorating and furnishing that appeared during this period all offered extensive advice on how to identify, purchase and use antiques.

The craze was current on both sides of the Atlantic. Clarence Cook declared in the well-known book, *Artistic Houses* (1883) that the interest in "old furniture" was "a fashion, that has been for twenty years working its way down from a circle of rich, cultivated people, to a wider circle of people who are educated, who have natural good taste, but who have not so much money as they could wish". The development of national consciousness that emerged around the time of the Philadelphia Centennial in 1876 provoked interest in past styles and indigenous antiques. Charles Allerton Coolidge, Francis H. Bacon, and Wilson Eyre were among those whose decorative work exhibited a respect for the Colonial and Federal eras.

Old furniture fulfilled a need to proclaim personal, social, and national affiliation. It suggested permanence in the home in opposition to the seemingly ever greater pace of change outside. Permanence additionally implied social status; old families had old things. Old furniture also had a romantic and emotional appeal, as H.J. Jennings in *Our Homes and How to Beautify Them* (1902) explained:

> Fashions have changed, beliefs have broadened, intellectual revolutions have taken place; yet the old chairs and cabinets and commodes remain to remind us .... Vita brevis, Ars longa. What stories they might tell us could they but speak, what gossip of long-ago romances and intrigues, of jealous quarrels, of tipsy, hot-blooded revels ending in tragedy, of elopements to Gretna Green, of all-night carousals, of high and reckless gaming, of all the excitement and stress and turmoil of a life and society that have passed away!

Sources for old furniture were plentiful. J.H. Elder Duncan, in *The House Beautiful and Useful* (1907) recommended "the quaint little second-hand furniture shops in Wardour Street and elsewhere" as useful places to go, although he admitted that it was no longer as easy to find bargains as it had been twenty years before. The painter Dante Gabriel Rossetti was a well-known customer of these shops and was one of the first people to start collecting the new antiques. He greatly admired English 18th century furniture for its simplicity and craftsmanship and according to Henry Teffry Dunn, his assistant, he "delighted to take an evening's walk through Leicester Square, visiting the various curiosity shops in that neighbourhood, or through Hammersmith, a district where many a Chippendale chair or table could be met with and bought for next to nothing, such things not being then in the repute that they have become since the taste for Queen Anne houses and fittings sprang up". What distinguished Rossetti's interiors in his house on Cheyne Walk from the earlier Antiquarian ones was that there was no precise historical theme. Gothic preferences were now supplemented by a liking for later objects and there was no evocation of any one period, just a generally old atmosphere, using "all conceivable superannuated designs".

The term "Antique Dealer" first appeared in London trade directories in 1886. By the turn of the century there were over 200 "Antique Dealers" listed for central London alone. In 1918 the British Antique Dealers' Association was established. Most large retail shops like Waring and Gillow and Heal's had antique departments. A great deal of publicity was given to this type of furniture. Articles were regularly published in both the trade press and in fashionable magazines.

Antiques were soon, however, in short supply. Ella Rodman Church, writing on the situation in America in *How to Furnish a Home* (1881), advised her readers to fill the many shelves of their artistic chimneypieces with bric-a-brac including "one's own or someone else's great-grandmother's candlesticks". If these were lacking, one was forced to visit "the Broadway bazaar, filled with antiques and supercilious clerks, with fabulous prices for the simplest articles". In 1884 the American magazine *Cabinet-Making and Upholstery* told its readers that "there is little doubt but the manufacture of antiques has become a modern industry". A massive trade in reproduction and period-style furniture flourished in both Britain and America until the middle of the 20th century.

The first serious book on furniture history in Britain, *An Illustrated History of Furniture* was published by a Wardour Street dealer, Frederick Litchfield, in 1892. The new kinds of books helped to assess authenticity; the new kind of dealer had to guarantee it. Early faking of old furniture, from the beginning of the 19th century onwards, consisted chiefly of making new pieces by reassembling old pieces of timber, or by carving plain old pieces. By the 1870s this practice was already ridiculed, as was the buying of "family portraits from Wardour Street". Charles Locke Eastlake also condemned the application of thick varnish with the aim of making furniture look old. Indeed, so widespread was the production of fakes or articles of dubious provenance that J.H. Elder Duncan declared: "Beyond a few dozen pieces of furniture made for royal households or ennobled families, where their history is preserved or known, it is unsafe to proclaim a single article that comes into the market as the authentic work of any known master".

An interest in antiques and period decoration was also fostered by the practice widespread in many late 19th century middle-class homes, of furnishing rooms in different styles according to prevailing fashions. This custom was equally, and perhaps not surprisingly, encouraged by the furniture trade, who produced vast catalogues of period styles promoting different styles for different rooms. Halls were typically decorated in Renaissance (Italian / Flemish / French) styles, dining rooms in Early English (Elizabethan / Jacobean) styles, drawing rooms in English or French 18th century styles (Chippendale / Adams / Louis XV or XVI), and bathrooms in Pompeian style. While it was widely accepted that these different styles might be appropriate to different rooms in the house, the resulting eclecticism was nevertheless often deplored. Mrs. Panton, for instance, in *Suburban Residences and How to Circumvent Them* (1897) attacked "the jumble of styles made by having an eastern-looking hall, an Old English dining room, a Queen Anne drawing room, and Moorish landing, which is inexpressibly dear to the would-be artistic decorator". And Jacob von Falke, whose *Art in the House* was published in Boston in 1879, observed in connection with the International Exhibition held in Vienna in 1873 that, "in so far as style is concerned the modern Frenchman dwells in the eighteenth century, he sleeps in that century likewise, but he dines in the sixteenth, then on occasion he smokes his cigar in the Orient, while he takes his bath in Pompeii, Rome". But, despite criticisms of this kind, eclecticism remained fashionable in wealthy artistic circles until the middle of the 20th century.

The aristocracy were more likely to furnish in a more historically consistent manner, often to provide a setting for their collections of art and antiques. Baron Ferdinand de Rothschild's massive English home, Waddesdon Manor in Berkshire, for example, was built in French Renaissance style but was furnished and decorated in French 18th century style so as to complement his family's fine collection of works of art of that period. Many of the interiors were designed to incorporate elaborately carved Rococo *boiseries* taken from houses in France. Several fashionable society decorators in the 20th century, such as Elsie de Wolfe, Sybil Colefax and later Madeleine Castaing and John Fowler, also advocated using antique furnishings although these were frequently combined with more modern elements in order to create a more eclectic but at the same time classically elegant style. The work of John Fowler, in particular, was extremely influential in promoting the English Country House style that has proved so enduringly popular in wealthy upper-middle-class circles since World War II.

For more middle income homeowners of the late 19th and early 20th century the choice of period furnishings was seemingly endless and the profusion of hybrid styles is extremely difficult to disentangle. But it was 18th-century English furniture which provided the mass of objects for the amateur collector and which most readily provided the comfort required of the new type of home. This period also had the additional advantage that many pieces could be labelled with the name of a designer. Chippendale was probably the best-known name and the most misused. H.J. Jennings explained:

> It may be taken for granted that a vast deal of the so-called "chippendale" furniture was not manufactured by Chippendale at all – was not even designed by him. And here it is permissible to say a word concerning the ignorance with which a great many people talk about this interesting but rather vague personality of the eighteenth century. When a few years ago the beauty and refinement of old cabinet-work came into more general recognition, they caught up the name of Chippendale, and have been

repeating it, they and their parrot-like successors – with the persistency of Poe's *Raven* ever since ... they prate about Chippendale, and fly into noisy raptures over any article, no matter how devoid of taste, that goes by his name.

One of the most successful manufacturers of reproduction furniture in East London this century carried the name Chippendale Workshops. With West End showrooms that stocked antique furniture alongside their own fine reproductions such firms did much to erode the distinction. Many people who became homeowners during the inter-war years in Britain were unconcerned about authenticity; what mattered was quality and durability.

During the 1950s young artistic couples setting up home began to collect second-hand Victorian furniture because it was cheap and well-made compared to the mass-produced furniture of the post-war period. This precipitated the craze for Victoriana in the 1960s. The revivalist and Authentic Decor movements of the 1980s have promoted a taste for the furnishings of many different periods and have encouraged the proliferation of antique shops and markets we see today.

JULIA PORTER

Selected Collections

Good collections of 19th- and 20th-century decorating books, periodicals and trade catalogues are available in the Geffrye Museum, and the Silver Studio Collection, Middlesex University, London, and in the design library of the Cooper-Hewitt Museum, New York. The National Monuments Record, London, holds a large collection of H. Bedford Lemere's photographs of late Victorian and Edwardian interiors, which demonstrate the exuberance of period styles. Several well-documented pieces of 19th century reproduction furniture are in the Victoria and Albert Museum, London.

Further Reading

There is no monograph devoted to this subject, but a useful survey of the history and origins of the collecting of antiques appears in Muthesius 1988. Additional and, at times, more revealing information can be found in contemporary decorating books, periodicals and trade catalogues.

Agius, Pauline, *British Furniture, 1880–1915*, Woodbridge, Suffolk: Antique Collectors' Club, 1978

Artistic Houses, Being a Series of Interior Views of a Number of the Most Beautiful and Celebrated Homes in the United States, 2 vols., New York, 1883–84; reprinted New York: Blom, 1971

Banham, Joanna, Sally MacDonald and Julia Porter, *Victorian Interior Design*, London: Cassell, 1991; as *Victorian Interior Style*, London: Studio, 1995

Calloway, Stephen, "The Lure of Antiques and the Modern Style" in his *Twentieth-Century Decoration: The Domestic Interior from 1900 to the Present Day*, London: Weidenfeld and Nicolson, and New York: Rizzoli, 1988, pp.141–213

Church, Ella Rodman, *How to Furnish a Home*, New York, 1881

Cooper, Nicholas, *The Opulent Eye: Late Victorian and Edwardian Taste in Interior Design*, London: Architectural Press, 1976; New York: Watson Guptill, 1977

de Wolfe, Elsie, *The House in Good Taste*, New York: Century, 1913; reprinted New York: Arno, 1975

Elder Duncan, J.H., *The House Beautiful and Useful*, London: Cassell, 1907

Falke, Jacob von, *Art in the House*, Boston, 1879

Gere, Charlotte, *Nineteenth-Century Decoration: The Art of the Interior*, London: Weidenfeld and Nicolson, and New York: Abrams, 1989

Jennings, H.J., *Our Homes and How to Beautify Them*, London: Harrison, 1902

Mayhew, Edgar de Noailles, and Minor Myers, Jr., *A Documentary History of American Interiors from the Colonial Era to 1915*, New York: Scribner, 1980

Muthesius, Stefan, "Why do we Buy Old Furniture? Aspects of the Authentic Antiques in Britain 1870–1910," in *Art History*, 11, June 1988, pp.231–254

Wharton, Edith and Ogden Codman, Jr., *The Decoration of Houses*, New York: Scribner, 1897; reprinted New York: Arno, 1975

Arabesque and Grotesque

Arabesque and Grotesque forms have been arguably the most popular and widely-used forms of ornament in the history of decoration and interior design. Originating in Roman times, they have played an important role in determining styles of surface decoration across several different cultures and nationalities and over many different periods. Versions of arabesque and grotesque motifs have also been used on a wide variety of two- and three-dimensional objects and in a range of different media including painted and printed designs, woven textiles, inlaid furnishings and engraved metalwork. Their use within interior decoration has been particularly significant, traversing the Renaissance, Mannerist and Neo-Classical periods, and encompassing the work of some of the most celebrated artists and designers from the 16th to the 19th centuries.

Although the descriptive adjectives *arabesque* and *grotesque* came into the vocabulary from different circumstances, they have a common source in Ancient Rome where a flowing, fanciful form of painted decoration incorporating scrolls, animals and flowers framing landscape scenes or mythological figures was used on walls and ceilings in the 2nd century BC and, to a lesser extent, in carved marble acanthus and vine scrolls, as well as in mosaics. These ornaments, especially scrolls and tendrils which acquired a religious significance, continued to be used in mosaics in Early Christian churches in Rome, Ravenna and Sicily, as well as in decoration in the Byzantine Eastern Empire. When the latter collapsed and was partly overrun by the Arabs they adopted many of these decorative characteristics while omitting human and animal forms. Hence the complicated interwoven and geometric patterns of Arabian and Moresque ornament which developed from around the 12th century. This, in turn, began to return to Europe in the form of patterns on damascened (inlaid with gold or silver) and engraved metalwork from Mesopotamia, Persia and Syria. Oriental carpets, too, with their repeating patterns of medallions and cartouches embedded in field patterns of flowing stems or with geometric strap patterns, may be regarded as another arabesque influence. Both metalwork and carpets were imported through Venice, and the velvets and damasks (another reference to Damascus) worn in Venetian paintings of the 15th century illustrate the vogue for arabesque ornament, which was given another and more important direction towards the end of the century in Rome.

Giorgio Vasari is the great source of information about

Arabesque and Grotesque: detail of satin bedtester, decorated with appliqué and embroidered with Renaissance design of strapwork and grotesques, French, c.1550

what he called "the new fashion of grotesques". In his famous *Lives of the Most Eminent Painters, Sculptors and Architects* he credited the painter Morto da Feltro with the introduction of the rediscovered 2nd century BC painted and stucco decoration on the walls and ceilings of the Imperial palaces of Nero and Titus, which by that time had become buried under accumulated earth so that they could be entered only through shafts as if they were *grotte* or caves. Hence the name *grotteschi*. Vasari described how Raphael and Giovanni da Udine were "struck with amazement [at] these grotesques ... executed with so much design, with fantasies so varied and so bizarre, with their delicate ornaments of stucco divided by various fields of colour, and with their little scenes so pleasing and beautiful". These light and airy, often fantastic, decorations introduced a freedom of expression to the late 15th century artists who viewed what remained of them by torchlight.

It is the name of Raphael that is most closely associated with the revival and development of grotesque decoration. In 1516 he was decorating two rooms in the Vatican for Cardinal Bibbiena; the smaller was painted in wax and was dark in colour because of the use of Pompeian red. Ovid's *Metamorphoses* provided the subjects of the little ceiling and wall scenes within painted frames, and cupids ride on chariots drawn by unlikely creatures. The walls and ceiling of the larger logetta are decorated with mythological scenes within cartouches and medallions which are surrounded by garlands of leaves, cherubs, birds, masks and hour-glasses against a white background, while *trompe-l'oeil* niches contain figures of the Seasons.

Raphael's next commission in this manner was for the more famous *loggie* in the Vatican for Leo X, a work with an extraordinary progeny. A gallery, originally open, was designed by Bramante but left unfinished when he died in 1514. Raphael completed the building and designed the overall decoration of the thirteen vaulted bays as an intricate arrangement of stucco and fresco decoration. Each bay is different in design, but there is an overall unity of concept and colour, and a varied arrangement of major elements such as cartouches and medallions on the walls, vaults and pillars. According to Vasari, this was executed largely by Giovanni da Udine under Raphael's direction, and he wrote with enthusiasm of the lifelike birds with their bright plumage, the vegetables and fruits, the garlands of flowers, the musical instruments, the fishes and sea-monsters that were all to be found in "the most beautiful, the most rare, and the most excellent painting that has ever been seen by mortal eye". Giovanni also worked with Raphael and Giulio Romano (who decorated an exquisite bathroom in this manner in Castel Sant'Angelo for Pope Clement VII) on the Villa Madama, a suburban residence for Leo X and Cardinal Giulio de'Medici. Work began in 1518, but the death of Raphael in 1520, followed by that of the Pope the next year, meant that only a fragment of the whole design was realised. Nevertheless, the portico with its delicate stuccowork on the walls and its vaulting painted with disciplined grotesque decoration, is among the finest examples of this brilliant style.

Another celebrated example is Pirro Ligorio's *Casina* in the Vatican for Pius IV, in which he had the assistance of Federico Barocci; but the fashion for grotesque decoration also spread to other Italian cities. Baldassare Peruzzi is credited with the appropriately named Sala detta del Magnifico in the Palazzo Vecchio, Florence, and there are endless examples in Tuscany and the Veneto in private palaces and villas. Among them reference must be made to Palazzo Farnese, Caprarola, where in the 1560s Taddeo and Federico Zuccari painted the ceilings of the huge rooms with mythological scenes set in elaborate grotesque decoration on a white ground. Each ceiling had to follow a detailed programme provided by Cardinal Alessandro Farnese. The famous open circular staircase leading up to them was painted by Antonio Tempesta in the 1580s; the walls and barrel vaulting are completely covered with grotesque panels, niches, large landscapes, and the crowning dome has three tiers of allegorical figures and *putti*, rising to the escutcheon of the Farnese family.

Italian artists worked in France and England. At Fontainebleau, Rosso Fiorentino from 1530 to 1540 and Francesco Primaticcio from 1540 to 1570 introduced elements of the grotesque in the Mannerist decoration for François I and founded a School of Fontainebleau continued by other artists, Ambroise Dubois, Martin Fréminet and Toussaint Dubreuil who worked for Henri IV and Marie de' Medici at the end of the 16th century. Grotesques still played a part in their designs. There was nothing comparable in England, but painted grotesque panels now at Loseley Park, Surrey, probably from a royal house (maybe Henry VIII's Nonesuch) and dateable to the 1540s, are very likely Italian in origin. The decorated pilaster strip, Roman in origin, in which repeated vase or candelabrum shapes are surrounded by freely flowing scrolls, tendrils and snakes, appeared in Italian paintings before the end of the 15th century, and it was used in inlaid choir stalls and marble wall monuments as well as in grotesque stucco decoration throughout the 16th century. It was this type of decoration that introduced grotesque ornament to other European countries. Simon Thurley in *The Royal Palaces of Tudor England* (1993) illustrates how such patterns as those engraved by Giovanni Pietro da Birago were closely followed in carvings in the Château de Gaillon in Normandy, while Margaret Jourdain in *English Interior Decoration* (1950) has made the connection between an engraving of a panel of grotesque ornament by Abraham de Bruyn and a chimneypiece at Boston House, Brentford, Middlesex. Hans Holbein's painting of *Henry VIII and the Barber-Surgeons* (1540) shows grotesque pilaster strips on the wall, and one by an unknown artist of *The Somerset House Conference* (1604) includes pilaster strips in the background and an imported oriental carpet on the table – a combination of grotesque and arabesque.

Henry VIII's break with Rome led to a change in European artistic currents and to the increased influence of Flemish and German pattern books, such as those by Vredeman de Vries and Wendel Dietterlin with their tortured versions of Mannerist decoration which included, *inter alia*, strapwork which, in a simplified form, could be used in woodwork and plasterwork. Some of these designs suggest why the term *grotesque* began to acquire a different meaning and *arabesque* became more commonly used. The flattened form of strapwork decoration, although related to grotesques, seems to have acquired some literally arabesque qualities, and the star-shaped patterns of ribs in some ceilings sometimes suggest an Eastern influence, while that in the Cartoon Gallery at Knole, Kent (early 17th century) could be a design for damask, although

Arabesque and Grotesque: engraving by Jean I Berain (1640–1711)

the wall pilasters are strongly Raphaelesque. The riotous exhibition of strapwork in the Great Hall at Hatfield House, Hertfordshire (c.1610) is an extreme example of what had happened to the graceful Italian *grotteschi* in their passage to England.

In France, versions of the grotesque were incorporated in the designs of Jean Berain, who designed architectural details, furniture, paneling and wall hangings in which fantastic architecture combined with sphinxes, satyrs, cupids and festoons. Similar designs were introduced in the tortoiseshell and brass marquetry furniture known as Boullework after the name of the royal *ébéniste* to Louis XIV, André-Charles Boulle, who collaborated with Berain in a publication, *Nouveaux Deisseins de Meubles et ouvrages* (from 1707) but the inlay technique was probably derived from imported damascened metalwork.

The decorative painter Andien de Clermont's work at Radnor House, Twickenham (c.1740–45) and Kirtlington Park, Oxfordshire (c.1745) is light-hearted Rococo-grotesque in style, but a more serious revival was prompted partly by the excavations at Herculaneum and Pompeii, and partly by the influx of architects from England and France who went to Rome to study Antique architecture and decoration; at the same time they rediscovered Raphael's *loggie*. James Stuart's Painted Room at Spencer House, London (1759) is an early example of the new trend, but Robert Adam was more accurate in his versions which were based on his own investigations with Charles-Louis Clérisseau in Rome (e.g., the Dining Room, Osterley Park c.1766–68; the Library at Kenwood, 1767–69; and the Dining Room, Shardeloes c.1761). Grotesque pilaster strips derived from the Vatican *loggie* and low relief wall panels in grotesque / arabesque style became hallmarks of the Adam style, in which such skilled painters as Biagio Rebecca collaborated. James Wyatt, again with Rebecca's assistance, worked in a similar style (e.g., the Cupola Room at Heaton Hall c.1772 and the Saloon at Heveningham Hall c.1797–99). The publication of George Richardson's *A Book of Ceilings in the Style of the Antique Grotesque* (1776) as well as the Adam brothers' *Works in Architecture* (1773–79) provided models for copying.

Clérisseau was able to take advantage of his studies with Adam to devise grotesque decoration in several countries. In Rome there was the coffee house at Villa Albani, (1764), in Paris one of the rooms in the Hôtel de la Reynière "dans le style arabesque" (c.1775); and he made designs for similar decoration in a Roman House at St. Petersburg (1773). Etienne de la Vallée also painted panels for the Hôtel de la Reynière and he published *Nouvelles Collection d'arabesques propres à la decoration des appartements* (1778). There was similar decoration in François-Joseph Bélanger's Pavillon de Bagatelle (1777) and for Marie-Antoinette at Fontainebleau (1780–85) by the Rousseau brothers. The exquisitely hand-blocked wallpapers designed by Jean Baptiste Fay and printed by J.-B. Réveillon in the 1780s made the style even more accessible. In Italy there are countless late 18th century examples of variants on the grotesque, although there too arabesque had become the favoured description. Stefano Tofanelli's decoration of the main rooms in Villa Mansi, Segromigno in the 1780s is an outstanding and imaginative sequence. In Rome the great rooms in Villa Borghese were systematically redecorated by Antonio and Mario Asprucci from 1781, and later by Luigi Canina.

It was a fashion that was easily absorbed into the Imperial taste of the early 19th century, exemplified by the work of Napoleon's favourite architects, Percier and Fontaine, and it was strong enough to survive for many decades. A more archaeological and boldly coloured revival of Roman styles of decoration, for example, had emerged c.1800 with the so-called Pompeian style, stimulated by new discoveries and excavations at Pompeii. Versions of this style appeared in Germany and France throughout the first and second quarters of the 19th century; Karl Friedrich Schinkel designed a Pompeian tea salon for Friedrich William IV in Schloss Charlottenburg (1820s) and Alfred Normand recreated a Pompeian interior for Prince Jérome Napoleon's Paris house (1854–59).

A more recent flowering of grotesque and arabesque ornament occurred among Renaissance Revival designers of the mid- and late 19th century such as the artist and designer Alfred Stevens, and his contemporary Godfrey Sykes. Much of Sykes's work, supervising the decoration of the South Kensington Museum (now the Victoria and Albert Museum), survives today, and illustrates not only the vigorous character of his Italianate grotesques but also the longevity and enduring appeal of this style.

DEREK LINSTRUM

See also Berain; Raphael; Udine

Further Reading

The standard account of the discovery of antique grotesque decoration appears in Dacos 1969. For useful surveys of the history and application of Grotesque and Arabesque ornament see Gruber 1993 and Pons 1993, both of which include extensive bibliographies.

Barasch, Frances K., *The Grotesque: A Study in Meanings*, The Hague: Mouton, 1971

Chastel, André, *La Grottesque*, Paris: Le Promeneur, 1988

Dacos, Nicole, *La Découverte de la Domus Aurea et la formation des Grotesques à la Renaissance*, London: Warburg Institute, 1969

Dacos, Nicole, *Le Logge di Raffaelo: Maestro e bottega di fronte all'antico*, Rome: Istituto Poligrafico dello Stato, 1977, 2nd edition 1986

Gruber, Alain, *Grotesken, ein Ornamentstil in Textilien des 16.–19. Jahrhunderts* (exhib. cat.), Riggisberg, Switzerland: Abegg-Stiftung, 1985

Gruber, Alain, "Grotesques" in Alain Gruber (editor), *L'Art Décoratif en Europe: Renaissance et maniérisme, 1480–1630*, Paris: Citadelles & Mazenod, 1993, pp.191–274

Jacqué, Bernard (editor), *Les Papiers Peints en Arabesque de la Fin du XVIIIe Siècle* (exhib. cat.), Rixheim: Musée du Papier Peint, 1994

Jessen, Peter, *Meister des Ornamentstichs*, 4 vols., Berlin: Verlag für Kunstwissenschaft, 1922–24

Pons, Bruno, "Arabesques" in Alain Gruber (editor), *L'Art Décoratif en Europe: Classique et Baroque, 1630–1760*, Paris: Citadelles & Mazenod, 1993

Schéle, Sune, *Cornelis Bos: A Study of the Origins of the Netherland Grotesque*, Stockholm: Almqvist & Wiksell, 1965

Ward-Jackson, Peter, *Some Main Streams and Tributaries in European Ornament from 1500 to 1750*, London: Victoria and Albert Museum, 1967

Warnke, Carsten-Peter, *Die ornamentale Groteske in Deutschland, 1500–1650*, 2 vols., Berlin: Spiess, 1979

Weigert, R-A., "L'Art Décoratif en France: Les 'grotteschi' ou grottesques: Leur adaptation et leur évolution du 16e siècle à la première moitié du 18e siècle" in *Information Artistique Culturelle*, vol.1, 1955–56

Arad, Ron 1951–

Israeli-born architect and designer

Ron Arad is not so much an architect and designer as a sculptor of furniture and spaces, whose work has pushed the range of acceptable materials and decorative details to their limits. A familiar figure within London's design avant-garde, he first worked in a broadly High-Tech manner. Subsequently, however, his name became associated with a post-punk or post-holocaust aesthetic. This association was particularly strong in his interiors of the late 1980s where his use of deliberately coarse industrial materials evoked dramatic, albeit somewhat brutal, images of destruction and decay. His furniture, characterised by oversized forms and salvaged materials, has an equally powerful and expressive presence. Arad has been described by the architect Richard Rogers as a "poet of technology", and his work exemplifies the ironies and contradictions of a post-modern age.

Born in Israel, Arad trained at the Belzalel Academy of Art in Jerusalem between 1971 and 1973, and then at the Architectural Association, London, where he studied under Peter Cook, the founder of the architectural group Archigram. After a brief period working in an architectural practice, he formed the design studio and furniture workshop, One-Off, with furniture entrepreneur Dennis Groves in 1981. One-Off grew to encompass gallery and showroom functions. Initially, Arad's aim was to produce individually customised designs; most furnished fashionable retail interiors or offices. But since then, One-Off has been commissioned to create whole interiors, and has worked with furniture manufacturers in Italy to make larger editions of Arad's furniture.

Many of Arad's most well-known pieces of furniture include found objects and materials salvaged from scrapyards, but he is highly selective about the objects he chooses and how they are manipulated. They are selected for particular reasons, such as their shape or their texture, and Arad has described his search for the most suitable items of wreckage as an art in itself.

One such found object, a red VW fender, appears in the 1987 interior of his Shelton Street One-Off showroom. The visitor enters through a roller shutter door into an antechamber of raw, welded steel which curls back to expose yet another welded skin, this one of sleek, chemically treated steel. The floor is made of multi-coloured concrete, coated with polyurethane to give the material a radiance. The only light entering the space comes through a lace-like tracery created by random applications of welding. Arad uses a blow torch like a pencil; his sketches are fast and immediate, and the light penetrating these squiggly lines unexpectedly reveals phrases in English and Hebrew. The remaining solid areas resemble animal and vegetable figures. Not surprisingly, Arad designed all of the showroom's furniture, as well as the pieces on display. The reception desk rests on steel strips which curve in opposite directions. The bar counter – lit from within – is composed of several sheets of metal, cut like filigree. A gallery space in the back of the showroom exhibits work by young designers who share Arad's interest in a rough, constructional aesthetic and in confronting technology and the machine. The actual furniture-making takes place in a Holborn welding shop. Arad's signature piece, the *Rover* chair, featuring a recycled leather seat salvaged from a British Rover car encased in a tubular steel frame, is one of the most celebrated pieces of furniture displayed in the showroom.

Arad has also designed a number of small shops and studios for the fashion industry. He was the interior architect on the Bureaux Clothing Group's design studio, located in a 19th century warehouse on the Thames side of the Metropolitan Wharf in London's Docklands. He designed the drawing boards out of plates of glass resting on tubular steel scaffolding which, in turn, are cantilevered from the main timber columns of the warehouse. The staircase is built out of railway sleepers, and its handrail – curved to resemble reeds blowing in the wind – was made from galvanized steel tubes. The balcony railing uses a similar vocabulary. Arad often collaborated with the designer Danny Lane on works involving glass, and in the rear of the studio Lane designed a screen of etched and clear glass to define a conference area. Arad's rough-edged granite conference table rests on criss-crossed railway sleepers and is surrounded by his horn chairs. Pyramidal lamp shades of rusted sheet steel, scored with welded spirals, carry light into the workspace.

A more public exposition of this raw, industrial aesthetic was revealed in his interiors for the clothes shop, Bazaar, in London's South Molton Street (1984). Huge broken slabs of concrete hung from rusty hawsers, and clothing-rails were supported by life-size cast-concrete figures. The atmosphere was one of dislocation, destruction and decay.

Arad's furniture designs, by contrast, are more ironic and playful. His *Big Easy* chair is featured in New York's Metropolitan Museum of Art's collection of 1980s furniture. The armchair consists of a large quantity of sheet steel welded into a form derived from old, overstuffed upholstered chairs. The steel is burnished to create a "soft" fabric feel and the hollow frame is filled with a ballast of sand so that it can be manipulated into a variety of positions, adjusting to the movements of its user.

Big Easy Volume 2 is another hollow armchair constructed from a single piece of sheet metal. Viewed from the front, its large cylindrical arms look like Mickey Mouse ears. The back is formed out of a concave sheet of steel, following the material's inherent curvature. The metal surface is chemically-treated and then waxed, giving it the appearance of elephant-hide, and the welded edges along the chair's seams suggest traditional piping. Surprisingly comfortable, the *Big Easy* series shows that comfort can be achieved using even the most unlikely of industrial materials.

The *Well-Tempered* chair, currently manufactured in limited numbers by Vitra Editions, is another variation on the overstuffed chair theme. Four sheets of steel are bolted together to form the chair's shape. The springy steel moves slightly with the user, creating a soft cushion out of the hard material. In describing the attractions of steel, Arad has said, "It's the easiest material to work in. I don't know of any other technique where you can do such big pieces. And it's friendly."

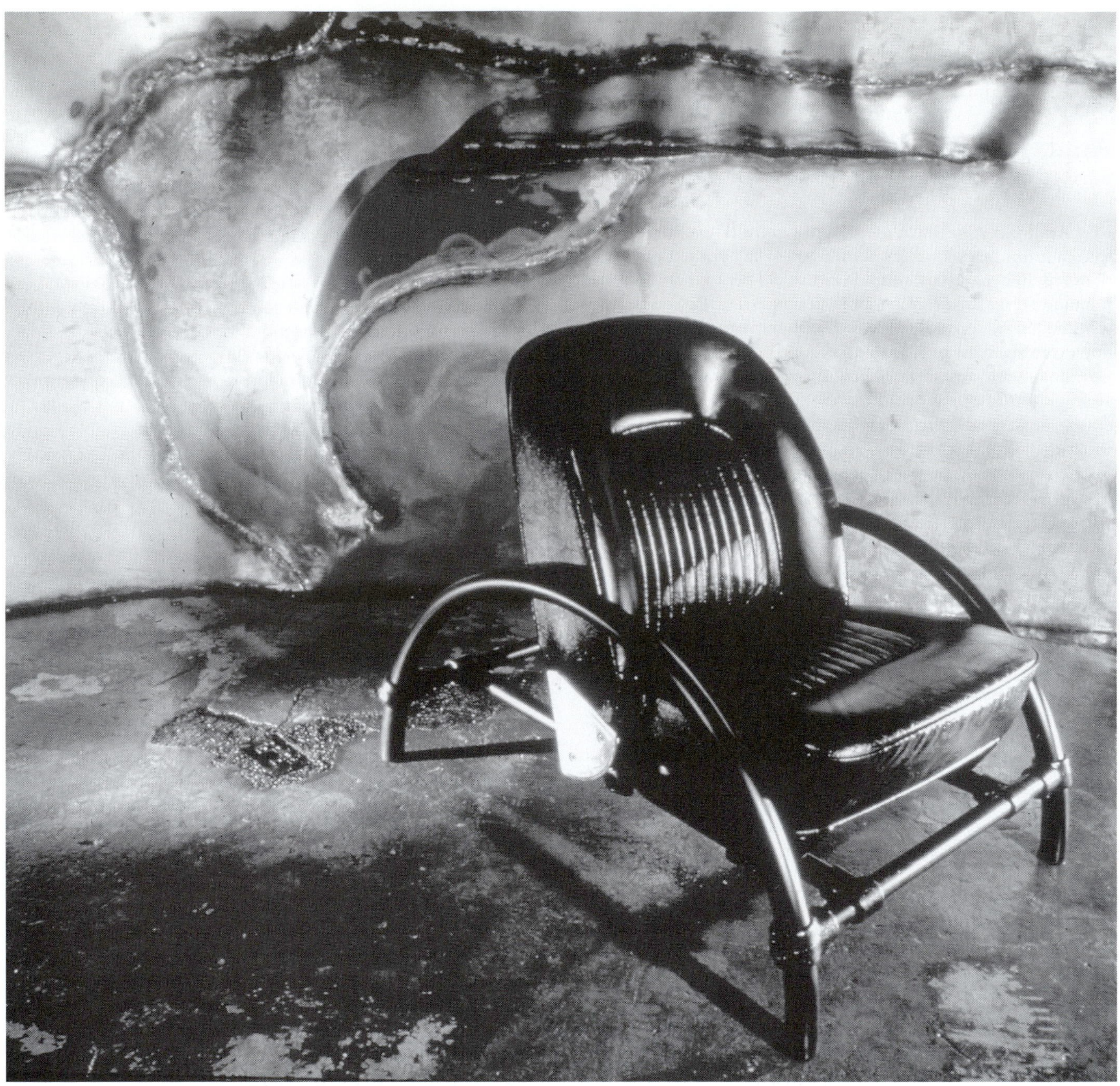

Arad: *Rover* chair, 1985

In recent years, Arad has moved towards the mass production of some of his designs. Originally produced as a limited edition in steel, the *Bookworm* bookcase system, for example, has been reinterpreted in translucent, pliable plastic for more general consumption and is being produced by Kartell, an Italian furniture manufacturer known for its innovative work with plastics. The worm-like bookshelf slithers across a wall in a path determined by the individual user. The modules come in ten-foot long coils and are supported vertically at twenty-inch intervals.

The *Metaply Collection* is part of a series of works designed specifically for mass-production, for the Aleph division of the Italian manufacturer, Driade. The table, chair and folding trolley are made of moulded, light coloured, walnut plywood. The materials and forms are reminiscent of work designed by Charles and Ray Eames in the 1950s and 1960s. But Arad adds spice to the organic, wood composition by contrasting the warm woods with the use of cold aluminium and steel, which serve as both structural and design elements. The table, known as *Fly Ply*, has a double set of retractable, insect-like legs that fold inconspicuously into the underside of the table so that it can alternate between cocktail and dining heights.

A *Suitable Case* was shown in Milan in 1993. The beautifully crafted wooden container opens to reveal unexpectedly a metal chair. Named the *London Papadelle*, after an Italian ribbon noodle pasta, the seat is made of ribbon-like woven metal mesh that rolls downwards into a "carpet". This "carpet" can be unrolled for an additional ten feet across the floor.

In 1989, Arad established the design and architectural practice Ron Arad Associates. In conjunction with his partner, the Canadian architect Alison Brooks, he designed the interiors of the foyers for the Tel Aviv Opera House. The building itself was designed by the Israeli architect Yacov Richter, with whom Arad had previously worked while he was student at the Architectural Association, and it was opened to the public in the autumn of 1994. Meanwhile, Arad has continued to expand his mass-produced furniture lines: smooth polished metal has replaced the battered sheet metal of his earlier days and he has added table accessories to his repertoire. Ron Arad Associates are also designing the interiors of restaurants in London, such as the new Belgo Centraal in Covent Garden (1994–95), and have designed boutiques in Milan, including Michelle Mabelle (1994).

Arad's skill lies in the combination of his first-hand knowledge of materials, which allows him to form mass and texture like a sculptor, and his conceptual abilities, which allow him to define space like an architect. He advocates a pluralist approach to design. He is not interested in the view that only some materials are acceptable, but actively promotes the idea that everything and anything that is available in the post-industrial world can be used in furnishings and interiors. The important criterion is how materials and objects are put together and combined. He has claimed that "the biggest influence on my work is my work", and that exploration has become the focus of his work.

SALLY L. LEVINE

Biography

Born in Tel Aviv, 1951. Studied at the Belzalel Academy of Art, Jerusalem, and at the Architectural Association, London. Lived and worked in London from 1973; co-founder with Caroline Thorman, of the design and production studio One-Off, with showrooms in Covent Garden and Holborn, 1981; established Ron Arad Associates architecture and design practice with Caroline Thorman and the Canadian architect Alison Brooks, 1989; founded the design and production unit Ron Arad Studio, Como, Italy, 1994. Guest professor, Hochschule, Vienna; guest editor of the 1994 *International Design Yearbook*. Arad has also supplied furniture and product designs for many international firms including Alessi, Driade, Kartel, Knoll International, Swatch, and Vitra International; he has participated in many group and solo exhibitions in Europe, Israel and Japan.

Selected Works

Examples of Arad's furnishings are in the Design Museum, and the Victoria and Albert Museum, London; the Metropolitan Museum of Art, New York; the Centre Georges Pompidou, Paris; the Tel Aviv Museum; and the Vitra Design Museum, Weil am Rhein.

Interiors

1984	Bazaar, South Molton Street, London (shop interiors and display system): Jean-Paul Gaultier
1986	Equation, Bristol (shop interiors)
1986	The Bureau, Metropolitan Wharf, London (design and fashion studio interiors)
1987	One Off studio, Covent Garden, London (furniture showroom and design studio interiors)
1988–94	New Tel Aviv Opera (foyer architecture and interiors)
1989–91	Ron Arad Associates, Chalk Farm Road, London (studio, gallery and workshops; conversion and interiors)
1993–94	Belgo Restaurant and Bar, London (interiors and furnishings)
1994	Michelle Mabelle, via della Spiga, Milan (shop refurbishment and interiors)
1994–95	Belgo Centraal, Covent Garden, London (restaurant, offices etc.; conversion and interiors)

Arad's furniture includes his *Rover Chair* (1985), the *Well Tempered Chair* (1985) the *Big Easy* series (1989), the *Metaply Collection*, and the *Suitable Case* and *London Papadelle* (1993).

Further Reading

Discussions of Ron Arad's early work appear in Sudjic 1989 and Vegesack 1990; for an account of his later work see Bullivant 1991 and *Ron Arad Associates* 1993. In addition, his work has regularly been featured in architectural and design journals worldwide.

Abrams, Janet, "Steely Grasp" in *World of Interiors*, May 1988, pp.164–69

Abrams, Janet, "Uneasy Edges" in *Architectural Record*, September 1988, pp.64–71

Arad, Ron (editor), *International Design Yearbook*, London: Calmann and King, 1994

Bullivant, Lucy, *International Interior Design*, New York: Abbeville, 1991

Dormer, Peter, *The New Furniture: Trends and Traditions*, London and New York: Thames and Hudson, 1987

Fiell, Charlotte and Peter, *Modern Furniture Classics since 1945*, Washington, DC: American Institute of Architects Press, and London: Thames and Hudson, 1991

Grant, Ian, "Restless Ron" in *Interior Design*, November / December 1989, pp.36–38

Knobel, Lance, *International Interiors*, London: Thames and Hudson, 1988

McDermott, Catherine, *Street Style: British Design in the '80s*, London: Design Council, and New York: Rizzoli, 1987

Moore, Rowan, "Furniture Writ Large" in *Blueprint*, December–January 1995, pp.3–6

Ron Arad Associates: One Off Three, London: Artemis, 1993

Sudjic, Deyan, *Ron Arad: Restless Furniture*, London: Fourth Estate, and New York: Rizzoli, 1989

Thackara, John (editor), *New British Design*, London and New York: Thames and Hudson, 1986

Vegesack, Alexander von, *Ron Arad* (exhib. cat.), Weil am Rhein: Vitra Design Museum, 1990

Architect, history and role of

The history of the role played by architects in determining the appearance of the interiors of buildings is a vast and complex subject and the extent of their involvement has changed quite radically over the past five hundred years. In 1812 the French architects Charles Percier and Pierre-François-Léonard Fontaine declared "Furniture is too much a part of interior design for the architect to remain indifferent to it", thus stressing their belief that architects should exercise overall control in the relationship between architecture, decoration and furnishings, even down to the placing of furniture as part of the total design. This was a concept that had been perfected in the second half of the 18th century by Robert and James Adam in whose major interiors virtually every element – including the ceilings and walls, chimneypieces and doors, moveable furniture and carpets, silverware and metalwork – all bore the mark of a single directing mind, and an all-embracing style and colour scheme. But such control was a comparatively new phenomenon and represented a culminating point in the rise of the professional architect, the idea of integrated design, and the relationship between designers and craftsmen, which had been developing since the 16th century.

Throughout the Middle Ages and for much of the Renaissance period, in most European countries the architect was usually a master-mason or artisan who had no expertise outside the sphere of building and only limited knowledge of recent developments within his own field. Although he was responsible for providing designs for the general plan for the building, the drawing of details such as the roof and woodwork were assigned to the master-carpenter and other craftsmen. The master-mason's contribution to the interior concentrated upon the built, fixed elements – notably the fireplace and the staircase – while the wood ceilings and panelling were the responsibility of the master-carpenter. Other work, such as the decorations and furnishings, were assigned to specialist craftsmen and painters, and more often than not it was the patron or client who exercised overall control of the building of his house and the shaping of its interiors.

With the publication of treatises on architecture, which appeared from the early 16th century, came the first step on the road towards the establishment of architecture as an educated and gentlemanly profession. The majority of these books, however, were principally based on a knowledge of Classical rules and the Orders and comparatively little attention was paid to interior details, although not surprisingly fireplaces featured quite prominently. Sebastiano Serlio (1475–1554), for example, whose writings were widely referred to and translated into several languages, offered designs for elaborate, canopied fireplaces which incorporated individual interpretations of classical motifs; he also included illustrations of doorways and ceilings. Andrea Palladio (1508–1580) provided plans and elevations of villas and town houses in his *Quattro Libri* (1570), but significantly he gave no indication of how the interiors might be treated. In his text he gave some general advice about flooring materials and ceilings, and he designed internal doorways and fireplaces, but there is no reason to suppose that he was consulted about the decoration of the rooms, even in such a residence as the Villa Barbaro at Maser, in which Paolo Veronese's frescoes so perfectly complement the architectural form and the spirit of the building.

Italian artists and architects were the first to take the lead in participating more fully in the design of interiors. Raphael (1483–1520) devised overall decorative schemes of stucco and paint, relating the spatial and decorative elements in a masterly fashion, in his work in the Vatican and the Villa Madama, and in the Farnesina. And Giulio Romano (c.1499–1546), at one time Raphael's assistant, developed an individual treatment of interiors and an assumption of overall control over the decoration of rooms in Mantua. He was able to ensure that all the different elements of a room, or of some decorative ensemble, were in the same style and created a unity. He made detailed drawings for mural decoration which could be realised either in fresco or tapestry, and he also made some designs for elaborately decorated furniture of an architectural character. But such control was comparatively rare and depended greatly on the character of the individual patron.

Outside of Italy, the more dominant role of the architect was initially evident in court circles, particularly in France. In the 1530s Francesco Primaticcio (1505–70), painter-sculptor-architect, who had worked with Giulio at Mantua, began work in the new rooms for François I at the Château of Fontainebleau, where woodwork, stucco and frescoes were combined in a riot of Mannerist decoration. The designs were executed by French, Italian and Belgian craftsmen who worked together and became proficient in the Franco-Italian Mannerist style. The application of this style to fireplaces, furniture and grotesque decoration permeated, for example, the published designs of Jacques Androuet DuCerceau the Elder (c.1515–85), and from the middle of the 16th century such books played a vital role in not only disseminating ideas throughout Northern Europe but also in underpinning the patron / architect / craftsmen relationship.

Louis Le Vau's (1612–70) appointment in the 1650s as overall controller of the building and decoration of the château of Vaux-le-Vicomte – described as "conjured up by a French architect-decorator and carried out entirely by Frenchmen" – marked another step towards artistic integration. Further steps were taken in 1662 when Jean-Baptiste Colbert (1619–83) re-established the royal Gobelins Workshops where the various artists and craftsmen all worked together under the artistic direction of Charles Le Brun (1619–90). The Gobelins was described by Sir Christopher Wren as "a School of Architecture, the best probably, at this day in Europe".

In England, the notion of integrated interior design was advanced by Inigo Jones (1573–1652) in the 1620s and 1630s. Jones produced many drawings of chimneypieces and overmantels, decorated compartmented ceilings, and carved or painted swags, grotesques and putti, as well as actual buildings, where a French taste, facilitated by the availability of published designs by Jean Barbet and Pierre Collot and encouraged by Henrietta Maria, Charles I's French queen, is clearly evident. This lavish and innovative form of decoration was developed by John Webb (1611–72), Jones's assistant, in the rich interiors of Wilton House of the 1640s. Webb also produced internal elevations for Lamport Hall and advised on the purchase of pictures for this house. But although it might be assumed that both Jones and Webb would have at least been consulted about furnishings for their decorated rooms, there is little evidence that they themselves provided designs for furniture, although a drawing by Webb from the mid-1660s does indicate a bed and balustrade in the French fashion as a central element in a bedroom intended for Charles II. Carvers and plasterers made their own detailed designs which were submitted to the architect and the patron for approval; painters of large-scale wall and ceiling decorations generally worked quite independently of the architect.

One of the first architects to be personally concerned with the design of not only furniture but also upholstery was Daniel Marot (c.1663–1752). Trained in France, Marot had a working knowledge of the Louis XIV style of decoration, but more important was his work as an all-round architect in Holland and England, where he designed rooms and furnishings for several major buildings including the palaces of Het Loo and Hampton Court. The Louis XIV style was reflected in

Marot's published designs for beds, chairs, pelmets and curtains, chimneypieces, wall panelling and bookcases, all of which tended towards a unified scheme of decoration and furnishing. By this time too, architects' designs for complete wall treatments were becoming popular in France as could be seen in the work of Gilles-Marie Oppenord (1672–1742), Robert de Cotte (1656–1735) and Jacques Gabriel (1667–1742), and in the plates of Jacques-François Blondel's influential *De la distribution des maisons de plaisance et de la décoration des édifices en général* (1737–38) which, in some cases, also included furniture as an integral element in the design of Rococo rooms.

During the course of the 18th century the architect became more entrenched as not only a knowledgable leader of a team of craftsmen but also as someone who could provide his own detailed interior designs. In England, John Talman (1677–1726) is credited with being the first such professional fully to integrate furniture, decoration and architecture, but the work of William Kent (1685/86–1748), who was active as an architect and designer as well as a decorative painter, is generally regarded as more important. Kent's most memorable interiors survive at Houghton, in Norfolk. Some of his designs for chimneypieces and architectural furniture as part of a total room treatment were published by John Vardy in 1744 who also made designs for furniture and produced some of the earliest known drawings for wall decoration which suggest the colours to be used. Vardy's designs were made for Spencer House, London, in 1755–57, a building for which James Stuart (1713–88) had made similar proposals. This significant step in an architect's total control of a room's decoration had already been taken in France and it was quickly adopted in England where a number of books on colour and painting, including Alexander Emerton's *Directions for Painting* (c.1753) and Robert Dossie's *Handmaid to the Arts* (1758) were available.

By this time, the role of the patron as director of proceedings was receding; the architect produced proposals for whole interiors to which the client could react, and the final appearance of the building was generally a compromise between these and the client's ideas. This development was encouraged by the greater attention paid to the making of drawings of interiors, generally in the form of an exploded ceiling or floor plan and four elevations, but sometimes as perspective views or as sectional drawings. This practice originated in France and Sir William Chambers, who was familiar with Parisian examples, made a sectional drawing of his proposals for York House (c.1759) which shows wall colours and patterns in detail, as well as major items of furniture which he evidently considered part of the overall design. Chambers also made it known that he wished to be consulted about Thomas Chippendale's designs for furniture in one of his houses "as I am really a very pretty connoisseur in furniture", and there is a reference elsewhere to "the assemblage and blending of couleurs [being] Great Principles of his [Chambers's] ... taste".

The assumption of greater architectural control culminated in the work of the Adam brothers, who collaborated with a team of master craftsmen including Thomas Chippendale, Joseph Rose and Matthew Boulton, but whose designs for complete rooms and furnishings were developed down to the smallest detail. Some 9000 of the drawings from their office, produced by a number of skilled draughtsmen including George Richardson, Joseph Bonomi, and Charles-Louis Clérisseau, are in Sir John Soane's Museum, London, and they represent the most important of all collections of architects' coloured designs for interiors. In France, a similarly comprehensive approach to interiors was taken by Percier and Fontaine whose precise and carefully studied creation of rooms, in which every item of furniture played a part and had its place in the overall picture, was based on Antique and Renaissance sources. Theirs was the quintessence of architects' interiors in which nothing should be changed. Their *Recueil de décorations intérieures* (1812) was well known to English architects and the influence of their furniture designs can be seen in Rudolph Ackermann's much referred to *Repository of Arts* (1809–28). The German architect Karl Friedrich Schinkel (1781–1841) also designed complete interiors and furniture. Like that of Percier and Fontaine, Schinkel's work reflected historical styles and motifs, but his designs were also strongly individual, often simple in their interpretation, and essentially part of the whole decoration.

Despite the pre-eminence of figures such as the Adam Brothers, Schinkel, and Percier and Fontaine, there was still much vying for precedence between architects and other tradesmen who specialised in interior work during the 18th and early 19th centuries. This was particularly the case where there was no actual building work to be done and internal alterations were often carried out by upholsterers who undertook to supply not only furniture, wallpaper, and textiles but could also provide a complete decorating service. The English upholsterers Thomas Chippendale and William and John Linnell collaborated with architects such as Robert Adam, but they also refurbished interiors independently: Chippendale worked at Mersham Le Hatch, Kent and David Garrick's villa in Middlesex, and the Linnells at Bowood House, Wiltshire. In France, a similar role was played by *marchands-merciers* such as Dominique Daguerre, who also had a showroom in London and worked at Carlton House. Many of these firms occupied large premises situated in fashionable districts of London and Paris and the sums paid out for their services were often very large, sometimes even exceding the cost of the building itself. Not surprisingly, this led to friction with the architectural profession. In 1824, the architect William Mitford claimed "The upholsterer's interest is in direct opposition to the architect's credit" (Thornton, 1978) and many architects were bitterly resentful of the influence wielded by upholsterers whom they regarded as purveyors of novelties and transient fashions.

This tension was particularly strong in the early part of the 19th century when upholsterers appear to have been in the ascendant and it subsided only in the second half of the century when it was replaced by a similar struggle with the emerging decorating trade. But by this time, the architectural profession had taken steps to bolster its position through a more formalised system of training and through the establishment of bodies such as the Institute (later Royal Institute) of British Architects (set up in 1834) which aimed to promote the "uniformity and respectability of practice" and which removed architects from building and decorative contracting, although not from the designing of decoration and furniture.

The mid-19th century spread of industrialisation in England brought with it an increasing gulf between commercial production and architect-designed work. Within critical circles, this gulf was widened further by the Gothic Revival's critique of contemporary mass-produced design which culminated in the latter part of the 19th century in the emergence of the Arts and Crafts Movement. Stemming from the philosophies of A.W.N. Pugin, John Ruskin and William Morris, this Movement sought to break down the divisions between art, architecture and craft and promoted the greater involvement of artists and architects in domestic design. It was a Movement dominated by architects – Philip Webb (1831–1915), Richard Norman Shaw (1831–1912), Thomas Edward Collcutt (1840–1924), John Dando Sedding (1838–91), W.R. Lethaby (1857–1931), Arthur Heygate Mackmurdo (1851–1942), M.H. Baillie Scott (1865–1945) and C.F.A. Voysey (1857–1941) – all of whom and many more had a far more "hands-on" approach to design and were frequently involved in the design of complete interiors including decorations, furniture and textiles. They also also designed for commercial Art manufacturers and Art firms.

The Aesthetic Movement of the late 1860s was another fashionable manifestation of total design, based on the creed that a truly beautiful and harmonious interior needed contributions from architects and painters. Its leading exponent was E.W. Godwin (1833–86) who would take over the responsibility for a whole house when he had the opportunity, designing its exterior, its decorations and furnishings, and even mixing the paints and choosing the pictures and ornaments. Another architect working in the Anglo-Japanese style was Thomas Jeckyll (1827–81); he too would undertake an entire commission to build, decorate and furnish, but the Aesthetic interior was promoted principally through commercial firms, such as Liberty's in London, which could supply a whole range of Artistic and Japanese-style goods.

The concept of total design was also evident in the work of various exponents of Art Nouveau, including the Belgian architects Victor Horta (1861–1947), Gustave Serrurier-Bovy (1858–1910), Paul Hankar (1859–1901) and Henry van de Velde (1863–1957). In van de Velde's own house (1895) he created a complete and totally integrated environment, designing the furniture, lighting fittings and even dresses for his wife. Similarly complete interiors were created by other Art Nouveau and progressive architects including Hector Guimard (1867–1942), Josef Hoffmann (1870–1956), Charles Rennie Mackintosh (1868–1928), H.P. Berlage (1856–1934) and Frank Lloyd Wright (1867–1959). Although many of these figures developed in different directions in the later phases of their careers, they all remained constant to the idea that the architect should be in control of the inside of a building as well as its exterior. Frank Lloyd Wright recalled, "I tried to make my clients see that furniture and furnishings not built in as integral features of the building should be designed as attributes of whatever furniture was built in". He spoke for many architects who believed in the integrity of interior design when complaining that "when the building itself was finished, the old furniture they possessed usually went in with the clients. Very few of these houses were anything but painful to me after the clients moved in and, helplessly, dragged the horrors of the Old Order along with them".

The notion of the architect-designer presiding over the interior fitments, decorations and furnishings has continued to shape the appearance of many of the seminal buildings of the 20th century with noteworthy examples being produced by many of the century's most celebrated Modernists. The Schröder House (1924) by Gerrit Rietveld, Mies van der Rohe's German Pavilion at the Barcelona Exhibition (1929), and the Eames House (1945–49) by Charles Eames might be included in this list. But the 20th century has also seen control over the interior increasingly wrested from the architectural profession by the growing influence of interior decorators.

Emerging in the late 19th century, the interior decorator took over many of the functions of the upholsterer, but whereas upholsterers were generally perceived as tradesmen, decorators were frequently drawn from the same social class as their clients and included many educated female practitioners. Notable pioneers were Elsie de Wolfe in America and Nancy Lancaster and Sybil Colefax in Britain. With fewer domestic houses being custom built by architects, decorators have become increasingly important since the mid- and late 20th century and their influence is widely reflected in popular interiors and lifestyles magazines. Architects, meanwhile, have become more closely associated with corporate clients, providing the interiors and corporate image for company headquarters and office buildings. The recent provision of professional training for decorators has also helped to put them on a par with architects and the late 20th century has witnessed the emergence of "interior-architects" whose training represents a blend of design and architectural skills.

DEREK LINSTRUM

See also Interior Design; Marchands-merciers; Upholsterer

Further Reading

Ackerman, J. S., "Architectural Practice in the Italian Renaissance" in *Journal of the Society of Architectural Historians*, XIII, 1954, pp.3–11

Airs, Malcolm, *The Making of the English Country House, 1500–1640*, London: Architectural Press, 1975

Colvin, Howard M., "The Architectural Profession" in *A Biographical Dictionary of British Architects, 1600–1840*, 3rd edition New Haven and London: Yale University Press, 1995

Jenkins, Frank, *Architect and Patron: A Survey of Professional Relations and Practice in England from the Sixteenth Century to the Present Day*, London and New York: Oxford University Press, 1961

Kaye, Barrington, *The Development of the Architectural Profession in Britain: A Sociological Study*, London: Allen and Unwin, 1960

Lever, Jill, *Architects' Designs for Furniture*, London: Trefoil, and New York: Rizzoli, 1982

The Role of the Amateur Architect (conference proceedings), London: Georgian Group, 1994

Saint, Andrew, *The Image of the Architect*, New Haven and London: Yale University Press, 1983

Scott, Katie, *The Rococo Interior: Decoration and Social Spaces in Early Eighteenth-Century Paris*, New Haven and London: Yale University Press, 1995

Thornton, Peter, *Seventeenth-Century Interior Decoration in England, France, and Holland*, New Haven and London: Yale University Press, 1978

Thornton, Peter, *Authentic Decor: The Domestic Interior, 1620–1920*, London: Weidenfeld and Nicolson, and New York: Viking, 1984

Thornton, Peter, *The Italian Renaissance Interior, 1400–1600*, London: Weidenfeld and Nicolson, and New York: Abrams, 1991

Walker, Lynne, "The Entry of Women into the Architectural Profession in Britain" in *Women's Art Journal*, vii, Spring–Summer 1986m pp.13–18

Wilton-Ely, John, "The Rise of the Professional Architect in England" in Spiro Kostof (editor), *The Architect: Chapters in the History of the Profession*, Oxford and New York: Oxford University Press, 1977, pp.180–208

Art Deco

Art Deco is a term used to describe design of the period 1920–40 which uses expensive and exotic materials, angular forms and luscious colours. It is a luxury style created by French *ensembliers* (a term adopted around 1911 to describe designers of entire interiors) in a successful bid to assert France as the world leader of interior decoration and high style. Although not generally used until the late 1960s, the term Art Deco derives from the lavish exhibition staged during 1925 in Paris – the Exposition Internationale des Arts Décoratifs et Industriels Modernes. The Exposition was an international display of temporary pavilions, built on the banks of the Seine in the grand tradition of world trade fairs.

The stylistic roots of Art Deco lie in the avant-garde of the turn of century, and in 18th-century and early 19th-century French furniture. Louis XV, Louise XVI, Consulate, Empire and Directoire styles were all revived and combined with a new, geometric form in design, developed in Glasgow and Vienna. At the turn of the century Charles Rennie Mackintosh and the Glasgow School had created a new style in interior design based on sparse Japanese interiors and the Scottish baronial style. The vertical, geometric forms used by Mackintosh for his fantastic chair designs in particular proved influential in mainland Europe. The designers of the Vienna Secession and the Wiener Werkstätte used similar shapes in their interior designs. At the Palais Stoclet, built between 1905 and 1911, Josef Hoffmann and the Wiener Werkstätte designed a luxury villa in the suburbs of Brussels using comparable, angular geometric forms and expensive materials. This stripped classicism was also explored by early 20th-century designers in Germany, particularly those exhibiting at the Paris Salon d'Automne in 1910. Designers linked with the Munich Deutscher Werkbund at the Salon showed a proto-Modernist form of interior design, for example Karl Bertsch, the Munich decorator, showed a lady's bedroom which was criticised by French experts for its lack of femininity but was a popular success with the public. This galvanised the French design establishment into action to ensure that their place as leaders in taste and fashion was maintained. The idea of holding an international exhibition devoted entirely to new design was born.

Due to the interruption of World War I the Exposition Internationale des Arts Décoratifs et Industriels Modernes did not take place until 1925, by which time, ironically, much of the impetus of French Art Deco had passed. One of the most extravagant constructions at the Exposition was Le Pavillon d'un Collectionneur which was designed by Pierre Partout and decorated by Jacques-Emile Ruhlmann and a team of prominent French designers, all members of the Société des Artistes Décorateurs which had been founded in 1901. Ruhlmann was the leading French *ensemblier* of the period, drawing upon past styles and combining this with Art Deco luxury. In the Grand Salon of the Pavillon hung a huge chandelier and the walls were covered with boldly patterned silk and topped by a classical entablature. The furniture in the room was based on French, 18th-century pieces and veneered with luxurious Macassar ebony. Ruhlmann continued to design in this extravagant Art Deco style throughout the 1920s and 1930s, always using the proportions of classical architecture and exclusive materials, including ivory, lizard-skin, shagreen, tortoiseshell and exotic hardwoods. He also undertook commissions for the Paris Chamber of Commerce and the cosmetics firm of Yardley. For the former he designed an imposing ballroom in the 19th-century Hotel Potocki. Chunky, ribbed pilasters line the walls, Cubist reliefs surround the mirrors and constitute the entablature. Grand chandeliers hang from the ceiling while a classically-inspired relief by Joseph Bernard decorates the main doorway.

Another important pavilion at the Exposition to showcase the work of French designers was that of the French Embassy, which consisted of 24 lavish rooms spread across two wings. Organised by the Société des Artistes Décorateurs and sponsored by the French government, the pavilion contained the soft Chambre de Madame furnished by André Groult. The velvet upholstery and curved, shagreen-covered, chest-of-drawers conjured up a feminine ambience. This contrasted with the modern reception area designed by Robert Mallet-Stevens. Art Deco was not only inspired by the French past. The sunrise motif used by Groult on the bed in the Chambre de Madame was probably inspired by ancient Egyptian art, a common source for designers following the discovery of Tutankhamen's tomb in 1922. The avant-garde painting style of Cubism was also an important influence on Art Deco. Indeed, there was a direct link between Cubism and interior design when, in 1912 at the Salon d'Automne the traditional designers Louise Süe and André Mare collaborated with the minor French Cubists Roger de la Fresnaye, Raymond Duchamp-Villon and Jacques Villon on the Maison Cubiste. This working partnership continued with the founding of the decorating firm, Compagnie des Arts Français in 1919. At the Exposition the Compagnie designed the Musée d'Art Contemporain to publicise their lavish room settings. The Parisian department stores who were to be so important in the promotion of the Art Deco style each sponsored a pavilion.

Galeries Lafayette's studio, La Maitrise, was headed by Maurice Dufrène. The lavish exterior of La Maitrise's pavilion was designed by a team of three architects – Georges Beau, Joseph Hiriart and Georges Tribout. The interior was designed by Dufrène and contained an exhibition hall plus five model interiors – a man's bedroom, salon, dining room, study and women's bedroom. The interior of Bon Marché's Pomone pavilion was designed by director Paul Follot, who had joined the department store in 1923. The Grand Salon of the Pomone pavilion was decorated with a bold mix of angular patterns and stylised flowers on the carpet, panels of the display cabinets and entablature. Au Printemps's Primavera was designed by director Charlotte Chauchet-Guillere. The Louvre's own Stadium Louvre was octagonal in outline plan, decorated with urns and carved and real plants with an exterior terrace. Inside

Art Deco: Grand Salon, Pavillon d'un Collectionneur, by Jacques-Emile Ruhlmann, 1925 Paris Exposition des Arts Décoratifs et Industriels

was the familiar mix of traditionally inspired furniture, finished with rare veneers.

One of the most important inspirations for Art Deco interior design was non-Western art. The exotic allure of African and Oceanic forms was exploited by Pierre Legrain in his design of a curved seat based on an Ashanti stool, exhibited at the 1923 Salon des Artistes Décorateurs, and a chair from the following year veneered in palmwood with parchment seating. Legrain contributed some important, exotically inspired furniture to the lavish interior of couturier and art collector Jacques Doucet's home, designed in 1929 at Neuilly. The villa contained important Art Deco furniture including a Japanese inspired, occasional table with sharkskin inlay by Rose Adler which supported an abstract, crystal sculpture by Gustave Miklos. Many of the pieces from the Doucet Villa can now be seen at the Virginia Museum of Fine Arts.

The exotic also inspired the rich variety of metalwork furniture and fittings produced by Art Deco designers. Armand-Albert Rateau created disturbing interiors using strange bird forms cast in bronze, which supported tables and were even used for taps. The apartment he designed for the couturier Jeanne Lanvin in Paris featured a low table with patinated bronze birds supporting a marble top, set in a bedroom hung with embroidered blue silk. The bathroom designed for the same commission featured a carved wall panel in stucco, decorated with a forest scene, the cream Siena marble bath and washbasin contrasted with the patinated bronze lights fittings, taps and mirror.

The adventurous use of colour was certainly an essential feature of the Art Deco interior and was partly inspired by the fashion for the exotic. This inspired the stage designs of Léon Bakst for the Ballet Russes. Serge Diaghilev's ballet, *Schéhérazade*, was performed in Paris in 1910, and the vivid colours, bold patterns and evocation of a distant, exotic land only heightened the contemporary fashion for Persian and Arabian themes. Modernist painters were also experimenting with colour and form at this time and certainly influenced Art Deco. Orphism was one movement which developed just before World War I in Paris. The chief exponents, Sonia and Robert Delaunay, liberated colour from the formal concerns of easel painting. Sonia Delaunay applied the experiments of Orphism to textile design during the 1920s, decorating their home with geometrically patterned rugs and furnishing fabrics in multi-coloured hues. Another group of painters to experiment with colour were the Fauves or Wild Beasts. The major artists in the group, Matisse, Derain and Vlaminck worked between 1905 and 1908 using vivid colours in amazing combinations. Such shocking contrasts were used by designers as a reaction to the insipid pastels of Art Nouveau.

The designer to best exploit an exotic atmosphere and

Art Deco: suburban lounge of the late 1930s; re-created in the Geffrye Museum, London

strong colours was Paul Poiret. He was originally a haute-couture designer who produced flowing dresses which liberated women from the corset. Poiret established the Atelier Martine in 1912 which was responsible for decorating his new shop, used to sell his own brand of perfume, Rosine. Poiret employed the Fauve artist, Raoul Dufy to design fabrics for his new firm. Young, working-class women were also used by Poiret to design bold, bright fabrics and surface patterns. The Atelier successfully designed and sold printed fabrics, wallpapers, ceramics, rugs and embroideries in addition to undertaking entire interior design commissions. The Atelier Martine designed three barges for the 1925 Exposition. These were painted on the exterior with exotic flowers and moored on the Left Bank of the Seine. Inside the *Amours* barge, the main living area was littered with huge cushions for informal seating, the walls were painted with palm trees and other strange flora which also decorated the carpeting. Poiret did not distinguish between textiles for clothing and textiles for the interior; this interaction between women's fashion and design typifies Art Deco. It was conceived as a style to challenge the masculine look of German, Modern design and wallowed in the decorative, the exotic and the amusing.

For political reasons Germany was effectively excluded from the 1925 Exposition because their invitation was not sent until it was too late for them to participate. America also refrained from participating in this show. Herbert Hoover, then Secretary of Commerce, claimed that American design was not in a position to offer "new and really original" design for international exhibitions although the real reason probably had more to do with costs than with aesthetics. Britain made a small contribution, with a pavilion designed by Easton and Robertson in Moorish style. The Exposition certainly ensured France's stylistic leadership of interior design and high fashion, and guaranteed the spread of the Art Deco style throughout the Western world, as visitors to the exhibition and the media carried news of the show.

The Art Deco style reached America partly through exhibitions of artifacts from Paris. In 1926 the Metropolitan Museum of Art in New York organised a touring exhibition of design objects and established a permanent gallery for the display of furniture bought at the Exposition. Department stores such as Saks, Macy's, and Lord and Taylor exhibited examples of French Art Deco after 1925. Thirty-six museums and department stores featured Art Deco furniture in their displays during 1925 to 1928. Brash and new, the Art Deco style was highly influential in America, and lent itself to the repeated, geometric patterns of mass production techniques pioneered in the US. Joseph Urban had emigrated to New York from Vienna in 1911 to set up a small design consultancy. In 1922 he established the Wiener Werkstätte of America, which produced geometric furniture and furnishings in the spirit of the Austrian prototype. Urban used the Art Deco style for the design of the Century of Progress exhibition in Chicago (1930). His Travel and Transport pavilion used the rising sun motif and the ziggurat profile. The Art Deco style was adopted for the design of buildings as diverse as modest hotels in Miami to New York skyscrapers.

The skyscraper was a building form introduced in New York during the 1870s and in Chicago during the following decade. During the 20th century skyscrapers were built in

Art Deco: block-printed wallpaper, 1933

every major American city and presented a unique interior design problem – how could the interior equal the sheer scale and magnificence of the exterior. Ely Jacques Kahn was one of the most prominent of America's interior designers of the time and created several impressive entrance lobbies including the Lefcourt Clothing Center on Wall Street, the Film Center and the Bricken Building, John Street. Two of the most important Art Deco buildings in New York are the Chrysler Building (1928–30) and the Empire State Building (1930–32). Designed by William Van Alen for the automobile corporation, the stepped exterior of the Chrysler Building is decorated with modern gargoyles and hub-caps. The lobby is decorated with rich red marble, Art Deco ironwork by Oscar Bach, and elevator doors veneered with light amber and dark brown woods in a geometric lotus design. The Empire State Building was designed by Shreve, Lamb & Harmon and built in stone with aluminium and nickel exterior decoration. The interior features Art Deco motifs from the zig-zag floor decoration to stepped balustrades and ceilings. Another key example of New York, high-rise Art Deco is the Chanin Building dating from 1929 on 42nd Street and Lexington Avenue. The interior decoration was orchestrated by Jacques Delamarre, head of the Chanin Construction Company. The 50th floor of the building featured an Art Deco auditorium and the 52nd floor an executive suite for the chairman, Irwin S. Chanin. This included an opulent bathroom tiled in cream, gold and green with a gold-plated sunburst over the geometrically engraved glass shower doors.

The Art Deco style influenced the interior design of office blocks and hotels throughout America. The Carew Tower, Cincinnati of 1931 by Walter W. Ahlschlager includes a resplendent Hall of Mirrors and Palm Court. However, by this date the influence of classic Art Deco, with its repeated, geometric forms, decorative ironwork and rich decoration was on the wane in America. It was gradually superseded by the Moderne, a combination of Art Deco and the Modern Movement which made an impact on the whole of the Western world through the Hollywood cinema and associated media during the 1930s and 1940s.

During the 1920s Art Deco was the dominant new style for Western European commercial buildings. After the 1925 Paris Exposition the style was linked with luxury and glamour, and with the world of Parisian haute-couture. Trent and Lewis's New Victoria Cinema in London (1929) features stepped, fan-shaped pillars, dramatised by concealed lighting to create an exotic ambience. London's Park Lane Hotel, built in 1927 by

Henry Tanner and decorated by Kenneth Anns, featured a graceful Art Deco ironwork mural in the foyer, complemented by silver painted furniture. Claridge's Hotel, also in London, was refurbished in 1930 by Oswald Milne using key aspects of the Art Deco style. The walls of the glamorous front entrance were painted primrose and the floor and steps were of Roman stone and Belgian black marble. The walls are punctuated by tall, gilded pillars, topped by illuminated fans. The ceiling is dominated by a chandelier which reflects in the blue and white mirrors, which are surmounted by stepped decoration. Extra decoration is added with delicate metal grilles, painted with cellulose gold. A burnished gold niche framed a sculpture of a deer against a tree by Milne, placed on a Lalique glass stand.

Such lavish design was rarely found in the domestic interior. It was only the very wealthy client who could afford such extravagance, particularly during the economic depression of the 1930s. Those who could afford to create a special Art Deco interior would commission interior decorators to execute the task. One example of this is the wealthy Dutch banker, David Van Buuren, who designed his own house in Brussels which was completed in 1928. After visiting the Paris Exposition in 1925 Van Buuren employed the Parisian decorating firm of Studio Dominique to decorate his living room. Dominique had been founded in 1922 by André Domin and Marcel Genevrière with a showroom at 104 Faubourg St. Honoré and executed work in Paris and Havana. The Van Buuren house features Dufy carpets, Lalique lighting and a specially designed black Canadian fireplace. (The house is now a museum open to the public on Monday afternoons.)

Outside France, the highly decorative and expensive style of Art Deco was usually seen only in specially commissioned cinemas, hotels and office blocks. It only reached a wider audience when it was combined with the simplicity of modern design in a style known as Moderne. This style was simpler and more chic and gradually supplanted Art Deco as the dominant influence on interior design in many parts of Europe and America. A commercial version that still had strong overtones of Art Deco gained mass popularity in the mid-1930s in Britain, where manufacturers and consumers had previously proved quite resistant to the appeal of Parisian ideas. The typical, modest-sized, semi-detached suburban home of the inter-war period often combined a Tudor Revival half-timbered exterior with lively Art Deco motifs on furnishings and interior details. These included rising suns which figured particularly in window-glass, mirrors and radio cabinets, and brightly coloured, geometric jazz patterns which were a favourite in wallpapers, carpets and upholstery fabrics, and tableware. The rare and exotic finishes characteristic of French Art Deco were replaced by mass-produced, modern materials. Popular furnishings included chunky or rounded sofas and matching armchairs covered with leather, velveteen or moquette, stepped, veneered cabinets and bookshelves, and geometric, coloured glass light-fittings. Such furnishings remained fashionable within middle-income sitting rooms until the outbreak of World War II and the introduction of rationing curtailed production within most areas of the home decorating industries.

ANNE MASSEY

See also Cinemas; Gray; Paris 1925; Rateau; Ruhlmann; Skyscrapers; Streamlining and Moderne

Further Reading

The literature on Art Deco and the designers associated with the style is immense, but useful general surveys appear in Brunhammer 1983, Duncan 1988, and Klein 1986. Arwas 1992 and Garner 1978 are standard reference works including numerous entries on individual decorators and designers. Bayer 1990 includes many excellent colour illustrations of surviving interiors.

Arminjon, Catherine and others, *L'Art de Vivre: Decorative Arts and Design in France, 1789–1989*, New York: Vendome, and London: Thames and Hudson, 1989

Arwas, Victor, *Art Deco*, 1980; revised edition New York: Abrams, and London: Academy, 1992

Barrett, Helena and John Phillips, *Suburban Style: The British Home, 1840–1960*, London: Macdonald, 1987

Battersby, Martin, *The Decorative Twenties*, 1969; revised by Philippe Garner, New York: Whitney Library of Design, and London: Herbert, 1988

Bayer, Patricia, *Art Deco Interiors: Decoration and Design Classics of the 1920s and 1930s*, London: Thames and Hudson, and Boston: Little Brown, 1990

Bayer, Patricia, *Art Deco Architecture: Design, Decoration and Detail from the Twenties and Thirties*, London: Thames and Hudson, and New York: Abrams, 1992

Bossaglia, Rossana, *Il Deco Italiano*, Milan: Rizzoli, 1975

Brunhammer, Yvonne, *Les Années "25": Collections du Musée des Arts Décoratifs* (exhib.cat.), Paris: Musée des Arts Décoratifs, 1966

Brunhammer, Yvonne, *The Art Deco Style*, London: Academy, 1983; New York: St. Martin's Press, 1984

Brunhammer, Yvonne and Suzanne Tise, *The Decorative Arts in France, 1900–1942 : La Société des Artistes Décorateurs*, New York: Rizzoli, 1990

Cabanne, Pierre, *Encyclopédie Art Déco*, Paris: Somogy, 1986

Caeymaex, Martine, *L'Art Deco en Europe: Tendances Décoratives dans les Arts Appliques vers 1925* (exhib. cat.), Brussels: Palais des Beaux-Arts, 1989

Duncan, Alastair, *Art Nouveau and Art Deco Lighting*, London: Thames and Hudson, and New York: Simon and Schuster, 1978

Duncan, Alastair, *Art Deco Furniture: The French Designers*, London: Thames and Hudson, and New York: Holt Rinehart, 1984

Duncan, Alastair, *American Art Deco*, London: Thames and Hudson, and New York: Abrams, 1986

Duncan, Alastair, *Art Deco*, London and New York: Thames and Hudson, 1988

Garner, Philippe, *The Encyclopedia of Decorative Arts, 1890–1940*, New York: Van Nostrand Reinhold, 1978

Heide, Robert and John Gilman, *Popular Art Deco: Depression Era Style and Design*, New York: Abbeville, 1991

Hillier, Bevis, *Art Deco of the 20s and 30s*, 1968; revised edition London: Herbert, 1985

Kjellberg, Pierre, *Art Déco: Les Maîtres du Mobilier*, Paris: L'Amateur, 1986

Klein, Dan, Nancy A. McClelland, and Malcolm Haslam, *In the Deco Style*, New York: Rizzoli, 1986; London: Thames and Hudson, 1987

Mandelbaum, Howard and Eric Myers, *Screen Deco*, New York: St. Martin's Press, 1985

Sharp, Dennis, *The Picture Palace and Other Buildings for the Movies*, London: Evelyn, and New York: Praeger, 1969

Tolstoi, Vladimir, *Art Décoratif Soviétique, 1917–1937*, Paris: Regard, 1989

Veronesi, Giulia, *Into the Twenties: Style and Design, 1909–1929*, London: Thames and Hudson, 1968

Weber, Eva, *Art Deco in America*, New York: Exeter, 1985

Art Furnishings

The term "Art", applied to furniture and decoration, refers to a style of domestic furnishing developed in Britain and America between the late 1860s and the mid-1880s. First coined by the critic Charles Locke Eastlake in 1867, the phrase Art Furniture initially referred to work that was architect- or artist-designed and that also involved a strong element of craftsmanship. Such pieces were therefore originally quite exclusive and expensive. Inevitably, though, these early associations lapsed and by the 1880s the word "Art" was being applied almost indiscriminately to wallpapers, ceramics and textiles, as well as furniture, to describe work that was not markedly different from that being produced by ordinary manufacturers at the time. In this sense Art Furnishings can be understood as both a continuation of and a commercial response to the reforms initiated by mid- and late-Victorian critics of architecture and design. Indeed, Art Furnishings have often been described as the first interior decoration style to reflect middle-class, as opposed to aristocratic taste, and their emergence coincided with the rise of the professional interior decorator and the increasing involvement of middle-class women as arbiters of taste and practitioners of design.

Stylistically, Art furnishings and decorations drew upon many sources. In the early phase elements derived from the reformed Gothic and Aesthetic styles, Japanese export goods, Islamic art, and European ornament in all its varieties were among the most important. Later, other features, notably those based on 18th-century English furniture, became more fashionable. But the central concern of Art Furnishings in both Britain and America was the demonstrable exercise of taste and it was perhaps this, rather than any purely stylistic feature that defined the phenomenon most clearly. Mainstream mid- and late-19th century styles of design were concerned above all with conspicuous consumption. Art Furnishings, on the other hand, appeared to reject such attitudes as vulgar and to value sensibility more than extravagance. In this respect, the emergence of Art Furnishings was closely linked to ideas popularised by Aestheticism whose most committed adherents not only decried the ugliness and ostentation of most manufactured goods but who likewise extolled the virtues of individuality over conformity and set great store by the exercise of an informed personal taste. For them, objects were to be appreciated not so much for their cost or status as for their intrinsic beauty, and the important thing was for the designer or consumer to be able to select from different periods or cultures judiciously and to combine the disparate elements harmoniously so as to create a coherent and beautiful whole. A similar outlook informed the production of Art Furnishings, many of which were actually used in Aesthetic homes and the purchase of which afforded visible proof of their owners' discrimination and taste.

The rise of Aestheticism in Britain, and with it a new emphasis upon the need for Art within the home, has been attributed to several factors, including the increasing acceptance of the design reforms set in motion in the 1840s, the influence of the writings of John Ruskin, the example of the many new public buildings and interiors then being constructed according to "reformed" Gothic principles, and the display of innovative design at the many national and international exhibitions held during the 1850s and later. Attention has also been paid to the effects of changing social and cultural values, and to the significance of increasingly liberal and anti-industrial tendencies among the country's professional and intellectual elite, in promoting an interest in art and beauty within the home. But perhaps of most importance within this context was the impact of the work of a small group of progressive architects and artist-designers and the growing appreciation of Japanese-inspired art and design.

Japanese goods were first exhibited in London at the International Exhibition of 1862 and were soon available from a number of retailers in the capital, notably Farmer & Rogers Oriental Warehouse, run by the young Arthur Liberty. Anglo-Japanese versions of the Oriental style were developed by designers such as Thomas Jeckyll, Christopher Dresser and E.W. Godwin during the late 1860s. A new freedom in the use of European ornament was demonstrated by Morris, Marshall, Faulkner & Co., both at the 1862 exhibition and in their prestigious commissions for the decoration of St. James's Palace and the Green Dining Room at the South Kensington Museum in 1866. Philip Webb's design for the latter was particularly significant, blending Gothic, Renaissance and modern elements into a scheme of subdued Pre-Raphaelite richness much more suitable for domestic applications than the ponderous Gothic then in vogue. Another distinctly artistic interior dating from the mid-1860s was D.G. Rossetti's house in Cheyne Walk, Chelsea. Rossetti decorated the interiors of his home with an informal and exotic mixture of objects from different periods which illustrated the value of antique furniture and carpets in producing rooms with an Aesthetic ambience. Underpinning these innovations and developments was the bedrock of reformist ideals espoused in the 1850s by the Government Schools of Design which gave a semblance of uniformity and order to the seemingly endless combinations of decorative design favoured by contemporary designers and manufacturers.

Publications played an important role in relaying these developments to a wider public, and two books, both written in the late 1860s were especially significant: *Gothic Forms Applied to Furniture, Metal Work and Decoration* by Bruce Talbert of 1868, and Charles Locke Eastlake's *Hints on Household Taste*, 1868. Talbert's book was aimed at the trade and proposed an architectonic style of furniture, termed Modern Gothic, which referred freely to Gothic within bold rectilinear designs. *Gothic Forms* brought this style to the attention of consumers on both sides of the Atlantic and his work was widely plagiarised although the principles which underlay it were not always understood: Talbert himself, for example, recommended simple materials with painted or incised surface decoration but cabinet-makers often interpreted these ornaments as inlay and veneer, a practice exemplified by the sideboard produced to his design by Holland & Sons for the Paris Exposition Universelle of 1867.

Hints on Household Taste fulfilled much the same function as *Gothic Forms* but its influence was immeasurably greater. The book was reprinted four times between 1868 and 1872 and it can justifiably be considered the single biggest influence on Art Furnishing. Declining to recommend any particular style, Eastlake distilled the ideas of the South Kensington Schools, the Gothic Revival architects and William Morris into a single philosophy of interior design, stressing the virtues of

Art Furnishings advertised by Henry Capel, London, late 1880s

simplicity, flat pattern and rectilinear forms. He addressed his ideas directly to the householder and was highly critical of professional decorators whom he accused of "the absurd love of change". His aim was to produce an environment that suggested continuity with the past in generalised terms and that stressed notions of simplicity, domesticity and homeliness.

There is little evidence of a commercial response to the above developments before the mid-1870s. Indeed the emphasis on amateurism and individual taste in *Hints* would seem to have precluded such initiatives. But from the mid-1870s the market for Art Furnishings was opened up in several ways. First, journals such as *The Builder*, the *Building News* and the *Art Journal* began discussing and illustrating new designs and, in so doing, stimulated wider demand for the style. Second, a steady stream of books and decorating manuals, mostly written by enthusiastic amateurs such as W.J. Loftie, Mrs. Orrinsmith and Mrs. Haweis, raised public consciousness about the importance of interior design. These publications were aimed at the professional middle classes and were supplemented by journals such as the *House Beautiful* in 1877 and *Decoration* in 1880. Third, a significant role was also played by London cabinet-makers like Gillows, Holland & Sons and William Watt, all of whom constructed suites of furniture for fashionable architects and later sold the same designs commercially. Watt's catalogue of 1877 featured many of Godwin's Anglo-Japanese designs while other firms in London and the provinces produced furniture more or less identical to that illustrated in Eastlake's *Hints*. Suitably artistic wallpapers and textiles also became more widely available during the 1870s. Morris & Co. increasingly concentrated their efforts in this area, firms like the wallpaper manufacturers Cowtan's imported Japanese embossed leather hangings, and retail outlets such as Liberty's, founded by Arthur Liberty in 1875, supplied imported Indian and Far Eastern textiles for the "Art" market.

Those consumers who did not wish to purchase their Art Furnishings from these specialist suppliers could patronise established decorators who soon began to supply versions of the style in pre-digested form. Many of the well-known metropolitan firms, including Jackson & Graham, Collinson and Lock, T. Knight & Sons, and James Shoolbred & Co., offered commercial variations of this taste. Shoolbred's, in particular, specialised in Art Furnishings and published an extensive catalogue in 1876 illustrating papers, furniture and suggestions for complete decorative schemes that has since become a standard sourcebook on the subject. Their designs came in a range of styles including the Anglo-Japanese, Modern Gothic and Renaissance, and although several bear a close resemblance to work produced by Godwin and the architect-designer T.E. Collcutt, they were produced in-house by Owen Davis utilising cheaper materials and machine-production techniques.

Despite their stylistic eclecticism, interiors furnished with Art Furnishings in Britain and America shared certain distinctive characteristics. As a general rule, the furniture was ebonised and gilded, lightly upholstered and displayed some evidence of revealed construction. Suites of matched furniture remained popular in dining rooms and bedrooms but there was a new move towards furnishing parlours, studies and smoking rooms with individual pieces in a variety of styles and towards mixing antique and modern furniture within the same scheme. Tastemakers also recommended a reduction in the density of decorative objects used within the interior, but the proliferation of "artistic" ceramics, metalwork and textiles produced by the Art Furnishings industry soon confounded their efforts. In fact, the quantity of objects to be found in "artistic" interiors was often identical to that in less fashionable rooms but their appearance, quality and distribution were significantly different. Art ceramics, for example, tended to be simple in shape, with decoration derived from Medieval, Renaissance and Islamic prototypes, and they were no longer arranged in picturesque groups on tables and case furniture, but were placed whenever possible on the shelves or brackets of overmantles and cabinets that were designed specifically for that purpose. The Aesthetic Movement's emphasis upon the importance of the contemplation of beauty also encouraged the isolated display of single objects such as paintings, sculptures or exotic curios, although how often the contents of the Art Furnished interior were subjected to the intense and self-conscious scrutiny suggested by their arrangement is open to question. And finally, the artistic interior was often flagged by totemic objects such as Japanese fans, Morris & Co. *Sussex* chairs, peacock feathers and oriental blue and white china – all widely lampooned in satirical journals like *Punch*.

The treatment of the architectural shell of these rooms also obeyed general principles. Architectural woodwork was usually quite conventional in form but was often painted in the same colours as furniture. Deeply moulded ceilings were frequently illustrated in the catalogues of professional furnishers, and the decoration of both ceilings and walls was given a new importance. Walls were generally divided into three horizontal bands – dado, fill and frieze – each given a separate decorative treatment that might include painted decoration, wallpaper and panelling. Ceramic tiles, either in panels or as continuous dados, were recommended in the catalogues of several decorating firms, but were generally expensive and were not widely used. Tertiary colour schemes, offset with gold, were common, and in time decorations became somewhat lighter in tone although white rooms were not widely accepted until the very end of the century. Several of these features survive in the interiors at 18 Stafford Terrace, Kensington, decorated some time after 1874 by its occupant, the political cartoonist Linley Sambourne. The furniture is a typical mixture of Talbert-style tables, sideboards and chairs, and genuine and reproduction Louis XVI antiques, while the decorations include generous use of embossed and gilded Japanese leather papers and Morris & Co. patterns.

The emergence of the Queen Anne style of domestic architecture led to a shift of emphasis within Art Furnishing. By the early 1880s, English 18th century styles – from George II to Robert Adam – had begun to replace Renaissance and Japanese styles as the favoured mode of furnishing. Colour schemes were generally lighter and brighter than in the 1870s and the elimination of cluttered surfaces was also carried further. Fitted furniture, inspired by 18th-century prototypes, was introduced both as a means of cutting down on the amount of dirt and dust within interiors and in order to open out the interior space. Increasingly Art Furnishings became more straightforwardly historicist and by the late 1890s, the original notions of simplicity and informality survived only as an ideal.

The introduction of Art Furnishings within North America occurred slightly later than in Britain but, initially at least, it developed along similar lines. Once again, Eastlake's ideas were extremely influential: *Hints* was published in Boston in 1872 and was widely available throughout the 1870s. Indeed, early American Art Furniture in the Modern Gothic manner was known as the "Eastlake Style", a term that Eastlake himself greatly disliked. Talbert's work was almost as popular, influencing among others the New York Art furnishers, Kimbel and Cabus, and the Philadelphia cabinet-maker Daniel Pabst. Pabst collaborated with the architect Frank Furness on Gothic furniture for several New York mansions, notably that of John Bond Trevor in Yonkers. But the key event in the popularisation of Art Furnishing in America was the Philadelphia Centennial Exposition of 1876. Several native firms showed furniture strongly influenced by Eastlake, and Collinson & Lock exhibited a number of Anglo-Japanese designs by Godwin, heralding the launch of Aesthetic styles within the avant-garde.

Despite the cultural and social hegemony of the East Coast, other centres of artistic activity emerged in the Midwest. Cincinnati was particularly rich in cabinet-makers and designers and a unique school of Aesthetic woodcarving developed at the Cincinnati School of Design under the instruction of Henry Linley Fry and Benn Pitman. Much of the best work was produced by women. Adelaide Nourse (later Pitman's second wife) and Emma Belper were both prominent in this field, and the work of 65 women carvers was exhibited by the Cincinnati School of Design at the Philadelphia Centennial.

Even more than in Britain, nostalgia played a leading role in American Aestheticism. The Centennial celebrations confirmed a growing interest in the nation's past and stimulated a taste for 18th-century Colonial furnishings. Clarence Cook, author of the influential *House Beautiful* of 1878, defended the liking for antiques on functional as well as aesthetic grounds. However, as in Britain, the desire to own old things reflected social anxieties more than practical considerations, and ownership of American antiques, in particular, was proof either of the family pedigree, or of aesthetic refinement in being able to pick out the object of quality from among the flotsam of second-hand furniture. With genuine antiques in limited supply, the fashion for reproduction furniture in 18th-century styles, known as the Colonial Revival, flourished and retailers like Sypher & Co. of New York responded quickly with advertising aimed at the Art market.

Art Furnishing has many claims to be the first "modern" form of interior design. Its appeal to middle-class taste, the new importance attached to named designers and retailers, and the network of publications and journals which evolved to inform the public about new developments all foreshadow the character of the market in the 20th century. But perhaps its most remarkable and enduring achievement was in the sphere of education, for within a few short years, a large section of the middle-class public were led to appreciate concepts of design quite alien to the understanding of the previous generation.

NICHOLAS SHADDICK

See also Aesthetic Movement; Colonial Revival; Eastlake; Kimbel and Cabus

Further Reading

Aslin, Elizabeth, *The Aesthetic Movement: Prelude to Art Nouveau*, London: Elek, and New York: Praeger, 1969

Burke, Doreen Bolger and others, *In Pursuit of Beauty: Americans and the Aesthetic Movement* (exhib. cat.: Metropolitan Museum, New York), New York: Rizzoli, 1986

Cooper, Jeremy, *Victorian and Edwardian Furniture and Interiors*, London: Thames and Hudson, 1987

Eastlake, Charles Locke, *Hints on Household Taste*, London, 1868, 4th edition 1877

Girouard, Mark, *Sweetness and Light: The Queen Anne Movement, 1860–1900*, Oxford: Clarendon Press, 1977; New Haven: Yale University Press, 1984

Hanks, David A. and Page Talbott, "Daniel Pabst, Philadelphia Cabinetmaker" in *Philadelphia Museum of Art Bulletin*, 73, 1977, pp.4–24

James Shoolbred & Co., *Designs for Furniture*, London, 1876

Kinchin, Juliet, "Collinson and Lock" in *Connoisseur*, 201, May 1979, pp.46–53

McClaugherty, Martha Crabill, "Household Art: Creating the Artistic Home, 1868–1893" in *Winterthur Portfolio*, 18, Spring 1983, pp.1–26

Madigan, Mary Jean Smith, "Eastlake-Influenced American Furniture, 1870–1890" in *Connoisseur*, 191, January 1976, pp.58–63

Pevsner, Nikolaus, "Art Furniture of the Eighteen-Seventies" in *Architectural Review*, 111, January 1952, pp.43–50

Pierce, Donald C., "Mitchell and Rammelsberg, Cincinnati Furniture Manufacturers, 1847–1881" in *Winterthur Portfolio*, 13, 1978, pp.222–29

Talbert, Bruce, *Gothic Forms Applied to Furniture*, Birmingham, 1868

Victorian and Edwardian Decorative Art: The Handley-Read Collection (exhib. cat.), London: Royal Academy, 1972

Art Nouveau

"Art Nouveau" is the generic term for a broad movement of style and ideas that embraced architecture, all the decorative and graphic arts, fashion, furniture and fittings right across Europe (and to a lesser extent, North America) in the years between 1880 and 1910. Art Nouveau is usually recognised by a distinct curvilinear quality,varying between subtle undulations of shape and an extravagant fantasy. It has a characteristic iconography of motifs and symbols abstracted from vegetation, and a repertoire of biomorphic forms; much of its imagery is directly or obliquely feminine. In a number of important cases this curvilinear and botanical stage was succeeded by a more geometrical manner, becoming something much closer to Modernism. If Art Nouveau is defined on formalist criteria it will probably be confined to the earlier manifestations associated with Brussels and Paris; but if it is regarded as a matter of taste and ideas, then a broader interpretation must be followed. The "broad movement" was also subject to a range of local or national variants, and an argument can be made that would advance the idea of a plural *Arts Nouveaux*. However the unity of a broad movement is not determined by formal characteristics alone, but by ideological, social and cultural use.

Historiographically, Art Nouveau has usually been treated as an intermediate phase, between the historicism of the 19th century and the Modernism of the 20th. But this story assumes that there is a simple single-line development from one stage to another, and is inadequate in both fact and theory. Today it seems best to consider Art Nouveau in its own terms, as an array of objects, interiors and buildings (etc.) to which a set of criteria can be addressed. These criteria concern the relations with history, technology, social significance, artistic means, formal vocabulary and clientele. No particular instance is likely to meet all the questions asked of it, but in the process of asking, a field of meanings is created. It is necessary to explore these meanings rather than define the objects.

This approach is especially appropriate to the study of interiors, which are not objects, but ensembles only gaining their full meaning when they are in use. Rooms are the spaces that make a range of human meetings possible; they both contain and help to form human behaviour. To investigate the Art Nouveau interior is also to explore a social moment. It is additionally appropriate because the creation of a harmonious ensemble, in which every feature is integrated with the next, was a deliberate and oft-repeated aim of this otherwise varied tendency. At its most complete, this integration began to abolish traditional distinctions between fine and applied arts, and between craft and industrial objects in favour of an intricate synthesis of all aspects of design. It passed over into the clothes and deportment of the men and women who used the rooms, and it was held to signify a new stage in social life. Hence the very names by which this domain came to be known – the "new art", "l'art nouveau", "Jugendstil", "Modernism", "Arte Joven" etc. The style is also associated with particular cities – including in addition to Paris, Brussels and Vienna, Glasgow, Budapest, Darmstadt, Munich, Barcelona, Turin, and Chicago – several of which underwent rapid growth in the 1890s and sought to establish their distinct modern character.

In what did this newness consist and what did it mean? It was partly an outcome of the demand, insistent throughout 19th-century Europe, for a new style of architecture appropriate to an industrial epoch and linked to a new building technology. In England, this demand went back to the year of the Crystal Palace (1851) and beyond. In that context, M.D. Wyatt could ask English architecture for " a vocabulary of its own, in which to speak to the world the language of [England's] power, and its freedom of thought and feeling." New methods of building were envisaged, such as W.V. Pickett's *New System of Architecture* (1845) which would be polychrome, curvilinear, prefabricated and distributed across the whole globe. The use of cast and wrought iron, later combined with steel joists and reinforced concrete, enabled architects to create interior spaces of great volume and delicacy. Ceramic and similar materials were developed which encouraged architects to treat the decoration of surfaces with a new freedom, independent of the underlying construction. Characteristic materials were terracotta, faience, artificial stone and enamelled iron – all capable of being used in strong or original colour. In this respect, Art Nouveau involved a reassessment of the relations between structure and decoration, with consequences for interiors as well as exteriors.

Art Nouveau was also related to developments in service technology. Throughout the later 19th century (at different rates in different places) oil lamps were replaced by gas lamps, mantels and flues were improved to get rid of greasy deposits, and finally electric light promised perfect cleanliness. Heating and ventilation were combined through the use of ducts, fans and extractors; steam central heating became common in the more expensive houses and apartments. Effective plumbing, with running hot water and flush toilets became widely available. Much of this technology originated in ship and railway design but was incorporated into domestic and other buildings during the 1890s. This vast improvement in services did not cause Art Nouveau, but it gave it occasion; both in the small example of lighting fixtures, and in the grand case of the Paris Metro. The workshops and showrooms of Vienna's Wiener Werkstätte (1903), for example, had electric lamps, washing facilities and water closets (*englische toiletten*) of such modernity that "many of those employed there ... found things so unfamiliar to begin with that they became a little shy, and none certainly had ever worked under such excellent conditions before" (Schweiger, 1984). Patrick Geddes, the Scots polymath, defined this in 1898 as the advent of the "neo-technic order" that would replace noisy and dirty "palaeotechnology" with "electricity, hygiene and art".

The new art was also an outcome of the re-evaluation of craft values in the face of industrial production. Though it was in many respects a repudiation of the Arts and Crafts Movement, it is very hard to imagine Art Nouveau without its predecessor. Some Art Nouveau craft work of the 1890s is of exceptional virtuosity – for example, the glass bowls and vases of Emile Gallé (1846–1904) – and this virtuosity is at the very opposite end of the scale of values from the homely qualities that the Arts and Crafts Movement promoted. Yet the latter Movement, as it developed in the course of the century, produced branches which are hardly to be distinguished from Art Nouveau. This is especially the case in England, where the Aesthetic Movement produced objects and interiors that all authorities agree are an important stage in the creation of the "new art". A very good example is the case of A.H. Mackmurdo (1851–1942), whose furniture and surface pattern work evinces Art Nouveau qualities, and whose writings advocate typical ideas and values.

Probably the most important debt that Art Nouveau owed to the Arts and Crafts Movements was the high value placed upon ordinary objects, and upon the necessity of seeking a synthesis between the useful and the beautiful. In particular, one can point to the ever greater significance attributed to decoration and the interior in English-language theory and criticism, all the way through from Pugin and Ruskin to Morris and Voysey. Where Art Nouveau differed from the Arts and Crafts Movement most strongly, was in social theory. The new style was openly progressive and anti-traditional, and developed no critique of capitalist modes of production and the division of labour, except in Belgium, in the pages of the journal *L'Art Moderne*.

The new style was also ideational. Though the precise signification of Art Nouveau varied according to country and context, it was always underpinned by a deep shift in philosophical, and therefore aesthetic, thought. This entailed a rejection of Positivism and a reassessment of intuitive and subjective modes of perception and knowledge. The language of Art Nouveau theory and criticism is often infused with vitalist descriptions of energy and life-force. This was enmeshed with what one writer has described as "the sense of the demise of an old society, coupled with an agonizing uncertainty as to what the form of the new society might prove to be ... The result was an enormous heightening of self-consciousness ... as a counterbalance to the positivist faith in exact science, a number of the young thinkers of the 1890s proposed to rely on 'intuition' (H.S. Hughes, *Consciousness and Society: The Reorientation of European Social Thought, 1890–1930*, 1979). Mackmurdo summed this up as "a strong advocacy of subjective art in all its branches ... giving our work a more abstract or mood-made character, than the more popular forms of art possess ... at all times quite consciously selective ... the exponent of sentiment whose immediate source lies in qualities rather than things" (*The Hobby Horse*, 1, 1883).

There is no direct road from the pages of a thesis to the design of a living room, but it is clear that this reassessment led to the rejection of Naturalism – although not nature – both in literature and in painting, and to a burgeoning interest in symbolic and abstract forms of expression. There are many areas of overlapping activity and theory between Art Nouveau and the Symbolist movement in painting. The decorative values of the visual arts were seen to be more significant than the narrative; the paradigm of expression was, above all, musical. The consequences of this for painting were profound, leading in time toward the development of non-figurative art; but they also led to a higher valuation of what had hitherto been regarded as merely decorative – wallpapers, textiles, tile patterns all took on greater signifying power. There is a convergence between what William Morris had earlier called the "greater" and the "lesser arts of life". The consequences for interior design were profound; a room might be called on to do the work hitherto deemed proper for fine arts. It should strive to "materialise the outward forms of my sensibilities" as Maurice Barrès wrote, in his *Culte de Moi* (1889).

Musical analogies form a major theme in art-theoretical and critical writing of the period, as do organic analogies. Musical composition provided an important model of synthetic unity and complete organisation, an idea that received philosophical support in the writings of Schopenhauer, and artistic validation in the writings and practice of Richard Wagner. Many examples could be cited; the treatment of melodic line in Wagner's *Tristan und Isolde* is strikingly suggestive of the sinuous wandering lines of Art Nouveau; and Debussy certainly made comparison between melodic "arabesque" and the principles of decoration. In English, the most significant statement of these beliefs will be found in Walter Pater's much quoted sentence, "In [music's] consummate moments, the end is not distinct from the means, the form from the matter, the subject from the expression; they inhere in and completely saturate each other; and to it, therefore, to the condition of its perfect moments, all the arts may be supposed constantly to tend and aspire" (*The Renaissance*, 1873). And a project such as the unbuilt Music Room for the "House for an Art Lover" (1901) by Charles Rennie Mackintosh (1868–1928) needs to be interpreted in terms of these analogies.

Mackintosh's drawings for this room also demonstrate to the highest degree that synthesis of all the parts which was the aim of Art Nouveau. The panels beside the fireplace were to have been by Margaret Macdonald, almost certainly in creamy white gesso with small touches of colour. The same creamy white would have extended to the white lacquered furniture

Art Nouveau: *Cromer Bird* block-printed cotton by A.H. Mackmurdo for the Century Guild, c.1884

and the decorative pillars. The bud-like motifs would have shown an inner purple red or dull pink, and the carpet would probably have been a light beige or silvery green: the lamp shades copper with coloured glass inserts, and the fire-irons plain polished metal. The panels in the window bays are probably embroidered on linen to designs by Macdonald. The Music Room was one of the typical sites of Art Nouveau interior decor.

The life sciences also provided analogies for the designer. With the growing rejection of historicism went a crisis in decoration; traditional motifs, patterns and ornament were felt to have no further meaning. The search for a new decorative style entailed a return to Nature, not as visual appearance, but as hidden structure. "The value to a designer of a scientific comprehension of the world is the insight it gives him into the possible variations of the original, and the inexhaustible sources of grace and beauty; whence so much that is new, and yet consistent, may be derived..." (Edward Forbes, 1851). The study of botany for ornamental purposes – known as Art Botany – became a major part of the drawing curriculum in British and some Continental schools of design, from the 1860s onward. Important pioneers of the new style, such as Christopher Dresser (1834–1904) and A.H. Mackmurdo had a scientific education. Among architects, Victor Horta, Antoni Gaudí, and H.P. Berlage are known to have had an informed interest in the life sciences. Books of scientific illustrations, such as Ernst Haeckel's *Kunstformen der Natur* (1899–1904) were in many studios, and the biomorphic element in Art Nouveau certainly derives in large measure from these sources. This is particularly true in domestic glassware, where the material lends itself to fluid treatment, and is well seen in the work of Louis Comfort Tiffany (1848–1933). However, this was not universal; the tendency to an informal naturalism was always present in French Art Nouveau.

The stylistic origins of Art Nouveau were diverse and extensive, including Celtic, Viking, Javanese, and above all Japanese decoration. These sources provided alternative examples of highly intricate decoration, without the cultural authority of historical precedence. Japanese structural carpentry, too, had a bearing on the treatment of wood by E.W. Godwin, Charles Rennie Mackintosh and Frank Lloyd Wright. Local and peasant traditions, too, played a part in the deployment of Art Nouveau through Eastern Europe and Russia. These latter interests were not so much anti-historicist, as ahistorical, part of an assumed "natural" folk-culture which had hitherto been overlaid with aristocratic and imported styles. Thus the New Art could be linked in one direction to global and imperial references, and in another to local or vernacular traditions. In each case, the aim was to find cultural models alternative to the former lines of European tradition.

All these theoretical concerns impelled designers and artist / craftworkers toward a style that rejected historical precedents (unless they were ancient or exotic), sought for models in other artistic disciplines and in a new concept of Nature, and which could embody a heightened self-consciousness. The bringing together of these concerns with new technical opportunities required a synthesis that was both imaginative and practical.

Art Nouveau was, more than anything, concerned with synthesis. This meant, at one level, creating a unity of style – a correlation of parts so that each detail contained within itself the germ of the whole ensemble. H.P. Berlage (1856–1934) described this as "a mutual agreement in art principle" such that a chair might be described in terms of a small building, and a small building in terms of a chair. The mental model here is, essentially, biological correlation between large and small features, such that just as an animal might be reconstructed from a few bones and a footprint, so a house might be deduced from a door-handle, two chairs and a balustrade. Here scientific methods defined by comparative anatomy combine with the Wagnerian *gesamtkunstwerk*. At the next level, it meant a synthesis of process, so that art, craft and industrial methods could be employed side by side to the one purpose; this may be seen as an outcome of British debates about the correct uses of hand and machine processes. And at the third level, the synthesis was between the demands of function and beauty (which was also of the binary balances between intellect and emotion, reason and intuition). This was a further stage in the long-running discourse that placed structure in relation to decoration. In 19th-century symbolic terms the balance between intellect / reason / structure and emotion / intuition / decoration was between supposedly masculine and feminine forces. This synthesis could only take place to the full in rooms, where spaces, objects and manners interact. At this deep symbolic level, Art Nouveau was concerned with gender relations.

At the level of immediate practice was the willingness on the part of artists and craftspeople to cross boundaries. An excellent example of this is Henry van de Velde (1863–1957), a painter who, having built and decorated his own house, designed his wife's wardrobe (in both senses of the word), and then became a designer for both craft and industrial production, and a leading theorist. Mackintosh was simultaneously a designer of buildings, interiors, furniture, textiles, and every detail of the household; finally a painter of some note. Peter Behrens (1868–1940) was first active as a painter, then as a graphic designer, branching out into applied arts and domestic architecture, finally becoming a major industrial designer and builder of factories. These are only the most prominent examples of a general tendency. Where all these domains intersected was in the design of interiors.

Another important question that needs to be answered is at whom was Art Nouveau addressed? Robert Schmutzler, whose *Art Nouveau* is one of the most complete studies, argues that it is "a style of the upper bourgeoisie, that of the cultured and urbane middle class in the heyday of classical capitalism. It is essentially the first genuinely universal style of a period which was no longer under the domination of the clergy or aristocracy." Conspicuous private consumption was certainly a feature of Art Nouveau commissions. The compact splendour of Josef Hoffmann's Palais Stoclet, Brussels (1905–11), takes the breath away; exotic woods, marbles, mosaic, copper, enamel and gold leaf are brought together with consummate taste. The house competes with Antoni Gaudí's Palacio Güell, Barcelona (1886–89), for the most expensive private commission of the epoch. But one should not assume that this social group was everywhere the same, or that it even had the same interests.

One persuasive analysis shows that in France the new art was perceived to be a modernisation of the Rococo in new conditions, a neo-conservative return to expensive craft values after the debacle of the Franco–Prussian war (Silverman 1989). This is particularly clear in the designs of Louis Majorelle (1859–1926), especially the series of restaurants he worked on between 1899 and 1905. The restaurant is another typical site for Art Nouveau, since it is a point where private and public worlds mingle in both fact and sentiment, and a restaurant is also a place for conspicuous consumption (in every sense of the word) and for the display of fashions. Majorelle's interior of the Restaurant Lucas-Carton, in the Place de la Madeleine, Paris (1905) demonstrates the Rococo aspect of Parisian Art Nouveau to the full, showing a characteristic delight in naturalistic detail and refined but entirely traditional craftsmanship. It is also, clearly, a strongly gendered space, devoted to a certain notion of the feminine. But these, it might be said, are exactly the aspects of Art Nouveau that were not transferable to the new century, and which prevented French designers from evolving the style toward industrial production.

Silverman aligns French Art Nouveau with an ideological struggle taking place between the traditional and the New Woman. Government circles encouraged the growth of the new art and identified it with a modern domesticity that was antagonistic to the undomesticated and autonomous New Woman (whose ideological profile was perceived to be scientific, Positivist and anti-clerical). The effect of this campaign was "to define and promote women as the natural allies of French luxury craftsmanship, and as the artificers of a unitary interior design". This is perfectly caught in some of the designs made by Georges de Feure and Eugène Gaillard and particularly in de Feure's boudoir designed for Bing's L'Art Nouveau pavilion (1900). But this interpretation suggests a defensive conservatism which does not match easily with the ideology of Catalan Modernismo (which had nationalist overtones); nor with Glasgow's imperial rapacity and colossal industrial undertakings. In Austria-Hungary, the Secession was at least partly an attempt to create a modern identity for an ancient regime. In Chicago and New York yet further assertions were being made. And none of these alliances explain the uses of the style in the cause of progressive politics and early socialism. That it should serve for the posters of the Italian Socialist Party and the headquarters of the Belgian Union of Socialist Workers is not surprising, since Art Nouveau was often conceived in Utopian terms, as a union between art and industry in the service of the future. This is clearly demonstrated in the connections established between radical politics and the new art in Belgium where the Belgian Union of Socialist Workers, or Maison du Peuple as it was known, was built by Victor Horta between 1895 and 1898.

The Maison du Peuple contained offices, meeting rooms and a large conference hall. The same ornamental motifs extend from pavement to roofline, in stone, brick and rivetted iron; structural elements such as the iron pillars, girders and brackets are left exposed and function as ornament, both within and without. Every detail seems to have been completely thought through. The plan fits a complicated building into an irregular site with great skill; the interiors were as plain, but as considered, as this façade, thus showing that Art Nouveau should not be thought of as invariably opulent. The destruction of this building in 1966 now looks like a piece of official vandalism.

In the United States, the new art was understood in rather different terms. In New York, and particularly in the work of Tiffany, it fits well within the range of European culture; but as developed in Chicago, with such designers as Louis Sullivan (1856–1924) and Frank Lloyd Wright (1867–1959), it was promoted as a democratic and American antidote to European aristocratic values. But within this context, America represents the geographical and ideological edge of the "field of meanings".

Elsewhere, the Art Nouveau style could be seen in popular commercial entertainment, in restaurants and tearooms, and in the major public services such as the Viennese tramway system, and most famously the entrances to the Paris Metro which were designed by Hector Guimard c.1900. As early as 1889 while a young teacher at the Ecole des Arts Décoratifs, Guimard had designed an exhibition pavilion called the Pavillon d'Electricité. Ten years later, a competition for new stations organised by the Metropolitan Company produced such poor entries that the committee turned to Guimard who had now a reputation as an ingenious and original architect. There followed a long battle with the municipal authorities who preferred academic architects; the new style was promoted by a new commercial / technical undertaking, in the teeth of older social forces. One contemporary journal wrote "His aim has been to avoid any ornamental motif borrowed directly from nature or, more specifically, flora. Here we shall find no decoration assuming the forms which exist in nature, neither flowers nor vegetation. M. Guimard is interested only in line; it is from the 'line' or from the arrangement of several lines that he draws all his effects." Guimard's entrances and balustrades perfectly illustrate the connection between abstract decorative draughtsmanship and industrial production typical of Art Nouveau; academic architecture has fallen through the gap in between them.

At its cheaper end, Art Nouveau is to be found in very ordinary urban situations. In the better terrace houses of Belfast, for example, one finds everywhere iron grates, mouldings, tiles, fireplaces and leaded windows with a "nouveau" character; the city enjoyed great prosperity in the early 1900s.

When we examine the uses of Art Nouveau, and look at its clientele and promotion, we begin to perceive why it was possible that such a tendency could be so widely disseminated and so characteristic of its period. All those groups looking toward the next century could align themselves around it, as iron filings align themselves round magnetic lines of force. Great wealth from the new industries, new technologies and building methods, liberal moral values, philosophical idealism, different feminisms, early socialist politics and new types of social relations based around all these, could find in Art Nouveau a focus of style and feeling, even while they might have nothing else in common. It is therefore most appropriate to think of Art Nouveau as the expression of a particular moment of modernity, in which a very wide coalition of interests and social groupings could, briefly, share. And it is possible to identify these around some contemporary activities.

The first of these activities is shopping. The growth of Art Nouveau coincides with the growth of department stores and specialised boutiques, and the style is frequently associated with particular names. Perhaps the most notable is Siegfried Bing's gallery L'Art Nouveau (established Paris, 1895) which commissioned or imported designs from Tiffany, van de Velde, Gallé, Lalique, Morris, Crane, Voysey and de Feure (as well as a host of others). But Liberty's (established London, 1875) is hardly less significant and gave the name of stile liberty to Italian Art Nouveau. The Magazin für Kunstgewerbe (Vienna 1875) was under the direction of Henry van de Velde from 1899. Other important names are La Maison Moderne (established Paris, 1897), and the Wiener Werkstätte showrooms (established Vienna, 1903). On the larger scale, major stores such as the Galeries Lafayette (established 1900), and similar emporia had Art Furnishing departments. Many of these major stores were themselves designed by Art Nouveau architects, including Messel's Wertheim Store (Berlin 1896), Horta's L'Innovation (1901), and Frantz Jourdain's La Samaritaine store (Paris 1905).

But shopping, especially for women, is a social activity of some importance. Where women of the 1890s were concerned, shopping was their principal point of entry into a public domain comprised not only of shops, but also of streets, boulevards, parks, tearooms, cafes, restaurants and transportation. Each one of these sites was a location for the new art, in the forms of street furniture, benches, shelters, kiosks, façades, doorways, shopfittings and interiors. Art Nouveau stands as a marker of a commercial modernity, and of an aspect of modern public life which was "feminine". A recent writer has remarked on "the invisibility of women in the literature of modernity"; but beyond literature, in the realm of things, a distinctly feminine domain was developed in and through Art Nouveau. Thus the style intersects with different aspects of

Art Nouveau: smoking room by Henry van de Velde for S. Bing's salon L'Art Nouveau, Paris, 1895

female emancipation and the discourse of femininity, and this discourse is deeply inscribed in its formal character, ambitions, promotion and marketing.

It does not now seem possible to reconstruct in detail the degree to which women were the direct buyers and commissioners of new designs. But it is clear that Art Nouveau was often addressed to women as if they were the principle customers. Further research might show non-architectural Art Nouveau to have been the first example of a style conceived in the modern terms of consumption and the buying power of women.

With consumption went publicity. Art Nouveau was deliberately promoted through illustrated art periodicals to an unprecedented degree. *L'Art Moderne* (Brussels 1881), *The Studio* (London 1893), *The Chap-Book* (Chicago 1894), *The Yellow Book* (London 1894) *Pan* (Berlin 1895), *Die Jugend* (Munich 1896), *Art et Décoration* (Paris 1897), *Deutsche Kunst und Dekoration* (Darmstadt 1897), *Dekorative Kunst* (Munich 1897) *L'Art Décoratif* (Paris 1898), *Ver Sacrum* (Vienna 1898), *Mir Iskusstva* (St. Petersburg 1899), are merely some of the widely distributed publications. Many more can be cited; all were concerned with the "artistic interior". The Art Nouveau style was also seen on posters and advertisements; most famously by Henri de Toulouse-Lautrec (1864–1901), Jules Chéret (1836–1932) and Alphonse Mucha (1860–1939). Art Nouveau should, therefore, be considered under the heading of "spectacle". And here should be noted the increased range of graphic techniques available for every kind of publication, and the use made of them by such Art Nouveau illustrators as Aubrey Beardsley (1872–98) and his many followers.

And third, closely connected to both shopping and publicity, were exhibitions. The phenomenon of large Expositions is now recognised as a gauge of national and regional ideologies; they existed then, as now, to promote social and political positions through the display of goods. The new art was an element in the promotion of the modern polity, as well as being an element of trade. Among the many exhibitions large and small, the following are certainly significant. Les Salons du Champ de Mars (Paris, from 1891), a regular exhibition venue which gave equal prominence to both the fine and applied arts. The 7th International Art Exhibition (Munich 1897) treated the applied arts with the same attention as painting and sculpture. The Decorative Arts Exhibition (Dresden 1897), at which Bing's exhibits, mainly designed by van de Velde, received an enthusiastic response. The 8th Secession Exhibition (Vienna 1900), organised by Josef Hoffmann of the Wiener Werkstätte, which brought the work of English and Scots designers into contact with the Werkstätte; especially that of the Glasgow Four and C.R. Ashbee. L'Exposition Universelle (Paris 1900), notable for Bing's pavilion with complete interiors designed by Eugène Gaillard, and Georges de Feure; and for an extensive display organized by the Central Union of Decorative Arts, which included Hector Guimard, Louis Majorelle, Emile Gallé and others. This was also the year in which the Metro, with entrances designed by Guimard, was brought into full operation. The Glasgow International Exhibition 1901, notable for the exhibits of the firm Wylie and Lochhead, and for connections established with Russia. The Decorative Art Exhibition, Turin 1902, with pavilions designed by Raimondo D'Aronco (1857–1932) brought quantities of the new art to Italy, not least work from Glasgow. The exhibits were subsequently seen in central and eastern Europe, in other shows. Many others might be cited.

In each and every one of these exhibitions, real or imaginary interiors were displayed, often made especially for the occasion. A study of these exhibits is a study of the developing idea of the modern interior; and this idea gains its point of maximum velocity in the years of Art Nouveau.

DAVID BRETT

See also Bing; Guimard; Horta; Maison Moderne

Further Reading

The literature on Art Nouveau is very extensive. Good general surveys appear in Madsen 1975, Schmutzler 1978, and Masini 1984. More specific accounts of Art Nouveau in particular countries are listed below.

Amaya, Mario, *Art Nouveau*, 1966; revised edition, London: Herbert, and New York: Schocken, 1985

Borisova, E.A. and Grigory Sternin, *Russian Art Nouveau*, New York: Rizzoli, 1988

Borsi, Franco and Hans Wieser, *Bruxelles, Capitale de l'Art Nouveau*, Rome: Colombo, 1971

Borsi, Franco and Ezio Godoli, *Paris 1900*, revised edition New York: Rizzoli, 1989

Bossaglia, Rossana, *Il Liberty: Storia e fortuna del Liberty italiano*, Florence: Sansoni, 1974

Bott, G., *Jugendstil* (exhib. cat.), Brussels: Palais des Beaux-Arts, 1977

Brunhammer, Yvonne, *Art Nouveau: Belgium / France* (exhib. cat.), Houston: Rice University Institute for the Arts, 1976

De Guffry, Irene, *Il Mobile Liberty Italiano*, Rome: Latera, 1983

Dierkens-Aubry, Françoise and Jos Vandenbreeden, *Art Nouveau en Belgique: Architecture et Interieurs*, Louvain: Duculot, 1991

Duncan, Alastair, *Art Nouveau and Art Deco Lighting*, London: Thames and Hudson, and New York: Simon and Schuster, 1978

Duncan, Alastair, *Art Nouveau Furniture*, London: Thames and Hudson, and New York: Potter, 1982

Eadie, William, *Movements of Modernity: The Case of Glasgow and Art Nouveau*, London and New York: Routledge,1990

Eri, Gyöngyi and Zsuzsa Jobbàgyi, *A Golden Age: Art and Society in Hungary, 1896–1914* (exhib. cat.), London: Barbican Art Gallery, 1983

Freixa, Mireia, *El Modernismo en España*, Madrid: Cátedra, 1986

Hiesinger, Kathryn B. (editor), *Art Nouveau in Munich: Masters of Jugendstil from the Stadtmuseum, Munich, and other Public and Private Collections* (exhib. cat.), Philadelphia: Philadelphia Museum of Art, 1988

Johnson, Diane Chalmers, *American Art Nouveau*, New York: Abrams, 1979

Kempton, Richard, *Art Nouveau: An Annotated Bibliography*, Los Angeles: Hennessey and Ingalls, 1977

Loze, Pierre, *Belgium, Art Nouveau: From Victor Horta to Antoine Pompe*, Ghent: Snoeck-Ducaju & Zoon, 1991

Madsen, Stephan Tschudi, *Sources of Art Nouveau*, 1959; reprinted New York: Da Capo, 1975

Madsen, Stephan Tschudi, *Art Nouveau*, London: Weidenfeld and Nicolson, and New York: McGraw Hill, 1967

Masini, Lara-Vinca, *Art Nouveau*, London: Thames and Hudson, 1984

Pevsner, Nikolaus and J. M. Richards (editors), *The Anti-Rationalists: Art Nouveau Architecture and Design*, London: Architectural Press, and New York: Harper, 1973

Russell, Frank (editor), *Art Nouveau Architecture*, New York: Rizzoli, and London: Academy, 1979

Schmutzler, Robert, *Art Nouveau*, 2nd edition New York: Abrams, and London: Thames and Hudson, 1978

Schweiger, Werner J., *Wiener Werkstätte: Designs in Vienna, 1903-1932*, London: Thames and Hudson, and New York: Abbeville, 1984

Selz, Peter and Mildred Constantine (editors), *Art Nouveau: Art and Design at the Turn of the Century*, 2nd edition New York: Museum of Modern Art, and London: Secker and Warburg, 1975

Sembach, Klaus-Jürgen, *Art Nouveau / Utopia: Reconciling the Irreconcilable*, Cologne: Taschen, 1991

Shimomura, Jun'ichi, *Art Nouveau Architecture: Residential Masterpieces*, London: Academy, and San Francisco: Cadence, 1992

Silverman, Debora L., *Art Nouveau in Fin-de-Siècle France: Politics, Psychology, and Style*, Berkeley: University of California Press, 1989

Troy, Nancy J., *Modernism and the Decorative Arts in France: Art Nouveau to Le Corbusier*, New Haven and London: Yale University Press, 1991

Weisberg, Gabriel P., *Art Nouveau Bing: Paris Style 1900* (exhib.cat.: Smithsonian Institution, Washington, DC), New York: Abrams, 1986

Artari Family

Italian family of stuccoists

The Artari family included a number of celebrated stuccoists who were active in Germany and England in the second and third quarter of the 18th century. The family originated in Arogno in Italy in the late 16th century; its history is extremely complex and confusing. Primary sources often refer to individual members by their surname only and although research undertaken by the historian Geoffrey Beard has gone some way towards clarifying certain important biographical details, there is still no catalogue defining the extent of each family member's work.

According to Beard, Giovanni Battista Artari was born in 1664 and married Caterina de Maini in 1688. His son, Carlo Giuseppe was born on 5 September 1692 and died on 27 May 1757. Another son, Adalbert, was born on 7 October 1693 and a record of the death of an Alberto Artari on 22 October 1751 may refer to this same Adalberto. There is also mention of another master called Giuseppe, the son of Domenico and Bartolomea Pianca, who was born on 20 September 1700. There is much to suggest that the stuccoist principally active in England was Carlo Giuseppe (1692–1757), and that it was the other Giuseppe (b.1700), perhaps a cousin of the former, who worked in Germany, especially since several sources record that a master with that name died in Cologne in 1769. Also, given the difficulties and time involved in foreign travel during this period, it seems unlikely that one master could have been active between 1729 and 1732 at Brühl and working contemporaneously in London (1729) and Essex (1730–31). Similarly, it is hard to believe that the same person who worked at the Pöppelsdorf Palace, near Bonn in 1744 was paid for work completed at Wimpole Hall and at the Radcliffe Camera in Oxford during the same period. Or that someone who was in Cologne between 1754 and 1757 was at the same time working in Warwickshire (1756–60). It seems altogether more plausible to suppose that after working with his father at Aquisgrana, Carlo Giuseppe settled in England while the younger Giuseppe continued to work in Germany developing his family's technical inheritance.

The earliest documented work by Giovanni Battista Artari is at Rastatt and is dated 1705. Giovanni's talent in rendering stucco with the same properties as marble is evident in the decorations executed for the Hofkirche in Rastatt, particularly in the Gloria of the Virgin on the high altar. He executed a large part of the sculptural work in the apse and chapels in Fulda Cathedral which was produced with Johann Neudecker the Elder in 1707. The extraordinary force of his work is apparent in the four colossal figures of the Fathers of the Church in the Monk's Choir. Following this he worked at Brühl and on the cupola decorations in Aquisgrana Cathedral (c.1720–30).

Adalberto Artari (b.1693) is probably the same Albert Artari active in 1724 with his brother, Joseph, at Sutton Scarsdale, Derbyshire, and at Ditchley in Oxfordshire. The Ditchley archives include a reference to a payment made for stucco executed by "two Mr. Artare".

Adalberto's elder brother Carlo Giuseppe enjoyed a considerable reputation in England and won the esteem of some of the most important English architects of the time. Between 1720 and 1724 he assisted another celebrated stuccoist, Giovanni (or Jacopo) Bagutti, on the sculptural decoration of the interiors of buildings designed by James Gibbs. These included the Octagon Room, Twickenham, the Church of St. Martin-in-the-Fields and the Church of St. Peter's in London, and the Senate, Cambridge. Their work consisted mainly of low-relief ornament executed in an elegant Rococo style. Carlo Giuseppe's activity in England is also documented in several payments made for work in various houses throughout the country and in London, including Houghton Hall, Norfolk (1726), and Castle Hill, Devon (1742). In some cases he was also paid for designs that he did not execute himself; he received two pounds and two shillings for a drawing for finishing the Temple of the Four Winds at Castle Howard, Yorkshire, in stucco in 1736 but the work itself was carried out by another craftsman, Vassalli. Several Italian masters were working in England during this period, although Artari and Bagutti were the most important, and together they played a significant role in bringing delicacy and refinement to the austere, classical style of architects such as Gibbs and Colen Campbell. Their work also had a strong influence on the beginnings of the Dublin school of stuccoists.

Between 1748 and 1761, the Giuseppe Artari active in Germany executed stucco-work after Biarelli's designs at Schloss Augustusburg, near Cologne which included decoration in the first floor State Room. The works executed for the Elector of Cologne's Residenz have unfortunately been destroyed, so Giuseppe's most important extant undertakings in Germany remain the stucco decorations for François Cuvilliés' Falkenlust Hunting Lodge, Brühl (1729–32) and those for the Cuvilliés' Pöppelsdorf Palace. The Pöppelsdorf stuccoes were produced with Carlo Pietro Morsegno and the Castelli brothers from 1744. The ceiling of the billiard room is especially noteworthy, as are the figures in the round on the chapel's altar and the frieze of the spire on the guards' hut in front of the palace. Giuseppe's extraordinary capacity for invention and virtuosity when handling refined Rococo themes is exemplified in these sculptural decorations.

LUCIANA ARBACE
translated by Antonia Boström

See also Plasterwork and Stucco

Biography

The Artari (Artaria, Artario) family settled at Arogno near Lugano in the Ticino in the late 16th century. All three of the most important members of the family, Giovanni Battista, Adalberto, and Carlo Giuseppe were active in England. Giuseppe Artari (b. 1700) was probably the family member active in Germany.

Artari, Giovanni Battista 1664–after 1730

Born in Arogno. The father of Adalberto and Carlo Giuseppe. Recorded at the Hofkirche, Rastatt, 1705, at Fulda Cathedral in 1707 together with G.B. Genone, and at Aquisgrana Cathedral, c.1720–30. Most of his career was spent in Northern Germany, the Netherlands and England. Married Caterina di Maini in 1688.

Artari, Adalberto (Adalbertus, Alberto) 1693–1751

Born in Arogno, 7 October 1693. Only his English career is known, where he worked with a brother, Joseph. Died 22 October 1751.

Selected Works

1724 Sutton Scarsdale, Derbyshire (stucco decoration)
1725 Ditchley, Oxfordshire (stucco decoration)

Artari, Carlo Giuseppe 1692–1757

Born in Arogno, 5 September 1692. Trained with his father, Giovanni Battista. Worked in Rome, Germany and Holland, before travelling to England c.1715. Worked on church decoration in London, at St Peter's, Vere Street, 1723–24, and at St Martin-in-the-Fields, 1722–26. Collaborated frequently with Giovanni Bagutti (1681–after

Carlo Giuseppe Artari: Octagon Room, Orleans House, Twickenham, Middlesex, 1720

1730) on country house interiors, and worked independently on the stucco decoration for several others from the 1720s; provided the unexecuted plans for a Temple of the Four Winds at Castle Howard, Yorkshire, 1736. Married to a Mary Gertrude. Died 27 May 1757.

Selected Works

c.1715	Duncombe Park, Yorkshire (stucco decoration)
1717–33	Clandon Park, Surrey (stucco ceiling in hall): 2nd Lord Onslow
1720	Octagon Room, Twickenham (stucco decoration)
1722–30	Senate House, Cambridge (stucco ceiling)
1725	Ditchley, Oxfordshire (saloon ceiling): George Henry Lee, 2nd Earl of Lichfield
1726	Houghton Hall, Norfolk (ceiling and frieze of Stone Hall): Sir Robert Walpole
1729–32	Cavendish Square, London (stucco decoration)
1730–31	Moulsham Hall, Essex (stucco ceiling of Great Room, stucco busts and figures)
1735	Parlington Hall, Yorkshire (stucco decoration in drawing room, hall, and staircase)
1737	Upton House, Banbury (stucco ceiling, statue of Apollo)
1737–38	Trentham, Staffordshire (stucco decoration in New Library)
1742	Castle Hill, Devon (stucco decoration, bas reliefs in Best Hall)
1743–44	Wimpole Hall, Cambridgeshire (stucco decoration)
1744–45	Radcliffe Camera, Oxford (stucco decoration)
1756–60	Ragley Hall, Warwickshire (stucco decoration in Great Hall): Lord Conway

Works attributed to Giuseppe Artari (b.1700)

1729–32	Hunting Lodge, Schloss Falkenlust, Brühl (stucco decoration): Clemens August, Elector of Cologne
1743–44	Pöppelsdorf Palace, Bonn (stucco decoration): Clemens August, Elector of Cologne
1748–61	Schloss Augustusburg, Brühl (stucco decoration in State Rooms and staircase figures): Clemens August, Elector of Cologne
1754–57	Erbdrostenhof (stucco decoration): Clemens August, Elector of Cologne

Further Reading

Beard 1983 includes a full catalogue of their career; Renard and Metternich 1934 are useful for Carlo Giuseppe Artari's German career.

Beard, Geoffrey, "Italian Stuccoists in England", in *Apollo*, LXXXI, July 1964, pp.48–56

Beard, Geoffrey, *Decorative Plasterwork in Great Britain*, London: Phaidon, 1975, pp.201–02

Beard, Geoffrey, *Craftsmen and Interior Decoration in England, 1660–1820*, Edinburgh: Bartholomew, and New York: Holmes and Meier, 1981

Beard, Geoffrey, *Stucco and Decorative Plasterwork in Europe*, London: Thames and Hudson, and New York: Harper, 1983

Hespe, R., in *Dizionario Biografico degli Italiani*, IV, Rome: Istituto della Enciclopedia Italiana 1962, pp.351–52

Gillam, S.G., "The Building Accounts of the Radcliffe Camera, Oxford", *Oxford Historical Society*, XIII, 1958

Kalnein, Wend Graf, "Das Kurfürstliche Schloss Clemensruhe in Poppelsdorf" in *Bonner Beiträge zur Kunstwissenschaft*, IV, 1956, pp.145–46, 151

Kurfürst Clemens August: Landesherr und Mäzen des 18. Jahrhunderts (exhib. cat.), Brühl: Schloss Augustusburg, 1961

Renard, Edmund, "Die Bauten der Kurfürsten Joseph Clemens und Clemens August", *Bonner Jahrbücher*, XCVII, 1896, p.54

Renard, Edmund and F. Wolff Metternich, *Schloss Brühl*, Berlin: Deutscher Verein für Kunstwissenshaft, 1934

Saumarez Smith, Charles, *Eighteenth-Century Decoration: Design and the Domestic Interior in England*, London: Weidenfeld and Nicolson, and New York: Abrams, 1993

Summerson, John, *Architecture in Britain, 1530–1830*, 1953, 9th edition New Haven and London: Yale University Press, 1993

Artists' Houses

Purpose-built artists' houses, designed by architects and incorporating the studio as a central feature within the structure of the house, were a distinctive feature of the art capitals of Europe and America in the later 19th century. Built at a time when it was not exceptional to find artists enjoying large incomes and social acclaim, these houses, sometimes called "studio houses", were often richly decorated in the fashionable tastes of the day.

A "studio" is by definition the place of work for an artist. In all periods an artist-craftsman would require both space and light, as well as further rooms for the storage and for the preparation of materials. The artists' "workshop" – in the classical writings of Vitruvius and Pliny the word *officina* was used – itself might also serve as a saleroom, if only in the sense that a patron or agent might come to observe a commission in progress.

The requirement for good steady light was particularly noted by the 1st century engineer Vitruvius in Book VI, chapter V of *De Architectura*. Vitruvius wrote of the importance of siting "picture galleries, embroiderers' workrooms and painters' studios [to the north] in order that the fixed light may permit the colours used in their work to last with qualities unchanged". Leonardo da Vinci also wrote that "Light should always come from the north, in order that it may not vary".

The artists' workshop or studio was also traditionally a place in which to make preparatory studies and a place of training for apprentices in the skills of a particular art trade. With the revival of interest in classical art during the 15th and 16th centuries, the study and imitation of antique sculpture became a central activity of the artist's studio. Vasari (1511–74) in his *Vite* (1550) referred to Francesco Squarcione, the master and adoptive father of Andrea Mantegna, having a collection of fragments and casts for the education of his gifted pupil.

During the Renaissance period the studio was a workshop and it differed little from other artisan workshops of the commercial quarters of cities. Some artists did own houses of substance; Vasari refers to a number of these which were designed by the artists themselves, such as that of Mantegna in Mantua. Vasari's own house in Arezzo survives with *trompe-l'oeil* architectural detail, decorative allegorical wall paintings and fashionable grotesque work carried out by the artist himself, perhaps both as a demonstration of his skill and imagination, and as proof of his comfortable status.

While the artistic elite of Europe in the succeeding centuries strove to maintain the intellectual image of the artist created by Vasari, the studio itself remained essentially the functional workroom. Indeed throughout the 18th century the painting rooms of distinguished painters were mostly built on as additions to their houses – with galleries for the combined display

Artists' Houses: Lord Leighton's studio London, 1890s

and storage of their paintings. As to the content of such rooms, paintings of that date and inventories of artists' property show that the attributes of the studio remained in the academic tradition of the Italian old masters, containing casts or fragments of antique sculpture as well as copies of the works of the old masters.

From the mid-19th century there was a significant rise in the number of studio houses designed by architects for the combined domestic and professional requirement of artists. The increasingly elegantly appointed studio was no longer an afterthought but the central element in the design and planning of such houses – what William Gaunt called the "luxurious core" around which the houses were built.

In England, Philip Webb (1831–1915), the associate of the Pre-Raphaelite Brotherhood and architect of the Red House for William Morris, designed several houses with studios during the 1860s, including one in Holland Park for the painter Val Prinsep (1838–1904). Solidly built of simple red brick in the new vernacular style, their decoration also tended to reflect the prevailing Arts and Crafts taste of their patrons – De Morgan tiles, Morris and Co. papers and furniture.

One of the best known, and most exotic, studio houses of the mid-19th century was the house built by Frederic Leighton (1830–96), later President of the Royal Academy. Leighton's plain red brick Italianate villa was built adjacent to Prinsep's house in Holland Park Road. It was designed in collaboration with the architect George Aitchison and the garden elevation was dominated by the studio window. The house was decorated throughout with ebonised woodwork, and turquoise blue De Morgan tiles lined the hall and the staircase walls. As Leighton became more successful and entertained more and more fashionably, he held receptions and musical recitals in his large studio with its terracotta coloured walls. Reflecting his travels in the Middle East and the taste for the exotic so evident in his paintings, in 1877–78 he added the domed Arab Hall. This was modelled on the reception hall of a Moorish Palace, La Zisa at Palermo, which Aitchison had drawn on a visit to Italy. The Arab Hall was decorated with Leighton's collection of 16th- and 17th-century Iznik and Syrian ceramic tiles.

A painter's subject interests were also often evident in the design sources for the studio house and its decoration at this date. The best example of this trend was the eccentric studio house in Hampstead belonging to one of Leighton's fellow Royal Academicians Lawrence Alma-Tadema (1836–1912). Tadema remodelled an older house in collaboration with the architect Alfred Calderon to create an essay in the Pompeian style that was highly appropriate for a painter famous for his classical subjects. His huge domed and vaulted studio had a ceiling lined with light-reflecting aluminium. The astonishing impact of the interior was said to conjure up visions of "all the luxury, the ivory, the apes and peacocks of the Roman civilisation with which his art was largely pre-occupied".

The architect who designed many of the more distinguished studio houses for the establishment artists of the later 19th century in Hampstead and Kensington was Richard Norman Shaw, R.A. (1831–1912). The house he built for Marcus Stone (1840–1921) on Melbury Road (1875) in Kensington exemplified the skill with which Shaw resolved comfortable and elegant domestic accommodation with the space and light required for the studio. The house was designed in the red brick Queen Anne style with cut and moulded brick dressings and white painted woodwork. The first floor is almost entirely given over to the studio, with three enormous oriel windows overlooking the street. The huge studio was furnished with 18th-century furniture – some of which appeared as props in his popular genre paintings – tapestries, ceramics and oriental carpets, which together gave the room the appearance of a grand "Old English" reception room. The characteristically grand interiors of these Kensington studios were recorded in a series of posed portrait photographs of "Artists at Home" taken by J.P. Mayall and published by F.G. Stephens in London and New York in 1884.

Similarly spendid studio homes were also built and decorated by artists in Europe and America. The vast Paris studio belonging to the painter Benjamin Constant contained many exotic Arabian features including, according to a contemporary report, "a choice collection of Moorish rugs and curtains of all sorts ... [which] ... transformed the place into quite a suggestion of a portion of the Alhambra itself". The American painter Frederick Church's house, Olana, was decorated in an even more self-consciously Aesthetic style. Perched high on a dramatic hillside site with spectacular views of the Hudson River valley, Olana was an astonishing mélange of colour, texture and form. Designed by Calvert Vaux (1824–95), it was built under Church's supervision in the 1870s with a new wing added in 1888–90. The dominant influences were once again Near Eastern and the interiors contained floors festooned with oriental rugs which also served as portières, wide arched openings decorated with stylised mozarabic floral stencilling in the spandrels, and numerous examples of elaborately carved dark wood furniture and gleaming brass bowls and ornaments. Olana exemplified both the theatricality and the artistic eclecticism that characterised artists' houses in the late 19th century.

The sudden evolution of houses of such individuality and increasingly studied interior decoration, often the result of close collaboration between artist and architect, is a remarkable phenomenon. Mark Girouard has suggested a helpful formula for the part explanation of the rash of such houses – in London at least. First, painters were becoming more interested in working in natural light. Second, the belief in "honest construction" that was widespread among more progressive architects in the second half of the 19th century encouraged an expectation that the studio should be "expressed" in the planning and exterior of the building. And third, there was considerably more money in art production – as much through reproduction rights as from originals. Indeed Andrew Saint's study of Richard Norman Shaw (1976) includes the observation that the artists, rather than the bankers, "were the real Nouveau riche" of Shaw's clients.

Of course, many artists failed to achieve great commercial success and occupied less distinguished studios. Some of these were modest but respectable speculatively built studio houses or flats, others were country retreats. And there were alsostudios closer in reality to the romanticised image of the Parisian garret of Puccini's *La Bohème*. Nevertheless, the more ambitious or commercially successful artists of this time set great store by the design and decoration of their studio houses. These artists were essentially engaged in an advertisement: the demonstration (or suggestion) of their success and position, and cultivated individuality. As the critic A.L. Baldry observed in his biography of Hubert Herkomer in 1904: "House Building became a fashion that any rising artist with a balance at the bank could not resist. He felt that he must surround himself with visible evidences of the appreciation in which he was held or there would be a danger that the public, all too ready to judge by externals, would pass him by as a failure, and prefer to him some of his more demonstrative competitors." And Albert Wolff, the influential critic of *Le Figaro* wrote of the smart Paris studios in 1886: "in our epoch the painter is no longer the labouring artisan who locks himself away in his studio behind a closed door – living in a dream, he has thrust his head foremost into the bustle of the world ... he has his day when his studio is transformed into a salon where he receives the elite of polite society".

JEREMY MUSSON

Selected Collections

Several artists' houses and studios have been preserved as memorials to their owners' lives and careers. Notable examples include the Rubens House, Antwerp; Leighton House, London; Olana, Hudson River Valley, New York; and the Musée Gustave Moreau, Paris.

Further Reading

For an introduction to the history of Artists' Houses in England see Walkley 1994 which also provides a gazetteer of principal works in London.

Artistic Houses, Being a Series of Interior Views of a Number of the Most Beautiful and Celebrated Homes in the United States, 2 vols., New York, 1883–84; reprinted New York: Blom, 1971

Banham, Joanna, Sally MacDonald and Julia Porter, *Victorian Interior Design*, London: Cassell, 1991; as *Victorian Interior Style*, London: Studio, 1995

Calloway, Stephen, "The Eclectic Aesthetes" in *House and Garden* (USA), February 1992, pp.100–05

Gere, Charlotte, *Nineteenth-Century Decoration: The Art of the Interior*, London: Weidenfeld and Nicolson, and New York: Abrams, 1989

Girouard, Mark, "The Victorian Artist at Home: The Holland Park Houses" in *Country Life*, 16 November 1972

Girouard, Mark, "The Victorian Artist at Home II: Chelsea's Bohemian Studio Houses" in *Country Life*, 23 November 1972

Goss, Peter L., "Olana, the Artist as Architect" in *Magazine Antiques*, October 1976, pp.764–775

Jones, Stephen, "Lord Leighton's Palace of Art" in *Magazine Antiques*, June 1989

Leopold, N.S.C., *Artists' Homes in Sixteenth Century Italy*, Ann Arbor: UMI, 1980

Milner, John, *The Studios of Paris: The Capital of Art in the Late Nineteenth Century*, New Haven and London: Yale University Press, 1988

Saint, Andrew, *Richard Norman Shaw*, New Haven: Yale University Press, 1976

Simon, Robin (editor), "Lord Leighton 1830–1896 and Leighton House: A Centenary Celebration" special issue of *Apollo*, 1996

Stephens, F. G., *Artists at Home*, London: Sampson Low, and New York: Appleton, 1884

Walkley, Giles, *Artists' Houses in London, 1794–1914*, London: Scolar Press, 1994

Zakon, Ronnie L., *The Artist and the Studio in the Eighteenth and Nineteenth Centuries* (exhib. cat.), Cleveland: Cleveland Museum of Art, 1978

Arts and Crafts Movement

Originating in Britain in the second half of the 19th century, the Arts and Crafts Movement was a broadly-based style that encompassed architecture, furnishings and every aspect of domestic design and whose influence was widely felt throughout the industrialised world. Its central tenets were the championship of architecture and the decorative arts as equal in status to the higher arts of painting and sculpture, the celebration of handwork and the revival of obsolete craft skills, and a belief in the moral and aesthetic supremacy of simplicity, fitness for purpose and honesty to materials. Yet for many of its most committed exponents, the Arts and Crafts Movement was not merely a style; it was also expressive of a whole way of life. Born out of the anti-industrial feeling that gathered momentum from the mid-19th century, it reflected a pervasive longing for a return to the simplicity and harmony of a vanished rural past. In this sense the Movement had a strong political dimension and many of its concerns anticipated the Modern Movement's belief that artists and designers should become more socially responsible and should play a more active role in the improvement of society as a whole.

The Movement took its name from the Arts and Crafts Exhibition Society which was formed in London in 1888 by Walter Crane, W.A.S. Benson, George Clausen, Holman Hunt, and T.J. Cobden-Sanderson. Many of its ideals, however, predated this event and its chief theorists prior to the 1880s were A.W.N. Pugin, John Ruskin, and William Morris.

Pugin was a staunch medievalist who promoted the revival of Gothic architecture and ornament in a new, archaeologically correct manner, and his work would at first sight seem to offer little to the future Arts and Crafts Movement. Yet in his writings Pugin laid the foundations for many later critiques of 19th-century design and society. In books such as *Contrasts; or, A Parallel Between the Architecture of the 15th and 19th Centuries* (1836), he portrayed architecture in industrial Britain as a dishonourable trade in the service of commerce and compared it to the higher calling that it had been in the Middle Ages when buildings were designed for the greater glory of God. Subsequent publications of the 1840s amplified this theme and asserted the debased nature of 19th-century Classical architecture and design when compared to the Pointed architecture of the 15th century.

Pugin's linking of style and society was of crucial importance to future members of the Arts and Crafts Movement. Moreover his dictums that "All ornament should consist of enrichment of the essential construction of the building" and that "There should be no features about a building which are not necessary for convenience, construction, and propriety" expressed a new attitude to decoration and placed a greater emphasis upon function that had a strong bearing on the development of Arts and Crafts philosophy. Furthermore, Pugin's practical involvement in a variety of media including metal, wood, clay, stained glass, wallpaper and textiles, served as an exemplar of a designer not only able to master many different skills but also willing to execute his designs himself rather than pass them down a production line.

Many of Pugin's ideas reached a wider audience in the writings of the art critic and social philosopher John Ruskin. Like Pugin, Ruskin was an outspoken critic of contemporary commerce and design and he berated the nouveau-riche of Bradford and Manchester for the inhumanity of their factories and for the poor quality of their manufactured goods. Imbued with a sense of art as a spiritually uplifting and socially improving activity, he championed the Gothic style in particular as a symbol of artistic freedom. "All noble ornamentation is the expression of man's delight in God's work" he wrote in the famous chapter on "The Nature of Gothic" in his book *The Stones of Venice* (1851–53), and his impassioned defence of medieval art was based not only on its truth to nature, and honesty of materials, but also on his belief in the rights of the individual worker to some form of self-expression. "The right question to ask", he wrote, "respecting all ornament is simply this: was it done with enjoyment – was the carver happy while he was about it". Such views, with their emphasis on the joy of labour and their preference for objects made by hand over those made by machines, exerted a major influence on the future Arts and Crafts Movement and underpinned much of its later thinking.

Ruskin's work was of enormous importance to William Morris who described "The Nature of Gothic" as "one of the few necessary utterances of our age". A key figure in the formulation of Arts and Crafts ideals, Morris was significant both for his practical involvement in the revival of craft practices and design and for his work as a theorist. Born in 1834, the son of a wealthy stockbroker, he embarked on several careers – the church, architecture, and painting – before he finally developed the skill in pattern design which was to become his forte. A decisive event in his determination to establish the decorating firm, Morris, Marshall, Faulkner & Co., was the experience of building his home, the Red House, near Bexleyheath, Kent. Designed in 1859 by his lifelong friend and collaborator, Philip Webb, the exterior of the house was vaguely Gothic in style, and was based on the vernacular domestic architecture and vicarages built by William Butterfield. The interior represented a collaborative endeavour with decorations by Morris, D.G. Rossetti and Edward Burne-Jones and heavy oak furniture designed by Webb. In many ways the Red House may be considered as the first house of the Arts and Crafts Movement; it also therefore represents its first interior.

In the Red House brick is not only used externally in an honest and unassuming manner of which Ruskin and Pugin might have approved, it is also a strong element in the interior where it is left similarly bare and exposed. The idea that exterior and interior should relate was soon to establish itself as a commonplace of the Arts and Crafts Movement. Just as brick is left uncovered so the construction of the roof is left open, rather than boarded over, and Webb seems to revel in the

Arts and Crafts Movement: sitting room, Great Tangley Manor, Surrey by Philip Webb; photographed in 1895

roughness and unevenness of the wide-boarded floors. Everywhere materials are left to speak for themselves, textures and colours contrasting the one with the other rather than being subsumed into an elaborate decorative scheme. Decoratively the house was decked out with painted friezes and stencilled patterns, and the main rooms were further adorned with embroidered hangings. The novelty of its interiors was noted by the artist William Bell Scott who visited the house shortly after its completion. He described "the dining-room or hall [which] had a fixed settle all round the walls, a curious music gallery entered by a stair outside the room, ... and no furniture but a long table of oak reaching nearly from end to end ... the adornment had a novel, not to say startling, character, but if one had been told it was the South Sea Island style of thing one could have believed such to be the case, so bizarre was the execution."

The exterior, by contrast, must have seemed much less remarkable. It was designed in the Gothic Revival style but its details suggested a building which had been added to, and altered, over several centuries. Gothic arches were seemingly filled in at later dates, and extensions made to create a rambling, asymmetrical and picturesque skyline and façade. Constructed out of red brick, the artisanal nature of the building also undercut the status implicit in the use of the Gothic style. And designed to be comfortable and convenient, rather than as a statement of its owner's wealth or social standing, it has subsequently been viewed as an important landmark in the beginnings of the Domestic, or Vernacular revival in architecture and interiors – a house designed from the inside out in contrast to the strictures of Classicism which often dictated symmetry, harmony and grandeur of proportions over convenience of arrangement and the comfort of rooms.

The building of the Red House convinced Morris of the need for well-designed and executed decorative work and, looking back on this period of his life in 1883, he recalled: "I got a friend to build me a house very medieval in spirit in which I lived for five years, and set myself to decorating it. We found, I and my friend ... that all the minor arts were in a state of complete degradation ... and accordingly in 1861 with the conceited courage of a young man, I set myself to reforming all that, and started a sort of firm for producing decorative articles." The firm was founded with Webb and the Pre-Raphaelite painters Edward Burne-Jones, D.G. Rossetti, and Ford Madox Brown as partners and initially named Morris, Marshall, Faulkner, and Company after its main financial backers. Though trading as a Limited company, the medieval guild ideal permeated its design practice and work was frequently produced collaboratively. In its first prospectus, it offered to undertake "any species of decoration, from pictures properly so-called, down to consideration of the smallest work susceptible of art beauty" and it is often considered as one of the first modern interior design firms.

Many of the company's earliest commissions were for ecclesiastical stained glass, as befitted the Gothicist credentials of its chief designers and the dominance of the Gothic style in the third quarter of the 19th century. Other important commissions from this period included schemes for the interiors of the Green Dining Room at the Victoria and Albert Museum (1866), rooms in St. James's Palace (1866–67), and work in colleges of Cambridge University. Morris himself also began to develop his skills as a designer of surface patterns early on in the company's history; his first wallpapers, *Trellis*, *Daisy*, and *Fruit*, were designed in 1862 and issued in 1864. Appalled by the highly illusionistic and overly ornate designs favoured by commercial manufacturers, he sought a more "honest" form of expression that would emphasise the two-dimensional nature of surface decoration and used shallow perspective and simple, naturalistic motifs held in formal repeats. Soon afterwards, he was employing the same principles in the design of textiles, carpets and rugs, using natural pigments and traditional dyeing techniques in place of the new, acrid colours created by advances in the chemical industry. As his skills developed so his interests expanded to include tapestry, embroidery, manuscript illumination, typography, furniture, and finally, printing.

Morris's devotion to medieval (and early Renaissance) designs, and the model of the Guild system made him an early advocate of conservation and in 1877 he and Philip Webb founded the Society for the Protection of Ancient Buildings (or "Anti-scrape" as it became known). The SPAB not only campaigned to save the historic fabric of old buildings from the ravages of insensitive restoration, it also exerted an important influence on contemporary architecture through its understanding of traditional, rational, methods of construction that had withstood the "test of time". And it was through the regular meetings of the SPAB, no less than through Morris's tireless design work for the firm, that the next generation of architects and designers came into contact with the new ideas that centered on the ideal of the pre-, or non-, industrial society. This generation was drawn initially from architects working in the practice of Richard Norman Shaw and in 1884 they formed the Art-Workers' Guild to act as a forum for the re-introduction and encouragement of those traditional methods of design and production that were in danger of dying out in the wake of widespread industrialisation. But because it was based on the model of a medieval guild with its Brothers and a Master, the Art-Workers' Guild was both semi-secret and highly selective and the Arts and Crafts Exhibition Society was formed to allow for the broader and more open display of objects created in the Arts and Crafts spirit.

The exhibitions included work by W.A.S. Benson, Walter Crane, William Morris, Heywood Sumner, Selwyn Image, W.R. Lethaby, C.F.A. Voysey, A.H. Mackmurdo, Henry Wilson, and Charles Rennie Mackintosh and many of the progressive young designers of the day. Though not overly prescriptive about the kinds of objects accepted, most of the work on display adhered to the principles of truth to materials and honesty of construction. And, despite the fact that after the first three annual shows of 1888, 1889, and 1890, profits dwindled and the regularity of the exhibitions was reduced, they were widely reported in the burgeoning new art periodicals of the 1890s and brought the Arts and Crafts Movement an international audience and following. The *Studio* magazine, in particular, became an increasingly active promoter of Arts and Crafts products and interiors. An American edition was brought out in 1897, and from 1898 to 1939 the magazine published a series of speculative numbers on topics such as "Modern British Architecture and Decoration", and from 1907, a yearbook on "Decorative Art". It continued to promote Arts and Crafts values in the face of Modernism well into the 1920s.

During the 1880s and 1890s, the political character of the Arts and Crafts Movement became more pronounced and the original mission to uphold the dignity of labour through the celebration of craft work became increasingly linked to a determination to improve the lot of the working man and to reform society generally. At the same time, however, many of those involved were forced to acknowledge the contradiction inherent in the fact that hand work was generally expensive to produce and that much of what was made was beyond the reach of the ordinary consumer. Morris himself, who became a Socialist in 1883, ultimately came to view his work as simply "ministering to the swinish luxury of the rich" but this represents too harsh a judgement of a Movement whose innovations had included the introduction of informal, open-plan and more comfortable interiors at a time when the opulence and excesses characteristic of French revivalist styles prevailed. And just as conservative Victorian taste revelled in the power of the machine to reproduce the historical furnishings of the past, so more progressive elements allied themselves with a real past – that of the yeoman farmer – that, due to the agricultural depressions of the late 19th century, was currently under threat.

A nostalgia for a simpler way of life and a growing dislike of modern cities led several Arts and Crafts designers to move out of London to the country. Morris had moved his family and part of his operations to Lechlade, in Gloucestershire in the 1870s. Similarly C.R. Ashbee who had established the Guild of Handicraft in 1888, moved to Chipping Campden in 1901, while Ernest Gimson and the Barnsley brothers moved to Sapperton in 1893. In forsaking more lucrative and socially rewarding careers as professional architects for the "simple life" of Cotswold craftsmen, designers such as Gimson, Ashbee, Powell and the Barnsley brothers led by example, and they formed a network of workshops producing the hand-crafted furniture and interior fittings for many of the Arts and Crafts houses built by Webb, W.R. Lethaby, Edward Prior, Halsey Ricardo, and others in the late 19th and early 20th century.

One of the best-known examples of these houses was Standen, in Sussex, built by Philip Webb in the early 1890s for the solicitor James Beale. Standen's exterior was designed in Webb's vernacular style around an existing Georgian farm-

Arts and Crafts Movement: *Daisy* wallpaper by William Morris, 1864

house. The interiors were left deliberately plain – Webb recommended a mixture of whitewash and plain painted surfaces – and the rooms were decorated with Morris & Co.'s wallpapers and textiles. Much of the furniture was designed by Webb, George Jack and W.A.S. Benson and was arranged in an informal manner. Benson also designed many of the electric light fittings, and it is important to remember that many Arts and Crafts interiors appeared lighter not simply because of the preference for lighter colour schemes, but also as a result of the more penetrative effects of the electric light bulb.

Webb's asymmetrical accretative plans where rooms were grouped for internal convenience rather than exterior display were not the only innovations in plan-form introduced by the Arts and Crafts Movement. Architect and fellow Guildsman Edward Prior developed what became known as the "Butterfly" plan, as at "The Barn", Exmouth of 1896–97, whereby the reception rooms were canted forwards at either end in such a way as to catch morning and then afternoon sun. Sometimes referred to as double sun-trap plans they were a development of the north-corridor plan where reception rooms were all south-facing (linked by a north corridor) to gain maximum sunlight. Given the emphasis on raising the standard of decoration and craftsmanship implicit in the Arts and Crafts Movement, together with the emphasis on the contribution of individual designer / craftsmen, changes in plan-form can often seem less important than the decorative revival of Morris and his followers. However this would be to ignore the very thing which so often gained the Movement an international reputation – that is to say the rational and intelligent planning of rooms and room use which it was hoped would partly transform social relations and shows the Movement at its most idealistic.

The most extreme, and influential example of this new form of planning was the advocacy of the "through-lounge" in what was known as "The Smaller Domestic House." The banishment of the conventional room at the front of a house, kept "for best," with its accompanying room to the rear used for all the day-to-day activities, was seen as a further attempt to create a more open, informal, and even democratic life-style and was a common feature of many of the houses of the Garden City Movement as found in Letchworth and Hampstead Garden Suburb. At its best, in the hands of a designer such as M.H. Baillie Scott, and when the house was large enough, the "through-lounge" was a further reminder of the Middle Ages and the tradition of the Hall house, sometimes complete with a Minstrels Gallery, and an inglenook fireplace to supply a "cosy-corner". However, when applied in large numbers, as was the case in Britain in the period immediately following World War I, the "through-lounge" proved less popular with users than with Arts and Crafts idealists, or ideologues such as the Socialist writer Edward Carpenter. Even where the client was believed to be in sympathy with the ideals of the Movement, as at a new house in Limpsfield for the Garnett family, the original plans for a great hall taken to the extreme of having a central open fire, were rejected in favour of a more usual L-plan with two storeys.

Nevertheless it was certainly this careful approach to planning as much as the simplicity and functionalism of the interior decoration which attracted the Prussian Government architect, Hermann Muthesius, while on appointment to the German Embassy in London. Muthesius wrote a number of articles in periodicals such as *Dekorative Kunst* praising the English Arts and Crafts Movement, and reviewing its major figures. On his return to Berlin he published a three-volume study of their work entitled *Das Englische Haus* (1904–05) which played a major role in disseminating the radical new approach to architecture and interiors. Moreover, where British architects and designers had been open to the charge of being anti-industrial, and even Luddite, Muthesius and the Germanic states saw the Arts and Crafts Movement as a model for "good design" that was capable of being mass-produced through the standardisation of designs and the rationalisation of the work processes. Elsewhere in the German states the Grand Duke Ernest-Ludwig of Hesse had established an Artists Colony at Darmstadt in 1899 with this very intention.

Involving many of the designers of the Vienna Secession such as Joseph Maria Olbrich, the Continental Arts and Crafts Movement tended to be characterised more by the English Free Style of Charles Harrison Townsend and Henry Wilson, or the ornate decorative schemes of Baillie Scott, which it misunderstood as English Art Nouveau. Indeed the English Arts and Crafts Movement generally was often seen as synonymous with Art Nouveau in Continental Europe, despite the fact that many of its principal exponents such as Walter Crane and W.R. Lethaby were vehemently opposed to this style. Similarly, to other British designers, like Baillie Scott and Charles Rennie Mackintosh, who were not as strongly influenced by the some-

Arts and Crafts Movement: design for drawing room with Liberty furniture by Leonard Wyburd, 1907

what severe and puritanical aesthetic espoused by members of the Arts and Crafts Exhibition Society, the Art-Workers' Guild and the SPAB, the overtly stylised, elongated forms, and semi-precious materials favoured by Art Nouveau clearly seemed part of the same Movement. However, in other parts of Europe, principally the Scandinavian countries, the Arts and Crafts Movement philosophy was more clearly understood.

In Sweden Carl and Karin Larsson decorated their simple wooden country cottage on the outskirts of Falun in light, simple, colours during the 1890s. In 1899 24 of the watercolours that Karl made of these interiors appeared in a book called *Ett Hem* (A Home). They were the first of many illustrations showing the influence of the Arts and Crafts Movement in Scandinavia and brought the Larssons to the attention of the *Studio* magazine in 1904. A large exhibition followed in Vienna in 1907 and in 1909 a collection of the Larssons' watercolours and their views on interior decoration were published in Germany in *Das Haus in der Sonne*. By 1912, 10,000 copies had been printed and future publications showed the development of the Larssons' tastes including the incorporation of 18th-century antique furniture, and an increasing emphasis on the rectilinear decorative schemes of the Secessionists and German designers. Although they were not strictly speaking practising designers, the Larssons' influence in Scandinavia was immense and touched fellow Swedes Herman Gesellius and Armas Lindgren and Eliel Saarinen of Finland. In Finland Axel Gallen-Kallela led the reformation of the interior along Arts and Crafts lines in a similarly vigorous manner.

Arts and Crafts interiors were to be found in both town and country houses and in richer and simpler versions. If Standen represents a pure Arts and Crafts interior in the vernacular style, then the so-called Peacock House designed by Halsey Ricardo represents an urban interior at its most jewel like with its use of "English Glass" developed by Edward Prior, tiles by William De Morgan, and sculpture by William Aumonier. Little wonder that Ricardo's client was the wealthy owner of one of the new department stores, Debenham's, making money partially out of selling the Arts and Crafts lifestyle.

Yet at the heart of the Movement as it developed in the 20th century was not only a deep divide over the benefits of hand production against machine production but also conflicting views about the extent to which Art was compatible with capitalism. Hence the work of many minor groups who operated commercially throughout Britain seems to have been all but ignored by the mainstream of the Movement. Under the umbrella first of the Cottage Art Association, and, from 1884, the Home Arts and Industries Association, hundreds of small regional groups were established which produced craft objects for the home and for sale. Regional classes were established aimed at the socially and physically disadvantaged, and the seasonally unemployed. Designs were often taken from part-works centrally distributed but in more innovative centres such as Newlyn, Keswick, Compton, and Southwold, small craft industries were created with their own distinct designs and designers. In essence small concerns like these spread the philosophy of early "Do-it-yourself" and craft as a leisure pursuit which became such a strong element of inter-war Britain and had an early champion in William Morris's daughter May. Indeed it is often remarked that women gained a measure of independence and recognition through the Arts and Crafts Movement and, while this may to some extent be true, it is also the case that their activities were seen as "home," "minor," or "lesser arts" compared with other areas such as furniture or architecture. Similarly, the work of the small regional classes was often seen as promoting the work of the amateur, rather than the skilled professional, a reputation which the crafts have struggled under ever since.

If European Arts and Crafts was attempting to re-create a pre-industrial past which in turn spawned a National Romanticism, as in the case of the Gödöllö craft workshops established in Hungary, then the United States was still creating its identity and the Arts and Crafts Movement suited its conditions wonderfully. As Gustav Stickley wrote in 1909 "we have no monarchs and no aristocracy, the life of the plain people is the life of the nation". Not only extreme simplicity but an accent on regionalism was a much greater feature of the Arts and Crafts influence as it came to affect the United States, where many small craft communities flourished briefly at the turn of the century.

The writings of Morris and Ruskin were bestsellers in North America and societies for the promotion of their ideas were set up in the 1890s. And in addition to the reproductions in the new art periodicals of the late 19th century, the American Arts and Crafts Movement was also supported by the visits of figures such as Walter Crane, and C.R. Ashbee, who became a close friend of Frank Lloyd Wright. Imbued with the frontier spirit, and less burdened by the baggage of conventional historical styles, American designers were free to be more Arts and Crafts in spirit than the European originators. To Ashbee, whose Guild of Handicraft furniture had been attacked by the *Studio* as "simplicity carried dangerously near triteness", the pioneer spirit of the United States seemed a perfect demonstration of the validity of Arts and Crafts principles. However, Americans also had a more open-minded attitude to the benefits of machine production which they viewed as the servant rather than the master of the designer. Nowhere was this more true than in the work of Wright who declared that "William Morris pleaded well for the simplicity as the basis of all true art. Let us understand the significance to art of that word – simplicity – for it is vital to the art of the machine."

Certain regions, notably the Northeast centered on Boston, the Midwest centered on Chicago, and the West Coast centered on San Francisco, developed their own distinct identities; the Boston Society of Arts and Crafts was founded in 1897 and operated much as the Arts and Crafts Exhibition Society had done in London. Similarly the magazine *The House Beautiful* (1896), was an equivalent of the *Studio* magazine. Among the principal figures in the United States version of the Arts and Crafts Movement were Elbert Hubbard and Gustav Stickley.

Hubbard had visited William Morris in England in 1893 to see the Kelmscott Press before his return to East Aurora, New York, where he established a craft community, the Roycrofters, which was to be one of the most successful of the American Arts and Crafts communities. This success was due in no small measure to Hubbard's earlier career as a soap manufacturer where he developed the mass-marketing techniques he was later to apply to craftwork. Hubbard's work commenced with the creation of a printing works, bindery and leather shop. Roycroft furniture, which began production in 1901, consisted of massive, simple, and unornamented oak pieces like the early furniture of Morris and Webb. Eventually Roycroft also added glass and metalwork products; the metalwork retained its hammered finish to subscribe to the notion of honesty in design. Janet Ashbee described Hubbard as "mostly Ruskin and Morris with a good strong American flavour". However this American flavour was often seen to be a genius for selling rather than producing, and in many ways Hubbard's determination to make the Roycrofters financially successful was at odds with the ideals of Ruskin and Morris. Nevertheless, Hubbard's entrepreneurial flair helped to spread the influence of the Arts and Crafts Movement across a much broader spectrum of different classes than in Britain.

A desire to reach a wide market also underlay the work of the furniture maker Gustav Stickley who, after meeting Voysey on a European trip in 1898, developed a simple, primitive style capable of being copied by readers of his numerous books and the magazine he established in 1901, entitled *The Craftsman*. This magazine showed interiors in every issue with, as he put it, "material surroundings conducive to plain living and high thinking". The magazine was supplied free as a way of gaining orders for furniture and other products. The interiors were all open-plan, with low ceilings and leaded windows, and featured wood-panelled walls with stencilled decoration and fireplaces with inglenooks. So ubiquitous did they become that Stickley designs for houses such as the Hawley Residence, Baltimore (1900) were readily called "Craftsman style". Like his European contemporaries Stickley organised his workshops on a guild basis, but the sheer volume of work he received enabled an expansion seemingly incompatible with such craft ideals. At its height Stickley employed more than 400 workers and developed a distinct idiom seen as part and parcel of the more indigenous Mission style. This association was in part because of its links with Spanish 18th century colonial churches, and in part due to Stickley's statement that "a chair, a table, a bookcase or bed must fill its mission of usefulness as well as it possibly can ... the only decoration that seems in keeping with structural forms lies in the emphasizing of certain features of the construction, such as the mortise, tenon, key, and dovetail." However, despite his statement that furniture should reveal "just what it is, how it is made, and what it is made for", in reality Stickley was not above using dowel joints, oak veneers, and plywood in his furniture to reduce costs while maintaining the appearance of the Arts and Crafts style.

In terms of the plan-form the architects of the Arts and Crafts Movement in the United States developed the house plan fully with the creation of open-plan houses. The style is most often associated with Wright's early Prairie houses of the Midwest; other notable architects wedded to Arts and Crafts notions included the practice of Greene and Greene in California. In Wright's case the Prairie house not only related to the landscape through the choice of materials but also through the long, low horizontals of the composition, with low-pitched roof and wide eaves, that mirrored the landscape of the midwestern states. The interior was conceived as a series of interpenetrating spaces as at the Ward Willits House of 1902, and the Robie House of 1909. Like Webb before him, Wright unified his designs by bringing materials used externally through to the interior. A common problem with the Arts and Crafts interior was the dilution of the simple uncluttered effect sought by the incorporation of the owner's own furniture and fittings which could be unsympathetic to the purity of the Arts and Crafts design language. Hence Wright designed many of his interiors with built-in light fittings and cupboards thus extending the designer's control over the character of the interior and effectively creating the modern notion of "lifestyling." Despite Wright's democratic concerns it was in practice left to the development of the wooden, open-plan, bungalow – often self-built and with furniture made from designs by Stickley – to be the ultimate expression of the Arts and Crafts ideal of the democratisation of the Arts. These simple, hand-crafted dwellings gave visible form to William Morris's desire for "an Art made by the people, for the people, as a happiness to the maker and the user."

JULIAN HOLDER

See also Ashbee; Crane; Gödöllő Colony; Greene; Inglenooks; Larsson; Lethaby; Morris & Co.; Muthesius; Scott; Stickley

Further Reading

Recent international surveys of the Arts and Crafts Movement appear in Anscombe 1991, and Cumming and Kaplan, 1991. For discussions of the theoretical bases of the Movement see Naylor 1990, and Stansky 1985. A comprehensive study of the Arts and Crafts in America appears in Kaplan 1987. All these texts include references to primary and secondary sources.

Anscombe, Isabelle and Charlotte Gere, *Arts and Crafts in Britain and America*, London: Academy, 1978

Anscombe, Isabelle, *Art and Crafts Style*, Oxford: Phaidon, 1991

Bowman, Leslie Greene, *American Arts and Crafts: Virtue in Design*, Los Angeles: Los Angeles County Museum of Art, 1990

Callen, Anthea, *Angel in the Studio: Women in the Arts and Crafts Movement, 1870–1914*, London: Virago, 1984; as *Women Artists of the Arts and Crafts Movement, 1870–1914*, New York: Pantheon, 1979

Carruthers, Annette, *Edward Barnsley and His Workshop: Arts and Crafts in the Twentieth Century*, Wendlebury, Oxfordshire: White Cockade, 1992

Carruthers, Annette and Mary Greensted, *Good Citizen's Furniture: The Arts and Crafts Collections at Cheltenham*, London: Lund Humphries, 1994

Clark, Robert Judson, *The Arts and Crafts Movement in America, 1876–1916*, Princeton: Princeton University Press, 1972

Comino, Mary, *Gimson and the Barnsleys: "Wonderful Furniture of a Commonplace Kind"*, London: Evans, 1980

Cumming, Elizabeth and Wendy Kaplan, *The Arts and Crafts Movement*, London and New York: Thames and Hudson, 1991

Davey, Peter J., *Arts and Crafts Architecture: The Search for an Earthly Paradise*, 2nd edition London: Phaidon, 1995

Harrison, Martin, *Victorian Stained Glass*, London: Barrie and Jenkins, 1980

Haslam, Malcolm, *English Art Pottery, 1865–1915*, Woodbridge, Suffolk: Antique Collectors' Club, 1975

Haslam, Malcolm, *Arts and Crafts Carpets*, London: David Black, 1991

Kaplan, Wendy (editor), *"The Art that is Life": The Arts and Crafts Movement in America, 1875–1920* (exhib. cat.: Museum of Fine Arts, Boston), Boston: Little Brown, 1987

Kaplan, Wendy (editor), *The Encyclopedia of Arts and Crafts: The International Arts Movement, 1850–1920*, New York: Dutton, and London: Headline, 1989

Lambourne, Lionel, *Utopian Craftsmen: The Arts and Crafts Movement from the Cotswolds to Chicago*, Salt Lake City: Peregrine Smith, and London: Astragal, 1980

Larmour, Paul, *The Arts and Crafts Movement in Ireland*, Belfast: Friar's Bush Press, 1992

MacCarthy, Fiona, *William Morris: A Life for Our Time*, London: Faber, 1994; New York: Knopf, 1995

Muthesius, Hermann, *The English House*, edited by Dennis Sharp, London: Crosby Lockwood Staples, and New York: Rizzoli, 1979 (German original, 3 vols., 1903–04, revised edition 1908–11)

Naylor, Gillian, *The Arts and Crafts Movement: A Study of its Sources, Ideals and Influence on Design Theory*, London: Studio Vista, and Cambridge: Massachusetts Institute of Technology Press, 1971

Parry, Linda, *Textiles of the Arts and Crafts Movement*, London and New York: Thames and Hudson, 1988

Stansky, Peter, *Redesigning the World: William Morris, the 1880s, and the Arts and Crafts*, Princeton: Princeton University Press, 1985

Trapp, Kenneth R. (editor), *The Arts and Crafts Movement in California: Living the Good Life* (exhib. cat.: Oakland Museum), New York: Abbeville, 1993

Volpe, Tod M. and Beth Cathers, *Treasures of the American Arts and Crafts Movement, 1890–1920*, New York: Abrams, and London: Thames and Hudson, 1988

Ashbee, C.R. 1863–1942

British architect, designer and design theorist

Founder of the Guild and School of Handicraft, C.R. Ashbee was a major force behind the Arts and Crafts Movement. His efforts to determine a place for the aesthetic and values of traditional craftsmanship in a modern industrial society exercised an important influence on British artistic and cultural life at the turn of the century. And in his own work he showed how the aesthetic of simplicity, which formed one aspect of the Arts and Crafts ideal, could progress from the hand-crafted to the machine-made, without any diminution of the tenets of the movement.

After studying history at Cambridge, where he was influenced by Ruskin, Morris and the Romantic socialist Edward Carpenter (1844–1929), Ashbee entered the office of the architect G.F. Bodley in 1883. In 1886 he moved into Toynbee Hall, the philanthropic University foundation in London's East End, where he offered a class on the writings of Ruskin. In an attempt to explore the dignity of labour, the following year his students executed a plasterwork panel for the dining room at Toynbee Hall which involved free-hand wall paintings punctuated by gilded modelled bosses and medallions. This collective endeavour prompted the establishment, in 1888, of the Guild and School of Handicraft. Partly inspired by A.H. Mackmurdo's Century Guild, Ashbee's idea of a craft school with a workshop at its centre was very much in tune with contemporary ideas on the teaching of art and craft and the technical education movement. By presenting the Guild as "artistic" decorators producing stained glass, furniture, fabrics and wallpaper that catered to advanced architectural tastes rather than the trade, he allied their work to the decorative art movements of the 1880s. The Guild also produced metal, silver and leatherwork, and as none of the pupils had any craft skills of their own, John Pearson, a metalwork instructor specialising in decorative repoussé work was employed. Other founder members included Fred Hubbard, responsible with Ashbee for decorative painting and general administration, and John Williams a metalworker. C.V. Adams, the cabinet-maker, was of particular significance in that he put Ashbee's ideas into practice organising a real co-operative workshop.

Early examples of the Guild's work were shown at the Arts and Crafts exhibition Society in 1888, and they also showed at the 1889 and later Arts and Crafts Exhibitions. Designs for furniture and metalwork for Riseholme Hall, near Lincoln, for Herbert J.Torr were followed by further commissions during 1889, including the design for a repoussé copper frame for Holman Hunt's *May Morning on Magdalen Tower, Oxford*. A large order in 1892 for panelling, decorative painting, leatherwork, metalwork and furniture – all to Ashbee's designs – for James Rankin's country house, Bryngwyn rescued the Guild from financial difficulties. As a result it was able to expand, and new recruits included Walter Curtis, Bill Hardiman and W.H.White. The latter were taught the techniques of modelling and casting in silver and their silver and metalwork was executed in a complicated Art Nouveau style.

Furniture was probably made from the earliest days of the Guild. Record books show that they made much the same types of furniture as trade cabinet-makers, and prices were comparable with those of firms such as Heal's and Harrod's who served the upper end of the middle-class market. They made occasional tables and chairs, cabinets of various kinds, sideboards, dining tables and chairs, desks and writing tables, and wardrobes and wash stands, but Ashbee did not like the many-shelved pieces like what-nots or overmantels, or elaborate upholstery. His admiration for vernacular and antiquarian styles encouraged the production of a limited number of traditional settles and trestle tables, but, on the whole, the Guild favoured heavy or fixed pieces such as cabinets to go against the wall. These pieces were unmistakably joiner's furniture, made of heavy members in explicit frame and panel construction; the usual woods were oak, basswood and walnut. Cabinets were solid and enclosed rather than open in structure, and the detailing was traditional; frame and panel elements were usually moulded and fielded, legs were often bracketed, and cornices were normal, with occasional resonances from the 16th and 17th centuries. While some pieces were quite plain and others – notably an oak cabinet for the New School at Abbotsholme whose doors were covered with a delicate design of undulating sprays of laurel interspersed with lines from Blake's writings – were painted. Ashbee's favourite form of decoration was coloured and gilded gesso applied sparingly to the wood. Compared with much light-weight, highly decorated trade furniture of the time, the overall character of these early pieces was of solid, traditionally constructed items with broad, restful surfaces.

Ashbee's later furniture was simpler and he was influenced particularly by the puritan sparseness of C.F.A. Voysey and Charles Spooner, both of whom exhibited at the Arts and Crafts Exhibition Society Exhibition of 1893. The enlarged Guild exhibited five pieces at the Society's Exhibition of 1896 and Ashbee's music cabinet in oak attracted considerable attention. In 1897, Ashbee was invited by the architect M.H. Baillie Scott to collaborate on the design of furniture and interior decorations for the dining room and drawing room of the Grand Duke of Hesse's palace at Darmstadt in West Germany. Ashbee was asked to design the light fittings and the Guild to make both fittings and furniture. Perhaps not surprisingly, Ashbee's work began to develop along the same lines as Scott's and the furniture of his mature period was boxy and rectangular in form, with clear, linear ornament. Cabinets were treated as boxes on legs; legs were more often than not square in plan and met the body without brackets; and almost all the carcase furniture was built up of simple planks. Gesso was abandoned and painting used only occasionally; instead Ashbee made great play with metalwork and inlay. Early, relatively discrete hinges gave way to long, wide, medieval-style straps of wrought iron, pewter or steel that ended in characteristically fleshy, natural forms. For inlays, Ashbee used the simple motif of rectangular or lozenge-shaped panels – two or three inches across – each inlaid with a conventionalised, almost linear plant design made from combinations of pewter, satinwood, ebony, holly and coloured woods. These panels were most effective on plain pieces of furniture, where they helped to relieve and enhance the puritanism of Ashbee's designs. By 1900 he was no longer content to produce austere or solid versions of existing furniture types and designs such as an oak and holly piano case (c.1900) demonstrate a new independence in his work.

For much of his career, Ashbee was also active as an architect and in the mid 1890s he designed several houses in Cheyne Walk, Chelsea. These included his mother's house, the Magpie and Stump (1893–94), whose complex and eclectic interiors served as a kind of showroom for the Guild and represent the most interesting example of their decorative work. The hall was a bare reddish room with little except the chimneypiece, whose panel of what appeared to be green tiles was in fact made up of plaques of plain and repoussé copper and coloured enamels, to catch the eye. The back wall was covered with an expanse of embossed leatherwork, incised, modelled and gilded by Bill Hardiman. The first floor drawing room was furnished with a mixture of antique and modern furniture and the walls were covered with papers in two tones of peacock blue. These papers were the most ambitious of the Guild's wallpapers and contained an undulating pattern of briar-like plant forms crowned by a frieze of Tudor roses and emblems of the wheel of fortune. The chimney breast was painted by Roger Fry, depicting a rather formal landscape garden, with a narrow canal. Ashbee drew upon the special skills of the Guild for the decorative metalwork of his copper and pewter fittings and the *Studio* compared the light fittings and the architectural metalwork to jewellery on a large scale. The dining room was long and austere. The walls were clad in plain wood panelling, painted a light colour and surmounted by a painted frieze, and the furnishings included rush-seated chairs and trestle tables.

After the Magpie and Stump, Ashbee's style of interior design, like his furniture, became more simplified as is evident in his Cheyne Walk houses of c.1898 and many of the small middle-class houses that he built in the country. His preferred form of decoration during this period was panelling, divided vertically, as in the hall at 39 Cheyne Walk, and if he could not panel then he would simply paint. For the frieze he liked a theme. If that were not possible then he would sometimes use plasterwork modelled in low relief, but never flat coloured pattern. Ashbee's fireplaces were typically austere and vertical and somewhat unhomely. They were sometimes made of cast iron, such as that in 39 Cheyne Walk. Rejecting the rich textures characteristic of advanced taste in the 1870s and 1880s, Ashbee also eschewed the cosy and nostalgic medieval ambience sought by contemporaries such as Baillie Scott. Nor was he interested in the subtle yet formal combinations of colour, tone and line favoured by Charles Rennie Mackintosh and the work of the Austrian school. He belonged instead to the mainstream of the English Arts and Crafts movement, designing reserved, light interiors where the character was given by panelling, a little plasterwork relief, and the careful handling of the chimneypieces; interiors which did not create an intense and separate atmosphere, but were continuous with the architecture; interiors which provide a setting for furniture without determining its character.

Towards the end of 1901, the lease on Essex House, London, where the Guild had been based since 1891, was nearing its end, and on Ashbee's return from America the Guild moved to Chipping Campden in Gloucestershire thereby conforming to the Romantic, rural ideal that was at the heart of much Arts and Crafts teaching. Soon after this move, Ashbee embarked on one of his most successful interior commissions for the library of Madresfield Court, Worcestershire. His clients, the 7th Earl of Beauchamp and his wife, were keen patrons of Arts and Crafts work and the library included light fittings by the Birmingham Guild of Handicraft. Ashbee's work was essentially that of embellishment and in 1902–03 he installed two single and one pair of double doors in oak. These were framed up in Ashbee's usual way and scattered among the panels were scenes appropriate to a library, carved in low relief by Alec Miller. The contrast between the broad framing and the carved panels, the vivid ornament on the pewter door furniture, and the delicacy of Miller's carvings attest to the skill and maturity of Ashbee's designs. A second stage of work – carried out in 1905 – involved decorating the ends of the two free-standing bookcases with carving. One end carried an image of the Tree of Knowledge and the other depicted the Tree of Life, thus encapsulating the contrast between sacred and profane learning through the imagery and decoration. These panels set the tone for the interior, replacing warmth and conviviality with an emphasis upon more philosophical ideas.

From the 1900s Ashbee was also increasingly active as a printer and designer of jewellery. After Morris's death in 1896 he acquired some of the Kelmscott Press equipment to start the Essex House Press; its first book, Cellini's *Treatises on Goldsmithing and Sculpture* (1898), translated by Ashbee, was dedicated to the Guild. Ashbee designed his own typeface, Endeavour, first used on *An Endeavour towards the Teaching of John Ruskin and William Morris* (1901). In the *Studio* winter number of 1901 to 1902 Aymer Vallance recognised Ashbee's pre-eminence as a designer of jewellery, and he was feted in Budapest in 1905. A laudatory account of the Guild appeared in *Kunst und Handwerk* (1907) but in the same year the Guild failed. Ashbee published an inquest entitled *Craftsmanship in Competitive Industry* in 1909. His *Should We Stop Teaching Art?* (1911) advocated government-endowed "small artistic workshops" run along similar lines to that of the Guild. From 1917 he was involved in town planning in Egypt and Jerusalem, but in 1924 returned to England and devoted himself to theorizing and his memoirs.

Like Voysey and Baillie Scott, Ashbee designed principally for middle-class urban and suburban homes. His aim was to bring reasonableness and simplicity to domestic living and his furniture offered a radical alternative to mainstream and cottage-style design. And if the demise of the Guild brought an end to these ambitions, it signalled not so much the failure of his designs as the impracticability of craft production in an era of mass production.

HILARY J. GRAINGER

See also Arts and Crafts Movement

Biography

Charles Robert Ashbee. Born in London, 17 May 1863, the son of Henry Spencer Ashbee, a city merchant and connoisseur of erotica. Educated at Wellington, and at King's College, Cambridge, 1883–86, where he became friends with Roger Fry and Goldsworthy Lowes Dickinson, and met the philanthropist Edward Carpenter. Married Janet Forbes c.1898: 4 daughters. Trained as an architect under the Gothic Revivialist G. F. Bodley, 1883–86. Resident at Toynbee Hall, a philanthropic foundation in London's East End, 1886; taught evening classes in drawing. Active as an architect and designer of furnishings, silverwork and jewellery from 1888. Founded the Guild and School of Handicraft, Toynbee Hall, 1888; Guild moved to Essex House, Mile End Road, London, 1891, and became a limited company, 1898; workshops moved to Chipping Campden, Gloucestershire, 1901; Ashbee established the School of Arts and Crafts, Chipping Campden, 1904 (active until 1914); Guild went into voluntary liquidation, 1908. Founded the Essex House Press, 1898. Travelled to the US in 1900, and again in 1909–10, when he met Frank Lloyd Wright. Professor of English, Cairo University, 1915–19. Adviser to the British government on the restoration of Jerusalem, 1919–23. Participated in numerous exhibitions including the Arts and Crafts Exhibition Society from 1888, and the Vienna Secession 1900, 1902, 1905 and 1906. Published several books on crafts and design. Member, National Trust; Council Member from 1896. Died in Sevenoaks, Kent, 23 May 1942.

Selected Works

Collections of Ashbee's architectural drawings are in the Drawings Collection of the Royal Institute of British Architects, the Chelsea Public Library, and the Victoria and Albert Museum, all London. The Victoria and Albert Museum also holds catalogues and Minute Books relating to the Guild of Handicraft for the period 1888–1907, an album of letters and printed ephemera, and original designs by Ashbee for furniture, metalwork, jewellery, etc. The Ashbee Journals (more than 50 volumes) are in King's College Library, Cambridge. Examples of Ashbee's furniture are in Cheltenham Art Gallery and Museum; examples of metalwork and jewellery are in the Victoria and Albert Museum.

Interiors

1887	Toynbee Hall, London (decoration of the dining room; with the Guild of Handicraft)
1892	Bryngwyn, Herefordshire (decorative scheme including a wall-painting and decorative frieze): James Rankin
1893	Magpie and Stump, 34 Cheyne Walk, London (building, interiors and furnishings; decorative work by Roger Fry, Christopher Whall and others): Mrs. H.S. Ashbee
1897–98	Grand Ducal Palace, Darmstadt, Hesse (design of light fittings; production of furniture and fittings designed by M. H. Baillie Scott): Grand Duke Ernest Ludwig of Hesse
1897–98	74 Cheyne Walk, London (building and interiors): F.A. Forbes
1898–99	39 Cheyne Walk, London (building, interiors and furnishings; frieze of Cheyne Walk by Fleetwood Varley): C.R. Ashbee
1902–03 & 1905	Madresfield Court, Worcestershire (library fittings and furniture; carving by Alec Miller): 7th Earl of Beauchamp
1905–07	Norman Chapel, Broad Campden, Gloucestershire (remodelling of the building, additions and interiors)
1905–07	De Szász House, Budapest, Hungary (building and interiors): Zsombar de Szász

1907–09 Villa San Giorgio, Taormina, Sicily (building and interiors; decorative carving by Alec Miller and Will Hart): Thomas Bradney Shaw Hellier

Ashbee's designs for furniture, decorative metalwork, silverwork, light fittings, embossed leathers and jewellery were carried out by the Guild of Handicraft, 1888–1907. He also designed pianos for Broadwood, c.1900, and cast-iron fireplaces for Falkirk Iron Co., 1897.

Publications

A Book of Cottages and Little Houses, 1906
Craftsmanship in Competitive Industry, 1909
Modern English Silverwork, 1909; new edition with introductory essays by Alan Crawford and Shirley Bury, 1974
The Guild of Handicraft, 1909
Should We Stop Teaching Art?, 1911

Further Reading

For a major, scholarly study of Ashbee's life, ideas and career, see Crawford 1985 which includes an Appendix of Ashbee's architectural commissions and a list of the works published by the Essex Press. Further details of work produced by the Guild of Handicraft appear in Crawford 1981, and a select bibliography appears in MacCarthy 1981.

Anscombe, Isabelle, *Arts and Crafts Style*, London: Phaidon, 1991
Catalogue of the Drawings Collection of the Royal Institute of British Architects, Farnborough: Gregg, 1969
Crawford, Alan, *C.R. Ashbee and the Guild of Handicraft* (exhib. cat.), Cheltenham: Cheltenham Art Gallery and Museum, 1981
Crawford, Alan, *C.R. Ashbee, Architect, Designer, and Romantic Socialist*, New Haven and London: Yale University Press, 1985
Cooper, Jeremy, *Victorian and Edwardian Furniture and Interiors*, London: Thames and Hudson, 1987
Gere, Charlotte, *European and American Jewellery, 1830–1914*, London: Heinemann, 1975; as *American and European Jewelry, 1830–1914*, New York: Crown, 1975
Krekel-Aalberse, Annelies, *Art Nouveau and Art Déco Silver*, New York: Abrams, and London: Thames and Hudson, 1989
MacCarthy, Fiona, *The Simple Life: C.R. Ashbee in the Cotswolds*, London: Lund Humphries, and Berkeley: University of California Press, 1981

Laura Ashley Ltd.

British manufacturer and retailer of home furnishings and clothing; established 1953

By 1985 the name of Laura Ashley was emblazoned above more than 180 forest green shop fronts from Tunbridge Wells to Tokyo, selling a complete Laura Ashley lifestyle. Fabrics, wallpapers, furniture, floor coverings and a range of accessories for the home as well as clothing were displayed in shop interiors intended to recreate an English Country House look, while glossy annual catalogues and books showed how customers could recreate the look for themselves.

Bernard Ashley provided the technical and entrepreneurial skills for the rapid and massive expansion of the firm, but it was Laura who was the design pioneer, finding sources of patterns in nature and the past, especially the Victorian period, for the fabric and wallpaper prints which were to become the firm's signature, together with its distinctive colour palette and the use of natural fabrics. Through the interiors of the Ashleys' own much photographed homes and lifestyle, she also associated the company with a style of decorating that sought to recreate a nostalgic, rural way of life whether lived in the English country house, rustic cottage or urban terrace.

Home furnishings were launched in the early 1970s when the company had already established a reputation for its romantically styled women's clothing. Some of the small scale designs used on dress fabrics were simply printed onto wallpaper and a wider width lightweight cotton, christened "Country Furnishing Cotton". Early collections included paisley and heraldic designs, but it was the monochrome, small scale florals, for example *Petite Fleur*, a sprig, and *Wild Clematis*, a design of trailing flowers and foliage, and geometrics such as *Nutmeg* which were successful in the long term. Some designs were available in positive and negative prints of each colourway: by the early 1980s the positive print was usually used on wallpaper, the negative on the coordinating fabric. This system, initially imposed by technical problems involved in printing in more than one colour, enabled easy coordination of wallcoverings and soft furnishings, and also hid any imperfections in the fabric with what were later dubbed "itsy bitsy prints". Patchwork quilts were a favourite source for prints, and also inspired the made up quilts sold in Laura Ashley prints. The homely, cottage look for which the firm became known in the 1970s is shown in the child's bedroom at Rhydoldog, where a patchwork quilt uses all the prints featured in the room: *Floribunda* covers the walls and ceiling while the cotton *Cottage Sprig* is used for the frilled curtains (available made to order from the early 1980s) and tablecloth. A larger scale print, *Meadow Flowers*, is used on the bed . These products were all sold very cheaply and appealed to young couples setting up home as well as to women who had already bought the "Laura Ashley" look in clothing and wanted to decorate their home in the same romantic, ruffled style.

Colour was another important element in identifying an early Laura Ashley interior. In contrast to the widely available garish florals and bright abstracts the company offered muted combinations of cream with a sludgy blue named "smoke", plum or terracotta, intended to evoke old vegetable dyes, while cherry, rose or moss with white gave a contemporary freshness to the prints. The names given to colours, and prints (from 1983), deliberately linked them to the countryside (e.g., *Dog Rose*, *Wild Strawberry*), or earlier periods of decoration (e.g., *Queen Anne's Needlework*).

Early prints were seen by the customer as particularly suitable for use in small bedrooms, bathrooms and nurseries. In 1983 the company introduced 13 larger scale prints, and some new wallpaper designs to work with them. They were printed on the carefully named "Drawing Room Fabric" to reinforce the message that Laura Ashley was suitable for downstairs rooms and master bedrooms, hanging at large windows and four-posters. The majority were florals, based on faded chintzes, such as *Blue Ribbons* and its accompanying wallpaper *Red Rose*, which were shown in the dining room of the Ashley's French château. A striking gold and burgundy print, *Venetia*, was also launched, together with upholstery fabric, rugs and tiles which coordinated with the main print collection.

These prints used the same colour palette as the existing

Ashley: Emma Ashley's bedroom at Rhydoldog in Wales, an early interior

small scale designs, and formed the backbone of the English Country House style which characterised the firm's output in the 1980s, in contrast to the cottage style of the 1970s. The change was partly to expand the market for the firm's products, but was also influenced by the Ashley's own changing tastes and new pattern sources. Master prints such as *Country Roses* were printed with a coordinating minor print of a rosebud on the same trellis ground, *Boudoir*, and used by Laura in the main bedroom at Rhydoldog . The elaborate hangings on the half tester, the traditional window treatment and the mass of cushions were all elements of the "Made To Order" lifestyle Laura Ashley could offer customers as far afield as Shrewsbury and San Francisco. This style had particular appeal in the USA where the company enjoyed a more upmarket image than in Britain. The firm was invited to decorate a house in Colonial Williamsburg.

The colour range also expanded: *Alba Roses*, a chintz launched in 1987, was available in butter yellow ("cowslip") and jade, and described as reproducing colours "kissed by the sun". Richer colours such as dark green, crimson, navy, burgundy and sand were especially popular in Owen Jones-inspired patterns such as *Mr. Jones*. The sources for new designs were also changing; *Cottage Sprig* had been inspired by a poster. Later prints were often reworked from historic textiles and wallpapers found by Laura in country houses (e.g., *Priory* from a fabric at Chatsworth) and museums (*Regatta*, a dress and furnishing fabric, was copied from a dress in collection at Platt Hall, Manchester; Tozer and Levitt 1983).

The expanding range of prints was also intended to "offer the possibility of achieving more sophisticated period ration" (Laura Ashley in the 1983 Home Decoration catalogue). *Salon* was used in this way, with a grisaille border and cut-out prints to create a print room at Rhydoldog. It was used again in the far more sophisticated surroundings of the Ashleys' Brussels house for the curtains and as a panelled wallpaper in the Salon, where the yellow scheme and cords and tassels on the goblet-pleated curtains recall Nancy Lancaster. But what identifies this room as a Laura Ashley interior is the large-scale floral chintz in a favourite combination of Ashley's, lilac and grey, used on the chairs, full-length fabrics and cushions.

This pattern was adapted from an 18th-century French silk and came from the "Laura Ashley Decorator Collection", launched in 1980. Although Ashley claimed the company aimed to make its prints as timeless as possible, customers' expectations of a Laura Ashley look did not move fast enough for her changing tastes and print research. The collection was sold initially through a London showroom and then interior design shops. Some were subsequently added to the main collection, e.g., the *Reveillon* prints, inspired by 18th-century French wallpapers, produced as wallpaper, chintz and satin weave fabric. These 18th-century patterns represent a definite move away from purely Victorian sources, and were often inspired by the grand interior schemes devised by Laura Ashley and her staff for the château at Remaisnil using patterns taken from *toiles de jouys* and floral silks. Not only did the prints become more sophisticated, interiors were also created based on contemporary sources. A carved bed original to the château was first shown in a fresh yellow and blue scheme with *Windspray* (based on an American stencil) at the windows and the striped wallpaper *Riviera*. Later the bed was used in Ashley's bedroom, the scheme inspired by a Sèvres plaque (Irvine 1987) using *Cirque* striped cotton battened on the walls, and for the bed drapes and curtains, whose pelmets copied an 18th-century drawing.

The range of fabrics was also expanded during the late 1980s, particularly for upholstery such as woven jacquard, ottoman, damask and checks. Furniture and home accessories were also built up from a "classic" loose covered sofa and armchair (*Montgomery*, introduced 1987) to include ranges of occasional and carcase furniture (for the bedroom and kitchen), and accessories included kitchenware, curtains and door fittings. Many of these ranges sold poorly and only served to dilute the company image which Laura Ashley, who died suddenly in 1985, had cultivated so carefully. Recent developments have included increased choice in window treatments and upholstered furniture, refocusing on the prints and colours with which the company is identified.

Few of the company's designs can be described as authentic reproductions. Even originals were copied, as at Charleston Farmhouse in England, the designs were adapted and recoloured onto a different fabric for sale in the shops. This collection was a rare venture into 20th-century sources for the firm – chapters on Modernism are always the last in the company's interior design books and concentrate on how "classic" florals can be used with checks and stripes. In the UK the company has been seen to grow from a family business selling cheap fabrics and wallpaper to a high street retailer with pretensions to be an interior decorator, but lacking the individuality and spontaneity sought by more sophisticated customers. It continues, however, to evoke a strong image of the past and rural life, and now has its own archive on which to draw, recolouring *Trefoil*, a 1980s print, for the 1995 collection.

CLARE TAYLOR

Further Reading

For a full range of Laura Ashley products see the firm's annual catalogues and promotional literature, particularly the *Laura Ashley Book of Interior Decoration*, 1983 and 1989. Additional useful sources of information appear in Ashley 1988, Dickson 1985, Gale 1987, and Sebba 1990 which is an authorized biography of the firm's founder.

Ashley, Nick and others, *Laura Ashley at Home: Six Family Homes and their Transformation*, London: Weidenfeld and Nicolson, 1988

Corbett-Winder, Kate, *Laura Ashley Living Rooms*, London: Weidenfeld and Nicolson, 1989

Dickson, Elizabeth and Margaret Colvin, *The Laura Ashley Book of Home Decorating*, 1982; revised edition, London: Octopus, 1985

Dumoulin, Marie-Claude, "Chez Laura Ashley", in *Elle*, 11 October 1976, pp.88–91

Finnerty, Anne, "Profile of Laura Ashley" in *Textile Outlook International*, January 1990, pp.77–94

Gale, Iain and Susan Irvine, *Laura Ashley Style*, London: Weidenfeld and Nicolson, 1987

Gandee, Charles, "Nick Ashley: Life after Laura" in *House and Garden* (UK), April 1991, pp.212

Irvine, Susan, *Laura Ashley Bedrooms*, London: Weidenfeld and Nicolson, 1987

Laura Ashley obituary in *The Times*, 18 September 1985

Mack, Lorrie and others, *Laura Ashley Guide to Country Decorating*, London: Weidenfeld and Nicolson, 1992

Sebba, Anne, *Laura Ashley: A Life by Design*, London: Weidenfeld and Nicolson, 1990

Tozer, Jane and Sarah Levitt, *Fabric of Society: A Century of People and their Clothes, 1770–1870*, Carno, Wales: Laura Ashley Ltd., 1983

Wilhide, Elizabeth, *Laura Ashley Windows*, London: Weidenfeld and Nicolson, 1988

Asplund, Erik Gunnar 1885–1940

Swedish architect and designer

Erik Gunnar Asplund is Sweden's greatest 20th-century international architect; he played a key role in Scandinavian architectural developments during the inter-war years, influencing colleagues such as Alvar Aalto. Initially working in the National-Romantic style, he adopted Neo-Classicism, a significant factor in this move being his tour of Italy in 1914.

Asplund's Neo-Classical style became increasingly pure, leading finally to his conversion to Modernism.

One of Asplund's earliest works was his interior for the Home Exhibition at Liljevalch's Art Gallery, Stockholm in 1917. The event was organised by the Swedish Society of Crafts and Design with a "social mission" to improve the design environment of the underprivileged urban proletariat. Although, not surprisingly, the show was not much visited by this group, critics singled out Asplund's atmospheric interior for its painstaking attention to detail – something that would become a trademark of all Asplund's work. The kitchen-living-bedroom space was decorated in light blue and white. Stained pine was used for the sturdy vernacular-inspired furniture, as well as for the ceiling and window frames. Rag-weave runners on the floor, a canary in a cage, and children's clothes drying by the stove, completed the homely feel. There were influences from both Carl Larsson's *Ett Hem* pictures as well as the continental Beidermeier style.

The 1920s saw Asplund's last commissions of representational, ceremonial furniture for civic buildings. His Neo-Classical furniture adorns the Councillors' Corridor in the Stockholm City Hall – a kind of waiting room with chairs, mirrors and a cupboard for coats. The grey and white lacquered birch chair with its straight lines and balanced proportions is particularly elegant. Grey painted cane is used for the seat and circular centre, framed by a square backrest. A cow's skull adorns the front edge of the seat. The leg of the adjoining table terminates in a horse's hoof. Asplund's Study at the 1925 Exposition des Arts Décoratifs in Paris continues this Neo-Classical theme. Its *pièce de resistance* was the luxurious *Senna* armchair with simplified Empire lines which was reissued by Cassina in the 1980s.

A central theme in Asplund's work is the transition from exterior to interior. This is featured in the Skandia Cinema, and perfected in the Stockholm City Library. The latter building consists of a cylinder on a cube, designed around the form of the innermost room – a typical Asplund strategy. The rotunda is lined with bookshelves centred on the circular lending desk. The stairs to this space begin at street level and gradually narrow as they proceed to the main reading level. On reaching the counter the visitor is struck by a sense of space and light. Asplund designed the furniture, shelving, lamps and door handles. About twenty different chair types were involved, each one having its own character, detailing, finish and specific function. They ranged from the Chief Librarian's *klismos*-inspired mahogany armchair, with leather upholstery and brass detailing, to its plainer stained birch counterpart in the Reading Room. The room's original colours were warm green, terracotta and yellow. Even the children's section has specially designed small-scale furniture. This is sturdy with a Nordic vernacular feel; the surface of the wood has a "brushed" tactile finish. A "Sandman" mural forms the atmospheric backdrop to the story room, with a ceiling painted in dark blue.

Asplund's architectural framework for the influential Stockholm Exhibition of 1930 marks his overnight conversion to Modernism – known as Functionalism in Scandinavia. This is also reflected in the furniture designed for the boardroom of the Swedish Society of Crafts and Design in the following year, although an echo of the curved Empire back of the library chair persists in the tubular steel seating. The armchair uses a minimum of tubing, but instead of being turned at right angles in the style of Le Corbusier, it follows a gently sweeping curve to the tip of the back leg. The up-market retailer Svenskt Tenn recently revived the design for a low tubular steel and leather hump-backed stool dating from 1933.

Significantly, Asplund's individual form of Modernism soon developed into a more gentle, traditionally based, humanist form of Swedish Functionalism. In his modest country cottage, Stennäs, the white unadorned-adorned living room conveys a homely and relaxed atmosphere. The room is dominated by an organic, grotto-like inglenook, and comfortable, white painted wood furniture – including a curvaceous sofa and a low table with a brown limestone top – frames the large panorama window.

Besides using colour and materials to create atmosphere, Asplund was very aware of how light can influence the perception of an interior, and of how, on entering a room, visitors react differently depending on how it is lit. The relation between windows and doors was therefore of considerable significance to him; there was also an awareness of how the placing of furniture influences behaviour and movement. In the Göteborg Law Courts, for example, the down-lighting of the main entrance hall creates a "distanceless" roof. Asplund also modified the standard measurements of the staircase steps, thereby forcing the agitated visitor to slow down and collect himself.

His chair for the "dock" ran counter to the stool specified in the design brief. Why, he argued, should someone who was innocent until proved guilty sit in a less comfortable seat than anyone else? Similarly, he saw no reason to exaggerate the dimensions of the Chairman's chair. This was made of hickory, with a T-shaped dark brown upholstered back. For more general use, Asplund designed a blond Thonet-inspired chair (made today by Cassina). Adorning the light wood panelled walls are textile hangings such as *Paragrafer* which featured paragraph symbols, exclamation and question marks, alluding to the difficult decisions to be made in the room. Elsewhere, cane furniture, large windows and pot-plants evoked the impression of a winter garden or conservatory.

The Woodland Crematorium shows further Asplund subtleties. The colonnade surrounding the main room echoes the loggia outside. The arched suspended roof and the bright frescoes (by Sven Erixson) intensify the sense of light and spaciousness. There are no formal religious symbols. The interior stresses the gallery surrounding the catafalque rather than the altar. Visitors sit on simple wooden pews, and their attention is captured by the limestone floor which was intended to provide something to focus on in difficult moments. In an adjoining room, wood panelling merges nearly invisibly into a bent laminate bench. These spaces convey a sense of intimacy and privacy. The Woodland Cemetery, with crematorium and three adjacent chapels, was a major and highly influential project. In 1994 it was placed on the UNESCO World Heritage List.

Asplund was, in the words of one Swedish critic, "more an artist-architect than a great innovator, a sensitive interpreter of a changing society in forms that expressed cultural continuity". His interiors and furniture may have sometimes veered towards being too precious. But they nevertheless express a unique psychological awareness and empathy, and it should be remembered that with few exceptions, Asplund's furniture was designed for specific purposes and settings. Since the 1980s, Asplund's timeless blend of classicism and Modernism has been the subject of renewed international interest and debate among both rationalists and Postmodernists. And he still represents a major source of inspiration for many of today's leading Scandinavian architects and designers.

DENISE HAGSTRÖMER

Biography

Born in Stockholm, 22 September 1885. Studied architecture at the Royal Institute of Technology, Stockholm, 1905–09: awarded travel scholarship, 1910, and travelled to Germany. Studied at the independent Klara School of Architecture under Carl Bergsten, Ivar Tengbom, Carl Westmann, and Ragnar Östberg, 1910–11. In private practice, 1911–40. Assistant lecturer, 1912–13, Special Instructor in Ornamental Art, 1917–18, and Professor of Architecture, 1931–40, Royal Institute of Technology, Stockholm. Also designer of furniture and interiors for public and private commissions. Married 1) Gerda Sellmann, 1918 (divorced 1934); 2) Ingrid Katarina Kling, 1934. Editor, *Arkitektur*, Stockholm, 1917–20. Died in Stockholm, 20 October 1940.

Selected Works

1913	Villa Selander, Örnsköldsvik (building and interiors): Selander family Villa Sturgården, Nyköping (building and interiors)
1914	Dr. Ruth's Villa, Kuusankoski, Finland (building and interiors): Kymmene Ltd.
1917	Home Exhibition of the Swedish Society of Arts and Crafts (interiors): Liljevalch's Art Gallery, Stockholm
1917–18	Villa Snellman, Djursholm, near Stockholm (building and interiors): Snellman family
1920	Workshops Society Exhibition, Stockholm (interiors)
1920–28	City Library, Stockholm (building, interiors, furniture): Stockholm City Council
1921	Stockholm City Hall (furniture)
1922–23	Skandia Cinema, Stockholm (remodelling of building and interiors)
1925	Exposition Internationale des Arts Décoratifs et Industriels Modernes, Paris (pavilion)
1931	Swedish Society of Arts and Crafts, Nybrogatan 7, Stockholm (fittings and furniture)
1932	Nationalmuseum, Stockholm (project for interiors)
1933–35	Bredenberg Department Store, Stockholm (building, fittings and interiors)
1933–37	Summer residence, Stavsnäs (building and interiors): B. Beckström
1934–37	Goteborg Law Courts (rebuilding and interiors)
1937	Stennäs House, Sorunda, Stockholm (building, interiors and furniture): G. Asplund
1940	Woodland Crematorium, South Cemetery, Stockholm (building, interiors and furniture)

Publications

Articles in *Arkitektur*, 1917–20
Articles in *Byggmästaren*, 1920–40
Acceptera, 1931

Further Reading

A well illustrated monograph is Caldenby and Hultin 1985. Wrede 1980 and Cruickshank 1988 are good English-language surveys of Asplund's career.

Alison, Filippo (editor), *Erik Gunnar Asplund: Mobili e oggetti*, Milan: Electa, 1985

Asplund 1885–1940 (exhib. cat.), Stockholm: Arkitekturmuseet, 1985

Blomberg, Erik, "Stadsbiblioteket i Stockholm", in *Svenska Slöjdföreningens årsbok*, 1928

Caldenby, Claes and Olof Hultin (editors), *Asplund*, Stockholm: Arkitektur Förlag, 1985; New York: Rizzoli, 1986

Constant, Caroline, *The Woodland Cemetery: Toward a Spiritual Landscape*, Stockholm: Byggförlaget, 1994

Cruickshank, Dan (editor), *Erik Gunnar Asplund*, London: Architects Journal, 1988

De Maré, Eric Samuel, *Gunnar Asplund: A Great Modern Architect*, London: Art and Technis, 1955

Doumato, Lamia, *Erik Gunnar Asplund: A Bibliography*, Monticello, IL: Vance, 1990

Engfors, Christina (editor), *Lectures and Briefings from the International Symposium on the Architecture of Erik Gunnar Asplund, 14–17 October 1985*, Stockholm: Swedish Museum of Architecture, 1986

Engfors, Christina, *E.G. Asplund, Architect, Friend and Colleague*, Stockholm: Arkitektur Förlag, 1990

"Erik Gunnar Asplund: September 22, 1885–October 20, 1940", in *Space Design* (special issue), Tokyo, October, 1982

Gunnar Asplund 1885–1940: The Dilemma of Classicism (exhib. cat.), London: Architectural Association, 1988

Holmdahl, Gustav and others (editors), *Gunnar Asplund, Architect: Plans, Sketches, and Photographs*, 2nd edition, Stockholm: Byggförlaget, 1981

Spark, D.M., *Gunnar Asplund*, dissertation, Newcastle: University of Newcastle, 1959

Wrede, Stuart, *The Architecture of Erik Gunnar Asplund*, Cambridge: Massachusetts Institute of Technology Press, 1980

Wrede, Stuart, *Woodland Crematorium; Woodland Chapel; Stockholm Public Library*, Tokyo: ADA, 1982 (Global Architecture 62)

Associated Artists

American interior decorating firm, 1879–1883

Associated Artists was created in 1879 by the partnership of Louis Comfort Tiffany (1848–1933), Samuel Colman (1832–1920), Lockwood de Forest (1850–1932) and Candace Thurber Wheeler (1827–1923). This partnership lasted four years, during which time the company (also called Louis C. Tiffany and Company) won many of the most prestigious American commissions of the period, including the redecoration of the White House in 1882.

Each of the partners managed a separate department in the firm, although they worked together closely to complete harmonious and luxurious interiors incorporating layered patterns, subtle colors and rich materials for some of America's most affluent clients. Tiffany directed the firm and was in charge of stained glass, Colman was consulted for color and flat patterns, de Forest oversaw carvings, furniture and wood decoration, and Wheeler supervised textiles.

Typical characteristics of the firm's interiors included the use of exotic motifs, such as those from Moorish or Near Eastern art, combined with East Indian and Japanesque features; layering and juxtaposition of patterns on the walls and ceilings; contrasts in light and dark and textures; delineation of rooms through the use of different decorative motifs and colors; and integration of paintings and pottery into decorative schemes. The most innovative creations of the firm were the inclusion of pale colors, with gradations from dark to light as the colors moved up the walls, the striking and abundant use of silver and gold details, and the augmentation of surfaces with extraordinary materials such as mother-of-pearl and metals on walls and ceilings as well as furniture.

Tiffany, Colman and de Forest began their careers as painters before turning their attention to the integration of artistic principles with interior decoration. Tiffany, who had studied painting under Colman, visited Europe and North Africa with him during the early 1870s. De Forest also travelled to Europe, Egypt, Syria and India, and in 1881, he established wood and metal workshops in Ahmadabad, India, in order to revive traditional Indian carved wood and perforated brass designs and crafts. These foreign tours, especially those in the Near East and North Africa, played a significant role in providing source material and inspiration for many Associated Artists designs.

Wheeler, who had learned spinning, weaving and knitting as a child, was inspired by a display of needlework from the South Kensington School of Art at the Centennial Exposition of 1876 in Philadelphia to organize the Society of Decorative Art in New York. Wheeler's Society, which was modeled on London's Royal Society of Art Needlework, sought to provide meaningful employment for women and to stimulate women's opportunities in artistic pursuits. It was Wheeler who first brought Tiffany, de Forest and Colman together as collaborators in artistic furnishings, when she invited these painters to teach her students design principles.

Associated Artists collaborated on some of the most important public and private commissions between 1879 and 1883, designing interiors for private residences and clubs as well as a curtain for a theater and the public rooms of an armory. Not only did the company work together to execute room decorations, but often the firm worked with other interior decorating businesses, such as Herter Brothers, within the same commissions. Specific rooms within a commission would be allocated to Associated Artists, while others were awarded to firms apparently in competition with them.

The two volume folio work, *Artistic Houses*, published 1883–84, covered some of the firm's most important commissions. This book not only illustrated some of their finest private interiors, but also detailed materials and color schemes. Other commissions completed by Associated Artists were described in monthly magazines and newspapers and heralded as some of the period's most creative and fashionable interiors.

Interiors by Associated Artists illustrated in *Artistic Houses* included Louis Comfort Tiffany's apartment; several rooms in the George Kemp house (1879), 720 Fifth Avenue; Hamilton Fish's drawing room, 251 East 17th Street; the drawing room in the John Taylor Johnston residence at 8 Fifth Avenue; and the dining room and parlor in the Dr. William T. Lusk house at 47 East 34th Street, all in New York. The firm also decorated the hall, library and parlor in the W.S. Kimball house in Rochester, New York, although only the hall and library were illustrated in *Artistic Houses*. Associated Artists had been selected by the new American president, Chester T. Arthur, to redecorate the White House's public rooms during the winter of 1882–83. A photograph of the East Room of the White House was reproduced in the book in addition to a detailed description of the firm's decoration of this room, the Blue Room, the State Dining Room, the Red Room and the corridor linking these public rooms.

Two further interiors, mentioned in *Artistic Houses* as the work of Samuel Colman, may also have been part of the collaborative work of Associated Artists: Colman's own house in Newport, Rhode Island and the decoration of walls and ceilings for the Henry G. Marquand residence at 68th Street and Fifth Avenue, New York. The interior decoration of this last commission was directed by the artist, decorator and stained glass designer, John La Farge, and included work by La Farge, Colman, Frederic Leighton and Lawrence Alma-Tadema, indicating the close cooperation among artists of this period.

Other private commissions executed by Associated Artists included the main rooms on the first floor of Nook Farm (Hartford, Connecticut, 1881), the residence of Samuel L. Clemens, known more familiarly as the author Mark Twain. These lavish interiors are the only rooms from a private residence executed by Associated Artists to have survived *in situ*. The firm also executed the interiors for the Cornelius Vanderbilt II residence, 1 West 57th Street.

The stage or drop curtain at the Madison Square Theater, New York, completed in 1879, was Associated Artists' first public commission. The design, a realistic landscape executed in appliquéd velvet and silk, was adapted from a painting by Mrs. Oliver Wendell Holmes, Jr. Although the production of the curtain was primarily under the auspices of Wheeler, the other partners in the firm contributed their expertise: Tiffany directed the construction of the 90 yard long curtain, Colman oversaw the color and de Forest was in charge of the materials. Unfortunately, the curtain was destroyed in a fire soon after it was installed.

In 1879, the company was awarded the commission to decorate the Veterans' Room and the adjoining Library for the Seventh Regiment Armory (66th–67th Streets between Park and Lexington Avenues), an army regiment made up of volunteers from New York's highest levels of society. The decoration of the building was completed by New York's finest interior decorating firms, including Associated Artists, Herter Brothers, Pottier & Stymus, Alexander Roux, Kimbel & Cabus, and Marcotte & Co. The interiors executed by Associated Artists, which opened 26 April 1880, were decorated in an Aesthetic style, combining Greek, Moorish, Celtic, Egyptian, Persian and Japanese ornament with militaristic motifs, such as chain mail, shields and allegories of war. The architect Stanford White and the painters George Henry Yewell (1830–1923) and Frank Millet (1846–1912) also collaborated on the decoration with Associated Artists. These opulent and luxurious rooms are two of the very few interiors completed by Associated Artists still extant.

A third public commission was the decoration of the halls and grand staircase for the Union League Club (Fifth Avenue and 39th Street) in 1880. Once again, the firm was one of many decorating companies contracted to execute the interiors for this private men's club. Associated Artists also supplied the draperies for the main public rooms, including three dining rooms, a picture gallery and a meeting hall.

All four members of Associated Artists designed wallpapers and ceiling papers for the firm of Warren, Fuller and Company, New York. Papers designed by Tiffany and Colman served as illustrations for an essay written by the art critic Clarence

Cook for a promotional booklet published by Warren, Fuller and Company, titled *What Shall We Do with Our Walls?* In 1881 the wallpaper firm sponsored a competition for designs for wall and ceiling papers for which Christian Herter, Edward C. Moore and Francis Lathrop served as judges. Candace Wheeler won first prize and her daughter, Dora, fourth, while second and third prizes were won by two other women who worked for Associated Artists, Ida Clark and Caroline Townsend. Wallpaper designs by Associated Artists were noteworthy for their integration of motifs taken from nature.

The partnership of Associated Artists dissolved in 1883, as Tiffany and the others decided to pursue their own interests. Candace Wheeler retained the name Associated Artists for her own decorating firm, which was primarily concerned with the design and manufacture of textiles and wall and ceiling papers. Under Wheeler's direction, the firm produced textile patterns for cottons, silks, embroideries, and even printed denims and helped women find employment in the arts. Clients included Mrs. Potter Palmer, Andrew Carnegie and Lily Langtry. Wheeler also arranged a business relationship with Cheney Brothers of Hartford, Connecticut, a manufacturer of silks, to produce designs by Associated Artists. In 1907, when Candace Wheeler was 80 years old, she closed Associated Artists, the source of some of the most innovative and luxurious textile decorations in the United States.

CATHERINE L. FUTTER

See also La Farge; Tiffany; Wheeler

Partnership of Louis Comfort Tiffany (1848–1933), Samuel Colman (1832–1920), Lockwood de Forest (1850–1932) and Candace Thurber Wheeler (1827–1923), established 1879; dissolved 1883. Name Associated Artists retained by Candace Wheeler for her own decorating firm; dissolved 1907.

Selected Works

Examples of the firm's work survive intact at the Mark Twain House, Hartford, Connecticut, and at the Seventh Regiment Armory, New York. Items designed by individual members of the firm are in the Metropolitan Museum of Art, New York. Many of their interiors are illustrated in *Artistic Houses*, 1883–84.

Interiors

1879	George Kemp House, New York (decoration and furnishings)
1879	Madison Square Theater, New York (embroidered stage curtain; mainly executed by Candace Wheeler)
1879–80	Veterans' Room and Library, 7th Regiment Armory, New York (decorations and furnishings, with Stanford White)
1880–81	Union League Club, New York (grand staircase and halls, and draperies for the main public rooms)
1881	William S. Kimball House, Rochester, New York (decorations and furniture)
1881	Mark Twain House, Hartford, Connecticut (decorations and furniture)
1881–82	Cornelius Vanderbilt II Mansion, New York (decorations and furniture)
1881–82	J. Taylor Johnson House, New York (decoration of the dining room)
1882–83	William T. Lusk House, New York (decoration of the dining room and parlour)
1882–83	The White House, Washington, DC (decoration of the public rooms, including the East Room, Blue Room, State Dining Room and the Red Room): President Chester Arthur

Further Reading

For a scholarly survey of the work of Associated Artists see Faude 1975.

The American Renaissance, 1876–1917 (exhib. cat.), New York: Brooklyn Museum, 1979

Artistic Houses, Being a Series of Views of a Number of the Most Beautiful and Celebrated Homes in the United States, 2 vols., New York, 1883–84; reprinted New York: Blom, 1971

Bradfield, Geoffrey N. and Connie Le Gendre, *Great New York Interiors: Seventh Regiment Armory*, New York, 1983

Burke, Doreen Bolger and others, *In Pursuit of Beauty: Americans and the Aesthetic Movement* (exhib. cat.: Metropolitan Museum, New York), New York: Rizzoli, 1986

Darbee, Henry (editor), *Mark Twain's House*, Hartford, CT, 1977

Duncan, Alastair, *Louis Comfort Tiffany*, New York: Abrams, 1992

Faude, Wilson H., "Associated Artists and the American Renaissance in the Decorative Arts" in *Winterthur Portfolio*, 10, 1975, pp.101–30

Faude, Wilson H., *The Renaissance of Mark Twain's House*, Larchmont, NY: Queens House, 1978

Schacter, Sophia Duckworth, *The Seventh Regiment Armory of New York City: A History of its Construction and Decoration*, M.A. thesis, New York: Columbia University, 1985

Williams, Virginia, "Candace Wheeler, Textile Designer for Associated Artists" in *Nineteenth Century*, 6, Summer 1980, pp.60–61

Audran, Claude III 1658–1734

French decorative painter, *ornemaniste* and tapestry designer

Claude III Audran played a critical role in the evolution of French decorative style in the late 17th and early 18th centuries. He displayed an amazing talent for artistic interpretation, applying forms such as arabesques, grotesques, Chinoiseries and *singeries* to a wide range of interior features. His best-known works were wall paintings, executed in oil and fresco for the French royal residences, and tapestry designs for the Gobelins. Unfortunately, few of his executed works survive and the large collection of drawings, purchased from his studio by Count Cronstedt and now in the Nationalmuseum, Stockholm, was relatively unknown before the 1940s. As a result, his reputation was for many years overshadowed by those of his more famous contemporaries. Yet closer study of his designs, in particular the arabesques, has revealed a freedom from academic restraint lacking in the work of other *ornemanistes* and designers such as Jean I Berain. The gaiety, playfulness and fantasy inherent in Audran's designs became hallmarks of the Rococo style.

Born in Lyon, the son of an engraver, Audran was trained by his father and his uncles, Claude II and Gérard Audran. Claude II had worked as a decorative painter under Charles Le Brun at Versailles and Audran followed in this role arriving in Paris to complete his training by 1684. The second half of the 17th century had witnessed a resurgence of academic classicism and the French court was dominated by the work of Charles Le Brun, Pierre Lassurance and François Mansart, the

Audran: Gobelins tapestry, *June*, c.1700

chief purveyors of the French classical Baroque style. At the same time, however, a growing interest in less formal styles of architecture and design was signalled by Louis XIV's demand for a new, more "youthful" set of interiors for the Ménagerie at Versailles.

Audran's work was well suited to this new style. His arabesques were not dissimilar from those of contemporaries like Berain but the individual elements seemed to have broken free of spatial constraint and to float with immaterial lightness and often in apparent isolation. Yet the compositions were also balanced and ordered, using cardinal and diagonal axes and well-defined bordered fields. In addition to arabesques, his favourite motifs were dancers, musicians, actors and balladeers (he greatly admired the work of the Italian Commedia dell'Arte); imaginary creatures and deities such as fauns, sphinxes, and winged goats; natural animals and birds; mythological gods and goddesses; and baldacchini, trellises, and canopies which provided a loose structure for his compositions. By 1699 he had also begun to introduce monkeys mimicking human activities and Chinese figures (*singeries* and Chinoiseries), a move that prefigured their full-scale adoption by ornamentalists during the first decades of the next century.

Like Jean I Berain, Audran never visited Italy and his inspiration derived from French sources such as historic embroideries, grotesques, and garden design (*broderies*). His early training as an engraver encouraged the use of two-dimensional compositions frequently involving bandwork, interlacing and scrolls. This highly ornamental style was ideally suited to both architectural decoration and tapestry design and Audran was awarded the first commission from the Gobelins workshops after their re-opening in 1699. His most important interior commissions were for decorative paintings at the royal châteaux of Marly, Meudon, La Muette and la Ménagerie at Versailles. His *singeries* at Marly were particularly influential and owed much to the example of Berain. His tapestry designs included the *Portières des Dieux* (1699–1711), a suite containing grotesque ornament and figures by Louis de Boulogne which was so successful that it was still being woven by the Gobelins factory in 1780, the *Douze Mois Grotesques* (1707–08), and borders for Charles Antoine Coypel's *Don Quixote* series (1716–17). He also produced designs for furniture, ceramics, musical instruments, embroideries, carpets, stained glass, gondolas, sundials, church vestments and even fireworks. His talents were enormously versatile and when he received his professional title of *maître* in 1692, he was described as a painter, sculptor, engraver and *enjoliveur* or embellisher.

A great portion of Audran's decorative work was executed by his team of assistants and pupils, the most celebrated of whom was the painter Antoine Watteau (1684–1721) who worked with him from 1707 after Audran's appointment as curator of the Palais du Luxembourg. Audran also collaborated with several other painters and designers including Jean-Baptiste Oudry (1686–1755) and Christophe Huet (1700–59). With much of his decorative work now lost, the best record of his style survives in his drawings.

Audran's most important contribution to interior design relates to his fusion of architectural membering and surface decoration, and to his freeing of design from academic dictates. Contemporary architects such as Pierre Le Pautre were becoming less and less interested in plasticity; columns began to disappear and pilasters were reduced to shallow strips. Walls became higher, ceilings flatter and doors and windows were integrated into the wall members so that decoration and function became indistinguishable. Wall compositions became a series of moving lines, fluttering on the surface as well as demonstrating the tension between the shallow three-dimensional ornament and the expanses of empty space on the wall. These compositions formed the perfect field for Audran and Berain's arabesques and naturalistic grotesque forms; exalted by their release from thickly-framed panels, these forms ran across and blended into borders and mouldings with a new freedom. This bold and innovative approach to decoration was an inspiration to the next generation of French artists and revealed possibilities that lay outside those dictated by their academic training. Audran's designs had "the relaxed, undidactic atmosphere of art that is free simply to be art: more bizarre than anything previously seen, deliberately not truthful, stirring neither patriotic nor moral strings, but beating drums for the sheer love of gaiety and noise" (Kalnein, 1995). Such work heralded the approach of the full-blown freedom of the Rococo.

MARGARET W. LICHTER

Biography

Born in Lyon, 25 August 1658, the son of the engraver Germain Audran (1631–1710). Taught by his father, and his uncles Claude II (1639–84) and Gérard (1640–1703). Working in Paris by 1684. Named Master Painter, Sculptor and Engraver, 1692. Active as a decorative painter in the Royal Palaces and worked at Anet (1698 and 1733), Versailles (from 1699), Fontainebleau (from 1703) and Marly (from 1704). Employed as a designer by the Gobelins tapestry factory from 1699 and was responsible for many notable tapestry series. Also designed stained glass, Savonnerie carpets (1711) and embroidery and church vestments. Appointed "intendant" at the Palais du Luxembourg, 1704; later set up his own tapestry factory there. Assisted by Antoine Watteau, 1707–09. Died in Paris, 27 May 1734.

Selected Works

Over 2000 drawings were acquired by the Swedish architect Carl Johan Cronstedt from Audran's estate; these are now in the Cronstedt collection in the Nationalmuseum, Stockholm. Additional designs and drawings are in the Cooper-Hewitt Museum, New York, and the Bibliothèque Nationale, the Louvre, and the Musée des Arts Décoratifs, Paris, which also contains Audran's ceiling from the Hôtel de Flesselles and panels from the Hôtel Peyrenc de Moras. Examples of Audran's tapestries are in the Mobilier National, Paris.

Interiors

1698 & 1733	Château d'Anet (painted decoration in the salon, grand cabinet, cabinet des muses, and cabinet des singes): Duc de Vendôme
1699	Versailles (petit chambre de Madame le Princesse de Conti)
c.1699 & 1708–09	Château Neuf, Meudon (decorations including various ceilings, and the Dauphin's apartment): Grand Dauphin
1699–1701	Château de la Ménagerie, Versailles (decoration of the apartment of the Duchesse de Bourgogne)
1703–32	Château de Fontainebleau (decorations)
1704–32	Château de Marly (*singeries*)
1704	Château de Sceaux (decoration of the apartment of the Duchesse du Maine)
1716–32	Palais du Luxembourg, Paris (decorations)
1720–32	Château de la Muette (decorations)

1723 Hôtel Angran de Fonspertius, Paris (decorations)
c.1724 Hôtel Peyrenc de Moras, Paris (decoration and panels of the Cabinet; with Nicolas Lancret)

Audran's tapestries included the *Portières de Dieux* (c.1699–1711), *Douze Mois Grotesques par Bandes* (1707–08), and borders for C. A. Coypel's *Don Quixote* series (1716–17).

Further Reading

For the most complete account of Audran's career see Weigert 1950.

Akerlund, Greta, "Audranstudier" in *Tidskrift für konstvetonskap*, 24, pt.3, 1942, pp.87–104

Duplesis, G., *Les Audran*, Paris, 1892

Gruber, Alain (editor), *L'Art Décoratif en Europe*, vol.2: *Classique et Baroque, 1630–1760*, Paris: Citadelles & Mazenod, 1992

Hautecoeur, Louis, *Histoire de l'architecture classique en France*, vol.3, Paris: Picard, 1951

Kalnein, Wend von, *Architecture in France in the Eighteenth Century*, New Haven and London: Yale University Press, 1995

Kimball, Fiske, *The Creation of the Rococo*, 1943; reprinted as *The Creation of the Rococo Decorative Style*, New York: Dover, and London: Constable, 1980

Pons, Bruno, "Le Décor de l'Appartement du Grand Dauphin au Château Neuf de Meudon" in *Gazette des Beaux Arts*, 117, February 1991, pp.59–76

Scott, Katie, *The Rococo Interior: Decoration and Social Spaces in Early Eighteenth-Century Paris*, New Haven and London: Yale University Press, 1995

Standen, Edith Appleton, *European Post-Medieval Tapestries and Related Hangings in the Metropolitan Museum of Art*, vol.1, New York: Metropolitan Museum of Art, 1985

Thiry, A., "L'Hôtel Peyrenc de Moras, Place Vendôme, architecture et décoration interieure" in *Bulletin de la Société d'Histoire de l'Art Français*, 1979, p.52–84

Weigert, R.-A., *Dessins du Nationalmuseum de Stockholm: Collections Tessin et Cronstedt* (exhib. cat.), Paris: Bibliothèque Nationale, 1950

Weigert, R.-A., "Quelques Travaux Décoratifs de Claude III Audran" in *Bulletin de la Société d'Histoire de l'Art Français*, 1955, pp.100–06

Weigert, R.-A. and J. Dupont, "Une Oeuvre de Claude III Audran à Clichy" in *Revue des Monuments Historiques de la France*, 1960, pp.223–32

Weigert, R.-A., *French Tapestry*, London: Faber, and Newton, MA: Branford, 1962

Australia

Whatever Britain's inchoate plans for the penal settlement of New South Wales in 1788, interiors in a European mould were envisaged, since Governor Arthur Phillip arrived in Sydney with a five-roomed oilcloth house, campaign furniture, crown glass and a portrait of Her Royal Highness the Duchess of Cumberland. Necessity and economy determined, however, that by 1796 "most of the comforts and not a few of the luxuries of life" had resulted from "communication with India and other parts of the world" (quoted in Serle, 1993). Robert Campbell, who represented an East India Company "house of agency", enjoyed "the parade and luxury of the eastern style of living" in his harbourside house in 1798 (quoted in Serle 1993). Until trading sanctions were introduced, India was a major source of household furnishings. Between 1810 and 1820 the market was glutted with goods including palampores, chintz and calico. Anglo-Indian furniture often appeared in the homes of settlers who had served in India: the quintessential example of Indian influence is Horsley, a cross-ventilated, verandahed bungalow built in the 1830s equipped with teak joinery, Regency dining chairs of Indian timber, a punkah and Indian servants. Besides importing Indian goods, enterprising colonists circumvented an embargo on trade with China to bring in ceramics, lacquerware and paperhangings adapted for the Western market, although their popularity was waning in Europe.

These chance Eastern imports and the appearance of American furnishings, sold by traders and whalers, do not obscure the fact that the first and subsequent migrants to both New South Wales and later settlements felt an urge to recreate the interiors they had known at home. Rare surviving pieces of colonial furniture and descriptions of interiors suggest that, whether imported or locally made, furniture of late Georgian design predominated in well-to-do colonial houses. Textiles were imported, as the finest still are today. 1800 saw the arrival of the first Governor's Lady, portraits of George IV and Queen Charlotte, fitted carpets and blue sprigged Spode teacups in Government House.

With the release of land – the traditional basis of status in society – to officers and civil servants, houses and their interiors grew more sophisticated. By 1812 the *Sydney Gazette* thought it relevant to satirize Neo-Classical decoration: "In the frame of a fashionable mirror, a crocodile watches; a companionable tiger crouches on a hearthrug; a sphynx supports us on a couch, and serpents twine round bedposts." Epitomizing such progress was Henrietta Villa, begun in 1816 by Captain John Piper, who was, according to the *Sydney Gazette* of 1823, "the most furnished and fashionable Corinthian in the colony". Piper's Neo-Classical interiors owed much to Sir John Soane, and sparse records point to chintzes, moreen, brass-inlaid furniture, mandarins with nodding heads and silver bought of George Purse, The Strand.

Disseminated in architectural pattern books, published designs for furniture and furnishings or via C.F. Bielefield's prefabricated *papier-mâché* mouldings, Greek Revival styles had a long run in Australia as they did in provincial Britain. John Taylor's *The Upholsterer's and Cabinet Maker's Pocket Assistant* (c.1825), George Smith's *The Cabinet-Maker, & Upholsterer's Guide* (1826) and J.C. Loudon's *Encyclopaedia of Cottage, Farm and Villa Architecture* (1833) are documented in the colony; Grecian sofas and tables were advertised for sale in the mid-1820s and descriptions of fashionable households focus on Greek Revival furniture, suggesting it was still in the vanguard of colonial fashion in the 1830s. There were English mahogany Grecian couches in the modest Government House and in the Grecian villas built by the civil establishment on fashionable Wooloomooloo Hill in that decade. As late as 1846 a Hobart cabinet-maker was offering to decorate after the "most approved Grecian" style as well as the much more fashionable "Parisian taste".

There was little consistency in architecture, decoration and furnishings, and Greek Revival furniture co-habited happily with "Louis" and Gothic Revival pieces, as well as with appealing locally-made mongrels. Regency and William IV designs gradually overtook Georgian ones, and inevitably former styles merged with early Victorian ones as furniture

Australia: Dome Room, Henrietta Villa, Sydney, c.1844; watercolour by Frederick Garling, Jr. (Mitchell Library, State Library of New South Wales)

thickened up and moved out from the walls as it did in British interiors.

Most settlers were groping towards an elegance they but dimly understood, and, while anxious to keep abreast of metropolitan, and largely English fashion, judged interiors in terms of what was reasonable in "this country at this stage of its existence" (G. Barrington, quoted in J. Cobley, *Sydney Cove 1791–1792*, Sydney, 1965). Nonetheless any interior could be annihilated with the words "It's quite colonial". Australia had no aristocratic class and was a small, socially and economically mobile society. The aspirant middle classes had mostly migrated to better themselves. They were not prodigiously rich. Almost everything was new and lacked patina as it did in the houses of Britain's new middle classes. Adelaide, settled in 1836, was later described as "a book one had never opened before, startling and new" (Douglas Pike, *Paradise of Dissent: South Australia, 1829–1857*, 2nd edition Melbourne: Cambridge University Press, 1967).

Isolation from the sources of supply made building and homemaking an unwieldy operation. Even relatively long-established families were sometimes slow to bother with curtains and carpets – their incomes, the climate and moths all played a part. When the depression of the 1840s struck, many interiors created in the prosperous 1830s were devastated. The collapse of a market dependent on a single staple, wool, and the cessation of transportation to the eastern colonies were both blamed, as household goods became "old acquaintances bought and sold twenty times over" (G.C. Mundy, *Our Antipodes*, London, 1852). Apart from a few outbreaks of short-lived grandeur, most of the interiors of respectable colonists at this time had much in common with the middle-class rooms recorded in England by Mary Ellen Best. New arrivals commented on their Englishness and overstuffedness and the non-observance of normal practice in hot countries. Amid the panic and promissory notes, Rococo Revival joined the Gothic Revival style, the latter receiving a fillip when adopted for a vice-regal residence.

As a result of official parsimony and competing calls on funds, it took roughly half a century for permanent Government Houses to appear in New South Wales, Tasmania and Western Australia. In the interim governors often lagged behind successful settlers in their domestic appointments and ability to influence public taste. This changed when three very different buildings appeared under the "Tudor Gothic"

Australia: Legislative Council Chamber, Parliament House, Melbourne, c.1856 (La Trobe Picture Collection, State Library of Victoria)

banner in Sydney (1837–45), Hobart (1854–58) and Perth (1859–62). Picturesque Gothic had been popular in vice-regal circles in the second decade of the century and the Gothic Revival's association with power and prestige provided the authority needed in a remote dependency – as the *Colonial Architect* remarked, "No style can have grander effect". Besides grandeur, these buildings had a backbone of official furniture, although changes of governors, who varied greatly in wealth, taste and personal chattels, constantly affected their interiors.

In Government House, Sydney, Edward Blore, architect to William IV and of Sir Walter Scott's Abbotsford, provided strong neo-Gothic detailing in the hall but less evidence of the style elsewhere. New South Wales being well established and in a depression, most furniture was acquired locally. An "Elizabethan" hall table and chairs were copied from Loudon and Neo-Classical rosewood drawing room furniture was purchased from the impoverished Colonial Secretary.

In Hobart the Government Architect, William Porden Kay, son of architect and decorator, Joseph Kay, and grandson of architect, William Porden, designed Government House and successfully argued for imported decorative schemes in all the public rooms. As a result Hobart's interiors were pure transplantations of British Establishment taste. While abroad in 1853 Kay was authorized to spend upwards of £2000 "on articles required in the completion and decoration of the building". These probably included the mouldings which reinforced the neo-Gothic character of the state interiors, including the dining room where the ceiling was coffered and stencilled with quarterings from the royal standard. The schemes for the main rooms (the panelled 18th century-style library failed to materialize), which were executed by a convict craftsman at a cost of

£823 almost certainly came from Messrs Trollope and Sons of Parliament Street, London. Trollope also provided £6126.15.6 worth of furniture including pairs of Boulle cabinets, Rococo overmantel mirrors and seat furniture for the drawing room. Puginesque pieces, including gasoliers for the dining room and ballroom were also acquired, and Rococo Revival chimneypieces supplanted those originally recommended.

Captain E.Y.W. Henderson, who designed Government House, Perth, had good contacts in England and was said to be a friend of Sir Charles Barry, architect of the Houses of Parliament, Westminster. He went to J.G. Crace, the fashionable London decorator who had worked with A.W.N. Pugin on the Houses of Parliament and now marketed Pugin's designs. Crace provided the actual ceilings for the hall (with coats of arms of the kings and queens of England), drawing room and dining room, Pugin wallpapers and one or more Pugin carpets. Chimneypieces, tiles, grates, fenders and hall lamp standards helped sustain the Gothic Revival character of the building internally, despite a Rococo Revival overmantel mirror, an 18th century French style chandelier and the inevitable cabriole-legged seat furniture in the drawing room.

Reverting to chronology, the late 1840s reveals that the various colonial economies were recovering, the future colony of Victoria was being settled and a new generation was taking the reins. 1851 was a watershed year. The discovery of gold in Victoria transformed Australia: the population increased dramatically, transportation of convicts ceased (except to Western Australia), new opportunities appeared as did a wealth of craftsmen who worked first on the public buildings being erected in the colony and later in the houses of those wishing to parade their success. Outstanding among public interiors was the Legislative Council Chamber in Parliament House, Melbourne (c.1856), designed by Peter Kerr, who had worked with Barry. Sculpture and architecture are fused in this monumental Corinthian interior, rich with symbols of Government derived from Roman antiquity.

Those who had come "before the gold" tended to look askance at the brash exuberance of new arrivals, but Louisa Anne Meredith who published an account of her visit to Victoria in 1861, was near the mark in saying that "the elegancies and refinements of civilized life are as well understood by the better classes in Victoria, as in Royal Victoria's loyal city itself; with perhaps a tint or two more of show, where the wealth of today is not the ancestral characteristic of the family, and the recent gilding is not toned down."

1851 proved a milestone in another way. A number of influential Australians marvelled at the Great Exhibition; they saw the triumphs of the Industrial Revolution it displayed and then returned to interpret the current fashion for Rococo Revival in their own way. Seduced by the Medieval Court at the Exhibition, Thomas Mort spent most of the 1850s transforming Greenoakes, Darling Point, into a "Gothic" building under Sydney's new architectural luminary, Edmund Blacket. Mort patronized at least four firms showing at the Great Exhibition: windows containing portraits of the Tudor kings and queens came from Hardmans of Birmingham; generous *carton pierre* mouldings for drawing room, dining room, library and corridor from George Jackson & Sons of London; M. Potts of Birmingham supplied neo-Gothic oak furniture, and Elkingtons furnished bronze casts. Greenoakes' hall, leading to the picture gallery, contained "ancient implements of war, representing with tolerable completeness the armour used by the English in olden time". Some of these relics, which included a valuable Italian 16th-century silver-inlaid suit of armour, were purchased by Mort in 1857 at the sale of the collection of the Earls of Shrewsbury at Alton Towers. A Pugin paper and a carving attributed to Grinling Gibbons contributed to interiors described as "quite old fashioned" and Elizabethan-looking seven years later.

Agents with London offices, particularly those involved in the pastoral industry, had long been buying furnishings for colonists, and in the wake of gold the practice grew: in 1859 Frederick Dalgety fitted out John Moffatt's Chatsworth House, the first of the Victorian "Bush Palaces" completely equipped from London. Everything from the *Encyclopaedia Britannica* to Alexis Soyer's cooking apparatus and patty pans was imported, with William Smee & Sons, rather than one of the "crack West End firms" or the "Cormorants of the Fashionable circle", supplying the furniture. Thus a shepherd who had started on £23 a year entertained Australia's first royal visitor, the Duke of Edinburgh, in 1867. Adequate bathrooms and plumbing determined who got the nod.

Most colonists stuck rigidly to the mid-century rules which dictated which woods appeared in which rooms and how furniture was arranged. Drawing rooms were focussed either on a central ottoman or a table on which objects were arranged radially around a vase of flowers, with an inner ring of chairs from a matched suite drawn up to take advantage of the source of light. At Mona Vale, Tasmania, the drawing room walls were hung with a rich moiré antique paper, in white and gold, the furniture was uniform throughout, the wood rosewood, the upholstery scarlet rep. Whether scarlet or the more popular grass green, glaring upholstery, produced with the virulent new analine dyes, was frequently combined with floral, foliate, striped, diapered, flocked or watered wallpapers and exuberant Brussels and Axminster carpets to create boldly patterned interiors.

The 1870s and 1880s saw the proliferation of grand houses in both town and country especially in gold-rich Victoria. The absence of major buildings seems to have kindled a passion for building in some colonists who had associated with the landed gentry in Britain and were keen to ornament their estates with houses redolent of ancient lineage and future dynasties. Anthony Trollope felt there was rarely "all the finished comfort, the easy grace coming from long habit" which distinguished country seats at Home. Though the likeness was there it existed with a difference.

At Werribee Park, Victoria, Thomas Chirnside demonstrated his apparent wealth and social standing in a two-storey Italianate mansion filled with 58 cases of furniture supplied by John Taylor & Son of Edinburgh in 1875 and augmented with a collection of Old Master paintings purchased from Christie's in 1881. His statuary included marble busts of the Prince and Princess of Wales by the English sculptor Marshall Wood, who had executed an over-lifesized statue of Queen Victoria for Parliament House, Melbourne. The identity of Werribee's decorator is unknown but the predominantly pale blue and gold decoration is reminiscent of the restrained schemes supplied shortly before by Jackson & Graham for Government House, Melbourne.

Australia: drawing room, Torrens Park, Adelaide, late 19th century (Mortlock Library of South Australiana, State Library of South Australia)

As in Tasmania, William Wardell, the architect of Government House, Melbourne, favoured placing the decoration and furnishing of the vast Italianate building in the hands of a well-established London firm, who could send out its own craftsmen: in fact "adopt the course most private persons take when they require the best class of furniture" (Lane and Serle, 1990). In the consequent uproar over the work going abroad, Jackson & Graham's schemes were shelved and only carpets and limited items of furniture were imported. High quality pieces in colonial woods were supplied by George Thwaites and James McEwan & Co., much to the chagrin of W.H. Rocke & Co., who started the furore. The furnishings having cost £30,000, the walls remained white for thirteen years. Living there later and freezing to death, Lady Tennyson described the building as "an enormous smart hotel", a "small Buckingham Palace" and "even bigger than India".

Whether it came from Wigmore Street or High Wycombe, imported furniture had lasting cachet, which resulted in Australian interiors becoming increasingly Europeanized, a fact borne out by figures for furniture exported to Australia. Henry Cooper, Filmer & Sons, Gillow & Co., Maple & Co., Saul Moss & Sons of Manchester, Sadgrove & Co., James Shoolbred & Co., William Smee & Sons, William Walker & Sons, together with Copelands, Jeffrey & Co., Hoock Frères of Paris, Minton & Co., and Daniel Walters were among those called upon as ambitious Australians trawled in fairly uncharted waters. Some combined decorating their interiors with a trip abroad and a visit to the Continent and went armed with advice from those who had preceded them. William Clarke, son of the largest landowner in Victoria, saved himself the trouble by patronizing Rocke and employed Schemmel & Shilton to decorate the interior of Rupertswood, his country seat near Sunbury in 1875.

Exhibitions, following the 1851 model, played an important role in interiors in the second half of the century and helped relay to colonists the dictates of new movements, in particular the Aesthetic Movement. While largely isolated from the intellectual ferment which ushered in Aestheticism and Art furnishing overseas, Australians were not in total purdah: Daniel Cottier established a branch of his firm in both New York and Sydney in 1873, with John Lamb Lyon as local manager. In 1875 visitors to the Melbourne Inter-colonial Exhibition (a dry

Australia: hall, Werribee Park; watercolour by A.C. Cooke, 1878

run for the Philadelphia Exhibition) were stunned by the "blaze of colour, the sheen of gold, the brilliancy of lacquer, the delicacy of enamel" in the Japanese exhibit, which occupied an entire gallery, and in 1878 a large shipment of Japanese works of art brought extravagant prices in Sydney. The Melbourne Exhibition of 1880 was said to have introduced Aestheticism and Artistic furnishing to the public at large. It certainly brought Oriental wares and household goods designed and / or decorated in a loosely Oriental manner to the attention of a large cross-section of society: lacquerware, a pair of cloisonné enamel jars, Oriental-inspired wallpapers and carpets, and porcelain and art pottery by Minton, Wedgwood, Royal Worcester, Doultons, Bretby and Brownfields were all on view.

Aestheticism had in fact already received the seal of approval in Melbourne at Joseph's Clarke's Mandeville Hall: begun in 1878, the year in which Thomas Jeckyll and Whistler's Peacock Room was completed, the decoration of Mandeville's interiors occupied Mr East from Gillow & Co. of London for a year. The decoration of the segmented drawing room ceiling was carried out in sage, salmon, buff and gold, and the walls were hung with an olive green silk designed by Bruce Talbert, above and below which was a frieze of silk and velvet embroidery and a dado of rose silken plush. The furniture was of satinwood and the floor was laid with a camel hair Persian rug. In the dining room the ceiling was panelled in oak and gold, and beneath a frieze depicting sporting scenes the walls were covered with richly-stamped leather. A massive oak chimneypiece was set with tiles and the silk curtains had dados and friezes of Utrecht velvet. The morning room, presented with some stylistic licence as an Indian room, embraced the fashion for exotic interiors.

The 1880s were an extravagant decade, with furniture warehousemen, decorators and leading stores such as David Jones of Sydney all strutting their stuff and offering pace-setters and others a wealth of Art Furnishings and Revival styles. Typical was William Cullis Hill of Melbourne, who, after training with Rocke, went out on his own and was soon informing "the patrician orders", via the *Melbourne Bulletin* of 1885, that they were Gillow's Australian agent and that "henceforth new designs would be released simultaneously in London and Melbourne". Cullis Hill, who mixed Oriental and Occidental furnishings promiscuously in his own interiors and, like many decorators, involved fine artists in his work, advocated a range of styles in a promotional juggling act. While invoking the names of Morris, Ruskin and Pater and writing piously of Old English, Queen Anne and fitness for purpose, he unblushingly recommended Louis-Quatorze, that "earthly paradise of ormolu". He advertised Art furniture, including pieces made to E.W. Godwin's designs, and employed about 80 workmen, including craftsmen brought out for the 1880 Exhibition, to produce Jacobean, Chippendale, Queen Anne or anything the public had a fancy for. A portière, a Persian rug, a furlong of Liberty silk or a suite in which every chair was of a different shape, size and colour were all within his grasp. W.H. Rocke & Co., who had long been scouring the fashion capitals of the world and offered a lavish promotional brochure, assumed an Aesthetic stance in 1880 with an advertisement lifted either from Mrs Orrinsmith's *The Drawing-Room* (London, 1877) or from the American Clarence Cook's *The House Beautiful* (1878).

In the 1880s Melbourne and Sydney swarmed with decorators: Paterson Brothers, who demonstrated their talents in the interior of the Exhibition Building in 1875 and in the library of Parliament House, Melbourne, and executed 14 by 40 foot murals of Sydney Harbour and Edinburgh during a romanticizing exercise at Villa Alba, Kew, about 1883, could boast that Hugh Paterson had trained with one Cornelius, described as a famous Scottish art decorator. While abroad in 1886 he had caught up with the most advanced taste and become acquainted with William Morris, Frederic Leighton, Walter Crane and many leading painters, decorators and scenic artists. Following this bout of self-promotion Paterson Brothers, together with S.W. Mouncey, were commissioned to introduce "the soft tints and faint colourings of artistic decoration" to Government House, Melbourne, in anticipation of the arrival of Lord and Lady Hopetoun in 1889. Lyon, Cottier & Co. was responsible for the new Aesthetic mural and ceiling decorations in Government House, Sydney and for major work at Cranbrook, Glanworth, Ginnagullah and Woollahra House, although Cottier had "banished all the Japanese stuff he used to be so fond of " by 1886. In the late 1880s Scottish-trained Andrew Wells was the firm's representative when the headquarters and residential suite of the English, Scottish and Australian bank in Melbourne were transformed into Australia's finest Gothic Revival interiors. America was represented among Art decorators by J. Clay Beeler, who trained at the Cooper Union art school. He was almost certainly responsible for the outstanding Aesthetic textiles and Eastlake sideboard at Mount Rothwell, Victoria, and was a member of the Society of Decorators and Painters established in 1904.

Maurice B. Adams, the designer of Bedford Park, was one English Queen Anne revival architect with an Australian clientele: when Charles Fairfax commissioned him to enhance a Sydney architect's design for Caerleon in the "Old English" style in the mid-1880s he ruffled local feathers, although a deferential press dubbed the style "New South Jacobean" and thought the result "as Australian as Riverina mutton".

While some colonists who had only recently created mid-Victorian interiors lay on their oars, the majority added at least a superficial Artistic overlay to conventional rooms and ignored Morris's call to make a bonfire of nine-tenths of what they owned. From the 1880s however, avant-garde architects were fretting about bows, rosettes, bandages, register grates and over-upholstered, unnavigable interiors. Added to this, well-to-do Australians were beginning to face the fact that they were not, and never would be, in the same league as the Devonshires, Astors, Fricks, Pierpont Morgans and Vanderbilts. Reeling from the depression of the 1890s and the recent imposition of land taxes and death duties, and feeling the results of the common lack of entail, they aligned their aspirations more closely with economic reality. This fortunately coincided with a growing concern for simplicity and fitness for purpose, which had its roots in the Arts and Crafts and "Health" movements and overlapped with growing nationalism and the limp, local version of Art Nouveau.

All styles were not equally pervasive: the vogue for Morris interiors in the 1880s and 1890s was most marked in South Australia where town and country houses of Robert and Joanna Barr Smith assimilated vast quantities of Morris goods. These houses are unique in the history of interior decoration in Australia for their wealth of Morris wallpapers and textiles, de Morgan tiles and Chinese export porcelain and for the fact that Morris himself, as well as W. Neville Ashbee, advised on their ever-changing interiors.

Morris's more central interest, the Arts & Crafts Movement, found expression in houses with face brick walls, high panelled dados, deep friezes and white plasterwork combined with ceilings supported on heavy bracketed beams. Native timbers were used for flooring and joinery, bays and inglenooks abounded, leather seats fixed by wrought iron nails were obligatory as was craftwork of variable quality. White, cream, blue, grey, purple and mauve dominated a limited palette. Some patronized Kosmic Co.'s "Liberty Rooms" in Sydney where Liberty wares shared space with local furnishings inspired by imported prototypes. Later Morris & Co.'s and Gustav Stickley's commercial ranges were available. Booloominbah, New South Wales, designed by the American-trained Horbury Hunt, was one of the more robust essays in Arts and Crafts, with interiors decorated by Lyon, Cottier and Co. displaying a wealth of indigenous motifs.

With nationhood about to become a reality, there were calls for Australian styles of decoration and a national school of decorative arts. Although his designs remained unpublished, Lucien Henri, the brilliant Frenchman who taught in Sydney during the 1880s, fostered the use of Australian motifs in decoration and produced a folio of plates in which flora and fauna were adapted to architecture and the applied arts. Ernest Wunderlich's embossed metal sheeting, patented in 1888 and decorated with Art Nouveau versions of national emblems actually introduced nationalism and hygienic surfaces into a wide cross-section of interiors. About 1903, at Purrumbete, Victoria, W.T. Manifold celebrated his pioneering forebears in a series of Art Nouveau murals which dominate the panelled open-plan living hall. There, Guyon Purchas expressed the most advanced architectural thought of the day and used local timber in carved newel posts and a screen beneath the minstrels' gallery; the furniture was by Liberty's.

The difficulty of creating distinctively Australian interiors in a country with such a short tradition was acknowledged, with many architects looking to America for models, as they have done ever since. American Romanesque interiors, featuring bespindled screens and round headed arches, and open-

Australia: drawing room, Government House, Hobart; mixed media drawing by H. Willson, 1856 (Tasmanian Museum and Art Gallery)

planned American bungalows were both gaining ground around the turn of the century, with some describing them as "almost" Australian. The expatriate Briton, John Sulman, argued, however, that neither England nor other nations were relevant to Australia – "we are just ourselves".

A growing sense of the country's history and an aversion to "groping among the ruins of Elizabethan and Queen Anne styles", as one authority put the case in 1890, for models for antipodean houses in the 20th century led some Australians back to their beginnings, and to Georgian interiors. Chief among them was the architect, William Hardy Wilson, who thought good taste had come to an end in 1820. He achieved the effect he wanted with Georgian-style joinery, panelling, parquetry floors of Australian timbers and with 17th- and 18th-century furniture ranged against plain walls. In his view such interiors were a step towards a harmonious, modern style of living and his expensive version of "good taste" has had a loyal following in conservative quarters ever since.

Wilson's ideas did not appeal to everyone: early this century Sir Rupert Clarke endorsed the overseas move towards flats when he moved into a new apartment in central Melbourne decorated in the Moorish style. Dame Nellie Melba, who returned shortly before World War I to transplant the informal elegance of the Edwardian English country house to Coombe Cottage, near Lilydale, Victoria, was more relaxed than Wilson: contributing to her electrically-lit, panelled music room was a Gothic fireplace, paintwork in two shades of green, a parquet floor, antique and reproduction furniture, an American grand piano and two sets of glazed chintz curtains and slip covers made in London.

Interior design and decoration was inhibited by the war, and the move towards simpler, healthier, more rational interiors was slow in the first two decades of the century: it was almost as if Australians had lost their nerve along with their money. By the 1920s Georgian Revival interiors, with their concomitant of antiques, seemed a safe investment and dominated Establishment houses until after World War II, in spite of architects like Robert Haddon and Harold Desbrowe Annear who were recommending open planning, built-in furniture, simplicity and restraint.

Sometimes it was an advantage to be an outsider. Walter Burley Griffin and his wife, the former Marion Mahony, who had previously worked with Frank Lloyd Wright, arrived from America in 1914 after winning the competition for the design of Canberra. A product of the Prairie School, Griffin attacked the lingering "mildew of mediaevalism" (Johnson 1977), put forward radical ideas and looked to nature and the landscape for inspiration. Their mature work included world-class interiors. The Café Australia, Melbourne (1915–16) – the country's first proto-modern interior – was an inspired amalgam, demonstrating their superb handling of space and concealed lighting as well as an ability to design all elements, including furniture and tablewares. The Capitol Theatre (1921–24) showed an imagination fired by the prismatic reflection of light on crystalline formations: cubes, triangles and stalactites of plaster concealed the mechanics of an ever-changing play of light in the main pillarless auditorium, which contrasted with the vaulted, cavernous lobby. The Capitol stood apart from Australia's later run of Hollywood-style theatres. The Griffins were also responsible for Newman College, Melbourne, including its furniture.

Late in the 1920s, after the 1925 Paris Exposition introduced a wide audience to Art Deco, Sydney Ure Smith's chic journal the *Home* (first published 1920) published the unflattering comments of some leading Sydneysiders on the continuing popularity of clutter, "Mission", fumed oak, "Jacobean", aspidistras, palms, spring roller blinds, panelled wallpapers, plate rails and other survivals. The *Home* continued to keep architects, fine artists, designers and the artistically-aware abreast of international fashion by publishing illustrations culled from the *Studio* and *Decorative Art* of interiors in London, Paris and New York. The occasional sub-Elsie de Wolfe or Syrie Maugham white-to-grey interior appearing locally was probably the result of such influences. Officialdom was unadventurous when fitting out Yarralumla, Canberra, in this decade to serve as the nation's premier vice-regal residence: directed to buy "first quality British", the "lady decorator", Ruth Lane-Poole, used local timbers although her purchases were mainly Georgian "Repro". More exciting were streamlined moderne interiors, which those who travelled could absorb on luxury liners.

Late in 1929, the year in which the Metropolitan Museum mounted an exhibition of modern decorative arts, based on the Paris model and planned by Eliel Saarinen, the *Home* announced that Modernism had reached Australia and heralded an interior containing furniture by DIM of Paris in "Pallisandre Verni" as Melbourne's first example of the style. Two months later a group of artists, led by Roy de Maistre, mounted a modest exhibition at Burdekin House, Sydney. Room settings with furniture based on Continental designs or adaptations of them were shown by de Maistre, Thea Proctor, Hera Roberts, Adrian Feint and Leon Gellert. Designs were based on the prism, cylinder, sphere, cone, cube and pyramid, preferred colours included ivory, grey, blue, black and yellow combined with judiciously chosen strong colours. The stress was on simplicity, functionalism and natural timbers, although painted furniture, with its long Arts and Crafts lineage, was also prominent.

In 1932 Paul Staal, Consul-General for the Netherlands, and his wife, Amelia, introduced what was probably the country's first full-blown collection of Modern European furniture to Sydney's diplomatic circuit and to readers of the *Home*. Their conventional house on Bellevue Hill was filled with steel and black wood furniture designed by Marcel Breuer and made by Thonet, Swedish glass light fittings by Giso of Rotterdam, a silver and ebony tea service by Begeer of Holland designed for the Wiener Werkstätte, and modern rugs and Dutch paintings. Marcel Breuer's Cesca cantilever chairs were covered with blue canvas.

Minimal migration, cosy complacency and the depression of the 1930s inhibited a general move towards Modernism although the ardent Melbourne Modernist, Robin Boyd, was later to say that the back-to-basics economy of the 1930s encouraged simplicity and functionalism. According to Boyd, students and young architects had converted to Modernism and Functionalism by 1934. Roy Grounds had begun designing functional interiors with built-in fitments which excluded many previously essential pieces of free-standing furniture and was also specifying copies of overseas furniture designs. Local designers were active, with Melbourne decorator Cynthia Reed offering modern craftwork, fabrics by Frances Burke and unstained, waxed furniture designed by the artist Sam Atyeo or by Frederick Ward, who later worked for Myers, a major department store. In 1933 Reed, Ward and Michael O'Connell showed furniture and handprinted hangings at an exhibition of British contemporary art sponsored by Keith Murdoch of the Melbourne *Herald*.

By 1935 the well-connected Marion Hall Best, "who studied with Proctor and had a hatred of cream, beige and porridge", caught the attention of the *Home* with an interior which included modern Sundour cretonne curtains, a Marion Dorn rug and a Franz Marc print. Then at the beginning of a long decorating / designing career, which covered importing, commissioning, marketing and promoting, Best studied first-year architecture, took a year-long course in interior decoration from New York and, on the eve of war, launched her own business in Sydney. She contributed a "Young Modern" and "Classic Modern" interior to David Jones's exhibition entitled "An Englishman's Home 1700–1941". Hampered by wartime shortages, she manufactured textiles and used designs by her sister, Doris Sweetapple, and others, together with furniture designed by Clement Meadmore.

The traditionalist Deric Deane had seen to the needs of Sydney's conservative enclave during the 1930s, and in the 1940s he was joined by Molly Gray, Merle de Boulay and Stuart Lowe. In Melbourne Reg Riddell served a similar clientele for many years as did the "lady decorator", Dolly Guy Smith. In 1949, the *Australian Home Beautiful* ran a major article on modern American home designs which anticipated how American styling would become synonymous with modernity. Peace gave impetus to interior decoration despite shortages and regulations. In the late 1940s the Hungarian architect, Steven Kalmar, began business selling custom-designed modern furniture and Dr. George Molnar opened Artes studios in Sydney.

The arrival in Sydney in 1948 of Viennese-born Harry Seidler, who had studied in America under Walter Gropius and Josef Albers and worked with Marcel Breuer in New York, consolidated the influence of Modernism. In the small Rose Seidler house (c.1950) open-planning, flexible subdivision of space, a lavish use of glass window walls, neutral colours contrasted with strong colour accents, a mural by the architect, and a sophisticated kitchen contributed to Seidler's "total sculpture". The furniture was from Herman Miller and Knoll International of New York or designed by Seidler and built by fellow Viennese craftsman, Paul Kafka. The chairs were by Charles Eames, Eero Saarinen and Hardoy. Family treasures, which were to enrich many houses of European post-war migrants, were banned by Seidler with the exception of ornate silver cutlery and tea services.

Post-war optimism brought faster change: following a trip abroad and exposure to modern theatre design, Best mounted an exhibition called "A Walk Through Europe" in her Woollahra studio. In Melbourne in 1949, the English-trained designer R. Haughton James, who had begun his crusade on behalf of good modern design a decade earlier in Sydney, organized a modern home exhibition. He enlisted Robin Boyd, whose "House of Tomorrow" gave the public their first close encounter with contemporary interiors, displaying furniture by Grant Featherston and showing great concern for functional lighting. James, Featherston and Joseph Burke, the Englishman recently appointed to the Melbourne Chair of Fine Arts, were

Australia: showroom of Marion Hall Best, c.1960 (Historic Houses Trust of New South Wales)

also active in the establishment of design bodies including the Society of Designers in Industry, which later joined with the Sydney Interior Design Association to form the Industrial Design Council of Australia. The Society of Interior Designers of Australia was formed in 1951 and by the 1960s schools of interior design and decoration were functioning. A foundation member of the Designers was Margaret Lord, who had worked in London before the war and wrote *Interior Decoration*, (Sydney 1944) which ran to four editions. Modern designers working for a mass market in the 1950s, some of whom have already been mentioned, included Gordon Andrews, Lester Bunbury and Douglas Snelling. Austrian cabinet-maker Schulim Krimper was producing superb hand-crafted pieces; hand-woven textiles were being made by the Sturt Workshops at Mittagong, New South Wales and by Eclarté, a Victorian firm which went to the landscape for colours and textures; and Florence Broadhurst was designing handprinted wallpapers.

Modernism had more than one face: Best, who made trips to Milan (1954), Japan (1957) and India and patronized Knoll International, assembled eclectic interiors using the world's finest products. But, for her, Modernism was essentially colour, large scale motifs from firms like the Scandinavian company Marimekko, shimmering oriental silks, lacquered rattan blinds, and brilliantly glazed walls, in contrast to interiors designed by many modern architects such as Boyd, whose mature work favoured non-featurism and pale, often limed timbers. Despite the different accent, Best was one of the few interior designers whom architects were able to work with – she spoke their language.

Although heavily reliant on American and European models, local furniture designers were forced to be innovative in the 1950s and early 1960s since the small local industry lacked the latest overseas technology. Furniture by leading overseas designers such as Breuer, Le Corbusier, Mies van der Rohe and Hans Wegner was available as licensed copies or near-plagiarized pieces. Scandinavian imports first appeared in minor outlets such as Guests of Melbourne and were later taken up by the big department stores. Danish Deluxe and *Mobler* were competing increasingly with local designers and Japan was attracting great interest, with Andersons of Melbourne a major outlet in the 1960s. When it came to public interiors Joern Utzon's inspired Opera House fell a victim to local mediocrity.

As Modernism faltered there was a lack of clear new directions. French-trained Leslie Walford was adding Gallic verve to Sydney's traditional interiors, and in Melbourne Riddell still held sway. The disillusioned turned again to revivals and romanticism and Australia was a prime market for overseas firms reproducing 19th-century wallpapers. This new historicism has resulted in academically correct conservation / restoration; an imaginative high-style Aesthetic decoration; and a rampant outbreak of nostalgia emanating from Laura Ashley's numerous outlets since 1977. Postmodernism has had a considerable presence, and some architects continue to create minimalist interior spaces which leave little place for anything beyond the built-in elements in their own designs. The late 1970s and rumbustious 1980s have, to some extent, been a replay of the 1870s and 1880s, with overseas firms such as David Hicks and Colefax and Fowler establishing outlets and with some of the world's major textile firms represented by local agents. Occasionally a client brought in a West Coast American interior designer or architect. The recession of the early1990s demolished some interiors created by the latest wave of overachievers. Today most Australian decorators and interior designers do their bi-annual swing around the world, taking in the latest American, English and Continental developments, soaking up the international glossies and, with few exceptions, producing modest versions of whatever homogenized, globalized style is currently fashionable.

Since 1788 almost every important overseas style of interior decoration has appeared in Australia, yet none has developed significantly in local hands. Indeed, some appear to have mutated on the voyage out. There have been quirky and resourceful individuals at work, but few heroics or soaring visions in major houses, which by and large have been restricted to the eastern and southern fringes of the continent. Although too isolated ever to penetrate the meaning of new styles, Australia was never sufficiently insulated to develop distinctive interiors as America did. A small population precluded the development of industrial traditions or skills and creative tumult and a lack of real money put a certain standard of interior out of reach. The colonies were linked initially to Britain and by the time Australia's outlook broadened to take account of America, copying had become a national way of life. The country has a high level of house ownership and a high ratio of rooms per person, and the average interior, even if undesigned, is extremely liveable. Yet at the highest level interiors have been and remain derivative – the creations of a "ship fed" people making tasty dishes from stale bread and largely unfussed by climate, landscape or commonsense. Money can still be spent with more satisfaction in London and New York than anywhere else in the world. An obsession with the rest of the world rather than a desire to discover what suits this corner of it has inhibited the growth of a national Australian style of interior decoration.

JESSIE SERLE

Further Reading

An excellent survey of the history of Australian interiors and Australian homes appears in Lane and Serle 1990 which also includes an extensive bibliography. Other useful general sources include Fahy and Simpson 1985, Forge 1981, and the various National Trust and Historic Houses guides.

Australian Council of National Trusts (editors), *Historic Homesteads of Australia*, 2 vols., Melbourne: Cassell, 1969–76

Australian Council of National Trusts (editors), *Historic Houses of Australia*, Melbourne: Cassell, 1974

Barker, Lady, *Letters to Guy*, London, 1885

Boyd, Robin, *Australia's Home: Its Origins, Builders and Occupiers*, Melbourne: Melbourne University Press, 1952, revised edition, 1987

Broadbent, James, *Aspects of Domestic Architecture in New South Wales*, 1788–1843, Ph.D. thesis, Melbourne: Australian National University, 1986

Cannon, Michael (editor), *Our Beautiful Homes: New South Wales*, Melbourne: Today's Heritage, 1977

Colonial Greek, Sydney: Historic Houses Trust of New South Wales, 1985

Craig, Clifford, Kevin Fahy and E. Graeme Robertson, *Early Colonial Furniture in New South Wales and Van Diemen's Land*, Melbourne: Georgian House, 1972

Evans, Ian, *The Australian Home*, Sydney: Flannel Flower Press, 1983

Fahy, Kevin, and Andrew and Christina Simpson, *Nineteenth Century Australian Furniture*, Sydney: David Ell Press, 1985

Forge, Suzanne, *Victorian Splendour: Australian Interior Decoration, 1837–1901*, Melbourne and Oxford: Oxford University Press, 1981

Hearth and Home, Sydney: Historic Houses Trust of New South Wales, 1988

Johnson, Donald Leslie, *The Architecture of Walter Burley Griffin*, Melbourne: Macmillan, 1977

Lane, Terence and Jessie Serle, *Australians at Home: A Documentary History of Australian Domestic Interiors from 1788 to 1914*, Melbourne: Oxford University Press, 1990

Lord, Margaret, *Interior Decoration: A Guide to Furnishing the Australian Home*, Sydney: Ure Smith, 1944

Lord, Margaret, *A Decorator's World*, Sydney: Ure Smith, 1969

Menz, Christopher, *Morris & Company: Pre-Raphaelites and the Arts and Crafts Movement* (exhib.cat.), Adelaide: Art Gallery Board of South Australia, 1994

O'Callaghan, Judith (editor), *The Australian Dream: Design of the Fifties*, Sydney: Powerhouse, 1993

Richards, Michaela, *The Best Style: Marion Hall Best and Australian Interior Design, 1935–1975*, Sydney: Art and Australia Books, 1993

Rocke, W.H., *Remarks on Furniture and the Interior Decoration of the House*, Melbourne, c.1874

Seidler, Harry, *Houses, Interiors and Projects, 1948–1953*, Sydney: Associated General, 1954

Serle, Jessie, "Asian and Pacific Influences in Australian Domestic Interiors, 1788–1914" in *Fabrications*, 4 June 1993, pp.56–107

Authentic Decor

"Authentic Decor" is the label often used to describe a more accurate approach to the study and restoration of period interiors and designs. This trend began in the late 1960s when new methods of research, the development of more scientific conservation techniques and the introduction of higher professional standards within museums and heritage organizations began to transform the field of historic preservation. It continued in the 1970s and 1980s when earlier restorations in many public buildings and museums were re-evaluated and often redone. Within this context, Authentic Decor in its purist sense has been the province of scholars and dedicated preservationists. But it has also had an important impact upon the commercial sector and certain sections of public taste, influencing not only the general fashion for period styles but also an interest in more historically accurate features and designs. And as the craze for period living has grown, large numbers of architects, craftspersons, consultants, manufacturers and salvage dealers now specialize in authentic reproductions suitable for either the grand historic interior or the more modest period home.

Public interest in historic preservation was fueled by many factors. In Europe, the devastation of World War II encouraged and expanded government protection of surviving historic properties. Patriotism and nostalgia for the perceived comforts of the pre-industrial past, which inspired turn-of-the-century antiquarians, maintained their hold on the popular imagination. Rebellion against the austerity of the modernist canon and contemporary minimalism – not to mention the cheap sterility of many second-rate modern structures – also played a major role. In particular, renewed respect for Georgian and Victorian buildings encouraged interiors which expressed the original architecture, rather than anachronistic open rooms created by gutting walls and cutting new windows. Scholarly attention to vernacular buildings and the work of seminal modern architects like Frank Lloyd Wright and Walter Gropius extended the scope of this concern. Perhaps most importantly, rising housing costs in the suburbs made decayed older buildings appealing to buyers willing to expend a little sweat equity. These "urban pioneers" brought energy, spending money and a certain cachet to old neighborhoods, making them attractive to second and third waves of increasingly affluent buyers. The townhouse squatters of the 1960s cleared the way for the campy Victorian revival of the early 1970s; but as even middle-class Victorian buildings gained prestige they soon shed the aura of camp, and the pursuit of authentic decor absorbed a new class of homeowners who never could have afforded to live in country houses or castles, the traditional haunts of preservationists.

Of course, purists winced at the efforts of well-intentioned amateurs, the often theatrical use of period style by prominent decorators like Mario Buatta and Mark Hampton, and the ersatz "Country House look" of the 1980s. Identifying the "right" interior mouldings, wallpapers, paint colors and floor-coverings with X-rays and microscopic analysis sometimes took on the character of a moral crusade, although in truth all restorations rely on the judicious use of an educated imagination. While entirely appropriate for historic sites and period rooms, this approach has proved too expensive, time-consuming and inflexible for most individuals. The formal furniture arrangements of the 18th century, for example, have little relevance to modern life. All but the most uncompromising owners have included modern appliances, heating and plumbing, even when well-disguised, and otherwise conscientious restorers are not always content to live in the darker, closer environments of the past. Many Victorian and Arts and Crafts homes restored in the 1970s and '80s, for example, while otherwise reverently researched and furnished, have been painted in pale hues more palatable to modern taste than their original murky tones. In contrast to the blithe remodelling projects of earlier decades, however, a sense of historical responsibility now impels many owners carefully to photograph, sample and measure original elements before any alterations are made.

In contrast to the enthusiastic support of architectural historians, many architects have expressed frustration with the rigidity of governmentally-imposed preservation guidelines, and architects and interior designers specializing in strictly authentic restorations remain relatively rare. Quite naturally, most are concerned first to create beautiful, liveable environments which please their clients, and to weigh authenticity against both the owners' needs and their own aesthetic interests. In general, designers working on older homes have preferred to reproduce the "feel" of the original design, preferably with some subtle, witty stamp of their own. By preservationist standards, most decorators' period interiors of the 1980s, while opulent and delightful, were also wildly overfurnished.

The preservation debate dates at least from 1789, when James Wyatt's over-zealous "restoration" of Salisbury Cathedral inspired a movement to preserve architectural monuments untouched; John Ruskin later became an influential proponent of this approach. Interiors were of less concern until the 1870s, when the Museum of Scandinavian Ethnography opened its first period rooms. These were of dubious accuracy, but their designers were probably the first to consult paintings and prints as sources for authentic interiors. The growing popularity of open-air and house museums and the burgeoning interest in antiques – especially in Britain and North America —encouraged the use of period styles, and by 1900 most books on interior design were essentially primers on historic furnishings. But early preservationists had little reliable information to guide their efforts, and their interiors were generally crammed with picturesque collections of antiques and reproduction furnishings arranged to suit contemporary taste. While a growing emphasis on scholarship, expressed in works like Henry Havard's *Dictionnaire de l'Ameublement* (1887–90), ensured that the details were often right, the effect remained essentially modern.

The wholesale purchase of period rooms – panelling, chimneypieces, mouldings, flooring and all – reached its apogee in the 1920s, by which time most major museums in Europe and America had installed at least a few. Opposition to this practice encouraged new guidelines for documenting and reconstructing interiors: the integrity of the original was to be preserved at all costs, and all new materials were to be clearly identifiable to future researchers. Promoted by influential leaders like William Sumner Appleton of the Society for the Preservation for New England Antiquities, these principles have remained the basis for nearly all later restorations. During the 1930s, researchers' efforts to identify original materials and mine estate inventories and other period documents for details of interior decoration began to bear fruit: John Fowler's early work on English country houses managed by the National Trust, for example, relied on careful study of historic fabrics, color schemes and furnishing plans, and has greatly informed the independent work of his decorating firm, Colefax & Fowler. Meticulous, focused research and scientific analysis are now considered essential for all professional treatment of historic interiors, although the staff of many freshly restored historic houses have faced consternation from traditional supporters with an attachment to the "wrong" wallpapers and furnishings. In a few cases, the original restoration itself is worthy of preservation as a document of early 20th century ideas and taste. Restorers must also grapple with the representation of a room's use over time: in many cases heirlooms and outmoded forms should ideally be combined with new pieces, and in older buildings, deciding which period to recreate can present a real quandary.

The last ten to fifteen years have also seen an explosion of literature on the history of interiors and the decorative arts. Mario Praz's *Illustrated History of the Interior* (1964) was a pioneering study in this field and was one of the first books to use paintings as important sources in the documenting of period decorations and furnishings. Numerous other scholarly texts have followed, amongst the most influential of which have been the books published by the English historian Peter Thornton (*Seventeenth-Century Interior Decoration in England, France, and Holland*, 1978; *Authentic Decor*, 1984; and *The Italian Renaissance Interior*, 1991) which have emphasised not only period illustrations but also the role of estate inventories and literary sources in helping to develop a clearer understanding of the arrangement and use of historic rooms. More recently, these have been supplemented by sourcebooks and manuals published by American and British heritage organizations such as the Society for the Preservation of New England Antiquities, and the National Trust, which are aimed at both a professional audience and amateurs. A more general readership has also been served by a large number of colour magazines including *Antiques*, the *World of Interiors*, and *Period Interior Decoration*, which feature articles on period homes.

The growth in books and magazines has been paralleled by a huge increase in the availability of reproduction patterns, furnishings and architectural features. Up-market decorating firms such as Colefax & Fowler and Cowtan and Tout have been producing copies of historical wallpapers and textiles for many years, but it is only since the 1970s that the taste for period styles has been reflected in the work of more commercial manufacturers. The British firm Laura Ashley led the way in the late 1960s with their small, sprigged and geometric fabrics based on early 19th century originals. Since then the market for period patterns has expanded enormously until virtually every new collection in the mid- and late 1980s included at least one historic design; even Habitat produced a range of Arts and Crafts textiles in 1992. In many cases these are not exact reproductions, and commercial patterns often involve alterations of scale and colour to suit contemporary tastes. But increasingly, with many of the more expensive products, authenticity has become an important means of ensuring sales.

JODY CLOWES

Further Reading

For general histories of heritage organisations in Britain and America see Jenkins and James 1994, and Murtagh 1988. The pioneering work of John Fowler in the restoration of historic interiors is discussed in Cornforth 1985 and Cornforth and Fowler 1974.

Aslet, Clive, *The Last Country Houses*, London and New Haven: Yale University Press, 1982

Beard, Geoffrey, *The National Trust Book of the English House Interior*, London: Viking, 1990

Cornforth, John and John Fowler, *English Decoration in the 18th Century*, London: Barrie and Jenkins, and Princeton, NJ: Pyne, 1974; 2nd edition, Barrie and Jenkins, 1978

Cornforth, John, *The Inspiration of the Past: Country House Taste in the Twentieth Century*, London and New York: Viking, 1985

Garrett, Elisabeth Donaghy, *The Antiques Book of American Interiors: Colonial and Federal Styles*, New York: Crown, 1980

Gilliatt, Mary, and Elizabeth Wilhide, *Period Decorating*, London: Conran Octopus, 1990; revised edition, 1993

Gilliatt, Mary, *Period Style*, Boston: Little Brown, 1990

Gross, Steven, *Old Houses: A National Trust for Historic Preservation Book*, New York: Stewart Tabori and Chang, 1977

Hewison, Robert, *The Heritage Industry: Britain in a Climate of Decline*, London: Methuen, 1987

Highsmith, Carol M. and Ted Landphair, *America Restored*, Washington, DC: Preservation Press, 1994

Hosmer, Charles B., Jr., *Preservation Comes of Age: From Williamsburg to the National Trust, 1926–1949*, 2 vols., Charlottesville: University Press of Virginia, 1981

Jenkins, Jennifer and Patrick James, *From Acorn to Oak Tree: The Growth of the National Trust, 1895–1994*, London: Macmillan, 1994

Murtagh, William J., *Keeping Time: The History and Theory of Preservation in America*, Pittstown, NJ: Main Street Press, 1988

Seale, William, *Of Houses and Time: Personal Histories of America's National Trust Properties*, New York: Abrams, 1992

Thornton, Peter, *Authentic Decor: The Domestic Interior, 1620–1920*, London: Weidenfeld and Nicolson, and New York: Viking, 1984

Tschudi-Madsen, Stephan, *Restoration and Anti-Restoration: A Study in English Restoration Philosophy*, Oslo: Universitetsforlaget, 1976

B

Baillie Scott, M.H. *See* Scott, M.H. Baillie

Baldwin, Billy 1903–1983

American interior decorator

Back in the mid-1930s, the New York society decorator Ruby Ross Wood declared amusedly of her slight, dapper young assistant, "Billy is small, but his sting is deep". The comment was directed justly at Billy Baldwin's thorny personality, but at its heart lay an unspoken promise. By the end of the next decade, Baldwin was well on his way to earning the nickname of his mature years, "the dean of American decorating". His hallmarks – strong silhouettes, tailored upholstery, printed cotton fabrics, fresh clear colors and whimsical *objets d'art* sternly organized – would define sophisticated taste in the United States in the 1960s.

Born at Roland Park, a prosperous suburb of Baltimore, Maryland, on 30 May 1903, William Willar Baldwin, Jr., was the eldest child and only son of W. W. Baldwin, an insurance broker, and his wife, Julia Bartlett, a foundry heiress. Destined for a comfortable if not luxurious life on the periphery of the horsey aristocracy of Baltimore, Baldwin dutifully went to Princeton University in 1922, only to leave two years later, under an academic cloud that he would later ascribe to a lack of interest in mathematics. Immediately he moved to New York City and worked, briefly and unhappily, as an insurance salesman, then, surprisingly, as a crime reporter at the *Baltimore Sun*.

Eventually, he ended up in the stockroom of the fashionable Baltimore decorators C.J. Benson and Company, where "the only thing I had to do was fold every single [fabric] sample and put it back on its rack after the client had taken it out and straighten the room every afternoon before I went home" (Baldwin, 1985). The color combinations into which he arranged those fabrics, however, impressed his employer, and after a few months' apprenticeship working on the houses of the local gentry, Baldwin, then 25, was hired as a staff decorator.

Soon he caught the attention of Ruby Ross Wood (1880–1950), an avant-garde if today little-known Manhattan decorator who ghost-wrote Elsie de Wolfe's 1913 decorating manual *The House in Good Taste* and espoused bed-ticking upholstery, Moroccan rugs, white painted floors and varnished card lampshades in an era of hidebound traditionalism. "If we ever recover from this goddamned Depression, I really think I would like to have you work for me," Wood reportedly said after seeing the colorful drawing room Baldwin decorated for a mutual friend: poison-green walls, yellow satin upholstered furniture, 18th century black-and-gold lacquer tables and Irish equestrian paintings with riders dressed in bright pink coats. Five years later, she did hire him, and excepting an assignment to the US Army Medical Corps during World War II, Baldwin remained in Wood's employ until her death in 1950. That year, he formed Baldwin, Inc., which was in operation under a variety of names – Baldwin and Martin, and Baldwin, Martin and Smith – until his retirement in 1973.

Instead of the brown-wood English conservatism or neo-Versailles frivolity that dominated the monied domestic interiors of mid-20th century America, Baldwin popularized leanly furnished, vibrantly accented rooms whose subtle luxury and textural interest were achieved by treating common materials with uncommon care. These optimistic, seemingly carefree interiors were especially appealing to the leaders of post-war American society, whose lifestyles emphasized moral freedom, youthful sophistication and household efficiency. According to Mark Hampton, Baldwin espoused a "light, immaculate, rather new look" with a "sleek, well-organized appearance" and "sparkling clarity", qualities that symbolized his belief in an independent American style.

"I am against the all-English house or the all-French house or the all-Spanish house", said Baldwin, who was the most prominent member of his field successfully to challenge the prevailing Europhilia in favor of developing a native American style that filtered its myriad cultural references through the prism of fresh-scrubbed modernity. "We can recognize and give credit where credit is due to the debt of taste we owe to Europe, but we have taste, too – in fact, we're a whole empire of taste. That is my flag and I love to wave it." His aesthetic jingoism was codified in two insightful manuals-cum-memoirs, *Billy Baldwin Decorates* (1973) and *Billy Baldwin Remembers* (1974).

Among his many clients were Jacqueline Onassis, Pamela Harriman, Greta Garbo, Barbara Hutton, the playboy Whitney Warren, the philanthropists Rachel and Paul Mellon, and the fashion mogul Hattie Carnegie. Much publicity was given to his interiors for two multi-house couples: Mary Wells Lawrence, an advertising agency founder, and her husband, Harding Lawrence, the president of Braniff Airlines (for whom Baldwin decorated four vast residences in as many years, in New York, Texas, Arizona, and France); and Kathryn Bache Miller, a banking heiress, and her husband, Gilbert Miller, a theatrical producer (for whom Baldwin decorated all or part of residences in England, Spain, and New York).

The most memorable project of Baldwin's many years as a decorator, however, was a small sitting room (c.1970), for Diana Vreeland, the flamboyant editor-in-chief of *Vogue* (US), and her husband, T. Reed Vreeland, a banker. Barely 15 feet square, the room was a cornice-to-baseboard panoply of vibrant scarlet-and-black flowered cotton chintz. The walls, furniture and curtains all were upholstered in the fabric, producing a lushly claustrophobic, vaguely alarming ambience that Mrs. Vreeland favorably compared to "a garden in hell".

Baldwin's innovation as a decorator was his development of elemental basics – some time-honoured, others his own designs – that could be used dependably in most situations, from tiny one-room flats to corporate offices to the houses of millionaires, and it seemed, with most any style of decoration, art or fabrics.

Less a strict formula than a Palladianesque philosophy of eternal harmony and comfort, these so-called "Baldwinisms" formed the core of many of his interiors. The major components were Louis XVI armchairs; deep, low, boxy sofas that recalled the streamlined creations of his idols Jean-Michel Frank and Syrie Maugham; handwoven fitted carpets with tiny geometric patterns (these greatly influenced the British decorator David Hicks); bulbous white plaster lamps à la Diego Giacometti; Chinese Coromandel screens, and Parson-style table, headboards and desks, made of wood tidily wrapped in clear-varnished rattan.

A particularly important piece of Baldwin furniture was the open bookcase that he designed in 1955 for the library of the songwriter Cole Porter. This was "one of the most famous rooms designed in America", according to the eminent architecture critic Brendan Gill, who greatly admired its walls, which were sheathed in tortoiseshell-finished leather. A towering skeleton of solid polished tubular brass set with ebony shelves, the bookcase was derived from a Directoire étagère that was purchased in the 1920s by Porter's wife, Linda. Like many of Baldwin's creations, it spawned a plethora of imitations.

In fabrics, Baldwin's preference was for bold colors, crisp motifs and relatively humble materials. "Cotton is my life", he told a reporter from *The New York Times* in 1965, at the height of his fame. So were linen and wool, which he deemed more suited to the pace of modern life than brocades and damasks.

The patterns of many of the fabrics that Baldwin designed were based on the works of 20th-century artists; all were manufactured by Woodson Wallpapers, an influential American fabric and wallcovering company owned by Woodson Taulbee, Baldwin's erstwhile companion. The leafy motif of a black-and-white printed cotton and matching wallpaper, for example, utilized a magnified detail from a pen-and-ink drawing by Henri Matisse that was owned by Baldwin. A Matisse still life of lemons and red and purple anemones inspired another popular wallpaper. Yet another owed a debt to the swirling patterns of a painting by Gustav Klimt.

Deep glossy walls were Baldwin leitmotifs. From 1946 to 1951, an aggressively shiny green was the dominant color of Baldwin's apartment at Amster Yard, an influential complex of renovated tenement buildings at 213 East 49th Street in New York. In his memoirs, he wrote that the color, an homage to Elsie de Wolfe, was copied by the painter from a gardenia leaf that "I had licked to a glisten".

Throughout the 1960s and early 1970s, he was especially fond of a color he called "Coromandel black-brown", a dark chocolate-colored enamel painted with a high-gloss, lacquer-like sheen. This, he said, soothed the "beams and bumps" of modern apartment buildings. It was used most prominently in Baldwin's own much photographed one-room apartment on East 61st Street, New York. He lived here from 1963 until 1979, when he moved permanently to a two-room cottage on the Massachusetts island of Nantucket.

Baldwin cited several influences on his work: Ruby Ross Wood, the French decorator Madeleine Castaing, and Dr. Claribel Cone of Baltimore, a pioneering collector of Impressionist art. Another was the 1930s California decorator Frances (Adler) Elkins, whose innovative synthesis of French Modernism, North African textiles and rough country furniture was largely ignored by the anti-Semitic, pro-Manhattan decorating press in the US. But the profoundest influence on Baldwin's style was an American fashion designer Pauline Fairfax Potter (known from 1954 as Baroness Philippe de Rothschild).

A Paris-born aesthete who met Baldwin when she moved to Baltimore as a teenager in 1925, Potter was known for calculatedly simple gestures that combined sophisticated rusticity with a theatrical sense of the surreal. "Her great gift was the unconventional use of conventional things," Baldwin told the writer Cleveland Amory in *Vogue* (US). Among her stylish affectations were bare windows "curtained" with giant potted camellia trees; 18th-century French lacquer commodes topped with crudely woven straw baskets for storing loose papers or magazines; cast-bronze faucet handles in the shape of lemons; and dining tables set with clumps of wild reeds and moss instead of cultivated flowers.

According to the American choreographer John Butler, a friend of Baldwin and Potter, it was the Dietrichian proportions of Potter's lower limbs that inspired the decorator's famous *Slipper* chair (also known as the *Lawson Slipper* chair). A diminutive descendant of a chair that Baldwin had adapted in the 1930s from the popular *Lawson* sofa, his low-slung *Slipper* chair featured a broad square seat and gently angled back that "small women and football linebackers find ... equally comfortable", the decorator said.

Traditionally upholstered in woven Madagascar grass cloth and cushioned with white duck, the chair was a Billy Baldwin hallmark. It appeared throughout his career in a variety of fabrics: white-piped beige canvas (Ellena du Wolcott Blair, Palm Beach, Florida, 1936); white sailcloth stencilled with sulphur-yellow orchids (John King Reckford, Montego Bay, Jamaica, 1938); white cotton trimmed with cobalt-blue tapes (Mary Runnells, Hobe Sound, Florida, c.1959); black leather (S.I. Newhouse, Jr., New York, 1965); flowered scarlet chintz

(Diana and T. Reed Vreeland, New York, c.1970); pink-and-blue tattersall (Kathryn and Gilbert Miller, Mallorca, Spain, c.1967), and apricot cotton (Maité and Don Plácido Arango y Arias, Madrid, 1972). One of the chairs is in the permanent collection of the museum of the Maryland Historical Society at Baltimore.

Baldwin's commercial projects were as emblematic of brisk, bandbox-perfect American chic as his residential work. These included the Woodward Gallery of Sporting Art at the Baltimore Museum of Art (1956); the Round Hill Club, Greenwich, Connecticut (1959); a Brighton Palace Mod beauty salon for Kenneth Battelle, the New York society hairdresser (1963); and a renowned redecoration of Tiffany and Company, the jewellers, which Baldwin furnished with rattan-wrapped furniture, white linen fitted carpeting and white wallpaper printed with a lively, neo-Persian pattern of black flowers and vines (1963).

He also designed stage sets, notably a lilac-and-white Adam-style drawing room for Gilbert Miller's production of the American premiere of William Douglas-Home's *The Reluctant Debutante* (1956). A little-known and now lost Baldwin design was a wood stand, in the shape of a slender fluted Greek column, for the America's Cup sailing trophy (1952).

Baldwin died of pneumonia at Nantucket Cottage Hospital, on 25 November 1983, aged 80.

MITCHELL OWENS

Biography

William Willar Baldwin, Jr. Born in Roland Park, Baltimore, 30 May 1903. Attended Princeton University, New Jersey, 1922–24. Worked as a staff decorator for C.J. Benson and Company, Baltimore, c.1928. Employed as a decorator by Ruby Ross Wood (1880–1950), 1935–50. Served in the US Army Medical Corps, 1942–43. Established his own decorating business, Baldwin Inc., 1950; later in partnership as Baldwin and Martin, and Baldwin, Martin and Smith; retired, 1973. Also designed stage sets, mid-1950s. Died on Nantucket Island, Massachusetts, 25 November 1983.

Selected Works

Baldwin's professional papers have disappeared. His work can be studied only though photographs, rare surviving interiors and home furnishings designs. His tables and upholstered furniture for Luten Clary Stern (1975) are now produced by Ventry Limited, of Locust, New Jersey. His brass bookcase for Cole Porter (1955) continues to be made by its original manufacturer, P.E. Guerin Inc., of New York.

Interiors

1955	Apartment 33A Waldorf Towers, 100 East 50th Street, New York (interior decoration and some furniture): Cole Porter
1959	Round Hill Club, Greenwich, Connecticut (interior decoration and some furniture)
1963	St. Regis Hotel, 2 East 55th Street, New York (interior decoration and some furniture): Barbara and William S. Paley
1963	Apartment., East 61st Street, New York (interior decoration): Billy Baldwin
1963	Kenneth Salon, 19 East 54 Street, New York (interior decoration and some furniture): Kenneth Batelle
c.1967	Miller Residence, Mallorca, Spain (interior decoration): Kathryn and Gilbert Miller
1968	Onassis Villa, Skorpios, Greece (interior decoration): Jacqueline and Aristole Onassis
c.1970	550 Park Avenue, New York City (interior decoration and some furniture): Diana and T. Reed Vreeland
1971	La Fiorentin, St.-Jean Cap Ferrat, France (interior decoration and some furniture): Mary Wells and Harding Lawrence
1972	2510 Foxhall Road, Washington, DC (interior decoration): Deeda and William McCormick Blair, Jr.
1979	22 Hussey Lane, Nantucket Island, Massachusetts (interior decoration and some furniture): Billy Baldwin

Baldwin designed the America's Cup trophy in 1952. He also designed a range of tables and upholstered furniture for Luten Clarey Stern in 1975 and a range of wallcoverings and fabrics for Woodson Wallpapers, New York in 1976.

Publications

There is no critical monograph on Baldwin; most informative sources relating to his life and career are his own writings, particularly *Billy Baldwin Decorates* and *Billy Baldwin Remembers*.

Billy Baldwin Decorates, 1973
Billy Baldwin Remembers, 1974
Billy Baldwin: An Autobiography (as told to Michael Gardine), 1985

Further Reading

Amory, Cleveland, "Who's Afraid of Elsie de Wolfe?" in *Vogue* (US), 1963, pp.116–22, 143

Brantley, Ben, "Billy Baldwin: An Original" in *W*, 4–11 December 1981, pp.13–18

Calloway, Stephen, *Twentieth-Century Decoration: The Domestic Interior from 1900 to the Present Day*, London: Weidenfeld and Nicolson, and New York: Rizzoli, 1988

"Cole Porter's Apartment: Country House on the 33rd Floor" in *Vogue* (US), 1 November 1955, pp.130–33

Cooper, Jeremy, "A Tribute to Billy Baldwin" in *Interior Design* (US), 58, September 1987, pp.296–99

Esten, John and Rose Bennett Gilbert, *Manhattan Style*, Boston: Little Brown, 1990

Hampton, Mark, *Legendary Decorators of the Twentieth Century*, New York: Doubleday, and London: Hale, 1992

Henry, Helen, "Billy Baldwin: From Baltimore, Charm" in *Baltimore Sun Magazine*, 17 November 1974, pp.20–23

O'Brien, George, "An American Decorator Emeritus" in *New York Times Magazine*, 17 April 1983, p.32

Owens, Mitchell, "Elegance of the 40's Rescued for the 90's" in *New York Times*, 22 April 1993, p.C1

Smith, C. Ray, *Interior Design in 20th-Century America: A History*, New York: Harper, 1987

Bamboo Furniture

In the Far East, the indigenous bamboo (*bambusa arudinacea*) has been an important material in house building, roofing, and in the making of simple furniture for many centuries. Its use in furniture-making can be traced to India in the 2nd century AD, although it is more commonly recognised as a product of China or Japan.

In the West there has been a fascination with the Orient for at least four centuries and this has been manifest in a number of ways. The particular taste for bamboo furniture started in 1757, when Sir William Chambers first published designs of it. Chambers's connection with Sweden is demonstrated by the existence of authentic Chinese bamboo furniture in some of the royal residences there.

Chairs were the main items to be given the bamboo treatment, although in many cases the bamboo furniture of the period was an imitation effect. Famous examples included bedroom chairs for David Garrick carved to imitate bamboo and painted a creamy white with the "knots" in green, while the Royal household at St. James's was supplied with "Bamboo elbow chairs ... very neatly japanned yellow ground and spotted rings".

The imitative process was popular into the early 19th century. Sheraton describes how beech was turned into chair parts which were then painted and flecked to imitate bamboo, while turned legs, fashioned to imitate bamboo, were used in a wide variety of furniture types. The exotic tastes of the Prince Regent gave a spur to the introduction of bamboo into the "Chinese" furnishings of the Royal Pavilion at Brighton, with many of the projects being produced in imitation of real bamboo. Some furniture examples supplied by Edward, Marsh and Tatham were made from a mix of real and imitation bamboo, combined with authentic lacquered panels.

The taste continued into the 19th century and was especially employed in making bedroom or fancy chairs. This furniture could well have been put into rooms which were decorated with wallpapers imitating bamboo and basket work. The example of the bamboo furniture supplied to the Chinese room at Claydon House c.1800 demonstrates this taste.

Although it gradually went out of high fashion during the first half of the century, by the mid-19th century bamboo was being imitated in materials other than wood. Cast-iron chairs painted to imitate bamboo caused particular consternation to the *Journal of Design*: "We really had imagined that society was getting tired of the conventional upholsterer's bamboo with its three black strokes and splashes to indicate foliations: but here it is breaking out in the most inveterate form, upon a material least of all calculated to support the attack".

It was the West's attraction to things Japanese following the opening up of the country from 1854 that eventually spawned a fresh demand for bamboo among other Oriental-style artifacts.

During the 18th century bamboo had been imported into America, and some manufacturers soon introduced imitation bamboo into their ranges. Samuel Gragg advertised bamboo fancy chairs in 1809, for example. Later in the 19th century firms such as the Vantine Emporium in New York were importing ready-made furniture from the East. On the other hand much allegedly oriental furniture, produced by businesses in several cities, was made from imported raw materials. These makers produced ranges of occasional furniture such as side tables, what-nots, flower stands, and the like. The Boston firm of James E. Wall seems to have specialised as a bamboo furniture-maker between 1881 and c.1895.

France also developed a business in bamboo furniture. In 1859 Joseph Cavoret applied for patents to protect his particular methods of imitating bamboo, while the business of Perret & Fils & Vibert made a speciality of bamboo furniture for export. They were particularly associated with a range of bamboo produced in three different colours – red, white, and black – which appears to have been successfully sold in America.

Imports of bamboo materials were soon made in England, and the first bamboo furniture-makers, Hubert Bill, seem to have been in business from 1869. By 1910 there were over 130 manufacturers working in the business of bamboo furniture. The bulk of the trade was situated in the East End of London, but the biggest establishment was founded in Birmingham. This city became a centre for the trade and large quantities of the fashionable products were made by the firm of W.F. Needham.

Needham's business started in 1886 and used his patent process to make a range called Ferrum Jungo. This method used a system of metal sockets and shoes which avoided the problems of splintering ends of poles and of the usual nailed joints coming loose. The business was so successful that by the mid-1890s Needham employed over 300 workers who produced over 4000 pieces of furniture per week.

In the last quarter of the 19th century there was a vogue for bamboo furniture based on the Japonisme style. Used in conjunction with lacquer panels and woven grass matting, it ideally reflected the Aesthetic tastes of the period. It was not only the fashion that made it popular however. Bamboo was lightweight, relatively inexpensive and decorative in its own right, while the tubular reed made it particularly appropriate for designers who were already attracted to using materials to produce vertical and horizontal forms.

Despite, or perhaps because of the considerable success of real bamboo furniture, it was still found that some manufacturers of more conventional furniture would use the imagery of bamboo in their products. George Hunzinger in New York produced chairs with turned legs in imitation of bamboo, and the European business of Thonet included bamboo styles in their range of bentwood furniture.

Throughout the 20th century, bamboo has continued to play a minor part in the repertoire of furnishings. Being lightweight and flexible, it was well-suited to the Contemporary furnishing style of the 1950s. In the 1980s it was seen as ideal for the conservatory-living style.

Bamboo has also had other roles to play in furnishings, since it was also suitable for interior decoration as well as for furniture. Split and varnished sections could be used for beading around panels, ceiling decoration, dados, cornices, and mantles, and even stair rods. It has been pressed into service for cornice poles, fire-screens, and shelving, as well as for the more common jardinières, chairs, and chair companions. The use of bamboo in cane-edge upholstery and bedding is also worthy of mention. It was used to provide a flexible but shape-retaining front or side edge to divans and sets of upholstered chairs prior to the ready-made spring unit which was complete with flexible metal edge built in.

CLIVE D. EDWARDS

See also Wicker Furniture

Further Reading

A well-illustrated survey of Bamboo Furniture in Europe and America appears in Walkling 1979 which also includes a long list of London manufacturers and importers of bamboo furniture.

Agius, Pauline, *British Furniture, 1880–1915*, Woodbridge, Suffolk: Antique Collectors' Club, 1978

Piper, Jacqueline M., *Bamboo and Rattan: Traditional Uses and Beliefs*, Oxford and New York: Oxford University Press, 1992

Walkling, Gillian, *Antique Bamboo Furniture*, London: Bell and Hyman, 1979

Walkling, Gillian, "Bamboo Furniture" in *Connoisseur*, 202, October 1979, pp.126–31

Barbet, Jean 1591–c.1654

French designer and architect

Jean Barbet was a French architect attached to royal circles who is best known for his book, *Livre d'Architecture d'Autels et de Cheminées* (1632), which was widely used as a source-book for fireplace designs both in his own country and in England and Sweden.

Little information relating to Barbet's life survives, but he is recorded as being in Rouen in 1616. From thence he travelled to Paris to work as an architect for Cardinal de Richelieu to whom he dedicated his *Livre*. The book contains twenty engraved designs depicting altars, fireplaces, mirrors and picture frames. The first edition was published in 1632 and met with such success that a second edition was issued in Paris and Amsterdam in 1641. The plates were engraved by Abraham Bosse who also worked as a painter and produced many charming views of fashionable Parisian interiors. The book's aim, stated in its foreword, was to show "ce qu'il y a de beau dans Paris" (that which is handsome in Paris). Although it included designs for other features, it became famed for its designs for chimneypieces in particular. Another edition containing simplified versions of Barbet's engravings also appeared in Amsterdam at about the same time, and his work was in part reproduced in Robert Pricke's *The Architect's Store House* (London, 1674).

Throughout the 16th century the chimneypiece was widely regarded as the most important feature of the room as it was locus of both warmth and light. Not surprisingly, therefore, it was the feature on which contemporary architects lavished most care and attention and it was the first part of the interior to warrant the production of ornamental pattern books devoted specifically to its design. The sheer size and style of fireplaces during this period, which typically had bold projecting surrounds that dominated the wall, also encouraged a demand for fresh ideas on how to incorporate them into interior schemes. The architect Philibert de l'Orme included some drawings of chimneypieces in his treatise of 1567 and other French designers such as Pierre Collot and Jean Le Pautre, and subsequently Jean I Berain and Jean Marot also published engravings of this kind. But to a large extent Barbet can be

Barbet: two designs for chimneypieces from *Livre d'Architecture*, 1641

viewed as a pioneer in this field and his *Livre* was the most celebrated sourcebook for much of the 17th century.

During the early 17th century, fireplaces were beginning to shed the massive and functional appearance that characterised earlier forms, but it is still possible to discern a certain lack of cohesion in Barbet's designs based as they were on existing Parisian forms. By the 1660s (after Barbet's death), French chimneypieces had evolved into a more refined, elegant structure with a lower, smaller opening and more simplified decor. This development can be seen in the designs of Jean Le Pautre, whose work was described as *à la Moderne*, and such fireplaces are distinct from Italian or Roman examples where the composition is more architectural and where the central frame is flanked by figures.

Barbet's designs were in the main executed in the bold Mannerist style associated with the School of Fontainebleau and often included strongly protruding figures, heavy garlands, sculptural putti and swelling volutes. He also, however, produced designs in a more sober style where the only embellishment was the architectural features. But it was his chimneypieces that extended from the floor to the ceiling – described as *à la Française* – where he combined the arts of painting, sculpture and architecture, that were most frequently imitated.

Barbet's work exercised a strong influence on the English architect Inigo Jones. By training and by inclination Jones was primarily drawn to Italian Renaissance architecture and he made several extended study trips to Italy to augment his knowledge of the Classical idiom. But he also sought inspiration from French sources for the interiors of his Palladian-style buildings. The eclectic nature of this approach arose partly from his recognition that Paris was then at the forefront of fashionable design but also from necessity. While the Italian treatises of Scamozzi and Palladio provided some information about mural decoration and the structure of ceilings, other elements of the interior were not discussed and for details such as ornament and architectural fitments Jones was forced to look to Northern European engravings. Much of Jones's work for the British court also coincided with the arrival in England of the French queen, Henrietta Maria, who brought with her a taste for French styles and French sources which were particularly important in his designs for the Queen's House, Greenwich, which was built in the 1630s. Some of the chimneypieces in the Queen's House represent exact borrowings from Barbet. Others illustrate how Jones rationalised Barbet's designs by modifying the use of the decorative elements. Where Barbet creates a heavy, somewhat cluttered-looking form by placing all the elements one on top of the other, Jones separates out the different sections of the fireplace to produce an altogether more classical design. The painting above the fireplace opening thus gains in importance and becomes an imposingly framed yet integrated part of the whole chimney surround.

The Double Cube room at Wilton House, designed by Jones and his pupil John Webb, also boasts a chimneypiece composed from different plates in Barbet's book, with the details combined in such a way as to make the borrowings less obvious. The fireplace includes heavy volutes and garlands in the lower section, while the square painting above is flanked by standing figures with Corinthian capitals and putti resting on a broken entablature. An even more remote example of Barbet's influence can be seen in the interiors of Skokloster, north of Stockholm, the castle built by Count Wrangel following his victories in the Thirty Years' War. Several of the chimneypieces are modelled on the plates in Barbet's book while certain of the ceilings are clearly indebted to the work of Jean Le Pautre. Moreover, Barbet's influence did not entirely fade away with the passing of the 17th century. His designs indirectly affected the drawings made by Lord Burlington in the late 1720s whose designs for fireplaces for the West Closet at Chiswick House were based on those used by Inigo Jones at Greenwich.

PIA MARIA MONTONEN

See also Chimneypieces and Chimney Furniture

Biography

Born in 1591 of a Norman family. Recorded in Rouen, 1616. Moved to Paris; worked as an architect for Cardinal de Richelieu, 1633; appointed Architecte du Roi, Touraine, 1642. Published designs for chimneypieces and other furnishings in the *Livre d'Architecture*, 1632. Died before 1654.

Publications

Livre d'Architecture d'Autels et de Cheminées, 1632; 2nd edition, 1641; as *A Booke of Archetecture*, 1670

Further Reading

There is no detailed study of Barbet's career but for a discussion of the influence of his engravings see Harris 1961 and Thornton 1978.

Andrèn, Erik, *Skokloster: Ett slottsbygge under stormaktstiden Slott*, Stockholm: Nordisk, 1948

Fuhring, Peter (editor), *Design into Art: Drawings for Architecture and Ornament: The Lodewijk Houthakker Collection*, vol.1, London: Philip Wilson, 1989

Harris, John, "Inigo Jones and his French Sources" in *Metropolitan Museum of Art Bulletin*, XIX, May 1961, pp.253–64

Harris, John and Gordon Higgott, *Inigo Jones: Complete Architectural Drawings* (exhib. cat.), New York: Drawing Center, and London: Zwemmer, 1989

Harris, John, *The Palladian Revival: Lord Burlington, His Villa and Garden at Chiswick*, New Haven and London: Yale University Press, 1994

Strange, Thomas Arthur, *An Historical Guide to French Interiors*, London: McCorquodale, 1903

Thornton, Peter, *Seventeenth-Century Interior Decoration in England, France, and Holland*, New Haven and London: Yale University Press, 1978

Wiebenson, Dora, *French Books: Sixteenth Through Nineteenth Centuries* (Mark J. Millard Architectual Collection, vol.1), Washington, DC: National Gallery of Art, 1993

Baroque

The Baroque style developed first in painting, before spreading to other media, at the end of the 16th century. Initially a style centred in Rome, the Baroque featured contrasts of dark and light and rich effects of colour and texture. A dramatic, theatrical style of art, the Baroque was often highly classical in iconography and subject matter, reaching its climax in the Apollo imagery adopted by Louis XIV of France. However, as the style spread northwards during the 17th century, it became more naturalistic in emphasis, culminating in the realism and

Baroque: gallery, Palazzo Colonna, Rome, 1572

floral decorative vocabulary of Baroque art in the Protestant Netherlands and in England. Baroque architecture, too, displayed this sense of drama with its boldly massed classical forms and powerful silhouettes. Interiors were dominated by a carefully planned sequence of rooms, each with a particular significance. Controlled contrasts of size, shape, colour and texture were at the heart of the effect of the formal Baroque state chamber.

The rapid development of trade with non-western cultures during the 17th century resulted in a flood of new and exotic materials to European cities which were quickly adopted by craftsmen to achieve the effects of novelty and surprise that were much prized during this period. For example, the English writer Aphra Behn, who possibly travelled to the Dutch Pacific colony of Surinam in the 1660s, described in her best-known work, *Oroonoko* (1688), the wonder felt by Europeans at their discovery of the richly coloured woods of the tropics: "The very wood of all these trees have an intrinsic value above common timber; for they are, when cut, of different colours, glorious to behold, and bear a price considerable to inlay withal."

The undoubted centre of the Baroque was Rome, where the Catholic Church used this powerful new style as a means of reasserting its authority in the wake of the challenge of the Protestant Reformation. However, while the emergence of a Baroque style in painting began in Italy late in the 16th century, the development of Baroque interiors can be traced to Rome during the 1620s, a decade that also saw the beginnings of the Baroque interior in France and the Netherlands. Therefore, although the influence of the Roman Baroque remained strong throughout the 17th century, even in the Protestant countries, each region developed its own version of the style. Indeed, in most cases Roman Baroque forms were used for their classical references, Rome having long been the centre of the antique world, rather than for their Catholic associations.

Among the early promoters of the Baroque in Rome were the Barberini family, whose most prominent member was Urban VIII, elected Pope in 1623. He was the principal patron of the sculptor Gianlorenzo Bernini, whose genius for creating dramatic architectural spaces and whose powerful modelling of the human form were to influence designers all over Europe.

Baroque: cabinet made for Madame de Maintenon, with *pietre dure* inlay, 17th century (Musées de la Ville de Strasbourg)

This influence was particularly strong in France, where the Barberini visited on several occasions, including a period of exile of family members in Paris from 1645 to 1653 when feeling ran strongly against them in Rome. Bernini visited France and supplied designs for the Louvre in the 1660s which profoundly influenced French Baroque architects. Baroque interior design responded to Bernini's famous baldacchino, or canopy, of St. Peter's in Rome, commissioned by Urban VIII in 1624. Its highly plastic, spirally turned columns revived from the late antique period were to be frequently used on cabinet furniture.

Bernini knew that Raphael had used the spiral column, signifying the architecture of the Biblical Temple of Solomon, on one of his cartoons for the *Acts of the Apostles* of 1514, which were designs for tapestries for the Sistine Chapel. These cartoons went first to Brussels for weaving into tapestries and then passed into the collection of Charles I of England early in the 17th century, ensuring their influence in northern Europe. This influence can be seen in the spiral columns of the marble chimneypiece for the Great Dining Room of Ham House, Surrey, executed in the 1630s by an English craftsman under the supervision of the Director of the Mortlake Tapestry works, Franz Cleyn, who had direct access to the Raphael cartoons.

The Baroque style represents a continuation of the classical tradition re-established in Western art during the Renaissance, and Italian Renaissance ideas of bringing order and regularity into architecture and interiors were developed much further during the Baroque period. The central unit of organization of living quarters was the apartment, the most important of which was the state apartment, a lavishly decorated suite of rooms prepared principally for show, for ceremonial functions, and for the reception of a monarch or guest of elevated rank. Thus Baroque apartments for private living were developed as separate entities from public apartments, a distinction that was unknown in the Renaissance.

Central to the Baroque apartment, whether private or state, was the placement of an impressive bed with expensive draperies, a representation of the wealth of the owner. In 1617 Lady Anne Clifford, Countess of Dorset and resident at Knole House, Kent, wrote in her diary of her "Green Cloth of Gold Bed" in the Great Chamber, which was used only for important family occasions such as the birth of a child or serious illness. Knole has several splendid state beds from the Baroque period, including a bed probably made for the marriage of the future James II in the 1670s by Louis XIV's upholsterer. The bed is hung with rich textiles made of gold and silver thread, with elaborately carved, upholstered stools en suite.

The arrangement of a bedchamber preceded by an antechamber (or "Drawing" chamber) and followed by a small closet (or private room) was in place by the early 17th century. This arrangement was first developed into a formalized plan in Rome, where a strict etiquette for the receiving and paying of visits according to the relative status of the host and the visitor was observed during the 1620s and 1630s. This etiquette governed social behaviour, which was dominated by the Church and the requirements of diplomacy. From Rome, this etiquette spread to the French court during the first half of the 17th century under Louis XIII, his formidable wife Anne of Austria, and their powerful Italian-born minister Cardinal Mazarin (born Mazarini). For example, when Cardinal Francesco Barberini visited Louis XIII in the Louvre, he was received by him in a state bed richly hung with red damask and marked off from the rest of the room by a balustrade.

Such a ceremonial use of the state bedchamber was to reach its apogee during the court rituals of Louis XIV, where the *levée* and the *couchée* of the king – that is, his ceremonial getting up and going to bed – were likened to the rising and setting of the sun. It was important that, when at court, aristocrats and ambitious courtiers attended such rituals, where behaviour was strictly regulated. In Molière's play *The Misanthrope* of 1666, one of his characters remarked: "I have come straight from the Louvre. Cléonte has been making a perfect fool of himself there at the leveé. Has he no friends who could in charity enlighten him as to how to behave?"

Therefore Baroque interiors were used as the settings for the rituals of formal etiquette, and even relatively modest apartments aped the arrangements at court. Living apartments assumed the form of a sequence of about five rooms, the grandest being on the *piano nobile*, or first floor, of a residence off a principal staircase. The first room was usually the largest in the apartment, a formal reception room (known as a *sala* in Italian, becoming the French *salle*) which could be used for formal dining. Often these rooms were furnished with a sideboard bearing an elaborate arrangement of plate and vessels.

Entertainments and dances could be held in this room when the tables and chairs for dining were cleared away. In Daniel Defoe's novel *Roxana* (1724), which was set in the time of Charles II, the lady Roxana explained how she rearranged her apartment for a grand party: "I had a large Dining-Room in my Apartments, with five other Rooms on the same Floor, all which I made Drawing-Rooms for the Occasion, having all the Beds taken down for the Day; in three of these I had Tables plac'd, cover'd with wine and Sweet-Meats; the fourth had a green Table for Play, and the fifth was my own Room, where I sat."

In a state apartment, the room beyond this first reception room was an audience chamber, furnished with a throne-like chair under a canopy, where formal visits took place. Seat furniture was arranged according to the status of the visitors, only the grandest of whom would be seated. This room assumed the function of the drawing room in a private apartment. Defoe's heroine Roxana described the essential furnishings of the smart middle-class drawing room as, "Pictures and Ornaments, Cabinets, and Peir-Glasses". Pier glasses were mirrors hung on the piers of masonry between the windows of the room, often above a side table, flanked by a pair of torchères, or candlestands, whose light was reflected in the mirror.

The Marquise de Rambouillet, the daughter of the French ambassador to Rome, became famous for the innovative decoration of her Paris town house during the 1620s. She introduced the practice of furnishing rooms with a unified suite of textiles, all of one predominant colour, and her apartment was arranged *en enfilade* – that is, all the doorcases of the various rooms were in alignment along the window wall of the apartment, creating an impressive vista. This arrangement, which became almost universally adopted in the Baroque apartment, threw into prominent view the furniture used against the pier. Therefore, as mirrors were luxury items in the 16th century, the pier glass with its accompanying suite of a table and two stands, often in sumptuous marquetry or japanned in imitation of Japanese lacquer, became important furnishings for the Baroque drawing room. The design of such furniture was developed in France, and richly sculptural designs for suites were published in the 1660s by the court designer Jean Le Pautre.

The third room in the Baroque sequence was normally a bedchamber. In state apartments the bed was a lavish and expensive creation of the upholsterer's art made primarily for show, whereas private apartments had beds which were actually slept in, often copying the grand design and draperies of state beds in less sumptuous materials. In some cases, such as the King's Apartments at Hampton Court, a state and private bedchamber were placed next door to one another. This practice was also used in Roman apartments in the 17th century. While the state bedchamber was the setting for ceremonial occasions, the private bedchamber was off-limits to all except close friends, family and servants, as was the closet (in French, *cabinet*), the small private sitting room beyond the bedchamber.

Because of its small size, being the smallest room of the Baroque apartment, the closet could be well heated in cold weather, unlike the larger rooms of the apartment, and richly decorated. The closet seems to have derived from the Italian Renaissance *studiolo* and was decorated to reflect the personal taste of the occupier, often containing favourite paintings and works of art. The English architect Christopher Wren visited the apartments of Anne of Austria in the Louvre in 1665, and he reported that her closet was richly hung with small landscape paintings. The Duchess of Orléans, the daughter of Charles I of England, had a white closet in the 1660s furnished with a marquetry cabinet veneered in ivory by the Dutch-born *ébéniste* Pierre Gole, the favourite cabinet-maker of Louis XIV. This example may have inspired the white closet of Ham House for the Duchess of Lauderdale, one of the two closets in her apartment. Next to the white closet was a second one arranged as a small private study where she wrote letters and drank tea with friends. Ham is remarkable for having four closets surviving from the 1670s with ceilings painted by Antonio Verrio, and one from the 1630s with a ceiling painted by Franz Cleyn. A fifth closet from the 1670s was situated off the library and functioned as a "study".

One principal function of the Baroque closet was to provide a private room for writing, whether it be diaries, love letters or diplomatic correspondence. Such activities required quiet surroundings and appropriate furniture to take place, and writing furniture became a new and fashionable form of furniture for the Baroque closet. Surviving records tell us that beautifully made bureaux and cabinets in marquetry of sumptuous woods or materials such as metal and tortoiseshell were also shown off in the drawing room (or audience chamber) of the Baroque apartment, along with rare and exotic objects of lacquer and porcelain. The most highly prized bureaux and cabinets were made in Paris and the Netherlands (Antwerp and Amsterdam), with craftsmen in other European cities following the models set by these leading centres.

One very important interior outside of the Baroque apartment itself was the gallery, a long, formal room that was usually the largest in a residence and used to display the art collection of the owner. Such galleries could be visited by members of the public without disturbing the household, as they were physically distinct from, although often adjacent to, the living apartments. In the Roman Palazzo Borghese, a sculpture gallery was in place by 1610 on the ground floor of the house. Shortly afterwards, and inspired by Italian example, Lord Arundel created a sculpture gallery on the ground floor of his London town house that was considered the finest in northern Europe by visitors such as the Flemish painter Peter Paul Rubens.

Increasingly during the 17th century, paintings became the focus of galleries. This was especially true of central Europe, where Italian and Northern works were hung from the ceiling to the floor, as illustrated in David Tenier's painting of Archduke Leopold of Austria's Gallery of 1651, now at Petworth House in Sussex. Prague Castle had a similar gallery recorded in a painting of 1702 by Johann Bretschneider (now in Nuremberg) showing the paintings framed in ebony, with a suite of seat furniture upholstered in blue around the walls of the room. In some Baroque galleries, especially in smaller houses where the collecting of great works of art was beyond the reach of the owner, portraits of ancestors were displayed on the walls.

In an extraordinary development of this theme, Cardinal Girolamo Colonna constructed a gallery in his Roman palazzo

Baroque: state bedroom, Chatsworth House, Derbyshire, 1690s

to glorify the exploits of a famous ancestor who had fought against the Turks in the Battle of Lepanto at the end of the 16th century. Begun in 1654, the gallery was not completed until 1702 and was designed in the manner of an ancient Roman triumph. A triumphal column (also a play on the family's name) raised on a dais at the far end of the gallery formed a focal point for the decoration, with ceiling paintings glorifying Marcantonio Colonna above a classically inspired interior with enormous gilt console tables with large carved figures of conquered Turks by Filippo Passarini, made in the 1690s. The highly theatrical quality of the Palazzo Colonna gallery marks the apogee of the Roman Baroque interior.

Displaying a shift of function is the Grand Galerie of Versailles, now known as the Hall of Mirrors because of its wall decoration in mirrored glass, which was relatively rare and very expensive in the 17th century. The gallery at Versailles was large enough to contain the assembled court for ceremonies and entertainments, and the reflection of chandeliers in the myriad glass panes made it particularly dazzling at night. Light was further reflected by the famous silver furniture in the gallery, consisting of pier suites as well as planters for the numerous orange trees and perfumers which kept the air sweet. The artist Charles Le Brun, who was head of the Gobelins manufactory set up in the 1660s to supply furnishings for the royal palaces, masterminded the Baroque interiors at Versailles for Louis XIV until his death in 1690.

In 1685 Louis had revoked state protection for Protestants, many of whom were well-to-do craftsmen and merchants, and in 1689 he had been forced to melt down the silver furniture of Versailles to pay for a disastrous series of military campaigns. These two events marked the beginning of a steady decline in the fortunes of France, which was gradually overtaken in wealth and prosperity by England and Holland by the end of the century. The period of 1660 to 1720 saw many country houses built and furnished in these two northern Protestant nations, which shared a common ruler in Prince William of Orange and which benefited from the exodus of Protestant craftsmen from France. In addition, both nations were becoming wealthy from colonial and Far Eastern trade, resulting in a flood of exotic materials into Dutch and English Baroque interiors. In an account of the city of Amsterdam, written in 1662, Melchior Fokken remarked upon the shop of Dirk Rijswijk, where one could purchase tables and cabinets made with exotic inlays of mother-of-pearl.

The most popular of these exotic materials, however, were lacquer and porcelain, and the leading collector of the day was Queen Mary, the English wife of William III. Daniel Defoe, who acted as a spy for William in the 1690s, wrote of Mary's collecting in *A Tour through the Whole Island of Great Britain* (1724–26): "The queen brought in the custom or humour, as I may call it, of furnishing houses with china-ware, which increased to a strange degree afterwards, piling their china upon the tops of cabinets, scrutores [writing cabinets], and every chimney-piece, to the tops of the ceilings, and even setting up shelves for their china-ware ..."

Queen Mary also collected objects of oriental lacquer, whereas William was a gardening enthusiast and a collector of Italian and northern paintings. Their apartments at Hampton Court and Kensington Palace were dominated by large galleries in which they displayed their collections.

In addition to their taste for collecting, William and Mary influenced northern Baroque interiors through their choice of court designer. This was Daniel Marot, the son of a French court architect and nephew of the leading *ébéniste* Pierre Gole, who was foremost among the Huguenot artists and craftsmen leaving France in 1685. Marot worked principally in the Netherlands for the rest of his long life, but he spent several years in England in the service of William III during the 1690s. Marot's Baroque style was disseminated in designs he began to publish in 1698 and featured highly elongated proportions of furnishings, most notably elaborate state beds, and the lavish use of textiles. Some of the motifs he used, as in the espagnolette mask, can be traced back to French court designers such as Jean Berain, but the distinctive tall, narrow proportions of his forms, surmounted by an arched, double-scrolled top, which appeared on everything from wall panelling to chair backs, attest to the widespread use of his designs in northern Europe.

As Marot's influence was felt most strongly in England and the Netherlands, it is sometimes difficult to distinguish between Dutch and English designs of this period. Marot's influence can also be seen in interiors from Sweden, northern Germany, Ireland, and even in Dutch and English colonies in the Americas and Asia, well into the 18th century. In most European countries, the powerful tradition of Baroque design extended into the first half of the 18th century, but a new, lighter style of interior design was already being formulated in France. In 1713, the year before the death of the old and ailing Sun King, Mme. de Maintenon, his second wife, remarked, "We have no more Court here ... other members of the royal family are never at Versailles." Indeed, the younger members of the court had removed themselves to Paris, where the building of private town houses with comfortable and luxurious apartments for the reception of friends became an aristocratic pursuit.

J.-F. Blondel's important guide to house-building, *De la Distribution des Maisons Plaisance* (1737–38) consolidated this already-established shift towards private living apartments in the 18th century, with a new style, the Rococo, rising to ascendency. By the 1740s the new style of France had largely superseded the Baroque in every fashionable centre in Europe, whereas in provincial areas or colonial outposts, the Baroque lasted a little longer. The development of private living areas, of interiors created to express individual taste, and of rooms differentiated by function are all key aspects of the development of European interiors that owe their origins to Baroque designers.

MEGAN ALDRICH

See also State Apartments

Further Reading

Baarsen, Reinier and others, *Courts and Colonies: The William and Mary Style in Holland, England, and America* (exhib. cat.), New York: Cooper-Hewitt Museum, 1988

Bauer, Hermann, *Barock: Kunst einer Epoche*, Berlin: Reimer, 1992

Blunt, Anthony, *Sicilian Baroque*, London: Weidenfeld and Nicolson, and New York: Macmillan, 1968

Blunt, Anthony, *Art and Architecture in France, 1500–1700*, 2nd edition Harmondsworth: Penguin, 1970

Blunt, Anthony (editor), *Baroque and Rococo: Architecture and Decoration*, New York: Harper, and London: Elek, 1978
Brusatin, Manlio and Gilberto Pizzamiglio (editors), *The Baroque in Central Europe: Places, Architecture and Art*, Venice: Marsilio, 1992
Downes, Kerry, *English Baroque Architecture*, London: Zwemmer, 1966
González-Palacios, Alvar, *Il Tempio del gusto: Le arti decorative in Italia fra classicismi e barocco*, part 1: *Roma e il Regno delle due Sicilie*, 2 vols., Milan: Longanesi, 1984; part 2: *Granducato di Toscana e gli stati settentrionali*, 2 vols., Milan: Longanesi, 1986
Grimschitz, Bruno, *Wiener Barockplaläste*, Vienna: Wiener Verlag, 1947
Gruber, Alain (editor), *L'Art Décoratif en Europe: Classique et Baroque, 1630–1760*, Paris: Citadelles & Mazenod, 1992
Hautecoeur, Louis, *Histoire de l'architecture classique en France*, vols.1 and 2, Paris: Picard, 1943–49
Hempel, Eberhard, *Baroque Art and Architecture in Central Europe*, Harmondsworth: Penguin, 1965
Minguet, Philippe, *France Baroque*, Paris: Hazan, 1988
Murray-Baillie, H., "Etiquette and the Planning of the State Apartments in Baroque Palaces" in *Archéologia*, CI, 1967, pp.169–99
Norberg-Schulz, Christian, *Late Baroque and Rococo Architecture*, New York: Rizzoli, 1985; London: Faber, 1986
Schindler, Herbert, *Europäische Barockklöster*, Munich: Prestel, 1972
Sedlmayr, Hans, *Österreichische Barockarchitektur, 1690–1740*, Vienna: Filser, 1930
Splendeur du Baroque: Soie, Or et Argent (exhib. cat.), Riggisberg, Switzerland: Abegg-Stiftung, 1994
Tapié, Victor-Lucien, *Le Baroque*, 7th edition Paris: Presses Universitaires de France, 1991
Thornton, Peter, *Baroque and Rococo Silks*, London: Faber, and New York: Taplinger, 1965
Thornton, Peter, *Seventeenth-Century Interior Decoration in England, France, and Holland*, New Haven and London: Yale University Press, 1978
Viale, Vittorio (editor), *Mostra del Barocco Piedmontese*, 3 vols., Turin, 1963
Walton, Guy, *Louis XIV's Versailles*, Chicago: University of Chicago Press, and London: Viking, 1986
Weigert, R.-A. (intro.), *Louis XIV: Faste et Décors* (exhib. cat.), Paris: Musée des Arts Décoratifs, 1960
Wittkower, Rudolf, *Studies in the Italian Baroque*, London: Thames and Hudson, and Boulder, CO: Westview, 1975
Wittkower, Rudolf, *Art and Architecture in Italy, 1600 to 1750*, 5th edition New Haven and London: Yale University Press, 1982

Basile, Ernesto 1857–1932

Italian architect and designer

Ernesto Basile is widely regarded as the most influential exponent of Italian Art Nouveau, known as *Stile Liberty*. Son of a distinguished architect, he was assistant professor of architecture in Palermo from 1877, and in 1888–90 taught architecture in Rome. He was the leading figure of Sicilian architecture and design at the end of the 19th century and was successful in several national competitions, designing many buildings in Sicily and Rome, including those for the Palermo exhibition of 1891–92; he also designed furniture. His modern style was developed after turning from sophisticated classical eclecticism to a personalised hedonistic Liberty style in the mid-1890s. He was aiming towards a renewal of architecture and to free it from the "vulgarity of the imitation of the past", though he paid particular attention to 12th-century Sicilian art and architecture, and to Viollet-le-Duc and William Morris's experiments in medieval revival. His Ribaudo's kiosk (1894) represents the beginning of this creative trend and was the first example of Art Nouveau architecture in Italy.

Basile's Modernist approach was to highlight the importance of the relationship between exterior architecture and interiors. He attempted to create a mutual dialogue between each detail of his projects: from the window-frames to the doors, from the metalwork to the murals, and from the ceiling to the carpets, as well as in the furniture. He also returned to the use of neglected craft traditions, such as wrought-iron work and stone carving.

The Sicilian Florio family had one of the largest fortunes in Europe and in their search for a cultivated identity they provided Basile with much patronage. He designed the Villino Florio (1899) in the Olivuzza park in Palermo for them; unfortunately most of the villa was destroyed by fire in 1962. Another commission was for the Villa Igiea (1899–1900), whose dining-room still survives, and illustrates Basile's understanding and use of modern elements. Here structure and ornament are successfully combined with a striking use of space and colour. The space is divided by a colonnade, and between the bow window and the main area of the room is a loggia overlooking Monte Pellegrino. Basile's attention to the harmonious combination of structural and ornamental elements is well illustrated here, as well as in the details such as the complicated light fittings, and in the design of single mirrors and doors whose decorative elements are repeated on the walls and the frieze supporting the ribs of the coved wooden ceiling. Other works in this style include the Utveggio House (1901) in Palermo. Among Basile's finest modern works are the Villino Fassini (1903), the Villino Basile (1903), the Municipal Palace of Liceta (1904), and Belmonte Palace (1906), and a vast number of interior designs which established his reputation internationally.

Basile is the only *Stile Liberty* architect to have had a long collaboration with a furniture firm. He worked with the Ducrot Company from 1899 to 1909. This firm was well established in the furnishing and cabinet-making fields, and its popular products were sold all over Italy. Although the firm continued to produce reproductions, Basile became artistic director of its modern work. This was important for Italian industrial design for it showed a new approach based on a recognition of the beneficial effect of the relationship between art and industry. Basile was in charge of two different kinds of furniture. The first consisted of richly carved and decorated unique pieces, designed for specific commissions and for exclusive interiors. The second kind was made up of cheaper furniture designed along geometric and functional lines. These pieces often formed part of a complete interior scheme, one of the most important of which was the oak workroom, shown at the Turin International Exhibition in 1902 under the joint name of Basile-Ducrot. In this scheme Basile combined oak and leather in an open structure characterized by a linear, modern design. The work was awarded a prize and was reproduced by Ducrot, with only minor changes, in hundreds of versions under the name of *tipo Torin'*.

At the Venice International Exhibition of 1903 Basile was in charge of the Naples and Sicily pavilion, where he demonstrated a familiarity with the work of Charles Rennie Mackintosh, especially in a mahogany armchair, decorated with gilded and impressed leather. This formed part of the same suite of furniture as the maple display-cabinet in which Basile stressed verticality, and eschewed all intrusive decoration, leaving only the top part of the structure as ornament.

The Milan Exhibition of 1906 was a milestone in the Basile-Ducrot collaboration. They exhibited a series of garden furniture called the *del carretto sicilian'* (after the Sicilian cart) which was inspired by Sicilian folklore and which recalls the colour and shape of this typically Sicilian vehicle. In his use of colour contrasts and carvings Basile is closely linked to a widespread European movement which looked back to earlier traditions. But, concurrently, Basile was also searching for a new more geometric and abstract language. This search culminated in his work in the dining room of the Villa Deliella, where surfaces and space are defined and articulated by line alone in a manner that echoes the style of Austrian designers like Josef Hoffmann.

As a designer in the *stile floreal'* (florid style), Basile's use of naturalistic imagery was controlled and selective and involved only the occasional use of stylized flowers and husks. His most original design in this style was a curious sideboard, exhibited at Milan in 1906, whose simple, square structure is animated by crabs and an octopus.

At the end of his career Basile returned to the eclecticism which he had previously depised. This move was mainly an attempt to satisfy the demands of patrons whose tastes ran more to revivalist than to modern designs. Nevertheless, his work retained the drama and individuality characteristic of his earlier years, and today he is justifiably remembered as one of the most innovative Italian designers of the early 20th century.

MARIELLA PALAZZOLO

Biography

Born in Palermo, 31 January 1857, the son of the architect Giovanni Battista Filippo Basile (1825–91). Studied at the University of Palermo, graduated 1878. Apprenticed to his father. Settled in Rome, 1881; assisted his father on various architectural projects; independent practice from c.1899. Assistant instructor in architecture, Scuola di Applicazione, Rome; director, then professor of architecture, Istituto Royale di Belle Arti, 1893; professor of architecture, University of Palermo, 1892. Designed furniture from c.1898. Exhibited at several national and international exhibitions including Turin, 1902, and Venice Biennale, 1903. Died in Palermo in 1932.

Selected Works

Interiors

1894 Ribaudo's Kiosk, Piazza Teatro Massimo, Palermo (building and interiors)
1899 Villino Florio all'Olivuzza, Palermo (building and interiors)
1899–1900 Grand Hotel Villa Igiea, Palermo (building and interiors)
1901 Utveggio House, Palermo (building and interiors)
1902 First International Arts Exposition, Turin (furnishings for the Ducrot stand)
1902–27 Palazzo Montecitorio (now Parliament Building), Rome (additions and interiors)
1903 Villino Basile, Palermo (building and interiors)
1904 City Hall, Licata (building and interiors)
1906 Palazzo Bruno di Belmonte, Spaccaforno (building and interiors)
1914 Municipal Palace, Reggio Calabria (building and interiors)

Basile designed the furniture and fittings for many of his buildings. He designed furniture and fabrics for Ducrot, 1899–1909.

Publications

Architettura, dei suoi principie e del suo rinnovamento, 1882; reprinted 1981

Further Reading

A full list of Basile's architectural works appears in Portoghesi 1980 which also includes references to primary and secondary sources. For a detailed account of his designs for Ducrot see Sessa 1980 and for a useful general discussion of Art Nouveau in Italy see Weisberg 1988.

Bairati, Eleonora and Rossana Bossaglia, *L'Italia Liberty*, Milan: Gorlich, 1973
Borsi, Franco, *L'Architettura dell'Unità d'Italia*, Florence: Le Monnier, 1966
Bossaglia, Rossana, *Il Liberty: Storia e fortuna del Liberty italiano*, Florence: Sansoni, 1974
Caronia Roberti, Salvatore, *Ernesto Basile e cinquant'anni di architettura in Sicilia*, Palermo: Ciuni, 1935
Damigella, Anna Maria, *Il Liberty nella Sicilia orientale*, Palermo, 1976
De Guttry, Irene and Maria Paola Maino, *Il Mobile Liberty Italiano*, Bari, 1983
Ernesto Basile e il Liberty a Palermo (exhib. cat.), Palermo: Herbita, 1987
Nicoletti, Manfredi, "Art Nouveau in Italy" in J. M. Richards and Nikolaus Pevsner (editors), *The Anti-Rationalists*, London: Architectural Press, and New York: Harper, 1973, pp.32–62
Nicoletti, Manfredi, *L'Architettura Liberty in Italia*, Rome and Bari: Laterza, 1978
Pirrone, Gianni, *Palermo Liberty*, Rome: Sciascia, 1971
Pirrone, Gianni, "Ernesto Basile and the Liberty Style in Palermo" in *Connoisseur*, March 1975
Pirrone, Gianni, *Studi e schizzi di E. Basile*, Palermo: Sellerio, 1976
Pirrone, Gianni, *Villino Basile, Palermo*, Rome: Officina, 1981
Portoghesi, Paolo and others, *Ernesto Basile Architetto* (exhib. cat.), Venice, 1980
Sessa, Ettore, *Mobile e arredi di Ernesto Basile nella produzione Ducrot*, Palermo: Novecento, 1980
Weisberg, Gabriel P., *Stile Floreale: The Cult of Nature in Italian Design*, Miami: Wolfsonian Foundation, 1988

Bathrooms

It is well known that the Greeks and the Romans took matters of personal hygiene seriously and adopted practices designed to promote health. The Minoan Palace of Knossos was equipped with bathtubs and running water (1600 BC), public toilets have been excavated in the ancient Greek city of Corinth, and every Roman city from North Africa to England had its public baths. But little is known about the origins of the domestic bathroom, in Europe at least, before the end of the 16th century.

During the 17th century matters of personal hygiene were dealt with in a variety of ways, but by the end of the century it was rare to find a bathroom, even in an important house. This does not mean to say the washing of the body was not important. In Britain and other European countries, at the upper end of the social scale, servants brought basins and ewers to a

Bathroom at Ashley Place, London, 1893

room where washing could take place and the items were taken away afterwards. The same situation applied to the wooden or copper bath tub used for bathing which was again removed after use. There is evidence to suggest at least some of the grand Elizabethan prodigy houses had bathrooms of a sort and attention has been drawn to Sir Francis Willoughby's plunge bath constructed in the sandstone underneath Wollaton Hall, Nottingham, in the 1580s (Beard, 1990).

In the second half of the 17th century bathrooms were beginning to be installed in grand properties, but they were still rare. During the 1670s a luxury *appartement de bains* was fitted at Versailles for Madame de Montespan, the king's mistress. In Britain, at a slightly later date, the Duchess of Lauderdale was busy developing the amenities at Ham House in Surrey and a small bathroom was installed which could be approached from her bedchamber via a spiral staircase. This was, however, a modest affair compared with the one constructed at Chatsworth House in Derbyshire which was probably there to impress visitors as much as anything else. Celia Fiennes noted in her journal that the room was luxuriously furnished with marble and had a white marble bath big enough for two people. Yet such rooms were definitely the exception rather than the rule and the bathroom as we know it did not make its appearance until well into the 19th century. The technology to raise water above ground level was available, but architects building country houses, in Britain at least, did not install running water above the ground floor; "cheap labour was available to transport water to all parts of the house and cold baths were regarded as efficacious to health" (Beard, 1990).

By the end of the medieval period most houses of any significance in Britain and on the Continent had primitive drainage systems of some sort to deal with the disposal of night soil. Small privies on upper floors were often connected by chute to the basement area and thence to an underground cesspool. Chamber pots were, however, extensively used by the more important members of a household, brought and taken away by servants and often kept in the pantry when not in use. The close stool was a more substantial alternative and consisted of a type of box with a lid which opened to reveal a ring-like seat over a fitted pan. In general they were relatively simple in terms of their form and construction but occasionally they could be more luxurious: an inlaid version is recorded at Hardwick Hall and a red velvet-covered example at Hampton Court. They are frequently mentioned in inventories from the period and seem to have been associated with, although not located in, bedchambers. At Bolsover Castle, Derbyshire, close stool rooms were located in corner turrets; at Ham House the same type of room could be found in small cubby holes behind wall hangings in two of the antechambers; at Petworth House the close stool rooms were located off a staircase. In France the small rooms which housed close stools were known as *garde robes*, which translated into English means wardrobe, literally rooms in which household effects were stored. On both sides of the channel these little rooms were the forerunners of the lavatory as we know it today and in France the term *garde robe* is still used to identify the room containing the toilet. Plumbed toilets with a flushing system were not introduced into houses until the second half of the 18th century. Toilets incorporating an S-bend filled with water were in use by 1775, following the patenting of such a device by Alexander Cumming, and a flushing water closet operated by a lever at the side was patented by Joseph Bramah in 1778. He installed flushing toilets at Audley End House in Essex in the 1780s using water from tanks installed on the roof. Again, however, progress regarding the installation of flushing toilet systems was slow and they did not become widespread until the second half of the 19th century.

Before 1870 bathing largely took place in a bedroom or dressing room using a receptacle brought in by servants and filled with water in the same way. Sponge bathing, which involved washing oneself with a sponge while standing in a shallow, water-filled tray, was a widespread practice, though hip baths, which allowed partial immersion of the body, provided a popular alternative. During the 19th century portable showers, which consisted of a tent-like structure erected temporarily in the bedroom with a water filled tank above, allowed the person taking the shower to pull a string which released the water which was eventually collected in the tray. It must have been a difficult process to control and an awkward one for the servants to arrange and manage. The development of plumbing technology, which allowed for the installation of a fixed-pipe hot water system, was introduced about 1870, and from this time bathrooms became, increasingly, a permanent feature of many homes in Britain. By 1900 only the smallest of houses in London were without a bathroom and the widespread adoption of this facility was fostered not only by the desire for status and "keeping up with the Jones's", but also by a positive attitude to hygiene and the prevention of ill-health.

Hot water heated in the kitchen area of the house by a solid fuel range could be piped to a reservoir tank in an airing cupboard and fed into wash basins, showers and bath tubs by a piped system with taps. Baths of the shape and type we are familiar with today were plumbed in and made of enamelled cast iron after 1880 and they could be either free-standing on elaborate feet or encased in mahogany. Houses belonging to people from the upper end of the social scale often had, in addition to the bath, plumbed-in shower units which provided horizontal and overhead jets of water.

Initially, bathrooms were created by converting bedroom space and they were relatively spacious rooms. They were looked upon as rooms to be furnished like any other rooms in the house and fireplaces, free-standing furniture including washstands, towel rails and small cupboards, ornamental woodwork, wallpaper, curtains and carpets were all introduced into furnishing schemes. Trade catalogues produced by firms such as Shanks of Barrhead in Glasgow and Doulton of Staffordshire showed spacious bathroom arrangements in their coloured illustrations. Even when bathrooms had become the norm in middle and upper class homes, however, many ladies continued to use their own bedrooms for washing. The Hill House at Helensburgh, in Scotland, designed by Charles Rennie Mackintosh for Mr. and Mrs. Blackie in 1904 and regarded as avant-garde by contemporary standards, had a significant house bathroom with bath and elaborate shower. The bedroom, however, just across the corridor, included a Mackintosh-designed washstand with beaten metal ewer and basin for Mrs. Blackie's use.

Even after the advent of the house bathroom in the 1870s,

it was unusual for the lavatory to be situated in the same room as the washing facilities, and indeed such an arrangement was frowned upon as being unhygienic and inappropriate. The toilet, it was recommended, should continue to be housed in a separate room. Water closets of a kind had been known and used since the end of the 16th century, but it was during the 19th century that the flushing toilet became a common feature of many homes in Britain, coinciding with the introduction of effective systems for the disposal of sewage which were implemented under the Public Health Acts of 1848 and 1870. The washdown toilet pan was developed, refined and patented towards the end of the 19th century and it still functions well at the end of the 20th century; the need for overhead cisterns, however, has long since disappeared as more efficient systems have been developed. While middle-class homes in the developing urban suburbs had bathrooms and toilets installed as a matter of course, many working-class homes went without such amenities until well into the 20th century, and it is only in recent decades that indoor toilets and bathrooms for all sectors of the population have come to be taken for granted.

Towards the end of the 19th century bathrooms shrank in size, and after 1900 they took on the more clearly defined look we recognise today. The elaborate bathroom furnishings of the 1880s were replaced with a simpler, more hygienic look, characterised by white fittings attached to the wall, walls with marble facings or washable tiles, washable wallpaper of tile design and marble tiled, cork or tile designed linoleum. These simpler schemes reflected the functional nature of the bathroom as well as promoting the notion of the hygienic home. In 1904, Hermann Muthesius praised the English for leading the way in the development of bathrooms, pointing out that bathrooms were being taken for granted in the United Kingdom when they were the exception rather than the rule in Germany.

By the middle decades of the 20th century Europe had been overtaken by America in matters of domestic hygiene, and 93.5 per cent of American urban dwellings had running water, 83 per cent had indoor toilets, and 77.5 per cent had bathing facilities by the 1940s. Yet, the provision of such facilities was a comparatively recent phenomenon. Baths had been a rarity in early and mid-19th century private homes and although American architects had begun to include bathrooms and water closets in their house plans during the 1850s and 1860s, their use was restricted to the wealthier sections of society. Andrew Jackson Downing's influential *Architecture of Country Houses* (1850), for example, included bathrooms and water closets in eight of thirteen villa designs whose building costs were estimated at between $4,600 and $14,000, but in only one of the thirteen cottages illustated. His and other pattern books of the period suggest that prosperous families living in rural or suburban areas fared better than their urban counterparts; in 1855 New York had only 1,361 baths to serve a population of 629,904 (Winkler 1989). Many of these baths were made of sheet metal and their surfaces were painted. By the 1870s cast-iron tubs with enamelled interior surfaces were available; the first were produced by the J.L. Mott Iron Works of Mott Haven, New York, in 1873. Mechanical flushing devices for toilets were also introduced during this period and by the late 1880s American manufacturers had perfected the porcelain, free-standing form whose basic design provided the model for many variations still in use today. The increasing popularity of one-piece, built-in baths and sinks towards the end of the century prepared the way for later modern, streamlined American bathrooms.

During the 20th century the bathroom has evolved at a relatively gentle pace and many of the features of bathrooms developed in the early decades of the century are recognisable in those in use today, even in bathrooms that have been recently installed. The concern for bathrooms to be functional and hygienic is as important now as it was in the early 1900s; washable surfaces are still seen as a priority. The variety of ceramic tiling and washable wallpapers available today is staggering, offering the consumer a wide choice of styles to suit personal tastes. It is interesting to note that as the Victorian period has been looked upon more favourably in recent years, so modern bathrooms have taken on a more late 19th century look. The desire for period detailing has given rise to a whole industry concerned with the reproduction of baths and bathroom fittings in the styles of the late 19th century with whirlpool technology available as an optional extra.

J. IAN COX

Further Reading

For a popular and anecdotal social history of bathrooms from ancient times to 1910 see Wright 1960. More detailed accounts relating to bathrooms and sanitary improvements in specific periods appear in Long 1993, and Winkler 1989. Several histories of water closets are also listed below.

Barrett, Helena and John Phillips, *Suburban Style: The British Home, 1840–1960*, London: Macdonald, 1987

Beard, Geoffrey, *The English House Interior*, London and New York: Viking–NationalTrust, 1990

Forty, Adrian, *Objects of Desire: Design and Society, 1750–1980*, London: Thames and Hudson, and New York: Pantheon, 1986

Garrett, Elisabeth Donaghy, *At Home: The American Family, 1750–1870*, New York: Abrams, 1990

Girouard, Mark, *Life in the English Country House: A Social and Architectural History*, New Haven and London: Yale University Press, 1978

Kira, Alexander, *The Bathroom*, New York: Viking, and Harmondsworth: Penguin, 1976

Lambton, Lucinda, *Temples of Convenience*, London: Gordon Fraser, 1978; New York: St. Martin's Press, 1979

Lambton, Lucinda, *Chambers of Delight*, London: Gordon Fraser, 1983

Long, Helen C., *The Edwardian House: The Middle-Class Home in Britain, 1880–1914*, Manchester: Manchester University Press, 1993

Palmer, Roy, *The Water Closet: A New History*, Newton Abbot, Devon: David and Charles, 1973

Reyburn, Wallace, *Flushed With Pride: The Story of Thomas Crapper*, London: Macdonald, 1969; Englewood Cliffs, NJ: Prentice Hall, 1971; reprinted London: Pavilion, 1989

Rudolfsky, Bernard, "Uncleanliness and Ungodliness: A Rapid Survey of Bathing Costumes and Bathroom History" in *Interior Design* (US), June 1984, pp.212–21

Winkler, Gail Caskey and Roger W. Moss, "How the Bathroom Got White Tiles ... and Other Victorian Tales" in *Historic Preservation*, February 1984, pp.33–35

Winkler, Gail Caskey, *The Well-Appointed Bath: Authentic Plans and Fixtures from the Early 1900s*, Washington, DC: Preservation Press, 1989

Wright, Lawrence, *Clean and Decent: The Fascinating History of the Bathroom and the Water Closet*, 1960; revised edition London and Boston: Routledge, 1984

Bauhaus

The German school of the Staatliches Bauhaus was founded in 1919 in Weimar, a town in East Germany. The school's first director was Walter Gropius (1883–1969) and the opening sentence of the Bauhaus manifesto, issued by Gropius in the founding year, set the educational goal: "The ultimate aim of all visual arts is the complete building!"

Throughout its existence (1919–33) the school's program was about bringing together all creative effort into one whole, to reunite all the disciplines of practical art – sculpture, painting, and crafts – as inseparable components of a new architecture. Architects, painters, and sculptors have always been craftsmen in the true sense of the word, hence a thorough training in the crafts was required of all students as the indispensable foundation for artistic production.

Bauhaus students began the course work with the *Vorkurs*, a basic design course of color and form, designed to assess and unleash their creative potential. The *Vorkurs* was unique in the quality of its theoretical teaching and the intellectual rigor with which it examined the essentials of visual experience and artistic creativity. Studio instruction covered architecture, painting, and sculpture, including all branches of the crafts. Students also took craft training, drawing, and painting (this department included the design of furniture and practical articles), and training in science and theory. What made the real difference, however, were the influential instructors Gropius brought to the school, among them Johannes Itten, Lyonel Feininger, Gerhard Marcks, Oskar Schlemmer, Georg Muche, Paul Klee, Wassily Kandinsky, László Moholy-Nagy, and Josef Albers.

Two international events took place at the Bauhaus in Weimar. One was the 1922 Constructivist and Dadaist Congress organized by Theo van Doesburg, a founder-member of the Dutch De Stijl group, with participants including El Lissitzky, Tristan Tzara, and Hans Arp. This confirmed the Bauhaus connections with the European avant-garde. The other event was the 1923 Bauhaus Exhibition which coincided with the annual Werkbund Conference, attended by no fewer than 15,000 people. Attending celebrities included Igor Stravinsky, and lectures were given by Gropius, Kandinsky, and J.J.P. Oud, and Schlemmer's *Triadic Ballet* and *Mechanical Ballet* were performed. The experimental house "am Horn" demonstrated most eloquently the capabilities of the school. Designed by Georg Muche, it was an exercise in the collaboration of the arts and crafts and a prototype of an inexpensive, mass-produced structure using the latest materials: a simple cubic mass framed in steel with a concrete infill. The innovative interiors were carried out entirely by Bauhaus workshops. The lighting fixtures, made in the metal workshops, were designed by Moholy-Nagy and the furniture designed by Marcel Breuer, at the time still a student. His kitchen design (1923) was truly revolutionary – a continuous work-surface with cabinets above and below, following the wall around a corner, and with the main work space in front of a window.

In 1925 the Bauhaus left the building in Weimar, designed in 1904–11 by Henry van de Velde, and moved to Dessau, where the city financed the construction of the school and housing for the instructors. The new building, designed by Walter Gropius in 1925–26, consisted of three wings: a school of design, workshops, and a student dormitory, the first two linked by a bridge over the street. In the bridge were the administrative offices, club rooms, and the office-studio of Professor Gropius. The atmosphere in Dessau was quite different from that at Weimar, and the Gropius building was streamlined, functional, and assertively modern inside and out. In Weimar the crafts lived on in a rejuvenated fashion; in Dessau a new kind of industrial designer was being trained. Now, however, the young masters taught in new ways and introduced new activities; former students were elevated to teaching positions: Herbert Bayer, Marcel Breuer, Hinnerk Scheper, Joost Schmidt, and Gunta Stölzl.

Oddly enough, until 1927 the Bauhaus lacked an architecture department. Gropius initially approached a reluctant Mart Stam, but the chair in architecture was eventually accepted by Hannes Meyer (1889–1954). Meyer's approach was different to that of Gropius. Of a leftist political philosophy, Meyer believed that the architect's job was to better society by designing functional buildings which would improve the condition of the common man. Under Meyer the architecture department assisted Gropius with commissions, including an experimental social housing project in the Torten-Dessau. The rationally planned housing estate was designed with standardized components, manufactured on-site for speed and economy of production and reduced transport costs.

Gropius resigned from the Bauhaus in January 1928 to return to full-time architectural practice. When Mies van der Rohe, his first choice for successor, declined, he named as director Hannes Meyer. Now the Bauhaus workshops conceived designs and products for sale to industry, making inexpensive and mass produced essential items like furniture. Town planning was taught by Ludwig Hilbersheimer (1885–1967). Meyer and Hilbersheimer encouraged the architecture students to concentrate not on a single family home but on the problems of mass housing. Despite the fact that the school, under the leftist Meyer, benefited from the success of the capitalist system and was in a good financial situation, Meyer's Marxism played into the hands of Bauhaus opponents. The Bauhaus in Dessau was accused of becoming a nest of Bolsheviks, and Meyer was forced out of the school, to the satisfaction of his adversaries. Meyer and a collective of loyal students left Germany for the Soviet Union and Meyer remained in Russia until 1936.

Mies van der Rohe (1886–1969) who replaced Meyer in August 1930, believed that architectural training was central to the school's curriculum. He created the department of interior design which combined the furniture, metal, and mural painting workshops, chaired by his collaborator Lilly Reich (1885–1947). In his teaching Mies stressed formal qualities and demanded elegance and aesthetic correctness.

The Nazis accused the school of being cosmopolitan and anti-German, equating Modernism with Communism. The school in Dessau was closed in September 1932 but Mies reopened the Bauhaus in Berlin, hoping to survive on income from patents, patrons, and student fees. When Hitler became Chancellor, Modernism was declared degenerate and all Modernists were banned from public activity. In April 1933, Staatliches Bauhaus finally closed.

Walter Gropius, Marcel Breuer, and Mies van der Rohe had

Bauhaus: Director's Office by Walter Gropius, 1925

considered furniture as integral to a unified architectural concept. Designs such as the *Barcelona* chair and the *Barcelona* ottoman of 1929, the cantilevered *Weissenhof* chair of 1927, the *Brno* chair of 1930, *Tugendhat* chair of 1930, *Wassily* chair of 1925, and the *Cesca* chair of 1927 were initially created within the context of specific interiors. They were included in the Bauhaus buildings of Dessau (1926), in the housing units at the Weissenhofsiedlung (1927), the German Pavilion at the Barcelona International Exhibition of 1929, and in Mies van der Rohe's Villa Tugendhat in Brno, Czechoslovakia (1930). The spatial experience was conceived as continuous, with interior and exterior to be integrated both visually and physically.

In 1925, inspired by the handlebars of his Adler bicycle, Breuer was the first to incorporate resilient tubular steel in the design of chairs with the *Wassily* chair, named after fellow teacher Wassily Kandinsky. The discovery of the chromed steel frame as a primary furniture structure led to further innovation. The pure geometry and clarity of form were achieved with the separation of the supporting and supported elements. Consequently, in line with the Modernist philosophy of honesty of expression and design solution, the furniture was reduced to essentials.

The invention of the cantilever chair, the chair without rear legs, was a symbolic event as well as a technological feat. The continuous loop of the tubular steel frame was a logical result of material properties and production techniques. The lack of legs eliminated all associations with the archetypal chair, the symbolic seat of paternal authority. The abolition of the solid, rooted supports, on which the primeval ruler elevated himself above his subjects, amounted to a democratizing gesture which rejected past hierarchical orders.

At the Weissenhof Siedlung exhibition, Mart Stam first displayed his gas pipe cantilevered side chair S33 of 1926. The chair was initially manufactured by L. & C. Arnold company, then reissued by Gebrüder Thonet. Mies van der Rohe also exhibited a cantilevered chair, Model No. MR 10, later named the *Weissenhof* chair, with steel tubes bent at the front into a coil that exploited the spring principle for resilience. A year later, in 1928, Marcel Breuer produced two more cantilever chairs, the Model No.B 32, named the *Cesca* after his daughter Francesca, and the Model No. B33, a derivative of the Mart Stam Side Chair. The chairs were manufactured by Gebrüder Thonet.

A number of the Bauhaus masters escaped the persecution of the Nazis and emigrated to the United States. Their arrival was prefaced by the 1932 exhibition on the new Internatonal Style, organized by Philip Johnson and Henry-Russell Hitchcock, held at the Museum of Modern Art in New York. This served as a catalyst for American architects to adopt the avant-garde style. Gropius, Breuer, Mies van der Rohe, Hilbersheimer, Moholy-Nagy, Bayer, and Albers settled in America where they profoundly influenced the building arts and their teaching.

While Thonet resumed production of the Bauhaus-era furniture in Europe after World War II, the products were introduced to the United States by Knoll Associates, known since 1957 as Knoll International, through the personal contact of Florence Knoll with Mies van der Rohe who was her professor at the Illinois Institute of Technology in Chicago.

During the 14 years of its existence, the Bauhaus succeeding in unifying the arts, and revolutionizing the world of industrial design and mass production. Never before, and perhaps never since, has there been such emphasis on the coexistence of artist and craftsman, designer and technician.

PETER LIZON

See also Breuer; Gropius; Mies van der Rohe; Modernism; Tubular Steel Furniture

Further Reading

An informative general history of the Bauhaus appears in Whitford 1984; for a discussion of its theories see Naylor 1985.

The Bauhaus: Masters and Students (exhib. cat.), New York: Barry Friedman, 1988

Bayer, Herbert, and Walter and Ise Gropius (editors), *Bauhaus 1919–1928* (exhib. cat.), New York: Metropolitan Museum of Art, 1938, London: Allen and Unwin, 1939; reprinted New York: Museum of Modern Art, and London: Secker and Warburg, 1975

Droste, Magdalena, *Bauhaus, 1919–1933*, Cologne: Taschen, 1990

Experiment Bauhaus (exhib. cat.), Berlin: Bauhaus Dessau, 1988

Franciscono, Marcel, *Walter Gropius and the Creation of the Bauhaus in Weimar: The Ideals and Artistic Theories of its Founding Years*, Urbana: University of Illinois Press, 1971

Hahn, Peter and others (editors), *Bauhaus-Archiv Museum: Sammlungs-katalog*, Berlin: Mann, 1981

Isaacs, Reginald R., *Gropius: An Illustrated Biography of the Creator of the Bauhaus*, Boston: Little Brown, 1991

Naylor, Gillian, *The Bauhaus Reassessed: Sources and Design Theory*, London: Herbert, and New York: Dutton, 1985

Neumann, Eckhard (editor), *Bauhaus and Bauhaus People: Personal Opinions and Recollections*, New York: Van Nostrand Reinhold, and London: Chapman and Hall, 1993

Richard, Lionel, *Encyclopédie du Bauhaus*, Paris: Somogy, 1985

Weltge-Wortmann, Sigrid, *Bauhaus Textiles: Women Artists and the Weaving Workshop*, London: Thames and Hudson, 1993

Whitford, Frank, *Bauhaus*, London: Thames and Hudson, 1984

Whitford, Frank and Julia Engelhardt (editors), *The Bauhaus: Masters and Students by Themselves*, London: Conran Octopus, 1992: Woodstock, NY: Overlook Press, 1993

Wingler, Hans M., *The Bauhaus: Weimar, Dessau, Berlin, Chicago*, 3rd edition Cambridge: Massachusetts Institute of Technology Press, 1976

Beckford, William 1760–1844

British antiquarian and connoisseur

Acutely sensitive to beauty as well as highly intelligent, William Beckford developed a lifelong interest in and knowledge of the arts, which helped to make him one of the most celebrated connoisseurs of his time. He also played an important role in the development of Antiquarianism in the late 18th and early 19th centuries, and the unique interiors that he created at Fonthill show him to have been a pioneer in the revival of Gothic styles of decoration and furnishing.

The circumstances of Beckford's birth and early upbringing made a significant contribution towards the formation of his wide-ranging collections and the settings he devised to show them off. As the sole heir to great wealth he was able to satisfy whatever desire he might have: either to acquire beautiful objects, or to erect buildings in which to display them, or to

Beckford: south end of St. Michael's Gallery, Fonthill, from *Graphical and Literary Illustrations of Fonthill Abbey* by John Britton, 1823

landscape the surrounding countryside. The atmosphere of costly magnificence that characterised Fonthill Splendens, his father's Palladian mansion in Wiltshire where he grew up, had a powerful effect on the formation of his own taste. In many ways it presented an ideal to strive to emulate, and at the same time, owing to a streak of perversity in Beckford's nature, something to react against. At first, on his coming of age, he was content to call in the architect John Soane to make small changes to the interiors at Splendens. By the mid-1790s, however, after he had returned from his enforced stay abroad, he decided to create a building in an entirely fresh style which should quite outdo Splendens in grandeur of conception. Over the next two decades, on one of the ridges of the Fonthill estate, he and his architect James Wyatt between them constructed an enormous neo-Gothic country house, Fonthill Abbey.

As its name implies, the Abbey was designed to suggest a monastic pile of the Middle Ages, though adapted to the needs of modern secular living. Like his near contemporary, Horace Walpole, Beckford wanted to incorporate in the interior design of his house faithful imitations of key elements from the late Gothic period: hence the fan vaulting in the Octagon under the central tower, and in three of its great arches the stained glass windows (commissioned from the firm of Francis Eginton and Son) which probably were influenced by Beckford's memory of those he had seen at Batalha Abbey in Portugal. In the two main galleries leading north and south from the Octagon further examples of stained glass and architectural features of Gothic inspiration again helped to reinforce the medieval atmosphere. The fan-vaulted ceiling of St Michael's Gallery, for instance, modelled in stucco, and painted and jointed to resemble stonework, was based directly on that of the Henry VII Chapel in Westminster Abbey.

In his overall scheme for the two galleries, however, Beckford subtly transformed the allusions to the Middle Ages from the religious and monastic to the knightly and chivalrous, with a linked heraldic and genealogical theme which allowed expression of all his most lofty pretensions to rank and his passion for heraldry. St Michael's Gallery was named for the knights of that order, from whom he claimed descent; and the other gallery (named for King Edward III) had at its centre a portrait of the king in his role as founder of the Order of the Garter. Here the arms of Beckford's gartered ancestors (he maintained he could trace his lineage back to John of Gaunt) were represented in the frieze of the entablature, while his own favourite devices of the Latimer cross and the Hamilton cinquefoil adorned the ceiling and formed the pattern of the carpet as well as being repeated even in the carving of the furniture

The whole decorative design – which might otherwise have appeared too severe and formalised – was brought alive by Beckford's individual touch, his flair for theatrical presentation. Since his early days at Splendens he had had a penchant for the exotic effect of brilliant colours. Now he could indulge it, allowing the crimson carpet to vie with the scarlet draperies that framed each of the bookshelf compartments, and setting off the scene with curtains of crimson and royal blue or purple trimmed with gold. At night the drama was heightened when candles were lit along the combined length of the two galleries, and their light reflected back again by the glass in the windows. The chief function of the galleries was to act as libraries, housing Beckford's magnificent collection of books: even here, though, the appearance of the fine calf bindings, stamped with the family crests and the ubiquitous cinquefoil, served a decorative purpose. Indeed the galleries provided a setting not only for his books but for all the other kinds of precious objects in his wide-ranging collection: Old Master paintings, ceramics both European and Oriental, silver and silver gilt, lacquer, ivories, enamels, hardstones mounted in superb metalwork. The cumulative effect was marvellously rich and eclectic, informed by Beckford's talent for securing pieces of quality, whether a priceless medieval chasse from the treasury of St Denis (put up for sale during the French Revolution) or a Florentine *pietre dure* table top which had been brought to Paris by Napoleon as part of the spoils from his Italian campaign.

In providing furniture for the galleries Beckford not only chose genuine antiques, but also commissioned pieces of antiquarian design which would accord with the prevalent late medieval atmosphere, suggesting a return to a vaguely defined point in the past when the Gothic was just giving way to Tudor Renaissance. By way of contrast, however, there was one particular room at the Abbey – the Grand Drawing Room, one of the last to be completed – where the decor and furniture owed inspiration to a single source – France – with superb examples ranging in period from the Rococo to the Neo-Classical, right up to the contemporary style of the First Empire. We owe our detailed knowledge of the layout and appearance of the interiors at the Abbey to the descriptions and illustrations in important books by John Britton and John Rutter which were published in 1823, just after Beckford had taken the decisive step of selling Fonthill to John Farquhar and had retired to Bath.

Although his achievements in Bath during the last twenty years of his life were inevitably on a smaller scale than before, yet the same traits which had been apparent in the decor and design of the monumental apartments at Fonthill Abbey were distinguished by observant visitors such as Henry Lansdown and Dr Waagen who came to admire Beckford's houses in Lansdown Crescent as well as the Neo-Classical Tower he had built at the highest point of his property on the hill behind. Dr Waagen commented on the exquisite taste which characterised the selection and display of the variety of pieces in his collection, while Henry Lansdown noted the effectiveness of Beckford's bold colour schemes and his dramatic use of drapery. In 1844, only a few months after Beckford's death, Edmund English brought out his *Views of Lansdown Tower*, illustrated by lithographs after originals by Willes Maddox. These reveal how the two main reception rooms – the Scarlet Drawing Room and the Crimson Drawing Room – and its two libraries managed to echo in miniature many of the preoccupations with colour and arrangement already seen at Fonthill. Even certain pieces of furniture, such as the chairs of "Fonthill design" depicted in the illustrations, hark back to the earlier period. Beckford, however (as James Lees-Milne has pointed out), would never allow his collections or his ideas about presenting them to remain static. Even in extreme old age he would be found trying out something quite novel, often perverse. As late as 1841 he had sold a number of his choice examples of 18th-century French furniture, to be replaced at the Tower by the cabinets, showcases and sideboards represented in the illustrations. In his correspondence of the time there are references to the creation of these new pieces in collaboration with his architect Goodridge, and directions as to how they should be made up in English's workshop.

Throughout his life Beckford had been in the forefront of taste, particularly with his imaginative reworking of themes from the Middle Ages both in architecture and interior design. He was also an original, imparting to his decorative schemes an individual touch of the theatrical and occasionally outrageous, which he maintained right to the end.

PHILIPPA BISHOP

See also Antiquarianism; Gothic Revival

Biography

Born at Fonthill Splendens, Wiltshire, 29 September 1760, son of the millionaire Alderman Beckford, Lord Mayor of London. Inherited a vast fortune on the death of his father in 1770; educated by private tutors and taught drawing by Alexander Cozens and music by Mozart. Married Lady Margaret Gordon, 1783 (died 1786): two daughters. Lived in Switzerland 1785–86; travelled to Spain and Portugal, 1787. Returned to England and commissioned the building of Fonthill Abbey, Wiltshire, from 1794; retired to Bath and built the Lansdown Tower, 1824–27. Member of Parliament for Wells, 1784–90; for Hindon, 1790–94 and 1806–20. Published several books during the 1780s and 1790s including the novel *Vathek*, 1786. Died in Bath, 2 May 1844.

Principal Works

Much of Beckford's prodigious collection of books, paintings and works of art from Fonthill Abbey was sold in 1823. Full details of the sale appear in Gemmett 1972; several items are now in the Victoria and Albert Museum. Landsown Tower, containing some surviving interiors, is managed by the Bath Preservation Trust. A large collection of Beckford's papers is in the Bodleian Library, Oxford.

Interiors

1788 Fonthill Splendens, Wiltshire (alterations including the picture gallery, tapestry room and parlour executed to designs by Sir John Soane): William Beckford

1794–1812 Fonthill Abbey, Wiltshire (building and interiors, designed by James Wyatt): William Beckford

1824–27 Lansdown Tower, Bath (building and interiors, built by Henry Edmund Goodridge): William Beckford

1824–37 19–20 Lansdown Crescent, Bath (remodelling and decoration of interiors): William Beckford

Publications

Biographical Memoirs of Extraordinary Painters, 1780
Vathek, 1786
Italy, with sketches of Spain and Portugal, 1834

Further Reading

The standard biography of Beckford is Alexander 1962. Detailed views of the interiors at Fonthill Abbey appear in Rutter 1822. For a full, scholarly account of Beckford's collecting habits, both at Fonthill and Lansdown Tower, see Wainwright 1989 which also includes many references to primary and secondary sources. A complete list of Beckford's own writings appears in Lees-Milne 1976.

Alexander, Boyd (editor), *Life at Fonthill 1807–1822*, London: Hart Davis, 1957
Alexander, Boyd, *England's Wealthiest Son: A Study of William Beckford*, London: Centaur Press, 1962
Alexander, Boyd, "William Beckford as Patron" in *Apollo*, July 1962
Alexander, Boyd, "Fonthill, Wiltshire, II" and "Fonthill, Wiltshire, III: The Abbey and its Creator" in *Country Life*, 1 and 8 December 1966
Bishop, Philippa, "Beckford in Bath", in *Bath History*, vol.2, 1988
Brockman, H. A. N., *The Caliph of Fonthill*, London: Laurie, 1956
Chapman, Guy, *Beckford*, 1937, revised edition London: Hart Davis, 1952
Crallan, Hugh, "Beckford's Houses in Bath" in *Architectural Review*, March 1968
English, Edmund, *Views of Lansdown Tower*, 1844
Fothergill, Brian, *Beckford of Fonthill*, London: Faber, 1979
Gemmett, Robert J. (editor), *Sale Catalogues of Libraries of Eminent Persons 3: Poets and Men of Letters*, London: Mansell, 1972
Gemmett, Robert J., *William Beckford*, Boston: Twayne, 1977
Harris, John, "Fonthill, Wiltshire I: Alderman Beckford's Houses" in *Country Life*, 24 November 1966
Lees-Milne, James, *William Beckford*, 1976, reprinted London: Century, 1990
Millington, Jon, *Guide to Beckford's Tower, Bath*, 5th edition, 1986
Oliver, John Walter, *The Life of William Beckford*, London: Oxford University Press, 1932
Rutter, John, *A New Description of Fonthill Abbey and Demesne*, 1822
Rutter, John, *Delineations of Fonthill and its Abbey*, 1823
Snodin, Michael and Malcolm Baker, "William Beckford's Silver" in *Burlington Magazine*, CXXII, 1980, pp.735–48 and 820–34
Wainwright, Clive, "Some Objects from William Beckford's Collection now in the Victoria and Albert Museum" in *Burlington Magazine*, CXIII, 1971, pp.254–64
Wainwright, Clive, *The Romantic Interior: The British Collector at Home, 1750–1850*, New Haven and London: Yale University Press, 1989
Wilton-Ely, John, "The Genesis and Evolution of Fonthill Abbey" in *Architectural History*, XXIII, 1980, pp.40–51

Bedrooms and Bedchambers

Given that human beings spend approximately a third of their lives in bed, it is not surprising to learn that the bedroom has occupied a significant position in the evolution of domestic living space in western culture. Its relative importance as a room within the home has, however, changed over time, and present-day conceptions of the bedroom as a private space for sleeping and intimacy are not always appropriate when considering the history of this room-type.

While bedrooms were a feature of some larger ancient Greek and Roman dwellings, the idea of a separate and distinctive bedroom to house a bed and thus afford a degree of privacy for the occupants does not appear to have occurred in the development of British homes until the mid-16th century. From the end of the medieval period until that time, the more significant members of a household slept in a bed in the corner of a room, or in an alcove. Such a room, known as a chamber, provided the occupant, or occupants, with a little privacy, but the room was essentially a multifunctional one affording accommodation for sitting, relaxing, studying, entertaining and sleeping – a type of bed-sitting room in fact. General purpose rooms of this type were common in the homes of the well-to-do throughout Europe at this time. In Britain, by about 1550, however, there is evidence to suggest bedrooms, or bedchambers as they were known, had come into common usage. Essentially, they represent the further separation of the chamber into the withdrawing chamber and bedchamber, the former a type of private sitting room and the latter a room containing a bed and largely for sleeping in. At Hardwick Hall, Derbyshire, built by Bess of Hardwick at the end of the 16th century, the pattern of important state rooms on the second floor involving the High Great Chamber, Withdrawing Chamber and the best Bed Chamber, reserved for the most important of guests, reflects the development of the bedroom in Britain up to this point in time.

In France the evolution of the bedchamber followed a different path, leading to an end result that was to prove influential abroad. In the early 17th century the French *chambre* was still a type of grand bed-sitting room in important houses, fulfilling all of the functions outlined above. The bed was the most significant item of furniture in the room and was often placed in an alcove. The room giving access to the *chambre* was a type of anteroom for visitors to the *chambre* to wait in before admittance, and leading off the *chambre* there would be a small *cabinet*, which compared with the anteroom was an essentially private room for the principal occupant of the *chambre* containing his or her most personal possessions. This suite of rooms, often directly linked to an important *salle* or saloon that fulfilled many of the functions of the hall in great English houses, gave rise to the so-called French apartment system that was closely linked to patterns of formal social behaviour established at the French court by Louis XIV at Versailles. In this system, the bedchamber became the innermost formal room of reception, and high-ranking individuals received visitors while in bed. The *coucher* and *levée* of the king were significant social rituals involving responsibilities designated to favoured courtiers. Tasks such as presenting the king with his night cap, conferred privilege and status on the person who carried out these duties and some responsibilities were regarded as more important than others. Such a system of access to the apartment and the bedchamber also conferred considerable importance on the bedroom as a room of reception and this was reflected in the elaborate schemes of decoration developed to reflect its position in the formal sequence of rooms.

The Continental apartment system developed in France influenced the evolution of the bedroom as a distinct room

Bedrooms: Blue Bedroom, Hardwick Hall, Derbyshire, late 16th century

with formal social functions in Britain, especially after the restoration of the monarchy in 1660. Here the bedchamber in important houses was always less public than it was in France, but in aristocratic circles French conventions were followed and in a number of the royal palaces bedrooms were established in the French manner with the bed strategically placed behind a balustrade. Surviving records indicate Charles II operated a system of privileged access to state bedrooms along the lines of the system practised in France. The majority of bedrooms established in this manner have long since disappeared, but an interesting example survives at Powys Castle in Wales, where the state bedroom was decorated for Charles II in about 1665.

The formal apartment system involving a suite of rooms leading off a central reception room influenced the development of house plans in Britain in the latter part of the 17th century. Good examples of this kind of arrangement can be seen today at Ham House in Surrey and at Hopetoun House in Scotland, although it must be stressed that the functions of these rooms and their furnishings have changed since their original designation. Not surprisingly, important bedrooms of this type were decorated lavishly with furnishings reflecting the importance of the rooms as rooms of reception. Beds had become highly prized pieces of furniture during the 16th century, as aristocratic life became more static. During the 17th century this tradition continued as architects and upholsterers chose to emphasise the bed as the focal point of a bedroom, giving the frame an architectural flavour and providing rich and expensive sets of hangings and covers. Most beds now stood with the head against the wall and the decorative treatment of the bed often influenced the decoration of an entire bedchamber, which tended to be furnished and decorated in a lavish but formal way with expensive suites of furniture consisting of chairs and stools lined up against the walls. Even in bedrooms that did not quite fit the state apartment category, beds were highly prized pieces of furniture with costly sets of hangings.

In the 18th century, in Britain at least, the nature of country house life changed and the important members of a household spent more of their time in designated public rooms and less time in apartments. The consequences of this change in social behaviour had repercussions for the planning of room layouts in country houses. More emphasis was given to the public rooms, and as a result the apartment diminished in significance, although it did not die out altogether. Instead, the apartment tended to evolve into a small suite of rooms involving a dressing room, bedroom and possibly a small closet. Apartments for important guests might involve two dressing rooms, one for the gentleman and one for the lady. Bedrooms thus became increasingly rooms for sleeping and intimacy, and the dressing room, often furnished as a sitting room or study, provided accommodation for social rituals associated with the toilet, getting dressed or preparing for bed.

Bedrooms were, by this time, becoming more private spaces and this is reflected in the number of bedrooms to be found on the first floor of houses built or developed during this period. State apartments could, however, still be found on the ground floor and a state bedroom might still be located at the end of an *enfilade*. The state apartments at Hopetoun House, designed by William Adam and decorated by his son John in the 1750s, culminated in an important state bedroom with dressing room attached; the focus of the main room was still a lavishly upholstered and draped state bed. By about 1770, however, state apartments organised along traditional lines were going out of fashion and state apartment rooms were being redecorated and furnished to provide the types of rooms that were in demand. Many ground floor state bedrooms thus changed function and what had been important state beds were removed to bedrooms upstairs. The state bed at Wimpole Hall, Cambridgeshire, was taken upstairs in 1781, and the same thing happened at Petworth in Sussex at about the same time. At Hopetoun the state bedroom was converted to a dining room at the beginning of the 19th century. By the end of the 18th century bedrooms, even the best ones, were nearly always located upstairs, and the bed, although still usually a four-poster with hangings, had declined in importance as a status symbol. Bedrooms had become rooms for sleeping in and they were furnished accordingly.

In the 18th century urban town house bedrooms were more often than not located on the first and second floors and beds were often placed in alcoves let into one wall. Plans and extant examples relating to town houses in London, illustrating this type of arrangement, survive to the present day, and it is interesting to see the continuing evolution of a practice that originated in medieval times. By the end of the 18th century bedrooms in homes at the upper end of the social scale were furnished comfortably with carpets and curtains and the most precious item of furniture (despite that fact that it was no longer the most important of status symbols) was still the four-poster bed with its related hangings. Both Chippendale and Sheraton included designs for beds in their influential pattern books. A gentleman's bedroom in a small town house of the period would probably have also contained items of furniture such as a mahogany clothes press, a dressing table and a cabinet which would have opened to reveal emplacements for a ewer and basin and a sliding shaving mirror.

In both town and country houses, the practice of locating bedrooms on the upper floors continued throughout the 19th century. The principal bedroom was normally located on the first floor and the 18th century practice of placing dressing rooms nearby continued. Increasingly the bedroom became the domain of the lady of the household, and although married couples still slept together, it was normal for the gentleman's dressing room to adjoin the main bedroom. There was also a growing tendency to site children's bedrooms near that of their parents when space permitted, although in town houses children's bedrooms had to be located on the floor above. In large houses there were separate corridors for the bedrooms of bachelor and lady guests. As guests were now expected to spend more of their time in the public areas of a house, these bedrooms were furnished with a desk and comfortable chairs in addition to the usual bedroom furniture but they were not expected to function as sitting rooms.

During the first half of the 19th century concern for the provision of a hygienic sleeping environment became manifest, a response to the large numbers of deaths caused by infectious diseases such as cholera. Bedrooms were perceived as possible havens of infection and there was a corresponding tendency to furnish them simply, a trend that was to develop as the century progressed. During the early decades of the century the bed was still of the four-poster variety, though half-tester beds where the canopy extended halfway down the length of the bed, also became popular. As health concerns came to the fore, beds of this type began to be replaced by metal bedsteads and by the 1870s four-posters and half-testers had become less desirable and were regarded as old-fashioned.

Many of the manuals of household taste – books of advice published for the edification of the female homemaker – made recommendations about the types of fabric which should be used for drapes, curtains and covers for the bed, and self-patterned cottons combined with lace were popular choices. Wallpapers were also common with an emphasis upon small, retiring patterns that would not hinder rest. Furniture for the bedrooms tended to be on the plain side compared with the heavily ornamented furniture found in downstairs rooms; a large wardrobe combined with a chest of drawers and a wash-stand, plus a couple of chairs would have generally sufficed. The wardrobe was often the largest piece of furniture in the room and was often constructed in three sections, one third of the space being for hanging and two thirds for underclothes and accessories. The door to the central compartment usually contained a mirror on the outside for dressing purposes. Mahogany was popular for bedroom furniture, but oak was also selected and indeed recommended by design reformers such as Charles Eastlake in his *Hints on Household Taste* (1868).

As bathrooms were still scarce, the washstand was an important item and many had marble tops and tiled backs to facilitate wiping down. Members of the household often washed in the bedroom or dressing room, so ceramic toilet sets were ubiquitous in these rooms. Eventually the washstand was replaced in many middle and upper class homes with a plumbed-in wash basin perhaps located in the corner of the room. Again, in an attempt to keep dust levels down and to promote a healthier environment, bedroom floorboards were scrubbed, swept and left uncarpeted, although rugs and carpet squares were used extensively to enhance the comfort of the room. Suites of matching bedroom furnishings designed in a variety of styles including the Queen Anne and Japanese were available from commercial manufacturers from the 1880s. And, towards the end of the century, furnishings became simpler still: it was not uncommon for bedrooms in progressive households to be painted white, a sure way of allowing accumulations of dust to be noted. Fitted furniture also became popular from about 1880 and was promoted by arbiters of taste such as R.W. Edis as being space-saving and hygienic. Hermann Muthesius noted the presence of fitted, built-in bedroom cupboards and dressing tables in many of the late 19th century houses that he visited and commented on their value in providing useful storage space, thereby helping to eliminate clutter (*The English House*, 1904). The same author summed up the character of the typical turn-of-the-century bedroom by noting that ideally it should foster a healthy environment but at the same time provide a room that the lady of the house could use as a private retreat in the absence of a boudoir.

In many ways the 20th century has seen few dramatic or overall changes in the evolution of the bedroom as a room type. Bedrooms have, however, tended to become smaller in size and fewer in number as the average family size has declined and separate dressing rooms have until recently all but disappeared. Styles of decoration and furnishing have altered as a variety of waves of popular taste have all had their effect on this room. As standards of living have risen in the post-war period, increasing amounts of disposable income have been expended on the decoration and furnishing of this type of domestic space. Particularly noticeable in recent years has been the fashion for "retro" styles, especially Victorian styles, and bedroom decoration has been much influenced by designer retailers such as Laura Ashley. Even in the 1990s, the fashion for bedroom furniture made from pine with complementary polished floorboards, rugs and chintz co-ordinated soft furnishings does not look like fading. It is interesting, however, that the country or vernacular look has not ousted the desire for comfort, and many contemporary bedrooms are centrally heated. In the same vein new house specifications are including master bedrooms with walk-in wardrobes and separate dressing rooms, sure signs not only of *fin de siècle* luxury but also another example of a revival of a custom that went out of fashion in the early part of the century.

J. IAN COX

See also Beds; State Apartments; State Beds

Further Reading

Barker, Lady, *The Bedroom and Boudoir*, 1878; reprinted with *The Drawing-Room* by Lucy Orrinsmith and *The Dining Room* by M.J. Loftie, New York: Garland, 1978

Conran, Terence, *The Bed and Bath Book*, London: Mitchell Beazley, and New York: Crown, 1978

Cruickshank, Dan and Neil Burton, *Life in the Georgian City*, New York and London: Viking, 1990

Eastlake, Charles Locke, *Hints on Household Taste in Furniture, Upholstery and other Details*, 1868, 4th edition 1877

Franklin, Jill, *The Gentleman's Country House and its Plan, 1835–1914*, London: Routledge, 1981

Garrett, Elisabeth Donaghy, *At Home: The American Family, 1750–1870*, New York: Abrams, 1990

Gilliam, Jan Kirsten and Betty Crowe Leviner, *Furnishing Williamsburg's Historic Buildings*, Williamsburg, VA: Colonial Williamsburg Foundation, 1991

Girouard, Mark, *Life in the English Country House: A Social and Architectural History*, New Haven and London: Yale University Press, 1978

Harris, Eileen, *Going to Bed* (The Arts and Living series), London: Victoria and Albert Museum, 1981

Irvine, Susan, *Laura Ashley Bedrooms*, London: Weidenfeld and Nicolson, 1987

Jackson-Stops, Gervase and James Pipkin, "Bedchambers" in their *The English Country House: A Grand Tour*, London: Weidenfeld and Nicolson, 1984; Boston: Little Brown, 1985

Kisluk-Grosheide, Danielle O., "A State Bedchamber in the Metropolitan Museum of Art" in *Magazine Antiques*, 133, March 1988, pp.662–67

Mayhew, Edgar de Noailles and Minor Myers, Jr., *A Documentary History of American Interiors from the Colonial Era to 1915*, New York: Scribner, 1980

Muthesius, Hermann, *The English House*, edited by Dennis Sharp, London: Crosby Lockwood Staples, and New York: Rizzoli, 1979 (German original 3 vols., 1904–05, revised edition 1908–11)

Osband, Linda, *Victorian House Style: An Architectural and Interior Design Source Book*, Newton Abbot: David and Charles, and New York: Sterling, 1991

Rivers, Tony and others, *The Name of the Room: A History of the British House and Home*, London: BBC Publications, 1992

Thornton, Peter, *Seventeenth-Century Interior Decoration in England, France, and Holland*, New Haven and London: Yale University Press, 1978

Thornton, Peter, *Authentic Decor: The Domestic Interior, 1620–1920*, London: Weidenfeld and Nicolson, and New York: Viking, 1984

Thornton, Peter, *The Italian Renaissance Interior, 1400–1600*, London: Weidenfeld and Nicolson, and New York: Abrams, 1991

Wright, Lawrence, *Warm and Snug: The History of the Bed*, London: Routledge, 1962

Beds

Beds in their simplest form are just raised platforms designed to support a reclining body. As old as the chair, they have also gone through an astonishing number of variations on the basic theme. In addition to reflecting the generally prevailing tastes of a period, they have also been associated with particular styles of textile draperies or added detail while the essential sleeping platform has substantially remained the same.

In ancient Egypt, beds were initially crude wooden frames lashed together, developing into sophisticated jointed frames, complete with a proper suspension system of leather thongs. These Egyptian beds were supported on short legs, usually in the form of a bull's foot and were often supplied with a separate head-rest, as headboards were uncommon. Examples of royal furniture have survived and demonstrate a high degree of design sophistication. The gold-covered canopy for Queen Hetepheres illustrates this. Designed as a simple frame with hooks for net curtains for the top and sides, it could be assembled or dismantled at will.

The Egyptians established type forms for beds that have remained ever since. Along with the simple supporting frame type, and the canopied bed, a version of a folding bed was found in the tomb of Tutankhamun.

In Classical Greece and Rome, the bed developed into a couch which was also used for reclining upon at mealtimes. Styles varied from simple bed platforms made from metal or wood, to sofas with high backs and arms. This style was continued in Byzantine times, often with an architectural emphasis in the design, but by the 12th century important beds were beginning to be furnished with testers and curtains, both for comfort and status.

The use of enclosures continued into the Middle Ages. In Northern Europe it became customary to use curtains and canopies supported in a variety of ways. In simple cases the curtains at the foot end would have been bundled up to give access to the bed as a day couch. In other examples the half tester often extended from the headboard over the bed. In Italy

Beds: Daniel Marot design for state bed with en suite portière, c.1690

it was common for the mattress to be laid on a low dais or floor with storage underneath, although the classical model of a mattress supported by two fulcra remained a type form until the 20th century. The four-poster bed was slowly developed from this type.

During the Renaissance the canopied four-poster bed remained popular, although there were beds with testers suspended from the ceiling, while some were fitted with a headboard instead. Until the mid-16th century fabrics had been important as decoration, and any woodwork was left rough and unfinished. After this time a taste for less fabric and more decorative exposed woodwork developed. Elaborately carved pillars and headboards reflect this change. The famous example of the Great Bed of Ware demonstrates the taste for detailed carving combined with inlaid panels at the headboard completed with a carved tester. Although often called four-poster beds, this name is not always an accurate description, as often the beds would be supported upon only two posts and a headboard.

In grand houses across Europe the state bed or *lit de parade* took an important position within the room, and it was usually the case that this bed was rarely slept in. Although the concept of state beds was ceremonial rather than functional, their designs were to have an influence on the style of ordinary beds. It was often the case that the architect responsible for the house interior would also have created the design for the state bed. Daniel Marot was known for his extravagant designs for beds, and the example of the State Bed at Melville (now in the Victoria and Albert Museum) appears to derive from his ideas.

The latter part of the 17th century saw the development of an informal bed type which contrasted greatly with the state bed of the period. These fantasy beds, which seem to have been designed for intimate rooms, were highly decorated with amazing drapery, inset mirrors and papier-mâché decoration. The Trianon de Porcelaine in Versailles (c.1670) had two examples of these fantasies.

For other situations box beds remained popular, as they were often built into the fabric of the house. This was often a sensible solution in cottages and farmhouses, where draughts and cold were frequent and fabric was scarce. However, they were not found only in the poorer homes since panelled bedrooms in well-to-do Netherlandish homes were themselves often furnished with this built-in form.

During the 18th century it was often the practice for husband and wife to use separate bedrooms. It became customary for the lady of the house to hold court in a more sumptuous room than her husband's; he would often sleep in a less attractive room. This meant a return to models based on stately examples. Beds became extremely tall and exuberant, surmounted by testers with most of the woodwork covered with fabric.

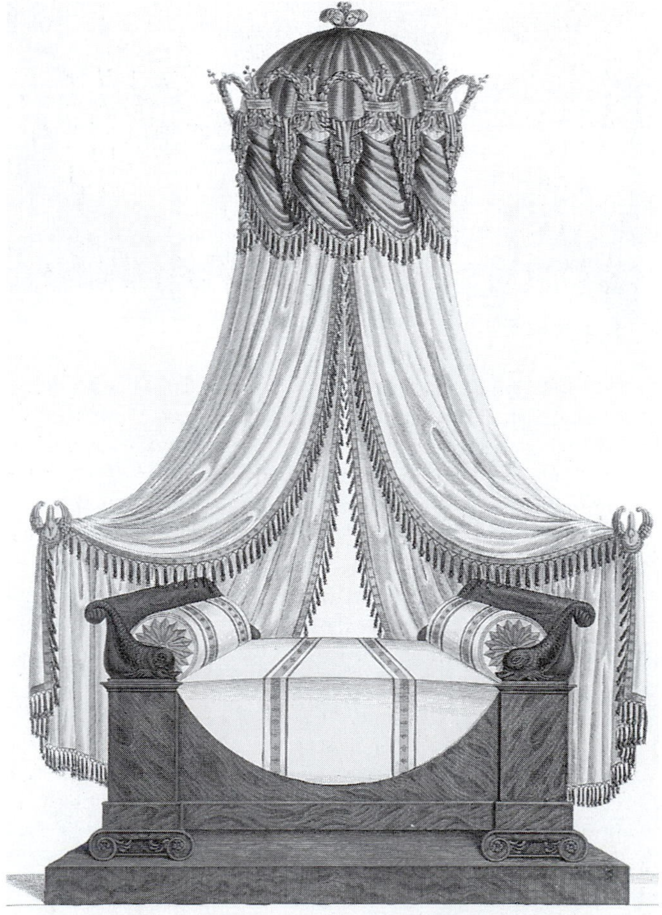

Beds: French canopied bed, *lit à dome*, 19th century

Beds: bedroom with metal bedstead designed by Liberty, London, 1890s

The differences between French and English styles continued throughout the century. The French preferred a box-like finish and shape, while the English influence was towards a domed top, ornamental valances and hangings that altered the essentially square shape of the frame. In either case, though, beds were now hung with expensive fabrics, and were more the realm of the upholsterers' art than the carvers'.

Many of the pattern books of the 18th century illustrate a variety of beds. The British upholsterers Ince and Mayhew produced some extravagant suggestions for Rococo beds, while John Linnell drew sketches of state beds. Thomas Chippendale supplied beds in all the fashionable styles: Dumfries House has a Rococo-style bed; Nostell Priory boasts a Neo-Classical bedstead, while the 1762 edition of the *Director* included designs for Chinese-style bedsteads. Chippendale's work for Harewood House demonstrates the unified theme where the bedstead has en suite window cornices to match the bed frame. Robert Adam's executed designs include an astonishing concoction devised for the re-modelled Osterley Park. It was criticised by Horace Walpole as being "too like a modern head-dress". In contrast, George Hepplewhite showed elegant bedsteads with restrained drapery combined with slender carved or reeded wooden posts. Altogether lighter in construction, the canopy itself was often pierced and carved. In another vein, Thomas Sheraton devised beds as various as a fascinating summer bed for a couple, and a design for a Grecian bed, complete with curtains and drapes.

Other bed designs continued the French taste for fabric dressing. These included the *lit à la polonaise* and the *lit à la turque*, often set into niches in panelled rooms, especially in France. The *lit à la polonaise* used curved iron supports which formed a fabric-covered dome and supports which could stand alone or be set into an alcove. The *lit à la duchesse* had a fabric tester attached at the back to the wall or ceiling which then extended the full length of the bed with no other support, whereas the earlier design called a *lit d'ange* used a flying tester or canopy which was smaller than the bed. The corona developed from this and has been a feature of bedrooms ever since. The French influence extended to *lits à l'anglaise* which had a three-sided level frame. This was designed for an alcove,

Beds: foam slab bed by George Nelson, 1950s

whereas the *lit de bateau* had just the two ends the same height.

The contemporary interest in mechanical furniture included beds, and a number of versions of hidden beds were devised. Some, like the one supplied to David Garrick's Hampton villa, had a mirror front and were painted to be en suite with cabinets. Others were less exotic and at their lowest level acted as folding beds for servants' rooms. Nevertheless many well-known makers produced this press bed form. The idea also developed into beds that were concealed as chests, library bookcases, and cabinets. A clear need for space-saving, as well as a taste for the metamorphic produced a whole range of folding beds, field beds and tent beds, many of which were ingeniously designed to be not only easily foldable but also portable.

During the 19th century, decorators and designers often looked to the past and introduced revivals of styles for interiors. Beds were no exception. In the early years of the century the influence of the Empire style continued to be felt through the works of designers such as Percier and Fontaine. During the 1820s there began to be a demand for Gothic designs, and in pattern books such as Nicholson's Practical Cabinet Maker, Upholsterer and Complete Decorator (1826), designs of four-poster beds are offered in both the Gothic and the Greek taste. The four-poster was giving way to the half- tester bed in a variety of designs. Some were Gothic with wooden frames and drapery, others were simply frames decorated with chintz dressings. Although generically called Arabian bedsteads, there were many variations. The famous Speaker's bed in the Palace of Westminster is an example.

During the 19th century demand for both hygiene and space-saving meant further developments in bed design. During the 1851 Exhibition, a number of iron bedsteads were displayed, some of which were fanciful reproductions while others were simply functional. The use of iron and brass for bed frames encouraged an elegant simplicity that has been revived in the latter part of the 20th century. Although initially produced from black painted iron, by the 1870s the metal bed was made from brass-sheathed iron which, with brass accessories, meant a much more attractive finish was obtainable. The idea of a full, or even half-tester, had nearly disappeared and was often replaced with hinged side screens which had thin muslin draped over.

The notion of a bedroom suite became popular, with bed frames being designed to match wardrobes and dressing tables. In America and Europe the wooden bed was revived. It might be with a elaborate headboard in a choice of styles or it could reflect other developments such as the Belter shaping method. In many cases the head and footboards were connected by iron rails which supported a bed frame and spring mattress. This mattress was a great advance on the various fillings that had been previously available.

Although brass remained popular, the revival of wooden beds was encouraged in part by the Arts and Crafts movement in England and America. The efforts of design reformers such as William Morris as well as retailers like Liberty and Co., Heal's and others, meant that there was a place for the simple oak bedstead. This demand resulted from the desire to integrate beds into a unified scheme. If not of plain wood, they might be painted in simple colours. The examples designed by Carl Larsson in Sweden and Charles Rennie Mackintosh in Glasgow bear witness to this style. In some case the beds were art works in their own right. William Burges's painted bed or the products of the Omega workshops illustrate this trend.

In the 20th century beds followed changing fashions. Art Nouveau produced bedsteads with swirling carvings or pictorial inlays. Art Deco's exotic creations ranged from Eileen Gray's lacquered boat bed, to steel and glass beds. Contrary to this display, the Modernists encouraged bed design in tubular metal utilitarian designs. Towards the end of this century the range of beds and bedsteads has increased widely to meet demands for stylistic variety. These have included frames of coloured aluminium, lacquer, plastic, metal, and wood, while electric beds, as well as water beds now have a place in the domestic bedroom. Changes in lifestyle have also meant that space-saving has once again become a consideration in bed-sits and flats so that the Japanese-inspired futon, the bunk bed, as well as convertible sofa-beds have found a ready market.

CLIVE D. EDWARDS

See also Bedrooms and Bedchambers; State Beds

Further Reading

An introductory survey of the history of Beds appears in Sparkes 1990 and a longer, more anecdotal, account is provided by Wright 1962. For information relating to specific types of beds see the specialised references below.

Beldegreen, Alecia, *The Bed*, New York: Stewart Tabori and Chang, 1991

Boynton, Lindsay O.J., "The Bed Bug and the Age of Elegance" in *Furniture History*, I, 1963, pp.13–31

Conran, Terence, *The Bed and Bath Book*, London: Mitchell Beazley, and New York: Crown, 1978

Eames, Penelope, *Furniture in England, France and the Netherlands from the Twelfth to the Fifteenth Century*, London: Furniture History Society, 1977

Edwards, Clive, "Press Bedsteads" in *Furniture History*, 26, pp.42–52

Harris, Eileen, *Going to Bed* (The Arts and Living series), London: Victoria and Albert Museum, 1981

Juin, Hubert, *Le Lit*, Paris: Hachette, 1980

MacQuoid, Percy and Ralph Edwards, *The Dictionary of English Furniture*, revised edition, 3 vols., 1954; reprinted Woodbridge, Suffolk: Antique Collectors' Club, 1983

Mehlman, F., "Brass and Iron Bedsteads" in *Antique Collector*, 51, January 1980, pp.46–49

Reynolds, Reginald, *Beds: With Many Noteworthy Instances of Lying On, Under or About Them*, New York: Doubleday, 1951; London: Deutsch, 1952

Sparkes, Ivan G., *Four-Poster and Tester Beds*, Princes Risborough: Shire, 1990

Thornton, Peter, "French Beds" in *Apollo*, March 1974, pp.182–85

Thornton, Peter, *Seventeenth-Century Interior Decoration in England, France, and Holland*, New Haven and London: Yale University Press, 1978

Thornton, Peter, "Beds, Canopies and the Lettuccio" in *The Italian Renaissance Interior, 1400–1600*, London: Weidenfeld and Nicolson, and New York: Abrams, 1991, pp.111–67

Wright, Lawrence, *Warm and Snug: The History of the Bed*, London: Routledge, 1962

Bed-sits

The existence of "digs", small rooms for couples and single-occupancy tenancies, has been a feature of the British rental housing market since the late 19th century with studios and one-room flats proliferating in the first decades of the 20th century. In post-war Britain, however, it was the need for rented accommodation among the recently arriving influx of foreign immigrants and for the new "youth" market that fuelled the classic phase of the growth of what has been termed "Bed-sitland". Although initially there were heavy concentrations of immigrants in Britain in the West Midlands and Bradford as well as a few other urban centres, almost a third of all immigrants arriving in the country after World War II settled in London. For such groups, unable to buy into the private housing market without capital, renting was the only option. Added to this, the renting of unfurnished accommodation lay beyond the pockets of the vast majority of immigrants.

Furnished accommodation in the form of single-room bed-sits tended to be centred in the inner city areas. In London's bed-sitland, the shared housing of digs and rooms was to become home to thousands of families. By using old, and now very often dilapidated housing stock, landlords also found that there were quick profits to be made from exploiting the very needy. A report in the *Kensington News* of 31 October 1958 commented on the Institute for Race Relations' Wickenden Report of the same year noting that, "during the period of a year nearly 70 companies were set up in North Kensington which let high-rented, over-crowded homes to coloured immigrants". Although attempts were made to curb the worst exploitative practices in London, by the London County Council for example, interviews conducted subsequently reveal that most tenants in rented rooms felt extremely insecure, the law allowing little or no protection against sudden eviction.

The psychological discomfort of bed-sit living for many immigrants and low-income tenants was matched by very poor physical standards of living. So flimsy was the re-structuring of earlier larger interiors that privacy was a particular problem. Furnished lets were not all subject to a regulated layout and the necessity of sharing cooking, washing and bathing facilities exacerbated the situation. Cheaply constructed partitions and poor facilities were matched, for the vast majority of tenants, by gloomy, drab decor. The cheapest wallpapers and linoleum were the best to be expected. Vagaries of tenancy rights meant that brightening up accommodation was either not permitted or simply not worth the effort with the result that many residents put up with whatever furniture and decorations the landlord had used. One interviewee remembers the standard West Kensington rented room as comprising a double bed, dressing table, Formica-topped table, two or three chairs, a wardrobe and a cot if you were lucky. Clothes were mainly kept in a suitcase and furniture was "second-hand and very shabby" (MacDonald and Porter, 1991).

In complete contrast to the furnished rooms inhabited by Britain's growing immigrant population was the bed-sitland of the 1950s and 1960s bachelor and single girl. Just as socio-economic trends in post-war Britain, and particularly the need for cheap labour, had encouraged immigration from abroad, so socio-economic patterns were associated with the rise in importance of the nation's youth population which, in turn, had a marked impact on housing patterns. A gradual reduction in family size in the years up to 1939, and the experiences of World War II (evacuation was especially significant), combined by the 1950s to give children greater freedom and to open up new possibilities. Post-war economic conditions provided many of the same children with new opportunities as young adults. Increased spending power created by the new technological high-wage society of the 1950s and 1960s produced a new group of young men and women whose affluence, for a while at least, fed back into the system that had helped to create them.

Like Pop music and the new youth fashion industry, the trend towards bed-sit living for the middle classes grew out of a whole new youth culture and at the same time depended upon the spending power of the affluent teenager and young working person. Leaving home to live independently expressed a need for autonomy, freedom, and a move away from the confines of traditional family living. Yet, like music and fashion, the bed-sit phenomenon was quickly assimilated into the mainstream and became a topic of considerable interest within the commercial sector and was the subject of much "how-to-do-it" advice from writers within the design establishment and home-interest journals.

A somewhat prescriptive attitude to interior design had already been adopted by bodies like the Council of Industrial Design (CoID) in official exhibitions such as *Britain Can Make It* (1946), and the Festival of Britain of 1951. A few years later, magazine articles and books devoted to the subject of bed-sit living began to proliferate. Indeed, so popular was writing on single-room living for the more affluent young person that it is possible to trace the history of their decoration and furnishing through such material. For the "single woman's bed-sit room in a block of flats" the CoID's *Furnishing to Fit the Family* (1947) advocated "the skilful use of built-in cupboards in walnut panelling on either side of the fireplace". Unit furniture also features very prominently and the CoID's author has the imaginary occupant sensibly insisting on "as little free standing furniture as possible" as well as a "fresh, light" colour to maximise a spacious atmosphere.

The important distinction between these kinds of bed-sits and the more traditional one-room tenancies was the emphasis upon newness, smartness and modernity. In place of the hand-me-down furnishings and make-do arrangements of low-income rentals, there was a stress on neat, compact living provided by new fitted and unit furnishings, and bright, co-ordinated textiles and wallpapers. "One-room living for Sandy and Jane is well ordered; their furniture divides the room into neat areas for eating, sleeping, cooking" ran a feature in a 1959 *Woman* magazine article. And the 1976 book, *Living in One Room* continued this theme: "Living in one room is becoming by necessity, a way of life for more and more people. And if the prospect doesn't inspire visions of comfort and space, the ideas in this book will. Open out the closet, get the sleeping space off the floor, have the storage disappear ... with foresight and planning you can keep pets, plants, even a roommate and still have an area for yourself". The increasing associations of bed-sit living with fashionable, youthful, urban lifestyles also meant that its design and decoration were often linked to modern youth, or alternative styles. Pop furnishings, such as blow-up chairs, bean-bags and brightly coloured posters were popular items in the 1960s and early 1970s, while futons and sofa-beds have become the fashionable adjuncts of bed-sits in more recent years.

HARRIET DOVER

Further Reading

Conran, Terence, *Terence Conran's New House Book*, London: Conran Octopus, and New York: Villard, 1985

MacDonald, Sally and Julia Porter, *Putting on the Style: Setting up Home in the 1950s* (exhib. cat.), London: Geffrye Museum, 1990

Marwick, Arthur, *British Society since 1945*, London: Allen Lane, 1982; 2nd edition Harmondsworth: Penguin, 1990

Naar, Jon and Molly Siple, *Living in One Room*, New York: Random House, 1976

Rivers, Tony and others, *The Name of the Room: A History of the British House and Home*, London: BBC Publications, 1992

Timmers, Margaret and others, *The Way We Live Now: Design for Interiors, 1950 to the Present* (exhib. cat.), London: Victoria and Albert Museum, 1979

Behrens, Peter 1868–1940

German architect and designer

After a first career as an artist, Peter Behrens was initially a leading figure in the Art Nouveau and Arts and Crafts movements. His early paintings concentrated on landscape, but in the 1890s he depicted modern industrial scenes. A little later he painted more Symbolist subjects, and made a speciality of woodcuts; his large coloured woodcut, *The Kiss* (1898), has become one of the best-known images of the Art Nouveau style. Like many of his generation, Behrens was drawn into applied art through a varied series of commissions to design lettering, porcelain, glass, cutlery jewellery, furniture and even so-called "reformed" dress for women. Gradually his activity as a painter declined.

Behrens exhibited applied art in Darmstadt in 1899, and received an invitation to join The Seven, a community of artists who were brought together under the patronage of the Grand-Duke Ernest-Ludwig II of Hesse. The aim was to establish Darmstadt as the leading centre of artistic activity in the field of architecture and design in Germany. Behrens took a prominent part in the exhibition which opened there in 1901 and which included the houses on the Mathildenhöhe which were at once the residences of the seven artists, and exhibits in themselves of a modern way of living. He designed his own house, the only one of the colony not by the Viennese architect Joseph Maria Olbrich.

The success of the Darmstadt artists' colony led to Behrens becoming Director of the School of Applied Arts in Düsseldorf in 1903, and he was given commissions to design a number of interiors for exhibitions – in Turin and Düsseldorf – and for important rooms in Hagen, as well as his second house, for Gustav Obenauer in Saarbrücken.

Following further major exhibition projects – for Dresden and Mannheim in 1906 – he was approached by the great electrical combine, the AEG, and engaged as artistic adviser on the design of arc lamps. Within a few years, however, Behrens's activity for the firm expanded to include the design of an enormous range of their products, the brochures and the typography used throughout the combine, their large factories and even the associated housing estates. His Turbine Hall of 1909 has become one of Behrens's best-known industrial works.

In his long and productive subsequent career, Behrens designed many houses, principally those in Hagen for Karl-Ernst Osthaus (1909–12), for Dr. Wiegand in Berlin (1911–12), for W. J. Bassett-Lowke in England (1923–25), and for Clara Gans in the Taunus mountains in 1931. He also

Behrens: dining room, Behrens house, Darmstadt, 1901

designed apartment blocks for Vienna City Council (1924–28), and for the Weissenhofsiedlung in Stuttgart (1926–27). His astonishingly prolific output included headquarters for the Mannesmann company Düsseldorf (1911–12), and for the Hoechst Dyeworks (1920–24), as well as the German Embassy in St. Petersburg (1912). His last project (1939) was a new AEG headquarters for Albert Speer's notorious and never realised *Nord-süd Achse* for Berlin.

Behrens's first house (1900–01) for himself, his wife, and their two children, has three principal rooms on the ground floor. A hall, from which the staircase rises, has wide sliding screens opening from it to a music room, which in turn is interconnected with the dining room through a broad arch. In this way, the whole of the ground floor might be opened up for musical evenings or parties. This open plan has been compared with that of Frank Lloyd Wright's first house at Oak Park, of the same period. The music room, said by Behrens to be the principal apartment of the house, was dark and intense, with armchairs, stools, and benches of black-stained birch, a gilded ceiling "like some old church dome", and blue mirror-glass on the walls which were decorated with red and grey marble. The piers on either side of the entrance to the dining room were decorated with stylised figures like Egyptian goddesses, and the piano, in grey maple, bore the Egyptian motif of spread wings. The floor was lower than that of the adjoining rooms, and the ceiling higher.

In sharp contrast, the dining room had japanned white furniture and panelling, with silver and crystal electric chandeliers suspended from the white ceiling, which was moulded with rhythmically interlaced lines. The carpet and other accents were wine red. Other rooms in the house were also colour-coordinated; the bedroom for Mrs. Behrens was predominantly yellow, and that of Behrens had violet-japanned poplar furnishings.

The Hamburger Vestibühl for the Turin Exhibition of 1902 was a crypt-like interior influenced by the writings of Friedrich Nietzsche, whose book *Also Sprach Zarathustra* was displayed in the room. It was a huge rectangular space surrounded by a massive arcade, which had huge voussoirs and keystones. Cross-vaults supported a flat ceiling pierced with a large rectangular opening, glazed with a yellow opalescent canopy. In the corners, by contrast, blue light filtered down from behind the arcade. Trailing plants hung down over a central, oblong, sunken pool with rounded ends, guarded by kneeling, winged figures in cement.

Following visits to Glasgow and Vienna, Behrens's style became lighter, more rectilinear and geometric, as in the interior of the restaurant Jungbrunnen for the 1904 Düsseldorf Exhibition. Here, and at the Oldenburg Exhibition buildings and at the Haus Obenauer (1905–06), "the admirable, cool spirit of the Greeks" was emulated. The interiors of the Concert Hall, and of the Delmenhorster Linoleumfabrik Pavilion at Dresden in 1906 developed this Neo-Classicism further, using spirals and other decorative motifs from Greek ceramics as flat surface wall patterns. In the sober, formal, sumptuous and rather heavy interiors of the Wiegand House in Dahlem (1911–12) for a client who was a classical archaeologist, this tendency was even more pronounced, with motifs such as a palmette derived from an Apulian painted amphora. The execution of the powerfully classical interiors of the German Embassy in St. Petersburg, also of 1911–12, were supervised by Ludwig Mies van der Rohe, acting as Behrens's site architect. "Under Behrens, I learned the grand form, if you see what I mean", Mies wrote later.

In his designs for the Mannesmann-Röhrenwerke in Düsseldorf (1911–12), Behrens took the practical step of working from the dimensions of an office desk and the space that it required. This unit and multiples of it was the basis for the construction of the entire building. An interior with furniture for working-class families was exhibited at the Trades Union Headquarters in Berlin in 1912.

In the 1920s, several of Behrens's interiors were Expressionist, the most commanding survivor being the hall of the Hoechst Dyeworks Headquarters (1920–24). Huge brick pillars, triangular in section, rise to support a roof lit by star-like skylights. The bricks are coloured, from the lightest and brightest yellow at the top, down through the spectrum to greens and blues at the bottom.

His Dombauhütte (a pavilion to exhibit religious art) at Munich of 1922 was attacked by the infant Nazi party for its violent polychromatic interior brickwork, Expressionist stained glass, and its tormented crucifix by Ludwig Gies. The Nazis succeeded in having it closed. The interior of the villa for Clara Gans in the Taunus (1931) was, by contrast, a major exercise in restrained, cubic Modernism, lavishly finished. The living room walls were lined with parchment, with a floor of dark ebonized bog-oak into which was laid a pattern of lines in white maple. The dining room walls and ceiling were panelled in rosewood, having a window to slide away to make the space continuous with the terrace.

Around the time of World War I, Behrens began writing and teaching on design and he became deeply involved with the Deutscher Werkbund. From 1922 to 1936 he taught architecture at the Vienna Academy and in 1936 he conducted architectural masterclasses at the Berlin Academy. His importance as a teacher and his work as an industrial designer have tended to overshadow his gifts as a designer of interiors and furnishings, but in both of these spheres he proved remarkably versatile.

ALAN WINDSOR

Biography

Born in St. Georg, Hamburg, 14 April 1868. Studied painting at the Geweberschule, Hamburg, and at the Künstschule, Karlsruhe; was a private pupil in the studios of Ferdinand Brütt, Düsseldorf and Hugo Kotschenreiter, Munich. Married Lilli Krämer, 1889 (died 1957). Active as a painter in Munich from 1890. Co-founder, Munich Secession, 1893; co-founder, Union of Arts and Crafts Workshops, Munich, 1897. Began designing furniture, porcelain and glass in the late 1890s. Joined the artists' colony, Darmstadt, with others including J. M. Olbrich, 1899. Commenced architectural work, 1900; in private practice, Berlin, from 1907. Founder-member of the Deutscher Werkbund, 1907. Employed as a designer and design consultant by electrical combine AEG, Berlin, from 1907. Director, Nuremberg Master Course, 1902; Director, Kunstgewerbeschule, Düsseldorf, 1903–07; Director, Academy of Art, Düsseldorf, 1921–22; Professor, Academy of Fine Arts, Vienna, 1922–36; Head of the Department of Architecture, Prussian Academy of Arts, Berlin, 1936–40. Exhibited at numerous national and international exhibitions including Turin 1902, St. Louis 1904, and Cologne Werkbund exhibition 1914. Pupil/assistants included Le Corbusier, Walter Gropius, and Mies van der Rohe. Published numerous books and articles on architecture and design. Died in Berlin, 27 February 1940.

Selected Works

Interiors

1900–01	Behrens House, Künstler-Kolonie, Darmstadt (building, interiors and furnishings)
1902	Exposition of Decorative Arts, Turin (exhibition display including vestibule, reception room and study)
1904	Building Exhibition, Düsseldorf (building, interiors and furnishings for the restaurant)
1904	City Library, Düsseldorf (decoration and furnishing of the Reading Room)
1905	Nordwestdeutsche Art Exhibition, Oldenburg (pavilions, showrooms and gardens)
1905–06	Gustav Obenauer House, Saarbrücken (building, interiors and furniture; remodelled the study/library 1910)
1906	Exhibition of Applied Arts, Dresden (buildings and interiors including a concert hall, vestibule and reception room, and the Delmenhorster Linoleumfabrik Pavilion)
1906–07	Klein carpet shop, Hagen (interiors)
1908–09	Schröder House, Eppenhausen, near Hagen (building and interiors)
1909–10	AEG Turbine Factory, Huttenstrasse, Berlin (building and interiors)
1910	Cuno House, Eppenhausen, near Hagen (building and interiors)
1911–12	German Embassy, St. Petersburg (building and interiors; supervised by Mies van der Rohe)
1911–12	Wiegand House, Dahlem, Berlin (building, interiors and furniture)
1911–12	Mannesmann Office Building, Düsseldorf (building, interiors and furniture)
1920–24	Hoechst Dyeworks, Frankfurt (building and interiors)
1922	Dombauhütte Craft Exhibition, Munich (pavilion and interiors)
1923–25	New Ways, Basset-Lowke house, Northampton (building and interiors)
1931	Clara Gans Villa, Kronberg, Taunus (building, interiors and furniture)

Behrens designed furniture, porcelain and glass from the late 1890s. He was employed by AEG to design lamps and other electrical appliances from 1907 and ultimately advised on all aspects of their corp rate identity including graphics and architecture.

Publications

Feste des Lebens und der Kunst: Eine Betrachtung des Theaters als höchsten Kultursymbols, 1900
Ein Dokument Deutscher Kunst: Die Ausstellung der Künstler-Kolonie in Darmstadt 1901, 1901
Behrens Schrift, 1902
Vom sparsamen Bauen: Ein Beitrag zur Siedlungsfrage, with Heinrich de Fries, 1918
Das Ethos und die Umlagerung der künstlerischen Probleme, 1921
Terrassen am Hause, 1927

Further Reading

A detailed and scholarly study of Behrens's architectural commissions, chronicling the work of his mid-career, appears in Anderson 1968 which also includes an extensive primary and secondary bibliography. For a survey of Behrens's life and work as a whole see Windsor 1981 which includes a discussion of his principal interiors and a select further reading list. An exhaustive account of Behrens's work as an industrial designer appears in Buddensieg and Rogge 1984.

Anderson, Stanford O., *Peter Behrens and the New Architecture of Germany, 1900–1917*, Ph.D. thesis, New York: Columbia University, 1968
Anderson, Stanford O., "Peter Behrens's highest Kultursymbol, the theater (the artists' colony at Darmstadt, Germany)" in *Perspecta*, 26, 1990, pp.103–42
Buddensieg, Tilmann and Henning Rogge, *Industriekultur: Peter Behrens and the AEG, 1907–1914*, Cambridge: Massachusetts Institute of Technology Press, 1984
Buderath, Bernhard (editor), *Peter Behrens: Umbautes Licht: Das Verwaltungsgebäude der Hoechst AG*, Munich: Prestel, 1990
Campbell, Joan, *The German Werkbund: The Politics of Reform in the Applied Arts*, Princeton: Princeton University Press, 1978
Doumato, Lamia, *Peter Behrens* (bibliography), Monticello, IL: Vance, 1983
Hoeber, Fritz, *Peter Behrens*, Munich: Müller & Rentsch, 1913
Hoepfner, Wolfram and Fritz Neumeyer, *Das Haus Wiegand von Peter Behrens in Berlin-Dahlem*, Mainz: von Zabern, 1979
Norberg Schulz, Christian, *Casa Behrens, Darmstadt*, 2nd edition Rome: Officina, 1986
"Peter Behrens: Haus Behrens 1901" in *Architectural Design*, no.1/2, 1980
Pfeifer, H-G., *Peter Behrens*, Düsseldorf: Beton, 1990
Schuster, Peter-Klaus, *Peter Behrens und Nürnberg*, Munich: Prestel, 1980
Weber, Wilhelm (editor), *Peter Behrens 1868–1940* (exhib. cat.), Kaiserslautern: Pfalzgalerie, 1978
Windsor, Alan, *Peter Behrens: Architect and Designer, 1868–1940*, London: Architectural Press, and New York: Whitney Library of Design, 1981

Bélanger, François-Joseph 1744–1818

French architect and designer of gardens and interiors

François-Joseph Bélanger was one of the most innovative designers of his generation. Trained as an architect, he was an important exponent of the early Neo-Classical style and was also noted for his work in landscape design. But he is best known for his interiors, and particularly the interiors of the small pavilions and bath-houses that graced the parks and gardens of his aristocratic and discriminating Parisian clientele. Many of these were designed in the newly-fashionable Etruscan manner, and Bélanger's skilful interpretations of this style, together with his championship of arabesque ornament and forms, exercised a strong influence on French interior decoration throughout the last quarter of the 18th century.

Bélanger was born in Paris, the son of a haberdasher, and was educated first at the Collège de Beauvais, studying physics under Abbé Nollet, and then at the Académie Royale d'Architecture where he studied architecture under Julien-David Leroy. He was a protégé of the influential collector and connoisseur, the Comte de Caylus, and he also spent time perfecting his draughtsmanship with the architect Pierre Constant d'Ivry. He is mentioned first in 1764 in the records of the Académie when he competed for one of the monthly prizes; in 1774 he applied unsuccessfully for membership. But his professional career had already begun in 1767 when he was appointed draughtsman to the Menus-Plaisirs du Roi. He designed a jewel cabinet for Marie Antoinette in 1769 that has been described as the first monument of the refined late 18th-century Neo-Classical style in furniture.

In the same year he met Sophie d'Arnould, the *prima donna* of the Paris Opéra. This was an important meeting for not only did Sophie d'Arnould become Bélanger's mistress but she was also well-placed to introduce him to a number of wealthy clients. These included the Prince de Ligne, for whom Bélanger worked on designs for the gardens of the Château de Beloeil in Belgium, and the Comte de Lauragais for whom he built a bath-house in the garden of his Paris house, the Hôtel de Brancas, c.1770. The bath-house was an unusual and well-publicized commission. Baths and bathing had become more common among the French aristocracy earlier in the century but Bélanger's bath-house represented a new building-type, resembling a free-standing temple or small-scale replica of the public baths of ancient Rome. It was embellished with four free-standing columns, recalling, according to Bélanger, one of the temples of Praeneste or one of those "which Palladio described and which existed at Pola in Istria". The interiors were extremely influential and included decorations by the sculptor Nicolas-François Lhuillier that recreated, amidst the grand columned interior, something of the style of the more intimate grotesque decorations, *à l'antique*, that Raphael and Giovanni da Udine had used in their work at the Vatican and other Roman palaces. This style of decoration, known as the arabesque, or Etruscan style, became so popular in Paris later in the century that even wallpapers, produced by firms such as J.-B. Réveillon, featured reproductions of arabesque and grotesque motifs.

The Comte de Lauragais was also a frequent visitor to England; he had his own stables at Newmarket and became a pioneer of the English garden in France. Bélanger went to England at least once – a notebook shows various sketches of English sites and in 1778 he designed a scheme for the gallery at Lansdowne House in London – and he too was interested in English landscape design. Indeed, although he was not the first French designer to plan gardens in the English style, his work at Beloeil, Bagatelle, Neuilly and Méréville did much to encourage the more widespread acceptance of this style of garden in France.

Bélanger also worked much for another Anglophile, the

Bélanger: Mademoiselle Dervieux's bathroom, Paris, c.1789 (Bibliothèque Nationale, Paris)

Comte d'Artois, who was the youngest brother of Louis XVI and for whom he designed the Château and park of Bagatelle in the Bois de Boulogne (1777). This commission included a small building, known as the Bagatelle, which was constructed in 64 days to win a bet and which became as famous as the Comte de Lauragais's bath-house. The scale of the building, as though befitting so precious a project, was kept small and deliberately underplayed its owner's rank. The main bedroom was conceived of as a tent, containing numerous military emblems including a cannon raised on its end to support the chimneypiece and heaps of cannon balls and grenades to fuel the stoves. Like the bath-house at the Hôtel de Brancas (1770), the walls of the Bagatelle featured elaborate arabesques and Bélanger was assisted in the execution of this work by his brother-in-law, Jean-Démosthène Dugourc, who painted the figurative elements and who went on to use this style of decoration in numerous subsequent decorative schemes.

Access to the Bagatelle was along a winding road, designed by a Scottish landscape architect, Thomas Blaikie, who was to remain busy at the site until the Revolution. Yet, if this was intended as an English garden, the result was distinctively French including numerous contrivances such as a grotto with a Gothic kiosk, a stone bridge with a pagoda, a Japanese bridge, and another pagoda which, like the bedroom of the house, was made in the form of a tent.

Nearby, Bélanger designed another garden complex – for the financier Claude Baudard de St.-James – which included a small brick house and several pavilions, kiosks and swings. The most celebrated of the garden features was the "Grand Roche", a massive rock carved to accommodate a bathroom, reservoir, grotto and gallery, and which was described as the "Eighth Wonder of the World". Claude Baudard de St.-James had previously engaged Bélanger to design the grand salon of his hôtel in the Place Vendôme. This interior still survives and includes elegant gilt and white panelling incorporating Corinthian pilasters, gilt trophies and garlands of flowers, and overdoors painted with mythological scenes by Jean-Jacques Lagrenée.

Bélanger was also responsible for the design and decoration of several other Parisian hôtels during this period, notably that of the hôtel on the rue des Capucins de la Chaussée-d'Antin (1787) which is asymmetrical in plan and whose elevation is decorated with free and scattered ornaments of a very mixed style. His most celebrated interiors, however, were created for another of his mistresses, the dancer Mlle. Dervieux, whom he subsequently married. In 1789 Bélanger added onto her house a dining room and a small wing containing a bathroom and boudoir. A coloured engraving of c.1790 shows the bathroom, with its sunken central pool and niches decorated with painted bas-reliefs, and a view through to the boudoir which contains a superb circular Beauvais carpet, furniture made by the Jacob firm, and an apsed alcove with a draped ottoman fitted into three sides. Like the interiors at the Château de Bagatelle, this pavilion was a refined and original exercise in the *Goût Etrusque* and featured liberal use of grotesque ornament. Its voluptuous setting formed the perfect backdrop for Mlle. Dervieux's celebrated soirées and complemented the personality of a client whose taste clearly ran to the theatrical and exotic: according to contemporary accounts, her bedroom was apparently hung with "elaborate banners covering the walls in the Arabian Manner".

During the Revolution Bélanger's fortunes were mixed. In 1787 he was elected to the States-General for the district of St.-Joseph but later he was imprisoned on suspicion of having helped some of the emigrés. In 1796 he joined the staff of the newly-formed Monuments Public but he did little work for this body. The two major works at the end of his career, both started in 1808, were quite different from his earlier commissions; one was a slaughterhouse, built at Rochechouart, known in Bélanger's drawings, the other was the dome of the Halle au Blé, executed in a combination of glass and iron. Bélanger had learned of the use of iron in England where he observed "it serves them in the absence of stone". But, at the Halle au Blé, glass was also used for the first time, and, if the use of iron was widely criticised, Bélanger himself was sufficiently proud of what he had done to write to Jacques-Louis David that this represented "a new conception for the first time".

Bélanger was dismissed from his post at the Monuments Public after writing an anonymous pamphlet attacking the administration of public buildings under Jarente de la Bruyère. However, after the restoration of the Bourbon monarchy he was back in favour, organising many public decorations including those for the entry of Louis XVIII into Paris in 1814, and was admitted to the Légion d'Honneur in 1815. He died in 1818 and was buried in the cemetery of Père Lachaise in Paris. His epitaph was appropriately grand and claimed that he was "superior to Kent in the gardens of Méréville / worthy follower of Michelangelo in the cupola of the Halle au Blé".

DAVID CAST

See also Dugourc; Etruscan Style

Biography

Born in Paris, 12 April 1744. Studied physics at the Collège de Beauvais under Abbé Nollet, and architecture at the Académie Royale d'Architecture under Julien-David Leroy and Pierre Constant D'Ivry, 1764–65. Married Mlle. Dervieux. Brother-in-law and pupil was the designer Jean Démosthène Dugourc (1749–1825). Visited England, 1766, where he probably met William Chambers (1723–96). Appointed dessinateur, Menus-Plaisirs du Roi, Versailles, 1767, inspecteur, 1777; premier architect to Comte d'Artois, 1777. Elected to the States General, district of St. Joseph, Paris, 1787; subsequently imprisoned as a royalist, 1794; named Commissaire de la Commune, 1795 and Architecte du Conservatoire, 1796. Organised several public decorations during the restoration, including that of the entry of Louis XVIII into Paris, 1814. Légion d'Honneur, 1815. Died in Paris, 5 January 1818; buried in the cemetery of Père-Lachaise.

Selected Works

An important collection of Bélanger's drawings and designs for his work at the Hôtel de Bagatelle are in the Archives Nationales, Paris. Additional manuscript material is in the Bibliothèque d'Art et d'Architecture, University of Paris. A list of his architectural commissions appears Gallet 1972.

Interiors

1770	Hôtel de Brancas, Paris (bath-house): Comte de Lauragais
1777	Hôtel de Bagatelle, Bois de Boulogne, Paris (building and interiors): Charles Philippe, Comte d'Artois
1777–79	Château de Maison, Neuilly-sur-Seine (remodelling and interiors, including summer dining room and gaming room): Charles Philippe, Comte d'Artois
c.1777	Hôtel de Mazarin, Paris (decoration including furniture and carpets): Duchesse de Mazarin
c.1780	Folie St. James and Garden, Neuilly-sur-Seine (house and park including the "Grand Roche" grotto and interiors): Claude Baudard de St.-James
c.1787	Château de Méréville (interiors including the hall, dining room, small saloon, billiard room, winter and summer salons; and gardens): Jean-Joseph de Laborde
c.1789	Hôtel Dervieux, Paris (additions and interiors including a dining room, bathroom and boudoir): Mlle. Dervieux
1808–13	Bélanger House, Santeny (building, interiors and gardens)
1808–13	Halle au Blé, Paris (dome)

Further Reading

Baillio, Joseph, "Hubert Robert's Decorations for the Château de Bagatelle" in *Metropolitan Museum Journal*, 27, 1992, pp.149–82

Barrier, Janine, "Les Voyages Outre-Manche de François-Joseph Bélanger" in *Histoire de l'Art*, 1990, no.12, pp.37–48

Braham, Allan, *The Architecture of the French Enlightenment*, Berkeley: University of California Press, and London: Thames and Hudson, 1980

Coutts, Howard, "French Eighteenth-Century Decorative Drawings in the Victoria and Albert Museum" in *Apollo*, 123, January 1986, pp.24–29

Duchesne, Henri-Gaston, *Histoire du Bois de Boulogne: Le Château de Bagatelle*, Paris: Schemit, 1909

Eriksen, Svend, *Early Neo-Classicism in France: The Creation of the Louis Seize Style*, London: Faber, 1974

La Folie d'Artois (exhib. cat.), Paris: Château de Bagatelle, 1988

Gallet, Michel, *Paris Domestic Architecture of the 18th Century*, London: Barrie and Jenkins, 1972; as *Stately Mansions: Eighteenth Century Paris Architecture*, New York: Praeger, 1972

Gjesdahl, Kerstin M., "La Folie Saint-James" in *Information d'Histoire de l'Art*, 1962

Hautecoeur, Louis, *Histoire de l'architecture classique en France*, vol.4, Paris: Picard, 1952

Michel, Christian, "The Theatre of the Comédiens Italiens" in Peter Fuhring (editor), *Design into Art: Drawings for Architecture and Ornament: The Lodewijk Houthakker Collection*, vol.2, London: Philip Wilson, 1989, pp.501–09

Scherer, François, "La Chambre à Coucher du Comte d'Artois à la Bagatelle, d'apres les Documents des Archives Nationales" in *Gazette des Beaux-Arts*, 105, April 1985, pp.147–54

Scott, Barbara, "A Delightful Bonbonnière: Mlle. Dervieux's Hôtel, Paris" in *Country Life*, 20 November 1980, pp.1902–04

Scott, Barbara, "Château de Bagatelle, Paris" in *Country Life*, 185, 16 May 1990, pp.142–44

Stern, Jean, *Á l'Ombre de Sophie Arnould: François Joseph Bélanger*, 2 vols., Paris: Plon, 1930

Belter, John Henry 1804-1863

American cabinet-maker and furniture manufacturer

John Henry Belter is considered to have been the foremost American cabinet-maker who worked in the Rococo Revival style. The combination of his innovative construction techniques and artistic genius resulted in forms that mark the crowning expression of the style.

Belter was born in 1804 near Osnabrück, Germany. Presumably he had already been well-trained as a cabinet-maker when he emigrated to New York City in 1833. His initial employers are unknown, but by 1844 his business on Chatham Street was listed in the New York City directories. Two years later, the shop moved to fashionable Broadway. A growing business resulted in store relocations further uptown, always on Broadway. By 1854 Belter also had a large factory on the Upper East Side. After his death in 1863, the business was continued by the remaining partners, brothers-in-law John, William, and Frederick Springmeyer, until bankruptcy closed it in 1867. Regrettably, the firm's records have never been discovered.

While it is likely that Belter worked in the Biedermeier, Grecian, and, perhaps, Gothic Revival styles in the early years of his career, his documented post-1845 American oeuvre is devoted solely to the Rococo Revival style. This revival originated in England in the 1820s, quickly moved to France, and appeared in Germany in the 1830s. Belter was obviously attuned to international trends and, with this foundation, created an individual style characterized by bold silhouettes and lush naturalistic ornament. In general, Belter modeled his forms after 18th-century Rococo furniture, but his adaptations reached new heights in furniture ornamentation.

Belter was not only an artist; he was a true designer who strove to create works of art that were striking, structurally sound, comparatively lightweight, and unusually durable. In appearance, these objects range from simple to complex, delicate to massive. Belter used traditional joinery techniques with solid and laminated wood to construct his wares. He called his furniture "pressed work," referring to the lamination process. It is the use of this bonded layering in combination with contoured shaping, intricate pierced decoration, and three-dimensional carving that characterizes Belter's work. He was not the first cabinet-maker to employ the lamination process, but he is credited with perfecting the technique and using it to achieve artistic distinction.

Belter was awarded four patents by the United States government. Although some of the methods described in the patents seem to have been used for years before gaining official recognition, the patents document Belter's manufacturing techniques and chronicle his career. The first patent, recorded in 1847, was for "Machinery for Sawing Arabesque Chairs." It described the equipment for holding a laminated chair or sofa back while a special saw cut out a design. His 1856 patent was for an easily assembled three- to five-piece laminated bed frame. Belter's third patent, "Improvement in the Method of Manufacturing Furniture," was approved in February 1858. While it fully described his lamination process, this patent specifically registered chair backs that curved in two planes. His final patent (1860) addressed the construction of a laminated bureau drawer and an unusual locking device.

Belter used thin layers of wood – as few as four, as many as 21, but often around ten – glued together with the grain of each layer at a right angle to the adjoining layer. Inner wood layers were less expensive varieties such as hickory, walnut, ash, and oak, whereas the outer layers were of rosewood, mahogany, or oak. These "sandwiches" were shaped and pressed in cylindrical cauls. Curved segments, including chair-backs, were cut from the formed wood. The laminated pieces, which were strong yet lightweight, were then yet able to be pierced and carved. To supply the essential depth for other ornamental carving, additional pieces of solid wood were employed. The completed ornamentation was realistic in appearance and encyclopedic in a variety that included flowers, fruit, vegetables, foliage, shells, birds, animals, putti, and figural busts. The backs of Belter's chairs were also carefully designed. The back and the rear legs fit flush into the seat rail and thereby display a beautifully veneered surface on a bold, curving silhouette.

Many of the same designs were used throughout Belter's relatively brief American career – including at least 75 distinct patterns within the typical armchair / side chair / sofa forms – but the scarcity of surviving labeled examples makes precise dating difficult. Few period records exist with appellative designations for the various Belter patterns, but names have been assigned using major collections as sources. These names reflect visual characteristics, original owners, object locales, or combinations thereof. For example, the *Rosalie* pattern is named for a house in Natchez, Mississippi, for which an *in situ* parlor suite was acquired in the late 1850s. Lacking openwork – but having carved flowers, foliage, and fruit (including grapes) — this originally may have been the "Grape Pattern" referred to on a rare Belter bill of sale to another client. "Arabasket," a similarly discovered Belter-coined term, could refer to a specific openwork pattern of scrolls, flowers, foliage, and fruit; a group of related patterns, or all patterns with openwork.

The influential American author Andrew Jackson Downing wrote in 1850 that "Modern French furniture" (Rococo Revival) was most appropriate for parlors and boudoirs. His comments coincide with the emerging trend of purchasing household furnishings en suite, and Belter made a specialty of matched parlor groups that included sofas and chairs of the same pattern, with complementary tables and étagères. As "Manufacturers of All Kinds of Fine Furniture" (according to a surviving label), J.H. Belter & Company also supplied objects for the dining room, the library, and the bedroom – mantels, mirror frames, and window cornices could be commissioned. Belter's showrooms gave clients a taste of his wares, but most of his sales were custom-orders, with the options of "extra carving," special wood finishes, protective fabric covers, and, if needed, packing crates. Belter's amazing design variety, albeit within the Rococo Revival *milieu*, appealed to a prosperous national clientele, principally from the Northeastern states, but occasionally from the South and Midwest. A handsome nine-piece group, without openwork, sold for about $700; more elaborately ornamented counterparts were priced upwards from $1100.

Several other cabinet-makers in New York City and

Philadelphia produced laminated Rococo Revival furniture. Comparative studies have clearly defined Belter's characteristics from those of his competitors. Amidst a challenging idiom, the works of the latter range from good to excellent, but Belter's designs are more exciting, his construction techniques are superior, his layers of lamination are thinner, and more numerous, and his carving is richer and more finely executed. Belter's expressive ornamentation, achieved through a judicious balance of machine technology and skilful, free-hand carving, exhibits a mastery of process that elevated the standards of craftsmanship for cabinet-makers working in the Rococo style.

ANNA T. D'AMBROSIO AND ED POLK DOUGLAS

See also Rococo Revival

Biography

Born Johann Heinrich Belter in Hilter, near Osnabrück (then Kingdom of Hanover), Germany, 1804. Trained as a cabinet-maker in Germany; emigrated to America, 1833. Established his own business and listed as John H. Belter, cabinet-maker, Chatham Street, New York, 1844. Listed as John H. Belter, manufacturer, 547 Broadway, 1852; opened a factory at 3rd Avenue and 76th Street, New York, 1854. Awarded 4 patents relating to the manufacture of furniture, 1847–60. Died in New York, 1863; the business remained in operation until 1867.

Selected Collections

Important examples of Belter's furniture are in the Metropolitan Museum of Art, the Brooklyn Museum and the Museum of the City of New York, all New York City; the Strong Museum, Rochester, New York; the Winterthur Museum, Delaware; and the Victoria and Albert Museum, London. A large group of furniture is also on view at Sewell House, Odessa, Delaware.

Further Reading

A comprehensive account of Belter's career and the firm's manufacturing processes appears in Schwartz 1980 which also contains a bibliography of primary and secondary sources. For more recent research see Douglas 1990.

Douglas, Ed Polk, "Rococo Revival: John Henry Belter" in *Nineteenth Century Furniture: Innovation, Revival, and Reform*, New York: Art and Antiques, 1982, pp.26–35

Douglas, Ed Polk, "The Furniture of John Henry Belter: Separating Fact from Fiction" in *Antiques and Fine Art*, November / December, 1990

Downing, Andrew Jackson, *The Architecture of Country Houses*, 1850; reprinted New York: Dover, 1969

Downs, Joseph, "John Henry Belter & Company" in *Magazine Antiques*, 54, Sept. 1948, pp.166–68

Dubrow, Eileen and Richard, *American Furniture of the 19th Century*, Exton, PA: Schiffer, 1983, pp.13–20

Franco, B., "John Henry Belter: A Rococo Revival Cabinetmaker" in *Nineteenth Century*, vol.6, pt.2, Summer 1980

Ingerman, Elizabeth A., "Personal Experiences of an Old New York Cabinetmaker" in *Magazine Antiques*, 84, November 1963, p.576

Jervis, Simon and others, *Art and Design in Europe and America, 1800–1900*, London: Herbert Press, 1987

Roth, Rodris, "A Patent Model by John Henry Belter" in *Magazine Antiques*, May 1977, p.1039

Schwartz, Marvin D., Edward J. Stanek and Douglas K. True, *The Furniture of John Henry Belter and the Rococo Revival*, New York: Dutton, 1980

Vincent, Claire, "John Henry Belter: Manufacturer of All Kinds of Fine Furniture" in Ian M.G. Quimby and Polly Anne Earl (editors), *Technological Innovation and the Decorative Arts*, Charlottesville: University Press of Virginia, 1974

Bennett, Ward 1917–

American sculptor, and furniture, interior and textile designer

Ward Bennett, born in New York, studied sculpture in the late 1930s in Paris with Constantin Brancusi, and painting in New York with Hans Hofmann in the early 1940s. In the later years of that decade he was apprenticed to and befriended by Le Corbusier. All of these experiences, along with a short stint as a fashion designer, were formative in the development of his work in the areas for which he is best known – interior design and product design. His training with such masters of control in modern art, architecture and design as Brancusi and Le Corbusier have given Bennett's work the rationality that has caused him to be identified as a practitioner of "reductivist Modernism" (Stern,1995).

About 1947 Bennett received his first interior design commission, from a family member. The apartment interior was published in the *New York Times*. Within a short time Bennett had opened his first interior design practice in New York. In the ensuing years he developed his distinctive vocabulary, which he describes as "intuitive, intellectual, and cultural" (Brown,1980). His artistic training has aided in the development of his reflective, minimalist style which often features well-chosen art and antique objects for his clients.

In 1960 Bennett made a splash with his conception of interiors for the recently completed Chase Manhattan Bank building in New York (Skidmore, Owings & Merrill), now regarded as a milestone for office spaces in the modern corporate era. Many of the floors were open-plan and enjoyed a freedom of space characteristic of the post-war modern period. Bennett's interiors for the executive offices were designed to take advantage of the larger spaces created on one side of the building through the off-center placement of the elevators. Most notable was the suite for David Rockefeller, the bank's president, which incorporated paintings and other works of art, furniture (some designed by Bennett) similar to the corporate-friendly style of Florence Knoll, and thoughtfully-chosen accessories. Bennett's connection with the art world compelled him to assist the bank in its development of a corporate art collection, a popular activity today but at that time a very radical investment. (The Chase Manhattan was also assisted in this endeavor by curator and later Museum of Modern Art director, Alfred H. Barr, Jr.)

After 1960, Bennett became heavily involved in furniture design, though innovative features of his interior settings, such as the conversation pit, were influential during that decade and the next. By 1970, the strain of his design commitments led to health problems, and Bennett became more selective in the commissions he accepted. In the 1970s and 1980s, Bennett was described as "the mentor of, and inspiration to, designers working in the industrial style," also known as the High-Tech movement, in interior design (Kron and Slesin,1978). This style was marked by the use of prefabricated materials and industrial fittings and objects in residential interiors. His Long Island summer home was his unofficial test-ground for unique uses for industrial supplies, such as incandescent light reflectors (used extensively in factories and warehouses) for home illumination, subway gratings to cover air ducts, and hospital fixtures in the kitchen and bath.

Following a Modernist credo, Bennett proclaims that "I keep interesting and good architecture. But if it's not interesting, I'm apt to destroy it to see if I can make it better." This can be seen in two simple but striking interiors he created for himself from the attics of Paris and New York apartment buildings. In his Paris home and studio, he gutted the former servants' quarters, created a white background with new walls and ceiling, and covered them with a linen / cotton fabric used for butchers' smocks. Other neutral elements such as a sisal floor covering provide a backdrop for his carefully chosen decorative and functional objects; he chose masculine objects for himself, such as leather-covered sofabeds, in strongly contrasting red and black color schemes, set into niches. His New York home and studio are at the Dakota, where he created a stepped space in the small interior to accommodate new plumbing. Black slate tiles and a red carpet continue his Paris color theme, as do neutral walls, black leather furnishings, and innovative, adjustable lighting – in the Paris apartment he used Le Corbusier's swivel lamps on walls and on furniture; at the Dakota he turned the photographic lighting equipment known as barn-doors into movable wall shades (another High-Tech detail). The decoration of his New York apartment at the Dakota, first completed in 1960, has been called his masterwork (Stern, 1995). He took the two pyramidal spaces atop the building and created a duplex, puncturing one wall with a two-story window that gives a diagonal view of Central Park. He colored the walls and floors with characteristic neutrals, which allowed for his art collection to mingle with Bennett-designed furniture, antiques, modern classics, and High-Tech selections.

Bennett's interiors over the past three decades, for the most part residential commissions in the United States and Europe, continue to be exercises in simplicity. He frowns on the collective work of his industry: "You should walk into a place and feel its ambience, not see that it has been done by some decorator in pastel this or lace that. I strongly disagree with, and disapprove of, most people who are doing interiors today. They are part of a big and fashionable industry – selling rugs and towels, color combinations, and pewter and bamboo. That's not for me." He still punctuates his interiors with strategically-chosen examples of modern lighting and furnishings, including pieces designed by Le Corbusier, Charles Eames, and by Bennett himself.

Bennett is well-known today for his numerous designs for home furnishings: he designed china, glassware, and furniture for Tiffany in 1963 and 1971, and flatware for Supreme (now Tole); he was commissioned by Bloomingdale's in 1986 to design flatware, tableware, and glassware for production by Sasaki; he has produced many designs for the furniture makers Brickel, Neocon, and Geiger International; and he has also produced jewelry and textile designs. All of Bennett's product designs, as do his interior designs, reveal his association with early Modernists, and share a rational, functional quality. Bennett was honored in 1985 with an award from the American Institute of Architects for his long and successful career in the design professions.

JENNIFER A. KOMAR

Biography

Born Howard Bennett Amsterdam in New York City, 17 November 1917. Studied sculpture at the Porto Romano School of Art, Florence, 1937; Académie de la Grande Chaumière and with Constantin Brancusi, Paris, 1937–38; and painting with Hans Hofmann, New York, 1943. Served in the United States Army, 1940–43. Apprentice in the studio of the architect Le Corbusier, Paris, 1947–50. Worked in the fashion industry as a designer, sketch artist and window dresser, in Paris and New York, 1930–45; free-lance jewellery designer, Mexico, 1945–46. Active as an interior designer in New York and Europe, from 1947; independent designer, New York, from 1950. Numerous designs for furniture post-1960. Visiting professor, Yale University, New Haven, Connecticut, 1962–63; instructor, 1969–71, and associate professor from 1971, Pratt Institute, Brooklyn. American Institute of Architects Award, 1985.

Selected Works

Archive material, and furniture by Bennett are in the Cooper-Hewitt Museum, New York. Additional examples of furniture are in the Museum of Modern Art, New York.

Interiors

1947	Penthouse apartment, New York (interiors): Harry Jason
1960	Chase Manhattan Bank, New York (office interiors; building by Skidmore, Owings & Merrill)
1962	Rubin apartment, Park Avenue, New York (interiors and refurbishment, with Earl Pope)
1964	Penthouse apartment, The Dakota, 1 West 72nd Street, New York (remodelling of interiors, decoration and interior design): Ward Bennett
1960s	Apartment, Paris (interiors): Ward Bennett

Bennett created more than 100 designs for furniture for Brickel Associates; his most well-known works include the 1148/58 *Mobius* range (1970), the *University Chair* for the L.B. Johnson Library, University of Texas (1971), and the *University 1550* chair (1979). He also produced a 22-piece furniture collection produced by Geiger International in 1990. His cutlery designs include the *Metro* (1977–78), the *Trylon* (1980), and the *Helex* (1981) ranges, all for Supreme Cutlery. Bennett also designed several furnishing fabrics for Brickel Associates from the mid-1970s.

Publications

Articles in *Interiors* (US), October 1952, November 1965, and January 1977; and in *Interior Design* (US), September 1972

Further Reading

Brown, Erica, *Interior Views: Design at its Best,* New York: Viking Press, and London: Thames and Hudson, 1980

Buehr, Wendy, "Ward Bennett's Bachelor Digs: An Artful Solution" in *Interiors*, 117, June 1958, pp.96–99

Friedmann, Arnold, John F. Pile and Forrest Wilson, *Interior Design: An Introduction to Architectural Interiors,* 3rd edition New York: Elsevier, 1982

Hatje, Gerd and Ursula, *Design for Modern Living*, New York: Abrams, 1962; London: Thames and Hudson, 1964

Kron, Joan and Suzanne Slesin, *High-Tech: The Industrial Style and Source Book for the Home*, New York: Potter, 1978; London: Allen Lane, 1979

Phillips, Lisa and others, *High Styles: Twentieth-Century American Design* (exhib. cat.: Whitney Museum, New York), New York: Summit, 1985

Smith, C. Ray, *Interior Design in 20th-Century America*, New York: Harper, 1987
Stern, Robert A.M., Thomas Mellins and David Fishman, *New York 1960: Architecture and Urbanism Between the Second World War and the Bicentennial*, New York: Monacelli Press, 1995

Bentwood Furniture

The use of bent wood for interior architecture has a long tradition. In England, J. Cumberland obtained, in 1720, the first patent, followed in 1768 by H. Jackson, and by J. Vidler, in 1794. In the United States in 1808, Samuel Gragg received his patent for the *Elastic Chair* in which the front legs, seat and back were stress-bent from a single piece of wood. In 1826, the Englishman Isaac Sargent succeeded in bending balustrade railings and window mullions with the aid of hot steam. Soon after, German-born John Henry Belter was investigating the steam-bending process in New York City. However, the most important contribution to the development of wood bending technology, its industrialization and its application in architecture was made by Michael Thonet (1796–1871).

In 1819 Thonet opened his first cabinet-making workshop in his birthplace, Boppard-am-Rhein, where the forests of the Rhine valley provided him with a good source of raw material. He began experimenting with the process of lamination of thin layers of wood, sliced along the wood fibers, cooked in glue and bent into shape. Thonet used this technique for the curved frames of his first chairs, assembled from continuous glued pieces and made in the Biedermeier style of the early 19th century. In comparison with other furniture-makers who used massive pieces of pre-cut wood, shaped, joined and glued, Thonet's method was more efficent, faster and cheaper.

To protect his innovative furniture-making methods, in 1840 Thonet applied in Prussia for a patent – an application which was rejected for the reason that it lacked innovation. A year later, however, in 1841, his patent application was accepted in Paris, and Thonet took part in the 1851 Great Exhibition at London's Crystal Palace, where he won a bronze medal for "innovation, originality and elegance of form".

The move of the Thonet company to Vienna, capital of the Austro-Hungarian empire was influenced by the receipt of commissions for the interiors of the palaces of Prince Liechtenstein and Baron Schwarzenberg. In 1853 Michael Thonet transferred the company ownership to his five sons, renaming it Gebrüder Thonet and moving it to the Mollard Mill in Vienna. After the installation of the first steam

Bentwood chairs and tables designed by Thonet, and shown at the 1851 Great Exhibition, London

machines to produce bentwood, the company employed 70 people.

In its material and structural continuity, and its simplicity, Gebrüder Thonet's steam bent laminated chair heralded the evolution of the modern chair. The Side Chair, *Model No. 14*, of 1857, made from moulded laminated wood and solid beechwood, with a wooden seat, anticipated the Modern Movement in its minimal use of materials, lightness of weight, and suitability for mass production, a phenomenon which began to penetrate commercial and domestic interiors.

The demand for furniture ensured Gebrüder Thonet's growth. The company's 1859 catalog lists 25 items for sale; in 1873 this had risen to 110, and by 1911 to 1,400. Bentwood products included coat hangers, sheet music stands, children's furniture, baby cribs, kneelers, barber chairs, rockers, tennis racquets, and sleds. The consumer chair, *Model No. 14*, consisting of only six individual pieces, had been developed and manufactured in the company's first factory which opened in Koryčany, in 1857. Other factories followed, also in Moravia because of the abundance in the area of quality woods. Between 1859 and 1914, 40 million *Model No. 14* chairs were produced, with Thonet employment growing to 25,000 workers in some 60 factories throughout Europe. A factory-line production system separated the stages of the manufacturing process, well in advance of the introduction of the Ford assembly line.

In 1898 the architect Adolf Loos designed a bentwood chair with a stained beechwood frame and woven cane seat. Based on Thonet's *Model No. 14* chair, Loos's chair, designed for Vienna's Café Museum, represented the first of the architect-designed bentwood products. The chair was manufactured by Jacob & Josef Kohn of Vienna. Due to its streamlined and functional appearance, the Café Museum was subsequently nicknamed "Cafe Nihilismus" by patrons. Loos expounded his theories in the essay "Ornament and Crime".

The interiors of Vienna's seminal Modernist building, the Postal Savings Bank (1904–06), were the result of collaboration between the architect Otto Wagner and his pupil Marcel Kammerer. The furnishings included a bentwood chair with square- profile frame, black lacquered finish, and metal feet; this chair, the *Model No. 6516*, was manufactured by the Gebrüder Thonet. Architect Josef Hoffmann designed two bentwood side chairs with plywood seats, one of which was made for his Sanatorium in Purkersdorf (1904); the other was exhibited at the Viennese Kunstschau, in 1908. It was, however, the *Sitzmaschine* (the machine for sitting), designed by Hoffmann in 1905, which stole the 1908 Kunstschau show. Like the two side chairs manufactured by Jacob & Josef Kohn of Vienna, it was made of stained, laminated wood, bent solid beechwood and turned wood with brass fittings; it also featured an adjustable back. Stringently geometric and based on machine aesthetics, Hoffmann's *Sitzmaschine* anticipates the *Red and Blue Chair* designed in 1917 by Gerrit Rietveld.

In his interiors Le Corbusier frequently used the *Wiener Stuhl* (Viennese Chair) developed by Gebrüder Thonet in 1904, with black lacquered bentwood frame and natural cane seat. Le Corbusier included this chair in his furnishings for the 1927 Weissenhof Housing Exhibition in Stuttgart.

The Finnish architect Alvar Aalto was, throughout his career, fascinated by wood, its structural as well as its aesthetic qualities. Aalto's exposed structural / architectural trusses, ceilings, lamps and chairs, evoke an age of architecture before the use of synthetics and plastics. His *Model 60* three-legged chair, with laminated bentwood birch frame and circular seat, designed in 1930, ostensibly rivalled in popularity Thonet's *Model No. 14* chair. The *Paimio Chair*, Model No. 41, from 1931, was designed for Aalto's Paimio Sanatorium, begun in 1929. The armchair has a bent, laminated birch frame and painted bent plywood seat. The design is revolutionary in the way greater pliancy is achieved by removing several layers of plywood veneer in the scrolls of the back and seat.

From 1945–46 the architect-designers Charles and Ray Eames contributed to the development of bentwood furniture with several innovative designs, including moulded plywood chairs, the *LCM* (Lounge Chair Metal) and the *LCW* (Lounge Chair Wood). The first had an animal-hide-covered moulded plywood seat and back, attached with rubber shock mounts to a chrome-plated bent tubular steel frame; the second, a stained moulded plywood seat and back attached with rubber shock mounts to bent plywood feet and back support. The *Lounge Chair and Footstool*, Model Nos. 670 and 671, conceived in 1956–57, were the Eameses' design for the luxury end of the market, with moulded plywood seat shells in rosewood veneer, leather covered foam- and down-filled cushions, on a swiveling cast aluminum base. Of generous proportions and of high quality materials, the *Lounge Chair* projects a sense of executive power. The Eameses' designs have been manufactured and marketed by the Herman Miller Company.

Since 1990 the Californian architect Frank Gehry has been developing a line of bentwood furniture characterized by the *Powerplay Chair*, made from bent and woven laminated wood. While he acknowledges the contribution of Thonet, Aalto and the Eameses in their innovative use of bentwood, Gehry wants to take it further by integrating the supporting and the supported (structure and seat) by forming it of the same lightweight interwoven wood strips in a basket-like pattern, thus giving the chair an extraordinary strength. Gehry's furniture is manufactured by the Knoll Group.

PETER LIZON

See also Thonet

Further Reading

The standard English-language history of Bentwood Furniture is Ostergard 1987.

Candilis, Georges and others, *Bugholzmöbel / Bent Wood Furniture*, 2nd edition Stuttgart: Kramer, 1984

Kane, Patricia E., "Samuel Gragg: His Bentwood Fancy Chairs" in *Yale University Art Gallery Bulletin*, XXXIII, Autumn 1971, pp.26–37

Ostergard, Derek E.(editor), *Bent Wood and Metal Furniture, 1850–1946*, New York: American Federation of Arts, 1987

Vegesack, Alexander von (editor), *L'Industrie Thonet: De la Création Artisanale à la Production en Série: Le Mobilier en Bois Courbé* (exhib. cat.), Paris: Musée d'Orsay, 1986

Wilk, Christopher, *Thonet: 150 Years of Furniture*, Woodbury, NY: Barron's, 1980

Zelleke, Ghenete, Eva Ottillinger and Nina Stritzler, *Against the Grain: Bentwood Furniture from the Collection of Fern and Manfred Steinfeld* (exhib. cat.), Chicago: Art Institute of Chicago, 1993

Berain, Jean I 1640–1711

French designer and *ornemaniste*

A designer of ornament, decorations, architectural fitments, furnishings, metalwork, tapestries and textiles, Jean I Berain was instrumental in the development of a new, less illustrative and more strictly decorative French Court style. Working in the latter years of the reign of Louis XIV, Berain's approach combined fantasy and exoticism with a tendency towards lighter, painted interior designs, and his work signified a move away from the grandiose and heavy Baroque style that had reached its zenith in the work carried out during the 1660s and after at Versailles. Employed as designer and draughtsman to the king ("Dessinateur de la Chambre et du Cabinet du Roi") from 1674, he was entrusted with the task of developing models from which other artists and craftsmen worked. These models included not only the decorations and costumes for all the royal ceremonies and entertainments but also designs for the interiors and furnishings of the royal palaces. The execution of these royal interiors did much to establish Berain's reputation among his contemporaries but, unfortunately, few have survived, and today he is remembered chiefly for the development of a new style of grotesque ornament that was influential in many parts of Europe and for his role in the evolution from Baroque to Rococo styles of design.

According to the Swedish royal architect, Nicodemus Tessin the younger, Berain was responsible for the design of the decorations of the Cabinet des Curiosité (c.1682) which housed Louis XIV's collection of antiques, jewels and cameos. The Cabinet was entered from the Salon de l'Abondance. The corners were embellished with pyramidal arrangements of ornate gilded shelves surmounted by putti carrying oval medallions adorned with painted or sculptural representations of Abundance, Magnificence, Symmetry, Cupid and Venus on a gilded background. The ceiling was in the form of a great dome, painted blue and decorated with golden flowers. In Tessin's opinion, the most striking feature was the use of mirrors on the walls and ceiling which reflected light from the windows, one of which was oval (*oeil de boeuf*). Berain also designed a sumptuous bureau for the room (untraced). Sadly, this spectacular interior was destroyed in the 18th century and only a drawing, which gives no decorative detail, survives.

Berain's work for the Dauphin's Cabinet de Monseigneur (1699) in the Château de Meudon has also been destroyed, and a degree of confusion surrounds this commission. According to the art historian Fiske Kimball this interior is represented in the painting by an unknown artist of *Le Grand Dauphin dans son cabinet* which is now in the collection at Versailles. Kimball's attribution, made in the 1940s, was based on the fact that the fireplace, the arabesque panel to its right and the bureau all appear to derive directly from Berain's engraved designs, thus establishing Berain as the author of the decoration as a whole. This view has been questioned by subsequent scholars but the similarities between these elements and Berain's models are undeniable, and while the precise identification of the room and its occupants may still remain a mystery, the painting is nevertheless a useful illustration of a Berainesque interior.

One of the few interior schemes designed by Berain to survive *in situ* can be seen in the Hôtel de Mailly, Paris, which

Berain: engraving, late 17th century

was executed by André Camot in 1687–88. A ceiling remains in the *chambre du lit* (also known as the *salon doré*) but the original wall and door panels were transferred to the Château de la Borde at Vernou-en-Sologne before World War I and reproductions are now in place. The decoration of the panelling is similar to the grotesques realised by Charles Le Brun at Vaux-le-Vicomte, but it does not have the suppleness and animation of other Berain designs. The ceiling is more original and is treated as a single surface. The arabesque structure of bandwork and acanthus is decorated with vines, masks, putti, "galant" motifs in medallions and portraits of Louis de Mailly and his wife surrounded by palms and laurels topped by the Marquis' crown. The decoration highlights the successful collaboration of designer and craftsman. Camot's experience in the execution of theatre and festival designs and his particular skill in imitating gilt-bronze is evident in the shimmering effect of the gold in the ceiling which, subtly highlighted in shades of brown, gives an astonishing sense of relief, so that the ceiling as a whole appears to be a decorative cage. The plain, pale background achieves a new significance as part of this illusion.

Determining the precise extent of Berain's own design work

and that which he delegated to his team of craftsmen is fraught with difficulties owing to the paucity of documentation. He certainly collaborated with other royal craftsmen and artists including the flower painter Jean-Baptiste Monnoyer (1636–99) with whom he worked on tapestries, and the ébéniste Alexander-Jean Oppenordt (c.1639–1715) who executed Berain's designs for the bureau in the Cabinet des Curiosité and a sarcophagus-shaped commode c.1690–95 (Wallace Collection, London). However, the promulgation of Berain's style and the widespread dissemination of his influence is largely attributable to the abundance and subsequent employment of his engraved designs.

Berain engraved only a limited number of designs himself, but about 300 prints were produced by designer-engravers such as Jean and Pierre Le Pautre and Daniel Marot. These engravings, many of which represent adaptations of his work, illustrate the extent of Berain's range not only in designs for ceremonies but also in designs for architectural features, furniture and decorative ornament, and include chandeliers, vases, ironwork, capitals, ceilings, fireplaces and above all panels of decoration. Yet it is undoubtedly as a result of the interpretation of his ideas via engravings that numerous unsubstantiated or erroneous attributions have been made in the past. Today, the frequent use of terms such as "Berainesque" or "in the style of Berain" reflects not only the pervasiveness of his influence but also the difficulties involved in attribution. The highly successful set of *tentures des grotesque* tapestries, designed for the Beauvais workshops c.1690 and still in production in 1725, are often referred to as "Berain Grotesques" but the actual cartoons were painted by Monnoyer. Nevertheless, the designs themselves clearly herald a new stylistic period and contain leafy trellises and fragile architectural constructions resting on slender colonettes that frame a central statue representing either Bacchus or Pan. The foregrounds are enlivened by colourfully attired figures such as animal tamers, dancers, acrobats and characters from the commedia dell'arte.

Berain's most original contribution to interior decoration and design lay in his influence on arabesque and grotesque ornament which provided a vital transitional link between Baroque and Rococo styles of design. Inspired by the forms in Antique wall decoration, grotesque ornament had been transmitted to France from Italy and was employed by, among others, Charles Le Brun at Vaux-le-Vicomte (late 1650s) and the Galerie d'Apollon in the Louvre (1660s). Berain was clearly aware of Le Brun's designs and had been employed to engrave plates depicting the decorations in the Louvre interior in the 1670s. Initially, his own work imitated the style of his immediate predecessors but he gradually developed a lighter and increasingly attenuated ornamental system which although related to the Renaissance *grotteschi*, was to lose the more muscular and sinister qualities inherited from 16th-century designs. The most representative of Berain's fantasies are characterised by the hierarchical nature of the decorative elements within a clearly defined structure and border. The framework is organised around a principal central scene or figure which is often situated within an architectural structure or under a suspended canopy. The remaining ornament and figures are distributed as single elements or additional scenes or groups. Berain employed a wide variety of motifs including animals, trophies, terms, swags, scrolls, acanthus and gods. His monkeys, in particular, represented a novel contribution to design and highlighted not only the move away from traditional grotesque figures such as chimera but also presaged the fashion for *singeries* that was to become such an important part of Rococo decoration and design. The Berainesque grotesque also influenced the sprightlier style of Rococo masters such as Claude III Audran, Claude Gillot, Pierre Le Pautre and others. But, unlike Rococo-style decoration, Berain's own designs remained on the whole symmetrical and were confined within a clearly defined geometric space. Thus, by the end of his lifetime, in comparison with the work of the new generation of ornamentalists, his style was considered old-fashioned. Nonetheless, it had entered the international repertoire of ornament and, as suggested by Jérôme de la Gorce, "Sans lui, l'esthétique de la première moitié du XVIIIe siècle aurait été sans doute différente." (Without him, the aesthetic of the first phase of the 18th century would have been, without doubt, very different).

CHRISTINE RIDING

See also Arabesque and Grotesque; Rococo

Biography

Born in Saint Mihiel, Lorraine, the son of a master gunsmith, in 1640. Family moved to Paris c.1645. Studied etching in his father's workshops. Married: 9 children including the designer Jean II Berain; Charles Le Brun was godfather to Berain's daughter Catherine. Active as a designer from mid-1660s; employed as an engraver by Louis XIV, 1670–74. Appointed Dessinateur de la Chambre et du Cabinet du Roi, 1674; appointed royal garden designer, 1677; given lodgings in the Louvre, 1679. Devised decorations and costumes for all the royal ceremonies and entertainments. Also designed decorations and furnishings for the royal palaces, tapestries, textiles, and metalwork. Published numerous engravings of designs for ornament and furnishings from 1659. Died in Paris, 24 January 1711.

Selected Works

Interiors

1682–85	Versailles (decoration, furniture and fittings for the Cabinet des Médailles and the Petite Galerie)
1687–88	Hôtel de Mailly, Paris (decoration of ceilings and panelling)
1688–89	Grand Trianon, Versailles (interiors)
1699	Château Neuf, Meudon (attributed: chimneypiece and panelling in the cabinet de Monseigneur): Grand Dauphin

More than 250 of Berain's designs for tapestries were woven, many by Louis-Gui Vernansal the Elder (1648–1728) and Jean-Baptiste Monnoyer (1636–99). His textile designs included embroideries for the Dauphin (1680), chair covers for the Dauphine (1695), silks for Nicodemus Tessin the Younger (1695) and silk portières for Versailles (1701). Some of his furniture designs were executed by Jean Oppenord and André Charles Boulle. His metalwork included a toilet service for the Dauphine (1680) and silver girandoles for Versailles (1700).

Publications

Diverses Pièces très utiles pour les Arquebuzières, 1659; 2nd edition 1667

Diverses Pièces de Serruriers, 1663

Oeuvres de Jean Berain, Recueillies par les soins du sieur Thuret, 1711

Further Reading

The standard, scholarly history of Berain's work appears in Weigert 1937 which includes a catalogue of his engravings. For discussions of Berain's work at Meudon see Kimball 1943, Gorce 1986, and Pons 1991.

Le Décor Berain (exhib. cat.), Paris: Musée des Tapisseries, 1960

Dee, Elaine Evans, "Prints in the Age of William and Mary" in *Magazine Antiques*, 134, December 1988

Gorce, Jérôme de la, "Aux Sources de l'Opéra Français" in *Connaissance des Arts*, July–August 1984, pp.28–35

Gorce, Jérôme de la, *Berain, Dessinateur du Roi Soleil*, Paris: Herscher, 1986

Gorce, Jérôme de la, "Berain Décorateur d'un Règne" in *Connaissance des Arts*, 418, December 1986, pp.106–09

Hautecoeur, Louis, *Histoire de l'architecture classique en France*, vol.2, Paris: Picard, 1949

Jean Berain (1640–1711) Ornemaniste et Dessinateur des menus-plaisirs de Louis XIV (exhib. cat.), Nancy: Musée des Beaux-Arts, 1961

Kimball, Fiske, *The Creation of the Rococo*, 1943; reprinted as *The Creation of the Rococo Decorative Style*, New York: Dover, and London: Constable, 1980

Lefort des Ylouses, R., "Des Dessins de Berain à le Bibliothèque et au Musée des Arts Décoratifs" in *Bulletin de la Société de l'Histoire de l'Art Français*, 1954, pp.39–46

Pons, Bruno, "Le Décor de l'Appartement du Grand Dauphin au Château Neuf de Meudon" in *Gazette des Beaux-Arts*, 117, February 1991, pp.59–76

Raggio, Olga, James Parker and Alice M. Zrebiec, "French Decorative Arts During the Reign of Louis XIV 1654–1715" in *Metropolitan Museum of Art Bulletin*, 46, Spring 1989, pp.1–64

Scott, Katie, *The Rococo Interior: Decoration and Social Spaces in Early Eighteenth-Century Paris*, New Haven and London: Yale University Press, 1995

Thornton, Peter, *Seventeenth-Century Interior Decoration in England, France, and Holland*, New Haven and London: Yale University Press, 1978

Weigert, R.-A., "Les Travaux Décoratifs de Jean Bérain à l'Hôtel de Mailly-Nesles" in *Bulletin de la Société de l'Art Français*, 1931, pp.167–174

Weigert, R.-A., *Jean I Berain: Dessinateur de la Chambre et du Cabinet du Roi, 1640–1711*, 2 vols., Paris: Edition d'Art et Histoire, 1937

Weigert, R.-A., "L'Art Décoratif en France: Les Groteschi ou Grotesques, leur Adaptation et leur Évolution: Jean I Berain" in *L'Information Culturelle et Artistique*, 1955, pp.100–06

Berlage, H.P. 1856–1934

Dutch architect and designer

H.P. Berlage, the foremost pioneer of modern architecture in the Netherlands, attained an international stature in the world of design that surpasses that of any other Dutch figure. In his debt are numerous 20th-century architects, among them Ludwig Mies van der Rohe, Peter Behrens, and members of the antithetical groups, the Amsterdam School and De Stijl. In his copious writings, based initially on the ideas of G.W.F. Hegel, E.E. Viollet-le-Duc, and Gottfried Semper, Berlage developed original proposals for the liberation of architecture and interior design from dependence on historical precedent. From his study of the geometric bases that underlie natural forms, he derived the motto "Unity in Diversity" and his goals of harmony, repose and equilibrium. His aesthetic notions were filtered through an ethical and political vision that foresaw an egalitarian society and therefore he intended his stylistic principles to be universally valid, free from the whims of passing fashion and materialistic ostentation.

Like many of his contemporaries, Berlage in each commission strove to attain a Gesamtkunstwerk. But unlike most, he himself was a Gesamtarchitekt, to coin a phrase. No project was too large – he developed extension plans for a number of Dutch cities, – or too small – he considered each piece of furniture a microbuilding. He created not only interior spaces and their containers, but designed many of the fittings, whether he was working on a public or private scale. His education from 1875 to 1878 at the Polytechnical School in Zurich, established by Semper, inclined him in this direction; he was trained in ornamental as well as architectural design and his final project there was for a *Kunstgewerbeschule und museum* (School and Museum of Arts and Crafts or Applied Art). Among his earliest executed works were a series of interiors for tasting bars run by the famous liquor firm of Bols; from 1886 to 1895, he created pubs in Amsterdam, Berlin, Bremen, Hamburg, Antwerp and Paris, which included both free-standing and built-in pieces, such as buffets, tables, and fireplaces. However, such establishments were not prophetic of the future products of this avatar of the Modern style; rather they demonstrated Berlage's skill in adapting the Dutch Renaissance mode.

Between 1891 and 1894, Berlage worked on a series of stage designs for the 17th-century masterpiece by Joost van den Vondel (1587–1679) – *Gysbreght van Aemstel*. In addition to exhibiting his debt to Semper's notion of the tectonic arts being based on four materials and techniques (ceramics, masonry, wood, and textiles – pottery, stereotomy, carpentry and weaving), these sets reveal Berlage's interest in the English Arts and Crafts movement; for example, sunflowers are a frequent motif and there are affinities with the work of C.F.A. Voysey. The two-dimensional patterns Berlage employed also resemble those devised by A.W.N. Pugin, although Viollet-le-Duc's interior "restorations" come to mind as well.

Berlage's mature furniture is simple, spare and sturdy, looking back to the Middle Ages but also to ancient Egypt, as Semper had previously done in a famous passage in *Der Stil in den technischen und tektonischen Künsten; oder Praktische Aesthetik* (Munich, 1860–63) referring to Pharaonic chairs. Through Semper also, Berlage had learned to appreciate the nature of materials, and his designs for objects in wood, metal, and textiles reflect his understanding of the structural and formal strategies that ideally are matched with each different substance. He prized the quality of *Sachlichkeit* (in Dutch, *zakelijkheid*), an untranslatable word that suggests focus on the necessary, the essential, the functional. These characteristics did not exclude the aesthetic pleasure and expressive qualities of ornament, however; it was left for later exponents of the *neue Sachlichkeit*, which Berlage detested, to purge all decorative impulses from interior design.

A product of his era, Berlage was also inspired by nature, and his decorative work belongs to one of the two Dutch manifestations of Art Nouveau – that called Nieuwe Kunst (New Art), characterized by rectilinearity, abstraction, symmetry, and severity, in contrast to the curvilinear branch, based in The Hague and inspired by French and Belgian work, with its elaborate whiplash curves and sensual forms. Berlage was one of the founders in 1900 of Het Binnenhuis (The Interior) in Amsterdam, the foremost purveyor of Nieuwe Kunst for the dwelling; he was among a very gifted cadre associated with that shop whose names constitute a roll of honor of *fin-de-siècle* Dutch decorative designers.

The house of 1898 in The Hague executed for his loyal client Carel Henny, is an excellent example of Berlage's approach to interior design. Planned around a double-height, skylighted stair hall, the Henny House has interior walls of soft red brick trimmed with glazed yellow, blue and white brick and with stone; for the first time in Berlage's domestic architecture the internal walls have been left unplastered to reveal the masonry and unite exterior and interior surfaces. Wooden floors and beams and wrought iron balconies complete the palette of materials. Tables, built-in cabinets, rugs and a grandfather's clock were all specially designed by Berlage for this ensemble.

Berlage was simultaneously engaged on two significant public commissions which have stylistic affinities with the Henny House: the Produce, Grain and Stock Exchange (Beurs, 1896–1903) for the capitalist merchants and traders of Amsterdam, and the headquarters of the Dutch Brotherhood of Diamond Workers (1897–1900) for the most advanced trade union in the Netherlands. The similarity in imagery and materials of two buildings for such vastly different constituencies tellingly illustrates Berlage's belief in an architecture of universal appeal, while the harmony of the interiors with the overall architectural concept demonstrates his fidelity to the *Gesamtkunstwerk*. Lighting fixtures, furniture (including, in the Beurs, specially designed brokers' booths) carpets, wallpaper, letterheads, logos, and calendars conform to the exquisitely sober style of Nieuwe Kunst. Berlage also believed in close collaboration with ornamentalists and craftsmen and both buildings have carved and tiled figurative decoration inside and out designed and executed by prominent artists such as Lambertus Zijl, Jan Toorop, and R.N. Roland Holst. Text is used aesthetically as well as didactically; the slogan *Proletariers Aller Landen Vereeniat U* (Workers of the World Unite!), spelled out in bright glazed tiles, is integral with the masonry of the multi-level stairhall of the Diamond Workers' headquarters. The ornamental patterns as well as the organization of the elevations and spaces were devised, according to a system of geometric proportions, based on the so-called Egyptian triangle, advocated by Semper and Viollet-le-Duc; after 1897, Berlage applied this system to all of his work, including the Henny House.

One of Berlage's most completely realized ensembles is the St. Hubertus Hunting Lodge that was commissioned in 1914 by a pair of his most faithful patrons, Hélène Kröller and her husband, A.G. Müller; indeed he executed a number of projects for this wealthy shipbuilding family. The lodge overlooks a pond in the wooded preserve of De Hoge Veluwe in Gelderland (today a national park). The imagery that governs the plan, massing and decoration of the lodge is based on the legend of St. Hubertus, the patron saint of hunting for whom it is named. The symmetrical plan suggests the antlers of the crucifix-bearing stag which guided the lost saint from the forest and effected his conversion to a life of service and piety; the six-storey tower that crowns the apex of the composition refers to the cross. Ceramic tiles placed in the walls reinforce the references. Dark wood wainscoting, floors, bookcases, desks and tables complement wall and ceiling surfaces of glazed and moulded brick and tile in green and the primary colors, white and black; the upholstery and carpets are the same hues. Chandeliers, clocks, fireplace utensils, metal-clad doors, and stained-glass windows designed by Berlage and his collaborators complete this thoroughly conceived and magnificently realized fantasy, the work by Berlage that is most closely allied to the current of Expressionism then being propagated in the Netherlands by his younger colleagues in the Amsterdam School.

Thanks to the municipal policy of Amsterdam which during the years 1915 to 1930 turned the new portions of the city into a *Gesamtkunstwerk*, Berlage's large-scale urbanistic plan for Amsterdam South (1903; 1915–17) is complemented by street furniture and bridges sympathetic to the larger ensemble, often designed by members of the Amsterdam School. Berlage himself was responsible for two of the many unique bridges that cross Amsterdam's numerous canals: the second Amstelbrug, of 1906, and the aptly named Berlagebrug of 1928–32.

One of the major architectural works of his last period is the Gemeentemuseum (Municipal Museum) in The Hague, completed posthumously in 1935 but designed over the years from 1919 to 1929. Here Berlage paid particular attention to the display spaces for decorative arts, of which the museum has a fine collection.

HELEN SEARING

Biography

Hendrik Petrus Berlage. Born in Amsterdam, 21 February 1856. Studied painting at the Rijksakademie van Beeldende Kunsten, Amsterdam, 1874–75; studied architecture at the Eidgenössische Technische Hochschule, Zurich, 1875–78. Travelled in Germany, 1879; in Italy, 1880–81; visited the USA, 1911. Married Marie Bienfait, 1887. Practised as an architect in Arnhem, Netherlands, 1879; worked in the office of the engineer Theodorus Sanders, Amsterdam, 1881–84; in partnership with Sanders, 1884–89; independent practice in Amsterdam and The Hague, 1889–1934. Active as a designer of furniture, ironwork, lighting and glass from the 1890s; opened Het Binnenhuis, a combined furniture and crafts workshop and saleroom, with Jacob van den Bosch and W. Hoeker, in 1900. Published several books and articles on ornament and design and, an acknowledged authority on modern architecture and design, he was a delegate at the first Congrès Internationaux d'Architecture Moderne (CIAM), Geneva, 1928. Awarded a Gold Medal, Royal Institute of British Architects, 1932. Died in The Hague, 12 August 1934.

Selected Works

The largest collection of drawings, designs and documentation relating to Berlage's work is the Berlage Archive, Nederlands Documentatiecentrum voor de Bouwkunst, Rotterdam. Examples of Berlage's furniture are in the Stedelijk Museum, Amsterdam, the Rijksmuseum Kröller-Müller, Otterlo, the Gemeentemuseum,The Hague, and the Centraalmuseum, Utrecht. A complete catalogue of Berlage's architectural projects and designs for decorative work appears in Polano 1988.

Interiors

1893–94 Arti et Amicitiae, Amsterdam (clubroom interiors and furnishings)

1894–95 De Nederlanden van 1845 Insurance Company Building, Amsterdam (building, interiors and furnishings)
1895–96 De Nederlanden van 1845 Insurance Company Building, The Hague (building, interiors and furnishings)
1896–1903 Stock Exchange (Beurs), Amsterdam (building, interiors and furnishings)
1897–1900 Headquarters of the Dutch Brotherhood of Diamond Workers, Amsterdam (building, interiors and furnishings)
1898 Villa Henny, The Hague (building, interiors and furnishings): Carel Henny
1900 Villa Parkwijk, Amsterdam (building, interiors and furnishings): Leo Simons
1914–20 St. Hubertus Hunting Lodge, Otterlo, Netherlands (building, interiors and furnishings): Kröller-Müller family
1919–29 Municipal Museum (Gemeentemuseum), The Hague (building and interiors)
1920–27 De Nederlanden van 1845 Insurance Company Building, The Hague (building, interiors and furnishings)

Berlage also designed furniture (much made in Het Binnenhuis workshop), graphics, textiles, lighting, metalwork and wallpapers.

Publications

"Over Architectuur" in *Tweemaandelijks Tijdschrift*, 11, 1896
Over Stijl in Bouw- en Meubelkunst, 1904; 2nd edition, 1908; 3rd edition, 1917
Gedanken über Stil in der Baukunst, 1905
Grundlagen und Entwicklung der Architektur, 1908
Studies over Bouwkunst, Stijl en Samenleving, 1910
Een drietal lezingen in Amerika gehouden, 1912
Amerikaansche Reisherinneringen, 1913
L'Art et la Société, 1921
"Het werk van den Amerikaanschen arch. Frank Lloyd Wright" in *Wendingen*, 11 (special issue, 1921)
De Ontwikkeling der moderne Bouwkunst in Holland, 1925
Het Wezen der Bouwkunst en haar Geschiedenis: Aesthetische Beschouwingen, 1934

Further Reading

Useful English-language studies of Berlage's work appear in Singelenberg 1972, and Polano 1988 which also includes a complete list of Berlage's writings and an extensive bibliography of primary and secondary sources.

Bock, Manfred and others, *Berlage in Amsterdam*, Amsterdam: Architecture & Natura, 1992
Eisler, Max, *Der Baumeister Berlage*, Vienna: Holzel, 1921
Gratama, Jan, "Dr. H.P. Berlage, Bouwmeester", 1925; reprinted in Manfred Bock, *Anfänge einer Neuen Architektur*, The Hague: Staatsuitgeverij, 1983
Grinberg, Donald I., *Housing in the Netherlands, 1900–1940*, Delft: Delft University Press, 1977
Gunnink, M., *St. Hubertus's Lodge: Designed by H.P. Berlage, Architect for the Kröller-Müller Family*, Otterlo: Kröller-Müller Stichting, 1985
"H.P. Berlage" in *Bouwkundig Weekblad Architectura*, (special issue), 51, 1934
Havelaar, Just, *Dr. H.P. Berlage*, Amsterdam: van Munster, 1927
Polano, Sergio (editor), *Hendrik Petrus Berlage: Complete Works*, New York: Rizzoli, 1988
Reinink, Adriaan Wessel, *Amsterdam en de Beurs van Berlage: Reacties van Tijdgenoten*, The Hague: Staatsuitgeverij, 1975
Searing, Helen, "Berlage and Housing, 'the most significant modern building type'" in *Nederlands Kunsthistorisch Jaarboek*, 25 (1974), pp.133–79
Singelenberg, Pieter, *H.P. Berlage: Idea and Style: The Quest for Modern Architecture*, Utrecht: Dekker & Gumbert, 1972
Singelenberg, Pieter, "Berlage in London: Holland House in Bury Street 1914–16", in *Bouwen in Nederland*, Leidse Kunsthistorisch Jaarboek, 1984, pp.407–25

Berlin School

The term "Berlin School" (Schmitz) refers to those architects who were active in Berlin during the last decade of the 18th century and who belonged to the circle of the Private Society of Young Architects, founded by Friedrich Gilly in 1799, or who were students of David Gilly at the private school of civil engineering he founded in 1793 (which became the State Academy of Civil Engineering in 1799). Of particular note are the architects Friedrich Gilly (1772–1800), Heinrich Gentz (1766–1811), and Carl Gotthard Langhans (1732–1808), but the young Karl Friedrich Schinkel (1781–1841) who came under the mantle of Friedrich Gilly's intellectual legacy in 1800, is also a significant figure. These architects were moulded by ideas of classicism and of "revolutionary architecture", but they also each developed individual forms in which the nature of their transposition of antique models (Greek as well as Roman) varied. While David Gilly's designs still included elements from the late Baroque, Gentz and, in particular, Friedrich Gilly detached themselves completely from this style. Their forms of architecture, influenced by the cube, the pyramid and the triangle, are generally labelled with the (questionable) term "revolutionary architecture". Although Berlin was the centre for these architects, they erected significant buildings outside Berlin and Prussia, such as David Gilly's Vieweg House in Brunswick (completed in 1804) and Heinrich Gentz's Weimar Castle (1801–03). Numerous plans were extant until 1945 and are reproduced in older monographic works. Like the Berlin buildings themselves, many of these documents were destroyed during the war.

David Gilly (1748–1808) was summoned by King Friedrich Wilhelm II to Berlin in 1788, where he had a formative influence on the young architects of the Berlin School. In 1796–97 he built the castle and the village of Paretz for crown prince Friedrich Wilhelm (III), which can be regarded as the most important work of his Berlin period. The "Paretz Sketchbook" – views and ground plans drawn up by Martin Friedrich Rabe – provides an impression of the original state and coloration of this work (M. Lammert). The building's exterior – a long, rectangular structure divided by offset ribbing and window axes with little architectural modelling – makes no reference to the structure of the interior. The exclusion of the flight of entrance steps beyond the actual entrance area and the separation of the vestibule represent an innovation when compared to magnificent Baroque stairways. Unfortunately, the building is destroyed and further indications of the interior design no longer exist.

Gilly's house for the publisher Vieweg was completed in Brunswick in 1804. Here the architect had to accommodate not only sumptuous living quarters, but also the premises of the publishing business. The offset ribbing arrangement of the exterior structure finds its correspondence in the interior's oval ground plan. The stairwell with its flight of entrance steps also has an oval ground plan. There is no information about the

Berlin School: staircase hall Weimar Castle, by Heinrich Gentz, 1801–03

original layout of the interior, which had already been altered many times by the 19th century. Restoration has shown that exposed remnants of paint originate from the 19th century. The interior designs of other buildings by David Gilly are not known, and his actual influence on his followers' structuring of interiors is therefore difficult to determine.

Gilly's son, Friedrich, had a lasting influence on his circle of friends and followers, including Schinkel, although owing to his premature death only a few of his architectural designs were realised. His design for the monument to King Friedrich II (1797) was particularly significant. Gilly can be regarded as the focal point of the Berlin School, as the decisive impulses came from him, and his death signified the end of the Private Society of Young Architects as a communal forum for discussion. However, both his father David Gilly and Carl Gotthard Langhans were already active in the years before Friedrich's period of activity and influence in Berlin. Although most of his designs concentrate exclusively upon the exterior of buildings and only a few drawings give an impression of his ideas for a building's interior (catalogue, Berlin 1984), it is clear from both photographs and drawings of completed projects (1794: drawings of the Hochmeister's Palace of Marienburg, East Prussia) and from his sketches and designs that Gilly's preoccupation with the interior design dates from the early period of his work.

The idea of a grave monument occupied him repeatedly and he planned its interior in a wide variety of forms. In 1791 he designed a pyramid (Oncken, plate 136) whose interior forms a large rotunda. Sixteen columns support a low tambour over a plain entablature, above which the vault of the cupola rises. The sarcophagus is located in the centre of the space, flanked by two sphinxes. Four rectangular air shafts illuminate the cupola. Echoes of a design for a mausoleum by Langhans Senior from 1784 (Schmitz, illus. p.33) are clear, but Gilly's design appears more monumental and is reduced to the essentials. In 1796, Gilly designed a tomb (Oncken, plate 19C), which he planned as a grotto with coffered barrel vaulting and a socle wall which juts out as a solid bench. Compared with this, the construction of space in a catacomb from c.1795 (Oncken, plate 21), which Gilly planned as a place of burial, appears more sumptuous. Powerful pillars support coffered girders, lateral passages cut like Gothic vaults into the vaulted surfaces between the girders. A deep door recess with a broad flight of stairs forms the entrance to the room on one long side of its rectangle; the room is illuminated only by a semi-circular window above the door. Just as these three mausoleum designs demonstrate clear differences – with common elements only appearing in the extensive abandonment of decoration – so the rest of Gilly's plans diverge from each other.

Gilly built up the plan for Berlin's National Theatre (1798–99) in some 40 sketches and designs, in which his search for a cohesively developed, unified interior is just as discernible as his variation of certain ordering and formal elements, for example, the positioning of the columns along the walls of the boxes and the design of the ceiling. The definitive design differs fundamentally from the earlier versions in its treatment of the walls of the boxes and in its ornateness and the working through of its decorative details (Oncken). The stage is covered by a star-shaped coffered barrel vault; the stalls are bordered by the fluent lines of the boxes' socle wall, decorated with a hanging palmette frieze. The middle box projects outwards and is thus accentuated. It is framed by columns that support an entablature that is decorated by a frieze and that runs along the plain walls of the boxes as a figural frieze. The ceiling is structured in a richly varied way; a segmented arch with organic and ornamental decoration spans the stalls. A half-barrel vault adjoins this, spanning the boxes adorned with a meander frieze and organic forms which run towards a central point.

Friedrich Gilly's concern with the interior design of residential buildings is evident from some of his plans, but what he planned for the external structure of these buildings is for the most part unknown. The walls of a vestibule (Oncken, plate 70b) are divided by Ionic columns, half-columns and pilasters, and the sections of this wall resulting from these divisions, lying above a cranked socle band, are further divided by an entablature decorated with festoons. Gilly also designed a garden room with an octagonal ground plan. A cranked socle strip and a horizontal ledge, which forms a transition to the vault, frame the space. The upper third of the wall of this room – which was possibly conceived as an anteroom – was decorated with incised reliefs. A variety of furniture designs, which had an influence on Schinkel's early designs, have also survived. But only a fraction of Gilly's designs are still available in the original; most have been missing since 1945. Moreover, hardly any of Gilly's plans were actually executed, yet his effect on friends and followers was profound.

Heinrich Gentz was one of Friedrich Gilly's closest friends and a co-founder of the Private Society of Young Architects. His Berlin Mint, built between 1798 and 1800 and demolished in 1886, was one of Berlin's important classical buildings; sadly, however, nothing is known of its interior design. Gentz proved himself as an interior designer primarily with Weimar Castle. Large sections of this castle were destroyed by fire in 1774. The work of rebuilding and newly constructing the castle using old stonework extended well into the 19th century. In close contact with Johann Wolfgang von Goethe, Gentz's chief designs were for the banqueting hall, the gallery (*Falkensaal*) and, most significantly, for the stairway in Weimar. Out of the narrow, low space of the gallery, a space which was also blocked off at either end, Gentz created a state room. He extended the room visually by having it open out into semi-circular niches on the short sides of its rectangle and he spanned the room, which had previously been flat-roofed, with a coffered barrel vault in the shape of a basket-arch. He let in small niches opposite the windows, and the two features together lent the room a lively rhythm.

While the proportions of the gallery had already been laid down, Gentz was able to intervene to a much greater extent in the layout of the stairway. Doric columns and a frieze of metopes and triglyphs running below the ceiling constitute the principal formal elements. The columns set off the actual run of stairs from the upper landing and also serve to support the ceiling above a powerfully-formed architrave. Three large reliefs by the Berlin sculptor Christian Friedrich Tieck (1776–1851) decorate the upper stairway and symbolise the influence of the sovereign. Tieck also created eight plaster statues in 1803 in close cooperation with Goethe, four of which were installed on the stairway. It is very likely that they were part of Gentz's overall conception. Areas of free-standing sculpture and reliefs create tense contrasts with the large sections of wall that are left free and unordered.

The banqueting hall occupies two floors and is surrounded by a series of columns that support galleries on the hall's short sides. The rhythm that is created by the series of columns is taken up by the succession of doorways and niches into which sculptural figures have been set. A griffin frieze that runs around the hall and the powerful, embellished architrave together provide a vertical counterweight to the columns which emphasise the horizontal. The design for the ceiling is not by Gentz, but by his predecessor in Weimar, Nicolaus Friedrich von Thonnet (1767–1845). The design of the rooms seems to be oriented towards a heightening of their splendour and of the ceremonial impression that they create. From the simple entrance hall and the stairway to the banqueting hall, Gentz moved towards a richer and more vibrant style of decoration and a predominance of elements in the Ionic style (Jericke and Dolgner).

With Goethe's cooperation, Gentz built a small theatre in Bad Lauchstadt (between Merseburg and Halle), the favoured spa of the Weimar court around 1800, that was opened in 1802. The theatre consists of a three-storey fly tower and a two-storey auditorium of the same width, which is served by a low entrance hall. The interior has a simple layout. The auditorium, which ends in a semicircle, has dress circle galleries at the back and galleries continue at the same height at the sides. The ceiling's barrel vaulting is decorated with fine ribbing, which has the effect of ruffled canvas. The auditorium is kept simple and all embellishment is sacrificed, except for paintings in the Pompeian style.

Gentz did not build anything else in Berlin until 1810 when he designed plans for the Princess Palace, although the only part of this building to be executed was part of the exterior's offset ribbing. Queen Luise's mausoleum in the grounds of the Palace of Charlottenburg was designed by Schinkel on King Friedrich Wilhelm III's own brief; Gentz was simply responsible for the construction as the leader of the court's planning department and building office (Hofbauamt). The layout of the repeatedly-extended interior cannot be traced back to him.

Carl Gotthard Langhans was of the same generation as David Gilly. Although the first buildings of his Breslau period, such as the former Hatzfeld Palace in Breslau (1766–73, fitting out of the interior until 1786), already betray a leaning towards classicism in their exteriors, their interiors are still clearly linked to the Rococo style. Director of the newly-created planning department and building office (Hofbauamt) in Berlin from 1788, Langhans was repeatedly enlisted by the court in the renovation of its castles, such as those in Rheinsberg and Potsdam (Marble Palace; Orangery). In 1788 he designed the Charlottenburg Palace's theatre, which was opened in 1791. The interior fittings were destroyed during major rebuilding work in 1902; few drawings or photographs show Langhans's interior design. The auditorium had three circles, supported by palm-shaped corbels. These, along with the ceiling with its false parapet and heavenly sea of clouds painted by Cunningham, constitute the only indication of the original design. In 1789–91 he created the Brandenburg Gate, his best-known work, a work which clearly shows Langhans's move towards classical forms and which betrays references to the Propylaeum in Athens.

Langhan's son, Carl Ferdinand Langhans (1782–1869), was a member of the Private Society of Young Architects. His buildings, which were erected after the Wars of Liberation, are oriented more towards Schinkel's work than towards that of Gilly's circle during the last decade of the 18th century. Works such as the New Theatre in Leipzig (1864–67) are thus no longer influenced by the Berlin School with its commitment to "revolutionary architecture".

The term Berlin School is problematic. The different architects each developed their own specific conceptions, which, in the realm of interior design, have mostly been only hazily preserved. Common ground between designs by the architects Friedrich Gilly and Heinrich Gentz, or especially between those of Langhans Senior and Langhans Junior, is hard to establish. The expression Berlin School may only indicate, therefore, that Gilly, Langhans and Gentz conversed with each other in the last decade of the 18th century and in the early 19th century and, united by the Private Society of Young Architects, sought new forms together, turning away from the formal vocabulary of the Baroque while rediscovering the architecture of the Greeks and Romans. A common formal programme, such as that in Schinkel's day, was not a feature of the Berlin School.

BETTINA JOST

Further Reading

Bollé, Michael, "Antiquities of Berlin? Carl Gotthard Langhans und die Architektur in Berlin um 1800" in *Das Brandenburger Tor, 1791–1991* edited by Willmuth Arenhövel and Rolf Bothe, Berlin: Arenhövel, 1991

Doebber, Adolph, *Das Schloss in Weimar: Seine Geschichte vom Brande, 1774 bis zur Wiederherstellung 1804*, Jena: Fischer, 1911

Friedrich Gilly, 1772–1800, und die Privatgesellschaft junger Architekten (exhib. cat.), Berlin: Berlin Museum, 1984

Hinrichs, Walther Th., *Carl Gotthard Langhans: Ein schlesischer Baumeister, 1733–1808*, Strasbourg: Heitz, 1909

Jericke, Alfred and Dieter Dolgner, *Der Klassizismus in der Baugeschichte Weimars*, Weimar: Bohlau, 1975

Lammert, Marlies, *David Gilly: Ein Baumeister des deutschen Klassizismus*, Berlin: Akademie, 1964; 2nd edition Berlin: Mann, 1981

Möller, Hans-Herbert (editor), *Das Vieweg-Haus in Braunschweig*, Hannover: Niedersächsisches Landesverwaltungsamt, 1985

Nerdinger, Winfried and others, *Revolutionsarchitektur: Ein Aspekt der europäischen Architektur um 1800* (exhib. cat.), Munich: Hirmer, 1990

Neumeyer, Fritz (introduction), *Friedrich Gilly: Essays on Architecture, 1796–1799*, Santa Monica, CA: Getty Center for the History of Art and Humanities, 1994

Oncken, Alste, *Friedrich Gilly, 1772–1800*, Berlin: Mann, 1981 (first published 1935)

Schmitz, Hermann, *Berliner Baumeister vom Ausgang des achtzehnten Jahrhunderts*, Berlin: Verlag für Kunstwissenschaft, 1914; reprinted 1925, 1980

Berlin Woolwork

Berlin woolwork was a type of counted thread embroidery on mesh canvas popular in western Europe and North America during the first three-quarters of the 19th century that was characterized by bright colors and naturalistic designs. In

Berlin Woolwork: design for three prie-dieu chairs from Henry Wood's *A Useful and Modern Work on Cheval and Pole Screens ... for Mounting Berlin Needlework*, 1846

domestic interiors Berlin woolwork was used for chair seats and backs, footstools, firescreens, sofa seats and backs, pillow covers, valances, table covers, rugs, framed pictures, and many smaller accessories.

Counted thread work on canvas has been done since ancient times. From the time the first printed pattern book appeared in Germany in 1523 until the early 19th century, counted thread patterns were printed in black and white on a grid background, with color changes indicated by different symbols in the squares. Needleworkers who wanted to work from a colored design had their canvases painted by professional artists, and then worked stitching over the paint. In 1804 a Berlin print-seller, A. Philipson, produced *Colorirte au 12 Blatt bestehende Muster* published by H. Kronberger-Frentzen. These were colored designs on point paper, a printed grid similar to graph paper. The patterns became generally available throughout western Europe within a year, but they were not as popular as expected.

In 1810 the Ludwig Wilhelm Wittich firm in Berlin began issuing patterns with hand-colored squares to designate colors. The Wittich patterns were, and still are, considered to be the best of their kind. The patterns soon became known as "Berlin patterns" and the resulting needlework was known as "Berlin work" or "Berlin woolwork". The patterns were exported to England, Russia, Sweden, Denmark, North America, Holland, Belgium, Switzerland, Italy, Spain, Portugal, Australia, and New Zealand. Publishers in Vienna and Paris soon began issuing patterns, and women's magazines such as *Godey's Lady's Book* (1830–98) included patterns as part of a continuing campaign to encourage women to occupy their time in making decorations for their homes. These patterns were often accompanied by instructions for doing the work.

The colored patterns were immensely popular with amateur embroiderers, who had only to match their yarn to the colors on the pattern and stitch over one warp / weft intersection of the canvas for each square on the pattern. Favored subjects were flowers, animals, sentimental figures, and popular paintings. Berlin patterns became very complex with realistic shading and detail.

Berlin woolwork pieces were executed with blunt tapestry needles primarily in the half-cross tent stitch or in cross stitch. Other canvas stitches were used, but the complexities of the shading in most of the patterns precluded the use of stitches that covered more than one square of the design. Small beads on silk threads were sometimes added to highlight portions of the design. Other variations included plushwork, introduced in the 1840s, consisting of long loopy stitches either left untrimmed or trimmed to create a fuzzy surface or a sculptured pile of three-dimensional birds or flowers. The sculpturing usually had to be done professionally. An imitation of black lace worked in silk or wool called "canvas lace work" was introduced also in the 1840s, and was used on cushions, ottoman tops, lamp mats, and table covers.

When Berlin patterns were first published, the work was done on silk canvas with silk thread. In the 1820s Berlin wool, or Zephyr Merino, yarns from Merino sheep in Saxony, were spun at Gotha in Germany, then dyed with natural dyes in Berlin. By the 1840s the wool was being produced in other countries. The wool had high bulk and only a little twist, and was available in various weights. It was softer and thicker than the crewel wool used for embroidery in the 18th century. The wools were dyed in bright colors to match the colored patterns, and became even brighter with the introduction of synthetic aniline dyes in 1856 by William Henry Perkin. The bright aniline colors were popularly called "gaslight" colors. The first was a purple known as "Perkin's mauve" followed in 1860 by magenta. Aniline dyes faded after exposure to light, but this did not diminish their popularity.

Although Berlin wool was soft, tight stitching on canvas made it suitable for upholstery, and it was not as subject to wear as the raised stitching of the earlier crewelwork. Since the work was done mounted on a frame, it was possible to do fairly large pieces without distortion. Some sofa seats and backs, and rugs were done, but smaller pieces were more common. Patterns designed specifically for pieces such as chair backs were shaped to fit. Heavy jute or cotton canvas was embroidered for upholstered furniture, and the finished work was mounted professionally. On many pieces the entire background around the design was covered with stitching, but sometimes the worked design was cut out and appliquéd, or sewed, to a cloth background. Designs could also be worked directly on cloth using the waste canvas method, in which the stitching was done over canvas laid on the cloth, and the canvas threads removed after the work was completed.

There was little attempt to relate Berlin woolwork upholstery designs to the style of the furniture on which they were mounted. The same naturalistic flowers could be found on any style of seating piece. In 1846 Henry Wood's *A Useful and Modern Work on Cheval and Pole Screens, Ottomans, Chairs and Settees for Mounting Berlin Needle Work* showed many styles of furniture all with similar floral-patterned upholstery. Firescreens and framed pictures often had copies of popular paintings, biblical lithographs, or famous persons such as the Prince of Wales and George Washington. The pictures resembled German and Austrian painting styles of the Biedermeier and Realist periods and the Troubadour style in France. Bird designs, usually parrots and macaws, were used for firescreens, cushions, and decorative panels. In the 1830s and 1840s floral wreaths and bunches of flowers were set on a light background. By the 1850s large flowers on a black background set off the bright colors. After 1850 there was a trend toward geometric designs in neo-Gothic style. These allowed for a greater variety of stitches, in particular the leviathan or railway stitch (now known as Smyrna cross) which covered four squares instead of one, and the perspective stitch in which graduated lengths formed a cube that appeared to be three-dimensional. Colors became more muted in the 1860s, and floral designs gave way to Greek key borders, folded ribbons, diaper patterns, ornamental scrolls, arabesques, and formalized acanthus and vine leaves. Large seating furniture was no longer covered with Berlin woolwork, as cushions and footstools predominated.

A perforated paper called Bristol board was introduced in the 1840s and was at first used for small items. From the 1870s to 1900 large mottoes and pictures worked in wool on Bristol board hung on walls in middle-class homes. Designs were printed directly on the paper, and the background was not filled in. Simple mottoes such as "Home Sweet Home" or elaborate renderings of the Lord's Prayer or the Ten Commandments were worked in shaded wools. A variation depicting ships known as "woolies" was done by British sailors. Even the paper Berlin patterns themselves were sometimes framed and hung as works of art.

Criticism was directed at Berlin woolwork from several sources. Since it dominated the needlework done by the middle and upper classes in western Europe and North America during its period of popularity, there was some complaint in the 1840s from church authorities that church needlework was suffering because the designs were not suitable for ecclesiastical use. The designs, which admittedly varied in quality, were attacked on artistic grounds by William Morris and others, particularly after the rise of the Arts and Crafts movement in the 1860s. Berlin work was considered too easy and simple-minded by some critics, a criticism that seems unjustified given the complex shading and multiple color changes required to execute most of the designs. Others decried the lack of originality on the part of the stitchers, also a somewhat unrealistic complaint since needleworkers have traditionally worked from designs created by others.

These criticisms did not have any effect on the needleworkers. The demise of Berlin woolwork, when it occurred in the 1870s, was the result of a new fad, art needlework, taking its place. William Morris, who established his own firm, Morris, Marshall, Faulkner & Co., in 1861, introduced the style in his own embroidery, and it was further advocated by the Royal School of Art Needlework, established in London in 1872. In America, Louis Comfort Tiffany and Candace Wheeler supported the new art needlework. The Philadelphia Centennial Exposition in 1876 had a large exhibit in the Women's Pavilion from the Royal School of Art Needlework that impressed many fairgoers with the new style. By 1900 the popular ladies' magazines had discontinued Berlin patterns, and few were published after that. Some needleworkers, however, continued to work from the old patterns until the 1930s when production of the Berlin wools was discontinued. In the late 20th century there has been renewed interest in collecting the old Berlin patterns and reproducing the work using modern materials.

CONSTANCE A. FAIRCHILD

See also Firescreens and Polescreens; Needlework

Further Reading

A detailed history of Berlin Woolwork, including an account of the designs and techniques, appears in Proctor 1972. For useful surveys see Morris 1962 and Warren 1976.

Karr, Louise, "Berlin Wool Work" in Betty Ring (editor), *Needlework: An Historical Survey*, 2nd edition Pittstown, NJ: Main Street Press, 1984

Morris, Barbara, *Victorian Embroidery*, London: Jenkins, 1962

Proctor, Molly G., *Victorian Canvas Work: Berlin Wool Work*, London: Batsford and New York: Drake, 1972

Swain, Margaret, "Stitching Triumphant" in *Country Life*, 185, 21 March 1991, pp.124–26

Vincent, Margaret, *The Ladies' Work Table: Domestic Needlework in Nineteenth-Century America*, Allentown, PA: Allentown Art Museum, 1988

Warner, Pamela, *Embroidery: A History*, London: Batsford, 1991

Warren, Geoffrey, *A Stitch in Time: Victorian and Edwardian Needlecraft*, Newton Abbot, Devon: David and Charles, 1976
Wood, Henry, *A Useful and Modern Work on Cheval and Pole Screens, Ottomans, Chairs and Settees, for Mounting Berlin Needle Work*, London: Ackermann, 1846

Biedermeier

The Biedermeier style dominated Central European tastes in furniture and interiors during the Vormärz, or Pre-March period, which lasted from the Congress of Vienna in 1814 and 1815 through to the March revolution of 1848. The Congress of Vienna signalled the end of the Napoleonic Wars and their attendant violence and instability, and the Austrian Empire – which included all of present-day Austria and Hungary, as well as much of the western part of what is now the Czech Republic – benefited enormously from increased prosperity and economic growth in the following years. Its capital, Vienna, became a natural magnet for the many craftsmen and artists, as well as the flourishing merchant classes who were exploiting their new-found freedom to trade and travel between states. Even as early as 1816, 875 independent master cabinet-makers were active in Vienna, and this figure had by 1823 risen to 951.

The name "Biedermeier" itself was coined some time after the period, and in fact was far from complimentary. "Biedermeier" is commonly attributed to the satirical writers Adolph Kussmaul (1822–1902) and Ludwig Eichrodt (1827–92). Their pseudonym, Gottlob Biedermaier, was a fictional author whose self-satisfied insularity symbolised all that was regarded as being negative about his era. "Bieder" means plain, everyday, and "Meier" (or Maier) is the German equivalent of the surname Smith. Hence the term was a scornful reference to the flourishing and newly-influential bourgeoisie with their largely materialistic values and their limited aspirations, during the first half of the 19th century. Although it was initially used in connection with literature and painting of the period, the appellation "Biedermeier" is today most often associated with furniture and the decorative arts.

In many ways the development of the Biedermeier style mirrors the arrival of the Industrial Revolution in Central Europe and its far-reaching changes in culture and society. No longer were fine furniture and furnishings the preserve of the aristocracy; a new market emerged with the rise of the bourgeoisie, at the same time as new production techniques were bringing down the cost of a wide range of luxury goods.

Although precise definitions of the style have been the subject of arcane debates among Austrian and German art historians for decades, Biedermeier furniture is generally held to be that produced in the Austrian Empire and the Germanic States in the late Neo-Classical period from around 1810 to 1830, and in the transitional period to the widespread adoption of Historicist styles from around 1830 to 1850. Neo-Classicism is often represented as an austere backlash against the extravagances of Rococo, but it was not a complete break with the past; many of the characteristics of that style lingered on in a diluted form in early Biedermeier pieces, in the form of bronze mounts and elaborate asymmetrical figurative ornament. The work of Benedikt Holl (c.1753–1833) is typical of this formative period. His pieces, including ladies' writing tables adorned with fine inlays, were in some ways a throwback to the traditions of technical virtuosity and exclusivity of the previous century, although there is in his work a clear shift toward the integration of decoration with structure which is characteristic of later "high" Biedermeier.

Many of the finest pieces of early Biedermeier furniture were executed as masterpieces; virtuoso demonstrations of a craftsman's skill and his maturity. These were frequently taken directly from the pattern books of the time, such as the *Cabinet-Maker and Upholsterer's Drawing Book*, published by Thomas Sheraton (1751–1806) in London from 1791 to 1793, and the *Modell- und Musterbuch für Bau- und Möbel-Tischler*, published in several editions by Marius Wölfer from 1826 to 1836. A distinctive secretaire by Adolph Friedrich Voight, who was active in Berlin between 1805 and 1826, is closely based on a published Sheraton design. It displays many of the characteristics of later Biedermeier furniture: an essentially simple design, borrowing lyre-form legs from the language of Neo-Classicism, and one which is immensely practical, combining as it does the functions of a writing desk and of a screen in the same piece.

This characteristic preoccupation with multi-purpose furniture was however not ingenuity merely for its own sake. Patterns of life were changing; an increasing urban middle class brought far higher population density – especially in Vienna, whose population grew from around 300,000 in the 1820s to 430,000 in 1857 – together with a higher level of ownership of luxury goods such as fine furniture. The result was an entirely practical fashion for space-saving and dual-purpose pieces. The new middle classes could not afford to furnish both lavish reception rooms and comfortable living areas separately; hence the popularity of pieces such as the *Couvertrahmen*, a traditional upholstered wooden frame which covered the bed and bedclothes, enabling the bedroom to be used as a semi-formal living room in the daytime.

The spending power of the middle classes also gave early Biedermeier another of its distinctive traits, in its rejection of expensive materials and labour-intensive processes for ones which were cheaper and more suited to the new, semi-industrial production techniques. Stained pear wood frequently serves as a substitute for ebony, for example. The cast bronze gilt mounts which echoed the earlier Empire style were copied in thin stamped brass plate, and patinated bronze castings were modelled in composition instead. Ultimately, this applied decoration died out completely; gilt mounts, for example, appear with declining frequency until around 1825; similarly, complex inlay and marquetry, which the early Biedermeier craftsmen had imitated with pen and ink, also diminished in popularity. Technological developments such as veneer cutting machines – which could produce continuous, large sheets of veneer by "peeling" wood from the outside surface of the log through to the heart wood – enabled designers and craftsmen to break free of the cost and limitations of traditional furniture manufacture. Veneers could be made more uniform in their grain and thinner, hence more elastic, making them ideal for covering complex curved surfaces.

The most successful craftsman and entrepreneur of the Biedermeier era was Josef Danhauser (1780–1829), who demonstrated the changing tastes and values of the period. His

Biedermeier: re-creation of a period interior by Rupert Cavendish Antiques, 610 King's Road, London SW6 2DX

Viennese Etablissement für alle Gegenstände des Ameublements (Establishment for all furnishing objects), established in 1807, was a huge concern, employing more than 130 workers within a year, whose catalogues listed such unlikely combinations as a pipe rack and rifle stand, as well as a vast range of the more orthodox items such as tables, chairs, settees, plant stands, washstands, desks and other miscellaneous pieces of furniture. Concentrating initially on luxury goods, it expanded its activities in 1814 to cover all types of furniture. While the sheer scale of his factory and showrooms – particularly after the move to the Karoly Palace in 1825 – indicate that the middle class was his main market, Danhauser also enjoyed the patronage of the aristocracy; he was responsible for the interior decoration of the Archduke Carl's palace in Vienna in 1822, and for Schloss Weilburg in nearby Baden at around the same time. After Danhauser's death in 1829, the company struggled on for a further ten years, after which it ceased trading. Although very few pieces survive that can be positively attributed to Danhauser's emporium, apart from those commissioned specifically for Schloss Weilburg, a wealth of graphic material remains which illustrates the diversity and imaginative use of form that typify his work. Drawings from his factory show more than 2,500 different designs, and indicate the gradual transformation of the Biedermeier style. The use of the Neo-Classical vocabulary became more and more bold, as small-scale decorative work diminished, so that, in his later designs, Danhauser has moved toward large scrolls and simplified lyre-forms, often serving as structural elements rather than superficial ornament. This tendency was reflected in Biedermeier designs generally; the lyre-form became a characteristic form for sofas and secretaires, and volutes – the spiral scrolls which adorn the capitals of classical columns – served as both visual and structural links between horizontal and vertical planes.

Another important figure was Michael Thonet (1796–1871) who, of all the furniture designers and craftsmen associated with the Biedermeier period, was the individual who most clearly grasped the new possibilities of industrial production, and whose work is most immediately familiar today. In the 1830s, he began experimenting with thin strips of beech and walnut veneer, glued together in a sandwich to form a new material which was tremendously versatile, as well as being very economical. This material could be formed into elaborate curves without waste, and, since it had no grain, was equally strong in all directions. Thonet found that solid wood could also be formed in this way, and it was his success with these techniques that led to his involvement in the decoration of the Liechtenstein Palace with the architect Carl Leistler (1805–57) between 1842 and 1849. Even today, Thonet's work is commonly seen in the ubiquitous and widely-copied bentwood cafe chair. While the bulk of Thonet's work came at the end of the Biedermeier period, and is frequently associated with the arrival of Historicism and the Second Rococo, it displays a preference for bold, decorative structure rather than simple embellishment, and in this respect is typical of high Biedermeier.

The primary influences on the Biedermeier interior were the general need to economise on space, and the shift from the conspicuous display of wealth that had characterised aristocratic tastes to the more modest, informal and above all comfortable style preferred by the middle classes. Indeed, the Biedermeier era was remarkable for the way in which the aristocracy emulated the increasingly independent and self-confident tastes of the emerging bourgeoisie, rather than vice-versa.

Colours in Biedermeier interiors were surprisingly vibrant, and were driven by the gradual technological advances in the use of pigments and dyes which enabled stronger and more saturated colours. Few examples of wallpapers and furnishing fabrics survive, owing to their inherent fragility; however, samples from the pattern books produced by the silk weavers, protected from the effects of light, illustrate a fondness for vivid, dazzling colours in bold, simple patterns. A favourite pattern both for wallpaper and printed and woven textiles is a broad stripe, often containing a repeated motif such as foliage or flowers, bordered by a narrower contrasting band, set on a neutral or contrasting background. As with furniture, there was a fascination for simulation; *trompe-l'oeil* mural painting simulated expensive relief plaster moulding, and mock watered-silk textile prints alluded to the real thing.

From the 1820s onward, textiles and drapery began to dominate the domestic interior. The vogue for elaborate festoon curtains soon spread to furniture, and the Josef Danhauser catalogues illustrate richly-upholstered sofas and chairs, and other furniture virtually enclosed in the folds of curtains and valances.

The rapid advance of urban development, and increasing industrialisation, was balanced by a nostalgia for nature and the natural world, a theme that had its seeds in the Romantic movement in art, literature and philosophy in the late 18th century. The image of an innocent, pre-industrial rural idyll was one to which writers of the Biedermeier era contributed with great enthusiasm, including Adalbert Stifter (1805–1868) in his novel *Der Nachsommer*. A similarly sentimental view of life in a subsistence economy was promoted in paintings by Biedermeier artists such as Rudolf Alt (also known as Rudolf von Alt; 1812–1905) and Ferdinand Georg Waldmüller (1793–1865). Its manifestation in the public sphere was represented by the Viennese obsession with parks, including the Prater and the Augarten, and in the private sphere by rich displays of indoor plants and flowers, together with a fashion for caged birds. Whether there were any buyers for the eccentric jardinière-cum-birdcage-cum-fishbowl illustrated in one of the Danhauser catalogues is unknown, however.

The Biedermeier style brought with it a domestic atmosphere which placed far more emphasis on comfort and family life than on external display of wealth. It was this private, introspective approach to domestic life that gave rise to the image of the stolid merchant Herr Biedermeier, too concerned with his own little materialistic world and too complacent to pay any attention to the momentous events in international affairs that were shaking the rest of Europe to its very foundations.

Biedermeier has in the past offered an easy target for critics. For some, it signalled the end of the age of craftsmanship, and the beginning of the slide into mass production. For others, it is a style of the philistine *nouveaux riches*, lacking the individual conviction and authenticity of "real" Neo-Classicism. In spite of this, the Biedermeier style had a major influence on successive generations of furniture designers. The work of the Vienna Secession in 1897 and the Wiener Werkstätte, established by Josef Hoffmann (1870–1956) in 1903, echoed both the theatrical aspects of late Biedermeier, and its attention to the practical concerns of production. The Art Deco style of the 1920s and 1930s owes an even more striking debt to late Biedermeier furniture, with its regular geometric solids and bold, simple vocabulary of form; indeed, some pieces of Art Deco furniture were straight copies of Biedermeier originals conceived a century before. Michael Thonet provided a model of elegance in design with efficiency in production that was frequently cited by architects of the Modern Movement, including Marcel Breuer at the Bauhaus, and the Swiss architect Le Corbusier.

DOMINIC R. STONE

Principal Collections

The Austrian Museum for Applied Art (Österreichisches Museum für angewandte Kunst), Vienna, holds an important collection of over 2,000 original drawings for furniture by Josef Danhauser and a number of pattern books illustrating decorative schemes for interiors by the *ornemaniste* and designer Franz Weiner. Collections of Biedermeier furniture and decorative objects are in the Austrian Museum for Applied Art, the Palais Liechtenstein, and the Wiener Glasmuseum, all in Vienna.

Further Reading

A useful introduction to the Biedermeier style appears in Stone 1990, and Wilkie 1987; Wilkie also includes a select bibliography. For a more detailed analysis, including information on textiles and ceramics as well as furniture and interiors, see Himmelheber 1989, which contains a long list of primary and secondary sources.

Berliner Biedermeier (exhib. cat.), Potsdam, 1973

Biedermeier in Wien, 1815–1848 (exhib. cat.), Vienna: Historisches Museum der Stadt Wien, 1990

Darby, Michael, "The Viennese at Home: Biedermeier Interiors" in *Country Life*, 165, 25 January 1979

Denvir, Bernard, "The Heroic Charm of the Bourgeoisie" in *Art and Artists* (UK), vol.13, pt.11, March 1979

Doderer, Otto, *Biedermeier*, Mannheim: Meyers, 1958

Eberlein, H. Donaldson and Abbot McClure, "The Biedermeier Style: Its Place in Furniture Design and Decoration" in *Good Furniture*, July 1916, pp.29–39

Feuchtmüller, Rupert and Wilhelm Mrazek, *Biedermeier in Österreich*, Vienna: Forum, 1963

Himmelheber, Georg, *Biedermeier Furniture*, London: Faber, 1974

Himmelheber, Georg, "Biedermeier Gothic" in *Furniture History*, 21, 1985, pp.121–26

Himmelheber, Georg (editor), *Biedermeier, 1815–1835* (in English), Munich: Prestel, 1989

Huey, Michael, "A Biedermeier Folio" in *World of Interiors* (UK), October 1993, pp.144–149

Josef Danhauser, 1805–1845: Gëmalde und Zeichnungen (exhib. cat.: Albertina, Vienna), Vienna: Osterreichischer Bundesverlag, 1983

Krüger, Renate, *Biedermeier: Eine Lebenshaltung zwischen 1815 und 1848*, Leipzig: Koehler & Amelang, 1979

Norman, Geraldine, *Biedermeier Painting 1815–1848: Reality Observed in Genre, Portrait and Landscape,* London and New York: Thames and Hudson, 1987

Ottomeyer, Hans and Ulrike Laufer, *Biedermeiers Glück und Ende: Die Gestörte Idylle,* Munich: Hugendubel, 1987

Pressler, Rudolf and Robin Straub, *Biedermeier-Möbel,* Munich: Battenberg, 1986

Spiegl, Walter, *Biedermeier Gläser*, Munich: Keyser, 1981

Stone, Dominic R., *The Art of Biedermeier*, London: Apple, and Secaucus, NJ: Chartwell, 1990

Vetter, Robert, "Herr Biedermeier in Vienna" in *Antiques*, December 1983, pp.698–705

Vienna in the Age of Schubert: The Biedermeier Interior 1815–1848 (exhib. cat.), London: Victoria and Albert Museum, 1979

Waissenberger, Robert (editor), *Vienna in the Biedermeier Era, 1815–1848*, New York: Rizzoli, 1986

Wilkie, Angus, *Biedermeier*, London: Chatto and Windus, and New York: Abbeville, 1987

Billiard Rooms

The origins of the billiard room, as of billiards itself, are obscure. Nothing is known of the game's precise beginnings, which some take back to ancient Greece, but plentiful allusions in the 16th and 17th centuries place its practice in France, where it may have originated, and England. In the 1670s the diarist John Evelyn, for example, noted billiard tables in houses which he visited in Ipswich and Deptford. In view of the scarcity of authentic examples from this early period, a record surviving from 1588 and stating that the Duke of Norfolk owned at Howard House "a billyard bord covered with a greene cloth wth a frame of beache wth fower turned postes", has great value. It is clear that the characteristic green colour of the table-covering material (possibly a visual reference to outdoor ball-games played with mallets on grass) was established early.

The beginnings of the billiard room as a space specifically set aside for the game are equally hard to trace. During the 16th century billiards was regarded as an important form of indoor exercise and Louis XIV was advised to play the game for this purpose. The bending positions required for stroke-play, and the measurements of the table itself – twelve feet long, six feet wide, two feet ten inches high, which became standard in England – make it easy to see why a large space, like a great hall or drawing room, might be preferred. Yet the advantages of social intercourse in such a room with non-playing members of a household had to be set against the disadvantages to the players of interrupted concentration, and to non-players of the noise of the balls.

A painting of about 1745 from Hogarth's circle (Christie's, London) shows gentlemen playing billiards in what looks like a specialised space. The table appears to be full-size, and no other furniture impedes the players' movements. Hats, wigs and swords hang on the wall and maces – the predecessors of cues – are in position in a rack further along it. Billiard rooms are also sometimes found in large country houses in France during this period. The designer Briseux advised placing them away from bedrooms on account of the noise, and the frequency of accidents led the architect J.-F. Blondel to recommend simple wooden panelling rather than paintings and mirrors as decoration.

In the later 18th century, as billiards became increasingly fashionable, and if space and funds allowed, rooms designed primarily or even wholly for the game might be added to the private house. An element of novelty or unconventionality which such a development might convey was signalled at Cairness House, Aberdeenshire, in 1793, when a billiard room was planned by James Playfair, working for Charles Gordon. This was a neo-Egyptian interior – the first in Britain – in an

Billiard Rooms: Moorish-style billiard room by S.C. Capes, Newhouse Park, St. Albans, Hertfordshire, 1897

otherwise Greek Revival house. On the Continent the billiard room shared in the taste for the grandiose represented by the French Empire style. A decorative scheme by Léger for a palatial French billiard room of the 1840s (Musée des Arts Décoratifs, Paris) shows how this style might convincingly provide the setting for a wide-spreading, architectonically-conceived billiard table with twelve legs joined by stretchers.

Social developments in the 19th century also affected the billiard room in several specific ways. With the introduction of modern urban lifestyles after the French Revolution and the Napoleonic Wars, billiard rooms were added to some of the famous 18th-century cafés in Paris and other cities. Paganini records himself in 1813–14 pursuing his taste for the game at a café in Milan. Though billiards had been played by men and women together and continued to be so enjoyed, the British trend towards the segregation of the sexes, which had long manifested itself in the fashion for men's clubs, began to develop a counterpart in larger houses with the provision of what were in effect male suites. Associations with gambling (which earned the game the moral disapproval of some Victorians) took billiards readily into this male domain and also carried overtones of a licence that was available to men but not to women. The pairing of the billiard room with the smoking room – another obvious "male" preserve – was well established by the mid-century, when Castle Carr, near Halifax, grouped library, smoking room and billiard room together in their own wing.

Many mid- and late-19th century billiard rooms were designed in extravagantly oriental, especially Moorish styles. This trend no doubt arose in part from the freedom of these styles from classical conventions – as Playfair's Egyptian design in 1793 had suggested; in part from their links with ways of life that to Western eyes appeared refreshingly outré; and in part from a straightforward delight in the exotic. An early "sultan's den" type of billiard room was laid out at Breadsall Priory, Derbyshire, for the hosier Francis Morley, by Robert Scrivener from 1861. Matthew Digby Wyatt produced a design in 1864 for 12 Kensington Palace Gardens, London, for the cotton magnate Alexander Collie. James Boucher's design for a mansion at 998 Great Western Road, Glasgow (1870s), included an "exotic" billiard room with walls of painted and gilded embossed leather. The Islamic styles spread to billiard rooms in America, an example being that in Mark Twain's house (1874), Hartford, Connecticut, where the walls were decorated with quasi-Moorish stencilled patterns.

In 1884 a fine "Indian" billiard room was created at Bagshot Park, Surrey, by John Lockwood Kipling for the Duke and Duchess of Connaught. Designer and clients all had intimate experience of India, and in addition to a "Hindoo" billiard-table that was constructed in London, a special authenticity was conveyed on the walls by 241 elaborate wood-carvings made at Lahore between 1885 and 1887 by Punjabi craftsmen.

One of the most delightful billiard rooms (now destroyed) to come from the period was at Newhouse Park, St. Albans (1883), designed by Silvester Capes. The room was recorded by Bedford Lemere in 1897, probably soon after its completion. A standard six-light fitting hangs over the table, fulfilling the unique requirement of the billiard room to have its main artificial lighting very low in the space. The room is decorated in a riot of idiosyncratic Moorish-style flat patterns on textiles and wood, and includes much fretted cresting and infilling; compartmentalised walls incorporate raised alcoves with cushioned sofas for spectators.

The artistic ingenuity and elaboration of examples such as Newhouse Park suggest that the late 19th and early 20th century represented the billiard room's heyday. After World War I the table might well find a place of consequence in a man's sitting room, but, increasingly the sexes were mixing for other types of recreation, notably bridge. The move towards smaller, more compact forms of housing also meant that there was often no longer the space available to accommodate the game. Today, the playing of billiards, or snooker, is most often restricted to sports hall and clubs.

JOHN SWEETMAN

Further Reading

Although Billiard Rooms are often mentioned in surveys of interior design, little detailed information has been published on this subject. For a general discussion of 19th and early 20th century styles of decoration see Forge 1981, Girouard 1978, and Sweetman 1988.

Cooper, Nicholas, *The Opulent Eye: Late Victorian and Edwardian Taste in Interior Design*, London: Architectural Press, 1976; New York: Watson Guptill, 1977

Cottle, S.H., "A Sport of Georgian Ladies: Gillow's Frou-Madame Tables" in *Country Life*, 167, 24 January 1980, pp.220–21

Edwards, Ralph, "Billiard Tables" in Percy MacQuoid and Ralph Edwards, *The Dictionary of English Furniture*, revised edition 3 vols., 1954; reprinted Woodbridge, Suffolk: Antique Collectors' Club, 1983

Forge, Suzanne, *Victorian Splendour: Australian Interior Decoration, 1837–1901*, Melbourne and Oxford: Oxford University Press, 1981

Franklin, Jill, *The Gentleman's Country House and its Plan, 1835–1914*, London: Routledge, 1981

Gere, Charlotte, *Nineteenth-Century Decoration: The Art of the Interior*, London: Weidenfeld and Nicolson, and New York: Abrams, 1989

Girouard, Mark, *Life in the English Country House: A Social and Architectural History*, New Haven and London: Yale University Press, 1978

Girouard, Mark, *The Victorian Country House*, revised edition New Haven and London: Yale University Press, 1979

Jennings, H.J., *Our Homes and How to Beautify Them*, London: Harrison, 1902

Sweetman, John, *The Oriental Obsession: Islamic Inspiration in British and American Art and Architecture, 1500–1920*, Cambridge and New York: Cambridge University Press, 1988

Bing, Siegfried 1838–1905

Naturalized French art dealer, publisher, entrepreneur and collector

Siegfried Bing (known as S. and mistakenly called Samuel) started his career in the arts as a ceramic manufacturer in Paris in the mid-1850s. He received a medal at the 1867 World's Fair, and a few examples of the pieces he produced can be found at the Adrien Dubouché Museum in Limoges. Following the Franco-Prussian War, Bing became an art dealer who specialized in the art of the Far East, and especially the art of Japan. His first shop, at 19 rue Chauchat, opened in time for the 1878 Paris World's Fair where Japan was extremely well represented. By the 1880s, after an extended trip to Japan, and as the demand for oriental art objects had turned into a craze known as *Japonisme*, Bing increased the scope of his business by opening several other shops that sold both modern and ancient Japanese arts and crafts. Between 1888 and 1891 Bing also published a magazine dedicated to the art of Japan, *Artistic Japan* (published simultaneously in French, English and German), and organized a series of Japanese art exhibitions which featured ceramics, paintings, and especially *ukiyo-e* prints. His shops became the mecca where many of the great collections of oriental art were formed (e.g., those of the Goncourt brothers, Philippe Burty, Henri Vever, Charles Haviland). And a passionate collector himself, Bing amassed an extraordinary collection which became a meeting ground for many of the *Japonistes*. It was totally dispersed after Bing's death in 1905.

By 1894, Bing had realized that his Japanese art business was not going to fulfil all his creative instincts. After a trip to the United States, where he went on behalf of the French government to study the level of culture, and after visiting several major American cities, Bing published his findings in *La Culture artistique en Amérique* (1895). He was especially impressed by the decorative work created by the workshops of Louis Comfort Tiffany and the Rockwood ceramic works in Cincinnati. This trip across the United States fired Bing's latent interest in design, and inspired his continuing quest to find the best arts and crafts workshops capable of producing the art objects he envisioned selling in his newly founded design gallery (e.g., the firms of Grueby and Co. in Boston or Clement Heaton in Neuchâtel, Switzerland).

Following a second exploratory trip in 1895, this time to Belgium in the company of the art critic Julius Meier-Graefe where they met the well-known designer Henry van de Velde, Bing decided to redesign his former Oriental art gallery at 19 rue Chauchat / 22 rue de Provence, and turn it into an emporium of modern design. The "new" gallery christened "L'Art Nouveau" opened in December 1895, and the exhibition became known as the "first Salon of Art Nouveau". The controversial exhibition was openly criticized in numerous

Bing: interior of room by Eugène Gaillard for the Art Nouveau Bing pavilion at the 1900 Paris Exposition Universelle, showing murals by José Maria Sert

articles in the daily French press for its support of a roster of foreign artists. This xenophobic sentiment was exacerbated by anti-semitic feelings which were always rampant, and had been made more acute by the Dreyfus "affair". Only a few advocates of Modernism came to Bing's support. Sympathetic critics and designers recognized that Bing commissions for entire room ensembles, such as those given to Belgian artists Henry van de Velde and George Lemmen, were the wave of the future. These interiors, along with stained glass windows, commissioned from the Nabis (including Edouard Vuillard, Paul Ranson, Pierre Bonnard, H.G. Ibels, Félix Vallotton, and Henri Toulouse-Lautrec) and executed by Tiffany in America, were installed in Bing's Art Nouveau gallery. *Papa Chrisanthème* by Toulouse-Lautrec (now housed at the Musée d'Orsay, Paris), was set above the entrance at 19 rue Chauchat.

This relationship with the firm of Tiffany in America was only one example of Bing's cooperative efforts with other design workshops in Europe and America, but it is special because it is the first time Bing forged an alliance with a designer and his craftsmen who created a group of objects under his entrepreneurial guidance. It was also a harbinger of Bing's foray into creative design after he opened his own ateliers in the same building as his gallery in 1898. Participants in the 1895 Art Nouveau Salon (which included painters, printmakers, glassmakers, jewellers, etc.) found Bing's exhibition challenging since it placed foreign artists alongside French ones. The 1895 Salon, which had expanded on the idea first tried in Brussels at the "Maison d'Art", demonstrated that all the arts were equally helping to professionalize the new field of interior design. Subsequent small exhibitions organized by Bing at his gallery were "one-man shows" of some of the artists who had been chosen for the first Salon of Art Nouveau. These included paintings, prints and design exhibitions. The show of paintings and prints by Edvard Munch (1896) did much to galvanize the avant-garde behind Bing while at the same time it alienated conservative painters and critics in France (as explained by Arne Eggum, "Munch tente de conquérir Paris, 1896–1900", in *Munch et la France*, Paris: Editions de la Réunion des Musées Nationaux, 1991, pp.199–203).

At the close of the 1890s, Bing's success as a tastemaker – albeit as a passive tastemaker since he was not in control of the design of the objects he exhibited – was further enhanced by his move from selling objects designed by others (fabrics and wallpapers by William Morris, metalwork by the English arts and crafts designer W.A.S. Benson or glass work by Tiffany) toward the production of pieces or total room ensembles by designers and artisans working in his own workshops. By

1898–99, Bing had renovated unused space at the back of his gallery on rue de Provence and rue Chauchat. He created *ateliers* where artisans fashioned furniture, other interior design objects, and jewellery from designs produced by a group of designers who worked on commission essentially for Bing. Bing's ultimate success among devotees of design reform climaxed with the construction and opening of his own pavilion: Art Nouveau Bing, at the Paris World's Fair of 1900. This building, constructed from the architectural design of André Arfvidson, and financed solely by Bing, incorporated modern room environments created by three of the major designers in his employ: Georges de Feure, Edward Colonna, and Eugène Gaillard. Although there was little press coverage in France and few pieces of furniture or entire room interiors seem to have sold in France, the rooms excited comment throughout the world and pieces sold to private collectors in Sweden and decorative arts museums in Copenhagen and Hamburg where they could be studied by young craftsmen. The First International Exhibition of Decorative Design in Turin (1902) was the last major design exhibition to which Bing contributed. Examples of his ceramics designed by de Feure and Colonna and executed by the firm of Gérard, Dufraisseix and Abbot (GDA) in Limoges were recognized. Bing received a prestigious "achievement" award, but the *Art Nouveau Bing* style had already been surpassed by the more angular and more modern style which ended in the Art Deco movement.

Two years later, in 1904, Bing sold his gallery and auctioned his Art Nouveau pieces. By 1905, worn out from years as a dealer, and with the oriental side of his business in the hands of his son Marcel (who was also a talented jeweller and had been in charge of the jewellery atelier at his father's gallery) Bing died. The sale of his private oriental art collection was held in Paris, 1906, bringing estimable prices and further adding to the prestige of Bing's connoisseurship. The Art Nouveau side of Bing's entrepreneurial achievements languished until the recent examination of the Art Nouveau period demonstrated his vital significance as a promoter and tastemaker.

GABRIEL P. WEISBERG

See also Art Nouveau; Colonna; Feure; Maison Moderne

Biography

Born in Hamburg, 1838. Worked in a ceramics factory, Paris, mid-1850s; opened an oriental warehouse, Paris, 1877; travelled to China and Japan, 1880; visited America, 1884. Visited Belgium where he met Julius Meier-Graefe and Henry van de Velde, 1895; returned to Paris and opened L'Art Nouveau, 1895, selling furnishings by French, Belgian, English and American designers; established his own studio and workshops for the production of furniture, furnishings and jewellery, 1898. Had his own pavilion at the Paris Exposition Universelle, 1900; exhibited again at Turin, 1902. Published several important works on Japonisme and Art Nouveau. Oriental side of the business taken over by his son Marcel, and L'Art Nouveau sold, 1904. Died in Paris, 1905; his collection of oriental art was sold in Paris, 1906.

Selected Works

Bing material, including the store's private catalogue that recorded all the available items and prices post-1900, and known as the Album de références de l'Art Nouveau, is in the Musée des Arts Décoratifs, Paris.

Interiors

1895 L'Art Nouveau, 22 rue de Provence, Paris (exhibition of interiors and furnishings): Siegfried Bing

1900 *Art Nouveau Bing*, Exposition Universelle, Paris (pavilion containing exhibition of interiors and furnishings): Siegfried Bing

Publications

Artistic Japan, 6 vols., 1888–91

La Culture artistique en Amérique, 1896; as *Artistic America*, 1970

Further Reading

A detailed study of Bing's career, including a list of his writings and a bibliography of primary and secondary sources, appears in Weisberg's *Art Nouveau Bing*, 1986. For a shorter account of the history of the L'Art Nouveau gallery see Troy 1991.

Dam, Peter Van, *Dossier Siegfried Bing: Oriental Art, Art Nouveau: Installations Modernes l'Art Nouveau Bing*, The Hague: Peter van Dam, 1985

Jullian, Philippe, *The Triumph of Art Nouveau: Paris Exhibition 1900*, New York: Larousse, and London: Phaidon, 1974

Koch, Robert, "Art Nouveau Bing" in *Gazette des Beaux-Arts*, vol.53, March 1959, pp.179–90

Mandell, Richard D., *Paris 1900: The Great World's Fair*, Toronto: University of Toronto Press, 1967

Silverman, Debora L., *Art Nouveau in Fin-de-Siècle France: Politics, Psychology, and Style*, Berkeley: University of California Press, 1989

Troy, Nancy J., *Modernism and the Decorative Arts in France: Art Nouveau to Le Corbusier*, New Haven and London: Yale University Press, 1991

Weisberg, Gabriel P., "S. Bing's Craftsmen Workshops: A Location and Importance Revealed" in *Source*, Autumn, 1983, pp.42–48

Weisberg, Gabriel P., *Art Nouveau Bing: Paris Style 1900* (exhib. cat.: Smithsonian Institution, Washington, DC), New York: Abrams, 1986

Weisberg, Gabriel P., "Félix Vallotton, Siegfried Bing and L'Art Nouveau" in *Arts Magazine*, vol.60, February 1986, pp.33–37

Weisberg, Gabriel P., "On Understanding Artistic Japan" in *Journal of the Decorative and Propaganda Arts*, vol.1, 1986, pp.6–19

Weisberg, Gabriel P., "S. Bing, Edvard Munch and L'Art Nouveau" in *Arts Magazine*, vol.61, September 1986, pp.33–37

Weisberg, Gabriel P., "S. Bing in America" in Weisberg and Laurinda S. Dixon (editors), *The Documented Image: Visions in Art History*, Syracuse: Syracuse University Press, 1987

Weisberg, Gabriel P., "Siegfried Bing and Industry: The Hidden Side of L'Art Nouveau" in *Apollo*, vol.78, November 1988, pp.326–29, 379

Blondel, Jacques-François 1705–1774

French architect and architectural theorist

Born in Rouen into a family of architects, Jacques-François Blondel was a key figure in the history of French mid-18th century design and taste. His work as an architect was limited to only a few commissions executed in Paris, Metz and Strasbourg. But as a professor of architecture he trained many of the leading Neo-Classical architects of the third quarter of the century including Etienne Louis Boullée, Claude-Nicolas Ledoux and Charles de Wailly, and his many publications, which included numerous plates drawn and engraved by Blondel himself, were enormously influential in explaining how to plan and decorate a modern building. The two activities of writing and teaching were closely intertwined. Publications such as *De la Distribution des Maisons de Plaisance* (1737), *Architecture Française* (1752–56), *Cours d'Architecture* (1771–72), and nearly 500 articles written for Diderot's *Encyclopédie*, announced or reflected subjects on which Blondel lectured at the École des Arts, the private architectural school that he opened in 1740, the Académie Royale d'Architecture where he taught after 1762, and in the short courses he offered to gentlemen (*cours elementaires*), designers (*cours de théorie*) and craftsmen (*cours de practique*) from 1754. Many of these subjects were also closely linked to interior decoration and design and he devoted much space to the discussion of features such as doors, windows, chimneypieces, ceilings, floors, principal pieces of furniture and the distribution and planning of rooms.

Blondel's lessons combined the traditional and the innovative. No iconoclast, Blondel usually began his public courses and texts by discussing the proportions and characters of the Orders, which he considered basic to the practice of architecture. He also respected Vitruvius, Palladio, and Scamozzi, whom he called "the Ancients," integrating their theories of proportion into his guidelines for composing both façades and spaces. On the other hand, *Maisons* reveals Blondel to be the first French architect to treat the pleasure pavilion as a building type worthy of sustained attention, to develop new room types (dining room, bath), and to promote new technology (flush toilets). What most distinguishes Blondel from his peers, however, was his conviction that the architect could influence the daily operation of a household; that it was proper for him to do so; and that, to do this well, he had to uncover the range of factors affecting the client, particularly the client's activities and those of his entourage. His approach embodies the essence, if not all the techniques, of what we now call design programming; and in his insistence that spaces be planned so that their users may move and function efficiently, he is entirely modern.

Blondel first treated interior decoration in Part II of *Maisons*, offering advice about each of the various parts of the dwelling in turn. The emphasis was on the building as a whole, however, not only because "architecture must always be superior to ornament" but because, as he said later, quoting Horace, "the fundamental principle of all the arts is unity" (*Cours*, vol. 3). To achieve this quality, Blondel counselled an interdependence of hierarchy (focus on architectural elements; build to a decorative crescendo), harmony (reflect a room's purpose in its decoration, its character and function with materials), and balance (temper symmetry with common sense). Proportion was highly important, not only as it contributed to hierarchy, but in the guide it offered (via the Ancients) for determining ratios of length to width to height for rooms and architectural elements. The principle of contrast, on the other hand, was not in his lexicon. Rocaille was used to ease the corners of panelling, the line of furnishings, and the pattern of locks and ironwork, but its free curves were never allowed to dominate the spaces and objects Blondel created or applauded. (Several of his contemporaries – Pierre Patte chief among them – credited his conservatism with returning French design to its classical roots.)

In *Architecture Française*, Blondel reiterated these views, and reproached those who ignored function and thought to develop beautiful plans by giving the rooms different shapes and arranging them symmetrically to right and left. After discussing room types and offering guidelines for their embellishment, he noted that the problems of layout tested the experience, intelligence, resources, and genius of an architect – the best decoration could not redeem inconvenience. General principles for interior spaces were recapitulated in the *Cours*: there should be reasonable variety in the shapes of the various rooms, a proportional relationship between height and width, a rational relationship of inside to outside. The interior treatment should reflect the status of the owner; spaces had to be convenient and suited to purpose; natural light should enter a library or gallery from high-placed windows, an *enfilade* should be side-lit by a rhythmic arrangement of tall windows.

Clients were at the heart of Blondel's approach. Layouts were to support their lifestyles. Room types – including the new bathrooms and toilets – were to increase their comfort. Decoration reflected their role in society. Servants were also clients of a sort, and the architect had to find ways to make their work more efficient (such as the uni-directional staircases proposed in *Maisons* to facilitate the serving and clearing of meals). The article "Cheminée" in the *Encyclopédie* used ratios to plan the height of a fireplace opening, but the height had both to obey the rules of proportion and allow those clustered around the fire to observe not only themselves but others elsewhere in the room. The principles which underlie Blondel's approach have lost little of their currency.

REED BENHAMOU

Biography

Born in Rouen, 8 January 1705, the son of the architect Jean François Blondel (1681–1756). Studied architecture under his uncle, François Blondel II (1683–1748); and later with Gilles-Marie Oppenord (1672–1742). Married 1) Marie Anne Garnier, 1729 (died 1755): two children including the engraver Georges François Blondel; 2) Marie Madeleine Balletti: son, the architect Jean Baptiste Blondel. Active as an architect in Paris by 1729. Established the École des Arts, an independent school of architecture, Paris, 1740. Member, Académie Royale d'Architecture, 1755; appointed professor, 1762. Practised as an architect in Metz, 1764–76. Author of numerous books on architecture from the 1730s, including the influential *Cours d'Architecture*, 1771–77. Died in Paris 9 January 1774.

Selected Works

Interiors

1745 Port St. Martin, Paris (decoration)
1748 Archbishop's Palace, Cambrai (building and interiors)
1748 Blondel House, rue de Croissant, Paris (remodelling of interiors)
1748 Hôtel de Choiseul, rue de Richelieu, Paris (decoration of the gallery)

Publications

De la distribution des maisons de plaisance et de la décoration des édifices en général, 2 vols., 1737–38; reprinted 1967

Discours sur la Manière d'Etudier l'Architecture, et les Arts qui sont Relatifs a celui de Bastir, 1747

Architecture Française; ou, Recueil des Plans, d'Élévations, Coupes et Profils, 4 vols., 1752–56; reprinted 1904–05
Discours sur la nécessité de l'Etude de l'architecture, 1754; reprinted 1973
De l'Utilité de Joindre à l'Etude de l'Architecture, celle des Sciences et des Arts qui lui sont Relatifs, 1771
Cours d'Architecture (with Pierre Patte), 9 vols., 1771–77
L'Homme du monde éclairé par les arts, 1774; reprinted 1973

Numerous articles on architecture and decoration for vols.1–7 of Denis Diderot and Jean le Rond d'Alembert (editors), *Encyclopédie*, Paris, from 1751

Further Reading

Benhamou, Reed, "Continuing Education and Other Innovations: An Eighteenth-Century Case Study" in *Studies in Eighteenth-Century Culture*, 15, 1986, pp.67–76
Benhamou, Reed, "Parallel Walls, Parallel Worlds: The Places of Masters and Servants in the 'Maisons de Plaisance' of Jacques-François Blondel" in *Journal of Design History*, 7, 1994, pp.1–11
Braham, Allan, *The Architecture of the French Enlightenment*, Berkeley: University of California Press, and London: Thames and Hudson, 1980
Cleary, Richard, "Romancing the Tome; or, An Academician's Pursuit of a Popular Audience in 18th Century France" in *Journal of the Society of Architectural Historians*, 48, June 1989, pp.139–49
Dézallier D'Argenville, A.N., "Jacques-François Blondel" in vol.1, pp.467–73 of *Vies des Fameux Architectes depuis la Renaissance des Arts*, 1788; reprinted, Geneva: Minkoff, 1972
Eriksen, Svend, *Early Neo-Classicism in France: The Creation of the Louis Seize Style*, London: Faber, 1974
Etlin, Richard A., "'Les Dedons': Jacques François Blondel and the System of the Home, c.1740" in *Gazette des Beaux-Arts*, XLI, April 1974, pp.137–47
Gallet, Michel, *Paris Domestic Architecture of the 18th Century*, London: Barrie and Jenkins, 1972; as *Stately Mansions: Eighteenth Century Paris Architecture*, New York: Praeger, 1972
Harrington, Kevin, *Architectural Relationships: Changing Ideas on Architecture in the "Encyclopédie", 1750–1775*, Ph.D. thesis, Ithaca, NY: Cornell University, 1981
Herrmann, Wolfgang, "Jacques-François Blondel" in his *Laugier and Eighteenth Century French Theory*, Appendix 9, London: Zwemmer, 1962
Kafker, Frank and Serena, *The Encyclopedists as Individuals: A Biographical Dictionary of the Authors of the Encyclopédie*, Oxford: Voltaire Foundation, 1988
Kaufmann, Emil, "The Contribution of J.-F. Blondel to Mariette's 'Architecture Français'" in *Art Bulletin*, 31, 1949, pp.58–59
Lejeaux, Jeanne, "Jacques-François Blondel: Professeur d'Architecture" in *L'Architecture*, 40, 1927, pp.23–27
Lejeaux, Jeanne, "Un Architecte Français: Jacques-François Blondel (1705–1774) in *La Revue de l'Art*, 52, 1927, pp.223–34
Middleton, Robin, "Jacques-François Blondel and the 'Cours d'Architecture'" in *Journal of the Society of Architectural Historians*, 18, 1959, pp.140–48
Prost, Auguste, *Jacques-François Blondel et Son Oeuvre*, Metz: Rousseau-Pallez, 1860

Boffrand, Germain 1667–1754

French architect and designer of interiors

Germain Boffrand played a significant role in the development of French architecture and interior decoration during the first half of the 18th century. His designs incorporated aspects of 17th-century French classicism and Italian Baroque, responded to the Rococo style of 18th-century Versailles and Paris, and ultimately contributed to the emergence of Neo-Classicism in France around the middle of the 18th century. His works were produced for noble and princely patrons in Paris, Lorraine and Germany, and included interior renovations, hôtels, pleasure pavilions and châteaux.

Boffrand often employed non-rectangular volumes, particularly ovals and circles, to create emphasis in a plan and a sense of continuity within a room. The Hôtel Amelot in Paris (1712–14) incorporated an oval entrance court, a trapezoidal vestibule flanked by two pentagonal spaces, and a projecting salon that carried this spatial dynamism through to the garden façade. The hunting lodge of Bouchefort near Brussels (1704–06), built for Max Emanuel of Bavaria, had an octagonal plan centered on a round, double-height salon articulated by two superimposed arcades. In two projects for La Malgrange (1712–17), a château near Nancy for Léopold, Duc de Lorraine, arcaded salons again dominated his designs, especially in the second version where a vast circular space marked the center of an X-shaped plan.

In the decoration of rooms, Boffrand sought a controlled dynamism in which the decorative articulation never dominated the architectonic conception. In the salon of the Hôtel d'Argenton in Paris (1704–05), built for one client and renovated around 1726 for another, a series of arches enframed the windows, doors, and mirrors, and the wall panels were punctuated with cartouches that enlivened but did not disrupt the regularity of the space. In a salon at the Petit Luxembourg in Paris (1709–11), redecorated for Anne de Bavière, princesse de Condé, Boffrand rounded the corners of the rectangular room, minimized the cornice, used the arcade motif rhythmically to unite doors, windows, and mirrors, and embellished the wall panels with delicate but strongly geometric patterns of gilded grotesque ornament.

Many of the devices explored in Boffrand's early work were reinterpreted in his most famous interior design, the Hôtel de Soubise in Paris. In 1732 Prince de Rohan commissioned Boffrand to renovate the hôtel on the occasion of his marriage to Marie-Sophie de Courcillon. The building had been substantially redesigned in 1705–09 by Pierre-Alexis Delamair, who provided a colonnaded entrance court and established a series of formal rooms arranged *enfilade* (with doors aligned on an axis). Boffrand's renovation, executed in 1735–39, both perpetuated a tradition of princely grandeur and met the standards of modern domestic distribution and decoration.

Boffrand designed two richly decorated *appartements de parade* (suites of formal reception rooms), one for the prince on the ground floor and one for the princesse directly above it. Each apartment culminated in an oval salon, located in a projecting, pavilion-like volume that Boffrand added to the corner of the building's garden façade. Boffrand also expanded and redecorated the less formal but equally elegant private living quarters adjacent to the grand apartments, in accordance with the functional specialization, convenience and intimacy that characterized 18th-century domestic planning. The new plans of the Hôtel de Soubise were published by Jacques-François Blondel in his 1752 edition of *Architecture Française*, and ten interior views were published by Boffrand himself in his 1745 *Livre d'architecture*.

The decoration of the Hôtel de Soubise incorporated work

Boffrand: oval salon, Hôtel de Soubise, Paris, 1705–09

by some of the most accomplished artists of the period, including the sculptor Jacques Verberckt and the painters François Boucher, Charles Natoire, Jean Restout, Charles Trémolières, and Carle van Loo. The decorative idiom of the apartments is Rococo, but Boffrand employed this light, lyrical vocabulary of curves, shells, foliage and dynamically shaped frames in a manner informed by both Baroque monumentality and cohesion and classical principles of regularity and harmonic proportion.

In the apartment of the prince, the *chambre de parade* (formal bedroom for receiving visitors), includes a bed niche set off by columns and pilasters, figured wall medallions invoking noble values such as wisdom and truth, and paintings of the loves of the gods. In the oval salon, eight arches rhythmically encircle the room and enframe the doors, windows, and mirrors. The spandrels between these arches contain white plaster bas reliefs by Lambert-Sigisbert Adam and Jean-Baptiste II Lemoine depicting personifications of various princely concerns, including poetry, music, justice, and astronomy. This apartment privileges tectonic form over opulent surface: gilding is used sparingly, painting is absent from the salon, and walls remain distinct from ceilings despite the rich mouldings that link them.

In the apartment of the princesse, gilding is used more extensively, the interplay of media and forms is more complex, and the program is focused more exclusively on the theme of love. In the *chambre de parade*, the loves of the gods are depicted in gilded wall medallions, in gilded cartouches in the corners of the ceiling cove, and by pairs of stucco figures perched at intervals upon the cornice. The oval salon in this apartment is probably the most famous of all 18th-century French interiors. As in the salon of the prince, eight arches enclose the doors, windows, and mirrors. But here the distinction between walls and ceiling is far more ambiguous: the arches are surmounted by gilded cartouches, which connect the arcade to a broad, undulating band of gilded openwork that encircles the room at cornice level. This band is punctuated above the cartouches by pairs of white stucco putti, and is connected by eight strips of gilded openwork to a gilded rosette in the center of the domed, sky-blue ceiling. In the spandrels between the arches, supported by pairs of gilded putti, are eight paintings by Charles Natoire depicting the story of Cupid and Psyche. In this room, Boffrand mobilized the arts of architecture, sculpture, and painting – as well as the dazzling visual and spatial effects of abundant mirrors, glass, and gilding – to create a very complex yet utterly coherent ensemble.

In the Hôtel de Soubise, as in all Boffrand's interiors, the architectural organization of space is discernible beneath the surface effects of ornament. The rooms are monumental in conception if not palatial in scale, and Boffrand used symmetry, rhythmic regularity, and contrasting colors and materials to maintain a visual and spatial clarity that was deliberately dissolved in the far more asymmetrical and atectonic schemes of such Rococo masters as Nicolas Pineau and Juste-Aurèle Meissonnier. Indeed, Boffrand participated in the criticism of the Rococo that began to pervade art and architectural theory in the 1740s. In his *Livre d'architecture* (1745), he condemned contemporary interiors as illogically composed, excessively luxurious spaces, tastelessly stuffed with fashionable bibelots. Many writers who similarly considered Rococo decoration to be a threat to the structural and aesthetic principles of good architecture, such as Jacques-François Blondel and Pierre Patte, praised Boffrand's buildings as paradigms of principled design.

Boffrand's work was governed by the classical concept of *convenance*, the stipulation that every aspect of a building be appropriate to its location, its usage, and the social status of its occupants. For Boffrand, a house was a manifestation of personality: "One can judge the character of the master of the house ... by the manner in which it is disposed, ornamented, and furnished" (*Livre d'architecture*, p.12). Boffrand's designs were portraits of his elite patrons, for both the interiors and their owners sought to fuse tradition and modernity, opulence and restraint, elegance and power.

MIMI HELLMAN

See also Boiseries; Rococo

Biography

Born in Nantes, 16 May 1667, the son of the architect-sculptor Jean Boffrand. Moved to Paris, 1681, and studied sculpture under François Girardon and architecture under Jules Hardouin-Mansart (1646–1708). Married Marie Leneveu de Beauval (died 1730): two sons and two daughters. Employed in the service of the Bâtiments du Roi, Paris, 1686–99; appointed curator of the royal archives, 1690. Active as an architect in Paris and Nancy from c.1700. Travelled to Belgium in the service of the Elector Max II Emanuel of Bavaria, 1705. Member, Académie Royale d'Architecture (first class), 1709. Appointed Premier Architecte to the Duc de Lorraine, 1711. Re-employed by the Bâtiments du Roi, Paris; served as Architecte de l'Arsenal and Architecte du Palais de Justice, 1712. Financial ruin following the collapse of the Banque Royale de Law, Paris, 1720. Active as an administrator and involved in several urban development schemes from 1720; appointed architect and director, Hôpital Général, Paris, 1724; joined the Department Ponts des Chausées, 1732, appointed Premier Ingénieur, 1742, and Inspecteur Général, 1743. Died in Paris, 18 March 1754.

Selected Works

A full list of Boffrand's architectural projects and decorative commissions appears in Gallet and Garms 1986. Examples of Boffrand's designs and architectural drawings are in the Archives Nationales, and the Bibliothèque Historique de la Ville de Paris, Paris, the Musée Historique Lorrain, Nancy, the Kunstbibliothek, Berlin, and the University Library, Wurzburg. Boffrand's Hôtel de Soubise is now occupied by the Archives Nationales; the Cabinet Vert from it is now installed in the Hôtel de Rohan, Paris.

Interiors

1704–05 Hôtel d'Argenton, Paris (building and interiors; redecoration of the salon, 1726)

1704–06 Hunting Lodge, Bouchefort, near Brussels (building and interiors): Elector Max II Emanuel of Bavaria

1707 Hôtel de Mayenne, Paris (remodelling interiors and decoration)

1708 Hôtel de Canillac, Paris (additions and interiors)

1709–11 Petit Luxembourg, Paris (building and interiors)

1709–22 Château de Lunéville, Lorraine (building and interiors; reconstruction and new chapel, 1719): Léopold, Duc de Lorraine

1712–14 Hôtel Amelot, Paris (building and interiors)

1712–14 Hôtel du Premier Président, Palais de Justice, Paris (renovation and interiors)

1712–17 La Malgrange, near Nancy (building and interiors): Léopold, Duc de Lorraine

1713 Hôtel de Seignelay, Paris (building and interiors)

1713	Maison de Elector of Bavaria, Saint Cloud (decoration): Elector Max II Emanuel of Bavaria
1714–17	Maison du Prince de Rohan, Saint-Ouen, near Paris (building and interiors)
1715–22	Palais Ducal, Nancy (building and interiors, including the Grand Salon)
c.1715–22	Arsenal, Paris (additions and interiors, including the Salon)
c.1716	Hôtel de Villars, Paris (decoration of the Salon)
1723	Palais de Justice, Paris (decoration of the Grand Chambre)
1729	Pavilion of the Duchess of Maine, Arsenal, Paris (building and interiors)
1735–39	Hôtel de Soubise, Paris (oval salons and decoration of the prince and princess's apartments): Prince de Rohan

Publications

Livre d'Architecture, 1745; reprinted 1969

Further Reading

The most comprehensive analysis of Boffrand's work appears in Gallet and Garms 1986 which includes essays on Boffrand's architecture, interiors and city planning, a section on decorative collaborations with C.J. Natoire, and an extensive bibliography.

Babelon, Jean-Pierre, *Musée de l'Histoire de France*, vol.1, in *Historique et Description des Bâtiments des Archives Nationales*, Paris: Imprimerie Nationale, 1958 (2nd edition 1968)

Babelon, Jean-Pierre, "Le Palais de l'Arsenal à Paris" in *Bulletin Monumental*, 128, 1970, pp.267–310

Babelon, Jean-Pierre, "Le Grand Appartement du Prince de Soubise" in *Cahiers de la Rotonde*, 1982, pp.44–98

Babelon, Jean-Pierre, *Du Palais Soubise au Caran: Le Siège des Archives Nationales*, Paris: Archives Nationales, 1988

Berckenhagen, Ekhart (editor), *Die französischen Zeichnungen der Kunstbibliothek Berlin: Kritischer Katalog*, Berlin: Hessling, 1970

Blondel, Jacques-François, *Architecture Française*, 4 vols., Paris, 1752–56; reprinted 1904–05

Brice, Germain, *Description de la Ville de Paris* (1752 edition), Geneva: Droz, and Paris: Minard, 1971

Gallet, Michel, Jörg Garms and others, *Germain Boffrand 1667–1754: L'Aventure d'un Architecte Indépendant* (exhib. cat.: Musée Carnavelet, Paris), Paris: Herscher, 1986

Garms, Jörg, *Studien zu Boffrand*, Ph.D. thesis, Vienna: University of Vienna, 1962

Garms, Jörg, "Le Projets de Mansart et de Boffrand pour le Palais Ducal de Nancy" in *Bulletin Monumental*, 125, 1967, pp.231–46

Garms, Jörg, "Der Grundriss der Malgrange I von Boffrand" in *Wiener Jahrbuch für Kunstgeschichte*, 22, 1969, pp.184–88

Garms, Jörg, "Les Nouveaux Dessins Lorrains de Boffrand: Leur Place dans l'Architecture de leur Temps" in *Bulletin de la Société de l'Histoire de l'Art Français*, 1990, pp.81–95

Hautecoeur, Louis, *Histoire de l'architecture classique en France*, vol.3, Paris: Picard, 1951

Kalnein, Wend von, *Architecture in France in the Eighteenth Century*, New Haven and London: Yale University Press, 1995

Kimball, Fiske, *The Creation of the Rococo*, 1943; as *The Creation of the Rococo Decorative Style*, New York: Dover, and London: Constable, 1980

Langlois, Charles-Victor, *Les Hôtels de Clisson, de Guise, et de Rohan-Soubise au Marais*, Paris: Schmidt, 1922

Mackenzie, Catherine, *The Ut Poesis Architecture of Germain Boffrand*, Ph.D. thesis, Toronto: University of Toronto, 1984

Pons, Bruno, "L'Hôtel de Seignelay" in *Monuments Historiques*, 162, 1989, pp.93–104

Scott, Katie, *The Rococo Interior: Decoration and Social Spaces in Early Eighteenth-Century Paris*, New Haven and London: Yale University Press, 1995

Simonin, Pierre, "Boffrand et la Décoration de l'Appartement du Duc Léopold au Château de Lunéville" in *Pays Lorrain*, LVI, 1975, pp.181–204

Boiseries

The term *boiseries* derives from *boiser*, the act of lining architectural surfaces with wood. Properly speaking, it includes any wood-paneled interior surface, whether ceiling, wall, or floor, but through convention it has become a synonym for vertical paneling. It is particularly associated with French carved and gilded paneling of the Louis XV and XVI periods but it is also used to refer to imitations of these styles in other countries such as the white and gilt saloon installed at Uppark, Sussex, in the early 1770s.

Made by *menuisiers en bâtiments* (members of the woodworkers' guild specializing in small-scale construction), *boiseries* consisted of flat panels (known as the field) held in place by tongue-in-groove framing of vertical (stiles) and horizontal (rails) units. Mounted on battens, they created a space between the wall and the wall treatment that both protected the wood from contact with damp masonry or caustic plaster, and provided recesses where valuables could be secreted in troubled times. Their method of construction and installation also allowed them to be demounted and reassembled. This portability has proved extremely helpful to modern museum curators intent on recreating period rooms, but it was also a useful feature in earlier times: provincial buyers frequently ordered their *boiseries* from Paris; and Parisians offered *boiseries* for re-sale. The advertisement of "72 feet of *boiseries*, 15 feet high, painted in arabesques by Watteau" carried by the *Annonces, affiches et avis divers* in July 1784 was not unusual.

Before the intervention of technology, paneling represented a material response to climate. In the France of the Middle Ages (as in England and across northern Europe), the insulating properties of wood mediated the cold and damp that could radiate from masonry walls, and enhanced the heat provided by primitive hearths and fireplaces. Practicality did not preclude embellishment, however; and the short, narrow panel fields of medieval *boiseries* generally carried geometric ornament and family crests, painted in bright colors and hung with tapestries. During the Renaissance period, improvements in fireplace construction and glazing lessened the importance of *boiseries* as insulation; advances in milling technology resulted in longer and wider panels; and evolution in the subjects and techniques of art led to more sophisticated designs. As in contemporary Italy, some French paneling was executed in pictorial marquetry; but the more important paradigm was the Italian integration of architecture, furnishings, and artwork seen in galleries at Fontainebleau begun by Rosso Fiorentino for François I and completed under Philibert de L'Orme and Francesco Primaticcio for Henri II (restored under Louis-Philippe in the 19th century).

By the middle of the 17th century, most walls were at least partially, and more often fully paneled; and French *boiseries* had assumed the character they would maintain, despite variations in detail, until the end of the Ancien Régime. This comprised a low dado surmounted by tall panels, usually extending to the cornice, but sometimes capped by a low attic or merged into a cove. The total height was generally around 5 meters. The prevailing shape was orthogonal: the asymmetric and freehand curves introduced during the Rococo period were never allowed to dominate the composition, and vanished when the country returned to classical prototypes around 1760.

In general, *boiseries* were modeled on architectural features and featured alternating wide and narrow widths. In classical styles, the narrow widths were often transformed into pilasters. The rhythmic arrangement, which spread symmetrically from centered fireplaces and accommodated windows and major passageways, was reinforced by building consoles at dado height and by disguising secondary entrances into rooms (as in the Queen's Cabinet Doré, Versailles). The dado was retained even during the curvilinear Rococo: its cap served the practical purpose of keeping furnishings away from the wall, and its height ensured that any decoration of the panel fields would be fully visible.

The character of the decoration reflected prevailing fashions or taste, the purpose of the room, and the financial resources of the owner. The simplest *boiseries* were of natural wood – typically, oak, fruitwood, walnut, or pine – finished with varnish. In the 18th century they were usually painted white, although pastel greens, pinks, and yellows became popular after 1730. Mouldings and ornament were often painted a contrasting colour or a lighter value of the panel hue. Both were also often gilded in grand rooms.

The panels were embellished in a variety of ways. Grandly-scaled ornament – trophées, cartouches, and heavy mouldings – were used in public rooms such as Louis XIV's Chambres de Parade at Versailles. Emblematic motifs, like musical instruments were a frequent device in music rooms. Small-scale arabesques, *singeries*, and Chinoiseries – executed in paint or lacquer – were popular for more intimate settings such as salons, cabinets, bathrooms, and boudoirs. At a time when artists were often closely involved in interior decoration, these decorations could be executed by a Christophe Huet (Hôtel de Rohan, 1735) or a François Boucher (whose *singerie* painted for Madame de Pompadour has disappeared). Other artists produced canvases to a size demanded by the *boiseries* (for example, Jean-Honoré Fragonard's *Progress of Love*, painted for Mme. Du Barry's pavilion at Louveciennes, now in the Frick Museum, New York). Overmantels, overdoors, and mirrored panels extended the decorative theme. *Boiseries* were also overlaid with gilded carving, as can be seen in the work executed throughout Versailles (Chambre de la Pendule, Mme. Adelaide's Music Room, Mme. Adelaide's Bath, etc.) by Antoine Rousseau and the Flemish *ornemaniste* Jacques Verberckt to the designs of Ange-Jacques Gabriel. Such work paid well; Verberckt received some 50,000 livres in 1735–36 alone.

The popularity of coloured *boiseries* led to the development of new techniques and formulae. The simplest approach to single-colour panels was a coat of whiting, polished and top-coated with the desired hue. For a more durable finish, the wood was prepared with two coats of hot glue and up to seven coats of whiting tinted with a little Prussian blue. The last coat of whiting was sanded with pumice before the oil-based colour was applied. For important installations, Ange-Jacques Gabriel specified a "chipolin" of multiple coats of whiting, colour, glue, and varnish. Lacquerwork required even more painstaking and time-consuming techniques. That each of these materials had its own unpleasant odour is suggested by the applause which greeted the "odourless" paint developed by vernisseur Dandrillon by the *Année littéraire* (1757–58). Called an "impression à la Grecque", this paint was probably similar to the encaustic (wax-based compound in which colours were fused with heat) attributed to Théodon Odiot and used by Gabriel at Choisy. Other "odourless" paints and stains were developed by Jean-Félix Watin, author of *L'Art du peintre, doreur, vernisseur* (2nd edition,1772).

By the last quarter of the 18th century, when entrepreneurs and inventors were creating a number of artificial products (including simulated marbles and building stones), the intricate ornament that had earlier required the skill of carvers like Verberckt could be imitated with a compound of parchment, gum arabic, gum dragon, water, and sawdust. Boiled to the consistency of oatmeal, this plastic wood was cast in moulds, attached to paneling with glue or screws, and painted (*Almanach sous verre*, 1780). In England, *boiseries* had long been imitated in stucco, or even papier-mâché as can be seen in the decoration of the saloon at Hartlebury Castle, Worcestershire, of c.1760. Concurrently, traditional *boiseries* fell from favour. Panels could be simulated with mouldings attached directly to the wall, and wallpaper, fabric, and imitation marble substituted for the panel field. The Empire period reduced paneling to a low dado, at best; and while the glories of earlier *boiseries* appeared to return with the Restoration, the old techniques of construction and decoration had vanished. However, *boiseries* enjoyed a brief revival during the last decades of the 19th century when interiors decorated in the Louis Quinze style became fashionable among a wealthy European and American clientele. These revivalist interiors included Baron Ferdinand de Rothschild's houses at Ferrières, near Paris, and Hamilton Place, London, which featured antique 18th-century French *boiseries*, and the châteauesque townhouses and Newport "cottages" built by Richard M. Hunt and decorated with Rococo-style *boiseries* designed by Ogden Codman, Jr.

REED BENHAMOU

See also Boffrand

Further Reading

Diderot, Denis and others, *Encyclopédie, ou, Dictionnaire raisonné des sciences, des arts et des métiers*, 17 vols., Paris, 1751–65

Hauteceour, Louis, *Histoire de l'architecture classique en France*, vol.3, Paris: Picard, 1951

Havard, Henry, *Dictionnaire de l'Ameublement et de la Décoration depuis le XIIIe siècle jusqu'à nos jours*, Paris, 1887

Janneau, Guillaume, *L'Epoque Louis XV*, Paris: Presses Universitaire de France, 1967

Kimball, Fiske, *The Creation of the Rococo*, 1943; reprinted as *The Creation of the Rococo Decorative Style*, New York: Dover, and London: Constable, 1980

Pons, Bruno, "Les Boiseries de l'Hôtel de Cressart, 18 Place Vendôme, au J. Paul Getty Museum" in *J. Paul Getty Museum Journal*, 9, 1983, pp.67–86

Pons, Bruno, *De Paris à Versailles 1699–1736: Les Sculptures Ornemanistes Parisiens et l'Art Décoratif des Bâtiments du Roi*, Strasbourg: Universités de Strasbourg, 1986

Pons, Bruno, "Jacques Verberckt (1704–1771), sculpteur des bâtiments du roi" in *Gazette des Beaux-Arts*, CXIX, April 1992, pp.173–88

Scott, Katie, *The Rococo Interior: Decoration and Social Spaces in Early Eighteenth-Century Paris*, New Haven and London: Yale University Press, 1995

Verlet, Pierre, *French Furniture and Interior Decoration of the 18th Century*, London: Barrie and Rockliffe, 1967

Vial, Henri, P. Marcel and A. Girodie, *Les Artistes décorateurs du bois*, 2 vols., Paris, 1912–22

Bonomi, Joseph 1739–1808

Italian architect and designer of interiors

Joseph (christened Giuseppe) Bonomi was one of the most important of a small but distinguished group of Continental Neo-Classicists who chose to settle in England, bringing a cosmopolitan sophistication which enlivened the native tradition, and playing a significant role in the Royal Academy and artistic life generally. His career in England of approximately forty years from 1767 spanned a period of rich variety and high achievement in English interior design, and Bonomi's own output reflects the full range of the fashionable alternatives: advanced Continental Neo-Classicism; the Greek Revival; the Adam Style; Pompeian. Despite this diversity, it would be a mistake to assume he was merely an adaptable follower of fashion; in all of them he developed his own personal idioms, sometimes displaying great originality and inventiveness. Bonomi is also important as one of the first architects in Britain to produce coloured interior perspective drawings of his designs, many of which gained prominence through their exhibition at the Royal Academy.

Bonomi was born in Rome and was educated at the Collegio Romano. He studied architecture with Antonio Asprucci and later with Marchese Teodoli. There is evidence to suggest he studied with Clérisseau too. He met James Adam while the latter was on his Grand Tour, and from 1763 he worked in Rome under contract for the Adam brothers, measuring antiquities and producing drawings for transmission to London. In 1767 they invited him to join their London office as one of a number of accomplished Italian draughtsmen on whom the firm relied for their finely worked presentation drawings. He remained with them until 1781 and a clause in his terms of employment precluded him from undertaking independent commissions during this part of his career.

Having had little success in launching a career in London, he returned to Italy in 1783. While there he became an associate of the Clementine Academy at Bologna and of the Academy of St. Luke in Rome. He also travelled in the South of Italy visiting Pompeii and Herculanium, and the Greek temples at Paestum, all of which were to provide fruitful sources for his subsequent designs, and usefully augmented his experience of ancient remains in and around Rome. He found little employment in Italy, but it seems likely that among the English travellers he met there were several who offered employment prospects in their native country. Thus in 1784 he returned to London, although he continued to exercise contact with artistic developments in Italy via his friends and relatives, and he appears to have entertained the desire eventually to secure a professional appointment and residence there.

One of Bonomi's major contributions to the interior designer's art was in helping to popularize the internal perspective drawing. Several of the finest of his own offerings in this genre were exhibited at the Royal Academy from 1783 onwards. Reynolds thought highly of him and in 1789 he was elected an associate of the Academy, on Reynolds's casting vote. The following year he tried unsuccessfully to gain full membership – having an eye on the vacant Professorship of Perspective – despite some influential support. Subsequently he made a number of other attempts to become a Royal Academician, all of which failed. Nevertheless, he continued to exhibit a series of outstanding drawings at their influential exhibitions.

There is a tradition that Bonomi was responsible for the interior perspectives which appeared in the Adams' *Works in Architecture* (vol.1 1773; vol.2 1779). There is no reason to doubt this as these illustrations have much in common with Bonomi's drawings of his own schemes. Significantly, they are quite different from the usual "folded down" elevations of a room's four walls which the firm usually used to depict its interior designs, or the sectional drawings used by many of the other leading British architects of this period. Bonomi's drawings recall the drama and strong chiaroscuro of Piranesi's illustrations, but they also share qualities with the virtuoso stage designs of the Bibiena family. Bonomi's internal perspectives helped found a tradition exploited so successfully by Sir John Soane and his assistants, and eventually adopted by many of the leading architects and interior designers of the 19th century.

The schemes depicted in Bonomi's interior drawings represent a highly individual and varied response to the current Neo-Classical taste. And while his exteriors were frequently severe to the point of ugliness, often he proposed sumptuous apartments behind them. Despite a working life spent almost entirely in England, always his work reflects his Italian training – and the avant-garde Neo-Classicism that evolved while he was a student – as well as his knowledge of that country's buildings, whether from antiquity, the Renaissance or post-Renaissance periods. Indeed, he was one of the few designers working in England before Soane who offered a serious alternative to the Adam style of interior.

Unsurprisingly, his early independent work is informed by his years in the Adams' office; for example, an unexecuted design for a dining room for Standish House, Lancashire of 1782, or the scheme for the Great Room of Montagu House, London of the late 1780s. But while he used many of their motifs, his work is more robust and avoids the brothers' fondness for distorting the proportions of the orders to the extent that they are reduced to mere decorative motifs. Another potent influence in his early interiors are the great baths of Imperial Rome. His tendency to specify vaulted ceilings springing from columns, domes and top lighting all draw unmistakably on this archaeological source, as is evident, for example, in his design for the gallery of an unidentified house, c.1782, and the design for the library of Lansdowne House, London, 1786.

Beginning in 1784, Bonomi spent several years completing the interiors of Packington Hall, Warwickshire, and building

Bonomi: design for Great Room for Mrs. Montagu, Portman Square, London, late 1780s

the church there. The patron was the 4th Earl of Aylesford, a gifted amateur architect who perhaps influenced the designs. Bonomi's work at the Hall included the Pompeian Gallery, executed in 1787, the largest and one of the earliest Pompeian schemes in England. A further variant on the Neo-Classical theme came in the interior of Packington church 1789–90. Here he combines thermal windows and a cross vault derived from Roman baths with squat Greek Doric columns – one of their earliest uses in England – and bare stone walls to produce a compelling and original interior. Greek references also appear in the entrance hall of Longford Hall, Shropshire, 1789–94, where the upper walls are decorated with casts of a Greek frieze, although the pedimented and columned screen to the staircase employs the Roman Doric order.

The drawings of Bonomi's schemes sometimes indicate a full complement of furniture as part of a carefully worked out architectural composition. In the unexecuted drawing room for Montagu House in London, c.1782, he specified familiar Adamesque motifs for sofas and oval mirrors which incorporate candelabra; for the Great Room of the same house, he designed a fitted carpet decorated in the manner of an antique mosaic floor. A remarkable set of *klismos* chairs in the Pompeian Room at Packington – probably designed by Bonomi – based on painted scenes from Greek vases, pre-date Thomas Hope's popularization of this form.

No doubt on Bonomi's recommendation, interiors which he designed were often executed by Italian decorators, painters and craftsmen, further strengthening the Continental flavour of Bonomi's Neo-Classicism.

CHRISTOPHER WEBSTER

See also Adam

Biography

Born in Rome, 19 January 1739. Educated at the Collegio Romano, Rome, and studied architecture under Antonio Asprucci and Marchese Teodoli. Married Rosa Florini, a cousin of the painter Angelica Kauffman (1741–1807): 3 sons including Ignatius (an architect) and Joseph (an Egyptologist and curator of the Soane Museum). Active in Rome from 1763; moved to England to work as a draughtsman for the Adam brothers, 1767 (remained in their employment until 1781); afterwards, assisted the architect Thomas Leverton (1743–1824). Active as an independent architect from c.1782; visited Italy, 1783; returned to England, 1784. Exhibited regularly at the Royal Academy of Arts, London, 1783–1806; elected an Associate, 1789. Associate of the Clementine Academy of Bologna, 1783; honorary architect to St. Peter's, Rome, 1804. Died in London, 9 March 1808.

Selected Works

An important collection of Bonomi's architectural designs, drawings and designs for interiors is in the Drawings Collection, Royal Institute of British Architects, London. A full list of his architectural commissions appears in Colvin 1995.

Interiors

c.1785–88	Packington Hall, Warwickshire (interiors, decoration and some furniture, including Pompeian Gallery): 4th Earl of Aylesford
1786	Lansdowne House, Berkeley Square, London (unexecuted designs for a library): William Petty, 1st Marquis of Lansdowne
1789	Townley Hall, Lancashire (unexecuted designs for a sculpture gallery): Charles Townley
1789–94	Longford Hall, Shropshire (building and interiors): Ralph Leeke
c.1790	Montagu (later Portman) House, Portman Square, London (ballroom): Mrs. Montagu
1793–1800	Eastwell Park, Kent (building and interiors): George Finch Hatton
1796–97	Lambton Hall, Co. Durham (interiors including library, dining room and picture gallery): William Lambton

Further Reading

Comparatively little has been written about Bonomi but an introduction to his career and a discussion of his drawings appears in Meadows's exhibition catalogue 1988.

Binney, Marcus, "Packington Hall, Warwickshire, III" in *Country Life*, CXLVIII, 23 July 1970, pp.226–29

Catalogue of the Drawings Collection of the Royal Institute of British Architects, Farnborough: Gregg, 1969

Colvin, Howard M., *A Biographical Dictionary of British Architects, 1600–1840*, 3rd edition New Haven and London: Yale University Press, 1995

"The Life and Work of Joseph Bonomi" in *Architect, Engineer and Surveyor*, 1843, pp.70–71

Meadows, Peter, *Joseph Bonomi, Architect* (exhib. cat.), London: Royal Institute of British Architects, 1988

Meadows, Peter, "Joseph Bonomi" in *Country Life*, 28 April 1988

Meadows, Peter and John Cornforth, "Draughtsman Decorator" in *Country Life*, 184, 19 April 1990, pp.164–68

Papworth, Wyatt, "Memoir" in *Transactions of the Royal Institute of British Architects*, 19, 1868–69, pp.123–34

Saumarez Smith, Charles, *Eighteenth-Century Decoration: Design and the Domestic Interior in England*, London: Weidenfeld and Nicolson, and New York: Abrams, 1993

Stillman, Damie, *English Neo-Classical Architecture*, London: Zwemmer, 1988

Bookcases

The storage arrangements for books was generally of little consequence until such time as there was a growth in book ownership. Book storage in the early period was crude but effective. Byzantine images show books stored flat on their sides in cupboards with solid doors. In monasteries and seats of learning, the storage of books was in specially designed fixtures, often with the volumes chained to them. For protection these open shelves were sometimes covered with a curtain. By the 16th century, the idea of a revolving bookcase or reading machine, was one response to a developing interest in reading and books, although it was still more common to store books in a secure chest.

By the 17th century, the growth in private book collections meant that there was a strong demand for proper storage facilities for books in a domestic environment. Free-standing bookcases were a response to this new need. These bookcases were based on a pattern that had a closed cupboard below surmounted with an open cupboard fitted with glazed doors. In this way the contents were on view, but protected and organised. On occasions when books were in use, or for ease of access in small rooms, wall-hanging shelves were introduced.

The end of the 17th century also saw a range of built-in bookcases which furnished the room in a particular architectural style. Examples exist of Daniel Marot's designs for a library in Holland which show plans for the careful integration of bookcases. In Italy architecturally detailed built-in bookcases were also introduced into private houses, while French architects were planning interiors with panelled walls, often incorporating bookshelves in parts of the scheme. If not built in, the *armoire-bibliothèque* with glazed doors was clearly designed for safeguarding books.

One of the most successful designs for book storage has been the bureau-bookcase. Simply put, it was a bureau desk with a bookcase surmounted upon it. This description belies the range of magnificent products of the late 17th and early 18th centuries. Initially made in walnut, the bookcase doors were usually either glazed or panelled. Although the bureau-bookcase was apparently first introduced in England, it soon found popularity in Holland, Italy and later on in America. This is not surprising as it was an extremely useful piece of domestic furniture, ideal for any location in a house.

In addition to the dual-purpose bureau-bookcases, the desire for free-standing architectural-style book cabinets developed. These were often decorated with fluted columns, pilasters, brackets and triangular or broken pediments: the Classical references indicating an association with learning. The use of fashionable mahogany timber meant that crisp carving and fine veneered finishes could be combined with glazed doors fitted with elegantly arranged bars to produce a powerful piece of furniture. The bookcases in Powderham Castle library supplied by the English cabinet-maker John Channon are extreme examples of the type.

The development of the wing or breakfront bookcase – a large bookcase with a central projection to house larger books with smaller sections on each side – seemed a natural progression. This style continued throughout the 18th century and has frequently been reproduced.

By the mid-18th century a gentleman's library might be too big to be stored in one or two bookcases, so the library room became more prominent. This room was specially fitted out with bookcases round much of the perimeter, and the design was often architecturally inspired to create a suitably studious atmosphere.

By Sheraton's time the fashionable bookcase had changed. They appeared to be narrower than previously with a higher base section and variety in the detailing. Their delicacy perhaps indicated that they were for use in drawing rooms rather than the library, especially as Sheraton made much of the selection of designs for the door tracery in his Drawing Book. This may have been a rather minor part of the design but was clearly important to Sheraton. In the same vein he was also influential in the taste for incorporating busts onto the frames of bookcases.

The 19th-century bookstand, a set of low open bookshelves on a base often fitted with castors, was indicative of a trend. Generally designed to stand against the wall, there were versions with open backs, glazed doors or cupboards, some being on feet, others on plinths. The 19th century also revived revolving bookcases, one particular patented model with an upright columnar action having considerable success. The idea in many variations continued into the 20th century.

Not surprisingly, it was at the Great Exhibition held in London during 1851 that one of the most impressive bookcases was displayed. It was produced by Carl Leistler of Vienna as a gift for Queen Victoria, and its usefulness as a bookcase was secondary to its value as an extraordinary *tour de force* of craftsmanship.

The influence of the Arts and Crafts Movement meant that bookcase designs might look like miniature architectural models. Norman Shaw's painted secretaire bookcase shown in London's 1862 Exhibition is an example. On the other hand, neo-Gothic bookcases were often based on functional units with simple inlaid decoration. Examples by A. W. N. Pugin and Charles Bevan show this form.

In the 20th century book storage developed upon unitary lines, with a number of designs being made on a modular basis. The minimal bookcase was an open carcase fitted with shelves, which could be made to any scale. The Minty range of sectional bookcases was relatively popular, but other models based on European types such as Plan furniture were less so. The functional idea of the Modernists meant that general items designed for a variety of tasks were preferred to specific objects for particular tasks. In the second half of the 20th century storage systems were developed that would store books and other items on open shelves. These systems, many of which were developed in Scandinavia, were based on ladders and brackets supporting shelves and small cupboards, and were particularly suited to open-plan interiors. Although a common solution to book storage problems is to have units built-in, one innovative product that was especially designed for a specific range of books was the Isokon Penguin "donkey". A small plywood bookcase designed to stand next to a chair, it was scaled to fit paperback books, especially the Penguin range.

The choice of bookcases is now as wide as the variety of styles that might require them, from Memphis to Makepeace, reproduction to Ron Arad: bookcases remain as important a symbol as they ever were.

CLIVE D. EDWARDS

See also Libraries

Further Reading

"Bookcases" in Percy MacQuoid and Ralph Edwards, *The Dictionary of English Furniture*, revised edition, 3 vols., 1954; reprinted Woodbridge, Suffolk: Antique Collectors' Club, 1983

Thornton, Peter, *Seventeenth-Century Interior Decoration in England, France, and Holland*, New Haven and London: Yale University Press, 1978

Walkling, Gillian, "Bookcases" in *Connoisseur*, CCI, August 1979, pp.268–71

Borra, Giovanni Battista (Giambattista)

1713–1770

Italian architect and draughtsman, engineer, engraver and painter

Following his work as architectural artist and topographer for a British-led expedition to the Levant in 1750 and 1751, Piedmont-born Giovanni Battista Borra quickly achieved a high level of recognition in England. This recognition was far greater than that which he received in his native Italy and is still to some extent evident today. Approximately half of the 200 drawings of ancient sites and monuments that Borra made on this trip served as the basis for a series of engravings published by Robert Wood, *The Ruins of Palmyra* (1753) and *The Ruins of Balbec* (1757). Both of these volumes attracted great interest from lovers of the ancient world. Borra's drawings of the architectural ornaments of Palmyra, in particular, proved to be an ideal source of patterns for interiors designed in the advanced Neo-Classical taste and, on his return from the Levant, his skills as a decorator were much in demand by wealthy landowners and aristocrats. English clients were also attracted to Borra's work by his knowledge of the Piedmont Baroque and the French-influenced Rococo.

A ceiling ornament from the sun temple of Palmyra, reproduced in Plate XIX/B of the Palmyra book, soon became an extraordinarily popular quotation from antiquity. Two years previously Horace Walpole had discovered a ceiling in the State Bedroom at Woburn Abbey decorated with this very motif. It consisted of a large central rosette bordered by a meander band, lying in a rectangular frame made up of fields of octagonal coffers which in turn are decorated with rosettes. Numerous richly varied interpretations of this ceiling pattern appeared in the second half of the 18th century – the most famous being Robert Adam's ceiling at Osterley Park, Middlesex – and many were produced either under the direct guidance of Borra himself or were copied from his designs. In February 1755 Borra was commissioned to produce plans for the redecoration of the State Apartment at Stowe, the Buckinghamshire home of Richard Grenville, Lord Temple (1711–79), for whom Borra also made two new designs for the south front of the house and by whom he was consulted over the Neo-Classical remodelling of the garden architecture. Lord Temple wanted new designs for the bipartite ceiling and frieze in the State Bed Chamber, as well as new chimneypieces here and in the adjoining State Dressing Room. The coffered section of the bedroom ceiling once again includes a variation on the popular decorative motif from Palmyra. But, instead of positioning a large patera above the central point of the room, Lord Temple used this position to display the Order of the Garter which had been bestowed on him a short time before and which gave the room the name – Garter Room – that it still bears today. As well as various antique-style ceiling decorations and architectural details, Borra was responsible for the design of the Baroque-style state bed which was in the form of a gilded baldachin and which was originally placed against the west wall of the room between Corinthian columns.

Borra's "Catholic Style" was much admired by aristocrats who championed the Tory cause, but he also attracted the patronage of the Duchess of Norfolk who was known to be a Jacobite sympathiser. The Duchess's husband, the 9th Duke of Norfolk, had chosen the Palladian architect Matthew Brettingham, a follower of Lord Burlington who was supported by the Protestant Whigs, to design his London house. And it was probably through Lord Temple, who was a friend of her husband, that the Duchess, whose taste dominated the interior decoration within Norfolk House, made contact with Borra. There was also an indirect connection with Piedmont through John Cuenot, a craftsman of French extraction who executed the wood-carvings and was possibly related to François Cuenot, who worked from 1660 for Carlo Emanuele II in Savoy as a sculptor and woodcarver. The music room of Norfolk House (demolished 1937 and reconstructed in the Victoria and Albert Museum) provides the best evidence of the house's exceptional interior decor which was developed chiefly from Borra's designs. The unusually free way in which different architectural and ornamental styles are combined is particularly striking, with English neo-Palladianism combined with Piedmont late Baroque and French Rococo.

The state rooms were reached via the central stairway whose skirtings on the first floor level were decorated in a rich, late Baroque style. They were finished with a stuccoed high relief in the form of trophy decorations hanging from large bows, a decoration which is reminiscent of Filippo Juvarra's wall decoration for the upper floor of the oval central room in the Stupinigi Hunting Lodge (1731), near Turin. On reaching the first floor, the visitor was led through a succession of magnificently decorated rooms. The plurality of styles – described by contemporaries as "whimsical" — reached its peak in the music room. Gilded wood-carvings in a French Rococo style decorate the alternately broad and narrow panelling and frame of the wall mirror above the marble fireplace (neither of the mirrors by Cuenot after Borra's design on the window side has been reconstructed). The formal plasticity of both the curved fireplace surround above its outwardly-turned supports, and the decorative elements such as the centrally-placed head of a woman – which appears to have derived from the work of the Baroque classicist Jean I Berain, and which is comparable to the wood-carved masks in the panelling as well as to the masks on the mirror frames and the head of Hermes on the fireplace in the former Green Damask Room – correspond neither to Baroque fireplace designs in Turin palaces nor to the latest trends in French Rococo design. The fireplace is still less indebted to English convention, and only the design of the ceiling in the Music Room can have been familiar to English visitors. The clearly-ordered Palladian ceiling decoration is readily identifiable as a variant of Inigo Jones's prototypical ceiling ornamentation in the Banqueting House at Whitehall, even though the geometrical fields of the ceiling are further decorated with Rococo cartouches of gilded stucco by the sculptor James Lovell with whom Borra had worked at Stowe.

In 1756, just a short while before his final return to Italy, Borra was commissioned to undertake alterations to the residence of Prince Ludovico di Carignano in Racconigi, near Turin. The early classical modification of Castello di Racconigi, which had been half completed following the Baroque plans of Guarino Guarini, also included the partial reworking of its interior design and its decoration. Borra's designs for the interior of the entrance hall (Salone d'Ercole) and its adjoining reception room (Salone di Diana) clearly demonstrate his knowledge of both antiquity and English neo-Palladianism. In stylistic harmony with the front entrance, the colonnade motif is taken up once again in the entrance hall in a neo-Palladian manner. A structure akin to a loggia, which reaches the bottom of the second floor, extends in front of the partition separating the two rooms, which lie one behind the other. This structure is formed by six free-standing Ionic columns which are arranged in pairs towards the centre and which support a passageway lined with balusters between the rooms to the sides. In contrast, the two walls which run the length of the entrance hall are structured and decorated in a late Baroque style. These walls rise up to the first floor and have alternate door openings with triangular pediments and niches with rounded pediments housing sculptures. The statues, modelled by the Lugano sculptor and stucco artist, Giuseppe Bolina, who was highly regarded in Piedmont, represent six of the twelve Labours of Hercules. The stucco war trophy mouldings above the niches closely resemble the forms on the staircase at Norfolk House.

With the fine stucco work that forms part of the interior of the neighbouring Sala di Ricevimento – also by Bolina – Borra looked back even more obviously to motifs that had proved their worth at Norfolk House. The overdoors above the entrance and the two pairs of side doors correspond to a large extent to the "monkey doors" of the Great Drawing Room that were carved by Cuenot. Only the main figurative motif, which had originally consisted of small, mischievous monkeys or Rococo *singeries*, was replaced by garland-bearing putti in the Sala di Diana. By contrast, the four colossally large medallions can be linked to the decoration in the Salle de la Guerre at Versailles, commissioned by Louis XIV and carried out by Antoine Coysevox; this link can be substantiated by Prince Ludovici's family tie with the French royal household. The two facing fireplaces are in the style of Guarini or may have been by Guarini himself (Gabrielli, 1972). Unlike the Baroque and Rococo style of the wall decoration, Borra used an anti-Baroque, antique motif for the ceiling. Around the middle field with its bas-relief, he arranged an ornament of intersecting circles with inlaid rosettes, a design that matches exactly another ceiling pattern from Palmyra which Borra recorded in the *Ruins*.

The tension in Borra's work resides not so much in the fact that he was willing and able to use several different styles simultaneously, but more in the breadth of his education, and in the open-minded and wide-ranging nature of his interest in architecture and its history. The results of this interest reached a wide public after the middle decades of the 18th century, and Borra's influence – felt most notably in the emergence of Neo-Classicism – is attributable primarily to the success of his published drawings.

OLGA ZOLLER

Biography

Born in Doglinai, Cuneo province, 27 December 1713. Trained under the architect Bernardo Vittone in Turin. Under Vittone's guidance, executed illustrations for Vignola's architectural treatise (unrealized), 1734, and drawings and prints for Vittone's *Istruzioni Elementari* (1760), c.1736. Studied at Turin University, graduated 1741. His practical manual, *Trattato della cognizione ...*, published 1748. Employed as architectural draughtsman by John Wood, James Dawkins and J. Bouverie on their archaeological expedition to the Levant, 1750–51. Returned to London in 1751, and provided the drawings for Wood's publications, *The Ruins of Palmyra* (1753) and the *Ruins of Balbec* (1757). Acquired several British patrons, including the Duke of Bedford, 1752, Richard Grenville, Lord Temple, 1752–55, and the 9th Duke and Duchess of Norfolk, 1755. Returned to Italy, 1756, and worked on interiors for the Castello di Racconigi, 1756–58. His designs were used for Palazzo Grassi (now Cocconito, Langosco), and Casale Monferrato (executed 1776). During the 1760s active as civil and sacred architect, and as engineer. Provided plans for the restoration of the fortifications of the citadel Alessandria, and hydraulic schemes. He died, probably in Turin, before 16 November 1770.

Selected Works

The most comprehensive collection of Borra's designs for interiors is in the library of the Society for the Promotion of Hellenic Studies, London, and in the Drawings Collection, Royal Institute of British Architects, London. 98 watercolours of the Levant are in the Mellon Collection, Center for Studies in British Art, Yale University. Borra's correspondence with Lord Temple is held at the Huntington Library, Santa Monica, and further manuscript sources are in the State and City archives, Turin. The Norfolk House Music Room is at the Victoria and Albert Museum.

Interiors

1740	Palazzo Isnardi di Caralgio, Turin (interiors with B. Alfieri)
1751	Woburn Abbey, Bedfordshire (interior decoration): Duke of Bedford
1752–55	Stowe, Buckinghamsire (State Apartment, State Bedchamber and Bed, State Dressing Room, Garter Room): Richard Grenville, Lord Temple
1755	Norfolk House, London (including Music Room): Duke and Duchess of Norfolk
1755	Stratfield Saye House, Hampshire (ceiling of dining room)
1756–58	Castello di Racconigi, near Turin (building and interiors including Salone d'Ercole, Salone di Diana, Sala di Ricevimento): Prince Ludovico di Carignano
1757	Palazzo Argentero di Bersezio, Perrone di San Marino, Turin (interiors)
1758	Palazzo di Città, Ivrea (building and interiors)
1760	Palazzo Turinetti di Pertengo, Turin (building and interiors)

Publications

Trattato della cognizione pratica delle resistenze geometricamente, 1748

Vedute principali di Torino disegnate in prospettiva, ed intagliate in rame dall' architetto Giambattista Borra, Parte prima, 1749

Vittone, Bernardo, *Istruzioni Elementari*, 1760 (engravings by Borra)

Wood, Robert, *The Ruins of Palmyra, otherwise Tedmor in the Desert*, 1753 (engravings after Borra)

Wood, Robert, *The Ruins of Balbec, otherwise Heliopolis in Colosyria*, 1757 (engravings after Borra)

Further Reading

Bernardi, Marziano, *Tre palazzi a Torino (Il Palazzo Carignano; Il palazzo dell'Accademia Filarmonica; La Villa della Regina)*, Turin: Istituto Bancario San Paolo di Torino, 1963

Cornforth, John, "Stratfield Saye House, Hampshire: The Seat of the Duke of Wellington, II", in *Country Life*, 17 April 1975, pp.982–85

Fitz-Gerald, Desmond, *The Norfolk House Music Room*, London: Victoria and Albert Museum, 1973

Fitz-Gerald, Desmond, "A history of the interior of Stowe", in *Apollo*, June 1973

Gabrielli, Noemi, *Racconigi*, Turin: Istituto Bancario San Paolo di Torino, 1972

Gibbon, Michael, "Stowe House, 1680–1779", in *Apollo*, June 1973, p.552ff

Gibbon, Michael, "The History of Stowe: XVIII Earl Temple and Giambattista Borra", in *The Stoic*, July 1973, pp.201–05

Harris, John, *Catalogue of the Drawings Collection of the Royal Institute of British Architects: Inigo Jones and John Webb*, Farnborough: Gregg, 1972

Hussey, Christopher, "The Opening of Woburn Abbey", in *Country Life*, 31 March 1955, pp.854–58

Rebaudengo, Dina, *Le isole di San Carlo e Santa Elisabetta*, Turin, 1979

Rebaudengo, Dina, *Le isole di San Giovanni Evangelista e San Giorgio*, Turin, 1981

Vitullo, Fulvio, *Torino di ieri e di oggi: I Palazzi della "Provvidenza", Perrone di San Martino, e della Cassa di Risparmio*, Turin: Cassa di Risparmio, 1959

Zoller, Olga, *Der Architekt und der Ingenieur Giovanni Battista Borra (1713–1770)*, dissertation, Bonn, 1993

Bossi, Antonio Giuseppe c.1700–1764

Italian stuccoist, sculptor and painter

Antonio Giuseppe Bossi was born in Porta Ceresio, near Lugano, at the beginning of the 18th century and came from a well-known family of Italian stuccoists. Trained as a sculptor and modeller, he also executed decorative paintings, frescoes and *scagliola*, and his work at the Würzburg Residenz in Germany includes some of the finest and most distinctive examples of stucco decoration in the High Rococo style.

In 1727–28 Bossi worked with Francesco and Antonio Quadri and Gina Battista Pedrozzi at the abbey of Ottobeuren, near Meuringen, producing elegant stucco decorations in the antechamber of the Imperial Hall, in the vestibules of various chapels and for the ceiling of the so-called Amigoni room. After this he moved to Magonga where it seems he came into contact with the older modeller Georg Hannicke, whose influence can be detected in much of the work that Bossi executed during the following years. Drawn to Würzburg by the work that was being undertaken in the Schönborn Chapel of the Cathedral, in 1733 he requested and was granted permission to join the team in charge of the decorations and was given the task of executing all the stucco work. He proved himself to be an artist of extraordinary skill and the Prince-Bishop Friedrich Carl von Schönborn appointed him court stuccoist at the end of the following year. Much of his activity over the next three decades was concentrated upon the decorations for the Würzburg Residenz where he worked, with only minor interruptions caused by ill-health, until just a few years before his death in 1764.

Bossi's work at the Residenz illustrates the full range of his stylistic development. In his earliest contributions, the impact of Northern Italian sculptural traditions, combined with

Bossi: Imperial Hall (Kaisersaal), Residenz, Würzburg, 1735–57

French and Viennese influences, are evident. His more mature works, however, reveal a more original language and the use of an unmistakably Rococo style. Moreover, always sensitive to the environmental and architectural characteristics of the spaces to be decorated, Bossi varied the distribution of the mass of ornament and the depth of the reliefs accordingly. His most important works, which also elicited the greatest praise from his contemporaries, were the ceiling of the Hall of Mirrors (1741), the Gallery (1743–44), the White Hall and the Main Staircase (from 1744), the hall facing the garden (1745) and the Imperial Hall (1750–51). The White Hall, or Salle des Gardes as it was also known, is a masterly example of Rococo decoration at its most delicate. The whole room is coloured in white and off-white, broken only by the subtle contasts of the brown doors and grey-black stove. It is dominated by Bossi's exquisite stucco work which covers large sections of the ceiling and walls in a lacy composition that includes swirling Rococo shells and foliage interspersed with emblems of war, insignia of nobility, flying cherubs and more dignified figures such as Mars and Bellona presented in an Arcadian pastoral setting. The restless energy and seemingly effortless ingenuity of the decoration contrasts with the tendency towards exaggeration and stylisation that is evident in later works dating from the last decade of his career.

Despite the remarkably skilful nature of the work at Würzburg, critical evaluations of Bossi's oeuvre are complicated by the fact that he employed a wide circle of assistants. At certain periods these numbered more than forty craftsmen including Giuseppe Vennino, and Bossi's relatives Maderno, Agostino, Ignazio and Carlo Bossi. These craftsmen often executed the actual decorations, following designs provided by Bossi in large drawings traced in charcoal. Some of Bossi's preparatory models have been preserved and illustrate the quality of his work; they were extremely precise and detailed indicating the completeness of his ideas even in early stages of a project. Bossi also executed frescoes at Würzburg and other important buildings. After training with the artist Rudolf Byss, he painted the ceiling of the Knights' Dining Hall in the Residenz in 1737, and in 1746–49 he executed frescoes in the large Hall in the Juliusspital (Hospital of St. Julian; destroyed).

Bossi was also very skilled in *scagliola* decoration and in sculpture in the round. He fashioned stucco sculpture in the Court Church (the altar of the Immaculate), and stucco figures in the wall-niches of the Imperial Hall at Würzburg representing Apollo, Neptune, Juno and Flora, whose forms were characterised by an impressive harmony, elegance and suppleness. These works made a strong impression on other artists active in the Residenz including the court sculptor, Johann Wolfgang van Auwera (1708–56), and the stuccoist Ferdinand Hundt.

As a result of the fame arising from his work for the Prince-Bishop Schönborn and for court palaces in other locations in the region (for example, Schlöss Werneck, 1744–52, the palace of Veitshöchheim, 1752–53, many churches in Gailbach, 1747–48, and at Gaukönigshofen near Ochsenfurt, 1751–52), Bossi received numerous other commissions from private patrons and religious institutions in Würzburg. In addition to the documented works, several schemes for the interiors and exteriors of buildings in the historic city centre have been attributed to him on stylistic grounds, although in some cases these must have been carried out by his assistants and imitators.

Bossi's genius brought a new direction and fresh impetus to the local tradition of stucco modelling in Würzburg, creating a tangible and characteristic Würzburg Rococo style that became justly famed throughout Germany. But, with the exception of the spectacular works in the Residenz, there is little of Bossi's signed work in the city that survives intact. Sadly, much was destroyed in the 19th century or was damaged during World War II and as a result we can only partially evaluate the true extent of his skills.

LUCIANA ARBACE
translated by Antonia Boström

See also Plasterwork and Stucco

Biography

Born in Porta Ceresio, near Lugano, Switzerland, c.1700, into a family of stuccoists. Active as a stuccoist in Germany from 1727. Appointed court stuccoist to Prince-Bishop Friedrich Carl von Schönborn, Würzburg, 1734. Died insane in Würzburg, 10 February 1764.

Selected Works

Interiors

1727–28	Abbey of Ottobeuren, near Meuringen (stucco decoration)
1733	Schönborn Chapel, Cathedral, Würzburg (stucco decoration)
1735–57	Residenz, Würzburg (stucco decoration in the Hall of Mirrors, the Gallery, the White Hall, the Staircase, the Garden Room, and the Imperial Hall)
1744	Schloss Werneck, near Würzburg (stucco decoration)
1751–52	Gaukönigshofen, near Ochsenfurt (stucco decoration)
1752–53	Veitschöchheim, near Würzburg (stucco decoration)

Further Reading

Bachmann, Erich, *The Würzburg Residence and Court Gardens*, 6th edition Munich: Bayerische Verwaltung der Staatlicher Schlosser, 1982

Beard, Geoffrey, *Stucco and Decorative Plasterwork in Europe*, London: Thames and Hudson, and New York: Harper, 1983

Blunt, Anthony (editor), *Baroque and Rococo: Architecture and Decoration*, New York: Harper, and London: Elek, 1978

Hitchcock, Henry-Russell, *Rococo Architecture in Southern Germany*, London: Phaidon, 1968

Landschreiber, Lars, "Sicherung des Vestibüls des Treppenhauses und Weissen Saales in der Residenz Würzburg" in *Deutsche Kunst und Denkmalpflage*, 1968

Lieb, Norbert, *Ottobeuren und die Barockarchitektur Ostschwabens*, Augsburg: Rosler, 1933

Sedlmaier, Richard and Rudolf Pfister, *Die fürstbischöfliche Residenz zu Würzburg*, 2 vols., Munich: Muller, 1923

Boucher, François 1703–1770

French painter, engraver, and designer of porcelain and tapestries

François Boucher was one of the most celebrated and prolific decorative artists of the 18th century, receiving numerous royal and private commissions at a time when France's influence on fashion and design was at its height. An artist closely associated with the reign of Louis XV, his work is considered by many to embody the indolence and hedonism of the social elite in the middle decades of the century. And although he was not a creator of the Rococo style, Boucher became one of its leading exponents and its popularity coincided with his most innovative and accomplished years.

Boucher was primarily a painter, but his natural affinity for decoration and ornament meant that his designs could easily be translated into a variety of decorative media. He worked directly for the Beauvais (from 1734) and Gobelins (from 1753) tapestry works, and for the Royal Porcelain Factory at Sèvres (1750s), and his designs continued to be used long after his personal involvement with these manufactories had ceased. He also published numerous suites of ornament, including the *Nouveaux Morceaux pour des paravants* (1737), the *Livre de Cartouches* and the hugely successful *Chinoiserie* series (from c.1740). These designs provided valuable source material for decorators throughout Europe and, reproduced on panels, fabrics, porcelain and in marquetry, they enhanced Boucher's reputation as effectively as the direct export of his canvases, tapestries and porcelain. His influence spread to many countries, including Britain and Italy, and can be seen as far afield as Sweden where the Chinoiserie interiors at Kina, Drottingholm, are clearly indebted to his designs.

Boucher's style was an amalgamation of artistic influences which included the Italian decorative tradition, the Flemish and Dutch schools, and in particular the work of the French painter, Antoine Watteau. Another more immediate stimulus was provided by the world of the theatre (Boucher executed several stage designs for the Opéra) whose influence is evident throughout his life-long association with the applied arts. Yet, ultimately, Boucher developed a highly personal style that is his alone. Characterised by the pursuit of pleasure and an atmosphere of gentle eroticism, he created a langorous dreamworld of mythologies, romantic pastorals and enchanted landscapes rich with reminiscences of Italy. And the sense of artifice was reinforced by the use of light and airy pastel shades, particularly powdery blues, pinks and lilacs, and the lack of perspectival depth.

The sensuous and decorative nature of this style appealed particularly to members of the closely interwoven world of the French court and the wealthy Parisian bourgeoisie, many of whom rejected the large-scale architectural decorations exemplified by Louis XIV's Versailles in favour of a more informal approach to interior design. Boucher's work was particularly well-suited to the relatively intimate scale of their city dwellings where the fashion for gilded panelling and mirrors often limited the space available for paintings to overdoors and areas above the wainscoting. The suite of large-scale paintings executed for the lawyer François Derbais for his hôtel in the rue Poissonière, Paris (c.1732–34) is without parallel in Boucher's work. His paintings were almost always executed for specific locations and formed part of an integrated decorative scheme where the function of the room and the intended decorative harmony between ornament, furnishings and painting dictated the subject and handling. The fact that many of these original settings have been destroyed and their contents dispersed to museums or private collections makes an appreciation of Boucher's contribution to interior design more problematic. A notable exception is the set of four grisailles paintings depicting the Virtues, which were commissioned for the *chambre de la reine* at Versailles where they remain to this day.

As part of the team of artists working on the redecoration of the Hôtel de Soubise, Paris (1738), Boucher was commissioned to paint seven overdoors which included mythologies, landscapes and pastorals. The most novel were the two pastorals *Le Pasteur Galant* and *Le Pasteur Complaisant* which reworked the tradition of idealised portrayals of shepherds' lives to concentrate upon the depiction of their amorous pursuits and pastimes. This genre was to become one of the mainstays of Boucher's career and the modernity of his approach to these subjects is demonstrated by his *Summer* and *Autumn* pastorals of 1749 (now in the Wallace Collection, London), which were inspired by contemporary pantomines performed by the Théâtre de la Foire. The *Venus* panel at the Hôtel de Soubise also illustrates Boucher's ability to adapt his compositions within the frequently complicated, fanciful shapes of Rococo frames.

Boucher became the favourite artist of Louis XV's mistress, Madame de Pompadour (1721–64), whose view of painting as primarily a decorative medium makes those works executed under her patronage especially interesting. Among her many commissions for interiors were Boucher's decorations for a Chinese boudoir at Bellevue and an octagonal boudoir at Crécy. Both châteaux have since been destroyed but several of Boucher's paintings, including the eight panels for the Crécy boudoir (now in the Frick Collection, New York), depicting allegories of human activities such as the Arts and Sciences, have survived. The use of children – as opposed to adults – in this series, largely attired in contemporary dress, was in keeping with the fashion of the 1750s but also represents Boucher's fondness for rosy-cheeked infants and putti many of whom feature in his most popular works. Boucher's masterpieces, *Le Lever* and *Le Coucher du Soleil* (1753 and 1752, Wallace Collection) were also commissioned by Madame de Pompadour, and were subsquently reproduced in tapestry form at the Gobelins. Devoid of action or drama, these "galant" mythologies exemplify Boucher's characteristic treatment of "noble" subjects in a lighthearted and sensuous manner. Both were more than ten feet high and were hung with pendant tapestries in Bellevue between 1754 and 1760. The striking effect of canvas and textile in the same design and on such a grand scale can unfortunately only be imagined as the tapestries have subsequently disappeared.

Boucher's mastery of tapestry design, both for wall hangings and upholstery, represents a microcosm of his style, subject matter and influence. His work dominated the output of the Beauvais factory from 1736, the date of his first designs, until the mid 1750s, and in 1755 he took over the prestigious role of Inspecteur at the Gobelins workshops. He adapted with habitual aplomb to the medium of silk and wool, producing designs full of attractive detail with blocks of colour kept to a minimum and boldly defined central figures. Boucher's passion for the exotic potential of Chinoiserie is beautifully expressed in the six designs *La Tenture chinoise* (1743) for Beauvais. His vision of China is less remote and mysterious that that of his contemporaries Antoine Watteau and Jean Pillement, and illustrates an emphasis upon sensuous and corporeal elements that is evident throughout his oeuvre. The series was rewoven many times between 1745 and 1775 and one set, dated 1764, was reputedly sent by Louis XV to the Emperor of China.

One of Boucher's last essays in tapestry design were the central details in the series named *Tentures de Boucher*. First produced in the 1760s, this series was woven by the Gobelins workshops for the music room at Croome Court, Worcestershire (now in the Metropolitan Museum of Art, New York). The designs include *trompe-l'oeil* medallions containing mythologies, set into a background featuring a crimson damask pattern and decorated with birds, garlands of flowers and trophies. The series proved hugely popular, and despite the growing influence of Neo-Classicism it continued to be woven for clients in Russia, Germany, England and Spain, although not in France. A set ordered in 1772 for Osterley Park, Middlesex, still remains *in situ* with a ceiling designed by Robert Adam and chairs upholstered with scenes from Boucher's *Les Amours Pastorales*, and it is perhaps within the context of this intimate room that the modern viewer can best appreciate Boucher's contribution to interior decoration and design.

Boucher's many imitators included his student and son-in-law, Jean-Baptiste-Henry Deshays de Coleville (1729–65) whose work, like that of Boucher's celebrated student Jean-Honoré Fragonard, is often attributed to Boucher and includes the decorative pendant overdoors of *La Musique* (Corcoran Gallery of Art, Washington, DC) and *Le Dessin*, sold at auction in May 1995. Boucher's own son, Juste-François (1736–82) worked in a pronounced Neo-Classical style and produced numerous engravings relating to many aspects of the decorative arts and interior design. Described at the time as "à la moderne" (in the modern style), his oeuvre included approximately 700 designs for beds, chairs, screens, balustrades and ornament published from the mid-1770s.

CHRISTINE RIDING

See also Rococo

Biography

Born in Paris, 29 September 1703, the son of a designer and master-painter, Nicolas Bouché. Probably apprenticed to his father c.1717–c.20; trained as an engraver, 1720; pupil of the artist François Lemoine c.1721–c.23; awarded first prize for painting, Académie Royale de Peinture et de Sculpture, 1723. Married Marie-Jeanne Buseau, 1733: 2 daughters and one son, the designer and engraver Juste-François Boucher (1736–82). Employed in making designs for engravings for Jean-François Cars c.1723–28. Travelled to Rome with the painters Carle, Louis-Michel, and François Van Loo, 1728–30. Active as a painter, engraver, and book illustrator, Paris, from c.1731; employed as a designer by the Beauvais Tapestry Works 1734–55; stage designs for the Opéra, Paris, 1739–48; produced designs for the Vincennes porcelain factory, from 1749, and remained involved with the factory after its move to Sèvres, 1753. Taught drawing and engraving to Mme. de Pompadour (1721–64), 1751, who remained his most important patron. Appointed Inspecteur sur les Ouvrages de la Manufacture des Gobelins, 1755. Elected Professor, Académie Royale, 1737; appointed Premier Peintre du Roi and Director, Académie Royale, 1765 (resigned 1768). Exhibited at the Paris Salon from 1741. Published several suites of Chinoiseries and ornament from late 1730s. Died in Paris, 30 May 1770.

Selected Works

Notable collections of Boucher's tapestries are in Osterley Park, Middlesex; the Musée des Arts Décoratifs, Paris; the J. Paul Getty Museum, Malibu; the Metropolitan Museum of Art, New York, which includes the tapestry room from Croome Court; and the Philadelphia Museum of Art. Examples of porcelain with designs after Boucher are in the Musée National de Ceramique, Sèvres.

Interiors

1732–34	Hôtel, rue de Poissonière, Paris (paintings for the salle de billiard): François Derbais
1738	Hôtel de Soubise, Paris (overdoors for oval salon)
1738–39	Versailles (paintings for the Galerie des Petits Appartements du Roi)
1741–43	Château de Choisy (paintings and overdoors)
1747	Château de Choisy (paintings for the Grand Cabinet des Jeux)
1748	Château de Fontainebleau (paintings for the Salle à Manger du Roi)
1753	Château de Fontainebleau (paintings for the ceiling of the Cabinet du Conseil)
1754–60	Château de Bellevue (paintings and tapestries for the Chinese boudoir)

Boucher's designs for tapestries included the *Fêtes Italiennes* (1736), the *Story of Psyche* (1741), *La Tenture chinoise* (1743), *Les Amours des Dieux* (1758), and the *Tentures de Boucher* (1764).

Publications (suites of ornament)

Diverse Figures Chinoises, 1731
Recueil de Fontaines, 1736; *Second Livre*, n.d.
Nouveaux Morceaux pour des paravants, 1737
Diverses Figures Chinoises, 1740
Livres d'Ecrans, n.d.
Livre de Cartouches, n.d.
Livre de Vases, n.d.

Further Reading

A detailed and scholarly study of Boucher's work, including discussions of his designs for tapestry and porcelain, a chronology and extensive bibliography, appears in Laing 1986.

Ananoff, Alexandre, *L'Oeuvre Dessiné de François Boucher (1703–1770)*, Paris: Nobele, 1966
Ananoff, Alexandre and Daniel Wildenstein, *François Boucher*, 2 vols., Lausanne: Bibliothèque des Arts, 1976
Ananoff, Alexandre and Daniel Wildenstein, *L'Opera Completa di Boucher*, Milan: Rizzoli, 1980
Borsch-Supan, Helmut, "François Boucher" in *China und Europa: Chinaverständnis in 17. und 18. Jahrhundert* (exhib. cat.), Berlin: Schloss Charlottenburg, 1973
Brunel, Georges, *Boucher*, London: Trefoil, and New York: Vendome, 1986
Hazelhurst, F. Hamilton, "The Wild Beasts Pursued: The Petite Galerie of Louis XV at Versailles" in *Art Bulletin*, 66, June 1984, pp.224–36
Hiesinger, Kathryn B., "The Sources of François Boucher's 'Psyche' Tapestries" in *Bulletin of the Philadelphia Museum of Art*, 72, November 1976, pp.7–23
Jacobson, Dawn, *Chinoiserie*, London: Phaidon, 1993
Jacoby, Beverly Schreiber, *François Boucher's Early Development as a Draughtsman, 1720–1734*, New York: Garland, 1986
Jean-Richard, Pierrette, *L'Oeuvre Gravé de François Boucher dans le Collection Edmond de Rothschild*, Paris: Editions des Musées Nationaux, 1978
Laing, Alastair (editor), *François Boucher 1703–1770* (exhib. cat.), New York: Metropolitan Museum of Art, 1986
Posner, Donald, "Mme. de Pompadour as a Patron of the Visual Arts" in *Art Bulletin*, 72, March 1990, pp.74–105
Scott, Katie, *The Rococo Interior: Decoration and Social Spaces in Early Eighteenth-Century Paris*, New Haven and London: Yale University Press, 1995
Standen, Edith A., "The Croome Court Tapestries" in James Parker and Edith A. Standen, *Decorative Art from the Samuel H. Kress Collection at the Metropolitan Museum of Art*, London: Phaidon, 1964, pp.7–21, 45–52
Standen, Edith A., "The 'Amours des Dieux': A Series of Beauvais Tapestries after Boucher" in *Metropolitan Museum Journal*, 19–20, 1984–85, pp.63–84

Boudoirs and Dressing Rooms

Dressing rooms emerged as one of the private rooms leading off the State Apartments in grand houses from the 17th century, but the precise origins and function of the boudoir are less clear. The term itself has been linked to the French word bouder meaning to pout or to be sulky, and it has been suggested that the boudoir was therefore originally a private withdrawing room or place in which to sulk. Among architectural historians, however, the term boudoir is generally accepted as deriving from "Bower", the name used to designate the second chamber within early medieval buildings. From quite an early period the bower had feminine connotations and was regarded as a room for ladies, but as houses became larger and their rooms more specialised, the second chamber increasingly served as a parlour and lost some of its distinction as an apartment exclusively for the use of women. With the provision of private or family apartments in the latter part of the 14th century, a Lord's Chamber or Parlour was added, often adjoining the sleeping chambers on the upper floors. A Lady's Chamber (or bower) was often provided in larger houses in proximity to the Withdrawing Room and, according to the historian Bannister Fletcher, probably answered the purpose of the best bedroom.

By the 15th century, the Withdrawing Room and Lady's Bower, which had previously contained beds, were both in many cases reserved as Sitting Rooms. The term "Lady's Bower" seems to have become obscure during the 16th and 17th centuries, and "chambers" came to denote bedrooms. During this period the boudoir was often indistinguishable from the closet, a small room or rooms off the bedroom that might serve as a dressing room, study or *garde-robe*, and that was a feature of both male and female sets of apartments.

By the mid-18th century a separate boudoir was a common

Boudoir at 3 West Halkin Street, London, 1891

feature in many larger aristocratic homes. In his *L'Art de Bâtir des Maisons de Campagne*, published in Paris in 1743, Charles-Etienne Briseux, for example, suggested that another small closet, called a boudoir, might be added to the "arrière cabinet" and the two "garderobes", which comprised the suite of rooms behind the bedchamber. Similarly, Victor, Marquis de Mirabeau, writing in *L'Ami des Hommes*, 1759, remarked that every great house should have suitable provision of "mezzanines, closets, garderobes and boudoirs". To a large extent this interest reflected an increased desire for privacy and relaxation among the owners of grand 18th-century homes, and the boudoir was perceived as a place in which to retreat from public gaze and the cares of public life. Its appearance was therefore frequently intimate and informal, in marked contrast to the formality of the decorations and furnishings used in State rooms. Nevertheless, boudoirs were often luxuriously and exotically appointed employing decorative schemes that were both imaginative and innovative. Madame de Pompadour, for instance, lavished especial care on the decoration of her boudoir at Bellevue (c.1748) which included costly embroidered silk hangings, and overdoors painted with chinoiseries by François Boucher. The boudoir owned by her brother, the Comte de Marigny, was decorated with "nudities", and the association of the boudoir with loose-living or erotic dalliance lasted for many years.

In Britain, the boudoir at Attingham Park, Shropshire, decorated in the late 1780s, serves as a fine example of ornament treated in the elegant Louis Seize style. The room is thought to have been painted by Louis-André Delabrière who was employed by the Daguerre company based in London from 1786. The boudoir at Shugborough, Staffordshire, dates from 1794. It is decorated with grey moiré wallpaper embellished with plain and cut-out floral borders supplied by the Eckhart Brothers of Chelsea, leading manufacturers of wallpaper in the late 18th and early 19th centuries. In both rooms the decorations reflect the most modish of tastes and they illustrate the extravagance with which such interiors were often treated.

While dressing rooms were used by both sexes throughout this period and later, by the 1780s several authors including Le Camus de Mesière, author of *Le Genie de l'Architecture*, were suggesting that the boudoir was a room for use by the women of the house only. This idea became even more firmly entrenched in the 19th century when Robert Kerr, author of the influential *The Gentleman's House*, described the boudoir as being "the private parlour of the mistress of the house". Gervase Wheeler, author of *Rural Homes, or, Sketches of Houses Suited to the American Life* of 1851, expressed a similar view when he declared it to be "a little gem of a room ... for the lady of the house", advising prospective builders "whether boudoir, book-room, or work-room, as its fair presiding deity may determine, let it have the sunniest aspect, the most charming prospect you can give it, for there will the taste that can best enjoy the enjoyable ... mostly congregate" (Thornton, p.219).

During this period the boudoir became firmly established as the feminine equivalent of the masculine study. While still a semi-private room it lost its connotations of dalliance and the daybeds, ottomans, and chaise-longues typical of earlier examples were replaced by more restrained furnishings such as light upholstered chairs and writing desks. Colour schemes were pale and overtly feminine in character and picturesque plans – "octagonal or oval or quaintly cornered" – were recommended. Boudoirs were also frequently given a distinguishing feature – a bay or an oriel window, and often had their own staircase. Male guests were rarely admitted, and an invitation to enter this room was occasion for remark. A male visitor to Lady Spencer's "sanctum sanctorum" at Althorp House in the 1870s described "a prettily furnished den. She showed me the many conveniences of her writing table, the pretty furniture and setting", while Henry James recorded being extended a similar privilege by the lady of the house during his visit to Egglesford Manor.

Within aristocratic houses the decoration of boudoirs continued to reflect a mixture of fashionable and personal tastes and were often still extremely splendid. An elaborately tented interior graced Queen Hortense's boudoir in her Paris residence in the rue Cerutti, illustrated in 1811, while the boudoir in Thomas Hope's Deepdene of 1807 was decorated in a fashionable Greek Revival style and included a chimneypiece of Mona Marble, a baldaquin supported over the sofa inspired by Charles Percier, and additional furniture designed by Hope himself. During the last quarter of the 19th century, boudoirs in artistic houses often favoured exotic effects inspired by Far Eastern decoration and design. The example in Mrs. Ellen Montagu's house at 96 Lancaster Gate, illustrated in a watercolour by Nicholas Chevalier in 1875, is furnished in the Aesthetic Anglo-Japanese taste and includes an extraordinary assemblage of genuine and fake oriental bamboo furniture and other lacquered goods. The boudoir at Clouds, the home of the Hon. Percy Wyndham and his family, was altogether less flamboyant, and had papered walls, white woodwork and plain, loosely draped curtains. The comparatively simple decorations and the elegant 18th-century English furniture conformed to progressive Arts and Crafts taste and were in marked contrast to the overtly feminine Louis XVI and Rococo Revival styles favoured in more mainstream boudoirs of this period.

In smaller, middle-class houses of the mid- and late 19th century, the boudoir was often no more than a secondary and smaller sitting room or parlour, and was reserved for the private use of the family, leaving the main drawing room for the entertainment of guests. According to Robert Kerr, "when the Drawing Room itself is very large, this arrangement has its advantages, but it is manifest that such a Boudoir is really a Morning Room". And he went on to declare that as regards its site or position within the house, the Boudoir should be regarded as a "Sitting Room and open ... from the principal corridor of the house" adding "It may be somewhat retired in situation ... although not restricted in free access, it being the lady's business room". In fact, what is often shown as the boudoir on 19th-century plans was in reality an additional small drawing room, and if the two were connected by communicating doors as was often the case in order to extend the drawing room for functions, then the resultant lack of privacy could not really justify definition of the room as a boudoir.

While descriptions of boudoirs continue to appear in decorating manuals of the Edwardian period, they clearly became increasingly anachronistic in modest-sized homes, and the use of the term seems to have been reserved for a few houses of grand pretensions that aped the lifestyle of an earlier generation. Even those houses which by today's standards would be considered opulent, with billiard rooms and servants' halls, rarely included boudoirs in their plans, although when they did appear they were still as large as any of the main reception rooms. More often, the need for a private, ladies or family room was met by the provision of a small sitting room which took on many of the connotations of intimacy and informality traditionally associated with boudoirs. Today, the term is rarely used other than ironically.

JOANNA MARSCHNER

Further Reading

Barker, Lady, *The Bedroom and Boudoir*, London, 1878; reprinted with *The Drawing-Room* by Lucy Orrinsmith and *The Dining Room* by M.J. Loftie, New York: Garland, 1978

Cornforth, John, "More than a Dressing Room" in *Country Life*, 186, 16 April 1992, pp.112–15

Franklin, Jill, *The Gentleman's Country House and its Plan, 1835–1914*, London: Routledge, 1981

Gere, Charlotte, *Nineteenth-Century Decoration: The Art of the Interior*, London: Weidenfeld and Nicolson, and New York: Abrams, 1989

Girouard, Mark, *Life in the English Country House: A Social and Architectural History*, New Haven and London: Yale University Press, 1978

Jackson-Stops, Gervase and James Pipkin, "Dressing Rooms, Cabinets and Closets" in their *The English Country House: A Grand Tour*, London: Weidenfeld and Nicolson, 1984; Boston: Little Brown, 1985

Joy, Edward Thomas, *Getting Dressed* (The Arts of Living series), London: HMSO, 1981

Kerr, Robert, *The Gentleman's House; or, How to Plan English Residences, from the Parsonage to the Palace*, 3rd edition, London, 1871; reprinted New York: Johnson, 1972

Thornton, Peter, *Authentic Decor: The Domestic Interior, 1620–1920*, London: Weidenfeld and Nicolson, and New York: Viking, 1984

Whitehead, John, *The French Interior in the Eighteenth Century*, London: Laurence King, 1992; New York: Dutton, 1993

Boulle, André-Charles 1642–1732

French cabinet-maker and sculptor

André-Charles Boulle's illustrious status within the history of European furniture has endured from his own lifetime to the present day. His name is not only synonymous with the technique of marquetry that he perfected, but with a genre of highly elaborate and skilfully executed furniture that reflected his patrons' passion for ostentatious display. Although his family originated from the Dutch-German border, Boulle is acclaimed as the first great French ébéniste and the most celebrated of Louis XIV's furniture makers and designers. Boulle was granted the title of *ébéniste, ciseleur, doreur et sculpteur du roi* (1672) allowing him the position of bronze founder and cabinet-maker. He exploited this dual role to design furniture marked by an unprecedented stylistic harmony between the form, marquetry and gilt-bronze mounts. Perhaps ironically, Boulle supplied very little furniture to Louis XIV himself, who seems to have preferred the work of Pierre Gole (c.1620–84) and Domenico Cucci (c.1635–1705). But Boulle executed work for other members of the royal family and private commissions for the nobility and bourgeoisie, as well as foreign royalty including Philip V of Spain.

Boulle was employed in the service of the Bâtiments du Roi, which was concerned with the furnishing and maintenance of the French royal palaces. On the evidence of the Bâtiment's accounts, it seems he was mainly responsible for the execution and restoration of marquetry and parquet floors and for the production of ornaments in gilt bronze. Between 1682 and 1683, Boulle was employed in the decoration of the Dauphin's Appartement de l'Aile du Midi, Versailles. The masterly conception and execution of the marquetry floor and wainscoting is said to have established his reputation among his peers. According to contemporary accounts, the *Cabinet* was decorated on the walls and ceiling with mirrors set in octagonal and square borders of gilt bronze on a ground of ebony, pewter and brass marquetry. The floor itself was of inlaid wood, embellished with many decorations including the emblems of the Dauphin and Dauphine. Yet the history of this magnificent decor is unclear. Most histories state that in the year following its completion the whole decorative ensemble was dismantled by order of the king and adapted for the Dauphin's new apartment on the ground floor of the palace. But a paper by J.C. Le Guillon given at the *Colloque Versailles* (1985) suggests that both Boulle and Pierre Gole, who had collaborated on the original decoration of the *Cabinet*, were commissioned to execute a completely new decor. The Dauphin's plan to economise and install the previous interior was abandoned because the two apartments differed in proportion. Le Guillon also suggests the possibility that the floor was adapted for another room in 1688. It is therefore uncertain whether contemporary sources describe the 1683 decoration or the completely new ensemble of 1684. The extent of Gole's involvement in Boulle's famous achievement is also unclear. The *Cabinet* itself fell into disrepair with the death of the Dauphin in 1711 and after subsequent refurbishments did not survive the 18th century.

Boulle's output is at once extraordinarily inventive and homogeneous. Its principal characteristics are sombre nobility and vigorous monumentality with elaborate and costly marquetry, wood veneers and gilt-bronze mounts. The lavish effect of such contrasting materials against the marble-lined walls or gilded white paneling of French palaces of the period is often lost in modern museum settings. Although he did not invent "Boulle marquetry" (called *tarsia a incastro*, of Italian origin, and employed in the German states) Boulle nevertheless developed it into a highly distinctive and personal style. The typical Boulle ensemble combines brass and tortoiseshell with those areas not decorated with marquetry veneered in ebony. The delicate designs of scrollwork and arabesques were cut, in a single layer or as a "sandwich" of layers, using a fret-saw probably only a millimetre in thickness. The brass and sometimes the shell were engraved for a richer appearance.

Brass on a ground of shell (*première partie*) or vice-versa (*contre-partie*) could be used to stunning effect on pairs of furniture pieces. Boulle often combined the two so that, for example on a wardrobe, the door panels were of *première partie* and the sides of *contre-partie*. Variations were introduced by using other metals – for example, pewter or copper – and materials such as mother-of-pearl and imitation lapis lazuli, and he also used painting or attached coloured foils (red, green and blue) to the reverse of the shell. Boulle not only worked to his own patterns but also to the designs of famous contemporary ornamentalists, including the fashionable grotesques and *singeries* of Jean I Berain. Boulle was also a master in polychrome wood marquetry, in particular the floral marquetry in favour during the 1680s. His masterpiece in this medium is the naturalistic panel which was remounted onto an English cabinet in the 18th century which is now in the Bowes Museum, County Durham. Other examples exist of panels in wood and shell / brass marquetry decorating the same piece and, more unusually, wood set into a ground of shell.

As a talented sculptor, Boulle incorporated sculptural elements into the general design of his work. Gilt-bronze mounts were made on a larger scale and in greater profusion and were given a dominant role which was new to furniture manufacture. All these works were original creations and of the highest quality; they were modeled by the finest sculptors of the day and cast in Boulle's workshop. Classical mythology was the predominant influence, a speciality being pictorial bas-relief mounts of Ovid's *Metamorphoses* (Apollo and Daphne, Apollo flaying Marsyas). Boulle also popularised the theme "Love triumphing over Time" in sculptural form for clocks.

If it is difficult to evaluate the role played by Boulle in the invention of furniture types such as the commode, the bas d'armoire and the bureau plat, which were all well represented in his oeuvre, his influence in the development of furniture styles is uncontested. Moving away from the simple, heavy forms produced by his contemporaries in the last decades of the 17th century, Boulle introduced lighter and more dynamic designs. This developed into the cabriole legs and swelling forms characteristic of his output between 1700 and 1725, heralding the Régence style. Examples which encapsulate Boulle's style and craftsmanship are the magnificent pair of commodes supplied in 1708 to the bedchamber of Louis XIV at the Grand Trianon and now at Versailles. A valuable source for his models and decorative details is the folio of engraved designs *Nouveaux Deisseins de meubles* … (1707–30) by Pierre-Jean Mariette,

Boulle: designs for desk, commode, and armoire

which includes clocks, inkstands, desks, cabinets, tables, mirrors and candelabra.

The longevity of furniture production in the manner of Boulle is one of its most unique aspects. The workshop itself employed four of Boulle's sons and accounted for over 80 years of production. Its direction was continued by Boulle's son Charles-Joseph (1688–1754) after Boulle's death in 1732. Numerous famous *ébénistes* were trained there, including some, like Etienne Levasseur (1721–98) who continued to restore and manufacture "Boulle" furniture independently. Levasseur and other craftsmen such as Philippe-Claude Montigny (1734–1800), specialised in pastiches of the Boulle style, occasionally reusing original marquetry panels. As none of the Boulle workshop's output was stamped, the inherent problem of attribution is exacerbated by such imitations.

The popularity of Boulle's style endured throughout the 18th century. Although it waned slightly during the Rococo period, the advent of Neo-Classicism encouraged a sense of nostalgia for the reign of Louis XIV and Boulle's furniture was the only type of its period to enjoy uninterrupted acclaim. Boulle's standing also remained undiminished in the 19th century, especially among English enthusiasts for French fine and decorative art, several of whom, like King George IV and the Marquess of Hertford, built up unrivaled collections of 18th-century French furniture. A portrait of George IV by Thomas Lawrence in the Wallace Collection, London, shows the king seated next to a Boulle pedestal table and inkstand; the table is now in the Crimson Room of Windsor Castle. The 4th Marquess of Hertford (1800–70) not only purchased many pieces of Boulle furniture but also commissioned seven replicas after his work, six of which were made by John Webb of New Bond Street, London. One, a copy of the Elector of Bavaria's desk (Louvre, Paris), remains in the Wallace Collection today.

CHRISTINE RIDING

See also Marquetry

Biography

Born in Paris in 1642, the son of an *ébéniste* of Flemish origin. Trained by his father. Married Anne-Marie Leroux in 1677: 7 children including Jean-Philippe (1678–1744), Pierre-Benoit (1680–1741), André-Charles II (1685–1745), and Charles-Joseph (1688–1754), all *ébénistes*. Active as an *ébéniste* by 1664; appointed Ébéniste du Roi and took over the lodgings of the cabinet-maker, Jean Macé, in the Louvre, 1672 (workshops enlarged in 1679, and c.1685); worked in the service of the Bâtiments du Roi from c.1672. Designs for furniture and bronzes published by Mariette after 1707. Business transferred to his sons, 1715. Amassed a vast collection of prints and drawings, including works by Le Brun, Cotelle, Loir, Polidoro, Enea Vico, Agostino Veneziano, Le Pautre, Jean Berain, and Jacques-Antoine Ducerceau, much of which was destroyed in a fire that gutted the Boulle workshops in 1720. Granted a royal pension, 1725. Died in Paris in March 1732. The workshops continued to be run by Boulle's four sons.

Selected Works

The output of the Boulle workshop was enormous and numerous items have been attributed to his hand. The more important collections of Boulle furniture are in the Wallace Collection, London; the Musée du Louvre, Paris; the château of Versailles; and the J. Paul Getty Museum, Malibu. Examples of Boulle's drawings are in the Musée des Arts Décoratifs, Paris. A list of Boulle's interior commissions for the Bâtiments du Roi and a list of his principal works appears in Pradère 1989.

Interiors

1672–75 Petite Chambre de la Reine, Versailles (marquetry daises)
1682–83 Appartement de l'Aile du Midi, Versailles (marquetry floor and wainscoting)
1684 Appartement de Monseigneur, Versailles (marquetry floor and wainscoting)

Publications

Nouveaux Deisseins de meubles ... (published by Mariette), 1707–30

Further Reading

The standard history of Boulle and the Boulle workshops appears in Samoyault 1979.

Fuhring, Peter, "Designs for and after Boulle Furniture" in *Burlington Magazine*, 134, June 1992, pp.350–62
Kimball, Fiske, "A French Regency Interior by Boulle" in *Burlington Magazine*, LXIX, 1936, p.93
Kimball, Fiske, The Creation of the Rococo, 1943; as *The Creation of the Rococo Decorative Style*, New York: Dover, and London: Constable, 1980
Massie, Frédéric, René Maubert and Patrick George, *La Marqueterie Boulle*, Paris: Biro, 1990
Pradère, Alexandre, "Boulle: Du Louis XIV sous Louis XVI" in *L'Object d'Art*, 1988, 4, pp.29–43
Pradère, Alexandre, *French Furniture Makers: The Art of the Ébéniste from Louis XIV to the Revolution*, Malibu, CA: Getty Museum, and London: Sotheby's, 1989
Raggio, Olga, James Parker and Alice M. Zrebiec, "French Decorative Arts during the Reign of Louis XIV 1654–1715" in *Metropolitan Museum of Art Bulletin*, 46, Spring 1989, pp.1–64
Ronfort, Jean-Nerée, "Le Fondeur Jean-Pierre Mariette et la Fin de l'Atelier de Boulle" in *L'Estampille*, September 1984
Ronfort, Jean-Nerée, "La Déclaration Somptuaire d'André-Charles Boulle et son Atelier" in *L'Estampille*, February 1985, pp.60–61
Ronfort, Jean-Nerée, "André-Charles Boulle, die Bronzearbeiten und Seine Werkstatt im Louvre" in Hans Ottomeyer, *Vergoldete Bronzen*, Munich: Klinkhardt & Biermann, 1986, pp.495–520
Samoyault, Jean-Pierre, *André-Charles Boulle et sa Famille: Nouvelle Recherches, Nouveaux Documents*, Geneva: Droz, 1979
Sargentson, Carolyn, "Markets for Boulle Furniture in Early Eighteenth Century Paris" in *Burlington Magazine*, 134, June 1992, pp.363–67
Verlet, Pierre, "A Propos de Boulle et du Grand Dauphin" in *Nederlands Kunsthistorisch Jaarbock*, 31, 1980, pp.285–88
Watson, F.J.B., *Wallace Collection Catalogues: Furniture*, London: Wallace Collection, 1956
Wilson, Gillian, "Boulle" in *Furniture History*, VIII, 1972, pp.47–69

Boyle, Richard. *See* Burlington, Earl of

Brenna, Vincenzo (Vinchentso) 1747–c.1819

Italian architect

Vincenzo Brenna lived and worked in several European countries, but the most fruitful period of his career was associated with Russia and, in particular, with St. Petersburg. It was here that he achieved his greatest success, becoming one of the leading exponents of Russian Classicism at the end of the 18th century.

Brenna began to work as an artist in his homeland, Italy. He trained in the studio of S. Pottsi who painted in a late Baroque style, and then continued his art education in France. Brenna's views on art were influenced by a study of antiquity, and an enthusiasm for the Renaissance. His first major works were measurements and sketches from paintings of Roman monuments – Nero's Golden Palace (1774 with the Polish artist F. Smuglevich) and the villas of Pliny the Younger, the so-called Laurentium (1777–78). The experience which he gained from copying arabesque and grotesque patterns and drawings on the theme of ancient mythology had a powerful influence on his subsequent work, and the extensive use of reworked motifs from antiquity is a characteristic feature of Brenna's designs in all his later projects.

In 1780 Brenna was invited to Poland by Count S. Pototsky and he worked there for several years on castle interiors and the palaces of leading magnates. In the frescoes and *plafonds* which he completed for August Chartorisky's palace in Natoline-Bazhantarni near Warsaw (1781), Princess Isabella Chartoriskaya Liubomirskaya's castle in Lantsut (1781), Marshal Stanislav Liubomirsky's estate in Grushchin (1781), the palace belonging to the Polish king's sister, Isabella Ponyatovskaya-Brannitskaya, in Warsaw (1782), and Rech' Pospolitaya's palace (1783), Brenna showed himself to be the master of polychrome painting.

In his spectacular decorative compositions, Brenna used the ornamental motifs which he had come to love, as well as turning to the legacy of Renaissance and Baroque artists. Brenna's paintings united classical principles with the Baroque effects of perspective painting and the illusion of expanding space.

Brenna's work as an artist and interior designer brought him wide renown. In 1784 he received an invitation from the heir to the Russian throne, the Grand Duke Paul, to go to Russia. He undertook the task of decorating the interiors of the splendid palace at Pavlovsk outside St. Petersburg, built by Charles Cameron. From 1786, Brenna took charge of the completion of the state rooms in the palace and he introduced several changes in its internal decoration and planning. Apart from introducing stucco moulding, friezes and *plafonds* into Cameron's interiors, Brenna drew up his own designs for many of the rooms. The interior design of the palace was completed in 1794. However, with the accession of Paul I to the throne in 1796, further work was begun on extending the palace and Brenna found himself in demand as an architect, subsequently becoming the first architect of the Imperial court. Work on the creation of new architectural and artistic interiors at Pavlovsk continued right up to 1801.

Brenna's interiors kept to classical forms. However, in contrast to Charles Cameron, who was an advocate of strict

Brenna: library, Pavlovsky Palace, 1786–1801

canons of style, Brenna favoured a saturated decorative style and put forward new methods which led people to view him as the precursor of the Empire style in Russian art. The decoration of the state rooms at Pavlovsk combines architectural elements, which act as the compositional basis for the interior design, with rich painted and relief decoration, decorative fabrics and *objets d'art*.

Triumphal motifs predominate among the themes of the bas-reliefs, marble statues and wide stucco friezes. Magnificent marble fireplaces, which Brenna transformed into complex architectural compositions, formed part of the single ensemble. The ornamental paintings, *plafonds*, gilded moulding and complex caisson ceilings were a no less significant part of the decoration. Brenna himself decorated the walls and *plafonds*, which were close stylistically to his Polish works; he also collaborated with the eminent artist and decorator Pietro Gonzaga, whom he invited specifically for the purpose and who decorated the interiors with frescoes and paintings containing the illusion of perspective. The Russian sculptors I.P. Prokofiev, M.I. Kozlovsky and I.P. Martos also worked on the palace's decoration. Brenna designed furniture for each room and his sketches show the breadth of his talent. Bureaus and writing desks were made from his designs, as well as other items made out of fine pieces of wood with gilded details standing out in relief against their background. Brenna's massive and rather heavy furniture is largely typical of the Pavlovsk period.

Another important undertaking by Brenna for Paul I was the reconstruction and decoration of the interiors of his palace at Gatchina near St. Petersburg, built by Antonio Rinaldi. The interiors were damaged during World War II and partially restored in the 1970s and 1980s. Brenna redecorated the main state apartments, including the Crimson and Chesmenskaya galleries, the Marble Dining Room, Paul I's Throne Room and the Empress' main bedroom. The decoration in these rooms, which included marble, bronze, gold and tapestries, is typical of Brenna's work. In designing the interiors of the state rooms at Gatchina, Brenna turned to the decorative methods of the Roman Empire and of 17th-century French Classicism, in order to emphasize the triumphal nature of the decoration and the might of the Russian Empire and its monarch. Features of the Empire style, which are typical of Brenna's art, appear more consistently here. There was a great deal of decorative stucco moulding and sculpture in the sumptuous architectural and painted decoration, including busts of Roman emperors, bas-reliefs on the theme of ancient history, copies of ancient works of art and original statues. Brenna's skill as a craftsman is evident in his compositions of military campaigns and the military motifs in the sculptures on the walls of the *Chesmenskaya* gallery.

Brenna's greatest achievement as architect and interior designer came with his work on the interiors of Mikhailovsky Castle (1797–1801; parts of the original building remain), which he built from initial designs by B.I. Bazhenov to be the Imperial residence in St. Petersburg. The plan of the castle, a square enclosing an octagonal inner courtyard, was proposed by Paul I himself and the Emperor devoted much attention to the completion of his grandiose project, spending vast sums on sumptuous decorations for the building.

In solving the spatial problems which the Mikhailovsky Castle posed, Brenna successfully combined rooms of all shapes and sizes: square, circular, triangular and oval halls all make up the state rooms and living quarters. He made extensive use of decorative materials for the rich architectural and artistic interior design. The palace's rooms were filled with works of art; paintings, sculpture and *objets d'art* played a crucial role in the decor. The interiors were decorated with ancient statues and sculptures by I.P. Prokofiev, who had worked with Brenna at Pavlovsk and Gatchina, as well as paintings by S.F. Shchedrin, A.E. Martinov, G.I. Ugriumov, Y.Y. Mettenleiter, A.Vigi, K.P. and J. Skotti, G.F. Dwain, and F. Smuglevich. The combination of coloured plate-glass with paintings, gilded carving and bronzes had never been attempted before. As in Brenna's earlier projects, decorative cloth, tapestries, silks, velvet upholstery and drapes all played a significant role in the decoration of the main interiors. Brenna also used coloured stone – his massive columns and wall facings were made of marble, porphyry and other types of stone.

The interiors of the Mikhailovsky Castle underwent repeated changes. Today the original internal decoration survives only on the main staircase, in the hall of the Resurrection, the Large Throne Room and the Raphael Gallery. The Mikhailovsky Castle became a symbol and monument of the Pavlovsk period and was the most significant of

Brenna's undertakings in Russia. As a mark of Brenna's services to Russian art, Mettenleiter painted an allegorical portrait of him on the *plafond* in the Raphael Gallery.

While working on the Mikhailovsky Castle, Brenna altered the interiors of the Winter, Tauride, Kamenny Ostrov and Marble Palaces, which belonged to the Imperial family. He redecorated and furnished a number of rooms in the Winter Palace (1796–98), using expensive materials, paintings and gilding as he had in the Mikhailovsky Castle. Brenna also made alterations to halls in the court Hermitage Theatre (1797). He restored Quarenghi's interior, stripped the dilapidated walls and repeated the ordered composition of his predecessor, although he did replace the columns with pilasters. The decoration of the Kamenny Ostrov Palace (1797) was equal to that of the Winter Palace. Brenna painted the main state rooms and furnished them with gilded furniture.

Brenna was frequently called upon to decorate the Imperial palaces and churches in St. Petersburg for funerals. After the execution of Prince Loudovic XVI, a decorative catafalque was built from a design by Brenna in the Polish Roman Catholic Church of St. Catherine (1793). Later, after the death of the Empress Catherine II, Brenna designed interiors for the Peter and Paul Cathedral (Fortress) and the Georgian Hall in the Winter Palace (1796).

The beginning of the 19th century marked a decline in Brenna's creative activities. In 1802, a year after the death of his patron and main client, Paul I, Brenna was dismissed and left Russia. He spent the last years of his life in France and Germany without work.

Brenna is renowned in the history of Russian art and architecture not only as an eminent architect and designer, but also as tutor to the greatest architect of the 19th century, Karl Rossi, the founder of the Russian Empire style who continued the artistic methods first employed by Brenna.

MARIA L. MAKOGONOVA
translated by Charlotte Combes

Biography

Born in Italy in 1747. Lived and worked in Rome during the 1770s; trained in the studio of S. Pottsi; published an album of drawings from Thermae, 1776. Active as an interior designer and architect in Poland from 1780. Moved to Russia, 1784; worked in the service of the Grand Duke Paul (later Paul I) on several royal palaces, dismissed 1802. Toured Europe with his pupil, Karl Rossi (1775–1849), 1802–05; retired to France. Died in poverty in Dresden, c.1819.

Selected Works

Interiors

- 1784–94 Pavlovsky Palace, Pavlovsk (design, decoration and furniture of the state rooms including the Italian Hall, Grecian Hall, and Grand Vestibule)
- 1796–98 Hermitage, St. Petersburg (restoration of interiors)
- 1796–98 Winter Palace, St. Petersburg (decoration and furniture)
- 1797 Kamenny Ostrov Palace, St. Petersburg (decoration and furniture for main state rooms)
- 1797–1800 Gatchina Palace, near St. Petersburg (redecoration of main state apartments; building by Antonio Rinaldi)
- 1797–1801 Pavlovsky Palace, Pavlovsk (enlargement and additions including the new Throne Room, Picture Gallery, orchestra room, and chapel)
- 1797–1801 Mikhailovsky Castle, St. Petersburg (building, interiors and furniture; assisted by Karl Rossi)

Further Reading

Belanini, Valeria, *Pavlovsk*, Moscow, 1987

Belyakova, Zoia, *The Romanov Legacy: The Palaces of St. Petersburg*, London: Hazar, and New York: Viking, 1994

Brumfield, William Craft, *A History of Russian Architecture*, Cambridge and New York: Cambridge University Press, 1993

Grimm, G.G., *Arkhitektura Perekytii Russkogo Klasitsizma*, St. Petersburg, 1939

Makarov, V.K. and A. Petrov, *Gatchina*, Leningrad: Iskusstvo, 1974

Shuiskii, V.K., *Vinchentso Brenna*, Leningrad: Lenizdat, 1986

Breuer, Marcel 1902–1981

Hungarian architect and designer

Marcel Breuer was the most famous student of the Bauhaus and is a key figure in the history of Modern architecture and furniture design. Progressive and forward-thinking in every area of his work, he produced some of the most enduring and iconic designs of the 20th century including his celebrated tubular steel and plywood chairs. He was also an early champion of mass-produced furniture, and he became an influential exponent of the International Style in his architecture and interior design.

Born in Hungary, Breuer was one of many art students wandering Europe in search of a sympathetic art school in the years following World War I. He studied briefly as a painter and sculptor at the Academy of Fine Art, Vienna, and in 1920, at the age of 18, he enrolled at the Weimar Bauhaus. He rose rapidly through the ranks of his fellow-students and was appointed to the teaching staff, along with the other rationalists, László Moholy-Nagy and Josef Albers, in 1923. He became head of the Bauhaus carpentry workshops in 1925 and used the workshops to develop prototypes of the furniture he designed.

His first chair was in wood and woven upholstery and was heavily influenced by the furniture of Gerrit Rietveld and members of the De Stijl group. From them Breuer learned to enjoy the constructional framework of his chairs, tables and beds. These could be hard and rectilinear but the supported elements that made contact with the body were soft and rounded. As his work developed, the supported elements became progressively softer, evolving from straight plywood sheets, through stretched canvas and curved plywood, finally to become upholstery on slats. As the supported elements became softer, the frames got lighter. At first this was achieved by using thinner wooden members; subsequently, it resulted from the use of lightweight metals. Breuer described how he purchased his first bicycle in 1925 and was so impressed by the lightness and strength of the frame that he began to experiment with tubular steel in the production of furniture. His *Wassily* chromium-plated tubular steel chair dates from this period and numerous other designs, including his famous *B32* cantilever chair, were produced between 1925 and 1928. While tubular steel chairs rapidly became almost commonplace among Modernist designers, Breuer's designs from the mid-1920s have never been surpassed and the *Wassily* and cantilever chair are still in production.

The Bauhaus served as Breuer's client as well as his

employer and in 1925 he was put in charge of fitting out the new Bauhaus building at Dessau. Breuer's tubular steel furniture was used in the canteen, in the assembly hall and elsewhere, and it was the first time his work had been produced on such a scale. He was also asked to design the interiors for some of the staff houses. Although these interiors can appear somewhat austere and characterless today, they demonstrate Breuer's liking for built-in units, such as cabinets and wall cupboards, which he designed as standardised modular components to facilitate mass-production. Mass-produced furniture was clearly not a new phenomenon, but Breuer's obvious appreciation of its advantages and his delight in the appearance of something that looked machine-made was unprecedented.

In 1928 he left the Bauhaus and opened his own office in Berlin. Numerous commissions for interiors followed in which he used chairs, tables and standardized storage units of his own design. In the Harnischmacher apartment (1929), for example, the study walls were lined with black lacquered wall-units and bookshelves and the room was furnished – like the dining room – with tubular steel chairs and the *B14* table which Breuer used in many subsequent interior designs. A year later, he designed an apartment space for the Deutscher Werkbund section of the 1930 Salon des Artistes Décorateurs, Paris. The overall theme of the Werkbund section was mass-produced design in architecture, furniture and household objects and Breuer made good use of materials such as linoleum, and simple features such as white blinds, fitted wardrobes and hanging wall units, while virtually all the furniture was tubular steel.

Following the rise of fascism, Breuer left Berlin and spent much of 1932 and 1933 travelling. During this period he built and furnished the Harnischmacher House in Wiesbaden. It was his first free-standing house and was much publicised. Tubular steel and black lacquered wood furniture were juxtaposed with white walls and light linoleum floors. He also began to develop aluminium furniture for retailing by the Wohnbedarf home-furnishing stores. His designs for dining chairs, armchairs, stacking tables and chaise longues, won a competition in Paris in 1933.

In 1935, the English architect F. R. S. Yorke invited Breuer to join him as his partner in London. Soon after arriving in London Breuer met Jack Pritchard, a founder of the Isokon furniture company that specialised in bending plywood. Breuer adapted the Paris aluminium chaise longue for production in plywood and the result is arguably the most elegant and justly celebrated of all his furnishings. It epitomises his approach to furniture design, including a frame of great technical sophistication that is obviously factory-made, a form designed to fit the body, and softness where there is contact. Other furniture for Isokon included a set of stacking tables, each made by folding a sheet of plywood, and plywood dining chairs which are clearly the precursors of the more sophisticated Eames dining chair of a decade later. This furniture was used in his interiors for the Isobar, a fashionable meeting place for architects and designers built in Hampstead in 1937.

The most important of the interiors produced by the Breuer and Yorke partnership were designed for the Gane Pavilion, Bristol, in 1936. This was an exhibition house, commissioned by the furniture manufacturers P.E. Gane, whose interiors served as showrooms for the company's modern furniture. The building itself illustrated a shift away from the strict geometry and hard edges of the International Style. It was an exercise in open and flexible planning with free-standing walls of rough masonry and no internal doors. Natural materials, such as stone and wood, were preferred; plywood walls and ceilings brought warmth and colour to the interiors and the plywood flooring was covered with simple rugs.

In 1937 Breuer settled in the United States, where he became professor of architecture at Harvard, and went into partnership with his old Bauhaus colleague, Walter Gropius. In 1939, he built his own house at Lincoln, Massachusetts, where the white painted timber tradition characteristic of New England architecture is combined with the rough masonry effects explored in the Gane Pavilion. The interior suggests a softening in his approach to domestic design and the space is organised over several levels linked by elegant steps.

Shortly after building this house, Breuer and Gropius designed a home for the Frank family in Pittsburgh. Described as the largest residence ever built in the International Style, it also represented one of Breuer's most complete interiors. Virtually all the contents – chairs, tables, wall units and light fixtures – were specially designed by him for the commission.

Breuer's next home, built in New Canaan, Connecticut, in 1947 is now probably his best-known project and it has become something of a mecca for aficionados of modern architecture. It is also one of his most dramatic designs and has a great cantilevered deck to take advantage of the New England summers. Both the plan and the construction are workmanlike, with a great brick chimney forming the core of the timber building. Gently sloping ceilings of pine boards, and floors of rush matting, continue the softening process.

Other projects from this period include the House for a Middle Income Family commissioned by the Museum of Modern Art and built in their garden in 1949. But it was the commission for the UNESCO Headquarters in Paris (1952–58) that established Breuer's reputation internationally as a major figure within the Modern Movement. Several substantial projects followed, including the St. John's Abbey and University at Collegeville, Minnesota (1953–61) and the Whitney Museum, in New York City. Both buildings have fine interiors but neither are as innovative or individual as his designs of the 1930s and 1940s. And it is for these houses and for his ground-breaking and beautiful pre-war furniture that Breuer will always be remembered.

JOHN WINTER

See also Bauhaus; Tubular Steel Furniture

Biography

Marcel Lajos Breuer. Born in Pécs, Hungary, 22 May 1902. Educated at Allami Föreáiskola, Pécs, 1912–20; studied painting and sculpture, Akademie der Bildenden Künste, Vienna, 1920; attended Bauhaus, Weimar 1920–24. Married 1) Martha Erps, 1926; 2) Constance Crocker, 1940: 2 children. Director of the carpentry workshop, Dessau Bauhaus, 1925–28. Active as an architect and designer of interiors and furniture, Dessau, 1925–28; Berlin, 1928–31; London (with F. R. S. Yorke), 1935–36. Controller of Design, Isokon, London, 1937. Emigrated to the US, 1937; became citizen, 1944. Associate Professor, Harvard University School of Design, Cambridge, Massachusetts, 1937–46. Established architectural and design practice from 1937; in partnership with Walter Gropius, Cambridge, 1937–41; principal, Marcel Breuer and Associates, New York, 1946–76. Fellow, American Institute of Architects: Gold Medal, 1968; Grande Medaille d'Or, French Academy of Architecture, 1976. Died in New York, 1 July 1981.

Selected Works

The Marcel Breuer Collection, containing much surviving correspondence, bills, contracts, drawings and photographs for the period up to 1951, is in the George Arents Research Library for Special Collections, Syracuse University, Syracuse, New York. For additional documentation relating to Breuer's work for the Bauhaus, see the Bauhaus Archive, Berlin; for Isokon, see the Pritchard Archive, School of Architecture, University of Newcastle, Newcastle upon Tyne; and for Thonet, see the Thonet Archive, Thonet Industries, York, Pennsylvania. Notable collections of Breuer's furniture are in the Victoria and Albert Museum, London, the Museum of Modern Art, New York, and the Staatliches Kunstsammlung, Weimar.

Interiors

1923	Haus-am-Ham, Bauhaus Exhibition, Weimar (furniture)
1925–26	Bauhaus, Dessau (furniture for the faculty buildings and furniture and interiors for the Masters' Houses)
1929	Harnischmacher Apartment, Wiesbaden (furniture and interiors)
1930	Apartment for a Boarding-House-Hotel, Deutscher Werkbund Section of the Salon des Artistes Décorateurs, Paris (furnishings and interiors)
1932	Harnischmacher House, Wiesbaden (building, furnishings and interiors)
1934–36	Doldertal Apartments, Zurich (building, furnishings and interiors; with Roth Brothers)
1936	Gane Pavilion, Bristol (building and interiors; with F. R.S. Yorke): P.E. Gane Ltd.
1937	Isobar, Isokon Flats, Hampstead (furnishings and interiors; with F. R.S. Yorke)
1937	Gropius House, Lincoln, Massachusetts (building and interiors, with Walter Gropius)
1938	Breuer House I, Lincoln, Massachusetts (building, furnishings and interiors; with Walter Gropius)
1939	Frank House, Pittsburgh (building, interiors and furnishings; with Walter Gropius)
1945	Geller House, Lawrence, Long Island (building, interiors and furnishings)
1947	Breuer House II, New Canaan, Connecticut (building, interiors and furnishings)
1949	Exhibition House, Museum of Modern Art, New York (building, interiors and furnishings)
1952–58	UNESCO Headquarters, Paris (building and interiors; with Pier Luigi Nervi and Bernard Zehrfuss)
1953–61	St. John's Abbey and University, Collegeville, Minnesota (building, interiors and furnishings; with Hamilton Smith)
1963–66	Whitney Museum of American Art, New York (building and interiors)
1967–69	Geller House II, Lawrence, Long Island (building, interiors and furnishings; with Herbert Beckhard)

Breuer began designing furniture in 1921. His designs for tubular steel furniture date from 1925, for aluminium from 1932, and for plywood from 1935. His designs were manufactured by several firms from the mid-1920s, including Thonet, Standard Möbel, Wohnbedarf, and Isokon. Certain classic pieces, such as the *Wassily* chair are currently made by Knoll International.

Publications

Sun and Shadow: The Philosophy of an Architect, edited by Peter Blake, 1955

Further Reading

The key text for the study of Breuer's interiors and furnishings, particularly for the period pre-1950, is Wilk 1981 which contains a bibliography intended to supplement and update the extensive primary and secondary material cited in Blake 1949.

Benton, Tim and Barbie Campbell-Cole (editors), *Tubular Steel Furniture*, London: Art Book Company, 1979

Blake, Peter, *Marcel Breuer, Architect and Designer* (exhib. cat.), New York: Museum of Modern Art, 1949

Buckley, Cheryl, *Isokon* (exhib. cat.), Newcastle upon Tyne: Hatton Gallery, 1980

Casper, Dale E., *Marcel Breuer: Twenty Years of Critical Comment, 1967–1987* (bibliography), Monticello, IL: Vance, 1988

Droste, Magdalena and Manfred Ludewig, *Marcel Breuer: Design*, Cologne: Taschen, 1992

Fehrman, Cherie and Kenneth, *Postwar Interior Design, 1945–1960*, New York: Van Nostrand Reinhold, 1987

Geest, Jan van and Otakar Máčel, *Stühle aus Stahl*, Cologne: Konig, 1980

Izzo, Alberto and Camillo Gubitosi (editors), *Marcel Breuer: Architettura, 1921–1980* (exhib. cat.), Florence: Centro Di, 1981

Jones, Cranston (editor), *Marcel Breuer: Buildings and Projects, 1921–1961*, New York: Praeger, and London: Thames and Hudson, 1962

Marcel Breuer: Architektur, Möbel, Design (exhib. cat.), Berlin: Bauhaus Archiv, 1975

Masello, David, *Architecture Without Rules: The Houses of Marcel Breuer and Herbert Beckhard*, New York: Norton, 1993

Neumann, Eckhard (editor), *Bauhaus and Bauhaus People*, New York: Van Nostrand Reinhold, and London: Chapman and Hall, 1993

Papachristou, Tician, *Marcel Breuer: New Buildings and Projects, 1960–1970 and Work in Retrospect, 1921–1960*, New York: Praeger, and London: Thames and Hudson, 1970

Smith, C. Ray, *Interior Design in 20th-Century America: A History*, New York: Harper, 1987

Stein, Richard G., *Marcel Breuer* (exhib. cat.), New York: Metropolitan Museum of Art, 1972

Whitford, Frank (editor), *The Bauhaus: Masters and Students by Themselves*, London: Conran Octopus, 1992; Woodstock, NY: Overlook, 1993

Wilk, Christopher, *Marcel Breuer: Furniture and Interiors*, New York: Museum of Modern Art, and London: Architectural Press, 1981

Wingler, Hans M. *The Bauhaus: Weimar, Dessau, Berlin, Chicago*, 3rd edition Cambridge: Massachusetts Institute of Technology Press, 1976

Britain

The movements in British interior design from the 15th to the 20th centuries are by nature indefinite due to overlapping influences, historical references, and guiding principles. Reflecting this inexactness is a classification system in which a variety of labels, derived from monarchs, stylistic references, designers, and typical woods, are used to identify similar and contemporary objects and interiors. Despite this confusion, there are recurrent themes: an overriding emphasis on the reinterpretation of styles derived both from foreign sources and from preceding periods of English history, and an increasing interest in domestic comfort and convenience. These themes characterize British design from the Renaissance to the present.

Within this broad framework, a sequence of stylistic periods

Britain: Long Gallery, Hardwick Hall, Derbyshire, 1590–96

is apparent. A shift from bare fairly utilitarian medieval interiors towards more humanistic Italian Renaissance and French Baroque styles is evident during the 15th to 17th centuries. In the 18th century, Palladian, Rococo, and Neo-Classical designers working in Britain borrowed, mixed, and reinterpreted contemporary and preceding Continental movements within an identifiably British framework. Revivalism reached its height in the mid- and late 19th century with Victorian styles which in turn sparked reform movements, including Aestheticism, Queen Anne, and the Arts and Crafts Movement. During the 20th century, the main thrusts of British design were represented by the English "Country House Style" as epitomized by Colefax & Fowler and Laura Ashley, and by the new modern schools, encompassing both international Modernist movements and British Modernism as promoted by *Daily Mail* Ideal Home Exhibitions and the Festival of Britain (1951).

The high points of this historic progression occurred during the 18th and 19th centuries, when the aristocracy and the newly prosperous upper-middle classes patronised a new breed of highly talented architects who not only designed the structure of buildings but also interior details, furniture, and decorations. As wealth and the demand for design expertise spread to other sections of society, the primacy of the architect-client relationship was overtaken by the rise of design professionals, whose status was legitimized with the establishment of the Government Schools of Design in 1836. In this sense, the growing cultural supremacy of Britain reflected in the careers of many of the country's most notable designers, including William Kent, Robert Adam, Thomas Hope, A.W.N. Pugin, William Morris, A.L. Liberty, and Charles Rennie Mackintosh, coincided with and paralleled the growth of the British Empire.

The gradual transition from Gothic church-derived decoration to a more humanistic secular orientation in interior spaces that took place during the 15th and 16th centuries reflected a shift in the peripatetic nature of medieval households towards a lifestyle and surroundings that celebrated the owner in a permanent way. In interior furnishings, the emphasis changed from portable items that were easy to dismantle and transport to objects and decorations that facilitated household ceremony and hierarchy.

The late medieval Gothic style predominated during this period. As a lord and his retinue traveled frequently, comparatively little attention was paid to fixed decoration, and movable furnishings such as plain oak pieces, tapestry wall-coverings, carpets as table covers, and thick rush floor-matting were typical. Folding chairs, trestle tables, stools, and folding beds with cushions were popular furniture pieces on account of their portability. Churches served as primary sources for the minimal ornament on architectural features, such as windows and doorframes, and on furniture, and decoration such as carved arches, tracery, floral forms such as vines and leaves, and human and animal representations was also borrowed from ecclesiastical models. The actual architecture of the Gothic home, however, differed from the stone churches of the period in the use of oak wall paneling and timbered ceilings. The carved and painted ornament on this paneling was often secular in nature, incorporating armorial devices, heraldic items, and portraits of kings, queens, and other notable contemporaries. Such ornament frequently embellished the principal bedchamber or the great hall, the latter serving as the social and administrative centre of the household.

British design of the early 16th century in many ways reflected the political developments of the period. Following Henry VIII's (1509–47) break with Rome, designers also broke free of ecclesiastical influences and introduced a more humanistic Renaissance style. During the reign of Elizabeth I (1558–1603), a symbolic progression of rooms which facilitated a life of continuous ceremony distinguishes the architecture of the period. Significant features included symmetrical layouts drawn from Italian Renaissance designs, ingenious manipulation of spaces, and an abundance of glass – the latter made possible by developments in engineering and which quickly became an Elizabethan status symbol.

As with architecture, Elizabethan interiors and objects employed a wider range of sources and more ornamentation than in the previous century. And while the influences themselves were often quite varied, a characteristic of much 16th-century woodwork, metalwork, and textiles is the richness of the surface decoration. Examples include elaborately-ornamented silver salts and commemorative cups, cushions embossed with pearls, tapestries of gold needlework, and colorful plaster friezes featuring allegorical references to mythological figures such as Diana, Ulysses, and Gideon. These motifs were inspired by Italian sources that had been adapted by German and Low Countries designers, and the result was a blend of native Gothic and foreign Renaissance styles.

The German painter Hans Holbein the younger (1497/8–1543) designed goldsmiths' work for Henry VIII from 1533 onwards. His designs were in the elaborate Italian Renaissance style incorporating acanthus leaves, arabesques, human heads, putti, and a lavish use of pendant pearls and encrustations of precious stones. Imported Flemish and German pattern books like those by Hans Vredeman de Vries, Wendel Dietterlin, Hans Brosamer, Virgil Solis, and Hans Collaert served as primary ornament sources for refugee Protestant craftsmen working in London. This influx of Continental influences and expertise energized native talent and greatly improved the availability of high-quality metalwork, furniture, and textiles.

Furniture tended to be massive, squat, and richly carved with a mixture of Gothic and Renaissance ornament. Sturdy balusters of cup-and-cover form were common in the legs of tables and supports for cupboards. Marquetry depicting buildings and foliage adorned expensive items such as Nonsuch chests and presentation tables. Elizabethan interiors continued the medieval tradition of using woven and embroidered textiles on tables and as wall coverings. Table covers and cushions had needlework patterns of flowers, foliage, and coiling tendrils. The majority of tapestry wall-hangings, with the exception of those produced by the workshop founded by William Sheldon in the early 16th century, were imported from the Low Countries and France. Sheldon's tapestries were naive in style and often featured figurative designs of Flemish origin that included birds, flowers, and landscapes.

The arrival of the Renaissance style and Continental craftsmen coincided with the introduction of imported objects suitable for households of varying classes. Local pottery and coarse green Weald glass served humble Elizabethan tables. Imported Chinese porcelain, Iznik pottery, German silver-mounted stoneware, and Venetian crystal glass or English imitations by immigrant Italians such as Giacomi Verzelini dressed the boards of the wealthy and fashionable.

Hardwick Hall, Derbyshire (1587–99) represents the finest of the great Elizabethan Power Houses. Designed by Robert Smythson (c.1535–1614), for Bess of Hardwick, it successfully integrated the most notable characteristics of 16th-century British architecture – symmetry, ingenious architectural "devices," and abundant use of glass – and incorporated diverse stylistic influences. Its symmetrical layout derives from Southern Renaissance prototypes; its tower and large grids of glass reflect the native Perpendicular Gothic tradition; and its interior ornament including obelisks and strapwork is modeled on examples published in Northern European pattern books.

Hardwick's interior layout and decoration, progressing from large, formal spaces, which visually trumpet familial status, to intimate chambers identifying their inhabitants' particular tastes and royal loyalties, reflect an aristocratic lifestyle of continuous ceremony and symbolic reference. As the great entrance hall includes an enormous plaster overmantel detailing the Hardwick family's coats-of-arms and coronets, so the high great chamber on the second floor includes a colorful plaster frieze depicting the goddess Diana and a court of animals – a symbolic reference to Elizabeth I. To complement the permanent surface decoration and for warmth, chamber walls were generously hung with tapestry series, floors were covered with rush matting, and table surfaces and bedsteads were adorned with expensive textiles. Otherwise the rooms were sparsely furnished and all the furniture – seating, tables, beds, buffets and cupboards – was arranged against the walls.

British interiors demonstrated an increasingly sophisticated assimilation of Italian Renaissance ideals – filtered through the work of Northern European designers – through the first part of the 17th century, and a growing dependence on French Baroque during the second. As the last vestiges of a peripatetic medieval lifestyle disappeared, an interest in achieving harmonious, unified interiors developed. Architects embraced classical principles of order and symmetry, blended with elegant French-inspired ornamentation and decorative touches. Mobility and symbolic ceremony were replaced by an emphasis upon comfort and aesthetic delight.

The introduction of new forms of furniture and the increased use of upholstery reflected these developments. New furniture forms – massive beds, elaborate buffets, cabinet-on-stands, writing-cabinets, and enormous candlestands – became more delicate and graceful, while upholstery – including silk,

Britain: Painted Hall, Chatsworth House, Derbyshire, 1690s

wool, leather, and tapestry wall hangings, bed and window hangings, and coverings for seat-furniture, tables, and floors – created soft, sumptuous effects.

By the 1620s, with the assimilation of Italian sources such as Palladio and Scamozzi, a sense of order, regularity, and discipline became the defining feature of larger domestic buildings. In his *Elements of Architecture* (1624), Sir Henry Wotton asserted that "Commoditie [convenience], Firmness and Delight" were the central elements of a successful home. Most crucial was a coherent progression of rooms, or specifically chambers and antechambers, arranged *enfilade* or in a row, which created interior vistas through aligned sequential rooms. This arrangement, derived from French examples, remained a favorite in Britain until the mid-18th century.

Upholstery played an important role in achieving a unified sequence within *enfilade* chambers. Typical furnishings included: seat-furniture, such as X-frame chairs with woodwork entirely masked by velvet or damask, "farthingale" chairs with seats and back-rests covered in leather or "Turkeywork," and Dutch chairs with high splat backs and rush seats; bedroom tables, covered with carpets and lace-adorned linens; and box-like bedsteads with flat testers, finials, and rich, heavy drapery. Pictures – portraits, maps, engravings – hung on top of wall coverings, and large cupboards dressed with silver and placed in dining rooms, furthered enhanced the lavish effect.

The combination of uniform architectural elements with extravagantly upholstered, French-inspired interiors reached a highpoint in the redecoration of Ham House and various of the buildings designed by the architect Inigo Jones (1573–1652). When the State Rooms at Ham House were refurbished in the late 1630s, the North Drawing Room was decorated entirely in white satin, embroidered most probably in gold, which matched the white and gilt paneling and radiated lightness, vibrancy, and glitter. Inigo Jones, the English master of classical architecture, was much influenced by Italian sources, and his interior ornament, including chimneypieces and ceilings, was derived from contemporary French designers such as Jean Barbet and Jean Cotelle. Jones's versatility as a designer and his successful integration of Italian and French elements won praise from royalty and he received commissions from Queen Henrietta Maria and James I, at Somerset House (1626), St. James's (1629–31), the Queen's House, Greenwich (1630–38), Oatlands (1636), and Whitehall (1630–38).

The restoration of Charles II in 1660 heralded the beginnings of the full-blown Baroque style and the imitation of Dutch and French decorative schemes. French designs, in particular, were extremely influential, and were much in demand by Royalists who had embraced Continental habits and tastes while in exile. And the Fire of London in 1666, which destroyed 10,000 Tudor buildings, meant that the new style was not exclusively confined to court circles. Simplified versions of French Baroque furniture – light, elegant, and commonly veneered with walnut – replaced much of the furniture that had been destroyed.

The third quarter of the 17th century, saw the introduction of Dutch-influenced floral marquetry, chests-of-drawers and cabinets on turned legs, chairs with caned seats, silver pieces embossed with floral garlands, Delftware, and imported Chinese and Japanese porcelain. But in spite of the new king's Dutch origins, and the arrival of Dutch cabinet-makers such as Gerrit Jensen, following the accession of William and Mary (reigned 1688–1702), French styles began to dominate British court design and a taste for French-styled gilt gesso side-tables with pillar legs, scrolled stretchers, and elaborate pendant aprons, tall chandeliers of carved and gilt wood, and chairs with cabriole legs and tall elaborately-carved backs emerged. This fashion for all things French reflected not only the fame of Versailles as pinnacle of European artistry and taste, it was also greatly encouraged by the influx of Huguenot craftsmen who departed France after the revocation of the Edict of Nantes (1685), and the success of the Franco-Dutch immigrant architect-designer Daniel Marot (c. 1663–1752).

Throughout the period, furniture progressed beyond its earlier oaken solidity and became more architectural in appearance, with sculptural carving, and vigorously ornamental surface decoration. Many designs incorporated lacquer, japanning, highly-polished veneers, and seaweed marquetry (suggesting French Boulle-work) to enhance surfaces. Tall, Marot-derived beds, as exemplified by the state bed at Melville (1685), had elaborate testers and cornices, and were richly draped with costly fabrics and trimmings. Elsewhere, the demand for stylish, comfortable furnishings for less formally decorated chambers led to the development of new types of furniture: the day-bed, sofa, wing-chair, free-standing toilet mirrors, and the fall-front writing cabinet or bureau.

A growing desire for opulence was met by the production of luxury items such as silver-coated furniture, and immense silver toilet sets, and by the increased use of gilding on woodwork, in particular carved Baroque bases for japanned or lacquer cabinets. English craftsmen and importers also responded to a new interest in the exotic: silversmiths produced Chinoiserie pieces and cabinet-makers mastered japanning. The English East India Company (established 1600) imported increasing quantities of Indian chintz and *pintados* (painted cottons), Japanese lacquer, and Chinese porcelain.

Overall, British Baroque interiors under the reign of James II and William and Mary were therefore more magnificent, yet at the same time more convenient than those in earlier great houses had been. Their design and decoration were still guided by the grand *enfilade* of chambers and the formal placement of furniture against walls, but a new emphasis on the use of rooms for specific purposes, such as dressing and dining, encouraged the introduction of new types of furniture. Displays of silver plate and porcelain became common. Similarly, mirrors, although still very expensive, played a more prominent role in decorative schemes. The "Triad" furnishing suite, consisting of a table, looking-glass, and pair of candle-stands, became a popular feature in grand interiors as did the liberal use of upholstery on walls, beds, and seat-furniture. Windows, which in Tudor times had generally had shutters, were now invariably hung with curtains.

The leading carver during the late 17th century was Grinling Gibbons (1648–1721). Gibbons's work exemplified the rich, sculptural nature of Baroque ornament, and he created paneling, picture frames, and overmantels with fluid, detailed carved festoons of flowers, leaves, and fruit. Exceptional Gibbons commissions include Petworth (1692), Burghley House (1682), and Kensington Palace (1691–93). He also worked with Christopher Wren on the redecoration of

Britain: ***A Family in a Palladian Interior*****, by Josef Nollekens, 1740** (Fairfax House, York)

William and Mary's State Apartments at Hampton Court Palace (1689–1702) creating some of the most sumptuous interiors of the period. Elaborate red damask and gold-trimmed upholstery was used to cover seat-furniture, windows, the king's bedstead, and the Privy Chamber canopy. Gilded and marbled-topped furnishings, all related to Marot designs and produced by cabinet-makers such as Gerrit Jensen, Thomas Roberts, and the Huguenot Jean Pelletier, were arranged against tapestry-covered walls. The overall effect was almost overwhelming in its use of three-dimensional ornament and rich, warm upholstery, and it represented the apex of the British Baroque style.

Outside of Court circles, many 17th-century interiors were quite plain and sparsely furnished as is suggested by an engraving of Samuel Pepys's library (1693) which shows a room lined with bookshelves but containing almost no other furniture or decoration and a plain wood floor. Provincial and less wealthy consumers were unable or possibly unwilling fully to embrace the extravagances characteristic of Baroque taste. Naive display slipware by Thomas Toft (d.1689), incorporating subjects such as Adam and Eve and Charles II hiding in the oak tree, was very popular among the middle classes, which perhaps indicates a distaste for the foreign grandeur associated with the Court.

The increasing confidence of British design during the 18th century mirrored the country's burgeoning expansionist ambitions and growing economic might. The relationship between Britain and the Continent became more equal as British designers began influencing interior fashion in both Europe and the North American colonies. They continued to borrow from historical sources and French styles, but they reinterpreted and mixed these elements in new and trend-setting ways. Finally, increased travel and the bilingual publication of popular pattern books, by, for example, Thomas Chippendale, Ince & Mayhew, the Adam brothers, and George Richardson, ensured the wide international dissemination of British ideas.

The various styles of this century have been classified in three ways: by monarch and period (e.g., Georgian and Queen Anne); by style or movement (e.g., Palladian, Rococo, Chinoiserie, Gothic and Neo-Classical); and by architect or upholsterer (e.g., Adam, Chippendale, Hepplewhite and Sheraton). Many of the leading architects and designers employed a variety of styles but an overriding concern for comfort and convenience defined interiors throughout the century. From the 1720s, there emerged a desire for smaller spaces better-suited to privacy, informal entertaining, and leisure pursuits such as cards and billiards. The use of dark woods such as mahogany, and the introduction of carpets and wallpapers further enhanced the warmth and intimacy of interior spaces, and architects additionally enlivened public and private rooms with elaborate wall and ceiling ornament in painted stucco and papier-mâché.

Subtle reinterpretations of earlier styles and shifts in furnishing practice more than bold stylistic innovation defined the reign of Queen Anne (1702–14). Rejecting elaborately-carved Baroque-style decoration and labored japanning, designers moved gradually towards greater simplicity. Cabinet-makers produced sleeker, more sophisticated forms incorporating stereotypical Queen Anne features such as the cabriole leg, curved chair backs, and smooth walnut surfaces. Perhaps to counterbalance this trend, the quality and quantity of objects – such as porcelain figures, vases, garnitures, and jardinières – increased. These were displayed on cabinets-on-stands, built-in cupboards, and overmantels. New furniture pieces, such as the *fauteuil de commodité* and *commode*, also emphasised the ideals of comfort and convenience.

By the 1720s, the Palladian style was in fashion. Strongly influenced by the classical ideas of Andrea Palladio and Inigo Jones, Palladianism's chief exponents adopted strict symmetry and minimal ornament in the design of exterior architecture. Palladian interiors, by contrast, were often sumptuously decorated, and included furnishings inspired by 16th- and 17th-century Italian prototypes that also incorporated elements of the provincial Franco-Dutch and late French Baroque styles that had originated during the last years of Louis XIV's reign. Palladian designers thus created a new amalgamation of late Renaissance architecture and highly-ornamented Baroque rooms.

The movement's high profile facilitated the spread of its ideals. Lord Burlington (1694–1753), who purchased Jones's Palladio drawings around 1720, and the architect Colen Campbell (1676–1729) initiated the cult of Inigo Jones. Their enthusiasm inspired other designers such as William Kent (1686–1748), Lord Burlington's protégé and the movement's most eminent designer, and John Vardy (d.1765). Key texts in disseminating Palladian doctrines included Kent's *Designs of Inigo Jones* (1727), William Jones's *The Gentleman's or Builder's Companion* ... (1739), Vardy's *Some Designs of Mr. Inigo Jones and Mr. William Kent* (1744), Batty Langley's *The City and Country Builder's and Workman's Treasury of Designs* (1740), and Isaac Ware's *Designs of Inigo Jones and Others*.

Colen Campbell's Wanstead House (1720), set the pattern for grand interiors for the next thirty years, and was the first large house built and decorated in the new Palladian style. By 1730, William Kent was producing even more splendid Palladian interiors – rich in stucco work, painted decoration, carved and gilt wood, and enormous marble chimneypieces – exemplified by his work for Lord Burlington at Chiswick House (late 1720s–36), and his designs for Sir Robert Walpole's Houghton Hall (c.1730). Kent's ornamentation was massive in scale and ebullient in spirit, incorporating motifs such as pediments, cornices, lion masks and paws, acanthus leaves, and swags derived from architecture or antique sculpture. His designs for doorcases and chimneypieces derived from Inigo Jones but his furniture was inspired by 16th- and 17th-century Roman and Florentine prototypes. Executed by leading cabinet-makers such as William Vile (1700–67) and Benjamin Goodison (d.1767), his furniture was massive and architectural. It included gilt side-tables and pedestals with thick scroll supports and decorative carvings of festoons, curling foliage, classical masks, putti, and gigantic shells; chairs with deeply carved legs and arms; and bedsteads, with shell-surmounted heads, covered in damask.

The a-tectonic and asymmetrical Rococo style was never embraced as fully in England as it was on the Continent, and British designers used it mainly in surface ornament rather than for whole interiors. Nevertheless, they developed a comprehensive and discernible vocabulary which included naturalistic ornament such as plant, bird, animal, and human imagery, splashing water, *rocaille* or rockwork, shellwork, fluid S-shaped curves, bright colors set off by white and gold, and copious use of mirrors. It was particularly well-suited to the design of objects, and its light and fanciful forms, together with its association with the sophisticated manners of the French court, and the publication of several useful Rococo pattern books ensured the style's wide diffusion in the mid-18th century. Matthias Lock's *A New Drawing Book of Ornaments* (1740), *Six Sconces* (1744), *Six Tables* (1746) and *A New Book of Ornament* (1752) served as standard Rococo design sources for cabinet-makers, silversmiths, and other makers of interior furnishings. Thomas Chippendale's *The Gentleman and Cabinet-Maker's Director* (1754) — an invaluable guide to genteel taste in London in the 1750s – further illustrated and inspired both standard Rococo furnishings and those diversified with playful Chinoiserie and Gothic elements. Such books were widely distributed, thereby guaranteeing the extensive acceptance of Rococo elements within British interiors.

At its most successful, the British Rococo possessed animated, rhythmic, sculptural qualities. Notable examples include: Paul de Lamerie's (1688–1751) fantastic silverwork; Spitalfields' sumptuous embroidered silks of the 1750s; Isaac Ware's French-styled Rococo interiors at Chesterfield House (1740s); John Linnell's chimneypiece and overmantel designed for Lady Coventry's dressing room at Croome Court (1758); and the fluid, richly-detailed Rococo display-pieces Chippendale produced for the Earl of Dumfries (1759–66). An exceptional all-embracing Rococo interior is Claydon House, Buckinghamshire (1757–71), designed by Luke Lightfoot, whose capricious stucco ceiling, wall, and overmantel work created a unified effect rare in British design.

Chinoiserie elements were also often incorporated into Rococo pattern books and interiors. The style became fashionable in Britain in the 1750s reflecting not only the growth of the British Empire, but also the increased exposure of British designers and consumers to influences beyond Europe. Yet, 18th-century Chinoiserie differed from its earlier 17th-century counterparts in two ways. First, it appropriated novel forms and ornament in addition to exotic surface decoration such as

Britain: drawing of Earl of Derby's house, by Robert Adam

japanning. Second, designers attempted more accurate renditions of oriental subjects. Lock and Chippendale pattern books illustrated how to integrate oriental ornament within furnishings, while William Chambers's *Designs of Chinese Buildings, Furniture, Dresses, Machines and Utensils* (1757) stimulated the incorporation of correct representations of Chinese elements within other areas of British design. The acceleration of trade with the Far East also galvanized the use of genuine oriental wares, such as porcelain, lacquerwork, screens, fans, painted silks, and wallpaper, and these elements were blended with Rococo and Chinoiserie ornament within fashionable mid-18th century interiors.

William Linnell (d.1763) and Thomas Chippendale (1718–79) were leading exponents of the Chinoiserie style. Linnell designed carved decoration furnishings for the interior of a Chinese pleasure pavilion in the grounds of Woburn Abbey in 1749. He also provided furnishings for a Chinese-style bedroom at Badminton House (1752). This interior, hung with oriental wallpaper, contained a spectacular pagoda-topped bed with dragon finials, a chimney-glass, eight lattice-pattern chairs, a commode, a dressing table, and two pairs of standing shelves, all japanned en suite in black, red, and gold. Chippendale skillfully blended picturesque Chinese elements with Rococo conceits, assimilating themes from Darly and Edwards's *A New Book of Chinese Designs* (1754) and creating designs that were more varied than those of either Lock or Linnell. Exceptional examples of Chippendale's Chinoiserie furniture were produced for Dumfries House, Scotland, where he supplied a pair of oval pier glasses, featuring a canopy that borders a bust of a mustachioed Chinese man, and a pair of gilt girandoles, Rococo in effect but Chinese in ornament with a Chinese man and ho-ho bird.

The first phase of the Gothic Revival surfaced in the 1750s and 1760s and was manifested in two parallel strands. The first of these involved leading designers such as Chippendale who adopted elements from the Gothic vocabulary alongside Rococo and Chinoiserie motifs as a means of introducing diversity within interiors. Their work reflected consumer demand for fanciful ornamentation more than a committed desire to create a genuinely Gothic effect. Its principal outlet was scrollwork ornament, patterned in cusps, ogees, lancets, and other shapes borrowed from Gothic tracery, on furniture.

The second strand of the Gothic Revival was more Antiquarian in character and involved direct borrowing from historical sources, the use of real medieval objects, and the rejection of popular design forms. Horace Walpole's Strawberry Hill (1747–96), a model for subsequent Antiquarian interiors of the late 18th and early 19th centuries, featured stained glass, carved woodwork and stone fragments, an armor collection, Gothic-inspired decoration with *trompe-l'oeil* wallpapers imitating stucco and tracery, and ancient and modern Gothic- and Elizabethan-styled furniture. Strawberry Hill's Holbein Room, decorated in purple and white with Gothic papier-mâché ceiling ornament, was a haunting divergence from mainstream Rococo, Chinoiserie, and Neo-Classical design.

The Neo-Classical style emerged in Britain around 1770 and dominated design in various guises until the 1820s. It grew out of French design of the 1750s which emphasized ornament directly inspired by the example of the ancient Roman interiors excavated at Herculaneum and Pompeii. But it rapidly developed a uniquely British character and soon became the preferred style for both public and private commissions. Designers adorned every aspect of an interior – from firedogs to ceiling patterns – with classical ornament so as to achieve a unified and harmonious effect, and the overall impression of such rooms was of a formal but colourful reverence for antiquity. The movement's most important designers were the architects Sir William Chambers, James "Athenian" Stuart, Robert Adam, Henry Holland, and Sir John Soane, and the cabinet-makers George Hepplewhite and Thomas Sheraton. Upholsterers, such as Ince & Mayhew, John Linnell, and Thomas Chippendale, immigrant marquetry masters such as Christopher Fuhrlohg and Pierre Langlois, and the ceramics manufacturer Josiah Wedgwood also played significant roles in realising Neo-Classical schemes.

William Chambers (1723–96) produced designs that, although lighter and more measured in ornament, bore a striking resemblance to the Palladian interiors of Kent and Vardy. The work of James Stuart (1713–88), co-author with James Revett of the influential archaeological sourcebook *The Antiquities of Athens* (1762), was by contrast quite severe and resembled designs associated with the French *goût grec*. Stuart's interiors for Spencer House, London, begun in 1759, demonstrate an eclectic, partly Grecian but mainly Roman-inspired, style which appears somewhat oppressive when compared with later work by Robert Adam. Stuart's furniture reveals an obsession with classical ornament and an aptitude for appropriating design from Roman temples for 18th century household use.

The Scotsman Robert Adam (1728–92), was Britain's foremost Neo-Classical architect, designing decorations, ornament, furniture, textiles, architectural features and interior arrangements, and creating a style (in partnership with his brother James) which swept through fashionable society during the 1760s and 1770s. Robert trained with the Italian architect and engraver, G. B. Piranesi, and the French architect C.-L. Clérisseau, in Rome, but his style developed in a less solemn manner than that of his French contemporaries. He used classical prototypes for architectural design and a full repertoire of classical motifs – swags and ribbons, fluting and paterae, ram's heads, sphinxes, griffins, chimeras, Greek key patterns, and Vitruvian scrolls – to create buildings and interiors that were wholly Neo-Classical in their forms, ornament, and restraint. He also enhanced the classical effect through a dynamic integration of materials and colors – in painted walls and ceilings, and surfaces such as marble and *scagliola* table tops and floors, and in gilding and elaborate metal door and furniture mounts. And he favoured grotesque decoration, incorporating medallions, rectangular-framed relief panels, arabesques and scrollwork that were inspired by ancient ruins and that enjoyed enormous popularity on the Continent. A fine example of Adam's grotesque interiors is the Etruscan room in Osterley Park (1776).

Two of Adam's most magnificent buildings were Syon House, begun in 1761, and Kedleston Hall (1758–77). Syon's great hall, with cream-white walls and a black and white marble patterned floor, epitomizes the classical ideal of pure, restrained ornament. Niches with classical sculpture surround the hall, stucco ornament of swags and medallions adorn the ceiling and walls, and Doric columns frame the doorcases. By comparison, the whole of Kedleston Hall reverberates with color – blue, green, yellow, and red on walls, ceilings, furniture, and upholstery, abundant gilding, *scagliola* flooring (whose design corresponds to ceiling stuccowork), and painted grotesque ornament.

The late Neo-Classical style – occasionally referred to as Hepplewhite – involved a shift towards greater simplicity and decorative refinement which was accelerated by popular books such as George Hepplewhite's *The Cabinet-Maker and Upholsterer's Guide* (1788) and Thomas Sheraton's *Cabinet-Maker and Upholsterer's Drawing Book* (1791, 1794). Hepplewhite (d.1786) demonstrated a union of elegance and utility through the simplification of Adamesque taste and the modification of early French Neo-Classicism; Sheraton (1751–1806) promoted delicate rectilinear forms and the highlighting of woods. Both featured flat, stylized Neo-Classical ornament – urns, medallions, paterae, swags, and pendants – and common features of furniture were bow- and serpentine-fronted chests and oval, heart-shaped, and shield-back chairs. Carlton House, created by Henry Holland (1745–1806) during the 1780s for the Prince of Wales, employed bold, large-scale ornament and epitomized the late Neo-Classical style. The style also had its practical side, and both Holland and Sir John Soane (1753–1837) designed furniture that was built into the architectural structure.

The architecture and interiors of many medium-sized villas and town houses during the late 18th and early 19th centuries were influenced by Picturesque theories, which celebrated the freedom, informality and irregularity of nature. These theories encouraged more informal living arrangements and asymmetrical house plans. Most importantly, they broke with the tradition of furniture being ranged around the perimeter of the room and promoted comfortable, irregular groupings in its center that facilitated conversation and less formal social intercourse. Publications which promoted this more relaxed style of living included Malton's *An Essay on Cottage Architecture* (1798), Bartell's *Hints for Picturesque Improvements in Ornamental Cottages* (1804), and Papworth's *Rural Residences* (1818).

Nineteenth-century design broadly separates into three periods, which while stylistically distinct, share commonalities of purpose and effect. The classically-inspired Regency phase of the early 19th century generally extended the stylistic prior-

Britain: drawing room from *The Decoration and Furniture of Town Houses* by Robert W. Edis, 1881

ities of 18th century "tasteful" Neo-Classicism. Victorian design, which spanned the period from the 1820s to the 1880s, adopted a broader range of revivalist motifs and consistently emphasized richness and texture. Finally, the mid-to-late 19th century reform movements argued strongly against the prevailing eclecticism and called for simpler treatments and a more "honest" approach to materials and design.

Throughout the century, however, there was greater emphasis upon the idea of home as a secluded and comfortable haven from the hazards and pressures of the outside world, as well as upon densely furnished schemes and conspicuous consumption. The century also saw the emergence of new markets in the form of the newly prosperous and fashion-conscious middle classes. Within this context, interior decoration became a major industry, supported by a vast literature of journals and home manuals that promoted popular styles and discussed design principles. Some of the best-known of these books were J.C. Loudon's *An Encyclopaedia of Cottage, Farm and Villa Architecture and Furniture* (1833; re-issued until 1867), Robert Kerr's *The Gentleman's House* (1864), Charles Eastlake's *Hints on Household Taste* (1868) and Macmillan's *Art at Home* series (published between 1878 and 1880). The widespread success of these books guaranteed the broad dissemination of different styles.

Reacting against against the excessive ornamentation within Adamesque interiors and the spindly elegance of Hepplewhite, Regency design was popular from the 1790s to the 1840s, and satisfied a taste for plain, pure surfaces, a reduction in the quantity of relief ornament, a reliance on painted decoration, and the use of furniture whose forms were based on antique prototypes. Greek Revival elements served as primary decoration in Regency interiors; but ornament and form derived from Chinese, Indian, Egyptian, and other exotic sources were also frequent embellishments. The style first appeared in works by Henry Holland, C.H. Tatham, Thomas Sheraton, and Sir John Soane. It reached its zenith in the work of Thomas Hope (1769–1831) whose book *Household Furniture and Interior Decoration* (1807) was extremely influential and whose designs were widely adapted and popularised by commercial cabinet-makers such as George Smith (d. 1826).

Hope's designs for furniture were strongly archaeological in flavor and drew upon his knowledge of ancient Greek, Roman and Egyptian sources. Other furniture, although less authentically antique, neverthless featured sabre legs, carved acanthus scrolls, inlaid palmettes and lion-paw feet, prompting Sir Walter Scott to remark in 1828, "An ordinary chair, in the most ordinary parlour, has now something of an antique cast – something of Grecian massiveness, at once, and elegance in its forms."

Regency's willingness to overlay formal classical structure with different stylistic and historical motifs culminated in the extraordinary interiors created by John Nash, Frederick Crace and Robert Jones for George IV at Brighton Pavilion (1815–23). The exterior of this building is Indian in style – featuring Picturesque groupings of minarets, porticoes, pillars, and Vathek caprices – but the symmetrically arranged interiors exude a dignified, differentiated exoticism. Indian, Chinese, and Egyptian quotations that include palm-tree columns, dragon-capped chandeliers, couches modeled after Egyptian boats, bamboo furniture, and a painted representation of a gigantic plantain tree, are coupled with an extensive use of mirrors and dramatic color schemes, and create an effect stunning in its richness.

High Victorian interiors can be broadly separated into Gothic Revival, Rococo Revival, and Renaissance Revival schools, but designers borrowed freely and simultaneously from each of these styles and others including Antiquarian, Neo-Classical, and Eastern-inspired design. The use of diverse patterns and textural embellishments on architectural structures, furniture, and all other decorative devices further complicated the visual impact that resulted from this stylistic mixing. Thus, rather than seeking unified effects, decorators and consumers attempted to balance varied color, pattern, and texture within comfortable, visually-stimulating rooms. To this end, the Victorians developed a uniquely British design movement characterized by rampant eclecticism.

The Victorian Gothic Revival developed as a nationalistic response to the foreignness of the classically-inspired Neo-Classical and Regency styles. Gothic, by contrast, was perceived as a native, ecclesiastical style and it had strong moral overtones. A.W.N. Pugin (1812–52), the style's major proponent, spearheaded a Reformed Gothic movement which insisted on the correct use of authentic medieval ornament and designs, honesty in construction and truth to materials. His ideas were disseminated in his published works, notably *Gothic Furniture in the Style of the 15th Century* (1835), *Contrasts; or, A Parallel Between the Architecture of the 15th and 19th Centuries* (1836; 1841) and *The True Principles of Pointed or Christian Architecture* (1841).

While designers from many different schools borrowed Gothic elements, Pugin, and the second generation of Gothic Revivalists such as William Butterfield, George Edmund Street, G.F. Bodley, and Philip Webb, created stylistically-uniform Gothic buildings with rambling, informal ground-plans. They revived the medieval Great Hall, which served as a seat of "old English hospitality" and functioned as the home's heart, to link other rooms and to provide a communal entertainment space, and used bold, chunky furniture such as Pugin's Glastonbury chairs and his massive cabinets with tracery and large brass hinges. Wall hangings of gilt leather with embossed patterns and stained glass in windows enhanced the Gothic effect. Notable Pugin interiors include Scarisbrick Hall (from 1837) and Eastnor Castle (from 1849). William Burges's (1827–81) Cardiff Castle (1869–81), represents the culmination of the Victorian Gothic Revival in its fantastic mix of Moresque detail and medieval painted decoration, carving, gilding, paneling, coffering, tiling, and architectural ornament.

Despite its morally superior stance, Gothic was never widely popular as a domestic style. Far more successful was the Neo-Rococo or Louis Quinze style, whose rounded forms and elaborate ornament were better-suited to the new priorities of comfort and display. Popular Neo-Rococo designs included heavily-stuffed, deeply-buttoned, and elaborately-trimmed furniture like balloon-back chairs with cabriole legs and curvaceous sofas. Ornament was similarly cumbrous and frequently included dense, bulging, sinuous foliage adapted from the acanthus ornament of the early 19th century. While originally for the very wealthy and embodying political connotations of the *ancien régime*, this plush domestic style dominated many drawing rooms and/or boudoirs – the feminine spaces of middle-class homes – by the 1840s; examples of the style within wealthy homes are Benjamin Dean Wyatt's (1775–1852) Belvoir Castle (c.1825–30), and Stafford House (c.1826–33). By the 1860s, the Rococo had developed into the *Louis Seize* revival, the High Victorian style most often associated with interiors brimming with densely-massed objects and ornament.

Another immensely popular style of the 1870s and later was the Renaissance Revival which had first emerged in the 1830s when it was used by Prince Albert for Osborne House on the Isle of Wight. This movement embraced a variety of revivalist idioms – many of which were not Renaissance-based and none of which were pursued with the fervor of the Reformed Gothic – and by the late 19th century, Victorian Renaissance interiors incorporated motifs from the Renaissance, Neo-Classicism, Louis Quatorze Baroque, Louis Quinze Rococo, and renewed Pompeian, Grecian, Turkish, and Egyptian styles. This "Free Renaissance" style, as it was known, also favored the use of different styles within different rooms. For instance, dining rooms or halls were typically "old English" and were decorated with paneling or leather wallhangings and pictures such as portraits. Drawing rooms, regarded as a more feminine domains, were more delicate in appearance and featured French or 18th-century Neo-Classical styles and soothing watercolors and landscapes. Reproduction furniture of virtually every period filled all parts of the home.

The Arts and Crafts Movement, the principal reform movement of the mid-to-late 19th century, represented a reaction to this eclecticism and a critique of the degeneracy of much mass-produced industrial design. Inspired by the writings of John Ruskin (1819–1900) and William Morris (1834–96), it championed the revival of obsolete craft skills, the use of natural materials and an emphasis upon simpler, vernacular forms. Though the name itself stemmed from the Arts and Crafts Exhibition Society founded in 1888, the movement grew out of the widespread critical dissatisfaction with the objects shown at the Great Exhibition of 1851. Its principles gained broader acceptance in the 1860s with Charles Eastlake's *Hints on Household Taste* (1868), through the work of Morris, Marshall, Faulkner & Company (founded in 1861, became Morris & Co. in 1875), and with the establishment in 1857 of the Victoria and Albert Museum whose mission was to promote standards of "good"design. Under its auspices, various design schools and design guilds were born, including the Century Guild (1882), Guild of Handicraft (1887), and Art-Workers' Guild (1884).

Although Arts and Crafts objects and interiors consistently emphasised fine workmanship, good design and native forms, individual designers and architects involved with the movement developed their own priorities and styles. The Aesthetic Movement, for example, championed by E.W. Godwin (1833–86), was strongly influenced by the lightness and elegance of Japanese forms, while the Queen Anne Revival, spearheaded by Richard Norman Shaw (1831–1912) and William Eden Nesfield (1835–88), drew on the vernacular traditions of the late 17th and early 18th centuries and favoured red brick, asymmetrical structures with a preponderance of Picturesque features such as tall chimneys and elongated windows. Queen Anne furniture was modelled on 18th-century prototypes and included tall display cabinets and corner cupboards featuring intricate mouldings, turned legs and stretchers, and gilt gesso naturalistic ornament. Designers such as Christopher Dresser (1834–1904), and C.F.A. Voysey (1857–1941) worked even more independently. Dresser produced designs for ceramics, wallpapers and textiles as well as furniture that explored the use of semi-abstract botanical and oriental forms. Voysey used a bright, light palette and simple unconventional patterns on his wallpapers and textiles and designed a range of simple, craftsmanlike furniture for cottage-style interiors such as those for his own house, The Orchard, Chorley Wood (1899).

Arguably the most celebrated Arts and Crafts interiors were designed by Morris & Co., the decorating firm founded by William Morris in association with Philip Webb (1831–1915), Dante Gabriel Rossetti (1828–82), and Edward Burne-Jones (1833–98), and others in 1861. The company produced solid oak furniture, wallpaper and textile patterns based on natural and historical sources, embroidered tapestries and bed hangings, and medieval-style stained glass. Their work was used for both important public commissions and town houses, for example the state rooms at St. James's Palace (1880–82) and the decoration of Aleco Ionides' house, 1 Holland Park (from 1880), as well as in more rustic settings like Philip Webb's Great Tangley Manor (1885–91) and Standen (1891–94)

Britain: library, Eaton Hall, Cheshire, c. 1882

where the interiors adhered more closely to the aesthetic of simplicity that characterized the later Arts and Crafts ideal. Moreover, Morris & Co.'s activities as a retailer and manufacturer exercised a strong influence on progressive upper-middle class tastes.

"New Art" or Art Nouveau emerged in the 1890s. The style's distinguishing features were its use of energized, swaying lines, deliquescent human figures, and tentacle-like flower and leaf motifs in surface decoration and eccentric, organic, curving forms. A watered-down version of the style was actively promoted by commercial manufacturers such as Liberty's (established 1875) which produced reasonably-priced furniture, textiles and wallpapers derived from the Arts and Crafts designs of artists like C.R. Ashbee, M.H. Baillie Scott, Archibald Knox and Voysey. Art Nouveau's most celebrated British exponent was Charles Rennie Mackintosh (1868–1928) but Mackintosh's style was more closely affiliated with that of the Viennese Secession and the International Modern Movement than with the work of his British contemporaries. Born and trained in Glasgow, he combined Scottish vernacular, Art Nouveau, and industrial functionalism in his architecture and furniture. He delighted in rectilinear formal effects and rounded, squat decoration such as his ubiquitous rose. His furniture designs evolved into square, heavy forms like the high-backed chair with a pierced oval backrail, used in the Tea Rooms at Argyle Street, Glasgow (1897–98). Mackintosh's interiors, notably those in the Glasgow School of Art (1896–99; 1907–09), Hill House at Helensburgh (1902–04) and multiple furniture designs, also prioritized stark architectural effect over comfort and convenience, and in his concern for design as artistic statement, he foreshadowed the interests of the 20th century.

The major developments in British design in the 20th century can be broadly classified as the continuation of the Arts and Crafts Movement, the development of the English Country House style, and emergence of the Modern Movement. The aesthetic characteristics of these programs ranged respectively from simple, rustic forms, to chintzy domesticity to functional minimalism. While individual designers created unified interiors in each of these styles, the mass of consumers selected elements from one or more movements and integrated them within a broader interior framework that included historicist ornament and antiques. The growth of retail chains devoted to both modern and revivalist designs further enabled customers to choose from various styles and to create interiors that reflected personal taste rather than a consistent style.

The Arts and Crafts ideals of high-quality workmanship and simple, straightforward design were perpetuated in the early part of the century by the designer and retail-store owner Sir Ambrose Heal (1872–1959) and the architect Edwin Lutyens (1869–1944). Heal's shop specialised in simple cottage-style furniture and freshly coloured textiles and he disseminated his ideas through publications such as *Plain Oak Furniture* (1898) and *Simple Bedroom Furniture* (1899) until the 1930s. Lutyens's designs, particularly those for Castle Drogo (1910–32), were also grounded in Arts and Crafts principles, but included additional ornamentation and touches of playful complexity to create more mannered effects.

The work of the Omega Workshops (1913–19) reflected more Modernist principles. Inspired by the Wiener Werkstätte and founded by Roger Fry, Vanessa Bell, and Duncan Grant, the Workshops used Fauvist and Cubist forms and axioms to create furniture, carpets and textiles decorated with brightly colored flat patterns. The Workshops' most important commissions include the Cadena Café in London's Westbourne Grove (1914) and a Post-Impressionist room in the Ideal Home Exhibition (1913). While occasionally classified as Arts and Crafts due to the Workshops' organizational structure, the designs themselves clearly suggest later Modernist movements.

The first sustained break with the Arts and Crafts tradition came with the English Country House style, which emerged in the 1930s with the establishment of the interior decorating firm Colefax & Fowler. Colefax & Fowler's clientele represented a wealthy social elite many of whom were intent on decorating their stately homes in a manner that was sympathetic to the age and history of the architecture. The firm's mixture of antiques with modern conveniences, their reliance on a subtle use of "old" paint colors to highlight features such as mouldings and plasterwork decoration, their revival of historic and traditional floral textile and wallpaper patterns, and their generous use of draperies and soft upholstery, were ideally suited to this task. Moreover, they formed the backbone of design principles which have gained post-war international popularity through the work of companies like Laura Ashley whose rustic chintz-style wallpapers and textiles have satisfied a more widespread taste for nostalgia and traditional living.

An interest in historical styles and references developed concurrently with the above-mentioned styles. Antique objects and revivalist design visually reinforced values of tradition, stability, and national pride, and antique or reproduction furniture from the 17th and 18th centuries was favoured in many fashionable turn-of-the-century homes. Firms such as Heal's and Liberty's established Antiques departments to service middle-class demand and the Ideal Home Exhibition (1920) and the British Empire Exhibition at Wembley (1924) both encouraged this anti-Modernist taste. The British Empire Exhibition featured a sequence of rooms furnished in the styles of 1750, 1820, 1852, 1888, and 1924. Popular architectural features included mock-Tudor timbered gable ends, heavy-paneled front doors, and wood-paneled halls and dining rooms.

British interpretations of international Modern Movements began with Art Deco of the 1920s and 1930s, and continued with British Modernism, Utility schemes, Pop, High-Tech and Postmodern design. But perhaps because of their foreign origins, or because of consumers' preference for cozy domesticity, none of these movements became firmly entrenched within the mass of British interiors. Rather, consumers tended to incorporate Modernist elements within rooms that were generally Country House or revivalist in style.

The British Art Deco Movement grew out of the 1925 Paris Exposition des Arts Décoratifs et Industriels and Art Nouveau. Art Deco designers rejected most historical references and used color and abstracted decoration, including motifs of chevrons, zigzags, and sunrises, as expressions of contemporaneity. Phyllis Barron (1890–1964), one of the British movement's most important textile designers, created hand-blocked fabrics of abstracted geometrical and floral patterns with Dorothy Larcher (1884–1952). Interior designer Syrie Maugham (1879–1955) juxtaposed white surfaces and mirrors. In the late 1930s, Art Deco design evolved into an extravagant, luscious style. The Dorland Hall Exhibition (1933) featured a boudoir with a glass chaise longue, silver-glass walls, and a glass floor by Oliver Hill. Suburban variations of Art Deco included bright, geometric Jazz-Age patterns for wallpapers and textiles, chunky or rounded sofas and matching armchairs covered with leather, velveteen or moquette, stepped veneered cabinets and bookshelves, and geometric coloured glass light-fittings.

Modernism, developed on the Continent under Le Corbusier, Mies van der Rohe, and designers associated with the Bauhaus school, favored modern materials such as concrete, tubular steel and glass, and mass-production technology to create pure, clean, sparsely furnished interiors. Serge Chermayeff (1900–96), the leading Modernist designer in Britain in the 1920s and 1930s, revolutionized British design with his incorporation of black glass, silver cellulose, macassar ebony, and abstract patterns. Chermayeff, who envisioned the elimination of ornament in the evolution of a pure style, designed strikingly plain interiors for the BBC (1932–34). The Design and Industries Association (DIA) and government commissions such as the Council of Industrial Design and the 1932 Gorell Report on Art and Industry actively promoted this minimalist aesthetic. Their efforts, however, had mixed results, with the broader adoption of Modernist designs by commercial manufacturers occurring only after World War II.

The premise that underpinned much post-war design was that scientific and technological advances as applied to the home could improve the quality of life through labor-saving and automation. The Festival of Britain (1951), while nominally devoted to celebrating Britain and its history, actually had a pervading sense of science fiction and displayed a consistent emphasis on science and technology as the means of modernizing the workings of the home. In many Festival exhibits, molecular, crystallographic, and atomic structures served as the basis for designs for textiles and other surface decoration for glass, packaging, pottery, and furniture. The Festival Pattern Group, for example, which represented 26

Britain: Joan and David, New Bond Street, London, by Eva Jiricna, 1994

manufacturers including Wedgwood, Goodearl Brothers, Chance Brothers, and London Typographical Designers, derived their ornament from the crystallographic structures of substances such as boric acid, insulin, aluminum hydroxide, and haemoglobin.

The Festival stimulated a general interest in "Contemporary Style" design among middle-class consumers. This style fused function and ornament in a playful manner, as epitomized by Robin Day's stackable *Hillestack* chairs and ubiquitous bold surface patterns, such as Lucienne Day's *Calyx*, on wallpapers, plastic laminates, and carpets. "Molecules" became a widespread decorative element – found on the feet of domestic appliances and furniture, and as surface ornament – throughout the 1950s.

By the mid-1960s, London had become a major centre of the youth-oriented Pop Movement which affected fine arts, fashion, and graphic and interior design. The Independent Group was at the forefront of Pop in the 1950s and members Alison and Peter Smithson created one of the earliest Pop interiors for the Ideal Home Exhibition (1956). This futurist house included organically-shaped rooms contained within an expendable plastic-plaster shell. Pop concepts of expendability and design pluralism challenged traditional notions of permanence and status. Designers created furniture constructed in cardboard, chipboard, and paper. Bright colors, strong geometric patterns such as targets and the Union Jack, and consumer-oriented motifs inspired by contemporary artists such as Oldenburg and Warhol decorated object surfaces. The radical youth culture of the late 1960s and early 1970s also encouraged the emergence of a psychedelic design style which drew upon the imagery and colors associated with experience of taking LSD as decorative sources. Designers blended hallucinatory motifs and colors with a variety of historical and artistic references including the illustrations of Aubrey Beardsley and Art Deco motifs and ornament. Nevertheless, the Pop and Psychedelic movements had only a marginal effect on domestic interiors through posters and other inexpensive, readily-available decorative items. Most middle-class homes retained either a revivalist, chintz, or 1950s "Contemporary" flavor.

Unlike the suggestive wit and modernity of Continental exponents such as Ettore Sottsass and the Memphis Group, much British Postmodernism, developed in the 1980s, has revealed a concern to preserve existing structures and a renewed interest in historical ornament and traditional craft techniques. The pastiche Georgian revivals of architects such as Quinlan Terry or the "classic" designs of the furniture maker David Linley are typical of this trend. The industrial home-furnishing style, known as High-Tech, is, by contrast, more modern in appearance and has proved more marketable. High-Tech interiors have incorporated steel furniture components, graph-based wallpapers and fabrics, and bulkhead lighting. The design concepts relate to the mid-20th-century work of Charles and Ray Eames and use ready-made industrial components to create personalized, contemporary interiors. Norman Foster and Nigel Coates represent the British movement's most influential designers, and Sir Terence Conran's Habitat and Conran's stores have served as the movement's major retailers.

While modern design movements continue to evolve, variations on the English Country House style and revivalism still reigns supreme, comfort and nostalgia – a veneration for the past no matter how recent or distant – remain guiding principles. Indeed, multiplicity has characterized British interiors from the turn of the 19th century through today, and reactions to the perceived detrimental impact of industrialization and the increasing significance of the middle class has clearly encouraged the celebration of individualism and personal taste. Retail design markets serving and directing *en masse* individual consumers in the 20th century have usurped the role of the architect-designers and design professionals of the 18th and 19th centuries.

ELIZABETH A. FLEMING

Further Reading

Airs, Malcolm, *The Tudor and Jacobean Country House: A Building History*, Stroud, Gloucestershire: Sutton, 1995

Barrett, Helena and John Phillips, *Suburban Style: The British Home, 1840–1960*, London: Macdonald, 1987

Beard, Geoffrey and Christopher Gilbert (editors), *Dictionary of English Furniture Makers, 1660–1840*, London: Furniture History Society, 1986

Beard, Geoffrey, *The National Trust Book of the English House Interior*, London and New York: Viking–National Trust, 1990

Calloway, Stephen, *Twentieth-Century Decoration: The Domestic Interior from 1900 to the Present Day*, London: Weidenfeld and Nicolson, and New York: Rizzoli, 1988

Colvin, Howard M., *A Biographical Dictionary of British Architects, 1600–1840*, 3rd edition New Haven and London: Yale University Press, 1995

Cooper, Jeremy, *Victorian and Edwardian Furniture and Interiors*, London: Thames and Hudson, 1987

Cooper, Nicholas, *The Opulent Eye: Late Victorian and Edwardian Taste in Interior Design*, London: Architectural Press, 1976; New York: Watson Guptill, 1977

Cornforth, John and John Fowler, *English Decoration in the 18th Century*, London: Barrie and Jenkins, and Princeton, NJ: Pyne, 1974; 2nd edition Barrie and Jenkins, 1978

Cornforth, John, *English Interiors, 1790–1848: The Quest for Comfort*, London: Barrie and Jenkins, 1978

Edwards, Ralph and L.G.G. Ramsey (editors), *The Connoisseur Period Guides to the Houses, Decoration, Furnishing and Chattels of the Classic Periods: I – The Tudor Period 1500–1603; II – The Stuart Period 1603–1714; III – The Early Georgian Period 1714–1760; IV – The Late Georgian Period 1760–1810; V – The Regency Period 1810–1830; VI – The Early Victorian Period 1830–1860*, 6 vols., London: Connoisseur, 1956–58; New York: Reynal, 1957–58

Gere, Charlotte, *Nineteenth-Century Decoration: The Art of the Interior*, London: Weidenfeld and Nicolson, and New York: Abrams, 1989

Girouard, Mark, *Life in the English Country House: A Social and Architectural History*, New Haven and London: Yale University Press, 1978

Girouard, Mark, *The Victorian Country House*, revised edition New Haven and London: Yale University Press, 1979

Gore, Alan and Ann, *The History of English Interiors*, Oxford: Phaidon, 1991

Gow, Ian and Alistair Rowan (editors), *Scottish Country Houses, 1600–1914*, Edinburgh: Edinburgh University Press, 1995

Holmes, Michael, *The Country House Described: An Index to the Country Houses of Great Britain and Ireland*, Winchester: Saint Paul's Bibliographies, 1986

Hussey, Christopher, *Early Georgian, 1715–1760*; *Mid Georgian, 1760–1800*; and *Late Georgian, 1800–1840* (English Country Houses, vols., 1–3), 1955–58; reprinted Woodbridge, Suffolk: Antique Collectors' Club, 1984

Jackson, Lesley, *"Contemporary": Architecture and Interiors of the 1950s*, London: Phaidon, 1994

Jackson-Stops, Gervase and James Pipkin, *The English Country House: A Grand Tour*, London: Weidenfeld and Nicolson, 1984; Boston: Little Brown, 1985

Jourdain, Margaret, *English Decoration and Furniture of the Early Renaissance (1500–1650)*, London: Batsford, 1924

Jourdain, Margaret, *English Interior Decoration, 1500 to 1830*, London: Batsford, 1950

Long, Helen C., *The Edwardian House: The Middle-Class Home in Britain, 1880–1914*, Manchester: Manchester University Press, 1993

MacCarthy, Fiona, *British Design since 1880: A Visual History*, London: Lund Humphries, 1982

MacQuoid, Percy and Ralph Edwards, *The Dictionary of English Furniture*, revised edition, 3 vols., 1954; reprinted Woodbridge, Suffolk: Antique Collectors' Club, 1983

Morley, John, *Regency Design, 1790–1840: Gardens, Buildings, Interiors, Furniture*, London: Zwemmer, and New York: Abrams, 1993

Mowl, Timothy, *Elizabethan and Jacobean Style*, London: Phaidon, 1993

Naylor, Gillian, *Arts and Crafts Movement: A Study of its Sources, Ideals and Influence on Design Theory*, London: Studio Vista: and Cambridge: Massachusetts Institute of Technology Press, 1971

Parissien, Steven, *Adam Style*, London: Phaidon, and Washington, DC: Preservation Press, 1992

Parissien, Steven, *Palladian Style*, London: Phaidon, 1994

Parissien, Steven, *The Georgian House*, London: Aurum Press, 1996

Saumarez Smith, Charles, *Eighteenth-Century Decoration: Design and the Domestic Interior in England*, London: Weidenfeld and Nicolson, and New York: Abrams, 1993

Snodin, Michael (editor), *Rococo: Art and Design in Hogarth's England* (exhib. cat.: Victoria and Albert Museum, London), London: Trefoil, 1984

Stillman, Damie, *English Neo-Classical Architecture*, 2 vols., London: Zwemmer, and New York: Harper, 1988

Thornton, Peter, *Seventeenth-Century Interior Decoration in England, France, and Holland,* New Haven and London: Yale University Press, 1978

Thornton, Peter, *Authentic Decor: The Domestic Interior, 1620–1920*, London: Weidenfeld and Nicolson, and New York: Viking, 1984

Thurley, Simon, *The Royal Palaces of Tudor England: Architecture and Court Life, 1460–1547*, New Haven and London: Yale University Press, 1993

Wood, Margaret, *The English Mediaeval House*, London: Phoenix House, 1965; New York: Harper, 1983

Brustolon, Andrea 1662–1732

Italian sculptor and carver

Described by Honoré Balzac as the "Michelangelo of wood", Andrea Brustolon was one of the most celebrated Italian woodcarvers of the late 17th and early 18th centuries. Active for much of his career in Belluno and Venice, he worked in an elaborate Baroque style and executed a wide range of furniture and carvings for wealthy aristocrats and Venetian churches. His father, Jacopo, was also a woodcarver, and it was from him that Andrea received his first training. He became particularly skilled in the carving of box and ebony, both of which were hardwoods and were extremely difficult to carve. Brustolon's mastery of these materials is further evidence of his technical prowess and skill.

A significant precedent for Brustolon's work is the extraordinary carvings of Francesco Pianta (1632–c.1692) in the Church of San Rocco, Venice. A letter of 1677 records that Brustolon was in Venice that year and that he met the Genoese sculptor, Filippo Parodi, during the course of his stay. Some drawings of antique Roman sculptures such as the *Laocoön* and the *Farnese Torso*, now in the Museo Civico, Belluno, support the suggestion that he made a trip to Rome c.1679. Brustolon could also have seen the works of Gian Lorenzo Bernini in Rome, and the sculptor's influence is detectable in a number of Brustolon's works during the following years. His highly personal style was also closely linked with Venetian traditions which are reflected especially in the overwhelmingly monumental character of his sculpture. And he also appears to have been influenced by the iconographic repertory of Northern European culture which may have provided the starting point for his own fanciful compositions.

Brustolon's figurative style is already apparent in his first documented work, the Altar of the Anime (Souls) in the Church of S. Florian in Pieve di Zoldo, near Belluno (1685–86). The wooden cone of the architectural structure is conceived on a rigorously classical foundation which is then masked by the complex interweaving of ornamental features such as curling leaves, cherubs and skulls. Two flayed telamones and two skeletons – symbols of temporal power – appear on the sides of the Altar. And the figures of two angels, carved in the round, are arranged on the cornice, crowning the central group of the Pietà.

Other sculptures are documented in the last decade of the 17th century, and Brustolon's ecclesiastical work includes carvings for several churches and convents in the Veneto. These include the group of angels for the church of San Fermo and the *Custodia* of Saint Teodora for the Augustinian convent in Feltre, both of which date from 1695 and were carved in the Belluno workshop where he worked with his father and his brother, Paolo (1664–c.1734).

In the first years of the 18th century Brustolon received his first important commission from patrician Venetian families. One of the statues from the "Venier suite", now in the Museo Correr, is inscribed "1706 And.s Brustolo.s Bellu.s F." This ensemble was produced for the Venetian nobleman, Pietro Venier, and demonstrates an exceptional technical virtuosity as well as a pleasing treatment of its subject. The suite consists of an assortment of sculpted furniture including twelve armchairs, two pedestals, several vase-stands, supports depicting Ethiopian slaves and Moors, groups of putti and caryatids, and a large group representing Hercules overcoming the Hydra with Cerberus. It was Brustolon's most celebrated work and the carving has such an unrestrained sculptural value that the practical function of the individual elements is completely obscured.

Preparatory studies in the Museo Civico have made it possible to authenticate numerous other secular works, including frames, chairs and wall panels, that are now in private collections. However, the authorship of the two famous suites of armchairs for the Correr family (Museo Correr, Venice) and for the Villa Pisani at Strà that are traditionally attributed to Brustolon has recently been called into question. The latter group, now in the Palazzo Quirinale, Rome, consists of twelve pieces, decorated with signs of the Zodiac and various naturalistic details, that symbolise the months of the year.

Documents published by Biasuz (1969) provide details of some of Brustolon's later works. These include two elegant angels carrying lamps in the Church of the Frari, Venice, and the Reliquary Tabernacle of Saint Innocentia made for Archbishop Antonio Polcenigo of Feltre (now in the Museum für Kunst und Gewerbe, Hamburg). Many commissions for religious institutions in Belluno followed in the last decade of his career, such as the Tabernacle for the Altar of the Rosary in the Church at Cortina d'Ampezzo (1724). Secular commissions included a box-wood group of statues on pedestals carved in low relief which were made for the Count Tiopo Piloni (1724). Once again a vivacity and freedom of invention are restored to subjects that hitherto had been strictly codified.

Brustolon's work was highly acclaimed by his contemporaries. Indeed, such was his fame that by the time of his death in 1732 he had a large number of followers and imitators whose work is often misattributed to Brustolon himself. These imitations rarely achieve the high sculptural quality of the artist's original works.

LUCIANA ARBACE
translated by Antonia Boström

Biography

Born in Belluno, 20 July 1662. Son of Jacopo Brustolon, a sculptor and woodcarver, with whom he first trained. Studied drawing and sculpture with Agostino Ridolfi (1646–1727), then entered the Venetian workshop of the Genoese sculptor, Filippo Parodi (1630–1702), 1677. Travelled to Rome, 1679; returned to Venice, 1680. Received commissions for suites of furniture from the Venier di S. Vio, S. Simeone and Pisani families in Venice, 1684–99. Completed the Altar of the Anime for the church of S. Floriano di Zoldo, 1685–86. Returned permanently to Belluno, where he set up a workshop with his father and brother Paolo, c.1699. In addition to decorative secular sculpture, furniture and frames, he executed much sacred sculpture for churches in Belluno and the surrounding area. Member of the Confraternità di S. Giuseppe, and Oratorio di S. Filippo Neri. Died in Belluno, 25 October 1732.

Selected Works

Brustolon's most important work is represented in the Museo Correr, and the Museo Ca' Rezzonico, Venice; the Quirinal Palace, Rome; and the Kunsthistorisches Museum, Vienna. The most comprehensive list of surviving, attributed, and lost works and earlier bibliography is in Biasuz and Lacchin 1928. Persicini 1882 has a full catalogue of works and documentary appendices.

1706 Venier Palace, Venice (now Museo Ca' Rezzonico, Venice; suite of sculpted furniture [the "fornimentoVenier"] including 12 armchairs; 9 Ethiopian slaves; 2 dead Moors; 1 standing Moor; 2 female caryatids; the Four Seasons; the Five Elements; 2 groups of putti; 2 pedestals; group of Hercules overcoming the Hydra with Cerberus with figures of Rivers and slaves): Pietro Venier

Attributed Works

Suite of 8 armchairs (now Museo Correr): Correr family

Villa Pisani, Strà (now Quirinal Palace, Rome; suite of 12 armchairs depicting the Months): Pisani family

Further Reading

Alberici, Clelia, *Il mobile veneto*, Milan: Electa, 1980, pp.162–84

Biasuz, Giuseppe and Enrico Lacchin, *Andrea Brustolon*, Venice: Zanetti, 1928

Biasuz, Giuseppe and Maria Giovanna Buttignon, *Andrea Brustolon*, Padua: Istituto Veneto di Arti Grafiche, 1969

Coleridge, Anthony, "Andrea Brustolon: Some Additions" in *Apollo*, March 1963

Coleridge, Anthony, "Andrea Brustolon at the Ca' Rezzonico", in *Bollettino dei Musei Civici Veneziani*, 4, 1963, pp.18–24

González-Palacios, Alvar "Il mobilio del' 700 veneto", in *Casa d'Oro*, 19, 1967, pp.145–52

González-Palacios, Alvar, *Il tempio del Gusto: Le arti decorative in Italia fra classicismi e barocco*, part 2: *Granducato di Toscana e gli stati settentrionali*, Milan: Longanesi, 1986, vol.1, pp.319–24

Honour, Hugh, *Cabinet Makers and Furniture Designers*, London: Weidenfeld and Nicolson, and New York: Putnam, 1969

Mariacher, Giovanni, "Nuovi appunti su Brustolon a Ca' Rezzonico e al Museo Correr", in *Bollettino dei Musei Civici Veneziani*, 10, 1965, pp.25–43

Martineau, Jane and Andrew Robinson, *The Glory of Venice: Art in the Eighteenth Century* (exhib. cat.), London: Royal Academy, and New Haven: Yale University Press, 1994, pp.32–33

Persicini, Petronio, *Andrea Brustoloni scultore bellunese: Notizie biografiche ed artistiche*, Padua: Stabilmento Prosperini, 1882

Buckland, William 1734–1774

American architect and carver

In colonial America, master builders, house joiners, and gentlemen were occasionally referred to as architects. Although many were distinguished for their technical expertise, ability to oversee a workforce, and basic knowledge of classical form and detail, few were architects in the strict sense of the word and fewer ventured into other areas of design. A notable exception is William Buckland, whose designs for public and private buildings and furniture in Virginia and Maryland justify his claim to the title, architect.

Buckland was born in the parish of St. Peter's-in-the-East, Oxford, England, in 1734 and trained as a joiner by his uncle James Buckland of London. On 4 August, 1755 – approximately four months after his apprenticeship expired – Buckland signed an indenture with Thomas Mason of Fairfax County, Virginia, agreeing to serve the former's "Executors or Assigns in ... Virginia" for four years. In turn Buckland received free passage to the colonies, food, lodging, and an annual salary of £20 sterling.

Thomas Mason acted as an agent for his older brother George, a prominent northern Virginia planter who had recently begun building Gunston Hall about ten miles south of Alexandria. Although the exterior walls of Gunston Hall probably were complete when Buckland arrived in November, it is likely that he designed the portico on the "south front." The portico closely resembles a garden temple in William Paine's *The Builder's Companion and Workman's General Assistant* (1758). Both designs are based on a hexagon and have Doric friezes, broad engaged pilasters, and Gothic arches.

The floor plan of Gunston Hall is similar to many other five-bay Virginia houses. On the first storey there is a wide central hall that accommodates the stair, and provides access to four rooms of approximately equal size. Both the hall and the southwest room are almost completely within the Palladian tradition. The hall has a Doric entablature and fourteen engaged pilasters, two of which act as imposts for elliptical arches. Functioning as a support for the floor at the top of the stair, the arches have keystones with toed back mouldings, a large pendant drop, and carved spandrel appliqués. The stair has intricately carved walnut brackets and newell posts and originally had a large frieze appliqué.

Buckland's acute understanding of classical form and detail was the result of his training and his familiarity with published designs. His estate inventory included fifteen architectural design books, furniture design books, and builders' guides. He probably purchased most of the books before leaving England, but at least four were acquired after his arrival. Buckland frequently borrowed designs from these sources. The acanthus appliqués on the windows and doors in the southwest room, for example, are based on the crossette appliqués on pl. 75 in Batty Langley's *The City &. Country Builder's and Workman's Treasury of Designs* (1740), a book Buckland owned.

The northwest room is one of the most fully developed interiors in the Chinese taste. Passion for Chinoiserie design was well established in English architecture before Buckland's move to Virginia, in part owing to publications such as William Halfpenny's *New Designs for Chinese Temples, Triumphal Arches, Garden Seats, Palings &c.* (1750) and George Edwards' and Matthias Darly's *A New Book of Chinese Designs* (1754). However, there is no design in these books that precisely matches Buckland's treatment of the windows and doors, which suggests that he was either working from memory or simply borrowing conventional "Chinese" details, such as scalloped cresting and imbricated consoles, from published sources. The only book in Buckland's library with similar details was Thomas Chippendale's *The Gentleman and Cabinet-Maker's Director* (1754).

For the execution of his designs, Buckland relied on local artisans. A suit for back wages filed by joiner James Brent provides information on tradesmen in Buckland's crew. On 6 July, 1763, Brent presented a list of outstanding wages and expenses incurred on Buckland's behalf including a "Pare Shoes" purchased for carver William Bernard Sears in 1759. Sears's son, Charles Lee, maintained that his father was indentured to Mason and that he executed the carving in Gunston Hall. The designs of the carved mouldings, appliqués, and other ornaments in Gunston Hall probably represent the collaborative efforts of Sears and Buckland; however, the former was entirely responsible for their interpretation in wood. Buckland and Sears also made at least four side chairs for Gunston Hall. Only a fragment of one survives, but its fret legs, carved brackets, and rail shaping are related to those of a Chinese chair illustrated on pl. 25 in Chippendale's *Director*.

Most of the interior work in Gunston Hall was completed when Buckland's indenture expired. On 8 November, 1759, Mason wrote, "I can with great Justice recommend him to any Gentleman ... I think him a complete Master of the Carpenter's &. Joiners Business both in Theory &. Practice." Mason's endorsement and social connections undoubtedly helped Buckland secure other commissions.

In 1761 Buckland moved to Richmond County, Virginia and settled near the town of Warsaw. By December of that year, he was working for John Tayloe II (1721–79), a wealthy planter who was either completing or remodeling his house, Mt. Airy. As at Gunston Hall, the masonry work probably was complete before Buckland's arrival. Although the interior of Mt. Airy burned in 1844, fragments of carved cornice moulding and three tables attributed to Buckland and Sears survive. The architectonic form of these tables and their carved details suggest that Buckland designed them to complement the interior woodwork in the house, much as he would have learned to do in England. One example is based on the sideboard table on pl. 38 of Chippendale's *Director*, but the large egg and tongue moulding, rope moulding, and circular fret match details in both Mt. Airy and Gunston Hall.

Buckland and Sears probably parted ways about 1765, after completing their work at Mt. Airy. Sears evidently moved to Loudoun County, Virginia and Buckland remained in Richmond County where his shop continued to produce furniture and architectural components and drawings. Between 1765 and 1771, Buckland took two apprentices and hired a "London Carver a masterly Hand." In November 1771, he and several of his tradesmen moved to Annapolis, Maryland to complete the large, five-bay townhouse that Edward Lloyd IV had recently purchased from Samuel Chase. Lloyd undoubtedly learned of Buckland from his father-in-law, John Tayloe II.

Lloyd's patronage enabled Buckland to escape the predominantly rural confines of Virginia's Tidewater region and move to a small, prosperous city during an unprecedented period of construction and renovation. At least fourteen townhouses were built in Annapolis between 1764 and 1774. Although Buckland's Maryland career lasted only three years, he has been erroneously credited with work on at least fifteen structures in the Annapolis vicinity and on Maryland's eastern shore. To date, only two houses and three public buildings can be firmly associated with his shop.

The woodwork on the first two floors of the Chase-Lloyd House occupied most of Buckland's workforce through April 1773. The floor plan features a wide central hall with an Ionic screen dividing the entrance from the stair. The stair rises from the center of the hall, divides at a landing with an ornately carved Venetian window, and terminates in a short hall with niches for sculpture. The dining room, which is the most ornate space in the house, has doors with gadrooned surrounds with floral appliqués in the crossettes, acanthus-carved trusses, pitched pediments with carved mouldings and frets, and Rococo frieze appliqués with bird heads and leafage derived from a design for a stair bracket on pl. 39 in Abraham Swan's *British Architect* (1745). The windows also have gadrooned surrounds, but they rest on paneled plinths with applied garlands of fruit and flowers.

The carving in the Chase-Lloyd House is attributed to Thomas Hall, a London artisan who was indentured to Buckland. Hall ran away in December 1773, but soon returned to his master's service. Judging from Buckland's advertisements for runaway servants – primarily bricklayers and plasterers – his workforce grew considerably after his arrival in Annapolis.

Unlike Buckland's previous work, the commission that he undertook for Lloyd's neighbor Mathias Hammond in 1774 involved furnishing both interior and exterior plans and elevations. Although construction may have begun in April, Buckland's death in December prevented him from seeing its completion. Nevertheless, evidence that Buckland designed the house is found in the final account of his estate and in artist Charles Willson Peale's depiction of Buckland working on the exterior elevations and floor plan. Despite Buckland's untimely death, the Hammond house was completed as drawn. With its two-storey, five-bay central block and half octagon wings, it is one of the most ambitious townhouses surviving from the colonial period. The large southeast room on the first floor has an ornate carved chimneypiece and three windows and doors, all with entablatures with carved trusses, mouldings, and appliqués. The latter are also based on pl. 39 in the *British Architect*, but the flow of the design and articulation of the leafage is more in the Neo-Classical taste. This stylistic shift may reflect the influence of Thomas Hall who worked in London during the late 1760s.

In addition to working on the Chase-Lloyd and Mathias Hammond houses, Buckland executed plans for a court house and prison in Caroline County, Maryland and received £25 for "expenses and services relative to the Public Building" in Annapolis. The latter may have referred to plans and elevations for the Senate Chamber in the State House. His Annapolis shop also produced a few pieces of furniture. The commissioners of the loan office paid him £16.12.6 for "one Large Double Desk" and miscellaneous repairs and his inventory listed table and picture frames.

During the 1750s and 1760s, Buckland referred to himself as a "house joiner" or a "house joiner and cabinetmaker," but in a letter written on 7 November 1772 he described himself as a "Citizen of the City of Annapolis ... Architect." This shift in self-perception was undoubtedly brought on by his growing prominence as a designer of domestic and public buildings and furniture. Today there is little dispute that Buckland was one of colonial America's greatest architects.

LUKE BECKERDITE

Biography

Born in Oxford, England, 1734. Apprenticed as a joiner to his uncle, James Buckland, London, 1749–55. Served indentures as a cabinet-maker and house-joiner under Thomas Mason, Fairfax County, Virginia, 1755–59. Active as an architect and carver in Richmond

County, Virginia, with workshops producing furniture and architectural components, from 1761. Moved to Annapolis, Maryland, 1771. Died in Annapolis in December 1774.

Selected Works

Examples of furniture attributed to Buckland's workshop are in the collection of the Museum of Early Southern Decorative Arts, Winston-Salem, North Carolina, and in the Colonial Williamsburg Foundation, Williamsburg, Virginia. Carving attributed to Buckland's workshop survives in Gunston Hall, Virginia, the Chase-Lloyd House, Annapolis, and the Mathias Hammond House, Annapolis. Notable design book collections related to Buckland are in the Redwood Library, Newport, Rhode Island, the Winterthur Museum, Delaware, the Metropolitan Museum of Art, New York, and the High Point Furniture Library, High Point, North Carolina.

Interiors

1755–63	Gunston Hall, Fairfax County, Virginia (south portico, interior and some furnishings): George Mason
1760	Truro Parish Glebe House, Fairfax County, Virginia (£93.2.0 received for unspecified work)
1761–64	Mt. Airy, Richmond County, Virginia (interior and some furnishings): John Tayloe II
1768	Richmond County Workhouse, Virginia (building and interiors)
1771–73	Chase-Lloyd House, Annapolis, Maryland (some exterior woodwork and interior): Edward Lloyd IV
1774	Mathias Hammond House, Annapolis, Maryland (exterior and interiors)
1774	Prison, Caroline County, Maryland (plans and elevations)
1774	State House, Annapolis, Maryland (£25 received for unspecified services, possibly plans for the Senate Chamber)

Further Reading

For the most recent studies of Buckland's work see Beckerdite 1982 and 1995.

Beckerdite, Luke, "William Buckland and William Bernard Sears: The Designer and the Carver" in *Journal of Early Southern Decorative Arts*, November 1982

Beckerdite, Luke, "William Buckland Reconsidered: Architectural Carving in Chesapeake, Maryland, 1771–1774" in *Journal of Early Southern Decorative Arts*, November 1982

Beckerdite, Luke, "Architect-Designed Furniture in Eighteenth-Century Virginia: The Work of William Buckland and William Bernard Sears" in *American Furniture*, Hanover, NH: University Press of New England for the Chipstone Foundation, 1995, pp.28–48

Beirne, Rosamond Randall and John Henry Scarff, *William Buckland, 1734–1774: Architect of Virginia and Maryland*, Baltimore: Maryland Historical Society, 1958

Brand, Barbara A., *The Work of William Buckland in Maryland, 1771–1774*, M.A. thesis, Charlottesville: University of Virginia, 1978

Buckland: Master Builder of the 18th Century, Gunston Hall, 1977

Davis, Deering, *Annapolis Houses, 1700–1775*, New York: Bonanza, 1947

Kimball, Fiske, "Gunston Hall" in *Journal of the Society of Architectural Historians*, 13, 1954, pp.3–8

Lounsbury, Carl, "An Elegant and Commodious Building: William Buckland and the Design of the Prince William County Courthouse" in *Journal of the Society of Architectural Historians*, 46, September 1987, pp.228–40

Monroe, Elizabeth Brand, *William Buckland in the Northern Neck*, M.A. thesis, Charlottesville: University of Virginia, 1975

Buffets, Cupboards and Sideboards

The basic need for receptacles for the purposes of storage and display has been fulfilled by the development of buffets, cupboards and dressers, and sideboards (or sideboard tables). These terms are mainly used to define pieces of furniture associated with rooms intended for eating – whether the hall, parlour or dining room. As a separate development – cupboards with fitted shelves for linen or pegs for hanging clothes are generally intended for bedrooms and became known as presses (*armoires* in France), while medieval "cubbordes of boxes" or "tills" were to develop into chests of drawers.

In the Middle Ages receptacles enclosed by doors were known in England as "aumbries" — the cupboards as such being an open structure of shelves or "bordes" on which were placed cups, both for use and for display. This corresponds to the French *buffet* – a term not apparently used in England with this meaning until the late 17th century. There are many illustrations and descriptions of these "riche cupbordes well and richly garnyshed" with silver and silver gilt objects. "Dressoirs" or dressers performed the same function, with the objects arranged in tiers according to the etiquette of the time and the status of the owner, "the largest firste, the richest in the myddis, the lightest before". By the early 16th century aumbries and cupboards had begun to combine as single pieces of furniture and the former term fell into disuse. They were often fitted into the panelling of a room, sometimes with canopies over them as can be seen in Holbein's drawing of Sir Thomas More and his family. If found in bedchambers they might have been described as "livery cupboards" after the nightly delivery of refreshments for a nobleman or his honoured guests.

When in use the shelves or tops of cupboards would be covered with a cloth from a variety of different materials, white diaper (with the ends falling down each side), damask, velvets or Turkey work. Closed aumbries for the storage of food had also appeared by the late 15th century – characterised by pierced panels with late Gothic tracery patterns, to be placed in the Solar or Great Hall.

Cupboards intended for the dining room, hall or parlour of the prosperous Elizabethan or Jacobean household developed as two-tier structures: either with an open lower section, with doors flanked by panels (often splayed) in the upper section; or with both upper and lower sections entirely enclosed. They often show the full range of Mannerist ornament – posts with bulbous "cup and cover" or figurative carving, low relief strapwork or inlaid decoration with arabesques. In France they inevitably show ornamental ideas derived from Fontainebleau. The chief purpose of these pieces was for the storage of utensils required for dining "cups and glasses to drink in, spoons, sugar box, viall and cruces for vinegar, oyle and mustard pot". The Court Cupboard which developed at the end of the 16th century was intended entirely for display: they derive from the French word *court* to distinguish them from their taller cousins. They consist of three open shelves supported by posts, sometimes with drawers in the frieze.

All three types of cupboards fell out of favour in the mid 17th century except in country areas where they frequently developed regional characteristics: in Wales the deuddarn or

Buffets from Vredeman de Vries' *Verscheyden schrynwerck*, 1630 (reprint of *Differents pourtraicts*, c.1585)

tridarn types; in northern England with distinctive variations in ornamental details. In more metropolitan circles they were replaced by marble-top side tables which were often supplied in pairs. Dining rooms in the grandest houses now contained virtually no cupboard or drawer furniture for storage; the sole purpose of these sidetables (or "sideboard tables") being to display plate in the renewed vigour of the Baroque style. New types of silver objects for the sideboard now emerged. In addition to purely ornamental pieces, the fountain and monteith were now used for rinsing glasses, the wine cooler and cistern were also used for rinsing glasses, while salvers and waiters were needed for the service of wine. In addition baskets for bread and cruet frames for condiments were now all to be found. The Hall of the Teutonic Knights in Berlin shows the style at its most extreme, while at Castle Howard in the early 18th century there were two sets of sideboard plate – one in white silver for everyday, the second in gilt for best. Lady Grisell Baillie descibed the essential items required for the well-appointed sideboard in the early 18th century: "Bread, Water Peper, Vinegar, ail, wines, Mustard, Shalot, Smal Beer, sugerr, Oyle, Sallad".

In more modest houses the dresser reappeared, generally consisting of a long narrow table with a deep frieze containing drawers, but sometimes with closed cupboards in the lower section. They also acquired superstructures with further open shelves intended for storage and display of earthenware or pewter.

The architectual and decorative styles of the early 18th century dictated the forms and ornament of such pieces of furniture as well as the etiquette and traditions of the time. Often the grander sideboard tables correspond to pier or side tables placed below mirrors and between mirrors in other rooms of the house. The Palladian style inspired "the sumptuous sideboard [which to] an ingenious eye has often more the air of an altar than a table", while Chippendale provided designs for whimsical variations in Rococo, Gothick and Chinoiserie tastes. Corner cupboards, in one or two stages, or on stands, or of the hanging variety, appear in the late 17th century, sometimes built-in to the panelling of a room. If they were open they were used for the display of china; if they had doors they were frequently japanned in imitation of lacquer. Alcove cupboards, both open and closed, served the same purpose, especially on the Continent. However, the appearance of glazed "china cupboards" by the mid century sounded the death knell of this former type.

The idea of a special recess in the dining room to accommodate a side table and sometimes tiers of shelves became a common enough feature in Continental Europe from the late

17th century. In England, where they appear more rarely, they are known as buffets. It was not until the early Neo-Classical period that semi-domed niches with a fitted side table (or sometimes three) became a feature. At Kedleston Hall, Derbyshire, Robert Adam designed just such a bespoke feature, also suggesting the ideal arrangement of the Scarsdale family silver, their knife boxes, jasper cistern and new-fangled *athenienne* or perfume burner. It was but a short step from here to the development of the matching five-piece suite: the sideboard table (often with a brass rail for hanging a protective cloth and for supporting candle branches), two pedestals with vases (for a variety of useful purposes), a wine cooler beneath, and a pier glass or mirror above. Hepplewhite illustrates such an arrangement in his *Cabinet Maker and Upholsterer's Guide* (3rd edition 1794, pl. 124). For less ambitious households new shaped sideboards, with hollow fronts and lateral drawers or cupboards, appeared from c.1780 from commercial firms like Gillows. With the emergence of the Regency style such pieces, inevitably Grecian, took on a new massiveness according to the taste of the time.

The 19th century saw the proliferation of new designs and styles for sideboards of all sorts, many intended for entirely new locations in the household or public building. Some of the most spectacular pieces shown at the international exhibitions were described as sideboards – the *Wines and Spirits* Sideboard by William Burges (1862), the Pet Sideboard by Bruce Talbert (1872). They ceased to belong exclusively to the dining room – drawing rooms now acquired pieces with identical features, often surmounted by vast mirrors and containing open shelves and glazed cupboards intended for the display of *objets d'art* of all kinds. Often these were supplied as part of a suite of furniture in a particular style – Gothic, Anglo-Japanese, "Artistic", New Art, or the revived 18th-century styles towards the end of the century. For the past hundred years the sideboard and cupboard have shown little development: storage and display problems have been resolved by different types of furniture.

JAMES LOMAX

See also Cabinets

Further Reading

Ames, Kenneth L., "The Battle of the Sideboards" in *Winterthur Portfolio*, IX, 1974, pp.1–27

Eames, Penelope, *Furniture in England, France and the Netherlands from the Twelfth to the Fifteenth Century*, London: Furniture History Society, 1977

Gilbert, Christopher, *English Vernacular Furniture*, 1750–1900, New Haven and London: Yale University Press, 1991

Glanville, Philippa, *Silver in Tudor and Early Stuart England*, London: Victoria and Albert Museum, 1990

MacQuoid, Percy and Ralph Edwards, *The Dictionary of English Furniture*, revised edition, 3 vols., 1954; reprinted Woodbridge, Suffolk: Antique Collectors' Club, 1983

Thornton, Peter, "Two Problems" in *Furniture History*, 7, 1971, pp.61–71

Thornton, Peter, *Seventeenth-Century Interior Decoration in England, France, and Holland*, New Haven and London: Yale University Press, 1978

Walkling, Gillian, "Sideboards" in *Connoisseur*, CCII, November 1979, pp.156–60

Bugatti, Carlo 1856–1940

Italian designer of furniture and interiors

Father of Ettore, the celebrated automobile designer, and the sculptor Rembrandt, Carlo Bugatti has been somewhat overshadowed by his sons and, with much of his work in private hands, his life and work are still comparatively little known. Born in Milan in 1856, he was active in a number of different media and worked variously as a designer of furniture, interiors and silverware and as a painter. His most significant work, however, was the furniture and interiors that he designed in the late 19th and early 20th centuries which combined exotic materials and rich decoration in a highly original and eccentric way. He participated in several of the major international exhibitions of this period and his emphasis upon craftsmanship was very much in keeping with the concerns of other 19th-century artists and designers. Yet, described as an "isolated genius", he was fiercely jealous of his independence; he did not ally himself with any particular group or movement and the radical individuality of his designs defies classification.

He was the son of the sculptor Giovanni Luigi Bugatti, whose diverse interests also included architecture and science, and it is not perhaps surprising that Carlo's career should have embraced several design disciplines. He studied art at the Brera Academy of Art in Milan, although in later years he tried to give the impression that he had received no formal training. An early interest in architecture gave way to a concentration upon furniture and interiors, and he then moved on to jewellery, sculpture and even musical instruments in the latter part of his career.

He viewed the design and making of furniture as a form of pure art and took pains to master the techniques appropriate to different materials. This facilitated a close understanding of the individual properties of each medium and allowed him to manipulate and exploit materials in a unique and highly personal way. The development of his furniture can be divided into three phases: in the first his work has been described as "quaint and whimsical"; in the second he became bolder, relying on the circle, or parts of the circle, as the foundation for the design; and in the third phase his work became increasingly fluid and sculptural in form.

Bugatti's earliest known furniture is the bedroom suite he designed and made as a wedding present for his sister in 1880. This suite consisted of a pair of chairs, a bed-head and footboard, and bedside cabinets. The pieces are constructed out of heavy, dark timber, and their geometric forms are alleviated only by asymmetrical features and the elaboration of the decoration. Applied wrought copper and fine fenestrations, combined with friezes of inlaid wood and ivory reflect the influence of contemporary fashions, and the impact of exotic Middle Eastern and Japanese styles, which were extremely popular during this period, are clearly evident in this work.

It was also during this phase of his career that Bugatti exhibited at the Italian Exhibition at Earl's Court, London (1888), where he was awarded a Diploma of Honour in recognition of the originality of his designs. In the same year he established his own workshops in Milan for the commercial production of his furniture. In 1900 he was commissioned to provide furniture for the Khedive's Palace, Istanbul, a project that underlined his skill in adapting the Moorish style for contemporary European furniture. In 1901 Bugatti executed his first complete interior, The Flowers Room, for the first Lord Battersea in London. Every detail of the room was subjected to Bugatti's discerning eye and the result was a sumptuous theatrical statement of pure opulence.

During the 1890s the second distinct phase of Bugatti's work had begun to emerge. The solid timber structure remained along with increasing use of materials such as vellum set against intricate inlaid metal borders and ornament inlaid in ivory and mother-of-pearl. But his style developed away from picturesque asymmetry towards more balanced geometric shapes and there was much greater emphasis upon the circle as the dominant form. A typical example is the desk in the Metropolitan Museum, New York.

The Decorative Arts Exhibition in Turin (1902) marked the beginning of Bugatti's third, "organic" phase. He exhibited furniture within complete room-sets that illustrated the type of decoration and accessories that would be appropriate for his work. Placed against a backdrop of panelled walls and richly patterned carpets, Bugatti's furniture was almost completely covered in vellum, and the vellum itself was also decorated. The most extravagant of his room-sets was the Camera del Bovolo or Snail Room which included a table and chairs and high-backed banquette seats whose forms were based on the snail-shell spirals. The furniture was extremely sculptural and combined sweeping curves with geometric decoration. Its extraordinarily eccentric style anticipates some of the African-inspired furnishings produced some twenty years later by Art Deco designers such as Pierre Legrain and Armand-Albert Rateau. In recognition of his originality, Bugatti received another Diploma of Honour for this work.

In 1904 Bugatti moved to Paris. His furniture business was sold to the Milanese firm of De Vecchi who continued to produce his work. Bugatti himself became more involved in producing designs for silverware, and an exhibition of his work in 1907 illustrates his unique ability to mix different materials harmoniously, displaying pieces with delicate combinations of silver, ivory and turquoise. He continued to exhibit designs at the Salon des Artistes Décorateurs in 1910 and 1911 but in 1913 his wife's ill-health forced him to leave Paris and he concentrated increasingly on painting. Lacking any pupils or direct imitators, he was nevertheless the only Italian designer of the late 19th and early 20th century to gain international recognition and acclaim, and his work stands out as virtually unique for its time.

RACHEL E. FRENCH

Biography

Born in Milan, 12 February 1856, the son of the sculptor Giovanni Luigi Bugatti. Studied architecture at the Accademia di Belle Arti de Brera, Milan, late 1870s. Married Therèse Lovioli in 1880 (died 1935): 1 daughter, and 2 sons, the automobile designer Ettore and the sculptor Rembrandt. Designed his earliest known furniture, 1880; established a commercial workshop for the production of furniture in Milan, 1888. Exhibited at several national and international exhibitions; awarded Diploma of Honour, Italian Exhibition, London, 1888, and Turin, 1902; silver medal, Exposition Universelle, Paris, 1900. Sold furniture-making business to De Vecchi and moved to Paris c.1904; took up painting. Exhibited silverware at the Galerie Hébrard, Paris, 1907, and at the Salon des Artistes-Décorateurs, 1910 and 1911. Moved to Pierrefonds c.1910; moved to Molsheim c.1937. Died near Molsheim in April 1940.

Selected Works

Much of Bugatti's work is in private collections but examples of his furniture can be seen in the Museum and Art Gallery, Brighton, Sussex, the Musée des Arts Décoratifs, Paris, and the Metropolitan Museum of Art, New York. A chair from the Camera del Bovolo is in the Brooklyn Museum, New York.

Interiors

c.1901	Bedroom for Cyril Flowers, 1st Lord Battersea
1902	International Exhibition of Decorative Art, Turin (four rooms, including the Camera del Bovolo or Snail Room)

Further Reading

A useful introduction to Bugatti's career is Haslam, 1979; the most extensive coverage of his work, including many archive photographs of his furniture, is Dejean 1982.

Anscombe, Isabelle, "The Amazing Bugattis" in *Connoisseur*, 201, August 1979, pp.224–29

Brunhammer, Yvonne and others, *Art Nouveau: Belgium / France* (exhib. cat.), Houston: Rice University Institute of the Arts, 1976

Bugatti, L'Ebé, *The Bugatti Story*, London: Souvenir Press, and Philadelphia: Chilton, 1967

Die Bugattis (exhib. cat.), Hamburg: Museum für Kunst und Gewerbe, 1983

Calloway, Stephen, *Twentieth-Century Decoration: The Domestic Interior from 1900 to the Present Day*, London: Weidenfeld and Nicolson, and New York: Rizzoli, 1988

Dejean, Philippe, *Bugatti: Carlo, Rembrandt, Ettore, Jean*, New York: Rizzoli, 1982

Haslam, Malcolm and others, *The Amazing Bugattis* (exhib. cat.), London: Design Council, 1979

Jervis, Simon, "Carlo Bugatti" in *Arte Illustrata*, no.3, 1970

Rutherford, Jessica, *Art Nouveau, Art Deco and the Thirties: The Furniture Collections at Brighton Museum*, Brighton: Royal Pavilion Art Gallery and Museums, 1983

Spadini, Pasqualina and Mario Paola Maino, *Carlo Bugatti: I mobili scultura* (exhib. cat.), Rome: Galleria dell' Emporio Floreale, 1976

Built-in Furniture

Furniture that is made as an integral part of the fabric of a building, or built-in as an addition, has a very long history. It has been an essential part of the Japanese interior for many centuries, and has been part of the Western furnishing environment since the earliest homes.

Among some of the earliest surviving furniture are the built-in bednooks, cupboards and "dresser" located in the Neolithic settlement of Skara Brae in the Orkneys. Constructed from stone at the same time as the house, this built-in furniture was an integral part of the interior as well as the fabric of the building. This tradition continued into medieval churches, where stone seats and benches were commonly built into walls of chapter houses and choirs. In medieval domestic dwellings, the use of fixed wooden benches was common in a range of houses up to the 17th century. In addition to benches, cupboards and beds were among other furniture that was built-in. The space-saving reasons are clear, but questions of hygiene in the case of food, and personal comfort and privacy in the case of beds, gave a range of reasons in addition to the cost savings that might be achieved by building in furniture during the construction of a house.

Changes in the use of built-in furniture occurred as the well-to-do became less peripatetic and demanded more versatile moveable furniture for their interiors, as opposed to the built-in items that were located in the less genteel sorts of dwellings. What this meant was that built-in furniture generally remained a less important form of furnishing in high-style interiors, yet continued to be highly important to the vernacular buildings. Indeed, built-in furniture was the rule in most commonplace buildings up to the 19th century.

The forms of built-in furniture often varied with the locality. In Devon, for example, farmhouses often had a kitchen with a fixed wooden bench under a window wall to be used in conjunction with a long table. A deep recess next to the fireplace had a large built-in cupboard which was used for storage and display, while a built-in corner cupboard was also on the other side of the hearth for storage. In the north of England, it was common to screen off the inglenook by a wooded seat called a heck or speer, built into a wall divider. The spice cupboards of the Lake District are an early indication of a pragmatic solution to a problem by using built-in storage. By building a cupboard in the wall where a fire was made, and fitting it with a tight door, the cupboard interior could be kept dry for salt, spices, etc., and yet remain convenient for cooking. These wall cupboards are also found in other parts of northern England from a later date.

The best known examples of historic built-in furniture are beds. Various arrangements of built-in beds have existed for many centuries, but it was in Scotland that the built-in wall or cupboard bed tradition was most strong. The box beds were clearly intended to provide privacy and a degree of warmth in a one- or two-room house. This Scottish custom remained in both the remote highland and island areas as well as in the lowland areas (for example in Robert Owen's New Lanark as well as urban tenement blocks) well into the 20th century.

In some cases wall and furniture were combined in that the built-in furniture in one room served as a wall on the other side. Sometimes these pieces were used in conjunction with an added partition wall. Long lateral settles, or large press beds were used in these cases, being common in North Wales and Ireland until the beginning of the 20th century. Another way of saving space and money, was by building-in a cabinet across a corner. J.C. Loudon's *Encyclopaedia* (1833) described such an item: "the shelves, which are supposed to be of deal, are let into the plaster; and the whole, outside, and inside, including the plaster between the shelves is painted of a wainscot colour. The cost will be considerably diminished by having the upper doors in single wooden panels."

Other built-in furniture of various kinds has also been part of the interior furnishings of vernacular houses. Hinged wall-mounted tables, larders, closets, alcove cupboards and a wide variety of specialist storage cabinets, often related to particular geographical areas are among the diverse range of built-in furniture.

However, not all built-in furniture was associated with the vernacular or common home. In the late 17th century, Cornelius Meyer (1629–1701) published designs for an amazing arrangement of built-in and folding fixtures and fittings to furnish his famous one-room fantasy. During the later 17th and 18th centuries, certain forms of high-style built-in furniture were in vogue. Room arrangements by such designers as Jean Berain and J.-F. Blondel often included luxurious beds built into niches, built-in buffets fitted into wall panelling, and sofas designed to fit into particular parts of the schemes in conjunction with the panelled wall designs. On a less grand scale, the built-in alcove was a feature of the first half of the 18th century. These display niches were often surmounted with a decorated semi-hemispherical head with pilasters framing the recess. These recesses became less popular with the decline of panelled walls, but have experienced a revival in some later 20th century interiors.

The development of libraries in the 17th century, and their wide acceptance in the 18th century, promoted a demand for book storage for which the built-in bookcase provided the ideal answer. In many instances they were contrived as part of the architectural shell of the room and were treated as such by the architect. The library at Ham House, Richmond (1670s) has built-in book storage as well as an integral writing cabinet. The library at the Hôtel de Lauzun, Paris, was devised so that books were stored in cupboards, whose doors were part of the integrated panelling scheme. Adam's magnificent Neo-Classical library at Osterley Park is an example of the grand architectural treatment that was popular in the 18th century.

During the 19th century, the American Shaker sects espoused the idea of built-in furniture. They produced elegant and functional built-in cupboards, chests and storage pieces designed to avoid clutter and display and to satisfy their creed of cleanliness and tidiness.

By the later 19th century the traditional built-in inglenooks of cottage homes were adapted to the Arts and Crafts-influenced middle-class tastes of the time. In addition to this revival there was a taste for built-in window seats and the so-called "cosy corner". The latter, which may have derived from medieval originals, were designed to be free-standing or built-in as an integral part of the wall. Cosy-corners often emphasised elaborate upholstery and carved features to promote an air of luxury and exoticism.

In contrast to the frivolous nature of the Victorian cosy-corner, at the turn of the 20th century, built-in furniture was seriously considered for its practical advantages. The taste for built-in wardrobes in the early 20th century was noted by the German architect, Hermann Muthesius. In his *The English House* he recorded that "built-in cupboards form a major element in the treatment of walls and are the most characteristic feature of the modern English bedroom". Although Muthesius warned against excessive built-in mania, he generally agreed with R.W. Edis, who, twenty years before, had recommended built-in cupboards in his *Healthy Furniture and Decoration*, as being hygienic. Muthesius added that they were also artistically advantageous "as they kept the room free and empty, so creating an impression of space and size". However, even such an apostle as Muthesius railed against the taste for built-in wash-stands which he considered were most unsuitable for their purpose.

During the 20th century, built-in furniture has developed from a vernacular necessity and a response to Victorian concerns with hygiene, to become a ubiquitous part of interior design and furnishings. The combination of apparent cleanliness, simple function, space-saving, and the integrated nature of built-in furniture meant that it satisfied most requirements on one level or another. The idea of built-in furniture was soon sold to the new generations of home-makers. Again the reasons were more often practical than aesthetic. Christine Frederick, in her *Household Engineering*, had designed a house that could be maintained solely by a housewife. No doubt influenced by developments in office and factory planning and layout, she achieved this improvement by reducing the size of rooms, and also in the extensive use of built-in furniture. Her main reason for using this form of furniture was that it never needed moving and it made cleaning simpler.

In contrast to the purely practical aspects of built-in furniture was the growing desire on the part of some architects for a modern integrated building incorporating shell, interior, and furnishings. Frank Lloyd Wright in his "In the Cause of Architecture" (*Architectural Record*, March 1908) pointed out the role of built-in furniture in this integration process: "The most truly satisfactory apartments are those in which most or all of the furniture is built in as a part of the original scheme". When this concept was combined with ideas of cleanliness, function, practicality, space-saving and convenience, it is easy to see how built-in furniture was espoused by the new generation of Modernist architects. For example, Le Corbusier in his Villa Savoye, Pierre Chareau and the Maison de Verre, and Rietveld's Schröder House demonstrate the remarkable cohesion that built-in furniture and fittings can give to an architectural concept. The concept of built-in went hand in hand with ideas of function and rationality, so it is no surprise to find that fitted furnishings were soon part of the repertoire of most advanced architects. From these radical examples, along with the ideas of scientific management, built-in furniture was to become one of the hallmarks of most Modernist interiors.

By the second half of the 20th century some of the pre-war Functionalist architects' ideas were used in a diluted form in general practice. Built-in furniture was to gain wide acceptance both in new building (especially flats) and in re-planned private interiors. In this period, flat dwellers were seen as particularly lucky in that built-in furniture was usually supplied as a matter of course.

In 1947 *Modern Homes Illustrated* praised built-in furniture as being labour-saving and space-saving, and for "living" it was seen as especially suitable for small homes. Traditional ideas were revived and recommended. A built-in sideboard between the kitchen and dining room, with a hatch and two-way drawers was seen as a valuable feature. Another reclaimed idea was to have cupboards built-in as a double wall between two bedrooms, so that one half served one room and the other half served the other room. This was successfully incorporated into English prefabricated housing after World War II.

In the second half of the 20th century, "built-in" furniture has become the norm for many parts of an interior. The availability of pre-prepared and packaged panels and parts all made to standard modules, in combination with the expansion of the DIY trade, has led to the irresistible rise of the fitted kitchen and bedroom. In addition, the boom in the DIY sector has encouraged home-makers to build in their own fixtures, whether shelves in alcoves or fully fitted kitchens. In Europe it is common for a residence to have very little free-standing furniture (except for chairs), the rest of the storage requirement being built-in. A more recent trend has been the fitting of customised furniture, designed for individual rooms and built-in by a joiner.

CLIVE D. EDWARDS

Further Reading

Calloway, Stephen and Elizabeth Cromley (editors), *The Elements of Style: A Practical Encyclopedia of Interior Architectural Details from 1485 to the Present*, London: Mitchell Beazley, and New York: Simon and Schuster, 1991

Gilbert, Christopher, *English Vernacular Furniture, 1750–1900*, New Haven and London: Yale University Press, 1991

Girouard, Mark, *The Victorian Country House*, revised edition New Haven and London: Yale University Press, 1979

Jervis, Simon, "Multum in Parvo" in *Furniture History*, XXI, June 1985, pp.126–31

Kinmonth, Claudia, *Irish Country Furniture, 1700–1950*, New Haven and London: Yale University Press, 1993

Long, Helen C., *The Edwardian House: The Middle-Class Home in Britain, 1880–1914*, Manchester: Manchester University Press, 1993

Meier-Menzel, H.J. and others, *Fitted Furniture*, London: Iliffe, 1967

Muthesius, Hermann, *The English House*, edited by Dennis Sharp, London: Crosby Lockwood Staples, and New York: Rizzoli, 1979 (German original 3 vols., 1904–05, revised edition 1908–11)

Bulfinch, Charles 1763–1844

American architect

No practitioner in design better represents America's Federal period than Boston's Charles Bulfinch. Born in the decisive year of 1763, when the Colonial period began its road to Revolution, he died in 1844, during a powerful era of expansion in the USA. Scion of an old Boston family, Bulfinch graduated from Harvard in 1781, just before the close of the Revolution, and entered young manhood in a time of great prosperity for Boston.

Interested in architecture, and somewhat familiar with its principles through a small but select library of architecture books owned by his grandfather, Bulfinch visited England, France, and Italy between 1785 and 1787. In England he became enthralled with the conservative Neo-Classicism then in the twilight of its popularity. He saw the work of William Chambers and the interior decorations of James Wyatt both at Heveningham Hall and at the Pantheon in London. In Paris he met Thomas Jefferson and the Marquis de Lafayette, who provided letters of introduction that admitted him to notable hôtels and châteaux. For several months he remained on the road in Italy, studying the classical ruins he had known heretofore in books in the Harvard library.

Back home in Boston he entered the field of design rather as a gentleman, enjoying, as he put it, a "season of leisure, pursuing no business, but giving gratuitous advice in Architecture." Among those he designed houses for was Joseph Barrell, a wealthy merchant and shipper. This villa summed up early the particular "style" with which Bulfinch was to captivate New England for an entire generation. Built of pinkish red-brick, with pine trim painted cold white, the Barrell house was in plan a rectangle, pierced by a semi-circular projection that rose from the ground, on above the second storey cornice line, and inside provided a saloon of that shape, rising a storey and a half and lighted by double bands of windows.

The plan is reminiscent of French houses of the time, with a succession of spaces climaxing in the saloon. As a surprise, a transverse hall featured a large "flying" staircase of wood, sweeping up in two ranges that united on a landing, then parted again to reach the second floor. Delicate composition ornaments appeared as Neo-Classical figures, urns, and swags and adorned the principal interiors as borders and also as ornament on door surrounds. The mantelpieces were marble. In the saloon a curved recess contained a stuffed satin *banquette*, with cushions laid against the wall. The pine floors were carpeted wall to wall. A bowed porch opened through the saloon's windows, giving a view over formal gardens and the river to Boston.

Barrell's house, the most ambitious of the early dwellings by Bulfinch, was considered the finest house in New England. Hardly had its paint dried when commissions came from the Secretary of War, Henry Knox, and also the fashionable beauty Mrs. Perez Morton. The latter's house was built of frame, somewhat resembling a traditional New England house, with embellishments. The interior, however, was very grand. Composition decorations were richly Adamesque with sunrays, pearl-beads, and garlands. The drawing room's coved ceiling was decorated with a deep swag of flowers.

Apparently Bulfinch accepted no fees for his work at this time. Possessed of family wealth, and living at home, he was a gentlemanly adviser, but one eagerly absorbing lessons in building from the tradesmen. From the first he had a strong affection for fine workmanship. His knowledge of construction grew, as his fascination with building increased. In 1796, at the zenith of Boston's post-Revolutionary boom, he persuaded his family to invest in a remarkable real estate development known as the Tontine Crescent, which he built a few blocks from the center of Boston. Tall and elegant, the Tontine houses were worthy of the Bath crescents that inspired them. Alas, in a temporary business slump, the Tontine Crescent threw Bulfinch and his kin into financial ruin.

All he had left was his architecture. He learned to charge fees, and though never a businessman, he struggled to make his projects support his family. Between 1796 and 1798 he completed his greatest public building, the Massachusetts State House, a direct although liberal borrowing from Chambers's Somerset House, which he had admired on his trip to England.

While the main influences on the structure are unquestionably English, Bulfinch also borrowed from A.-J. Gabriel's façades on the Place de la Concorde in Paris, and somewhat from the national capitol of the time, New York's Federal Hall, by Pierre Charles L'Enfant. The latter seems to have inspired a princely touch in interior decoration, which was rare in Bulfinch. The General Court, which stands behind a long columned porch, has colonnaded galleries and rich arcades fashioned into ashlar reminiscent of stonework; it is domed and embellished with elaborate Neo-Classical composition ornament set against smooth plaster walls. *Guilloche*, garlands, modillions, rosettes, Ionic-capped pilasters, immense bursts of leaves and flowers all characterize both General Court and Senate. Wood trim by comparison is somewhat plain, although finely moulded. Presumably the surfaces have always been white, as they usually are today, although it would not be hard to imagine the flat walls tinted, to emphasize the splendors of the composition ornament.

Row houses, churches, mansions, country residences, a prison, and remodelings of colonial buildings were projects he completed with distinction. His plans were often innovative, largely English, with French touches. The design themes of the interiors were nearly always the same, employing flat plaster, with composition embellishments. For the New South Church in Boston he devised a dome in plaster on lath, with deep spandrels; lesser groin vaults gave to the side aisles and altar area drama in light and shadow. At the Church of the Holy Cross, the ceiling is a shallow barrel vault crossed by smaller barrel vaults springing from Corinthian pilasters and lighted by arched windows.

Ironically, the best representative of his interiors is a painting which is one of the most valuable documents of America's Federal era, Henry Sargent's *The Dinner Party* (Museum of Fine Arts, Boston). It shows an interior – a ground floor dining room – in the Tontine Crescent. Spare in ornament, the room has a plaster cornice in white, against butter-yellow walls, with mahogany-grained doors and white mantel and door trimming. The floor is covered wall to wall with an ingrain carpet; red silk is swagged over the two windows, unlined, with light passing through it where a shutter is open. Gilt-framed pictures hang high on the wall, lined up like soldiers. Gentlemen sit at a long mahogany table, beneath the light of an Argand chandelier that awaits movement up or down by way of a counterweight device in its chain.

Making a living was hard on Bulfinch. At one point he went to prison for his debts. He accepted a salaried public office in 1799, in which he served for many years, designing and building privately all the while. In 1817, when President James Monroe visited Boston on his New England tour, Bulfinch was his guide. So delighted was the president with Bulfinch's work that he offered him the position of architect of the US Capitol, which was then under construction.

With a substantial salary, Bulfinch moved to Washington, DC, where he worked for the government until 1830. He proved as adept with monumental architecture as with the domestic mode that had made him famous. Bulfinch built the Capitol's central rotunda on the east side and the Library of Congress on the west; the building externally is in harmony with the French Neo-Classicism of the wings, already underway, and was originally crowned with a tall, bulbous dome that, while it appears characteristic of Bulfinch, was not his preference but that of the building committee.

His rotunda, with its echoes of the Pantheon in Rome, survives today complete. It is at once a very simple and an august interior, carried out in marble, with a majesty of form, light, and shadow that makes it one of the greatest of all American public interiors. The excellence of Bulfinch's taste in design, detail, and quality of workmanship are evident everywhere. Note for example the lobbies to the rotunda, with their chaste Corinthian columns in pale gray marble; their delicacy of design and skill in execution is worthy of fine statuary. Light pours into the space through a high-placed ring of windows and spills onto pilasters, classical panels, and patterned marble floors.

The Library of Congress chambers, which no longer exist, were workrooms surrounding a central reading room two storeys high, with Corinthian pilasters and columns along the walls. The shallow, sky-lit ceiling was decorated with composition work in Neo-Classical motifs. For this interior Bulfinch designed a Neo-Classical stove in iron, a column topped by an urn.

Bulfinch is best-remembered for his houses and for the Massachusetts State House. However, it was after his move to Washington that he really proved himself an architect. Already in his fifties, he made a distinguished place for himself comparable to that of any architect in the nation. Today's west front of the Capitol, with its porch that once opened off the reading room of the Library of Congress, is known as the Bulfinch Front.

WILLIAM SEALE

Biography

Born in Boston, Massachusetts, 8 August 1763. Educated at Harvard University, 1778–81 (M.A. 1784). Toured Europe, visiting England, France and Italy, 1785–87; met Thomas Jefferson and the Marquis de Lafayette in Paris. Married his cousin, Hannah Apthorp, 1788 (died 1841): 7 children. Worked as an accountant for a local Boston merchant, 1787. Practised as an architectural adviser on an amateur basis, Boston, from the late 1780s. Following the failure of the Tontine Crescent development, suffered financial ruin and practised as a professional architect, Boston, from 1796. Accepted salaried post as Chair of Boston's Selectmen and Superintendent of Police, 1799; appointed supervising architect for the United States Capitol Building, Washington, DC, 1817; lived in Washington, DC, 1817–30. Retired to Boston, 1830. Died 4 April 1844.

Selected Works

Important collections of Bulfinch's drawings and designs are in the Library of Congress, Washington, DC. Numerous archive photographs of Bulfinch's buildings, including views of interiors, are in the Connecticut Historical Society, Hartford, and manuscript material relating to his work on the Harrison Gray Otis House and the Derby House is in the Essex Institute, Salem, Massachusetts.

Interiors

1792–93 Joseph Barrell House, Somerville, Massachusetts (building and interiors)
1793 Charles Bulfinch House, Boston (building and interiors)
1793–94 Theater, Boston (building and interiors)
1793–96 Tontine Crescent, Boston (buildings and interiors)
1793–96 State House, Hartford, Connecticut (building and interiors)
1795–96 Harrison Gray Otis House I, Boston (building and interiors)
1795–97 State House, Boston (building and interiors including the Representatives Room, Senate Chamber and Council Chamber)
1795–99 Elias Hasket Derby House, Salem, Massachusetts (building and interiors)
c.1796 James Swan House, Dorchester, Massachusetts (building and interiors)
1796 Perez Morton House, Roxbury, Massachusetts (building and interiors)
1800–02 Harrison Gray Otis House II, Boston (building and interiors)
1803–04 Thomas Amory House, Boston (building and interiors)
1805–08 Harrison Gray Otis House III, Boston (building and interiors)
1811 Essex Bank (now Salem Fraternity Building), Salem, Massachusetts (building and interiors)
1818–29 US Capitol, Washington, DC (rebuilding and completion of work by Benjamin Henry Latrobe, and interiors)
1829–32 State House, Augusta, Maine (building and interiors)

Further Reading

For a scholarly survey of Bulfinch's career see Kirker 1969 which includes a detailed account of his principal works, and appendices listing minor commissions, attributed works, public buildings erected after Bulfinch's designs, and the contents of his architectural library.

Brainard, Newton C., *The Hartford State House of 1796*, Hartford: Connecticut Historical Society, 1964
Brown, Frank Chouteau, "The Joseph Barrell Estate, Somerville, Massachusetts: Charles Bulfinch's First Country House" in *Old-Time New England*, 38, January 1948, pp.53–62
Brown, Glenn, *History of the United States Capitol*, 2 vols., Washington, DC: Government Printing Office, 1900–03; reprinted New York: Da Capo, 1970
Bulfinch, Ellen Susan (editor), *The Life and Letters of Charles Bulfinch, Architect*, 1896; reprinted New York: Franklin, 1973
Harmon, Robert E., *Charles Bulfinch: A Bibliography*, Monticello, IL: Vance, 1979
Kimball, Fiske, *Mr. Samuel McIntire, Carver: The Architect of Salem*, 1940; reprinted Gloucester, MA: Peter Smith, 1966
Kirker, Harold and James, *Bulfinch's Boston*, 1787–1817, New York: Oxford University Press, 1964
Kirker, Harold, *The Architecture of Charles Bulfinch*, Cambridge, MA: Harvard University Press, 1969
Kirker, James, "Bulfinch's House for Mrs. Swan" in *Magazine Antiques*, LXXXVI, October 1964, pp.442–44
McLanathan, Richard B. K., "Bulfinch's Drawings for the Maine State House" in *Journal of the Society of Architectural Historians*, XIV, May 1955
Morison, Samuel E., *The Life and Letters of Harrison Gray Otis, Federalist*, 2 vols., Boston: Houghton Mifflin, 1913
Nylander, Richard, "The First Harrison Gray Otis House" in *Magazine Antiques*, CVII, June 1975, pp.1130–41
Pickens, Buford, "Wyatt's Pantheon, the State House in Boston and a New View of Bulfinch" in *Journal of the Society of Architectural Historians*, 29, May 1970, pp.124–31
Pierson, William H., Jr., *The Colonial and Neo-Classical Styles* (American Buildings and Their Architects, vol.1), New York: Doubleday, 1970
Place, Charles A., *Charles Bulfinch: Architect and Citizen*, 1925; reprinted New York: Da Capo, 1968
Stoddard, R., "A Reconstruction of Charles Bulfinch's First Federal Street Theater, Boston" in *Winterthur Portfolio*, 6, 1970
Whitehill, Walter Muir, *Boston: A Topographical History*, Cambridge, MA: Harvard University Press, 1959

Bullock, George 1782/83–1818

British sculptor and cabinet-maker

George Bullock is celebrated as one of the most innovative cabinet-makers active during the Regency period. It was his individualistic ability as a designer which distinguished the furniture made in his workshops from that of his contemporaries.

Details about Bullock's early life remain vague, but he appears to have been born in Birmingham where he followed in his mother's footsteps as a wax modeller. His earliest known work is a wax relief of the great collector Henry Blundell executed in 1801, by which date it is assumed that Bullock had arrived in Liverpool. By 1804 he had begun to practise there as a cabinet-maker as well as a sculptor and had various work-

Bullock: drawing room window curtain from Ackermann's *The Repository of Arts*, April 1817

shops in the city until 1814, when he became fully established in London. Bullock's reputation rests principally on this final phase of his career (1814–18) during which time he created some of his most characteristic furniture and when he executed his major commissions.

Bullock never entirely discarded sculpture and continued to make busts even while presiding over his grand establishment and newly built workshops in Tenterden Street, London. As well as furniture, Bullock designed interiors, textiles, light fittings, silverware, ceramics and chimneypieces. These last were made of the so-called Mona marble (mainly green like *verde antico* and red) from the quarries he owned on Anglesey. Although Bullock did not publish a self-promoting pattern book, he was, from the start, a skilful publicist and made good use of the Liverpool press to announce new developments in his career. Later, from 1816–17, he contributed eight attributed and five anonymous designs to the monthly series on "Fashionable Furniture" which appeared in Ackermann's *Repository of Arts*. This would have been an excellent publication in which to introduce to a wider audience his furniture, chimneypieces and interiors.

Bullock is first noted as a cabinet-maker in partnership with William Stoakes; together in 1804 they advertised as "General Furnishers and Marble Workers". In December that year Bullock designed a Gothic drawing room for the Marquess of Cholmondeley, for whom he also supplied furniture and mock armour. In the *Liverpool Chronicle* (4 September 1805) Bullock took the "opportunity of acquainting his Friends, and more particularly those ... who have expressed a desire to see the Rich Gothic Furniture, Armour &c WHICH HE HAS DESIGNED AND EXECUTED FOR LORD CHOLMONDELEY ... previously to their being removed to Cholmondeley Castle". Throughout his career, Bullock moved easily between the Gothic, Old English (Antiquarian) and Neo-Classical styles. A rosewood and brass inlaid table (National Museums and Galleries on Merseyside), acquired by Sir William Cumming in the 1819 sale following the closure of Bullock's workshop, is a Neo-Classical variant of an oak Gothic-revival table designed for Battle Abbey, c.1817 (now in the Victoria and Albert Museum, London).

Although Bullock does not appear to have received any formal artistic training, he benefited from being taken up by such discerning figures as the Liverpool poet, patron and art historian William Roscoe and Henry Blundell, also of Liverpool. It was perhaps from Blundell's substantial collection of antique sculpture that Bullock learned the Classical vocabulary he adapted so naturally in his London-period furniture. For example, Blundell owned a restored relief *Girl Before a Round Temple* (National Museums and Galleries on Merseyside) a detail of which Bullock drew and turned directly into the pattern for a marquetry panel. Other immediately identifiable influences on Bullock's artistic development were

Thomas Hope's *Household Furniture* (1807) and the published designs of Piranesi and Percier. However, on every occasion where these debts can be established, it is also the case that Bullock has effected a distinctly personal transformation.

The most important source for our understanding of Bullock as a designer is an album of tracings known as the Wilkinson Tracings (City Museum and Art Gallery, Birmingham). On more than 200 sheets, there are hundreds of designs for furniture, silver, monuments, metalware, mounts, "buhl" marquetry, chimneypieces and interiors. The cover states these are "from designs of the late Mr George Bullock 1820". These, or another version, remained in his workshop after his death. The Wilkinson Tracings offer a broad overview of Bullock's mature achievements in the full range of styles which he employed. They also record the names of several clients, including those such as Mr. Sone (sic), Mrs. Barron, Lady Spencer, Sir Henry Bunbury and Lady Ormond for whom no other evidence of patronage survives.

A good idea of the appearance of a Bullock interior can be gained from the Drawing Room Window Curtain in Ackermann's *Repository*. The design shows elaborate curtains either side of a bold "dwarf cabinet" with brass grilles and marble slab, on top of which sits a bronze colza lamp. In common with major designers from the previous century such as William Kent and Robert Adam, Bullock clearly saw the importance of being involved with every aspect of the interiors he created.

Bullock's London career was brief but successful. The Prince Regent had already been patron of the Liverpool Academy, where Bullock had been the first president. In 1814, Queen Charlotte gave a cabinet by Bullock to Princess Sophia of Gloucester and there is other evidence of Royal patronage. On many of his better known commissions Bullock worked alongside the architect William Atkinson, including at Abbotsford, Biel, Gorhambury and Scone. His work at Abbotsford connected Bullock with Walter Scott's literary circle and strengthened his involvement with the nascent Antiquarian movement, to which the writer was such a central figure. It is, however, another Atkinson / Bullock commission that perhaps crowned his career.

In 1815 Bullock was chosen by the Prince Regent to supply the furniture and all the other domestic requirements for Napoleon and his entourage who were to be exiled on St Helena. As architect at the Board of Ordnance, Atkinson was responsible for the house. This well-documented commission saw Bullock designing a suite of interiors, all fully furnished and lavishly upholstered in fashionable Regency period taste. Bullock supplied a wide range of furniture, some in the British oak of which he was a keen advocate, but much in mahogany inlaid with ebony (which he also favoured) and also some ebonised and brass inlaid pieces.

Several features combine to distinguish Bullock's furniture. In design many of his cabinets, tables and chairs have a boldness dictated by an artist's creative eye rather than by more purely practical considerations. His choice and combination of materials created a powerful and striking effect: for example, in the contrasting use of oak and ebony on his clearly delineated marquetry, the designs for which were often inspired by British plant forms. In general, his treatment of flat pattern can be seen as anticipating the approach, later in the century, of designers such as A.W.N. Pugin and Owen Jones.

A year after Bullock's death, having lost the driving inspiration of his forceful personality, his workshop was sold up. Much of the stock-in-trade (including marquetry panels, partly made up furniture, patterns for metalwork and design drawings) was acquired by the London cabinet-making trade. Thus, features of his style were immediately circulated and began to be incorporated into the production of Bullock's talented, but less inspired contemporaries. His distinctive furniture design was also disseminated by admirers such as Richard Brown (*Rudiments of Drawing Cabinet and Upholstery Furniture*, second improved edition, 1822) and Richard Bridgens (*Furniture with Candelabra*, 1826).

Bullock's work and personality were much admired by his friends. As Richard Brown wrote: "The late Mr Bullock was the only person who ventured into a new path ..." (*Rudiments* ..., under pl. XXV). And Sir Walter Scott observed: "he had a taste rarely found in that profession in which such sums of money are expended to make more barbarous and costly monstrosities ..." (Wainwright, 1988).

MARTIN P. LEVY

Biography

Born in Birmingham, 1782/83. In Liverpool by 1801; working as a sculptor, modeller and cabinet-maker by 1804; trading as Bullock and Stoakes with William Stoakes from c.1805 (partnership dissolved 1807); involved with the mining of Mona Marble in Anglesey from c.1806; in partnership with J. M. Gandy as "architects, modellers, sculptors, marble masons, cabinet-makers and upholsterers" from 1809; established in London as a sculptor, furniture maker, and proprietor of the Mona Marble Works from 1814. Continued to practise as a sculptor and exhibited at the Liverpool Academy and the Royal Academy, London. Contributed designs to Ackermann's *Repository of Arts* 1816–17. Died 1 May 1818; workshop closed 1819.

Selected Works

Examples of Bullock's furniture are owned by the Walker Art Gallery and Sudely Art Gallery (National Museums and Galleries on Merseyside) Liverpool, and by the Victoria and Albert Museum, London. An important album, containing more than 200 sheets of designs for furniture, silver, monuments, chimneypieces and interiors, known as the Wilkinson Tracings, is in the City Museum and Art Gallery, Birmingham.

Interiors

1805	Cholmondeley Castle, Cheshire (furniture and armour for the Gothic drawing room): Marquess of Cholmondeley
1814–19	Blair Castle, Perthshire (furniture): Duke of Atholl
1815	Longwood, St. Helena (furniture and fittings for Napoleon's use)
1816	Tew Park, Oxfordshire (furniture and fittings): Matthew Robinson Bouton
1816–19	Abbotsford, Roxburghshire (furniture and fittings): Sir Walter Scott
1816–17	Battle Abbey, Sussex (furniture and fittings): Sir Godfrey Webster

Further Reading

The most comprehensive account of Bullock's work, including a full bibliography, is Wainwright 1988. A full list of Bullock's commissions appears in Beard and Gilbert 1986.

Beard, Geoffrey and Christopher Gilbert (editors), *Dictionary of English Furniture Makers, 1660–1840*, London: Furniture History Society, 1986, pp.126–28
Coleridge, Anthony, "The work of George Bullock, Cabinet-Maker, in Scotland" in *Connoisseur*, CLVIII, 1965, pp.249–252 and CLIX, pp.13–17
Collard, Frances, *Regency Furniture*, Woodbridge, Suffolk: Antique Collectors' Club, 1985
Edwards, Ralph, "George Bullock as a Sculptor and Modeller" in *Connoisseur*, July 1969
Glenn, Virginia, "George Bullock, Richard Bridgens and James Watts's Regency Furnishing Schemes" in *Furniture History*, 1979, pp.54–67
Joy, Edward T., "Identifying a Regency Cabinet: A Recently Discovered Piece by George Bullock" in *Country Life*, 168, 21 August 1980, pp.646–68
Levy, Martin P., "George Bullock: Some Sources for Identifying his Furniture" in *Apollo*, June 1987
Levy, Martin P., "George Bullock: A Regency Cabinetmaker Reassessed" in *Magazine Antiques*, June 1988, pp.1392–1403
Levy, Martin P., "George Bullock's Partnership with Charles Fraser, 1813–1818, and the Stock-in-Trade Sale, 1819" in *Furniture History*, 1989, pp.145–213
Levy, Martin P., "Ditton Park, Berkshire" in *Country Life*, 11 January 1990, pp.70–73
Wainwright, Clive, "Walter Scott and the Furnishing of Abbotsford" in *Connoisseur*, January 1977
Wainwright, Clive and others, *George Bullock: Cabinet Maker*, London: Murray, 1988

Buontalenti, Bernardo 1531–1608

Italian architect, designer and engineer

The chief architect of the Florentine Medici family in the second half of the 16th century, Bernardo Buontalenti worked in various media and his activities covered every area of courtly life. Trained as a painter and architect in the circle of Salviati, Bronzino and Vasari, he also worked as an engineer and he is even reputed to have designed a perpetual motion machine. His interest in scientific and mechanical studies was shared by his patron, Grand Duke Cosimo, and his work for the Medicis frequently involved jobs where such expertise was essential. Buontalenti's understanding of waterworks was the key to his fantastic designs for the Boboli Gardens Grotta Grande, and the layout of the grounds at Pratolino, and his elegant and eccentric designs for these projects were no less influential than his designs for masques and silver and hardstone vessels. He worked in a refined but energetic proto-Mannerist style and his work was both flamboyant and grand. Surviving examples and drawings illustrate his wit and artistic independence, qualities that were all the more unusual at a time when grace was a codified virtue and the undisputed authorities were classical forms.

Buontalenti's earliest work for the Medici household was as a planner of festivals at the wedding of Francesco I and Johanna of Austria in 1565; the Medici nuptial masque consisted of a fully realised naval battle. He was also involved in the renovation of the Casa di Bianca Capello which he decorated with a delightful festooned, scrolled and figured sgrafitto fresco on the street façade in 1567. Such pleasing accomplishments were rewarded by Francesco I with a commission to design a villa and its grounds, the Pratolino. Sadly the main building of the villa was destroyed in 1822, but plans and a lunette painting by Giusto Utens of 1599 as well as visitors' descriptions survive. The French essayist Montaigne was deeply impressed on his arrival in 1581 and commented favourably on the time and care that had gone into creating such a complex. A lake and waterfalls were engineered so that even during the summer water levels were constant. Much of the ornamentation of the extremely elaborate waterworks was mechanised and the grottoes were installed with moveable scenery. The gardens also contained organs, topiary, an aviary, a maze and numerous examples of statuary and fountains. On one of the lawns there were hidden sprinklers from which an automated shepherdess would gather water in a bucket while a small satyr played his pipes. The grounds were designed to be an entertainment and the landscape was fashioned accordingly. The villa rose above symmetrically laid-out gardens. The chapel is still standing; it is a small, graceful domed structure that Buontalenti would repeat with modifications later in his Tribuna in the Uffizi. Pratolino is an excellent example of the harnessing of intricate fancy to complex mechanics for which Buontalenti was so celebrated.

The Uffizi was Vasari's last Medici project and he did not live to see its grandeur realized. His students Buontalenti and Alfonso Parigi inherited the job and carried it through to completion. Among the many buildings incorporated within the Uffizi was Buontalenti's octagonal domed Tribuna (1574–89). The design included clerestory windows, which the earlier Cappella at Pratolino had not. And the interior was ornamented from floor to the ceiling. The marble floor was patterned to divide the space into a graceful ground plan articulating each block of the interior space corresponding to its segment of the unifying dome. The revetment on the floor was imitated up the walls and around the window niches in paint, wooden and plaster mouldings and *pietre dure*. The dome itself was painted brilliant blue with gold-leaf, starry scales. The connection and contrast between the solid geometry of the floor and the dizzy illusionism of the roof lent a sense of gravity and airiness to a small and powerful room. Buontalenti's controlled seriousness may have been informed by his interest in fortifications for which he also drew plans. Such sombre effect was perhaps not his favoured design product, but it was evidently a part of his more rigorous Renaissance formalist vocabulary – a part he would express again in his designs for the Cappella de' Medici, San Lorenzo.

Another triumph of decorative extravagance and technical virtuosity is the Boboli Gardens complex (1583–93). Buontalenti took over the general plans from Tribolo and worked in conjunction with Bartolommeo Ammanati who was architect of the extension project of the Pitti Palace. Vasari had also been involved in the planning stages but his designs for the façade of the grotto do not survive and were never completed. The grotto, known as the Grotto Grande, is arguably Buontalenti's masterpiece. Flat lintels over columns make up the niched lower elevation which was crafted into a loggia with three arches while, in the interior, the free handling of forms explore the Renaissance concept of the grotesque. Exaggerated or stylized natural elements are carefully aggregated in unnatural volumes and combinations. According to the historian Eugenio Battisti, "The symbolic and pictographic language of the grotesque voices such marvellous ideas! But unfortunately it follows no glossary, no syntax, no conventional, united plan. Sometimes it has a relationship with the material whose soul it attempts to reveal; it articulates itself in the vaguest ways as the material suggests; it does not speak aloud by hints without explaining. And at least in certain of its forms, for example crystal, it expresses itself in a wide variety of formal tendencies which always demand new images and alternative technical solutions for displaying them."

Although Buontalenti's grotto does follow a united plan, the intention was to surprise and dissemble at every opportunity. The basic materials are plaster, stone, sponge, pumice and shell. Their textures ripple and blend into one another, agitating the heavier outlines of the forms they describe. The shapes are therefore a kind of three-dimensional *trompe-l'oeil*, and the rocks, waves, and stalactites prove on closer inspection to be a community of human and animal figures. The challenge of interpreting the forms and their relationship to the supporting walls, surrounding spaces and materials was further complicated when the grotto was first constructed due to Buontalenti's masterful manipulation of light. There are no windows and the only source of light is the oculus in the ceiling. The plans originally adapted this space for a crystal fishbowl; the light was meant to filter through the water and crystal and the shadows of small fish would have thrown a dappled, undulating pattern over the entire interior thereby creating a striking underwater effect. In the event, this project proved too complicated but fountains and other mechanized props contributed to the transformational power of the place. The grotto was also to have been the setting for Michelangelo's statues of the Slaves, and it contained Bernardino Poccetti's frescoes of Pyrrha and Deucalion.

Buontalenti's work in the Grotta Grande suggests a sense of drama and theatre that is also evident in his festival productions. The baptism of Filippo de' Medici, for example, was a stunning spectacle. Buontalenti modified the interior of the Baptistry of San Giovanni adding two silvered, balustraded staircases in a platform over the medieval font. The existing columns were to be hidden by pilasters built on volutes. These created niches for the Ammanati stuccoes finished and installed for the occasion. A screen was also rigged in front of the lower gallery giving the plans a particularly Roman accent. Ideas from the Pantheon and Bramante's villa architecture are visible in Buontalenti's plans which pre-date the wider influence of Roman architecture in Tuscany.

The exterior of the Baptistry was similarly dressed. The "Gates of Paradise" were hidden by a temporary portico designed as a triumphal arch which suggested Constantine's in its design and its decorations. The newly made oval double font and its *pietre dure* table were also Buontalenti's and they formed the centrepiece of the ceremony. No expense was spared and the festival grew naturally into a huge civic event. In addition to the hunting and feasting that were organized, elaborate decorations were ordered to complement the rituals. Buontalenti was called on for these arrangements as well and he produced model or "counterfeit" creatures out of wood, cloth, clay, and wax, each capable of movement or the spectacular emission of fireworks. Such displays were not to be enjoyed frequently by Florentines as they were extraordinarily costly. But the weddings of Virginia de' Medici to Cesare d'Este in 1585, and of Ferdinando I de' Medici to Christine of Lorraine in 1589 were on a similar scale. The 1589 wedding was a reprise of earlier naval battles for wedding celebrations, but the extravagant *concetto* was vastly expanded in its execution. The bride was led through the streets of Florence which had been decorated with triumphal arches celebrating the past of both families and the parades, pageants, masques, banquets, ballets and musical intermezzi were ceaseless. The lavish culmination was staged at the Pitti Palace in the courtyard leading to the Boboli Gardens. The area was flooded to accommodate eighteen galleys from which victorious Christians played their parts and took a Turkish fort.

Because these celebrations are impossible to re-visit, and the drawings are so brief a guide, Buontalenti's contributions to the artistic culture of his age are generally measured by more enduring monuments. His skill in *pietre dure* design stands out as brilliant and pioneering. The Capella de' Medici was decorated entirely with stone and semi-precious revetments cut into the heraldic emblems and mottoes of the twelve league cities of Tuscany, based on their Etruscan precedents. Even in this monumental and dark setting, the decoration maintains an element of chivalric pageantry which makes permanent the presence of the families who sponsored such displays. The heaviness and endurance of the rock itself defies the transience of the festivals and politics that are left on paper and in archives. Regrettably, such a monument can only hint at the fully realized creations of such a diverse and curious mind.

MELI COSTOPOULOS

See also Grottoes and Shellwork

Biography

Born in Florence, 1531. Training is unknown, but his fresco of *Christ on the way to Emmaus*, in S. Miniato al Monte, Florence, is dated 1547. Taken under the protection of the Medici family; probably learned painting and architecture in the circle of Francesco Salviati, Agnolo Bronzino and Giorgio Vasari. Appointed tutor to Francesco de' Medici, whose passion for scientific studies he shared; remained in Medici family's service for the rest his career from c.1557–1608. Accompanied Francesco de' Medici to Spain in 1562–63; appointed engineer to the Medici, 1568. Worked on Medici villas and grottoes, 1580–97. Designer of silver and hardstone vessels, and porcelain for the Grand-ducal factory, 1575–87. Died in Florence in 1608.

Selected Works

The largest number of Buontalenti's architectural drawings and decorative designs are in the Uffizi, Florence (c.200); others are in the Louvre, Paris; Victoria and Albert Museum, London; Chatsworth House, Derbyshire; and in Rome and Florence.

1565	Decorations for the marriage of Francesco I and Johanna of Austria: Grand Duke Cosimo I de' Medici
1567	Casa di Bianca Cappello (renovation, sgraffito façade, and interiors): Francesco I de' Medici
1569–80	Medici villa, Pratolino (gardens, grotto, fountains, houses): Francesco I de' Medici
1574	Designs for funeral of Cosimo I (catafalque, decorations): Grand Duke Francesco I de' Medici
1574–80	Casino di S. Marco, Florence (building and interiors): Grand Duke Francesco I de' Medici
1574–89	Tribuna, Uffizi, Florence (interior, central table and cabinet) Grand Duke Francesco I de' Medici
1575–90	Medici Villa, Petraia: Grand Duke Francesco I de' Medici

1577 Baptismal font for Prince Filippo de' Medici: Grand Duke Francesco I de' Medici
1583–93 Grotta Grande in the Boboli Gardens, Florence
1585 Design of theatrical events for marriage of Virginia de' Medici and Cesare d'Este: Grand Duke Francesco I de' Medici
1589 Design of theatrical events for marriage of Ferdinando I de' Medici and Christine of Lorraine: Grand Duke Francesco I de' Medici
1594–1602 Cappella de' Medici, S. Lorenzo, Florence (interior marble decoration)

Further Reading

A useful survey of Buontalenti's drawings in the Uffizi and further bibliography is in Botto 1968. For detailed documentation and an account of the architectural and iconographical aspects of Pratolino see Zangheri 1979. See Heikamp 1964 for the Tribuna.

Berti, Luciano, *Il principe dello studiolo: Francesco I dei Medici e la fine del rinascimento fiorentino*, Florence: Edam, 1967

Borsook, Eve, "Art and politics at the Medici court, I: The funeral of Cosimo I de' Medici", in *Mitteilungen des Kunsthistorischen Institutes in Florenz*, XII, 1965–66, pp.31–54

Borsook, Eve, "Art and politics at the Medici court, II: Baptism of Filippo de' Medici in 1577" in *Mitteilungen des Kunsthistorischen Institutes in Florenz*, XIII, 1967, pp.95–114

Botto, Ida Maria, *Mostra di disegni di Bernardo Buontalenti (1531–1608)* (exhib. cat.), Florence: Uffizi Gabinetto Disegni e Stampe, 1968

Giusti, Annamaria, *Splendori di Pietre Dure: L'Arte di Corte nella Firenze dei Granduchi* (exhib. cat.), Florence: Giunti, 1988

Gurrieri, Francesco and Judith Chatfield, *Boboli Gardens*, Florence: Edam, 1972, pp.26–29, 38

Heikamp, Detlef, "La Tribuna degli Uffizi come era nel Cinquecento", in *Antichit Viva*, 3, 1964, pp.11–30

Heikamp, Detlef, "The Grotto Grande in the Boboli Gardens, Florence", in *Connoisseur*, 199,1978, pp.38–43

Morrogh, Andrew, *Disegni di architetti fiorentini, 1540–1640* (exhib. cat.), Florence: Uffizi Gabinetto Disegni e Stampe, 1985, pp.131–60

Nagler, Alois Maria, *Theatre Festivals of the Medici, 1539–1637*, New Haven: Yale University Press, 1964, pp.79–89

Saslow, James M., *The Medici Wedding of 1589: Florentine Festival as Theatrum Mundi*, New Haven and London: Yale University Press, 1996

Silvani, Gherardo, "Vita del Signor Bernardo Buontalenti" in Paola Barocchi (editor), *Francesco Baldinucci, Notizie dei professori del disegno da Cimabue in qua*, vol.7, Florence: SPES, 1975

Smith, W, "Pratolino" in *Journal of the Society of Architectural Historians*, 1961

Wright, David R., "The Medici villa at Olmo a Castello: Its history and iconography", Ph.D. thesis, Princeton: Princeton University, 1976

Zangheri, Luigi, *Pratolino: Il giardino delle meraviglie*, 2 vols, Florence: Gonnelli, 1979, 2nd edition, 1987

Burges, William 1827–1881

British architect and designer

William Burges was one of the leading exponents of Britain's mid-19th century Gothic Revival, and an architect who was responsible for some of the most extraordinary interiors of the period. Heavily influenced by the French architect Viollet-le-Duc, and by A.W.N. Pugin, his architectural and interior designs were the antithesis of the graceful and coherent classicism of the 18th century, which Burges called "the dark ages of art". Instead, he was an uncompromising advocate of medieval design and worked in a distinctive style that became known as "Burgesian gothic". Most of his designs were inspired by historical precedent but they were also often enlivened by a quirky and humorous individualism. Indeed, his vivid interiors frequently border on the fantastic and are bright with gilding, painting, stained glass, furniture and textiles. His rooms are warm and rich with red, gold and green generally dominant. The overall effect is occasionally overwhelming, but never gloomy or dull.

Burges's projects were nearly always highly elaborate and he paid great attention to each detail of his buildings, and to each stage of the design process. In many schemes this would include designing not only the structure, but also its decoration and furnishings. No doubt because of this, Burges was a costly architect to employ and many of his most spectacular proposals, such as those for London's new Law Courts, or for cathedrals in Edinburgh, Lille or Brisbane, would have proved prohibitively expensive. Burges himself was also possessed of a comfortable private income and so could afford to be exacting and uncompromising in his designs. Consequently few buildings by him exist.

He travelled extensively in Europe and the Middle East throughout his career, measuring and drawing buildings. Many details of these buildings appeared in his subsequent work and he adopted a skilfully eclectic approach to decoration and design. His principal source of inspiration was medieval European architecture, especially that of 12th- and 13th-century France. But he was also interested in Arab architecture and design and was an early champion of Japanese art which he likened to the art of the Middle Ages in that it was uncontaminated by industrialisation.

Burges's early works were completed during the period in which he was articled to the architect Edward Blore and in partnership with Henry Clutton. His first major independent commission came in 1863 with a competition for rebuilding the Cathedral of St. Fin Barre in Cork, Ireland. The main influence in this project is 13th-century French Gothic and, despite its comparatively small size, the cathedral is built on a grand scale. Sculptural decoration always played a large part in Burges's designs and there are over 1200 pieces at Cork alone. Equally lavish are his two major churches at Studley Royal and Skelton in Yorkshire, and his restorations at Waltham Abbey. With such commissions Burges became an important figure in the renaissance of stained glass manufacture and his churches glow with colours. Their furnishings, such as choir stalls, pews, lecterns and so on, are designed in a bold, muscular style that is highly individual.

Burges's domestic designs were equally opulent, and although the commissions to build and decorate Knightshayes Court, Devon, and Gayhurst, Buckinghamshire, were not completed, Burges's drawings record the richness and colourfulness of his projected interiors.

His most important patron was the 3rd Marquess of Bute, a wealthy and cultured aristocrat who shared his architect's vision of the medieval past. Bute commissioned Burges to transform his Welsh seat, Cardiff Castle, from a small, plain historic house into a neo-Gothic fantasy. It was a project that would last the rest of Burges's life. Beginning with the Clock

Burges: library, Tower House, 9 Melbury Road, London, late 1870s

Tower in 1869, Burges created some fifteen interiors of extraordinary splendour within five towers reminiscent of the architecture of fairy-tales.

All Burges's interiors had themes and at Cardiff the rooms were inspired by incidents from classical and medieval literature and history, depicted in mural paintings, tiles and stained glass. The designs were realised by his team of artisans which included, among others, the sculptors Thomas Nicholls and Ceccardo Fucigna, the painters Horatio Lonsdale, Frederick Smallfield and Fred Weekes, and the stained glass artist G. Saunders. This talented group worked with Burges on many of his most important schemes. One of the principal interiors at Cardiff was the Summer Smoking Room. Burges designed an impressive dark encaustic tiled floor covered with tiled panels which was inspired by the medieval work at Westminster Abbey; the walls were covered with tiled panels illustrating the legends of the zodiac, painted by Smallfield in delicate tones of pale blue, pink and gold. The chimneypiece, a characteristically dominant design featuring a massive hood, was carved with scenes of courtly love by Nicholls before being painted and gilded.

Some of the rooms at Cardiff Castle included Burges furnishings. The Library (1875–81) remains the only interior to survive intact and includes bookcases and desks made by Gillow and carved by the Bute workshops. Lord Bute's Sitting Room, the Bachelor Bedroom and the Summer Smoking Room also included examples of Burges's textiles, usually made of crewelled serge with Gothic diaper and band designs. Nevertheless, there is little in the way of conventional Victorian upholstered comfort which was always subordinated to the medieval appearance of Burges's rooms. His interest in Middle-Eastern styles culminated in the Arab Room which is lined with marble, has *mishabaya* shutters fitted to the windows and a spectacular richly gilded and painted Muqarnas ceiling. Burges would prepare detailed drawings, cartoons and models for his interiors which would be used by decorators such as Harland and Fisher, and later by Campbell and Smith who worked on several of his schemes.

At Castell Coch, another commission for the Marquess of

Bute in Glamorgan, Burges's academic approach to the restoration of the structure was combined with a more personal style in the interiors which, like those at Cardiff, are elaborate Gothic fantasies. The drawing room is particularly impressive and has a dramatic domed ceiling decorated with birds and butterflies against a sky-blue background. This room was completed after Burges's death by his assistants J.S. Chapple and William Frame.

During the 1870s Burges also began creating his own home in Kensington. Tower House, in Melbury Road, was an astonishing tour de force of his thoughts and ideas and was described as "massive, learned, glittering, amazing" and "strange and barbarously splendid". The rooms at Tower House were not as large as those at Cardiff Castle or Castell Coch, but they demonstrate how Burges was equally comfortable working on a small scale. Indeed, many of the interiors have an intricate jewel-like quality. The Library, whose walls are lined with the witty *Alphabet* bookcases, is dominated by another of his massive chimneypieces, as is the adjoining Drawing Room. Both chimneypieces were carved by Thomas Nicholls, and the walls and ceiling of the Drawing Room were decorated with legendary and mythical lovers, painted by Fred Weekes, echoing the romantic theme of the *Roman de la Rose*.

Burges's passion for Gothic pervades every aspect of his work as a designer. His furniture, in particular, was strongly influenced by 13th-century French precedents and many pieces featured intricate and detailed paintings of mythical or historical scenes. Several pieces were exhibited in the Medieval Court at the International Exhibition of 1862 where they excited much interest and praise. The *Yatman* cabinet (now in the Victoria and Albert Museum) of 1858 is a typical example of his work – colourful, highly decorated and amusing. Painted neo-Gothic furniture is often described as Pre-Raphaelite in deference to the early pieces decorated by Morris, Marshall, Faulkner & Co. but Burges's interest in this style clearly predated that of his contemporaries by several years. Nevertheless, unlike other decorators or cabinet-makers, Burges's furniture was only made to commission and his designs were never repeated or mass-produced.

By the time Burges died in 1881, the Gothic Revival was more or less a spent force. However, the legacy of Burges's own work endured, for not only did he create some of the most memorable interiors of the period, his interest in medieval techniques was later revitalised by the Arts and Crafts movement.

MATTHEW WILLIAMS

See also Gothic Revival

Biography

Born in London, 2 December 1827, the son of Alfred Burges, a successful marine engineer. Studied engineering at King's College, London; articled to the architect Edward Blore in 1844; moved to the office of Matthew Digby Wyatt (1820–77) in 1849. From 1851 in partnership with Henry Clutton; in independent practice, London, from 1857. Made successful competition designs for Lille Cathedral, 1856, and Crimea Memorial Church, Constantinople, 1857; from 1858 designed furniture, jewellery and metalwork, and later wallpapers and stained glass; main interiors from mid-1860s. Member of several antiquarian and artistic societies including the Medieval Society, from 1857, and the Hogarth Club, 1858–63; delivered Royal Society of Art's Cantor Lectures on "Art Applied to Industry", 1864, and published extensively on antiquarian subjects in the *Gentleman's Magazine*, the *Ecclesiologist*, and *Annales Archeologiques*. Exhibited furniture at the 1862 International Exhibition, London. Died in London, 20 April 1881.

Selected Works

A complete list of Burges's secular and ecclesiastical commissions appears in Crook *William Burges* 1981. A large collection of his designs for buildings and interiors, including many drawings for furniture and decorations at Buckingham Street and Tower House, is in the Drawings Collection of the Royal Institute of British Architects, London; 9 albums of sketches are in the Prints and Drawings Department of the Victoria and Albert Museum, London. An additional collection of drawings is in Trinity College, Hartford, Connecticut. Important collections of Burges's furniture and metalwork are held at the Victoria and Albert Museum, the Fitzwilliam Museum, Cambridge, the Cecil Higgins Art Gallery, Bedford and at Knightshayes, Devon.

Interiors

1858–71 15 Buckingham Street, London (decoration, fittings and furniture): William Burges
c.1858–62 Treverbyn Vean, Cornwall (decorations and chimneypieces): Lt. Col. C.L. Somers Cocks
1858–65 Gayhurst, Buckinghamshire (alterations, fittings and furniture): Lord Carrington
1864–79 Worcester College, Oxford (hall and chapel)
1867–74 Knightshayes Court, Devon (decorations and furniture): Sir J. Heathcote-Amory
1869–81 Cardiff Castle, Glamorgan (alterations, extensions, decoration, fittings and furniture): Marquess of Bute
1871–77 Harrow School, Middlesex (speech room)
1875–81 Castell Coch, Glamorgan (reconstruction, decoration and fittings): Marquess of Bute
1875–81 Tower House, Melbury Road, London (building, decoration, fittings and furniture): William Burges

Burges's numerous designs for furniture include the *Yatman* cabinet (1858), *King René's Honeymoon* cabinet (1861–62), *Narcissus* washstand (1865–67), *Zodiac* settle (1869–71), *Alphabet* bookcases (1876), *Philosophy* cabinet (1878–79) and the *Vita Nuova* washstand (1879–80). His wallpapers were produced by Jeffrey & Co, and his tiles by Minton & Co. and W. B. Simpson. He also designed jewellery and metalwork, stained glass and painted decoration.

Further Reading

The most extensive bibliography, including a list of Burges's own writings, appears in Crook *William Burges* 1981. Burges's Cantor Lectures were published as a book, *Art Applied to Industry*, in 1865.

Cooper, Jeremy, *Victorian and Edwardian Furniture and Interiors*, London: Thames and Hudson, 1987

Cornforth, John, "Knightshayes Court, Devon" in *Country Life*, 1 August 1985, pp.314–18

Crook, J. Mordaunt, "Patron Extraordinary: John, 3rd Marquess of Bute" in *Victorian South Wales* edited by P. Howell, London: Victorian Society, 1971

Crook, J. Mordaunt, "Knightshayes, Devon: Burges versus Crace" in *National Trust Yearbook 1*, 1975–76

Crook, J. Mordaunt and others, *The Strange Genius of William Burges* (exhib.cat.) Cardiff: National Museum of Wales, 1981

Crook, J. Mordaunt, *William Burges and the High Victorian Dream*, London: Murray, and Chicago: University of Chicago Press, 1981

Girouard, Mark, *The Victorian Country House*, revised edition New Haven and London: Yale University Press, 1979

Handley-Read, Charles, "William Burges" in Peter Ferriday (editor), *Victorian Architecture*, London: Cape, 1963; Philadelphia: Lippincott, 1964

Handley-Read, Charles, "Notes on William Burges's Painted Furniture" in *Burlington Magazine*, 1963, pp.496–509
Handley-Read, Charles, "Aladdin's Palace in Kensington: William Burges's Tower House" in *Country Life*, 17 March 1966, pp.600–604
Handley-Read, Charles, entry on William Burges in *Catalogue of the Drawings Collection of the Royal Institute of British Architects*, vol.B, London: Gregg, 1969
Haweis, Mary Eliza, *Beautiful Houses*, London: Sampson Low, 1882
Pullan, R.P., *The House of William Burges,* London, 1886
Pullan, R.P., *The Designs of William Burges*, London, 1886
Pullan, R.P., *The Architectural Designs of William Burges*, London, 1887

Burlington, Earl of 1694–1753

British architect and connoisseur

Lord Burlington was perhaps the most influental patron of the arts and architecture in early 18th century England. Of Anglo-Irish origins, he was appointed Lord Treasurer of Ireland and Lord Lieutenant of the East and West Ridings of Yorkshire by George I in 1715. His wealth and position at court enabled him to patronize a number of architects and designers, most notably William Kent (1685/86–1748). He also promoted the architectural designs and ideas of the Italian architect Andrea Palladio (1508–80) and in so doing established the pre-eminence of Palladian Neo-Classical architecture, essentially a reaction to the perceived "unpatriotic" and licentious Baroque tradition exemplified by Wren, Hawksmoor and Vanbrugh.

The young Burlington acceded to the family titles on the premature death of his father in 1704. His interest in the arts was most likely kindled by his mother, a noted patron in her own right and, like most aristocrats, he completed his education with the Grand Tour. It was between this Tour in 1714–15 and his second visit to Italy in 1719 that he was converted to the idea of a new architecture based on the tenets of Palladio. The catalyst for this was undoubtedly the publication in 1715 of two seminal works in English architectural history. The first was volume 1 of the three-volume *Vitruvius Britannicus*, mainly a collection of engravings of 17th and early 18th century English country houses by the Scottish architect Colen Campbell (1676–1729), and the second was the first full English edition of Palladio's *I Quattro Libri dell' Architettura – The Four Books of Architecture* – edited by immigrant Italian architect Giacomo Leoni.

During Burlington's Grand Tour his London home in Piccadilly, Burlington House, was being extensively altered and refurbished by the architect and Baroque traditionalist, James Gibbs and a plan of the house appeared in the first volume of *Vitruvius Britannicus.* Burlington subsequently dismissed Gibbs and employed Campbell to oversee the continued refashioning of his London home. The Earl himself now determined to seek out the work of Palladio at first hand and this resulted in his second visit to Italy in 1719.

Andrea Palladio had drawn his inspiration from the buildings of classical antiquity and especially those of the 1st-century architect and engineer Vitruvius. Palladio wished to free Italy from the Gothic influence and lead architecture back to "correct proportions". Introduced into England a hundred years earlier by Inigo Jones – the "British Vitruvius" of Campbell's title – Palladianism was anglicized by Burlington and his protégés and developed into a distinctive style which set the tone of English architecture and interior decoration for the ensuing half century.

Burlington acquired a number of Palladio's unpublished drawings while in northern Italy and visited the best examples of his built repertoire. He also met William Kent there and so began the partnership which lasted until Kent's death in 1748. Burlington commissioned Kent to paint a number of ceilings in Burlington House. These included the *Banquet of the Gods* in the Great Saloon, the *Assembly of the Gods* in what is now the Secretary's Room and an *Apotheosis of Inigo Jones* in a third room (now over the main staircase).

Burlington, meanwhile, was developing his architectural ideas with the construction of three major buildings, the Dormitory of Westminster School in London, Petersham Lodge in Surrey and Tottenham Park in Wiltshire, the latter based on the layout of Palladio's Villa Poiana. It was in these buildings that Burlington established the principles of English Palladianism, notably the use of four symmetrical wings to the main house (rather than the two used in a traditional Palladian villa) and the associated multi-level roofscapes.

Chiswick House is the apogee of Burlington's interpretation of Palladio's aesthetic. It also introduced the villa into the English vernacular, a style of domestic architecture which has endured. Although relying on Palladio's Villa Capra (Rotonda) for inspiration, with its coffered domes and half-domes, Chiswick incorporates significant variations, for example the use of thermal windows and the octagonal dome and hall of the *piano nobile* (first floor). Probably never intended as a dwelling house, the villa was described as "the beautiful model" by Horace Walpole and can be considered an architectural masterpiece. William Kent was entrusted with the interior decoration which, though sombre, incorporates traditional classical mouldings: egg and dart, Greek key and Vitruvian scrolls as well as Inigo Jones-inspired triangular pediments over the doorways. The opulent ceiling in the Blue Velvet Room, with Kent's painting of *Architecture with Attendants* in the centre is clear testimony to the growing abilities of Burlington's protégé.

It was at Chiswick also that Burlington and Kent initiated the change from the formality of the Italian Renaissance garden to one which emphasized a natural landscape of vista and perspective. Kent was to develop these ideas more radically in his later landscape gardening work.

The Grand Assembly Rooms in York (1731–32), funded by public subscription, enabled Burlington to interpret his ideas in a public building. Again he drew inspiration from Palladio, who had executed a design for a hall "suitable for festivals and entertainment". This design in turn was based on a description in Vitruvius's work of a hall built in the "manner of the Egyptians". Intensely classical with its colonnaded hall lit by clerestory (high-level) windows, the Assembly Rooms reflect the grandeur of ancient Rome, not only in concept but also in interior detailing. The design of the secondary spaces – square, rectangular, round, a double-apsed entrance hall, with one room leading into another – was echoed later in the work of Robert Adam. The concept of the Egyptian Hall, with its long and short axis, displaced the cube-shaped hall hitherto

Burlington: interior of Chiswick House, 1730

employed in domestic architecture and was copied throughout Europe. As a final act of patronage Burlington donated the magnificent Venetian chandeliers and chimneypiece.

Burlington also commissioned the publication of a number of architectural volumes which added to his reputation as an arbiter of taste. Kent's *Designs of Inigo Jones*, based on the Earl's collection of Jones's drawings, was published in 1727 and Burlington's own *Fabbriche antiche* followed in 1730. This contained Palladio's unpublished drawings of ancient buildings which Burlington had purchased during his second visit to Italy.

Burlington retired from public life in 1733 and spent most of his remaining years at Chiswick and his Yorkshire estates at Londesborough. His ideas provoked a mixed response during his lifetime. The strong contrast between the severity and restraint of Palladian exteriors and their often lavish and ornate interiors, for example, was frequently criticised and contemporaries also complained that Palladian houses were dark and gloomy owing to the wide spaces between windows (as, for example, at Houghton Hall, Norfolk). Nevertheless, the partnership between Burlington and Kent marked a turning point in English architecture and, although some doubt still exists about the exact contribution of each, there is no doubt that, whether considered as architect or patron, Lord Burlington exercised a profound influence on the English architectural tradition. As Kent wrote to him in 1732, "What you and I do, it may be esteemed a hundred years hence, but at present does not look like it." Time has proved kinder than Kent's pessimistic forecast.

NICHOLAS NUTTALL

See also Kent

Biography

Born Richard Boyle in London, 25 April 1694; succeeded as 3rd Earl of Burlington and 4th Earl of Cork with large estates in Yorkshire and Ireland, 1704. Travelled to Italy on a Grand Tour, 1714–15; visited Vicenza to study the work of Palladio, 1719; first architectural projects date from c.1721. Married Dorothy Savile, 1721. Appointed Lord Treasurer of Ireland and Lord Lieutenant of East and West Ridings of Yorkshire, 1715; made a Privy Councillor, 1729; made a Knight of the Garter, 1730; resigned all political appointments in 1733 and devoted the remainder of his life to intellectual pursuits and architecture. Published scholarly works on Inigo Jones (1727) and Andrea Palladio (1730). Died in London, 4 December 1753.

Principal Works

A collection of Burlington's architectural plans and drawings is in the Drawings Collection of the Royal Institute of British Architects, London. Manuscript material, including correspondence, is held at Chatsworth, Derbyshire, and Althorp, Northamptonshire.

Interiors

c.1721 Tottenham Park, Wiltshire (building and some interiors): Charles, Lord Bruce
1722–30 Westminster School, London (dormitory)
c.1723 29 Old Burlington Street, London (building and some interiors): General Wade
1726–27 Warwick House, St. James's, London (internal alterations): Lord Bruce
c.1730 Foxhall, Charlton, Sussex (banqueting hall)
1730 Northwick Park, Worcestershire (remodelling including entrance hall): Sir John Rushout
1730 Chiswick House, London (building and interiors; with William Kent): Lord Burlington
1731–32 Assembly Rooms, York (building and interiors)
c.1734 Holkham Hall, Norfolk (building and some interiors; with William Kent, including north dressing room): Earl of Leicester
1747 Kirby Hall, Northamptonshire (building and interiors; with Roger Morris)

Publications

The Designs of Inigo Jones (with William Kent), 2 vols., 1727
Fabbriche antiche disegnate da Andrea Palladio, 1730

Further Reading

The most recent, scholarly account of Burlington's career appears in Harris 1994 which also includes numerous references to primary and secondary sources.

Arnold, Dana (editor), *Belov'd by Ev'ry Muse: Richard Boyle, 3rd Earl of Burlington and 4th Earl of Cork*, London: Georgian Group, 1994

Barnard, Toby and Jane Clark (editors), *Lord Burlington: Architecture, Art and Life*, London and Rio Grande, OH: Hambledon, 1995

Carré, Jacques, *Lord Burlington, 1694–1753: Le Connaisseur, le mecen l'architecte*, Clermont-Ferrand: Adosa, 1993

Colvin, Howard M., *A Biographical Dictionary of British Architects, 1600–1840*, 3rd edition New Haven and London: Yale University Press, 1995

Cornforth, John, "Chiswick House, London" in *Country Life*, 16 February 1995, pp.32–37

Craig, Maurice, "Burlington, Adam and Gandon" in *Journal of the Warburg and Courtauld Institutes*, 17, 1954

Harris, John, *The Palladian Revival: Lord Burlington, His Villa and Garden at Chiswick*, New Haven and London: Yale University Press, 1994

Lees-Milne, James, "Lord Burlington in Yorkshire" in *Architectural Review*, July 1945

Lees-Milne, James, *Earls of Creation: Five Great Patrons of Eighteenth-Century Art*, 1962; reprinted London: Century Hutchinson, 1986

Parissien, Steven, *Palladian Style*, London: Phaidon, 1994

Pfister, Harold F., "Burlingtonian Architectural Theory in England and America", in *Winterthur Portfolio*, II, 1976

Rosoman, Treve, "The Decoration and Use of the Principal Apartments of Chiswick House" in *Burlington Magazine*, 127, 1985, pp.663–77

Wilson, Michael I., *William Kent: Architect, Designer, Painter, Gardener, 1685–1748*, London: Routledge, 1984

Wilton-Ely, John (editor), *Apollo of the Arts: Lord Burlington and his Circle* (exhib. cat.), Nottingham: University Art Gallery, 1973

Wittkower, Rudolf, *The History of the York Assembly Rooms*, York, n.d.

Wittkower, Rudolf, *Palladio and English Palladianism*, London: Thames and Hudson, 1974; New York: Thames and Hudson, 1983

Burns, Robert 1869–1941

Scottish painter and decorative artist

During his long career the Edinburgh artist Robert Burns worked in many different media and styles. His work ranged from decorative oil paintings in a late Pre-Raphaelite style to German-inspired advertisments, from Symbolist book illustrations to elaborately worked metalwork. One medium, however, which Burns returned to repeatedly was interior decoration.

Burns's interest in interior decoration began during the years 1889–91 which he spent studying in Paris. The Nabis were the new influence in French art at this date and Burns would probably have seen and admired their mural paintings. On returning to Edinburgh in 1892 he became involved with Patrick Geddes's Edinburgh Social Union, helping to paint murals in the Old Town tenements which Geddes was renovating. Burns's murals – scenes from Celtic and Arthurian legend – have since been painted over, but similar paintings by his friends and colleagues still survive.

Burns's involvement in interior design continued after he left Geddes's circle; he exhibited several mural and stained glass designs in the Royal Scottish Academy annual exhibitions - including in 1919 a sketch for the decoration of an, as yet untraced, music room. In 1900 he was commissioned by the Glasgow architectural firm Salmon and Gillespie to design mosaics for a house at 22 Park Circus in Glasgow.

Interior decoration commissions were limited, however, by Burns's other commitments. From 1908 he was head of the Painting and Drawing department at Edinburgh College of Art and he was working as a fine artist, specialising in moody landscapes of East Lothian and in Austrian-inspired interior scenes. In 1919 however, he left his job at the art college and in the following year resigned his associateship of the Royal Scottish Academy, choosing instead to concentrate on applied and commercial art.

This break left him free to accept the commission for which he is now best known, the interior decoration of the flagship premises of D.S. Crawfords, an Edinburgh-based chain of restaurants and tea rooms. The decoration of this eating place, which contained several different restaurants, grill rooms and cafes, took from 1923 until 1927 and the resulting interiors became an important part of Edinburgh social life, described by Edwin Muir in 1935 as "places more strange than a dream" (*Scottish Journey*). The consciously artistic tea room had been very popular in Scotland since the 1890s when Miss Cranston commissioned George Walton and Charles Rennie Mackintosh to decorate the interiors of her Glasgow tea rooms. Novel interior decoration, especially when it created an otherworldly atmosphere, drew customers; David Crawford's aim in employing Burns was "to create an environment which would attract the best class of customer" ("A caterer's experiment", *Commercial Art*, August 1926).

Crawfords Tea Rooms were made up of two buildings, one on Princes Street, the other on the adjoining Hanover Street, which were linked by a large room called the Oak Hall. This hall was one of the first rooms to be decorated by Burns and contemporary photographs show that it was not conceived as a unified scheme. The only obviously artistic elements are two painted panels over the fireplaces, a series of bas reliefs and a curtain appliquéed with the Crawfords logo. These have to compete with heavy oak panelling, classical columns, plaster urns, a paisley patterned carpet and shaded candelabra-style wall lights. If Burns's involvement in the interiors had stopped at this point it would be difficult to understand why he was praised by contemporaries as an artist who proved that "the commonplace can be recreated enticingly uncommon when embued with spirited design" (E.A. Taylor, *The Studio*, 1925 p.36).

However, the Chinese Room, a banqueting room on the first floor, completed towards the end of 1926, provides a total contrast, justifying Burns's reputation as an interior designer. In this room Burns gave his attention to every detail – basing the scheme around a magnificent set of painted panels depicting the wreck of the Spanish Armada off the coast of Scotland. These panels, which covered two facing walls, were inspired by Japanese screens of the Edo period. They are predominantly gold, black and red, with full-sailed galleons foundering against black rocks, the sea spray, anemones and barnacles picked out in tooled gold leaf over modelled plaster. The remaining walls were hung with woven oriental textiles that set off two elaborate lacquered and veneered cabinets which were designed by Burns and made by the Edinburgh firm Whytock and Reid. The room is conceived as an integrated scheme – from the stepped-back ceiling and the air conditioning grills to the lacquer coal boxes and specially painted china, everything was made to fit the oriental theme. The contrast between these two rooms is dramatic and the evidence which remains of the other rooms suggests that either Burns gained confidence as the project developed, or that at some point his role changed from that of an artistic adviser enlivening an existing scheme to that of a full blown interior designer.

Burns did not work alone in these schemes but brought in a number of younger artists, many of whom had been students at Edinburgh College of Art. These artists were responsible for working up Burns's sketches into either finished works of art – at least one of the fireplace panels was painted by Burns's protégé W.R. Lawson – or into measured drawings to give to manufacturers. The artists were given little scope for individual creativity. Burns was ultimately responsible for every design, even choosing the colouring of the letters on the bronze hanging signs outside (Letter from D.S. Crawford to the sculptor Pilkington Jackson who had notional responsibility for the hanging signs, National Library of Scotland).

The newly refurbished tea rooms were very favourably received, receiving several eulogistic reviews in *The Studio*. This was to be Burns's last interior commission, however. He received no more commissions from Crawfords, though he continued to design advertisements for them, and in 1929 he suffered a stroke which confined him to bed for six months. While recovering he began to work on a series of book illustrations for his patron Alexander Hunter Crawford which were to take him the rest of his life.

Crawfords Tea Rooms were refurbished in Scandinavian style in the 1960s and have since been broken up into separate shops. Various panels and pieces of furniture survive in the National Gallery of Scotland, the Royal Scottish Academy and in several private collections.

JANE LINDSEY

Biography

Born in Edinburgh, 9 March 1869. Studied painting at the South Kensington Schools, London, and at the Académie Delécluze, Paris, 1889–91. Active as a mural painter with Patrick Geddes's Edinburgh Social Union, 1892. Worked as a painter and commercial artist, producing designs for stained glass and interiors, from c.1893. Elected Associate of the Royal Scottish Academy, 1902 (resigned

1920). Head of Painting and Drawing, Edinburgh College of Art, 1908–19; active as a painter of landscapes. Concentrated upon applied and commercial art from c.1920; suffered a stroke, 1929; active as a book illustrator from 1929. Exhibited frequently at the Royal Scottish Academy, Royal Society of Painters in Water Colours, Royal Glasgow Institute of the Fine Arts, and Aberdeen Artists' Society, between 1893 and 1926. Died in Edinburgh, 30 January 1941.

Selected Works

Panels from the Chinese Room, Crawfords Tea Rooms, are in the Royal Scottish Academy, and some pieces of furniture are in the National Gallery of Scotland, Edinburgh. Examples of Burns's paintings and illustrations are in the Hunterian Gallery,Glasgow, and the National Gallery of Scotland, Edinburgh.

Interiors

1900 22 Park Circus, Glasgow (mosaics)
1923–27 Crawfords Tea Rooms, Princes Street and Hanover Street, Edinburgh (interiors including the Oak Hall and the Chinese Room)

Burns's designs for furniture were made by Whytock and Reid, Edinburgh.

Further Reading

Caw, Sir James, *Scottish Painting, Past and Present*, Edinburgh: Jack, 1908

Forrest, Martin A., *Robert Burns, Artist and Designer* (exhib. cat.), Edinburgh: Bourne Fine Art, 1982

Irwin, David and Francina, *Scottish Painters at Home and Abroad, 1700–1900*, London: Faber, 1975

Macmillan, Duncan, *Scottish Art, 1460–1990*, Edinburgh: Mainstream, 1990

Stirton, Paul, *Robert Burns, Limner* (exhib. cat.), Edinburgh: Fine Art Society, 1978

Byzantine Interior Design

The word "Byzantine" refers to the culture of the Byzantine Empire which was founded by the first Christian Roman emperor Constantine in c.330 AD, and lasted for over a thousand years until it was conquered by the Muslim Ottomans in 1453. The term is also used to describe the art and architecture of the Greek, Russian, Armenian and other Orthodox Churches which have perpetuated the formal conventions of the Byzantine era during the post-medieval period to the present day. Centred on its capital city Constantinople, situated between Europe and Asia on the Bosphorus, Byzantium was at the height of its power under the emperor Justinian in the 6th century. The Empire reached as far as Persia in the east, included the upper reaches of the Nile and the hinterland of the North African Mediterranean coast to the south, stretched along the northern Mediterranean coastline from Gibraltar, encompassing the Italian and Balkan peninsulas and extended as far north as the northern shores of the Black Sea.

Despite the duration and extent of Byzantine influence, the principal elements of Byzantine art and architecture were remarkably constant. The greatest threat to representational art occurred in the 8th century when the controversy of Iconoclasm and the triumph of the image emphasised the iconic character of Byzantine pictorial art. With Greek as the imperial language, the Byzantines regarded themselves as the legitimate heirs of the Greeks of Antiquity and responsible for integrating Christian Orthodoxy into their Classical heritage. Also influenced by the Orient, their philosophy was concerned with defining the indefinable and led to a consuming interest in the finer points of religious doctrine, in which ceremony was given important symbolic functions. The edicts of emperor Constantine VII Porphyrogenitus (913–959), *De Ceremonis* and *De Administratione*, provide insights into the contribution expected from the architectural context and from the visual arts in conveying the symbolic aspects of ceremony. The greater part of written sources and surviving examples of Byzantine culture relate, therefore, to an ecclesiastical context; the secular and domestic aspects of Byzantine civilization are still largely underestimated.

The Byzantines modified and made their own contributions to the Graeco-Roman tradition. The re-use of Roman columns and carved capitals, sometimes alongside their own, serves as a demonstration of their lack of distinction between the two cultures. However, their lack of respect for architectonic principles as seen, for example, in their treatment of carving which tends to obscure the definition between the capital and the abacus, demonstrates the Byzantine preference for ornament. Their favoured building material was brick, with which they perfected the use of pendentives and unsupported semidomes to carry hemispherical domes. A unique achievement of this method, in terms of scale, is Justinian's church dedicated to Holy Wisdom, Hagia Sophia (532–537) in Constantinople. The dome in square plan, as exemplified in the 11th-century church of Hosios Loukas in Phocis, has served continually since Iconoclasm as a model for both the monastic and secular church in Orthodox cultures.

In contrast to the brickwork of the exterior, the magnificence of church interiors was intended to evoke the splendours of the Heavens on earth. On ground level, the brickwork was concealed under marble revetment, slices of marble applied as veneer on the wall giving mirrored patterns of veining. In the upper registers, mosaics of ornamental friezes and biblical scenes, and later narrative schemes of wall painting, covered the brick structure. Most of these forms of treating the internal surfaces are to be found in the Monastery in Chora (converted to the Kariye Djami) in Constantinople, which belongs to the first half of the 14th century. Byzantine descriptions praise church interiors for the quality and colour of effects of light reflected off the polished polychrome surfaces of marbles, mosaic, and ritual objects of enamel, gold and other burnished metals.

Comparatively little material relating to domestic architecture survives from the earliest period of the Byzantine Empire, and it is assumed that the constructions were less permanent than their Roman equivalents. The surviving material on imperial palaces is in the form of written accounts, mostly by Western visitors, notably by the Bishop of Cremona, Liudprand (922–972), by Eudes de Denil (visited the capital under Comnene rule in 1147) and by the Frankish crusaders in 1204, Robert de Clari and Villehardouin. Owing to the ceremonial structure of religion and government, the imperial court required a complex of buildings. The Byzantine Palace was therefore an elaboration of the Roman villa plan found at Tivoli and Piazza Armerina and anticipates the Alhambra and

Byzantine: Sala di Ruggero, Palace of the Normans, Palermo, Sicily, c.1170

the Topkapı Sarayı. Byzantine palaces dating from the early 5th century have been excavated at Lausos and Antiochus, but the most important are the imperial palaces in Constantinople. The site of the Bucoleon, founded by Constantine, stretches from the Hippodrome to the sea walls and accommodated up to 20,000 people.

The second imperial palace in Constantinople dates from the 12th century and was built by the Comnene dynasty on the Theodosian walls at the point of the Golden Horn, commanding the sea, the city and the hinterland. The plan of both was similar, with a great number of buildings housing state rooms, private apartments, military quarters, offices of administration and of government and workshops supplying the court community, arranged around gardens, terraces and connected by stairs, colonnades and covered passages. Western visitors were struck by the number of richly furnished chapels and shrines housing venerated relics, by the imposing scale and magnificence of the bronze doors and porphyry floor of the main entrance, the Chalke Gate, and by the mosaics in the imperial apartments depicting Byzantine emperors and their achievements. Descriptions also emphasise the use of precious metals for functional purposes, such as silver used for floors, door hinges and for the chains of hanging lamps. The furnishing of the Room of Porphyry hung with silks epitomises the importance attached to costliness by the Byzantines, for only children born in this bedchamber were entitled to ascend the throne.

The sources are not specific on the furnishing and arrangement of interiors. In an imperial bedchamber, the focus of attention was not the bed but a central fountain in the form of a peacock from which the water flowed in channels to the four corners of the room. Formal banquets were taken on couches in basilican halls, the largest containing nineteen cubicles for the couches aligned on each side of the principal couch in an apse. From the evidence of representational art, such as the mosaic of empress Theodora and her suite in the apse of San Vitale in Ravenna, it can be seen that textiles hanging from rings on poles served as adaptable partitioning in large halls. Floors were of polished stone or marble, inlaid in geometric patterns. The throne of Maximian of the early 6th century (Ravenna, Archaeological Museum) suggests that ceremonial seating furniture of wood was elaborately carved and inlaid with sculpted ivory plaques. Due to the formality of conduct at court, it appears that little attention was given to other forms of seating. Carved ornament, whether in ivory, wood or stone, was generally executed in shallow relief with drilled holes. Typical ornament relied on geometric pattern, often making repeated use of roundels and interlacing, and favoured motifs included scrolled vines, sharp-leafed acanthus, the peacock and symbols of Christianity, imperial insignia such as the double-headed eagle and elements assimilated from Eastern and Oriental sources.

The impression the Byzantines' predilection for automata left on Western visitors features frequently in accounts of Byzantine interiors. Dishes of food in the great dining halls as well as lamps were operated automatically and the most memorable was the raising aloft of the Emperor himself, seated on his fabulous gilded throne, blazing with jewels.

By the 13th century, the plan of an imperial residence had developed into a narrow, rectangular building with vaulted halls superimposed on several floors. The ruined Palace of Pophyrogenitus, also depicted on the Theodosian walls, has a three-storey elevation ornamented externally with polychrome treatment of the ashlar. The principal apartments were raised onto the first floor. The remains of the imperial palace of the Nymphaion, Kemalpasa near Izmir, inhabited by the emperor John III Vatatzes exiled at Nicaea during the Latin occupation of Constantinople after 1204, is similar and the near contemporary palace at Mistra offers a more complete example. An impression of the marble revetment and mosaic decoration of these Byzantine medieval interiors can be obtained from the heavily restored Sala di Ruggero (1170) in the Palace of the Normans in Palermo, Sicily.

The appreciation of Byzantine art and architecture has had a chequered history. Relations between western Europe and Byzantium were not as antagonistic as the history of the perpetual religious disputes might suggest. Byzantium was renowned for its luxury and exoticism, and objects from Byzantium, often in the form of diplomatic gifts, were highly prized in the West. The late 8th-century silk with the charioteer motif from the tomb of Charlemagne (now divided between Aachen and Paris, Musée Cluny), the 9th-century silk discovered in 1827 in the tomb of St. Cuthbert in Durham Cathedral and the fragments of the 11th-century textile found in the tomb of Edward the Confessor (now London, Victoria and Albert Museum, Textile and Dress Collection 2,3,4–1944) are some examples of the prestige attached to Byzantine textiles in the western medieval world.

Another channel for the dissemination of Byzantine art in the West were the Crusades, and many ecclesiastical treasuries in Venice and in the Kingdom of the Francks were filled with items looted during the Sack of Constantinople by the Fourth Crusade in 1204. As a measure of how these objects were valued in the West, many of them were subsequently mounted in metalwork or incorporated into jewellery and regalia by secular rulers, among whom the Medicis and Louis XIV of France were renowned for their collections.

Following the Ottoman conquest of Constantinople in 1453, access to Constantinople and to other Christian sites in territories of the former Byzantine Empire was closed to Christians. Consequently, the regard for Classical Greece maintained in the Orthodox tradition of the Byzantine Empire was marginalised in the Humanist Renaissance of western Europe. During the Neo-Classical era, European Byzantine monuments and sites, such as St. Mark's, Venice, and later the church on Torcello, and the ecclesiastical buildings of Ravenna and Sicily (San Vitale, Ravenna; San Apollinaire, Classe; the churches at Monreale and Cefalù, Sicily, and the Palace of the Normans, Palermo) were perceived as extraneous achievements of the medieval period. And it was only with the scholarly interest in the classification of historical styles that emerged in the mid-19th century that Byzantine art began to be accepted as a distinct category. Owen Jones's *Grammar of Ornament* (1865), which includes a chapter devoted to Byzantine ornament illustrated with three plates, represents one of the first pattern books to reflect the revival of interest in the art of Byzantium. The author of this section acknowledged the pioneering publication of Christian monuments in Constantinople, W. Salzenberg's *Alt Christiliche Baudenkmal vom Constantinopel*, which had been published in Berlin in

1854 as a result of Western European concern for the crumbling Ottoman Empire. And with the increasing enthusiasm for decorative polychromy and dense pattern came a reappraisal of Byzantine colour and interlaced patterns.

Nevertheless, archaeological interest in Byzantium was never developed to the same extent as it was for other cultures, and the art of Byzantium did not stimulate a revival which resulted in stylistic consistency. The hemispherical forms and geometric ornament and polychrome decoration were viewed as synonymous with Norman, Ottonian and Carolingian art in the revived Romanesque style. When Byzantine elements were accentuated, it was usually for political or religious purposes. Representative examples frequently quoted are Paul Abadie's Sacre Coeur in Paris (1875–1919) and John Francis Bentley's Westminster Cathedral (1894–1903), the seat of Roman Catholicism in the United Kingdom, with ivory inlaid choirstalls designed by Ernest Gimson. This also accounts for the use of Byzantine forms and non-Christian motifs as appropriate for synagogues and other Jewish buildings, exemplified in the Jewish synagogue in Berlin. In the United States, the architect H.H. Richardson (1838–86) blended Byzantine influences with the Romanesque Revival, and Charles Vogue's *Byzantine Architecture and Ornament* was published in Boston in 1890. The contribution to the progressive reform movements of the late 19th century – the Arts and Crafts movement and Art Nouveau – is yet to be evaluated.

The popular perception of Byzantium remained shrouded by myth and fable and the taste for brightly coloured and gilded mosaic decoration and for luxurious materials characteristic of the end of the 19th century made Byzantium one of the sources for fantasy. The episodes of Homer's *Odyssey* depicted in mosaic by Gaetano Meo in the dome of the double-storeyed central hall in Sir Ernest Debenham's house built by Halsey Ricardo at 8 Addison Road, Kensington in London (1905–07) reflects a concept of Greek decoration that was far from authentic. The revival of mosaic decoration owed as much to Arab as to Byzantine decorative schemes and the distinction between Christian and Muslim cultures became confused in the vogue for Orientalism. An example was the decoration in glass mosaic by Tiffany for a chapel at the Chicago World's Columbian Exposition of 1893 and this popular fashion can still be seen in the mosaic and marble interiors of the London Railway's Criterion Eating Room (1874) on Piccadilly. The mosaic decoration in the apse of the Guards Chapel, remodelled by G.E Street in 1875–78, reflects an academic dimension of the Byzantine Revival that also has yet to be fully evaluated.

CLAIRE BRISBY

Further Reading

General information and bibliographies on Byzantine interiors can be found in surveys and histories of the art and architecture of the period. Recent, more specialist sources include Maguire 1989, and Rodley 1994, and the specialist essays on individual aspects of Byzantine art in Buckton, 1994.

Beckwith, John, *Early Christian and Byzantine Art*, New Haven and London: Yale University Press, 1993

Boyd, Susan A. and M.M. Mango (editors), *Ecclesiastical Silver Plate in Sixth-Century Byzantium*, Washington, DC: Dumbarton Oaks, 1992

Buckton, David (editor), *Byzantium*, London: British Museum Press, 1994

Cutler, Anthony, *The Hand of the Master: Craftsmanship, Ivory, and Society in Byzantium 9th–11th Centuries*, Princeton: Princeton University Press, 1994

Hamilton, J. Arnott, *Byzantine Architecture and Decoration*, 2nd edition London: Batsford, 1956

Johnstone, Paul, *The Byzantine Tradition in Church Embroidery*, London, 1967

Kitzinger, Ernst, *Byzantine Art in the Making*, London: Faber, and Cambridge, MA: Harvard University Press, 1977

Krautheimer, Richard, *Early Christian and Byzantine Architecture*, 4th edition Harmondsworth: Penguin, 1986

Maguire, Eunice Dauterman and others, *Art and Holy Powers in the Early Christian House*, Urbana: University of Illinois Press, 1989

Mango, Cyril, *Byzantine Architecture*, 1976; revised edition New York: Rizzoli, 1985, London: Faber, 1986

Mark, Robert and Ahmet S. Cakmak (editors), *Hagia Sophia from the Age of Justinian to the Present*, Cambridge and New York: Cambridge University Press, 1992

Martiniana-Reber, Marielle, *Lyon Musée Historique des Tissus: Soieries Sassanides, Coptes et Byzantines Ve-XIe Siècles*, Paris, 1986

Rice, D. Talbot, *Byzantine Glazed Pottery*, Oxford: Clarendon Press, 1930

Rice, D. Talbot (editor), *The Great Palace of the Byzantine Emperors*, Edinburgh: Edinburgh University Press, 1958

Rice, D. Talbot, *The Art of the Byzantine Era*, London: Thames and Hudson, 1963; New York: Praeger, 1966

Rodley, Lyn, *Byzantine Art and Architecture: An Introduction*, Cambridge and New York: Cambridge University Press, 1994

Weitzmann, Kurt, *Late Antique and Early Christian Book Illumination*, London: Chatto and Windus, and New York: Braziller, 1977

Wessel, Klaus, *Byzantine Enamels from the 5th to 13th Century*, Greenwich, CT: New York Graphic Society, 1968

C

Cabinets

Originally a small private room, often planned to house a personal collection, a cabinet is now considered as a case for displaying or storing objects. Cabinets are usually distinct from cupboards in that they have drawers, and distinct from chests of drawers in that they have doors. This can present difficulties in description as the types and styles of cabinets can vary enormously.

They originated from the early simple coffers, chests, and cupboards that were found in the ancient world. These fulfilled the requirement for storage, but were not necessarily attractive. The Spanish *vargueno* from the 16th century is an early example of a moveable cabinet that also had a stand to display it upon. It has been said that this model was the first type of cabinet in the true sense. Originally used as church furniture, its particular arrangement made it useful for other situations: supported on a trestle stand, the dropfront, the drawers and small cupboards inside made it ideal for a number of uses. Although the first mention of the cabinet as an item of furniture appears to date back to a French record of 1528, by the early 17th century cabinets were one of the main items of a fashionable interior and were considered to be a reflection of status as well as a focal point of the room. The desire to display meant that the cabinet was placed in a prominent position within either the main bedchamber, withdrawing room or gallery. Ham House, Surrey, has a large ivory cabinet in the principal bedchamber, which is indicative of the costly materials, impressive techniques and high value that was placed upon cabinets in the 17th century. Cabinets were sometimes made in pairs to double the effect or they were displayed with a table *en suite*.

Many cabinets attained the status of works of art in themselves, being finely veneered, painted or inlaid with precious materials. The wide variety of finishes and settings including painting, inlaying, marquetry, *pietre dure*, tortoiseshell, metal inlays, and other embellishments such as mirrors, mouldings, and carving also meant that the status of the maker assumed greater importance. The term cabinet-maker reflects this changed role.

The centres of excellence of this trade in the 17th century were Antwerp and Augsburg. Augsburg continued to produce show-piece cabinets for over a century, with the famous *Wrangelschrank* being the epitome of their craft. In Antwerp an international trade developed in exclusive cabinets often veneered in ebony with painted inside doors.

Oriental cabinets were introduced into Europe early in the 17th century and although not always lacquered, this particular finish was the most popular. In both France and England the lacquered or japanned cabinet was usually intended to sit upon a stand, often exuberantly carved and gilded or silvered.

Towards the end of the 17th century the highly decorated Baroque-inspired cabinet fell out of favour and was replaced by a larger, flatter, squarer cabinet on a stand. This was decorated with veneers, used to produce floral marquetry designs. Amsterdam and The Hague became centres for specialists in this field of decorative wood veneer. Jan van Mekeren's Amsterdam workshops produced some of the most outstanding work. With the influence of the Dutch court, this taste spread to England, and cabinets on stands decorated either in floral or geometric marquetry were considered high-style.

In France the Royal workshops encouraged production of exotic pieces. Pierre Gole's cabinets on stands with fully formed figures supporting a cabinet with drawers are an example of this exclusive patronage, while the Dutch cabinet style was interpreted by cabinets on stands wholly finished in ebony. These have been particularly associated with Jean Mace. Another exotic taste was established by André-Charles Boulle, whose work with metal and tortoiseshell inlays was widely admired.

Just as exotic was the work of Italian cabinet-makers who produced cabinets finished with *pietre dure*. The diarist, John Evelyn, purchased panels of *pietre dure* and had them mounted into a cabinet, while the famous Beaufort cabinet represents a marvellous example of the process. This cabinet was commissioned by the Duke of Beaufort in 1726 to be inset with *pietre dure* panels from Florence. Other parts of Italy specialised in different cabinet styles. Naples specialised in ebony and ivory cabinets, specifically for the Spanish taste.

Each part of Europe had its own specialty. In Egerland (once Germany, now Hungary) there developed cabinets with drawers or sections in the interior, with doors carved with low relief panels. More generally in Germany there was a taste for white or ivory-finished cabinets. Particularly attractive was japanned decoration applied on a white background.

During the early 18th century, the flowering of the Rococo taste was witnessed throughout Europe. In Italy, cabinets sometimes developed into top-heavy edifices balanced on side

Cabinets: ebony cabinet with inlay and marble plaques by Henri Fourdinois, Paris, 1860s; awarded Grand Prix, 1867 Paris Exposition Universelle

tables, although the work of cabinet-makers such as Pieta Piffetti was oddly magnificent. A more practical, but no less exuberant version of Rococo was found in German cabinets. The large secretaire cabinet, often asymmetrical, crested and covered in marquetry and bronze mounts was a typical product of the period.

In England the taste for Rococo was less well established, but the cabinets of makers such as John Channon reveal an interest in this style of decoration. The cabinet on a stand continued as a type-form through the century. Whether designed to display rare marbles, exotic marquetry, glass paintings or other expensive materials, the idea of impressive display was never far away.

Cabinets for other special purposes were also developed during the 18th century. The china cabinet was a term used both by Thomas Chippendale and Ince and Mayhew to describe units for the display of china. Glass doors indicated display, while storage required solid doors. Print cabinets were low, rectangular cases with doors and sliding shelves designed to be pulled out for examination of the contents. Collectors' cabinets were planned to house particular collections, for example, medals, minerals, birds' eggs and so on.

During the 19th century cabinets were made in a great variety of shapes and styles depending upon the fashionable revived taste. The early Regency particularly offered smaller side cabinets set on plinths or short legs. Useful for storage, they again offered a surface suitable for decoration. Dark timbers combined with brass, white on black penwork, lacquered panels or even pleated fabric, all offered a decorative finish.

Most spectacular however, were the cabinets designed for the international exhibitions that were a feature of the century from 1851. These magnificent cabinets were not intended for sale; rather they were an opportunity for a cabinet-making firm to display their skills and demonstrate the quality of their workmanship. The English makers Jackson and Graham showed a cabinet and mirror in the Paris Exhibition of 1855, which was nearly fourteen feet high, encrusted with enrichments and ornament much of which was gilded. More restrained was the Adam-style cabinet shown by Wright and Mansfield in the Paris Exhibition of 1867. One of the most remarkable examples of this genre is the carved fruitwood and ebony cabinet made by Henri Fourdinois. An example of consummate skill, it took six years to complete and was also displayed in Paris in 1867.

These exhibition pieces were often unique, but there was a growing demand for cabinets for the home. A particular cabinet from the mid to end of the 19th century was the side cabinet. The type probably derived from the French *meuble d'appui* or the smaller Regency cabinets, and was available in a wide variety of styles. These cabinets still had a function but were often made with highly decorated marquetry panels, ormolu mounts, marble tops and the like.

For Gothicists and Arts and Crafts designers the cabinet was an ideal vehicle for displaying their particular taste. William Burges's painted cabinets, J.P Seddon's architect's cabinet with panels painted by Pre-Raphaelite artists and William Morris and Philip Webb's *St George* cabinet give an indication of this trend.

Another development was the work of reformers such as Charles Eastlake and Bruce Talbert. The progressive style of their work was defined by inlay, carving and a trend towards elementarism. The style of cabinets was pushed further by E.W. Godwin who had helped to develop an Anglo-Japanese style characterised by cabinets decorated with Japanese carvings and giving a lighter delicate feel. This led into a more commercial Art furniture movement, both in England and America.

The 20th century has seen the continuation of the cabinet as a furniture form. The results have been varied. Arts and Crafts influence has maintained the cabinet in its traditional role, with makers such as C.R. Ashbee using it as a vehicle for crafts objectives. Other designers, Koloman Moser for instance, introduced their particular style into the form, Art Deco designers revived the use of exotic materials on cabinets, and subsequent practitioners like Piero Fornasetti used the cabinet as a basis for art work.

In contrast to these decorative cabinets was the Modernist ideal of reducing storage to a minimum function. Hence, box-like cabinets were part of a complete storage programme. The work of architects such as Walter Gropius, Charles and Ray Eames, Robin Day, as well as products such as the Plan range illustrate this. In the last quarter of the century, the choice of styles, as well as the eclectic nature of interiors has meant a revival of historical images offering reproductions of classic cabinets, a development of the Modernist cabinet into mainstream popular models as well the idea of a cabinet being continually adapted to a variety of decorative aesthetics.

CLIVE D. EDWARDS

See also Buffets, Cupboards and Sideboards

Further Reading

A detailed history of cabinets appears in Riccardi-Cubitt 1992 which also includes a full bibliography.

Alter, D., "Augsburger Kabinettschränke" in *Die Weltkunst*, October 1976

Himmelheber, Georg, *Kabinettschränke*, Munich: Bayerisches Nationalmuseum, 1977

Jervis, Simon, "A Tortoiseshell Cabinet and its Precursors" in *V & A Album*, IV, no.4, October 1986

Kjellberg, Pierre, *Le Mobilier Français*, 2 vols., Paris: Le Prat, 1978–80

Lunsingh Scheurleer, T.H., "The Philippe d'Orléans Ivory Cabinet by Pierre Gole" in *Burlington Magazine*, June 1984

MacQuoid, Percy and Ralph Edwards, *The Dictionary of English Furniture*, revised edition, 3 vols., 1954; reprinted Woodbridge, Suffolk: Antique Collectors' Club, 1983

Mundt, Barbara (editor), *Schatzkästchen und Kabinettschrank* (exhib. cat.), Berlin: Staatliche Museen, 1990

Radcliffe, Anthony and Peter Thornton, "John Evelyn's Cabinet" in *Connoisseur*, CXLVII, April 1978, pp.254–62

Riccardi-Cubitt, Monique, *The Art of the Cabinet, Including a Chronological Guide to Styles*, London and New York: Thames and Hudson, 1992

Rogers, Phillis and John Hayward, *English Cabinets*, revised edition, London: HMSO, 1972

Wood, Lucy, *Catalogue of Commodes*, London: HMSO, 1994

Cabinets of Curiosities

"Cabinets of curiosities" were collections of natural and artificial objects, popular in educated and aristocratic circles in 16th and 17th century Europe – they are sometimes referred to by their German name, *Wunderkammer*. The term "cabinet" can refer to the collection, or to the room, or a specially worked cupboard in which the collections were stored and presented. Cabinets of curiosities were emphatically private collections, corresponding with the "closet" or cabinet in the scheme of a palace or country house as the most private of withdrawing rooms. Many of the most influential cabinets were formed by university professors as a teaching resource for natural sciences; but as they became fashionable they were acquired by monarchs and cultivated by many with pretensions to learning. Cabinets could be both encyclopedic in content as well as arranged to impressive visual effect. Dr. Johnson defined a museum in his 1755 *Dictionary* as "a repository of learned curiosities" and a number of significant private cabinets became the foundation for the great public collections of the 19th century.

In 1594 Francis Bacon (1561–1626) wrote of the essential requirements of a learned gentleman. He listed a good library and a well-stocked garden with a menagerie: "so you may have in a small compass a model of universal nature made private". A gentleman, he said, required "a goodly, huge cabinet ... wherein whatsoever the hand of man by exquisite art or engine has made rare in stuff, or form or motion: whatsoever singularity, chance or the shuffle of things hath produced: whatsoever Nature has wrought in things that want life and may be kept, shall be sorted and included".

Bacon's description of the type of rarity that was prized in such collections is an indication of both their scope and their function. The curiosities were the objects of study, comparison, learning and conversation. While cabinets might include paintings, fragments of classical sculpture, as well as antique coins, they were also likely to contain precious stones, shells and other exotic objects from distant lands and objects of a perceived historical or mythological significance.

The collecting of curiosities has a long tradition in Western Europe. Pliny the Elder described collections of semi-precious stones preserved in temples; Suetonius noted that the Emperor Augustus had such rarities in his palace as the bones of giants and the weapons of fabled heroes. In the medieval period natural curiosities had found their way into churches alongside the relics of saints. Durandus described ostrich eggs in churches "and other things of the like kind which cause admiration and are rarely to be seen ... that by their means the people may be drawn to church and have their minds more affected". During the Renaissance in Italy the revival of interest in classical literature led to a corresponding interest in the surviving small objects of that historical period: coins, inscriptions, and other archaeological fragments.

The range of the contents of such cabinets of the 16th and 17th centuries was broad and is surprisingly all-encompassing to the modern eye, used to the narrow specialisms of museums and collectors in the later 19th and 20th centuries. Indeed, "the very traits of diversity and miscellaneity which serve in our eyes to impair the serious intent of these collections were essential elements in a programme whose aim was nothing less than universality" (MacGregor, 1983).

Cosimo de Medici (1519–74) and his sons had a collection renowned for its ethnographic content, with objects from South America, Africa, India and Japan. John Evelyn described it in 1644 as containing: "hundreds of admirable Antiquities, Statues of Marble and mettal, vassas of porphyry", also, "antique habits, as that of Chineze Kings, the sword of Charlemain (and) ... such rare tourneries in Ivory, as are not to be described for their curiosity". The Medici family were also patrons of Ulisse Androvandi (1522–1605), Professor of Botany and Natural History at the University of Bologna, who published a series of important reference works on zoology and mineralogy, derived from the collections of his own cabinet.

One of the great princely collections outside of Italy was that of Rudolf II (1552–1612) at Hradschin in Prague, where four whole rooms were filled with the curiosities of art and nature. If he was unable to acquire a work of art he admired for his collection he had it copied by skilled artists. His collection was dispersed in the 17th century.

Olias Worm (1588–1654) in Copenhagen, Denmark, where he was Professor of Latin and of Medicine, formed one of the most important collections in northern Europe, which after his

Cabinets of Curiosities: Bonnier de la Mosson's physical sciences cabinet, by Jean Courtonne, 1739–40

death passed to the royal cabinet. There is a published catalogue of 1642, which includes fossils, plants, "sea unicorns" and parts of mermaids, as well as Egyptian antiquities and other ethnographic material. A contemporary observer noted: "many royal persons and envoys visiting Copenhagen ask to see the museum on account of its great fame and what it relates from foreign lands, and they wonder and marvel at what they see".

Certain private cabinets became the founding collections of important museums. The famous collection of the Tradescant family of Lambeth became the foundation for the Ashmolean Museum (1683), while the British Museum was created from the cabinet of curiosities of over 100,000 items collected by Sir Hans Sloane (1660–1753), physician to the governor of Jamaica, the Duke of Albemarle.

At the height of their popularity, the cabinets were intensely personal fields of operation. Always seen as a source of education, like a library in a well appointed house or palace, they were also for relaxation; John Ray was shown the cabinet of the Elector Karl Ludwig at Heidelberg in 1663: "after dinner his highness was pleased to call us into his closet, and shew us many curiosities ... (including) an excellent and well digested collection of ancient and modern coins and medals of all sorts in which the prince himself is very knowing". Similarly, John Evelyn on his travels wrote in his *Diary*, in 1644, that he visited: "Signor Angeloni's study: where with greater leysure we survey'd the rarities, his cabinets and medaills especially". But perhaps one of the most engaging descriptions of the sheer enjoyment of collected objects comes in his *Numismata*, in 1697: "nothing can be pleasanter than to see a circle of these virtuosi about a cabinet medals, descanting upon the value, rarity and authenticalness of the several pieces that lie before them."

JEREMY MUSSON

Further Reading

Useful essays on the subject in English are in Impey and MacGregor 1985. For a comprehensive bibliography see Balsiger 1971. Much scholarship is in Italian; for the classic study see the 1974 Italian edition of Schlosser (1st German edition 1908).

Balsiger, Barbara Jeanne, *The Kunst- und Wunderkammern: A Catalogue Raisonné of Collecting in Germany, France, and England, 1565–1750*, Ann Arbor, MI: University Microfilms, 1971

Bazin, Germain, *The Museum Age*, New York: Universe, 1967

Findlen, Paula, *Possessing Nature: Museums, Collecting, and Scientific Culture in Early Modern Italy*, Berkeley: University of California Press, 1994

González-Palacios, Alvar (editor), *Objects for a "Wunderkammer"* (exhib. cat.), London: Colnaghi, 1981

Impey, Oliver and Arthur MacGregor (editors), *The Origins of*

Museums: The Cabinet of Curiosities in Sixteenth- and Seventeenth-Century Europe, Oxford: Clarendon Press, and New York: Oxford University Press, 1985

Liebenwein, Wolfgang, *Studiolo: Die Entstehung eines Raumtyps und seine Entwicklung bis um 1600*, Berlin: Mann, 1977

Lugli, Adalgisa, *Naturalia et mirabilia: il collezionismo enciclopedico nelle Wunderkammern d'Europa*, 2nd edition Milan: Mazzotta, 1990

MacGregor, Arthur (editor), *Tradescant's Rarities: Essays on the Foundation of the Ashmolean Museum, 1683*, Oxford: Clarendon Press, and New York: Oxford University Press, 1983

Miller, Edward, *That Noble Cabinet: A History of the British Museum*, London: Deutsch, 1973

Philippovich, Eugen von, *Kuriositäten / Antiquitäten*, Braunschweig: Klinkhardt & Biermann, 1966

Pomian, Krzysztof, *Collectors and Curiosities: Paris and Venice, 1500–1800*, Cambridge: Polity, 1990

Prinz, Wolfram, *Die Enstehung der Galerie in Frankreich und Italien*, Berlin: Mann, 1970

Riccardi-Cubitt, Monique, *The Art of the Cabinet, Including a Chronological Guide to Styles*, London and New York: Thames and Hudson, 1992

Scheicher, Elisabeth, *Die Kunst- und Wunderkammern der Habsburger*, Vienna: Molden, 1979

Schlosser, Julius von, *Die Kunst- und Wunderkammern der Spätrenaissance*, Leipzig: Klinkhardt & Biermann, 1908 (Italian translation, *Raccolta d'arte e di meraviglie del tardo Rinascimento*, Florence: Sansoni, 1974)

Schnapper, Antoine, *Collections et collectionneurs dans la France du XVIIe siècle*, vol.1, Paris: Flammarion, 1988

Cameron, Charles c.1745–1812

British architect and interior designer

The ambitious son of a carpenter and builder, Charles Cameron was first apprenticed to Isaac Ware, then spent the years 1767–69 in Rome, studying and measuring and drawing antiques with the aim of producing a work that would establish him as an authority on the architecture and decoration of antiquity. Having been trained in the Palladian tradition, he first planned his work as a new edition of Burlington's *Fabbriche antiche* (1730) as well as correcting and continuing Palladio's work on antiquity. He was also influenced by the works of Giovanni Battista Piranesi. His publication *The Baths of the Romans* was published in 1772 after his return to England. The work received mixed reviews, but the plates were admired.

Cameron failed to achieve the success of such predecessors as Robert Adam, and after various vicissitudes he went to Russia in 1778. Catherine the Great was impressed by his publication and his knowledge of antiquity and, having been frustrated in her desire for a Roman house by the French architect Charles-Louis Clérisseau (1721–1820), she made Cameron her architect. Cameron spent the rest of his life in Russia, producing palaces and interiors for the Empress and her successors in the current Neo-Classic style. The works were shaped by his Palladian background as well as his first-hand knowledge gained in Rome. Furthermore Clérisseau's designs of 1773 for a Roman House as well as over 1,170 drawings of antique subjects had been bought by Catherine and were used by Cameron in his various works.

Cameron produced a series of brilliant interiors for the palace at Tsarskoe Selo, including the Green Dining Room of 1780–83, which had raised stucco decoration in the Clérisseau style, but is exaggerated in size and scale and lacks the grace and subtlety of Adam's work based on the same ancient and Renaissance sources of *grotteschi*, inset plaques and urns. The decoration of the door panels was smaller in scale, more successful and less "provincial" in appearance. Cameron's surviving drawings are more delicate and subtle, so the differences may be due to the artists and workmen who executed the work. Cameron's decoration of the 5th Apartment of 1782–84, containing Catherine's bedroom with inset Wedgwood plaques with gilded bronze embellishments, glass panels and mirrored surfaces, is far more successful and original. It has the delicacy of the works of Adam but with the added richness of shining metal and coloured moulded glass. Other rooms had delicate detailed silk panels recalling Clérisseau and Adam. None of these rooms was original in shape as they were primarily the redecoration of Rastrelli's old palace.

Cameron's exteriors for the Agate Pavilion 1782–85 and the Cameron Gallery (1783–86) were Palladian in style combined with severe Neo-Classicism. The interiors were decorated with rich materials, including, besides flat glass over coloured felt, malachite, agate, and moulded glass columns, all of which produced a richness and brilliance of colour – particularly blue and gold and black and terracotta – and a variety of textures and surfaces that was lacking in Neo-Classical interiors in England and Germany.

Cameron's work for Grand Duke Paul at Pavlovsk (from 1781) is perhaps the architect's most complete work (now completely restored). The Palladio-inspired exterior is square, with a dome, but the rich interiors were inspired by the Pantheon and Roman baths and have various geometrical room shapes with domes and niches. The Grecian Hall, for example, with its great Corinthian columns, niches and elaborate stucco ceiling resembles Adam's work at Kedleston. Any lack of subtlety is more than compensated for by the richness and colour of the decoration and the wide variety of precious and shining materials. The furniture, too, is elaborate in style and primarily by Russian designers, perhaps using Cameron's designs.

Cameron's Russian works are brilliant examples of the Neo-Classical style as it spread from Italy, France, and England. His use of a wide variety of rich, precious and colourful materials is unparalleled in the development of Neo-Classical interiors.

THOMAS J. MCCORMICK

Biography

Born in London, c.1745, the son of Walter Cameron, a Scottish carpenter-builder. Apprenticed to his father in 1760; subsequently became a pupil of the architect Isaac Ware. Lived in Rome from 1767, collecting material for a new edition of Lord Burlington's *Fabbriche antiche* (1730), published as *The Baths of Rome*, 1772. Returned to London by 1769. By 1778 had established himself in Russia as court architect to Empress Catherine II; worked chiefly on the royal palaces. Married Catherine Bush by 1784. Dismissed from service by the Grand Duke Paul after the Empress's death, 1796; re-employed as an official architect on the accession of Paul's son in 1801; made Architect to the Admiralty in 1802. Died in St. Petersburg early in 1812.

Cameron: Great Hall, Agate Pavilion, Tsarskoe Selo, 1782–85

Selected Works

A large collection of over 100 drawings by Cameron is held by the State Hermitage Museum, St. Petersburg. An album of designs is in the Alexander Palace Museum, St. Petersburg; 10 additional designs are in the Museum of the Academy of Arts, St. Petersburg; and 37 drawings relating to the Palace of Pavlovsk are in the Palace Archives, Pavlovsk. A design for a ceiling is in Sir John Soane's Museum, London.

Interiors

1780–83 Great Palace, Tsarskoe Selo, Russia (1st Apartment including the Salon Blue, Green Dining Room, Chinese Room, Bedroom and Music Room): Empress Catherine II

1781–84 Great Palace, Tsarskoe Selo, Russia (4th Apartment including the Salle des Arabesques and the Salle de Lyon): Empress Catherine II

1781–96 Palace of Pavlovsk, Pavlovsk, Russia (completed by V. Brenna: interiors including the Italian Hall, Grecian Hall, Cabinet de Toilette and gallery): Grand Duke Paul

1782–84 Great Palace, Tsarskoe Selo, Russia (5th Apartment including the Silver Cabinet, Blue Tabatière, Mauve Bedroom, Boudoir, Raphael Room and Cabinet of Mirrors): Empress Catherine II

1782–85 Agate Pavilion, Tsarskoe Selo, Russia (building and interiors including the Agate and Jasper Rooms, Great Hall and Cabinet de Toilette): Empress Catherine II

1783–86 Cameron Gallery, Tsarskoe Selo, Russia (building, interiors and furniture): Empress Catherine II

1790–1800 Batourin Palace, Ukraine, Russia (building and interiors): Count Mikhail Razoumovsky

Publications

The Baths of the Romans Explained and Illustrated, with the Restorations of Palladio Corrected and Improved, 1772 (new issues 1774 and 1775)

Further Reading

The standard monographs on Cameron are Taleprorskii 1939, Loukomskij 1943, and Rice and Tait, 1967, all of which include select further reading lists.

Colvin, Howard M., *A Biographical Dictionary of British Architects, 1600–1840*, 3rd edition New Haven and London: Yale University Press, 1995

Loukomskij, George, *The Palaces of Tsarskoe-Selo*, 1928; edited by Richard Garnier, London: Heneage, 1987

Loukomskij, George, "Charles Cameron" in *Royal Institute of British Architects Journal*, August 1936

Loukomskij, George, *Charles Cameron*, London: Nicholson and Watson, 1943

Loukomskij, George, "Charles Cameron" in *Architectural Review*, January 1943

Rae, Isobel, Charles *Cameron, Architect to the Court of Russia*, London: Elek, 1971

Rice, T. Talbot and A.A. Tait, *Charles Cameron: Architectural Drawings and Photographs from the Hermitage Collection* (exhib. cat.), London: Arts Council, 1967

Robinson, John, "A Dazzling Adventurer: Charles Cameron, The Lost Early Years" in *Apollo*, January 1992, pp.58–78

Shvidkovsky, Dmitri, *The Empress and the Architect: British Architecture and Gardens in the Court of Catherine the Great*, New Haven and London: Yale University Press, 1996

Stroud, Dorothy, *Henry Holland: His Life and Architecture*, London: Country Life 1966; South Brunswick, NJ: A.S. Barnes, 1967

Taleporovskii, V.N., *Charl'z Kameron*, Moscow, 1939

Campen, Jacob van 1595–1657

Dutch painter and architect

A native of Haarlem, Jacob van Campen was admitted to the Guild of St.Luke in his native city in 1614 after training as a painter. His first recorded design for a building is for a double house on the Keizersgracht in Amsterdam (1625) for Balthazar and Joan Coymans. He may have been partly responsible for the design of the Huis Ten Bosch (House in the Woods) near The Hague (c.1629–52); but Pieter Post (1608–69) was nominally the architect although van Campen is known to have supervised the decoration of the Oranjezal, the large central cruciform-shaped space rising to a dome in which the decorations, painted by Jacob Jordaens and other artists, are in a pompous Baroque manner commemorating the Triumph of Prince Frederik Hendrik. The allegorical programme for these decorations had been prepared by Constantijn Huygens, the Prince's secretary, and through him van Campen was introduced to Prince Johan Maurits van Nassau, from whom he received the commission to design the Mauritshuis in The Hague c.1633. Once again, Post seems to have been largely responsible for the execution of the building, and his drawings are the only record of the original interiors, which were destroyed by fire in 1704; but it is known that the vestibule was decorated with murals of Brazilian landscapes. An engraving of 1660 shows that the ceiling of the main apartment was painted with allegorical scenes in panels, and that there were heavily carved garlands on the walls, but the reconstruction after the fire was in the Louis XIV style.

Van Campen designed a number of residences as well as the Nieuwe Kerk at Haarlem (1645), but his masterpiece is the Amsterdam Stadhuis (Town Hall), which was known as "the eighth wonder of the world". The phenomenal growth of Amsterdam began at the end of the 16th century. Between 1600 and 1640 the population of the city had increased at least fourfold, its area had trebled, and it had become the world's most important trading centre. Fulsome comparisons were made between the onset of this golden age and the benefits brought to Rome by Augustus during the years of peace when he restored the arts to their former splendour. In Amsterdam, too, peace, supported by prosperity, was seen as an opportunity to encourage the arts, to embellish the city, and to confirm the fundamental importance of law and justice. It was in this climate that a decision was taken to erect a palatial building symbolic of the city's wealth and serving the dual purpose of a court of justice and the seat of the city council. Van Campen was chosen as architect and his design was approved in 1648.

At the centre of the plan is the great first-floor *Burgerzaal* (Citizens' Hall). This was inspired by the Roman basilican form, with two storeys of giant Corinthian columns; the programme of its decoration is the glorification of Amsterdam as the centre of the world. The marble floor is inlaid with maps of the Eastern and Western hemispheres, and Universal Harmony is the general theme, with sculptured references to Strength, Wisdom and Good Government. Above the four arches leading off to the galleries are the four elements, Earth, Water, Air and Fire, and higher up are figures emblematic of Peace, Prudence, Justice, Atlas, Vigilance and Moderation. Apart from the painted ceiling and coloured marble in the two doorways, all this is white, and it is only in the smaller rooms leading off the galleries that colour forms part of the decoration.

The sculpture, which forms an integral part of the whole design while providing a carefully worked out iconography, is the work of Artus Quellinus (1609–68), an artist born in Antwerp who had trained in his native city and later studied in Rome under the guidance of François Duquesnoy. His work at Amsterdam, although Baroque in spirit, complements van Campen's formal classical architecture surprisingly well.

The most interesting aspect of the plan is the integration within the whole of the rooms required for the dispensation of justice according to a traditional ritual. The *Burgerzaal* and the rooms at the north and south ends together form one cross-axis dedicated to the process, although the former had many other daily and ceremonial uses. Within the various rooms devoted to justice, decoration played an important part. Prisoners accused of serious criminal cases were interrogated in the *Pijnkamer* (Torture Chamber) on the ground floor. The object was to obtain a confession and representations of methods of torture – flogging, shinscrews and thumbscrews – are carved as decoration in the vaulted ceiling. On the day of execution the condemned man was brought to the *Vierschaar* (Court of Justice), a claustrophobic, coffinlike space, entering through bronze doors on which are depicted emblems of punishment; when they closed shut behind him they were fastened by a serpent. On the long wall the officials sat on a marble bench under the Eye of God, which looked unwaveringly at the prisoner. The caryatids supporting the entablature are in the form of captive women, and between them are large carved panels of appropriate subjects. Everything is of deathlike white marble in this panorama presented to the prisoner as he faces his judges. Finally he was turned to face the Secretary at the end of the room to hear his fate; if he looked up he could see weeping children and a skull. There was little need for further edification within this marble drama; but as the condemned man passed through the final room and out to the scaffold his last sight would have been of four great two-edged swords inlaid in the marble floor.

Van Campen, after a disagreement, withdrew from the building in 1654 and died three years later without seeing the completion of his masterpiece. He was succeeded by Pieter Post, but not all van Campen's designs for decorative painting were completed. Quellin died in 1668, but he had already handed over to Rombout Verhulst (1624–98) and other capable sculptors. The building was officially inaugurated with great ceremony and much rhetoric in 1655, although work went on for several years. Then, in 1808, Louis Napoleon, the short-lived king of Holland, recognised its pre-eminence among the public buildings in his capital by appropriating it as a royal palace – a status it still has.

DEREK LINSTRUM

Biography

Born in Haarlem, Netherlands, 1595. Trained as a painter. Member, Guild of St. Luke, Haarlem, 1614. Active as an architect from 1625. Associate of the Dutch humanist Constantijn Huygens. Died in 1657.

Selected Works

A list of Campen's architectural commissions appears in Swillens 1961.

c.1629–52 Huis ten Bosch, The Hague (decoration of the Oranjezal; building by Pieter Post)

1633 Mauritshuis, The Hague (building with Pieter Post; internal decorations including the vestibule)

1648–54 Stadhuis (now Royal Palace), Amsterdam (building and interiors; completed by Pieter Post)

Further Reading

Buchbinder-Green, Barbara Joyce, *The Painted Decorations of the Town Hall of Amsterdam*, Ph.D. thesis, Evanston, IL: Northwestern University, 1974

Fremantle, Katharine, *The Baroque Town Hall of Amsterdam*, Utrecht: Haentjens Dekker & Gumbert, 1959

Fremantle, Katharine and Willy Halsema-Kubes, *Beelden Kijken: De Kunst van Quellien in het Palais op de Dam*, Amsterdam: Koninlijk Paleis, 1983

Kuyper, W., *Dutch Classicist Architecture: A Survey of Dutch Architecture, Gardens, and Anglo-Dutch Relations from 1625 to 1700*, Delft: Delft University Press, 1980

Rosenberg, Jakob, Seymour Slive and E.H. ter Kuile, *Dutch Art and Architecture, 1600–1800*, 3rd edition New Haven and London: Yale University Press, 1993

Schama, Simon, *The Embarrassment of Riches: An Interpretation of Dutch Culture in the Golden Age*, New York: Knopf, and London: Collins, 1987

Swillens, P.T.A., *Jacob van Campen: Schilder en bouwmeester*, Assen: Van Gorcum, 1961

Terwen, J.J., "The Buildings of Johan Maurits van Nassau" in E. van den Boogaart (editor), *Johan Maurits van Nassau-Siegen, 1604–1679: A Humanist Prince in Europe and Brazil*, The Hague: Maurits van Nassau Stichting, 1979

Weissman, A.W., "Jacob van Campen" in *Oud Holland*, 20, 1902

Candid, Pieter 1548–1628

Flemish painter, sculptor, architect and designer of tapestries

Born Pieter de Witte (or de Wit), Pieter Candid was a Flemish painter, sculptor and architect active in Florence and Munich in the latter half of the 16th century, who together with Friedrich Sustris was responsible for establishing the Italian Mannerist style of painting and decoration in South Germany.

According to the contemporary historian Carel van Mander, Candid was born in Bruges c.1548, the son of Pieter de Witte, a tapestry maker. In 1558 his father moved to Florence to work for the Grand Duke, Francesco I de Medici, and changed the family name to Candido. Pieter Candid was trained as a painter and worked under the direction of Giorgio Vasari. An early commission dating from c.1569 was for a fresco in the chapel of San Luca in the church of SS. Annunziata, Florence; the work itself may have been carried out by one of Candid's pupils, Giovanni Fedini. Soon afterwards, Candid assisted Vasari with the decorations in the Sala Regia in the Vatican (1569), and later with the decoration of the interior of the Dome of Florence Cathedral, c.1572.

In 1576 Candid was made a member of the Accademia del Disegno in Florence and in 1583 he was given an official position there. Several important commissions date from this period. In 1578 he produced an altar painting for the Cathedral in Volterra; in 1585 he painted a fresco of the Madonna and St. Jerome and St. Michael for the church of San Niccolo del Cepo; and in the same year Francesco I commissioned him to paint a series of portraits of members of the Medici family. But in 1586 he was called to Munich by Wilhelm V, Duke of Bavaria (reigned 1579–92) on the recommendation of the sculptor Giovanni da Bologna. Candid remained in Munich for the rest of his life, completing a range of important and varied commissions, many in association with the painter and designer Friedrich Sustris whom he had met previously in Florence. He worked with Sustris on the decoration of the Antiquarium, or classical museum, in the Residenz, supplying a number of paintings of allegorical subjects that were set into the ceiling amidst the rich Italianate grotesque decorations supervised by Sustris. A sketch exists for an allegory of Hope (Spes) from this scheme. Candid is also recorded as working on the Grottenhalle at the Residenz which was mainly designed by Sustris.

When Wilhelm turned to religion and began to support the Jesuit order, Candid received a number of associated commissions. An altar painting of the Martyrdom of St. Ursula for the Church of St. Michael was executed in 1588, and no less than eight other commissions for the Jesuits were carried out during these years. In 1595 he produced an altar painting for St. Ulrich, Ugsburg; in 1600 another for the Capuchin Church in Munich. And later, in 1620, he executed a large painting depicting the Ascension of the Virgin to celebrate the military victory at Weissenberg that stood on the high altar of the Frauenkirche, the Cathedral of Our Lady, Munich, until 1858.

Candid was also active as a sculptor, and as a designer of sculptures that were produced by his workshop. The attribution of many of these works is unclear but notable examples include the statue of Perseus in the centre of the garden of the Grottenhalle (although this piece is also associated with Sustris), the Allegory of Bavaria in the Rotunda of the Hofgarten executed by Hans Krumper, and the Mausoleum of the Emperor Ludwig of Bavaria in the Frauenkirche, erected by Krumper in 1619–22.

Throughout this period Candid was also active as a designer of tapestries, a branch of art that was particularly encouraged by Wilhelm's successor, Maximillian I. From c.1604 until 1614 Candid was engaged on two series of twelve tapestries, one of grotesques and the other commemorating the deeds of Otto von Wittelsbach, the 12th-century founder of the Bavarian ducal line. These were made for the Residenz and are now preserved in the Burg Traunitz, Landshut, where Sustris had previously worked in 1573–80. A second series of tapestries, woven between 1612 and 1614, depicted the Twelve Months, the Four Seasons and Day and Night. In 1614 Candid began work on a series of Heroes and Heroines from the Old Testament and from classical history for the Kaisersaal in the Residenz; the painter Hans Kappler assisted in the preparation of the cartoons. Despite the fact that later historians have sometimes described these tapestries as vulgar and heavy, this series arguably represents Candid's finest achievement in this medium. Whether working on a grand scale or, as with the Seasons, more intimately, Candid's great strength lay in his ability to incorporate all the richness of Italian decoration in the borders and edges of his tapestries, while at the same time employing the more simplified figurative systems demonstrated in Raphael's Sistine Chapel tapestries in the central sections. This approach prepared the way for the grand style later used in Rubens's tapestry designs.

Candid was also responsible for several painted decorative schemes. These included decorations in the Altes Schloss at Schleissheim (1617), and a set of allegorical ceiling paintings in the Goldener Saal in the Augsburg Rathaus, or Town Hall of 1619. The latter were executed by the local Augsburg painter Matthias Kager (1575–1634).

Candid's style, particularly in some of his designs for statuary, owes much to the Mannerist tradition of sculptors such as Giovanni da Bologna. But the style of his drawings, many of which survive, appears closer to the Northern Italian style of artists like Paolo Veronese combined with strong influences derived from his study of High Renaissance masters such as Raphael and Michelangelo. Like Sustris, he played an important role in introducing the Italian style to the Munich court and in popularising a refined and colorful style of art that led naturally and easily into the German Baroque.

DAVID CAST

See also Sustris

Biography

Born Pieter de Witte (or de Wit) in Bruges, 1548, the son of a tapestry maker. Moved with his father to Florence, 1558, and trained as a painter. Worked under Giorgio Vasari (1511–74) in Rome and Florence, 1569–74. Member, Accademia del Disegno, Florence, 1576. Active as a tapestry designer under Jan van der Straet (1523–1605), Florence, c.1576. Active as a painter in Volterra, 1578, and Florence, 1585. Summoned by Duke Wilhelm V of Bavaria to Munich, 1586, where he worked as a painter in the Residenz under the direction of Friedrich Sustris (c.1540–99). Active as a painter of altarpieces from the late 1580s, and later as a sculptor; designed tapestries for the Munich workshops of Hans van der Biest from 1604. Continued to work as a painter in Munich until the 1620s. Died in Munich, 1628.

Selected Works

1569	Sala Regia, Vatican (painted decoration under the direction of Vasari)
1586	Antiquarium, Residenz, Munich (painted decoration under the direction of Sustris)
1586	Grottenhalle, Residenz, Munich (grotto decoration under the direction of Sustris)
1617	Altes Schloss, Schleissheim (painted decoration)
1619	Town Hall, Augsburg (designs for decorations for the Goldener Saal)

Candid's tapestries included a series of grotesques (1604–15); a series commemorating the deeds of Otto von Wittelsbach (c.1604–11); a series of the Twelve Months, the Four Seasons, and Day and Night (1612–14); and a series representing Old Testament Heroes and Heroines (begun 1614).

Further Reading

Burresi, Mariagiulia, *Pieter de Witte* (exhib. cat.), Volterra: Fotoimmagine Volterra, 1994

Mander, Carel van, *The Lives of the Illustrious Netherlandish and German Painters, from the First Edition of the Schilder-boeck (1603–1604)*, edited by Hessel Miedema, 2 vols., Doornspijk: Davaco, 1994

Volk-Knuttel, Brigitte, *Wandteppiche für den Münchener Hof: Nach Entwürfen von Pieter Candid* (exhib. cat.: Bayersichen Nationalmuseum), Munich: Deutscher Kunstverlag, 1976

Volk-Knuttel, Brigitte, *Peter Candid, Zeichnungen* (exhib. cat.), Munich: Staatliche Graphische Sammlung, 1978

Volk-Knuttel, Brigitte, "Candid nach Schwarz" in *Münchner Jahrbuch der Bildenden Kunst*, 39, 1988, pp.113–32

Candles, Candle-holders and Candle-stands

Until 1800, artificial lighting in interiors was almost completely dependent on candles, a form of illumination that was always costly since good wax candles were very expensive. Tallow candles (made of animal fat) and rushlight (meadow rush soaked in fat) were less expensive but smelt badly and were quickly consumed. This meant that candle-holders were rare objects in ordinary households and even in larger houses there were surprisingly few.

Over the centuries many terms have been used to designate hanging and standing candle-holders. Although the historical terminology is often confusing, three different types can be discerned: the candlestick to place on a flat surface; the sconce to hang on the wall; and the chandelier which is suspended from the ceiling. Designs of candle-holders and -stands changed over the centuries and followed fashion. Major artists and interior designers contributed designs, among them Albrecht Dürer, Christoph Jamnitzer, Jean Berain, Daniel Marot, Johann Michael Hoppenhaupt, Juste-Aurèle Meissonier, Robert Adam, and Augustus Pugin. These designs were often carried on by others and produced in more than one country.

A basic form of lighting was the lantern, a receptacle for a light-fixture, enclosed partly by small panes of glass or translucent material to protect the candle from drafts, set in a frame of metal or wood. Lanterns were hung in important passages, staircases, and halls; side lanterns were attached to walls.

Probably the best-known support for candles, usually singly, is the candlestick, a free-standing support with a nozzle into which the candle is inserted. The stem is often in the form of a baluster, column, or human figure and over the centuries this has produced considerable variety. Materials, too, have varied considerably, notably metal – brass, silver, Sheffield plate, or pewter – but also including ivory, rock-crystal, glass, Delftware, porcelain, and wood.

Candlesticks for ecclesiastical purposes normally have prickets (spikes) rather than nozzles to hold the candles. The chamber candlestick, with a short stem, wide pan, and a handle, was intended for the bedroom. A candlestick for more

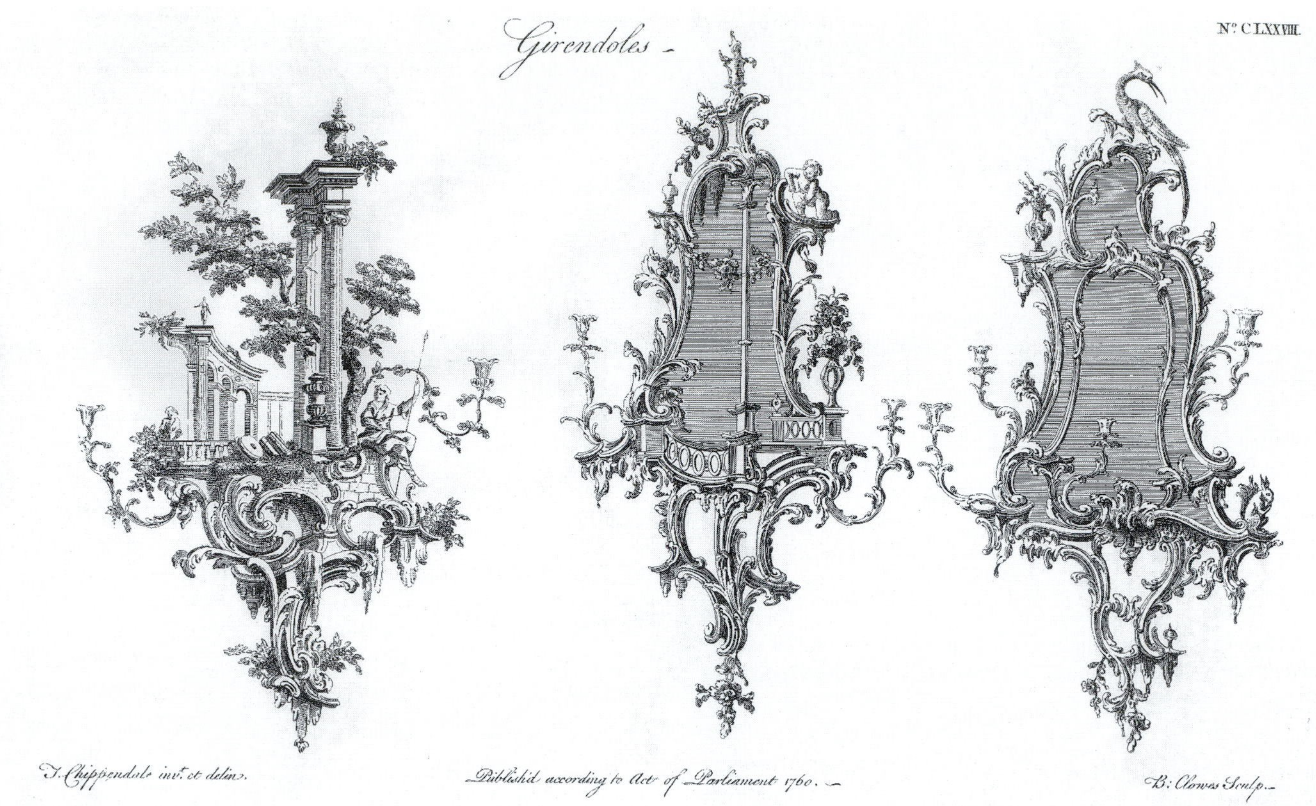

Candles: designs for girandoles by Thomas Chippendale from *The Gentleman and Cabinet-Maker's Director*, 1762

than one candle, generally with six branches, is called a candelabrum; *candélabre* in French.

The etymology of lighting can be confusing, to say the least. During the Middle Ages, and even up to the 16th century, the term "candlestick" was occasionally applied to what we call a chandelier – a hanging light fixture with several branches suspended from a ceiling or roof. Originally the French term for candlestick, the name chandelier (from the French *chandelles*, tallow candles) has also been used for a wall-light or sconce. In England, these hanging fixtures were generally known as hanging candlesticks or branches and it was not until the 18th century that the term chandelier came into use in England. After the mid-18th century they became known in France as *lustre*, a term also employed in England.

Chandeliers were generally made of brass or carved and gilded wood; and the most precious ones were of silver and rock-crystal. The earliest surviving chandelier dates from the 11th century – a large hanging ring onto which the candleholders are attached. In the 15th century a type was developed with a moulded stem and several branches in one or two tiers; this was made well into the 18th century. From the late 17th century onwards, pyramidal chandeliers made of rock-crystal became fashionable. A century later rock-crystal was replaced by cut glass and Venice became a centre of production.

The sconce, or wall-light, consists of one or more branches springing from the lowest point on a reflector back plate. Like candlesticks, they have come in a wide variety of materials, including silver, pewter, carved wood, earthenware, and cut glass, sometimes combined with other materials such as enamel or embroidery. A looking-glass in a wooden or silver frame occurs as a backplate from the late 17th century onwards, often pleasingly shaped, sometimes decorated with a chased armorial device or monogram. Occasionally the branch takes the form of a human arm, the hand holding a socket or a scroll on which the socket is placed. Sconces were used for general illumination, but for activities such as reading, sewing, or writing, additional light from a candlestick or girandole was necessary.

The girandole, a pyramidal candelabrum, derives from the Italian *girandola* a type of firework like a horizontal Catherine wheel. In the late 17th century it referred to an elaborate type of candelabrum with pendants of cut crystal or glass, forming a pyramid of light – as described in the French royal inventories of 1660. In the 18th century the term girandole applied to all candelabra as well as to chandeliers and lustres, with or without crystal pendants. In mid-18th century England it referred in particular to large carved and gilt-wood sconces in the Rococo style; also to a wall bracket with mirror back. Later in the century the mirror was often circular and convex and was sometimes used alone.

To elevate a lamp or candle to a convenient height, a torchère or portable stand was often employed. Normally these were made in the form of a table with a tripod base, turned or baluster shaft, occasionally in the form of a human figure, and a small, circular, square, hexagonal, or octagonal top with moulded border, often adjustable in height. Occasionally torchères were made in the form of a Negro holding up a circular tray. This type, originating from Italy, was fashionable during the second half of the 17th century and often called a *guéridon*, the French name for a Negro pageboy.

The most valuable torchères were made in silver, but they were more often in wood, enlivened with sculptural details such as gesso work, lacquer, or marquetry. Although torchères were primarily candle-stands, they have also been used to support objects such as vases or dishes. From around 1670 into the 18th century, torchères were often made in pairs, or *en suite* with a table and mirror, or with a cabinet. In 14th- and 15th-century France the word *torchère* or *torchière* referred to a type of candlestick which was larger than usual. Later the word was also used for a large candelabrum and, in the last quarter of the 17th century it became what it is today, a stand on which a candlestick or candelabrum could be placed.

ELOY KOLDEWEIJ

See also Lights and Lighting

Further Reading

Bacot, H. Parrott, *Nineteenth Century Lighting: Candle-Powered Devices, 1783–1883*, West Chester, PA: Schiffer, 1987

Butler, Joseph T., *Candleholders in America, 1650–1900*, New York: Crown, 1967

Cooke, Lawrence S. (editor), *Lighting in America: From Colonial Rushlights to Victorian Chandeliers*, revised edition Pittstown, NJ: Main Street Press, 1984

Eveleigh, David J., *Candle Lighting*, Aylesbury: Shire, 1985

Gilbert, Christopher, James Lomax and others, *Country House Lighting, 1660–1890* (exhib. cat.), Leeds: Leeds City Art Galleries, 1992

Hoos, Hildegard and others, *Kerzenleuchter aus acht Jahrhunderten*, Frankfurt: Museum für Kunsthandwerk, 1987

Hughes, G. Bernard, "Fashions in English Candlestands" in *Country Life*, 14 December 1967, pp.1586–87

Jarmuth, Kurt, *Lichter leuchten im Abendland: Zweitausend Jahre Beleuchtungskörper*, Braunschweig: Klinkhardt & Biermann, 1967

Michaelis, Ronald F., *Old Domestic Base-Metal Candlesticks from the 13th to 19th Century*, Woodbridge, Suffolk: Antique Collectors' Club, 1978

Symonds, R.W., "Candle Lighting in the 18th Century" in *Antique Collector*, April 1952, pp.52–58

Thornton, Peter, "Lighting" in *Seventeenth Century Interior Decoration in England, France, and Holland*, New Haven and London: Yale University Press, 1978, pp.268–81

Wechssler-Kümmel, Sigrid, *Schöne Lampen, Leuchter und Laternen*, Heidelberg: Keysersche, 1962

Cassina

Italian furniture manufacturer; established 1927

Cassina is one of an influential group of family-owned Italian businesses that have dominated avant-garde and High-Style furniture manufacturing in the post-war period. Based in Meda, near Milan, since the 18th century, by the 1930s the Cassina family was producing upholstered pieces for major Milanese department stores such as La Rinascente and Mobilificio di Fogliano. Under the inspired partnership of the brothers Umberto and Cesare, the marketing possibilities of modern design were fully exploited by the company. By restructuring the production and distribution systems (partly aided by a large naval order between 1947–52) they were able to capitalise on the post-war growth of Italian and international middle-class elites who were increasingly interested in modern, stylish furniture by major Italian and international designers. After early collaborations with Paolo Buffa and Franco Albini, the firm turned to the prolific architect-designer Gio Ponti, and the practice of producing design-led pieces for which Cassina is now famed began.

Ponti's *Distex* armchair combined 1950s angularity with upholstered Italian élan and the *Superleggera* side chair, a synthesis of traditional and contemporary styles, was a particular international success which Cassina has mass-produced since 1957.

During the 1960s the Italian furniture industry embraced the new materials and technologies of an increasingly imaginative and uninhibited era and Cassina's continuing collaborations with the new generation of Italian designers advanced this process. Cassina particularly excelled at producing sophisticated contemporary models that nevertheless still had traditional appeal. Examples of this furniture include the 1963 Vico Magistretti *892* chair made in beech or walnut with a stained or lacquered finish, and the plush, yet modernistic leather pieces designed by Mario Bellini in the 1960s such as the *Cab* chair of 1967 which has zips up the sides of the leather-covered steel skeleton. Luxury and comfort also combine in the designs by Tobia and Afra Scarpa such as the model *917* of the early 1960s.

By purchasing the exclusive reproduction rights from the heirs of Charles Rennie Mackintosh, Gerrit Thomas Rietveld, Erik Gunnar Asplund, Frank Lloyd Wright, Le Corbusier, and Charlotte Perriand, Cassina created a collection of masterpieces of late 19th- and 20th-century furniture design named the "Cassina i Maestri." The Le Corbusier chaise longue of 1929 was the first classic piece to be reproduced by Cassina (since 1965). The work of reconstructing the furniture pieces LC1, 2, 3 and 4 was carried out by Cassina when Le Corbusier was still living and other models were added in 1974, 1978 and 1985 under the supervision of the Fondation Le Corbusier with the collaboration of Charlotte Perriand. Coloured versions of some of the pieces were introduced in 1985 using pastel colours close to shades illustrated in Le Corbusier's original palette and which matched the taste of the 1980s.

Each piece of furniture in the "Cassina i Maestri" collection bears a copy of the signature of the author, a production number, information on the materials used and the original design, biographical details of the designer and a bibliography and list of museums and galleries which have exhibited the piece. Through its commitment to authenticity, and by promoting such classic pieces as the Corbusier *Grand Confort*, chaise or the Rietveld *635 Red and Blue* chair of 1918 (first reproduced in 1978) Cassina has cleverly tied in its own products with the celebration of the grand tradition of European Modernism. Many of the interiors associated with the "designer decade" of the 1980s would inevitably feature a Cassina reproduction of a Corbusier chaise longue or a Mackintosh Hill House ladder-back chair.

Some of the company's own most renowned pieces of furniture were produced during the Italian design renaissance of the 1970s and 1980s. These include the *Aeo* chair by Paolo Deganello of the early 1970s with its soft slung form, or the *Manhattan Sunrise* sofa by Gaetano Pesce of 1980, inspired by pop sculpture and the Manhattan skyline. Vico Magistretti's

Cassina: *Superleggera* chair designed by Gio Ponti in 1955

1981 *Sinbad* armchair marks a continuing interest in the manufacture of luxury designs. Inspired by brightly-edged English horse blankets, this sumptuous sofa combines innovative materials with rich colour, and evokes a sense of effortless luxury. It is a Modernist interpretation of comfort allied with wealth and style, as are Magistretti's *Maralunga* chair and ottoman and the Mario Bellini series of marble tables.

Many of these innovative pieces were launched by Cassina at the annual Milan Furniture Fairs, and their showroom in Milan is a showpiece of contemporary Italian exhibition- and retail-expertise. An international team of designers has also been called upon, such as in the famous *Wink* armchair by Japanese designer Tokiyuki Kita. On the death of Umberto Cassina in 1991, Vico Magistretti remarked on the opposing yet complementary skills of the two Cassina brothers: "Umberto decided how and when to manufacture while Cesare selected the designs, thus creating a perfect management division". Cassina was brought into the American Steelcase Group in the late 1980s.

SUSAN HOYAL

See also Ponti

Further Reading

Cassina's work is illustrated in most histories of 20th-century furniture; another useful source is the firm's own catalogues, particularly for the 1970s onwards.

"Cassina: The Image" in *Ottagano*, 92, September 1989, pp.146–49

Fiell, Charlotte and Peter, *Modern Chairs*, Cologne: Taschen, 1993

Hiesinger, Kathryn B. and George H. Marcus III (editors), *Design since 1945* (exhib. cat.), Philadelphia: Philadelphia Museum of Art, and London: Thames and Hudson, 1983

Licitra Ponti, Lisa, *Gio Ponti: The Complete Work, 1923–1978*, Cambridge: Massachusetts Institute of Technology Press, and London: Thames and Hudson, 1990

Modern Chairs, 1918–1970 (exhib. cat.: Whitechapel Gallery, London), London: Lund Humphries, and Boston: Boston Book and Art, 1971

Pasca, Vanni, *Vico Magistretti, Designer*, New York: Rizzoli, and London: Thames and Hudson, 1991

"La Saggezza di Umberto" in *Ottagano*, 104, September 1992, pp.61–64

Santini, Pier Carlo, *Gli Anni del Design Italiano / The Years of Italian Design: Ritratto di Cesare Cassina* (in Italian and English), Milan: Electa, 1981

Sparke, Penny, *Italian Design, 1870 to the Present*, London: Thames and Hudson, 1988; as *Design in Italy*, New York: Abbeville, 1988

Cassoni

In current usage, "cassone" refers to the several styles of large chests used as decorative furniture in wealthy Italian Renaissance homes. Household inventories suggest that these massive forms were most often grouped in bedchambers, flanking either beds or walls in the otherwise sparsely furnished interiors. They also indicate, however, that the term cassone was not used consistently during the period; at any rate scholarship has not yet reached any conclusions about its precise meaning between about 1400 and 1600. In fact it appears only rarely before 1500, and was little used in southern Italy even after that date. A much more common term, *forziere*, generally referred to painted or leather-covered chests reinforced with iron straps, but cassone was also occasionally used to describe these. The distinction may have been refined in later years, as the carved walnut chests characteristic of the high Renaissance seem not to have been described as *forziere*.

As dowry chests, cassoni were an important focus of marriage preparations and ceremonies, although it should not be supposed that all cassoni were made for weddings. Many exhibit two families' coats of arms, usually placed symmetrically on the stiles or the side panels, and carved or painted figures on the stiles sometimes serve as armorial supporters. Later examples in the style of antique sarcophagi often display arms where classical Roman carvers would have placed inscriptions or portraits. A cassone in the Victoria and Albert Museum depicts the family arms of Elisabetta Gonzaga impaled by those of her husband, Guidobaldo di Montefeltro, but most armorial designs are less graphically suggestive. Despite the arms which document their marriage, this is a simple board chest decorated with paint and gilding and was probably not made for their wedding – unless it was part of a group including several grander examples. Dowry chests were usually commissioned in pairs, but patrician families owned large numbers of cassoni: Isabella d'Este, for example, arrived in Mantua for her wedding in 1490 with 13 painted chests. But it is likely that the corpus of cassoni which survive – nearly all richly decorated with panel paintings, gilding, inlay or carving – presents a distorted picture. Chests with painted panels, in particular, were rarely mentioned in inventories or depicted by artists. Even less elaborate cassoni, however, were expensive and treasured possessions. Most were lined with fabric, and a

Cassoni: painted cassone from the workshop of Apollonio di Giovanni (c.1416–65), showing the meeting of Solomon and the Queen of Sheba

few were painted in imitation of brocade, which suggests that fine textiles sometimes decorated the exterior.

Because Italian women's direct inheritance was increasingly restricted after the 13th century, the dowry took on added importance. Packed in paired cassoni, dowry goods were carried to the conjugal home in public wedding processions which literally described the transfer of wealth between newly allied families. This practice, which seems to have been confined to the aristocracy and the upper-middle classes, continued as late as the mid-15th century in Florence. In procession, extravagant cassoni intimated the dowry's value without actually displaying its contents publicly, and served as vehicles for social competition. Although in most cases the bride's father commissioned these, after about 1450 this was often the groom's responsibility. Cassoni presented as a groom's marriage gift could still be paraded through the streets, if less formally.

The workshops which produced cassoni responded slowly to new artistic developments, and the flat, even patterning of Gothic chests remained popular outside Florence and Siena into the late Quattrocento. Iron straps were less common after 1400, but the façade division they imposed – usually tripartite – was retained in many later chests. In Venice and the Adige Valley, "engraved" designs were cut into softwood with hot needles and filled with pigment; cypress, which repels insects, was favored. Venetian workshops also specialized in gesso relief, gilded and painted in vibrant colors. Both types were essentially mass-produced: engraving was laid out with templates, and mould-made relief elements were easily rearranged. Tin-leaf, varnished yellow, could replace gilding, which was more expensive than even painting or carving. The imagery on these richly textured chests included the iconography of chivalric courtship: female archers and heart-struck men, lovers at a fountain and falconers on horseback. On later cassoni, symbols of the garden of love gave way to painted narratives from Ovid, Boccaccio, Petrarch, classical mythology and biblical subjects. Storiated panels could be confined within moulded quatrefoils or roundels or extend across the façade; side panels often continued the tale. Paired cassoni were conceived as a seamless narrative or developed a relationship between two subjects. Apollonio di Giovanni's workshop (1446–63) specialized in such painted cassoni, and served clients from all the great Florentine families. Although little is known about other workshops' production, individual cassone panels have been attributed to Sandro Botticelli, Domenico Veneziano, Jacopo del Sellaio and Paolo Schiavo, among others.

The stories illustrated on cassoni offer a complex view of marriage, and often represent cautionary tales rather than romantic statements. The brutal rapes of Lucretia and the Sabines may have been reminders of wifely duty: submission, fidelity and childbearing. Dido and Griselda modeled devotion, while Callisto and Daphne showed the risks of passion. In general, cassoni panels imply that romantic love is fraught with danger, while loyalty and selflessness are heroic choices. These messages were later supplanted by epic classical themes, but they should not be underestimated. Many Renaissance Italians believed that images seen during pregnancy would influence the child, and the paintings of Paris and Helen found inside the lids of several paired cassoni were probably charms for beautiful children. Storiated panels may have offered similar spells for a successful marriage.

In the second half of the 15th century, cassoni became larger and more architectural in form, with coffered, moulded lids and tall plinths. Walnut chests with intarsia decoration remained popular throughout Italy after 1470 into the 16th century, but by the early 1500s cassoni *a moda di tomba* were all the rage in Tuscany and Rome. Carved in high relief with caryatids or dolphins bulging on each corner, broad volutes, classical mouldings and lions'-paw feet, these chests show the influence of sculpture rather than painting. Their strongly Mannerist façades, often crowded with writhing, heroic figures, were left unpainted: dark walnut was preferred, gilded sparingly if at all. Little progress has been made in attributing carved cassoni, but Rome was probably a center for their production. Both carved and intarsia cassoni were made as pairs, often "right and left handed" for symmetry.

According to Vasari, the cassoni tradition led to the use of *spalliere* – framed, rectangular panels used as friezes – as well as other painted furniture, and furnishings were often conceived in tandem to create a unified effect. For a 1515 wedding, Andrea del Sarto's workshop was commissioned to paint two panels to hang above a pair of carved walnut cassoni, and similar panels were used throughout the bedchamber. The painted walls of the Palazzo Davanzati in Florence echo the motifs on early marriage cassoni: the arms of a husband and wife, roses, lilies, fruit trees and peacocks – emblems of Juno, to whom wedding vows were sacred.

19th-century antiquarians and art collectors were fascinated by cassoni, which they collected avidly. William Morris and Philip Webb's *Saint George* cabinet (1861) is a direct, if romantic, interpretation of painted cassoni, and inspired many Victorian designers' fanciful "medieval" furniture. Unfortunately, the restorations undertaken by early collectors also tended to be fanciful: new carcasses were constructed to support painted panels, gesso relief was replaced and gilding added, especially on walnut chests where little or none may have been evident. Along with the removal of panels to be hung as paintings, these improvements have created tremendous obstacles to connoisseurship. Scholars' interpretations of individual panels' original context often differ substantially, and in many cases the material evidence which could resolve the issue is long since lost.

JODY CLOWES

See also Chests; Renaissance

Selected Collections

Important collections of cassoni are at the Victoria and Albert Museum, London; at the Museo Nazionale del Bargello, Museo Bardini and Museo Stibbert, Florence; and at the Metropolitan Museum and Frick Collection, New York.

Further Reading

The most up-to-date English survey of the cassone is in Thornton 1991, with good illustrations and further bibliography. Schiaparelli 1908 (1983) and Schubring 1915 remain classic studies of the subject. Klapisch-Zuber 1985, Lydecker 1987, and Witthoft 1982, are useful for discussions of the social context of *cassone.*

Baskins, Cristelle, L., *Lunga pittura: Narrative Conventions in Tuscan Cassone Painting circa 1450–1500*, Berkeley: University of California Press, 1988

Callmann, Ellen, *Apollonio di Giovanni,* Oxford: Clarendon Press, 1974

Faenson, Liubov, *Italian Cassoni from the Art Collections of Soviet Museums*, Leningrad: Aurora, 1983

Ferrari, Maria Luisa, *Cassoni rinascimentali,* Milan: Arti Grafiche Ricordi, 1964

Frederickson, Burton B., *The Cassone Paintings of Francesco di Giorgio*, Malibu, CA: Getty Museum, 1969

Klapisch-Zuber, Christiane, "The Griselda Complex: Dowry and Marriage Gifts in the Quattrocento", in her *Women, Family, and Ritual in Renaissance Italy*, Chicago: University of Chicago Press, 1985, pp.213–246

Lydecker, John Kent, *The Domestic Setting of the Arts in Renaissance Florence*, Ph.D. thesis, Baltimore: Johns Hopkins University, 1987

Pope-Hennessy, John and Keith Christiansen, "Secular Painting in 15th century Tuscany: Birth Trays, Cassone Panels and Portraits", in *Metropolitan Museum of Art Bulletin*, New York, Summer 1980, pp.12–55

Schiaparelli, Attilio, *La casa fiorentina e i suoi arredi nei secoli XIV e XV*, 1908; reprint edited by Maria Sframelli and Laura Pagnotta, 2 vols., Florence: Le Lettere, 1983

Schubring Paul, Cassoni: *Truhen und Truhenbilder der Italienischen Frührenaissance: Ein Beitrag zur Profanmaleri im Quattrocento*, 2 vols., Leipzig: Hiersemann, 1915–23

Thornton, Peter, "Cassoni, forzieri, goffani and cassette: Terminology and its Problems", *Apollo*, CXX, October 1984, pp.264–51

Thornton, Peter, *The Italian Renaissance Interior, 1400–1600*, London: Weidenfeld and Nicolson, and New York: Abrams, 1991

Witthoft, B,. "Marriage Rituals and Marriage Chests in Quattrocento Florence", in *Artibus et Historiae*, vol.5, 1982, pp.43–59

Castaing, Madeleine 1897–1992

French interior decorator and antique dealer

Decorator, antique dealer and connoisseur of modern art, Madeleine Castaing was the most influential exponent of the eclectic decorating style that emerged in fashionable circles in the post-war period. During the mid and late 1930s a number of experts and connoisseurs had come to the conclusion that modern furniture did not have the scale and presence to hold its own in an important interior. This view was encapsulated in the furniture historian Ralph Edward's article of 1936 entitled "Old Furniture and the Modern Background" (published in the magazine *Decoration*) which predicted the mixing of styles that was to become fashionable after the war. Raymond Mortimer's article, "Modern Period Character Mania: The Alternative to Period Style", (*Decoration*, 1937) not only endorsed this theme, it defined and developed it further. Mortimer also emphasised the role of the decorator as arbiter of taste, proclaiming: "Having accepted the principle of mixing styles – aesthetic judgment supplanting period consistency – we realize that all things that are good of their kind do not necessarily mix. They must have been conceived in the same spirit – have some abstract aesthetic relationship".

Castaing was particularly well-placed to make such judg-

Castaing: dining room for Madame Ferenzi, Paris, 1948; watercolour by Aleksandr Serebriakov

ments. Her credentials as an interior decorator were strongly underpinned by her professional skills as an antique dealer and by her serious interest in modern art. She moved in the inner circle of Parisian artistic life, combining her reputation as an arbiter of taste with a more cerebral involvement in supporting and promoting the Lithuanian Expressionist painter Chaim Soutine. Furthermore, her knowledge of period and modern styles was coupled with considerable artistic flair, and, as a result, her expertise and judgment were eagerly sought after by a wealthy Parisian clientele.

Castaing's first antique shop opened in the rue du Cherche Midi in 1941, when Paris was under the shadow of German occupation, but it was with her new premises, established at the corner of the rue Jacob and the rue Bonaparte in 1947, that she is most closely associated. The situation all over Europe was still intensely grim during this period and yet a pent-up creative energy, suppressed through the years of war and its aftermath, produced an extraordinary renaissance in the arts of living. Thus, Castaing's first decorative commissions coincided not only with Dior's "New Look" that was to revolutionize fashion, but also with the important fresh direction taken by interior decoration in England that was led by John Fowler and Nancy Lancaster.

The Castaing shop was extremely distinctive. The exterior was painted black and the low-set windows offered a view of a dimly-lit, rambling interior containing a seemingly careless arrangement of furniture and *objets d'art* of every description and value ranging from museum-quality antiques to fleamarket finds. Castaing aimed to create an impression of private rooms from which the occupant had just departed – in other words, of rooms that were not overly formal or immaculately tidy. The stock was unpriced and Castaing parted with her favourite pieces only with huge reluctance and for very substantial prices. This did nothing to diminish their desirability for her devotees, among whom she was proud to name the artist and film director Jean Cocteau. She insisted that she must feel a total rapport with her clients and she brought a dedicated perfectionism to the achievement of the desired effect.

Almost impossible to categorize, the Castaing style consists of an apparently random mixture of furniture from all periods, with wallpaper and textiles in a subtle blend of nostalgia and modern chic. A pared-down, simple architectural framework showed the antique furniture to great advantage, though she sometimes indulged in dramatic touches, like marbled wallpaper, for her own front hall, or woven canework wall-panels at the Villa Santo Sospiro. The element of chic makes the French version of post-war eclecticism quite distinctive. Castaing's own designs, coupled with an unrivalled eye for quality and individuality, made her interior schemes inimitable, and her patrons were prepared to accept her wilfullness and the enormous cost of her ideas in the knowledge that only she could create this particular neo-19th century look with total conviction.

The Castaing revival style was a mixture of Neo-Classical, Biedermeier and Regency, combined with judicious touches of Second Empire buttoned upholstery and papier-mâché inspired by the evocative descriptions in Balzac's novels. She was responsible for stimulating interest in English mahogany among French decorators. Any suggestion of scholarly antiquarianism was put to flight by her bold use of colour; much black, with sienna, grey, "Pompeian" red and sky-blue, and her particular favourite "Castaing green", like turquoise water, which she used for the walls of her shop. Her signature touches were a taste for flowered needlework, and striped carpets of her own design with low seating in quilted satin and lacquered coffee tables, also her own designs. The shock factor was provided by the frankly esoteric in the form of staghorn furniture or oversize painted shell chandeliers.

The effect was quite unlike the austere correctness of the Regency Revival or the claustrophobic stage-setting of "Victoriana", with wax or woolwork fruit under glass domes, as espoused by posing undergraduates largely as a joke. Smart "Victoriana", created by artists and fashion people – Digby Morton, Lady Ashton and John French in London, and Carlos de Beisteguy, who was responsible for the famous pastiche, Château de Groussay, in Paris – was quite different, and can be seen as a parallel strand to Castaing's work. "I don't care about periods", she remarked, "If a room is finished and there is no life to it, there is nothing there". Her decorating philosophy was exemplified in her Parisian apartments – the ghostly *prémises* full of cobwebby and shrouded furniture, like Miss Havisham's dining room from Charles Dickens's *Great Expectations* – and at Lèves, the Castaing's country property near Chartres.

CHARLOTTE GERE

Biography

Born in Paris, 1897. Married Marcellin Castaing. Worked as an interior decorator and opened her first antique shop in Paris, 1941; business moved to premises at the corner of rue Jacob and rue Bonaparte, 1947. Died in Paris, 1992.

Selected Works

Business records and drawings relating to Madeleine Castaing's decorating commissions remain in the hands of the firm, now known as the Fondation Castaing, which is based in the rue Bonaparte premises, Paris.

Further Reading

Boyer, Marie-France, *Paris Style: The Private Apartments of Paris*, London: Weidenfeld and Nicolson, 1989

Calloway, Stephen, *Twentieth-Century Decoration: The Domestic Interior from 1900 to the Present Day*, London: Weidenfeld and Nicolson, and New York: Rizzoli, 1988

Gere, Charlotte, *Interiors* (sale cat.), London: Christie's, 17 November 1994, pp.117–18

Hampton, Mark, *Legendary Decorators of the Twentieth Century*, New York: Doubleday, and London: Hale, 1992

Melikian, Souren (editor), *The Art of Interior Decoration*, London: Hachette, 1963

Cast-Iron Furniture

During the 19th century cast-iron furniture was a characteristic feature of many domestic interiors. It was designed to be especially suitable for gardens, conservatories and halls, although useful and purely decorative items could also be found in other parts of the Victorian home. Garden benches and tables, hall stands, stick and umbrella stands, jardinières, wash stands, radiator covers, *objets d'art* and mirror frames, were all manufactured in large quantities and there was a thriving home and export market in Great Britain, although the United States, Germany and a number of other European countries were also important centres of production.

During the 18th century cast iron was used within the home environment, but its application was largely restricted to the manufacture of cooking pots, oven ranges and grates. It was during this period, however, that companies such as Coalbrookdale in Shropshire, and Carron in Falkirk, were established in Britain, and it was to be only a matter of time before they turned their hand to the production of furniture. In the early years of the 19th century the virtues of cast iron as a material had been fully recognised by architects, and its incorporation into the design of the Brighton Pavilion and its use by Paxton in the Crystal Palace project is well known. The development of cast-iron furniture was a spin-off of the decorative architectural ironware business established by firms like Coalbrookdale. Furniture production at Coalbrookdale was introduced in the early 1830s alongside the manufacture of a range of so-called artistic wares and they produced everything from cake plates and inkstands to the large and imposing hall stands already mentioned. A number of eminent artists and designers worked for the company including the sculptor John Bell whose Coalbrookdale iron *Andromeda* was shown by the firm at the Great Exhibition in 1851. Critics commented on this exhibit favourably saying "as an example of casting it may take rank with the best specimens in the Exhibition." Bell also designed the *Deerhound* hall table, a commissioned piece where the deerhounds, which provide the four supports for the table top, bear on their chests the arms granted to John Hargreaves of Blackburn, Lancashire. This elaborate and imposing item, clearly demonstrating the firm's capability, was shown at the Paris International Exhibition in 1855. Christopher Dresser also worked for the Coalbrookdale company and a number of designs for hall stands, hall chairs and garden benches can be attributed to him. A pioneer of industrial design, Dresser was well aware of the considerable potential embodied in cast iron as an ideal material for the manufacture of furniture.

As a substance cast iron had many advantages which made it suitable for the manufacture of furniture. As an alloy of iron and other materials, its crystalline structure enabled it to be poured into moulds when in molten form. The process by which castings could be produced was, and still is, relatively simple, involving sand moulds and carved wooden templates. Simple objects such as solid and pierced decorative panels could be produced straightforwardly in two-part moulds, though more complex objects might involve three-part moulds or even a lost-wax process. It will perhaps be obvious that the great virtue of cast iron lay in the fact that it could be moulded to take on almost any form. The tractability of cast iron and the simple technology needed to produce three-dimensional objects meant that decorative items of almost any form could be produced to identical standards, repetitively and at an economic cost. The early 19th-century preoccupation with bringing the garden into the home and the cult of naturalism, which was to reach its zenith during the High Victorian period, provided the foundry industry with the stimulus to produce goods which would satisfy the demand for garden, conservatory and hall furniture. The writer J.C. Loudon in his *Encyclopaedia of Cottage, Farm and Villa Architecture* (1833) recommended the use of cast-iron furniture for halls on the grounds that it was cheap and practical, and illustrated examples of hall chairs in various styles. The majority of the furniture items were made from prefabricated panels which could be bolted together to produce the desired object.

In stylistic terms the items conformed to the Victorian taste for heavy ornamentation, and in this respect the medium responded well to the reproduction in cast iron of naturalistic, Gothic, Renaissance and Neo-Classical repertoires of ornament. It had the added advantage of being able to be finished in a variety of ways and painted finishes and bronzed metallic effects were not uncommon. Indeed in certain cases the user might not even know the object was made from cast iron at all, as the finishing process could hide the nature of the core material. Garden benches and conservatory benches, one of the commonest types of cast-iron furniture, were usually made from three panel components, two for the sides and one for the back, the seats more often than not being made from wooden slats. The panels often took the form of logs, with branches and twigs smothered in foliage – this was considered to be a very appropriate form of decoration given the object's likely location. Hall stands on the other hand were often made from panels where the ornamental detail was more formal or even abstract in nature. In both cases, however, the objects were functional, decorative, sturdy and were easily capable of withstanding wet environments and heavy usage.

While the products of some of the foundries which displayed items at the Victorian exhibitions held in Europe and America received critical acclaim and the firms were awarded medals for their efforts, many design critics poured scorn on the cast-iron furniture produced in the mid part of the century. A.W.N. Pugin criticised the excesses of ornament found on many cast-iron objects in the 1830s and as late as 1868 Charles Eastlake wrote "all cast iron ornament is bad in style". Although tractability had been one of cast-iron's fundamental assets in terms of its application to the production of a wide range of objects, it was this very property which eventually led to the resultant objects being so heavily criticised. With hindsight this criticism seems unfair. In many respects it was an admirable industrial material with a potential that was fully exploited by foundry entrepreneurs. Certainly if sales and usage are anything to go by, decorative cast-iron furniture was popular with a wide range of consumers.

Many companies protected their designs by registering them with the patent office, and surviving examples often bear the diamond registration marks used to mark items between 1842 and 1883. The simple code embodied in the diamond gives information related to the day, month and year of registration. After 1883 the marks "Rd. No." (registered number) followed by a series of digits may be found. Both of these sources of information are useful when research is being carried out on an item today. Some companies marked objects with their own cypher or mark and this is indeed true of Coalbrookdale products where a small rectangle on the underside of an object will reveal the name.

One category of furniture incorporating cast-iron components is 19th-century patent furniture. The first patent for a metal bed was taken out in 1849 and the major bedhead components were made from cast iron. But, in the late 1850s, when steel tubing became available, cast-iron bedsteads were superseded by tubular steel ones. More successful, however, was the range of tables designed for specific purposes. Carter's patent Literary Machine, sold by J. Carter of 64 New Cavendish Street, Portland Place, London provides a good example of such a table. It consisted of a small round circular table top made of mahogany, supported by a tubular metal stem and with a moulded cast-iron cruciform base. From beneath one side of the top an arm projected which supported an adjustable surface which acted as a book rest. Many of these industrially-made novelty objects combined technical ingenuity with modern materials and the use of cast-iron components for structural support and decorative ornamental detail represented an interesting and valid use of the material.

The demand for cast-iron furniture had fallen by the end of the century as fashions changed, and this is reflected in the reduced number of designs shown in the foundry trade catalogues. It is only in recent years that cast-iron furniture has made a comeback as interest in the Victorian period has grown and conservatories have once again become popular features of late 20th century homes. Many of the cast-iron seats and tables made today are reproductions of designs first introduced in the 19th century.

J. IAN COX

Selected Manufacturers

Manufacturers involved in the production of Cast-Iron furnishings included the following: William Bullock and Co., West Bromwich; the Coalbrookdale Company, Shropshire; the Carron Ironworks, Falkirk; Walter Macfarlane and Co., Glasgow; and The James Foundry Co., Staffordshire. American producers included the Miller Iron Co., Providence, Rhode Island; J. L. Mott Ironworks, New York and Chicago; and Robert Wood and Co., Philadelphia.

Selected Collections

Specialist collections of British Cast-Iron furniture can be seen at the Falkirk Museum, Falkirk, Stirlingshire, the Victoria and Albert Museum, London, and the Coalbrookdale Museum of Iron, Telford, Shropshire.

Further Reading

Ames, Alex, *Collecting Cast Iron*, Ashbourne: Moorland, 1980

Fearn, Jacqueline, *Cast Iron*, Princes Risborough: Shire, 1990

Gay, John, *Cast Iron: Architecture and Ornament, Function and Fantasy*, London: Murray, 1985

Himmelheber, Georg, *Cast-Iron Furniture*, London: Philip Wilson, 1996

Lawley, Ian, "Art and Ornament in Iron: Design and the Coalbrookdale Company" in Nicola Hamilton (editor), *Design and Industry: The Effects of Industrialisation and Technical Change on Design*, London: Design Council, 1980, pp.18–21

Lister, Raymond, *Decorative Cast Ironwork in Great Britain*, London: Bell, 1960

Raistrick, Arthur, *Dynasty of Iron Founders: The Darbys and Coalbrookdale*, London: Longman, 1953

Schiffer, Herbert, Peter, and Nancy, *Antique Iron: American and English Forms, Fifteenth Through Nineteenth Centuries*, Exton, PA: Schiffer, 1979

Snyder, Ellen Marie, "Victory over Nature: Victorian Cast-Iron Seating Furniture" in *Winterthur Portfolio*, XX, Winter 1985, pp.221–42

Celtic Revival

The Celtic Revival had a particular vogue during the last two decades of the 19th century and the period leading up to World War I in the 20th. At its zenith, Grant Allen in the *Fortnightly Review* of 1893 could claim that it was the Celtic spirit that lay behind most innovations in Western culture, fixing on examples as diverse as Socialism, Methodism and the Eisteddfod. Like most of the ideological movements of the period, it embraced all aspects of culture, and although its most successful form was in literature, particularly that of Yeats and the Irish literary revival, it was also evident in many interiors and furnishings of the period. In discussing early 20th century styles, *The Lady's Realm* of 1905 (vol XVIII, p.228) commented that "fumed oak and inlays of ebony and ivory point to a Celtic origin, and many town houses are furnished throughout on this scheme of decoration."

There had been considerable interest in the Celtic peoples among antiquarians of the 18th century, but the intellectual origins of the Celtic Revival proper may be traced to research and debate in philology, archaeology and racial theory during the second half of the 19th century. It was from writers like Ernest Renan and Thomas Carlyle that a notion of Pan-Celtic identity and culture was established. Celticism appeared as an expression of the marginal or peripheral cultures at the north-western extremity of Europe, where the Celtic peoples had been driven in the early Middle Ages by successive invasions. Racially and culturally, Scotland, Ireland, Wales, the Isle of Man, Cornwall and Brittany were felt to have a common ancestry distinct from the rest of Britain and France. Such speculations and new scientific discoveries surfaced in the later 19th century among the national and religious disputes in the countries of the so-called Celtic fringe. In this respect the Celtic Revival could be described as a manifestation of National Romanticism which thrived during the same period in central Europe and Scandinavia. Celticism was viewed as a tribal phenomenon with a great literary and musical tradition; it was argued that the oral culture emanating from this Celtic Spirit had been overwhelmed and marginalised by the onset of industrialisation and urban growth, although it had managed to prevail in traditional rituals, crafts and festivals.

One of the principal aids to the Celtic Revival in the visual arts was the archaeological discoveries of the mid to late 19th century and the presentation of important finds in publications and museum displays. The Tara Brooch and the Ardagh Chalice, for example, discovered in Ireland in 1850 and 1868 respectively, were copied by several metalworkers (notably Waterhouse and Co. of Dublin and, slightly later, Edmond Johnson), the designs eventually being used on objects as diverse as dishes, tea sets and the paraphernalia of the gentleman's desk. It was the publication of Celtic decoration, however, particularly those patterns from manuscript illumination, which created a repertoire of designs that could be applied to a range of media and contexts. Among the decorative arts featured in "artistic" interiors of the period, Celtic designs were particularly popular for metalwork, stained glass, stencilwork, textiles and carving. A further boost to the Revival was the appearance of such crafts in International Exhibitions of the period, particularly those in America where cities such as Chicago, host to the World's Columbian Exposition of 1893, had a large Irish population.

Given the emerging consciousness of Irish identity, it is not suprising that Celtic designs should have been prominent in works produced under the aegis of the various Arts and Crafts associations in Ireland. The Dun Emer Guild, for example, set up in 1902 by Evelyn Gleeson and the two Yeats sisters, Lily and Elizabeth ("Lolly") took its name from "Emer", the wife of the ancient Celtic hero Cu Chulainn. Much of the imagery used in their textiles, carpets and book illustration was derived from the traditional Celtic vocabulary of interlace patterns and stylised dragons. The most celebrated craftsman of the Irish Arts and Crafts Movement was Harry Clarke, a stained glass artist and book illustrator, whose work was influenced by Celtic patterns while also being heavily dependent on the febrile stylizations of Aubrey Beardsley and the late Symbolists. Alongside the craftworkers of the Dun Emer Guild he was employed on several collaborative schemes such as the Honan Chapel in Cork in which the unifying element was the protean Celtic interlace pattern, found on glass, stone, metal and textile.

Working from the Isle of Man between 1889 and 1901, H.M. Baillie Scott developed an integrated style of interior decoration, inspired largely by William Morris but exploiting a richer sense of an ancient tribal past that was redolent of popular ideas of the Celt. This style gained great international prestige when Baillie Scott's designs for the Palace at Darmstadt were published in *The Studio* in 1898. In 1901 Scott won the top prize in the competition for a house for an Art Lover, with a design based on similar principles, although very little of it was explicitly "Celtic". The designer who did most to bring the styles and motifs of the Celtic Revival into the mainstream was Baillie Scott's Manx collaborator, Archibald Knox (1864–1933). Between 1899 and 1912 Knox designed two lines for Liberty's, Cymric and Tudric ware, which exploited the elaborate interlace pattern of Celtic ornament. Initially applied to plate and candlesticks, the designs which Liberty's promoted as "suggestive of a more remote era than this", were soon to be found on picture frames, wall mirrors, clocks, cigarette cases, belt buckles and jewellery. Such was the popularity of the two-dimensional Celtic interlace that it was also applied to the firm's carpets, textiles and ceramics.

The association of Celtic culture with Ireland and hence Catholicism, could explain why evidence of the Celtic Revival, with its range of suitably sinuous forms, was not more pronounced in the Glasgow Style interiors of Charles Rennie Mackintosh and his associates. Although Glasgow had a large Catholic community, it was largely composed of recent immigrant Irish or Highland workers who lacked the wealth and political clout to impinge on the world of the International New Art. In Edinburgh, on the other hand, Catholicism was not so socially problematic and it was here that Celticism found its most vociferous and active exponent, the maverick Patrick Geddes (1854–1932). The periodical *The Evergreen*, one of the numerous illustrated art magazines of the 1890s, was a mouthpiece for Geddes and the artists and designers sympathetic to Celticism. Among the latter was Phoebe Traquair who provided a direct link with the Irish Arts and Crafts Movement, having trained in Dublin.

What distinguished Geddes from his Irish counterparts was his commitment to large-scale mural schemes to put over his aesthetic and cultural ideals. There are, however, very few documented or surviving Celtic interior schemes by this group, a notable exception being Ramsay Garden in Edinburgh (1893–95) undertaken by a number of craftworkers under the direction of Geddes and the artist John Duncan. As well as private flats which made up the bulk of this development, the self-governing student hostel incorporated a large common room decorated with extensive Celtic knotwork and a series of twelve murals on the spritual history of the Gael, which in Geddes's view extended to the Arthurian cycle and to modern figures like Charles Darwin.

A recurring theme in the writings of the Celtic Revival was the emphasis on the separate development and character of the early Celtic church. Given the national and political context in the wake of Catholic Emancipation, therefore, it is not surprising that the more important decorative schemes should have been applied to ecclesiastical interiors, in Ireland notably St Brendan's Cathedral (Loughrea, c.1902–20), and the Honan Hostel Chapel (Cork, c.1916). Equivalent examples in Scotland would be the Catholic Apostolic Church decorated with murals by Phoebe Traquair (Edinburgh, 1895–97), and St. Conan's Kirk (Argyll, 1907–30).

Irish Home Rule in 1921 confirmed the popularity of the Celtic Revival as a national style based on true sources. Not surprisingly therefore, Celtic-inspired decoration has persisted in Ireland throughout much of the present century and it is still possible to see new decorative schemes in public and private buildings which deploy Celtic motifs alongside other symbols as the expression of an independent, native Irish culture.

PAUL STIRTON AND JULIET KINCHIN

Further Reading

Boardman, Philip, *The Worlds of Patrick Geddes: Biologist, Town Planner, Re-educator, Peace-Warrior*, London: Routledge, 1978

Bowe, Nicola Gordon, "The Arts and Crafts Society of Ireland (1894–1925), with particular reference to Harry Clarke" in *Journal of the Decorative Arts Society*, no.9, 1985

Cumming, Elizabeth, *Arts and Crafts in Edinburgh, 1880–1930* (exhib. cat.), Edinburgh: Scottish National Portrait Gallery, 1993

Cumming, Elizabeth, *Phoebe Anna Traquair*, Edinburgh: Scottish National Portrait Gallery, 1993

Edelstein, T.J. (editor), *Imagining an Irish Past: The Celtic Revival, 1840–1940*, Chicago: University of Chicago Press, 1992

Martin, Stephen A., *Archibald Knox*, London: Academy, 1995

Sheehy, Jeanne, *The Rediscovery of Ireland's Past: The Celtic Revival, 1830–1930*, London: Thames and Hudson, 1980

Stirton, Patrick, "Patrick Geddes in Edinburgh" in *Newsletter of the Charles Rennie Mackintosh Society*, no.60, Winter 1992, pp.9–11

Tilbrook, Adrian J. and Gordon House (editors), *The Designs of Archibald Knox for Liberty & Co.*, revised edition Shepton Beauchamp, Somerset: Richard Dennis, 1995

Chairs

In its widest sense the chair holds a special position in the interior as it is the only item designed to support people. It is not a coincidence that the parts of a chair often has human attributes, for instance, arms, legs, feet, back, and seat.The variety of chairs that has developed over 4000 years of furniture use testifies to the importance of this furniture type. Chairs ranging from simple stools to elaborate thrones represent aspects of social history, the most common being the indicator of status.

The range of chairs appears to be endless. Apart from those indicating position or status, there are others intended for a wide variety of special purposes. These include dining, sleeping, rocking, relaxing, praying, reclining, exercising, and sewing. In addition, the selection is further extended by methods of construction including fixed, folding, wheeled, and skidded. Also the choice of materials in chair-making has ranged from marble to plywood, and from coal to glass.

In Egypt, seats were derived from backless stools, initially having framed seats with carved bulls' legs to the front, and then to armchairs by the 4th dynasty (c.2600–2500 BC). The best-known example of an Egyptian seat is Tutankhamun's gold throne, both as a model of furniture-making and also as the embodiment of the symbolic authority of the chair. On a more mundane level, stools remained popular, often designed with braced struts and a white paint finish. Folding stools were also used: they often had hide seats, and cross-frames decorated as carved ducks' heads inlaid with ivory.

In ancient Greece, seating arrangements were based on a range of stools and chair types. Stools were basic four-legged versions or box-like constructions. In addition there was the

Chairs: designs for chairs by the firm Poirer et Remon, Paris, late 19th century

diphros, a four-legged stool with stretchers. The famous *klismos* chair form, originally with well-proportioned outward-curving legs and a back panel at shoulder height, gradually developed a top-heavy back board, thus making it rather clumsy in appearance. The Romans developed the *curule-sella curulis* – a seat with arms and no back. This was an important precursor of the folding chair or *faldstuhl* and the X-chair.

In the Byzantine period chairs and thrones remained important and were now based on a box shape with back. X-framed chairs, sometimes made of metal, were fitted with a slung leather seat. Combinations of desk and lectern were significant, indicating the importance of manuscripts and reading.

Chairs remained a sign of rank and the style of chair reflected its occupant's position within society. The throne of the Emperor Maximian which was covered with carved ivory plates indicates this status. Thrones were the ultimate symbols of authority: examples include the English Coronation chair, Dagobert's bronze throne, and the silver throne of King Martin of Aragon.

During the Middle Ages, chairs developed in England, France and the Netherlands, based on a box-like panelled structure, possibly derived from chest construction. Chair types, including simple turned chairs with pegged members and box-seated chairs, were decorated with carving, applied mouldings and arcading. In conjunction with these patterns the X-framed chair remained a favoured model.

Chairs developed from a box-panelled shape gradually began to be less heavy, more open, and usually fitted with arms. They were given a slight rake to the back, but the legs remained straight. Joiners continued to make chairs, often adorning them with prestigious ornament inlaid into the backs of such "joyned" chairs.

The chair developed a greater number of variations in the 16th century. The *caquetoire* was a French-style chair designed for conversation, while the farthingale chair developed in England and Europe. The name farthingale is a modern description for a broad seated side chair or back stool introduced in the latter part of century and common for the next 100 years throughout Europe. It was used for casual seating and dining and for the latter purpose would be covered in leather.

During the 17th century chair types continued to proliferate. Regional variations became important with such examples as the Yorkshire and Derbyshire chairs. These were identified by a variety of arcaded backs and particular turnings. In America the regional types included the Boston chair, a leather-seated chair with a broad central splat, while the Brewster chair from New England was a spindle-backed rush-seated chair with high posts and decorative finials. Though known as early as the 15th century, the chair-table was not popular until the 17th century. It was a wooden armchair with a large hinged back which could be let down for use as a table. The settle was sometimes further developed into a combination piece, with the back turning into a table (called a monk's bench). The thrown chair with highly turned parts was an example of the turner being employed to make chairs in this period.

Chairs continued to be made in massive and solid forms, but there was a growing demand for comfort and luxury. The result of this was the beginning of upholstery, the earliest examples being simply based on stretched coverings over a frame. This developed into the X-frame chair which was supplied with loose cushions. By the Restoration, twist turning had become a typical feature of the period, and the tall-backed walnut chairs with caned seats and back panels were easily recognisable. Constructionally they were not always so sound, since in many cases, seat-rails were simply placed on top of the legs and dowelled instead of being tenoned in between. However, the introduction of the splayed back leg does show some consideration for the possibility of over-balancing. The double-scroll Flemish leg changed to a Dutch bandy-leg which gradually led to the cabriole shape. By the 1690s an inverted cup and trumpet was used for legs on tables, tallboys and cabinets. Castors, using leather or wood rollers were introduced around this time. Daybeds or couches, with six legs, had cane, carved or turned-wood decoration to match the chairs. Settee-backs were divided to give the effect of chairs joined together, and for dining chairs, drop-in seats and the stuff-over method were both used.

Queen Anne chairs were noticeably restrained in their added decoration, although the most important feature to emerge from this period was, without doubt, the cabriole leg. Introduced in the late 17th century, and perfected at the beginning of the 18th, the cabriole leg, with its uniting of two opposing curves, was seen as the epitome of the curvilinear design. Compound curves were introduced into the hoop backs of chairs, and stretcher braces disappeared as construction techniques improved.

Chair types continued to increase. Hall chairs with hard seats, often decorated with coats of arms, became important. The *sgabello* chair, derived from Italian originals, and often fitted with a shell-shaped back was also used for halls and entrances. Upholstered easy chairs with embroidered coverings, and upholstered wing-chairs with padded arms and backs demonstrated a renewed desire for bodily comfort as well as the avoidance of cold draughts.

The vernacular types continued to develop, especially with the Windsor chair. This traditional chair form made with a solid wood seat and stick back was known in England and America from the early 18th century and has continued as a type-form ever since. The regional variations are wide and give credence to the idea of a lively local design tradition. Indeed, in the second half of the 20th century the Windsor chair has been used in traditional and contemporary interiors.

Around 1700, Daniel Marot introduced a style of chair with a narrow back which enclosed a vertical solid vase or splat, and is sometimes known as a Queen Anne chair. The introduction of cabriole legs changed chair construction by removing the stretcher bars. The construction method demanded a wider knee which soon became a favourite place for carved decoration. Other technical changes occurred: shoe-pieces for backs were now pinned and glued to back rails, and seat rails were rebated to accept drop-in seats. Chairs had broader seats and the cabriole legs were finished in a ball and claw foot.

During George II's reign, legs became even more elaborate having high relief carving and decorated seat rails with solid splats replacing pierced ones. These features remained essentially the ingredients of wooden armchairs throughout the mid-century. There were innovations and changes of scale and detail in line with changes in taste. An example was the introduction of the square-section leg with stretcher bars; the ladder-back dining chair; fretted and latticed work in the Chinese style, and various Gothic motifs.

Numerous designers have been credited with particular chair styles. Robert Adam's French influence is apparent in his chair designs based on the oval back and taper-turned leg, whereas the Neo-Classical influence was found in the round, or rectilinear style of backs.

Hepplewhite introduced the shield-back, oval, and heart shapes for chair backs which are often supported by the upward elongation of the back legs. Thomas Sheraton's chairs were generally designed with square backs and frequently had square-section legs which were slightly tapered. For economy or a particular effect many of these chair types were often made from beech with a painted finish.

Throughout the 18th century the range of chair types continued to develop. Many of these were again special-purpose models. The gouty chairs for example, were designed to allow invalids to self-propel the chair around a room, while library chairs were especially designed for supporting a book and assisting the reader. Upholstered armchairs referred to by Ince and Mayhew as burjairs (bergères) were popular, as they allowed for informal relaxation. Sheraton stipulated that they should have caned back and arm frames and loose cushions; this style was popularly revived in the early and mid 20th century.

The development of fancy chairs began in the late 18th century, when a taste arose for the lightweight but decorative chair. Sheraton encouraged the style, while in America, Hitchcock introduced a late Sheraton-style chair of light weight having a cane or rush seat, often painted in black with gold or stencilled decoration, which was very successful.

Regency chairs can be identified by their dark, glossy wood offset by brass inlay, trellis-work galleries, lion's paw feet, masks, star-shaped bolt heads and studs. Angularity of shapes was often accentuated by reeding on chair legs and cabinets as it was considered that ancient furniture was nearly always angular. The chairs often took on extravagant proportions or highly decorated forms to make them appear lavish in conception and execution. Motifs such as dolphins and chimera, as well as more restrained images derived from classical devices, were common.

Victorian chairs were characterised by the revivals that formed the styles of interiors, including the Gothic, the Elizabethan, and the Rococo, but from the 1850s onwards, upholstered lounge suites of no particular pedigree were popular. These comprised a sofa, a pair of spoon-back chairs and a number of smaller balloon-back side or dining chairs. These suites remained available well into the next century in one form or another and were a middle-class status indicator. During the period 1850–1900, two new chair designs were introduced that are seen as typically Victorian. These were the balloon-backed dining or bedroom chair and the *prie-dieu* or kneeling chair.

Nineteenth-century chairs display Janus-like features. On the one hand they were often based on revivals of past styles. The *Glastonbury* chair for example, was a 19th-century term for a type of chair based on a 16th century model supposedly based on a model made for the Abbot of Glastonbury. On the other hand they often incorporated interesting and new technology which was hidden within the chair. The use of metal springs was a very important step in the search for resilience and comfort, while the easy chair, with an internal frame of iron strips often in combination with springing, created a comfortable and relaxing chair.

In the same vein were a wide range of reclining chairs, often based on patent methods, which varied from medical principles to sumptuous elegance. Rocking chairs also developed in this period, usually with an emphasis on a combination of comfort and technology. Rockers were made in wood or metal; they were mounted on curved skids or on spring platforms and achieved great success in Europe and the United States. Patentees also devised new methods of construction, including the important knock-down technique, especially advantageous in the export business.

Arts and Crafts designers frequently returned to vernacular models for their chair designs. The Morris *Sussex* chair is one example, and the ladderback chair with horizontal rails, which was originally associated with country chairs, was taken up as the epitome of a simple chair. William Morris's armchair, with cushioned back and seat, and an adjustable rake to the back, was the precursor to many variations produced ever since. Particularly popular in the United States they were called Morris chairs for many years. The Arts and Crafts influence was also important for reconsidering the idea of the total interior. In terms of chairs this meant that architects were involved in designing chairs to complement interior schemes. The work of Gustav Stickley and Frank Lloyd Wright in America and C.F.A. Voysey in England clearly demonstrate this tendency.

One of the most important examples of change in chair design and making were the products and production methods of the Thonet company. Their laminated and later the bentwood products have become internationally known as examples of simple, elegant and cheap chairs. The conscious decision to manufacture in bulk, to export worldwide, to use machinery and semi-skilled labour, and to produce designs that have since been seen as type-forms of chairs was revolutionary. Although the range of Thonet products was very wide, the classic *No. 14* chair remains an icon for designers today. It has been associated with the International Style of the 1920s to 1930s, has experienced a revival in the 1960s and 1970s in eclectic interiors supplied by Habitat and their like, and in the 1990s the models are still used as a basis for simple chairs, even if made from metal or plastic.

During the 20th century the chair has become an icon of style and design movements. Many architects have designed chairs, often as a complement to their architecture and interior work; very often these designs coexisted, bearing little relation to the commercial styles available to the majority. This is partly because much of an architect's time is involved in contract work rather than domestic design. Examples of individual designers will be found in other parts of this book, but mention must be made here of some of the most important. Some experimented with new artistic ideas, others developed new materials and design approaches, yet others returned to the essence of craft to develop their designs.

One of the major features of 20th-century furniture design, particularly of chairs, is the understanding that furniture items stand in a given space and, in the case of chairs, often remain unoccupied for much of their life. Their sculptural value in an

Chairs by Arne Jacobsen, the *Egg* and the *Swan* for Fritz Hansen, late 1950s

interior is therefore quite important. Designers as varied as Charles Rennie Mackintosh, Gerrit Rietveld and Harry Bertoia all acknowledged in different ways this role for a chair. Mackintosh used the chair in a way similar to early Frank Lloyd Wright chairs, to enclose a dining space, for example. Rietveld and his famous *Red / Blue* chair used his design to evaluate grids and planes in relationship to each other and beyond that within the space in which the chair stands. In 1952 Harry Bertoia, who trained as a sculptor, devised the wire chairs which have since carried his name. These particular chairs clearly show an understanding of the needs of the open-plan interiors of that time and remain elegant examples of the sculptural possibilities of chairs.

The second strand in 20th-century chair design was the application of materials towards a Modernist ethic. In the Bauhaus the seminal work of Marcel Breuer was an enormous challenge to convention and resulted in the famous *Wassily* chair and the ground-breaking cantilever chair. From the same inspiration were the chairs of the architect Mies van der Rohe. His *Barcelona* chair from 1929 is often seen as a "design classic" which epitomises the tenets of Modernism in its purity of form, lack of applied decoration and fine materials.

Many other early 20th century architects devised furniture for their interiors, often in collaboration with a partner. Le Corbusier and Charlotte Perriand are one such team, as were Charles and Ray Eames. Among many experiments using a variety of materials, their work on plywood chair frames is very significant. The resulting three-dimensional plywood chair seats and backs were revolutionary.

Plywood and laminated wood were also the favoured materials of the Finnish architect Alvar Aalto. His experiments with cantilever forms made in beech and birch were in contrast to the metal forms of the Bauhaus and the main Modernist movement.

After World War II, other materials began to feature in chair design. Aluminium was successfully used by Ernest Race in his *BA* chairs but was not destined to be a widely favoured material. More successful in the long term was the role of plastics. Often associated with the Pop movement and the 1960s, plastic chairs have been developed in an enormous variety of styles and forms. On the one hand the potential of plastics has been explored in injection-moulded units such as Robin Day's polypropelene chair and some Italian studio designs, while on the other hand, many commercial manufacturers have used fibreglass or polystyrene shells for a range of chairs for the mass market.

The benefits accruing from other technology, such as plastic foams, have also influenced the design of chairs. Some "chairs" have been created to exploit the material into a variety of sculptural shapes, while others have used the material to reproduce traditional style upholstery at a mass market level.

A third strand of chair design in the 20th century is the importance of craft and material. The work of Carlo Bugatti, Jacques-Emile Ruhlmann, Maurice Dufrène, and Pierre Chareau all emphasise the chair as a vehicle for exotic decoration, fabric or special effect. In another vein is the more influential role of Scandinavian chair-makers in the post-war period. Designers such as Hans Wegner, Arne Jacobsen, and Bruno Mathsson have produced enduring chairs which have combined hand skills and machine work, as well as reflecting a simple attitude to materials and decoration.

Other examples of this craft work are Wendell Castle (USA) and John Makepeace (UK). Both are interested in the effects that can be achieved by materials, but both have also looked at added decoration and have moved towards a Postmodern ethic.

In the Postmodern era of the 1980s and 1990s, chairs again became icons of style. Whether it is Memphis with a riot of colour and pattern, Philippe Starck and a playful approach to chair design, Tom Dixon making chairs from found objects, or Ron Arad's unconventional use of materials, the chair will continue to be a challenge for future generations of designers.

CLIVE D. EDWARDS

See also Bentwood Furniture; Jacobsen; Stools; Tubular Steel Furniture

Further Reading

For a detailed history of American chairs see Forman 1988; a detailed account of English regional chairs appears in Cotton 1990. Surveys of modern chairs appear in Benton 1979 and Ostergard 1984.

Baker, Hollis S., *Furniture in the Ancient World: Origins and Evolution, 3100–475 B.C.*, London: The Connoisseur, and New York: Macmillan,1966

Benton, Tim and Barbie Campbell-Cole (editors), *Tubular Steel Furniture*, London: Art Book Company, 1979

Cotton, Bernard D., *The English Regional Chair*, Woodbridge, Suffolk: Antique Collectors' Club, 1990

Dunbar, Michael, *Windsor Chairmaking*, New York: Hastings House, 1976; London: Stobart, 1977

Fiell, Charlotte and Peter, *Modern Chairs*, Cologne: Taschen, 1993

Forman, Benno M., *American Seating Furniture, 1630–1730*, New York: Norton, 1988

Gloag, John, *The Englishman's Chair: Origins, Design and Social History of Seat Furniture in England*, London: Allen and Unwin, 1964

Graham, Clare, *Ceremonial and Commemorative Chairs in Great Britain*, London: Victoria and Albert Museum, 1994

Jarry, Madeleine, *Le Siège Français*, Fribourg: Office du Livre, 1973

Kane, Patricia E., *300 Years of American Seating Furniture: Chairs and Beds from the Mabel Brady Garvan and Other Collections at Yale University*, Boston: New York Graphic Society, 1976

MacQuoid, Percy and Ralph Edwards, *The Dictionary of English Furniture*, revised edition, 3 vols., 1954; reprinted Woodbridge, Suffolk: Antique Collectors' Club, 1983

Mayes, Leonard John, *The History of Chairmaking in High Wycombe*, London: Routledge, 1960

Meadmore, C., *The Modern Chair*, New York: Van Nostrand Reinhold, 1979

Modern Chairs, 1918–1970 (exhib. cat.: Whitechapel Gallery, London), London: Lund Humphries, and Boston: Boston Book and Art, 1971

Ostergard, Derek E., *Mackintosh to Mollino: Fifty Years of Chair Design*, New York: Barry Friedman, 1984

Ostergard, Derek E. (editor), *Bent Wood and Metal Furniture, 1850–1946*, New York: American Federation of Arts, 1987

Pallot, Bill G.B., *The Art of the Chair in Eighteenth-Century France*, Paris: ACR–Gismondi, 1989

Please be Seated: Fifty Years of Innovative Seating Design (exhib. cat.), St. Paul: Goldstein Gallery, University of Minnesota, 1984

Steinbaum, Bernice, *The Rocker: An American Design Tradition*, New York: Rizzoli, 1992

Thornton, Peter, *Seventeenth-Century Interior Decoration in England, France, and Holland*, New Haven and London: Yale University Press, 1978

Vegesack, Alexander von, *Deutsche Stahlrohrmobel: 650 Modelle aus Katalogen von 1927–1958*, Munich: Bangert, 1986

Wilk, Christopher, *Thonet: 150 Years of Furniture*, Woodbury, NY: Barron's, 1980

Yates, Simon, *An Encyclopedia of Chairs*, London: Apple, 1988

Chambers, William 1723–1796

British architect, designer and theorist

Sir William Chambers was regarded as the most successful architect of the second half of the 18th century; he was also the most travelled and mixed freely with the more progressive Continental architects and theorists on his numerous trips abroad. Yet today he is frequently viewed as an establishment figure and, in comparison with that of his more fashionable contemporary, Robert Adam, his work is often deemed to have been quite conservative. An able administrator, he is also remembered as a key figure in the Office of Works and as a founder-member and first treasurer of the Royal Academy of Arts. He was the author of numerous books on architecture and design including *A Treatise on Civil Architecture* (1759) which was the most widely read of all 18th-century academic treatises, and he did more than anyone else prior to Sir John Soane to bring new dignity and prestige to the architectural profession in Britain.

Born the son of a Scottish merchant, Chambers spent much of his childhood in Gothenburg, Sweden. Destined for a mercantile career, he worked for the Swedish East India Company from 1739 to 1749, during which period he made a number of trips to China. This rare first-hand experience of the inhabitants and topography of China made him something of a celebrity in Sweden and London. The lengthy sea voyages also gave him the opportunity to study mathematics and languages, and, more importantly, books on architecture.

In 1749, at the age of 26 and with modest savings from his years in business, Chambers embarked upon an architectural career. He enrolled at Jacques-François Blondel's Ecole des Arts in Paris where he made contact with many figures who played an important role in development of Franco-Italian Neo-Classicism. Between 1750 and 1755 he was in Rome almost continuously where he was taught by the French Neo-Classicist Charles-Louis Clérisseau and where he met many of the more progressive artists, theorists – including G. B. Piranesi – and patrons of the day.

He returned to London in 1755 to launch his career. However, despite a thorough grounding in the most sophisticated Continental ideas, professional success was not immediately forthcoming. The publication of *Designs of Chinese Buildings, Furniture, Dresses*, etc. in 1757, produced in part to "put a stop to the extravagances that daily appear under the name Chinese", enjoyed only limited success in England, although its influence was much more substantial abroad. French editions appeared in 1757 and 1776 where it encouraged the continuing popularity of Chinoiserie, and German editions were published in the 1770s and 1780s. The book was "rediscovered" in Britain in the early 19th century when the interiors of the Prince of Wales' Brighton Pavilion encouraged a renewed interest in Oriental and Chinoiserie styles of design.

Chambers produced several designs for Chinoiserie garden buildings and interiors in the 1760s and 1770s, but it was as a designer in the classical idiom that he was most significant. His

Chambers: design for entrance hall of Gower House, Whitehall, 1765–74

earliest designs, such as the unexecuted monument for the Prince of Wales (1751–52), were, by English standards, cosmopolitan and sophisticated. Another design, for Harewood House (1756), also shows the influence of his French training. But the rejection of this design in favour of a tamer and more conservative Palladian scheme executed by John Carr probably discouraged Chambers from further essays in this style and for much of the remainder of his career he too adopted the current Palladian repertoire, enlivened only occasionally by a sparing use of French details. While a knowledge of contemporary Parisian interiors is evident in Chambers's design for the Gallery at Kew (1757), he developed a personal but distinctively English style for the design and decoration of his subsequent classical buildings.

In comparison with the work of the Adam brothers, Chambers used decoration sparingly, especially on walls. These were sometimes left plain, as in Dundas House, Edinburgh (1771–74), or were articulated with panels formed by thin mouldings. The walls of entrance halls might include niches with sculptural figures. Occasionally, as in Gower House, London (1765–74), he might use Adamesque motifs, but Chambers always left plenty of blank space between the decorated areas. Ceilings, by contrast, were much richer. Early examples, such as Roehampton, Surrey (c.1761) continue the essentially Palladian tradition of using robust mouldings to divide the ceiling into a series of compartments; the compartments themselves contained a series of relatively heavy Palladian or Neo-Classical motifs. For taller spaces he often specified a deep cove. In later examples, the decoration is more delicate and, although Chambers continued to exercise a fondness for geometric compartments, the motifs within are more refined. The gallery at Milton Park (1770–76), has an almost Rococo lightness, while in other interiors, such as those at Somerset House, Chambers develops a more masculine version of the Adam repertoire.

Chambers's role in developing the scope or extent of the architect's involvement in interior design was also significant. Whereas previously architects's drawings had usually been produced in monochrome or had depicted a single room in isolation, Chambers produced a series of coloured sectional drawings which illustrated decorative schemes for the complete building. These drawings were produced either by his own hand, or by his pupils and assistants, and one of the earliest examples is the unexecuted design for York House, London (1759) which shows details such as chimneypieces and mouldings and rooms hung with a variety of coloured, patterned silks or wallpaper. Numerous references to colour schemes also occur in drawings or correspondence related to executed commissions.

Chambers also designed furniture for some of his buildings such as Charlemont House, Dublin (1763–75) and Blenheim Palace where he carried out alterations between c.1766 and c.1775. More often he designed chimneypieces, for example at The Hoo, Hertfordshire (c.1762) and Peper Harrow, Surrey (c.1765–75). But a letter to Lord Melbourne of 1773 suggests that Chambers took a close personal interest in the way in which his buildings were furnished. He writes: "Chippendale called upon me yesterday with some Designs for furnishing the rooms which upon the whole seem very well but I wish to be a little consulted about these as I am really a very pretty connoisseur in furniture ...". It is likely that Chambers acted as a consultant, overseeing the furnishing and decoration of a number of his houses.

Chambers's *Treatise on Civil Architecture* was described by Horace Walpole as the "most sensible book and the most exempt from prejudice that ever was written on that science". It was certainly one of the most widely read, with further editions appearing in 1768 and 1791, when the text was amended and the book was renamed *A Treatise on the Decorative Part of Civil Architecture*; additional versions were published after his death in 1825, 1826, 1836 and 1862. The bulk of the text was concerned with the exteriors of buildings, but much was also relevant to the decorative use of orders within interiors and it contains sections of chimneypieces, ceilings, and drawings illustrating the proportions of rooms. Nevertheless, there were comparatively few illustrations and it was essentially a theoretical treatise rather than a pattern book supplying specific models that could be imitated. Its influence on interior design was necessarily, therefore, limited, and ironically it was his illustrations of Chinoiserie, rather than classical designs that proved most significant within this context.

CHRISTOPHER WEBSTER

See also Chinoiserie

Biography

Born in Gothenburg, Sweden, 23 February 1723, the son of a Scottish merchant. Educated in England; returned to Sweden to join the Swedish East India Company, 1739. Made three voyages to the Far East: to Bengal, 1740–42; to Canton, 1743–45; and to China, 1748–49. Embarked on career as an architect; studied at Jacques-François Blondel's Ecole des Arts, Paris, 1749; travelled to Italy and studied in Rome with Charles-Louis Clérisseau, 1750–55. Married Catherine More in Rome, 1753; at least one daughter. Established architectural practice in England, 1755. Appointed architectural tutor to the Prince of Wales (later George III); joint architect (with Robert Adam) at the Office of Works, 1761; Comptroller of Works, 1769; Surveyor General and Comptroller, 1782. Published several books on architecture, gardens and design. Member, Swedish Academy of Sciences, 1766; Knight of the Polar Star, Sweden, 1770: subsequently allowed to assume title of British knight; Fellow, Royal Society, 1776. Regular exhibitor, Society of Arts, London, 1761–68; founder-member and treasurer, Royal Academy of Arts, London, from 1769. Died in London, 8 March 1796; buried in Westminster Abbey.

Selected Works

A complete catalogue of Chambers's architectural and decorative work appears in Harris 1970. Important collections of designs and drawings are held in the drawings collection of the Royal Institute of British Architects; Sir John Soane's Museum, London; the Victoria and Albert Museum; and the Royal Library, Windsor; and also in the Avery Library, Columbia University, and the Metropolitan Museum of Art, New York. A large number of Chambers's letters are in the Manuscripts Collection, Royal Institute of British Architects; four letter-books, containing copies of professional correspondence dated 1769–75, are in the British Museum.

Interiors

1757–c.63 Kew Gardens, Surrey (garden buildings with some interiors): Princess Augusta and George III

1758–76 Casino, Marino House, near Dublin, Ireland (building and interiors)

1760–64 The Hoo, Kimpton, Hertfordshire (interior alterations, bridge and gateway)

1762–76 Buckingham Palace (formerly Buckingham House), London (remodelling, additions and interiors including the saloon and the Octagon library): George III
1763–75 Charlemont House, Dublin (building and interiors including furniture): 1st Earl of Charlemont
1764–70 13–22 Berners Street, London (town houses, interiors and decoration of no. 13): William Chambers
c.1765–75 Peper Harrow, Surrey (alterations, additions, new villa and interiors): 3rd and 4th Viscounts Midleton
1765–74 Gower House, Whitehall, London (building and interiors including the hall, eating room, great drawing room and staircase): 2nd Earl of Gower
1766–75 Blenheim Palace, Oxfordshire (garden buildings, and internal decorations including the grand cabinet, state bedchamber and Duchess's dressing room): 4th Duke of Marlborough
1767–72 Woburn Abbey, Bedfordshire (rebuilding of the South Wing and interiors including the eating rooms and library): 4th Duke of Bedford
1768–72 Ampthill Park, Bedfordshire (additions and redecoration of principal rooms): 2nd Earl of Upper Ossory
1771–76 Milton Park, near Peterborough, Northamptonshire (alterations and interiors including the gallery, dining room, tea room and green library): 4th Earl of Fitzwilliam
1776–82 Somerset House, Strand, London (building and plan, completed by James Wyatt): Office of Works

Publications

Designs of Chinese Buildings, Furniture, Dresses, Machines and Utensils, 1757
A Treatise on Civil Architecture, 1759; 3rd edition, *A Treatise on the Decorative Part of Civil Architecture*, 1791
Plans, Elevations, Sections and Perspective Views of the Gardens and Buildings at Kew in Surrey, 1763
Dissertation on Oriental Gardening, 1772

Further Reading

A comprehensive account of Chambers's life and career appears in Harris 1970 which also includes references to primary and secondary sources; for a more recent scholarly study see Harris 1996.

Beard, Geoffrey, "Chambers at Kew" in *Apollo*, August 1963
Colvin, Howard M., *A Biographical Dictionary of British Architects, 1600–1840*, 3rd edition New Haven and London: Yale University Press, 1995
Edwards, A.T., *Sir William Chambers*, London: Benn, 1924
Goodison, Nicholas, "William Chambers's Furniture Designs" in *Furniture History*, 26, 1990, pp.67–89
Hardwick, T., "Memoir of the Life of Sir William Chambers" in *Treatise on Civil Architecture*, 1825
Harris, John, "Sir William Chambers and His Paris Album" in *Architectural History*, 1963, pp.54–90
Harris, John, *Sir William Chambers: Knight of the Polar Star*, London: Zwemmer, and University Park: Pennsylvania State University Press, 1970
Harris, John and Michael Snodin (editors), *Sir William Chambers, Architect to George III*, New Haven and London: Yale University Press, 1996
Jacobson, Dawn, *Chinoiserie*, London: Phaidon, 1993
Martienssen, H.M., "Chambers as a Professional Man" in *Architectural Review*, April 1964
Saumarez Smith, Charles, *Eighteenth-Century Decoration: Design and the Domestic Interior in England*, London: Weidenfeld and Nicolson, and New York: Abrams, 1993
Snodin, Michael (editor), *Sir William Chambers: Catalogue of Architectural Drawings in the Victoria and Albert Museum*, London: V&A Publications, 1996
Watkin, David (editor), *Sale Catalogues of Libraries of Eminent Persons*, vol.4, London: Mansell, 1972

Chareau, Pierre 1883–1950

French architect and designer

The architect and furniture designer Pierre Chareau made a significant contribution to Modernism in France in the period between the two world wars. Today, his reputation rests largely on the design of one house, the Maison de Verre, which was completed in 1932.

Born in Bordeaux in 1883, the young Chareau was employed as a draughtsman in the Paris office of the English furniture manufacturers, Waring and Gillow, from the age of 16. Waring and Gillow's furniture was craftsmanlike and well-made and Chareau remained with the firm for a total of ten years, learning his trade.

On returning from military service in 1919 he established his own practice in Paris as an architect and furniture designer. His early chairs had massive wooden seats with dramatic grainy veneers, but within a couple of years his forms had become more assured. The Bergère chair of 1921 was also slightly Neo-Classical. By 1923 Chareau was exploring the idea of moving parts – sliding screens, drawers that rotated from a hinge at one corner, tables with leaves, and cots with dropping sides. This was an interest that remained with him all his life and that reached its climax in the Maison Verre.

In 1924 Chareau opened a shop called La Boutique in which to sell his furniture. He also began a long association with the metalworker Louis Dalbet during this year. Dalbet encouraged Chareau to experiment with metal frames, and the desks and tables from this period began to be supported by black steel flats. Chareau and Dalbet also produced a series of light fittings using flat sheets of alabaster and steel framing. Chareau's work was becoming more adventurous and he began to collaborate with avant-garde filmmakers and Modernist architects such as Bernard Bijvoet, Robert Mallet-Stevens and Francis Jourdain. Influenced by the Bauhaus, Chareau and Dalbet began to abandon flat metal framing in the late 1920s in favour of steel tubes.

Chareau obtained his first architectural commission in 1927 and he employed Bernard Bijvoet as his assistant. The commission was for a clubhouse at Beauvallon which was also furnished throughout with Chareau's designs. All trace of the traditional elements in his furniture had disappeared; the chairs were mostly framed in light steel, and the tables and fitments were hard-edged and aggressively rectangular.

The following year Chareau was commissioned to design a house for Dr. Dalsace whose wife was the niece of Chareau's Beauvallon client. Once again Chareau called in Bijvoet and Dalbet to work with him and together they produced the Maison de Verre (completed in 1931) which is Chareau's masterpiece and one of the great interiors of the 20th century.

The Dalsace's site in the rue Saint-Guillaume in Paris would have daunted most designers. It was located at the back of a courtyard which contained an 18th-century house. This had to be demolished to make way for the new building but the top two floors had to be retained because they belonged to a different owner who refused to move! Chareau inserted a frame of riveted steel and the two new external façades were made entirely of glass. The windows had clear glass and steel frames and the remainder of the building was enclosed by rectangular glass bricks. The design accorded with Dr. Dalsace's belief that as much daylight as possible should enter the house.

The interior of the Maison Verre is "High-Tech" two generations before its time. It contains an exposed steel frame whose joints are revealed, studded white rubber floors, window opening devices celebrated as conspicuous pieces of machinery, staircases with elegant minimalist steel handrails and extensive use of bright primary colours.

The building is entered up a short flight of steps at the side of the courtyard. The entrance floor was reserved for Dr. Dalsace's medical practice and had free-flowing partitions weaving in and out of the free-standing exposed H-section steel columns. The plan is very deep, and full-height pivoting glass panels introduce additional light into the interior. A wide staircase leads into the magnificent double height living rooms on the first floor. The free-standing steel columns are painted bright red and all their rivets are revealed. The living room is furnished with Chareau's chairs and bookcases; display cases and cabinets show Dalbet's black metalwork to its best advantage. The family bedrooms are situated on a gallery; movable screens of perforated metal or glass and movable bookcases provide a layout that can be constantly changed and bedrooms can open up to become living rooms, bathroom or terrace as needed. Everything is extremely complex, although many of the swivelling partitions do not reach the floor or ceiling suggesting that privacy was not deemed a priority in the Dalsace family.

After the completion of the Maison de Verre, Chareau's architectural opportunities were limited. He designed interiors for the LTT Telephone and Telegraph company in 1931–32 but the effects of the Depression meant that there were few chances for large projects in Europe, and with the onset of war Chareau left France for the United States where he lived for the remainder of his life. His most significant commission in America was the house and studio that he designed for the painter Robert Motherwell in 1947. This was a typically spare and restrained design involving the conversion of a Long Island Quonset hut to which Chareau added a mezzanine and some nice wood detailing, but no more.

The influence of the Maison de Verre has been immense in recent years. Unlike Le Corbusier's villas, the Dalsace family continued to occupy the house for many years and a younger generation of architects and designers could view the house with all its original furnishings and decorations in place, looking very much as it had when Chareau first designed it. Among those who were particularly impressed were many young English architects of the 1970s and 1980s and it is tempting to see the Maison de Verre as the source of the ideas that were later developed in Piano and Rogers's Pompidou Centre, in Eva Jiricna's Joseph Shops, and in the work of James Stirling.

JOHN WINTER

See also Modernism

Biography

Born in Bordeaux, 3 August 1883. Studied painting, music and architecture at the Ecole des Beaux-Arts, Paris; apprenticed to, and then employed as a draughtsman and designer by Waring & Gillow Furnishings, Paris, 1899–1914. Married Dolly Dyte, 1904. Served in French Army, 1914–19. Established his own design and architectural practice, Paris, 1919–40; opened shop La Boutique, selling furniture, 1924; worked with Bernard Bijvoet, 1925–35; emigrated to New York, 1940; practised in New York until 1950. Founder-member, Union des Artistes Modernes, and CIAM, 1929. Regular exhibitor at the Salon des Artistes Decorateurs, Paris, during the 1920s; exhibited at the Salon des Arts Décoratifs, Paris, 1925; Exposition Internationale, Paris, 1937. Died in New York in 1950.

Selected Works

Examples of Chareau's designs, and drawings for decoration are in the Musée des Arts Décoratifs, Paris and in the Museum of Modern Art, New York.

Interiors

1918–19	Apartment, rue Saint-Germain, Paris (furnishings and interiors): Dr. and Mrs. Dalsace
1924	Villa Hyères, France (furnishings): Vicomte and Vicomtess de Noailles
1925	Exhibition, Salon des Arts Décoratifs, Paris (interiors and furniture for "Suite for an Ambassador" and "Dining Room for a Colonial Habitation")
1927	Golf Club, Beauvallon, France (building and interiors with Bernard Bijvoet): Emile Bernheim
1928	Grand Hôtel de Tours, Tours (interiors including smoking/games room and bar)
1928–32	Maison de Verre, rue Saint-Guillaume, Paris (building, interiors and furniture, assisted by Bernard Bijvouet and Louis Dalbert): Dr. and Mrs. Dalsace
1931–32	Compagnie du Téléphone, rue de la Faisanderie, Paris (remodelling of offices and furnishings)
1937	Djemel Anik Country House, near Rambouillet (building and interiors)
1939	Soldat Colonial Foyer, Grand Palais, Paris (decorations and furnishings)
1940–50	Exhibition layouts for the French Cultural Center, New York
1947	Robert Motherwell House, East Hampton, Long Island (studio conversion and furnishings)

Chareau designed much furniture and lighting, and some textiles, from c.1919.

Publications

Meubles, 1929

"La Creation artistique et l'imitation commerciale" in *L'Architecture d'aujourd'hui* (Paris), September 1935

Further Reading

Many of Chareau's interiors are illustrated in *Les Arts de la maison, Interieurs français*, and *Interieurs VI*. The most comprehensive study of Chareau's work is Vellay 1985. A select bibliography, and a chronology of Chareau's life, appears in Taylor 1992.

Brunhammer, Yvonne, *1925* (exhib. cat.) Paris: Presses de la Connaissance, 1976

Brunhammer, Yvonne and Suzanne Tise, *The Decorative Arts in France, 1900–1942: La Société des Artistes Décorateurs*, New York: Rizzoli, 1990

Duncan, Alastair, *Art Deco Furniture: The French Designers*, London: Thames and Hudson, and New York: Holt Rinehart, 1984

Fillion, Odile, "A Look at Pierre Chareau: Inside the Maison de Verre" in *Architecture-Interieure-Créé*, April/May 1983

Fleg, Edmond, "Nos Décorateurs, Pierre Chareau" in *Les Arts de la Maison*, Winter 1924, pp.17–27

Frampton, Kenneth, "Maison de Verre" in *Perspectiva*, no.12, 1969, pp.77–126

Gopnik, Adam, "The Ghost of the Glass House" in *New Yorker*, 9 May 1994, pp.54–71
Herbst, René, *Un Inventeur, l'Architecte Pierre Chareau*, Paris: Editions du Salon des Arts Ménagers, 1954
"A House of Glass in Paris: Architect Pierre Chareau" in *Architect and Building News* (London), 13 April 1934
Lugnier, Michel, "Le Corbusier, Mallet-Stevens, Chareau and Some Others" in *Architecture française*, October 1975
Pierre Chareau, Architecte: Un Art Intérieur (exhib. cat.), Paris: Centre Georges Pompidou, 1993
Rogers, Richard, "La Casa di Verro di Pierre Chareau" in *Domus* (Milan), October 1966
Taylor, Brian Brace, *Pierre Chareau: Designer and Architect*, Cologne: Taschen, 1992
Vellay, Marc and Kenneth Frampton, *Pierre Chareau, Architect and Craftsman*, New York: Rizzoli, and London: Thames and Hudson, 1985
Vellay, Marc and Bernard Bauchet, *La Maison de Verre: Pierre Chareau*, Tokyo: ADA, 1988

Chermayeff, Serge 1900–1996

Russian-born architect and designer

Serge Chermayeff is perhaps best known for his design work in Britain in the late 1920s and 1930s, during which time his output evolved from a style heavily influenced by the geometric motifs of French Art Deco towards the more austere, Functionalist aesthetic of the Modern Movement for which he became a leading protagonist. As a result of his emigration to the United States in 1939 he played a significant role in furthering Modernist ideology in architectural and design circles across the Atlantic.

During his early career in Britain he found employment at Ernest Williams Ltd., a London firm of interior decorators, from 1924 to 1927. During this time he also designed theatre sets for Gerald du Maurier, a line of work which came to fruition in his first large-scale interior design commission, for the Cambridge Theatre, London, in 1930. Much of his early work derived from school and family connections and, having been introduced to Lord Waring by his father-in-law, he was appointed in 1928 as Director of the Modern Art Studios of the firm of Waring and Gillow in Oxford Street, London. His first major enterprise during his time at the company was the mounting of the 1928 Exhibition of Modern Art in Decorating and Furnishing. This large show included a suite of ten rooms by Chermayeff which echoed the rich decorative ensembles of the French ateliers seen at the influential 1925 Exposition des Arts Décoratifs et Industriels in Paris. As far as Waring and Gillow was concerned the exhibition marked a turning away from eclectic historicism, which had been the hallmark of its craftsmen, towards a more contemporary outlook. This found favour both with the *Architectural Review* and the Design and Industries Association, two agencies which did much to introduce Modernism to a wider, if relatively specialist, audience. The exhibition also marked Chermayeff's links with the French designer Paul Follot, who contributed designs for ten rooms, a partnership that resurfaced in 1931 in their interior designs for the French liner *SS Atlantique*.

By 1929 Chermayeff began to lean more heavily towards the tenets of the Modern Movement, having encountered a number of leading Modernists, including Erich Mendelsohn, during his travels in Europe. He had also fallen under the influence of the British artist-designer Eric Gill, who instilled in him the strong sense of social purpose in design which had pervaded the work and thought of design reformers from the mid-19th century onwards. He became friendly with leading fine artists of the day including Ben Nicholson, Henry Moore, Barbara Hepworth and Paul Nash, echoing the links between the visual arts commonly found in avant-garde circles on the Continent.

One of the most notable projects with which he was concerned in the early 1930s was the interior decoration of the British Broadcasting Corporation's newly-erected Broadcasting House in Langham Place, London. Chermayeff worked alongside Raymond McGrath and Wells Coates, and his designs exuded the clean lines and forms of the Modern Movement. An important part of the aesthetic derived from the tubular steel furniture commissioned from Practical Equipment Ltd (Pel) whose managing director, Captain Carew, was highly influential in promoting in Britain Modernist ranges to compete with those imported by Thonet and other European companies. He was also concerned with the exploration of new materials and clean, modern forms in his bakelite radio designs for Ekco Ltd., using the possibilities of plastic to produce an appropriately radical design for the new medium of broadcasting.

Another important example of Chermayeff's commitment to Modernist interior design could be seen at the landmark Dorland Hall Exhibition of British Industrial Art in relation to the Home of 1933. Chermayeff's Weekend House, exhibited by Plan Ltd, included entrance hall, living-dining room, kitchen, two bedrooms and bathroom. The design was structurally conceived for economic mass-production. The frames of all the windows and the screen to the dining recess were of anodised stainless steel, while a further large partition was faced with walnut ply in a clear varnish. The floors throughout the single-storey house were of white linoleum and the furniture, although of dark oak, used chromium-plated tubular steel and unit-based structures where appropriate. As Chermayeff himself wrote in an uncompromisingly propagandist essay in *Design for To-Day* in July 1933, "the discoveries of science have changed and improved our living conditions. These forces have brought into being a profusion of new materials which demand a new technique and expression".

Also significant in Chermayeff's Modernist oeuvre was the his auditorium for the De La Warr Pavilion at Bexhill-on-Sea on which he collaborated with Erich Mendelsohn. He was in partnership with Mendelsohn between 1933 and 1936, the two having become friends well before Mendelsohn's emigration from Germany. With its extensive use of modern materials, glass and white stucco finishes, the De La Warr Pavilion embraced a fresh vision of potential patterns of leisure for a new society. However, despite the attention gained from his work at Bexhill and other commissions (including W. and A. Gilbey's Camden Town, London, office building (1937) and the research laboratories for ICI in Manchester (1938), in the unsettled economic and political climate of the late 1930s Chermayeff's private practice in Britain folded, as did many others chasing few commissions in straitened times.

After Chermayeff emigrated to the United States his career

Chermayeff: flat at 24 Upper Brook Street, London, 1935

took on a more distinctly pedagogic flavour with key educational appointments at Brooklyn College, the Institute of Design in Chicago, the Massachusetts Institute of Technology, and Yale University. His interests were more centred upon debates surrounding urban and environmental design issues, as well as writing which resulted in a number of significant texts published between the early 1960s and the 1980s. Although still involved with interior design in the post-war years, albeit generally within a wider environmental context, his commissions in this sphere of design were more limited. Among the best known were those for British Railways offices at the Rockefeller Center, New York (1950) and the Chermayeff House in New Haven, Connecticut (1962).

JONATHAN M. WOODHAM

Biography

Born Sergei Ivanovitch Issakovitch, in Grozny, Azerbaidzhan, Russia, 8 October 1900. Resident in England from 1910: naturalized, 1928; emigrated to the United States, 1939: naturalized, 1946. Educated at Royal Drawing Society School and Harrow School, London, 1910–17; studied art and architecture in Europe, 1922–25. Married Barbara Maitland May, 1928; two sons, the graphic designer Ivan Chermayeff, and the architect Peter Chermayeff. Journalist for the Amalgamated Press, London, 1918–23. Chief designer for decorators Ernest Williams Ltd., London, 1924–27; director of Modern Art Department, Waring and Gillow furnishers, London, 1928–29; co-founder, furniture retailer Plan Ltd., 1932 (sold 1936). Active as a designer of furniture, clocks, rugs, textiles and radios from 1930s. Established own architectural and design practice in London, 1933–39 (partnership with Erich Mendelsohn, 1933–36), in San Francisco, 1940–41, and in New York, 1942–46; in partnership with Heywood Cutting, 1952–57. Professor of Design, Brooklyn College, New York, 1942–46; President of the Institute of Design, Chicago, 1946–51; lecturer, Massachusetts Institute of Technology, Cambridge, 1953–62; professor of architecture, Harvard Graduate School of Design, 1953–62; professor, Yale University, 1962–71, emeritus from 1971. Gropius Lecturer, Harvard University, 1974; Distinguished Visiting Professor, Ohio State University, Columbus, 1979. Fellow of the Royal Institute of British Architects and the American Institute of Architects. Died 8 May 1996.

Selected Works

The Serge Chermayeff Archive is in the Avery Library, Columbia University, New York. A comprehensive list of Chermayeff's architectural projects and designs appears in Plunz 1972.

Interiors

1928	Exhibition Layouts, Waring and Gillow, London
1930	Chermayeff Apartment, London (interiors)

1930 Cambridge Theatre, Seven Dials, London (interiors)
1931 *S.S.Atlantique* (ship interiors; with Paul Follot)
1932–34 British Broadcasting Corporation, Broadcasting House, London (interiors; with Wells Coates and Raymond McGrath)
1933 Exhibition of British Industrial Art in Relation to the Home, Dorland Hall, London (Weekend House interiors and furnishings)
1934–35 De La Warr Pavilion, Bexhill-on-Sea, Sussex (auditorium interiors; with Erich Mendelsohn)
1935 Nimmo House, Chalfont St. Giles, Buckinghamshire (building and interiors; with Erich Mendelsohn)
1937 Heywood-Lonsdale flat, Connaught Place, London (interiors and furnishings)
1938 Chermayeff House, Bentley, near Halland, Sussex (building and interiors)
1944 *Design for Use* (exhibition layouts), Museum of Modern Art, New York
1950 British Railways Offices, Rockefeller Center, New York (with Ketchum, Gina and Sharpe)
1962 Chermayeff House, 28 Lincoln Street, New Haven, Connecticut (building and interiors)

Chermayeff designed tubular steel furniture for Pel (1931–32); Unit furniture for Plan Ltd. (1932–36); lighting for Best and Lloyd (1930s). He produced radio cabinet designs for Ecko (1930s) and carpet designs for Wilton Royal Carpet Factory, Salisbury (from 1929).

Publications

A list of Chermayeff's writings appears in *Design and the Public Good*, 1982.

Colour and its Application to Modern Building, 1936
Community and Privacy: Toward a New Architecture of Humanism (with Christopher Alexander), 1962
Shape of Community: Realization of Human Potential (with Alexander Tzonis), 1971
Design and the Public Good: Selected Writings, 1930–1980, edited by Richard Plunz, 1982

Further Reading

Benton, Tim and Barbie Campbell-Cole, *Tubular Steel Furniture*, London: Art Book Company, 1979
Bertram, Anthony, *The House: A Machine for Living In*, London: A.&C. Black, 1935
Carrington, Noel (editor), *Design in the Home*, London: Country Life, 1933
"House at Chalfont St. Giles" in *Architectural Review*, November 1935
"House near Halland, Sussex" in *Architects' Journal*, 16 February 1935
Klein, Dan, "The Look of '34" in *Connoisseur*, 210, May 1982, pp.118–22
"Offices and Factories" in *Architectural Design and Construction* (London), June 1938
Plunz, Richard, *Projects and Theories of Serge Chermayett*, Cambridge: Massachusetts Institute of Technology Press, 1972
"Serge Chermayeff" in *The Designer* (London), December 1980
Sharp, Dennis and others, *Pel and Tubular Steel Furniture in the Thirties*, London: Architectural Association, 1977
Thirties: British Art and Design Before the War (exhib. cat.), London: Arts Council of Great Britain, 1979
Tilson, Barbara, "Modern Art Department, Waring and Gillow, 1928–1931" in *Journal of the Decorative Arts Society*, 8, 1984, pp.40–49
Tilson, Barbara, *Erich Mendelsohn 1887–1953*, London: Modern British Architecture, 1987

Chests

Chests are essentially barriers: they mark the boundaries of ownership, and protect valuable goods from damage or theft. Light basketwork chests have been made throughout history – the ancient Egyptians used them, and China exports quantities of inexpensive wicker hampers today – but wooden chests have addressed the need for security as clearly as that for storage. In the Middle Ages many chests were really strong-boxes, with stout oak or walnut construction, multiple locks, and imposing metalwork; softwood chests were often virtually wrapped in iron. Substantial medieval households commonly owned 75 or more; in 1405 the Duchess of Burgundy had 154 chests stashed in just one room. Inventories of the period reveal a fascinating array of goods stored in chests: coin, plate and precious jewelry, of course, but also linens, silks, furs, chapel vestments, candles, books and papers, armor, weapons, banners, even grain and spices. Most early chests had undifferentiated interiors, but vertical dividers were not uncommon. Cypress or cedar chests were often specified for linens, and aromatic herbs might be tucked in to help deter insects; small compartments were sometimes built in for these herbs. By the 18th century chests were commonly lined with paper to protect their contents from dirt and insects.

Portability is the chest's second virtue. Although many variations have been devised, two forms are basic to the Western tradition: flat-topped chests with legs, and domed-lid chests that sit directly on the ground or on a low stand. Domed lids were designed to dispel water, and were often covered with leather as a protection against the weather after Islamic craftsmen introduced Spanish Leather into Europe in the 14th century. Iron handles were fixed to the sides for easy handling, and flat bottoms allowed them to be conveniently stacked and strapped to a cart. This type is still recognized as a travelling trunk, although late versions covered with velvet were often highly impractical. A few wheeled chests survive; in Japanese homes of the early- to mid-Edo period, chests with wooden wheels were rolled away to store bedding during the day. Footed chests were better-suited to storage on damp floors of earth, brick, or stone, but awkward to move. Still, a surprising number survive with iron handles, and even massive footed chests seem to have been loaded into large packing boxes called *bahuts* and carted away when medieval nobility decamped.

Carts or bearers were also weighed down with chests for weddings: elaborate dowry or marriage chests advertised the social position of a bride's family, and together with their contents, they generally represented women's only personal wealth within marriage. Marriage chests were probably used in most ancient cultures which instituted dowries: the famous silver casket of Secundus and Projecta from 4th-century Rome offers a tantalizing hint of their form. The Italian cassone of the 14th through 16th centuries are among the few marriage chests which can be confidently identified; these typically depicted the arms of both families, and their decoration was often playfully erotic. Korean brides' chests of the Yi Dynasty included symbols of fertility and prosperity in the design of their metal fittings, and in China similar chests were lacquered red, the color of good fortune. Most Western marriage chests were denoted as such by the initials and dates included in their decoration. Because of their symbolic value, marriage chests (also called hope chests or trousseaux) survived in use much longer than other types.

Chests were the most important pieces of case furniture in medieval Europe: they were omnipresent even in modest homes, and grand manors had chests in every room. Flat-topped chests served as seats, tables, or even beds in addition to providing storage; placed against walls and padded with cushions, they suggested the later box-settle. Chests were often set along the foot or side of a bed as a combined step, table and bench. One long chest or a row of smaller ones ranked at bedside created the impression of a large platform bed. The chest's role diminished gradually in the 15th century, as feudal life became more stable and forms like the open cupboard and cabinet were introduced. They were supplanted by chests of drawers in fashionable interiors by about 1650, although chests continued to be showcased in provincial areas into the mid-19th century. Today only toy chests and cedar chests for woolens are in regular use, although old-fashioned trunks and painted "country" chests are still favored as accents and occasional tables.

The most primitive chests were hollowed-out logs, sawn on one side to lie flat and secured with iron bands; this type was used as a collection box by the early church. Domed lids are vestiges of this technique, to judge from surviving board chests with thick curved lids cut from logs. Luxurious chests with sophisticated joinery, veneering and inlay were made as early as the 4th Dynasty in Egypt, and survive in quantity from later burials. Those in common materials were painted to imitate ebony, ivory, gilt and marquetry. Many were made with gabled lids or lids that slope to a gentle arch at one end, like the roof of a shrine, and nearly all stand on legs. They were "locked" by lashing cord around fat knobs on the lid and carcass and applying a seal to the cord. Greek and Etruscan chests generally resembled Egyptian models, but Pliny listed a wide variety of woods unused in Egypt. Imported citron was apparently most favored, and Pliny sneered at painted imitations of its grain. The Roman *arca* were being edged out by *armarium* (wardrobes) by the Hellenistic period, but chests of board or frame-and-panel construction were common articles in Byzantium, painted or decorated with marquetry and veneer. The most splendid were veneered with carved ivory.

In most of medieval Europe, metalsmithing was more advanced than carpentry, and wrought iron was used extensively to decorate and reinforce board chests. Paint (often on a gesso ground) was much more frequently used than surviving examples suggest, and brilliant reds, greens, blues and gold were favored. Chip carving was widely used in the Romanesque period, and sustained its popularity in Scandinavia and Germany into the modern era. A chest's stiles or sides could be extended to form board feet; these were sometimes softened with carved brackets, but most footed chests were starkly rectilinear. After about 1200, however, Gothic tracery and linenfold carving contributed to more unified, architectural designs. Spanish Gothic resembled that of the rest of Europe, but under the Islamic influence, Spain also developed a mosaic-style inlay called Mudéjar for chests and other furniture. Panel and frame construction was adopted in the 15th century and became standard for European oak chests, with carved and painted decoration which usually articulated the framed structure. In Paris, walnut was increasingly preferred for finely carved furniture, and by the 15th century the feet of French chests were often replaced by a solid plinth. Most were decorated with bays of architectural ornament, but some of the finest examples were carved with chivalric scenes that spanned the entire façade. Italian chests of the same period also displayed fine carving, but moulded gesso ornament, brightly painted and gilded, seems to have been especially popular in Italy. This treatment, while much less expensive than carving, gave a similarly rich effect. It was often combined with inset painted panels in early Renaissance cassoni.

Inspired by antique sarcophagi, 16th-century Italian furniture shops developed the plinth chest into a new form. The most elaborate high Renaissance cassone were carved in deep relief with friezes of classical scenes, caryatids at each corner, lions' paw feet and deeply moulded lids. This type was not widely imitated outside Italy, although carved Renaissance ornament was readily adapted for the older plinth form. Italian intarsia, or marquetry, spread quickly throughout Europe in the 16th century and was particularly influential for German and Netherlandish chests, which evolved into bold architectural forms. By the mid-17th century, however, the chest was eclipsed by sophisticated cabinets and chests of drawers. Joiners tried to compete by offering chests with two drawers near the base, or tall stands to prop them up to cabinet height – but the cabinet-makers' day had dawned. Although Gothic Revival and Arts and Crafts designers admired the decoration of medieval chests, the forms they favored – like the cupboard, or cabinet on stand – were more complex. Today only antique or heirloom chests still hold pride of place.

Jody Clowes

See also Cassoni

Further Reading

Burr, Grace Hardendorff, *Hispanic Furniture from the Fifteenth through the Eighteenth Century*, revised edition New York: Archive Press, 1964

Eames, Penelope, *Furniture in England, France and the Netherlands from the Twelfth to the Fifteenth Century*, London: Furniture History Society, 1977

Fairbanks, Jonathan and Robert Trent, *New England Begins: The Seventeenth Century* (exhib. cat.), Boston: Museum of the Fine Arts, 1982

Gilbert, Christopher, *English Vernacular Furniture, 1750–1900*, New Haven and London: Yale University Press, 1991

Hayward, Helena (editor), *World Furniture: An Illustrated History*, New York: McGraw Hill, 1965; London: Hamlyn, 1969

Jenning, Celia, *Early Chests in Wood and Iron*, London: HMSO, 1974

MacQuoid, Percy and Ralph Edwards, *The Dictionary of English Furniture*, revised edition, 3 vols., 1954; reprinted Woodbridge, Suffolk: Antique Collectors' Club, 1983

Odom, William, *A History of Italian Furniture from the Fourteenth to the Early Nineteenth Centuries*, 2 vols., 1918; reprinted New York: Archive Press, 1966

Richter, G.M.A., *The Furniture of the Greeks, Etruscans and Romans*, London: Phaidon, 1966

Wickman, Michael, *Korean Chests: Treasures of the Yi Dynasty*, Seoul: International Tourist Publishing, 1978

Chimneypieces and Chimney Furniture

Chimneypieces first developed when the Normans began building fireplaces against the walls of their multi-storeyed castles in the 12th century, although central fires remained common in poorer European homes before 1600. The earliest were only slightly recessed, with angled flues that required massive, sloping hoods. These were usually conical, supported by pillars or projecting corbels, and looked somewhat like huge tents pitched against the wall. In small chambers they could be fitted into a corner, where they were less obtrusive; in vernacular and cottage architecture, corner hearths have survived into the 20th century, particularly in Scandinavia and Latin America. After 1250 deeper hearths with vertical flues permitted smaller hoods, and by the early 1300s construction improvements had made them virtually unnecessary. But the hood was slow to disappear, especially in northern Europe. The bulky conical form was gradually replaced by a flat, truncated pyramid, which remained typical from about 1400 through the mid 16th century. Both types were usually plastered and brightly painted: coats of arms and mottoes were favored motifs, and in Italian villas chimneypieces were integrated into extensive painted friezes. As hoods became less prominent, fireplace surrounds in grand rooms were articulated with four-centered or Tudor arches of wood or stone, moulded profiles, and carving, especially on the spandrels and lintel.

During the 16th century wall fireplaces became widespread, and rough versions were simply built with deep timber or stone lintels flush to the wall. But money did not guarantee comfort, and domestic life in poor and wealthy homes alike revolved around the fireplace in cold weather and at night, making the chimneypiece a natural focus for decoration. Renaissance architects kept tinkering with the pyramidal hood, and by 1525 important chimneypieces were transformed into elaborate architectural confections with waisted sides, carved figures, mouldings and full entablatures. Pillars and corbels became classical pilasters, columns, or caryatids, and eventually the vestigial hood was completely dissolved in sculptural ornament. Mantelshelves were incidental elements as yet, although deep mouldings made convenient homes for small items. Architects and contractors lavished attention on emphatic, projecting chimney breasts and overmantels that grazed the ceiling, retaining the chimneypiece's traditional height and mass for symbolic and artistic effect, rather than practical necessity. Even fully-recessed fireplaces, neatly framed with mouldings, could be expanded with illusionistic mural decoration. The Italians preferred richly colored polished marble, while the rest of Europe relied chiefly on wood, limestone or painted plaster; but in either case the glistening carved and moulded surfaces were at their best in the evening, enlivened by deep shadows and flickering firelight.

Before glazed tiles became fashionable in the 17th century nearly all hearths were brick or stone, and the back wall was frequently protected by a cast-iron fireback. These could be quite ornate, and many examples included heraldic motifs, a date, and the owner's initials; in provincial areas firebacks remained important into the mid 19th century. Firedogs, or andirons, were first developed for open hearths, and their ancient animalistic form underlies even the most fantastic later designs. In addition to logs, firedogs could support crossbars or even stands for jugs of wine. Most were iron, but brass, steel, or silver reflected the light brilliantly. Their prominent position made them ideal showcases for fine metalwork, and by 1600 firedogs were often purely ornamental, their massive pillars extending halfway to the fireplace lintel. Small, plain andirons called "creepers" served for shorter logs, and preserved the symmetry of their decorative cousins. Tongs, billet hooks and forks were used to handle burning logs, and shovels and brushes cleared the ashes; a bellows was especially useful if the fire was used for cooking. Handled tools could be supported with hooks just inside the chimneypiece, but in many households they were simply propped nearby when not in use. Such tools were increasingly sold en suite with the firedogs as the 16th century wore on. In very wealthy homes, a hierarchy of silver-, brass- and iron-handled hearth equipment marked each room's relative importance.

Architects' engravings of chimneypiece designs were widely circulated and copied after 1630; most originated in Paris, and designs by French Baroque architects like Jean Barbet, Jean Le Pautre, and Daniel Marot contributed to the development of a truly international style. The preferred form was a flat, projecting chimney breast terminating in a cornice at the ceiling, with a related cornice surrounding a lowered fire-opening. This integrated, logical, and relatively simple structure could be extended to the wall panelling, while rich embellishments – scrolled cartouches, pediments, and naturalistic carving – maintained the chimneypiece's dominance. In complex schemes paintings and tapestries were specially fitted in the overmantel. Toward the end of the 17th century large (and extremely costly) mirrors were available to the French aristocracy; as they became less precious, mirrors usurped all other types of ornament for the overmantel. In the Netherlands, conservative taste retained protruding chimney breasts that suggested hoods; combined with fashionably emphatic cornices, these evolved into deep mantelshelves ideal for displaying porcelain. A fabric valance was usually hung below the shelf to trap smoke. Most wealthy patrons preferred colored marbles by this period, but wood, rougher stone and plaster were more common. The walls of 17th-century Dutch and Spanish hearths were often lined with bright, easily cleaned tin-glazed earthenware tiles, and this fashion spread rapidly to England and northern France.

Late 17th-century firedogs became shorter in proportion with the hearth, and balusters, pyramids, urn or flame shapes and enormous, gleaming globes replaced more ornate types. As wood became scarcer and more expensive in Britain, many fireplaces were re-fitted for coal, and newly built hearths were considerably smaller to accommodate the new fuel. Iron fire-baskets, raised on firedogs or their own legs, had appeared by the mid 16th century, and gradually evolved into compact grates which burned coal efficiently. Two forms were typical from the early 18th-century: hob-grates of iron crossbars supported by solid cast-iron sidepieces, or hobs; and free-standing dog-grates, which were suspended between prominent side pillars resembling firedogs. Elegant fenders and fire-screens – usually of pierced or latticed metal – were developed by 1750 to prevent hot coals from rolling into the room. Fenders were also convenient resting places for fire equipment. Coal required a shovel, poker and tongs, which might be

Chimneypieces: drawing room, Loseley House, Guildford, Surrey, c.1570

supplemented by brushes and bellows; fuel was stored out of sight in baskets or, by the Georgian period, in metal coal-scuttles. It was not until after 1850 that decorative coal-scuttles emerged from the closet as part of the hearth's kit.

Fireplaces designed for coal-grates could be compact and somewhat austere, at least by comparison to the extravagant designs of the 17th century. Fine chimney surrounds in 18th-century British townhouses often relied on carefully selected marble and simple mouldings for their effect. Marble "cheeks" or slips, inserted between the stiles and the grate, were judiciously chosen to complement the surround. In North America and on the Continent, improvements to the wood-burning grate eliminated most of the smoke and, like British coal fires, permitted much smaller fireplaces. This reduced scale suited the Rococo environment's intimacy and delicate, fluent use of line. Fullblown Rococo chimneypieces relied on gilt (or, less often, silvered) mirror frames, candle-sconces, and carved or applied foliate ornament to dissolve their mass, and their creamy white or veined marble was critical to the room's color scheme. Matching hearth furniture added to the unified effect, and the splendid sculptural firedogs, or *chenets*, made by 18th-century French bronze-workers were in demand throughout Europe. *Chenets* were essentially ornamental, and in this sense closely related to the evolving fashion for garnitures. For very grand chimneypieces, specially designed firebacks, mantel friezes, columns and busts were also produced in gilt-bronze.

Late Georgian architects advocated precisely symmetrical central chimneypieces, ideally flanked by windows and facing a door. Whenever possible they eliminated the projecting chimney breast and outlined the fireplace with shallow, subdued marble or wooden mouldings; light classical motifs, carved or moulded of composition, were the favored ornaments. By 1790 the overmantel had been reduced to a spare frame for paintings or mirrors. Wallpaper and fabric hangings extended above prominent mantelshelves, which held careful arrays of paired candleholders, vases, figures and – almost always – a clock. Tin-glazed earthenware tiles were popular slip facings, and the slips themselves were incorporated into many of the new register grates: these filled the entire opening, and adjusted to regulate the draft. Register grates were sometimes offered with hinged shutters to replace the traditional chimneyboard. Hob- and dog-grates, however, remained

Chimneypieces: *Cheminées à la Moderne* and *Cheminées à l'Italienne*, by Jean Le Pautre, 1660s

popular outside Britain and are still used in large fireplaces. Grates were offered in a wide variety of designs; although polished steel and brass were more prestigious, the market was dominated by cast iron. Franklin stoves, in use in the United States by 1785, originated as a hearth surround, liner and grate cast in one unit. These developed into enclosed wood and coal stoves, which soon found almost universal favor among the middle class – everywhere but in Britain.

By 1810, the chimneypiece had been stripped to essentials. Flat slabs of reeded marble or painted wood, their corners punctuated by square tablets, created a severe classical effect, and polished ornaments and hearth furniture shone against the preferred soft white, grey or black veined marble. Overmantels were often omitted – even in the finest rooms – in favor of independently framed paintings or mirrors. Short mirrors reaching just above the top of the mantel ornaments were elegant and much cheaper than the enormous vertical glasses favored by the wealthy. On less restrained chimneypieces, Greek and Egyptian Revival motifs were picked out with applied composition or gilt metal, and sleek freestanding columns supported the mantelshelf. Splayed hearth walls, which improved the draft, caught on slowly by mid-century, and low stone curbs were also introduced during this period; combined with a mesh fire-screen, curbs could replace the fender. They were generally designed to match a moulded marble or stone surround. Iron hearth furniture was routinely polished with graphite, or "black-lead"; if the hearth walls were brick or stone, they might be black-leaded while in use, then whitewashed for summer.

Carved ornament began creeping back by 1840 on the broad spandrels of Gothic Revival and rounded "Romanesque" arches. But many early Victorians simply draped their old-fashioned chimneypieces with fringed or tasseled velvet, silk or lace in a vaguely Turkish manner – although the style actually originated in France. Deep flounces on the mantelshelf became almost obligatory after 1840, and often chimneypieces were completely curtained when not in use. This style prevailed until the 1860s, as historicism developed in earnest: bulky Renaissance Revival forms renewed the chimneypiece's sculptural prominence, and the Aesthetic emphasis on collecting encouraged huge overmantels packed with fancy brackets, mirrors and cabinets. Late Victorian chimneypieces also shouldered a moral burden as the "heart" of the home, and cozy hearths increasingly symbolized refuge from the pressures of modern life. Designers and manufacturers responded with goods in a bewildering variety of styles.

Aesthetic motifs like the sunflower and peacock were applied freely to commercial hearth furniture, and "encaustic", transfer-printed and "art" tiles were specially made for hearths, fireplace slips and mass-produced register grates. Entire chimneypieces were available in cast iron from about 1850, and trade catalogues bulged with ready-made overmantels for the middle-class.

Arts and Crafts Movement designers also concentrated their energies on the fireplace, designing hand-painted tiles, hand-forged firedogs, hammered copper hoods and wood, stone or brick chimneypieces inspired by medieval, folk and – in the United States – colonial architecture. Richard Norman Shaw was among the first to rediscover the inglenook, which became a signature element in Arts and Crafts interiors; in place of a built-in inglenook, one could purchase a fender specially fitted with leather seats. Ironically, this emphasis on large, old-fashioned chimneypieces coincided with the rise of central heating.

By 1900 the fireplace was shrinking again, and the overmantel virtually disappeared within the next decade. Light Adamesque surrounds, simple facings of plain tiles, and flat expanses of marble or glass appealed to the modern taste for expensive restraint. Fire tools were sold with matching, freestanding racks, as they rarely fit in newer fireplaces. Electric fires were introduced in the 1920s, and both streamlined versions and the illusionistic "Magicoal" were installed like fireplaces; by the mid 1930s, louvered, polished metal vents concealed their electric coils. In Europe, sleek hoods bridged the taste for modern and vernacular-style architecture. Modern architects preferred asymmetrical fireplaces with sweeping, horizontal lines and stepped tiers or flat, flush surfaces, and they generally eschewed the mantelshelf. In open-plan interiors, flues might be re-routed to leave a clear view over the fireplace. Simpler solutions devised in the 1950s included egg-shaped revisions of the cast-iron stove and island fireplaces, in which the fire is built on a low pedestal below a freestanding or partially engaged hood. Both of these remained stylish through the 1960s – the stoves in bright enameled colors, and the fireplaces richly surfaced with rough stone, slate, mosaic or glazed tile. Sunken conversation pits often centered on these pared-down hearths. In the early 1980s Postmodern architects began designing coloristic fireplaces based on classical elements and a loose, witty approach to 1930s style, but these have proved less influential than the recent interest in authentic decor.

Since the 1970s, salvaged and reproduction chimneypieces have become immensely popular for both new and old homes. Glass shutters offer a compromise between aesthetic effect and the recent concern for energy efficiency.

JODY CLOWES

See also Barbet; Stoves

Further Reading

A concise history of English Fireplaces and Chimneypieces appears in Gilbert and Wells-Cole 1985. For information relating to European examples see Thornton 1978 and Thornton 1991, and for a study of American Fireplaces see Kauffman 1972.

Calloway, Stephen and Elizabeth Cromley (editors), *The Elements of Style: A Practical Encyclopedia of Interior Architectural Details from 1485 to the Present*, London: Mitchell Beazley and New York: Simon and Schuster, 1991

Cornforth, John and John Fowler, *English Decoration in the 18th Century*, London: Barrie and Jenkins, and Princeton, NJ: Pyne, 1974; 2nd edition, Barrie and Jenkins, 1978

Fearn, Jacqueline, *Cast Iron*, Princes Risborough: Shire, 1990

Gilbert, Christopher and Anthony Wells-Cole, *The Fashionable Fireplace, 1660–1840* (exhib. cat.) Leeds: Temple Newsam House, 1985

Hills, Nicholas, *The English Fireplace: Its Architecture and the Working Fire*, London: Quiller Press, 1985

Kauffman, Henry J., *The American Fireplace: Chimneys, Mantelpieces, Fireplaces, and Accessories*, Nashville: Nelson, 1972

Kelly, Alison, *The Book of English Fireplaces*, Feltham: Country Life, 1968

Laing, Alastair, "The Eighteenth-Century English Chimneypiece" in Gervase Jackson-Stops (editor), *The Fashioning and Functioning of the British Country House*, Washington, DC: National Gallery of Art, 1989

Lemmen, Hans van, *Tiles in Architecture*, London: Laurence King, 1993; as *Tiles: 1000 Years of Architectural Decoration*, New York: Abrams, 1993

Long, Helen C., *The Edwardian House: The Middle-Class Home in Britain, 1880–1914*, Manchester: Manchester University Press, 1993

McDonald, Roxana, *The Fireplace Book*, London: Architectural Press, 1984

Mariacher, Giovanni, *Camini d'ogni tempo e paese*, Milan: Valardi, 1958

Mayhew, Edgar de Noailles and Minor Myers, Jr., *A Documentary History of American Interiors, from the Colonial Era to 1915*, New York: Scribner, 1980

Parissien, Steven, *Fireplaces*, London: The Georgian Group, 1992

Parissien, Steven, *Regency Style*, London: Phaidon, and Washington, DC: Preservation Press, 1992

Parissien, Steven, *Palladian Style*, London: Phaidon, 1994

Thornton, Peter, *Seventeenth-Century Interior Decoration in England, France, and Holland*, New Haven and London: Yale University Press, 1978

Thornton, Peter, *The Italian Renaissance Interior, 1400–1600*, London: Weidenfeld and Nicolson, and New York: Abrams, 1991

West, Trudy, *The Fireplace in the Home*, Newton Abbot: David and Charles, 1976

Wilhide, Elizabeth, *The Fireplace*, Boston: Little Brown, 1994

Wright, Lawrence, *Home Fires Burning: The History of Domestic Heating and Cooking*, London: Routledge, 1964

China

The subject of traditional Chinese interiors is many faceted and reflects the long continuous cultural development throughout the nearly ten thousand years of China's history. It is perhaps because the notion of interior decoration is somewhat more Western in concept that the subject has not been approached with any comprehensive study to date. Perhaps, too, it is because the romantically idealized view of a traditional Chinese interior differs so vastly from that of the general Chinese populace. A narrow study of any cultural aspect must embrace important relationships with its history, philosophies and religions, political and economic structures, social structures and moral codes, art and architecture, and foreign influences. This introductory survey will touch upon these various

China: *The Night Revels of Han Xizai* (detail), 12th-century copy of painting attributed to Gu Hongzhong, Five Dynasties period, 10th century; hand scroll, ink and colours on silk

factors to understand better how traditional Chinese interiors fit into the concept of interior decoration.

The essay begins with a review of the historical background. Excavations in central China at Hemadu reveal that timber frame construction had already developed nearly 7,000 years ago. These long buildings probably provided shelter for tribal communities who hunted and fished for food. Since Neolithic times, dwellings were optimally sited in relation to the sun, and sat upon built-up platforms of rammed earth.

Depictions on Shang dynasty (16th–11th century BC) bronzes and stone carvings illustrate figures resting on their haunches or sitting on woven mats with low tables set in front of them. Numerous examples of lacquered furniture – low tables, armrests, beds, chests – have been excavated from tombs dating the Eastern Zhou period (770–256 BC) and are representative of those that were used in the daily life of the aristocratic ruling class. The aesthetics and structural conceptions of furniture excavated from the former state of Chu, active during this period, demonstrate designs which blend simplicity with elegance. Their surfaces are often colorfully patterned with contrasting red and black lacquer, and were sometimes simultaneously decorated with relief and incised carving. Eastern Zhou bronze lamp stands have also been excavated which, besides their functionality, have a high artistic sculptural quality. Decorative patterns for doors and windows noted in the contemporaneous Chu dictionary (*Chuci*) also reflect an early architectural woodworking tradition that was to last for thousands of years.

During the Han dynasty (206 BC–220 AD) furniture continued to characterize a lifestyle at ground level. Woven mats, used for sleeping as well as sitting, had also become a standard of measurement for rooms, like the *tatami* which still exists in present-day Japan. Wall murals and stone engravings illustrate low couches, or platforms, elevating a master or special guests in a distinguished seat of honor; decorated screens were often placed behind the couch. Besides the honorific and decorative use of the screen, the literal terminology "windscreen" (*pingfeng*) also implied its functional use to provide protection against drafts. Although clothing was the principal means of keeping warm, excavated materials, as well as early records from the earlier Zhou period, indicate that bronze braziers and fire pits built into the floor were also used to provide a localized heat source during the cold winters. Bamboo-plaited baskets, clothes racks, granaries, and cabinets as well as utensils for eating and drinking and writing materials that are known from this period are all of excellent workmanship. These pieces also reflect the thoughts of the Han dynasty philosopher, Yang Xiong, who wrote: "Substance without beauty is rough, and beauty without substance is futile. Their combination, however, is an external exemplification of eternal principles."

Tomb pottery models of buildings, as well as stone engravings from the Han period, convey more information relative to the contemporary architecture of houses, pavilions, and watch towers. Small houses were commonly raised on stilts, and were divided into three bays which opened to a courtyard. A pottery relief brick depicting an estate at Chengdu illustrates an entire compound surrounded by a wall with tiled eaves. A gate on the southern wall opens to a three-bay building with no interior divisions. Screens and curtains would have been used to divide and enclose the open space to protect from drafts and sunlight.

During the Han dynasty China's domain expanded and brought her into contact with nomadic tribes in more remote regions. The influences from this exposure were further popularized by the Han emperor Lingdi (reigned 168–188 AD) who had a strong fascination with foreign curiosities, including the folding stool, which was then termed a "foreign" or "barbarian" seat (*huchuang*). These portable seats were commonly used by nomadic tribes in the more remote northern and western regions, and were also used for mounting and dismounting horses. Today it is generally thought that the popularization of the *huchuang*, as well as the simultaneous

China: *Meeting with the Matchmaker*, woodblock print, illustration to *Jin Ping Mei*, published Ming dynasty, Chongzhen period, 1628–42

eastward migration from India of the raised dais associated with Buddhist art influenced the shift in seating from mat to chair level over the next few centuries. After the Han dynasty a greater variety of seating furniture began to appear; however, these seats were primarily used to elevate priests or high officials in distinguished positions of honor.

During the Tang dynasty (618–907 AD) the sphere of China extended once again to distant foreign lands, and considerable influence was assimilated from Middle Eastern cultures. At this time raised seating around high tables had become more common among aristocratic circles. A Chinese-style armchair, preserved from this period at the Imperial Treasury in Nara, Japan, is made from zelkova with tapering square-cut members and finished with a dark lacquer. This chair also closely resembles armchairs illustrated in Buddhist wall paintings at Dunhuang from the same period. Tang pottery figurines and paintings often depict ladies sitting upon high hour-glass shaped stools, as well as elaborately carved stools. The popularization of the raised box platform for seating is reflected in many representations in paintings and wall murals such as those from Dunhuang. These latter records also depict such platforms arranged with canopies, which mark the advent of the canopy bed.

The 10th century painting *The Night Revels of Han Xizai* illustrates a series of scenes representing the official Han Xizai which were recorded by the court painter Gu Hongzhong in an attempt to discredit Han Xizai's licentious activities. This record of revelry has also become a highly valuable reference for the material culture of the Tang and Five Dynasties periods. Some of Han Xizai's guests sit upon large couch beds surrounded with decorative railings. Men sat on yokeback chairs draped with silk chair covers, some with feet pendant, others sitting with legs crossed. Ladies sat on large round stools. Food and wine was served upon high tables. Large standing screens were decorated with painted panels and provided space division. Canopy beds were draped with brocaded silks, and high racks stood at one end to provide a place to hang bed covers and clothes.

Architecture and furnishings of the Song dynasty (960–1279) are both considerably lighter and airier in structure than that of the preceding Tang and Five Dynasties periods. This stylistic shift was likely due as much to severe timber shortages, necessitating more resourceful use of materials, as it was to the overall intellectual and artistic climate of what is considered to be one of China's most glorious periods. New techniques and tools emerged which permitted the use of smaller components firmly secured to one another with ingenious systems of wooden joinery. The Song architectural treatise *Yingzao fashi* documents a fully developed building system which was to change very little in the following centuries. During this period, the chair height mode of living had become assimilated into common life. Paintings also record that many of the traditional furniture forms, which in modern times have been popularized as "Ming-style," were actually already developed by this time; however, virtually no extant pieces of Song period furniture are known to have survived. Nevertheless, both the traditional furniture styles and furniture arrangements which are considered "classical" today were likely established during the enlightened age of the Song dynasty.

Concepts about traditional Chinese interiors are mostly sourced from extant examples of traditional furnishings, visual reference materials, and literary writings from the Ming dynasty and afterwards. Many more furnishings from the Ming (1368–1644) and Qing (1644–1911) periods have survived, including furniture made from lacquer, hardwoods, bamboo, rattan, and roots. Of these, those made of tropical hardwoods have survived in the greatest numbers because of their general characteristics of durability and resistance to decay. In recent decades, collections formed of late Ming and early Qing tropical hardwood furniture reveal a variety of simple, elegant, and robust designs that rival the world's best furniture-making traditions.

In 1567, because of the depletion of silver from the Imperial treasuries, the ban on maritime trade was lifted in order capitalize on Spanish silver coming into the Philippines from Central America. It is simultaneously at this time that furnishings made of tropical hardwoods such as *huanghuali* begin to appear in much greater quantity. Chinese cargo ships frequented ports in Southeast Asia, including Hainan Island and the Spanish-controlled Philippines where goods were traded for silver, as well as for precious hardwoods. It is after

China: hall with a couch, opening onto a garden; gouache painting from *Essai sur l'architecture chinoise* (Bibliothèque nationale, Paris)

the lifting of the ban that Fan Lian notes in his *Record of Things Seen in Yunjian*:

> When I was young I never saw any fine quality hardwood furniture such as desks and large chairs. The rich people only had square tables in gold-colored transparent lacquer or in gingko wood. Mo Tinghan and the sons of the Gu and Song families began to buy a few fine quality hardwood objects from Suzhou and bring them to Yunjian [Songjiang]. During the Longqing and Wanli periods (1567–1620) even lower officials began to use fine quality hardwood furniture in their homes. Cabinetmakers from Huizhou opened shops in Yunjian, making wedding furniture and other objects. The wealthy people would not use elm (*ju*) wood and had their beds, cabinets, and tables made from *huali*, burl wood, ebony, *jichi* wood, and boxwood. It became fashionable to spend thousands of *taels* on a single piece. Even policemen who owned a house would decorate a room with wooden partitions. In their gardens they have flower pots and bowls of goldfish. Inside they would have a good quality wooden desks and a horsetail whisk for dusting the room they called their study, but what books they studied is open to question.

Although the Ming government was struggling with its depleted treasuries, the passage above reflects a flourishing merchant economy during the late Ming period that was to last for several decades. Anxious antipathy is also reflected here about the *nouveau riche* merchants and low officials who were leading extravagant materialistic lifestyles in some sort of imitation of the literati officials. This situation was quite contrary to traditional sumptuary regulations and fundamental social principles of state and, in fact, was to spur numerous publications on connoisseurship and taste from various members of the literati. Perhaps the most renowned of these was Wen Zhenheng's *Treatise on Superfluous Things*. This work contains a number of ideas regarding the propriety or unsuitability of interior furnishings and interior arrangements in terms of "elegance" (*ya*) or "vulgarity" (*su*), grouped together with ideas about garden arrangements, trees and flowers, fish and birds, clothing and ornament, boats and carriages, vegetables and fruits, incense and teas, brushes, paper and ink, and the care and hanging of paintings. For the late Ming literati, the idea of interior design fits into an entire lifestyle of elegant refinement. Nonetheless, the chapter devoted to furniture opens:

> When the men of old made tables and couches, although the length and width were not standardized, they were

China: album leaf attributed to Qiu Ying illustrating *Dream of the Western Chamber*; Ming dynasty (15th–16th century)

invariably antique, elegant and delightful when placed in a studio, or for sitting up, lying down or reclining. In moments of pleasant relaxation they would spread out classic or historical texts, examine works of calligraphy or painting, display ancient bronze vessels, dine or take a nap, as the furniture was suitable for all these things. The men of today make them in a manner which merely prefers carved and painted decoration to delight the vulgar eye, while the antique pieces are cast aside, causing one to sigh in deep regret.

Relative to arrangements, Wen repeatedly advises the reader to avoid excesses in numbers of pieces in a room or tables cluttered with objects. It was considered to be of poor taste to hang a set of four paintings on the walls of a single room. The placement of flowers on the desk in a study was utterly unacceptable. The appropriate use of furnishings according to the size of the room as well as according to the season was also part of the general formula for elegant taste.

The publication of illustrated books and novels was also popularized during the late Ming period. These woodblock print illustrations often depicted interior scenes which can be used as reference for interior design and the arrangement of furnishings. A late Ming woodcut from the novel *Jin Ping Mei* illustrates such a scene. (Ironically, this novel features a wealthy merchant, typical of the late Ming period, who epitomizes those despised by the contemporary literati.) Three steps lead up from a garden courtyard onto an open-front building with carved balustrade railings; the back and the side walls otherwise enclose the space. Although the perspective and proportion is somewhat distorted by the traditional "bird's-eye" viewpoint, the panel between two columns near the center-line of the room should separate the room into two equal spaces. The long side table with sharply upturned ends and end panels decorated with *ruyi* is centered against the central dividing wall panel. Laid out upon its surface are an incense box, a censer and a vessel with incense tools; set out on one end is a flowering sprig arranged in an antique vase. A scroll painting of a figure hangs against the wall above the table. A typical Ming period table of minimalistic form is placed against the side wall and supports a small decorative screen framing a Dali marble panel. In this particular scene a matchmaker is about to introduce a prospective couple, and thus three handsome yokeback chairs have been specially set out and arranged for the occasion. Master Ximen Qing, the prospective groom, occupies the seat of honor which is centrally arranged to face out onto the courtyard. The prospective bride takes the position in the more distant of the adjacently arranged chairs; the matchmaker is showing Ximen her lovely feet. There are literally thousands of such illustrations from the Ming and Qing periods which are just as rich in interpretive detail. However, the source of these publications was mostly concentrated in Zhejiang, Jiangsu, and Anhui, and thus it must be borne in mind that these illustrations mostly reflect the architecture and furnishings from wealthy estates in those southerly regions.

A major point in the evolution of decorative arts is marked by the reign of Qianlong (1735–95) during the Qing dynasty. Like other emperors he highly venerated the knowledge of the ancients and, with dominating influence in the Imperial Workshops, effected archaistic tendencies in the decorative arts to communicate this devotion. Qianlong also loved a precious tropical hardwood called *zitan* and monopolized its few remaining supplies. *Zitan* is an extremely dark and heavy wood; because of its scarcity, however, popular furniture often imitated its appearance with a coating of a deep reddish-black semi-transparent lacquer, or was made from another similar but much more available dark wood called *hongmu*. Scarcities of rare hardwoods also resulted in the production of decorative furnishings composed from mixed materials which were often artistically conceived, as well as the use of thin veneers of rare hardwoods facing softwood cores. Qianlong's expeditions into Burma near the end of the 18th century also reinvigorated the trade route to the southwest resulting in large supplies of highly-figured marble coming out of the nearby Dali region in Yunnan province; those figured like traditional landscape paintings were often given inscriptions, framed and hung on walls; secondary panels became extremely fashionable as decorative inlays for furniture.

A manuscript in the Bibliothèque Nationale in Paris contains a set of gouache paintings depicting interiors of houses in Beijing. These paintings, dated to the 18th century, illustrate the formalized interiors and decorative furnishings of the elite at that time. In one, the relationship of the interior to the walled garden courtyard and to the distant landscape visible through the moon gate has a striking effect. It is not really clear where the interior begins or ends until one has descended the outermost terrace. Inside however, the spaces are divided with lattice partitions made up of mixed woods. The upper panels are decorated with small paintings and calligraphy, and the lower panels with archaic designs typical of the period. The decorative brackets visually reinforce the juncture of the horizontal and vertical panels. Their carved openwork design of angular scrolling is also another archaistic tendency derived from the decoration of early bronzes. A couch-bed set at the center emphasizes the symmetrical layout. Its railings are ornamented with panels of Dali marble. The refined elegance and formal atmosphere of this space differs greatly from the robust and rounded decoration found in the late Ming architecture at Anhui to be discussed below.

Western missionaries were also gaining more respect at court for their knowledge, and often presented the court with gifts of Western decorative art and introduced European Baroque architecture. After the Opium War in 1840, Western influences were even more pronounced. An eclectic blending of Chinese and Western decorative motifs can be witnessed in furnishings from this period, especially in the larger cities and coastal regions where there was more frequent contact. In remote inland areas, Western influence was hardly noticed until recent times. Deteriorating economic conditions and a severely weakened political structure in the 19th century contributed to a general decline in quality in the decorative art produced at that time.

Having briefly reviewed the historical background, the next section focuses upon a discussion of traditional Chinese architecture. Chinese society may be loosely defined as a class society which, outside of the Imperial circles, was traditionally divided into four classes. These followed, in descending rank, military and scholar-officials; merchants; artisans; and peasants, although actually, these divisions do not reflect the much broader diversity of the Chinese population, nor the interplay between them. Chinese society was also strongly influenced by Confucian principles since the tumultuous Warring States period (476–221 BC). These principles were eventually codified into a system of social morals by which society could govern itself based upon virtuous rule throughout a hierarchical network of relationships. These relationships of man to elders, wife to husband, son to father, etc., evolved into a complex system of social protocol which in turn influenced interior space division as well as furniture arrangements. Gender division was also a factor, and a husband of wealth and rank often had a wife and several concubines who all occupied separate quarters.

Sumptuary regulations – ranging from the use of personal ornament to the size and architectural style of housing – provide a means of differentiating rank and class in Chinese society. The type of jade ornament and decorative motifs that a person was permitted to wear were restricted according to rank. During the Song dynasty it was decreed that only the emperor could use beds of red lacquer. Buildings with curved roofs were reserved for government buildings and homes of high-ranking officials. It was decreed by the Ming court, that "officers of the first grade to the third grade can build halls of seven bays, from the sixth to ninth grades, the beams can only be decorated with black color." During the Qing dynasty, imperial sumptuary regulations stipulated that the houses of common people could not exceed three bays, or *jian*, houses of officials seven, temples nine, and palaces eleven. The status of the master was thus represented by the size and decoration of his house.

The courtyard house was the typical form used by the majority of the population and, according to archaeological evidence, existed as early as the Han dynasty (206 BC–220 AD). Walled courtyard houses encouraged families to live together as a family unit. In many areas of the country, common houses were arranged with a sleeping room to the left of the main room which was traditionally reserved for the parents. Children would sleep in a room on the opposite side. Such an ordering also recognized hierarchy, significance, and seniority which was further emphasized as additional rooms were added.

Courtyards and buildings were situated along an axially oriented pattern. Depth along a longitudinal axis in the courtyard houses of the wealthy also reflected a similar hierarchical pattern. The most public spaces were housed in the front including the kitchen, store rooms, and rooms for servants. Movement along the axis away from this common space was a passage to more private domains, with the last hall on the axis of the courtyard serving as the living quarters for the oldest generation, and those along the side halls for the children. A main reception hall was generally more highly decorated than the side halls, and functioned as a ceremonial hall for worshipping ancestors as well as for various seasonal ceremonies,

China: group of *huanghuali* furniture from the Woman's Quarters; from the exhibition *Masterpieces from the Museum of Classical Chinese Furniture*

weddings, or funerals. The courtyard was used primarily for circulation space between rooms and halls. Large estates also had enclosed gardens with water and rock gardens filling the space with life. Large trees provided shade, scent and fruit; decorated pavements and small pavilions accommodated outdoor spaces for the placement of tables and chairs and provided a refreshing atmosphere for relaxation, circulation and recreation.

Chinese architecture typically utilizes post and beam construction. After raising a foundation of rammed earth, a wood framework was erected usually consisting of an odd number of bays, or *jian*. The frame and roof trusses were joined with elaborate systems of wood joinery able to sustain the forces of common earthquakes. The adoption of the sweeping upcurved roof lines appears to have been an aesthetic preference which imparts an uplifting visual effect to lighten the mass of the large overhanging tiles roof; of course, the additional expense of such construction was only afforded by those of wealth and rank. The floors often remained earthen, or were overlaid with stone tile.

The spaces between the posts along the outside walls were generally filled with some variety of masonry on the back and sides, and narrow wood panels filled the spaces along the front. These modular panels were either solid wall panels, or served as window or doors. Open-work lattice windows, often detachable, let light and air into the rooms, and served a striking decorative purpose. The infinite variations of decorative lattice patterns were periodically re-covered on one side with a semi-transparent oiled paper which could be purchased in the local markets. In more temperate regions, simple reed or bamboo curtains were hung between the supporting posts and rolled up during the day.

Large interior spaces were frequently divided with curtains, fixed partitions, or movable folding screens. The latter were often pasted with paper and painted with countless beautiful designs. In the Qing dynasty, precious treasure cabinets also were used as room dividers in the homes of wealthy. One side was flat and the other side fitted with many small and different sized shelves for the display of precious antiques and treasures. Sometimes they were made completely open so that the treasures could be appreciated both from front and back.

The diverse climatic and geographical conditions affected the architecture of buildings and their styles. In the cooler climate of northern China, where dust storms were also frequent, dropped ceilings were often added, to enclose the open roof space and maintain temperature, as well as to provide a shield from dust and dirt filtering in through the roof. Buildings in rainy areas tended to have large overhanging roofs. Those in high altitudes where rain was scarce were the opposite, with high stone walls and flat-topped buildings. In the northwestern regions of China, where rainfall is also scanty, and timber scarce, subterranean housing was common.

Because of the cold climate in northern China, the interiors of houses also generally incorporated a raised brick platform called a *kang*. These hollow platforms were often heated from the inside with fire, and, in larger estates, a series of *kangs* in adjacent rooms were connected with a system of flues to a central furnace. The *kang* varied in size, from those of single bed size to large platforms which provided sufficient space for an entire family. These were not only slept upon, but used during the day as warm sitting platforms and arranged with low furniture such as *kang* tables and cabinets. Thus the early mat level culture did not entirely disappear, but is evidenced even in modern times as a continuation of a somewhat elevated mat level.

In the more temperate southern regions such as Jiangsu and Zhejiang, where the hot season was much longer than the cold season, the relationship of the interior to the exterior is less well defined. Walls of carved or lattice wooden window panels could be opened to outside terraces. Halls often had an open front, entered by a portico, with exquisitely carved woodwork. The colors were generally warm gray, with whitewashed walls. The woodwork was covered with a chestnut color or dark red or transparent paint. The general feeling was sedate and subtle, designed to create an intimate, pleasant environment for peaceful and harmonious family life.

In southern China, the rainy season is called the "mold rains" because of the propensity of household items to mildew during times of little sunlight and high humidity. Much more attention to ventilation was required, and few items could be stored directly on the cooler ground floor.

In Anhui province many two-storey houses dating from the Ming dynasty (1368–1644) are still found which formerly belonged to wealthy merchants. They are typically constructed with a light well that permits daylight to illuminate a small interior courtyard as well as the surrounding rooms that were fitted with latticework windows. The balustrades of Fang Wentai's house are richly carved, and the curved profile forms a comfortable bench along the light well wall inside each of the surrounding rooms. The roofs of houses in this region were constructed so as to drain rain water into small pools at the center of the front interior courtyard, just inside the main door where guests enter the house. The tapered post and upcurved beam architecture is robust with spirit. The main members of the elaborately framed roof structures were shaped rounded and smooth, while the corbels and other secondary elements were crisply carved. Such *yinyang* balancing juxtapositions are frequently integrated throughout many aspects of the Chinese culture. The wood was once finished with oil to highlight the grain patterns.

Entering the household of a wealthy family, one might be greeted with a large horizontal sign in the frieze above the doorway with carved characters suggesting an auspicious wish or noble sentiment. During the Ming and Qing dynasties, the latticework of doors was so full of intricate patterns that the door was more a work of art than an article for daily use. Latticework panels often had various auspiciously-shaped openings or panels into which landscapes, or birds and flowers were painted, along with a short poem. Often precious hardwoods were used for these interior elements, including *huali*, *zitan*, *hongmu*, golden flecked *nanmu*, cassia, boxwood, cypress, fragrant fir, etc. The most highly prized latticework was inlaid with jade or enamel. Decorations in domestic houses and those of minority nationalities were also extremely rich in variety, boasting many ingenious creations using local materials and suited to local conditions.

Interiors might be similarly varied, but, throughout China, the central room of a dwelling has traditionally served ritual as well as secular purposes. It may be a simple room, or rather grand and lavishly decorated. The central room commonly has a high, long table placed against the back wall where ancestral tablets, images of gods and goddesses, and various ceremonial vessels and utensils are arranged. A large decorative painting flanked by a pair of vertical couplets was usually hung above the table. Periodic offerings of food and incense acknowledge patrilineal descent and communal links. Due to the high ceilings with exposed beams blackened by the burning of incense and dim lighting from the single entrance, these halls usually had a sobering atmosphere. However large the family and dwelling became, this room was accepted as joint property never to be divided. The room was multi-functional and served ceremonial purposes from birthday celebrations to funerals. In the late Ming period novel *Jin Ping Mei*, the great hall of Ximen's residence was rearranged for a final tribute to his deceased wife with side tables set out as formal altar tables. During the Qing dynasty, a square table was customarily placed in front of the long side table with two chairs formally placed on either side. In the central room of more modest dwellings, and at meal time, the square table was brought forward into the central part of the room where chairs, stools, and benches were gathered around for seats.

In another episode from the novel *Jin Ping Mei*, Ximen gives a banquet for his friends and relatives; the scene is represented in an illustration. The large hall is set out with tables and large decorative screens facing one another. Candles on lamp stands illuminate the space for the evening's entertainment. Modular square tables were often placed side by side to make up long banquet tables. On such formal occasions the tables were draped with brocade frontals and the chairs with chair covers. A less formal side of Chinese life occurred around the square "Eight Immortals" table. Because the Eight Immortals were known for their fun-loving joviality, the name has come to characterize the family entertainment – dining, playing games, chatting, drinking, etc. – that often occurred around the central square table.

In the homes of wealthy families, the kitchen was not central to the household and was staffed by servants. Meals were served wherever the master or the mistress of the household might fancy – in the bedroom, the study, or perhaps under a flowering tree in the garden. In the common dwellings of the general populace, however, the kitchen hearth was a central element in the home, as well as the dwelling of the kitchen god who watched over the family activities and reported annually to the heavenly emperor on their behavior. These stoves were generally fitted with a small shrine and decorated with auspicious imagery.

The idealized Chinese interior is most closely associated with the traditional scholar's study, an example of which is represented in a woodblock illustration dating from the Kangxi period (1662–1722). The study reflects the Confucian ideal of a highly educated class of moral and virtuous officials well-versed in the classics, and expert in the four traditional arts of calligraphy, painting, poetry and music. A large painting table served as a desk and was central to the studio. In the 12th century, Guo Xi described a scholar preparing to write a poem or brush a painting: "On days when he was going to

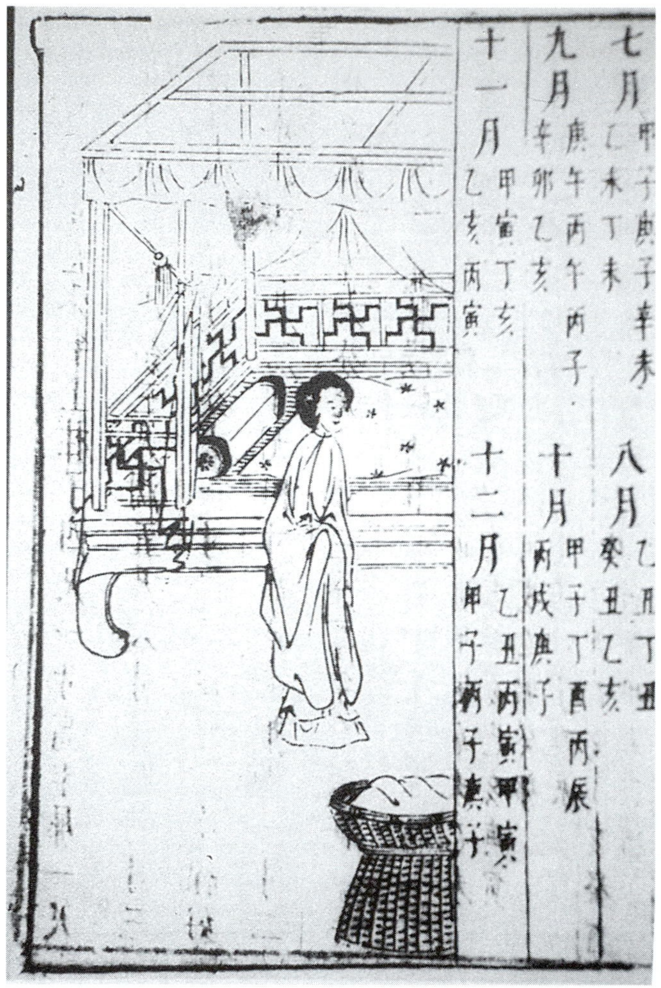

China: canopy bed; woodblock illustration to the carpenters' manual, *Lu Ban Jing*, Ming dynasty

paint, he would seat himself at a clean table, by a bright window, burning incense to right and left. He would choose the finest brushes, the most exquisite ink, wash his hands, and clean the inkstone, as though he were expecting a visitor of rank. He waited till his mind was calm and undisturbed, and then began."

"A clean desk by a bright window" not only reflected an ideal relative to interior arrangements, but also the desired empty state of mind from which creative production can arise. The studio was often simply furnished. A footrest was placed below the table in front of the master's chair. Those with massaging rollers stimulated the circulation and excited the internal state for creative production. Elegant cabinets were filled with books, scroll paintings, and treasured writing utensils. A couch, or daybed, placed along a wall provided a place for quiet relaxation, as well as a platform to entertain a friend while playing enchanting music on the *qin*.

Footrests raised the feet away from the cool earthen or masonry floors; footrests fitted with warming brazier pans were also used during the cold seasons and, during the summer, footrests with cool stone panels provided some relief from the stifling heat. In southern China, with its milder winters, portable braziers were commonly used to provide a localized source of heat. They also served as portable stoves for warming wine and preparing small delicacies. Low, bronze braziers, as well as brazier pans that fitted into low wooden stands were common; large, square ones were set out for special receptions or garden gatherings. Various charcoals were made of animal bone and dung. Fragrant flowers were added to refined charcoal blends and moulded into auspicious shapes that, when burned, perfumed the air and spread symbolic wishes.

The arrangement of the master's bedroom can be discerned in a painting by Qiu Ying of Master Zhang's bedroom from the well-known story *Dream of the Western Chamber* (*Xixiang ji*), as well as from the above mentioned jottings on elegant taste by the late Ming arbiter of taste, Wen Zhenheng. Concerning the master's bedroom, Wen notes: "Place the bed (*ta*) facing south. The half of the room behind the bed where people do not go should be used for such things as a brazier, clothes rack, washbasin, dressing case, and reading lamp. In front of the bed place only a small table with nothing on it, two small square stools, and a small cupboard containing incense, medicine, and delightful curiosities. The room should be refined, elegant, and not too cluttered. If too ornate, it will be like a ladies' room and unsuitable for a recluse sleeping in the clouds and dreaming of the moon."

Wen Zhenheng's passage provides an interesting juxtaposition with the furniture arranged in the ladies quarters which was generally provided as part of the dowry trousseau. Such furniture was considerably more ornate and decorated with traditional symbolic rebuses wishing for the newlywed bride to bear male children with the implied promise of sustaining the lineage and providing security and wealth for the future. Canopy beds were often carved with such auspicious decoration. The top rail of a late Ming dynasty *huanghuali* washbasin stand, formerly in the Museum of Classical Chinese Furniture, is crisply carved with *lingzhi* fungus and scrolling grass. The central panel is decorated with magnolia blossoms, symbolic of a beautiful woman, and the exposed seed pods represent fertility. Small jars of soap and cosmetics were placed upon its narrow, beaded shelf. A *huanghuali* towel rack in the same collection, dated to the 18th century, is decorated with an aquatic scene of mandarin ducks in a pond among lotus flowers in their various stages of development. Mandarin ducks, which mate for life, together with the lotus flowers, imply a wish for a long harmonious marriage with male offspring. A *huanghuali* mirror stand in the collection is decorated with plum blossoms which foretell of beauty rejuvenated with the arrival of springtime, and thus appropriate for a lady's cosmetic case.

The architectural canopy bed, enclosed with colorful brocade draperies hung from the inside, became a room within a room to provide privacy and warmth inside cold, drafty quarters. During the cold season, its enclosed spaced could also be used as a small room for dining, socializing, and other daily activities. Larger alcove beds additionally contained a small sitting area in front of the bed platform where a small table and stool might be placed. Such beds could be dismantled, so as to ease their installation and relocation. Similar beds were also built-in to the room structure during construction.

A poet of the Tang dynasty recommended that for a well planned residence, a sixth of the total area should be assigned to the house, half to lakes and ponds, and a third to plantations of bamboo. In both the temperate seasons and temperate regions, these outside areas were equally used as living space as were the interior spaces. Decorative screens, tables, and chairs were commonly moved into the garden according to the occasion. During the hot summer evenings, gauze-lined enclosures arranged on the veranda furnished with a daybed, incense stand, stool, and side table served as comfortable sleeping quarters.

In summary, the Chinese "traditional interior" perhaps should be considered as a "traditional living space." It was relatively flexible, and furnishings were grouped in accordance with the occasion as well as with the season. Although there were deeply rooted folk traditions among the common people who lived in simpler dwellings, the idealized concepts of "living spaces" really fall under a broader umbrella of "elegant living" defined by the ruling elite and the refined tastes of the literati. These tastes, or aesthetics, were based upon fundamental and dynamic principles of nature whereby beauty be blended with function, and simplicity be balanced with elegance.

As modern China races forward with a strong fascination towards the sciences, technologies and arts of the Western world, so the influences of Western architecture, furniture, interior design, and fashion will slowly become assimilated into Chinese culture. Presently, however, the state of interior design in China appears rather muddled to both a Western or a Chinese eye. However, like the previous Han and Tang periods when foreign influences have been highly fashionable, even greater artistic periods have flowered. Today China is once again in the process of rediscovery, and only the yet untold future will tell how the deeply rooted Chinese aesthetic will prevail.

CURTIS EVARTS

Further Reading

Berliner, Nancy and Sarah Handler, *Friends of the House: Furniture from China's Towns and Villages*, Salem, MA: Peabody Essex Museum, 1996

Chen Wanli, *Zhongguo Chuantong* (Chinese Traditional Architecture), Hong Kong, 1991

Clunas, Craig, *Chinese Furniture*, London: Bamboo, 1988

Clunas, Craig, *Superfluous Things: Material Culture and Social Status in Early Modern China*, Cambridge: Polity, and Urbana: University of Illinois Press, 1991

Ecke, Gustave, "A Group of Eighteenth-Century Paintings of Beijing Interiors" in *Journal of the Classical Chinese Furniture Society*, 3, Summer 1994, pp.60–69

Gernet, Jacques, *Daily Life in China on the Eve of the Mongol Invasion, 1250–1276*, New York: Macmillan, and London: Allen and Unwin, 1962

History and Development of Ancient Chinese Architecture, Beijing: Institute of the History of Natural Sciences, Chinese Academy of Sciences, and Science Press, 1986

Journal of the Classical Chinese Furniture Society, Renaissance, CA: Classical Chinese Furniture Society, 1990–94

Knapp, Ronald G., *The Chinese House: Craft, Symbol, and the Folk Tradition*, Hong Kong: Oxford University Press, 1990

Liu, Laurence G., *Chinese Architecture*, New York: Rizzoli, and London: Academy, 1989

Tian Jiaqing, *Classic Chinese Furniture of the Qing Dynasty*, London: Philip Wilson, 1996

Wang Shixiang, *Classic Chinese Furniture: Ming and Early Qing Dynasties*, Hong Kong: Joint Publishing, and San Francisco: China Books and Periodicals, 1986

Wang Shixiang, *Connoisseurship of Chinese Furniture*, 2 vols., Hong Kong: Joint Publishing, and Chicago: Art Media Resources, 1990

Wang Shixiang and Curtis Evarts, *Masterpieces from the Museum of Classical Chinese Furniture*, San Francisco: Tenth Union, 1995

Wen Zhenheng, *Zhang wu zhi* (Treatise on Superfluous Things), 1615–20

Zhang Yinwu, "A Survey of Chu-Style Furniture" in *Journal of the Classical Chinese Furniture Society*, 3, Summer 1994, pp.48–59

Chinese Export Wares

Although the term "export wares" suggests a predominantly one-way trade, the truth is very different. Long before the 17th- and 18th-century European craze for all things Oriental, a flourishing trade was carried on between the Chinese and traders from the Near East, with the great trading port of Canton established and noted for its wealth. It is probable that the first examples of Chinese goods for export found their way to the West via these Near Eastern markets. Porcelain and lacquerwork items brought to Europe before 1600 were treated as rare and valuable objects, but cannot be said to have been a significant influence on the domestic interior.

This situation changed dramatically during the 17th century with the expansion of European trade. The Dutch East India Company (established 1597) imported large quantities of primarily blue and white porcelain; but despite the legacy of Chinese "manufactured" items such as ceramics, lacquerwork, and ivory, it was in raw materials such as tea and silk that the greatest trade was carried on. Until the mid 17th century porcelain exports from China were, with rare exceptions, indistinguishable from those wares designed for the domestic market.

During the first half of the 17th century the most popular type of porcelain to be exported was the blue and white Kraak, and it is arguably the first type to have been purchased in sufficient quantities to have had a definable influence on the contemporary interior. It is characterised by a thick glossy glaze particularly liable to chipping along any sharp edges on the pieces. The blue underglaze decoration is applied thinly, and so has a watery quality. Variety of decoration is enormous, but is noted for the surfaces of pieces being divided into panels containing individual scenes of birds, animals, or Chinese religious motifs. This ware was avidly collected by European royalty such as Mary II at Hampton Court, and by the Elector of Brandenburg at Oranienburg near Berlin. There is also evidence that the lesser nobility were equally interested. In Wycherley's play *The Country-Wife* (c.1675) Lady Fidget exclaims, "We women of quality never think we have china enough".

During this period lacquerwork also became better known in Europe. The complex technique used the sap of the tree *Rhus vernicflua*. The earliest type to reach the West, known to the Chinese as *Kuan Cai* ("engraved polychrome") and to the British as Bantam Work, involved coloured decoration previously engraved or carved in intaglio into a background layer of lacquer. Two screens in red lacquer given to Archduke Leopold

Chinese Export Wares: painted panel showing Chinese workshop with pots, screens and lacquer artefacts, late 18th century

of Austria by the Jesuit Fathers when he was elected Emperor in 1700 are examples of this process which also contain early signs of Western influence in their double-headed eagle decoration. The lacquerwork industry was strengthened by the closure of Japan (previously seen as the source of the best lacquerwork) to Western traders after 1639.

Later Kraak porcelain shows evidence of subjects designed specifically for Europe, such as decoration depicting tulips and other types of European flower. The quality of porcelain exported from China improved dramatically after 1650, with a heavier, thicker body than kraak. Blue and white porcelain continued to be shipped, the shapes borrowing from Chinese prototypes but adapted to suit Western tastes. Examples include garnitures of vases catering to the European fashion for matching sets of mantelpiece ornaments, and large vases to be displayed on the floor or, as at Dyrham Park, Gloucestershire (1710 inventory), in fireplaces during the summer.

By the early years of the 18th century a slow decline in the popularity of blue and white porcelain had begun. Fascination with Japanese culture sponsored a fashion for so-called *Imari* ware decorated in both underglaze and overglaze colours, and often lavishly gilded. The closed Japanese market once again favoured the Chinese, Chinese *Imari* being a significant export during the early 18th century.

During this period enamelled wares became more prominent in their influence on the Western interior. These wares were decorated in the predominantly green *famille verte* enamels from the first decade of the 18th century, whilst the *famille rose* was introduced from the 1730s.

The new colours were used for new forms. Birds, dogs, and lions as well as human figures were exported in pairs as decoration for European cabinets and mantelpieces, as well as a huge variety of more or less utilitarian items such as cups, mugs, and teapots.

The passion for collecting porcelain soon began to exhaust the space available on mantelpieces however, and we know that as early as 1708 the modestly wealthy Squire Blundell of Lancashire was ordering furniture having "steps" for the display of his china. The supply of furniture designed to display china became quite an industry in itself during the 18th century; Thomas Chippendale for example illustrating examples in his *Director* of 1762 (3rd edition).

The lacquer industry also prospered through the adoption of new techniques. The process of *Kuan Cai* was superseded during the 18th century by painted lacquerwork and the familiar gold-on-black style of decoration more suited to bulk production of both furniture and smaller decorative items such as boxes, screens, and fans. Imported lacquerwork screens were mounted in ormolu to form larger pieces of furniture, or used as wall panels, as in the case of the china closet built for Mary (later Queen Mary II of England) at Honselaardijk, Holland in 1686.

By the mid 18th century the growth in demand for porcelain made to special order was becoming a significant aspect of trade. Pieces from the early years of the 18th century are usually only distinguishable as "special" by the addition of coats of arms, or small details in the form of decorative cartouches, most often applied underglaze in cobalt blue; but the trade in armorial porcelain developed very rapidly. For much of the century the great families of Europe and America were supplied with often lavish porcelain decorated with personal arms. This trend was aided by the increased palette of colours available to the Chinese potter; a fine example is the exquisite service created for Leake Okeover during the 1740's, the polychrome onglaze enamel design covering virtually the entire surface of the ware.

Blank pieces were also decorated to local taste in Europe, and there is evidence that the East India companies periodically employed artists (most famously Cornelis Pronk) to develop designs. Much more common, however, was the use of well-known engravings by leading artists and caricaturists. These were sent East to be used by the Chinese potters. Subject matter ranged from satirical themes to gently erotic scenes for private consumption. Dinner ware and other items for societies, guilds, and companies were also made to special order, such as the large blue and white service ordered from Canton by the Mutual Assurance Company of Philadelphia in 1812. The service was used for dinners following meetings of the Board of Directors.

Chinese ceramics made for export during the last half of the 18th century presage a sharp decline in the popularity of the ware. A reliance on designs "borrowed" or adapted from those of European manufacturers (particularly porcelain factories) is noticeable. The figure groups and dinner pieces of Meissen, Sèvres, Strasbourg, and Chelsea were all copied. It is ironic that Chinese potters found themselves decorating pieces with designs reflecting a European pastiche of their own culture. This trend continued into the 19th century, for example with the ordering of massive porcelain pagodas to complement the decoration of the Royal Pavilion in Brighton.

During the late 19th century, the Aesthetic Movement encouraged a revival in all things oriental which once again led to large-scale exports, with retailing firms in Europe like Liberty's specialising in the trade. Large scale "Mandarin" vases were imported to complement (even dominate) the domestic interior, while the smaller "Ginger jars" decorated in underglaze blue and white frequently fetched very high prices.

GRAHAM MCLAREN

See also Lacquer and Japanning; Porcelain Rooms

Further Reading

The most useful recent surveys of Chinese Export Wares are Clunas 1987, and Medley 1989; both include further reading lists.

Ayers, John, Oliver Impey and J.V.G. Mallet, *Porcelain for Palaces: The Fashion for Japan in Europe 1650–1750*, London: Oriental Ceramic Society, 1990

Clunas, Craig (editor), *Chinese Export Art and Design*, London: Victoria and Albert Museum, 1987

Feddersen, Martin, *Chinese Decorative Art: A Handbook for Collectors and Connoisseurs*, London: Faber, and New York: Yoseloff, 1961

Godden, Geoffrey A., *Oriental Export Market Porcelain and Its Influence on European Wares*, London: Granada, 1979

Gordon, Elinor (editor), *Chinese Export Porcelain: An Historical Survey*, New York: Universe, 1975; London: Bell, 1977

Howard, David S. and John Ayers, *China for the West: Chinese Porcelain and Other Decorative Arts for Export Illustrated from the Mottahedeh Collection*, 2 vols., London: Philip Wilson, and New York: Sotheby Parke Bernet, 1978

Howard, David S. (editor), *A Tale of Three Cities: Canton, Shanghai and Hong Kong, Three Centuries of Sino-British Trade in the Decorative Arts*, London: Sotheby's, 1997

Jörg, C.J.A., *Porcelain and the Dutch China Trade*, The Hague: Nijhoff, 1982

Jourdain, Margaret and R. Soame Jenyns, *Chinese Export Art in the Eighteenth Century*, London: Country Life, and New York: Scribner, 1950

Matos, Maria Antónia Pinto de, *Chinese Export Porcelain from the Museum of Anastácio Gonçalves, Lisbon*, London: Philip Wilson, 1996

Medley, Margaret, *The Chinese Potter: A Practical History of Chinese Ceramics*, 3rd edition Oxford: Phaidon, 1989

Oort, H.A. van, *Chinese Porcelain of the 19th and 20th Centuries*, Lochem: Tijdstroom, 1977

Schiffer, Herbert, Peter, and Nancy, *Chinese Export Porcelain: Standard Patterns and Forms, 1780–1880*, Exton, PA: Schiffer, 1980

Chinoiserie

Chinoiserie is a wholly European style whose inspiration is entirely oriental. True Chinoiseries are not pallid or incompetent imitations of Chinese objects. They are the tangible and solid realizations in the West of "Cathay", an imagined land, created over the centuries by travellers' tales and by careful scrutiny of its inimitable products of embroidered silk, lacquer screens and porcelain bowls, carried to Europe by the East India trade. The craze for the orient and all things Chinese that gripped Europe in the second half of the 17th century incorporated these exotic treasures into the Baroque decorative schemes then fashionable in the West. Porcelain vases were displayed in a quite un-Eastern fashion, towering and clustering on cabinets and chimneypieces, or mounted in silver or ormolu. The glowing hues of the embroidery were hung on bedsteads which rose to the height of the ceiling, and were capped with great plumes of feathers, while at Versailles, where Louis XIV collected oriental works on a vast scale, the glitter of lacquer replaced the silver furniture melted down to finance the king's disastrous wars. Under Louis XIV, Versailles became the arbiter of fashion for all Europe. There Chinoiserie was given the royal imprimatur, and from there it spread as a court style to Germany, and from Germany to Scandinavia, Russia, and the rest of Europe. A more fantastic and playful view of China – also present in mainland Europe's Chinoiserie images – added a sense of whimsical eccentricity to the style in England.

Seventeenth-century interiors throughout Europe were sparsely furnished. Furniture needed to make an impact, and lacquer – whether imported from the East, or "japanned" by local craftsmen, who attempted to emulate the lacquer-makers' art using home-grown ingredients – was highly favoured. The method was minutely described in *A Treatise of Japanning and Varnishing* (1688) by John Stalker and George Parker, and japanning became a fashionable pastime with English ladies who japanned anything, even walnut furniture. In Germany, two of the finest japanners of the 17th century, Gerhard Dagly and Maximilan Schnell, produced furniture and bibelots of outstanding worth, while Dutch lacquer copies were of such high quality that they were easily mistaken for the real thing.

Chinoiserie: *grande singerie*, Chantilly, by Christophe Huet, 1735

Imported lacquer screens were cut up to line the walls of small dressing rooms and closets, often used for the new diversion of taking tea. The earliest surviving example of a *lackcabinett* (c.1660) is at Rosenborg Castle, Copenhagen. In England, Burghley, Chatsworth and Hampton Court all had lacquer rooms before the century was out. Baroque-style lacquer rooms were found in Germany (Chinesische Zimmer, Neue Residenz, Bamberg, 1705), while the Baroque Indianisches Lustschloss (Pilnitz, c.1720) and a Japanisches Palais (Dresden, c.1715) show the confusion of names typical of the geographical indifference and topological uncertainty that underpinned Chinoiserie.

Seventeenth-century pottery throughout Europe strove to emulate the porcelain imported from China. Dutch pre-eminence was marked in the Delft potteries, which mimicked the blue-and-white Ming colours but on new Baroque forms – pagoda-shaped tulip stands, lobed dishes, sets of vases – and with new decoration too, moving from Chinese designs to pure Chinoiserie scenes, often taken from engravers' manuals or illustrations in travel books. In France, Rouen produced polychrome dishes decorated with Chinoiserie subjects, while at Nevers Chinese ornament was applied to both Baroque and Chinese shapes, albeit with an air of French orderliness completely lacking in the originals. English Delftware was manufactured at Lambeth and Bristol in the 1680s, while at Fulham John Dwight was granted a patent in 1672 for the manufacture of "transparent earthenware commonly known by the name of Porcelaine or China." Between about 1670 and 1685 engraved Chinoiserie motifs were popular on English silver, and from the mid-century imitative designs by English needle-workers, in the Chinese manner or "after the Indian fashion", made their appearance on the counterpanes and curtains of the Stuart household. Chinoiserie tapestries were woven in Soho c.1700, while in France both Gobelins and Beauvais produced notable suites of Chinoiserie tapestries in the 18th century

In the first decades of the 18th century artists and designers found that Chinoiserie's clear, bright colours, amusing and fantastic motifs, and asymmetric design were all shared by the new Rococo style, and combined these with purely European Rococo motifs, often in the same work. The result was so felicitous and so popular that it became one of the Rococo's most notable features. The few Chinoiseries produced by Antoine Watteau set the course for Rococo Chinoiserie throughout Europe. His decorative scheme for the Cabinet du Roi, Château de la Muette, (c.1718) presented a distinctly Gallic and frivolous view of Chinese life. The ironic tone struck by Watteau was taken further by Christophe Huet when he produced a Chinoiserie *singerie* of Watteau's scene in the *grande singerie* at Chantilly (1735). About 1748, Huet decorated the salon chinois and the boudoir at the Château de Champs with a series of vignettes of Chinese and exotic birds for Madame de Pompadour. Madame de Pompadour's Château at Bellevue was decorated by François Boucher, who infused his highly individual Chinoiserie style with the sensuality common to all his work. At Bellevue he devised a Chinese boudoir and painted two *paysages chinois* for the drawing room. As Boucher's influence spread across Europe his painting *A Chinese Fishing Party* became a favourite theme for Chinoiserie designers, and little Chinese figures fishing under a willow tree ornamented the luxurious trinkets of the rich. From 1740, many suites of Boucher's Chinoiserie engravings were issued. All were widely copied and adapted, used for statuettes in bronze and terracotta, gold and enamel snuff-boxes, overdoors and painted panels, and designs on porcelain in factories from Meissen to Lowestoft.

The last great French designer of Rococo Chinoiseries, Jean-Baptiste Pillement, worked in practically every major city in Europe, from London to Warsaw, designing with equal facility and *joie de vivre* a Chinoiserie study for the king of Poland, a pavilion at Cintra in Portugal, floral designs for silks and cottons, and hundreds of designs for enchanting "Chinese ornaments" complete with bells, dragons, birds, monkeys, shells, and Chinamen wearing upside-down flowers instead of hats. These were engraved and translated into fields as various as marquetry, textiles, tiles, wallpapers and room decoration. Between about 1755 and 1760, Pillement prints were published in London as well as in Paris, and up to 1774 he continued to produce prints of Rococo Chinoiseries in large numbers.

Painted Chinoiserie rooms remained fashionable up to the 1770s. Costly alternatives used satins and embroideries from India and painted silks from China to line the walls. From 1750 toile de Jouy, a cotton fabric decorated with engraved copperplates of little vignetted scenes, often Pillementesque Chinoiseries, was extensively used, not only to line the walls, but also to cover chairs and beds. Few of these rooms have survived, although examples of the fabrics are preserved in textile collections, and textile companies today have reissued document prints of the 18th-century designs. Wallpapers filled any gap caused by the huge demand for printed cottons, and by 1750 boldly-drawn and brightly-coloured Chinoiserie papers were fashionable. Lacquer reflected the mid-18th century taste for pure colours with red and polychrome lacquers generally preferred to black. *Vernis Martin*, a French version of lacquer, was produced in response to the demand for colour in furniture and decoration. By the 1760s a more severe Neo-Classical style was in fashion and Japanese lacquer was favoured above all others as colours grew more restrained and black and gold returned to fashion.

The wild enthusiasm for Chinoiserie encountered north of the Rhine contrasted with the restrained Frenchification of the style that ruled in France. The German princelings were passionate Sinophiles, and their family connections throughout Europe ensured the spread of the style. Frederick the Great's most notable essay in architectural Chinoiserie, the Chinese Tea House (Potsdam, 1757) is much more fantastic than its Gallic equivalent. Its cupola is topped by a gilded Chinese figure holding an umbrella, while life-size gilded sandstone Chinese musicians are placed on its veranda. In Sweden, the Queen, one of Frederick's sisters, was given an entire Chinese pavilion as a birthday present: Kina – China – whose exquisite interiors embody a mixture of European Chinoiserie designers, the French represented by Boucher and Watteau, the English by William Halfpenny and William Chambers. Another of Frederick's sisters, the Margravine of Bayreuth, built a summer palace, Schloss Eremitage, which had a Chinese kiosk in the garden, drawing rooms decorated with *singeries*, butterflies, Chinamen, and flowers, and a mirror room. The Amalienburg Pavilion (Nymphenburg) has Chinoiserie scenes in blue and

Chinoiserie: state bedroom, Nostell Priory, by Thomas Chippendale, c.1750

white in three of its rooms, the Hundekammer, the Retirade and the kitchen.

Chinoiserie interiors were considered sublimely appropriate to house and display the collections of oriental porcelain that every German princeling was amassing. A few such *porzellan zimmers* survived until World War II. The earliest and most noticeable (Schloss Charlottenburg, outside Berlin) has been restored. True porcelain was first produced at Meissen c.1710 and spread from there across Europe. Chinoiseries formed an important part of the porcelain decoration of all factories, whether in blue and white, polychrome enamels, or gold-leaf. Most of Meissen's useful ware was decorated with the so-called *Indianisches blumen*, emphatically-coloured, fancifully-drawn flowers deriving from the peonies and chrysanthemums first seen on the Chinese *famille vert* and *famille rose* wares imported to Europe.

The fretwork, bells and dragons of Cathay made an early appearance in Russia. Monplaisir, Peter the Great's summer palace in the grounds of Peterhof Palace, had a scarlet lacquer cabinet, since restored, with gilt Chinoiserie scenes and brackets holding porcelain. Catherine the Great's so-called Chinese Palace at Oranienbaum (1762) has an *enfilade* of state rooms with a number of Rococo Chinoiserie interiors: painted, lined with silk, decorated with beads, and inlaid with wood. A complete Chinese village erected in the grounds of Tsarskoe Selo is a rare survivor of a vogue for Chinoiserie garden follies that spread from England to every country in Europe.

Italy had early embraced Chinoiserie. Venetian lacquer, known and admired in the 17th century, reached its apogee in the 18th, and is still produced today. Early 18th-century lacquer designs were directly inspired by the Far East, with red or black ground colours decorated in gold with an assortment of exotic subjects. Some notable lacquer rooms (Palazzo Reale, Turin c.1725) follow the model found elsewhere in Europe, while the native style of fresco decoration extended its subject matter to include Chinoiseries too (Villa la Barbariga, Stra). At the Villa Valmarana, Vicenza, decorated by G.D. Tiepolo (c.1757), the Foresteria is frescoed with large Chinese scenes given a particularly Venetian quality of richness and lightness. Further south, the king and queen of Naples created a porcelain room at their royal palace at Portici (c.1757), featuring groups of brightly enamelled porcelain Chinamen in high relief. The entire decorative scheme was repeated at the king's palace at Aranjuez, Spain. In Sicily, the Villa la Favorita, also known as the Palazzina Cinese, has fresco decoration in a Pompeian Chinoiserie style, where richly attired mandarins and pagoda-roofed fretted pavilions replace the Roman temples and classical maidens of the Pompeian style.

In England, Chinoiserie decoration, largely suppressed in the early 18th century by the emphatic and narrow dictates of the Burlington school, was liberated by the Rococo. But unlike

France, where Chinoiserie had been seamlessly absorbed into the sophisticated body of the Rococo style, in England it was a quite independent element, a wild and frivolous changeling of the parent style. This was due to another key difference: patronage. Rococo Chinoiserie in England was not the exclusive plaything of the rich and well-born. It was the compilers of pattern books and carvers who were responsible for the vitality of English Chinoiserie and for its wild popularity in the 1750s. By 1765 the craze was on the wane, although the new style, Neo-Classicism, did not eclipse it entirely. Both Robert Adam and William Chambers produced refined Chinoiserie designs and used the style for interiors. Chambers's *Designs of Chinese Buildings, Furniture, Dresses, etc.* (1757) was considered the most authentic of the pattern books of Chinoiserie designs that appeared in the 1750s. The first was *New Designs for Chinese Temples, Triumphal Arches, Garden Seats, Palings etc.* by William Halfpenny, quickly followed by his *Rural Architecture in the Chinese Taste* (1752), a year that also saw the first pattern book devoted to Chinoiserie designs for interiors, Matthias Lock and Henry Copland's *A New Book of Ornaments in the Chinese Taste* (1752). This was followed by *A New Book of Chinese Designs Calculated to Improve the Present Taste* (1754) by Matthias Darly and George Edwards. Here were designs for furniture, chimney furniture, vases and stands, as well as illustrations of landscapes and ornaments useful for japanners, porcelain painters, and embroiderers. These designs appeared on printed cotton and on Bow porcelain, and some were reprinted in 1762 in *The Ladies Amusement, or the whole art of Japanning made easy* by Robert Sayer. Darly's and Edwards's designs were also appropriated in *Chinese Architecture* (Paul Decker, 1769). The best known patternbook, Thomas Chippendale's *Gentleman and Cabinet-Maker's Director* (1754), included designs for "Chinese Chippendale" furniture. This not only has decidedly "Chinese" ornamentation of pagoda cresting or pierced and fretted galleries. Its shape is different with a square and angular outline and straight legs. Most furniture made in the Chinese taste was of mahogany, a wood that took carved decoration extremely well, but the large frames of looking-glasses were generally of soft wood, mostly gilded, occasionally japanned.

By 1750 a Chinese bedroom and dressing room was considered the height of fashion. The most famous, decorated c.1753 at Badminton House for the 4th Duke of Beaufort, by John Linnell, had a suite of japanned furniture: eight chairs, two knee-hole dressing tables, probably two mirrors, a commode and two pairs of standing shelves, apart from its glory, the bed.

Chinoiserie: engraving from *A Collection of Designs for Household Furniture* by George Smith, 1808

Square in shape, japanned in scarlet, canopied by a black and gold pagoda roof, hung with bells and ornamented with dragons, this spectacular bed has a latticed headboard as high as the top of its posts. Perhaps the most brilliant ensemble of Chinoiserie japanned furniture still in place is at Nostell Priory, Yorkshire, where Chippendale decorated the state bedroom and dressing room, and two adjoining closets. Chinese bedrooms were generally lined either with printed linen or wallpaper. The cost of imported Chinese wallpapers encouraged the production of local versions, inspiring patterns still produced. Some country houses in England still have rooms hung with mid-18th century "Indian paper", Saltram House, Devon, being a notable example.

The more extravagant and inventive path of English Chinoiserie Rococo is exemplified at Claydon House, Buckinghamshire, where great carved ho-ho birds perch on the cresting of the classical doorcases, fabulous cranes roost, and winged dragons swish their barbed tails. The so-called Chinese room on the first floor has an entire wall devoted to an astonishing tea-alcove, a realisation in three dimensions of the airy fancies seen on porcelain or lacquer, a kind of pagoda-pavilion carved in wood and painted a glistening white, where among the bursting flowers, shells, scrolls, bells and diaper-work, a miniature Chinese family sits round a tea-table, each raising a carved arm in stiff salute, while on the table the meticulously carved tea equipage waits. Luke Lightfoot, a little known carver of genius, is responsible for these, the most extraordinary Chinoiseries in England.

The techniques of Chinoiserie decoration were attempted in America as soon as they had been tested in Europe. From the 1760s Chinoiseries appeared on copper-plated printed textiles and wallpapers, while the James Reid House, Charleston (1757) and Gunston Hall, Fairfax County, Virginia (1758), boasted Chinoiserie interiors contemporary with their equivalents in England.

George IV was England's greatest devotee of Chinoiserie in the 19th century and the design of the Chinese drawing-room (c.1790) at Carlton House, his London house, was seen as the paragon of Georgian Chinoiserie taste. Its architect, Henry Holland, had re-imported Sir William Chambers's "Chinese design" to England from France, where it had been sharpened with Gallic sophistication and good breeding. But it was a combination of opulence with a kind of barbaric splendour that dominated the furnishings of that most extraordinary of Chinoiserie palaces, the Royal Pavilion at Brighton. Its first decoration, c.1801, by the firm of Frederick Crace, was in the established tradition of Chinoiserie taste. Delicate, light and fanciful bamboo, fretwork, and *treillage* were combined with sophisticated ground colours, like scarlet and purple, to provide a scheme that was gay, light-hearted and rather old-fashioned in its air of Rococo charm. In 1815 the interiors were remodelled, and a more powerful, bizarre but disciplined richness replaced the tinsel and toylike brilliance of the first style. Scaly dragons and metallic snakes, lotus-shaped gasoliers, gilded palm-tree pilasters, combined with rich colours and grand furniture to produce an astonishing and exhilarating effect. By this stage the Crace firm's knowledge of Chinoiserie was augmented by the work of Robert Jones, who was responsible for many of the designs. The dramatic finale of the decorative scheme, the Music Room, represents the summit of the Crace firm's achievement. Blazing with crimson and gold Chinese landscape murals framed by gigantic serpents and winged dragons, it is like a huge lacquer box lit by water-lily and dragon-shaped gasoliers.

The Prince Regent's championing of Chinoiserie was in the old style of court art, and he collected only the finest examples. But new industrial techniques of mass production made for a wider participation in the taste. Transfer-printed Chinese-style designs on tableware, especially blue and white, were cheap and popular by the 1830s. A favourite was the Willow Pattern, developed about 1795 by Josiah Spode. The 19th century Rococo revival introduced mass-produced Chinoiserie motifs onto wallpaper, textiles and furniture. About 1870, the Queen Anne revival returned lacquer and japanned cabinets and bureaux, Delft and Nanking China to fashion.

Chinoiserie's most notable achievements in the 20th century are in places of public amusement, where its sense of opulence and fantasy can be given unbridled rein. Public parks, music halls, theatres, cinemas and hotels, even cruise liners, have all embraced the style. The Grand Theatre, Clapham (designed by E.A. Woodrow c.1900, recently restored) has a Baroque exterior and a Chinese interior, complete with dragons, and boxes shaped like pagodas. But it was the cinema, of which Grauman's Chinese Theatre in Hollywood itself is perhaps the most conspicuous example, that gave Chinoiserie new life in the 20th century. Chinoiserie was employed by cinema designers from La Pagode in the rue Babylone, Paris, to the Palace, Southall, West London, while in Seattle, Washington, the 2,400-seater cinema, the 5th Avenue, is a grand example of the subverted authenticity that has always provided Chinoiserie with its richest soil.

DAWN JACOBSON

See also Boucher; Chambers; Lacquer and Japanning; Pillement

Principal Collections

Important Chinoiserie interiors survive in many European houses and collections. French examples include: the Salon Chinois, Château de Champs, Champs-sur-Marne; La Grande Singerie, Musée Condé, Chantilly; and Le Salon Pillement, Château de Crâon, Haroué, near Nancy. German examples include: Schloss Favorite, Baden Baden; the Chinese Room, Neue Residenz, Bamberg; Schloss Charlottenburg, Berlin; the Amalienburg and Pagodenburg Pavilions, Schloss Nymphenburg, Munich; and the Chinese Tea House, Sans Souci, Potsdam. British examples include: the Chinese Room, Claydon House, Buckinghamshire; the Chinese Rooms, Saltram, Devon; the Royal Pavilion, Brighton, Sussex; and the State Bedchamber and Dressing Room, Nostell Priory, Yorkshire. Italian examples include the Palazzina Cinese (Villa Favorita), Palermo, Sicily; the Porcelain Room, Museo e Gallerie Nazionale de Capodimonte, Naples; and the Lacquer or Chinese Room, Palazzo Reale, Turin. Russian examples include the Chinese Palace (now China Palace Museum), Tsarskoe Selo, near St. Petersburg. Scandinavian examples include the Kina Slott (Chinese Pavilion), Drottningholm, Sweden.

Further Reading

A thorough introduction to the origins and development of Chinoiserie can be found in Honour 1961 which includes annotated notes on many of the important primary and secondary sources. The most recent and comprehensive survey is Jacobson 1993 which also contains a full bibliography and a guide to the major European and North American collections.

Ayers, John, Oliver Impey and J.V.G. Mallet, *Porcelain for Palaces: The Fashion for Japan in Europe, 1650–1750*, London: Oriental Ceramic Society, 1990
Belevitch-Stankevitch, H., *Le Goût Chinois en France au Temps de Louis XIV*, 1910; reprinted Geneva: Slatkine, 1970
Bourne, Jonathan (editor), *Lacquer: An International History and Collectors' Guide*, Marlborough: Crowood Press, and New York: Abrams, 1984
China und Europa: Chinaverständnis und Chinamode im 17. und 18. Jahrhundert (exhib. cat.), Berlin: Schloss Charlottenburg, 1973
China's Influence on American Culture in the 18th and 19th Centuries (exhib. cat.), New York: China Institute in America, 1976
Conner, Patrick, *Oriental Architecture in the West*, London: Thames and Hudson, 1979
Cornforth, John, "A Role for Chinoiserie?" in *Country Life*, 7 December 1989, pp.144–51
Honour, Hugh, *Chinoiserie: The Vision of Cathay*, London: Murray, 1961; New York: Dutton, 1962
Hussey, Christopher, *Early Georgian, 1715–1760* (English Country Houses, vol.1), 1955; reprinted Woodbridge, Suffolk: Antique Collectors' Club, 1984
Impey, Oliver, *Chinoiserie: The Impact of Oriental Styles on Western Art and Decoration*, London: Oxford University Press, and New York: Scribner, 1977
Jacobson, Dawn, *Chinoiserie*, London: Phaidon, 1993
Jarry, Madeleine, *L'Exoticisme dans L'Art Décoratif Français au Temps du Louis XIV*, Paris, 1957
Jarry, Madeleine, *Chinoiserie: Chinese Influence on European Decorative Art, 17th and 18th Centuries*, New York: Vendome, and London: Philip Wilson, 1981
Morley, John, *The Making of the Royal Pavilion, Brighton: Designs and Drawings*, London: Sotheby, and Boston: Godine, 1984
Morley, John, *Regency Design, 1790–1840: Gardens, Buildings, Interiors, Furniture*, London; Zwemmer, and New York: Abrams, 1993
Setterwall, Åke and others, *The Chinese Pavilion at Drottningholm*, Malmö: Allhem, 1974
Sullivan, Michael, *The Meeting of Eastern and Western Art, from the Sixteenth Century to the Present Day*, London: Thames and Hudson, and Greenwich, CT: New York Graphic Society, 1973
Verlet, Pierre, *French Furniture and Interior Decoration of the 18th Century*, London: Barrie and Rockliffe, 1967

Chintz

Strictly speaking chintz is a type of painted or printed cotton. It differs from printed calico (a far humbler fabric) in that it is finer in quality, firmer and more tightly woven, sometimes with a glazed finish. It boasts multivarious designs and has been used for soft furnishings, bedcovers and hangings, and curtains. And it has occasionally been used for clothes.

Chintz is not only a type of fabric, the term has also come to be identified with a particular style of interior design. "Chintz!", wrote Frank Lewis in his early history of the subject published in 1935, "What a pleasant sounding name – what pleasant thoughts it brings to the mind – the old country cottage with its old grandfather clock, the burnished copper warming pan, and those gaily coloured chintz curtains. The country house with its bright chintz covers, so reminiscent of home and all it means. Truly, chintz may be said to represent the feeling of the Englishman and his home, as it really is." Lewis's words highlight the association that has developed between chintz and Englishness, particularly in the world of interior design. This association is, if anything, even stronger today and has contributed greatly to the international popularity of traditional floral patterns produced by firms such as Arthur Sanderson & Sons, Colefax and Fowler, and Laura Ashley.

Chintz first arrived in western Europe from India, and although many of the early designs suggest Persian influences, it is considered to be of Indian origin. The name has Hindi roots and stems from the word *Chitte* or *Chit* which means speckled or painted cloth. During the 16th, 17th and 18th centuries, the designs in the better kind of Indian chintzes were often painted; other varieties included painted areas within block-printed outlines, and printed patterns.

The early European traders in the East used the brightly coloured cloths as barter to obtain spices from the Malay peninsula. The earliest evidence for their use in Europe dates from the 1570s and 1580s when they are mentioned in the wills of wealthy citizens living in Marseilles. These particular samples were brought by the overland route but almost simultaneously other consignments were reaching Lisbon and Amsterdam by sea. The first examples arrived in England as booty in captured ships. An important cargo aboard the Portuguese *Madre di Dios*, including *chittes*, calicoes, lawns, quilts and carpets, was captured by a British privateer in 1592 and brought to Devonport. The interest and enthusiasm generated by these cloths (also known as "pintados" after the Portuguese word meaning speckled cloth) encouraged the establishment of the British East India Company in 1600.

Initially chintzes or "pintados" employed native Indian styles. But as the commercial possibilities became more evident, trading companies began to commission special designs to suit European taste. The Mughal Emperor Akbar introduced craftsmen from Turkey, Persia, China and Italy to instruct his workmen, and in 1669 the English East India Company began sending actual patterns for Indian cotton-painters to copy. Many of these patterns were floral and included both tree and branchwork designs as well as all-over floral repeats. Other designs were copies or adaptations of European models, including the work of established designers such as Jean Berain. But craftsmen rarely produced exact replicas of the designs that they were shown. Instead they produced their own interpretations which resulted in the beautiful and exotic stylisations of flora and fauna that have proved so appealing to European tastes.

The attractions of chintz were manifold. Previously, the only fabrics available were linen, hemp, silk and wool, all of which were heavy and expensive. Also, the colours in these fabrics tended to fade with age, or lost their brilliance when washed. Chintzes, by contrast, were bright and fresh, reasonably priced and light in weight. They offered an alternative furnishing fabric that was attractive, hardwearing and washable, and, for the first time, beautiful textiles were no longer the prerogative of the very rich.

Demand for such goods soon became overwhelming, especially in England and France. Originally, they were regarded as an exotic curiosity but by the 1680s they had become widely admired and sought after commodities. Not surprisingly, there were many European printed imitations. In 1648, Benoit Ganteume, a master playing-card maker, together with Jacques Bavilles, a master engraver, set up the first cotton printing company in France. Others quickly followed and when Marseilles became a free port in 1669, the first Provençal prints were produced.

The rapidly increasing popularity of chintz and other printed cottons posed a growing threat to the established textile industries – especially silk – and numerous restrictions on imported and locally-produced goods imposed in France between 1686 and 1759 sought to protect native industries and restrict the supply of foreign work. These included the banning of all cotton imports in 1691, and subsequent bans of chintz in 1720 and 1734. Nevertheless, chintz still managed to find its way into France and, if anything, the bans served only to heighten demand and strengthen its appeal. Highly placed leaders of fashion openly defied the 1691 decree. The Marquise de Pompadour, for example, commissioned a portrait from Hubert Drouais in which she is shown wearing a dress made of chintz. She also made a particular point of decorating her Bellevue château with chintz and made gifts of it to her friends. The less privileged had to be more clandestine and punishments for breaking the law were severe, ranging from fines and imprisonment to years in the galleys and even death. Even so, people of high rank continued to acquire chintz through smuggling and to use it in their homes.

British consumers were just as enamoured of chintz as their French counterparts. In 1663, the fashion-conscious Samuel Pepys recorded: "After many tryells bought my wife a Chinte; that is a paynted Indian calico for her to line her new study, which is very pretty." The early British imitations were very poor quality and so initially posed no threat to other textile producers. Increasingly, however, silk weavers were affected not only by the falling-off in popularity of their products but also by the arrival of an influx of Huguenot weavers fleeing France after the 1685 revocation of the Edict of Nantes. After much agitation an Act of 1701 forbade the use of printed cottons. Successive legislation imposed yet more restrictions and fines, and a total ban on the use of printed cottons for clothes or furnishings was not relaxed until 1774 when the use of cottons manufactured in Britain was allowed. As in France, however, chintz was still much sought after and quite large quantities were smuggled in from Holland.

The first chintzes sent to America came from Britain and were favourably received. Fashionable and influential figures, such as Thomas Jefferson and Governor Penn of Philadelphia, who had spent time in Europe, brought samples back with them initiating a vogue for chintz hangings and upholstery. After the Revolution, however, British fabrics were boycotted. This created an opening for French suppliers who stepped in to meet the growing American demand for gaily coloured printed cottons.

The 18th century was the heyday of chintz in Europe, witnessing not only the production of many beautiful designs but also the emergence of cotton as an important furnishing fabric. "Pintados" and imported cloths were frequently used as wall and bedhangings as well as on furniture. A bedroom in the Château Borély, Marseilles, contains wallcoverings made from Indian flowering-tree bedspreads that were installed between 1775 and 1780, while two other rooms are hung with chintz yardage, the design consisting of small sprigs and treelets. The fabric was set into panelled walls and secured with beading. Interiors entirely furnished with chintz were also very popular in England, particularly in bedrooms, the best-known surviving examples being the hangings made for the "Garrick Bed" now in the Victoria and Albert Museum. These chintzes were sent from India in 1774 as a gift to the wife of the actor, David Garrick, and includes two pairs of curtains and valances featuring designs based on the flowering tree. Numerous quilts and palampores, often designed to match sets of hangings or curtains, were also imported during this period. Some of these were also used as covers for furniture, such as tables, stools and cupboards.

A major figure in the development of European chintz was Christophe-Philippe Oberkampf who established a printing works and a cotton spinning and weaving mill at Jouy-en-Josas, near Versailles, in 1760. In addition to their celebrated Toile de Jouy fabrics, the factory produced numerous Indian-style floral patterns of very high quality which were greatly admired and used in many wealthy French interiors. Robert Hendry, a Scottish colour maker and engraver, spent considerable time at Jouy and brought the secrets of their dying and manufacturing processes to Britain. The popularity of chintz patterns during the Georgian period is evident from the many designs used for both wallpapers and textiles, although they tended to be used for informal areas such as small sitting rooms, cabinets and bedrooms.

The revival of interest in early 19th century designs that occurred in the late Victorian period was spearheaded by William Morris whose earliest printed textiles were copies of traditional floral patterns. The delicate colouring and stylized naturalism of these patterns contrasted sharply with the acidic hues and overtly realistic appearance of mid- and high-Victorian commercial textile designs. Morris himself went on to develop his own distinctive style, derived both from nature and from historic designs, and his printed textiles were eagerly sought after in "artistic" Arts and Crafts homes. A taste for more traditional chintz designs re-emerged in the mid-20th century when it was closely associated with the English Country House style. This style was developed by the decorating firm Colefax and Fowler who pioneered the use of period colours and patterns in interiors that were intended to evoke the grace, elegance and comfort of the Georgian period. They reproduced many historic textiles and their use of glazed floral chintzes has become one of the company's hallmarks.

Today, chintz can refer both to a style – rustic 18th and early 19th century English – and to printed cottons. Up-market producers of chintz fabrics include G.P. & J. Baker, Osborne & Little, and Jane Churchill. In the work of firms such as Laura Ashley, Sandersons, Liberty and John Lewis, the style has gained even broader appeal and chintz lines are often marketed with matching or co-ordinating wallpapers. In France, Boussac and Manuel Canovas both design and produce fine chintz fabric, while in the United States one of the major chintz producers is Brunschwig & Fils. Expensive, hand-blocked designs are still made and demand outstrips supply.

MARLENE COHEN

See also Printed Textiles

Further Reading

The standard history of Chintz up to the 19th century is Irwin and Brett, 1970.

Beer, Alice B., *Trade Goods: A Study of Indian Chintz*, Washington, DC: Smithsonian Institution Press, 1970

Brédif, Josette, *Classic Printed Textiles from France, 1760–1843: Toiles de Jouy*, London: Thames and Hudson, 1989; as *Printed French Fabrics*, New York: Rizzoli, 1989

Bunt, Cyril G.E. and Ernest A. Rose, *Two Centuries of English Chintz, 1750–1950*, Leigh on Sea, Essex: F. Lewis, 1957

Clabburn, Pamela, *The National Trust Book of Furnishing Textiles*, Harmondsworth: Penguin, 1989

English Chintz (exhib. cat.), London: Victoria and Albert Museum, 1960

Howell Smith, A.D., *Brief Guide to Western Painted, Dyed and Printed Textiles*, revised by Muriel Clayton, London: Victoria and Albert Museum, 1938

Irwin, John and Katharine B. Brett, *The Origins of Chintz*, London: Victoria and Albert Museum, 1970

Lewis, Frank, *English Chintz*, revised edition Leigh on Sea, Essex: F. Lewis, 1942

Montgomery, Florence M., *Printed Textiles: English and American Cottons and Linens, 1700–1850*, London: Thames and Hudson, and New York: Viking, 1970

Montgomery, Florence M., *Textiles in America, 1650–1870*, New York: Norton, 1984

Percival, MacIver, *The Chintz Book*, London: Heinemann, and New York: Stokes, 1923

Phillips, Barty, *Fabrics and Wallpapers*, London: Ebury, and Boston: Little Brown, 1991

Schoeser, Mary, *Fabrics and Wallpapers*, London: Bell and Hyman, and New York: Dutton, 1986

Schoeser, Mary and Celia Rufey, *English and American Textiles from 1790 to the Present*, London and New York: Thames and Hudson, 1989

Chippendale, Thomas 1718–1779

British designer and upholsterer

Thomas Chippendale is indisputably the most famous cabinet-maker ever to have emerged from Britain. His reputation is international, and during the 19th century, so overwhelming that admiration for the joiner's son from Otley in Yorkshire grew into an adulatory cult which seemed to ignore the existence of any other contemporary British cabinet-maker. Chippendale was certainly one of the leading cabinet-makers of the time but his apparent pre-eminence is due to his publication in 1754 of *The Gentleman and Cabinet Maker's Directory*. This collection of 161 folio plates engraved largely by Matthias Darly and a small number by T. and J.S. Müller of Chippendale's furniture designs, was instrumental in finally disseminating the Rococo style throughout Britain, a country which had adopted the Continental style unwillingly and slowly a century after the rest of Europe. Furniture designs, although available in Europe for the previous 200 years, had never been published on such a scale before, and, as a consequence, Chippendale emerged from relative obscurity to become the best-known cabinet-maker of his day.

Although Chippendale would have received a traditional and thorough training as a cabinet-maker, it is unlikely that he would have worked at the bench himself after the business moved to St. Martin's Lane in 1754. The firm employed up to 50 skilled men and his contribution would have been to direct them, monitor the quality of their work and above all design for them. Designs from the *Director* were disseminated throughout Britain, with provincial cabinet-makers using it as a sourcebook either for a complete design or for various elements to be used in their own output. It was twice reissued by Chippendale, with the final third edition containing 200 plates. When the Third Edition was advertised in 1763, a French version entitled *Guide de Tapissier, De L'Ebéniste* was offered "for the convenience of Foreigners". Whilst extremely rare, copies of the book have been traced to contemporary collections in France, Germany and one in the Imperial Russian Library, suggesting some influence in Russian court furniture.

The *Director* continues to be reprinted to this day, not just as an academic exercise, but as a reference book for practising cabinet-makers. The notes to the plates and the scale measurements mean that the designs can be used as the basis for working drawings, and technical advice on setting out the work, mitering and methods of construction show Chippendale's awareness of how a working cabinet maker would use the book.

The trade card of Chippendale and Rannie read "Cabinet-maker and Upholsterers" and the upholstery side encompassed a far wider range of commercial activity than would be considered normal today for such a trade. In 1747, Robert Campbell's *London Tradesman* described a typical Upholder as having "not only Judgement in the Materials, but Taste in the Fashions ... Skill in the Workmanship ... and set up as a Connoisseur in every Article that belongs to a house".

In addition to the business of designing and making furniture, Chippendale's accounts list a number of services provided to his clients: he was responsible for hanging paper in patrons' houses and colouring on site. Sir Edmund Knatchbull complained "As to the Man who putt up & colourd the Green Paper he was not above two days at work & did it extreamly bad" (Mersham correspondence, January 1771). Chippendale also assumed the responsibilities of an interior decorator in that he counselled his clients on the appropriateness of their decisions. Lady Knatchbull was advised to install in her dressing room "Large Berjairs as We think it would be of propriety in one room". The firm continued to advise in the time of Chippendale the Younger when asked by Ninian Homes as to whether the ceiling of his drawing room should be white or "painted in different colours", what sort of wallpaper to hang saying "I leave you to choose the paper since you are a better judge of what is proper for such a room".

Actually decorating the rooms was not something that the firm undertook. Responsibility for such things rested traditionally with other tradesmen, and when Chippendale did send a painter, such as at Harewood and Nostell Priory, "Brewer the Painter" spent his time colouring wallpaper. A number of houses had cartridge paper hung by Chippendale's workmen which they then coloured by hand. The colouring was either in stripes or in an all-over wash and was popular since it avoided the tax levied on manufactured papers. The same blue colour, known as "verditer" was popular both as a wall covering and as a pasted lining paper for drawers, although Chippendale's firm was more often in the habit of lining drawers with a

No CLXXIX

A Design for a Chimney Piece

T. Chippendale inv. et delin. Publish'd according to Act of Parliament 1762 M Darly Sculp.

Chippendale design for chimneypiece from *The Gentleman and Cabinet-Maker's Director*, 1762

marbled paper. Lady Knatchbull's dressing room was hung with verditer paper and then fashionably pasted with engravings. Chippendale also designed wallpaper for Harewood in account 4 September 1776, now lost. Oriental wallpaper was generally obtained by the clients themselves, since it was hard to come by and Chippendale's firm was responsible for the hanging only. At Harewood, however, Chippendale was able to supply eighteen sheets for the sum of £12 15s 0d. Carpets were supplied – the floor plan of the premises in 1803 shows a carpet room and the sale of stock in 1766 included carpets. He hired out furniture for various periods of time and also arranged carriage and storage for his patrons, especially during the time a house was being renovated or redecorated. He repaired and restored furniture to the degree of providing a new handle for a coffeepot for Sir Edward Knatchbull.

Marble slabs were imported for resale, china and glassware supplied for washstands, writing and dressing tables. Bedhangings and bedding were supplied to Dumfries House, Harewood and David Garrick's villa. The Garrick bed is the only one to retain its original chintz hangings, made up by Chippendale from illegally imported Indian Chintz. Loose covers to protect expensively upholstered furniture were routinely supplied, curtains and blinds for windows and at Paxton House, Berwick, Scotland even a complete bell system to communicate below stairs.

Lack of evidence means that Chippendale's early career cannot be clearly traced. Between his baptism at Otley Parish church in Yorkshire on 5 June 1718 and his marriage to Catherine Redshaw at St. George's chapel, Hyde Park, London on 19 May 1748, nothing is known. Where he learned his trade as a cabinet-maker and designer is pure speculation, although over the years it has come to be said that he worked initially for his father, a local "joyner" and subsequently for the local gentry such as Henry Lascelles of Harewood and for the Fawkes family of Farnley. He is reputed to have worked for the Winn family at Nostell Priory, Yorkshire which would have been around 1740–45. The young architect James Paine also worked for Sir Rowland Winn at Nostell from 1736 and the two must have met. Paine studied at Hogarth's St. Martin's Lane Academy in London and could well have introduced Chippendale to this circle of artists and designers who were at the forefront of the dissemination of the Rococo style in England. Alternatively, Chippendale could have received instruction in drawing from a professional tutor – Matthias Darly, who engraved 98 of the plates in the first edition of the *Director*, and whose family probably shared a house with Chippendale, advertised in 1748 in the *Daily Advertiser* for tradesmen to attend his evening drawing classes.

The finest collection of *Director* period furniture is at Dumfries House, Ayrshire, Scotland for the 5th Earl of Dumfries where most of the furniture invoiced for in May / June 1759 and in 1763 and 1766 survives. It is the best documented of his earlier period. The first edition of the *Director* in 1754 had a large proportion of plates with Chinese elements (64 out of 161). By 1762 and the third edition, this was down to 43 out of 200 as interest waned, but Dumfries House was supplied with some spectacular Chinoiserie pieces, most notably a pair of oval pier glasses surmounted by a bust of a mandarin with coolie hat.

By including a number of Gothic designs in the *Director*, Chippendale risked being associated with a style in danger of becoming outdated and frivolous. Originally appearing as an antidote to the strictures of Palladianism in the 1740s, it had never been a mainstream style, being confined either to the antiquarian or to the merely decorative. However, Chippendale's inventive re-interpretation of the genre gave it new credibility: Chippendale's firm supplied only a few pieces in the Gothic style but other cabinet-makers continued to work in the Gothic manner. Four library bookcases made for Sir Rowland Winn's London house in 1766, with Gothic glazing bars taken from a *Director* plate are a rare example.

Furniture supplied to Nostell Priory, Yorkshire (Sir Rowland Winn) and Aske Hall, Yorkshire (Sir Lawrence Dundas) best illustrate Chippendale's transition to the Neo-Classical. Sir Rowland Winn seems to have held an influential position in Chippendale's affairs – letters at Nostell Priory indicate that he worked to advance Chippendale's career by recommendation and described his own patronage as a "friend's protection". Although the *Director* designs are rooted firmly in the Rococo tradition, many of the details in the plates – caryatid supports, ram's heads and lion masks among many others, point the way forward to his later Neo-Classical work, with the library table at Nostell acting as a stepping stone between the two styles.

Harewood House, owned by Edwin Lascelles, is where his mature "Adam" period style can best be seen. Chippendale's initial visit to the house was in the summer of 1767 and the first furniture was delivered in April 1769. The entire contract most likely exceeded £10,000 and there survive some nine full and six incomplete sets of seat furniture in the Neo-Classical taste. There is a remarkable group of inlaid marquetry furniture including the incomparable library table, now at Temple Newsam House, Leeds. This writing table, with its classical inlaid decoration and applied English ormolu mounts, when compared with the writing table supplied to Nostell Priory around 1766 which has almost entirely carved decoration, marks Chippendale's complete shift away from his earlier *Director* style. His conversion to the Neo-Classical taste was eased by the emulation of certain of Adam's design motifs: Chippendale's library chairs of 1768 at Nostell Priory retain the lyre back splat and oval patera in the top rail of Robert Adam's chairs supplied to Osterley Park, Middlesex c.1767.

By the late 18th century, it was expected that architects would be involved in the furnishing of rooms in the buildings they had designed so as to achieve a continuity of style within the building. They were more influential than upholsterers or cabinet-makers since theirs was considered a superior art and consequently, one which brought higher social standing. Thus, while architects such as Wyatt or the Adam brothers took an active role in designing the furniture for their interiors themselves, this was something for which they charged. Chippendale, however, was able to offer the service nominally free of charge, i.e., within the price of supplying the furniture itself. This gave a certain commercial advantage. Nevertheless Chippendale's aristocratic patrons such as Sir Rowland Winn and Sir Edward Knatchbull demonstrated a cavalier attitude to settling their debts which resulted in a lifetime of financial insecurity. Towards the end of Chippendale's career, as his son took on more of the practical responsibilities in the firm, the financial situation stabilised somewhat. It is fortunate that superlative furniture continued to be made as the business passed to the succeeding generation in the person of Thomas Chippendale the Younger.

PAUL HARDY

Biography

Baptised in Otley, Yorkshire, 5 June 1718, the son of a joiner. Apprenticed to his father; trained in the workshop of the joiner and cabinet-maker Richard Wood of York; possibly taught design by Matthias Darly (fl.1741–72) who shared his house, 1753, and who engraved most of the plates for the *Director*. Married 1) Catherine Redshaw, 1748 (died, 1772): 9 children including Thomas Chippendale the Younger (1749–1822) who took over the business after his father's death; 2) Elizabeth Dixon: 3 children. Active in London as a designer and upholsterer from 1748; opened first premises 1749; moved to Somerset Court, 1752; new premises in St. Martin's Lane in partnership with James Rannie, 1754; partnership dissolved on Rannie's death, 1766; Chippendale Haig & Co. formed in partnership with Thomas Haig and Henry Ferguson, 1771. Designed a vast quantity of furniture, carpets and wallpaper for his own and other firms, and for the influential pattern book *The Gentleman and Cabinet-Maker's Director*, published in several editions from 1754. Member, Royal Society of Arts, 1760. Died in Hoxton; buried 13 November 1779.

Selected Works

A portfolio of over 140 drawings ascribed to Chippendale is in the Victoria and Albert Museum, London which also holds designs by Matthias Lock for the *Director*. Two albums of drawings, including almost all Chippendale's drawings for the first edition of the *Director* are in the Metropolitan Museum of Art, New York. Approximately 700 items of furniture designed by Chippendale survive; notable examples are in the Victoria and Albert Museum, Temple Newsam House, Leeds, and Nostell Priory, Yorkshire.

Interiors

1759–66	Dumfries House, Ayrshire (furniture, wallpapers and curtains): 5th Earl of Dumfries
1763–66	Aske Hall, Yorkshire (furniture including a suite made by the Chippendale firm designed by Robert Adam): Sir Lawrence Dundas
1766–85	Nostell Priory, Yorkshire (furniture, wallpapers and curtains): Sir Rowland Winn
1767–78	Harewood House, Yorkshire (furniture, wallpapers and curtains): Edwin Lascelles
1767–79	Mersham Le Hatch, Kent (decorations and upholstery): Sir Edward Knatchbull
1768–78	Garrick's Villa, Hampton, Middlesex (furniture, wallpapers and curtains): David Garrick
1768–79	Burton Constable, Yorkshire (saloon furniture): William Constable
1772–75	Brocket Hall, Hertfordshire (furniture): Viscount Melbourne
c.1772–76	Newby Hall, Yorkshire (furniture for the Tapestry Room): William Weddell
c.1774–91	Paxton House, Berwick-on-Tweed (furniture): Ninian Home
1777–79	Petworth House, Sussex (beds and hangings): Earl of Egremont

Publications

The Gentleman and Cabinet-Maker's Director, 1754, 2nd edition 1755, 3rd edition 1762; reprinted 1966

Further Reading

The most comprehensive and scholarly monograph on Chippendale, including a complete catalogue of his work, is Gilbert 1978. The 1968 issue of *Furniture History*, published to commemorate the 250th anniversary of Chippendale's birth, includes articles on several important commissions and prints the complete texts of Chippendale's letters and accounts for Harewood, Nostell Priory and Mersham Le Hatch.

Boynton, Lindsay and Nicholas P. Goodison, "Thomas Chippendale at Nostell Priory" in *Furniture History*, 4, 1968, pp.10–16

Boynton, Lindsay, "Thomas Chippendale at Mersham Le Hatch" in *Furniture History*, 4, 1968, pp.81–104

Boynton, Lindsay, "The Furniture of Thomas Chippendale at Nostell Priory, I, II" in *Burlington Magazine*, CXI, May and June 1969, pp.281–85, 351–60

Brackett, Oliver, *Thomas Chippendale: A Study of his Life, Work and Influence*, London: Hodder and Stoughton, 1924; Boston: Houghton Mifflin, 1925

Coleridge, Anthony, *Chippendale Furniture: The Work of Thomas Chippendale and His Contemporaries in the Rococo Taste, 1745–1765*, London: Faber, and New York: Potter, 1968

Fitz-Gerald, Desmond, "Chippendale's Place in the English Rococo" in *Furniture History*, 4, 1968, pp.1–9

Gilbert, Christopher, "Chippendale's Harewood Commission" in *Furniture History*, 9, 1973, pp.1–32

Gilbert, Christopher, "The Subscribers to Chippendale's 'Director': A Preliminary Analysis" in *Furniture History*, 10, 1974, pp.41–51

Gilbert, Christopher and Karin Moon, "Chippendale's Upholstery Branch" in *Leeds Art Calendar*, 74, 1974, pp.26–32

Gilbert, Christopher, *The Life and Work of Thomas Chippendale*, 2 vols., London: Studio Vista, and New York: Macmillan, 1978

Gilbert, Christopher, "Chippendale's Patrons in Yorkshire" in *Magazine Antiques*, 199, 1 January 1991, pp.308–23

Hall, Michael and Roger Whitworth, "Chippendale in his Setting" in *Country Life*, 187, 1993, pp.68–73

Thomas, G.Z., "The Invention of Chinese Chippendale, I, II," in *Connoisseur*, CLXVII, February and March 1968, pp.127–32, 200–06

Vance, Mary, *Thomas Chippendale: A Bibliography*, Monticello, IL: Vance, 1985

Cinemas

With the first "electric theatres" dating from early in the 20th century, soon after the invention of "moving pictures", cinemas were one of the first modern building types. Although there are some notable exceptions, it is their interiors that are of greatest interest, rather than the characteristically box-like exterior forms. Films were first shown in converted rooms or halls, then featured as additions to the live programmes in theatres or music halls, or vaudeville theatres in America. The earliest purpose-built cinema interiors were merely rectangular halls with a stage and screen at one end, often with a barrel-vaulted roof. Decoration, if any, consisted of moulded plasterwork ribs or panelling effects. English examples that have survived are the Electric in Portobello Road, London (1905) and the Electric Palace in Harwich, Essex (1911). The English Cinematograph Act of 1909 led to more purpose-built cinemas appearing as it insisted on quite specific provisions, such as a separate fire-resistant projection box. In the United States early cinemas were known as nickelodeons and were most often store-front theatres with rows of hard seats.

From about 1912 cinemas, which were taking over in popularity from theatres, became increasingly theatrical in style, with the inclusion of boxes and balconies and elaborate Baroque or Neo-Classical decoration. In Britain, World War I, and the restrictions on building in force until 1921, limited the supply of new, larger buildings to meet the increasing demand for cinemas, resulting in the conversion of numerous theatres. Their interiors were updated and the provision of a circle became standard.

The Regent in Brighton (1921), by Robert Atkinson, was Britain's first "super" cinema and also the first notable cinema by a well-known architect. While traditional in design, its classical Italianate interiors show the influence of the American "hard-top" school (so called in contrast to the "atmospheric" school described below) and its principal proponent, Thomas Lamb. Lamb was a Scottish-born architect responsible for designing hundreds of cinemas in the United States. In New York he created the first of the vast, elaborately decorated, "movie palaces" or "picture palaces". These included many on, or near, Broadway from the 1914 Strand Theatre to the 1919 Capitol, with over 5,000 seats. His designs for the Loew Corporation spread his work right across to the west coast. The opulent interiors were derived from the decorative classicism of Robert Adam, or from French Renaissance and Empire designs, with rich effects from gilt or gold leaf and marble, combined with deep carpets and crystal chandeliers. Lobbies were at least as grand as the auditoria, lined with marble columns and culminating in wide curving staircases. Other designers followed suit. The architects Rapp and Rapp, working mainly in Chicago, were famous for their "Sun King" style, first used for the foyer of the 1921 Tivoli Theatre, taken directly from the Chapelle Royale at Versailles.

The 1920s also saw the first of the so-called "atmospheric" cinema interiors. John Eberson, an Austrian-born architect working in America, developed a way of creating, within the auditorium, the illusion of being out-of-doors, under an open sky. This was done through the use of lighting, combined with stage-set building façades and rooftops, often covered in artificial vegetation, built around the auditorium walls and proscenium arch. Lighting effects might change the colour of the "sky" from that of sunset to dawn, with moonlight and stars between and projected clouds drifting across the sky. Lights behind the mock building fronts made them appear more three-dimensional, and the subdued level of lighting overall hid the artificiality and added to the sense of mystery. The Houston Majestic (1923) was the first, having the appearance of an Italian Renaissance garden complete with vines, statues and stuffed birds. Eberson was influenced by the Spanish Colonial architecture of Florida and Texas as well as European styles, and many of his atmospherics were Spanish or Moorish in inspiration. His mosque-style Avalon (1927) in Chicago added to the illusion with a ladies lounge in the form of a harem and ushers wearing costumes of the French Foreign Legion. Such fantasies fed on and enhanced the element of escapism inherent in watching the films themselves. The success of this particular form of fantasy encouraged many other designers to create atmospherics, even Thomas Lamb. In London four Astoria cinemas were built as atmospherics, with interiors by Somerford and Barr. They included the Brixton Astoria (1929), now the Academy, and the Finsbury Park Astoria (1930), latterly the Rainbow Theatre, with a mixture of styles from Moorish to Baroque. John Eberson himself designed one atmospheric in Europe, the Rex in Paris (1932). This is one of the few that still operates as an atmospheric, including a cloud machine.

From the beginning of the 1920s cinema designers became increasingly eclectic in their sources of inspiration. From 1922, following the discovery of Tutankhamen's tomb, the Egyptian style, the subject of many earlier revivals, became wildly popular in all areas of design. Architects Meyer and Holler built Grauman's Egyptian Theatre (1922) in Hollywood with a winged-scarab sounding board and sunburst grille above the proscenium arch and Karnak-like columns covered in Egyptian tomb paintings. Grauman's Chinese Theatre (1927), also in Hollywood, is better known. However, it is less authentic than the Fifth Avenue Theatre (1926) in Seattle whose auditorium is a duplicate of the throne room of the Imperial Palace in Peking. Many other American cinemas incorporated dragons, serpents and even buddhas into often unbearably elaborate "oriental" schemes. The Palace in Southall, London (1928) by George Coles, complete with Chinese interior, is the only

Cinemas: foyer, New Victoria, Westminster, by E. Wamsley Lewis, 1930

example of a Chinese-style cinema in Britain in spite of the potential influence of the Brighton Pavilion.

Pre-Columbian American cultures provided another source of inspiration for American cinema designers, having been popularized through Aztec and Mayan exhibitions such as that of 1893 in Chicago and of 1915 in San Diego. The 1915 Aztec Theatre in Eagle Pass, Texas incorporating linear, geometric decoration derived from Mexican Mitla masonry, was followed by the Aztec Theatre in San Antonio, Texas (1926). This featured a replica of a sacrificial calendar stone in the foyer along with funerary urns lining the walls. The proscenium arch is topped by a lintel decorated with a feathered serpent panel and sun symbol. Mayan theatres followed in Los Angeles in 1927 and Denver in 1930. In the former the decoration is synthesised to form an all-over surface effect.

Examples of other more localised design influences survive. In America Hispanic and Pueblo styles were popular in the Southwest and taken up by the Boller Brothers. Their KiMo Theatre in Albuquerque (1927) combines the Native American and Hispanic cultures in tiles and frescoes. In Europe the closest equivalent is the Filmtheater Tuschinski (1919) by H.L. de Jong in Amsterdam, possibly influenced by the native Indonesian styles of the Dutch colonies.

It was Germany that influenced developments in Europe in the next decade, bringing modernity into cinema design. Although Gunnar Asplund, a pioneer of Scandinavian Modernism, had designed an influential cinema in Stockholm in 1922, the Scandia, it was only an interior for a pre-existing building. As such it was a traditional rectangular shape and its decor, while comparatively simple in contrast to most cinemas of that date, was very much derived from 19th-century Scandinavian classicism. Fritz Wilms, in his Berlin cinemas of the 1920s, such as the Luna Filmpalast, led the way in a new simplicity of interior design relying on broad curving sweeps of often unadorned concrete. Erich Mendelsohn's 1926 Universum in Berlin showed the new modern Functionalism at its best. Hans Poelzig, in his Babylon Cinema (1928) had also moved to a large scale simplicity after his earlier Grosses Schauspielhaus (1919), both in Berlin. Their use of lighting inside and out to emphasise the structural forms was to be very influential during the 1930s. The New Victoria of 1930 in London, by E. Wamsley Lewis, shows a direct German influence.

With the change to the "talkies" in the late 1920s a new era of cinema began. Good acoustics and sightlines became more important. Fan-shaped auditoria with plaster coving and sound boards catered for these needs. The stripped-down geometry and dynamic curves of International Modernism were combined with the decorative elements of Art Deco – wave patterns and fan shapes, concealed coloured strip lights and new, or newly adapted, materials such as holophane lighting, chrome, faience tiles, vitrolite, and mirror glass. The 1930s was the decade of the Odeons in England, with their characteristic house-style based on standardised design elements. The auditoria were generally large curved spaces with the walls and ceilings sculpted with broad bands of plain plasterwork, curved in plan or section, often converging on the proscenium arch. Illuminated organ consoles were a popular additional feature. The foyers and ancillary rooms, such as cafes, were often more elaborately decorated with specially designed seating and upholstery, and even clocks and carpets incorporating the Odeon brand name in their design. Harry Weedon was the most prolific Odeon architect and contributed to the overall stylistic unity of the Odeons. The Muswell Hill Odeon, 1936 by George Coles, in London, with its "cash register"-effect auditorium is a good surviving example.

Eclecticism continued into the 1930s, but Art Deco became the dominant style for cinemas. This popular form of Modernism suited the cinema industry very well and even found its way into film set design. Two other important designers of this period, working in England, who specialised in decorative schemes for cinema interiors illustrate both trends. These were John Alexander, whose designs survive to indicate original colour schemes, and Theodore Komisarjevsky. The Northwick cinema in Worcester of 1938 shows John Alexander's Art Deco style at its best with stylised mythical figures in a chariot either side of the proscenium and a pink, peach, and gold colour scheme. The Russian-born Komisarjevsky produced several amazingly richly decorated and glowingly coloured interiors. These were a continuation of the 1920s eclectic fantasies and included the Granada Tooting (1931), a Venetian Gothic gilded fantasy, and the Granada Woolwich (1937). This was a variation on the same theme, with additional elements from French Gothic cathedrals.

These were rivalled by the American Art Deco fantasies such as the Hollywood Pantages (1930) by B. Marcus Priteca, with its zig-zag excesses, or the Oakland Paramount (1931), by Timothy L. Pflueger, a classic of Art Deco with hidden lighting effects creating a Fountain of Light in the foyer and Columns of Incandescence framing the stage. The Radio City Music Hall in the Rockefeller Center in New York, (1932) by Donald Deskey, was the largest movie theatre ever built and the last of the real movie palaces. The famous golden arches of the auditorium are preceded by a foyer with a vast 60 by 40 foot mural behind the stair, depicting a mythical landscape.

From these heights decline was perhaps inevitable. After World War II cinema attendances fell and few new cinemas were built. Many existing cinema interiors were sub-divided or converted to other uses, if they survived at all. Those built since then tend to be either diluted versions of the Odeons or plain boxes.

DIANA HALE

See also Art Deco

Selected Collections

Illustrations and documentation relating to British cinema interiors can be found in the following collections: Drawings Collection, Royal Institute of British Architects, London, and Cinema Theatre Association Archives, London. Substantial holdings of photographic records are also in the Greater London Record Office, London, and the National Monuments Record Centre, Royal Commission on the Historical Monuments of England, Swindon and London, which contains the Maltby Collection of photographs of Odeon cinemas. A provisional list of surviving "listed" cinemas in England appears in the *Cinema Theatre Association Bulletin* 1994. Material relating to American cinema interiors is held by the Theatre Historical Society, Chicago, and important examples are listed in Naylor 1981 and 1987.

Further Reading

For a gazetteer of UK surviving cinemas and a full bibliography see Atwell 1980; a useful study of US cinemas appears in Naylor 1987.

Albrecht, Donald, *Designing Dreams: Modern Architecture in the Movies,* New York: Harper, 1986; London: Thames and Hudson, 1987

Atwell, David, *Cathedrals of the Movies: A History of British Cinemas and Their Audiences,* London: Architectural Press, 1980

Bayer, Patricia, *Art Deco Interiors: Decoration and Design Classics of the 1920s and 1930s,* London: Thames and Hudson, and Boston: Little Brown, 1990

Binney, Marcus, "Greatest Surviving Atmospheric: Restoration of the Atlanta Fox Cinema, Georgia" in *Country Life,* 25 March 1982, pp.796–98

Clegg, Rosemary (editor), *Odeon,* Birmingham: Mercia Cinema Society, 1985

Eyles, Allen and Keith Skone, *London's West End Cinemas,* Sutton, Surrey: Premier Bioscope, 1991

Eyles, Allen, *Gaumont-British Cinemas,* London: British Film Institute, 1996

Hall, Ben M., *The Best Remaining Seats: The Story of the Golden Age of the Movie Palace,* New York: Potter, 1961

"The Listed Cinemas Steadily Grow" in *Cinema Theatre Association Bulletin,* 1994, pp.6–7

Naylor, David, *American Picture Palaces: The Architecture of Fantasy,* New York: Van Nostrand Reinhold, 1981

Naylor, David, *Great American Movie Theaters,* Washington, DC: Preservation Press, 1987

Preddy, Jane, *Glamour, Glitz, and Sparkle: The Deco Theatres of John Eberson,* Chicago: Theatre Historical Society of America, 1989

Sharp, Dennis, *The Picture Palace and Other Buildings for the Movies,* London: Evelyn, and New York: Praeger, 1969

Clein, Francis 1582–1658

German decorative painter and designer of tapestries and ornament

Francis or Franz Clein (Cleyn, Kleyn) was a German painter, tapestry designer and ornameniste active in Denmark and Britain in the early 17th century. He was born in Rostock in Mecklenburg-Schwerin in 1582, the son of the goldsmith Hans Clein from whom he learned the basics of drawing and engraving. A promising student, by 1611 he was working in the service of Christian IV of Denmark. A portrait of Christian IV is dated 1611, and between 1618 and 1623, following a decisively significant four-year study trip to Italy, Clein was employed on the decoration of several royal residences including Fredericksborg, Christiansborg and Kronborg. He also worked at Rosenborg Castle in Copenhagen where he decorated the Queen's chamber and painted Italianate grotesques in the king's writing closet.

During his stay in Italy, Clein was introduced to the distinguished virtuoso, Sir Henry Wotton and on his return to Copenhagen he met Sir Arthur Anstruther, the English ambassador to Denmark. In 1623, Clein travelled to England, arriving with letters of introduction to the Prince of Wales, the future King Charles I, from both Anstruther and Wotton. He was warmly received by Charles's father, James I, who appointed him artistic director of the newly-established Mortlake tapestry works, founded in 1620 by Sir Francis Crane on the model of the Royal Tapestry Works of Henry IV. Clein was granted a pension of £100 a year, but almost immediately he had to return to Denmark to finish projects that he had begun for Christian IV. By 1625, however, the year that Charles I ascended to the throne, he was back in England where he lived and worked for the remainder of his life.

Clein's first project was to provide designs for the triumphal arch erected for the ceremonial entry into London of Henrietta Maria, Charles's bride, under the supervision of the Surveyor-General Inigo Jones. He was also employed on the decoration of the Queen's apartment at Old Somerset House, and at Wimbledon House, both royal residences where the work was directed by Jones. Clein's knowledge of Italian design was extremely useful to Jones, and his work clearly complemented the new classical style of architecture and interiors that Jones introduced to the Stuart court. It also appealed to other

Clein: North Drawing Room, Ham House, Surrey, 1637

members of the court and there are records of Clein's involvement at several aristocratic and great houses in the 1620s and 1630s. At Holland House, Kensington, for example, he not only decorated the gilt room but also designed some items of furniture including a set of Italian *sgabello*-type chairs that featured shell-shaped backs and classicising swags, masks and pendant ornament. Other versions of these chairs were used at Ham House where Clein was working in the 1630s; an example survives in the Victoria and Albert Museum, London. Additional commissions of this period include decorations at Carew House, Parsons Green, Bolsover Castle, and Stoke Bruerne, Northamptonshire, for Sir Francis Crane.

Clein's most important interior work was carried out at Ham House, near Richmond, between 1637 and 1639 for William Murray. Although the history of the early decoration of this house is somewhat unclear, Clein appears to have been responsible for the four inset panels depicting naked putti in the North Drawing Room, one of which includes a motif borrowed from Van Dyck. He also executed the highly elaborate decoration in the little Miniature Room, or the Green Closet, where the spandrels around the central panel of the ceiling were painted with a form of Italianate grotesques, and the long panels on the cove between the cornice and ceiling was decorated with landscapes containing putti, based on originals by Raphael's assistant, Polidoro da Caravaggio. Clein was also responsible for the design of a fireplace and chimneypiece and the finely carved and gilded balustrade on the Great Stairs.

Throughout this period, he was also busy at Mortlake. The first tapestries woven by the factory had been from Flemish designs, but changing fashions ushered in a taste for Italian models, particularly after the purchase of the Raphael cartoons in 1623. Clein's skill in designing ornament and grotesques was particularly well-suited to this style of work and c.1625 he produced copies of Raphael's cartoons with new, more elaborate borders including putti climbing twisted columns and festoons of fruits and terms, that were greatly admired. A set of these tapestries is now in the Mobilier National, Paris. Clein was also responsible for other designs, the most popular being a sequence of six or seven hangings depicting the tale of Hero and Leander; sets of these tapestries survive in the Swedish Royal Collection, Stockholm, and in the Primatial Palace, Bratislava.

Much of Clein's work as a tapestry designer and decorative painter was curtailed by the outbreak of Civil War in 1642, and although he seems to have retained his houses, first at Mortlake and later at Covent Garden, where he spent most of his later years, he was never again involved in such grandiose projects as those on which he had been engaged previously. Instead he worked chiefly as an engraver of ornament and designer of illustrated books. In 1632 he had provided the illustrations for an edition of Ovid's *Metamorphoses* (reprinted in Paris in 1637), and he also designed plates and ornamental frontispieces for John Ogilvy's editions of classics such as Aesop's *Fables* (1651), Virgil (1654, 1658) and Homer (1660). Although somewhat less numerous, Clein's suites of ornament were no less admired. He published the *Septum Liberales Artes* (1645), *Quinque Sensuum descriptio* (1646), *Varii Zophori figuris animalium* (1645) and *Several Borders of Grotesk Works Useful of Painters* (1654). All demonstrate a thorough understanding of the repertoire of Baroque ornament and include numerous grotesque and acanthus friezes and panels, incorporating many birds and animals.

Given the fact that so little of Clein's interior work survives, and that some of his finest decorations, such as those in the Queen's Chamber at Old Somerset House which were much vaunted by the courtier Edward Norgate, are known only through descriptions, it is hard to judge the extent of his influence or skill as a designer. Indeed, the high praise accorded Clein by his contemporaries – one critic described him as "the most famous of painters, the miracle of the century" – sometimes seems inflated. Yet, he clearly played an important role in giving practical expression to the Italianate ideas espoused by Inigo Jones, and, along with that of Jones, Clein's work did much to help establish the classical style as the official style within court circles during the 1620s and 1630s.

DAVID CAST

Biography

Franz Cleyn. Born in Rostock, Mecklenburg-Schwerin, in 1582, the son of the goldsmith Hans Clein. Studied in Italy, c.1612–17, where he met Sir Henry Wotton and Sir Arthur Anstruther. Married: children included the painters Francis Clein the Younger and John Clein, and the miniaturist Penelope Clein. Employed in the service of Christian IV of Denmark, c.1611–23, executing decorative schemes for several royal castles. Appointed designer to the Mortlake tapestry factory, London, 1624; active there until c.1657. Permanently resident in London from 1625; also active as a designer of interiors and decorative painter. Published several suites of ornament from 1645. Active as an illustrator of books from the 1630s, producing plates for Ovid's *Metamorphoses* (1632), Aesop's *Fables* (1651), Virgil (1654, 1658) and Homer (1660). Died in London, 1658.

Selected Works

Examples of tapestries after Clein's designs are in the Primatial Palace, Bratislava, the Mobilier National, Paris, and the Royal Collection, Stockholm. Examples of Clein's decorative work survive at Ham House, near Richmond, Surrey, and a chair attributed to Clein is in the Victoria and Albert Museum, London.

Interiors

1618–23	Rosenborg Slot, Copenhagen (decoration of the interiors, including the Queen's chamber): Christian IV
c.1625	Old Somerset House, London (decoration of the Queen's cabinet): Queen Henrietta Maria
after 1625	Holland House, London (interiors and some furniture)
1630s	Stoke Bruerne, Northamptonshire (decoration): Sir Francis Crane
1637–39	Ham House, near Richmond, Surrey (decoration and interiors, including the North Drawing Room and the Green Closet): William Murray

Clein worked for the Mortlake tapestry factory from 1624 to c.1657 and his work included cartoons and borders for Raphael's *Acts of the Apostles* (c.1625), and suites of *Hero and Leander* (completed 1636), *Horses*, and the *Five Senses*.

Publications

Septum Liberales Artes, 1645
Varii Zophori figuris animalium, 1645
Quinque Sensuum descriptio, 1646
Several Borders of Grotesk Works Useful of Painters, 1654

Further Reading

The most detailed English-language account of Clein's work in England appears in Thornton and Tomlin, "Franz Cleyn at Ham House", 1980. Information relating to his career in Denmark appears in Heiberg 1988.

Beckett, Francis, "The Painter Frantz Clein in Denmark" in *Memoires de l'Académie Royale des Sciences et des Lettres de Danemark*, series 7, no.2, 1936

Beckett, Francis, *Kristian IV og Malerkunsten*, Copenhagen, 1937

Croft-Murray, Edward, *Decorative Painting in England*, vol.1, London: Country Life, 1962

Heiberg, Steffen, *Christian IV and Europe* (exhib. cat.), Hillerød: Frederiksborg slot, 1988

Moore, Cathan, Christopher Rowell and Nino Strachey, *Ham House*, London: National Trust, 1995

Thornton, Peter, *Seventeenth-Century Interior Decoration in England, France, and Holland*, London and New Haven: Yale University Press, 1978

Thornton, Peter and Maurice Tomlin, *The Furnishing and Decoration of Ham House*, London: Furniture History Society, 1980

Thornton, Peter and Maurice Tomlin, "Franz Cleyn at Ham House" in Gervase Jackson-Stops (editor), *National Trust Studies*, London: Philip Wilson, 1980

Weilbach, Philip, *Kunstnerleksikon*, vol.1, Copenhagen: Aschenhoug, 1947

Clérisseau, Charles-Louis 1721–1820

French architect, painter and designer of interiors

Charles-Louis Clérisseau is an important figure in the genesis and diffusion of the Neo-Classical style in architecture and decoration in the middle and later 18th century in Italy, France, England, Germany, and Russia. His exact relationship to Giovanni Battista Piranesi and J.J. Winckelmann, major figures in the revival of interest in antiquity, and to his pupils and associates including Robert and James Adam, William Chambers, Friedrich Wilhelm von Erdmannsdorff and Thomas Jefferson, has been the subject of much debate. Equally as important is his precise role in the creation and spread of the Neo-Classical decorative style known in France as the Style Louis XVI, Pompeian or Arabesque, as the Adam in England, the Cameronian in Russia and Jeffersonian in America. While there is no doubt that he played a major part in the study and adaptation of ancient and Renaissance decorative details, particularly the arabesque and grotesque in the creation of a new decorative style, the early beginnings will never be completely clear.

Clérisseau trained as an architect in Paris and at the French Academy in Rome. He spent 17 years in Italy studying and drawing ancient and Renaissance architecture, emphasizing the decorative details as well as the architectural forms. These became the basis of the Neo-Classical style of decoration. He imparted his knowledge to his pupils, particularly Robert Adam who, with Clérisseau's help, created the Adam style, skilfully combining ancient and Renaissance motifs in an original and delicate new creation. Clérisseau's great wealth of drawings, made throughout his long career, sold by him to Catherine the Great of Russia in 1779, are closely related to Adam. What may be his earliest decorative work is the decoration of the coffee house of the Villa Albani in Rome (1764) which is described as having Ionic pilasters with elegant arabesques and tiny bas-reliefs in white and scenes derived from antiquity. Winckelmann, who played a major role in Clérisseau's obtaining the commission, wrote that Clérisseau was also to execute large landscapes of the antiquities of Dalmatia and Southern Italy, but these may not have been carried out. The vicissitudes of the Villa and its various restorations make it unclear how much of Clérisseau's work has survived.

The other early decorative design by Clérisseau is the fantastic Ruin Room, painted about 1766 in the monastic cell of Père Thomas Le Sueur in the monastery, now convent, of S. Trinità dei Monti, Rome to resemble an ancient ruin inhabited by a monk, complete with crumbling walls, other decorative and architectural details, and a ruined vaulted ceiling. Originally it contained furniture in the ancient style, a sarcophagus desk and an upturned capital for a chair. Called one of "the wonders of Rome" it still exists, as do the drawings and descriptions of it in the Hermitage Museum, St. Petersburg. Executed in bright colours of reds, blues, greys, and greens, it is an exact and convincing evocation of classical antiquity. It is a tour de force of Neo-Classicism and continues a tradition of less archaeologically-correct painted ruin rooms stretching back to the Renaissance.

Considering Clérisseau's reputation as a pioneer of Neo-Classical decoration, very few of his works were executed and most of those were late in his career. His Roman house for Catherine the Great of Russia of 1773 was not built. The plans which survive resemble an enormous Roman bath set into Hadrian's Villa at Tivoli; it was rejected for this reason. The drawings of the interior resemble the works of his pupil Robert Adam and contain walls divided by niches, delicate arabesque panels and inset classical scenes, features which also appear in many of the imaginative drawings by Clérisseau among the 1,170 drawings purchased by Catherine. These later inspired the Russian works by Charles Cameron.

Clérisseau's designs for salons for two hotels for Laurent Grimod de la Reynière, Paris, 1775–77 and 1780–82 were executed, and much of the second one survives today in the Victoria and Albert Museum, London. The earlier one seems to have elements which were transferred to the second one, about which we know more. It consists of a rectangular room with large panes of arabesques with classical oval scenes of the life of Ulysses in the centre and small roundels above rectangular plaques, framed by arabesque patterns with urns, scrolls, flowers, birds, and drapery. These large panels are separated by thin rinceau strips. All of this decoration, which is painted on flat panels (not in stucco relief like many of the Adam works), is carried out in colour shades of pink, grey, blue-grey, green, and Pompeian red against a white background. The Ulysses ovals are in full colour. The tall rinceau panels are in gold and grey. Much of the actual painting was executed by Etienne de la Vallée, later Lavallée-Poussin, although the general scheme and probably much of the detail was done by Clérisseau.

Clérisseau's last important commission was between 1792 and 1794. It involved the decoration of the great hall and adjoining room at the Palace of Weimar. It was not executed, but a drawing of the hall exists. It consisted of a rectangular room with balconies on all four sides supported by giant Corinthian columns surmounted by a rinceau frieze. The walls were to be divided into panels with friezes and decorative areas above crowned by a cornice of swags. The adjoining room was to be decorated with arabesque panels alternating with ruin scenes.

Clérisseau's greatest importance is as a teacher of other architects and in his thousands of drawings of ancient decorative and architectural details and designs in the antique style. Nearly all of these are undated. His exact role in the creation of the Adam style will probably never be clear. He seems to have worked on various Adam projects in in the early 1770s while he was in England and it is suggested that he was then influenced by their work. Although Clérisseau is credited with introducing the arabesque style into France, the earliest dated examples are the panels at Bagatelle by François-Joseph Bélanger (1744–1818), a friend of Clérisseau's. And it was Giovanni Battista Piranesi who was the first to show the new archaeologically-correct *grotteschi* or arabesque as wall decoration in his *Diverse maniere d'adornare i cammini* of 1769.

THOMAS J. MCCORMICK

See also Adam; Arabesque and Grotesque

Biography

Baptized in Paris, 28 August 1721. Student under Germain Boffrand (1667–1754) at the Académie Royale d'Architecture by 1745: awarded the Grand Prix 1746; attended the French Academy, Rome, 1749–54. Remained in Italy until 1767 where he was active as a draughtsman, painter and designer of interiors and gardens; met G. B. Piranesi and Winckelmann; acted as tutor to Robert Adam (1728–92), 1755–57 and travelled with him to Diocletian's Palace, Spalato (Split, former Yugoslavia), 1757, and collaborated on Adam's book on the palace (published 1764). Returned to France, preparing plates for a book on Antiques (published 1778), 1767. Travelled to England, 1771; prepared designs for the Adam brothers. Resident in France by 1775, where he worked as an architect, painter and designer of interiors. Advised Thomas Jefferson on the building of the State Capitol, Virginia. Member, Academy of Rouen, 1810; Legion d'Honneur, 1815. Regular exhibitor, Society of Artists, and Royal Academy, London. Died in Auteuil, 19 January 1820.

Selected Works

The largest collection of Clérisseau's drawings, including unexecuted designs made for Catherine the Great, is in the Hermitage, St. Petersburg. Additional smaller collections of drawings are in the Fitzwilliam Museum, Cambridge, the British Museum, and Sir John Soane's Museum, London. Panels removed from Ashburnham Place, Sussex are from the decoration of the Hôtel Grimod, and are now in the Victoria and Albert Museum, London.

Interiors

1764	Villa Albani, Rome (decoration of the coffee house)
c.1766	Monastery, Santa Trinità dei Monti, Rome (decoration of the Ruin Room): Père Thomas Le Sueur and Père Jacquier
1773	Roman House, St. Petersburg (unexecuted designs for the building and interiors): Empress Catherine II
1774	Lansdowne House, London (garden alcove, and unexecuted design for the gallery): Marquess of Lansdowne
1775–77	Hôtel Grimod de la Reynière, rue Grange-Batelière, Paris (salon decoration): Laurent Grimod de la Reynière
1776–89	Palais du Gouverneur, Metz (building and interiors)
1780–82	Hôtel Grimod de la Reynière, rue Boissy d'Anglas, Paris (salon decoration): Laurent Grimod de la Reynière
1792–94	Palace of Weimar (unexecuted designs for the salon and hall)

Publications

Antiquités de la France: Première Partie: Monuments de Nismes, 1778; revised edition by J.G. Legrand, 1804

Further Reading

A comprehensive analysis of Clérisseau's life and career appears in McCormick 1990 which includes numerous references to primary and secondary sources.

Braham, Allan, *The Architecture of the French Enlightenment*, Berkeley: University of California Press, and London: Thames and Hudson, 1980

Charles-Louis Clérisseau (1721–1820): Dessins du Musée de l'Ermitage, Saint Petersbourg (exhib. cat.), Paris: Musée du Louvre, 1995

Croft-Murray, Edward, "The Hôtel Grimod de la Reynière: The Salon Decorations" in *Apollo*, 77, 1966, pp.377–83

Fleming, John, "The Journey to Spalato" in *Architectural Review*, 123, 1958, pp.102–07

Fleming, John, *Robert Adam and His Circle in Edinburgh and Rome*, London: Murray, and Cambridge, MA: Harvard University Press, 1962

Gallet, Michel, *Paris Domestic Architecture of the 18th Century*, London: Barrie and Jenkins, 1972; as *Stately Mansions: Eighteenth Century Paris Architecture*, New York: Praeger, 1972

Kalnein, Wend von, *Architecture in France in the Eighteenth Century*, New Haven and London: Yale University Press, 1995

Lejeaux, Jeanne, "Charles-Louis Clérisseau, Architect et Peintre des Ruines, 1721–1820" in *Revue de l'Art*, LIII, April 1926

McCormick, Thomas J. and John Fleming, "A Ruin Room by Clérisseau" in *Connoisseur*, 159, 1962, pp.239–43

McCormick, Thomas J., "Virginia's Gallic Grandfather" in *Arts in Virginia*, 4, 1964, pp.2–13

McCormick, Thomas J., "Piranesi and Clérisseau's Vision of Classical Antiquity" in Georges Brunel (editor), *Piranèse et les Français* (conference papers), Rome: Elefante, 1978

McCormick, Thomas J., *Charles-Louis Clérisseau and the Genesis of Neo-Classicism*, Cambridge, MA: Massachusetts Institute of Technology Press, 1990

McCormick, Thomas J., "Monastic Caprices: The Monastery of Trinità dei Monti: The Ruin Room by Charles-Louis Clérisseau" in *FMR*, XIV, no.71, December 1994, pp.31–44

Middleton, Robin and David Watkin, *Neoclassical and 19th Century Architecture*, New York: Abrams, and London: Academy, 1980

Stillman, Damie, "The Gallery for Lansdowne House: International Neo-Classical Architecture and Decoration in Microcosm" in *Art Bulletin*, LII, 1970, pp.75–80

Closets

The closet was a small room, usually annexed to a bedchamber, gallery or library, that would now probably be called a study or an office. Also known as a *cabinet* in France, or as a *camerino*, *cameratta*, *studio* or *studiolo* in Italy, closets were very personal, intimately-sized rooms that were tucked away in the innermost reaches of a house, not easily accessible from the more public spaces. These rooms were variously used: as strong rooms in the Middle Ages where a rich householder would safeguard valuables; as an office in which to keep documents (private and business); as a study for learning and meditation (common in the papal apartments at the Vatican and at

Closets: Queen's Closet, Ham House, Surrey, c.1670

Avignon and among the clergy); as a treasury for the contemplation of art objects; or simply as a room in which friends could be entertained informally.

Medieval closets were spartan rooms appointed to suit the particular requirements of each inhabitant. During the Renaissance in Italy, closets (*studii*, or *camerinii*) increasingly became cherished havens for rich men of learning in which they could meditate, read and write, as well as store and display their growing collections of art, antiquities and curiosities. These *studii* were to some extent inspired by the writings of classical authors which contained references to the private studies or libraries in which they worked. Petrarch called his closet his "solitudo". According to contemporary inventories secular closets were already common in rich Italian houses in the early 15th century. The Medici residence on the Via Larga in Florence (1440), for example, contained at least three closets. Merchants and businessmen also had *studii*. A merchants' handbook of 1569, *Della Meratura et del Mercante Perfetto*, recommended placing one close to the bedchamber and another, a *scritorio*, at some distance from the domestic areas of the house so as not to disturb the family with business matters.

Although the main motives of the 15th-century Italian closet were secrecy, privacy and solitude, they could also be quite richly decorated so as to do justice to the impressive collections of books, miniature paintings, and antiquities such as medals, coins and small statues or vases and gems that were housed there. Proper shelving was introduced, great emphasis was placed on the effective display of objects, and ceilings were often lowered to better suit the intimate proportions of the room. Within wealthy houses and palaces, closets were among the most expensively and sumptuously decorated rooms: Pietro de Medici's closet in the family residence on the Via Larga was famously opulent, as was that of his contemporary Federigo da Montefeltro, the Duke of Urbino. The Duke of Urbino's *studiolo* is probably the best known Renaissance example of its kind. It was used to house the Duke's priceless collection of theological manuscripts, medical treatises, Greek texts, and library of classical and contemporary writings, and the walls were richly decorated in fine pictorial intarsia (inlaid woodwork) above which portraits of famous men and allegories were painted.

During the 16th century the Italian closet became a more public space. Contemporary collectors' *studii* were opened up to selected members of the public who had appropriate letters of introduction, many of whom came to see the art on display. This practice was especially prevalent in Venice; Francesco Sansovino, a 16th-century Venetian writer, compiled a list of *casa aperte*, open houses in Venice with *studii* of interest.

In northern Europe the closets in great houses fulfilled similar functions. Closets were alternatively dressing rooms, venues for informal gatherings or secret meetings, or served as an escape route from the main apartment as many closets had access to the backstairs. These stairs performed another important role: they enabled servants to pass in and out of the bedchamber via the adjacent closet without having to cross the main rooms of the house. Although closets were still quite private, by the 17th century they had become more luxuriously appointed. Great care was lavished on their decoration and, unlike more public rooms, whose furnishings were dictated by contemporary convention, closets were often decorated in a more personal, but at the same time, fanciful or experimental fashion.

Closets were located at the farthest end of the row of rooms that made up the formal apartment in a great house. They were often furnished with dressing tables, tea tables, and increasingly comfortable seating such as easy chairs or *fauteuils de commodité*. Daybeds and sofas were also typical. The informality of the closet gave householders the opportunity to experiment with more outlandish decorative schemes. Chinese themes were popular, as were glass or mirrored wall panels; Francis Bacon even noted a cupola. The Duchess de Valentois took informality to an extreme, furnishing her closet with piles of cushions.

The opulence with which some 17th-century closets were decorated was symptomatic of the social aspirations of the householder. Many great houses were built to accommodate visiting royalty, either because the owner already had connections with the royal court or because he hoped to acquire them. The closet in the Queen's apartment at Ham House was decorated with red satin brocade hangings, gold and striped silk. Catherine of Braganza's own closet was decorated with sky-blue damask wall hangings with divisions of gold lace.

Towards the end of the 17th century many European great houses followed the French model in having two closets or cabinets; a larger closet served as a reception room for select company, and a smaller, more private closet was for very close friends or solitude. Louise de la Vallière, one of Louis XIV's mistresses, could seat 18 people in her grand cabinet; Madame de Maintenon's grand cabinet could accommodate 29 people, and the king's grand cabinet could house his entire privy council when he wished to discuss affairs of state. In England, the Duchess of Lauderdale had two closets adjacent to one another at Ham House. The larger "white" closet was lavishly decorated and very public; her "private" closet was more intimately, although still quite richly appointed, and was small and intended as a study.

Developments in collecting also influenced the appearance of closets. By the second half of the 17th century, a marked interest in scientific learning was matched by a growing fascination with the fine arts and collecting. Collections were divided into large and small objects; larger objects such as statuary and paintings were distributed in rooms such as the gallery, while smaller objects were displayed on shelves and in cabinets in the closet. The Green Closet at Ham House (1637–39) was exotically decorated so as to complement the collection of small treasures displayed there. Closets with art collections that were used for study were often located alongside libraries or galleries. The art collections of so-called "virtuosi" or "dilettanti" (terms used to describe a late 17th or early 18th century equivalent to the Renaissance humanist), were sometimes well-known and were a magnet for other cognoscenti or for educated visitors making a Grand Tour.

By the last quarter of the 18th century the functions of rooms had become less rigidly determined, and closets, libraries and galleries were used more diversely for recreational purposes. Corsham Court (1760s), for example, had a library with a cabinet en suite that doubled as a saloon and withdrawing room. Similarly, as bedrooms became more private, closets were used increasingly as dressing rooms or private studies. Many of the functions previously served by women's closets were transferred to the boudoir in the late 18th and 19th centuries. By the beginning of the 19th century the closet had all but disappeared and it survived only in great houses as a relic, or reminder of a more codified way of life.

MAREIKE VON SPRECKELSEN

See also Studioli

Further Reading

Cornforth, John and John Fowler, *English Decoration in the 18th Century*, London: Barrie and Jenkins, and Princeton, NJ: Pyne, 1974; 2nd edition, Barrie and Jenkins, 1978

Girouard, Mark, *Life in the English Country House: A Social and Architectural History*, New Haven and London: Yale University Press, 1978

Jackson-Stops, Gervase and James Pipkin, "Dressing Rooms, Cabinets and Closets" in their *The English Country House: A Grand Tour*, London: Weidenfeld and Nicolson, 1984; Boston: Little Brown, 1985, pp.181–198

Thornton, Peter, "Closets" in *Seventeenth-Century Interior Decoration in England, France, and Holland*, New Haven and London: Yale University Press, 1978, pp.296–303

Thornton, Peter and Maurice Tomlin, *The Furnishing and Decoration of Ham House*, London: Furniture History Society, 1980

Thornton, Peter, *The Italian Renaissance Interior, 1400–1600*, London: Weidenfeld and Nicolson, and New York: Abrams, 1991

Whitehead, John, *The French Interior in the Eighteenth Century*, London: Laurence King, 1992; New York: Dutton, 1993

Coates, Nigel 1949–

British architect and designer

Attempts to categorise Nigel Coates's activities as an architect and designer are revealingly unsatisfactory. An architect who embraces teaching and theory, building, interiors, furniture and product design, Coates's work is not so much unified by a consistent style or aesthetic, but by an expressive approach that sets out to explore richer possibilities for the architecture of our cities in the late 20th century. It reflects the vibrant multi-layered cacophony of urban life and its vivid collision of past and present.

Coates's built projects are a series of interiors and buildings realised in Japan and Britain since the mid-1980s. They are instant urban monuments with the patina of history, like The Wall, literally a monumental stone wall that looks as though it could be part of some Roman ruin uncovered in the centre of Tokyo and converted for the use of some futuristic corporation; or like the Knightsbridge Jigsaw fashion store where a giant copper column (is it some antique relic or part of an ornate aircraft?) announces the shop's street presence, while a monumental terrazzo staircase draws customers upstairs into a room that seems to be modelled on the salone of an Italian palazzo. Or like the restaurants in Schipol airport that explore the artificial world of the airport and the promise of flight with surreal simulations of exotic locations. Exploiting the power of visual metaphor, ricocheting across the barriers of high and low art and sampling across time and cultures, Coates's environments characteristically set out to engage the user on the level of the imagination as well as functional "reality".

Coates first studied architecture at Nottingham University but it was his immersion in the dynamic atmosphere of the Architectural Association (AA) in the 1970s, where Coates was first a student and later taught, that the formative influences converged. At the time the AA, under the directorship of Alvin Boyarsky, was run more as a forum for the exchange of ideas with an international outlook than as a conventional school. Coates was drawn to the experimental work of Swiss architect Bernard Tschumi who brought a political dimension to architecture, and an approach based in the visual arts that was to have a profound effect on Coates. Tschumi introduced Coates to the work of the anarchic French group, the Situationists, who saw the city as a theatre of experience and superimposed maps of the imagination onto the geography of the city to create a new dimension of urban experience.

At the same time Coates, who was awarded a scholarship to Rome University in 1978, began to explore other disciplines to enrich his approach to architecture. He was influenced by the narrative structure of film – in particular the work of Pasolini – and also by 18th-century Italian garden design, where the garden is conceived as a stage for a series of choreographed events and the visitor as a participant creating their own narrative from their experience.

These ideas crystallised in a series of projects for London carried out first in collaboration with Tschumi and then with students from Unit 10 at the AA, which Coates took over teaching from Tschumi in 1979. In 1983 Coates formed a group of self-styled architectural anarchists with eight of his Unit 10 students who called themselves NATO, an acronym for Narrative Architecture Today.

In a series of catalytic projects including Albion, Ecstacity and Giant Sized Baby Town – typically the name came from a song by the punk group Bow Wow Wow – NATO attacked the sterility of urban planning and controlled zoning, and promoted a scrambled vision of the city as playground, offering residents a rich arena of possibilities. They celebrated the conflicting energies of urban life, the possibilities of change and the regeneration of industrial buildings, drawing as much on the Situationists' dream maps of the city as the subversive concerns of punk and street culture.

In keeping with their sympathy with youth subcultures, NATO's ideas were broadcast in magazine format: large newsprint pages overspilling with frenzied expressionistic drawings of the city in a state of flux, combined with charged texts that borrowed as much from the manifestos of the Italian Futurists as youth culture.

NATO's ad hoc approach to urban design and concern with imaginative regeneration were in tune with current directions in the visual arts, design and fashion: in particular the design movement led by Tom Dixon whose furniture was built from industrial parts salvaged on the city's streets and recycled with decorative euphoria. It also reflected the concerns of sculptor Tony Cragg whose work drew new imagery from found objects, and the designs of fashion designer Vivienne Westwood which plundered pageant and the dressing-up box as freely as the illicit and fetishistic.

In 1985 NATO held an exhibition "Gamma City" at the AIR gallery in London. The show began on the street with the zebra crossing extended to lead into the show, literally and symbolically breaking down the barriers between street and

Nigel Coates: L'Arca di Noè, Sapporo, Japan, 1988

gallery, and NATO's work and the real world. Inside provocative polemic recast the city as a chaotic collage of dreams, subcultures and romanticised decay, celebrated in a jumble of the spare parts of urban life. Overhead televisions flashed Gamma city slogans: "Gamma-city is not a style but a political, social and aesthetic attitude based on crumbling signs and processes ... Exchanges is a basic act of architecture and its space the street. Gamma streets double-up as home, market, factory, bar switching old images for new uses".

Critics incited by the celebration of post-industrial fantasies, the scrapyard and the slum, and the parade of imagery drawn from youth subcultures regarded NATO's work as lacking serious intent and noted the impossibility of bridging the gap from paper to reality. But to read NATO's proposals as blueprints for the city was to miss the point: its intention was to challenge the accepted authority of a tired Modernism and open new ways of thinking.

It was not in Britain that Coates was first able to move from paper architecture to the built project. This opportunity was provided by the booming entertainment and fashion industries of Tokyo in the mid-1980s which proved a voracious consumer for Coates's sophisticated theming and theatrical vision through the contracts entrepreneur and self-styled "architectural producer", Shi Yu Chen and his company CIA, Creative Intelligence Associates.

In 1985 Coates formed the partnership Branson Coates with architect Doug Branson to realise his first Tokyo commission, the Metropole, a restaurant in a former garage conceived as fantastical stage set layered with classical references sampled across time and cultures. This was followed by Caffé Bongo with an aircraft wing strapped to the façade celebrating the mythology of flying and the exchange of ideas around the world. The Hotel Otaru Marittimo was a hotel in the port of Otaru in the north of Japan where guests were invited to go on a voyage through rooms recalling the city's history as much as the imaginative possibilities of travel. In Japan too, Coates realised his first building, the L'Arca di Noè. This was a restaurant and bar in the city of Sapporo that took the form of an Ark, a massive concrete structure that looked as though it had been chiselled from a rock, playfully exploiting the triangular site on the island of Hokkaido.

If it seems extraordinary that Coates's built projects, so Western, even Eurocentric in their references, should find an audience in Japan, arguably such high-octane flamboyance was an end in itself in an all-consuming consumer culture. Prompted by Si Yu Chen, Japanese backers were able to translate Coates's prowess for attention-grabbing prominence into commercial success. The other side of this coin is, of course, a swift turnover of ideas and obsolescence reflected in the short lifespan of Coates's projects in Japan.

The developer's urge for instant gratification generates difficulties of its own, perhaps most apparent in the Penrose Institute, a contemporary art gallery, or as Coates described it an "art silo" housed in a glass tower attached to The Wall and funded by its developers. While the comparatively sober glass structure revealing the lift in its core seemed to mark a new direction for Coates, the desire to create a landmark takes precedence over the gallery spaces it contains.

With his built projects Coates continued the collaborative working method established with NATO, inviting artists and designers to participate in interiors which energetically encapsulated current directions in British design and the decorative arts. Collaborators have regularly included the artists Stuart Helm and Adam Lowe, and the designer Tom Dixon as well as members of the original NATO group.

Coates views the different perspectives incorporated in a collaboration as opposed to a building with a single author as vital to the creation of what he describes as "a harmonious discord". In Coates's conception the multiplicity of voices is mirrored by the multiple-possibilities offered to the inquiring visitor.

Coates's office also designs much of the furniture used in his interiors. In fact new designs frequently arise from the needs of a particular architectural project. The Noè range was designed for the Arca di Noè and has a similar primitive rough-hewn feel; while the Slipper range is an update on a Victorian boudoir chair designed for Liberty's shoe department. The eroticised anthropomorphism characteristic of Coates's furniture recalls the work of Italian architect Carlo Mollino and his witty fusions of furniture and the human body, and even the surreal imagery of Salvador Dalí. For Coates, Mollino also represents a significant model for the role of author, an architect whose work encompasses different spheres of activity from furniture to a building and whose vision is vibrantly enriched by reference to sphere of the imagination.

JANE WITHERS

See also Postmodernism

Biography

Born in Malvern, Worcestershire, 2 March 1949. Studied architecture at the University of Nottingham, 1968–71, and at the Architectural Association, London, 1972–74. Awarded a travelling scholarship to Rome, 1978. Employed as a unit master at the Architectural Association, 1979–89; course master, Bennington College, Vermont, 1980–81. Founder member, NATO (Narrative Architecture Today), 1983. Founding partner, with Doug Branson, Branson Coates Architecture, London, from 1985. Interior and architecture commissions in Japan, from 1985; appointed house architects to Jigsaw, 1988, and Liberty, 1992 (both London). Received Japan Inter-Design award, 1990. Numerous lectures on architecture in Britain and abroad; frequent exhibitor at national and international exhibitions.

Selected Works

Examples of Coates's drawings, and one of his chairs is in the Victoria and Albert Museum, London. A complete list of Coates's architectural and interior commissions up to 1990 appears in Poynor 1989.

Interiors

1985	Metropole Restaurant, Tokyo (interiors and furnishings)
1986	Caffé Bongo, Parco Department Store, Tokyo (façade, interiors and furnishings)
1986	Bohemia Jazz Club, Takeo Kikuchi building, Tokyo (interiors and furnishings)
1986–87	Jasper Conran Shops, London and Dublin (interiors)
1988	Katharine Hamnett Shops, Glasgow and London (interiors)
1988	Jigsaw shops, London and Bristol (interiors)
1988	L'Arca di Noè restaurant building, Sapporo (building, interiors and furnishings)
1989	Hotel Otaru Marittimo, Otaru, Japan (interiors)
1990	Katharine Hamnett Shop, Tokyo (interiors)
1990	The Wall, Nishi Azabu, Tokyo (building and interiors)
1991	Taxim Restaurant, Istanbul (interiors)
1993	Nautilus and La Foret Restaurants, Schipol Airport, Amsterdam (interiors)
1993	Art Silo (Penrose Institute), Tokyo (building and interiors)
1995–96	Geffrye Museum, London (extension and exhibition layouts)
1996	Bargo bar/restaurant, Glasgow (interiors and furnishings)

The majority of Coates's interiors include custom-made furnishings. His furniture designs have been commercially produced by the Japanese firm Rockstone from 1987, the London firm SPC from 1988, and the Italian firm Bigelli, from 1989.

Publications

Nigel Coates: ArkAlbion and Six Other Projects, introduction by Brian Hatton, 1984
"Metropole Restaurant, Tokyo" in *Architecture and Urbanism*, 185, February 1986
"Street Signs" in John Thackara (editor), *Design After Modernism: Beyond the Object*, London and New York: Thames and Hudson, 1988, pp.95–114
Ecstacity, 1992

Further Reading

For a stimulating and detailed discussion of Coates's work see Poynor 1990 which includes a select bibliography, a list of Coates's writings and a chronological list of projects.

Bangert, Albrecht and Karl Michael Armer, *80s Style: Designs of the Decade*, New York: Abbeville, 1990
Calloway, Stephen, *Designs for Interiors* (exhib. cat.), London: Victoria and Albert Museum, 1986
Crysler, Geig, "Architectural Dandyism in the Age of Mass Media" in *New Art Examiner*, 16, Summer 1989, pp.32–34
Dormer, Peter, "Nigel and the Others" in *Blueprint*, 22, November 1985
Fawcett, Anthony (editor), *Zaha Hadid, Nigel Coates: New British Interiors*, Kyoto: Kyoto Shoin, 1991
Fitoussi, Brigitte, "Barroco in Tokyo" in *L'Architecture d'Aujourd'hui*, 253, October 1987, pp.81–83
McDermott, Catherine, "Anarchic Architect" in *Creative Review*, April 1986
McDermott, Catherine, *Street Style: British Design in the 80s*, London: Design Council, and New York: Rizzoli, 1987
"Nigel Coates (recent work)" in *Architectural Design*, 62, December 1992, pp.73–96
Okagawa, M., "Restaurant, Tokyo" in *Architectural Review*, CLXXIX, June 1986
Poynor, Rick, "Coates Rebuilds the Ark in Japan" in *Blueprint*, 44, February 1988
Poynor, Rick, *Nigel Coates: The City in Motion*, London: Fourth Estate, and New York: Rizzoli, 1990
Thackara, John (editor), *New British Design*, London and New York: Thames and Hudson, 1986

Coates, Wells 1895–1958

Canadian architect and designer

Wells Coates was at the forefront of modern architecture and design in inter-war Britain. He was an engineer by training, and his lack of a conventional architectural education was undoubtedly a source of some insecurity, but his understanding of materials and industrial processes informed his design thinking, and was a fundamental influence on his utilitarian aesthetic.

Coates's earliest domestic commission as an interior designer was the refurbishment of 1 Kensington Palace Gardens (1931), where he replaced the ornate late-Victorian interior with rather "moderne" furniture and fittings almost all to his own design. Although the refurbishment was characterised by flush surfaces and plain finishes, it was not without decorative touches. A frieze of ballet figures by John Armstrong was painted on the ballroom wall; the dressing table in the master bedroom was equipped with "rotatable" tinted mirrors; and the steel legs of the dining table were encased in green glass. Doors were done away with and bay windows hidden behind sliding silk screens, a device Coates also used at Charles Laughton's flat in Gordon Square (1931), and which was clearly influenced by Japanese interiors. As was to become clear later, it was built-in furniture that most preoccupied Coates when designing interiors, and here was no exception; a single built-in unit in the drawing room brought together the radio, gramophone, cocktail-cabinet and bookcase. Despite the striking "before and after" views of the house which appeared in the architectural press, it was Coates's belief that "design must begin from the interior *plan* ... as generator", and it is for his subsequent experiments in interior planning, as well as a more International Modern style, that he is best remembered.

The Isokon flats on Lawn Road in Hampstead (1933) firmly established Coates as one of the leading protagonists in the UK of what became known as the International Style. As he was, to some extent, client *and* architect (having co-founded the Isokon company in 1931), the building allowed him to explore his own design philosophy and affirm his commitment, until then simply theoretical, to the advantages of flat living; the socially responsible use of land, provision of communal services, use of standardized parts etc. Designed as "ready-to-live-in" dwellings, the flats sought to relieve their single, mainly middle-class, occupants from the unnecessary encumbrance – as Coates saw it – of furniture ownership. Indeed, writing in the *Architectural Review* in 1932, Coates had argued that; "Furniture in the dictionary sense will take its place in the logic of construction, becoming an integral part of architecture". Nevertheless, like many architects, he undoubtedly also relished the opportunity of perhaps avoiding his designs being compromised by their occupants' furniture choices. Each of the 22 "minimum" flats occupied only 271 square feet (25 square metres), and was equipped with standardized built-in furniture, designed for maximum economy of space. Unlike the furniture at Kensington Palace Gardens, that at Lawn Road made no concessions to decoration, its aesthetic being derived from its function, as well as the appearance of the modern materials from which it was constructed. Of these, plywood was the most prevalent, making up the sliding table, stools, built-in bookcase units and doors, although tubular steel was also in evidence, forming the sub-frame of the table.

This seminal experiment in minimum living was taken a stage further in Coates's own flat at 18 Yeoman's Row, Knightsbridge (1935), where he again made great use of uncompromisingly modern built-in furniture. Of equal significance here, however, was his use of a "2-1" section. The living area occupied most of the flat on the top floor of the terraced house, while a smaller space at the rear of the flat was subdivided horizontally to provide two sleeping galleries on one level and a kitchen and bathroom on the other. A keen yachtsman, Coates was undoubtedly influenced by the design of boats: sleeping areas were entered via utilitarian ladders, while services were hidden behind sliding hatches. At Palace Gate (1937–38), arguably his most important building after Lawn Road, Coates was able to apply some of the thinking behind Yeoman's Row to a large-scale residential development. Designed around an ambitious "3-2" section – where the height of two living rooms was equal to three bedrooms – the flats were equipped with an abundance of built-in furniture (now also serving as room dividers), again executed in a spare Modernist idiom. Although Coates did design some rather conventional loose wooden furniture for the model Palace Gate flat shown in Bristol in 1936, the flats as built did not offer as complete an environment as those at Lawn Road.

Coates also designed some notable interiors outside the residential sphere. Indeed, it was his factory and shop interiors for the Cresta Silks chain (1929–32), and more specifically his use of plywood in them, which had first impressed Jack Pritchard and led to the formation of the Isokon company. At a time when plywood was generally seen as a cheap and inferior alternative to solid wood, Coates exploited its intrinsic properties to produce modern, standardized shop fittings, entirely free of decoration.

The dramatic effects studios at Broadcasting House (1931) gave Coates the opportunity to design his most futuristic interiors. Despite the building's rather half-heartedly modern exterior (designed by Val Myer), the British Broadcasting Corporation wanted the studios to embody the modernity of the broadcasting medium, and, as such, Coates was probably less restricted by aesthetic convention than on any other project. His essentially engineering-based, aesthetically-spare interiors were characterised by the use of extremely modern materials – notably, anodised aluminium alloy – and ingenious purpose-designed fittings, some of which became standard broadcasting equipment. While the lack of any conventional sort of decoration could be put down to the demanding technical requirements of a broadcasting studio, the interiors, through the use of bold curved forms, displayed an extremely expressive quality.

Most of the furniture Coates designed throughout his career was for specific interiors, although he was also responsible for a number of pieces which secured a wider exposure. These included simple plywood bookcase units of the type used at Lawn Road, and some elegant, albeit slightly formulaic, tubular steel furniture for Practical Equipment Ltd (Pel), first used at Coates's Embassy Court in Brighton (1934). It was for the design of radio cabinets, however, that Coates received widespread and popular recognition. As at the BBC, there were few firmly established aesthetic conventions to which he needed to adhere, and his most famous and successful model, the circular Ecko AD65 (1934), is today widely recognized as a mark of the up-to-date 1930s interior.

In the years following World War II, Coates was involved in a wide variety of projects in both Britain and Canada, including housing and hotel developments, town-planning, and product design. However, all but one of the architectural commissions – the "Telekinema" at the Festival of Britain (1951) – failed to materialise and in 1955, Coates finally accepted an invitation to teach at Harvard.

While Lawn Road and Palace Gate undoubtedly represent significant contributions to Modernist thinking, other projects, such as Embassy Court (which featured decorative pictorial murals by Edward McKnight Kauffer), do not sit quite as comfortably alongside the work of the established European "masters". Nevertheless, between the wars, Coates was one of only a handful of individuals in Britain committed to modern design, and, through his few extremely significant buildings, as well as an important series of radio broadcasts, he played a pivotal role in the introduction of Modernism to Britain.

ANTHONY HOYTE

See also Isokon; Plywood Furniture

Biography

Wells Wintemute Coates. Born to Canadian parents in Tokyo, Japan, 17 December 1895. Studied engineering at the University of British Columbia, Vancouver, 1913–15 and 1919–21; and for a Ph.D. at the University of London, 1922–24. Served as a lieutenant, Canadian infantry, 1915–17; pilot, Royal Air force, 1917–18; Wing Commander, Royal Air Force, 1939–45. Married Marion Grove, 1927; one daughter, Laura. Draughtsman and journalist in London and Paris, 1923–26; engineer / architect, Chrysede Textiles Company, London and Cornwall, 1927–28. Settled in London 1929; in private practice as a designer and architect, 1929–39, 1945–52, and 1956–58; in partnership with David Pleydell-Bouverie, 1933–34; with Patrick Gwynne, 1935–39; with Jacqueline Tyrwhitt, 1949–52; with Michael Lyell, 1954–56; architect / planner, Iroquois New Town, Ontario, 1952–54; visiting professor, Harvard University; resumed private practice, London, 1956–58. Designed furniture and interiors from late 1920s; radios and electrical appliances from c.1932; aircraft interiors and experiments with transportation from late 1940s. Consultant for Isokon from 1931; member, Twentieth Century Group and Unit One 1933–35; founder-member, Modern Architecture Research Group, 1933–34. Published many articles on architecture and design during the 1930s. Numerous honours, including Fellow, Royal Institute of British Architects, 1938; Royal Designer for Industry, 1944; Officer, Order of the British Empire (OBE), 1944. Died in London, 17 June 1958.

Selected Works

A large collection of Coates's architectural drawings and designs is in the Drawings Collection, Royal Institute of British Architects; examples of his furniture are in the Victoria and Albert Museum, London. A list of his principal architectural and design commissions appears in Cantacuzino 1978.

Interiors

1929–32 Cresta Silks Factory and Shops, Welwyn Garden City, London, Birmingham, Brighton, Bromley (buildings, furniture and fittings): Cresta Silks

1931 1 Kensington Palace Gardens, London (interiors, furniture and fittings)

1931 Studios, British Broadcasting House, London (furniture, light-fittings and broadcasting equipment): British Broadcasting Corporation

1931 34 Gordon Square, London (flat conversion and interiors): Charles Laughton

1933 Lawn Road Flats, Hampstead, London (building and interiors): Jack Pritchard and Isokon

1934 Embassy Court, Brighton (building and interiors)

1934 Sunspan House, Daily Mail Ideal Home Exhibition, London (prototype building with David Pleydell-Bouverie, and furniture and fittings)

1935 Studio flat, 18 Yeoman's Row, London (interiors, furniture and fittings): Wells Coates

1936 Hampden Nursery School, Holland Park, London (building, interiors, furniture and fittings)

1937–38 10 Palace Gate, Kensington, London (building and interiors)

1947 British Overseas Aircraft Corporation (BOAC) (aircraft interiors)

1950–51 Telekinema, Festival of Britain, London (building and interiors)

Publications

"Broadcasting House" with Walter Goodesmith and F.R.S. Yorke in *Architectural Review*, 72, January 1932, pp.42–78
"Furniture Today – Furniture Tomorrow" in *Architectural Review*, 72, 1932, pp.29–34
"Response to Tradition" in *Architectural Review*, November 1932
"Modern Shops and Modern Materials" in *Building*, December 1932
"Design in Modern Life: Modern Dwellings for Modern Needs" with Geoffrey Boumphrey in *Listener*, 24 May 1933
"The Conditions for an Architecture for Today" in *Architectural Association Journal*, April 1938, pp.447–57

Further Reading

Useful and thorough surveys of Coates's life and career appear in Cantacuzino 1978, and Cohn 1979 which was edited by Coates's daughter and includes many references to material in the family archive. Cantacuzino also includes a full list of Coates's writings and broadcasts, and a primary bibliography relating to his principal commissions.

Banham, Reyner, "Isokon Flats" in *Architectural Review*, July 1955
Boumphrey, Geoffrey, "The Designers, 6: Wells Coates" in *Architectural Review*, 179, 1936, pp.45–46
Buckley, Cheryl, *Isokon* (exhib. cat.), Newcastle upon Tyne: Hatton Gallery, 1980
Cantacuzino, Sherban, *Wells Coates*, London: Gordon Fraser, 1978
Catalogue of the Drawings Collection of the Royal Institute of British Architects, Farnborough: Gregg, 1969
Cohn, Laura (editor), *Wells Coates: Architect and Designer 1895–1958*, Oxford: Oxford Polytechnic Press, 1979
Collins, Michael (editor), *Hampstead in the Thirties: A Committed Decade* (exhib. cat.), London: Camden Arts Centre, 1974
"The Double Tragedy of Architect Wells Coates" in *House and Garden* (UK), September 1980
Hiesinger, Kathryn B. and George H. Marcus III (editors), *Design Since 1945* (exhib. cat.), Philadelphia: Philadelphia Museum of Art, and London: Thames and Hudson, 1983
Prus, Timothy and David Dawson, *A New Design for Living: Design in British Interiors, 1930–1951* (exhib. cat.: B2 Gallery, London), London: Lane Publications, 1982
Read, Herbert (editor), *Unit 1: The Modern Movement in English Architecture, Painting and Sculpture*, London: Cassell, 1934
Richards, J.M., "Wells Coates 1895–1958" in *Architectural Review*, 124, December 1958, pp.357–60
Sharp, Dennis and others, *Pel and Tubular Steel Furniture in the Thirties*, London: Architectural Association, 1977
Thirties: British Art and Design Before the War (exhib. cat.), London: Arts Council of Great Britain, 1979
Yorke, F.R S. and Frederick Gibberd, *The Modern Flat*, London: Architectural Press, 1937; revised edition, 1950

Cockerell, Samuel Pepys 1753–1827

British architect

Descended on his mother's side from the diarist Samuel Pepys, S.P. Cockerell is one of the least-studied architects of late 18th and early 19th-century England. Trained in the architectural office of Sir Robert Taylor, and an exact contemporary of John Soane, Cockerell followed on the heels of Adam, Dance, Holland, and Wyatt. His practice included country houses, churches, and government buildings, for which he designed interesting and significant interiors. He built upon the Neo-Palladian interior vocabulary of the earlier 18th century, upon Adam's newer classicism, and upon contemporary French interiors, and became the first English architect to mix Indian, Gothic Revival, and Neo-Classical styles for exotic interior effects. Cockerell exhibited great skill in spatial distribution and sequencing, the plans of his houses being among the most sophisticated of the late Georgian and Regency periods.

Cockerell's concern for the design of interiors expressed itself in practical counsel to his son, the architect Charles Robert Cockerell, as the latter passed through Paris in 1817, returning from his investigation of temples in Greece. Cockerell wrote: "Decoration [provides] the most extensive employment [in England] and you will ... find more importance attached to the decoration of a Saloon than to the building of a Temple; if you can therefore bend to the consideration of what is called the fittings up of the interior of the best Hotels and Palaces of Paris, the graces of their *Meubles* and the harmony of their Colours in Hangings painting and Gilding you may be the general Arbiter of taste here."

In his domestic floorplans Cockerell disposed rooms with great cleverness in planning and circulation. At Middleton Hall, Carmarthenshire, Wales (c.1793–95), he juxtaposed multiple circulation systems. The major public rooms revolved asymmetrically about a small central vestibule, or circulation cell, from which the servants could quickly radiate in any direction, while public circulation moved in a perimeter, or ambulatory, route that led sequentially from one principal room to the next. The main suite of rooms, along the garden front, was connected by a formal, French *enfilade*. Similar planning systems appeared in other Cockerell residences, such as Admiralty House, London (1786–88), Wyndham House, Salisbury (1788), and Sezincote, Gloucestershire (c.1805).

Cockerell also developed an interesting system of articulating space by gender. The ground floor of his houses often included a "Gentleman's suite" and a nearby library, "masculine" interiors that he gave rectilinear shapes, plain walls, and the bold, architectural mouldings of the older, Neo-Palladian style. His most notably "masculine" interiors were, appropriately, the public rooms of Admiralty House, London, the official residence of the Lord High Admiral of the Royal Navy. In a Cockerell house, the most distinctly "feminine" space was the Lady's Saloon, a room in which the mistress of the house spent her time and entertained company. It usually occupied the center front of the first, or chamber, storey. Both Middleton Hall and Daylesford (1788–93) in Gloucestershire had such rooms. The Lady's Saloon at Daylesford survives. It is a jewel-like space, ornamented with a highly restrained version of the Adam style, with stucco ornamentation gilded and painted in pale blues. The room is a rotunda, with a double-shell dome supported on slender columns with palm-tree capitals, behind which alternate wall piers, mirrors, and niches. The lower dome is pierced by an oculus through which one views a *trompe-l'oeil* sky painted on the upper dome and illuminated by concealed windows. Cockerell's particular uses of the older Neo-Palladian style, and the newer classicism of the Adam style, seem to indicate his personal critique of these major, interior decorative trends of 18th-century England. He considered the robust classisism of the Neo-Palladian style to be appropriate for masculine interiors, and the delicate classicism and attenuated proportions of the Adam style to be appropriate for feminine ones.

Cockerell also exhibited an eclectic appreciation for past

Cockerell: interior of Dome Room, Daylesford, Gloucestershire, 1788–93

styles in his ecclesiastical interiors. At the Tickencote Parish Church in Rutland, he restored and rebuilt a 12th-century church and its interiors in a revived Norman style (1792); at Banbury Church, Oxfordshire, (1792–97), he designed a new building, but with the nave based on Christopher Wren's St. Stephen Walbrook, London (1672–79), a kind of "Baroque revival" interior. Cockerell's appreciation for and adaptation of the earlier stylistic vocabularies of 18th-century Neo-Palladianism and 17th-century Wren-Baroque was quite unusual at a time when both had generally passed from favor.

Cockerell's critical adaptation of previous styles also opened for him the possibility of re-using earlier decorative and architectural elements within his interiors. In the public rooms of Admiralty House, he re-used a series of fine, carved-marble mantlepieces from an earlier, 18th-century London residence. While this decision accorded well with the "revived" Neo-Palladian boldness of his Admiralty interiors, it would have been almost unthinkable, say, for Adam or Soane, with their near-mania for the total design of interiors in every detail. But Cockerell could also completely detail a space by designing all its decorative accessories. For the inner hall at Admiralty House, he not only designed all the interior architectural elements but also a superb cast-iron stove in the symbolically appropriate form of a Roman naval, or rostral, column with ships' bows protruding from it.

Cockerell's most notable contribution to the design of English architecture and interiors was his introduction of an exotic eastern vocabulary based on Indian sources. This was invented for two "nabob" clients returned from India: Warren Hastings, the controversial Governor-General of Bengal, and his own brother, Sir Charles Cockerell, an official in the East India Company. The houses of both men, on nearby estates in Gloucestershire, involved extensive remodelings of, and additions to, earlier buildings, an exercise at which Cockerell was particularly adept. At Daylesford, Hastings's country house, the Indian influence was confined primarily to the interiors. The exterior is quietly classical with only a hint of Indian influence in the dome of the garden front. Hastings brought back from India paintings, fabrics, jeweled mementos, Persian armour, and suites of gilt and ivory furniture decorated with tiger heads, the latter given him by the Begums of Oudh. As a setting for these treasures, Cockerell blended Indian and Neo-Classical forms to create interiors at once splendid and restrained: cornices of gilded lotus leaves, mantlepieces carved with palm trees, elephants, and Eastern allegorical figures, and draperies of muslin edged with silver spangles and "beetle wings." Hastings's Indian furniture was augmented with satinwood and painted furniture by Ince and Mayhew of London.

Sezincote (1805 onwards), the country house of Cockerell's brother, was the first complete English country house in the "Indian" style. The exteriors are ornamented with *chattris*, *chuijas*, minarets, scalloped arches, and an onion dome. The interiors are a skilful and eclectic blending of Neo-Classical, Indian, and Gothic forms. Cockerell excelled in the design of staircases; that at Sezincote is perhaps his best. One approaches through Gothic-arched doors into the hall, where a divided "imperial" staircase with Greek anthemion balustrades leaps overhead on pierced, cast-iron beams. The hall is lighted from above by vast, classically-detailed clerestory windows alternating with channeled, Byzantine pendentives which support a classical dome inside, and a copper-sheathed onion dome on the roof. The saloon, with its great bow window, has a deep, coved ceiling of gilded, interlacing Gothic arches. Sir Charles Cockerell's bedroom, in an octagonal pavilion attached to the main house by an arcade, was fitted up to emulate an Indian tent supported on ornamental spears.

The exotic interiors of Daylesford and Sezincote, though they exhibited a certain Neo-Classical restraint, acted as precursors to the Anglo-Indian interiors of the Prince Regent's Brighton Pavilion and the many exotic Regency interiors which followed. Though Cockerell's career needs more study, it is safe to say that his sensitive and studied eclecticism, with its revival and mixing of multiple historical styles, predicted many of the important trends of the later 19th century.

PATRICK A. SNADON

Biography

Born in London, 6 January 1753. Related through his mother to the diarist Samuel Pepys; his father was John Cockerell and his son was the architect C.R. Cockerell (1788–1863). Pupil of Sir Robert Taylor from 1768; took over Taylor's office after his death in 1788. Appointed District Surveyor, St. George's, Hanover Square, 1774;

clerk of works, Tower of London, 1775; clerkship, Newmarket, 1780–82. Appointed Inspector of Repairs to the Admiralty, 1785; surveyor, Foundling and Pulteney estates, London, 1788 (resigned 1808); obtained surveyorship, Victualling Office, 1791; surveyorship, East India Company, 1806; surveyor, sees of Canterbury and London, 1811–19; surveyor, St. Paul's Cathedral, 1811–19. Co-founder, Architects' Club, London, 1791. Pupils included the architects B.H. Latrobe, William Porden, C.H. Tatham, and C.R. Cockerell. Died in London, 12 July 1827.

Selected Works

A collection of Cockerell's drawings is in the Royal Institute of British Architects, London. A full list of Cockerell's architectural commissions appears in Colvin 1995.

Interiors

1786–88 Admiralty House, London (building and interiors)

1788–93 Daylesford House, near Moreton-in-Marsh, Gloucestershire (building and interiors; some furniture by Ince and Mayhew): Warren Hastings

c.1793–95 Middleton Hall, Carmarthenshire, Wales (building and interiors): Sir William Paxton

1799–1802 St. Margaret's Church, Westminster (repairs and redecoration)

c.1805 Sezincote House, near Moreton-in-Marsh, Gloucestershire (building and interiors): Sir Charles Cockerell

Further Reading

There is no monograph on S.P. Cockerell; information relating to his interior work can be found in articles on specific houses.

Betjeman, John, "Sezincote, Moreton-in-Marsh, Gloucestershire: Its Situation, History, and Architecture Described" in *Architectural Review*, 69, 1931, pp.161–66

Catalogue of the Drawings Collection of the Royal Institute of British Architects, Farnborough: Gregg, 1969

Colvin, Howard M., *A Biographical Dictionary of British Architects, 1600–1840*, 3rd edition New Haven and London: Yale University Press, 1995

Ginger, Andrew, "Daylesford House and Warren Hastings" in *Georgian Group Annual Report*, 1989

Hussey, Christopher, "Sezincote, I, II" in *Country Life*, LXXXV, 13 and 20 May, 1939, pp.502 and 528

Hussey, Christopher, *Late Georgian, 1800–1840* (English Country Houses, vol.3), 1958; reprinted Woodbridge, Suffolk: Antique Collectors' Club, 1984

Norton, Paul F., "Daylesford: S.P. Cockerell's Residence for Warren Hastings" in *Journal of the Society of Architectural Historians*, 22, 1963, pp.127–33

Watkin, David, *The Life and Work of C.R. Cockerell*, London: Zwemmer, 1974

Cocktail Cabinets

The cocktail cabinet was a fashionable novelty in the domestic furnishing of the inter-war period. It brought a whiff of urbanity, sophistication and glamour into middle-class life, where its entry into the modern suburban lounge marked the acceptance of drinking as a respectable social activity. The cocktail cabinet was not gender specific, unlike its ancestor, the more general drinks cupboard, which formerly would have demarcated the room it occupied as distinctively masculine.

The cocktail drink itself emerged together with the night-clubs which opened following World War I. According to H. Craddock, the barman at the London Savoy Hotel who compiled *The Savoy Cocktail Book*, it was named after a legendary Mexican princess called "Cocktel" and made of a mixture of different ingredients mostly with alcoholic content. To the "bright young set" the cocktail meant emancipation and a hedonistic lifestyle, but to the older more traditional generation it represented an affront to British values of class and taste. Gin, the main ingredient in a "martini" cocktail was thought of as a cheap working-class drink only associated with the "public" – the pub, while vermouth had dubious Latin connotations. Both the wine cupboard and the "smokers cabinet" had respectable and gentlemanly precedents, but a cocktail cabinet was seen as conspicuous consumption and in poor taste. Middle-class manuals preached against the "vulgar" show of large quantities of drinks and tobacco, claiming it made the home too much like a public bar.

With the greater emancipation of women, precipitated by World War I, drinking and smoking were no longer considered an exclusively male indulgence. The custom of separating the sexes after a dinner party, leaving the men to smoke and drink in the dining room, became as outdated as the smoking-jacket. In the inter-war period the informal cocktail party became a popular and fashionable alternative to the dinner party. By the 1930s the cocktail cabinet was a much more acceptable and general piece of furniture, displacing the inherited Victorian parlour piano and standing as a symbol of modernity alongside the gramophone.

Because of its lack of pedigree the cocktail cabinet has not been categorised as an antique and therefore has been of little interest to collectors. Examples only started to be cited in books and added to museum collections towards the end of the 1960s when a return of interest in historic styles began to include the 20th century. Art Deco revivalism was presaged by a Musée des Arts Décoratifs exhibition in Paris – *Les Années Vingt Cinq* held in 1965. While traditionalists and strict Modernists have not considered the cocktail cabinet of any interest, some 20th-century historians have recognised it as a worthy subject, both as a typical item of inter-war decorative art as well as an aspect of modern material culture. In *Art Deco* (1968), just one in a large wave of publications coinciding with the fashion for Art Deco interior design, Bevis Hillier refers to the inter-war period as "the cocktail age", and features on the back cover an illustration of a "cocktail cabinet" made from a converted grandfather clock, demonstrating a humorous disregard for good taste.

The cocktail cabinet took a variety of forms – often as a two-tier arrangement of cabinet over a cupboard or on a stand, legs, plinth or single column. Sometimes it was discreetly built-in to a wall or a range of fitments; occasionally it was incorporated into a trolley to make it mobile. Styles varied from the severely functional with nothing but the grain of a natural wood veneer to relieve modern square lines, to the flamboyantly ornamental with fluted and contoured fronts. The craftsmanship available in the inter-war period and modern styling also combined fashionable blonde veneers with contrasting geometric marquetry. More lavish examples were covered completely in mirrored glass. The typical cocktail cabinet interior was mirrored and illuminated by concealed lighting, fully fitted with an array of chrome cocktail shakers, the characteristic triangular stemmed glasses, decorative cherry picks and

Cocktail cabinet in maple, 1935

lemon squeezers. While some flamboyantly flouted their purpose in modern styling or were jokey conversions of unlikely pieces such as grand pianos, others were discreetly disguised to match the style of the interior, fashioned in modern or reproduction styles. Cabinets designed for the purpose could disguise their function discreetly behind closed doors or announce it in different ways. Hosts could enjoy orchestrating the opening of the "bar" at an opportune moment to reveal an illuminated peach mirrored interior in its full chrome and cut-glass glory. Some versions included gadgets that slid an inside section into view as a flap was lowered providing a glass topped "bar" to mix the drinks, imitating in miniature the dramatic effect of the cinema organ rising from the pit.

The cocktail cabinet was reintroduced in a new form in the 1950s following the austerity period after World War II when nothing but the most functional furniture was produced. As soon as a competitive market reappeared and once the relaxation of design restrictions would allow, the furniture industry looked for new "selling points" to attract the popular market. As a result a small version of a cocktail cabinet was integrated with the sideboard to become a standard part of the dining set. More often than not the cabinet remained empty because people couldn't afford to keep it stocked with drinks or preferred to go to the pub for a drink. Nevertheless it alluded to a glamour consumed through the cinema but not previously made available for inclusion in the working-class home. With the growing popularity of DIY (do-it-yourself), Spanish holidays, the availability of plastic coated laminates and quilted leatherette, the built-in cocktail bar became a fixture in many 1950s and 1960s living rooms.

The recent revival of cocktail bars and drinks has been for consumption in public and has not stimulated the production of a new type of domestic cocktail cabinet, with the consequence that it now remains a period piece.

JUDITH ATTFIELD

See also Art Deco; Streamlining and Moderne

Further Reading

For a history of cocktail cabinets see Attfield 1990.

Attfield, Judy, "Pram Town" in Judy Attfield and Pat Kirkham (editors), *A View from the Interior*, London: Women's Press, 1989

Attfield, Judy, "The Empty Cocktail Cabinet" in Tim Putnam and Charles Newton (editors), *Household Choices* (exhib. cat.: Victoria and Albert Museum, London), London: Middlesex Polytechnic, 1990

Battersby, Martin, *The Decorative Twenties*, 1969; revised by Philippe Garner, New York: Whitney Library of Design, and London: Herbert, 1988

Battersby, Martin, *The Decorative Thirties*, 1969; revised by Philippe Garner, New York: Whitney Library of Design, and London: Herbert, 1988

Hillier, Bevis, *Art Deco of the 20s and 30s*, 1968; revised edition, London: Herbert, 1985

Klein, Dan, *All Colour Book of Art Deco*, London: Octopus, 1974

MacDonald, Sally and Julia Porter, *Putting on the Style: Setting Up Home in the 1950s* (exhib. cat.), London: Geffrye Museum, 1990

Codman, Ogden, Jr. 1863–1951

American architect and interior decorator

Ogden Codman, Jr. was one of the most prestigious American interior designers of his generation. His clients included some of the wealthiest and most influential East Coast families of the time and his name has become closely associated with what has been termed the opulence of the "gilded age" of decoration. He was also an important arbiter of taste and together with the author and society hostess Edith Wharton he wrote *The Decoration of Houses* (1897) which was the model for many subsequent primers on interior design. The dominant influences on his work were historical, and he borrowed freely from 18th-century French, English and American styles. His interiors were light and informally elegant, and featured white painted panelling, simple flowered fabrics and cream-coloured antique furniture. At a time when the dominant fashion was for over-elaboration and density in both decoration and furnishings, this style was classically simple and restrained.

Codman had already established a reputation as an architect and decorator among an élite clientele when he collaborated with Wharton on *The Decoration of Houses*. The two had met in 1893 when Mrs. Wharton (as he always addressed her) hired him to update the interiors of her seaside cottage, Land's End, in Newport, Rhode Island. Codman, who was born into an old Boston family, was in his mid-thirties and was

Codman: drawing room of his own house, 7 East 96th Street, New York, 1912

already worldly and sophisticated, having spent his adolescence in Europe. Upon his return, he lived with John Hubbard Sturgis, a Boston-area architect who was also his uncle and, as the designer of Land's End, may have provided his nephew with an introduction to Wharton. Codman also studied a number of 18th-century American houses, including his ancestral home outside of Boston, The Grange, which he would later remodel and redecorate. To this informal education in architecture, he added a year of study at the Massachusetts Institute of Technology school of architecture and an apprenticeship with two architectural firms. In a sense, this was a typical architectural education for his era, mixing formal institutional study with the older traditions of apprenticeship and first-hand, observational knowledge. He was able to open his first office in Boston by 1891 and followed with New York and Newport offices in 1893. The range of European and early American references which he gained during these years stayed with him in all his design work and is clearly reflected in his collaboration with Wharton who had similar sensibilities about weaving American and European influences into her life.

Over the next two decades, Codman went on to build or remodel several dozen residences in Boston, Newport, New York, Washington, and Providence, but he was never fully accepted into the first rank of architects. Instead, his lasting impact emanates from his notable interior design work, such as the ten bedrooms for Cornelius Vanderbilt II at The Breakers, Newport (1895), the interiors for John D. Rockefeller's Kykuit, Pocantico Hills, New York (1908), the Martha Codman House, Berkeley Villa, Newport (1910), and the Archer M. Huntington House, New York 1913–15 – for the last two of which he also designed the building – and several collaborations with Elsie de Wolfe between 1910 and 1920.

These designs reflect the assumptions and precepts presented as a design philosophy to a broader public in *The Decoration of Houses*: a call for decoration that is simple and structural, creating a harmonious unity while simultaneously referencing selected historical styles of American and European houses of the 16th, 17th, and 18th centuries. The book is nothing short of a primer, with every interior element addressed in short chapters ranging from rooms in general, to walls, doors, windows, fireplaces, entrances, halls, stairs, special function rooms and even a section on "bric-a-brac".

It is tempting to consider Codman's and Wharton's principles as a proto-modern aesthetic: an insistence that houses are "mechanisms for living", that "the supreme excellence is simplicity" and that architecture and interior design should be unified, but to do so misses the essence of their generation. For over twenty years, interior decoration in America had meant domestic trappings of mass-produced items ranging from rugs and draperies to ornamental china, statues, oriental motifs with Colonial Revival furniture, much if not all of which was given popular credence by the displays of 1876 Centennial Fair in Philadelphia. Wharton called other interior designers "upholsterers" who "crammed every room with curtains, lambrequins, jardinières of artificial plants, wobbly velvet covered tables littered with silver gew-gaws, and festoons of lace on mantle pieces and dressing tables". Both Codman and Wharton, helped sweep away this vision by encouraging an aesthetic of simplicity and restraint as good taste, of interior design as "appropriate" to the sense of the building, its functions and its owners. Much of what they proclaim, with great authority, as "good design" must be seen as an antidote to this earlier idiom. While they professed to be addressing a broad American public, the tone and examples employed clearly articulated their vision for a late 19th-century wealthy lifestyle whose social customs and large staffs were waning by the early years of the modern era. This new aesthetic would reach a mass audience only through the trickle-down effects of followers and popularizations over the next few decades. Toward the end of his life, Codman gave a major archive of his office papers and drawings to the Metropolitan Museum of Art in New York and his substantial catalogue raisonné of French châteaux – which encompasses 36,000 photographs and 400 notebooks – to the French Ministry of Cultural Affairs.

By 1920, Codman, who had made numerous trips to Europe to procure furnishings for his clients, closed his New York office and returned to live out his life in France. As if to sum up his life, he designed and built a grand château, La Leopolda, near Villefranche (1929–31), combining aspects of Italian and French house and garden design, quoting historical motifs, and employing a sense of classical order and proportion that were the hallmark of his career.

While it has never been entirely clear what role each played in the writing of *The Decoration of Houses*, 25 years later Codman remembered that he did the work and Wharton just "polished" the sentences. While they did not always agree on issues of design (she once referred to one of his buildings as a "mud hut"), they maintained a correspondence into the 1930s when they lived only 80 miles apart as expatriates in southern France. Whatever their individual contributions, the book remained a standard text for the next 40 years, only succumbing to the change in lifestyles and means of production that occurred after World War II.

RONALD J. ONORATO

See also de Wolfe; Interior Design

Biography

Born in Boston, 19 January 1863. Educated in Dinard, France, where his family lived from 1874–84; returned to America in 1882; studied architecture at the Massachusetts Institute of Technology, Cambridge, 1883–84. Married Leila Howard Griswold, 1904. Apprenticed to various Boston architectural firms, including Andrews, Jacques and Ranton, 1886–87; practised independently in Boston as an architect and interior decorator from 1891; opened a New York office in 1893 and moved to New York permanently shortly thereafter. Published *The Decoration of Houses* with Edith Wharton, 1897. Executed many architectural projects and commissions for interiors during the 1890s and early 1900s. Closed the New York office in 1920 and spent the remainder of his life in France. Died at the Château de Grégy, Brie-Comte-Robert, near Paris, 8 January 1951.

Selected Works

Codman's personal papers, early architectural drawings, and family records are in the Codman Family Manuscripts Collection, Society for the Preservation of New England Antiquities, Boston. Business records, later architectural drawings and records are in the Department of Prints and Photographs, Metropolitan Museum of Art, New York. Other architectural plans and drawings are in the Avery Library, Columbia University, New York, and additional archival material is in the Ogden Codman Manuscript Collection, Boston Athenaeum.

Interiors

1893–94	Land's End, Newport, Rhode Island (redecoration and interiors): Edith Wharton
1894	Harold Brown House, Newport, Rhode Island (interiors): Harold Brown
1895	The Breakers, Newport, Rhode Island (decoration of 2nd and 3rd floor rooms): Cornelius Vanderbilt II
1896–97	Nathaniel Thayer House, Edgemere, Rhode Island (interiors)
1900	Villa Rosa, Newport, Rhode Island (building and interiors): E. Rollins Morse
1900	170 Beacon Street, Boston (interiors): E. Howard Gay
1904	High Wall, Prides Crossing, Massachusetts (building and interiors): Oliver Ames
1910	Berkeley Villa, Newport, Rhode Island (building and interiors): Martha Codman
1910	131 East 71st Street, New York (alterations and interiors): Elsie de Wolfe
1913–15	Archer M. Huntington House, New York (building and interiors)
1916	Hautbois, Jericho, Long Island (building and interiors): Walter Maynard
1929–31	La Leopolda, Villefranche-sur-Mer, France (house and interiors): Ogden Codman, Jr.

Publications

The Decoration of Houses, with Edith Wharton, 1897; reprinted 1975

Gravestone Inscriptions and Records of Tomb Burials in the Central Burying Ground, Boston Common, and Inscriptions in the South Burying Ground, Boston, 1918

La Leopolda: A Description, 1939

Further Reading

The most recent comprehensive survey of Codman's work, including a chronology, full bibliography and list of commissions, appears in Metcalf 1988.

Codman, Florence, *That Clever Young Boston Architect*, Augusta, ME: privately printed, 1970

Craig, Theresa, *Edith Wharton: A House Full of Rooms: Architecture, Interiors, and Gardens*, New York: Monacelli Press, 1996

Doumato, Lamia, *Ogden Codman, Jr.: A Bibliography*, Monticello, IL: Vance, 1989

Drake, Stuart A., *Ogden Codman, Jr., 1863-1951*, MA thesis, Cambridge, MA: Harvard University, 1973
Jones, Stephen, "Understated Style" in *Country Life*, 183, 8 June 1989, pp.292–95
Lewis, Arnold, James Turner and Steven McQuillan, *The Opulent Interiors of the Gilded Age*, New York: Dover, and London: Constable, 1987
Lewis, R.W. B., *Edith Wharton: A Biography*, New York: Harper, and London: Constable, 1975
Menz, Katherine Boyd and Donald McTernan, "Decorating for the Frederick Vanderbilts" in *Nineteenth Century*, vol.3, pt.4, Winter 1977, pp.44–50
Metcalf, Pauline C., "Interiors of Ogden Codman, Jr. in Newport, Rhode Island" in *Magazine Antiques* (USA), vol.118, pt.3, September 1980, pp.486–97
Metcalf, Pauline C., "Ogden Codman and The Grange" in *Old Time New England*, 71, 1981, pp.68–83
Metcalf, Pauline C., "Victorian Profile: Ogden Codman, Jr.: A Clever Young Boston Architect" in *Nineteenth Century*, vol.7, pt.1, Spring 1981, pp.45–47
Metcalf, Pauline C., "Elegance without Excess" in *Bulletin of the Preservation League of New York*, Winter 1986
Metcalf, Pauline C. (editor), *Ogden Codman and the Decoration of Houses*, Boston: Godine, 1988
Monkhouse, Christopher, "Napoleon in Rhode Island" in *Magazine Antiques*, January 1978, pp.190–202
Sutton, Denys, "The Sharp Eye of Edith Wharton" in *Apollo*, 103, January 1976, pp.2–12
Wilson, Richard Guy and others, *The American Renaissance, 1876–1917* (exhib. cat.), New York: Brooklyn Museum, 1979

Coffee Tables

The coffee table is emblematic of the rise of popular modern styling in the mid-20th century domestic interior. The feature that most distinguished a typical "coffee table" from the more generic "occasional" table, apart from its larger size and lower height, was the conspicuousness of its central position in front of easy chairs and settees, forming the nucleus of the sitting area. During the height of its popularity its most common form was rectangular and low, echoing the horizontal emphasis of modern architecture. Just as the cocktail cabinet was the set-piece denoting modernity and sociability in the 1930s suburban house, the coffee table was its equivalent in the 1950s "Contemporary" idiom of domestic decor.

It has been claimed that the coffee table was an American invention. Its popularity in the United States may in part be explained by the adoption of a less formal open-plan lifestyle where it formed the focus of the living room and replaced the dining table for informal eating in front of the television.

By the mid-1940s, among the more progressive style-conscious American furniture manufacturers, the coffee table had become a vehicle for novel and experimental designs. The sculptor Isamu Noguchi's version designed for the Herman Miller Company was clearly intended to give an abstract aesthetic dimension to the modern interior. With its asymmetrical carved wood base and heavy plate glass amorphous top, it clearly set out to transcend mere furniture and make its presence felt as a piece of sculpture. In contrast, Charles Eames's 1946 moulded plywood range of coffee tables were rather like large trays on legs and the ultimate in functionalism. Both his and Noguchi's designs were displayed at the Museum of Modern Art (MOMA) in New York in 1946, which thus acknowledged the coffee table as a modern furniture type and securing a place for these tables as design classics of the Modern Movement.

Popular American versions appeared in geometric as well as the organic free-forms translated from abstract modern art, and in every imaginable shape from boomerangs, amoebas, kidneys, and blobs, to guitars and artists' palettes. It is not surprising that the exuberant variety of its popular forms should have been condemned as excessive by Edgar Kaufmann, American "good design" guru and Director of MOMA. In the conclusion to *What is Modern Interior Design?*, one of a series of didactic MOMA publications he wrote in 1952, Kaufmann exemplified the perfect interior as one in which: "We see no fur throws, no free-form coffee tables".

In Britain the craze for coffee bars and Italian cappuccino coffee coincided with the popularization of the coffee table during the 1950s, though it had started to appear in a variety of guises and versions much earlier on in the period immediately following World War II. Firms that could not get the necessary permits or materials to manufacture furniture while timber was in short supply from 1945, were eased back into peace-time production by being allowed a "Fancy Goods and Domestic Equipment" licence. This permitted them to make small items such as trays and mirrors which only required modest quantities of timber. With the addition of thin, spindly legs using a minimum amount of wood "off-cuts" and waste, a tray could become a small table. The firm of David Joel produced just such an item with a glass top displaying a souvenir map of the American landings in Normandy, and called it a "coffee table" hoping to appeal to the American market.

Another early example, was the *Cloud Table*, designed by Neil Morris and produced by H. Morris and Co. of Glasgow from 1946, exploiting the design possibilities of plywood. It consisted of an abstract amoeba-shaped top faced in walnut on turned tapered legs. An ornamental striped effect was obtained by the bevelled edge exposing the natural colours of the contrasting wood laminations. Morris also designed the *Long John* which came complete with a foam rubber cushion so that it could be adapted from a coffee table to a low bench.

Other early British versions of coffee tables in the "Contemporary" style selected from the Council of Industrial Design's Index of approved designs, appeared in 1952 in Noel Carrington's *Design and Decoration in the Home*, claiming to be the first survey of interior design after the restrictions of the Utility Period. Apart from a rather restrained "boomerang"-shaped table designed by A.M. Lewis for Liberty, it also featured a "nest of coffee tables" designed by Hulme Chadwick for Frank W. Clifford Ltd. Although in style these small tables were presented as the new fashionable "coffee table" type with their brass-tipped tapered "toothpick" legs, the fact they appeared in a "nest" suggests an adaptation of a traditional form. It was occasional tables that habitually came in sets; while the coffee table was essentially a single piece. The concept of suites of furniture conformed to a more traditional pattern of furnishing where the nest of occasional tables was positioned discreetly, strategically but unobtrusively stowed away against a wall or alongside an easy chair to be brought out when needed for perching tea cups or ash trays. The more typical coffee table demanded attention and defined the centre "hot" spot of the room – the focus of social conviviality, leisure and relaxation.

The first G-Plan catalogue produced by Gommes of High Wycombe in 1954 included a transitional coffee table, significantly labelled a "cocktail table" and accessorized with a typical 1930s chrome cocktail shaker and triangular stemmed glasses. Its revolutionary break from tradition offering single "units" rather than complete sets and suites of furniture, aimed at the younger, more fashion-conscious generation proved to be very popular.

Hille was another, among the more up-market firms, to break from tradition in the post-war period and go on to produce avant-garde design. Their designer Robin Day, who distinguished himself by winning a MOMA competition in 1949, was responsible for some of the most forward-looking developments in English furniture design during the 1950s and 1960s. Day turned out a number of coffee table designs for Hille, in a variety of geometric forms from triangles to ovals, using moulded plywood and highly figured veneers on simple inset timber or metal-rod legs.

By the mid-1950s the coffee table had become a standard item of furniture in the British domestic interior. Its presence marked the notional centre point of the seating area, suggesting conversation and social interaction rather than the more introverted and traditional arrangement of easy chairs radiating around the fireplace. During the 1960s when central heating took over from the fireplace, it was the coffee table that almost replaced the hearth as the altar to domesticity. It defined the room as "Contemporary" and provided a space for the display of the accoutrements of ideal modern home living, style awareness and leisure through the display of items such as coasters, "coffee table books", exotic house plants, statuettes and ornaments.

The symptomatic nature of the coffee table, which made it a signifier of modernity in the domestic landscape, was evident in its appearance as one of the central motifs of the "Homemaker" dinner service brought out by Ridgway Potteries in 1955. With its striking surface pattern of black on white featuring a boomerang coffee table with black tapered legs, "Homemaker" proved popular enough to continue to be sold by Woolworths until 1967 and has since become a mid-century period icon among collectors.

Alongside the consumption of modern style furniture, period and reproduction furniture has continued to be popular in Britain to the present day. Although the coffee table is strictly a modern type-form, it has been adapted to match in with reproduction style furniture, acquiring in the process such travesties as cabriole legs and "antique" finishes. Among the many hybrids, one of the more recent is the stripped pine "genuine antique" coffee table made out of old kitchen tables with cut down legs, which have in turn been reproduced. Although no longer at the forefront of furnishing fashion, coffee tables continue to be popular items in today's domestic interiors.

JUDITH ATTFIELD

See also "Contemporary" Style

Further Reading

Burns, Mark and Louis DiBonis, *Fifties Homestyle*, New York: Perennial, and London: Thames and Hudson, 1988

Garner, Philippe, *Contemporary Decorative Arts from 1940 to the Present Day*, Oxford: Phaidon, and New York: Facts on File, 1980

Greenberg, Cara, *Mid-Century Modern: Furniture of the 1950s*, New York: Harmony, 1984; London: Thames and Hudson, 1985

Hine, Thomas, *Populuxe: The Look and Life of America in the 50s and 60s, from Tailfins and TV Dinners to Barbie Dolls and Fallout Shelters*, New York: Knopf, 1986; London: Bloomsbury, 1987

Jackson, Lesley, *The New Look: Design in the Fifties*, London and New York: Thames and Hudson, 1991

Ward, Mary and Neville, *Living Rooms*, revised edition London: Macdonald, 1970

Colefax & Fowler

British interior decorators; established 1934

Colefax & Fowler is one of the foremost British interior decorating firms of the 20th century and their work has had a significant impact on many other designers and manufacturers in the post-war period. The company's style was strongly influenced by three figures: Sybil (or Sibyl) Colefax, Nancy Lancaster, and the decorator John Fowler. Together, they created a distinctive house style that has since become synonymous with the English Country House style. This style combined a respect for tradition with an emphasis upon comfort and simplicity, and by adapting the choicest elements from the decorative styles of the past – predominantly the 18th and early 19th centuries – its exponents sought to create an ambience of gracious and timeless elegance. Several other firms have also promoted this style but none as successfully as Colefax & Fowler; their work has come to epitomise the best of English taste and enjoys a reputation for quality and discernment worldwide.

The origins of the company date back to 1933 when the society hostess, Sybil Colefax embarked upon a career as a "lady decorator among friends" in collaboration with certain Bruton Street antique dealers. In this respect, Colefax was following the example set by Elsie de Wolfe in New York. De Wolfe had played a pioneering role in promoting the involvement of women in the world of interior decoration by establishing herself as the first professional female decorator in the period leading up to World War I. Like de Wolfe, Colefax courted clients from the upper eschelons of society and entertained many of London's fashionable and intellectual elite at Argyll House, her home in Chelsea. Cecil Beaton described her drawing room in his book *The Glass of Fashion* (1954), noting the use of pale, mixed colours such as almond, light green, grey and opaque yellow, and admiring its simplicity and attention to detail.

In 1934, Sybil founded Colefax & Co. with premises at 29 Bruton Street, and the company gained in stature with the arrival of the promising young decorator John Fowler in 1938. Having trained as a decorative painter, Fowler had run the painting studio of the home furnishings section of the department store Peter Jones from 1931, before establishing his own

Colefax & Fowler: Nancy Lancaster's living room, Haseley Court, Oxfordshire, c.1959

business in premises in Chelsea in 1934. In contrast with the Modernist aesthetic of the 1930s, Fowler's personal style was characterized by simplicity and an eye for period furniture which had been sharpened during his association with the antique dealer Margaret Kunzer. He endorsed the use of traditional English furnishing materials such as Norfolk rush matting and striped cottons, and he also had a liking for the Toiles de Jouy printed cottons from France. In describing his work, he adopted the expression "pleasing decay" which was coined by John Piper in the *Architectural Review* of 1947, and commissions included schemes at Blenheim for the Duchess of Marlborough.

In 1944 the company moved to larger premises at 39 Brook Street – the house designed and owned by the 19th-century British architect Sir Jeffry Wyatville. Sybil Colefax retired due to illness and the financially ailing company was bought by Ronald Tree as a parting gift for his wife Nancy, the future Mrs. Lancaster, after their divorce. The American-born Nancy Lancaster acknowledged the importance of the role played by the company's principal decorator by revising the firm's name to Colefax & Fowler, and in 1950 the two began the creative professional partnership which consolidated the company's house style.

Described as "the unhappiest unmarried couple in England", Lancaster and Fowler had quite different, but complementary approaches to interior design. Brought up in the American South, Nancy had no patience with the painful formality and inconvenience of English aristocratic life and she introduced the concept of comfortable living into England in the two stately homes – Kelmarsh in Northamptonshire, and Ditchley Park in Oxfordshire – that she and Ronald Tree had occupied. She also had a strong dislike for showy sumptuousness and she used fresh colours to emphasise architectural features and faded fabrics and furniture to create a mood of timelessness and casual elegance. Frequently, the furnishings were left to fade naturally in sunlight but in some cases, the ageing of fabrics was precipitated by dyeing them in tea. Into this classic period environment were integrated the comforts of modern services and she created connecting bathrooms which were carpeted and furnished as extensions of the bedroom. Her drawing rooms at Ditchley, Haseley and her London flat in Avery Row became showpieces for the Colefax & Fowler style, mixing grandeur and elegance with understatement and comfort.

The emphasis on understatement in Lancaster's work countered the more flamboyant aspects of Fowler's work. Fowler's decorative schemes of the 1950s were founded on his sense of colour and on his instinctive balancing of contrasts, of pattern, texture and scale. Thus, he avoided co-ordinating colour schemes and relied instead on juxtapositions of related tones. His palette consisted of distinctive yellows, blues, pinks, apricots and natural greens, and he mixed large-scale floral designs with sprig patterns, checks and stripes. Fabrics played an especially important role in his interiors, and curtains, pelmets and upholstery were often treated extravagantly. An early predilection for the Regency style resulted in the use of generously swagged pelmets hung from exaggeratedly large poles, while his enthusiasm for the Baroque-style draperies illustrated in the 17th-century interiors engraved by Daniel Marot broadened his repertory of curtain treatments and informed his use of decorative braids, fringes and tassels to emphasise form. Fowler's work has sometimes been likened to that of a couturier, especially in its attention to detail, and his friendship with the society dress designer Hardy Amies may well have influenced features such as his use of contrasting piping, his fondness for pleating and gathering in upholstery and on straight-sided lampshades, and his technique of covering round tables with fabrics that fell in loose folds down to the floor. His strong sense of pattern also informed his interest in picture-hanging and his formula of arranging pictures in symmetrical groupings with the frames suspended by decorative cords from rosettes, bows and tassels has been repeated in numerous other decorators'schemes. The inspiration for his work lay in the past, many of the motifs for his fabrics and wallpapers were taken from period samples found in the houses he was decorating. He described himself not as a designer but as an "architectural decorator", and if his approach to history was sometimes more intuitive than archaeological, it nevertheless proved enormously appealing and strongly influenced later attitudes to decoration and period styles.

The novelty of Colefax & Fowler's approach lay in their ability to enhance period features, while at the same time adapting them to suit the greater informality of contemporary lifestyles. This approach quickly found favour with the English aristocracy, and the firm's clientele included many wealthy and titled customers who occupied historic houses themselves and who were eager to preserve their heritage. Among their more prestigious commissions were Daylesford, Wilton, Tyninghame and Chequers, and the decoration of the Audience Room at Buckingham Palace.

Fowler's knowledge of and sensitivity to period styles also attracted the attention of the National Trust and from the late 1950s he became increasingly involved, on a personal basis, with the restoration of interiors in their care. His work at Clandon, Surrey, from 1968, represents one of the most comprehensive schemes with which he was associated and illustrates his concern to capture the feeling of the room in the period to which it was restored, even if this was sometimes at the expense of historical accuracy. Thus, in the Saloon at Clandon, he added a third shade of blue to complement the two original tones uncovered in paint-scrapes, and the overmantel was marbleised to match the fireplace. Such "improvements" would clearly be unacceptable to purists today, but Fowler's work nevertheless did much to foster new standards of professionalism within the Trust and encouraged the use of skilled craftsmen and firms with long traditions of specialist work. Moreover, his frequent use of paint-scrapes foreshadowed the more scientific investigation of historic colours developed by Trust consultants such as Ian Bristow, while Fowler's emphasis upon the importance of historic lifestyles has strongly influenced the studies of "authentic decor" pioneered by the scholar Peter Thornton. From 1969, following his retirement from Colefax & Fowler, Fowler's energies were exclusively devoted to assisting the Trust. He worked on more than 25 of their houses and his book, *English Decoration in the 18th Century*, written with John Cornforth and published in 1974 (revised 1978), represents a summary of his long experience in this sphere and remains a standard textbook on historic interiors and design.

John Fowler died in 1977 but Colefax & Fowler has remained remarkably true to the spirit of his style. Now run by Tom Parr, who has been chairman since 1960, the company has built up an important archive of designs for wallpapers, fabrics and trimmings gathered from previous commissions. Many of these are now manufactured commercially, and Fowler's *Old Rose* pattern is one of their best-selling chintzes. Historical sources also remain the key to the new collections of designs which include the adaptation of period wallpapers from the archives of the Musée des Arts Décoratifs, Paris. However, the company's market has broadened considerably, and having started out as a small partnership offering a professional decorating service to an exclusive elite, its commissions now include jets and yachts as well as large town and country houses. And it provides an increasing number of textiles and wallpapers for sale to a wider public in its retail outlets in England and abroad.

In recent years, Colefax & Fowler has continued to expand. With three showrooms in London, they also have outlets in New York, Paris, and Sydney. The company was floated on the London Stock Exchange in 1988, and a year later it acquired Jane Churchill, a more commercial producer of traditional-style designs, and Kingcome Sofas, the manufacter of upholstered seating.

The crisp sprigged wallpapers, floral chintzes and blue and gold floral carpets that exemplify Colefax & Fowler's work have been copied by many other manufacturers and designers and the company has spawned many imitators. The influence of Fowler himself resonates in the work of those who were closely associated with him in the 1950s, including that of the decorators Nina Campbell in London, and Mario Buatta and Keith Irvine in New York. Indeed, Colefax & Fowler has been particularly successful in America and their style is acknowledged in numerous interiors by East Coast decorators such as Mark Hampton and David Easton that have responded to their clients' nostalgia for an ennobling past. But the company has also been influential in more commercial spheres. Features such as elaborate curtain treatments, flounced lampshades and tablecloths, and ubiquitous chintz and sprig designs are now widely available from firms like Laura Ashley, and cheaper, mass-produced versions of the Colefax & Fowler house style are a familiar sight in many urban professionals' homes.

CLAIRE BRISBY

See also Interior Design

Further Reading

An authorized history of Colefax & Fowler appears in Jones and Dickson 1989. For additional information on the career of John Fowler see Cornforth 1983 and 1985.

Anscombe, Isabelle, *A Woman's Touch: Women in Design from 1860 to the Present Day*, London: Virago, and New York: Viking, 1984

Becker, Robert, *Nancy Lancaster: Her Life, Her World, Her Art*, New York and London: Random House, 1996

Calloway, Stephen, *Twentieth-Century Decoration: The Domestic Interior from 1900 to the Present Day*, London: Weidenfeld and Nicolson, and New York: Rizzoli, 1988

Cornforth, John, "John Fowler (1906–77): 1. Prince of Humble Elegance; 2. Comfort and Pleasing Decay" in *Country Life*, CLXXIII, 28 April and 19 May 1983, pp.1092–95 and 1308–11

Cornforth, John, *The Inspiration of the Past: Country House Taste in the Twentieth Century*, London: Country Life, and New York: Viking, 1985

Dickson, Elizabeth, "English Elegance" in *Elle Decor*, Winter 1990, p.38

Hampton, Mark, *Legendary Decorators of the Twentieth Century*, New York: Doubleday, and London: Hale, 1992

Jones, Chester and Elizabeth Dickson, *Colefax & Fowler: The Best in English Interior Decoration*, London: Barrie and Jenkins, and Boston: Little Brown, 1989

McLeod, Kirsty, *A Passion for Friendship: Sibyl Colefax and Her Circle*, London: Joseph, and New York: Penguin, 1991

Morris, Susan, "Design for Living: A History of the Interior Designers Colefax and Fowler" in *Antique Collector*, November 1993, p.74–75

"Nancy Lancaster" obituary in *The Times* (London), 20 August 1994

Smith, C. Ray, *Interior Design in 20th-Century America: A History*, New York: Harper, 1987

Colombo, Joe 1930–1971

Italian painter, architect, sculptor and designer

Joe Columbo was one of Italy's foremost modern designers. Trained as an artist at the Accademia di Belle Arti di Brera, and subsequently as an architect at the Politecnico di Milan, he was initially active as an avant-garde painter and sculptor, joining the fine art group Movimento Nucleare, and the Concrete art movement between 1951 and 1954. He later worked as a designer of both furniture and interiors. Bold and innovative, his designs were simple, flexible, brightly coloured, functional and appropriately futuristic for the times. His work was highly regarded by both critics and other design professionals, and was notable for its uncompromising modernity, its use of new materials, especially plastics, and for its development of modular and mass-produced living units.

Colombo became interested in furniture, lighting and interior design in the early 1960s. He had already been working as an architect for several years and it was no doubt his experience of working on the interiors of buildings that prompted his involvement in design. This involvement also gave him an opportunity to experiment with new materials and to put into practice his ideas about the domestic environment. Accordingly, he opened his own office in Milan in 1961 and worked as a freelance designer for a number of progressive furniture manufacturers including La Linea and La Rinascente, lighting companies such as O'Luce, and the specialist plastics firm, Kartell and Bayer Plastics. Success was not long in

Colombo: Total Furnishing Unit, 1972, comprising four units: kitchen, bathroom, cupboard and bed-and-privacy unit; shown at the exhibition *Italy: The New Domestic Landscape*, Museum of Modern Art, New York

coming. In 1963 he received an award from the Italian National Institute of Architecture for his interiors for the Hotel Pontinental in Sardinia, and in 1967 the New York department store, Gimbel's, held a special Joe Colombo week promoting some of his most popular works. These included his ergonomic series of *Universale* chairs which had injection-moulded plastic seats and adjustable legs to suit both adults and children, and his *Spider* light which was the first lamp to use the halogen bulb for non-industrial purposes.

Colombo's background in sculpture clearly influenced his approach to furniture design and encouraged experiments that were to revolutionize the function and appearance of furniture in the 1960s. His *Tube* chair of 1970, for example, transcended traditional ideas of what a chair should be and blurred the distinctions between furniture and sculpture. It consisted of four tubes that could either be clipped together, or rolled inside one another, to modify the arrangement of seating or for storage. It was made of white plastic polyurethane and had mustard acrylic upholstery.

It was Colombo's championing of new materials such as injection-moulded plastics and plastic laminates that was especially influential. The historian Penny Sparke has described the impact that this had on Italian furniture design: "The shiny surfaces and voluptuous curves they [Colombo's furniture] created symbolically transformed plastic from a cheap into a luxury material, and earned [Italy] a reputation as the first country to find a truly modern idiom. No longer was it merely an imitation of other more expensive materials, but one with its own seductive aesthetic – determined for the most part by its own production process" (Sparke, 1988). By way of example, she illustrates the ABS stacking chair, designed for Kartell in 1965. The bright emerald green colour and sleek contours of this chair denote both modernity and sophistication. Furthermore, the form has been shaped by its production; the hole in the back which gives the chair its distinctive appearance is also essential to the release of each chair in the vacuum-forming process.

From the late 1960s Colombo became interested in new concepts of domestic organisation. In collaboration with the designer Ignazia Favata, he developed a system of co-ordinated, flexible structures, composed of four mobile units – "Kitchen", "Cupboard", "Bed and Privacy" and "Bathroom" – which created a "total" living environment. Based on space travel research, these units were intended to meet every domestic need and although the appearance of the individual components seems somewhat futuristic today, the overall concept was undeniably practical. A version of this system was installed in Colombo's own apartment in Milan, and his experiments culminated in the "Rotoliving Unit" exhibited posthumously at the Museum of Modern Art's exhibition, *Italy: The New Domestic Landscape*, held in New York in 1972. By this time, Colombo's interest in individual furnishings and plastics had been replaced by a concern with the utopian, humanistic needs of environmental design that examined what he perceived as three key relationships: that between the city and the dwelling unit, between green spaces and the dwelling unit and between the dwelling unit and man.

Design could never therefore exist in a vacuum. Its social and technological roles were always of paramount importance, and in his work for interiors Colombo was determined to achieve the most effective use of materials to create objects that could be mass-produced without aesthetic compromise. His work was never simply decorative, and right up to his untimely death at the age of 41, he strove to make his designs relevant to the age in which he lived.

JANICE WEST

Biography

Born Cesare Colombo, in Milan, 30 July 1930. Studied painting at the Accademia di Belle Arti di Brera, to 1949; studied architecture at the Politecnico di Milan, 1950–54. Active as a painter and sculptor, Milan, 1950–55; joined the Movimento Nucleare (founded by Enrico Baj and Sergio Dangelo 1951); founder-member, Arte Concreta group, Milan, 1955. Took over the family electrical equipment business, 1959; ran his own design office, Milan, 1962–71. Designed furnishings, lighting, ceramics and electrical appliances for many firms including Arflex, Elco, Kartell, O'Luce, La Rinascente, Candy and Zanotta. Exhibited at numerous national and international exhibitions including the Milan Triennale 1954, 1964 and 1967, and Museum of Modern Art, New York, 1972. Received many awards including: IN/ARCH Award, National Institute of Architecture, Rome, 1963; Silver Medal, Milan Triennale, 1964 and 1967; Compasso d'Oro, Milan, 1967; Association of Industrial Designers Award, New York, 1968. Died in Milan, 30 July 1971.

Selected Works

The Joe Colombo Archive, containing designs, correspondence and business records, is in the Joe Colombo Studio, Milan. Collections of Colombo's furniture and lighting are in the Stedelijk Museum, Amsterdam, and the Metropolitan Museum and Museum of Modern Art, New York.

1963 Hotel Pontinental, Golfo dell'Asinara, Sardinia (interiors and furniture)
1964 *Elda 1005* Easy Chair: Comfort
1965 *Spider* Lamp: O'Luce
1966 *Supercomfort 1000* Easy Chair: Comfort
1966–67 Magnetic Furniture System: La Rinascente
1967 *Universale* Seating: La Rinascente
1967–68 *Box 1*, combined bedroom / study / living room furniture unit: La Linea
1968 Eurodomus Exhibition, Turin (display stand and furniture)
1970 *Tube* Chair: Zanotta
1971–72 *Total Furnishing Unit* ("Rotoliving Unit") Museum of Modern Art, New York (exhibition display and furniture)

Publications

New Form Furniture: Japan, with Sori Yanagi and others, Tokyo, 1970

Further Reading

A chronology of Colombo's works, together with a full list of his writings, exhibitions, awards and an extensive bibliography, appears in Favata 1988.

Ambasz, Emilio (editor), *Italy: The New Domestic Landscape* (exhib. cat.), New York: Museum of Modern Art, 1972
Bellini, A., "Interview mit Joe Colombo" in *MD Möbel Interior Design*, January 1966, pp.135–36
Fagone, Vittorio (editor), *I Colombo: Joe Colombo 1930–1971, Gianni Colombo 1937–1993*, Milan: Mazzotta, 1995
Favata, Ignazia, *Joe Colombo and Italian Design of the Sixties*, London: Thames and Hudson, and Cambridge: Massachusetts Institute of Technology Press, 1988
Grassi, Alfonso and Anty Pansera, *Atlante del Design Italiano: 1940–1980*, Milan: Fabbri, 1980
Hiesinger, Kathryn B. and George H. Marcus III (editors), *Design Since 1945* (exhib. cat.), Philadelphia: Philadelphia Museum of Art, and London: Thames and Hudson, 1983
Joe Colombo Retrospective (exhib. cat.), New York: Galliera Gallery, 1976
Modern Chairs, 1918–1970 (exhib. cat.: Whitechapel Gallery, London), London: Lund Humphries, and Boston: Boston Book and Art, 1971
Sparke, Penny, *The Design Sourcebook*, London: Macdonald, 1986
Sparke, Penny, *Italian Design, 1870 to the Present*, London: Thames and Hudson, 1988; as *Design in Italy*, New York: Abbeville, 1988

Colonial Revival

The colonial past and the tradition of colonial design have exerted a strong and persistent influence on American society since the War of Independence. During the late 19th and early 20th centuries, however, that historical awareness dramatically increased. In a style now defined as Colonial Revival, designs from the 17th and 18th centuries, as well as those from the Federal era, were revisited, reproduced, and adapted for modern life.

The origins of the Colonial Revival rested in the economic change and social upheaval of the 19th century. Many Americans worried that the nation heroically created by the Founding Fathers was in a state of decay. Industrialization, immigration, and the moral crisis of the Civil War all threatened the established order and national sense of identity. The Colonial Revival represented a material response to these changes, and reflected a longing for the security and simplicity of an idealized past.

One of the earliest manifestations of the Colonial Revival was a campaign begun in the 1850s to restore George Washington's home, Mount Vernon. The Colonial Revival expressed tremendous reverence for the leaders of the Revolution, and great value was assigned to places they knew and objects they used. Tourists connected with the spirit of the Founding Fathers by visiting their homes, and taking part in a more virtuous past made palpable in honest, hand-crafted surroundings.

In its association of morality with handcraftsmanship, the Colonial Revival may be seen as part of the Arts and Crafts movement. The colonial era was lauded as a time of artisans' pride in their independent creation; objects made by colonial craftsmen came to symbolize the dedication and democratic fervor of their time. Colonial designs became prescriptions for moral living, purifying and elevating everyday life through a connection to America's exalted youth. The evils of modern, industrial life could be reformed by recreating the domestic environment of the past.

Furthermore, new immigrants could be taught America's history and democratic values by visiting restored colonial homes. In the 1920s museums across the country opened permanent exhibitions of Americana – the Metropolitan Museum in New York, for example, opened its American wing in November 1924 with displays of early furniture – and promoted the artistic, historic, and didactic value of their collections. Colonial objects were tools for creating a shared national culture, helping assimilate visitors into the American tradition.

The International Centennial Exposition in Philadelphia in 1876 helped to spread the popularity of the Colonial Revival. Exhibitions included the New England Farmer's Home with "colonial kitchen," a display that purported to represent early American domestic life. Costumed guides led throngs of visitors through an interior including a hearth, settle, spinning wheels, and furniture with historical associations. The colonial kitchen was juxtaposed with a Modern Kitchen, which attracted relatively little notice. Indeed, the Colonial Revival may be seen as a reaction against Victorian household goods. Critics dismissed modern furnishings as fussy, poorly-made copies of European designs. Historical eclecticism was condemned, and Americans were urged to decorate in an indigenous style suited to their colonial heritage.

Clarence Cook, a leading proponent of the Household Art movement, praised the simplicity and usefulness of colonial furniture, and his *The House Beautiful* (1878) contained a view of Charles McKim's restoration of the 18th-century Robinson house kitchen in Newport, Rhode Island. The Robinson kitchen featured a Chippendale mirror, William and Mary caned armchair, Windsor chair, and enormous fireplace surrounded by tiles over a brick hearth. McKim was an early advocate of colonial architecture, and with his partners William Rutherford Mead and Stanford White, a leading proponent of the Shingle Style. An American adaptation of the English Queen Anne Style, the Shingle Style is closely allied to the Colonial Revival. Shingle Style houses were nostalgic, often using broad living halls, large chimneys, inglenooks, beamed ceilings, sash windows, and fanlights. Simplicity, amplitude, and a sense of comforting shelter characterized the Shingle Style and Colonial Revival architectural shell.

Hearths like that designed by Charles McKim became virtual icons of the Colonial Revival. Obsolete in an age of central heating, the open fireplace became the symbolic heart of the house. Its welcoming warmth and light created a sense of security and romance, an escape to a more simple time. Period literature described the fireplace as the family altar.

Other Colonial Revival objects assumed a heightened importance, including tall-case clocks and spinning wheels. "My Grandfather's Clock," an acclaimed song from 1876, helped popularize the outdated timepiece at the time of the Centennial. Its ponderous ticking and old-fashioned form evoked both present and past time. Similarly, the spinning wheel became a potent symbol of the past, and was virtually ubiquitous in the Colonial Revival house. Advocates of Household Art championed the spinning wheel. In *Stepping Stones to Happiness* (1897), Harriet Prescott Spofford promoted the "clear beauty" of the wheel, describing it as "a real object for an artist." The Daughters of the American Revolution, an elite genealogical society, adopted the spinning wheel as part of its insignia, reflecting its position that American women fought the Revolution by spinning and weaving homespun for their fighting men. Even fragments of the spinning wheel were valued, as shown by a group of armchairs manufactured in the 1880s from old spinning and flax wheels parts: flyers decorated the crestrails, wheels formed the backs, and trestles were incorporated into the legs.

Inevitably, as admiration for the Colonial period grew, new industries emerged to meet the demand for Colonial furnishings. Makers of colonial adaptations and reproductions, practitioners of colonial style handicrafts, and antiques dealers all profited from and disseminated the Colonial Revival. The earliest pieces of reproduction furniture date from the mid-century when, according to one contemporary observer, "Mayflower furniture [was] becoming common" (Rhoads, 1977). By the 1880s, the taste had become more widespread and a writer in the *Decorator and Furnisher* of November 1883 declared that "the Chippendale or Colonial Style is a favorite in new designs for interiors" and that it had ousted the fashion for Eastlake and Early English furnishings. By this date reproductions of colonial furniture were being produced across the country, from large midwestern factories like the Century Furniture Company of Grand Rapids, Michigan, to smaller shops like Sypher and Company, and Ernest Hagven of New York City. Among the best-known reproductions were those produced by Wallace Nutting Period Furniture of Framingham, Massachusetts.

Nutting, a retired Congregational minister and self-styled "poet-capitalist," championed the Colonial Revival. He collected rapaciously, and used antiques as models for his high-quality reproductions. His collection also appeared in photographs he produced of colonial interiors. The photographs were tremendously popular, and helped expose Americans to the precepts of Colonial Revival decoration. Nutting focused on the design and historical associations of early American furnishings rather than their means of production. However, other figures in the Colonial Revival combined their interest in colonial objects with a rediscovery of traditional handcrafts. Of particular note are the embroideries and furniture produced in Deerfield, Massachusetts. In 1896 local women established the Society of Blue and White Needlework.

They traveled through the Connecticut River Valley studying colonial embroidery, seeking to preserve and replicate the patterns and skills of the past. All the Society's embroidery initially was stitched with blue and white linen thread, yet soon other natural dyes were introduced. The success of the Society spurred the creation of the Deerfield Society of Arts and Crafts, which produced hand-crafted reproduction furniture. The blue and white of the Deerfield embroideries were typical of Colonial Revival color schemes; Colonial Revival decorators favored subdued tones, such as pale yellow, pearl gray, and the historically evocative "Williamsburg blue."

Unlike other passing fashions, the Colonial Revival did not fade away with the advent of the new century. It was still popular for much of the first two decades of the 20th century and although decorators like Elsie de Wolfe professed herself bored with the style in 1915, she nevertheless furnished some of the bedrooms in Stanford White's Colony Club with colonial reproductions. Modernist critics, however, were more categorically hostile. Lewis Mumford's *Sticks and Stones* (1924) attacked the style as inappropriately historicist, as did the champion of Modernism, Henry-Russell Hitchcock. But Colonial Revival has refused to disappear. It continues with great vitality, informing modern life, and fulfilling Americans' need to articulate a continuity with their past. It remains the most popular historical style in contemporary home decoration.

MADELINE SIEFKE ESTILL

Selected Collections

Examples of Colonial Revival furnishings and interior schemes can be viewed in the period rooms at the Winterthur Museum, Delaware, and Colonial Williamsburg, Virginia.

Further Reading

For comprehensive and stimulating histories of the Colonial Revival see Axelrod 1985 and Rhoads 1977, both of which include detailed bibliographies.

Axelrod, Alan (editor), *The Colonial Revival in America*, New York: Norton, 1985

Burke, Doreen Bolger and others, *In Pursuit of Beauty: Americans and the Aesthetic Movement* (exhib. cat.: Metropolitan Museum, New York), New York: Rizzoli, 1986

Harmon, Robert B., *The Colonial Revival in American Architecture: A Brief Style Guide*, Monticello, IL: Vance, 1983

Harmon, Robert B., *The Shingle Style in American Architecture: A Brief Style Guide*, Monticello, IL: Vance, 1983

Kaplan, Wendy, "R.T.H. Halsey: An Ideology of Collecting American Decorative Arts" in *Winterthur Portfolio*, 17, 1982, pp.43–53

Kaplan, Wendy (editor), *"The Art That is Life": The Arts and Crafts Movement in America, 1875–1920* (exhib. cat.: Museum of Fine Arts, Boston), Boston: Little Brown, 1987

Marling, Karal Ann, *George Washington Slept Here: Colonial Revivals and American Culture, 1876–1986*, Cambridge, MA: Harvard University Press, 1988

Monkhouse, Christopher, "The Spinning Wheel as Artifact, Symbol, and Source of Design" in Kenneth L. Ames (editor), *Victorian Furniture*, The Victorian Society in America, 1983

Rhoads, William B., *The Colonial Revival*, New York: Garland, 1977

Rossano, Geoffrey L., *Creating a Dignified Past: Museums and the Colonial Revival*, Lanham, MD: Rowman and Littlefield, 1991

Roth, Rodris, "American Art: The Colonial Revival and Centennial Furniture" in *Art Quarterly*, 27, 1964, pp.57–81

Scully, Vincent J., Jr., *The Shingle Style and the Stick Style: Architectural Theory and Design from Richardson to the Origins of Wright*, revised edition New Haven: Yale University Press, 1971

Colonna, Edward 1862–1948

German designer and decorator

Circumstances conspired to deprive Edward Colonna of his position as a pioneer in the development of the curvilinear Art Nouveau style. His seminal publication, *An Essay on Broom-Corn*, dating from 1887, a revolutionary booklet of meandering Art Nouveau designs produced while he was working in Dayton, Ohio, was in the style of modest, small-scale publication which had come to be associated with the Arts and Crafts Movement rather than with the international avant-garde with which Art Nouveau was to be identified. And almost at once nearly the entire stock of booklets was destroyed in a fire in the storage warehouse. Colonna's wavy, interlaced designs are inspired by the stalks of corn used to make a corn-broom (a besom or rustic farmyard broom). Strongly reminiscent of the designs of Louis Sullivan, the Chicago architect, the booklet predates experimental work of a very similar kind by architects in Belgium like Victor Horta and Henry van de Velde. Colonna's ideas seem to have inspired the "Broomcorn" table silver designed for Tiffany & Co. by T. Curran in 1890. Colonna was to remain essentially faithful to this organic curvilinear inspiration throughout the greater part of his career, only turning to a modified geometric manner in keeping with French Art Deco in the 1920s.

Errors of biographical information in the Paris Salon catalogues even deprived Colonna of his true nationality and it was only with the series of articles published by Martin Eidelberg in the late 1970s that the details of his life and career were unearthed. Colonna was born near Cologne in Germany, and after architectural studies in Brussels, which he commenced at the very early age of 15, he went to New York at the age of 20 to work in Louis Comfort Tiffany's decorating company Associated Artists. In 1885 he was appointed chief designer at the Barney & Smith Manufacturing Company, a factory making railway wagons in Dayton, Ohio. From there he went to Montreal, where he set up his own studio and supplied railway wagon designs for the Canadian Pacific Railway. It was towards the end of his period in Montreal that he made his first jewellery.

Meanwhile the great entrepreneur Siegfried Bing (German-born but by now established in Paris) was investigating American decorative art for his book, *Artistic America*, which was published to coincide with the opening in 1895 of his Parisian gallery. The famous Maison de l`Art Nouveau at 22 rue de Provence was to give its name to the very movement with which Colonna's name is associated. Bing was already an admirer of Sullivan and Tiffany, and of Edward Moore, the inventive director of Tiffany & Co.; Colonna was among the rising young designers to be recruited by Bing for L`Art Nouveau, along with Eugène Gaillard and Georges de Feure.

For Bing, Colonna produced a flow of scintillating Art Nouveau designs. The metalwork and jewellery stand out as notably controlled among the female heads and sinuous bodies with flowing hair and drapery from the more flamboyant of his contemporaries, for example, René Lalique and Georges Fouquet. The furniture mounts are exquisite jewel-like pieces, but still perfectly appropriate to their purpose. The same control is evident in the furniture, ceramics, wallpaper and textile designs. Colonna might start with a flower motif, but the development of his designs was always in the direction of complete abstraction.

Bing's venture was extensively reported in design and decoration periodicals and the display at the Paris Centennial Exhibition in 1900 was regarded as a triumph for the gallery and its designers. Colonna created a salon complete with furniture and all its decoration. Bing had urged him to "eschew the bulky, box-like forms of British and Belgian furniture and instead to apply a modern decorative vocabulary to the light, graceful forms of Louis XV", an acknowledgment of the Rococo inspiration that is at the heart of the Art Nouveau style.

After the celebrity of his Parisian career Colonna returned in about 1902 to obscurity in North America – from 1903 his work ceases to feature in decorative art publications – but he was very influential in America where he made silverware designs for leading Arts and Crafts-inspired manufacturers like Marcus & Co., confirmation of the duality of the *Broom-Corn* essay. In 1925 Colonna returned to France and settled in the south, where he spent his time in collecting and dealing and carving in alabaster. He died in Nice in 1948.

Colonna's work is well represented in museum collections (particularly the Musée des Arts Décoratifs in Paris), mainly by individual ceramics and metalwork. There is a strong emphasis on the jewellery, the area on which his modern reputation principally rests. A collection of his designs for jewellery is preserved in the Public Library in Newark, New Jersey. For his work as an interior designer it is best to consult the illustrations recording Bing's presence at the Paris 1900 exhibition, where the effect of the complete ensemble can be appreciated. Gabriel Weisberg's 1986 exhibition catalogue includes a full bibliography of these sources, and reproduces photographs of the salon from the Bing archive material in the library of the Musée des Arts Décoratifs. The bibliography also lists all of Martin Eidelberg's invaluable articles on Colonna.

CHARLOTTE GERE

See also Art Nouveau; Bing

Biography

Born Edouard Klönne in Müllheim, near Cologne, 27 May 1862, the son of a bookdealer. Studied architecture in Brussels, 1877–81. Moved to New York, 1882; worked with Louis Comfort Tiffany (1848–1933) 1883; worked with the architect Bruce Price, 1884–85; chief designer for Barney & Smith Manufacturing Company, Dayton, Ohio, 1885. Married Louise McLaughlin, daughter of the architect James McLaughlin, 1887. Moved to Montreal, 1888, and worked for the Canadian Pacific Railway. Active as a designer of furniture, decoration and textiles from the late 1880s. Moved to Europe, 1898, and worked for Siegfried Bing's L'Art Nouveau gallery, 1898–1903; designed furnishings for Bing, jewellery for Henri Vever, and ceramics for Gérard, Dufraissex & Abbot; returned to Canada, 1902, and worked as an interior decorator and antique dealer; returned to Europe 1908; moved back to New York, 1913. Settled in Nice, France, 1925, and worked sporadically as an antique dealer and carver of alabasters but was increasingly confined to bed through ill health. Published an influential work, *Essay on Broom-Corn*, New York, 1887. Died in Nice, 14 October 1948.

Selected Works

An important collection of Colonna's designs, drawings, photographs, letters and personal memorabilia is in the Newark Museum and Library, New Jersey. Examples of Colonna's furniture and ceramics are in the Dayton Art Institute, Ohio. Additional items of ceramics and of jewellery are in the Musée des Arts Décoratifs, Paris, and examples of textiles are in the Museum of Applied Art, Vienna.

Interiors

1885–88	Barney & Smith Manufacturing Company (interiors of railway carriages)
1888–90	Canadian Pacific Railway (interiors of railway carriages)
1890	Van Horne House, Montreal (remodelling of interiors, including the main salon): William Van Horne
1900	Exposition International, Paris (salon and music room for S. Bing's pavilion)
1903	King Edward Hotel, Toronto (decoration and furnishings)

Publications

An Essay on Broom-Corn, 1887

Further Reading

The only monograph, and the most comprehensive account of Colonna's career, is Eidelberg 1983, which includes numerous references to primary and secondary sources. A useful introduction to Colonna's designs for jewellery appears in Gere 1975.

Brunhammer, Yvonne and others, *Art Nouveau: Belgium / France* (exhib. cat), Houston: Rice University Institute for the Arts, 1976

Duncan, Alastair, *Art Nouveau Furniture*, London: Thames and Hudson, and New York: Potter, 1982

Eidelberg, Martin, "Edward Colonna's 'Essay on a Broomcorn': A Forgotten Book of early Art Nouveau" in *Connoisseur*, 176, February 1971, pp.123–30

Eidelberg, Martin, *Edward Colonna* (exhib. cat.), Dayton, OH: Dayton Art Institute, 1983

Fish, Michael, "A Farewell Tour of the Van Horne Mansion" in *Habitat* (Canada), XVI, 3, 1973, pp.22–24

Gere, Charlotte, *European and American Jewellery, 1830–1914*, London: Heinemann, 1975; as *American and European Jewelry, 1830–1914*, New York: Crown, 1975

Krekel-Aalberse, Annelies, *Art Nouveau and Art Deco Silver*, London: Thames and Hudson, and New York: Abrams, 1989

Silverman, Debora L., *Art Nouveau in Fin-de-Siècle France: Politics, Psychology, and Style*, Berkeley: University of California Press, 1989

Weisberg, Gabriel P., *Art Nouveau Bing: Paris Style 1900* (exhib. cat.: Smithsonian Institution, Washington, DC), New York: Abrams, 1986

Commodes

According to Thomas Sheraton, who defined the commode in his *Cabinet Dictionary* of 1803, the word was "from the French and signifies a woman's head dress. In cabinet making it applies to [a] piece of furniture chiefly for ornament, and to stand under a glass in a drawing room ... It is sometimes used more agreeably to its derivation, and signifies such commodes as are used by ladies to dress at, in which there is a drawer

Commodes: Thomas Sheraton design for a commode, 1794

fitted up with suitable conveniencies for the purpose ...." His definition captures the merging of functional and decorative purpose that this piece was devised to serve.

Like all storage units, the commode is based on the coffer, or trunk. Its development can be traced to the late 16th century, when English and Continental cabinet-makers developed the chest-of-drawers by approaching the box from the front rather than the top, and dividing its volume into accessible units held in place by runners or plates. In France, their *commodité*, or convenience, was not recognized linguistically until the early 18th century. The oldest French reference dates to 1708, when the Duc d'Antin mentioned that he had seen two commodes that Guillemart was making for the king's bedroom at Marly, and that each cost 310 *livres*. The name took some time to catch on. Writing a letter about presents given at court in 1718, the Duchesse d'Orléans felt constrained to tell a friend that, "A commode is a big table with big drawers [and] beautiful decorations." An object that so combined beauty and function was irresistible, however; by 1740, commodes were as popular with the bourgeoisie as with the nobility.

This development coincided with the rise of the curvilinear Rococo, and the revolution in form sparked new construction methods. As forms became increasingly plastic, cabinet-makers often found it necessary to commission scale models from a sculptor. Templates cut to conform to the model were laid along the fronts and sides of the piece as it was carved from the plank, to ensure that the complex curves of these areas would be bilaterally identical.

These techniques allowed such innovative cabinet-makers as Antoine Gaudreau and Charles Cressent to transform the commode's appearance. Marble tops became standard. Legs were lengthened and curved, straight fronts and sides made parabolic. Drawers concealed the frame that held them in place. The number of full-length drawers rarely exceeded two, half-width drawers disappeared, and drawers could be concealed by doors. Most important, fronts were decorated as unbroken areas, covered with floral marquetry in exotic woods, and overlaid with interlacing ormolu arabesques.

By 1745, decoration had overtaken function. Moved from the bedroom to the salon, the commode was generally surmounted by a mirror, and used to balance the mass of the fireplace and mirrored overmantel. When straight lines returned in the Neo-Classical Louis XVI period, commodes were sometimes combined with *encoignures* (corner cabinets), and given convex ends. At the same time, the façade was typically arranged in three vertical sections of geometric marquetry outlined with ormolu or brass moulding, drawers were concealed behind doors, and the piece was brought lower to the floor.

Although England had had the chest-of-drawers since the late 16th century – Lawrence Abelle had built a "cubborde of boxes" in Stratford-upon-Avon in 1595 – the appearance of the decorative and explicitly labeled commode coincided with the emergence of "French taste" around the middle of the 18th century. The best known examples are provided by Thomas Chippendale in his *Gentleman and Cabinet-Maker's Director*, the third edition of which (1762) illustrated two "French commodes," four "French commode tables," five "commode tables," and a comparable "buroe dressing table." All had a decidedly Rococo appearance, although their fronts were more serpentine than parabolic, and their sides generally straight. Commodes remained in fashion throughout the Late Georgian period, the dominant form being that of the demi-lune (half-round). Most provided some storage with narrow drawers set into the apron or with shelves hidden by concave doors; others were purely decorative, such as the elaborately veneered unit attributed to John Linnell executed for Osterley Park. The vogue ebbed toward the end of the century. George Hepplewhite, in the *Cabinet-maker and Upholsterer's Guide* (3rd edition, 1794), showed one "commode" and one "commode dressing table," both part of the "dressing apparatus." Sheraton included a "commode" and a "dressing commode" in *The Cabinet-Maker and Upholsterer's Drawing Book* (3rd edition, 1802); defined it in the *Cabinet Dictionary*, as we have seen, offering two examples; and omitted it from the incomplete *Cabinet Encyclopedia* (1804).

The term commode was not applied to furniture in America, but it can be related on both formal and functional levels to the lowboy. Highly decorated examples from Philadelphia workshops resemble commodes produced by craftsmen in the Dauphiné and other French provinces.

REED BENHAMOU

Further Reading

For a detailed and scholarly study of Commodes see Wood 1994 which includes a long introductory survey of the subject and numerous references to primary sources.

Bedel, Jean (editor), *Dictionnaire illustré des Antiquités et de la brocante*, Paris: Larousse, 1983

Havard, Henry, *Dictionnaire de l'Ameublement et de la Décoration depuis le XIIIe siècle jusqu'à nos jours*, 4 vols., Paris, 1887 ("Commode")

Hayward, John Forrest, *Chests of Drawers and Commodes in the Victoria and Albert Museum*, London: HMSO, 1960

MacQuoid, Percy and Ralph Edwards, *The Dictionary of English Furniture*, revised edition, 3 vols., 1954; reprinted Woodbridge, Suffolk: Antique Collectors' Club, 1983

Symonds, R.W., "English Commodes in the French Taste" in *Connoisseur*, January 1957, pp.16–20

Verlet, Pierre, *French Furniture of the Eighteenth Century*, Charlottesville: University Press of Virginia, 1991 (French editions 1956, 1982)

Wood, Lucy, "English Commodes in the French Taste in the Lady Lever Art Gallery" in *Magazine Antiques* (US), CXLIII, June 1993, pp.902–11

Wood, Lucy, *Catalogue of Commodes: Lady Lever Art Gallery*, London: HMSO, 1994

Conran, Terence 1931–

British entrepreneur and interior designer

Terence Conran has made his passions into his life's work. And in the spheres of design, food and retailing he has been without doubt one of the most influential figures of his age. Indeed, when many of the cultural movements of the last decades are examined there is often a thread that leads back to Conran. His inspirations have included the Bauhaus, English Arts and Crafts, Danish Modernism, Mediterranean exuberance, ethnic styles, peasant simplicity, and truth to materials. He has applied these enthusiasms exhaustively in all his businesses and, in so doing, he has transformed the way millions of people live.

Born into a middle-class family, he was brought up in Esher, Surrey, and was educated at Highfield and Bryanston public school. He went on to study textile design at London's Central School of Art in 1949 and 1950, where he was influenced by Eduardo Paolozzi, with whom he shared a fascination for popular culture. Showing an early preference for the world of commerce over academia, he was tempted away from the Central School before graduating by a job offer from the architect and designer Dennis Lennon. Between 1950 and 1952 he produced textiles designs, the magazine *Rayon and Design*, furniture for the Ridgeway Hotel, Lusaka, and murals for the Festival of Britain. Following an exhibition in Simpson's *Ideas and Objects for the Home*, he founded Conran and Company, manufacturing furniture and accessories.

A first visit to France in 1953 was to prove extremely influential, laying the foundations for the Francophilism that has remained with him ever since. In November 1953 he was part of a joint venture in a cafe called The Soup Kitchen which marked his debut in the catering industry; a year later he went solo when he designed and opened The Orrery restaurant in 1954.

1956 saw the founding of The Conran Design Group working in graphics, exhibitions, furniture and interiors including the shop Bazaar, for Mary Quant. Other ventures of that year were the establishment of Conran Contracts and Conran Fabrics, and the production of Conran's first book, *Printed Textile Design*. He has since gone on to publish numerous books on furnishings and interiors and *The House Book* of 1974 became a best-selling guide to home design.

Increasingly frustrated with the resistance that his work encountered among retail buyers, Conran and his third wife Caroline decided to open their own shop and on 11 May 1964, Habitat opened its doors at 77 Fulham Road, South Kensington. Habitat's aim was to provide low-priced furnishings in a simple Modern style. It was an immediate success, striking exactly the right note with a younger generation anxious to distance themselves from post-war austerity and eager for a new kind of lifestyle. After two years of good trading, Conran opened a second branch in Tottenham Court Road, which was followed by a rapid expansion across the country.

In 1968, the Conran businesses merged with Ryman, the stationery and office equipment group. Habitat mail order was launched in 1969. But by 1970 deep fissures had opened up in the newly joined company causing Conran to buy back

Habitat from Ryman although he had to leave behind Conran Contracts, Fabrics, Design, and the Thetford factory. He founded the design practice, Conran Associates, and the Neal Street Restaurant in 1971. By 1972, the Habitat chain was 12 strong and in the following November, The Conran Shop was born on the site of the original Habitat showrooms. Conran took Habitat to Paris in 1973, and then on to New York in 1977 where it traded as Conran's. The turn of the decade saw Habitat with 47 stores and in 1981 it was floated on the London stock exchange to become a Public Company. A further spurt of growth was achieved through a merger with the retail giants, Mothercare.

During 1983, Habitat-Mothercare acquired Heal's, and Conran Octopus was formed as a joint publishing venture with Paul Hamlyn. The ill-fated Butler's Wharf property development was initiated at the same time and the Conran Roche architectural practice was formed with Fred Roche. Terence Conran was knighted in the New Year's Honours list.

With none of his energy or enthusiasm for new projects dimmed, Conran bought Michelin House with Paul Hamlyn in 1985, and in 1986 Habitat Mothercare merged with British Home Stores to form Storehouse which also included NOW, and Richard Shops, and which had a combined turnover in excess of £1 billion. The Conran Shop expanded into Michelin House in 1987 but elsewhere the company's financial problems were mounting. Storehouse's profits had dropped by 29 per cent by 1988 and there were several attempted takeovers. After a two-year period of wrangling and in-fighting, and many failed attempts to reverse the group's dwindling performance, Conran stood down as Chairman of Storehouse in 1990 and bought The Conran Shop out of the group.

At an age when he might not unreasonably have been expected to retire from business, Conran decided to begin again. And with the singular determination that he had always shown he started to build up a restaurant business which went on to include Bibendum, The Oyster Bar, the Blueprint Cafe, Le Pont de la Tour, La Cantina, The Chop House, Quaglino's, and the enormous Mezzo. At the same time he expanded The Conran Shop group, established a Contracts division, started an architectural and design consultancy, CDP, and remained involved with the Design Museum and a variety of publishing projects. When Habitat celebrated its 30th birthday in May 1994, Conran was accorded the tribute of guest of honour and was welcomed back by the assembled throng as a returning hero.

The apparent contradictions in his nature are intelligible only when it is remembered that Conran is in every sense a Modernist. This term has become somewhat debased, but when it is understood in its original, early 20th century sense, it begins to explain how Conran can be on the one hand sybaritic and indulgent, and on the other a puritanical wielder of Occam's Razor. Modernism is also at the heart of his tenacious determination to improve the quality of people's lives through their environment in an essentially democratic manner. He has always understood just how much "Design" his public could tolerate but has never been cynical or contemptuous towards his customers. Nevertheless his involvement with first the Boilerhouse Project, and later the Design Museum, shows him to have been deeply concerned with issues relating to the education and improvement of public taste and to the promotion of high standards within design. The Boilerhouse project, funded by the Conran Foundation between 1982 and 1986, consisted of a series of changing exhibitions, temporarily housed in the Victoria and Albert Museum, that explored some of the most celebrated icons – be they designers or artefacts – of the 20th century. They provoked enormous interest and excitement among the public and professional critics and designers alike and their success led to establishment of the Design Museum, that has been housed in its own building on Shad Thames since 1989.

On a personal level, Conran can be wily and sharp-witted but he has a scrupulous honesty which derives from a totally secular moral code. He can enforce a stringency that comes close to meanness but in the next instance can be generous and thoughtful. Considering his great wealth he lives well within his means. Money has only ever been his tool, the fuel necessary to make his projects run. His twin passions are his businesses and his life, and because he has never made any clear separation between work and leisure, he can appear indefatigable. Restless when not at his desk or immersed in one of his many businesses he drives ever onward.

Despite the fact that he describes himself primarily as a designer, Conran's real skill is as an editor, having always gathered around him a team of talented devotees who share his beliefs and codes. In this sense he is a true charismatic, able to inspire loyalty and optimism in his employees, many of whom have gone on to achieve considerable success in their own right. Conran is also one of the great retail innovators of our time and many of the aspects of shopping that we now take for granted started in Habitat or one of the other businesses that he either designed or advised. The Conran Shop in London is often praised as one of the most inspiring and beautiful home furnishing shops in the world. It is also one of the principal outlets for international Modern design promoting goods that range from design classics by giants such as Le Corbusier, Marcel Breuer and Mies van der Rohe to new work by contemporary designers like Matthew Hilton, Pascal Mourgue and Philippe Starck. The success of the Fulham Road shop has spawned offshoots in Paris and Tokyo and further branches are planned in north London, Glasgow, Hamburg and other European cities.

Conran has been receptive to many diverse influences but he has nevertheless always retained a peculiarly English point of view, save in his tireless fight against what he has perceived as the impoverishment of the English visual tradition. It is all the more remarkable that a man who has no formal design qualifications and severely impaired sight in his left eye should have so shaken the taste of nations. The perceptions and practices of the British design establishment and many sections of the British public have been so fundamentally changed as a result of Conran's influence that one is reminded of the old adage that "in the valley of the blind, the one-eyed man is king".

CRAIG ALLEN

See also Good Design Movement; Habitat

Biography

Terence Orby Conran. Born in London, 4 October 1931. Educated at Bryanston School, Dorset, 1944–49; studied textile design at the Central School of Arts and Crafts, London, 1949–50. Married:

1) Brenda Davison, 1952 (divorced); 2) Shirley Ida Pearce, 1955 (divorced, 1962): two sons, furniture designer, Sebastian and clothes designer, Jasper; 3) Caroline Herbert, 1963 (separated): two sons, Tom and Edmund, and one daughter, Sophie. Textile designer for the Rayon Centre, London, 1950–51; interior designer, Dennis Lennon studio, London, 1951–52; established freelance furniture design practice, Conran and Company, and worked for many firms including John Lewis Partnership, Edinburgh Weavers, and Simpsons of Piccadilly, 1952–56; founder-proprietor (with Ian Storey) of Soup Kitchen Restaurants (London), 1953–56; founder-director (with John Stephenson), Conran Design Group, London, 1956–71: Chair of Conran Design Group from 1971; founder-director from 1964, and Chair from 1971 of Habitat furnishing stores; Joint-Chair, Ryman Conran Ltd., 1968–71; Chair, Conran Stores, Inc., since 1977; Chair, Jasper Conran fashion company, London, from 1977; Director from 1979, and Chair, 1981–83, J. Hepworth and Son, London; Chair, Habitat Mothercare Ltd., London, from 1982; Director, Conran-Roche architectural and city planning firm, London, from 1982; Chair, Conran Octopus publishing company, London, from 1983; Chair, Butlers Wharf Development, London, from 1984; Director of Michelin House Development, London from 1985, and Chairman, Bibendum Restaurant, from 1986; Director of British Home Stores plc, and Savacentre Ltd., London, from 1986. Numerous restaurants from 1986, including Quaglino's and Mezzo (1995). Founder-trustee, Conran Foundation for design and industry, from 1982, and the Design Museum, London, from 1989. Member, Royal Commission on Environmental Pollution, 1973–75; Council Member, Royal College of Art, London, 1978–81, and since 1986; Advisory Council Member, 1979–81, and Trustee since 1984, Victoria and Albert Museum, London. Awarded Presidential Medal, 1968, 1975, and Bicentenary Medal, 1983, Royal Society of Arts, London; Society of Industrial Artists and Designers Medal, London, 1980; *Daily Telegraph* / Association for Business Sponsorship award, London, 1982. Received a Knighthood, 1983; made Honorary Fellow, Royal Institute of British Architects, 1984.

Publications

Printed Textile Design, 1957
The House Book, 1974
The Kitchen Book, 1977
The Bed and Bath Book, 1978
The Cook Book (with Caroline Conran), 1980
Terence Conran's New House Book, 1985
The Conran Directory of Design (edited by Stephen Bayley), 1985
The Soft Furnishings Book, 1986
Terence Conran's France (with Pierrette Pompon Bailhache and Maurice Croizard), 1987
Terence Conran on Design (with Elizabeth Wilhide), 1996

Further Reading

For the most recent biography and account of Conran's career see Ind 1995.

Appleyard, Bryan, "The Man who Outgrew his Habitat" in *Sunday Times Magazine* (UK), 13 December 1987, pp.60–66
Bayley, Stephen, "Mr. Habitat" in *Architectural Review*, 162, November 1977, pp.287–89
Black, Misha, *Public Interiors*, London: Batsford, 1960
Faulkner, Thomas (editor), *Design 1900–1960*, Newcastle: Newcastle Polytechnic, 1976
Garner, Philippe, *Twentieth-Century Furniture*, Oxford: Phaidon, and New York: Van Nostrand Reinhold, 1980
Gosling, David and Barry Maitland, *Design and Planning of Retail Systems*, New York: Whitney Library of Design, and London: Architectural Press, 1976
Hennessy, Elizabeth, *The Entrepreneurs*, Newbury, Berkshire: Scope, 1980
Hirst, Arlene, *Metropolitan Home*, April 1990
Ind, Nicholas, *Terence Conran: The Authorized Biography*, London: Sidgwick and Jackson, 1995
MacCarthy, Fiona, *All Things Bright and Beautiful: Design in Britain 1830 to Today*, London: Allen and Unwin, 1972
Phillips, Barty, *Conran and the Habitat Story*, London: Weidenfeld and Nicolson, 1984
Wilhide, Elizabeth and Andrea Spencer, *Original Home Design: The Secret of Style on a Budget*, London: Conran Octopus, 1989

Conservatories

The modern-day conservatory which serves as an additional sitting room built onto the garden side of the house has its roots in the orangeries and glasshouses, constructed for the cultivation of exotic or out-of-season plants and fruits, that first appeared in the 17th century. These buildings used a variety of means, including warmed air flues, peat or charcoal fires and coverings of rush or woven matting, to cosset the delicate plants and were often rectangular in form with large windows to admit sunlight. John Evelyn is often cited as the first person to use the term "conservatory", which he did in 1664 when it was still fully interchangeable with orangery and greenhouse. His travels in France and Italy also revealed how the cultivation of tender plants was deeply entrenched in the social fabric of aristocratic life. Leiden Botanical Garden (1599) and the palace at Heidelberg (built by Salomon de Caus in 1619) represent early designs for winter shelters where walks could be taken accompanied by the fragrance of orange blossom and fruits. And a substantial orangery built at the Villa Aldobrandini, Frascati (before 1646), with tall shuttered windows below an upper smaller tier fitted in between the ceiling vaults, is a large and handsome structure which would have impressed itself on the procession of eminent travellers who continued to visit the villa in the late 17th and early 18th centuries.

French taste, inspired by Italian gardens, developed at Vaux-le-Vicomte and Versailles towards a unified house and garden conception to which André le Nôtre, gardener to Louis XIV, contributed so importantly. Orange trees still held pride of place in English formal gardens with continuing French influence through André Mollet at Queen Henrietta Maria's Wimbledon Manor House where a large garden house was "... fitted for the keeping of Oringe Trees". Another enthusiast, Philip Stanhope, 2nd Earl of Chesterfield, housed orange and lemon trees and winter greens in a handsome pedimented summerhouse at Bretby, Derbyshire, which was admired by Celia Fiennes on her travels in 1698. Wollaton (1696) and Chatsworth (1697) were two of many examples that must have been affected by King William's heavy tax on glass, a miscalculation that was fortunately short-lived and repealed within three years.

Several royal orangeries or glasshouses from this period are still in existence. The glasshouse at Hampton Court is in the form of a long brick and tiled-roof structure, and was designed in simple and unadorned style by Sir Christopher Wren to look southwards over the new Dutch garden laid out in William and Mary's reign. Queen Anne's orangery at Kensington Palace (1704) is a detached building and has been attributed variously to both Wren and Vanbrugh but its balanced elegance with two

Conservatory at Dudley House, Park Lane, London, 1890

circular end rooms and a linking central space leaves no reason to dispute its claim to be one of the finest buildings of its type to survive. Unlike most other orangeries of this date whose interiors were generally plain, the interior at Kensington Palace was enhanced by semi-circular columns interspersed with niches for statuary and it was regularly used by the Queen for winter promenades and supper parties.

The 18th century has been described as the golden age of the greenhouse when horticulture and botanical gardens flourished in Sweden, Germany, Holland, England, France and Italy. The influence of Picturesque theories which revolutionised British garden design in the last part of the century also helped to encourage the building of conservatories. Humphry Repton, a leading figure in the Picturesque movement, developed many ideas for classical and "Gothic" style conservatories in his *Observations on the Theory and Practice of Landscape Gardening* (1803), and an increasing fascination with nature – both wild and cultivated – encouraged an interest in breaking down the rigid distinctions between the house and its interiors and the garden outside. Many fanciful structures date from this period among the most striking being the Indian or Moghul style greenhouse and pavilion built at Sezincote, Gloucestershire (c.1805) by Samuel Pepys Cockerell which made extensive use of new techniques such as cast iron and bronze and large sheets of glass.

The manufacture of cast iron and sheet glass transformed glasshouse design by permitting improved lighting and windows and structures of much greater size. But given that glass was once again subject to heavy duties, costs were high and conservatories remained the prerogative of the very rich until the tax was repealed in 1845. Shortly before this, Joseph Paxton, then head gardener at Chatsworth House, had designed the Great Conservatory in collaboration with Decimus Burton to house the 6th Duke of Devonshire's tropical plant collection. He introduced a "ridge and furrow" glazed construction which enabled him to produce the largest glass building in existence, measuring 277 feet long, 123 feet wide and 67 feet high. Ten years later, Paxton's miraculous Crystal Palace was erected in 22 weeks using the same system and housed the 1851 Great Exhibition in Hyde Park. In this building Paxton increased the overall dimensions to 1,848 feet by 408 feet, a work of genius that made him a popular hero. Applied interior decoration was devised to a simple formula by the colour theorist and architect Owen Jones, who used three primary colours of red for the underside of the girders, yellow for the columns and blue to emphasise the recessed areas in concave surfaces.

Paxton's Crystal Palace may have been inspired by Decimus Burton's Palm House at Kew (1848) which was another vast free-standing glasshouse, and there was clearly considerable cross-fertilisation of ideas between the two men. More traditional examples of country house conservatories were built in England by members of the Wyatt architectural family, including the greenhouse at Doddington Park, Gloucestershire (1797–1817), and Wollaton Hall, Nottinghamshire (c.1804), but the Scottish Kibble Palace, designed by Boucher and Cousland in 1865 and now erected in Glasgow Botanic Garden, followed the innovative materials and style used by Burton and Paxton. The Royal Palace at Laeken, Belgium had a similarly spectacular curvilinear winter garden designed by Alphonse Balat in 1876.

The emphasis in America was on public parks and gardens, and Boston's Public Gardens contained two successive camellia houses before 1850 – a much earlier date than the conservatory in Central Park, New York of 1899. Philadelphia and Pittsburgh were among many cities to create similar "leisure centres" during the mid and late19th century, while private owners, whose enthusiasm for horticulture was spurred on by a treatise written by A.J. Downing in 1844, added their own conservatories to the mansions along the Hudson River and elsewhere.

While many of the conservatories built in the grounds of larger country homes were still primarily intended for promenading and nurturing exotic plants, the mid and later Victorian period also saw a shift away from the "gardener's conservatory" to the "architect's conservatory" which gave priority to the social uses of the room. These rooms generally led off one of the back reception rooms and were used as places for informal entertaining, smoking or as a quiet retreat. They were comfortably furnished with lightweight rattan or wicker tables and chairs, and might have parquet or tiled floors covered with Turkey carpets or rugs. And as the actual business of planting was increasingly relegated to a separate greenhouse, the greenery was confined to arrangements of potted plants. Grander versions of these domestic conservatory-living rooms could be found in the large winter gardens that were so characteristic a feature of late 19th century fashionable resorts and hotels, where afternoon tea and refreshments were served.

Arts and Crafts and Cottage Style architects of the early 20th century on the whole neglected conservatories in favour of open loggias or verandas, furnished with rustic pieces such as a dresser, settle and simple rush-seated chairs. Such spaces could be used in summer for eating or even sleeping and were ubiquitous in brick-built, vernacular-style country homes.

The current revival of the conservatory is a comparatively recent trend and dates back only to the last twenty years. It has been motivated principally by the desire to provide additional living space and once again the conservation of plants takes second place to the provision of a garden or sitting room. Separate greenhouses may provide the amateur or professional gardener with their home-grown exotic species, but garden centre pot-grown plants offer an alternative solution for immediate decorative effects. Garden room furnishings are usually light and portable with loose cushions for sofas and chairs and windows fitted with roller or Venetian blinds. But when conservatories are used as a family sitting or eating room (a situation made possible by the provision of all-year-round central heating), their furnishings may not differ greatly from those in other areas of the house.

Standard ranges of conservatories have been manufactured since the late 19th century but the number of firms involved in this trade has expanded greatly since the 1970s. Most companies produce items that can be adapted to different sites, but better results can generally be achieved by using firms that offer design by architects or other trained designers who can apply principles of proportion, unity, detail and scale in relation to the main building.

ELAINE DENBY

Further Reading

A general history of the development and uses of conservatories and greenhouses in Europe and America appears in Woods and Warren 1988 which also includes a detailed bibliography. Boniface 1982 includes numerous contemporary photographs from the late 19th century onwards as well as a concise but informative survey of the subject. For a more detailed study see Kohlmaier and von Sartory 1986 which features an illustrated catalogue raisonné of more than a hundred historic conservatories, and Marrey and Monnet 1986 which provides an excellent social history of the subject.

Boniface, Priscilla, *The Garden Room*, London: HMSO, 1982

Dickson, Elizabeth (editor), *The English Garden Room*, London: Weidenfeld and Nicolson, and Boston: Little Brown, 1986

Gere, Charlotte, *Nineteenth-Century Decoration: The Art of the Interior*, London: Weidenfeld and Nicolson, and New York: Abrams, 1989

Girouard, Mark, *The Victorian Country House*, revised edition New Haven and London: Yale University Press, 1979

Hibberd, Shirley, *The Amateur's Greenhouse and Conservatory*, London, 1878

Hix, John, *The Glasshouse*, London: Phaidon, 1996

Kerr, Robert, *The Gentleman's House; or, How to Plan English Residences, from the Parsonage to the Palace*, 3rd edition London, 1871; reprinted New York: Johnson, 1972

Kohlmaier, Georg and Barna von Sartory, *Houses of Glass: A Nineteenth-Century Building Type*, Cambridge: Massachusetts Institute of Technology Press, 1986

Koppelkamm, Stefan, *Glasshouses and Wintergardens of the Nineteenth Century*, London: Granada, and New York: Rizzoli, 1981

Lemmon, Kenneth, *The Covered Garden*, London: Museum Press, 1962

Long, Helen C., *The Edwardian House: The Middle-Class Home in Britain, 1880–1914*, Manchester: Manchester University Press, 1993

Loudon, John Claudius, *Remarks on the Construction of Hothouses*, 1817

Marrey, Bernard and Jean-Pierre Monnet, *La Grande Histoire des Serres et des Jardins d'Hiver: France 1780–1900*, Paris: Graphite, 1984

Muijzenberg, Erwin W.B.van den, *A History of Greenhouses*, Wageningen: Institute for Agricultural Engineering, 1980

Rutherford, Alison, "A Garden in the Parlour: Victorian Miniature Greenhouses" in *Country Life*, CLVII, 3 April 1975, pp.836–87

Vance, Mary, *Garden Rooms and Greenhouses: A Bibliography*, Monticello, IL: Vance, 1983

Woods, May and Arete Swartz Warren, *Glass Houses: A History of Greenhouses, Orangeries and Conservatories*, London: Aurum Press, and New York: Rizzoli, 1988

Constructivism

Russian Constructivism first emerged at the beginning of the 1920s. Over the following decade it developed into a broad and influential movement covering architecture, industrial and exhibition design, typography, theatre and cinema design, and the applied arts. The new movement actively drew artists from different disciplines who were united by a search for aesthetic ideals and artistic forms to express the social progress that was taking place in Russia after the revolution. They saw their task as the creation of a spatial environment which would organise the new way of life. The design of interiors, furniture and everyday items became essential to the creative practice of Constructivism and to the realization of an idea which saw art as a constructor of life, showing the way forward for architecture and real practical work in industry.

Vladimir Tatlin (1885–1953) occupied a central position in the development of Constructivism and he was the first to give expression to the new interior in his experimental project for the monument to the Third International (1919). Tatlin's structure symbolized a rejection of decorative form in favour of ascetic expediency and the role of engineering, technical forms and new materials in formulating the new style. The spiralling framework of the construction supported three rooms placed on top of each other – a conference hall and two centres for administration and information respectively. In his own description of these interiors, Tatlin spoke of a space that could transform itself dynamically and of multi-functional equipment. It was an idea subsequently much used by other architects.

The Working Group of Constructivists which was formed in 1921 in the Moscow Institute of Artistic Culture by A. Rodchenko, V. Stepanova, A. Gan, the brothers V. and G. Stenberg, K. Medunetsky, and K. Ioganson played a crucial role in establishing the movement. The group's theoretical treatise was written by Alexei Gan and later developed in greater detail in his book *Constructivism* (1922). The group's initial creative aspirations, which had started out as abstract aesthetic experiments with form, centred on functional design for living leading to the creation of objects for everyday use. The practice spread widely within the Higher Artistic and Technical Workshops (later Institute), an educational institution where the faculties of art, architecture and industry all came together to make experimental models of standard furniture for private houses and public buildings. Particular attention was paid to the artistic problem of form, which was considered in close connection with the social and ethical role that the object was to play in the new society.

The work of Alexander Rodchenko (1891–1956), El Lissitzky (1890–1941), Tatlin and other professors, and of their students in the Workshops, in designing furniture and other domestic objects played an important role in establishing a new type of art – that of industrial design. Their first designs were shown at the annual exhibition of 1923, and included three categories of objects: those that could be folded (a folding bed), items that performed several functions (a bed which also served as an armchair) and objects that involved movement (a moveable display window on an "endless" track). Once they had mastered the creation of new types of furniture, the Constructivists moved on to more complicated projects concerning the internal environment.

The discipline of multi-functional furniture and equipment design was taught by Lissitzky, who first introduced Europe to the term Constructivism in 1922. However, the most significant achievements in this field are linked with the work of Rodchenko in the Metalwork faculty. Furnishings for a Workers' Club, based on the use of multi-functional constructions and including standard furniture types, different sorts of moveable boards and screens for displaying posters, slogans, photographs and slides, and lamps to direct light where it was most needed, were made for the Paris Exposition Internationale des Arts Décoratifs et Industriels Modernes (1925) from drawings by Rodchenko. The fact that the furniture was painted white, black, grey and red reinforced the simplicity of the forms and the asceticism of the club's artistic interior, thereby expressing the aesthetic ideal of Constructivism.

Rodchenko actively developed the new methods for the organisation of objects in the environment in the second half of the 1920s, when he was in charge of producing different furniture designs for the many workers' clubs that were being built at the time. To popularize his ideas, Rodchenko published his designs for models and became involved in designing sets for the theatre and cinema, including *The Journalist* (1924), *The Doll with Millions* (1927), *Albidum* (1928) and the play *Inga* (1929), which showed contemporary office and living interiors. All his sets had rational furniture where every component was a carefully reworked and experimental model of the new furniture that could be folded away and used for several purposes.

Tatlin had a different approach to furniture design. In 1927 a soft bentwood chair was made under his direction. Unlike his contemporaries, who relied on industrial technology and the use of tubular steel in furniture construction, Tatlin chose to work with organic materials. The slightly elastic chair was constructed from curved switches of wood which bent to create a spring and form a chair that could support the whole body from legs to elbow and back rest. In comparison to the chairs designed by Mart Stam (1926) and Mies van der Rohe (1927), Tatlin's chair is less technological – it is assembled entirely by hand. The antifunctionalism, sculptural nature and anthropomorphism of Tatlin's forms make his relationship to material and furniture design similar to the approach adopted by Alvar Aalto.

In the early stages of the development of Constructivism, the renewal of principles of interior design was mainly linked to experimental projects and exhibition models. It was only in the mid-1920s, when real construction was resumed in Russia, that the conditions were created for the artist-Constructivists, who had worked in the field of industrial design, to join forces with the architect-innovators. Their collaboration was officially sealed in 1925, with the formation of the Society of Contemporary Architects (OSA.), which included among its members Alexander (1883–1959), Leonid (1880–1933) and Viktor Vesnin (1882–1950), Moisei Ginzburg (1892–1946), A. Nikolsky (1883–1953) and their followers, as well as a group of designers.

The "functional method" (A. Vesnin, Ginzburg) lay at the basis of Constructivism in architecture. It was an extensive programme which sought to make a building as functional and practical as possible. Having linked their art to the task of organising the necessary processes for living, the architects worked on designing houses and public buildings which would demonstrate the new social relationship and emphasise the new attitudes to life, work and leisure.

First and foremost, Constructivist architects sought to create a rational and comfortable internal environment, which would unite all the rooms with their different purposes into one single organism that was itself determined by its function. Design followed the principle of revealing the "inside on the outside": from working out a free and often asymmetrical plan of a building, its constructive basis and interior, to the exposure of its volume. In its best examples, Constructivism was able to solve architectural problems by revealing the internal structure of a building on the outside and by giving the internal space a practical and artistic interpretation.

Constructivism reached its fullest aesthetic potential, and its most interesting functional and technical solutions, in public buildings. The new social task meant that the architect had to design buildings that could hold mass activities, meetings and performances. In order to meet these demands, huge rooms were designed where the internal space could be altered and where the ceilings were not dependent on the support of pillars.

Architectural Constructivism announced itself in the competition designs for the Palace of Labour project (1923, Vesnin brothers), where the aims of the new method were successfully realized for the first time. The building, which comprised two volumes – a cylinder and a tower – was conceived inside as a system of halls and auditoria which could be adjusted to form one colossal room by using wrought-iron screens. Thus the internal space acquired at one and the same time a sense of unity and differentiation according to function.

In designing the main, oval hall, the Vesnins turned to the form of the amphitheatre which they saw as a democratic alternative to the traditional tiered design. The first actual example of this idea was the auditorium in the Palace of Culture in the Moscow-Narvsky region of Leningrad (1924–27, A. Gegello, D. Krichevsky). The subsequent use of the amphitheatre design in public buildings and places of entertainment, where the foyer and lobbies also fed into the main auditorium, led to a number of interesting solutions (Government Building in Alma-Ata, Kazakhstan, 1928–1930, M. Ginzburg, I. Milinis; Palace of Culture at the Likhachev Factory in Moscow, 1932–37, Vesnin brothers). Within the theatre, the emphasis was more on a circular auditorium which joined onto the stage. Out of necessity part of the stage became an extension of the amphitheatre (competition designs for the theatre in Kharkov, 1931, Vesnin brothers).

In Constructivist architecture, a building's interior was determined by simple undemonstrative forms which expressed the aesthetic ideal of Constructivism and which, in turn, dictated the strict choice of method. The introduction of new technical solutions and the extensive use of reinforced concrete, steel and glass enabled the Constructivist architects to experiment widely in the organisation of the internal environment. Interiors were constructed according to the principle of interpenetrating spaces "flowing into one another" and this led to the illusion of a compositional play within the building. On moving through the building, the interaction of the various elements, which all served different purposes, created calculated effects from perspectives that were constantly changing. In their designs for the Kharkov theatre, the Vesnins put the lobby, foyer and the auditorium all on one axis, treating them as a complete unit without partitions which would have isolated them. As a result, the entrance and the stage appeared to be visibly linked. The idea of an internal space which remains complete and is not broken up was effectively realized in the work of Ivan Leonidov (1902–59). In his project for the House of Industry in Moscow (1929–1930), he drew up a plan of a typical floor in an office building where the walls were replaced by plants which delineated the areas for work, rest and sport. Leonidov was responsible for introducing the popular practice of covering walls with large windows. This was intended to create a sensation of unity between the internal and external environments, and of the abundance of light and air. Similar methods were also developed by Ginzburg and the Vesnin brothers.

Artists' experiments with form at the beginning of the 1920s exerted a considerable influence on the architectural practice of the Constructivists. The interiors designed by the Vesnin brothers and I. Golosov (1883–1945) for the Zueva Club in Moscow (1927–28) were greatly enhanced by the introduction of methods taken from painting – by the contrasts of simple geometric volumes and curvilinear forms – and by features such as round columns, stairs, galleries and rib vaulting. Emphasis was consciously placed on the architectonics of space by exploiting the potential of the materials themselves in terms of colour and *faktura* (texture).

Colour was exploited by the Constructivists as one means to organise space and increase its expressive qualities. As early as 1923–25 Tatlin conducted the first experiments along these lines, trying out new colours and their combinations. On the basis of these experiments, Tatlin devised standard interiors for apartments. The aesthetic, emotional and psycho-physical effects of a building's interior design were used extensively for the first time by Ginzburg in the Government Building in Alma-Ata). The artist Sheper was invited from the Bauhaus to help work out colour solutions for the interiors of the living quarters of the employees of the Commissariat of Finance (Narkomfin, 1928–30, Ginzburg, and Milinis). The artists P. Likin, A. Kolodin and V. and G. Stenberg were also actively involved in the interior design of the Likhachev factory's Palace of Culture.

Attracted by the prospect of creating new types of buildings, the Constructivists devoted much of their time to the problem of housing, including planning communal housing blocks. The popularity of the idea of the full socialization of the home environment led to a number of competitions and construction projects where kitchens and subsidiary rooms were removed from flats; the living quarters, which were reduced to a minimum, were then linked to the main complex of social amenities by covered walkways. Within the students' communal block in Moscow (I. Nikolaev, 1929–30), the functions of the eight-storey sleeping quarters, housing a thousand sleeping compartments / rooms, and of the public block, were strictly delineated. The interiors of the latter (the lobby, reading room and sports complex) had their own expressive features.

The idea of "typification" or standardisation emerged in the mid-1920s. This led to intensive work on developing standard living units and to an increase in sectional planning. In 1927 a competition launched by OSA to design the new communal dwelling revealed a tendency to rethink the entire structure of a building. The most successful entry was a project by Ginzburg; this proposed a new type of flat – a spatial unit that was divided into rooms on two levels, each with different functions. The split level meant that the living quarters had ample space and that the internal central corridors could cut through the storey, so making for economical use of the building's volume.

Towards the end of the 1920s, a number of different government planning organisations began to research the standardization of housing for workers based on rational designs, under the direction of Ginzburg. Small flats were to be equipped with standard furniture, including multi-functional items and purpose-built equipment. The internal space in some of the units was to be divided by using folding metal screens. These were tried out in the "transitional" house types which had a block with six different versions of living units and a communal block with kitchens and a kindergarten. Five such communal houses were built in Moscow, Saratov and Sverdlovsk. Among these was the house built for the Narkomfin employees. The main living quarters had several flat modules to suit different families. Units comprising a tall common room (5 metres) and a bedroom (2-3 metres), were the most consistent and effective realization of the principle of interpenetrating spaces. The two-storey structure meant that the building only needed two internal corridors. Differences in the height and size of the rooms were matched by a rational use of windows – narrow ribbon windows in the bedrooms and tall glass screens in the common rooms. Le Corbusier in 1925 was the first to suggest the idea of a contemporary small flat with problems of space solved by having two storeys, but the idea was realized in the Narkomfin building, where the problem of the internal environment was seen as a complex task involving the exploitation of all the possibilities of colour and the new rationalist furniture.

The work of the Constructivists in designing space-saving living units was an important stage in the standardization of flats which was subsequently continued by other architects elsewhere. Unfortunately, the opportunity did not exist in Russia for many interesting experiments to be fully realized. In the mid-1930s Soviet architecture took an abrupt about turn towards traditionalism. The period of experimentation had come to an end.

MARIA L. MAKOGONOVA
translated by Charlotte Combes

Further Reading

Useful surveys including references to more specialized sources appear in Elliot 1987, Gray 1962, Kopp 1985, and Lodder 1983.

Andel, Jaroslav and others, *Art into Life: Russian Constructivism, 1914–1932*, New York: Rizzoli, 1990

Brumfield, William Craft, *The Origins of Modernism in Russian Architecture*, Berkeley: University of California Press, 1991

Cooke, Catherine "'Form is a Function X': The Development of the Constructivist Architect's Design Method" in Catherine Cooke (editor), *Russian Avant-Garde Art and Architecture*, London: Academy, 1983

Elliott, David (editor), *Rodchenko and the Arts of Revolutionary Russia*, New York: Panttheon, 1987

Gray, Camilla, *The Russian Experiment: Russian Art, 1863–1922*, London: Thames and Hudson, and New York: Abrams, 1962; as *The Russian Experiment in Art*, 1971; revised by Marian Burleigh-Motley, London and New York: Thames and Hudson, 1986

The Great Utopia: The Russian and Soviet Avant-Garde, 1915–1932 (exhib. cat.), New York: Guggenheim Museum, 1992

Khan-Magomedov, S.O., *Aleksander Vesnin and Russian Constructivism*, New York: Rizzoli, 1986

Khan-Magomedov, S.O., *Pioneers of Soviet Architecture*, New York: Rizzoli, 1987

Khan-Magomedov, S.O., *Les Vhutemas*, Paris: Regard, 1990

Kopp, Anatole, *Constructivist Architecture in the USSR*, London: Academy, and New York: St. Martin's Press, 1985

Lissitzky, El, *Russia: An Architecture for World Revolution*, Cambridge: Massachusetts Institute of Technology Press, and London: Lund Humphries, 1970
Lodder, Christina, *Russian Constructivism*, New Haven and London: Yale University Press, 1983
Quilici, Vieri, *L'Architettura del Costruttivismo*, Bari: Laterza, 1969
Shvidkovsky, Oleg A. (editor), *Building in the USSR, 1917–1932*, London: Studio Vista, and New York: Praeger, 1971
Starr, S. Frederick, *Melnikov: Solo Architect in a Mass Society*, Princeton: Princeton University Press, 1978
Strigalev, A.A. and I.V. Kokkinaki (editors), *Konstantin Stepanovich Melnikov*, Moscow: Iskusstvo, 1985

Consumerism

Before the 19th century interiors were decorated by craftsmen who provided materials on a bespoke basis for the wealthy. With the rise of the bourgeoisie and the impact of mass production in the second half of the 19th century, items to decorate the interior became available through shops, most notably the department store. Department stores were gigantic buildings which housed a vast array of consumer goods in various sections or departments. In terms of interior design they were important not only for the supply of furniture and furnishings, but also in the creation of taste and fashion from the 1880s onwards through the use of the lavish displays of room settings and the design of the shop interiors themselves.

The first purpose-built department store in London was Selfridge's, built by Gordon Selfridge using his knowledge of American stores in 1909. This Empire Revival style building reflected the American fascination with the French Beaux Arts. The building was entirely open-plan as it was constructed using a steel frame. This enabled the consumer to browse, to roam around the shop experiencing the luxury on offer without feeling the necessity to buy. This differentiates the department store from the bespoke craftsman's premises where fixed prices would not be on display. Selfridge's great rival, Harrod's, was founded in 1849 on Brompton Road, Knightsbridge, expanding rapidly throughout the late 19th century to its current size on a 4.5 acre site providing 14 acres of selling space on five floors. In common with most department stores, a massive range of goods were on sale from luggage to food to perfumes. In 1883 there was a fire and Harrod's was rebuilt. An article in the *Chelsea Herald* described the household furnishings area, and in particular the range of lighting: "But this is not all that is to be found here, for there is a big show of lamps, from those burning benzoline and costing a few pence, to the delicately painted china varieties, for the drawing room or boudoir, and as a direct contrast there are lanterns for stable use and the burglar's bull's-eye". Harrod's exported its goods worldwide using the mail-order catalogue to aid choice.

Paris also witnessed a boom in the opening of department stores with Au Bon Marché in 1872, Les Grands Magasins du Louvre in 1877, Au Printemps in 1881 and La Samaritaine in 1903. At Les Grands Magasins customers could buy exotic, decorative objects, textiles and carpets imported from Albania, Syria, Mauritius and Martinique. At Au Bon Marche antique furniture could be bought, plus a wide range of reproduction pieces. The Parisian department stores were also important in the promotion of Art Deco during the 1920s. Les Galeries Lafayette opened its *atelier d'art moderne* in 1921, directed by leading decorator Maurice Dufrène and christened La Maitrise. The atelier manufactured furnishings, fabrics, carpets and accessories designed by Dufrène and his team which were displayed in the windows of the department stores, in sumptuous room settings and illustrated on the pages of catalogues.

By the 1930s the heyday of the department store was over, as smaller, more specialised shops began to compete and the economic depression curtailed consumer spending. During this period the consumer began to be taken more seriously with the foundation of the American Consumers' Association, financed by members' subscriptions, which gave advice about consumer goods to potential buyers. A similar organisation was founded in Britain in 1957: the Consumers' Association publishes *Which?* and *Shopper's Guide* to arm consumers with useful advice.

During World War II choice in terms of furnishing the home was limited for the consumer with the introduction of rationing and official good taste. It was not until the 1950s that a consumer boom developed in America followed by Western Europe. The Contemporary Style and a popular Modernism, inspired by Scandinavia and the Cranbrook Academy, hit the shops. In terms of consumerism, the new trend for Do-It-Yourself (DIY) made a huge impact. Before the 1950s there had been a tradition of home carpentry, whereby the male of the household would build modestly sized furniture or erect shelves. During the 1950s this type of activity became more commercialised with more decorating materials and goods on offer and more leisure time to indulge in creating a stylish home. By the end of the 1950s sales of DIY tools and accessories in America had an annual turnover of $12 billion.

In Britain new magazines were launched to advise the DIY enthusiast and advertise the new range of products. This included *Do It Yourself*, launched in Britain in March 1957, which included plans and instructions for ambitious building projects including beach chalets and three-piece suites. The materials for creating your own dream home were sold through a new type of shop. Previously sold by the hardware store, the goods now became available from shops such as the Texas chain, established during the 1950s. Texas Homecare began as a family business in 1911, manufacturing wooden fireplaces. In 1954 the company opened several shops selling wallpapers and paint. In 1972 Texas opened its first warehouse for the large-scale provision of materials for home improvements, and by the late 1980s there were almost two hundred such outlets. The market for such goods for the amateur decorator has partly been stimulated by simple-to-use emulsion paints and readily available wallpapers. For example, in 1948 sales of wallpapers in Britain totalled only 43.9 million rolls; by 1958 the volume was 115.4 million rolls. The mass availability and convenience of such decorating materials has been complemented by a growth in popular literature on the subject. For example, the Home News editor of the *New York Times*, Betty Pepis, published *How to Be Your Own Decorator* in 1962 and journalists Mary Derieux and Isabelle Stevenson advised in *The Complete Book of Home Decorating* in 1956: "Start an indexed scrapbook in which you can collect magazine articles, advertisements of new types of equipment and furnishings, room pictures and color schemes which appeal to you. Don't be afraid to give expression to your own taste in making your selections. It is *your* home." The idea that the interior decoration of a house was symbolic of individual taste and an empty canvas for amateur design is peculiar to the post-war era and stems from the burgeoning commercialisation of DIY. This emphasis on the consumer and individual taste also contributed to the demise of Modernism in interior design and the adoption of a more pluralistic approach.

ANNE MASSEY

See also Do-It-Yourself; Furniture Retail Trade

Further Reading

Adburgham, Alison, *Shops and Shopping, 1800–1914: Where, and in What Manner, the Well-Dressed Englishwoman Bought Her Clothes,* 2nd edition London: Allen and Unwin, 1981

Forty, Adrian, *Objects of Desire: Design and Society, 1750–1980,* London: Thames and Hudson, and New York: Pantheon, 1986

Johnson, David, "The History and Development of Do-It-Yourself" in *Leisure in the Twentieth Century*, London: Design Council, 1977

Marling, Karal Ann, *As Seen on TV: The Visual Culture of Everyday Life in the 1950s*, Cambridge, MA: Harvard University Press, 1994

Marrey, Bernard, *Les Grands Magasins des origines à 1939*, Paris: Picard, 1979

Miller, Michael B., *The Bon Marché: Bourgeois Culture and the Department Store, 1869–1920*, Princeton, NJ: Princeton University Press, and London: Allen and Unwin, 1981

Pasdermadjian, Hrant, *The Department Store: Its Origins, Evolution and Economics,* London: Newman Books, 1954; New York: Arno, 1976

Tise, Suzanne, "Les Grands Magasins" in Catherine Arminjon and others, *L'Art de Vivre: Decorative Arts and Design in France, 1789–1989*, New York: Vendome, and London: Thames and Hudson, 1989

Wilson, Elizabeth, *Hallucinations: Life in the Post Modern City*, London: Radius, 1988

"Contemporary" Style

"Contemporary" was the adjective used in Britain during the 1950s to describe the new self-consciously modern style of interior design which achieved widespread popularity shortly after World War II. The emergence of the "Contemporary" style during the early post-war years was very much an international trend, however, and in many respects Britain was rather slow off the mark in adopting the new aesthetic compared to other countries such as Denmark, Sweden, Finland, Italy and the US, who rapidly emerged during the late 1940s as the new design superpowers of the post-war era. The British public did not really begin to embrace "Contemporary" design actively until the Festival of Britain in 1951, and for this reason, because "Contemporary" design in the UK is so closely associated with the Festival of Britain, it has also been dubbed the Festival style.

Another evocative phrase coined at the time was "The New Look". This phrase, which crops up repeatedly in product advertisements from this date, was co-opted from the world of haute couture following the launch of Christian Dior's revolutionary new collection of spring 1947. By the mid 1950s the use of the phrase "The New Look" had declined, however, as it became less appropriate to keep referring to what was now a well established style as "New". Other terms which were used contemporaneously, or which have been adopted retrospectively to describe the "Contemporary" style have usually been specific to certain countries or regions or to limited aspects of the style. These include California Modern and Organic (both specific to the US), Scandinavian Modern (applied exclusively to the furniture and furnishings produced in Finland, Denmark, Sweden and Norway), and Neo-Liberty (a term used only in Italy, where parallels were drawn between "Contemporary" design and the revival of interest in Art Nouveau, which had been known in Italy as Stile Liberty because of its association with the London department store, Liberty's). Although no one single term was adopted internationally at the time to define the new style,the word "Contemporary" was frequently used in North America as well as in Britain and it is on the basis of this widespread contemporary usage that this adjective is now applied retrospectively to characterise international developments in design between 1945 and the early 1960s.

During the 1920s and 1930s the two prevailing styles of progressive interior design were the Modern and the Moderne, the latter being a blatantly decorative pastiche of the former. Whereas the Modern and the Moderne reflected two ideological extremes – "less is more" (in the words of Mies van der Rohe) versus "l'art décoratif" – the early post-war "Contemporary" style represented the successful fusion of the functional and the ornamental. "Contemporary" design was more accessible than early Modern Movement architecture, and it became popular because it struck a balance between the clinical and the expressive. During the late 1940s and early 1950s, for example,the houses of Richard Neutra, a key figure in the development of the California Modern style, and in the transition between first generation Modernism and second generation "Contemporary" design, were singled out in the media for their human qualities.In these dwellings the concept of the house as a machine for living in was reconciled with the impulse to create a building that could be enjoyed as a work of art. The crucial difference was that, while fulfilling the Modern Movement precepts of functionalism, simplicity and truth to materials, "Contemporary"design acknowledged the vital humanising role of visual stimulation and aesthetic variety within the interior. Combining clean lines and a sense of spaciousness with stimulating colourways and abstract patterns, "Contemporary" design was a relaxed and expressive style which established a middle ground between the austerity and high seriousness of Modernism and the playfulness and frivolity of Jazz Moderne.

"Contemporary" architecture and "Contemporary" furniture and furnishings developed hand in hand during the early post-war period, with the latter being produced as a direct response to the former. New buildings were noticeably lighter and airier than in the past, lighter both physically in terms of how they were constructed, and aesthetically in terms of the amount of natural light entering the interior. Furniture, too, became proportionately lighter as a result, the heavier structures of the inter-war years appearing out of place and unbalanced in these new surroundings. Even the tubular steel framed

"Contemporary" Style: interior from *Daily Mail Ideal Home Book*, 1956

furniture of Marcel Breuer and the bent laminated wood furniture of Alvar Aalto, revolutionary and fresh though they had seemed during the1920s and 1930s, looked a trifle cumbersome in the "Contemporary" interior of the late 1940s. Not until a new range of lightweight, pared down and more skeletal designs had been developed and put into production after the war did furniture design catch up with, and successfully complement, the new style of interior architecture. This was why the spidery plywood and metal dining and lounge chairs of Charles Eames (the LCM and DCM ranges produced by Herman Miller from 1946) were so popular during the early years after the war.

A typical "Contemporary" building, such as the Case Study Houses sponsored by *Arts and Architecture* magazine in the Los Angeles area over a twenty-year period between the mid 1940s and the mid 1960s, was constructed using a post and beam framework made of steel bars, with thin cladding infill panels and large sheets of glass sheathing the exterior. In the proto high-tech Case Study Houses of Craig Ellwood and Pierre Koenig, the steel beams were left exposed on both the interior and the exterior, and formed an integral part of the overall aesthetic. This was truth to materials taken to an extreme. Sometimes, as in the Farnsworth House by Mies van der Rohe and Philip Johnson's Glass House, designed in 1946 and 1949 respectively, the cladding material was exclusively glass, and the "Contemporary" house was transformed into a transparent floating pavilion. Needless to say, the increased use of glass in post-war architecture had a dramatic impact on the interior. It broke down the conventional barriers between the interior and the exterior of the house, and it brought the landscape inside the building so that it could be experienced with greater immediacy. In the early post-war houses of Richard Neutra, such as the Moore House in Ojai, California, 1952, the architect dispensed entirely with window frames in the corners of certain rooms. Instead they had invisible mitred glass butt joints which provided an uninterrupted view of the surrounding landscape.

Many of the same basic principles of design were applied to the construction of larger buildings such as apartment blocks, schools and offices, although here a reinforced concrete grid structure was usually adopted in the place of steel beams. Concrete, both poured and prefabricated, played an increasingly important role in post-war architecture. The 1950s also witnessed the birth of Brutalist architecture, but in terms of interior design it was rare to find exposed concrete, other than concete insulation blocks, used as a surface finish on the interiors of buildings until the 1960s. The exceptions to this were the giant concrete shell structures created by architects such as Pier Luigi Nervi in Italy and Eero Saarinen in the US as sports arenas and transport terminals, where concrete was used as both a structural and a decorative, sculptural material.

In the best "Contemporary" houses there was usually a remarkable coherence between the design of the interior and the exterior of the building. This was partly due to the legacy of Frank Lloyd Wright who, although no longer a major player himself after the war (with the exception of his final masterpiece, the Guggenheim Museum in New York, completed posthumously in 1959) had an enduring influence on the younger generation of architects practising during the 1950s. Of particular significance were his ideas about organic design, and about the importance of treating the interior and exterior of the building as a unified whole. It was largely as a result of Wright's example that architects of the 1950s paid such close attention to the finishes and decoration applied to the interiors of their buildings. A typical Wrightian characteristic was to leave areas of exposed masonry on the interior in order to create coherence and continuity between the inside and the outside of the house. As well as concrete blocks, other forms of masonry used as cladding materials on "Contemporary" buildings included brick and stone. These were frequently left unadorned on both the interior and the exterior rather than being plastered, painted or rendered. Architects of the time were keen to explore the visual effects created by juxtaposing materials with contrasting surface textures, so areas of exposed masonry were often to be found in the same room as areas of smooth wood in the form of tongue and groove boards or veneered plywood panels.

The approach of the Danish architect Arne Jacobsen to the design of his buildings during the 1950s illustrates another way in which "Contemporary" architects were influenced by the total design ideas of Frank Lloyd Wright from earlier in the century. In a truly organic building, not only was minute attention paid to the interior layout and to surface finishes, but also to the design of all the furniture, fittings and accessories. In the case of Jacobsen's St Catherine's College in Oxford, completed in 1964, this attention to detail extended right through from the landscaping of the grounds, to the design of the special high-backed chairs at the high table in the dining room, to the seating in the lecture theatre, to the light fittings in the study bedrooms. Jacobsen himself was personally responsible for virtually every detail of the scheme, and the all-embracing nature of his vision pervades the whole project. Although few other architects were quite so meticulous, this type of attention to detail, whether in the selection of existing products or the commissioning of new designs from others, was not at all uncommon during the 1950s and was a distinguishing feature of "Contemporary" design.

Because so much new housing and so many new schools and local amenities were needed in both Europe and America immediately after the war, buildings began to be designed on a modular basis so that they could be quickly constructed on-site using prefabricated components. This naturally affected their internal arrangement as well. The use of a reinforced concrete or steel bar structural framework in place of load-bearing walls also had a significant effect on interior design because it meant that there were fewer interior dividing walls. This led to a surge of interest in open-planning during the 1950s and 1960s, and to its widespread usage in both private dwellings and in public and commercial buildings. Neither open-planning nor curtain wall windows were new developments of the 1950s – both were a legacy of the Modern Movement – but what was different about the post-war period was the new freedom with which these discoveries and technical advances were exploited. This was a time of unparalleled daring and experiment in the use of light and space within the interior, particularly in the US where some of the most adventurous work was carried out. Whether adopted in full strength or in watered-down form, American "Contemporary"architecture was to have a major influence internationally on the development of the post-war interior. This was equally true in the field of offices and commercial buildings as in domestic dwellings, where the innovative work of architects such as Eero Saarinen and Skidmore, Owings and Merrill resulted in a new corporate aesthetic which was adopted by big business throughout the world.

Many American "Contemporary" houses were either L-shaped, X-shaped or T-shaped as a result of the implementation of ideas about zoning. Zoning was a practice which became popular in the US during the late 1940s whereby different or conflicting areas of activity were isolated into separate wings or branches of the house, so that an activity requiring quiet would not be disturbed by a noisy activity. The most common example of this was the separation of areas of daytime activity such as the kitchen and living room, from areas of night-time activity such as the bedrooms and bathroom. The same thinking was also applied to the work / study areas and relaxation areas, with offices, workshops or studios being distanced from the children's playroom or the main living room where noise-generating activities, such as listening to or making music and watching television, took place. Whatever their layout, however, "Contemporary" interiors were usually economically planned, with each room being created on a scale and placed in a location best suited to its purpose. In American "Contemporary" houses it became common to find the kitchen, dining room and living room designed as one continuous free-flowing space. This open plan multi-purpose living room was almost invariably the largest room in the house. It was often extremely long and sometimes, in two storey houses, unusually tall as well. Full or partial double-height ceilings were popular at this date, as were open-tread stairs, which usually led directly from the living room to the first floor, sometimes to a mezzanine or balcony area overlooking the main room. Asymmetry was often the natural outcome of this form of arrangement, not only in the placing of fixtures such as fireplaces and staircases but in the grouping of furniture, such as tables and seating, as well.

During the 1950s there was probably greater freedom and flexibility in interior design than there had ever been before. For architects and designers "Contemporary" design was the embodiment of creative release. Filling the void caused by the war and reflecting the new feeling of optimism felt by many people, the "Contemporary" style rapidly achieved widespread popularity. Commercial success led in turn to further development and expansion. The market for "Contemporary" furniture and accessories grew rapidly during the early 1950s. Lighter, leaner and more spindly, "Contemporary" furniture was made of materials such as narrow-gauge steel rods and tapering turned wood. In the UK Ernest Race's ball and spoke *Antelope* chairs, which were originally designed as public seating for the Festival of Britain, typified the "Contemporary" style. Bent plywood was used extensively for seats and seat-backs, and because of advances in technology during the 1940s, the wooden laminates used were now much thinner than during the 1930s, and there was greater flexibility in terms of the shapes into which they could be moulded. In addition to Charles Eames's classic plywood chairs for Herman Miller, Arne Jacobsen's plywood *Ant* and *Series 7* chairs were produced by Fritz Hansen in Denmark from 1952, while in Britain Robin Day's *Hillestak* chairs for Hille, and the *Jason* range of dining chairs designed by the Danish-born Carl Jacobs for Kandya, both dating from 1951,became all-pervasive in "Contemporary" interiors of the time. Most of these chairs were stackable, and many were available with a choice of either metal or wooden legs, and could be purchased in a range of natural wood finishes as well as in mix and match colourways.

In terms of the new shapes seen in furniture, lighting and accessories of the 1950s, the main distinguishing characteristic of the "Contemporary" style was its strongly organic curvilinear quality, which was taken to extremes in the anthropomorphic creations of Carlo Mollino and the boldly aerodynamic designs of other Italian furniture designers. Wood was treated as if it was totally malleable, and in chair design considerable attention was paid to minute details of contour and outline. Rounded square and rounded triangular seats and seat backs were particularly prevalent, as in Hans Wegner's three-legged dining chairs and table for Fritz Hansen, and Ilmari Tapiovaara's *Domus* chair for Asko, both made of plywood. Later in the decade, after Charles Eames had mastered the use of plastic for shell seating by reinforcing it with fibreglass, there were apparently no limits on the shapes and structures that could be created. Ultimately this led to the *Tulip* range of pedestal chairs and tables designed by Eero Saarinen for Knoll, in which the traditional four legs were replaced by a single stem. Whatever materials were used, however, exaggerated contours were a common feature of furniture design. This freedom of expression meant that asymmetrical forms, such as cloud-shaped, kidney-shaped or palette-shaped coffee tables, gained widespread acceptance, and unconventional structures,

"Contemporary" Style: living room, Rose Seidler House, Sydney, Australia, c.1950

such as three-legged chairs and tables, were not uncommon either.

However, the impulse towards the organic did not exclusively determine the form of furniture in the 1950s. Between the turn of the 19th century when the organic and naturalistic Art Nouveau style had dominated design, and the middle of the 20th century when organic abstract "Contemporary" design developed, the Modern Movement had intervened. Modernism had an enduring impact on the thinking of the architects and designers who were working during the 1950s, many of whom had been trained during the inter-war years. Rectilinear forms in buildings and furniture were an expression of Modern Movement principles, as was the desire to perfect structures that were modular and which could be made from prefabricated components. These impulses influenced the development of storage furniture during the late 1940s and 1950s, in particular the unit furniture and the Storage wall shelving systems devised by George Nelson and Charles Eames. Interestingly it was these designers who were at the same time creating such strongly organic seating designs for Herman Miller, including the moulded fibreglass swagged legged chair designed by Nelson, and the bent wire chairs designed by Eames. One of the most interesting characteristics of 1950s design was this counterpoint and interplay between the creation of geometric structures and buildings, and organic furniture and accessories.

Although there were common characteristics which pervaded the "Contemporary" style internationally, it was interpreted in a highly distinctive way and given very different emphases in each individual country depending on the circumstances which prevailed. In Britain the "Contemporary" style was playful and somewhat quirky. It was strongly coloured by the fact that it was associated with an attitude of determined gaiety as the country struggled to break out of a demoralising period of post-war austerity, and self-consciously endeavoured to raise its spirits. Even the Government admitted that the Festival of Britain of 1951 was a propaganda exercise intended to act as "a tonic to the nation". The furnishing fabrics designed by Lucienne Day for firms such as Heal's during the 1950s typify the spirit of the time, especially *Calyx*, produced for the Festival, and it was in the field of surface pattern design – wallpapers, plastic laminates and carpets included – that Britain made its most original contribution to the development of the "Contemporary" style. The bold progressive abstract patterns commissioned by the wallpaper firm, John Line, and the textile manufacturer, David Whitehead, from leading British artists and designers of the day were particularly significant, and were much favoured by architects for use in "Contemporary" interiors.

The Italian interpretation of the "Contemporary" style was, if anything, even more idiosyncratic than that of the British. Isolated during the 1930s because of the political situation which prevailed, Italian architects and designers made a vigorous recovery after the war, re-establishing contacts with the international design fraternity through the launch of the prestigious Milan Triennale exhibitions in 1948. In visual terms, however, they continued to pursue an independent path after the war and throughout the 1950s they went their own way in defiance of what was going on elsewhere as part of the mainstream international "Contemporary" design movement. Designers who typify this spirit of independence include the architect and furniture designer, Carlo Mollino, with his bizarre and theatrical taste for anatomy and aerodynamic forms; Piero Fornasetti, with his concept of total decoration involving the application of printed patterning to all the surfaces of an interior, including the furniture and accessories; Gio Ponti, who celebrated both tradition and modernity in his work, and who tried his hand in many different media, including ceramics, glass, enamels and furniture; and Gino Sarfatti, who set up his own lighting firm, Arteluce, which led the world in the creation of fantasy lighting. It seems ironic that, although the Italians clearly appreciated the mainstream – the remarkable creative showcase offered to the international community every three years by the Milan Triennale exhibitions is an indication of this – when it came to what they chose to create and produce for themselves, they clearly felt at liberty to go their own way. To design purists, much Italian design of the 1950s seems completely over the top. It was certainly very spirited.

This was very different from the situation in Scandinavia, where there was a much deeper commitment to the social and moral principles underlying "Contemporary" design, and a genuine belief that good design improved the quality of life of those who came into contact with it. In Scandinavia many of the leading applied art manufacturers, such as the Finnish glass firm, Iittala, had already begun to adopt modern design during the 1930s, so the switch to making products exclusively in the "Contemporary" style after World War II was perhaps not so great as elsewhere. However, even taking this into account, the design transformation which took place in the three leading Scandinavian countries – Sweden, Denmark and Finland – over a forty year period between the 1920s and the 1960s is still remarkable. Also noteworthy is the fact that, although each country retained its own distinct design identity during the1950s, there was a natural corporate identity to the Scandinavian Modern version of the "Contemporary" style. To receptive customers in other countries Scandinavian Modern design represented the ultimate in refinement and sophistication: it was a symbol of creativity tempered by restraint. Designers such as Tapio Wirkkala in Finland (glass,furniture and metalwork), Stig Lindberg in Sweden (ceramics and textiles), and Finn Juhl and Poul Henningsen in Denmark (furniture and lighting respectively) were internationally revered. Distinguished by superb quality materials and high standards of craftsmanship, the Scandinavian Modern aesthetic was all-embracing; it shaped the line of furniture and glass; it dictated the colour, weave and pattern of soft furnishings; and it determined the shape and texture of every domestic accessory in the home, whether useful or purely ornamental.There was thus a remarkable coherence to the Scandinavian Modern "Contemporary" style, and when diverse individual objects were brought together within an interior, they complemented each other because there was a natural affinity and a sympathy between them.

Architecture and furniture design were the fields in which the Americans excelled during the 1940s and 1950s, but the US, being so large geographically, and being such a cultural melting pot in terms of its social make-up, was bound to result in greater diversity of expression. The exiled architects from the Bauhaus strengthened the force of European influence on the East Coast and in the Chicago area where they settled, while architects based on the West Coast looked across the Pacific to Japan and south to South America for inspiration. The influences on American architecture and interiors of the 1950s were as diverse as the origins of the designers themselves: Eero Saarinen from Finland; Richard Neutra from Austria; Mies van der Rohe, Walter Gropius and Marcel Breuer from Germany; and Japanese Americans such as the sculptor and lighting designer, Isamu Noguchi. Of all the eclectic foreign influences on American interior design in the1950s, the influence of Japan was one of the strongest. The exchange had begun in earnest earlier in the century as a result of contacts established by the much-travelled Frank Lloyd Wright. Richard Neutra visited Japan during the 1930s, and the buildings he saw there were to have a decisive effect on the development of his future work. Neutra in turn influenced a whole group of younger generation California-based architects, who espoused the aesthetics of Japan even more closely: Craig Ellwood in particular, but also Charles Eames, Pierre Koenig and Raphael Soriano. Modular rectilinear post and beam structures with flexible screen-like wall divisions were the main expression of Japanese influence on California Modern interiors; Eames even used *tatami* mats on the floor in his own home at Pacific Palisades in Los Angeles.

This brief survey of "Contemporary" design during the 1950s highlights the importance of assessing the style internationally. It is particularly important to distinguish between the rather narrow British definition of "Contemporary" design as a fashion associated with the Festival of Britain, and "Contemporary" design as a description of a much more widespread international phenomenon, Modernism in a revised form, the Modern Movement in a human guise.

LESLEY JACKSON

Further Reading

The most recent account of the origins and history of the "Contemporary" style and interiors within an international context appears in Jackson 1994; this book also includes a lengthy bibliography of primary and secondary sources, and a useful guide to important buildings and museum collections in Europe and North America. Additional information on product design can be found in Jackson 1991. For a discussion of 1950s mass-produced furnishings and interiors within British middle- and lower- middle-income homes see MacDonald and Porter 1990.

Les Années Cinquantes (exhib. cat.), Paris: Centre Georges Pompidou, 1988

Banham, Mary and Bevis Hillier (editors), *A Tonic to the Nation: The Festival of Britain 1951*, London: Thames and Hudson, 1976

Borngräber, Christian, *Stilnovo: Design in den 50er Jahren*, Frankfurt: Fricke, 1979

Burns, Mark and Louis DiBonis, *Fifties Homestyle*, London: Thames and Hudson, and New York: Perennial, 1988

Cantacuzino, Sherban, *Modern Houses of the World*, London: Studio Vista, and New York: Dutton, 1964

Carrington, Noel, *Design and Decoration in the Home*, London: Batsford, 1952

Castelli, V. (editor), *Il Design Italiano degli Anni '50*, Milan: IGIS, 1981
Crosby, Theo and Monica Pidgeon, *An Anthology of Houses*, London: Batsford, and New York: Reinhold, 1960
Eidelberg, Martin, *Design 1935–1965: What Modern Was*, Montreal: Musée des Arts Décoratifs, and New York: Abrams, 1991
Fehrman, Cherie and Kenneth, *Postwar Interior Design 1945–1960*, New York: Van Nostrand Reinhold, 1987
Gobyn, Ronny (editor), *Les Fifties en Belgique* (exhib. cat.), Brussels: Didier Hatier, 1988
Greenberg, Cara, *Mid-Century Modern: Furniture of the 1950s*, New York: Harmony, 1984; London: Thames and Hudson, 1985
Harling, Robert (editor), *The House and Garden Book of Small Houses*, London: Condé Nast, 1961
Hiesinger, Kathryn B. and George H. Marcus III (editors), *Design Since 1945* (exhib. cat.), Philadelphia: Philadelphia Museum of Art, and London: Thames and Hudson, 1983
Jackson, Lesley, *The New Look: Design in the Fifties*, London and New York: Thames and Hudson, 1991
Jackson, Lesley, *"Contemporary": Architecture and Interiors of the 1950s*, London: Phaidon, 1994
McCoy, Esther, *Case Study Houses 1945–1962*, Los Angeles: Hennessey and Ingalls, 1977
MacDonald, Sally and Julia Porter, *Putting on the Style: Setting Up Home in the 1950s* (exhib. cat.), London: Geffrye Museum, 1990
McFadden, David Revere (editor), *Scandinavian Modern Design, 1880–1980* (exhib. cat.: Cooper-Hewitt Museum, New York) New York: Abrams, 1982
Mundt, Barbara, and others, *Interieur und Design in Deutschland 1945–60* (exhib. cat.), Berlin: Kunstgewerbemuseum, 1993
Nelson, George and Henry Wright, *Tomorrow's House: A Complete Guide for the Homebuilder*, New York: Simon and Schuster, 1945
Pearce, Christopher, *Fifties Source Book*, London: Virgin, 1990
Sembach, Klaus-Jürgen., *Contemporary Furniture*, New York: Architectural Book Publishing, and London: Design Council, 1982
Smith, Elizabeth A.T. (editor), *Blueprints for Modern Living: History and Legacy of the Case Study Houses*, Cambridge: Massachusetts Institute of Technology Press, 1989

Corridors

Corridors have been an important means of communication in the domestic house for centuries. They have taken various forms, from underground passages to covered walkways, to wide galleries hung with tapestries and portraits, or narrow, snake-like spaces intended to separate and segregate the classes and the sexes from one another.

One of the earliest examples of corridors is described by T. A. Heslop in his discussion of Orford Castle, Suffolk built in 1165 by King Henry II. The castle is laid out with a public reception room and kitchen in the centre and a corridor leading to a private chamber on the ground floor. The first floor is of a similar layout with a private chamber at the end of a private corridor. Such a system allowed for greater privacy for the inhabitants who could retire away from the activity of the central hall and public rooms, from the noise and smells, and close their doors against draughts.

In early medieval houses there is evidence to suggest that while most consisted of one or two rooms opening onto one another, corridors were sometimes used to connect separate rooms. Examples of this in French towns of the early 13th century have been cited by Büttner and Meissner in their *Town Houses of Europe* (1983). In the Castle of Courcy, built between 1225 and 1240, underground passages connected the defensive walls and the lodgings therein with the central keep, most probably for reasons of defense. Evidence of external corridors, or pentices, has been documented in early 14th century houses in England such as Goodrich Castle, Herefordshire, c.1300, and covered passageways were sometimes arranged around a cloister.

In Italian palazzi of the 15th century, such as the Florentine Palazzo Strozzi, by Giuliano da Sangallo begun in 1489 and not finished until 1536, access to the various rooms of the house is from wide loggias on the ground and first floors which open on the central courtyard. This arrangement suited the warm climate of Italy, and made it possible for the inhabitants to pass from one room to another, without travelling through the primary rooms. Such open loggias or covered passageways were common in courtyard houses of the middle and upper classes throughout the Renaissance.

It is not until the mid- to late 17th century, however, that corridors were given a great deal of consideration by architects and theorists. Around this time corridors came into favour because they could increase the separation between the servants and the family of the house. Such social segregation was considered to be important in the structure of the domestic house and would continue to be so until late in the 19th century. As early as 1624 Henry Wotton in his *The Elements of Architecture*, criticised the *en suite* system in which rooms were designed so as to open on to one another. In a similar arrangement, called the *enfilade* system, the doors of each room are aligned with each other, thereby providing a grand and impressive view through the connected rooms.

Sir Roger Pratt's design of Coleshill, Berkshire, of c.1657 is important as it combined Palladian ideas with the practical needs of a domestic English house. It is arranged as a double pile house with the public rooms in the centre and the private rooms branching off on all four corners. A corridor runs the length of the house through the middle, thereby eliminating the need to walk through the various rooms. Thus residents and servants could pass efficiently through the house without disturbing the occupants in each room. Corridors could limit unwanted interruptions and encounters. As rooms became more specialized in the 18th and 19th centuries, corridors helped to ensure that each room was kept as a separate and more private space. Corridors, together with the servants' back stairs, were also an important means of isolating the servant class from the house owner and his family.

For reasons of social propriety and privacy, the British increasingly abandoned the long *enfilades* of rooms in favour of corridors. The French were also beginning to design more intimate private spaces, although they were slower to relinquish the *enfilade* of rooms. For example in the Hôtel Crozat, in Paris of 1700–02, by Bullet, while suites of rooms continue to open onto each other, a corridor is placed between suites allowing an alternative route to the bedrooms, thereby affording more privacy. Similarly corridors provided access to private suites of rooms assigned to household members.

Thus corridors became not only the connecting threads between rooms and suites of rooms, but also the means of detaching those spaces. They grew more highly developed as the social hierarchy of servants and masters grew more pronounced and divided, and they provided links between the two social spheres. Corridors were most specialized in 19th-century England. In larger houses, respective corridors were assigned to the family, to the female servants, to the male servants, to the bachelors and to the young women of the house. Such a system was intended to protect against the mingling of the sexes and the classes except in assigned spaces. The floor plans illustrated in Robert Kerr's book *The Gentleman's House* of 1865 clearly identify these areas, which were built into the grander houses by architects such as William Burn and Anthony Salvin. Such sophisticated arrangements of rooms and thoroughfares reflected the intricately structured and carefully ordered social life of Victorian England and were never instigated with such rigour in Europe.

By the turn of the 20th century as houses shrank in size and fewer and fewer servants were employed, the isolating aspect of the corridor was no longer required. Modern domestic house plans, such as those by Frank Lloyd Wright in America, H.M. Baillie Scott in England, Adolf Loos in Austria and Le Corbusier in France, were based on a free flow of space from room to room which was just what corridors had inhibited. Most frequently, corridors are now associated with vast impersonal institutions or dark and musty passages. They are no longer the spine which structures the domestic house but an occasionally necessary means of access.

MARGARET BIRNEY VICKERY

See also Planning and Arrangement of Rooms

Further Reading

Blunt, Anthony, *Art and Architecture in France, 1500–1700*, 2nd edition Harmondsworth: Penguin, 1970

Bold, John, "Privacy and Plan" in John Bold and Edward Cheney (editors), *English Architecture, Public and Private: Essays for Kerry Downes*, London and Rio Grande, OH: Hambledon, 1993, pp.107–20

Büttner, Horst and Gunter Meissner, *Town Houses of Europe*, New York: St. Martin's Press, 1983

Evans, Robert, "Figures, Doors and Passages" in *Architectural Design*, 1978, pp.267–78

Franklin, Jill, *The Gentleman's Country House and its Plan, 1835–1914*, London: Routledge, 1981

Girouard, Mark, *Life in the English Country House: A Social and Architectural History*, New Haven and London: Yale University Press, 1978

Heslop, T.A., "Orford Castle, Nostalgia and Sophisticated Living" in *Architectural History*, 34, 1991, pp.36–58

Hitchcock, Henry-Russell, *Architecture: Nineteenth and Twentieth Centuries*, 3rd edition Harmondsworth: Penguin, 1968

Holberton, Paul, *Palladio's Villas: Life in the Renaissance Countryside*, London: Murray, 1990

Kerr, Robert, *The Gentleman's House; or, How to Plan English Residences, from the Parsonage to the Palace*, 3rd edition London, 1871; reprinted New York: Johnson, 1972

Lavedan, Pierre, *French Architecture*, 2nd edition London: Scolar Press, 1979

Long, Helen C., *The Edwardian House: The Middle-Class Home in Britain, 1880–1914*, Manchester Manchester University Press, 1993

Wood, Margaret, *The English Mediaeval House*, London: Phoenix House, 1965; New York: Harper, 1983

Cortona, Pietro da 1596–1669

Italian painter and architect

Born Pietro Berrettini in 1596 in the town of Cortona, Pietro da Cortona, with Bernini and Borromini, was one of the principal exponents of Roman Baroque. Trained as a painter, he worked in a variety of different media including fresco painting, architectural decoration and architecture. He is often remembered today primarily as an architect but, like Bernini, he approached architecture in a more painterly manner than most of the architects of his generation. And his fame is based as much upon his architectural decoration as upon his architecture.

Cortona's early work is derivative of that of Lanfranco, Correggio, and his idol, Raphael. However, his own style developed quickly and is apparent in his most famous fresco, the ceiling of the grand salon of the Palazzo Barberini in Rome which he executed between 1633 and 1639. This commission is almost exactly contemporary with the design of S. Luca e S. Martina, Cortona's most mature architectural work, and consequently the period repesents the apogee of Cortona's career. The Barberini ceiling required a painting on a colossal scale; the room is approximately 16 metres wide by 22 metres long (52 by 72 feet). Cortona's fresco is a virtuoso performance of illusionary quadratura painting portraying the Triumph of Divine Providence and the claims of the Barberini family to immortality. It is unique in its fusion of sacred content with dynastic allegory and in the technical mastery of the painting. And it was so successful that it influenced decoration in the great palaces of the Catholic world for the next hundred years.

The Barberini ceiling occupies a position in Baroque decoration roughly equivalent to that of Michelangelo's Sistine Chapel ceiling in the High Renaissance. Whereas Michelangelo had used a painted architectural system to divide and compartmentalize his ceiling, Cortona used the same device to unify the various frescoed scenes that sweep between, in front of, and behind the painted architectural framework. Cortona simplified Michelangelo's complex system of ribs and panels into four great painted architectural ribs that rise from the corners of the room to carry a single colossal rectangular frame in which the most important figures of the fresco are located. This central scene, and the four that occupy the panels in the cove beneath it, work with the architectural framework to suggest three spatial layers: the foreground layer which includes the figures that overlap the frame and which read as if they are below it, the frame itself with its *ignudi* and medallions, and the sky and the figures above and behind the architectural frame. Both the architectural framework and the painted scenes emphasize the play of elements in depth. And equally significantly, Cortona eschews individual articulation of elements in favor of a sweeping, moving, dynamic unity of all the parts. These are the characteristics that clearly establish the ceiling as a Baroque rather an a Renaissance masterpiece.

The layered approach to interior design that is characteristic of the Barberini ceiling fresco is also apparent in Cortona's architectural masterpiece of the same period, the church of S. Luca e S. Martina, in Rome. In almost all his architectural work, Cortona combined straight, crisp elements with lushly curving, sensuous ones and the façade of S. Luca e S. Martina is no exception to this practice. Here Cortona used these elements to express an equilibrium of space and mass: the interior spaces seemingly push out between the rigid corner piers to form curving wall planes. The façade also features the same layering of architectural elements that is the hallmark of the treatment of the interior walls, suggesting that it is composed of a series of architectural planes superimposed upon each other. The various layers are unified by material and color; all are constructed of the rough, golden travertine that was Cortona's favorite building material.

The plan of the church is basically a Greek cross, with the domed, central, vertical axis roughly equal in height to the length of the two horizontal axes. The wall zone is capped by a continuous entablature that carries the eye around the complex interior and gives it unity. Beneath the entablature the wall is made up of three separate superimposed planes, all rendered in white stucco. The outer one runs behind the columns and entablature of the middle plane. The inner one is defined by the projecting pilasters and entablatures of the crossing piers. The back and forth play of these wall systems gives the interior its richly sculptural character.

The half domes of the apses and the dome above the crossing are decorated with heavy sculptural features: powerful ribs are superimposed upon a coffered surface and aedicular window frames, flanked by consoles and capped with broken pediments which break into the coffered surfaces. The coffers seem to disappear behind the ribs, emphasizing the layered character of the design.

Discussion of Cortona's significance as a decorator is incomplete without some mention of the shift in manner that is visible in his later works. Chief among these are the five rooms he decorated during the 1640s for the Medici in the Pitti Palace, their ducal palace in Florence. These rooms illustrate a dramatic change in style from the Barberini ceiling. Early in the work, Cortona went to Venice to study the work of Veronese. In Venice, he was impressed by the ceilings of the great Venetian salons. Henceforth, the sweeping, overlapping, unified, quadratura composition that characterizes the Barberini ceiling would give way to richly sculpted stucco architectural frames decorated with life-size figures in the round, usually in white in contrast to the gilded architectural frame, forming precise, if heavy, compartments for individual painted pictures. Cortona has returned to an organizational system much closer to that of Michelangelo. Moreover, the palette used for the pictures is strongly Venetian; glowing bright colors play against skies of blue and gold. Cortona was never tempted by the chiaroscuro of the Caravagisti; instead his color is much more closely related to that used by Bernini in his architectural decoration. The Pitti Palace rooms were to prove singularly important in the history of interior decoration; they constitute the prototypes for the French style of Charles Le Brun which was copied widely throughout Europe.

C. MURRAY SMART, JR.

See also Baroque

Biography

Pietro Berrettini. Born in Cortona, 1 November 1596, the son of a stonemason. Trained at Andrea Commodi's studio, c.1610–12. Went to Rome with Commodi, 1612; moved to Baccio Ciarpi's studio, 1614. Met the Florentine artists Cigoli, Passignano and Ciampelli; Cardinal Giulio Sacchetti and his brother Marcello, Cortona's main patrons from 1623, were in the papal circle of the Barberini and Cassiano del Pozzo. First important commission from Marcello Sacchetti, 1626. Active as an architect, late 1620s. Active for Barberini family from 1632. Festival regalia for "Quarantore" (S. Lorenzo in Damaso, Rome), 1633. Church architecture from 1634. Accompanied Cardinal Giulio Sacchetti to Bologna, and briefly visited Venice, 1637. Summoned to Florence by Grand Duke Ferdinand II de' Medici, 1637, returning to Rome, December ?1637. In Florence, 1640–47. Settled in Rome, 1647. Received important commissions from Pope Innocent X, c.1651. Under Alexander VII (Pope, 1655–67) active as architect of Roman churches; abandoned secular decoration. Presented design to Louis XIV for east façade of Louvre (rejected), 1664. Principal of Accademia di San Luca, 1634–38. Died 16 May 1669; buried in church of S. Luca e S. Martina, Rome.

Selected Works

Cortona's ceiling decorations at Palazzo Barberini and Palazzo Doria-Pamphilij survive *in situ.*

Interiors

c.1616	Villa Arrigoni (now Muti), Frascati (fresco decoration)
1622–23	Palazzo Mattei, Rome (frescoes in the gallery): Mattei family
1626–29	Villa Chigi (formerly Sacchetti), Castel Fusano, near Ostia (gallery ceiling and chapel): Marcello Sacchetti
1633–39	Palazzo Barberini, Rome (Great Salone ceiling, and tapestries): Cardinal Barberini
1634–69	SS Luca e Martina, Rome (building and interiors)
1637	Palazzo Pitti, Florence (Sala della Stufa): Grand Duke Ferdinand II de' Medici
1641–47	Palazzo Pitti, Florence (5 rooms: Venus, Jupiter, Mars and Apollo, Saturn): Grand Duke Ferdinand II de' Medici
1651–54	Palazzo Doria-Pamphilij, Rome (ceiling of gallery): Pope Innocent X

Further Reading

Briganti, Giuliano, *Pietro da Cortona; o, Della pittura barocca*, 2nd edition Florence: Sansoni, 1982

Campbell, Malcolm, *Pietro da Cortona at the Pitti Palace: A Study of the Planetary Rooms and Related Projects*, Princeton: Princeton University Press, 1977

Chiarini, Marco, "The Decoration of the Palazzo Pitti in the Seventeenth and Eighteenth Centuries", in *Apollo*, CVI, September, 1977, pp.178–89

Fabbrini, Narciso, *Vita del. Cav. Pietro da Cortona*, Cortona, 1896

Haskell, Francis, *Patrons and Painters: A Study in the Relations Between Italian Art and Society in the Age of the Baroque*, revised edition New Haven and London: Yale University Press, 1980

Posse, H., "Das Deckenfresko des Pietro da Cortona im Palazzo Barberini", in *Jahrbuch der Preussischen Kunstsammlungen*, XL, 1919

Vitzthum, W., "A Comment on the Iconography of Pietro da Cortona's Barberini Ceiling", in *Burlington Magazine*, 1961, pp.427–33

Wittkower, Rudolf, *Art and Architecture in Italy, 1600–1750*, 5th edition New Haven and London: Yale University Press, 1982

Cotte, Robert de 1656–1735

French architect

Robert de Cotte was arguably the most important French architect and designer in the early 18th century. His work is particularly associated with the period after 1715 of the regency of Louis XV, known as the Régence. Like many architects of the time de Cotte was a member of the workshop of Jules Hardouin-Mansart, working there by 1676. He was to become Mansart's most valued assistant in the Service des Bâtiments du Roi, especially after 1699 when Mansart was named Surintendant and enlarged the Bureau des Desseins which supplied the Bâtiments with drawings and designs. In 1699 de Cotte was named Architecte Ordinaire, Mansart's second in command, in the offices Mansart set up at Versailles, Marly and Paris. And when Mansart died in 1708, de Cotte was appointed his successor, Premier Architecte, a position that he held for the next 25 years. His output was prodigious, and in addition to the works executed for the court, de Cotte ran a thriving private practice serving both French and foreign patrons. It was largely through his efforts that the French court style began increasingly to supplant the influence of Italian architecture and design in Europe during this period.

De Cotte was born into a family of builders. His grandfather had been architect to Louis XIII, his father was also an architect, and in 1677 he married one of Mansart's sister-in-laws thus allying himself to one of the most powerful architectural dynasties in France. In 1702 he received *lettres de noblesse* from Louis XIV. In addition, like many other architects of the period, de Cotte amassed a large personal fortune through various speculative building projects. His family's rapid rise through the social hierarchy culminated with the career of his son, the architect Jules-Robert de Cotte (1683-1767) who purchased the estate and title of Baron de Réveillon from the Marquis d'Argenson.

De Cotte's early work was clearly indebted to the example of Mansart, especially in the various urban plans that he supervised. At the Place Vendôme, Paris (1700–35), for instance, Mansart had been responsible for a first design but the final octagonal plan was determined by de Cotte. The same scheme was repeated at the Place du Dôme des Invalides; once again Mansart had prepared the initial design in 1676 but when the square was being finished in 1698 de Cotte supervised the work and was able to fix the final form that it would take. And at Lyon, at the Place Bellecour (1711–13), Mansart's visionary plan was rejected in favour of a simpler and more practical design prepared by de Cotte.

De Cotte's private projects for hôtels and town houses date from the second decade of the 18th century and were especially numerous after 1720 when the boundaries of Paris expanded westwards. Here again de Cotte followed Mansart's classical model but he adapted this model to suit the demands of propriety and expense. At the Hôtel de Lude, Paris (1710), his first private house, the owner was a successful banker and much attention was paid to the idea of display; at the Hôtel d'Estrées (1711–13), the plan was more concerned with convenience, with the various apartments being made suitable for a range of different functions. In both cases, the exteriors were devoid of columns and pilasters and were plain and reserved. The same was true of the designs for the Hôtel de Torcy, Paris (c.1713), and for those of the Hôtel du Maine (1716–19) where de Cotte set all the various elements including the end pavilions and the entrance front under one large, simple roof.

The exact nature of de Cotte's contribution to interior design is quite difficult to determine. From the time of his promotion to Architecte Ordinaire, he had at his disposal a large team of talented assistants the most well-known of whom were the designer Pierre Le Pautre and the sculptor François-Antoine Vassé. These assistants were responsible for committing de Cotte's ideas to paper and there has been considerable speculation as to the extent of de Cotte's involvement within interiors. Contemporaries sometimes questioned whether he was responsible for any of the designs produced by the Bâtiments du Roi, but the historian Robert Neuman, who has made a detailed study of de Cotte's drawings, suggests that he played an important role in the broad conception of the interior detailing. He normally determined the design of the architectural framework, the subdivision of the wall panels or other components, and the location of relief carving, paintings and mirrors. The finer details and decorative elements were provided by one of the dessinateurs working in the Bâtiments, or a sculptor in an independent workshop who worked up de Cotte's preliminary sketches into full-scale drawings. De Cotte's sketches of chimneypieces and overmantels for his own apartment in Paris (1721–22) also suggest that he continued to play an active part in the design of some decorative features. And finally, he imposed a house style upon his dessinateurs so that even when the drawings were executed by other hands they were clearly indebted to his overall conception and ideas.

De Cotte's approach to architecture and design marked a new phase in the history of architectural theory. This was elaborated in his ideal of *la belle architecture* which shows his work to have been less dependent upon classical rules deriving from ancient or Renaissance prototypes than on the exercise of good judgment and taste. Certain terms were deemed especially important: *bienséance*, or decorum, an idea of the clear relationship of the form and purpose of a building; *convenance*, an idea closely related to *bienséance* which argued that all the parts of a building, the exterior elevation, the location of the rooms, the choice of materials and the decoration of the interior, should suit the needs, the social status and wealth of the patron; and *distribution*, the proper planning of the rooms which was considered the most important responsibility of the architect. His concern with decorum and appropriateness led de Cotte to regard each commission as what has been called a typological problem and to argue that each building could be said to have its own tradition of planning and iconography. The influence of these ideas is evident in Jacques-François Blondel's important treatise, the *Cours d'Architecture* (1771–77), which developed the notion of *distribution* in particular, and which grouped all kinds of buildings under the three general categories of private dwellings, public buildings and ecclesiastical edifices.

During the 1720s de Cotte was involved in the design of three Episcopal Palaces outside Paris, at Châlons-sur-Marne (1719–20), at Verdun (1724) and at Strasbourg (1731–35). In keeping with prevailing codes of social hierarchy and decorum, the Bishop's apartment at Strasbourg was modest, but that for the king, the Grand Appartement, was more lavish and was set

Cotte: design for lacquered room, 1717

along the river side of the building. De Cotte also prepared several designs for palaces for European nobility. Few were built but all had longitudinal axes in the plans and radiating avenues for the gardens similar to those at Versailles. The buildings were variations on simple French plans: a simple block at the Château de Rivoli (c.1700) built for the Duke of Savoy; a U-shaped plan at Chanteloup (c.1711) built for the Princess Orsini; and a central plan at the Château of Poppelsdorf, Bonn (1715–23), and at the Château of Tilbourg in the Netherlands (c.1715). All these plans included imposing state rooms but, unlike the designs of the previous century, they also included more functional arrangements in the private rooms and connecting corridors that offered some privacy.

In 1715 de Cotte planned two palaces for the grandson of Louis XV, Philip V of Spain. Buenretiro I was devised as a simple U-shaped building, while the design of Buenretiro II was in the form of a vast cross that could accommodate two sets of apartments (joined by a single set of dressing rooms) which were intended to be inhabited alternately in summer and winter. Although these proposals were unexecuted, they had a significant impact on architectural design in Italy and were the starting point for Luigi Vanvitelli's Royal Palace of Caserta, Naples (1751–74).

De Cotte was in charge of several ecclesiastical projects, the most notable being the decoration of the chapel at Versailles (1708–10) and the decoration of the choir of Notre Dame, Paris (1708–14); much of the work in these two schemes was carried out by Vassé and Le Pautre. He also designed several large complexes of buildings including the Parisian garrisons for the Mousquetaires Noires (1699) and the Mousquetaires Gris (1716–20).

Many of de Cotte's buildings have been demolished or, like the Episcopal Palace at Strasbourg, have been substantially altered. Yet, the evidence from surviving works, drawings and contemporary accounts suggests that he was skilled in designing a simple, balanced form of architecture that was well-suited to the new breed of client who required comfort as well as a setting appropriate to public life. While much of his architectural language was quite traditional or familiar, his interiors illustrate the introduction of a more varied style of organisation. And in the work of his assistants, like Vassé, the decorative details and ornament are less two-dimensional and include much bolder reliefs than that characteristic of the older classical style of French architecture. This work heralds the arrival of the Rococo style of design.

DAVID CAST

Biography

Born in Paris in 1656, the son of an architect, Charles de Cotte. Trained as a stone-mason. Married the sister-in-law of Jules Hardouin-Mansart (1646–1708), 1677: son, the architect Jules-Robert de Cotte (1683–1767). Working in the offices of Jules Hardouin-Mansart by 1676; travelled to Italy with the architect Jacques V Gabriel, 1689; appointed Architecte Ordinaire, and director, Départment de Paris, and director, Académie Royale d'Architecture, 1699; succeeded Hardouin-Mansart as Premier Architecte du Roi, 1708–34. Ennobled by Louis XIV in 1702. Died in Paris, 15 July 1735.

Selected Works

The de Cotte Collection, comprising several thousand documents, drawings and designs issued by de Cotte's office, is divided between the Bibliothèque Nationale, and the Bibliothèque de l'Institut de France, Paris. For a full account of de Cotte's architectural commissions see Neuman 1994.

Interiors

1703 Hôtel de Lionne, Paris (interior remodelling): Chancellor de Pontchartrain

1708–09 Château Neuf, Meudon (interiors including the Dauphin's apartments)

1708–10 Chapelle Royale, Versailles (decoration, with A. Vassé)

1708–14 Notre Dame, Paris (decoration of the choir, with A. Vassé)

1709 & 1721–22 Château de Saverne, Alsace (decoration, including the Appartement de Parade)

1711–13 Hôtel d'Estrées, Paris (building and interiors): Duchesse d'Estrées

1713–19 Hôtel de la Vrillière (later Hôtel de Toulouse), Paris (remodelling of original building by F. Mansart; interiors with A. Vassé)

1714 Hôtel de Gramont, Besançon (interiors)

c.1715–17 Buenretiro I and Buenretiro II, outside Madrid (unexecuted designs for the building and interiors): Philip V

1716–17 Electoral Palace, Bonn (interiors)

c.1716–19 Hôtel du Maine, Paris (building and interiors): Duc and Duchesse du Maine

1717 Hôtel de Bourvalais, Paris (remodelling and interiors including the Grand Salon)

1719–20 Palais Episcopaux, Châlons-sur-Marne (building and interiors; unfinished)

1721–22 Hôtel de Cotte, Paris (building and interiors)

1721–35 Cabinet des Medailles, Bibliothèque du Roi, Paris (with Jules-Robert de Cotte; not completed until 1741)

1724–35 Palais Episcopaux, Verdun (building and interiors; not completed until 1739)

1725–36 Versailles (remodelling of interiors, including the Chambre de la Reine, and the Salon d'Hercule, with A. Vassé)

1731–35 Palais Rohan, Strasbourg (building and interiors including the Chambre du Roi; not completed until 1742)

Further Reading

The most recent and comprehensive account of de Cotte's career appears in Neuman 1994 which also includes an extensive bibliography of primary and secondary sources. For details of de Cotte's involvement with interiors in particular, see Babelon 1927, Kimball 1943, Ludmann 1981 and 1985, and Pons 1990 and 1991.

Babelon, Jean, *Le Cabinet du Roi; ou, Le Salon Louis XV de la Bibliothèque Nationale*, Paris: van Oest, 1927

Bordeaux, Jean-Luc, "La Commande Royale de 1724 pour l'Hôtel du Grand Maitre à Versailles" in *Gazette des Beaux-Arts*, 104, 1984, pp.113–26

Bottineau, Yves, "Philip V and the Alcázar at Madrid" in *Burlington Magazine*, 98, 1956, pp.68–75

Brunel, Georges, "Würzburg: Les Contacts entre Balthasar Neumann et Robert de Cotte" in *Actes du XXIIe Congrès International d'Histoire de l'Art, Budapest 1969*, Budapest: The Congress, 1972

Exposition de Dessins et de Souvenirs de Robert de Cotte, Premier Architecte du Roi, Paris: Hôtel des Invalides, 1937

Guiffrey, Jules, *Comptes des Bâtiments du Roi sous le Règne de Louis XIV, 1664–1715*, 5 vols., Paris: Imprimerie Nationale, 1881–1901

Hautecoeur, Louis, *Histoire de l'architecture classique en France*, vols. 2–3, Paris: Picard, 1949–51

Hautmann, Max, "Die Entwürfe Robert de Cottes für Schloss Schleissheim" in *Münchner Jahrbuch*, 6, 1911, pp.256–76

Iberville-Moreau, José-Luc d', *Robert de Cotte: His Career as an Architect and the Organization of the Services Des Bâtiments*, Ph.D. thesis, London: University of London, 1972

Jestaz, Bertrand, *Le Voyage d'Italie de Robert de Cotte*, Paris: Boccard, 1966

Kimball, Fiske, *The Creation of the Rococo*, 1943; reprinted as *The Creation of the Rococo Decorative Style*, New York, Dover, and London: Constable, 1980

Ludmann, Jean-Daniel, "Projets de Robert de Cotte et de l'Agence des Bâtiments du Roi pour la Ville de Lyon" in *L'Art Baroque à Lyon*, Colloque Lyon, 1972, Lyon, 1975, pp.375–97

Ludmann, Jean-Daniel, *Le Palais Rohan de Strasbourg*, 2 vols., Strasbourg: Dernières Nouvelles, 1979–80

Ludmann, Jean-Daniel, "Nouveaux Documents sur l'Hôtel du Doyenné du Grand Chapitre, Actuel Evêche de Strasbourg" in *Cahiers Alsaciennes d'Archeologie, d'Art et d'Histoire*, 23, 1980, pp.73–88

Ludmann, Jean-Daniel and Bruno Pons, "Nouveaux Documents sur la Galerie de l'Hôtel de Toulouse" in *Bulletin de la Société de l'Histoire de l'Art Français*, 1981, pp.115–28

Ludmann, Jean-Daniel, *Les Grand Appartements du Palais Rohan de Strasbourg*, Strasbourg: Musées de Strasbourg, 1985

Marcel, Pierre, *Inventaire des Papiers Manuscrits du Cabinet de Robert de Cotte*, Paris: Champion, 1906

Marie, Alfred and Jeanne, *Versailles au Temps de Louis XIV: Mansart et de Cotte*, Paris: Imprimerie Nationale, 1976

Neuman, Robert, "French Domestic Architecture in the Early 18th Century: The Town Houses of Robert de Cotte" in *Journal of the Society of Architectural Historians*, 39, 1980, pp.128–44

Neuman, Robert, *Robert de Cotte and the Perfection of Architecture in Eighteenth-Century France*, Chicago: University of Chicago Press, 1994

Pons, Bruno, *De Paris à Versailles 1699–1736: Les Sculpteurs Ornemanistes Parisiens et l'Art Décoratif des Bâtiments du Roi*, Strasbourg: Universités de Strasbourg, 1986

Pons, Bruno, "Hôtel Robert de Cotte" in Bruno Pons and Anne Forray-Carlier (editors), *Le Faubourg Saint Germain: Rue de Bac*, Paris: Délégation à l'Action Artistique de la Ville de Paris, 1990, pp.98–102

Pons, Bruno, "Le Décor de l'Appartement du Grand Dauphin au Château Neuf de Meudon" in *Gazette des Beaux-Arts*, 117, February 1991, pp.59–76

Reinhardt, Ursula, *Die Bischöflichen Residenzen von Châlons-sur-Marne, Verdun und Strasbourg: Ein Beitrag zum Werk des Ersten Königlichen Architekten Robert de Cotte (1656–1735)*, Basel, 1972

Scott, Katie, *The Rococo Interior: Decoration and Social Spaces in Early Eighteenth-Century Paris*, New Haven and London: Yale University Press, 1995

Cottier, Daniel 1838–1891

Scottish interior decorator, stained-glass designer and antique dealer

Daniel Cottier was appropriately described as a man who "thought in Continents" and his influence as an interior decorator, stained-glass designer and dealer in fine and decorative arts was felt not only in Britain, but in North America and Australia. His impact spread outwards from the fashionable elites of Scotland, and by 1873 he had established offices and partnerships in London, Sydney, Melbourne and New York, backed up by a European network of agents and contacts. In all these centres Cottier played a leading role in disseminating the artistic ideas of the Aesthetic Movement, establishing a contemporary taste in interiors, and introducing paintings of the Barbizon and Hague Schools to homes of the international art-buying public.

Cottier traded on a sophisticated colour sense which was rooted in technical skills acquired in the 1850s during his Glasgow apprenticeship as a stained-glass artist and house painter (probably with Cairney & Son). There followed a couple of years in London where, at the Working Men's College in Red Lion Square, he absorbed Ruskin's fiery invective and witnessed the inception of Morris, Marshall & Faulkner. Returning to Scotland in 1862 he worked for two years as an assistant manager with Field & Allan, leading stained-glass artists in Edinburgh, before setting up on his own account as a "glass painter and mural decorator" luring the talented Andrew Wells to join him. Typical of Cottier's charismatic, outgoing personality was the instant friendship he struck up on a train journey with the collector John Forbes White, which resulted in a series of interior and stained glass commissions in Aberdeen. Even more significant for Cottier's subsequent career as a dealer was White's interest in contemporary Dutch and French painting, and his connections with prominent European artists, collectors and dealers.

Cottier kept on the Edinburgh studio until 1869. By this time he had also established himself back in Glasgow where he had completed a formative series of daring, polychromatic church interiors in collaboration with the architects John James Stevenson (1831–1908), William Leiper (1839–1916) and Alexander "Greek" Thomson (1817–75). In his decoration of Stevenson's Townhead Church (1865–66) Cottier clearly demonstrated his receptivity to the work of Burges, Morris and Jones. The strongly coloured stencilling and stained glass complemented the architecture with an assured blend of muscular Gothic, classical and exotic styles. Equally startling were the colour combinations and boldly geometric designs applied to Leiper's Dowanhill Church (1865–66). Like Cottier, Leiper was not long returned from London where he had been a fringe member of the Burges-Godwin set, whose influence was apparent in the use of painted arcading, ringed shafts and miniature rooves in the theatrical pulpit and in the star-studded blue ceiling. The third of these ecclesiastical commissions, the elaboration of Thomson's overall design for the interior of Queen's Park Church (1867–69), established Cottier as a "consummate colourist". To his former mentor, the London artist Ford Madox Brown, it was a revelation, and demonstrated the extent to which Cottier had outstripped his London training with "a range of performance beyond that of any other modern artist. Here line and colouring are suggestive of paradise itself. I now know what all along has been wrong with my ceilings. Well done Glasgow! I put ... this Thomson-Cottier church above everything I have seen in modern Europe" (*Glasgow Evening Times*, 19 October 1893).

In 1869 Cottier moved his main base to London, initially in partnership with old friends from Glasgow – John McKean Brydon, Bruce Talbert and William Wallace. He was no longer confining his energies to glass painting and decorative work but broadening out to encompass the manufacture of furniture, textiles and painted ceramics. Being close to the heart of the leading Aesthetic circles enhanced his reputation. It was he, for example, who first gave Rhoda and Agnes Garrett studio space and a grounding in decorative design, perhaps on account of his working friendship with their relative J.J. Stevenson. During frequent trips to the Continent he began dealing in contemporary Dutch and French painting, and persuaded the dealer Van Wisselingh to become manager of the London Gallery. Through this connection the Dutch artist Matthijs Maris came to live with Cottier in 1877, producing both paintings and stained glass for the firm's various outlets. At the same time Cottier was continuing to work back in Scotland on a series of striking villa interiors in a mature Aesthetic style (Cairndhu, Helensburgh; Colearn House and Ruthven Towers, Auchterarder).

Having been born into a seafaring family in the west of Scotland, Cottier was no stranger to international trade and travel, and throughout his life cultivated the air of an old sea-dog, apparently looking "more like an ideal coasting skipper than an artist." He took advantage of rail and steamer routes to expand his affairs into an international market, and in 1873 set up an Australian operation, Lyon & Cottier, with branches in Sydney and Melbourne. The ground had been prepared by John Lamb Lyon, a fellow apprentice in Glasgow and London who had emigrated in 1861. The long-term side effects of working with noxious pigments and processes combined with the notoriously dank weather in the west of Scotland made emigration appealing on health grounds for many decorators. Cottier himself suffered from a recurrent rheumatic fever (which eventually killed him), and both Andrew Wells and Charles Gow spent a convalescent spell working for him in Australia before returning to Glasgow. The firm was instantly successful and an extensive folio of designs now in the Mitchell Library, Melbourne, suggests that they virtually monopolised high-class commissions for decorative work there during the 1870s and 1880s.

Cottier's New York branch established in 1873 was also a runaway success, helped by Clarence Cook as publicist. In a series of magazine articles subsequently published as a best-selling book *The House Beautiful* (1878), Cook repeatedly praised the firm's Artistic furnishings. Some designs were in fact versions of Godwin's furniture which Cottier had initially imported and later manufactured in New York. On significant Aesthetic interiors like the Boston Trinity Church and the New York Union League Club, Cottier worked alongside American designers John La Farge and Louis Comfort Tiffany. This side of Cottier's business is well documented in the catalogue *In Pursuit of Beauty* (1986) which also mentions interiors for the homes of F. W. Stephens and Joseph Decker and furniture for

Catherine Lorillard Wolfe's Newport, Rhode Island "cottage". The North American operation was managed and subsequently owned by James Smith Inglis who had followed Cottier from Glasgow in 1873.

Wherever he went Cottier attracted a following and connected with the most interesting artists, architects, designers, critics and collectors around. His various enterprises provided a magnet for a younger generation of talent, and a stepping-stone to other practices. In particular, untried Scottish designers seeking openings in London or abroad received a ready welcome. Cottier also helped to bring on indigenous talent in America and Australia, which would eventually oust British firms like his own from their pre-eminent position. In Glasgow, his contribution to the pool of decorative skills and successful collaboration with adventurous patrons added to the growing reputation of the city as an international centre for progressive design. Integrated schemes incorporating self consciously "artistic" paint effects and distinctive stained glass were hallmarks of both Cottier interiors and the subsequent Glasgow Style. The atmospheric qualities and subtle coloration of painters like Corot and the "grey School" of Dutch painters whom Cottier promoted, enriched the visual vocabulary of interior designers such as George Walton, Charles Rennie Mackintosh, the Macdonald sisters and George Logan. Many of the decorators and stained-glass artists (Hugh McCulloch, Charles Gow, Andrew Wells) who went on to employ or work with Mackintosh and his associates had emerged from the Cottier stable.

JULIET KINCHIN

Biography

Born in Glasgow, 1838. Apprenticed to the stained-glass manufacturer David Kier (1802–64), Glasgow; attended lectures at John Ruskin's Working Men's College, London, c.1860–62. Married Marion Field, 1866. Worked for stained-glass manufacturers Field and Allan, Edinburgh, 1862–64. Established his own studio, with Andrew Wells, George Street, Edinburgh, 1864; active as a stained-glass designer and interior decorator, Glasgow, 1867–69; established Cottier & Company Art Furniture Makers, Glass and Tile Painters, London, 1869; listed as Cottier & Co., Upholsterers, Fine Cabinet Makers, Glass Stainers, Art Rooms, 144 Fifth Avenue, New York City, 1873; set up decorating and furniture business with John Lamb Lyon (Lyon & Cottier) with branches in Sydney and Melbourne, 1873. Designed furniture and interiors from c.1870; active as a dealer in paintings in London and New York from 1873. Died in Jacksonville, Florida, 1891; British and American business managed by James Inglis, 1873–1907; Cottier & Co. survived until 1915.

Selected Works

Few records, drawings or authenticated examples of Cottier's work in Europe and America survive, but examples of his stained glass are in the Victoria and Albert Museum and in situ in a number of churches, including the Cathedral of Saint Machar, Aberdeen, Trinity Church, Boston, and the Church of the Incarnation, Madison Avenue, New York, and in secular settings at Harvard University, and the New York Society Library. An extensive folio of designs relating to his work in Australia is in the Mitchell Library, Melbourne.

Interiors

1865–66	Townhead Church, Glasgow (stained glass and stencilled decoration; building by J.J. Stevenson)
1867–69	Queen's Park Church, Glasgow (stained glass and decoration; building by A. Thompson)
1870s	Cairndhu, Helensburgh, Scotland (interiors)
1870s	Colearn House, Auchterarder, Scotland (interiors including stained glass): Alexander Mackintosh
1878	New York Society Library, New York (stained glass, Green Memorial Alcove)
1880s	Memorial Hall, Harvard University (stained glass)
1881	Union League Club, New York (library interiors including furniture and stained glass)
early 1880s	F.W. Stephens House, New York (interiors)
early 1880s	Joseph Deckers house, New York (interiors)

Further Reading

A biography and long bibliography of primary and secondary sources appears in Burke 1986. For additional information on Cottier's stained glass see Gould 1969 and Harrison 1980. Examples of Cottier's furniture are illustrated in Cook 1878, and illustrations of some of his American interiors appear in *Artistic Houses*, 1883–84.

Artistic Houses, Being a Series of Interior Views of a Number of the Most Beautiful and Celebrated Homes in the United States, 2 vols., New York, 1883–84; reprinted New York: Blom, 1971

Burke, Doreen Bolger and others, *In Pursuit of Beauty: Americans and the Aesthetic Movement* (exhib. cat.: Metropolitan Museum, New York), New York: Rizzoli, 1986

Cook, Clarence, *The House Beautiful: Essays on Beds and Tables, Stools and Candlesticks*, New York, 1878; reprinted Croton-on-Hudson, NY: North River Press, 1980

Donnelly, Michael, *Glasgow Stained Glass: A Preliminary Study*, Glasgow: Glasgow Museums and Art Galleries, 1981

Elliott, Charles Wyllys, *The Book of American Interiors*, Boston, 1876

Forge, Suzanne, *Victorian Splendour: Australian Interior Decoration, 1837–1901*, Melbourne and Oxford: Oxford University Press, 1981

Girouard, Mark, *Sweetness and Light: The Queen Anne Movement, 1860–1900*, Oxford: Clarendon Press, 1977; New Haven: Yale University Press, 1984

Gould, Brian Merton, *Two Van Gogh Contacts: E.J. Van Wisselingh, Art Dealer; Daniel Cottier, Glass Painter and Decorator*, London: Naples Press, 1969

Harrison, Martin, "Contemporary Art Glass One Hundred Years Ago" in *Glass*, 6, January 1975, pp.36–39

Harrison, Martin, *Victorian Stained Glass*, London: Barrie and Jenkins, 1980

Haweis, Mary Eliza, *The Art of Beauty*, London, 1878, 2nd edition 1883; reprinted New York: Garland, 1978

Hobler, Margaret H., *In Search of Daniel Cottier, Artistic Entrepreneur, 1838–1891*, M.A. thesis, New York: Hunter College, 1988

Crace & Son

British firm of decorators, designers and cabinet-makers, 1768–1899

In the 18th century in Britain, the work of the interior designer could be done by several different types of craftsmen, including cabinet-makers and upholders. This work involved the design and supply of furniture and soft furnishings; the re-gilding of furniture and frames; the restoration and re-hanging of pictures; and often the entire arrangement of an interior scheme. Into this category fell Edward Crace, a leading coach decorator of Long Acre, Covent Garden, London, when he established a decorating business in 1768. The Crace firm of decorators was to be remarkable for its longevity and the breadth of its work. It was continued by five successive generations until its closure in 1899 by John Dibblee Crace, the great-great-grandson of Edward.

As a successful coach decorator, Crace was able to draw upon an established client base among the gentry and aristocracy for his new venture into interior decorating. Information on his career is sparse, and only one interior by him has been recorded, in an oil painting by the studio of Zoffany. This was of the main interior of the Pantheon in Oxford Street, London, built in 1770–72 by the architect James Wyatt as a public meeting place in the new Neo-Classical style. In the Zoffany painting, Edward Crace's decoration is clearly visible beneath the vast central dome, including large *giallo antico* columns painted in *scagliola* and the principal decorative features of pendentives in grisaille work with arabesques supporting cameos in the antique manner. Horace Walpole likened these to Raphael's decoration at the Vatican. It is known that Edward Crace also supplied a large suite of gilt furniture for the Pantheon, although this has since disappeared, along with the building itself.

By 1778 Edward Crace had become curator of the extensive paintings collection of George III, and his eldest son, John Crace, took over the running of the Crace decorating business at 55 Great Queen Street, London. John Crace, who was assisted in business by his good looks, extrovert personality, and early marriage to an heiress, seems to have had about fifteen regular employees, including a cousin of the same name. While bills in the Victoria and Albert Museum archive indicate that he executed much routine painting and decorating work during the 1780s, by 1794 he had become a member of the team working for John Soane at the Bank of England. Crace designed a ceiling in the Breakfast Room of 12 Lincoln's Inn Fields (now part of Sir John Soane's Museum), which he decorated c.1794 for Soane. It has been recovered from beneath many layers of paint. The ceiling of the Back Parlour at Soane's country house, Pitzhanger Manor in Ealing, has been repainted recently to Crace's design after a watercolour by J.M. Gandy. This was executed c.1802. Both ceilings were of trellis design with vines and flowers, following an established French Neo-Classical type.

By 1790 John Crace was decorating interiors at Carlton House, the legendary London house of the Prince of Wales, demolished in 1827. The architect was Henry Holland, with whom John Crace worked closely on a number of occasions. In 1794 Crace was joined by his eldest son, Frederick, then 15 years old, who was noticed by the Prince for his skill in gilding the staircase at Carlton House. Frederick later remarked that his father's contribution to the history of English interiors had been to reintroduce the decorative techniques of graining, marbling, and illusionistic painting. All these techniques the Craces learned while working at Carlton House alongside the French decorative artists Jean Jacques Boileau and his assistant, Louis Delabrière. The Italian *scagliola* artist Bartoli was also an influence. The Crace decoration at Carlton House was unfortunately lost by 1806 in a new scheme of decoration, directed by Walsh Porter.

In 1793 Thomas Sheraton had published the Chinese Drawing Room of Carlton House, the work of Henry Holland the architect and Crace the decorator and contemporary to their Chinese Dairy at Woburn Abbey, Bedfordshire (finished c.1789). John Crace not only collected Chinese *objets d'art* but had a considerable library of topographical books on the Orient. This knowledge was put to use by the Prince of Wales between 1801 and 1804 in the first phase of Chinoiserie decoration at the Royal Pavilion, Brighton, the Prince's famed pleasure palace on the Sussex coast where he entertained lavishly. A number of boldly drawn and coloured designs for the Pavilion in the Cooper-Hewitt Museum in New York can be attributed to John Crace by virtue of their similarity to the painted interior of the Woburn Dairy. In addition to designing and executing interiors for the Prince, John Crace also imported a considerable number of Chinese objects, lacquer, and furniture for the Pavilion.

Frederick Crace was also much involved during this phase of decoration at Brighton. He seems to have acted as foreman for his father's men, although one interior designed by him in 1801 is known. This was a tented bed alcove, with en suite breakfast and dressing rooms in the newest French manner, illustrating his precocious talent. The light, sure touch and sophisticated use of colour developed by Frederick Crace while working at Brighton Pavilion distinguish his later interiors. Typically, the Prince became dissatisfied with his early exercise in Chinoiserie and decided to re-do the Pavilion interiors, beginning in 1815. Until c.1822 this work was led by Frederick Crace, with some 34 assistants. The most spectacular of these interiors, and the masterpiece of Crace, was the gas-lit Music Room, completed in 1820, with mural panels in imitation of scarlet and gold lacquer (executed by a specialist French painter), Chinese-style gasoliers based closely upon Chinese export glass, and a large domed ceiling decorated with silvered "dragon" scales. The interior has been restored, replete with a carpet re-woven to Crace's designs, after a severe arson attack in 1975 and damage from a hurricane in 1987; the original suite of furniture by Bailey and Saunders survives in the Royal Collection. The Music Room was the most talked-about interior in Europe in its day, not least for the entertainments which took place within it.

Shortly after completing the Music Room, the then-George IV transferred Frederick Crace to Windsor Castle, which was being extensively remodelled by Jeffry Wyatville. Contemporary newspaper accounts and diaries suggest that Crace executed a great deal of painting and gilding, although few specifics are known about this work. Crace did, however, contribute to the new Rococo Revival and Gothic interiors by Wyatville, including the State Rooms where a teenager named Augustus Welby Pugin was employed in designing furniture. The experience of Windsor seems to have sparked an interest in the Gothic on the part of Frederick Crace, who went on to decorate a townhouse for the novelist and antiquary Edward Bulwer-Lytton in a heraldic style, followed by heraldic decorations in the state rooms of Taymouth Castle, Perthshire, Scotland, in conjunction with his eldest son, John Gregory Crace.

J.G. Crace began working for his father in 1825 at the age of 16, acting as the firm's foreman. In 1830 he inherited cash and property from his mother's estate, enabling him to become a full partner with his father, trading as "Frederick Crace & Son" from 14 Wigmore Street (renumbered to 38 in 1859), Cavendish Square, London, premises they occupied from 1827 until 1899. At the time of their partnership, J.G. Crace had

Crace & Sons: state drawing room, Knebworth House, Hertfordshire, 1844

become worried about the state of the business. His father had been occupied for some time almost exclusively with commissions for George IV, who was notoriously slow in paying his bills, and their country-house clientele had fallen off. The younger Crace was determined to rebuild the business, beginning with new showrooms at Wigmore Street.

As he and his father considered French decoration to be superior to that in England at the time, he went to Paris on a study-tour of contemporary French interiors in 1837, returning to decorate a principal showroom in the French Renaissance style. Invitations were then sent out to prospective clients inviting them to a series of open-house evenings which proved to be very successful. Among the first, and certainly the most important, of J.G Crace's patrons, was Andrew Spencer Cavendish, the 6th Duke of Devonshire, who employed Crace from 1840 until the mid-1850s, beginning at Devonshire House in London and his seat, Chatsworth, in Derbyshire. For the former, Crace redecorated the Saloon in a sumptuous mixture of French Baroque and English Palladian motifs, while at Chatsworth he created a private library for the Duke, who wished to have a room in the "new style" of decoration, what Crace was to term "Old French". The wall and ceiling decoration was inspired by French Neo-Classicism in its arabesques of pastel colours, while a suite of maple and amaranth marquetry furniture was designed by Crace for the room. Crace later remarked it was the Duke who had suggested he add cabinet-making to his business, and workshops in Little Welbeck Street and Welbeck Mews, behind the Wigmore Street showrooms, were established.

In 1841 Crace had collaborated with his father in designing a suite of state rooms for Taymouth Castle, decorated to receive the young Queen Victoria and Prince Albert on a state visit. At Taymouth Crace began what was to become a life-long interest in the Gothic style of decoration, which was strongly reinforced by his introduction in 1843 to A.W.N. Pugin by Lord Shrewsbury when both were working at Alton Towers, Staffordshire.

Also in 1843, Crace travelled to Munich and was greatly excited by the rich use of polychromy he found there in the Neo-Classical interiors of Leo von Klenze and his team of decorative artists. Crace presented his findings in a lecture to the Royal Institute of British Architects, in which he recognised that the use of contrasting bold colours could enhance the effect and clarify the structure of architecture and interiors, especially when combined with the use of repeated decorative patterns. This approach to interiors was followed by Crace for the rest of his career.

By early in 1844 J.G. Crace had entered into a decorating partnership with A.W.N. Pugin, and their joint commissions were still in progress at the latter's death in 1852. Pugin's passion and genius for medieval design had an immediate impact upon the Gothic style of Crace, while Crace provided his years of experience in decorating with a long-established and well-known family firm, as well as his strong interest in the proper use of colour in interiors. This is demonstrated clearly in a letter Crace wrote to *The Builder* in 1855, responding to criticisms of the Saloon at Chirk Castle, Clywd, which he had decorated with Pugin in 1846–48. He defended his scheme of a strong blue ceiling with green and gold walls, saying the colouring had been chosen by him to harmonise with the existing collection of portrait paintings, whose varnish had yellowed, concluding that, "Any two colours may be brought together by a proper modulation of tone, and interposition of suitable contrast between them." This concisely sums up the Crace approach to interiors throughout the 19th century.

The later 1840s were, for J.G. Crace, dominated by his work in conjunction with Pugin. In 1846 Frederick Crace & Son were officially awarded a contract by the Office of Works for decorating the new Palace of Westminster. This work was to continue for more than twenty years, encompassing the supplying of an enormous number of wallpapers, carpets and textiles, as well as executing painted interior decoration to Pugin's designs.

Crace worked closely with the Pugin "team" of Minton, Myers, and Hardman, all of whom collaborated in the production of the Medieval Court at the London Exhibition of 1851 where the Gothic style of Pugin and his colleagues achieved its greatest public acclaim. Elegant furniture with coloured marquetry from one of Pugin and Crace's most satisfying collaborations, Eastnor Castle, Herefordshire (1849–50) was exhibited, along with a large oak cabinet (now in the Victoria and Albert Museum) and many other objects.

Crace amassed a large number of sketches and designs by Pugin in his workshops which were used by the firm as the basis for their Gothic furniture production until well into the 1860s, while Pugin-designed textiles and wallpapers were supplied by the Crace firm until its closure in 1899. In this way, the imprint of Pugin upon the firm's work was large. However, Crace remained committed to the practice of other styles of decoration, aside from the Gothic. Owing to the influence of his son and successor, John Dibblee Crace, he experimented with the Renaissance and Islamic styles, for example. An Islamic character was given to the refreshment room of the Manchester Art Treasures Exhibition, held in 1857 in Trafford Park, and decorated by Crace. It was doubtless the success of this enterprise that led to his being awarded, at the last minute, the contract to decorate the controversial exhibition building for the London Exhibition of 1862.

In 1862 the reputation of the Crace firm was undoubtedly at its height. J.G. Crace not only decorated the exhibition building but was a principal exhibitor and a juror. He went on to international acclaim at the 1867 Exposition in Paris, receiving a medal from the Imperial Commission. Through these exhibitions his eldest son, John Dibblee Crace, was introduced to the public by means of his subtle but rich designs for furniture in the Gothic and Renaissance styles. In 1877 J.D. Crace became a partner with his father, and the two remained on the closest terms until the elder's death in 1889, when the younger man remarked that much of his pleasure in the business was lost.

The artistic talent of J.D. Crace was, in many respects, similar to that of his grandfather Frederick Crace. It was a precocious talent, resulting in a rapid but delicate style of draughtsmanship and a predilection for subtle colour combinations. J.D. Crace was certainly influenced by the colour theory of his father, but his passion for Italian interiors of the 16th century resulted in his own book on the subject, *The Art of Colour Decoration*, in 1912. Here he put forth his view that no artists before or since had produced better architectural decoration than those of the Italian Renaissance and Mannerist periods. He came to know these interiors intimately through frequent study-tours to Italy throughout his life.

J.D. Crace was fortunate in finding a wealthy patron who shared his views in the person of the 4th Marquess of Bath. Crace and Lord Bath collaborated in designing a series of state and private rooms at Longleat House, Wiltshire, beginning in 1874. By the time work was finished, in 1882, these interiors ranked among the finest examples of the Renaissance Revival in Europe, and they comprise the most complete example of the work of the Crace firm. Not only ceiling and wall decoration, but curtains, upholstery, fittings and furnishings remain *in situ*, all executed by Crace's men to his designs, in conjunction with the ideas and suggestions of Lord Bath.

Of the state rooms on the first floor of Longleat, J.D. Crace's masterpiece is the State Dining Room, begun in 1875, with a ceiling based upon the Great Council Chamber of the Ducal Palace in Venice. Jackson & Sons of Rathbone Place, London, executed the gilded mouldings of the ceiling panels in "composition", into which some of Lord Bath's collection of Venetian paintings was inserted, while the walls were decorated with antique gilded and silvered Spanish leather. On the ground floor, in the private rooms of the east range of the house, Crace decorated the Red Library in 1879 in the manner of Giulio Romano, whose work he much admired. Throughout the ground floor rooms were marquetry doors and fittings of walnut and fruitwoods in delicate arabesques designed by Crace and made by a workshop in Florence.

J.D. Crace had little sympathy for the Arts and Crafts designers, whom he called the, "false prophets of modernism". He was intrigued by the medievalism of Morris & Co., but found their emphasis on rustic, vernacular design to be an affectation. Instead the interiors he executed at Longleat during the 1870s and 1880s reveal a decorative artist steeped in the mainstream of European art and confident in his use of historical styles. As he remarked in *The Art of Colour Decoration*, the decorators of the past, "met the various problems which surface decoration set before them. They are always the same problems; differing perhaps in extent, or in detail, but the same in principle." This remark certainly expressed the view of the great majority of designers working in the 19th century, when historicism played a major role. For example, Crace designed a spectacular series of interiors in the French Renaissance style, including furniture made of ebony and ivory, in the 1890s for William Waldorf Astor in order to celebrate the wealth and prominence recently achieved by his patron.

Nor was the work of the Crace firm confined to country houses and palaces. During the 1870s, when the firm was at its largest with 101 regular employees, the greatest number of sales was for small amounts of textiles and wallpapers, sometimes sent as far as Montreal, Macao, and Australia, to middle-class clients. Civic and institutional commissions had always formed an important aspect of the work of the Crace firm, and this was continued by J.D. Crace, most notably in his highly successful re-decoration of Leeds Town Hall in the 1890s after the original scheme by his father had become blackened by smoke.

For several reasons, J.D. Crace decided to close the family firm in 1899 and act as a consultant from his house at 15 Gloucester Place, London, until his death in 1919. His son was not interested in continuing the business, and many of the principal artists and craftsmen hired by his father had retired without training successors. Moreover, the new century was to prove hostile to the way of life of the Craces' major clients and to the grand manner of decoration they practised. The obscurity of the reputation of the Craces throughout much of the 20th century suggests that the firm would not have flourished alongside the designers of the Modern Movement.

MEGAN ALDRICH

See also Gothic Revival; Pugin

Selected Works

Several hundred signed drawings by members of the Crace family survive in various public collections: the principal holdings are in the Department of Prints and Drawings, Victoria and Albert Museum, and the Drawings Collection, Royal Institute of British Architects (both London); the Department of Drawings, Prints and Photographs, Metropolitan Museum of Art, and the Cooper-Hewitt Museum (both New York); and the Royal Pavilion, Art Gallery and Museums, Brighton. Additional manuscript material, including an unpublished biography of John Crace by his son Frederick and the Mostyn-Crace collection, is in the Victoria and Albert Museum.

Interiors

1770–72 Pantheon, Oxford Street, London (decoration: interiors by James Wyatt)

c.1789–95 Carlton House, London (decorations including the Chinese Drawing Room): Prince Regent, later George IV

c.1794 12 Lincoln's Inn Fields, London (decoration of the breakfast room): Sir John Soane

1801–22 Brighton Pavilion, Sussex (decorations and furniture, including the Entrance Hall, Music Room and Tent Room): Prince Regent, later George IV

c.1802 Pitzhanger Manor, Ealing (decoration of the back parlour): Sir John Soane

1840–44 Chatsworth, Derbyshire (interiors and furnishings, including the library): 6th Duke of Devonshire

1840–44 Devonshire House, London (interiors and furnishings; redecorated by J.D. Crace in 1892): 6th Duke of Devonshire

1841–42 Taymouth Castle, Perthshire (interiors including the State Drawing Room, Small Drawing Room, Gallery, Library, Grand Hall, Tapestry Rooms and bedroom): 2nd Marquess of Breadalbane

1844 Knebworth House, Hertfordshire (interiors and furnishings, including the Library, State Drawing Room and Bedroom): Sir Edward Bulwer-Lytton

1846–69 Palace of Westminster, London (decorations and furnishings with A.W.N. Pugin)

1849–50 Eastnor Castle, Herefordshire (interiors and furnishings with A.W.N. Pugin, including the Drawing Room): 1st Earl Somers

1852–57 Abney Hall, Cheadle, near Manchester (interiors and furnishings including the Drawing Room, Dining Room, Library and Prince Consort's Bedroom): James Watts

1854–55 Windsor Castle, Berkshire (State Rooms for Emperor Napoleon III and Empress Eugénie): Queen Victoria

1857 Leeds Town Hall (decoration and furnishings; redecorated by J.D. Crace in 1894)

1862 International Exhibition, London (decoration and furnishings)

1874–82 Longleat, Wiltshire (interiors including the Saloon, State Drawing Room, Ante- Library and Red Library, and State Dining Room): 4th Marquess of Bath

1879	Pompeian Room, Ickworth House, Suffolk (decoration): 3rd Marquess of Bristol
1895–96	18 Carlton House Terrace, London (interiors and furniture): William Waldorf Astor

Publications

J.G. Crace, "The History of Paperhangings", a lecture published in the *Royal Institute of British Architects Proceedings*, 1839

J.G. Crace, "On the Decoration of Some Buildings at Munich", a lecture published in the *Royal Institute of British Architects Proceedings*, 1850–51

J.G. Crace, "The Decoration of Chirk Castle" in the *Builder*, 1853, p.449

J.G. Crace, "On the Decoration of the International Exhibition Building" in the *Journal of the Society of Arts*, 11 April 1862, pp.339–43

J.G. Crace, "On Colour" in the *Builder*, 30 November 1867, pp.874–75 and 7 December 1867, pp.888–89

J.D. Crace, "Household Taste" in *Furniture Gazette*, 17, 11 March 1882, pp.167–69 and 1 April 1882, p.203

J.D. Crace, "Augustus Welby Pugin and Furniture" in *Royal Institute of British Architects Journal*, 5, 1894, pp.517–19

J.D. Crace, *The Art of Colour Decoration*, 1912

Further Reading

The definitive study of the Crace firm is Aldrich 1990 which includes detailed accounts of all aspects of the family's work and numerous references to primary and secondary sources relating to particular commissions. For further details of the firm's work at Brighton see Morley 1984, and for A.W.N. Pugin's designs for Crace see Wedgwood 1985.

Aldrich, Megan, "Gothic Interiors of the 19th Century: John Gregory Crace at Abney Hall" in *V & A Album*, 5, 1986, pp.74–86

Aldrich, Megan, "Fit for an Emperor at Windsor: J. G. Crace at Windsor Castle" in *Country Life*, 8 December 1988, pp.56–59

Aldrich, Megan, "The Marquess and the Decorator: J. D. Crace at Longleat House" in *Country Life*, 7 December 1989, pp.162–67

Aldrich, Megan (editor), *The Craces: Royal Decorators, 1768–1899*, London: Murray, 1990

Aldrich, Megan, *Gothic Revival*, London: Phaidon, 1994

Aldrich, Megan, "John Gregory Crace" in Colin Matthew (editor), *The New Dictionary of National Biography*, Oxford: Oxford University Press, forthcoming

Catalogue of the Drawings Collection of the Royal Institute of British Architects, Farnborough: Gregg, 1972

Crook, J. Mordaunt and M.H. Port, *The History of the King's Works*, vol.6: 1782–1851, London: HMSO, 1973

Flower, Sibylla Jane, "Knebworth House" in *Country Life*, 177, 31 January 1985, pp.244–48 and 7 February 1985, pp.320–23

Morley, John, *The Making of the Royal Pavilion, Brighton: Designs and Drawings*, London: Philip Wilson, 1984

Port, M.H. (editor), *The Houses of Parliament*, New Haven and London: Yale University Press, 1976

Rosoman, Treve, "The Pitzhanger Story" in *Traditional Interior Decoration*, 2, October / November 1987

Rowan, Alastair, "Taymouth Castle, Perthshire" in *Country Life*, 8 October 1964, pp.912–16 and 15 October 1964, pp.978–81

Wainwright, Clive, "Eastnor Castle II" in *Country Life*, 20 May 1993, pp.90–93

Wedgwood, Alexandra, *A. W. N. Pugin and the Pugin Family* (catalogue of drawings), London: Victoria and Albert Museum, 1985

Crane, Walter 1845–1915

British illustrator, painter and designer

Walter Crane was one of the most influential figures in the British Arts and Crafts Movement, occupying a position of importance second only to that of his friend and mentor, William Morris. And, like Morris's, Crane's talents were as prolific as they were versatile. Trained first as an engraver, he became hugely successful as a graphic artist and illustrator of children's books; he was also active throughout his life as a painter, exhibiting regularly at London's Royal Academy, and he designed several hundred patterns for wallpapers, textiles, stained glass, and ceramics. He was also responsible for the design and execution of painted friezes, mosaics and relief panels within several actual interiors. And finally, he published numerous articles and books championing the unity of the arts and crafts and was a dedicated and able administrator of various art schools and exhibition societies. His work was greatly admired in the UK and he was one of the few British designers in the late 19th century to achieve international renown, particularly in Eastern Europe and the United States.

Born in 1845, the son of the painter Thomas Crane, Crane was educated first on an informal basis by his father, and then apprenticed to the political radical, printer and wood-engraver, W. J. Linton, in 1859. It was Linton who gave him his first experience of book illustration, and in 1865 Crane began designing his own books for children, known as Toy Books, for the publisher George Routledge. Early contact with the work of Morris and his associates, and an awareness of the views propounded in books like C.L. Eastlake's *Hints on Household Taste* (1868), encouraged an interest in the decorative arts and by the end of the 1860s Crane had become thoroughly conversant with current ideas on interior decoration and design. Not surprisingly, therefore, many of his Toy Book illustrations of this period reflect the influence of fashionable, artistic styles, and depict interiors containing features such as Japanese screens and fans, blue and white china, 18th-century furnishings, and oriental rugs that were much admired by followers of the Aesthetic and Queen Anne schools of design.

These illustrations were highly praised by architects and artists and, given their wide circulation, they actively helped to disseminate a taste for new and progressive styles of furnishing in many middle- and upper-middle class homes. They also led to a closer practical involvement in interior design when Crane was approached in 1876 by Metford Warner, the proprietor of the wallpaper manufacturers Jeffrey & Co., with a commission to adapt some of the Toy Book plates as nursery wallpapers. Crane proved to be a skilled and prolific designer of wallpapers of all kinds and Jeffrey & Co. printed more than fifty of his designs. Like Morris, who was clearly a strong influence on his work, Crane frequently made use of interwoven floral patterns. But, unlike Morris, his wallpapers also featured bird and animal forms, such as peacocks, swans, deer and rabbits, and examples such as the *Peacock Garden* (1889), *Cockatoo* (1891), and *Cockatoo and Pomegranate* (1899) patterns, all demonstrate his versatility in incorporating pictorial elements within a floral design. Several of his patterns, like *Woodnotes* (1886), and *Golden Age* (1887) included human figures and were derived from the classical style that he had previously used in designs for Wedgwood ceramics and for many of his large oil paintings. Others, like the *National Arms of England, Scotland and Ireland* (1902) appear to have been influenced by medieval heraldry. The majority were highly complex, containing numerous colours and much linear activity. As a result they were not only expensive to produce but also sometimes criticised for a lack of reticence that was deemed inappropriate in wallpaper. Nevertheless, they won numerous awards both in England and abroad, and despite the fact that Crane himself decried it as a "decorative disease", his designs were an important influence on the sinuous, vegetal style associated with continental Art Nouveau.

From the late 1870s, Crane designed relief panels and friezes for several actual interiors. Much of this work was executed in plaster and gesso. The work at Coombe Bank, near Sevenoaks, Kent, for example, included an elaborate, classical-style gesso ceiling depicting the signs of the zodiac, for the saloon. This project also included a chimney breast, mantel, andirons and fender, and Crane produced painted decorations for the window shutters and doors, and a frieze of decorative figures that was intended to complement the owner, Dr. William Spottiswoode's, collection of Venetian pictures. In 1880, Crane designed another series of panels based on the zodiac theme that were executed in plaster for the stairwell of Stewart Hodgson's London house in South Audley Street. He also designed four mosaic panels depicting the Elements for the drawing room; an earlier commission in this medium was for a frieze in Lord Leighton's Arab Hall.

Another important project dating from 1880 was Crane's work at 1 Holland Park. Enlarged by Philip Webb, the interiors of this famous house were entirely decorated by Morris & Co. and it contained many of the firm's finest embroideries, textiles and tapestries, as well as a plethora of antiques, paintings and other works of art. Crane's contribution consisted of decorations in the dining room where he devised a lacquered, gesso and plaster ceiling, inspired by the *Rubáiyát of Omar Khayyám*, and a gesso frieze illustrating scenes from *Aesop's Fables*. In 1883, he painted a three-foot high, oil on canvas, frieze, depicting the early Norse settlers in America, for the dining room of an American house, Vinland, in Newport, Rhode Island. And at Clare Lawn, East Sheen, he designed more painted friezes containing figures representing the arts, entertainment, and learning, for the picture gallery, drawing room and library (1888–90). Crane's last major interior project was for the home of the railway magnate, Sir Weetman Pearson, at Paddockhurst, Sussex (1896–97), where he devised a plaster frieze for the dining room illustrating "a sort of playful symbolic history of locomotion and transport, from the earliest period to the present time", and which included representations of not only ox-carts, boats and automobiles, but also Lady Pearson's silver bicycle!

Crane's versatility as a designer led to his involvement in many media. He designed stained glass, for example, for the windows of the library at Vinland, the picture gallery doors at Clare Lawn, and the Church of Agapemone, Stamford Hill, London. He also designed some spectacular embroidered hangings, sewn by workers at the Royal Art School of Needlework and subsequently exhibited to much acclaim at the Philadelphia Centennial in 1876. His designs for printed cottons were manufactured by Edmund Potter & Co., and

Crane: interior of Crane's house, 13 Holland Street, London, 1890s

Thomas Wardle, his woven textiles were made by John Wilson, and he designed one tapestry, based on his *Goose Girl* illustration, which was commissioned by Morris & Co. and woven at their Merton Abbey works where Crane's stained glass had also been made.

The sheer diversity of his talents makes Crane's style difficult to summarize, but his strength as a designer of two-dimensional works lay in his ability to translate complex visual images into simplified linear designs and to create dynamic patterns out of colour combinations ranging from the subtle to the lively. His three-dimensional reliefs appear to rely more on his admiration for classical or Renaissance prototypes, where balance and clarity of form play a primary role. But perhaps Crane's greatest impact on interior design came through his work for the Arts and Crafts Exhibition Society, his lectures and demonstrations of art and craft techniques, and his publications on the decorative arts and design. In 1888 Crane became a founder-member and president of the Arts and Crafts Exhibition Society, whose aims were to showcase the work of craft-workers and designers, and to inform and educate the public to demand higher standards of craftsmanship and design. Under Crane's leadership, the Society mounted annual exhibitions from 1888 to 1890, and every third year thereafter, and he became a dedicated champion of good quality design. His lecture topics also included practical advice and exercises on topics such as plaster reliefs and embroidery. Much of his writing focused on the unity of the arts and crafts, and, like Morris, he was a firm believer in the creativity of hand-work and in the importance of beauty in improving the lot of society as a whole. These ideas were publicised in books, such as *The Claims of Decorative Art* (1892), *The Bases of Design* (1898), *Line and Form* (1900), and *Ideals in Art* (1905), where they were able to reach a far wider audience than that of his fellow-designers. And finally, as part-time Director of Design at the Manchester School of Art (1893–96), and as Principal of the Royal College of Art (from 1898), Crane also had a significant effect on design education in England.

DOUGLAS G. CAMPBELL

See also Arts and Crafts Movement

Biography

Born in Liverpool, 15 August 1845. Apprenticed to the wood-engraver W.J.Linton, London, 1859–62; worked with printer Edmund Evans & Co. from 1863. Married Mary Frances Andrews 1871: one daughter, Beatrice, and two sons, Lancelot, and the architect Lionel Crane. Travelled in Italy 1871–73. Exhibited oil paintings at the Royal Academy, London, from 1862; designed Toy Books for George Routledge & Sons 1865–76; ceramics from 1867; interior decoration, wallpapers, tiles and embroideries from mid-1870s; Art Superintendent of London Decorating Co. 1880; designed printed and woven textiles and from late 1880s. Work exhibited at many national and international exhibitions including the Philadepphia Centennial, 1876. First retrospective exhibition at the Fine Art Society, London, 1891 (toured US and Europe until 1896); exhibited Hungary 1900, Vienna 1901, and Turin 1902. An active member of several artistic and political societies including the Art-Workers' Guild (1884), the Socialist League (1885), the Fabian Society (1886) and the Arts and Crafts Exhibition Society (President 1888–1893 and 1896–1912). Lectured and published extensively on the decorative arts from the 1890s; part-time Director of Design at the Manchester School of Art, 1893–96; Principal of Royal College of Art, London, from 1898. Awarded Albert Gold Medal, Royal Society of Arts, 1905. Died in London, 14 March 1915.

Selected Works

A large collection of Crane's designs for decorative work is in the Victoria and Albert Museum. The Museum also houses collections of his wallpapers, textiles and ceramics. Other important holdings of Crane's work are the Whitworth Art Gallery, Manchester (wallpapers and textiles); the City Art Gallery, Manchester (wallpapers and ceramics); Royal Borough of Kensington and Chelsea Libraries and Arts Service, London (decorative designs); William Morris Gallery, Walthamstow (wallpapers and designs); and the Wedgwood Museum, Stoke-on-Trent (ceramics).

Interiors

1875	52 Prince's Gate, London (boudoir: decorative frieze): T. Eustace Smith
1877–79	Arab Hall, Leighton House, Holland Park Road, London (Arab Hall: mosaic frieze): Frederic Leighton
1878–80	Coombe Bank, Sundridge, Sevenoaks (saloon: gesso and painted decoration): Dr. William Spottiswood
1880	1 Holland Park, London (dining room: ceiling, frieze and overmantel): Alecco Ionides
1888–90	Clare Lawn, East Sheen, Surrey (picture gallery, library and drawing room: decorative friezes and stained glass): Sir Francis Wigan
1890s	13 Holland Street, London (decorations and furniture): Walter Crane
1896–97	Paddockhurst, near Crawley, Sussex (drawing room: stucco panels and frieze): Sir Weetman Pearson

Crane designed wallpapers for Jeffrey & Co.; tiles for Maw & Co.; tiles and ceramics for Pilkington's Tile & Pottery Co.; and ceramics for Josiah Wedgwood & Sons. His designs for printed cottons were produced by Edmund Potter & Co., Thomas Wardle & Co., and Birch Gibson; woven textiles by John Wilson & Sons; carpets by Templeton & Co.; tapestries by Morris & Co., and A. H. Lee & Sons. He also designed embroideries for the Royal School of Art Needlework.

Publications

A Catalogue of a Collection of Designs by Walter Crane ... with Prefatory Notes by the Artist, London: Fine Art Society, 1891
"Decorative Plaster Work" in *Royal Institute of British Architects Transactions*, vol.VII, 1891
The Claims of Decorative Art, 1892
"The English Revival of Decorative Art" in *Fortnightly Review*, vol.52, December 1892
The Bases of Design, 1898
"The Work of Walter Crane with Notes by the Artist" in *Art Journal Easter Art Annual*, 1898
Line and Form, 1900
Ideals in Art: Papers, Theoretical, Practical, Critical, 1905
An Artist's Reminiscences, 1907
William Morris to Whistler: Papers and Addresses on Art and Craft, 1911

Further Reading

For a recent study of Crane's work see Smith and Hyde 1989. The most comprehensive lists of Crane's publications appear in Spencer 1975 and Burke 1986, which also include many references to primary and secondary sources.

Anscombe, Isabelle, *Arts and Crafts Style*, London: Phaidon, 1991
Burke, Doreen Bolger and others, *In Pursuit of Beauty: Americans and the Aesthetic Movement* (exhib. cat.: Metropolitan Museum, New York), New York: Rizzoli, 1986
Crane, Anthony, "My Grandfather, Walter Crane" in *Yale University Library Gazette*, vol.31, 1957
Exhibition of Victorian and Edwardian Decorative Arts, London: Victoria and Albert Museum, 1952
Kaplan, Wendy, *"The Art that is Life": The Arts and Crafts Movement in America, 1875–1920* (exhib. cat.: Museum of Fine Arts, Boston), Boston: Little Brown, 1987
Konody, Paul G., *The Art of Walter Crane*, London: Bell, 1902
Oman, Charles C. and Jean Hamilton, *Wallpapers: A History and Illustrated Catalogue of the Collection of the Victoria and Albert Museum*, London: Sotheby Publications, and New York: Abrams, 1982
Parry, Linda, *Textiles of the Arts and Crafts Movement*, London and New York: Thames and Hudson, 1988
Smith, Greg and Sarah Hyde (editors), *Walter Crane: Artist, Designer and Socialist* (exhib. cat.: Whitworth Art Gallery, Manchester), London: Lund Humphries, 1989
Spencer, Isobel, *Walter Crane*, London: Studio Vista, and New York: Macmillan, 1975
Stephens, F.G., "The Designs of Walter Crane", in *The Portfolio*, 1890, pp.12–19
Vallance, Aymer, "Walter Crane's Paper-Hangings" in *The Studio*, vol.4, 1894–95
Von Schleinitz, Otto, *Walter Crane*, Leipzig: Velhagen & Klasing, 1902

Curtains: Bedhangings and Window Curtains

Before the 17th century, documented references to window curtains are rare. The size of windows and the use of wall-hangings and bedhangings to create warmth and comfort moderated their use, and when recorded they are usually described as made of a warm and draught-excluding wool fabric such as the "courteynes of grene saye" used in the three most important interiors in a London house in 1509, or those of yellow saye recorded at Canons Ashby about fifty years later. Darnix curtains "for the windowes" in an important bedchamber were reported in the Hardwick Hall Inventory of 1601 (as were some for Chatsworth). In the same room at Hardwick another set of "curtins of damask and sarscenet for the windowes", and at Cockesden in 1610 for the "wyndoes, 2 curteans of greene cotton" were probably hung to reduce light. The richly decorated and sophisticated interiors of

Renaissance Italy used shutters, wicker and linen screens to exclude light and draughts. By the early 17th century, window curtains were found in the grandest and most fashionable interiors, notably in Italy and France, when the word *rideaux* came into general use. However, they were not generally regarded as necessary fittings until later in the century, and many windows had no curtains until well into the 18th century.

The influence of Italian architecture and style, which had spread throughout Europe by the beginning of the 17th century, not only led to the appearance of larger windows in new classically-inspired buildings, but also promoted the Renaissance ideal of harmony and a unity of decorative effects in interiors. This was created first by architectural ornament and fittings, and enhanced by the textile hangings and upholstery of which Paris had become the leader of fashion by the 1630s. Seat upholstery, bedhangings, wallhangings and portière curtains were often made of the same fabric and trimmings, but window curtains (although they might be of the same colour) were generally fashioned from a different fabric. Soft furnishings in the Princess of Orange's luxurious closet at The Hague were described in a 1632 inventory as being all of green velvet, whereas the window curtains were made of a green silk taffeta. One curtain per window was most common until the later 17th century, although two would be more symmetrical when open. Two windows close together, with the curtain on each drawn to the opposite side, could create the same effect, as many Dutch interiors and a series of engravings of Parisian interiors in the 1630s (Thornton, 1978) illustrate. The 1654 Inventory of Ham House in Surrey describes divided curtains in several rooms with window curtains matching the wallhangings – probably examples of an advanced taste, influenced by the pre-Civil War court fashions of Charles I. When the house was redecorated in the 1670s, divided curtains were fitted in the principal rooms and in 1679 they were also recorded in the elegant interiors of Dublin Castle. In 1673 an article in the *Mercure Galant* (which kept Parisians informed of the latest gossip and changes in fashion) described divided curtains as the latest fashion, although it was most likely that the article was affirming that single curtains were no longer considered to be acceptable (Thornton, 1978).

Inventories of aristocratic and gentry houses in England during the 17th century record references to curtains of "stripte stuff", darnix (a coarse patterned woollen material), saye (a lightweight serge), and other woollen stuffs. Indian painted cottons, known as "pintadoes" or "chintes" were being imported by the East India Company and in 1682 the "Calleco Chamber" at Cowdray – including the window curtains – was entirely fitted out with them. In 1623 Lord Howard of Naworth paid 49 shillings for "4 ells of mingled [i.e., shot] taffeta to mak a curtin". Sarsne (a thin silk taffeta) was also popular, being particularly suitable for sun curtains.

Window curtains seem largely to have been fitted to regulate the access of light at this time, hence the use of thin but elegant fabrics. These straight curtains were hung from thin iron rods and rings which were clearly visible. The rods were occasionally gilded and sometimes had a decoratively scrolled or curled end. The curtains were usually sewn directly onto rings or hung from tapes looped over the rod. They were not as wide as modern curtains, so the effect was somewhat thinner and flatter when drawn, and they seem to have hung to just below the window. By the third quarter of the 17th century, rods were masked by a matching or contrasting textile pelmet, which in a bedchamber, with matching valances on the bed, created more decorative unity. Inward-opening leaded windows were being widely replaced by sliding sashes which were easier to open when curtains were installed, and some embellishments were being added, such as fringe along the bottom and braid to the sides.

Around 1690, the smartest and most fashionable curtains took on a new form as upholstery effects (led by the example of the French court of Louis XIV) became richer, and window curtains followed the pattern of the draped upholstery effects on beds and wallhangings, with flounces, festoons and swagging. These new "pull-up" curtains were drawn straight up or lowered by cords sewn to the back of the curtains, through pulleys set into the embrasure at the top of the window or in a pulley-board. The pelmet to mask this mechanism could be of fabric, or one of wood (known most commonly as a "curtain cornice") was often carved to match other architectural features in a room or the cornice of a bed. These were usually covered with the same fabric of which the curtain was made, and both types could be decoratively edged with a contrasting braid ("lace") or hung with fringe. Designs for four different and elaborate curtains of this type were published by the Huguenot architect Daniel Marot, and were probably inspired by what he had seen in France before he fled as a religious refugee in 1685.

Marot's illustrations for window treatments are very decorative: one has a shaped, scalloped-edged pelmet, the curtain with lappet-shaped edges outlined with braid and fringe. Another has flounced, ruffled edges to the top edge of the pelmet and another is trimmed along the bottom in this manner with additional fringe, and is drawn up so that tails drape at either side and tassels hang in the spaces between the furbelows. These curtain types were being made for English royal palaces by the end of the century: among the 1699 Hampton Court Estimates are details of white silk damask being ordered for the King's Closet, with white silk cord and tassels. Reference is also made to "covering cornices". The pelmet with scalloped edges was used in England until the 1740s, and examples survive in America: wool tape of different widths and colour could be applied to curvilinear pelmets in decorative patterns of scrollwork, strapwork and volutes, reflecting contemporary taste in ornament.

Most of the principal rooms at Dyrham Park, fitted out in the 1690s, had pull-up curtains, with pelmets being specified for two rooms as "Window Curtains" that were "to be made to draw up". These were still made of lighter fabrics and contrasting colours for the rooms, with the richest materials on the walls and beds, such as yellow wallhangings with red and white window curtains or the "painted Sattin Window Curtains & vallains" for the Damask Bed Chamber, where the portière curtains were made of the same damask as the rest of the textile furnishings. Velvet, the most expensive and heaviest fabric, was not generally used for window curtains, but in the best bedchamber, where crimson and yellow velvets were used for bedhangings and portières hung against tapestries, the window curtains were made of yellow damask, generally considered the next best thing. White damask, used also at Ham House, was employed with crimson "strip'd velvet"

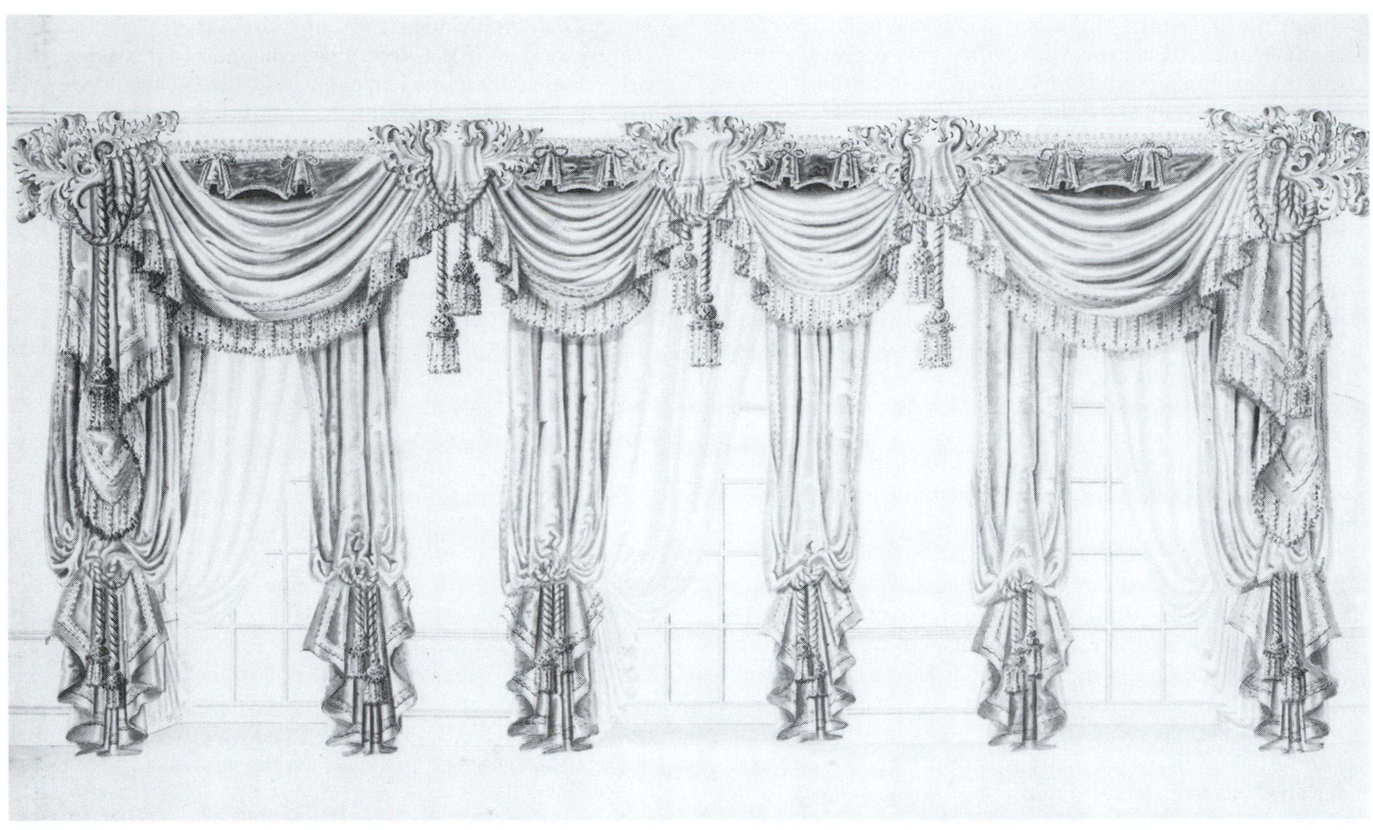

Curtains: scheme by Gillow & Co., 1820

upholstery. Silk fabrics were used for the grandest bedchambers, anterooms and closets, as at Ham House, but "Stuff", serge and cheney, and other fine worsted fabrics, were used for "parlours" where dining took place, and libraries, as at Dyrham. Divided curtains with pelmets were also present, such as those of "blew serge" in the Great Hall.

Divided curtains continued to be used in grand interiors, acquiring a new sophistication with the development of a pulley system to draw them. An interior view of c.1730, of a grand reception room at Wanstead House (by William Hogarth, Museum of Art, Philadelphia), which had been built in the 1720s in the Palladian style, has simple draw curtains with the rod on display. In 1705, the French refugee upholsterer Lapierre, who did work at Hampton Court Palace, charged the Duke of Montagu for two sets of window curtains of blue camlet "to draw upon pulley Rodds", and in the following year, for 76 yards of green silk cord with five green tassels to draw curtains. Cords (usually described as "line") and tassels in the 18th century were treated as important decorative accessories for both pull-up and draw curtains. They were made in the same basic material as the curtain, either silk, worsted, linen or of mixed fibres, and usually colour co-ordinated. Rods and other hardware were considered similiarly, such as the gilded rods specified for the Dining Room curtains at Temple Newsam in 1735, with a gilded brass pulley, gilded hooks to hold up the rods and "36 large polished brass Rings Gilt".

Against the architectural backdrop of the lavish Baroque style in Europe, and the slightly later, more austere Palladian style in England and America, the most important and lofty interiors were fitted out with pull-up curtains, where the ornamental woodwork of the window architraves would be exposed when they were drawn up. Increasingly, the fabric of which they were made was colour co-ordinated with the rest of the interior of which they had become an intrinsically decorative facet. The Duke of Cumberland's suite of four rooms at Hampton Court Palace, which were completed in early 1733, had "draw-up window curtains" in two rooms of "blue Florence Taffeta", co-ordinated with blue mohair hangings, seat and bed upholstery. The upholsterer Sarah Gilbert's bill describes the brass rings (or "Os") and the lead weights (or "plumbetts"), usually pear-shaped (although round-shaped weights have been found in surviving festoon curtains supplied by Chippendale to the Tapestry Room at Newby Hall), and three different types of "binding lace", braid, and silk line which were used to make up each curtain. The Chiswick House Inventory of 1770 describes interiors which may have survived from three decades previous, where "festoon Window Curtains" of silk lustring are colour matched in interiors with velvet and tapestry wallhangings.

Curtains of this type were being described as "festoon" window curtains in England by the middle of the 18th century, and were so ubiquitous that in inventories between the 1760s and late 1780s the term was often not specifically used (Westman, 1993). In America they are generally described as "Venetian" curtains. In the Neo-Classical interiors of this period, the fuller, more bunched festoons in use earlier in the century were not considered so desirable, as surviving "festoon" curtains at Osterley Park demonstrate. In the grandest rooms, hung with damasks or brocades (velvet was not so fashionable), curtains were now being made of the same fabrics and, probably to protect them from the damaging effects of sunlight, were usually lined, often with a glazed tammy (a fine worsted fabric) which was richly coloured to match the facing fabric. Blinds were generally installed with festoon curtains to do the job that curtains had earlier, such as the wooden-slatted Venetian blinds at Audley End House, brown Holland roller blinds at Appuldurcombe Park (c.1780 Inventory) or the "Spring blinds" at Chiswick House (1770 Inventory).

The silk face and tammy lining of the surviving Etruscan Room curtains at Osterley are bound together along the sides and edges with a patterned braid or "lace", concealed by the heading of a silk fringe. On the back of each, four lengths of narrow silk tape are stitched, with small brass rings attached, about 8 to 9 inches apart through which the silk cords ("line") were passed, creating three evenly-spaced swags when drawn. The numbers of these lengths of tape could be varied to create less or more swags, depending on the size of the window and the effect desired. The plumbetts were covered with the lining fabric and stitched onto the base of each of the silk tapes on the reverse. Attached by rings to the base of the cords, these weights would influence the shape of the swags when drawn up, making them neater, and allow the curtains to be fully lowered. A large silk tassel was also divided to hang on the end of the silk line, which was looped around a pair of gilt brass cloakpins and which fixed the curtains in position.

The shape and finish of curtain cornices increasingly matched those of beds in the best bedchambers. The Boughton inventory of 1718 describes the State Room window curtains with cornices of white damask with a white fringe. Chippendale's *Director* includes a plate of carved cornices for beds and windows, and the Gallery at Harewood House still displays spectacular examples of the firm's work, with curtain cornices carved and painted to imitate the effect of festooned silk with fringed valances. In the middle decades of the century curtain cornices took on the curvilinear lines of the Rococo and could be ornamented with *rocaille*, or pierced. Gothick interiors provided their own ornamental vocabulary for cornices for window curtains, and those provided for Neo-Classical interiors in a severe and basic box form were ornamented with appropriate classical motifs, enriched perhaps by cresting of scrolled acanthus or anthemion, or, as in one Parisian example of 1773, with military trophies. Occasionally no cornice was supplied, as in the Great Drawing Room and dining room at Audley End, where a braid might be applied along the top of a curtain which would be gathered in small box-pleats and pinned to the pulley board behind.

Formal damasks, generally *en suite* with the rest of the room, were favoured during the early part of the century, but damasks of a more naturalistic floral flavour (sometimes of three colours) were popularised by the Rococo taste. In England such damasks were used at Brocket Park and Audley End in the 1770s. Fabrics used at Osterley for other window curtains include "Decca work", an Indian embroidered cotton used for Mr. and Mrs. Child's bedchamber, which was lined with silk. Thomas Chippendale provided festoon curtains for the drawing room of William Constable's London town house of "Blue mixt damask", lined with blue tammy, with "mixt" line and tassells. Fringe, when used, was often applied only along the bottom of the curtains, or could be broader across the bottom and narrower along the sides. Alternatively, it could run only part way up the sides. It could also be dyed in narrow widths of different colours, such as the crimson, white and green fringe used to trim the three-colour damask festoons in the Great Drawing Room at Audley End in the 1760s. Lustring (a crisp plain coloured silk) was used widely by the end of the century, as were watered silks and tabberary, a striped fabric with alternating bands of watered and satin weave mixed silk. Worsted fabrics, such as moreen and camlet, which could be plain, striped or stamped with a watered or patterned effect, were also popular, particularly in America. Printed chintzes, increasingly available from the middle of the century with the development of new technology, were widely used on both sides of the Atlantic, particularly in bedchambers, parlours and drawing rooms. In 1770 a "Chintz Bed Chamber" in the old house at Chiswick had "Chintz festoon Window Curtains Lin'd".

Another form of window curtain popular in England and America from the middle to the end of the 18th century was described in England as "drapery" or "in drapery" and in America as "festoon" curtains. These would be hung from a pelmet board but divided, and the rings would be sewn on diagonally behind so that when the cords were drawn the curtains were pulled up towards the outer corners of the window, forming "draped festoons" with tails at the sides. Zoffany's portrait of Sir Lawrence Dundas (c.1769) depicts curtains of this type, made of blue damask with a matching fringe, and Thomas Chippendale's firm made two similar curtains for Mersham-le-Hatch in 1767.

After the 1770s upholstery became increasingly important. This was particularly evident in Parisian interiors, where new and elaborate curtain types were created through the inventive cutting and combining of fabrics and colours, enriched with trimmings hung from rods, with a pelmet of "drapery" swathed over a decorative pole or hung in a festooned form with tapering tails, but with draw curtains hung below from rods. The walls of Empire-style rooms were hung all round with these draperies, of which the window curtains formed an intrinsic part. In the 1780s Henry Holland's work at Carlton House for the Prince of Wales demonstrated the richness of these new effects. The most intricate and extravagant of the hanging schemes would have two different weights of fabrics, usually in two colours with the heavier for the drapery, running across the top of the window and decoratively draped over a pole, and the lighter used for the secondary areas which could be festooned swags or a divided pelmet hanging beneath the drapery. Both elements would be richly trimmed.

Divided curtains and "drapery" were the height of fashion throughout Europe and America by c.1800: designs shown by Thomas Sheraton in his *Cabinet Directory* (1803) illustrate the new window drapery with elaborate valances and trimmings, and he noted that festoon curtains were less favoured in "genteel houses" than "the French rod curtains" hanging straight. The rod allowed divided curtains to overlap slightly where they met; two pulleys on one side and one on the other, with cords operating the draw function from one side, created a system that was used well into the 20th century. Draped pelmets, perhaps with sun-curtains or blinds, were also popular; Thomas Jefferson ordered "Drapery for the tops of 4

Curtains: Gothic curtains designed by A.C. Pugin from Ackermann's *The Repository of Arts*, 1826

windows ... no curtains being desired" for Monticello in 1808. Many were related to the newly fashionable floor-length windows, and "continuous drapery", spanning a number of adjacent windows, was popular until 1830; it never totally went out of fashion and was revived again at the end of the 19th century. An early example is the scheme provided for the Dining Room of Attingham Park in 1805 by Gillows. Such draperies needed to be protected from the damaging effects of sunlight, and blinds were standard additions, as were sun-curtains of muslin (plain or figured), taffeta or some other semi-transparent fabrics hung from a thin inner rod, which could be partly drawn to one side. These could be coloured, embroidered, trimmed with fringe or have shaped edges.

Rings and rods increasingly became the focus of fashionable ornament, and the curtain cornice vitually disappeared for some years during the early decades of the 19th century. Some schemes hung from rods, but the tails were draped over large cloak pins stamped with stylised rosettes or other appropriate ornament. Imperial eagles were employed in the grandest schemes, surmounting the whole arrangement and grasping the edge of a pelmet in their claws. The head of Apollo, from which the folds of the drapery radiated, was used in the Crimson Drawing Room at Carlton House. Decorative rods took the form of a Roman spear or Roman fasces, and after 1814 Prince of Wales feathers were incorporated in the vocabulary of ornament – which also included elaborate finials and terminals shaped in popular classical ornaments of the period such as the anthemion or acroteria, outsize cloakpins and rings, and brackets to support gilt or mahogany and rosewood rods, which became thicker by the 1830s.

Contemporary theories of complementary colours also appear to have influenced the fashioning of upholstery, and particularly curtains, during the first three decades of the 19th century. Many plain fabrics, boldly coloured with contrasting linings and trimmings were draped over rods, with the curtains beneath held back over large-scale cloak pins, and after 1820 by tiebacks consisting of heavy looped cord with large tassels. Bright lemon or egg yolk yellow, scarlet, red and blue were all popular colours, and could be joined in combinations such as crimson damask with a blue embossed calico. Other recommendations included light blue silk lined with pink taffeta with gold trimmings, yellow with lilac or geranium pink. A more austere combination of scarlet and black was used in the Long Gallery at Castle Howard and the Queen's Breakfast Room at Buckingham House. These colour and textural contrasts could be repeated in the trimmings and tie-backs, which could be made wholly of silk or worsted, or a combination of the two. Red and heavier fabrics tended to be obligatory for dining rooms, while lightweight fabrics were for drawing rooms, boudoirs and bedrooms. The most expensive and exclusive fabrics were still silk velvets, "superfine cloths" (closely woven woollen fabric with a fine nap), silk damasks and satins. Cheaper alternatives were moreen, Manchester (cotton) velvets and chintzes, with a wide range of patterns, from large landscapes to small seaweeds, often used for linings, and including floral, Chinoiserie, classical and Gothic designs. Cotton dimity was another fabric that became increasingly fashionable during the first three decades of the 19th century.

A larger range of trimmings became available, of which gold was the most frequently recommended. Interlacing gimps (used for borders) were made of vellum covered with silk thread in various sizes and degrees of elaboration. Bordered fringes could have richly decorative "hangers" of small balls, or balls interspersed with tapered long drops or spools, and might have a wide netted heading. "Bullion" fringe consisted of lengths of tiny joined balls set before a double spun cord fringe at regular intervals, and tassels were made with similar combinations, in different sizes for hanging from draperies and for use as tiebacks. All trimmings were often in contrasting colours to match those of a curtain scheme.

From the beginning of the 19th century, published manuals and periodicals played an important role in disseminating information about new fashions throughout Europe and America among the burgeoning middle classes. George Smith's *Collection of Designs for Household Furniture and Interior Decoration* of 1808 illustrates the hierarchy of newly fashionable styles. Designs for the Egyptian style were " ... proper for Dining-rooms and Libraries"; the Etruscan style was for "secondary rooms, with draperies of plain coloured calicoes or small chintz with fringes of worsted", and the Chinese was for grandeur when "the curtains should be made wholly of silk or velvet and in either case embroidered in yellow to imitate gold". Rudolph Ackermann's *Repository* popularised the mature Empire style of Percier and Fontaine in England, as did the *Workwoman's Guide* (1838) in America. Also following the French lead, J.C. Loudon's *Encyclopaedia* of 1833 promoted the "Grecian" taste in draperies with simple designs of straight hanging panels of heavy material hung from large brass or wooden rings on rods with elaborately turned finials, in a manner that continued in fashion in middle-class houses for three decades. From the 1820s, the historical revival styles which were to dominate interior design for the rest of the century began to appear in increasing numbers of books, trade catalogues and periodicals. The Gothic was a highly creative and reforming strand, while the "Renaissance" or "modern" French style incorporated most outpourings of the classical tradition in drapery, including the revived "Louis Quatorze" and "Louis Quinze" styles. The latter dominated mainstream fashion in the middle decades of the century and again during the 1890s throughout much of Europe and America.

About 1840, the lambrequin – a flat pelmet of shaped outline, often fanciful and with long tails at the sides – appeared. It could be hung from poles or from decorative cornices and generally replaced draped and festooned headings. One of the most fashionable shapes was known as the "Vandyke" which could be used for all the medieval-inspired and exotic styles, but, as many contemporary French publications illustrate, simply by varying the shape and trimmings, lambrequins could also be made to express the whole gamut of popular styles.

A wide variety of fabrics in many price ranges also became increasingly available, such as mixed damasks, moreens, wool velvets and repps. The best rooms continued to be fitted with silks or wool, with the heavier fabrics still being used in libraries and dining rooms, often in crimson or deep olive green. Seventeenth- and 18th-century silk damask designs in Baroque and Rococo patterns were rewoven using new technology, as were 17th-century fabrics such as brocatelle and chenille and "tapestries" for upholstery. Chintzes began to go out of fashion by the 1860s, except for use in bedrooms.

The layers of different fabric weights, embellished with long, trailing braid, fringe, cord, tassels and tiebacks, attracted the antipathy of mid- and late 19th century design reformers who attacked the unnecessary complexity of contemporary curtain schemes, and the use of heavy fabrics and lavish trimmings as repositories of dust and vermin. C.L. Eastlake praised the new cretonnes (an unglazed printed cotton) in preference to chintz in his influential *Hints on Household Taste* (1868), and recommended a heavy ribbed fabric with broad horizontal stripes which needed no lining or trimmings and which could recreate the simplicity of early curtains. Fabrics of this type were imported from North Africa by firms such as Liberty's of London. They were further promoted by designers like E.W. Godwin and Bruce Talbert who published illustrations during the 1870s of sparsely furnished interiors in a reformed Gothic or Japanese-inspired taste with curtains hanging in two lengths to the floor from simple brass rings and rods without blinds or sun-curtains. Eastlake and other writers in England and America also recommended that curtains should be sewn onto rings, without pleating. And for the first time in almost two hundred years, the emphasis on decorative unity within interiors was replaced by a self-conscious eclecticism in fashion, where window curtains could be of a different fabric from other soft furnishings in a room, or different in colour or pattern.

The late 1880s saw a mainstream revival of traditional drapery styles which used more fabric and became more complex in their cutting and arrangement. In the trade these hangings, whose use extended to the covering of doors and mantlepieces, were generically known as "French drapery". The reaction followed in the 1890s, led in England by architects working in the Baroque revival style, and in America by Edith Wharton and the architect Ogden Codman whose book, *The Decoration of Houses* (1897) suggested treating windows as part of an interior's architectural fittings rather than obscuring them with draperies. Interior fashions inspired by the Baroque period and what became known in America as the Beaux-Arts style led to an aristocratic vogue for expensive

Curtains / Bedhangings: French canopied bed set in an alcove, design by Marsaux, Paris, 19th century

reproductions of antique textiles, particularly French *toiles*, brocades and fabrics woven with silver and gold threads which were used for simpler window curtains. Popular colours during this decade were red and old rose.

The 20th century has been marked by rapid changes in technology and fashion, with patterns of taste changing at an ever faster rate, decade by decade. At the beginning of the century there was widespread interest in aspects of the Neo-Classical style, with the Adam, Colonial, Empire and Louis XVI styles being generically interpreted. Textiles often favoured pastel colours, especially green, blue and pink, and were combined with white walls and stripped woodwork. Window-curtains generally hung straight, with simple valances and some sort of undercurtain. The American decorator, Elsie de Wolfe, popularised many of Wharton and Codman's ideas in her book, *The House in Good Taste* (1913), and emphasised a kind of elegant simplicity, including harmonious colours and good proportion, which was based on a liking for the classical styles of the 18th and early 19th centuries.

Within these interiors curtains hung to either the sill or the floor, with simple scalloped valances or none at all. Their form changed little until the 1980s, but the type and design of fabrics reflected changing fashions. Arts and Crafts-influenced rooms favoured Morris patterns or rough linens and muslins; new, Art Nouveau-style designs were followed by a taste for 17th-century patterns which was particularly strong from the 1920s. Old English Tudor and Jacobean designs made in machine-woven tapestries, or printed on cretonnes and heavy linen, were very popular, as was reproduction crewel embroidery. Modernist, Art Deco designs were often not markedly different from more traditional examples, except that the motifs were generally more stylised and geometric. Horizontal stripes and chequer patterns were quite popular in 1930s flats and middle-class houses, and by the postwar period trimmings had virtually disappeared. Traditional methods of block and cylinder printing were replaced by screen printing, with older designs being rescaled to suit the size of modern interiors.

One of the most significant developments of the past twenty years has been the growing interest in historic styles of upholstery, curtaining and decoration. Emerging in the wake of the English Country House style, pioneered by decorators such as Sybil Colefax and John Fowler, fashionable lifestyle magazines like the *World of Interiors* have plundered the taste of the 18th and 19th centuries to recreate elaborate window treatments including patterns re-woven from old documents and period features such as rich trimmings, festoons and scalloped draperies. These, together with the chintzy, cottage styles popularised by firms like Laura Ashley in the 1970s and 1980s, have become increasingly popular, and today an enormous variety of pleated, gathered, festooned and draped styles are available to the fashion-conscious consumer.

DORIAN CHURCH

Further Reading

Information relating to the treatment of curtains for beds and windows can be found in many of the better period surveys such as Thornton 1978 and 1984, Parissien 1992 and Winkler 1986. An overview of the history of the subject appears in Brightman 1972 and Gibbs 1994. For a more detailed treatment see Cummings 1961, which contains scholarly essays on both bedhangings and window curtains, and articles relating to particular periods.

Agius, Pauline (editor), *Ackermann's Regency Furniture and Interiors*, Marlborough, Wiltshire: Crowood Press, 1984
Brightman, Anna, *Window Treatments for Historic Houses, 1700–1850*, Washington, DC: National Trust for Historic Preservation, 1972
Clabburn, Pamela, *The National Trust Book of Furnishing Textiles*, Harmondsworth: Penguin, 1989
Cooke, Edward S., Jr. (editor), *Upholstery in America and Europe from the Seventeenth Century to World War I*, New York: Norton, 1987
Collard, Frances, "Curtains Up" in *Country Life*, 183, 20 April 1989, pp.194–97
Cornforth, John and John Fowler, *English Decoration in the 18th Century*, London: Barrie and Jenkins, and Princeton, NJ: Pyne, 1974; 2nd edition Barrie and Jenkins, 1978
Cummings, Abbott Lowell, *Bed Hangings: A Treatise on Fabrics and Styles in the Curtaining of Beds, 1650–1850*, Boston: Society for the Preservation of New England Antiquities, 1961
Dornsife, Samuel, "Design Sources for Nineteenth Century Window Hangings" in *Winterthur Portfolio*, 10, 1975, pp.69–99
Gibbs, Jenny, *Curtains and Drapes: History, Design, Inspiration*, London: Cassell, 1994
Grier, Katherine C., *Culture and Comfort: People, Parlors, and Upholstery, 1850–1930* (exhib. cat.), Rochester, NY: Strong Museum, 1988
Jameson, Clare (editor), *A Pictorial Treasury of Curtains and Drapery Design 1750–1950*, Sessay, Yorkshire: Potterton, 1987
Mayhew, Edward de Noailles and Minor Myers, Jr., *A Documentary History of American Interiors from the Colonial Era to 1915*, New York: Scribner, 1980
Parissien, Steven, *Curtains and Blinds*, London: Georgian Group, 1992
Parissien, Steven, *Regency Style*, London: Phaidon, and Washington, DC: Preservation Press, 1992
Rosoman, Treve, "Swags and Festoons" in *Traditional Interior Decoration*, Autumn 1986
Schoeser, Mary and Celia Rufey, *English and American Textiles from 1790 to the Present Day*, London and New York: Thames and Hudson, 1989
Thornton, Peter, *Seventeenth-Century Interior Decoration in England, France, and Holland*, New Haven and London: Yale University Press, 1978
Thornton, Peter, *Authentic Decor: The Domestic Interior, 1620–1920*, London: Weidenfeld and Nicolson, and New York: Viking, 1984
Walkling, Gillian, *Upholstery Styles: A Design Sourcebook*, New York: Van Nostrand Reinhold, 1989
Westman, Annabel, "English Window Curtains in the Eighteenth Century" in *Magazine Antiques* (US), June 1990
Westman, Annabel, "Festoon Window Curtains in Neo-classical England: An Analysis and Comparison" in *Furniture History*, 29, 1993, pp.80–87
Winkler, Gail Caskey and Roger Moss, *Victorian Interior Decoration: American Interiors, 1830–1900*, New York: Holt, 1986

Cuvilliés, François 1695–1768

Belgian architect and designer

The architect and designer of interiors and furnishings François Cuvilliés was one of the principal practitioners of the French Régence and Rococo styles in Bavaria. To these styles he added his own sense of fantasy and his knowledge of indigenous south German preferences in architecture. His decorations in the Amalienburg Pavilion and in the Munich Residenz represent some of the most breathtaking and splendid examples of Rococo interiors to survive today.

Cuvilliés's exposure to French styles came through his contact with the Parisian designer Germain Boffrand and the Munich architect Josef Effner while he was employed as court dwarf in the service of the Francophile Elector Max Emanuel of Bavaria who was then living in exile in Bouchefort. Cuvilliés's skill as a draughtsman came to the attention of the Elector and by 1715, when Max Emanuel returned to Munich, Cuvilliés was employed full-time in that capacity by Effner. From 1720 to 1724, under the Elector's auspices, Cuvilliés trained with the architect Nicolas-François Blondel in Paris. His career as an independent architect flourished in Munich from the mid-1720s until his death. Much of his best work was for the Wittelsbach court; he was appointed chief court architect towards the end of his life.

One of Cuvilliés's first major commissions was at the Augustusburg Summer Palace, Brühl, where he worked on several projects for the Elector Clemens Augustus, prince-archbishop of Cologne. These projects included the Elector's Chinoiserie-style Indianisches Kabinett and the little hunting lodge of Falkenlust at Brühl. But the most magnificent of his designs was a suite of rooms, known as the Yellow Apartment (1728–30), whose principal rooms were arranged on the *enfilade* system and included a dining room, an audience room, a bedroom and a music cabinet.

The dining room was a long rectilinear space overlooking the garden and, like the other rooms in the apartment, carried ivory *boiseries* delicately carved and gilded with decorations relating to the theme of dining. Ceres, goddess of the earth, and Bacchus, god of wine, appear on cartouches while grape vines and wine carafes intermingle with floral motifs. Two corners of the dining room are bevelled and carry large niches of salmon-coloured marble holding basin fountains, adorned with gilt putti and swans, for the cooling of wine. The only other colours added to the room are from painted overdoors fitted into gilt frames and from the soft brown tones of the parquetry floor. There is gilt stucco on the cove of the ivory ceiling, and a Venetian chandelier illuminates the room.

The elegant dining room at Brühl is subdued and the *boiseries* do not include the sinuously curving tops so typical of French Rococo examples. The palette is also quite narrow – limited to ivory and gold – and Cuvilliés restrains the witty decorative detailing to specific sections of the room.

The ivory and gilt *boiseries* in the bedroom at Brühl are

Cuvilliés: Hall of Mirrors, Amalienburg Pavilion, Nymphenburg, 1734–39

more exuberantly carved. A French-style sleeping alcove, with a mirrored back wall and enclosed by yellow satin draperies, is the dominant feature of the room. Two bevelled and mirrored wall segments flank the alcove. A marble fireplace with a mantle for the display of *objets d'art* is placed below one of the mirrors. The carved and gilt panelled doors have delicate moulded surrounds in the fashion of the day. Two small ancillary rooms, a dressing room and a *garde-robe*, complete the ensemble.

Cuvilliés's most famous work, and a gem of Bavarian Rococo, is the splendid Amalienburg garden pavilion in the park of the Nymphenburg Palace, Munich (1734–39). Cuvilliés was joined in the creation of the Amalienburg by the master Bavarian artists the stuccoist, Johann Baptist Zimmermann, and Joachim Dietrich, carver of *boiseries* and furniture maker. Built for the Elector Karl Albrecht and his wife Amalie, it was intended as a retreat especially for the Electress and court ladies, who hunted game with bow and arrows from a circular space on the pavilion's roof that is surrounded by a fine decorative iron railing. The elegant sculpted entry overdoor shows Diana, goddess of the hunt, and "hunting" and the bounty of nature provide the thematic imagery of the pavilion.

The single-storeyed Amalienburg pavilion is constructed of brick stuccoed and painted white. The exterior surfaces are drafted and dominated by large windows and slender Ionic pilasters. Inside, the plan has a central circular Mirrored Salon which cuts entirely through the structure with a door to the garden on either side. Two other major rooms, arranged again on the *enfilade* plan, lie to either side of the Mirrored Salon – the retiring rooms of the Elector and Electress with adjacent cabinet. Service rooms at the back include a splendid warming kitchen covered with Delft tiles.

The Mirrored Salon is pale blue in colour and is encased in silvered *boiseries* and arched mirrors in sinuous Rococo frames that are surmounted by a wide band of silvered stucco that encircles the room. From this hang elaborate garlands which festoon the mirrors, and Rococo patterning consisting of cartouches and diamonds vies with lively still-lifes of the hunt and the abundance of nature. The decorative band is surmounted by a smaller, simpler stuccoed cove whose ground is painted ivory, like the ceiling. Perched on its top ledge are four handsome semi-nude female figures (Diana, Ceres and companions) who dangle a leg over the side and lean upon a tree that sways into the vault where silvered birds in flight are seen. Romping putti, elegant fountains, pheasants and other game complete this uppermost figural level of the decoration and a Venetian chandelier in a stucco medallion at the ceiling's centre rounds off the decoration of the room as a whole.

The jewel-like interiors of the Amalienburg shimmer with light from the silvered decoration reflected in the multiple mirrors by day and by night. It is a paradisical image, much like that of the *fêtes galantes* of Antoine Watteau or the Baroque garden in which it sits. Cuvilliés's architectural conception, along with the crisp stucco work of Zimmermann and the carved *boiseries* of Dietrich give a lightness to the interiors. The images are grounded in nature and stem from traditional Bavarian folk art as well as from the Rococo style of French masters such as Germain Boffrand and Juste-Aurèle Meissonnier.

Cuvilliés created several magnificent interiors for the Wittelsbach court Residenz in Munich, beginning with the decoration of the Reiche Zimmer carried out from 1729. His most celebrated commission, the Residenz theatre, where he was assisted by Dietrich, Zimmermann, and the sculptor J.B. Straub, is the quintessential court theatre of the period. Horseshoe in plan, it contains loggia on four levels and a magnificent royal box, decorated with carved and gilded palm trees opposite the stage. Term figures, palms, rocaille motives, and stuccoed draperies in vivid red decorate the loggia which also held sconces for hundreds of candles.

Cuvilliés's fertile imagination received a warm reception in Bavaria and his knowledge of the current French style, together with his adaptability to local sensibilities, allowed him to create a series of unsurpassed masterworks in architecture and interior design. His work reached a wider audience through an influential series of books of ornamental engravings. The first series, published in Munich from 1738, comprised thirty suites of six plates and included cartouches, frames, designs for ceilings and wall elevations with panelling and furniture. From 1745, a second series included more cartouches, panels of ornament, furniture designs, vases, mirrors, chandeliers, picture frames and much else. The impact of these engravings was felt throughout Central Europe and they influenced not only the design of architectural features but also that of furniture and porcelain. Like his interiors, Cuvilliés's engravings show him to have had complete and inspired mastery of the Rococo style and his work compares favourably with the most celebrated of contemporary French designers.

BEVERLY F. HEISNER

See also Rococo; Zimmermann

Biography

Born in Soignies-en-Hainaut, near Brussels, Belgium, 1695. Son was the architect François-Joseph-Ludwig Cuvilliés (1731–77). Entered the service of Max II Emanuel (elector of Bavaria 1679–1726) as court dwarf, Brussels, 1706; moved to Munich and worked for Max II Emanuel as a military engineer, 1716; studied architecture in Paris, 1720–24, partly with Nicolas-François Blondel (1683–1756); appointed court architect, Munich, 1725, alongside current court architect Josef Effner (1687–1745); served as supervising architect to electoral court, Munich, 1730–53; appointed director of architecture to Elector Maximilian III Joseph, 1763. Also active as an independent architect from the mid-1720s working in Bonn (1728), Mergentheim (1734), and Kassel (1749); revisited Paris, 1754–55. Published *Livres de Cartouches*, an influential series of designs for ceilings, wall elevations and furniture, Munich, 1738. Died in 1768.

Selected Works

Interiors

1728–30 Schloss Augustusburg, Brühl (Yellow Apartment including dining room, audience room, bedroom, and music cabinet): Elector Clemens August

1729–37 Schloss Falkenlust, Brühl (building and interiors): Elector Clemens August

1729–37 Residenz, Munich (interiors including the Reiche Zimmer, Green Gallery, staircase): Elector Karl Albrecht

1734–39 Amalienburg Pavilion, Nymphenburg Park, near Munich (building and interiors, with J.B. Zimmermann and J. Dietrich): Elector Karl Albrecht

1750–53 Residenz Theatre, Munich (building and interiors, with J. B. Zimmermann, J. Dietrich and J.B. Straub)

1756–57 Schloss Nymphenburg, near Munich (reconstruction of main salon, with J. B. Zimmermann)

Publications

Livres de Cartouches, Series I, 1738; Series II, 1745; Series III, 1756

Further Reading

A comprehensive analysis of Cuvilliés work appears in Braunfels 1986 which includes many illustrations of interiors, a list of works, and an extensive bibliography. For a detailed and scholarly account of Cuvilliés' work at Brühl see Hansmann 1972 and 1974.

Aufleger, Otto and Karl Trautmann, *Die Reichen Zimmer der Königl. Residenz in München*, Munich: Werner, 1893

Binney, Marcus, "Schloss Brühler" in *Country Life*, 30 November and 7 December 1972

Braunfels, Wolfgang, *François de Cuvilliés, Ein Beitrag zur Geschichte der Künstlerischen Beziehungen zwischen Deutschland und Frankreich*, Würzburg: Mayr, 1938

Braunfels, Wolfgang, *François Cuvilliés: Der Baumeister der galanten Architektur des Rokoko*, Munich: Süddeutscher, 1986

Gaillenui, Jean-Louis, "Falkenlust Pavilion" in *World of Interiors*, July 1995, p.58–63

Hager, Luisa, *Nymphenburg: Palace, Park, Pavilions*, Munich: Bavarian Administration of State-Owned Castles, 1964

Hansmann, Wilfried, *Das Treppenhaus und das Grosse Appartement des Brühler Schlosses*, Düsseldorf: Schwann, 1972

Hansmann, Wilfried, *Schloss Falkenlust*, Cologne: Schauberg, 1972

Hansmann, Wilfried, "Die Stuckdecken des Gelben Appartements im Schloss Augustusburg zu Brühl" in *Beiträge zur Rheinischen Kunstgeschichte und Denkmalpflege*, vol.16, Düsseldorf: Rheinland Verlag, 1974, pp.241–68

Harris, Dale, "Schloss Falkenlust in Germany: The Intimate Grandeur of a Rococo Hunting Lodge" in *Architectural Digest*, 49, March 1992, pp.197–98

Kurfürst Clemens August, Landesherr und Mäzen des 18. Jahrhunderts: Ausstellung im Schloss Augustusburg zu Brühl, Cologne: Schauberg, 1961

Laing, Alastair, "Palaces of the Empire" in Anthony Blunt (editor), *Baroque and Rococo: Architecture and Decoration*, New York: Harper, and London: Elek, 1978, pp.281–87

Lieb, Norbert, *Barockkirchen zwischen Donau und Alpen*, 1953; 2nd edition Munich: Hirmer, 1969

Mellenthin, Horst, *François Cuvilliés' Amalienburg: Ihr Bezug zur französischen Architekturtheorie*, Munich: Institut für Kunstgeschichte, 1989

Schick, Afra, "François Cuvilliés and Joachim Dietrich: The Furnishing of the Treasury in the Munich Residenz" in *Burlington Magazine*, June 1996, pp.393–95

Thon, Christina, *Johann Baptist Zimmermann, als Stukkator*, Munich and Zurich: Schnell & Steiner, 1977

Wolf, Friedrich, *François de Cuvilliés: Der Architekt und Dekorschöpfer*, Munich: Historischer Verein von Oberbayern, 1967

Cuypers, P.J.H. 1827–1921

Dutch architect, city planner, designer and restoration expert

Dubbed "the Dutch Viollet-le-Duc" because he followed the rationalist principles and proportional systems, based on an analysis of Gothic structures, formulated by the French architect and theorist who befriended him, P.J.H. Cuypers might as appropriately be called the "Dutch Pugin", to whose writings he was introduced by the Roman Catholic intellectual (and his future brother-in-law), J.A. Alberdingk Thijm (1820–89). Like Pugin, both men dreamed of a pre-Reformation Utopia based on morality, truth, and beauty where architecture as the mother of the arts would reveal the divine order. Cuypers believed fervently in the ideal of the *Gesamtkunstwerk* and took it as his responsibility to be concerned with every aspect of design, from the most modest piece of furniture to the most grandiose conception of the building. In each detail, no less than in the plan and structure, the architect, inspired by his faith, would express the sacred nature of his vocation.

In 1862 Cuypers visited London to examine the work of Pugin and G.G. Scott and became a member of the Ecclesiological Society. His architecture has affinities with the work of William Butterfield and G.E. Street, while his decorative designs might be compared not only to those of Pugin but also of William Morris, and he readily accepted Ruskin's advocacy of a wealth of ornament derived from stylized natural forms. Furthermore, Cuypers shared with his British colleagues a fervent admiration for indigenous medieval architecture and an abiding commitment to reviving the decayed crafts of his native land. The foremost restorer of historical buildings in the Netherlands, he lavished particular care on the interiors which, although totally sympathetic to the period in which the original work was executed, nevertheless reveal his own characteristic genius for architectural decoration.

Cuypers was trained at the Academy of Fine Arts in Antwerp (1846–49) where he studied painting and sculpture as well as architecture, a decision that would stand him in good stead in his future evocations of the ideal of the "total work of art." Although that training was chiefly based on the classical tradition, the independent Cuypers was prescient in his early preference for Gothic structures and techniques. And he echoed Pugin in his argument that medieval architecture rather than the current French classicism was the only appropriate model for the Netherlands on the basis of custom, climate, and materials. His obvious talent secured for Cuypers the Academy's Prix d'Excellence, despite the fact that he submitted a neo-Gothic church design. After receiving his diploma, he made a trip to study and measure medieval buildings on the Rhine.

In 1850 Cuypers commenced practice in his native Roermond in the southern Netherlands, where the population was predominantly Catholic; when the Dutch government restored the episcopal hierarchy in 1853, his career as a builder of ecclesiastical structures was launched. (He designed more than 300 churches, often accompanied by rectories; unfortunately, many of them have been demolished with the decline of religious worship.) That same year he established, with F. Stoltzenberg, a group of ateliers for the creation and production of "Christian art" (*Christelijke kunst*) that would furnish in complementary medieval style the religious buildings that he was asked to design, for – again like Pugin – he found the fittings and decorative items then available to be inappropriate. Modelled after the masons' lodges and guilds of the Middle Ages, his workshops would eventually employ more than eighty designers and craftspersons to execute, variously, windows, altars, pulpits, confessionals, pews, vestments, chalices, stations of the cross, chasubles, lamps, and wall decorations in diverse materials like wood, stone, plaster, wrought iron, precious metals, tile, mosaic, terracotta, paint and stained glass. From Roermond these products found a ready market abroad, for they were displayed at international exhibitions – often receiving recognition in the form of medals. Further, Cuypers's example stimulated the founding of about a dozen other ateliers for applied arts in his native city.

When Cuypers moved to Amsterdam in 1865, he continued to use his own workshops, situated adjacent to his former house and studio, to embellish and complete his new constructions and his numerous restorations throughout the Netherlands and in Germany. During the 1870s and 1880s, he was particularly active in the area of furniture making, preparing interiors for government buildings in The Hague, for the Rijksmuseum, and for various private residences, and he established a branch of Cuypers & Stoltzenberg in Amsterdam. In 1894 he returned to Roermond and started a new firm, Cuypers & Co., with his son Joseph, also an architect-designer.

Almost single-handedly, Cuypers regenerated, or perhaps more correctly, transformed, the brickmaking industry; this was necessary because the use of unplastered, high-quality brick, once the primary building material of the Netherlands, had declined under the influence of Beaux-Arts architecture, as had the knowledge of bricklaying. Cuypers encouraged the manufacture of bricks of different formats and shapes, and of diverse hues like green, purple, and yellow as well as the time-honored red, and he trained masons to fashion complex ribbed vaults in brick, enlivening interiors through polychromy and distinctive profiles. The Church of the Sacred Heart (Vondelkerk) in Amsterdam (1870–73), is an example of one of the most dazzling of the surviving sanctuaries.

Influenced by Alberdingk Thijm, whose numerous writings urged the recovery of the symbolic dimension of architecture, Cuypers developed ornament that expressed theological and historical meanings; he would extend this concept of *architecture parlante* to secular work as well. The Rijksmuseum, a commission won in competition in 1876, was the first 19th-century building in the Netherlands to have a decorative program so carefully and thoroughly conceived from the iconographical standpoint, to the extent that it rivals in complexity of imagery and variety of material the major public buildings of London, Paris, Munich, and Berlin. He was aided in the formulation of the program by the Hon. Victor de Stuers (1843–1916), chief of the Arts Section in the Interior Ministry from 1875 to 1901, a Roman Catholic, and a strong supporter of Cuypers's innovations. The exterior is resplendent with relief carvings, tile murals, and stone and metal – iron, zinc, copper, bronze – sculptures and details that glorify the history and art history of the Netherlands and celebrate both famous and anonymous practitioners of the fine and useful arts; the stone portraits of Cuypers and de Stuers imitate those that often decorate medieval churches. The façades thus offer hours of visual pleasure and instruction.

Within, the visitor encounters not only the collections of paintings, sculpture, furniture, ceramics, textiles, armor, dolls' houses, and the like, but a rich tapestry of polychromatic patterns that sympathetically evoke the historical context of the works on display. Mosaics on the floor symbolize the material world, the middle zone of the wall represents the social world, and the upper walls and vaults the intellectual world; much of the painted decoration is the work of Georg Sturm. The stenciled friezes and vault paintings have affinities with those created by English Arts and Crafts designers as well as those by Viollet-le-Duc, and in some cases cover the iron beams that Cuypers incorporated into his structure. Regrettably, much of the decoration was whitewashed at a later time, but since the 1980s portions of the original colors and motifs have been restored. The enormous stained-glass windows, however, continue to glow in the antechamber with rich harmonies of colored light; after a competition, the London glazier W.F. Dixon won the commission to depict a program devised by Cuypers. The three large windows depict Painting, Architecture and Sculpture, the smaller ones Poetry and Music, and Wisdom and Theology.

Like the Victoria and Albert Museum, the Rijksmuseum embodied as well as exhibited examples of applied art, and served as a training ground for designers and craftsmen no less than a repository for objects which they might emulate. In 1877 Cuypers had set up in the building shed of the museum a workshop where draughtsmen and sculptors were taught to conceive and execute symbolic decoration; in 1879 this became the official school of applied arts "Quellinus," and moved to quarters in Cuypers's former house on the Vondelstraat; in 1883 the school settled into a new building, also designed by Cuypers. In 1881 two additional places of instruction were established for the Rijksmuseum – the State School for Drawing Instructors and the State School for Applied Art. Cuypers had argued that the lack of skilled practitioners in the northern Netherlands, which required the importation of decorative artists and craftsmen from Belgium, England, and Germany to complete some of the museum's decoration, was an obstacle to the development of an architecture worthy of his native land, and he did his best to ensure training to overcome the deficit.

The extensive decorative program of the vast Central Station, 1882–86, was accomplished by pupils from these schools as well: references to travel and allusions to the cities and countries served by the Dutch railways abound on its external surfaces, while the various waiting rooms within, including one exclusively for the use of the Royal Family, beguile the waiting passengers with a visual feats of imagery, color, and texture; the complex and somewhat moralizing allegories were devised by Alberdingk Thijm. The structural, formal and decorative vocabulary of both the Rijksmuseum and the Central Station is an eclectic mixture of Neo-Gothic overlaid by Northern Renaissance, filtered through the decorative inventions of English Gothic Revivalists and of Viollet-le-Duc. Calvinists and liberals who experienced these public buildings would have found a single-minded reference to medieval architecture too "Papist", so Cuypers, like his contemporaries in other countries, invented a national style that combined profane and religious elements from the 13th through the 16th centuries.

Château De Haar, at Haarzuylens in the province of Utrecht (1892–1912) comprises one of Cuypers's most triumphant ensembles. Nominally a restoration, this, the largest castle in the Netherlands, is actually a new and very personal creation, especially as regards the interiors. The 15th-century building was in ruins when in 1892 Cuypers was invited to rebuild it. There was nothing left of the original decor nor were there documents on which to base his designs; the result, which took fifteen years to execute, is a magnificent series of imaginative and elegant spaces lovingly and lavishly detailed to suggest his own vision of the Middle Ages.

Cuypers also participated in determining the layout of some of the extensions that were developed after the fortification walls of the city were demolished in mid-century. In particular the Vondelstraat, which many of his colorful house façades still front, and the sites on which the Rijksmuseum and the Central Station are located, demonstrate his skills applied to town planning. A member of the city council during his last years in Amsterdam, he was appointed to the commission for public works, where he could apply his expertise.

Cuypers also represented the council on the committee for secondary education; as demonstrated above, instruction of artists and artisans was a high priority. Many designers and craftsmen who gained fame during the late 19th and early 20th centuries emerged from Cuypers's office or from the schools he was responsible for founding. J.L.M. Lauweriks and K.P.C. de Bazel worked for him until 1895, when they renounced Catholicism for Theosophy and established their own Atelier for Architecture and the Applied and Decorative Arts, and such renowned decorative artists as L. Zijl, G.W. Dijsselhof, C.A. Lion Cachet, and Theodoor Nieuwenhuis attended the Rijksmuseum Schools where Cuypers taught the history of art as well as essentials of design. In the reinvigoration of the crafts and applied arts in the Netherlands, Cuypers was indisputably the most important figure of his generation, and his influence in that arena was profound and long-lasting.

HELEN SEARING

Biography

Petrus (Pierre) Josephus Hubertus Cuypers (Cuijpers). Born in Roermond, Netherlands, 16 May 1827. Educated at the Belgian Academy of Fine Arts, Antwerp, 1846–49: won Prix d'Excellence, 1849. Married Antoinette Alberdingk Thijm: son was the architect Joseph Cuypers. Established architectural office, Roermond, 1850. Active in the restoration of historic buildings in the Netherlands and other countries, especially Germany, throughout his career. Founded firm for the design and production of church furniture and liturgical fittings with F. Stoltzenberg, 1853. Moved his practice to Amsterdam, 1865; founded Rijksmuseum School (later Quellinus School), 1865; set up additional schools to train draughtsmen, sculptors, decorative artists and craftspersons, 1879 and 1881. Elected to Amsterdam Council. Exhibited furniture at the Art Applied to Industry Exhibition, Amsterdam, 1877, and at many international exhibitions abroad. Returned to Roermond, 1894. Died in Roermond, 3 March 1921.

Selected Works

An important collection of furniture, painting, sculpture, drawings and other documents related to Cuypers's career is in the Roermond Museum, situated in his former house and atelier.

Interiors

1850–52 P.J.H. Cuypers House, Maastrichterweg, Roermond (building, interiors and furnishings)
1860 & 1886–89 Church of Our Lady of the Immaculate Conception ("De Posthoorn"), Amsterdam (building and interiors)
1870–73 Church of the Sacred Heart (Vondelkerk), Amsterdam (building and interiors)
1876–77 Double House "Nieuw Leyerhoven", 73–75 Vondelstraat, Amsterdam (building and 1890 and interiors)
1876–86 & 1906–15 Rijksmuseum and Director's House, Amsterdam (building and interiors)
1877–79 Knights' Hall, Binnenhof Palace, The Hague (restoration)
1881 Double House, 77–79 Vondelstraat, Amsterdam (building and interiors)
1882–86 Central Station, Amsterdam (building and interiors with A.L. van Gendt)
1890 School for Drawing Teachers, Hobbemastraat and Hobbemakade (building and interiors)
1892–1912 Château De Haar, Haarzuylens (restoration and interiors with Joseph Cuypers)

Publications

Le Château de Haar à Haarzuylens, with Frans Luyten, 1910

Further Reading

The only monograph on Cuypers was published in Amsterdam in 1917. For a more recent study of his work see Hoogewoud and others 1985.

Cuypers, Joseph T.J., *Het Werk van P.J.H. Cuypers*, Amsterdam: Van Holkema & Warendorf, 1917

Hoogewoud, Guido and others, *P.J.H. Cuypers en Amsterdam: Gebouwen en Ontwerpen 1860–1898*, The Hague: Staatsuitgeverij, 1985

Kiers, Judijke and Fieke Tissink, *The Building of the Rijksmuseum: Design and Message*, London: Scala Books, 1992

Stuers, Victor E.L. de, *Le Musée National à Amsterdam, Amsterdam*, 1897

Czech Cubism

Theo van Doesburg writing in the Modernist architectural journal, *Het Bouwbedrijf*, in the mid 1920s was a keen though critical advocate of Czechoslovak experiments in architecture and design. He saw the contemporary development of Functionalism there as "trailblazing" whereas Czech Cubism, developed by architects and designers fifteen years earlier, was written off as a form of mere decorativism, as a "simple replacement" of Secessionism and as a misguided departure into "aestheticism" and "individualism." For the greater part of this century van Doesburg's views held sway: Czech Cubism was first eclipsed by the Modern Movement and then shrouded by the aesthetic dictates of Stalinist and post-Stalinist culture in Czechoslovakia. But with the rise of interest in Czech culture abroad since the "Velvet Revolution" of 1989 and post-modern fascination with semantics and decoration, Czech Cubism has enjoyed a thorough reassessment and rehabilitation.

The first signs of Cubist architecture and design in Bohemia were found around 1910. It developed, perhaps paradoxically, as both a product of Czech bourgeois affluence and as an avant-garde (and sometimes nationalist) rejection of the Viennese Secessionist principles formulated by architects such as Otto Wagner who affirmed "purpose, construction and poetry." Josef Chochol and Pavel Janák, both architects, formulated spiritualist philosophies of design and a dynamic ideal of planar form derived, in part, from Cubist art. Initially, Czech Cubism took form on the pages of the artistic journals published in Prague. But from 1912 these ideas began to be translated into actual designs by a group of architects and designers working and exhibiting with an alliance of artists, the Group of Plastic Artists, which formed in that year. Early significant designs included Janák's reconstruction of a house (the Fára House) in Pelhřimov of 1913. This design, a richly plastic façade of sculpted planes cloaking a conventional apartment house, is typical of the initial years of Cubist architecture in Bohemia.

At this time a number of architects also began producing designs for furniture. Janák, Josef Gocár and Otakar Novotný's furniture reflect their interest in oblique planes, prisms and triangular forms. In most designs this fascination prevailed over concerns for material or technique. The heavy sculptural forms of these wooden, upholstered chairs and glass and wood cabinets demanded ingenuity on the part of the cabinet-makers employed to realise the designs. So while having apparently "modern" origins in Cubism, these chairs and other pieces of furniture were, in such terms, conservative. In effect Czech Cubism's radical aspect lay in the intellectual declarations and the visionary sketches made by its leading advocates. Janák, in particular, rejected utilitarian and quotidian concerns for spiritual expression in his poetic declarations published in the Czech artistic press before World War I. These designs for furniture before 1918 were largely commissioned by patrons of the artistic avant-garde in Prague: figures like Vojta Novák, a theatre director, and Vaclav Vilém Stech, an art critic. But Czech Cubism did find popular form through Artel, a progressive decorative arts workshop established in Prague in 1908. The ceramic, glass and metal-ware designed by Artel members took a variety of forms including traditional folk arts (echoing growing Czech nationalist sentiment at the time) and the radical Modernism of Cubist designs. Vlastislav Hofman, for example, sought to realise a decorative Cubism by deforming traditional ceramic forms in a series of services and vases. The surfaces of these Artel products were transformed with angled planes and trimmed edges.

In 1914 Czech Cubism underwent a shift that has been described as a move to "monumentalism" and "decorativism." The angular, planar forms exploited in pre-war designs by Gocár and Janák evolved into circles and curves. This style, known as "Rondo-Cubism," was adopted as a national style in 1918 when the new Czechoslovak state emerged and its practitioners became prominent figures in the architectural profession. Cubism had since its arrival in Bohemia been characterised as part of the national heritage, a modernisation of the dynamism of the Baroque. But the new national style, often including elements of vernacular architectural forms, was a form of popularism designed to meet the national mood. The dynamism which had characterised pre-war Czech Cubism was replaced by weighty geometric forms and an emphatic use of colour (often in the new national colours, red, white and blue). The Legionnaires' Bank in Prague designed by Gocár in 1922, an example of "official" patronage of this style, has an oppressive, classical symmetry with massive circular decorative forms bolted onto its façade and an overbearing decorative interior scheme. Rondo-Cubism marked the last phase in the development of Czech Cubism. Lasting little more than a decade the entire movement was short-lived. But a number of influential architects after 1918 began their careers under its influence: Chochol was an active proponent of Functionalism in Bohemia in the 1920s; and, in the case of Jirí Kroha, his early experiments in the Czech Cubist idiom formed a foundation for successful practice in Stalinist Czechoslovakia. His designs for Brno University Library of the early 1950s, for example, reflect roots in Cubism.

The number of new buildings built in the early pre-1918 phase of Czech Cubism was small. And the Cubist aspect of these buildings was often a matter of modelling the façade while the organisation of interior space often conformed to convention. The façade itself was the focus of theoretical discussion among these architects and designers. In 1912 Janák wrote an essay entitled "Renewal of the Façade" published in *Umelecky mesícník* (*Arts Monthly*) in which he celebrated the plastic and dynamic handling of form on the front of a building as the "movement of matter." The organisation of space according to Cubist "principles" was to some degree an unresolved intellectual challenge. Pablo Picasso and Georges Braque's painterly mission to "unfold" the subjects of their paintings in time and space was essentially at odds with architecture which by definition requires the fixing and framing of space. Simply to regard the façade of a building, as Janák claimed in his 1912 essay, as a large picture plane failed to acknowledge the Cubist challenge to space and volume. This problematic relationship with Cubism seems even more pronounced when considering the later "Rondo-Cubist" style. This aesthetic, forged on circles, rings and cylinders – the geometry of perfection and wholeness – seems in conflict with the fragmented, splintered and even "kinetic" aesthetic of Cubism in painting.

To some extent, therefore, the designation "Cubist" was a misnomer. For while it is undeniable that analytical and synthetic Cubism developed in France was a major influence on the work of key figures in Prague like Janák (who saw paintings by Picasso and Braque acquired by the Czech collector, Vincenc Kramář, in 1911), a broad range of other influences and shared enthusiasms can also be traced. Before 1918 Czech Cubism seems to have been a hybrid conglomeration of different themes and concerns. Futurist enthusiasms for simultaneity, modernity and velocity as well as for the Gothic for its particular synthesis of technology and fantasy (notable in the "diamond" vaults found in late Gothic churches of Southern Bohemia and Moravia), were strongly expressed by Chochol in his 1913 essay "On the Function of the Architectural Detail." A further, and probably more significant point of intellectual congress was with German Expressionist architects. The Deutscher Werkbund Exhibition in Cologne in 1914 holds a significant place in the history of Expressionist design largely due to Bruno Taut's Glass Pavilion. Four rooms in the Austrian pavilion dedicated to Bohemian art and industry were designed in a Cubist style by Novotný. He was warmly applauded by contemporary German supporters of Expressionism for bringing a slavic "energy" that might "speed up the pulse" of German design. Similarly the celebration of the crystalline structure of the prism and the pyramid in Janák's writings echoed the Expressionist poems of Paul Scheerbart and the drawings of crystalline buildings by Wenzel Hablik (a Bohemian graduate of the Prague Academy of Arts) in Germany. In fact, the contemporary critic, Václav Vilém Stech preferred, with some reservations, the moniker "Czech Expressionism" as the appropriate description of this new style of design in Bohemia. Perhaps Stech was right: Janák and his colleagues' essays published at the moment of the appearance of Cubism in Bohemia are a strong call for individual creativity and free expression in design above all technical and utilitarian considerations; in other words, an appeal to the "inner" man characteristic of Expressionism in Europe.

Despite the attention to the façade and the relatively conservative planning of space (and consequently the social vision of these architects), furniture designs best display the more experimental and dramatic achievements of Czech Cubism. The designers abandoned contemporary Secessionist fashion of the interior as *Gesamtkunstwerk*. In fact, many contemporary photographs of interiors arranged by Gocár, Novotný and Janák show their striking pieces in rather conventional arrangements accompanied by rather banal bourgeois furnishings such as vernacular ceramics and floral patterned carpets. More importantly, the individual object – be it a chair, a table or a lamp – was claimed to be a work of art in its own right. The Czech Cubists viewed their furniture designs as expressions their own aesthetic vision. In the early phases of Czech Cubism these angular, sculptural pieces of furniture lacked any applied ornament and, consequently, had a rather monumental and even sometimes primitive appearance. Ornamental effects were replaced by the sculptural quality of the object itself. Its forms were essentially abstract, making no reference to historical ornamental languages or to nature. Nor were these objects in keeping with the prevailing principles of good design established by influential theorists such as Gottfried Semper who stressed that form should be derived from materials or technological process. For instance, craftsmen constructing Gocár's designs for a table shown at the first exhibition of the Group of Plastic Artists, had to make bevelled, hollow forms that mimicked the seemingly "cast" and inevitably heavy shapes suggested by the architect's drawings. In fact, the drawings and other representations of Czech Cubist furniture were often better expositions of their attitudes to art and design than the resulting pieces. Fluid, expressive sketches or photographic images capturing the object from unexpected angles seemed to suggest deformation and spatial instability whereas the actual realised object was often disappointing, its presence static and monumental.

Czech Cubist designs testify to the sense of complexity and confusion experienced by a generation of architects and designers in the 1910s in their search for the modern. As Milena Lamarová has argued, "Cubism was recognised not as a style or a dogma, but as the point of departure for the modern perception of the world." Although the designs and writings of Janák, Gocár and Chochol were strongly marked by a sense of departure from the past and, in particular, from historicism and naturalism, they manifested a sense of uncertainty about where the future would lie. And as van Doesburg's views indicate, Czech Cubism was eclipsed by the Modern Movement in the 1920s. In one sense, however, the Czech Cubists anticipated a Postmodernist approach developed by figures like Ettore Sottsass of the Memphis group in the 1980s, which regards furniture as discursive, contemplative objects rather than as practical and functional things.

DAVID CROWLEY

Selected Collections

A large collection of "Cubist" furniture, including examples by Josef Chochel, Josef Gočár, Vlastislav Hofman, Pavel Janák, Jirí Kroha, Otakar Novotný and Rudolph Stockar, is in the Museum of Decorative Arts, Prague. Furniture and designs by Antonín Procházka are in the Moravia Gallery, Brno. The National Technical Museum, Prague, holds a substantial collection of architectural drawings and designs by members of this group; archive photos including views of contemporary interiors and exhibitions are in the Stenc Collection, National Institute for the Protection of Heritage and the Environment, Prague.

Further Reading

For an excellent, well-illustrated, English-language study of Czech Cubism, which includes a chronology, a detailed bibliography, and biographies of the main designers involved, see Vegesack 1992.

Behal, V., "Czech Cubism in Arts and Crafts 'Artel-Studio for the Plastic Arts in Prague' and 'The Prague Art Workshop'" in *Kosmas: Journal of Czechoslovak and Central European Studies*, (Vienna) 17, 1988

Burkhardt, François and Milena Lamarová, *Cubismo Cecoslovacco: Architetture e Interni*, Milan: Electa, 1982

Czechoslovkia Cubism: The World of Architecture, Furniture and Craft (exhib. cat.), Tokyo: Parco, 1984

Gočár, Josef, P. Janák and F. Kysela, *Tschechische Bestrebungen um ein Modernes Interieure*, Prague, 1915

Herbenová, O. and Milena Lamarová, *Czech Cubist Interior* (exhib. cat.), Prague: Museum of Decorative Arts, 1976

Lamač, Miroslav, *Cubisme tchèque*, Paris: Centre Georges Pompidou, 1992

Lamarová, Milena, "The Bohemian Cubist Avant-Garde: The Cubist Phenomenon in Architecture and Design" in *Architectural Association Quarterly*, 13, 1982

Margolius, Ivan, *Cubism in Architecture and the Applied Arts: Bohemia and France, 1910–1914*, Newton Abbot, Devon: David and Charles, 1979

Slapeta, Vladimír, *Czech Functionalism, 1918–1938*, London: Architectural Association, 1987

Slapeta, Vladimír, "Cubism in Prague" in *Daidalos*, 39, March 1991, pp.64–71

Svaché, Rostislav and Jan Sekera, *Devětsil: The Czech Avant-Garde Art of the 1920s and 30s* (exhib. cat.), London: Design Museum, 1990

Vegesack, Alexander von (editor), *Czech Cubism: Architecture, Furniture and Decorative Arts, 1910–1925*, New York: Princeton Architectural Press, and London: Laurence King, 1992

Wirth, Zdeněk, *Joseph Gočár*, Geneva: Meister der Baukunst, 1930

D

Dairies

Traditionally dairies have been part of farm architecture. A special room was set aside for the storage of milk and the production of cream, butter, and cheese. Large manor houses and stately homes ran their own dairies to supply the needs of the house. This was the state of affairs until the middle of the 19th century when dairy factories began to emerge to supply the ever-growing towns.

The need for dairies to have clean interiors has made tiles an integral part of dairy architecture. Delftware tiles made in Holland and Britain were used in dairies to provide more hygienic wall surfaces. Tiled dairies emerged during the course of the 17th century, such as Queen Mary's dairy at Hampton Court which was completed in 1689 with large blue-and-white tiles made in Delft. At the time Daniel Defoe recorded that "the Queen has also a Dairy, with all its conveniences, in which her Majesty took great delight", and the watercolourist Mary Ellen Best has left us an accurate picture painted in the 1830s of the former 18th-century dairy at Howsam Hall near York where Delftware tiles cover the wall and the front of the stone dresser. Delftware tiles were also used in the former dairy built in 1779 at Brocklesby Park, Lincolnshire, where they ran in a double row above the marble dresser.

Wedgwood began the manufacture of Queen's Ware tiles during the 1780s and these proved popular for the interiors of dairies. 18th-century Wedgwood tiles have a hard cream body covered with a transparent glaze which if desired could be printed and painted on the glaze and were more durable than the more brittle and softer Delftware tiles.

A number of Georgian architects took a specific interest in designing dairies either as individual buildings in their own right or as part of larger farm complexes. Sir John Soane, Henry Holland, and S.P. Cockerell put their minds to style-conscious but at the same time functional and practical dairies.

Soane designed a free-standing dairy in 1783 in an archaic Greek style for Philip Yorke in the grounds of Hamels Park, Hertfordshire. This had a thatched roof which gave the dairy the idyllic rustic appearance favoured at the time, but it was also functional as the thatched roof helped to keep the temperature inside more constant.

Holland became somewhat of a specialist with his dairies at Althorp and Woburn. The dairy at Althorp, Northamptonshire, built in 1786–88 for Countess Spencer, has its walls covered with Wedgwood tiles. The marble-topped dresser and tables still have their original Wedgwood dairy bowls and vases. He also designed the unusual Chinese Dairy at Woburn for the Duke of Bedford in 1791. Despite its exotic appearance, it is functional with a veranda around the building to deter direct sunlight and tiles in the interior to cover the walls below the marble dresser and the floor for cleanliness.

More exotic influences can be seen in the dairy at Sezincote, Gloucestershire, designed by S.P. Cockerell in the Moorish style in 1808, with tiled walls, stained glass, and a fountain in the centre. Just to show that he could design in any style, an alternative unexecuted design for a dairy at Sezincote in the Gothic style has survived.

The interest by the highest echelons of society in the dairy as part of the notion of the ideal pastoral life was highlighted by the French queen Marie Antoinette at the end of the 18th century when she would play at being a dairymaid at her small model farm Le Hameau at Versailles and the dairy at Rambouillet. However she did not set the fashion for this as is sometimes supposed. In England this was a trend already established to which the examples at Hampton Court, and later Hamels, Althorp, Woburn, and Brocklesby testify.

J.C. Loudon comments on dairy design in his *Encyclopaedia of Cottage, Farm and Villa Architecture* of 1833, and cites the dairy at Alnwick Castle as a good functional example with its veranda, thatched roof, white marble shelves, and white glazed tiles.

The fashion for state-of-the-art dairies continued in the Victorian period but was now linked to colourful machine-made decorative tiles. If the Georgian dairies had often been plain in their wall decoration with white or cream-coloured tiles, the Victorian dairy became highly decorative and polychromatic, as can be seen in the wonderfully preserved example at Windsor.

The dairy at Windsor was built under the direct patronage of Prince Albert, and shows all the best that could be incorporated into dairy architecture at that time. The dairy was built between 1858 and 1861 according to a design by John Thomas with an interior consisting of stained-glass windows, painted woodwork, statues, fountains, and walls covered from top to botton with colourful block-printed Minton tiles, moulded ceramic panels with rustic scenes, and a frieze with ceramic portrait medallions of the Royal family. The non-slip ceramic floor has special channels beneath marble-topped tables down which water can be sluiced for cleaning, while the windows incorporate an early form of double glazing to control the temperature. There are perforated tiles in the ceiling to allow for the circulation of air.

Not all Victorian dairies were tiled. The model dairy at Manderston, Berwickshire, designed by John Kinross in 1900 is built in an Early English Gothic style. It has a vaulted roof with a marble floor and walls that also make for excellent hygienic surfaces.

Numerous dairy factories sprang up throughout the second half of the 19th century, such as the one at Crouch Hill, London. One of the best preserved examples of this type is to be found in Dresden, Germany. There the Pfund Dairy was built in 1892 and tiled in a functional way. The great showpiece however is the large dairy shop which has a complete ceramic interior with tiled walls, ceiling and floor. The walls have elaborately painted scenes and designs on tiles made by Villeroy & Boch showing cherubs engaged in the processing of butter and milk, including tinned condensed milk which, among other places, was exported to Britain.

In Britain dairy factories would run chains of shops well into the 20th century, such as the Buttercup Dairy shops in Scotland and the Maypole shops in England. Figurative and decorative tiles were a standard part of the shop interiors and entrances. Contemporary dairy factory design is perhaps more hygienic then ever before, but less remarkable in its interior design with much use of plain tiles and stainless steel work surfaces showing the influence of the increasing effect of complex government regulations.

HANS VAN LEMMEN

See also Tiles

Selected Works

Notable examples of purpose-built domestic dairies survive in England at Althorp, Northamptonshire; Brocklesby Hall, Lincolnshire; Sezincote, Gloucestershire; Windsor Castle, Berkshire; and Woburn, Bedfordshire. The most celebrated French example is at Rambouillet.

Further Reading

A useful discussion of English dairies with particular reference to those decorated by Wedgwood and Sons appears in Kelly 1965.

Carrot, R.G., "The Hameau de Trianon: Migie, Rousseau and Marie-Antoinette" in *Gazette des Beaux-Arts*, CXIII, 1989, pp.19–28

"Cream of Dresden" in *World of Interiors*, November 1991, pp.96–101

Du Prey, Pierre de la Ruffiniere, *John Soane: The Making of an Architect*, Chicago: University of Chicago Press, 1982

Gere, Charlotte, *Nineteenth-Century Decoration: The Art of the Interior*, London: Weidenfeld and Nicholson, and New York: Abrams, 1989

Jonge, C.H. de, *Dutch Tiles*, London: Pall Mall Press, and New York: Praeger, 1971

Kelly, Alison, *Decorative Wedgwood in Architecture and Furniture*, London: Country Life, 1965

Lambton, Lucinda, *Beastly Buildings: The National Trust Book of Architecture for Animals*, London: Cape, and Boston: Atlantic Monthly Press, 1985

Loudon, J.C., *Encyclopaedia of Cottage, Farm and Villa Architecture and Furniture*, 1833

"Prince Albert's Dairy" in *Architectural Review*, 146, December 1969, pp.414–16

Robinson, John Martin, *Georgian Model Farms: A Study of Decorative and Model Farm Buildings in the Age of Improvement, 1700–1846*, Oxford: Clarendon Press, 1983

Stroud, Dorothy, *Henry Holland: His Life and Architecture*, London: Country Life, 1966; South Brunswick, NJ: A.S. Barnes, 1967

"A Wedgwood Dairy in a French Collection" in *Connoisseur*, August 1957

Davis, Alexander Jackson 1803–1892

American architect and designer

Alexander Jackson Davis was one of the leading American revival architects during the period from 1835 to the Civil War, working first in a Greek Revival style with his partner Ithiel Town (1784–1844), and then on his own in a Gothic Revival style. A major proponent of the integration of the building within its landscape setting, once he began to design on his own, he also believed in relating every function of the building to its interior appearance: he thus anticipated a later generation's concern with total design. His specific furniture designs, while few in number, are exquisite proof of his feel for the spirit and shape of the Gothic buildings on which he drew for inspiration.

Originally trained as a lithographer, at the age of 20, Davis was directed toward architecture by John Trumbull, the president of the American Academy in New York. Following several years as an apprentice, he began work as an architectural draughtsman, and showed an early interest in the design of country houses. His work attracted the attention of the highly successful Greek Revival style architect, Town, and the older man offered him a partnership in 1829. Davis was well aware of the ideas of the Oxford Movement that had swept through England, and he incorporated its spirit in major urban residences, churches, and public buildings, with the earliest major example of the form of English Collegiate Gothic being the Town and Davis's main building for New York University. In later years, Davis was to base his design for the Great Hall at the University on the Chapel of Henry VII at Westminster.

When Town retired from active practice, Davis turned his attention to more rural cottage designs, where he could indulge his taste for the Picturesque. He wrote and illustrated *Rural Residences* in 1837, with the support of many of the business and artistic leaders of the day. His practice flourished, with such major commissions as the 1838 residence for William Paulding, formerly called Knoll and now known as Lyndhurst. In addition to designing the exterior and the basic organization of the rooms – the normal way of working at the time – Davis designed every interior detail himself. He contracted with a furniture-making firm, Burns and Tranque, and with wallpaper designers and mantel artisans. He designed the walls so that the plaster would appear to be ashlar stonework; he used *trompe-l'oeil* graining in the passageways; he created built-in furniture to house objects meant for display. For the actual furniture, particularly for the major first floor public rooms, he created more than fifty designs for such objects: those for both

Davis: study for Neo-Greek double parlour in a New York house, c.1845 (New-York Historical Society)

wheelback and pointed chairs for the dining room epitomize his inventive taste.

When the building was expanded in 1864, the new owner hired Davis both to harmonize the additions with the original structure and to add some furnishings to replace some of those that had been removed. Some of the pieces are a little heavier, indicating that his Pugin-inspired designs were modified by the more ornate Victorianism that was probably demanded by the patron. The octagon dining table and heavier chairs are the main surviving examples of that modified Gothicism.

When dealing with public buildings, Davis also tried to integrate the interior design and the furnishings, with even stronger attention to function. This interest is best exemplified in his designs for a schoolhouse that was included in his later versions of *Rural Residences*, rather than in his completed college buildings for Virginia Military Institute, New York University, or the several other college buildings that Davis designed and saw to completion. His basic school design included a concentric seating arrangement facing the raised teacher's platform, in a room with skylights replacing conventional windows. By doing so, he provided more wall space for chalkboards, maps, and shelving, while avoiding the distraction of observing what was happening outdoors. He even devised a storage space for coats and hats in a hallway under the bell tower. The design was so well received that the American Common School Society illustrated his design on the cover of their 1839 brochure and recommended it as the preferred form of schoolhouse design.

Much of Davis's best known work is through his collaboration with Andrew Jackson Downing, and the perspectival views and renderings of residences, garden seats, and various outbuildings that appeared in Downing's *The Architecture of Country Houses* in 1850. The two men remained partners in various projects from 1838 to 1852, when Downing died. Though the designs Davis produced through the partnership was exterior rather than interior, they reflect the coordination of all design elements that was the hallmark of his pioneering overall design concept. Until the Civil War, when declining demand and changes in taste pushed Davis's fame into history, his impact on ecclesiastic, rural domestic, school, and public architecture and design was tremendous. Although he lived until 1892, Victorian exuberance, changing political and social configurations, and a distaste for the moral basis that always accompanied Davis's commentary on his work, combined effectively to end his career thirty years before he died. All that remained was his work on the design and landscape for the group of houses that formed the Llewellyn Park Association at Belleville, New Jersey, where he lived most of the last years of his life. This project catered to a small group of like-minded businessmen who sought a retreat near, but not part of the city.

A new interest in overall design, not in the particulars of his eclectic taste or morality, finally created a new interest in Davis in the mid-20th century.

DAVID M. SOKOL

Biography

Born in New York, 1803. Educated at the Antique School, Philosophical Society (later merged with the Academy of Design), and at the Athenaeum, Boston, 1827; subsequently at the American Academy of Fine Arts, New York, and New York Drawing Association. Served as apprentice designer under Josiah R. Bradley, New York; draughtsman, Ithiel Town's office, New York, 1826; partner with Town, New York, 1829; opened own office New York, 1844. Designed illustrations for the writer on landscape gardening and house furnishing, Andrew Jackson Downing (1815–52), 1838–52; published *Rural Residences*, 1837. Designed furniture for specific commissions from the late 1830s. Died in New York, 1892.

Selected Works

The principal manuscript sources for Davis's work are in the Davis collections of the Avery Library, Columbia University, the Metropolitan Museum of Art, the New-York Historical Society, and the New York Public Library, all in New York, and in the Winterthur Museum, Delaware. Examples of Davis's furniture survive *in situ* at Lyndhurst, Tarrytown, New York. A full list of Davis's executed and unexecuted architectural projects appears in Peck 1992.

Interiors

1833	United States Customs House, New York City (building and interiors; with Ithiel Town)
1835–37	New York University Chapel, Washington Square (interiors; with Ithiel Town)
1838–42	Knoll, Tarrytown, New York (building, interiors and furniture): William and Philip R. Paulding
1842	Angier Villa, Medford, Massachusetts (building and interiors, in consultation with A. J. Downing)
1842–44	Wadsworth Atheneum, Hartford, Connecticut (building and interiors, with Henry Austin)
1842–49	Joel Rathbone House, Kenwood, New York (farmhouse, gate lodge and some furniture)
1854	Grace Hill, Brooklyn, New York (building, interiors and furniture): Edwin C. Litchfield
1855–59	Ericstan, Tarrytown, New York (building and interiors): John J. Herrick
1857	Gate Lodge, Llewellyn Park, West Orange, New Jersey (building and interiors)
1864–67	Lyndhurst (formerly Knoll), Tarrytown, New York (remodelling, additions, interiors and furniture): George Merritt

Publications

Rural Residences, 1837; reprinted 1980

Further Reading

A detailed study of Davis's work appears in Donoghue 1982 which includes an extensive bibliography of primary and secondary sources. A more recent collection of essays, including a study of Davis's work at Grace Hill and Lyndhurst, appears in Peck 1992 which also contains a list of all Davis's executed and unexecuted architectural projects.

Andrews, Wayne, *Architecture, Ambition and Americans: A Social History of American Architecture*, 1955; revised edition, New York: Free Press, and London: Collier Macmillan, 1978

Caine, Rebecca and Amelia Peck, "The Artistic Career of Alexander Jackson Davis" in *Magazine Antiques* (US), 142, November 1992, pp.704–13

Davies, Jane B., "Alexander J. Davis: Architect of Lyndhurst" in *Historic Preservation*, 17, 1965, pp.54–59

Davies, Jane B., "Blandwood and the Italian Villa Style in America" in *Nineteenth Century*, 1, 1975, pp.11–14

Davies, Jane B., "Gothic Revival Furniture Designs of Alexander J. Davis" in *Magazine Antiques* (US), 111, 1977, pp.1014–27

Donoghue, John C., *Alexander Jackson Davis, Romantic Architect*, New York: Arno Press, 1982

Doumato, Lamia, *Alexander Jackson Davis* (bibliography), Monticello, IL: Vance, 1980

Downing, A.J., *Cottage Residences*, 1842, revised edition, 1873; reprinted Watkins Glen, NY: Library of Victorian Culture, 1967

Downing, A.J., *The Architecture of Country Houses*, 1850; reprinted New York: Da Capo, 1968

Harmon, Robert B., *Greek Revival Architecture in America and the Designs of Alexander Jackson Davis: A Select Bibliography*, Monticello, IL: Vance, 1981

Newton, Roger Hale, *Town and Davis, Architects: Pioneers in American Revivalist Architecture, 1812–1870*, New York: Columbia University Press, 1942

Peck, Amelia (editor), *Alexander Jackson Davis: American Architect 1803–1892* (exhib. cat.) New York: Metropolitan Museum of Art, 1992

Pierson, William H., Jr., *Technology and the Picturesque* (American Buildings and Their Architects, vol.2), New York: Doubleday, 1978

Stevens, Louise C., "A.J. Davis and American Classicism" in *Magazine Antiques*, 136, December 1989, pp.1320–35

Day, Lucienne 1917–

British textile and wallpaper designer

During the 1950s Lucienne Day was arguably the leading British surface pattern designer of the day. Day was one of Britain's few designers to achieve an international reputation, and her work was in demand in both North America and continental Europe, in particular West Germany. Although primarily a designer of printed textiles, she also produced patterns for wallpaper, carpets and tableware. She counted among a sizeable and articulate group of designers in the immediate post-war period who, educated in the ideas of the Bauhaus, believed it part of their role to get good, affordable modern designs into ordinary homes.

Day was trained, first, at Croydon School of Art, and then at the Royal College of Art. When she left in 1940 her incipient career was put on hold by the war, although she taught part-time and did some design work for the dress trade. By 1946–47 she was getting enough design work to enable her to give up teaching, and was exhibiting her fabrics regularly at the Cotton Board's Colour, Design and Style Centre in Manchester, set up in 1940 to encourage industry to invest in good design and to raise public awareness of well-designed goods. In 1948 Day received an important commission for two chintz designs from Alastair Morton, Artistic Director of Edinburgh Weavers, a company with a reputation for high-quality innovative furnishing fabrics designed to complement modern developments in architecture. In their turn, the two designs (*Florimel* and *Elysian*, 1949) brought Day's work to the attention of Heal's who commissioned a design in a similar style (*Fluellin*, 1950).

The Festival of Britain in 1951 provided many young

Day: *Calyx* fabric, 1951, manufactured by Heal's

designers, Lucienne Day included, with an important showcase for their most innovative work. When her husband, the furniture designer Robin Day, was unable to find a really modern, yet moderately priced, furnishing fabric to complement the furniture in his section of the *Homes and Gardens* Pavilion at the Festival, Day persuaded Heal's to print one of her designs, *Calyx*, especially for it. The company was initially sceptical that such an abstract design could possibly have any commercial appeal but were proved wrong. *Calyx* was a huge success, especially in the US, where it sold to more than 200 leading North American decorators through Greeff Fabrics Inc. of New York. Inspired by contemporary abstract art, *Calyx* is a highly original pattern and justifiably regarded as a landmark in the history of 20th-century design. It took a gold medal at the 1951 Milan Triennale and won the coveted International Design Award of the American Institute of Decorators in 1952, the first time that the award had gone to a British designer. It spawned a number of imitations, sold for some ten years and helped to establish Day's international reputation.

Following the success of *Calyx*, Day received further commissions from Edinburgh Weavers and other leading British textile manufacturers such as Sanderson's and Liberty, but her name became inextricably linked with that of Heal's. Although never contractually bound to the company, she worked for them almost exclusively, designing four to six furnishing fabrics a year from 1952.

Day's work for Heal's falls into a number of distinct stylistic groupings. During the first half of the 1950s she was widely imitated and did much to popularise the abstract style, contributing to a revolution in the taste of the British consumer. In addition to purely abstract patterns, many of Day's designs of that period (*Trio*, 1954 and *Herb Antony*, 1956 are prime examples) were based on abstracted plant forms, representing a radical reworking of the English chintz tradition. Her colour palette – a limited range of bright colours sharply contrasted – was equally innovative. In Day's later work for Heal's (*Apex*, 1967 or *Sunrise*, 1969, for example) the startling colour combinations and uncompromising geometry form a stark contrast to the relatively small-scale, sometimes whimsical early abstract designs. Partly these patterns grew out of her general move in the direction of more large-scale designs, but they also met the company's demand for patterns to satisfy the growing contract market of the 1960s.

Many of Day's designs counted among Heal's critical as well as commercial successes. Four early ones – *Ticker-tape, Spectators, Linear* and *Graphica* – jointly took the prestigious Grand Premio at the Milan Triennale in 1954, an exhibition dominated throughout the 1950s by Scandinavian design. *Triad* (1955) was used in all the bedrooms of the reconstructed Strand Palace Hotel in London and in the Leofric in Coventry, one of Britain's most modern hotels of the period, while *Ducatoon* was awarded a gold medal at the California State Fair of 1959, testifying to the enduring popularity of Day's work in America.

Day began designing wallpapers, an obvious corollary to textile design, in 1951 when the British manufacturer John Line commissioned a design (*Provence*) from her to be included in a range of modern wallpapers called "limited editions". It was shown at the Festival of Britain, together with three others which she designed for Cole & Sons. Between the mid-1950s and mid-1960s Day produced occasional designs for inexpensive, machine-printed wallpapers manufactured by Crown and, in 1954, the German firm Rasch Tapetenfabrik – one of the earliest producers of Modernist wallpapers, who had put out a range for the Bauhaus years before – also began to commission wallpaper designs from her. In contrast to other designers of the period who were producing large figurative patterns, Day preferred wallpaper to be recessive, especially if it were being used in a scheme which also included patterned textiles and possibly patterned carpets, and the majority of her designs were simple one- or two-colour abstract linear patterns.

An exhibition of Rasch artists at Osnabrück Museum in 1956, which included Day's work, led to an invitation from Rosenthal Porzellan AG to design patterns for their new "Studio Line" tableware shapes, launched in 1955 and designed by leading international designers such as Raymond Loewy (US) and Tapio Wirkkala (Finland). Day worked for Rosenthal for ten years from 1957, the only British representative on their design team. Back in the UK, in the late 1950s, she extended her design repertoire to include carpets and table linens. Both were successful in capturing a market not hitherto notable for innovative design. Her first Axminster design, *Tesserae*, for Tomkinson's Ltd. of Kidderminster, was named one of twelve products of outstanding design in 1957, while a set of glass cloths for Thos. Somerset & Co. of Belfast took the same award in 1960.

By 1960 Day was as well known in Europe as in Britain, a fact which is evident from the many features and full-length articles on her work which appeared in the pages of such journals as *Bonytt* (Norway), *md: moebel und decoration* and *Gebrauchsgraphik* (Germany). In 1962 she was elected a Royal Designer for Industry in recognition of her contribution to British design and exports.

Day gave up designing for industrial production in the mid-

1970s and now designs pieced silk wall-hangings known as silk mosaics which are made to commission and for exhibition.

JENNIFER HARRIS

Biography

Born Désirée Lucienne Conradi, in Coulsdon, Surrey, January 1917. Trained at Croydon School of Art, 1934–37; studied design, Royal College of Art, London, 1937–40. Married the designer Robin Day (b.1915) in 1942: 1 daughter. Tutor, Beckenham Art School, 1942–47. Active as a freelance commercial designer of textiles from 1947 to 1970s; supplied designs for Cavendish Textiles (John Lewis Partnership) from 1947, Edinburgh Weavers, 1948–52, and Heal's c.1950–1970s. Designed wallpapers for John Line & Sons Ltd. from 1951, for Crown Wallpapers, 1954–64, and for Gebr. Rausch & Co., Bramsche, mid-1950s. Designed porcelain decorations for Rosenthal ceramics, 1957–59. Worked, with Robin Day, as design consultant to the John Lewis Partnership, 1962–87. Active as a designer of wall-hangings and silk tapestries from 1970s. Exhibited at the Festival of Britain, London, 1951. Elected Royal Designer for Industry, 1962; Master of Faculty of Royal Designers for Industry, 1987–89.

Selected Works

Collections of Day's textiles and wallpapers are in the Victoria and Albert Museum, London, and the Whitworth Art Gallery, Manchester.

Further Reading

A well-illustrated and informative monograph on Day is Harris 1993 which includes a select bibliography and a checklist of her designs for Heal's, Edinburgh Weavers, and British Celanese.

Banham, Mary and Bevis Hillier (editors), *A Tonic to the Nation: The Festival of Britain 1951*, London: Thames and Hudson, 1976

Carrington, Noel, *Design and Decoration in the Home*, London: Batsford, 1952

Goodden, Susanna, *At the Sign of the Fourposter: A History of Heal's*, London: Heal & Son, 1984

Harris, Jennifer, *Lucienne Day: A Career in Design* (exhib. cat.), Manchester: Whitworth Art Gallery, 1993

MacCarthy, Fiona, *British Design Since 1880: A Visual History*, London: Lund Humphries, 1982

MacCarthy, Fiona and Patrick Nuttgens, *Eye for Industry: Royal Designers for Industry, 1936–1986*, (exhib. cat: Royal Society of Arts, London), London: Lund Humphries, 1986

Schoeser, Mary, *Fabrics and Wallpapers*, London: Bell and Hyman, and New York: Dutton, 1986

Sparke, Penny (editor), *Did Britain Make It? British Design in Context, 1946–86*, London: Design Council, 1986

Stewart, Richard, *Design and British Industry*, London: Murray, 1987

Day Beds and Chaises Longues

Day beds and chaises longues are essentially frontally elongated seated units. Closely related to beds and sofas, they differ from the first in that they are for daytime use and from the second in that they are intended for a single person. They have their roots in the low, rectangular banquet couches and beds used in ancient times and, given that lounging or sleeping during the day is traditionally an activity restricted to the leisured classes, they have been a fashionable feature in many wealthier homes since their introduction in the late 16th century. Unlike more formal types of seating, they have also been associated mainly with private and intimate settings such as boudoirs and bedrooms. They have been constructed from a variety of woods and other media, and were almost always upholstered or fitted with cushions. Their design has reflected changing fashions and styles, but as an emphasis upon comfort – which began in the 18th century – became more significant, so the body-conforming qualities of day beds and chaises longues became more pronounced. This tendency reached its apogee in the deep-buttoned, highly-sprung examples produced in the last decades of the 19th century but is still evident in some of the stark modern designs which appear to be composed along the abstracted lines of the human torso. Some of the most contemporary models appear more like functional sculpture than furniture.

Day beds have their antecedents in many cultures of the ancient world. Ceremonial couches in the form of attenuated animal bodies, the back serving as the resting surface, have been found in ancient Egyptian tombs, including that of Tutankhamun. Most evidence points to their having been used primarily in embalming and funerary rites; to what extent they might have served other functions is unclear, yet their form is undeniably associated with other, later examples of day beds. Ancient Greek and Roman sculptures, reliefs, and vase paintings dating back to the 6th century BC depict innumerable examples of the popular banquet couches, or *klines*. These furnishings had a two-fold purpose: they could be used to sleep upon, or, lined up end to end and with small tables with food and wine by their side, they served as recliners for those who were dining. It has been suggested that this double function was imported from the Near East, but regardless of the exact origin, this use became the standard custom for festive occasions in Greek and Roman times.

Similar early examples are known to have existed in the Far East. In China the *ta*, or couch – as distinct from the *chuang*, or bed – has been one of the most important types of furniture for centuries. It was a central feature of a man's study, and was given special attention by Ming writers addressing issues of taste; the *chuang* served a comparable function for wealthy women. Even after upright or high seating was introduced in the 8th century, the *ta* remained a common piece of furniture upon which one could kneel or recline. Before the 18th century, decorative emphasis was placed on the textiles which adorned the relatively simple *ta*, but after this period the focus shifted to surface embellishment, chiefly lacquered designs. As is the case with other cultural artifacts emanating from the Far East, substantial symbolic meaning was attached to the *ta*; they were part of the moral and aesthetic discourse of the period.

Day beds existed in Europe from at least the Middle Ages, although their use did not become commonplace until the 16th century. The form seems to have evolved out of the *couche* or *couchette* (the French *coucher* means to go to bed), a simple type of bed which served both night-time and daytime use. By the 17th century a distinction appears to have been made between couches and day beds, the latter now bearing a single slanted endboard or arm (versus one on each end) against which one rested. However, this terminology was occasionally confused, and one finds the word couch applied by English writers to the single- as well as double-ended type. French commentators also called both versions *lits de repos* (literally,

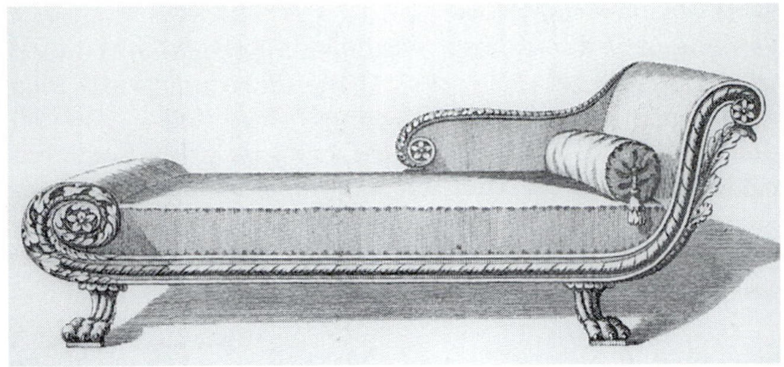

Day Beds: Grecian Squab by Thomas Sheraton, 1803

day bed) or *reposoirs*, but these terms were most often applied to those with a single end.

Perhaps the more important distinction between the two is in their use. Day beds became the less formal type of furniture, while couches evolved into objects of ceremony, often bearing elaborate canopies. By 1700, day beds had become essential furniture for most fashionable ladies and were usually installed in bedrooms or closets where they could be used for relaxing and lounging during intimate conversations with other ladies and friends. As comfort and ease became more important concerns, they increasingly became vehicles for the most sophisticated arts of the upholsterer. Their basic structure up until this time had been of a low, narrow and rectangular palette raised on four to eight shaped or turned feet, featuring drop-in or loose cushions, and bolsters or pillows for added comfort. The endboard was vertical or slanted, sometimes hinged, and a few rare and exceptionally elaborate examples were designed with flying testers and mirrors built into the endboards. Frames were of wood, often with a caned back and seat. Typically, day beds were placed with a long side against the wall, and on occasion they were made en suite with a double-ended couch and / or sofa (a couch with a back as well as sides). They were always an indication of status and wealth.

Chaises longues are a type of day bed or *lit de repos* which evolved in France in the early 18th century. Their name (literally "long chair"), also betrays their close resemblance to chairs, having upright backs and elongated seats. To maximize comfort, their backs were nearly always rounded (in which case the period appellation was duchesse) and they were deeply upholstered or caned, and fitted with soft loose cushions. If the foot was surrounded by a low curving back, the piece was said to be *en bateau* or *en gondole*. If the chaise longue was made in two or three sections which could be separated as individual seating units – a stool and an armchair, for instance, it was then referred to as a *duchesse brisée*. In fact by the mid-18th century *duchesses brisées* had superseded chaises longues in popularity, their form allowing for flexibility of use, and they began to be copied abroad by furniture designers like the British cabinet-maker George Hepplewhite. Other 18th-century variations on the general chaise longue form include *turquoises* or *sultanes* (double endboards of equal height, with or without loose cushions), *veilleuses* (full sloping back which wrapped around three sides), and *meridiennes* (double, outward scrolling endboards of equal height, with or without loose cushions). The *récamier* is simply another term for *meridienne*, popularized by the beautiful and widely celebrated one owned by Madame Juliette Récamier.

With the increasing influence of Neo-Classicism at the end of the 18th century, many furniture types including day beds adopted the newly fashionable antique forms. Cabinet-makers on both sides of the Atlantic loosely copied Greek and Roman prototypes, sometimes calling their pieces "couches", but often simply applying whatever name was currently in vogue. There were *récamier* sofas, Grecian squabs, chaises longues, among others. As before, these furnishings were generally used in boudoirs and were sometimes specially designed to fit into a niche or alcove. The French architects François-Joseph Bélanger, and Percier and Fontaine, both designed rooms with elaborately tented or draped day beds set into the recesses in the walls.

During the 19th century, furniture arrangements became less formal, and reception rooms were increasingly regarded as the precinct of the ladies of the house and were decorated in appropriately feminine styles. As a result, the chaise longue, in particular, moved out of the bedroom and became a popular item of furniture in sitting rooms and parlours. It was ubiquitous in the densely furnished drawing rooms of the late Victorian period and its design was well-suited to the plush fabrics and deep-buttoned styles that were fashionable in wealthier homes. Day beds were still mainly located in private areas but became more complex. Mechanized designs made their debut, as did multiple-use designs some of which combined a reclining surface with storage units, and others which converted from a sofa into a day bed by removing a front rail. As exotic oriental styles became fashionable in the last quarter of the century, ottomans and divans also proved immensely popular, especially in Moorish-style sitting rooms, studios and smoking rooms.

A renewed interest in day beds both as an expression of the inherent beauty of the human form and as a measure of modern cultural values has marked designs of the 20th century. The simple and eloquent day beds of designers such as Le Corbusier, Marcel Breuer, and Charles Eames have streamlined and open structures of industrial materials like steel tubing and plywood. Additionally, the futuristic and amusing models of Olivier Mourgue, Joe Colombo, and even Roberto Matta have emphasized standardization of form, the use of materials developed post-war, and the sculptural possibilities of furniture. Like many furniture designs of recent decades, day beds and *chaises longues* are manufactured today largely with comfort, manoeuvrability, and ease of maintenance in mind.

MARGARET W. LICHTER

Further Reading

Baarsen, Reiner and others, *Courts and Colonies: The William and Mary Style in Holland, England and America* (exhib. cat.), New York: Cooper-Hewitt Museum, 1988

Baker, Hollis S., *Furniture in the Ancient World: Origins and Evolution, 3100–475 B.C.*, New York: Macmillan, and London: The Connoisseur, 1966

Beldegreen, Alecia, *The Bed*, New York: Stewart, Tabori and Chang, 1991

Carlos, A. Rosas, "Strange Bedfellows" in *Connoisseur*, 221, September 1991, pp.116–17

Clunas, Craig, *Chinese Furniture*, London: Bamboo, 1988

Jarry, Madeleine, *Le Siège Français*, Fribourg: Office du Livre, 1973

MacQuoid, Percy and Ralph Edwards, *The Dictionary of English Furniture*, revised edition, 3 vols., 1954; reprinted Woodbridge, Suffolk: Antique Collectors' Club, 1983

Sparke, Penny, *Domestic Furniture* (Twentieth-Century Design series), London: Bell and Hyman, 1986; as *Furniture*, New York: Dutton, 1986

Thornton, Peter, "Sofas and Daybeds" in his *Seventeenth-Century Interior Decoration in England, France, and Holland*, New Haven and London: Yale University Press, 1978, pp.210–17

Watson, Francis (introduction), *The History of Furniture*, edited by Anne Charlish, New York: Morrow, and London: Orbis, 1976

Decorating Manuals

Although information relating to interior design and decoration has been disseminated in various forms since the Renaissance period – as individual engravings, as prints bound in book form, and in treatises on art, architecture and ornament – decorating manuals are predominantly a feature of the 19th and early 20th centuries. They should also be seen as distinct from pattern books or compilations of existing rooms and furnishings in aristocratic homes, both of which flourished in most parts of Europe during the 18th and 19th centuries. Generally profusely-illustrated, pattern books were usually produced by architects and designers and were intended as copy-books of decorative examples for other professionals and the trade; notable examples include anthologies such as Thomas Hope's *Household Furniture and Interior Decoration* (London 1807) and Percier and Fontaine's *Recueil de décorations intérieures* (Paris 1801). Publications such as J.-F. Blondel's *De la Distribution des Maisons de Plaisance et de la Décoration des édifices en général* (Paris 1737–38) were more theoretical but were still mainly directed at a specialist audience. Decorating manuals, by contrast, had a much wider circulation, were frequently more text-based and were usually directed at a non-professional as well as professional readership.

Greater interest in interior decoration developed during the first decades of the 19th century as an outgrowth of the Industrial Revolution. Economic expansion brought an increased production of material goods. By 1840, newly wealthy industrialists and prosperous middle-ranking workers were in a position to indulge in home furnishing and decoration, previously the prerogative of the upper classes alone. While works like J.C. Loudon's *Encyclopaedia of Cottage, Farm and Villa Architecture and Furniture* (London 1833) followed the example of treatises and books from preceding centuries by providing exemplary types of design, there was also a much stronger emphasis upon consumers of architecture and design, and a new educational tone began to enter such publications. Authors of the emerging Victorian period, faced with a multitude of decorative styles, ornamental patterns and new materials, felt the need to explain design options to the growing numbers of consumers.

The interiors of important houses continued to be profiled, as can be seen in Louis Normand's *Paris Moderne ou Choix de Maisons* (Paris 1837–42), but the rise of popular new styles, and the resultant eclecticism, was featured in such diverse works as François Thiollet's *Nouveau Recueil de Menuiserie et de Décorations Intérieures* (Paris 1837), Richard Bridgens's *Furniture with Candelabra and Interior Decoration* (London 1838), and Samuel H. Brooks's *Designs for Cottage and Villa Architecture* (London 1839). Many of these books were still principally read by architects and members of the trade but publications such as Mrs. William Parkes's *Domestic Duties* (London 1825 and New York 1831) whetted the middle-class public's appetite for discussions on the decoration and philosophy of interiors.

The London Great Exhibition of 1851 brought redirections in writings on interior decoration, to accommodate the design reform movement. Decorating manuals were now imbued with the need to "improve taste" and educate the consumer. Manufacturers and purchasers alike required more information and guidance on how to combine sound design principles with appropriate adornment. Consumers were asked to consider issues of domestic presentation and comfort. In addition to professional architect-designer authors, a new category of writer, the "professional" (albeit usually unpaid) adviser, now emerged. Several of these authors were women, and interior decoration came to be regarded increasingly as an activity that was not only sanctioned for women but that also came naturally to the female sex. Two titles exemplify the split in gender approach, Isabella Beeton's *Book of Household Management* (London 1861) and Robert Kerr's *The Gentleman's House* (London 1864). No book was more influential in its advice, in Britain and particularly in America, than Charles Eastlake's much reprinted *Hints on Household Taste* (1868). Significantly, this work was a recasting of articles previously published in general interest magazines (the *Cornhill Magazine*, *Queen*, and the *London Review*), and it was clearly intended to have a fairly wide appeal. Its author's promotion of quality and simplicity in interior decoration, complete with directives and exhortations on avoiding purely fashionable effects, as well as its readable, accessible style, was echoed in many subsequent manuals.

Although many titles from Britain were reprinted in America, independent publishing on decoration was plentiful in the United States, particularly in the 1850s and 1860s. Andrew Jackson Downing's *The Architecture of Country Houses* (New York 1850) and Gervase Wheeler's *Rural Homes; or, Sketches of Houses Suited to American Life* (New York 1852) provided practical, masculine perspectives. The increasing numbers of female consumers could turn to Miss Leslie's *Lady's House Book* (Philadelphia 1854) and a popular work by educators Catherine Beecher and her sister, Harriet Beecher Stowe, *The American Woman's Home* (New York 1869), for a more moral, advisory tone.

By the 1870s, the development of "how-to" decorating manuals was fuelled by a growth in literacy and disposable incomes. There was a consequent increase in these publications as guides to "appropriate" furnishing. Contemporary books surveyed the multiplicity of design styles available to consumers, complete with the mixing of antique and new pieces. An example of this is C.J. Richardson's *The Englishman's House from a Cottage to a Mansion* (London 1870). The artistic nature of current decorative fashions can be seen in Eugène Viollet-le-Duc's *Habitations modernes*, 2 vols. (Paris 1875–77) and Harriet Spofford's *Art Decoration Applied to Furniture* (London 1878). Macmillan's "Art at

Home" series, introduced from 1876 to 1878 and including W.J. Loftie's *A Plea for Art in the House* (London 1876) and *The Dining Room* (London 1878), was especially popular and provided a room-by-room guide to the decoration and furnishing of the fashionable home. Other books also increasingly emphasized newly fashionable styles. Works such as Robert Edis's *The Decoration and Furniture of Town Houses* (London 1881) and Clarence Cook's *The House Beautiful* (New York 1878) advocated the composition of interiors according to prevailing late Victorian "artistic" taste. Agnes and Rhoda Garrett, who had successfully established their own interior decoration firm, published their trend-setting opinions in *Suggestions for House Decoration* (London 1876, US edition 1877).

Lighter treatments of walls, furniture and colours can be seen in manuals that stress such contemporary design solutions over revivalist-inspired interiors, as in one of Mrs. Haweis's most acclaimed guides, *The Art of Decoration* (London 1881). By 1888, even the lower orders were to be instructed in appropriate furnishing and decor from guides such as Mrs. J.E. Panton's frequently consulted manual, *From Kitchen to Garret* (London 1887). This guide advised young housewives on everything from how to decorate within a budget to the correct arrangement of place-settings. And Mrs. Panton herself also wrote a regular column for a number of women's magazines and offered a more personal service with consultations available by mail or visits.

Publications from the last decade of the 19th century dealt with the new realities of modern life. Decorating manuals such as Mrs. Orrinsmith's *The Drawing Room* (London 1877), and Rosamund Watson's *The Art of the House* (London 1897) stressed schemes for important rooms, and were not concerned with large houses exclusively. Other books, however, like Edith Wharton and Ogden Codman's *Decoration of Houses* (1897), which strongly influenced Elsie de Wolfe's later *The House in Good Taste* (1913), still emphasised aristocratic styles, in particular those of the French 18th century. Works from this time championed the young professional decoration industry and cited design goals based on simplicity and efficiency. Nevertheless, no one viewpoint or longed-for national style prevailed. Battles raged in newspapers and periodicals over the correct handling of interior decoration. Books reflected popular stances, as in a work by critic H.J. Jennings, a solid despiser of the newborn Art Nouveau style, who illustrated his *Our Homes and How to Beautify Them* (London 1902) with interiors by prominent, established furnishing firms such as Waring & Gillow. The exchange of ideas across Europe can also be seen in Hermann Muthesius's *Das Englische Haus* (Berlin 1904–05) which praised British commercial production and creations by the Arts and Crafts Movement.

The quickened pace of mechanization, and subsequent innovations in lighting, heating and sanitary conveniences required explanation in another wave of books. Many of these early 20th century manuals were concerned with the effective integration of these innovations into domestic settings. Edwardian interiors, influenced by William Morris and revivalist styles, can be seen in W.S. Sparrow's *Hints on House Furnishing* (London 1909). Good photographic images of interiors became more widely available for use in books. However, the impact of the Modern Movement altered approaches to interior furnishing, with spokesmen such as Adolf Loos and architect Le Corbusier scorning older modes of decoration. Interestingly, the types of middle-class decorating manuals established during the 19th and early 20th century survive to some extent to the present day. They exist as guides to specific styles, the works of individual designers, or design firm approaches. Books about interior decoration still dispense lifestyle advice and provide views of interior arrangements for consumer inspiration.

PAULA A. BAXTER

See also Eastlake; Loudon; Magazines and Journals; Muthesius

Publications

In the absence of a general survey on Decorating Manuals, the most useful starting point is often the individual publication itself: for a selected list see below. A detailed discussion of late 19th and early 20th century British examples appears in Neiswander 1988.

Barker, Lady, *The Bedroom and the Boudoir*, London, 1878; reprinted with *The Drawing-Room* by Lucy Orrinsmith and *The Dining Room* by M.J. Loftie, New York: Garland, 1978

Beecher, Catharine E. and Harriet Beecher Stowe, *The American Woman's Home; or, Principles of Domestic Science, Being a Guide to the Formation and Maintenance of Economical, Healthful, Beautiful, and Christian Homes*, New York, 1869; reprinted New York: Arno, 1971

Beeton, Mrs. [Isabella Mary], *Book of Household Management*, London, 1861; reprinted London: Chancellor Press, 1982

Cook, Clarence, *The House Beautiful: Essays on Beds and Tables, Stools and Candlesticks*, New York, 1878; reprinted New York: Dover, 1980

de Wolfe, Elsie, *The House in Good Taste*, New York: Century, 1913; London: Pitman, 1914

Eastlake, Charles Locke, *Hints on Household Taste in Furniture, Upholstery and Other Details*, London, 1868; 4th edition 1877; reprinted New York: Dover, 1969

Edis, Robert W., *The Decoration and Furniture of Town Houses*, 2nd edition London, 1881; reprinted, with introduction by Christopher Gilbert, Wakefield: EP, 1972

Falke, Jacob von, *Art in the House: Historical, Critical, and Aesthetical Studies on the Decoration and Furnishing of the Dwelling*, Boston, 1879

Garrett, Rhoda and Agnes, *Suggestions for House Decoration in Painting, Woodwork and Furniture*, London, 1876; reprinted with *The Art of Decoration* by Mary Eliza Haweis, *Dress* by Margaret Oliphant, and *Music in the House* by John Hullah, New York: Garland, 1978

Haweis, Mary Eliza, *The Art of Decoration*, London, 1881; reprinted, with *Suggestions for House Decoration* by Rhoda and Agnes Garrett, *Dress* by Margaret Oliphant, and *Music in the House* by John Hullah, New York: Garland, 1978

Kerr, Robert, *The Gentleman's House; or, How to Plan English Residences, from the Parsonage to the Palace*, London, 1864; 3rd edition 1871, reprinted New York: Johnson, 1972

Loftie, W. J., *A Plea for Art in the House, with Special Reference to the Economy of Collecting Works of Art, and the Importance of Taste in Education and Morals*, London, 1876; 2nd edition 1877

Orrinsmith, Lucy, *The Drawing-Room: Its Decoration and Furniture*, London, 1877; reprinted with *The Bedroom and Boudoir* by Lady Barker and *The Dining Room* by M.J. Loftie, New York: Garland, 1978

Panton, Jane Ellen, *From Kitchen to Garret: Hints for Young Householders*, London, 1887

Spofford, Harriet Prescott, *House and Hearth*, New York, 1891

Wharton, Edith and Ogden Codman, Jr., *Decoration of Houses*, New York, 1897; reprinted New York: Arno, 1975

Further Reading

Burke, Doreen Bolger and others, *In Pursuit of Beauty: Americans and the Aesthetic Movement* (exhib. cat.: Metropolitan Museum, New York), New York: Rizzoli, 1986

Cooper, Nicholas, *The Opulent Eye: Late Victorian and Edwardian Taste in Interior Design*, London: Architectural Press, 1976; New York: Watson Guptill, 1977

Gere, Charlotte, *Nineteenth-Century Decoration: The Art of the Interior*, London: Weidenfeld and Nicolson, and New York: Abrams, 1989

Girouard, Mark, *Sweetness and Light: The Queen Anne Movement, 1860–1900*, Oxford: Clarendon Press, 1977; New Haven: Yale University Press, 1984

McClaugherty, Martha Crabill, "Household Art: Creating the Artistic Home, 1868–1893" in *Winterthur Portfolio*, 18, Spring 1983, pp.1–26

Neiswander, Judith A., *Liberalism, Nationalism and the Middle-Class Interior: The Literature on Domestic Decoration in England, 1870–1914*, Ph.D. thesis, London: Westfield College, University of London, 1988

Weiss, Jo Ann, *Clarence Cook: His Critical Writings*, Ph.D thesis, Baltimore: Johns Hopkins University, 1976

Delafosse, Jean-Charles 1734–1789

French *ornemaniste* and architect

Trained as a sculptor, under the carver Jean-Baptiste Poulet, Jean-Charles Delafosse later worked as an architect and designer. By 1767 he was describing himself as professor of drawing at the Académie of Saint-Luc, and he was appointed assistant professor of geometry and perspective in 1777. His architectural commissions included two houses erected in the rue Faubourg Poissonière in Paris between 1776 and 1783. Yet of far greater importance as far as the history of interior design is concerned was his work as an engraver of designs for ornament. He published approximately 500 plates, illustrating numerous architectural features and almost every type of domestic furniture, which were not only enormously influential in France but which were also issued in several editions abroad. Like his contemporary, Jean-François Neufforge with whose work his is sometimes compared, he developed an uncompromising, almost brutal form of classicism, and today he is regarded as one of the originators of the massive Louis XVI style.

The majority of Delafosse's engravings were published under the title *Nouvelle Iconologie Historique*, a work that was the result of many years study and that included designs prepared over several years. The first edition was issued in 1768 and comprised 111 plates; a second edition containing 258 plates appeared in 1771 and by 1785, with the publication of a third edition, Delafosse's oeuvre amounted to nearly 400 plates. The engravings initially consisted of a series of designs for trophies. To these were added designs for fireplaces, monuments, fountains, consoles, vases, friezes, medallions, cartouches, pendules, chandeliers and furniture of all kinds.

The engravings in the *Iconologie* were tied together by a complex and comprehensive iconography, interpreted in the lengthy prefaces in which Delafosse explained his aim as to represent the whole world in allegorical terms. He focused on themes such as the four elements, the four parts of the world, and the four seasons, but despite the grandiosity of this endeavour the iconography is as times more confused than consistent. The plate representing England, for example, is a cluttered composition with a collection of symbols of somewhat dubious applicability; masks and leopards appear among the three architectural orders along with military equipment, a papal tiara and a chained crown. Although this mixing of traditional representation with images drawn from his own imagination is what constitutes much of Delafosse's appeal, contemporaries were not surprisingly quite critical of such tendencies and the architect and theoretician Jacques-François Blondel described him in 1774 as "a man of genius but inconsistent". This inconsistency is perhaps most evident in the engravings of trophies dedicated to the nations, where the subjects were clearly subordinate to the designs and where there seems to have been little serious intention to incorporate what was known of each nation at the time, especially concerning exotic cultures.

The designs themselves drew heavily on ancient sources and represented a personal and innovative reworking of classical ornament that provided a seemingly endless variety of source material for craftsmen of many kinds. This ornament included versions of the Greek fret, twisted columns, foliated scrolls, garlands of laurels and roses, rams' heads, bucrania and lions' masks, some drawn in a style that echoed the heaviness of Baroque design, but the majority illustrating the severity of early Neo-Classical design. The second edition was especially important in disseminating the Louis XVI, or transitional style, and its designs for trophies, vases and chandeliers, combined elements of ancient decor in a tasteful, sober and accessible manner. The third edition was less original but was no less influential. It related more specifically to furniture, and combined antique motifs with curving Rococo profiles embodying the traditional period of 1760–1770. Several of the motifs from the first and second editions were used to decorate the exterior and interior of the Hôtel Titon, which Delafosse began in 1776. Lions' snouts and laurel branches, for example, are featured on the main entrance, while friezes of foliage appear between the storeys, and in the entrance passage, two niches protect antique urns decorated with interlaces and laden with festoons.

Many of Delafosse's architectural compositions bear a close resemblance to the work of the Italian engraver, Giovanni Battista Piranesi. Only the most unorthodox of French designers of this period were susceptible to the Piranesian rich decorative scheme, so this affinity was quite unusual. Moreover, its origins were somewhat unclear for it is not known whether Delafosse ever visited Italy. Nevertheless, several of the engravings in the 1771 *Iconologie* reveal specific borrowings from Piranesi although they also retain a distinctive character that is clearly Delafosse's own.

Delafosse's other books of trophies, published between 1776 and 1785, and in particular the *Attributs d'Amour*, also seem to have enjoyed considerable popularity and the designs were often executed, especially in marquetry. Pictorial marquetry first appeared on French furniture in the mid-18th century and remained fashionable throughout the reign of

Louis XVI. Delafosse played an important role in the spread of this fashion during the 1770s. His engravings were sold by the gilder Jean-Félix Watin and by several dealers such as Daumont, in the rue Saint-Martin, and Chereau, in the rue des Mathurins, and were clearly copied by a number of ébénistes, bronziers and other craftsmen. A table stamped by Adrien Delorme, now in the Victoria and Albert Museum, for example, has a top veneered with a design copied from the frontispiece to Delafosse's *Livre de Trophées Contenant Divers Attributs Pastorals*. Other pieces in the Wallace Collection also contain marquetry incorporating the same aforementioned frontispiece while an anonymous writing desk is decorated with a military trophy made to Delafosse's design. Nevertheless, the cost of reproducing the intricate detail and elaborate decoration typical of Delafosse's work was prohibitive even for the wealthiest patrons, and Félix Watin, who also dealt in furniture, offered to supply his customers with simplifications or substitutes of Delafosse's designs. Prints after Delafosse were also owned by the Sèvres factory, and Franz Ignaz Günther copied some of his vases for the Nymphenburg garden in Munich, c.1770.

Delafosse is remembered chiefly as an *ornemaniste*, whose engravings encouraged a taste for antique motifs – notably bucrania, heavy drapery, and serpents – among contemporary ébénistes, bronziers and silversmiths. His work is also characterized by extensive use of garlands – laurel, oak and floral. But unlike the more elegant offerings of Rococo designers, these are drawn in a compact style and it is this architectural heaviness, directly inspired by ancient examples, that also distinguishes the early massive form of the Louis XVI style from later kinds of Neo Classicism.

PIA MARIA MONTONEN

Biography

Born in Paris in 1734. Apprenticed to the carver Jean-Baptiste Poulet, director of the Académie de Saint-Luc, Paris, 1747. Worked in Corsica and Paris. Active as a designer of ornament and furnishings from 1767; architectural commissions date from the late 1770s. Appointed professor of drawing, Académie de Saint-Luc, 1771; made assistant professor of geometry and perspective, 1777. Published numerous engravings, including the *Nouvelle Iconologie*, from 1768. Member, Académie of Bordeaux, 1781. Died in Paris, 11 October 1789.

Selected Works

A collection of Delafosse's designs for chimneypieces and other architectural ornament is in the Musées des Arts Décoratifs, Paris. Additional drawings are in the Kunstbibliothek, Berlin, the Victoria and Albert Museum, London, the Cooper-Hewitt Museum, New York, and the Ecole Nationale des Beaux-Arts, Paris.

Interiors

1776–83 Hôtel Delbarre (later Titon), 58 faubourg Poissonière, Paris (building and interior fitments)

1776–83 Hôtel Delbarre (later Goix), 60 faubourg Poissonière, Paris (building and interior fitments)

Publications

Nouvelle Iconologie Historique, 1768; 2nd edition, 1771; 3rd edition, 1785

Further Reading

For a recent, scholarly study of Delafosse's engraved work see *Fragments énigmatiques* 1994.

Bellaigue, Geoffrey de, "Eighteenth Century French Furniture and its Debt to the Engravers" in *Apollo*, January 1963, pp.16–23

Bellaigue, Geoffrey de, "Engravings and the French Eighteenth-Century Marqueteur" in *Burlington Magazine*, May 1965, pp.240–50, and July 1965, pp.357–362

Eriksen, Svend, *Early Neo-Classicism in France: The Creation of the Louis Seize Style*, London: Faber, 1974

Fragments énigmatiques: Allégories de Jean-Charles Delafosse (exhib. cat.), Paris: Musée des Arts Décoratifs, 1994

Fuhring, Peter (editor), *Design into Art: Drawings for Architecture and Ornament: The Lodewijk Houthakker Collection*, vol.2, London: Philip Wilson, 1989, pp.496–98

Gallet, Michel, "Jean-Charles Delafosse, Architecte" in *Gazette des Beaux-Arts*, 61, March 1963, pp. 157–64

Gallet, Michel, *Paris Domestic Architecture of the 18th Century*, London: Barrie and Jenkins, 1972; as *Stately Mansions: Eighteenth Century Paris Architecture*, New York: Praeger, 1972

Hautecoeur, Louis, *Histoire de l'architecture classique en France*, vol.4, Paris: Picard, 1952

Kaufmann, Emil, *Architecture in the Age of Reason*, Cambridge, MA: Harvard University Press, 1955

Lavallet, Geneviève, "L'Ornemaniste Jean-Charles Delafosse" in *Gazette des Beaux-Arts*, 1929, pp.158–69

Mosser, Monique, "Trois Colonnes Hiéroglyphique de Jean-Charles Delafosse" in *Revue de l'Art*, 73, 1986, pp.65–66

Pressouyre, Sylvia, "La Poetique Ornamentale chez Piranèse et Delafosse" in Georges Brunel (editor), *Piranèse et les Français* (conference papers), Rome: Elefante, 1978

Watson, F.J.B., *Wallace Collection Catalogues: Furniture*, London: Wallace Collection, 1956

Wiebenson, Dora and Claire Baines, "Oeuvres de J.Ch. Delafosse" in *French Books: Sixteenth Through Nineteenth Centuries* (Mark J. Millard Architectural Collection, vol.1), Washington, DC: National Gallery of Art, 1993.

Delaunay, Sonia 1885–1979

Russian painter and designer

Sonia Delaunay was a pioneering painter who successfully applied abstract art forms to interior design. Between 1905 and 1925, with her second husband Robert Delaunay, she evolved the theory of Simultaneous Contrasts, creating abstract paintings by juxtaposing pure blocks of colour to produce both harmony and dissonance. Delaunay's colour relationships were calculated using mathematical precision combined with theoretical ideals. These complex ideas were integrated into all aspects of her work, reflecting her belief that there was no clear boundary between art and design.

Her departure into diverse media directed her down a different path from that taken by most other avant-garde artists of her time. Although her important perspectives contributed to similar theories then developing in Germany, Russia and Holland, they had a more personal application. Delaunay widened her experience of what art was and developed new approaches and definitions through her designs.

The first embroidery she created, in 1909, was considered to be a breakthrough in her development: the expressive potential of the satin stitch wallhangings was liberating. As a painter she was always concerned with surfaces, and the structure of the embroidery allowed her to explore surfaces in a new way, breaking with the conventions of her academic training to use colour more freely. From this point Delaunay explored many media and always remained intrigued by the surfaces and patterns of other cultures, both ancient and modern.

Her earliest interior designs were those for her own home, begun when her son was born in 1911 and when domestic life grew increasingly important. From their onset the highly individual interiors were extensions of her paintings: theories of colour and form were successfully transferred to walls, ceilings and fabric without losing either aesthetic expression or practicality. Art came out of her daily experiences and could, therefore, be fed back into everyday items, transforming them with complete validity. When making an appliqué cover for her son's crib, she created a design with the same intensity of colour and form as her paintings. The cover was far ahead of its time and was declared to be Cubist; her explorations in abstraction developed more intensely from this point. Working with textiles encouraged her to experiment, and she went on to create curtains, cushion covers, and lampshades, items that allowed her to explore her fascination with surfaces. She continued to explore colour theory while experiencing a constant interplay between her painting and her environment. This cross-fertilization, combined with travel, added new confidence to her work.

Her reputation for innovative interior design grew as she applied her theory of Simultaneous Contrasts to various surfaces, and she went on to combine these developments with architectural form. A large-scale church mural was the first of many commissions in which she successfully combined art and architecture. She was to receive many mural commissions, on both a large and small scale, throughout her life.

In 1918 Delaunay established Casa Sonia a small shop in the most fashionable area of Madrid. Its modern interior was simple: while walls and raffia flooring provided a perfect foil for the colourful objects on sale: the cushions, lampshades and painted accessories stimulated commissions to design domestic interiors for wealthy Spanish clients. On a grander scale she conceived dramatic colour schemes for the Petit Casino which opened in Madrid in 1919. The recognition gained in Spain preceded her return to France, enhancing her reputation. A commission to design a book shop, Au Sans Pareil, in Neuilly brought a great deal of publicity. The strength of the geometric designs established her in Paris as an interior designer of distinction.

The 1925 Exposition des Arts Décoratifs et Industriels placed France firmly at the forefront of new movements in art and design, and Delaunay was undoubtedly one of the major successes of this event. Her Boutique Simultanée encapsulated the aims of the exhibition and fused architecture, fine art, and design into one small space, gaining her international acclaim.

Not content to keep repeating herself, Delaunay went on to design furniture. Seating was upholstered in her fabrics and contrasting wood veneers were formed into Simultaneous surfaces. Together with matching carpets and rugs they provided the perfectly integrated scheme. As always, these pieces were practical, designed to complement a client's lifestyle. This ability to meld aesthetics with function in an uncomplicated way represented a humane balance between the austere Modernism of Russian and German design, and the sophisticated and glamorous Art Deco interiors of the same period.

Delaunay evolved a method of manipulating textiles which related them to the function of architecture, and walls were covered with her fabrics to emphasize a room's structure. This greater focus on the entire wall surface led to the further development of wall decoration – impressive hangings and murals explored the structural possibilities of materials in order to integrate them more fully with the building. Her designs for the cinema and theatre employed the same attention to colour and form which she manipulated to echo the mood of the production. Her synthesis of interiors, furniture, and costumes showed a mature understanding of multiple design fields. This creativity led to business commissions and collaborations which investigated the concept of "public" art. The 1937 Exposition Internationale des Arts et Techniques Appliqué à la Vie Moderne in Paris brought two commissions for murals, one of which earned her a medal.

Her daring and her technical control continued to bring public appreciation in her later years. In the 1950s she returned to textiles and designed curtains and tapestries. Both the Gobelin and Aubusson tapestry works produced a number of her large-scale designs with their carefully balanced colour combinations. Her artistic integrity was never compromised as she was able to treat all media with equal validity. The technicalities were the same and the fascination with colour, so essential to her life, had no limits. She placed it everywhere; using its transforming qualities to add movement and vibrancy to everyday existence.

The innate talent that was evident in 1901, and still productive in the 1970s, earned Sonia Delaunay a widespread reputation as a distinguished artist and designer. Her vision and commitment, which dramatically influenced modern interiors by expanding the boundaries of what was possible, was formally honoured: she was granted a number of prestigious awards including the Grand Prix Ville de Paris (1973) and the Légion d'Honneur which she received in 1975.

BRENDA KING

Biography

Sonia Ilinichna Delaunay-Terk. Born Sarah Stern in Gradizhsk, Ukraine, 14 November 1885. Moved to St. Petersburg to live with her maternal uncle, 1890; adopted his surname, Terk. Educated in St. Petersburg until 1902; studied drawing and anatomy under Ludwig Schmidt Reutter at the Kunstakademie, Karlsruhe, 1903–04; studied painting at the Académie de la Palette, Paris, 1905. Married 1) Wilhelm Uhde, 1908 (divorced 1910); 2) the French painter Robert Delaunay, 1910 (died 1941): one son. Active as a painter and graphic artist, Paris from c.1905; involved with embroidery from c.1909; began designing bookbindings, lampshades, curtains, mosaics, posters, and interior schemes, c.1913. Lived in Portugal (1915–16) and Spain (1917–18) during World War I; opened the Casa Sonia, Madrid, to sell her designs, 1918; met Sergei Diaghilev and designed costumes for his production of *Cleopatra* in London, 1918. Returned to Paris, 1920, and became closely associated with Dada and Surrealism. Opened a fashion atelier with Jacques Heim, Paris, 1924; designed interiors and furniture, and from 1923 increasingly concentrated on textile design. Almost exclusively involved with painting from c.1931. Moved to Grasse, Provence, 1941; returned to Paris, 1945. Member, Abstraction-Création group, 1932; founder-member with Robert Delaunay and others, Salon des Réalités Nouvelles,

1939, and Groupe Espace, 1953. Exhibited at numerous national and international exhibitions including the Paris Exposition des Arts Décoratifs et Industriels, 1925, and the Paris Exposition Internationale des Arts et Techniques Appliqués à la Vie Moderne, 1937. Received Grand Prix de l'Art Féminin, Salon International de la Femme, Cannes, 1969; Grand Prix, Ville de Paris, 1973. Chevalier des Arts et Lettres, 1958; Officier, Légion d'Honneur, 1975. Died in Paris, 5 December 1979.

Selected Works

Examples of Delaunay's textiles and designs are in the Musée de l'Impression sur Etoffes, Mulhouse and the Centre de Documentation de Costume, Paris. Examples of her furniture are in the Musée des Art Décoratifs, Paris and additional works including paintings and sculpture are in the Centre Georges Pompidou, and the Musée National d'Art Moderne, Paris.

1911 Appliqué cot quilt
1918 *Cleopatra* ballet costumes for Diaghilev's Ballets Russes, London
1921 19 Boulevard Malesherbes, Paris (decoration and furniture): Robert and Sonia Delaunay
1922 Au Sans Pareil, Neuilly (shop interior)
1925 Citroën B12 car (styling and decoration)
1925 Boutique Simultanée, Exposition des Arts Décoratifs et Industriels, Paris (layout and interiors, textiles and furniture)
1937 Exposition Internationale des Arts et Techniques Appliqué à la Vie Moderne (murals in the Palais des Chemins de Fer and Palais de l'Air; with Robert Delaunay)
1957 Salon de l'Automobile, Paris (exhibition stand for Maison Berliet)

Publications

"Tissus et tapis" in *L'Art International d'Aujourd'hui*, 15, 1929
Compositions Couleurs Idées, 1930
Robes-Poémes, 1969
Alfabeto, edited by R. Marconi and G. Niccolai, 1970
Nous Irons Jusqu'au Soleil, 1978
The New Art of Color: The Writings of Robert and Sonia Delaunay, edited by Arthur A. Cohen, 1978

Further Reading

Anscombe, Isabelle, *A Woman's Touch: Women in Design from 1860 to the Present Day*, London: Virago, and New York: Viking, 1984
Baron, Stanley and Jacques Damase, *Sonia Delaunay: The Life of an Artist*, New York: Abrams, and London: Thames and Hudson, 1995
Cohen, Arthur A., *Sonia Delaunay*, New York: Abrams, 1975
Damase, Jacques, *Sonia Delaunay: Tapis et oeuvres graphiques* (exhib. cat.), Paris: Demeure, 1970
Damase, Jacques, *Sonia Delaunay: Fashion and Fabrics*, London: Thames and Hudson, and New York: Abrams, 1991
Delaunay (Sonia et Robert) (exhib. cat.), Paris: Musée d'Art Moderne de la Ville de Paris, 1985
Dorival, Bernard, *Sonia Delaunay: Sa Vie, son oeuvre, 1885–1979*, Paris: Damase, 1980
Lassaigne , Jacques and others, *Sonia Delaunay: Tapisseries* (exhib. cat.), Paris, 1972
Lhote, André and others, *Sonia Delaunay: Ses peintures, ses objets, ses tissus simultanés, ses modes*, Paris: Libraires des Arts Décoratifs, 1925
Madsen, Axel, *Sonia Delaunay: Artist of the Lost Generation*, New York: McGraw Hill, 1989
Todd, Dorothy and Raymond Mortimer, *The New Interior Decoration*, 1929; reprinted New York: Da Capo, 1977

Delftware

Delftware is the name given to a type of tin-glazed pottery produced in Holland from the early 16th century; the name derives from the Dutch town of Delft which became one of the most important centres for the production of this type of ware from the mid-17th century. The name is also sometimes applied to similar tin-glazed wares produced elsewhere in northern Europe, especially in England, where it is known as English Delftware.

Dutch tin-glazed pottery was derived directly from Italy. By 1512, or possibly earlier, the Italian potter Guido Andries had established a pottery workshop in Antwerp. Its productions consisted mainly of drug jars with simple geometric designs, tiles (good examples of which can be found at The Vyne, in Hampshire) and small altar vases. The colours were Italianate: blue, yellow, orange, green, but dominated by a very dark blue. Production of tin-glazed pottery quickly spread from Antwerp, particularly in the northern Netherlands, and soon established its own distinct style, subject matter and methods of production. This expansion was largely the result of the political and economic upheaval during the war between Spain and the Netherlands. The fall of Antwerp in 1585 led to a mass migration north and this undoubtedly included potters who were looking for a more favourable economic climate in which to work. Tin-glaze techniques were introduced to Middleburg in 1564 by one of Andries's sons, and the towns of Gouda, Rotterdam, Delft, Haarlem, Amsterdam and Frisa were all to become thriving centres for Delftware in the second half of the 16th century, producing both pottery and tiles.

The range of forms made in Delftware for domestic use was extensive. One of the features of the Delftware industry was its ability to respond to new tastes and fashions. It was quick to recognise the increasing demand for tablewares in the 17th century. The functional type of pottery known as *wit-goet*, or white wares, made in vast quantities, was derived from Italian models: simple jugs, fluted bowls, plates and other domestic pieces can often be seen depicted in contemporary paintings by artists such as Vermeer. These functional domestic wares were mostly undecorated, but glazed in an extra thick tin-glaze known as *dubblewit* (double white). The *Wapengoet* fulfilled a demand from the upper classes for fine quality heraldic ware featuring family coats of arms. Notable among the ornamental wares produced in Delftware were various flower vases, such as the *tulipiere*, specially made for displaying tulips, and gadrooned sunflower bowls, often with crudely painted borders of tulips and sunflowers.

Tiles are one of the most characteristic products of Delftware and were made in vast quantities. The political annexation of the Netherlands to Spain had brought the former into contact with a much wider use of tiles, and production of Delftware tiles and their use in interiors dramatically increased throughout the 17th century. They began to be used in entrance halls, passageways and staircases to a height of about one metre so as to protect clothing from white-washed walls. It was a small step from there to the tiling of kitchens, fireplaces and then entire rooms. It was during this period that very large tile paintings were used for walls. Compared to other forms of wall covering, such as wall-painting or tapestry, tile panels had the advantage of economy,

Delftware: panel of Dutch tiles with biblical scenes, made in Rotterdam, mid-18th century (such tiles were used in fire-places in farmhouses); National Tile Museum, Otterlo, Netherlands

hygiene and bright lasting colour. Splendid flower panels are probably the best known of these.

Large quantities of tiles were exported to England, France, Spain, Portugal and South America. In England William and Mary ordered tiles and pots for the decoration of Hampton Court, and Delftware was also sent to France for the Trianon de Porcelaine where it created a vogue for blue and white ceramics. Architects of churches and palaces in Germany and Eastern Europe also commissioned large quantities of tiles from Holland. Tile-decorated rooms survive intact, notably in France at the Château de Rambouillet (1715–34), and at the Amalienburg, Nymphenburg, Munich (1734–39), both supplied by the De Ross factory (1666–1854) which dominated Delft tile production from the mid 18th century onwards. Collectively, production of Delftware was on a massive scale and, from the mid-17th through the 18th centuries Delft had probably the largest ceramics industry in Europe. It made fine, decorative ceramics available to many people and would have had an impact on most Dutch, and many other European, interiors in the homes of lower middle class people upwards.

Early in the 17th century many potteries began to abandon the hot maiolica colours for a blue and white scheme made fashionable by the vogue for Chinese porcelain, imported in quantity by the Dutch East India Company, founded in 1609. In 1615 there was a large auction of Chinese porcelain in Delft, and from this time onwards, Delftware potters all over the Netherlands began to imitate or integrate Chinese designs and subjects into their work. For example, *Wanli* borders of Buddhist symbols began to appear, juxtaposed with Dutch madonnas and baskets of fruit; soon Chinese figures, landscapes and flowers were imitated and the Chinese maze pattern became one of the standard corner motifs used on tiles.

However, although Chinese porcelain was of major importance stylistically, Dutch forms and subjects are nearly always clearly recognisable. Perhaps due to the influence of the Dutch Calvinists, who were opposed to any form of ornament, art in Holland became much more secular and realism dominated the work of contemporary artists, such as Vermeer, de Hooch and van Ruisdael. This tradition is reflected in Dutch Delftware painting which was, compared to Italian maiolica, sparser in colour, less elaborate in design and typically based on subjects from everyday life: flowers, bowls of fruit, contemporary landscapes and scenes of rustic life. Many Delftware painters were also fine artists. Frederick van Frijtom, for example, who decorated some of the finest plaques and plates, was also a highly respected landscape painter in his own right.

After about 1750 the high artistic standards and quality of craftsmanship which had characterised the previous century began to tail off, as Delftware faced increasing competition from German porcelain and English creamware. Some factories fell back on wares popular in the 17th century, others produced novelty wares, such as vases in the forms of fiddles, shoes or sledges, fussily decorated with landscapes in blue and white. By the 19th century only two tin-glazed earthenware factories survived in Delft. Dutch Delftware, however, had been extraordinarily successful in its ability to reflect the taste and needs of the day, with a high degree of elegance and craftsmanship. Production of traditional Delftware has continued to this day on a modest scale in Holland by factories such as Tichelaars at Makkum and De Porceleyne Fils at Delft.

DARRON DEAN

See also Tiles

Further Reading

A useful introduction to Delftware tiles appears in Lemmen 1986 which also includes a short list of collections and further reading.

Austin, John C., *British Delft at Williamsburg*, Williamsburg, VA: Colonial Williamsburg Foundation, 1994
Britton, Frank, *London Delftware*, London: Horne, 1987
Dam, Jan Daniel van and others, *Dutch Tiles in the Philadelphia Museum of Art*, Philadelphia: Philadelphia Museum of Art, 1984
Dam, Jan Daniel van, *Nederlandse Tegels*, Amsterdam: Veen / Reflex, 1991
Horne, Jonathan, *A Catalogue of English Delftware Tiles*, London: Horne, 1980
Jonge, C. H. de, *Dutch Tiles*, London: Pall Mall Press, and New York: Praeger, 1971
Lemmen, Hans van, *Delftware Tiles*, Princes Risborough: Shire, 1986
Lemmen, Hans van, *Tiles in Architecture*, London: Laurence King, 1993; as *Tiles: 1000 Years of Architectural Decoration*, New York: Abrams, 1993
Ray, Anthony, *English Delftware Tiles*, London: Faber, 1973

De Morgan, William 1839–1917

British designer of ceramics and tiles

William De Morgan was arguably the most celebrated designer and manufacturer of ceramics and tiles associated with the Arts and Crafts Movement in the late 19th century. He trained first as a painter at the Royal Academy Schools but in 1861 he gave up this ambition and began to design stained glass. Two years later he met William Morris who commissioned De Morgan to provide designs for tiles as well as stained glass. Morris's tile designs were very simple diaper patterns mainly in blue and white, derived from medieval manuscript illumina-

De Morgan: panel of six tiles, 1880s

tions and engravings in old herbals. Technically, however, they were often imperfect and by c.1869 De Morgan was experimenting with tile production on his own. He was also becoming increasingly disillusioned by the overriding control that Morris exercised over the colours used in the production of De Morgan's stained glass designs. So, using the technical knowledge of J.T. Lyon, he began to manufacture his own glass. Production was short-lived largely due to a fire at his Fitzroy Square premises in 1872.

De Morgan was at heart an inventor with a basic knowledge of chemistry, and his interest was roused by the iridescence that appeared on his glass when the yellow stain of silver was overfired. This interest led to the rediscovery of lustre, a technique that had a long history dating back to 10th-century Iraq during the Abbasid period. It was also used in the Hispano Moresque wares of the early 14th century and Italian maiolica in the 15th and 16th centuries, but after this time it fell out of favour and by the 19th century it had all but disappeared. Basically lustre is a fine metallic deposit on the surface of a ceramic object brought about when a metallic oxide (silver, gold, copper) loses its oxygen (reduction) in the firing. De Morgan's early lustre tiles were mainly restricted to a coppery red but later he was able to produce tiles with two or three lustre colours – red gold, yellow gold, and pearly silver – on the same tile. The effect produced by the play of light reflected on the uneven density of metal was little short of magical.

Concurrent with his experiments in lustre, De Morgan was designing and making tiles that showed a strong Morris influence. He had also taken over the production of a number of Morris's designs, initially using white blanks imported from Holland, and later, as his production techniques improved, tile blanks that he made himself. The influence of Morris on late 19th century design was, of course, enormous and his taste for the simplicity of medieval art and craftsmanship eventually influenced architecture, decoration, embroidery, and even music. De Morgan's interest in patterns derived from simple country flowers was clearly indebted to Morris's example but he also had a taste for fantasy and devised any number of fantastic animals and birds, as well as ships, sometimes as single tiles, and sometimes as repeat patterns with foliage or as pictorial panels. These latter tiles and panels were sold for framing, frequently in symmetrical pairs, or were incorporated into domestic fireplace surrounds. Tiles were also becoming increasingly popular in other areas of the domestic interior during this period and De Morgan's work was often used in bathroom dadoes, in entrance halls and in other locations where hygiene was considered important. The architect Halsey Ricardo, who was De Morgan's partner between 1888 and 1898, also made extensive use of tiles on the exterior of his house in Addison Road, not only because rain washed them clean but also because they retained their colour permanently. Another important use for De Morgan's tiles was in the interior decoration of ships, first the Tsar of Russia's private yacht, *Livadia* (launched 1880), and then ten liners for the Peninsular and Orient Steam Navigation Co. between 1882 and 1900. Some of the original drawings for these commissions and a number of duplicate panels have survived.

Many of the tile panels used in ships depicted stylised and fantastic views of some of the countries and ports that the P. & O. liners frequented. These views were not only intended as an expression of Imperial pride, they also reflected a broadening of the sources of inspiration available to designers in the late 19th century. The pattern books of Owen Jones, the artifacts gathered from all over the world and displayed at the great International Exhibitions from 1851, and the wider-buying policy of the South Kensington Museum, all encouraged a greater eclecticism in Victorian design. De Morgan was most interested in Islamic design. He had a thorough understanding of its principles and applied them frequently in his own work, particularly the ogee form which he used as a controlling construction in his designs. From c.1870 he was also experimenting with the deep cobalt, turquoise and olive green colours that were typical of Turkish and Persian glazes and which had never been used in Britain before. Théodore Deck in France and Cantagalli in Florence were involved in similar experiments and revived many of the same colours at around the same time. Unlike many other late 19th century ceramic manufacturers, however, De Morgan does not seem to have been interested in Japonisme, and equally he made no attempt to experiment with Spanish *cuenca* techniques even though certain of his clients and contemporaries – notably the architects Norman Shaw at Cragside, and G.E. Street at the American church in Rome – used them occasionally.

De Morgan's strength was as a designer of patterns for tiles.

The seemingly arbitrary way his patterns run over the shapes of his three-dimensional pottery offended later studio potters, but the idea of the unity of form and decoration was largely irrelevant to a 19th-century designer. The shapes of his thrown pots were designed on paper and much of his decorative work was executed on bought-in commercial wares. He employed a small permanent staff of four workers for the decoration of pots and dishes and some of the panels, but the tiles were decorated by a team of six girls. Often friends such as Halsey Ricardo and Dr. Thompson, were called in to help out or even to contribute the occasional design, but De Morgan did not allow his regular decorators to do any designing. The kilns were designed by De Morgan himself and drawings for many of these are in the Victoria and Albert Museum as are sketches for grinding mills and sieves and even roof trusses and a revolving grate. He also devised a system of gears for a bicycle. His knowledge of production was widely recognised; the Egyptian Government invited him to visit Egypt and to report on pottery production in 1893.

De Morgan tiles were never aimed at the mass-market. They were hand-crafted as opposed to factory-made and so inevitably they were expensive and were therefore always used in wealthy houses and often only in principal rooms. Cheaper versions were available for bedrooms and lesser areas. A plain 6 inch tile cost one shilling and threepence (6p) in 1887 compared with a similar product by Maw & Co. at fourpence (1.5p), and a decorated 6 inch tile was two shillings and sixpence (12.5p) compared with Maw & Co.'s version at sixpence halfpenny (2.5p).

By 1907 De Morgan had decided to give up pottery. He had already embarked upon a new career with the publication in 1906, at the age of 67, of the first of seven immensely popular novels. By this time too, his designs already appeared old-fashioned and sales had declined. Apart from his writing, he and his wife, the painter Evelyn Pickering, devoted much time to the support of the Suffragette movement and De Morgan was an ardent pacifist. In view of this it is sadly ironic that his death in 1917 should have been caused by a bout of trench fever which he caught from a friend who was visiting him on leave from France.

JON CATLEUGH

See also Tiles

Biography

William Frend De Morgan. Born in London, 16 November 1839; the son of the mathematician Augustus De Morgan. Studied art at the Royal Academy Schools, London, 1859. Married the painter Evelyn Pickering in 1888. Designs for stained glass and tiles from c.1863; worked for Morris & Co., 1863–72; established own pottery business in Cheyne Row, Chelsea, 1871; moved to Merton Abbey, Surrey, 1882; new factory at Sands End Pottery, Fulham, 1888. In partnership with the architect Halsey Ricardo, 1888–98; new partnership with Charles and Fred Passenger and Frank Iles, 1888–1907. Retired as a potter, 1905; Fulham factory closed, 1907; business continued under the Passengers and Iles until 1911. From 1906 pursued a successful career as a novelist. Died 15 January 1917.

Selected Works

The largest collection of De Morgan's designs is in the Victoria and Albert Museum which has more than 1200 sheets of original drawings; many of these are for dishes, pots and other decorative objects but at least 800 are for tile patterns and tile panels. Another 91 tracings and a sketchbook are in the Museum and Art Gallery, Birmingham. These museums also hold collections of De Morgan's ceramics and tiles. Other collections of De Morgan's work are housed at Old Battersea House, London; Fitzwilliam Museum, Cambridge; Leighton House, London; and William Morris Gallery, Walthamstow. Examples of De Morgan's tiles, employed in fireplaces or as small panels, were used in many Aesthetic and Arts and Crafts interiors.

Interiors

c.1879	Leighton House, Holland Park Road, Kensington (tiles for the hall, stairway and Arab Hall): Frederic Leighton
1882–1900	Tiles for the interiors of 10 liners built for the Peninsular & Orient Steam Navigation Company
1888	1 Holland Park, London (tiled porch and fireplace tiles): Alecco Ionides
1904	8 Addison Road, London (tiles for the exterior, fireplaces and interior): Sir Ernest Debenham

Stained glass, tiles and painted furniture for Morris & Co., 1863–72.

Further Reading

The most complete account of De Morgan's tiles is Catleugh 1983 which includes a chronology of his life and numerous illustrations of his designs, individually and *in situ*.

Barnard, Julian, *Victorian Ceramic Tiles*, London: Studio Vista, and Greenwich, CT: New York Graphic Society, 1972

Catalogue of Works by William De Morgan in the Victoria and Albert Museum, London: HMSO, 1921

Catleugh, Jon, *William De Morgan Tiles*, London: Trefoil, and New York: Van Nostrand Reinhold, 1983

Gaunt, William and M.D.E. Clayton-Stamm, *William De Morgan*, London: Studio Vista, and Greenwich, CT: New York Graphic Society, 1971

Greenwood, Martin, *The Designs of William De Morgan*, Ilminster, Somerset: Dennis and Wiltshire, 1989

Lockett, Terence A., *Collecting Victorian Tiles*, Woodbridge, Suffolk: Antique Collectors' Club, 1979

Morris, May, "Reminiscences of William De Morgan" in *Burlington Magazine*, August and September 1917

Pinkham, Roger, *Catalogue of Pottery by William De Morgan*, London: Victoria and Albert Museum, 1973

Sparrow, Walter Shaw, "William De Morgan and His Pottery" in *The Studio*, 15 September, 1899

Stirling, Mrs. A.M.W., *William De Morgan and His Wife*, London: Butterworth, and New York: Holt, 1922

Young, Hilary, "The Drawings of William De Morgan" in *Magazine Antiques*, June 1989

Design Reform Movement

Design reform has been a continuing theme throughout the history of design in most parts of Europe since the Industrial Revolution. The design reform movement in Britain came about as a reaction to a general fear that industrialisation had led to a lowering of aesthetic standards, since the preoccupations of the craftsman had little to do with the demands of industrial production. In addition to any cultural damage that might ensue from lower standards, it was feared that they would weaken Britain's position in world trade. Hence the arguments put forward by early design reformers, while motivated by a spiritual and moral concern for the development of industrial culture, often also cited the excellence of continental education and industrial practice as compared with that in Britain, and the commercial ramifications of this situation. Reformers perceived a two-fold problem: first, in the education of designers, which was either non-existent or wholly inappropriate; and second, in the low expectations of the producer and consumer. The tactics they adopted were therefore geared towards the reform of design education, and also the education of public taste.

The earliest recognition of the importance of design in industry came not from Britain, surprisingly, perhaps, given her pre-eminent position in world trade during the mid-19th century, but from Continental Europe. As early as 1725, for instance, the reorganisation of the Academy of Art in Vienna made specific reference to the need to promote the country's products abroad, and the same principle informed Friedrich Anton Freiherr von Heinitz's (1725–1802) reform of the Berlin academy in 1790; its manifesto stated that its intention was "to contribute to the well-being of the arts in general as well as to instigate and foster home industries, and by influencing manufacture and commerce, improve them to such an extent that the taste of Prussian artists will no longer be inferior to that of foreigners" (Pevsner, 1940). The end of the Napoleonic wars, and the rapid increase in trade across Europe in the early 19th century as a consequence, accelerated the shift away from territorial struggles between nations towards commercial rivalry, and served to heighten concerns about national competitive advantage.

The concept of the artist in industry was therefore not a new one when, in 1835, William Ewart (1798–1839), Member of Parliament for Liverpool, established a Select Committee "to enquire into the best means of extending a knowledge of the arts and principles of design among the people (especially the manufacturing population) of the country; also to enquire into the constitution of the Royal Academy and the effects of institutions connected with the Arts" (Bell, 1963). Ewart's ideas were strongly influenced by those of Benjamin Robert Haydon (1786–1846), a painter who had campaigned throughout the late 1820s and 1830s for the establishment of a school of design. It was the Select Committee of 1835 which gave rise to the first such institution. This school had in fact begun to be set up before the committee even published its recommendations, in August 1836. Its council was drawn entirely from members of the Royal Academy, which previously had viewed the reformers' campaign with some distrust, and so the new school had a rather compromised status from its very inception. In its early years it was beset by argument and criticism, and its first director, John Buonarotti Papworth (1775–1847), lasted just 18 months in the post.

Papworth's replacement at the School of Design, William Dyce (1806–64), was to have a far greater impact on design reform in Britain. Dyce was a shrewd campaigner, who was able to invoke the now familiar commercial argument for design training, although it is clear that his motivations were at least as much aesthetic and spiritual. He had worked in Rome, where he had been impressed by the group of German painters known as the Nazarenes. The Nazarenes had become disillusioned with the academic approach to art education promoted at the Vienna Academy, and had established a commune in a deserted Italian monastery. Their austere outlook and stress on objective drawing from life influenced Dyce. In 1837 he was appointed to the Edinburgh Trustees' Academy, and undertook a study tour of schools in France and Germany on behalf of the Council of the London School of Design, during which he developed his views on both the need for a new system for training designers in Britain, and the basis of the curriculum that they should follow. He wrote: "the studies of an elementary school must be undergone by pupils who are to become designers for industry; and in the present state of things it may be asked, where are the means of engaging in these studies to be found? Why, nowhere. There is at present no elementary school suited to the wants of a designer for industry" (Dyce, 1853). More than most reformers, Dyce also had a subtle understanding of the need not only for good design education, but also for industry to recognise the value of design: "It may appear incredible, but I assert it without fear of contradiction, that there are very few if any instances in Great Britain, of industrial artists who are employed as responsible persons; that is, to whose judgment manufacturers give the least deference; whose productions can be looked upon as original works; or who are allowed even to have a voice as to the mode in which the patterns they are employed to make should be executed" (Dyce, 1853).

It was Dyce's cogent argument that encouraged the Government to invest in and expand the School of Design. By the time he left the School of Design in 1843, there were six regional branch schools, and a Normal School – a school for teacher training – had been established within the London school.

The single most important figure in design reform in Britain in the mid 19th century was Henry Cole (1808–82). It was Cole who was most successful in mobilising public opinion and the establishment, using three key channels: publications, exhibitions and museums, and the design schools. Although Cole was a highly influential figure, and worked closely with Prince Albert in the latter's capacity as the President of the Royal Society of Arts, he realised that, in order to succeed, design reform had to filter down through all levels of society. It was largely due to Cole's efforts that the design reform movement broadened its horizons and took on Dyce's implicit understanding that design could not exist in a vacuum; the demand for good design had itself to be cultivated, both among manufacturers, and among the buying public.

As a result of his tireless campaigning, Cole was asked in 1848 to make a report on the Schools of Design. His conclusion was that no-one had responsibility for the schools, and that they had lost direction. Cole himself became chairman of the Schools of Design in 1851 and subsequently, in 1852, Secretary of the new Department of Practical Art. During the same period he published an influential magazine, the *Journal of Design*, which carried articles by sympathisers such as Dyce and Owen Jones (1809–74). Cole was an energetic and versatile campaigner who could turn his hand to a wide range of enterprises as the need arose. He was involved to varying degrees in design, manufacturing, publishing, and organising exhibitions, specifically the 1851 Exhibition, which marked a turning point in the development of industrial design as a professional discipline in Britain. The Great Exhibition, although a commercial success, underlined the bankruptcy of industrial art to reformers; it was dominated by the naturalism and eclecticism that they despised. However, even for Cole, some of the exhibits were worthy examples of industrial design, and a selection was bought with the profits of the exhibition, to be housed in a Museum of Manufactures. This collection formed the nucleus of the collection established in South Kensington in 1852, that was renamed the Victoria and Albert Museum in 1899, and that was the inspiration for similar museums in continental Europe, notably Paris, Stuttgart and Vienna.

Another strident critic of the uncontrolled application of ornament and decoration to industrial products was the painter and designer, Richard Redgrave (1804–88), who lectured at the School of Design from 1846 onwards. Between 1849 and 1852, Redgrave edited the six editions of Cole's *Journal of Design*, and through its pages helped develop the principles of a new industrial aesthetic. Redgrave inherited the Dyce concept of studying nature and making abstractions based on the principles of geometry, and of using these abstractions, rather than historicist motifs, to create designs for industry. He was not concerned with craftsmanship, but with reproducibility, and saw the skill of the designer as residing in his ability to select and arrange materials, rather than technical virtuosity.

As with many campaigning movements, the aims of the design reformers are easier to describe in the negative than in the positive; that is to say, they described and ridiculed the many examples of what they saw as debased and vulgar design far more often than they upheld examples of good and proper design. Many of their ideas are manifest, however, in the work of A.W.N. Pugin (1812–52), a fervent critic of eclecticism and a devout Catholic who took his lead from Gothic architecture. Pugin's *bêtes noires* were *trompe-l'oeil* and other forms of pretence or artifice, such as veneered mahogany. His work on the Medieval Court at the Great Exhibition was praised by the design reformers, although the stridency of his views – expressed in his books, including *The True Principles of Pointed or Christian Architecture* (1841) – meant that he was often marginalised both as a designer and as a theorist.

This raises the question of how strong an impact the design reform movement actually had on manufacturing and design. In the short term, the teachings of Redgrave and the design orthodoxy preached by the South Kensington Schools certainly encouraged the more progressive sections of the wallpaper and textile industries, in particular, to abandon overtly naturalistic effects in favour of simpler, conventionalised designs, and from the mid-1850s stylised floral and diaper patterns proliferated at the more expensive end of the market. Similarly, the influence of Pugin and Owen Jones helped to inspire a fashion – albeit shortlived – for authentic Gothic and Moorish designs which went some way towards weakening the stranglehold of foreign, historicist styles. Yet, despite the emphasis on machine production, the majority of designers involved in the movement for design reform were still producing expensive, handcrafted work and their influence was therefore quite limited. And, large sections of the public proved quite resistant to the aesthetic of simplicity and conventionalisation and continued to purchase furnishings and decorations that were richly endowed with meretricious carving and ornament. Indeed, it was not until the last quarter of the 19th century, when a second generation of architects and designers such as Bruce Talbert, Christopher Dresser, and Lewis Foreman Day produced more popular forms of reformed Gothic and Anglo-Japanese design, that the principles of design reform began to enter the commercial sphere and even then the appeal of such work was generally restricted to upper-middle-class, progressive tastes.

Meanwhile, design reformers in Britain frequently cited the superiority of either continental design education, or of the manufactured products themselves, as an argument for action. Ironically, many of the foreign governments were facing the same problems and proposing similar solutions. Britain's economic power and naval dominance had clearly given rise to complacency in the first half of the 19th century, and the sheer capacity of its manufacturing industry led some French economists in the 1820s to argue that France should not attempt to compete with Britain in output, but to maintain its superiority in terms of design and craftsmanship. Many British manufacturers simply bought or copied their designs from France; and Dyce asserted that "Every one admits, that the great evidence, which we find in France, of the cheaper kinds of manufacture, is due to the ample opportunities of study provided for the common people" (Dyce, 1853).

Germany too was increasingly active in international competition, and gradually became the focus of anxiety among design reformers and industrialists in both France and Britain, who each sent numerous committees to examine the provision for education of artists in industry. A British committee visiting southern Germany in 1896 found that "numbers of illustrated books, besides large quantities of almanacs and Christmas cards, intended for the English-speaking markets, are printed, and the success of this industry is no doubt largely due to the [...] ready supply of well-trained artistic operatives" (HMSO 1896).

Design reform has continued to resurface as a theme in Britain and across Europe during the 20th century. On an aesthetic level, the rise of Functionalism after World War I and its dominance in the avant-garde of design theory through to the 1960s vindicated the reformers in their desire to find an aesthetic appropriate to the age of mass production. On a more prosaic level, however, industrial design as a professional discipline has had a rather more ambivalent response from industrialists and the general public alike.

Some of the initiatives promoted by Dyce, Cole and the other design reformers developed into highly influential establishments themselves, notably the Victoria and Albert museum and the Royal College of Art, which emerged from the School of Design, and have ironically come under fire from latter day reformers who would like to see more dynamic agents for change. Many of the arguments put forward for good design in industry and investment in design education in the intervening period have strong echoes of the design reform debate, which begs the question whether any real progress has been made in the last century and a half. Quite clearly, however, the debate has had a profound effect on the manufactured environment, and it seems that the economic and cultural arguments for good design and design training will continue to be rehearsed as long as the context in which they operate continues to evolve.

DOMINIC R. STONE

See also Good Design Movement; Owen Jones

Further Reading

Surveys of the history of the Government Schools of Design, the South Kensington Schools and the role played by the Victoria and Albert Museum appear in Bell 1963, Macdonald 1970 and Morris 1986. For a study of reforming influences in France see Tise 1991.

Banham, Joanna, Sally MacDonald and Julia Porter, *Victorian Interior Design*, London: Cassell, 1991; as *Victorian Interior Style*, London: Studio, 1995

Bell, Quentin, *Schools of Design*, London: Routledge, 1963

Bonython, Elizabeth, *King Cole: A Picture Portrait of Sir Henry Cole, KGB, 1808–1882*, London: Victoria and Albert Museum, 1982

Cooper, Anne, *For the Public Good: Henry Cole, his Circle and the Development of the South Kensington Estate*, Ph.D. thesis, Milton Keynes: Open University, 1992

Dyce, William, *Instruction on Art in Foreign Schools*, London, 1853

Forty, Adrian, *Objects of Desire: Design and Society, 1750–1980*, London: Thames and Hudson, and New York: Pantheon, 1986

Frayling, Christopher, *The Royal College of Art: One Hundred and Fifty Years of Art and Design*, London: Barrie and Jenkins, 1987

Frayling, Christopher and Claire Catterall (editors), *Design of the Times: One Hundred Years of the Royal College of Art* (exhib. cat.: Royal College of Art, London), Shepton Beauchamp, Somerset: Richard Dennis, 1996

Heskett, John, *Design in Germany 1870–1918*, London: Trefoil, 1986

Jervis, Simon, *High Victorian Design*, Woodbridge, Suffolk: Boydell, 1983

Jones, Owen, *The Grammar of Ornament*, London, 1856

Journal of Design and Manufactures, London, 1849–52

Macdonald, Stuart, *The History and Philosophy of Art Education*, London: University of London Press, 1970

Morris, Barbara, *Inspiration for Design: The Influence of the Victoria and Albert Museum*, London: Victoria and Albert Museum, 1986

Naylor, Gillian, *The Arts and Crafts Movement: A Study of its Sources, Ideals and Influence on Design Theory*, London: Studio Vista, and Cambridge: Massachusetts Institute of Technology Press, 1971

Pevsner, Nikolaus, *Academies of Art, Past and Present*, Cambridge: Cambridge University Press, and New York: Macmillan, 1940; reprinted New York: Da Capo, 1973

Redgrave, Richard, *Report on Design*, London, 1852

Tise, Suzanne, *Between Art and Industry: Design Reform in France, 1851–1939*, Ann Arbor: UMI Research Press, 1991

Deskey, Donald 1894–1989

American interior, furniture, product and packaging designer

Although originally trained in the United States, Donald Deskey was much influenced by his time in Paris where he studied in the early 1920s, thus experiencing directly many facets of contemporary European design and fine arts practice. Of considerable influence for him, as for a number of designers in 1920s America, was the famous 1925 Exposition Internationale des Arts Décoratifs et Industriels Modernes, held in Paris, which did much to popularize the Art Deco style. It provided an important stimulus for Deskey's lavish interior decorative schemes for Radio City Music Hall (completed 1932) in the Rockefeller Center, New York City. Although such luxurious designs have been portrayed subsequently by many historians as the high point of his career, it is important to remember that Deskey also did much to promote in America something of the more austere and functionalist aesthetic of the avant-garde European Modernists whose work he had also encountered. Indeed, he had visited the Bauhaus in Germany and was a keen admirer of the work of artists and designers associated with De Stijl in Holland. However, his designs may perhaps best be summarised as exhibiting traits of both European decorative and functionalist tendencies, blended with the symbolism of progress evidenced in the forms and features of the American streamlined aesthetic of the 1930s.

Deskey's interest in French design was paralleled by the mounting in the United States of a touring exhibition of a selection of designs from the 1925 Exposition, commencing at the Metropolitan Museum, New York, in 1926. This decorative aesthetic soon became a fashionable style, bolstered in 1928 by two major department store exhibitions, at Macy's and Lord and Taylor's in New York. Like a number of other American designers who came to prominence in the later 1920s, Deskey was involved in the window display of fashionable stores; as the profits of these stores dropped in the recessionary years, designers were brought in to stimulate flagging sales. For the Saks Fifth Avenue store Deskey made dramatic use of cork and metal as a backdrop for the display of fashionable merchandise (1926–27); for the Franklin Simon store he introduced corrugated and galvanized iron, copper and brass as a setting for the sale of goods. This exploration of the fresh aesthetic possibilities of contrasting materials came to typify much of his interior design work of the later 1920s and 1930s. Apart from the use of chromium-plated metal in furniture and fixtures design, he also used plastics which, as he stated in an article in *Modern Plastics* in December 1934, had a practical as well as aesthetic role, being impervious to the damaging effects that might be wrought by the alcoholic cocktails of the Prohibition era. He also explored the decorative and expressive potential of glass in both architecture and furniture; in the former he deployed glass bricks to provide interesting effects in indirect lighting and in the latter glass was used to emphasise the possibilities of transparency and structure.

Building on the early critical success of his designs for hand-painted decorative screens and lighting, he undertook commissions for the interiors of apartments belonging to a number of prominent and influential New Yorkers. Perhaps unsurprisingly, given his earlier window display commissions, these included that of Adam Gimbel, President of Saks. Gimbel's apartment (1927) boasted cork walls, a copper ceiling, linoleum floor, pigskin chairs, a living room which explored the decorative possibilities of aluminium, and a hall which made imaginative use of stainless steel and vitrolite. Other celebrated New York clients included Abby Aldrich Rockefeller, for whom Deskey designed a private print gallery and boudoir in her West 54th Street residence (1929–31). With its clean, austere forms and sense of spatial clarity this was much more in tune with the progressive Modern Movement tendencies of the European avant-garde. More typical of his work as a whole, and inclining more towards the streamlined Modernism of a number of his American contemporaries, was his design for the apartment of George and Eleanor Rand (1930).

He also exhibited his work at the influential American Designers' Gallery in which he played a prominent role, as he did in the American Union of Decorative Artists and

Deskey: Radio City Music Hall, New York, 1931–32

Craftsmen (AUDAC). Like their counterpart, Contempora Inc., these two organisations were established in the later 1920s in order to promote modern decorative arts and design in the United States, much along the lines of European groups such as the Wiener Werkstätten and the Werkbunds in Austria and Germany or the Société des Artistes Décorateurs in France. Although the activities of such American propagandist organisations were seriously curtailed by the Wall Street Crash of 1929 they did much to foster a new climate for modern design in the United States in the years leading up to World War II.

At Radio City Music Hall (1931–32), part of the Rockefeller Center in New York, Deskey sought to promote American modernism, commissioning a number of renowned sculptors and painters to provide a rich decorative ambience in one of the most lavish interior schemes of the 1930s. Having won the limited competition for the project, he collaborated with many fellow members of AUDAC in the design of the foyer, auditorium, smoking and powder rooms and other public spaces. He himself contributed designs for some of the wallpapers and coverings (including a design based on tobacco-oriented motifs, printed on aluminium foil, loosely drawing on Cubist motifs), carpets, furniture and lighting designs. As well as bakelite and aluminium in the furniture, he also made extensive use of mirrors and glass fitments as a means of creating a sense of spaciousness. Of considerable significance for the establishment of Deskey's subsequent reputation were his designs for Samuel L. "Roxy" Rothafel's apartment, also in the Radio City Music Hall complex. ("Roxy" was the impresario of stage and radio shows who was the driving force behind Radio City Music Hall.) The interiors were imbued with a distinctly Moderne flavour in their exploration of the decorative possibilities of aluminium, bakelite, glass, cherry wood panelling, lacquer, and even gold-leafed ceilings which hinted at memories of the French artistes-décorateurs of the 1920s.

Deskey also featured significantly in designs for the New York World's Fair of 1939–40, designing the Focal Exhibits for the Communications and Transportations Zones. Both incorporated multimedia presentations and revealed the levels of sophistication which were expected of professional designers by the late 1930s. At the same exhibition he was also commissioned to produce interiors for the House of Jewels, one of the most popular exhibits at the Fair, as well as interiors for the Maison Coty Pavilion which were strikingly reminiscent of contemporary film sets. By this time Deskey's design practice clearly embraced a wide range of commissions in various design media, reflecting the growing professional status of, and demands made on, industrial designers in the United States.

After World War II Deskey's designs were in tune with the corporate ethos of the International Style and among the commissions he worked on were packaging designs for Proctor and Gamble (1949–76), packaging and interiors for Johnson and Johnson (1959) and Wall Street Club interiors on Chase Manhattan Plaza, New York (1960–62). This reflected a move away from artistic personality to all-but-anonymous design professional which, with a number of notable exceptions, became common practice in the post-war years.

JONATHAN M. WOODHAM

See also Streamlining and Moderne

Biography

Born in Blue Earth Minnesota, 23 November 1894. Studied architecture at the University of California, Berkeley, 1915–17; studied painting, Art Institute of Chicago, 1918–19; California School of Fine Arts, San Francisco, 1919–20; Ecole de la Grande Chaumière, Académie Colarossi, and Atelier Leger, all Paris, 1920–22. Served in the United States Army 1917–18. Worked as a graphic designer and co-founder, with Charles Howell, of an advertising agency, New York, 1921. Lived in Paris, 1921–22 and 1925–26. Married 1) Mary Campbell Douthett, 1923 (divorced 1946): 2 sons; 2) Katharine Godfrey Brennan, 1952. Returned to America and active as a designer of interiors, furniture, textiles, light fittings and glassware from 1927. Established his own design company with Philip Vollmer, Deskey-Vollmer Inc., New York, 1927; partnership dissolved c.1931; in private practice from 1931; formed Donald Deskey Associates, c.1943; branches in London, Brussels, Milan, Copenhagen, and Stockholm by 1950; retired as President, 1976. Instructor in art, Juniata College, Huntingdon, Pennsylvania, 1923–25; Professor of Industrial Design, New York University, 1930–36; lecturer, Massachusetts Institute of Technology, Harvard University, and other universities. Work displayed at many exhibitions including the Chicago Century of Progress, 1933; Exposition Internationale des Arts et Techniques Appliqués à la Vie Moderne, Paris, 1937; and World's Fair, New York, 1939. Co-founder and Fellow, American Society of Interior Designers; Member, American Architectural League, and Royal Society of Art. Died in Vero Beach, Florida, 29 April 1989.

Selected Works

The Donald Deskey Collection, containing numerous drawings, company records and brochures, manufacturers' catalogues, correspondence and photographs, is in the Cooper-Hewitt Museum, New York. Examples of Deskey's furnishings are in the Metropolitan Museum of Art and the Cooper-Hewitt Museum, both New York, and Yale University Art Gallery, New Haven.

Interiors

1926–27	Display windows, Fifth Avenue, New York: Saks and Company
1927	Adam Gimbel apartment, Park Avenue, New York (interiors and furniture)
1929–31	Abby Aldrich Rockefeller apartment, West 54th Street, New York (interiors including picture gallery, ceramics room, print room, dressing room and bathroom)
1930	Helena Rubenstein apartment, Fifth Avenue, New York (interiors including drawing room, bedrooms, and dressing rooms)
1931–32	Radio City Music Hall, Rockefeller Center, New York (interiors and furnishings): Samuel L. (Roxy) Rothafel
1932	Roxy apartment, Radio City Music Hall, Rockefeller Center, New York (interiors and furnishings): Samuel L. (Roxy) Rothafel
1933–35	Richard H. Mandel house, Mount Kisco, New York (building and interiors with Edward Durell Stone)
1934	Eleanor Hutton Rand apartment, Washington Mews, New York (interiors and furnishings)
1937	Hollywood Turf Club, Inglewood, California (interiors): Harold Anderson
1948	*S.S. Argentina* (interiors of ship's staterooms and public areas): Moore- McCormack Lines
1959–60	Marco Polo Club, Waldorf-Astoria Hotel, New York (interiors and furnishings)

Publications

"The Rise of American Art and Design" in *The Studio*, 1933

Further Reading

The definitive monograph on Deskey is Hanks and Toher 1987; it contains a long bibliography including a full list of Deskey's writings and numerous primary sources, a chronology of his life and work, and a select list of manufacturers for whom Deskey supplied designs.

Bayer, Patricia, *Art Deco Interiors: Decoration and Design Classics of the 1920s and 1930s*, London: Thames and Hudson, and Boston: Little Brown, 1990

Davidson, Gail, "Donald Deskey" in Mel Byars and Russell Flinchum (editors), *50 American Designers*, Washington, DC: Preservation Press, forthcoming

Davies, Karen (editor), *At Home in Manhattan: Modern Decorative Arts, 1925 to the Depression* (exhib. cat.), New Haven: Yale University Art Gallery, 1983

Duncan, Alastair, *American Art Deco*, New York: Abrams, and London: Thames and Hudson, 1986

Ferretti, Fred, "Requiem for Radio City Music Hall" in *New York Times Magazine*, 19 February 1978, pp.16–18, 20, 22–24, 26

Greif, Martin, *Depression Modern: The Thirties Style in America*, New York: Universe, 1975

Hanks, David A. and Jennifer Toher (editors), *Donald Deskey: Decorative Designs and Interiors*, New York: Dutton, 1987

Klein, Dan, Nancy A. McClelland, and Malcolm Haslam, *In the Deco Style*, New York: Rizzoli, 1986; London: Thames and Hudson, 1987

Komanecky, Michael, "The Screens and Screen Designs by Donald Deskey" in *Magazine Antiques*, 131, May 1987, pp.1064–77

Loring, John, "Above Radio City Music Hall" in *Architectural Digest*, 41, July 1984, pp.66–71

"Radio City Music Hall, Rockefeller Center", in *Architectural Forum*, February 1933, pp.153–64

Wilson, Richard Guy and others, *The Machine Age in America, 1918-1941* (exhib. cat.), New York: Abrams, 1986

Desks

Although known in Ancient Egypt and China, the desk in this period was merely a writing slab supported upon the knees. The earliest desks, in the sense of a supported surface, appear in Byzantium. They were little more than table tops fitted with a chest-like lower part and a lectern above, which could be angled to suit the writer. Clearly, the common use for desks at this time was in religious establishments where illuminated manuscripts were prepared, but the term "desk" originated in the Middle Ages and has since been applied to a range of writing and reading furniture such as lecterns, bureaux and secretaires.

While social conditions limited the spread of education and the growth of large numbers of written documents, the need for a private desk was limited. In the Middle Ages shallow boxes with sloping lids were used. These were known as scriptorie and remained the norm well into the post-medieval period.

By the 16th century, the notion of a portable table desk was developed. These were often elaborately decorated as they may well have been part of the furnishings of cabinets of curiosity. Inventories of Charles I's property include a "faire deske richly embroydered with silver and silk wherin is a silver inke pott and sand box".

The development of desks from writing boxes followed two paths. One was based on the fall-front *vargueño* (*escritorio*), an early form of the fall-front desk that was to become popular all over Europe. The *vargueño*-inspired desk inevitably followed the prevailing decorating fashions through a long history. In the late 17th century these fall-front cabinets, sometimes known as escritoires, were very fashionable, having a range of drawers and pigeon holes arranged around a central cupboard. Examples exist in marquetry and lacquer, but they eventually tended to decline in favour of bureau cabinets. By the mid 18th century the *secretaire à abattant,* a cabinet-like piece which has a vertical fall-front for writing upon, found great success as a design in France. These vary widely in finish, but usually have a fitted section behind the desk flap and a cupboard below, often a marble slab is fitted to the top. During the Louis XVI period this form of desk was made in a smaller, more delicate shape, with the desk cabinet fitted onto legs or an open stand and used as a framework for luxurious decoration.

The form was adapted to the tastes of Empire and Biedermeier during the early 19th century and revivals of the 18th century models were also made in the mid to late 19th century. The modern wall unit having a rectangular cabinet with a drop flap is the distant relative of one of the most inspired desk designs.

The second path was based on the angled front slope of writing boxes. Initially these were mounted on stands: subsequently the whole desk was mounted on a chest of drawers or on a stand to create a bureau desk. The imaginative reversal of the lid hinging was designed to allow the lid to drop down onto lopers to form a writing surface. The developments from this type were numerous versions of bureaux, which although providing writing space, are really a different category of furniture.

A third development was based on the adaptation of a table to create a variety of desk forms that, like the ones above, are still used today. The growth of polite society, a more literate public and better communication systems, encouraged writing which required new furniture forms. The initial development was based on the plan of two pedestals (usually with drawers) surmounted with a table top. Hence storage and writing were both catered for. The so-called *bureau Mazarin* was one of the first of these forms, being popular at the end of the 17th century, both for its practical use and also as an opportunity for luxurious decoration. In contrast to the Mazarin desk was the *bureau plat*, a flat writing table with drawers in the frieze. These again presented an opportunity for luxurious finishes; some of the most illustrious were made by Charles Cressent. This form was sometimes combined with a *cartonnier*, an extension which could be used as a matching filing cabinet.

This latter form was popular in France throughout the 18th century. In England and America the writing bureau (often in combination with a top cabinet) remained popular as did a range of table bureaux or portable desks.

The pedestal desk was also developed either into a library desk or a kneehole desk. The kneehole desk was often on a small scale and was ideal for private apartments and boudoirs, whereas, due to the development of libraries in private houses, the library desk became an important symbol of wealth and taste. Indeed most of the well-known cabinet-makers of the 18th century produced fine examples. Chippendale made a superb mahogany library desk for Nostell Priory and published

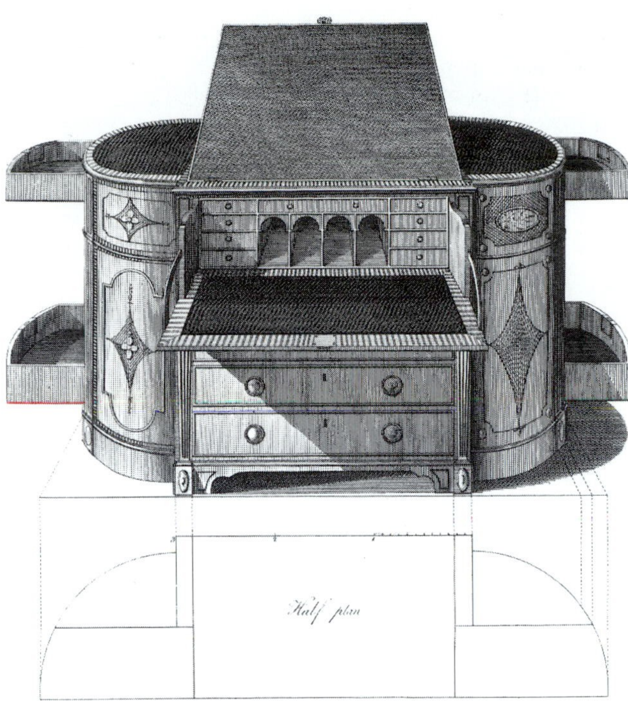

Desks: library table by Thomas Sheraton, 1793

a design for a quite exotic writing desk-table in the *Director* of 1762. John Channon is credited with making perhaps the most extravagant library tables which are fitted with superb mounts and ingenious construction methods. The pedestal desk form remains popular today, made in a variety of sizes suited to differing situations.

In France, a taste developed for delicate writing desks such as the *secretaire en pente*, a free-standing table with a flap used as a lid when closed and a writing surface when open. The *bonheur du jour*, a term first encountered in the 1770s, refers to a small writing table with a shallow superstructure of shelves or pigeon holes, especially designed for ladies' use. Sheraton's Harlequin desk table is somewhat similar, although his example has a hidden superstructure that rises when required.

Towards the end of the 18th century the fascination with mechanics and furniture found fertile ground in desk design. A simple example might be the *Secretaire à la bourgogne*, a French mechanical desk with one part rising to reveal a range of small drawers while the other part hinged forward as a writing surface. However, it was the work of David Roentgen and Jean-François Oeben that was to produce some of the most spectacular mechanical desks of the period. The famous Bureau du Roi, made for Louis XV, took advantage of the new cylinder top as well as a number of ingenious secret mechanical devices to become one of the world's most famous pieces of furniture.

In the same vein were a range of desks that incorporated the solid cylinder front, or a tambour. The *bureaux à cylindre* were designed so that as the writing slide was pulled forward, so the cylinder front would roll back revealing the desk interior. This was a fine example of the most skilful cabinet-making.

Sheraton devised cylinder desk / bookcases, some of which were intended for the use of two persons and demonstrated something of the desire for ingenuity that his Harlequin design had done previously. In the same vein were the mechanical desks devised by Giovanni Socchi c.1810 in which a compact oval table converted into a desk and chair.

In the late 18th century a distinctive desk form was developed and named after Carlton House. The design usually follows an elegant library table base with drawers in its frieze, which is surmounted with a gallery of smaller drawers or pigeon holes. It has an instantly recognisable D-shaped profile.

During the 19th century a range of adaptations and copies were made of earlier desk models, but there were a number of innovations as well. The well-known Davenport compact desk is one such example. These were made in the full range of Victorian materials and finishes. It was also during this period that the requirements of business produced a demand for office desks rather more substantial than the simple clerk's desk which was still recognisable as a derivative of the medieval table desk. The market was particularly strong in the United States and the products of the W.S. Wooton Patent Desk Company helped many businesses organise themselves efficiently. The Wooton desk was among the first to incorporate a variety of features related to filing, storage, and security; its swing-out front sections were adapted subsequently in British models as well as in the 20th century "home office".

Wooton's desks were exported, along with their less exotic partners, the rolling-top office desk. This desk, a feature of many Sheriff's offices in the Wild West, soon became popular in European business houses.

The 20th century has witnessed an amazing development in all forms of furniture, including desks. In the early part of the century, while Frank Lloyd Wright was developing metal desks with integral chairs for the Larkin building, the Arts and Crafts movements were using traditional shapes to experiment with their particular design and decoration. For example, desks by Koloman Moser and C.R. Ashbee are different in design but often have the same basic form.

The Art Nouveau and Art Deco movements influenced shape and decoration dramatically, but the basic function of the pedestal or table desk remained unchanged. In the same way the Modern Movement influenced styling and choice of materials, for example, the tubular-framed desk, but the shapes often remained the same. This is not surprising, as desks are essentially work-stations and as such must ultimately remain suited to the human form.

CLIVE D. EDWARDS

Further Reading

For numerous pictorial references see Bridge 1988. A full bibliography appears in Dietrich 1986.

Berman, Anne E., "Antiques: Early American Writing Furniture" in *Architectural Digest*, 52, June 1995, pp.214–19

Bridge, Mark, *An Encyclopedia of Desks*, London: Apple , 1988

Dietrich, Gerhard, *Schreibmöbel: Vom Mittelalter zur Moderne*, Munich: Keyser, 1986

Gloag, John, "Design for Correspondence" in *Connoisseur*, CXCI, January 1976, pp.14–19

Hayward, J.F., *English Desks and Bureaux*, London: HMSO, 1968

MacQuoid, Percy and Ralph Edwards, *The Dictionary of English Furniture*, revised edition, 3 vols., 1954; reprinted Woodbridge, Suffolk: Antique Collectors' Club, 1983

Ormond, Leonee, *Writing* (The Arts and Living series), London: HMSO, 1981

Symonds, R.W., "Back to Back Writing Tables" in *Country Life*, 13 September 1956, pp.533–34

De Stijl

The Dutch artists' group and journal known as "De Stijl" was founded in Leiden by Theo van Doesburg in 1917. Strongly influenced by the paintings of Piet Mondrian, much of the work produced by the group relied on flat, geometric areas of primary colours arranged within a matrix. This approach was applied to architecture, furniture, textiles, graphics and other media. And De Stijl interiors were similarly characterised by flat of areas of colour applied directly to the walls to produce a visual effect on the architectural space. They contained comparatively little furniture which was arranged in a linear pattern in this space-colour composition. The principles of this use of colour and the effect achieved ultimately varied from artist to artist. The fact the De Stijl group was made up of painters and architects was the principal reason for a dualistic approach to interiors.

Moreover, interiors were not initially a specific theme for the members of the group. The articles in the periodical *De Stijl* (1917–31) deal mainly with the relationship between painting and architecture, and the interior is mentioned only in passing. For this reason the attention to furniture and other interior components which help define interior design is a neglected aspect of the De Stijl interior. The well-known exceptions to this rule are the interiors of the furniture designer / architect Gerrit Rietveld.

Some De Stijl members were more preoccupied, at both a theoretical and practical level, with interiors than others. Those with the most clearly defined vision of the interior which was proclaimed in word and deed, are the painters Theo van Doesburg and Vilmos Huszár, and Rietveld. The painter Bart van der Leck was of great importance in the first steps towards a symbiosis of painting and architecture, though for him, Mondrian and the architects Robert van t'Hoff, J.J.P. Oud and Jan Wils, interiors were a topic with which they were only indirectly involved in the 1920s. Beside the official De Stijl members there were architects both at home and abroad who worked in the same style. Sometimes these were imitators, like P.J.C. Klaarhamer, S. van Ravesteyn, Félix Del Marle and Robert Mallet-Stevens, but in a few cases, such as in the work of Piet Zwart and El Lissitzky, their contributions had a fruitful impact on the formation of the De Stijl interior.

The development of the De Stijl interior spans roughly the period 1917–1928, from the setting up of the magazine to the year in which the last issues appeared. The personal positions of most members were subject to constant change. There is a clear watershed in 1921–23 when individual visions changed and the communal endeavour became dominant. In those years Oud broke with Van Doesburg and *De Stijl* because he could not agree with the painterly attitude which wanted to dis-

De Stijl: Aubette cafe and cinema by Theo van Doesburg, Strasbourg, 1927–28

mantle the structure of architecture by means of painting. At the end of the 1920s the design of interiors was very much determined by the New Architecture (*het Nieuwe Bouwen*), which forced the influence of Neo-plasticism (*de Nieuwe Beelding*) into the background.

The concern of De Stijl painters with the interior and their consequent collaboration with architects issued from their joint desire to unite various disciplines under the umbrella of architecture. In this they were extending the tradition of the 19th-century ideal of communal art which had been propagated in the Netherlands by the architect H.P. Berlage. The desire for collaboration and the attempt to gain a place for painting which was incorporated in, rather than separate from social life, was one of the main sources of this ideal. Besides this there was an inspirational impulse to reform life through redesigning the living environment, giving preference to the universal and collective over the arbitrary and individual. Use of abstract painting, harmony through the union of opposites, the destruction of architectural construction by means of painting, technical achievements and standardisation would on the one hand avoid echoes of the past and actually introduce the new life, and on the other and make the "well-planned" interior an off-the-peg product accessible to all.

During his De Stijl period Rietveld did not formulate any theoretical background for his work. However, his furniture designs already expressed a design ideology which did not restrict itself to designing an object but broadened into a general view of space and an ideological social position. Through the design and construction of furniture Rietveld tried to make a link with the space in which it was set. In addition his designs reflect a predilection for mechanisation and standardisation intended to make the furniture more affordable. Gradually his view of space developed towards interior design. In his approach to architecture the interior was more a starting point than a result. He wanted to make people aware of the notion of space, not as the content of a shape, but as a part of the overall space. The design of the furniture, which he had incidentally produced before joining De Stijl and which visually occupied and enclosed no space, also fitted in with that view. It is apparent from his work that he was not opposed to the use of colour in interiors, but his solo activity indicates that he was certainly not over-eager for a painter to be become involved. This does not detract from the fact that in the first half of the 1920s he was heavily influenced by the De Stijl painters in his choice of colours. The colour reduction which van der Leck had arrived at in his work as a result of his process of abstraction, was adopted by Rietveld; despite the fact that in his interiors he was never converted to the exclusion on principle of other than primary colours.

In 1922 van Doesburg met the architect Cornelis van Eesteren, with whom he worked intensively the following year on the design of the *Hôtel Particulier* (a residence for the Paris gallery owner Léonce Rosenberg) and two other architectural designs, *Maison Particulière and Maison d'Artiste*. The experiments with Van Eesteren bear witness to a changed view of the use of colour in architecture. Separate blocks of colour give way to a use of colour which focused on the surfaces and volumes of the architecture and which sought to highlight them.

In 1924 van Doesburg published the article "Towards a Neoplasticism" in *De Stijl*, on the subject of modern architecture. Its content was undoubtedly inspired by his architectural experiments with van Eesteren. Simultaneously van Doesburg's speculations were realised by Rietveld in the house which he designed for Truus Schröder-Schräder in Utrecht. The ground plan of the first floor of the Rietveld Schröder House (1924) is completely open. This area contained the living space. The dividing walls are movable, making the space multi-functional and a large part of the furniture is built in. The walls are coloured, making wallcoverings unnecessary. Ornaments and decorative items have been avoided in order to show the essence of the architecture (space) to maximum effect. The interior is light because of the daylight which floods in through the many large glass surfaces. However, this interior is more a reflection of an attitude to life in which awareness, sobriety, efficiency and economy are central, than a product of monumental art.

The first issue of *De Stijl* in 1928 was called the Aubette issue. It was devoted entirely to the conversion of the 18th century Aubette building in Strasbourg as an entertainment venue, which was supervised by van Doesburg. Unlike earlier examples of De Stijl interiors, the internal walls and parts of the walls are treated as separate contrasting vehicles of the compositions, with the structure of the architecture being followed rather than dismantled.

Although fruitful results were initially achieved in joint projects by van Doesburg, Oud and Wils, and Huszár, Wils and Zwart, demarcation was the rock on which the ideal of collaboration foundered. This did not mean that there was no belief in the role of painting in architecture. However, the moment the notion of the art of painting was abandoned and interpreted more widely as colour compositions in architecture, new potential uses for the future seemed to emerge. Nor was it any longer the painter who by definition determined the colour scheme or conversely the architect who was the sole purveyor of architecture focused on painting. As van Doesburg had defined it in *De Stijl* in 1924, in a joint article with van Eesteren,"Vers une construction collective", it must be the work of "the constructor of the new life".

MARIJKE KUPER
translated by Paul Vincent

See also Rietveld

Selected Works

Examples of furniture by Pieter Klaarhamer and Piet Zwart are in the Gemeentemuseum, The Hague; the largest collections of furniture by Gerrit Rietveld are in the Stedelijk Museum, Amsterdam and the Centraal Museum, Utrecht. Numerous designs, photographs and documentation relating to the work of Theo van Doesburg are in the van Doesburg Archive, part of the collection of the Rijksdienst Beeldende Kunst, The Hague. Additional archive photographs and documentation relating to the De Stijl group are in the Nederlands Architectuurinstituut, Rotterdam.

1917–18 Bruynzeel House, Voorburg (bedroom; decoration and carpets by Vilmos Huszár, furniture by Pieter Klaarhamer)
1922 Hôtel Particulier, Paris (building and interiors by Theo van Doesburg, in collaboration with Cornelis van Eesteren)
1924 Schröder House, Utrecht (interiors and furnishings by Gerrit Rietveld, in collaboration with Truus Schröder-Schräder)
1926–28 Café l'Aubette, Strasbourg (remodelling and interiors by Theo van Doesburg)

Further Reading

Many of the more scholarly studies of the De Stijl group and its members have been published in Dutch but a good English-language account of their interiors, including numerous archive photographs, appears in Troy 1983. The standard monograph on the Schröder house is Overy 1988. For studies of individual architects and designers see Küper and van Zijl 1992 (Rietveld), Ex and Hoek 1985 (Huszár) and van Straaten 1988 (van Doesburg).

Blotkamp, Carel, *De Stijl: The Formative Years, 1917–1922*, Cambridge: Massachusetts Institute of Technology Press, 1986
Blotkamp, Carel, *Mondrian: The Art of Destruction*, London: Reaktion, 1994; New York: Abrams, 1995
Ex, Sjarel and Els Hoek, *Vilmos Huszár Schilder en Ontwerper 1884–1960*, Utrecht: Reflex, 1985
Fanelli, Giovanni, *De Stijl*, Rome: Laterza, 1983
Friedman, Mildred (editor), *De Stijl, 1917–1931: Visions of Utopia* (exhib. cat.: Walker Art Center, Minneapolis), New York: Abbeville, and Oxford: Phaidon, 1982
Jaffé, H.L.C., *De Stijl 1917–1931: The Dutch Contribution to Modern Art*, London: Tiranti, 1956; Cambridge, MA: Harvard University Press, 1986
Kuper, Marijke, *Rietveld als meubelmaker: Wonen met Experimenten, 1900–1924* (exhib. cat.), Utrecht: Centraal Museum, 1983
Kuper, Marijke and Ida van Zijl, *Gerrit Th. Rietveld 1888–1964: The Complete Works*, Utrecht: Centraal Museum, 1992
Kuper, Marijke, "De Stijl" in E. Bergvelt, F. van Burkom, K. Gaillard (editors), *Nederlandse interieures van neorenaissance tot postmodernism*, Rotterdam, 1996
Overy, Paul and others, *The Rietveld Schröder House*, London: Butterworth, and Cambridge: Massachusetts Institute of Technology Press, 1988
Overy, Paul, *De Stijl*, London and New York: Thames and Hudson, 1991
Overy, Paul and Peter Vöge, *The Complete Rietveld Furniture*, Rotterdam: 010, 1993
Oxenaar, R.W.D., *Bart van der Leck tot 1920 een Primitief van de Nieuwe Tijd*, thesis, The Hague: Rijksuniversiteit te Utrecht, 1976

Straaten, Evert van, *Theo van Doesburg: Painter and Architect*, The Hague: SDU, 1988

Straaten, Evert van, *Klare en Lichte, gesloten ruimten geaccentueerd door diepe en pure Kleuren, het werk van Theo van Doesburg in de Architectuur*, thesis, Amsterdam: Vrije University, 1992

Straaten, Evert van (introduction), *Bart van der Leck: "een Toepassend Kunstenaar"* (exhib. cat.), Otterlo: Kröller-Müller Museum, 1994

Troy, Nancy J., *De Stijl's Collaborative Ideal: The Colored Abstract Environment, 1916–26*, Ph.D. thesis, New Haven: Yale University, 1979

Troy, Nancy J., "Mondrian's Designs for the Salon de Madame Bienert, à Dresedin" in *Art Bulletin*, 62, December 1980, pp.640–47

Troy, Nancy J., *The De Stijl Environment*, Cambridge: Massachusetts Institute of Technology Press, 1983

Deutscher Werkbund

German design and industries association; established 1907

Founded in Munich in October 1907 by Peter Bruckmann, Peter Behrens, Hermann Muthesius, Josef Maria Olbrich, Fritz Schumacher and Richard Riemerschmid, the Deutscher Werkbund was a professional coalition of designers and industrialists dedicated to the improvement and promotion of German design. Inspired by Muthesius, who had earlier warned of the commercial dangers of backwardness in design, its motivations were as much economic as aestheric, and, unlike the Arts and Crafts Movement, it did not seek to revive the romantic notion of handicraft but encouraged a closer cooperation between designers and industry. The Werkbund also considered the education of designers and retailers to be vital, and to this end it organised programmes of evening lectures and supporting exhibitions to help raise public awareness about design issues, subsidised a number of industries and founded a Museum of Industrial Design in Hagen.

By 1909 membership, which was by invitation only, had risen to 700 and included the architects Henry van de Velde, Ludwig Mies van der Rohe, Walter Gropius, Marcel Breuer and Friedrich Neumann. By 1914 it had grown to 1,870 and included most of the leading designers, architects, industrialists, craftspeople, teachers and publicists of the time. The Werkbund also produced a yearbook (1912–20), held annual conferences, and in 1914, staged a major exhibition in Cologne. From 1925 to 1934, the Werkbund published a magazine, *Die Form*, and in 1927 it organised an exhibition of housing at Stuttgart, building a model suburb with Mies as its architectural director. However, the Werkbund lacked theoretical coherence. Its belief in the cultural value of quality could be interpreted in many different ways and from the outset the organisation was characterised by fundamental disputes.

Some industrialists quickly recognised the commercial advantages of producing tasteful, modern goods. Emil Rathenau hired Peter Behrens in 1907 to design a new corporate system for the AEG which embraced factories, graphics, products, showroom and office interiors, and workers' estates. The Werkbund Yearbooks included contemporary designs for automobiles, factories, steamship interiors, railway coaches and illustrated the variety of approaches to interior design. These ranged from Bruno Paul's elegant interior for a Lady's Bedroom for the Westend House, Berlin 1909, to Walter Gropius's Gentleman's Study 1912, where the furniture revealed an interest in clean, geometrical forms, while still retaining a feeling for handcraftsmanship in the highly polished treatment of wood and in the upholstery of the chair.

In 1909 the Werkbund's interest in objects for a wider market was reflected by Riemerschmid and Bertsche's development of Typenmöbel furniture in Munich, whose interchangeability of parts allowed 800 different permutations and combinations. Manufactured in large quantities and therefore relatively cheap, the furniture nevertheless had an individuality and character of its own, without betraying the use of machinery in its production. In comparing the chairs in Karl Bersch's study, executed by the Deutsche Werkstätten für Handwerkskunst at Dresden-Hellerau in 1909–12 and those by Behrens in Darmstadt in 1901, it is difficult to guess which one had been machine-made. Although most Werkbund designers acknowledged the effectiveness of both the machine and hand tools in achieving quality, their interiors reveal that an insistent bias towards craft remained. The work from Karl Schmidt's Dresdener Werkstätten shows this clearly. Paul Schultz-Naumburg was typical of the majority of leading designers who chose to eschew advanced theory in favour of a more conservative position. He encouraged continuity through the adaptation of earlier styles to suit modern conditions. His bedroom, executed by the Saalecker Werkstätten, contained Biedermeier and Neo-Classical elements, especially in the couch, table, light fittings and heavily draped windows. Fischer and Riemerschmid also sought continuity, but they drew their inspiration from regional craft traditions.

The architecture of the 1914 Cologne Werkbund Exhibition exposed a polarisation between sober classicism and imaginative individualism. Interior design also showed that formal unity, so important to the cultural reform movement, remained elusive. Hoffmann's room, with its Regency stripes and strangely mannered chairs, showed the refinement of the Wiener Werkstätte giving way to a fussiness verging on the decadent. The interior of Muthesius's pavilion for the Hamburg-America shipping line proved that while his theories were advanced, his practical designs tended towards Neo-Classicism, so popular since the turn of the century. In contrast to the curving organic lines of the exterior of van de Velde's Werkbund Theatre, the foyer and interior theatre remained largely based on rectangular constructional features while his design for a living room, with its Art Nouveau chairs and carpet, presented a mixture of styles. Gropius's Hall, designed for Hermann Gerson of Berlin, appeared heavy and conventional and curiously at odds with the transparent clarity and daring fenestration of his Model Factory, constructed at Cologne. A wide range of historical and regional forms were evident. Behrens displayed Neo-Classical furnishings for the German Embassy in Leningrad and Paul Ludwig Troost showed his Neo-Baroque style dining room for the Bremen-Oldenbeurg House. Lucien Berhard designed an Empire style bed for a luxurious room by the Deutsche Werkstätten. Runge and Scotland's room was decorated with heavily patterned wallpaper, carpet and fabrics and included marble-topped tables and carved chairs. This richness was echoed in the

Deutscher Werkbund: community room in block of flats by Walter Gropius, with tubular steel furniture by Marcel Breuer, Berlin, 1931

heavily upholstered furniture and patterned décor of the Summerhouses by Max Heindrich and Berhard Stadlet. Wilhelm Lossow and Max Kuhne sought to invest the Saxon House with regional identity by using local craftsmen to create wrought-iron gates and screens. While the exhibits manifested divergences in practice, the annual conference debated the underlying theoretical tensions, namely the relative importance of individual design (supported by van de Velde) and *Typisierung* (or standardisation of good form and good taste), supported by Muthesius.

A change of direction was evident in the 1920s when, responding to the circumstances of post-war Germany, the Werkbund concerned itself more closely with social needs and contributed to a number of rebuilding schemes. In 1927 they organised the Weissenhof Seidlung Exhibition in Stuttgart where, under the supervision of Mies van der Rohe, Modernist architects and designers tackled the problem of mass-housing and in so doing revealed their desires for humanity and their belief in a broader vision of the new social order. Mart Stam's 1925 cantilever tubular steel chair with leather seat and back rest was shown with Mies's own *Weissenhof* cantilever chair in wicker and tubular steel. Similar Werkbund exhibitions followed in Breslau in 1929 and Vienna in 1932. Gropius's Weissenhof house included tubular metal beds by Le Corbusier and Alfred Roth, that could be folded away during the day. However, not all chair design in the 1920s made use of dramatically new materials, and, in comparison to wood, metal was expensive. The Rasch Brothers therefore used steamed and moulded plywood, which was in every way as significant as tubular steel – providing an all-plywood suite for one of Mies's flats at Weissenhof. Adolf Schneck in Stuttgart and Ferdinand Kramer in Frankfurt, while showing a clear understanding of the International Style, adopted a less dogmatic attitude to revolutionary materials. Using composite boards, faced with veneer or painted in brightly coloured enamel, their furniture was precise in constructional and technical details and therefore "modern" in appearance. It could be dismantled and readily assembled for easy transportation. Schneck illustrated a room in *Wie Wöhnen*? published by Der Eiserne Hammer (1929): this influential book, brought together a collection of reasonably priced furniture for the low income householder, emphasising cheap and simple arrangements.

Other interiors by Marcel Breuer and Walter Gropius reflect the aesthetics and philosophy of the International Style and in their communal rooms for a ten-storey apartment block (Werkbund Exhibition, Paris, 1931, and Deutsche Bauausstellung, Berlin, 1931), they endeavoured to realise their ideal of how people might live in a new society in which leisure facilities and swimming pools might be shared. Another important area of Werkbund reform during this period was in the design and equipping of kitchens, especially those designed by Grete-Schutte-Lihotsky and Ernst May for the massive rehousing schemes undertaken in Frankfurt in the early 1930s. However, with the advent of the Third Reich, the Werkbund split into opposing factions. Its more conservative members sought an accommodation with the Nazis which was fiercely opposed by Gropius and his ex-Bauhaus associates Wilhelm Wagenfeld and Martin Wagner and in 1934 the Werkbund was formally dissolved. It was revived again in 1947, since when it has been responsible for the design of several important buildings and displays, notably the German Pavilion at the Brussels Exposition Universelle in 1958. Eschewing unjustified criticism of superficiality and narrowness of approach, its longstanding promotion of simplicity and clarity in design was successful in permanently changing the appearance of the average domestic interior. Greatly admired in other countries as an efficient promoter of good industrial design, the Werkbund formed the model for other similar organisations in Austria (1910), Switzerland (1913), Sweden (1910–17), and the Design and Industries Association in Britain (1915).

HILARY J. GRAINGER

See also Muthesius

Publications (journals)

Jahrbücher des Deutschen Werkbundes, 1912, 1913, 1914, 1915, 1917, and 1920
Die Form, 1922 and 1925–34
Werk und Zeit, from 1952

Further Reading

A scholarly survey of the history and ideas of the Werkbund, including a discussion of the major figures and design, architecture and interiors, appears in Burckhardt 1980. For an analysis of the Werkbund within a political context see Campbell 1978.

Benton, Tim and others, "Part 6: Industry, the Werkbund and German Design from the Machine" in Tim Benton, Stefan Muthesius and Bridget Wilkins, *Europe 1900–1914: The Reaction to Historicism and Art Nouveau*, Milton Keynes: Open University Press, 1975

Burckhardt, Lucius (editor), *The Werkbund: Studies in the History and Ideology of the Deutscher Werkbund, 1907–1933*, London: Design Council, and Woodbury, NY: Barron's, 1980

Campbell, Joan, *The German Werkbund: The Politics of Reform in the Applied Arts*, Princeton: Princeton University Press, 1978

Giedion, Sigfried, *Mechanization Takes Command: A Contribution to Anonymous History*, New York and Oxford: Oxford University Press, 1948; reprinted New York: Norton, 1969

Heskett, John, *Design in Germany, 1870–1918*, London: Trefoil, 1986

Hoffmann, Ot (editor), *Der Deutsche Werkbund: 1907, 1947, 1987*, Berlin: Ernst, 1987

Junghanns, Kurt, *Der Deutsche Werkbund: Sein erstes Jahrzehnt*, Berlin: Henschelverlag, 1982

Kirsch, Karin, *The Weissenhofsiedlung: Experimental Housing Built for the Deutscher Werkbund, Stuttgart, 1927*, New York: Rizzoli, 1989

Schwartz, Frederic J., *The Werkbund: Design Theory and Mass Culture before the First World War*, New Haven and London: Yale University Press, 1996

Zwischen Kunst und Industrie: Der Deutsche Werkbund (exhib. cat.), Munich: Staatliches Museum für Angewandte Kunst, 1975

de Wolfe, Elsie 1865–1950

American interior decorator

Elsie de Wolfe was a pioneer of the profession of interior decoration in America. For almost half a century her rooms were copied and her pronouncements repeated in the magazines that shaped popular taste across the country. Her combination of antique furniture, modern colours and convenience, encompassed in her design philosophy – Simplicity, Suitability and Proportion – remains one of the most popular styles of decorating today.

In 1895, the magazine *The Outlook* published an article by Candace Wheeler entitled "Interior Decoration as a Profession for Women". In 1897, the Hewitt sisters, friends of de Wolfe, launched their museum of decorative arts and design, the Cooper-Hewitt, which inspired contemporary designers. In the same year, Edith Wharton and Ogden Codman published *The Decoration of Houses*, in which they equated natural good taste with English, Italian and French models from the Renaissance onwards, but particularly 18th-century French, and urged a rejection of contemporary revivalism. The book advocated interiors in which proportion, architectural unity, and propriety were emphasised. Renaissance and Neo-Classical furniture and architecture provided the preferred vocabulary. Wharton and Codman's ideas greatly influenced de Wolfe, whose early travels in France were to lead to a lifelong passion for the country and a considerable knowledge of its decorative arts. She modified them in her work as a writer and interior decorator to produce interiors of clarity, simplicity and lightness which were markedly different from those of the Victorian era, and which were well-suited to the burgeoning aspirations, confidence and success of North America, both economically and industrially.

De Wolfe's first decorating project was in 1897 with the decoration of the house that she shared with the wealthy theatrical agent Elizabeth Marbury in Irving Place, New York. De Wolfe revitalised the interior by stripping away the Victorian features. In the dining room the wainscoting, the corner doors, the ceiling mouldings and the bases and tops of the other mouldings were all painted white, which later became a de Wolfe trademark. The hanging chandelier, the Delft plates, the tapestries and the grandfather clock all vanished. The scatter of small oriental rugs gave way to a single plain carpet. New dining chairs with painted frames and transparent cane backs, from France, replaced the heavy oak pieces with cut velvet seats. Clever use of mirrors, over the fireplace and behind the wall sconces, another frequently used de

de Wolfe: Colony Club, New York, trellised tearoom, 1913

Wolfe device, lightened the room further. The transformation of Irving House from cluttered interiors typical of contemporary American taste to scenes of elegance and airiness, coincided with the emergence of de Wolfe and Marbury as significant figures in New York high society. The house was seen by a stream of important visitors and they were impressed.

In 1904 de Wolfe left an unsuccessful career on the stage where she had attracted little acclaim for her acting but plenty for her dress sense and elegance, to launch herself as a decorator. In 1905 Stanford White, the leading New York Beaux-Arts architect, secured for her the contract to decorate the city's new Colony Club, open only to women. This was the first time a public interior had been designed by a professional decorator and not an architect or antique dealer. De Wolfe rejected both the current fashion for 18th century American Colonial and the taste for the Neo-Classical revival that followed the Chicago World Columbian Exposition of 1893. Instead she was inspired by the elegant interiors she had seen in English country houses that she had visited in the 1880s. Walls were painted soft, pale colours, antique furniture acquired from England and France was light, comfortable, undistracting and easily moved if required for a special event. Large print chintzes, another popular de Wolfe adaptation, were brought from England for the bedrooms. The tea room was decorated as a conservatory with green painted trellis work, tiled floor and wicker furniture. Her scheme was a success; she became famous as the "Chintz lady" and further commissions followed.

In 1909 she hit upon the idea of a show house that would demonstrate her style of decoration, create some publicity and earn some money. With Ogden Codman as collaborator, she tore apart and rebuilt a New York brownstone on East 71st Street, and transformed it. Since brownstones were still the most common and characteristic style of New York house, de Wolfe and Codman's work attracted great interest and before long they were kept fully employed by owners of other brownstones who wanted similar transformations.

By 1911, de Wolfe was established as one of the most influential tastemakers in the country. In 1913, she received a commission from the multi-millionaire art collector, Henry Clay Frick. Frick had been impressed by the display of 18th-century French fine and decorative art that had been recently bequeathed as the Wallace Collection in London. Having decided to found a similar institution in America he commissioned the architectural firm of Carrere and Hastings to design a Renaissance palace on Fifth Avenue to house the collection of

18th-century French paintings and furnishings which he formed with the advice of the English dealer Joseph Duveen. William Allom, Duveen's decorator, was responsible for the public areas on the ground floor, but Frick commissioned de Wolfe to decorate and furnish the private family rooms on the first floor. She worked for a ten per cent commission of costs, and it is said that these totalled between one and three million dollars. This commission took de Wolfe into a new league both financially and professionally, and she went on to decorate numerous interiors for America's wealthy families.

Increasingly, de Wolfe left the running of the New York business to associates and employees (the company filed for bankruptcy in 1937) while she herself concentrated on a select group of individual clients. Among these was the publisher Condé Nast who employed her throughout the 1920s in New York, and Paul Louis Weiller, the aircraft manufacturer, in France. In 1936, she was asked by King Edward VIII to advise on the redecoration of Buckingham Palace, but this project was abandoned after the king's abdication. She remained friends with the exiled Duke and Duchess of Windsor, however, and in 1938 she helped the Duchess of Windsor redecorate Château de la Croë on Cap d'Antibes in the South of France.

De Wolfe established a working pattern for subsequent interior decorators to follow. She travelled extensively in Europe to gather antique furniture and fabrics. She wrote articles and books and carried out commissions. From the 1890s she had a home in France in Versailles, at the Villa Trianon; she died there in 1950. Always deeply attached to France, she received the Croix de Guerre, and the Légion d'Honneur for her work in World War I. Her taste for "old French" set a standard. A group of professional decorators emerged during the 1920s and 1930s, in America and England, eager to emulate her success. Ruby Ross Wood (1880–1950) who began her professional life as a journalist, ghost-writing de Wolfe's magazine articles that became the book *The House in Good Taste* in 1913, went into the business herself, establishing her own highly successful decorating firm in the 1920s. Nancy McClelland and "Sister" Parish were also clearly inspired by her and Syrie Maugham (1879–1955) and Lady Sybil Colefax (1875–1950) were among her English followers.

De Wolfe pioneered the eclecticism that still characterises much interior decoration today, using contemporary art in traditional settings, and, even quite late in her life, introducing new and unexpected materials: plastic and glass, fur throws, leopard and zebra prints. What she discovered was not a new style but a new sense of the way a house should function – a synthesis of comfort, practicality, and tradition that was in tune with the new century. She used familiar materials to forge something original, a combination of antique elegance and modern convenience that would be known for decades as the Elsie de Wolfe look. Today the American Society of Interior Designers still calls its annual prize for interior design the Elsie de Wolfe Award.

VICTORIA BROACKES

See also Interior Design

Biography

Born in New York in 1865. Attended school in New York; lived in England, 1879–86. Returned to New York in 1886 and employed as an actress by Charles Frohman. Several stage successes during the 1890s; retired from the theatre in 1904. Established herself in New York as an interior decorator in 1905 and executed many commissions over the next 30 years; interior decorating business declared bankrupt in 1937. Published several articles on interior decoration which appeared as *The House in Good Taste*, 1913. Volunteer nurse in France, 1916–18; awarded the Croix de Guerre, and the Légion d'Honneur. Shared homes in New York and Paris with the theatrical agent, Elizabeth Marbury from 1892 to early 1920s; married Sir Charles Mendl in 1926 and lived mainly in France until 1940; lived in Beverly Hills, California, 1940–44; returned to Paris in 1946. Died in Paris, 12 July 1950.

Selected Works

Interiors

1897–98	Irving Place, New York (remodelling and decoration of interiors): Elsie de Wolfe and Elizabeth Marbury
1905–07	Colony Club, 120 Madison Avenue, New York (decoration)
1910	131 East 71st Street, New York (alterations and decoration in collaboration with Ogden Codman, Jr.)
1910	123 East 55th Street, New York (interiors): Elizabeth Marbury and Elsie de Wolfe
1913	Frick House, Fifth Avenue, New York (decoration of the private rooms): Henry Clay Frick
1920s	Various commissions for Condé Nast, New York
1940	House, Benedict Canyon Drive, Beverly Hills: Sir Charles and Lady Mendl (Elsie de Wolfe)
1946	Villa Trianon, Versailles (renovation and redecoration): Sir Charles and Lady Mendl (Elsie de Wolfe)

Publications

"Chateau in Touraine" in *Cosmopolitan* (USA), February 1891

"Stray Leaves from My Book of Life" in *Metropolitan* (USA), XIV, 1901

The House in Good Taste, 1913

Recipes for Successful Dining, 1934

After All (autobiography), 1935; reprinted 1974

Further Reading

An important source of information about de Wolfe's early career is *The House in Good Taste* 1913, which contains several contemporary photographs of her interiors. The most recent biography, Smith 1982, elaborates and corrects the version that appears in de Wolfe's own account of her life, *After All* 1935.

Bemelmans, Ludwig, *To the One I Love the Best*, New York: Viking, 1955

Campbell, Nina and Caroline Seebohm, *Elsie de Wolfe: A Decorative Life*, New York: Panache, 1992; London: Aurum, 1993

Doumato, Lamia, *Candace Wheeler and Elsie de Wolfe, Decorators: A Bibliography*, Monticello, IL: Vance, 1989

Esten, John and Rose Bennett Gilbert, *Manhattan Style*, Boston: Little Brown, 1990

Green, Robert L., "The Legendary Ruby Ross Wood" in *Architectural Digest*, October 1979

Hampton, Mark, *Legendary Decorators of the Twentieth Century*, New York: Doubleday, and London: Hale, 1992

Massey, Anne, *Interior Design of the Twentieth Century*, London and New York: Thames and Hudson, 1990

Metcalf, Pauline C. (editor), *Ogden Codman and the Decoration of Houses*, Boston: Godine, 1988

Platt, Frederick, "Elsie de Wolfe: The Chintz Lady" in *Art and Antiques*, III, September 1980, pp.62–67

Smith, Jane S., *Elsie de Wolfe: A Life in the High Style*, New York: Atheneum, 1982

Dining Rooms and Eating Rooms

Compared to some of the other rooms within the house dining rooms have a relatively short history. The term itself did not acquire its modern meaning until the second half of the 17th century and was not generally accepted until well into the 18th century. Prior to this it was not usual to set aside a room solely for eating, even in wealthy homes. In medieval hall houses the family ate their meals along with their servants in the great hall using trestle tables and benches that could be cleared away to free the room for other uses. It was also usual during this period for the family to sit at a separate table, placed on a dais at one end if they were particularly grand. From the 14th century, a greater desire for privacy emerged, and separate family rooms were created behind the screen of the great hall; two living rooms on the ground floor and a sleeping apartment above. The family then ate in one of the living rooms, known as the parlour, but they continued to use portable furniture until the 16th century.

Wealthy households also required a larger room for more ceremonial meals during the 16th century since entertaining large numbers of guests was regarded as an important sign of rank during this period. Long dining tables were used, with guests seated in a strict order according to their position within the social hierarchy and meals consisted of numerous courses and lasted anything up to five hours. But by the 17th century society was becoming more exclusive. It was no longer regarded as a mark of favour to be entertained in as large a company as possible, and dining was on a smaller and more intimate scale, although mealtimes themselves were still quite formal occasions and were subject to numerous conventions and rules. This period also saw the development, particularly in England and Holland, of heavy pieces of furniture connected with dining that could not easily be moved from one room to another. These pieces included massive oak buffets, heavy draw-leaf tables, and built-in buffets and shelves.

The buffet originated in the open shelves that had previously been used to support the plate and wine and became a vast piece of furniture consisting of an enclosed section or cupboard below and stepped shelves above. At meal times the top of the cupboard was covered with a linen cloth and wine and plate were displayed; during other parts of the day these were cleared away and the surface was left bare. The table was equally massive and was solidly constructed from thick planks of wood supported on heavily carved legs. For the first half of the century, it was usual to protect the surface with a table carpet (generally of Turkish origin) and a white linen cloth was laid on top at mealtimes. Rectangular draw-leaf tables, which allowed the head of the household, or a guest of higher rank, to sit at the head of the table with a more elaborate chair, were also common during this period. By the late 17th century, however, circular or oval gate-leg tables with falling leaves were preferred, particularly in England and Holland. These could be folded down and taken away or placed against the wall when not in use. By this time too, the buffet had fallen from favour and was replaced in the early 18th century by more elegant sideboards that often had a top made out of marble or some other material that was easy to wipe clean.

The introduction of large permanent items of furniture encouraged the emergence of separate dining rooms as places that were used exclusively for eating and such rooms began to appear from the late 17th century. But it is important to stress that throughout this period dining rooms might still sometimes be used for other purposes and also that meals were frequently taken on small tables set up in other rooms.

While Great Chambers and halls were often hung with tapestries, panelling and gilt leather hangings were preferred for early dining rooms as these did not retain the smell of food. In grand houses panelled walls might also be hung with family portraits. In 1690, Celia Fiennes described the dining room at Lowther Castle as being wainscoted in oak, while the dining room at Chippenham Park had three windows with a looking glass on each pier, set into the wainscot. In houses of this kind, a Great Dining Room was one of the principal rooms and occupied a central position within the house. Ceremonial dinners involved the use of side tables from which the servants served the food and wine. But when the family dined alone meals were taken in the common eating room or dining parlour.

The Marble Dining Room at Ham House, Twickenham, represents one of the earliest uses of the term in England. Added in 1675, it occupied a central position on the ground floor and was flanked by the Duke and Duchess of Lauderdale's apartments. It had a black and white marble floor in the Dutch manner and gilt leather hangings. The furnishings included three oval tables, 18 walnut chairs and two cedar side-tables with marble tops that were placed in recesses either side of the main door. Such rooms were becoming increasingly common in new houses during the early 18th century and by the 1720s even town houses in the provinces sometimes included dining rooms. This development is indicative of the general move towards rooms with more specific uses and away from the multi-purpose rooms that had prevailed before. An early example of such increased specificity is Sir Robert Walpole's house, Houghton (from 1726), which even included a breakfast room and supper room as well as a splendidly appointed dining room on the *piano nobile* that was designed by William Kent.

The 18th-century English practice of decorating the main public areas, including the dining room, as a suite of rooms did not apply in France. Although by the early 18th century the *salon* had become the *salle à manger* for formal dinners and banquets in the larger houses in France, most meals were taken in an anteroom. Robert Adam, in the *Works in Architecture*, 1773–79, explains that this difference between England and France was due to the different amounts of time spent on dining; in England dining, and more particularly drinking after the meal, was a protracted affair and therefore the decoration of the room was important, whereas in France the company soon removed to another apartment.

Parquet floors became fashionable in the mid 18th century; the dining room at Ham House had its marble floor replaced with one of parquetry c.1756. But as the century progressed and floor carpets became more widespread, Turkey or mock turkey Wilton carpets began to be used for the centre of the room. The introduction of Rococo styles meant that stucco and plasterwork decoration replaced wood panelling, and the decoration was applied to form a series of vertical panels, painted white or a pale colour. Dining rooms were also increasingly used as a place in which to hang paintings, with sporting

Dining Rooms: ***Our Dining Room in York*****, watercolour by Mary Ellen Best, 1838**

themes, portraits and still-lifes proving especially popular. Paintings were commonly hung within the fields of plaster-work panels but another variation was Robert Adam's treatment of the Dining Room at Osterley (c.1766) where the panels themselves were painted with scenes of ruins.

Large tables, or sets of tables as they were called, had become fashionable by around 1780. These enabled larger numbers of people to be entertained and demonstrate the increasing importance placed on dining as a social function. Formality, both in the terms of the way that meals were served and in table manners, was an essential part of the proceedings. (A detailed description of a dinner party in the early 19th century appears in Johanna Schopenhauer's *A Lady Travels*, 1988.) The use of large tables also meant that the room could not be used for anything else, although it was still common for the chairs to be placed against the wall when not in use. By the 19th century they began to be left drawn up to the table, but this was not a fixed rule.

As separate dining rooms became more firmly established there followed an important development in their decoration and furnishings which was to become prevalent throughout much of Europe and North America during the 19th century. This development was related to the growing tendency to distinguish between the light, feminine character of the drawing room and the sombre, more masculine tone of the dining room. Within this context, dining rooms were increasingly furnished with heavier, more robust styles of furniture, usually made of dark woods such as mahogany. Sideboards often had pedestals at either end, with urns which contained water and the drawer below was lined with lead so that wine glasses could be rinsed. Chair seats were frequently covered in leather, with red being the favoured colour. Curtains were usually of woollen cloth and were not as elaborate as the drapery treatments employed in the drawing room, and less use of upholstery generally, at a time when it was becoming more important in other areas of the house, helped make the dining room seem more masculine.

A typical example of an early 19th century middle-class dining room furnished in the "modern" or Greek style appears in Mary Ellen Best's watercolour of her dining room at York (c.1840). The room has green and white wallpaper with a formal striped pattern. The curtains are red woollen, moreen cloth with a simple fringe, and the chair seats are covered with black horsehair, a cheaper alternative to leather. The table is laid out in the old-fashioned manner which involved serving several courses together. And the floor has a fitted Brussels carpet although it was still common at this date to carpet the centre of the room only and show floorboards around the edge.

The distinction between male and female rooms and styles of decoration extended to most middle-class homes by the mid 19th century and became even more pronounced by the 1860s and 1870s when dining rooms became even more sombre. Colour schemes were rich and dark, and walls were decorated in deep reds and browns and hung with flock wallpapers or imitation embossed leathers. Gothic, Northern Renaissance and Jacobean styles were popular for furnishings which were once again massive, and the room was generally dominated by a large sideboard with deeply carved decoration often incorporating vines and grapes or hunting themes.

By the early 19th century dinner was served between six and seven o'clock and mealtimes became later as the century progressed. Dinner was still, however, a formal occasion requiring a change of clothes, and women retired to the drawing room after the dessert leaving the men to enjoy their port and cigars. During the mid-century a new method of serving food, known as *à la Russe*, which had been taken up by wealthier households some years earlier, became more widepread in middle-class homes. Instead of all the main dishes being arranged on a central table, the dessert was placed down the centre of the table before the meal began while the preceding dishes were brought in one at a time. Each course was served separately, with the food being served to diners by servants who carried the dishes around the table. Whereas previously the tablecloth had been removed for the dessert, it now remained in place throughout the meal, and the presence of the dessert as a decoration led to a great quantity of raised dishes being employed. Another consequence of this new method of serving was that more servants, especially ones who were highly skilled at waiting at table, were required. The ritual of dining became more pronounced and the dinner party became both an important social function and a means of demonstrating wealth and status among the middle and upper classes.

Most middle-class town dwellers in England lived in terraced housing where the rooms were symmetrically arranged above one another over several storeys. There were usually two rooms on each floor. As the kitchen was in the basement, the dining room was on the ground floor, but the drawing room was usually on the floor above. The staircase leading from the ground floor to the first floor played a significant role in the ritual of dining, and its decoration was therefore a matter of some importance. In large country houses arrangements were rarely as convenient. The kitchen was often located in a separate wing, and access to the dining room was through long corridors and passages. This had the practical advantage of taking cooking smells out of the house but it also frequently resulted in the food being cold before it reached the table. Hot plates and warming devices, placed in serving rooms adjacent to the dining room, were introduced in the early 19th century in an attempt to overcome this problem. Continental city apartments did not have as many separate dining rooms, and anterooms were still often used for dining. A useful comparison of floor plans of flats and houses in London, Paris and Vienna in the 19th century appears in D.J. Olsen's, *The City as a Work of Art*, 1986.

Although the dining room was the only room used for the main meal, food and drink were consumed in other rooms at other times of the day. Large country houses might include a breakfast room for informal meals not just breakfast, and even urban terrace houses sometimes had a breakfast room included in the back extension on the ground floor. Afternoon tea became an important institution from the 1840s; it was taken in the drawing room as were tea and coffee after dinner and sometimes a light supper too.

The formal tendencies in the decoration and use of the dining room continued, though to a lesser degree, into the 20th century. Speculative housing of the 1920s and 1930s always included a separate dining room, although as the numbers of servants decreased, devices such as the serving hatch began to appear. Masculine styles of decoration still prevailed, with Tudor and Elizabethan influenced furniture, often in a dark stained oak, proving popular in the inter-war years.

Although the Modern Movement challenged these notions, it was not until the 1950s and 1960s that the character of the dining room underwent a dramatic change, often ceasing to exist altogether. The dominant influences then came from the US and Scandinavia for open-plan interiors. Dining took place in a dining area or alcove rather than a separate room. Informality was taken a step further in the 1960s and 1970s when the influence of shops such as Habitat promoted the farmhouse kitchen, sometimes with a French influence, using a large, scrub-top table for dining and stripped pine dressers instead of a sideboard. By the 1980s and 1990s there was no longer a strict rule about separate dining rooms; some homes preserve them if formal dinner parties are given frequently, but many do not, and in many contemporary households meals are eaten in front of the television.

MARGARET PONSONBY

Further Reading

Arminjon, Catherine, "The Art of Dining" in Catherine Arminjon and others, *L'Art de Vivre: Decorative Arts and Design in France, 1789–1989*, New York: Vendome, and London: Thames and Hudson, 1989, pp.144–69

Beeton, Mrs. [Isabella Mary], *The Book of Household Management*, London, 1861; reprinted London: Chancellor Press, 1982

Belden, Louise Conway, *The Festive Tradition: Table Decoration and Desserts in America, 1650–1900*, New York: Norton, 1983

Berger, Diane L., *The Dining Room*, New York: Abbeville, 1993

Brears, Peter and others, *A Taste of History: 10,000 Years of Food in Britain*, London: English Heritage, 1993

Brett, Gerard, *Dinner is Served: A History of Dining in England, 1400–1900*, London: Hart Davis, 1968; as *Dinner is Served: A Study in Manners*, Hamden, CT: Archon, 1969

Clark, Clifford E., Jr., "The Vision of the Dining Room: Plan Book Dreams and Middle Class Realities" in Kathryn Grover (editor), *Dining in America, 1850–1900*, Amherst: University of Massachusetts Press, 1987, pp.142–72

Collard, Frances, "Summoned by Dinner Bells" in *Country Life*, 1 April 1993, pp.45–47

Dunbabin, Katherine M. D., "Triclinium and Stibadium" in William J. Slater (editor), *Dining in a Classical Context*, Ann Arbor: University of Michigan Press, 1991

Edis, Robert W., *The Decoration and Furniture of Town Houses*, 2nd edition London, 1881; reprinted, with introduction by Christopher Gilbert, Wakefield: EP, 1972

Franklin, Jill, *The Gentleman's Country House and its Plan, 1835–1914*, London: Routledge, 1981

Garrett, Elisabeth Donaghy, "The American Home IV: The Dining Room" in *Antiques* (US), 126, October 1984, pp.910–22

Garrett, Elisabeth Donaghy, "The Dining Room" in her *At Home: The American Family, 1750–1870*, New York: Abrams, 1990

Gilliam, Jan Kirsten and Betty Crowe Leviner, *Furnishing Williamsburg's Historic Buildings*, Williamsburg, VA: Colonial Williamsburg Foundation, 1991

Girouard, Mark, *Life in the English Country House: A Social and Architectural History*, New Haven and London: Yale University Press, 1978

Grow, Lawrence (editor), *The Old House Book of Kitchens and Dining Rooms*, New York: Warner, 1981

Huls, Mary Ellen, *Architecture and Interior Design of Dining Halls: A Bibliography of Periodical Literature*, Monticello, IL: Vance, 1986

Jackson-Stops, Gervase and James Pipkin, "Dining Rooms" in their *The English Country House: A Grand Tour*, London: Weidenfeld and Nicolson, 1984; Boston: Little Brown, 1985

Jenkins, Susan, "Dining in State: Towards a Greater Simplicity" in *Apollo*, 138, September 1993, pp.164–69

Loftie, M.J., *The Dining Room*, London, 1878; reprinted with *The Drawing-Room* by Lucy Orrinsmith and *The Bedroom and Boudoir* by Lady Barker, New York: Garland, 1978

Olsen, Donald J., *The City as a Work of Art: London, Paris, Vienna*, New Haven and London: Yale University Press, 1986

Paston-Williams, Sara, *The Art of Dining: A History of Cooking and Eating*, London: The National Trust, 1993

Thornton, Peter, "Dining Rooms" in his *Seventeenth-Century Interior Decoration in England, France, and Holland*, New Haven and London: Yale University Press, 1978, pp.282–92

Thornton, Peter, *The Italian Renaissance Interior, 1400–1600*, London: Weidenfeld and Nicolson, and New York: Abrams, 1991

Do-It-Yourself (DIY)

"Do-It-Yourself" or – in its abbreviated form – "DIY", emerged as a household expression during the 1950s, and owes its popularity, as a phrase at least, to a movement which developed in America. Recognized on a world-wide basis today as a symbol for the pursuit of home-improvement through self-contribution, DIY unites under its banner an integrated network of manufacturers, publishers, retailers, promoters and consumers.

Any attempt to measure how far this movement as a whole has affected the design of the post-war domestic interior, however, is problematic; for DIY encompasses such a complex web of supply, promotion, sales and individual activities that identification of fixed patterns is virtually impossible. In spite of this, it is evident that since the end of World War II, householders have become more and more involved in the design and construction of their home environment, and it is clear that this contribution to domestic interior design, although difficult to pin down in general terms, deserves due recognition.

In the course of acknowledging the importance of these ventures, however, a number of questions need answers: why, for instance, has "self-contribution" to the domestic interior become so important to the householder in the post-war years?; whose ideas have "home-improvers" chosen to follow?; and what part has the DIY movement played in moulding a continuum of consumer practices?

A comprehensive building programme, in the immediate post-war period, spread private suburban dwellings across vast tracts of the US, extolling the dream of home-ownership to a receptive public in its wake; and as the economy boomed and full employment returned to America, the dream, for the many citizens who were able to take advantage of the new financial security, turned to reality.

The upheaval and disruption caused by World War II meant that "home", for civilians, ex-servicemen and government officials alike, symbolised security and stability. It is perhaps not surprising, therefore, that householders readily took on the guise of home-makers – increasingly devoting themselves to nurturing and generally "improving" their properties.

New advances in technology, coupled with the introduction of new materials, assisted home-makers in realising their aims. New technology, in fact, was instrumental in contributing to the rise of DIY in a number of ways. Improved technology reduced working hours, for instance, and thus was indirectly responsible for increasing the time which could be devoted to leisure activities. In the process, however, the new automated, push-button world of work also deprived employees of both physical labour and the opportunity of expressing individuality. Americans had traditionally regarded leisure as something that must be earned and "leisure without effort" hinted at idleness, luxury and immorality. Work, on the other hand, was looked on as being something that was morally good. To engage in do-it-yourself, therefore, indicated a fusion of work and leisure, which, within the context of the home environment, helped to satisfy both psychological and physical needs. At home couples could spend their leisure time, as Richard Horn has put it, "... in a purposeful, physically demanding project that [they] initiated and completed" (Horn,1985).

By far the most direct and significant contribution of the new technological innovations to the home-improver, however, was the introduction (around 1945) of the lightweight portable electric drill. Compact, uncomplicated and convenient, the drill, with its added accessories, surpassed the versatility of any tool that was then available, and, when used in conjunction with such new materials as hardboard, chipboard and Formica, both enhanced and simplified the DIY process for the consumer.

Servicing consumer demand for home repair, construction and decorating equipment was furnished by an industry that transcended mere suppliers. The combined efforts of manufacturers, DIY shops, magazines and exhibitions instigated and promoted a continual flow of new products which were designed to assist the home-improver in tackling mundane and adventurous projects alike. Emulsion paint, for instance, affected decoration – wallpaper could now be painted over or left out of the decorating plan altogether. Adhesive polystyrene, vinyl and ceramic tiles were as "easy as A.B.C. to fix" according to the advertisements, and should the absolute novice ever feel deterred from getting involved in DIY help was at hand in the form of *U-May-Kit* yourself furniture which

DIY: covers from *Do It Yourself* magazine, October 1957 and December 1958

promised that all you needed for successful completion was "a hammer and a screwdriver".

It was probably the commercial side of DIY that set it aside as a movement in its own right, for "doing-it-yourself", in a creative sense, was certainly not a new concept – nor was it peculiar to America. Late 19th century British magazines such as *Amateur Work Illustrated*, had praised the practice of self-help as did the *Amateur Mechanic* series of publications in the early part of the 20th century. In light of these examples, and especially when the war-time "make-do-and-mend" activities are taken into account, it could be argued that do-it-yourself, in Britain at least, was simply a continuation of the Arts and Crafts tradition. As F. J. Camm put it in *Practical Householder*, October 1956, "Do-It-Yourself is an expression of the ingenuity, enterprise and self-reliance of the individual, and in the age of automation it is good that fundamental arts and crafts are not being lost."

During the late 1950s and early 1960s British magazines such as *Do It Yourself* (first published 1957) and *Practical Householder* enjoyed a boom period. "In the space of three years", the editor of *Do It Yourself*, David Johnson, proudly boasted in March 1960, "it is no mean achievement to have reached a readership of something like 3,750,000 monthly." There is no evidence to suggest, however, that the blueprints included in these magazines for major projects like, for instance, "building your own refrigerator" were carried out by readers *en masse*; it is far more likely that householders borrowed general ideas which would contribute to a modern interior look – ideas that were also supported by similar imagery in the media in general.

Blackouts, heavy "Victorian" furniture, brown varnished doors and green distempered walls had provided an ambience of darkness and heaviness within the majority of Britain's domestic interiors during the war years. In stark contrast "lightness and brightness" in every sense of the phrase, therefore, was seen as desirable by a public which had been deprived of these qualities for so long. The shortage of new houses in Britain until the late 1950s, however, meant that buyers had to take what they could get, which often meant older properties. Do-it-yourself magazines presented anti-Victorian and pro-modern interior campaigns with great relish. "Transforming an ugly Victorian house into a charming contemporary and comfortable home" was a task requiring "originality and skill", Roger Smithells remarked in *Do It Yourself*, March 1957. People were advised how to cover over their staircase banisters and panelled doors and give them the "modern" look. Everything had to be smooth, flush and probably painted white. J.R. Burt's "New Doors for Old" feature, in *Do it Yourself*, April 1957, for instance, encouraged the reader to "Give your doors that new look with hardboard panels. Flush doors give the whole house a sleek well groomed appearance. The out of date panelled door tends to provide a series of dust-collecting ledges that are a nuisance to the busy housewife."

Despite the similarities here to the stark, clutter-free interiors promoted by the Modern Movement in the 1930s, this was not an attempt by the public to follow any fixed philosophy; householders were clearly defining the "modern" interior not so much by what it *was*, but by what it *wasn't* – dark and brown. Doing-it-yourself may not have provided all the answers for those engaged in trying to present a Contemporary or modern look to their homes in the immediate post-war years, nor did it allow householders the privilege of claiming, that "we have arrived", but it certainly encouraged them to say "we are on our way."

Perhaps the progressive and golden-age of DIY will remain forever locked in the 1950s and 1960s, for in the eclectic, "mix and match", Postmodern world of the DIY superstores – such as the British chain Texas who opened their first warehouse in 1972 and had nearly 200 outlets by the late 1980s – that was to follow, almost anything, including the purchase of ready-made furniture and previously potted plants, was now to count as DIY This would seem to speak less of doing-it-yourself and more, as the chain store of a similar name would imply, of trying to "do-it-all". Nonetheless, DIY, at any level of consumption and practice, continues to provide a vehicle through which householders can retain some degree of self-expression while at the same time remaining in touch with current interior design trends. As Alan Tomlinson pointed out, "the DIY phenomenon is not class or gender specific. It is not only the hi-tech specialist who does the carpentry: it is the bus driver, the nurse, the postman," and it is clear that ever since DIY arrived householders have made, and will continue to make, carefully measured contributions, over a long period of time if necessary, towards the construction of their own home environment.

SCOTT ORAM

See also Consumerism

Further Reading

Banham, Reyner, "Happiness is a Warm Pistol Grip" in *Leisure in the Twentieth Century*, London: Design Council, 1977

Brooks, Colin, "The Amateur Mechanic and the Modern Movement" in *Leisure in the Twentieth Century*, London: Design Council, 1977

Clarke, John, and Chas Critcher, *The Devil Makes Work: Leisure in Capitalist Britain*, London: Macmillan, and Urbana: University of Illinois Press, 1985

Do-It-Yourself, London, first issue 1957

Horn, Richard, *Fifties Style: Then and Now*, New York: Beech Tree, and Bromley, Kent: Columbus, 1985

Ideal Home Exhibition (exhib. cat.), London: Design Museum, 1993

Johnson, David, "The History and Development of Do-It-Yourself" in *Leisure in the Twentieth Century*, London: Design Council, 1977

Oram, Scott, *"Common Sense Contemporary": The Ideals and Realities of the Popular Domestic Interior in the 1950s*, M.A. thesis, London: Royal College of Art / Victoria and Albert Museum, 1994

Tomlinson, Alan, "Home Fixtures: Doing-It-Yourself in a Privatised World" in Alan Tomlinson (editor), *Consumption, Identity and Style: Marketing, Meanings and the Packaging of Pleasure*, London and New York: Routledge, 1990

Doors

Doors may be said to fall roughly into two types – namely interior and exterior doors – and their size and shape will largely depend on the period of the building concerned. Similarly, door furniture, hinges, handles, locks and knockers, will also reflect the particular use and status of the door and the building of which it forms a part.

Originally there were two main methods of constructing doors: ledge-and-brace or batten doors, and panelled doors. Exterior doors tended to be of the ledge-and-brace design, which meant the door was constructed from a number of vertical planks (ledges) held together by a Z-shaped brace nailed to the back of the door. Such sturdy items formed the basis for almost all doors prior to the late 17th century; Tudor doors, for example, were made from wide oak planks strengthened by a second set of planks laid across the back at right-angles. This version was called a double-boarded or cross-boarded door. Interior doors were usually panelled and their construction was lighter and more technically complex than the ledge-and-brace design. Thus they were more expensive and required the skills of a joiner, rather than a carpenter, to construct a wooden framework into which the panels were set.

Seventeenth-century interior doors were rather simple, consisting first of two and then four panels, which reflect the ordered classical interiors of the period. By the late 18th century, however, the six-panelled Georgian door was uniform in most houses, although thin four-panelled doors with no mouldings remained the standard servant area fittings on the upper floors of wealthier houses.

Since exterior doors are, by their very nature, strong and heavy, their decoration tends to be of a more robust form. Tudor door fittings were basic, with wooden latches and handles operated by string and main doors decorated by flattened nail heads, although the grander houses did have some lighter doors with a frame filled with wooden linenfold panels. By the 17th century, however, exterior doors were increasingly embellished by classical stone surrounds of columns, pilasters and pediments. The grander the house the more impressive the entrance: front doors were placed at the tops of steps, or covered with shaped wooden canopies painted white, such as those still to be seen in Queen Anne's Gate, London.

An important feature of the 18th-century exterior door was the fan-light which served to increase the amount of light let into the front hall. It gradually reduced the size of the front door and probably encouraged the Victorian taste for the stained-glass front door which was so familiar a feature of domestic housing at the turn of the century. During the second quarter of the 19th-century, glass was also being used (mainly in French and German houses) in internal doors to conservatories, glass-houses and vestibules. Folding doors were especially popular in 19th-century houses as they enabled rooms to be opened up, and sliding doors were probably introduced by the end of the century.

Interior doors reflected these stylistic changes, but because interior doors were protected from the elements they could be finely decorated with unusual inlaid woods such as holly and cherry, painted scenes or carved mouldings. If the wood was of good quality like ebony, it was left bare or polished; this was the case at Chiswick House where the panelled doors designed by William Kent were simply varnished and their decorative moulding picked out in gold leaf. The moulding was usually carved in sections and may have been in the form of beading, egg-and-dart or the acanthus leaf pattern. Main doors were painted to blend in with decorative schemes, such as the painted doors in fashionable Pompeian interiors designed by Robert Adam at Osterley Park, London. During the Greek Revival of the early 19th century, doors were further embellished by fluted pilasters and curved panelling, and the door handles, finger-plates and locks were increasingly elaborate.

By the late 19th century, mass production and the eclectic tastes of the period ensured that doors came in every shape and size. Moreover, the revival of fashions from the past saw the reintroduction of old methods of manufacture: American Beaux-Arts interiors, for example, featured oak-plank doors decorated with carved wooden swags, garlands and cartouches; Queen Anne Revival doors had shelves above them where ceramic plates and vases were crammed in to look authentic. The mass production of domestic furniture and the vast range of different pattern books suddenly on the market also meant that most people could afford to have a relatively smart front door.

In order for a door to function, hinges, handles and locks are required. The earliest hinges were called strap-hinges (known in North America as a cross-garnet hinge), which was a T-shaped hinge usually made of wrought iron, with the cross bar fixed vertically to the door frame. These substantial hinges were nailed rather than screwed to the woodwork and could be rather decorative. In the 18th century, interior doors were fitted with either H- or L-shaped hinges, again with nails rather than screws, the best examples being hand-cut until the introduction of machine-made screws in the 19th century. Other hinges to appear during this period were the hidden and rising-butt hinge. The hidden hinge, as its name suggests, has the fixings set into the frame of the door and sunk into the door surround or architrave. The pivot, or pintle (the pin running through the two parts of the hinge allowing it to swing) made the door more decorative. The rising-butt hinge, which appeared in Britain c.1750, was spirally pivoted so that the door raised up as it opened, thus clearing a fitted carpet and dropping down again when still to stop draughts.

The use of door locks was relatively unknown before the 16th century since they were expensive, cumbersome and considered a luxury by the majority of home-dwellers. The earliest locks in use were rim locks, also known as box locks. They were fitted onto the surface of the door (internal doors were too thin to support an internal mechanism) and were usually covered by a wooden, iron or brass box, hence the name. Rim locks were the standard type used in British and North American houses until the mid-18th century when the mortise lock appeared. These locks were designed to fit into a slot, or mortise, cut into the frame of a panelled door. Doors were also secured by sliding barrel bolts and heavy, wrought iron bars to secure the main front doors of the grander houses.

The design of door furniture such as handles, escutcheons, finger-plates and knockers or letter-boxes for front doors, developed relatively late in comparison to hinges and locks. Some noticeable exceptions were the Neo-Classical escutcheons Robert Adam designed which featured classical swags and lion heads; and fretted brass fingerplates were common in the 19th century, as were ceramic door-handles. Particularly fine examples of surviving decorative door furniture are the elaborate brass Gothic designs produced by A.W.N. Pugin for the Palace of Westminster, and Art Nouveau finger-plates made from hammered copper, brass or silver.

Doors are useful for the historian in many ways in that, like fireplaces, they will usually reflect contemporary tastes in interior decoration long after rooms have been changed and walls covered over. Where and when they do survive, their paint-layered surfaces remain a valuable indicator of changing fashions. As for knob, knockers and handles, they may be called "door furniture", but as a recent style article in *The Times* declared, "in fashion terms, they are clothing accessories" for the fashion conscious.

RACHEL KENNEDY AND TREVE ROSOMAN

Further Reading

Amery, Colin (editor), *Period Houses and their Details*, London: Architectural Press, and New York: Whitney Library of Design, 1974

Amery, Colin (editor), *Three Centuries of Architectural Craftsmanship*, London: Architectural Press, and New York: Nichols, 1977

Calloway, Stephen and Elizabeth Cromley (editors), *The Elements of Style: A Practical Encyclopedia of Interior Architectural Details from 1485 to the Present*, London: Mitchell Beazley, and New York: Simon and Schuster, 1991

Parissien, Steven, *Doors*, London: Georgian Group, 1992

Period Doors, Colchester: Essex County Council, 1986

Saumarez Smith, Charles (introduction), *London Doors*, photographs by Charles Viney, Harpenden: Oldcastle, 1989

Tanner, Henry, *Old English Doorways: A Series of Historical Examples from Tudor Times to the End of the XVIII Century*, London: Batsford, 1903

Dorn, Marion 1896–1964

American textile, wallpaper and interior designer

Marion Dorn is best known for the work she did in Britain during the 1920s and 1930s when she was a leading figure in the re-assessment of the function of textiles in the interior. Her textiles were to be seen regularly in the architecture and design press of the day, chosen by architects and interior designers as important components of their creations. She was one of the first female textile designers to establish her design business as a limited company (1934) to facilitate her varied collaboration with large textile manufacturers, architects, interior designers and private clients. Her most celebrated output was in rug design and her success in this area continued when she returned to the United States in 1940.

Dorn settled in Britain in 1923, and designed and made batiks, a medium she had begun to work in when she lived in New York State with her first husband, the painter and potter Henry Varnum Poor. Her batiks were reviewed favourably in *Vogue* in 1925; conceived as fine art pieces, they were compared to tapestries or murals. In contrast to most of her contemporaries Dorn produced batiks on a large scale, designing decorative hangings or curtains which were used as focal

Dorn: interior of Ralph Rayner's home, Ashcombe Tower, 1937, with rugs, curtains and upholstery fabrics by Dorn

points in the homes of clients such as Noel Coward and the Countess of Lathom.

Dorn designed her first rugs in the mid 1920s and by the end of the decade exhibited them at the Arthur Tooth Gallery in London alongside rugs by her partner and future husband, Edward McKnight Kauffer. It was Dorn's practice to design rugs exclusively for particular customers or to produce limited editions; these were usually hand-tufted for her by the Wilton Royal Carpet Factory. Her contribution towards raising the status of the rug within the interior was unequalled by any of her contemporaries. She promoted the use of her rugs as fixed points within a space, around which other components were arranged; this was particularly the case in larger spaces such as hotels and ocean liners. Dorn was commissioned for various projects by the Savoy Company throughout the 1930s, beginning with a number of rugs for the re-decoration of Claridge's Hotel by Oswald P. Milne in 1932. The design of a circular carpet for the hexagonal lobby was dominated by directional lines in shades of light and dark brown on a fawn ground, the design suggested routes through the space. The following year Dorn produced designs for carpeting and rugs for Oliver Hill's Midland Hotel, Morecambe. The rugs for the lobby, with their directional design of waves, represented perfectly the hotel's seaside location. They also provided an important focus around which furniture was arranged. As with all her commissioned work Dorn produced rugs which in terms of design and colouring were in perfect sympathy with their surroundings. The Midland Hotel rugs in brown, ivory and brick-red complemented Hill's colour scheme of beige-pink walls, polished cement terrazzo floor and furniture of weathered sycamore. Hill continued to commission textiles from Dorn throughout the 1930s.

On several occasions the architect and interior designer Brian O'Rourke approached Dorn for suitable textiles for his schemes. In 1932 she designed a group of rugs for his decoration of Mrs. Robert Solomon's music room. Two years later he used Dorn's rugs to indicate different functions within one space in his scheme for the interiors of the Orient Line's ship the *Orion*. These designs were praised by *Shipbuilding and Shipping Record* as providing the basis around which everything else was hinged. Dorn's willingness to meet the needs of her clients is evident in the work chosen by O'Rourke for Ashcombe Tower, the house he designed for the Member of Parliament Ralph Rayner in 1937. The architect and client visited Dorn's studio in Lancashire Court off New Bond Street, London, to choose the most appropriate rugs and fabrics. The theme of their choice was texture, with a herringbone weave for the furniture, horizontal striped fabric for the curtains and textured rugs.

A desire for aesthetic interest in textiles provided by means of texture rather than surface pattern made Dorn's work an obvious choice for many Modernist designers. Pattern in Dorn's rugs was often achieved by the use of contrasting textures, the combination of hand-tufting with flat weaving was used to good effect in several designs, such as the large cream rug with a linear tufted design which Syrie Maugham used in her own "all-white" drawing room in 1931. A similar design was used by Serge Chermayeff in his scheme for a flat in London. The popularity of Dorn's work with architects is illustrated by the press coverage she received in journals such as the *Architectural Review* and *The Studio*. Her fabrics would often be designed to enhance the architectural design of a building, and the rugs provided a limited but appropriate focus of pattern. As Dorothy Todd commented, Dorn aspired to provide "a floor service" for her clients, preferring wherever possible to plan her designs in relation to the room for which they were intended. This worked particularly well when she was able to act as the designer of a complete interior scheme as when she worked for the writer Arnold Bennett in 1931, and for the actress Diana Wynyard in 1936.

Dorn worked with the leading textile manufactures of the day, including Warner & Sons, Old Bleach Linen, Edinburgh Weavers and Donald Brothers. She operated as either a freelance designer of printed and woven textiles, or she commissioned these firms to produce fabrics to her designs which were then sold under the name of her own company, Marion Dorn Ltd.. The woven fabrics produced for her were popular with interior designers. Gordon Russell Ltd. used Dorn's tufted leaf fabric *Hasta*, woven by Edinburgh Weavers in the interior of the Prince of Siam's London flat in 1937, and Ian Henderson used two weaves (*Lodore* and *Dorn Upholstery*) in his design for Jean de Casalis's flat in 1936. Her printed textiles were often chosen as curtains and upholstery for the cabins of ocean liners; *Scallop Shell*, a hand-screen printed fabric was used in the bathrooms for Cunard's *Queen Mary* in 1936. As her experience of designing for hand-screen printed fabrics developed, simple motifs such as birds, leaves and flowers received a more sophisticated treatment. Her approach became more painterly with dashes of colour used to suggest rather than define shapes; this stylistic approach, combined with a more classical subject matter, dominated her later work of the late 1930s.

Dorn returned to America in 1940, and although she never enjoyed the huge acclaim she had received in Britain, she continued to run a successful freelance business. She was employed by Edward Fields Carpets on the basis of her British reputation. Throughout the 1950s Dorn produced designs for Fields which were based on the reproduction of pattern derived from other flooring materials, such as marble, parquet and stone paving. Her work for Fields culminated in the design for a large oval rug for the Diplomatic Reception Room at the White House in 1960. She also developed her freelance work in wallpaper design which had begun towards the end of her stay in Britain; she produced designs for Katzenbach and Warren, Bassett and Vollum, A.H. Jacobs and Imperial. Wallpapers such as *Master Drawings* and *Cameo* (both produced by Katzenbach and Warren in 1949) represented the trend for bold, striking patterns used in limited spaces. In contrast she also produced simple designs such as *Persian Linen* (Imperial, 1952), based on a woven fabric, which was used for larger spaces. Her fabric designs for companies such as Greeff, Goodall Fabrics and Schumacher demonstrated her ability to react quickly to current trends. Dorn continued her practice of producing designs that were conceived in sympathy with the work of architects and interior designers. She received an Honorary Fellowship from the Society of Industrial Artists in 1957 for her "unique and quite outstanding contribution to British textiles".

CHRISTINE BOYDELL

Biography

Marion Victoria Dorn. Born in San Francisco, 25 December 1896. Trained as an artist; graduated from Stanford University, California, BA in education (graphic art), 1916. Married 1) Henry Varnum Poor, 1919 (divorced 1923); 2) Edward McKnight Kauffer, 1950 (lived with him from 1923; he died 1954). Settled in London and worked as a freelance designer from 1923; designed batiks from 1923, rugs from 1926, carpets from 1928, printed and woven textiles and wallpapers from the early 1930s. Associated with several textile and carpet manufacturers including Wilton Royal Carpet Factory, Warner & Sons, Donald Brothers, Old Bleach Linen, and Edinburgh Weavers; established her own company, Marion Dorn Ltd., with workshops and showrooms in London, 1934. Moved to New York, 1940; active as a freelance designer of textiles, wallpapers, and interiors, supplying designs for companies including Edward Fields Carpets and Katzenbach and Warren; retired to Morocco, 1962. Exhibited at Dorland Hall, London, 1933, and at the Paris Exhibition, 1937. Honorary Fellow, Society of Industrial Artists of Great Britain, 1957. Died in Tangier, 23 January 1964.

Selected Works

For a recent monograph on Dorn's work see Schoeser 1996. A catalogue raisonée appears in Appendix 1 of Boydell 1992, which also includes the locations for surviving works. Examples of Dorn's rugs and textiles are in the Victoria and Albert Museum and the Museum and Art Gallery, Brighton; 20 designs for rugs survive in the archive of the Wilton Royal Carpet Factory.

Interiors

1931	Complete interior scheme for Arnold Bennett
1932	Claridge's Hotel, London (interiors by Oswald P. Milne; rugs by Dorn)
1933	Midland Hotel, Morecombe (building and interiors by Oliver Hill; rugs and carpets by Dorn)
1933–35	Savoy Hotel, London (rugs and carpets)
1934–35	*S. S. Orion* (interiors by Brian O'Rourke; rugs by Dorn): Orient Shipping Company
1935	Flats, Embassy Court, Brighton (interiors by Wells Coates; carpets by Dorn)
1936	Complete interior scheme for Diana Wynyard
1936	*Queen Mary* (printed textiles for the bathrooms): Cunard Shipping Company
1937	Ashcombe Tower (building and interiors by Brian O'Rourke; rugs and textiles by Dorn): Ralph Rayner, M.P.
1960	White House, Washington, DC (rug for the Diplomatic Reception Room)

Further Reading

A lengthy bibliography of primary and secondary sources related to Dorn's life and work appears in Boydell 1992; for surveys of her career within published sources see Schoeser 1996 and Boydell 1989 and 1995.

Anscombe, Isabelle, *A Woman's Touch: Women in Design from 1860 to the Present Day*, London: Virago, and New York: Viking, 1984

Boydell, Christine, "Women Textile Designers in the 1920s and 1930s: Marion Dorn, a Case Study" in Judy Attfield and Pat Kirkham (editors), *A View from the Interior: Feminism, Women and Design*, London: Women's Press, 1989, pp.57–70

Boydell, Christine, *Marion Dorn: A Study of the Working Methods of the Female Professional Textile Designer in the 1920s and 1930s*, Ph.D. thesis, University of Huddersfield, 1992

Boydell, Christine, "The Decorative Imperative: Marion Dorn's Textiles and Modernism" in *Journal of the Decorative Arts Society*, 19, 1995, pp.31–40

Boydell, Christine, *Architect of Floors: Modern Art and Marion Dorn Designs* (exhib. cat.), London: Heinz Gallery, 1996

Hunt, Anthony, "The Artist and the Machine" in *Decoration of the English Home*, January–March, 1938, pp.28–33

Mendes, Valerie, "Marion Dorn, Textile Designer" in *Journal of the Decorative Arts Society*, 2, 1978, pp.24–35

Patmore, Derek, "Diana Wynyard's Flat: Marion Dorn, Interior Decorator" in *The Studio*, 112, 1936, pp.334–35

Thackeray, Ann, "Marion Dorn and Carpets in the 1930s" in *Leisure in the Twentieth Century*, London: Design Council, 1977, pp.14–19

Thirties: British Art and Design Before the War (exhib. cat.), London: Arts Council of Great Britain, 1979

Todd, Dorothy, "Marion Dorn: Architect of Floors" in *Architectural Review*, 72, 1932, pp.107–14

Draper, Dorothy 1889–1969

American interior designer

Dorothy Draper was one of the first modern interior designers in the first half of the 20th century and, by 1934, she had appeared on more American magazine covers (*Time*, *Life*, etc.) than even First Lady, Eleanor Roosevelt. Her fame resulted from her pioneering success in commercial design, a newly created offspring of architecture and interior decorating, and her creative, affordable interior design solutions during the restrictions of World War II quickly established her as a heroine to American housewives. A champion of professional women, Draper forged a path for women in the work-place and began defining the boundaries of the emerging Interior Design profession. And according to *Harper's Bazaar* (1941), she was "brisk, iconoclastic, inventive, unapologetic, and successful".

Born Dorothy Tuckerman on 22 November 1889, Draper was raised an Edwardian debutante within the safe, yet sometimes restrictive, confines of Tuxedo Park, New York, an elite community founded in part by her parents, Paul and Susan (Minturn) Tuckerman, who traced their family history to colonial Connecticut. Dorothy attended Brearley in Manhattan, a private finishing school, but had no specific technical or artistic training. Throughout her career, she depended mainly upon

Draper: Coty Beauty Salon, New York, 1941

imagination and common sense augmented by extensive travel.

In 1912, she married Dr. George Draper, who became the personal physician of Franklin D. Roosevelt, after Roosevelt was stricken with poliomyelitis. Though this introduced a lasting and influential relationship between Dorothy Draper and Eleanor Roosevelt, the demands of his work isolated George Draper from his family. The Drapers' marriage ended in 1930 leaving Dorothy with the unwelcome image of a social divorcee, which remained with her for the rest of her life. In order to confront her new social position, she underwent psychoanalysis, which she later claimed greatly liberated her sense of design and color.

Barbara E. Scott Fischer of the *Christian Science Monitor* (1941) described Draper as tall, tailored, and as decisive as a man, and later 20th century feminists may well count Draper among the early, trailblazing, career women. Although she received financial support to start her business from her parents, it was her masterful manipulation of men, materials, and the media that made her a monumental success. Her first venture, the Architectural Clearing House, founded in 1925, had the goal of introducing the "proper" architect to the "proper" client, and was a triumph. Draper's own duties ranged from detailed discussions of plans with architects and builders and giving ideas on everything from storage bins to roof terraces, from the inspection of radiators to the spacing of windows. Although Draper initially felt intimidated by architects because of their superior education, she soon achieved a sense of equality both from design and financial standpoints. But her growing success, and the new self-confidence that it gave interior decorators, was increasingly regarded as a threat by architects as they perceived a portion of their profession slipping away. This rivalry culminated in 1952 at the Association of Interior Decorators Dinner honoring Frank Lloyd Wright, when the famous architect openly criticized decorators, by referring to them as "inferior desecrators," and named Draper specifically. Present in the audience, Draper rose, and politely ended his diatribe. This confrontation between two national heroes set the stage for a struggle between the professions that continues even today.

Despite jealousy from both architects and her fellow decorators, by 1939 a large proportion of the American public perceived Draper as the undisputed spokesperson for the Interior Decorating profession. She entered the Hall of Fame in 1933 for her decorating of the River Club and was chosen as sole representative in decoration by the National Federation of Business and Professional Women. In addition, a media deluge kept her name on the lips of more housewives than any other decorator in history. She wrote two books on the subject – *Decorating is Fun!* (1939) and *365 Shortcuts to Home Decorating* (1968) – took to the airwaves with her own radio show, *Lines about Living*, and was encouraged to take charge of *Good Housekeeping's* "Studio for Living" section in June 1941. After being interviewed in 1939 by *Vogue* and *Harper's Bazaar* in her own Bandbox Apartment on 3rd Avenue, her popularity became international. Commissions were hers for the choosing; she accepted residential projects like the Walter Winchell estate, but turned down the Duke and Duchess of Windsor and President and Mrs. Eisenhower because their projects were too small.

During World War II, a majority of decorators were forced to close their doors or to cut their payrolls drastically. Draper, however, seized the moment and used her talents to aid the war effort. With the national economy completely devoted to the war, she utilized all of her media tools to reach out to the American housewife and breathe hope and optimism into days otherwise shrouded in loneliness and death. Because of the fear of air-raids, the citizens of New York City were asked to board up their windows; Draper advised the public how to conceal such eyesores. Her burlap and heavy drapery treatments became the fashion overnight. In addition, her programs, such as, "How to Buy a House for Under $500, Furniture Included," "A Christmas Celebration for $4.05," and "How to Decorate and Recycle the Home Interior" aided in maintaining morale on the homefront.

Draper created dramatic interiors through imagination, attention to function and a creative interpretation of historical sources. It was not uncommon in her work to see American Federal motifs in predominantly Roman Imperial interiors or juxtapositions of Italian Renaissance damasks and tropical designs. While the majority of her work was in New York, Draper's commissions stretched across three continents: the United States, South America and Europe.

After decorating a series of three personal dwellings in New York, one of which included the "Upside-down" House (1923), named because she created a garden terrace on the top floor in order to make room for a garage, Draper established a traditional approach to domestic design through fidelity to historical periods. Draper's interiors in the 1920s were conventional and similar to those of other decorators. Her Imperial Roman lobby at the Carlyle Hotel, 35 East 76th Street (1928), demonstrated her attention to history and was her first large commercial commission. In the 1930s, however, she began to expand her historical repertoire to include the Modern Movement. During this period, she also completed her course of psychoanalysis and her unique style emerged. In 1934, she unified a city block, Sutton Place tenement apartments, both without and within, by combining black with dead white trim and a variety of boldly colored doors. This project brought high society back to Sutton Place South, and was a great financial success.

Two years later, Draper was commissioned to design the Hampshire House Hotel, 150 Central Park West, out of a field of 154 decorators. It was the largest commission to date entrusted to a woman. At the Hampshire House Draper demonstrated a new design vocabulary, characterized by bolder contrasts and a greater sensitivity to the patterning of architectural surfaces. In addition, she designed her famous *Cabbage Rose* pattern for both fabric and wallpaper. Inspired by Georgia O'Keeffe, she dispensed with traditionally delicate motifs and produced patterns of heroic size. Confident of the success of the *Cabbage Rose* design, Schumacher produced over a million yards and it was one of the company's all-time best-sellers. In 1941, Draper outpaced all her contemporaries with her design for the Coty Beauty Salon in New York. For the first time, she combined a Modernist's use of space with exaggerated historical motifs and highly unconventional color schemes. Massive dead-white Baroque ornamentation framed doors and appeared as balustrades against blue and cherry-red walls and accents. Such combinations were extremely innovative and with the Coty commission, Draper defined a new interior type, since the beauty salon was a recent addition to the commercial market.

Her most spectacular foreign project, which generated a $30,000 fee – the largest commercial contract in the world to date – was the Quitandinha Resort in Petrópolis, near Rio de Janeiro, Brazil, completed in 1944. Consisting of a hotel and casino, the Resort was also the first project into which she introduced regional themes and motifs. She designed custom-made furniture, extruded in shape from the floor plan, and used out-scaled Baroque scroll work and chandeliers nearly 15 feet in height to create breathtaking spaces. Again, she produced a fabric line, *Brazilliance*, which was Schumacher's most famous line to date.

In 1954 Draper designed the still-extant cafeteria in the Metropolitan Museum of Art in New York. The space is basically a Roman atrium featuring columns and an impluvium or pool located in the center of the space. She gave the space an unarchaeological twist by designing great, swooping, strap-metal chandeliers. In 1958, Draper further refined her unorthodox style at the International Hotel, Kennedy Airport. Here, she designed large floor patterns which she extruded up to create large-scale custom-made furniture. One of the more spectacular pieces was a serpentine sofa, predecessor to the curved modular sectional of the 1970s. In a set of tables with X-shaped metal legs, Draper revealed the influence of Modernist furniture designers like Mies van der Rohe and Eero Saarinen.

Little is known of Draper's design process. On the larger commissions such as the hotels, for which she designed everything from furniture to the buttons on the bellman's cuff, she apparently executed rough conceptual sketches to create a basic sense of atmosphere and furniture placement, and then had her artist, Glenn Boyles, produce more detailed renderings under her verbal guidance. Final approval often required many attempts. Her staff comprised an impressive group drawn from various applied arts colleges and included the designers Lester Grundy and Ted Stewart and social secretary Belle Clark. The designers were often given projects immediately after Draper's initial visit; as long as the client was aware of her involvement within the process, it was unnecessary for her to be physically present on site. In addition, Draper carried all of her contractors in a "little black book," which became a compilation of some of the best craftspeople in the business, all of whom were fiercely loyal to her.

Other Draper commissions included: the Gideon Putnam Hotel in New York (1933); the Arrowhead Springs Resort in California (1939); the Camellia House at the Drake Hotel in Chicago (1940); the Delnor Hospital in St. Charles, Illinois (1940); Mayflower Hotel in Washington, DC (1940); Kerr's Department Store, Oklahoma City, in which she was able to increase the selling space by over 40 per cent (1944); Fairmont Hotel in San Francisco, in which Draper collaborated with architect Julia Morgan, (1945); the Versailles Dinner Club in New York (1945); and the Greenbrier Hotel in White Sulphur Springs, West Virginia (1946). In addition, Draper received design commissions for railway interiors and floating hotels as well as the interior of the 1952 Packard automobile, Convair Airline Interiors, and the packaging for *In the Pink* perfume for Gimbel's Department Stores.

For a woman once so well-known, it is hard to believe that today Draper is virtually forgotten. In many respects, she may be the quintessential interior designer. She created a unique style, promoted herself successfully within the domestic and commercial arenas, and stood face to face with male business tycoons, whom she described as "cowards when it comes to color." She opened the door for women in the work-place and began defining the field of modern American commercial Interior Design. In describing Draper, she said it best herself: "Be critical, never humble."

JOHN C. TURPIN

Biography

Born Dorothy Tuckerman in Tuxedo Park, New York, 22 November 1889. Educated at Brearley School, New York; received no formal design training. Married George Draper, 1912 (divorced 1930). Active as an interior designer in New York from the 1920s; established the Architectural Clearing House, 1925; received many commissions for hotels and restaurants, apartment buildings and department stores from the 1930s; interior design business sold in 1960. Published extensively on design and decoration; appeared on her own radio show, *Lines about Living*, 1940–41; director of the "Studio for Living" section in *Good Housekeeping* magazine, 1941. Designed fabrics and wallpapers for Schumacher from the mid-1930s, and furniture from the 1940s. Died in New York, 1969.

Selected Works

Interiors

1923	"Upside-down" House, New York (interiors)
1928	Carlyle Hotel, 35 East 76th Street, New York (Imperial Roman lobby)
1933	Gideon Putnam Hotel, New York (interiors)
1934	Sutton Place Apartments, New York (interiors and exterior colour scheme)
1936	Hampshire House Hotel, 150 Central Park West, New York (interiors)
1940	Camellia House, Drake Hotel, Chicago (interiors)
1940	Mayflower Hotel, Washington, DC (interiors)
1941	Coty Beauty Salon, New York (interiors)
1944	Kerr's Department Store, Oklahoma City (interiors)
1944	Quitandinha Resort, Petrópolis, near Rio de Janeiro (interiors and furnishings)
1945	Versailles Dinner Club, New York (interiors and furnishings)
1946	Greenbrier Hotel, White Suphur Springs, West Virginia (interiors and furnishings)
1954	Metropolitan Museum of Art, New York (restaurant interiors and furnishings)
1958	International Hotel, Kennedy Airport, New York (interiors and furnishings)

Draper's textile designs included *Cabbage Rose*, *Braziliance*, and *Scatter Floral* fabrics for Schumacher, and *Stylized Scroll* for Waverley.

Publications

"From the Inside Looking Out" in *House and Garden* (US), 51, June 1927, p.90
"Planting in the Sky" in *House and Garden* (US), 53, May 1928, pp.82–87
"Before the Plans are Drawn" in *House and Garden* (US), 54, November 1928, p.84
Decorating is Fun!, 1939
"A House in One Room Designed by Dorothy Draper" in *House and Garden* (US), 90, September 1946, pp.86–87
365 Shortcuts to Home Decorating, 1968

Further Reading

The standard monograph on Draper is Varney 1988.

"Dorothy Draper" in *Current Biography*, 2, 1941 Yearbook, pp.237–38
Flanner, Janet, "The Amazing Career of Dorothy Draper" in *Harper's Bazaar*, January 1941, pp.89–90
Goss, Jared, "Designing Women" in *Elle Decor* (US), 6, April–May 1995, pp.114
Hampton, Mark, *Legendary Decorators of the Twentieth Century*, New York: Doubleday, and London: Hale, 1992
McMullen, Frances, "Mrs. Draper, Home Stylist" in *Woman's Journal*, 15, March 1930, pp.16–17
Massey, Anne, *Interior Design of the Twentieth Century*, London and New York: Thames and Hudson, 1990
Owens, Mitchell, "Larger than Life: Dorothy Draper's Outsize Grandeur" in *Elle Decor*, I, September 1990, pp.54–56
"Re-Styled Buildings" in *Business Week*, 5 September 1936, p.34
Roe, Evelyn, "Giving Style to Real Estate" in *Christian Science Monitor*, 25 August 1937, p.6
Schroeder, Francis (editor), "Draper in Oklahoma" in *Interiors* (US), 103, April 1944, pp.50–51
Tate, Allen and C. Ray Smith, *Interior Design in the 20th Century*, New York: Harper, 1986
Towne, Charles, "A New Service for Those About to Build" in *Country Life*, 49, November 1925, p.42
Varney, Carleton, *The Draper Touch: The High Life and High Style of Dorothy Draper*, New York: Prentice Hall, 1988

Drawing Rooms

As a room-type, the modern drawing room retains a schizophrenic quality, split somewhere between a "gala" space and a family sitting room, which reflects what Edith Wharton once termed its "mixed ancestry" (*The Decoration of Houses*, 1897). Its development can be traced back to a small apartment, linked to the principal bed chamber, which provided a degree of privacy from the communal life of the medieval Great Hall. This type of "withdrawing" room lacked specialised furniture and created an indeterminate but relatively intimate space into which all or part of a small company

Drawing Room, Durham House, London, 1887

could temporarily withdraw. In the Apartment system of processional "shewed" interiors introduced to grand British houses from France and the Low Countries in the late 17th century, the drawing room continued to function primarily as a buffer zone in the sequence of State rooms, playing a supporting role in relation to the more glamorous State bed chamber and Baroque dining room.

By the early 18th century, however, this kind of drawing room occasionally co-existed with, and was subsequently modified by, the influence of more grandiose European models, in particular the Italian *salone*. In its original form the *salone* was a multi-storeyed space dedicated to large-scale gatherings and formal entertainment, and was characterised by bold, showy decor with minimal furnishings. Inspired by this prototype, the expanded British drawing room, and the "saloon" to which it was often closely linked, assumed a higher profile and more distinct character. A typical example is the barnlike "parade" space of the Great Drawing Room at Hopetoun created in the mid 18th century. Such a showpiece was reserved for large-scale formal entertainment rather than day-to-day use. The moveable furniture was set out in symmetrical order against the walls. Key signifiers of major expenditure were the pure white marble fire-surrounds, the colossal yardage of silk damask for upholstery and wall coverings, the glass mirrors with sconces for dozens of wax candles, elaborate plasterwork on the ceiling, and extensive gilding on the interior ornament and matching furniture. Similarly, the lofty saloon in a house like Robert Adam's Culzean Castle (1780s), with its spectacular westward vista out to sea, provided a climax to the staircase and sequence of public rooms on the first floor; typically it was circular or oval in plan, with a coved, and elaborately decorated ceiling. Although such glamorous schemes were few and far between, they were significant in formalizing many of the decorative conventions subsequently associated with the middle-class drawing room.

By the end of the 18th century a more Picturesque approach began to free up the disposition of the furnishings. Greater flexibility in the way the room could be used and the introduction of a diversified range of seating and tables allowed for varied groupings of people and activities. Apart from being the main reception room for both casual callers and formal entertainment, it was also becoming the space where the women of a household, and in some cases the children, would spend much of their time during the day. When there was company, family and guests would assemble there in more formal mode to be shuffled into order of precedence before the ritual procession through to the dining room. Later in the evening the gentlemen would rejoin the ladies in the drawing room for tea, cards and informal conversation to round off the day. The custom of women withdrawing from the dining room, leaving the men to get on with prolonged bouts of drinking, began to wane in Europe and America in the mid to late 19th century (but appears to have remained entrenched in Scotland).

While a party in summer might fall into little detached groups scattered all over the apartment, in winter the company tended to form into one large cluster around the fire. In many cases it was easier to shut up drawing rooms altogether out of season, removing textile wallhangings to storage. In fact the vast majority of people could not afford a highly specialised sequence of rooms, particularly a drawing room which tended to take up more square footage and window frontage than any other interior. Heating, lighting and maintaining such large rooms for occasional use was a formidable task. Case-covers shrouded the precious upholstery most of the time, and candle-light was kept to a minimum.

In its evolved 19th-century form, elements of the stately saloon-type drawing room were to become effectively merged with the pre-existing tradition of a more family-oriented living space, in a curious blend of formality and informality. With the quest for comfort intensifying throughout the 19th century it is not suprising to find that larger houses often accommodated an additional Small Drawing Room, (sometimes labelled the Morning Room) as an escape from the chilly formality of the State apartments. This smaller room might be equipped with draught- and fire-screens for sitting cosily near the fire, a book-case for reading matter, and a breakfast table for light meals. The main drawing room, on the other hand, was equipped with greater quantities of lighting, mirrors and seating for formal evening entertainment, along with the necessary accoutrements for tea and cards. Often such rooms would be furnished en suite on the principal floor so that the spaces could be interconnected by folding doors for large parties.

The drawing room assumed new and increased importance as the focus of the 19th-century cult of bourgeois domesticity, embodying family values and the civilizing influence of the home. An emphasis on cultural and artistic values was frequently symbolized through decorative schemes featuring the Muses or musical trophies, and through inclusion of the relevant furniture and props. The various table tops would be liberally scattered with small artworks, work- and drawing-boxes, writing equipment, folios of prints and drawings, and books of poetry or novels. Most commonly a piano, music stand and canterbury signified a musical household, while needlework skills were signalled through the presence of a spinning wheel, sewing table or embroidery frame; portfolios, easels, a small bookcase and writing desk were further indicators of artistic and literary activity. As the furnishing of the drawing room was, among other things, about the art of self-presentation and the reception of visitors, it was particularly important for young unmarried women to make their accomplishments evident. Private tutors and various ladies' magazines or books gave instruction in a wide range of decorative skills or "fancy work" which could occupy endless hours and be used to beautify the domestic interior – crafts such as chip-carving, pokerwork, staining, stencilling china or glass painting and repoussé metalwork. The most well-established and widespread of such domestic arts was needlework. There were aristocratic and genteel models to follow, as demonstrated by the survival in the drawing room of numerous historic samplers, "sewed" seat covers and embroidered boxes or frames.

There was widespread agreement that the drawing room's arrangement be left to the lady of the house. Within the home, it was perceived as the most "feminine" of the key rooms, providing an explicit and elaborate contrast to the "masculine" dining room. The picturesque variety of the drawing room's seating, cabinets and tables was in marked contrast to the restrained and formal symmetry associated with the dining room. Materials of a perceptibly higher quality were used and the reflective glitter of the gilding, the silky fabrics, elaborate veneers and mirrored or French-polished surfaces to be found in the drawing room were deliberately played off against the "solid" and unadorned materials in more masculine schemes. Upholstery was usually of velvet or silk-damask as opposed to horsehair, leather or plain repp; grates would often be of bright-cut or inlaid steel rather than brass or iron, and the furniture predominantly of rosewood or walnut, embellished with decorative inlays, carved detail and gilding. The proliferation and complexity of objects in the drawing room, and the variation of mass and outline in their grouping, expressed notions of civilizing "refinement". Accents of deep subtle colours, variegated patterns, or the application of veneers could all enhance a luxuriant effect. In particular, the availability and range of household textiles and wallpapers, formerly the preserve of aristocratic households, had been transformed by technical innovations. Although for the most part spun and woven by machine, textiles still retained associations of richness and refinement. The protective, womb-like muffling of the drawing room in layers of curtains, carpets, fluffy rugs, frilly lampshades, cushions and padded upholstery all gave the space a distinctive sound and feel aimed at inducing a state of physical and mental comfort.

Being the showpiece of the home, watercolour, printed and photographic images of the drawing room proliferated in the 19th century. The impact of such representations was intensified by the fact that they were designed to be looked at and enjoyed within the context of the drawing room itself. Photograph albums and stereoscopes or magnifying glasses encouraged an appreciation of intricate visual detail. The art of systematic looking was also encouraged through recording the drawing room in watercolour and pencil sketching, an activity deemed entirely appropriate for the context of the space. Small bookcases and reading lamps in most drawing rooms equipped avid novel-readers to consume literary descriptions of domestic interiors. Novels were considered suitably lightweight reading matter for an interior which was supposed to entertain idle hours.

The mirrors over fireplaces and pier tables which dominated most drawing room schemes constantly reflected women's appearance back to them and women were often depicted against the backdrop of a drawing room. Indeed, they were encouraged to see themselves as part of the drawing room scheme, and to match their figure, complexion and dress to the domestic environment. Not suprisingly, therefore, drawing rooms were frequently sucked into the negative comment surrounding the topic of women and fashion. As with the clothes they wore, women were often criticized for "dressing up" their drawing rooms to be attractive. The apparently random accumulation of small decorative objects was a particular butt of criticism.

As the showcase for artistic discrimination and individual taste, the drawing room accommodated collecting interests focused on small, exquisite and rare or curious items. Contemporary photographs show vast numbers of such items strewn around the table tops, in and under display cabinets, and stashed into the nooks and crannies of towering overmantels or hanging shelves. It was felt that such objects would stimulate the imagination and refined conversation, providing an informal education through the emanation of moral sentiment, history and cosmopolitan culture. Some items had a clear iconic and symbolic value, while others such as framed photographs and jewellery reflected more sentimental and personal interests. The "Chinamania" which reached its height in drawing rooms of the 1880s and 1890s was a competitive and fashionable pastime for both men and women. In less affluent homes the projection of artistic taste could be relatively cheaply paraphrased with a few bits of bric-a-brac and mass-produced china.

Within the home generally, and the drawing room in particular, women were expected to create an oasis of light and calm. Furnishings which were light in colour and form could provide a material analogy for the hygienic and spiritual purity of the household. The drawing room usually had more windows than any other room, and ideally a southerly aspect with a view upon which great importance was placed. The regenerative, colourful and sensual power of nature certainly enhanced the concept of the drawing room as an antidote to the drab world of work, and as an "unsullied" environment feeding the imagination and spirit. Nature was introduced directly to the drawing room through dried and cut flower arrangements, potted plants with elaborate jardinières, and collections of natural objects such as shells or semi-precious stones. In the 1850s and 1860s fern cases and aquaria were particularly in vogue. Still-life or landscape pictures could be displayed either on the walls or in albums. Gardens were also evoked indirectly through conventionalized ornament derived from nature. Drawing room carpets, upholstery and wallpaper were frequently floral in design and at a more abstract level the generally curvaceous, swelling forms of the furniture triggered similar associations.

Historical and foreign styles were used to conjure up the appropriate sensual qualities and social nuances for a drawing room, the most popular undoubtedly being an 18th-century French look creating an impression that was organic, glitzy and cushioned, with overtones of aristocratic refinement. Chinoiserie or the more exotic 18th-century styles were frequently recommended as a means of releasing the imagination, while a touch of Moresque and Oriental added a discreet hint of colourful luxury, mystery and sensuality. Drawing rooms of the 1880s and 1890s were characterized by an increasingly eclectic blending of styles and materials, and a self-conscious integration of old and new elements, though the overall emphasis was still very much on 18th-century styles. This mish-mash was to be given coherence and made "home-like", through the individual taste of the owner.

The cult of simplicity, which developed from the 1880s and continued into the 20th century, entailed a paring down of the drawing room's ornamental features and the thinning out of its contents. "Artistic" drawing rooms popularised a new, more reductivist aesthetic, while even in less self-consciously artistic households, social change was rendering the historical baggage and function of the drawing room obsolete. Simplified, more open planning was leading to greater continuity between adjacent interiors, and, like the hall and library, the drawing room was now increasingly furnished as a family "living room". Various authors on household taste in the 1920s referred to "the passing of the drawing room", not least because ladies were "fast becoming men", and therefore did not need a space into which to withdraw. The preferred terms were "living room", "sitting room" or "lounge". The usage of these labels was more linked to style and class connotations than clear differences in the purpose served by the room. While the familiarly lumpen and cosy forms of the three-piece suite marked the rise of the lounge and sitting room, the drawing room was generally distinguished by references to 18th-century styles with their overtones of genteel and elegant living. From its sumptuous Victorian and Edwardian heyday the drawing room had been diminished to a label which then, as perhaps now, persisted only "amongst a few who still have early Victorian tendencies".

JULIET KINCHIN

See also Parlours

Further Reading

Banham, Joanna, Sally MacDonald and Julia Porter, *Victorian Interior Design*, London: Cassell, 1991; as *Victorian Interior Style*, London: Studio, 1995

Carruthers, A. (editor), *The Scottish Home*, Edinburgh: National Museum of Scotland, 1996

Cornforth, John, *English Interiors, 1790–1848: The Quest for Comfort*, London: Barrie and Jenkins, 1978

Forge, Suzanne, *Victorian Splendour: Australian Interior Decoration, 1837–1901*, Melbourne and Oxford: Oxford University Press, 1981

Franklin, Jill, *The Gentleman's Country House and its Plan, 1835–1914*, London: Routledge, 1981

Garrett, Elisabeth Donaghy, *At Home: The American Family, 1750–1870*, New York: Abrams, 1990

Gere, Charlotte, *Nineteenth-Century Decoration: The Art of the Interior*, London: Weidenfeld and Nicolson, and New York: Abrams, 1989

Girouard, Mark, *Life in the English Country House: A Social and Architectural History*, New Haven and London: Yale University Press, 1978

Grier, Katherine C., *Culture and Comfort: People, Parlors, and Upholstery, 1850–1930* (exhib. cat.), Rochester, NY: Strong Museum, 1988

Jackson-Stops, Gervase and James Pipkin, "Withdrawing Rooms" in their *The English Country House: A Grand Tour*, London: Weidenfeld and Nicolson, 1984; Boston: Little Brown, 1985

Loudon, J.C., *An Encyclopaedia of Cottage, Farm and Villa Architecture and Furniture*, London, 1833

Mayhew, Edgar de Noailles and Minor Myers, Jr., *A Documentary History of American Interiors from the Colonial Era to 1915*, New York: Scribner, 1980

Muthesius, Hermann, *The English House*, edited by Dennis Sharp, London: Crosby Lockwood Staples, and New York: Rizzoli, 1979 (German original 3 vols., 1904–05, revised edition 1908–11)

Orrinsmith, Lucy, *The Drawing-Room: Its Decoration and Furniture*, London, 1877; reprinted with *The Dining Room* by M.J. Loftie and *The Bedroom and Boudoir* by Lady Barker, New York: Garland, 1978

Thornton, Peter, *Authentic Decor: The Domestic Interior, 1620–1920*, London: Weidenfeld and Nicolson, and New York: Viking, 1984

Thornton, Peter, *The Italian Renaissance Interior, 1400–1600*, London: Weidenfeld and Nicolson, and New York: Abrams, 1991

Dresser, Christopher 1834–1904

British designer

A pioneer of modern design, Christopher Dresser was one of the most radical and prolific designers of the 19th century. His output included ceramics, glass, metalwork, furniture, carpets, fabrics, wallpapers and every aspect of interior decoration. He was one of the first designers to be professionally trained for industry and he worked for at least sixty of the most forward-looking Victorian manufacturers. His designs were well-known in Europe, America and Japan and his wallpapers were produced in America and Germany where they exercised a decisive influence on the development of Modernism. Finally, he was also an influential writer on botany, design and interior decoration. He stressed the importance of function and simplicity, as well as subdued colouring and restrained ornamentation in interiors, and his theories were regarded as among the most advanced of his day.

Dresser also prioritised the role of the designer within manufacturing. He was one of the first European designers to imprint his signature next to the maker's mark and during the early 1860s he pioneered the elevation of design and interior decoration to the status of an art. This development in turn encouraged the emergence of terms such as Art furniture, Art pottery and Artistic or Aesthetic interiors. And although little of Dresser's own work within interiors has survived, his ideas are fully documented in the numerous publications he produced from the early 1860s which provided ample advice on the decoration of ordinary middle-class homes.

Dresser's style was based on a general affinity with Early English medieval art and on his admiration for oriental and Japanese art. But he was never dogmatic in his adoption of past styles, and his free mixing of historical pastiches with ideas from diverse cultures gave rise to a highly personal manner that was closely attuned to the spirit of the times. His championship of Japanese art was particularly important and he played a leading role in the introduction of the Anglo-Japanese or Modern English style in the last third of the 19th century. In 1876–77 he became the first European designer actually to visit Japan and he established a number of trading companies which presented Japanese art and architecture on a larger scale to the British public. He also published one of the first European books on Japanese art in 1882 which consolidated his campaign for the acceptance of Japonisme. He particularly admired the simplicity of construction and subtlety of colour in Japanese interiors and design. In place of the early Victorian emphasis upon polychromy, he advocated the use of secondary and tertiary tones. Primary colours were permissible in decorative patterns on walls and ceilings but when viewed from a distance they should give the impression of a natural bloom "similar to that of the peach, where all the colours of the rainbow combine".

Dresser: wallpaper for Sanderson, c.1878

These views were propounded in his writings, which were enormously influential. Dresser's early publications represented the first thorough discussion of interior design and became popular reading long before those of contemporaries such as C.L. Eastlake, William Morris or E.W. Godwin. Indeed, Dresser's influence was arguably far more widespread than that of most other craft-oriented architect-designers, for although Dresser, like Morris, preached the gospel of art for the masses, he also appreciated the advantages of machine production and his enormous output reached a far larger audience through the techniques of mass-production and modern industry. And similarly, although his ideas were not publicly acknowledged by Morris or other Aesthetes, Dresser was largely responsible for promoting the ideal of the "aesthetic interior" which gained momentum during the 1860s and 1870s. He placed special emphasis upon the need for carefully chosen colour schemes and suggested particular combinations for different rooms. His ideas for a drawing room, for example, included blue or multicoloured ceilings, citrine or yellow-orange walls, maroon or purple dadoes, and bronze-green doors surmounted by black architraves – colours that were intended to inspire "purity, activity and enlightenment".

He also presented a programme for a blue study and a red dining room, "suggesting strength and beauty", and a purple nursery and olive breakfast room, "inspiring feelings of repose and gladness" respectively. For kitchens and rooms intended for manual work, he recommended buff or dark yellow tones. These distinctive colours became the favoured palette of the Aesthetic Movement and had become so popular by the 1880s that Gilbert and Sullivan's satirical opera *Patience* employed the phrase "greenery-yallery" to signify the taste of the Movement.

Dresser's treatment of ceilings was particularly distinctive. He strongly disapproved of the fashion for whitewashed ceilings and advocated instead the abundant use of colour, especially blue. His ceiling decorations also always complemented the treatment of the wall and he designed some of the first matching frieze-fill-dado-ceiling papers, produced by the wallpaper manufacturers Jeffrey & Co. from 1871. He also often employed relief materials such as Linoleum Muralis and was one of the first designers to produce patterns in the Anglo-Japanese style for the Lincrusta Walton (from 1876) and Anaglypta (from 1887) firms. Some of his most sophisticated hand-painted ceilings were incorporated in the interiors (some of which are still *in situ*) he created for Thomas Shaw's Allangate Mansion, in Halifax, where the rich, oriental-style patterns in iridescent shades of green, turquoise, blue and gold, were said to have cost its owner some £3,500. And following his return from Japan in 1878, Dresser promoted the adaptation of Japanese ceilings with overlapping floral patterns superimposed with an open framework of joists which became increasingly widespread in Britain during the 1880s and 1890s.

For walls, he recommended plain colours or tinted decorations, sometimes enriched with a simple powdered pattern or a wallpaper in "subdued colours", as greatly preferable to the naturalistic patterns featuring large bunches of flowers combined with animals or human figures that were characteristic of much commercially produced work. He argued that allegorical symbolism could be most successfully embodied in stylised or abstract ornamentation, and that the motifs should have a bilateral arrangement and "in all cases consist of flat ornament" and of "small, simple repeated parts, which are low-toned or neutral in colour". The majority of his designs were in his favoured Anglo-Japanese style incorporating grill or lattice patterns combined with diaper or overlapping floral patterns and sometimes including exotic insects or birds. After his tour of Japan, Dresser launched a series of papers printed in various shades on plain, brown sugar-papers, and most of the wallpapers from the latter period of his career expanded on this colour scheme. His output was prodigious and by the time of his death he had designed more than a hundred papers for over 17 different manufacturers in Europe and America.

Dresser's designs for carpets were equally numerous. Rejecting the naturalistic designs that were still commonplace in the third quarter of the 19th century, he argued that carpets should be restrained in colour and that they should serve as a background to the furnishings and contents of the room. From 1862 he championed the use of geometrical and conventionalised Oriental patterns and advocated designs based on the principles of geometry that, he believed, reflected the way that plants and flowers should appear when viewed from above. Most of his own carpets contained patterns based on radiating leaf and floral forms, framed by scrolls or banded borders at their edges. Some examples included a slight relief imitating the *ton sur ton* effect of Chinese rugs and, like Morris, Dresser clearly hoped to make Britain independent of the carpets imported from the East. He also helped to reform the design of floorcoverings in America and in 1873 he was commissioned to produce a government report on design "applied to objects and to houses" that included many useful comments on carpets and rugs. His personal output included several hundred carpet designs the majority of which were produced as double-cloth Brussels carpets and as "spool" Axminster rugs by John Brinton Ltd. and by John Crossley.

Dresser was also active as a designer of furnishing fabrics and designed lace produced by Edward Cope, silk and woollen damasks and worsted woollen fabrics by W. & C. Ward and by Norris & Co. (later Warner & Co.), cotton damasks for John Wilson and Sons, Lotus fabrics for Arthur Liberty, cretonnes for Steiner & Co., and towels, bedspreads and quilts for Barlow and Jones and others. Barlow and Jones's *Empire* quilt (1887) and *Colombian* quilt (1893), produced to commemorate Queen Victoria's Golden Jubilee and the discovery of America, were particularly admired and proved highly popular.

Stylistically, Dresser lamented the general "want of simple structure, want of simple treatment, [and] want of simplicity of effect" in British textiles, and he proposed simple and conventionalised motifs such as circles, diapers, vertical and diagonal stripes as suitable for hanging fabrics. He also stressed that the laws governing the design of textiles were identical to those for carpets and that hanging fabrics should follow the rules applied to wallpapers – namely a bilateral arrangement of themes. Several of his designs were in the Anglo-Japanese style and his use of layered compositions, made up of ground and superimposed motifs which derived from his admiration of Japanese textiles, was far ahead of his time. These layered and juxtaposed patterns proved extremely influential and made an important contribution to the reform of ornamental design in Britain.

Dresser also designed furniture, metal fittings, stained glass and all the objects required to decorate a house. His designs for furniture date from the late 1860s and although the history of his early work is still quite obscure, some of his pieces may have been produced by C. L. Eastlake's Art Furniture Company (fl.1869–71). Like Eastlake, Dresser advocated built-in ensembles and admired Japanese and Early English and medieval prototypes and emphasised principles of sound construction with minimal carving and upholstery. Unlike Eastlake, however, he disliked the prevalent Neo-Renaissance and reformed Gothic styles which he regarded as unsuited to a modern Protestant society. And although much of Dresser's Art furniture was frequently referred to as Anglo-Japanese, it also reflected a sifting of ideas from Early English, Egyptian, Islamic and Greek sources and, in its constructional honesty, angularity and simplicity, it represents a highly individual and radical departure from ordinary Victorian furniture. Pieces such as tables and chairs often appear quite sturdy and robust, and sometimes incorporate lattice panel backs and intricate substructures which contrast solid and void and the regular with the irregular in the characteristic Anglo-Japanese manner. Much of Dresser's furniture was also painted in ebony and lacquer tints with deeply incised and gilded borders and the cabinet doors sometimes included grotesque or humorous motifs such as stylised owls, cranes and frogs. When Dresser established the Art Furnishers' Alliance Co. in 1880 production was turned over to Chubb & Sons who also made the pieces designed for Bushloe House that date from this period.

Dresser's designs for brass, copper and cast-iron objects, including candle-holders, lamps, kettles, trays, coalboxes in mixed metals, and cast-iron andirons, fireplace surrounds and hall furniture, formed another essential element of his artistic interiors. His cast-iron furniture illustrates once again his willingness to embrace modern materials and methods of production and included some particularly distinctive coat-stands, hall tables, chairs and benches that featured spiky foliage and angular scrolls combined with elliptical mirrors and roundels. He also supplied elegant fireplace overmantels with ebonised shelves containing his colourful ceramics and glass vases, as well as stained-glass windows in muted and delicate colours containing spiky leaf ornament and Anglo-Japanese motifs. Finally, Dresser recommended that all the frames and curtain poles in the room should be ebonised to complement the furniture and to provide an artistic contrast with the wallpapers and paint colours. Curtains were to be loosely draped from "a simple and obvious pole". Such ideas represented a radical departure from the usual preference for ponderous gilt frames and elaborate curtain arrangements and anticipated the practice of modern decorators. Above all, Dresser aimed to free his furnishings and decorations from the straitjacket of historicism and to create a "new style" which would make "every homestead artistic in the true sense of the word".

WIDAR HALÉN

See also Aesthetic Movement; Art Furnishings

Biography

Born in Glasgow in 1834. Enrolled at the Government School of Design, London, 1845. Married Thirza Perry, 1854: 13 children. Lectured at School of Design, Marlborough House, 1854–68; appointed Professor of Botany, 1859; received honorary doctorate from the University of Jena, 1860. Established as a leading commercial designer of ceramics, wallpapers and textiles by mid-1860s; produced designs for metalwork, furniture and cast iron from the 1870s; glass from the 1890s. An authority on Japanese art, he visited Japan at the invitation of the Japanese government, 1876; returned with stock for Tiffany & Co. Founded Dresser and Holme, importers of Japanese goods, 1879; appointed "art superintendent" for Linthorpe Art Pottery 1879–82; established Art Furnishers' Alliance 1880 (closed 1883). Exhibited at many national and international exhibitions including London 1862, 1871 and 1872; Philadelphia 1876; and Paris 1878. A prolific writer and lecturer he was editor of the *Furniture Gazette*, 1880–81, and wrote many articles on ornament, colour and design. Died in Mulhouse, France, 24 November 1904.

Selected Works

A sketchbook of Dresser's original designs, dating from the 1860s, is in the Ipswich Museum, Suffolk; two volumes of tracings from his studio of the same period are in the Victoria and Albert Museum, London; the Metropolitan Museum of Art, New York has an album of 40 coloured designs dating from the 1880s for wallpapers, ceramics, stained glass, textiles, and for the ornamental treatment of plants. Documentation and artwork relating to his designs for ceramics is in the Minton Archive, and the Archive of Josiah Wedgwood & Sons, Stoke-on-Trent. Further documentation relating to Dresser's work can be found in the Nikolaus Pevsner Papers, Getty Center for the History of Art and the Humanities, California. Examples of Dresser's textiles, ceramics, wallpapers, glass and metalwork are in the Victoria and Albert Museum.

Interiors

1870	Allangate Mansion, Halifax, Yorkshire (decorations and furnishings): Thomas Shaw
1879–80	Bushloe House, Leicester (decorations and furnishings): Hiram B. Owston
1880	Chubb & Son, 128 Queen Street, London (dining room and office furniture): George Hayter Chubb

Dresser produced designs for over 60 commercial manufacturers in England, France and the US. The principal companies with whom he was associated included: ceramics for Minton & Co., Josiah Wedgwood & Sons, Linthorpe Art Pottery, and Old Hall Earthenware Co.; metalwork for Elkington & Co., Hukin & Heath, James Dixon & Sons, and Benham & Froud; glass for James Couper & Sons; textiles for W. & C. Ward, Warner & Sons, Liberty & Co., and F. Steiner & Co.; carpets for John Crossley & Co., and John Brinton; wallpapers for William Woollams & Co., Jeffrey & Co., Frederick Walton & Co., Lightbown Aspinall & Co., John Line & Sons, and Zuber et Cie.

Publications

The Art of Decorative Designs, 1862
Development of Ornamental Art in the International Exhibition, 1862
Principles of Decorative Design, 1873; reprinted 1973
Studies in Design, 1874–76
Japan: Its Architecture, Art and Art-Manufactures, 1882; reprinted 1977
Modern Ornamentation, 1886

Numerous articles on ornament, decoration and design in contemporary journals such as the *Art Journal*, the *Builder*, *Journal of the Society of Arts*, and the *Furniture Gazette*.

Further Reading

A scholarly monograph on Dresser is Halén 1990 which includes a full primary and secondary bibliography and a full list of the manufacturers with whom Dresser was involved.

The Aesthetic Movement and the Cult of Japan (exhib. cat.), London: Fine Art Society, 1972
Anscombe, Isabelle, "Knowledge is Power: The Designs of Christopher Dresser" in *Connoisseur*, May 1979, pp.54–59
Aslin, Elizabeth, *The Aesthetic Movement: Prelude to Art Nouveau*, London: Elek, and New York: Praeger, 1969
Burke, Doreen Bolger and others, *In Pursuit of Beauty: Americans and the Aesthetic Movement* (exhib. cat.: Metropolitan Museum, New York), New York: Rizzoli, 1986
Bury, Shirley, "The Silver Designs of Dr. Christopher Dresser" in *Apollo*, December 1962, pp.766–70
Collins, Michael, *Christopher Dresser 1834–1904* (exhib. cat.), London: Camden Arts Centre, 1979
Cooper, Jeremy, *Victorian and Edwardian Furniture and Interiors*, London: Thames and Hudson, 1987
Dennis, Richard and John Jesse, *Christopher Dresser 1834–1904: Pottery, Glass, Metalwork* (exhib. cat.), London: Fine Art Society, 1972
Dryden, Annamarie, "Bursting Buds" in *Country Life*, 20 August 1992, pp. 46–47
Durant, Stuart, *Christopher Dresser*, London: Academy, and New York: St. Martin's Press, 1993
Halén, Widar, "The Dresser Pattern Books from Charles Edward Fewster's Collection" in *Journal of the Decorative Arts Society*, vol.12, 1988, pp.2–9

Halén, Widar, *Christopher Dresser*, London: Phaidon, 1990; 2nd edition 1993
Pevsner, Nikolaus, "Christopher Dresser, Industrial Designer" in *Architectural Review*, LXXXI, 1937, pp.183–86
Tilbrook, Adrian, "Christopher Dresser's Designs for Elkington & Co." in *Journal of the Decorative Arts Society*, no.9, 1985, pp.23–28

Dufour et Cie.

French wallpaper manufacturers, 1797–1865

The name of Dufour et Cie. dominated French wallpaper production at the outset of the 19th century. The company's early success was based upon its application of Neo-Classical ornament to wallpaper design and coincided with a period when the popularity of the Empire style was at its height. Dufour also became known for its spectacular panoramic or scenic decorations, wallpapers containing large illusionistic and non-repeating pictorial designs that covered the walls of a room with a continuous scene. These decorations were akin to murals or paintings in appearance and, requiring many hundreds, and sometimes thousands of blocks to print, they represented outstanding examples of technical virtuosity the like of which was never rivalled, before or since.

Joseph Dufour was born in 1757, the son of a carpenter, at Tramayes, close to Mâcon in Burgundy, France. Nothing is known about his training, but by 1789 he was based in Lyon. At this time Lyon was the European capital of the silk trade and a principal centre of textile production. It was also an important centre for the manufacture of wallpaper, but wallpaper was still not widely used during this period. Dufour worked for the Ferrouillat factory – a major producer of wallpaper – and he became a partner in 1792. Unfortunately, the business suffered during the revolutionary riots of 1793–94 and closed down in 1797.

Following this event Joseph Dufour set up his own factory in Mâcon later that year in association with his brother Pierre. At the same time he kept certain interests in the Lyon wallpaper business. It seems that Pierre was in charge of the administration of the business while Joseph managed the workshops. They secured the services of Jean-Gabriel Charvet (1750–1829), who was already active in the wallpaper industry in Lyon, to prepare designs and drawings for the block-cutters. The company's figures for 1800 show that it quickly achieved a substantial turnover grossing a total of 119,164 francs. Pierre left the company, which was then registered as Joseph Dufour & Cie, and Dufour's cousin Antoine took over the administrative side.

By 1804 the business was thriving and employed 90 workers, and Dufour issued his first panoramic decoration entitled *Les Sauvages de la Mer Pacifique* (or *The Voyages of Captain Cook*) which was designed by Charvet and sold together with a 48 page booklet describing the different scenes and detailing the exotic flora and fauna. At the same time, a rival manufacturer, Jean Zuber & Cie., launched *Les Vues de Suisse*, and these two panoramic designs were probably the first to be produced in colour. Both decorations were featured at the Exposition des Produits de l'Industrie at the Louvre in 1806 where they aroused much interest and critical acclaim. Dufour's work was singled out for especial praise, with one commentator declaring that "New wallpaper decorated with subjects drawn from Captain Cook's voyages counts perhaps among the most unusual work created in this field." But the Mâcon-produced wallpaper did not win an award, whereas Zuber's decoration received a silver medal.

In 1808 Dufour established a workshop in Paris, at 17 rue de Beauvau in the faubourg Saint-Antoine, an area containing numerous cabinet-makers' workshops and where J.B. Réveillon and his successors had been working since 1763. Dufour appears to have employed Xavier Mader from the time he arrived in Paris. Mader managed the drawing and engraving workshops until 1823 and it was he who introduced the distinctive Neo-Classical look to the company's products which were not widely known until this time. His firm engravings resulted in a style that was as rigorous as it was elegant, and which could be seen as early as 1808 in the classically-inspired series of grisaille figures representing the months (*Les Mois*) drawn by Evariste Fragonard, in the Greek deities that appeared in the *Galerie mythologique* (1814), and in the Empire-style drapery decorations and friezes containing *trompe-l'oeil* representations of ruched and gathered muslin and silks that continued to be produced well into the 1820s.

Dufour's draperies were an extraordinary exercise in verisimilitude and proved popular in many Empire and Biedermeier interiors of the early 19th century, but it was the panoramic decorations which brought the business its great success. Its most notable works included *Les rives de Bosphore* from around 1812, *Les monuments de Paris* (1812–14), and *Psyché & Cupidon* (1815). These last two panoramics were especially original. The first contained a frontal composition and artificially aligned the most well-known Parisian monuments along the banks of the Seine. The second built up a complex narrative in twelve individual tableaux, printed in sepia or grisaille, illustrating scenes in the Cupid and Psyche story. The series was designed by the artists Louis Lafitte (1770–1828) and Méry-Joseph Blondel (1781–1853) and featured elegant, life-size Neo-Classical figures who inhabit palatial marble halls containing carefully rendered Empire-style furniture and ornament and massive architectural features and mosaic floors based on those discovered at Herculaneum and Pompeii. *Les paysages de Télémaque dans l'île de Calypso* (c.1818), *Les Incas* (around 1818) and *Les Fêtes Grecques* (1818) demonstrate the depth and quality achieved artistically, which was recognized when the firm was awarded a silver medal at the Exposition des Produits de l'Industrie in Paris in 1819.

In 1821 Joseph Dufour's daughter married Amable Leroy of Lyon and the name of the company was changed to Joseph Dufour & Leroy in the following year. Xavier Mader left the business in 1823 to set up his own venture. Dufour & Leroy continued to produce panoramic scenes, such as *Paul & Virginie* (c.1824), *Les Voyages d'Anthénor* (c.1820–25), and when Joseph Dufour died on 15 January 1827 his son-in-law continued in the tradition, launching *Les Campagnes des armées françaises en Italie* (c.1829), *Renaud & Armide* (1831) and *Les paysages pittoresques* (c.1832), before selling the company to the Lapeyre & Drouard factory in 1835.

If Dufour's production of panoramic scenes is well known

and demonstrates the creativity and technical and artistic strengths of the business, we are now beginning to be better able to define and to date the rest of the factory's output, thanks to an album of samples in the Musée des Arts Décoratifs in Paris. These samples, together with examples at the Musée du Papier Peint de Rixheim and artwork preserved at the Bibliothèque Forney in Paris, have established the image of a manufacturer totally mastering a rich and sumptuous French Empire style which continued to have popular appeal long after 1815 and which explains the success of the company's output both in France and abroad during this period.

BERNARD JACQUÉ
translated by Philippe Barbour

Selected Works

The major collection of Dufour et Cie.'s wallpapers is in the Musée des Arts Décoratifs, Paris. Additional examples are in the Musée de Papier Peint, Rixheim, Victoria and Albert Museum, London, the Whitworth Art Gallery, Manchester, and the Cooper-Hewitt Museum, New York.

Further Reading

While there is no complete catalogue of work produced by Dufour et Cie., a catalogue raisonné of the panoramic decorations appears in Nouvel-Kammerer 1990 which also includes an extensive bibliography of primary and secondary sources. The most recent English-language survey of their work appears in Hoskins 1994.

Alcouffe, Daniel, Anne Dion-Tenenbaum and Pierre Ennes, *Un Age d'Or des Arts Décoratifs, 1814–1848* (exhib. cat.), Paris: Réunion des Musées Nationaux, 1991

Clouzot, Henri, *Les Chefs d'Oeuvres du Papiers Peints: Tableaux-tentures de Dufour et Leroy*, Paris, 1931

Clouzot, Henri, *Le Papier Peint en France du XVIIe au XIXe siècle*, Paris: van Oest, 1931

Clouzot, Henri and Charles Follot, *Histoire du Papier Peint en France*, Paris: Moreau, 1935

Crick, Clare, "Wallpapers by Dufour et Cie." in *Connoisseur*, 193, December 1976, pp.310–16

Entwisle, Eric A., *French Scenic Wallpapers, 1800–1860*, Leigh-on-Sea: F. Lewis, 1972

L'Etoffe du Papier Peint (exhib. cat.), Rixheim: Musée de Papier Peint, 1995

Guibert, Mireille, *Catalogue des Papiers Peints (1800–1875) de la Bibliothèque Forney*, Paris: Bibliothèque Forney, 1980

Hoskins, Lesley (editor), *The Papered Wall: The History, Patterns and Techniques of Wallpaper*, London: Thames and Hudson, and New York: Abrams, 1994

Jacqué, Bernard and Odile Nouvel-Kammerer, *Le Papier Peint Décor d'Illusion*, Schirmeck: Gyss, 1986

Kammerer-Grothaus, Helke, "Bildtapeten des Klassizismus" in *Zeitschrift des Deutschen Vereins für Kunswissenschaft*, XXXVII, 1/4, 1983

Nouvel, Odile, *Wallpapers of France, 1800–1850*, London: Zwemmer, and New York: Rizzoli, 1981

Nouvel-Kammerer, Odile (editor), *Papier Peints Panoramiques*, Paris: Flammarion, 1990

Teynac, Françoise, Pierre Nolot and Jean-Denis Vivien, *Wallpaper: A History*, London: Thames and Hudson, and New York: Rizzoli, 1982

Trois Siècles de Papier Peint (exhib. cat.), Paris: Musée des Arts Décoratifs, 1967

Watkin, David, "Some Wallpapers by Dufour" in *Apollo*, 64, June 1967

Dugourc, Jean-Démosthène 1749–1825

French designer of furniture, textiles, interiors and ceramics

Jean-Démosthène Dugourc was one of the leading French designers of the last decades of the 18th century. He seems to have been responsible for the introduction of a wide variety of delicate styles that became current in the last years of the *ancien régime*, particularly the refined version of the Classical style called the *Style Étrusque*.This was based on discoveries of Classical antiquities at Pompeii and Herculaneum, and tended to eschew the elaborate gilt and bright colours of much 18th-century decoration in favour of severe outlines, sharp profile decoration and sombre colours (especially, yellow and chocolate brown) reminiscent of Greek vase decoration. In addition, Dugourc was particularly important in the designing of three-dimensional objects and the propagation of French styles abroad. However, as he was neither a professional architect nor a manufacturer (except for a short space of time just after the beginning of the French Revolution), his significance has until recently remained largely unrecognized, and has only recently been revealed through documents and the study of his drawings. These latter include an important album of drawings in the Musée des Arts Décoratifs, formerly in the collection of Sir Richard Wallace, and the now-dispersed archive of the silk-weaving firm of Tassinari et Chatel at Lyon, the successor firm to one of Dugourc's long-standing patrons, Camille Pernon.

The basis of all historical research on Dugourc is given by two autobiographies or *mémoires* that he wrote in 1800, just after he had left Republican France, and in 1823, when he was reduced to begging a pension from the Crown. He was born in 1749, the son of a high-ranking official in the household of the Duc d'Orléans, a cousin of the king and owner of the Palais Royal in Paris. He apparently took some lessons with the Duke's son, the Duc de Chartres, later to become famous as Philippe Egalité, who voted for the death of the king in 1793 and was himself executed in 1794. A visit to Rome in 1765, where he encountered Winckelmann, was cut short by the death of his mother, but left him with an abiding love of Classical antiquity. He learnt his proficiency in the arts of painting, sculpture and engraving with the painter and engraver Saint-Aubin, laying the foundations of his skill in draughtsmanship. His first recorded work is an allegory of the marriage of the Dauphin to Marie-Antoinette in 1770, known through an engraving by Ingouf. Throughout his career he seems to have been able to fall back on drawings and engravings of fine art subjects as a sideline to his career as a designer.

In 1776 Dugourc married a sister of the Neo-Classical architect François-Joseph Bélanger (1744–1818), and although she was to die in 1785, Dugourc's relationship with his brother-in-law seems to have lasted until the end of the century, and brought him close to one of the most advanced and innovative of all 18th-century French designers. Bélanger is believed to have re-introduced the arabesque style into interior decoration, and it would seem that one of Dugourc's first decorative commissions was the painting in 1777 of small-scale human and semi-human figures in the arabesque wall decoration of Bagatelle, the pleasure pavilion of the king's youngest brother, the Comte d'Artois. Many of the interiors of

Dugourc: design for a bed in an alcove

Bagatelle were in an extraordinarily refined and fantastic taste, including a bedroom with hangings imitating a military tent complete with a stove in the form of a pile of cannon balls and grenades, and must have had enormous influence on Dugourc's development as an interior designer.

Among Dugourc's earliest recorded designs were interiors in the Chinese taste for the Duchesse de Mazarin, another client of Bélanger, who wanted a suitable setting for her collections of Oriental porcelain. Dugourc also seems to have contributed to theatre design as early as 1779, when he began what he called the "total reform" of theatrical costumes. In 1780 he commenced his long involvement with the royal family when he became draughtsman to the king's younger brother, the Comte de Provence, and produced designs for the inauguration of the Count's theatre at Brunoy, built to the designs of the architect Chalgrin, including a vestibule painted to imitate a garden surrounded by trelliswork in front of trees. He also produced theatrical designs for the king of Sweden.

By 1781 Dugourc was working with Camille Pernon, an eminent silk manufacturer at Lyon. His designs included wall hangings with decoration in the arabesque manner and others with an out-of-doors character showing birds sitting in trees. Chairs and chair covers with similar decoration complemented these designs. Some of the furniture he designed was made by the leading chair-maker of the day, Georges Jacob, and some chairs made by him for the celebrated hôtel of Mademoiselle

Dervieux have straight legs supporting a frame with an acanthus border, and a general lightness of style that marks a refinement of the heavy Neo-Classicism which had by then become current. In 1784 Dugourc was appointed designer to Garde-Meuble de la Couronne, the organization responsible for the furnishing of the royal palaces, and a set of chairs and a bed for Louis XVI made to his design survive at the château of Compiègne. Dugourc also seems to have provided designs for the famous royal jewel cabinet created for the queen in 1787, and a wax model close to his designs survives in the Walters Art Gallery, Baltimore; the top of this model comprises tall panels decorated with flat Pompeian-type figures in the Etruscan style. He also claimed to have provided designs for ormolu mounts for the gilders Pierre Gouthière and François Rémond, as well as designs for the clockmaker Godon. An important drawing in the album in the Musée des Arts Décoratifs shows an elegant Neo-Classical side table supporting a whole range of ormolu goods, including a candlestick in the form of female terms, identical to a pair now in the Wallace Collection, London.

Much of Dugourc's time in the 1780s seems to have been spent in preparing an amazing range of decorative schemes for royal and aristocratic patrons throughout Europe, few of which were executed, although his drawings survive to show his extraordinary powers of invention. In 1784 he prepared designs for interiors for Catherine the Great of Russia, her son Grand Duke Paul, and General Lanskoi, all of which show extensive use of silk hangings which would presumably have been supplied by Pernon. In 1786 he prepared a whole range of designs for the Spanish Court, including a room in the Gothic taste, complete with tracery, and a Turkish saloon for the palace of the Prado, as well as an Egyptian room and Etruscan gallery for the Escorial. In 1789 he prepared Neo-Classical designs for a Throne Room in the royal palace at Madrid.

Much of Dugourc's patronage naturally fell away at the time of the French Revolution, and he seems to have had difficulty in finding outlets for his extravagant talents. He is recorded as operating a wallpaper factory with Etienne-Alexandre Jacques Anisson-Duperon, who was guillotined in 1794, and also ran a factory making playing cards in which the Kings, Queens, and Knaves were replaced by *Génies*, *Libertés* and *Egalités* according to Republican taste. He also ran a glass factory and produced designs for one of the Paris porcelain factories, about which little is known. However, his capacity for producing luxury items continued, as is shown by his design of 1799 in the Hermitage, St. Petersburg, possibly for the gilder Rémond, for mounting a hard-stone bowl on a frame consisting of four eagles with outstretched wings. Such designs prefigure the severe classical style of Percier and Fontaine.

Dugourc continued to provide designs for the court of Spain, including some of the furnishing in 1799 for the celebrated Casita del Labrador (worker's cottage) at Aranjuez, a garden pavilion, which includes a billiard room hung with silk hangings by Pernon designed by Dugourc based on Raphael's famous arabesque designs in the Vatican. In 1800 he accepted an offer to work for the Bourbon king of Spain, Charles IV, and appears to have acted as a representative at the Spanish court for the firm of Pernon. The war in the Peninsula led to his return to France in 1813, just in time to profit from the Bourbon restoration of 1814, when he became official designer for public ceremonies. In 1816 he regained his former title of designer to the Garde-Meuble de la Couronne and continued to produce designs for royal occasions and interiors, including the refurnishing of the Throne Room at the Tuileries. He died in Paris on 30 April 1825.

Dugourc's main achievement was to develop the Neo-Classical taste beyond the severe *goût grec* of the 1760s and 1770s into an elegant and adaptable style that did not neglect the possibilities of using other styles – Chinese, Turkish or Gothic – in the creation of fantasy interiors in which every detail contributed to the overall effect of the whole. His willingness to design for manufacturers gave a boost to the prestige of French taste and luxury goods abroad, and helped the propagation of the late Louis XVI style in other countries. It is possible to see in his work both the seeds of the severe Empire style of Percier and Fontaine, with its emphasis on austere decoration based on Roman military emblems, and the fantastic lattice work and Chinoiserie of the Brighton Pavilion in England, the whole prefiguring the stylistic diversity of the 19th century.

HOWARD COUTTS

See also Bélanger; Etruscan Style

Biography

Born in Versailles, 23 September 1749, only son of François Dugourc, controller in the household of the Duc d'Orléans. Travelled to Rome c.1765 where he met J.J. Winckelmann; returned to Paris and studied under the engraver Saint-Aubin c.1766. Married Marie-Anne-Adélaide, sister of the architect François-Joseph Belanger (1744–1818) in 1776 (died 1785). First decorative commissions, 1777; designed furniture for leading cabinet-makers from late 1770s. Appointed designer to the Comte de Provence, 1780; worked with the Lyon silk manufacturer, Camille Pernon, 1781–90; appointed designer to the Garde-Meuble de la Couronne, 1784; opened a wallpaper factory with Etienne-Alexandre Jacques Anisson-Duperon, c.1790. Provided designs for Catherine the Great and the Russian court from 1784; and for the Spanish court from 1786; worked in Madrid for Charles IV from 1800; returned to France c.1813; appointed official designer of public ceremonies, 1814; regained former title, designer to the Garde-Meuble de la Couronne, 1816. Petitioned Louis XVIII for a pension, 1823. Died in Paris, 30 April 1825.

Selected Works

Important collections of Dugourc's designs for interiors, furniture and textiles are in the Musée des Arts Décoratifs, Paris, and in the Musée des Arts Décoratifs, Lyon. Both museums also hold examples of Dugourc's furniture and textiles.

Interiors

1777	Hôtel de Bagatelle, Bois de Boulogne, Paris (part of the wall decoration; building and interiors by F.-J. Bélanger): Charles Philippe, Comte d'Artois
c.1777	Hôtel de Mazarin, Paris (Chinoiserie decoration): Duchesse de Mazarin
1780	Château de Brunoy (interiors including the theatre and vestibule): Comte de Provence
1785	Château de Compiègne, near Paris (decoration of a bathroom and some furniture for the Royal Apartments): Louis XVI
1786	Escorial, Madrid (designs for an Etruscan Gallery, Egyptian, Chinese and Turkish rooms): Charles IV

1786 Prado, Madrid (designs for a French cabinet, Gothic and Turkish rooms): Charles IV
1790 Apartment for the Duke and Duchess of Alba, Madrid (designs for interiors)
1799 Casita del Labrador, Aranjuez (interior and furnishings)
1818–24 Throne Room, Tuileries (interior decoration and furnishings): Louis XVIII

Publications

Mémoires, 2 vols., 1800

Further Reading

A detailed account of Dugourc's work including his designs for interiors appears in Arizzoli-Clementel and Baulez 1991 which includes a reprinting of Montaiglon's *Autobiographie* and numerous references to primary and secondary sources.

Un Âge d'Or des Arts Décoratifs, 1814–1848 (exhib. cat.), Paris: Grand Palais, 1991

Arizzoli-Clémentel, Pierre and Christian Baulez, "De Dugourc à Pernon: Nouvelles Acquisitions Graphiques pour les Musées" in *Les Dossiers du Musée des Tissus* (Lyon), 3, December 1990–March 1991

Brière, G., "Dessins du Dugourc au Musée de Versailles" in *Bulletin de la Société de l'Histoire de l'Art Français*, 1909, pp.213–20

Brière, G., "Notes Complémentaires sur J.D. Dugourc" in *Bulletin de la Société de l'Histoire de l'Art Français*, 1910, pp.313–19

Duret-Robert, François, "L'un des Créateurs du Néo-Classicisme: Jean-Désmosthène Dugourc" in *Connaissance des Arts*, May 1989, pp.98–95

Gastinet-Coural, Chantal, "À Propos du Palais D'Albe" in *L'Objet d'Art*, 242, December 1990, pp.65–95

Gastinet-Coural, Chantal, "Le Décor Textile de la Salle du Trône" in *Les Dossiers du Musée des Tissus* (Lyon), 1, October 1987–January 1988

Hartmann, Simone, "Les Dessins de Jean-Démosthène Dugourc dans la Collection Tassinari et Chatel à Lyon" in *Travaux de l'Institut d'Histoire de l'Art de Lyon*, cahier no. 4, 1978, pp.63–66

Hartmann, Simone, "L'Ornemaniste Jean (Démosthène) Dugourc: Précurseur de l'Empire" in *L'Estampille*, June 1978 (9), pp.30–35

Hartmann, Simone, "Fabriques et Jardins Dessinés par Jean-Désmosthène Dugourc dans la Collection Tassinari et Chatel à Lyon" in *Bulletin de la Société de l'Histoire de l'Art Français*, 1980, pp.211–18

Junquera, Juan José, *La Decoratión y el Mobiliario de los Palacios de Carlos IV*, Madrid, 1979

Montaiglon, Anatole de, *Autobiographie de Dugourc*, Paris, 1877

Sancho, José Luis, "Proyectos de Dugourc para Decoraciones Arquitec Tonicas en las Casitas de el Pardo y el Escorial" in *Reales Sitios*, 101–02, 1989, pp.21–36

Trevise, Duc de, "La Réapparation de Dugourc" in *La Renaissance de l'Art*, 1925, pp.75–84

Vallespin, Isabel Morales, "Proyectos Arquitectonico de Dugourc para el Futuro Carlos IV" in *Reales Sitios*, 100, 1989, pp.73–76

Dummy Boards and Chimney Boards

Dummy boards are essentially life-size character representations, that were painted onto wooden cut-outs which were designed to be self-supporting. The cut-out dummy board figures appear to be descended from the traditions of *trompe-l'oeil* and illusionistic painting. They are part of a tradition of representation that showed reality as an illusion. In addition, they provided images of self-representation and were apparently very amusing.

Dummy boards appear to have their origins in early 17th century Holland where artists such as Gysbrechts, van Hoogstraten, and Bisschop produced lifelike cut-outs of everyday objects which were intended to amuse. They could be seen to have derived from the shadowy figures that are sometimes found in the background of Dutch paintings of interiors.

Originally the work of professional painters, by the mid 18th century they were popular enough to sustain the livelihood of many a sign painter. One such painter, John Potts of London, had a trade card with a representation of Queen Elizabeth I, complete with an inscription offering dummy boards for halls, stairways, and chimneys.

The mention of chimney boards gives a clue to some of the uses that dummy boards have been put to within an interior setting. Indeed the painted chimney board designed to fill the

Dummy Board figure, English, c.1690

fireplace during the summer months is a very close relative of the dummy board. While this seems an eminently practical purpose, the use of dummy boards in halls and stairways is more ambiguous and many fanciful reasons have been put forward for their use. Possible explanations for the dummy board have included their use as aunt sallys and fairground targets; to provide an image of a security guard in an empty house; to act as door stops; to double as firescreens, and to act as silent companions. There may be a grain of truth in many of these suggestions.

Although there are many different types of dummy boards, they can be classified under several headings to help explain their use. The first group are single figures. These were generally of full-size women, children or men. The dress and accompanying accessories often indicate status. A maid might have a broom or kettle, while a child might be holding a toy. Wealthy images were depicted by their dress or fashionable accessories. The use of single figures was explained by the Dutch painter Houbraken. He said the idea of a dummy board was so that a silent companion would be a presence in an empty space. Houbraken intended them to be placed in a corner of a room or at the end of a vestibule so that they appeared to greet someone, just as a living person might.

The second group could be called "sweeping maids". Interestingly, although they often seem to represent a maid, upon closer examination they can be found to be a lady in sumptuous clothes underneath a servant's apron. An early example from the inventory of Cobham Hall (1672) lists such an item as "piece of ye Dutchesse of Richmond at length cut out". Some of the most attractive examples are designed as pairs. These were often of children, usually a boy and a girl, which are sometimes oddly displayed standing in front of a fire grate.

The third group are soldiers dressed in full uniform. It is likely that they were used for recruiting purposes, but examples have been used in domestic interiors. It is recorded that a dummy English grenadier provided much amusement in 18th-century Philadelphia by frightening visitors in a particular home.

The fourth group are low-life characters produced in the latter half of the 18th century for use in public pleasure gardens, and for outdoor entertainment. Similar examples of animals were also used in private gardens, again for providing amusement.

From these descriptions it can be seen that dummy boards provided examples of indoor entertainment as well as exemplifying a continuing fascination with questions of illusion and reality, and materialism. In terms of interiors, they were clearly a successful component, as not only were they valued in the 17th and 18th centuries, but were revived in the mid 19th century, and again in the 1920s and 1930s. Even in the contemporary interior, their decorative value has been acknowledged.

Not to be confused with dummy boards, but often seen as similar, are painted chimney boards. Used from the mid-17th century, these were fitted panels that would fill the fireplace void during summer months when the fire was not in use. They not only improved the appearance of the fireplace, but also acted as protection against falling soot and draughts. Either made from boards or panels in a similar way to dummy boards, or painted on stretched canvas like pictures, they were ideally suited for painted decorative treatments. Some often featured simple motifs of objects, such as flowers and plants, while others might be painted to match the decor of the room. Yet others represented an animal, a child, an oriental, or a pastoral scene.

Examples are not uncommon in America, but in England there are relatively few survivors. In Osterley Park House chimney boards exist for the fireplaces in the Taffeta bedroom and the Etruscan room, both being decorated en suite. At Audley End House, the Adam rooms also have chimney boards which clearly form part of the original decoration of the rooms.

In France, the chimney board was known as a *devant de cheminée*. Famous painters have produced such fine examples that they have sometimes been framed and presented as easel paintings rather than the chimney board they started life as: Chardin's *The White Table-Cloth*, Oudry's *Dog with a Porcelain Bowl*, and Tessier's *White Porcelain Bucket* are fine examples of the genre of illusionistic painting applied to the chimney board.

CLIVE D. EDWARDS

Further Reading

A useful introduction to Dummy Boards and Chimney Boards is Graham 1988 which also includes a short bibliography and a list of important collections in Great Britain.

Ayres, James, *The Art of the People in America and Britain* (exhib. cat.), Manchester: Cornerhouse, 1985

Conway, Michael, "Dummy Board Figures" in L.G.G. Ramsey (editor), *The Concise Encyclopedia of Antiques*, vol.5, New York: Hawthorn, 1961

Cuming, H. Syer, "On Picture Board Dummies" in *Journal of the British Archaeological Association*, vol.30, 1874, pp.66–71, 325–27

Edwards, Ralph, "Dummy-board Figures: An Early Reference" in *Country Life*, 6 November 1926

Fletcher-Little, Nina, "Pictures on the Hearth: Painted Fireboards in American Homes" in *Country Life*, 4 January 1973

Gilbert, Christopher and Anthony Wells-Cole, *The Fashionable Fireplace, 1660–1840* (exhib. cat.) Leeds: Temple Newsam House, 1985

Graham, Clare, *Dummy Boards and Chimney Boards*, Aylesbury: Shire 1988

Jourdain, Margaret, "Dummy Board Figures" in *Country Life*, 4 December 1926

MacQuoid, Percy and Ralph Edwards, *The Dictionary of English Furniture*, revised edition, 3 vols., 1954; reprinted Woodbridge, Suffolk: Antique Collectors' Club, 1983

Perry, Edward, "Figures for the Fireplace" in *Country Life*, 3 October 1957

Scott, Amoret and Christopher, *Dummy Board Figures*, Cambridge: Golden Head Press, 1966

Silent Companions: Dummy Board Figures of the 17th through 19th Centuries (exhib. cat.), Rye, Sussex: Historical Society, 1981

E

Eames, Charles 1907–1978

American architect and designer

Architect and designer Charles Eames and artist Ray Kaiser teamed up together at Eliel Saarinen's Cranbrook Academy in Michigan in 1940, where Ray had come to study weaving and where Charles had been appointed head of the Department of Industrial Design. They were married the following year, the start of a unique creative collaboration which would continue until Charles's death in 1978. While each had their own areas of expertise – Ray in the fields of painting, sculpture, graphics and textile design; Charles in the fields of architecture, three-dimensional design and technology – the fruits of their partnership, which included films, exhibition design and toys, as well as furniture, architecture and interior design, were the direct result of the creative energy which arose from their personal and professional relationship.

Charles Eames came to prominence in 1940 after winning first prize with Eero Saarinen in the Museum of Modern Art's "Organic Designs in Home Furnishings" competition. This led to further experiments with moulded plywood, which the Eameses realised had tremendous potential for embodying organic, sculptural, curvilinear forms. War-related work designing plywood splints, litters and gliders led directly to the design of plywood furniture after the war, produced initially by the Molded Pywood Division of Evans Products Company in Venice, California, from 1945–46, but subsequently manufactured from 1947 onwards by the Herman Miller Furniture Company of Zeeland, Michigan. The Eameses' plywood chairs were revolutionary technically, aesthetically and ergonomically, and they rapidly became icons of modern American post-war design. The chairs were produced in two different heights – a dining chair and a low lounge chair – and with two alternative frames, either plywood or tubular steel, hence the codes. Brought to public notice as a result of an exhibition called "New Furniture by Charles Eames" held at the Museum of Modern Art (MOMA) in 1946, the chairs were greeted with enthusiasm by Contemporary architects such as Richard Neutra because, with their lightweight frames and sculptural forms, they perfectly complemented the new open-plan domestic interiors of the day. Quality of manufacture and attention to detail were hallmarks of Eames's designs for Herman Miller, and the plywood series was distinguished by its attractive and sometimes exotic veneers, which added colour and pattern to sculptural form. The chairs were followed in 1946 by a wavy plywood folding screen, and by a series of circular, rectangular and square tables, the latter with folding metal legs, all distinguished by the way in which they successfully united functionalism with expressive shapes.

In 1948 Charles Eames entered another MOMA-sponsored event, the International Competition for Low-Cost Furniture, and it was this which led to the development of his moulded plastic shell chair, produced from 1950 onwards. The chair was originally conceived as being manufactured from stamped metal components, but when this material and method of production proved impractical, the designer teamed up with Zenith Plastics. This resulted in the development of a lightweight moulded fibreglass and polyester shell which sat on either tubular steel legs or sculptural steel rod understructure, available in a variety of combinations, including a rocking chair version. The plastic shell had integral colouring and was produced in a variety of shades; it could also be padded and upholstered. Both armchair and and sidechair versions were produced, the resulting series being extremely versatile, suitable for both domestic and commercial interiors, as well as public buildings such as schools.

The plastic chair was followed shortly afterwards in 1951 by the wire mesh chair, not dissimilar in its aesthetic to Harry Bertoia's wire *Diamond* chair for Knoll, Herman Miller's main competitor in the field of Contemporary furniture. The wire mesh chair was produced with the same range of bases as the plastic chair, including the wire structure known as the *Eiffel Tower*. Its sculptural origins were clearly expressed through its form and its open wire mesh structure. Like Eames's earlier designs, the wire chair was not only practical but highly photogenic, particularly when photographed en masse in arrangements and groupings which emphasised its status as a work of art as well as a piece of furniture. As the Eameses themselves were responsible for overseeing the firm's publicity photographs, for the graphic design of their advertisements and even for the design of the company's showrooms, this meant that they exerted a large degree of control over the identity with which their products were associated. When a customer bought an Eames chair for their office or home, they were buying an image as well as an object. Although by comparison with some of the more mannered and exaggerated Contemporary furniture on the market during the 1950s,

Eames: interior of Case Study House no. 8, 1940s

the Eameses' designs were relatively understated, they made a signficant visual contribution to the interiors in which they were used, and they were widely employed by other architects.

The influence of the Eameses on interior design is not limited to furniture, however. In 1945 they had been asked by John Entenza, editor of the influential Los Angeles-based *Arts and Architecture* magazine, to contribute a design to the Case Study House programme that the magazine was promoting after the war. Ray Eames designed many of the covers for *Arts and Architecture* during the late 1940s, and the magazine itself served as a vehicle for the progressive ideas of the Eameses and their circle. In addition to working with Ray on the design of their own house (Case Study House no.8), Charles Eames also collaborated with Eero Saarinen on the design of a house for John Entenza (Case Study House no.9). The Eames house, completed in 1949, was and still is hugely influential, both as a piece of architecture and as a personal statement by the Eameses about their outlook on life. It is a steel framed structure built on a modular grid system using mass-produced off-the-peg industrial components. The steel structure, which includes some diagonal cross-bracing, is left exposed on both the interior and the exterior, and is clad with a mixture of glass and cemesto panels. The exterior is black and white with blocks of bright pure primary colours in red, yellow and blue. Interior walls juxtapose tongue and groove wooden cladding with large flat veneered plywood panels, and areas of painted plaster, the steel joists and decking of the roof being left exposed on the ceiling. In some ways, therefore, the house was an early example of high-tech, although the way in which the interior was decorated and furnished was highly idiosyncratic and represented a unique expression of the Eameses' personalities and interests.

Ray's abstract paintings were suspended from the walls and the ceiling of the dramatic double height living room; vinyl tiles were laid on the floor, on top of which were placed Japanese *tatami* mats and wool and animal skin rugs; Charles's furniture was also dotted around. However, the main impact within the interior was the eclectic collection of multi-cultural artefacts and found objects, both natural and man-made, carefully arranged throughout the house. These gave the house an exuberant and celebratory atmosphere, and set the interior ablaze with pattern and colour. The Eames house was recorded by the couple themselves in their fascinating short film, *House: After Five Years of Living*, made in 1955. The film, which is composed of a kaleidoscope of still images of views and close-ups compiled from hundreds of 35mm slides, is accompanied by music by Elmer Bernstein. There is no commentary; the slides follow the sequence and the rhythm of the music, the effect being highly poetic. It was through this film that the creativity of the Eameses in its fullest sense reached a wider audience, and in particular their unique way of combining art, architecture, design and film.

Charles Eames's partnership with Herman Miller continued for many years, so that over time the name of the company became almost synonymous with that of its leading designer. His later designs included the luxurious *Lounge Chair* and *Ottoman* of 1956, with its plywood rosewood veneered frame and cushioned leather upholstery; and the *Aluminium Group* of 1958, a series of chairs with cast aluminium frames across which specially designed plastic cloth was stretched. In addition to chairs, Eames also designed storage furniture, including a flexible, modular, knock-down storage system called the *Eames Storage Units* (ESU), produced from 1950. This highly functional steel angle-framed system had an industrial aesthetic, and was equally suitable for the office and the home. A choice of decorative plastic-coated panels (available in black, white and primary colours) and veneered or dimpled plywood panels could be installed, the varied visual effects of which gave the units a cheerful appearance. Within this basic framework, cupboards, drawers and shelves could be inserted in a variety of configurations and, as on the Eames house, exposed cross-bracing was used as part of the structure and as well as an element of the decoration. As with so many of the Eameses' designs, ideas derived from this system were widely adopted by other manufacturers during the ensuing decades, so their influence on the post-war interior was both direct and indirect.

LESLEY JACKSON

See also "Contemporary" Style; Herman Miller Inc.

Biography

Charles Ormond Eames, Jr. Born in St. Louis, Missouri, 17 June 1907. Awarded an architectural scholarship, Washington University, St. Louis, 1925–28. Married 1) Catherine Davey Woermann, 1929 (divorced 1941): one daughter; 2) Ray Bernice Alexandra Kaiser, 1941. Visited Europe and saw the work of Modernist architects Mies van der Rohe, Walter Gropius, Le Corbusier and Henry van der Velde, 1929. Active as an architect, in partnership with Charles M. Gray and Walter E. Pauley, St. Louis, 1930–34. Travelled and worked in Mexico, 1934–35. Returned to St. Louis, and resumed architectural practice in partnership with Robert T. Walsh, 1935–36. Designed furniture and architectural fittings from mid 1930s. Awarded fellowship in architecture and design, Cranbrook Academy of Art, Bloomfield Hills, Michigan, 1938; instructor in design, 1939; head of Department of Industrial Design, 1940. Moved to Los Angeles, and established architectural and design practice in partnership with his wife, Ray, 1942–45; practice moved to Venice, California, 1945–78. Formed Molded Plywood Division of Evans Products Company, Los Angeles, 1944; employed as consulting designer by the furniture manufacturers, Herman Miller Inc., Los Angeles, from 1947. Active in exhibition design from 1949; involved in film-making from 1950. Lecturer, California Institute of Technology, Pasadena, 1953–56; Charles Eliot Norton Professor of Poetry, Harvard University, Cambridge, Massachusetts, 1970. Received numerous prizes and honours including Gold Medal, American Institute of Architects, 1957, Elsie de Wolfe Award, with Ray Eames, American Society of Interior Designers, 1975, and Gold Medal, Royal Institute of British Architects, 1979. Fellow, Royal College of Arts, London, 1960; Member, American Academy of Arts and Sciences. Died in St. Louis, 21 August 1978.

Selected Works

The Eames Archive, containing an extensive collection of letters, drawings, photographs and films, is in the Library of Congress, Washington, DC. Notable holdings of Eames's furniture are in the Museum of Modern Art, New York, and the Philadelphia Museum of Art, Philadelphia.

Interiors

1936 Meyer House, Huntleigh Village, Missouri (building, interiors and furniture; with Robert T. Walsh): John Philip and Alice Meyer

1945–49 Eames House and Studio, 203 Chautauqua, Pacific Palisades, California (building, interiors and furniture; with Eero Saarinen)
1945–49 John Entenza House, 205 Chautauqua, Pacific Palisades, California (building, interiors and furniture; with Eero Saarinen)
1947–49 Herman Miller Showroom, 8806 Beverly Boulevard, Los Angeles (building and interiors)
1949 *An Exhibition for Modern Living*, Detroit Institute of Arts (office room display)
1950 *Good Design Show*, Museum of Modern Art, New York (exhibition design and installation)
1950 Billy Wilder House, Beverly Hills, California (unexecuted project for building and interiors)
1952 Philip Dunne Office, Twentieth Century-Fox Studios, California (interiors and furniture)
1960 Time-Life Building, Rockefeller Center, New York (lobby interiors and furniture)
1961 *Mathematica* exhibition, for IBM, California Museum of Science and Industry, Los Angeles (exhibition layout and installation)
1964 IBM Exhibit, World's Fair, New York (pavilion and exhibition design)
1965 *Nehru: His Life and His India*, Ahmedabad, India; New York; London; Washington, DC; and Los Angeles (exhibition layout with Alexander Girard)
1975 *The World of Franklin and Jefferson*, American Revolution Bicentennial Touring Exhibition, Paris, Warsaw, London, New York, Chicago and Los Angeles (exhibition layouts and installation)

The Eames office produced numerous designs for furniture including Molded Plywood furniture, 1945–46, Eames Storage Units, 1950, Wire Chairs, 1951, Stacking Fiberglass Chair, 1955, Lounge Chair and Ottoman, 1956, Aluminium Group furniture, 1958, Time-Life Chair, 1960, Tandem Sling Seating, 1962, and Soft Pad Chair, 1969. All Eames furniture was produced and distributed through Herman Miller Inc. from 1946.

Publications

"Design Today" in *Arts and Architecture*, September 1941
"Organic Design" in *Arts and Architecture*, December 1941
"General Motors Revisited" in *Architectural Forum*, June 1971

Further Reading

A detailed and well-illustrated, authorized account of the work of Charles and Ray Eames and their design practice, including a chronological study of the main projects and design for graphics, film and exhibitions as well as interiors and furniture, appears in Neuhart 1989. For a recent study focusing on the firm's furnishings see Kirkham 1995; a monograph on the Eames house appears in Neuhart 1994.

Baroni, Daniele, "Charles Eames and the Methodology of Design" in *Ottagono*, June 1981, pp.8–85
Caplan, Ralph, *The Design of Herman Miller*, New York: Whitney Library of Design, 1976
Caplan, Ralph and Philip Morrison, *Connections: The Work of Charles and Ray Eames*, Los Angeles: Wight Art Gallery, 1976
Clark, Robert Judson (editor), *Design in America: The Cranbrook Vision, 1925–1950* (exhib. cat.), New York: Abrams, 1983
Drexler, Arthur, *Charles Eames Furniture from the Design Collection*, New York: Museum of Modern Art, 1973
Hiesinger, Kathryn B. and George H. Marcus III (editors), *Design since 1945* (exhib. cat.), Philadelphia: Philadelphia Museum of Art, and London: Thames and Hudson, 1983
Jackson, Lesley, *"Contemporary": Architecture and Interiors of the 1950s*, London: Phaidon, 1994
Jackson, Neil, "Metal-Frame Houses of the Modern Movement in Los Angeles" in *Architectural History*, 32, 1989, pp.152–72
Kirkham, Pat, *Charles and Ray Eames: Designers of the Twentieth Century*, Cambridge: Massachusetts Institute of Technology Press, 1995
McCoy, Esther, *Case Study Houses 1945–1962*, 2nd edition Los Angeles: Hennessey and Ingalls, 1977
Modern Chairs, 1918–1970 (exhib. cat.: Whitechapel Gallery, London), London: Lund Humphries, and Boston: Boston Book and Art, 1971
Neuhart, John and Marilyn, and Ray Eames, *Eames Design: The Work of the Office of Charles and Ray Eames*, New York: Abrams, and London: Thames and Hudson, 1989
Neuhart, John and Marilyn, *Eames House*, Berlin: Ernst, 1994
Noyes, Elliot, "Charles Eames" in *Arts and Architecture*, 63, September 1946, pp.26–44
Spaeth, David A., *Charles Eames Bibliography*, Monticello, IL: Vance, 1979
Steele, James, *Eames House: Charles and Ray Eames*, London: Phaidon, 1994

Eastlake, Charles Locke 1836–1906

British design theorist and architectural historian

Although he trained as an architect, Charles Locke Eastlake never actually executed any buildings and his chief claim to fame was as a theorist and author. His *History of the Gothic Revival*, published in 1877, still remains an important treatise in the study of Gothic architecture, while his earlier publication, *Hints on Household Taste* (1868), was arguably the most significant of many contemporary books on decoration and design. A combination of philosophical and practical advice, this book set stylistic standards in the production and consumption of domestic furnishings and was hugely influential on both sides of the Atlantic. Indeed, it was so popular in the United States that, by 1886, it had been reprinted seven times.

Hints on Household Taste represented an expanded version of articles previously published in the early 1860s in the British journals *Cornhill* and *Queen*. In it Eastlake attempted to lay the foundation for an understanding of good design that would establish criteria for discrimination and taste. "If I am thus enabled," he wrote in the introduction, "even indirectly, to encourage a discrimination between good and bad design in those articles of daily use which we are accustomed to see around us, my object will be attained". And by this exercise of taste the "recent degradation" that he perceived in English manufacture could be halted and reversed.

Eastlake's approach to the design and style of furniture and interiors was clearly much influenced not only by the writings of mid-century Gothic Revivalists such as A.W.N. Pugin and John Ruskin, but also by those of a second generation of designers and critics including Bruce Talbert, G.E. Street and Owen Jones, all of whom argued for honesty of construction and propriety of ornament in the design of furnishings. Building on these ideas, Eastlake codified the basic tenets of "good design" as simple, functional forms, honesty in construction, and ornamentation that is subordinate to the object. His belief in the fitness of form to function was reflected in his view that "To fulfill the first and most essential principles of good design, every article of furniture should, at first glance, proclaim its real purpose", while his emphasis upon simplicity arose from a belief that "The best and most picturesque furniture of all ages has been simple in general form ... Its main outlay was always chaste and sober in design, never running into extravagant contour or unnecessary curves". Ornament was not completely disavowed, but he contended that it should be appropriate to both the form of the object that it decorated and the material out of which it was made and so indicate "by its general character the material that it enhances". Nevertheless, he did not recommend a slavish following of these theories but advocated some flexibility, if necessary, in order to achieve a pleasing design, declaring that "a little alteration in the details gives a picturesque character to such articles of furniture".

Eastlake designed only a few pieces of furniture himself which were made up for him by the London cabinet-makers Jackson and Graham. Much of this work was sturdy and rectangular in shape and loosely derived from medieval prototypes. Decoration was generally limited and was confined to details such as incised lines, geometric patterns, shallow carving and functional yet decorative metalwork accessories such as Neo-Gothic strap hinges. In comparison with the high finish and complex carving found on most commercial cabinet-makers' work, Eastlake's designs appeared remarkably severe and a particularly robust-looking cabinet was likened to a rabbit-hutch by a caricaturist in the satirical magazine *Punch*. Nevertheless, the Eastlake style was widely imitated by many more progressive firms, and several American manufacturers, notably Herter Brothers and Kimbel and Cabus from New York, and Daniel Pabst of Philadelphia, were influenced by his work.

Eastlake's line drawings of furniture in the first editions of *Hints* clearly favour the Modern Gothic style derived from the work of architect-designers such as G.E. Street, Norman Shaw, and J.P. Seddon and subsequently popularised in Bruce Talbert's *Gothic Forms Applied to Furniture* (1868). In later editions, Eastlake substituted other styles such as Elizabethan and Anglo-Japanese, explaining that "artistic taste in the 19th century [is based] upon eclecticism rather than one tradition". Thus, although he admired the integrity of medieval furniture, he believed his theories could be applied to any kind of furniture and his philosophy of design emphasised a generic canon that could be used to conceive a number of fashionable styles.

Although he argued for the unification of the arts and crafts, unlike many reformers Eastlake did not totally eschew the use of machines but he did "deplore ... the misapplication of machine technology to create a surfeit of tasteless ornamentation" (Madigan). Nevertheless, the rectilinear outlines and incised decoration that were seen as characteristic of his designs were easily married to machine technology, and furniture factories, especially in the midwestern United States, were quick to adopt Eastlakean forms and to advance them using the author's name. Indeed, the word "Eastlake" became so closely coupled with mass-produced – and often inferior – furniture that Eastlake felt himself compelled to discredit this association, declaring in the fourth edition of *Hints*, "I find American tradesmen continually advertising what they are pleased to call 'Eastlake' furniture, with the production of which I have had nothing to do, and for the taste of which I should be very sorry to be considered responsible".

Much of *Hints on Household Taste* is taken up with the discussion of contemporary furniture, but the book was also a practical treatise that addressed home decoration in general. "There is no reason", Eastlake wrote, "why true principles of design should not be found in the humblest objects of household use" and to help his readers achieve this, he advised on every element of the interior, ranging from the choice of furnishings appropriate to particular rooms to specific items such as tableware, ornaments, picture frames, ceramics, metalwork and upholstery. He also praised the work of particular firms, recommending encaustic tiles by Maw & Co., furniture by his own cabinet-makers Jackson and Graham, and the wallpapers by Jeffrey & Co., and he was one of the first to publicise the merits of wallpapers by the decorators Morris, Marshall, Faulkner & Co. His views on pattern were especially influential. He emphasised the importance of flat patterns for two-dimensional surfaces such as walls and floors, advocating simple, unshaded designs containing conventionalized flowers and foliage that would "neither belie their flatness nor solidity". His own wallpaper, *Solanum*, produced by Jeffrey & Co., adheres admirably to these precepts and contains a trailing fruit and foliage pattern that appears to be indebted to Morris's designs.

Addressed to an upper-middle class, non-specialist readership, *Hints on Household Taste* proved extremely popular in England and was reprinted three times before an American edition was available. Its impact in the United States was unprecedented. Acceptance of the Aesthetic Movement in America was materially inspired by the book, and its author was championed as a leading arbiter of artistic taste. A host of similar books on domestic decoration and furnishing followed in its wake and Eastlake's writing influenced many other authors, such as Clarence Cook, author of *The House Beautiful* (1878), and Harriet P. Spofford, author of *Art Decoration Applied to Furniture* (1877). The seminal nature of its significance was highlighted by Spofford who declared, "Not a young marrying couple who read English were to be found without *Hints on Household Taste* in their hands, and all its dicta were accepted as gospel truth".

ANNA T. D'AMBROSIO

See also Aesthetic Movement; Art Furnishings

Biography

Born in Plymouth, 11 March 1836, the nephew of the painter Sir Charles Lock Eastlake PRA (1793–1865). Articled to the architect Philip Hardwick; studied at the Royal Academy Schools and awarded Silver Medal for drawing, 1854. Married in 1856. Travelled extensively in Europe between 1856 and 1859. Exhibited architectural projects at the Royal Academy, London, 1855–56, but never practised formally as an architect; worked as administrator and journalist after this date. Appointed Assistant Secretary to the Royal Institute of British Architects, 1866; Secretary, 1871–78; Keeper of the National Gallery, London, 1878–98. Regular contributor of articles on decoration and design to the *Cornhill Magazine*, the *Queen*, and the *London Review* in the 1860s; published his most influential work, *Hints on Household Taste*, in 1868. Designed a small number of wallpapers, furnishings and interior fittings from the late 1860s. Fellow, Royal Institute of British Architects, 1869. Died 20 November 1906.

Selected Works

Eastlake's main impact was as an arbiter of taste but he designed a small amount of furniture for Jackson and Graham, and wallpapers for Woollams, and Jeffrey & Co., examples of which are in the Victoria and Albert Museum, London. Manuscript material relating to Eastlake is in the library of the Royal Institute of British Architects, London.

Publications

Hints on Household Taste, in Furniture, Upholstery and Other Details, 1868; 4th edition 1877; reprinted 1969
A History of the Gothic Revival, 1871; edited by J. Mordaunt Crook, 1970
Lectures on Decorative Art and Art-Workmanship, 1876
The Present Condition of Industrial Art, 1877

Eastlake's articles on furniture and decoration for the *Cornhill Magazine*, the *Queen*, and the *London Review* were recast and reissued in *Hints*, 1868.

Further Reading

For an overview of Eastlake's career see Crook 1970. More detailed information relating to his influence in America appears in Madigan 1973 and 1975. For a biography and detailed bibliography see Burke 1986.

Aslin, Elizabeth, *Nineteenth Century English Furniture*, London: Faber, and New York: Yoseloff, 1962
Burke, Doreen Bolger and others, *In Pursuit of Beauty: Americans and the Aesthetic Movement* (exhib. cat.: Metropolitan Museum, New York), New York: Rizzoli, 1986
Crook, J. Mordaunt, "Eastlake's Career" in *A History of the Gothic Revival*, reprinted, New York: Humanities Press, 1970, pp.18–29
Gloag, John, "Introduction" to *Hints on Household Taste*, reprinted, New York: Dover, 1969
Harmon, Robert B., *The Eastlake Style in American Architecture: A Brief Style Guide*, Monticello, IL: Vance, 1983
Lasdun, Susan, "Keeping One's House in Order: Victorian Magazines and Furnishing Taste" in *Country Life*, 160, 9 September 1976, pp.672–73
"The Late Charles Locke Eastlake" in *Royal Institute of British Architects Journal*, 14, 1906–07, p. 59
McClaugherty, Martha Crabill, "Household Art: Creating the Artistic Home, 1868–1893" in *Winterthur Portfolio*, 18, Spring 1983, pp.1–26
Madigan, Mary Jean Smith, *Eastlake-Influenced American Furniture, 1870–1890* (exhib. cat.), Yonkers, NY: Hudson River Museum, 1973
Madigan, Mary Jean Smith, "The Influence of Charles Locke Eastlake on American Furniture Manufacture, 1870–90" in *Winterthur Portfolio*, 10, 1975, pp.1–22
Madigan, Mary Jean (Smith), "Eastlake-Influenced American Furniture, 1870–1890" in *Connoisseur*, 191, January 1986
Pevsner, Nikolaus, "Art Furniture of the Eighteen-Seventies" in *Architectural Review*, January 1953, pp.43–50
Scherer, Barrymore Laurence, "The Gothicist: Shades of Charles Locke Eastlake" in *Connoisseur*, 213, July 1983, pp.74–79

Edinburgh Weavers

British textile manufacturers, 1929–1963

Edinburgh Weavers was established as an experimental subsidiary of Morton Sundour Fabrics in 1929. Although only based in Edinburgh for two years – the firm was subsequently based in Carlisle – the name was maintained as it remained synonymous with raised standards of design for household furnishings. Alastair Morton first became involved with the venture in 1932 and was soon its artistic director and chief designer. A painter and a convinced Modernist, he set out to apply modern thinking to textile design and interior design as a whole.

Coming from a family firm with a long-standing devotion to the manufacture of top quality materials, Morton envisaged that Edinburgh Weavers would provide furnishing fabrics to complement modern developments in architecture. Many traditional fabrics were completely unsuitable for modern interiors and nullified the carefully conceived schemes. Progressive architects were demanding fabrics that would enhance their stark interiors and the architectural press regularly carried articles which blamed uncaring manufacturers for failing to comprehend their needs. At this time a number of fine artists were also promoting the need for a greater unity between art and design; in particular they felt there could be a greater harmony between modern architecture and abstract art. They thought that by designing textiles that embodied the same visual values as Modern Movement architecture they would obviously be in keeping with modern interiors. Morton was aware of these developments and consequently always used the most interesting professional designers and fine artists: those who had devised a new aesthetic language appropriate for an increasingly industrialised society. By offering them an opportunity to engage with industry and work in a different medium he presented them with new forms of stimulus while he gained fresh design ideas.

The year 1937 was a crucial one for the firm. In October Morton launched a range of "Constructivist Fabrics" to an interested and intrigued London press. This range became the most outstanding achievement of Edinburgh Weavers' pre-war days and was a unique experiment in textile manufacturing. Morton's understanding of the most progressive art trends greatly influenced his work in textiles; in particular it conditioned his choice of artists to design for him. They would initiate visual ideas which he would develop into a fabric. Designs by Ben Nicholson, Barbara Hepworth, Ashley Havinden and others, were transformed into richly textured woven fabrics. These particular artists were chosen because their work embodied principles of modern design, showing the same rhythmic balance of pure forms. Some of the artists, notably Nicholson, felt the need to combine art with daily life; by offering artists the opportunity to design for mass-production Morton felt he was helping to satisfy that need. The fabrics designed by Ben Nicholson and Barbara Hepworth were considered to be way ahead of their time and were acclaimed as a breakthrough in textile design.

Nicholson's design *Vertical* was considered to be still worthy of production after World War II. Nicholson took infinite care in proportioning his designs, building them up in the same manner that he used to develop his paintings. He was meticulous when conceiving their tonal values and textural contrasts; possessing a clear conception of the way a textile differed from other visual forms, he could accurately visualise how the finished cloth would look in use. *Vertical* was a woven rayon and cotton damask and was produced in three separate colour versions and white on white. In varying tones of white the main body of the cloth contained sections that were bounded by contrasting weaves and textural yarns. The whole piece was vertically traversed by a widely spaced satin stripe of either red, blue, or green. At the time it was stated that the all white version epitomised that subtlety of contrast in the surface texture for which Edinburgh Weavers was acclaimed.

Morton had a thorough understanding of the weaving process, and it was his interest in the surface texture of the fabrics which gave Edinburgh Weavers its hallmark. He believed it was unnecessary for the commissioned artist to have any knowledge of cloth construction since this was the realm of the specialist weaver. When faced with an artist's design Morton would sometimes contemplate it for weeks before he felt ready to translate it into cloth. He had the ability to hand weave and combined the best of craftsmanship with the cost-effective benefits of the machine. When necessary he could spin the yarn by hand in order to gain the effect he sought, which might be three-dimensional or transparent. He often used hand-weaving as he felt it was a vital transitional stage in the evolution of an industrially produced textile. Morton's combined talents as a designer, painter, craftsman and manufacturer equipped him particularly well to translate the ideals of the Modern Movement into textile design. He insisted that handling the materials was a vital stage in production and certainly there was no rigid, mechanical appearance about these fabrics. Edinburgh Weavers produced numerous magnificent textiles that were machine made versions of Alastair's hand-weaving.

Like his father, James Morton, he believed there should be a truly modern style in furnishing fabrics, and by the end of 1937 Edinburgh Weavers had established an enviable reputation in this field. The *Constructivist* range was considered to have placed furnishing fabric onto the same level as painting and architecture. The firm also used top designers to produce a range of knotted carpets in avant-garde designs.

After the war years and following a lull in trade, a revival in the firm took place. This phase is characterised by a greater inventiveness and boldness of design. A wide variety of artists became interested in Morton's ability to translate the essence of their work into woven or printed patterns, whatever the medium of their original idea. Artists who collaborated with him included Elisabeth Frink, Hans Tisdall, Keith Vaughan, and Joe Tilson. The textiles of the 1950s show evidence of an increased awareness of the possibilities of colour: the result of more sophisticated dyeing techniques combined with striking developments in the fine arts of that period.

As a result of working with many distinguished artists, Morton had a very clear idea of how he thought things should be done. By 1939 Edinburgh Weavers was far ahead of any producer of contemporary fabrics in Britain. His range of exciting fabrics won him the greatest recognition both at home and abroad: he was elected a Royal Designer for Industry in 1960 and Edinburgh Weavers won major design awards both for their woven and printed textiles. In the 1960s the firm was taken over by Courtaulds.

BRENDA KING

Selected Works

Collections of textiles produced by Edinburgh Weavers are in the Scottish National Gallery of Modern Art, Edinburgh, the Victoria and Albert Museum, London, and the Whitworth Art Gallery, Manchester. Additional examples, artwork and archival material relating to the firm are in Courtauld's Textile Design Library, Courtauld's Textiles, London.

Further Reading

Alastair Morton and the Edinburgh Weavers: Abstract Art and Textile Design, 1935–46 (exhib. cat.), Edinburgh: Scottish National Gallery of Modern Art, 1978

Gleadell, Colin, "Abstraction, Art and Design" in *The V & A Album*, 1988, pp.47–52

King, Brenda, *Modern Art in Textile Design, 1930–1980* (exhib. cat.), Manchester: Whitworth Art Gallery, 1989

MacCarthy, Fiona and Patrick Nuttgens, *Eye for Industry: Royal Designers for Industry, 1936–1986* (exhib. cat.: Royal Society of Arts, London), London: Lund Humphries, 1986

Mendes, Valerie, *The Victoria and Albert Museum's Textile Collection: British Textiles from 1900 to 1937*, London: Victoria and Albert Museum, and New York: Canopy, 1992

Morton, Alastair and others, *The Practice of Design*, London: Lund Humphries, 1946

Morton, Jocelyn, *Three Generations in a Family Textile Firm*, London: Routledge, 1971

Thirties: British Art and Design Before the War (exhib. cat.), London: Arts Council of Great Britain, 1979

Egypt, ancient

Protected by water and sand, Ancient Egypt was little subject to outside influences; conservative, it recapitulated the basic patterns of its buildings, space planning, furnishings, and decoration through the millennia. Its building forms reiterated the past, even when new materials would have permitted a different expression.

Because forests were exhausted early in Egyptian history, pre-dynastic dwellings were built of vegetal materials: columns of lashed papyrus, roofs of palm leaves, walls hung with woven mats, the whole sometimes sealed with mud. The pressure of the mud-reinforced roofs probably produced an outward roll at the top of the thin reed walls, a concave quarter-circle that would later be recapitulated in stone as the characteristic "gorge" cornice known as a *cavetto* or bird's beak. By the time of the Old Kingdom, plant materials were largely replaced by sun-dried bricks, a material used for hovels and palaces alike. Strength was provided by limestone lintels. To prevent displacement from this load, walls were made thicker at the bottom than at the top, or "battered." This resulted in exterior walls which slanted outward from top to bottom, a shape which was also translated into stone construction. Vertical support was provided by lashed papyrus or by palm tree trunks tied together for greater strength, which produced the effect of vertical convex ribs, or "reeding." This, too, was often imitated in stone pillars, although it could be reversed (fluted) or even omitted if the column were to be enriched with carving or painting. In addition, papyrus flowers and buds were conventionalized as capitals, the first forming a bell-shaped or "campaniform" capital (which has also been interpreted as a cluster of palm branches), the second resembling a long and somewhat sagging cap. Both types are represented in the Hypostyle Hall of the Great Temple of Ammon, at Karnak in Thebes, built during the New Empire.

By the time of the New Empire, temples had become elaborate walled complexes that used site and scale to induce a feeling of reverence in worshippers. Plans varied, but in general the temple, with its façade of immense, slope-sided pylons, was approached from a broad axial walkway delineated by rows of columns or sphinxes. Behind the pylons was an open and colonnaded court which led to a hall dominated by immense, closely set columns. Chapels and ritual rooms were located to the rear of the rectangular or L-shaped structure. The areas within the temple were stepped down in height to provide clerestory lighting; skylights were also used. Columns and walls were generally decorated with bas-reliefs, incised carving, or brightly painted motifs outlined in black.

Residences were composed of interlocking or adjacent rectilinear spaces. In cities, where land was scarce, dwellings could be three storeys high. Country properties expanded horizontally behind protecting walls of mud-brick, a watchman's lodge set near the gates. Within these walls, the self-sufficient estate consisted of living quarters, service areas, a chapel, and gardens. Service areas, such as the kitchens, bakery, brewery, servants' quarters, and storage cellars, were to the rear of the house. Separate structures were provided for granaries, stables, cattlesheds, kennels, and workshops for carpentry and spinning. The main dwelling unit, zoned into public and private areas, was entered through an antechamber leading to a reception area, the ceiling of which was raised above adjacent rooms on painted columns to provide clerestory lighting on one or more sides. Window openings elsewhere were generally small and high, in order to limit the heat and glare of bright sun. The adobe walls were probably plastered and painted with colors derived from plant and mineral materials in hues that included earth tones (rust, henna, bone, dull gold, and brown), light and dark green, light and dark blue, soft purple, bright yellow, and pink. Decorative painting was applied to columns, and entryways accented with painting or carving. Except in public rooms, where mosaics might be laid, floors were likely to be of beaten earth, sometimes covered with mats woven of reeds or palm fiber. Private areas consisted of drawing rooms, bedrooms, and sanitary facilities that included toilets, shower rooms, and spaces for oiling and massage. Stairwells led to a roof-top loggia that provided additional space for work, relaxation, and sleeping.

Of the three types of tomb built for both royal and wealthy Egyptians, the earliest was the walled or underground *mastaba*, built to simulate a house plan, with a central area for the sarcophagus and smaller rooms for funerary offerings. Increasing concern for the security of the remains led to the development of pyramid and rock-hewn tombs, whose interior space planning was limited to an elaborate system of long, low corridors, the principal corridor leading to chambers for the caskets and funeral furniture. In all tombs, hieroglyphs and scenes of ritual and daily life executed in paint, incised carving, and bas-relief filled the walls and ceilings.

Free-standing furniture was uncommon, the floor or built-in platforms being used for most sitting and sleeping. Tomb furnishings and decorations tell us, however, that two types of stool had evolved by the beginning of the Old Kingdom (?2700–?2150 BC), one woven of papyrus (wicker construction), the other made of wood and given a low back. By the New Empire, stools with straight, simply turned legs were also seen. These were strengthened with stretchers and accented with struts set in a pattern that combined straight and angled pieces.

Folding stools were introduced in the Middle Kingdom. The frame was generally mortised, and the cane or rush seat was sometimes covered with a loose cushion that could be covered in woven cloth, rush, leather, or skins. Wooden seats that were "scooped" or "dipped" to imitate the shape of earlier, leather sling-seats appeared during the New Empire; their X-shaped frames were stabilized by low stretchers similar to sled runners, and carved to end in the form of animal legs and paws, or a duck's head. Surface decoration was usually painted, although inlay in ivory, ebony, and the pottery-like faience was also seen; patterns included frets, chevrons, and a range of highly stylized motifs derived from nature, such as papyrus and lotus flowers or leopard skin.

Armless chairs, and box-like armchairs, often with backs and arms of equal height, were common by the Middle Kingdom (?2040–?1670 BC). Variations in the seating heights of stools and chairs occurred in all periods, but this was especially true of the New Empire, when 9-inch high seats were popular. Royalty, however, sat on high-legged chairs, supporting their feet on footstools. Chairlegs were typically in the form of an animal's front and back limbs, particularly those of the lion and jackal; these were usually raised on pegs, perhaps so that they might appear to rest on (rather than disappear into) a floor mat. Such chairs often incorporated the same stretcher-and-strut designs used on straight-legged stools. Seats were usually flat but could be scooped like those of folding stools. Chairbacks were raked, the angle reinforced by vertical supports that ran from the rear of the seat to the back of the top rail; as construction techniques improved, some seatbacks were even given a slight concavity. Comfort was increased by thick pads, upholstered and made long enough to curl over both the top rail and front seat rail. Again, painted and inlaid decoration were used; and pieces intended for royalty could be gilded.

Beds were more likely to have a footboard than a headboard, and tended to slope downwards toward the floor. The sleeper's head was supported on a U-shaped wooden headrest attached to the frame. Legs could be simply turned or, like seating pieces, carved in the form of front and rear animal legs. Hinged beds made to fold in the middle had developed by the New Kingdom (?1570–?1080 BC) period, and indicate a more peripatetic lifestyle.

Round, oblong, or square tables were supported on three or four legs. Storage was provided by woven baskets; various sorts of chests, some on high legs, like tables; and by small, wooden caskets. Tops were lifted into place and secured with a leather thong wrapped around a large-headed peg.

Because it was difficult to obtain planks of lumber, craftsmen made wooden furniture by joining many small pieces of wood. Species ranged from the domestic acacia and sycamore-fig to the imported tamarisk, cedar, cypress, juniper, ebony, yew, and olive. Mortise-and-tenon joints might be protected with copper sheathing, as they were on the tomb furniture of Queen Hetephras, which is totally covered in gold leaf. These pieces, now in the Cairo Museum, included a bed, throne, and storage box, assembled under a collapsible canopy. Furnishings made of vegetal materials were woven or coiled. Decorative techniques included inlay, painting, gilding, carving, veneering, and turning.

Linen-making was practiced from predynastic times. Improved methods of spinning and weaving, including an upright loom, were introduced at the end of the Middle Kingdom, but even early linens have a weave so fine they can be mistaken for silk.

Egypt was rich in copper and gold, the latter naturally alloyed with varying amounts of silver and electrum, and its craftsmen showed considerable skill in making both decorative and utilitarian objects from these metals. Bronze was not introduced until the New Kingdom, and Egyptians made little use of iron. The New Kingdom developed the art of coloring gold in tones ranging from pink to crimson.

Hand-built pottery produced in predynastic times is sometimes thought superior to that made on the potter's wheel, a technique introduced at the beginning of the Old Kingdom. Egyptian ceramicists are perhaps best known for faience – a pottery-like substance made of crushed quartz that could be cast, carved, shaped, and fired. The first faiences were blue or green in color; white, yellow, violet, red, and black glazes were eventually developed. Highly sophisticated glassworking appears in the New Kingdom, when glass was cast to imitate semi-precious stones for inlay in jewelry and furniture. Even in predynastic times, vases were made of stone, and these became increasingly common after the introduction of the hand-cranked lathe known as a flintborer. Decorative stone vessels were produced from alabasters, porphyries, breccias, and diorites selected for their attractive formations; some were carved to imitate leaf forms.

Many motifs, particularly the geometrics, were either purely ornamental or, like the spiral – associated with Thoth (the ibis-headed god of truth) and symbolizing the breath and spirit – were so stylized that their symbolic content was subordinate to their decorative value. Among those that retained symbolic importance were animal forms associated with gods, such as the hawk-god Horus or Anubis the jackal; the ankh, which was a symbol of life; the aten, or sun-disk, sometimes depicted with rays ending in human hands; lotus and papyrus blossoms, which denoted Lower and Upper Egypt, respectively; and the winged globe, which was associated with Horus and served as a symbol of protection. Such motifs reflect the integration of the earthly and the eternal in Egyptian culture. Religion – particularly the belief in an afterlife that was a continuation of life on earth – was of primary importance to Egyptian art and architecture. The need to provide kings with resting places worthy of the gods they were assumed to be led to the design of the pyramids that characterise the period. The assumption that images had the power to bring about events caused both king and subject to fill burial chambers with favorite possessions, and render every surface with carved and painted images of activities they wished to occur in the hereafter.

Peculiar to the culture that evolved it, Egyptian design has not had the influence of that of Ancient Greece or Rome, but this does not mean that it has no legacy. Ghiberti, Mantegna, and Raphael are among the Renaissance artists who used Egyptian motifs; and it is an important, if minor, component in 19th- and 20th-century design.

In France, the revival was sparked by Napoleon's expedition to Egypt in 1798; and the sketches and artifacts brought back by the 160 scientists and artists who accompanied his armies inspired French designers. Under the supervision of Vivant Denon, the Sèvres porcelain manufactory made a table piece that represented various Egyptian temples connected by an avenue of ram-headed sphinxes. An accompanying sugar bowl, its handle ending in a head adorned with a *kaffiyeh* (head-dress), was glazed with individually authentic hieroglyphs rearranged for design effect. In England, thanks to Nelson's victory over the French navy in 1798, the revival was as much patriotic as exotic. A dining room set in Egyptian style made for Lord Sandwich by Gillow was only one of several such commemorations.

In most cases, the Egyptian gloss on Empire and Regency designs was carried by easily recognizable motifs grafted onto conventional furniture forms. Thomas Sheraton showed the pharaonic head on a lady's work table, a canopy bed, and curtain tiebacks in the *Cabinet Encyclopedia* (1804), but broke from the mould in a chair with finials in the shape of dromedary heads. Thomas Hope took what he believed to be a more archaeological approach in *Household Furniture and Interior Decoration* (1807), in which he illustrated Egyptian-style furnishings he had designed for his house on Duchess Street around 1800. George Smith (1783–1869) showed an armchair based on the Egyptian prototype of front and rear animal legs in *Household Furniture* (1808).

Although it faded rapidly in France, increasing Anglo-Egyptian trade and tourism kept the style alive in England. Among the British visitors to Egypt was Owen Jones, author of *The Grammar of Ornament* (1856), who found in the conventionalised Egyptian motifs an antidote to excessive decoration. Several Arts and Crafts designers accepted this view, carrying the trend into the first quarter of the 20th century. Around 1857, William Holman Hunt executed a chair with a scooped seat and angled struts based on an Egyptian stool in the British Museum, even repeating the struts in the chairback where structure became decoration. In 1884, the Liberty Furnishing and Decorating Studio followed Hunt's lead, producing both three- and four-legged stools (known as Thebes stools) patterned on the museum's Egyptian holdings. That collection also attracted E.W. Godwin, whose work adapted rather than replicated the ancient furniture forms. The discovery of the tomb of Tutankhamun in 1922 by Lord Carnarvon and Howard Carter sparked both a series of exuberant motion picture palaces in Art Deco America, and Bertram Goodhue's relatively restrained Los Angeles public library. Within a few years, however, such fantasies were superseded by the intellectualized approach of the Bauhaus émigrés; and even the 1967 Paris exhibition of Tutankhamun's treasures failed to excite another revival.

REED BENHAMOU

See also Egyptian Revival

Further Reading

Aldred, Cyril, *The Egyptians*, revised edition London and New York: Thames and Hudson, 1984

Aronson, Joseph, *The New Encyclopedia of Furniture*, New York: Crown, 1967

Baker, Hollis S., *Furniture in the Ancient World: Origins and Evolution, 3100–475 B.C.*, New York: Macmillan, and London: The Connoisseur, 1966

Birren, Faber, *Color for Interiors, Historical and Modern*, New York: Whitney Library of Design, 1963

Conner, Patrick (editor), *The Inspiration of Egypt: Its Influence on British Artists, Travellers and Designers, 1700–1900* (exhib. cat.), Brighton: Brighton Museum, 1983

Cottrell, Leonard, *The Lost Pharaohs: The Romance of Egyptian Archaeology*, revised edition London: Evans, 1961

Curl, James Stevens, *Egyptomania: The Egyptian Revival*, Manchester: Manchester University Press, 1994

Desroches-Noblecourt, Christiane, *Tutankhamen: The Life and Death of a Pharaoh*, New York: New York Graphic Society, and London: The Connoisseur, 1963

Durant, Will, *Our Oriental Heritage* (The Story of Civilization, vol.1), New York: Simon and Schuster, 1954

Killen, G., *Ancient Egyptian Furniture*, Warminster, Wiltshire: Aris and Phillips, 1980

Treasures of Tutankhamun (exhib. cat.), London: British Museum, 1972

Egyptian Revival

As one of the first exotic styles, along with the Gothic, to challenge the supremacy of Classical design, the Egyptian Revival reached its peak in interior design during the late 18th and early 19th centuries. While already existing in the later Roman Empire and re-emerging during the 1920s, partly inspired by the discovery of Tutankhamun's tomb, Egyptomania or *Egyptiennerie* achieved a particular popularity through the publications following Napoleon's campaign in Egypt in 1798. This event coincided with new tastes for monumental and richly ornamental forms associated with the literary and associational concerns of Romanticism. However, quite unlike its Greek and Roman equivalents, the Egyptian Revival never represented a coherent movement with ethical and social implications, and should be seen as one of those sporadic waves of European taste in design, often linked to archaeological enquiry. The study of Egyptian art and architecture, moreover, has continued to inspire a keen awareness of abstraction in design and of a decorative vocabulary of great sophistication right up to the present time.

Even before the Roman conquest of Egypt in 30 BC, the forms, rituals and architectural concepts of Egyptian civilization were being gradually absorbed into the classical world. Apart from the subsequent introduction of the mystery cults of Isis and Osiris, with their temple decoration, during the Empire, Hadrian may be regarded as one of the first Egyptian revivalists with the creation of the Canopus area of his villa at Tivoli, dating from around 130 AD. While certain motifs, such as obelisks and sphinxes recur frequently in funerary design during the Middle Ages, the Arab conquest of Egypt in 641 made access by Europeans difficult for many centuries. Apart from Bernardino Pintoricchio's esoteric fresco scheme featuring the bull Apis in the Borgia Apartments (1492 – 95), derived from Roman sources as well as Egyptian material in the growing Vatican collections, travel books on Egypt from the 16th century onwards began to provide fresh inspiration for artists and designers. Predictably, the more methodical archaeological activities of the 18th-century Enlightenment introduced a new seriousness in levels of information and interpretation, outstandingly represented by Frederick Norden's *Voyage de l' Egypte et de Nubie* (1755) and the *Recueil d'antiquités égyptiennes, étrusques, grecques, romaines et gauloises* (1752–67) of the highly erudite Comte de Caylus who first analysed the aesthetic features of Egyptian art as representing one of the cultural roots of European civilization with properties of grandeur, primitiveness, simplicity and massiveness.

The very first concerted attempt to create a fully integrated style of interior design according to Egyptian principles, supported by more radical theories of abstraction than those of de Caylus, was to occur within this intellectual context. During the early 1760s, the Venetian designer G.B. Piranesi produced a highly original painted interior in the Egyptian taste for the Caffè degli Inglesi in the Piazza di Spagna, Rome. In this work, long since vanished but recorded in two etched plates along with 11 fanciful chimneypiece designs in the same mode published in his testament of design, *Diverse maniere d'adornare i cammini* ... (1769), Piranesi used a variety of motifs derived from the Vatican collections and past publications. His justification for this style in the prefatory essay of the *Diverse maniere*, moreover, represented an exceptional understanding of Egyptian processes of abstraction from natural forms. While Piranesi's interior excited little enthusiasm at the time – the artist Thomas Jones described it in 1766 as "fitter to adorn the inside of an Egyptian sepulchre, than a room of social conversation" (quoted in B. Ford, editor, "The memoirs of Thomas Jones", *Walpole Society*, XXI, p.54) – within the next two decades tentative signs of a sophisticated stylistic revival are seen for the first time, mainly in the decorative and applied arts. Apart from A.R. Mengs's Camera dei Papiri in the Vatican (c.1770), Piranesi's etched Egyptian compositions in the *Diverse maniere* were used as an ornamental quarry for designers as diverse as François-Joseph Bélanger, Pierre Gouthière and Josiah Wedgwood.

By the 1790s Neo-Classical taste for a more severe and monumental expression can be seen in the Billiard Room of Cairness House, Grampian, Scotland (1793) by James Playfair with its stepped chimneypiece and battered doorcases. Also after visiting Rome in the mid-1780s, as well as Egypt itself in 1796, the British designer Thomas Hope was to produce the most accomplished interior of the entire revival with his *Egyptian or Black Room*, devised between 1779 and 1801 for his London house in Duchess Street (demolished 1850) and illustrated in a plate published in his *Household Furniture and Interior Decoration* of 1807. Apart from his ingenious furniture, some pieces of which survive in the Faringdon Collection at Buscot Park, Oxfordshire, Hope employed a particularly vigorous colour scheme involving "that pale yellow and that blueish green which hold so conspicuous a rank among the Egyptian pigments; here and there relieved by masses of black and gold" (*Household Furniture*, 1807).

By the time that Hope had published this exceptional interior, he was able to pay tribute to new and unparalelled sources of archaeological information; namely the lavish books based on the expedition made by a commission of scholars, scientists and surveyors on Napoleon's 1798 Nile campaign in *Description de l'Egypte* (20 vols., 1809–28) and Baron Vivant Denon's equally lavish *Voyage dans la basse et la haute Egypte* (1802). These works were to impel the revival as far as the third decade of the new century, as reflected initially in the

Egyptian Revival: Thomas Hope's Egyptian Room, Duchess Street, c. 1800 (from *Household Furniture and Interior Decoration*, 1807)

applied arts ranging from the suite of furniture made by F-H-G. Jacob-Desmalter to designs by Charles Percier for Denon himself in 1809 (published in Percier and Fontaine's *Recueil de décorations interieures*, Paris, 1801) to the ambitious *Service Egyptienne* in Sèvres of 1810–12, ordered by Napoleon (Apsley House, London). The closeness of these forms to the newly published finds is often in marked contrast to the imaginative licence shown by Piranesi, and even Hope. Moreover, the emerging Egyptian Revival taste proved to be as international a style as the Pompeian and Greek counterparts, represented in furniture designed by the Sienese Agostino Fantastici, and the British Charles Heathcote Tatham.

By the second decade of the 19th century, architects had begun to follow suit with designs for civic, commercial and engineering structures, but the Egyptian style had the most extensive application of all to funerary and cemetery buildings. Meanwhile interior designs in the taste were extensively applied to Masonic temples throughout the century on both sides of the Atlantic, a particularly late example being the Chapter Room in the Royal Arch Chapter of the Scottish Freemasons in Edinburgh, produced in 1900 by P.L.B. Henderson.

Earlier in the century the High Victorian phase of the revival found a place in the campaign for improved art education, exemplified by the Egyptian Court by Owen Jones and Joseph Bonomi in the Crystal Palace, rebuilt at Sydenham after the London Great Exhibition of 1851 (destroyed 1936). Egyptian motifs also fulfilled a major role in Owen Jones's magnificent *Grammar of Ornament* (1856) which repeated Piranesi's respect for the Egyptian genius in natural abstraction. Later on, Christopher Dresser was to draw attention to functional properties he discerned in Egyptian utensils and furniture in his *Principles of Decorative Design* (1873), as well as producing several chairs based on ancient prototypes.

During the 20th century the influence of basic Egyptian forms and patterns has continued to recur, transcending the more ephemeral impact on jewellery and costume of Howard Carter's sensational discovery of Tutankhamun's tomb at Thebes in 1922. Certain formal influences have affected interior design, as reflected in such outstanding Art Deco works as the foyer of Oliver P. Bernard's Strand Palace Hotel, London, of 1930 (destroyed 1967–68; parts now in the Victoria and Albert Museum, awaiting display), while the most persistent of all revivalist images, the pyramid form, has found its expression internally as well as externally in the work of the American architect I.M. Pei, notably in the controversial Louvre Extension of 1989.

JOHN WILTON-ELY

See also Percier and Fontaine

Further Reading

The most recent scholarly study of the Egyptian Revival appears in Curl 1994 which also includes a lengthy bibliography of primary and secondary sources. For additional information on the Egyptian Revival in France see *Egyptomania* 1994.

Bohdan, Carol L., "Egyptian-Inspired Furniture, 1800–1922" in *Art and Antiques*, 3, November–December 1980, pp.64–71

Carrott, Richard G., *The Egyptian Revival: Its Sources, Monuments and Meaning, 1808–1858*, Berkeley: University of California Press, 1978

Clayton, Peter A., *The Rediscovery of Egypt: Artists and Travellers in the Nineteenth Century*, London: Thames and Hudson, 1982

Conner, Patrick (editor), *The Inspiration of Ancient Egypt: Its Influence on British Artists, Travellers and Designers, 1700–1900* (exhib. cat.), Brighton: Brighton Museum, 1983

Curl, James Stevens, *The Egyptian Revival: An Introductory Study of a Recurring Theme in the History of Taste*, London: Allen and Unwin, 1982

Curl, James Stevens, *Egyptomania: The Egyptian Revival*, Manchester: Manchester University Press, 1994

Dresser, Christopher, *Principles of Decorative Design*, 1873; reprinted London: Academy, 1973

Egyptomania: L'Egypt dans l'Art Occidental, 1730–1930 (exhib. cat.), Paris: Musée du Louvre, 1994; as *Egyptomania: Egypt in Western Art, 1730–1930*, Ottawa: National Gallery of Canada, 1994

Harmon, Robert B., *The Egyptian Revival in American Architecture: A Brief Style Guide*, Monticello, IL: Vance, 1982

Honour, Hugh, "The Egyptian Taste" in *Connoisseur*, CXXXV, 1955, pp.242–46

Humbert, Jean-Marcel, *L'Egyptomanie dans l'art occidental*, Paris: ACR, 1989

Jones, Owen, *The Grammar of Ornament*, 1856; reprinted New York: Van Nostrand Reinhold, 1972, London: Studio, 1986

Morley, John, *Regency Design, 1790–1840: Gardens, Buildings, Interiors, Furniture*, London: Zwemmer, and New York: Abrams, 1993

Pevsner, Nikolaus and Susan Lang, "The Egyptian Revival" in Nikolaus Pevsner, *Studies in Art, Architecture and Design*, vol.1, London: Thames and Hudson, and New York: Walker, 1968, pp.212–48

The Sphinx and the Lotus: The Egyptian Movement in Decorative Arts, 1865–1935 (exhib. cat.), Yonkers, NY: Hudson River Museum, 1990

Syndram, Dirk, "Interieurs im Ägyptischen Stil: Englische und Deutsche Innendekoration im Frühklassizismus" in *Kunst und Antiquitäten*, 6, 1989, pp.34–45

Watkin, David, *Thomas Hope and the Neo-Classical Idea*, London: Murray, 1968

Wilton-Ely, John (editor), *G.B. Piranesi: The Polemical Works*, Farnborough: Gregg, 1972

Wilton-Ely, John, *Piranesi as Architect and Designer*, New Haven and London: Yale University Press, 1993

Wittkower, Rudolf, "Piranesi and Eighteenth-Century Egyptomania" in his *Studies in the Italian Baroque*, London: Thames and Hudson, and Boulder, CO: Westview Press, 1975, pp.259–73

Empire Style

"My favourite style is – I cannot deny it – a style which offers easy game to caricature", wrote Mario Praz, the historian and apologist of the early 19th century Empire style. "It is a common criticism that it is cold, stiff, that there is something funereally monotonous in its eternal sphinxes, its swans, its goats' and lions' feet ... A style for *parvenus*, with all that bronze gilt ornament on shining, heavy mahogany, that ostentation of richness in its crudest form, gold".

Napoleon I's domination of the European scene was relatively brief in historical terms, but his influence, directly or indirectly, on taste was quite extraordinary. The Empire style was conceived and developed over a short period, and yet it became a fashion not only in France, but in Italy, Spain, the Netherlands, Russia and Sweden as well as in England. Like the associated Regency style, it has been revived more than once and retains its popularity up to the present day. It has continued to offer inspiration to furniture designers and decorators, and yet in origin it was a style consciously developed by Napoleon and his artistic advisers to symbolise his dreams of imperial grandeur and the planned mastery of Europe.

The ground had already been prepared before the Revolution. The dramatic paintings by Jacques-Louis David had extolled the heroes of the Classical past – Socrates, Brutus, Hector and the widely admired group of the Horatii (which was to serve as a model for a clock) – and David himself was a leading figure in the circles influenced by the pre-Revolution fashion for the Antique which was only to intensify over the next two decades.

After 1795 France was ruled for a time by a Directoire consisting of three Directors; but in 1799, following the return of the then General Bonaparte from his Egyptian campaign, there was a change in the constitution when three Consuls, of whom Bonaparte was nominated the First, were appointed at the head of the government. Four years later he became Emperor. Hence the nine years of the Directoire and the Consulate were a transitional period politically and artistically between the *ancien régime* and the Empire. Stylistically, there was not a marked change at first from the late Louis XVI fashions. Architects such as François-Joseph Bélanger, Louis-Martin Berthault and Alexandre-Théodore Brongniart had been trained in the old school, and they still had contributions to make despite the rapid rise of Charles Percier and Pierre-François-Leonard Fontaine. The Jacob firm that had been patronised by Louis XVI and Marie-Antoinette was still the leading furniture-maker, and all these were associated with significant decorative commissions during the years of the Directoire and the Consulate.

David's *The Loves of Paris and Helen*, which was commissioned in 1788 by the Comte d'Artois (later Charles X), may be seen as a model for the many designs for bedrooms which began in 1798 with that of Mme. Récamier which became the talk of Paris. This famous room contains a classical statue on a pedestal, a tripod table or candlestand derived from Antiquity, a scroll-ended couch, all set against a draped background and, conceived by Louis-Martin Berthault and Fontaine, this Directoire design set a fashion for such theatrical compositions. The Récamier bedroom may be seen in a partial arrangement in the Louvre, but Robert Smirke's delicate

Empire Style: Salon de Musique, Malmaison, 1812; watercolour by Auguste Garneray

watercolour in the Royal Institute of British Architects Drawings Collection, London, captures well the combination of the Antique and feminine elegance.

On the other hand, the first Parisian townhouse of Bonaparte and his wife Josephine in the rue Chantereine introduced the military or masculine character that was to be incorporated in fashionable decoration. The beds had cannons as corner-posts and hangings simulating a tricolour tent, while the stools were modelled on military drums. Other furniture made for the Bonapartes at this time included the writing desk designed by Percier and now in the Grand Trianon, Versailles, which was lavishly ornamented with ormolu mounts and bronze figures in a manner that was to become typical of Empire furniture; but this too, although more overtly deriving from Antique sources in the detailing, was a development from late Louis XVI furniture. The tents and draperies in these rooms and in those at Malmaison, the most important pre-Empire commission, remained a characteristic of Empire decoration, largely because they were capable of creating a rich effect that could be assembled in a short time. Wallpaper simulating draperies became fashionable for the same reason.

Similarly, the fine furniture made by Georges Jacob and his two sons, Georges II and François-Honoré-Georges Jacob-Desmalter, was calculated to give an impression of luxury and richness with the highly polished mahogany and the applied ormolu mounts. Napoleon's blockade against the import of products from England and her colonies meant that the supply of mahogany was reduced, and so it was used sparingly and as a veneer over an oak or walnut frame. Improvements in the design of the circular saw meant that thinner layers could be cut and so smooth surfaces and sharp angles became characteristic of Empire furniture. At the same time the veneered surface was highly polished to enhance the grain.

Apart from Percier and Fontaine, who wrote in their *Recueil* that "It is a delusion to believe that there are shapes preferable to those which the Ancients have handed down to us", the most influential figure in matters of art and taste during the Empire was Dominique Vivant, Baron Denon. His official position was director of the Musée Napoleon and of the Monnaie des Médailles; but he played an important part in major decorative schemes such as Percier and Fontaine's new apartments on the south front of the Tuileries. He was also largely responsible for adding to the decorative vocabulary; it was the publication in 1802 of engravings made from his drawings of Egyptian buildings and decoration, obtained during Napoleon's campaign in 1798–99, that provided the sources for the sphinxes and other Egyptian motifs that became popular. Percier and Fontaine included a clock and a secretaire-bookcase in the *forme egyptienne* with Osiris-headed terms in their *Recueil*; other products of this fashion are the portico with palm columns added on the Emperor's instructions to the Hôtel de Beauharnais, Paris in 1806, the

Sala Impero in Palazzo Massimo, Rome, and the Sèvres Egyptian Service made in 1810–12 and now in Apsley House, London.

It was after the Egyptian campaign that Bonaparte returned to Paris and was made First Consul. Fontaine was instructed quickly to restore the Tuileries as a residence, at first using silk hangings and porcelain that had belonged to Marie-Antoinette. During this period Percier and Fontaine were also commissioned to remodel and decorate Malmaison but after Napoleon seized the throne and proclaimed himself Emperor in 1804 there was a new initiative to restore the splendour of the French court. Even when there was an opportunity to buy back furnishings taken from the royal palaces during the Revolution it was made clear that "His Majesty wants to create the new, not to order the old". Factories were re-opened, craftsmen were given loans to start up in business again, and a greater richness of colour and elaboration of ornament succeeded the generally elegant Neo-Classicism of the Directoire and the Consulate.

By 1813 Napoleon had decorated and furnished all his residences with furniture made by the Jacob family, Gobelins tapestries, Savonnerie carpets, Sèvres porcelain and Thomire bronzes. The throne room at Fontainebleau gives a good idea of the effect he wanted, with much symbolism of large N's, imperial eagles and Bonaparte bees; while the Emperor's and Empress's apartments at Fontainebleau and Compiègne are among the best surviving examples of what was provided for him at the height of his glory by Percier and Fontaine and their associates. The Emperor's bedroom at Fontainebleau is largely gold with gilded Jacob furniture, while that of the Empress has a patterned silk as wall hangings. At Compiègne the rich and sombre library was also furnished by the Jacobs, while the Empress's dining room is a relatively modest room with marbleised walls and plainer Jacob furniture. Two other Parisian residences could match the royal palaces, the Hôtel de Beauharnais (now the German Embassy) where Napoleon's stepson Eugène de Beauharnais and his sister, Queen Hortense, lived, and the Hôtel de Charost (since 1814 the British Embassy) where Pauline (Bonaparte) Borghese entertained. Both still retain their decoration and furnishings.

Napoleon's second marriage, to Princess Marie-Louise in 1810, was a signal for more redecoration and refurnishing, this time in an even more luxurious and richly imperial style. The Emperor's bedroom at Compiègne was hung with crimson silk, and the bed was crowned by a great gilded eagle and flanked by gilded corner posts supporting busts of Minerva. The rest of the furniture was heavily gilded and covered with the same crimson silk, while the new Empress was given a bed made of gilded cornucopia, with large gilded angels holding up the drapes which hang from a gilded crown topped with white feathers. Not to be outdone, the ex-Empress refurnished some of the rooms at Malmaison, including her bedroom which became an oval tent, with scarlet draperies embroidered in gold, upheld by small columns of gilded wood. The gilded bed had swans at the head and cornucopia filled with fruit at the foot, behind which white and gold draperies hung from a gold crown on top of which a golden eagle had settled on a spray of gilded roses.

Napoleon's occupation of Italy prompted more redecoration and refurnishing in the palaces that were to receive him. In Rome, the Quirinale from which the Pope had been evicted underwent changes orchestrated by Carlo Finelli to conform to the imperial taste around 1811. In Venice the Ala Napoleonica e Nuovissima was constructed by Giuseppe Maria Soli and Lorenzo Santi from 1810 to 1813 in Piazza San Marco, with decorations by Giuseppe Borsato and Giovanni Carlo Bevilacqua; and on the Venetian mainland some parts of the large Villa Pisani, Strà were redecorated by Gianantonio Antolini after Napoleon had bought the building in 1807 as a residence for Eugène de Beauharnais, Viceroy of Italy.

The Emperor had every intention to found a dynasty and to guarantee the future of his Empire, so whenever possible he exalted members of his family, first giving them Royal titles then arranging advantageous marriages, and finally putting them on thrones from which he had temporarily succeeded in toppling the legitimate monarchs. Thus there were Napoleonic courts in Italy, Germany, Holland and Spain, each with its several palaces which had to be refurnished. Consequently, there is a curious similarity in royal palaces in all these countries even today. Joseph Bonaparte became king of Spain, and Napoleon commissioned Percier and Fontaine to design an elaborately detailed small room which was fabricated in Paris and then transported to Aranjuez, including mirrors and painted panels. Louis Bonaparte was made king of Holland and he took over Amsterdam Town Hall as his palace, making Jean Thibault responsible for the alterations and for decorating and furnishing in the Empire style. The work itself was executed by four Dutch craftsmen. After Napoleon's downfall the building continued to be the royal palace and the collection of Empire furniture is the finest outside France.

Elisa Bonaparte married the Prince of Lucca and became Grand Duchess of Tuscany, acquiring five palaces including Villa Reale, Marlia, where a Salotto Impero was created, and Palazzo Pitti, Florence which was completely redecorated in 1810–13 with wall-hangings, bronzes, tapestries and carpets from Paris. Again, the furniture was made by local craftsmen, thus contributing to the prevalence and continuity of the Empire style in Italy. Joachim Murat, the husband of Caroline Bonaparte, became king of Naples and he lavishly redecorated the palaces at Caserta and Portici; the Bourbons were overwhelmed when they returned and saw the result. Sweden was not a part of the Empire, but the style was taken there when General Bernadotte, one of Napoleon's Marshals, was elected Crown Prince, and subsequently became king in 1818. Rosendal, close to Stockholm, is the finest example of the Empire style in Scandinavia but Swedish craftsmen and the painter Pehr Emanuel Lundelius were in charge; only the carpets and clocks were imported from France, the furniture and silks being produced in Sweden. The Russian court quickly adopted many of the style's characteristics, to which it could add the lavish use of malachite from Siberian quarries. And in England, in 1822 Rudolph Ackermann commented on one of the designs in his *Repository* that the "taste for French furniture is carried to such an extent, that most elegantly furnished mansions, particularly the sleeping-rooms, are fitted up in the French style".

George IV admired the Empire style, and one piece of furniture in which he took especial pride was a gift from the newly restored French king, Louis XVIII. Known as the *Table des Grands Capitains*, it was commissioned by Napoleon in 1806 from the Sèvres manufactory. Made of hard-paste porcelain with gilt bronze mounts, the stem is in the form of a bundle of pikes, while the porcelain top represents Alexander the Great surrounded by scenes of his victories and an outer circle of profiles of twelve other commanders from Antiquity; but it was not completed until 1812 and Napoleon had little pleasure from what was intended to be another act of self-glorification identifying himself with the military heroes of the past. As a symbolic gesture, George IV chose to be portrayed by Sir Thomas Lawrence in his Coronation robes with his hand resting lightly on this table as if to underline, with an item of furniture, the Emperor's downfall.

There were several Empire revivals in the late 19th and early 20th centuries and the style has retained its popularity up to the present day. During the 1920s and 1930s, the taste was greatly stimulated in France by the connoisseur Paul Marmottan whose outstanding collection of Empire furnishings is now on public display in the Musée Marmottan, Paris. The English Vogue Regency flourished during the same period and was similarly encouraged by collectors such as Edward Knoblock who had purchased many items of furniture at the sale of Thomas Hope's country home, Deepdene. More recently, tent-rooms and swagged draperies were revived during the late 1980s by fashionable decorators.

DEREK LINSTRUM

See also Percier and Fontaine; Jacob / Jacob-Desmalter Family

Selected Collections

The Musée Marmottan, Paris, specialises in work of the Directoire and Empire periods and contains many designs and examples of furnishings and decorations. Notable examples of Empire Style furnishings and interiors survive in France in the Château de Malmaison, the Hôtel de Beauharnais, Paris, the Château de Compiègne, and the Château de Fontainebleau; in Germany in the Schloss Wilhelmshölme, Kassel, and the Schloss Charlottenhof, Potsdam; in Italy in the Pitti Palace, Florence, and the Royal Palace, Caserta, Naples; in Russia in Mon Plaisir, Peterhof, St. Petersburg; and in Sweden in Rosendal, near Stockholm.

Further Reading

Good general introductions to the Empire Style appear in Aprà 1972 and Grandjean 1966; a more detailed account including a long bibliography appears in Groer 1986. For an account of the style in Italy and Scandinavia see Brosio 1967 and Groth 1990.

Aprà, Nietta, *Empire Style, 1804–1815*, London: Orbis, 1972; New York: World, 1973

Brosio, Valentino, *Ambienti italiani dell'Ottocento*, 2nd edition Milan: Vallardi, 1967

Curl, James Stevens, *The Egyptian Revival: An Introductory Study of a Recurring Theme in the History of Taste*, London: Allen and Unwin, 1982

Draper, James David, *The Arts Under Napoleon* (exhib. cat.), New York: Metropolitan Museum of Art, 1978

L'Empire: Musée Marmottan, Paris: ABC Décor, 1971

Foucart, Bruno, "L'Empire de Série" in *L'Objet d'Art*, 3, January 1988, pp.44–45

Groer, Léon de, *Decorative Arts in Europe 1790–1850*, New York: Rizzoli, 1986

Groth, Håkan, *Neoclassicism in the North: Swedish Furniture and Interiors, 1770–1850*, London: Thames and Hudson, and New York: Rizzoli, 1990

Grandjean, Serge, *Empire Furniture, 1800 to 1825*, London: Faber, and New York: Taplinger, 1966

Hubert, Gérard, "Napoleon and Josephine at Malmaison" in *Connoisseur*, CXCIII, December 1976, pp.259–70

Ledoux-Lebard, Denise, "Josephine and Interior Decoration" in *Apollo*, CVI, July 1977, pp.16–23

Ledoux-Lebard, R. and G., "La Décoration et L'Ameublement de la Chambre de Mme. Récamier sous le Consulat" in *Gazette des Beaux-Arts*, October 1952, pp.175–219 and June 1953, pp.299–312

Mansel, Philip, *The Eagle in Splendour: Napoleon I and His Court*, London: George Philip, 1987

Percier, Charles and Pierre-François-Léonard Fontaine, *Recueil de décorations intérieures, comprenant tout ce qui a Rapport à ameublement*, 1801, 2nd edition 1812; translated as *Empire Stylebook of Interior Design*, New York: Dover, 1991

Pinto, Sandra, "The Royal [Pitti] Palace from the Lorraine Period to the Present Day" in *Apollo*, CVI, September 1977, pp.220–31

Praz, Mario, *On Neoclassicism*, London: Thames and Hudson, 1969

Sassone, Adriana Boidi and others, *Il Mobile dell'Ottocento*, Novara: Istituto Geografico de Agostini, 1988

Stewart, Patrick L., "The American Empire Style: Its Historical Background" in *American Art Journal*, X, November 1978

Erdmannsdorff, Friedrich Wilhelm von

1736–1800

German architect

Friedrich Wilhelm von Erdmannsdorff is one of the most important German architects of the mid- and late 18th century, during the transition from the late Baroque to the Neo-Classical styles (at first Roman and later Greek). His patron, Prince Leopold Friedrich Franz of Anhalt-Dessau (1740–1817) sent him to Italy in 1761, and they travelled together to England in 1763 and Italy in 1765–66. The neo-Palladian houses and new English informal gardens which they saw were to play major roles in Erdmannsdorff's works for the prince and others. Equally, if not more important were the Italian journeys, where he became a pupil of the French architect-artist-archaeologist Charles-Louis Clérisseau (1721–1820) in the study of ancient monuments and decoration which would be the basis for his later architectural works in Saxony. He also met in Rome J.J. Winckelmann, the leading writer on classical art, and the printmaker Giovanni Battista Piranesi, and in Naples Sir William Hamilton, the great collector of ancient art.

On his return to Germany Erdmannsdorff first designed new interiors, particularly the Festsaal of the Prince's town palace at Dessau; this was in a classical style, with great Corinthian columns, inset classical-style reliefs and friezes above the doors and a rinceau cornice. A circular study was decorated in stucco with painted medallions. All of these resembled Clérisseau's designs, as well as the work of Robert Adam which Erdmannsdorff had probably seen in England. However, Erdmannsdorff's decoration was less delicate and refined. The architect's major work for the prince was the palace and gardens, including pavilions, at Wörlitz (1769–98). The exterior in the English Palladian style was probably influenced by Henry Holland's Claremont of 1769, but the result was slightly heavier. The plan was also Palladian in its clarity of parts, but the decoration of the rooms with their raised stucco decoration derived from the antique, and the inset painted scenes were in the new classical style of Clérisseau and Adam, but again less delicate. The fireplaces were based on the designs of Piranesi. Certain details were derived from Robert Wood's study of the Roman remains at Palmyra. The influence of the wall paintings of Pompeii is evident, particularly in the frescoes in the library, with their inset scenes and portraits of ancient and modern figures in the antique style. The Grand Saal shows the influence of Pompeii in its stucco and painted decoration combined with details from the Carracci's 17th-century Farnese Galleria and the Roman acanthus frieze from the Villa Medici. Although a major example of the Neo-Classical style in Germany, the room's overly rich decoration and multiplication of details make for a certain heaviness, and it lacks the refinement of the work of Adam. Furniture for the palace in the classical style was designed by David Roentgen. While most of the palace was decorated with classically-inspired works there was also a Chinese room.

This profusion of styles is even more evident in the pavilions scattered throughout the gardens, the first landscape garden in Germany. Most of these are classical and are freely based on such buildings as the Pantheon and the Temple of Tivoli; some are more severe and Palladian in character. One was even in the Gothic style. Many of these pavilions have elaborate interiors, such as the elegant dome of the Pantheon. The most interesting is the Villa Hamilton, also known as the Villa Stein (1791–94), with its Pompeian decoration, stucco work and ceiling paintings. The decoration was inspired by engravings of the recently excavated buildings at Herculaneum. The interior included ruin paintings by Clérisseau, classical reliefs designed by John Flaxman for Wedgwood, copies of Raphael frescoes, and Greek *klismos* chairs which are among the earliest examples in this style.

Erdmannsdorff's later work in Berlin at the Royal Palace (1787–89) is flatter and less brittle, relying more on painting and less on raised stucco decoration. The classical scenes are larger in size as are the panels of decoration, and there is more of a feeling of Raphael than the antique. This is particularly apparent in the Speisesaal. In some rooms the ceilings resemble those at Wörlitz in their profusion of small and fussy classical details inspired by Roman stuccos and wall paintings, but in others, such as the one in the Königskammern, there are vast areas of empty space contrasting with the large classical scenes and *grotteschi* decoration. It is only in such rooms as the Goldener Kammer in the Schloss Monbijou, Berlin (1788–89) that one returns to the large rectangular or arabesque and *grotteschi* panels of decoration without the intrusion of classical scenes. The feeling here is reminiscent of the work of Erdmannsdorff's teacher Clérisseau in his design for the Hôtel Grimod de la Reynière and the Roman House for Catherine the Great.

Erdmannsdorff introduced the latest artistic and architectural thinking into Germany in his buildings, gardens and, most importantly, in his classically-inspired interiors, which were based on ancient sources often combined with the Renaissance and Baroque classical motifs. These interiors also often included furniture specifically designed for the rooms, which added to his vision of classical antiquity.

THOMAS J. MCCORMICK

Biography

Born in Dresden, 18 May 1736. Studied mathematics, history, philology, natural sciences and philosophy at the University of Wittenberg, 1754–57; made study trips to England and Holland in 1763; visited Italy, where he met Charles-Louis Clérisseau, G.B. Piranesi, J.J. Winckelmann and William Hamilton, in 1761–63, 1765–66, 1770–71. Met Prince Leopold Friedrich Franz of Anhalt-Dessau in 1756; acted as his artistic adviser, agent and architect from 1757. Active as an architect and designer of interiors from late 1760s; designed some furniture from c.1766. Summoned to Berlin in 1787 and worked in the service of Friedrich Wilhelm II of Prussia. Further travel throughout Germany and Italy, 1787–80. First artistic director of the Dessau institute of copper engraving, 1796–1800. Died in Dessau, 9 March 1800.

Selected Works

Interiors

1765–70 Schloss Dessau, Dessau (remodelling of interiors)
1769–98 Schloss Wörlitz, Wörlitz (building, interiors and some furniture, gardens and pavilions including the Nymphaeum 1767–68, Villa Hamilton 1791–94, Temple of Venus 1793–94, Pantheon 1794–96, Temple of Flora 1797–98,): Prince Leopold Friedrich Franz
1774–80 Schloss Luisium, near Dessau (building and interiors)
1777 Court Theatre, Dessau (building and interiors)
1780 Schloss Georgium (building and interiors)
1786 Sanssouci, Potsdam (decoration of the bedroom and workroom in the King's apartments): Friedrich Wilhelm II
1787–89 Royal Palace, Berlin (remodelling and decoration of the King's apartments): Friedrich Wilhelm II
1794 Theatre, Magdeburg (building and interiors)

Further Reading

A recent study and catalogue raisonné of Erdmannsdorff's work is Kadatz 1986. A detailed discussion of his most celebrated commission, Wörlitz, appears in Harksen 1973.

Gaillemin, Jean-Louis, "Allez à Worlitz" in *Connaissance des Arts*, 483, May 1992, pp.106–17
Grote, L., *Führer durch den Wörlitzer Park*, Dessau, 1929
Harksen, Marie-Luise, *Erdmannsdorff und seine Bauten in Wörlitz*, Wörlitz: Orienbaum & Luisium, 1973
Harksen, Marie-Luise, "Die Arbeiten von Erdmannsdorff in Potsdam und Berlin 1786 bis 1789" in *Dessauer Kalender*, 1974
Hempel, Doris (editor), *Friedrich Wilhelm von Erdmannsdorff, 1736–1800: Leben, Werk, Wirkung*, Wörlitz: Orienbaum & Luisium, 1987
Hirsch, Erhard, *Dessau-Wörlitz: Zierde und Inbegriff des 18. Jarhrhunderts*, Munich: Beck, 1985
Kadatz, Hans-Joachim, *Friedrich Wilhelm von Erdmannsdorff*, Berlin: Bauwesen, 1986
Reinhard, Alex, *Schlösser und Gärten um Wörlitz*, Kohlhammer, 1988
Riesenfeld, Erich Paul, *Erdmannsdorff: Der Baumeister des Herzogs Leopold Friedrich Franz von Anhalt-Dessau*, Berlin: Cassirer, 1913

Errard, Charles c.1606–1689

French painter, engraver and architect

Charles Errard was one of the most important artists of his time and precisely why his name is so little known outside France today remains a mystery. Errard was a close friend of the painter Nicolas Poussin, and his work represents a continuation of Poussin's classical tradition; he dominated artistic production in Paris in the mid-17th century. He was involved in all the major royal palaces ranging from the Fontainebleau to Versailles, he occupied senior positions at Court and at the French Academy in Rome, and he exercised a decisive influence on French decoration in the period leading up to the supremacy of Charles Le Brun.

Born in Nantes in about 1606, Errard made frequent, extended trips to Italy throughout his long career. He spent a total of almost thirty years in Rome where he was able to immerse himself in the study of antique monuments and ornament which he greatly admired. His first visit took place between 1627 and 1637 when he trained as a painter in the workshop of Poussin. He returned again in the early 1640s and in 1666 he was appointed head of the Académie de France in Rome where he remained until 1683. Errard's major works, however, were executed in France. In 1640 he was active in Paris, providing historical scenes for tapestries, and in 1643 he was appointed Peintre Ordinaire du Roi and granted a pension and lodgings in the Louvre. Several important commissions ensued and he was entrusted by Cardinal Mazarin with the decoration of the Palais Royal, the residence of the young Louis XIV. His interiors for the theatre were greatly admired as were his stage sets for performances by the Italian opera which he executed with the help of his assistants Sève and Noël Coypel. In 1648 Errard decorated a private house in the Quai Notre Dame with scenes from Ovid's *Metamorphoses*, and during the mid-1650s he was involved in the decoration of the private apartments of the King, Cardinal Mazarin and the Queen's mother in the Louvre. The ceiling of the dowager Queen's apartments were praised in Saville's *Antiquités de la Ville de Paris* as being the last example of gallantry and magnificence in court decoration. Unfortunately, however, only fragments of Errard's work have survived, namely the pilasters decorated with arabesques which are now in the Palais Luxembourg.

As official Peintre du Roi, Errard was put in charge of all the decorative work at the Tuileries and Fontainebleau as well as the Louvre, and he subsequently directed work at Versailles (1661). His closest assistants were the sculptor Marsy and Noël Coypel, and in 1656 Errard and Coypel painted the ceiling of the Grand Chambre in the Parlement de Rennes. This was one of Errard's most impressive endeavours. Unlike the Baroque decorations that he had seen in Rome which included vast illusionistic expanses of sky, Errard's ceiling was divided into compartments containing painted figures within medallions surrounded by gilt wood frames. The allegorical figures are delineated in profile using strict rules of perspective. This style must have appeared quite old-fashioned by this date, but alternatively it can be viewed as a move towards a purer form of classicism. Other areas of the ceiling are filled with grotesque ornament painted on a gilded surface. This type of decoration had become increasingly popular in Northern Europe following the widespread publicity accorded the discovery of ancient examples in Nero's Domus Aurea and the work of painters such as Raphael and Giovanni da Udine in the Vatican Loggia and other palaces in Rome. But once again Errard did not slavishly follow antique precedents but used grotesque ornament in a freer and more purely entertaining manner. The Rennes commission was followed in 1657 by work in the theatre of the Tuileries, and later by projects at Versailles, S. Germain-en-Laye and Fontainebleau. Errard also decorated various private houses during this period, notably those belonging to the financiers Le Charron, La Bazinière, and Catalan.

In addition to his work as a painter, Errard also devoted much of his time to publishing books and suites of ornament. Together with Fréart de Chambray, he translated Palladio's four books of architecture during the 1640s, and in 1650 he illustrated Chambray's *Parallèle de l'Architecture antique et de la moderne*. He also translated Leonardo's *Trattato della pittura* which he illustrated with engraved paintings after Poussin; published in 1651, this was the first printed version of Leonardo's treatise. Also in 1651 he published three suites of Baroque ornament dedicated to the Queen Christina of Sweden: *Divers Ornements* (eight plates), *Divers Trophées* (six plates after Polidoro da Caravaggio), and *Divers Vases antiques* (twelve plates). Some time after 1655 he published six plates showing the interiors of the Louvre entitled *Ornements des appartements de la Reine au Vieux Louvre*, and during his time as head of the French Academy in Rome he designed the ornaments for Bellori's *Vite* (1672).

The period between 1653 and 1661 was the most successful and busy time of Errard's career, but from the early 1660s his reputation was increasingly eclipsed by that of the rising star, Charles Le Brun. Errard continued to receive commissions for work at S. Germain and Fontainebleau but the most important projects were awarded to Le Brun. And when Le Brun was made a member of the Conseil des Bâtiments, a position that would have given him a decisive say in much of Errard's work, Errard left Paris to take up his official appointment in Rome.

Given the paucity of Errard's surviving work, it is hard to arrive at an accurate evaluation of his talents as a decorative painter and designer, and he is generally remembered today only for his use of grotesque ornament. Within a broader context, however, with his cosmopolitan and scholarly background, Errard must have had an indirect but nevertheless important influence on the French Academic style attributed to and embodied by Le Brun.

PIA MARIA MONTONEN

Biography

Born in Nantes c.1606. Trained as a painter in Rome from 1627. Returned to Nantes, before travelling to Paris, 1637. After a second Roman trip, appointed Peintre Ordinaire du Roi in Paris, with pension and lodgings at the Louvre, 1643; appointed Peintre du Roi, 1644. Founder-member of the Académie Royale, 1648: treasurer, 1651; rector, 1655; director 1657. Directed and designed decorations and operas at royal palaces in Paris and at Saint-Germain-en-Laye, Fontainebleau and Versailles, 1661, and produced designs for tapestry and theatre. Translated Palladio's *Four Books of Architecture*, 1650, and Leonardo da Vinci's *Trattato della pittura*, 1651; published several books of ornament, 1647–51. Church architect in Paris, c.1663. Married 1) Marie de la Rue (died 1661); 2) daughter of Claude Goy, 1675. Appointed head of the French Academy in Rome, 1666. Member of the Academy of St. Luke, Rome. Returned to France, 1683. Died in 1689.

Selected Works

1643 Palais Royal (theatre): Cardinal Mazarin

1644 Hôtel de Senneterre (Grande Galerie paintings)
1648 Hôtel Charron, Paris (Cabinet; scenes from Ovid's *Metamorphoses*): Jean Charron
1654–55 Louvre, Paris (painted and arabesque decoration in apartments of the King, Cardinal Mazarin, and Queen Mother): Louis XIV
1656 Parliament (now Palais de Justice), Rennes (ceiling decoration, with Noel Coypel)
1657 Tuileries, Paris (salle de théâtre, with Noel Coypel)
1658 Hôtel de la Bazinière, Paris (paintings, together with Le Brun, Le Sueur, Boulogne): Bertrand de la Bazinière
1658 Hôtel Séguier (chambre l'alcove): Chancellor Pierre Séguier
1662–63 Palais Royal, Paris (chambre l'alcove): Duc d'Orléans
1662–65 Petit Château, Versailles (arabesques): Louis XIV

Publications

Brevarium Romanum, 1647

Parallèle de l'architecture antique et de la moderne (with Roland Fréart de Chambray), 1650

Parallèle de l'architecture antique avec la moderne, suivant les dix principaux auteures qui ont écrit des cinques ordres, edited by Charles Antoine Joubert, 1766

Recueil de vases antiques, de trophées et de divers ornements, 1651 (three suites: "Divers Ornements"; "Divers Trophées" and "Le Recueil des Divers Vases antiques")

Receuil [sic] *de divers vases antiques par Charles Errard*, Rome, 1680

Ornements des appartements de la Reine au Vieux Louvre, Paris, n.d.

Further Reading

Berger 1993 and 1994 are useful for general surveys of Errard's royal commissions. Beresford 1994 has an important catalogue and bibliography.

Beresford, Richard C., *Domestic Interior Decoration in Paris, 1630–1660: A Catalogue based on the written sources*, Ph.D. thesis, London: Courtauld Institute of Art, 1994

Berger, Robert W., *The Palace of the Sun: The Louvre of Louis XIV*, University Park: Pennsylvania State University Press, 1993

Berger, Robert W., *A Royal Passion: Louis XIV as Patron of Architecture*, Cambridge and New York: Cambridge University Press, 1994

Blunt, Anthony, *Art and Architecture in France, 1500–1700*, 2nd edition Harmondsworth: Penguin, 1970

Dacos, Nicole, *La Découverte de la Domus Aurea et la formation des Grotesques à la Renaissance*, London: Warburg Institute, 1969

Hautecoeur, Louis, *Histoire de l'architecture classique en France*, vol.3, Paris: Picard, 1951

Lapauze, Henry, *L'histoire de l'académie de France à Rome*, vol.1., Paris: Plon-Nourrit, 1924, pp.1–67

Marcel, Pierre, *Charles Le Brun*, Paris: Plon, 1910

Nexon, Yannick, "L'Hôtel Séguier: Contributions à l'Étude d'un hôtel parisien au XVIIe siècle", in *Bulletin Archéologique du Comité des Travaux Historiques et Scientifiques*, 16, 1980, pp.143–77

Nexon, Yannick, "La collections de tableaux du Chancelier Séguier" in *Bibliothèque de l'Ecole des Chartres*, 140, 1982, pp.189–214

Sainte Fare Garnot, Nicolas, *Le décor des Tuileries sous la règne de Louis XIV*, Paris: Réunions des Musées Nationaux, 1988

Sainte Fare Garnot, Nicolas and Emmanuel Jacquin, *Le Château des Tuileries*, Paris: Herscher, 1988

Thuillier, Jacques, "Charles Errard, Peintre", in *Gazette des Beaux-Arts*, March 1963, pp.151–172

Thuillier, Jacques, "Propositions pour I: Charles Errard, peintre" in *Revue de l'Art*, 40–1, 1978, pp.158

Etruscan Style

The conscious search for a contemporary style of expression under Neo-Classicism during the late 18th century in Britain is supremely demonstrated by the creation of the Etruscan Style in interior design. While ostensibly derived from the shapes, motifs and colours of antique vases (initially misunderstood as Etruscan and later recognised as largely Greek), it also drew inspiration from Renaissance grotesque ornament and material discovered at Herculaneum and Pompeii.

An interest in Etruscan culture and art, while it can be traced back to the theorists of the Italian Renaissance, was first seriously developed by the Scottish 17th-century historian Sir Thomas Dempster whose pioneering researches were posthumously published in 1723–25. By this time a growing patriotic movement in 18th-century Italy led to the foundation of the Accademia Etrusca at Cortona in 1726 and the Museo Guarnacci at Volterra in 1750. By the 1760s, excavations and the accumulated publications of scholars such as Gori, Passeri, Guarnacci and the Comte de Caylus, assumed a new significance for early Neo-Classical designers searching for fresh sources of inspiration. The architect and engraver G.B. Piranesi, partly inspired by his friend Thomas Jenkins's excavation in tombs at Corneto (modern Tarquinia), portrayed the Etruscans as Rome's chief source of inspiration in his polemical work *Della magnificenza ed architettura de' Romani* (1761) when countering the arguments of the Greek Revivalists, led by the eminent German scholar J.J. Winckelmann.

"Etruscheria" swiftly became "Etruscomania", and owing to the confusion of evidence, extravagant claims were made concerning the respective influences of Greeks and Etruscans on Roman culture. The Scottish antiquary James Byers was preparing a history of the Etruscans (posthumously published in 1842) during the 1760s when his engraved plates were in circulation, while Piranesi, in 1765, issued three etchings of wall decorations from tombs at Corneto and Chiusi. Both authors were in regular correspondence, meanwhile, with the distinguished connoisseur Sir William Hamilton in Naples who was assembling his first major collection of antiques, chiefly found in Southern Italy. This material was published between 1766 and 1776 in the lavish four-volume *Collection of Etruscan, Greek and Roman Antiques*, under the authorship of the scholar Baron d'Hancarville, with the express aim of providing inspiration for contemporary designers.

The potter Josiah Wedgwood was already familiar with proof plates of Hamilton's publication by the 1760s and applied the term "Etruscan" to certain basalt vases made to imitate that civilization's bronze vessels. This particular ceramic material was also the basis for other wares decorated with encaustic and enamel paintings, closely based on Hamilton's plates and described as being in the "Etruscan style". From 1769, when Wedgwood and his partner Thomas Bentley opened "Etruria", their factory at Burslem, Staffordshire, they also introduced antique plaques and large cameos, advertised as in "black basaltes with Etruscan burnt-in grounds". In 1773 their *Catalogue of Cameos, Intaglios, Medals, and Bas Reliefs, with a General Account of Vases and Other Ornaments after the Antique* included "Etruscan" ornaments as "fit either for inlaying, as medallions, in the panels

Etruscan Room, Osterley Park, Middlesex, 1775–76

[sic] of rooms, as tablets for chimneypieces, or for hanging up as ornaments in libraries ... or as pictures for dressing rooms".

Wedgwood's intentions were to be swiftly adopted and by 1771 James Wyatt had produced what is now generally accepted as the first Etruscan Style interior, within a modest fishing pavilion on the Thames at Fawley Court, Buckinghamshire. This room, probably carried out by Biagio Rebecca – one of the decorative artists most associated with the style – has pale green walls which are given the appearance of being hung or inlaid with antique figures, medallions and plaques after Wedgwood. In 1773 the Adam brothers, with their customary entrepreneurial skill, swiftly applied the style in a dressing room for the Countess of Derby in Grosvenor Square, London. Their engraved designs (frequently issued in colour) for the ceiling and chimneypiece appeared in Volume II of their *Works in Architecture* (1779), in which they flagrantly claimed to have invented the style. They did, at least, identify the style by name and defined its essential characteristics as involving the colour, i.e. terracotta and black, and style of the ornament "both evidently taken from the vases and urns of the Etruscans" (*Works*, 1779, Preface, p.2.).

For all their opportunism, the Adams' work, represented in at least eight Etruscan interiors, designed between 1773 and 1780, should be seen as a considered response to Piranesi's call for a modern style in interior design, based on a broadly eclectic use of Antiquity, in his highly influential folio *Diverse maniere* (1769). In this publication the Venetian designer had recognised the potential for transposing vase motifs for other decorative functions and at least two of his opening plates show this principle applied to wall compositions with chimneypieces, clearly influencing the Adams' Etruscan interiors. The finest and most complete of these to survive is the dressing room at Osterley Park, Middlesex, carried out for the banker Robert Child and his wife Sarah mainly around 1775–76. This integrated scheme, probably painted by Pietro Maria Borgnis, in colours of terracotta and black on a blue-grey ground, involves not only the four walls, two doors and ceiling (with roundel by Antonio Zucchi) but also its carpet (no longer extant), eight chairs, a chimney-board, a pole-screen, and the curtain cornices of the two windows. While in 1778 Horace Walpole scathingly noted the Wedgwood influence, Mrs. Lybbe-Powys perceptively remarked in 1788 on the room's debts to Herculaneum.

In addition to those at Derby House and Osterley, other Etruscan rooms by the Adams included a partially-surviving one at 20 Portman Square; a small room under the garden-front staircase, also at Osterley; and others, no longer surviving, are recorded at Cumberland House (1780), "Mr Adamson's parlour" (possibly at the Adelphi), both in London, as well as at Harewood House and Byram House, both in Yorkshire. A number of imitations followed, the most distinguished being Thomas Leverton's entrance hall at Woodhall Park, Hertfordshire, of the 1770s.

By the 1780s painted interiors after the Antique in France had been absorbed into the Louis XVI style, as introduced by the Adams' colleague C.L. Clérisseau (he is also documented in 1764 as having produced an "Etruscan room" for Cardinal Albani in Rome, no sign of which survives). But a more specifically Etruscan manner appears in interiors by F.J. Bélanger and J.D. Dugourc (notably those at Bagatelle), as well as in furniture by Georges Jacob, executed for Marie Antoinette's Laiterie at Rambouillet in 1787 and described as "de forme nouvelle de genre étrusque".

In England, meanwhile, the Etruscan Style underwent a new and particularly astringent interpretation by Wyatt in a small anteroom at Heveningham Hall, Suffolk, completed before 1784 for Sir Gerard Vanneck. The residual traces of illusionistic devices from Herculaneum and use of the "Grottesque", as seen at Osterley, are here replaced by a system of composition involving pale green walls with white wood and plaster enrichments as a particularly austere context for terracotta figurative panels, mainly derived from Hamilton's *Antiquities*. The integrated painted furniture includes a pair of highly idiosyncratic candelabra, based on urn forms, in opposing niches.

By 1791–95 Hamilton's second collection of vases was published, as delineated by the artist Wilhelm Tischbein. This work revealed an awareness of their Greek origins, although the original misconception persisted and C.H. Tatham, writing from Rome to Henry Holland in 1796, described these latest illustrations as being "in the Etruscan style, precisely copied from Sir William Hamilton's Vases and adapted to small rooms and cabinets ..." (C. Proudfoot and D. Watkin, "A Pioneer of English Neo-classicism" in *Country Life*, 20 April 1972, pp.918–21). However, by then the fresh revelations at Pompeii were already encouraging bolder and more colourful interior schemes while the change from "Etruscomania" to "Etruscology" in Italy was being impelled by the magisterial researches of Luigi Lanzi. Only thereafter did the Etruscan Style appear as one among many historicising modes of expression, such as in 1834 when Pelagio Palagi and Carlo Bellosio created an Etruscan room in the Castello Reale di Racognigi, near Turin, for King Charles-Albert of Piedmont, reflecting the heavy opulence of the late Empire style.

JOHN WILTON-ELY

See also Adam; Wedgwood

Selected Collections

Examples of Etruscan style interiors survive in England at Fawley Court, Buckinghamshire; Woodhall Park, Hertfordshire; Osterley Park, Middlesex; and Heveningham Hall, Suffolk.

Further Reading

A concise history of the Etruscan Style in Britain appears in Wilton-Ely 1989 which also includes references to primary and secondary sources.

Barocchi, Paola and Daniela Gallo (editors), *L'Accademia Etrusca, Cortona* (exhib. cat.), Milan: Electa, 1985

Bloch, Raymond, *The Etruscans*, London: Thames and Hudson, and New York: Praeger, 1958

Cornforth, John, "Heveningham Hall, Suffolk" in *Country Life*, 17 June 1993, pp.62–64

Croft-Murray, Edward, *Decorative Painting in England, 1537–1837*, vol.2, London: Country Life, 1970

Les Étrusques en Europe (exhib. cat.), Paris: Grand Palais, 1992

Fothergill, Brian, *Sir William Hamilton, Envoy Extraordinary*, London: Faber, and New York: Harcourt Brace, 1969

Hardy, John and Caroline Andrew, "The Essence of the Etruscan Style" in *Connoisseur*, 205, November 1981, pp.225–27

Hardy, John and Martin Tomlin, *Osterley Park House*, London: Victoria and Albert Museum, 1985

Harris, Eileen and John Martin Robinson, "New Light on Wyatt at Fawley" in *Architectural History*, XXVII, 1984, pp.263–67

McCormick, Thomas J., *Charles-Louis Clérisseau and the Genesis of Neo-Classicism*, Cambridge, MA: Massachusetts Institute of Technology Press, 1990

Stillman, Damie, *The Decorative Work of Robert Adam*, London: Academy, and New York: St. Martin's Press, 1973

Wilton-Ely, John, "Vision and Design: Piranesi's 'Fantasia' and the Graeco-Roman Controversy" in Georges Brunel (editor), *Piranèse et les Français* (conference papers), Rome: Elefante, 1978

Wilton-Ely, John, "Pompeian and Etruscan Tastes in the Neo-Classical Country-House Interior" in Gervase Jackson-Stops (editor), *The Fashioning and Functioning of the British Country House*, Washington, DC: National Gallery of Art, 1989, pp.51–74

Wilton-Ely, John, *Piranesi as Architect and Designer*, New Haven and London: Yale University Press, 1993

F

Federal Style

The Federal Style, which began around 1785, takes its name from the post-revolutionary period in which the United States established its federal government. Its architecture is a greatly simplified version of buildings by Robert Adam. Its furnishings are comparable in style and workmanship to contemporaneous English designers, thanks to the availability of their pattern books and the influx of craftsmen from the British Isles. The Federal Style was quickly overlaid, and then replaced, by the Greek and Roman prototypes of the Classical Revival. Because of this rapid evolution, authorities divide on the duration of the period. Some extend it to 1830, by which time the erosion of Neo-Classical antecedents was complete; but the character of the style is better captured if the line is drawn around 1810, when this influence was disappearing but discernible.

The War of Independence interrupted the natural evolution of American furnishings and architecture as the country turned its attention to survival, and craftsmen joined the army or produced its goods. The end of the war saw not only built-up demand, but the necessity to increase manufacturing and commerce to make the new nation self-supporting. A wave of immigration helped to swell the population, and a rising prosperity based on trade increased the audience for designed products.

Furniture makers reacted quickly. In an announcement of March 1790 illustrated with a Hepplewhite shield-back chair, London-trained George Shipley notified the readers of the New York *Daily Advertiser* that his workmen made furniture in "the neatest, and most fashionable manner," and that mahogany planks and logs were for sale in his yard. Like Shipley, many craftsmen had become entrepreneurs, retailing lumber and hiring journeymen – Scottish immigrant Duncan Phyfe had some 100 workers at his shop in New York. Others began to specialize in the new techniques required by the changing style, producing veneers or inlaid designs. As a result, popular forms were standardized, the use of machines increased, and some artisans set up merchandising warehouses to sell their own work and that of others.

Competition for jobs was fierce at all levels. In Philadelphia, which had over 120 cabinet- and chair-makers in the 1790s, tensions between journeymen and masters led first to a labor strike and then to the publication of *The Journeymen Cabinet and Chair-Makers Philadelphia Book of Prices* (1795). In 1796, the journeymen won their demand for a six-day week and a median wage of a dollar for an eleven-hour day. Their price book reveals the average number of days required to produce various furnishings (and thus the complexity of their construction), and the mark-up imposed by the masters when work was sold. Among the longest to produce, was a "circular bureau" (nine and a half days), among the shortest a "splatt back chair" (just under two days). Mark-ups ranged from 25 per cent for a square card table to 50 per cent for a dining table, 4 x 5 ($8.08 for labor, $16.05 retail), and averaged around 30 per cent.

Although the United States was no longer a colony, English prototypes continued to dominate its furniture design, reinforced by pattern books, imported furnishings, and immigrant artisans. The basic texts of the trade were Thomas Shearer's *The Cabinet-Makers' London Book of Prices* and George Hepplewhite's *The Cabinet-Maker and Upholsterer's Guide*, both published in 1788, and Thomas Sheraton's *The Cabinet-Maker and Upholsterer's Drawing Book* (1791–93). Like the pieces illustrated in these works, American furniture was finely proportioned and small in scale, with straight and tapering legs. Its surfaces were veneered, inlaid, and occasionally embellished with low-relief carving.

American craftsmen were more likely to interpret than to copy, however. If Salem carver Samuel McIntire modeled the set of oval back sidechairs made for Elias Hasket Derby in 1798 on Plate 8 of the 1794 edition of Hepplewhite's *Guide*, he marked them as his own by carving his signature grapes and grape leaves on the front legs. Similarly, a sofa attributed to Jacob Sanderson of Salem, and perhaps carved by McIntire in 1802 or 1803, drew on Sheraton's 1791 *Drawing Book* for its silhouette and on Plate 6 of Shearer's *London Book of Prices* for the basket design that decorates its top rail. (Sidechair and sofa are held by the Winterthur Museum.) New York chair-makers produced a variety of square chairbacks patterned on Plate 36 (no. 1) of the *Drawing Book*. Additionally, Americans regularly supplemented the Neo-Classical motifs they shared with England – swags, urns, paterae husks, palmettes, classical figures – with the eagles and shields that celebrated the national identity.

Although Federal pieces integrate Hepplewhite and Sheraton designs, many authorities have developed criteria to distinguish the two sub-styles, even as they admit that "Hepplewhite-Sheraton" is a realistic nomenclature. American

Federal Style: McIntire Room in the Winterthur Museum, Delaware

Hepplewhite chairs have oval, shield-, or heart-shaped backs, frequently incorporating a draped motif; Sheraton chairbacks are squared, the top rail broken by a straight, raised section. The legs of Hepplewhite pieces are generally square and tapered, often carved, fluted, or inlaid, and ending in spade feet; Sheraton-style legs are more frequently round-sectioned and reeded, with a thimble-shaped foot. Hepplewhite arm stumps rise in a concave curve from the front leg or side rail and, in upholstered pieces, form a nailer for the fabric cover; Sheraton arm stumps rise straight from the front leg and, in upholstered pieces, stand free of the upholstered edge. A sideboard with a serpentine front – and, thus, concave ends – is a Hepplewhite; straight or segmental fronts mark the piece as a Sheraton, as do convex ends. Architectonic looking-glasses flanked by twin colonnettes are identified with Sheraton, although he shows only one wall mirror (Plate 50, *Cabinet Dictionary*, 1803) which, while rectangular, is not in the columnar style. Finally, there is a greater use of pediments, smooth bracket feet, and contrasting woods in Sheraton casepieces.

The regional variations that had marked colonial furniture continued after the war. These could include construction methods. In Salem, Massachusetts, chairs were often braced with triangular, horizontally grained blocks, while Philadelphia used quarter-round, vertically grained blocks. Regional variations could also include a preference for certain forms (such as the square chairback popular in New York); and there were individual artisanal signatures such as McIntire's grapes and the extremely fine inlay which English immigrant John Seymour and his son Thomas patterned to make the eye see movement. Baltimore craftsmen are perhaps the most idiosyncratic, known not only for their black-and-gilt finishes but for the *verre églomisé* panels (glass painted with gold and black on the reverse side, and usually representing allegorical figures) found almost nowhere else.

A few furniture types, such as the lowboy, disappeared from the lexicon, while specialized pieces were developed to make life more comfortable and convenient. Chief among these were the tent or canopy bed; the window seat; the rocking chair; the open-arm "lolling chair" (for unknown reasons, also called the

Martha Washington); basin stands; worktables to hold a lady's writing and sewing equipment; and canterbury stands to hold her music. Dining rooms, newly important to social life, saw the introduction of sideboards, knife boxes, cellarettes, and sectional dining tables assembled from from a centre drop-leaf supplemented with half-round side tables and held together with brass clips. The importance of dining as social activity is corroborated by the number of arm- and sidechairs (in sets of up to 24) ordered from the various workshops.

The new style required more sophisticated woodworking techniques, and these were made possible by machine-cut nails and refinements in sawing technology. Bowed and serpentine doors and panels were built up from vertical strips laid over a caul carved from the solid; curved drawers were constructed rather like brick walls, being made of small sections of wood laid horizontally and glued together. Surfaces were almost always veneered, and often inlaid. Mahogany and satinwood were the materials of choice, although other contrasting woods could be used, their colors further differentiated with cross-banding and stringing. The line of leg and edge was often stressed with fluting or reeding, the change from the convex to the concave beginning around 1800; and the unity of form and surface was emphasized with wax or (after 1800) a French polish (shellac dissolved in spirit).

If Federal Style furnishings resembled English prototypes, Federal architecture did not. For economic and cultural reasons, the Neo-Classical movement sparked by Robert and James Adam in the 1760s had little impact in either colonial or federal America. What versions of the Adam style that did reach these shores tended to come from popularizing builders' manuals, such as William Pain's *Practical House Carpenter* of 1766 and *Practical Builder* of 1774. In any case, America favored the traditional styles of the early Georgian period in its dwellings and those of Continental Europe in its public structures. While a recognizably "Federal" architectural style developed by the late 1780s, it rather quickly yielded to the Classical Revival that emphasized form over applied detailing.

The typical Federal façade was clapboarded and symmetrical, its centrally located entrance a composition of six-paneled door, framing pilasters, and elliptical fan light, sometimes sheltered by a porch or portico. The door opened into a hall in which the staircase still held pride of place, although its balusters and handrails were newly attenuated and its stair-edge detailing simplified. The rooms beyond this hall were generally square or rectangular in plan, even if dining rooms could be given a niche to accommodate a sideboard. Interior doorways were often pedimented, and enriched with fine-scaled paterae, swags, or urns.

Fireplaces were similarly decorated. Usually of wood, occasionally of marble, these were often the most Adamesque element within the structure. Typically, a small, relief-carved panel was centered under the mantelshelf, and surrounds were embellished with applied or carved designs. An especially elaborate example, carved by McIntire for Elias Hasket Derby and salvaged when the Derby house was demolished in 1815, exhibits an exemplary vocabulary of stiff-leaf, swags, fluting, garlands, classical figures, guilloches, rosettes, acanthus leaves, and lyres; only McIntire's signature vine, here rather naively executed, lacks the refinement necessary to Neo-Classical ornament. (The fireplace surround is now in the Metropolitan Museum of Art, New York.) Other fireplaces, like some architectural trim, incorporated composition ornament purchased from London exporters.

Full panelling was retained only on the fireplace wall (although it was disappearing even here); the wainscot on the remaining walls rose to the level of the dado and whitewash, paint, or wallpaper was used between dado and cornice moulding. In grander houses the walls of the principal rooms would be papered, the papers often imported from England or France. During the late 18th century wallpaper was often plain with elaborate festoon or floral borders at cornice level and around the wainscotting and doors. After 1800, striped or floral papers were preferred and geometric and Neo-Classical motifs were common. The wealthiest houses used scenic or panoramic papers produced by French companies such as Dufour et Cie. and Zuber et Cie. Walls were generally broken by tall, nine-over-nine windows distributed more or less evenly across the façade (six-over-six units, sometimes triple-hung, eventually became standard).

Reception and bedroom floors generally consisted of wooden planks that were either left plain or were painted or stencilled. Hall flooring could be made of white or patterned marble or stone, and kitchen and service areas often used brick underfoot. Floorcoverings were quite varied and included painted canvas floorcloths with marble or geometric patterns and carpets. Loomed carpets were available to the wealthy after the 1790s and were usually patterned with scrollwork, polygonal shapes or floral and Neo-Classical motifs. They were generally cut to fit the shape of the room and were laid wall to wall and fixed to the floor with tacks.

Revealing the economic level of the owners, ceilings ranged from whitewashed boards, to plain plaster, to decorative work executed with plaster of Paris, putty, or papier-mâché. The backgrounds of elaborate ceilings could be strongly coloured, their swags, guilloches, and arabesques picked out in white, but this treatment diminished in importance after the turn of the century.

Many of the accessories that decorated Federal rooms – among them looking-glasses, picture frames, statuettes, porcelain, and earthenware – were imported, usually from England, but sometimes from France, Germany, or Holland. Still, a substantial number of looking-glass frames were domestically produced, particularly after 1800. (Polished glass was invariably imported, and usually imported as mirror, that is, silvered; there was only one silverer in New York in 1817, and even so late as 1872, the United States did not produce mirrored glass.)

More than many other pieces, looking glasses tended to retain the shapes of the Chippendalian Colonial style. Even in 1820, American merchants and makers offered (and presumably sold) frames with swan-necked pediments and bottoms cut in intricate but unidimensional curves, the whole oddly embellished with such symbols of the time as urns, swags, husks, and eagles. Other domestically produced forms were more genuinely Neo-Classical: the convex glasses that, despite their lack of candleholders, are known in America as girandoles; and those made in the "columnar" style associated with Sheraton. Many of the latter are topped by a entablature decorated with balls, and have a decorative panel of arabesques, bas-reliefs, seascape, or portrait at the top of the glass. Other looking glasses were hung within U-shaped stands and, depending on size, were placed on either the floor or a dressing table.

If looking glasses were primarily foreign in origin, Federal clocks were primarily domestic. Like many mirror frames, however, tall clock cases were transitional in styling, mixing curved pediments with paterae, string inlay, and smooth bracket feet. Shorter versions were made to be placed on mantels, brackets, and shelves. Still, it was during this period that American clockmaking took a new turn, with the development of small and relatively inexpensive wall and shelf clocks. Around 1802, Massachuetts clock-maker Simon Willard developed an eight-day wall clock called the "banjo" because of its shape, much copied then and later. Some four or five years later, Eli Terry of Connecticut set up a factory with water-powered machinery, where he eventually produced thousands of wooden clock mechanisms.

The purely Neo-Classical phase of the Federal period lasted only some twenty years. By 1815, it had been submerged by the flamboyant lines and neo-archaic forms of English Regency and French Empire design that inspired the dual Greek Revival / American Empire period. One major source of inspiration for the new approach was *The London Chair-Makers' and Carvers' Book of Prices for Workmanship* (1802) and its supplement (1808). Of the Federal furniture makers, only Phyfe – who had experimented with the Greek and Roman idiom as early as 1805 – survived the change in styles.

REED BENHAMOU

See also Bulfinch; McIntire

Selected Collections

Examples of Federal Style furniture and some period rooms can be seen in the following museums: Winterthur Museum, Delaware; Baltimore Museum of Art; Boston Museum of Fine Arts; Brooklyn Museum, and Metropolitan Museum of Art, New York. Celebrated examples of Federal Style architecture and interiors survive in the Gardner-Pingree House, Boscobel, New York, and in the Harrison Gray Otis House, Boston.

Further Reading

The standard history of Federal Style furniture is Montgomery 1966. Well-illustrated surveys of interiors of this period appear in Garrett 1980, and Garrett 1992 which also includes a list of houses open to public view and a bibliography.

Boyd, Sterling, *The Adam Style in America, 1770–1820*, New York: Garland, 1985

Davidson, Marshall B. and Elizabeth Stillinger, *The American Wing at the Metropolitan Museum of Art*, New York: Metropolitan Museum, 1985

Fairbanks, Jonathan L. and Elizabeth Bidwell Bates, *American Furniture: 1620 to the Present*, New York: Marek, and London: Orbis, 1981

Garrett, Elisabeth Donaghy, *The Antiques Book of American Interiors: Colonial and Federal Styles*, New York: Crown, 1980

Garrett, Wendell, *Classic America: The Federal Style and Beyond*, New York: Rizzoli, 1992

Garvan, Beatrice B., *Federal Philadelphia, 1785–1825: The Athens of the Western World* (exhib. cat.), Philadelphia: Philadelphia Museum of Art, 1987

Gorvy, Brett, "American Classics" in *Antique Collector*, February 1993, pp.44–49

Harmon, Robert B., *The Federal or Adamesque Style in American Architecture: A Brief Style Guide*, Monticello, IL: Vance, 1982

Lahikainen, Dean, "The Gardner-Pingree House, Massachusetts" in *Magazine Antiques*, 137, March 1990, pp.718–29

Mayhew, Edgar de Noailles and Minor Myers, Jr., *A Documentary History of American Interiors from the Colonial Period to 1915*, New York: Scribner, 1980

Montgomery, Charles C., *American Furniture: The Federal Period in the Winterthur Museum*, New York: Viking, 1966; London: Thames and Hudson, 1967

Parissien, Steven, *Adam Style*, London: Phaidon, and Washington, DC: Preservation Press, 1992

Peirce, Donald C. and Hope Alswang, *American Interiors: New England and the South*, New York: Brooklyn Museum, 1983

Pierson, William H., Jr., *The Colonial and Neo-Classical Styles* (American Buildings and Their Architects, vol.1), New York: Doubleday, 1970

Feure, Georges de 1868–1943

Dutch designer, painter and lithographer

Georges de Feure was the adopted name of Georges Joseph van Sluijters. He was born on 6 September 1868, in Paris, the son of a Dutch architect, Jan Hendrick van Sluijters and his Belgian wife. Although he was one of the most significant artistic figures in France between 1890 and 1905, much of de Feure's career is shrouded in mystery and he died in poverty, largely forgotten, in 1943.

De Feure's family fled France in 1870 after the outbreak of the Franco-Prussian War, moving from place to place in Holland and Belgium, wherever Jan could find employment. Apart from a brief period attending evening classes at the Royal Academy of Architecture, Amsterdam, in 1886, Georges's only formal education was at the Jesuit boarding school in Hilversum which he left in 1883. Between 1883 and 1886 he worked as a clerk in Utrecht and Dordrecht, as a bookseller's assistant in The Hague, and an odd-job man at an Amsterdam theatre where his duties ranged from bill-posting, scenery painting, and wardrobe assistant to part-time acting.

Arriving in Paris in 1889, he found lodgings in Montmartre where he associated with the painters, writers and musicians who crowded the café-cabarets of that area. During the next decade he established a reputation as a major graphic artist. Beginning with caricatures and illustrations for humorous or popular literary magazines such as *Fin de Siècle*, *Le Messager français*, *Le Boulevard*, and *La Butte*, he went on to produce cover designs and illustrations for books such as *Le Rêve* by Emile Zola (1888), *Fémines* by Octave Uzanne (1896), and, most significantly, *La Porte des Rêves* by Marcel Schwob (1898). He also worked in watercolour and gouache, producing work that was strongly influenced by Symbolist literature and painting.

By 1892 he had mastered the techniques of colour lithography, producing small edition prints as well as posters for magazines, groceries, circuses and café-cabarets. Many of these show pale, mysterious, often threatening women in a restricted palette of browns, greens and rose; others in a more garish palette of yellows, reds and blues are perhaps less successful. Although he might have been influenced by the poster artists Jules Chéret, it is unlikely that de Feure studied under him.

Heavily Symbolist in content, the principal themes of many

of de Feure's graphic works were the *femme fatale* or Sapphic love. During this period he exhibited at the Expositions des Peintres Impressionistes et Symbolistes (1892 and 1895); the Salon de la Rose & Croix (1893 and 1894); the Salon de Cent (1894-95); the Salons de la Société Nationale des Beaux-Arts in Paris (1894–98) and Brussels (1895). He held his first one-man show in Paris in 1894.

Around this time de Feure also appears to have developed an interest in the decorative arts. He was associated with André Marty in the establishment of l'Artisan Moderne, c.1894, for which he designed such disparate objects as a lithographed lampshade, tables, a table-rug, and the silvered bronze cane-handle of abstract whip-lash design between 1895 and 1896.

In 1899 Siegfried Bing invited de Feure to play a major role in the creation of what would become the single most significant exhibit at the Paris Exhibition of 1900. The Pavillon de L'Art Nouveau Bing was a single-storey structure with a façade decorated with canvases painted by de Feure, of female figures in contemporary dress as allegories of architecture, sculpture, metalwork, jewellery, pottery, glasswork and leatherwork. Of the six interior spaces in the Pavillon, de Feure was responsible for the total design of the dressing room and boudoir, as well as the stained-glass windows representing the Four Seasons.

In de Feure's dressing room, curtains of Japanese silk, furniture of natural Hungarian ash and wall coverings of figured silk in grey / blue, grey / mauve, grey / green decorated with white copper fittings, appeared "like a field of flowers under the moonlight". His boudoir was even more acclaimed. The wall covering was of grey silk brocade with a floral pattern, reflected in the silk embroidered gilded beechwood furniture, with a subtly carved floral decoration. The white marble fireplace was designed in the form of stalks supporting the mantelpiece. In this quintessentially feminine room de Feure combined 18th-century influences, with the ébéniste tradition of fine craftsmanship and the contemporary fascination with naturalistic organic forms associated with Art Nouveau.

Perhaps spurred on by this success, de Feure established his own atelier in partnership with the German architect Theodor Cossmann in 1901. He immediately received a commission for the interior of part of the Restaurant Knoss on the Boulevard des Italiens, where large panels of female figures were framed with green enamelled brickwork. At the same time he was engaged in designing porcelain for the Limoges company of Gérard, Dufraisseix & Abbot, which included teapots, jugs, cups, saucers, toothpick holders, trays, figurines and sweet-boxes, with floral designs or human figures in green and rose-mauve on a white ground. These were exhibited at the International Exhibition in Turin in 1902. He also continued to design furniture and decorations for Bing.

In recognition of his importance, de Feure was made a Chevalier of the Légion d'Honneur in 1901. Two years later he showed over 150 paintings as well as decorative art objects in Bing's gallery, including a fascinating series of landscapes – another new departure. Sadly, this venture was not a financial success, and due to increasing financial difficulties Bing's shop closed in 1904. A year later de Feure's company also closed.

Much of the remainder of de Feure's career is impossible to trace. He is known to have married in England in 1915, having divorced his first wife whom he had married in 1897, and he was working in France again by 1929 where he stayed for the rest of his life. Later commissions included furniture and interiors for the Vionnet fashion house (1923), for which he designed 18 differently styled changing rooms. And in 1925 he designed and decorated the pavilion of Roubaix and Tourcoing at the Paris Exposition Internationale des Arts Décoratifs et Industriels Modernes, which was the showcase for French Art Deco. But despite developments in his style, de Feure's most distinctive work was essentially a product of fin-de-siècle Paris, to which he had made a major contribution in every aspect of the decorative arts.

BRIAN J.R. BLENCH

See also Bing

Biography

Georges Joseph van Sluijters. Born in Paris, 6 September 1868, the son of a Dutch architect. Family fled Paris, 1870, and lived in various towns in Amsterdam and Belgium. Educated at boarding school in Hilversum until 1883; attended the Rijksakademie voor Beeldende Kunsten, Amsterdam, 1886. Had two sons with Pauline Dornec, 1890 and 1891; married Marguerite Guibert, 1897 (divorced); second marriage, 1915. Lived in Paris from 1889; worked as an illustrator and painter during the 1890s; first one-person exhibition, 1894. Associated with André Marty's L'Artisan Moderne, c.1894, and began designing furniture and decorative art items. Head of the design department for Siegfried Bing's shop L'Art Nouveau, Paris, 1900–04; ran his own studio, L'Atelier de Feure, in partnership with the German architect Theodor Cossmann, 1901–05. Worked for a period as a stage designer in England. Active in Paris as a decorator and designer of furniture, textiles, ceramics and metalwork, from c.1923. Exhibited at the 1900 Paris Exhibition, 1902 Turin Exhibition, and 1925 Paris Exhibition. Founder-member, Société Moderne des Beaux-Arts, 1900, and Salon d'Automne, 1902. Chevalier, Légion d'honneur, 1901; Officier, Légion d'honneur, 1923. Died after a long illness in Paris, 26 November 1943.

Selected Works

Examples of de Feure's furniture are in the Musée des Arts Décoratifs, Copenhagen, and the Musée des Arts Décoratifs, Paris. Examples of his stained glass are in the Virginia Museum of Fine Arts, Richmond.

Interiors

1900	Pavillon de L'Art Nouveau Bing, Exposition Universelle, Paris (boudoir and dressing room; interiors and furnishings)
1901	Restaurant Knoss, Paris (dining room; interior and furnishings)
1908	Maison Kreiser, Paris (interiors and furnishings)
1923	Madeleine Vionnet's showrooms, Paris (interiors and furniture)
1925	Exposition Internationale des Arts Décoratifs et Industriels Moderne (Roubaix and Tourcoing Pavilion; design and decoration)

De Feure designed furniture for Maison Fleury in 1894, furnishings, stained glass and painted decoration for Bing, 1900–04, porcelain for Gérard, Dufraisseix & Abbot in 1902, and furnishings, textiles, frescoes, and lighting for Manufacture Française de Tapis et Couverture, early 1920s.

Further Reading

For a comprehensive monograph on de Feure see Millman, 1993, which includes a full bibliography.

Fréchet, André, "Une grand maison de couture moderne: Madeleine Vionnet, Decorateur: Georges de Feure" in *Mobilier et Décoration d'Interieurs*, 5, August–September 1923, pp.3–11

Jullian, Philippe, *The Triumph of Art Nouveau: Paris Exhibition 1900*, Oxford: Phaidon, and New York: Larousse, 1974

Millman, Ian, "Georges de Feure: A Turn of the Century Universal Artist" in *Apollo*, CXXVI, November 1988, pp.314–18

Millman, Ian, "Georges de Feure et la Maison de Couture Madeleine Vionnet" in *Bulletin de la Société de l'Histoire de l'Art Français*, 1990, pp.309–20

Millman, Ian, *Georges de Feure 1868–1943*, Zwolle: Waanders, 1993

Mourey, Gabriel, "Round the Exhibition, 1: The House of 'Art Nouveau Bing'" in *Studio*, XX, August 1900, pp.169–81

Troy, Nancy J., *Modernism and the Decorative Arts in France: Art Nouveau to Le Corbusier*, New Haven and London: Yale University Press, 1991

Weisberg, Gabriel P., *Art Nouveau Bing: Paris Style 1900* (exhib. cat.: Smithsonian Institution, Washington, DC), New York: Abrams, 1986

Fireplaces. *See* Chimneypieces

Firescreens and Polescreens

The firescreen is an adjustable or fixed screen designed to protect persons seated in a room from the direct heat of an open fireplace. It can also be pushed in front of the fireplace when not in use, to serve as a decorative element. Firescreens first appeared in the 17th century, having been used in England as early as the reign (1625–49) of Charles I. They were part of a general trend towards greater numbers and varieties of furniture pieces in the houses of the wealthy and middle classes in England, North America, and continental European countries.

Firescreens were finely crafted pieces of furniture suitable for the most formal room settings. In addition, the screen panels of needlework, tapestry, beadwork, leather, or painted wood were highly decorative. Tapestry was often used when the screen was part of a matching set of furniture and hangings. However it was as vehicle for the display of needlework that the firescreen has maintained its popularity even to the present day. Canvaswork petit-point (tent stitch) was most often used, but crewel embroidery in wool on linen was also suitable since the screens were not subject to wear. Pictorial scenes, floral arrangements, ornamental maps, genealogical charts, and family coats of arms were mounted on the side of the panel facing into the room away from the fire. Succeeding generations often replaced the needlework in old screens with work of their own. Berlin woolwork pictures were used in the 19th century, and embroidery in a mix of styles has been employed in the 20th century.

In Great Britain and North America firescreens were made from designs by Chippendale, Hepplewhite, Sheraton, and other furniture designers of the late 18th and early 19th centuries. Chippendale polescreens, in particular, were elegantly made with tripod legs, claw feet, and Chinoiserie fretwork.

There were three main kinds of firescreens. The polescreen, with a sliding screen on a turned upright pole, four to five feet tall, supported on a tripod base, was also known as a screen-stick in the late 17th century. The screen, often of needlework or beadwork, was at first rectangular, but oval and shield shapes became fashionable in the late 18th century. In some cases the tripod was replaced by a solid base, and the screen became a banner of velvet or other fabric with tassels that hung from a bar on the upright pole. In the early 19th century some English polescreens were made in the French Empire style with claw, ball, or scroll feet and Egyptian motifs, inspired by Napoleon's campaign in Egypt. When the pole was fitted with a shelf to hold a candlestick, it was called a polescreen candle-stand. Small candle polescreens less than two feet high were made to sit on tables and shield a candle flame.

The horse or cheval screen, consisted of two uprights, each balanced on trestle feet, with a rectangular panel between. The panel was either fixed in place or made to slide up and down in grooves in order to adjust the height. The word horse in this instance indicates a large object, often used in connection with mirrors. Thomas Sheraton in his *The Cabinet-Maker and Upholsterer's Drawing-Book* 3rd edition, 1802, states that horse screens were about three feet six inches in height and about 19 inches in breadth. Elaborate carving and gilding were often used on these screens until the end of the 18th century, when lighter and simpler screens were in vogue. Needlework, tapestry, beadwork, or paintings were used for the panel in designs that included Chinoiserie, classical figures, flowers, and landscapes. Horse screens used in America were generally imported from England.

The third type was the small folding screen consisting of two panels on legs that were hinged together to stand upright when set at an angle. In the 17th century folding screens with painted leather panels were made, chiefly in Spain, but also in France and the Low Countries. After the restoration of Charles II (1660) leather screens in continental style were made in England. Needlework was also used for the panels.

Variations included the firescreen desk, a shallow drop-front desk box set vertically between footed uprights, serving as a firescreen and a desk. When closed, the desk appeared similar to the horse screen. The front panel dropped down to form a horizontal writing surface with storage area for paper and pens. These date from the 1780s. In the early 19th century they sometimes had a wooden panel extending almost down to the floor. The firescreen table, made from the mid 18th century, was a four-legged tea table, the screen being a sliding frame attached to the two back legs and covered with a heavy fabric or a painted panel of Japanned metal. Hand-held screens resembling flat fans on sticks also protected the face from the fire.

Like the open fire that it is designed to screen, the firescreen has become a purely decorative feature in the modern house. The flat screen surface is still eminently suitable for the display of needlework or small pieces of tapestry. Some new screens in period styles are being made for historic houses and other formal room settings. Crewel embroidery and canvaswork of all kinds continue to be made by 20th century needleworkers who find the firescreen a convenient means of display.

CONSTANCE A. FAIRCHILD

Further Reading

Gilbert, Christopher and Anthony Wells-Cole, *The Fashionable Fireplace, 1660–1840* (exhib. cat.) Leeds: Temple Newsam House, 1985

Joy, Edward, *A Pictorial Dictionary of British 19th Century Furniture Design*, Woodbridge, Suffolk: Antique Collectors' Club, 1977

MacQuoid, Percy and Ralph Edwards, *The Dictionary of English Furniture*, revised edition, 3 vols., 1954; reprinted Woodbridge, Suffolk: Antique Collectors' Club, 1983

Sackville-West, T., "Firescreens" in *Antique Collector*, 49, March 1978, pp.90–93

Wood, Henry, *A Useful and Modern Work on Cheval and Pole Screens, Ottomans, Chairs and Settees, for Mounting Berlin Needle Work*, London: Ackermann, 1846

Fischer von Erlach, Johann Bernhard

1656–1723

Austrian architect

Johann Bernhard Fischer von Erlach was the Imperial architect of the Hapsburg emperor in Vienna at the end of the 17th and early 18th century. His late Baroque style in architecture and interior decor is an amalgam of the Italian Baroque, with which he was familiar from study in Rome, and the French Baroque and newly developed Rococo which he knew from books and travel. Also a sculptor, Fischer von Erlach designed palaces, sculptural monuments, and many churches which provide much of the extant evidence regarding his ideas on interior decoration.

A scholar of the history of architecture, Fischer von Erlach published a landmark illustrated text called *Entwurff einer historischen Architektur* (Historic Architecture), 1721. Historicism infused his architecture. But he was a man of his times and chose his decorative formats to match the dignity and purpose of the individual works he conceived.

An early work, the Ancestral Hall of the Althan Family at their Schloss Frain, Moravia (1688) is a monumental free-standing oval hall rising to a soaring oval cupola. Set into the vault are ten vertically placed oval windows which light the ceiling's illusionistic frescoes, depicting the history of the family, painted in 1695 by Johann Michael Rottmayr. The walls of the lower register alternate French windows and wall segments that are articulated by two Corinthian pilasters with a large niche, holding statues of famous members of the Althan family within them. A filigree of white stucco floral motifs, surrounding bas-reliefs, covers the other wall surfaces.

In 1696–1700, Fischer von Erlach designed a City Palace for Prince Eugene of Savoy, commander of the Imperial armies. Twelve original exterior bays are articulated by giant Ionic pilasters. Entry is through a vaulted vestibule whose walls are covered with delicate Rococo stucco work. A well-lit stairhall to one side gives access to the upper storeys of the palace. The first flight of stairs is flanked by four large atlantes (carved by Giovanni Giuliani) and opens through the entire palace. Fischer von Erlach's use of decorative balustrades, the open character of the stairhall, and the use of sculpted atlantes was to resonate in the interior decor of other later palaces of the Viennese 18th century.

Another magnificent staircase is to be found in the Batthyány Palace, Vienna. This staircase consists of three flights and is symmetrical, and it occupies the whole of the right-hand side of the central area of the Palace. It is approached through the vestibule which contains four pairs of heavy Tuscan columns, holding up nine cross-vaults, supported at the walls by rusticated pilasters. Unlike the vestibule, however, whose stark and severely undecorated style evokes an air of monumental simplicity, the staircase is richly and elegantly decorated and is enriched by vases and niches with shell motifs and masks that recall the ornament of 17th-century Holland.

Outside of Vienna, Salzburg is the site of the largest number of works by Fischer von Erlach. One of them, the University Church (Kollegienkirche), 1696–1707, is representative of his ideas on sacred design. Its powerful façade is composed of a convex central section flanked by towers. Giant Ionic pilasters, stuccoed garlands, and roofline figural sculpture decorate a façade whose surfaces are painted in umbers and beige.

In plan the University Church is a cross set within a rectangle. There is a Latin dome over the crossing and four oval chapels, with galleries above, lie on the corners. The monumental interior, stuccoed and painted entirely in white, soars vertically above a stone floor. Giant Corinthian pilasters rise on 14-foot bases to create Roman triumphal arch motifs along the barrel-vaulted nave. These terminate in an entablature whose frieze is a running band of Antique motifs in stucco, designed by Fischer. Between the pilasters double niches, each containing a life-size sculptural figure of a saint, were placed.

The interior is well-lit from large arched windows, from the dome, from oval "bull's-eye" windows (a Fischer favorite) in the apse and on the entry wall, and from oculi cut into the vaults of the chapels. Here the architect is following an 18th-century preference in the North for well-lit interior spaces. The orchestration of decoration culminates in the apse. Set behind a traditional balustrade, the high altar is flanked by two free-standing Palladian columns. The altar, although not Fischer's original conception, perfectly fits the space. A stucco glory of clouds and angels, with the Immaculate Virgin in the center, covers much of the wall surface and surrounds two large windows on the back wall.

The commission for the Imperial votive Saint Charles Borromeo Church (Karlskirche) in Vienna, 1715–38, came from Emperor Charles VI. Its iconographic program both embraces the life of the emperor's patron saint and aggrandizes the Imperial family. The historiated entry façade carries a Roman-style portico connected by concave wall segments, before which colossal Trajanic columns stand, to low bell towers. A broad Latin dome covers the large oval congregational space of the interior. To this centralized space, rectangular arms are appended on the cross axes and, on the diagonal axes, smaller rectangular chapels with galleries above, are inserted. The church's interior space has a rich complexity similar to that found in Italian Baroque architecture. All of the openings into the principal space are arched. Fischer von Erlach's familiar giant-order Corinthian pilasters standing on high bases elegantly encircle the room. Single storey paired free-standing columns mark the entry into the cross arms.

Fischer von Erlach: central oval hall, Imperial Library, Vienna, 1722–30

Differing from Fischer's usual church interiors, both pilasters and columns are of dark veined marble and their capitals are richly gilt.

To complete the decorative ensemble of the St. Charles Borromeo church interior, as was true of secular interiors of the period, sculpture was added. Fischer orchestrates figures of saints and angels, stucco swags and other ornaments within the interior. Also, he gives rich sculptural expression to those other two basic church accessories – the pulpit and the organ loft and its casing. In the extended choir and apse, the high altar too is given definition through a sculptural ensemble (white and gold in color). Between marble Ionic columns, a statue of St. Charles Borromeo ascending to heaven is seen.

Among the many impressive libraries built during the Austrian Baroque period, Fischer von Erlach's Imperial Library, Vienna, 1722–30, is the best-known and most monumental in scale. A wing of the Imperial Hofburg Palace, the Library's spatial conception is based on Fischer's knowledge of Ancient Roman architectural forms. The longitudinally placed oval central hall (dimensions 77 metres by 14 metres) is flanked by rectangular wings sub-divided into two sections by free-standing marble columns and enclosed circular stairways. The stairs lead to the second storey balustraded gallery which is held by carved and gilded wooden brackets in the wings and by free-standing tapered wood piers in the central oval hall. Built-in bookshelves made of finely carved and gilt wood reach from the marble floor, through the gallery level, to the springing of the vaults.

The imagery of the Imperial Library's centralized oval hall celebrates the Hapsburg Dynasty. A marble statue of the ruling emperor, Charles VI, patron of the Library is placed in the center of the space as defined by a medallion pattern on the marble floor. Statues of the Emperor's ancestors stand on high podia before the tapered piers of the gallery. The enormous ceiling fresco, lit by bull's-eye windows, was painted by Daniel Gran in 1730. It is filled with allegorical imagery alluding to the power of the emperor and to his patronage of the arts and learning.

The many Imperial commissions Fischer von Erlach received suited his taste for large-scale projects, which, while alluding to the past, successfully incorporated the latest aesthetic impulses from Baroque architecture.

BEVERLY F. HEISNER

Biography

Born in Graz, baptized 20 July 1656, the son of the sculptor Johann Baptist Fischer. Trained as a sculptor in his father's workshop. Went to Rome, 1671; worked under the architect and painter Phillip Schor, and in the studio of Bernini; employed as Schor's assistant in Naples, 1783. Married 1) Sophia Konstantin Morgner: 5 children including the architect Joseph Emanuel Fischer von Erlach (1693–1742); 2) Franziska Sophia Willer, 1705. Active as an architect in Vienna and Graz from 1687 and also in Salzburg from the 1690s. Appointed architectural tutor to Joseph, elder son of the Emperor Leopold I, 1689; joined the court of the Emperor Joseph, 1694; raised to the nobility, 1796; appointed chief inspector of court buildings, Vienna, 1705. Travelled to England and Holland, 1704; and to Venice, 1707 and 1717. A scholar of architectural history, he published the influential *Entwurff* in 1721. Died after a long illness in Vienna, 5 April 1723.

Selected Works

For a complete list of Fischer von Erlach's architectural works see Aurenhammer 1973.

Interiors

1688–95 Schloss Frain, Moravia, Czechoslovakia (ancestral hall)
1690–93 Althan Garden Palace, Rossau, Vienna (building and interiors)
c.1693 Hunting Lodge, Engelhartstetten (building and interiors)
1694–1702 Dreifaltigkeitskirche, Salzburg (priest's house and college; building and interiors)
1696–1700 City Palace of Prince Eugene of Savoy, Vienna (building and interiors)
1696–1707 Kollegienkirche, Salzburg (building and interiors)
1696–1711 Schönbrunn Palace, Vienna (plans, building and interiors)
1698–1705 Batthyány Palace, Vienna (building and interiors)
1700–09 Klesheim Palace, Salzburg (buildings including garden house and interiors)
1710–16 Trautson Garden Palace, Vienna (building and interiors)
1715–38 Karlskirche, Vienna (building and interiors)
1716–18 Herzogenburg Convent, Lower Austria (central part of east wing, great hall and staircase)
c.1716–19 Hofburg Palace, Vienna (project for revisions)
c.1720 Schwarzenberg Garden Palace, Vienna (alteration and interior decorations)
1722–30 Imperial Library, Hofburg Palace, Vienna (building and interiors)

Publications

Entwurff einer historischen Architektur, 1721; 2nd edition, 1725; reprinted with English translation Farnborough, 1964

Further Reading

An authoritative study of Fischer von Erlach's work appears in Sedlmayr 1976.

Aurenhammer, Hans, *Johann Bernhard Fischer von Erlach* (exhib. cat.), Vienna: Schroll, 1957
Aurenhammer, Hans, *J.B. Fischer von Erlach*, London: Allen Lane, and Cambridge, MA: Harvard University Press, 1973
Buchowiecki, Walther, *Der Barockbau der Ehemaligen Hofbibliothek in Wien*, Vienna: Prachner, 1957
Franz, H.G., *Die Deutsche Barockbaukunst Mährens*, Munich: Bruckmann, 1943
Frey, Dagobert, *Johann Bernhard Fischer von Erlach*, Vienna: Holzel, 1923
Grimschitz, Bruno, *Wiener Barockpaläste*, Vienna: Wiener Verlag, 1944
Hagen-Dempf, Felicitas, *Die Kollegienkirche in Salzburg*, Vienna, 1949
Hempel, Eberhard, "Jugendwerke Fischers von Erlach" in *Kunstchronik*, 10, 1957, p.338
Hempel, Eberhard, *Baroque Art and Architecture in Central Europe*, Harmondsworth: Penguin, 1965
Ilg, Albert, *Leben und Werke Fischers von Erlach*, Vienna: Konegan, 1895
Kreul, Andreas, *Die Barockbaumeister Fischer von Erlach: Bibliographie zu Leben und Werk*, Wiesbaden: Harrassowitz, 1988
Kunoth, Georg, *Die Historische Architektur Fischers von Erlach*, Düsseldorf: Schwann, 1956
Lanchester, H.V., *Fischer von Erlach*, London: Benn, 1924
Lorenz, Hellmut, "Das 'Lustgartengebäude' Fischers von Erlach: Variationen eines Architektonischen Themas" in *Wiener Jahrbuch für Kunstgeschichte*, 32, 1979, pp.59–88
Moisy, P., "Fischer von Erlach et les Architectes Français" in *Art de France*, 3, 1963

Passmore, Edward, "Fischer von Erlach, Architect to a Monarchy" in *Journal of the Royal Institute of British Architects*, 58, 1951, pp.452–75

Sedlmayr, Hans, *Johann Bernhard Fischer von Erlach*, 1956; reprinted Vienna: Herold, 1976

Weber, Nicolas Fox, "Baroque Splendours of Vienna's Schwarzenberg Palace" in *Architectural Digest*, 47, September 1990, pp.116

Zacharias, Thomas, *Joseph Emanuel Fischer von Erlach*, Vienna: Herold, 1960

Floorcloths

The term floorcloth is a slightly problematic and misleading one. In the 18th century it referred to any treated or untreated cloth laid on the floor, and included materials such as baize and drugget which were frequently used to cover more expensive carpet, especially in dining areas. By the 19th century, however, floorcloth was more often used to describe cloth treated with an evaporating oil and painted to make it waterproof. Such cloth was also called oilcloth or waxcloth, and it is to these materials that the term floorcloth usually refers today.

The precise origins of floor oilcloths are still obscure. While there are references to painted cloth and to "oyl" cloth in the 15th and 16th centuries there is no clear evidence that they were used on floors until the early 18th century by which time they appear to have become common in both Britain and America. In 1728, the estate inventory of Massachusetts governor, William Burnet, referred to two painted oil floorcloths. In 1738, the *Encyclopedia of Architecture* warned against using painted floorcloths because they would trap moisture and promote rot in the wood flooring. In 1750, the writer Dr. Samuel Johnson recorded his disdain at a friend's efforts to impress him with a new and brightly painted floorcloth. And in 1760, the *Maryland Gazette* carried an advertisement for one John Winters that claimed he could "paint floorcloths as neat as any imported from Britain."

The early floorcloths were usually made in two-to-three-yard squares of linen, hemp or cotton and had to be seamed together for larger sections. The process of sizing the cloth and covering it with successive layers of paint was done by hand as was the painting of the designs which were either stencilled or painted freehand. Popular patterns included plaited mat, Turkey carpet and a variety of Neo-Classical designs. During the mid and late 18th century painted floorcloths were frequently used in passages, on stairs and in entrance halls. Their waterproof properties also made them suitable as a protective covering for expensive carpets under sideboards and tables in dining rooms. A fine example dating from the 1780s survives from the hall at Workington Hall, Cumbria, and another floorcloth imitating a luxurious oriental carpet is recorded in the Attingham Park sale catalogue of 1827 as having been used in the Grand Dining Room.

The earliest recorded factory for making floorcloths was established by Nathan Smith in Knightsbridge, London. His 1763 patent indicates that there was already a commercial trade in floor oilcloth, but that he intended to introduce a new process for its manufacture. Smith is credited not only with the first factory, but also with the first printing block for creating designs on the floorcloth. By the end of the 18th century, there were at least twenty floor oilcloth factories in England, and by the end of the first decade of the 19th century, there were several in the United States as well.

The Industrial Revolution had a major impact on the production of floor oilcloth. The technological advance of the flyshuttle in the early 19th century meant that wider lengths of canvas could be produced. In sailmaking centers like Dundee and Kirkcaldy in Scotland, weaving factories began to produce heavy canvases in widths of 18 to 24 feet specifically for the floorcloth trade. This meant that seamless wall-to-wall floorcloths could be produced.

In August 1842, the London *Penny Magazine*, published by the Society for the Diffusion of Useful Knowledge, reported, "A Day at a Floorcloth Factory" (pp.337–344) and gave a full account of the manufacturing process. Canvas was stretched on large vertical frames and men working on scaffolding brushed and troweled both sides of the canvas with sizing. After drying, it was pumiced and a second coat was added, allowed to dry and pumiced again. Successive layers of thick paint were then applied with each layer drying thoroughly before the next was added. The cloth resembled a flexible, well-tanned hide by the time it was ready for its final sanding, painting and decorating.

In a manner similar to wallpaper printing, patterns were applied with wooden blocks that were usually eight to 24 inches square. Separate blocks were used for each color, but they could not overlap because the paint was so thick it would have created an uneven surface. In the final step, the floorcloth was hung in large, heated drying rooms and required six months or more of "curing" or "seasoning."

While 18th-century floorcloth had been made largely by hand and was frequently found in the homes of the well-to-do, 19th-century industrialization made floorcloth more affordable and it appeared in the homes of the middle class, and, by the end of the century, even the poor. Popular designs were usually imitative of tile, marble, or carpet. One outcome of the printing process was that the designs looked as if they were based on a dot matrix. This is because in order to cover large color areas, channels were cut into the wood blocks to give them "teeth" to hold the ink. The resulting pointillistic pattern resembled the woven texture of carpet. In 1851 at the Great Exhibition, the judges' criticism of this effect led the Scottish firm of Nairn to create blocks with a much smaller grid of squares. When all the color blocks had been printed, they used a "mash block" to blend the areas and give overall even coverage. Finally they used a block with metal strips to outline the different color sections and give them more definition.

By the end of the 19th century, most of the procedures for creating floor oilcloth had been mechanized. Although it continued to be marketed well into the 20th century, it was eventually superseded by the new development of linoleum.

There were various experiments in the early 19th century with rubber-based floor coverings, and Kamptulican, patented in England by Englishman Elijah Galloway in 1844, was one such effort. But it was expensive and never achieved the widespread acceptance that linoleum was to have. Linoleum was invented by another Englishman, Frederick Walton, in about 1860. Legend has it that one day Walton peeled off a skin of oxidized linseed oil from the top of an open paint jar. Playing

Floorcloths: trade advertisement showing a variety of linoleums from Whiteley's of London, mid-19th century

with the rubbery film gave him the idea that eventually led to his invention of linoleum. He named it from the Latin *linum* for flax and *oleum*, for oil.

Basically linoleum is oxidized linseed oil mixed with ground cork dust, gums and pigments which are then pressed through heavy metal rollers onto a canvas backing. Walton set up his first factory in 1864 in Staines, near London, and by 1866 the Linoleum Manufacturing Company was reporting steady sales. By 1869, they were exporting their product to the Continent and the United States.

The advantages of linoleum over oilcloth were that it was thicker, more waterproof, resilient, and much longer-wearing. Its popularity was such that the older oilcloth trade began to imitate it. In 1877 Walton instituted legal proceedings against the Nairn Company for infringement of his product and trade-name. But in 1878 the British Courts ruled against him. Walton had never actually registered the name linoleum. The ruling stated that even if he had, he could no longer have exclusive use of the name since linoleum had become a commonplace term and was the only way to describe the product.

Although Walton was soon in competition with numerous rivals, his company continued to expand their markets and sold their patents to firms in Germany, France and the United States. Walton went to the United States in 1872 and spent two years setting up the American Linoleum Manufacturing Company on Staten Island. He named the factory and company town he created "Linoleumville." Other American firms founded to make oilcloth soon began to make linoleum as well.

The next major technological improvement was the introduction of "inlaid" linoleum. Earlier linoleum had been all one color, which had offered an advantage over oilcoth because it would hide wear. When designs were wanted, the linoleum was painted much like the oilcloth and eventually showed the same kind of wear. In 1882, Walton created a way for the color patterns to go all the way through to the back thus greatly expanding the life of the material.

The first experiments with inlaid linoleum were done by hand, but by 1892 Walton had successfully mechanized production and in 1898 he set up his own manufacturing company, Greenwich Inlaid. Inlaid linoleum was long-wearing, but it was also more expensive and the earlier painted versions continued to be produced.

By 1910 there were prominent linoleum firms in Germany, France, the United States and Canada that competed with the older British companies. In America one of the most important was the Armstrong Cork and Tile Company. It began producing linoleum in 1908 and eventually came to dominate the American industry.

Linoleum was a world-wide product in other ways as well. Linseed oil came largely from South America, cork came from Spain and Portugal, jute came from Pakistan and India and was processed into the canvas backing in Scotland. Linoleum was also used world-wide, especially where the British Empire had established footholds. World War I greatly disrupted this network, but it quickly re-established itself in the post-war period.

In the 1910s cheaper felt-based versions of linoleum were developed. Congoleum is the best known example and it enjoyed wide popularity as a cheap substitute for linoleum. It did not wear as well or as long and was not as waterproof, but it was so cheap, it could be easily replaced. It was especially popular in rug-like widths and its patterns often imitated carpet. Armstrong's version of it was called "Quaker Rugs."

Linoleum remained one of the most popular floor coverings from the 1870s to the 1960s, but was eventually replaced with plastic-based products. Today most of what people call "linoleum" is vinyl floor covering.

The appeal of linoleum was that it was practical, durable, decorative, waterproof, inexpensive and easy to clean. It was also considered sanitary and therefore suited to bathrooms, nurseries, and kitchens. Unlike the earlier oilcloth, it was resilient, which gave it sound-proofing qualities and made it more comfortable. It was promoted for businesses and factories where people had to stand for long periods. A special grade of thick, solid-color linoleum called "Battleship" was developed and used on both American and British naval vessels as well as on yachts and ocean liners. It was so durable that it also became popular for use in government buildings including post offices, courthouses and schools.

The decorative qualities of linoleum also proved especially appealing. It offered "art" at an affordable price and was produced in an amazing variety of designs; by 1918 Armstrong was advertising 380 different patterns and added new ones every year. Most were imitative of other materials and popular lines included mosaic, tile, parquetry, granite, marble, and carpet designs. This imitative quality led to criticism and elitists scorned linoleum as a cheap and inartistic material. Nevertheless, linoleum was incredibly popular. Mass production had made it widely available; mass advertising had made it well known, and popular taste made it a success. Linoleum was the "democratic floor covering" of its age.

PAMELA H. SIMPSON

See also Floorcoverings

Further Reading

Useful introductions to the history and manufacture of painted and printed floorcloths can be found in Von Rosenstiel and Winkler 1988, Parks 1993, and Gilbert 1987. For numerous illustrations and more detailed discussion of late 19th and 20th century examples see various trade journals, particularly *Builder*, 1888–1922, *Building News*, 1895–1905, *Carpet and Upholstery Trade Review*, 1877–1918, *Journal of Decorative Arts*, 1895–1921, and *Ladies Home Journal*, 1912–30.

Ayres, James, "Simple Floors and Floor Coverings" in *Traditional Homes*, June–August 1985

Blackman, Leo and Deborah Dietsch, "A New Look at Linoleum, Preservation's Rejected Floor Covering" in *Old House Journal*, January 1982, pp.9–12

Bristow, Ian, "Painted Floorcloths in the 18th Century" in *Society for the Preservation of Ancient Buildings News* (UK), 11, no.2, 1990

Gilbert, Christopher, James Lomax and Anthony Wells-Cole, *Country House Floors, 1650–1850*, Leeds: Leeds City Art Galleries, 1987

"How Linoleum and Oilcloths are Made" in *Scientific American*, 97, 13 July 1907, pp.128–30

Little, Nina Fletcher, *Floor Coverings in New England Before 1850*, Sturbridge, MA: Old Sturbridge Village, 1967

Mehler, William A., Jr., *Let the Buyer Have Faith: The Story of Armstrong*, Lancaster, PA: Armstrong World Industries, 1987

Muir, Augustus, *Nairns of Kirkcaldy: A Short History of the Company, 1847–1956*, Cambridge: Heffer, 1956

Parks, Bonnie W., "Floorcloths to Linoleum: The Development of Resilient Flooring" in Michael Auer (editor), *The Interiors Handbook for Historic Buildings*, vol.2, Washington, DC: Preservation Press, 1993

Von Rosenstiel, Helene, *American Rugs and Carpets from the Seventeenth Century to Modern Times*, New York: Morrow, and London: Barrie and Jenkins, 1978

Von Rosenstiel, Helene and Gail Caskey Winkler, *Floor Coverings for Historic Buildings*, Washington, DC: Preservation Press, 1988

Walton, Frederick, *The Infancy and Development of Linoleum Floorcloth*, London: Simpkin Marshall, 1925

Floorcoverings

There is a fundamental difference in the attitude of eastern and western societies regarding the use of floorcoverings. In eastern countries, and in many tribal societies, the floorcovering is treated as part of the furniture, and many activities are carried out by householders while seated on the floor. Street shoes are left at the door, and bare feet or soft slippers are worn in the house. In western societies rugs are used decoratively to add color to rooms, define room areas, and add warmth to cold floors. Bare feet and slippers are considered too informal for social wear, street shoes are commonly worn in the house, and only children use the floor. As a result, floorcoverings in the west are subject to heavier wear. Fine carpets are commonly used in rooms such as parlors and dining rooms where they do not receive the heavy foot traffic of the house, while utilitarian rugs and carpets are used in other areas of the house.

Animal skins were probably the first floorcoverings, followed by coarse plain weave fabrics and mats. Mats were woven of reeds, straw, rushes, palm leaves, bamboo, or other locally available fibers, and served for sleeping, eating, and other activities. A mat weaving process similar to basketry was used in Mesopotamia as early as c.5200 BC. The usual methods of making matting were to join bundles of fiber together by a twined thread or to weave the fibers in a simple plain weave.

In tropical areas *tapa*, or beaten bark cloth, was also used. Matting was the most commonly used floorcovering in Europe from the 16th to the 18th century. Tudor portraits frequently show rooms with traditional rush matting on the floors and samples of 17th century bullrush matting have been discovered at Hampton Court. During the Restoration period, these thick utilitarian floorcoverings were replaced by more finely-woven and decorative, often brightly-colored examples imported from Portugal, North Africa and Holland, and a Kensington Palace inventory of 1697 notes Portuguese mats in the principal bedchambers as well as the King's Drawing Room and Privy Chamber. By the second half of the 18th century, matting was confined to areas such as passages and halls but it was revived again during the Victorian and Edwardian periods when cheap Oriental mats flooded the European market.

In early times bed furniture was rare, and floorcoverings often served as bedding for persons sleeping on the floor. With regard to use, there was little distinction made between rugs, carpets, and blankets. The word rug itself is derived from the Scandinavian word *rugga* which meant a wool covering for the bed or body.

The earliest carpets were flat-surfaced weaves. The tapestry weave, in which the pattern is formed by discontinuous weft threads, is believed to be the oldest. The kilims of Turkey, Persia, the Caucasus, and Turkestan, as well as Indian dhurries and American Navajo rugs are woven by this method. Kilim designs incorporate many traditional motifs having symbolic meaning. Another flatwoven rug, the Soumak, was made in the Middle East and the Caucasus as early as the 7th century BC. In this weave, which is a variation of brocade, the weft threads are wrapped around pairs of warp threads in a lateral direction making a herringbone pattern on the surface and leaving many loose threads on the back.

Tapestry rugs, called *tapis sarasinois*, were first made in Aubusson, France, in the 8th century by Moors living there. The production of tapestry rugs and wall hangings increased in the 13th century when artists from Flanders moved to Aubusson. Aubusson production after the French Revolution was limited to carpets and upholstery. Aubusson has become the generic name for French flatwoven carpets.

Non-woven wool felt rugs have been used for at least 2000 years in Asia. They were made by nomads in Central Asia and Mongolia as yurt furnishings, and were exacted as tribute by the Chinese who used them as cushion covers and kneeling mats. Felt rugs were often decorated with appliqué, and embroidery in bold designs. A felt rug called namda, or numdah, has been made in India for many centuries. Recent namdas, exported to the west, have large chain stitch embroidery designs.

The pile rug or carpet is more durable than the flatwoven rug, and is the most commonly used floorcovering in temperate regions of the world. Carpet looms are generally the same as those used for tapestry. The pile is created during the weaving process by a series of threads knotted around the warp threads between rows of straight wefts. The symmetrical Ghiordes knot, used mainly in Turkish and Caucasian rugs, and the asymmetrical Persian (Sehna) knot, used in Persian, Central Asiatic, Indian, and Chinese carpets, are the two types of knots used. After each knotted row a weft thread is carried across the full width of the loom and beaten into place. When the carpet is finished the pile is cut to an even surface, and a fringe is formed of the warp ends. The pile gives the rug softness and creates an insulation barrier over the cold floor.

Floorcoverings: knotted wool pile carpet, Ushak, Turkey, 17th century

The earliest pile rug now extant was found frozen in the Pazyryk tombs of the Scythians in the Altai Mountains of Siberia. It is now housed in the Hermitage in St. Petersburg. This rug, which dates to c.500 BC, is very sophisticated in design and technique, leading scholars to believe that pile rug weaving in Central Asia developed as early as 2500 BC. From very early times the nomads of Central Asia and Mongolia used pile rugs as floors in their tents and yurts. Although there is a gap in the historical record of extant specimens until 1200 AD, rugs have been made continuously from the time of the Scythians and are mentioned by travellers and other writers. 13th-century fragments found in Turkey demonstrate that geometric patterns forming the basic design structure of rugs in that area were already well established.

Nomadic rug weaving is done by women on portable looms that can be rolled up and transported from place to place. The rugs are not large, and it was not until weavers settled in cities that large rugs on high vertical looms could be woven. Rugs are woven from bottom to top in either flat or knotted pile weave. The most commonly used material is sheep's wool, although in some regions goat's or camel's hair is used. Luxury carpets made in Persia or China may have a silk pile. Natural dyes were used exclusively until the late 19th century when aniline dyes were introduced from Europe. Aniline dyes are not colorfast, and many rugs with these dyes have faded.

When Marco Polo passed through Anatolia in the 13th

Floorcoverings: drawing room, The Close, Winchester, 1847; watercolour by Beatrice Olive Corfe

century, he described Turkish rugs as the finest in the world. Turkish rugs had geometrically stylized designs. The city of Ushak was an important center of carpet-making by the 16th century, and supplied the export market. Ushak carpets had two main types of design – medallion or star. Some Turkish rugs had borders of often meaningless Kufic script lettering. Writing was considered to have magic properties, and was incorporated into rugs and other decorative objects without regard to the literal meaning of the script.

When Oriental rugs were first imported into Europe from Turkey in the 14th century they were considered too valuable to put on the floor, so they were draped on tables, cupboards, and chests as decoration. Many paintings of the 14th through the 17th centuries, particularly those of Hans Holbein the Younger and Lorenzo Lotto, show such table rugs. This practice continued throughout the 17th century and carpets remained rare items with only rich and high-ranking persons having carpets underfoot. Oriental rugs were used on floors of wealthy homes in North America from the 18th century onward but they were still sufficiently rare that visitors often hesitated to walk on them. The carpet was placed in the center of the room as a showpiece, with tables and chairs arranged around the perimeter against the wall.

Rug making spread with Islam throughout Central Asia, the Middle East, India, China, North Africa, and the Iberian peninsula. Distinctive designs were developed in each place. Oriental rugs were named by their point of origin, although in some cases the name was that of the trading city (i.e., Samarkand), rather than the home of the weaver. The carpet trade with the west has continued through political upheavals and changes in consumer taste. Western consumer preference has affected both the design and coloring in carpets made for market since carpets were first exported.

Traditions of rug making were highly developed in Persia by the 16th century. The Safavid rulers in Persia established court workshops that produced densely woven carpets in naturalistic designs designated as medallion, garden, flower, vase, animal, or hunting carpets depending on the principal motifs. Many designs were influenced by Persian court painters who supplied cartoons for weaving patterns. Flower designs characterized the regional and village carpets of Persia.

Magnificent carpets were woven for the palace and other buildings in the new capital of Isfahan during the reign (1587–1628) of Shah 'Abbas I. During this time Persian carpets were first exported to Europe, where they were called "Polonaise carpets" from the mistaken idea that they were made in Poland. The finest Persian carpets were woven in the 16th through the 18th centuries. After 1850 weavers worked mainly for export to the west, and designs lost their originality. The introduction of aniline dyes in the 1870s had a further detrimental effect on quality. In 1934 the Iranian government prohibited the export of inferior quality carpets. 20th-century carpet weaving centers in Iran include the cities of Herez, Sultanabad, Tabriz, and Tehran.

Persian-style carpets were also made in China, but Chinese rugs had, and still have, a distinctive style of their own. They tend to have symbolic floral or geometric designs with the motifs much more widely spaced. Often the pile is sculptured so that the motifs stand out in relief. Color schemes are pale with yellow, blue, and white predominating in large areas of solid color. Chinese rugs have a soft pile that is not as resistant to wear as other oriental rugs.

Moorish influence produced two types of folk rugs in the Iberian peninsula, the Alpujarra rug of Spain, and the Arraiolos rug of Portugal. The Alpujarra, named after a city near Granada, is a coarse, heavy rug worked in loops similar to a hooked rug, and had its first use as a bed cover. The Arraiolos is a flat embroidered rug worked in long-legged cross stitch on a jute canvas backing. The design motifs and composition of these rugs are similar to Persian carpets and mosaic tile floors.

Hand-knotted pile rugs in Baroque style were made in France at Savonnerie. The original factory was established by Louis XIII in 1627 at the site of an ancient soap factory in

Chaillot, and was the most important European manufacturer of knotted pile carpets. Production was limited to the court until 1768 when the carpets were made available to private individuals. Savonnerie became a generic name for this type of French carpet, which was the prototype for western carpet design. In 1825 the Savonnerie factory was incorporated into the Gobelins tapestry works.

The most distinctive rug in Scandinavia is the *rya*, or *ryijy*, worked in a knotted pile weave technique that goes back to the Bronze Age. In the Middle Ages *ryas* were used as cloaks and bed covers, and now in modern times they are used on floors or hung on walls. The *rya* is woven with single rows of pile separated by 10 to 20 weft rows. The long pile hides the unknotted areas. Sometimes the knotting is worked by hand on a prewoven background that has holes spaced at the proper intervals. Originally made from wool in natural colors, the *rya* has evolved into a colorful work of art in the 20th century.

Less expensive alternatives to imported carpets were developed in Europe and North America. In the 18th and 19th centuries, painted canvas floorcloths were used in affluent American homes including those of George Washington and Thomas Jefferson. Designs were copied from carpets, marble floors, and stenciled patterns. The cloths were imported from England, or were made locally by sign and coach painters. Floorcloths went out of use when linoleum and vinyl floors became common, but they have recently been revived for period interiors.

Woven rag rugs were common in early America, and remain popular in rural areas where they are woven on home looms. The rag rug has a weft made of narrow strips cut from old clothes or other rags and is woven on a cotton warp in plain weave. The rags may be dyed to form stripes or woven as is to make a multicolor hit-and-miss design. Rag rugs were often used to cover expensive pile carpets in heavily trafficked areas or were sewn together to form wall-to-wall carpeting or covering for stair treads. They are very durable and are easily laundered.

The 19th-century hooked rug also utilized used cloth, primarily wool, cut into strips and hooked into a linen, cotton, or jute backing to form raised loops on the face of the rug. The loops were left uncut, giving the rug a tight, somewhat curly appearance. Hooked rugs were noted for their somewhat naive floral and pictorial designs, although many were made from commercial patterns. Usually made by housewives, they were sometimes also made by sailors on board ship or resting in port. They are now made by home craftsmen. A related type of rug developed in England, the latch-hook, is worked in pre-cut yarn pieces with a special latch-hook tool. It has a cut pile, and resembles a short-pile *rya*.

Braided rugs also use wool rags sewn together and braided into a continuous strip. The strip is coiled into a flat, oval rug and the coils stitched edge-to-edge to hold them together. Braided rugs can also be made of rope or cord. Large braided rugs are extremely heavy, and provide good insulation on cold floors.

Embroidered canvaswork, or needlepoint, rugs are another alternative to expensive carpets. They are usually worked in wool using the half-cross tent stitch or the cross stitch on a canvas background. In the 16th and 17th centuries they were made by amateur needleworkers in imitation of Turkish carpets and were used on tables. In the 18th century floral patterns predominated, and canvaswork rugs were used on floors. Berlin woolwork designs were popular in the 19th century.

Floorcoverings: designs for stone or painted floors by John Carwitham, from *Various Kinds of Floor Decoration*, 1739

Handmade rugs continue to be made in the 20th century, mainly by artists and home craftsmen. The Arts and Crafts movement of the late 19th century led by William Morris revived interest in the rug as an art form. Recently museum reproduction canvaswork rugs have been worked in China for sale in the west. These are large rugs, worked on a vertical frame by several people. Commissioned reproduction oriental pile rugs using natural dyes are now being woven in India for sale in American galleries.

The Industrial Revolution in the 18th century saw the introduction of machine-woven carpeting. There were three basic kinds of machine-woven rugs in England: Wilton, Axminster, and velvet. Wilton first produced Brussels carpeting, a durable carpet with the pattern formed on the surface by uncut looped warp threads on a woven foundation of linen, jute, or cotton. Cut pile Wilton carpeting was developed from this technique. The Wilton loom used a Jacquard system of perforated cards (invented 1805), and after the 1850s a Bigelow power loom. The number of colors was limited, but very intricate patterns with great clarity could be produced on the cut pile surface.

Axminster carpets, also named for a town in England, had a large choice of stylized geometric or floral designs and colors. The Axminster carpet, originally knotted by hand in the oriental manner, had a cut pile and a heavily ribbed back. The three types of Axminster carpet were designated chenille Axminster, spool Axminster, and gripper Axminster, based on the type of loom used.

Velvet carpets had a simpler weaving technique than the other two and were characterized by a large number of possible texture effects, including plushes, uncut loop piles, and sculptured effects.

The increased availability of manufactured carpets in the late 18th century and throughout the 19th century caused floorcoverings of this kind to become more common in European and American interiors. Machine-made carpeting was used as a substitute for, or in combination with, imported Oriental carpets. Nevertheless, these floorcoverings were still sufficiently expensive to warrant the use of protective covers in the form of small rugs or druggets made of plain, coarse woollen cloth that were placed over areas where wear was most likely to occur. Dining rooms and breakfast rooms were particularly susceptible to spills and stains, and druggets, frequently coloured to match the other furnishings, were often placed under tables or sideboards. Protective covers were also placed around fireplaces to catch falls of soot and powdering cloths were used in bed and dressing rooms to save the carpet from hair or powder. By the mid 19th century druggets decorated with needlework borders sometimes served as a cheap substitute for more expensive carpets and were used on their own either on stairs or in rooms where there was no other floorcovering.

Manufactured rugs were made in a variety of shapes – square, rectangular, or round – and loose-fitting rugs had the advantage of being able to be turned and reversed to equalize wear. Fitted carpets, made in strips cut to accommodate the shape of the room and tacked to the floor, were fashionable by the second half of the 18th century, and in 1806 Thomas Sheraton observed that "since the introduction of carpets, fitted all over the floor of a room, the nicety of flooring anciently practiced in the best houses, is now laid aside". The architect Robert Adam designed some particularly fine examples with boldly-coloured patterns whose design complemented that of the decorations and architectural features within interiors such as Syon House, Middlesex (1768–69). Mid-19th century design reformers such as Charles Eastlake criticised the taste for fitted carpets as both unhygienic and dishonest and advocated a return to scatter rugs that did not mask the construction of the floor and that could be removed and beaten for more effective cleaning. Hall runners were generally loose, while stair runners were either tacked to treads and risers or threaded under rods fastened at the foot of each riser. Cheap druggets and mats were placed at outside doorways for wiping boots and shoes before entering the house.

Machine-made carpets have proliferated in the 20th century, with advances in manufacturing processes causing reductions in price. The wall-to-wall carpet, which is cut to fit the room and tacked permanently to the floor, has changed from a symbol of luxury and prestige to a commonplace item in homes and public buildings. In the early 1950s the invention of high-speed tufting machines and the introduction of rayon, nylon, polypropylenes, and polyesters as carpet material caused a revolution in the carpet industry. By the 1980s carpets were of superior quality to those of the early 1950s and cost only about half as much.

Large tufting machines make carpeting with hundreds of individual needles stitching simultaneously through a backing material, and may be as much as 15 feet wide. A secondary backing material is added to hold the tufts in place. Foam rubber, sponge, or vinyl cushion may also be added. Carpet can be made plain or patterned in a number of different pile treatments. The pistol tufter, a tool that shoots wool through a canvas web backing, was introduced in the 1980s, and is used to make intricate designs similar to tapestry.

Other machine-made carpets include knitted and needlepunch rugs. Knitted rugs are worked on three sets of needles, and have a foam backing added after the knitting is done. These rugs are usually solid color or tweed. Needlepunch carpet is a flat, utilitarian indoor / outdoor carpet formed of unspun fibers meshed into a pre-woven fabric by the action of hundreds of barbed needles. It is made of weather-resistant polypropylene and can be printed with colorful designs. Indoor / outdoor carpet lacks the aesthetic appeal of soft pile carpeting, but it has provided a means of covering bare floors in areas where pile carpeting would not be practical or affordable.

CONSTANCE A. FAIRCHILD

See also Floorcloths; Floors

Further Reading

An excellent introduction to the history and use of Floorcoverings appears in Gilbert, Lomax and Wells-Cole 1987. Additional bibliographical sources are cited in Von Rosenstiel and Winkler 1988. For more detailed information on particular types of carpets and rugs see specialist histories.

Ayres, James, *The Shell Book of the Home in Britain: Decoration, Design and Construction of Vernacular Interiors, 1500–1850*, London: Faber, 1981

Baker, Patricia L., "Carpets" in Jennifer Harris (editor), *5000 Years of Textiles*, London: British Museum Press, 1993, pp.118–33

Beard, Geoffrey, *The National Trust Book of the English House Interior*, London: Viking, 1990

Beattie, May H., *Carpets of Central Persia*, London: World of Islam Festival Publishing, 1976

Black, David (editor), *World Rugs and Carpets*, Feltham, Middlesex: Country Life, 1985

Cornforth, John and John Fowler, *English Decoration of the 18th Century*, London: Barrie and Jenkins, and Princeton, NJ: Pyne, 1974; 2nd edition Barrie and Jenkins, 1978

Erdmann, Kurt, *Seven Hundred Years of Oriental Carpets*, Berkeley: University of California Press, and London: Faber, 1970

Faraday, Cornelia Bateman, *European and American Carpets and Rugs*, 1929; revised edition Woodbridge, Suffolk: Antique Collectors' Club, 1990

Gilbert, Christopher, James Lomax and Anthony Wells-Cole, *Country House Floors, 1660–1850*, Leeds: Leeds City Art Galleries, 1987

Haslam, Malcolm, *Arts and Crafts Carpets*, London: David Black, 1991
Jacobs, Bertram, *Axminster Carpets (Hand-Made) 1755–1957*, Leigh-on-Sea: F. Lewis, 1970
Jarry, Madeleine, *The Carpets of the Manufacture de la Savonnerie*, Leigh-on-Sea: F. Lewis, 1966
Jarry, Madeleine, *The Carpets of Aubusson*, Leigh-on-Sea: F. Lewis, 1969
King, Donald and David Sylvester, *The Eastern Carpet in the Western World from the 15th to the 17th Century* (exhib. cat.), London: Arts Council of Great Britain, 1983
Little, Nina Fletcher, *Floor Coverings in New England Before 1850*, Sturbridge, MA: Old Sturbridge Village, 1967
Mayorcas, M. J., *English Needlework Carpets, 16th to 19th Centuries*, Leigh-on-Sea: F. Lewis, 1963
Roth, Rodris, *Floor Coverings in 18th-Century America*, Washington, DC: Smithsonian Press, 1967
Sherill, Sarah B., "Oriental Carpets in 17th and 18th Century America" in *Magazine Antiques* (US), 109, pp.142–67
Tennant, Emma, *Rag Rugs of England and America*, London: Walker, 1992
Thornton, Peter, *Seventeenth-Century Interior Decoration in England, France, and Holland*, New Haven and London: Yale University Press, 1978
Thornton, Peter, *Authentic Decor: The Domestic Interior, 1620–1920*, London: Weidenfeld and Nicolson, and New York: Viking, 1984
Verlet, Pierre, *The Savonnerie: Its History: The Waddesdon Collection*, Fribourg: Office du Livre, 1982
Von Rosenstiel, Helene, *American Rugs and Carpets from the Seventeenth Century to Modern Times*, New York: Morrow, and London: Barrie and Jenkins, 1978
Von Rosenstiel, Helene and Gail Caskey Winkler, *Floor Coverings for Historic Buildings*, Washington, DC: Preservation Press, 1988
Winkler, Gail Caskey and Roger Moss, *Victorian Interior Decoration: American Interiors, 1830–1900*, New York: Holt, 1986

Floors

The earliest floors were of tamped earth, and in many contexts rudimentary earth floors have continued in use into the 20th century. Spanish colonials in Mexico and the American southwest sealed earth floors with blood, but oil or whitewash offered less grisly alternatives. Plasters of lime or mud, dung and straw, often decoratively painted or incised, were a common medieval treatment for earth floors, and survive in folk houses around the world. Nomadic peoples used matting or rugs for temporary floors, a custom that has died hard in the floor-oriented cultures of Africa and Asia where carpets, mats and cushions have traditionally been primary furnishings. Because of this, although glazed tile floors were used in Asia (especially Persia) from the 6th century BC, they were both rarer and less magnificent than surviving tiled walls. In 19th-century Japan, the secondary entrances of most farmhouses still opened on earth-floored rooms used for work, storage and food preparation. Shoes were removed before stepping up to the main floor, an austere wooden or bamboo platform or, in cold or damp regions, earth padded with layers of chaff and straw; either type would typically be covered with *tatami* matting.

Many of the elegant Hellenistic houses excavated in Delos reveal tamped earth floors (which were surely painted or sealed) butted against beautifully painted walls. The upper floors of better Greek houses were wooden planks, but plasters of clay and rushes were also used over wooden joists. Bricks, terracotta tiles and stone slabs were used for lower levels throughout the ancient Mediterranean, but the Greeks also devised composition floors, recommended by Vitruvius as "very inexpensive and yet serviceable." Rubble, charcoal, and finally cement mortar were layered over compacted earth; smoothed and polished, the result was a glossy pavement which absorbed spills and retained warmth. Greek "black-stone" floors of lava cement colored with charcoal could be set with marble pieces in imitation of true mosaic. Similar polished concrete floors were favored by the Romans, who also laid rough terrazzo floors in service areas. Finely finished terrazzo (sometimes with lead strips separating fields of color) was used extensively in later Italian villas, and became fashionable in Victorian public buildings and residential entryways as wealthy travellers returned from their Italian tours. Today terrazzo is used primarily in public and commercial buildings.

Cobblestone is an ancient solution, durable and extremely cheap, and patterned cobblestone floors precede the development of mosaic flooring. By the 2nd century BC Greek mosaicists were using finely cut stone tesserae and small pieces of glass to create strongly colored, naturalistic designs. Mosaic was highly developed by the Romans and used throughout the empire; the floors of Imperial buildings and large villas often mirrored ceiling designs, and occasionally marked the placement of furniture. Epic battles and mythological scenes composed in fine mosaic were usually bordered with coarser tesserae, and reserved for the finest rooms. All-over geometric patterns and informal fields of tesserae were more common, and substantially less expensive. The influence of classical mosaic in medieval Europe and the Islamic world, however, was largely limited to religious buildings.

Marble was imported in great quantities for Roman public buildings during Augustus's reign, and laid in geometric patterns which echoed the interior's rhythms. By Nero's time shaped tiles cut from colored stone, *opus sectile*, created complex designs with little relationship to the architecture. Marble, stone, or brick was used for raised *hypocaust* floors, which were heated through under-floor passages. Although basic to Roman bath-houses after the 1st century BC, this innovation was not used in private homes until the Christian era, and rarely even then. Hypocaust floors were more common in Rome's chilly British outposts, but the Saxons abandoned them, preferring their smoky central fires. In northern China, the Ming aristocracy laid polished black flagstones over heating pipes; in Korea heated stone or ceramic tile floors were sometimes sealed with varnished paper.

Early medieval floors in Europe were generally earth, or brick laid on edge in a herringbone pattern. Flagstone or wooden blocks were preferred in the public rooms of wealthier homes, and upper floors were wood plank, usually oak. Marble floors, while rare until well after the Carolingian period, appeared regularly by the 14th century. The most common were checkered in black and white or "woven" patterns of thin monochrome strips, although finer floors, especially in churches, were laid with rich mosaic designs. Marble floors inlaid with resin compounds were developed during the 13th century, but as the resin lacked durability this technique was short-lived. Thick layers of dry straw insulated the feet from cold brick or stone in winter; in hot weather, fresh greens were cooling. Wooden platforms could also provide areas of relief from hard, cold floors.

Stamped, unglazed red earthenware tiles were used for the floors of Charlemagne's palaces, and remained popular in Germany, Switzerland, Austria and the Netherlands until about 1700; grey and red tiles of this type were often laid in checkered patterns. Plain unglazed tile floors were more common, and could be polished to a shine. Lead-glazed tiles were introduced on the Continent in the mid 12th century through Islamic Spain, and simple square or hexagonal tiles were widely available by 1300. These were usually yellow, green, brown or black, plain or in sets with continuous patterns. Many Cistercian churches had floors of shaped tiles glazed in these colors, giving the effect of *opus sectile*. Heraldic, animal and geometric motifs were favored on "inlaid" earthenware tiles, the best examples of which were laid in French and English churches from the 13th and 14th centuries. Islamic craftsmen in Spain also produced white tin-glazed tiles with intensely colored designs, but these were only used for floors in the finest houses; Luca della Robbia's celebrated tin-glazed tile floor at Piero de Cosimo de Medici's palace sparked a brief vogue for similar pavements, particularly in Italy, France and the Netherlands. After the 16th century, most tin-glazed tiles were blue and white in imitation of Chinese porcelain, and the Netherlands became the major center for their production.

Glazed pavements fell out of fashion by about 1650. The Italian marble quarries were newly re-opened, and colored marble laid in antique patterns became the rage; inspired by the Italians, Louis XIV installed them at Versailles. Large slabs were used, and although most marble floors were still laid in simple alternating patterns, fantastic, richly colored *opus sectile* floors were installed in many Baroque palaces, particularly in France and Germany. Parquet and marquetry floors could be equally grand, if more fragile, and were better suited for upper rooms. The radiating central motifs and complex, curved borders of ballroom and great hall floors in the French royal palaces were influential throughout Europe, especially in Germany, but simpler, geometric parquet floors were more usual. By 1720 wood floors were in general use and marble, stone or tile paving were increasingly confined to halls and stair landings, a pattern which lasted into the 1920s. Matting – common on medieval floors – was banished to private chambers, and bare floorboards, waxed or scoured, prevailed until fitted carpets became available after 1750. Most early floors were hardwood, but fir and pine became usual – in progressively narrower boards – as the European forests were depleted. On occasions the boards were painted, a practice that was well-established in England by the 17th century and which was intended as a cheaper alternative to parquetry or marquetry. Few painted floors survive, but one of the finest examples in Britain can be seen in the Tyrconnel Room at Belton, Lincolnshire. Paint or parquet were also sometimes used to border a carpet, especially in England, a strategy which regained popularity in the late 19th century.

Inspired by archaeological discoveries, Neo-Classical designers renewed enthusiasm for marble floors in the halls and reception rooms of the rich. *Scagliola*, an imitation marble made from cement and colored marble chips or pigment, also proved quite popular from the mid-18th century although this material was quite fragile and cracked easily underfoot. John Carr laid *scagliola* floors on the landing of the staircase in Fairfax House, York, in the 1750s while a more celebrated example survives in Robert Adam's anteroom at Syon House (1761) where the elaborate design of the *scagliola* floor echoes that of the ceiling and was derived from an illustration by Sebastiano Serlio.

Gleaming, pigmented *scagliola* or stucco floors, plain or patterned, were considered elegant throughout 18th-century Europe but, as the 19th century progressed, the price of fitted carpeting fell and this style of flooring gradually replaced earlier forms. Fitted carpets remained fashionable until the 1870s when writers like Charles Eastlake began advocating varnished hardwood and loose oriental carpets as a more artistic and "honest" treatment. Despite the trend towards hardwood, Scandinavians continued to prefer pine boards, smoothed and whitened with lime, well into the 20th century.

Before 1870, most American floors were also softwood: unfinished planks could be protected with a layer of sand, swept into decorative patterns for special occasions, but paint was tidier. The American architect A.J. Downing recommended staining every other board for a lively striped effect, if carpet was out of reach. Although Aesthetic tastemakers scorned manufactured carpet, parquet and hardwood planks were expensive, and softwood floors increasingly condemned as unhygienic. As an alternative, "wood-carpet" — thin hardwood "parquet" glued to a muslin backing – could be tacked down over an existing floor. Wood-carpet borders and medallions were also available, and as the price was comparable to carpet it was widely used to refurbish older homes. Washable surfaces like linoleum or oilcloth were often nailed over softwood floors in service areas, but were not recommended for public rooms.

Encouraged by A.W.N. Pugin, the English ceramics firm Minton & Co. first introduced its Gothic Revival "geometric" and "encaustic" tiles in 1842; in red, blue, fawn and dull yellow, these remained popular for halls and vestibules for over 50 years. Victorian factories produced tiles in dazzling variety, but plain unglazed red tiles were favored for floors, especially in Europe and America. After the 1870s, small square and hexagonal "mosaic" tiles were sold in sheet units with light classical motifs, borders, and even mottoes, and "sanitary" black and white tiles of this type became standard for conservatories and bathrooms. Although a wide array of industrially produced floor-coverings were available by the turn of the century, most designers continued to recommend dark polished hardwood scattered with rugs. By the 1930s paler wood finishes, cork tiles and composition floors were fashionable for modern interiors, and Frank Lloyd Wright's dramatic use of stone inspired many stylish Americans to install flagstone or slate floors. The American Colonial Revival also renewed interest in wide pine boards. But the informal lifestyles and inexpensive synthetics of the post-World War II era kept most floors buried under wall-to-wall carpeting, rubber, vinyl, or linoleum until the 1970s, when interest in natural hardwood flooring was rekindled.

JODY CLOWES

See also Floorcoverings; Mosaic

Further Reading

A concise history of Floors appears in Gilbert, Lomax and Wells-Cole 1987.

Ayres, James, *The Shell Book of the Home in Britain: Decoration, Design and Construction of Vernacular Interiors, 1500–1850*, London: Faber, 1981

Calloway, Stephen and Elizabeth Cromley (editors), *The Elements of Style: A Practical Encyclopedia of Interior Architectural Details from 1485 to the Present*, London: Mitchell Beazley, and New York: Simon and Schuster, 1991

Cornforth, John and John Fowler, *English Decoration in the 18th Century*, London: Barrie and Jenkins, Princeton, NJ: Pyne, 1974; 2nd edition Barrie and Jenkins, 1978

Eames, Elizabeth S., *English Medieval Tiles*, London: British Museum Press, and Cambridge, MA: Harvard University Press, 1985

Fischer, Peter, *Mosaic: History and Technique*, London: Thames and Hudson, and New York: McGraw Hill, 1971

Gilbert, Christopher, James Lomax and Anthony Wells-Cole, *Country House Floors, 1660–1850*, Leeds: Leeds City Art Galleries, 1987

Lemmen, Hans van, *Tiles in Architecture*, London: Laurence King, 1993; as *Tiles: 1000 Years of Architectural Decoration*, New York: Abrams, 1993

Little, Nina Fletcher, "Decorations Under Foot: Painted Floors in Early New England" in *Country Life*, 3 January 1974, pp.32–34

Long, Helen C., *The Edwardian House: The Middle-Class Home in Britain, 1880–1914*, Manchester: Manhester University Press, 1993

Parissien, Steven, *Floors*, London: The Georgian Group, 1991

Pilling, Rosalind, "Wooden Floors in Evolution" in *Traditional Homes*, February 1987

Thornton, Peter, *Seventeenth-Century Interior Decoration in England, France, and Holland*, New Haven and London: Yale University Press, 1978

Thornton, Peter, *Authentic Decor: The Domestic Interior, 1620–1920*, London: Weidenfeld and Nicolson, and New York: Viking, 1984

Thornton, Peter, *The Italian Renaissance Interior, 1400–1600*, London: Weidenfeld and Nicolson, and New York: Abrams, 1991

Wight, Jane, *Mediaeval Floor Tiles*, London: Baker, and New York: St. Martin's Press, 1975

Fontainebleau, School of

A milestone in the development of French decorative arts, painting and sculpture, the School of Fontainebleau (a label first coined in the 19th century) refers to an elegant and highly ornamental style of painting and interior decoration distinguished by the use of high relief stucco combined with painted panels. Developed primarily at the instigation of François I for the decoration of interiors at the Château of Fontainebleau near Paris, between 1528 and 1558, the Fontainebleau style can also be found at the Grotte de Meudon (1552), the Château d'Écouen (c.1540), in the tombs of chapels throughout the Ile-de-France and in a number of châteaux in the Loire valley.

The development of this distinctively French style, strongly influenced by Italian Mannerist painting, was to bring France into the Renaissance, moving away from the Gothic and forging a link between the restraint of Classicism and the excesses of Baroque. Fontainebleau became the medium through which France assimilated ideas from Southern Europe and adapted them for her own use. Sculpture and painting complemented each other – the central motifs were painted, the cartouches in low relief and framing devices, such as strapwork (the imitation of interlacing leather straps) in high relief. With its sense of drama and exaggeration of style, Mannerism was well suited to the ornamentation of interiors. Contrived rather than natural, it broke with classical composition in its use of vivid colour, its distorted forms, incorporating scenes from mythology, garlands of flowers, baskets of fruit, Mediterranean draperies and sensuous nudes.

For around one hundred years Fontainebleau was an important centre for the decorative arts, employing Italian painters together with some of the finest French and Flemish artists and craftsmen of their time – stucco workers, woodcarvers, gilders, stone masons, tapestry weavers, bronze casters and printers – and providing a training ground for French sculptors, decorators and painters. Distinguished visitors included the sculptor and goldsmith Benvenuto Cellini, who made a magnificent gold salt cellar for François I.

Until the release in 1528 of François I from captivity in Madrid, Fontainebleau had been little more than a hunting lodge of the Capetian kings. Favouring it in preference to the Loire, he ordered it to be redesigned, under the direction of master mason Gilles Le Breton. The addition of apartments and galleries occurred somewhat haphazardly over a period of time, starting with the Cour Ovale and the Cour du Cheval Blanc, linked by a wing which incorporated the fine Galerie François I. Behind a simple façade the interiors were to be elaborately designed. In 1530, inspired by the Italian humanist princes and the desire for prestige, François I invited the Florentine master artist Giovanni Battista Rosso (1494–1540), known as Rosso Fiorentino, to decorate the new rooms. Rosso, who had worked under the Florentine painter Andrea del Sarto, moved to Rome in 1524 (where he acquired Mannerist leanings and use of ornament), to Venice after the Sack of Rome in 1527 and thence to Fontainebleau.

Francesco Primaticcio (1504–70), a pupil in Mantua of Giulio Romano (whose contributions to Fontainebleau included tapestry designs which were woven in Brussels), gained his decorating skills working with Romano on the Palazzo del Te. Influenced by Parmigianino, he introduced a more restrained style of Mannerism than that of Rosso. Summoned by François I in 1532, he took over as Director of Works to the King on Rosso's death in 1540 and also contributed designs for enamels, sculpture and architecture.

Nicolò dell'Abate (c.1512–71) trained in Bologna under Correggio and Parmigianino, where his designs for palace interiors combined stucco with deep-focus landscapes and friezes of figures in the foreground. He arrived at Fontainebleau in 1552 to assist Primaticcio, bringing his own vibrant use of colour, fantasy, sensuality and illusion and a particular talent for painting frescoes. Although little remains of his decorative work, he contributed much to the ensuing French painting and landscape tradition.

The 64-metre Galerie François I, started in 1534, was Rosso's greatest achievement at Fontainebleau. After his death in 1540 the lively decoration, strongly influenced by Raphael, was completed by Primaticcio. The walnut panelling, with carvings by Francisco Scibec de Carpi, was replaced during the

19th century and the stucco and fresco decoration restored in the 1960s and 1970s. The window bays were interspersed with antique casts, brought to France by Primaticcio who visited Rome in 1540 and returned with antiques and plaster casts of classical statues in the Belvedere Court of the Vatican to be cast in bronze. These, and others resulting from a visit to Rome in 1552 and placed in the Jardin de la Reine and the Cour de la Fontaine, prompted Giorgio Vasari to describe Fontainebleau as "a new Rome". Rosso and Primaticcio collaborated on the decoration above the wainscot. Mannerist in style, it included dramatic stucco figures of men and women, satyrs, angels, putti, masks and garlands of fruit, surrounding frescoes of mythological scenes executed predominantly in green and mauve with yellow, grey-blue and pink. Frescoes showed scenes in the life of François I, including L'Eléphant Royal, an allegorical reference to the wisdom of royalty, decorated with *fleurs de lys*, the letter "F" and ostrich feathers, the symbol of justice. There is an innovative use of strapwork and the ceiling is panelled and highlighted in gilt. The galerie was badly restored during the reign of Louis Philippe, and Rosso's work is chiefly known through many superb drawings.

The adjoining Appartement des Bains was an innovation in France, inspired by Ancient Roman baths with their stuccos, cartouches and grotesques, was influenced by Rosso and directed by Primaticcio.

Running along the southern wing of the Cour du Cheval Blanc, destroyed in 1738, the Galerie d'Ulysse was completed in 1570 after Primaticcio's death. In place of Rosso's strapwork Primaticcio favoured the use of small-detailed grotesque ornament, possibly influenced by the Vatican Loggie and the Volta d'Orata of the Golden House of Nero. The ceiling was decorated with small panels of figures, elegant, elongated women. Drawings show how Mannerist tricks were played with space and perspective.

The superb Galerie Henri II, also known as the Salle de Bal, survives in its restored form. It was decorated by Primaticcio assisted by Nicolò dell'Abate. The space between the ceiling and the ten windows was decorated with frescoes which show eight mythological groups which are echoed in the recesses.

Under the patronage of Henry IV who revived the decorative painting of palaces, and Marie de Medici, a Second School of Fontainebleau evolved in the late 16th century, though it lacked the brilliance and innovation of the First. Chief protagonists were the Flemish artist Ambroise Dubois (1542–1614); Toussaint Debreuil (1561–1602) and Martin Fréminet (1567–1619). Subject matter included images from the *commedia dell'arte* and women at their toilette, while colours were more subtle, with more tonal contrast.

Subsequent rulers, notably Marie-Antoinette and Napoleon, who described Fontainebleau as "the house of the centuries", ordered many restorations and changes and little remains today. It is in the field of interior design and the training and inspiration of skilled craftsmen that the School of Fontainebleau left its mark. Although much of the decoration has been overpainted, badly restored or simply destroyed, the decorative tenets of Fontainebleau spread through Northern Europe. Demand for highly decorated interiors was created through drawings and technically superb prints and the designs and innovations, notably Rosso's strapwork, were taken up by woodcarvers, enamellers, tapestry weavers, even armourers.

JACQUELINE GRIFFIN

The school of Fontainebleau was established under the direction of the Italian painter, Rosso Fiorentino (c.1494–1540), invited to France by François I, c.1531. Rosso was succeeded by another Italian, the Bolognese artist Francesco Primaticcio (1504–70), c. 1532, who had trained under Giulio Romano at the Palazzo del Te in Mantua. In 1552 Nicolò dell'Abate (c.1509–71) arrived at Fontainebleau, where he remained until his death in 1571. Together with a large workshop, they created a series of galleries and apartments, decorated with painted and stuccoed ornament executed in an attenuated and elegant Mannerist style. Combining strapwork and grotesques in its formal vocabulary, this established the predominant style of the Fontainebleau school. Primaticco was also active for Catherine de' Medici on memorial and religious sculpture, 1560–70.

Selected Works and Drawings

At Fontainebleau:

1533–39	Chambre du Roi (Primaticcio: decoration)
1534–37	Galerie François I (Rosso: fresco and stucco decoration)
c.1535	Pavillon de Pomone (Rosso and Primaticcio: fresco and stucco decoration)
1535	Porte dorée (Primaticcio: painted decoration)
1535–40	Pavillon de Poêles (Rosso: Salle Haute, Grande Galerie, Galerie Basse)
1537	Chambre de la Reine (Rosso and Primaticcio: decoration)
1541–44	Chamber of the Duchesse d'Etampes (Primaticcio: painted decoration)
1541–47	Appartement des Bains (Primaticcio: painted decoration)
1542–70	Galerie d'Ulysse (Primaticcio and Nicolò dell' Abate: arabesques and stucco)
1543	Vestibule of the Porte dorée (Primaticcio: painted decoration)
1544	Grotto of the Jardin des Pins (Primaticcio: painted decoration)
1545	Cabinet du Roi (Primaticcio: painted and stucco decoration)
1551–56	Galerie Henri II or Salle de Bal (Primaticcio and Nicolò dell'Abate: painted decoration)
1568	Wing of the Belle Cheminée (Primaticcio: painted decoration)

Other locations

c.1540	Château d'Écouen (chimneypiece for Salle du Pins; Primaticcio): Anne, Connétable de Montmorency
1552	Grotto of Meudon (Primaticcio): Catherine de' Medici

Further Reading

For an accessible introduction in English see the *School of Fontainebleau* 1965; Chastel 1975 includes a series of scholarly essays on the subject.

Béguin, Sylvie, *L'École de Fontainebleau: Le manierisme à la cour de France*, Paris: Gonthier-Seghers, 1960

Béguin, Sylvie, *Rosso e Primaticcio al Castello di Fontainbleau*, Milan: Fabbri, 1966

Béguin, Sylvie and others, *L'École de Fontainebleau* (exhib. cat.), Paris: Grand Palais, 1972

Béguin, Sylvie, Jean Guillaume and Alain Roy, *La Galerie d'Ulysse à Fontainebleau*, Paris: Presses Universitaires de France, 1985

Bologna, Ferdinando and Raffaello Causa, *Fontainebleau e la maniera italiana* (exhib. cat.), Florence: Sansoni, 1952

Chastel, André (editor), *L' Art de Fontainebleau*, Paris: Editions du Centre National de la recherche Scientifique, 1975

Dimier, Louis, *Le Primatice, peintre, sculpteur, et architecte des rois de France*, 2nd edition Paris: Michel, 1928

Herbet, Felix, "Graveurs de l'École de Fontainebleau", *Annales del Societé historique et archéologique du Gâtinais*, 1896–1902; articles reprinted Amsterdam: Israel, 1969

Johnson, W. McAllister, *Prolegomena to the Ulysses Gallery and the School of Fontainebleau*, Ph.D. thesis, Princeton: Princeton University, 1965

Johnson, W. McAllister and others, *L'École de Fontainebleau* (exhib. cat.), Paris: Grand Palais, 1972

Lövgren, Sven, *Il Rosso à Fontainebleau*, Stockholm, 1951

The School of Fontainebleau: An Exhibition of Paintings, Drawings, Engravings, Etchings and Sculpture, 1530–1619, Fort Worth Art Center / University of Texas Art Museum, 1965

Zerner, Henri, *The School of Fontainebleau: Etchings and Engravings*, New York: Abrams, and London: Thames and Hudson, 1969

France

Although French interior decoration assumed a widespread influence outside France in the 17th and 18th centuries, it only really began to take a place in the main European artistic tradition during the reign of François I in the 16th century. Prior to this period, Late Gothic rooms were often richly furnished and decorated – as may be seen in contemporary book illustrations – and the most important fixed element was the fireplace, usually with projecting corbels which supported a hood. Viollet-le-Duc described several examples in his *Dictionnaire* (1858–68), singling out especially those in the mid-15th-century house of Jacques Coeur in Bourges, with their elaborately sculpted decoration, and the enormous triple fireplace featuring richly carved capitals and representations of angels supporting shields, which was installed in the Palais des Contes, Poitiers, in the 14th century for Jean, duc de Berry. The importance of the fireplace in a room was to remain a characteristic of French decoration until the 19th century.

Stone vaulting was used in such 14th-century royal buildings as the Château de Vincennes and the Conciergerie in Paris, but there is a rare domestic example of a decorative use over the 15th-century staircase in the Hôtel de Bourgogne in Paris, in which the four ribs are in the form of leafy oak branches spreading over the surface of the masonry. In general the timber construction of the floors or roofs above the rooms was left exposed and decorated, sometimes with carvings, sometimes with panelling, and often with painted patterns. This feature remained typical, even after underdrawn ceilings were introduced; two fine late examples are the 16th-century Salle des Gardes in the Château de Fontainebleau and the early 17th-century Grande Salle of the Hôtel de Sully in Paris.

Floors were generally paved with tiles laid in geometric patterns, as in ecclesiastical buildings, but these have rarely survived. The bare walls were usually plastered and covered with tapestries or painted hangings which could be packed and transported from place to place since the life of the Court and nobility was peripatetic. It was customary to change them four times a year, according to the season, together with the oriental carpets and the cushions. Tapestries were also draped over tables and beds. Tournai and Arras were the centres of manufacture, especially in the 15th century, and the latter town gave its name outside France to wallhangings in general; Shakespeare had both Polonius and Falstaff hiding behind an arras. The museum in the late 15th-century Hôtel de Cluny, Paris, contains notable examples of tapestries, including the famous *milles-fleurs*, so-called because the backgrounds are filled with scattered flowers surrounding the groups of courtiers and animals.

Other forms of mural decoration were also used. The Chambre du Roi in the Château de Vincennes was described in the middle of the 15th century as being worked with gold and faced with wooden panelling, while the vaulting of the Grande Salle was panelled with chestnut which acted as insulation. The Chambre Verte in the Palais de la Cité in Paris was panelled with Irish oak which was believed to repel spiders and thus prevent cobwebs. Some rooms at Vincennes are thought to have retained the original painting from the late 14th century, and undoubtedly painted decoration was often used. Viollet-le-Duc wrote extensively about the various techniques and patterns that were used in the 13th to 15th centuries, and he made use of this knowledge in his restoration work at the Château de Pierrefonds as well as in ecclesiastical buildings. The 14th-century frescoed walls in the Palais des Papes at Avignon are covered with a sumptuous combination of painted draperies for a dado, quatrefoil frames separated by little aedicules as a frieze, and between them an overall pattern of giant vine scrolls. This scheme was possibly painted by Italian craftsmen, and it is with the importation of two outstanding Italian artists, Giovanni Battista Rosso (known as Rosso Fiorentino 1495–1540) and Francesco Primaticcio (1504/5–70) by François I in the 1530s that French decoration moved into a new and important phase.

In 1528 Gilles Le Breton was commissioned to rebuild the Château de Fontainebleau and to create a new gallery as a link with the old convent. Two years later Rosso was summoned from Florence to undertake the decoration of the new rooms, and in 1532 Primaticcio, who had worked with Giulio Romano at Palazzo del Te, Mantua, joined him. In François I's earlier châteaux at Blois (1515) and Chambord (1519) elaborate façades concealed interiors that had been furnished in the traditional manner with ornate fireplaces and tapestries. At Fontainebleau, however, this model was reversed. The exterior was relatively plain while the interiors were elaborately and permanently decorated. The Galerie François I is the least altered of the apartments for which Rosso and Primaticcio were responsible, although it too has suffered some changes and restorations. The lower parts of the walls of this 64-metres-long gallery are panelled in walnut with carvings by Francisco Scibec de Carpi (replicated in the 19th century); above is a riot of Mannerist-inspired decoration, of stucco figures of Parmigianino-like men and women, of putti, satyrs and angels, disconcertingly varied in scale, of garlands of fruit and of masks, and of large mythological scenes in fresco. Into all this Rosso and Primaticcio seem to have introduced the strapwork ornament that was to become popular in Northern Europe and which even survived in an elegant form of bandwork in 18th-century decoration. Restoration during the 1960s revealed that the original colouring of the frescoes was predominantly green and mauve, with smaller areas of salmon pink, pale yellow and slate blue. The ceiling of this remarkable room is compartmented, geometrically panelled and highlighted with gilt.

France: Palais des Papes, Avignon, 1334–62

Primaticcio also decorated the King's Bedroom, which the English ambassador to France described to Henry VIII (who was eager to have all the details of François's palace building and decoration) as "very singular as well with antical borders as costly ceilings and a chimney right well made", as well as the Queen's Bedroom, both of which have lost their decoration. The room of the Duchesse d'Etampes and the staircase to the Royal Apartments retain most of the original work which is in the same Mannerist style as the Galerie with huge attenuated nude figures flanking frescoed panels of mythological subjects. Sebastiano Serlio (1475–1554) was another importation from Italy. He arrived at Fontainebleau in 1541 where he designed an open loggia, now known as the Galerie Henri II or Salle de Bal; this was completed to a revised design made by Philibert de l'Orme (1514–70) who became Superintendent of Buildings in 1547. He changed the ceiling from a vaulted one to the present flat wooden one divided into square and octagonal coffers. This was executed in 1550 by Scibec de Carpi. Primaticcio, this time working with Nicolò dell'Abate (c.1512–71), was responsible for the decoration of this gallery, but all these rooms, including the Galerie d'Ulysse which was destroyed in 1738, were executed by artists – French, Italian and Belgian – who became proficient in this Italo-French Mannerist style and formed what became known as the First School of Fontainebleau, an enterprise that played a major part in establishing the Renaissance in France.

Towards the end of his life François I resolved to rebuild the Louvre, and Pierre Lescot (1500/10–78) was commissioned to make the design in preference to Serlio. After François's death in 1547 Henri II confirmed the appointment and Jean Goujon, the leading sculptor of the time, worked with Lescot on the interiors. These included the Salle des Cariatides, in which the four figures based on those on the Erechtheum and forming a porch facing the throne, are still in place. The ceilings of the main rooms, especially of the Grande Antichambre or Salle Henri II, were elaborately carved by Scibec de Carpi and heavily gilded in a manner that foreshadows the opulent interiors of the 17th century. Thomas Coryate, writing in 1611, thought "a stranger upon the first view thereof, would imagine it were beaten gold".

The work of the painters of the Second School of Fontainebleau, who worked for Henri IV, has largely disappeared; but from engravings and a few survivals it appears that the three artists (Ambroise Dubois 1542/3–1614, Toussaint Debreuil 1561–1602, and Martin Fréminet, 1567–1619) were still working in a Mannerist style well into the 17th century. According to Anthony Blunt, at this time private patrons continued to indulge in the "fantasies of Late Mannerism, not, it is true, quite as wild as those of the previous decades, but still ignoring the logical style encouraged by the King" (Blunt, 1970). The Mannerist character is clear enough in the designs for fireplaces, furniture and grotesque decoration made and published by Jacques Androuet DuCerceau the Elder (c.1515–c.1585) after he had visited Rome in the 1540s. How many of his fantastic designs, overloaded with ornament, were executed is unclear, but his publications helped make Italianate design fashionable in France. This influence may be seen, for example, in the Burgundian furniture associated with the name of Hugues Sambin (c.1520 –c.1601/2), who also published a book of extraordinary term figures. Two of DuCerceau's grandsons, Salomon de Brosse (1571–1626) and Jean Androuet DuCerceau (c.1585–c.1650), were the architects for the Palais du Luxembourg for Marie de Médici, the Queen-Regent, which was begun c.1614.

Hardly anything remains of the original decoration in the Palais de Luxembourg, but there are survivals, such as the panels painted by Theodore van Thulden. The most important decorations, the Rubens series of 21 allegorical paintings based on the life of Marie de Médici, once in one of the galleries of the Luxembourg, have long since been removed to the Louvre. Salomon de Brosse was responsible for work in several châteaux and Parisian hôtels, but his most important interior was the Salle des Pas Perdus in the Palais du Parlement, Paris (now Palais de Justice), which was constructed between 1618 and 1624. This austere stone hall (reconstructed after destruction during the Commune in 1871), with its giant Doric columns and black and white chequered floor, was de Brosse's attempt to recreate the grandeur of the basilicas of Ancient Rome, and it introduced a new seriousness into French Classical public and ecclesiastical architecture and decoration, which was apparent too in the work of François Mansart (1598–1666). The only one of Mansart's buildings in which the decoration has survived is the Château de Maisons (1642), but this shows an austere Classicism which does not rely on gilding or colour for its effect. There is a noble Antique air about the Roman Doric vestibule and the monumental staircase beyond that is almost a reproach to the excessive ornamentation of more or less contemporary and later interiors. Nevertheless, Mansart could also charm, as in the small Cabinet aux Miroirs with its pretty painted and inlaid decoration, its domed ceiling with stucco grotesques and painted putti, and its patterned marquetry floor in which pewter and bone were also used. This is the earliest surviving example of a mirror room.

Along with the adoption of the visual characteristics of Italian Renaissance architecture, there was a growing appreciation and application of its order, regularity, harmony and proportion. The Marquise de Rambouillet's pioneering of these qualities in the remodelling from 1619 of her Parisian hôtel has been discussed by several authors (notably Thornton 1978), and evidently her innovations were observed, admired and imitated, even by Marie de Médici at the Luxembourg. The Marquise's Chambre Bleue, in which the wall coverings, paintwork and furnishing fabrics were all of shades of the ubiquitous colour, seems to have been regarded as revolutionary in its harmony and uniformity. We are assured by an early 18th century writer that her decorations and arrangement of rooms were imitated in "all well ordered and splendid houses".

The most splendid Parisian hôtel of the 1640s was the Palais Mazarin. Some of the decoration still showed Mannerist influences but the finest room, the Galerie Mazarine (which survives in the Bibliothèque Nationale), was the work of the Roman painter, Giovanni Francesco Romanelli, who created in 1646–47 what has been described as "a type of decoration blending in a novel manner classical and Baroque elements … Romanelli may be said to have combined the classical pattern of the Farnese ceiling with the rich stucco effects achieved by Pietro da Cortona in the Palazzo Pitti" (Blunt, 1970), a combination more palatable to a French public. The Cardinal's library was moved after his death to a wing of the Palais de

France: Galerie François I, Fontainebleau, 1534–37

l'Institut, built in the 1660s as the Collège des Quatre Nations by Louis Le Vau (1612–70), who had earlier shown his skill as a designer and decorator in the Hôtel Lambert (1639–44). The Cabinet de l'Amour, Cabinet des Muses and, above all, the innovative Galerie revealed a control and harmony between the clearly defined decorative elements, the bronze and gold stucco reliefs of the Labours of Hercules, the painted landscapes by Jacques Rousseau and the ceiling painted by the Rome-trained Charles Le Brun (1619–90) which was "the most ambitious piece of Baroque illusionism to be executed in France".

Le Vau was also the designer of the Hôtel de Lauzun (1656) which has richly modelled and gilded decoration and ceilings attributed to Le Brun, all in the most luxurious taste. Opulence from floor to ceiling could hardly go further than in these rooms in which no surface is left unadorned. Other Parisian hôtels of the mid-century, such as the Hôtel des Ambassadeurs de Hollande (Pierre Cottard 1657–60, now the seat of the Fondation Paul Louis Weiller) which retains a gilded gallery with stucco putti and a *trompe-l'oeil* ceiling painted by Michel Corneille, and the Hôtel Beauvais (Antoine Le Pautre, 1654–60, now the headquarters of the Association pour la Sauvegarde de Paris), of which the staircase was decorated by the Flemish sculptor Van der Bogaërt (known as Martin Desjardins), show the influence of the Cardinal's Baroque taste in the Palais Mazarin.

Le Vau was appointed Premier Architecte du Roi in 1654, and he began work at the Louvre, collaborating with Romanelli and the stuccoist, Michel Anguier; but then in the following year he received the important commission for the Château de Vaux-le-Vicomte for the government financier Nicolas Fouquet. The centrepiece of the plan is a great oval drawing-room, two storeys high, which Le Brun and his collaborators decorated in a manner close to Pietro da Cortona's combination of painting, stucco and gilt in the Palazzo Pitti. But it was nonetheless "a totally French achievement, conjured up by a French architect-decorator and carried out entirely by Frenchmen" (Thornton, 1978). The story of Fouquet's downfall as a consequence of daring in his château to emulate the grandeur and luxury of the royal household is well known, and the young Louis XIV not only confiscated Vaux but also took over Fouquet's artists. Le Brun became Premier Peintre du Roi, and in 1663 he was made responsible for decorating parts of the Louvre, including the rebuilt Galerie des Rois (renamed the Galerie d'Apollon) after a disastrous fire. This was a development of his work at Vaux, and in 1665 Christopher Wren wrote admiringly about the current work in the Louvre where he could watch artists and craftsmen engaged "in Carving, Inlaying of Marbles, Plaistering, Painting, Gilding &c. Which altogether make a School of Architecture, the best probably, at this Day in Europe".

Although work continued at the Louvre until 1680, Louis XIV concentrated on the Château de Versailles, turning it from a hunting lodge into Europe's greatest palace and an influential if not quite emulable model in other European countries. The history of its transformation and the many artists involved has been written many times and the complexities of its decorations can only be summarised here. Le Brun's first work at Versailles was in the Grands Appartements, in which the ceilings were a similar combination of stucco, paint and gilt to that of the Galerie d'Apollon. The walls were covered either with patterned velvet or coloured marbles, and the floors too were patterned with marble. Le Vau's *Escalier des Ambassadeurs*, which formed the approach to these rooms (each of which contributed in its painted allegorical decoration to the theme of Apollo or the Sun King) was panelled with marble and painted with *trompe-l'oeil* architecture not unlike that in the Sala Regia in the Palazzo del Quirinale, Rome. The painted ceiling over the staircase contributed to the general theme. The whole was demolished in 1752 but the not dissimilar although less elaborate Escalier da la Reine (1670–81) has survived.

Le Vau died in 1670 and Jules Hardouin-Mansart (1646–1708) was appointed his successor. He and Le Brun were responsible for the Galerie des Glaces, of which the design was approved in 1678 and the work completed six years later. The bays of this 80-metres-long gallery are defined by 24 red marble pilasters with gilt bronze bases and capitals which, instead of one of the Classical orders, used an innovation, an *ordre français*, with symbolic fleurs-de-lis and suns. Above the richly coloured and mirrored walls is Le Brun's vaulted ceiling in which the paintings represent mythologised incidents in Louis's life, classicised so that he assumes the guise of a Roman emperor accompanied by all the gods and goddesses of Antiquity. This is the quintessence of decoration put to political service. At each end of the gallery a triumphal arch leads into the Salon de la Guerre and the Salon de la Paix. The rich effect of the marble and gilded stucco in these two rooms yields in each case to a dominating decorative element over the fireplace; in the former a huge oval sculptured panel of an equestrian Louis XIV by Antoine Coysevox (1640–1720), and in the latter a later painting by François Lemoine (1688–1737) of Louis XV bestowing peace on Europe. Anthony Blunt compares this famous suite of rooms to a Roman precedent, Palazzo Colonna, but concludes the Versailles ceiling is "less illusionistic, the compartments of the walls are more rectilinear, the carved trophies more classical. This is as far as the French could go towards Baroque at this period" (Blunt, 1970). It was, however, a considerable distance.

The furnishing of the royal palaces assumed a symbolic role as an expression of the magnificence of Louis XIV and France, and it became a part of the political strategies of Jean-Baptiste Colbert (1619–83) who had helped overthrow Fouquet and became Intendant des Finances in 1661 and Contrôleur General in 1665. The Gobelins workshops had been founded in 1622 by Henri IV to manufacture tapestries; this remained one of its principal functions, but in 1662 the enterprise was reorganised with Colbert as superintendant and Le Brun as artistic director, and it then became the Manufacture Royale des Meubles de la Couronne. One of Colbert's aims was to improve the standards of craftsmanship in France so as to reduce or put an end to imports from abroad; fashion, in clothes as well as in decoration and furnishing, was all promoted with this in view. The best designers and craftsmen were recruited by Le Brun, in order to create tapestries, carpets, brocades, mirrors, furniture of gold and silver, or inlaid with *pietre dure* to match the richness of the interior. Jean Le Pautre, who published engravings of designs for furniture in the 1660s, was an important figure, as was Jean Berain (1640–1711) who was Dessinateur du Roi from 1682 to 1711

France: Salon de Guerre, Versailles, 1678–84

and provided the designs for ornaments in Le Brun's Galerie d'Apollon in the Louvre. The most celebrated of the cabinet-makers was André-Charles Boulle (1642–1732) who was created Premier Ébéniste du Roi. He was skilled in working with metal and wood, but his name is inevitably linked with the elaborate marquetry of tortoiseshell, brass and ebony he used in opulent cabinets, commodes and bureaux which incorporated complicated grotesques and arabesques. Boulle too published some of his designs in *Nouveaux Deisseins de meubles* ... (1707–30), one of the many publications showing ornaments and complete rooms which, as Christopher Wren observed, would "give our Country-men Examples of Ornament and Grotesks, in which the Italians themselves confess the French to excel".

By this time the influence of French design was spreading well outside the country's boundaries. Travellers were noting and generally admiring the new ideas about decoration and the arrangement of rooms, the French Baroque style was becoming available to all through the increased number of publications such as the many illustrated by members of the Le Pautre family, and craftsmen were beginning to take their skills abroad. By 1634 it was said that in The Hague "The ladies and gentlemen are all Frenchified in French fashion", and both architecture and decoration were following suit. The Stadholder, Frederik Hendrik, Prince of Orange, had spent a year at the French court and returned full of admiration for what he had seen. The Mauritshuis in The Hague, the residence of Prince Johan Maurits van Nassau which dates from around 1633, had an obviously French quality both outside and inside, as had the Burgerzaal in Amsterdam's Town Hall, begun in 1648, with its cool classicism and allegorical sculptures.

Louis XIV's revocation of the Edict of Nantes meant that many Huguenots, including skilled craftsmen, left France for the Protestant Holland and England. Among them was Daniel Marot (c.1663–1752), a pupil of Berain. Marot went to Holland where he was commissioned to design the staircase and other apartments at Slot Zeist for the cousin of William of Orange and a former ambassador to France. He then entered the Stadholder's service and worked with Jacob Roman on the interiors of the palace of Het Loo in 1692, before travelling to England with William and his Stuart wife, Princess Mary, after their accession to the English throne. Marot continued to work in Berain's manner, but he added an increased elaboration in the hangings and upholstery of his furniture, especially of the great state beds with monumental testers in which he specialised; these are illustrated in his *Nouveau Livre d'Appartements* (1702). The Marot style became fashionable in England as well as Holland, and he worked at Kensington Palace, Hampton Court and Ham House. One of Marot's innovations, the porcelain cabinet designed to display collections of blue and white ware on tiers of shelves, became a characteristic of Dutch interiors which was also adopted, with more moderation, in English rooms, especially over corner fireplaces.

Meanwhile at Versailles Louis XIV had begun a new project which, whatever the original intention, was to mark a change in interior decoration. This was the single-storey Grand Trianon, a small palace designed by Jules Hardouin-Mansart and built in 1687. Guy Walton writes that "as walls and windows rose at Trianon, the curtains to hang on them were being woven in Lyon, and at the royal manufactories old furniture was being restored and new made to fill the rooms" (Walton, 1986). From start to finish the building took seven months, and the interiors were quite different from those in Versailles itself. Walton comments that whether "it was because the finishing of the interiors ... coincided with a serious international crisis which called for the diversion of some funds ... or simply that Trianon was intended to contrast sharply with the heavy grandeur of the Apartments at Versailles, or even that the king wanted the fastest possible completion of work ..., Louis apparently said 'Paint everything white. No gilt or colour for the walls of Trianon'. The new white decor came at a time when the architectural articulation of the interior walls had reached a new level of refinement ... while a lightening of feeling was achieved by the increasing delicacy of purely decorative elements such as floral and architectural ornament". Whatever the explanation, the result seems to foreshadow the king's instruction to Mansart more than ten years later regarding the decoration of the duchesse de Bourgogne's apartments in the Ménagerie at Versailles to offer "a certain youthfulness, a certain playfulness, introduced into what we are doing".

The Grand Trianon apartments and others from the turn of the century were more private in character than the magnificent state apartments, and illustrate the first moves in the transition from Baroque to Rococo. The walls are lined with wood panelling, *boiseries*, which were generally painted white and gold. Mirrors were incorporated in the panelling, frequently replacing paintings over the fireplace, which remained the central feature in the arrangement of the room. The tendrils and scrolls of the formerly fashionable painted arabesques became less formal as they were translated into curling shapes which became part of the framing of panels and mirrors. Scrolls, masks and shells were introduced, although there was still a classical framework within the rooms even if the pilasters were panelled rather than being fluted or decorated with arabesques.

Louis XIV died in 1715. He was succeeded by his great-grandson, Louis XV, a minor, and from 1715 to 1723 the country was governed by the Regent, Philippe, Duc d'Orléans. During this period the political and artistic focus of the court moved from Versailles to Paris and a non-monumental form of decoration became fashionable. There was less formality, more comfort, and a new group of designers was emerging. Robert de Cotte (1656–1735) had become Premier Architecte in 1681, but because of financial crises the number of royal commissions had been declining during Louis XIV's last years, and de Cotte and his colleagues were more often employed on private residences (*hôtels particuliers*), especially during the 1720s when Paris was expanding and noblemen were no longer required to be resident at Versailles. One of the most splendid of these early 18th century interiors was in the Hôtel de Toulouse, which had been built as the Hôtel de la Vrillière by Mansart (1633–34); de Cotte collaborated with François-Antoine Vassé (1681–1736) in redecorating the Galerie Dorée with a painted ceiling by François Perrier, mirrors, and enriched doorcases and chimneypieces. In the Palais Royal, Gilles-Marie Oppenord (1672–1742) redecorated Mansart's Galerie d'Enée, and in 1732 Jean-Baptiste Leroux (c.1677–1746) fitted out the gallery of the Hôtel de Villars with a profusion of Rococo filigree-framed mirrors, the elaboration of which was reflected in the design of the coved ceiling.

Oppenord created many interiors which earned him a reputation that was only increased by the posthumous publication of three volumes of his designs. More valuable are two publications which encapsulate early 18th century taste in decoration, architecture and garden design, Jacques-François Blondel's *Distribution des Maisons de Plaisance* (1737) and Charles-Etienne Briseux's *L'Art de bâtir des maisons de campagne* (1743). Appropriate decoration for each room in the house is prescribed, and this can be matched with rooms that have survived, either *in situ* or in collections at the Musée Carnavalet and the Musée des Arts Décoratifs.

A major figure in the first half of the 18th century was Germain Boffrand (1667–1754), who was apprenticed to Jules Hardouin-Mansart. Not only was he employed by several important clients to build or remodel their hôtels in Paris, but he was also a speculator involved in developing parts of the faubourgs Saint-Germain and Saint-Honoré and the Place Vendôme. It was he who, in his interiors, created a complete fusion of forms in which the structural lines became blurred and walls and ceiling merged into a unity of *boiseries*, mirrors, windows and doors. Boffrand developed this mastery from his early designs for salons in the Petit Luxembourg (1709–11) and La Malgrange (1712–17) near Nancy, where he worked for almost twenty years from 1702, to the perfection of the oval salon in the Hôtel de Soubise (1735–39) back in Paris, in which the decorative elements, the mirrors, putti, cartouches, are all fused into an undulating but carefully disciplined perpetual motion. Despite the freely flowing curves of this exquisite decoration in the rooms created for the Prince and Princesse de Soubise, the skeleton on which it was hung was still symmetrical although the classical elements themselves were no longer used. The fully developed Rococo did not begin until designs such as those of Juste-Aurèle Meissonnier (1695–1750) appeared when "through the hardening established lines of the French interior, about 1730, rustled a fresh breeze, bringing new life and movement. The novelty and import were recognised by contemporaries, who within a generation were to call it the *goût nouveau* or the *genre pittoresque* and to remark on its most striking characteristic, asymmetry — 'le contraste dans les *ornemens*'" (Kimball, 1980). Meissonnier's designs were published, some during his lifetime and others after his death, but he was more influential on Rococo decoration in Germany and Austria than in France where a more restrained version was preferred.

More to the taste of Parisian society was the work of

France: design for vestibule and salon by Jacques-François Blondel, from *De la distribution des maisons de plaisance*, 1737–38

Nicolas Pineau (1684–1754), who trained under Jules Hardouin-Mansart at the Gobelins and worked in Russia for Peter the Great for more than ten years. In the palace of Peterhof he "displayed great artistic tact and exquisite taste in decorating long panels with trophies of arms, globes, astronomical instruments, signs of the zodiac, musical attributes, palm fronds, flower garlands, scallop shells, foliate scrolls and other grotesque motifs". After more than twenty years in St. Petersburg, Pineau returned to Paris in the late 1720s and collaborated with a number of architects on interiors of hôtels. One example that has survived is in the Hôtel des Maisons (c.1750), and another is in 26 rue Cambon. Both reveal a delicate line in the curving tendrils and interlacing natural forms of the elegant, restrained Rococo that recalls Blondel's praise of "MM. Pineau, Lange and Verberckt [who] have contributed in rendering our dwellings worthy of the admiration of unprejudiced nations". Certainly by this time French decoration was becoming European by adoption since it was widely admired, although examples such as the Drawing Room at Chesterfield House (1747–52) and the Music Room at Norfolk House (1753–56) were exceptional in England.

In the rooms of the Régence and the early years of Louis XV's reign, the fireplace remained the main focus, as it had been since the Middle Ages. Usually it was made of marble and over it was placed an overmantel mirror which was often matched by others above marble-topped console tables. The flooring was patterned in marble or marquetry, or it was wooden blocks. The ceiling was generally flat and plain, with a chandelier hanging from a central ornamental rose. Michel Gallet has described the elaborate process of painting the *boiseries*, which entailed five operations. White and gold was the most common combination, but fashions changed. In the 1730s pale yellow was favoured and described as jonquil, sulphur, straw or lemon; blue and lilac were popular complementary colours for the hangings. Another process was *vernis Martin*, a brightly painted and lacquered finish invented in 1730; it was usually a bright green. Illusionist decoration was sometimes found, especially in staircases, but it was relatively rare. An outstanding example is the painted staircase hall in the Palais Royal (1755–60) by Pierre Contant d'Ivry (1698–1777) who decorated several rooms for Philippe, Duc d'Orléans. In less magnificent interiors, paintings became a part of the overall wall design, generally being placed as an overdoor panel; pastoral scenes were popular.

In the 1730s the court once again became active as a patron, although Louis XV lacked his great-grandfather's enthusiasm. A new generation of artists came to the fore. Ange-Jacques Gabriel (1698–1782) and Jacques Verberckt (1704–71) both worked at Versailles. First came the Petits Cabinets, dating from the late 1720s, in which the *boiseries* were delicately carved and some were finished with a *vernis Martin*. Soft colours were used, "*petit vert, jonquille, lilas et gris de perle*", and there was no gilding except in the frames of mirrors and paintings. The Petits Appartements, a conception of Mme. de Pompadour which consisted of a private suite of a small salon, a library, a bedroom and a boudoir, were constructed in the 1750s and painted white and gold. Fontainebleau too received attention in the 1750s when the Cabinet du Conseil was redecorated with panelling painted with allegorical figures set inside Rococo frames and hung with floral garlands. François Boucher, Carle van Loo, Jean-Baptiste Pierre and Pierre-Joseph Peyrotte were the artists. There was similar decoration in the

Hermitage of Mme. de Pompadour at Fontainebleau, where Verberckt was in charge.

The Gobelins tapestry workshop had reopened in 1699 and it continued to provide fine pieces until competition from wallpapers and the general adoption of Neo-Classicism, with which tapestries did not easily fit, caused its decline. In 1775 François Boucher was appointed director, and his designs were used for the sets in the rooms that Robert Adam designed for them at Osterley Park, Newby Hall, Moor Park and Croome Court. The elegant, fanciful Rococo lent itself to the inclusion of exotic elements. A taste for Chinoiserie had produced the Trianon de Porcelaine, a ceramic-faced building designed by Le Vau at Versailles for Louis XIV and Mme.de Montespan (1670–71) and there are many references to furnishings *à la chinoise* in 17th-century inventories.

Berain's designs for grotesques occasionally included oriental motifs. In 1719 Antoine Watteau painted a series of oriental figures for the Château de la Muette, and Christophe Huet added monkeys to Chinamen in the *Grande Singerie* he painted in 1735 for the Château de Chantilly. Around the same time Andien de Clermont was introducing simian figures in his decorations in English houses, at Kirtlington Park and Wilton House. There are more monkeys in the Hôtel de Rohan's Cabinet des Singes (c.1750) by Huet, who decorated the Salon Chinois at the Château de Champs for Mme. de Pompadour, whose protégé, François Boucher, designed a series of tapestries, *Tentures chinoises*, which were woven at Beauvais. Chinoiserie decoration continued to be popular in various media throughout Louis XV's reign, and Jean-Baptiste Réveillon, the leading producer of wallpapers, was using Chinese subjects as well as Pompeian up to the time of the Revolution.

By the 1750s a change in taste had occurred, first in architecture and then in decoration, and a reaction against the Rococo was asserting itself. The newly awakened interest in Antiquity was reinforced by the influence of Mme. de Pompadour and her brother, the Marquis de Marigny, who was appointed Directeur des Bâtiments in 1746. After two years in Italy he returned in 1751, an opponent of Baroque and Rococo architecture and decoration and a convert to the Antique. Francis Watson has drawn attention to the well-known portrait of Mme. de Pompadour by François-Hubert Drouais, in which "the transitional style is admirably exemplified in almost every piece of furniture with which she is surrounded. The cabriolet form of the stool, the undulating lines of the sofa and the curved and splayed legs of the gueridon table beside her, all still hark hack to the Louis XV style, but the prominent goats' heads and heavy swags with which the table is mounted and the strictly rectilinear shape of the work-box with its handle in the form of a Roman victor's wreath are in the new Neo-Classic taste" (Watson, 1956).

Young French artists at the Académie de France in Rome were inspired by the discoveries at Herculaneum and Pompeii, and they were encouraged by Marigny's instructions that they should be given studies "*pour corriger le mauvais goût d'ornement qui subsiste aujourd'hui*". But it was some time before the Rococo lost its curl and wilted – or straightened up. Verberckt was faithful to it until the end, and Gabriel was still designing *boiseries* and trophies for Madame Adélaide's Salon de Musique in 1767. However, the Petit Trianon at Versailles, intended for Mme. de Pompadour by Louis XV, but completed only in 1768 after her death, marked a change. Curves on plan, in section and in decoration had disappeared. Straight lines were the rule, and acanthus scrolls had replaced Rococo tendrils; vases and medallions were incorporated in the wall panels, and white and grey predominated in the cool classical rooms. But at the same time as these changes were taking place, there was a partial return in the decoration of some Parisian hôtels, and more particularly in public buildings such as the Ministère de la Marine (Gabriel 1762–72) and the Monnaie (Jacques-Denis Antoine 1768–75) to the pre-Rococo style of Louis XIV's reign. The two styles, both looking back but to widely separated periods, one to the 17th century and one to Republican Rome, existed side by side during the 1760s.

The popularity of the newly discovered interest in the Antique as a design source can be measured by the success of the publication in 1768 of Jean-Charles Delafosse's *Nouvelle Iconologie Historique*, a collection of engravings of classical ornament which had to be reprinted within three years. A casino designed by François-Joseph Bélanger (1744–1818) for the Marquis de Lauragais in 1769 abandoned all the elements of Rococo decoration and introduced a wall articulation of Ionic pilasters. *Scagliola* was used in the Doric pilastered dining room of the Hôtel de Botterel-Quintin (attrib. Pérard de Montreuil c.1780). Although the salon in the Hôtel d'Uzès (1768) by Claude-Nicolas Ledoux (1736–1806), now in the Musée Carnavalet, might seem still to be recalling something of the splendour of Louis XIV, there is a monumental Roman quality with Palladian undertones in his other work; in Mme. du Barry's pavillon at Louveciennes (1771), the dining room has apsidal ends, a partly coffered ceiling, and walls lined with giant order grey marble pilasters with gilded Corinthian capitals. Ledoux incorporated rotundas, coffered domes, muses and vases in the geometrically planned Hôtel Hocquart (1765) and Hôtel de Montmorency (1769), and even the 73-year-old Gabriel followed the fashion when, in 1771–72, he made a design for a Cabinet du Conseil at Versailles in which the only decorations were Corinthian pilasters. The *palais abbatial* at Royaumont (1785–89) by Louis le Masson (1743–1830) derives from Palladio's Villa Capra in plan, but its interiors, especially the Galerie Dorique, display an austere nobility with stone walls and the eponymous columns.

The credit for the re-introduction of grotesque decoration is given to Charles-Louis Clérisseau (1721–1820), who had returned to Paris in 1768 from Rome, where he had assisted Robert Adam in recording vast quantities of classical ornament and decoration as well as becoming acquainted with the Raphaelesque decorations in the Vatican and the Farnesina. He had collaborated with Bélanger in decorating the Pavillon de Lauragais in the late 1760s, and his elegant arabesque / grotesques in the Hôtel Grimod de la Reynière c.1775 had immediately set a fashion. Possibly he was also consulted by Bélanger about the decoration of the Pavillon de Bagatelle (1777–78) for the Comte d'Artois; in the small rooms there are grotesques in stucco and on painted panels, and Jean Dugourc, who executed the stuccowork, used a similar technique in the nearby Folie St. James (1778) where the entrance hall is painted with *trompe-l'oeil* architecture, statues and urns. Another outstanding interior of this date is the boudoir from the Hôtel de Sérilly (now in the Victoria and Albert Museum),

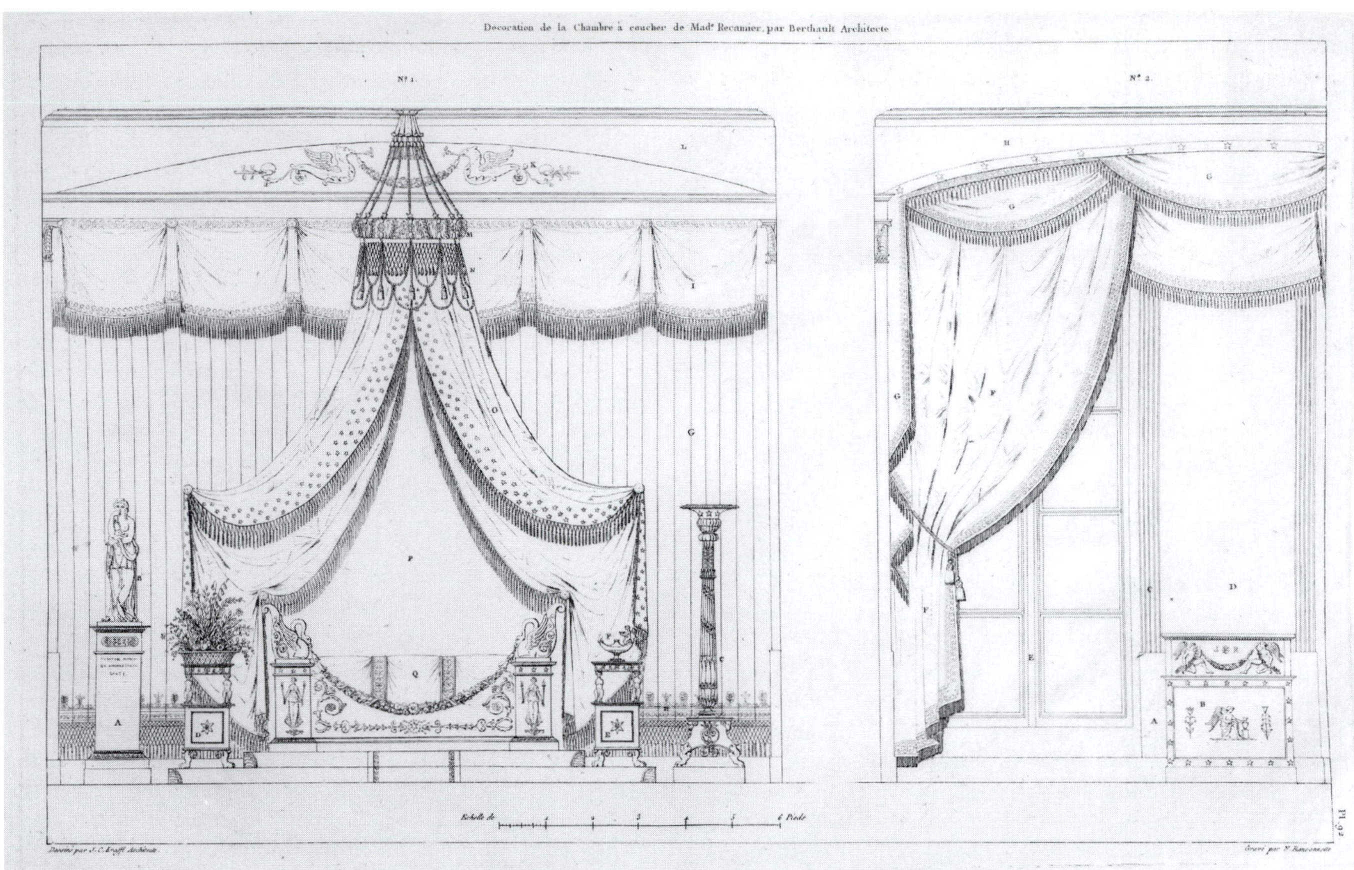

France: design by J.-C. Krafft for Madame Récamier's bedroom, 1798

which was decorated by Jean-Siméon Rousseau, using a Pompeian style with coloured and gilt composition ornaments; Clodion (1738–1814) supplied the handsome chimneypiece. To some extent this decoration reflects the influence on Bélanger and some of his contemporaries of the work of the Adam brothers in England, which was widely known through the 1773 publication of their designs, some of which Bélanger knew from first-hand experience.

After the arrival of Marie-Antoinette in 1774, Richard Mique (1728–94) and the brothers Rousseau had taken over from Gabriel and obeyed the Queen's taste for elegant floral decoration. According to the historian Wend Kalnein, "flowers swamped everything ... carving, paintings, hangings, clothes, and furniture. Festoons of flowers, still lifes of fruit and flowers, and cherubs playing with flowers". An enchanted flower garden was painted between a *trompe-l'oeil* Ionic colonnade in the Pavillon de Musique de Madame (Jean-François Chalgrin 1739–1811); but by 1780 when this was created, even the Court of Louis XVI and Marie-Antoinette had succumbed to the taste for Antiquity. Sphinxes, vases and medallions, as well as elegant arabesque / grotesques appeared at Versailles, as in the Cabinet Doré (1783), and at Fontainebleau, where the exquisite Cabinet de Toilette and Salon du Jeu were completed in 1785. In the former the delicate arabesques are painted on gold and silver grounds alternating with mirrors and the furniture was inlaid with mother-of-pearl; in the latter much of the decoration is grisaille, with richer colours on the doors and overdoors.

The chaos of the Revolution brought an era to an end, but once its worst effects were over there was a continuation of the fashions that had been evolving in the late Louis Seize years. The paintings of Jacques-Louis David presented a brave image of the classical past in which furnishings and draperies were based on Antique models but could also be taken as sources for contemporary apartments. The Neo-Classical taste and the cult of the Antique were only intensified, although there was an element of eclecticism in the borrowing from Greek, Roman and Egyptian sources. Many of the same architects, such as Bélanger, Louis-Martin Berthault (?1771–1823) and Alexandre-Théodore Brongniart (1739–1813) — the last was to design the major public building in Paris during the Empire, the Bourse with its majestic Roman interior – were still working and continuing an established 18th-century tradition.

New publications offered models for decoration, such as Charles Normand's *Nouveau Recueil en divers genres d'ornemens et autres objets propres à la décoration* (1803) and P.N. Beauvallet's *Fragmens d'architecture, sculpture, et peinture dans le style antique* (1804). But the most important and influential source of inspiration was the *Recueil de décorations intérieures* (1801 and 1812) by Charles Percier and Pierre-François-Leonard Fontaine, the architects favoured by Napoleon, since they could interpret his imperial ambitions in decoration and furnishing. From the very beginning of his rise to power, while he was still General Bonaparte, the future Emperor was commissioning designs for furniture which, despite its lavish ormolu mounts and bronze figures characteristic of the first phase of Empire design, was nevertheless derived from late Louis Seize pieces. Again, the tented rooms in Bonaparte's first Paris residence in the rue Chantereine and, more famously, in the Château de Malmaison, were following the Comte d'Artois's 1777–78 example at Bagatelle where Bélanger had designed the bedroom with walls and ceiling draped in blue and white striped material edged with gold.

The remodelling and decoration of Malmaison represents the first phase of the Empire taste which combines a military theme with a generally restrained and elegant Neo-Classicism associated with the short-lived Directoire regime. Like all Napoleon's projects, the work had to be completed in a short time, which meant that draperies and paint were used to create an almost instant effect with simulated marbles, grisaille instead of elaborate plasterwork, and painted canvas rather than laboriously woven tapestries. At the same time Percier and Fontaine were restoring the Tuileries palace for use as an official residence. Where decoration had survived the treatment of the Revolutionaries, it was retained, and what remained of Marie-Antoinette's furnishings and decorations was reused. But Napoleon also resembled Louis XIV in encouraging the setting up of new factories to produce the furnishings needed to restore the splendour of the French court, helping the economy while contributing to the imperial image.

It was on Napoleon's instructions that silk weaving was revived at Lyon where Jean Dugourc (1749–c.1825), who had worked with his brother-in-law, Bélanger, at Bagatelle, made some of the finest designs, including a blue and silver brocade with a pattern of myrtle and ivy leaves which was used in 1802 in the Empress Josephine's Drawing Room. Records show that strong colours were popular; yellow and silver in her Music Room, and brown, blue and gold in the Emperor's grand cabinet. Spectacular panoramic wallpapers were being manufactured by Jean Zuber and Joseph Dufour, but wallpapers seem not to have satisfied Napoleon; he is said to have flown into a rage when he found some had been used at Fontainebleau which was being prepared for a Papal visit.

Before his downfall, Napoleon had decorated and furnished all his residences, the Tuileries and the Elysée Palace, Fontainebleau and Compiègne, Saint-Cloud and Rambouillet with furniture made by the Jacobs, including the famous beds created for the two Empresses, Joséphine and Marie-Louise, with Gobelins tapestries (although apparently his short reign allowed time only for one set to be completed), with carpets made in the Savonnerie factory or at Aubusson, and with Thomire bronzes and Sèvres porcelain. Most of these furnishings were classical in inspiration with ornaments derived from Antiquity, although there was a short-lived Egyptian fashion. But the Napoleonic image was spread to other European countries where members of the Bonaparte family were placed temporarily on usurped thrones; hence its influence in Holland, Spain and Italy.

Despite the constant wars between England and France in the 18th and early 19th centuries, there was considerable reciprocal influence between the two countries on their styles of decoration and furniture. Sir William Chambers and Robert Adam, François-Joseph Bélanger and Charles-Louis Clérisseau alone formed a quartet in which there was a general exchange of ideas, while Henry Holland clearly had an affinity with French Neo-Classicism. Thomas Chippendale's *The Gentleman and Cabinet-Maker's Directory* (1754) contains designs strongly influenced by French Rococo furniture, and Adam interiors were frequently furnished with *bergère* chairs and *bombée* commodes either bought in Paris or based on French pieces. Before the Revolution the Prince of Wales (later George IV) was buying furniture through Guillaume Gaubert (who had been employed as a decorator at Chatsworth) and Dominique Daguerre, a prominent Parisian *marchand-mercier*, and French artists were employed at Carlton House – Jean-Jacques Boileau, Jirouard Le Girardy, Louis-André Delabrière (to whom the delicate Bagatelle-like painted arabesques at Attingham Park have been attributed) and Alexandre-Jacques de Chantepré. The Prince was a great collector of French furniture, favouring that of Louis XVI date, but he also took a keen interest in the latest Parisian fashions, and there are many similarities between Regency and Empire furniture designs. Anglo-French reciprocity is a complicated subject, but one aspect of it, apart from Carlton House, is the revival in England in the 1820s of French Rococo decoration which was generally referred to as "Louis Quatorze" although it was more accurately "tous les Louis". Benjamin Dean Wyatt (1775–1852) at Apsley House, Belvoir Castle, Crockford's Club and York (now Lancaster) House, Sir Jeffry Wyatville (1766–1840) at Windsor Castle, and the little known Jonathan Ritson in the White and Gold Room at Petworth House, all incorporated skilful recreations of Rococo decoration, sometimes making use of old *boiseries*, but more often using composition, plaster and papier-mâché, a decade or more before there was a similar revival in Paris, but it came into its own again with the Second Empire.

The 1834 Exposition des Produits de l'Industrie Française in Paris raised a question that was being asked in other countries too, "Are we Greek, or Roman, or Gothic? are we returning to the Renaissance style or that of Louis XIV, or Louis XV, or the Empire? Have we one of our own?" The exhibits displayed in this and subsequent exhibitions reflected the eclecticism that characterised 19th-century taste all over Europe. A comfortable version of the Empire style persisted well into the 1830s. The Style Troubadour or *à la cathédrale* were two aspects of a taste for the Middle Ages which was displayed in Jacob Petit's *Recueil de décorations intérieures* (1831) which includes most of the styles then available; so did another publication, Théodore Pasquier's *Dessins d'ameublement* (1835) in which comfortable upholstered chairs and ones with spiky Gothic tracery backs exist side by side with heavily draped windows and hybrid fantasies of wall treatment.

The 1844 Exposition des Produits included a Salon Louis XV by Georges Monbro, and designs of the same date by Fernand Léger in the Musée des Arts Décoratifs illustrate a hierarchy of rooms in varying degrees of "*tous les Louis*" style. These range from an elaborate ballroom with herm figures supporting the ceiling beams and a marquetry floor, through a white and gold salon with heavily draped curtains, a dining room with Renaissance buffets, to astylar minor rooms. But a return to the 18th century was given an impetus after Napoleon III married Eugénie de Montijo in 1853. She made a cult of Marie-Antoinette and, as Mario Praz wrote, "became an interior decorator out of emulation of her idol and combined modern comfort with 18th-century elegance. She

France: wallpaper, c.1870

mixed sofas and chairs, over-stuffed with navel-like buttons, with authentic Louis XVI pieces and modern imitations of them made by cabinet-makers so clever that only the experts can distinguish these precise imitations from authentic 18th-century furniture". The result was known as Louis XVI-Impératrice, or the Second Empire style. The results of this mixing and matching could be seen at their best in the Château de Saint-Cloud and in the Tuileries. Both of these palaces were destroyed in 1871, the first by the Prussians and the other by the Parisians, but the apartments are recorded in detailed watercolours by Benedic Masson and J.-B. Fortune de Fournier. In the New Louvre, Hector Martin Lefuel (1810–80) created a suite of three apartments for the Empress which have survived to illustrate the Second Empire taste at its most opulent.

It was a taste that attracted followers of different classes. In a modified form, especially in the furniture, it was popular with the haute bourgoisie who appreciated its combination of comfort and history, and revivalist features were relatively easy to manufacture in plaster and paint. Wealthy families, such as the Rothschilds, might not yet have built up their substantial collections of pre-Revolution royal furniture, but they could buy 18th-century *boiseries*, bronzes and furniture, or items from any other historical period, to install in their great mansions and town houses. Of these, Ferrières in France (1853–59), Mentmore (1850–55), and Waddesdon Manor (1876–90) in England are the best known. The first two were designed by Sir Joseph Paxton (1801–65), and the last, which is largely furnished with decorations and furnishings brought from France, was actually designed by a Frenchman, Hippolyte-Alexandre-Gabriel Destailleur (1822–93). At Ferrières, Eugène Lami, who made watercolours of the rooms, was in charge of the decoration which ranges stylistically from Louis XIII to Louis XVI.

The Emperor's decision in 1857 to restore the ruined castle of Pierrefonds brought Eugène-Emmanuele Viollet-le-Duc (1814–79) into the Imperial circle. Best known as the restorer of countless medieval churches and cathedrals, he was the greatest living authority on medieval decoration and furnishings. He found favour with the Empress who championed his design for the Paris Opéra. Nevertheless, this commission was given to Charles Garnier, whose opulent interiors epitomise the pleasure-loving society of the Second Empire, as do the interiors of Alfred Armand's adjacent Grand Hôtel de l'Opéra (1862). But as well as public buildings, such as Garnier's Opéra, and the Palais de Justice by Louis Duc (1802–79), Napoleon III's reign witnessed the transformation of the old fabric of the city by Georges-Eugène Haussmann (1809–91) and the erection of new building types including railway stations, the central markets at Les Halles and the *grands magasins*. In all of these buildings, iron and glass were used to create new structural forms which did not derive from historical precedents, even if the skins with which they were clad often derived some elements from the past. The vast internal spaces of such *magasins* as au Bon Marché (1873–76) by Louis-Charles Boileau (1812–76) and Gustave Eiffel (1832–1923) and du Printemps (1881–89) by Paul Sedille (who also designed the Rococo auditorium of the Théâtre du Palais Royal c.1880) illustrate a new spatial concept combined with stylistically eclectic decoration; the ironwork in the latter was brightly coloured, and bronze, marble and terra-cotta were all employed in the decoration. But the monumental Salle de Lecture in the Grands Magasins du Louvre (1881) reverted to the First School of Fontainebleau for its elaborate decoration that recalls the spectacular Hôtel de Paiva (1863–66).

The Second Empire came to an end in 1870, but the standards of luxury and opulent display that characterised its architecture and decoration were upheld, even surpassed, during the Third Republic that followed. The new interiors in the Palais du Luxembourg, created to house the Sénat in 1879, continued what Napoleon III had begun in the old Salle du Trône which became the Salle des Conférences and was encrusted with heavily modelled Renaissance / Baroque decoration, dazzlingly gilded and painted by Jean Alaux, Henri Lehmann and Adolphe Bruce. The Palais de Justice, which had been partly destroyed during the Commune uprising in 1871, was rebuilt and decorated in a richer manner than before; the Salle d'Audience of the Première Chambre Civile is the most magnificent of the new interiors with a heavily modelled ceiling reminiscent of the Doge's Palace in Venice, painted by Paul Baudry (1828–86) and Elie Delaunay (1828–91), two of Garnier's team at the Opéra. The Hôtel de Ville, which had been completely destroyed in 1871, was rebuilt (1873–83) in a rich Renaissance style by Théodore Ballu (1817–85) and Edouard Deperthes with grandiose reception rooms glittering with gold and painted by Puvis de Chavannes, Jean-Paul

Laurens, Benjamin Constant and more than forty painters and sculptors whose work took its place in the overpowering Renaissance / Baroque interiors. Puvis also contributed painted decorations in the Grand Amphithéâtre of the Nouvelle Sorbonne (1885–89) designed by Henri-Paul Nenot (1853–1934) and the secularised Pantheon (1885).

"Tous les Louis" retained its popularity for theatres, such as Stanislas Louis Bernier's Opéra-Comique (1893–98) and the Théâtre Grevin (originally Joli) designed in 1900 by Antoine Bourdelle with paintings by Gustave-Joseph Chéret, and as an international style for hotels and restaurants. It had little to fear from Art Nouveau which had been developing at Nancy around the figures of Émile Gallé and Louis Majorelle. This style was introduced to Paris by Hector Guimard (1867–1942) who had visited Belgium in 1895 and been impressed by the work of Victor Horta and Paul Hankar. Pieces of furniture in the new style designed in Nancy by Majorelle and decorated with marquetry by Victor Prouvé were shown at the 1900 Exposition in Paris, as were whole room settings by Edward Colonna and Georges de Feure and others in Siegfried Bing's Pavillon de L'Art Nouveau. Five years earlier La Maison de l'Art Nouveau (Louis Bonnier) had been opened in the capital to sell fabrics, glass, pottery and furniture from Nancy and from other countries.

In Guimard's buildings, iron was used in the curvilinear, interlacing forms to which it was suited, both externally and internally, as in Castel Béranger (1894–98), a 36-apartment house in which the entrance doors and staircase balustrades had twisted, sinuous shapes distantly related to the natural forms and twining tendrils of Rococo frames and panels. His designs for fireplaces, mirrors and furniture were all similarly flowing. The same principles were carried into structural forms as in the Salle de Concert Humbert de Romans, Paris (1897–1901) in which the root-and-branch-like frames were exposed as a part of the interior design, reaching up to support a ceiling pierced with yellow glazing. Clusters of electric bulbs, like fruit, hung from the branches. The rooms in his own home, Hôtel Guimard (1909–12), were completely based on curvilinear forms in their decoration and furniture; more attractive is the staircase in Hôtel Mezzara (1910–11) with a characteristic but elegant iron balustrade. The designs Guimard made for the entrances to the Paris Métro from 1899 to 1904 lent publicity to Art Nouveau. This style enjoyed a vogue in glass, pottery, fabrics, graphics and jewellery, but it had little direct effect on interior design, although a commercialised version was used in restaurants such as Maxim's (Louis Marnez 1899), Lucas Carton (1901), the Wagenende brasserie (c.1902), and in Henri Sauvage's fin-de-siècle decorations in the Café de la Paix. The Grand Magasins du Printemps was remodelled c.1907 by René Binet, who created a great free-standing staircase with sweeping lines in the decorative balustrade, and the Magasins Jansen was also redecorated by Sauvage; but there was little enthusiasm at the time for Art Nouveau which soon faded away until it was rediscovered and became a cult fifty years later.

The Paris Exposition des Arts Décoratifs of 1925 was the showcase for the last *style de luxe*; namely Art Deco. But just as the exhibition itself had been planned for 1914, the appearance of Art Deco too had been delayed. Paul Poiret, the couturier, had opened his own decorating business in 1911

France: lady's bedroom by André Groult, 1925

under the name of the Atelier Martine, and at first the influence of Léon Bakst and the Ballets Russes was strong. Oriental luxury and strong colours, dim lighting, low divans with tasseled cushions, were typical of the furnishings displayed in Poiret's showroom, but although some of the comfortable aspects remained in the designs of the 1920s there was also a reinterpretation of the form and character of Louis Seize, Directoire and Empire furnishings. The materials used were characteristic of the exotic tastes favoured by fashionable, wealthy society of the 1920s, and included sycamore, ebony, shagreen, lacquer, enamel and silvered bronze. Marquetry was also used, sometimes inlaid with ivory or mother-of-pearl, a fashion known to Marie-Antoinette. Sometimes furniture was painted – grey, gold or silver – which was an effect that was also much favoured in decorative schemes as a whole and perhaps harked back to late Louis XVI taste and the Salle d'Argent in the Elysée palace.

The Art Deco style was closely associated with the world of haute couture. Jeanne Lanvin commissioned Albert-Armand Rateau to decorate her house in the rue Barbet-le-Jouy and her boutique in the faubourg St. Honoré, and Madeleine Vionnet filled her house with lacquer screens and furniture by Jean Dunand. Jacques Doucet, who collected post-Impressionist, Cubist and Surrealist works of art, brought together leading Art Deco designers to furnish an apartment in Neuilly in 1927. These included Pierre Legrain who made furniture of sycamore and chrome, Clément Rousseau who was fond of shagreen and lacquer, Marcel Coard who used sheets of parchment, layers of tinted glass, mirror and inlays of amethyst and mother-of-pearl, and Eileen Gray (1879–1976) who graduated from the manufacture of elegant lacquered screens and small pieces of furniture to complete interiors. One of Gray's most notable Art Deco ensembles was for the Paris apartment of the couturier Suzanne Talbot (1919–22) which featured satiny white walls, a silvered floor and luxurious Deco-style furnishings. Gray subsequently went on to work in a sparse Modernist style designing angular tubular steel furniture and compact built-in fittings for her own villa at Roquebrune in the south of France (1926–29) and for the Paris apartment of the architect Jean Badovici (1930–31).

Other leading Art Deco designers were Jacques-Emile

France: office interior by Andrée Putman, 1995

Ruhlmann (1879–1933) and André Groult (1884-1967). Ruhlmann's Pavillon d'un Collectionneur was one of the highlights of the 1925 exhibition and contained a large circular salon whose walls were covered with silk, featuring a large repeated pattern of classical urns and formalised flowers and birds. The principal decorative elements were a huge crystal chandelier complemented by related wall lights, and a large panel, *Les Perruches*, by Jean Dupas over the fireplace. The basic idea is no different from that of an 18th-century room; and Groult's furniture and decoration also followed an 18th-century formula, even if the colours, paintings and fashionable character were of the 1920s.

The Esprit Nouveau Pavilion at the 1925 Exposition presented a different sort of interior in the copy of one of the cells of Le Corbusier's Immeubles-Villas housing project with its machine aesthetic. Le Corbusier's early work from Villa Fallet (1907) until Villa de Mondrot (1931) was largely domestic, although he regarded the Villa Schwob at La Chaux-de-Fonds (1916–17) as the first acceptable work in his canon. In *Vers Une Architecture* (1923) he wrote that "the decorative arts are now at the dangerous height which goes before a fall ... exquisite ovals where triangular doves preen themselves or one another, boudoirs embellished with 'poufs' in gold and black velvet, are now no more than the intolerable witnesses to a dead spirit. These sanctuaries stifling with elegancies ... are an offence". The Villa Schwob and the Esprit Nouveau Pavilion offered an alternative, "machine for living in", which was to be developed more fully in Villa Savoye, Poissy (1928–31) in the open planning and the austere, undecorated forms of the internal spaces that opened up to the surrounding landscape through continuous windows, and in which each permitted item of furniture was a part of the architectural image. Corbusier's intolerance of his client was revealed in an article in *L'Esprit Nouveau* (1921): "When the architect hands over the keys of the house, his heart sinks. He knows that the owner ... will have no compunction in smothering the walls with intemperate wallpapers which will unbalance the spaces, in cluttering the rooms with any old furniture which will annihilate the value of the volumes and in hanging up paintings and prints which will upset the order required by the architect".

The appeal of stripped, functional, impersonal interiors was limited. The millionaire collector Carlos de Beisteguy commissioned Corbusier to design an apartment for him in the Champs Elysées in the early 1930s which included an elegant staircase that spiralled gracefully around a central glass newel; but the novelty quickly wore off and within a year Beisteguy called the apartment an "uninhabitable machine", and filled it with Baroque furnishings. In his château at Groussay he installed a quite different spiral staircase in the sumptuous double-height library that was filled with predominantly Neo-Classical objects and furnishings arranged with a theatrical Baroque opulence. Of the two, Groussay has been more influential than the Villa Savoye in the eclectic world of haute couture decoration revealed in the pages of *Maison et Jardin*.

The post-war styles such as "Contemporary" and Pop were largely British and American phenomena, but the French designer Olivier Mourgue (b.1939) embraced the more futuristic elements of 1960s design in his sets for the cult film, *2001: A Space Odyssey* (1967). These featured Mourgue's foam-padded *Djinn* seating (1964) whose low curved shapes were based on exaggerated amoeboid forms.

Since the 1970s, Postmodernism has been strongly in evidence in the work of interior designers such as Andrée Putman, Jean-Michel Wilmotte and Philippe Starck. Andrée Putman (b.1925) has an international reputation as one of France's most elegant and stylish designers, and she has designed numerous apartments and showrooms for top fashion designers Yves St. Laurent, Karl Lagerfeld and Thierry Mugler, and has worked on the interiors of many hotels, galleries, museums and government offices. One of her most widely publicised commissions was the Paris office of Jack Lang, the Minister of Culture (1984), where golden-blonde, drum-shaped Postmodernist furniture and High-Tech lamps were dramatically combined with traditional 18th-century gilt panelling and chandeliers. Official encouragement was also given to other Postmodernist designers when the French President, François Mitterand, commissioned Jean-Michel Wilmotte (b.1948) and Ronald Cécil Sportes (b.1943) to decorate the private apartments of the Elysée Palace in 1983. Once again the setting was traditional, and the decoration, inspired by Viennese design of the 1900s, Art Deco and High-Tech, creates a striking mix of the antique and the contemporary. Philippe Starck's witty interpretations of the streamlined Deco and Moderne style have also proved very popular in the United States where he has supervised the decoration and furnishings of several innovative and much-acclaimed hotels: the Paramount (1990) and the Royalton (1988) in New York, and most recently, the Delano in Miami Beach (1995).

DEREK LINSTRUM

Further Reading

Alcouffe, Daniel, Anne Dion-Tenebaum and Pierre Ennes, *Un Age d'Or des Arts Décoratifs, 1814–1848* (exhib. cat.: Grand Palais, Paris), Paris: Réunion des Monuments Nationaux, 1991

Arminjon, Catherine and others, *L'Art de Vivre: Decorative Arts and Design in France, 1789–1989*, New York: Vendome, and London: Thames and Hudson, 1989

Arwas, Victor, *Art Deco*, 1980; revised edition New York: Abrams, and London: Academy, 1992

Babelon, Jean Pierre, *Demeures Parisiennes sous Henri IV et Louis XIII*, Paris: Le Temps, 1965; new edition Paris: Hazan, 1991

Béguin, Sylvie and others, *L'École de Fontainebleau* (exhib. cat.), Paris: Grand Palais, 1972

Binney, Marcus, *The Châteaux of France*, London: Mitchell Beazley, 1994

Blunt, Anthony, *Art and Architecture in France, 1500–1700*, 2nd edition Harmondsworth: Penguin, 1970

Boyer, Marie-France, *Paris Style: The Private Apartments of Paris*, London: Weidenfeld and Nicolson, 1989

Brunhammer, Yvonne and Suzanne Tise, *The Decorative Arts in France, 1900–1942: La Société des Artistes Décorateurs*, New York: Rizzoli, 1990

Chadenet, Sylvie, *Les Styles Empire et Restauration*, Paris: Baschet, 1976

Eriksen, Svend, *Early Neo-Classicism in France: The Creation of the Louis Seize Style*, London: Faber, 1974

Feray, Jean, *Architecture Intérieure et Décoration en France, des Origines à 1875*, Paris: Caisse Nationale des Monuments Historiques et des Sites, 1988

Gallet, Michel, *Paris Domestic Architecture of the 18th Century*, London: Barrie and Jenkins, 1972; as *Stately Mansions: Eighteenth Century Paris Architecture*, New York: Praeger, 1972

Hauteceour, Louis, *Histoire de l'architecture classique en France*, 7 vols., Paris: Picard, 1943–57

Inventaire du Fonds Français, Paris: Bibliothèque Nationale, 1930–

Jean-Richard, Pierrette, *Ornemanistes du XVe au XVIIe siècle: Gravures et Dessins* (exhib. cat.), Paris: Musée du Louvre, 1987

Kalnein, Wend von, *Architecture in France in the Eighteenth Century*, New Haven and London: Yale University Press, 1995

Kimball, Fiske, *The Creation of the Rococo*, 1943; reprinted as *The Creation of the Rococo Decorative Style*, New York: Dover, and London: Constable, 1980

Ledoux-Lebard, Denise, *Les Ebénistes Parisiens du XIXe Siècle (1795–1870): Leurs Oeuvres et leurs Marques*, 2nd edition Paris: Nobèle, 1965

Pradère, Alexandre, *French Furniture Makers: The Art of the Ebéniste from Louis XIV to the Revolution*, Malibu, CA: Getty Museum, and London: Sotheby's, 1989

Scott, Katie, *The Rococo Interior: Decoration and Social Spaces in Early Eighteenth-Century Paris*, New Haven and London: Yale University Press, 1995

The Second Empire, 1852–1870: Art in France under Napoleon III (exhib. cat.), Philadelphia: Philadelphia Museum of Art, 1978

Silverman, Debora L., *Art Nouveau in Fin-de-Siècle France: Politics, Psychology, and Style*, Berkeley: University of California Press, 1989

Slesin, Suzanne and Stafford Cliff, *French Style*, New York: Potter, and London: Thames and Hudson, 1982

Thornton, Peter, *Seventeenth-Century Interior Decoration in England, France, and Holland*, New Haven and London: Yale University Press, 1978

Troy, Nancy J., *Modernism and the Decorative Arts in France: Art Nouveau to Le Corbusier*, New Haven and London: Yale University Press, 1991

Verlet, Pierre, *French Furniture and Interior Decoration of the 18th Century*, London: Barrie and Rockliffe, 1967

Verlet, Pierre, *Styles, Meubles, Décors, du Moyen Age à nos jours*, 2 vols., Paris: Larousse, 1972

Walton, Guy, *Louis XIV's Versailles*, Chicago: University of Chicago Press, and London: Viking, 1986

Watson, F.J.B., *Wallace Collection Catalogues: Furniture*, London: Wallace Collection, 1956

Weigert, R.-A., (introduction), *Louis XIV: Faste et Décors* (exhib. cat.), Paris: Musée des Arts Décoratifs, 1960

Frank, Jean-Michel 1895–1941

French interior decorator and furniture designer

Jean-Michel Frank was one of the most highly regarded of the generation of designer-decorators in Paris who spanned Art Deco and Modernism, although his career lasted little more than ten years. He combined technical perfectionism, ("..one doesn't work in centimetres but in millimetres") and a preference for luxurious, unusual and rare materials, in keeping with the *ébéniste* tradition, with a puritan's taste for simplicity, achieved by sparse furnishing and minimal decoration. His work exemplified Robert Mallet-Stevens's dictum: "You can most luxuriously install a room by unfurnishing it".

Jean-Michel Frank: Vicomte Charles de Noailles' salon, Hôtel Bischoffsheim, Paris, 1929

The hallmark of Frank's early style is his novel treatment of wall surfaces. These were plain, without divisions or mouldings and were covered either in squares of vellum, or in marquetry, painstakingly constructed from split rye straw (a revival of a traditional craft), or painted white. Later he was to favour plain wood panelling, much of it salvaged, often with doors set flush without mouldings. Bathrooms could be lined with marble or travertine. His early furniture was rectilinear, reviving the geometric shapes pioneered by Koloman Moser in Vienna, and included sofas, low, rectangular tables and folding screens. Frank would sometimes incorporate fruitwood furniture of Louis XVI style and later used overstuffed armchairs and sofas with plain upholstery.

There is little evidence that Frank actually made any furniture, but his partner, Adolphe Chanaux, was a consummate cabinet-maker who had worked with André Groult and Jacques-Emile Ruhlmann. He may have introduced Frank to the decorative possibilities of the shagreen and gypsum veneers he favoured for the surfaces of tables and cabinets. They employed a range of craftsmen at their La Ruche workshops: a Spanish vellum specialist, a Hungarian shagreen expert, a team of traditional cabinet-makers and four or five women working on straw marquetry. Leather was provided by Hermès and carpets, textiles and rock-crystal for lamps were also supplied by appointment, from the highest-quality sources. From the mid-1930s, Frank collaborated actively with artists from his social circle. The sculptors Alberto and Diego Giacometti contributed innovative designs for lamps, vases and mirror frames in white plaster and patinated bronze; Christian Bérard, the painter, introduced colour and decorative pattern into wall decorations (particularly the architectural *capriccios* employed at the Guérlain Institute) and carpet design; Emilio Terry broadened and enlivened the range of furniture designs with Neo-Classical shapes and Greek ornament. In addition, his interiors were often embellished with folding screens with designs by Bérard, Filippo de Pisis and Salvador Dalí.

Frank was left with an independent income after the tragic early deaths of his parents and gravitated towards artistic social groups. In Venice he met Diaghilev and his circle who included Stravinsky and Picasso. Shortly after, he fell under the spell of the elderly South American arbiter of taste, Mme. Eugenia Errazuriz, whose maxim was "Throw out, and keep throwing out! Elegance means elimination." He also met Vicomte and Vicomtesse Charles and Marie-Laure de Noailles, his first important clients, and their circle who included Jean Cocteau, Luis Buñuel and Man Ray. Frank must have met most of his clients through private introduction and by recommendation; he belonged to no design groups and did not exhibit at the salons. He did receive regular media coverage, however, which no doubt helped to publicize his work.

His first published schemes and furniture designs were for his own apartment on the rue de Verneuil, his first collaboration with Adolphe Chanaux, in 1927–28. The drawing room and bedroom were almost indistinguishable; both had plain walls and ceilings totally lined with bleached straw marquetry. The flush doors were similarly decorated, although those in the bedroom had panels of sunburst effect. In both rooms he made use of low tables, veneered in shagreen or irregular gypsum tiles, boxy stools and chairs and half-height screens. The long, rectangular drawing-room sofa in white leather was exchanged for a built-in bed on a plinth, heaped with cushions. His library and dining room were, in complete contrast, hung with full-length net curtains and furnished with traditional, Louis XVI chairs.

Frank's association with the de Noailles included decorations for their villa at Hyères in the South of France, schemes whose details are now lost. Arguably his most important commissions were the rooms for their 18th-century Paris house, the Hôtel Bischoffsheim. The high-ceilinged salon was stripped of mouldings and lined throughout with squares of creamy parchment, resembling blocks of warm stone. Heavy, beige silk curtains hung the full height of the room and burnished bronze doors were recessed into the walls. The fireplace was faced with a vertical brickwork of mica tiles. A rectilinear sofa and club armchairs in bleached, white leather gleamed against a deep chocolate carpet. There were wall cabinets with veneers of straw marquetry in fan-shaped panels and low tables in bronze or shagreen veneer on which sat lamps formed of irregular lumps of rock crystal and asymmetrical slices of ivory. Relations between Frank and his clients were to deteriorate when they hung paintings on the walls and introduced the clutter of their personal effects.

At much the same time, 1929–30, Frank created modern rooms within another historic building, the 16th-century palazzo of the Pecci-Blunts near Rome. For their library, also used as a music room, he created a plain oval, lacquered white, whose book recesses, lined with straw marquetry and illuminated with concealed top lights, alternated on one side with full-length windows of equal size and on the other, with doors also decorated with straw marquetry. Tub-shaped armchairs and a sofa with curved ends were of pearwood, upholstered in beige leather; they were served by elegant gilt-bronze side-tables.

Frank had a number of couturiers as friends and clients. In the late 1920s he decorated the Paris apartment of Elsa Schiaparelli on the Boulevard St. Germain. In her white-painted salon he used new, rubberized textiles for the white curtains and green upholstered chairs, in combination with an enormous orange leather sofa. Black framed tables with glass tops and black porcelain in the dining room must have created a startling effect; no wonder that Chanel, a more conservative friend of Frank, "shuddered as if she were passing a cemetery". In 1936, Frank fitted out the showrooms for Lucien Lelong and Schiaparelli in the Place Vendôme, in a more restrained traditional style. His frilled draperies, plain, pale carpet and the pale sofas and boudoir chairs with their ruched valances and frivolous ear-tassels perfectly complemented the exuberant, Rococo decoration of the salon.

The same ear-tasselled chairs are used to furnish Baron Roland de L'Epée's extraordinary cinema-ballroom, published in 1939, perhaps Frank's most famous interior. Each wall was painted a different pastel shade with a matching, overstuffed rectangular sofa on gilt, spiral-carved legs set before each except for the pink wall. This was set with a sofa upholstered in Schiaparelli's "Shocking"-pink satin, in the form of the actress Mae West's lips from the design by Salvador Dali. Above it hung a white plaster disc, with a relief design by Alberto Giacometti, which hid the cinema projector lens. In the corners on either side stood two circus boxes with barley-twist balustrades, upholstered in purple velvet. The floor was fitted with a dark red carpet which could be rolled back for dancing. The effect was highly theatrical, betraying the influence of the Surrealist artists with whom Frank collaborated.

In 1937 Frank furnished a living room for the New York apartment of Nelson Rockefeller which had been designed by the architect Wallace K. Harrison. The walls were sheathed from floor to ceiling in polished oak with minimal mouldings and flush cupboard doors. Fireplaces at either end of the room were surrounded by murals by Matisse and Léger, and works by Picasso hung on the walls. Frank supplied an Aubusson carpet patterned with stylized leaves on a solid ground, designed by Christian Bérard, which added further colour to the room. He also provided overstuffed sofas and armchairs with delicate cabriole legs in the Louis XVI style and his hallmark low tables. Diego Giacometti designed lampstands and firedogs in bronze and a gilt, console table supported on abstracted human arms sprouting leaves. A similar decorative treatment was used later in George Born's apartment in Buenos Aires.

Frank created some of his most radically modern interiors for the Templeton-Crocker apartment in San Francisco; somewhere between Ocean-liner style and 1950s Modernism. There were a dining room and breakfast room furnished entirely in lacquer by Jean Dunand and a bathroom with streamlined fitments and floor in black Belgian marble and metal-framed granite walls. The split-level bedroom had a mirror-panelled wall and a platform bed set into a flight of carpeted steps. Most extraordinary of all was the living room, as large as a hotel concourse, which was also used as a music room. The windows alternated with mirror panels around the high walls and there were banks of bushy plants in troughs beneath them. The furniture was uniformly low; boxy, geometric armchairs and sofas, several partly enclosed by half-height screens. There were rectangular, reclining seats and floor cushions, rough-hewn X-frame stools and stone-paved floors strewn with animal skins and Navaho rugs; an electrifying combination of Functionalist chic and American Frontier style.

STELLA BEDDOE

See also Surrealism

Biography

Born in Paris in 1895; the great-uncle of Anne Frank. Trained as a lawyer. Travelled extensively in Europe, 1920–25; active as a decorator and designer of furniture from c.1925; collaborated with cabinet-maker Adolphe Chanaux from 1927; made designs for the theatre and ballet, 1929–35; opened a shop with Chanaux selling furnishings at 147 rue du Faubourg St. Honoré, 1932. Left France for Argentina via Lisbon, 1939; worked as a decorator in Buenos Aires, 1939; moved to New York, 1940; lectured at the Parsons School of Design and worked with backing from the interior design firm McMillen. Committed suicide in New York, 1941.

Selected Works

Much of Frank's work is in private collections; examples of his furniture are in the Museum and Art Gallery, Brighton, and the Musée des Arts Décoratifs, Paris. His interiors and furnishings survive, intact, in the Rome apartment of Comtesse Pecci-Blunt and Nelson Rockefeller's apartment, New York.

Interiors

1924–33	Villa de Noailles, Hyères (furniture and decoration): Vicomte and Vicomtess de Noailles
1927	Frank apartment, rue de Verneuil, Paris (furniture and decorations): Jean-Michel Frank
c.1928	Schiaparelli apartment, Blvd. St. Germain, Paris (furniture and decoration): Elsa Schiaparelli
1929	Hôtel Bischoffsheim, Place des Etats-Unis, Paris (furniture and decoration): Vicomte and Vicomtess de Noailles
1930	Pecci-Blunt apartment, Rome (furniture and decoration): Count and Countess Pecci-Blunt
1935	Georges Born apartment, Paris (furniture)
1935	Couturier's showrooms, Place Vendôme, Paris (furniture and decoration): Elsa Schiaparelli
1936	Apartment, Paris (furniture and decoration): Mlle. Estevez
1936	Couturier's showrooms, Paris (furniture and decoration): Lucien Lelong
1937	Jean-Pierre Guérlain's apartment, Paris (furniture and decoration)
1937–38	Rockefeller apartment, 5th Avenue, New York (furniture): Nelson A. Rockefeller
1937–38	Templeton-Crocker apartment, San Francisco (furniture and decoration)
1937–38	Helena Rubinstein's apartment, Paris (furniture)
c.1939	Guérlain Institute, Paris (furniture and decoration)
c.1939	Cinema ballroom, Paris (furniture and decoration): Baron Roland de L'Epée
c.1939	Georges Born apartment, Buenos Aires (furniture and decoration)

Further Reading

The literature on Frank is sparse, confusing and contradictory. The only monograph, Sanchez 1980, has excellent plates but the text is unsatisfactory.

Auerbach, A., "The Relevance of Jean-Michael Frank" in *House Beautiful* (U.S.), October 1969

Cabanne, Pierre, *Encyclopédie Art Déco*, Paris: Somogy, 1986

Calloway, Stephen, "Perfectly Frank" in *House and Garden* (USA), 1990

Calloway, Stephen, *Baroque Baroque: The Culture of Excess*, London: Phaidon, 1994

Cayeaux, G., "The Modernism of Jean-Michel Frank" in *House and Garden*, 1929

"Chez M. Jean-Michel Frank" in *Art et Industrie*, March 1928

Duncan, Alastair, *Art Deco Furniture: The French Designers*, London: Thames and Hudson, and New York: Holt Rinehart, 1984

Esten, John and Rose Bennett Gilbert, *Manhattan Style*, Boston: Little Brown, 1990

Hampton, Mark, *Legendary Decorators of the Twentieth Century*, New York: Doubleday, and London: Hale, 1992

Jullian, Philippe, "L'Hôtel de Charles de Noailles" in *Connaissance des Arts*, October 1964

Lannes, R., "Exegèse Poétique de Jean-Michel Frank" in *Art et Décoration*, May 1939

Lassaigne, J., "L'Oeuvre de Jean-Michel Frank" in *Art et Industrie*, November 1945

Rutherford, Jessica, *Art Nouveau, Art Deco and the Thirties: The Furniture Collections at Brighton Museum*, Brighton: Royal Pavilion Art Gallery and Museums, 1983

Sanchez, Léopold Diego, *Jean-Michel Frank*, Paris: Regard, 1980

Schiaparelli, Elsa, *Shocking Life*, New York: Dutton, and London: Dent, 1954

Smith, C. Ray, *Interior Design in 20th-Century America: A History*, New York: Harper, 1987

Todd, Dorothy, "Interiors by Jean Frank" in *Good Furniture Magazine*, September 1929

Truex, Van Day, "Jean-Michel Frank Remembered" in *Architectural Digest*, September–October 1976, pp.71–5, 170–1

Frank, Josef 1885–1967

Austrian architect and designer

Born in Austria, Josef Frank became one of the most important and influential exponents of modern design in Sweden and his work made a strong impact on Scandinavian Modernism. He grew up in the culturally vibrant and eclectic atmosphere of turn-of-the century Vienna where he was exposed to the work of the Thonet company and the designers associated with the Wiener Werkstätte as well as the philosophies of Freud and Wittgenstein. Viennese design was also strongly influenced by the ideas of the English Arts and Crafts Movement at this time and especially the work of Charles Rennie Mackintosh and William Morris. Frank himself also greatly admired the clear and simple architecture of Leon Battista Alberti on whom he wrote his doctorate. He declared that man's ideal dwelling is the garden city with one-family houses set in their own gardens.

Frank's first furniture was designed in the 1910s. He was initially influenced by Vernacular and Biedermeier design. However, these influences were soon replaced by that of traditional English furniture and he also became fascinated by the forms associated with Chinese and Japanese design. Increasingly he felt that the models for all furniture lay in English prototypes; they only needed to be adapted to new environments and freed from their nationalistic and historic associations. In 1925, while he was still living in Vienna, he established an interior design co-operative together with Oscar Wlach called Haus und Garten for whom he produced many of the furnishings that would later become classics for the Swedish firm Svenskt Tenn. These included a light Chinese style cane-seat chair, Egyptian stools, an English Rococo armchair and functional sideboards. Facing growing hostility from the Nazis, Frank moved to Sweden with his Swedish wife Anna Sebanius in 1934 where, but for a sojourn of four years in New York between 1942 and 1946 during which he was associated with the New School of Social Research, he remained for the rest of his life.

Frank's move to Sweden was to prove decisive for the history of Swedish interior design. He was invited to work as chief designer for Svenskt Tenn, a company established in the 1920s by Estrid Ericsson. Together Frank and Ericsson produced work that represented a striking alternative to the cold, cubist Swedish Functionalism that was so much in evidence at the time. And in stark contrast to mainstream Swedish design, their room exhibited at Liljevalch's Gallery in

Josef Frank: living room for Svenskt Tenn, c. 1950

1934 included cretonnes blossoming on deep, over-sized, sofas that had soft rounded edges, tables with marble tops, teak furniture, an abundance of cushions and a leopard-skin rug on the floor. Always concerned with the same basic forms, Frank developed his ideas further in the 1940s and 1950s. He particularly liked the shape of the vitrine (a glass-fronted cabinet), admiring both its lightness and the fact that it stands on tall feet or legs leaving a large area of space between the floor and wall visible. Frank's version seems to almost float in mid-air as it is supported on its stand by only a turned ball in each corner. He also worked with the traditional four-poster or canopied bed and updated the Baroque "cabinet of curiosities" in a plain but powerfully elegant "cupboard with 19 drawers". Works such as these exercised a powerful influence on contemporary design and the introduction to an exhibition held at the National Gallery in Stockholm in 1952 declared: "One can very well ask if anyone has had a stronger impact on the formation of Swedish furniture and interior design than … Austrian Josef Frank".

Frank's attitude to interior design is deeply rooted in his ideas about housing. As an architect he was a pioneer Functionalist belonging to the radical circle of Modernist architects working in Vienna in the 1920s. But in his designs for interiors he rejected this approach. Indeed, the very essence of his approach to interior design was that the interior of a house should not conform to its exterior. He believed that the fast busy life led by modern people required its antidote and that it was only in cosy, comfortable surroundings as opposed to Modernist or Artistic interiors that they would be able to relax.

Frank also maintained a sharp distinction between works of art and objects for use. Art, he claimed, was something finished, whereas the home should be a living organism whose furnishing is an ongoing process. He called this process "Accidentism", meaning that surroundings should be designed as if they had come about by chance, and declared "A room where one can live and think freely is neither beautiful, nor harmonious nor photogenic". Frank also disliked monochrome surfaces, describing their immediate impact as unsettling; patterned surfaces, by contrast, were praised as calming because they beguiled and intrigued the observer. He therefore advocated the free use of different patterns and colours in upholstery, curtains and carpets – and his own designs for textiles included bold forms taken from nature and bright colours – but declared that walls should be whitewashed to maintain a balance in the modern house. Furniture should not attempt to become part of the architecture by being static but should be small, light and movable. Individual pieces should be placed wherever they are needed at the time and should never be larger than is required or they risk running contrary to the basic aesthetic principle of economy. Large furniture makes the room look small, whereas small furniture makes it appear large. Following these principles Frank created nonconformist interiors for free-thinking individuals. The seats and backs of his chairs are never square since "anyone choosing for himself a chair with a square seat harbours totalitarian sympathies in some corner of this heart". And another classic item designed for Svenskt Tenn was a sofa table of amboyna wood, the top of which has edges that float irregularly outwards like a puddle of water. The surface of the wood was extremely important to Frank who claimed that wood is to the craftsman what colour is to the painter. Hence, his furniture was never stained, and if on occasions it was painted this was in accordance with the colour scheme of a particular room.

Despite his humble and retiring personality, Frank harboured no false modesty about his achievements: "I have saved Swedish interior design and created the Scandinavian style. Before me Bauhaus was the only inspiration". He also showed that furniture, in the true sense of the word, cannot be achieved through formulas, and that the designer must have real creative ability in order to produce furniture with character. Frank's own creativity was inspired by the past and he created furniture that was not only modern but also timeless. He introduced colour and pattern into the Swedish home, transforming it into a jungle of trees exploding with flowers, fruit and vegetables. And if the work sold by Svenskt Tenn catered for an elite, wealthy clientele, its influence reached a far wider audience than its immediate customers and continues to do so today.

PIA MARIA MONTONEN

Biography

Born in Baden bei Wien, near Vienna, 15 July 1885. Received a Ph.D, 1910. Married Anna Sebanius, 1912. Active as an architect and designer of interiors and furniture in Austria and Germany from 1910; worked in Sweden from 1934. Professor of Building Construction, Wiener Kunstgewerbeschule, 1919–25; taught at New School for Social Research, New York, 1942–46. Founded interior design cooperative, Haus und Garten, Vienna, with Oskar Wlach, 1925–34. Chief designer at Svenskt Tenn, Stockholm, 1932–67. Awarded the Grand Austrian National Prize for Architecture, 1965. Exhibited at Paris 1925, Stuttgart 1928, Paris 1937, and New York World's Fair 1939. Died in Stockholm, 8 January 1967.

Selected Works

A large collection of Frank's drawings and designs for furniture and textiles, photographs and additional documentation, is in the Svensk Tenn archive, Stockholm. Examples of furniture are in National Museum, Stockholm, and the Museum of Decorative Art, Vienna.

Interiors

1912	Museum for Eastern Asian Art, Cologne (interiors)
1927	Villa Claeson, Falsterbo (building and interiors)
1927	Villa Carlsten, Falsterbo (building and interiors)
1929–32	Villa Beer, Vienna (building and interiors)
1932–66	Interiors for Svenskt Tenn
1936	Villa Bunzl, Falsterbo (building and interiors)
1936	Villa Wehtje, Falsterbo (building and interiors)
1937	Exposition International, Paris (interiors for Svenskt Tenn and Haus und Garten)

Publications

Architektur als Symbol, 1931
"Rum och Inredning" in *Form*, 1936, pp.217–225
"Accidentism" in *Form*, 1958, pp.161–66

Further Reading

Boman, Monica (editor), *Svenska Möbler 1890–1990*, Lund: Signum, 1991

Feuerstein, Günther, *Vienna, Past and Present: Arts and Crafts, Applied Art, Design*, Vienna: Jugend & Volk, 1976

Johansson, Gotthard, *Josef Frank, Tjugo år i Svenskt Tenn*, Stockholm: Nationalmusei, 1952

Josef Frank: Inredning (exhib. cat.), Stockholm: Millesgården, 1994

Hård af Segerstad, Ulf, *Modern Scandinavian Furniture*, London: Studio, and Totowa, NJ: Bedminster, 1963

McFadden, David Revere (editor), *Scandinavian Modern Design, 1880–1980* (exhib. cat.: Cooper-Hewitt Museum, New York), New York: Abrams, 1982

Spalt, Johannes, *Josef Frank: Möbel, Geräte und Theoretisches*, Vienna: Hochschule für Angewandte Kunst, 1981

Spalt, Johannes and Hermann Czech, *Josef Frank 1885–1967*, Vienna: Hochschule für Angewandte Kunst, 1981

Spalt, Johannes and Otto Kapfinger, *Josef Frank 1885–1967: Stoffe, Tapeten, Teppiche*, Vienna: Hochschule für Angewandte Kunst, 1986

Stritzler-Levine, Nina (editor), *Josef Frank, Architect and Designer: An Alternative Vision of the Modern Home* (exhib. cat.: Bard Graduate Center, New York), New Haven and London: Yale University Press, 1996

Wänberg-Eriksson, Kristina, *Josef Frank: Livsträd i Krigens Skugga*, Lund: Signum, 1994

Woodham, Jonathan M., *Twentieth-Century Ornament*, London: Studio Vista, and New York: Rizzoli, 1990

Frankl, Paul 1887–1958

Austrian-born furniture designer and author

Trained as an architect in his native Vienna and later in Berlin, Paul Frankl also studied at art schools in Paris and Munich before emigrating to America in 1914. During his early years in America he worked for the theatre but his main creative interest was furniture and domestic interiors, and it was in these spheres that he rose to prominence both as a practitioner and writer. At the forefront of Modernist American design in the 1920s and 1930s, and embracing both moderne and streamlined forms, Frankl not only fought to achieve recognition for the designer's central role in the decorative arts, but also pioneered the search for a modern aesthetic that would reflect the rapidly changing lifestyle of big-city America.

Frankl theorised about a distinctly "modern American" style, unrelated to outdated and inappropriate revivalist models, but in practice it was difficult for designers to overlook the strong design trends coming from Europe. A visit to Japan early in his career proved deeply significant, and many of his pared-down interiors, several of which include the use of delicate screens and coloured lacquer finishes, suggest a Japanese influence.

Frankl: bedroom furniture from *Form and Re-Form*, 1930

He rose to fame in the late 1920s for his "sky-scraper furniture"; a series of tall stepped bookcases, desks and combination units, in which he emulated the horizontality and profile of early stepped skyscrapers, thus achieving an "American" form unmistakably reminiscent of the urban skyscape. These dramatic, geometric pieces, devoid of ornament, were custom-made pieces made from expensive materials, often polished woods defined with a contrasting material such as metal-leaf, ebonized wood or coloured lacquer. A large combination bookcase and desk (1927) made of California redwood trimmed with black, or a lacquered skyscraper dressing-table (c.1928) featuring a tall mirror set between stepped-back cabinets of drawers and cupboards with silver handles, are fine examples of his singular invention during this period. Frankl argued that his skyscraper furniture responded to the exigencies of apartment living, where floor space and storage were at a premium, although lack of space was probably not a concern for the socially elite customers who visited the Frankl Galleries, which he had opened on Madison Avenue, New York in 1924.

Frankl's work began to receive critical attention in home and furnishing magazines, and a whole room of his skyscraper furniture was featured among the work of American and European designers in R.H. Macy & Co.'s 1927 "Art in Trade" exhibition. He promoted his own and other Modernist designers' work from the Frankl Galleries, and was also a founder and active member of the American Designers' Gallery, established in 1928, and the American Union of Decorative Artists and Craftsmen (AUDAC) formed in 1930. Although these groups were short-lived, mainly due to the economic depression, both aimed to raise the profile and status of decorative artists, bringing their work to public attention through exhibitions. *The Annual of American Design 1931*, produced by AUDAC, included chapters by leading members such as Kem Weber and Frank Lloyd Wright, with Frankl contributing the section "The Home". Frankl's books *New Dimensions* (1928) and *Form and Re-Form* (1930), both lavishly illustrated, mainly with dramatically photographed interiors of his own and other designers' works, were important in promoting new American design and theory.

As Frankl himself wrote, his skyscraper furniture represented only one phase of his creativity, but he was much aggrieved at the derivative and shoddy mass-produced versions of his work that later appeared. He was committed, theoretically at least, to the notion that the machine was the tool, not the slave, of a creative designer and could be harnessed to mass-produce functional objects with clean and simple lines. Nevertheless, he was unable in *Machine-Made Leisure* (1932) to find an easy solution to the modern dilemma of "deplorable" machine-made objects. He argued for the training of designers for industrial applications but admitted his own furniture was custom-made in the craftsman tradition for an elite and sophisticated clientele.

His writings confirm his strong opposition to the practice of producing furniture in historical styles, such as pseudo-Renaissance, which he saw as totally removed from the lifestyle of modern America. Frankl's appreciation of the rapidly changing social conditions of men and women in the urban environment led him to suggest a far more flexible and practical approach to interior design. His ideas for a new cost-effective house to be designed by AUDAC for the 1933 Chicago Century of Progress Exposition included strong collaboration between architect and designer, making walls function as furniture with hanging and storage space, practical bathrooms and kitchens, and built-in space-saving furniture inspired by the interiors of contemporary ocean liners.

In his own furniture he moved on to embrace a more horizontal aesthetic, claiming that skyscrapers were a "passing fad" and that American life was fundamentally horizontal, which he equated with speed, both of change and movement. Closely in touch with the changing designs of automobiles, liners, gadgets and electrical products, Frankl continued to create unique furniture, accessories and interiors using a variety of materials. He promoted the use of new industrially produced materials like Bakelite and Formica, and made imaginative use of the creative possibilities of cork, glass and mirrors. He was vehement, almost Ruskinian, in his belief that materials should be true to their nature – insisting that man-made materials should not masquerade as wood or metal, while natural materials should reflect their true characteristics.

Frankl's creative life was marked by several stylistic changes, but he was consistently aware of the visual and aesthetic potential of carefully juxtaposed materials, textures and colour. In a 1932–33 streamlined easy chair he contrasts a dark leather upholstered frame with thickly textured beige fabric cushions, and the shiny angular frame of an early 1930s chair is upholstered with matte black leather. He successfully used thin cork veneer in furniture he designed for the Johnson Furniture Co. and was excited by the potential of thick rattan which he heated and bent to detail low glass-topped tables or form the frames for outdoor furniture. In 1938 he published

Space for Living, a book on interior design which was illustrated with photographs of his clients' homes.

While continuing to design and write, Frankl also demonstrated his dedication to the decorative arts through teaching. He lectured at the Metropolitan Museum of Art, and taught at New York University and later at the University of Southern California, Los Angeles.

MARY PESKETT SMITH

Biography

Paul Theodor Frankl. Born in Vienna in 1887. Studied in Vienna, Paris, Munich, and Berlin. Settled in the United States, 1914. Opened a retail furniture shop, the Frankl Galleries, New York, 1924. Lectured and wrote on furniture and interior design. Founder-member of American Designers' Gallery, 1928, and American Union of Decorative Artists and Craftsmen, 1930. Active as a designer in New York and California. Published several books on design. Died in New York, 1958.

Publications

New Dimensions: The Decorative Arts of Today, 1928; reprinted 1975
Form and Re-Form: A Practical Handbook of Modern Interiors, 1930; reprinted 1972
Machine-Made Leisure, 1932
Space for Living: Creative Interior Decoration and Design, 1938
American Textiles, 1954

Further Reading

Algozer, Sharon Ann, *Paul Theodor Frankl: American Interior and Furniture Designer*, MA thesis, University of California at Riverside, 1990
"American Modernist Furniture Inspired by Sky-Scraper Architecture" in *Good Furniture Magazine*, 27, September 1927, pp.119–27
Bayer, Patricia, *Art Deco Interiors: Decoration and Design Classics of the 1920s and 1930s*, London: Thames and Hudson, and Boston: Little Brown, 1990
Byars, Mel, "What Makes American Design American?" (introduction) in R.L. Leonard and C.A. Glassgold (editors), *Modern American Design by the American Union of Decorative Artists and Craftsmen*, reprinted New York: Acanthus Press, 1992
Davies, Karen, *At Home in Manhattan: Modern Decorative Arts, 1925 to the Depression* (exhib. cat.), New Haven: Yale University Art Gallery, 1983
Fehrman, Cherie and Kenneth, *Postwar Interior Design, 1945–1960*, New York: Van Nostrand Reinhold, 1987
Mignennes, Pierre, "Un Artiste Décorateur Américain: Paul Th. Frankl" in *Art et Décoration*, 53, January 1928, p.49
Potter, Durwood, "Paul Frankl" in Mel Byars and Russell Flinchum (editors), *50 American Designers*, Washington, DC: Preservation Press, forthcoming
Robinson, Cervin and Rosemary Haag Bletter, *Skyscraper Style: Art Deco New York*, New York: Oxford University Press, 1975
Smith, C. Ray, *Interior Design in 20th-Century America*, New York: Harper, 1987
Wilson, Richard Guy and others, *The Machine Age in America, 1918–1941* (exhib. cat.), New York: Abrams, 1986

Furniture Retail Trade

During the 19th century the nature of the purchase of domestic furniture and furnishings changed radically. The growth in demand, not only from an expanding population, but also from a growing class of citizens who wanted to express themselves through their furnishings and decoration meant that changes in the distribution system were essential.

The old arrangement of the maker also being the supplier to the customer took a long time to die out. For wealthy clients it was *de rigueur* in the 18th and 19th centuries to visit showrooms of the direct supplier, who in many cases was able to offer a complete interior furnishing and decoration service. The importance of this relationship was noted in 1747 when it was suggested that the upholsterer was "that man on whose judgement I rely for the choice of goods; and I suppose he has not only judgement in the materials but taste in the fashion and skill in the workmanship".

However for the majority of the new strata of customers, the rise in the 19th century of the retail store, which was able to supply fashionable furniture and furnishings, provided the route to establishing a home. Inevitably these new consumers had little idea about how to furnish and what to purchase, so they were even more reliant on the retailer. Although general stores and cabinet-making and upholstery businesses were able to meet some of this new demand, two new breeds of retailer developed. These were department stores and specialist furnishing stores, established in the main cities; many were to become household names in the 19th century. Pratts of Bradford, Robson's of Newcastle, Wylie and Lochhead of Glasgow, Maples, Shoolbred, and Waring and Gillow of London, are a sample of the specialist furniture suppliers that developed substantial retail businesses. Visits to department stores such as Fraser, Lewis's, and Harrod's became a favourite shopping experience. These firms were very conscious of the need to develop and inspire customer demand, and to this end they produced a range of innovative methods to inspire customers and make sales. The use of window displays to attract customers was to become widespread. The construction of room settings within the store allowed customers to visualise a complete scheme before it was made up in their home. These sorts of firms were able to design and supply the whole range of house furnishings as well as often supplying bathroom equipment, central heating, kitchen requisites and other items.

One of the most successful tools these specialist firms developed was the illustrated catalogue and estimates of schemes. These productions could range from a simple single sheet listing the proposed selection of goods to a full-scale illustrated catalogue complete with a variety of estimates for varying sizes of house and price ranges of merchandise. In addition, the opportunity to pay for goods on deferred terms – hire-purchase – was soon encouraged, although its heyday was not until the 20th century.

In the late 19th and early 20th centuries in the United States furniture purchases were often through mail-order catalogues. Any item of furniture could be purchased from the catalogues of Sears-Roebuck or Montgomery Ward and be dispatched to any part of the country. From this business there developed a range of department stores that supplied furniture, among other items; these stores have now become major forces in American furniture retailing. The large shopping malls in North America are often anchored to a Sears, Simpsons, Eatons or Macy's store. These businesses have enormous influence over contemporary American taste.

In England it was the development of multiple furnishing stores such as the Times Furnishing Co., John and William Perring, Cavendish Woodhouse and others, that were to use the idea of credit purchase as a major incentive to buy furniture. These stores generally carried a more limited range of stock and would concentrate on cabinets, upholstery, bedding and carpets, leaving other specialists to supply wallpapers and kitchen and bathroom fittings, etc. Their growth was great between the wars, so that by 1939 they controlled some 20 per cent of the retail furniture trade. In the latter part of the century these firms continued to grow either organically or by amalgamation. By the 1980s their concentration into two or three large groups meant that choice was often relatively restricted. For example at the height of the 1980s boom the Harris Queensway group controlled more than 750 outlets with an estimated 13 per cent of the total market.

In contrast to these stores, during the 20th century there was a small coterie of independent shops that promoted "modern design". Heal and Sons had been one of the first to introduce ranges of furniture intended for a particular group of customers. They were followed by businesses such as Dunns of Bromley, Bowmans of Camden Town and Oscar Woollens of Finchley. The efforts of these and other firms in promoting Modern design were far in excess of their physical size. In some cases other companies attempted to take some of this exclusive market; Waring and Gillow established a "Modern furniture department" under Serge Chermayeff, and Fortnum and Mason also tried to tap this trade.

The post-World War II period was characterised by a continuation of the previous methods of furnishings and the growth of a range of specialist furnishing businesses which were more akin to an interior decorator type of trade than the high street image. These were often single stores with their own identity but they might belong to bulk buying groups to improve their profitability. They were often members of the National Association of Retail Furnishers and took pride in their quality of service and supply.

During the later part of the 20th century there was another development, the concept stores. This new form of business was established to develop a new market, namely the younger, more design-conscious and affluent customers of the 1960s and onward. The Habitat range of stores was the most obvious example of this development, whereby one particular taste is catered for under one roof. Terence Conran had recognised that there was a need for stores that would sell a complete ambience or lifestyle, and after his initial success others entered that market at various levels. Sometimes these were small independent companies with one branch, others, like the Ethan Allen company in America, moved towards the decorator end of the trade, while yet others might be multiple businesses with world-wide interests such as the Roche-Bobois company.

Alongside the boom in DIY (Do-It-Yourself), there has also been an expansion in the market for self-assembly furniture. Increasingly this has been sold by warehouses and DIY superstores giving an advantage to customers in terms of price and availability. The success of these outlets encouraged the idea of furniture superstores. Based on the warehouse principle and self-selection, a vast array of cabinets, dining room furniture and three-piece suites are on display with a smaller selection of other items. These businesses trade on price advantage and quick delivery, but offer little in the way of service, and in England eventually lost their appeal. In the United States they continue to be a favoured furniture outlet, where sophisticated displays and selling systems are combined with stock delivery or take-away systems.

One particular furnishing business was able, however, to combine the advantages of superstore-style trading with a very particular ethos of design and management. This is IKEA. Originating in Sweden, the company is now the largest furniture retailer in the world. In 1993 the company operated 111 stores in 24 countries, employed 20,000 workers and had world-wide sales of £2.2 billion. By offering competitively priced and well designed and made products IKEA has been able to meet a wide range of demands from a large cross section of the public across the world. A significant part of their business is the production of a comprehensive catalogue published in ten different languages but always offering the same range of goods.

Other Scandinavian enterprises supplying interior products and furniture based on a particular design ethic include the famous NK department store in Stockholm and Den Permenante in Copenhagen, both renowned as centres of design excellence.

The continual growth of the domestic furniture market has meant that there is more and more demand for choice. To satisfy this there has now developed a range of furniture retailers who are specialists in particular fields, whether these are inspired by price, design, style or image. These shops may specialise, for example, in 18th-century reproduction furniture, Shaker-style interiors, a chic contemporary or a country house image. Whatever the case, this attention to particular niches of the market will ensure that the role of the retailer remains an important part of the creation of an interior.

CLIVE D. EDWARDS

Further Reading

Adburgham, Alison, *Shops and Shopping, 1800–1914: Where, and in What Manner, the Well-Dressed Englishwoman Bought Her Clothes*, 2nd edition London: Allen and Unwin, 1981

Banham, Joanna, Sally MacDonald and Julia Porter, *Victorian Interior Design*, London: Cassell, 1991; as *Victorian Interior Style*, London: Studio, 1995

Edwards, Clive, *Twentieth-Century Furniture: Materials, Manufacture and Markets*, Manchester: Manchester University Press, 1994

Goodden, Susanna, *At the Sign of the Fourposter: A History of Heal's*, London: Heal and Son, 1984

Johnson, David, "The History and Development of Do-It-Yourself" in *Leisure in the Twentieth Century*, London: Design Council, 1977

Pasdermadjian, Hrant, *The Department Store: Its Origins, Evolution and Economics*, London: Newman, 1954; New York: Arno, 1976

Phillips, Barty, *Conran and the Habitat Story*, London: Weidenfeld and Nicolson, 1984

Sheridan, Michael (editor), *The Furnisher's Encyclopaedia*, London: National Trade Press, 1955

Tilson, Barbara, "Modern Art Department, Waring and Gillow 1928–1931" in *Journal of the Decorative Arts Society*, 8, 1984, pp.40–49

G

Gabriel, Ange-Jacques 1698–1782

French architect

The Gabriel family already had a long history of service to the crown when Ange-Jacques succeeded his father Jacques (1667–1742) as First Architect to King Louis XV (Premier Architecte du Roi). He held this position for 33 years (1742–75), eventually retiring with great professional and personal honors at the age of 77. Well-known as the principal French architect working at mid-century, Gabriel was responsible for a number of building projects. These include: Châteaux at Compiègne and Saint Hubert, the small Pavillon Français, Le Butard and Petit Trianon, and important additions to existing Royal residences at Versailles, Fontainebleau, Choisy, and Paris. The seemingly impossible list of accomplishments credited to him includes not only the building projects themselves, but also their interior decor, as well as renovated interiors for almost all of the royal residences.

Gabriel's role as an interior designer has engendered much debate due to the strong spirit of collaboration that existed between the architect and his decorative sculptors (*sculteurs*). This is particularly relevant to his relationship with Jacques Verberckt (1704–71) and Antoine Rousseau (1710–82), with whom Gabriel worked on many projects. An examination of the drawings of architectural interiors executed by Gabriel and conserved in the Archives Nationales, Paris makes it clear, however, that Gabriel played a considerable role in shaping the taste of interior design of his time. And this time heralded a transition from the elegant exuberance of the Rococo to a more reserved academic classicism much championed by Gabriel.

Gabriel first emerged as an interior designer at Versailles when he contributed plans for the newly refurbished Queen's bedroom (Chambre de la Reine) in 1735. Although working in conjunction with his father and Robert de Cotte, the young Gabriel envisioned the long, narrow panels that included gilded medallions at both ends and in the center. These panels framed large mirrors mounted over the chimneys, which were ornamented with gilded palm tree motifs. The bedroom was originally renovated for Queen Marie Leczinska; Gabriel would later alter his own decor to include emblematic references to Queen Marie Antoinette. He continued a blatantly Rococo approach to architectural interiors when he was commissioned by Louis XV to transform his whole private apartment at Versailles (1738–75). Here the white walls and ceiling of the King's bedroom were ornamented by carved, gold-gilded panels (*boiseries*) which incorporated trophies, busts, medallions and an array of vegetal motifs that give the room a feeling of lightness and gaiety. Although clearly conforming to the Rococo taste of the time, Gabriel avoided the asymmetrical inventions of Gilles-Marie Oppenord, Nicolas Pineau and Juste-Aurèle Meissonnier, in favor of a more symmetrical and ordered interior decor. In the King's Council Chamber at Versailles of 1755, considered a magnificent example of Gabriel's Rococo phase, he already shows a stronger approach with the large, very three-dimensional medallions surmounting heavily outlined panels decorated with cherubs acting out the role of the King. Classical-style consoles link the cornices between the wall and the ceiling, which is now free of ornamentation.

It is in his small pavilions that Gabriel's natural inclination towards a statelier, more classical approach becomes apparent. This appears first at the Pavillon du Butard and the Pavillon Français, both dating from 1750, but may be seen most dramatically in his unabashed masterpiece, the Petit Trianon. Begun for Madame de Pompadour in 1763 but not completed until after her death (1764), this reserved square building has a flat balustraded roof and a minimum of exterior decoration which includes pilasters and engaged columns in the Corinthian order. The dignity and symmetry of the exterior elevations were echoed in the interior rooms designed by Gabriel and carved by Honoré-Guibert, a new *sculteur* associated with the "goût grec" chosen to replace the Rococo Verberckt and Rousseau. In the salon de compagnie one finds long, plain, painted wall panels decorated quite sparingly at the bottom with garland crowned medallions and a running spiral motif. The chapel of the Petit Trianon is even more classical in its inspiration. The altar area is supported by consoles and flanked by Ionic columns that support a rounded pediment. The rest of the room is covered with totally unadorned wooden wainscoting, with only simple garlands appearing above round arched niches. Gabriel's dramatic change of style reflected the general change of taste in France at this time from the playful fantasies of the Rococo age to the more serious Neo-Classical. This was a change first initiated by Louis XV and Madame de Pompadour but more often associated with Louis XVI.

Gabriel: Chambre de la Reine, Versailles, from 1735

Appropriately, the classical elements in his large-scale late projects were stronger and grander than in his small pavilions. Free standing and engaged columns in the Doric, Ionic and Corinthian orders may be seen throughout the École Militaire, a project first conceived in 1750. They are incorporated into plain, almost austere rooms, as may be seen in the chapel of the infirmary, where exaggerated guttae and garlands in the circular dome form almost the only ornamentation. Classical orders are again the focus in the much more elaborate interior of the Opéra at Versailles (1770). Here gilded Corinthian columns, three storeys high, flank the stage and balcony areas, while smaller Ionic columns surround the theater on the third floor. A cartouche held by angels and rays of light surmounts the stage area, while sphinxs, shells, trophies, garlands and putti holding crowns are all incorporated into the richly colored and gilded decor. Although many of these motifs could be found in his earlier Rococo interiors, they are used here in a much stronger, more powerful manner. Louis XV's magnificent opera, carved by Pajou, overwhelmed royal visitors when it was inaugurated on the occasion of the marriage of the Dauphin and Marie Antoinette.

Considered his most dazzling triumph in terms of architectural interiors, the Opéra at Versailles was a fitting note on which Gabriel could retire. He did this in 1775, shortly after the death of his patron and friend Louis XV. He was sickly and almost blind by this time but had ample reason to be proud of his success. Even so, with all of his accomplishments Gabriel was often criticized by his contemporaries for borrowing from other artists and spending too much on his projects. There is no doubt, that he depended on an array of architects and sculptors at the Royal Building Works (Bâtiments du Roi) to assist him in his many commissions. His brilliance was at assimilating the best of the ideas that were most popular at the time and incorporating them into buildings of great taste and beauty.

KATHLEEN RUSSO

Biography

Born in Paris, 23 October 1698, the son of Jacques Gabriel (1667–1742), Premier Architecte du Roi. Trained by his father; enrolled at the Académie de l'Architecture, Paris, 1728. Married Catherine de la Motte, 1728: 3 children. Worked as an architect on royal buildings under his father from 1729. Member (first class), Académie, and succeeded his father as Contrôleur of Versailles, 1735; appointed Premier Architecte du Roi, and Director, Académie Royale, 1742; retired, 1775. Died in Paris, 4 January 1782.

Selected Works

Large numbers of Gabriel's drawings are in the Archives Nationales, Paris. A full list of his architectural commissions appears in Tadgell 1978.

Interiors

1738–75 Palais de Versailles (renovations and additions including the completion of the right wing, and interiors including the state apartments, private apartments, and the Chambre de Conseil, 1755)

1744 Place Royale, Bordeaux (completion of work by Jacques Gabriel; interiors include panelling by Verberckt)

1746 Château de la Muette, near St. Germain (renovations)

1747–82 Château de Compiègne (renovations and additions, including new apartments for the king and queen and dauphin: completed posthumously)

1749 Château de Fontainebleau (renovations, additions and Great Pavilion)

1750 Pavillon Français, Palais de Versailles (building and interiors)

1750 Le Butard (hunting lodge), near Versailles (building and interiors)

1750–68 École Militaire, Paris (building and interiors including the chapel, library, exercise room, governor's apartment and council chamber)

1751–55 Château de Fontainebleau (additions, renovation of the King's Bedroom and the Council Chamber)

1753 Hermitage, Choisy (building and interiors)

1755–74 St. Hubert, near Rambouillet (additions to hunting lodge, including the Great Circular Salon)

1761–68 Petit Trianon, Opera House, and Hermitage for the Trianon, Palais de Versailles (buildings and interiors)

1772–73 Château de Fontainebleau (renovations and additions, including the Comtesse du Barry's salon)

1773 Château de Bellevue, near Paris (dining room)

Further Reading

A recent scholarly account of Gabriel's career, incorporating detailed sections on his work at the Royal residences, appears in Bottineau and Gallet 1982, which also includes notes of the drawings related to his principal projects and a full bibliography. For an English-language study of his work see Tadgell 1978.

Bottineau, Yves, *L'Art d'Ange-Jacques Gabriel à Fontainebleau, 1735–1774*, Paris: Boccard, 1962

Bottineau, Yves and Michel Gallet, *Les Gabriel*, Paris: Picard, 1982

Boucher, Th.-G., "Les Théâtres des Palais Royaux" in *Monuments Historiques de la France*, 4, 1978

Braham, Allan, *The Architecture of the French Enlightenment*, Berkeley: University of California Press, and London: Thames and Hudson, 1980

Chamchine, B., *Le Château de Choisy*, Paris: Jouve, 1910

Connolly, Cyril, and Jerome Zerbe, *Les Pavillons: French Pavilions of the Eighteenth Century*, London: Hamish Hamilton, and New York: Macmillan, 1962

Cox, H. Bartle, *Ange-Jacques Gabriel (1698–1782)*, London: Benn, and New York: Scribner, 1926

Fels, Edmond, conte de, *Ange-Jacques Gabriel: Premier Architecte du Roi*, 2nd edition Paris: Laurens, 1924

Gallet, Michel, *Paris Domestic Architecture of the 18th Century*, London: Barrie and Jenkins, 1972; as Stately Mansions: Eighteenth Century Paris Architecture, New York: Praeger, 1972

Gromort, Georges, *Ange-Jacques Gabriel*, Paris: Freal, 1933

Hauteceour, Louis, *Histoire de l'architecture classique en France*, vol.4, Paris: Picard, 1952

Lacour-Gayet, R., *L'École Militaire*, Paris, 1973

Laulan, Robert, *L'École Militaire de Paris: Le Monument, 1751–1788*, Paris: Picard, 1950

Quarré, P., "Le Palais des Etats de Bourgogne" in *Provence Historique*, 88, April–June 1972, pp.92–105

Racinais, Henry, *Un Versailles Inconnu: Le Petits Appartements des Roys Louis XV et Louis XVI au Château de Versailles*, Paris: Lefèbvre, 1950

Tadgell, Christopher, "Gabriel's Grands Projects" in *Architectural Review*, CLVII, March 1975, pp.155–64

Tadgell, Christopher, *Ange-Jacques Gabriel*, London: Zwemmer, 1978

Galleries

The history of galleries concerns the evolution of two distinct but nonetheless closely related rooms: the Long Gallery and the Gallery for the display of art. Long galleries were an important feature of grand houses from the 16th to the early 18th century, while galleries for the display of art developed from the late 17th century and paved the way for the public art gallery as it is known today.

Long galleries originated in France in the late Middle Ages as covered walks, sometimes open on one side, with a view through to a garden or courtyard. Their principal function was to provide an area for exercise and they evolved in response to physicians' convictions that walking was good for health. While the extensive grounds and garden surrounding great houses afforded ample opportunities for exercise outside, covered walks were an ideal way to take exercise in bad weather and, in winter months, offered a refuge from cold and rain.

Enclosed 16th-century galleries were long, narrow spaces that sometimes served as a corridor between the separate wings of a house or ran along its entire length. Some country houses had two galleries built one above the other. This is the case at The Vyne, Hampshire, which boasts England's oldest long galleries. The lower gallery was open and loggia-like while the upper gallery, which survives intact, was closed and had walls lined with linenfold panelling that was decorated with painted grotesques, crests, arms, and initials. Thornbury Castle (1520) also had an upper and lower gallery but these were designed as a two-storey cloister walk, surrounding three sides of an enclosed garden, the fourth side being attached to the main body of the house. These cloister-style galleries were in essence exercise circuits and often had fireplaces to warm walkers in cold weather.

Exercise or "communicating" galleries as they were also known, were built in increasing numbers in wealthy houses all over Europe throughout the 16th century. They were gradually integrated into the main body of the house but were usually built along the outer wall to guarantee a view. In England, the changing decoration of galleries reflected their growing importance. Initially, the walls were often hung with tapestries and the floors were covered with rush matting but they contained little or no furniture thus emphasising their role as a place for parade and exercise as opposed to comfort. From quite an early period, however, they were also being used to display paintings. Henry VIII's gallery at Hampton Court contained nineteen paintings from his collection and set a precedent that other members of the court gradually began to follow. Paintings collected for galleries during the 16th and early 17th

Galleries: Long Gallery, Aston Hall, near Birmingham, early 17th century

centuries were mainly portraits (a peculiarly British phenomenon) and were chiefly intended as a diversion during exercise. They generally depicted existing family members and ancestors, but might also include monarchs and famous historical figures and served as both inspiration to the viewer and as proof of the household's good connections. Bess of Hardwick, for example, hung portraits of past kings and queens as well as members of her own family in the Long Gallery at Hardwick Hall, Derbyshire, in the 1590s and the Brown Gallery at Knole contained a huge series of uniform portraits of medieval kings and remote family ancestors by Jan van Belkamp, a Flemish artist working in England in the early 17th century.

As painting collections grew, galleries became increasingly opulent in their decoration and furnishings and even began to approach the magnificence of the great chambers in palaces and country houses. In the great "prodigy" houses of the Elizabethan and Jacobean periods, the ideal sequence of rooms included a great chamber, a withdrawing chamber, a best bed chamber and a gallery en suite. Galleries were usually located on the same floor as the great chamber but were sometimes sited on the floor above as at Hardwick or Worksop Manor (1580) where the second floor long gallery measured 212 by 36 feet, had a continuous glass lantern and stood fifty feet above the ground providing magnificent views of the local landscape.

Increasingly, galleries developed ever more diverse functions, offering a supplementary space for entertainments and recreational activities such as music, masques, and games such as billiards, shuttlecock and shovel-halfpenny. Lord Petre's gallery at Ingatestone in Essex contained a large table or "shuffle-board", as well as six paintings, nine painted shields, chairs and stools.

Galleries were also a common feature in wealthy Italian houses in the 16th century where they were based on the French example. François I's gallery at Fontainebleau proved to be hugely influential in Italy as Italian artists had been largely responsible for its decoration. The gallery at the Palazzo Spada in Rome (1548–49), designed by the architect Il Baronino, was inspired by Fontainebleau as was the gallery at the Montebello family castle in Piedmont (1512), an Italian province closely linked to France.

Although European galleries had originated primarily as exercise and entertainments rooms, in Italy they rapidly evolved as a space in which to house growing collections of paintings, curios and antiquities that had become too large to store in the collector's private *studiolo* or closet. It was customary to have the gallery annexed to the *studiolo*, which acted as a treasury or office from which the collector or specially employed curator could study and manage the collection. An early 17th century treatise by Giulio Mancini entitled *Considerazioni sulla pittura* actually advises on the management of painting collections in galleries. These collections were often so densely hung that decorative wall hangings were unnecessary.

By the late 17th century, European galleries included some of the most lavishly appointed and influential interiors of their time: the gallery in the Farnese Palace in Rome (1597–1660) decorated by Annibale Carracci, and the Galerie des Glaces at Versailles (1678) both fall within this category. And this opulence reflected the changing function of the gallery which was increasingly regarded as the place in which to display properly substantial collections of art. European monarchs had individually amassed celebrated collections of paintings, sculptures and other *objets d'art* and their activities were emulated by the aristocracy and wealthier members of the bourgeoisie. There was already a general preference for Italian Renaissance artists ("old masters") as can be seen in David Teniers' painting of the *Picture Gallery of Archduke Leopold Wilhelm of Austria* (1647) which shows framed paintings by Raphael, Giorgione and Titian, and these were added to during the 18th century with collections of classical statuary and works by Dutch masters.

In England, discriminating collectors, known as virtuosi or dilettanti, were rich, cultured individuals who had invariably started collecting while on their European Grand Tour, and many of their collections have formed the basis of Britain's national heritage. The sizeable collection of Elias Ashmole, for example, who was considered the greatest virtuoso of his time, became the Ashmolean Museum in Oxford. And Lord Burlington, also a celebrated virtuoso, displayed the spoils of his Grand Tour in the purpose-built villa, Chiswick House, whose interiors were decorated by William Kent, and which can be regarded as one of the first free-standing public galleries. Other important "art" galleries of this period include the 2nd Earl of Egremont's gallery at Petworth (1754) which housed its owner's collection of antique sculpture, and Robert Adam's sculpture gallery at Newby, Yorkshire (1760s).

By the mid 18th century, picture and sculpture galleries were important features in almost every wealthy house of considerable size. Owners of these houses, proud of their collections of paintings and objects were prepared to show complete strangers with the appropriate letters of introduction around their more formal reception rooms, and galleries, in particular, proved a popular attraction for country house visitors. Some even had their own guidebooks, and the gallery at Petworth was apparently constantly filled with copyists, foreign visitors, cognoscenti or the simply curious. But by the end of the century it was becoming increasingly common for owners to want to live with their treasures rather than to confine them to a specific room. Paintings were scattered throughout the house and were grouped according to size or theme to suit the function and decoration of different rooms. Within this context, galleries became a place in which to hang old-fashioned portraits of ancestors and those paintings that were not suitable for more important rooms. And as country house architecture became more compact and their inhabitants spent more time in town, the sumptuous private galleries characteristic of earlier times became less of a priority. Similarly, by the Victorian period, the function of the long gallery as a place of recreation and indoor exercise was served both by the library-sitting room and by billiard rooms.

MAREIKE VON SPRECKELSEN

See also Picture Frames and Picture Hanging

Further Reading

Cornforth, John and John Fowler, *English Decoration in the 18th Century*, London: Barrie and Jenkins, and Princeton, NJ: Pyne, 1974; 2nd edition Barrie and Jenkins, 1978

Girouard, Mark, *Life in the English Country House: A Social and Architectural History*, New Haven and London: Yale University Press, 1978

Jackson-Stops, Gervase and James Pipkin, "Long Galleries" in their *The English Country House: A Grand Tour*, London: Weidenfeld and Nicolson, 1984; Boston: Little Brown, 1985, pp.101–20

Thornton, Peter, *Seventeenth-Century Interior Decoration in England, France, and Holland*, New Haven and London: Yale University Press, 1978

Thornton, Peter, *The Italian Renaissance Interior, 1400–1600*, London: Weidenfeld and Nicolson, and New York: Abrams, 1991

Waterfield, Giles (editor), *Palaces of Art: Art Galleries in Britain, 1790–1990* (exhib. cat.), London: Dulwich Picture Gallery, 1991

Wood, Margaret, *The English Mediaeval House*, London: Phoenix House, 1965; New York: Harper, 1983

Garnier, Charles 1825–1898

French architect

"What kind of style is this?" demanded the Empress Eugènie of the young architect whose design for the Paris Opéra had been selected in competition in 1861; "It is not a style: it is neither Greek, nor Louis XVI, nor even Louis XV". Charles Garnier, forgetting protocol, replied "those styles have had their time. It is Napoleon III, yet you complain". The building was not completed until 1874, by which time the Second Empire had collapsed and the Emperor and Empress were in exile; but the Opéra is not only Garnier's masterpiece but also the supreme monument to the remarkable reign which had seen the transformation of Paris with the newly imposed pattern of boulevards, impressive public buildings and open spaces. Internally and externally it symbolises the 18 glittering imperial years. As for the style, it draws most heavily on Michelangelo and the Baroque theatre.

Garnier was the son of a blacksmith, but he attended various classes and schools until he was able to obtain entry to the École de Dessin in Paris in 1838, and then four years later he was admitted to the École des Beaux-Arts. In 1848 he won the Grand Prix de Rome and began a period of five years study in the Villa Medici. In 1851 he made a tour of Southern Italy and Sicily, and evidently he was impressed by the Pompeian frescoes he saw. He made brilliant gouache copies of a number of them, which reveal an interest in vivid polychromy as well as in the scenographic nature of much Pompeian decoration with its different planes and framed views in perspective. His

Garnier: staircase, Opéra, Paris, 1861–75

final *envoi* in 1852 was a restoration study of the Temple of Jupiter at Aegina, once again rendered in rich polychromy which, he admitted, was speculative rather than based on archaeological evidence. The effect is astonishing, but undoubtedly decorative.

At first after returning to Paris there was little to suggest that seven years later he would be the winner of the prestigious Opéra competition which immediately placed him among the leaders of his profession. In *Charles Garnier's Paris Opéra*, Christopher Curtis Mead has provided a detailed account of the background to the competition and of the genesis and construction of the magnificent building in which the auditorium occupies only a small part of the total area. As Edwin Sachs suggested in *Modern Opera Houses and Theatres*, "the audience and its entertainment perhaps only had a subsidiary place in the general conception" (Sachs, 1897). He also pointed out that the plan allowed "an extensive vista in nearly every direction [and was] one of the greatest achievements ever accomplished in the planning of a public building". These vistas are integrated in the theatrical spaces that begin in the relatively sober Grand Vestibule in which homage is paid to four composers, Lully, Rameau, Gluck and Handel.

This leads to a slightly higher level which brings the operagoer into a complicated sequence of levels and perspectives that can be likened only to the theatrical designs of the Bibbiena family which have been described as "uninhabitable dream spaces that could not but become vulgar in the reality of stone". Garnier too has often been accused of vulgarity, but he handled with imagination and panache the way in which each space is extended visually into the next through dividing screens, and how light is used to heighten the theatrical quality by contrasting brightness and darkness. All the vestibules, foyers and corridors are ultimately leading from and to the Grand Escalier, the apotheosis of the staircase and the focal point of the plan rather than the auditorium itself. In *Le Théâtre* (1871) Garnier wrote at length about his conception of the staircase as "a sumptuous and lively place [where] the decorative arrangement is elegant [and] the animation that reigns on the steps is an interesting and lively spectacle. Finally, by disposing fabrics or hanging draperies, girandoles, candelabra or chandeliers, then marble and flowers, colour everywhere, one will make of this ensemble a sumptuous and brilliant composition that will recall in real life some of the splendid dispositions that Veronese fixed on his canvases".

The ceiling of the heavily modelled Grand Foyer was painted by Paul Baudry in a complex iconographical programme after studying Michelangelo's work in the Sistine Chapel, while the Avant Foyer ceiling was executed in mosaic by Salviati and Facchina with elaborate arabesques and mythological figures. The ceiling of the auditorium was painted by Eugène Lenepveu, but regrettably this was covered up in 1964 when Marc Chagall was commissioned to paint a substitute. The auditorium itself, heavily modelled and subfuscly gilded, despite its richness and red drapings and upholstery, tends to be an anticlimax after the splendour of the approach to it. At the back of the 47.75 metres deep stage Garnier placed the Ballet Room, a sumptuously decorated and gilded apartment which can be opened up to the stage to add another dimension and an additional 20 metres to the depth.

Garnier took complete control of the decoration, believing "the painted and sculptured decoration derives from and depends on the architectural composition ... the architect, to conserve the general harmony ... must impose on the artist not only the exact dimensions, but also the subjects, the silhouettes, the general tones, the effects and the style of the composition". Presumably he exercised similar control over the decoration of his other Opéra house, the small one at Monte Carlo which dates from 1878 and seats only 500. A top-lit foyer which serves both house and casino has a peristyle of red columns with gilded capitals, which supports an upper gallery above which the deep coves of the ceiling are covered with painted arabesques. Gold, bronze, yellow ochre and red are the predominant colours in the auditorium which has something of the character of the Rococo 18th-century German court theatres. Like them, it has a prominent royal box in the centre of the back wall, domed, crowned and garlanded. The rest of the decoration is similar to that in the Opéra, with broken pediments, arabesque pilaster strips, caryatids framing the doorways, and naked figures balancing precariously on the heavy cornice brackets. Painted allegorical scenes fill the vacant spaces on the ceiling, and above all hangs a gigantic chandelier. Edwin Sachs circumspectly appraised it as a "luxurious and highly decorated piece of work [constructed for] visitors on pleasure bent, and by habitués of the gambling saloons" (Sachs, 1897).

DEREK LINSTRUM

See also Second Empire Style

Biography

Jean-Louis Charles Garnier. Born in Paris, 6 November 1825, the son of a blacksmith. Studied at the École de Dessin, 1838; entered the architectural atelier of Jean-Arnould Léveil, 1840; moved to the atelier of Louis Hippolyte Lebas (1782–1867), 1840–42; enrolled at the Ecole des Beaux-Arts, 1842. Won the Grand Prix de Rome, 1848; studied in Italy and was a Pensionnaire, Académie de France, at the Villa Medici, Rome, 1849–53, where he met Gustave-Rudolphe Boulanger, Paul Baudry and Jules-Eugène Lenepveu; visited Greece and Turkey in the company of the writer Edmond About, 1852. Married Louise Bary, 1857: 3 sons. Active in Paris as an architect from 1854. Won the commission for the Paris Opéra, 1861. Held many government posts and appointed Inspecteur Général des Bâtiments Civils, 1877–96. Elected to the Institut de France, 1874; president of the Société Centrale des Architectes, 1889–91 and 1895–97; member, Commission des Monuments Historiques, 1895–98. Awarded Gold Medal, Royal Institute of British Architects, London, 1886. Contributed numerous articles to the *Moniteur Universal* during the 1860s. Died in Paris, 3 August 1898.

Selected Works

The Fonds Garnier, in the Bibliothèque de l'Opéra, Paris, contains all his surviving manuscripts, much private and official correspondence, numerous building reports, and many newspaper and journal articles. The remainder of his archive, including his architectural library, and watercolours and sketches executed on his travels, is in the Bibliothèque de l'Ecole des Beaux-Arts, Paris.

Interiors

1861–74 Opéra, Paris (building and interiors)
1872–73 Villa Garnier, Borgidhera, Italy (building and interiors)
1878–79 Cercle de la Librairie, Paris (building and interiors)
1878–81 Hôtel Hachette, Paris (building and interiors)
1878–81 Casino, Monte Carlo (building and interiors)

1882–83 Panorama Valentino, Paris (building and interiors)
1883–84 Panorama Marigny, Paris (building and interiors)

Publications

A Travers les Arts, 1869
Le Théâtre, 1871
Le Nouvel Opéra de Paris, 4 vols., 1878–81

Further Reading

A detailed and scholarly account of Garnier's work at the Paris Opéra appears in Mead 1991 which also includes a chronology of Garnier's career, a guide to archival sources and an extensive bibliography of primary and secondary sources.

L'Art en France sous le Second Empire (exhib. cat.), Paris: Grand Palais, 1979

Chesneau, Ernest, "La Décoration de l'Opéra: Peintures de M. Paul Baudry" in *Paris Journal*, 28 August, 1874

Doumato, Lamia, *Charles Garnier, 1825–1898* (bibliography), Monticello, IL: Vance, 1988

Garnier, Louise, "Charles Garnier par Mme. Garnier" in *L'Architecture*, 38, 1925, pp.377–90

Kahane, Martine and Thierry Beauvert, *The Paris Opéra*, photographs by Jacques Moatti, New York: Vendome, 1987

Lavezzari, E., "Le Nouvel Opéra" in *Revue Générale de l'Architecture*, 32, 1875, pp.30–33

Mead, Christopher Curtis, *Charles Garnier's Paris Opéra: Architectural Empathy and the Renaissance of French Classicism*, Cambridge, MA: Massachusetts Institute of Technology Press, 1991

Middleton, Robin and David Watkin, *Neoclassical and 19th Century Architecture*, New York: Abrams, and London: Academy, 1980

Pinchon, Jean-François, *Catalogue de l'Oeuvre de Charles Garnier en Dehors de l'Opéra de Paris*, M.A. thesis, Paris: University of Paris-Nanterre, 1981

Pinchon, Jean-François, "L'Example de Baudry and Garnier" in *Monuments Historiques*, 123, 1982, pp.67–71

Revel, J.F., "Charles Garnier, Dernier Fils de la Renaissance" in *L'Oeil*, 99, 1963, pp.2–11, 30

Sachs, Edwin O., *Modern Opera Houses and Theatres*, vol.2, 1897; reprinted New York: Blom, 1968

Sédille, Paul, "Charles Garnier" in *Gazette des Beaux-Arts*, 20, 1898, pp.341–46

Steinhauser, Monika, *Die Architektur der Pariser Oper*, Munich: Prestel, 1969

Steinhauser, Monika, "Le Palais Garnier, Cathédrale Mondaine du Second Empire" in *Les Monuments Historiques de la France*, 1974, pp.81–96

Garnitures de Cheminée

The French term, *garniture de cheminée*, or mantel garniture, applies to any set of ornaments designed for the mantelshelf of a chimneypiece. Such ensembles first gained popularity in the latter part of the 17th century but they remained a common feature of fashionable interiors well into the 19th century. Traditionally, they comprised two, three, or five Chinese porcelain vases or beakers, generally of alternating baluster and cylindrical form. Later versions, however, increased both the number of pieces and the types of media employed. Different ceramics (principally Delftware), silver, ormolu, and hardstones such as blue-john became popular, and they occasionally featured candlesticks, perfume-burners, pot-pourri, vases, and even clocks. A key feature of every example was their symmetry of design and disposition, and they provided a balanced and harmonious arrangement of ornaments that occupied a prominent position within the room.

The evolution of garnitures is closely bound up with the overall development of ceramics as a central element within the decoration of interiors. Indeed, their first wave of popularity during the late 17th century occurred when the mania for imported porcelain was at its height. During this period the collecting and display of exotic and costly Chinese and Japanese wares in particular became an extremely fashionable pastime, and porcelain was not only massed within interiors, but small rooms – known as china closets – were also designed specifically for collections of these wares. The royal house of Orange-Nassau, with its easy access to goods imported by the Dutch East India Company, is usually credited with spreading the craze for porcelain collecting, and wherever members of this family settled, impressively rich displays of export porcelains were installed. Queen Mary II introduced the fashion to England and, with the assistance of Daniel Marot, created some of the most elaborate installations of porcelains of the period.

The formal arrangement of precious objects on the walls of interiors was also an activity that had been adopted by Italian architects in the late 16th century. According to the historian Peter Thornton, this habit "conformed to the Renaissance sense of order that was already so strikingly embodied in the current Italian architecture" (Thornton, 1978). As this trend towards orderliness spread northward, so did the aesthetic of displayed ceramics. Certain distinct features of Baroque architecture such as pronounced overdoors, cornices, and mantelshelves conveniently served as ideal surfaces upon which to position porcelains. An inventory of the Stadtholder's residence of 1632 lists numerous precious objects mounted on various types of shelves. Similar arrangements were to be found in England as well where such displays were recognised as being Dutch in origin: the Earl and Countess of Arundel, for example, referred to their china closet as their "Dutch Pranketing Room".

Concurrent with the growing appeal of formal arrangements of precious and rare objects, was the increased flow of Oriental ceramics into Europe, and eventually America. Although a few isolated examples had appeared in Europe as early as the 14th century, it was not until the establishment of the Dutch (1597), English (1660) and French (1664) East India Companies, that a flourishing commercial trade in Oriental porcelains began to develop. This trade increased rapidly throughout the late 17th and 18th centuries, but was ultimately stemmed by changing tastes, a fall in the quality of imported goods, and the growth of competitive European porcelain manufacturers.

Most of the early Oriental wares exported to Europe were bowls and dishes, and by the mid-17th century these also included the accoutrements for tea and coffee drinking. Vases are mentioned for the first time in the Dutch East India Company's records in 1636 (Charleston, 1975). However, the fashion for grouping vases on mantels did not arise until the last third of the century when it first emerged in the Netherlands. Initially, mantel garnitures were "free combinations of types" (Cocks, 1989); they then evolved into the five-, seven-, and even nine-piece sets made by the Chinese for the West. These goods were produced solely for export and the taste for garnitures as a type of decoration was a specifically European phenomenon; the only sets made by the Chinese for their own purposes were sacred ones designed for temples, and which included two vases, two candlesticks, and a perfume-burner.

Early sets of *garnitures de cheminée* mostly consisted of blue and white, *famille verte*, and *famille rose*, Chinese porcelains; armorial and pseudo-armorial pieces were also very popular and were specially ordered. By 1670, however, Europeans were making imitations in silver and Delftware (or *faience* – tin-glazed earthenware) to meet the rapidly growing demand, and were decorating them in styles that corresponded to the changing whims and fashions of their clientele. Various Dutch and French factories produced huge quantities of ornamental ceramics, including mantel garnitures, that were modelled in Baroque forms and decorated with Baroque motifs. Strapwork and arabesque ornament were much-used, distinctively European decorations, and Western variations of Chinese patterns, collectively known as Chinoiseries, were also popular. The Meissen factory in Germany produced garnitures in porcelain with a variety of decoration as early as 1720, and the English factories at Chelsea and Bow followed suit in the 1750s. The Sèvres manufactory was also making garnitures by the mid 18th century, and some examples are known to have included wall sconces for hanging on either side of the fireplace *trumeau*. Perfume-burners and pot-pourri vases made an appearance towards the end of the century when they were featured in fashionable Neo-Classical interiors: Wedgwood, for example, producing several types of garnitures derived from ancient Greek and Roman vases.

Whatever the style or exact composition of garnitures, by the early 18th century they were widely considered to be basic decorative components within the fashionable interior, and were no longer simply discrete collectable items but formed part of the overall scheme of a room. Glazes and colours were co-ordinated with those of the wallcoverings and fabrics, and novel types of shelving units and consoles – some moveable, others part of the architectural structure – were developed. The confinement of porcelain displays to the perimeters of rooms corresponded to the contemporary practice of lining furniture against the walls. Tables and smaller items were moved too often to provide suitable display space, and even when furniture was moved permanently into the centre of rooms towards the end of the century, the emphasis on mantels and overdoors as the location for ceramics returned as the fashion for shelves and consoles waned.

Given that wealthy women were often important collectors of ceramics, up until c.1760 ornamental porcelains were often placed in rooms occupied chiefly by women. Thus the style of garnitures frequently followed the style of decoration adopted in those private apartments where women spent much of their time. The proliferation of Chinoiserie decoration on porcelains, for example, reflected the rage for bedrooms and dressing rooms or boudoirs designed in the Chinese style. This feminizing tendency began to reverse, however, during the third quarter of the 18th century and Wedgwood's use of more erudite subjects was more in keeping with the masculine flavour of Neo-Classical interiors by Robert Adam and his contemporaries. These interiors were highly integrated and mantel garnitures were usually co-ordinated with architectural features and other decorative elements within these schemes. It was also deemed essential that a room's decoration be consonant with its function and location within the hierarchy of the house plan, and mantel garnitures that occupied a prominent position on the chimneypiece did much to advance this philosophy.

From the second half of the 18th century *garnitures de cheminée* also began to be produced in a greater variety of materials. Matthew Boulton's ormolu pieces were a popular choice for mantels, and blue-john was used extensively after 1743 when the first substantial deposit was mined near Castleton in England. Likewise, other hardstones and marble were conducive to turning and carving into the classical shapes then in vogue. Silver was also desirable, and was worked into more intricate designs than ceramics, but it tended to be used for decorations on tables than for mantelpieces. In France, gilt-bronze mantel clocks braced by a pair of candelabra began to supersede the traditional set of vases for the mantel.

To summarize, mantel garnitures were present in Northern European interiors from the late 17th to the early 19th centuries. Their increasing popularity conformed to that of export wares generally and they represented one among several methods of displaying porcelains within the interior. Whole rooms were devoted to such displays, and all types of shelving and consoles were designed to support individual and grouped pieces. Ornamental ceramics were placed not only on mantels, but also on the tops of cabinets, within fireplaces (during the summer months only), over doors, and under buffets, cabinets and tables. The excitement first generated by exquisite delicacy of Oriental porcelains gave rise to a new generation of ceramic decorations and forms, and the evolution of *garnitures de cheminée* parallels that of the early history of Western ornamental ceramics.

MARGARET W. LICHTER

Further Reading

Baarsen, Reinier and others, *Courts and Colonies: The William and Mary Style in Holland, England, and America* (exhib. cat.), New York: Cooper-Hewitt Museum, 1988

Charleston, Robert J., "Porcelain as Room Decoration in Eighteenth-Century England" in Elinor Gordon (editor), *Chinese Export Porcelain: An Historical Survey*, New York: Universe, 1975; London, Bell, 1977

Clunas, Craig (editor), *Chinese Export Art and Design*, London: Victoria and Albert Museum, 1987

Cocks, Anna Somers, "The Nonfunctional Use of Ceramics in the English Country House During the Eighteenth Century" in Gervase Jackson-Stops (editor), *The Fashioning and Functioning of the British Country House*, Washington, DC: National Gallery of Art, 1989, pp.195–214

Gordon, Elinor (editor), *Chinese Export Porcelain: An Historical Survey*, New York: Universe, 1975; London: Bell, 1977

Thornton, Peter, *Seventeenth-Century Interior Decoration in England, France, and Holland*, New Haven and London: Yale University Press, 1978

Whitehead, John, *The French Interior in the Eighteenth Century*, London: Laurence King, 1992; New York: Dutton, 1993

Gaudí, Antoni 1852–1926

Spanish architect and designer

Antoni Gaudí's unique approach to design is perhaps best summarized in his maxim that "Originality is the return to the origin." His work had an organic quality in which structure is the form, and form is structural. A eucalyptus tree which grew in front of his studio in Barcelona was his metaphor: the tree supports its branches, the branches its twigs, the twigs its leaves; the parts and the whole grow harmoniously with no need of external support. Whether designing building structures, ornamentation, ironwork or furniture, Gaudí's art was rich and varied. His work was the result of his interest in the origins of structure and resulted in works of functional sculpture.

Although best known for his unfinished church, Barcelona's Sagrada Familia, Gaudí had an active career, with commissions covering a wide range of design projects. He was greatly influenced by the work of Eugène Viollet-le-Duc whose principle of "equilibrium" grew out of his extensive work in restoring and renovating Gothic buildings. Yet Gaudí's approach to structural integrity went beyond Gothic, which required buttresses to guarantee stability. Gaudí's masonry structures were self-sufficient. His formal vocabulary consisted of ruled surfaces of double curvatures such as paraboloids, hyperboloids and helicoids. He believed that nature's forms and structures were based on these same geometries and, therefore, they were realistic forms, not artificial abstractions. And coming from a long line of boilermakers, he was accustomed to transforming flat sheets of copper into curved and double curved forms.

In 1885 Gaudí received a commission to design the mansion of Don Eusebio Güell at 3–5 Calle del Conde del Asalto (almost opposite Picasso's studio at No. 8) in an old downtown section of Barcelona. Gaudí used marble throughout the interiors of the Güell mansion, including arcades of parabolic marble arches carried on round columns and ceilings of marble slabs carried by exposed iron beams. The rooms were ornamented by elaborate woodwork detailed in the Moorish tradition. Gaudí produced original, delicate metalwork and wrought-iron decoration, such as convex metal grills which looked like sails in the wind. The high central room, with its organ and minstrels' gallery, was the dominant feature of the house and rose to a blue-tiled parabolic-domed ceiling. He also designed some of the furniture for the bedroom, most notably a chaise-longe with twined metal legs, which reveals his liking for extravagant, curvilinear motifs. In reassessing the functional needs of a dressing table, he added a lower surface to be used for lacing shoes to his animated, asymmetrical piece.

Gaudí's relationship with Don Eusebio Güell was to prove fruitful, as the same client employed him on many subsequent projects. In 1887, Gaudí designed the gatehouse at Finca Güell in Avenida Pedralbes. The Dragon Gate displayed an inventive exploitation of various forms of metal, including woven wire fabric. Built in tensile, curvilinear forms, the gate was a semi-transparent organization of the delicate interwoven planes. Gaudí's first-hand metal-working experience (having worked in his father's coppersmith shop) provided a solid base for his experiments with metals. Gaudí also designed the stables at Finca Güell. Here, to face the cupola, he used broken tile as a mosaic technique for the first time. This technique was to be exploited by Abstract Expressionists more than fifty years later.

Ceramic tilework was favored in many of Gaudí's projects. At the Parc Güell, in 1908, he decorated the playground's curving benches with bits and pieces of broken ceramic tile mosaics to resemble the waves of the sea. By this time Gaudí's work had developed into such highly warped surfaces that the use of the typical square Spanish tile would have been impossible. These abstract mosaics share a spirit of delight with the work of painters such as Paul Klee or Wassily Kandinsky. The Parc Güell project mainly consisted of landscape design, but included several small buildings and subsidiary construction. The built forms were not based on any historical style, but emulated slanting tree trunks whose actual shape resulted from the careful technical analysis of the forces involved. The Parc was a place of fantasy, filled with colonnades, porticos and grottoes of pre-cast concrete blocks made to look like natural stone rubble. The lock plates on the gates had grotesque personalities. By exaggerating the enormous nail heads and oversized keyholes, Gaudí created fantastic, gargoyle-like creatures.

In 1901 Gaudí received Barcelona's first annual Architectural Prize for the design of the Casa Calvet, an apartment house for the heirs of Pedro Martin Calvet, but the project is most memorable for its ironwork detailing and furniture. After the building was completed in 1899, he designed the popular Calvet chair for an office in the building. In this early example of "free-form" furniture, Gaudí sought to design a piece that would support a human body at rest. Anticipating concerns for ergonomically-correct chairs, the seat and back were designed to cradle the human body. Its animal-like composition was similar to contemporary Art Nouveau furniture, which imitated antelopes or insects. The chair's front legs were turned out like classical ballet's second position; the back legs were a sinuous reversed S-curve. The director's desk was a substantial and massive wooden piece, complimented by bric-a-brac shelving.

Gaudí's next major secular project was the renovation of the Casa Batlló in Barcelona in 1904–06. Gaudí altered the main rooms, creating bright, open spaces with the use of articulated stone members. The windows on the first floor showed extraordinary plasticity; the ovoid stone surrounds were detailed with slender bony columns. Fragments of blue and green glass in abstract patterns highlighted the upper windows. The interior doors were small, set in large hinged panels which could be opened for formal occasions or in order to move furniture. The wall and ceiling surfaces gave a look of total motion, like waves of the sea. Gaudí inverted expectations in the detailing of the staircase, placing wooden treads between ceramic risers and baseboards. Since the court was wider at its top, Gaudí arranged the ceramic tiles on the walls in a graduated color flow with the lightest-colored tiles at the bottom to illuminate the lower floors. Gaudí designed much of the home's furniture. Highly functional, his pieces reinforced the pattern of curves that characterized the interior.

Casa Milá was built in Barcelona for Rosario Segimón de Milá between 1906 and 1910. This apartment house occupies an obtuse-angled site, in contrast to the traditional urban grid. Gaudí's study and keen understanding of structure freed him to design a highly individual work. The internal skeleton was built of widely separated piers which replaced the need for interior bearing partitions. As a result, Gaudí could place his walls anywhere and create rooms of any configuration. The resulting plan was highly original, with no right-angled corners; no two floors or apartments were the same. The main rooms flowed into one another, each one decorated with its own pattern of whirlpools and sand dunes on the plaster ceilings and shell-like forms on the doors and door trim. Gaudí repeatedly worked with the same group of tradesmen who, trained in his methods of design and construction, were able to achieve the free, spontaneous quality which made his work so special.

Although not widely exhibited, Gaudí's work was represented at the Paris Exhibition of 1878, at the Naval Exhibition of 1887 at Cadiz, and at the 1888 International Exhibition in Barcelona.

Gaudí continually experimented with materials, particularly ironwork. His fascination with the intrinsic character of metals and his complex and imaginative approach to decoration led him to find ways to curve wrought and cast iron on the fence at the Casa Vicens to make it appear like lively plants. Reinterpreting the Spanish tradition of *rejas* (grille-work), he gave the entrance gate at the Teresan School a spiky character. The iron door at Bellesguard looked like it was made of ribbons sewn together, and the lion of the city decorated the top of the door grille at the Casa Fernández-Andrés of León. Gaudí's work challenged the view to grasp the enormous possibilities of form and space, and materials and techniques.

Gaudí's talent was an intensely personal one. From his innovations in structure to his experiments with furniture, his voice stands out for its expressive and eccentric tone. His work is characterized by his preoccupation with organic form and his enthusiasm for surface texture. Gaudí was an artist of design, his approach resembling the impulses of painters and sculptors. Not surprisingly, his tile mosaics and metalwork have influenced artists outside of the design fields. Gaudí's body of work is a symphony, where each project, like each line of orchestration, is composed to be part of a greater whole, bringing a visual excitement to its environment.

SALLY L. LEVINE

See also Art Nouveau

Biography

Antoni Gaudí y Cornet. Born in Reus, near Tarragona, 25 June 1852. Studied architecture at the Escuela Provincial de Arquitectura, Barcelona, from 1873; graduated Dip. Arch., 1878. Worked with various architects in Barcelona, 1874–82; collaborated on electric street lighting project, 1878–80; practised as an independent architect in Barcelona from 1882. Withdrew from all secular commissions c.1915 to concentrate on the Sagrada Familia, Barcelona (1883–1926). Died in Barcelona following a road accident, 10 June 1926.

Selected Works

A catalogue raisonée of Gaudí's designs and drawings, including a chronology of his life and work, appears in Collins 1983. Examples of Gaudí's architectural drawings, decorative designs and furniture are in the Gaudí Museum, Parc Güell, Barcelona.

Interiors

1878 Comillas Pantheon, Comillas, Santander (furniture)
1886–89 Palacio Güell, Barcelona (building, interiors and some furniture): Eusebio Güell
1898–1904 Casa Calvet, Barcelona (building, interiors and furnishings): Calvet family
1900–14 Parc Güell, Barcelona (design of the grounds, pavilions, and park furniture): Eusebio Güell
1902 Café Torino, Barcelona (interior decoration including relief panels)
1904–06 Casa Batlló, Barcelona (remodelling, interiors and furniture): José Batlló y Casanovas
1906–10 Casa Milá, Barcelona (building and interior decoration): Doña Rosario Segimón de Milá

Further Reading

The literature on Gaudí is vast; a full bibliography including a descriptive listing of approximately 1800 items up to the 1970s appears in Collins 1973.

Bassegoda Nonell, Juan, *Antonio Gaudí: Vida y Arquitectura*, Tarragona: Caja de Ahorros Provincial, 1977

Bassegoda Nonell, Juan, *Obras Completas de Gaudí*, 2 vols., Tokyo: Rikyosha, 1979

Bassegoda Nonell, Juan, *El gran Gaudí*, Sabadell: Ausa, 1988

Borras, Maria Lluisa, "Casa Batlló, Casa Milá" in *Global Architecture*, 17, 1972

Collins, George R., *Antonio Gaudí*, New York: Braziller, and London: Mayflower, 1960

Collins, George R., *A Bibliography of Antonio Gaudí and the Catalan Movement, 1870–1930*, Charlottesville: University Press of Virginia, 1973

Collins, George R. and Juan Bassegoda Nonell, *The Designs and Drawings of Antonio Gaudí*, Princeton: Princeton University Press, 1983

Dalisi, Riccardo, *Gaudí Furniture*, Woodbury, NY: Barron's, 1980

Descharnes, Robert, *Gaudí the Visionary*, New York: Viking, and London: Stephens, 1971

Flores, Carlos, *Gaudí, Jujol y el Modernisimo Catalan*, 2 vols., Madrid: Aguilar, 1982

Hitchcock, Henry-Russell, *Gaudí*, New York: Museum of Modern Art, 1957

Martinell, César, *Gaudí: His Life, His Theories, His Work*, Cambridge: Massachusetts Institute of Technology Press, 1975

Puig Boada, Isidro, *El Pensament de Gaudí: Compilació de Textos i Comentaris*, Barcelona: Colegio de Arquitectes de Catalunya, 1981

Ráfols, Fontanals José, *Gaudí*, Barcelona: Canosa, 1929

Sola-Morales, Ignasi de, *Gaudi*, New York: Rizzoli, 1984; London: Academy, 1987

Sweeney, James Johnson and José Luis Sert, *Antoni Gaudí*, revised edition London: Architectural Press, and New York: Praeger, 1970

Torii, Tokutoshi, *El Mundo Enigmático de Gaudí*, 2 vols., Madrid: Instituto de España, 1983

Zerbst, Rainer, *Antoni Gaudí i Cornet: A Life Devoted to Architecture*, Cologne: Taschen, 1988

Gehry, Frank O. 1929–

Canadian architect and furniture designer

Frank O. Gehry is one of the most innovative and highly regarded architects of the late 20th century. Initially renowned as an experimental architect of the spontaneous Californian school, he has gained international standing as a designer of several prestigious and exuberant cultural centres in the United

States, Europe and Japan. He approaches buildings as if they were sculptural objects, expressive, spatial containers; and he has described the manipulation of the interior as "an independent, sculptural problem and no less interesting than the design of the container itself." His work is informed by a close association with contemporary American artists and sculptors which has helped to break down the historic divisions between art and architecture, and by his wish to escape the limitations of "the rectangular box". His buildings and interiors, although fiercely expressive, are also the fruit of successful collaborations with client, partner or artist.

Gehry was born Ephraim Goldberg in Toronto, of Jewish parents. His father moved to California to sell pinball and slot machines in 1947. As a child Gehry had been fascinated by the materials of his grandfather's hardware store and at one period his father had a furniture company. Gehry also cites a lecture given by the Finnish architect, Alvar Aalto when Gehry was 16 as a formative memory. He studied architecture at the University of Southern California and attended the Harvard Graduate School of Design. After graduating he went to work with large commercial firms such as Victor Gruen who built shopping centres in Texas and William Pereira, responsible for Los Angeles Airport. In 1961 he worked in Paris but returned to Los Angeles to open his own office in 1962 which he runs today as the firm of Frank O. Gehry Associates.

The free spirit of the West Coast of America permeates his early works which are an improvised fusion of high- and low-tech and easy, haphazard collisions of shapes and materials. In the studio-house (1970–72), built for a friend, the painter Ron Davis, the interior, trapezoidal plan and elevations exaggerate the perspectival distortions of right-angled room spaces. The architect plays with the interior space in homage to the artist's experiments with perceived reality. The shed-cum-factory exterior of corrugated metal encloses a softer, wood-panelled interior with exposed beams, lofts and staircases. A warmth and freedom lends an air of informality to spatially ambiguous complexity.

The interior office space of the Mid-Atlantic Toyota Offices, Glen Burnie, Maryland (1978) breaks up the internal space into abstract shapes using inexpensive materials, perhaps reminiscent of Russian Constructivism. Chain-link fencing, which was to become a prominent feature of Gehry's later work, and sheetrock (plasterboard) walls form irregular spaces for workers, and skylights and carefully arranged divisions bring daylight to every part of the interior.

It is in his own house in Santa Monica that Gehry iconoclastically bonds semi-industrial ugliness with high art. Mixing hostility with domestic homeliness, the house is perhaps a metaphor for America itself. The house is built up around the shell of an existing 1920s California "dumb little house". The pink walls are partly retained, yet deconstructed and surrounded by an encasement of corrugated metal, chain-link-fencing and raw plywood, materials normally associated with an industrial landscape or loose residential backyards. The interior emphasises a sense of the makeshift and unstructured by using unpainted, rough wooden walls, textures and surfaces. "I am not interested in finishing work," Gehry has declared, "but am interested in the work's not appearing finished, with every hair in place, every piece of furniture in its spot, ready for photos. I prefer the sketch quality, the tentativeness, the messiness ... the appearance of in progress." The dining room is a glazed extension of the original house which also remains a strong presence in the kitchen's south wall. Brick fireplaces are surrounded by raw plywood walls in the living room where a seating area is made from industrial felt-covered, foam-rubber cushions. The partially stripped walls of the second floor master bed-sitting room again reveal the original framework of the old house and the dialogue between outdoor and interior spaces continues with transparent walls, floors and ceilings creating unexpected views. The windows are large-scale to encourage space, light, comfort. They are also intended to dominate the supposed chaos. One corner-window stirred associations with Duchamp's *Nude Descending a Staircase* and Gehry tried to rotate the corner "so as one walks around it, the window would rotate."

Symbolic (perhaps subliminal) natural forms, particularly fish- and snake-forms have also permeated Gehry's interiors and designs. They include *Fish Lamps* made from smashed shards of ColourCore, the Fishdance Restaurant in Japan in the form of a giant, semi-erect fish, and Snake Lights and serpentine staircases proliferate in his work. Gehry's *Easy Edges* series of abrasive, corrugated cardboard furniture, produced between 1969 and 1979, has also made a significant contribution to furniture design. Intended as the ultimate solution to the search for an inexpensive modern chair, the series included rockers, a high chair, and the *Wiggle* side chair. It not only gained critical acclaim but was also commercially successful; however, Gehry withdrew it from circulation because he did not want to be famous as a furniture maker. *Easy Edges* were reissued in 1982 at the request of the Bloomingdale's store. Gehry's next series, entitled *Experimental Edges* was also constructed out of cardboard, and despite its "punk" irreverence and political liberalism, aspired to the status of high art. There has been considerable cross-fertilisation between Gehry's architecture and his furniture designs and it has been noted that some of his buildings appear not only sculptural but also like large pieces of furniture. The Chapel at Loyola Law School, for example, is panelled in stained plywood and the Winton guest house of 1984–86 is clad in Kasota stone which Gehry wants to look like plywood. Here also he clusters his one-room units into village-like groups of buildings, a theme he returns to continually, especially in his private houses.

In Rebecca's Restaurant, Venice, California, Gehry creates a surreal flamboyance in a small, 60-seater restaurant populated by a menagerie of large crocodiles, an enormous glass, octopus-chandelier, fish lamps and leafless, wooden trees. The materials – glass, copper and onyx – are crafted and do not appear cheap or gaudy; the rich colours are predominantly white, orange and green.

"Why should buildings always be boxes? I suggest the use of objects as 'found' design, to construct colossal things as seriously as buildings are built." So stated Gehry's friend, the sculptor Claes Oldenburg with whom he collaborated (together with Oldenburg's wife, Coosje van Bruggen) on the Chiat / Day advertising agency building. The exterior of this building comprises a complex of individual forms that also function as sculptures: a white boat, central, black binoculars and a red forest-form. Ironic and funky, fusing high and low taste, the interiors of this 1980s media building are equally remarkable. There are three separate media rooms, each designed in contrasting materials of sheet metal, cardboard and dark red Finn plywood. The cardboard room has furniture in *Experimental Edges* style. The walls are surfaced in corrugated blocks of cardboard and a shaft of California light enters by means of an oculus, piercing the womb-like space. The room is zany and unorthodox yet it also functions perfectly as an acoustically silenced office and is ideal for this self-reverentially creative and unashamedly commercial environment. The lights are in the form of snakes or giant, pop-art-like bulbs, and the furniture is formed from rough tree-trunks; they serve as functional objects, as art and as sculpture.

A direction towards monumentality is realised in the Vitra Design Museum, Weil am Rhein, Germany, 1989 where Gehry's fascination with one-room buildings attains grandeur. The project was commissioned by Ralph Fehlbaum, director of the Vitra furniture company who wished to house his collection of industrially designed furniture in a purpose-built museum adjacent to his factory, shops and showroom and sculptures by Oldenburg and Coosje van Bruggen. The exterior is a disarming mixture of serpentine and angular architectural sculpture, contrasting sheet steel "like an old oil-can" with white, plastered surfaces. In contrast, the interior is breathtakingly calm. Light floods into the building from an ascendant, cruciform window in the glass roof. The central, two-storeyed exhibition space contains a play of openings and light sources against which the full, sculptural values of the chairs are enhanced and informally displayed. The serenity of this museum's church-like interior surely marks Gehry's long-standing love of Romanesque church architecture as well as Le Corbusier's Ronchamp chapel. A sanctuary is distilled from chaos.

In 1991 Gehry designed another highly individual furniture series for Knoll International which was produced from woven, maple strips. Three years of technical and artistic experimentation resulted in five chairs, two tables and an ottoman, named after ice hockey terms (Gehry's favourite sport), which were inspired by wooden crates and bushel baskets. *Hat Trick, Power Play, High Sticking,* each weigh perhaps no more than six pounds. They demonstrate Gehry's desire to create a chair where the seats and backs are no longer independent of the frame and no upholstery is required. Sculptural, distinctive, and experimental, the furniture, like his architecture, marries individualism with a sympathetic responsiveness to materials and user.

Gehry's most recent commissions have included further buildings for Vitra, the Walt Disney Concert Hall, the American Center, Paris, and the Euro-Disney Entertainment Center, Marne-la-Vallée. Currently in progress is the Guggenheim Museum, Bilbao, Spain where he is incorporating a road bridge and a high gallery space with catwalks that will provide views into the gallery and out over the city and the river. The building will use local materials and skills. This intention, like much of Gehry's work itself, appears to represent the finer aspects of American culture, generosity, humanitarianism, and freedom.

SUSAN HOYAL

Biography

Frank Owen Gehry. Born Ephraim Goldberg, in Toronto, 28 February 1929. Family moved to Los Angeles, 1947. Studied architecture at the University of Southern California, Los Angeles, 1949–51 and 1954; studied city planning at the Graduate School of Design, Harvard University, Cambridge, Massachusetts, 1956–57. Served in the United States Army, 1955–56. Married: 2 sons. Architectural designer, Victor Gruen Associates, Los Angeles, 1953–54; planner and designer, Robert and Company Architects, Atlanta, 1955–56; designer and planner, Hideo Sasaki Associates, Boston, 1957; architectural designer, Pereira and Luckman, Los Angeles, 1957–58; worked on planning, design and project direction, Victor Gruen Associates, 1958–61; project designer and planner, André Remondet, Paris, 1961. Principal, Frank O. Gehry Associates, Los Angeles since 1962. Designed interiors and exhibition layouts from the 1960s; produced furniture from 1969; involved in stage set design. Assistant Professor, University of Southern California, Los Angeles, 1972–73; visiting critic, University of California at Los Angeles, 1977 and 1979; Professor of Architecture, Yale University, New Haven, Connecticut, 1979 and 1982; Eliot Noyes Professor, Harvard University, 1982, 1985, 1987, 1988, 1989. Received numerous prizes and awards including the Pritzker Architecture Prize, 1989. Fellow: American Institute of Architects, 1974; American Academy and Institute of Arts and Letters, 1987; American Academy and Institute of Arts and Sciences, 1991.

Selected Works

For a full list of Gehry's architectural and design projects see Arnell and Bickford 1985. Examples of Gehry's furniture are in the Museum of Modern Art, New York, and the Vitra Design Museum, Weil am Rhein, Germany.

Interiors

1968	O'Neill Hay Barn, San Juan Capistrano, California (building and interiors)
1970–72	Ron Davis Studio and House, Malibu, California (building and interiors)
1974	Rouse Company Headquarters, Columbia, Maryland (building, interiors and fixtures)
1977	Berger, Berger, Kahn and Shafton, Law Offices, Los Angeles (interiors and furniture)
1978	Mid-Atlantic Toyota Offices, Glen Burnie, Maryland (office interiors)
1979–87	Frank O. Gehry House, Santa Monica, California (building, interiors, furniture and fittings)
1981–84	Law School Building, Loyola University, Los Angeles (building, and remodelling of library interior)
1982	Wosk Residence, Beverly Hills, California (building and interiors)
1983	Norton House, Venice, California (building and interiors)
1984–86	Rebecca's Restaurant, Venice, California (interiors, fittings and furniture)
1984–86	Winton Guest House, Wayzata, Minnesota (building and interiors)
1986	Schnabel Residence, Brentwood, California (building and interiors)
1986	Chiat / Day offices, Venice, California (building, interiors and furniture; with Claes Oldenburg and Coosje van Bruggen)
1986–89	Fishdance Restaurant, Kobe, Japan (building, interiors and furnishings)
1987–89	Vitra Design Museum, Weil am Rhein, Germany (building and interiors)
1988	Euro Disneyland Entertainment Center, Marne-la-Vallée, near Paris (building and interiors)
1989	Walt Disney Concert Hall, Los Angeles (building and interiors)

1990 University of Minnesota Art Museum, Minneapolis (building and interiors)
1991 Guggenheim Museum, Bilbao, Spain (building and interiors)

Gehry's first furniture designs, for dayrooms at Fort Benning, Georgia, date from 1954. His celebrated corrugated cardboard furniture was produced between 1969 and 1973, and included the *Easy Edges* range of 1972 (reissued as *Rough Edges* in 1982). In 1991 he created a collection of furniture for Knoll International. Gehry's *Rykba* fish lamps, and his Snake lamps were produced by Formica in 1984.

Publications

Interview in *Angels and Franciscans: Innovative Architecture from Los Angeles and San Francisco*, edited by Bill Lacy and Susan deMenil, 1992

Further Reading

The literature on Gehry is extensive; a major study of his work, including a definitive bibliography up to 1985, appears in Arnell and Bickford 1985. For information relating to more recent works see Bletter 1986, Boissière 1990, and Steele 1993.

Arnell, Peter and Bickford, Ted (editors), *Frank Gehry: Buildings and Projects*, New York: Rizzoli, 1985

Bletter, Rosemarie Haag and others, *The Architecture of Frank Gehry*, New York: Rizzoli, 1986

Boissière, Olivier, *Gehry, Site, Tigerman: Trois Portraits de l'Artiste en Architecte*, Paris: Moniteur, 1981

Boissière, Olivier and Martin Filler, *Frank Gehry: Vitra Design Museum*, New York: Rizzoli, and London: Thames and Hudson, 1990

Davidson, Ellen, *Frank Gehry: New Bentwood Furniture Designs* (exhib. cat.), Montreal: Montreal Museum of Decorative Arts, 1992

Futagawa, Yukio (editor), *Frank O. Gehry*, Tokyo: ADA, 1993 (Global Architecture 10)

"Gehry Residence in Santa Monica" in *GA Houses* (Tokyo), no.6, 1979

Grandee, Charles K., "Catch of the Day: Fishdance Restaurant" in *Architectural Record*, January 1988

Jencks, Charles, "Frank Gehry, The Deconstructivist" in *Art and Design*, May 1985

Jencks, Charles (editor), *Frank O. Gehry: Individual Imagination and Cultural Conservatism*, London: Academy, and New York: St. Martin's Press, 1995

Nairn, Janet, "Frank Gehry: The Search for a 'No Rules' Architecture" in *Architectural Record*, June 1976, pp.95–102

"Norton House, Venice, California" in *Architectural Record*, mid-April 1985

Nulli, A., "Vitra Design Museum, Weil am Rhein" in *Domus*, February 1990

Phillips, Lisa (introduction), *Shape and Environment: Furniture by American Architects* (exhib. cat.), New York: Whitney Museum of American Art, 1982

Richardson, Sara S., *Frank O. Gehry: A Bibliography*, Monticello, IL: Vance, 1987

"Schnabel Residence" in *GA Houses* (Tokyo), no.29, August 1990

Steele, James, *Schnabel House: Frank Gehry*, London: Phaidon, 1993

Stephens, Suzanne, "Frank O. Gehry and Associates" in *Progressive Architecture*, March 1980

Sudjic, Deyan, "One Man and His Museum" in *Blueprint*, November 1989

Vegesack, Alexander von, *Vitra Design Museum*, Tokyo: GA Design Center, 1993

George IV 1762–1830

British monarch, collector and patron

"I am hard at work upon my mansion at Carlton House ... I am adding and building considerably to it, and hope on yr. Return you will not think me a bad architect", wrote the young Prince of Wales to his brother in 1783. But the talents of the future King George IV lay in his skill in interior design.

That skill was exhibited principally in four sites: Carlton House, where he lived from about 1785 to the mid 1820s; the Royal Pavilion, Brighton (1780s–1826); Buckingham Palace, where rebuilding began in 1825; and at Windsor. Windsor Castle was made habitable by about 1828, but he was never able to live in the rebuilt Buckingham Palace. Thus it is in his princely residences, Carlton House and the Brighton Pavilion, that one is able to study the development of his taste, although the two kingly residences represent its culmination.

At first he employed Henry Holland as his architect. Carlton House was a confused congeries of old buildings to which Holland brought a sense of order and rationality; and the marine villa at Brighton was acquired as a mere holiday residence for the heir to the throne. The need to amend these inadequate structures to accommodate the princely household, and to find the best arrangement, called for frequent modifications; and the interior decorator's perpetual search for perfection that induced the patron to discard half-executed schemes, stamped the Prince as a man of fickle taste.

The prince was, however, consistently an admirer of French taste, as was Holland. In 1785 Horace Walpole recognised the French derivation of the ornamentation at Carlton House, striking in its "august simplicity", though this must have owed at least as much to Holland and his French craftsmen as to the Prince. But constant alterations were made in the interiors, the Prince experimenting with the juxtaposition of complementary colours in furnishings. He employed successive French decorators, first Guillaume Gaubert until about 1787 and then the *marchand-mercier* Dominique Daguerre, who furnished a Chinese Saloon designed by Holland in 1789, the first of a series of Chinoiserie essays.

Thus in 1805–07 a Chinese room at Carlton House (whether the original or another is unclear) was decorated at a cost of £1,375: the walls of carmine, with eight large figure panels; the doors black, with gold ornamentation; the ceiling, echoed by the carpet, with a lilac border, and central dragon on a green ground. Such schemes rarely survived long enough to be recorded visually: in May 1806 it was reported that "Although Carlton House as finished by Holland was in a complete & new state", the Prince had "ordered the whole to be done again under the direction of Walsh Porter who has destroyed all that Holland has done & is substituting a finishing in a most expensive & motley taste" (Farington Diary, 3 May 1806).

Just as the Prince's experiments with Chinoiserie at Carlton House paved the way for his Brighton Pavilion work, so similar experiments in Gothic – another exotic style employed at the time to arouse particular sensations – preceded the restoration at Windsor Castle referred to below. A cast-iron Gothic Conservatory with plaster fan-vaulting (inspired by Henry VII's Chapel, Westminster Abbey), the panels between the vaulting ribs filled with coloured glass, designed by Thomas Hopper about 1807, has been perpetuated on paper, but a slightly earlier Gothic Library left no pictorial record. Among works carried out by John Nash in 1814 was a new Gothic Dining Room. These rooms enabled the Prince to indulge his fondness for armorial shields as a decorative feature, also found in stained glass added in 1817 to the skylight of the Grand Staircase, and subsequently widely used for Gothic ornament, as in the Houses of Parliament.

James Wyatt's structural alterations at Carlton House in 1804–05 gave scope for wholesale schemes of redecoration superintended by Walsh Porter, a connoisseur who strongly influenced the Prince. Magnificent textiles replaced mural painting, enabling the Prince's growing collection of easel paintings (mainly of the English and Netherlands schools) to play an integral role in the decoration. Drawing inspiration from ancient Rome, Porter achieved sumptuousness. Adjacent apartments were brought into harmony as in the two Blue Velvet Rooms, and in the *enfilade* of rooms on the basement floor garden front (continued after Porter's death in 1809) with scarlet curtains and furnishings ornamented in black velvet and scarlet-bordered yellow carpets. And Porter declared that "I have not added or branched out into a single thing that was not plan'd by the Prince himself (not me)" (Aspinall, *Corr. of Pr. of Wales*, no.2078).

The Prince's fastidious supervision is established by the number of models made both of parts of rooms and of furniture, and the submitting of numerous patterns for textiles, glass and flooring for his selection. A carpet for the Ballroom was made in 1792 "after a design given by his Royal Highness" (PRO, HO73/19). His enthusiasm for Sèvres porcelain was expressed in the introduction of quasi-permanent garnitures in his rooms, as well as displays of *déjeuners* and small items. Similarly he acquired ornamental pieces of gold (or silver-gilt) plate for permanent display, and, with his friend and adviser Lord Yarmouth (later 3rd Marquess of Hertford), was a keen collector of the then *démodé* Boulle furniture, actually ordering new pieces. Likewise, although he bought furniture in the fashion of the day, he snapped up French furniture of the finest quality in unfashionable earlier styles as far back as Louis XIV, whom he admired as a role model.

As an escape from Court life, the prince took a house at Brighton in 1786. Henry Holland quickly added a new north wing, linked to the existing south wing by a circular saloon, and introduced bow windows, adorned with Ionic *scagliola* columns. The prince's Gallic taste was commented on: the library, "fitted up in the French style", with a brilliant yellow paper; *scagliola* columns in the dining room, painted in yellow and maroon with a sky-blue ceiling. The saloon, with paintings by Biagio Rebecca was in Holland's Berrington style. About this time, the house began to be called the prince's "marine pavilion", a term borrowed from the Comte d'Artois's lately-built *pavillon de Bagatelle* in the Bois de Boulogne, Paris.

At Brighton, the Prince lived less formally than in his town palace; his house likewise was less inhibited. His long-standing interest in Chinoiserie found ample scope here. The gift of "a very beautiful Chinese paper" in 1802 is said (Brayley, *Her Majesty's Palace at Brighton*, 1838) to have decided him to employ it in constructing a Chinese gallery out of two of Holland's rooms, made redundant by new extensions, but this may not have been the earliest Chinoiserie at the Pavilion. Seized with enthusiasm for the alterations, the Prince decided to decorate it wholly in the Chinese style; he told an intimate that he had chosen it "because at the time [during the French Revolution] there was such a cry against French things, etc. that he was afraid of his furniture being accused of jacobinism" (*Lord Granville Leveson Gower: private corr.*, 1916). Chinoiserie fittings and furnishings were brought from Carlton House, and new ones acquired. Chinese papers were hung in the principal rooms, "the Prince assisting in fixing up and cutting out the Birds, etc. on the paper in the Saloon" (Crace ledgers), bamboo panelling was effected in wood or in paper, lacquer cabinets and bamboo furniture installed, ornaments imported direct from China: a new, or at least a modified fashion in interior decoration. Many of the decorations painted by Crace are taken directly from Chinese porcelain or textiles, rather than from the Westernised tradition. In the sequel, ideas for creating a Chinese exterior also were abandoned in favour of the more substantial forms of Mughal architecture when John Nash reconstructed the building in 1814–21.

Nevertheless, the internal changes and the new rooms at the Pavilion were still Chinoiserie, though in a rather different style, and with Indian touches. Indeed, in retrospect, the period 1815–c.1819 appears as one of decorative experimentation. The Prince supervised the work closely, as the Crace ledgers show: thus in July and August 1815 he was attended by teams of assistants "putting in patterns" in the North and South Drawing Rooms, and ordering technical experiments and successive changes in colour; subsequently he arranged the hanging of papers; and in 1818 he himself sketched the bamboo and bows design for decorating the convex covering of the end walls of the Music Room. One of the most interesting experiments was the combining of decorative marbling, as practised at Carlton House, with Chinoiserie, but it was soon abandoned, to be followed into limbo by gay, colourful Rococo designs in the saloon and drawing rooms associated with the Craces' rival painter, Robert Jones.

Grandest of the interiors of this period were two new immense domed rooms, one for eating (largely Jones's designs), the other for music (principally decorated by the Craces), the most spectacular of George's works; and it is particularly with these that the final, more sumptuous style of decoration is associated. Princess Lieven, familiar with the Russian imperial palaces, commented: "I do not believe that, since the days of Heliogabalus, there has been such magnificence and such luxury" (quoted in Clifford Musgrave, *Regency Furniture*, 1966). Their remarkable ceilings were highly original in form, the music room's dome resting on a double coving above an octagon, that of the Banqueting room having a convex coving above a more conventional arrangement of spandrels, with a fantastic central chandelier (strictly, gasolier) ringed by lotus flowers upheld by dragons, and suspended from a dragon in the dome that cost £5,600. This opulence with its Mughal flavouring, was echoed in the redecoration of the lesser rooms, creating a measure of harmony throughout: scarlet and gold predominate, gold in profusion. Intricate carving, gilded or silvered, glittered in a hundred mirrors; porcelain in the richest mounts proliferated.

The Brighton Pavilion was a seaside amusement; as Regent

from 1811, with full powers from 1812, the Prince required residences of state. The increasing grandeur of Carlton House may be seen as responding to this need, but the building was too ramshackle structurally and too public – "in a street" – to serve permanently for a ruler made conscious of his unpopularity. St James's Palace could still be used for state ceremonies, but his father had resided in Buckingham House ("The Queen's Palace") and Windsor Castle. The deaths of his mother and father, in 1819 and 1820 respectively, opened the possibility of reconstructing those palaces whenever the government would provide the means. In these two great undertakings of his reign, George IV reverted to his habitual francophilia, encouraged by a new artistic adviser, Sir Charles Long (later Lord Farnborough).

To make Windsor Castle a convenient modern residence, Long drew up a blueprint executed by Jeffry Wyatville; the young A.W.N. Pugin was employed to design appropriate furniture in the increasingly fashionable Gothic style. But the king's French predilections were expressed in a Grand Reception Room in a revived, somewhat indeterminate retrospective style (miscalled "Louis XIV"), for which Long purchased 18th-century Rococo *boiseries* in Paris, while the semi-state apartments, with much material from Carlton House re-used, echoed that palace's French tone. The younger Wyatts were employing a similar Louis style in York (later Sutherland, now Lancaster) House, London and Belvoir Castle, Leicestershire. Although the king took up residence in the castle in 1828, much still remained to do at his death.

In London, funds were found to start rebuilding the Queen's Palace in 1824, a work entrusted to Nash. The king determined the character of the plan, and then, as work progressed, developed his ideas on the interior decoration. At first he had intended it simply as his town residence, but in 1826 decided that it would make an excellent state palace in which to hold his courts, so that the decoration was enriched, at an additional estimate by 1828 of £51,000, quite apart from sculpture, and impressive parquet floors in the French manner (only one of which, in the Bow Room, was ultimately installed). "Whenever I saw [the King]", Nash recalled, "it generally happened that he ordered some alteration" (House of Commons, *Report on Buckingham Palace ...*, 1831). There was some attempt at economy by re-using chimneypieces and furnishings from Carlton House, from whence many of the decorative ideas derived: *scagliola* or marbling was employed very extensively both for walling and for columns and pilasters in bright colours ("Raspberry-coloured pillars without end", complained a Whig socialite – *Creevey Papers*, ed. Maxwell, 1904). The proliferation of panels in high relief, though a development of Holland's overdoors, was regarded by contemporaries as a new development in interior decoration. As at Brighton, the ceilings of the State Apartments formed a remarkable feature, with bold concave or convex covings, often with huge scrolled brackets supporting the rich central coffering, the sculptured friezes and profuse gilding of the ornaments creating an effect of the greatest magnificence. A contemporary journal observed: "It is, indeed, not easy to conceive anything more splendid", describing them as "a style new in this country, partaking very much of the boldest style, in the Italian taste, of the 15th century" (*Fraser's Magazine*, 1830). Uncompleted at his death, Buckingham Palace displayed only the more substantial decorative features of George IV's taste.

In an eclectic age, the patron was able to choose from a wide variety of styles, and to choose the instrument (architect, decorator, painter) most appropriate for his purpose. George IV employed a range of such men, but he ultimately determined the work they accomplished. Rooted firmly in late 18th century French classicism, his taste nevertheless embraced and enhanced the more exotic forms employed at the time, and he declined to observe a strict uniformity of style in furnishing his rooms, creating grand but harmonious interiors by a carefully considered combination of diverse elements.

M.H. PORT

See also Henry Holland

Biography

George Augustus Frederick. Born in London, 12 August 1762, eldest son of George III. Married 1) Maria Fitzherbert, 1785 (marriage declared invalid); 2) Princess Caroline of Brunswick, 1795 (separated 1796; she died 1821): one daughter. Served as Regent when his father George III was declared permanently insane, from 1811. Succeeded to the throne, 1820. Died at Windsor, 26 June 1830.

Further Reading

Bellaigue, Geoffrey de, "The Furnishings of the Chinese Drawing Room, Carlton House" in *Burlington Magazine*, CIX, September 1967

Bellaigue, Geoffrey de and Pat Kirkham, "George IV and the Furnishing of Windsor Castle" in *Furniture History*, 1972

Bellaigue, Geoffrey de, "George IV and French Furniture" in *Connoisseur*, June 1977, pp.116–25

Bellaigue, Geoffrey de, *Carlton House: The Past Glories of George IV's Palace* (exhib. cat.), London: Queen's Gallery, 1991

Cornforth, John, "Fit for a Prince" in *Country Life*, 28 March 1991, pp.66–69

Hibbert, Christopher, *George IV* (biography), Harmondsworth: Penguin, 1976

Morley, John, *The Making of the Royal Pavilion, Brighton: Designs and Drawings*, London: Sotheby Publications, and Boston: Godine, 1984

Morley, John, *Regency Design, 1790–1840: Gardens, Buildings, Interiors, Furniture*, London: Zwemmer, and New York: Abrams, 1993

Stroud, Dorothy, *Henry Holland: His Life and Architecture*, London, Country Life, 1966; South Brunswick, NJ: A.S. Barnes, 1967

Watkin, David, *The Royal Interiors of Regency England: From Watercolours First Published by W.H. Pyne in 1817–1820*, London: Dent, and New York: Vendome, 1984

George & Peto (Sir Ernest George 1839–1922 and Harold Ainsworth Peto 1854–1933)

British architects and interior designers; firm established 1876; became George and Yeates 1892

Ernest George was one of the most prolific and successful of late Victorian domestic architects. His town houses in Harrington and Collingham Gardens, Kensington, of the late 1880s, were described by Hermann Muthesius as "'among the finest examples of domestic architecture to be seen in London", and his country houses, which ranged in style from

George & Peto: sitting room, 9 Collingham Gardens, London, 1883–84

Queen Anne, Elizabethan, Jacobean and Tudor, to Neo-Georgian, were no less successful. Throughout his career, George was committed to architectural partnership, setting up his first practice with fellow Royal Academy student Thomas Vaughan in 1861. Their commissions included commercial, domestic and some ecclesiastical work, and various of their country houses, such as Rousdon, Devon (1872–76), rehearsed the Great Halls with a floor to ceiling hooded stone fireplace, minstrels' gallery and long manorial windows, that were to be a speciality of George's work in the 1880s and 1890s.

In 1876, after the early death of Vaughan, George entered into partnership with Harold Ainsworth Peto, fifth son of the celebrated public works and railway contractor, Sir Samuel Morton Peto. Trained in both building and architecture, Peto, according to George, was not a draughtsman, "but had all the feeling of an artist". His taste and business acumen, together with his interest in interior, furniture and later garden design, made a perfect contribution to the 19-year partnership which was to be the most spectacularly successful period of George's career.

The strength of George & Peto's practice did not lie in the formation of a progressive doctrine such as the Arts and Crafts Movement, but in their emphasis upon high quality in materials and craftsmanship. George & Peto's interiors were invariably designed in an effort to create picturesque effects, to give the impression of a house lived in by many generations in which the charm of "olden days" was combined with modern conveniences, as at Poles, Hertfordshire (1890–92). Where appropriate, George designed furniture himself, much of it forming part of integrated schemes and built *in situ,* as at Rousdon and in the Morning Room at Glencot, Somerset (1887). Free-standing, individual pieces were never direct copies, but rather slightly simplified versions of existing pieces with which he was familiar drawn from sources ranging from the medieval period to the mid 18th century. Guy Dawber recalls that George "always impressed upon clients the importance of keeping to some uniform scheme of furniture design in keeping with the architecture of the house with which it was to be associated."

George & Peto's own designs for furniture show a high level of scholarship, historical expertise and structural integrity. They were both enthusiastic collectors of old furniture and *objets d'art*, as evidenced by the interiors of their own homes and their office at 18 Maddox Street, London. The interior decoration of George's house, Redroofs, Streatham Common (1887–88), was subservient to the superb collection of Renaissance furniture, pictures and tapestries. Peto specialised in Old English Oak, detailing his collections in *The Boke of Iford* (1917). They purchased furniture and furnishings on behalf of clients and were prepared to combine genuine examples of early furniture and applied design with examples of contemporary craftsmanship, as at the Yellow House, London (1892), designed for Peto's friend, the furniture connoisseur Percy MacQuoid. At Osmaston Manor, Derbyshire (1886), the antique furniture and tapestries were supplied by Joseph Duveen, while the plasterwork was executed by Walter Smith.

The scope of the practice widened dramatically after 1876, with many commissions plainly coming through the Peto family's connections with the worlds of art, commerce and construction, notably the Peto Brothers' timely speculation in Harrington and Collingham Gardens, South Kensington, with which George & Peto confirmed their success as advanced domestic architects. Their superbly conceived designs, executed between 1880 and 1888, represent the extremist point of late Victorian individualism. The range of plain Queen Anne was extended to include something of the picturesque brio of the old Flemish and German town houses, sketched and painted by George on his frequent tours to Northern Europe. The interiors tended to eschew the orthodox upper-class house plan, in favour of greater variety. In all the houses the stairs are of oak, and there is much dark panelling contrasting with rich hooded stone chimneypieces, white ornamental strapwork, beamed or coffered ceilings and stamped leather or otherwise Aesthetic wall coverings. In style, George & Peto's varied and individual schemes borrowed from almost every school and epoch of the early Northern Renaissance; the decoration is most prodigal on the highly carved friezes and fireplace arches. Small panels of Holbeinesque painted glass are introduced for picturesque effect, and porches have mosaic floors in Dutch tradition. While the detailing responds to the Aesthetic Movement, with Jeffrey & Co. wallpapers designed by J.D. Sedding and Walter Crane, and tiles by De Morgan, the quality of workmanship in the panelling, door furniture, and the carving of the interior schemes, reflect George & Peto's concern for craftsmanship.

The interior of 37 Harrington Gardens was calculated to create a fine setting for Sir Walter Richard Cassel's collection of paintings, while No. 39 was built for the celebrated dramatist W.S. Gilbert. Here, a dramatic stepped gable surmounted by a ship prepared the visitor for an interior richly ornamented in a style with consistent with the Northern Renaissance character of the house. The porch, with its rich carving in high and low relief, with quaint little sculptured caryatids playing music, leads through an unpolished oak door into the vestibule. The latter, with its mosaic floor, oak panelled walls and fluted frieze, has a moulded rib plaster ceiling. The oak panelled hall includes a characteristic floor-to-ceiling chimneypiece in carved stone, fronting a Dutch blue-tiled inglenook where Gilbert periodically hung his hams. In the hall window are panels of glass, painted by Lavers & Westlake, but unfortunately the stamped poppy paper by Jeffrey & Co. has been removed. Another whimsical feature is provided by mottoes above the ground floor doors; these included the saying "And those things do best please me, that fall preposterously" above the drawing room, and "All hope abandon ye who enter here" over the entrance to the dining room. The latter was originally decorated by Howard & Sons, and has a wooden overmantel, and a ceiling with small gilt-edged panels between beams which rest on merrily carved corbels. The drawing room, opening out into the garden, has a strapwork ceiling and hooded alabaster chimneypiece to the west, sculpted after the manner of the 16th century, rather like those of "the old French castles". The panelling is of rosewood. The boudoir is at half landing level, and affords a small plaster oriel projecting into the hall. On the first floor, the billiard room with white toned panelling below red surfaced walls (originally decorated by Howard & Sons) and Gilbert's oak panelled library-cum-study, which retains its corner fireplace, high panelling and gold-stamped leather paper (originally red and gold). The radiator grills were brass repoussé panels by J. Starkie Gardiner.

Special interest attaches to the interior of 9 Collingham Gardens, it being Harold Peto's original house. It is quite naturally one of the most individual buildings in the development. Built in 1883–84, it adopts the Jacobean style, which sets it apart from its neighbours, and the interior decoration and appointments more than adequately compensated for any lack of extravagance in the plan. There were "many good bits of German glass", introduced into the windows, and antique tiles and panels in the hearths. The hall has an angled hooded stone fireplace with ingenious early Renaissance style carving and Dutch tiles, the whole carried up to the low pitched oak ceiling. Original beams of timber made up the staircase arcade which has vigorous Jacobean detailing. The dining room has an attractive stone arched inglenook and the beams of the ceiling rest on carved corbels, one depicting a jester. The walls were originally covered with 16th-century stamped and gilded leather, above an oak dado. All the decorative ironwork was executed by Ellis and Rice. In 1889, Peto moved to 7 Collingham Gardens. During his occupancy the interior, remarkable for its rich, dark and heavy Jacobean detailing, historicist panelling and coffered ceilings, provided the perfect context for Peto's collection of *objets d'art*, and the furniture, in particular, revealed his love of Renaissance work. The lofty sitting room, occupying a storey and a half in height, in original warehouse / shop fashion, was especially luxurious, with old stained glass in the windows, a music gallery and antique tapestries above the panelling.

George & Peto's country house interiors varied according to the style of the house, but invariably involved a good deal of oak, with elaborate relief decoration with figure and scroll decorations, and stone fireplaces elaborately sculpted with Neo-Renaissance decoration. The interior decoration of Woolpits, Surrey (1885–88), for Sir Henry Doulton, employed terracotta. While this material lent itself well to patterned forms in chosen places, the work of George Tinworth, one of Doulton's leading craftsmen, pre-empted the banality of mere repetition. He carved the panel over the entrance door in the porch, with "Abraham Receiving the Angel's Visit" and also a fine terracotta chimney breast over the inglenook, which included a panel with carvings, "suggestive of domestic employments and hospitality". In the dining room, George & Peto created a classical setting appropriate for Tinworth's bas-relief of *The Sons of Lydippe*, placed above the fireplace. By far the most impressive display of Doulton Ware was in the billiard room, where it was combined with "impasto" to rich effect.

In their designs for the principal rooms of Sir Andrew Barclay Walker's yacht, *Cuhona* (1882), George & Peto chose to ignore any maritime connotations, instead deliberately treating the yacht as just another domestic interior. The salon, 24 by 20 feet, was richly carved in dark oak, the panels above the dado line carved in wood and lacquered a dull gold, were separated by fluted and carved pilasters. The ceiling was painted by G.F. Malins. A rich curtain enabled the limited space to be divided – an arrangement often favoured by George & Peto to convert halls into more intimate areas – into a drawing and dining room. The side of the curtain facing the drawing room was maize brocade, the reverse, stamped velvet. A mirror, surmounting the fireplace, was another device to extend the limited space. The sideboard, piano, writing tables, chairs and even the wine glasses were all specially designed by George & Peto to accord with the scheme. The sofas were covered with antique Persian rugs. The state rooms were all treated differently, the Ladies' Room had walnut dados with cretonnes above, while the other rooms were panelled to the ceiling. The boudoir, considered to be the "most perfectly finished of any part of the boat" had a rosewood dado, surmounted by hangings of *velours cisele* in pale terracotta and maize. The ornaments here were all old carved ivory figures, Netsuke and old coloured oriental porcelain. The panelling and cabinet work for these aesthetic interiors were from the shops of Messrs T. Lawrence & Sons.

Peto retired from the practice to concentrate on landscape gardening and interior design in 1892 and in the same year George entered into his final partnership with Alfred Bowman Yeates. George and Yeates designed Jacobean and Elizabethan interiors for North Mymms, Hertfordshire and in 1891–93, they undertook the alterations and refurbishment of West Dean Park, Sussex. Here the Great Hall was a comfortably furnished area, overlooked by an oak balustraded bedroom corridor. Other large country house commissions followed: Crathorne Hall, Yorkshire (1903–06), Eynsham Hall, Oxfordshire (1904–08) and Putterbridge Bury, Hertfordshire (1889–91). All included a great deal of oak panelling and characteristic carving, although more sober in feel. Their series of interior schemes in London included the design of the public apartments on the ground floor of Claridge's Hotel (1894–98). The hotel's smoking room was timber-beamed, with a lofty stone chimney piece, half-panelled walls and an intricate light fixture; the billiard room had an elaborate frieze. The ladies drawing room, with its deep white ceiling and fireplace, created a fresh airy atmosphere and was reminiscent of their highly successful Flemish Renaissance work of the 1880s.

HILARY J. GRAINGER

Selected Works

A large collection of George and Peto's drawings is in the Drawings Collection, Royal Institute of British Architects, London.

Interiors

1881–82	35 & 37 Harrington Gardens, London (buildings and interiors): Walter Richard Cassel
1882–83	39 & 41 (formerly 19 & 20) Harrington Gardens, London (buildings and interiors): W.S. Gilbert
1882–83	*Cuhona* yacht (interiors, furnishings and fittings): Sir Andrew Barclay Walker
1883–84	9 Collingham Gardens, London (building and interiors): Harold A. Peto
1885	7 Collingham Gardens, London (building and interiors): W.H. Peto
1885–88	Woolpits, Peaslake Road, Ewhurst, Surrey (building and interiors): Henry Doulton
1886	Osmaston Manor, Derbyshire (restoration and furnishings): Sir Andrew Barclay Walker
1887	Glencot, Wells, Somerset (building and interiors): William Sampson Hodgkinson
1887–88	Redroofs, Streatham Common, London (building and interiors): Ernest George
1889–90	6 Carlton House Terrace, London (alterations and redecoration): C.H. Stanford
1889–91	Shiplake Court, Henley-on-Thames, Oxfordshire (building and interiors)
1890–92	Poles, Ware, Hertfordshire (building and interiors): Edmund Smith Hanbury
1891–93	West Dean Park, Singleton, near Chichester, Sussex (additions, alterations and redecoration by George and Yeates): William Dodge James
1892	The Yellow House, Palace Court, London (building and interiors): Percy MacQuoid
1897	Claridge's Hotel, London (interiors including the ground floor public apartments and the principal staircase)
1904–08	Eynsham Hall, Witney, Oxfordshire (building and interiors): James Francis Mason
1908–11	Putterbridge Bury, Lilley, Hertfordshire (building and interiors): T.M. Clutterbuck

Further Reading

A detailed study of George & Peto's work appears in Grainger 1985 which includes a complete catalogue of their architectural and interior commissions and an extensive bibliography of primary sources.

Aitchison, George, "Presentation of the Royal Gold Medal to Ernest George: Address Delivered to the General Meeting of the RIBA, Monday 22 June 1896" in *Journal of the Royal Institute of British Architects*, 25 June 1896, pp.469–71

Darcy Bradell, T.A., "Architectural Reminiscences, 3: Fugaces Anni" and "Conclusion" in *The Builder*, 5 January 1945, pp.6–7 and 12 January 1945, pp.27–29

George, Sir Ernest, "An Architect's Reminiscences" in *The Builder*, 13 May 1921, pp.622–23

Gleeson-White, J.W., "The Revival of English Domestic Architecture III: The Work of Mr. Ernest George" in *The Studio*, 1896, pp.147–58

Gleeson-White, J.W., "The Revival of English Domestic Architecture V: The Work of Messrs. George & Peto" in *The Studio*, 1896, pp.204–15

Grainger, Hilary J., *The Architecture of Sir Ernest George and his Partners c.1860–1922*, Ph.D. thesis, Leeds: University of Leeds, 1985

Richardson, Margaret, *Architects of the Arts and Crafts Movement*, London: Trefoil, 1983, pp.59–69

Germany

Two points play an important role in the consideration of German architecture and interior design. First, from AD 899 to 1805, the "Holy Roman Empire of the German Nation" embraced a total of over 300 autonomous Länder (territories) and cities. So, for this reason the following account is not limited geographically to the region occupied by Germany at the end of the 20th century. Second, during World War II a great many works of art, and in particular a great many of the most significant interiors, were destroyed. Thus our knowledge of German decoration and design must often be based on descriptions and illustrations of examples that no longer exist.

Little is known about German interior decoration of the Early Middle Ages. The earliest surviving documentary evidence dates from around 1200 and consists chiefly of allusions in epic literary texts produced at the German courts. These contained descriptions of imaginary fortified castles and Pfalzen or Imperial palaces, referring to chapels and shared living spaces as well as larger halls for special festivities and private chambers (*Kemenaten*). Walls of castle interiors were often hung with carpets or textiles or decorated with murals, usually depicting subjects from mythology, history, or courtly poetry. Particularly important were the large fireplaces and splendid candelabra, of which only a few ecclesiastical examples survive, including those in Aachen and Hildesheim cathedrals. The focal point of an interior would be a bed, used for sitting and reclining as well as for sleeping. Contemporary literature invariably describes them as richly decorated and very comfortable, qualities also evoked in the miniature showing Solomon's bed that decorates the late-12th-century manuscript of Herrad von Landsberg's *Hortus deliciarum*.

Few secular decorative objects or pieces of furniture are known from the High Middle Ages. The Neuburg in Unstrut, one of the seats of the Landgraf of Thuringia, and the residence of the Babenbergs at Klosterneuburg, both dating to around 1200, have, for example, retained part of their architectural decoration, and the Kaiserpfalz at Gelnhausen still has a fireplace mantel with elaborate wickerwork patterning. Representative examples of simpler interior decoration are to be found in Burghausen – a dining room that could be heated, a ground floor hall (1250–1300) and, in Babenhausen, a 13th-century Romanesque ground floor hall. Early 13th century wall paintings depicting the Quest for the Holy Grail are to be found at Burg Rodeneck near Brixen.

Textiles were generally imported from Sicily, Byzantium, or Persia, as shown by cloths used to wrap relics that have survived in the Servatius Treasury in Siegburg. Although woven textiles were produced in Germany by the 13th century, embroidered cloths and knotted carpets were more likely to be used to decorate residential quarters, mostly produced at courts, monasteries, and in convents. Three carpets from 1300–30 with scenes of the Tristan legend have survived in the monastery of the Dukes of Braunschweig at Wienhausen near Celle, while wall-coverings with 22 scenes from the Tristan legend can be found in London's Victoria and Albert Museum, made in Lower Saxony in 1350–1400.

Monasteries and convents on the Lüneberger Heide still possess an extensive collection of Early Gothic furniture. In addition to the usual fixed cupboards, there are many examples of the type of dowry chest presented to a convent by a nun on her arrival, used not only as containers but also as seats and beds. Initially simple in design and decoration, their front panels became increasingly elaborate, attesting to the wealth of the owner. Cupboards, portable tables, and simple forms of seating were also to be found in late medieval monasteries and convents, while folding chairs became more common during the course of the 14th century.

Important political changes in the mid-13th century affected interior decoration. As the German emperor's influence declined, cities took over from the court as the sources of power and supporters of the arts. The bund van der düdeschen hanse, a closed association of approximately 200 cities pledged to mutually supportive trading arrangements, established in 1358, ensured a marked improvement in the economy and increased political self-confidence. Nonetheless, it was the fortified castles that first adopted the formal language of Gothic architecture. Aspects of vaulting, the decorative use of tracery, and particular forms of columns and capitals were transferred from the ecclesiastical sphere for incorporation into secular architecture, examples of which can be found in many fortified castles along the Rhine. The knights of the Deutscher Orden, who effectively mediated in German political life between the emperor, the trading cities, and the church, also drew on this style of building for their fortified castles: Marienburg, East Prussia (1339–1407, by Conrad von Jungingen), or Burg Allenstein.

New architectural forms also appeared in some public buildings erected by the newly enriched cities, for example the Fürstensaal in the town hall at Breslau (1350–late 1400s). Also notable in this respect were the assembly rooms and ceremonial halls used by the guilds of merchants and craftsmen. Great emphasis was placed on the interior decoration, which often incorporated typical Gothic decorative devices such as crockets or tracery. The town hall of Lüneberg, a city grown rich on the salt trade, is an outstanding example: the council chamber, completed in 1320, had glass windows and richly painted decoration, and its walls were later panelled. The collection of silver was housed in cupboards decorated with tracery; every rich German city possessed such a collection, which it used as a status symbol to prove its investment capabilities and to demonstrate its silversmiths' skills. The Fürstensaal in the town hall of the free imperial city of Goslar, renowned for its mining industry, retains the painted decoration it received in about 1520 as well as two candelabra made by the sculptor Hans Witten in about 1500 and fixed benches for the use of councillors. The Hansasaal, Cologne's town hall, has its principal wall richly decorated with figures and ornaments and showing the "Nine Heroes" (1349). The south of Germany also has many sumptuously appointed town halls, including Zug, with its decoratively carved hall of 1507–09.

In the houses of the emerging middle class there seems initially to have been little in the way of architectural decoration, and all that has survived are structural elements and some foundation walls. Such houses were half-timbered (the oldest surviving example is the 14th-century assembly house in Quedlinburg), sometimes with a basement floor in stone or, particularly in north Germany, of red brick. In the 14th century these styles gave rise to a distinct type of middle-class German house, featuring a large, usually two-storey, entrance hall, with several separate rooms and a stone side wing or annexe, which initially housed individual quarters and provided a fire escape. Storage space was provided under the roof and there were stables in the yard. During the 15th century rooms tended to acquire distinct functions. The living room, a feature first found in south Germany, was also adopted in the north. Increasingly, the entrance hall developed into a reception area.

From the 14th century rooms were often panelled and, in south Germany, frequently heated by a stove covered with clay tiles worked in relief or decorated with figures; this feature spread to central and north Germany in the mid-15th century. Late medieval furniture, in particular chests and cupboards, was increasingly elaborately carved. Apart from its painted decoration, which has often not survived, the furniture of the late 15th century is distinguished by wavy and X-shaped ornamentation, seemingly in an attempt to soften the strict geometrical forms of High Gothic. Of particular interest is the Dürer cupboard in the Wartburg, the front of which is decorated with carved reliefs after woodcuts by Albrecht Dürer. The leading German craftsmen of this period were famous in their own right, for example Jörg Syrlin the Elder, who carved the high altar in Ulm Cathedral.

Medieval household utensils were generally of wood or clay. From the 13th century, Siegburg and the southern part of Lower Saxony were centres of stoneware production, while from the 15th century implements made of tin were more commonly found in wealthier households. Nuremberg and Silesia were the main centres of production. The use of bronze casting in the production of candelabra and ewers for washing the hands is known from the High Middle Ages. This process was subsequently used for door-knockers and circular candelabra. Bowls were mostly embossed and decorated with low relief work. Wrought iron was used for decorative additions to doors such as lanterns or gratings, and windows were seldom glazed. From the 14th century, drinking glasses came from Bohemia, the southern part of Lower Saxony, or Italy, and mirrors from Lübeck. Leather was used for containers or binding. Unique to the Middle Ages were beautifully-worked caskets that were both functional and works of art.

From the political point of view, the Middle Ages in Germany may be said to have ended with the death of the Emperor Maximilian I (reigned 1493–1519), known as "the last knight". The accession of his grandson, who became Charles V (reigned 1519–56) heralded a new era. Leading German artists were Albrecht Dürer (1471–1528), Albrecht Altdorfer (c.1480–1538), and Hans Burgkmair (1473–1531), all from the south of Germany, signalling a shift in the 16th century in the location of the most important German art centres. The south, enriched through the work of its craftsmen and trade, became increasingly important, with special emphasis on Nuremberg, Augsburg, and Regensburg. Through the wide-ranging and profitable activities of the trading house of Fugger and the Welser bank, some of the middle classes achieved a power and wealth that outshone that of many princes. An increase in trade with Italy and Spain established connections which led to German artists undertaking journeys to Italy. The fall of the House of Burgundy, which had previously influenced matters of taste at the German courts, also prompted a degree of aesthetic reorientation, resulting in a new language of form and new types of ornamentation. At first, the basic shapes evolved during the Middle Ages for everyday objects and for furniture were often retained and were merely decorated in a new style. Later, bolder changes included more attention to surfaces, while geometric pattern gave way to classicizing arabesques or floral motifs, formal qualities which first emerged in the products of goldsmiths, leather embossers, and cloth makers.

New designs were disseminated through printed books and sheets, most strikingly in the case of table centrepieces, or drinking vessels in the shape of coconuts, elaborate shells, and horns in gold or silver. A new generation of artist-engravers emerged: Albrecht Altdorfer and Hans Brosamer designed various objects for goldsmiths.

In the realm of cabinet-making, the most important designs included those devised by the Viennese court cabinet-maker Augustin Hirschvogel (1503–53). This culminated in the emergence of deutsches Rollwerk and the arabesque. The first books of patterns for textiles and embroidery also appeared at this time, published by Peter Quentel of Cologne, Jörg Gastel of Leipzig and, in 1534, Johann Schwarzenberger and Heinrich Steyner of Augsburg.

With the decline of the Hansa cities in the 16th century, the wealth of some parts of north Germany was redistributed and agriculturally rich areas prospered. After the end of the Schmalkaldian War (1547) and other religiously motivated disputes, a general improvement set in, partly encouraged by the arrival of gold from Central and South America. The fortified castle was no longer central to architectural developments, but was replaced by the Schloss (palace) whose principal function was residential rather than defensive. Many Renaissance palaces afford a good survey of the architecture of this period, among them Heidelberg, Stuttgart, and Mainz, but few have complete interiors. Most palaces retain only the built-in elements – fireplaces, door lintels, and ceilings – since most of their furniture was destroyed during the Thirty Years' War (1618–48).

The German Renaissance was initiated by the Italian Renaissance from which it repeatedly borrowed and adapted, without ever attaining the grandeur of its model. Around 1600, however, there was a marked increase in artistic influence from Flanders and Holland. There, in the circle of the artists Hans Vredeman de Vries (1527–1606?) and Cornelis Floris (1513–75), a new style emerged which Germany adopted and which was popularized by architects such as E. van der Neer. Its ornamental decoration embraced elements of the grotesque and the fantastical, often recalling the appearance of rocks, hence the term Knorpelstil (literally "cartilege style"), and often combined with metal mounts and Rollwerk. The purest adaptation is to be found in the 1593 *Architectura* by Wendel Dietterlin (c.1550–99), followed by the *Architectura Civilis* of 1628 and *Architectura Privata* of 1641 by Josef Furttenbach, which are typical products of the Mannerist style.

A particularly versatile exponent of the German Renaissance was the Dutch painter, decorator, and architect Friedrich Sustris (c.1540–99). Trained under Giorgio Vasari in Florence, he was commissioned by Hans Fugger in 1568 to decorate a series of rooms in the latter's Augsburg residence. He worked for the dukes of Bavaria at Burg Trausnitz near

Germany: Green Lacquered Room, Residenz, Würzburg, 18th century

Landshut and finally in Munich, where he supplied designs for sculpture, stucco work, decorations for court festivities, and even architectural plans. His masterpiece is the Munich Jesuit church of St. Michael.

A number of south German palaces contain particularly rich interiors, the most notable of which is at Landshut (1534–46) which was the first pure Renaissance palace to be built in Germany. A strong Italian influence is detectable in the severely architectonic arrangement of the Italian chamber and the barrel-vaulted hall and, in particular, the wall articulated with bands of coloured stone. Equally impressive is the Festsaal in the Fugger palace at Kirchheim an der Mindel, with carved ceiling and doors by Wenzel Dittrich (1585) and figures decorating the fireplace and niches (1582–85) by Hubert Gerhard and Carlo Pallego.

North Germany was influenced more by Holland than by Italy. The concentration of many splendid buildings along and near the River Weser gave rise to the term "Weser Renaissance", although this style was to be found also in Westphalia, on the Baltic coast, in Hesse, and in Brandenburg. Exceptionally rich in figurative decoration, it is at its most impressive when used for memorials and tombstones. Secular examples include the Goldener Saal in Schloss Bückeburg, where the court sculptors Ebert the Younger and Hans Wolff carved the Götterpforte in 1605, drawing on the Mannerist style of Dietterlin. At Schloss Wilhelmsburg in Schmalkalden (1585–89), where the interior decoration was carried out by, among others, the Dutch court sculptor Wilhelm Vernucken, the influence of Floris and Vredeman de Vries is detectable in both the painted and sculptural elements. In the Weisser Saal there is stucco work, and carpets once hung on the walls; in the Riesensaal there were *trompe-l'oeil* caryatids and biblical and mythological scenes. The coffered ceiling of the banqueting hall is inset with 90 paintings on canvas by J. vom Hoffe. The painted decoration of the window recesses is by Van der Borcht, who was close to the Dutch circle. Books of Dutch motifs remained a significant source of design until the late 17th century.

Renaissance staircases continued to draw on traditional Gothic forms. Beginning with the late Gothic spiral staircase in the Frauenhaus in Strasbourg, the development led by way of the model of the Château of Blois, to the Wendelstienen (spiral stones) of Schloss Hartenfels in Trogau which was built by C. Krebs in 1533–36.

Unlike its French equivalents, German Renaissance furniture retained a number of Gothic forms. Through the use of pillars, gables, and coffering, these relatively simple objects received an architectonic stamp, while a variety of wood inlays enriched their surfaces. Cabinets were designed to contain a particular collection of curious, rare, or valuable objects, with smaller cabinets made for private individuals and larger, grander ones for use at court. Examples of these are the Prussian cabinet now in the Kunstgewerbemuseum, Berlin, and the cabinet made in Augsburg in 1625–32 for King Gustavus II Adolphus of Sweden.

In the ornamentation of stucco ceilings and carvings, Knörpelwerk and Rollwerk endured into the 1670s and 1680s. However, the true German Renaissance may be said to have come to an end in the Goldener Saal of Augsburg's town hall, decorated by Elias Holl and Mathias Kager. With its gilt coffered ceiling, niches with figures, and rich architectural decoration, it draws on Venetian models and anticipated the splendour of the Baroque.

The Thirty Years' War (1618–48), during which large parts of south Germany and Brandenburg were laid waste, marks a definitive caesura in German history and the history of its art. The style of the Baroque era in Europe was determined by Calvinist Holland (which had become rich through the war and expanding worldwide trade) and by Catholic, Counter-Reformation Rome. In 1650, looking for a new orientation, Germany drew on the examples of Holland and Italy as it had during the Renaissance and adopted the modern style of the Baroque.

Germany's most significant connections with Holland and Italy were largely dynastic or political. The Governor of the Netherlands came from Hesse Nassau; in 1646 Luise Henriette of Orange married the Grosse Kurürst Friedrich Wilhelm of Brandenburg, while her sister Henriette Katharina (1637–1707) became the wife of Johann Georg II, Prince of Anhalt-Dessau. All three commissioned important palaces: respectively, Schloss Oranienstein near Diez (1672–84), enlarged by Daniel Marot in 1696–1709); Schloss Oranienburg to the north of Berlin (built by J.G. Memhardt and M.M. Smidts in 1651, enlarged by J.A. Nehring from 1688), and Oranienbaum near Dessau (built by Ryckwaerts in 1688–98). Oranienstein retains splendid stucco work and a ceiling painting by Jan van Dyck. Oranienbaum still has a number of pieces of contemporary decoration, such as a Dutch leather wallcovering, from the Dessau Stadtschloss of 1661, a Brussels wall carpet after a design by Peter Paul Rubens made in the workshop of Franz van der Hecke, and a basement room of c.1690 decorated with Dutch tiles. Oranienburg has unfortunately lost all its original fittings. A fine ceiling painting and tiled dining room of this period is to be found in the royal Schloss Caputh near Potsdam, built in 1673 by Philipp de Chièze.

The first phase of German Baroque, lasting to around 1715, reveals strong Italian-Dutch influences and at the Berlin court a number of decorators were working in the classically imbued style. Johann Arnold Nehring (1659–95) was not only active in building work carried out at the Schloss at Potsdam but also designed, together with the artist Eggers, the Alabastersaal, notable for its clear articulation, a decorative cycle on the theme of the Kurfürst for the Residenz in Berlin, and a chapel for Schloss Köpenick. Dutch influence is even more clearly detectable in a number of tiled rooms, such as those in Schloss Hünefeld near Osnabrück, or in the Amalienburg in Munich (Cuvilliés, 1725). Many examples survive showing the use of Dutch leather wall coverings, as at Hunefeld or in the monastery Zur Ehre Gottes in Wolfenbuttel. Carpets made in Brussels were widely popular, as they had been during the Renaissance, and in 1688 a German carpet factory was established in Berlin by Philip Mercier.

Italian influences can be seen in the Residenz commissioned by King Wilhelm I's grandfather, Duke Ernst August of Hanover who in 1685 had travelled in the Veneto. Leading Italian artists were employed. The gallery and orangery built in 1694–1700 in Herrenhausen has painted decoration by T. Giusti and D. Grana. In 1670 the Venetian Lorenzo Bedogni took over the decoration, followed by G. Arighini and the stucco master G.B. Tornelli.

Ten years earlier the Kurfürstin Henriette Adelaide of Bavaria, a native of Turin, had commissioned Agostino Barelli to build the palace of Nymphenburg outside Munich as a suburban villa. Italian architects received many such commissions in Germany for some years after this. Enrico Zuccalli (1642–1724) from Ticino, who provided the designs for many palaces, and in particular for the Baroque interiors of Schloss Lustheim near Schleissheim and for Der Favorite, assumed control of the building work at Nymphenburg in 1673. In a further phase of building, starting in 1701, under the direction of Zuccalli and A. Vascardi, the palace was enlarged and partly redecorated following the example of Dutch palaces such as Het Loo, Rijswijk. For the large hall, Johann Anton Gumpp painted scenes from the life of Diana, Goddess of the Hunt, with stucco decoration by the Milanese F.A. Appiani.

While the strict classical architecture of building styles and furniture design followed the Dutch early Baroque, stucco work and painted decoration was usually executed with reference to Italian models. Stucco work was notable for its sculptural and symmetrical forms, with figures and fruit frequently worked in the round and sometimes coloured. Ceiling paintings made up of several individual canvases were set into the stucco; only rarely were they painted in fresco. This was the great age of German Baroque, and the leading architects responsible for interiors included Johann Friedrich Nette (1672–1714), who worked at the Ludwigsburg in Württemberg and in the palaces of Anhalt, together with Schlüter and the stucco master Giovanni Simonetti (1652–1716).

Around 1700 the first celebrated German fresco painters and stucco masters emerged, most either from south Germany or from the north of Italy. In accordance with traditional guild practices, craftsmen and architects tended to come from the same family and during the 17th and 18th centuries a number of families simultaneously provided stucco masters, painters, and architects, in some cases working together on the same commission.

While wooden ceilings and, to some extent, wooden walls had been painted during the Renaissance, in the Baroque era such painted decoration was incorporated into thematic programmes to which both stucco masters and painters contributed. Initially paintings were executed on canvas and inset into the ceiling. While a room in Schloss Lustheim at Schleissheim, decorated under the direction of Zuccalli, was already entirely painted in fresco in the 1680s, the high point occurred in the 18th century. Such schemes created a compelling illusion or appeared to attempt to defy architectural space. The first such ceiling painting in a German palace was executed by Vittorio Andrea Aloisius in 1656–57 at Schloss Iburg.

The 700-square-metre fresco cycle of 1751–53 by Giambattista and Giandomenico Tiepolo that decorates the grand staircase of the Residenz at Würzburg is something of an exception. Alongside the usual allegories of the Four Seasons, and mythological, historical and religious scenes, there is also an apotheosis of the prince-bishop who commissioned the work. Similar features can be found at Pommersfelden and in the Herrenhaus at Hasselberg near Altenkrempe, which has a Glorification of Count von Dernath by J.G. Simola, of about 1710. These celebrations of absolute power were derived from the notion of the state expounded by the French king Louis XIV. Initially, the example of the French court at the Château of Versailles impressed German rulers less for its architectural and decorative style than for the symbolism embodied in the *enfilade* system of interiors, and the use of allegories of Mars, Apollo, and Diana which embodied the idea of the ruler as the centre of the state.

The German Empire consisted of numerous small principalities, and the minor princes were keen to have their own status immortalized by artists and architects. In 1694 Duke Anton Ulrich of Braunschweig, ruler of some 200,000 subjects, commissioned the building of Schloss Salzdahlum from the architects Lauterbach and Hermann Korb, the theatre painter J.O. Harms, and various Italian stucco masters. It proved to be the largest German palace erected during the 17th century, and, as if taking a cue from the palace theatre (for which the duke himself wrote plays), illusion was intended to replace reality. Virtually everything was made of timber, even the apparent marble being merely stained wood. Nonetheless, there were also examples where the use of authentic materials was insisted upon. The court at Hanover commissioned solid silver furniture from the renowned Augsburg silversmith family of Biller, who also published engravings. A gilt display buffet made for the Grosse Kurfürst for use in the Stadtschloss in Berlin, was intended to highlight the wealth and power of its owner and in times of hardship might be used as a reserve fund, as were many gold dinner services.

The advent of German High Baroque dates from around 1715 and is comparable to the French Régence. Eschewing Italian-Dutch influences, German art demonstrated a new readiness to follow French examples, and an important conduit was the work of Paris-trained Joseph Effner (1687–1745), who was involved in the building of the Munich Nymphenburg and who was to influence Bavarian architecture for several decades. In place of the strongly plastic elements of the Italian approach to decoration, Effner used the shallow ornamental ribbons or strips of the strapwork style, Bandelwerkstil. The decoration of the northern antechamber in the main Nymphenburg building was executed by the Paris-trained court cabinet-maker J.A. Pichler in strap- and lattice work, interspersed with victory trophies and symbols of the Arts. Simultaneously, work on the stucco reliefs of the copestones of the windows (1726) was being executed by the Parisian sculptor Charles Dubut, by G. de Grof from Antwerp, and by the Italian Giuseppe Volpini.

It was in architecture, rather than in interior decoration, that the French made the greatest impact. Richer and more elegant interiors contrasted with the heavy style of the Baroque as French architects and decorators became involved in German projects. German architects, meanwhile, reciprocated by travelling to France. The palaces initiated by the Schönborn family in Würzburg, Pommersfeldern, and Mainz (Der Favorite, 1700–24), all drew heavily on the classicism of French Baroque in a style that is architectural rather than relating to the decorative arts.

French Rococo was adopted in Germany around 1735–40 and was strongly influenced by the engravings of Jacques de Lajoüe, Nicolas Pineau (1684–1754), and Juste-Aurèle

Meissonnier (1695–1750), and the elegant furniture designs of Gilles-Marie Oppenord (1672–1742). These designs featured shell-like *rocaille* ornament that was asymmetrical in form and arranged in accordance with C- and S-curves. Unlike France, German Rococo was used not only for interiors but also for external façades. French designs were independently interpreted and an autonomous style evolved, centred on Berlin, Munich, and Saxony. In Berlin, the principal representatives of this style were the architect G.W. Knobelsdorff (1699–1753), cabinet-maker Johann August the Elder (1710–81), and the court painter Antoine Pesne who also worked in palaces such as the Neue Palais and the Stadtschloss at Potsdam, at Sanssouci, and in Breslau and Rheinsberg. In Munich the leading exponent was architect and designer François Cuvilliés (1695–1768). In Saxony the most significant work was executed by Johann Christoph Knöffel (1686–1752) and Friedrich J.M. Stengel.

In Bavaria planar surfaces were filled entirely with carving and stucco work. In Prussia a more restrained version of Rococo was employed, with greater use of unornamented surfaces and, from 1750, the adoption of naturalistic features, as in the Voltaire Room at Sanssouci. The designs had a greater unity than was to be found in Early Baroque: furniture, panelling, and ceilings were devised in relation to each other and executed through the collaboration of craftsmen, stucco masters, and architects. In the case of Potsdam-Sanssouci (1744), the distinctive styles of Knobelsdorff, Hoppenhaupt, and August Nahl are detectable in the vestibule and the garden room, while J.A. Hülsmann contributed stucco work, carvings, and panelling, and J.M. Kambli and J.F. and H.W. Spindler the furniture (the latter also drawing on the designs of Hoppenhaupt). Antoine Pesne contributed his idiosyncratic "empty" frescoes. At the Residenz in Munich Cuvilliés worked alongside J.B. Zimmermann and the cabinet-makers Wenzeslaus Miroffsky and Joachim Dietrich; at the Residenztheater he worked with the sculptor Johann Richard Straub (1704–84).

It is characteristic of Rococo architecture and design, as of Baroque, that palaces and park buildings became smaller and associated with specific functions. This is evident in Ruhesitze or pavilions such as Mon Repos in Bayreuth; in Gartenschlösser, palaces set in large gardens, such as the Belvederes in Vienna and Weimar; in Jagdschlösser, hunting lodges, such as Falkenlust near Brühl; and in Lustschlösser, pleasure palaces, such as Monplaisir in Wolfenbüttel, or Ludwigslust.

Porcelain and lacquer cabinets also became popular from the late 17th century. Initially, Far Eastern porcelain, lacquer trays, silks, and individual art objects from Holland were acquired for such displays; later porcelain of German origin as well as Chinese lacquer furniture were increasingly used. Fine examples of such East Asian rooms are to be found in Schloss Weilburg, Schloss Arnstadt, Nymphenburg, and Bayreuth. Augustus the Strong had already commissioned designs from Pöppelmann for the Chinese Palace (1715–86) and the Indian-style Lustschloss at Pillnitz (1720–21). Most of the porcelain in such collections would have been supplied by the porcelain factory in Meissen, established in 1710. A number of other porcelain factories were subsequently founded: at Nymphenburg (1761), Höchst (1756), Ludwigsburg (1758), Fürstenberg (1747), Vienna (1717) and Berlin (1761), mostly supplying the various courts. Faience was widely acquired by the bourgeois and aristocratic markets. In 1661 the Dutch established their first ceramics factory in Germany at Hanau, followed by Braunschweig, Kassel, Berlin, Ansbach, Nuremberg, and Strasbourg. During the 18th century large display kilns were built, fine examples of which are to be found at Schönbrunn and at the monastery of St. Florian.

Another elaborate form of display took the form of cabinets decorated with intarsia – a form of inlay combining precious woods and ivory – and examples are to be found at Ludwigsburg and Wolfenbüttel. Of particular interest is the Amber Room, produced using East Prussian amber for the Schloss in Berlin and, in 1717, presented as a gift to Russia. French silk was the favoured wall covering for display rooms, with more rarely embroidered wallhangings (as in the Löwenburg in Kassel), wood panelling, or even feathers (as in Schloss Moritzburg, c.1725). Use was also made in the early period of fine vari-coloured marble incrustation (as in the marble cabinet of 1712 in Ludwigsburg), and around 1720–30 highly polished artificial marble was favoured and used for pillars (as in the Kaisersaal in the Residenz in Würzburg, or the Gartensaal at Sanssouci, Potsdam), entrance areas and, less frequently, living quarters.The more expensive artificial marble became a status symbol.

A further invention of the Baroque and Rococo eras was the Schönheitsgalerie, gallery of beauty, in which portraits of the ladies of the court were displayed. Rooms devoted to the celebration of hunting (as at Ludwigsburg, 1712) were less common, although entire palaces might be devoted to hunting, as at Augustusburg or at Hubertusburg in Saxony. Opportunities for bathing were rare in palaces, since most baths were found in specially designed buildings: the Badenburg in Munich, for example, or the Marmorbad in Kassel, designed by Pierre Etienne Monneot in 1722–28. Around 1710–20 the elaborate court ceremonial also conditioned the decoration of the Paradeschlafzimmer, state bedroom, with canopied beds and elaborate cupboards. Examples have survived in the Residenz of Munich, Schönbrunn and at Kassel.

The staircase was the hallmark of the owner of any palace, its impact achieved by refined architectural design and rich materials – at Bruchsal and in Salzdahlum there is even a grotto under the stairs. As in almost no other type of interior, with the exception of churches, the attempt was made to create a total work of art, with the intention that painting, sculpture, ornamentation, and architecture should combine to create a spatial and theatrical experience An early example is to be found at Schloss Moritzburg in Zeitz (1657–78), by J.M. Richter the Elder and Younger.

Monasteries occupied a special place within German cultural life. Abbots and bishops were worldly as well as religious leaders, and monasteries, often closely tied to princely families, usually followed secular models, apart from a tendency to display allegories of saints in their ceilings and wall paintings. Renowned ecclesiatical residences were to be found at Würzburg, Mainz, and Brühl. Especially attractive Rococo decoration is to be found in the palace of the Prince-Abbot in Kempten in the Allgäu and in the hunting lodges designed by Schlaun at Clemenswerth and Falkenlust.

The parts of a monastery most readily suited for worldly display were the library, the Kaisersaal, the Prälatur, and the refectory. Next to the chapel itself, the library was the most richly appointed interior, and most libraries had a gallery. Important examples can be found at the Benedictine monastery at Einsiedeln (1738 with stucco by Feichtmayr) and at Fürstenzell (c.1745, by J. Deutschmann, M. Günther, and Zeiller). The three-storey library of the Duchess Anna Amalia of Weimar, created by A.F. Strassburger (1761–66), was clearly intended above all for display, whereas the circular library built for Friedrich II at Sanssouci, with intarsia and elegant Rococo ornamentation, was reserved for purely private study and therefore less functional.

No significant independent bourgeois style of interior decoration existed at this time. In the cities, important architectural commissions were associated only with the palaces of highly placed court officials. Even those bourgeois buildings dating from the second half of the 18th century (the Ermelerhaus in Berlin, Haus Köppelmann in Lippstadt, the Rotes Haus in Monschau, 1762–65) followed models established by the court, albeit in a simplified form. A rare example of a type of interior decoration indebted to both rural and urban tradition is to be found in the architect Schlaun's own house, the Rüschhaus in Münsterland (1745–48).

With the buildings and interiors of Schloss Solitude and of Mon Repos, by Phillippe de La Guépière (1715–73), German architecture rejected the elaborate characteristics of Baroque and Rococo and adopted elements of classicism. An example of interior decoration from the transitional period, the Goldener Saal at Ludwigslust, the Residenz in Mecklenburg (1772–76), with ornamentation made of papier-mâché, already anticipates the rigorous articulation of classicism. In the 1760s purely classical schemes of interior decoration appeared, for example in Schloss Richmond near Braunschweig (1768) where the court architect Karl Christoph Fleischer articulated the space of the severe and symmetrical central oval room by means of bronze-toned pilasters interspersed with delicate arabesques and grisaille medallions with scenes of the Labours of Hercules. At Schloss Wörlitz the architects F.W. Erdmannsdorff and Friedrich Franz von Anhalt-Dessau drew directly on English architecture, interior decoration, and technical achievements. The stucco decoration in the dining room is in the Adam style, the chairs are copies of styles devised by Chippendale, and there are Wedgwood basalt ware vases grouped around the walls.

Attempts were made to incorporate the naturalness, beauty, and utility demanded by the Enlightenment using an idealized image of the Antique, an approach which influenced the contemporary visual arts as much as it was reflected in Winckelmann's interpretation of contemporary archaelogical discoveries or in the adaptation of the values of antiquity in the idylls and pastoral poetry of Lessing and other German writers. Classicizing motifs such as urns, rams' heads, and garlands were adopted with enthusiasm, inspired by the engravings of Piranesi and the drawings by Clérisseau. Ornamentation became subordinate to architecture.

In the decorative arts, reactions to the rediscovery of antiquity were reflected not only in the design of porcelain and stoves in classical forms but also in the evolution of the Landschaftszimmer or landscape room, intended to remind its owner of travels in Italy. Landscapes in the style of Claude Lorrain or Adam Elsheimer were painted on the walls or printed onto wall-coverings, as is the case in the Behnhaus in Lübeck (re-designed in 1800 by J.C. Lille). Occasionally exotic motifs were also employed, particularly after the publication of George Forster's account of his voyages around the world. Examples are to be found in the Turm Kabinett in the small palace on the Pfaueninsel in Berlin (1794, by Brendel). Chinese salons and mirrored cabinets remained fashionable; examples from this period are to be found in Wörlitz or at the Luisium in Dessau. The use of silver and gold elements or marble wall facings had, by now, virtually ceased.

Early classicism, established in Germany by the late 1770s, is also termed Zopfstil (plait or braid style), alluding to its frequent use of garlands and festoons, although this never attained the splendour associated with French interior decoration under Louis XVI. Such decorative schemes were generally implemented on a small scale, as seen in numerous examples from bourgeois interiors. A number of small manor houses in north Germany also have elegant classical interior decoration: in Herrenhaus Tüttendorf, in Schierensee, and in Altenholz, all with delicate stucco work by Michel Angelo Taddei.

As forms became comparatively simple and more architectonic, materials became more valuable; for example, the lavish examples of furniture from the renowned Neuwied firm of Abraham and David Roentgen, which imported items from Russia and France, and the furniture made of precious woods designed by Gontard for the Marmorpalais which had inlays of Wedgwood porcelain and of painted lacquer from the Stobwasser factory in Braunschweig.

Towards the end of the century German classicism became even more severe, dispensing almost entirely with ornamentation. This was similar to what was known in other parts of Europe as the Empire style, but such a name is not appropriate for German classicism as it never ceased to retain its practicality. The leading theorists, architects, and designers of German classicism were based in Berlin: Karl von Gontard (1731–91) designed the richly stuccoed Festsaal in Schloss Friedrichsfelde (1786) and the unadorned staircase in the military orphanage in Potsdam (1771–78); Carl Gotthard Langhans (1732–1808) is notable for a series of clearly articulated oval rooms, such as those in Schloss Bellevue (1791), and the decoration of the Marmorpalais in Potsdam.

Another new architectural form was the public bath, which emerged during the second half of the 18th century. The English city of Bath may have served as a model for such famous resorts as Bad Lachstät. There were a number of particularly elegant German Kurgebäude for those taking the cure, such as the interiors of the Palais and the salon building at Bad Doberan (respectively 1806–09 and 1819–21) by C.T. Severin.

While classical German furniture drew initially on French and English models, around 1800 it evolved a style of its own. In place of the furniture partially painted in subdued pastel colours that was typical of the 1780s, wood emerged in its own right, often bearing bronze mounts in the Antique style. Key items of this period were the chest of drawers and the escritoire, both frequently assuming forms reminiscent of architecture. Especially fine birchwood escritoires were produced around the Baltic coast.

The Napoleonic occupation of many parts of Germany and the demise, in 1806, of the Holy Roman Empire, hindered the rapid evolution of an autonomous German style. Only in Kassel, in the residences of Jérôme of Westphalia, brother of Napoleon, and in the powers tied to France such as Württemberg and Bavaria did the owners of palaces undertake any more ambitious rebuilding or redecoration. Among the furniture brought to Kassel, French pieces dominated; in Munich the French architect Puille redecorated certain rooms. At Ludwigsburg, starting in 1806, substantial alterations were implemented: the architect N.F. von Thouret was commissioned to decorate the Neues Corps of the Logis, where he collaborated closely with J. Klinckerfuss, a pupil of Roentgen, and the sculptor A. Isopi. The decoration has elements in common with the French and Russian Empire style and is among the best interior decoration to be created in Germany during this period.

German architecture revived slowly after the end of the Napoleonic occupation, with a new generation of architects not emerging until the 1820s. The leading architect, Karl Friedrich Schinkel, also contributed substantially to the design and decoration of interiors, for example in the Schloss Charlottenhof at Potsdam (1827–28) in which he sought to adapt to contemporary requirements the conception of a villa built in antiquity. Charlottenhof has a vestibule with a double staircase reminiscent of the staircases in the Luisenmausoleum at Charlottenburg or in the Neues Museum in Berlin. Apart from a room with a tented roof, the interior decoration is classicizing in style. One room is entirely decorated with Italian copper engravings, another painted in the "Pompeii red" inspired by the frescoes uncovered in excavations at Pompeii. At Tegel, Schinkel created an elegant vestibule with specially designed pillars and a hall for plaster casts of Antique statues. In a neighbouring building there were sculpted figures by Thorwaldsen and Rauch. Classicized buildings and interior decoration are to be found in the Roman Baths at Potsdam, and in the Orangery at Neustrelitz (1842), painted with motifs taken from the work of Raphael.

Furniture as well as entire decorative schemes were adopted from Antique forms. The dominant motifs in ornamentation were palmettes and acanthus leaves, with arabesques prominent in decorative painting. While the most favoured colours around 1800 were still pastels, subsequently ever more saturated colours were used and the overall colouring of rooms during the early 19th century became darker.

During the Biedermeier period – so-called after an invented literary figure – more attention was paid to interior decoration, comfort being a prime concern. Smaller living quarters required furniture that was practical and simple, and corner and folding tables were introduced. Woods such as walnut, mahogany, and sometimes stained pine, were especially popular, and a huge variety of chair types emerged. Cabinetmakers in Vienna proved especially inventive. Display cabinets and sideboards became objects of domestic curiosity, housing items of memorabilia, as well as decorative art. Other items included pieces made of iron such as flower pots, crosses, and ink wells, from the foundries of Gleiwitz and Berlin who also made spiral staircases; lamps with thin shades (Lithophanien); vases and decorative bowls in porcelain, made by Schumann (Berlin), Tiersch and Altwasser (Silesia); cut and coloured glass; decorative cloths and cushions embroidered at home. Lithographs and works in watercolour or gouache were displayed on the walls.

Germany: hall, Schloss Charlottenhof, Potsdam, by K.F. Schinkel, 1827–28

Inexpensive objets d'art and objects intended for display became accessible to a bourgeois market, among them the crater vases produced by the Königliche Porzellan Manufaktur in Berlin, and the Warwick vase worked in silver by J.G. Hossauer to patterns provided by Schinkel. The aim was to encourage German craftsmanship, which at the time was making little use of the latest technology. As a result of support from the Prussian court, Berlin gradually emerged as a centre of decorative arts and industry.

Among the most important architects working in Munich during the first half of the 19th century were Leo von Klenze and Friedrich von Gärtner. Gärtner designed not only classical interiors (Residenztheater, 1823), but also frequently cited Early Italian Renaissance motifs in exterior façades. In Braunschweig after 1831, T. Ottmer decorated the Residenzschloss (destroyed in 1961), a work already pointing to late classicism in its extensive ornamentation. In 1837–40 Georg Moller decorated the interiors of the palace in Wiesbaden. Drawing on the example of the rotunda of Schinkel's Altes Museum in Berlin, itself an adaptation of the Pantheon in Rome, Moller created a domed room with niches which were filled by sculpted figures by Schwanthaler.

The era of political Restoration brought a return to past traditions and styles. Whereas architects and designers had previously looked towards classical Italian models or to the Antique, after 1815 Gothic began to exert its appeal. Neo-Gothic interiors in combination with gardens were to be found in the Gotisches Haus in Wörlitz (1773) and the Meierei on the Pfaueninsel (1795). Like Chinese temples (Wilhelmshöhe), Moorish mosques (Schwetzingen), or ruins (the theatre at Sanspareil), these were regarded as embodiments of the exotic. The effects were generally a painterly combination of pseudo-

Gothic and the grotesque, similar to the designs popularized in England by William Halfpenny.

The first neo-Gothic castles included Landsberg (1836–40) by A.W. Doebner and K.A. Heidloff); Albrechtsburg and Reinhardsbrunn in Saxony (1827–35, by G. von Eberhard and Heidloff). Although Schinkel, who also built in this style, designed Neo-Gothic furniture, he mainly used old pieces in his interiors to evoke a sense of age and tradition. The building of Stolzenfels on historic ruins is ultimately to be understood as an act of reconstruction of the sort previously attempted in 1799 by Friedrich Gilly in his aquatint illustrations of the East Prussian fortress of Marienburg. During the completion of Cologne Cathedral (1842–80), systematic research into medieval Gothic was pursued. The secular counterpart is to be found in the decoration of the Wartburg near Eisenach. Here, the old decoration was partially restored and supplemented and the artist Moritz von Schwind painted a renowned Wartburg fresco. The decoration was completed in 1902–06 with the addition of glass mosaic by A. Oetken in the Elisabeth-Kemenate.

Later examples of Gothic Revival architecture in Germany include Marienburg near Hildesheim (1857–67, by Hase, with decoration by Edwin Oppler); the fortress at Wernigerode (1862–68); the hunting lodge at Letzlingen (1843) by King Friedrich IV and F.A. Stüler; and Schloss Drachenburg (1884), one of many Rhine fortresses. The success of this style is explained not only by the painterly effect but also by its appropriation as a national German style that was regarded, in the aftermath of the Napoleonic Wars, as anti-French. Among the books and volumes of designs published on Gothic architecture during the first half of the 19th century were K.A. Heidloff's *Ornamentik des Mittelalters* (1832–52) and Becker and Hefner-Alteneck's *Kunstgewerbe und Gerätschaften des Mittelalters* (1852).

A Rococo Revival was to be found in Russia by the late 1820s, in architectural projects commissioned by Tsar Nicholas I and his consort Charlotte of Prussia from the architect A.I. Shtakenschneider. It was probably Shtakenschneider who encouraged the Rococo decoration of the Imperial guest apartments in the Orangery at Potsdam (1851–64, by F. Stüler and Hesse), which had originally been built in the style of the Italian Renaissance, even including a Raphael Room with copies of famous paintings by the artist. In Vienna the Rococo Revival appeared at approximately the same time, sometimes drawing on French models, as in the decoration of the Lichenstein Majoratshaus, by F.A. Leistler. It was a style that was reflected in developments in the decorative arts and in the ornamentation of furniture, but it resulted in few great building projects. A late example is Schloss Linderhof. While earlier examples of Rococo Revival tended, unlike the 18th-century Rococo, to use ornament symmetrically and to combine Rococo and classical elements, this later instance incorporates an excess of ornamentation that is more theatrical than historical.

Although German Historicism may be found to have had precedents in the early 19th century, it emerged more strongly after the death of Schinkel and especially after 1850. Alongside the Neo-Gothic and the Rococo Revival, styles associated with the Renaissance were also popular. While Leo von Klenze and Schinkel had pre-empted such styles (respectively, in Palais Beauharnais of 1816, and in Palais Redern of 1832), the first high-point of the German 19th-century Neo-Renaissance is to be found in the Residenz at Schwerin of 1843–57, designed by Stüler and G.A. Demmler, based on the Loire châteaux. At Schwerin, above all in the panelled Ahnengalerie and the stuccoed throne room, classical ornamentation was partially combined with that derived from the Renaissance. Another important representative of the Neo-Renaissance style was Gottfried Semper (1803–79), the key historicist architectural theorist, architect, and decorator. Among his most important buildings were the Gemäldegalerie (1847–54) and the Opera in Dresden (1871–78); the polytechnic and the observatory in Zürich (1858–64) and new plans for the Hofburg and the Burgtheater in Vienna (1869–1903). While not rejecting the stylistic mixture of the mid-19th century, Semper also emphasised the need for a meaningful use of space and ornament.

Although it had been acceptable to use the Rococo Revival in interior decoration in a Neo-Gothic schloss, as in the royal Villa Berg near Stuttgart of 1845–53, or to combine Tudor and Rococo decorative styles, a much closer adherence to historical fidelity was now required. One of the most knowledgeable proponents of this idea was Duke Georg II of Meinigen, who assembled artists and craftsmen at his court, one of their aims being to create buildings in historicizing styles mostly tending to Neo-Renaissance. Alongside the leading 19th-century academies of Munich, Berlin, Karlsruhe, and Düsseldorf, the true centres for the dissemination of new architectural and decorative styles were the regional schools of applied arts, the Kunstgewerbeschulen and the technical universities, the Technische Universitäten. Those in Prague (established c.1803) and Vienna (1815), where leading architects and craftsmen often held teaching positions, were especially significant.

The interplay of industry, research, and artistry resulted in many innovations in interior design, including inexpensive textiles, pressed glass, stone pasteboard for use in place of stucco, pre-coloured terracotta to imitate carving work, linoleum, rubber, aluminium, and brass. It is significant that these new materials were often used as substitutes for natural elements. Increasing mechanization made the production of elaborate furnishing forms relatively inexpensive and mass-production became a key aspect of Historicism. As had been the case in the Baroque era, the appearance of the materials used counted for more than their authenticity. The decoration of interiors with ornaments and knick-knacks made this virtually inevitable, but it is necessary to distinguish between the houses and apartments of the upper bourgeoisie, where very valuable works of art might be found, and those of the lower classes, where copies of such works appeared, made with simple materials and poorly worked – silver-plated tin goblets, prints imitating oil paintings, plaster busts, and imitation bronze sculptures (Ladenbronzen). Of particular importance were the exhibitions of decorative art and, above all, the international exhibitions, which had a considerable influence on Germany's stylistic development.

Between 1860 and 1900, the Neo-Renaissance established itself as the leading style in German-speaking Europe. The centres of this development were Vienna and Munich where large exhibitions had promoted this style – respectively the Weltausstellung of 1873 and the Kunstgewerbeausstellung of 1876. After the removal of the Viennese fortifications in 1858, the Ringstrasse replacing them was planned as a centre of cultural and political life. The scheme included buildings in Neo-Gothic and Neo-Classical style (respectively, the town hall and the Parliament). In the case of the Burgtheater, the new wing of the Hofburg, and the Opera House (the latter of 1861–69 by Eduard Van der Nüll and August von Siccardsburg), both architecture and interior decoration drew on models from the Florentine and Venetian Renaissance. German Neo-Renaissance architecture also looked to the Flemish Renaissance and, at a later date, to the German Renaissance (above all the "Weser Renaissance", an example of which is the Palais Schack in Munich, built in 1872 by L. Gedon).

Many publications served to guide taste, among them Georg Hirth's *Das deutsche Zimmer der Renaissance* (1880) and *Das deutsche Zimmer der Gotik und Renaissance, des Barock und Rococo* (1886). The most explicit form of stylistic quotation in later German 19th-century decoration is to be found in wood panelling on walls and in coffered ceilings. The Neo-Renaissance style reached its high-point and its end in the historicist interiors of the Makart-style, called after the painter Hans Makart and characterized by especially dark colouring, rich drapery, and opulent ornamentation, as in Makart's paintings.

In the late 1880s the Baroque Revival and a new Rococo Revival – the so-called "third Rococo" – attained a popularity comparable to that of the Neo-Renaissance. While Rococo Revival, promoted by Princess Eugénie of France, had a considerable impact in the realm of fashion, it was relatively unsuccessful in interior decoration, although examples are to be found in some of the palaces built for Ludwig II of Bavaria – Schloss Linderhof by Georg Dollmann and others (with decoration, from 1870, by Franz Seitz and Eugen Drollinger) and Schloss Herrenchiemsee (1878–86). The façade, mirrored hall, and principal bedroom of the latter were modelled on the Château de Versailles, the copy far outshining the original in its excess of ornamentation. The Festsaal of Schloss Bückeburg is oriented more towards historical forms, with artificial marble, a fresco, and Rococo stucco work.

There remained a considerable difference between the decoration of private, bourgeois interiors, and that of public buildings, but a notable element of display now entered the private sphere. As a result of the ennobling of members of the bourgeoisie enriched through industry, the villa and the country house took on a special importance. Countless villas were built for factory owners, partly in competition with the houses of rich gentlemen farmers who did not wish to be outdone. Particularly elaborate examples of villas in a historicist style are the Lenbachhaus and the Villa Stuck in Munich (both built for successful artists) and the Villa Hügel in Essen (1870–72, by Rasch) – hardly distinguishable in their interior decoration from the houses of the landed nobility. Even in the apartment blocks built from the 1860s onwards an attempt was made to adapt elements from more expansive architectural projects, by adding elegant staircases and by decorating them with stucco work, paintings, lanterns, wall fountains, and reliefs; later there were elaborately designed lifts. Stuccoed ceilings and double doors were regarded as essential everywhere except in apartments opening on to backyards.

The interior decoration of public buildings such as town

Germany: entrance of Klein carpet shop, Hagen, by Peter Behrens, 1906–07

halls, universities, schools, and ministries aimed for a sense of dignity and status. After 1871 the predominantly Neo-Baroque interiors of courts of justice became more sumptuous, as if to underline their role in the new Imperial constitution. Examples are to be found in the Imperial court in Leipzig and the courts in the Schöneberg, Mitte, and Moabit districts of Berlin. Offices of the bureaucracy in general, as an expression of an era of Parliamentarianism, presented architects with a specific task. Yet another was represented by buildings of great cultural significance – opera houses and theatres – such as the Musikverein in Vienna and the Festspielhaus in Bayreuth. To these must be added a series of museums, some of which have in part retained their decoration, such as the Kunsthalle in Hamburg (Neo-Renaissance, 1863–68, by G.T. Schirrmacher and H. von der Hude) and, in Berlin, the Nationalgalerie (Neo-Classical, 1866–76, by A. Strack and Stüler). The interiors of the Bodemuseum in Berlin, meanwhile, were executed in the styles of various art historical eras.

Around 1895 Historicism attracted increasing criticism: it was argued that in its excess of ornamentation, the Neo-Renaissance stifled architecture, while the production methods employed were mechanical and superficial. The reaction of the furniture industry was to produce items decorated with simpler leaf and floral forms adopted from those of the French Art Nouveau. But at a more fundamental level no change occurred until the emergence of the group of architects assembled by the Grand Duke of Hesse in Darmstadt. These architects, who

Germany: hall, Zuckerkandl House, Berlin, by Hermann Muthesius, 1914

included Joseph Maria Olbrich, Hermann Obrist and Peter Behrens, committed themselves to a programme of radical reform, breaking with tradition, freeing architecture from superfluous stucco work, and opposing mechanical mass-production. Authentic materials were to be used in interior decoration. Around 1900 many of these architects built houses for themselves in Darmstadt, but these houses, with their unified style and special fittings, were considered elitist. The Jugendstil (named after the Munich weekly periodical founded in 1896) also employed leaf and floral forms but stylized them into almost geometrical shapes, resulting in more abstract forms approaching those favoured by the later Art Deco movement. In the work of the designer Henry van de Velde, however, inspired by his native Belgian Art Nouveau, the sweeping forms were softened and became more economical. His furniture designs were elegant and simple but relied on the use of expensive materials.

In Vienna a number of architects and painters were associated with the Secession (1897–1907). The most progressive of these was Adolf Loos (1870–1933). His Haus am Michaelerplatz and his American Bar Wien were designed to be free of ornament and to achieve their effect purely through their architectural form and the quality of the materials used, an approach propounded in his essay of 1908, "Ornament und Verbrechen" (Ornament and Crime). In the extravagant Secession building erected in 1897–1898, Joseph Maria Olbrich combined a simple basic form, with a dome covered in stylized laurel leaves, while Otto Wagner created a forward-looking interior in his glass-roofed central hall for the Vienna Postsparkasse (Postal Savings Bank) of 1904–06. Josef Hoffmann (1870–1956) who, in 1910, was to become the founder of the Österreichischer Werkbund, built a large number of villas and sanatoria. His designs for textiles and furniture partially reveal the influence of Scottish designer Charles Rennie Mackintosh. In planning the Palais Stoclet near Brussels (built 1905–11), he collaborated on the interior with the Viennese painter Gustav Klimt. A number of important schemes for interior decoration were produced by his friend and collaborator Koloman Moser.

English Arts and Crafts architecture also proved a source of great inspiration for Hermann Muthesius (1861–1927), whose book *Das Englische Haus* (1904–05) had a significant influence on the planning of garden cities in Germany as well as on interior decoration, even though Muthesius himself generally built private villas. Schulze-Naumburg's Palais Cecilienhof in Potsdam (1913–17) draws directly on English models.

Around 1900, alongside the many luxurious schemes of Jugendstil interior decoration, new demands and new decorative programmes arose in response to the widespread housing shortage. From 1893 a specially designed type of apartment block was built in Berlin by Alfred Messel and subsequently by Paul Mebes and others, which offered a more economical use of space, better sanitation, and more pleasant living rooms. The furnishing for such apartments became the province of the newly established Werkschülen (factory schools) and of organizations such as the Vereinigten Deutschen Werkstätten. The first German garden city, Hellerau, was built for workers in the Dresden factories by Muthesius (1908), H. Tessonow (houses and theatre, 1910–11) and Riemerschmid (workshops, 1911). All three architects were also involved in work on interior decoration, to which the furniture designers Schlecta and Wytrlik contributed.

In 1907 the Deutscher Werkbund was founded as an alliance of established artists and industrialists. Functioning as an advisory body, it provided new ideas on matters of design. The functional construction of furniture and inexpensive programmes of interior decoration served as a counter-movement to the elitist Jugendstil. New working-class residential districts were often built in a similar sort of "rural" style as that employed for many villas, with architecture expected to imitate a certain form of rusticity while promoting a healthier way of life.

In spite of its reliance on simplicity, the formal variety of German Jugendstil is clearly demonstrated in the fitting out of shop interiors (known now only through plans and photographs): Peter Behrens (1868–1940), chief designer and architect at AEG, designed the company's principal showroom in Berlin in 1910; August Endell (1871–1925), who adopted a Moorish-influenced Jugendstil, designed the Salamander shoe shop in Berlin in 1915 and the Elvira photographic studio in Munich in 1897; Messel, Riemerschmid and van de Velde redesigned the Berlin art gallery of Keller und Reiner; and in 1899 van de Velde designed a salesroom for the Havana company. The highpoint of technical innovation was the interior of the automat restaurant on Friedrichstrasse in Berlin (1904–05).

The interior decoration of department stores was particularly noteworthy, although the majority of these have not survived (an exception is the Kaufhaus zur Straussen in Görlitz). A highly influential architect in this area was Alfred Messel, who was engaged by the Berlin department store Wertheim. With his architectonically conceived interior courtyards, he created an imposing, yet still functional, architecture where techniques and materials such as marble incrustation and gilt bronze were used for both interior and external decoration. World War I brought many developments in German interior decoration and design to a halt. The re-orientation of the 1920s pointed in a variety of directions.

Following the emergence, in 1905–20, of Expressionist artist groups such as Der Blaue Reiter and Die Brücke and the literary association Der gläserne Kette, an Expressionist form of architecture evolved, turning above all to crystalline forms, the first examples appearing around 1919. Otto Bartning and the brothers Wassili and Hans Luckhardt created several interiors in this style. The use of pointed shapes in combination with brick is characteristic of the work of the north German architect Fritz Höttger, examples of which are to be found in Böttgerstrasse, Bremen, 1926–27, and the Chilehaus, Hamburg. In 1929–31 Hans Poelzig decorated the staircase and the façade of the Haus des Rundfunks in Berlin and is also known for his cave-like interior for the city's Grosses Schauspielhaus (1918–19). Founder-director of the Bauhaus School of architecture and design, Walter Gropius (1883–1969) was also interested in crystalline forms, as is evident in his work at the Holzhaus Sommerfeld (1920) and the Haus Otto in Berlin (1921–22). Erich Mendelsohn, meanwhile, designed angular furniture for his idiosyncratic Einsteinturm in Potsdam, built in 1920–21.

Expressionist buildings were erected throughout the 1920s, but from 1925 a new movement was underway, centred on the Bauhaus in Dessau and later in Weimar, led chiefly by the architects Walter Gropius, Mart Stam, and later Mies van der Rohe, who designed new furniture: key examples were Stam's *Freischwinger* or suspended chair, and the *MR* chair by Mies. In contrast to the Jugendstil era, design and manufacture were contemporaneous, and new combinations of materials were introduced, such as leather and steel.

During this period there was a strong interest in housing for workers combined with a leaning towards the traditional prewar forms which resulted in designs such as Grete Schütte-Lihotzky's "Frankfurt kitchen" and the contemporary estates of houses for workers in Frankfurt am Main designed by Ernst Meys. Such estates, and also those in Berlin (Siemensstadt, Weisse Stadt,1929–31), show that this development had lost none of its relevance decades later. The large architectural exhibition held in 1927 at the Weissenhof in Stuttgart represented both a simple and a more sophisticated standard of living, and architects such as Behrens, Stam, Gropius, and Le Corbusier designed houses and schemes of interior decoration for this event.

While industrial mass production remained prominent, particularly in the manufacture of textiles and pottery, there was also great emphasis on the individual artist-made object. Lilly Reich, for example, produced excellent textiles, Gunta Stölzl was known for her carpets and Gerhard Marcks for ceramic sculpture. There were also occasional examples of wall painting, as in the Bauhaus staircase. Oskar Schlemmer devised a mural for the country house at Mattern near Potsdam, designed in 1934 by Scharoun. Bruno Taut, who in 1924 published *Die neue Wohnung*, was noted for his particularly colourful treatment of walls. Rudolf Steiner's Anthroposophy system of mystical philosophy embraced ideas on decoration relating to the colour, materials, and geometry of interiors and exteriors. Examples of architectural projects accommodating these ideas are the second Goetheanum near Basle (1923–28) and numerous buildings by Hans Scharoun, including the Philharmonie in Berlin (1963).

Far less radical than the work of the Bauhaus, and consequently a great deal more popular with the German public during the 1920s, were the architectural forms of the Heimatstil. Fixed fittings, of the kind initially introduced by the Deutscher Werkbund, were modified and further developed by Bruno Paul during the 1930s. A leading influence by this period was the Reichsheimstättenamt (Imperial Office for Homes), under the direction of Robert Ley. The National Socialist regime especially encouraged the design of simple timeless furniture. At the 1934 Deutsche Siedlungs-Ausstellung held in Munich, extremely simple, even Spartan furniture was shown, the so-called "settler furniture", intended above all for young families. The Reichsausstellung Schaffendes Volk, held in Düsseldorf in 1937, showed interior decoration schemes intended for the bourgeoisie which were formally more elaborate and sometimes also ornamented, often in imitation of older patterns, though retaining an essentially unpretentious character. This sort of somewhat bleak simplicity was also to be found in the interiors of buildings designed for the governing cadres, as at the country houses of Carinhalle in Brandenburg, "Berghof" at Obersalzburg, and the Reichskanzlei in Berlin.

While it is true that Ludwig Troost continued to employ a simple Art Deco style, he nonetheless combined this with intarsia, using precious materials and expensive textiles. The illusion of a certain solidity in furniture and interiors was evoked by means of free borrowings from the Baroque, known as the Mastaba style, and Renaissance coffering. Brown and green dominated most colour schemes. Despite public rejection of the Bauhaus's ideas, its practical achievements were eagerly copied, above all in the realm of industrial design. The interiors of public buildings such as the Haus der deutschen Kunst in Munich, and the airport at Tempelhof outside Berlin followed classical models, while dispensing with ornamentation, appearing as a result both timeless and unostentatious. A favoured facing material was travertine and, more distinctively, marble.

After World War II there was a return to the ideas of the Deutscher Werkbund and of the Bauhaus. Because of the dearth of fresh materials and the extensive destruction of houses and apartment buildings, the first postwar furniture exhibitions, in 1949 (Neues Wohnen in Cologne and Wie wohnen in Stuttgart), showed items that were extremely simple, even primitive, often made of plywood. Leading designers of this period were Hans Schwippert, Otto Bartning, Paul Renner, Egon Eiermann, Hans Scharoun, Bruno Taut, Lilly Reich, and Hermann Henselmann.

During the 1950s German interior decoration and design followed American and Scandinavian models. Organic forms, natural and durable materials (teak and linen, for example) and ergonomic chairs and beds from Scandinavia remained in

Atrium of Haas Haus, Vienna, by Hans Hollein, 1985–90

the forefront into the 1960s. Popular American innovations included artificial materials (such as foam rubber, synthetic fibres, imitation leather) and coloured veneers. Furniture designed by Charles Eames, Harry Bertoia, and Eero Saarinen was especially fashionable, the US firm of Knoll International in Stuttgart producing versions of such designs or devising interior decoration for homes in collaboration with German architects. Leading German furniture designers included Egon Eiermann, Sep Ruf, Hans Gugelot, Herbert Hirche, and Eduard Ludwig.

Furniture of the 1950s and 1960s was not only smaller and lower than in the past, but also gave an overall impression of greater lightness. Tubular steel supports were often used, for instance, in the interior of the Hilton Hotel in Berlin (examples now in the Berlin Museum). More thought was given to developing space-saving forms of furniture – folding beds, combined dining and living rooms, integrated desk-tables or room dividers. Typical of German design of this period was the kidney-shaped table (designed in 1952 by Heinz Vetter) and the cone-shaped lamp, sometimes used in clusters. Furniture forms often recalled the paintings and sculpture of Hans Arp, Willi Baumeister, Ernst Wilhelm Nay, and Victor Vasarely.

Although there was little experimentation in political life during the Adenauer period (1949–63), the model city quarter of West Berlin, the Interbau (initiated in 1957), represents something of an exception. German and foreign architects were engaged to design both outer structures and their interiors. Staircases and assembly halls were used for display (as in the case of the Schillertheater in West Berlin), their decoration often incorporating wall sculptures or inner or outer murals.

After the formal division of Germany in 1949, the German Democratic Republic in the East looked initially to much the same models as did the Federal Republic in the West. The principal distinction was the imposition in the GDR of standard furniture designs, a Socialist-planned economy favouring standardization. Because the intention was to offer inexpensive furniture, cheap materials were used, often resulting in a decline in quality. The range of choice in furnishings, as in types of new residential accommodation, was limited, although great attention was paid to the design of public buildings, in which display invariably served a political, often propagandist, purpose. It was only during the 1970s that an attempt was made to catch up with international standards, notably in the building of the Palast der Republik in the centre of Berlin and in the Interhotels erected in various East German cities.

In the West the 1960s designs now readily termed modern had a traditional counterpart in the so-called Gelsenkirchen Baroque, a robust form of furniture and interior decoration, notable for its allusion to past styles, its reliance on forms evolved during the 1930s, and a somewhat uncertain sense of design. In line with the attempt to appeal to a largely working-class market, the style was named after a centre of the German mining industry.

During the 1960s a simpler, more geometric building style evolved, which was also reflected in interior decoration. In the now popular bungalows (Kaiserbungalow, by Sep Ruf) the design of walls and windows was of particular importance, although this was also true of public buildings, as demonstrated by the interiors of the Deutsche Oper and the Reichstagsgebäude in West Berlin (both 1961–72, by Paul Baumgarten). The West Berlin shopping arcade, the Europacenter (1963–65, by Werner Düttmann and Egon Eiermann), was notable for the restrained elegance of its reflective surfaces and coloured glass chandeliers.

While, on the one hand, an architecture favouring the use of substances such as wood, glass, and visible concrete evolved, architects also tended to use an increasing number of objects made of plastic and other artificial materials. Characteristic of 1960s interior decoration and furnishing were the fitted cupboard or wardrobe, the television console, the extendable sofa, and the low coffee table. Particularly popular were Verner Panton's plastic stacking chair (1960–67, for Vitra) and objects in spherical form (ash trays, televisions, lampshades).

With the advent of the mid-1970s oil crisis there emerged a need for an entirely new approach. A heightened awareness of the environment in combination with a preference for natural materials had a marked impact on interior decoration – wooden floors, fabric or cork floor coverings, and brown and green tones were favoured. An example of the transition between the garish colours of the early 1960s and the subdued tones of the end of the decade is to be found in the carriages of the Deutsche Bundesbahn's Inter-City trains which are decorated in orange, brown and green.

It is difficult to speak of an independent and distinctive German design in the 1970s and 1980s since national developments invariably emerge from interaction with a wider, international context. The futuristic metal forms employed in the Internationales Congress Centrum in Berlin (1975–79, by R. Schüler and U. Schüler-Witte) were to be found in public buildings of this period, but they were unpopular. The design of interiors incorporating solid wood, brick, and sisal floor covering, such as the library of the Philosophy Faculty of the Freie Universität in West Berlin (1982–83, by Hinrich and Inken Baller), may be seen as a reaction to such criticism.

The leading representative of Postmodernism in German interior decoration and design is Hans Hollein. His schemes for the interiors of shops in Vienna range from interiors for the candle-seller Retti (1964–65) to interiors for the jeweller's Schullin (1981–82), with its Egyptian ambience, and the Austrian Travel Agency, where decorative motifs allude to palms, mosque, and a Rolls-Royce. Hollein likes to combine a variety of stones (marble, sandstone) with polished metal or metal alloy. Other examples of Postmodern architecture and design in Germany are James Stirling's Wissenschaftszentrum in Berlin and his Staatsgalerie for Stuttgart. In the designs of the Viennese Coop Himmelblau, interiors and exteriors are merged, deconstruction itself being elevated to a method of design. The Pentagon design group of Cologne is also important, in particular for its original response to the influence of the Memphis design group and Italian Postmodernism in general. Leading contemporary design firms include Vorwerk, makers of carpets (which has collaborated with many architects), Vitra and Techta who both make office furniture.

MARCUS KÖHLER
translated by Elizabeth Clegg

Further Reading

Bauer, Margrit, Peter Märker and Annaliese Ohm, *Europäische Möbel von der Gotik bis zum Jugendstil*, Frankfurt: Museum für Kunsthandwerk, 1976

Bergdoll, Barry, *Karl Friedrich Schinkel: An Architecture for Prussia*, New York: Rizzoli, 1994

Binding, G. (editor), *Das deutsche Bürgerhaus*, Tübingen, 1959–86

Brix, Karl, *Baukunst der Renaissance in Deutschland*, Dresden: Verlag der Kunst, 1965

Campbell, Joan, *The German Werkbund: The Politics of Reform in the Applied Arts*, Princeton: Princeton University Press, 1978

Feldmeyer, Gerhard G., *The New German Architecture*, New York: Rizzoli, 1993

Günther, Sonja, *Das deutsche Heim: Luxusinterieurs und Arbeitermöbel von der Gründerzeit bis zum "Dritten Reich"*, Giessen: Anabas, 1984

Hempel, Eberhard, *Baroque Art and Architecture in Central Europe*, Harmondsworth: Penguin, 1965

Heskett, John, *Design in Germany, 1870–1918*, London: Trefoil, 1986; as German Design, 1870–1918, New York: Taplinger, 1986

Himmelheber, Georg, *Biedermeier, 1815–1835* (in English), Munich: Prestel, 1989

Hitchcock, Henry-Russell, *Rococo Architecture in Southern Germany*, London: Phaidon, 1968

Hitchcock, Henry-Russell, *German Renaissance Architecture*, Princeton: Princeton University Press, 1981

Hubala, Erich, *Renaissance und Barock*, Frankfurt: Umschau, 1968

Kadatz, Hans-Joachim, *Deutsche Renaissancebaukunst*, Berlin: Verlag für Bauwesen, 1983

Kreisel, Heinrich and Georg Himmelheber, *Die Kunst des deutschen Möbels*, 3 vols., Munich: Beck, 1968–73

Selle, Gert, *Geschichte des Designs in Deutschland*, Frankfurt: Campus, 1994

Thornton, Peter, *Authentic Decor: The Domestic Interior, 1620–1920*, London: Weidenfeld and Nicolson, and New York: Viking, 1984

Watkin, David and Tilman Mellinghoff, *German Architecture and the Classical Ideal, 1740–1840*, Cambridge: Massachusetts Institute of Technology Press, and London: Thames and Hudson, 1987

Whitford, Frank, *Bauhaus*, London: Thames and Hudson, 1984

Wilkie, Angus, *Biedermeier*, London: Chatto and Windus, and New York: Abbeville, 1987

Zukowsky, John (editor), *The Many Faces of Modern Architecture: Building in Germany Between the World Wars*, Munich and New York: Prestel, and London: Thames and Hudson, 1994

Gibbons, Grinling 1648–1721

British carver and sculptor

Grinling Gibbons was the most famous carver of his generation. From his arrival in England from Holland in about 1667 he helped establish the fashion for flamboyant Dutch-style carving which dominated the decoration of the late 17th century interior.

Gibbons probably trained in the workshop of Arnold Quellin (or Artus Quellinus) in Amsterdam. Quellin and his sons were involved in the decoration of the impressive Town Hall in Amsterdam. Gibbons first came to notice in March 1671 when John Evelyn showed a piece of his work to Charles II and, according to Evelyn, the king "cast his eye on the Worke but he was astonish'd at the curiositie of it, & .... considered it a long time." From this point on, Gibbons was commissioned to work at a number of royal palaces, commencing in 1677 in the King's Eating Room and Queen's Audience Chamber at Windsor Castle and continuing into the reign of William and Mary at Kensington Palace, Whitehall, St. James's and Hampton Court. Gibbons worked for the Board of Works as part of a team of carvers and decorators supervised by Sir Christopher Wren as Surveyor-General of the King's Works. But he was granted personal recognition in 1682 when he was given the official role of Surveyor and Repairer of Carved Work at Windsor by Charles II and a salary of £100 a year. He received further royal favour in 1693, when William III appointed him Master Sculptor and Carver in Wood to the Crown.

The royal commissions undertaken by Gibbons rank among his most important work and they helped establish his predominant influence in interior decoration. The virtuoso decorative carvings in limewood or oak which he carved in the form of overmantels and overdoors at Windsor, Hampton Court and Kensington Palace created a considerable impact at the time and were termed "incomparable" by contemporaries such as Evelyn. Gibbons and his studio also put their stamp on other interior decorative features, including carved door frames, picture frames, and marble chimneypieces. The bills of 1676–77 for the work at Windsor Castle (where Gibbons worked with Master Sculptor and Carver Henry Phillips) specify: "Severall sorts of Carved workes ... performed upon the Chimney peeces Pedestalls and picture frames of the Kings Greate and Little Bedchambers". His most exuberant work was reserved for the King's Chapel, Windsor (1680–82), carvings of sprays of palm and laurel which John Evelyn struggled to describe in 1683 as "stupendous and beyond all description .... the incomparable carving of our Gibbons, who is without controversie the greatest master both for invention and rareness of work that the world ever had in any age."

At Whitehall Palace from 1685 Gibbons supplied a carved chimneypiece surmounted by a crown and coat of arms for the Great Bedchamber and a marble altarpiece for the chapel which he worked on with Artus Quellinus. Gibbons was also responsible for a number of interior decorative features at Kensington Palace, including a pair of gilt overmantels in the Queen's Gallery, carved in 1691 with drapes and festoons. At Hampton Court, Gibbons and his team worked extensively on the new State Apartments built for William and Mary from 1689 to 1694, including carved door and window mouldings and overmantel and overdoor decorative fruit and floral drops. In the Chapel Royal in 1699 Gibbons carved the decoration for a reredos designed by Sir Christopher Wren.

Royal commissions were prestigious and an excellent showcase for skills, as contemporaries were able to visit palaces and admire Gibbons's work. After her visit to the King's Chapel, Windsor, in 1698 the diarist and traveller Celia Fiennes wrote of "the exactest workmanship in the wood carving ... the pattern and masterpiece of all such work both in figures, fruitages, beasts, birds, flowers all sorts, soe thinn the wood and all white natural wood without varnish ... here is a great quality."

Gibbons was also employed by the crown as a virtuoso carver and he was commissioned to carve exceptional pieces – for instance the panel sent as a gift in 1682 to Cosimo III, Grand Duke of Tuscany (the so-called *Cosimo* panel). In addition, William III commissioned him to decorate the catafalque erected in Westminster Abbey for the funeral of Queen Mary.

Queen Mary's catafalque was not Gibbons's only funerary work: he carved more than 30 funerary monuments in his workshop from the late 1670s onwards, including the important stone monuments of Robert Cotton (dated 1697) and the first Duke of Beaufort (dated 1700) in St. Paul's Cathedral.

Not all Gibbons's work, however, involved royal commissions; the fashion for carved work made popular by his work in royal palaces led to commissions for other important patrons. Gibbons's first major non-royal commission was for Charles Seymour, 6th Duke of Somerset, at Petworth House in Sussex, where he supplied a pair of elaborately carved picture frames and pendants for the Carved Room. He also worked at Badminton House, Gloucestershire, for the 1st Duke of Beaufort, where he carved a decorative overmantel for the great parlour incorporating dead game, woodcock and partridge. He carved one of his most beautiful commissions for Anne, Duchess of Buccleuch, at Dalkeith House who paid £800 to "Mr. Grin Gibbons for carving a marble Baster-leaf", of the story of Neptune and Galatea; a skilfully carved plaque, which is probably Gibbons's best work in marble. Similarly, at Blenheim he worked with decorative marble for Sarah, Duchess of Marlborough, and in 1712 he supervised eight men to work marble for the niches in the Saloon.

Gibbons also worked on several religious commissions. From 1696 to 1697 he carved two banks of choir stalls, the bishop's throne and stall in stone, oak and limewood at St. Paul's Cathedral, and he worked on the case and screen of the great west organ. His work for St. James's, Piccadilly, is typical of the type of carving Gibbons supplied for churches: Evelyn describes the "flowers & garland about the walls".

Grinling Gibbons undoubtedly played a key role in the history of late 17th century interior decoration. His richly decorated carving, teamed with Baroque painted rooms by Antonio Verrio (for instance at Burghley House) set the standard for the grand style of decoration in noble houses and palaces at this period. His style of carving was much admired throughout his life and he was believed with justification by contemporaries to be "incomparable".

SUSAN JENKINS

Biography

Born in Rotterdam, the Netherlands, 4 April 1648. Trained as a woodcarver, possibly in the Quellin workshops, Amsterdam or Antwerp, c.1665. Settled in England, c.1667. Married c. 1670: 5 sons and 6 daughters. Worked as a ship's carver, Deptford; "discovered" by John Evelyn and introduced to Charles II and Christopher Wren, c.1670. Active as a carver from the early 1670s, and as a sculptor and carver of monuments from the mid-1670s. In partnership with Arnold Quellin, 1681–83. Appointed Surveyor and Repairer of Carved Work, Windsor Castle, 1682; appointed Master Sculptor and Carver in Wood, 1693; appointed Master Carpenter to the King's Works, 1719. Admitted to the freedom of the Drapers' Company, 1672; appointed Renter-Warden, 1705: acted as Master, 1718–20. Died in London, 3 August 1721; buried at St. Paul's, Covent Garden.

Selected Works

Examples of Gibbons's drawings, mainly for projects at Hampton Court, are in Sir John Soane's Museum, London. Additional drawings and manuscript sources are listed in Beard 1989. Examples of Gibbons's carved work in wood can be seen at Blenheim Palace, Hampton Court, and Petworth House. The *Cosimo* panel is in the Pitti Palace, Florence.

Carvings

1676–92 Trinity College, Cambridge (library)

1677–78 Windsor Castle, Berkshire (carvings for various rooms, including the King's Eating Room and the Queen's Audience Chamber)

1681–82 *Cosimo* panel, for Cosimo III, Grand Duke of Tuscany

1690–91 Kensington Palace, London (carvings in Queen Mary's bedchamber, and frames for chimney glasses)

c.1692 Petworth House, West Sussex (Carved Room)

1697–1719 Hampton Court, Middlesex (carving for the King's Staircase, and in various interiors including the Chapel Royal, the King's bedchamber, and the music room)

Further Reading

The standard account of Gibbons's career appears in Green, 1964. For a more recent scholarly study see Beard 1989 which includes a chronology, a list of carved works, a list of monuments, and an annotated bibliography of primary and secondary sources.

Beard, Geoffrey, "Some English Wood-Carvers" in *Burlington Magazine*, CXXVII, October 1985, pp.686–94

Beard, Geoffrey, *The Work of Grinling Gibbons*, London: Murray, 1989

Beard, Geoffrey, "Grinling Gibbons" in *Magazine Antiques*, 135, June 1989, pp.1444–55

Colvin, H.M. and others, *The History of the King's Works*, vol.5: *1660–1782*, London: HMSO, 1976

Esterly, David, "Grinling Gibbons: The Final Experiments" in *The King's Apartments: Hampton Court Palace*, special issue of *Apollo*, August 1994, pp.32–39

Esterly, David, *Grinling Gibbons* (exhib. cat.), London: Victoria and Albert Museum, forthcoming

Green, David, *Grinling Gibbons: His Work as Carver and Statuary 1648–1721*, London: Country Life, 1964

Mowl, Tim, *Elizabethan and Jacobean Style*, London: Phaidon, 1993

Oughton, Frederick, *Grinling Gibbons and the English Woodcarving Tradition*, London: Stobart, 1979

Parker, James, "A Staircase by Grinling Gibbons" in *Metropolitan Museum of Art Bulletin*, June 1957, pp.229–36

Stewart, J. Douglas, "New Light on the Early Career of Grinling Gibbons" in *Burlington Magazine*, CLXVII, July 1976, p.508

Symonds, R.W., "Grinling Gibbons the Supreme Woodcarver" in *Connoisseur*, CVII, April 1941, pp.141–47

Thurley, Simon, *The Royal Palaces of Tudor England: Architecture and Court Life, 1460–1547*, New Haven and London: Yale University Press, 1993

Tipping, H. Avray, *Grinling Gibbons and the Woodwork of his Age*, London: Country Life, and New York: Scribner, 1914

Gillow & Co.

British upholsterers, cabinet-makers and makers of furniture; established c.1728; amalgamated as Waring & Gillow 1903

The famous furnishing business of Gillow of Lancaster (later Waring and Gillow) holds an important place in the history of furniture and furnishings. Not only were they among the longest established businesses in the trade who also held an enviable record of maintaining production of quality products, but their legacy of the Gillow Archive is also of great impor-

Gillow: design for a bedroom, c.1820

tance. The archive, housed at Westminster City Libraries, is an unsurpassed source of design and business history for much of the 18th and 19th centuries. The archive, parts of which date from 1731, includes account books, day books, cash books, bill books, drawing books, packing books, accounts and letters. However, the Estimate sketch books which date from the 1760s are perhaps the most valuable as they give detailed drawings of items, prices, materials, and list the name of the makers and the customer. This record is invaluable for considering provenance as well as building a picture of both taste and trade. In addition, during the last quarter of the 18th century the firm began the practice of stamping furniture items with their name which has been another valuable aid to identification.

The firm was established in 1728 by Robert Gillow who finished his apprenticeship and became a freeman of Lancaster in that year. The choice of Lancaster as a base for the business was eminently sensible. The importance of the port as a centre for the receipt of raw imports and for the export of finished goods made it ideal for an entrepreneur furniture-maker. Trade with the West Indies meant that finished furniture would be exported, and rum and sugar, as well as the all-important mahogany timber, would be imported through the port. This Atlantic trade was later followed by trading on the Baltic route which ensured supplies of oak and pine for the company.

In 1757 Richard Gillow, the eldest son, was taken into the business, having been trained as an architect; in 1769 another son, Robert, took over the running of the London branch which had been established some four years previously. Both these members of the family brought to the business differing skills which were invaluable in developing the firm. Robert Gillow died in 1772 but the family remained in control until 1814. This period under the management of Richard Gillow was one of the firm's most prosperous periods. Many large commissions were carried out for country houses, including Workington Hall, Cumbria, Tatton Park, near Manchester, and Farnley Hall, Otley. It was also a time of innovation in furniture design. Richard Gillow patented a method of extending dining tables by using a system of slides, and the firm also developed revolving bookshelves and the well-known small chests with writing slopes, allegedly called after the original customer, Captain Davenport.

In 1807 Gillows were described as being "among first grade manufacturers in London; their work is good and solid though not of the first class in inventiveness and style". In Lancaster similar comments were made. "Mr. Gillow's extensive warerooms, stored with every article of useful and ornamental mahogany furniture, are well worth the attention of strangers, as they are said to be the best stocked of any in this line, out of the metropolis". Both these comments reflect the demands of the solid, middle-class customers who were the mainstay of the Gillow business.

Although these favourable comments might have been encouraging, by the beginning of the 19th century trade was poor, particularly as the West Indies trade, which had been a mainstay of the business, declined rapidly. With the firm under new management from c.1814, they turned their attention to developing other parts of the trade, particularly commercial and institutional customers. Among many important commissions, the supply of furniture for the New Palace of Westminster was perhaps the most important. Indeed during the 1840s Gillows worked with Pugin furniture designs, many of which were to be reused for years to follow.

Gillows were represented at the 1851 Exhibition, and in 1863 they received the Royal Warrant as cabinet-makers to the Queen. Their involvement with exhibitions continued, and at the 1872 London International Exhibition they showed an oak sideboard (*Pet*) designed by Bruce Talbert, and a cabinet for display of Doulton reliefs designed by Charles Bevan. Talbert also designed a folding chair for the firm (c.1873) that remained available for some years. Other important designers associated with Gillows include T.E. Collcutt and E.W. Godwin.

In a vein similar to but less exalted than the Houses of Parliament contract, they also supplied furniture and fittings for work for the other Houses of Parliament (Cape Town), the new Law Courts, the St. Pancras hotel and other Midland railway hotels. They became important contractors for government buildings, museums, and exhibitions world-wide including work in Australia, India, the United States, Russia, Germany and France.

Despite the involvement of important contemporary designers, the 19th century middle-class taste for reviving designs, such as the Regency revival, meant that Gillows, with their retrospective records were well placed to meet the demand.

Although Gillows took over the bankrupt firm of Collinson and Lock in 1897, and had diversified into other work, including the fitting and furnishing of luxury yachts and ships (e.g., the Royal yacht *Victoria And Albert*, and Tsar Alexander III's yacht *Lividia*), there were financial problems. In 1903 a casual business partnership with the firm of S.J. Waring became official through takeover and the Waring and Gillow business was established.

In the 20th century the new business extended its manufacturing work to furniture and ship fitting as well as developing a retail business. The business of fitting out liners such as the *Lusitania*, *Caronia*, and *Queen Mary* cushioned the firm against the worst effects of the Depression. In 1906 Waring and Gillow opened a retail furniture store in Oxford Street, London and they had soon built up a reputation for high quality furnishing and interior decoration. A rather conservative initial approach to design was complemented by the founding of a Modern Art Department for the store in 1928. This was an important landmark in 20th century interior design. The appointment of Serge Chermayeff as director was perceptive, while a similar venture was being opened by Gillows in Paris under the direction of Paul Follot. Follot designed the Waring and Gillow exhibit at the 1929 Salon des Artistes-Décorateurs.

In 1932 another financial collapse led to a restructuring, but in 1953 the business was finally taken over and broken up, and in 1962 the Lancaster workshops were closed, effectively bringing to an end a remarkable enterprise.

CLIVE D. EDWARDS

Selected Works

The Gillow Archive, containing day-books, sales ledgers, order books, estimate sketch books, accounts and correspondence, is held by Westminster City Library, London. Additional collections of designs are in the City Museum and Art Gallery, Lancaster, and the Victoria and Albert Museum, London. Examples of Gillow furniture survive *in situ* at Tatton Park, Cheshire; Workington Hall, Cumbria; and Broughton Hall, Yorkshire.

Interiors

1771	Heaton Hall, Lancashire (furniture)
1786–90	Farnley Hall, Otley (furniture)
1788–89	Workington Hall, Cumbria (furniture for the dining room, hall, and billiard room, and some upholstery): John Christian Curwen
1810–12	Parlington Hall, Aberford (furnishings for bedrooms, library, dining room and study): Richard Oliver Gascoigne
1811–12	Tatton Park, Knutsford, Cheshire (furniture and upholstery for the library, bedrooms and dressing rooms): Wilbraham Egerton
late 1840s	Houses of Parliament and New Palace of Westminster, London (furniture)

Further Reading

For a recent scholarly history of Gillow see Boynton 1995.

Beard, Geoffrey and Christopher Gilbert (editors), *Dictionary of English Furniture Makers, 1660–1840*, London: Furniture History Society, 1986
Boynton, Lindsay, "Sir Roger Newdigate's Commodes" in *Antique Collector*, 1991, pp.12–15
Boynton, Lindsay, *Gillow Furniture Designs, 1760–1800*, Royston, Hertfordshire: Bloomfield Press, 1995
Burkett, Mary and others, *A History of Gillows of Lancaster*, Lancaster: Lancashire County Museum Service, 1984
Coleridge, Anthony, "The Firm of Gillow & Co. at Blair Castle" in *Connoisseur*, 157, 1964, pp.88–93
Collard, Frances, *Regency Furniture*, Woodbridge, Suffolk: Antique Collectors' Club, 1985
Gilbert, Christopher, *Furniture at Broughton Hall* (exhib. cat.), Leeds: Leeds City Art Galleries, 1971
Gillow's: A Record of a Furnishing Firm During Two Centuries, London: Harrison, 1901
Goodison, Nicholas and John Hardy, "Gillows at Tatton Park" in *Furniture History*, 1970, pp.1–40
Hall, Ivan, "Patterns of Elegance: The Gillows' Furniture Designs I" in *Country Life*, CLXIII, 8 June 1978, pp.1612–15
Hall, Ivan, "Models with a Choice of Leg: The Gillows' Furniture Designs II" in *Country Life*, CLXIII, 15 June 1978, pp.1740–42
Nichols, Sarah, *Gillow and Company of Lancaster, England: An Eighteenth Century Business History*, M.A. thesis: Newark: University of Delaware, 1982
Nichols, Sarah, "Gillows of Lancaster: The Role of the Upholsterer" in *Abbot Hall Quarterly Bulletin*, June 1984, pp.7–11
Nichols, Sarah, "Furniture Made by Gillow & Co. for Workington Hall" in *Magazine Antiques*, June 1985, pp.1353–59
Nichols, Sarah, "A Journey Through the Gillows Records" in *Antique Collector*, February 1986, pp.36–39
Nichols, Sarah, "A Pair of Gillows' Curricle Chairs: Lancaster or London?" in *Leeds Art Calendar*, 101, 1987, pp.10–16
Reynolds, S., "The Gillow Family and Their Furniture" in *Nineteenth Century*, 4, Winter 1978, p.69–74
Tilson, Barbara, "Modern Art Department, Waring and Gillow, 1928–1931" in *Journal of the Decorative Arts Society*, 8, 1984, pp.40–49

Girard, Alexander 1907–1993

American architect, interior, furniture and textile designer

Although born in New York, Alexander Girard grew up in Florence, Italy where he acquired the informal first name of "Sandro". He was trained as an architect in London at the Architectural Association, graduating in 1929 and winning a Florence Traveling Scholarship. He established an office in Florence but gave it up to take up further study at the Royal School of Architecture in Rome graduating there in 1931. He returned to New York and maintained an architectural office there from 1932 to 1937 when he moved to Detroit, where he practised architecture and interior design and operated a retail showroom. In 1947 he moved his office and showroom to the wealthy suburb of Grosse Pointe, Michigan where he also designed his own spacious and comfortable house, remarkable for an interior using strong color tones of orange, yellow, blue, magenta and purple along with thoughtfully displayed objects from his growing collection of folk art. Objects from Mexico and South America, paper kites and Victorian decorative objects contributed to the overall effect.

In 1943 Girard was the designer of a cafeteria for the International Detrola Corporation in Detroit and also worked for a time as an industrial designer for that firm. His Detrola table radio was one of the first radios to escape from the habit of disguise in anachronistic cabinets based on historic (often Gothic) furniture. In 1946 he was the interior designer for several projects including offices and a cafeteria for the Ford and Lincoln motor companies in Detroit.

He was associated with the architect Eero Saarinen on several projects including the General Motors Research Center in Detroit, the Irwin Miller residence in Columbus, Indiana and was a member of the winning team in the competition for the St. Louis Memorial, which was ultimately built as a great arch gateway to the American west on the bank of the Mississippi River. Other clients included the Cummins Engine Company of Columbus, Indiana, John Deere Co. (for an historic exhibit at their corporate offices) in Moline, Illinois, and the Detroit Institute of Arts for the 1949 exhibit *For Modern Living*. Girard became known for a number of exhibit designs including *Design for Modern Use, made in U.S.A*, (1950), *Good Design*, (1954), *Textiles and Ornamental Arts of India* (1955), all at the Museum of Modern Art in New York, and the traveling exhibition *Nehru: His Life and His India* (1965) designed in collaboration with Charles Eames.

Girard's relationship with Eames, established during his Detroit years while Eames was at Cranbook Academy, near Detroit and the subsequent relationship with George Nelson, the Design Director for Herman Miller, the leading American maker of modern furniture, led to Girard's 1952 appointment as the Design Director of a textile division established by Herman Miller. The three designers worked together as a team to shape the design philosophies and policies of Herman Miller, forming what came to be regarded as a prime example of the role that outstanding design can play in the success of a manufacturing firm.

Girard's efforts in finding sources and directing the development of lively color and strong, generally geometric pattern made the textiles offered by Herman Miller unique in their color and variety. He was also the designer of showrooms for Herman Miller in Grand Rapids, Michigan and in San Francisco. In 1953 he moved to Santa Fe, New Mexico and built there an office and residence that became a showcase for his colorful folk art collections that eventually grew to include some 100,000 objects, now held by the Girard Foundation.

In 1961 he was responsible for the establishment of a retail shop in New York known as Textiles and Objects (T & O) which featured his fabric designs along with many small decorative objects that reflected his interest in folk art. He continued an interior design practice with commissions for restaurant design that included the New York restaurants of La Fonda del Sol (1960, with a South and Central American theme) and L'Etoile (1966, with a French theme). Girard's restaurant projects included, along with interior design, development of related graphics, table settings, and small details down to the ash trays and matchbooks.

In 1965, Girard took over all visual design for Braniff International airlines and designed all their airport facilities, graphics, and aircraft interiors. His aircraft color schemes, which involved painting the planes in unconventional bright solid colors (such as yellow, pink and violet), were both startling and spectacular. For Braniff, he designed a complete line of furniture for use in interiors which was then introduced as part of the Herman Miller furniture product line in 1966. Although spectacular and colorful, this product group did not achieve commercial success and was withdrawn after a short time.

Girard was the recipient of many honors and awards including an honorary Royal Designer for Industry diploma from the Royal Society of Arts, London (1965) and a gold medal from the American Crafts Council (1985). Girard is now best known for his role as a colorist and for his development of varied and imaginative decorative patterns. Girard's folk art collection now occupies a wing of the International Folk Art Museum in Santa Fe.

JOHN F. PILE

Biography

Alexander Hayden Girard. Born in New York City, 24 May 1907. Studied at the Architectural Association School, London, 1925–29; Royal School of Architecture, Rome, 1930–31; New York University, 1932–35. Employed in several architectural offices in Rome, Florence, London, Paris and New York, 1929–32; active as an independent architect and designer in Florence, 1930, New York, 1933–37, and Detroit, 1937–52; settled permanently in Santa Fe, New Mexico, 1953. Design director, textile division, Herman Miller Inc., Zeeland, Michigan, from 1952. Active as a designer of exhibitions from late 1940s. Established Girard Foundation for collections of toys and folkcraft objects, Santa Fe, 1961: donated to the State of New Mexico, 1978; opening of the Girard Wing of the Museum of International Folk Art, Santa Fe, 1982. Received numerous prizes and awards including Medal of Honor, American Architectural League, New York, 1962 and 1965; Elsie de Wolfe Award, American Institute of Interior Designers, 1966; Allied Professions Award, American Institute of Architects, 1966; and Gold Medal, American Crafts Council, 1985. Honorary Royal Designer for Industry, Royal Society of Arts, London, 1965. Died in Santa Fe, 1993.

Selected Works

Examples of Girard's textiles and furnishings are in the Museum of Modern Art, New York. His collection of children's toys and folk art is in the Museum of International Folk Art, Santa Fe.

Interiors

1930	G. Uzielli Apartment, Florence, Italy (interiors)
1946	Ford Motor Company, Dearborn, Michigan (office interiors)
1948	Girard Residence, Grosse Pointe, Michigan (building and interiors)
1952	Rieveschel House, Grosse Pointe, Michigan (building and interiors)
1953	Herman Miller Inc., Grand Rapids, Michigan (showroom)
1955	*Textiles and Ornamental Arts of India*, Museum of Modern Art, New York (exhibition layout)
1958	Irwin Miller House, Columbus, Indiana (building by Eero Saarinen; interiors by Girard)
1958	Herman Miller Inc., San Francisco (showroom)
1959–60	La Fonda del Sol, New York (restaurant interiors and furnishings)
1961	Herman Miller Inc., New York (Textiles and Objects shop interiors)
1965	Braniff International Airline, Dallas, Texas (corporate visual programme including airport facilities, aircraft interiors and furnishings)
1965	*Nehru: His Life and His India*, Ahmedabad, India; New York; London; Washington, DC; and Los Angeles (exhibition layout, with Charles Eames)
1966	L'Etoile, New York (restaurant interiors and furnishings)
1982	*Multiple Visions*, Girard Wing, Musuem of International Folk Art, Santa Fe (inaugural exhibition layouts)

Girard designed textiles and wallpapers, 1952–64, and a furniture range, 1967, for Herman Miller Inc., Zeeland, Michigan; glassware, ceramics and leather goods for Georg Jensen Inc., New York, 1955.

Publications

The Magic of a People: Folk Art and Toys from the Collection of the Girard Foundation, 1968

Further Reading

A bibliography appears in Larsen 1975.

Caplan, Ralph, *The Design of Herman Miller*, New York: Whitney Library of Design, 1976

Fehrman, Cherie and Kenneth, *Postwar Interior Design, 1945–1960*, New York: Van Nostrand Reinhold, 1987

Hiesinger, Kathryn B. and George H. Marcus III (editors), *Design since 1945* (exhib. cat.), Philadelphia: Philadelphia Museum of Art, and London: Thames and Hudson, 1983

Larsen, Jack Lenor, "Alexander Girard" in *Design Quarterly*, 98–99, Walker Art Center, Minneapolis, 1975, pp.31–40, 61–62

Lockwood, Charles, "A Perfectionist at Play" in *Connoisseur*, 212, January 1983, pp.92–98

"Out-Manoeuvering the Pain Plane" in *Interiors* (US), 125, February 1966, pp.99–105

Pool, Mary Jane and Caroline Seebohm (editors), *20th Century Decorating: Architecture and Gardens: 80 Years of Ideas and Pleasure from House and Garden*, London: Weidenfeld and Nicolson, and New York: Holt Rinehart, 1980

Pulos, Arthur J., *The American Design Adventure, 1940–1975*, Cambridge: Massachusetts Institute of Technology Press, 1988

Storey, W. R., "International Decorators of Today: Alexander Girard" in *The Studio*, July 1938

Giulio Romano (Giulio Giannuzzi) c.1499–1546

Italian painter, architect and designer

The pupil of Raphael, inheritor of his studio and the only influential artist of his period to be born in Rome, Giulio Romano created some of the most memorable and important decorations of his time and occupies a central position in Renaissance interior decoration of the first half of the 16th century.

Born some time between 1492 and 1499, Giulio was immersed in the material and historical fabric of Rome from the very beginning of his life. He grew up surrounded by visual stimuli; even the street on which he was born was overshadowed by one of the most significant of the city's monuments, Trajan's column. And the nationalistic, political upheavals that dominated the first few years of the century – namely the declaration of the Roman Republic in 1511 and the expulsion of the French in 1512 – must have influenced his attitude towards the vast, decaying monuments of ancient Rome. The juxtaposition of ancient and modern buildings which characterised the city's appearance during this period is later reflected in his startling decorative schemes, particularly in the Palazzo del Te.

Giulio Romano's training under Raphael not only established his credentials as an artist, they also enabled him to develop his own artistic ideas. The *Battle of Constantine* fresco

(1520–21) for the Sala di Constantino in the Vatican is an example of Raphaelesque ideas translated into Giulio's style which, in turn, was derived from Roman sarcophagi reliefs. Unlike most other Italian artists of this period, including Raphael, Giulio's interest in Roman Antiquity can be traced to specific Roman sources. And as the more flamboyant Mannerist style began to take root, especially in Florence, Giulio's own brand of Mannerism was based in Roman Classicism. Roman Classicism also appealed because of its formality. The Villa Lante, built for Baldassare Turini da Pescia c.1523, demonstrates a lightness and simplicity of design which are indebted to formal classical design solutions.

In October 1524 Giulio left Rome for Mantua to work for Duke Federigo II Gonzaga. Mantua was a city of 40,000 inhabitants and was both prosperous and politically strategic. Federigo was extremely ambitious and instituted a programme of building that would reflect the wealth and importance of the city. Giulio was offered overall control of this programme and the prospect of unprecedented artistic freedom and power no doubt strongly influenced his decision to work for Federigo.

Giulio's most famous commission for the Duke was the Palazzo del Te (1526–31). The resulting decoration reflects not only the ambitions of his patron and the Gonzaga family but also those of Giulio himself. No area is left undecorated and the effect is a sumptuous display of gold, colour and marble and an overwhelming affirmation of Ducal wealth.

There were two phases of decoration. The first, carried out between 1526 and 1529, was the decoration of the north-east apartment and the Sala di Psiche. Based on the story of Cupid and Psyche, the scheme is dominated by a fresco of the marriage ceremony, while two windowless walls are united by one continuous narrative of the wedding feast. In the second phase (1530–35), Giulio uses decorative schemes to emphasise the power and status of his patron. The walls are filled with representations of Roman triumphs and demonstrations of Olympian strength. In the Sala dei Venti, the Gonzaga badge, Mount Olympus, appears in the centre of the ceiling, and the room includes 16 medallions depicting scenes of hunting, fighting, and struggles between gladiators arranged under the twelve signs of the zodiac.

The Sala dei Giganti indicates the sheer scale of ideas and techniques that Giulio was capable of. There are no breaks between walls or ceiling and the scheme has no start or finish. Even the door has been painted out. The frescoes depict the battle between the giants and the gods as the giants attempt to storm Olympus. In a triumph of *trompe-l'oeil* painting, the dome appears to collapse as classical columns crash down upon the heads of the giants.

The decoration of Te was complemented by the work Giulio undertook between 1536 and 1540 redecorating the Palazzo Ducale in Mantua. Of particular interest is the Camerino degli Uccelli which displays grand design on a miniature scale. A mirror vault crowns an elaborate architectural scheme through which is woven an equally elaborate decorative scheme of classical architecture, putti, satyrs and beasts. Giulio continued to work on a grand scale in the Appartamento di Troia which was designed to house Federigo's paintings by Titian.

Not all Giulio's decorative work comprised scenes of artful, yet meticulously contrived, frivolity and flattery. In 1540, Federigo died and Giulio became painter to his brother, Cardinal Ercole Gonzaga. This change of patron naturally led to a change of emphasis in thematic composition.

Giulio already had some experience of non-secular work. Around 1532 he had undertaken a commission to decorate the apse of Verona Cathedral. His painted an Assumption of the Virgin whose design was not dissimilar to that of his work in the Sala dei Giganti at Te. Indeed, so shocking were the twelve apostles that one contemporary observer railed against "the indecency of the caricature with which he portrayed those holy men". His work for Cardinal Ercole demonstrates a more serious approach, particularly in his work on the reconstruction of Mantua Cathedral (1544). And at San Benedetto Po the decoration is polychromatic with a restricted decorative scheme set within a geometric linear system.

Giulio Romano was the least derivative of all the Italian painters of the period. Despite, and perhaps partly because of his training under Raphael, he was a maverick artist whose originality of design reflects the relative independence allowed him by his tutor. He was a keen individualist who did not return the favour of artistic freedom to his own pupils. Instead he preferred glorious artistic isolation and the certainty of absolute artistic supremacy in Mantua.

DORCAS TAYLOR

See also Mannerism; Trompe-l'Oeil

Biography

Born Giulio Pippi in Rome c.1499. Apprenticed to Raphael as a young boy, working with him in the Vatican *Stanze* and loggias, c.1509–20. After Raphael's death he contributed to the interior of the Villa Madama in Rome, c.1520, and to the completion of the *Stanze*, until c.1525. Employed as architect, and designer of interiors, pageants and the applied arts for the Gonzaga family in Mantua, from c.1524. Became citizen of Mantua, 1525; appointed Vicar to the Court and Superior General of Gonzaga buildings and streets of Mantua (city architect), 1526. Married in 1529: 2 daughters and 1 son. Built his own house in Mantua from 1538. Died in Mantua, 1 November 1546.

Selected Works

1514–24	Vatican Palace, Rome (fresco decoration, Sala dell'Incendio and Sala di Constantino): Pope Julius II
1526–31	Palazzo del Te, Mantua (architecture and fresco decoration including the Sala dei Cavalli, Sala dei Giganti, Sala delle Aquile, Loggia di Davide, Sala di Psiche, Sala of Attilio Regulus, Loggia della Grotta, Loggia delle Muse): Duke Federigo II Gonzaga
1530	Pageant for entry of Emperor Charles V to Mantua (painted decorations): Duke Federigo II Gonzaga
1531	Pageant for marriage of Duke Federigo II Gonzaga and Margherita Paleologo (painted decorations): Duke Federigo II Gonzaga
1536–38	Cabinet of Caesars, Palazzo Ducale, Mantua (interior decoration, Appartamento di Troia): Duke Federigo II Gonzaga
1538–44	Giulio Romano House, Mantua (building and interiors)
c.1544	Palazzo Pippi, Mantua (building)
c.1544	Cortile della Cavallerizza (building): Duke Federigo II Gonzaga

Further Reading

For a comprehensive biography, catalogue, and further bibliography see Hartt 1958. Verheyen 1977 is the most complete account of the Palazzo del Te. For recent scholarly essays see *Giulio Romano* 1989.

Brown, Clifford Malcolm, "The Decoration of the Private Apartment of Federico II Gonzaga on the Pino Terreno of the Castello di San Giorgio", in Carlo Marco Belfanti (editor), *Guerre, stati e città: Mantova e l'Italia Padana dal secolo XIII al XIX*, Mantua: Arcari, 1988, pp.315–43
Chambers, David and Jane Martineau (editors), *Splendours of the Gonzaga* (exhib. cat.), London: Victoria and Albert Museum, 1981
Forster, Kurt and Richard J. Tuttle, "The Palazzo del Te", in *Journal of the Society of Architectural Historians*, XXX, December 1971, pp.267–93
Forster, Kurt and Richard J. Tuttle, "The Casa Pippi: Giulio Romano's House in Mantua", in *Architectura*, 3, 1973, pp.104–30
Giulio Romano (exhib. cat.), Milan: Electa, 1989
Giulio Romano: Atti del Convegno Internazionale di Studi su "Giulio Romano e l'espansione europea del Rinascimento", Mantua, 1–5 October 1989, Mantua: Accademia Nazional Virgiliana, 1991
Gombrich, Ernst, "The Sala dei Venti in the Palazzo del Te", in *Journal of the Warburg and Courtauld Institutes*, 13, 1950, pp.189–201
Hartt, Frederick, "Raphael and Giulio Romano, with Notes on the Raphael School", in *Art Bulletin*, 25, 1944, p. 67ff
Hartt, Frederick, "The Chronology of the Sala di Constantino", in *Gazette des Beaux-Arts*, series VI, 36, 1949, pp.301–08
Hartt, Frederick, "Gonzaga Symbols in the Palazzo del Te", in *Journal of the Warburg and Courtauld Institutes*, 13, 1950, pp.151–88
Hartt, Frederick, *Giulio Romano*, 2 vols., New Haven: Yale University Press, 1958; reprinted New York: Hacker, 1981
Leland Hunter, George, "Scipio Tapestries now in America", *Burlington Magazine*, 29, 1916, pp.56–66
Magnusson, Borje, "A Drawing for the Façade of Giulio Romano's House in Mantua", in *Journal of the Society of Architectural Historians*, 47, June 1988, pp.178–84
Martin, Ursula W., *Giulio Romano: A Working Bibliography*, Santa Monica, CA: Getty Center, 1989
Thornton, Peter, *The Italian Renaissance Interior, 1400–1600*, London: Weidenfeld and Nicolson, and New York: Abrams, 1991
Venturi, Adolfo, "Pitture nella Villa Madama di Giovanni da Udine e Giulio Romano", in *Archivio storico d'arte*, 2, 1889, p. 157 ff.
Verheyen, Egon, "Die Sala di Ovidio im Palazzo del Te", in *Römisches Jahrbuch für Kunstgeschichte*, 12, 1969, pp.161–70
Verheyen, Egon, *The Palazzo del Te in Mantua: Images of Love and Politics*, Baltimore: Johns Hopkins University Press, 1977

Glasgow School

At the close of the 19th century Glasgow witnessed a distinctive flowering of the applied arts allied to a new emphasis on the design of artistic interiors. The Glasgow Style emerged initially at the Glasgow School of Art in the early 1890s and reached its peak around the turn of the century, before fading by 1910. This singular style is characterised by an economy of line and ornament and is inspired by natural forms; its sudden appearance in the "Second City" of the British Empire was all the more striking for its industrial and commercial context.

The pivotal figure of the Glasgow Style was the architect and designer Charles Rennie Mackintosh (1868–1928); he played a significant role in the invention of the style's distinct visual language. His interior design work gave real expression to the notion of the interior as a work of art. It was Mackintosh's Glasgow School of Art building, completed in 1899, that provided the inspirational setting for the emerging style. However, Mackintosh took almost no personal interest in the development of the broader Glasgow Style. He did not teach at the School of Art and his focus remained steadfastly on his own work. His contribution in the context of the School must be seen as part of a collaborative partnership involving his fellow students and friends Herbert MacNair and the two Macdonald sisters, Frances and Margaret. And the work of this group (The Four) itself should be considered in relation to developments in design instruction within the School.

In 1885 the appointment of Francis H. Newbery as headmaster gave a new emphasis to design instruction within the School of Art. His enthusiasm for the Arts and Crafts movement and background in teaching at South Kensington, allied to an enthusiastic support of individuality, underpinned his ambitions for the School. In 1893, the technical art studios were opened, offering courses in glass staining, repoussé, metal working, stone carving and book binding. As the decorative arts gained greater prominence, the first graphic works by The Four began to appear. Combining stylized plant and human forms to ambiguous and challenging effect, they were given an uncertain reception when first exhibited. By the middle of the decade, the Macdonald sisters, working in the new studios, had translated these graphic experiments into the applied arts, producing beaten metal candlesticks, mirror frames and sconces. If the establishment reaction to their work was occasionally hostile, the work of The Four clearly inspired their fellow students and laid the foundations for the Glasgow Style. With Newbery's encouragement the style rapidly became established within the School. A common linear quality appeared in the work of the decorative art studios with stylized plant forms, birds and butterflies becoming key motifs. The excesses of Continental Art Nouveau were avoided in favour of a tighter, sparer linear quality.

Although Mackintosh played a part in these developments, almost all of his own decorative art production was completed in connection with specific interior commissions. The Macdonald sisters were both full-time students at the School, while Mackintosh was an evening class student and working to further his professional architectural career. His contribution to the emergence of a Glasgow Style within the context of the Glasgow School of Art was not as significant as the part he played in the development of the Glasgow Style interior.

In 1896, the Glasgow tea room proprietor Kate Cranston opened her new premises on Buchanan Street. Tea rooms on Argyle Street followed in 1897. The interiors of both featured the work of Mackintosh and his contemporary, George Walton. For many Glaswegians and visitors to the city alike, these tea rooms were their only brush with the "artistic" Glasgow interior, and they had considerable impact. Walton had formed his company of Ecclesiastical and House Decorators in 1888. Through the early 1890s he had been working towards increasingly integrated interiors, expanding his firm's output from painting and paper hanging to include furniture, textiles, metalwork and stained glass manufacture. As the more experienced of the two, Walton was given overall responsibility for Buchanan Street. Mackintosh's contribution was limited to the provision of stencilling in the stairwell and two interiors. His uncompromising and symbolically-charged schemes did not sit altogether happily with Walton's more

Glasgow School: design for a bedroom by George Logan, c.1904

conventional work. At Argyle Street, Walton again retained overall control while Mackintosh designed all the furniture. These interiors were some way short of absolute stylistic unity, but the work of the two designers did display a common freshness and originality and, in the interiors designed by Walton alone, demonstrated what could be achieved by giving a single designer responsibility for every aspect of an interior design.

The tea rooms were Walton's last major contribution to the Glasgow scene. He had departed for London before the completion of Argyle Street. Mackintosh was left to take centre stage. In 1898 he designed his first white domestic interior at Westdel, a house in Queen's Place, Glasgow. One of the beautifully executed drawings for the scheme was shown in Glasgow the following year, and its exhibition was followed by a number of Glasgow designers exhibiting scenes for interiors which were self-consciously artistic in style: none more so than George Logan's fairy-tale interiors. Logan was chief designer for the Glasgow furnishing firm of Wylie and Lochhead, and it was this firm which attempted to harness the new style to more commercial ends.

At the Glasgow International Exhibition of 1901, the firm commissioned a pavilion containing three interiors, each designed in its entirety by one of their designers. Logan contributed the library, E.A. Taylor the drawing room and John Ednie the bedroom. None of these designers is known to have undertaken a complete interior scheme before this date and the opportunity to do so now must have sprung from Wylie and Lochhead's ambition to be seen at the forefront of modern interior design and to capitalise on the growing reputation of the Glasgow Style work being produced at the School of Art. The designers involved would certainly have been aware of Mackintosh's increasingly sophisticated interior schemes produced around 1900, evidenced in the deliberate arrangement of the furniture and the "tendency towards the straight up" in the design of the furniture itself, while the colour schemes of greens, pinks and purples link them to the earlier Cranston tea room schemes.

Wylie and Lochhead did not require their customers to commission complete interiors. The commissions that they did undertake following the exhibition were more piecemeal, with the existing possessions of the client often competing with the introduction of a new stencilled frieze or suite of furniture. The Glasgow Style interior on Mackintosh's rigorous model failed to materialise in any quantity in the city. Ironically, one of the most complete of the post-exhibition Wylie and Lochhead interiors was completed not in Glasgow but suburban Birmingham. Mackintosh alone developed a sufficiently sympathetic, if limited, set of clients to allow him to produce interiors that were in themselves works of art. But by 1910, Mackintosh was nearing the end of his productive years in Glasgow. Two of the three designers responsible for the Wylie and Lochhead exhibition rooms had left the company, while at the Glasgow School of Art the vigour and invention that had been so much a part of the early Glasgow Style had been dissipated. The Glasgow Style, it seems, ultimately promised more than it achieved.

DANIEL ROBBINS

See also Mackintosh; Walton

Further Reading

Billcliffe, Roger and Peter Vergo, "Charles Rennie Mackintosh and the Austrian Art Revival" in *Burlington Magazine*, CXIX, November 1977

Burkhauser, Jude, *Glasgow Girls: Women in Art and Design, 1880–1920* (exhib. cat.: Glasgow City Art Gallery), Edinburgh: Canongate, 1990
Cooper, Jeremy, *Victorian and Edwardian Furniture and Interiors*, London: Thames and Hudson, 1987
Cummings, Elizabeth, *Glasgow 1900: Art and Design* (exhib. cat.), Zwolle: Waanders, 1992
Eadie, William, *Movements of Modernity: The Case of Glasgow and Art Nouveau*, London and New York: Routledge, 1990
The Glasgow Style 1890–1920 (exhib. cat.), Glasgow: Glasgow Art Gallery and Museum, 1984
Helland, Janice, *The Studios of Frances and Margaret Macdonald*, Manchester: Manchester University Press, 1996
Kaplan, Wendy (editor), *Charles Rennie Mackintosh*, New York: Abbeville, 1996
Larner, Gerald and Celia, *The Glasgow Style*, Edinburgh: Harris, and New York: Taplinger, 1979
Moon, Karen, *George Walton, Designer and Architect*, Oxford: White Cockade, 1993
Nuttgens, Patrick (editor), *Mackintosh and His Contemporaries in Europe and America*, London: Murray, 1988

Gobelins Tapestry

French tapestry workshop; established 1663

The village of Gobelins, on the outskirts of Paris, derived its name from the Jean Gobelin family of scarlet-dyers who established a workshop there c.1440. A tapestry workshop was established in the Boulevard St. Marcel close to the old dyeworks in 1607 by two Flemish weavers, François de la Planche of Oudenarde and Marc de Comans of Antwerp. They took over the property of the Gobelins family and their Italian associates, the Canayes. These workshops were purchased on behalf of King Louis XIV in 1662 by the finance minister Jean Baptiste Colbert, in order to establish the Manufacture Royale des Meubles de la Couronne (Royal Factory for the Furnishings of the Crown) to make furnishings for the king's palaces. Charles Le Brun, artistic director of Nicolas Fouquet's Maincy tapestry workshop at Vaux-le-Vicomte was appointed artistic director in 1663. Le Brun's principal task was to produce designs for tapestries and other types of furnishings and have them executed correctly.

In 1667 the Gobelins workshop was organized under letters patent incorporating it as the Manufacture Royale des Gobelins. Approximately 250 craftsmen including tapestry weavers, painters, bronze workers, furniture makers, and others were employed to provide furnishings for the royal residences, particularly the Palace of Versailles. The Gobelins tapestry workshop became the most important of its time.

The tapestry workshop had one low-warp and three high-warp workshops. From 1665 onward the factory had its own dyeworks using mainly vegetable dyes with mineral mordants. The weavers and their families lived in houses with gardens, an arrangement that lasted until the 20th century. Apprentices were given instruction in drawing before they began to specialize. They could become master-craftsmen after a six-year apprenticeship and four years of service.

Weavers in the Gobelins workshops had more freedom in executing designs with regard to choice of color than had been usual in Renaissance workshops. Le Brun made his designs in oils specifically for tapestry in the classical Baroque style, and did not attempt to copy paintings. He had a large team of painters who prepared cartoons and models. Each painter had his own specialty and worked on specific elements of the design such as architectural subjects, animals, or scenery.

In 1664 the first tapestries, a set of portières, *The Fames* and *Mars* originally started at Maincy, and *The Acts of the Apostles* from cartoons by Raphael, were completed. That Le Brun was well acquainted with the Italian style is evident in *The History of Alexander*, a series with wide, intricate borders and a large range of colors.

Until the year 1683, multiple copies were made of each set of tapestries produced at the Gobelins workshops so they could be sent as royal gifts to other European countries. These were intended as propaganda to impress other rulers with the greatness of the king. For twenty years the major part of the resources of the manufactory were used exclusively for this purpose.

Colbert died on 6 September, 1683, and his successor, the Marquis de Louvois, kept Le Brun, who had fallen from royal favor, nominally in charge, but the Controller of Buildings, M. de la Chapelle-Bessé, took over actual direction of the workshop. The old spirit of grandeur and opulence was replaced by one of economy. Work was stopped on *The History of the King*, a series of fourteen tapestries based on the life of Louis XIV designed by Le Brun and begun in 1665, which required a great deal of gold thread. A set of these is now in the Mobilier Nationale in Paris. The weavers turned to copying master painters, notably Raphael, Giulio Romano and Nicolas Poussin.

Le Brun died in 1690 and was succeeded by the painter Pierre Mignard, who himself died in 1695. Mignard changed the role of Gobelins tapestry from historical and political display to one of entertainment and amusement, using pleasant themes and fables.

From 1694 to 1699 the Gobelins workshops were closed down because of the exhaustion of the royal treasury as a result of the War of the League of Augsburg. After reopening in 1699 they produced only tapestries. Following the reopening, the workshop was under control of the Superintendent of Buildings with an artistic director in charge of design. These included Robert de Cotte, 1699–1735; Jean-Baptiste Oudry, formerly director of the Beauvais factory, 1736–55; François Boucher, 1755–70; and Noël Hallé, 1770–83. Oudry's chief interest was in "verdures", or landscape themes based on nature. He insisted on exact reproduction of the artists' cartoons, a policy that caused great conflict with the weavers who considered it a prerogative of their craft to interpret designs in their own way, as they had previously. The weavers gave in, but the conflict continued until Oudry's death in 1755.

Gobelins tapestries in the 18th century were intended to please the elegant society of the day. *Scenes from Opera, Tragedy and Comedy* and the *Gods' Sequence* were the most notable. With the weaving of *The Story of Don Quixote* after a design by Charles-Antoine Coypel in 1714 the center scene of the tapestry was reduced in size, and an elaborate *alentours*, or decorative border, was introduced. The *alentours* simulated a damask panel with garlands, ribbons, birds, etc., and came to fill a major part of the tapestry. *The Gods* set by Boucher begun in 1758 with *alentours* by the flower painter Maurice

Gobelins Tapestry: Louis XIV visiting the workshop, c.1644

Jacques was the finest of this type. Leading French painters provided cartoons, but the tapestries again had to compete with oil paintings for wall space. By the 1770s the Gobelins workshop was making pastoral scenes for furniture upholstery in order to compete with Beauvais, which had increasingly focused its production on furniture covers.

Under the director of the dyeworks, Jacques Neilson (director 1768–84), the color range of dyes was increased by use of fugitive vegetable dyes in order to reproduce the colors of oil paintings. Neilson was head of the low-warp factory and introduced this and other technical improvements to obtain higher quality and fidelity of reproduction without increase in cost. Unfortunately the dyes on surviving tapestries have faded badly.

In the 1770s the factory adapted its production to Neo-Classicism under the painter, Pierre-François Cozette. The factory closed temporarily in 1793 and was reorganized in 1794 following the French Revolution. The Comité de Salut Public (Republican Committee of Public Safety) examined the subjects of tapestries in production, condemning 120 as reactionary and 136 as frivolous. Many residences and public buildings were sacked by the revolutionaries, and their tapestries destroyed.

Napoleon's government in 1805 instructed the Gobelins workshop to choose subjects from the history of France, particularly from the Revolution, and increase production to furnish the imperial palaces. Several sets on Napoleonic themes were executed from 1806. Director Charles-Axel Guillaumot introduced chemical dyes, again increasing the color range to match that of paintings. These colors were also subject to fading. Chevreul, director of the laboratory from 1824 to 1889, developed 14,400 shades of silk that enabled the weavers to make faithful copies of paintings by old masters and contemporary artists such as Ingres and Horace Vernet. Throughout the 19th century and on until the 1940s the Gobelins tapestries were copies of every type of painting.

During the Second Empire of Napoleon III, from 1852 to 1870, the Gobelins workshop again served as a factory for the production of tapestries for the imperial residences. The factory was nearly ruined by fire in the 1871 insurrection of the Commune of Paris and the fall of the Second Empire, but it survived and continued producing historical tapestries. Jules Guiffrey, the administrator and artistic director from 1885 to 1908, tried to revive interest in tapestries by changing designs from copies of paintings to something more appropriate to the tapestry medium, but he was unable to convince the cartoon artists and dyers to accept this. In 1911 Gobelins gave up the use of natural colors and adopted bright colored synthetic dyes based on anthracene that proved even more fugitive. Director Gustave Geffroy's finely detailed copies of Impressionist paintings have all faded to dull greys and wine tints. The factory returned to natural colorfast dyes in 1939.

The Gobelins and Beauvais workshops amalgamated into the Manufacture National de Beauvais aux Gobelins in the 1930s. Since 1937 the Gobelins factory has been a branch of the Mobilier National and works only for the French government, producing tapestries for government buildings.

Constance A. Fairchild

See also Tapestries

Further Reading

The massive and authoritative history of the Gobelins Tapestry factory is Fenaille, 1903–23.

Fenaille, Maurice, *Etat Général des Tapisseries de la Manufacture des Gobelins depuis son Origine jusqu' a nos jours, 1600–1900*, 6 vols., Paris: Hachette, 1903–23

Manufacture Nationale des Gobelins: Etat de la Fabrication 1900 à 1990, Lyon: Collection Mobilier National, 1991

Meyer, Daniel, *L'Histoire du Roy*, Paris: Editions de la Réunion des Musées Nationaux, 1980

Standen, Edith Appleton, *European Post-Medieval Tapestries and Related Hangings in the Metropolitan Museum of Art*, 2 vols., New York: Metropolitan Museum of Art, 1985

Stein, Fabian, *Charles Le Brun: La Tenture de l'Histoire du Roy*, Worms: Wernersche, 1985

Weigert, R.-A., *French Tapestry*, London: Faber, and Newton, MA: Branford, 1962

Gödöllő Colony

One of the more far flung reaches of English Arts and Crafts influence was the colony which formed at Gödöllő, to the north of Budapest in Hungary, at the beginning of this century, where a group of artists, craftsmen and craftswomen gathered to form the Gödöllő Workshop.

Aladár Körösfői-Kriesch, a painter and designer, had moved to Gödöllő with his family in 1901. In 1904 the Ministry of Culture donated the looms of a bankrupt weaving factory and charged him with reviving the skill of weaving in Hungary by setting up a school of weaving. The graphic artist and designer Sándor Nagy, who moved there in 1907, was joined by others, including workers from the weaving factory. Traditional techniques were revived and only natural dyes were used. As well as carpets and tapestries, the Workshop soon expanded to produce embroideries, frescoes, furniture, leatherwork, ceramics, mosaics and stained glass. Other artists involved included Leo Belmonte, Rezho Mihály, Laura Kriesch, Jenö Gyorgy Remsey, István Zichy, Mariska and Carla Undi, Árpád Juhász, Ervin Raáb and Endre Frecskai. Some were primarily painters rather than designers, and there was also a school of sculpture, directed by Ferenc Sidló. Also associated with the colony were the architect István Medgyaszay and the designer turned architect, Ede Thoroczkai Wigand. Medgyaszay built studio houses for Sándor Nagy and Leo Belmonte in Gödöllő. The Workshop rapidly achieved national and international success, through displays at exhibitions. This resulted in commissions for fittings and furnishings for several major architectural projects in the period up to World War I. These included the Nemzeti Salon, an exhibition hall of 1906–07, and the Academy of Music, 1907, both in Budapest, and the Cultural Palace of 1912, in Marosvásárhely (now Tirgu Mures in Romania).

In wishing to revive the unity of art and life, while combining strong spiritual beliefs with social conscience, the members of the Gödöllő Colony were heavily influenced by the writings of John Ruskin and William Morris, as well as Nietzsche and Tolstoy. Ideas of the value of community spirit and of the simple life had become increasingly popular across Europe, particularly in artistic and intellectual circles. Körösfői-Kriesch wrote a book on Ruskin and the Pre-Raphaelites, in 1905, *Ruskinröl és az angel praerafaelitekról*, and said that "most art is to be found where art encounters life, in the spirit of Ruskin". Emphasis was therefore put on the applied arts and on integrating all the arts to create the *gesamtkunstwerk*. Living in such an environment would then further encourage a productive and fulfilling existence.

In Hungary at the beginning of the 20th century, this idealistic and philosophical approach coincided with both a political desire to find a means of expressing a national identity – as in many other European countries around this time, Finland for example – and a social policy to revive cottage industries and improve the lives of the rural peasantry. Their ability to find a combined solution to these various needs accounts for the success of the Workshop. The Gödöllő circle placed more emphasis on their social role than the Wiener Werkstätte or the Deutscher Werkbund, their nearest equivalents at the time, and were possibly more successful in achieving their social aims than Morris. They involved the wider community by providing training in craftwork and by employing local people in the workshop. However they did not always aim to achieve the Arts and Crafts ideal of the unity of designer and maker.

In their own work they combined motifs and patterns from Hungarian folk art with myths and fairy tales. They studied regional art and architecture and collected examples of folk art. They also popularised the use and display of such work in interiors. Thoroczkai Wigand created a museum of Székely folk art in his flat in Buda and Körösfői-Kriesch contributed an article on peasant art to the *Studio* magazine of 1911. The folk arts of the various Hungarian regions had been studied and indeed exhibited throughout the world from the 1850s onwards, but were only now seen as "art" and as exemplifying the ethical value of integrating art into the everyday life of local communities.

In deriving from a tradition which predated industrialisation and the pervasive influence of the Austro-Hungarian Empire, these arts had symbolic value in reflecting the origins of the Hungarian people and were seen as a valid source for a new national style. Carved and flower-painted beams and furniture, wooden columns with carving derived from Transylvanian grave posts, curtains and carpets with stylised patterns, all showing the influence of folk art, can be seen in the interiors of the studios of Körösfői-Kriesch and Sándor Nagy of 1905. Nagy's studio was exhibited at the 1905 Art Lover's Exhibition, with another version as "The Home of an Artist", shown to great acclaim, at the Milan International Exhibition of 1906. Here the interior was designed by István Medgyaszay with a beamed ceiling and carved wooden columns and balustrade. The furniture was by Sándor Nagy and embroideries by Laura Kriesch.

The series of frescoes by the Gödöllő master Mariska Undi in the Népszálló, or People's Hotel in Budapest, of 1911, shows scenes of peasant life in the various regions of Hungary, including many examples of folk art and costume. In Gödöllő tapestries and stained glass, patterns and motifs abstracted from peasant carvings and embroideries were often combined with figurative subjects. These might portray actual peasant life, shepherds and women in national dress (Körösfői-Kriesch's *Women of Kalotaszeg* tapestry of 1908), or be based

Gödöllő Colony: design for a Home of the Artist, 1906 Milan Esposizione Internazionale

on myths of the origins of the Hungarian people. The latter show heroes such as Attila the Hun or depict Hun-Magyar stories such as *The Hunt of the Magic Deer* or the life of Toldi, a popular hero, from the poems of János Arany (tapestry by Sándor Nagy of 1917). In many examples, such as Nagy's stained-glass window for the Hungarian Exhibition Hall at Venice (1909) with its reconstruction of the wooden palace of Attila the Hun, ancient heroes were shown wearing Transylvanian costumes or living in Kalotaszeg or Székely houses, or sometimes incorporating Transdanubian (another region of Hungary) elements in the architecture. Such subjects were already popular in the fine arts but depicted in a more realistic, historicist style than the stylised, decorative approach used by the Gödöllő designers. As many of the original myths had Asian and even Mughal sources, Islamic motifs, already prevalent in Hungary from the years of Turkish rule and preserved in folk art, were a strong additional design influence. This can be seen, for example, in Körösfői-Kriesch's decoration of the vaulted entrance hall of the Marosvásárhely Cultural Palace.

The combination of these exotic and vernacular sources, together with the international influence of Art Nouveau, gives a unique flavour to the best work of the Gödöllő designers. While some of their work shows strong medievalising tendencies, in other examples, such as the Academy of Music interiors, the Art Nouveau or Jugendstil element is more evident. Here the Körösfői-Kriesch murals show the Viennese influence of Klimt, as does the geometric gold ornamentation of the rest of the interior. Other works by Körösfői-Kriesch, such as the mosaic fountain depicting *The Siege of Aquileia* in the Hungarian Pavilion at Venice of 1909 and his mosaic for the Mexican National Theatre of 1908–21, show similar geometric influence. Such influence was of course evident in Hungarian Art Nouveau interiors of the period, and as other artists were often involved in these commissions as well as members of the Gödöllő Workshop, their work was often only a part of the overall result. In some of Körösfői-Kriesch's painted figurative panels and the work of Sándor Nagy generally, there is less Jugendstil influence and a more lyrical feeling, comparable to English Pre-Raphaelitism and Arts and Crafts designs. This is particularly true of Nagy's stained glass such as the *Kisfaludy* panel of 1907 and the series of windows he designed for the Cultural Palace at Marosvásárhely, of 1912, carried out by Miksa Róth whose studio worked on most of the stained glass and glass mosaics designed by the Gödöllő Workshop. The subjects of these windows were taken from Székely folk ballads, including one showing Kata Kádár, a Hungarian Ophelia, mixing Christian symbols with pagan and magical elements. Their strong compositions and intricate designs, making much use of leading and jewel-like colours, combined with their symbolic content make them some of the most effective work of the Gödöllő Colony, as is the Cultural Palace as a whole.

Sándor Nagy had earlier designed a window, *Hunting Gentry*, for the theatre at Vezsprém by Medgyaszay of 1907, in a lighter style with more clear glass, which combined with the simplicity and general lightness of the interior does seem more modern in design than the later but more archaic and medieval Cultural Palace. Nagy's later work in the 1920s for public commissions became increasingly academic. He remained in Gödöllő, and took charge of the weaving workshop after Körösfői-Kriesch died in 1920, although the rest of the workshop closed down. The outbreak of World War I had put an end to commissions and some members had already moved on.

DIANA HALE

See also Arts and Crafts Movement

Selected Collections

Documentation and examples of work by members of the Gödöllő Colony are in the Museum of Applied Art, and the National Gallery of Hungary, both in Budapest, and in the Local History Collection, Gödöllő City Museum, Hungary.

Further Reading

For a complete history of the Gödöllő workshops see Gellér and Keserü 1987; a shorter introductory account appears in Keserü 1988.

Éri, Gyöngyi and Zsuzsa Jobbágyi, *A Golden Age: Art and Society in Hungary, 1896–1914* (exhib. cat.), London: Barbican Art Gallery, 1989

Gellér, Katalin, "Hungarian Stained Glass of the Early 20th Century" in *Journal of Stained Glass*, XVIII, no.2, 1986–87, pp.204–05

Gellér, Katalin and Katalin Keserü, *A Gödöllő i Müvésztelep* (The Gödöllő Artists Colony), Budapest: Corvina, 1987

Gellér, Katalin, "Romantic Elements in Hungarian Art Nouveau" in Nicola Gordon Bowe (editor), *Art and the National Dream*, Dublin: Irish Academic Press, 1993

János, Gerle, Attila Kovács and Imre Makovecz, *A Szazadfordulo magyar epiteszete* (Hungarian Architecture at the Turn of the Century), Budapest: Szépirodalmi Konyvkiadó, 1990

Keserü, Katalin, "Decorative Arts and Sources of Architectural Symbolism" in *Journal of the Decorative Arts Society*, 11, 1987

Keserü, Katalin, "The Workshops of Gödöllő: Transformations of a Morrisian Theme" in *Journal of Design History*, 1, no.1, 1988

Keserü, Katalin, "Vernacularism and its Special Characteristics in Hungarian Art" in Nicola Gordon Bowe (editor), *Art and the National Dream*, Dublin: Irish Academic Press, 1993

Levetus, A. S., "Hungarian Architecture and Decoration" in *The Studio Yearbook of Decorative Art*, London: The Studio, 1912

Magdolna, Lichner (editor), *Tapestries in the Collection of the Museum of Applied Arts*, vol.2, Budapest: Museum of Applied Arts, 1989

Godwin, E.W. 1833–1886

British architect, furniture, interior and theatre designer

The intimate of J.M Whistler and Oscar Wilde, E.W. Godwin was one of the most successful and innovative architects and designers of his generation. A key figure in the development of late 19th century Aestheticism, he pioneered the use of Anglo-Japanese styles in decoration and furniture design and created interiors that were remarkable for their subtle blend of colours and their simple, uncluttered lines. He was also one of a small group of Victorian designers whose work was admired abroad. His designs for furniture, in particular, were frequently copied in the United States and he exercised an important influence on progressive Austrian and German taste. More recently, he has been hailed as a forerunner of Functionalism, and his emphasis upon form rather than ornament or style prefigures many of the ideas associated with the Modern Movement.

Godwin's early work was executed in a fairly conventional Ruskinian mode and the commissions for Northampton (1861) and Congleton (1864) Town Halls represent successful, if not wholly original, exercises in the popular Italianate and French Gothic styles. By the late 1860s, however, he had begun working in a much more independent and eclectic manner. This development was mainly due to his growing appreciation of Japanese art, an enthusiasm that, in time, was to have a decisive influence on every aspect of his work. He had begun collecting oriental china in the 1850s and shortly afterwards he reputedly became the first person in England to decorate his home in a Japanese way. The walls of his Bristol house at 21 Portland Square were painted in plain, pale colours and hung with Japanese prints, while his collection of blue and white vases stood on straw matting that covered the floors. An interest in Japonisme is also evident in his work for the Earl of Limerick at Castle Dromore, Co. Limerick (1866–73). While the exterior of this building was still strongly medieval in appearance, the interiors, for which Godwin designed the decorations and much of the furniture, contained elements that were far more radical. A scheme for the drawing room includes a frieze of fruit trees and female figures dressed in kimonos, alternating with panels of William Morris's *Trellis* wallpaper, above a plain, sage-coloured wall. Other rooms were painted in shades of pale peach, soft blues and grey and the furniture included chairs made in oiled wainscot oak, that were upholstered in natural calf decorated with simple embossed roundels of Japanese origin.

The influence of Japanese sources is even more pronounced in the furniture that Godwin produced for his London chambers in 1867. He described this work as an attempt to design pieces "by the grouping of solid and void and by more or less broken outline". The result was a collection of strikingly minimal buffets, tables and chairs whose highly rectilinear appearance was inspired by the example of the domestic fitments and woodwork illustrated in Japanese prints. Each piece was constructed on the basis of a symmetrical arrangement of straight vertical and horizontal lines. Surface decoration was kept to the bare minimum and was confined to panels of embossed leather paper and geometric, incised gold lines.

Godwin's earliest furniture was made in ebonised deal. Later, polished walnut and mahogany sometimes replaced the

Godwin: design for sideboard, c.1870

ebonized finish and his furniture of the 1870s and 1880s illustrates a move away from the strict vertical and horizontal emphasis towards more attenuated, curving lines. By this time, Godwin was working in a variety of styles. The celebrated *Butterfly Cabinet* (1877), which formed the centrepiece of the Collinson and Lock display at the 1878 Paris Exposition Universelle, designed in collaboration with J.M. Whistler, has much in common with the popular Queen Anne style, while a catalogue of Godwin's work published by the cabinet-maker William Watt (1877) includes examples of Greek, English Renaissance and Egyptian-style furniture alongside his favourite Anglo-Japanese. The eclecticism of this approach is perhaps characteristic of 19th-century attitudes to design. But, unlike his contemporaries, Godwin never attempted to reproduce period styles exactly and his work is remarkably free of the historicism that dominated the age. Moreover, his commitment to functional simplicity resulted in light and economical designs that, beside the elaborately carved and excessively ornamented furniture produced by the majority of mid-Victorian commercial firms, appear remarkably unfussy and restrained.

Godwin's work was much in demand among the more Aesthetically-inclined residents of fashionable areas such as Chelsea, Hampstead and Bedford Park and through his writings and his furniture he did much to foster a more self-consciously artistic approach to the decoration and furnishing of the upper-middle-class home. From the 1870s he was also devising complete interior schemes. In several of these he was responsible for not only designing the furniture and wallpapers and mixing the paints but also for supervising every detail of the contents right down to the pictures and tableware. Sadly, none of these interiors survives, but his notebooks record features such as Japanese-style overmantels and wall-treatments. Many of his other commissions came from friends, and his clients included the actress Lily Langtry, the Countess of Lonsdale, and the sculptor Princess Louise. The climax to his career, both as architect and decorator, came with the series of artists' studio-houses that he built in Tite Street, Chelsea, between 1877 and 1879. These included Whistler's White House and a studio home for the painter Frank Miles. The latter house contains a large recessed inglenook and an elegant staircase whose open fretwork balustrade and brass-capped finials recall the Oriental-style furniture with which Godwin was involved at the time. A number of his interiors were reviewed in the press and, judging from contemporary descriptions, their appearance was markedly artistic and evoked an atmosphere of spaciousness and calm. Godwin's own home at Taviton Street (1874) exemplifies the simplicity of his style. The walls were painted subtle shades of yellow, cream and grey, Japanese matting covered the dado and the floor, the furniture was light and undecorated, and the soft, cretonne draperies hung in loose, elegant folds. Such artful economy was almost unheard of and comprised a radical alternative to the density of pattern and furnishings that was normally to be found in late Victorian rooms.

The interiors devised for Oscar Wilde, the high-priest of Aestheticism, represent a fitting end to Godwin's involvement in this field. On this occasion Godwin was not responsible for the structure, but he designed some items of furniture and all the decorations, over which he took enormous care. The project also demonstrates the important role that colour played in his work. With the exception of the Japanese leather papers used in the drawing room, wallpapers were eschewed and each room had its own combination of softly harmonizing paint hues. The dining room was painted with variations on enamel-white and contained a suite of Godwin's Greek-style furniture over which Wilde enthused, "each chair is a sonnet in ivory, the table is a masterpiece in pearl". The drawing room was gold and the entrance hall was grey and white. Upstairs, the colour combinations included pink with apple-green, and dark blue with pale blue-green. Such attention to detail exemplifies the Aesthetic quest for beauty, and the house epitomised the ideal of the "House Beautiful" to which the more committed adherents of Aestheticism aspired. What also makes these and Godwin's other interiors so unusual is their delicacy and clarity. It is frequently said that the Aesthetic Movement ushered in a taste for pale colours and emptier rooms but more often than not artistic interiors were strongly patterned and just as densely furnished as their more conventional counterparts. In Godwin's work, by contrast, there is a real attempt to create interiors that were light, convenient and uncluttered. This endeavour was little short of revolutionary.

JOANNA BANHAM

See also Aesthetic Movement; Art Furnishings

Biography

Edward William Godwin. Born in Bristol, 26 May 1833. Articled to William Armstrong, city surveyor, architect, and civil engineer, Bristol. Married 1) Sarah Yonge, 1859 (died, 1865); lived with the actress Ellen Terry, 1868–75, one daughter and one son, the theatrical designer Edward Gordon Craig; married 2) Beatrice Philip, 1876,

1 son (Beatrice Philip married the painter James McNeill Whistler, 1888). Established own architectural practice, c. 1854; received first commission, c. 1855; made successful town hall competition designs for Northampton, 1861, and Congleton, Lancashire, 1864; in architectural partnership with Henry Crisp of Bristol, 1864-71: opened London office of Godwin & Crisp, 1865; established Art Furniture Company to manufacture his designs for furniture, 1867 (company failed, 1867); from 1867 designed furniture, tiles, pottery, fabrics, wallpapers, and stained glass for several British firms; main interior designs from mid-1870s; from 1880 worked increasingly on design of costumes and sets for the theatre; consultant on historic dress, Liberty's department store, 1883. Regular contributor of articles on furniture and interior decoration to the *Architect* and *Building News*, both London, from 1867; prolific writer on subjects such as historical architecture, Shakespeare, and dress reform. Exhibitions (furniture): Universal Exhibition, Vienna, 1873; Centennial Exhibition, Philadelphia, 1876; Exposition Universelle, Paris, 1878. Died 6 October 1886.

Selected Works

No complete catalogue of Godwin's work exists but the most comprehensive list of his architectural commissions appears in the RIBA catalogue (1973) which includes 783 working plans and drawings of 158 separate works. More than 5,000 pages of sketches, including designs for interior schemes, wallpaper, furniture, textiles, ironmongery, wall decorations, and stained and painted glass are held in the Prints and Drawings Department of the Victoria and Albert Museum, London. The museum's Department of Furniture and Interior Decoration also holds a large collection of his furniture. Other important collections of furniture are the City Art Gallery, Bristol and the Hunterian Art Gallery, University of Glasgow. The Public Records Office in London holds all Godwin's registered designs for furniture, wallpaper and textiles.

Interiors

1861	Northampton Town Hall, Northamptonshire (building, interiors and furniture)
1864	Congleton Town Hall, Lancashire (building and interiors)
1866–73	Dromore Castle, Co. Limerick, Eire (building, interiors and furniture): Earl of Limerick
1867	23 Baker St., London (interiors and furniture): E.W. Godwin
1870	Castle Ashby, Northampton (Chinese Bedroom)
1871	Fallows Green, Harpenden, Hertfordshire (building, interiors and furniture): E.W. Godwin
1874	Taviton Street, London (interiors and furniture): E.W. Godwin
1877–78	White House, Tite Street, Chelsea (building and interiors; with J.M. Whistler): J.M. Whistler
1878	Studio, Kensington Palace (building and interiors): Princess Louise
1878	33 Tite Street, Chelsea (building and interiors): Frank Miles
1884	16 Tite Street, Chelsea (interiors and furniture): Oscar Wilde

Godwin designed furniture for his own Art Furniture Company (1867), Collinson & Lock (c.1872–75), Gillow's (1874–76), Green & Kind (c.1861), W.A. & S. Smee (c.1883), William Watt (c.1867–86) and Waugh & Sons (1876). His best-known pieces include the *Lucretia* cabinet (1873), the *Monkey* cabinet (1876) and the *Butterfly Suite* (1877). He also designed wallpapers for Jeffrey & Co., Lightbown Aspinall & Co., and James Toleman & Sons; silk damasks for Warner & Sons and carpets for Waugh & Sons; tiles for Minton & Hollins, and Burnmantofts; and stained glass, staircases and whole interiors for William Watt (from 1877).

Publications

Art Furniture, from designs by E. W. Godwin, with Hints and Suggestions on Domestic Furniture and Decoration, with William Watt, 1877

Artistic Conservatories, with Maurice B. Adams, 1880

Numerous publications in *The Architect* and *Building News*.

Further Reading

The most useful account of Godwin's interior work appears in Aslin 1986. For an extensive bibliography, including a full list of Godwin's writings, see Williamson 1992; a biography and select list of contemporary reviews appears in Burke 1986.

Aslin, Elizabeth, "E.W. Godwin and the Japanese Taste" in *Apollo*, December 1962, pp.779–84

Aslin, Elizabeth, "The Furniture Designs of E.W. Godwin" in *V & A Bulletin*, 3, October 1967, pp.145–54

Aslin, Elizabeth, *The Aesthetic Movement: Prelude to Art Nouveau*, London: Elek, and New York: Praeger, 1969

Aslin, Elizabeth, *E. W. Godwin: Furniture and Interior Decoration* (exhib. cat.), London: Murray, 1986

Bence-Jones, Mark. "An Aesthete's Irish Castle: Dromore Castle, Co. Limerick" in *Country Life*, 136, 12 November 1964, pp.1274–77

Burke, Doreen Bolger and others, *In Pursuit of Beauty: Americans and the Aesthetic Movement* (exhib. cat.: Metropolitan Museum, New York), New York: Rizzoli, 1986

Catalogue of the Drawings Collection of the Royal Institute of British Architects, Farnborough: Gregg, 1973

Girouard, Mark, "Chelsea's Bohemian Studio Houses: The Victorian Artists at Home", part 2 in *Country Life*, 152, 23 November 1972, pp.1370–74

Hall, Michael, "Chinese Puzzle: Chinese Bedrooms at Castle Ashby, near Northampton, Decorated by E.W. Godwin" in *Country Life*, 25 July 1991

Harbron, George Dudley, *The Conscious Stone: The Life of Edward William Godwin*, London: Latimer House, 1949

Hyde, H. Montgomery, "Oscar Wilde and his Architect" in *Architectural Review*, 109, March 1951, pp.175–76

Lambourne, Lionel, *The Aesthetic Movement*, London: Phaidon, 1996

O'Callaghan, John. "The Fine Arts Society and E.W. Godwin." *FAS 100*. Fine Arts Society, London. 1976

Pevsner, Nikolaus, "Art Furniture of the 1870s" in *Architectural Review*, 111, January 1952, pp.43–50

Soros, Susan (editor), *E. W. Godwin* (exhib. cat.), New York: Bard Graduate Center, forthcoming

Williamson, Nancy Burch, *Edward William Godwin and Japonisme in England*, Ann Arbor: UMI, 1992

Witt, Cleo and Karin Walton, *Furniture by Godwin and Breuer* (exhib. cat.), Bristol: Bristol City Art Gallery,1976

Good Design Movement

The idea that there is an identifiable and common standard of "good design", agreed between experts and bestowed upon the consumer, is common to all areas of design and is most prevalent in interior design. A body of literature stipulating what was current good taste in interior design has existed since the 18th century and the emergence of the pattern book and magazine. During the mid 1790s the *Magazin fur Freunde des guten Geschmacks* (Magazine for Friends of Good Taste) was published in Leipzig and carried the Neo-Classical style throughout Europe in the form of coloured plates. The banker

Thomas Hope attempted to reform British taste with his book, *Household Furniture and Interior Decoration Executed from Designs by Thomas Hope*, published in 1807. Hope illustrated the interior of his own London home and other classical examples with descriptions and stark line-drawings. However, it was not until the second half of the 19th century and the onset of mass production and the proliferation of the middle-classes that taste became an issue of grave concern for aesthetic reformers. An important collection of critical writing, published from the mid 19th century onwards, dealt with the thorny question of taste. Writers and design theorists appointed themselves as guardians of the aesthetic well-being of the nation.

The best-known exponent of this new phenomenon was John Ruskin, the leading architectural and art critic of Victorian Britain. His *Seven Lamps of Architecture*, published in 1849, spelt out his views. In the chapter "Lamp of Truth" Ruskin decreed that materials should be used honestly; the decorative paint finishes, so popular in the 19th century, were pilloried. Ruskin argued that art and architecture should imitate nature, or a least adapt forms common in the natural world. Like several influential designers of the period, including A.W.N. Pugin, Ruskin also looked back to the Middle Ages and vaunted the style of 14th-century England as the only true style.

Ruskin's work influenced Charles L. Eastlake, whose best-seller, *Hints on Household Taste, in Furniture, Upholstery and Other Details* was first published in 1868. This was one of the first books to be aimed primarily at the amateur decorator. The material had first appeared in print as articles in the *Cornhill Magazine* and the *Queen*. Eastlake's book was very popular, running to seven editions in America where an "Eastlake Style" emerged. In *Hints on Household Taste* Eastlake, in common with taste-makers before and after him, defined good design in terms of what was bad. Eastlake laid a great deal of blame for the popularity of vulgar taste at the door of the decorator, always an unpopular figure among design reformers. Eastlake objected to the influence of fashion over home decoration and the Victorian love of complex decoration and polychromy. *Hints* was followed by numerous other books and manuals on taste and by the last decades of the century the literature on interior decoration and design had become extremely extensive. The furniture makers Rhoda and Agnes Garrett, for example, published an advice manual for the home entitled *Suggestions for House Decoration in Painting, Woodwork and Furniture* in 1876. In it they proposed that one must look back to the past for the best architecture and design. The Garrett sisters' propensity was, however, not for the medieval but for Queen Anne. Across the Atlantic, Frank Alvah Parsons, founder of the New York design school, typifies American writing on the subject of good taste and the interior. He equates good design with European, classical styles of the past. For Parsons, the home should be more a testimony to one's good taste than a place to relax, a view shared by the American decorators Edith Wharton in *The Decoration of Houses* of 1897 and Elsie de Wolfe in *The House in Good Taste* of 1913.

During the early 20th century the Georgian period began to supplant the Gothic and Queen Anne as the most desirable to imitate. Decorator Edward J. Duveen's *Colour in the Home, With Notes on Architecture, Sculpture, Painting and upon Decoration and Good Taste* was published in 1911 with 32 colour illustrations of ideal interiors. Duveen concurred with Eastlake in dismissing fashion : "A delight in new impressions, a love of change are characteristic of the simple and uneducated". In keeping with all the writers covered, Duveen was concerned with the aesthetics of interior decoration on moral grounds. From Ruskin onwards, design writers have emphasised that the adoption of "good taste" reveals the existence of an advanced civilization and healthy nation.

The shared vision of good taste in interior decoration which informed much official activity during the 20th century was the Modern Movement. For example, the British government offically adopted Modernism during World War II with the Utility scheme. Britain's involvement in the war had severely depleted materials and led to a shortage of labour for the manufacture of consumer goods. The Board of Trade could not completely halt furniture production as replacements were needed for families who had been bombed out. Therefore, furniture was allocated on a points system according to need. Prices were fixed by the Government, as was style and materials. The Government's view of what constituted well-designed furniture was informed by the pre-war activities of the Council for Art and Industry. Their 1937 report on "The Working Class Home: Its Furnishings and Equipment" had condemned surface ornament and period revivals. Good design was defined as: "... items in which the design was simple, of good proportions and without dust-collecting features". This definition was shared by the official committee which introduced the Utility scheme in 1942. The designer Gordon Russell chaired the Design Panel and welcomed the opportunity to influence mass taste. Consumers had little choice but to buy Utility, and, when restrictions were lifted in 1948, the popular Tudor revival styles were again manufactured. However, supporters of Modernism built on the experience of the Utility experiment officially to encourage good taste with the establishment in 1944 of the Council of Industrial Design (CoID).

The first public manifestation of the CoID was an exhibition held at the Victoria and Albert Museum in 1946 entitled "Britain Can Make It". This consisted partly of room settings for ideal families, ranging in social class from coal miner up to television broadcaster. Many visitors to the exhibition found the furniture dull and too reminiscent of wartime Utility. At the Festival of Britain in 1951 the CoID again attempted to influence public taste with the creation of the Contemporary Style, a watered-down Modernism which drew on the Arts and Crafts movement as well as current Swedish design. At the South Bank site, which formed the focal point of the exhibition in London, the CoID vetted all furniture and displayed a Design Index, through which visitors could browse to learn what the recommended good designs on offer were. The CoID moved to a new headquarters in Haymarket, London in 1956 and continue to promote good design to manufacturer and consumer alike through the magazine *Design*, exhibitions and televised awards.

In America similar efforts were made by museums to promote good design. For example, the Walker Art Center, Minneapolis established an "Everyday Art Gallery" in 1944 to show well-designed consumer goods to the public, and interior designer Alexander Girard organised an influential exhibition of home furniture and furnishings entitled "For Modern Living" in 1948 at the Detroit Institute of Arts. However, with the impact of Pop during the 1960s and the subsequent decline of Modernism, the notion that one, idealised standard of taste should prevail became discredited. A new plurality of style and the dominance of the consumer has led to the decline of a singular notion of good design.

ANNE MASSEY

See also Design Reform Movement; Russell

Further Reading

Bayley, Stephen, *Taste: The Secret Meaning of Things*, London: Faber, and New York: Pantheon, 1991

Dover, Harriet, *Home Front Furniture: British Utility Design, 1941–1951*, Aldershot, Hampshire: Scolar Press, 1991

Forty, Adrian, *Objects of Desire: Design and Society 1750–1980*, London: Thames and Hudson, and New York: Pantheon, 1986

Pevsner, Nikolaus, *Academies of Art, Past and Present*, Cambridge: Cambridge University Press, 1940

Smith, C. Ray, *Interior Design in 20th-Century America: A History*, New York: Harper, 1987

Sparke, Penny (editor), *Did Britain Make It? British Design in Context 1946–86*, London: Design Council, 1986

Gothic Revival

Gothic Revival architecture is noted for its dramatic shapes and silhouettes, its irregular massing, and its use of vertical elements such as pinnacles and towers. This irregularity of shape and outline lent itself readily to picturesque effects in landscape gardens and on the exterior of country houses. However, such architectural qualities cannot be translated directly into the design of interiors, where the box-like space of a room acts to contain overly plastic forms. Therefore, the Gothic Revival interior, from its beginnings in the 18th century, relied upon architectural ornament and polychromy to create a medieval effect.

By the middle of the century, the use of the Gothic style had become established in domestic architecture in Britain through the efforts of a small group of dedicated gentleman-amateur architects. It was in this context that the Gothic Revival interior began to be developed. The first important group of Gothic Revival interiors were those created by Horace Walpole at his country house, Strawberry Hill, in Twickenham, Middlesex, the first complete house in the style. The ground-breaking interiors of the house are described in Walpole's *Description of Strawberry Hill*, published in 1774 and enlarged in 1784, and recorded in a series of watercolours he commissioned from John Carter in 1788, the first systematic record of house interiors known. Walpole began to remodel the modest Thameside villa in 1750. By 1753, work on the early interiors of the Great Parlour, Library and Stairwell was underway.

The designs of the early interiors at Strawberry Hill were based upon varied sources. Some features, such as ogee-arched windows and pendant friezes, were derived directly from Batty Langley's *Antient Architecture Restored and Improved* of 1741–42, re-issued in 1747 as *Gothick Architecture*. After further experience of the Gothic style, however, Walpole came to refer to Langley's "bastard Gothic", because the forms he illustrated were not derived from real medieval buildings. Other designs, as in the lace-like traceried chimneypiece of the Great Parlour, were the product of the imagination of Richard Bentley, a member of Walpole's "Committee of Taste" who assisted him.

Gothic Revival: Cabinet, Strawberry Hill, Twickenham, 1784

The library, designed in 1753–54 by Walpole's close friend John Chute, established the direction Walpole was to pursue – namely, towards a more literal use of Gothic motifs derived from the antiquarian books on medieval architecture that he owned. For example, the bookcases of the Library were designed using a 17th-century print by Wenceslas Hollar of the choir screen of Old St. Paul's Cathedral in London as a source. Increasingly, the Strawberry Hill interiors were designed around the collections of antiquarian objects they contained. This was the case with the Holbein Chamber (designed 1758), the guest bedroom at Strawberry Hill, named in honour of the copies of miniatures attributed to Holbein that hung on its walls. The room was furnished with other objects dating to the reign of the Tudors, and the associations provoked by the objects within Walpole's interiors played an increasingly important role in the design of his house. In this, Walpole was anticipating developments in interior design within the Romantic Movement of the 19th century.

The prophetic role of Walpole as regards the Gothic Revival is indicated by his late interiors at Strawberry Hill. The Gallery, designed in 1760 with the assistance of Thomas Pitt,

Gothic Revival: Great Drawing Room, Eaton Hall, Cheshire, by Alfred Waterhouse, 1887

has a high ceiling decorated with gilded papier-mâché "vaults" copied from those of Henry VII's chapel at Westminster Abbey. The dramatic, enlarged scale of this interior, and its literal derivation from a late medieval source, were echoed in the interiors created by Sir Roger Newdigate at his seat, Arbury Hall in Warwickshire, from c.1755 to 1788. Newdigate, who had attended Westminster School, relied almost exclusively on the elaborate Late Gothic vaulting of Henry VII's Chapel at Westminster Abbey as a source for a series of remarkable plasterwork ceilings executed in the 1760s. The lavishly detailed interiors at Arbury went beyond those at Strawberry Hill in their fidelity to medieval models. Newdigate was assisted by Henry Keene, Surveyor to the Fabric of Westminster Abbey, who worked with plaster casts to ensure that the detail of the Arbury interiors was "correct" Gothic.

The novelty of the style, and the fame of Walpole's Strawberry Hill, inspired the use of the Gothic from Ireland to Russia, although the Gothic Revival was to remain primarily a phenomenon of the English-speaking world. Castle Ward in Northern Ireland (c.1760–64), the Gothic House in Wörlitz, Saxony (1770s), and the Church at Chesme Palace for Catherine the Great (c.1780), all demonstrate the rising popularity of the Gothic style. For example, the Gothic House at Wörlitz was begun in 1773 for the von Anhalt-Desslau family at a time when German Neo-Classicism was in full progress. It provided a picturesque view in a landscape garden. Late Gothic sources in Germany and Italy were used for the designs, but the exterior Stair Tower bears a strong resemblance to the architecture of Strawberry Hill, as does the design of the Ante-Chapel interior, painted with tracery and saints in niches in grisaille work resembling the famous Stair Hall of Walpole's house. Strawberry Hill also exerted an influence on the interiors of Petershof, a Gothic-style country house designed for the Russian tsar Nicholas I by a Scottish architect, Adam Menelaus, in 1825.

It was Walpole who promoted the work of the professional architect James Wyatt by recommending him to a friend and fellow antiquary, Thomas Barrett, as the architect to remodel Barrett's country house in Kent, Lee Priory, c.1785–90. The house was demolished, but part of the Library has been installed in the Victoria and Albert Museum in London. This room demonstrates that Wyatt, too, looked to the Chapel of

Henry VII at Westminster Abbey as a source, although his borrowing was neither as literal nor as detailed as that of Walpole and Newdigate. Of Lee Priory, Walpole made the observation that it was, "a child of strawberry, prettier than the parent."

Wyatt was the leading architect of the day with an enormous professional practice and several important government appointments, including that of Surveyor to Westminster Abbey, succeeding Henry Keene. Through his extensive (and controversial) restoration work on Gothic cathedrals such as Salisbury, Wyatt gained a greater structural understanding of Gothic architecture than that of Walpole, which he translated into interiors at Windsor Castle for George III (1800–04) and at a number of country houses in England and Ireland. Among these, it is the legendary interiors of Fonthill Abbey in Wiltshire, created to suit the tastes of the eccentric and exceedingly wealthy connoisseur, William Beckford, that exerted the greatest influence upon contemporaries.

Fonthill Abbey was originally intended to be a sumptuous "folly" within the vast park of the Beckford estate, inspired by the younger Beckford's adolescent fantasies about the Middle Ages and fueled by the fact that a medieval friary had once stood on the site. By 1798 Wyatt was exhibiting designs for this, the largest house of the Gothic Revival, which collapsed in a thunderstorm in 1825, three years after Beckford had sold it. Fortunately the interiors were recorded in several publications, most notably John Britton's *Graphical and Literary Illustrations of Fonthill Abbey* and John Rutter's *Delineations of Fonthill*, both in 1823. At Fonthill, Wyatt perfected his architecture of effects, and nowhere was this more evident than in the design of the interiors.

Fonthill was entered by means of a 30-foot door which opened onto an enormous hall with a hammerbeam ceiling and with lancet windows and stone details in the Early English Gothic borrowed from Salisbury Cathedral, not far away. The effect of light on the stained-glass windows of the entrance hall was described as "sublime" by Rutter. At the top of the stone staircase was the octagonal hall, one hundred feet high, at the centre of two exceedingly long and richly decorated galleries which housed the bulk of Beckford's famous collection of manuscripts, furniture, and art objects. The walls of the two galleries were deep crimson, while purple and gold draperies and upholstery increased the effect of sumptuousness. The rich colouring and vast scale of the Fonthill interiors were to be highly influential on the next generation of Gothic Revivalists. These were led by Wyatt's pupil William Porden, the architect of the enormous Gothic pile Eaton Hall, in Cheshire, begun c.1804, and Wyatt's nephew, Sir Jeffry Wyatville, who was knighted for his work at Windsor Castle in 1828.

The reign of George IV saw many interesting developments in the Gothic Revival. The sale of Fonthill Abbey and the remodeling of Windsor to become the most lavish royal residence in Europe helped to increase the popularity of the Gothic style. So did the publication of a number of books on the subject, including the first accurate account of the development of Gothic architecture in the Middle Ages, Thomas Rickman's *An Attempt to Discriminate the Styles of English Architecture*, which went through seven editions from 1817 to 1881. John Britton published many topographical volumes on Gothic monuments, while a French-born architectural draughtsman

Gothic Revival: wallpaper by A.W.N. Pugin

named Auguste-Charles Pugin published elegantly drawn illustrations of Gothic architectural detail. His best known work was *Specimens of Gothic Architecture* of 1821–23. At last, accurate illustrations of real medieval architecture were available to a wider public, who began to adopt the style for more modest houses by simplifying Gothic ornamental details.

Rickman, Britton and A.C. Pugin's publications quickly reached the New World, where the Gothic had taken root by the turn of the 19th century. The first Gothic "villa" in North America is credited to A.J. Davis, a prominent New York City architect, in 1832, but Davis's most famous Gothic building was Lyndhurst, in Tarrytown, New York, a country house built in 1838–42 and enlarged in 1864–67. Details of the house were taken directly from Rickman and A.C. Pugin, while Davis's furniture began to show the influence of the younger Pugin who was probably the most important designer and architect within the entire Gothic Revival.

A.W.N Pugin began his career by designing Gothic furniture and fittings for George IV at Windsor in 1827 at the age of 15. Pugin's furniture for the State Dining Room included sideboards and an elegant suite of low-backed, upholstered rosewood chairs with Gothic details in gilt, made by Morel and Seddon. Although he later disliked the Gothic designs of the 1820s, the two men worked at the forefront of Gothic design of this period and their designs were popularised in Ackermann's *Repository of Arts*, the leading design journal of the day. During the 1830s the younger Pugin developed his ideas on design, culminating in his most important publication, *The True Principles of Pointed or Christian Architecture*, of

1841. This impassioned manifesto, linking design and the state of 19th-century society, had a powerful influence upon all subsequent Gothic Revivalists.

The immediate impact of Pugin upon interiors, however, was not so much theoretical as decorative. Instead of the reliance upon ecclesiastical architecture shown by Walpole and subsequent Gothic Revivalists (which Pugin felt to be inappropriate to domestic interiors), and instead of the vast scale and sublime effects used by the followers of James Wyatt, Pugin's Gothic interiors were distinctly domestic in character, with scaled-down ornamental details and a rich scheme of colouring derived from his study of medieval manuscripts and decorative art, Netherlandish paintings of the 15th century, and actual medieval buildings. Even in the relatively large interiors of the New Palace of Westminster, his most important commission, the scale and character of the rich Gothic interiors he designed were suggestive of the residence of a medieval king – the function of the palace until the reign of Henry VIII.

During the 1840s and early 1850s, Pugin worked closely with a team of craftsmen and manufacturers, including John Hardman for metalwork, Herbert Minton for ceramics, and the builder George Myers, and he actually formed a partnership in 1844 with a leading London decorator, John Gregory Crace, for the furnishing and decoration of houses in the Gothic style. A small but significant group of houses were redecorated by the Pugin-Crace partnership, including several (Abney Hall, Cheshire; Leighton Hall, Welshpool; and Lismore Castle, Ireland) that were finished by Crace after Pugin's premature death in 1852. The Crace firm continued to produce designs by Pugin, particularly for textiles and wallpapers, until its closure in 1899.

By means of this "team" surrounding Pugin, his direct influence on interiors extended well into the 1860s, when a new generation of Revivalists formulated a type of Gothic known as "Reformed" under the influence of the Gothic Revival architect G.E. Street. Foremost among them was Richard Norman Shaw. Shaw had been Street's principal assistant from 1859 to 1862, and when he set up his own practice he began to develop a style of design deriving from Pugin's *True Principles* – namely, with an emphasis on revealed construction, truth to materials, and a reduced vocabulary of ornament. The essentials of this style of Gothic, which quickly spread to the New World in the designs of firms such as Kimbel and Cabus, were used principally for furnishings and interiors rather than for architecture, and it favoured the effects of simple geometric cutting and carving in wood (chiefly oak) in panelling and furniture, giving an abstract, somewhat primitive effect. Instead of the richly patterned wallpaper designs of Pugin, often derived from textiles of the Italian Renaissance, Reformed Gothic interiors featured walls hung with woven woollen textiles with simplified naturalistic motifs in deep colours. Bruce Talbert, a Scottish designer, made the Reformed Gothic style popular by means of his publications, especially in *Gothic Forms Applied to Furniture, Metal Work and Decoration for Domestic Purposes* (1868). It is possible to view Reformed Gothic as a precursor to the Arts and Crafts Movement in the sense that it relied upon vernacular sources and was a style suited to the middle classes, whereas the work of Pugin and Crace was essentially for aristocratic patrons.

In the London Exhibition of 1862, two newcomers, William Morris and William Burges, had displayed Gothic furnishings of a distinctly bold and primitive character that was far removed from the sophistication of Pugin's work, and that was distinct in its lavish schemes of decorative and narrative painting from the Reformed Gothic designers. Morris, whose furnishing firm was to become world-famous, displayed a distinct Medievalism in his early designs of the 1860s but quickly moved on to more naturalistically inspired forms of ornament. Burges, however, forged an original Gothic style that was more in tune with Continental European developments. In this, he was greatly influenced by Eugène Viollet-le-Duc, the most important French Gothic Revivalist.

Born in 1814, two years after the younger Pugin, Viollet-le-Duc grew up in Paris at the height of the Romantic Movement. He was involved in the Revolution of 1830, the year before Victor Hugo published *The Hunchback of Notre Dame*, a novel set in Paris of the 15th century which did so much to popularize the study of Gothic architecture in France. Initially Viollet experimented with an unarchaeological form of Gothic known in France as the Style Troubadour which to a great extent paralleled the romantic and picturesque developments in England of the same period. Later he evolved a highly original interpretation of the Gothic style.

In common with James Wyatt, Viollet-le-Duc had acquired a knowledge of Gothic architecture by working on the restoration of the great French churches and cathedrals of the Middle Ages. This was during the 1840s and 1850s. In 1858 Viollet began to publish a series of works on Gothic architecture and decorative art which were widely read and used. His most important Gothic interiors – which were mixed with other styles, including the Byzantine and Early Christian – were created at the Château de Pierrefonds in Picardy, restored and remodelled for Napoleon III from 1858 until the latter's overthrow in 1870.

The powerful colour combinations, extensive use of polychromy, and original mixing of ancient styles of decoration seen at Pierrefonds inspired Ludwig II of Bavaria to build Neuschwanstein, and William Burges was inspired by Pierrefonds to remodel Cardiff Castle for the Marquess of Bute. Both these late Gothic Revival castles were begun in 1869; both featured an almost overpowering use of polychromatic decoration; and in both can be seen the mixing of ancient styles promoted by Viollet-le-Duc. At Neuschwanstein, the Early Christian and Romanesque motifs were used in combination with the "troubadour Gothic" created by Ludwig's team of designers, while at Cardiff Burges created brilliantly original interiors with strong Islamic overtones.

Despite the brilliance of Burges's Gothic designs, he found few patrons. His interior schemes were expensive to execute and were increasingly out of sympathy with the tenor of his times. Reviews of the Great Exhibition (1851) had hinted that the majority of the public, while appreciating the exciting work of Pugin and his team, found his personal brand of "True" Gothic somewhat too ecclesiastical for mainstream, domestic use. By the early 1870s the Gothic style was becoming less and less fashionable for interiors, and in a review of the London Exhibition of 1871, the lack of Gothic exhibits was noted. (This was just two years after Cardiff Castle was begun.) In 1881 the magazine *The Builder* reported that Gothic furniture was going out of favour, while in October of 1886 *The Cabinet*

Maker made the observation that, "the Gothic furniture which Welby Pugin endeavoured to foist upon the public now sells for a song." Gothic Revival architecture still lingered, especially within ecclesiastical or collegiate contexts, but the style was all but extinct in fashionable domestic interiors by the mid-1880s.

MEGAN ALDRICH

See also Beckford; Burges; Ludwig II; Pugin; Style Troubadour; Talbert; Viollet-le-Duc

Further Reading

The literature on the Gothic Revival is extensive. Useful surveys appear in Mahoney 1995 and Aldrich 1994 both of which include specialist bibliographies; Aldrich also includes a list of important surviving buildings and examples of the Gothic Revival style.

Aldrich, Megan, *Gothic Revival*, London: Phaidon, 1994
Andrews, Wayne, *American Gothic: Its Origins, Its Trials, Its Triumphs*, New York: Random House, 1975
Atterbury, Paul and Clive Wainwright (editors), *Pugin: A Gothic Passion*, New Haven and London: Yale University Press, 1994
Blondel, Nicole, "Néo-Gothique" in Alain Gruber (editor), *L'Art Décoratif en Europe: Du néoclassicisme à l'Art Déco, 1760–1930*, Paris: Citadelles & Mazenod, 1994
Clark, Kenneth, *The Gothic Revival*, 1928; 3rd edition London: Murray, and New York: Holt Rinehart, 1962
Cooper, Jeremy, *Victorian and Edwardian Furniture and Interiors*, London: Thames and Hudson, 1987
Eastlake, Charles Locke, *A History of the Gothic Revival*, 1871; edited by J. Mordaunt Crook, Leicester: Leicester University Press, 1970
Germann, Georg, *The Gothic Revival in Europe and Britain: Sources, Influences and Ideas*, London: Lund Humphries, 1972; Cambridge: Massachusetts Institute of Technology Press, 1973
Gothick, 1720–1840 (exhib. cat.), Brighton: Royal Pavilion, Art Gallery and Museums, 1975
A Gothick Symposium, London: The Georgian Group, 1983
La "Gothique" Retrouvé avant Viollet-le-Duc (exhib. cat.), Paris: Hôtel de Sully, 1979
Harmon, Robert B., *The Gothic Revival in American Architecture: A Brief Style Guide*, Monticello, IL: Vance, 1982
Howe, Katherine S. and David B. Warren, *The Gothic Revival Style in America, 1830–1870* (exhib. cat.) Houston: Museum of Fine Arts, 1976
Hunter-Stiebel, Penelope, *Of Knights and Spires: Gothic Revival in France and Germany*, New York: Rosenberg and Stiebel, 1989
Macaulay, James, *The Gothic Revival, 1745–1845*, Glasgow: Blackie, 1975
McCarthy, Michael J., *The Origins of the Gothic Revival*, New Haven and London: Yale University Press, 1987
Mahoney, Kathleen, *Gothic Style: Architecture and Interiors from the Eighteenth Century to the Present*, New York: Abrams, 1995
Richardson, Douglas Scott, *Gothic Revival Architecture in Ireland*, 2 vols., New York: Garland, 1983
Vance, Mary A., *Gothic Revival in Architecture, Art, and Literature* (bibliography), Monticello, IL: Vance, 1985
Wainwright, *Clive, The Romantic Interior: The British Collector at Home, 1750–1850*, New Haven and London: Yale University Press, 1989

Goût Grec

The term *goût grec* has come to describe those objects created during the first phase of the Neo-Classical movement in France, specifically between c.1755 and 1765, and hence preceding "le style Louis XVI." The term is a contemporary one, cropping up in diaries and art criticism of the period, but its meaning varied and it was not often used in contexts that were literally correct. The objects defined by the term *goût grec* are characterized by somewhat heavy proportions, straight lines, and the use of classical ornament such as festoons, urns, scrolls, and Greek meander patterns. They demonstrate a strident enthusiasm for the ancient world, its precepts and artistic accomplishments, and betray the anti-Rococo sentiment which was developing at this time.

By the 1740s rumblings about the excesses and license of the Rococo style were being heard, and a movement began among several factions of the art world calling for greater stability, balance, and an adherence to common standards. There was also a measure of nostalgia contributing to this reaction, a longing for the glories of the period of Louis XIV, when France's artistic supremacy was one of the country's greatest achievements. The monarchy had reached the height of its popularity about 1748 with the end of the War of Austrian Succession, but proceeded then to enter a period when long-standing resentments between king and parliament, state and church, and Paris and the provinces surfaced. There was measurable unrest both politically and socially.

The most significant developments and disaffection occurred in the intellectual field, where figures such as Voltaire, Montesquieu, and Diderot produced works which systematically attacked certain foundations of French society – the monarchy, the Catholic church, and the judicial system. The Enlightenment called for the triumph of human reason and a rejection of the frivolity and privilege associated with the Rococo style. There was nothing logical about French art and interiors of the earlier part of the century, and this was unacceptable to the current generation of intellectuals.

The *éminence grise* of Neo-Classicism was the Comte de Caylus (1692–1765), an antiquarian who published his important collections of antiquities and waged an anti-Rococo campaign through lectures given at the Académie de Peinture et de Sculpture and the Académie des Inscriptions. His effect on architecture has been disparaged, but there is no contesting the significant influence his published collection had on the decorative arts. Designers of furniture and other household objects found a treasure of ornament and motifs here, a new vocabulary for their work. Others in Caylus's circle were the Abbé Leblanc, credited with being the first to publish a direct attack on Rococo style, in 1745; the collector Pierre-Jean Mariette, who wrote a stinging obituary of Meissonnier; and Abbé Barthélemy, curator of the Cabinet de Médailles.

Besides these promoters of "l'Antiquité" there were the "philosophes," those who openly and nostalgically praised French tradition and the "good taste" of the previous century. Prominent among this group was Jacques-François Blondel (1705–74), an architect, architectural theorist, and lecturer at the Académie. Blondel also established his own architecture school, the first outside of the Académie, where he exercised considerable influence, and contributed to Diderot's *Encyclopédie*. He believed in the separation of architecture and sculpture on buildings, and espoused functionality, symmetry, solidity, and avoidance of superfluous ornament.

In the meantime, France had been continuing to send

promising native sons to Italy to study its arts and architecture. A circle of young artists at the Académie de France in Rome began in the 1740s to develop a strong, new vision of architecture which relied not only on antiquity, but also on Baroque design, for its inspiration. Jean-Laurent Legeay was among the most talented of this group, and he produced highly dramatic works where humans are dwarfed by monumental ruins and the presence of the past is almost overwhelming. These young artists in due course returned to France, and Legeay's appointment as professor at the Académie in Paris, in 1742, ushered in a welcome freshness and revived academic interest in classicism. The first hints of Neo-Classicism were beginning to be manifested in the work of this new generation.

Another to make the pilgrimage to Rome, although in a different capacity, was the Marquis de Marigny, the brother of Madame de Pompadour. The latter had urged her brother to make the trip as preparation for his impending appointment as Directeur des Bâtiments, and he spent nearly two years there, from 1749 to 1751, in the company of Abbé Leblanc, the architect Jacques-Germain Soufflot (1713–80), and the designer and engraver Charles-Nicolas Cochin (1715–90). Marigny was at least a partial convert to *l'Antiquité* – the extent of his admiration is the subject of differing opinions – but he flatly rejected the Baroque, and official taste was thus directed. Considerable debate has centered on the issue of whether the Marquis's voyage marked the beginning of the anti-Rococo movement, but it should be emphasized that the evolution of Neo-Classicism was a process which developed on several fronts, as outlined above.

It is important to mention the excavations at Pompeii and Herculaneum (1754), the temples of Greece (1758), and Paestum (1764), for a steady stream of information about these remains was published over the course of several decades in Europe, exciting general interest. These rediscoveries of the art and architecture of ancient Greece and Rome provided another important source for contemporary artists and architects, as well as designers of everything from clothing and jewellery to stage sets. Also, one must note the growing predilection for architecture and objects in the English style during this time: "Anglomanie" was exceedingly influential in matters of French taste. The English had maintained keen interest in Classical design throughout the earlier part of the century and it cannot be assumed that this went unnoticed or unappreciated by the French.

The first artistic field to exhibit changes in the direction of Neo-Classicism was architecture. French Rococo architects and designers had not rejected all the features of classical design, thereby providing a window for hybrid interiors of the mid-century which appear to bridge Baroque with early Neo-Classicism. The full acceptance of such schemes is demonstrated by Blondel's praise of Pierre Contant d'Ivry's interiors in the Palais-Royal, dating to 1755–57. These rooms blend Classical architectural features in a Baroque vein with tempered Rococo ornament and furnishings: there are strongly articulated columns and pilasters and Roman arches of stately proportions, all embellished with floral garlands, putti, and frilly shells.

Soon following this development was a proliferation of accessories and *objets d'art* in the "Greek taste." The publication of numerous books of classical ornament, both directly copied from Greek and Roman prototypes and imaginative interpretations, had provided designs for easy copying by goldsmiths and mount-makers. Ornament preceded form and structure, which led eventually to adoption by sculptors and painters of the new aesthetic. In fact, it is this vogue for superficial and unbounded "Greek" decoration that led to harsh criticism of the early Neo-Classical manifestations. Some contemporaries bemoaned the silly fashion for everything "à la grecque" and condemned all but the most serious interpretations of antiquity.

There is one early interior with its furnishings which is commonly cited as a prime example of *goût grec*. It is the study designed c.1756 by Barreau de Chefdeville, Caffiéri, Leroy, and Le Lorrain for the Parisian collector Ange-Laurent de Lalive de Jully. The ebony and gilt-bronze furniture, which has survived to this day (Musée de Chantilly), is massive and rectilinear, and sports ornament inspired by Greek architectural motifs – deep fluting, Vitruvian scrolls, lion pelts, and *cordes à puits*, heavy rope-like garlands. While the ornament is in a pure classical idiom, the structure of the pieces owes a debt to Baroque design in its resemblance to pieces by A.-C. Boulle. Indeed, a hallmark of much early Neo-Classical furniture design is its resemblance to the monumental works created under Louis XIV. The study itself has not survived, but descriptions tell of a new sort of decorative scheme, novel in the components as well as the manner in which they were all put together.

Lalive de Jully and Cochin believed this room to have prompted the mania for the *goût grec*, and despaired that so much abuse of the serious study of antiquity should have resulted from this example. But they also recognized the influence information about Pompeii and other excavation sites had on this fashion. An oft-quoted passage from Baron de Grimm's *Correspondance littéraire* (1763) suggests the degree to which this fad spread: "Depuis quelques années, on a recherché les ornements et les formes antiques; le goût y a gagné considérablement et la mode en est devenue si générale que tout se fait aujourd'hui *à la grecque*" (In the years since the discovery of antique ornament and antique forms, the taste for such things has grown considerably and the fashion has become so general that today everything is in the "Greek" mode).

While the actual meaning of the term *goût grec* in contemporary usage varied, it is generally acknowledged today that the description "Greek" was often loosely attached to anything inspired by antiquity. *Goût grec* and *style antique* were synonymous, partially because of the historic veneration of the Greeks and the assumption that ancient Roman architecture was merely derived from that of Greece. It has been contended, too, that the expression *goût grec* really just meant that something was in a non-Rococo style. The logic of this may be clearer when one understands that the Rococo and the new Neo-Classical style existed side-by-side for several decades, and the "Transitional" period leading to Louis XVI was largely characterized by the application of Neo-Classical ornament to basic Rococo forms. It would not be until the late 1760s that the sober, elegant, and lighter Louis XVI style epitomised by architects such as François-Joseph Bélanger and Jean Démosthène Dugourc and that represented the next phase of Neo-Classicism, would fully emerge.

MARGARET W. LICHTER

See also Neo-Classicism

Further Reading

The Age of Neo-Classicism (exhib. cat.: Royal Academy, London), London: Arts Council, 1972

Catalogue historique du cabinet ... de M. De Lalive, Paris, 1764

Dacier, Emile, *Le Style Louis XVI*, Paris: Larousse, 1939

Eriksen, Svend, "La Live de Jully's furniture à la grecque" in *Burlington Magazine*, CIII, 1961 pp.340–46

Eriksen, Svend, "Marigny and 'Le Goût Grec'" in *Burlington Magazine*, March 1962, pp.96–101

Eriksen, Svend, *Early Neo-Classicism in France: The Creation of the Louis Seize Style*, London: Faber, 1974

Felice, Roger de, *Le Meuble Français sous Louis XV*, Paris: Hachette, 1920

Honour, Hugh, *Neo-Classicism*, Harmondsworth: Penguin, 1968

Kalnein, Wend von, *Architecture in France in the Eighteenth Century*, New Haven and London: Yale University Press, 1995

Kimball, Fiske, "Les Influences anglaises dans la formation du style Louis XVI" in *Gazette des Beaux-Arts*, V, 1931, pp.231–55

Kimball, Fiske, "The Beginnings of the Style Pompadour, 1751–59" in *Gazette des Beaux-Arts*, XLIV, 1954, pp.58–64

Verlet, Pierre, *French Furniture and Interior Decoration of the 18th Century*, London: Barrie and Rockcliffe, 1967

Watson, F.J.B., *Wallace Collection Catalogues: Furniture*, London: Wallace Collection, 1956

Watson, F.J.B., *Louis XVI Furniture*, London: Tiranti, and New York: Philosophical Library, 1960

Whitehead, John, *The French Interior in the Eighteenth Century*, London: Laurence King, 1992; New York: Dutton, 1993

Graves, Michael 1934–

American architect and designer

Michael Graves was born in Indianapolis and trained as an architect at the University of Cincinnati and at the Graduate School of Design at Harvard University where he graduated in 1959. He worked briefly in the office of George Nelson in New York before winning a Prix de Rome fellowship which made it possible for him to work at the American Academy in Rome from 1960 until 1962. On his return to the United States he accepted a teaching position in the architectural school at Princeton University and, in 1964, established his own architectural practice in Princeton.

He became known in the 1970s for his work in a loose affiliation with the architects called "The New York Five" or, as they were informally known, "The Whites" in recognition of the highly abstract, white painted geometric forms of their architectural design. This was a style of late Modern work suggesting a devotion to the puristic principles of the International Style Modernism of the late 1920s and early 1930s. Graves's work soon separated itself from that of the Fives with an increasing introduction of decorative elements, historic references and a use of varied color, generally in a range of hues and pastel tints unlike the reserved color uses of Modernism.

As the term Postmodernism came into use, Graves came to be viewed as a key figure in this development although he would not regard the term as fully appropriate to his work, preferring the word "figurative" for his architecture. Among the projects that first brought him to prominence were several houses and their interiors and a number of interior projects including a clinic in Fort Wayne, Indiana (1971) where strong color and original mural painting gave the spaces a highly individualistic character. In 1981 and 1982, he contributed furniture designs to the Milan-based Memphis venture including the *Plaza* dressing table and the *Stanhope* bed, designs with a strong connection to Art Deco precedent.

From 1980 to 1986, Graves was active as a designer for the Sunar Hauserman furniture firm designing offices and showrooms in a number of cities including New York, Chicago, Houston, Dallas and London. These showroom interiors were colorful and full of unusual and imaginative forms that ranged from decorative to somewhat eccentric. Graves was also the designer of furniture produced by Sunar Hauserman so that these showrooms and their contents were influential in bringing Graves's work to the design professions in an influential manner.

The 1983 Portland city office building, a commission won through a national competition, was a major building project, widely published and sufficiently controversial in character to elicit the statement from one architectural critic that it had "set American architecture back by fifty years". It was the use of non-functional, strictly decorative elements and the seemingly arbitrary use of colors and bands of trim that made the building a striking example of Postmodernism, inevitably to be praised by those admiring of this direction but condemned by the entrenched adherents to the doctrines of Modernism. An increasing flow of work has come to Graves as he has come to be regarded as a key figure in current architecture and design in America. Most of his architectural projects incorporate interiors of his own design. Among the most striking are the 1982 San Juan Capistrano Library, the Clos Pegase Winery in Napa Valley (1984) with its hints of the 18th century design of Ledoux, the large Humana office building in Louisville (1985) and various projects for Walt Disney ventures including corporate headquarters in Burbank, the Walt Disney World Dolphin and Swan hotels in Orlando, Florida, and the 1989 Hotel New York at Euro Disneyland in France.

In addition to continuing work in furniture design, Graves has been active in the development of various other products for household interior use such as tableware, carpets, textiles, small clocks and the well-known 1985 tea-kettle for Alessi known as "fledgling" for the metal bird-whistle perched on its spout. Graves has established a retail shop in Princeton near his home and office where a variety of products of his design are offered for sale, and a mail-order catalog offers these products as well. The items offered include jewelry, watches, leather goods, lamps, picture frames and woven wool blanket-scarves. Graves's sketches and drawings have been widely published, admired and collected.

Recent commissions include a number of libraries, theaters, office buildings, college and university projects and exhibition design projects. The work includes projects in Taiwan, Japan, Belgium and in many American cities. Graves's designs for the expansion of the Whitney Museum of American Art in New York have been widely published and have excited much discussion as a result of the way in which the strong Postmodern character of the addition would contrast with the existing building by Marcel Breuer.

Graves has been an active teacher of architecture at a

number of universities and is the winner of many honors and awards including membership in the American Academy of Arts and Letters.

JOHN F. PILE

See also Postmodernism

Biography

Born in Indianapolis, Indiana, 9 July 1934. Studied at the Department of Architecture, University of Cincinnati, 1954–58; graduate student, Harvard University, Cambridge, Massachusetts, 1958–59; awarded the Prix de Rome and studied at the American Academy, Rome, 1960–62. Married 1) Gail Devine (divorced): 2 children; 2) Marie Lucy James (divorced 1977). Lecturer, 1962–63, Assistant Professor, 1963–67, Associate Professor, 1967–72, and Schirmer Professor of Architecture since 1972, Princeton University. Established his own architectural office, Michael Graves, Architect, Princeton, and Principal since 1964. Also active as a painter, muralist and designer with numerous designs for furniture, textiles, lighting and tableware from the mid-1970s. "Graves Design", product design department of Michael Graves, Architect, launched, 1991; opened retail shop for the sale of his own furnishings and products, Princeton, 1994. Has taught at many colleges in North America: Visiting Fellow, Institute for Architecture and Urban Studies, New York, 1971–72; Visiting Professor, University of Texas at Austin, 1973 and 1974, University of Houston, 1974 and 1978, New School for Social Research, New York, 1975, and University of California at Los Angeles, 1977. Numerous awards including 9 American Institute of Architects National Honor Awards from 1975, Louis H. Sullivan Award, 1994. Member, American Academy and Institute of Arts and Letters, 1991.

Selected Works

Interiors

1967	Hanselmann House, Fort Wayne, Indiana (building and interiors)
1969	Benacerraf House, Princeton, New Jersey (building and interiors)
1971	Ear, Nose and Throat Associates Medical Office, Fort Wayne, Indiana (building and interiors)
1971–73	Alexander House, Princeton, New Jersey (building and interiors)
1972	Snyderman House, Fort Wayne, Indiana (building and interiors)
1975	Plocek House, Warren Township, New Jersey (building, interiors and furnishings)
1976	Schulman House, Princeton, New Jersey
1977	Graves Warehouse / House conversion, Princeton, New Jersey (interiors and furnishings; refurbished 1982)
1980–86	11 Sunar Hauserman Furniture Showrooms and Offices, various locations including New York, Chicago, Dallas, Los Angeles, London (buildings, interiors and furnishings)
1982	San Juan Capistrano Library, California
1982	Newark Museum, New Jersey (building and interiors)
1982	Emory University Art Museum, Atlanta (renovation and interiors)
1983	Portland Building, Portland, Oregon (building and interiors)
1984	Clos Pegase Winery and Residence, Napa Valley, California (buildings and interiors)
1984	Diane Von Furstenberg Boutique, Fifth Avenue, New York (interiors and furnishings)
1985	Humana Building, Louisville, Kentucky (building and interiors)
1986	Shiseido Health Club, Tokyo (building and interiors)
1986	Crown American, office building, Johnstown, Pennsylvania (building, interiors and furnishings)
1986	Disney Company Headquarters, Burbank, California (building, interiors and furnishings)
1987	Walt Disney World Dolphin and Swan hotels, Lake Buena Vista, Florida (buildings, interiors and furnishings)
1987	15 Lenox Showrooms and Galleries, various locations including Florida and New York (buildings, interiors and furnishings)
1989	Hotel New York, Euro Disneyland, Marne-la-Vallée, France (building, interiors and furnishings)

Graves has been a prolific designer of furnishings and other products and many of his buildings and interiors have contained examples of his work. His furniture includes collections produced by Sunar Hauserman, 1977–87; many designs for Memphis, including *Plaza* dressing table (1981) and *Stanhope* bed (1982), during the early 1980s; the *MG2* and *MG3* club chairs by Saways & Moroni (1985); and the *Kyoto Collection* for Arkitektura (1989). His textiles include carpet designs for the *Dialog* collection for Vorwek (1987). He has also designed tableware, including the celebrated "fledgling" teapot (1985), for Alessi and ceramics produced by Swid Powell, including 1985 *Big Dripper* coffee pot.

Further Reading

The literature on Graves is extensive. The standard monographs covering his architectural projects which include numerous illustrations of interiors are Arnell 1982 and Nichols 1990. For a study that concentrates on Graves's work as a designer see Abrams which also contains a select bibliography of books and articles relating specifically to this area.

Abrams, Janet and others, *Michael Graves*, Berlin: Ernst, 1994

Archer, B.J. and Anthony Vidler, *Follies: Architecture for the Late-Twentieth-Century Landscape*, New York: Rizzoli, 1983

Arnell, Peter, Ted Bickford and Karen Vogel Wheeler (editors), *Michael Graves: Buildings and Projects, 1966–1981*, New York: Rizzoli, 1982

Casper, Dale E., *Michael Graves, Architect: Periodical Articles, 1967–1987* (bibliography), Monticello, IL: Vance, 1988

Collins, Michael and Andreas Papadakis, *Post-modern Design*, London: Academy, and New York: Rizzoli, 1989

"Dolphin and Swan Hotels, Walt Disney World" in *Architectural Design* (special issue), July/August 1988

Dunster, David (editor), *Michael Graves*, New York: Rizzoli, and London: Academy, 1979

Five Architects: Eisenman, Graves, Gwathmey, Hejduk, Meier, New York: Oxford University Press, 1975

Harmon, Robert B., *Building with Symbols: The Architectural Work of Michael Graves: A Selected Bibliography*, Monticello, IL: Vance, 1981

Jencks, Charles, *Kings of Infinite Space: Michael Graves and Frank Lloyd Wright*, revised edition London: Academy, and New York: St. Martin's Press, 1985

Macrae-Gibson, Gavin, *The Secret Life of Buildings: An American Mythology for Modern Architecture*, Cambridge: Massachusetts Institute of Technology Press, 1985

"Maison Snyderman" in *Architecture d'Aujourd'hui*, August / September 1976

"Michael Graves" in *Space Design* (special issue), April 1983

Nichols, Karen Vogel, Patrick J. Burke and Caroline Hancock (editors), *Michael Graves: Buildings and Projects, 1982–1989*, New York: Princeton Architectural Press, and London: Architecture Design and Technology Press, 1990

Papadakis, Andreas (editor), *The Post-modern Object*, London: Art and Design, and New York: St. Martin's Press, 1987

Phillips, Lisa (introduction), *Shape and Environment: Furniture by American Architects* (exhib. cat.), New York: Whitney Museum of American Art, 1982

Powell, Kenneth, *Graves Residence*: Michael Graves, London: Phaidon, 1995

Gray, Eileen 1879–1976

Irish architect and designer of interiors, furniture and textiles

Eileen Gray's reputation and status as a designer has, like her work, been through several phases. Her early lacquered furniture was highly sought after by wealthy Parisian patrons of Art Deco, while her later minimalist, black and chrome furniture, reproduced since the 1970s by Zeff Aram in London and Andrée Putman in Paris, has been an inspiration for a new generation of style-conscious designers. Today, she is often hailed as a pioneer of modern design. Yet, for Gray herself, it was her architectural work that was most significant and it is in the interiors of her two major buildings that her particular brand of humane Modernism, with its sensitive detailing and ingenious functionalism, triumphs. Her small, inventive legacy of furniture, rugs, lighting, room schemes and houses reflects both her perfectionism and her responsiveness to the evolving materials and shifting themes of the early and mid 20th century.

Born in Ireland into an aristocratic and artistic family, Gray travelled widely in Europe as a child before enrolling to study painting and drawing in London at the Slade School of Art. She became interested in furniture and oriental lacquerwork during her many visits to the South Kensington Museum (now the Victoria and Albert Museum) and joined D. Charles's Dean Street Street lacquer restoration workshop between 1900 and 1902. From 1902 to 1905 she studied in Paris at the Atelier Colarossi and the Académie Julian and settled there in 1907.

Fuelled by the interest generated by the display of Japanese antiques and crafts at the Exposition Universelle of 1900, Paris had attracted several Japanese craftsmen including the lacquerwork artist Seizo Sugawara with whom Gray subsequently trained. She began her career by producing decorative panels and screens, followed by furniture, desks, bookcases and beds, designed in a contemporary idiom, and which she exhibited at the prestigious Salon des Artistes Décorateurs from 1913. Undaunted by the technical vicissitudes of lacquer, she responded to its need for high standards and recognised its affinity with a luxurious, but at the same time austere, Modernist aesthetic. Her most celebrated piece of this period was the *Le Destin* folding screen of 1914, an exotic fusion of symbolist, figurative and abstract Deco styles, that was commissioned for the newly refurbished apartment of the Paris couturier and collector Jacques Doucet.

Gray worked in London during World War I, but returned to Paris in 1918 where she extended her sphere of interests to include interior decoration, designing a spectacular apartment in the rue de Lota for the wealthy milliner, Suzanne Talbot between 1919 and 1922. This innovative commission has been described as the epitome of Art Deco and combined luxury furniture with avant-garde work. It included geometrical light fittings made out of ostrich eggs, parchment and lacquer, draped animal skins, abstract rugs, lacquered "brick" screens, and exotic, salmon-pink chairs. The centrepiece was the gondola-shaped *Pirogue* day bed, finished in patinated bronze lacquer, which stood on twelve arched feet as if awaiting a 1920s odalisque. Throughout, African and Oriental influences converge with a sleek, Parisian opulence.

In 1922 Gray opened the Galerie Jean Désert, an exclusive showcase for her furniture, screens, lamps, mirrors and Modernist hangings in the rue du Fauboug Saint Honoré for which she also designed the minimalist façade. Although the shop was never a commercial success – it closed due to financial losses in 1930 – Gray numbered among her clients some of the most fashionable and glamorous figures of the day including Elsa Schiaparelli, the Maharajah of Indore and the Countess of Oxford. The weaving workshop which produced some of Gray's most coveted designs for rugs, hangings and carpets, was run by her companion and partner, Evelyn Wyld.

The geometric, almost painterly style of Gray's textiles was clearly indebted to Cubist and De Stijl influences and by the mid 1920s her work was becoming increasingly Modernist in appearance. Her furniture began to exploit more utilitarian forms, and, eschewing earlier Art Deco effects such as tortoiseshell, silver leaf, tasselled lacquer, mother of pearl inlay and ivory carving, she turned to industrial materials like tubular steel, sheet aluminium and glass. Not surprisingly, the austerity of her new style was not universally admired by her existing clients, and the bedroom / boudoir for a house in Monte Carlo, exhibited at the 1923 Salon des Artistes Décorateurs, provoked some hostile criticism. But it attracted much more favourable comment within avant-garde circles and the Dutch De Stijl magazine, *Wendingen*, published an issue in 1924 that was entirely devoted to a laudatory exposition of her work.

Encouraged by the Romanian architect Jean Badovici, Gray embarked upon a number of architectural projects whose severely functional appearance seems to have evolved out of the abstract and constructivist principals of her furniture. From 1926 to 1929 she designed and built E-1027, a villa overlooking the sea at Roquebrune in a remote part of the South of France. Admired by Le Corbusier, this building is unequivocally Modernist in form, but it is the interior that defines Gray's principal contribution to the Modern Movement. The rooms were clean, sparse and comfortable, the space was multifunctional, and the furnishings include some of her most inventive and flexible items, such as the *Transat* and *Bibendum* chairs, swivelling mirrors, adjustable tables, deckchairs that also act as indoor chairs, and alternate day and night lights. Devoid of pattern, the decoration is restricted to areas of monochrome with a deep blue in the rugs, and luxurious touches such as padded white leather upholstery, and lacquer and glass, co-exist with industrial materials like perforated steel, celluloid, felt and cork. Gray's aim was to create a harmony between architecture, interior space, and fittings in a humane Modernist idiom.

Her interiors for Badovici's studio apartment in Paris were an exercise in designing for compact living. Using devices such as concealed storage areas in the ceiling, and mirrors to create an illusion of space, she organised a complete home containing kitchenette, bar, bathroom, bedroom and office within a space of no more than 40 square metres.

Gray's only other completed architectural commission was a house called Tempe à Pailla at Castella in the South of France. This house reveals her growing preoccupation with the idea of a fully integrated, reductionist, living space, and uses compact, built-in furniture with sliding doors and windows. Flexibility was emphasised with a wardrobe that could extend if extra space were needed and a step that doubles as a drawer.

Gray: apartment for Suzanne Talbot, Paris, 1922

The canvas-backed, S-shaped outdoor chair folded up for storage and the dining table adapted to coffee-table height. Tempe à Pailla was later puchased by the painter Graham Sutherland.

A founder-member of the Union des Artistes Modernes, Gray continued to explore functionalist and egalitarian ideals in the mid- and late 1930s with projects such as designs for storage units, the Tube House of prefabricated metal, and a Centre des Vacances including a restaurant / cafe, open-air theatre, housing and a recreational area for young people. Grey lived in semi-retirement after World War II and it was not until the 1970s that her work began to enjoy belated acclaim. Reproductions of her furniture, rugs and light fittings proved particularly popular in the High-Tech interiors of the late 1970s and 1980s and original pieces are highly sought-after collector's items today.

SUSAN HOYAL

Biography

Eileen Moray Gray. Born at Brownswood, Enniscorthy, County Wexford, 9 August 1879, the daughter of Baroness Gray. Educated at the Slade School of Art, London, 1898–1902; trained in lacquerwork at D. Charles furniture workshops, 92 Dean Street, Soho, 1900–02; studied drawing at the Atelier Colarossi and the Académie Julian, Paris, 1902–05; studied furniture making and lacquerwork with the Japanese craftsman Seizo Sugawara, Paris, 1907–14. Independent furniture and interior designer from 1908; textile designer and architect from 1926. Joint owner of lacquerwork and furniture studio, with Sugawara, in London, 1915–17, and Paris, 1918–22; proprietor of the furniture showrooms and interior decorating service, Galerie Jean Désert, Paris, which she ran with Evelyn Wyld, 1922–30 (Wyld resigned 1927); worked on architectural projects with Jean Badovici from 1926. Founder-member of the Union des Artistes Modernes; exhibited at Salon des Artistes Décorateurs, and Salon d'Automne, Paris, during the 1920s, and Exposition Internationale, Paris, 1937. Honorary Royal Designer for Industry, Royal Society of Arts, London, 1972; Fellow, Institute of Architects, Ireland, 1973. Died in Paris, 31 October 1976.

Selected Works

A checklist of Gray's complete works appears in Adam 1987. A collection of architectural drawings, glass negatives of houses and furniture, working papers, notebooks and correspondence (1913–37) is held in the Archive of Art and Design, Victoria and Albert Museum, London. Examples of her furniture are in the Musée des Arts Décoratifs, Paris.

Interiors

1919–22 Apartment, rue de Lota, Paris (interiors and furnishings): Suzanne Talbot (Mme. Mathieu-Lévy)

1923 Salon des Artistes Décorateurs, Paris (bedroom-boudoir for a Monte Carlo studio)

1925–28 Apartment, 21 rue Bonaparte, Paris (interiors and furnishings): Eileen Gray

1926–29 E-1027, Roquebrune, Cap Martin (building, interiors and furnishings; with Jean Badovici): Eileen Gray

1930–31 Studio / Apartment, 17 rue Châteaubriand, Champs Elysées, Paris: Jean Badovici
1932–34 Tempe à Pailla, Castellar, near Menton (building, interiors and furnishings): Eileen Gray
1937 Exposition Internationale, Paris (project for a Centre des Vacances, in Le Corbusier's Pavillon des Temps Nouveaux)

Furniture

Gray designed numerous items of furniture and lacquered screens from 1913; her many designs for textiles and lighting date from the early 1920s. Well-known furnishings include *Le Destin* (1914), *La Nuit* (1919) and the *Block* (1925) lacquered screens; the *Pirogue* day bed (1919–20); the *Bilboquet* and *Lotus* tables (both 1915); and the *Transat* chair (1925). Much aluminium furniture, including the *E-1027* table, was produced for her house of the same name.

Publications

"La Maison Minimum", with Jean Badovici, in *L'Architecture d'Aujourd'hui* (Paris), 1930

Further Reading

An introduction to Gray's work, including a chronology of her life and a select reading list, appears in Garner 1993. For a full bibliography see Doumato 1981.

Adam, Peter, *Eileen Gray, Architect / Designer: A Biography*, London: Thames and Hudson, and New York: Abrams, 1987
Anscombe, Isabelle, *A Woman's Touch: Women in Design from 1860 to the Present Day*, London: Virago, and New York: Viking, 1984
"L'appartement de Suzanne Talbot" in *L'Illustration*, 7, 1933
Badovici, Jean, "Maison en bord de mer" in *Architecture Vivante* (Paris), 1929
Collection Eileen Gray (sale cat.), Sotheby's, Monaco, 25 May 1990
Doumato, Lamia, *Eileen Gray 1879–1976* (bibliography), Monticello, IL: Vance, 1981
Duncan, Alastair, *Art Deco Furniture: The French Designers*, London: Thames and Hudson, and New York: Holt Rinehart, 1984
Eileen Gray: Pioneer of Design (exhib. cat.), London: Heinz Gallery, 1972
Garner, Philippe, *Eileen Gray: Design and Architecture 1879–1976*, Cologne: Taschen, 1993
Johnson, J. Stewart, *Eileen Gray, Designer 1879–1976* (exhib. cat.), New York: Museum of Modern Art, 1979
"Lacquer Walls and Furniture Displace Old Gods in Paris and London" in *Harper's Bazaar* (New York), September 1920
Lakah, Paula and others, *Eileen Gray*, Berlin: Giessen, 1979
Loye, Brigitte, *Eileen Gray 1879–1976: Architecture, Design*, Paris: Viguier, 1984
Rykwert, Joseph, "Eileen Gray: The Houses and an Interior" in *Perspectiva* (New Haven), 9, 1971
Schlumberger, Eveline, "Interview with Eileen Gray" in *Connaissance des Arts*, 258, 1973
Sparke, Penny, *Domestic Furniture* (Twentieth-Century Design series), London: Bell and Hyman, 1986; as Furniture, New York: Dutton, 1986
Teitelbaum, Mo, "Lady of the Rue Bonaparte", *Sunday Times Magazine* (London), 22 June 1975
Wils, Jan and Jean Badovici, article in *Wendingen* (Amsterdam), no. 6, 1924

Greece, ancient

A discussion of interiors in Ancient Greece should begin by mentioning two defining conditions. First, Classical Greece was a world where life was lived outdoors. Second, decoration was integral to the forming of all Greek material culture – the Greeks used rich ornamentation and vivid colours in all their fabrication, whether of tools, clothes or buildings. There was no division between major and minor arts; no lines separated sculpture, architecture and decoration. Interior decoration, therefore, becomes a category of little relevance in this context.

Classical Athens had great building programmes of immense importance; these symbolised, made concrete, commemorated and enabled to be formed the great public events of social life. There were the *stadion* and the *oedion*, the places between buildings for great histories to be declaimed and the theatres for tragedies to be performed. In this way the spaces of the city were formed and inhabited; yet it was not a world of indoors. Even though the Athenians (in contrast to their peninsular rivals the Spartans) developed new building forms for everything in their young democracy, life was still conducted *en plein air*. The great Athenian law court, the *heliaia*, held 1,500 people – a minimum jury size numbered 201 citizens. Yet the court's walls were only about one metre high. Public life was visible, observed. The need to succeed, which defined the citizen, was as visible as the shame of failure. Civic rules – laws, agreements, and even the payments and contracts to build the famous temples – were chiselled in stone and set up outdoors.

With the citizenry spending its life outdoors – whether engaged in drama, politics, religion or law – solid public buildings in the city were particular objects. They were storehouses of one sort or another, and were not dedicated to human action. Seeing such places as objects of enclosure, there is a resonance with the boxes and chests which, for classical Greeks, signified the lives of women. And women were non-citizens; invisible in the civic agenda and its life.

Classical culture was defined by sets of opposites, and of these none ran deeper than that between citizen and non-citizen. All the aforementioned comments about "Athenian life", therefore, refer exclusively to the smallish minority of the male population who were citizens. Civic life and work took place outdoors. The farmer-citizen who took up arms for his *polis* (his city-state) in time of need, was their ideal model (as it would, millennia later, be that of the US Founding Fathers). Indoors was the realm of children and of women (whose principal occupation was weaving); of food, sex and sleep.

The greatest of the Classical Greek solid treasure chests, the Parthenon, epitomised this Athenian sensibility. Its outside, a columnar, rhetorically-clad skin (rather than a set of façades) was the most exposed and visible form in the city, an icon of civic unity. Its interior, dark and mysterious, clothed and shrouded the great image of their civic goddess Athena (known as *Parthenos*). The Parthenon was highly decorated with carved and gilded ceiling bosses glinting in the dim light far above the eye. Within the encircling double columns, deeply coloured patterning, fretwork ornament and an array of honeysuckle and palmette patterns, gilded bronze rails and grills could be discerned. But all this was for the goddess rather than the populace. The public ceremonies and processions, including the sacrifices at the great altars, like the attention of the human pilgrim, were all outdoors.

The temples were exquisitely formed storerooms. The Parthenon, uniquely, had two utterly different such spaces: one literally for the civic treasure, and another for Pheidias' vast figure of Athena all covered in ivory and gold. These stuffy, enclosed, airless boxes symbolise treasure; even more they symbolise motherhood and the link with the earth. (Athens' mythical ancestor, the child king Erekthonios was, as an infant, kept in a chest on the *akropolis*.)

Public life gave form to the immortality of the *polis*; in the *agora*, where the citizens governed themselves, and on the *akropolis* where their enduring greatness was celebrated. And, in their irresistible urge to polarise, private life was modest and simple, the hidden realm of necessity and of individual mortality. The city, then, was an almost Oriental mixture of splendidly formed and gilded public buildings in the midst of mean, ill-grouped housing.

Within the city streets, private spaces were indistinguishable: whether of new (5th century BC) opulence or of aching poverty. They all lay beyond the blank thresholds, outside which – in Athens at least – the citizens were *isoi*, equals in a politics structured by democratic *isonomia*. Inside the private world, beyond the high, windowless domestic walls, lived the women and servants. "A wife's business," said Xenophon in *Oikonomikos*, "will be to stay indoors." The rude, domestic forms were simple to an extreme: quarters for the women (where the domestic belongings were stored in chests), places for the preparation of food and cooking round the court (with small cells for storage of provisions), and men's quarters off the court (often with direct private access to the street); perhaps also a yard for domestic animals. All this spread away from the civic-monumental centre as an Indian or Yemeni town of today.

The larger courtyard dwelling was a miniature city, the yard its *agora* where the household freely mingled – if there were no strangers present. (Women of the household would not be in the court if there were male visitors.) It was surrounded by a colonnade onto which opened the rooms, often really formed with walls just back and sides. It was open to the sun and sky (main rooms to the northwest of the court to catch the sun), but quite cut off from the public realm beyond. It was centred on the peristyle of slender columns with, occasionally, a delicately patterned mosaic carpet.

Whatever the curtilage of the household, and it was often not rectangular, the dwelling inevitably centred on this strictly rectangular peristyle court, always the largest unit in the house. The Athenian suburb of Olynthus, for example, laid out exactly while the Parthenon was coming to completion in the later 5th century BC, was made up of ordered streets of back-to-back courtyard houses (separated only by a narrow lane), strung between wide avenues. Sometimes (but our only firm evidence is post-classical, notably from 4th-century Delos), two-storey homes could be centred on a magnificent double-height court with a colonnaded gallery running round the upper level.

In the classical 5th century BC, columns were wooden posts, floors usually cemented or just hardened earth, and the wonderfully decorative wall ornamentation and mosaic pavements of later years were still extremely rare. There was great restraint in domestic decoration, walls being strongly coloured, often in red. The predominant colours were still those archaic earth hues: white, yellow, red and black. There would be very few movable furnishings – though wonderfully restrained and elegant craftsmanship formed the noble beds, tripods, chests and chairs seen in their vase paintings and other representations. Fabrics of all kinds must have covered walls, enclosed colonnades, draped furniture and formed bedding.

In the next century, domestic luxury began to develop; it was not unusual for walls to be divided by highly ornamented dados, a metre from the floor, into dark bases and lighter higher areas, capped with painted friezes of egg-and-dart, meander, Greek key or other repeating elements, often now exploring a wider range of colours. Perspective painting, well-known in the classical period (though none remains), must have permeated the private realm, probably in murals of tempera on plaster, in the generations before the famous wall perspectives and *trompe-l'oeil* paintings of Rome and Pompeii.

But, whether descriptions derive from the 5th century BC or from later times when Athens had become a cultured backwater (like Cambridge to Rome's London), they always only refer to the one major interior space beyond the court: the *andron*. This room, often translated as "dining room" means, of course, the men's room. The women's quarters, the *gynaikeion*, were separate; and, if the household was affluent enough, they were upstairs, even including a room called *parthenon* or room of the virgins, being the one where sexual intercourse was taboo. Married women never penetrated the *andron* and the only women permitted within this area were servants or prostitutes.

Greek public life was exterior; Greek private life, beyond the *andron*, was considered so insignificant as to be invisible and certainly beyond the realm of interior design. The basic *andron* had fixed benches round the three sides, forming space for a dozen or more to recline. Here the men ate, reclining, spitting and throwing the food debris onto the floor, where it could be washed away towards a street drain. In larger houses, on top of the cemented raised brick platforms which often made a horseshoe shape of the *andron*, there would also be couches whereon they held their *symposia*, parties where they drank, flirted, fondled prostitutes (both male and female), talked, boasted and ate.

On the whole, domestic interiors were plain. The houses had mostly plastered unbaked brick walls on stone bases, with a steep wooden stair to an upper storey with a clay floor, and covered in a tiled, pitched roof. The rammed earth ground floor sometimes had a cemented finish which could be polished and occasionally decorated with mosaic, which might pick out the fixed position of the few important elements like couch or bed. Movable furniture existed only in the wealthiest of households where its design was of exquisite elegance and proportion, and it was made in chosen woods, perhaps inlaid, and with metal fixings.

Although fabrics were surely at the essence of the Greek interior, they have proved almost impossible to reconstruct, and their meaning, both sensual and cerebral, can only be guessed in a parallel study of the draping and revealing of Greek bodies with clothing. Curtains were used in place of doors and hangings were often perfumed. All women wove, and designs were both woven and printed onto cloth. Greeks also loved tents: nationally, the tent of Xerxes, won in battle, was an important Athenian icon; more domestically, splendid canopies were erected in gardens and at the *akademia* for *symposia*.

Greek houses also had kitchens, sometimes with flues, and washrooms, sometimes with terracotta basins. But virtually no clues survive as to the disposal of bodily waste in Classical interiors. Athens was a densely packed carpet of ill-drained courtyard-houses with inadequate latrines. The terrifying plague, more deadly than the Spartans, was no respecter of class or affluence; in its epidemic of 430 BC, it took as one of its last victims Athens' greatest leader, Perikles.

JOHN MCKEAN

Further Reading

For a comprehensive bibliography of Greek architecture see Dinsmoor, 1975. An authoritative study of ancient Greek furniture appears in Richter 1966.

Baker, Hollis S., *Furniture in the Ancient World: Origins and Evolution, 3100–475 BC*, New York: Macmillan, and London: The Connoisseur, 1966

Boardman, John (editor), *The Oxford History of Classical Art*, Oxford and New York: Oxford University Press, 1993

Dinsmoor, William Bell, *The Architecture of Ancient Greece*, 3rd edition London: Batsford, and New York: Norton, 1975

Kriesis, Anthony, *Greek Town Building*, Athens: National Technical University, 1965

Lawrence, A.W., *Greek Architecture*, 4th edition, revised by R.A. Tomlinson, Harmondsworth: Penguin, 1983

Ling, Roger, *Classical Greece*, Oxford: Phaidon, 1988

Martienssen, R.D., *The Idea of Space in Greek Architecture*, 2nd edition Johannesburg: Witwatersrand University Press, 1964

Pasztory, Esther, "Hellenic Identity and Athenian Identity in the Fifth Century BC" in Susan J. Barnes and Walter S. Melion (editors), *Cultural Differentiation and Cultural Identity in the Visual Arts*, Washington, DC: National Gallery of Art, 1989

Richter, G.M.A., *The Furniture of the Greeks, Etruscans and Romans*, London: Phaidon, 1966

Salonen, Armas, *Die Möbel des alten Mesopotamien*, Helsinki: Tiedeakatemian, 1963

Greene, Charles 1868–1957, and Greene, Henry 1870–1954

American architects, interior and furniture designers

Influenced by the ideology of the Arts and Crafts Movement, the designs of Charles Sumner Greene and Henry Mather Greene established the standard for the development of the California bungalow in the early decades of the 20th century. The Greenes were skilled as both architects and craftsmen in their own right. Their early work reflected their strong debt to Asian influences as well as a preference for residential commissions, which particularly suited their emphasis on complete aesthetic control. Their rigorous standards of craftsmanship and use of rich materials, combined with a masterful sense of space and detail, resulted in some of the most significant examples of American architecture and interior design from this period.

Early in life, with their father intent on establishing their architectural vocation, the two brothers were sent to a manual training school opened by Calvin Milton Woodward, a student of William Morris. Through the teachings at this school, the Greenes quickly absorbed the elements of Morris's philosophy and gained a particular respect for the elemental properties of various materials including wood and metals, thereby establishing the basis for their own approach to design. In 1891, after two years of study at the Massachusetts Institute of Technology, the brothers engaged in an architectural apprenticeship in Boston where they were first exposed to the arts of Asia through visits to the Boston Museum of Fine Arts. Their interest in the arts of China and Japan was further enhanced by a visit to the Japanese pavilion at the Chicago 1893 World's Columbian Exposition. As with Frank Lloyd Wright, another young architect visiting the Exposition, the simple lines and uncluttered spaces of the Japanese structures were ultimately to inspire the brothers towards a vocabulary in American architectural design that was greatly unlike the Neo-Classical ornamentalism of the Beaux-Arts school.

Soon after leaving the Exposition, the brothers travelled to Pasadena, California and found the cultural and natural environments particularly suitable for the development of their work. Their first few commissions involved an unusual combination of Shingle, Mission, and Neo-Classical styles that met with varying degrees of success. By 1901, their designs, including Charles's for interior furnishings, continued to develop in the face of other potential influences such as the work of C.F.A. Voysey, Will Bradley, Frank Lloyd Wright, and Peter Behrens, all of whom were becoming known through publications such as *International Studio Magazine and Ladies Home Journal*. Of particular importance to the changes in the Greenes' work was Gustav Stickley's *The Craftsman*, which heralded the most significant period of American Arts and Crafts philosophy. A few months after the first issue of *The Craftsman* appeared, the Greenes selected a number of pieces of Stickley furniture for the interior of the James A. Culbertson house (1902) in Pasedena, and began to experiment with built-in seating, contrasting bands of dark wood and tan-colored wall surfaces, and simple linear patterns for leaded windows. By 1903, with the construction of a house for his sisters-in-law, Martha, Violet, and Jane White, Charles began producing his own furniture designs for clients. Reflecting the growth of the American Arts and Crafts movement, during the next few years the Greenes increasingly developed the possibilities of a completely integrated structure which included their involvement in such details as the design or selection of furnishings, fabrics, pottery, and metalwork.

The Jennie A. Reeve (1904) and the Adelaide M. Tichenor residences (1904) in Long Beach, California both exemplify this development in the refinement of their interior design work. The Reeve interior still strongly reflects the vision of Stickley in Charles's rectilinear designs for the furniture, but other details, such as the delicately executed stylized patterns of the leaded glass and the forms of the copper light fixtures, betray the Greenes' attraction to Japanese-style elements. Through an understanding client and a free rein to control all aspects of the commission, the Tichenor residence became their first fully integrated bungalow which included a more mature expression of their creativity and interest in oriental motifs. The furniture for the house shows a departure from Stickley's severe lines with gently rounded Asian cloud-like forms which softened the designs and became a signature of their work in the period before 1909. The once angular forms became highly sculptural expressions of cabinetwork, revealing a sophistication and originality that were the Greenes' own. In addition, Charles's experimentation with varying widths of lead overlays for stained-glass panels provided new opportunities for the depiction of branches, vines, and other naturalistic motifs in a manner unlike, yet complementary to, the often geometric patterns preferred by Henry.

By 1905, as the Greenes continued to gain commissions and had established offices in both Los Angeles and Pasedena, the brothers turned to the firm of Peter and John Hall to execute their designs for furniture, and the firm of Harry Sturdy and Emile Lange for their complex stained-glass work. Aided by these talented craftsmen who could meet their high standard of workmanship, the Greenes quickly completed a number of commissions which won them recognition not only in Pasedena, but throughout the United States. During the next few years, the refinement of their work continued in such commissions as the additions and alterations to the Van Rossem House (1906), the Theodore Irwin House (1906), and the furnishings for Dr. William T. Bolton (1906). The Bolton furniture marked the first occurrence of their trademark square ebony "pegs" in joinery and marked a move away from the use of ash and oak to the richer teaks and Honduras mahoganies that characterized the interiors of their elaborate bungalows of the following three years.

Between 1907 and 1909, wealthy Easterners who were drawn to the pleasant climate of southern California offered the Greenes substantial commissions which resulted in some of the most elaborate and significant expressions of their mature style. The unlimited budgets of these few "ultimate bungalows" allowed the Greenes full control over all aspects of the design, including furnishings, textiles, and landscaping. These commissions include the residences for Freeman A. Ford (1907), Robert Blacker (1907), David B. Gamble (1908), and William R. Thorsen (1909). These homes show the Greenes' enthusiasm for sculpted wood and Asian motifs to the fullest; all exhibit similarities in their emphatic presentation of joinery and structural beams, expansive and flowing plans, and their integration of exterior spaces through extensive sleeping porches, terraces, and balconies. Although much larger than the Greenes' relatively simple shingle and stone houses of the previous years, these structures maintained a similar intimacy that resulted from their uncluttered simplicity and the Greenes' fastidious attention to detail. Art glass lanterns, windows, and ceiling panels provided indirect lighting through naturalistic and stylized patterns that were echoed in furniture inlays of ebony, silver, and fruitwood, appliqué for curtains, and painted or carved friezes that highlighted the wood-paneled walls. In typical Arts and Crafts style, earth-tones of faded gold and browns predominated, intended to harmonize with the natural wood finishes seen through the interior and exterior. The impact of these residences was felt throughout the nation over the next several years, inspiring other architects to offer their own, often much more modest versions of the Greenes' California bungalows.

In 1910, following Charles's year-long visit to England with his family, the brothers began designing a number of structures that were ultimately never to be constructed. Within a few years, due to the extreme costs of their demanding craftsmanship, combined with the public's generally declining interest in the vocabulary of the Arts and Crafts style, the Greenes' work began a gradual transformation. Following the completion of the Culbertson residence (1911) – their last commission which provided for complete interior furnishings – the brothers continued to work on an irregular basis. In 1916, Charles moved to Carmel, California to pursue other interests, and in 1922 their association was formally dissolved. During the 1920s, both brothers continued their independent work, often revising schemes for earlier clients. Charles continued producing designs for furniture, often highly carved with Chinese-derived imagery, while Henry concentrated on his architectural practice which began to exhibit the subtle influence of the Spanish Colonial Revival. However interesting, the work of their later years never equaled the complete vision and deft touch of their earlier bungalows which reflected a devotion to the supreme development of the Arts and Crafts home as a totally integrated environment.

KEVIN W. TUCKER

See also Arts and Crafts Movement

Charles Sumner Greene. Born in Brighton, Ohio, 12 October 1868. Educated at Calvin Milton Woodward Manual Training School, St. Louis; studied architecture, Massachusetts Institute of Technology, Cambridge, 1888–91. Married Alice Gordon White, 1901: 5 children. Worked for architects H. Lawford Warren, then for Winslow and Weatherall, 1891–94. Visited England, 1901 and 1910–11. Established architectural partnership with Henry Mather Greene, Pasadena, California, 1894–1903, Los Angeles, 1903–06, Pasadena, 1906–22. Active as a designer of furniture and furnishings from c.1903. Moved to Carmel, California, 1916; practised independently as a designer of furniture from 1922. Died in Carmel, 11 June 1957.

Henry Mather Greene. Born in Brighton, Ohio, 23 January 1870. Educated at Calvin Milton Woodward Manual Training School, St. Louis; studied architecture, Massachusetts Institute of Technology, Cambridge, 1888–91. Married Emeline Augusta Dart, 1899: 4 children. Worked for architects Stickney and Austin, then for Shepley, Rutan and Coolidge, Boston, 1891–94. Established architectural partnership with Charles Sumner Greene, Pasadena, California, 1894–1903, Los Angeles, 1903–06, Pasadena, 1906–22; practised independently as an architect, Pasadena, from 1922. Died in Altadena, California, 2 October 1954.

Selected Works

The Greene and Greene Library and Archives, containing drawings, designs, company records and books, is held by the University of Southern California, Los Angeles. Examples of Greene and Greene's furniture are in the Gamble House, Pasadena, the Los Angeles County Museum of Art, and the Oakland Museum.

Interiors

1902	James A. Culbertson House, Pasadena, California (building and interiors)
1903	Josephine Van Rossem House, Pasadena, California (building and interiors; additions, 1906)
1903	Martha, Violet and Jane White House, Pasadena, California (building and interiors)
1904	Jennie A. Reeve House, Long Beach, California (building and interiors)
1904	Adelaide M. Tichenor House, Long Beach, California (building, interiors and furnishings)
1906	Theodore M. Irwin House, Pasadena, California (building, interiors and furnishings)
1907	Robert R. Blacker House, Pasadena, California (building, interiors, and furnishings)
1907	Freeman A. Ford House, Pasadena, California (building, interiors and furnishings)

1908 David B. Gamble House, Pasadena, California (building, interiors and furnishings)
1909 Charles M. Pratt House, Ojai, California (building, interiors and furnishings)
1909 William R. Thorsen House, Berkeley, California (building, interiors and furnishings)
1911 Cordelia A. Culbertson House, Pasadena, California (building, interiors and furnishings)

The Greenes designed furniture and furnishings for their buildings from c.1903; their furniture was executed by Peter and John Hall, and their stained glass by Harry Sturdy and Emile Lange.

Further Reading

For a comprehensive descriptive account of Greene and Greene's architectural and design commissions, and full primary and secondary bibliographies, see Makinson 1977–79.

Bosley, Edward R., *Gamble House: Greene and Greene*, London: Phaidon, 1992

Bowman, Leslie Greene, *American Arts and Crafts: Virtue in Design*, Los Angeles: Los Angeles County Museum of Art, 1990

Clark, Robert Judson (editor), *The Arts and Crafts Movement in America, 1876–1916*, Princeton: Princeton University Press, 1972

Current, Karen, *Greene and Greene: Architects in the Residential Style* (exhib. cat.), Fort Worth, Texas: Amon Carter Museum of Western Art, 1974

Doumato, Lamia, *The Greene Brothers* (bibliography), Monticello, IL: Vance, 1980

Greene and Greene: The Architecture and Related Designs of Charles Sumner Greene and Henry Mather Greene, 1894–1934, Los Angeles: Municipal Art Gallery, 1977

Kaplan, Wendy (editor), *"The Art that is Life": The Arts and Crafts Movement in America, 1875–1920* (exhib. cat.: Museum of Fine Arts, Boston), Boston: Little Brown, 1987

Makinson, Randell L., *A Guide to the Work of Greene and Greene*, Salt Lake City: Peregrine Smith, 1974

Makinson, Randell L., chapter on Greene and Greene in Esther McCoy, *Five California Architects*, New York: Praeger, 1975

Makinson, Randell L., *Greene and Greene*, 2 vols., Salt Lake City: Peregrine Smith, 1977–79

Makinson, Randell L., *David B. Gamble House, Pasadena, California*, 1908, Tokyo: ADA, 1984 (Global Architecture 66)

Marks, Alan, "Greene and Greene: A Study in Functional Design" in *Fine Woodworking*, 12, September 1978

Trapp, Kenneth R. (editor), *The Arts and Crafts Movement in California: Living the Good Life* (exhib. cat.: Oakland Museum), New York: Abbeville, 1993

Gropius, Walter 1883–1969

German architect and designer

After training as an architect in Charlottenburg and Munich, Walter Gropius entered the Berlin practice of Peter Behrens in 1907. Gropius subsequently acknowledged the significance of this apprenticeship, stating "I owe him much, particularly the habit of thinking in principles ... endowed with willpower and a penetrating intellect ... moved more by reason than emotion." These qualities also characterised Gropius's own approach to architecture and interior design after he established his own Berlin office in 1910.

In conjunction with Adolf Meyer, one of Gropius's first designs to attract international interest was the Model Factory built for the 1914 Deutscher Werkbund exhibition. In a radical use of new materials, Gropius enclosed two corner staircases in a wall of glass. This marked an end to the division between interior and exterior in architecture, and a consequent unity between the building's interior space and surrounding environment.

The concern to resolve divisions – between arts and crafts, theory and practice – characterizes Gropius's teaching at the Bauhaus, where he was installed as Director in 1919. The principles that Gropius outlined in the first Bauhaus manifesto stressed the need for collaboration in solving design problems, the link between design and industrial technology, and "the common citizenship of all forms of creative work and their logical interdependence on one another."

This "benign regeneration of design" (Fitch 1960) fell into two important phases during Gropius's time at the Bauhaus. As Master of Form and Colour in the Technical Workshop from 1921 to 1925, he introduced the basic laws of design in relation to form, colour and proportion. Among the early successful products of the course were the first examples of Marcel Breuer's furniture, which combined innovative use of cheap, durable raw materials with an easy adaptability to commercial mass production.

When the school moved from Weimar to Dessau in 1925, Gropius oversaw the building of a new Bauhaus. All the functions of the school were combined under one roof, with the canteen, auditorium and theatre areas being noteworthy. In an economic use of space, these three rooms could be opened out into one large "play area" for social functions. The auditorium showed the collective subordination of all the arts to *Bauen* (building) incorporating Breuer furniture, lamps by the Technical Workshop, and murals by the Decorative Workshop.

In tandem with the design of the school, Gropius created five Masters' Houses nearby, to house the teaching staff. Here the corridor is done away with as an internal feature, with Gropius continuing to wrestle with problems of space and layout. Large windows along one wall made the rooms light and airy, with the placing of the furniture completing the "unity" of the interior according to the Bauhaus model. Breuer chairs were included, and cupboards and cabinets, made of different kinds of stained and polished wood, added to the visual stimulus for the inhabitant.

On return to private practice, Gropius embarked on the design of furniture for the Feder stores in Berlin (1929). Bauhaus features of easy assembly, standardized, interchangable components, and the substitution of a handmade for an industrial finish, are prominent. Of equal significance was Gropius's appointment as Director of Design for the 1930 Werkbund exhibition in Paris, where his prototype for a high-rise flat was the centrepiece of a display of German industrial products. The hall, living room and study echo the Masters' Houses with their economic deployment of Breuer furniture, and a new feature was the open-work metal staircase.

Increasing political hostility from the Nazi government saw the tailing off of his practice and Gropius moved to London in 1934. Engaged by Jack Pritchard's Isokon company, Gropius completed buildings in partnership with Maxwell Fry, particularly Impington village school near Cambridge. When Isokon established a furniture subsidiary in 1935, Gropius was appointed Controller of Design. He exhibited prototypes for a sofa, armchair and mirror glass fireplace in Flat 37 at a

Gropius: interior of Sommerfeld House, with Adolf Meyer and Joost Schmidt, Berlin, 1920–21

Manchester department store, but none of these reached production. Elliott's suggestion that Gropius's spell in England was a "transitional phase", seeking to establish "a rational methodology for the solution of design problems", is apt (Elliott, 1974).

Gropius emigrated to the US in 1937 to take up a Professorship of Architecture at Harvard. He collaborated with Breuer in the construction of the Gropius house at Lincoln, Massachusetts, "shaping the patterns of life through building." The interior was entirely open-plan, providing for better air circulation, and large windows were again used to expand the interior space. The relationship of the interior to the surrounding environment was stressed by a colour scheme of white, grey, earth and red. The interior was kept cool by means of external ovehangs, and almost all the fixtures were factory made, most strikingly the iron spiral stairway. Furnishings included Breuer's famous *Isokon* long chair.

Shortly after Gropius founded The Architects Collaborative (TAC) in 1946, he completed his first significant post-war design at the Harvard Graduate Center (1949–50). The layout of student dormitories, and the open-plan dining room and lounge at the heart of the building again reflects the experiments in the Dessau Bauhaus, and Gropius's continuing insistence on inter-disciplinary cooperation and the exchange of ideas.

Focusing on his work with TAC from 1952, Gropius maintained his interest in industrial design, witnessed in the 1963 Rosenthal Ceramics factory at Selb, Germany. The interior of this prefabricated structure was laid out in a flexible manner so that the firm had space to incorporate future technical innovations. This layout eliminated inefficient use of space and any friction in the manufacturing process. At the same time, architectural stimulation was provided for the worker engaged on repetitive tasks, with the tiles of individual workshops painted in primary colours. Furthermore, a greenhouse, with trees, bushes, flowers and birds was incorporated in the centre of the factory space, to provide a natural counterpoint to the mechanistic environment.

Buildings like the Rosenthal factory underpin Gropius's reputation as an important pioneer of 20th century architecture, which often obscures his achievements in furniture and interior design. László Moholy-Nagy provided a most effective summary of Gropius's career in 1945, stating that "Fearlessly and uncompromisingly he defended the principles on which the Bauhaus was built: that art and architecture which fail to serve for the betterment of our environment are socially destructive by aggravating instead of healing the ills of an iniquitous social system".

JONATHAN BLACKWOOD

See also Bauhaus; Modernism

Biography

Born in Berlin, 18 May 1883. Studied architecture at the Königliche Technische Hochschule, Munich, 1903–07. Married 1) Alma Mahler (divorced); 2) Ise Frank; one daughter. Chief assistant to Peter Behrens (1868–1940), Berlin, 1907–10. Established his own architectural practice, Berlin, 1910; designed furniture and interiors from c.1913. Served in the military, 1914–18. Appointed Director, Staatliche Bauhaus, Weimar, 1919; Director, Dessau Bauhaus, 1925. Resumed private practice, Berlin, 1928; Vice-President, Congrès Internationaux d'Architecture Moderne (CIAM), 1929–57; moved to London and worked in private practice with Maxwell Fry, 1934–37; controller of design, Isokon furniture company, London, 1935. Settled in the United States, 1937; Professor of Architecture, Graduate School of Design, Harvard University, Cambridge, Massachusetts, 1937: Chair, 1938–52; Professor Emeritus, 1952. Worked in partnership with Marcel Breuer (1902–1981), 1938–43; established his own firm, The Architects Collaborative (TAC), Cambridge, Massachusetts, 1946. Published extensively on architecture and design. Received numerous honours and awards including: Royal Gold Medal, Royal Institute of British Architects, 1956; Gold Medal, American Institute of Architects, 1959; Grand State Prize of Architecture, 1960. Died in Boston, 5 July 1969.

Selected Works

Interiors

1911–12	Fagus Factory, Alfeld (building and interiors with Adolf Meyer)
1913	World's Fair, Ghent (interiors)
1913–14	German Railroad Sleeping Car (interiors)
1913–14	Werkbund Exhibition, Cologne (building and layout of interiors with Adolf Meyer)
1920–21	Adolf Sommerfeld House (building and interiors with Adolf Meyer and Joost Schmidt)
1925	Director's House, Bauhaus, Dessau (building and interiors)
1925	Gropius Residence, Dessau (building and interiors)
1925–26	Bauhaus Building, Dessau (building and interiors)
1929	Feder Furniture Stores, Berlin (building, interiors and some furniture)
1930	Werkbund Exhibition, Paris (building and layout of interiors and some furniture)
1936	Levy House, London (building and interiors with Maxwell Fry)
1936	Impington Village School, Cambridgeshire (building and interiors with Maxwell Fry)
1937	Gropius House, Lincoln, Massachusetts (building and interiors with M. Breuer)
1938	Breuer House I, Lincoln, Massachusetts (building, furnishings and interiors; with M. Breuer)
1939	Frank House, Pittsburgh (building and interiors with M. Breuer)
1949–50	Harvard Graduate Center, Cambridge, Massachusetts (building and interiors with TAC)
1963	Rosenthal Ceramics Factory, Selb, Germany (building and interiors with TAC)

Publications

Programm des Staatlichen Bauhauses, 1919
Idee und Aufbau des Staatlichen Bauhauses, 1923
Editor, *Neue Arbeiten in Bauhauswerkstätten*, 1925
The New Architecture and the Bauhaus, 1935
Bauhaus, 1919–1928 (with Herbert Bayer and Ise Gropius), 1938
Rebuilding Our Communities, 1945
Architecture and Design in the Age of Science, 1952
The Scope of Total Architecture, 1955
Editor, with others, *The Architects Collaborative 1945–1965*, 1965
Vertical City, 1968
Apollo in the Democracy: The Cultural Obligation of the Architect, 1968

Further Reading

The standard monograph on Gropius is Isaacs 1991 which includes numerous references to primary and secondary sources. Elliott 1974 is an indispensable guide to the years in England.

Berdini, Paolo (editor), *Walter Gropius*, Bologna: Zanichelli, 1983

Busignani, Alberto, *Gropius*, London: Hamlyn, 1973

Droste, Magdalena, *Bauhaus, 1919–1933*, Cologne: Taschen, 1990

Elliott, David, *Gropius in England*, London: Building Centre Trust, 1974

Fitch, James Marston, *Walter Gropius*, New York: Braziller, 1960; London: Mayflower, 1961

Franciscano, Marcel, *Walter Gropius and the Creation of the Bauhaus in Weimar: The Ideals and Artistic Theories of its Founding Years*, Urbana: University of Illinois Press, 1971

Gropius, Ise, and James Marston Fitch (introduction), *Walter Gropius: Buildings, Plans, Projects, 1906–1969*, Lincoln, MA: Ise Gropius, 1972

Isaacs, Reginald R., *Gropius at Harvard*, Berlin: Bauhaus-Archiv, 1983

Isaacs, Reginald R., *Gropius: An Illustrated Biography of the Creator of the Bauhaus*, Boston: Little Brown, 1991

Nerdinger, Winfried, *Walter Gropius* (in German and English), Berlin: Mann, and Cambridge, MA: Harvard University Busch-Reisinger Museum of Art, 1985

Neumann, Eckhard (editor), *Bauhaus and Bauhaus People*, New York: Van Nostrand Reinhold, and London: Chapman and Hall, 1993

Pritchard, Jack, "Gropius, the Bauhaus and the Future" in *Journal of the Royal Society of Arts*, 117, January 1969, pp.55–94

Richard, Lionel, *Walter Gropius: Architecture and Society*, Paris: Linteau, 1995

Wingler, Hans Maria, *Walter Gropius, Werk und Persönlichkeit*, Darmstadt: Bauhaus-Archiv, 1963

Grottoes and Shellwork

A grotto is an artificial cave, either designed or decorated to simulate a natural cave, or to evoke the mythical associations of caves as dwelling places of the gods. Although most examples formed part of the garden and in this sense were exterior architectural features, several were adjoined to large houses or were installed in the basement levels, and most also served as semi-habitable rooms and included decorations made of pebbles and shells and specially designed furnishings.

Natural caves were traditionally identified with springs and the source of rivers, and their symbolic associations are well-known. They were represented in classical mythology either as the homes for gods and spirits, or as places of transition between this and other worlds. In the Christian era the cave became associated with the nativity and the tomb of the resur-

Grotto at Woburn Abbey, Bedfordshire, c.1630

rection, and with the ascetic tradition of the hermit, retired from active life for the purpose of contemplation.

In ancient Rome the artificial grotto was a familiar garden feature of the grander villa. Grottoes were traditionally built as places of cool retreat from the heat of the day, for rest or contemplation, sometimes as banqueting rooms, often with fountains. The taste for both rustic grottoes and the more formal architectural "nymphaea" – shrines dedicated to nymphs – was revived in Renaissance Italy, as part of the wider revival of the ideal of classical civilisation. Popular features of larger-scale gardens in France and Germany, and throughout Europe, in the 16th and 17th centuries, grottoes became an essential ingredient of the picturesque landscape garden in England, when they were prized for their classical associations and evocation of the "Sublime".

The appeal of the grotto has always been the expressive use of natural materials in its decoration: natural rocks, shells, minerals and glass, as well as water. The delight of the patron or designer was found chiefly in the ingenuity with which natural aesthetic effects could be recreated, and new aesthetic effects created by using natural materials or forms. John Woolridge in *Art of Gardening* (1677) observed the Mediterranean tradition of the grotto and recommended it to the English "to repose ourselves in the time of our summer faint heats" ... "it is a place that is capable of so much pleasure and delight, that you may bestow not undeservedly what cost you please on it by paving it with marble or immuring it with stone or Rock-work either natural or artificial to resemble the excellencies of nature". Nature was tamed, and at the same time its wildness and irregularity celebrated in such schemes. One famous description appears in Alberti's treatise *De re aedificatoria* (1485): "the ancients used to dress the walls of their grottoes and caverns with all manner of rough work, with little chips of pumice or soft Tybertine stone which Ovid calls the living pumice: and some I have known daub them over with green wax, in imitation of the mossy slime which we always see in our moist grottoes. I was extremely pleased with an artificial grotto which I have seen of this sort, with a clear spring of water falling from it; the walls were composed of various sorts of sea-shells lying roughly together, some reversed, some with their mouths outwards, their colours being so artfully blended as to form a very beautiful variety."

The evidence of ancient ruins and the references to grottoes in classical literature were the sources for the design and decoration of the grottoes of the Italian Renaissance. The same central themes therefore applied: the associations with water; iconographical associations with nymphs and sea gods; irregular rock forms, even if confined to the central fountain; and the purpose of the grotto as a place of retreat and contemplation.

An important surviving example of the grotto of the later 16th century, designed by the Mannerist architect Bernardo Buontalenti (1531–1608) is the Grotta Grande (1583–93) of the Boboli Gardens, in Florence, which was completed for the Grand Duke Francesco I de' Medici. The external form was classical, a central arched opening beneath a triangular pediment. The edges and outline of this classical form were deliberately disordered with irregular artificial incrustation. Within, a series of smaller grottoes were connected by a passage. In the first were placed four sculptures, "rough hewn" figures of slaves, by Michelangelo; in the third grotto there was a mosaic wall fountain with the figure of Venus by Giovanni da Bologna. And "it is only when the eye has grown accustomed to the dim light that it becomes aware of the countless shells on the pedestals of the statues and on the walls" (Lotz, 1995). It was a bizarre and new creation, drawn with reference to the imagined classical past; indeed it appeared almost to have emerged from the ground as an excavation. According to Naomi Miller, "the overwhelming impression is that of a ruin resurrected; it is the *idea* of antiquity incarnate" (Miller, 1982).

Consistently popular as garden features throughout Europe in the later 16th and 17th century, the grotto was usually part of a highly formal symmetrical garden arrangement or at the end of a walk or vista – such as the Grottoes of Venus and Diana (1560–75) in the Villa D'Este at Tivoli. They were also important settings for sophisticated fountains and waterworks as in the magnificent architectural Grotte de Thetis at Versailles, built 1664–72. It was in England in the 18th century that the grotto became a popular feature of the "picturesque" landscape movement. As in the Renaissance period, the evocation of the classical world was important, but at the same time the irregular naturalistic qualities were increasingly valued. An external form would sometimes be almost hidden in the landscape, "a rude structure" seemingly carved from rock, while within the grottoes might be gloriously decorated with shells, flints and other minerals. The taste for the "Sublime" experience in the mid 18th century was stimulated by the contrasts and ambiguity of the grotto, curiosity and "astonishment" combined.

The grotto built by the poet Alexander Pope at Twickenham between 1719 and 1725 was one of the first fashionable grottoes of this period. It was a place of contemplation, and at once a challenge to the senses and an inspiration to the spirit, rich in classical allusion. Pope's grotto was, and is, entirely subterranean. It was described by an anonymous contemporary in 1747:

> The grotto is an irregular vault and passage, open at both extremities, and further illuminated by two windows to the front. In passing along it, we are presented with many openings and cells, which owe their forms to a diversity of pillars and jambs, ranged after no set Order or Rule, but aptly favouring the Particular designs of the place; they seem, as roughly hew'd out of Rocks and Beds of mineral strata, discovering in the fissures and angular breaches, variety of flints, spars, ores, shells, etc.

The visual impression for the visitor was not, however, static. First, water was observed: "among [the minerals and ores] the stream issuing from the spring of water .. distributed to a diversity of purposes". Second, "to still more increase the delight" pieces of mirrors had been concealed in obscure places to reflect, as Pope himself wrote in a letter to a Mr. Blount in 1725, "a lamp .. [which when] .. hung in the Middle, a thousand pointed Rays glitter and reflected over the place".

The 18th-century English grotto could also serve as an element in an iconographic sequence as in the landscape gardens at Stourhead, in Wiltshire. These gardens were laid out for the banker Henry Hoare in the 1740s, with a series of garden buildings and temples in the classical idiom. Intended to inspire contemplation, they culminated in a dramatic circular and domed grotto (1748) built of ancient-looking dark-coloured tufa rock – the grotto survives today. The floor was made of pebbles laid in concentric patterns, and within the central chamber lay the figure of a sleeping nymph, in painted lead, over a spring pool with a continual cascade – Hoare referred to the grotto as "the temple of the nymph". A second figure within the grotto complex – a finely modelled figure of a River God by Cheere – prompted this observation from Horace Walpole: "the most fortunately placed grotto is that at Stourhead where the river bursts from the urn of its god, and passes on its course through the cave".

Grottoes were often decorated with shells and stones. Professionally executed shell decoration was popular in France from the 16th century and numerous examples of Nymphaea and grottoes whose walls were encrusted with shells followed. One of the earliest such edifices was the grotto in the Bastie d'Urfé (1535) whose interior was covered with arrangements of shells and pebbles. Later examples included the Nymphaeum of the Maisons-Lafitte (1642), designed by François Mansart, and the shell cottage in the royal park at Rambouillet built by the Duc de Penthiève for his widowed daughter-in-law, the Princesse de Lamballe. Known in the 1730s as *rocaille*, shellwork was used both as a decorative material, covering walls and surfaces with a rough, irregular finish, and as an inspirational motif in ornament and design. The engravings of designers such as Juste-Aurèle Meissonnier illustrate many types of *boiseries*, wall decoration, frames and other carved decoration whose curved, scallop shapes clearly echo those of shells. And as forms such as rocks, corals, and shells became more popular, *rocaille* effectively gave its name to the new style of interior decoration known as Rococo that emerged in many parts of Europe from the second quarter of the 18th century.

However, it was in England that the passion for shell decoration really took hold. It was frequently carried out by enthusiastic amateurs. Mrs. Delaney, one of the principal arbiters of taste in the mid 18th century, often referred to the new fashion for shell-collecting and for decorating summer-houses and grottoes with shells gathered on beaches in her letters. "I have got a new madness, I am running wild after shells", she declared and went on, "the beauty of shells is as infinite as flowers, and to consider how they are inhabited enlarges a field of wonder that leads one insensibly to the great Director and author of these works".

There is perhaps no better example of the "madness" for shells than the incomparable shellwork grotto at Goodwood in

Sussex (1739) which was obsessively decorated by Sarah, Duchess of Richmond and her daughters. Thousands of shells were used, many collected in the South Seas by Captain Knowles of HMS *Diamond*, and shells covered the entire room – including the remarkable vaulted and coffered ceiling – with geometric patterns and motifs of stars and flowers. A similarly striking interior, containing unique hand-made decorations of feather and shellwork was made by the Misses Jane and Mary Parminter for their cottage orné, A La Ronde in Devon (1810–11), and such is the sophistication of these schemes that it is hard to credit that they were done by amateurs.

By the middle of the 19th century grottoes and shellwork interiors had become curiosities and represented a popular middle-class tourist attraction. Shells themselves, however, continued to serve as the inspiration for furnishings well into the 20th century. Thomas Chippendale's *Director* had illustrated several examples of fanciful scallop and shell chairs, and shellwork also appeared on some of the early 19th century furniture in the Brighton Pavilion. But it was in the 1920s and 1930s that such furnishings once again became fashionable. The French *couturier*, Helena Rubinstein's neo-Rococo Paris apartment included some extravagant examples of chairs designed by André Mare in the form of a shell and finished in lacquered silver leaf, and distorted shell-shape furniture and sculptures appeared in several Surrealist and neo-Baroque settings of the 1920s and 1930s. More recently, shells and pebbles formed an important feature as table arrangements in David Hicks's interiors of the 1970s.

JEREMY MUSSON

See also Buontalenti

Selected Collections

Notable examples of grottoes and shellwork interiors in England survive at A La Ronde, Devon, Goodwood House, Sussex, and Woburn Abbey, Bedfordshire; in France at the Bastie d'Urfé, Maisons-Lafitte, Château Rambouillet, and the Nymphaeum, Jouy en Josas; in Germany, at the Schloss Nymphenburg, and the Alte Residenz, Munich, and the Weissenstein Palace, Pommersfelden; and in Italy in the Boboli Gardens, Florence, Villa Castello, Florence, and the Villa Giulia, Rome.

Further Reading

A detailed discussion of the development and fashion for grottoes in Britain, including a gazetteer, appears in Jones 1974; information on Italian and Renaissance grottoes can be found in Miller 1982 and Lazzaro 1990. For a recent survey of the use of shellwork in interior decoration and furnishings see Mauries 1994.

Acidini, Christina Lucinat and Lauro Magnani (editors), *Arte del Grotte*, conference proceedings, 17 June 1985, SAGEP, Genoa

Aubin, R. A., "Grottoes, Geology and the Gothic Revival" in *Studies in Philology*, 32, 1934, pp.408–16

Coffin, David R., *Gardens and Gardening in Papal Rome*, Princeton: Princeton University Press, 1991

Cornforth, John, "An Extravagance of Shells" in *Country Life*, CLXIV, 24 August 1978, pp.495–98

Cornforth, John and John Fowler, "Ladies' Amusements" in their *English Decoration in the 18th Century*, London: Barrie and Jenkins, and Princeton, NJ: Pyne, 1974; 2nd edition, Barrie and Jenkins, 1978

Cox, Ian (editor), *The Scallop: Studies of a Shell and Its Influence on Humankind*, London: Shell Transport and Trading, 1957

Harris, Dale and Sally Sample Aall, *Follies and Fantasies: Germany and Austria*, New York: Abrams, 1994

Heikamp, Detlef, "The 'Grotta Grande' in the Boboli Gardens, Florence" in *Connoisseur*, 199, no.299, 1978, pp.38–43

Heydenreich, Ludwig H., *Architecture in Italy, 1400–1500*, revised by Paul Davis, New Haven and London: Yale University Press, 1996

Howe, Bea, "A La Ronde" in *Country Life*, 3 March 1966

Howley, James, *The Follies and Garden Buildings of Ireland*, New Haven and London: Yale University Press, 1993

Hunt, John Dixon and Peter Willis, *The Genius of the Place: The English Landscape Garden, 1670–1820*, London: Elek, and New York: Harper, 1975

Jones, Barbara, *Follies and Grottoes*, 2nd edition London: Constable, 1974

Jourdain, Margaret, "Shellwork Rooms and Grottoes" in *Country Life*, 95, February 1944, pp.241–43

Lambton, Lucinda, *An Album of Curious Houses*, London: Chatto and Windus, 1988

Lazzaro, Claudia, *The Italian Renaissance Garden*, New Haven and London: Yale University Press, 1990

Lotz, Wolfgang, *Architecture in Italy, 1500–1600*, New Haven and London: Yale University Press, 1995

Mauries, Patrick, *Shellshock: Conchological Curiosities*, London: Thames and Hudson, 1994

Miller, Naomi, *Heavenly Caves: Reflections on the Garden Grotto*, London: Allen and Unwin, and New York: Braziller, 1982

Guimard, Hector 1867–1942

French architect and designer

Hector Guimard was the most important and original French exponent of the Art Nouveau style in architecture – which, with characteristic assurance, he termed "Style Guimard." His most famous designs are the sinuous cast-iron entrances to the Paris Métro stations (from 1900), yet the interiors which he created for residences and apartment buildings are among his most compelling and coherent statements. Like his Belgian contemporaries Victor Horta and Henry van de Velde, Guimard insisted that a structure's interior and exterior create a unified expression, and he was not content to leave this unity to chance. Whenever possible he designed not only fireplaces, window grilles, and banisters for his buildings, but also their hardware, wallpapers, curtains and furnishings. The enveloping totality of his interiors might have been stifling except for Guimard's mastery of taut line and soft color. His best rooms were sinewy and light, held in tension with their own peculiar rhythmic logic.

As a young man, Guimard was attracted to Viollet-le-Duc's interpretation of the Gothic revival. He did not really find his stride until 1895, when he visited Horta's Hôtel Tassel (Brussels, 1893). His interiors for the apartment building Castel Béranger (Paris, 1894–98) were completely reworked upon his return and directly incorporated many of Horta's ideas, particularly his extensive use of iron, stained glass and smooth, fluid forms inspired by plant-life. Both Guimard and Horta disdained naturalistic floral or leaf ornament, preferring the abstract linear character of stems, stalks and branches. But whereas Horta's whiplash line is consistently urgent, abrupt and quick, Guimard's is langourous and vegetal, its brief rushes interrupted with curled, knotted pauses like the growth nodes of a stem. His characteristic branching ornament is both powerfully suggestive and unfamiliar: as a result, his interiors create the impression of a comprehensible alien world. Inspired by Viollet-le-Duc, Guimard aspired to use modern materials "honestly" – he often, for example, left the rivets in his ironwork visible. He also experimented with unusual combinations of materials for textural or pictorial effect. However, his designs – which were usually conceived as drawings or clay models – make it clear that materials were always secondary to "Style Guimard."

The vestibule of Castel Béranger was dominated by a fantastic, asymmetrical wrought-iron gate, but its overall effect depended on a complex confluence of elements: iron pilasters snaking upward into arches; stained-glass windows, sheet-metal strapwork, and mosaic floor tiles which echoed the gate's undulating line; and ceramic wall panels in thick, swirling relief. Glazed in coppery green, these panels lend a cool, dark, grotto-like quality, and their indefinite design seems almost to have been frozen in mid-swell. In the stairwells, Guimard installed irregular grids of glass brick. His distinctive line found its way into the Castel's stair carpeting, wallpapers and embossed Lincrusta-Walton wall panels, fireplaces, mouldings, even the doorknobs and lockplates. Much of the iron and woodwork was painted, and the hand-tinted plates in Guimard's album promoting the Castel recall its soft palette of peach, sage green, pine, dusky gold, pale blue and yellow against white. The surviving stained glass, while more vivid, is in similar hues. One of Guimard's first tenants, the painter Paul Signac, described his new home as "Eccentric ... but gay, practical and bright."

For the Maison Coilliot in Lille (1898–1900), Guimard used warm, strong yellows, greens and blues, and wrapped the hallway with enamelled lava blocks whose incised patterns were related to the enamelled iron panels in the Métro entrances. These rough blocks offered a textural contrast to the hall's rippled stained glass, carved woodwork and moulded stucco. The fireplace for Maison Coilliot was also made from lava, glazed tawny gold and fitted with a strikingly elaborate cabinet in pearwood with enamelled glass. Two shelf units flanked the fireplace, and slender vining supports rose from these to a broad, glassed cabinet that spanned the chimney's width. Twining above this, the supports terminated in small curved shelves for art objects. Guimard rarely designed new forms, but his vigorous, elastic line could transform clichés like the Victorian parlor cabinet into remarkably original pieces. His use of asymmetry, moreover, was carefully balanced. A few exceptions verged on the bizarre: a bench for Castel Béranger had a high, serpentine back which incorporated display shelves and a small corner cabinet, and several of his sideboards and overmantels also sprouted shelves from thin, branching extensions. These rank among his most dramatic linear gestures, with an exuberance comparable to the Métro streetlamps.

In general, however, Guimard's furniture was surprisingly restrained. His own desk, an L-shaped wedge laid over two independent cabinets, has sometimes been admired as a precursor of modern Functionalist furniture. The vigorous, grasping arms of his boudoir chairs express muscle as graphically as the best Rococo examples; and his dining chairs use their structure as line, spilling over in wave-like carved flourishes at critical junctures. On beds and wardrobes, Guimard confined ornament to the edges and corners, leaving wide expanses untouched. The looping cast-metal hardware was always of his own design. Although the Castel Béranger furniture was mostly mahogany, he later turned to fruitwoods (especially pear), whose fine grain responds well to carving. The quality of cabinetwork produced in his studio was consistently excellent. Guimard's perfectionism and intricate designs, of course, resulted in very steep prices.

While not technically built-in, the Maison Coilliot fireplace cabinet was clearly custom designed. Guimard also offered furniture of his own design to tenants at the Castel, an option he later provided only for private residences. The Castel Henriette in Sèvres (1898), Hôtel Nozal (1902) and Hôtel Mezzara (1910; both Paris) were among the most important commissions for which Guimard provided furnishings. He equipped Castel Henriette's dining room with a table and chairs, a tall chandelier cradling both candles and electric light in a teardrop-shaped cage, and a massive sideboard and overmantel which grazed the moulded stucco frieze. Later cabinetwork was more unified: the lower two-thirds of his own oval dining room (Hôtel Guimard, Paris, 1909–12) were fitted with continuous pearwood panels which incorporated shelves, a mirrored cabinet with an inset marble shelf, and a china cupboard with glass doors. Although richly carved, the panels and cabinets – now housed in the Musée des Arts Décoratifs, Paris – flow gently into one another, without the spiky tendonous quality seen in Guimard's earlier furniture. Above them, an embossed frieze was set below long tongues of moulded stucco ornament. In the center of the room hung a chandelier with two layers of beaded fringe, and the windows were draped with open mesh curtains to reveal the stained glass. The carpet was decorated with an all-over composition of interlaced line. This reserved, luxurious interior in Guimard's mature style was in stark contrast to those in the Castel Béranger.

Photographs reveal Guimard's eclectic use of decorative objects and floral arrangements, which was entirely in keeping with Aesthetic taste. The shelves in his office were filled with small figural sculptures, vases and ripe, informal bouquets; a landscape painting hung inside the overmantel. For staged photos of Castel Béranger's apartments, he hung striped cotton or lace curtains and a Toulouse-Lautrec poster, placed a Japanese figurine in a mantel niche, and set cushions and potted palms on the floor. Guimard placed his own vases – the ancestors of his designs for Sèvres – alongside gracefully dishevelled piles of books.

Perhaps Guimard's most intriguing interior was the auditorium of the Humbert de Romans (Paris, 1897–1901), designed as a concert hall. A broad octagon, its exposed, branching steel structure brilliantly evoked both a forest and a cathedral while preserving its essentially industrial character. The steel supports were veneered in red mahogany, and the ceiling was decorated with moulded ornament painted in graduated shades of orange. Electric light bulbs hung in floral clusters from the corners of the open structure. Unfortunately, the little-used auditorium was demolished some time between 1905 and 1908.

Guimard hoped personally to inspire a renaissance in French architecture and design, but his ambition was doomed to fail. Nevertheless he remained faithful to the "Style

Guimard." His last Paris building, an apartment house, was completed well past the flowering of Art Nouveau in 1928.

JODY CLOWES

See also Art Nouveau

Biography

Hector Germain Guimard. Born in Lyon, 10 March 1867. Studied at the École des Arts Décoratifs, Paris, 1882–85, and subsequently at the École des Beaux-Arts, Paris. Married Adeline Oppenheim, 1909. In practice as an architect from 1888; and designed a full range of furnishings, including furniture, ironwork, carpets, stained glass and wallpaper, from c.1890. Travelled in England and Belgium, 1894–95, meeting Victor Horta and Paul Hankar in 1895. Commissioned to design the entrances for the Paris Métro from 1900. Participated in many national and international exhibitions including the Exposition Universelle, Paris, 1900, the Paris Exposition de l'Habitation, 1903, and the Exposition des Arts Décoratifs et Industriels, Paris, 1925. Founder-member of the Société des Artistes Décorateurs; exhibiting from 1904 and Vice-President, 1905. Taught at the École des Beaux-Arts, Paris, from 1896. Chevalier de la Légion d'Honneur, 1929. Moved to New York, 1938. Died in New York, 20 May 1942.

Selected Works

A vast collection of designs, drawings, watercolours and manuscript material – known as the Fonds Guimard – is in the Musée des Arts Décoratifs, Paris, which also contains an important collection of Guimard's furniture. Additional collections of furniture, including work from the Hôtel Guimard, are in the Musée des Beaux-Arts, Lyon, and the Musée d'Orsay, Paris, whose holdings also include examples of Guimard's designs for metalwork, lighting and stained glass. A collection of architectural drawings is in the Avery Library, Columbia University, New York, and the Cooper-Hewitt Museum, New York, contains examples of Guimard's textiles and archival material relating to his work. A collection of drawings and a copy of *Le Castel Béranger*, including 65 colour plates and numerous archival photographs of the interiors, is in the Bibliothèque des Arts Décoratifs, Paris.

Interiors

1888	Au Grand Neptune (restaurant), quai d'Autueil, Paris (interiors)
1893	Maison Jassedé, avenue de Clamart (now avenue Charles de Gaulle), Paris (building, interiors and furnishings): Charles Jassedé
1894–98	Castel Béranger, Paris (building,interiors and furnishings): Elizabeth Fournier
1897–1901	Salle Humbert de Romans, Paris (building, interiors and furnishings)
1898–1900	Maison Coilliot, Lille (building, interiors and furnishings): Louis Coilliot
1898–1900	Castel Henriette, Sèvres (building, interiors and furnishings): Mme. Hefty
1902	Hôtel Nozal, Paris (building, interiors and furnishings)
1903–05	Jassedé Apartment Building, Paris (building, interiors and furnishings)
1905	Castel Orgeval, Villemoisson, near Morsang-sur-Orge (building, interiors and furnishings)
1909–12	Hôtel Guimard, 122 avenue Mozart, Paris (building, interiors and furnishings): Hector Guimard
1910	Hôtel Mezzara, Paris (building, interiors and furnishings)
1930	La Guimardière, Vaucresson (building, interiors and furnishings; incomplete): Hector Guimard

The majority of Guimard's buildings included custom-made furniture, metalwork, textiles, wallpapers and stained glass. He also designed porcelain for the Sèvres manufactory between 1899 and 1904, tiles for Alexandre Bigot, c.1902, and ironwork made by the Fonderies de Bayard et Saint-Didier, c.1907.

Publications

Le Castel Béranger: L'Art dans l'Habitation Moderne, 1898

"An Architect's Opinion of 'l'Art Nouveau'" in *Architectural Record*, 12, 1902, pp.127–33

Fontes artistiques pour constructions, fumisterie, articles de jardins et sepultures, style Guimard, 1907

Further Reading

A recent comprehensive account of Guimard's career, which includes a full bibliography and numerous illustrations and archive photographs of his work, is Thiébaut 1992. A complete list of his architectural projects appears in Frontisi 1985.

Blondel, Alain, *Hector Guimard, fontes artistiques*, Paris: Galerie du Luxembourg, 1971

Brunhammer, Yvonne, *Hector Guimard, 1867–1942: Architektur in Paris um 1900* (exhib. cat.), Munich: Villa Stuck, 1975

Brunhammer, Yvonne, *Art Nouveau: Belgium / France* (exhib. cat.), Houston: Rice University Institute for the Arts, 1976

Culpepper, Ralph, *Hector Guimard: Bibliographie*, 2nd edition Paris: Société des Amis de la Bibliothèque Forney, 1975

Dierkens-Aubry, Françoise and Jos Vandenbreeden, *Art Nouveau en Belgique: Architecture et Interieurs*, Louvain: Duculot, 1991

Doumato, Lamia, *Hector Guimard* (bibliography), Monticello, IL: Vance, 1981

Duncan, Alastair, *Art Nouveau and Art Deco Lighting*, London: Thames and Hudson, and New York: Simon and Schuster, 1978

Frontisi, Claude, *Hector Guimard: Le Castel Béranger*, Paris: Academy, 1980

Frontisi, Claude, *Hector Guimard, Architectures*, Paris, 1985

Graham, F. Lanier, *Hector Guimard* (exhib. cat.), New York: Museum of Modern Art, 1970

Naylor, Gillian and Yvonne Brunhammer, *Hector Guimard*, London: Academy, and New York: Rizzoli, 1978

Pionniers du XXe Siècle: Guimard, Horta, van de Velde (exhib. cat.), Paris: Musée des Arts Décoratifs, 1971

Plantin, Yves and Alain Blondel, "Hector Guimard: La Salle Humbert de Romans" in *L'Architecture d'Aujourd'hui*, 43, 1971, pp.17–18

Rheims, Maurice and Georges Vigne, *Hector Guimard*, New York: Abrams, 1988

Thiébaut, Philippe (editor), *Guimard* (exhib. cat.), Paris: Musée d'Orsay, 1992

Thiébaut, Philippe, *Guimard: L'Art Nouveau*, Paris: Gallimard, 1992

Vigne, Georges, *Hector Guimard et L'Art Nouveau*, Paris: Hachette, 1991

H

Habitat

British home furnishings retailer and manufacturer; established 1964

Habitat, an international chain of home furnishing stores, was founded with the incorporation of Habitat Designs Ltd. on 14 January 1964. The first Habitat shop, which opened to the public on 11 May 1964 at 77–79 Fulham Road, London, was situated in the ground floor and basement of a new development "at the junction of Sloane Avenue and Fulham Road" and sold furniture, kitchen goods, fabrics, carpets, china and glass under the banner of "good practical design". It brought with it an innovative approach to retailing which equated furnishing with fashion by rejecting the formal and often dreary environments of traditional furniture stores in favour of exciting "modern" design, in-store music, amateur staff and self-selection shopping.

The influences on Habitat ranged from Mary Quant's Bazaar boutique and Woolland Brothers' Modern Interiors department in Knightsbridge to Madame Cadec's cookware shop in Soho, Heal's furniture in Tottenham Court Road, Abacus in Dunmow and numerous other boutiques around London such as Primavera on Sloane Street. Comparable developments to Habitat in Europe and North America would include Design Research in Boston and IKEA in Sweden.

The founders of Habitat Designs Limited (who included Terence Conran, the designer and manufacturer; Caroline Conran, the former home editor of *Queen* magazine; Pagan Taylor, a former fashion model; and John Mawer, the managing director of Conran Furniture Limited) were inextricably linked to London's post-war culture of art, design, fashion and journalism and sought to bring the glamour of magazine "lifestyle" into the home via the high street. Large plate glass windows extending from floor to ceiling presented the shop directly to the street like a double page spread from a colour supplement. The shop's immediate success was partly due to the visual integrity of the shop's Corbusier-style interior design – by architect Oliver Gregory – and its imaginative warehouse-style displays of super-abundant merchandise.

Habitat goods included sturdy modern British furniture manufactured in pine and ash by Thetford-based Conran Furniture Limited; colourful striped and floral textiles produced by Conran Fabrics Limited; modern furniture and tableware from Scandinavia and Italy; bentwood and "rustic" furniture; traditional French cookware; Polish enamelware; Afghan rugs and coir matting; Japanese paper lanterns; German audio equipment; and Swiss tablelights.

A press release of the time announced, "We hope we have taken the footslogging out of shopping by assembling a wide selection of unusual and top quality goods under one roof" indicating the previously disparate nature of such goods and crucially how the "editing" process of magazine production might constitute a retailing philosophy. The editor-in-chief of Habitat was Terence Conran who chose goods for the arbitrary qualities of "good design", "good taste", and "good living" – criteria derived variously from 19th-century design reform, Bauhaus functionalism, Elizabeth David's *French Provincial Cooking* and Design Council rhetoric.

In 1966 a second Habitat shop opened in London at 156–158 Tottenham Court Road. This followed a similar scheme to the Fulham Road store by occupying the ground floor and basement of the building and keeping the space light and airy. Walls and ceilings were painted white, tiled floors were covered in coir matting, white painted brick piers supported natural beech shelving and stock was displayed on simple trestle tables and white painted metal towers. The interior design scheme and merchandise of Habitat suggested a vision of domestic living which was transferable from the shop to the home and vice versa. A vision which mixed modern with traditional, high design with vernacular crafts, and urban with rustic. The often highly coloured Pop merchandise, which had first emerged in Carnaby Street boutiques such as Gear, contrasted starkly with the white and natural background of the shop.

In 1969, by which time there were five shops in England and one in Toronto, Habitat merged, through H.J. Ryman Limited, with Lupton Morton Furniture, a private mail-order company based at Wallingford in Oxfordshire, which manufactured simple, modern domestic furniture with names such as *Campus*. These designs were incorporated into the Habitat range and formed the basis of a new mail-order catalogue called *Creative Living: Habitat by Post*. The range of goods expanded accordingly to include toys, gardening equipment and electrical appliances which prescribed a clearly defined middle-class lifestyle. The company also began to engage with the cult of DIY (do-it-yourself) by introducing decorating tools

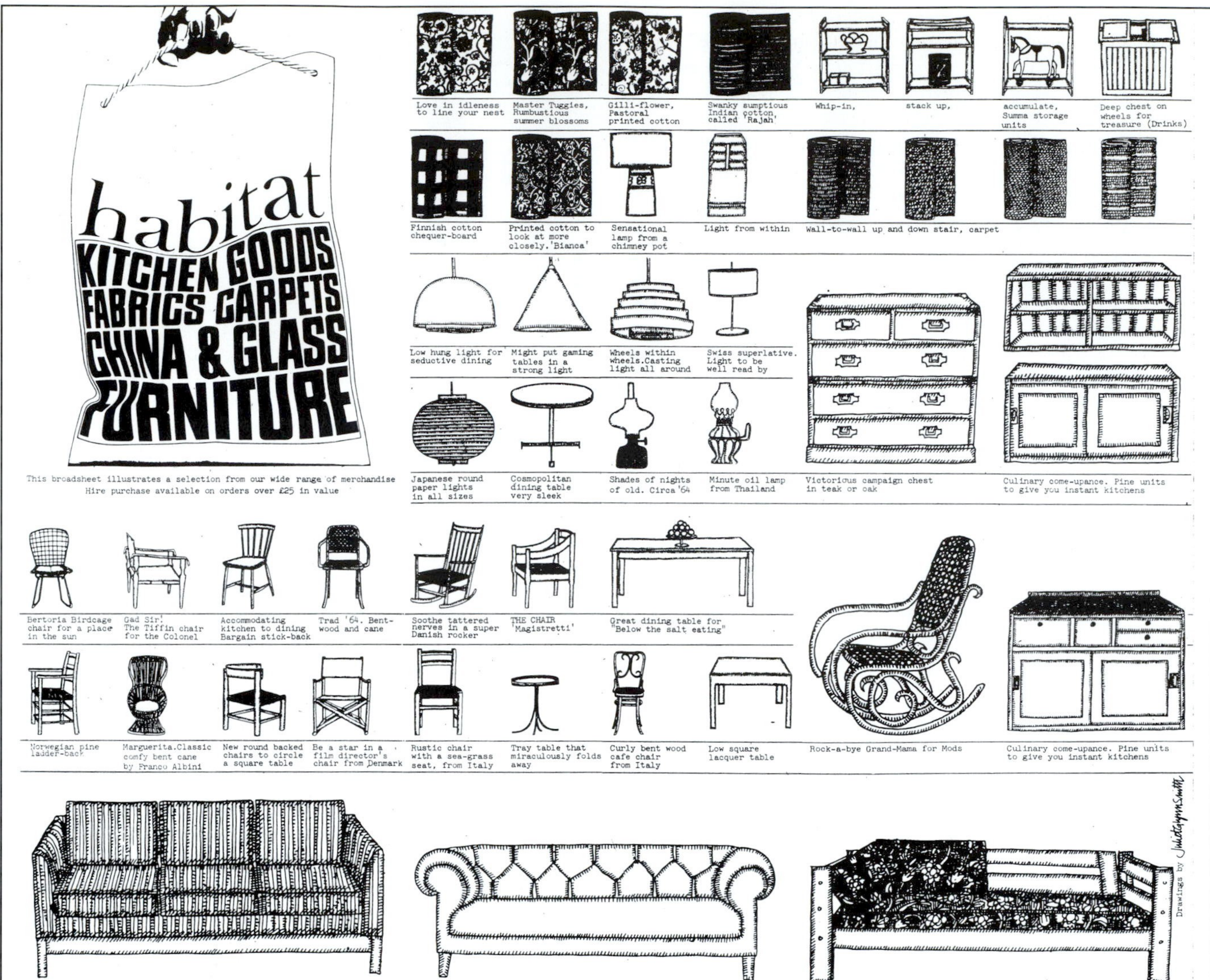

Habitat: an early brochure

and materials, a new range of Habitat paints in 16 colours, simple whitewood furniture, wall hessian and cork tiles.

The second annual Habitat catalogue, published for 1971, was supported by an advertising campaign running across broadsheet newspapers and magazines such as *House and Garden*, *Nova* and *Good Housekeeping*. The layout for the catalogue went "from one room's furniture and accessories to another – just like walking through a house" and established a format which continued annually until 1989. The third annual catalogue of 1972 included "specially commissioned prints by David Hockney and Peter Blake", *Lollo* foam furniture, Tefal non-stick saucepans and "a smoked acrylic digital clock" – goods which proposed a lifestyle that engaged with contemporary art and modern technology. The Pop minimalism of this era is evoked by the work of David Hockney and bears direct comparison with the art direction of Habitat in the early 1970s. At the same time the particular aesthetic of art gallery spaces began to shape the scenography of domestic interiors in the catalogue.

In 1973 the first Habitat shop on Fulham Road was transformed into The Conran Shop – "a super elegant design store specialising in the more expensive end of the home furnishing market" – while Habitat moved into the former Gaumont Palace cinema on the Kings Road. In the same year the first French Habitat opened in Paris through a relationship with Prisunic and an acclaimed high-tech warehouse shed was designed and built by architects Ahrends Burton Koralek at Wallingford, Berkshire.

Through the 1970s new stores opened across the UK, USA, France and Belgium. The first American Habitat – named Conran's – opened in New York in 1977. Designed like a supermarket with wide aisles and a row of check-out tills, Conran's brought take-away and flatpack furniture into an arena that preferred home delivery and high levels of customer service. Nevertheless the chain expanded across the East Coast with moderate success until closing in 1992.

In 1981 Habitat was floated on the stock exchange and in 1982 it was merged with Mothercare to form the Mothercare/ Habitat Group plc. The group was enlarged by the subsequent acquisition of Heal's and Richard's in 1983. In 1986 the

Habitat / Mothercare Group merged with British Home Stores to form Storehouse plc. Ironically the "designer decade" was a low point for Habitat in terms of product design and quality, though the company retained the slogan of "good design at good prices" Out-of-town retail developments increasingly became the focus of corporate strategy which further eroded the company's credibility as a design-led retailer.

In 1990 Terence Conran left Storehouse whence a new merchandising and marketing division, Habitat International, was set up to introduce new product designs, global sourcing and central buying in an attempt to gain economies of scale and an international brand image. The mail-order operation was closed down and the annual catalogue was briefly replaced by a lower pagination seasonal "magalogue". Through the 1990s Habitat has made a steady return to the centre of the home furnishing arena by responding to changes in fashion and maintaining an emphasis on style and quality rather than design and price. In 1992 Habitat was bought by the Amsterdam-based Stichting Ingka Foundation which has invested in a comprehensive program of store refurbishments, re-locations to in-town sites and high quality catalogues.

BEN WEAVER

See also Conran

Selected Works

Archive collections documenting the history of Habitat from the 1960s to the 1990s are in the National Archive of Art and Design, Victoria and Albert Museum, London. The most important of these is the Habitat UK Ltd. Archive, which consists of 130 boxes of material including press cuttings, a complete run of the company's catalogues, photographs of products, printed material, in-house magazines, printed ephemera, books, photographs and video tapes. Additional documentation is in the John Maltby Archive which contains the photographs and daybooks of the photographer regularly commissioned by Terence Conran during the 1960s, and in the Paul Reilly collection of speeches and articles, which includes the speech given at the opening of the Conran factory in Thetford.

Further Reading

For a survey of the early history of Habitat see Phillips 1984. The best source of information relating to the company's work in more recent years is the Habitat catalogues and brochures, copies of which are in the Habitat Archive.

Bure, Gilles de, *Habitat, 20 Ans de Quotidien en France* (exhib. cat.: Musée des Arts Décoratifs, Paris), Paris: Aveline, 1993

Gilliatt, Mary, *English Style*, London: Bodley Head, 1967; as *English Style in Interior Decoration*, New York: Viking, 1967

Gosling, David and Barry Maitland, *Design and Planning of Retail Systems*, London: Architectural Press, and New York: Whitney Library of Design, 1976

Hewitt, John, "Good Design in the Market Place: The Rise of Habitat Man" in *Oxford Art Journal*, 10, no.2, 1987, pp.28–42

Hillier, Bevis, *The Style of the Century, 1900–1980*, London: Herbert, and New York: Dutton, 1983

Ind, Nicholas, *Terence Conran: The Authorized Biography*, London: Sidgwick and Jackson, 1995

MacCarthy, Fiona, *All Things Bright and Beautiful: Design in Britain 1830 to Today*, London: Allen and Unwin, 1972

Phillips, Barty, *Conran and the Habitat Story*, London: Weidenfeld and Nicolson, 1984

Weaver, Ben, *Habitat Designs Limited: Lifestyle Retailing and the Media, 1963–1973*, M.A. thesis, London: Victoria and Albert Museum / Royal College of Art, 1995

Wilhide, Elizabeth and Andrea Spencer, *Low Cost, High Style*, London: Conran Octopus, 1986

York, Peter, *Modern Times: Everybody Wants Everything*, London: Heinemann, 1984

Halls and Vestibules

Domestic halls originated as secular meeting places presided over by community leaders, nobility and royalty in the early Middle Ages. Halls evolved to fulfil a diversity of functions: reception space, living room, dining room, assembly room, games room, music hall, court, council room and parliament.

One of the earliest surviving halls is the throne room of King Ramiro I of the Asturias at Naranco in Spain, dating from the 9th century. It is fairly small in dimension, with doors that open to loggias at either end for addressing assemblies. "Great" halls of this type were the most important rooms in medieval princely or noble residences and quickly became the epicentre of all substantial households in medieval Europe. They varied enormously in size, ranging from the vastness of Westminster Hall (239 by 67 feet) to the more compact Oakham Hall in Rutland (65 by 44 feet). Early medieval halls were vaulted and aisled like churches until more sophisticated joinery practices allowed wide span roofs, first arch-brace and later hammer beam in construction, negating the need for supporting colonnades regardless of the hall size. Within these halls, European kings, princes and noblemen administered justice, presided over matters of state and hosted huge receptions as well as community festivities. Guests were entertained with great ceremony and the scale of the entertainment and lavishness of the hospitality was a direct reflection of the status, wealth and generosity of the householder. As the main room of the house, castle or palace, the hall was also the room in which the entire household (sometimes as many as 200 people) ate and slept, although the lord and his family had private rooms off the main hall into which they could retreat. At mealtimes, the householder and his guests sat at one end of the hall with their staff before them. From the 13th century it became customary for the lord's table to be raised on a platform / dais so that he was clearly visible to all in the room.

The layout of medieval halls was in essence geared to the moment when the lord and his household sat down to eat together. The entrance from the kitchen was customarily at the end of the hall opposite to the family's table and was deliberately grand. At Penshurst Place in Kent (1341), for example, it consisted of a series of three large arches through which the food was carried in a ceremonial procession the entire length of the hall to the lord's table. At Dartington Hall in Devon (1390), there were also three arched entrances to the hall, the central one from the kitchen, and the flanking two from the pantry where bread was stored and from the buttery where beer and candles were dispensed. Towards the end of the 14th century these "triumphal" arches were frequently screened off to exclude draughts from the kitchens. Initially these screens were moveable, but they soon became a permanent, ornamental feature taking over the role of the arches as ceremonial entrance passage. As they were set slightly away from the entrance and were beautifully carved and extremely solid in

Halls: Great Hall, Shiplake Court, Oxfordshire, by George & Peto, 1891

structure, the next logical stage in their evolution was to construct a music gallery over them, so that the food could enter the hall to a fanfare of music, and so that music could be played after the meal for the entertainment of those present.

Hall fireplaces evolved in a similarly dramatic way to the kitchen entrance, especially on the Continent where the medieval functions of the hall persisted longer than in Britain. Fireplaces were usually built along the longest wall in the hall – halls in the early Middle Ages were heated by fires in the centre of the room, the smoke being released via a louvre in the roof – and evolved as increasingly ornate showpieces. The great hall at Poitiers Castle (1384–88), for example, had an elaborately carved triple fireplace, topped by a screen of arches, perforated by glazed tracery, and a balcony. Equally impressive was the fireplace in the hall of Jacques Coeur's house in Bourges (1443) which was of staggering proportions and boasted ornamental detail, including turrets, and a carved frieze of huntsmen, knights and donkeys. Medieval halls were customarily hung with tapestries and other movable treasures. Weapons and shields bearing coats of arms were also displayed. Their presence was essentially practical – to arm the lord's knights in the event of a crisis and to keep track of the weaponry stock as many were quite valuable – but they also served as decoration.

Although the great hall persisted as a dining area throughout the 16th century, the lord and his family had retreated from the communal mealtimes into private chambers by the 14th century, a trend first established by royalty. In the absence of the lord, his senior staff occupied the high table. The gradual retreat of the householder from the communal sphere to his great chamber above the hall reinforced existing hierarchies. It set the householder apart from his staff, who were now quite literally beneath him at mealtimes, and the dimensions of the great chamber increased at the expense of those of the great hall as a result. At Hardwick Hall in Derbyshire (designed in the 1590s by Robert Smythson for Bess of Hardwick) the hall, though monumental in scale and rising over two floors, was considerably smaller than the great chamber. Here Bess of Hardwick dined in state and received royal envoys in the most lavish of circumstances. The hall still functioned as the servants' dining room and Bess of Hardwick's absence from meals was compensated for by an enormous coat of arms over the fireplace, flanked by two full-sized plasterwork relief stags.

The great hall at Hardwick had other notable characteristics that set it apart from other contemporary interiors. Hardwick was designed with very narrow side elevations and the hall runs the entire width of the building, along the central axis, with rooms arranged on either side and above it. The ceiling is flat, an unusual feature, due to the rooms above, and the traditional wooden screen / music gallery was replaced by a screen supported by four carved Doric columns, derived from an engraving by Sebastiano Serlio. This music gallery also served as a connecting passage between the private dining and withdrawing rooms on the first floor from which Bess could monitor the activities of her staff.

Despite its monumental proportions, Hardwick had an unusually rational and sophisticated plan. The rationalisation of the English country house interior as a reflection of the architectural order of the exterior became more widespread in grand houses following the Restoration of the monarchy in the latter half of the 17th century. This was partly due to the influence of foreign models. Dutch houses were particularly influential as their compact practical solutions to domestic life, sweeping the servants' quarters and service rooms into the basement or below stairs, combined well with the stylistic vocabulary of Palladian classicism in English country houses. Also, the combined effects of economic restrictions and the fact that the rich often had responsibilities at court, necessitating properties in town as well as in the country, meant that households generally became smaller. Where possible, house plans were symmetrical, with the most important rooms at the centre. Halls became smaller to the extent that some were mere vestibules, neat reception areas for visitors and tradesmen as was common in European homes. The marble hall at Petworth, Sussex (1692) is an example of such a continental-style vestibule; its modest dimensions appear slightly out of place in the otherwise huge house.

In spite of such economies of scale, small vestibules did not become widespread in England due to the popularity of the symmetrical French formal house plan in the early 18th century. The French plan concentrated the public rooms of the house along the central axis, with state and private apartments arranged in symmetry to either side. An early application of elements of the French plan, a "state centre" with flanking apartments, can be seen at Coleshill House, designed in 1650 by Roger Pratt for his cousin Sir George Pratt. At Coleshill, the hall rises over two storeys and is connected to the great chamber on the first floor by a staircase. Once the servants had been banished from the hall, however, the householder and guests no longer needed to dine symbolically above them and the great chamber, renamed the Saloon after the French term *salon* and the Italian *salone*, could be placed on the same level as the great hall. The great hall was itself raised above ground level on the *piano nobile*, necessitating a grand staircase at the entrance of the house.

It was the architect Sir John Vanbrugh who exploited the formal continental plan to its fullest and most ostentatiously Baroque potential. He created a hall of epic proportions at the Duke of Marlborough's house, Blenheim in Oxfordshire (1705–20). It is topped by a clerestory lantern, 67 feet high, decorated with painted military trophies and a painting depicting the apotheosis of the Duke in commemoration of his outstanding military career. The hall had a music gallery high above the entrance to the saloon, as was traditional. The hall was used for huge gatherings at seasonal festivities, while the saloon was used for more stately occasions. The great hall at Castle Howard, also by Vanbrugh, is equally theatrical, although inspired by a musical as opposed to military theme. The richly painted and decorated hall is crowned, cathedral-style with a dome and cupola.

The dramatic scale and exuberance of Baroque architecture was never completely accepted in England, but Lord Burlington's revival of Palladian architectural principles proved more palatable as they revisited an architectural vocabulary that had already been established in the previous century by Inigo Jones. The basic plan of the formal house did not change however, simply the stylistic vocabulary and the relationship of scale and proportion. The stone hall at Houghton Hall in Norfolk, designed for Robert Walpole by Colen

Campbell and William Kent in the early 1700s, was a perfect cube rising, as was customary, over two storeys. The hall was decorated with stone carvings and high relief plasterwork, consisting in part of hunting imagery as Houghton was mainly used as a hunting lodge by Walpole and his political allies. By the mid 18th century, the aristocracy and professional classes socialised more readily in the public assembly rooms in fashionable town and city centres. The formal house plan, therefore, became less important as attitudes towards individual room functions became more flexible due to the slight relaxation of social convention. Yet, although people enjoyed socialising outside the domestic sphere, assemblies were also given at home, with dancing, music, tea and cards after dinner. The state rooms of private houses were opened up to provide the assembly space, effectively creating a circuit of rooms around a first floor balcony. In town houses where space was at a premium, the hall was marginalised and the stairs from the hall to the first floor became a more important feature, and were often situated in the centre of the house.

The compact town house plan with its small hall and dominant staircase circuit was easily adapted to equally compact country houses such as Harleyford Manor, built in 1755. Here the hall accommodates a grand staircase which all but subordinates the function of the hall as a reception space, necessitating a tiny vestibule at the front entrance in order to receive visitors. Various types of hall staircase were popular: oval, circular and cantilevered, always top-lit. At Hagley Hall (1752) overlapping staircase circuits were required to circumnavigate successfully the two separate sets of assembly rooms in the east and west wings of the house.

The revival of the old Baronial Hall which was to become so striking a feature of much mid- and late Victorian country house architecture began in the second quarter of the 19th century. Based on medieval and Elizabethan models, these rooms were inspired by a romantic nostalgia for "old English hospitality" and the social and religious stability of a bygone age, and they provided a space for communal gathering where the lord and his tenants could once again come together for ceremonial meals and entertainments. The Gothic revivalist A.W.N. Pugin was a great admirer of settings of this kind and designed a number of Great Halls in buildings such as Scarisbrick (from 1837) all decorated in a suitably authentic medieval style. Another Gothic hall, built by Sir John Boileau at Ketteringham, Norfolk (1840) was described as "fit for the hospitalities of the chivalrous ages", and was used for dances for the gentry, dinners for the tenantry and an annual servants' dance. Elizabethan and Jacobean styles also proved popular in the first half of the century with notable examples at Charlecote Park (1848) and Knebworth (1840s); the latter had a staircase and banqueting hall, both hung with armour and decorated with heraldic devices in the ancient tradition.

Increasingly, however, large Victorian halls were perceived as a useful additional space for the entertainment of family members and friends. They gradually took on the role of informal living or games rooms, containing large fireplaces, comfortable furniture such as armchairs, writing tables and sofas, musical instruments, and recreational facilities such as billiard tables and books. They were also a place in which guests could gather prior to meals, the descent from the first-floor rooms via a grand staircase acting as a showcase for the ladies dressed in their finery. The apogee of the living-hall came in the last quarter of the century in the work of Renaissance revivalist architects such as Norman Shaw and the London firm of George & Peto whose great hall at Shiplake Court, Oxfordshire (1891), combines the scale and splendour of an old English prototype with the informality and comfort of a more modern dwelling. The fashion for such rooms was also fuelled by the Arts and Crafts interest in vernacular building types and they continued to appear well into the Edwardian period. However, the post-war economic strictures that hastened the demise of the country house lifestyle also helped put an end to the hall as a large, independent space, and in most modern homes it is simply a small vestibule providing access to a passageway or leading directly to the main rooms of the house.

MAREIKE VON SPRECKELSEN

Further Reading

Ames, Kenneth L., "Meaning in Artefacts: Hall Furnishings in Victorian America" in *Journal of Interdisciplinary History*, 9, Summer 1978, pp.19–41

Ames, Kenneth L., "First Impressions" in his *Death in the Dining Room and Other Tales of Victorian Culture*, Philadelphia: Temple University Press, 1992

Franklin, Jill, *The Gentleman's Country House and its Plan, 1835–1914*, London: Routledge, 1981

Gere, Charlotte, *Nineteenth-Century Decoration: The Art of the Interior*, London: Weidenfeld and Nicolson, and New York: Abrams, 1989

Girouard, Mark, *Life in the English Country House: A Social and Architectural History*, New Haven and London: Yale University Press, 1978

Girouard, Mark, *The Victorian Country House*, revised edition New Haven and London: Yale University Press, 1979

Jackson-Stops, Gervase and James Pipkin, "Halls" in their *The English Country House: A Grand Tour*, London: Weidenfeld and Nicolson, 1984; Boston: Little Brown, 1985

Rivers, Tony and others, *The Name of the Room: A History of the British House and Home*, London: BBC Publications, 1992

Scully, Vincent J., Jr., *The Shingle Style and the Stick Style: Architectural Theory and Design from Richardson to the Origins of Wright*, revised edition New Haven: Yale University Press, 1971

Thompson, Michael, *The Medieval Hall: The Basis of Secular Domestic Life, 600–1600 AD*, Aldershot: Scolar, 1995

Wood, Margaret, *The English Mediaeval House*, London: Phoenix House, 1965; New York: Harper, 1983

Hardouin-Mansart, Jules 1646–1708

French architect

The posthumous reputation of Jules Hardouin-Mansart has suffered from the multiplicity of his activities, which were chiefly carried out in the service of Louis XIV, first as Premier Architecte du Roi and then as Surintendant des Bâtiments. His role was certainly as much civil servant and organiser as designer, but this should not blind us to his creative input in many spheres – not just interior decoration but also monumental architecture both religious and secular, engineering, town planning and garden design.

Hardouin-Mansart: Salon de l'Oeil-de-Boeuf, Versailles, 1684

The great-nephew of the leading mid-17th century architect François Mansart, in whose atelier he studied and whose surname he adopted, Hardouin-Mansart first rose to public notice at the Château de Clagny at Versailles (1673–79), designed for the king's mistress Madame de Montespan, after which he was quickly engaged to work in the main palace itself. The marble revetments of the first interiors there with which his name can be associated – the Escalier de la Reine (1680), her Salle des Gardes (1679–81) and the Salles de Venus and de Diane in the Grand Appartement (finished 1684) – follow the general effect of heavy magnificence evident elsewhere in the ceremonial interiors of the palace established under the artistic aegis of the Premier Peintre du Roi, Charles Le Brun.

It was around this time, however, in the design of the Galerie des Glaces (the Hall of Mirrors from 1678), a collaboration between Hardouin-Mansart and Le Brun, that we can see the emergence of the former's distinctive style in interiors. Here he put to good use his experience at Clagny, whose most celebrated internal feature was an elaborate gallery. In the Hall of Mirrors the emphasis is on purely architectural values, on simplicity and light. Le Vau's exterior envelope of the palace was extended and revised to allow taller, arched windows. Combined with the mirrors on the opposite wall, these flood the gallery with illumination to give the best possible viewing conditions for Le Brun's cycle of paintings on the vault above. The general *ordonnance* of the interior is rich but restrained – the arcades of windows and recessed mirrors are enclosed within a modified Corinthian order, whose unbroken entablature and regular bay rhythm provide an undistracting framework to emphasise the great length of the room and the depictions of the king's victories on the ceiling.

Such ambitious interiors were necessarily collaborative efforts. Hardouin-Mansart was evidently happy to work with decorative painters – Le Brun and Mignard contributed to the decoration of his own house in Paris (1674). But the Bâtiments du Roi was a huge organisation, and he had many draughtsmen and other architects working under him. Many design decisions must have been taken by them rather than by Hardouin-Mansart, even if they all had to be passed by him before execution, and this must have been even more the case after he was made Surintendant des Bâtiments in 1699. It may be that he himself never executed his own drawings – certainly, none of the drawings which have survived are in his hand. This makes problematic the attribution of many of the interiors carried out at Versailles. On the basis of his study of the surviving drawings, Fiske Kimball effectively denied all attribution of interiors after 1684 to Hardouin-Mansart, identifying the designer with the particular draughtsman in each case, especially Lassurance and, from 1699, Pierre Le Pautre. We do know that in the case of the Grand Trianon Hardouin-Mansart was away from Versailles in 1687 when the crucial decisions affecting the design of the exterior (at least) were taken, and that the building's appearance as we see it today is largely due to to his subordinate Robert de Cotte and to ideas emanating from the king himself (Jestaz, 1969).

Nevertheless, there are distinctive features common to much of the decorative work carried out under Hardouin-Mansart throughout his career which mean that it is possible to isolate the contribution he made to interior design independently of those in his employ. We can trace, for instance, an interest in the use of varied room shapes, first seen in the tiny hunting lodge, the Château du Val, that he designed for the king at Saint Germain-en-Laye in 1674, and which recurs in the Salon Ovale of the Petits Appartements du Roi (1692) and the Appartement d'Hiver at the Ménagerie (1698–99).

We can also distinguish, as in the Hall of Mirrors, a concern to introduce a properly architectural framework for interiors – not just for vestibules, but also the inner rooms of apartments. This is seen in the Appartement du Roi of 1684 (the bedchamber of which is now incorporated in the Salon de l'Oeil-de-Boeuf) and in the Petits Appartements of 1692. Often, interiors are enclosed and controlled by a full pilaster order with ornament concentrated in the frieze; even where this is not the case, key physical elements, such as doors and chimneypieces, are placed in a regular bay system determined by the height and spacing of window apertures.

On a more strictly decorative level we can also see a distinctive use of mirror glass, often filling to entablature height the chimney breast and bays answering to window openings. In a turn typical of the intricate taste of the last decades of the 17th century, and one which would be copied in many palace interiors elsewhere on the continent, these mirror bays could be used to set off curios and pieces of porcelain set on consoles – an idea proposed in 1692 for the Petite Galerie and carried out in the Cabinet du Conseil and at the Menagerie.

In the 1690s there developed a new, lighter approach to design. This was partly necessitated by the financial crises induced by the wars of the later part of Louis XIV's reign, a period when the silver furniture in the Grand Appartement was melted down and the Gobelins factory closed. However, it was also the reflection of a new concern for practicality and comfort, first seen in the dependencies of the main palace. In the Grand Trianon (from 1687) the interiors were not gilded and the panelling was painted plain white or grey; at the Ménagerie (1698–99) the king rejected designs with elaborate painted ceilings offered by Hardouin-Mansart for the apartment of the young Duchesse de Bourgogne, asking for simplicity and youthfulness, "de l'enfance répandue partout" (Hautecoeur, 1948).

The desire for increased lightness was seen not only in simplified materials but also in general design, with a new emphasis on height and airiness. Heavy vaults and entablatures were reduced; on walls horizontal impost divisions were gradually eroded and *boiserie* mouldings refined – frame elements began to be extended by vegetal and arabesque carving to invade field areas, linking the full wall height in a continuous chain of motifs. The key element in this reformulation of the domestic interior was the new, low type of chimneypiece "à la Royale" (as engraved by Le Pautre) installed in the King's Pavilion at Marly in 1699 and then in the remodelled Appartement du Roi at Versailles in 1701.

The Salon de l'Oeil-de-Boeuf as formed in this remodelling can be taken as representative of this last stage of Hardouin-Mansart's contribution to interior design. Elements such as the pilaster order with its entablature are retained from the 1680s, but the fireplace is low with a very tall overmantel mirror. Polychrome marbles have given way to a simpler gold and white colour scheme; lighting is facilitated by the oval window which lends the room its name (the same device had been used in the central salon at Marly); lastly, the vault is not painted but has a frieze of playing children which seems like a direct echo of the aging king's desire for a light and youthful note to be introduced into his surroundings.

Hardouin-Mansart's crowning architectural achievement, the Chapel at Versailles, is, as a religious building, outside the remit of this essay. In any case, the decorative work in its interior was completed after his sudden death in 1708. Nevertheless, it should be noted that the design as a whole, though monumental, again shows the search for greater lightness and simplicity characteristic of his decorative work in general.

It may be justified to speak of the effect of earlier work at Versailles being that of a "striking whole" which, in its details, "offers little in either painting, sculpture or architecture, which is of the first quality in itself" (Blunt, 1970). But this is surely not true of the interiors created under the Surintendance of Hardouin-Mansart: through the refinement of form and modelling they ushered in a new style – the Rococo – which would provide a formal and conceptual framework for much 18th-century decorative art.

DAVID CRELLIN

Biography

Born in Paris, 16 April 1646. Trained with his great-uncle, François Mansart, inheriting his large collection of plans and drawings. Worked independently from 1666; designed residence in new town of Versailles, 1669. In service of Louis XIV from 1673. Appointed Royal Architect and member of the Royal Academy, 1675; Premier Architecte du Roi, 1681; Surintendant des Bâtiments du Roi, 1699. Active on projects at Versailles and Trianon, from 1678 until the end of his career in the 1680s. Also worked on eccesiastical buildings and town planning, such as the Place Vendôme in Paris, 1680–98. Died in Marly, 8 May 1708.

Selected Works

Interiors

1673–75	Hôtel de Ville, Arles
1673–79	Château de Clagny, near Versailles (building and interiors): Madame de Montespan
1674–75	Château de Sceaux: Jean-Baptiste Colbert
1674–75	Pavillon du Val, near St. Germain-en-Laye (building and interiors): Louis XIV
1676–91, & 1699	Dôme des Invalides, Paris (with Libéral Bruand)
1676	Versailles (pavilions for Grove of Fame): Louis XIV
1678–89	Versailles (Galerie des Glaces; with C. Le Brun): Louis XIV
1679	Marly, Château: Louis XIV
1685	Château de St. Cloud (building and interiors)
1685	Pont Royal, Paris (with Jacques Gabriel)

1687 Grand Trianon (Grands Appartements, Cabinet de Madame de Maintenon): Louis XIV
1689–99 Versailles (chapel): Louis XIV
1698–99 Ménagerie, Versailles (interiors)

Further Reading

Berger 1985 and Walton 1986 give useful overviews of Mansart's career at Versailles. Kimball's several studies cover all aspects of his activities.

Berger, Robert W., *Versailles: The Château of Louis XIV*, University Park: Pennsylvania State University Press, 1985

Berger, Robert W., *A Royal Passion: Louis XIV as Patron of Architecture*, Cambridge and New York: Cambridge University Press, 1994

Blunt, Anthony, *Art and Architecture in France, 1550–1750*, 2nd edition Harmondsworth: Penguin, 1970

Bourget, Pierre and Georges Cattaui, *Jules Hardouin-Mansart*, Paris: Freal, 1960

Doumato, Lamia, *Jules Hardouin-Mansart* (bibliography), Monticello, IL: Vance, 1981

Hautecoeur, Louis, *Histoire de l'architecture classique en France*, vol.2, Paris: Picard, 1949, pp.527–688

Jestaz, Bertrand, "Le Trianon de marbre ou Louis XIV architecte" in *Gazette des Beaux-Arts*, ii, 1969, pp.259–86

Kimball, Fiske, "The Development of the Cheminée à la Royale", in *Metropolitan Museum Studies*, vol.5, 1936, pp.259–80

Kimball, Fiske, "La transformation des appartements de Trianon sous Louis XIV", *Gazette des Beaux-Arts*, vol.19, 1938, pp.87–110

Kimball, Fiske, "The Creation of the Style Louis XIV", in *Art Bulletin*, vol.23, 1941, pp.1–15

Kimball, Fiske, *The Creation of the Rococo*, 1943; reprinted as *The Creation of the Rococo Decorative Style*, New York: Dover, and London: Constable, 1980

Kimball, Fiske, "Mansart and Le Brun in the genesis of the Grande Galerie de Versailles", in *Art Bulletin*, XXII, 1949, pp.1–6

Mabille, G., "La Ménagerie de Versailles", in *Gazette des Beaux-Arts*, vol.83, 1974, pp.1–36

Marie, Alfred, "Les chambres de Louis XIV au Grand Trianon et à Marly", in *Bulletin de la Société de l'histoire de l'art français*, 1938, pp.190–96

Thornton, Peter, *Seventeenth-Century Interior Decoration in England, France, and Holland*, New Haven and London: Yale University Press, 1978

Walton, Guy, *Louis XIV's Versailles*, Chicago: University of Chicago Press, and London: Viking, 1986

Heal's (Heal and Son Ltd.)

British furnishings manufacturers and retailers; established 1810

Heal's has long been synonymous with the promotion of fine craftsmanship and good taste in furniture and interior design. Under the direction of Sir Ambrose Heal (1872–1959), great-grandson of the firm's founder, who designed furniture for the company from 1896 until his retirement in 1953, the store pioneered many developments in retailing and manufacture. These included introducing the work of individual designers to the market, modernising shop design and layout, and manufacturing well-designed furniture, fabrics and lighting at affordable prices. In effect, Heal's helped to promote a taste for modern design among a new, younger and often intellectual middle-class audience, while at the same time maintaining high aesthetic standards and commercial integrity.

Heal and Son was founded in 1810 by John Harris and his brother Ambrose Heal as a firm of feather dressers for mattress-making in Leicester Square, London. Heal moved the firm to Tottenham Court Road in 1818 to be near other furnishing businesses. John Harris Jr. took control in 1840 and expanded the shop, promoting the "Heal bed" and moving into bedroom furniture. He also exploited the benefits of innovation and advertising and in Christmas 1866, the company issued "invitations" in Charles Dickens's *Once a Year* for the public to come to Heal's to see furniture "as it would appear in their own rooms". The room-set has subsequently become the convention for furniture retailing display.

Ambrose Heal, Jr. joined the firm in 1893. Prior to this he had been educated at Marlborough and the Slade School, and then served an apprenticeship as a cabinet-maker with Messrs. Plucknett of Warwick from 1890 to 1893. Armed with this training he combined a visionary sense of design with a canny, commercial aptitude. His sincere, simple oak furniture was strongly influenced by the English Arts and Crafts movement and the timeless ideals of Cotswold craftsmen such as Ernest Gimson and Edward Barnsley. Unlike many of his contemporaries, however, Heal was not opposed to mechanisation and he was convinced of the value of machine tools to assist in the mass production of good design.

Heal's distinctively English style soon began to make its mark, helped by the firm's imaginative retailing techniques. In addition to producing catalogues, in 1898 the company commissioned Gleeson White, editor of the Arts and Crafts magazine *The Studio*, to write a brochure with illustrations by C.H.B. Quennell, which Heal's published under the title *A Note on Simplicity of Design in Furniture for Bedrooms with Special Reference to Some Recently Produced by Messrs. Heal and Son*. The booklet was widely praised for its usefulness and artistry. Heal's had embarked on its promotion of tasteful, modern design by allying itself with the aesthetic elite and by means of fine typography and illustration.

Ambrose Heal joined the Arts and Crafts Exhibition Society in 1906, exhibiting his range of fumed oak bedroom furniture which was named after English seaside towns such as St. Ives and Newlyn. Other pieces carried inlaid mottoes or bore the distinctive chequered black and white, inlaid border which became a feature of Heal's advertising for more than thirty years from 1902. A commission for the Hotel Standard at Norrkoping, Sweden, helped promote the modern style, and established a long-standing and fruitful relationship between Heal's and Scandinavia. In 1900 examples of his furniture were shown at the Paris Exhibition. In the same year Ambrose Heal took over the directorship of advertising and introduced the new corporate logo of the four-poster bed. Heal was to commission the best illustrators, graphic designers and photographers in advertisements, catalogues and exhibition posters, and invitations.

In 1913 Ambrose Heal became chairman and, until his retirement in 1953, he exercised complete control over every aspect of the store. A landmark in shop architecture was heralded by the new building by Cecil Brewer at 195–196 Tottenham Court Road. Colonnaded and clad in Portland stone, the new building had windows from floor to ceiling on the façade which let in large amounts of daylight and which gave shoppers and passers-by a good view of the inside of the shop. The signs on the exterior had crafted lettering by Percy J. Smith and painted ironwork plaques by Joseph Armitage advertising the skills of Bedding Makers, Carpet Dealers, Cabinet Makers and Upholsterers; the centrepiece announces the catchphrase "At the sign of the four-poster."

With his fellow-director, Hamilton Smith, and Cecil Brewer, Heal was a founder-member of the Design and Industries Association in 1915 which became the Council of Industrial Design, and was later re-formed as the Design Council. Heal's became a "showcase" for the association with members' work on sale transmitting its ideals of "truth to materials" and "fitness of purpose" to a broad middle-class audience.

The Mansard Gallery, on the top floor, was a highly innovative and influential means of raising the profile of progressive art and design. Significant exhibitions such as Sacheverell Sitwell's show of Picasso, Derain, Utrillo, Matisse and Modigliani in 1919 and exhibitions of the early chromium-plated metal furniture by Mies van der Rohe and Marcel Breuer and works by other continental designers and the British firm Isokon, were displayed in the gallery. Indeed, it was the stylish metal furniture and lighting, often designed by Heal and manufactured by the company, which proved a commercial success during the tough times of the 1930s. By means of innovation and imaginative retailing the store survived a difficult period.

Scandinavian furniture was brought to Britain by Heal's throughout the 1920s and the store also launched the sale of Orrefors glass and Finnish furniture, including pieces by Alvar Aalto. Ambrose Heal produced one-off, "signed edition" examples of his finely crafted, detailed classics. Cleverly promoted, economy lines from Heal's in the 1930s anticipate the functional Utility designs of the next decade. Ambrose Heal was knighted in 1933, thereby raising the profile and status of the design profession and their work in Britain at this period.

After World War II Heal's was a significant presence at the Britain Can Make It exhibition of 1946 at London's Victoria and Albert Museum, and at the Festival of Britain of 1951 which included plywood and moulded furniture by Christopher Heal, son of Ambrose, and several designs from their textiles department which was rapidly gaining a name in the field. Striking and novel fabrics in the optimistic and gay spirit of the late 1940s and 1950s by designers such as Lucienne Day, Helen Close, and Jane Edgar eventually evolved into the vivid, explosive textiles of the 1960s designed by Barbara Brown, Howard Carter and Peter Hall. Heal's textiles were highly successful in the 1960s and Heal Textil GmbH was also established in Stuttgart. Heal's continued to promote contemporary and international design throughout this period under the chairmanship of Anthony Heal. A further extension was opened in 1962 with 11,000 square feet of open-plan showroom space.

The arrival of imitators and rivals, such as Habitat, on the furniture retailing scene increasingly threatened Heal's share of the market in the 1970s and 1980s and in 1983 the store was purchased by Sir Terence Conran's Habitat / Mothercare Ltd., later to become Storehouse Plc. After Storehouse's demise in the troubled 1980s, a management buyout acquired ownership of the store. The current Heal's (still at Tottenham Court Road, and with a new showroom in Fulham Road) aims to emphasise its core values of "style, quality and exclusivity" in the light of its impressive heritage.

SUSAN HOYAL

Selected Works

The Heal's archive, containing several hundred volumes of press-cuttings, daybooks, catalogues, correspondence, ledgers and other company records covering the period from the late 19th century to the late 20th century, is in the National Archive of Art and Design, Victoria and Albert Museum, London. Examples of Heal's furniture are in the Victoria and Albert Museum; numerous illustrations appear in the firm's catalogues, reprinted 1972.

Further Reading

An introduction to the company's work appears in their authorized history, Goodden 1984. For a more detailed and impartial analysis of Heal's between the wars see Benton 1978.

Anscombe, Isabelle, *Arts and Crafts Style*, London: Phaidon, 1991

Astley, Stephen, "Head Over Heal's" in *Traditional Interior Decoration*, 1, Autumn 1986, pp.162–72

Benton, Tim, "History of Taste 6: Up and Down at Heal's: 1929–35" in *Architectural Review*, February 1978, pp.109–116

Boumphrey, Geoffrey, "The Designers 1: Sir Ambrose Heal" in *Architectural Review*, LXXVII, July 1935, pp.39–40

Cooper, Jeremy, *Victorian and Edwardian Furniture and Interiors*, London: Thames and Hudson, 1987

Garratt, Pat, "The Stuff of Dreams" in *The World of Interiors*, May 1990, pp.47–54

Goodden, Susanna, *At the Sign of the Fourposter: A History of Heal's*, London: Heal and Son, 1984

Gloag, John (introduction), *A Booklet to Commemorate the Life and Work of Sir Ambrose Heal, 1872–1959*, London: Heal and Son Ltd., 1972

Heal's Catalogues, 1853–1934 (reprint); Newton Abbot: David and Charles, 1972

Jackson, Lesley, *The New Look: Design in the Fifties*, London and New York: Thames and Hudson, 1991

Thirties: British Art and Design Before the War (exhib. cat.), London: Arts Council of Great Britain, 1979

Health and Hygiene

All architecture is an index of attitudes towards health and hygiene as one of its basic functions is to shelter its users from physical and social danger. However, building interiors are particularly clear manifestations of the complex interaction between health and space. Such concerns have played an important role in shaping much progressive 20th-century domestic design, and since the 1920s Modernists such as Le Corbusier have championed an aesthetic of cleanliness in both the layout and planning of interiors and in the pared-down appearance of their decorations and furnishings. But an emphasis upon the need for more hygienic styles of living and a corresponding interest in healthier interiors pre-dates this period and has its origins in the sanitary and health reforms of the mid- and late 19th century.

Concerns about health peaked in the 1870s and 1880s following revelations about the direct connections between architectural design and illness. The "domestic sanitarians", as they were called in both England and North America, pointed to the lack of ventilation, supposedly dangerous materials, and poor drainage to explain the spread of infection as the century progressed.

These concerns represented the second stage of the reformers' agenda. Sanitarians during the mid-century had concentrated their efforts on large-scale municipal improvements such as the sewers and the Embankment (in the case of London), and had focused on working-class housing. Edwin Chadwick's pivotal *Report on the Sanitary Condition of the Labouring Population of Great Britain* of 1842 had given credence to environmental explanations for health. It was not until after the postulation of the germ theory in the 1860s by Louis Pasteur that sanitarians pointed explicitly to the role of interior domestic space in disease transmission.

At the heart of the Victorian debate over health throughout the English-speaking world was the issue of ventilation, fired by a continued faith in the miasma theory of disease transmission even after the formulation of the germ theory. Tuberculosis and many other deadly diseases were thought to be spread through bad air; as a result, sanitarians prescribed well-ventilated rooms and corridors, insisting that both water closets and bedrooms have windows. The placing of sanitary facilities next to the exterior walls of houses was therefore also advised, as this allowed for windows and the thorough ventilation of drainage pipes.

In order to avoid drafts, architects also prescribed the use of the ventilating tube, a device which was first adopted by hospitals and schools. This tube or pipe was inserted directly into the exterior wall of a building and provided fresh air to interiors without the discomfort of drafts; the supply was regulated by a lid at the mouth of the pipe. The most popular model of ventilating tube was called "Tobin's tube".

The Victorian obsession with fresh air is perhaps most clearly illustrated by the history of hospital architecture. The ideas of Florence Nightingale, a dedicated miasmatist, led to the popularity of the "pavilion" plan hospital: a central administration building, flanked by long, narrow, open wards. This interior arrangement of alternating beds and windows was believed to reduce the transmission of disease among patients through the circulation of fresh air in the ward's interior.

The planning of middle-class houses in the 19th century also presupposed notions about health and hygiene, a factor reflected in the near obsessional interest in the growing specialisation of individual rooms. Most middle-class interiors, for example, included a special "sick-room" for use when family members were ill. Experts advised householders to furnish this room carefully, advocating simple textile and wallpaper patterns and quiet crockery that would not excite or disturb the feverish patient. Ordinary bedrooms were also considered particularly important to health as it was believed that people were most vulnerable to disease when they were asleep, and once again much attention was paid to the suitability of furnishings. Dust-retaining surfaces and materials were to be avoided and the elaborate bed-hangings and draperies fashionable in the second and third quarters of the 19th century were increasingly eschewed in favour of more simple treatments and beds made of polished oak, cast iron or brass. Brass and iron bedsteads had been in production since the 1830s but gained new popularity in the 1880s and 1890s in recognition of the fact that they did not harbour dust and could be easily cleaned.

Predictably, nurseries were also frequent targets for sanitarians' reforms and their recommendations included wipeable surfaces, such as oil-based paints and linoleum, for walls and floors, and plain painted furnishings. The important role played by bedrooms and nurseries in relation to health was underlined by publications such as Catherine Gladstone's *Healthy Nurseries and Bedrooms, including the Lying-in Room* of 1884.

However, it was not only the sleeping rooms, but the entire middle-class house that was affected by changing notions of health and hygience, particularly with regard to decorations and building materials. Up until the 1860s, wallpapers frequently used pigments that were manufactured with arsenic which heightened the brightness of the colours, particularly in shades of bright green. Experts believed that these papers emitted toxic fumes that were responsible for a long list of common illnesses. Several well-publicized cases of childhood sickness and even death resulting, so it was believed, from arsenic poisoning led to the introduction of non-arsenical or arsenic-free wallpapers. The invention of washable, so-called "sanitary" wallpapers, in the 1870s, whose designs were printed with oil based pigments that were impervious to water, was another welcome improvement, but many sanitarians still disapproved of wallpapers. W.H. Corfield, for example, recommended using tiles in every room; Douglas Galton, an expert on hospital design, proposed walls of metal or cement. In 1875, Benjamin Ward Richardson advanced an entire city, "Hygeia", built on subways carrying fresh air. The interiors of Hygeia's houses consisted of a washable glazed brick.

The promotion of healthier living environments was also a major concern in the work of many architects and designers associated with the Arts and Crafts Movement, concerned as they were about the effects of industrialization and urbanization on the home. Queen Anne style architecture, for example, placed a premium on natural illumination and materials, features that were admired not only for their picturesque appearance but also for their encouragement of supposedly healthier lifestyles. The Movement's emphasis upon handcrafted, vernacular interiors also marked a move away from the densely furnished and upholstered styles popular in the High Victorian period and fostered the use of simpler forms and finishes such as stained oak.

Poor drainage was considered the most dangerous of common building flaws and the most difficult to improve. This included everything from the inappropriate placement of water closets to the design of sewer traps. Sanitarians drew attention to the common mistakes in publications such as T. Pridgin Teale's *Dangers to Health: A Pictorial Guide to Sanitary Defects* of 1878. There is evidence that middle-class women were largely held responsible for the healthiness of their own homes; in America, this attitude was best expressed in Harriette M. Plunkett's *Women, Plumbers, and Doctors: or, Household Sanitation* of 1885.

In general, concerns about health affected every scale of decision-making about domestic architecture and its relation to the city. After about 1850, in fact, the row or terrace house was largely usurped in popularity by the detached, single-family house, especially in North America, fuelled by an attempt to escape the supposedly disease-ridden, crowded city, among other factors. Suburban development, resort architecture, including both hotels and vacation houses, spas, athletic complexes, and the movement for public parks (especially in America) were also given a considerable boost by the assumption that nature and natural environments could function as spatial correctives to city living. Sleeping porches and plants in middle-class houses are among the material vestiges of this belief.

New suburban houses like those constructed in Bedford Park, London, in the 1870s were far less constrained by the size and shape of their sites than the row or terrace house of the central city. One of the healthier aspects of these houses was that the kitchens were located on the main floor, rather than in the basement. Advertising for Bedford Park and other Victorian suburbs emphasised the neighbourhood's healthy aspects and low death rates.

A major arena for the discussion of healthy interiors was the International Health Exhibition held in London in 1884 which included vast displays of heating and cooking equipment, clothing, machinery, food, ambulances, lighting, furniture and baths. A principal theme of this exhibition was the design of healthy houses and their contents, and among the most popular exhibits were the sectional models representing an "improved" and "ordinary" house which were open for public tours. One of the exhibition's organisers was the architect Robert Edis. Best known as the designer of the British pavilion at the World's Columbian Exposition in Chicago in 1893, Edis also had a substantial architectural practice in London and lectured and published widely on the subject of healthy furniture and decoration. In his most well-known book, *Decoration and Furniture of Town Houses* (1881), he insisted that the design of furnishings and wallpaper had a powerful impact on personal health. He detested commercially-produced furniture and warned against the dangers of deep carving and mouldings, the accumulation of useless ornaments, and the use of plush fabrics and upholstery as harbourers of dirt and dust. In their place he recommended fitted furniture with tops that reached to the ceiling to avoid dust traps, or furniture that stood on legs to facilitate dusting underneath, and loose floor-coverings that could be aired and beaten regularly. Edis's model room for the exhibition, displayed by the cabinet-makers Jackson and Graham, also exemplified his idea of treating rooms as a single architectural gesture rather than as a collection of isolated articles.

In some ways 20th-century interiors have generated less concern about health issues than the previous era, probably due to stricter municipal codes preventing the widespread transmission of foul air and sewage. By about 1900, floor plans of houses in England and North America were typically much more open, allowing the free movement of air between rooms and an increased transmission of light.

The 20th-century hospital, too, has been shaped by large-scale social reforms. Its plan, however, has become more closed. An arrangement of cellular rooms along a double-loaded corridor has replaced the open wards of the pavilion plan and medical technology and pharmaceuticals have largely displaced fresh air and sunlight as general treatments for disease. Nevertheless, light-coloured walls and easily washable materials are still used in hospitals.

Healthier living conditions were promised by the architects of the International Style during the 1920s, such as Le Corbusier and Richard Neutra. In retrospect, however, their buildings offered few real innovations in terms of health and hygiene. The sleek, undecorated surfaces of Modernism, popularized after World War II in the ubiquitous ranch house, were showcases for high standards of housekeeping. In the name of health, a near mania for domestic appliances developed in the decades following World War II.

Our current debate over "sick building syndrome" – modern buildings that unintentionally generate illnesses – recalls in many ways the destructive powers attributed by Victorians to houses and cities. An "environmental" approach to health thus predates modern architecture by several generations, rather than emerging, as is often implied, from the energy crisis of the 1970s.

ANNMARIE ADAMS

Further Reading

A stimulating discussion on the relation of notions of health and hygiene to design appears in Forty 1986.

Adams, Annmarie, *Corpus Sanum in Domo Sano: The Architecture of the Domestic Sanitation Movement, 1870–1914*, Montreal: Canadian Centre for Architecture, 1991

Adams, Annmarie, "The Healthy Victorian City: The Old London Street at the International Health Exhibition of 1884" in Zeynep Celik, Diane Favro and Richard Ingersoll (editors), *Streets: Critical Perspectives on Public Space*, Berkeley: University of California Press, 1994, pp.203–12

Cassedy, James H., "Hygeia: A Mid-Victorian Dream of a City of Health" in *Journal of the History of Medicine and Allied Sciences*, 17, 1962, pp.217–28

Douglas, Mary, *Purity and Danger: An Analysis of Concepts of Pollution and Taboo*, 1966; reprinted London and New York: Routledge, 1992

Edis, Robert W., *The Decoration and Furniture of Town Houses*, 2nd edition 1881; reprinted, with introduction by Christopher Gilbert, Wakefield: EP, 1972

Forty, Adrian, "The Modern Hospital in France and England" in Anthony D. King (editor), *Buildings and Society: Essays on the Social Development of the Built Environment*, London: Routledge, 1980, pp.61–93

Forty, Adrian, *Objects of Desire: Design and Society, 1750–1980*, London: Thames and Hudson, and New York: Pantheon, 1986

Girouard, Mark, *Sweetness and Light: The Queen Anne Movement, 1860–1900*, Oxford: Clarendon Press, 1977; New Haven: Yale University Press, 1984

Long, Helen C., *The Edwardian House: The Middle-Class Home in Britain, 1880–1914*, Manchester: Manchester University Press, 1993

Muthesius, Stefan, *The English Terraced House*, New Haven and London: Yale University Press, 1982

Neale, Shirley, "Robert William Edis, 1839–1927, Decorator and Furnisher" in *Victorian Society Annual*, 1985–86, pp.12–20

Stevens, Edward F., *The American Hospital of the Twentieth Century*, revised edition New York: Dodge, 1928

Stone, May N., "The Plumbing Paradox: American Attitudes toward Late Nineteenth-Century Domestic Sanitary Arrangements" in *Winterthur Portfolio*, 14, Autumn 1979, pp.284–309

Tomes, Nancy, "The Private Side of Public Health: Sanitary Science, Domestic Hygiene, and the Germ Theory, 1870–1900" in *Bulletin of the History of Medicine*, 64, Winter 1990, pp.509–39

Wright, Gwendolyn, *Moralism and the Model Home: Domestic Architecture and Cultural Conflict in Chicago, 1873–1913*, Chicago: University of Chicago Press, 1980

Heating

Further Reading

Bruegmann, Robert, "Central Heating and Forced Ventilation: Origins and Effects on Architectural Design" in *Journal of the Society of Architectural Historians*, XXXVII, October 1978, pp.143-60

Caspall, John, *Making Fire and Light in the Home pre-1820*, Woodbridge, Suffolk: Antique Collectors' Club, 1987

Cornforth, John and John Fowler, "Light and Heating" in their *English Decoration in the 18th Century*, London: Barrie and Jenkins, and Princeton, NJ: Pyne, 1974; 2nd edition Barrie and Jenkins, 1978

Gilbert, Christopher and Anthony Wells-Cole, *The Fashionable Fireplace, 1660–1840* (exhib. cat.) Leeds: Temple Newsam House, 1985

Mayhew, Edgar de Noailles and Minor Myers, Jr., *A Documentary History of American Interiors from the Colonial Era to 1915*, New York: Scribner, 1980

Thornton, Peter, *Seventeenth-Century Interior Decoration in England, France, and Holland*, New Haven and London: Yale University Press, 1978

Wright, Lawrence, *Home Fires Burning: The History of Domestic Heating and Cooking*, London: Routledge, 1964

See Chimneypieces; Stoves

Heaton, Clement John 1861–1940

British stained glass, enamel, furniture and wall-coverings designer

The eldest son of Clement Heaton, the founder of the firm of stained glass manufacturers and interior decorators, Heaton, Butler and Bayne, Clement John Heaton was brought up at a time when that firm was producing progressive work and was carrying out important secular and ecclesiastical commissions, collaborating in particular with the architects, Alfred Waterhouse Richard Norman Shaw and Sir Arthur Blomfield.

Heaton joined his father's firm in 1880 becoming a partner after the latter's death in 1882. Friction over the company's commercial practices which, according to Heaton, were leading to a general lowering of standards in quality, led him to renounce his share in 1886. The terms of the break-up contract prevented Heaton from designing or making stained glass for a period of 15 years. This restriction left him with no other choice than to pursue experiments which he had already started with other techniques such as cloisonné enamel, mosaics, *opus sectile*, plaster and metalwork.

Heaton combined, to a high degree, practical scientific knowledge and technical resourcefulness with the creative talents of an artist. He invented both new processes and the machinery with which to carry them out, in the fields of cloisonné and embossed wall-covering in paper and cloth.

As an artist Heaton was inspired by the teaching of Ruskin and William Morris and was an early exponent of the ideals of the Arts and Crafts movement. He passionately believed in the essential unity of all arts and that the artist should be closely involved in the execution of his designs. Thus, in the field of stained glass he was opposed to the prevailing practice by which artists supplied cartoons without being involved in the execution of their design. Throughout his life Heaton remained craft-orientated, setting up his workshops in beautiful rural surroundings to achieve quality of life as well as work.

Heaton: staircase, Museum of Art, 1895–1906, Neuchâtel, showing cloisonné detail

The first signs of artistic originality appear in the work Heaton carried out in his own technique of cloisonné. He eliminated firing and substituted enamels with coloured cements which were set between a web of metal walls and grew hard as they were drying. The result was a matt surface as opposed to the shiny surface of real enamels. The advantage of this hybrid process, which was patented in 1886, was its potential for the decoration of architecture. It could be applied on a large scale to walls as well as used to decorate smaller items in copper, such as vases, plaques, chargers and jardinières. By the early 1890s, Heaton had developed a distinctive style which exploited the expressive power of line surrounding flowing stylised patterns inspired by nature. The colours he used were soft and cool, predominantly delicate greens and blues. His work achieved recognition at the Arts and Crafts Exhibition Society exhibitions; at the Society's 1890 exhibition the Duke of Westminster acquired a vase in Heaton cloisonné. The same year Heaton was elected to the Art-Workers Guild. From 1892 Liberty started retailing Heaton cloisonné wares.

The frequent claims that Heaton was a close associate of the

Century Guild (1882–88) are, so far, unsupported by any contemporary document relating to the Guild. These statements might be founded on brief notes made some 50 years later in 1932 by Arthur Heygate Mackmurdo, one of which relates to a Heaton cloisonné piece he owned (now in the Colchester and Essex Museum). Heaton's major work in the field of decoration was the staircase and vestibule of the Museum of Art and History in Neuchâtel (1895–1906), which he undertook in collaboration with the painter Paul Robert. Heaton achieved artistic unity by integrating the three large allegorical paintings by Robert into the surrounding architectural framework by devising a rich, varied and innovative decorative scheme. The chased copper plaques, cloisonné decor, plaster work and embossed wallcovering which decorate the dadoes, walls, friezes, archways and coves exemplify Heaton's fascination with textures and the tactile quality of surfaces. The decoration of the Museum was published in the *Studio* (1899). In Great Britain and Ireland the surviving works in Heaton cloisonné on walls are a tympanum showing St. Peter Raising Tabitha, in Blomfield's extension of the church of St. Peter at Eaton Square, London, and two scenes showing Christ and Angels at the church of St. Michael and All Angels at Clane, near Dublin. Both date from 1892.

By the early years of the century Heaton's workshop was well established and very busy executing official and private commissions both in Switzerland and France. In 1904 another article about his work appeared in the *Studio*. Heaton had by then successfully exhibited in Paris where Bing also sold his work. In 1900 Heaton's workshop started to make furniture decorated with marquetry designs influenced by the Nabis. The influence of the latter also appeared in the three windows on the theme of the seasons in the Temple of St. Aubin (1903). In 1902 Heaton was free again to resume work in stained glass and over the following 13 years he executed more than 100 windows for Swiss churches and museums. The quality of the glass he used was a constant concern to him and he may have benefited from the research in this field carried out by his younger brother, Noel (1874–1955), a chemist. Noel had succeeded their father at the head of a separate company, Heaton and Co., which had been set up to supply materials for colouring glass. Among the most important windows of these years are those for the Collegiale of Neuchâtel (1905) and for the cathedral of Lausanne (1906).

Although Heaton received official commissions from the Swiss government, for example, four rooms in the Federal Palace (1901) were decorated with his embossed "linealis" wall-paper, it seems he was refused permission to carry out his own large mosaic designs for the National Museum in Zurich on the grounds that he was a foreigner, despite the fact that they had been accepted by the architect. Possible disappointment over this, coupled with the complete loss of his workshop in a disastrous fire in 1914, led him to emigrate to the United States, where he had already developed strong contacts with the architect Ralph Adams Cram.

From then on, Heaton devoted his life to stained glass. His work in America displayed a more conservative approach, dominated by the tradition of the Gothic revival. The windows of the church of the Blessed Sacrament in New York (1918) were the first major commission of his early US years. After his death, Heaton's workshop was carried on by his son Maurice (1900–90) who was a highly original and experimental creator of glass works in his own right.

ANNE CERESOLE

Biography

Born in Watford, Hertfordshire, 21 April 1861, the son of Clement Heaton (1824–82), founder of the stained glass manufacturers and interior decorators, Heaton, Butler & Bayne. Attended Heatherley School of Fine Art, London, 1886; apprenticed to the stained glass manufacturers, Burlison and Grylls, 1886. Married 1) Lise Flore Favre, 1884 (died 1886): 1 son; 2) Rose Marie Junod, 1888: 5 daughters and 1 son, the stained glass manufacturer Maurice (1900–90). Joined his father's firm 1880; partner, 1882; resigned 1886. Established Heaton Cloisonné Mosaics Ltd., 1887. Settled in Neuchâtel, Switzerland, with a workshop at 10 rue de Collegiale, 1893; opened a workshop in Paris, 1903; moved the Neuchâtel workshop to Villaret near Comondrèche, 1908 (destroyed by fire, 1914). Emigrated to the United States where he was active as a stained glass designer; opened a workshop in Brooklyn, New York, 1914; established workshop at Valley Cottage, near Nyack, New York, 1917. Designed stained glass, 1880–86, and from 1902; active as a designer and manufacturer of cloisonné enamel, mosaics, embossed wallcoverings and plaster and metalwork from the mid-1880s; designed furniture, 1900–05. Took out patents for Heaton Cloisonné, ornamental mouldings and "linealis" embossed wallpaper, 1886. Exhibited: selected Arts and Crafts exhibitions 1888–1910; Paris Salon 1898–1900; Exposition Universelle, Paris, 1900. Appointed Master of the Art-Workers' Guild, 1890; resigned, 1898. Published articles on cloisonné enamel and mosaic and was an authority on French medieval stained glass. Died in New York, 1940; his workshop was taken over by his son Maurice.

Selected Works

Important archive collections relating to Heaton's work are in the Museum of Art and History, and the University of Neuchâtel Library, Switzerland, and in the Marquand Library of Art and Architecture, Princeton University, New Jersey, which has approximately 2000 items including drawings, watercolours, correspondence and lecture notes. Examples of Heaton's work are in the Staatliche Kunstgewerbemuseum, Berlin, the Victoria and Albert Museum, London, the Museum of Art and History, Neuchâtel, and the Musées des Arts Décoratifs, Paris.

Stained glass, cloisonné and decorations

1892	St. Peter's, Eaton Square, London (tympanum in cloisonné)
1892	St. Michael and All Angels, Clane, near Dublin (cloisonné decorations)
1895–1906	Museum of Art and History, Neuchâtel, Switzerland (decoration of the landing and staircase)
1897 & 1901	Palais Federal, Bern, Switzerland (four rooms including mosaic and "linealis" mural decoration)
1902	Temple of Cornaux, Switzerland (stained-glass windows)
1903	Temple of St. Aubin, Switzerland (stained-glass windows)
1905	Collegiale, Neuchâtel, Switzerland (stained-glass windows)
1907	St. Thomas's Hospital, London (cloisonné panels and stained glass)
1908	Museum of Art and History, Neuchâtel, Switzerland (3 windows in the hall)
1909	Museum of Art and History, Geneva, Switzerland (stained-glass window in the entrance hall)
1918–39	Numerous stained-glass windows for churches in USA

Publications

"The Use of Cloisonné for Decoration in Ancient and Modern Times" in *Journal of the Society of Arts*, 3 April 1891, pp.375–89

"Notes on the Practice of Pictorial Mosaic" in *Journal of the Royal Institute of British Architects*, IX, 12 April 1902, pp.299–304
"The Precious Windows of Chartres" in *Journal of the Royal Institute of British Architects*, XIII, no.5, 13 January 1906, pp.117–28
"Cloisonné Enamels by a Worker in the Art" in *Brooklyn Museum Quarterly*, II, No.2, July 1915, pp.301–310
"Beauty of Design and the Pictorial Element in Stained Glass" in *Art and Archaeology: The Arts Throughout the Ages*, XXII, nos.1 and 2, July 1926, pp.3–11 and 46

Further Reading

There is no catalogue raisonné of Heaton's work but the most comprehensive list appears in the forthcoming exhibition, Neuchâtel 1996.

Ceresole, Anne and others, *Clement John Heaton* (exhib. cat.), Neuchâtel: Museum of Art and History, 1996
"Décoration du Musée de Neuchâtel" in *L'Art Décoratif*, October 1899 –March 1900, pp.101–02
"Die Dekoration des Kunstmuseums in Neuchâtel" in *Dekorative Kunst*, III, December 1899, pp.95–96
"L'Exposition des 'Arts and Crafts' à Londres" in *Art et Décoration*, January –June 1900, pp.25–31
Faulkner, Herbert W., "A Remarkable Guild of Art Workers at Neuchâtel" in *New York Herald* (Paris edition), 13 September 1903
Grasset, Eugène, "Papiers Peints" in *Art et Décoration*, January –June 1897, pp.121–24
Mobbs, Robert, "The Decoration of the Musée des Beaux-Arts at Neuchâtel" in *The Studio*, 16 January 1899, pp.254–60
Mobbs, Robert, "M. Clement Heaton and His Work" in *The Studio*, 15 August 1904, pp.212–29
Verneiul, M. P., "L'Email et les Emailleurs" in *Art et Décoration*, January –June 1904, pp.48–49 and 53
Walker, Howard, "Notes on Stained Glass and the Art of Clement Heaton" in *American Architect*, 136, September 1929

Hepplewhite, George died 1786

British cabinet-maker

The importance of George Hepplewhite is founded upon his pattern book *The Cabinet-Maker and Upholsterer's Guide; or, Repository of Designs for Every Article of Household Furniture, in the Newest and Most Approved Taste*. The title of the pattern book clearly shows the intention to illustrate the wide range of available designs; it was not intended to introduce new or avant-garde ideas. The work was also valuable to decorators and designers as it showed plans of rooms "shewing the proper distribution of furniture".

Hepplewhite died in 1786 so did not live to see the publication, which is now assumed to have been executed by his wife Alice. The first edition was published in 1788. This must have been well received, as a second edition came in 1789. The desire to be up to date resulted in a third edition being published in 1794. This included rectangular backed chair designs which replaced some of the more curvaceous and less fashionable ones from the previous editions.

With over 300 designs, the *Guide* was the first to show furniture in the Neo-Classical style and therefore perpetuated and popularised the Adam style. The influence of Adam can be seen in the shapes of the back splats, and the use of urns, vases, petals, drapery, wheat ears, and rosettes.

The designs were intended to "unite elegance with utility", and to avoid "articles whose recommendation was mere novelty". Hepplewhite's other stated intention was to provide designs that would be of use to foreigners as well as "our own countrymen and artisans whose distance from the metropolis makes even an imperfect or superficial knowledge of its improvement acquired with much trouble and expense." It is therefore clear that the pattern book was not just for high-style use. Although the designs were not copies of Adam, demand for patterns of the Neo-Classical style must have been great, so this work was simply a codification of styles for the trade's use.

The most famous items were chairs which included the oval back, the wheel back, the heart and shield back chairs, all with either straight or tapered legs. In addition, Prince of Wales feather and wheat-ear motifs were his hallmark. Detailed recommendations included suggesting that shield back chairs ought to be upholstered as they were usually intended for drawing rooms.

Sofa designs were often made to appear en suite with chairs and the early Georgian idea of using joined chair backs for settees was revived. The combination of elegance and utility is seen in Hepplewhite's designs for sofas. They are particularly delicate but are more practical than Adam's due to the deeper seats.

The sideboard, with a central table flanked by urns, which was established by Adam, was continued by Hepplewhite, but he developed a new type-form when he integrated the table and pedestals into one piece. This was ideal for the smaller house, and practicality was again stressed with fitted wine storage and a heated section for plates. Hepplewhite considered that the sideboard was an important piece of furniture for the dining room, to the extent that he suggested the room was incomplete without one.

Elegance and utility again combine in Hepplewhite's designs for secretaire cabinets. Planned with a base like a chest of drawers and the front top drawer opening downwards to form a writing shelf, and with the upper section using glazed doors with bars echoing the classical-style motifs of the chairs, it has become a classic of its type.

Four-poster beds with slender posts continued the Chippendale tradition and were often supplied with decorative cornices. Few of these have survived, so most Hepplewhite beds are decorated with fabric valances.

It is important to remember that Hepplewhite was generally designing for the small private domestic interior, not for the large-scale country or town house that Adam often involved himself with. Hence his decoration was restrained and thus avoided too dramatic an effect. For friezes of tables, Hepplewhite suggested simple vertical fluting moving away from the Adam emphasis on classical detail. Table tops were simplified from the Adam by using only one motif with small festoons.

Hepplewhite did make some excursions towards the fanciful tastes of the period. The design for Rudd's Reflecting Dressing Table is an example of the taste for furniture specifically designed for a particular purpose, in this case to use a combination of moveable mirrors to enable the occupant of the

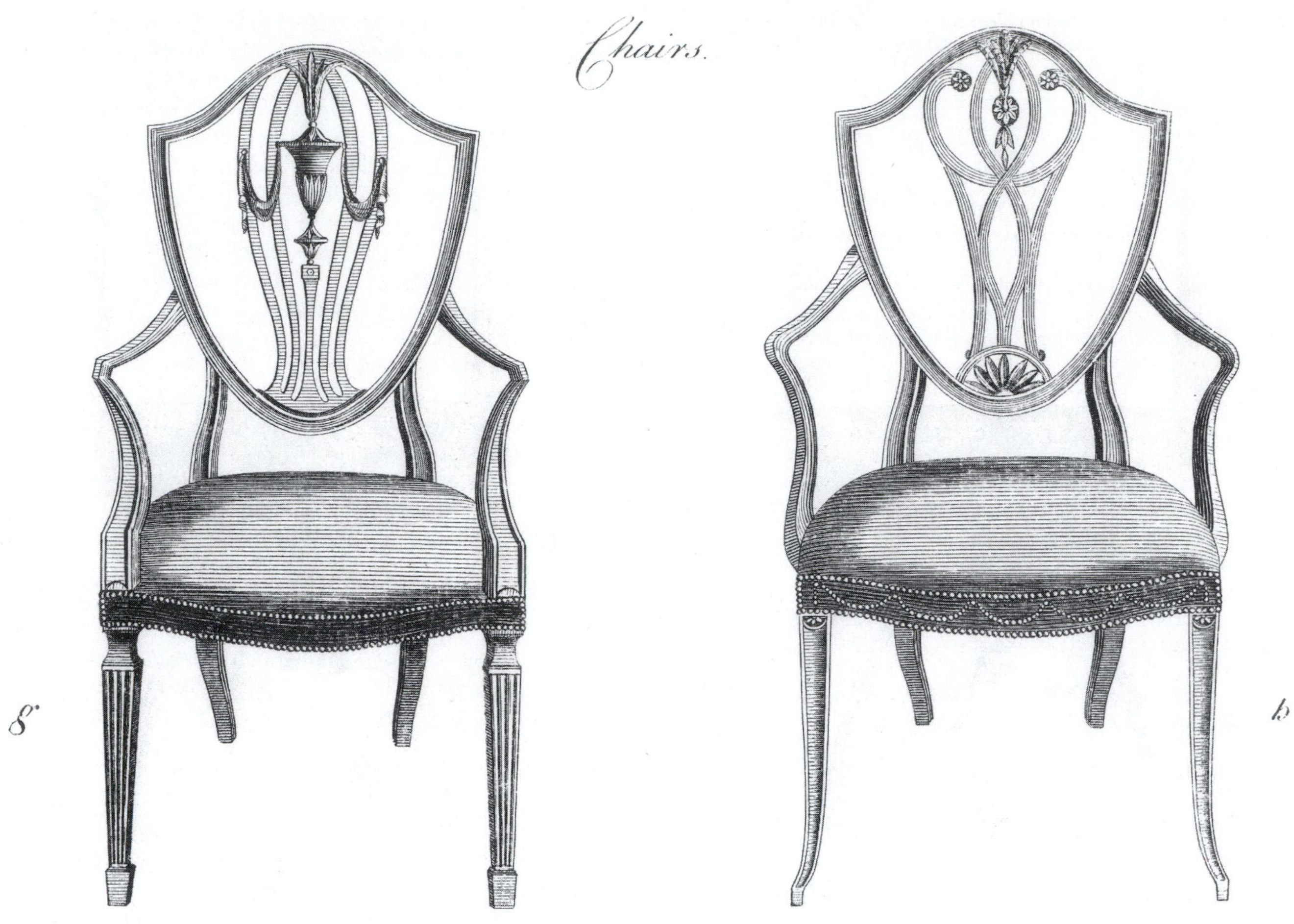

Hepplewhite: designs for shield back chairs, a plate from *The Cabinet-Maker and Upholsterer's Guide*, 1794

table to see him or herself from most angles. A different taste was catered for by Hepplewhite's illustrated designs for library furniture, for example tables or bookcases, which might be ornamented with a vase or bust on the top.

The important role of pattern books in disseminating designs is shown by the *Guide's* particular influence. Faithful copying of Heppelwhite designs was carried out in North Germany, Italy, and Portugal while in Denmark it was ensured that the pattern books were available for the Royal Furniture Emporium. In Sweden the popular box-like form of sofa design was clearly influenced by Hepplewhite and in the new United States, the impact on the Federal style was often literal. The example of John Shaw and his interpretation of the Hepplewhite style in Annapolis demonstrates this well.

Although there had been some sporadic interest by collectors in the later 18th century furniture, it was not until the 1870s, when a general revival of 18th-century decoration occurred, that a Hepplewhite revival became inevitable. The response to the demand was on two levels. The high-class comprehensive manufacturing firms of the West End of London produced fairly faithful copies, and the East End trade made less accurate but nonetheless passable imitations for a wide market. Hepplewhite's wider place in the market was confirmed by the re-issue of the *Guide* by Batsford in 1897. The elegance and compactness of many Hepplewhite designs has meant that they have been copied or adapted for the reproduction market ever since.

CLIVE D. EDWARDS

See also Pattern Books

Biography

An obscure figure, Hepplewhite may have been apprenticed to Gillows. Active as a cabinet-maker, trading at Redcross Street, Cripplegate, London, before 1786. Business continued by his widow, Alice Hepplewhite, after his death in 1786. Folio volume of *The Cabinet-Maker and Upholsterers's Guide*, published posthumously in 1788.

Publications

The Cabinet-Maker and Upholsterer's Guide, 1788, 1789, 1794; 3rd edition reprinted 1969

Further Reading

For a general introduction to Hepplewhite's work and influence see Collard 1985. Numerous examples of furniture in the Hepplewhite style are illustrated in Hinckley 1987.

Beard, Geoffrey and Christopher Gilbert (editors), *Dictionary of English Furniture Makers, 1660–1840*, London: Furniture History Society, 1986

Bell, J. Munro, *The Furniture Designs of George Hepplewhite*, London: Gibbings, 1910; New York: McBride, 1938

Collard, Frances, *Regency Furniture*, Woodbridge, Suffolk: Antique Collectors' Club, 1985

Edwards, Ralph, *Hepplewhite Furniture Designs*, London: Tiranti, 1947

Edwards, Ralph and Margaret Jourdain, *Georgian Cabinet-makers, c.1700–1800*, 3rd edition London: Country Life, 1955

Hinckley, F. Lewis, *Hepplewhite, Sheraton and Regency Furniture*, New York: Washington Mews, 1987; London: Tauris, 1990

Morley, John, *Regency Design, 1790–1840: Gardens, Buildings, Interiors, Furniture*, London: Zwemmer, and New York: Abrams, 1993

Musgrave, Clifford, *Adam and Hepplewhite and Other Neo-Classical Furniture*, London: Faber, and New York: Taplinger, 1966

Parissien, Steven, *Adam Style*, London: Phaidon, and Washington, DC: Preservation Press, 1992

Ward-Jackson, Peter, *English Furniture Designs of the Eighteenth Century*, London: Victoria and Albert Museum, 1984

White, Elizabeth, *Pictorial Dictionary of British 18th Century Furniture Design: The Printed Sources*, Woodbridge, Suffolk: Antique Collectors' Club, 1990

Herman Miller Inc.

American furniture and design company; established 1923

Herman Miller was founded as a traditional furniture company called Michigan Star Company in 1905, and was reorganized and renamed in 1923. Under the leadership of Dirk Jan DePree, it became a pioneer in contemporary design, standardization, marketing, and the development of office and industrial environments. It remained a closely-knit family business until 1970 when a second generation of DePrees made it a public company.

Like most of its Grand Rapids counterparts, the firm started out producing individual pieces of case furniture and sets of hand-crafted bedroom suites for such major outlets as Sears Roebuck & Co., in styles that were often indistinguishable from those of its competitors. Designs were derivative and based on assumptions of what the public would accept; they were also often conservative. The pieces were sold directly through department stores and wholesale distributors, where they were presented by manufacturers' representatives who might be selling a variety of products and with no particular knowledge about any individual item.

Herman Miller was able to turn the industry on its head and to even redesign the practice of interior design in the United States, not only because of the superior designers that were hired, but also through the firm's receptivity to innovation in all aspects of the business. Beginning in 1930, when DePree first hired Gilbert Rohde (1884–1944), a freelance designer committed to modern furniture, on a royalty rather than a fee basis, the company began to change. Rohde challenged the prevailing notion that one needed large suites, and designed a four-piece modern bedroom set, without legs, and using plastics. At the same time, the larger pieces provided much-needed storage space for contemporary – and especially apartment – living. Within a few years, Rohde also got Miller to start using upholstery and metal as integral parts of their contemporary line. Also a pioneer of the concept of systems, Rohde introduced the idea of standardization that would allow hundreds of products to come out of a handful of components.

Changes in marketing and distribution soon followed, with seminars and training for sales staff and the establishment of the soon-to-be-copied external showroom. Leasing space in the Merchandise Mart in Chicago, Miller undertook the unusual practice of keeping the showroom open all year around, instead of only during the major quarterly shows, as was then customary. By presenting the products directly to architects and designers, the firm was able to both reach the public most receptive to its modern designs and to remove the steep commissions that had traditionally gone to the department store or distributor.

After Rohde's death in 1944, George Nelson (1908–1986) took the lead in designing many of the firm's products, and also in leading DePree towards a clear design philosophy. He instituted a greater degree of standardization, developed the concept of wall storage, and recommended volume production. While many of his individual designs and his technological innovations became classics, it is the wall storage system, with space for books, music components, etc., that has been his most lasting contribution in the eyes of the public. Recognizing the advantages of a leadership position, he convinced the company to issue its 1948 catalog with heretofore unidentified dimensions and fabrics listed, and to sell the catalog as a volume on contemporary design. The impact on the firm was incalculable: the first edition quickly sold out, and the public came to know both Herman Miller and the names of its designers in their own right.

As Nelson was unafraid of competition, he brought innovative designers such as Charles Eames, and artists like Isamu Noguchi to the attention of the firm, some as full-time staff and some working on contract or commission. Eames began a life-long but non-exclusive relationship with Miller in 1946. Eames and his wife Ray were pioneers in the use of plastics, resins, tubular steel, and other materials, inventing and designing whole new forms of seating furniture as they experimented both with materials and their potential. But in spite of the familiarity of designs such as the *Shell* chair, the *Chaise*, and the *Tandem Sling* seats, it is the fact that they have been used in such large numbers that has caused them to be so strongly imprinted on the contemporary mind. Entire universities and libraries are furnished with the Eames stacking shell chairs, airports throughout the world use the tandem sling seats, and their winged plywood chairs fill countless business and home offices. Working on the cutting edge of technology, Eames's designs helped the firm leap to the forefront of the institutional market, and the adaptation of their designs to various uses enabled Miller to respond to corporate America with unheard-of rapidity.

In the 1960s the inventor / designer Robert Propst took the

Herman Miller: items of furniture showing parabolic leg table by Isamu Noguchi, plywood screen by Charles Eames, and cabinet and clock by George Nelson

firm beyond its residential and large corporate bases, by introducing the concept of environmental design through the use of both individual components and specialized products. Work space configurations, created after long and intensive studies of psychology, office behavior, and the properties of materials, became known under such names as Action Office, and were created in the Ann Arbor based research center that Propst conceived. A second generation of this form of system development produced new environments for such specialized institutions as hospitals, where new modular, portable, and adjustable units can accommodate the traditional need of sanitation, storage and patient handling. Other Miller design solutions are so far from the concept of interior design that their story belongs more to the history of engineering and manufacturing.

JOHN F. PILE

See also Eames; Nelson

Selected Works

Archive material, including photographs, manuscripts and designs, is housed at the Herman Miller Resource Center, Ann Arbor, Michigan. Examples of furnishings manufactured by the firm are in the Metropolitan Museum of Art, and the Museum of Modern Art, New York.

Further Reading

A history of the Herman Miller company appears in Caplan 1976. For more detailed information on individual designers and their work see separate monographs and catalogues.

Caplan, Ralph, *The Design of Herman Miller*, New York: Whitney Library of Design, 1976

Greenberg, Carla, *Mid-Century Modern: Furniture of the 1950s*, New York: Harmony, 1984; London: Thames and Hudson, 1985

Guelft, Olga, "Nelson / Eames / Girard / Propst: The Design Process at Herman Miller" in *Design Quarterly*, 98–99, 1975, pp.11–19

Hanks, David A., *Innovative Furniture in America from 1800 to the Present*, New York: Horizon, 1981

Hanks, David A. and Derek Ostergard, *Gilbert Rohde* (exhib. cat.), New York: Washburn Gallery, 1981

Hiesinger, Kathryn B. and George H. Marcus III (editors), *Design since 1945* (exhib. cat.), Philadelphia: Philadelphia Museum of Art, and London: Thames and Hudson, 1983

Jackson, Lesley, *"Contemporary": Architecture and Interiors of the 1950s*, London: Phaidon, 1994

Kirkham, Pat, *Charles and Ray Eames: Designers of the Twentieth Century*, Cambridge: Massachusetts Institute of Technology Press, 1995

Miller, R. Craig, *Modern Design in the Metropolitan Museum of Art, 1890–1990*, New York: Abrams, 1990

Nelson, George, *Storage*, New York: Whitney Publications, 1954

Nelson, George, *George Nelson on Design*, New York: Whitney Library of Design, 1979

Phillips, Lisa (introduction), *Shape and Environment: Furniture by American Architects* (exhib. cat.), New York: Whitney Museum of American Art, 1982

Please be Seated: Fifty Years of Innovative Seating Design (exhib. cat.), St. Paul: Goldstein Gallery, University of Minnesota, 1984

Stein, Margery B., "Teaching Steelcase to Dance" in *New York Times Magazine Business World*, 1 April 1990

Herter Brothers

American interior decorators and furniture manufacturers, 1859–1906

Herter Brothers, under the leadership of Gustave and Christian Herter, was one of the United States' leading 19th-century cabinet-making and interior decorating firms. An 1871 Herter Brothers bill of sale for a cabinet in the collection of the Currier Gallery of Art described its services as purveyors of "Rich & Plain Furniture, Curtains and Curtain Materials, Wood Mantels, Looking-glasses, Frames, Cornices & Clocks, Mosaics and Marqueterie, Architectural Decorations and fittings of Banks and Offices, Wall Decorations in Fresco, Wood, Tapestry, and Paper." Its most productive years were between 1858, when young Gustave Herter took over a firm originally established by Erastus Bulkley, and 1883, when Christian Herter died.

Numerous prominent investors, industrialists, and institutions commissioned work from Gustave and Christian Herter. They included Ruggles S. Morse (Portland, Maine, c.1860); Henry Probasco (Cincinnati, 1860–68); LeGrand Lockwood (Elm Park, Norwalk, Connecticut, c.1869–70); Darius Ogden Mills (Happy House, Millbrae, California 1869–70, 1880 and New York City, 1880); Milton S. Latham (Thurlow Lodge, Menlo Park, California, 1872–73); William H. Vanderbilt (New York City, 1869–71, 1878, 1879–82); the White House (1875); Mark Hopkins (San Francisco, 1875–80); Reed and Barton (Philadelphia, 1876); Tiffany & Co. (Paris, 1878); J. Pierpont Morgan (New York City, 1880–82); Jay Gould (New York City, 1882); and Arabella Worsham Huntington (New York City, 1881–84).

Julius Gustav [sic] Alexander Hagenlocher Herter (born Stuttgart, Kingdom of Württemberg, 14 May, 1830; died New York City, 29 November, 1898) and Christian Augustus Ludwig Herter (born Stuttgart, 8 January, 1839; died New York City, 2 November, 1883) were trained in Stuttgart as cabinet-makers. They joined the great wave of immigration from German principalities to the United States following the political and economic upheavals there in the late 1840s. Gustave Herter arrived in New York City in 1848 and gravitated almost immediately to New York's fashion center on lower Broadway in Manhattan. Soon thereafter he was working with Auguste Pottier (1823–96) in the firm Herter, Pottier & Co.(1851–53), and in a partnership with the established New York cabinet-maker Erastus Bulkley in the firm Bulkley & Herter (1851–58). In 1858, Herter took over Bulkley & Herter and named it after himself, Gustave Herter.

By 1859 his younger brother Christian was also in New York. In 1864 Christian joined Gustave's firm, which they then named Herter Brothers. The two brothers operated Herter Brothers in partnership until 1870, when Gustave retired and returned to Stuttgart to live until 1892, and Christian became the principal in the firm, a role he maintained until 1882 when ill-health compelled him also to retire. William Gilman Nichols (d. 1909), first in partnership with long-time Herter employee William Baumgarten (1845–1908), and then acting alone, continued the firm until 1906, but under his tenure it never enjoyed the success of its earlier years.

Herter Brothers' best known years coincide with a unique

Herter Brothers: Japanese parlour in the William H. Vanderbilt residence from Edward Strahan's *Mr. Vanderbilt's House and Collection*, vol. 1, 1883

moment in American history. First, Herter Brothers benefited from owners who were well trained in Württemberg under the lingering traditions of its rigorous German guild system, as, no doubt, were some of its employees. In New York, Herter workers' fine cabinet-making techniques were unfettered by traditional German shop practices. Herter Brothers furniture was made with uncompromising sensitivity to design, construction, and detail. It encompasses a full vocabulary of construction techniques, including panel and frame construction for case pieces, carving, marquetry, inlay, incising, turning, gilding, painting, and ebonizing.

Second, the firm thrived in an era of unparalleled American prosperity. Investors and industrialists eager to mark their social ascendancy commissioned Herter Brothers to decorate their residences in keeping with their aspirations or new status. The results, such as the William H. Vanderbilt residence at 640 Fifth Avenue, were uncompromisingly complete and luxurious.

Lastly, the firm thrived in a business climate that was being revolutionized by improved communication and transportation methods. Railroads, including the transcontinental railroad completed in 1869, which joined California to the East, made it possible for the Herters to execute commissions beyond New York City. The telegraph system and the Atlantic cable facilitated communication and enabled the firm to link European suppliers with American clients located from coast to coast. Faster ocean travel also facilitated both clients' and the firm's links with Europe.

Gustave and Christian Herter were synthesizers of European taste and fashion. They keenly followed European styles, adapting them to the preferences of their American clients. Whether reinterpreting an 1851 sideboard created by Parisian master Alexandre George Fourdinois for the 1853 New-York Crystal Palace Exhibition as Gustave Herter did, or looking at the work of James Lamb of Manchester and other English designers as Christian did in the 1870s, the brothers remained conversant with the latest styles, moving seemingly effortlessly through French Renaissance and Louis XIV styles, through Pompeian and neo-Grèc modes, to English reform and Anglo-Japanese designs. As the firm's designs evolved, so, too, did its furniture materials: walnut, maple, oak, mahogany, cherry (sometimes stained or painted to imply ebony or Japanese finishes), and rosewood, the most lavish, were used, often in combination on the same piece.

The firm's facility with different design vocabularies was due in large part to its continuing close ties to Europe, including a period in 1869 when Christian Herter lived in France. Herter Brothers bought ceiling and decorative wall panels in Paris from Pierre-Victor Galland for LeGrand Lockwood and William H. Vanderbilt, textiles in France for Vanderbilt and others, clocks and sculpture from Ferdinand Barbedienne's Paris foundry for Henry Probasco and Vanderbilt; and interior fittings from Guéret Frères for Milton S. Latham.

With few surviving Herter Brothers interiors (the Ruggles S. Morse house and Elm Park, the LeGrand Lockwood residence, are notable exceptions), the firm's reputation rests largely on its furniture, most notably its marquetry and mother-of-pearl designs made under Christian Herter's leadership in the late 1870s and early 1880s. In this furniture, the firm successfully combined traditional western forms with Anglo-Japanese ornament richly interpreted in contrasting abstract patterns of dark and light marquetry. It was during these years that the firm also completed its most ambitious commission, the Vanderbilt residence located on Fifth Avenue between 51st and 52nd streets. Designed entirely by the firm, including the exterior, it was an elaborate progression of Pompeian, Renaissance, Moorish, Japanese, and Chinese styles carefully orchestrated in exotic woods, mother-of-pearl and minerals, and elaborately decorated surfaces and textiles. The Vanderbilt residence was Christian Herter's last great commission and the culmination of his career. It affirmed the integrity of Herter Brothers work, its originality, and the consummate craftsmanship for which the firm remains justly known.

KATHERINE S. HOWE

See also Aesthetic Movement

Selected Works

The Herter Brothers Business Papers, 1891–1906, form part of the Joseph Downs Collection of Manuscripts and Printed Ephemera, in the Winterthur Library, Delaware; additional archive material is in the R. G. Dun & Co. Collection, Baker Library, Harvard University Graduate School of Business Administration, Cambridge, Massachusetts. Examples of Herter Brothers furniture are in the Los Angeles County Museum of Art, Brooklyn Museum, and Metropolitan Museum of Art, New York, Museum of Fine Arts, Houston, and the Wadsworth Atheneum, Hartford, Connecticut; Herter Brothers interiors survive at the Victoria Mansion, Portland, Maine. An account of the firm's principal interior design commissions appears in Howe 1994.

Interiors

c.1860	Ruggles S. Morse residence, Portland, Maine (decorations and furnishings): Ruggles Sylvester Morse
c.1869–70	Elm Park, Norwalk, Connecticut (decoration and furnishings): LeGrand Lockwood
1869–70 & 1880	Happy House, Millbrae, California (decoration and furnishings): Darius Ogden Mills
1869–71 &1878–82	William H. Vanderbilt residence, 640 Fifth Avenue, New York (interiors and furnishings)
1872–73	Thurlow Lodge, Menlo Park, California (decoration and furnishings): Milton Slocum Latham
1875 & 1902	The White House, Washington, DC (furnishings for the Red Room; plasterwork and carving, East, Green, Red and State Dining Rooms)
1875–80	Mark Hopkins residence, San Francisco (decoration and furnishings): Mark and Mary Hopkins
1880–82	J. Pierpont Morgan residence, 219 Madison Avenue, New York (alterations, decoration and furnishings): J. Pierpont Morgan
1881–84	Arabella Huntington residence, 4 West 54th Street, New York (bedroom suite)
c.1882	John Sloane residence, 997 Fifth Avenue, New York (parlour and library: decoration and furnishings): John Sloane
1882	Jay Gould residence, 579 Fifth Avenue, New York (furniture)
1883	Oliver Ames residence, 335 Commonwealth Avenue, Boston (drawing room: decoration and furnishings): Oliver Ames

Further Reading

The most detailed scholarly account of the Herter Brothers' work appears in Howe 1994; this book also includes numerous archive photographs of the firm's interiors, a chronology, an extensive primary and secondary bibliography, and a list of archival sources.

Artistic Houses, Being a Series of Interior Views of a Number of the Most Beautiful and Celebrated Homes in the United States, 2 vols., New York, 1883–84; reprinted, New York: Blom, 1971

Boehm, Mary Dutton, "Herter Brothers and the William H. Vanderbilt House", M.A. thesis, New York: Cooper-Hewitt Museum and Parsons School of Design, 1991

Bordes, Marilyn Johnson, "Christian Herter and the Cult of Japan" in Robert Judson Clark (editor), *Aspects of the Arts and Crafts Movement in America*, special issue, *Art Museum Record*, Princeton University, 34, no.2, 1975, pp.20–27

Burke, Doreen Bolger and others, *In Pursuit of Beauty: Americans and the Aesthetic Movement* (exhib. cat.: Metropolitan Museum, New York), New York: Rizzoli, 1986

Cook, Clarence, *The House Beautiful: Essays on Beds and Tables, Stools and Candlesticks*, New York: Scribner, 1878

Hanks, David A., *Christian Herter and the Aesthetic Movement in America* (exhib. cat.), New York: Washburn Gallery, 1980

Hanks, David A., "Herter Brothers: Art in Furniture Design" in *Journal of Decorative and Propaganda Arts*, Spring 1986, pp.32–39

Howe, Katherine S., Alice Cooney Frelinghuysen and Catherine Hoover Voorsanger, *Herter Brothers: Furniture and Interiors for a Gilded Age* (exhib. cat.), New York: Abrams, 1994

Kimbro, Edna E., "The California Commissions of Herter Brothers, Interior Designers, New York City", senior thesis, Santa Cruz: University of California, 1986

King, Robert B. and Charles O. McLean, *The Vanderbilt Homes*, New York: Rizzoli, 1989

Nichols, William Gilman, *In Memory of Christian Herter. Born Jan. 8, 1840* [sic], *Died Nov. 2, 1883*, New York, 1883

Nineteenth-Century America: Furniture and Other Decorative Arts (exhib. cat.), New York: Metropolitan Museum of Art, 1970

Strahan, Edward (Earl Shinn), *Mr. Vanderbilt's House and Collection*, 4 vols., Boston: Barrie, 1883–84

Hicks, David 1929–

British designer of furnishings and interiors

David Hicks is arguably the best-known of all post-war British interior decorators and designers. Trained in fine art at the Central School of Arts and Crafts, he was one of a second generation of young designers whose interest in contemporary design heralded a move away from the faded elegance characteristic of the traditional "English Country House" style that had dominated up-market British interiors since the 1930s. Hicks's trademarks were strong colours, crisp outlines, and bold, geometric carpet and fabric designs. But his interest in modern design was tempered by a fondness for antiques and, like the designer Michael Inchbald whose work Hicks greatly admired, his skill was in combining these two elements to create a distinctive and highly personal style. With offices in Britain, Australia, Belgium, France, Germany, Pakistan and Switzerland, his ideas have reached many parts of the globe and his work has been particularly influential in the United States. Moreover, his numerous books on decoration and design have helped to ensure that his ideas have reached a far wider audience than the wealthy and exclusive group that makes up his decorating clientele.

Hicks's career as an interior designer began in 1954 when he redecorated his mother's house in South Eaton Place, London, and photographs of his work were featured in the magazine *House and Garden*. These pictures attracted the attention of Mrs. Rex Benson, the ex-wife of the publisher of Condé Nast. The two worked together on the design of her flat and this led to numerous small jobs, mainly re-upholstery work. In 1956, Hicks went into partnership with the antique dealer Tom Parr – Parr subsequently took over the running of the decorators Colefax and Fowler – and they opened their shop, Hicks and Parr, in Lowndes Street, Chelsea. In 1959 he opened his own shop, David Hicks Ltd., also in Lowndes Street, and continued both retailing and designing. But in 1963 he closed the Lowndes Street shop and worked from his house in St. Leonard's Terrace. Sixteen years later he opened another shop at 101 Jermyn Street which featured four, frequently restyled, room settings, through which customers had to pass to reach the main body of the shop. The shop also doubled as the headquarters of Hicks's international interior design business; he had numerous shops and associates in Europe and Asia dedicated to the dissemination of his design ideas. He designed everything from textiles, ceramic tiles and furniture to cufflinks, carrier bags and a church, but he was also concerned to employ other designers to widen the range of possibilities for his clients. However, unless they were associates, these designers worked under the company name. Hicks himself created interiors for such notable projects as the Q4 room on the liner *Queen Elizabeth II* and beauty salons for Helena Rubinstein.

In 1960 he married Lady Pamela Mountbatten and the home that he created for their early married life is a fine example of the eclectic Hicks style. The house, called Britwell Salome, in Oxfordshire, was built in 1728, and initially Hicks wanted to maintain the 18th-century quality of the rooms, keeping the furniture to a minimum and placing all the chairs against the walls. But gradually, the austerity and rigour of his plans were modified and increasingly he used the house to experiment with new interior effects before presenting them to clients. A description of the house appears in his book, *Living – with Taste*. The decoration of the library was particularly dramatic with matt black walls, white ceiling and woodwork, and books bound in shades of red and purple. The bathroom was also somewhat unconventional in appearance; the bath was placed centrally between two chairs and the overdoors were of *faux* granite. But the most important element of this room was the carpet; based on Persian mosaic designs, it was Hicks's first geometric carpet.

These geometric designs were to become something of a Hicks trademark and were highly influential in the United States. Billy Baldwin (1903–83), the leading American post-war interior decorator, wrote that Hicks "had revolutionised the floors of the world with his small-patterned and striped carpeting", and a beige, black and white carpet with another geometric design was used in Hicks's collaboration with the American designer Mark Hampton for an East 89th Street apartment. This project also included white plastic chairs by the British designer Max Clendinning, a 19th century marble fireplace, and black walls lit by uplighters. It was simpler than the typical Hicks style, lacking the decorative details that he delighted in, but it was very "Sixties" in appearance and very much of its time.

Another of Hicks's enthusiasms was for arrangements of personal collections of objects on small tables and sideboards. He called these arrangements "table scapes" and he created

Hicks: his own house, Villa Verde, Portugal, 1988

numerous small groups consisting of objects of vertue, shells, stones and other natural objects, or souvenirs and mementoes, ephemera and anything else that fitted into his theme or colour scheme. Many clients were happy to use Hicks's collections but he nevertheless tried to encourage them to devise their own creative arrangements and add them to the interior themselves.

Another example of Hicks's theatrical use of colour is a Chelsea dining room illustrated in Mary Gilliatt's *English Style* (1967). Hicks took as his inspiration the Durbar Hall in Jaipur; the walls of this room were painted orange with black and white borders and the carpet was aubergine. The table was dressed in orange and white but the drinking glasses were blue. Lighting was provided by a spotlight in the centre of the ceiling and a jug that had been converted into a table lamp.

Hicks was evangelical about interior design, and in the 1970s he produced an inspirational series of books dealing with each room of the house in turn. The ideas presented in the books were based on his own work but he understood that many of his readers had limited incomes and the examples were modified accordingly. In 1970 he was presented with a

Design Council Award. He diversified into designing womenswear in 1982. He summarised his own view of his contribution to interior design thus: "My greatest contribution as an interior designer has been to show people how to use bold colour mixtures, how to use patterned carpets, how to light rooms and how to mix old with new" (*Living – with Taste*, p.72).

JANICE WEST

Biography

David Nightingale Hicks. Born in London, 25 March 1929. Trained at the Central School of Arts and Crafts, London, 1938–42. Served in the Royal Army Educational Corps, 1949–51. Married Lady Pamela Mountbatten, 1960: 3 children. Independent designer from 1953; founder-principal, with Tom Parr, of Hicks and Parr decorating firm, 1956–59, David Hicks Ltd. from 1959, and David Hicks Marketing Ltd. with branch offices in Switzerland, France, Belgium, Germany, Pakistan and Australia, from 1970; also active in New York. Designed textiles and carpets from 1960; clothing and fashion accessories for the Association of Japanese Manufacturers from 1977; womenswear collections from 1988. Published numerous books on decoration and design from the mid-1960s. Member and Master, Worshipful Company of Salters; Fellow, Royal Society of Arts, London. Received Design Council Award, London, 1970. Homes in London and Portugal.

Selected Works

Hicks's designs for public interiors include the original nightclub on the Queen Elizabeth II liner (1969), Raffles nightclub in Chelsea, beauty salons for Helena Rubinstein Ltd., and 10 Peter Evans Eating Houses. He has also designed numerous domestic interiors including several for his own family such as his mother's house in South Eaton Place, London (1954), his country house Britwell Salome, Oxfordshire (1960), and his villa in the South of France (late 1960s). Good illustrations of his interiors are featured in his books.

Publications

David Hicks on Decoration, 1966
David Hicks on Living – with Taste, 1968
David Hicks on Bathrooms, 1970
David Hicks on Decoration with Fabrics, 1971
The David Hicks Book of Flower Arranging, 1976
David Hicks: Living with Design (with Nicholas Jenkins), 1979
David Hicks Garden Design, 1982
David Hicks Style and Design, 1987

Further Reading

Calloway, Stephen, *Twentieth-Century Decoration: The Domestic Interior from 1900 to the Present Day*, London: Weidenfeld and Nicolson, and New York: Rizzoli, 1988

"David Hicks: Style and Design" in *Studio*, 164, November 1962, pp.182–87

Garner, Philippe, *Contemporary Decorative Arts from 1940 to the Present Day*, Oxford: Phaidon, and New York: Facts on File, 1980

Gilliatt, Mary, *English Style*, London: Bodley Head, 1967; as *English Style in Interior Decoration*, New York: Viking, 1967

Hampton, Mark, *Legendary Decorators of the Twentieth Century*, New York: Doubleday, and London: Hale, 1992

Levin, Angela, "At Home with David Hicks" in *You: The Mail on Sunday Magazine*, 6 March 1983, pp.42–45

Patterson, S., "The Bigger the Challenge the Better I Like it" in *Réalités*, March 1970

Vinson, R. H., "La Salle de Bains de David Hicks" in *Connaissance des Arts*, November 1972

High-Tech

The term "High-Tech" has often been used to describe the Modernist style of architecture developed from the 1960s by British architects such as Norman Foster, Richard Rogers, Nicholas Grimshaw and Michael Hopkins. But it can also be applied to a style of interior design that flourished in the 1970s and 1980s and that found favour with fashion-conscious consumers on both sides of the Atlantic. This style celebrated the aesthetic of industrial production by introducing elements such as steel scaffolding, office furniture and factory flooring into the domestic interior. At its most extreme it represented a purist version of minimalist chic that contrasted sharply with both the historicism of late 20th century revivalist styles and the pluralism and irony of Postmodernism.

The emergence of High-Tech coincided with a growing disillusionment on the part of architects and designers with the achievements of the Modern Movement. But unlike those styles which turned to the past for inspiration, High-Tech retained a strong belief in the possibilities provided by the modern world and was aggressively optimistic about modern technology and the quality of modern design.

Within other spheres, notably industry, the term High-Tech denotes sophisticated production methods such as atomic energy, silicon chips and robotic control. Within design, however, the emphasis is frequently upon hand-crafting, and a High-Tech interior is often painstakingly constructed by craftsmen with the intention of looking machine-made. The essence of High-Tech is that it celebrates the way in which objects and interiors are made, and they frequently include exquisite, jewel-like joints and junctions, and materials such as shiny metal and glass, sometimes supplemented by brightly coloured studded rubber, that suggest transparency, lightness or modernity. The early adherents of High-Tech believed that architecture had been outstripped by other industries and felt compelled to try to bring the building industry up-to-date, often by importing techniques and methodologies from other spheres. Transport was an especially popular source of inspiration, and architects borrowed the imagery of rounded corners from the car industry, stressed-skin construction from the aerospace industry, and spars and tension cables from yacht-builders and shipyards.

Precursors of the High-Tech movement included work by Buckminster Fuller, Jean Prouvé, the California Case Study houses and, above all, the Charles Eames house built in Pacific Palisades, California, in 1949. The Eames house was assembled from mass-produced components, and its innovative interior was ordered by the open-web steel joists of the ceilings that formed a striking backdrop to the collection of modern furnishings and paintings displayed within. Twenty years elapsed before other designers developed the ideas embodied in this house.

In architecture, the generally accepted starting point of High-Tech is the Reliance Controls factory in Swindon designed by Team 4, a group of architects that included Norman Foster and Richard Rogers, and which was completed in 1967. The factory is executed in an unornamented minimalist style and represents a lightweight version of earlier buildings by Mies van der Rohe. Richard Rogers, working with Renzo Piano, went on to design the Georges Pompidou Centre in Paris in 1977 which is one of the most well-known High-Tech buildings and which propelled the style into the big time. All the apparatus for servicing the building is boldly displayed on the exterior and the interior walls were designed to be moveable. The high-point of High-Tech architecture occurred with the completion in the mid-1980s of Rogers's Lloyd's insurance building in London, and Norman Foster's Hong Kong and Shanghai Bank in Hong Kong. Both buildings have modern, functional offices surrounding vast barrel-vaulted atria – a feature that has been widely imitated in other office buildings – with access to the different levels provided by futuristic, zig-zag tiers of escalators.

Interior designers were quick to pick up on elements of these architects' work, and soon began to employ imagery borrowed from industrial design. The case of the Czech-born designer, Eva Jiricna, is a notable example. She worked with Rogers on the fittings and furnishings of the restaurant for the Lloyd's building, and also designed a series of shops for the clothes designer, Joseph Ettedgui, that often featured stunning glass and metal staircases suspended from a complex web of stainless steel. Jiricna's work brought the aesthetic of High-Tech to the smart world of fashion retailing, and so successful were her Joseph interiors that other up-market retail chains, including Joan and David, and Vidal Sassoon, soon commissioned her to create High-Tech shops all over Europe and America. They came to represent the ultimate in high-fashion chic.

Although the High-Tech aesthetic was particularly well-suited to office and retail interiors, by the late 1970s elements of this style had also begun to appear within the domestic sphere. Initially, this trend was to be seen in architect-designed homes. Michael Hopkins's steel-framed house in Hampstead (1975), for example, contained an open-plan interior that featured exposed metal girders and living spaces demarcated by Venetian blinds instead of walls. The American architect, Peter de Bretteville's two family houses in Laurel Canyon, Los Angeles (1977) were similarly spare and were furnished with rectangular blocks of foam covered in yellow plastic, and Helmut Shulitz's Beverly Hills and Hollywood homes extend the High-Tech theme with interiors containing open wells and minimalist, boat-type, trim. But it was the publication in 1978 of Joan Kron and Suzanne Slesin's book, *High-Tech: The Industrial Style and Source Book for the Home*, that signified the formulation of a coherent, more commercial High-Tech domestic style. This book not only illustrated notable High-Tech interiors, – for instance the designer Joseph Paul D'Urso's minimalist New York apartment which included steel-mesh walls and hospital doors – and goods produced for industrial use placed in the home, it also provided the names and addresses of stockists where these products could be obtained. It included staircases in checker plate, laboratory beakers for the dining table, wire refrigerator shelving for bookcases, poultry cages as storage units, and car wheels as coffee tables, and the world of industrial products was ransacked for anything that might be used within the home. Another much-used source of inspiration was the office environment and as distinctions between the workplace and the home became less clear the functional efficiency embodied in the High-Tech style became increasingly popular among young professionals in the late 1970s and 1980s. The British retailer Habitat's range of all-black furniture, launched in 1979, exemplified the mass-marketing of this trend.

High-Tech did much to counteract the nostalgia of much 1970s and 1980s design and it produced some of the century's most notable buildings, with interiors as impeccably crafted as the exteriors. But by the mid-1980s, the industrial character of the style had lost ground within avant-garde circles. Its minimalist strand, however, has endured. Indeed, the legacy of the High-Tech movement is a style that continues to use modern materials, such as polished metal and reflective glass, but in an increasingly simple and pared-down fashion. This has become an aesthetic of exclusion which strives to produce a look that, by virtue of its very sparseness, will appear classic and timeless. Whatever the merits of this development, it has been achieved at the expense of much of the energy and vitality that was originally associated with the High-Tech style.

JOHN WINTER

See also Jiricna

Further Reading

Bangert, Albrecht and Karl Michael Armer, *80s Style: Designs of the Decade*, New York: Abbeville, and London: Thames and Hudson, 1990

Chaslin, François and others, *Norman Foster*, Paris: Electa Moniteur, 1986

Davies, Colin, *High Tech Architecture*, New York: Rizzoli, and London, Thames and Hudson, 1988

"Joe D'Urso: The Mastermind of Minimalism" in *Metropolitan Home* (US), June 1981

Kron, Joan and Suzanne Slesin, *High-Tech: The Industrial Style and Source Book for the Home*, New York: Potter, 1978; London: Allen Lane, 1979

McDermott, Catherine, *Street Style: British Design in the 80s*, London: Design Council, and New York: Rizzoli, 1987

Manser, José, *The Joseph Shops: Eva Jiricna*, London: Architecture Design and Technology Press, and New York: Van Nostrand Reinhold, 1991

Massey, Anne, *Interior Design of the Twentieth Century*, London and New York: Thames and Hudson, 1990

Hildebrandt, Johann Lukas von

1668–1745

Austrian architect

Johann Lukas (or Lucas) von Hildebrandt is considered one of the finest architects and interior designers of the early 18th century Austrian Baroque period. Born in Genoa, he trained there and then in Rome under the Baroque architect, Carlo Fontana. Hildebrandt moved to Vienna, the capital city of the Austro-Hungarian Empire, in 1696. His career flourished, and, encouraged by his patrons, the architect assimilated the French Rococo style and through commissions all over the Empire became familiar with indigenous Austrian traditions in architecture. Hildebrandt's style is an amalgam of Italian, French, and Austrian sources which are brought together to produce original, often witty, and sophisticated designs for both churches and palaces.

The architect's aristocratic clients were at that time engaged

Hildebrandt: entrance hall, Upper Belvedere, Vienna, 1721–22

in building dwellings of two types: the garden palace and the city palace. Typically, a Viennese city palace sits on a narrow street between contiguous structures, has a long intricately decorated "show" façade, is entered via an ornamental stairway (Hildebrandt was one of the prime inventors of this form), and has major rooms for entertaining placed on the *piano nobile* (one storey above ground level).

The Daun-Kinsky Palace, 1713–16, is one of Hildebrandt's most characteristic designs. The street façade carries tapered giant Ionic pilasters reaching from the *piano nobile* through the third storey. Richly sculptural window surrounds (in stucco), an entry-way flanked by atlantes, and a horizontal roofline that is punctuated by figural statuary complete the exuberant exterior. It is a direct prelude to the interiors which likewise incorporate the architectural orders, sculpture and, in addition, painting to create the unified effect sought in Baroque decor.

Within the Daun-Kinsky Palace an octagonal foyer leads to an oval vaulted *sala terrana* overlooking one of the two interior courts that lie on the main axis between the palace's two long wings. To the left is the palace's most innovative interior, an ornamented stairhall (a stairway that fills an entire room). It leads to the main rooms, including the oval two-storeyed marble salon which lies above the *sala terrena*.

In the oblong stairhall, single flights of stairs lie directly above one another. They are flanked by windowed corridors on the court side. An Atlas figure, like those on the exterior, guards the entry to the stairs. These figures are a leitmotif of the Viennese Baroque, symbolically referential to the power of the inhabitant of the palace. The stairs proceed upward beneath a series of low cupolas stuccoed with delicate Rococo strapwork. The wall side of the stair is punctuated by niches filled with marble statues. The balustrade, opposite, is a series of carved stone scrolls. After one long flight of stairs, the space opens vertically through the rest of the building to a frescoed ceiling painted by the Italian master, Marcantonio Chiarini.

For his patron, Prince Eugene of Savoy, Hildebrandt designed the double garden palace, the Lower Belvedere (1713–16) and Upper Belvedere (1721–25). The garden palace type, used only seasonally, is a free-standing structure placed in a landscaped setting. The single storeyed Lower Belvedere, a residence, sits at the bottom of a hill. A French Baroque garden runs up the hill to the much larger multi-storeyed Upper Belvedere, designed to house the Prince's extensive art collection. Marble revetted Grand Salons, overlooking the garden, lie in the center of each of the palaces. There, in the Lower Belvedere, marble inset with figural bas-reliefs is used to face the fireplaces, overmantel, and door surrounds. Colorful illusionistic frescoes cover the rest of the walls and ceiling. Iconographically the narrative imagery alludes to Prince Eugene's military prowess or to his patronage of learning and the arts.

Other important rooms in the Lower Belvedere include a mirrored cabinet, which follows the French taste for delicately painted *boiseries* between walls of mirrors. The mirrors reflected the Prince's porcelain collection which was displayed on wall brackets. The coved ceiling is covered with delicate stuccoed putti cavorting among garlands of flowers and other Rococo ornamentation. The long marble gallery has stucco ornamentation over a slightly barrelled ceiling vault. One wall is divided into bays by tapered pilasters. Niches holding life-sized sculpture are set between them. The room's short ends are covered with large mirrors inset in marble frames that match the wainscoting. The other long wall holds large windows overlooking the garden.

The Upper Belvedere has two formal entries, on the garden side and on the court side. They incorporate, from the garden, a vestibule of atlantes beneath white stuccoed sail vaults. From the court, a *porte-cochère* gives access to a double staircase with marble putti holding bronze lanterns that leads directly to the Marble Salon. Overhead and on the walls a program of white Rococo stucco ornament continues. In the Marble Salon, salmon colored paired pilasters with gilded Corinthian capitals line the space, octagonal in form, which rises two storeys to a frescoed vault.

Hildebrandt built several churches, the most important of which is the Dominican Church of St. Lawrence at Gabel in Bohemia (1699–1711). Its interior decor has been marred by fire, but the plan, a composite of centralizing and longitudinal elements has the tremendous energy of his many monumental stairhalls (e.g., at the Monastery of Gottweig, and the Weissenstein Palace). A pattern of separate vaulted spaces of different sizes are interconnected by torsion vaults.

Hildebrandt's mature style represents the synthesis of elements from Italian Baroque architecture, French Rococo, and imaginative Austrian indigenous art. His interiors are modulated from formal monumental Grand Salons, used for audiences and lavish entertainments, to more intimate delicately articulated cabinets reserved for private usage. His ingenious recourse to fine stucco work and fresco painting gave a lively and often light-hearted touch to interiors that reflect the cultivation of the arts in Viennese culture of the early 18th century.

BEVERLY F. HEISNER

See also Staircases

Biography

Born in Genoa, 14 November 1668. Studied architecture in Genoa; continued his studies in Rome under Carlo Fontana c.1690, where he also trained as a military engineer. Married Francesca Johanna Perpetua Geist, 1706: 8 children. Commenced his architectural career in Italy, 1693–95; active as a military engineer in the service of Prince Eugene of Savoy in Piedmont, 1695–96. Moved to Vienna, 1696; employed as Councillor to the Court, 1698; appointed court architect, 1700. Ennobled by the Hapsburg Court, 1720. Named first court architect after the death of Fischer von Erlach (1656–1723). Died in Vienna, 16 November 1745.

Selected Works

A list of Hildebrandt's architectural commissions appears in Grimschitz 1959.

Interiors

1697–1715 Mansfeld-Fondi (later Schwarzenberg) Palace, Vienna (building and interiors including the chapel and rooms in the west wing; completed by J.B. and J.E. Fischer von Erlach)

1699–1711 Dominican Church of St. Lawrence, Gabel, Bohemia (building and interiors)

1701–17 Ráckeve Palace, Czepel, Hungary (building and interiors)

1702, 1708–09, 1723–24 City Palace of Prince Eugene of Savoy, Vienna (building by Fischer von Erlach; additions and interiors by Hildebrandt)

1705–06 Starhemberg-Schönburg Garden Palace, Vienna (designs for building and interiors; building completed by Franz Jänggle, 1711, interiors completed by others, 1721)

1705–11 Schönburg Garden Palace, Vienna (alterations, additions, interiors and garden)

1709–10 Archbishop's Residence, Salzburg (additions and interiors)

1711–15 Weissenstein Palace, Pommersfelden, Germany (building by Johann Dientzenhofer; stair pavilion and central pavilion including grotto, vestibule and Imperial Hall by Hildebrandt)

1712–25 Schönborn Country House, Göllersdorf (restoration, redecoration, garden, pavilions and orangerie)

1713–16 Daun-Kinsky Palace, Vienna (building and interiors)

1713–16 Lower Belvedere, Vienna (building and interiors including the marble salon, marble cabinet, frescoed salon and marble gallery)
1720–44 Prince-Bishop's Residence, Würzburg (building by Johann Balthasar Neumann; stair pavilion by Hildebrandt)
1721–25 Upper Belvedere, Vienna (building and interiors including the vestibule and stairhall and marble salon)
1721–27 Mirabell Palace, Salzburg (renovations, additions and interiors including the stairhall and marble hall)
1724–39 Monastery of Göttweig, Göttweig (east wing and stairhall)
1725–32 Schlosshof Palace, Marchfeld (additions and interiors and chapel)

Further Reading

Aurenhammer, Hans, "Ikonographie und Ikonologie des Wiener Belvederegartens" in *Wiener Jahrbuch für Kunstgeschichte*, 17, 1955, pp.86–108
Aurenhammer, Hans, *J.B. Fischer von Erlach*, London: Allen Lane, and Cambridge, MA: Harvard University Press, 1973
Bachmann, Erich, *The Würzburg Residence and Court Gardens*, 6th edition Munich: Bayerische Verwaltung der Staatlicher Schlosser, 1982
Brinckmann, Albert E., *Von Guarino Guarini bis Balthasar Neumann*, Berlin: Deutscher Verein für Kunstwissenschaft, 1932
Fox Weber, Nicholas, "Baroque Splendours of Vienna's Schwarzenberg Palace" in *Architectural Digest*, 47, September 1990
Franz, Heinrich Gerhard, *Studien zur Barockarchitektur in Böhmen und Mähren*, Brno: Rohrer, 1943; reprinted Nendeln, Liechtenstein: Kraus, 1976
Freeden, Max H. von, *Balthasar Neumann: Leben und Werk*, 1953; 2nd edition Munich: Deutscher Kunstverlag, 1963
Freeden, Max H. von, *Residenz Würzburg*, Munich: Deutscher Kunstverlag, 1952
Grimschitz, Bruno, *Wiener Barockpaläste*, Vienna: Wiener Verlag, 1944
Grimschitz, Bruno, *Das Belvedere in Wien*, Vienna: Wolfrum, 1946
Grimschitz, Bruno, *Johann Lucas von Hildebrandt*, Vienna: Herold, 1959
Hager, Werner, *Die Bauten des Deutschen Barocks, 1690–1770*, Jena: Diederichs, 1942
Harris, Dale, "The Art in Social Climbing: Staging the Drama of Ascent on the World's Six Greatest Staircases" in *Connoisseur*, 215, September 1985, pp.108–13
Hegemann, Hans W., *Die Deutsche Barockbaukunst Böhmens*, Munich: Bruckmann, 1943
Hempel, Eberhard, *Baroque Art and Architecture in Central Europe*, Harmondsworth: Penguin, 1965
Hofmann, Walter, *Schloss Pommersfelden*, Nuremberg: Carl, 1968
Keller, Harald, *Das Treppenhaus im deutschen Schloss- und Klosterbau des Barock*, Ph.D. thesis, Munich: University of Munich, 1929
Kerber, Ottmar, *Von Bramante zu Lucas von Hildebrandt*, Stuttgart: Kohlhammer, 1947
Knopp, Norbert, *Das Garten-Belvedere*, Munich: Deutscher Kunstverlag, 1966
McKay, Derek, *Prince Eugene of Savoy*, London: Thames and Hudson, 1977
Schuckmann, Angelika von, "The Starhemberg-Schönburg Garden Palace in Vienna" in *Apollo*, CIII, January 1976, pp.26–33
Sedlmayer, Hans, *Johann Bernhard Fischer von Erlach*, 1956; reprinted Vienna: Herold, 1976
Sedlmayer, Richard and Rudolf Pfister, *Die fürstbischöfliche Residenz zu Würzburg*, Munich: Müller, 1923
Wagner-Rieger, Renate, "Die Piaristenkirche in Wien" in *Wiener Jahrbuch für Kunstgeschichte*, 17, 1955, pp.49–62
Wenzel, Werner, *Die Gärten des Lothar Franz von Schönborn*, Berlin: Mann, 1970

Hill, Oliver 1887–1968

British architect and interior designer

Oliver Hill was once regarded as a lightweight figure because of his frequent changes of style, but his ability to find solutions appropriate to the requirements of each individual design commission without resort to dogma can now be seen as pragmatic and desirable rather than facile. He designed interiors for houses, apartments and public buildings which combined traditional attitudes to craftsmanship and materials with a Modern aesthetic, avoiding an uncompromisingly Functionalist approach, but including many design innovations. He also succeeded in bringing modern design to a wide public during the 1930s, particularly through his work on important Modernist exhibitions. And although Hill was part of the fashionable milieu of interior decorators of the 1920s and 1930s, his approach was fundamentally architectural and avoids any hint of superficiality.

Hill had little opportunity to execute much work before World War I, and his career only really began in the 1920s. This was also his most eclectic period, and his early houses are neo-Georgian (Sandhill, Aldeburgh, 1923–25) or neo-Vernacular (Cock Rock, Croyde, 1925–26, Knowle, Warwickshire 1923–29) in style. These buildings, together with the town houses and few commercial buildings of this period, show the influence of Edwin Lutyens, a family friend whose work Hill had admired from his schooldays. It was Lutyens who recommended that Hill gain experience working in a builder's yard, where he developed a love of textures and materials. The country house interiors are generally traditional and simply furnished, with picturesque details such as vast chimneypieces, and the occasional unusual and flamboyant touches in use of materials or colour (blue mosaic baths at Woodhouse Copse, Holmbury St. Mary, 1924–26 and Knowle). Such individual touches became increasingly dominant through the decade but from the very beginning showed a desire to specify details down to the cushions and curtains.

In Hill's London apartments and town houses, designed for wealthy clients with fashionable pretensions, there was the opportunity for extravagant show and experimentation. These commissions were seen as typifying the style satirised by Osbert Lancaster as Vogue Regency, but in fact they demonstrate considerable originality and a keen interest in Modernism. The Devonshire House apartment for Sir Albert Levy contained numerous Modernist features. It had a grey and black mirrored glass-walled entrance hall – albeit inset with leading suggesting classical arches and pilasters. The dining room, with the exception of the chairs, was formed entirely of different coloured marbles, with bands of colour providing the only ornament, uplit by onyx candelabra standing in each corner and with a vast slab of marble on a metal frame supporting a verdite table top. The music room was lined with laminated wood sheets of grey walnut from floor to ceiling, painted by George Sheringham with landscape scenes, delicately foreshadowing the style of the bolder Art Deco landscapes of Clarice Cliff pottery. The scenes included a pagoda to accompany a display of Levy's Oriental jade and crystal. Hill had always been interested in Chinese objects, particularly ceramics, and these were often incorporated into his interiors as well as being a source for some of his favourite yellow and green colour schemes.

In the late 1920s the influence of Hollywood can perhaps be detected, in some of Hill's Spanish hacienda style houses, such as Marylands, Hurtwood, of 1928–29, as well as in his use of mirror cladding and his exotic bathrooms. These include the grey mirror-lined bathroom for Lady Mount Temple at Gayfere House, its glass shelves displaying blue glass objects and even the bath faced in strips of mirror, although lined with gold mosaic.

A visit to the 1930 Stockholm Exhibition opened Hill's eyes to the lightness and elegance of Scandinavian Modernism. His lack of preconceptions and unpolemical disposition allowed him to move increasingly towards a successful interpretation of this new style, designing furniture and commissioning work from artists and designers to provide additional modern furnishings and decoration. His first supposedly Modernist house, Joldwynds (1930–37) had light and plainly furnished interiors, with a curved glazed stair tower fitted with striped curtains by Marion Dorn and included an all-white dining room. However the furniture he designed found little favour with his clients, who complained about its large scale and concern for appearance rather than comfort, and the rooms appear rather bleak and box-like.

Landfall (1936–38) is a more genuinely Modernist house, glass fronted on the garden elevation, and with the hall between the dining room and large living room given a curved interior wall. The client, Mr. Ashton, who seems to have encouraged a radical approach, wanted a circular room. Folding doors allowed it to be opened up to give one large space. The uncluttered interior, with built-in fittings such as a drinks cupboard and radiogram, also had rugs by Marion Dorn and furnishings by Betty Joel and Alvar Aalto. In a letter to Ashton, Hill wrote that he liked to incorporate different coloured walls within a room, harmonizing them according to the light within, so he evidently did not often subscribe to an all-white interior. Here the colours seem to have included pinks and beiges. Some of Hill's wall finishes of this period were combed to give texture and he used the wonderfully named "Marb-L-Cote" on occasion.

In 1930 Hill set up the Rondo company to display and market modern decorative art. The company sponsored the Ariadne's Bath display at the 1930 Ideal Home Exhibition, a controversial exhibit designed by Hill. Although short-lived as a business venture, Rondo presumably opened up to Hill the possibilities of exhibition design and also helped his contacts with artists and designers. In 1933 Hill was responsible for the overall presentation of exhibits at the Exhibition of British Industrial Art in Relation to the Home. This popular exhibition, held at Dorland Hall and chiefly organised by Christopher Hussey, included Serge Chermayeff's Weekend House and the Wells Coates / Isokon Minimum Flat. Hill's own exhibits included a glass room, carried out by Pilkington's as a showpiece rather than a practical proposition, and the famous Stone Dining Room with stone walls incised with nudes by Eric Gill, and stone floor, table, sideboard and stools. This was later installed in Hill's own house in Cliveden Place, where the sitting room of 1938 also incorporated nudes by Gill, this time white line drawings on charcoal grey paper covering the chimney breast and protected by glass. An example of Hill's eclectic brand of Modernism, this room also featured a built-in fitting including a chaise-longue covered in dark green velvet and a radiogram, displays of Chinese porcelain, and a Chinese rug. The walls were panelled in pale cedar wood and the colour scheme was pale yellow and grey-blue.

Hill: bathroom, North House, London, 1929–33, with *Seaweed* ceiling paper designed by Edward Bawden

The Ideal Home exhibition was followed in 1934 by the less successful Contemporary Industrial Art in the Home, also at Dorland Hall, at which Hill fell out with the Modernists over the luxurious nature of his exhibits, such as a snakeskin-covered piano.

For the 1937 Paris Exhibition Hill designed the British Pavilion and organised the displays representing modern British life, commissioning artists such as Eric Ravilious and Edward Bawden to provide backgrounds, as well as work by Raymond McGrath, Mary Adshead and others. The interior was modern and forward looking, anticipating both the Festival of Britain (1951), and, in its large photo-mural display, Alvar Aalto's Finnish Pavilion interior at the 1939 New York World's Fair.

In addition to his domestic work Hill also successfully worked on public buildings. The Midland Hotel of 1932–33 at Morecambe was one of the first public buildings in Britain in a Modern style, a "marine fantasia", according to *Country Life*, incorporating reliefs by Eric Gill, including one of Odysseus and Nausicaa, and a medallion depicting Triton; a spectacular three-storey concrete and blue and white metal spiral stair with blue rubber treads; murals of *Day* and *Night*, by Eric Ravilious, occupying the whole of the circular wall of the café not occupied by window; shell-pink vitrolite-topped tables and steel-framed chairs in the cafe; and an entrance hall floored with sand-coloured stone and silver mosaic strips to resemble the sea rippling across a beach, with huge circular rugs by Marion Dorn continuing the wave theme, as do the colours of the blue and silver curtains.

Although his Modernist ideas were continued in designs for schools and an interesting public house built in 1939, Hill's commissions began to dry up from the late 1930s and those he did carry out after World War II show a reversion to Lutyenesque styles. His own country residences were restorations of older houses, first Valewood and then Daneway, where he spent his later years in an apparently joyous rural idyll. The interiors housed his own varied collections of objects and furnishings, put together in original ways, in conjunction with some startling colour schemes – including lime green, bright yellow and pink at Daneway. Hill's love of life was evident throughout all his work and does much to explain its fascinating variety.

DIANA HALE

Biography

Born in London, 15 June 1887. Educated at Uppingham; worked for 18 months in a builder's yard; trained with the architect William Flockhart, 1907–10, while also attending evening classes at the Architectural Association. Established his own architectural practice, 1910. Served in the London Scottish Regiment 1914–18. Resumed architectural practice from 1918; designed furniture and fittings from 1920s; established the Rondo company retailing modern decorative art, 1930; supervising architect for several national and international exhibitions during the mid-1930s. Associate, Royal Institute of British Architects, 1921; Fellow, 1923. Wrote extensively on architecture and design; published frequently in *Country Life*. Married Margaret Beverley, 1953. Appointed MBE (Member, Order of the British Empire), 1952. Died 29 April 1968.

Selected Works

A large collection of Hill's architectural drawings and designs are in the Drawings Collection, Royal Institute of British Architects, London; manuscript material is in the RIBA library.

Interiors

1926–30 Devonshire House, Piccadilly, London (interior decoration; music room paintings by George Sheringham): Sir Albert Levy
1928–29 Marylands, Hurtwood (building and interiors)
1929–33 Gayfere House, Westminster, London (building and interiors): Lord and Lady Mount Temple
1929–33 North House, Westminster, London (building and interiors): Robert Hudson M.P.
1930–37 Joldwynds, Holmbury St. Mary, Surrey (building and interiors including furniture and fittings): Lord Justice Wilfred Greene
1932–33 Midland Hotel, Morecambe, Lancashire (building and interiors; murals by Eric Ravilious, plaster reliefs by Eric Gill)
1932–33 213 King's Road, London (alterations and decorations): Mrs. Syrie Maugham
1933 British Industrial Art Exhibition, Dorland Hall, London (general design including the entrance hall, first gallery, stone dining room and glass room)
1936–38 Landfall, Poole, Dorset (building and interiors): Mr. Ashton
1937 British Pavilion, Exposition Internationale des Arts et Techniques Appliqués à la Vie Moderne, Paris (design of pavilion and display)

Publications

"Architect's Autobiography" 12 parts in *Building*, XXIV–XXV, 1949–50
Fair Horizon: Buildings of Today, 1950
Scottish Castles of the Sixteenth and Seventeenth Centuries, 1953
Caroline, 1625–1685 (English Country Houses, vol.4), with John Cornforth, 1966; reprinted 1985

Further Reading

A catalogue of Hill's architectural and interior commissions appears in Powers 1989 which also includes a complete list of Hill's writings and selected references to primary and secondary sources.

Battersby, Martin, *The Decorative Thirties*, 1969; revised by Philippe Garner, New York: Whitney Library of Design, and London: Herbert, 1988
Catalogue of the Drawings Collection of the Royal Institute of British Architects, Farnborough: Gregg, 1973
Gradidge, Roderick, "The Architecture of Oliver Hill" in *Architectural Design*, XL, 1979, pp.30–41
O'Donovan, Dermod, "The Work of Oliver Hill" in *Decoration*, III, 1935, pp.28–31
Powers, Alan, *Oliver Hill: Architect and Lover of Life 1887–1968* (exhib. cat.), London: Methuen, 1989
Powers, Alan, "Oliver Hill as Exhibition Designer" in *Thirties Society Journal*, 7, 1989, pp.28–39
Thirties: British Art and Design Before the War (exhib. cat.), London: Arts Council of Great Britain, 1979

Hoffmann, Josef 1870–1956

Austrian architect and designer

Josef Hoffmann always considered himself an architect even though much of his work was interior design. He believed in the idea of design as an all-embracing discipline that encompassed everything from pattern and fashion design to interior design, architecture and landscape architecture. This is what for many years he taught at the Vienna Kunstgewerbeschule and what during sixty years he practised himself. He would use the same formal device for a small object, a piece of furniture, or a building, as with the undulating wall profile of his pavilion at the Paris Exposition Internationale des Arts Décoratifs (1925), which had its correspondence in furniture and metal coffeepots.

Exhibitions were of major importance in Hoffmann's oeuvre and contributed significantly to his eventual worldwide renown. At the outset of his career he designed pieces of furniture, rooms, and entire exhibition installations for the Vienna Secession, that highly successful association of avant-garde artists where he had close contacts with influential painters like Gustav Klimt, Carl Moll, and Kolo(man) Moser. From such fellow artists and interested visitors to the early Secession exhibitions Hoffmann received his first commissions, including the design of several houses and their interiors at the small housing estate of the Hohe Warte in a suburb of Vienna.

Hoffmann's earliest works such as the Apollo candle shop in Vienna and his designs for members of the Wittgenstein

Hoffmann: dining room, Palais Stoclet, Brussels, 1905–11; murals by Gustav Klimt

family (forestry offices and dwelling at Hohenberg, Lower Austria, and interiors at the Bergerhöhe nearby) show him under the spell of curvilinear Art Nouveau and the English Arts and Crafts movement. But around 1900 the earlier exuberance in form and colour is replaced by great restraint, a predominance of rectilinearity, and colour schemes of white and black. Three interiors from the year 1902 well represent this phase: the apartment for Max Biach, the rooms for Fritz Wärndorfer, and the rooms of the 14th exhibition of the Vienna Secession. For this exhibition Hoffmann created a barrel-vaulted main room flanked by upper galleries which through wide openings between piers permitted views down at Max Klinger's Beethoven sculpture in the centre of the main room. Gustav Klimt painted his Beethoven frieze for the left gallery, and Hoffmann himself contributed two striking, because completely abstract, *sopraporta* reliefs in cut plaster.

Fritz Wärndorfer, a young well-to-do industrialist who had met Hoffmann through the Secession, became not only his enthusiastic client and friend but also a business partner. In 1903, inspired by C.R. Ashbee's Guild of Handicraft, they, along with Kolo Moser, founded the Wiener Werkstätte. Moser withdrew from the enterprise in 1907 to concentrate on his work as painter, but during the four years of his involvement he designed furniture and interiors in such close collaboration with Hoffmann that at times it is impossible to know who did a certain piece. Generally Hoffmann's designs are more restrained. During the almost three decades of the Wiener Werkstätte's existence its numerous artists and craftsmen created a wealth of works in all areas of the decorative arts; they were also responsible for furnishing and decorating many apartments and the small Fledermaus cabaret (1907), for mounting exhibitions, and, as long as Hoffmann was in charge of a separate architectural department, for providing designs of buildings. Three examples show Hoffmann and the early Wiener Werkstätte at their best: the Purkersdorf Sanatorium (1904), the Hochreith Hunting Lodge (1906), and the Palais Stoclet in Brussels (1905–11).

The building Hoffmann created at Purkersdorf had an exterior of dramatic simplicity, revolutionary for its date in the manner in which it presented a composition of cubic shapes without any historic reminiscences. The mostly white interiors, done jointly by Hoffmann and Moser, were characterised by spatial generosity and formal and coloristic reticence, with a reliance on the square as the predominant element. Hoffmann, who usually designed on gridded paper, in Vienna jokingly became known as "Quadratl Hoffmann" (Hoffmann of the little squares). At Hochreith, near Hohenberg, Lower Austria, Karl Wittgenstein, the industrial magnate and generous supporter of the Secession, had an existing lodge remodelled and furnished by Hoffmann who created a new entry and vestibule as well as a main room divided into two sections. The walls and ceiling of this carefully proportioned room were panelled in highly polished Maracaibo wood, and its furniture was strictly coordinated with the squarish grid of the wall panels which were framed by the same gilt mouldings as the furniture. Carl Otto Czeschka, Richard Luksch, and Kolo Moser contributed works of art to these rooms which heightened their sumptuousness and aesthetic appeal.

The same atmosphere of sophisticated richness that characterises the Hochreith rooms pervades the whole of the large Palais Stoclet, built, furnished, and appointed down to the last detail for two ideal clients, the extremely wealthy and distinguished art collector Adolphe Stoclet and his wife Suzanne. Here again, Hoffmann included works from a number of artists in his interiors. The Stoclet dining room, with marble walls, furniture in black macassar wood, large mosaic panels by Gustav Klimt, and a spatial and formal treatment to enhance these, became one of the most admired secular interiors of the 20th century. It forms the climax of an extremely artful sequence of rooms for entertaining on the ground floor, just as the master bedroom and the richly appointed large (6m by 5.8m) bathroom – marble-clad with black and malachite inlays and mosaic insets – are the high points on the upper floor. Never during the remainder of his career did Hoffmann surpass the achievement of the Stoclet ensemble, though he came close to it in the apartment for Moriz Gallia (1913) and in three large suburban houses at Vienna, the Ast House (1909–11), the Skywa / Primavesi House (1913–15), and the Knips House (1924–25). But by the time these houses and their interiors and furniture were carried out, Hoffmann's style had changed noticeably.

This change can be observed by comparing the numerous exhibition installations Hoffmann designed over the years. They demonstrate a move away from the rigorous purism of the early years toward greater decorative richness and a personal reinterpretation of the classical vocabulary; this tendency is clearly recognisable at the Vienna Kunstschau (1908), at the Austrian Pavilion for the International Art Exhibition in Rome (1911), and even more strikingly at the Austrian Pavilion for the Cologne Werkbund exhibition (1914) which attracted much attention by the stylistic unity of its interiors, although except for the reception room, these were not done by Hoffmann himself, but by invited colleagues – often former pupils.

At the same time, however, Hoffmann proved his versatility by designs of folkloristic inspiration. For Otto Primavesi, a banker and, for a while, financial supporter of the Wiener Werkstätte, he designed a large country house at Kouty (Winkelsdorf) in the Praded (Altvater) mountains of Moravia (1913–14) using the local techniques of loghouse construction and thatching. The interiors too, through lively colors and a great deal of dynamic decoration by means of applied, painted wooden strips, often forming lozenges, echoed the strong forms and colours of Moravian folk-art which Hoffmann admired and collected. In addition, these spiky forms may have owed something to the Expressionist movement in the visual arts, for Hoffmann always kept up with the latest artistic developments. Several exhibitions and rooms for private clients designed after the end of World War I show his awareness of Expressionism, and later of the various tendencies that contributed to the Modern Movement.

Hoffmann's personal forte, however, remained the feeling for sophisticated decorative effects and an infallible taste in the selection of materials, patterns, and colors. This is as true for the Knips House – with its convincing employment of transparency and of contrast between plain surfaces and highly decorated elements – as for the boudoir Hoffmann designed for the Exhibition of Arts and Crafts in the Austrian Museum for Art and Industry (1923). The boudoir with its alluring, slightly orientalising sofa niche was later shown in New York and at the 1925 Paris exhibition for which Hoffmann also designed the remarkable Austrian Pavilion. The Pavilion's top-lit main exhibition gallery had boundaries that were visually dissolved by the floor-to-ceiling glazing of showcases. On the inside these cases were covered in yellow, on the outside they displayed white flowery decorations on delicate black subdivisons. Hoffmann's contribution to the Paris exhibition also included a tea-room and a smoking room as well as a gallery for Austrian printing and publishing firms. For the successful completion of the Paris installation Hoffmann relied on the collaboration of Oswald Haerdtl and Max Fellerer, two senior assistants, who, like so many other former students or employees such as Robert Mallet-Stevens, later became major architects and interior designers in their own right.

Hoffmann's last major interior designs once more were done in connection with exhibitions. Not only was he in charge of the general arrangement of the 1930 Werkbund exhibition in Vienna, he also designed for it the great central hall – covered by a pleated, top-lit velum with inclined sides – and its flanking display corridors as well as the adjoining café with a large terrace. The idea of a display corridor was taken up again in the Arts and Crafts Gallery of the exhibition Austria in London at Dorland Hall in 1934. In the same year Hoffmann designed the Austrian Pavilion for the Biennale in Venice, with Robert Kramreiter as partner for the execution. Sixty years after its opening, this recently restored building, small yet monumental, dignified yet graceful, with proportions derived from the square, still fulfills its function perfectly. The sequence of its contrasting yet interacting spaces, from the open travertine-framed portal and vestibule, down a few steps into the galleries on either side, and finally into the open sculpture court, in its simplicity is as sophisticated and effectual as Hoffmann's great exhibition pavilions of earlier years.

To the end of his life Hoffmann never ceased designing. He left a vast legacy of objects, pieces of furniture, and drawings that, like his surviving buildings, bear testimony to the strength of his talent and the fecundity of his creative imagination. He was held in high professional regard internationally as indicated by his numerous foreign honors and decorations, and the fact that he contributed the entry on modern interior decoration to the 14th edition (1929) of the *Encyclopaedia Britannica*. While the important role he played in Austria is generally realised, his extensive impact abroad remains to be fully appreciated.

EDUARD F. SEKLER

See also Art Nouveau; Moser

Biography

Josef Franz Maria Hoffmann. Born in Pirnitz, Moravia (now Brtnice, Czech Republic), 15 December 1870. Studied architecture under Carl von Hasenauer and Otto Wagner at the Academy of Art, Vienna, 1892–95; awarded the Rome Prize, 1895. Married 1) Anna Hladik, 1903; 2) Karla Schmatz, 1925: 1 son. Worked with Joseph Maria Olbrich in the studio of Otto Wagner, Vienna, 1896–97; in private practice in Vienna, 1898–1956. Professor, Vienna School of Applied Arts, 1899–1936; founder-member, the Secession Group, 1897; founder (with Koloman Moser and Fritz Wärndorfer) of the Wiener Werkstätte, 1903; director (with Gustav Klimt) of the Kunstschau, Vienna, 1908–09; co-founder and director, Austrian Werkbund, Vienna, 1910; director Künstlerwerkstätte, Vienna, 1943–56. Awarded honorary doctorates from the Technische Hochschule in Dresden, Berlin and Vienna. Received the Légion d'Honneur, Paris, 1926. Died in Vienna, 8 May 1956.

Selected Works

A catalogue raisonné of Hoffmann's work, including designs for furniture and interiors as well as architectural projects, appears in Sekler 1985. Examples of Hoffmann's architectural drawings and decorative designs are held by the Academy of Fine Arts, Vienna and by the Austrian Museum of Applied Art, Vienna. Archival material can be found in the Wiener Werkstätte Archive, Austrian Museum for Applied Art, which also holds the best collection of Hoffmann's furniture, and in the Archive of the Association of Austrian Artists, Secession, Vienna.

Interiors

1898 Ver Sacrum Salon, Secession Exhibition, Vienna (decoration and furniture)
1899 Apollo candle shop, Vienna (entrance and furnishings)
1899 Bergerhöhe, near Hohenberg, Lower Austria (remodelling of the interiors): Paul Wittgenstein
1899–1902 Exhibition designs for the Secession, Vienna (decoration and furniture)
1901–03 Kolo Moser House, Hohe Warte, Vienna (building and interiors) Carl Moll House, Hohe Warte, Vienna (building and interiors) Hugo Henneberg House, Hohe Warte, Vienna (building and interiors)
1902 Max Biach Apartment, Vienna (remodelling and furnishings)
1902 Wärndorfer House, Vienna (interiors including smoking room, nursery, gallery, dining room; with Koloman Moser): Fritz Wärndorfer
1903–11 Ast House, Hohe Warte, Vienna (building and interiors): Edouard Ast
1904 Purkersdorf Sanatorium, Purkersdorf (building, interiors and furnishings; with Koloman Moser)
1905–11 Palais Stoclet, Brussels (building and interiors): Adolphe Stoclet
1906 Hochreith Hunting Lodge, near Hohenberg, Lower Austria (building, interiors; with Koloman Moser): Karl Wittgenstein
1907 "Die Fledermaus" Cabaret, Vienna (remodelling of interior and furnishings)
1909–11 Ast House, Vienna (building, interiors and furnishings)
1913–15 Skywa / Primavesi House, Heitzing, Vienna (building, interiors and furnishings): Josefine Skywa and Robert Primavesi
1913–14 Primavesi House, Winkelsdorf, Moravia (building, interiors and furnishings): Robert Primavesi
1914 Austrian Pavilion, Deutsche Werkbund Exhibition, Cologne (building and selected interiors)
1915–16 Knips Apartment interiors, Vienna (interiors including anteroom, living room, smoking room, boudoir, dressing room, bedrooms, studies): Sonja Knips
1923–24 Ast House, Velden on the Wörthersee (building and interiors): Edouard Ast
1924–24 Knips House, Dobling, Vienna (building, interiors and furnishings): Sonja Knips
1925 Austrian Pavilion, Exposition des Art Décoratifs, Paris (building and interiors; with Oswald Haerdtl and Max Fellerer)
1928–29 Graben Café, Vienna (remodelling of interiors and furniture)
1930 Austrian Section, International Exhibition, Stockholm (interiors)
1934 Austrian Pavilion, Biennale, Venice (building and interiors; with Robert Kramreiter)

Further Reading

The most scholarly and comprehensive account of Hoffmann's career is Sekler 1985 which also contains a complete list of Hoffmann's architectural projects and writings; the most up-to-date bibliography appears in the Italian edition of this book, 1991. For more detailed information on the Palais Stoclet see Muntoni 1989, and on Hoffmann's designs see Noever 1992.

Baroni, Daniele and Antonio D'Auria, *Josef Hoffmann e la Wiener Werkstätte*, Milan: Electa, 1981

Baroni, Daniele and Antonio D'Auria, *Kolo Moser: Graphic Artist and Designer*, New York: Rizzoli, 1986

Behrens, Peter, "The Work of Josef Hoffmann" in *Architecture* (UK), 2, 1923, pp.589–99

Brunhammer, Yvonne, *Art Nouveau: Belgium / France*, Houston: Rice University Institute for the Arts, 1976

Fenz, Werner, *Kolo Moser: International Jugenstil und Wiener Secession*, Salzburg: Residenz Verlag, 1976

Gebhard, David, *Josef Hoffmann: Design Classics* (exhib. cat.), Fort Worth, TX: Fort Worth Museum and Art Gallery, 1982

Greer, Nora Richter, "Furnishings: Josef Hoffmann" in *American Institute of Architects Journal*, April 1983

Gresleri, Giuliano (editor), *Josef Hoffmann*, New York: Rizzoli, 1985

"Josef Hoffmann: Palais Stoclet, 1905" in *Architectural Design* (UK), 1–2, 1980

Kallir, Jane, *Viennese Design and the Wiener Werkstätte*, London: Thames and Hudson, and New York: Braziller, 1986

Meyer, Christian (editor), *Josef Hoffmann: Architect and Designer, 1870–1956* (exhib. cat.), Vienna: Galerie Metropol, 1981

Muntoni, Alessandra, *Il Palazzo Stoclet di Josef Hoffmann*, Rome: Multigrafica, 1989

Neuwirth, Waltraud, *Josef Hoffmann: Bestecke für die Wiener Werkstätte*, Vienna: Neuwirth, 1982

Noever, Peter (editor), *Josef Hoffmann Designs*, Munich: Prestel, 1992

Schweiger, Werner J., *Wiener Werkstätte: Designs in Vienna, 1903–1932*, London: Thames and Hudson, and New York: Abbeville, 1984

Sekler, Eduard F. and Robert Judson Clark, *Josef Hoffmann 1870–1956, Architect and Designer* (exhib. cat.), London: Fischer Fine Art, 1977

Sekler, Eduard F., *Josef Hoffmann: The Architectural Work*, Princeton: Princeton University Press, 1985; Italian edition, Milan: Electa, 1991

Vergo, Peter, "Fritz Wärndorfer and Josef Hoffmann" in *Burlington Magazine*, CXXV, 1983, pp.402–10

Vergo, Peter, *Art in Vienna, 1898–1918*, 3rd edition London: Phaidon, 1993

Viladas, Pilar, "Josef Hoffmann Revisited" in *Interiors* (USA), September 1979

Holland, Henry 1745–1806

British architect

Although Henry Holland's practice was not the largest of his day, he created a decorative style that proved extremely influential, appealing to aristocratic patrons, the leaders of taste, and appropriate in smaller country houses and town dwellings. Like his chief patron, George Prince of Wales (later King George IV), Holland, brought up in the tradition of the francophile Sir William Chambers, was an enthusiast for the classicising French late 18th century Louis Seize style. This he assimilated with Greek and Roman models found in the latest works of scholarship or obtained from drawings he himself commissioned. He did not visit France until 1785, though he closely studied French design in such publications as those of Blondel, Patte, Dumont, Gondoin and Neufforge. Italy he never visited, but made use of G.B. Piranesi's etchings; and in 1794 commissioned Charles Heathcote Tatham to collect antique and contemporary specimens and make drawings. For Greece, there were Desgodetz's or Stuart and Revett's studies of the antiquities of Athens and Ionia.

Holland established his reputation by his work on a gentlemen's club, Brooks's, in St. James's Street, London, a favourite resort of the Whig aristocracy; the Prince of Wales became a member in 1783. Holland had bought the site, so when Brooks took it up for his club in 1776, he was naturally given the commission. His work here was strongly marked by contemporary French classicism. The refined decoration, best exhibited in the Great Subscription Room, more restrained than that employed by Holland's leading English contemporaries Robert Adam or James Wyatt, is characterised by its lowness of relief. Even the great Venetian window is treated as a Roman arch in low relief with semi-columns, and circular features above the side windows (which he repeated externally on the greenhouse at Woburn); the ceiling is a simple but impressive segmental vault divided into nine panels by narrow guilloche bands. The chimneypiece of white marble is likewise treated simply, surmounted by a large glass framed in three panels and a carved relief above, a device Holland particularly adopted. The mahogany doors, luxurious but restrained, have reeded panels, ebony handles with mother-of-pearl stars, and painted elliptical overdoors.

At Berrington Hall, Herefordshire (1778–83), Holland combined ideas from Piranesi's Roman engravings with Greek details culled from recent publications of source material. The hall retains its delicate but complex colouring, with grey-white and pale blue walls; a great arch, its soffit covered in terracotta and biscuit, creates directional ambiguity; the stairs rise in another direction, under a lantern dome, the pink ceiling panelled in pale blue, the mouldings gilded, as at Brooks's. More elaborate in its decoration than most of Holland's work, Berrington anticipates the splendours of Carlton House, yet it is more restrained than the late work of Adam or Paine. Duck-egg blue or green, terracotta and flesh shades, bistre, and gilding are extensively employed, together with columns in *scagliola*. The decoration culminates in the drawing room with its richly ornamented ceiling – cupids and sea-horses in high relief between gaily painted medallions by Biagio Rebecca – and marble chimneypiece with a sculptured frieze supported by herms. A similar combination of relief (foliage swags) and painting obtains in the dining room ceiling. The boudoir is an early essay in Louis Seize, the segmental ceiling's panels distinguished by colour rather than relief, but with an exedra in James Wyatt's manner, marked off by lapis-lazuli *scagliola* columns and a scalloped concave ceiling. Holland's mastery of contemporary English fashions is further exhibited in the library, a completely integrated design similar to Robert Adam's Nostell Priory.

The francophile character of Holland's work at Brooks's Club proved highly congenial to the Prince of Wales. Endowed in 1783 with his grandmother's somewhat ramshackle Carlton House, Pall Mall, London, the Prince rapidly invited Holland to enlarge and reorganise it. For this major undertaking, where there was already a French clerk of works, Guillaume Gaubert, Holland engaged a French assistant, J.P.T. Trecourt, French craftsmen, including Alexandre-Louis Delabrière, T.H. Pernotin and other decorative painters (from whom John Crace learned the art), and Jean Prusserot (wood-carver), and the *marchand-mercier* Dominique Daguerre. Several of them had lately been employed at the Pavillon de Bagatelle, Paris, for the Comte d'Artois, Louis XVI's brother. In 1785 Holland himself went to Paris.

The 20th-century historian Peter Thornton regards Holland's Carlton House as "an almost pure expression of Parisian taste of the 1780s". Holland's contemporary, Horace Walpole, however, while appreciating that Holland's ornament was new to England, saw it rather as a delicate synthesis of modern French and antique, having "more freedom and variety than Greek ornaments, and though probably borrowed from the Hôtel de Condé, and other new palaces, not one that is not rather classic than French ... How sick one shall be, after this chaste palace, of Mr. Adam's gingerbread and sippets of embroidery" (to Lady Ossory, 17 September 1785). Holland's decorations, however, were soon superseded by new princely preferences, and few illustrations of them are known. Only the hall and staircase survived largely unchanged, the hall recalling that at Berrington, but of a more Roman character, *scagliola* columns supporting entablatures and friezes flung across segmental arches on each side, flanked on the longer sides by niches containing sculptures *à l'antique*. Holland's Chinese drawing room (perhaps inspired by Chinoiserie at Bagatelle), known from the illustrations in Sheraton's *Cabinet-Maker and Upholsterer's Drawing Book* (1791) and furnishings now in Buckingham Palace, is not essentially different from his Neo-Classical work, marked by flat panelling, rectilinear furniture with rounded ends, and exquisite detail of ornamental carving.

The Prince also acquired a seaside villa or "Marine Pavilion" at Brighton, which Holland greatly enlarged in 1787, and further in 1795 and 1800–03. Contemporary descriptions (for Holland's work has been lost in subsequent alterations) again stress the French character of the work, which included paintings by Rebecca in the grand saloon. In his last period, Holland reworked much of the interior in Chinoiserie, the painting carried out by John Crace (1754–1819) – employed at Carlton House – and his son Frederick (1779–1859).

For the Prince's brother, the Duke of York, Holland enlarged James Paine's York (previously Featherstonhaugh, subsequently Melbourne, and then Dover) House, Whitehall, in 1787–90, creating in the courtyard an exquisite circular

Holland: boudoir, Berrington Hall, Herefordshire, 1778–83

vestibule in which Doric *scagliola* columns support a dome, a plan probably derived from J.-F. Neufforge, and remodelling several of the rooms. At the same period Holland was working for Lord Spencer, at Spencer House, London, and also at Althorp, Northamptonshire, both conspicuous aristocratic rendezvous. Similarly, he was much employed on houses belonging to the Duke of Bedford, most extensively at Woburn, where overdoors by George Garrard in naturalistic high relief were introduced in the suite of South rooms, and much built-in furniture to Holland's designs, including the library bookcases with convex features at the corners and characteristic mirrors with relief panels above; while a Chinese dairy (1787) was again decorated by Crace.

The most perfect statement of Holland's Neo-Classicism, however, is to be found in a smaller country house, Southill, which he reconstructed in 1796–1803, for the brewer and radical Whig politician, Samuel Whitbread: the most complete fusion of the English Palladian tradition with antique (Greek and Roman) and contemporary French elements. Neo-Classical ornament is combined with a naturalism (seen notably in the reliefs and paintings of the over-doors) inspired by contemporary science. The ceilings exhibit restraint, ornamented with severely rectangular panels of rich mouldings in low relief: except in the dressing room or boudoir (where Delabrière was employed to paint decorations), ceiling-painting is eschewed. The chimneypieces generally have Holland's characteristic rather low form and restrained sculptured enrichments, often based on specially commissioned drawings from the antique taken in Rome, varying in richness to correspond with the character of the room. Above them hang his usual gilt-framed mirrors surmounted by panels in relief. His furniture is characterised by the same rectangularity as his ceiling decorations, but he employed concave or convex ends, or colonnettes at the corners of cabinets, commodes or bookcases, after a Louis Seize fashion. Some Southill designs are contained in his sketchbooks in the library of the Royal Institute of British Architects, London.

This melding of French classicism with elements of Greek and Roman antiquity created a masculine, restrained style of great elegance and purity, characterised by precision and refinement: an aristocratic manner, employing an innovatory vocabulary governed by traditional syntax. His furniture, much of which was built-in, formed an extension to the architectural decoration of his rooms, dependent upon framed panels distinguished by good proportions rather than elaborate mouldings or ormolu enrichments. Although he did not, as has sometimes been stated, introduce *scagliola* in England, he used it extensively (employing the Italian craftsman Dom Bartoli), and his work at Carlton House saw the revival of marbling, and painting in imitation of bronze. His Chinoiserie, although governed by the same fundamental rules as his Neo-Classical work, exhibited an alternative vocabulary that was widely taken up.

M.H. PORT

See also George IV

Biography

Born in London, 20 July 1745, the son of the master builder Henry Holland (1712–85). Married Bridget Brown, daughter of the landscape gardener Lancelot "Capability" Brown (1716–83), 1773: 5 children. Trained in his father's building yard in Fulham. Practised as an architect from 1770 and worked with Capability Brown from 1771; assisted by the architect John Soane and the designer Charles Tatham, 1772–78. Appointed clerk of works at the Royal Mews, Charing Cross, 1775; surveyor to Bridewell and Bethlehem Hospitals; employed as architect by the Prince of Wales, 1782–93. Visited Paris, 1785. Founder-member of the Architects' Club; Fellow of the Royal Society of Antiquaries. Died in London, 17 June 1806.

Selected Works

Two sketchbooks relating to Holland's work at Carlton House, and a volume of drawings (mainly of interior decoration) are in the Drawings Collection of the Royal Institute of British Architects, London; another sketchbook is in Sir John Soane's Museum, London; records of the accounts for Holland's work at Althorp are in the archive, Althorp, Northamptonshire. The most comprehensive list of his architectural commissions is in Colvin 1995.

Interiors

1776–78	Brooks's Club, St. James's, London (building and interiors, including the Great Subscription Room): Lord Brooks
1778–83	Berrington Hall, Herefordshire (building and interiors): Thomas Harley MP
1783–96	Carlton House, London (remodelling and interiors): Prince Regent
1785–92	Spencer House, London (internal alterations, including red dining room and small drawing room): 2nd Earl Spencer
1786–87, 1795, 1800–03	Marine Pavilion, Brighton (alterations and interiors): Prince Regent
1787–90	Featherstonhaugh (now Dover) House, Whitehall, London (additions and interiors): Duke of York
1787–89	Althorp, Northamptonshire (recased house and remodelled interiors, including gallery, library, yellow drawing room, south drawing room, blue boudoir, and some furniture): 2nd Earl Spencer
1787–1802	Woburn Abbey, Bedfordshire (additions, alterations and interiors, including library, eating room, sculpture gallery and Chinese dairy): 5th Duke of Bedford
1796–1803	Southill House, Bedfordshire (remodelling and interiors, including new drawing room, dining room, entrance hall, sitting room, boudoir, and library, and some furniture): Samuel Whitbread

Further Reading

A comprehensive survey of Holland's life and work is Stroud 1966. Bellaigue 1991 provides a detailed account of his involvement at Carlton House and many of his royal interiors are illustrated in Watkin 1984.

Bellaigue, Geoffrey de, *Carlton House: The Past Glories of George IV's Palace* (exhib. cat.), London: Queen's Gallery, 1991

Catalogue of the Drawings Collection of the Royal Institute of British Architects, Farnborough: Gregg, 1973

Collard, Frances, *Regency Furniture*, Woodbridge, Suffolk: Antique Collectors' Club, 1985

Colvin, Howard M., *A Biographical Dictionary of British Architects, 1600–1840*, 3rd edition New Haven and London: Yale University Press, 1995

Hodson, H.B., "Holland the Architect" in the *Builder*, 13, 1855, p.437

Hussey, Christopher, *Mid Georgian, 1760–1800* (English Country Houses, vol.2), 1956; reprinted Woodbridge, Suffolk: Antique Collectors' Club, 1984

Morley, John, *The Making of the Royal Pavilion, Brighton: Designs and Drawings*, London: Sotheby Publications, and Boston: Godine, 1984

Morley, John, *Regency Design, 1790–1840: Gardens, Buildings, Interiors, Furniture*, London: Zwemmer, and New York: Abrams, 1993

Stroud, Dorothy, *Henry Holland: His Life and Architecture*, London, Country Life, 1966; South Brunswick, NJ: A.S. Barnes, 1967

Watkin, David, *The Royal Interiors of Regency England: From Watercolours First Published by W.H. Pyne in 1817–1820*, London: Dent, and New York: Vendome, 1984

Watson, F.J.B., "Holland and Daguerre: French Undercurrents in English Neo-Classical Furniture Design" in *Apollo*, XCVI, October 1972, pp282–87

Holland and Sons

British cabinet-makers, upholsterers and decorators, c.1815–1947

Holland and Sons was one of the largest and most celebrated furnishing firms in Britain in the 19th century. Renowned for the scope and variety of its work, the company initially favoured Neo-Classical and Gothic styles and later 18th century revivalist and Renaissance styles. 237 volumes containing detailed records of the firm's commissions, accounts and designs are preserved in the National Archive of Art and Design, London, and represent a unique record of both the workings of a successful Victorian cabinet-maker and of wealthy Victorian taste.

The history of Holland and Sons dates back to at least 1815 when Stephen Taprell and William Holland are first mentioned as in business together at 25 Great Pulteney Street, London, under the name of Taprell and Holland "cabinet makers etc." While little is known of Taprell, documents in the Victoria and Albert Museum point to a family connection between William Holland and the famous Regency architect, Henry Holland. Taprell and Holland's growing reputation led to its first major commission to furnish the Athenaeum, London, in 1824. The club was furnished throughout from designs by Decimus Burton in the Grecian Style; much of the furniture remains in place today. The firm went on to work for a number of other gentlemen's clubs. The most notable was the Reform Club, the first club to be built and decorated throughout in an Italian Renaissance manner, but they also provided furniture for the Army and Navy Club on Piccadilly, and other London venues including the Oxford and Cambridge, and the Carlton clubs.

Following several changes of address, the firm's name was changed to Holland and Sons in 1843, and was amended again to William Holland and Sons in 1846. In 1850 they were listed in trade directories as occupying premises at 19 Marylebone Street with workshops in Lower Belgrave Street, Pimlico, and in 1852 the main offices moved to 23 Mount Street where it is possible that Holland's took over the cabinet-makers, Thomas Dowbiggin and Co. whose past commissions had included the state throne for Queen Victoria's coronation (1837). Holland's themselves received the Royal Warrant early in Victoria's reign and supplied furniture to Balmoral, Buckingham Palace and Windsor Castle at various dates throughout the 19th century. Between 1840 and 1845 the company was involved in the commission to furnish the Queen's new house at Osborne on the Isle of Wight; much of their work has since been dispersed to other royal residences such as Sandringham.

During the 1840s, Holland's and the rival firm, Gillows, were awarded the tender to manufacture furnishings and upholstery for the New Palace of Westminster to the revived Gothic designs of A.W.N. Pugin. This contract led to almost 300 further Government commissions, and Holland's retained and were still using Pugin's designs well into the 1870s.

By 1850 the company had grown to a considerable size and the census for the following year records James Holland, upholsterer and son of William, as employing 350 men. In the mid 1850s the firm's workshops were described by Matthew Digby Wyatt as being "among the best mounted in London, exhibiting all recent improvements as to process of manufacture ... introducing machinery to a large extent ... with workshops so excellent and so well arranged with every known appliance for good and cheap production." The company was also strongly committed to improving standards of furniture design but declared a great drawback to be the "great want of designers, draughtsmen and modellers, in fact, of all directors of art. The very few who can assist demand are paid such excessive rates that their services are dispensed with except on important occasions". Nevertheless, Holland's themselves employed top British and Continental designers throughout the 19th century including Henry Whitaker in the 1840s, J.K. Collings in the 1850s, and G.E. Street in the 1860s, and the firm's success is partly attributable to the quality of their designs.

Holland's also scored several notable successes at various International Exhibitions. In 1851, the company received a prize for their massively proportioned chimneypiece and bookcase in the Italian Renaissance style. In 1855, they exhibited a neo-Renaissance ebony cabinet and stand designed by the celebrated German architect and theorist, Gottfried Semper which was purchased five years later by the South Kensington Museum. And in 1867, they received another prize for their *Pericles* sideboard, exhibited at the Paris Exposition Universelle and designed by Bruce Talbert whom they employed from 1866 until his death in 1881. Although the sideboard's name – derived from the quotations from Shakespeare that decorate the superstructure – had classical allusions, its form was in the reformed Gothic style and its decoration included liberal use of features such as marquetry quatrefoils and trefoils, and crockets and finials. Made of polished oak and fruitwood, it was praised by the *Art Journal* as "certainly the most distinguished among competing Gothic works". It was purchased by the Empress of France and, much more recently, it fetched a record price for a piece of Victorian furniture when it was sold at Christie's in January 1986.

However, royal commissions and exhibition pieces are hardly representative of the everyday business conducted by the firm which also undertook much more mundane and even minor tasks ranging from the furnishing of provincial houses to delivering two dozen buttons to a home in Oxford Square. Like many successful upholsterers they offered an enormous variety of services and the company's day books provide a fascinating record of jobs that included supplying display cases to the British Museum, erecting and decorating the stands for Edward VII's coronation procession, and even mending the lock on A.A. Milne's basement door. They also served as auctioneers, sanitary engineers, surveyors, a furniture repository and house and estate agents, and in their capacity as undertakers the firm arranged the funerals of the Duke of Wellington, the Duchess of Kent, Princess Sophia and Lord Leighton.

During the last decades of the 19th century, Holland's was able to meet the challenge of a public who demanded increasingly varied and novel styles by drawing upon past commissions for inspiration. Their catalogue of 1896 states: "Having secured the assistance of well-known artists we are at all times ready to submit designs for rooms of special objects and we have also the advantage of numerous old models, collected during many years." The plates show furniture and interiors in the Louis XIV and 18th- century styles, Moorish styles which were "in much request for the Smoking Room where comfort is looked for", and the Italian Renaissance style which "peculiarly lends itself to interior architecture, and is seen nowhere to better advantage than in the Hall or Dining Room". Nevertheless, the numbers of workmen employed by Holland's steadily declined. The Pimlico workshops were acquired by Morris and Co. in 1887, and by 1900 little cabinet-making, with the exception of special items, was undertaken by the firm.

NERIDA C.A. AYLOTT

Selected Works

The Holland and Sons archive containing over 200 ledgers, day books and account books, the majority covering the period 1824–1942, is in the National Archive of Art and Design, Victoria and Albert Museum, London. Examples of Holland and Sons furniture are in the Victoria and Albert Museum, and remain *in situ* at Buckingham Palace, the Reform Club, and the Palace of Westminster, London, and Osborne, Isle of Wight.

Interiors

Holland and Sons worked on interiors at several London clubs, including the Athenaeum (1824), the Reform, the Army and Navy, Oxford and Cambridge, and the Carlton, during the mid-19th century. Also provided furniture for several royal houses, including Windsor Castle, Osborne House, and Buckingham Palace. The company was a major contractor for H. M. Works in the late 19th century and worked on the Palace of Westminster and other government buildings, and supplied furniture and decorations for the Great Western Railway and the Royal Academy, London.

Further Reading

There is no published monograph on Holland and Sons, but an unpublished typescript of their history by the furniture historian Edward T. Joy is in the collection of his widow, Mrs. Edward Joy. Information relating to the early history of the firm can be found in Jervis 1970.

Agius, Pauline, *British Furniture, 1880–1915*, Woodbridge, Suffolk: Antique Collectors' Club, 1978

Allwood, Rosamond, "Luxury Furniture Makers of the Victorian Period" in *Antique Collecting*, June 1988, pp.4–8

Allwood, Rosamond, *Dictionary of Nineteenth Century British Furniture*, Woodbridge, Suffolk: Antique Collectors' Club, forthcoming

Beard, Geoffrey and Christopher Gilbert (editors), *Dictionary of English Furniture Makers, 1660–1840*, London: Furniture History Society, 1986

Hunting, Mary Ann, "The Reform Club in London: A Nineteenth-Century Collaboration" in *Magazine Antiques*, CXLX, June 1994, pp.878–85

Jervis, Simon, "Holland and Sons and the Furnishing of The Athenaeum" in *Furniture History*, VI, 1970, pp.43–61

Joy, Edward T., "Holland and Sons and the Furnishing of Osborne House" in *Antiques*, XCIX, April 1971, pp.580–85

Kirkham, Pat, *The London Furniture Trade, 1700–1870*, Leeds: J.S. Maney and Furniture History Society, 1988

Massie, Mary Ann Hunting, *The Furnishing of the Reform Club Interiors: A Collaboration between Charles Barry, Holland and Sons and the Reform Club Members*, M.A. thesis, New York: Cooper-Hewitt Museum, 1990

Symonds, R.W. and B.B. Whineray, *Victorian Furniture*, London: Country Life, 1962

Hollein, Hans 1934–

Austrian architect, designer and artist

Trained as an architect in Vienna and the United States in the 1950s, Hans Hollein has endeavored to express his personal commentary on society through all the visual arts, from jewelry design to performance art. In the 1960s, Hollein produced collages criticizing the modern urban landscape; shortly after, he combined his individuality, his understanding of the human psyche, of modern materials, and high craftsmanship together in memorable structures devoted to the new consumer society. His designs were informed and influenced by his Viennese predecessors, the turn-of-the-century progressive architect / designers Adolf Loos, Otto Wagner, and Josef Hoffmann. Hollein formally paid tribute to them in his 1986 reconstructive installations for the exhibition *Vienna: Dream and Reality, 1870–1930*, held at the Künstlerhaus, Vienna.

Hollein's rebellion against Modernism has placed him with the Postmodernists, who critiqued modern architecture and design through their anti-rational architecture and furnishings for an intellectual, cynical contemporary society. The meanings of Hollein's work, however, reside both in and beyond the surface – beyond the mere referencing of historical sources in anti-rational ways – characterized by creative, successful spatial solutions and novel uses of materials. Hollein's best interiors bring together diverse historical and psychological sources to create interiors that are both innovative and manipulative.

With his statement "Architecture is not the satisfaction of the needs of the mediocre, is not an environment for the petty happiness of the masses ... architecture is an affair of the elite" (Collins and Papadakis, 1989), Hollein has conveyed his understanding of his audience. Hollein's architectural commissions have concentrated in the areas of shopping, art, travel, and commerce, with structures serving a culturally sophisticated, financially secure audience; these situations have allowed him to develop interiors for those who can appreciate "aesthetically upgraded post-industrial objects" (Collins and Papadakis, 1989). He has explored the layers of meaning these structures and their interior spaces can hold.

Among his most striking architectural accomplishments in terms of original and evocative spatial arrangements are the municipal museum at Mönchengladbach, Germany and the Museum of Modern Art in Frankfurt. Hollein has also been very successful in dealing with existing spaces for new uses, with striking results: in the sensitive but expressive remodeling

Hollein: Schullin Jewelry Shop II, Vienna, 1981–82

of a medieval town hall in Perchtoldsdorf that preserved centuries-old frescoes of former mayors, and in the architectural carving of a breathtaking central atrium for a Madrid bank from the interior of three 19th-century apartment buildings, while still preserving the original façade. Hollein secured, with successes such as these, the prestigious contemporary architecture award, the Pritzker Architecture Prize, in 1985.

Where these architectural projects employ blatant deception (placing new contents inside old packaging) Hollein's well-known interiors, on the other hand, are subtle manipulations of the expectations of customers through his uses of real and *faux* materials. Hollein does this through his designs for interiors that evoke a surface response as well as a deeper intellectual or psychological one. In Hollein's Austrian Travel Agency in Vienna of 1976–79, he employs objects such as palm trees, an Indian pavilion, airplane wings and ocean liner railings that have an immediate association for the traveler. However, Hollein elevates these pedestrian travel-poster images by creating them in expensive, uncharacteristic materials such as marble, bronze, and mahogany. As with many of his interiors, he juxtaposes exquisite materials with industrial ones, such as aluminum, Formica, acrylic, and frosted glass. On another level, Hollein quotes the vision of one of his Viennese architectural forefathers: his Doric column, representing travel in Greece and Rome, is a reference to Adolf Loos's unrealized columnar design for the Chicago Tribune building competition in 1922, though Hollein altered the original reference through his transformation of the column at the halfway point into a column of steel. As well, his metallic palm trees refer to the fantastic palms created by John Nash for the Royal Pavilion at Brighton. In his discussion of this interior, the architect Mark Mack has made the distinction between Hollein and his fellow Postmodernists: "Hollein offers a functional and metaphoric spatial organization with a semantic content, in direct contrast to the stage-set architecture of Charles Moore and Michael Graves" (Mack, 1979).

In his 1982 design for the interiors of the Schullin Jewelry Shop in Vienna (his second shop for Schullin), Hollein catered again to the culturally and financially elite, and filled the interior with provocative, luxurious elements appropriate to the shop's function. Hollein recognized the customer's base instinct to be drawn towards the glittery objects at the entrance to the shop, whose door (with square perforations in perspective, à la Josef Hoffmann) was surmounted by a curved, blade-like object on two supports that resembled a primitive weapon. These ignited consumer desires were fanned in the front room of the shop, where a sharply diagonal floor and matching light poles of exotic woods reinforced the customer's yearning and led him or her into the back room, where a ghostly, ethereal, almost holy atmosphere pervaded through the use of white marble flooring, gold leaf, and soft light, a reassurance to the consumer of the validity of his or her possible purchase. Hollein manipulated his audience once again by mixing the precious with the base (such as *faux* marble and chrome-plating), and layered meaning through his deceptively simple selection of motifs and materials, subtly producing what can only be called a ritualistic interior.

Hollein has been able to infuse the objects he has designed most directly with semantic importance; the purchasers of these objects are expected to recognize and appreciate their significance beyond the mere decorative or utilitarian. In 1981, Hollein was one of eleven internationally-recognized architect / designers who were asked to design a tea and coffee *piazza* to be produced by Officina Alessi (the avant-garde section of Alessi) on a suggestion from Alessandro Mendini. The use of an architectural term for a functional object reinforces the Postmodern sense of architectural spatial arrangement applied to familiar forms. Hollein chose an aircraft carrier to define the placement of his tea service components, a continuing exploration of a theme he developed in an absurdist photomontage from 1964 called *An aircraft carrier in the Austrian wheatfields*, that gave added meaning to his service beyond the historical or architectural references of his fellow *piazza* designers.

Hollein's furniture designs have blended the serious with the whimsical, and, like his interiors, looked to the art-historical past. In 1981 he was one of eight non-Italians to produce designs for the inaugural Postmodern Memphis collection; Hollein's *Schwarzenberg* side table, the most symmetrical, controlled piece of the group, featured a stepped top and luxurious blond wood, recalling the Biedermeier furniture designs made for the Austrian elite of the early 19th century. His *Marilyn* sofa for Poltronova, produced in 1984/85, is layered with references: to Marilyn Monroe (inspiration for the original lip-shaped red Marilyn sofa of the 1960s, designed by Studio 65 for Gufram), to Art Deco blond wood furniture used in the era of the screen goddess, and to Biedermeier.

Hollein's early European commissions and the Austrian predecessors he has quoted have allowed him to develop his particularly exquisite brand of Postmodernism. Hollein has escaped the American trap Mack describes as "the rapid turnover of businesses in America [which] promotes rapidly built spaces and material hollowness" (Mack 1979). In a description of one of his interiors Hollein seems to sum up his entire creative philosophy: "I think you should have complexity in simple things, and simplicity in complex things. And if you can overlay both, I think that is the ideal." (*Architectural Record*, September 1994, p. 84).

JENNIFER A. KOMAR

See also Postmodernism

Biography

Born in Vienna, 30 March 1934. Studied at the Department of Civil Engineering, Bundesgewerbeschule, Vienna, 1949–53, then at the School of Architecture, Academy of Fine Arts, Vienna, 1953–56, Dip.Arch.; studied in the US: architecture and planning at the Illinois Institute of Technology, Chicago, 1958–59; M.Arch., College of Environmental Design, University of California, Berkeley, 1960. Worked in various architectural offices in the US, Sweden and Germany; in private practice in Vienna, since 1964; consultant designer to various corporations in Austria, France, Italy, Japan and the US, including Herman Miller, Alessi, Memphis, Baleri, Knoll International, and Yamagiwa, since 1966. Professor of Architecture, Academy of Fine Arts, Düsseldorf, Germany, since 1967; head of the School and Institute of Design, since 1976, and leader of the master class in architecture, since 1979, at the Academy of Applied Arts, Vienna; Visiting Professor, Yale University, New Haven, Connecticut, since 1979. Author of numerous articles on design and architecture and editor of *Bau* magazine, Vienna, 1965–70. Received numerous prizes and awards including the Grand Austrian State Award, 1983, German Architecture Award, 1984, and Pritzker Prize, 1985. Honorary Fellow, American Institute of Architects, 1981; Member, Royal Swedish Academy of Fine Arts, Austrian Chamber of Architects, German Chamber of Architects, League of German Architects.

Selected Works

Examples of Hollein's designs and drawings are in the Museum of Modern Art, Vienna, and the Avery Library, Columbia University, New York. Examples of his furniture and furnishings are in the Art Institute, Chicago, the Victoria and Albert Museum, London, the Minneapolis Institute of Arts, the Museum of Modern Art, New York, and the Centre Georges Pompidou, Paris.

1964–65	Retti Candle Shop, Vienna (façade and interiors)
1967–69	Richard L. Feigen Gallery, New York (building and interiors)
1970–72	Carl Friedrich von Siemens Foundation, Nymphenburg, Vienna (building and interiors)
1970–75	Siemens Headquarters Building, Munich (building and interiors)
1971–72	Section N interior furnishing shop, Vienna (interiors)
1972–82	Städtiches Museum, Abteiberg, Mönchengladbach (building and interiors)
1973	Museum of Modern Art, Villa Strozzi, Florence (interiors)
1974	Schullin Jewelry Shop I, Vienna (façade and interiors)
1976–79	Austrian Travel Agency Central Office and 3 branch offices, Vienna (building, interiors and furnishings)
1977–78	Museum of Glass and Ceramics, Tehran (building and interiors)
1981	Beck Department Store, Munich (building and interiors)
1981	Museum of Applied Art, Vienna (extension)
1981–82	Schullin Jewelry Shop II, Vienna (façade and interiors)
1981–83	Beck Shop, Trump Tower, New York City (interiors and furnishings)
1983	National Museum of Egyptian Civilization, Cairo (layout and interiors)
1985–90	Haas Haus Complex, Vienna (building and interiors)
1987	Banco Santander Headquarters, Madrid (building and interiors)
1987–91	Museum of Modern Art, Frankfurt (building and interiors)
1989	Fukuda Motors Building, Tokyo (building and interiors)

Hollein's design work includes stage designs and numerous designs for furniture, jewellery, lamps, sunglasses, lighting and household appliances. His furniture includes the *Roto-desk* made by Herman Miller (1966), the *Mitzi* and *Marilyn* sofas made by Poltronova (1981 and 1985), the *Vanity* dressing table for Möbel Industrie Design (1981), the *Schwarzenberg* table produced by Memphis (1981), and the *Sigmund Freud* divan (1984). Hollein also designed the *Aircraft Carrier* tea-service for Alessi (1980–81), and has produced jewellery designs for A.E. Köchert and Cleto Munari, and tableware designs for Swid Powell.

Publications

"Rudolf M. Schindler: Ein Wiener Architekt in Kalifornien" in *Aufbau*, March 1961

"Transformations" in *Arts and Architecture*, May 1966

"Architecture" in *Aujourd'hui Art et Architecture*, May/June, 1966

"Neue Konzeptionen aus Wien" in *Bau*, 2/3, 1969

"All is Architecture" in *Architectural Design*, February 1970

"Position and Move" in *Space Design*, April 1976

"Messages" in *Japan Architect*, June 1976

Otto Wagner (Global Architecture 47), 1978

Design: Man Transforms, 1989

Paolo Piva: Design & Architektur, with Wilhelm Holzbauer and Sergio Polano, 1991

Further Reading

Alexander, Dorothy, "Schullin: Jewel Shop in Vienna" in *Interiors* (US), February 1977, pp.70–73

Bode, Peter M. and Gustav Peichl, *Architektur aus Österreich seit 1960*, Salzburg: Residenz, 1980

Capella, Juli and Quim Larrea, *Designed by Architects in the 1980s*, New York: Rizzoli, and London: Mitchell, 1988

Collins, Michael and Andreas Papadakis, *Post-modern Design*, London: Academy, and New York: Rizzoli, 1989

Davey, Peter, "Hollein in Munich" in *Architectural Review*, June 1981

Esherick, Joseph, *Hans Hollein / Walter Pichler: Architektur* (exhib. cat.), Vienna, 1963

Fehlig, Teresa Anne, *Hans Hollein: A Bibliography*, Monticello, IL: Vance, 1988

"Furniture Showroom, Vienna" in *Architectural Review*, 915, May 1973, pp.107–10

"The Glass Museum, Tehran, Iran" in *Architectural Review*, 1006, December 1980, pp.374–77

"Haas Haus" and "Elementary School at Kohlergasse" in *GA Document* (Tokyo), 30, 1991

"Hans Hollein: Austrian Travel Agency, Vienna" in *Architecture and Urbanism*, January 1979, pp.31–46

"Hans Hollein: Portrait" in *Architecture Intérieure*, April–May 1983, pp.96–105

Hans Hollein: Métaphores et Métamorphoses (exhib. cat.), Paris: Centre Georges Pompidou, 1987

Hans Hollein: Work and Behaviour, Life and Death, Everyday Situations (exhib. cat.), Venice: Venice Biennale, 1972

Isozaki, Arati and Richard Fuchs, "Recent Works of Hans Hollein" in *Architecture and Urbanism*, 1, 1984, pp.27–72

Jencks, Charles, *The Language of Post-Modern Architecture*, New York and London: Rizzoli, 1984

Mack, Mark, "Extracting and Recombining Elements: Austrian Travel Agency, Vienna, and Townhall, Perchtoldsdorf, Austria" in *Progressive Architecture*, December 1979, pp.76–83

Mackler, Christoph, *Hans Hollein*, Aachen, 1978

Pehnt, Wolfgang, "Architektur als Collage" in *Hans Hollein: Museum in Mönchengladbach*, Frankfurt: Fischer Taschenbuch, 1986

Pettena, Gianni, *Hans Hollein: Works, 1960–1988* (English edition), Milan: Idea, 1988

Powell, Ken, "Museum of Modern Art, Frankfurt" in *Architectural Design*, November–December, 1991

"Richard Feigen Gallery: Hans Hollein" in *L'Architecture d'Aujourd'hui*, 151, August–September 1970

"Schullin Jewellery Shop 2" in *Architecture and Urbanism*, 1, 1984, pp.59–65

Spens, M., "Hollein's Vienna" in *Architectural Review*, November 1985, pp.58–63

Hope, Thomas 1769–1831

British architect, collector and connoisseur

Born in Amsterdam into a wealthy and cultivated family of bankers, Thomas Hope travelled extensively on the Continent before settling permanently in England in 1795 where he established himself as a patron of the arts. Hope's Grand Tour of 1787–95 took in Turkey, Egypt, Syria, Greece, Spain, Portugal, France, and Germany. Later excursions included Egypt (1797), Athens (1799), Naples (1802), Rome (1803) and Italy (1815). An amateur architect, collector and connoisseur, Hope was also a competent draughtsman producing an eclectic and highly personal range of designs for interiors and furnishings that incorporated Greek, Roman and Egyptian elements, with an admixture of Indian or Turkish features. While his practical involvement with architecture and interiors was confined to his own two houses, his publications and engravings were influential and well-known. He also played an important role in efforts to improve standards of design by education and actively promoted Greek Revival principles and an archaeologically correct version of the Neo-Classical taste.

Hope had begun to assemble his important collection of antique and modern art, purchasing sculptures from Flaxman and a number of antique statues and Egyptian pieces, during his Grand Tour. In 1799 he bought a house built by Robert Adam in Duchess Street, Portland Place in which to display these pieces, adding items purchased from Sir William Hamilton's second collection of vases in 1801. Hope made substantial alterations to this property c.1800 and, fired by a desire to influence and educate contemporary taste, he opened it to the public, issuing tickets of admission to Royal Academy members in 1804. In 1819 he added a Picture Gallery of his own design in which he displayed the collection of Dutch and Flemish pictures belonging to his brother Henry Philip Hope. This room was decorated in an advanced Neo-Classical style and contained complementary classical-style furniture also designed by its owner.

In 1807 Hope published *Household Furniture and Interior Decoration Executed from Designs by Thomas Hope* which contained general views of the principal interiors of the Duchess Street house as well as measured drawings of individual pieces of furniture. The spare, linear style of the engravings in this book was clearly indebted to the drawings of Flaxman and was paralleled by the style of illustrations in Percier and Fontaine's *Recueil* (1801). Hope's intention was that his book should serve as a sourcebook for designers and craftsmen. It did not include a plan of the house, but a contemporary sketch-plan was drawn up by the antiquary Francis Douce sometime before 1819. This plan is now in the Bodleain Library and offers additional information relating to Hope's ideas and the Duchess Street decorative schemes.

Apart from the Picture Gallery the interiors included a Sculpture Gallery, a second Picture Gallery suggestive of a Greek temple, and Indian and Egyptian rooms. According to Richard Westmacott's *British Galleries of Painting and Sculpture* of 1824, the chief elements of the decoration of the Egyptian Room (described as the "Black Room") were black with gilt ornaments. The background colours of the walls, ceiling, and upholstery were blue-green and pale yellow which

Hope: boudoir, The Deepdene; watercolour, 1818

Hope described as colours that "uphold conspicuous rank among Egyptian pigments". Paintings were set in plain frames studded with Piranesian Egyptianising stars. The decoration of the Flaxman Room which housed Flaxman's sculptures of Aurora and Cephalus was, by contrast, classical. The Indian Room was designed to display four large paintings of buildings in India by Thomas Daniell and contained "a low sofa after the Eastern fashion ... [a] ceiling, imitated from those panels in Turkish palaces ... [and] a canopy of trellis work, or reeds tied together with ribbons". Three further rooms were used for the display of Greek vases. Every room was decorated in bright, strongly contrasting colours and was furnished with Hope's archaeologically correct furniture imbued with an esoteric symbolism that was to become highly characteristic of his designs. The house was demolished after his death by his son in 1850.

Hope's activity as a collector was accompanied by an active participation in the politics of art. He had been elected a Fellow of the Society of Antiquaries in 1794 and in 1800 he became a member of the influential and learned Society of Dilettanti. In the same year as he opened his Duchess Street mansion to the public, Hope published a pamphlet entitled *Observations on the Plans and Elevations Designed by James Wyatt* ... in which he attacked Wyatt's Neo-Classical vocabulary and unreservedly promoted Greek Revival principles.

In 1807 Hope bought The Deepdene, a country house in Surrey, and was engaged in its remodelling and improvement until his death in 1831. While the architectural components of the house were mostly classical, the planning was essentially asymmetrical and picturesque. The styles of the interiors and furnishings were, in parts, similar to Hope's London house and included much classical statuary and an Egyptian room that was decorated "with a quantity of dull red paint" and that contained a bed copied from a plate in Denon's *Voyage dans la Basse et la Haute Égypt* (1802). In the Small Drawing Room (also referred to as the Boudoir) and the Library, wallpaper was used to create an architectural effect. Apart from the ceiling cove, the Small Drawing Room was entirely devoid of architectural decoration. The walls were covered with an "Etruscan" pink printed paper that contained classicising details such as arabesques and garlands picked out in black and brown in the dado and frieze. Architectural emphasis came from the green Mona marble chimneypiece, the architectonic overmantel, and the silk-hung baldachino that framed an ottoman whose design was closely related to similar furnishings illustrated by the French Empire decorators Percier and Fontaine. Deepdene was subsequently remodelled and enlarged in an Italianate style by Hope's son, Henry Beresford Hope. The house was demolished and the contents were dispersed in 1917.

Hope played an important role in disseminating Neo-Classical ideas and in promoting an ideal of archaeological correctness among contemporary architects and decorators; George Smith's *Designs for Household Furniture* (1808) was probably directly influenced by his visits to Duchess Street. But ultimately Hope influenced taste more by the general example of his seriousness of attitude and method than by the provision of specific models for imitation. Following the sale of Deepdene there was renewed interest in his designs. Many items from his collection were purchased by the playwright Edward Knoblock who recreated a number of celebrated Regency interiors in the 1920s and 1930s, and Hope's work exercised a strong influence on the Regency Revival in Britain during the second quarter of the 20th century.

BRIDIE DORNING

See also Neo-Classicism; Vogue Regency

Biography

Born in Amsterdam, the Netherlands, in 1769, the eldest son of a wealthy merchant. Travelled extensively in Europe and the Middle East, 1787–95. Moved permanently to England in 1795 where he established himself as a connoisseur and patron of the arts. Married Louisa Beresford 1806: 3 sons, Henry Thomas (founder of the Art Union), Adrian John, and Alexander James Beresford Hope (President of the Royal Institute of British Architects, 1865). Elected a Fellow of the Society of Antiquaries, 1794; a member of the Society of Dilettanti, 1800. Opened his London home, on Duchess Street, to the public as a lesson in taste, 1804; subsequently published several influential books on costume, architecture and interior design, including *Household Furniture* (1807) which illustrates furnishings that he designed for Duchess Street and The Deepdene, Surrey. Died in London, 3 February 1831.

Selected Works

Hope's practical work was confined to the furnishing and decoration of his own houses. Examples of his furniture are in the Victoria and Albert Museum, London, the Royal Pavilion, Brighton, the Ashmolean Museum, Oxford, and Lord Faringdon's collection at Buscot Park, Oxfordshire. An illustrated copy of Britton's *History of the Deepdene* is in the Drawings Collection of the Royal Institute of British Architects, London. The contents of the Deepdene, including much of Hope's collection, are featured in the Christie's, London, sale catalogue of 1917.

Interiors

1799	Duchess Street, London (interiors and furniture): Thomas Hope
1807	The Deepdene, Surrey (interiors and furniture): Thomas Hope
1818–19 & 1823	The Deepdene, Surrey (enlargements): Thomas Hope
1819	Duchess Street, London (alterations, including a sculpture gallery, two picture galleries, Indian room, Egyptian room, Flaxman room, and three rooms for the display of Greek vases): Thomas Hope

Publications

Observations on the Plans and Elevations Designed by James Wyatt, Architect, for Downing College, Cambridge ..., 1804
Household Furniture and Interior Decoration Executed from Designs by Thomas Hope, 1807; reprinted 1970
Costume of the Ancients, 2 vols., 1809
An Historical Essay on Architecture, 2 vols., 1835

Further Reading

The most comprehensive account of Hope's life and work, including a list of his designs and publications, appears in Watkin 1968.

Ackermann, Rudolph (editor), *Repository of Arts*, 1, no.VI, 1823
Baumgarten, Sandor, *Le Crépuscule néo-classique: Thomas Hope*, Paris, 1958
Britton, John, *History, etc., of the Deepdene: Seat of Thos. Hope Esqr.*, 1821–26
Britton, John, *Illustrations of the Deepdene: Seat of Thos. Hope Esqr.*, 1826
Christie, Manson & Woods Ltd., *Sale Catalogues*, vol.VI, nos. 98–102, July–August 1917
Collard, Frances, *Regency Furniture*, Woodbridge, Suffolk: Antique Collectors' Club, 1985
Crook, J. Mordaunt, *The Greek Revival: Neo-Classical Attitudes in British Architecture, 1760–1870*, London: Murray, 1972
"The Deepdene" in *Country Life*, v, 1899
Harris, John, *Regency Furniture: Designs from Contemporary Source Books, 1803–26*, London: Tiranti, and Chicago: Quadrangle, 1961
Morley, John, *Regency Design, 1790–1840: Gardens, Buildings, Interiors*, Furniture, London: Zwemmer, and New York: Abrams, 1993
Symonds, R.W., "Thomas Hope and the Greek Revival" in *Connoisseur* (UK), vol.CXL, 1957
Watkin, David, *Thomas Hope and the Neo-Classical Idea*, London: Murray, 1968
Wellesley, Gerald, "Regency Furniture" in *Burlington Magazine*, vol.LXX, no.410, May 1937

Horta, Victor 1861–1947

Belgian architect and designer

Together with Henry van de Velde and Gustave Serrurier-Bovy, Victor Horta was one of the originators and leading practitioners of Belgian Art Nouveau. In common with the foremost European designers of the period, he promoted the idea of buildings and their interiors as total works of art (*Gesamtkunstwerk*) and concerned himself with every aspect of design from the architectural structure to the smallest interior details, including furniture, furnishings, carpets, stained glass, chandeliers, door handles and domestic utensils. In his mature work of the 1890s and later, he developed a new style based on a synthesis of several different influences. These included the structural emphasis of French Rationalism promoted by Viollet-le-Duc, formal elements from the English Arts and Crafts Movement, and shapes and forms derived from nature. Horta's architecture and interior design provided a three-dimensional equivalent to the two-dimensional linear inventiveness of contemporary painters and graphic designers like A.H. Mackmurdo, Jan Toorop, Aubrey Beardsley and Fernand Khnopff, all of whom shared his feeling for natural forms combined with a deliberate freshness and exoticism.

Horta: Tassel House, Brussels, 1892–93

Horta first studied music, later entering the Ghent Academy to study drawing and architecture (1874–77). In 1878 he worked in the studio of Paris architect and decorator Jean Dubuysson, before being admitted to the Académie des Beaux-Arts in Brussels in 1881. After working as a draughtsman for Alphonse Balat (1818–95), a Neo-Classical eclectic architect, Horta produced his first independent work. This unremarkable group of three houses in Ghent, 1885, drew on Belgian traditional architecture for inspiration and in no way presaged the innovative Tassel House, built in Brussels in 1892 and 1893.

Described as "a work of complete assurance, outstanding for its synthesis of architecture and the decorative arts and its declaration of new formal principles", (William J. Curtis, *Modern Architecture Since 1900*, 1982) the Tassel House was the first of a series of extravagant and spectacular town houses designed for a wealthy, urbane, fin de siècle clientele with exotic tastes. The principal innovation of these houses lay not in the design of their restrained stonework façades, but in their spatial planning and decoration. Spacious stairwells and long internal vistas through dining rooms and glazed, interior winter gardens were common elements. In order to allow plenty of light into the office and study of the Tassel House, Horta contrived a series of changes of level on each floor, linked by a central stair-corridor with light wells on either side. Cast-iron columns carried the loading. The resulting openness of structure and exciting spatial fluidity created an unprecedented lightness in the centre of such a narrow house. The staircase was particularly innovative, with its frank expression of the metal structure and its sinuous, tendril-like ornamentation transforming gradually into the vegetal shapes of banisters, patterned stucco walls and floor mosaics, glass and woodwork. This continuity, suggestive of organic growth and tension, invoked contemporary interests in "empathy" and organic symbolism.

In the Van Eetvelde house (1895), Horta carefully orchestrated a processional route from the front door to the salon, again involving a series of changes of level, in order to impress the visitor with spatial drama. A great circular double-height space covered by a colourful, top-lit glazed dome, was devised as a central living area and communication core for the house. Here the use of sinuous shapes of iron, wood and plaster, suggest climbing stalks and clinging tendrils, and produced the effect of a suddenly fossilized conservatory. In the Aubecq house (1889–1902) Horta linked together a suite of polygonal rooms into a subtly modulated flow of space. American architects, such as Frank Lloyd Wright provided the sources for this approach to internal space, but it was Horta's exploitation of the structural possibilities of iron and steel, allowing the dematerialization of internal walls and different floor levels, which added a completely new dimension. Mirrors created further spatial ambiguity, as instanced at top of the staircase in Horta's own house and office at 23–25 rue Américaine (1898).

In the Hôtel Solvay (1895), designed for the industrialist and chemist Armand Solvay, Horta's credo was successfully expounded throughout the scheme: in the linking of interior volumes, in the furniture and fittings (all extant) and in the treatment of the façade, where an appropriately linear ornament was displayed. Light fittings were all consistently designed as flowering plants with long, upright or nodding stems terminating in sprays of metal or glass petals holding conspicuously naked bulbs. They entwined themselves around the stair rails, rose gracefully from the sides of fireplaces, or drooped in elaborate clusters from ceilings, flooding light over the carved wood furniture and walls. In these houses Horta's Art Nouveau detailing allowed him to use his preferred materials such as iron and steel for structural emphasis, in close conjunction with the costly materials expected of a sumptuous interior: marble, stained glass, Liberty silks, gold, bronze, mosaic, Padouk and pine, mahogany and bilinga. In the dining room of his own house the honey tones of the elegantly fashioned ash furniture harmonise with the copper picture-rails and painted decoration. White-enamelled bricks were used in place of wallpaper and the floor covering is wood parquet with a mosaic border with copper inlay to echo the linear motifs of the painted ironwork supports. Horta's elegant style created an ambiance of luxury which is not associated with the more austere "honesty" of van de Velde's furniture and interiors.

Horta's Maison du Peuple (1895–98; now demolished), built as the headquarters of the Belgian Socialist Party,was intended to provide labourers with a meeting place equal to the dwellings of the bourgeoisie. Constraints in the requirements and funding for the building presented a challenge. Two large public spaces were needed; a cafe, where people could meet daily and talk, and a large auditorium for party meetings and stage presentations, that was capable of seating 2000 people.

Several offices and smaller meeting rooms were also required, and as much of the street frontage as possible had to be used for shops. The site was a difficult one, the overall shape of the building being dictated by the circular Place Emile Vandervelde, and the two streets that enter it at an angle. The façade was designed as a continuous, but irregular series of mostly concave curves and was constructed in masonry, iron and glass. The integration of material, structure and expressive intentions was most successful on the interior, especially the main auditorium at the top of the building where the roof was formed from a sort of hammer-beam system in steel, with gracefully inclining curving girders carrying the galleries at half their height. The foliate iron decoration swarms energetically over the gallery railings. The auditorium was enclosed only by glass or by thin infill panels creating a volumetric lightness which recalls some early 19th century engineering structures, while at the same time anticipating 20th-century developments. This interior is one of the few which successfully combine Art Nouveau decoration with a genuinely Art Nouveau curvilinear structure to form an organic unity.

The 1901 Brussels department store, L'Innovation, shows the extent to which the structural elements of the metalwork, externally as well as internally, were even more affected by a curvilinear aesthetic. Here, as in the Grand Bazaar in Frankfurt (1903), Horta was concerned to exploit the new possibilities offered by steel and glass to create large internal spans and allow for wide openings.

In about 1905 Horta abandoned the Art Nouveau style, and in 1912 he became a Professor at the Académie des Beaux-Arts, later serving as its Director. In 1913 he was made a baron. He lived in America from 1916 to 1918, returning to Brussels after the war. His later architecture, well represented by his concrete Palais des Beaux-Arts (1920–25), was classical and severe, in contrast to his earlier work, which was to prove more influential in the development of modern architecture.

HILARY J. GRAINGER AND SUSAN HOYAL

See also Art Nouveau

Biography

Born in Ghent, 6 January 1861. Studied architecture at the Academy of Fine Arts, Ghent, 1874–77, and at the Academy of Fine Arts, Brussels, to 1881. Married 1) Pauline Heyse, 1881 (divorced 1906); 2) Julia Carlsson, 1908. Apprenticed to the architect-decorator Jean Dubuysson, Paris, 1878–80; assistant in the office of King Leopold I's architect, Alphonse Balat (1818–95), Brussels, 1884–85 and worked intermittently with this firm until 1892. In private practice, Brussels, 1886–1915; lived in London, 1915 and in the US, 1916–18; returned to Belgium and resumed practice in Brussels, 1919–47. Appointed lecturer in design at the Université Libres, Brussels, 1892, and professor of architecture, 1902–15; professor, Academy of Fine Arts, Brussels, from 1912, and director 1923–25, 1926–29, 1930–31; professor of Fine Arts, Académie Royale de Belgique, 1919; professor of architecture, Institute of Fine Arts, Antwerp, 1920. Exhibited at numerous international exhibitions including Tur in 1902, and Paris 1925. Received several prizes for architectural projects, 1887–92; awarded Légion d'Honneur, 1926; Ordre de la Couronne, 1936. Died in Brussels, 11 September 1947.

Selected Works

A chronology of Horta's life, including a complete list of his architectural projects, appears in Borsi and Portoghesi 1991. Much of the documentation relating to his practice and his career was sold for scrap in 1946 and has been destroyed, but some archival material survives in the Victor Horta Papers held at the Musée Horta, Brussels.

Interiors

1892–93	Tassel House, Brussels (building, interiors and furnishings)
1893	Autrique House, Brussels (building, interiors and furnishings)
1895–1900	Hôtel Solvay, 224 Avenue Louise, Brussels (building, interiors and furnishings)
1895–98	Maison du Peuple, Place Emile van de Velde, Brussels (building and interiors)
1895–1900	van Eetvelde House, 4 Avenue Palmerston, Brussels (building, interiors and furnishings)
1898	Horta House and studio (now Musée Horta), 23–25 rue Américaine, Brussels (building, interiors and furnishings)
1899–1902	Aubecq House, 520 Avenue Louise, Brussels (building, interiors and furnishings)
1901–03	L'Innovation Department Store, Brussels (building and interiors, with the sculptor Van der Stappen)
1902	Belgian Pavilion, International Exposition of Decorative Arts, Turin
1903	Grand Bazaar Department Store, Frankfurt (building and interiors)
1903	Waucquez Department Store, 20 rue de Sables, Brussels (building and interiors)
1903	Max Hallet House, 346 Avenue Louise, Brussels (building and interiors)
1909	Wolfers Store, 11–13 rue d'Arenberg, Brussels (building and interiors)
1920–25	Palais des Beaux-Arts, Brussels (building)
1925	Exposition des Arts Décoratifs, Paris (Belgian Pavilion building and interiors)

Publications

Considérations sur l'Art Moderne, 1925
L'Enseignement Architectural et l'Architecture Moderne, 1926

Further Reading

The most recent monograph on Horta, which includes excellent recent and archive photographs of his principal interiors and a full bibliography, is Borsi and Portoghesi 1991.

Borsi, Franco and Hans Wieser, Bruxelles, *Capitale de l'Art Nouveau*, Rome: Colombo, 1971

Borsi, Franco and Paolo Portoghesi, *Victor Horta*, London: Academy, and New York: Rizzoli, 1991

Brunhammer, Yvonne, *Art Nouveau: Belgium / France* (exhib. cat.), Houston: Rice University Institute for the Arts, 1976

Delevoy, Robert L., *Victor Horta*, Brussels: Elsevier, 1958

Dierkens-Aubry, Françoise, *The Horta Museum, Brussels Saint-Gilles,* Brussels: Crédit Communal, 1990

Doumato, Lamia, *Baron Victor Horta* (bibliography), Monticello, IL: Vance, 1981

Dulière, Cécile (editor), *Victor Horta: Mémoires*, Brussels: Ministère de la Communauté Française de Belgique, 1985

Henrion-Giele, Suzanne, *Horta* (exhib. cat.), Brussels: Musée Horta, 1973

Hoppenbrouwers, Alfons and others, *Victor Horta Architectonographie*, Brussels: Confédération Nationale de la Construction, 1975

Kaufmann, Edgar, "224 Avenue Louise" in *Interiors* (USA), February 1957, pp.88–93

Loyer, François and Jean Delhaye, *Victor Horta: Hôtel Tassel, 1893–1895*, Brussels: Archives d'Architecture Moderne, 1986

Loze, Pierre, *Belgium, Art Nouveau: From Victor Horta to Antoine Pompe*, Ghent: Snoeck-Ducaju & Zoon, 1991

Madsen, Stephan Tschudi, "Horta: Works and Style of Victor Horta before 1900" in *Architectural Review*, 118, December 1955, pp.388–392
Oostens-Wittamer, Yolande, *Victor Horta: L'Hôtel Solvay / Victor Horta: The Solvay House*, 2 vols., Louvain-la-Neuve: Institut Superièur d'Archéologie et d'Histoire de l'Art, 1980
Oostens-Wittamer, Yolande, *Horta en Amérique*, Brussels: Hossmann, 1986
Pionniers du XXe Siècle: Guimard, Horta, van de Velde (exhib. cat.), Paris: Musée des Arts Décoratifs, 1971
Portoghesi, Paolo, *Victor Horta* (Global Architecture 42), Tokyo: ADA, 1976
Puttemans, R. and others, *Victor Horta*, Brussels, 1964
Russell, Frank (editor), *Art Nouveau Architecture*, New York: Rizzoli, and London: Academy, 1979
Selz, Peter and Mildred Constantine (editors), *Art Nouveau: Art and Design at the Turn of the Century*, 2nd edition New York: Museum of Modern Art, and London: Secker and Warburg, 1975
Thiebault-Sisson, "The Innovator: Victor Horta" in *Art et Décoration*, 1, 1897; republished in Tim and Charlotte Benton and Dennis Sharp (editors), *Form and Function*, London: Crosby Lockwood Staples, 1975

Horti, Pál 1865–1907

Hungarian designer

Pál Horti's early death and perhaps even his nationality as a Hungarian account for the fact that he is a relatively unknown figure in the history of interior design. Yet his designs at the height of his career in the late 1890s and early 1900s were warmly regarded by his contemporaries in Europe and the United States. One commentator viewing his schemes for the Hungarian Pavilion at the Turin Exhibition in 1902 described them as "original expressions of the new movement in Hungary". Furthermore, they have become increasingly understood as key works in the national movement for design reform in Hungary in the 1900s and as important international conveyors of Art Nouveau.

Horti was born Pál Hirth into an artisanal family in Pest at the beginning of a great phase of growth in the Hungarian capital and the opening of a so-called "golden age" in Magyar culture. Following the Compromise, a political agreement made between Hungary and Austria in 1867 which extended some autonomy to the Magyars in return for loyalty to the newly founded Dual Monarchy, Magyar nationalism flourished in all fields of culture. This took a variety of forms from neo-Romantic Vernacularism at the turn of the century which invented an idyllic vision of Hungarian life in the isolated rural region of Transylvania to the Modernism of industrial investment and urban growth advocated by a confident bourgeoisie. In his career Horti also displayed his nationalism in a variety of ways. In the late 1890s he relinquished using his German-sounding name in favour of its Hungarian equivalent and while his mature designs share characteristics found in Belgian and English work of the period, they also make reference to vernacular traditions in their wooden constructional forms and traditional peasant embroidery. In fact, in 1902 *The Studio* reported that Horti (and Istvan Gróh) had been commissioned by the Minister of Commerce to tour rural Hungary giving advice to village potters on modern glazing and decorating techniques. The results of this venture combining traditional forms with modern skills were of "the highest artistic merit".

Horti: interior designed for the Hungarian pavilion, 1902 Turin Esposizione Internazionale

After completing his training in a vocational school in Budapest where he studied drawing and furniture design, Horti resolved to become a painter. In the 1880s he studied in Munich, London and Paris. Although his studies and the exhibition of his work did not bring him great acclaim, it nevertheless helped Horti secure a position as a lecturer in painting at the Budapest School of Applied Art (Iparrajzikola) in 1890. As the influence of the English Arts and Crafts Movement began to spread in artistic circles in the city, Horti was again attracted to the applied arts and, in fact, in 1895 returned to Munich to study different graphic techniques in the design of decorative patterns. Following the principles of design reform movements found across Europe, Horti's curiosity led him to experiment with a wide variety of materials and techniques. He learned, for example, not only how to design ceramic vessels but also how to throw, glaze and fire his projects. He established a close relationship with some leading Hungarian manufacturers such as the Nagybecskerek textile factory.

Horti's mature style of design emerged relatively rapidly in the course of the 1890s. While his early works displayed a strong strain of historicism, often derived from Rococo sources, he established a decorative language in a series of designs for flat decorative patterns used in stained glass and carpets exploiting arabesques, exaggerated floral motifs and strong tonal contrasts that became recognised as a Hungarian variant of Art Nouveau. Horti's major works were a small number of designs for interiors. In touch with the spirit of the *Gesamtkunstwerk* (total work of art) found in the oeuvre of the leading Viennese Modernists such as Josef Hoffmann, his unified interiors were marked by a strong aesthetic sensibility. A 1902 prize-winning interior designed for a Society of Applied Art (Magyar Iparmüvészeti Társulat) exhibition and made by the firm of Vukovics and Kaufmann, for example, came entirely from Horti's drawing board. An oblong shape recurred throughout this design both as a motif and as a proportional principle; his furniture designs were emphatically undecorated though Horti exploited the expressive qualities of the constructional elements of his furniture designs such as joints; and his designs were richly coloured.

Horti was responsible for a number of interiors for various Hungarian pavilions at international exhibitions in the early years of the new century. His designs featured at the Paris Exposition Universelle in 1900 where he was awarded a gold medal for his carpets and furniture, as well as his ornamental designs. Such was his reputation as an important advocate for Art Nouveau, that in 1904 he was asked (with the support of a small group of architects and designers including Geza Maroti and Ede Thoroczkai Wigand) to oversee the design and installation of the Hungarian display at the St. Louis International Exhibition. Reinforcing the peculiarly Hungarian mix of Art Nouveau and the vernacular, the façade of this display was styled as a Transylvanian country house with characteristic wooden fencing and a Székely gate. Horti reported the successes of the Hungarian display to his compatriots in a ringing article in the pages of *Magyar Iparmüvészet* (Hungarian Applied Art). In this report he also claimed that the measure of the Hungarian success could also be taken in the "brilliant contract offers" that he and his colleagues received from American companies. While little is known about these offers, Horti did create a number of furniture designs for American manufacturers including a large, wooden upholstered chair. This low, simple design, known as a "Morris Chair", was part of a library suite commissioned by Oscar Onken Co. of Cincinnati in 1905.

In April 1906 Horti travelled to San Francisco from where he planned to travel to Mexico then across the Pacific to Japan and China and through Asia collecting works for display in the Budapest Museum of Applied Arts. He succeeded in making only part of this journey. In Mexico he caught Yellow Fever and while he continued his voyage, he died in May 1907 in Bombay. His grave in Budapest was testimony to his high reputation among his colleagues, for it was designed by sculptor Ede Telcs and decorated with a mosaic panel by Miksa Róth.

DAVID CROWLEY

Biography

Born Pál Hirth in Pest, 1865. Studied drawing and furniture-making in Budapest. Trained as a painter in Munich, London and Paris, 1880s. Appointed lecturer in painting, Budapest School of Applied Art, 1890. Active as a designer of ornament, textiles, furniture and interiors from the mid-1890s. Exhibited at the Paris Exposition Universelle, 1900, and the St. Louis International Exhibition, 1904. Travelled to San Francisco and South America, 1906. Died in Bombay, May 1907; buried in Budapest.

Selected Works

1900	Exposition Universelle et Internationale, Paris (Hungarian Pavilion interiors, carpets and furniture)
1902	Esposizione Internazionale d'Arte Decorativa Moderna, Turin (Hungarian pavilion, building and interiors)
1904	Louisiana Purchase Exposition, St. Louis (Hungarian pavilion layout and display)

Publications

"St. Louis kiállitás" in *Magyar Iparmüvészet*, 1904, pp.249–313

Further Reading

Crowley, David, "Modernity and Tradition in Hungarian Design at the Turn of the Century" in *Design and Culture in Hungary and Poland 1890–1990*, Brighton: University of Brighton, 1993

Dömötör, István, "Horti Pál" in *Magyar Müvészet*, 1908, p.107

Éri, Gyöngyi and Zsuzsa Jobbágyi, *A Golden Age: Art and Society in Hungary, 1896–1914* (exhib. cat.) London: Barbican Art Gallery, and Miami:Center for the Fine Arts, 1989

Gerk, János, Attila Kovács and Imre Makovecz, *A Századforduló Magyar Epíteszete*, Budapest: Szépirodlnii Könyvkiadó, 1990

Koós, Judith, "A Hungarian Pioneer of Art Nouveau: Pál Horti" in *Ars Decorativa*, no.2, 1974, pp.173–90

Koós, Judith, *Horti Pál élete és Müvészete 1865–1907*, Budapest: Kiadó, 1982

Hotels

The evolution of the hotel followed the evolution of travel and in the sense that we use the word today – "a superior kind of inn" – it dates only to 1765 when some sophistication was replacing the plain necessities of the inn. A short list of late 18th century hotels may give some idea of their levels of comfort and efficiency of management as most were the subject of recommendation by literary travellers. Unfortunately, though, little indication of their interiors was recorded. The Rotes Haus in Frankfurt, which housed royalty, and the Drei Mohren in Augsburg were well-known. The latter was rebuilt in 1722–23 with a Rococo and pilastered exterior. It housed a ballroom which, as many expert stuccoists were working in Augsburg at the time, may well have had a correspondingly decorative interior scheme. In France, little remains of the large and famous Dessin's Hotel complex in Calais (1768) or of the Henri Quatre in Nantes (1782). The Lion Hotel at Shrewsbury had an assembly room added about 1775–80; it was plain but elegant, with an apse at one end and semicircular-headed windows.

From ancient times spring waters have been recognised for their medicinal qualities, and by the early part of the 19th century the spas in Europe, named after Spa, a town in Belgium, were becoming popular centres for health-seekers. This attracted entrepreneurs with a mercenary interest in building accommodation to house these visitors. One of the first spa hotels was the Badischer-Hof at Baden, converted from a Capuchin monastery by the Neo-Classical architect Friedrich Winbrenner in 1809. The church was turned into a majestic banqueting hall with music and conversation rooms; the former cloister was transformed into a dining hall, being covered by a gigantic barrel vault supported by 18 giant Doric columns, with galleries on three floors. This monumental space was lit by a skylight and in the later 19th century was turned into a staircase hall. Although much extended, the hotel still survives recognisably. At Wiesbaden, architect and developer J.C. Zais designed the Hotel Vierjahreszeiten (1817–18) as part of a symmetrical town centre plan. It had 150 rooms, 44 baths, and a banqueting hall to seat 124 "adorned by a spectacular array of columns" (Watkin, 1984). Only vestiges remain after destruction in World War II. A comparable English complex was built in Plymouth as the Royal Hotel and Athenaeum (1811–19) incorporating a large Dining or Tea

Room for Assembly, a Commercial Room, Billiard Room, suites of sitting, dining and bedrooms (with scant provision of sanitary accommodation), a Bar and Coffee Room, as well as a Theatre. The building was designed in the Neo-Classical style by the architect John Foulson. Other popular spa towns of this period, including Bath, Brighton and Leamington, also had hotels; the best example still in use is the Regent Hotel, Leamington Spa (1819) by C.S. Smith, a pupil of Sir Jeffry Wyattville.

In 1825 the first steam railway was opened between Stockton and Darlington in the north of England and almost instantly revolutionised travel on land. Steam-powered transport increased the pace of life, affecting the construction of buildings, the development of technology, and the mobility of the populace wherever the railroads spread. The hotel world entered a period of accelerated development which, except in time of war, has scarcely slowed. The United States, Canada, France, Belgium, and Germany all opened railway systems within the space of ten years.

Hotels in the United States had, from their first introduction at the end of the 18th century, been large and fitted out with all the available amenities. The first in New York was the City Hotel (1794–96) with 73 rooms on five floors though "really no more than two houses". Boston's Exchange Coffee House (1806–09) by architect Asher Benjamin, was larger, with seven storeys, a domed atrium with classical pillared galleries, and 200 apartments. The ballroom had three domes and 12 Corinthian columns and the dining room was over 70 feet long. The Tremont House, Boston (1827–30) became a landmark in hotel quality. It was designed by Isaiah Rogers and was featured in some detail in Charles Dickens's *American Notes* of 1842. Dickens commented on the "boarders, both married and single, many of whom sleep upon the premises" as though this was unusual, but in America there was already a tradition of residential hotel accommodation which offered a permanent way of life far less easily achieved by the private individual. The Tremont House had 170 rooms and could seat 200 in its dining room. Its management was innovative in training staff to be respectful to the customers, and in providing room keys, proper curtains, a rug, and, best of all, a piece of soap with the washing water. Having seen the Tremont House, J.J. Astor briefed Rogers to design him a New York hotel which would exceed it in size and quality. The result, the Astor House (1832–36), had 309 rooms, 17 basement bathrooms, and privies on the upper floors, and was described as "the marvel of the age". Some classical Greek Doric design elements persisted, corridors as well as rooms were carpeted, and American black walnut – perennially a favourite joinery timber – was widely used for fittings.

On both sides of the Atlantic large hotels proliferated, providing varying degrees of luxury. The United States has always tended to excel in matters of size and was usually first with new types of equipment. Bed springs, which had been invented in Massachusetts in 1831, were not mass-produced for a further 40 years, but thereafter made a great contribution to comfort. Steel-framed buildings and hydraulic or electrically powered "rising rooms" added greatly to the possibilities of height and size. Well-known pioneering hotels of the time were the Palmer House, Chicago (1870) which burnt down, and the Palace Hotel, San Francisco (1875) destroyed in the earthquake of 1906 in spite of precautions against fire.

Summer and resort hotels in the middle of the 19th century catered for great numbers of people; for many, their accommodation may have been a small bedroom with access to a distant bathroom and meal service in a vast dining room. Figures cited for the Mount Vernon Hotel at Cape May, New Jersey (1853–56) were 9½ feet square for the bedroom and 425 feet long for the dining room, so it is not difficult to understand the popularity of family suites or private cottages with their own bathrooms. The Mount Vernon, timber framed and generally sparsely furnished, had been planned to accommodate 2100 guests but it too burnt down even before final completion. Saratoga Springs in New York State, with its spring waters and race track, became fashionable in the 1860s. Saratoga's United States Hotel, which was rebuilt in 1875 following a fire, claimed to be the largest hotel in the world. Nearby, the Grand Union Hotel by J.A. Wood, architect, vied for the same distinction and boasted a 305-foot dining room to serve 1400 people. In addition, it had 12 acres of carpet, an acre of marble tops and tiles, and a mile of covered piazzas. Crystal chandeliers, black walnut stairs, and a steam-powered elevator by the Otis brothers were listed by the local press when the whole property was sold after the owner's bankruptcy.

In Canada, the hotel network followed closely on the construction of the Canadian Pacific Railway. Plain and basic designs such as the first Vancouver Hotel (1887) by Thomas Sorby were overtaken by the tourist-orientated enterprises of CPR Hotels. The firm's first project was the Banff Springs Hotel (1888) designed by the New York architect Bruce Price and executed under the direction of the company president Cornelius Van Horne, for whom impressive planning and design were matters of policy. It was a first step in the development of the "château style" and attracted international interest in its siting and amenities. The Château Frontenac, Quebec (1893) by the same architect, was soon redecorated and refurbished by Kate Reed whose taste for European antiques and *objets d'art* was allowed full rein in other CPR hotels including the Place Viger Hotel, Montreal; the Empress, Victoria, British Columbia; Royal Alexandra, Winnipeg; and Glacier House, Mount Stephen House, and Chalet Lake Louise, all in the Rockies. All Mrs. Reed's schemes were planned in detail down to harmonising or matching linen. The overall effect was a successful blending in the interiors of domestic comfort and pleasant atmosphere with monumental scale and historical allusions.

New mid-century European hotels were substantially less spectacular in capacity and size than their Northern American counterparts and were developing from a totally different background in which a network of hotels already existed with long-established standards arising from visits by royalty, nobility, or gentry who required comfort, good food, and service. Interiors followed the fashions of the times with a leaning towards classical grandeur and much ornamental detail in the large public spaces. Good representative examples existed in Paris beginning with the Grand Hôtel du Louvre (1855), which had 700 bedrooms and the great advantages of originating under the general benevolence of Napoleon III and of being designed in the Second Empire style. The architects, A.

Armand, J. Hittorf, C. Rohault de Fleury and A. Pellechet, had the earlier Great Western Hotel in London as a model on which to expand and improve. The Grand Hôtel survived until it was replaced in 1927 by another hotel. The Hôtel de Crillon had different origins, having been built originally behind the majestic colonnade of the Place de la Concorde by L. Trouard as a Parisian town house in 1765. It was not put to use as a hotel until 1909 and the interiors of many of the main rooms were skilfully remodelled in 1912 by H. Destailleur in Louis XVI style. The *belle époque* ambience can be savoured in the Continental (now Intercontinental) built in 1878 to designs by H. Blondel and influenced by Charles Garnier. It retains magnificent Second Empire interiors, and features luxurious sculpture and red and gold painted and gilded columns. A Moorish room imitated the details and decor of the Alhambra in Granada.

Monaco's Hôtel de Paris (1862) was developed four years before the railway connection, by Francis Blanc who already ran the casino and was also able to succeed with the hotel. It was enlarged by Dutrou in 1865. Its rotunda entrance hall, with a glazed dome and sculpted naiads and tritons, now incorporates much of the lavish 1908 remodelling by Edouard Niermans. The Hôtel de l'Ermitage in the same area dates from 1890 and shows local architect J. Marquet indulging in a delightful confection of stained glass and Art Nouveau in the cast iron rotunda, used as a winter garden. The oval Louis XIV dining room ceiling was designed by A. Levasseur and painted by G. Ferrier. The town of Menton eastwards along the coast had developed ten years previously with several Baroque / Rococo / Moorish six-to-eight storeyed hotels, now used as apartments and offices, but of which the Riviera Palace, designed by Abel Glena, is perhaps the most interesting. This had a columned entrance hall and a small integral theatre originally with a sliding roof to be open or closed as required. Nice, to the west, has remained more fashionable than Menton, and the memorable Negresco (1912) is another example of Niermans's work with a large glazed dome over the Salon Royal on the ground floor supported by paired Ionic columns and scrolled iron cantilever brackets made by Gustave Eiffel, designer of the Eiffel Tower. The central chandelier by Baccarat is similar to one supplied to the Tsar of Russia and the Savonnerie carpet is claimed to be the biggest ever made. The same architect executed a design much resembling this salon for the Palace Hotel in Madrid at the earlier date of 1909.

Switzerland built up a reputation for hotel management which has never been surpassed and which created its own hierarchy. Johannes Baur, whose hotels Baur en Ville and Baur au Lac, Zurich (1837 and 1844), are still in existence, was among the pioneers of the Swiss hotel establishment. Alphonse-Rodolphe Armelder opened the Grand Hotel Richemond in Geneva (1875) and three generations later it is still run by his family. A restored Art Deco façade conceals eclectic interiors in Louis XV, Louis XVI, Empire and Napoleon III styles. In St. Moritz Johannes Badrutt had first built the Engadiner Kulm, and, as the resort expanded his son Caspar carried on the family enterprises with the Palace (1896). His architects Chiodera and Tschudi departed from classical models on his instructions which resulted, in Raymond Flower's words, in a "combination of mountain schloss and baroque château, with gingerbread features such as turrets and arrow-slits, all topped by a great tower". The resulting profile, restored after serious fire which destroyed the tower in 1967, adds distinction to St. Moritz just as the interior Victorian Gothic pine-panelled public rooms, with more than a touch of the required Baronial manner, attracted the noble and the rich. The original Badrutt hotel which was incorporated in the present palatial one, was supplied in 1878 with hydro-electricity generated from the river Inn and this was used to light the dining room – the first electric light in Switzerland, we are told. The new building was short on private bathrooms – three only in a total of 140 bedrooms plus one more for communal use on each of three floors. A ladies' drawing room, a men's smoking room, a library, and a billiard room augmented the large dining and ballrooms.

César Ritz epitomised the skill and attention to intricate detail needed to produce service of the highest possible standard. From Switzerland and the Côte d'Azur he came in 1889 to manage the Savoy in London and was later involved with the Carlton. His co-operation with architect Charles Mewès resulted in the creation of several hotels which took his name, in Paris, Madrid, and London. Ritz hotels which had no direct connection with César multiplied, in much the same way as Bristol hotels did during the 18th century and later, which claimed no contact with the eccentric Earl-Bishop of Bristol other than a certain standing derived from this persistent traveller's name.

The Grand Hotel in Stockholm (1874) has had a long and consistent history as an important asset to Sweden's capital. Architect Axel Kumlien designed it with neo-Renaissance exterior, the main banqueting hall being influenced by Brunelleschi's church of San Lorenzo, Florence. The basement Porcelain Café, with slightly Moorish references, had walls and ceiling lined with lime green tiles. These interiors disappeared with the 1898 alterations from which the white and gold Mirror Room emerged which survives today. Designer Thure Steuberg went to Versailles for his model, adding gilded Corinthian columns and a small stage. The resulting room accommodated the most important Swedish functions until 1929 when the next Stockholm Town Hall presented an equally distinguished setting in a modern idiom.

Two central European spa hotels have survived in partially changed form. The Grand Hotel Pupp takes up the spa theme in 1893 in the long-established town of Carlsbad (Karlovy Vary) which was well accustomed to visitors. The Pupp family, after years of assembling a central site adequate for their ambitious plans, commissioned Viennese architects Ferdinand Fellner and Hermann Helmer to develop their land to include a Festival Hall and Restaurant (1905–07) flanked by two hotel wings totalling 270 rooms. Neo-Baroque characterises the interiors in the form of the rich stuccowork, which abounded in the Austro-Hungarian Empire. Politics and wars disrupted the old luxurious spa life and, after numerous vicissitudes, the hotel found itself by the late 1950s known as the Grandhotel Moskva as it remained until 1989. Unsympathetic restoration after a fire spoiled the south side, although much else has fortunately been preserved as has a certain amount of historical atmosphere. The Hotel Gellért in Budapest was completed in 1918, the work of Artur Sebestyén, Izidor Sterk and Armin Hegdüs; the interior work was under the direction of Ferenc

Szjaba. The main hotel rooms have largely been modernised with little character, but the adjoining medicinal baths, with original tiling, sculpture, and faience work as well as a sliding roof, retains the Art Nouveau character in the main bath halls area.

Also in the 20th century the Hotel Metropol, Moscow (1905), is surprisingly the work of an Englishman, William Walcot, who was commissioned by the financier and art patron Savva Marmontov to prepare designs and carry out the work for the new hotel even though he had not been a winner in a previous competition for the project. The hotel turned out to be a success which lasted until the October Revolution in 1917. Its Art Nouveau-flavoured interiors, called *style moderne*, are attributed to A.E. Erikson and were augmented by other Neo-Classical and neo-Baroque schemes.

In Britain the advent of the railways brought with it the introduction of the railway hotel. Notable in London were the Great Western Royal, Paddington (1852) by Philip Hardwick, the Grosvenor, Victoria (1861) by James Knowles, the Charing Cross (1863), by E.M. Barry, and the Midland Grand Hotel, St. Pancras (1876) by Sir George Gilbert Scott. Interiors improved from the barn-like coffee room at the Great Western through the heavily carved stonework in the hall of the Grosvenor to the high Victorian Gothic at St. Pancras, with intricately decorated and painted structural wrought iron work, a world away from its contemporaries on the Continent. Scottish resort hotels were opened when rail systems reached northwards, in part-classical, part-baronial styles and throughout the country good railway and non-railway hotels were built to provide a very acceptable level of accommodation and service.

American tourists and businessmen took full advantage of easier long distance travel at home and abroad and returned with many ideas and plans. Lifts, electric power, centrally-fired heating, telegraph and telephones were installed, new fashions and manners were observed, and hotels became skyscrapers. Rooms multiplied in number, aiming at 1000 or more – the Stevens in Chicago reaching 3000 – against the norm in, for example, Switzerland of about 300 for large hotels. Historicism dwindled except for the occasional fantasy such as the Moorish style Tampa Bay Hotel, Florida (1891) by J.A Wood, which, eccentrically, depended for some of its steel reinforcement on unwound cable from old submarine telegraph lines and cable car wires. A number of rural sites inspired more designs in the vernacular idiom and Frank Lloyd Wright produced not only the outstanding Imperial Hotel in Tokyo but also the Arizona Biltmore, Phoenix, in which he supplied design ideas direct to the builder Albert Chase McArthur in 1929. The Greenbrier, White Sulphur Springs, West Virginia should be mentioned as one of the most prestigious resort hotels in the United States, with a long history and many transformations. It was completely refurbished after World War II, re-opening in 1948 with attention to every small detail in the sophisticated, elegant classical-cum-Victorian interior by Dorothy Draper.

Fashion in hotel decoration before and after World War II often adopted the English Country House style, which was suitable for both renovating older buildings and fitting out new hotels. The Dorchester, Park Lane, London (1931), by W. Curtis Green, was one of the latter and opened to great acclaim for its highly successful interiors, charming and comfortable as well as lavish and extremely well-equipped. Five main suites were decorated by five different designers with the Oliver Messel Suite being regarded as the most notable. This was restored closely to its original state with the help of Messel's sometime assistant, John Claridge, in the 1989–90 redecoration.

The Midland Hotel, Morecambe, was designed as a railway hotel by Oliver Hill in 1933, replacing the early 1848 North Western Hotel. The design is unique in its complete commitment to the Modern Movement of which it is an excellent example, with sculpture and relief work by Eric Gill, a mural by Eric Ravilious, and specially designed rugs by Marion Dorn. Under private ownership it has now been restored after years of deterioration.

In recent decades travel has come within the reach of many and the railway hotel industry in a large part of the world is able to provide the traveller and tourist with reliable plumbing and heating, usually an en suite bathroom, comfortable beds, adequate cupboards and shelves, telephone, and a television set to supply world-wide news. An increase in outdoor activities and sightseeing has reduced the need on the regular tourist circuits for impressive rooms, although in existing historic buildings they are certainly regarded as assets. Pacific islands, Indian palaces, and African safari are accessible at the higher end of the scale and the state-run *paradores* and *pousadas* in Spain and Portugal have pioneered current conservation policies in restoring and adapting outstanding historic buildings for hotel use. Commercial hotel chains which standardise planning, equipping, and catering have played an important part in making the timid traveller feel more at home in strange places. The United States has again led the field as such familiar names as Hilton and Sheraton with their corporate design styles repeated in many different parts of the world bear witness. Air travel and motoring on a continental scale have provided the mobility which underpins the entire scene.

ELAINE DENBY

Further Reading

A useful introduction to the history of hotel architecture is Watkin 1984 which also includes many original views and illustrations of interiors and a geographical index of the major European hotels from 1800 to 1930. Donzel 1989 contains a geographical index of hotels in America and Canada and a short further reading list. More detailed information about individual hotels can be found in some of the numerous commemorative publications produced by the hotels themselves.

Arnold, Wendy, *The Historic Hotels of London: A Select Guide*, revised edition London: Thames and Hudson, 1989

Arnold, Wendy, *The Historic Hotels of Paris: A Select Guide*, London: Thames and Hudson, and San Francisco: Chronicle Books, 1990

Borer, Mary Irene Cathcart, *The British Hotel Through the Ages*, Guildford: Lutterworth Press, 1972

Carter, Oliver, *An Illustrated History of British Railway Hotels, 1838–1983*, Silver Link Publishing, 1989

Denby, Elaine, *Grand Hotels*, London: Reaktion, forthcoming

Donzel, Catherine, Alexis Gregory and Marc Walter, *Grand American Hotels*, New York: Vendome, and London: Thames and Hudson, 1989

Limerick, Jeffrey, Nancy Ferguson and Richard Oliver, *America's Grand Resort Hotels*, New York: Pantheon, 1979

Ludy, R. B., *Historic Hotels of the World*, Philadelphia: McKay, 1927
Meade, Martin, Joseph Fitchett and Anthony Lawrence, *Grand Oriental Hotels*, London: Dent, and New York: Vendome, 1987
Montgomery-Massingberd, Hugh and David Watkin, *The London Ritz: A Social and Architectural History*, London: Aurum, 1980
Ott, Thierry, *Palaces: Une Histoire de la grand hôtellerie suisse*, Yens sur Morges: Cabédita, 1992
Pevsner, Nikolaus, *A History of Building Types*, Princeton: Princeton University Press, and London: Thames and Hudson, 1976
Taylor, Derek, *Fortune, Fame and Folly: British Hotels and Catering from 1878 to 1978*, London: IPC Business Press, 1977
Watkin, David, *Grand Hotels: The Golden Age of Palace Hotels* (introduction by Jean d'Ormesson), London: Dent, 1984

I

Ince and Mayhew

British cabinet-makers and upholsterers, 1759–1804

The prominent and long-lasting partnership of William Ince and John Mayhew began in 1759 in premises opposite Broad Street, in Carnaby Market, London. Both partners were young men not long out of their apprenticeships. Mayhew had served his time with William Bradshaw an upholsterer, and Ince trained with John West, a cabinet-maker of some repute. This valuable combination of the two main furnishing skills would stand them in good stead in the development of their business. Not only did they have the advantage of a good training, but by taking over the premises and part of the stock of an established business they ensured themselves a substantial start in trade.

Almost immediately after embarking upon their business they began to publish designs, as a way of advertising their business and creating trade, no doubt following Chippendale's successful example. In a listing in the *Gentleman's Magazine* of 13 July 1759 it was recorded that: "A general system of useful and ornamental furniture by Mess. Ince and Mayhew, [is] publishing in numbers at 1s each". The venture was initially to have had 160 plates but the difficulty of meeting deadlines for regular publication made the partners decide to amalgamate the designs and add a small metalwork section to make 101 plates. This was published in book form in 1762 under the title *The Universal System of Household Furniture*. The layout of the volume is directly based on Thomas Chippendale's *Director*, and Matthias Darly, who engraved most of the plates for Chippendale, was also responsible for those in the *Universal System*.

Although the designs were based on an interpretation of the Rococo style they have their own characteristics. Ward-Jackson has defined some of them as having "the frequent use of elaborate symmetrical patterns, half Gothic and half Rococo, executed in fretwork and applied blind to panels or used as an open-work filling for a frame" (Ward-Jackson, 1984). Some of the designs in their pattern book owe a little to contemporary French taste, especially in upholstery. For example, a design for a bergère chair with a bolster, and a couch with three graduated cushions at the back reflect contemporary and fashionable French taste. It is also noteworthy that the title page and notes of the *Universal System* were translated into French, no doubt intended to indicate a knowledge of the prevailing fashionable taste as well as a desire to spread their markets abroad.

The criteria that were employed by tradesmen and customers to ensure a furnishing scheme that was both functional and attractive were clearly defined. In the preface to the pattern book it was remarked that: "In furnishing all should be with propriety. Elegance should always be joined with a peculiar neatness through the whole house, or otherwise an immense expense may be thrown away to no purpose either in use or appearance."

The pattern book was apparently successful, even though Chippendale had published his third edition of the *Director* in 1762. Sheraton considered that the *Universal System* had "been a book of merit in the day, though much inferior to Chippendale which was a real original, as well as more extensive and masterly in Design".

As well as being a partnership of cabinet-maker and upholsterer, the business was also divided upon other skills. Ince was the partner who dealt with the designing, while Mayhew supplied capital and managerial skills. This division of labour appears to be one of the first conscious attempts explicitly to separate the profession of designing from the running of the business. Mayhew, for example, dealt with Sir William Chambers, the supervisor of commissions for the Duke and Duchess of Marlborough. On another occasion it was Mayhew who attended to Boulton and Fothergill's complaints about faulty glass. Although Mayhew was considered to be the entrepreneur and financial manager of the partnership, his supervision of the accounting side of the business appears to have left a lot to be desired; he made out only nine partnership balance sheets in the 45 years of trading.

Ince's early interest in design is evidenced by his subscription to Chippendale's *Director* in 1754 and his ownership of important architectural treatises. He was the main contributor of designs to the *Universal System* and his skills were also required for patterns to be published in a joint trade venture entitled *Household Furniture in Genteel Taste* (1760).

As with many 18th-century comprehensive furnishing firms, the partners were also dealers. Specific mention of glass and furniture for export, runs parallel to such offers as "An assortment of French furniture consign'd from Paris for immediate sale very much under the original cost, which may be seen at their warehouse Broad Street Soho".

The partnership was clearly well-thought of and highly

Ince and Mayhew: design for a dressing room, 1762

respected both by its customers as well as its employees. In 1775, Ince and Mayhew asked for apprenticeship fees of £210, a record for a furniture-making fee, which is indicative of their high reputation. They were also employed by many of the most important architects and clients of the time.

Although the partners initially employed a Rococo style, in their work for Adam at Croome Court they developed a Neo-Classical manner of design which was to be highly valued. In 1768 Lady Shelburne noted the details of a visit to the partnership in her diary. "To Mayhew and Inch [sic] where is some beautiful cabinet work and two pretty cases for one of the rooms in my apartment, and which though they are only deal, and to be painted white, he charges £50.00 for". In 1775 the firm supplied an important satinwood and marquetry commode for Robert Adam's patron the Earl of Derby. This was one of a range of superb commodes finished with marquetry work, exotic veneers and ormolu mounts that are now associated with them.

Both Mayhew and Ince were elected as directors of the Westminster fire office for various periods of office. This connection no doubt helped the firm secure a 1792 order for 18 new chairs for the office. However it was not an easy commission, as the board of Directors told Ince and Mayhew that "the charge of making desk and chairs is high and wish to refer it to their consideration".

The partnership also supplied furniture to the instructions of Henry Holland for Carlton House in the 1780s. This encouraged the development of a squared off classical style which later evolved into typical Regency forms. The partnership formally continued until 1799, but they remained in business in a reduced way until 1804 when Ince died. Mayhew continued trading under the partnership title until 1808.

CLIVE D. EDWARDS

Selected Works

Examples of Ince and Mayhew's furniture survive *in situ* at Cobham Hall, Burghley House and Caledon Castle; a marquetry cabinet made for Kimbolton Castle, Huntingdonshire is now in the Victoria and Albert Museum. Only one drawing can be firmly attributed to the firm (Victoria and Albert Museum) but miscellaneous bills and accounts survive in country house archives including Burghley. A full list of the firm's commissions appears in Beard and Gilbert 1986.

Interiors

1761–1803 Cobham Hall, Kent (bedroom and seat furniture): 3rd and 4th Earls of Darnley

1764–94 Croome Court, Worcestershire (furnishings; interiors by R. Adam): 6th Earl of Coventry

1767–79 Burghley House, Lincolnshire (furnishings for private apartments): 9th Earl of Leicester

pre-1773–93 Blenheim Palace, Oxfordshire (furnishings for private apartments; interiors by W. Chambers): 4th Duke of Marlborough

1783–96 Caledon Castle, Co. Tyrone, Ireland (furniture, carpets and curtains): 1st Earl of Caledon
1787–92 Daylesford House, Gloucestershire (furnishings; building and interiors by S.P. Cockerell): Warren Hastings
1787–93 Woburn Abbey, Bedfordshire (furnishings for bedrooms): 5th Duke of Bedford

Publications

The Universal System of Household Furniture, 1762; reprinted with preface by R. Edwards, 1960

Further Reading

No monograph on Ince and Mayhew exists but a survey of the firm's history appears in Kirkham 1974, with further details in Kirkham 1988. For a list of their principal commissions see Beard and Gilbert 1986.

Beard, Geoffrey and Christopher Gilbert (editors), *Dictionary of English Furniture Makers, 1660–1840*, London: Furniture History Society, 1986

Boynton, Lindsay, "The Furniture of Warren Hastings" in *Burlington Magazine*, CXII, August 1970, pp.508–20

Heckscher, Morrison H., "Ince and Mayhew: Two Biographical Notes from New York" in *Furniture History*, 10, 1974, p.63

Kirkham, Pat, "The Partnership of William Ince and John Mayhew 1759–1804" in *Furniture History*, 10, 1974, pp.56–59

Kirkham, Pat, *The London Furniture Trade, 1700–1870*, Leeds: Furniture History Society and J.S.Maney, 1988

Snodin, Michael, *Rococo: Art and Design in Hogarth's England* (exhib. cat.), London: Victoria and Albert Museum, 1984

Ward-Jackson, Peter, *English Furniture Designs of the Eighteenth Century*, reprinted London: Victoria and Albert Museum 1984

White, Elizabeth, *Pictorial Dictionary of British 18th Century Furniture Design: The Printed Sources*, Woodbridge, Suffolk: Antique Collectors' Club, 1990

India

From the dissolution of the Roman Empire, India's wealth had always been greater than that of Europe, and when traders began to bring back tales of the opulence of the new Mughal dynasty from the mid-15th century, the interest of the West grew. Before long, imported Indian goods and designs began to influence Western products – particularly textiles. With the colonisation of the subcontinent, this influence became reciprocal and the history of Indian design and interiors from the 16th century to the present day includes a rich vein of cross-fertilization between East and West. This essay examines that cross-fertilization.

The arrival of the Mughals in India dates from the defeat by Babur of Ibrahim Lodi at the battle of Panipat in 1526. This victory enabled Babur to claim the Delhi Sultanate. Babur consolidated his position by a second victory over the Hindu rulers at Khanua in 1527 and only after this was he able to survey his new kingdom and its contents. Little remains of Babur's building projects, although he is known to have employed 680 masons on one building at Agra alone, and to have laid out at least one garden, the Ram Bagh at the fort in Agra. Much of the time he lived in tents like his Central Asian ancestors. He was succeeded by his son, Humayan in 1530, but as he was in exile from 1540 to 1555 and died in 1556, Humayan had little opportunity to build, although his brother Kamran built an extensive palace in Lahore on the banks of the Ravi.

Early Mughal works are mosques and tombs for favoured persons, such as the Jamali Kamali Masjid and tomb (1528–36) and the tomb of Adham Khan, c.1562. From Humayan's reign remain the ruins of the Purana Qila, the old fort, begun as the first Mughal capital city, the sixth of the seven Islamic Delhis. A mosque (1541) and a three-storey octagonal pavilion known as the Sher Mandal survive from this period. Due to his sudden death, Humayan was unable to plan his tomb during his own lifetime, which was the Mughal tradition. Instead it was commissioned and built in the 1560s by his senior widow, Haji Begum, who employed an architect, Mirak Mirza Ghiyas specially brought from Persia for the purpose. Standing in the centre of a garden, it was to become the first in the series of great Mughal tombs and buildings. The design combines elements from 15th-century Delhi tombs of the Sayyid and Lodi sultans on a new and massive scale. An elaborate geometric structure is complemented by decorative surface decoration on the façades, emphasized by the use of three different colour stones. William Finch, an English merchant, visited it in 1611 and described the building as "spread with rich carpets ... a rich semiane (coloured tent) over head". Other Mughal buildings, typical of the early period of Mughal architecture, stand in the same garden.

Such was the wealth of the state during this period that monumental building programmes could be undertaken and completed. Palace complexes in Delhi, Agra, Fatepur Sikri, Allahabad and Lahore were built by the Mughals in the late 16th and 17th centuries. These complexes included gardens and pleasure and hunting pavilions.

The Jahangir Mahal, in the Agra Fort, was built in 1570 by Akbar and is the only palace apartment which survives from his time. He was also, however, responsible for building work in the forts at Allahabad and Lahore, in the fort and palace at Ajmer, and in his summer palace at Mandu on an elevated plateau in central India, as well as his masterpiece, Fatepur Sikri near Jaipur, where he was able to put his philosophical, religious and architectural ideas into practice. Akbar began this palace complex in 1571, but he had abandoned it by 1585, when he transferred his capital to Lahore, and never returned. Water problems may have been a factor in its decline, but it is more likely that it was a result of Mughal architectural prodigality: a frontier slash-and-burn mentality that involved building magnificently and lavishly and then moving on when the building was found no longer suitable or convenient.

Jehangir built the Khamba pavilion at Nizamuddin, now part of New Delhi, in 1623. The small, white marble pavilion is seen as prefiguring the architecture of Shah Jarhan's reign and the Taj Mahal. Jehangir also made alterations to the fort in Lahore and is responsible for the Bari Khwabgah (sic), the large bedroom, among other interiors.

Shah Jahan (ruled 1638–48) was mainly responsible for the Red Fort in Delhi and also for interiors in the fort in Agra including the Khas Mahal and the Anguri Bagh garden and pavilion. He also commissioned the building of the Taj Mahal I (after 1631 to mid-17th century) one of the crowning achievements of Mughal architecture. Private domestic architecture was simpler than the royal complexes, although the arrangements were not dissimilar, but furnished on a lesser

India: column, Fatepur Sikri

scale. Furnishing was often minimal, with low thrones, or mattresses and bolsters brought in as required, and the rooms decorated with rare and precious textiles which were removed and stored when not required. This type of interior remained more or less the same until the widespread arrival of European manufactured goods by the beginning of the 19th century, and the increasing use of European-style furniture within India began to change the appearance of Indian interiors around the same time. Shah Jahan's buildings often included the use of semi-precious stones embedded into the walls, as in the Taj Mahal; others could not afford to copy this, but Rajput princes often used a similar but cheaper method of decoration, with multi-coloured glass inserts. Few domestic interiors of the 16th and 17th centuries are still extant, with the exception of some of the royal palaces mentioned above, and some in palaces in Rajasthan where even the rare 15th-century interior may remain, although much altered.

The enormous wealth of the Mughal emperors attracted craftsmen from many countries to the royal ateliers. The Mughal *karkhana* (workshops) were attached to the major centres of government such as Agra, Delhi and Lahore, and in them the artisans, goldsmiths, painters and weavers produced artifacts for the court. The craftsmen usually worked in family units, fathers passing on skills to their sons. Provincial centres followed the Mughal model, each workshop answering the need of a particular noble or ruler. Commercial centres also existed for particular products traded with the rest of India and exported to Iran, the Middle East and (with the increasing involvement of the European East India Companies) to the West.

The impetus was two-way trade; crafts also came from Europe during the Mughal period and influenced the work of the Mughal *karkhanas*. European royal gifts had a bearing on the Mughal style in painting and the decorative arts. A fusion of indigenous Indian and imported Iranian and European styles took place. *A Deposition from the Cross*, for example, copied by a Mughal artist in Lahore in about 1598 from a Flemish print, was made under the personal supervison of Prince Jehangir. The ceaseless flow of European artefacts to the Court, the strong Iranian cultural and political ties, and the arrival of European and Iranian artisans, who were taken into the emperor's workshops to join the Indian Hindu and Muslim craftsmen there, profoundly influenced the style and decoration of objects, and seems to have been responsible for the creation of entirely new industries.

In India the idea of art for art's sake was unknown until the Mughal emperors. Courts, temples and export markets to east and west motivated Indian art, as well as the everyday needs of its population.

The stability that developed during Akbar's reign, from 1556 onwards, and the attendant wealth generated, allowed him to encourage the manufacture in the royal workshops of copies of artefacts that appealed to him, things that came from abroad, or for which there was a demand. Court-patronized crafts were unparalleled; architects, builders and craftsmen were brought to Mughal cities not only from all over India but also from other parts of Asia. Due to political disturbances in Italy in the 16th century, Italian architects worked in many other parts of the world, seeking royal or imperial patronage. In France, Portugal, England, in the Spanish West Indies and Goa, knowledge of Renaissance architecture and design, even if not widespread or long lasting, arrived in this manner. Italian and Portuguese architects were working in Goa from the mid-16th century onwards, and European artisans may also have travelled inland to the Mughal court.

Government-sponsored design workshops – an idea not developed in Europe until Louis XIV in the 17th century at Versailles – produced combinations of indigenous Indian and traditional Islamic designs. Specialised designers conceived each work of art, causing for the first time in India a separation between the craftsman and his inspiration, an emphasis on the individual versus the anonymous. Pile carpets, wall hangings, floor coverings, tent-panels, ivory and mother-of-pearl inlay on wood were some of the items introduced or improved under Akbar's court workshops.

In 1592 the English had captured a large Portuguese ship the *Madre de Dios* and had found it to contain a cargo of incredible wealth, including porcelain, jewels, spices, silks, calicos, carpets, quilts and dyes. The size of this prize encouraged English merchants to press for the formation of the English East India Company (established 1600) to open up the profitable trade to the east.

The Portuguese had been the first European colonisers to build extensively in India – in Goa – where Don Alfonso de Albuquerque created a thriving settlement with domestic, administrative and religious buildings from 1510 onwards. A previous Portuguese "factory" and settlement had been at Cochin in the south. Early buildings were wooden, fortified with palisades, but by the middle of the 16th century Daman, Diu and Bassein contained many stone buildings, chief among which was the Basilica of Bom Jesus in Old Goa.

Goa contained many religious buildings, both convents and monasteries. The Portuguese had assigned responsibility for the conversion of the Goans to Christianity to European-based monastic orders, such as the Franciscans and later the Jesuits, so the design of Goa's churches followed contemporary European styles. Most were built at the cusp of the late-Renaissance / early-Baroque style. The most important – Bom Jesus – was built by the Jesuits between 1594 and 1605 in a style derived from Vignola's Gesu church in Rome. Bom Jesus and other churches were designed for preaching, and similar façades, with superimposed classical pedimented fronts, can be seen throughout the parts of the colonial world where the Jesuit order was established.

Almost all Goa's churches have Baroque interiors with gilded altarpieces. Paintings on wood were usually by local artists, many assisted by Italians, whereas those few that were painted on canvas were imported from Europe. Wooden statues were the norm, as western India is largely forested, although some imported stone statues do exist.

Domestic architecture also followed Portuguese precedents. The Indo-Portuguese aristocracy developed a version of the Portuguese town house and plantation house adapted for a tropical climate, and this style was repeated throughout Portugal's colonies. The officially encouraged policy of intermarriage with local people also meant that an Indo-Portuguese style of domestic architecture developed in their colonies from quite early on. By contrast, the "factories" of the Dutch, English, French and Danish colonisers in India in the early period were institutional, almost male-only enclaves and had little architectural influence on their surroundings. It was not until the 18th century, when the journey became less costly and the political situation more secure, that more women began to travel to India and an indigenous European domestic achitecture began to develop in and around the enclaves of the colonists.

Danish, Dutch, French and English settlements followed the Portuguese. The Dutch already had a fort at Cochin, where the Dutch palace existed from the 16th century. A Jewish synagogue there had existed from very early on, and was decorated with blue and white export tiles brought from China in the 18th century.

In Surat, the Portuguese, Dutch (1616), British (1612) and French (1668) erected factories; long, low, defensive buildings, facing inwards onto courtyards, acting both as dwellings and warehouses. Built first in mud and brick, and later in more permanent materials, they provided communal living, as in a college or mess. None of these early European factories survive; they are known now only from drawings and engravings.

European colonisers had been able to establish footholds in India relatively easily as the arrival of the earliest settlers actually pre-dated that of the Mughals. The Portuguese had established themselves on the west coast of India in the 1490s, while the first Mughal emperor arrived in 1526. To the local Indian population the regime of one foreigner appeared little different from that of another. The European colonists might even have seemed preferable as, initially, they were interested only in establishing trading relations, while the Mughals actively sought to impose political and possibly religious hegemony over the subcontinent.

★

Early in the 16th century merchants of the Portuguese East India Company, already established at Goa, began to look to Bengal in eastern India, motivated by commercial and religious considerations. In 1536, after many attempts, they gained a foothold, setting up trading posts at Satgaon and Chittagong and controlling the customs houses there. They gradually ousted the Arabs from their key position in the eastern sea trade and the period of European dominance began. In the 16th and 17th centuries a three-way trade existed, with textiles from the Indian subcontinent being used as barter for spices from South East Asia. Europeans had to break into the textile market if they were to procure the spices which were their main prize. The most favoured commodity demanded in exchange for textiles at Dacca, the capital of Bengal, was gold and silver bullion, giving the Bengali merchants the ability to trade with the rest of the subcontinent with a freedom they had not known before.

The Portuguese, who had established the trading post at Hooghly in the 16th century, were mainly interested in richly embroidered backstitched quilts, bed-hangings made in and around Satgaon, the old mercantile capital of Bengal on the banks of the river Saraswati. These were used in Europe as bed-covers, highly prized in England as well as in Portugal. (The earliest reference to Bengal quilts is recorded in 1618 in the English records of the East India Company, but the Frenchman, Pyard de Laval, visited Bengal in 1607 and described the embroideries there). The Portuguese were themselves often represented on the embroideries, as well as in temple reliefs, as an exotic motif.

In 1632 the increasingly hostile relations between the Portuguese and their Arab hosts culminated in the siege and fall of the Portuguese settlement at Hooghly. Thereafter Portuguese influence and power in Asia declined and their role was taken over by other Europeans, anxious to avail themselves of India's merchandise. Nevertheless, the Portuguese never entirely disappeared from Bengal, where their descendants are still found, having intermarried with the local population.

Little furniture was used in India before the arrival of the European colonisers, with the exception of the *charpai* or *charpoi*, the archetypal Indian bed. The Portuguese in the 16th century were the earliest colonisers to use Indian artisans, and the carvers of wood and ivory who embellished temples and palaces now diversified to provide items for the Portuguese Asian export market, such as portable communion tables and church furnishings. These would be decorated with Christian motifs and subsidiary Indian designs and are known to have existed from the 1580s.

Portuguese-designed furniture was hardwood with inlaid Mughal decoration. Ivory caskets were produced in Sri Lanka for dispatch to Portugal as diplomatic gifts – these, and Communion tables, are the earliest datable examples of Indo-Portuguese furniture design. Furniture was assembled in Goa from different production centres in India, including Sind, Gujerat and the Deccan, for shipment to Europe. Both the Portuguese and later the Dutch took part in this trade.

Ebony was prized for its hardness, durability and grain, taking a brilliant polish and providing a dark, lustrous background for applied decoration in ivory and bone. Rattan, or cane, first appeared in the Indo-Dutch export trade furniture in the 17th century and within a generation was known all over Europe. Indian-made furniture continued to be almost solely for the European market until the 18th century, when increasing numbers of European settlers created a demand for furniture for the home, as opposed to the export market. Local craftsmen re-interpreted models from imported pattern books.

The English and the French rapidly expanded their ports along both coasts during the 17th century. With these new ports came an increased demand for goods. As pre-industrial India was still 90 per cent rural, it was largely the village farmers and craftsmen who supplied the market. Indian wares flooded European shops and warehouses, creating fashions in design and changing styles in every field. Textiles were among the most important exports: chintz, calico, gingham, muslin, silk, satin, velvet and brocade as well as quilts, embroideries and carpets. For three hundred years a steady flow of Indian fabrics exported to Europe increased in popularity and demand.

In the latter part of the 17th century in Europe the fashion was for complete sets of Indian hangings, in chintz, embroidery, or a combination of both techniques. These sets were almost certainly entirely designed for the export market and might comprise wallhangings, bed-curtains with valances and coverlet, perhaps matching chair and cushion covers and small carpets to surround the bed. Some purchasers were content to acquire only a coverlet, or chintz yardage to line a small room, such as was bought by Samuel Pepys in 1663 and mentioned in his diary. The attraction of these Indian chintzes lay in the brilliance and fastness of their colours and the fineness of their designs, and such was their popularity that Louis XIV banned their sale in France in the late 17th century. As a result, textile workers set up in Provence, which was a separate administrative area until the French Revolution. Various enterprises began reproducing the fabrics in Nimes, Tarascon and Marseille, calling them "indiennes" after their country of origin, the name by which they are still known in France, although in England they are called Provençal prints.

In textile design Gujerat and Bengal were the main bulk producers and suppliers, and had the sites from which transportation overseas was easiest. *Kanthas* from Bengal were also produced commercially for export, with biblical scenes for a foreign clientele and double-headed eagles for Spain in the 16th century. Bengal embroideries were exported from very early times. Tome Pires in his *Suma Oriental* states that as early as 1515 the exports from Bengal included "very rich and beautiful bed canopies of cut-cloth work [appliqué] in all colours, and wall hangings like tapestry", and they formed part of the royal household in Portugal by 1570.

Printed cottons from India were known in England in the 16th century or earlier. The word calico, which means painted cotton cloth, entered the English dictionary in 1540 and the word chintz, derived from *chitt*, in 1614.

During the 17th and 18th centuries foreign travellers witnessed the wealth and prosperity of Dacca, and its flourishing commerce based on the production of cotton goods. Gradually the East India Company set up an extensive system of procurement. It took two years before orders for selected samples or "musters" at different factories could reach London for the two major sales in March and September. Decisions of the Court of Directors in East India House were communicated to remote weaving centres in the Subah of Bengal through the Governor General and Council at Fort William in Calcutta and its factories. By the mid-18th century every town and almost every village had its looms worked on a joint-family basis. Medium grade cloths of all types provided the bulk of the piece-goods exported to Europe.

The finest silks and muslins (plain, figured in the loom, or needle embroidered) were reserved for the Mughal courts of Delhi and later Murshidabad. These translucent muslins suited Muslim rulers, with their lavish tastes, and provided a desirable alternative to Qur'anic restrictions on the use of pure silk by men. Jamdani muslin was lavished with the best techniques and designs of the Persian masterweavers settled in India. In the period of the European Companies, the best Bengal muslins came from Dacca and Santipore. The *tasar* and other wild silk embroideries of Satgaon in Hooghly district had been a major export commodity in the age of Portuguese supremacy, but declined thereafter.

As trade became more highly competitive in the 18th century, the agents of the European companies and other private merchants farmed out their orders to weaving villages and tried to buy export orders in direct sales. Therefore by 1751 more direct supervision was considered necessary. The British introduced standardisation of the product for export to Europe, thereby dispensing with the outstanding quality possible in the limited quantities required for the royal courts.

Textile design in Bengal did not only consist of woven muslins. At Dacca, *chipikars* or block printers printed cotton prayer shawls for Hindu rituals and shrouds for Muslim funerals, applied gold and silver leaf to wedding garments and printed the outlines for *khasida* embroideries. Indian textiles were not only woven and printed but also embroidered. Chamba *rumals*, Bengal *kanthas*, Punjab *phulkaris*, Kashmir shawls, Bihar *sujani* quilts are just some of the names that are widely known. In Bihar the appliqué technique for commercial purposes was mostly confined to canopies, tents and large walled enclosures, a form of decorative art which derived from the originally nomadic Mughals and could assume vast city proportions. Mughal tented encampments were extremely elaborate. They usually had two sets of tents, one of which was sent ahead to be set up. These were organized like small towns and each person had his alloted place. Jehangir's quarters were a fort of painted wood and canvas 300 yards in diameter and included a harem and a mosque.

Historical and religious conditions applicable in Bengal (and differing from the rest of India), meant that the influences on the arts were different. At the beginning of the 18th century conditions at the Mughal capital, Delhi, were no longer conducive to the employment of artists, and the consequent dispersal of painters led to the establishment of a school of provincial Mughal painting in Bengal, at Murshidabad, which soon acquired distinctive characteristics of its own. Within the ambiance of the newly independent court, a demand for the trappings of aristocratic life resulted in the development of crafts, such as metalwork, ivory and textiles, in which the decorative motifs stemmed from Mughal, rather than local artistic traditions – although it is at the landlord and middle-class level that the distinctions between Hindu and Muslim cultural icons were most sharply made. However, during the 18th century particularly, Hindu rajas and zamindars involved with the Mughal court, adopted aspects of Persian culture in its Mughal forms. The transmission of visual form from the courtly to the village level again indicated the cohesion of the culture. Murshidabad also supported a flourishing school of ivory carving, which has a history in India dating back at least to the Mahabharata. During the colonial period this craft flourished wherever culture was high enough to support such luxuries. Ivory sheeted wooden caskets were among the early state and diplomatic gifts of the Portuguese period, some showing Christian scenes. Eastern India is known to have had an ivory carving tradition from at least the 10th century. It became important in the 18th century when Murshidabad was a major regional capital, with the decline of the Mughal powers in Delhi. The National Trust at Powis Castle in Wales has Lord Clive's ivory and partly coloured chess set, made in Murshidabad in about 1760. The industry seems always to have been dependent on the level of local patronage; at the end of the 18th century the focus changed from Murshidabad, with the decline of the Nawabs' court no longer the regional capital, to nearby Berhampore, an army cantonment town where the increased demand for ivory was from Europeans, as Fanny Parks noted when in Berhampore in 1836.

Sandalwood inlaid with bone and ivory was used in both furniture design and later for decorative chess sets. The two major centres of furniture-making at this time were Murshidabad in Bengal and Vizagapatam in south India, each close to an administrative centre of the East India Company and both with traditions of ivory carving, veneering, and, in Madras, inlaying wood. Vizagapatam was a large and important furniture-making centre for elaborate and intricately inlaid furniture popular with European purchasers in the 18th century. In both these centres, local craftsmen, experienced in working for foreign markets, were known for their ability to work from "musters" (patterns), and to copy unfamiliar objects.

Indian furniture in the 18th century generally followed the styles of Chippendale and later Hepplewhite and Sheraton. In Bengal the ivory workers of the Murshidabad court produced ivory furniture strongly influenced by the Neo-Classical style. In Vizagapatam, furniture was either wood with ivory inlay, or was veneered with sheets of ivory on a wooden core. Ivory was decorated by incising a pattern and filling the depressions with black lac. The monochrome black, on work for Europeans, is probably due to the monochrome engravings they provided for the craftsmen to copy, or possibly due to less exuberant taste. Later examples of furniture, from Berhampore, are of ebony with ivory embellishments. The size and importance of the market in providing European-style furniture is demonstrated by the wealth of the Kat Gola complex near Murshidabad, a large early 19th century Neo-Classical mansion and grounds built on the profits from the making of European-style furniture.

★

In the 18th century the power of the centre in Delhi began to decline and various regional centres of influence and patronage developed. These included the states already carved out by the Rajputs and Marathas in western India, and the Muslim states of rulers such as the Nawab of Murshidabad in Bengal, the Nizam of Hyderabad in the Deccan, the Nawab of Arcot, and later Tippoo Sultan, in the South. The Rajput and Maratha states were traditional opponents to the Mughals in Delhi. The Muslim rulers on the other hand, had earlier been feudatories of the Mughals in Delhi but were able to set themselves up as rival power centres as conditions in the centre weakened. Conditions in the Mughal Court were no longer conducive to the kind of patronage required by artists and painters, and they moved to seek work and patronage elsewhere. A thriving school of Mughal-derived painting developed in Murshidabad. The Rajputs developed not only a style of painting but also an architecture in which a successful and aesthetic synthesis of Mughal and Hindu art became Rajput art. These regional styles originated in Delhi but mutated as they reached the provincial courts. Examples from this period in Rajasthan are the palaces of Kotah, Bundi and Dungapur, all with interiors of the period. In the South, Tippoo's winter palace in Bangalore was frescoed, as was his summer palace at Seringapatam, still extant but recently in need of repair, which was decorated with fresco murals of his victories.

An early example of planned city layout is the city of Jaipur. Jai Singh, the ruler of what would come to be known as Jaipur, abandoned his fortified rock palace of Amber in the early 18th century to lay out the new city in the 1720s. The grid plan was used, and although such high standards of town planning had been known two thousand years earlier (as evidenced by excavations at Mohenjo Daro, in present-day Pakistan), this is the first known major example in the recent historical era. Jai Singh may have had access to European books on architecture known to have been circulating in India, and certainly one building in Jaipur of this period exists which has a very European façade to the street, with alternating triangular and segmental pediments to the windows. Jai Singh also built the astronomical observatory at Jaipur, and another almost identical building exists in Delhi. To his reign dates the Diwan-i-Am and other interiors of the city palace in Jaipur. But, apart from these rare examples, architecture and design in India continued to follow oriental norms; domes on religious (Islamic) buildings incorporated squinches, arches were ogival, and labour was often seasonal.

At this period, although the activities of the French and British colonisers were becoming more evident in India, the connection between European and Indian thought on the matters of architecture and design was very much a matter for individual rulers and their tastes and interests. There was much greater interest in European astrological and navigating instruments, which were of a high standard and had always been much sought after. The ruler of Mandvi in western India financed a young man, Ram Singh, to go to England to learn various trades, such as watch-making, and he set up workshops on his return to India, various European technical crafts being practised in Mandvi during this period.

★

In addition to Bengal, colonisers had settled earlier in the south, around Madras and Tanjore where the major architectural and design influences were French and British. Unlike the parsimonious East India Company, the French state provided impressive residences for their governors in Pondicherry in the south and later in Bengal at Chandernagore. Thus the magnificent Baroque Government House in Pondicherry (founded 1674) which was commissioned by Dupleix, built in 1752 and destroyed by the British in 1761, was rebuilt in the Rococo style from 1766 onwards, while the governor's house in Chandernagore in Bengal was in the Neo-Classical style.

After the conquest of Pondicherry, the British led in matters architectural as well as in commerce. Although the French had built earlier in the 18th century, the major architectural contributions of the British began after 1750.

Calcutta had become the site of the East India Company factory in eastern India in 1690. The new Fort William was begun in 1758, after the Battle of Plassey. Bricklayers and carpenters recruited from England acted as instructors for local Indian labour. By 1780 Calcutta was known as a "city of palaces", and the more settled existence necessitated a variety of different building types; churches, town halls, residences, tombs, monuments, official, legal and administrative buildings and a Mint went up rapidly in a Neo-Classical style mainly derived from the architectural books of James Gibbs, written much earlier in the century, and others. The administrative Writers Building existed by the 1780s. In 1794 the Government House, Council House, Accountant General's Office and Supreme Court had all been built, only to be replaced within ten years by even grander edifices.

Alongside official architecture, domestic building developed. Rich merchants' town houses, designed in the manner of Palladian town palaces, required 50 to 100 servants to function. Increased mercantile expansion allowed the inhabitants to live lavishly. Sophisticated country or garden houses flourished around the large cities from the middle of the 18th

India: interior in Impey household showing Lady Impey with her servants, c. 1780; watercolour by Shaykh Zain al-Din

century. Their design may have been influenced by the books of architecture of Andrea Palladio, or later James Gibbs and John Nash – with the addition of very wide verandas on the south side for shade, and *punkas* (cloth ceiling fans, aiding air circulation) – but the usual bungalows were more rustic. As the name suggests, they originated in Bengal but were also built in northern India and in the south, adapting to local conditions. In the beginning clay and thatch were used. These materials would be replaced later on by stone walls and roof tile; the character changing from *cutcha* (raw, unfinished, unripe) to *pukkha* (finished, ripe, complete).

Two gouaches painted c.1782 for Sir Elijah and Lady Impey show fashionable European interiors in Calcutta in the late 18th century. Sir Elijah Impey was Chief Justice of Bengal and the Impeys were important art collectors, connoisseurs and patrons. One interior shows Lady Impey in her bedroom, giving instructions to her household staff. The bed is tucked away in an alcove. The French windows are hung with fashionable balloon shades, the floor is covered with a large patterned carpet with a distinctive border, the wheel-back chair set against the wall is in the style of Adam, the dressing table and its mirror are draped in the manner fashionable in England at the time (as shown in the portrait by Zoffany of Queen Charlotte with two of her children). The other interior shows the large nursery furnished much more sparsely. French windows lead from a semi-circular bay onto a veranda, the floor is covered with a simple striped *dhurrie* and the children's beds have posts at each corner to support the mosquito nets. The Impeys are among those families whose collections provide important documentary evidence in the history of European art in India, as are the collections of the Clive family, now at Powis Castle in Wales, or the works commissioned by Marquis Wellesley, Governor General from 1798 to 1805. Many European artists were also working in India at this period, including Chinnery who eventually moved to China and later died there. Devis and the Daniells are among the best

India: the Judges' bungalow, Madura, 19th century

known of the British artists, and a portrait by Reynolds remains still in Calcutta.

Architecture and design commissions remained in the hands of military engineers until the 1820s, when a course in civilian architecture was introduced. Previous to that, study of Belidor's *La Science des Ingénieurs* and consultation with patrons had been considered adequate training. This system had produced, for example, the new Government House, Calcutta (1799–1803) for Marquis Wellesley by Charles Wyatt, a member of the Bengal Engineers and one of the Wyatt architectural dynasty, who had been inspired by James Paine's project for Kedleston Hall in Derbyshire which had been published. John Garstin, also a Bengal Engineer, designed the circular storage *gola* (meaning round) at Bankipore in Bihar (1784–85) – as a means of preventing famine – and also the Calcutta Town Hall (1805–13).

Architecture and design also celebrated military successes, as with the circular temple of St. John in Calcutta, commemorating the second Rohilla war. The Banqueting Hall at Madras built c.1803 for Lord Clive by the Danish-born astronomer and mathematician John Goldingham, remembered the Freedom of Amiens. In the same year the Neo-Classsical British Residency at Hyderabad was begun by Samuel Russell of the Madras Engineers. Like the Government House, Calcutta, it was intended for extravagant state occasions. Elsewhere, at Lucknow, General Martin's yellow stucco palace-cum-tomb had no parallel in Europe; neither did Garstin's *gola*.

As British political power in India increased, Neo-Classicism became the preferred architectural style. It was fashionable in the mother country, and its adherents felt that it was well adapted for the tropical climate. Also, the overtones of classical antiquity suggested an association with imperial Greece and Rome which cannot have been absent from the minds of the colonisers and their architects.

By the end of the 18th century, smaller towns outside

Calcutta were developing. Barrackpore, the country seat of the Bengal governor, was a military cantonment. Officers usually lived in bungalows and soldiers in tents. This new urban pattern developed to meet the military's need for mobility and speed. Troops were located away from the old forts in permanent camps. Building was planned around a large open space, or *maidan* for gatherings and parades. Bankipore in Bihar, Meerut in northern India and Berhampore grew up in much the same way; a large brigade station with a very full European cemetery containing Neo-Classical tombs and monuments rivalling the Park Street cemetery in Calcutta. Nearby Murshidabad's European palace, with its Indian Neo-Classical interiors, was built on the river front by Bengal Engineers in Neo-Classical style between 1817–20.

From the 16th century onwards Italian architects were in service with the Portuguese in Goa, but the majority working in India were British and Irish. Tiretta, the East India Company's architect in Calcutta in the late 18th century, was an Italian architect. European architectural books circulated; the works of James Gibbs, James Paine, the Adam brothers and William Chambers were all known, as well as Leoni's editions of Alberti and Palladio, Vauban's plans for fortifications and the works of Vignola.

In the areas colonised by the British, many churches derived their plan from that of James Gibbs's St. Martin in the Fields, included in his 1728 *Book of Architecture*; these included St. Mary in Poona, (1825), St. John, and St. Andrew in Calcutta and St. George and St. Andrew in Madras. The latter church was designed after drawings by Thomas Fiott de Havilland and contained a memorial statue by John Flaxman. Catholic churches, especially in Goa, often followed the Baroque, Vignola-derived, style popular in southern Europe. Skinner's church in Delhi is in a more Northern Italianate, Tuscan style.

The Gothic style was rarely used at this period, except, in a very early example, at the garrison church at Fort William, Calcutta, in the late 18th century. St Paul's Cathedral (1829–47) in Calcutta, an early example of Victorian Gothic, has interesting stained glass by Sir Edward Burne-Jones, and is more or less the first example of the revival of this taste. Thereafter, however, Gothic was to become the official style.

Neo-Classicism dominated European architecture in India until the middle of the 19th century; Madras was the "Grecian city". The Greek Revival was introduced into the Presidency towns by William Nairn Forbes (Calcutta Mint) and Thomas Cowper (Town Hall, Bombay). Both had been inspired by Stuart and Revett's measured drawings of Greece – Forbes's Doric order on the Calcutta Mint derived from the Parthenon. The earlier generation of architects, Garstin (b.1756) and Wyatt (b.1758) were firmly rooted in the Palladian style, whereas Cowper (b.1780) and Forbes (b.1796) were Greek Revivalists, a more directly historic style. Many of those working in India in various capacities were Scots, and as Edinburgh was a city almost rebuilt in the Greek Revival style at the end of the 18th century, this doubtless influenced their choice. The change in emphasis occurred c.1820 simultaneously in India, Europe, Britain and the United States. The engineers in India worked in the same antique Grecian manner as their colleagues in Europe and the former "western colonies".

★

In the early 19th century, the artist Robert Home was appointed Court Painter in Lucknow, and "school of Home" thrones, chairs and furniture designs flourished across northern India and survived, at least in Benares, until as late as 1880. Thrones however, normally maintained their traditional Indian shapes. Often octagonal, they were made as portable objects, to be used in camp as well as at court, the upper section lifting off the base.

The Victoria and Albert Museum possesses the famous Tipu's tiger, c.1795, the world's best known mechanical toy, made for Tipu Sahib, Sultan of Mysore, 1782–99. French artisans were employed in his court workshops, contributing to the renaissance of crafts Mysore enjoyed during his reign. Tiger motifs adorned most of Tipu's possessions. His cannon and mortars were cast in the form of tigers, and the covering over his tomb is the mock print of a tiger skin. The tiger head finial of rubies, diamonds and emeralds from his throne is at Powis Castle in Wales. It was given by Marquis Wellesley to Lord Clive's daughter-in-law, who had become a keen collector of material related to Tipu Sultan during her stay in India, searching out his relics immediately after the siege of Seringapatam in 1799. Indian princes had always understood the importance of the image and of "face", but Tipu Sultan was possibly the first Indian ruler to develop the use of a logo identifying his personal possessions as part of his cult of personality.

European influences had formed a small component of the imperial style of painting and decoration from the first half of the 17th century, but it was not until the 19th century that we find them affecting the manner and form, as distinct from the content, of the indigenous tradition. The Vizagapatam style of furniture and decoration in south India remained important until the end of the 18th century. Magnificent pieces, such as those commissioned by two generations of the Clive family and now in Powis Castle in Wales, were made there.

The Vizagapatam style fell out of favour in the 19th century when more middle-class Europeans began to come to India. This furniture was expensive, had to be commissioned to order and was also unable to stand up to the rigours of the constant moves necessitated by the frequent transfer of administrators and officials around the country. Important officials who had arrived in the 18th century lived in style and commissioned furniture to take back to Europe on their return. The early 19th century watershed saw the arrival of administrators without capital, who bought their furniture at auction when they arrived in India and sold it when they left. Interiors and furnishings became more bourgeois. Furniture began to adapt to the needs of the middle classes, often becoming portable and usually finished in a simpler manner with a black Indian shellac finish known as French polish. Indians in the large urban areas, and particularly in British India, now also began to use more furniture, usually following English styles. Department stores and furniture companies also developed in British India, in Calcutta, Bombay and Madras, to cater for the needs of more middle-class British administators. In the early part of the century designs were based on the English Regency style, while in the mid-century they followed the mid-Victorian Rococo Revival style.

Travelling furniture, pieces bound with brass corners and edges to prevent damage, was popular. The reclining armchair with swivelling or sliding footrest section and caned seat was also developed at this time. Beds had reeded, turned tapering legs, bulbous reeded supports (for mosquito curtains) and spindled railings.

In the early 19th century, Lord Wellesley's new, grand Government House was built in Calcutta and it is known later to have contained a large suite of furniture, made in India, in the French Regence Revival style, a style which had been popularised by Wellesley in the interiors of his London residence Apsley House – which he later sold to the Duke of Wellington. Some of this furniture is still in the Government House, Calcutta and some is in a private collection in London. The visit of Edward, Prince of Wales to India in 1876 necessitated the purchase of a suite of Louis XVI chairs from Paris for the Government House, Calcutta. Some of these are also now in the same London private collection.

By the late 19th century, furniture manufacturing and retailing shops existed in major cities such as Calcutta, where the firm of Lazarus and Tomlin produced Rococo Revival furniture to order. Calcutta's Whiteway and Laidlaw department store provided movable "campaign" style furniture for those out of town. These pieces could be easily dismantled and moved about from place to place. Furnishings were also available by mail-order from catalogues for those administrators in "up-country" bungalows. Their differing needs gave rise to a particular style of life, with gardens arranged with plants in pots, for easy transportation to the next posting, and readily transported furniture.

Design and architecture for the urban middle classes became much more important in the 19th century. Nineteenth-century households in India had much of the clutter of a Victorian home in England. For the Indian wealthy, there was lavish display including, for the aristocracy, even glass and crystal furniture in certain instances. Much of this was manufactured in Belgium and transported to India, and a suite is still extant at the palace in Udaipur. Particularly in Bombay and Calcutta, some sections of society became so prosperous that they commissioned and influenced design. In Bombay the Parsis were an immensely wealthy and influential community originally from Persia, as were the Marwaris, originally from Rajasthan. The Marwaris had made their fortunes in Calcutta, but retained homes in their ancestral districts of Mewar and Shekawati in Rajasthan, incorporating large traditional house complexes called *haveli*, often elaborately frescoed inside and out, with frescoes based on Indian and European themes.

British successes in the early part of the 19th century meant that territorial jurisdiction now extended into the first range of the Himalayas, at a height of about 7,000–8,000 feet. The government began to develop "hill stations" in these regions, with their alpine-type climate, as recuperation centres for British soldiers in India, and they later developed into summer resorts. The hill station bungalow developed as an alpine adaptation of the plains bungalow, similarly furnished with simple interiors. Later the development of the railway system meant that the whole machinery of government could be transferred from Calcutta, the capital, to Simla the summer capital, for eight months of the year. An enormous summer residence for the Viceroy, and others almost as large for important officials such as the governors of the states and the Chief of the Army Staff, were constructed there in timber and brick in the Elizabethan or Jacobean Revival style popular at the end of the 19th century. Suburban Surrey was recreated 8,000 feet up in the Himalayas, with interiors typical of the "English country house" of the end of the century.

Although the arrival of the railways had made the annual move to the hills easier, this peregrination had been an annual event from the 1830s when the annexation of these territories had taken place. The British had continued the Mughal tradition of moving through the country in tented encampments. Emily Eden wrote about her brother's period as Governor General in India in the 1830s; the retinue housed in his tented encampment numbered some 12,000 persons. The use of tented encampments continued to be important throughout the 19th century, culminating in the Coronation Durbar of 1911, when all the Indian Princes and King George and Queen Mary were housed in an enormous tented encampment at the site of what was to become New Delhi.

The impact of Indian design in Britain, which was particularly strong in the second half of the 19th century, was complex, creating new markets and in turn affecting design in India. But ultimately, and perhaps inevitably, increased demand led to a decline in standards.

Benefiting from Cornwallis's permanent land settlement of 1790, which increased the revenue of land-owners, the landed aristocracy, the rajas and the zamindars devoted their new prosperity to the cultivation of European tastes by furnishing their palaces in what they took to be the style of the colonial mansions erected for the East India Company's merchants and officials. Even Bengal's major goddess, Durga, was housed under a Regency style portico with Corinthian columns, such was the influence of European design. Hindu religious ceremonies increased in grandeur after the establishment of British rule and landowners lavished much larger sums on ceremony than before. The Hindu gentry and rural aristocracy derived their status and importance from conspicuous consumption and by religious philanthropy; they still do so today in certain areas.

By the 1870s people were fearing deterioration in quality, loss of artistic integrity and the destruction of traditional modes of production in the decorative arts in India. George Birdwood, Professor of Medical Science and founder of the Victoria and Albert Museum, Bombay, talked about this at the Paris Universal Exhibition in 1878: "Indian collections are now also ... [becoming] ... more overcrowded with mongrel articles, the result of the influences on Indian art of English society, missionary schools, schools of art, and international exhibitions and, above all, of the irresistible energy of the mechanical productiveness of Manchester and Birmingham, and Paris and Vienna". Birdwood had a romantic image of the Indian craftsman living in a democratic village community working with simple tools in his own home. His anxiety about the dangers of market exploitation and official encouragement of industrial development in India was identical to that of contemporary design critics and the leaders of the Arts and Crafts movement in England. India came to represent an ideal artisan society which had long disappeared in Europe. The importance of these arguments was not lost on the Nationalist leaders in India. A few decades later the same ideas were used effectively in the *swadeshi* (home industry) campaigns of 1905–10 and further elaborated by Mahatma Gandhi in the 1920s and 1930s.

Following their introduction in England, Schools of Art

were established in Madras, Bombay and Calcutta in the 1850s and in Lahore in 1875. The British debate about the purpose of Art Schools – whether as training grounds for artisans or institutions providing a generalized artistic education – had an added complexity in India. Their practical purpose was to provide a new generation with useful and employable skills in the industrial and ornamental arts – a vocational training for those in the expanding middle classes who were unable to undertake a literary or scientific education. During the 1870s and 1880s there was much debate on the state of Indian crafts. In Calcutta there were token attempts to support a few surviving traditional art industries, but there was also a new emphasis on training in the techniques of Western academic art.

Indian art schools were doomed from the start because of the conflicting ideological imperatives which had brought them into existence. Their failure to recruit artisans – who could afford neither the time nor the fees – encouraged students with a taste for European academic art, and they became the purview of the gentry. The Calcutta Art School, for example, was a haven for unemployed graduates. By the end of the 19th century, the Calcutta Art School had also become associated with the developing Nationalist movement. E.B. Havell, the Director from 1896 to 1906, an ardent critic of British policy on the arts, encouraged the study of India's own fine art traditions and supported the painter Abadindranath Tagore's development of a new "Indian style" of painting.

In Lahore, Lockwood Kipling (1837–1911) took charge of the new Mayo School of Craftsmen, helped to set up the influential *Journal of Indian Arts and Industry*, and worked with the American designer Lockwood de Forest to promote the export of Indian design. Kipling was the Municipal Architect of Bombay and Curator of the Lahore Museum from its inception in 1875 to 1893. He had trained as an artist in London and was closely associated with English art circles – his sister-in-law was married to Edward Burne-Jones. Kipling was instrumental in bringing English mid-Victorian sensibilities to India and, later, a knowledge of the Arts and Crafts movement. He realised the importance of craftsmanship and India's enormous design heritage, and almost single-handedly revived the craft of the stonemason in Bombay. He also designed and installed, with the help of Indian artisans, an Indian billiard room for the Duke of Connaught at Bagshot Park, Surrey, and a dining room for Queen Victoria at Osborne House on the Isle of Wight, as well as the Durbar room at Elvedon House in Suffolk for the Maharaja of the Punjab.

In the 19th century many of the Indian princes used their energies and revenues to build large new palaces in European styles, using British architects, such as Sir Swinton Jacob, among whose other works is the Art Museum in Jaipur. Udaipur and Mysore are examples of 19th-century palace complexes which show the influence of European taste, as do several of the Palaces of the Nizam in Hyderabad.

By the end of the century, Indian princes had also come to emulate the fashions and lifestyles of their British overlords. Factory-made fabrics from distant Europe displaced traditional textiles. Men's headwear and garments became more uniform. Some Indian rulers took to wearing western clothes. Under the British umbrella, myriad communities had moved to the new cities of Calcutta, Kanpur, Bombay and Madras. The ease of the journey to India, with the opening up of the Suez Canal, meant that a flood of Europeans travelled out to India to seek work, particularly Scottish and Irish nannies, raising generations of the aristocratic and the wealthy in India, burdening them with nicknames such as Baby and Bubbles and leaving them with a taste for Europe, including copies of French châteaux and Italian villas. The architecture the British left throughout the subcontinent is a testimony to their presence, but their cultural impact remained limited, and it is easy to overestimate the extent to which the mass of Indian art or society was influenced by the West before 1947. After the decline in arts and crafts in the late 19th century, a revival took place in the earlier part of the 20th century, helped in part by the artistic aspect of the Bengal Renaissance, and later by the political counterpart to this.

The Coronation Durbar of 1911 was the catalyst for the decision to build a seventh Delhi – New Delhi – moving the capital from Calcutta, which was felt to be too far from the centre of the country. Sir Edwin Lutyens, along with Sir Herbert Baker, was commissioned to design and develop the new capital, a project which occupied him until the 1930s. Lutyens had long been looking for a grand project where he could develop his ideas on classicism. The most important domestic building of the complex is the Viceroy's Lodge, now known as the Rashtrapati Bhavan, and the official residence of the President of the Republic. Lutyens studied many examples of Indian architecture and combined them successfully, synthesising the English Baroque Revival style of the early part of the century with elements from Hindu architecture. It was furnished in the Edwardian Country House style, mixing European antiques and decorations with caned *bergère* suites of furniture. Lutyens was closely involved with all the interior planning, even down to designing some of the chandeliers in the children's bedrooms himself.

"Lutyens Baroque" was the official British style of the 1920s and 1930s, but Art Deco was preferred by avant-garde collectors and Rajput princes, and unlike in Europe, the style did not suddenly end at the outbreak of World War II, but lingered on into the late 1940s and early 1950s. Its popularity was enhanced by the fact that it was perceived initially as a non-British style whose origins derived from non-European sources. This was an important consideration for independent rulers living in a society where the coloniser was omnipresent, even if not officially recognised as being so.

During the period following the end of World War I, many Indian princes became assiduous travellers to Europe – especially France where Art Deco originated – and purchased numerous items of furniture and objects in the Art Deco style to be shipped out to India. Several palaces were built in the Art Deco style and examples in both Jaipur and Jodhpur have Art Deco interiors, as well as some in the smaller states such as Orcha and Dungapur. Jodhpur has the Umald Bhavan palace, built between 1929 and 1940, which was the largest private residence in the world, with Art Deco furnishings, interiors and murals by the Polish artist Stephan Norblin. The Maharaja of Morvi also built a new palace in this style. Art Deco buildings were still being put up in Calcutta into the 1950s. Also exceptional is the Bauhaus palace of the Maharaja of Indore built in the 1930s by a German architect with Bauhaus / moderne interiors featuring furniture by Jacques-Emile Ruhlmann, Le Corbusier, Louis Sognot, Eileen Gray and others.

India: Durbar Hall, Viceroy's House, New Delhi, by Edwin Lutyens and Herbert Baker, 1931

Art Deco, "Lutyens Baroque", and much Victorian clutter, lingered on into the late 1940s and even into the early 1950s, in Calcutta. The Modern Movement was significant in India only after World War II. An attempt in the 1930s to introduce the Modern style into India by the architect Walter Burley Griffin proved abortive. But in the post-war period, French influences became important – Le Corbusier was invited to plan and build the new capital of the Punjab at Chandigarh from 1951 – as did Scandinavian design. Modernist furniture, copied by Indian carpenters, was derived from "Scandinavian modern" models , American design magazines and British "Festival of Britain" period furniture. These trends lingered on well into the 1970s.

One of the leading figures of the Bengal Renaissance, Rabindranath Tagore, the poet and Nobel Prize laureate, established a craft programme to increase interest in Indian design at Santiniketan, his country estate in Birbhum District in Bengal which he turned into a university. Within the university at Santiniketan, he established a Craft Department. Kala Bhavana was the College of Fine Arts and Silpa Bhavana the Hall of Industries or crafts. At the beginning a graphic art and craft workshop, Vichitra Studio, was set up at Kala Bhavana, where teachers and students learned and practised various decorative arts and crafts such as alpana, lacquer work, calico painting, batik work, bookbinding and illumination, also wood-engraving and mural decoration. As these so-called "craft" activities were always overshadowed by the art programme, they were eventually moved to Silpa Bhavana in Sriniketan, a sister campus related to rural development, education and organization.

Rabindranath Tagore at one time had a keen desire to build a craft-based educational system in Sriniketan, based on the "Sloyd" system in Sweden. Staff were sent to Sweden to study the system and in 1934 and 1935 two Swedish weavers came and taught at Santiniketan and Sriniketan. The 1933 catalogue mentions the products available: *dhurries*, carpets and curtains, for which they also took orders, as well as for upholstery. These designs and items were non-traditional, catering for the needs of the newly-educated upper- and middle-class consumers wanting indigenous, as opposed to foreign, manufactured items.

The Silpa Bhavana products were very influential in India in the 1930s and 1940s among the educated elite. Their Art Nouveau flavour managed to reconcile East with West, art with craft, and personal creativity with mass production. Decline and stagnation took hold in Silpa Bhavana in the late 1940s and early 1950s after Tagore's death. Tastes had changed, and by then the movement had outlived its context. It was overtaken by the concerted effort, in the 1950s, of the newly independent government to re-equip the traditional handicraft sector to meet new demand. Traditional units were more resourceful in making quality products and had greater technical range. The Indian public wanted simpler, less ornamental and more functional design.

In the late 1950s, the Government of India invited the American designers Charles and Ray Eames to recommend a programme of design training as an aid to small industries. Out of this grew the National Institute of Design, founded in Ahmedabad in 1961, designed to function as "an autonomous national institution for research, service and training in industrial design and visual communication".

In the late 1950s, the American architect Edward Durell Stone (1903–78) designed the new American embassy in Delhi (1954–58), where he combined American Modernism with elements from Mughal architecture, surrounding the building with pierced Mughal screens. By the 1970s, however, a much more confident generation of architects and designers had grown up in India who had never been confined within the strait-jacket of colonialism. Notable among them are Charles Correa, architect of the Cidade de Goa in Goa, and Laurie Baker, the British-born Trivandrum-based architect. Both Correa and Baker have attempted to tackle the perennial Indian problem of finding a solution to the widespread lack of affordable middle-class housing.

Indian architects and sculptors, such as Satish Gujral, have also designed embassies in Delhi, and hotel design has become important with the growth of tourism. Significant among the new hotel interiors are the redecoration of the new wing of the Taj in Bombay, by the Hong Kong-based designer Dale Keller (who has since built the new palace for the Sultan of Brunei), and the interiors of the Intercontinental Hotel in New Delhi 1951–58, by Durga Bajpai and Piloo Mody.

Whereas in Europe and America one of the reactions to Modernism had been the Postmodern classically influenced style, the new generation of architects and designers in India has returned to its ethnic roots; low divans, stools and other types of furniture referring to Indian history now fill New Delhi colonial bungalows and exist cheek-by-jowl in Bombay high-rise apartments with shiny chrome and glass furniture.

The large amounts of money pouring back into India from Indians working overseas has also influenced styles in architecture and design as has the upsurge in numbers of the vast new urban middle class, estimated at some 150–200 million people, whose buying power is beginning to count. Several new or recently founded design magazines in Delhi and Bombay disseminate the work of leading architects and designers and shape the taste of this newly prosperous class. However, as far as the general level of taste is concerned, the stage of development in design resembles the situation which existed in western Europe after World War II and which continued well into the 1950s, when many things were in short supply and most people made do with whatever was available.

GERALDINE SMITH-PARR

Further Reading

Amery, Colin and others, *Lutyens: The Work of the English Architect Sir Edwin Lutyens* (exhib. cat.), London: Arts Council of Great Britain, 1981

Archer, Mildred, *India Observed: India as Viewed by British Artists, 1760–1860* (exhib. cat.: Victoria and Albert Museum, London), London: Trefoil, 1982

Architecture in India, Paris: Electa Moniteur / France, 1985

Baroda, Maharaja of, *The Palaces of India*, London: Collins, and New York: Vendome, 1980

Bayly, C.A. (editor), *The Raj: India and the British, 1600–1947* (exhib. cat.), London: National Portrait Gallery, 1990

Chaudhuri, Sukanta (editor), *Calcutta: The Living City*, 2 vols., Calcutta and New York: Oxford University Press, 1990

Cooper, Ilay, *The Painted Towns of Shekhawati*, Ahmedabad: Mapin, and Middletown, NJ: Grantha, 1994

Fermor-Hesketh, Robert (editor), *Architecture of the British Empire*, London: Weidenfeld and Nicolson, and New York: Vendome, 1986
Head, Raymond, *The Indian Style*, London: Allen and Unwin, and Chicago: University of Chicago Press, 1986
Huyler, Stephen P., *Village India*, New York: Abrams, 1985
The Indian Heritage: Court Life and Arts under Mughal Rule, London: Victoria and Albert Museum, 1982
Irving, Robert Grant, *Indian Summer: Lutyens, Baker, and Imperial Delhi*, New Haven and London: Yale University Press, 1981
Jayakar, Pupul (foreword), *Festival of India in the United States*, New York: Abrams, 1985
Losty, J.P., *Calcutta, City of Palaces: A Survey of the City in the Days of the East India Company, 1690–1858*, London: British Library / Arnold, 1990
Lutyens, Mary, *Edwin Lutyens*, revised edition London: Black Swan, 1991
Metcalf, Thomas R., *An Imperial Vision: Indian Architecture and Britain's Raj*, Berkeley: University of California Press, 1989
Michell, George (editor), *Architecture of the Islamic World: Its History and Social Meaning*, London: Thames and Hudson, and New York: Morrow, 1978
Michell, George, *The Royal Palaces of India*, London: Thames and Hudson, 1994
Morris, Jan, *Stones of Empire: The Buildings of the Raj*, Oxford and New York: Oxford University Press, 1983
Murphy, Veronica, *Origins of the Mughal Flowering Plant Motif*, London, 1990
Nilsson, Sten, *European Architecture in India, 1750–1850*, London: Faber, 1968; New York: Taplinger, 1969
Patnaik, Naveen, *A Second Paradise: Indian Courtly Life, 1590–1947*, New York: Doubleday, 1985
Pott, Janet, *Old Bungalows in Bangalore, South India*, London: Pott, 1977
Punja, Shobita, *Museums of India*, Hong Kong: Odyssey Guides, 1991
Quraeshi, Samina, *Lahore: The City Within*, Singapore: Concept Media, 1988
Skelton, Robert, *Rajasthani Temple Hangings of the Krishna Cult from the Collection of Karl Mann*, New York: American Federation of Arts, 1973
Slesin, Suzanne and Stafford Cliff, *Indian Style*, London: Thames and Hudson, and New York: Potter, 1990
Smith-Parr, Geraldine, *Palladianism in India*, M.A. thesis, London: Courtauld Institute of Art, 1984
Smith-Parr, Geraldine, articles on Architecture in India during the Colonial Period; Decorative Arts in India during the Colonial Period; and Furniture in India during the Colonial Period, in Jane Turner (editor), *The Dictionary of Art*, London and New York: Grove, 1996
Swallow, Deborah and John Guy (editors), *Arts of India, 1550–1900*, London: Victoria and Albert Museum, 1990
Tadgell, Christopher, *The History of Architecture in India: From the Dawn of Civilization to the End of the Raj*, London: Architecture Design and Technology Press, 1990
Tillotson, G.H.R., *The Rajput Palaces: The Development of an Architectural Style, 1450–1750*, New Haven and London: Yale University Press, 1987
Tillotson, G.H.R., *The Tradition of Indian Architecture: Continuity, Controversy, and Change since 1850*, New Haven and London: Yale University Press, 1989
Tillotson, G.H.R., *Mughal India*, London: Viking, and San Francisco: Chronicle Books, 1990
Vance, Mary A., *Architecture in India* (bibliography), Monticello, IL: Vance, 1987
Wacziarg, Francis and Aman Nath, *Rajasthan: The Painted Walls of Shekhavati*, London: Croom Helm, 1982

Inglenooks

The inglenook is an ubiquitous feature of the late Victorian and Edwardian interior. Serving both decorative and practical functions, these built-in fireside seating areas had antecedents in the interiors of the 16th and 17th centuries. Inglenooks appear in drawing rooms, dining rooms and halls in both Britain and the United States. They are a feature of Richard Norman Shaw's "Old English" and "Queen Anne" styles, the American Shingle Style and were particularly important within the context of the Arts and Crafts movement on both sides of the Atlantic.

Although the use of seat furniture immediately adjacent to the fire had a precedent in the fireside positioning of benches and settles in the great halls of manor houses of the 16th and 17th centuries, it was in fact with the Arts and Crafts movement that the inglenook lost its purely practical aspect and became an integral part of contemporary interior schemes. The incorporation of the inglenook into late Victorian and Edwardian plans for domestic housing came about for both logistical and emotional reasons. Often central to the plan of the Arts and Crafts house, the inglenook can also be viewed as the psychological heart of the home. Equally, it provides a microcosmic view of many of the connotations and associations of the movement's philosophy for interior decorative schemes.

The Arts and Crafts movement had gathered pace in England in the 1880s and had been given its impetus by a number of designers, architects and theorists key among whom were William Morris and John Ruskin. The movement's practitioners sought to provide an alternative to the harshness of life in 19th-century Britain. A central tenet of the Arts and Crafts designer's creed was to ameliorate ordinary people's lives, bringing greater harmony into their living and working conditions through an improvement both of the work process itself and of its products. Indicting the machine age as being responsible for both the loss of personal freedom and poor standards of design, Arts and Crafts advocates paradoxically saw the way forward in a return to the practice of craftsmanship along the lines of the medieval guild system. In this way, the close identification of a way of life with the creation of objects and buildings and their interiors meant that the movement became very largely focused on the domestic. It is against this background that the key significance of the inglenook to contemporary schemes should be viewed.

Perhaps one of the finest examples of an Arts and Crafts inglenook is the one in the Great Parlour at Wightwick Manor near Wolverhampton (1897). Here the fireplace and surround dominate one wall, and form a typical alcove with built-in seating. As happens elsewhere, the Wightwick parlour inglenook provides a secluded seating area and makes a neat enclave in an otherwise vast gallery.

Of all the Arts and Crafts architects to incorporate inglenooks in their schemes, it was H.M. Baillie Scott who really championed their use. Baillie Scott advocated using plain brickwork hearths, simple fire-baskets and oak settles in the inglenook's alcove. His work reflected the desire to build according to a simplified but idealised version of the traditional country manorhouse. His schemes, in which the fireplace is usually of central importance illustrated the cherished

Inglenook in a house in Rugby, designed by Barry Parker; photograph c.1904

belief that not only the comfort but the aesthetic charm of a room depended on the situation and appearance of the fireside area.

In addition to its dominance in the interior of the typical Arts and Crafts scheme, the inglenook fireplace was often of indirect importance to the exterior of such houses. Richard Norman Shaw's "Old English" style typified by Cragside, built during the 1880s near Newcastle, combines a fusion of styles and uses very imposing Tudor chimney stacks to give the house something of a quaint manorial feel. Here it seems that the exaggerated height of the chimneys signifies the most important element of the rooms indoors.

In Britain, the Queen Anne and in the United States, the Shingle styles also referred to an architectural past and reflected it in the use of large open fireplaces in drawing rooms, dining rooms and libraries. In such schemes, wooden chimneypieces with shelves displaying plates and pottery were built into large recesses which were made to accommodate oak benches or settles on either side of the fire.

The incorporation of discrete seating areas provided by inglenooks in interiors in both Britain and the United States, paradoxically goes hand in hand with one of the innovative aspects of late 19th- and early 20th-century interiors: the use of open-plan design. Within interiors of this kind, the inglenook fits perfectly as it allows for privacy, and the much sought after Arts and Crafts quality – cosiness – without compromising the fluidity of the large open room. The British architects Parker and Unwin even went as far as commenting that, "if your big room is to be comfortable, it must have recesses" (Kaplan, 1989).

The inglenook's central status in the Arts and Crafts interior reveals the extent to which the twin notions of hearth and home have remained as deeply entrenched emotional issues within attitudes towards the domestic environment and its culture. Above all, its popularity as an integral part of late 19th- and early 20th-century interior schemes points to the importance of addressing questions of symbolism and meaning when evaluating any aspect of design relating closely to personal life.

HARRIET DOVER

See also Arts and Crafts Movement; Scott

Further Reading

Anscombe, Isabelle and Charlotte Gere, *Arts and Crafts in Britain and America*, London: Academy, 1978

Gere, Charlotte, *Nineteenth-Century Decoration: The Art of the Interior*, London: Weidenfeld and Nicolson, and New York: Abrams, 1989

Girouard, Mark, *Sweetness and Light: The Queen Anne Movement, 1860–1900*, Oxford: Clarendon Press, 1977; New Haven: Yale University Press, 1984

Girouard, Mark, *The Victorian Country House*, revised edition New Haven and London: Yale University Press, 1979
Harper, Maureen, "The Revival of the Settle and Inglenook" in *Decorative Art Society Journal*, 12, 1988
Kaplan, Wendy (editor), *The Encyclopedia of Arts and Crafts: The International Arts Movement, 1850–1920*, New York: Dutton, and London: Headline, 1989
Kaufmann, Edgar, "Precedent and Progress in the Work of Frank Lloyd Wright" in *Journal of the Society of Architectural Historians*, XXXIX, May 1980, pp.145–49
Long, Helen C., *The Edwardian House: The Middle-Class Home in Britain, 1880–1914*, Manchester: Manchester University Press, 1993
Saint, Andrew, *Richard Norman Shaw*, New Haven: Yale University Press, 1976
Scully, Vincent J., Jr., *The Shingle Style and the Stick Style: Architectural Theory and Design from Richardson to the Origins of Wright*, revised edition New Haven: Yale University Press, 1971

Intarsia

The term intarsia causes some confusion as it is derived from the Italian word which refers to all kinds of inlay (including marquetry). It is accepted that intarsia is a particular form of decoration for furniture and architectural panels that is distinct from other types of wood decoration, including inlay, certosina and marquetry. It is, in fact, an inlay process which builds up a pictorial design by setting timber pieces 3mm to 6mm thick into recesses cut into a solid ground. The process was intended to provide colour by using stained or shaded timbers set against a dark background.

Generally, intarsia incorporates *trompe-l'oeil* perspective designs, often using humanistic motifs such as books, globes, and other trappings of Renaissance learning. Motifs also included architectural perspectives of imaginary buildings, both complete and in ruins, and it was these that could be found in both furniture and architectural woodwork.

Intarsia appears to have originated in Siena in the 14th century and was initially used for the decoration of religious buildings. The first recorded use was in the choir stalls of Orvieto Cathedral. This was the work of Giovanni Ammannati who died c.1340. Later examples can be found in the chapel of the Palazzo Publico Siena executed by Domenico di Niccolo de Cori (1415–28). The process matured in Florence and was at one time considered equal to painting. Giorgio Vasari in his *Lives of the Artists* gives details of artists who worked in the medium and credits Francesco di Giovanni as the originator of the process. He also notes that Brunelleschi taught perspective to artists by using intarsia examples.

The religious use of intarsia continued and both the choir stalls of Siena Cathedral (1503) and the doors of Raphael's Stanze in the Vatican (1514–21) are examples of this continuing church patronage. Both were executed by Fra Giovanni da Verona of whose work Vasari comments: "Fra Giovanni executed not only the surrounding panelling, but also some very fine doors and chairs, with perspective studies, which won him generous praise and rewards from the Pope". Although this work was planned to complement Raphael's paintings, designs might be supplied by contemporary painters. It is known that Piero della Francesca provided designs for the intarsia work in the Sacristy of Modena Cathedral, while Lorenzo Lotto designed the intarsia screen for the church of Sta. Maria Maggiore at Bergamo.

Apart from the religious applications of intarsia it was also used in secular decoration, for cabinets and *cassoni*, but also for decorating interior wall panelling. Perhaps the most famous use in a domestic room was the decoration of the Studiolo of Federigo da Montrefelto, in the Ducal Palace at Urbino. Constructed c.1470 and still *in situ*, the small room is enlivened by amazingly skilled intarsia decoration. The *trompe-l'oeil* effect is achieved by creating the illusion of half-open cupboards with their contents tantalizingly on display, shelves with lifelike objects and architectural detail which is featured all round the room. A similar example by Francesco di Giorgio for the Palazzo Gubbio is now located in the Metropolitan Museum of Art in New York.

In Italy, by the mid-16th century intarsia was moving out of high fashion and gradually became a craft rather than the high art it had once been. Work in hard-stones replaced the supremacy of wood.

The strong influence of Italy meant that intarsia became attractive to South German cabinet-makers. The high quality intarsia work from Augsburg and Nuremberg was evidence of their expertise in the field. The famous Wrangelschrank made in Augsburg during 1566 is a fine example of the cabinet-maker's skill. Unlike much of the Italian work preceding it, the designs were Mannerist, incorporating strapwork, animals, and birds, within an imaginary architectural ruin. Intarsia can often be found on the back and top as well as the front and sides of a cabinet, clearly an indication of prestige.

More typical is the example of the cabinet dated 1561, made by the Master HS, which demonstrates a close connection with the Italian tradition. Three central panels are decorated with an inlaid design, based upon architectural perspective. Renaissance designs were being produced in Germany for use by craftsmen, such as those by Peter Flötner. The Augsburg intarsia workers often used the printed designs of the type produced by Lorenz Stör, who published woodcut designs in his *Geometria et Perspectiva* in 1567.

As in Italy, intarsia was also occasionally used for panelling. An example is the panelled room from the Schloss Haldenstein, in Switzerland, which is now in the Kunstgewerbe Museum in Berlin. This has a deep frieze ornamented with inlaid architectural scenes.

From Germany the influence of intarsia decoration spread further north. Towards the end of the 16th century, parts of the Low Countries had developed the skills to use intarsia work, particularly Zeeland and Antwerp, both using the imaginary architectural scene to decorate the fronts of cupboards and chests. In England, the well-known Nonsuch chests were made up from a form of intarsia, and often incorporated architectural scenes in their front panels. With the development of the marquetry process, which was much more adaptable, intarsia became redundant.

Intarsia should not be confused with the Islamic-influenced process of certosina. This is a 15th-century Italian inlay process which uses wood, metal, bone, and shell, cut into small polygons and arranged geometrically on a surface.

CLIVE D. EDWARDS

Intarsia: Studiolo of Federico da Montefeltro, Palazzo Ducale, Urbino, c.1470

See also Pietre Dure

Further Reading

A detailed and well-illustrated survey of the history and techniques of intarsia in Europe appears in Flade 1986; this book also includes a lengthy bibliography of primary and secondary sources.

Beblo, Hans, *Die Intarsia und ihre Techniken*, Augsburg, 1966

Bruggemann, Erich, *Kunst und Technik der Intarsien*, Munich: Callwey, 1988

Fiorentino, Alessandro, *L'Arte della Tarsia a Sorrento, Naples*, 1982

Flade, Helmut, *Intarsia: Europäische Einlegekunst aus sechs Jahrhunderten*, Munich: Beck, 1986

Grentz, Georg, *Intarsien-Arbeiten*, Heidelberg, 1968

Jackson, F. Hamilton, *Intarsia and Marquetry*, London: Sands, and New York: Scribner, 1903

Kossatz, Gert, *Die Kunst der Intarsia*, Dresden: Verlag der Kunst, 1954

Phillips, John Goldsmith, "The Private Study of Federigo da Montefeltro: A Masterpiece of Fifteenth Century Trompe-l'Oeil" in *Bulletin of the Metropolitan Museum of Art*, XXXVI, January 1941, pp.3–23

Smith, H. Clifford, *The Inlaid Room from Sizergh Castle* (The Panelled Rooms 4), 2nd edition London: Victoria and Albert Museum, 1925

Thornton, M.J., "Tarsie: Design and Designers" in *Journal of the Warburg and Courtauld Institutes*, XXXVI, 1973, pp.377–82

Tormey, A. and J. Farr Tormey, "Renaissance Intarsia: The Art of Geometry" in *Scientific American*, CCXLVII, 1982, pp.116–22

Interior Design, history and development

Before the 20th century the profession of "interior decorator" or "interior designer" did not exist. Interiors would exceptionally be designed by architects but more usually by tradesmen such as the cabinet-maker, upholsterer or retailer. Key examples include Waring and Gillow or Lenygon and Morant, who specialised in buying and selling antiques, rather than interior design specifically. It was during the early years of the 20th century that the profession of interior decorator emerged, to be superseded by that of interior designer in the post-war era.

The role of interior decorator has traditionally been a feminine one, of adviser and confidante working from natural instinct rather than professional training. Before World War I

Interior Design: the London drawing room of Mrs. David Bruce, decorated by John Fowler

interior decoration was established as an acceptable way for women to earn a living. The decorator was responsible for the selection of suitable floor- and wall-coverings, furniture, furnishings, lighting and overall colour-scheme for pre-existing rooms. The decorator would not undertake structural alterations which were the responsibility of an architect. Interior decoration has never shared the status of architecture or interior design, being regarded as a lowly branch of fashion. This is due to the ephemeral nature of much of the work and the fact that the profession was dominated by women in its early days.

During the 19th century decorating the home was regarded as an acceptable past-time for the middle-class married woman, and women played a major part in the Arts and Crafts movement. The translation of this traditional role into a profession began in America, where women were less restricted by social convention. Candace Wheeler, founder of the Society of Decorative Art of New York City and of Associated Artists, encouraged women to enter the world of interior decoration in her article "Interior Decoration as a Profession for Women" in the Christian magazine, *The Outlook* in 1895. Interior decoration achieved greater status in 1897 when novelist Edith Wharton and architect Ogden Codman published *The Decoration of Houses*, which established a standard criteria for judging "good taste". Such good taste consisted of any French, English or Italian architecture from the Renaissance to the 18th century, with a particular emphasis on the latter. Codman and Wharton also worked as interior decorators in New York, emphasising the qualities of harmony and good proportion in their work. This inspired Elsie de Wolfe, another pioneer of interior decoration in America. She practised in New York from 1897 onwards, decorating the Colony Club and Henry Clay Frick's private apartments on Fifth Avenue. She travelled to Europe frequently to obtain antiques for her clients, mingled socially with them and adhered to Codman and Wharton's dictates about classical proportion and the desirability of 18th-century French furniture.

During the inter-war years a group of professional interior decorators emerged in America and Britain to enjoy great success. Among them were Nancy McClelland, Eleanor Brown (McMillen) and Ruby Ross Wood in America and Betty Joel in Britain. Joel used mainly Art Deco and Moderne furniture and effects in her commercial interiors. The two women who were to contribute most towards the development of interior decoration as a profession in Britain, Syrie Maugham and Lady Sybil Colefax, worked largely on commissions for the decoration of private houses. After her marriage to the novelist Somerset Maugham failed, Syrie Maugham trained in the antique department at Fortnum and Mason's before establishing her own business in the late 1920s. Her most distinctive and influential interior was the "All White" room she created for her London home in c.1929–30. Actually decorated in tones of cream and beige, the room featured a large Moderne mirror screen, a Marion Dorn abstract rug and off-white, Louis XV chairs. In contrast, the work of her rival Lady Sybil Colefax was inspired by the English Country House look. Heavy chintzes and solid furniture were a feature of the Colefax interior from 1933 onwards. In 1938 she formed a business partnership with John Fowler, an expert in 18th-century decoration and influential figure in the world of authentic, period decor. Fowler was chief adviser for the National Trust's restoration of Syon House, Middlesex and Wilton House, Wiltshire during the post-war years. Schemes such as these were featured in British and foreign periodicals throughout Fowler's long career, contributing to the popularity of the English country house look from the 1930s onwards. Interior decoration therefore acquired the reputation for accurately restoring or recreating past styles.

While past styles provided an important source of inspiration for many interior decorators, that of Surrealism also played an important role in the 1930s. For example, France's leading interior decorator Jean-Michel Frank designed the Cinema Ballroom for Baron Roland de l'Epée using a startling colour scheme. The carpet was bright red and each of the four walls had a separate colour – pink, pale blue, sea-green and yellow. The theatre-boxes were draped with purple velvet framing the ultimate Surrealist seating, Salvador Dalí's *Mae West Lips* sofa of c.1936. The sofa was based on his painting, *Mae West* (1934). British versions were commissioned by the foremost collector of Surrealist art, Edward James, for Monkton House near Chichester, and an example is housed in Brighton Museum. In America interior decorators such as Dorothy Draper and Rose Cumming were also influenced by Surrealism.

By the 1930s the profession of interior decoration was well established in America, with the American Institute of Interior Decorators (now the American Society of Interior Designers) founded in 1931 and trade journals launched. *Home Furnishing* was established in 1929 and *The Decorators' Digest* in 1932. More men now worked as interior decorators, some of whom had received some formal training and adopted a more commercial approach. Terence Harold Robsjohn-Gibbings had been trained as an architect and was brought to America by Charles Duveen, the antique dealer and brother of the art dealer Joseph Duveen. Robsjohn-Gibbings set up in practice on Madison Avenue, New York City in 1936 and undertook commissions for California jeweller Paul Flato in a mixture of Scandinavian modern and period styles. The rise in status of the interior decorator was interrupted by World War II, and the subsequent shortages of materials. By the 1950s the emergence of interior design as professional practice challenged the hegemony of interior decoration. Key interior decorators to emerge during the post-war years include David Hicks in Britain and Albert Hadley in America. Hadley was an admirer of the work of Eleanor Brown and joined McMillen Inc. in 1956. In 1962 Hadley joined Mrs. Henry Parish II as a partner, and the firm of Parish-Hadley undertook many commissions to restore or recreate period interiors throughout the 1960s and 1970s.

While post-war interior decorators catered for the wealthy client in the creation of luxurious, domestic surroundings frequently with a period flavour, a new breed of architects undertook interior designer commissions for commercial and modern interiors. For the first time in the history of design, America was now at the forefront in terms of stylistic leadership. While Modernism had originated in Europe during the 1920s and 1930s, the migration of émigrés to the US during the war and the official American encouragement of Modernism established their cultural leadership. Much interior design work executed during the 1950s and 1960s in America was the work of architects. For example, the architectural practice of Skidmore, Owings and Merrill (SOM) designed one of the most important post-war office buildings – Lever House, New York in 1950-52 complete with open-plan offices. SOM became established as world leaders of the contract interior market, that is, interiors designed for commercial as opposed to domestic purposes. Offices designed by SOM for the Chase Manhattan Bank, Pepsi Cola and the Connecticut General Life Insurance Company under the direction of Davis Allen were classically modern in style. In terms of domestic interiors, architect-designer Alexander Girard designed the Rieveschel house in Grosse Pointe, Michigan in 1952 with Corbusian ramps and built-in furniture to create a fluid interior space. Much use was made of natural light while fur rugs and plants served to blur the distinction between interior and exterior as a key modern architect, Philip Johnson, had done with his Glass House in New Canaan, designed in 1949.

The American modern style had an enormous influence throughout Europe by means of film, television and magazines as did the concept of the architect-designed interior. For example, in London the Architects Co-Partnership designed a house in 1956 bearing all the hallmarks of the modern style: built-in furniture and storage, a scattering of free-standing lamps and the integration of indoors and out with a sliding glass door leading to a balcony. This style was established by architects trained in the International Style, the classical Modernism of the 1930s. The interior designer was yet to emerge, even though other design areas were receiving recognition, for example, commercial artists were now graphic designers. The transformation of interior decoration into interior design was marked with the changing titles of societies and journals. For example, the Incorporated Institute of British Decorators, founded in 1899 added "and Interior Designers" to its title in 1953 and were eventually to drop "Decorator" altogether in 1976 to become the British Institute of Interior Design. During 1987 it merged with the Chartered Society of Designers. Across the Atlantic the American Institute of Interior Decorators was founded in 1931 and transmuted into the American Society for Interior Designers during the 1970s. Journals followed a similar trend with the American periodical *Interior Design and Decoration*, founded in 1937, becoming simply *Interior Design* during the 1950s. In 1940 *The Interior Decorator* became *Interiors*. A further indication of the emergence of interior design as a profession can be found in the extent of training provided. In Britain by 1968 five art colleges ran diploma courses in interior design and the Royal College of Art had created a department of Interior Design. In America the Fashion Institute of Technology, New York introduced a course for interior designers in 1951. By the 1970s most American colleges offered courses in interior design.

In terms of professional practice in Britain, interior design played an important part in the 1980s retail boom. Fitch and Co. were responsible for the design of the interiors of Top Shop and Top Man at Oxford Circus, London during the 1970s and Midland banks and Debenhams during the 1980s. Fitch were important in terms of the development of interior design as they were specialists in this field, rather than architects who also designed interiors. In 1985 British design turnover was over one billion pounds, with interior design contributing 35 per cent of the business. Interior design had become an important part of the corporate identity of any company, whether it be a retail chain or a building society. The questioning of international modern architecture during the same era also put more emphasis on interior design. With the impact of Postmodern design from the mid-1970s onwards and the more recent experiments of Deconstructivism, interior design formed an exciting showcase for such developments. For example, the work of British designer Nigel Coates exemplifies the verve of recent interior design. His Metropole restaurant in Tokyo of 1986 combined elements of the London gentlemen's club, classical columns and *trompe-l'oeil* paintings to create an exhilarating interior. Interior design is now a well-established profession, enjoying a distinct identity from architecture in the commercial sector.

ANNE MASSEY

See also Architect; Upholsterer

Further Reading

There is no extended account of the evolution of the interior design profession but useful overviews concentrating on the emergence of the decorator appear in Cornforth and Fowler 1978, Calloway 1988 and Massey 1990. For a feminist perspective highlighting the role of women decorators see Anscombe 1984 and McNeil 1994.

Anscombe, Isabelle, *A Woman's Touch: Women in Design from 1860 to the Present Day*, London: Virago, and New York: Viking, 1984

Calloway, Stephen, *Twentieth-Century Decoration: The Domestic Interior from 1900 to the Present Day*, London: Weidenfeld and Nicolson, and New York: Rizzoli, 1988

Cornforth, John and John Fowler, "The Concept of the Decorator" in their *English Decoration in the 18th Century*, London: Barrie and Jenkins, and Princeton, NJ: Pyne, 1974; 2nd edition, Barrie and Jenkins, 1978

Cornforth, John, *The Inspiration of the Past: Country House Taste in the Twentieth Century*, London: Viking-Country Life, 1985

Gardner, Carl and Julie Sheppard, *Consuming Passion: The Rise of Retail Culture*, London: Unwin Hyman, 1989

Garrett, Stephen, "Interior Design: An Enquiry into Current Training, Prospects and Practices" in *Design*, August 1959

McNeil, Peter, "Designing Women: Gender, Sexuality and the Interior Decorator c.1890–1940" in *Art History*, 17, December 1994, pp.631–57

Massey, Anne, *Interior Design of the 20th Century*, London and New York: Thames and Hudson, 1990

Wharton, Edith and Ogden Codman, Jr., *The Decoration of Houses*, 1897; reprinted New York: Arno, 1975

Ireland

Interior design in Ireland may be summed up in the overall relaxed informality of the arrangement of rooms and a love of excess of ornamentation, particularly in plasterwork during the 18th century. If there is such a thing as an Irish style it is essentially a country house one, and it is in the rural parts of Ireland that survivals of the unique characteristics of interior design may be found both in the vernacular interiors of the country cottage or farmhouse and in the great country houses.

As a result of its unsettled history – marked out by rebellion, civil war, famine and more recently, the destruction caused by greater affluence – few domestic interiors in Ireland have survived intact with their original decorative schemes and contents or with the accumulation of objects and styles from succeeding generations. The number of houses of any significance that have descended in the same family with their contents intact may be counted on the fingers of two hands. The surviving interiors date from after 1700 and are generally to be found in buildings of the 18th century. The period of peace that followed the Battle of the Boyne in 1690 brought about a spate of house building after the destruction that marred the previous centuries and the relative prosperity of the 18th century allowed for more lavish decoration to be undertaken. The professional training of designers and craftsmen in drawing at the Dublin Society's School, established in 1746, contributed to the improvement in standards of design and decoration.

Specifically regional elements are found in the vernacular country cottage and farmhouse interiors. The rudimentary cabins and cottages constructed along traditional lines form a continuous history from earliest times well into the 20th century. The interiors were sparsely furnished, partly due to poverty but also because since the 16th century there has been a shortage of native timber. Locally available alternatives were used in the construction of cabins, such as turf (peat), clay or wattle and daub with roofs thatched in straw, reeds or flax. The interiors of these long, low houses, usually one room deep, were whitewashed and the floors were earthen or of a mixture of pebbles and flagstones. The hearth was the functional centre of the house around which the seating was arranged often with stone hob seats and built-in benches. The most inventive aspect of these interiors was the way the furniture formed an integral part of the construction of the interior: two pieces of furniture such as a cupboard and dresser acted as a room divider or were literally built-in as part of a partition wall. A door could be placed in between to create a separate room. This room was usually a bedroom but in the 19th century modest farmhouses were extended to include a parlour in imitation of the houses of the gentry. Another common feature was the bed alcove situated close to the hearth and curtained off.

The interiors of many cottages were painted in dark brown, green, ox blood or black halfway up the wall and whitewashed above. The larger pieces of furniture, dressers and settles, were always painted, stained or grained and often painted in contrasting bright colours.

The most important surviving interiors from before 1600 are at Malahide Castle, Co. Dublin, which contains a 15th-century medieval great hall in its original form which continued to be used as a dining room. Although re-roofed and partly

Ireland: wooden staircase from Eyrecourt Castle, Co. Galway, c.1660

altered in the 19th century, the dimensions of the hall, the vaulted undercroft and carved corbel heads are original. In the medieval core of the castle is the Oak Room with walls covered in carved and stained oak paneling with strapwork decoration, scenes from the Old Testament, and a Flemish carving of the Coronation of the Virgin. Carrick-on-Suir Castle, Co. Tipperary built c.1568 contains a brightly lit long gallery on the *piano nobile*. The plasterwork ceiling is decorated with geometrical strapwork and the frieze contains an iconographic scheme that demonstrates the loyalty of the 10th Earl of Ormonde to Queen Elizabeth I. The portrait of Elizabeth is placed in a roundel between fluted pilasters and is flanked by personifications of Equity and Law that are set in niches on either side. The gallery is dominated by a limestone chimneypiece that breaks the frieze and has an elaborately carved overmantel that displays the Ormonde arms. Originally the walls were covered in tapestries that may have been woven in Kilkenny where the 8th Earl of Ormonde established a manufactory employing Flemish weavers.

The construction of Portumna Castle, Co. Galway, now a ruin, in 1618 marks the arrival in Ireland of more fully-fledged Italian Renaissance decoration. The gateway is in the form of a classical triumphal arch and the doorcase is decorated with strapwork and obelisks. However, these advances were interrupted by the political upheavals of the 17th century. The most significant event took place in 1662 when the Duke of Ormonde was made Viceroy; his patronage ensured that the classical style was established in the great public building schemes he undertook, but similar developments in domestic architecture would have to wait.

After 1700 house building took on a new importance in Ireland. The strength of Dutch influence, after the triumph of William of Orange in 1690, may be seen in both urban and country houses. Sash windows were introduced at this time and high-pitched gable-roofed houses with wainscoting and corner chimneypieces decorated with blue and white Delft tiles were commonplace in Dublin. Only a few of these interiors survive with such early chimneypieces and paneling; the best preserved example is 48 Montpelier Hill.

The most important interiors of the early 18th century are at Beaulieu, Co. Louth, which combines a mixture of medieval, Dutch and English classical influences as well as rare painted ceilings. The great central two-storey hall is a descendant of the medieval hall. This contains a large chimneypiece with overmantel incorporating a topographical view of Drogheda. The triumphal arch theme is suggested by the arched central doorway which is flanked by wooden Corinthian pilasters and decorated with carved timber trophies, musical instruments and coats of arms. The drawing room, dining room and study are wainscoted throughout with bolection-moulded paneling. The drawing room ceiling is compartmented with garlands of flowers and leaves framing an oval central panel that contains a *trompe-l'oeil* view of a Baroque colonnade with urns in niches and a cloudy sky with flying putti in the manner of Antonio Verrio (1639–1707).

Dutch influence was quickly supplanted and the building of Castletown, Co. Kildare, which began in 1722, represents a definitive shift to Italianate taste. Castletown remains the largest house in Ireland, its interior design and decoration took up most of the 18th century and any discussion of taste or interior decoration in Ireland is dominated by its overwhelming influence. The architectural shell of the house was designed along palazzo lines by the Italian Alessandro Galilei (1691–1737) for William Conolly (1662–1729), the Speaker of the Irish House of Commons. Conolly wanted Castletown to show off his wealth and status but also to be a patriotic expression of national pride. Bishop Berkeley (1685–1753) was influential in the design and planning of the interiors and he may have suggested the inclusion of the long gallery. In a letter to Berkeley, Sir John Perceval (d.1748) refers to the design and decoration of Castletown: "... recommend to him the making use of all the marbles he can get of the production of Ireland for his chimneys, for since this house will be the finest Ireland ever saw, and by your description fit for a Prince ... I would examine the several woods there for inlaying my floors, and wainscot with our own oak, and walnut; my stone stairs should be of black palmers stone, and my buffet adorned with the choicest shells our strands afford. I would even carry my zeal to things of art: my hangings, bed, cabinets and other furniture should be Irish, and the very silver that ornament my locks and grates should be the produce of our mines" (M. Craig and others, *Country Life*, 1969, p.724–25).

The hall was designed by Sir Edward Lovett Pearce (d.1733) who visited Italy and studied the writings of Palladio. (Pearce's annotated copy of the *Quattro libri dell'architettura* still exists.) The entrance hall at Castletown is articulated with Ionic columns on the ground floor and an idiosyncratic Corinthian order in the form of tapering pilasters with carved wooden capitals of baskets of flowers and fruit at gallery level. The gallery has a delicate wrought-iron balustrade and the plasterwork on the coved ceiling with bold Greek key pattern is reminiscent of earlier 17th century work. Documentary evidence and paint scrapes indicate that the hall has always been painted white. Thus there is a spectacular contrast with the polished black limestone chimneypiece and black and white chequered floor. The entrance hall of Pearce's fully executed Palladian villa at Bellamont Forest, Co. Cavan, contains busts of Roman emperors set in *oculi*; here Pearce repeats the Greek key pattern in the coved ceiling.

Richard Castle (c.1690–1751) came to Ireland from Hesse-Cassel in 1728 and worked for Pearce on the Parliament House, Dublin. After Pearce's death Castle dominated Irish country house architecture and he was commissioned to design most of the significant interiors of the 18th century including Westport, Co. Mayo; Carton, Co. Kildare; Powerscourt, Co. Wicklow (interiors destroyed); Russborough, Co. Wicklow; and Leinster House, Dublin. The interiors at Russborough are the best preserved and an impression of their original arrangement may be established since much of the contents of the house, notably the furniture and pictures, were donated to the National Gallery of Ireland in the Milltown Bequest.

Russborough was built in 1741; the state rooms (hall, saloon and music room) have lavish late Baroque stucco ceilings that are largely the work of the Lafranchini brothers, stuccodores from Ticino who worked in Ireland for most of their careers. Paolo (1695–1770) and Filippo Lafranchini (1702–79) worked with Richard Castle at Carton; Summerhill, Co. Meath; and 85 St. Stephen's Green, Dublin. They probably worked with other foreign or Irish craftsmen, as the stylistic variations in the decoration at Russborough are great, ranging

Ireland: Saloon, Carton, Co. Kildare, 1739–45

from the controlled and balanced Lafranchini work in the saloon to the overwhelmingly crowded plasterwork on the staircase which must have been the work of their studio. The lavish plasterwork spills over the cornices and down the walls. In the drawing room the elaborate plaster cartouches were executed to frame four seascapes by Claude-Joseph Vernet (1714–89). Each room (except the dining room) has a four foot high mahogany dado which acted as a backdrop for the heavily carved mahogany furniture and gilded mirrors that were originally designed for the house. Dark San Domingo mahogany is used lavishly throughout the house in the doorcases, staircase and geometrically patterned floors which are unusual in Ireland. The hall has a polished black limestone chimneypiece, an established feature of the hall of an Irish country house. The walls of the saloon are covered with mid-19th century Genoese cut velvet which survived in the house and was conserved under the direction of Lady Beit in the 1950s. In the saloon the chimneypiece flanked by terms with a panel showing Androcles and the lion was carved in London by Thomas Carter the younger (similar to one at Uppark, Sussex); the inlaid marble mantelpiece in the boudoir is by Pietro Bossi who worked in Dublin. The scale of the interiors decreases dramatically on the first floor. In comparison with the robust proportions below there is a doll's house quality upstairs with superb details in the paneling, doorcases and chimneypieces.

Only the ceiling of the saloon and the Chinese room at Carton, Co. Kildare remain as they were in the 18th century. The interiors were remodeled by Richard Castle in 1739 and in that year the Lafranchini executed the stucco work in the saloon depicting the *The Loves of the Gods*. The engraved sources for this ceiling and its connections with the saloon ceiling at 85 St. Stephen's Green, Dublin, also by Castle and the Lafranchini are fully described in Joseph McDonnell's *Irish Eighteenth-Century Stuccowork and its European Sources* (1991). The florid Lafranchini plasterwork decoration soon gave way to the Rococo of Robert West (d.1790) whose best work is in the staircase hall of his own house 20 Lower Dominick Street, Dublin and at 86 St. Stephen's Green. Michael Stapleton (fl.1770–1801) was the most important Irish Neo-Classical stuccodore of the late 18th century. Working in the style of Robert Adam, Stapleton created delicate interiors covered in finely detailed plasterwork on the ceilings and walls using moulds and freehand work. He repeated the designs in several rooms, for example in the Wedgwood room at Lucan House, Co. Dublin and 17 St. Stephen's Green and at Powerscourt House both in Dublin. Robert Adam (1728–92) designed the interiors for Headfort, Co. Meath in 1771; the coloured drawings for these interiors are in the collection of the Yale Center for British Art.

The interiors created by Emily, Duchess of Leinster (1731–1814) at Carton and her sister Lady Louisa Conolly (1743–1821) at Castletown are among the most important surviving interiors of their type. In 1759 Emily purchased some hand-painted Chinese paper depicting scenes of everyday life and landscapes. The large panels were framed on the walls with borders made in a Chinoiserie design and the smaller panels were cut out in irregular shapes and arranged around the borders. A carved and gilded Chinoiserie fillet frames the wall below the cornice and above the dado. The gilded Rococo overmantel is sumptuously carved with tiny brackets that would originally have carried Chinese jars, snuff bottles or figurines frames the chimneypieces. One of the most delightful interiors in Ireland is to be found in the park at Carton. During the 1760s, the Duchess of Leinster created a *cottage orné* with a shell room in the style of the one at Goodwood, Sussex. The walls, coved ceiling and central lantern are decorated in patterns of shells, with coral and shells suspended from the rafters. Mirrored glass is set into the walls and there is a rocky grotto.

Lady Louisa Conolly was inspired by her older sister in the decoration of Castletown. For instance, each designed and made a print room and each employed the Lafranchini stuccodores. In 1759 the Lafranchini were employed to decorate the staircase hall at Castletown with family portraits, masks representing the four seasons and Vesta (the goddess of the hearth), as well as grotesque heads, Chinese dragons, cornucopiae and shells, symbolic of the four elements. Paintings were set into plasterwork frames. The cantilevered Portland stone staircase was built under the direction of Simon Vierpyl (c.1725–1811) and the brass banisters that contrast with the white stucco ornamentation were made by A. King of Dublin in 1760. In 1768 Lady Louisa set about creating a print room using favourite prints and decorative borders. This remains one of the most elaborate print rooms to have survived without alteration since the 18th century.

The state rooms at Castletown were redecorated in a rigid Neo-Classical style to designs attributed to Sir William Chambers (1723–96). The dining room and drawing rooms contain compartmented ceilings, chimneypieces and door cases in the manner of Chambers. The cabinet-maker Richard Cranfield (1713–1809) carved the pier glasses in the dining room in the form of fruiting vines appropriate in a room presided over by Bacchus. The Dublin firm of Thomas Jackson were responsible for much of the rest of the carving and gilding in the house. The remaining state rooms form an *enfilade* comprising saloon, drawing room, closets and state bedroom. The red drawing room contains a set of Chinese Chippendale seat furniture that was made in Dublin and pier glasses in the style of Chambers. 18th and early 19th century textile wall coverings have rarely survived *in situ* but in this room the walls are covered in red French damask that dates from the 1830s.

The long gallery was redecorated in the Pompeian style under the direction of Lady Louisa Conolly in the mid-1770s. It was to be used as an informal drawing room. The gallery is illuminated by three Venetian glass chandeliers and four exceptionally large sheets of French mirrored glass. The room was originally filled with furniture, commodes by Pierre Langlois, tables by John Linnell, bookcases (now at Barons Court, Co. Tyrone), a billiard table and musical instruments. The walls and fields of the ceiling are painted lavender blue, with gilded cornice and frieze against a red background. Charles Reuben Riley (c.1752–98) and Thomas Ryder (1746–1810) carried out the decorative painting. They covered the walls with Raphaelesque grotesque decoration and the twin themes of love and marriage are celebrated in the murals which derive from engravings in d'Hancarville's *Antiquités Etrusques, Grèques et Romaines* (1766–67) and Montfaucon's *L'antiquités expliquée et representée en figures* (1719). Painted interiors were not unusual, and some survive in Dublin town houses in Fitzwilliam Square and Merrion Square (notably no.49) and at Lyons, Co. Kildare, which was painted with Claudian landscapes by Gaspare Gabrielli (fl.1803–1833) in 1806.

Sir William Chambers's designs for Lord Charlemont's Marino Casino were published in his *Treatise on Civil Architecture* (1759) and executed by Simon Vierpyl. Nothing of the original furniture, pictures or contents survive at the Casino. The interiors suffered severe damage during the early part of this century and the chimneypieces were removed. The quality of the plasterwork and joinery that remains is outstanding and gives some indication of what must have been perfect early Neo-Classical interiors. The hall takes the form of an atrium in a Roman villa. It originally housed marble sculpture and is appropriately painted white. The hall compensates for its small scale by the use of receding coffering in the semi-circular apse that gives an illusion of depth, as does the detailed plasterwork on the ceiling and frieze. The plasterwork throughout the main interiors is filled with classical references. The theme of Apollo representing the arts, and his attribute the lyre may be found in details of the stone carving on the exte-

Ireland: Long Gallery, decorated in the Pompeian style, Castletown, Co. Kildare, 1770s

rior and in the plasterwork inside. The lyre dominates the central panel of the compartmented ceiling in the hall, along with Mercury's caduceus. The frieze is decorated with garlands of flowers and musical instruments, both symbols of festivity. The saloon continues the Apollo theme with his mask in a sunburst against a blue background in the centre of a white coved ceiling. The original blue and white colour scheme in the saloon has been restored. Extensive paint scrapes were carried out at the Casino and documentary evidence is extant for the interiors in the Charlemont Manuscripts (Royal Irish Academy), making the Casino one of the best documented buildings of the 18th century.

In the 1790s James Wyatt (1746–1823) created the grandest Neo-Classical interiors in Ireland at Castle Coole, Co. Fermanagh. The interiors are remarkable for the quality of the joinery, and the plasterwork and the textiles are outstanding. That they have survived in such good condition is a tribute to the tradition of rigorous housekeeping now continued by the National Trust. John Preston (fl.1807–25), the finest Dublin upholsterer, supplied elaborate curtains with intricate borders, fringes and tassels, suites of gilded furniture in Greek Revival style and a magnificent State Bed hung with scarlet silk curtains. Joseph Rose (1745–99) executed the plasterwork and there are six chimneypieces by Richard Westmacott (1747–1808).

Two other interiors have survived virtually intact from the 1820s. The drawing room at Newbridge, Co. Dublin, contains the furniture and curtains made by the Dublin firm of Mack, Williams and Gibton in 1828 and the collection of pictures is arranged as it was in the 1830s. At Killadoon, Co. Kildare the drawing room retains its 1820s French green and gold wallpaper, original red curtains, flounces and gilt pelmets.

Sir Richard Morrison (1767–1849) and the stuccodore James Talbot (fl.1802–1808) excelled in decorative plasterwork. Morrison and his son William Vitruvius Morrison (1794–1838) created opulent Regency interiors at Ballyfin, Co. Laois, Baronscourt, Co. Tyrone and Borris House, Co. Carlow with richly encrusted coved ceilings and screens of *scagliola* columns. The dining room at Carton, Co. Kildare and the entrance hall at Fota, Co. Cork demonstrate their mastery of interior spaces.

At Lismore Castle, Co. Waterford, part of the interior deco-

Ireland: Red Drawing Room, Newbridge, Co. Dublin, early 19th century

ration was designed by the Gothic Revivalist A.W.N. Pugin (1812–52) and the work was carried out by J.G. Crace (1809–89) in 1850. The Banqueting Hall has an ecclesiastical air with choir stalls, perpendicular Gothic windows and stained glass. The walls and timbers of the open roof are richly stenciled. Pugin and Crace also worked on the Great Hall at Adare, Co. Limerick.

Humewood, Co. Wicklow was designed by William White (1825–1900) in 1866. It contains the most virtuoso Gothic Revival interiors surviving in Ireland. The staircase hall is dominated by a pair of polished black marble columns and heraldic stained glass, however the rooms are relatively small in scale and the ceilings were painted by an Italian artist Grispini. Humewood was finished by James Brooks (1825–1901) the church architect who adapted his French 13th-century Gothic to domestic use in the design of the banqueting hall. The paneling and the ironwork in the gun room anticipates later Arts and Crafts developments.

The mid-19th century was dominated by the influence of Ruskinian Gothic and the work of Sir Thomas Deane (1792[-1871) and Benjamin Woodward (1816–61) who formed a partnership in Cork in 1851. Ruskin greatly approved of their work with its Byzantine Revival vocabulary and for the freedom they gave to their stone carvers, Charles Harrison (1835–1903) and the O'Shea brothers (fl. 1846–64). The great staircase of the Kildare Street Club was destroyed in 1971 and Woodward's achievement in domestic architecture may be fully appreciated at Clontra, Co. Dublin. In 1862 the interiors were decorated by John Hungerford Pollen (1820–1902) in a series of Pre-Raphaelite fresco cycles. Above the internal staircase a knight in armour and his lady drink a stirrup cup. The *Seven Ages of Woman* decorate the end walls of the drawing room and in the dining room frescoes depict *Spring Morning and Autumn Evening*. The timber construction of the high-pitched roofs is left exposed and the space between the rafters is decorated with birds, flora and fauna. On the walls is Celtic interlace, probably the earliest use of this Celtic Revival motif in an interior scheme.

The Arts and Crafts Movement in Ireland had a rich life, notably in enameling, stained glass and ecclesiastical interiors. Domestic interiors such as those at Belle Isle, Co. Fermanagh and on a modest scale at Baytown Park, Co. Meath with exposed beams, paneling and stained glass are rare.

Sir Edwin Lutyens (1869–1944) remodeled interiors at Howth Castle, Co. Dublin, adding a library with oak paneling and bookcases. He created a series of romantic vaulted interiors at Lambay Castle, Co. Dublin, using pale grey limestone and contrasting white rendered walls.

Iveagh House, Dublin contains some of the finest neo-Rococo and Italianate interiors of the late 19th century. The staircase was designed by J.F. Fuller (1835–1924) and the decoration of the walls in Algerian onyx, alabaster and marble in the staircase hall and ballroom are to designs by William Young (1843–1900).

Eclectic late-Victorian and Edwardian taste is reflected in the work carried out by Dublin firms of professional decorators and house fitters that flourished at the turn of the century. Many of these firms survived into the 1960s and 1970s reproducing a variety of neo-Georgian and neo-Rococo interiors. The largest firm of decorators was Millar and Beatty Ltd., with branches in Grafton Street, Dublin and in Londonderry, where they employed more cabinet-makers and upholsterers than any other firm. They specialized in reproducing French Rococo Revival, Sheraton and Chippendale style interiors and reproduction furniture. In 1905 they advertised a range of interiors in *The House Beautiful*; one in the "New Art" style comprised of imported American mass-produced furniture and fittings as well as Donegal and Cork (Youghal) carpets and linoleums in Art Nouveau patterns. Millar and Beatty designed an interior for the Irish section at the St. Louis Exhibition in 1904.

Maguire and Gatchell were decorators, lighting specialists and suppliers of bathroom fittings (their work is perfectly preserved at Killineer House, Co. Louth). They also sold jewel safes and strongrooms at their showrooms in Dawson Street, Dublin and were pioneers in modern forms of central heating.

H. Sibthorpe & Sons' early work included fitting out the Kildare Street Club (c.1860) in robust plaster friezes and corbelled beams. They are more usually associated with the variations of Rococo such as their own "Marie Antoinette style" and Louis Seize decoration. Sibthorpe provided the more popular neo-Adamesque that fitted in with existing 18th-century plasterwork. At 18 Parnell Square, Dublin, they added gilded friezes and lincrusta mouldings with paintwork in the manner of Angelica Kauffmann. Their Neo-Classical work is best preserved at Coolmore, Co. Cork. There, the drawing room wallpaper has stenciled decoration in red and green, and medallions of classical figures painted on a blue ground. Sibthorpe specialized in decorative painting and created a Rococo painted ceiling and gilt interiors in the Royal Train for the visit of Edward VII in 1904. Sibthorpe continued their work as the leading decorators in Ireland until the 1960s. Other notable professional decorators were Pilkingtons of Kildare Street and J.F. Keatinge & Sons Ltd., who were founded in the 1882 and ceased trading in 1994.

Textiles were designed, manufactured and sold by Walpole Brothers Ltd. of Dublin, Belfast and London. The firm was founded in 1766 and supplied hand-woven Irish double damasks and linens often with hand embroidery made by the Royal Irish Linen and Damask Manufacturers. Whyte & Sons specialized in glass and china and household goods as did the great Dublin department store Pim Brothers Ltd. of South Great Georges Street, established in 1841. Combridge & Co. Ltd. were picture framers, gilders and stationers who specialized in decorative bookbinding and library fittings. Cramer, Wood & Co. sold musical instruments and a range of pianos for the cluttered Victorian interior.

Several country house interiors were redecorated in the grand manner although none with such opulence as Castle Forbes, Co. Longford. Beatrice, Countess of Granard was assisted by two firms of architects, Frederick Foster of London and Kaye, Parry & Ross of Dublin, who were employed to execute her ideas. The French interior decorator Fernand Allard and the firm of Lenygon and Morant of 31 Old Burlington Street, London, were more influential in the design of the interiors. Allard designed the hall and staircase which is lined with grey ashlar. The London decorators fitted out Cunard liners at this time and they designed the dining room, lined with oak paneling and a *trompe-l'oeil* ceiling of an open dome. The drawing room is an English Palladian room in the manner of William Kent. Lavish ceilings were imported and an 18th-century ceiling was inserted in the drawing room depicting an allegory of the *Genius of Architecture*. In the library Faith, Hope and Charity preside with the Four Seasons set in each corner of the ceiling.

At Birr Castle, Co. Offaly, Anne, Countess of Rosse (the founder of the Victorian Society) reinterpreted some of the most beautiful Victorian rooms in Ireland in the skillful arrangement of furniture, flowers and pictures. The ballroom is hung with Victorian green and gold damask patterned wallpaper and during the 1940s Lady Rosse hung red flock wallpaper in the dining room and restored the dado. In the 1950s Luttrellstown Castle, Co. Dublin was transformed in the grand manner by the Hon. Mrs. Aileen Plunket who created interiors of great elegance with the help of the English decorator, Felix Harbord, a pupil of Sir Albert Richardson. A mixture of styles was brought together in the 18th and 19th century rooms. These incorporated a Baroque painted ceiling by Sir James Thornhill (1675/6–1734) and grisaille paintings by Peter de

Gree (d.1798) of allegorical scenes depicting *Mercury introducing the Arts and Industry to Ireland.*

In the post-war years a number of houses were decorated by their owners who relied on their own good taste. Dunsany Castle, Co. Meath with Neo-Classical plasterwork by Michael Stapleton was elegantly redecorated by Lady Dunsany with impeccable taste and individual style. A new delicacy was introduced in the warm colours used and the arrangements of Sèvres porcelain and pictures. Russborough was bought by the Beits in 1951 and Sir Alfred and Lady Beit restored the house to form a backdrop for one of the finest private collections of art in the world.

International Modernism began to filter into the design of domestic interiors in the Dublin suburbs during the 1930s. Robinson and Keefe designed semi-detached "Sunshine" houses at Dollymount, Dublin, that retained a traditional internal plan but had unadorned white walls, windows and doors with decorative glazing bars, and tiled chimneypieces. Walter Gropius visited Ireland in 1936. The greatest Irish exponent of his theories was Michael Scott (1905–1989). Scott's house Geragh, near Dun Laoghaire was designed in 1937–38, exemplifying the Gropius style in the severity of its white interiors and tubular steel furniture. The Australian architect and designer Raymond McGrath (1903–1977) was appointed to the Office of Public Works and was responsible for the redecoration of many public buildings, including Aras an Uachtarain (President's Official Residence) in a neo-Georgian style incorporating 18th-century plasterwork and designing carpets based on the ceiling decoration. McGrath did much to revive Donegal Carpets and Waterford Glass. Eileen Gray (1879–1976), the creator of some of the most spectacular Parisian interiors of the 1920s, was born in Ireland and during the 1960s some of her abstract carpet designs were reproduced and manufactured in Ireland.

In the 1950s two significant events took place; the Hon. Mr. and Mrs. Desmond Guinness bought Leixlip Castle, Co. Kildare, and in 1958 they re-established the Irish Georgian Society. At this time very few people in Ireland appreciated Irish interiors, and the redecoration of Leixlip was important in that here for the first time a specifically Irish look was recreated using heavily carved 18th-century Irish furniture. The style may be characterized by an overall simplicity, the use of strong colours, blues, reds and brilliant white, the dramatic placing of furniture and the rejection of fussiness and upholstery. This was a highly architectural style that respected the structure of interiors, windows were left uncurtained, layers of flaking paintwork left untouched and furniture unrestored. Shells, prints and books were collected, arranged alongside doll's houses and the ubiquitous fresh green or golden autumnal beech leaves. This new aesthetic of the informal, unrestored yet grand interior was well-suited to Irish houses that had been neglected for generations. These ideas were disseminated through the Irish Georgian Society in the rescue projects that it sponsored, most importantly at Castletown, where repainting was done with sensitivity. Entire rooms were shown to the public in an untouched state. In the conservation work that the society undertook in Dublin this minimal intervention left the rooms essentially undecorated, and this may best be seen at 13 Henrietta Street where the Casey family have maintained the purity of a very grand but unrestored interior. Many influential English and American decorators visited Leixlip and Castletown and were greatly influenced by these ideas.

This renewed interest in historic interiors encouraged many country house owners to restore their family property. Desmond FitzGerald, Knight of Glin, was a kindred spirit of the Guinnesses in the revival of interest in Irish interior design and furniture. Glin Castle, Co. Limerick has been carefully restored and provides a unique setting for a collection of Irish furniture and pictures. In Dublin the large houses in the unfashionable north inner city had been turned into tenements in the 19th century. This slow decline has been arrested and although many of the finest interiors have been lost, among those that survive there have been some remarkable restorations. Since the 1960s a dozen houses have been rescued or restored, particularly in North Great Georges Street and Henrietta Street.

PAUL CAFFREY

Further Reading

McParland 1989 is an essential reference work for the 20th-century literature on Irish architecture and interior design.

Bence-Jones, Mark, *A Guide to Irish Country Houses*, revised edition London: Constable, 1988

Casey, Christine and Alistair Rowan, *North Leinster: The Counties of Longford, Louth, Meath and Westmeath* (Buildings of Ireland series), London and New York: Penguin, 1993

Craig, Maurice, *Classic Irish Houses of the Middle Size*, London: Architectural Press, 1976; New York: Architectural Book Publishing, 1977

Craig, Maurice, *Dublin 1600–1860*, London: Penguin, 1992

Curran, C.P., *Dublin Decorative Plasterwork of the Seventeenth and Eighteenth Centuries*, London: Tiranti, 1967

Danaher, Kevin, *Ireland's Vernacular Architecture*, 2nd edition Cork: Mercier Press, 1978

De Breffny, Brian and Rosemary Ffolliott, *The Houses of Ireland*, London: Thames and Hudson, and New York: Viking, 1975

Georgian Society Records, vols.1–4, Dublin: Georgian Society, 1909–13

Glin, The Knight of, David J. Griffin and Nicholas K. Robinson, *Vanishing Country Houses of Ireland*, 2nd edition Dublin: Irish Architectural Archive, 1988

Guinness, Desmond and Jacqueline O'Brien, *Great Irish Houses and Castles*, London: Weidenfeld and Nicolson, and New York: Abrams, 1992

Guinness, Desmond and Jacqueline O'Brien, *Dublin: A Grand Tour*, London: Weidenfeld and Nicolson, and New York: Abrams, 1994

Harris, John, *Headfort House and Robert Adam*, London: Royal Institute of British Architects, 1973

Kinmonth, Claudia, *Irish Country Furniture, 1700–1950*, New Haven and London: Yale University Press, 1993

Larmour, Paul, *The Arts and Crafts Movement in Ireland*, Belfast: Friar's Bush Press, 1992

McDonnell, Joseph, *Irish Eighteenth-Century Stuccowork and its European Sources*, Dublin: National Gallery of Ireland, 1991

McParland, Edward, *James Gandon: Vitruvius Hibernicus*, London: Zwemmer, 1985

McParland, Edward, *A Bibliography of Irish Architectural History*, Dublin: Irish Historical Studies, 1989

McParland, Edward and others, *The Architecture of Richard Morrison and William Vitruvius Morrison*, Dublin: Irish Architectural Archive, 1989

Sheehy, Jeanne, *The Rediscovery of Ireland's Past: The Celtic Revival, 1830–1930*, London: Thames and Hudson, 1980

Williams, Jeremy, *A Companion Guide to Architecture in Ireland, 1837–1921*, Blackrock, Co. Dublin: Irish Academic Press, 1994

Isokon

British furniture manufacturers, 1931–1939

Founded in 1931 by Jack Pritchard and Wells Coates, the Isokon company was one of only a handful of inter-war British forays into Modernism. Pritchard, then working for the Venesta Plywood Company, had come across Coates's shop interiors for the Cresta Silks chain (1929–32), where plywood was used, not as a cheap substitute for solid wood as was generally the case, but as a truly modern material. Pritchard subsequently commissioned Coates to design a house for his own family on Lawn Road in Hampstead; a brave decision considering that the engineer and former *Daily Express* journalist had not, at that point, had anything substantial built. Through discussion about what was the most socially responsible use of land in London, the project eventually developed into a block of "minimum" flats, and the Isokon company was founded principally to manage its erection and promotion. (The name "Isokon" was coined because of Coates's preference for drawing his designs in isometric projection.)

Completed in 1934, the monolithic concrete structure, with its bold external staircase and access galleries, and which the one-time resident Agatha Christie likened to a cruise liner, represents one of the first appearances in the UK of what was to become known as the International Style. The internal planning of the building was equally revolutionary. The flats were designed as complete "ready-to-live-in" dwellings specifically for young single people with few possessions. It was Coates's belief that furniture, like the plumbing system, should become part of the fixtures of a dwelling, rather than be taken from home to home. Moreover, built-in multi-purpose furniture would ensure a more economic use of space; an important consideration in a modern city. Each of the 22 minimum flats – consisting of a living / bedroom, kitchen, bathroom and dressing room – occupied only approximately 271 square feet (25 square metres), and was comprehensively equipped with standardized built-in furniture, most of it manufactured from plywood.

Perhaps because simplicity and lack of ornament in home furnishings are today not unusual, it is easy to overlook the significance of the Lawn Road interiors, which, as Nikolaus Pevsner noted, made no "compromises with convention". The undisguised use of modern materials, such as plywood and tubular steel, which had not yet entered the everyday vocabulary of the home, and the inclusion of built-in furniture (which effectively removed choice from the resident) were indeed unconventional design decisions – especially in England, which lagged behind the rest of Europe in its acceptance of Modernist ideas. References to the more established European "masters", particularly Le Corbusier, abound in contemporary descriptions of the building, although, as one commentator has noted, Coates's enthusiasm for built-in furniture may have been influenced as much by the traditional architecture of Japan, where he was brought up, as by Continental Modernism.

Nevertheless, the notion of minimal living, or *Existenzminimum*, had a great deal of currency among Modernist sympathizers, having been advocated at the 2nd meeting of the Congrès International d'Architecture Moderne (CIAM) in Frankfurt in 1929, as one solution to Europe's housing problems. While Coates and Pritchard were undoubtedly inspired by the socialist rhetoric of policies such as this, the Isokon flats were beyond the means of those most in need of new housing. Indeed, simply to ensure their erection, the flats were pitched at the middle-class *cognoscenti*.

The Lawn Road flats quickly became a focus for Hampstead's intellectual and artistic communities, themselves soon to be augmented by an émigré population fleeing Germany. While Coates clearly played a very important role in the formation and direction of Isokon, it was the involvement of a number of these émigrés – Walter Gropius, Marcel Breuer and Lázló Moholy-Nagy – which has done most to ensure the company's enduring significance in the eyes of design commentators.

Pritchard invited Gropius to England to design a new block of flats (in partnership with E. Maxwell Fry), to be built in an affluent suburb of Manchester. In the event, this project, as well as a small development planned for Birmingham and a much-celebrated scheme for Windsor, fell through due to lack of funds, and Isokon focused its attention on its furniture operations. The company had been involved in marketing Coates's plywood bookcases as early as 1933, but the formation of the Isokon Furniture Company in 1935 effectively marked the transition from architecture to furniture. More significantly, it also signalled the adoption of *moulded* plywood construction over more conventional techniques. The new company's Bauhaus-inspired philosophy – which stated that form should be determined by function rather than superimposed ornament – stressed Isokon's commitment to plywood, which, Pritchard felt, offered more "traditional English comfort" than the arguably more austere tubular steel furniture from the Continent. Nevertheless, the modernity of plywood was emphasised through reference to its use in the aircraft industry.

Gropius became Isokon's Controller of Designs, although only one of his designs was ever manufactured. But it was his insistence that his former Bauhaus colleague, Marcel Breuer, join the design team that proved an important contribution to the company's work. Breuer set about exploiting plywood's intrinsic properties through the re-design of an aluminium chaise-longue he had designed for Wohnbedarf in 1933. The resulting *Long Chair* (1936) demonstrates Breuer's thorough understanding of the material and bears comparison with the furniture of Alvar Aalto. Like much of Aalto's furniture, the Long Chair consists of a single sheet of moulded plywood supported on thick laminated wood leg-forms. Its significance arises, in part, from the fact that, like Aalto's *Paimio* chair, it could not have been manufactured from solid wood and did not try to pretend it was. Moreover, it illustrates very effectively the state-of-the-art of plywood technology in 1936: not until the advent of stronger adhesives would it be possible to mould plywood into complex compound curves.

Apart from a set of nesting tables and a *Short Chair*, Breuer's other designs for Isokon were less satisfactory; their originally simplistic designs were compromised by the need for lateral bracing which gave them a heavy and overworked appearance. It is perhaps for this reason that Isokon furniture has not entered the canon of "classics" to the same degree as many pieces by Le Corbusier, Aalto and Breuer himself. Nevertheless, Breuer's work for Isokon – which also included the Isobar restaurant in the Lawn Road flats – rates among the

Isokon furniture designed by Marcel Breuer, c.1936

most successful realisations of Modernist ideals in the UK, and represents a conscious attempt to tailor those ideals to the perhaps rather spurious notion of Englishness.

In 1937, a shortage of architectural commissions in the UK led Gropius to seek work in the United States; he was followed shortly afterwards by Breuer. Production of Breuer's furniture continued, but the onset of war in 1939 effectively halted the company's supply of timber from Estonia. After the war, Pritchard made several attempts to restart the company, even manufacturing a number of new designs by Ernest Race. Without the enviable Modernist credentials of Gropius, Breuer or Moholy-Nagy (who had designed Isokon's graphics) behind him, however, Pritchard met with little success and the company eventually folded. Nonetheless, between the wars, Isokon was at the cutting-edge of design practice. The mere presence of Gropius *et al.* clearly makes Isokon significant, but the company's modest output continues to look as original and uncompromisingly modern today as it did sixty or so years ago.

ANTHONY HOYTE

See also Wells Coates; Plywood Furniture

Selected Collections

Documentation, correspondence and manuscript material relating to Isokon is in the Pritchard Archive, School of Architecture, University of Newcastle, Newcastle-upon-Tyne; drawings and designs for furniture by Wells Coates are in the Drawings Collection, Royal Institute of British Architects, London. Examples of Isokon furnishings are in the Victoria and Albert Museum, London, the School of Fine Arts and Music, University of East Anglia, Norwich, and the Pritchard Archive, University of Newcastle.

Further Reading

A concise history of Isokon's work appears in Buckley 1980.

Banham, Reyner, "Isokon Flats" in *Architectural Review*, July 1955

Buckley, Cheryl, *Isokon* (exhib. cat.), Newcastle-upon-Tyne: Hatton Gallery, 1980

Cantacuzino, Sherban, *Wells Coates*, London: Gordon Fraser, 1978

Carrington, Noel, *Design and Decoration in the Home*, London: Batsford, 1952

Collins, Michael (editor), *Hampstead in the Thirties: A Committed Decade* (exhib. cat.), London: Camden Arts Centre, 1974

Hoyte, Anthony, "Why Gropius Didn't Sell" in *Design Review: The Journal of the Chartered Society of Designers*, 1, Winter 1991, pp.40–45

Pritchard, Jack, *View from a Long Chair: The Memoirs of Jack Pritchard*, London and Boston: Routledge, 1984

Prus, Timothy and David Dawson, *New Design for Living: Design in British Interiors, 1930–1951* (exhib. cat.: B2 Gallery, London), London: Lane Publications, 1982

Sembach, Klaus-Jürgen, *Into the Thirties: Style and Design, 1927–1934*, London: Thames and Hudson, 1972

Thirties: British Art and Design Before the War (exhib. cat.), London: Arts Council of Great Britain, 1979

Wilk, Christopher, *Marcel Breuer: Furniture and Interiors*, New York: Museum of Modern Art, and London: Architectural Press, 1981

Isozaki, Arata 1931–

Japanese architect and designer

Arata Isozaki was Japan's leading interpreter of Postmodern trends from the West in the early 1970s when he established personal contacts with Peter Cook in London, Hans Hollein in

Vienna, and Peter Meier and Peter Eisenman in New York. A prolific essayist as well as designer, Isozaki attacked Modern architecture in several books. In the process, he challenged the dominant modern Japanese synthesis, devised by an older generation trained in the 1930s and led by Kenzo Tange and Kunio Maekawa, of trabeated concrete-framed buildings expressive of traditional Japanese carpentry.

From 1954 to 1963 Isozaki was a member of Kenzo Tange's Team and Urtec. Under the stimulus of Metabolism, he enlarged traditional column brackets to the scale of major urban elements in Cities in the Air (1960–62), and used ruined Greek columns to support giant lattice beams in City in Ruins (1962) which extended in a free system of towers over a chaotic Tokyo. These proposals anticipated the big-beam style of his trabeated beam compositions during the 1960s after he left Tange.

Isozaki's career is punctuated by sudden shifts in style every ten years. This periodicity resulted in a succession of style phases: from the big-beam expression in raw concrete of the 1960s, much of the work being at Oita, Kyushu, where Isozaki was born; to the mannerism of the 1970s, which was followed in the 1980s by international eclecticism, which in turn launched into schizoid eclecticism and hyper-tech in the 1990s. Mannerism was present in one form or another in all the phases, in the exaggerated enlargement of structural beam elements in the 1960s, 45 degree geometry and space bridges, which was succeeded in the 1970s, immediately after Expo '70, Osaka, by a Postmodern orientation that exploited obsessive compositions of neo-Platonic pure forms such as cubes, cylinders and spheres. In the 1980s this mannered idiom flowered into an energetic international eclecticism, with motifs drawn from contemporary styles and sometimes the early Modernism of the 1920s and 1930s, and often looked back across Western architectural history to Claude Nicolas Ledoux, 16th-century Italian Mannerism and Andrea Palladio. By the 1990s, international eclecticism became more *ad hoc* and arbitrary and led to a Schizoid eclecticism that combined motifs that broke up the presumed normalities of integrated form. At the same time, Isozaki experimented with a hyper-tech expression as the occasion demanded. In all of this, Isozaki mirrored the ongoing cultural schizophrenia and confusion of Japan in an era of unprecedented economic growth characterised by a deep obsession with Western culture.

The structuralism of Isozaki's early interiors, where the material was raw concrete, gave way to the use of polished marble, red Indian sandstone, rusticated granite, reflective aluminium panels and silver tiles. From the 1980s on, Isozaki used colour more, and contrasted rough natural textures with smooth artificial materials, together with mirrors and glass blocks.

In his early big-beam works at Oita, the interiors were defined by beams, with the primary material exposed concrete. The entry hall and reading spaces of the Oita Prefectural Library (1962–66) resulted from the placement of exceptionally large U-shaped off-form concrete beams resting on other hollow beams or bedded in cross walls. As with the earlier mega-structure proposals, the primitive structure of the beams defined the character of the interior spaces. These were dynamic and directional in the Oita Library; for the Oita Branch of the Fukuoka Mutual Bank a spine bridge under diagonal roof beams energised the white interior assisted by bright vivid reds and blues.

The Fukuoka Bank Headquarters, Fukuoka (1968–71) had a suite of remarkable rooms: the meeting room had concentric squares inscribed on the walls and ceiling, the subdued lighting adding to the hypnotic effect of its identical walls; the boardroom in full-blown High-Tech with curved aluminium panels and prominent air nozzles had a decidedly science fiction unreality; but most arresting of all was the large Surreal eye at one end of a black and white chequered floor.

The Kitakyushu City Museum of Art (1972–74), with its twin gun barrels, was notable for its square die-cast aluminium panels and polished marble floors, which produced an effect of public magnificence. Like the previous big-beam concrete works the spaces were the result of the structural scheme. The Museum of Modern Art, Takasaki (1971–74) was clad in polished aluminium panels and based around a composition of cubes which supplied universal frames for the temporary objects on display. The interiors were a remarkable tour de force, with architecture, sculpture and interior design merged in a total work. It explored such typical Mannerist devices as false perspective, dissonant scale and the decaying form. Most notable was the main staircase which was treated in such a way that the edges appear to merge with the polished walls, rising in infinite axial extension to the cylindrical half-landing. Within the first floor lobby, smaller rooms were inserted within the main cube as a Mannerist play on the room-within-a-room theme. The most striking object is a superbly executed stepped marble platform at the far end of the entrance lobby; its perverse perspective and over-large steps made it appear much smaller. Traces on the ceiling and walls of the lecture hall disrupted it.

In the 1970s, semi-cylindrical barrel vaults, inspired by Palladio, took the theme of infinite uni-axial extension and combined it with plastic and passive form which was acted on by powerful external forces. The arbitrary character of such works (a question mark for a golf club), reflected Isozaki's preoccupation with linguistics. On this occasion, the Golf Club barrel vault was moulded into a sign for Isozaki's puzzlement over why the Japanese are obsessed with golf. The best vaulted composition was the Hayashi House, Fukuoka (1976–77), which, like a fragment of plumbing, consisted of a leading vault feeding into two small extensions which covered the main living area and sleeping quarters. The entrance foyer had mirrors on the two facing walls which multiplied the image of the entry's circular vault. The effect was both arresting and disorienting – a similar illusion was achieved in the Mickey Mouse canopy of the Team Disney Building (1991).

Tsukuba Center Building, Tsukuba (1979–83) had Isozaki's most important interiors in the 1980s. So great was the totality of its conception it is difficult to separate the interior from the exterior design, especially the ironic sunken Campidoglio. Besides Michelangelo, the project owed much to Isozaki's fascination with Ledoux at that time, especially the Salt Works at Arc-et-Senans, which was echoed in the banded columns and rusticated masonry; this was repeated in the concert hall and lobby areas where refined polished surfaces touched rough stone facings in a contest between natural and man-made. Dipping into history, Isozaki refers to Karl Friedrich Schinkel in the night sky ceiling of the banquet hall. At Tsukuba, Isozaki engaged in a wide use of historical motifs assembled in a contrived Mannerist way with inversions, reverse perspective effects, traces projected from inside imaginary rotated cubes on walls and ceilings to undermine the surface appearance, and subversive angled pavilions, all of which contributed to a pervasive feeling of unease and anxiety. Tsukuba Center was brilliant and marvellously sophisticated, yet underneath it all it was hollow. For all its classical allusions, the classical was subverted in a virtuoso display of architectural facility.

In the Los Angeles Museum of Contemporary Art (1981–86) Isozaki returned to the earlier Fukuoka Bank Headquarters to use red Indian sandstone and to a quieter aesthetic of neutral interiors lit from above that retreated before the art objects on display. It was a mixture of Palladio and Egypt with its palms and pyramids. Because the museum was set below the plaza, light was introduced through the roof through pyramid-shaped skylights and translucent ceilings. As was to be expected, Isozaki's wavy Marilyn Monroe silhouette dominated the entry and lower court.

The Art Tower Mito, Ibaragi (1986–90) was less restrained. Its 100 metre high symbol tower was pure hyper-tech. The hexagonal concert hall casually repeated the vault of Sir John Soane's Breakfast Parlour at 13 Lincoln's Inn Fields. It is refined and elegant with precise timber-panelled seating terraces and creamy walls and ceiling. The tower lobby was Viollet-le-Duc Gothic structuralism in hyper-tech mode with its great angled steel tubes springing from plated columns. The cylindrical Theatre repeated the restrained grey exterior but it was deepened to a metallic blue. Sandwiched between, the entrance hall was lit by an inverted triangular onyx window whose shape overturned structural logic. The walls of the conference hall were decorated with voluminous drapes.

The Disney Building at Lake Buena Vista, Florida (1987–91), was extremely successful and was typical of Isozaki's mature 1990s style. It was calm, assured, less intense, but the earlier Mannerism was still evident in the Dadaist entrance lobby, in the 36 metre high truncated cone and rotated cubes whose forms were disguised by decorative areas of colour and lines. The curtain wall of the 250 metre axial block was converted to a reflective tartan grid of blue and white stripes and squares. The great sun dial connective space was punctured by an elevated bridge which recalled Isozaki's earlier dynamic interpenetrating forms in the 1970s, but, in the 1990s, structure gave way to colour and pattern, and squares were repeated endlessly in subdividing windows and as isolated openings. The impact of the truncated open cone depended on the circling movement overhead of sun and shadow on its brown surface with the yellow gnomon acting as a kind of Dadaist ornament or joke.

Isozaki's interiors show a typical Postmodern concern for widening the design vocabulary to enrich it beyond the limited functionalist scope of Modernism. His excursions into European architectural history are filtered through the agency of ideas from neo-Dada, Marcel Duchamp, Man Ray, and Shuzo Takiguichi. Isozaki's interiors are subversive in intent in relation to Modernism. His elevation of personal experiences to do with death and disintegration mean that his forms shatter, and what seems most solid disintegrates in order to reveal the darkness beneath the surface of things. His ultimate concern is with emptiness in what is an intense and highly intellectual method.

Isozaki's subversive attack on conservative culture manifest in his Dadaist bias towards ambivalent structured works and the imposition of a Western Mannerist metaphysic of unease and instability reflected the Japanese contemporary condition. As language has its rules, so architecture gains by the breaking and inversion of its grammar. In his recourse to the past, unlike 19th-century eclectics, Isozaki has aimed less at mimicking the past than at turning it inside out in order to drain it of meaning.

PHILIP DREW

See also Postmodernism

Biography

Born in Oita City, 23 July 1931. Graduated from the Architectural Faculty, University of Tokyo, 1954. Married the sculptor Aiko Miyawakiin, 1972. Worked with Kenzo Tange's Team and Urtec, Tokyo, 1954–63. Established his own architectural practice, Arata Isozaki and Associates, Tokyo, 1963; has also continued to collaborate with other architects and studios and was chief architect with Kenzo Tange for the Japan World Exhibition, Osaka, 1970. Designed textiles and furnishings from the mid-1970s. Has taught widely in the United States including visiting professorships, University of California at Los Angeles, 1969, Columbia University, New York, 1976 and 1979, Harvard University, Cambridge, Massachusetts, 1981, and Yale University, New Haven, Connecticut, 1982. Juror for the Pritzker Prize, New York, 1979–84. Numerous prizes and awards including Annual Prize, Architectural Institute of Japan, 1967 and 1975; *Interiors* Award, New York, 1983; Mainichi Art Award, Tokyo, 1983; Gold Medal, Royal Institute of British Architects, 1986. Honorary Fellow, American Institute of Architects, 1983; Honorary Member, Bund Deutscher Architekten, Germany, 1983; Member, Accademia Tiberina, Italy, 1978; Honorary Fellow, Royal Institute of British Architects, 1994; Honorary Academician, Royal Academy of Arts, 1994.

Selected Works

Interiors

1962–66 Oita Prefectural Library, Oita City (building and interiors)
1966–67 Fukuoka Mutual Bank, Oita City (building and interiors)
1968–71 Fukuoka Mutual Bank Headquarters, Fukuoka (building, interiors and furniture)
1971–74 Museum of Modern Art, Takasaki, Gunma (building and interiors)
1972–74 City Museum of Art, Kitakyushu, Fukuoka (building and interiors)
1973–74 Fujimi Country Club, Oita City (building and interiors)
1973–74 Kitakyushu Central Library, Kitakyushu, Fukuoka (building and interiors)
1979–83 Tsukuba Center Building, Tsukuba Science City, Ibaragi (building and interiors)
1981–86 Museum of Contemporary Art, Los Angeles (building and interiors)
1981–86 Björnson Studio-House, Venice, California (building and interiors)
1983–85 Palladium Club, New York City (building and interiors)
1983–90 Sant Jordi Sports Palace, Barcelona, Spain (building and interiors)
1986–90 Art Tower Mito, Mito Ibaragi (building and interiors)
1987–90 Kitakyushu International Conference Center, Fukuoka, Japan (building and interiors)
1987–91 Team Disney building, Buena Vista, Florida (building and interiors)

1990–94 The Center of Japanese Art and Technology, Krakow, Poland (building and interiors)
1991–92 Guggenheim Museum, Soho, New York City (additions and interiors)
1991–94 Museum of Contemporary Art, Nagi, Okayama, Japan (building and interiors)
1991–95 Kyoto Concert Hall, Kyoto, Japan (building and interiors)
1993 La Casa del Hombre (House of Man), La Coruña, Spain (building and interiors)

Isozaki has also designed dinnerware for Swid Powell; rugs for Vorwerk (1988); furniture including the *Marilyn* chair and table by ICF (1973–83), *Fuji* cabinets by Memphis (1981), and bed exhibited at the Milan Triennale in 1985; and jewellery by Cleto Munari (1986).

Publications

Kukan-e (Towards Space), Tokyo, 1971
Kenchiku no Kaitai (The Destruction of Modern Architecture), 1975
Shuho-ga (collected writings 1969–78), Tokyo, 1979
Kenchiku-no-Chiso (critical essays), Tokyo, 1979
Kenchiku Angya (Architectural Pilgrimage Series, with photographer Kishin Shinoyama), vols.1–12, Tokyo, 1980–92
Post-Modern Genron (The Principles of Post Modernism), Tokyo, 1985
"The Paradox of Tradition" in *Kagu: Mobilier Japonais*, Angers, 1985
Post-Modern no Jidai to Kenchiku (The Post Modern Era and Architecture), Tokyo, 1985
"The Current State of Design" in *International Design Yearbook* 4, New York, 1988
Kenchiku no Seijigaku (The Politics of Architecture), Tokyo, 1989
Seikimatsu no shiso to kenchiku (Thoughts and Archtiecture at the Turn of the Century), dialogue with Koji Taki, Tokyo, 1989
Kenchiku to iu Keishiki (Formalizing Architecture), Tokyo, 1991

Further Reading

There are several monographs on Isozaki; a good recent general book is *Arata Isozaki: Architecture 1960–1990*, 1991 which includes critical essays, a biography, a list of his principal buildings, projects and exhibitions and an extensive bibliography of primary and secondary sources.

"Arata Isozaki: Square, Cube and Rectangle" in *Japan Architect*, 51, March 1976
"Arata Isozaki: Cylinder and Semicylinder" in *Japan Architect*, 51, April 1976
Arata Isozaki: Architecture, 1960–1990, New York: Rizzoli, 1991
"Arata Isozaki, 1985–1991" in *Space Design* (Tokyo), part 1, special issue October 1991; part 2, special issue November 1991
Arata Isozaki: Works 30, Architectural Models, Prints, Drawings, Tokyo: Rikuyo-sha, 1992
Barattucci, Brunilde and Bianca Di Russo, *Arata Isozaki: Architetture, 1959–1982*, Rome: Officina, 1983
Bognar, Botond, *Contemporary Japanese Architecture: Its Development and Challenge*, New York: Van Nostrand Reinhold, 1985
Bognar, Botond, *The New Japanese Architecture*, New York: Rizzoli, 1990
Boyd, Robin, *New Directions in Japanese Architecture*, New York: Braziller, and London: Studio Vista, 1968
Capella, Juli and Quim Larrea, *Designed by Architects in the 1980s*, New York: Rizzoli, and London: Mitchell, 1988
Drew, Philip, *The Architecture of Arata Isozaki*, New York: Harper, and London: Granada, 1982
Drew, Philip, *The Museum of Modern Art, Gunma, 1971–1974*, London: Phaidon, 1996
Frampton, Kenneth, "Arata Isozaki's MOCA" in *Domus*, November 1986
Frampton, Kenneth, *Arata Isozaki*, Tokyo: ADA, 1991
Hollein, Hans, "Position and Move" in *Space Design*, April 1974
Mendini, Alessandro, *Arata Isozaki*, Tokyo: ADA, 1993 (Global Architecture 69)
The Prints of Arata Isozaki, 1977–83 (exhib. cat.), Tokyo: Gendai Hanga Center, 1983
Richardson, Sara, *Arata Isozaki, Post-modern Master* (bibliography), Monticello, IL: Vance, 1987
Ross, Michael Franklin, *Beyond Metabolism: The New Japanese Architecture*, New York: McGraw Hill, 1978
Stewart, David B., *The Making of a Modern Japanese Architecture: 1968 to the Present*, Tokyo and New York: Kodansha, 1987
Stewart, David B. and Higime Yatsuka, *Arata Isozaki: Architecture, 1960–1990*, New York: Rizzoli, 1991
Suzuki, Hiroyuki, "The Dismantling of History" in *Space Design*, October 1991
Taylor, Jennifer, "The Unreal Architecture of Arata Isozaki" in *Progressive Architecture*, September 1976
White, Anthony G., *Arata Isozaki and Fumihiko Maki: A Bibliographic Update*, Monticello, IL: Vance, 1990

Italy

Following the decline of the Roman empire and with the rise of Christian patronage, medieval Europe passed through the Early Christian, Byzantine, and Romanesque periods into the styles and stages of Gothic art and architecture. In Italy semi-independent city states developed, many based on trading and banking activities and represented in other commercial centres of western Europe. A rebirth of classical ideas arose in the 14th century from the rediscovery of classical literature; the works of Dante, Petrarch, and Boccaccio stimulated a new age of intellectual enquiry, philosophical and scientific. Against this background of wealth and the pursuit of knowledge, profound changes were about to take place which would leave indelible impressions on history until the Industrial Revolution.

In Florence, the powerful Medici banking family, engaged in local affairs spasmodically since 1296, encouraged patronage of the arts. In company with like-minded families – Pitti, Rucellai, and Strozzi – they pursued vigorously the emerging ideals of the Renaissance. A new cultural spirit made use of the classical past to inspire the future; evidence of ancient Rome sparked the search for new rules of design.

Because they had applied this new thinking to commerce and art in advance of any competitors, the Italian states had accumulated reserves of wealth. Beyond Medici dominance in Florence, other princely banking and trading families such as Farnese, Gonzaga, Este, and Sforza spent lavishly on public building works which contributed to civic pride and amenity. Prosperous citizens spent well on their own homes, as private sector building was thought to honour the community. Education improved and the invention of printing spread freedom of thought. Tuscany, too, made use of these new facilities in the transformation of art and architecture.

Although in some parts of Italy – including Sicily and particularly the Venetian Republic – medieval styles persisted into the 16th century, Florence and Rome were invigorated by the climate of change known as the Renaissance. Key Florentine protagonists, Leon Battista Alberti (1404–72) and Filippo Brunelleschi (1377–1446), defined geometric systems of proportion and perspective, Brunelleschi having studied in Rome after the turn of the century. His dome for Florence Cathedral (1420–34) harmonized classical motifs and new structural methods with a Gothic church – one of the first expressions of the Renaissance. In 1485 Alberti, more academic in approach, published his *De Re Aedificatoria*, setting out a design ideal "that nothing could be added, diminished or altered, but for the worse". Vitruvius's *De Architectura* was printed in 1486. Written in the reign of Augustus (27 BC–14 AD), it was not translated into Italian until 1521, becoming a lasting source of classical inspiration for many generations. The young theorists, chiefly Andrea Palladio (1508–80), Giacomo Barozzi da Vignola (1507–73), and Vincenzo Scamozzi (1552–1616) studied and interpreted Vitruvius and codified rules and proportions of the five ancient Orders of Architecture – Tuscan, Doric, Ionic, Corinthian, and Composite. Ideal proportions of the human body were mathematically formulated and used to great effect by Alberti and Brunelleschi.

New elements were added to the Renaissance vocabulary, principally a new form of dome with its supporting pendentives and the balustrade with its candelabra-like or vase-shaped balusters. Decorative treatments included rusticated stonework, fashionable initially for the external walls of early Florentine palaces and sometimes transformed into a painted feature for interiors. Much was owed to artists, sculptors, and other craftsmen and many of the architects started in this way, Brunelleschi as sculptor, Ghiberti as metalworker.

Many of Brunelleschi's designs were built after his death. The Pazzi Chapel at Santa Croce, Florence (1429–46) demonstrates early Renaissance qualities of deceptive simplicity and balance, achieved in a scheme of grey stone classical dressings and mouldings set into near-white plastered backgrounds. Mouldings and oculi are offset by limited frieze decoration and roundels of glazed terracotta reliefs coloured by Luca della Robbia, decoration serving architecture to achieve unity. Secular building took perhaps even greater steps forward – palaces were less fortified than before and housed enormous wealth in terms of building and contents.

The Ducal Palace at Urbino (c.1444–82), which entered the Renaissance after the appointment of Luciano Laurana as architect by Federico di Montefeltro in 1465, relies on elegance and purity of line. Doorcases and hooded carved fireplaces provide centres of interest in otherwise restrained, white plaster backgrounds. In the Sala degli Angeli, the well-known frieze of the chimneypiece bearing gambolling angelic putti is the work of Domenico Rosselli. The palace also contains outstanding intarsia work in the doors and cupboards of the studiolo designed at least in part by Botticelli. Portraits from the studiolo and most of the furnishings have been scattered to collections and museums, but in spite of the empty rooms, traces of influence from Piero della Francesca, Alberti and Laurana who was probably familiar with Diocletian's Palace at Spalato (Split), add to Federico's achievement.

The first Medici villa in the High Renaissance style was built at Poggio a Caiano, designed by Giuliano da Sangallo (1443–1516) and completed in 1485 for Lorenzo de' Medici. Instead of the usual central cortile, there is a two-storey barrel-vaulted hall with coffered gilded stucco ceiling. Lorenzo's son, Pope Leo X, commissioned the frescoes which were started in 1521 by Francabiagio and finished in a second stage in about 1579 by Allori. Pontormo and Andrea del Sarto contributed to the overall scheme which recorded allegorically various events in Medici family history. Most apartments in the villa suffered 19th-century redecoration, but the great hall survives.

Donato Bramante (1444–1514) worked as a painter under Laurana at Urbino and in mid-life changed to an architectural career in which he exercised wide influence in his handling of space as the chief component of interior design.This was initially demonstrated in the Tempietto in Rome, a small circular "temple" in the courtyard of S. Pietro in Montorio, 1502.

The Palazzo Venezia with its loggia dating from 1467–71 and completed after 1500, grew into the first great Renaissance palace in Rome, home to Paul II and his magnificent collections. Its architect is unknown but attributions have been made to Alberti, Rossellino, and Giuliano da Maiano.

The new ways of thinking fostered an interest in the domestic interior, the layout of rooms, and their fittings and furnishings. Relative stability in society allowed for improvements in convenience and privacy to an extent never practicable in medieval times. The stringing together of rooms reached from a main hall and dining space had, by the mid-15th century, been overtaken by more ingenious planning. Larger town houses were mostly planned round an open courtyard which was often colonnaded to provide protection from the weather and easy access. Planning of country villas was less restricted and symmetry more easily achieved where land was available and the need for defence had diminished. Windows could be placed looking outwards over the landscape, radically affecting the outside appearance and giving freedom of internal and external design.

Before the advent of the Baroque style, rooms were usually rectangular, possibly with flat beamed ceilings on upper floors and for smaller rooms. These would coexist with vaulted or deeply coved ceilings if height was a consideration and, where additional space was required, columns could be introduced for structural and visual reasons. The supporting ceiling members may have been exposed or concealed by a suspended ceiling, with decorated soffit. From the 16th century ceilings became elaborate, with gilded carved wood coffering in geometric shapes, until Baroque outlines began to take over. A number of the Palazzo Vecchio rooms in Florence dating from the 1480s have elaborate ceilings, for example the Sala dei Gigli and the Audience Room, the latter by the Del Tasso brothers.

Doors and windows had architraves in stone or plaster, with varying degrees of carving or stucco decoration. Pilasters in classic styles with entablatures or pediments might, in the most luxurious surroundings, be in marble or *scagliola*. Windows were by this time usually glazed and shuttered. Chimneypieces formed the focal point and gave owners, architects, and sculptors opportunity to show their talents. Fireplace accessories could also be stylish and decorative: sculpted figures or simple architectural forms in worked iron, steel and bronze.

Fired earth in the form of thin bricks or tiles was the most usual flooring, in geometric shapes in simple but effective patterns, particularly the enduring herring-bone. Terrazzo, a mix of marble chippings with stucco and stone dust spread with a trowel and polished when dry, was one alternative, and marble, laid in patterns using varied natural colours came at

Italy: Camera degli Sposi, Palazzo Ducale, Mantua, frescoes by Andrea Mantegna, 1465–74

the top of the scale, in ecclesiastical buildings even more than the imposing palazzi. Timber was another medium for flooring, particularly on upper floors where there was less likely to be a problem with damp. Patterns were produced from naturally contrasting woods, but the finest intarsia inlays were reserved for chests, doors, and cupboard fronts.

Before the Renaissance, Italian furniture seems to have been generally primitive in comparison with the work produced by sculptors, painters, metal, and leather workers. A medieval tradition of church-furniture making did exist, but such fine quality woodwork was slow to enter the domestic market. Cassoni or chests were perhaps the most common pieces, for storing, securing, and carrying personal and household belongings, painted more often than carved until the early 16th century fashion for deeply cut relief panels of scenes sometimes taken from the engravings of famous painters. Carved walnut chests dating from c.1560, with gesso and gilded surrounds to the panels, can be seen in London's Victoria and Albert Museum, and the Museo del Castello Sforzesco, Milan, possesses a fine Lombard chest with intarsia panels.

Chairs varied from the throne-like, upholstered and tasselled ones for the nobility, descending according to rank through smaller, cushioned versions to simple ladder-backs, the older X-form chairs, and finally to wooden stools. The amount of carving and decoration varied considerably, the most ornate being the most likely to have been preserved. Tables with columned or balustered underframes and fixed tops took the place of earlier trestle types, and, for the grand interior, inlaid marble tops on carved and gilded bases gave splendid opportunities to artists and craftsmen during the 16th century.

Beds ranged from the planks-on-trestles primitive type up through the *lettiera* with frame and headboard to those with posts, testers, valances, and curtains. Evidence of these refinements exists in contemporary paintings, for example, Sodoma's *Alexander Visiting Roxana* in the Farnesina, Rome (1512) shows a bed of magnificent architectural design, although no surviving examples are recorded. Bed-hangings, mattresses, pillows, sheets, and bedcovers were all in use, with wall and door curtains to subdue draughts and give added privacy. Italy produced fabrics of great variety, in wool, silk, linen, and cotton. Patterns were woven or embroidered; cotton with painted patterns was imported, probably as Indian chintz via Portugal. Summer and winter curtains were sometimes hung to suit the seasons and mosquito nets provided protection.

Michelangelo (1475–1564) and Raphael (1483–1520) worked contemporaneously in Florence and then in Rome, and were key figures in the Renaissance but were orientated by great difference of temperament in separate stylistic directions. Raphael spent many years on the papal apartments, the stanze and loggie in the Vatican Palace, for the Medici Pope Julius II, creating a magnificent parade of Pompeian interiors based on ancient models but brought to Renaissance life by the artist's impeccable skill and freshness of vision. Michelangelo had also been called to Rome by Pope Julius in 1505, three years before Raphael, painting the Sistine Chapel as a vast story of the Creation and man's relation to God (1508–12). In his architectural design for the Laurentian Library, Florence, his unorthodox treatment of the classical orders demonstrated his adherence to the innovative style we now call Mannerism. The library staircase, completed later by Giorgio Vasari (1559), introduced scrolls, exaggerated balusters, and a wanton ingenuity in the combination of outer flights of straight edged steps flanking curved and recurved steps in the central flight. The pilasters on window surrounds have reverse tapers, from top to bottom, an unmistakable departure from High Renaissance handling of established elements. Classical motifs had burst out of theoretical restraints with curved, scrolled, and broken pediments, vigorously-posed figures, strongly emphasized cornices and the addition of acanthus leaves and grotesques. These features, augmenting Michelangelo's earlier freedom of expression in the well-known sculptures and in the completion of the Sistine *Last Judgment* finished in 1541, exerted widespread influence. Michelangelo's Mannerist style affected Italy and northern Europe as the precursor of the Baroque. In Rome, Baldassare Peruzzi (1481–1536) showed a brilliantly executed Mannerist style in the interiors of the Villa Farnesina (1509–11) and the Palazzo Massimo (1533–36) with *trompe-l'oeil* scrolls and stuccoes.

Mannerist tendencies reached Mantua in the 1520s where Giulio Romano's frescoes for the Palazzo del Te incorporated influences absorbed while working with Raphael and Giovanni da Udine in Rome during the preceding decade. The classical reliefs in the Mantua Palazzo's Sala degli Stucchi came from the same Raphael school, but in the famous Sala dei Giganti, Giulio eliminated the frieze and covered the walls entirely with the apocalyptic collapse of huge sections of the composite order of architecture on top of writhing giants. Restraint is abandoned in favour of dramatic energy. Francesco Primaticcio worked as assistant to Romano on the frescoes and used his experience to very good effect, moving to the France of François I where, at Fontainebleau, he and Rosso Fiorentino transformed the interior of the Château in a manner far more elegant than that of the Palazzo del Te.

In the Veneto, Gothic had given way more slowly to the reborn classical style, but the change, once started, expanded quickly. The first work of prime classicist Andrea Palladio was the Villa Godi at Lonedo c.1537 where a repertory of landscape, grotesque, and illusionist relief, all in fresco, decorates the *piano nobile* interiors executed by Gualtiero dall'Arzere, Battista del Moro and Giambattista Zelotti.

Palladio's Villa Caldogno near Vicenza, contains lackadaisical atlantes figures in grisaille holding up a painted cornice, ignored by Gianantonio Fasolo's groups of pastoral figures in their intervening frescoed panels. Many Palladian palaces and villas in the Vicenza area followed in the 1540s and 1550s, all assuming fresco treatment as the main constituent of their interior decoration. Architectural influences from Raphael and Bramante reached Palladio through Michele Sanmicheli (1484–1559), reinforcing the classical strands of Renaissance networks. Fresco as a medium remained popular over a very long period. Many painters were employed on Palladio's interiors, and the extent to which his strictly classical work dominated the overall effect varied. At the Villa Barbaro, Maser, Paolo Veronese may not have adhered to the principles of Palladio's forthcoming *Quattro Libri dell Architettura* (1570) for his painted architecture, but their collaboration resulted in an undoubted masterpiece. Another Palladian interior, the Teatro Olimpico, Vicenza (from 1580), unites three-dimensional illusory architecture with a real Roman-inspired interior, completed by Scamozzi, in the form of a permanent stage set showing in detail three diverging city streets disappearing in false perspective to far distances behind a front screen based on a Corinthian triumphal arch.

In Rome, meanwhile, the Catholic church was in turmoil, with the Counter-reformation and the Council of Trent engaged in recovering ground lost to the Lutheran Reformation. The Papacy was deeply involved with the spiritual and physical reconstruction of the Church. Church building proceeded energetically and began to embody a powerful new iconography helpful to its re-establishment. Changes of style seen in the work of Michelangelo, Giovanni da Udine, and Giulio Romano continued to develop in freer modelling and greater use of heavily gilded mouldings. It was a time of many transitions and confusions before a clear conception of the Baroque emerged, led by Italy in spite of its fragmented political structure and its uneven absorption of differing aesthetic trends.

The Third Loggia and the Sala Paolina in the main palace and the Casino of Pius IV (c.1561) and the Villa di Papa Giulio all demonstrate proto-Baroque features and indicate a constant building programme originating from the Vatican. Between Mannerism and Baroque the line is not well defined but there is common agreement that the rule books of the Renaissance were no longer dictating every architectural detail. Giant orders and oval plans entered the repertory, and painting, still with a strong illusionary content, spread freely into available spaces without always being confined to definite compartments.

The growth of an innovative style practised by a limited number of architects and artists in the 16th century had been nurtured by Michelangelo. Others leading beyond Mannerism to form the full-blown Baroque are headed by Carlo Maderno (1556–1629), nephew of Domenico Fontana, designer of the Palazzo Barberini and a robust pioneer of the movement which was still concentrated in Rome. With his nephew, Francesco Borromini (1599–1667) he began work in 1625 on the palace for the family of Pope Urban VIII. Its completion in 1633 by Giovanni Lorenzo Bernini (1598–1680) established unequivocally the presence of Baroque design. The frescoed coved ceiling in the Barberini salone by Pietro da Cortona (1596–1669) was started in 1633. It conveyed in allegorical terms the triumph of the Church through the instrument of Divine Providence in the shape of the Barberini Pope Urban, symbolized in the centre of the ceiling by the three bees of his coat of arms. Painted architecture, garlands and greenery, putti, and mythical beasts intertwine with angelic and human figures, focusing on the corona of the Pope.

Italian Baroque made interior design, sacred and secular, into a heightened setting, theatrical in feeling, for which the

Italy: Galleria Farnese, Palazzo Farnese, Rome, 1597–1603

outside approach had prepared strong expectations. Bernini was to be the ideal practitioner in this art, although his years of preoccupation with St. Peter's piazza and its colonnades resulted in disappointingly few secular interiors. The Vatican's Sala Regia (1663–66) is a monumental staircase in which highly developed skill in the handling of inadequate and irregular space overcomes the drawbacks of the site, giving a worthy ceremonial means of access from the Pope's private apartments or from the Sala Regia to the main portico of the church. Correction of asymmetry and increase of effect through manipulation of perspective devices together with adroit placing and lighting of his equestrian statue of the Emperor Constantine show what Bernini could do in spite of unpromising conditions. False perspective had been used previously by Borromini in the Palazzo Spada (c.1653) and before that to Antonio da Sangallo's entrance to the Palazzo Farnese. Here, at the end of the 16th century, Annibale Carracci executed the complex painted ceiling of the Farnese Gallery. It owes much to Michelangelo's Sistine Chapel ceiling, but is composed with greater intricacy, leading up in a framework of quadratura from a sumptuous modelled amd gilded frieze below the cornice to groups of grisaille herms and atlantes who appear to bear another painted cornice. Groups of life-like figures and large imitation easel paintings carry the design upwards to the crowning centrepiece, *The Triumph of Bacchus and Ariadne*. Lanfranco and Guercino in Rome maintained the Baroque manner of ceiling painting during the 1620s for the Villa Borghese and Casa Ludovisi respectively.

A very different variation of the style was created by Guarino Guarini (1624–83), a Theatine monk who was in Rome undergoing his novitiate during the 1640s. Church building was a function of this order which often trained its own architects and which found in Guarini an eccentric individual talent. Starting from the full Baroque scene created by Bernini, Borromini, and Cortona, he was also influenced by Moorish design, probably having visited Spain and Portugal, but himself supplied the complicated mathematical schemes which he transformed into decidedly original buildings. The management of intricate spaces and the introduction of subtle lighting effects take the place of elaborate surface decoration, but even with a certain austerity there is no suggestion of weakened drama.

Piedmont in northern Italy gained the services of another architect trained in Rome, Filippo Juvarra (1678–1736) who again became known for his churches, chief among which is the Superga on a hilltop just outside Turin. His major domestic work included the Palazzo Madama (1718–21) with its fine double staircase and sculptured detail, compared by Anthony Blunt to the Escalier des Ambassadeurs at Versailles. Stupinigi, a magnificent hunting lodge in the countryside a few miles away, was designed for his patron, Victor Amadeus II of Savoy and begun in 1729. It rises from an irregular star-shaped ground plan, centred on an oval ballroom, with a very large hexagonal court and wings positioned at diagonal angles. The tall galleried ballroom, apsed and pilastered with all the established Baroque characteristics of scrolls, wayward pediments, shells, urns, and putti in grisaille and quadratura, shows nevertheless a slight retreat from the most overwhelming exaggerations. Juvarra, like many of his contemporaries, maintained close control over the interior design and finishes, supervising and possibly executing some of the work himself. Lightness of colour in the *Triumph of Diana* ballroom ceiling and elsewhere may have been enhanced by the Venetian artists Giuseppe and Domenico Valeriani, indicating a definite bias towards the greater elegance and fancy that were to come. Among the last great Italian masters of the Baroque, Juvarra was still able to hold his own in relation to the rising French tide.

In 1720, Turin became the capital of the so-called Kingdom of Sardinia, being previously a substantial trading and commercial city under the Counts of Savoy. Benedetto Alfieri (1700–67) succeeded Juvarra as architect to the king and designed a series of small rooms and cabinets in the Royal Palace, many for the private use of the queen. A *cabinetto Cinese* indicates the extent to which Baroque was being superseded here by Rococo tastes.

Genoa had evolved its own branch of Baroque design. An early start in the first half of the 16th century had produced the High Renaissance palaces of the Strada Nuova to which the Palazzo Doria-Tursi (now Municipio), begun 1564 by Rocco Lurago, and the Palazzo Bianco (1565), by G. Orsolino and D. Ponzello, were later added. Steeply rising sites encouraged monumental double staircases but decorative virtuosity was reserved for the great rooms where fresco was still the preferred medium. In the Palazzo Bianco, flamboyant decoration in the late 17th and early 18th centuries was carried out by Domenico Piola and Lorenzo de Ferrari. This was largely destroyed in World War II but has since been restored in its original Baroque spirit. The Palazzo Rosso (1671–67) by Matteo Lagomaggiore, fared better and contains, within its hundred or more rooms, mature Rococo decorative treatments. The bedchamber has much white and gold with mirror-panelled doors, paintings in gilded wall frames, and a fine saucer-domed bed recess. C-scrolls and more white and gold feature in the Sala della Primavera.

Borderlines between Baroque and Rococo are not governed by date but arose from historic circumstance, variable resources, and artistic influences. Neither Florence nor Venice had fully rejected their classical Renaissance inspiration to assimilate Mannerism and subsequent Baroque. Florence was too deeply immersed in the culture which had originated there to embark on such radical changes once Michelangelo had concentrated his main activities in Rome, where the Papacy had attracted the available creative talent. Venice, too, failed to develop the full panoply of Baroque due, as Anthony Blunt has stated, to the ghosts of Palladio and Scamozzi hanging heavily over it in the 17th and 18th centuries. Instead, greater continuity of Palladian classicism existed, with little acknowledgement of the freedom of design which was altering the streets and palaces of Rome. Even the one grand essay in Venetian Baroque, S. Maria della Salute (1631–82), by Baldassare Longhena, retained a strong classical basis to support the large scrolled buttresses below the dome, each surmounted by a statue, which give such predominant character to this great octagonal church on the Grand Canal.

Interiors in the great palaces adhered more closely to the current Roman fashion, but this was not innovative and tended to cling to Renaissance grandeur. In the Sala del Maggior Consiglia of the Palazzo Ducale, the redecoration of 1577 produced works by Veronese, Palma Giovane, and Tintoretto. The later *Paradise* of Tintoretto (1588) claims to be the largest painting on canvas in the world and the overwhelming effect of a chamber so decorated is certainly Baroque in spirit. The Albrizzi, Rezzonico, and Pesaro palace interiors are particularly noteworthy, but the slow drift towards a lighter Rococo approach to decoration can be discerned. The quality of light and impressionistic colours of the Venetian painters continued to delight the eye without the need for excessive splendour.

Italian supremacy over the European artistic scene had been taken for granted since Renaissance times, but during the reign of Louis XIV (1643–1715) France usurped Italy's lead. The building of Versailles set the seal on French autonomy in art and architecture. Quality of workmanship and artistic excellence were deployed using French talent educated at the French Academy in Rome, established in 1666. Gradually Louis XV and Louis XVI styles replaced magnificence with the elegance and fantasy of the Rococo, although Italian artists, craftsmen, and architects continued to work throughout western Europe and to diffuse their influence in a way that was not easily superseded. Grand Tourism in the 18th century maintained strong links, and, in England, enriched country houses and art collections, not just through purchase of Italian artefacts but by way of the teams of painters, sculptors and stuccoists who were engaged on the interiors of English great houses.

A sense of direction was lacking in Italy in this period, as it came under French rule for a time in the north and Spanish Bourbon royalty in the Kingdom of the Two Sicilies in the south. Before moving to the mixture of late Baroque and Rococo of Naples and Sicily, a view of Venice and the mainland in the 18th century should be taken. The Villa Valmarana dei Nani, near Venice, was begun in 1669, probably by Antonio Muttoni, but acquired its famous frescoes after the property was bought by the Valmarana family. In the 1740s and 1750s, the Tiepolos, Giambattista and his son Giandomenico, decorated the main house and the guest house or foresteria in free and confident manner, fulfilling the prime purpose of much Italian fresco which aims to make important rooms extend into larger spaces, creating at the same time an autonomous work of art. Giambattista Tiepolo's *Sacrifice of Iphigenia* in the central salon is probably the work of most distinction, but in the Stanza della Villegiatura, another interior is framed in illusionist Venetian Gothic design which contains surprising Neo-Classical hints. The guest house frescoes are generally considered to be by Giandomenico, and contain distorted, slightly sinister Chinoiserie figures and motifs of Rococo character. The architectural settings were

Italy: Salottino di Porcellana, Palazzo Reale, Pórtici, 1757–59 (now Capodimonte, Naples)

painted by Mengozzi Colonna and the work was probably finished in 1757.

The Palazzo Labia, in Venice, was built from about 1720 onwards by Andrea Cominelli and Alessandro Tremignon for the Labia family. Again, Gianbattista Tiepolo frescoed the grand ballroom, which has some very impressive pedimented doorways, window surrounds, and traditional fluted Corinthian pilasters in fluent Palladian language. This architecture was augmented by Mengozzi Colonna's quadratura and left Tiepolo to depict on the ceiling *Genius Putting Time to Flight*, and within the painted arches on the walls his favourite subjects, Antony and Cleopatra, in legendary scenes. Comparison of the Tiepolos with Veronese, the artist whose influence on them was so strong, shows the greater mastery of the earlier painter but also illustrates the shift of style to a lightness in line and colour and the loosening of compositional relationships.

A completely different social structure greeted the traveller in late 17th century Naples and Sicily, and talent in art and architecture was by no means so plentiful. The Kingdom of the Two Sicilies was from 1734 ruled by Charles VII, son of Philip V of Spain and Elizabeth Farnese, known on succession to the Spanish throne as Charles III. In Naples, Ferdinando Sanfelice (1675–1748) was designing churches in the main but also built palaces where intricately planned staircases vied with each other in their elaborate geometry. In the Palazzo Serra di Cassano (1720–38) an entrance staircase starts at ground level with twin flights which twist and turn to form a bridge giving access to the *piano nobile*. This is in a style far distant from anything found further north. Sanfelice and Antonio Vaccaro (1681–1750) continued to design in ecclesiastical Baroque but employed for secular purposes ideas incorporating Rococo ornament. Vaccaro's cloister of S. Chiara convent in Naples (1739–42), executed entirely in maiolica, is of very worldly appeal. Octagonal piers with spiralling vine designs in yellow, blue and green support pergolas with living vines forming a shady roof. The floor tiles of a nearby fountain depict painted fish under water. Following the French example in royal patronage of manufacture, Charles in 1743 started the royal porcelain factory at Capodimonte where, in addition to *objets d'art* and porcelain for domestic use, a Porcelain Room, now in the Capodimonte Museum, Naples, was created for the Palazzo Portici (1757–59), inspiring examples in Holland, Germany and Austria. Some Porcelain Rooms were merely for the display of collections but this one was completely lined with the material, with finely modelled panels of Chinese figures, gilded mouldings, and tall mirrors among Rococo flowers, trophies, birds, and butterflies, more than 3000 pieces of porcelain.

Charles also imported two Rome-trained architects, Ferdinando Fuga (1699–1781) and Luigi Vanvitelli (1700–71) for an extensive public works programme of which much was left unfinished. Outside the Royal Palace at Caserta by Vanvitelli the long flat entrance front demonstrates an abandonment of Baroque spatial values and indicates reconsideration of classicism. Inside, however, the main entrance vestibule and stairs retain not only monumental scale but clearly express movement and drama, a swirling coffered dome over the upper level vestibule which commands a view of the grand axial composition. Versailles was obviously a source of inspiration as Charles was a grandson of Louis XIV and had seen the palace at first hand. Furnishing in the palace at Caserta (1780) follows Louis XV and XVI styles and provided a gilded bath with gold taps for the queen. Later First Empire furnishing in the Appartamento Nuovo includes magnificent French furniture, a Roman-style stone bath and an alabaster dressing table centred on a pedestal fountain for perfumed water.

Sicilian variants of Baroque and Rococo in Palermo and Catania had, at the end of the 17th century, drawn directly on Roman ideas. The Oratory of S. Zita, Palermo was decorated in 1685–88 by Giacomo Serpotta (1656–1732) in immensely skilful high relief stuccoes. The design encompassed three-dimensional frames recessed to hold deeply modelled scenes of religious subjects, the frames being set against a stucco mock drapery held by numerous putti and ornamented with scrolls, shells, military trophies, and swags of fruit. The centrepiece on the end wall represents the Battle of Lepanto when Christians defeated Turks, and all is naturalistically created to very small scale – a technique used earlier in the century in Palermo Cathedral. The Palazzo Gangi, Palermo by an unknown architect dates from at least 80 years later but is an equally surprising survival of the fantastic Rococo. The ceiling of the Gangi Galleria degli Specchi consists of an inner curved and pierced dome-like stucco framing above which is a second domed surface brightly lit to emphasise its painted scenery by Gaspare Serenario (d.1759). Lavish gilded Rococo ornamentation and dark panels furnish the walls while maiolica floor tiles are painted with scrolls, leopards, and landscapes. Window shutters decorated on the reverse give a continuous decorative scheme when closed. Adjacent rooms complete an unexpectedly sophisticated suite, used as a location for the film *Il Gattopardo*. The *salone* was painted by Elia Interguglielmi who died in 1773.

Another eccentricity, this time in Catania, involves work by Francesco Battaglia at the incomplete Palazzo Biscari. In a preliminary exterior flourish he perched two small square pagoda-roofed pavilions on a conventional terrace and proceeded to decorate the *gran salone* in an effusion of Rococo stucco. The coved *rocaille* ceiling is pierced to form a musicians' gallery, revealing the well-lit painted dome above, full of flying figures. The musicians' staircase is also clad in *rocaille* stucco with an accompanying wrought-iron balustrade in lightweight swirls which might easily be at home in an Art Deco context.

The status of France as leader of taste in the 17th and 18th centuries was supported by interchanges with Italian artistic culture. In the 17th century Bernini had submitted designs for the Louvre, painters led by Primaticcio were employed on the French royal palaces, and French art students maintained contact through their academy in Rome. French Rococo design scarcely outlived the Revolution and classical academicism persisted, ready to inspire the next formulation of principles. Italy's alternative to Rococo concentrated yet again on painting and stucco. The reappearance of classicism – Neo-Classicism – in Italy was spasmodic, and since its use in interiors had never entirely disappeared, it lacked the novelty it afforded the French.

Giovanni Battista Piranesi (1720–78), a Venetian living in Rome, published sets of engravings from 1748 onwards of views of Rome, its antiquities, and the curiously named

Diverse maniere. He came under many influences from the later Baroque period. The Bibienas and the Valeriani brothers were stage designers, Juvarra and Fischer von Erlach were architects and Gian Paolo Panini was a painter and teacher – all of whom could have sparked off the romantic element in Piranesi's vision. Excavations at Herculaneum and Pompeii had begun in 1738 which disclosed previously unknown ancient interiors; these also changed stylistic direction.

J.J. Winckelmann (1717–68), whose study was Greek art and the ideals of "noble simplicity and calm grandeur" and whose infuential *History of Ancient Art* was published in 1764, encouraged partisanship in the Greece-versus-Rome argument which he headed as a counterpoise to Piranesi. The enthusiasm at the end of the century for collecting ancient art and sculpture led to the building of new museums in topical versions of the old formula. Papal patronage under Pius VI added rooms to the Vatican Museum, most notably the Sala Rotonda (1776–80), providing a circle of shell-headed niches for antique statues ranged round a central fountain. The Sala delle Muse and the Sala a Croce Greca complete the suite of Neo-Classical rooms by Michelangelo Simonetti (1724–81) whose source of inspiration was likely to have been Herculaneum. Pietro Camporese (1726–81) and his son Giuseppe (1763–1822) both worked at the Vatican Museum on new sculpture galleries (1786), Giuseppe being credited with successful blending of academic background with the current Neo-Classical motifs. A more formal expression of Neo-Classicism was Raffaele Stern's (1774–1820) design for the Braccio Nuovo, the new wing which was built between 1817 and 1822 incorporating a modified interpretation of Winckelmann's principles but described by Georgina Masson in 1965 as "cold nineteenth century classicism".

In Rome, Carlo Marchioni (1702–86), talented in all aspects of sculpture, engineering, architecture, and design, provided a setting for Cardinal Albani's collection of antique sculpture in the Villa Albani. His facility in a number of design styles reflected Roman love of display but did not inhibit his choice of the Neo-Classical architecture for this purpose.

Napoleon's ventures in northern Italy gave status to Milan as a capital city, encouraging new design and building. The city's principal architect Giuseppe Piermarini (1734–1808) used Neo-Classicism with elegance and skill in extensive works at the Royal Palace, on the design of La Scala opera house, and in the Villas Ducale and Reale at Monza, all principally in the 1780s, although he was criticized by the theorist Francesco Milizia for too much magnificence. Milizia is connected with a later designer, whom he taught and who worked almost exclusively in the Veneto, Giovanni Antonio Selva (1751–1819). Selva was well-indoctrinated by Milizia and also by his extensive travels through Italy with sculptor Antonio Canova whose monuments later became almost synonymous with Neo-Classicism. Works by Selva include the Venetian opera house, La Fenice (1790–92); the Teatro Nuovo, Trieste; Villa Manfrin, Treviso; and Palazzo Dotti, Padua.

Also in the north, the interior of the Palazzo Milzetti, Faenza, built by Giuseppe Pistocchi between 1790 and 1800, places special emphasis on the local traditions of painting, sculpture, and decoration. Felice Giani (1758–1823), experienced in Napoleonic decoration at the Tuileries, Paris, and Malmaison, and accustomed to working in all parts of Italy, contributed paintings in the Galleria and Sala degli Sposi to achieve, in combination with Raphaelesque stucco work by Antonio Trentanove, one of the finest intact Neo-Classical interiors in the region.

The introduction of the Empire style was approved by the new ruling establishment, many of whom were familiar with the style through close connection with France. Napoleon's Egyptian campaign of 1798–99 focused attention on Egyptian antiquities, and a translation of Baron Denon's account of the expedition was available in Italian by 1808. The inclusion of Pharaohs, pyramids, hieroglyphs, and sphinxes in the Sala Impero, Palazzo Massimo, Rome in Egyptian Revival fashion is an admirable example. Naples under Murat, also from 1808, was the scene of Empire decoration in the Italian manner with the Appartamento Nuovo (1807–45) in the Royal Palace, Caserta containing the Sala di Marte by Antonio de Simone, with extensive use of marble and heroic bas-reliefs as main wall decorations executed by Villareale, Monti, and Masucci. The frescoed ceiling vault of the Triumph of Achilles is by Raffaelle Galliano. In the king's apartment the rooms for the king and for Murat have superb canopied Empire beds, carved and inlaid in mahogany and gilded bronze, with accompanying tables, chairs, and commodes. Similar furniture by Percier and Fontaine who exerted such powerful influence on the whole range of Empire interior design had been imported from Paris by Caroline Murat for the earlier old Royal Palace in Naples.

Palermo is the site of a unique building that is almost a folly. The Palazzina della Favorita or Palazzina Cinese on the outskirts of the city, was built in 1799 as a summer villa for King Ferdinando IV and Queen Maria Carolina who had, the previous year, fled from Naples on Nelson's flagship. Allegedly, they acquired the idea of a "Chinese" style from a successful Chinese setting to a banquet they gave for Nelson. The exterior is unresolved, with heavy, plain columns supporting upturned eaves hung with tiny bells, but the real attraction is inside where architect Giuseppe Venanzio Marvuglia (1729–1814) exercised his considerable skill on Pompeian, Turkish, and Chinese rooms, now well restored and glowing with pleasing colour. Comparison with Brighton Pavilion is unavoidable, although the Palazzina was conceived on smaller and more modest lines, entirely lacking in the rich and sophisticated background which the Prince Regent so much enjoyed in Brighton. In the ballroom of the Royal Palace in Palermo (c.1815) the shallow barrel-vaulted ceiling, frieze, pilastered walls, and traditional dado hark back to the Italian Renaissance but a Neo-Classical statement is clearly intended, if not achieved. The heaviness of would-be Empire furniture underlines the decline of a style which owed so much to elegance and crispness of finish.

Also relevant to Italian Neo-Classical design is a study of interiors by Italian architects and decorators at Pavlovsky Palace, St. Petersburg. Giacomo Quarenghi (1744–1817), Vincenzo Brenna (1747–1819) and Karl Rossi (1775–1849) all left oeuvres which, restored after serious World War II damage, provide a body of work including furniture and other contents, equal to any Neo-Classical source in Italy.

After 1815, the eclipse of Napoleon affected fashions in decoration and design and although Italian Neo-Classicism persisted by way of a few substantial examples, it no longer survived as a mainstream style. It had been a product of

Italy: Palazzo Reale, Caserta, Sala di Marte, 1807

imported French culture and although its archaeological basis was not forgotten, the clean-cut academic approach to design was being invaded by more romantic aspirations. Although individual architects were no longer making international reputations, some distinguished buildings were constructed, particularly theatres and opera houses, and town planning received attention on a classical scale even if, as in Florence, such schemes were not completed.

Some painters were able to assimilate a stylistic change of direction. The Bolognese painter Pelagio Palagi (1775–1860), who developed also as architect and designer of interiors and furniture, was in the forefront of this transition. In borrowing from architectural styles of the past, historicism combined in the first half of the 19th century strong romantic and eclectic elements. An interest in literature was translated into three-dimensional substance, the novels of Sir Walter Scott being a popular source. The improvement of communications and resulting spread of ideas gave wide freedom of choice which characterized design styles in Italy as elsewhere for most of the rest of the century. From ancient Roman, Greek, and Egyptian models the field was extended to include Moorish, Gothic, and Oriental, with even indigenous Rococo, Baroque, and Renaissance design being searched for inspiration as nostalgia took the place of innovation.

Palagi's abilities had been recognized early, and in 1806 Count Aldrovandi sent the young painter to study in Rome. A series of attributed drawings of romanticized Neo-Classical vases decorated with symbolic subjects must have been inspired by Piranesi and indicates further affinity with Giani and Fuseli. In Rome, Palagi worked with Felice Giani on the redecoration of the Quirinale for Napoleon, but his major achievements were for the king of Sardinia, Carlo Alberto, for whom he improved two royal palaces in Turin. In the Castello at Racconigi, about 40 kilometres to the south, Palagi began to design in 1832 a fine bathroom on the ground floor and rooms with their furnishings for the *piano nobile*, incorporating a reception hall, an Apollo Study, and an Etruscan Cabinet. The Etruscan Cabinet was one of his greatest successes, carried out with help from Carlo Bellosio, with frescoed ceiling, coved frieze, and wall panels, dark backgrounds, and gold or yellow figures. Palagi's fine drawings for furniture show derivation from Percier and Fontaine with caryatids, lion heads and palmettes much in evidence. He favoured the use of bronze to obtain a fine finish, employing French and Milanese foundries for the work. Another source of French influence was through E.A. Petitot who had enlarged the vocabulary of ornament taken from both ancient and recent periods. By this time Palagi had amassed a substantial collection of antique art which is now in the municipal collections at Bologna.

Palagi's interiors at the Royal Palace in Turin (1835–57) expanded into rich Neo-Renaissance treatments with Corinthian orders and coffered ceilings. Robust carving and gilding with heavily draped curtains and brilliant chandeliers accomplished the transition into a mid-century style which in Britain would be described as Victorian. The Ballroom contains ceiling panels painted entirely by Palagi who also designed carved doors for the Council Chamber which were carried out by Capello, Ferrero, and Marielloni. The elaborately carved gilt furniture in this room shows Palagi's most eccentric vein, but his fertile imagination restored some of the status Italian design had possessed at the time of Juvarra. The staircase of the Palace was redecorated for Vittorio Emmanuele II in 1864–65, dominated by a statue of Carlo Alberto by Vincenzo Vela in a Renaissance-type niche and tabernacle and supported by stuccoes and paintings which celebrated the history of the House of Savoy.

The popularity of cafes and restaurants presented opportunities for smaller-scale work catering for a wider public. Turin's Ristorante del Cambio was elegantly renovated by Lorenzo Panizza in 1850 and a cartoon of Cavour still exists above the table where he used to sit, marking the move towards Italian unity which took a further 20 years to achieve. The Caffe Pedrocchi in Padua (1816–31), designed by Antonio Gradenigo (1806–84), and Giuseppe Jappelli (1783–1852), a pupil of Selva, is a Neo-Classical building of character. It was extended on ground and first floors into Egyptian, Etruscan, Moorish and Gothic rooms, with a finishing touch in the Sala Rossini of painted harps above gold-starred walls. According to one historian, it was "the handsomest 19th-century cafe in the world".

The interior of La Scala opera house in Milan was redecorated in 1830 by Alessandro Sanquirico (1774–1849) in a white and gold scheme, anticipating the Late Empire Throne Room at Caserta (1839–45) by Gaetano Genovese (1795–1860), assisted by Angelini and Tommaso Arnaud. At the same time Genovese was extending and remodelling the Royal Palace in Naples, also for Ferdinand II.

Little pioneering work marked Italian interiors in the troubled political climate leading to unification in 1870, after which the new Kingdom of Italy required far fewer royal palaces. The glazed galleries or arcades made possible through advancing technology, although not strictly ranking as interiors, housed shops and other urban facilities in a novel way. The Galleria Vittorio Emmanuele in Milan, dating from the 1860s, is probably the best-known with its cruciform plan and central glazed dome designed by Giuseppe Mengoni (1829–77), and its carefully detailed arcades below long curved glass roofs. Genoa competed, with an even longer Galleria Mazzini (1871) and both were important achievements in the use of glass and iron to define enclosed space.

Representing an entirely opposite design approach is the Palazzo Municipale in Padua (1880). The architect Camillo Boito (1836–1914), was an enthusiast for medieval studies, but this building can only be called eclectic, combining *Rundbogenstil* and Pompeian features as well as Gothic. It succeeds in conveying a feeling of vigour absent in much contemporary Italian architecture. Further historicism in the form of Moorish extravagance deriving from the Alhambra, surfaced in the Villa Panciatichi (c.1875), previously the Castle of Sammezano at Rignano sull'Arno, with much coloured tile work, fretted screens, and Moorish arches alongside fan vaulting and ogee pediments. Upholstered divans were covered with Genoa velvet and damask, gestures towards the prevalent idea of comfort even in such an eccentric setting.

A new and expressive form of architecture and decoration appeared at the end of the 19th century. The obsessive massing of clutter on every available surface was diminishing and ostentation was being replaced by more domestic amenities, made practicable by improvements in technology. The long-cherished language of fresco had given way to patterned papered walls hung with gilt-framed oil paintings or watercolours and mirrors. Fitted carpets were an accepted floor covering, particularly in the north, and curtains took an important place in middle-class interiors. Surviving domestic backgrounds for Cavour, Manzoni, Verdi, and d'Annunzio all breathed such atmosphere of convenience and comfort, as also does the small bedroom of Pope Leo XIII in the Vatican, although he did have immediate access to grander spaces in his Torre Leonina with eclectic interiors designed and painted by Ludovico Seitz in the 1880s.

Italy took its place in Art Nouveau history by staging the highly successful Turin Exhibition of 1902. The style had acquired national variations in character, but the emphasis at Turin was on the flowing line and naturally-derived shapes of flowers and plants. A contradiction of this trend was the mannered work with a touch of brutalism by Carlo Bugatti (1856–1940) in his disc-backed chair and in the snail-shell motif of his Snail Room design. The firm of Ceruti in Milan which employed Gaetano Moretti, and Eugenio Quarti, a Milanese cabinet-maker, had exhibited Mackintosh-inspired furniture with inlays of mother-of-pearl, silver, and gilt bronze at the Paris Exhibition of 1900. Ernesto Basile designed in a more severe vein for the Ducrot furniture firm in Palermo. Mackintosh's Scottish influence shows again in Antonio Tagliaferri's design for the Santa Teresa Pharmacy in Milan, well-preserved in an equally interesting Art Nouveau building of 1905. Few of the more orthodox Art Nouveau interiors remain, but among them is the Casa Fenoglio, Turin by Pietro Fenoglio (1903), deriving from Victor Horta and displaying good woodwork, coloured glazing, and metal balustrading. Italian work tended to be more restrained than French or Belgian examples and to use geometric curves more than the free whiplash motifs usually identified with the style.

A little-known Art Nouveau survival which continued under construction long enough to break into riotous Art Deco is the spa of Salsomaggiore Terme near Parma. The two main centres of interest in the town are the Grand Hotel des Thermes (begun 1901) designed by Luigi Broggi and now the Palazzo dei Congressi, and the Terme Berzieri, the amazing spa building itself (1914–23), under architects Giulio Bernardini and Ugo Giusti. The hotel, still a fine example of the Stile Liberty, synonymous with Italian Art Nouveau, provided 300 bedrooms for international royalty, rulers, and society. Alessandro Mazzucotelli, one of the finest decorative metal-

Italy: Lord Battersea's bedroom, London, by Carlo Bugatti, c.1901; photograph by James Hyatt

work artists, executed the hotel's entrance canopy metalwork in the contemporary style he was also using in Milan. Gottardo Valentini was responsible for interior painting in *stile floreale* in which he was not entirely at home but he progressed to more confident work for the Terme at San Pellegrino and the Gambrinus Cafe, Milan. Mazzucotelli's other work included electric light fittings for the Palazzo Castiglione, Milan (1901–03), designed by the well-known architect Giuseppe Sommaruga (1867–1917), for his engineer friend Ermenegildo Castiglione. It was in Stile Liberty throughout, introducing asymmetric accents into a basically symmetrical classical plan. Interior surfaces were enriched by juxtaposed texturing and animated by decorative figures and plant forms. Nudes were removed soon after completion for modesty's sake.

The Terme Berzieri spa at Salsomaggiore represents above all a triumph of close collaboration between architect Ugo Giusti (1880–1928) and decorative designer / painter Galileo Chini (1873–1956) after Bernardini's retirement. Chini was also artistic director of the Chini Ceramics Works and this connection played a substantial part in determining much of the character of the Terme Berzieri decor. Marble, travertine, faience, maiolica, coloured glass, and iron, not forgetting mural painting and stucco, were all assembled, often in zoomorphic forms, with oriental symbolism which possibly represents a search for health and fertility. Overtones of Gustav Klimt and the Viennese Secession are evident but inventiveness and quality are not always consistent. After completion of the Terme building the partnership worked on extending the Grand Hotel des Thermes from 1924–27 where accommodation was needed for gala entertainments. Chini was well attuned to oriental influences, having spent three years in Bangkok from 1911 onwards, and he now blended this experience with an interpretation of the Alhambra based, in all probability, on the earlier one he could have visited at Sammezano. Much of the frescoed decoration was painted by Chini himself and has since been restored. There is also a Sala delle Cariatidi where Chini covered earlier painting by Gottardo Valentini, and the Red Tavern bar, with matching reddish lacquered furniture made, along with some striking chandeliers, by Franco Spicciani in Lucca.

The consolidation of Art Deco at the 1925 Paris Exposition Internationale des Arts Décoratifs et Industriels Modernes indicated once again the lead held by France. Italy was less sympathetic to Art Deco than it had been to Art Nouveau, and although its recognized idiom was used to fit out some lavish rooms, these followed rather than led the style. Milan was the centre of much of the Art Deco which appeared, but no great upsurge materialized. G.B. Gianotti in the 1920s designed an interesting dining room with adaptations of Neo-Classical volutes and anthemions; Tomaso Buzzi started the 1930s with a mix of slightly Cubist, slightly oriental bedroom furnishings, and Gigioti Zanini in 1933 made opulent use of geometric and sunburst motifs. Franco Albini followed the trend for built-in furniture and unusual colour combinations when designing for aviator Arturo Ferrari a dressing room introducing some Modernism and combining brown and yellow striped silk with pink lacquering on the dressing table, pink silk, and a large zebra-skin pillow on the sofa.

The growth in Germany of the Modern Movement and the Bauhaus made little impression on Italian design before the International Style was appropriated by the Fascist Party in the 1930s. Clean lines, tubular steel, glass, and abstract wall decoration by Giuseppe Terragni for the conference room in the Casa del Fascio, Como (1932–36) announced a new departure, but the mixture of politics and aesthetics was short-lived.

Post-war reconstruction absorbed Modernist ideas which also took in Le Corbusier and Frank Lloyd Wright. Design was rethought in terms of straightforward production of homes to remedy war damage. However, interior design received some stimulus from London's Festival of Britain exhibition in 1951 and simultaneously designers in Italy were applying revived Internationalism with elegance and flair. Milan again became a focal point and the centre of a booming industry manufacturing domestic furniture and fittings, employing first-rate designers, with great success in the export market. Names such as Nervi, Ponti, Fornasetti, and Magistretti appeared in international periodicals and good design had become news. *Domus* magazine, founded and edited by Gio Ponti (1891–1979) had helped to widen the market, spreading the language of plain wood, deep-textured rugs, uncluttered shelving and storage units, and areas of strong colour. Ponti's furniture designs were manufactured by the firm Cassina, as were those by Vico Magistretti and Mario Bellini. Ponti and Fornasetti worked together on commercial and domestic interiors which often incorporated wittily printed patterns on hard and soft materials, as in the Appartamento Luccano, Milan, 1950 where silk curtains carried printed patterns of manufacturers' labels and silk-upholstered chairs were covered with book-backs and mock woodgrain prints. A "casa di fantasia", illustrated in a 1952 *Domus* issue, contained elaborate Fornasetti iconography of the antique gods. Small painted ceramic panels by Romano Rui and a mirror door decorated with the Bacchus story by the distinguished artist Edina Altara both represented Italian traditions.

Despite the eminence of Milanese designers and manufacturers, Italy failed to maintain its leading position of the 1950s for long. Speed of communication meant speed of fashion trends and an ethos of disposable furniture and entire interiors made a brief appearance. The architect / designer Andrea Branzi (b.1938) led the Archizoom group in Florence in 1966 to break away from the American and Scandinavian influenced mainstream "Contemporary" style, mixing Art Deco and Pop Art in an attempt to attract young buyers who would spend for amusement on fake fur and cardboard chairs. They also sampled Deconstructivism and experimented briefly with other interior fashions. A "green" conservation philosophy in the next decade slowly affected views on design which were also accommodating computerization and High-Tech construction methods.

Two Italian design groups attracted special attention following the 1972 New York exhibition, Italy: The New Domestic Landscape. The exhibitions had commissioned designers Ettore Sottsass (b.1917), Mario Bellini (b.1935) and Joe Colombo (1930–71) to create micro-environments. Their minimum space modules exhibits offered flexibility and new techniques for instant changes of lifestyle. Ponti's successor as *Domus* editor, Alessandro Mendini, formed the Studio Alchymia, Milan, in 1976, which Sottsass then joined and which, with its personnel of young, avant-garde designers, was funded by Artemide on a serious commercial basis. Their stated inspiration combined performance art, left-wing politics, and bizarre furniture but they nevertheless produced exciting designs. Soon Sottsass left the Studio to form his own independent Memphis Group which exhibited for the first time at the 1981 Milan Fair. Bright nursery colours, plastic materials, and zany ideas, made immediate appeal and the Carlton room divider shown at the Fair was instantly confirmed as a Memphis icon.

Having been overtaken by British, American and Japanese designers, the position of Italy in Modern and Postmodern design today gives some cause for concern, and a degree of conservatism based on revivalist styles seems to be gaining influence among the more up-market interior decorators. The concept of integrating interior and exterior design seems to be losing ground – a problem Palladio would have appreciated.

ELAINE DENBY

Further Reading

Thornton 1991, González-Palacios 1993, Praz 1969 and Hiesinger and Marcus 1983 are each useful, well-illustrated overviews of Italian interiors in successive periods, and provide further reading.

The Age of Neo-Classicism (exhib. cat.: Royal Academy and Victoria and Albert Museum, London), London: Arts Council of Great Britain, 1972

Alberici, C., *Il mobile veneto*, Milan, 1980

Beard, Geoffrey, *Stucco and Decorative Plasterwork in Europe*, London: Thames and Hudson, and New York: Harper, 1983

Branzi, Andrea, *The Hot House: Italian New Wave Design*, London: Thames and Hudson, and Cambridge: Massachusetts Institute of Technology Press, 1984

Brosio, Valentino, *Mobili italiani dell'ottocento*, Milan: Vallardi, 1962

Brosio, Valentino, *Lo stile Liberty in Italia*, Milan: Vallardi, 1967

Castelnuovo, Enrico, *Il Gusto Neogotico* (exhib. cat.), Turin, 1980

Civiltà del' 700 a Napoli, 1734–1799 (exhib. cat.: Museo di Capodimonte, Naples), 2 vols., Florence: Centro Di, 1979–80

González-Palacios, Alvar, *Il Tempio del gusto: Le arti decorative in Italia fra classicismi e barocco*, part 1: *Roma e il Regno delle due Sicilie*, 2 vols., Milan: Longanesi, 1984; part 2: *Granducato di Toscana e gli stati settentrionali*, 2 vols., Milan: Longanesi, 1986

González-Palacios, Alvar, *Il gusto dei principi: arte di corte del XVII e del XVIII secolo*, Milan: Longanesi, 1993

Heydenreich, Ludwig H., *Architecture in Italy, 1400–1500*, revised by Paul Davis, New Haven and London: Yale University Press, 1996

Hiesinger, Kathryn B. and George H. Marcus III (editors), *Design since 1945* (exhib. cat.), Philadelphia: Philadelphia Museum of Art, and London: Thames and Hudson, 1983

Lotz, Wolfgang, *Architecture in Italy, 1500–1600*, New Haven and London: Yale University Press, 1995

Massobrio, Giovanna and Paolo Portoghesi, *Album degli anni Venti*, Bari: Laterza, 1976

Morazzoni, Giuseppe, *Il mobile neoclassico italiano*, Milan: Görlich, 1955

Ottino della Chiesa, Angela, *L'età neoclassica in Lombardia* (exhib. cat.), Como: Nani, 1959

Praz, Mario, *On Neoclassicism*, Evanston, IL: Northwestern University Press, and London: Thames and Hudson, 1969

Raimondi, Giuseppe, *Italian Living Design: Three Decades of Interior Decoration, 1960–1990*, New York: Rizzoli, 1988; London: Tauris Parke, 1990

Sabino, Catherine and Angelo Tondini, *Italian Style*, London: Thames and Hudson, 1985; New York: Potter, 1995

Sato, Kazuko, *Alchimia: Never-Ending Italian Design*, Tokyo: Rikuyo-sha, 1985

Schlosser, Julius von, *Die Kunst- und Wunderkammern der Spätrenaissance*, Leipzig: Klinkhardt & Biermann, 1908 (Italian translation, *Raccolta d'arte e di meraviglie del tardo Rinascimento*, Florence: Sansoni, 1974)

Schottmüller, Frida, *Wohnungskultur und Möbel der italienischen Renaissance*, Stuttgart: Hoffmann, 1921

Thornton, Peter, *The Italian Renaissance Interior, 1400–1600*, London: Weidenfeld and Nicolson, and New York: Abrams, 1991

Waddy, Patricia, *Seventeenth-Century Roman Palaces: Use and the Art of the Plan*, New York: Architectural History Foundation, 1990

Wichmann, Hans, *Italien Design 1945 bis heute*, Basel: Birkhäuser, 1988

J

Jackson and Graham

British cabinet-makers and upholsterers, fl.1836–1885

Jackson and Graham were arguably the most important, and certainly the most publicised of any of the high Victorian cabinet-making firms. Listed as in business by 1836, the firm occupied premises at 37 Oxford Street in the heart of London's West End, and specialised in furniture that was aimed at the luxury end of the market. They were best-known for their elaborate and finely wrought French and Renaissance-style cabinets, decorated with marquetry or ebony inlaid with ivory, that were exhibited to high acclaim at numerous International Exhibitions. Several of these pieces were designed by prestigious architects such as Bruce Talbert. Their in-house designers included Peter Graham and Alfred Lorimer and they were one of the first London establishments to employ a foreign designer, the Frenchman Eugène Prignot who worked for the firm from 1849. By the mid 1870s they were also providing a complete interior decorating service and had commissioned a range of oriental-style carpets, wallpapers, curtains and other furnishings from Owen Jones.

Prignot was responsible for Jackson and Graham's first prize-winning cabinet at the Crystal Palace exhibition of 1851. For much of this period French designers were generally perceived as superior to their British counterparts and, encouraged by Jackson and Graham's lead, numerous other firms began to use their services. Indeed, by the International Exhibition of 1855, the influx of foreigners engaged by London firms prompted Matthew Digby Wyatt to declare that "it is a subject for congratulation that foreigners of such talent should be at work among us" and their influence was widely thought to have raised standards of design. Jackson and Graham's entry in the 1855 exhibition was a cabinet designed by Prignot in the florid Louis XVI style. The scale, elaboration and opulence of this work epitomised the design of successful Victorian exhibition pieces. It was made up of two parts; the upper part comprised a vast mirror enclosed within an ornate, columned, carved wooden frame, and the lower section contained the cabinet and was decorated with sculpted figures made of gilt cast brass. No fewer than 40 modellers, gilders, metal-chasers and other craftsmen, including the Italian carver Claudio Colombo, were involved in the execution of this work; the brass castings were made in Birmingham and the porcelain plaques were decorated by the Minton firm. The cabinet was hailed by Wyatt as being "the first really noble piece of cabinet-makers' work involving excellence in all the most difficult processes of the manufacture which has been executed in this country". The firm was awarded a Gold Medal of Honour and the cabinet was subsequently purchased for the nation by the South Kensington Museum for £2000.

Jackson and Graham's entry in the 1867 Paris Exposition Universelle was designed by Alfred Lorimer. While the majority of British firms preferred light finishes involving satinwood and gold, this piece was made of ebony. Wyatt felt that the exhibit was "the finest in the exhibition: richly inlaid with ivory, lapis lazuli and excellently engraved". A similar cabinet was shown at the International Exhibition of 1871 where, once again, it was lauded as "one of the most superb pieces of decorative cabinet work".

Bruce Talbert's *Juno* cabinet was designed for the firm's stand at the Paris exhibition of 1878. Made in ebony inlaid with ivory, this piece reflects the influence of fashionable Aesthetic styles. The structure is strongly geometric with an emphasis upon vertical and horizontal lines and the decoration includes classicising details and a pedimented frieze containing representations of Juno and Minerva. It also displays the two leitmotifs of Aestheticism, namely the peacock in the centre of the pediment and lilies in the door panels in the base. Another highly acclaimed design, it was awarded a Grand Prix and was purchased by the Viceroy of India before ultimately arriving at the Victoria and Albert Museum.

Although these exhibition pieces did much to enhance the reputation of the firm as a leader in luxury furnishings, the individual items themselves were produced mainly for show and Jackson and Graham's commercial success rested more firmly on the popularity of their less elaborate furniture and their carpets and wallpapers, several of which were designed by Owen Jones. Jones also re-designed their shop front in 1867 and collaborated on a number interior projects including a billiard room for James Gurney in Regent's Park of c.1870 and the hugely prestigious commission to furnish and decorate the Palace of the Khedive (Viceroy) at Cairo.

As business grew the company expanded and by 1880 they were occupying larger premises that took in the whole of nos. 29 to 38 Oxford Street. By this time, too, they had increased their range of activities to include every aspect of house furnishing and decoration and they provided the furniture and fittings for a number of London restaurants in the mid 1870s. They also offered services that ranged from house letting, appraisals and sales, to the storage of contents.

An article in G.P. Bevan's *British Manufacturing Industries*, written by J.H. Pollen in 1876, describes Jackson and Graham as a typical example of a successful furnishing firm. The article describes the range of operations undertaken at their Oxford Street premises and notes the construction of "an elaborate cabinet of marquetry in patterns of Oriental character, after designs by the late Mr. Owen Jones". By this time Jackson and Graham were one of the largest furniture-making businesses in the country, employing between 600 and 1000 hands, depending on the pressure of work at different times of the year, and had a weekly wages bill of close to £2000. They were also one of the first British firms to use machinery, introduced in the 1850s, and in 1862 they advertised that they were "fitted with all means and appliances to ensure superiority and economise cost". Nevertheless, the company was not always beyond reproach, and in 1873 the *Furniture Gazette* criticised "a bedroom suite of furniture painted black, relieved with white etc., in stripes which we consider in bad taste. Black is a most objectionable colour for a bedroom and when it is striped like the panels of a cab, it makes the matter worse". In 1881, however, they were commended by the *Builder* for their "production of cheap furniture of artistic design" which "endeavoured to meet the requirements of those who cannot afford to furnish their houses in Italian, French or Chippendale furniture." And the writer continues, "They are making some very excellent buffets and other furniture of exceedingly simple design, the lines of the framework being relieved by plain flutings and moulded work ...[as well as]... suites of bedroom furniture, made in pine and stained green with black mouldings; some excellent painted bedroom furniture all produced by machinery at reasonable cost." This furniture represented a departure from their earlier French and Renaissance styles and was clearly stimulated by the fashion for Artistic styles promoted by rival firms such as William Watt, James Shoolbred & Co., and Collinson and Lock. The attempt to enter more mainstream commercial markets did not, however, solve the financial problems that had begun to beset the firm, and in 1885 they were taken over by Collinson and Lock who were in turn absorbed by Gillows in 1897.

NERIDA C.A. AYLOTT

See also Talbert

Selected Collections

The principal collection of Jackson and Graham furniture is in the Victoria and Albert Museum, London, which includes Eugène Prignot's 1855 cabinet and Bruce Talbert's *Juno* cabinet of 1878; the museum also holds examples of the firm's wallpapers designed by Owen Jones. An album of sketches and designs for decorations and interiors for Jackson and Graham attributed to Jones is in the Whitworth Art Gallery, Manchester.

Further Reading

There is no monograph on Jackson and Graham; the most detailed history of the firm's work is included in Allwood's forthcoming *Dictionary*. For more general information see Allwood 1988 and Aslin 1962.

Allwood, Rosamund, "Luxury Furniture Makers of the Victorian Period" in *Antique Collecting*, June 1988, pp.4–8
Allwood, Rosamund, *A Dictionary of Nineteenth Century British Furniture*, Woodbridge, Suffolk: Antique Collectors' Club, forthcoming
Aslin, Elizabeth, *19th Century English Furniture*, London: Faber, 1962
Collard, Frances, "The Juno Cabinet" in Christopher Wilk (editor), *Western Furniture 1350 to the Present Day*, London: Victoria and Albert Musuem, 1996
Cooper, Jeremy, *Victorian and Edwardian Furniture and Interiors*, London: Thames and Hudson, 1987
Jervis, Simon, *High Victorian Design*, Woodbridge, Suffolk: Boydell, 1983
Kinchin, Juliet, "Collinson and Lock" in *Connoisseur*, 201, May 1979, pp.49–53
Pollen, John Henry, "Furniture and Woodwork" in G.P. Bevan, *British Manufacturing Industries*, London, 1876
Rogers, Phillis, *English Cabinets* (revision of edition by John Hayward), London: HMSO, 1972

Jacob / Jacob-Desmalter Family

French furniture makers, c.1765–1847

The Jacob dynasty spanned eighty years of activity from Georges I (1739–1814) to Georges Alphonse (1799–1870). Georges I, the founder, was born at Cheny of Burgundian parentage, but he soon left for Paris where he was apprenticed to Louis Delanois (1731–92), who is said to have been one of the first Parisian chair-makers to adopt the Louis Seize style. A pair of armchairs illustrated by Svend Eriksen from a suite dating from c.1770 are stamped with the names of both Delanois and Jacob; at that time the former is said to have been turning out around 2000 pieces a year (Eriksen, 1974).

Jacob became a *maître menuisier* in 1765, and he was soon being employed by such fashionable clients as Mme. Geoffrin. He was one of the few superior 18th-century craftsmen to work both in *menuiserie* (carving from the solid wood) and *ébénisterie* (veneered furniture). In 1781 he was appointed "chair maker in ordinary to Monsieur" (i.e., the Comte de Provence, later Louis XVIII). Among the furniture in the Louvre is an armchair, a part of a suite made for the Comte in 1785; they are painted *lilas clair ... rechampe en blanc*. In 1782 Jacob's gilded *lit à la romaine* made for Carl August Herzog von Zweibrücken-Burkenfeld, was a sensation when it was exhibited in his workshop before being delivered to Schloss Karlsberg. In 1786 he became *fournisseur des Menus Plaisirs*, which gave him a place in the Royal Household, and in the following year he made a suite of chairs, stools and tables for Marie-Antoinette's *laiterie* at the Château de Rambouillet from designs made by Hubert Robert, the painter of ruin scenes; they were described as *du genre étrusque* and anticipate by many years some of the Jacob firm's later designs.

Georges I is credited with introducing the sabre leg c.1790 and the use of mahogany for chair-making in France. There is an element of fantasy in some of his designs, such as the chairs made for the Duc de Choiseul which were probably intended for his pagoda at Chanteloup; but on the other hand a large number of chairs were supplied by him before the Revolution to Fontainebleau and the Tuileries for anterooms and the offices of minor officials, and these show a simplicity and elegant utility which point the way to the Directoire taste. The collection of the Queen includes beds and chairs made by Jacob, including a number of the so-called *fauteuils à l'anglaise*, mahogany chairs with pierced backs enriched with gilt bronze beadings.

In 1796 Georges I made over the business to his two elder sons. Georges II took over the administration and François-Honoré-Georges, who added the name of Desmalter (a family property in Burgundy) to that of Jacob, became the artistic and technical director. The firm took the name of Jacob frères and continued to work from the building in the rue Meslée which Georges I had acquired in 1775. The Revolutionary years had brought disaster to furniture-makers who had lost their patrons, and in 1791 the old guilds, including the *ébénistes* and *menuisiers*, were abolished. However, the Jacob frères survived, and during the Consulate and the Empire they enjoyed great patronage which began when the then-General Bonaparte took a house in Paris in the rue Chantereine, which the Jacobs decorated and furnished. This introduction to the future Emperor led to the important commission to work with his favourite architects Percier and Fontaine, at Malmaison, furnishing it in the elegant Directoire style with some military additions. At the same time in 1799–1800 they were employed to furnish the empty apartments in the Tuileries in a suitably grand style.

Georges II died in 1803 and left Jacob-Desmalter to direct the firm's fortunes and use his own stamp alone on the vast quantity of furniture he was producing. At that time they had sixteen workshops, which covered the complete range of trades -- for joinery work in buildings and in furniture, figure carving, ornamental carving, turning, painting and gilding, veneering, inlaying, polishing, bronze founding, moulding, bronze working, gilding on metal, tapestry weaving and locksmiths' work. In his survey of the firm, Serge Grandjean, quotes a document in the Archives Nationales which reveals that in 1807 Jacob-Desmalter was employing 350 workmen and that one third of the firm's output was for export (Grandjean, 1966). By 1810 the number of workmen had apparently risen to nearly 800.

The great years of the Empire produced more orders for refurnishing the palaces at Compiègne and Fontainebleau, Versailles and the Tuileries, and a great quantity of fine furniture, including most of the famous pieces which figure in any account of Empire furniture, was made by Jacob-Desmalter, who enjoyed the Emperor's confidence and special patronage. After the first rush of orders leading up to Napoleon's coronation, there was a second when he married Marie-Louise in 1810. Even so Jacob-Desmalter was declared insolvent in 1813. However, he recovered and after complaining that this setback was largely due to the Continental blockade which was ruining his business, the Emperor issued a decree allowing the firm to trade with England, even though the two countries were at war. This allowed Jacob-Desmalter to increase his export trade through such middlemen as Dominique Daguerre who supplied furniture to the Prince of Wales. Jacob pieces went as far away as Brazil.

The firm continued to be successful during the post-Empire years. Jacob-Desmalter retired in 1825 when his son, Georges Alphonse, who had trained as an architect under Charles Percier, took over the business. In his first year he supplied a cylinder-top desk to George IV (now at Buckingham Palace), elaborately veneered in satinwood and purplewood with gilt bronze ornaments and very much in the Percier-Fontaine style. He was still working in the Empire style in 1837 when he made a pair of night tables for Queen Marie-Amelie to complement her bedroom in the Grand Trianon at Versailles, but at the same time he provided an *étagère* with fretted panels and turned balusters in a more electic taste. Georges-Alphonse directed the business until 1847 when he handed over to Joseph-Pierre-François Jeanselme, who then took his place among the leading *ébénistes*.

DEREK LINSTRUM

See also Empire Style; Percier and Fontaine

Selected Works

The Jacob family's more important commissions included furniture for the châteaux of Malmaison, Compiègne, Fontainebleau, Versailles and the Tuileries. Notable collections of their work are in the Musée du Louvre, Paris, Buckingham Palace, London, and *in situ* at Compiègne, Fontainebleau, and Versailles.

Further Reading

Duret-Robert, François, "Juliet et ses Meubles" in *Connaissance des Arts*, 498, September 1993, pp.112–15

Eriksen, Svend, *Early Neo-Classicism in France: The Creation of the Louis Seize Style*, London: Faber, 1974

Foucart, Bruno, "L'Empire de Serie" in *L'Objet d'Art*, no.3, January 1988, pp.44–55

Gaigneron, Axelle de, "Palais Rohan: la Memoire de Napoléon" in *Connaissance des Arts*, 494, 5 April 1993, pp.4–6

Grandjean, Serge, *Empire Furniture 1800 to 1825*, London: Faber, and New York: Taplinger, 1966

Groer, Léon de, *Decorative Arts in Europe, 1790–1850*, New York: Rizzoli, 1986

Ledoux-Lebard, Denise, "The Refurnishing of the Tuileries under the Consulate" in *Apollo*, September 1964, pp.199–205

Lefuel, Hector, *Georges Jacob*, Paris: Morance, 1923

Lefuel, Hector, *François-Honoré-Georges Jacob-Desmalter*, Paris, 1927

Moulin, Jean-Marie, "La Chambre à Coucher et le Boudoir de l'Impératrice Marie-Louise à Compiègne" in *Revue du Louvre et des Musées de France*, 34, 1984, pp.326–36

Watson, F.J.B., *Louis XVI Furniture*, London: Tiranti, and New York: Philosophical Library, 1960

Jacobsen, Arne 1902–1971

Danish architect and designer

A pioneer of Danish functionalism, the architect Arne Jacobsen was one of the best-known and most highly esteemed exponents of the modern International Style. He was responsible for many of Denmark's most celebrated modern buildings and, a firm believer in the integration of architecture with interior design, he often also exercised overall control of the fittings and furnishings within his buildings. He designed furniture, flatware, glass, lighting and textiles, and several of his chairs are now widely regarded as classics of 20th century Modernist design.

Born in Copenhagen in 1902, Jacobsen trained as a mason

Jacobsen: *Ant* chair, 3-leg version

before studying architecture at the Royal Danish Academy of Fine Arts from which he graduated in 1927. He worked in the office of the city architect Poul Hansen from 1927 to 1930, and established his own architectural and design practice in Copenhagen in 1930 where, apart from a short period during the war years, he remained active until his death. He was also active as a teacher and was professor of architecture at the Academy of Arts from 1956.

A participant in the 1925 Paris Exposition des Arts Décoratifs et Industriels, Jacobsen was strongly influenced by the work of Le Corbusier, Walter Gropius and Mies van der Rohe. These influences were manifest in the project for a House of the Future that he exhibited at the Danish Building Exhibition in 1929. The house was a bold circular two-storey structure, and the uncompromising modernity of Jacobsen's approach was evident not only in its design but also in the provision of contemporary facilities such as garaging for cars and a helicopter landing pad. The Bauhaus inspiration is even more marked in the Rothenborg House that he designed the following year and in his designs for the Bellevue Housing Development where he provided furniture and fixtures for the theatre, restaurant and public swimming pool. While still at the Copenhagen Academy Jacobsen formed a life-long friendship with the Swedish architect Gunnar Asplund. Asplund's influence was evident particularly in the more expressive version of Modernism that Jacobsen embraced in the late 1930s and 1940s which combined details and materials used in traditional Nordic architecture with the simplicity and precision of the International Style.

Following the German occupation of Denmark, Jacobsen fled to Sweden in 1943 where he remained until 1945. During this period he continued to produce furniture and began designing textiles, glassware, lighting and tableware. His textiles were designed in collaboration with his wife, Jonna Jacobsen, and the patterns exhibit a strong element of naturalism.

During the post-war period, Jacobsen's architectural work became infused with influences from the industrialised European nations and the United States. At the same time, a new style was emerging in Danish furniture design. The architect Finn Juhl propounded the view that as well as being functional, furniture should have a sculptural quality. Jacobsen was also becoming interested in new materials and methods of production, and from 1950 he began designing furniture for mass production. His light, plywood and tubular steel three-legged stacking chair was conceived for factory production. The back and seat, moulded from one piece of plywood, clearly shows the impact of earlier examples by Charles and Ray Eames, yet the character of the design remained distinctively Scandinavian. The chair was named the *Ant*, after the sculptural form of the back; in Germany it was known by the nickname, the *Violin*. Its overall lightness meant that it was easy to move and stack, and its modest cost and simple maintenance made it especially popular for public seating areas such as restaurants and airports. It was subsequently produced in several different versions; some included arms and castors, but the most important modification was the addition of a fourth leg and the introduction of colour on the back. The *Ant* chair was awarded a Grand Prix at the 1957 Milan Triennale and, like Eero Saarinen's *Womb* chair, and the Eameses' *Shell* chairs, it has become closely identified with its creator. The *Ant* series has been in continuous production by A / S Fritz Hansens, who have manufactured all of Jacobsen's furniture designs, since 1955.

Many of Jacobsen's other chairs illustrate a similarly sculptural quality which, nevertheless, does not lessen their strongly utilitarian character. The *Swan* and *Egg* chairs were originally designed for the SAS Royal Hotel in Copenhagen (1958–60). This glass-sheathed building, reminiscent of Skidmore, Owings and Merrill's Lever House in New York, represents one of Jacobsen's most important and best-known architectural commissions for which he designed not only the exterior but also all the interior fitments and furnishings. A similarly complete commission was his design for St. Catherine's College, Oxford (1960–64), where he devised every detail of the interiors including the lighting, textiles, cutlery and tableware. Both projects exemplify his ideal of the building as a total work of art.

Jacobsen's *Egg* chair has a fibreglass seat shell, upholstered in foam and covered in fabric or leather, supported on a swivelling star-shaped base of cast and polished aluminium. It also has an adjustable tilting mechanism and is accompanied by a footrest to enhance comfort; designed in 1959, it is still in production today. In contrast with the Egg's high, curving back which almost completely encases the sitter, the *Swan* is a more horizontal design with armrests in the form of bird's wings, outstretched as if for flight. Both chairs underline Jacobsen's ability to rupture conventions, but in so elegant and understated a fashion that their radicalism is barely noticeable. His work exemplifies the aim of many 20th-century Modernists to create a modern yet comfortable chair whose design complements the shape of the human body. He was also typically Scandinavian in his love of organic forms, natural materials, and nature generally from which he drew much of his creative energy. And his designs for furniture, lighting, glassware, tableware and other domestic items resulted in the production of many design classics that have been compared to works of art. The fact that these items were for everyday use and sold at affordable prices has greatly enhanced their influence on domestic interior design.

PIA MARIA MONTONEN

Biography

Born in Copenhagen, 11 February 1902. Studied at the School of Applied Arts, Copenhagen, graduated 1924; studied architecture at the Royal Danish Academy of Fine Arts, Copenhagen, 1924–27. Married the textile designer Jonna Jacobsen: two sons. Worked in the office of the city architect Poul Hansen, Copenhagen, 1927–30; private architectural practice, Copenhagen, 1930–71. Lived in Sweden, 1943–45. Designed furniture from 1932; textiles, glassware, lighting and tableware from 1943: designed for Graucob Textilen, August Millech, C. Olesen, A. Michelsen, Fritz Hansen, Louis Poulsen Company and others. Professor of architecture, Royal Danish Academy of Fine Arts, 1956–71. Received many prizes and honours including Silver Medal, Paris Exhibition, 1925, Eckersberg Gold Medal, Royal Danish Academy of Fine Arts, 1936, medal of honour, Danish Architectural Association, 1962, and gold medal, Académie d'Architecture de France, 1971. Honorary Corresponding Member, Royal Institute of British Architects; Honorary Fellow, American Institute of Architects. Died in Copenhagen, 24 March 1971.

Selected Works

Interiors

1929 House of the Future, Danish Building Exhibition, Copenhagen (building and interiors with Flemming Lassen)
1930–31 Rothenborg House, 37 Klampenborgvej, Copenhagen (building and interiors)
1937 Bellevue Theatre and Gammel Bellevue Restaurant, Copenhagen (buildings, furniture and fittings)
1937 Jacobsen Country House, Gudmindrup Lyng, Denmark (building, interiors and furniture)
1937–38 Stelling House, Gammel Torv 6, Copenhagen (building and interiors)
1938 Thorvald Pedersen's House, Klampenbors (building and interiors)
1940–42 Town Hall, Søllerød (building, furniture and fittings; with Flemming Lassen)
1948 Poulsen and Company, Copenhagen (office interiors and furnishings)
1952–56 Munkegaard School Vangedevej, Gentofte (building, furniture and fittings)
1955 Town Hall, Rødovre (building, furniture and fittings)
1955 Jespersen and Son Office Building, Copenhagen (building and interiors)
1956 Jurgensen House, Vedbaek, Copenhagen (building and interiors)
1957 "Round" House, Sjellands, Odde (building, interiors and some furniture)
1958 Town Hall, Glostrup (building, furniture and fittings)
1958–60 SAS Royal Hotel and Air Terminal, Copenhagen (building, furniture and fittings)
1960–64 St. Catherine's College, Oxford (building, furniture and fittings)
1962–69 Hamburgischen Elektrizitätswerk, Hamburg (building and interiors)
1966–78 National Bank of Denmark, Copenhagen (building and interiors Hans Dissing and Otto Weitling)
1970–73 Town Hall, Mainz (building and interiors with Otto Weitling)

Jacobsen's design work included textiles and wallcoverings for C. Olesen Company (1942–43); furniture for Fritz Hansen Company (from 1932) including the *Ant* chair (1951–52), *Egg* chair (1959), and *Swan* chair (1959); lighting fixtures produced by Louis Poulsen Company (from 1955); silver and stainless steel for A. Michelsen (from 1957); and *Cylinda* tablewares for Stelton Company (1962).

Further Reading

For a catalogue raisonné of Jacobsen's work see Rubino 1980.

Arne Jacobsen: Architecte et Designer Danois 1902–1971 (exhib. cat.), Paris: Musée des Arts Décoratifs, 1987
Faber, Tobias, *Arne Jacobsen*, New York: Praeger, and London: Tiranti, 1964
Fehrman, Cherie and Kenneth, *Postwar Interior Design, 1945–1960*, New York: Van Nostrand Reinhold, 1987
Hiesinger, Kathryn B. and George H. Marcus III (editors), *Design since 1945* (exhib. cat.), Philadelphia: Philadelphia Museum of Art, and London: Thames and Hudson, 1983
Jackson, Lesley, *The New Look: Design in the Fifties*, London and New York: Thames and Hudson, 1991
Jackson, Lesley, *"Contemporary": Architecture and Interiors of the 1950s*, London: Phaidon, 1994
Karlsen, Arne, *Made in Denmark*, New York: Reinhold, 1960
Kastholm, Jørgen, *Arne Jacobsen*, Copenhagen: Høst, 1968
McFadden, David Revere (editor), *Scandinavian Modern Design, 1880–1980* (exhib. cat.: Cooper-Hewitt Museum, New York), New York: Abrams, 1982
Pedersen, Johan, *Arkitekten Arne Jacobsen*, Copenhagen: Arkitektens Forlag, 1954
Richardson, Sara S., *Arne Jacobsen, A Danish Master: A Bibliography*, Monticello, IL: Vance, 1989
Rubino, Luciano, *Arne Jacobsen: Opera Completa*, Rome: Kappa, 1980
Skriver, Poul Erik, *Arne Jacobsen: Architecture, Applied Art* (exhib. cat.), London: Royal Institute of British Architects, 1959
Skriver, Poul Erik, "Royal-Hotel-Copenhagen" in *Arkitektur*, 4, December 1960, pp.209–48
Skriver, Poul Erik and others, *Arne Jacobsen: A Danish Architect*, Copenhagen: Ministry of Foreign Affairs, 1971–72
Solaguren-Beascoa de Corral, Félix, *Arne Jacobsen*, 3rd edition Barcelona: Gili, 1992
Tarschys, Rebecca and Henry End, "Arne Jacobsen: From Stainless Steel Flatware to the Royal Hotel in Copenhagen" in *Interiors*, 122, October 1962, pp.112–21

Japan

To understand the basic principle that underlies Japanese interior design, it helps to keep in mind the words of the legendary founder of Chinese Daoism, Laozi, who maintained that "the reality of a building is not the roof and the walls but the space to be lived in." Over the centuries, Japanese architects have followed this principle in the construction of both religious

Japan: narrative picture scroll showing scene known as *yadogiri*, from the *Tale of Genji* scroll, Heian period, 12th century

architecture, such as temples and shrines, and secular buildings, including palaces, castles and the homes of people of all classes. Using wood, bamboo and paper as their principal working materials, they have produced buildings which on the outside are plain and austere enough to blend with their natural surroundings, while on the inside show a deep reverence for the space they enclose.

Traditionally, Japanese buildings are not large, but their relative emptiness and the easy mobility of the various furnishings, create a sense that space is not something static, but somehow alive and changing. A typical Japanese room contains relatively little furniture and wall decoration, a fact that caused many Westerners visiting Japan from the late 19th century onwards to label them stark, austere and uncomfortable. What furnishings there are – futon mattresses, cushions, screens and the like – are generally light and portable, and when rearranged or removed, transform the size, form and nature of the room; a living room becomes a bedroom, for example.

Sliding doors, made from wood and paper, separate the rooms and are often all that stands between the interior of the building and the garden outside. These doors are easily detached, allowing an expansion and contraction of the space within the building, and, in addition, opening up the interior to the world outside. Unlike many cultures, where space is divided up by solid walls, creating a sharp distinction between "inside" and "outside", in traditional Japanese buildings space is a flexible concept, and no real differentiation exists between interior and exterior space.

A high regard for natural materials also characterizes Japanese architecture and interior design. Wood, of which the Japanese islands have plentiful supplies, has always been Japan's chief building material, and is ideal for constructing the airy buildings necessary in this hot and humid country. Traditionally, Japanese buildings have been constructed around a large, strong central wooden pillar, sunk deep into the ground and supporting the roof and walls. This ensured that during the earthquakes that regularly rock Japan, only the central pillar swayed with the movements of the earth, with the rest of the house being suspended and thus protected from the shock.

The Japanese have never attempted to cover up this central pillar or any other of the structural elements of the building, choosing to leave the wood, bamboo, reed, or clay walls in their natural state, perhaps out of gratitude to the materials for their protective qualities, but more likely in appreciation of their inherent beauty. Left exposed, the pillars, beams, lintels, and other elements which make up the interior of a Japanese home, create a wealth of textural variation as well as a mass of horizontal and vertical wooden lines that divide up the surfaces of the room. This linear effect extends to the floor, which is made up of several rectangular straw *tatami* mats, their dark borders dividing the floor into a rhythmic patchwork. Bright colours are very rare in a Japanese interior, the most predominant tones being different shades of brown and grey and the white of the paper doors and windows.

The earliest form of secular buildings constructed in Japan were the shallow pit dwellings of the prehistoric Jomon Period (10,000–300 BC). These pits were dug two to three feet into the ground, with four posts planted into the ground, supporting four horizontal beams, rafters and a ridge pole. Onto this frame was placed a great thatched roof, made from grass bark and leaves, which reached right down to the ground. Inside was an open hearth for warmth, with the only light entering through a small hole which served as a doorway and some ventilation gaps below the roof. Inhabitants spread straw husks on the floor for sitting and sleeping.

During the Yayoi pariod (300 BC–300 AD), when rice cultivation was introduced from the continent to Japan, inhabitants shifted towards wetter regions of the country and, although pit dwellings were still common, the wealthier members of society began to construct houses on a raised floor, with large gabled roofs, similar to the raised-floor houses of Southeast Asia. These dwellings were single cells of space, much drier that the pit dwellings, but similarly dark inside. Little is known about the interiors, except that for comfort and warmth, residents covered the wooden floors with thin mats of plant fiber, animal skin or cloth.

Throughout the 4th and 5th centuries, Japan interacted increasingly with China and the Korean peninsula, and absorbed much of the culture and technology of the Asian mainland. In part, this absorption was of religious ideas and customs, often relating to burial practices, but it was also an important period for various secular developments, such as improvements in pottery, ironworking, weaving and agriculture. One contribution to the lifestyle of the nobility of the period was the introduction of the continental bed to the Japanese home for the first time. This structure, made of a wood or bamboo framework and covered with straw, mats or cloth, was used solely by the nobility of the period and never became widespread in Japan.

From the 7th century Japan was fascinated by the powerful civilization of Tang China (618–908), and, over the next two centuries or so, embarked on a period of importation and imitation of things Chinese, including the writing system, governmental structure and city planning. Buddhism, with its art and architectural tradition, was also embraced, bringing with it continental artistic and technological innovations that overflowed into the secular realm. Chinese customs and habits were emulated, particularly by members of the Japanese upper classes, who took to wearing Chinese-style dress and employing chairs, folding stools and other sitting devices in their homes. However, as with the continental beds, these chairs were not widely used by the populace as a whole.

The Heian Period (794–1185), which is generally regarded as the classical age of Japanese art and literature, brought about significant developments in architecture and interior design. During this time, the Imperial Court was at its cultural zenith and still enjoyed some degree of political power. The Court lived in the city of Heian-kyo, now known as Kyoto, in a palace compound surrounded by stone walls, isolating the aristocratic inhabitants from the population outside. The palace buildings themselves were made almost exclusively of wood in what is known as the *shinden* style, a style modelled after Chinese palace architecture. This style contained a main chamber and one or more outer buildings, all of which were connected by covered or open corridors. Each building contained a main room surrounded by verandas which were sheltered by the broad eaves of the roof.

These verandas, which were incorporated into secular buildings from earlier Shinto (the native animistic Japanese religion) shrine architecture, had the practical function of enabling residents to watch the outside world from a position protected from the sun and rain. They were also important in a social and psychological sense as they were spaces that were neither inside or outside the house. The veranda could be made part of the interior by the simple action of sliding open the wooden doors separating it from the interior of the house. Conversely, closing the same doors made the veranda a part of the exterior. As they had such a unique, flexible role, these spaces were considered to be areas free from the social status associated with the rooms within the house.

The interiors of these buildings were very dark as little light was able to enter, and, because of their relative openness to the elements, were fairly cool in the summer but bitterly cold during the winter months. As can be seen from the various picture scrolls that depict Heian palace interiors, these residences were largely free of bulky furnishings, as Chinese-style furniture generally failed to appeal to the Japanese. Instead, the floors of these buildings were made of wooden planks, and on them were scattered rectangular straw mats known as *tatami*. These soft, woven mats, measuring approximately 180cm by 90cm and finished with a decorative edging, were a little larger than the circumference of a lying human figure and were employed as bedding or seats as the occasion required.

Some time during this period, sliding doors covered with opaque Chinese paper appeared in these residences. Known as *fusuma* doors, these paper doors served not only as cupboard doors and room dividers, but also as canvases for Chinese-style paintings which provided some of the decoration in the rather sombre apartments. In addition, folding screens made of wood, bamboo, and paper were used as decorative room dividers, or placed on the verandas as protection from the sun. They were also employed by the emperor as screens behind which he sat to address lower-ranking people. Blinds made of reed and bamboo also served as curtains or dividers, and, like the mats, they featured decorative edging and were drawn up with the aid of attractive silk tassels. Other features of the Heian aristocrat's room were low Chinese-style tables, lamps, and curtains which hung on movable T-frames.

Interestingly, much of the decoration of the aristocratic residences of the Heian period was provided by the rich clothing of the courtiers. In particular, women wore several layers of gorgeous silk kimono of various colours and designs, which revealed their rank, wealth and level of cultural awareness at once. In the cold weather, these garments also served as bed clothes and they were occasionally left draped over screens as a temporary ornament.

In the 12th century, battles raged throughout Japan between various military clans, culminating in the victory of the Minamoto family who transferred the capital to Kamakura on the east coast of Japan and established military rule. Over the next few centuries, during the Kamakura (1185–1336) and the Muromachi periods (1336–1574), Japan was ruled by various military regimes, and the imperial court, though still wielding some cultural influence, lost its political power. Not surprisingly, the nature of the arts and lifestyle of the nation underwent a shift from the elegant, somewhat effete style of the imperial court to the more practical nature of the warrior. In dress, the multi-layered, flowing robes of the courtiers were replaced by lighter, shorter kimonos which allowed more freedom of movement. In architecture, the ruling war lords chose to reside in more practical dwellings, eschewing the complex *shinden* style of residential architecture, in which single units of living space were separated by corridors, in favour of a more concentrated residence, in which one large main chamber was divided up into smaller units of space.

These divisions were made possible by a major innovation – the square wooden pillar, which replaced the circular columns of earlier architecture. These pillars, arranged in rows throughout the main hall, served as posts to which were fitted lintels and sills, enabling the easy installation of sliding screen doors. Such doors, which slide behind each other on a pair of grooves in the sill, were a Japanese invention, and had existed in the Heian period, in the form of the *fusuma* mentioned above. During the Kamakura period, doors were increasingly made with a translucent Japanese paper, known as *washi*, which allowed the gentle diffusion of exterior light into the room and throughout the building. These doors were light and easily detached and were often removed to create a large reception room on special occasions. Exterior doors could also be drawn apart to provide a view of the garden outside, acting as a type of frame around a real natural scene. However, such thin, insubstantial partitions had several disadvantages, as they offered little privacy to the residents and allowed considerable draughts to travel through the residence during cold weather.

The floors of domestic interiors also changed significantly, perhaps because of the more active lifestyles of the warriors and their families. The straw *tatami* mats, previously a single, movable furnishing, were now fitted together to cover completely the wooden floor, a development which strongly influenced the shape, function and decoration of the Japanese room. First, as *tatami* are of a more or less standard size, rooms had to be built to match the dimensions of a certain number of mats, a trend that has continued to the present day. In addition, their soft, fragile surface did not permit the use of heavy furnishings, such as dressers, tables and chairs, which would have dug into and torn the mats. For the same reason, outdoor shoes could not be worn inside the house, leaving the surface of the mats clean enough to sit and lie down on. As a consequence, silk and cotton cushions served as seats, and dining tables were low, most often square or rectangular in shape, with a glossy lacquer finish. In the winters they were fitted with a heating device on their undersides and covered

Japan: drawing of *tokonoma* alcove from *Japanese Homes and their Surroundings* by Edward S. Morse, 1886

with a heavy blanket, under which each person could huddle for warmth. From the early 16th century onwards bedding, in the form of mattresses filled with layers of wadded cotton, was laid out on the mats. These mattresses, or futons, were rolled up and stored in adjacent cupboards when not in use.

Since much of everyday life was conducted on *tatami*, the typical posture of a Japanese indoors is a kneeling position, a fact which explains why many of the furnishings and structural features, such as the ceilings, decorative lintels and beams, as well as door handles and fitted desks, are so low. Most of the decorations of the room, including paintings on sliding doors and portable screens and flower arrangements, were also placed at a low eye level, as they were meant to be appreciated from a kneeling position.

Another significant development in these warrior residences was the addition of three new features to the study chamber, or *shoin*, resulting in a new style of interior design known as the *shoin* style. These new elements were an alcove, a set of staggered shelves, and a window with a fitted desk. All constructed out of wood, as immovable parts of the structure of the room, these elements became key parts of the Japanese interior. The alcove, or *tokonoma*, served as a display space for valuable Chinese-style hanging scrolls of calligraphy and ink paintings and for ceramic and metal vases and other luxury artefacts. Often an elegant flower arrangement was placed in the alcove to suit the season, occasion or character of any expected guest. These floral displays, known as *ikebana*, or "living flower", had their origins in Buddhist temples where they were placed at the altar for worship. Gradually, they began to appear in secular interiors and came to represent a piece of nature living inside the room, reinforcing the idea that there is no real distinction between the inside and outside worlds.

The staggered shelves, often located next to the alcove, were also erected for the display of artefacts. On the shelves, the owner placed a miniature bonsai tree, a carving in some natural material such as wood or even jade, a piece of porcelain or pottery, or a valuable lacquer box or bowl. The desk was often located in front of a window giving onto the garden, providing inspiration for the composition of poetry or Chinese-style ink paintings, both of which were considered highly cultured pursuits during this period. On the desk, therefore, a lacquer ink box was almost always present, containing brushes and inkstone, and a container for the water needed to prepare the ink. These lacquer boxes often bore natural motifs, such as flowers, grasses and birds, or scenes from literary classics, and were often decorated using sprinkled gold and mother-of-pearl inlay.

During the Kamakura and Muromachi periods, the custom of tea drinking, borrowed from China, became widespread in Zen Buddhist temples and among the warrior class. As a part of the entertainment of the period, tea gatherings were held at the homes of the wealthy, often in the *shoin* rooms mentioned above, or in Chinese-style pavilions, known as *sukiya*, in the garden. The host often used such gatherings as an opportunity to display his treasures, including Chinese paintings, ceramics, metalwork and lacquer, in the alcoves and on the shelves. In the case of the shogun, connoisseurs of Chinese artefacts were employed both to authenticate and catalogue these treasures and to formulate rules for their display. Two such men were Noami (1397–1471) and Soami (1472–1523) who worked for the shogun Ashikaga Yoshimasa (1436–90), a keen tea drinker and collector of Chinese artefacts. These men were knowledgeable art historians responsible for arranging the shogun's collection of lacquer, porcelain, ink paintings and other treasures to create a sumptuous background to the serving of tea. In this role, they were perhaps Japan's first interior designers.

Late in the Muromachi period, tea gatherings developed into what is generally known as the tea ceremony, or *chanoyu*, a form of tea drinking heavily influenced by Zen Buddhism. The warrior rulers, who had moved their capital back to Kyoto and lived in the Muromachi area, increasingly renounced their political responsibilities to take up refined pastimes such as calligraphy, poetry, Noh theatre and tea drinking. The highly cultured Ashikaga Yoshimasa employed a Zen monk, Murata Juko (1423–1502), as his tea master. In contrast to the refined style of the connoisseurs mentioned above, Juko emphasized the Zen principles of simplicity, humility, and harmony with nature, introducing an aesthetic known as *wabi*, a sort of "symbolic poverty", into the world of tea. Under Juko and the two other major tea men who are said to have formulated the tea ceremony, Takeno Joo (1502–55) and Sen no Rikyu (1522–91), tea drinking was transformed into a spiritual act, and the setting played a key role.

These tea masters encouraged the drinking of tea in rustic tea huts, which were ideal manifestations of the *wabi* aesthetic. Built in imitation of traditional thatched farmhouses, but on a smaller scale, the *wabi* teahouse generally contained four and a half *tatami* mats of floor space. The interior was extremely austere and empty, the only features being a small depression in the floor for the charcoal brazier and an alcove for the display of a scroll and simple flower arrangement. To achieve the desired rustic effect, structural materials were often left in their natural state, the walls of rough clay and straw, the wooden pillar and exposed rafters providing visual and textural variation as well as a sense of natural simplicity. The windows, made of translucent paper, merely permitted a gentle light to enter the room, and their placement at irregular intervals around the walls was deliberately asymmetrical, but nonetheless well balanced. The overall effect was natural and calming, with no ostentation which might distract the mind. Such tea houses or tearooms began to appear in castles,

Japan: Nijo Castle, Kyoto – interior of room with paintings attributed to Kano school, 1603

temples and the homes of the wealthy, serving at once as a place to serve tea to guests and as a spiritual refuge.

Of the great tea masters who designed these tearooms, Sen no Rikyu is regarded as the most influential. He created the most intimate of tearooms, often only two mats in size, enough for the host and one guest, and placed the guest on the mat of honour in front of the alcove while he served the tea from a subordinate position. His manner of decorating the tearoom interior came closest to the *wabi* ideal. Often, he chose to arrange a single flower in a handmade bamboo vase on the pillar at the side of the alcove, or simply shook cherry or plum blossoms onto a dish filled with water to create a simple but powerful display of nature within the tea room.

One of his pupils, Furuta Oribe (1543–1615) was also a celebrated tea master and designer, and his tea rooms were characterized by numerous windows, which he employed, along with the arrangement of the *tatami* mats, to transform the host's seat into a sort of stage. One of his successors, Kobori Enshu (1579–1647), was another notable tea master, who was also famed for his designs of buildings and gardens as well as for his love for antiques. His style is often regarded as a blending of the *shoin* room with the grass tea hut, since many of his tea rooms featured sliding doors and shelves laden with valuable antiques alongside posts and other wooden features with their bark intact.

The 16th century was a time of civil wars in Japan, and the country was ravaged by the armies of feudal lords battling with each other for supremacy. During the latter half of the century, many of the most powerful lords constructed great castles to protect themselves and to assert their authority. These castles were generally built on high ground and featured stone foundations surmounted by several storeys of wooden structure and tiled roofs. Many castles were burnt to the ground during the feuding, but judging from the interiors of those which have survived, the rooms inside displayed the characteristics of *shoin* style architecture, but often with sumptuous decoration. The interior of Nijo Castle in Kyoto, built by the feudal lord who finally established peace in 1603, Tokugawa Ieyasu (1542–1616), is an early 17th century example of the rich ornamentation enjoyed by the top military men of the land in the late 16th and early 17th centuries. In many of the reception rooms, the walls and *fusuma* doors were almost entirely covered with bold paintings, and the motifs, such as eagles and tigers, symbolizing power and bravery, were meant to intimidate visitors to the lord's castle.

These particular paintings are the work of the Kano school

Japan: print showing interior of pleasure house, by Torii Kiyotada, c.1720–50

of painters who had been active in the Muromachi period but continued to paint as official artists for the military rulers well into the Edo Period (1603–1868). In Japan, it is almost impossible to separate painting from interior design, as Japanese paintings tend to function either as a decorative section of the structure of the room itself or, in the case of movable screens, as part of the furniture. Many warlords employed their own official painters to produce works for their castles, the most elaborate of which involved gold leaf backgrounds and expensive pigments. In addition, the ceilings of the main halls were also gorgeously decorated with geometric painted designs, sections of the wooden walls were finely carved and elaborate metal ornamentation was also fitted to the pillars and beams. A great part of the warlord's wealth went into the decoration of his chambers, and yet the room itself contained little furniture.

The Edo period began when Tokugawa Ieyasu unified the country and moved the capital to present-day Tokyo. During this period, Japan was in a state of relative peace and prosperity, although the warrior class, who were still nominally in charge of the government, found themselves deprived of their martial role and gradually lost their financial and cultural influence. As the nation became increasingly settled and urbanized, the need for castles disappeared, and the wealthy took to building less ostentatious residences. One villa in Kyoto, built for an imperial prince around 1636, is one of the finest examples of early Edo period architectural design and brings together many of the elements of *shoin* and tearoom architecture. Known as the Katsura Imperial Villa, this elegant residence contains about 40 rooms arranged in an asymmetrical pattern, the main rooms all facing southeast and rooms at the back being used for circulation. Few of the rooms were assigned any specific function, many of them resembling simple tearooms with their unpainted wooden elements and rather empty interiors. In many of these elegant chambers the plain, linear appearance is enhanced only by an ink painting on the wall or sliding door or by decoration such as a repeated leaf pattern on the fusuma doors. Although the overall effect of this interior is one of reserve and simplicity, it must be remembered that, in this aristocratic residence, the materials and craftsmanship were undoubtedly of the finest quality and were by no means cheap.

The artistic developments of the Edo period owe less to the aristocracy or military rulers than to the exuberant culture of the townspeople, who, led by merchants, were enjoying increasing wealth. In Edo, the pleasure quarters and theatres became the focus of artistic energy and feature in much of the art of the time, especially in the colour wood block prints that have come to characterize the period. Some such prints by artists such as Torii Kiyotada (fl. 1720–50) show the interiors of pleasure houses in the Yoshiwara district of Tokyo, depicted using a strong sense of perspective, borrowed from Western paintings and engravings. These scenes show plentiful space, with the screen doors being drawn open to expand the main room and reveal the other rooms in the building. Furniture is typically sparse, with the occasional small table and lamp, and often the only decoration appears on the screen doors, in the form of abstracted natural motifs and geometric patterns.

The Edo period brought little change in the development of Japanese interiors, although the type of interiors mentioned above became increasingly available to the lower-class townspeople, who were becoming more prosperous. However, due to the increasing crowdedness in cities, many pleasure houses, shops and domestic residences began to feature a second storey, which often served as storage space. The second storey was reached by means of free-standing wooden staircases, which originated in rural areas and appeared in urban shops and houses in the late Edo period. These structures were often disturbingly steep and rather bulky, but they did provide additional storage space. In most cases, they were fitted with cupboards with sliding doors as well as small drawers with metal handles, and were generally used to hold goods and supplies or household articles. Around this time, large wooden storage trunks and cabinets known as *tansu* also began to be used for the storage of clothing and other personal possessions.

Throughout most of the Edo period, Japan had fairly successfully managed to shut out the rest of the world, but when, in the mid-19th century, American and European gunboats appeared off the coast demanding that Japan open up its ports, the island nation was forced to reconsider its isolationist attitude. In 1868, the military government which had ruled Japan for over 250 years collapsed and power was handed over to the Emperor. This new government embarked on an extensive programme of modernization, reorganizing the nation following Western technology, government, communications methods and customs. Western architecture was also absorbed, more as a building technique than for its aesthetic qualities, and many foreign architects were imported to Japan to teach their skills, while Japanese architects were sent abroad to train. However, Western-style buildings were neither practical in Japan's hot, humid climate, nor did their styles suit Japanese taste, and although some of the wealthier, more "modern" Japanese took to wearing Western clothes and using chairs and other Western furnishings in their home, the average Japanese person's lifestyle remained largely unchanged.

In the late 19th century, while Japan was frantically absorbing information from the West, many Europeans became equally fascinated with Japan and its art. In a phase generally known as Japonisme, Europeans, and later Americans, eagerly bought up imported Japanese art objects such as wood block prints and the porcelain, lacquer articles, fans and kimonos which featured increasingly at the international exhibitions of the late 19th century and early 20th century. These prints and decorative objects, with their novel motifs and compositions, inspired many Western painters, most notably James McNeill Whistler (1834–1903), Édouard Manet (1832–83) and Claude Monet (1840–1926) as well as Art Nouveau designers such as Émile Gallé (1846–1904) and Charles Rennie Mackintosh (1868–1928). Japanese artefacts also began to feature prominently in European interiors, often arranged in ways that would have no doubt surprised the Japanese, and many objects and motifs which were not part of Japanese interior design were given new roles in the Western room. For example, large porcelain jars, decorated in a very un-Japanese flamboyant manner, were often lined up on mantlepieces already crowded with other art objects, while fans, which in Japan were rarely used as decoration in the home, were displayed on walls and shelves as exotic ornaments. Westerners were also greatly charmed by portable folding screens, lacquer boxes and fine metalwork sculptures, all of which inspired many European imitations.

In the 20th century, modernization and Westernization continued to a great extent, and after World War I, the modern architecture movement reached Japan. The Japanese increasingly designed their homes in European styles, both modern and traditional. The interiors generally mixed traditional Japanese and Western-style rooms, the latter often being used for the entertainment of guests, while the old-style rooms were often where the family really lived. It was during this time that many Western architects came into contact with Japanese architecture, often by means of exhibition buildings at world fairs and expositions. Some, such as Frank Lloyd Wright (1867–1959) visited Japan to learn about Japanese architectural design, while many Japanese architects went to study under European architects such as Walter Gropius (1883–1969) and Le Corbusier (1887–1965), thus creating a great exchange of ideas on both interiors and exteriors.

During World War II many of Japan's cities were burnt to the ground, and after the war Japan was forced to rebuild itself, largely under the influence of its former enemy, the United States. This resulted in the Americanization of Japanese architecture, with many architects substituting reinforced concrete, metal and glass for the traditional wood. Elements of interior design began to transform, often for practical reasons. For example, in many homes, sliding doors began to be made with glass instead of paper, so are less easily damaged. Most buildings now have glass windows set in a metal frame, rather than paper and a wooden frame, thus letting in more light in while keeping out the cold. Most Japanese homes, and many hotels and restaurants, have kept the traditional *tatami* mats, however, and living space is still measured according to number of *tatami*. However, many homes have at least one carpeted Western-style room, most commonly a living room or dining room, which is also equipped with Western-style tables and chairs, as well as televisions and other electrical goods. Ironically, in the United States and many European countries, an interest in practical, minimalistic interiors has led many people to look to Japan for ideas, resulting in the increasing appearance of futons, portable wooden screens and paper lamps in Western homes.

It was also mainly after World War II that Japanese interior designers became recognized as artists, many of them having found new, exciting methods of expressing traditional Japanese ideas of space and line. Major architects, such as Kenzo Tange (b.1913) and Isozaki Arata (b.1931), who have combined Japanese and Western ideas of architectural design, have attracted much attention throughout the world for their original works. Another important figure, Kazuo Shinohara (b.1925), considered to be one of Japan's most influential house designers, conducted extensive research into the tradi-

Japan: House under High Voltage Lines by Kazuo Shinohara, 1981

tional Japanese house and the Japanese concept of space. His most famous buildings include Umbrella House (1961), which harks back to a late 16th century umbrella-structure tea house by Sen no Rikyu, and his House under High Voltage lines (1981), which features a solid, round central pillar, sliding glass doors opening onto a veranda and abundant interior space, all modern in style and material, but Japanese in conception.

Another of Japan's foremost architects, Tadao Ando (b.1941), also creates highly modern exteriors and interiors with a strong Japanese sense of line and space. One of his most interesting works is the Koshino Residence built in 1981 almost entirely with reinforced concrete and glass on a hillside near Kobe. Despite its modern design and the use of Western-style furniture, the living room retains many traditional Japanese elements, such as matting on the floor, low placement of the chairs and lacquer tables. More significantly, Ando left the concrete interior walls undecorated, a decision reminiscient of tea house interiors with their rough, unpainted clay walls. The room also features a large, rectangular window looking right onto the slope of the hillside, bringing together the interior of the house with the world outside.

MEHER SHONA MCARTHUR

Further Reading

Banham, Reyner and Hiroyuki Suzuki, *Contemporary Architecture of Japan, 1958–1984*, London: Architectural Press, and New York: Rizzoli, 1985

Clarke, Rosy, *Japanese Antique Furniture: A Guide to Evaluating and Restoring*, New York: Weatherhill, 1983

Coaldrake, William H., *The Way of the Carpenter: Tools and Japanese Architecture*, New York: Weatherhill, 1990

Drexler, Arthur, *The Architecture of Japan*, New York: The Museum of Modern Art, 1955

Engel, Heinrich, *The Japanese House*, Rutland, VT: Tuttle, 1964

Fujika, Michio, *Japanese Residences and Gardens: A Tradition of Integration*, Tokyo: Kodansha, 1982

Hashimoto, Fumio (editor), *Architecture in the Shoin Style: Japanese Feudal Residences*, Tokyo: Kodansha, 1981

Hibi, Sadao, *Japanese Detail: Traditional Architecture, Gardens, Interiors*, London: Thames and Hudson, 1989

Inoue, Mitsuo, *Space in Japanese Architecture*, New York: Weatherhill, 1985

Ishimoto, Tatsuo and Kiyoko, *The Japanese House: Its Interior and Exterior*, New York: Crown, 1963

Itoh, Teiji, *The Essential Japanese House: Craftsmanship, Function and Style in Town and Country*, New York: Weatherhill, 1967

Itoh, Teiji, *Traditional Domestic Architecture of Japan*, New York: Weatherhill, 1972

Itoh, Teiji, *Traditional Japanese Houses*, New York: Rizzoli, 1983
Kirby, John, *From Castle to Teahouse: Japanese Architecture of the Momoyāmā Period*, Rutland, VT: Tuttle, 1962
Lee, Sherman E., *Japanese Decorative Style* (exhib. cat.), Cleveland: Cleveland Museum of Art, 1961
Matsunaga, Yasumitsu, *Kazuo Shinohara*, New York: Rizzoli, 1982
Morse, Edward S., *Japanese Homes and their Surroundings*, 1886; reprinted New York: Dover, 1961
Okawa, Naomi, *Edo Architecture: Katsura and Nikko*, New York: Weatherhill, 1975
Sasaki, Hiroshi (editor), *The Modern Japanese House: Inside and Outside*, Japan Publications, 1970
Slesin, Suzanne and others, *Japanese Style*, London: Thames and Hudson, and New York: Potter, 1987; as The Essence of Japanese Style, Thames and Hudson, 1994
Takakuwa, Gisei, *Shoji: The Screens of Japan*, Tokyo: Mitsumura Suiko Shoin, 1961
Ueda, Atsushi, *The Inner Harmony of the Japanese Home*, New York: Kodansha, 1990
Yoshida, Tetsuro, *The Japanese House and Garden*, revised edition London: Pall Mall, and New York: Praeger, 1969

Jefferson, Thomas 1743–1826

American statesman and architect

Best known for his political achievements as author of the American Declaration of Independence (1776) and third President of the United States (1801–09), Thomas Jefferson also made lasting contributions to American architecture through his designs for the Virginia State Capitol, Richmond; Monticello, his country estate in Albemarle County; and the University of Virginia, Charlottesville. Inspired to create an American architecture that would win worldwide respect for his young country, he remodelled and furnished dwellings for himself in Paris, New York, and Philadelphia as well as the President's House in Washington, DC. Monticello, his first architectural project, occupied Jefferson's attention for more than forty years. He is reported to have said that "architecture is my delight, and putting up and pulling down, one of my favourite amusements".

Jefferson was the eldest son of the surveyor Peter Jefferson, and was raised in rural central Virginia. Jefferson was a voracious reader with knowledge of seven languages, including Greek and Latin, and his early knowledge of architecture came chiefly from books. About 1768, Jefferson acquired James Gibbs's *Book of Architecture* (1728) while a student at the College of William and Mary in Williamsburg. His later architectural library included five editions of Andrea Palladio's *Quattro Libri*; Jefferson was said to have called this work "the Bible". He also owned Robert Morris's *Select Architecture* (1755). Two of Morris's designs, Plates 2 and 37, may have influenced the first scheme for Monticello.

Erected on land Jefferson inherited from his father, Monticello was begun in 1768. Jefferson chose a site on a low mountain and named it "Monticello", meaning little mountain in old Italian. Monticello's architectural consequence was quickly recognized. The Marquis de Chastellux, who visited in 1782, noted that "Mr Jefferson is the first American who has consulted the Fine Arts to know how he should shelter himself from the weather". Relatively little is known about the furnishings of the earliest period as few survive. Among these are an English-made Queen Anne card table and a tall desk made in Virginia.

Jefferson's knowledge of architecture and art expanded greatly during five years of diplomatic service in Paris. He wrote in 1787 that "from Lyons to Nîmes I have been nourished with the remains of Roman grandeur". The Maison Carrée at Nîmes in fact inspired Jefferson's design for the Virginia State Capitol, whose classical Roman vocabulary Jefferson thought appropriate for the American republic.

Jefferson also admired much of modern Parisian architecture, particularly the Hôtel de Salm with its single storey and dome. He rented the recently completed Hôtel de Langeac (demolished in 1842) designed by Chalgrin at the corner of the Champs-Elysée and the rue de Berri. The oval saloon was decorated with a ceiling painting by Jean-Simon Berthélmy of the rising sun.

The Hôtel de Langeac was entirely outfitted by Jefferson, and its furnishings reveal much about his taste. His choices for four different suites of chairs and various tables suggest that he appreciated elegance and simplicity. Mahogany *fauteuils à la reine* with sabre legs attributed to the famous Georges Jacob are so streamlined they are often mistaken for later Directoire works. The Hôtel de Langeac dining room featured consoles, a dining table that could seat twenty, and patinated and decoratively carved chairs upholstered in blue silk, probably woven in Lyons. The suite may have been made by Jacques Upton who had a shop nearby. Jefferson also acquired three gaming tables, a number of table tops, and an architect's desk with a movable top called a *table à la tronchin*.

Jefferson returned from France in the autumn of 1789. While Secretary of State under President Washington, he lived briefly in New York City in 1790, making modifications to the house he occupied there in Maiden Lane. When the government moved its headquarters to Philadelphia, Jefferson rented an elaborate residence at 234 High Street which he also modified to suit his requirements, adding a book room, stable, garden house, and bed alcove. His French furnishings and sizeable art collection, mainly copies of Old Masters, were installed in tiers throughout the house.

In 1794 Jefferson wanted to leave "the hated occupations of politics" and return to "my family, my farm, and my books". He concentrated his attention toward enlarging Monticello from eight to 21 rooms. The double-storeyed porticos were knocked down but three rooms from the original house were incorporated into the new house. The revised Monticello included features he had seen in France: two narrow staircases rather than a single grand stair (which Jefferson thought too expensive), bed alcoves, a dome, and privies. For comfort and convenience Jefferson also added a dumbwaiter to carry wine from the wine cellar to the dining room, double-acting doors between the entrance hall and parlour, and a dual-faced clock that could be seen in the entrance hall as well as outside on the east portico.

Monticello's new scheme demonstrated a sophisticated understanding of both modern and ancient architecture. The entablatures were much influenced by great Roman buildings that Jefferson had studied in books by Desgodetz, Fréart de Chambray, and Jombert. The entablature of the Temple of Fortuna Virilis became the entablature for his bed chamber, the

Temple of Jupiter for the parlour, and the Temple of Antoninus and Faustina for the entrance hall.

Jefferson designed double-height spaces for the public rooms (the entrance hall, parlour, dining room, and tea room), the third-floor dome room, and his own bed chamber. A "sanctum sanctorum" of bed chamber, cabinet of study, book room, and conservatory helped protect Jefferson's privacy.

Although Monticello's Roman Neo-Classical exterior was spare, its interior furnishing was intricate. Judging by inventories and accounts, Monticello was crowded with furniture and works of art hung in tiers in the public rooms. The eclectic furnishings were acquired over a long period of time from a variety of sources in Williamsburg, Paris, London, Philadelphia, and New York. After Jefferson's financial resources diminished when he retired from the presidency in 1809, a great deal of furniture probably designed by Jefferson was made by several talented slave cabinet-makers. These plain works demonstrate Jefferson's preference for practical and elegant solutions.

Jefferson's last architectural work was the design of the University of Virginia which he helped to found in 1819 and called the "hobby of his old age". A central-domed Rotunda looking west to the mountains housed the university's library and was flanked by two rows of pavilions for professors, each of a different design and architectural order, connected by student rooms.

SUSAN R. STEIN

Biography

Born in Shadwell, Goochland (now Albemarle) County, Virginia, 13 April 1743, the eldest son of a landowner and surveyor. Studied law at the College of William and Mary, Williamsburg, Virginia, from 1760; became a barrister in 1767. Self-taught in architecture. Active in politics from the late 1760s; drafted the American Declaration of Independence, 1776. Elected Governor of Virginia, 1779; lived in Paris from 1784 and as US Minister to France, 1785–89; first US Secretary of State, 1790–93; US Vice-President, 1797–1801, and President, 1801–09. Helped found the University of Virginia, 1819. Died at Monticello, near Charlottesville, Virginia, 4 July 1826.

Selected Works

The largest collection of Jefferson's architectural drawings is the Coolidge Collection of Thomas Jefferson Manuscripts, held by the Massachusetts Historical Society, Boston. Jefferson's papers are dispersed among many repositories. The principal collections are in the University of Virginia, Charlottesville, the Massachusetts Historical Society, and the Huntington Library, Pasadena.

Interiors

1768–82 Monticello, near Charlottesville, Virginia (building and interiors): Thomas Jefferson
1785–99 Virginia State Capitol, Richmond
1796–1809 Monticello, near Charlottesville, Virginia (remodelling of building and interiors): Thomas Jefferson
1806–12 Poplar Forest House, Bedford County, Virginia (building and interior fitments)
1817–26 University of Virginia, Charlottesville (buildings and interior fitments)

Publications

There are several collections of Jefferson's writings; the best, though incomplete, is Boyd.

Notes on the State of Virginia, 1785
The Papers of Thomas Jefferson, edited by Julian P. Boyd, 19 vols., 1950–
Writings (Library of America), edited by Merrill D. Peterson, 1984

Further Reading

There are numerous histories of Monticello; for an informative recent account see Stein *The Worlds of Thomas Jefferson*, 1993.

Adams, William Howard (editor), *The Eye of Thomas Jefferson* (exhib. cat.), Washington, DC: National Gallery of Art, 1976
Adams, William Howard, *Jefferson's Monticello*, New York: Abbeville, 1983
Berkeley, Francis Lewis, Jr. and Constance E. Thurlow, *The Jefferson Papers of the University of Virginia*, Charlottesville: University of Virginia Library 1950; supplement 1973
Cote, Richard C., *The Architectural Workmen of Thomas Jefferson in Virginia*, Ph.D. thesis, Boston: Boston University, 1986
Granquist, Charles L., *Cabinetmaking at Monticello*, M.A. thesis, Oneonta: State University of New York, 1977
Hitchcock, Henry-Russell and William Seale, *Temples of Democracy: The State Capitols of the USA*, New York: Harcourt Brace, 1976
Kimball, Fiske, *Thomas Jefferson and the First Monument of the Classical Revival in America*, Washington, DC, 1915
Llewellyn, Robert and Charles L. Granquist, *Thomas Jefferson's Monticello*, Charlottesville: Thomasson Grant, 1983
McLaughlin, Jack, *Jefferson and Monticello: The Biography of a Builder*, New York: Holt, 1988
Nichols, Frederick Doveton, *Thomas Jefferson's Architectural Drawings*, 4th edition Boston: Massachusetts Historical Society, 1978
Norton, Paul F., *Latrobe, Jefferson, and the National Capitol*, New York: Garland, 1977
O'Neal, W.B. *Jefferson's Buildings at the University of Virginia*, Charlottesville: University of Virginia Press, 1960–
Rice, Howard C., Jr., *Thomas Jefferson's Paris*, Princeton: Princeton University Press, 1976
Sowerby, E. Millicent, *Catalogue of the Library of Thomas Jefferson*, 1952; reprinted Charlottesville: University Press of Virginia, 1983
Stein, Susan R., *The Worlds of Thomas Jefferson at Monticello*, Charlottesville: Thomas Jefferson Memorial Foundation, 1993
Stein, Susan R., "Furnishings at Monticello" in *Magazine Antiques*, July 1993, pp.70–79
Stein, Susan R., "Jefferson's Museum at Monticello" in *Magazine Antiques*, July 1993, pp.80–85
Waddell, Gene, "The First Monticello" in *Journal of the Society of Architectural Historians*, 46, March 1987, pp.5–29

Jeffrey & Co.

British wallpaper manufacturers, 1836–c.1928

For almost half a century Jeffrey & Co. was one of the foremost producers of wallpaper in England, in terms both of the quality of their products and their influence on designers, decorators, and other manufacturers at home and abroad. To a large extent the firm's reputation for innovation and quality can be attributed to Metford Warner (1843–1930), who joined as a junior partner in the mid-1860s. It was Warner, for example, who introduced the practice of commissioning work from established and progressive architects and designers such as Walter Crane, E.W. Godwin, Christopher Dresser, Bruce Talbert and C.F.A. Voysey, and who championed the re-evaluation of wallpaper as art. However, the foundations of the

Jeffrey & Co: London showrooms

firm's success were laid long before Warner's arrival, during a period of amalgamation and consolidation.

Jeffrey & Co. were first established in East London as Jeffrey, Wise & Co., c.1836. It underwent several changes of name (Jeffrey & Wise, 1839; Jeffrey, Wise & Horne, 1842; Horne & Allen, 1843; Jeffrey, Allen & Co., 1848) before taking on the title of Jeffrey & Co. in 1858, and although little is known about the firm's early history, it seems by this time to have already been established as an innovative concern, located at Kent and Essex Yard, Whitechapel. As Jeffrey & Wise it is credited with being one of the first London firms to install a cylinder printing machine and, at a time when it was virtually impossible to clean most wallpapers (other than by rubbing them gently with bread) Jeffrey & Wise was listed as being the "sole maker" of a type of washable paperhanging first developed by Crease & Co. earlier in the century.

By 1851 the firm was printing private commissions for the London furnishers and decorators, Jackson & Graham, and it seems likely that, in common with other manufacturers, it was also importing French wallpapers – possibly in association with a Robert Horne, who became a partner c.1842. It is also clear, both from illustrations in *The Journal of Design and Manufactures* (1849–52) and from descriptions of the exhibits it displayed in the Great Exhibition of 1851, that, by mid-century, Jeffrey & Co. was producing a wide range of products to suit almost all sections of the market.

In 1862, trading as Jeffrey & Co., the firm exhibited at the International Exhibition in London and in 1864 it amalgamated with Holmes & Aubert, another established manufacturer, whose Islington premises it enlarged and occupied until the late 1920s. This merger enabled Jeffrey & Co. to take over production of Holmes & Aubert's high-quality hand-prints, flocks and leaf-metal printed papers and enhanced the firm's reputation substantially.

Soon afterwards Jeffrey & Co. was commissioned by Jackson & Graham to print the series of elaborate papers designed by Owen Jones for the Khedive's (Viceroy's) Palace in Cairo. This was an important and prestigious commission but, in the long term, it was the firm's association on its own account with prominent 19th-century artists, architects and designers which led to its being a major influence.

When Metford Warner joined in 1866 Jeffrey & Co. was already printing the first wallpapers designed by William Morris for his decorating company Morris, Marshall, Faulkner & Co. The following year it printed several designs by Christopher Dresser and the firm's main exhibit at the International Exhibition in Paris was a pilaster decoration designed by Owen Jones. Despite these connections, most of Jeffrey & Co's output was either based on French originals or designs supplied by block-cutters and was largely indistinguishable from the myriad papers produced by other reputable firms; that is, arabesque and chintz designs in the French style, flocks of various kinds, imitations of marbling and wood-grain and other papers for a general middle class market.

However, when Charles Eastlake criticised English wallpaper manufacturers in the first edition of his book *Hints on Household Taste* (1868) Warner (himself an accomplished draughtsman and colourist) decided to try a different approach and commissioned designs from several leading British architects, none of whom had designed for this medium before.

Although some of the first wallpapers produced from their designs received a mixed reception in the trade press, others, for example Eastlake's *Solanum* (1869) and E.W. Godwin's *Bamboo* (1872), proved highly successful. The *Bamboo* pattern, for instance, was especially popular in the United States where samples survive *in situ* in the Major Goodwin parlour, now installed in the Wadsworth Atheneum, Hartford, Connecticut. Moreover, Warner's departure from established practice marked the beginning of a new phase for Jeffrey & Co., raising awareness of the firm's products and associating its name with well-known members of an influential artistic elite. This factor must have had some bearing when, at Warner's insistence, wallpapers were displayed for the first time at the annual Exhibition of Fine Arts in London in 1873. Previously they had only been shown at exhibitions of industrial goods.

This not inconsiderable achievement helped to place Jeffrey & Co. at the centre of a new surge of confidence in the abilities of the home industry, previously perceived as deficient in design flair when compared to its French counterpart, and by the mid-1890s Warner had commissioned patterns from numerous artists and architects, including Walter Crane. Crane's first design, a nursery pattern, was machine-printed by the firm in 1875 and he went on to design more than 60 of its wallpapers.

It is unlikely that many of Crane's papers were themselves financially profitable. Indeed, in 1894, Crane (whose designs were often particularly eccentric) was asked to make his pattern repeats smaller and reduce the number of colours. Nevertheless their reflection of avant-garde ideas and their capacity to win major awards at international and other exhibitions (for which they were often specially commissioned) secured Jeffrey & Co's position as the leading manufacturer of "Artistic" wallcoverings for a discerning market.

As a result, the firm's reputation became closely linked with the hand production of luxury items for consumers who could afford wall decorations with large-scale, highly-coloured patterns, designs printed on or decorated with gold leaf, elaborate flocked papers, embossed and stamped leather wallcoverings and highly-decorated imitation leather papers. However, Warner took care to ensure that, in addition to providing "advanced" patterns and those which satisfied traditional taste, the firm also catered for a less well-off market, producing decorations which, although cheaper, reflected current fashionable styles. Many of these were designed by or had patterns heavily influenced by the work of professional freelancers, including Lewis F. Day, Alan Vigers and A.F. Brophy, and groups such as the Silver Studio.

By 1900 Jeffrey & Co. had won nine gold medals and numerous other awards at international and other exhibitions – several in Paris and the US – was exporting to the USA, Australia and Scandinavia as well as Europe, and its products were reviewed regularly in the trade press and in publications aimed at fashionable consumers throughout the Western world.

Jeffrey & Co. is reputed to have manufactured the first imitation leather paper produced in the UK – embossed with a design by Bruce Talbert – and is also credited with having first marketed co-ordinating wallpapers designed specifically for decorative schemes which divided the wall horizontally into dado, filling and frieze. In 1871, Christopher Dresser supplied the firm with a series of designs of this kind, together with complementary ceiling patterns, predating the better known tripartite scheme by the architect Brightwen Binyon, issued by Warner in 1875. A similar arrangement, designed by Walter Crane, won a prestigious award for the firm at the Philadelphia Centennial Exhibition (1876) – stimulating demand for a fashion which subsequently became widespread in all sections of the market and remained popular at the cheaper end into the 20th century.

Jeffrey & Co.'s papers were imitated widely from the 1870s and by the turn of the century the firm was competing with manufacturers whose machine-printed papers, often inspired by Jeffrey & Co. originals, were satisfying a mass market which required a high turnover of stylish products at low prices. The firm's success at the Franco-British Exhibtion in 1908, where it won the Grand Prix for Walter Crane's *Macaw*, and reviews of its products in the trade press indicate that it was seen to be still in the first rank until the mid-1920s. However, despite the opening of a showroom in central London, Warner, who had been sole proprietor since 1871, found it difficult to maintain the firm's independence in the face of changing fashions and market conditions. Moreover, his sons lacked his business acumen and entrepreneurial flair and, shortly after his retirement in 1924, Jeffrey & Co. was taken over by the Wall Paper Manufacturers Ltd., a joint-stock company that dominated the British industry from 1899. By 1927 manufacture and distribution of the Jeffrey patterns had been transferred to Arthur Sanderson & Sons Ltd., which continues to print many of Jeffrey & Co.'s designs.

CHRISTINE WOODS

See also Crane

Selected Collections

Designers working for Jeffrey & Co. included Walter Crane (1845–1915), Lewis Foreman Day (1845–1910), Christopher Dresser (1834–1904), E.W. Godwin (1833–86), Owen Jones (1809–74), William Morris (1834–96), Bruce Talbert (1838–81) and C.F.A. Voysey (1857–1941). Substantial holdings of Jeffrey & Co. wallpapers can be found in the following collections: Temple Newsam House, Leeds; Public Records Office, and Victoria and Albert Museum, London; Manchester City Art Gallery and Whitworth Art Gallery, Manchester; Cooper-Hewitt Museum, New York; Nordiska Museet, Stockholm.

Further Reading

For a chronology of Jeffrey & Co. and an extensive bibliography see Burke 1986.

Banham, Joanna, *A Decorative Art: 19th Century Wallpapers in the Whitworth Art Gallery* (exhib. cat.), Manchester: Whitworth Art Gallery, 1985

Burke, Doreen Bolger and others, *In Pursuit of Beauty: Americans and the Aesthetic Movement* (exhib. cat.: Metropolitan Museum, New York), New York: Rizzoli, 1986

Entwisle, E.A., *Wallpapers of the Victorian Era*, Leigh-on-Sea: Lewis, 1964

Halén, Widar, *Christopher Dresser*, London: Phaidon, 1990

Hoskins, Lesley (editor), *The Papered Wall: The History, Patterns and Techniques of Wallpaper*, London: Thames and Hudson, and New York: Abrams, 1994

Jeffrey & Co., *Illustrations of the Victorian Series*, London, 1889

Lynn, Catherine, *Wallpaper in America from the Seventeenth Century to World War I*, New York: Norton, 1980

Oman, Charles C. and Jean Hamilton, *Wallpapers: A History and Illustrated Catalogue of the Collection of the Victoria and Albert Museum*, London: Sotheby Publications, and New York: Abrams, 1982

Sugden, Alan V. and J.L. Edmondson, *A History of English Wallpaper, 1509–1914*, London: Batsford, 1926

Woods, Christine, *Sanderson, 1860–1985* (exhib. cat.), London: Arthur Sanderson & Sons, 1985

Woods, Christine, "A Marriage of Convenience: Walter Crane and the Wallpaper Industry" in Greg Smith and Sarah Hyde (editors), *Walter Crane: Artist, Designer and Socialist* (exhib. cat.: Whitworth Art Gallery, Manchester), London: Lund Humphries, 1989

Jiricna, Eva 1939–

Czech interior designer and architect

Eva Jiricna has gained an international reputation as a designer of innovative and elegant shop interiors for the fashion industry. Often categorised as "High-Tech" – a label that Jiricna herself rejects – her work exemplifies a chic, Modernist aesthetic that exploits the use of industrial materials such as aluminium, matt black cladding and tensioned-steel cables, combined with classic, minimalist forms. The influence of this style has extended far beyond the narrow world of retailing and the sparseness and understatement of her interiors has been widely emulated by contemporary architects and designers in Britain and abroad.

Jiricna's background was firmly rooted in the Modern Movement. Born the daughter of an architect in Zlin, the new town created for the Bata shoe empire in Czechoslovakia, she grew up surrounded by modern furniture in a modern house in a modern city. And she has described her dismay when she moved away from home and observed with horror the kitsch interiors inhabited by other people. She trained as an architect at the Technical University in Prague and, after working in Czechoslovakia for a short period, she was invited to England to join the Greater London Council for a six-month work assignment. While she was in London the Russian tanks entered Prague and Jiricna decided to make London her home, to the great enrichment of the city.

During the 1970s she worked on the design for a large marina at Brighton. Only part of the marina was built, but the project served as a second apprenticeship, providing an opportunity for her to learn the practicalities of architectural work in England, to perfect her English, and to gain an appreciation of quality materials and a love of the detailing of boats and their rigging that was evident in many of her later projects.

In 1979 Jiricna was commissioned to design a shop in London's fashionable South Molton Street for the clothes designer Joseph Ettedgui. The Ettedguis also asked her to design their flat in Sloane Street. By this time her mature style was already formed and these interiors featured hard-edged, machine-made materials used in a frankly industrial way, and combined the precision of a watchmaker with a shiny glamour that had not been seen in Europe since the early interiors of Le Corbusier some fifty years before. They attracted much publicity and were an instant success. Jiricna established her own practice and her career was on its way.

In 1982 she re-designed the interior of her own apartment in London's Belsize Park. While the colours in her shops were deliberately kept neutral so as to show off the clothes, the colours in this small apartment were bright and mirrors were used to provide a sense of space. Nevertheless, as in all her work, the design was underpinned by a rational, clear plan.

Meanwhile, the relationship with Joseph Ettedgui proved increasingly productive as he branched out into different activities. The Le Caprice restaurant in Arlington Street represented a new building type and Jiricna's polished and glamorous high-tech interiors were well-received by the restaurant's affluent and high-profile clientele.

Jiricna and Ettedgui's next joint project was the Kenzo shop in London's Sloane Street. This interior retains the monochrome finish and the precision characteristic of the earlier South Molton Street shop and colour is confined to the fitting rooms. But a rich wooden floor with graceful curving steps gives the Sloane Street interior an air of more traditional quality as well as being the first example of Jiricna's winning way with staircases. The next project – Joseph Pour la Maison – was almost next door. This shop marketed an entire lifestyle, selling clothes, furniture and food all under the same roof. The Mallet-Stevens chairs used in the restaurant, for instance, were also on sale in the shop and the divisions between merchandise and fittings were almost indistinguishable. These and other chairs were displayed on "Profilit" shelves, like standard products, but the shelves themselves were made of glass bent to a channel section to give structural rigidity and suggest the imagery of an impossibly chic warehouse. Eileen Gray mirrors, a jewellery showcase as exquisite as the jewellery it displays, and the minimalist background for the clothes, all impart an atmosphere of confident, unforced quality.

The Joseph shop in the Fulham Road, built in 1988, set the scene for the most well-known of Jiricna's interests, the metal staircase with glass treads, hung from stainless steel rods. While most aspects of her shop interiors are reticent so as not to compete with the goods on sale, her staircases are more autonomous, each a hedonistic tour de force. The 1989 Joseph shop at 26 Sloane Street contains a two-storey staircase and takes the concept to its extreme. Engineered by Matthew Wells, it is a stainless steel structure of understated complexity with thin members supporting treads of etched glass. It makes going upstairs an adventure and challenges shoppers to work out the means of support. The elaborate structure has a great number of joints, each one celebrated with beautiful craftsmanship, and gives the impression that – given the right size allen key – it could be disassembled and taken away with the other merchandise.

With success came other clients: the Captain's Restaurant in the Lloyd's Building designed with Richard Rogers, the Way-In department at Harrod's designed with Jan Kaplicky, a series of shops worldwide for Joan and David with Art Deco overtones, and hairdressing salons for Vidal Sassoon. In most of these interiors it is the staircases that are most memorable, and in the commission for Legends night club in Old Burlington Street, Jiricna demonstrated her confidence with this feature by making the suspended staircase curved on plan. Situated beneath a waving ceiling of aluminium rods and placed

Jiricna: interior of Joseph shop, Fulham Road, London, 1988

between drums of perforated stainless steel, it is an extravagant gesture that makes the setting uniquely memorable.

JOHN WINTER

See also High-Tech

Biography

Eva Magdalena Jiřičná. Born in Zlin, Czechoslovakia, 3 March 1939, the daughter of an architect. Studied architecture at the Czech University of Technology, Prague, to 1963, and the Academy of Fine Arts, Prague. Married Martin Holub, 1963 (marriage dissolved 1973). Settled in London, 1968. Architect with the Greater London Council Schools Division, 1968–69; associate, Louis de Soissons Partnership, 1969–78; established interior design practice with David Hodges, 1978; worked independently, 1982–84; formed Jiricna Kerr Associates with Kathy Kerr, 1984; re-formed as Eva Jiricna Architects, 1986. Designed numerous shop, restaurant and club interiors throughout the 1980s; collaborated with Richard Rogers on the interiors of the Lloyd's building, London, and Jan Kaplicky on the refurbishment of Harrods' Way-In. Honorary Fellow, Royal College of Art, 1990; Member, Royal Institute of British Architects, 1991; Member, Prague Presidential Council, 1993. Awarded Royal Designer for Industry, 1991; Commander, Order of the British Empire (CBE), 1994.

Selected Works

Jiricna's work has been regularly illustrated in design and architecture journals, especially *Blueprint*, *Designers Journal*, and *Architectural Review*.

Interiors

1979–80	Joseph, South Moulton Street, London (interiors): Joseph Ettedgui
1980	Flat, Sloane Street, London (interiors): Joseph Ettedgui
1981–82	Flat, Belsize Park, London (building and interiors): Eva Jiricna
1981–82	Kenzo, Sloane Street, London (interiors)
c.1982	Le Caprice restaurant, Arlington Street, London (interiors)
1984	Lloyd's Headquarters, London (interiors, including Captain's Restaurant, with Richard Rogers Partnership)
1985	"Way In" Harrods, Knightsbridge, London (interiors with Jan Kaplicky)
1987–94	Joan and David retail outlets, London, Paris, Montreal, Toronto, and shops throughout the US (interiors)
1988	Vitra shop, Weil am Rhein, Germany (office refurbishment and landscaping)
1988	Legends nightclub, London (refurbishment and interiors)
1989	Joseph, Sloane Street (interiors)
1992–93	Design Council, London (refurbishment and interiors)
1994	Library Extension, De Montfort University, Leicester (building and interiors)

Further Reading

Cooper, Maurice, "The Deceptively Simple Style of Eva Jiricna" in *Blueprint*,1, October 1983, pp.14–15

Glancey, Jonathan, "Interior Design: Graphic Design Studio, Wimbledon, London" in *Architectural Review*, CLXXVII, February 1985, pp.60–71

Glancey, Jonathan, *New British Architecture*, London: Thames and Hudson, 1989; New York: Thames and Hudson, 1990

"Joseph Steps Up" in *Blueprint*, November 1988, pp.34–35

"Kenzo Shop, Sloane Street; Belsize Park Flat" in *Architectural Design*, 54, no.3–4, 1985, pp.18–21

McDermott, Catherine, *Street Style: British Design in the 80s*, London: Design Council, and New York: Rizzoli, 1987

McGuire, Penny, "Eva Jiricna's Own Home" in *Architectural Review*, 174, July 1983, pp.65–68

McGuire, Penny, "High Priestess of High Tech: the Immaculate Eva Jiricna" in *Designer*, July–August, 1983, pp.19–20

McQuiston, Liz, *Women in Design: A Contemporary View*, New York: Rizzoli, and London: Trefoil, 1988

Manser, José, *The Joseph Shops: Eva Jiricna*, London: Architecture Design and Technology Press, and New York: Van Nostrand Reinhold, 1991

Pawley, Martin, *Eva Jiricna: Design in Exile*, London: Fourth Estate, and New York: Rizzoli, 1990

"Practical Pictorial: Eva Jiricna: Hi-Tech Style that Wins Competitions" in *Royal Institute of British Architects Journal*, 89, November 1982, pp.2–3

Richardson, Sara, *Eva Jiricna, Jiricna Kerr & Associates: A Bibliography*, Monticello, IL: Vance, 1989

Stern, Robert A. M. (editor), *The International Design Yearbook*, New York: Abbeville, and London: Thames and Hudson, 1985–86

Joel, Betty 1896–1985

British furniture, textile and interior designer

The designer and interior decorator Betty Joel's furniture and interiors were strongly influenced by French styles and reflect the geometrical inspiration of Art Deco mingled with the smoothness and glamour of the Moderne. She established her furniture-making business, Betty Joel Ltd., with her husband David just after the end of World War I in 1919. The company acted as manufacturer as well as retailer and had a factory in Hayling Island, Essex, and a shop at 177 Sloane Street, London. The emphasis was upon quality in both design and manufacture; David Joel had been in the navy and craftsmen yacht-fitters who used traditional joinery and cabinet-making techniques were employed to make the company's early furniture.

Initially the designs represented a stripped-down Arts and Crafts style with neo-Georgian overtones. But by the 1930s Joel had developed a more dashing Modernistic manner. Her work has often been described as an English version of the elegant Moderne style embodied in the work of French furniture designers such as Süe et Mare, and it featured simple, Modernist shapes veneered in luxurious materials like walnut, Macassar ebony, rosewood and ivory. She specialised in using "Empire" woods, the term used to describe woods that came from what are now called the Commonwealth countries and which included Indian laurel, Australian silky oak, and Indian greywood. These unusual materials made even the most traditional designs look fresh and interesting.

Joel's bedroom set, exhibited at the British Art in Industry exhibition at the Royal Academy in 1935, attracted considerable interest and acclaim. And many of her patrons came from the very highest ranks of society and included several members of the royal family – Lord Louis Mountbatten commissioned her to decorate fully and to furnish his London penthouse, and Queen Elizabeth the Queen Mother bought furniture from her while still the Duchess of York – as well as the Savoy Hotel Group for whom she worked on several occasions during the 1930s. But Joel's aim was not simply to provide interior design and furniture for the wealthy; she made a point of also stock-

Joel: living room with chaise longue and rug, early 1930s

ing well-designed but moderately priced furniture to serve a fashionable but more bourgeois clientele.

During the mid 1930s the business expanded. Joel commissioned the architect H.S. Goodhart-Rendel to build a new, larger works on the Kingston by-pass, closer to London than her previous works had been. She also opened a new showroom at 25 Knightsbridge with a façade designed by Goodhart-Rendel. By this time the company not only imported raw materials but also used foreign manufacturers to produce their designs. For, example, a Betty Joel carpet now in the Victoria and Albert Museum was made in China specially for the firm. The design is geometric with bands of cream, circles of red and lines of maroon on a sand-coloured background.

The new showroom sold furniture and textiles designed by other designers as well as those by Joel herself. For instance, in 1937 they featured chairs covered with Aubusson tapestries by the French textile artist Anna Zinkeisen. They also imported prints by artists such as Raoul Dufy and Henri Matisse and a variety of decorative objects that would complement Joel's designs, as well as more utilitarian objects like radios and electric heaters. The shop served as her headquarters and clients could buy furniture and accessories from stock or commission interior design projects on any scale.

A typical example of the Joel interior was illustrated in Derek Patmore's influential book *Colour Schemes for the Modern Home* (1933). It features natural-coloured, grained, Canadian pine walls and a yellow ceiling. The furniture includes a pink canoe-shaped sofa and ziggurat bookcases with painted red shelves. A similar shape is used in a dressing table of 1931 now in the Victoria and Albert Museum, which is made of Australian oak with ivory handles.

Joel's main achievements were to promote the elegance of the modern French style in Britain and to widen the scope of the interior designer to include industrial design products, particularly those that were labour-saving. She was also well-known for her striking geometric carpets that were finer and denser than others of the time. But despite her success in the early and mid 1930s, her career as a designer came to a somewhat abrupt end when she retired from the business in 1937. The firm itself continued into the 1950s, run by her former husband, David Joel, who revived many of her designs and whose book, *The Adventure of British Furniture*, provides an account of her work.

JANICE WEST

Biography

Born in Hong Kong in 1896, the daughter of Sir James Stewart Lockhart, a senior government official. Educated in England. Married David Joel (divorced 1937). Lived in England and active as a designer of furniture and interiors from c.1919; designed carpets from early 1930s. Established Betty Joel Ltd. with David Joel, 1919; workshops at Hayling Island, near Portsmouth, retail outlet in Sloane Street, London; opened large new showrooms in Knightsbridge, c.1925; refurbished with façade and new factory in Kingston-on-Thames designed by H.S. Goodhart-Rendel, 1937. Retired, 1937; company continued under the management of David Joel. Exhibited at British Art in Industry Exhibition, Royal Academy, London, 1935. Died near Andover, Hampshire, 21 January 1985.

Selected Works

Betty Joel Ltd. carried out a number of private commissions, including a bedroom for the Countess of Iveagh at Eleveden Hall, and work for Lord Mountbatten (c.1937), the Duchess of York, and Winston Churchill. Her commercial decorating projects included work for the Savoy and St. James's Palace Hotels, shop interiors for Mary Manners, Reillon Frères, and Bramah, and a number of company boardrooms. Many of these interiors and furnishings are illustrated in *The Studio* 1927–37, in Patmore 1938, and Joel 1953. Examples of her furniture are in the Victoria and Albert Museum, London.

Publications

"At Last a Modern Period" in *Colour*, 2, 1929, pp.23–24

"A House and a Home" in John de la Valette (editor), *The Conquest of Ugliness*, London: Methuen, 1935, pp.87–97

"Antiques and the Modern Setting" in *The Studio*, 109, 1935, pp.302–09

"Space Saving in a Small Flat" in *The Studio*, 112, 1936, pp.89–90

"The Coming of the Modern Flat" in *The Art Centre Gazette*, 1, no.1, March 1936, pp.5–6

Further Reading

The standard account of Joel's furniture appears in Joel 1953. For a more critical analysis of her work and the organisation of the firm see Wilk 1995.

Anscombe, Isabelle, *A Woman's Touch: Women in Design from 1860 to the Present Day*, London: Virago, and New York: Viking, 1984

Battersby, Martin, *The Decorative Thirties*, 1969; revised by Philippe Garner, New York: Whitney Library of Design, and London: Herbert, 1988

Bayer, Patricia, *Art Deco Interiors: Decoration and Design Classics of the 1920s and 1930s*, London: Thames and Hudson, and Boston: Little Brown, 1990

Boumphrey, G., "The Designers 5: Betty Joel" in *Architectural Review* (London), 78, 1935, pp.205–06

Joel, David, *The Adventure of British Furniture, 1851–1951*, London: Benn, 1953; revised edition as *Furniture Design Set Free: The British Furniture Revolution from 1851 to the Present Day*, London: Dent, 1969

Patmore, Derek, "British Interior Architects of Today 6: Betty Joel" in *The Studio*, 104, 1932, pp.276–77

Patmore, Derek, *Decoration for the Small Home*, New York and London: Putnam, 1938

Thirties: British Art and Design Before the War (exhib. cat.), London: Arts Council of Great Britain, 1979

Wilk, Christopher, "Who was Betty Joel? British Furniture Design Between the Wars" in *Apollo*, CXLII, July 1995

Johnson, Philip 1906–

American architect

Starting out as a critic and writer and then becoming an architect in the Modernist and then Postmodernist vein, Philip Johnson has skilfully followed every twist and turn of style in the design world, finally, in his late eighties, promoting Deconstructionism.

Johnson originally studied classics and philosophy at Harvard, but his great passion was architecture and he was one of the instigators of the 1932 Modern Architecture exhibition at New York's Museum of Modern Art which first introduced the International Style to America. In 1940, he returned to Harvard, this time to the architecture school which was then under the control of Walter Gropius. While still a student Johnson designed and built a house for himself which revealed the direction that he was to follow for the next 15 years. This direction was strongly influenced by that of Mies van der Rohe whom Johnson had invited to America in 1937 to design a house in Wyoming. Mies's Wyoming house was never built, but Johnson's first project owes much to its design, and even more to Mies's court houses of the early 1930s. Johnson surrounded his site with a wooden wall, put a single large window across it to separate interior and exterior space and furnished it with Mies furniture arranged in a very formal manner.

In 1949 Johnson designed a second house for himself, in New Canaan, Connecticut. It is his most famous building and one of the century's most celebrated examples of modern architecture. Since settling in Chicago, Mies had designed an all-glass house at Plano, Illinois and Johnson picked up the idea and built his own version. As he had been a critic before becoming an architect, Johnson was an extremely knowledgeable designer and readily acknowledged his sources, not only Mies, but also Karl Friedrich Schinkel, Claude-Nicolas Ledoux, and the paintings of Ben Nicolson. The New Canaan Glass House was a single space with a polished brick floor, a circular brick core containing bathroom and fireplace, a Nadelman sculpture and Mies's Barcelona furniture. When Johnson found curtainless glass walls oppressive at night, he installed floodlights to illuminate all the surrounding trees, turning the house into a belvedere in the forest.

A single room glass pavilion is no place for weekend guests, so Johnson balanced the glass house with a brick box. Within this brick box he gave the first hints of the way that his architecture would develop, for inside the bedroom is a curvilinear false ceiling apparently supported on false pillars – features that acknowledge a debt to the work of Sir John Soane. Johnson's liking for historical references ran counter to the dominant trends within the Modern Movement which aimed to avoid any overt reference to the past.

The New Canaan House was much admired and brought Johnson a succession of architectural commissions. Most of these were family dwellings and so lack the magic openness of his own house, but even so they are some of the most habitable domestic residences in the United States, combining private rooms where occupants can do what they like with big open living rooms furnished with formally placed Mies furniture.

Johnson collaborated with Mies himself in the design of the Seagram Building on New York's Park Avenue and in 1958 he put the finishing touches to the building with the design of the Four Seasons Restaurant. This interior is Johnson at his best. Lavish, formal, opulent and hedonistic, it uses Mies's *Brno* chairs in a setting of machine age richness. Curtains are great swathes of anodised aluminium, and the ceiling is marked by a hanging sculpture by Lippold.

In the 1956 design for the Boissonnas House, Johnson faced a new problem, namely clients who would not accept Mies furniture throughout as they already had a fine collection of antiques. Johnson's response was to design a house based on a regular grid of brick piers like Louis Kahn's de Vore house. Johnson sensed that the Miesian approach was on the wane in America and he began exploring new directions.

The New York State Theatre in the Lincoln Center of 1964 has a clear plan and, as always with Johnson, beautiful lighting. Despite a quantity of plush, it has the heaviness of the stripped classicism reminiscent of Italian designers working under Mussolini. This Neo-Classicising tendency became more pronounced in the extension that he designed in 1966 to McKim, Mead and White's Boston Public Library. At this stage Johnson appears to have lost some of his early impetus, but his partnership with John Burgee in 1967 started him off in a confident new direction with big corporate clients.

The 1973 IDS Center in Minneapolis introduces the "Crystal Court" or great interior which, as well as being the entrance to an office building, is a shopping mall and a meeting place for the town. The late 1970s saw stylistic experimentation; Thanksgiving Square in Dallas shows a love of pure geometry, with a spiral chapel containing a few folding chairs and an altar consisting of a great cube of Carrara marble standing on a circular plinth of red granite. The Crystal Cathedral in Garden Grove, California returns to the glasshouse idea but on a tremendous scale, seating 4000 and being cooled by fountains. Most famous of the buildings of this period is the 1978 design for the AT&T Headquarters in New York, an overtly classical design with touches of Postmodern irony: "we yearn for some richness" Johnson said, but the design is too heavy for the richness to be properly enjoyed.

As his career progressed Johnson's work became increasingly eclectic, mixing the modern notions that he had so fully embraced at its start with references to the past. When the vogue for Postmodernism passed he used his position at the Museum of Modern Art to promote the designers of Deconstructionism. Skilled and ever sensitive to the mood of the moment, Johnson has always promoted the style of the day, but has equally always moved on before it could grow stale.

JOHN WINTER

Biography

Philip Cortelyou Johnson. Born in Cleveland, Ohio, 8 July 1906. Educated at Harvard University, Cambridge, Massachusetts, 1923–30; studied architecture under Walter Gropius (1883–1969) at Harvard Graduate School of Design, 1940–43. Director, Department of Architecture, Museum of Modern Art, New York, 1930–36 and 1946–54. In architectural practice, Cambridge, 1942–46, and New York, 1954–64; partner: Philip Johnson and Richard Foster, New York, 1964–67; with John Burgee, as Johnson / Burgee Architects, New York, 1967–83, John Burgee Architects with Philip Johnson, New York, 1983–91. Established new practice, Philip Johnson Architects, New York, 1992. Trustee, Museum of Modern Art since 1958. Received numerous prizes and awards since 1950 including Gold Medal, American Institute of Architects, 1978, Gold Medal of Honor, with Mies van der Rohe, Architectural League of New York, 1960, Pritzker Architecture Prize, 1979. Fellow, American Institute of Architects, and American Academy of Arts and Letters. Curated several important modernist exhibitions at the Museum of Modern Art including Mies van der Rohe, 1936, and Deconstructivist Architecture, 1988; author of many influential books and articles on architecture.

Selected Works

Interiors

1942	Philip Johnson House, Cambridge, Massachusetts (building, interiors and garden)
1949–present	Philip Johnson House ("Glass House"), New Canaan, Connecticut (building and interiors, and additions including Guest House, 1949 and 1953, Lake Pavilion, 1962, Painting Gallery 1965, Sculpture Gallery 1970, Studio 1984, Lincoln Kirstein Tower 1985, and Visitors Pavilion 1994; furnishings by Mies van der Rohe)
1953	Alice Ball House, New Canaan, Connecticut (building and interiors)
1958	Seagram Building, Park Avenue, New York (building and interiors including the Four Seasons Restaurant; with Mies van der Rohe and Kahn and Jacobs)
1963	Museum for Pre-Columbian Art, Dumbarton Oaks, Washington, DC (building and interiors)
1964	New York State Theatre, Lincoln Center, New York (building and interiors; with Richard Foster)
1966–73	Boston Public Library, Boston (additions and interiors; with John Burgee)
1972–76	Pennzoil Place, Houston (building and interiors; with Wilson, Morris, Crain and Anderson)
1973	IDS Center, Minneapolis (building and interiors including the Crystal Court; with Edward F. Baker Associates)
1978–84	American Telephone and Telegraph Corporate Headquarters, New York (building and interiors)
1979	Crystal Cathedral, Garden Grove, California (building and interiors)
1979–85	Transco Tower and Park, Houston (building and interiors)
1981–84	Republic Bank, Houston (building and interiors)
1984	Pittsburgh Plate Glass (PPG) Corporate Headquarters, Pittsburgh, Pennsylvania (building and interiors)
1986	500 Boylston Street Office Building, Boston (building and interiors)
1991	Museum of Television and Radio, New York (building and interiors)

Publications

Johnson's collected papers are in the Archives of the Museum of Modern Art, New York.

Modern Architects, with others, 1932
The International Style, with Henry-Russell Hitchcock, 1932
Machine Art, 1934
Mies van der Rohe, 1947; 2nd edition, 1953; 3rd edition, 1978
Writings, edited by Robert A.M. Stern, 1979
Deconstructivist Architecture, with Mark Wigley, 1988

Further Reading

The literature on Johnson is very extensive. A useful study of his early work appears in Hitchcock 1966; for an illustrated catalogue of his later work see Knight 1985. There are several monographs, the most recent being Schulze 1994. For a detailed discussion of the Glass House see Whitney and Kipnis 1993; in a series of recent interviews Johnson discusses his major commissions in Lewis and O'Connor 1994.

Harmon, Robert B., *Philip Johnson and American Architecture: A Selected Bibliography*, Monticello, IL: Vance, 1979
Heyer, Paul, "Philip Johnson" in *Architects on Architecture: New Directions in America*, New York: Van Nostrand Reinhold, 1993

Hitchcock, Henry-Russell (introduction), *Philip Johnson: Architecture 1949–1965*, New York: Holt Rinehart, and London: Thames and Hudson, 1966
Jacobus, John M., *Philip Johnson*, New York: Braziller, and London: Prentice Hall International, 1962
Jencks, Charles, *Late-Modern Architecture and Other Essays*, London: Academy, and New York: Rizzoli, 1980
Knight, Carleton III (introduction), *Philip Johnson / John Burgee: Architecture 1979–1985*, New York: Rizzoli, 1985
Lewis, Hilary and John O'Connor, *Philip Johnson: The Architect in His Own Words*, New York: Rizzoli, 1994
Miller, Nory, *Johnson / Burgee: Architecture*, New York: Random House, 1979; London: Architectural Press, 1980
Noble, Charles, *Philip Johnson*, reprinted London: Thames and Hudson, and New York: Simon and Schuster, 1972
Owens, Craig, *Philip Johnson, Processes: The Glass House 1949 and the AT&T Corporate Headquarters 1978* (exhib. cat.), New York: Institute for Architecture and Urban Studies, 1978
"Philip Johnson" in special issue of *Architecture and Urbanism* (Japan), 6, 1979
Robertson, Bryan, *Johnson House: New Canaan, Connecticut*, Tokyo: ADA, 1972 (Global Architecture 12)
Schulze, Franz, *Philip Johnson: Life and Work*, New York: Knopf, 1994
Whitney, David and Jeffrey Kipnis (editors), *Philip Johnson: The Glass House*, New York: Pantheon, 1993

Johnson, Thomas 1714–after 1778

British carver and furniture designer

Thomas Johnson's description of himself in the dedicatory epistle of his "Collection of Designs" (1758) as "an Englishman ... who possesses a truly anti-Gallic spirit ..." and his membership of the anti-Gallican Society, which had been founded "to oppose the insidious arts of the French nation", belies the fact that the source of the style in which he worked, was to a large extent quintessentially French. Mortimer's *Universal Director* of 1763 records Johnson as "carver, teacher of drawing and modelling and author of a book of designs for chimneypieces and other monuments and of several other pieces." His working life was spent at various workshops in or near the Soho district of London, including Queen Street, Seven Dials, Grafton Street and Charlotte Street. His designs show him to have been one of the most creative interpreters of the Rococo in Britain and "with their startling lines and varied imagery, they presented a fresh and ingenious vision" (Hayward, 1964).

One of Johnson's most important contributions was to introduce into the British design repertory elements derived from mainstream, Continental European Rococo. As a creative artist, he was less interested in plagiarising the designs of others than some of his contemporaries, but he did study engraved designs, particularly of French and other Continental ornamentalists, and many of his ideas and motifs were derived from designers such as Jean Berain and Bernard Toro. François Cuvilliés (court architect to the Elector of Bavaria) may also have provided a source for motifs, a suggestion reinforced in plate 13 of Johnson's "Collection of Designs" (1758), which contains designs for candlestands, one of which introduces a pair of dolphins entwined around the central support. Yet despite his adaptation of the most advanced Continental

Thomas Johnson: design for mirror from "Collection of Designs", 1758

Rococo work, Johnson's designs are characterised by a naturalism that would have been unthinkable to French designers. A number of his creative ideas, such as a console table (plate 20 in his "Collection of Designs"), are formed of leafless trees with realistically dripping icicles and a barking hound counterpoised with C-scrolls and vigorous raffle leaves.

The full potential of Johnson's skill as a designer was revealed in his publication *Twelve Gerandoles* of 1755. As it became more fashionable to dine later, so girandoles or wall lights became necessary fittings for stylish interiors. Nevertheless, few designs for girandoles had been published until this time and as their form was not severely curtailed by function, a master carver such as Johnson could exploit his originality and skill to the full. Helena Hayward describes these items as "among the potentially more exciting products of the Rococo age", and in this instance the designs revealed Johnson's independence of French examples and the fertile range of his motifs. The designs are taut, jagged and spiky, the outlines pierced by leafless twigs and spurting or dripping water. Scrolls and columns support the structures, but are subsumed in a range of decorative detail. Chinoiseries play little part in the decorative schemes and a rustic mood prevails, with watermills, boats, peasants and a donkey forming prominent elements of the designs. A recurring decorative theme, which contributes to this vigorous, rustic, and unidealised air, is Johnson's frequent use of scenes derived from Francis Barlow's illustrated publications of *Aesop's Fables* (1666 and 1687), such as, "The Wolf in Sheep's Clothing" or "The Bear and Two Travellers".

Johnson produced a far wider range of motifs for carvers' pieces than his contemporaries, such as Matthias Lock or Thomas Chippendale. In a series of 53 engravings for chimneypieces, looking glasses, picture frames, console tables and other items published between 1756 and 1757, Johnson included among his rustic scenes, some Chinoiseries, trophies, pendant arms and caryatids – motifs, which were later to find their way into the designs of his contemporaries. It may have been as a result of Johnson's influence that in the third edition of *The Director* (1762), Chippendale included more than one hundred designs for carvers' pieces, far more than in previous editions.

Rococo was almost never favoured as an architectural style in Britain, save for garden buildings. Palladian houses, however, were frequently internally decorated and furnished with wild interpretations of the style in plaster or carved and gilded wood. Rococo was also often thought appropriate for the decoration of bedrooms, dressing rooms or rooms with orchestrated views over parkland. In terms of interior furnishing schemes, Johnson and his London contemporaries usually produced designs, which were conceived as isolated items. This approach contrasted with French methods, in which all the elements in an interior, including the ceiling, wall panelling, chimneypiece and console tables were planned as a unified whole. However, as well as creating individual designs for carvers' pieces, Johnson also produced designs for ceilings, walls and chimneypieces, the latter comprising one of the most important features of the 18th-century interior. For example, in Johnson's series of plates published in 1758, which, with modifications and additions, became *One Hundred and Fifty New Designs* in 1761, he includes several ideas for chimneypieces with elaborate overmantel mirrors, a design for a ceiling and a design for the side of a room. Nevertheless, Johnson treats the panels of the room as mere surface ornament, comprising a series of flattened, Rococo *boiseries* hung with trophies of musical instruments, centred on a chimneypiece with overmantel mirror, rather than as architectural elements. This scheme is the only known example of a fully worked out interior by Johnson, as well as being the only English engraving of the period to show a scheme for carved boiseries. And it demonstrates that he was happier designing individual pieces than dealing with the complexities of a unified interior, unlike French ornamentalists such as Nicolas Pineau.

The effect of Johnson's designs on furniture making and furnishing schemes was felt beyond Britain, and after his lifetime. *One Hundred and Fifty New Designs* (1761) was one of the most influential English pattern books in Philadelphia, and according to Gregory Landrey, "Numerous examples of eighteenth century (American) carving attest to the popularity of Johnson's designs, especially those based on Barlow's engravings" (Landrey, 1993). Johnson's publication was reprinted in 1834, with his name erased, and under the spurious title *Chippendale's Designs for sconces, Chimney and Looking glass frames, in the Old French style*. The printer, John Weale, clearly intended to capitalise on Chippendale's reputation as the author of the best known and most impressive pattern book of its day. Nonetheless, Johnson's designs, albeit fraudulently misattributed, were instrumental in the promotion of the "old French" style, as the revived Rococo was called, in interior furnishings in Britain in the second quarter of the 19th century.

No single piece of carved furniture has been directly attributed to Thomas Johnson, although he may have worked exclusively as a specialist carver to a cabinet-maker and upholsterer called George Cole, who supplied a number of houses, including Corsham Court, Wiltshire, Blair Castle and Dunkeld House, with elaborate, carved pieces in the style of Johnson's engravings. It is these engravings of his designs, however, which provide the key to his achievement. As Gervase Jackson-Stops has stated, "they were among the most influential of the period" and were "highly individual in their extravagant asymmetry, often approaching a truly oriental abstraction of design" (*The English Country House: A Grand Tour*, 1984).

ROBIN D. JONES

See also Rococo

Biography

Born in London; baptized 13 January 1714. Trained as a carver; active in workshops in Queen Street, Soho, by 1755; subsequently occupied workshops in Seven Dials, Grafton Street, Charlotte Street and Tottenham Court Road; described as a "Carver, Teacher of Drawing and Modelling" and author in 1763. Supplied furnishings to several specialist cabinet-makers and upholsterers, including George Cole. Published several influential books of engraved designs from 1755. Last recorded in 1778.

Selected Works

The largest collection of Johnson's drawings for furniture, ceilings, grates, and silver, is in the Victoria and Albert Museum, London. Examples of furniture attributed to, or after, Johnson's designs, and supplied by the London upholsterer George Cole, are at Corsham Court, Wiltshire, Dunkeld House and Blair Castle. Additional pieces are in the Victoria and Albert Museum, London, and Temple Newsam House, Leeds, and in the Philadelphia Museum of Art. For a more comprehensive list of works see Beard and Gilbert 1986.

Publications

Twelve Gerandoles, 1755
Glass, Picture and Table-Frames; Chimney Pieces, Gerandoles, Candlestands, Clockcases, Brackets, and Other Ornaments in the Chinese, Gothick and Rural Taste, plates published 1756–57; volume ("Collection of Designs"), 1758
Household Furniture in the Genteel Taste, 1760
A New Book of Ornaments, 1760
One Hundred and Fifty New Designs, 1761
A New Book of Ornaments (not same as 1760 book), 1762
A Brief History of Free Masons, 1784

Further Reading

Definitive accounts of Johnson's work appear in Hayward (Tiranti) 1964 and (Connoisseur) 1964.

Beard, Geoffrey and Christopher Gilbert (editors), *Dictionary of English Furniture Makers, 1660–1840*, London: Furniture History Society, 1986

Coleridge, Anthony, *Chippendale Furniture: The Work of Thomas Chippendale and His Contemporaries in the Rococo Taste, 1745–1765*, London: Faber, and New York: Potter, 1968

Hayward, Helena, *Thomas Johnson and English Rococo*, London: Tiranti, 1964
Hayward, Helena, *Thomas Johnson and Rococo Carving*, London: Connoisseur Yearbook, 1964
Hayward, Helena, "The Drawings of Thomas Johnson in the Victoria and Albert Museum" in *Furniture History*, V, 1969, pp.1–115
Hayward, Helena, "Newly Discovered Designs of Thomas Johnson" in *Furniture History*, XI, 1975
Heckscher, Morrison, "Gideon Saint: An Eighteenth Century Carver and his Scrapbook" in *Metropolitan Museum of Art Bulletin*, XXVII, February 1969, pp.299–310
Landrey, Gregory, "The Conservator as Curator: Combining Scientific Analysis and Traditional Connoisseurship" in Luke Beckerdite (editor), *American Furniture*, Hanover, NH: Chipstone Foundation and University Press of New England, 1995, pp.149–50
Snodin, Michael (editor), *Rococo: Art and Design in Hogarth's England* (exhib. cat.), London: Victoria and Albert Museum, 1984
Ward-Jackson, Peter, *English Furniture Designs of the Eighteenth Century*, London: HMSO, 1958
White, Elizabeth, *The Pictorial Dictionary of British 18th Century Furniture Design: The Printed Sources*, Woodbridge, Suffolk: Antique Collectors' Club, 1990

Jones, Inigo 1573–1652

English architect and designer

Inigo Jones was the dominant figure in the visual arts of early Stuart England. He contributed as much to interior decoration as to architecture and the court masque, and, in looking at his total achievement, his decorative work provides a link between those two other fields in which he is more often remembered.

A crucial component of the more disciplined classicism which Jones introduced to English design was the subordination of decoration to a proper architectural control. As he wrote in 1615, "In all inuencions of C[a]ppresious ornaments on must first designe ye Ground, or ye thing plaine, as yt is for youse, and on that, varry it, addorne it. Compose yt wth deccorum according to the youse, and ye order yt is of ...". In designing interiors, Jones was faced with the problem that Palladio, his chief guide on stylistic decorum, had not laid down clear rules. He therefore needed to make his own reconciliation of architectural propriety with current decorative trends, which he did by distinguishing between the levels and types of ornament appropriate for exteriors and interiors. Whereas the outside of a building should be correct and sober, "Sollid, proporsionable according to the rulles, masculine and unaffected", inside the desire for rich effect allowed a more free interpretation of the classical orders. Although Jones was critical of the "Composed ornamentes wch Proceed out of ye aboundance of dessignes, and wear brought in by Mihill Angell and his followers", he admitted that they were "of necesety to be youced" for "stucco or ornamentes of chimnie piecces, or the innerparts of hoases". He thought their use was also sanctioned by what he knew of "the Cimeras [rooms] yoused by the ansientes"; certainly, by comparing contemporary work with Roman remains, he was able to justify the decorative idioms developed by Renaissance architects (extracts quoted from Harris and Higgott, 1989).

Inigo Jones: sketch elevation for a chimneypiece for Oatlands Palace, Surrey, 1636, with alternative overmantel designs

The success of Jones's interior schemes was dependent on the ability and sophistication of the decorative artists he employed. He was helped by a period of relative peace on the Continent during most of James I's reign and by the ambitious diplomatic strategy of the king. Diplomats such as Sir Henry Wotton (1568–1639) and Sir Balthazar Gerbier (1592–1663) were a means of contact with Continental craftsmen and artists, particularly Protestants from the Low Countries, who were more able to execute Jones's designs according to his intentions (Thornton, 1978).

From what little evidence remains, it appears that in the first years after his second return from Italy in 1614 Jones's decorative schemes relied on his knowledge of Italian work. Two drawings of 1618–19 of a marble fireplace at Arundel House in London probably designed by Jones show a boldly architectural arrangement, the broken segmental pediment of the overmantel enclosing a cartouche supported by a mask and garlands (Girouard, 1962). We know little else about the interiors carried out for Lord Arundel, although there are tantalising glimpses of the galleries designed to house his collections of paintings and sculpture in Daniel Mytens's portraits of the earl and countess, painted before 1618 (now at Arundel Castle). In the background of the portrait of the countess can be seen an Italianate shell-backed *sgabello* chair, probably designed by Jones and similar to still-extant examples designed by Franz Cleyn (1582(?)–1657/8) (Thornton and Tomlin, 1980). This is the only evidence we have of any furniture designed by Jones, and raises the fascinating question of the extent of control that he exerted over the contents of the rooms he designed.

The chief problem in assessing Jones's contribution to interior decoration lies in the almost total lack of its survival. We are lucky that the Banqueting House at Whitehall Palace (1619–22), his most ambitious secular interior scheme, survives in something approaching its original condition (there is also the Queen's Chapel at St. James's Palace of 1623–27).

The first aspect of the Banqueting House interior to strike the visitor is the way the discipline of the classical orders coordinates it with the exterior, the two equal storeys and seven regularly-spaced bays of the main façades being echoed inside. However, since the 17th century many of the individual elements of the interior have to some degree been altered – a reflection of the vicissitudes of use to which it has been subjected. A 1773 view of the northern end (reproduced Charlton, 1964:35) shows the wooden gallery flat-fronted before it was altered to support an organ loft in 1829–37, together with what may have been Jones's original door surrounds. Today's unpedimented and slightly anaemic surrounds are also probably 19th-century, as the engraving shows the principal door to have had a broken pediment enclosing the Le Sueur bust of James I now displayed in the building's undercroft. Though less elaborate, it is an arrangement reminiscent of Jones's unexecuted design for the "great doure" preserved at the RIBA. The use of an Ionic columned surround and Jones's favourite motif of a broken pediment enclosing a cartouche makes this drawing the ancestor of the grandiose portals designed by his pupil John Webb for Wilton House and Greenwich Palace (Harris and Higgott, 1989).

Although the Whitehall interior was painted plain white on the structural completion of the building in 1622, its decoration was probably left unfinished for economy. Copious gilding, particularly of the ceiling, was carried out later in 1635–36 – surely part of Jones's original intention, it illustrates the rich interior effect he thought desirable. The ceiling, the most striking decorative feature, was the first English compartmented beamed ceiling to be designed with classically moulded frames and, taking up the Venetian tradition of elaborate wooden *soffitti*, is an instance of the overwhelmingly Italian influences seen in Jones's decorative work at this time (Harris and Higgott, 1989; Held, 1970). Although Rubens's nine canvases glorifying the reign of James I were probably not commissioned until the artist's 1629–30 stay in London, Jones must always have intended the ceiling to frame such painted scenes and almost certainly devised their iconographical programme himself (Strong, 1980). To judge the intended effect of the interior, one should remember that for important ceremonies the lower storey was hung with Mortlake tapestries, probably a lost set woven after the Raphael *Acts of the Apostles* bought by James I (Palme, 1956). The combined splendour must have been overwhelming.

The Queen's House, Greenwich, begun for Anne of Denmark in 1616 but whose interior fitments were executed for Henrietta Maria between 1633 and 1640, is the other surviving secular building by Jones. Only three ceilings and some wall decorations partially survive from his day. While the Hall and Cabinet have flat compartmented ceilings like the Banqueting House, the Bedchamber has a deep cove, following the guidelines set by Palladio for varying room heights and ceiling types in houses (Palladio I:xxiii-xxiv). The ceiling and the wooden galleries in the Hall retain their original paintwork in white (now faded to grey-green) and gold, giving some indication of what the original treatment of the Banqueting House may have been like. The importance of decorative paint effects in Jones's schemes is hinted at in the accounts for work carried out for Henrietta Maria at Somerset House, where in 1628–29 the New Cabinet Room was given an elaborate treatment in gold, white and blue bice with marbling and grotesque panels, all carried out by Matthew Goodrich (active 1616/17-c.1654) (Colvin, 1982; Croft-Murray, 1962).

Like the Banqueting House, the interiors at Greenwich relied for their effect partly on the contribution of the figurative arts. In 1639–40 Zachary Taylor carved pedestals for statues from the royal collection to go in the Hall; the pieces at Greenwich included the lost Bernini bust of Charles I (Colvin, 1982:121; Chettle, 1937:34). As at Whitehall, it is likely that Jones conceived the programme of *Peace and the Arts* for the Hall ceiling canvases by Orazio Gentileschi (c.1636–38, now at Marlborough House) (Bissell, 1981). Elsewhere in the house, canvases by Gentileschi and other Continental artists, for which frames were being carved by Matthew Goodrich from 1633, formed a major part of the decorative schemes (Colvin, 1982:119). A Giulio Romano *Daedalus and Icarus* was incorporated into the ceiling of the Bedchamber (Chettle, 1937:37-38), while in the Cabinet were canvases commissioned from Jacob Jordaens. A draft of instructions sent by Jones to Jordaens in 1639 about the Cabinet illustrates the close control he maintained: he tells the painter which scenes from the story of Cupid and Psyche are to be depicted and advises him in matters such as iconography, lighting and measurements (Bissell, 1981; Keith, 1936–37).

None of the chimneypieces designed for the Queen's House remain *in situ*, though there is probably one surviving example removed to Charlton House, Greenwich (Newman, 1984). Jones's drawings of fireplaces intended for Greenwich and Henrietta Maria's other palaces in the 1630s show him coming under contemporary French decorative influences, particularly the engraved designs of Jean Barbet and Jean Cotelle, and it is possible that the increasingly Gallic flavour of Jones's Italian-based classical style may have been encouraged by the circles around Charles I's French queen. The variety of these designs form a striking contrast to his earlier work (Harris, 1961; Harris and Higgott, 1989; Thornton, 1978).

Paradoxically, the best impression to be had today of Jonesian interior decoration is in the state apartments of Wilton House, Wiltshire, designed not by Jones himself but by John Webb (1648–52). Their nobility of conception and occasional crudities of execution bear witness both to Jones's synthesising genius and to the cultural constraints under which he worked.

DAVID CRELLIN

See also John Webb

Biography

Baptized in London, 19 July 1573, the son of a clothmaker. Apprenticed to a joiner, St. Paul's Churchyard; described as a "picture maker" in 1603; active as a designer of sets and costumes of court masques and theatricals, often in collaboration with Ben Jonson, c.1598–1640; practised as an architect from c.1608. Visited France, 1609. Appointed Surveyor to Henry, Prince of Wales, 1610. Travelled in Italy with 2nd Earl of Arundel, 1613–14, where Jones acquired drawings by Andrea Palladio and Vincenzo Scamozzi. Appointed Surveyor of the King's Works to James I, 1613; Surveyor-General, 1615. Responsible for many of the principal royal residences and palaces from 1616; designs for interiors date from c.1619. Pupil was the architect John Webb (1611–72). Elected a Member of Parliament, 1621. Died London, 21 June 1652.

Selected Works

The largest collections of Jones's architectural drawings are in the Royal Institute of British Architects, London and at Worcester College, Oxford. Additional important but smaller holdings are in the Devonshire Collection, Chatsworth, Derbyshire and the Ashmolean Museum, Oxford. A chronology of works and projects appears in Harris and Higgott 1989.

Interiors

1616 & 1633–40	Queen's House, Greenwich Palace, Greenwich (building and interiors; completed by others): Queen Anne of Denmark, and Queen Henrietta Maria
1618	Arundel House, Strand, London (sculpture gallery and some interior fittings): 2nd Earl of Arundel
1619–22	Banqueting House, Whitehall, London (building and interiors): James I
1623–31	St. James's Palace, Westminster, London (additions and interiors including the Queen's Chapel, the Queen's Bedchamber and Sculpture Gallery)
1628–36	Somerset House, Strand, London (Queen's Cabinet Room, and Queen's Chapel; Queen's Bedchamber 1630–32; and Cross Gallery 1635–36)
1636–38	Oatlands Palace, Weybridge, Surrey (interiors including the Queen's Cabinet, Queen's Bedchamber, and Lower Gallery)
1637	Whitehall Palace, London (new Masque Room)

Publications

The Most Notable Antiquity of Great Britain, Vulgarly Called Stone-Heng, edited by John Webb, 1655

Inigo Jones on Palladio (facsimile of Jones's annotated Palladio), 2 vols., 1970

Further Reading

The most recent and authoritative study of Jones's work, including a detailed discussion of his work in interiors, a chronology and a select further reading list, appears in Harris and Higgott 1989. For a study of his work as Surveyor-General, including his involvement in the building and decoration of the royal palaces see Colvin 1982.

Bissell, R. Ward, *Orazio Gentileschi and the Poetic Tradition in Caravaggesque Painting*, University Park: Pennsylvania State University Press, 1981

Charlton, John, *The Banqueting House, Whitehall*, 1964; revised edition, London: Historic Royal Palaces, 1994

Chettle, G.H., *The Queen's House, Greenwich*, London: London Survey Committee, 1937

Colvin, H.M. and others, *The History of the King's Works*, vol.4: *1485–1660*, part 2, London: HMSO, 1982

Croft-Murray, Edward, *Decorative Painting in England, 1537–1837*, vol.1, London: Country Life, 1962

Girouard, Mark, "The Smythson Collection at the RIBA" in *Architectural History*, 5, 1962, pp.53,63

Harris, John, "Inigo Jones and his French Sources" in *Bulletin of the Metropolitan Museum*, May 1961, pp.253–64

Harris, John , *Catalogue of the Drawings Collection of the Royal Institute of British Architects: Inigo Jones and John Webb*, Farnborough: Gregg, 1972

Harris, John, Stephen Orgel, and Roy Strong, *The King's Arcadia: Inigo Jones and the Stuart Court* (exhib. cat.), London: Arts Council of Great Britain, 1973

Harris, John and A.A. Tait, *Catalogue of the Drawings by Inigo Jones, John Webb and Isaac de Caus at Worcester College, Oxford*, Oxford and New York: Oxford University Press, 1979

Harris, John and Gordon Higgott, *Inigo Jones: Complete Architectural Drawings* (exhib. cat.), New York: Drawing Center, and London: Zwemmer, 1989

Haslam, Richard, "The Queen's House, Greenwich" in *Country Life*, 184, 10 May 1990, pp.88–91

Held, J., "Rubens' Glynde Sketch and the Installation of the Whitehall Ceiling" in *Burlington Magazine*, 112, 1970, pp.274–81

Keith, W. Grant, "The Queen's House, Greenwich" in *Journal of the Royal Institute of British Architects*, 44, 1936–37, pp.943–47

Lees-Milne, James, *The Age of Inigo Jones*, London, Batsford, 1953

Newman, John, "Strayed from the Queen's House?" in *Architectural History*, 26, 1984, pp.33–35

Orgel, Stephen and Roy Strong, *Inigo Jones: The Theatre of the Stuart Court*, 2 vols., London: Sotheby Parke Bernet, and Berkeley: University of California Press, 1973

Palme, Per, *Triumph of Peace: A Study of the Whitehall Banqueting House*, Stockholm: Almquist & Wiksell, 1956

Strong, Roy, *Britannia Triumphans: Inigo Jones, Rubens and Whitehall Palace*, London: Thames and Hudson, 1980; New York: Thames and Hudson, 1981

Summerson, John, *Inigo Jones*, Harmondsworth: Penguin, 1966

Thornton, Peter, *Seventeenth-Century Interior Decoration in Britain, France, and Holland*, New Haven and London: Yale University Press, 1978

Thornton, Peter and Maurice Tomlin, *The Furnishing and Decoration of Ham House*, London: Furniture History Society, 1980

Jones, Owen 1809–1874

British architect and designer

Architect, designer and authority on pattern and historic ornament, Owen Jones is best-known today for his encyclopedic *Grammar of Ornament* (1856), a publication which both reflected and influenced the ideas of British mid 19th century design reformers and which had a significant impact on High Victorian taste. The *Grammar of Ornament* is also well-documented as an important source for Art Nouveau designers, and as a contributory influence on the work of certain Modernists, particularly Frank Lloyd Wright. However, this achievement should not be seen in isolation, but as one result of a much larger project concerning the rational application of ornament in architecture and design.

Jones's interest in architectural decoration and polychromy was stimulated by his travels in the "Orient" – Greece, Istanbul and Egypt – which he made in the early 1830s in the company of the French architect Jules Goury, and later the Egyptologist Joseph Bonomi. Both these men were classicists interested in the use of colour in Greek and Egyptian architecture. In 1834

Jones travelled to Spain, where with Goury he began to make a detailed study of the Alhambra Palace in Seville. Goury died six months into the project but Jones completed the work and returned to England where he published the results of their research as *Plans ... of the Alhambra* (1836–45). The printing of this monumental two-volume work presented considerable technical difficulties and was not a commercial success. But despite this, the book had a widespread influence among architects and designers. First, it established Islamic architecture and design as worthy of serious study, whereas previously it had been regarded as merely exotic or picturesque. Second, the many detailed and strongly coloured illustrations of Islamic ornament provided designers not only with a new decorative idiom, but also with novel solutions to basic problems concerning the decoration of interiors and objects. The design of geometric patterns, the division of interior walls into three zones of dado, fill and frieze, and the use of ceramic tiles as wall decoration are among the innovations which his work suggested. Moreover, many of the principles that Jones observed in the Alhambra – for example, the exclusive use of primary colours in the major features of a decorative scheme – were equally applicable to other styles of ornament.

Jones's clear and structured analysis of Islamic ornament and the spectacular chromolithographic colouring of the plates ensured that the book was well received in the architectural press and Jones became closely associated with Islamic art in the public mind. However, there was no immediate revolution in taste; the Gothic style with its nationalistic and Christian associations continued to serve the aspirations of mid-Victorian society better than the art derived from Muslim culture. Jones himself combined Islamic exterior details with Italianate architecture in his work at nos.8 (1843) and 25 Kensington Palace Gardens (1845) and prepared designs for highly coloured ceiling decorations in the same houses using a mixture of Islamic and Renaissance motifs. He also designed a number of retail interiors in central London (Crystal Palace Bazaar, 1858, and Osler's Showrooms, 1859) using his own interpretations of Islamic ornament in the late 1850s, and during the 1860s he designed a series of rooms at 16 Carlton House Terrace for the millionaire Alfred Morrison. The surviving coffered ceilings from this scheme, installed by Jackson and Graham, are a fine synthesis of Islamic geometric decoration and Victorian craft skill and were highly praised by the *Builder* in 1874. But in general, the "Moorish" style remained an exotic counterpoint to mainstream Western architecture and a contributory influence on the design of textiles, wallpapers and ceramics.

Jones's book on the Alhambra also brought him to the attention of Henry Cole, and through Cole he became involved with the Government Schools of Design and the organisation of the Great Exhibition of 1851. Jones was responsible for the interior decoration of Joseph Paxton's Crystal Palace. He devised a colour scheme of radical simplicity, based both on his experience of Islamic art and also on his interest in the physics of colour, particularly his reading of Chevreul's *The Principles of Harmony and the Contrast of Colours* (in French, 1839; English edition, 1854) and the work of the English colourist George Field. Developing the notion that the primary colours were the basis of all successful ornament, Jones devised a scheme of red, blue and yellow which he believed would maximise the sense of interior space by combining at a distance to produce a soft white light. Using Field's theory of colour harmony, he distributed the colours in a ratio of blue 8: red 5: yellow 3, painting the faces of the girders blue, the soffits and undersides of the beams red, and projecting components yellow. This disposition of colour was augmented by the use of red cloth behind the handrails of the galleries to produce a diffusion of colour described by the *Illustrated London News* as "comparable to the work of Turner".

Owen Jones: Greek design from *The Grammar of Ornament*, 1856

Jones also took charge of the signage at the exhibition (another red accent in the scheme) and the arrangement and distribution of the exhibits. It is tempting to suppose that the "Bazaar-like" ambience noted by contemporaries may also have derived from Jones's taste for the Orient but there is no direct evidence for this. At the end of the exhibition Jones was commissioned to design several of the architectural Courts which formed part of the permanent display of the re-opened building at Sydenham in South London. His Egyptian, Roman, Greek and Alhambra Courts (1853–54) were a popular success and also provided the raw material for his most celebrated publication, the *Grammar of Ornament*. This impressive compendium surveyed the history of ornament from prehistory to the Renaissance and included 37 "propositions" or laws governing the appearance and distribution of ornament which were formulated in collaboration with contemporary authorities such as Cole, M.D. Wyatt and J.B. Waring. Endorsed by the backing of the design establishment, the book became a staple part of the teaching in the Government Schools of Design and quickly became an indispensable source book for all those involved in the application of surface patterns.

The success of the Crystal Palace decorations established Jones as the leading British authority on the decoration of iron and glass architecture. Matthew Digby Wyatt sought his advice on the decoration of Paddington Station (1854) and the iron arabesque in the end walls of the train shed, although not actually designed by Jones, certainly demonstrate his influence. Jones himself designed several iron-framed structures in the decade after 1851 – notably St. James's Hall (1855–58) and the Crystal Palace Bazaar (1858). Both buildings featured iron and glass construction, but Jones abandoned the simplicity of the Great Exhibition scheme in favour of more complex polychromatic decorations featuring mirrors, coloured glass, and stencilled motifs derived from plant forms.

In the last years of his life Jones became increasingly involved in activities at South Kensington, both as a teacher and as the designer of interior decorations for the South Kensington Museum (now the Victoria and Albert Museum). He also expanded his practice to include the design of textiles and wallpapers working for firms such as Townsend, Parker & Co., Jeffrey & Co., and Warners. Many of his patterns were inspired by Persian prototypes and by the examples illustrated in A.W.N. Pugin's *Floriated Ornament* (1849). All adhered to the principles outlined in the *Grammar* that "all ornament should be based upon a geometrical construction" and that flowers and other living objects should be replaced by "conventional representations ... sufficiently suggestive to convey the intended image to the mind, without destroying the unity of the object they are employed to decorate". The result was a highly stylised rendering of nature with flat, symmetrical motifs arranged in mechanically plotted rows. The construction of flat patterns from the observation of natural forms, known at the time as "Art-botany", was subsequently criticised for producing somewhat rigid designs but the method rapidly became established as a standard strategy within the South Kensington circle, with Christopher Dresser being its most skilled and best-known exponent.

Owen Jones's work has often been contrasted with that of the Gothic Revivalists on the grounds that the anti-industrialism of Pugin and his followers was at odds with Jones's attempt to operate within the commercial world. But, aesthetically, the generation that began to produce mature work during the 1830s and 1840s had much in common despite differences in ideology. Colour, patterns, and the rational application of newly discovered styles of ornament were the central concerns of a whole generation of British architects and designers. Jones's contribution to this development was to provide a theoretical framework that permitted the new styles to enter the mainstream of design.

NICHOLAS SHADDICK

See also Design Reform Movement

Biography

Born in London, 15 February 1809. Apprenticed to the architect, Lewis Vulliamy (1791–1871), 1825–30; studied at the Royal Academy Schools, London, from 1829; travelled with the French architect Jules Goury in France and Italy, 1830; Egypt, 1832–33; Istanbul, 1833; and Spain, 1833–34. Brother-in-law was the architect James W. Wild. Mainly active as a designer of tiles, wallpapers, and mosaics during the 1840s; began designing linens in the 1850s, and silks in the 1870s; involved in the decoration and design of many private and public interiors from the 1840s. Appointed Superintendent of Works of the London 1851 Exhibition in 1850; from 1852 employed as a lecturer and expert in the Department of Science and Art, London, and appointed Director of Decorations for the Crystal Palace in Sydenham, opened 1854. Lectured and wrote extensively on the principles of design, colour and ornament, publishing the *Plans ... of the Alhambra* (1836–45) and *The Grammar of Ornament* (1856). Awarded gold medals for furniture exhibited at the Paris Exposition Universelle, 1867, and the International Exhibition in Vienna, 1873. Fellow, Royal Institute of British Architects, 1843; Royal Gold Medallist, 1857. Died 19 April 1874.

Selected Works

There is no complete catalogue of Jones's work but the most comprehensive list appears in Lever 1973 which mentions numerous drawings for architectural and interior projects. Designs for tiles, wallpapers and textiles are held in the Prints and Drawings Department of the Victoria and Albert Museum, London; wallpaper pattern books produced for Townsend, Parker & Co., and Jeffrey & Co. are in the Archive of Arthur Sanderson & Sons Ltd., Uxbridge; and a logbook of attributed sketches and schemes for interiors executed for Jackson & Graham is held by the Whitworth Art Gallery, Manchester.

Interiors

1843–47 8 Kensington Palace Gardens, London (building and decorations): John Mariott Blashfield

1845–47 25 Kensington Palace Gardens, London (building and decorations): John Mariott Blashfield

1850–51 Crystal Palace, Hyde Park, London (interior decoration)

1852–54 Crystal Palace, Sydenham (decoration with Joseph Paxton including the Greek and Alhambra Courts)

1855–58 St. James's Hall, Piccadilly (building and interior decoration)

1858 Crystal Palace Bazaar, London (building and interiors)

1864 Oriental Court, South Kensington Museum, London (decoration)

1865–67 16 Carlton House Terrace, London (interior decoration and furniture): Sir Alfred Morrison

1872 Eynsham Hall, Oxford (building, interiors and some furniture)

Jones worked for many commercial manufacturers and his designs included wallpapers for Townsend & Parker, John Trumble & Sons, Leeds, and Jeffrey & Co.; furniture and interior decoration for Jackson & Graham; and textiles for Erskine Beveridge & Co. and Warner & Sons.

Publications

Plans, Elevations, Sections and Details of the Alhambra, with Jules Goury, 1836–45

Designs for Mosaic and Tessellated Pavements, 1842

Examples of Encaustic Tiles, 1844

The Fine Arts in the Crystal Palace, 1854

The Grammar of Ornament, 1856; reprinted 1972, 1986

Lectures on Architecture and the Decorative Arts, 1863

Examples of Chinese Ornament, 1867

Further Reading

The most comprehensive list of Jones's publications and a full bibliography of primary and secondary sources appears in Burke 1986.

Burke, Doreen Bolger and others, *In Pursuit of Beauty: Americans and the Aesthetic Movement* (exhib. cat.: Metropolitan Museum, New York), New York: Rizzoli, 1986

Catalogue of the Drawings Collection of the Royal Institute of British Architects, Farnborough: Gregg, 1973

Darby, Michael, "Owen Jones and the Eastern Ideal", PhD. thesis., Reading, England: University of Reading, 1974

Darby, Michael and David Van Zanten, "Owen Jones's Iron Buildings of the 1850s" in *Architectura*, 1974, pp.53–75

Darby, Michael, *The Islamic Perspective: An Aspect of British Architecture and Design in the 19th Century* (exhib. cat.), London: Leighton House Gallery, 1983

Day, Lewis F., "Victorian Progress in Applied Design" in *Art Journal*, 1887, pp.185–202

Durant, Stuart, *Ornament: A Survey of Decoration Since 1830*, London: Macdonald, and Woodstock, NY: Overlook Press, 1986

Jervis, Simon, *High Victorian Design*, Woodbridge, Suffolk: Boydell, 1983

"The Late Mr. Owen Jones" in the *Builder*, 9 May 1874, pp.383–85

Schoeser, Mary, *Owen Jones Silks*, Braintree: Warner & Sons, 1987

Sugden, Alan V. and J.L. Edmondson, *A History of English Wallpaper, 1509–1914*, London: Batsford, 1926

Sweetman, John, *The Oriental Obsession: Islamic Inspiration in British and American Art and Architecture, 1500–1920*, Cambridge and New York: Cambridge University Press, 1988

Wainwright, Clive and Charlotte Gere, *Architect-Designers: Pugin to Mackintosh* (exhib. cat.), London: Fine Art Society, 1981

Juvarra, Filippo 1678–1736

Italian architect

In 1703, when he was only 15 or 16, Filippo Juvarra left his native Messina for Rome, to study architecture as an apprentice in Carlo Fontana's studio. In Rome he studied ancient, Renaissance, and Baroque works with equal enthusiasm. His great gifts as draughtsman and designer were soon apparent, and in 1708 he entered the service of Cardinal Ottoboni as a stage designer. In 1714, Victor Amadeus of Savoy offered him a post at his court in Turin as "First Architect to the King," a post he would keep until his death in 1736.

Soon after arriving in Turin, his fame had spread throughout Catholic Europe. He was sought out to do royal commissions in Austria, Portugal, France and Spain. However, the major portion of his work is in Piedmont, in and around its capital. The quantity of work he produced is truly prodigious. In Turin alone, he designed five churches, four royal residences, and four large palazzi, as well as whole quarters of the Baroque city. Of these projects, the ones for which he is most famous are the renovation and façade of the Palazzo Madama (1718–21), La Superga (1717–31), the hunting lodge at Stupinigi (1729–33), and the Chiesa del Carmine (1732–35).

It is very difficult to categorize Juvarra's style; in fact, his encyclopedic knowledge of historical and contemporary works allowed him to tailor his style for each commission to whatever seemed most suitable. In its stylistic variety, his work is a precursor of the eclecticism that is characteristic of the 19th-century approach to design. The client and the particular location of the work were of paramount importance in shaping the character of Juvarra's buildings. In royal commissions in town and for commissions of state significance such as the Palazzo Madama and La Superga, Juvarra's work is formal, the façades are richly articulated, and the French influence is particularly clear. When the commissions were for rural settings or for parish churches such as the hunting lodge at Stupinigi and the Chiesa del Carmine, the work is much more playful, spatially experimental, and Italian / Austrian in character.

At the Palazzo Madama, Juvarra is responsible for the front façade and the grand foyer containing the stairs to the staterooms on the *piano nobile*. It had been the intention of the Madam Reale, the widow of Victor Amadeus I, completely to reconstruct the existing 14th-century castle, but only the central nine bays of Juvarra's 19 bay design were executed. Although it is apparent that the design of the façade was directly influenced by the Palace at Versailles, Juvarra improved upon his model. The proportion of base to wall to cornice is much better; the *piano nobile* dominates the design; and the architectural decoration is much more sculptural and more clearly articulated. Although it borrows freely from France, the effect of the façade is completely Italian; the composition owes much more to Bernini than to Louis Le Vau.

It is the interior of the grand foyer that is of greatest interest, however. It is a single great two-storeyed space, covered with a barrel vault, which runs completely across the front of the building. On either side of the entrance and perpendicular to it, a monumental stair doubles back on itself to return to the central axis and entry to the grand salon on the upper floor. The plan of this double staircase foyer was probably inspired by a Le Vau design for the Louvre; yet, like the façade, its decorative treatment is completely Italian in feeling. The sculptural stair balustrade, the curving forms used at the landings, the stucco decoration which combines lush naturalistic motifs with flat classical elements, and, in particular, the decoration of the barrel vault which superimposes a series of ribs and frames on a coffered surface are clearly inspired by the decoration of Pietro da Cortona.

In contrast to the dignity and grandeur of the Palazzo Madama, the hunting lodge at Stupinigi seems almost frivolous. The Palazzo Madama is Baroque, while the Stupinigi lodge is Rococo. The functional parallel of this royal hunting lodge, located some six miles away from Turin, to Versailles is obvious; yet there is virtually nothing French about this building. Its plan is a combination of Italian and Austrian ideas. Juvarra's mentor, Fontana, had designed a villa with a central pavilion with radiating wings; similarly, the typical Austrian *lustschloss* form as popularized by Fischer von Erlach invariably featured a dominating central pavilion with lower wings to each side. Juvarra borrowed this formal idea and made it his own by extending the wings to create an hexagonal entry courtyard. The base is suppressed so that the staterooms can open directly to the court in front and the garden behind. The exterior architectural decoration is simplified and flattened. All emphasis is placed on the central pavilion which has monumental arched windows and doors in Rococo frames and a complex faceted dome that is particularly Germanic.

In contrast to the restrained simplified exterior decoration, the interior of the grand salon is an illusionistic fantasy and a spatial tour de force. The pavilion is two-storeyed in height

Juvarra: Saloon, Stupinigi, 1729–33

and oval in plan with its long axis perpendicular to the direction of entry. In its center is inserted a square formed by four tall slender piers placed on the diagonal. Between the piers and the curving outer wall a balcony curves in and out in a series of sensuous double curves. The piers rise the full height of the space to support a plaster domical vault over the central space and four apsidal vaults over the gallery spaces. All vaults and all wall surfaces are frescoed with quadratura paintings that echo the doubly curving lines of the balcony edges. The color scheme plays bright pastels against creamy white background surfaces in a way that seems to negate the realism of the painting in favor of an obvious scenographic theatricality. Juvarra's early work as a stage designer obviously influenced this mature work, and he achieves a paradox: a space that is seemingly weightless and delicate while remaining grandly monumental.

C. Murray Smart, Jr.

Biography

Born in Messina, Sicily, 1678, the son of a goldsmith. Reputedly studied for the priesthood (ordained 1703) but also studied architecture. Worked in the studio of the architect Carlo Fontana (1638–1714), Rome, 1703–14; taught at the Accademia di San Luca, 1706–08 and 1711–12; worked as a theatre and scene designer, 1714–18. Active as an architect, Turin, and appointed First Architect to Victor Amadeus II of Savoy, 1714–36. Made several more visits to Rome; travelled to Portugal 1719–20; visited Paris and London, where he met Lord Burlington, 1720; employed to design the Royal Palace, Madrid, 1735. Member, Accademia di San Luca, 1707. Died in Madrid, 31 January 1736.

Selected Works

Numerous drawings by Juvarra for furniture, vases and other ornament are preserved in the Museo Civico and the Biblioteca Nazionale, Turin, which also holds 2 albums of scene designs and many drawings from Juvarra's Roman period. Additional collections of drawings are in the Kunstbibliothek, Berlin, the Victoria and Albert Museum, London, the Biblioteca Nacional, Madrid, and the Metropolitan Museum of Art, New York. For a complete register of Juvarra's architectural commissions see Viale 1966.

Interiors

1716	Palazzo Birago di Borgaro, Turin (building and interiors)
1716	Palazzo Martini di Cigala, Turin (building and interiors)
1717–31	Church and Monastery, Superga, Turin (building and interiors)
1718	Castello Reale, Rivoli (building and interiors including the salone; not completed)
1718–21	Palazzo Madama, Turin (remodelling and interiors including the grand staircase)
1720s	Scala delle Forbici, Palazzo Reale, Turin (building and interior)
1720s	Royal Palace, Turin (modelling of theatre)
1729–33	Stupinigi Hunting Lodge, near Turin (building and interiors)
1732–35	Chiesa del Carmine, Turin (building and interiors)
1735	Royal Palace, Madrid (building and interiors; executed in a reduced form)

Further Reading

The standard monograph on Juvarra is Boscarino 1973 which includes an extensive bibliography of primary and secondary sources. For a catalogue of Juvarra's Roman drawings see Millon 1984; an exhaustive discussion of his work as a scene designer appears in Viale Ferrero 1970.

Barghini, Andrea, *Juvarra a Roma: Disegni dall'Atelier di Carlo Fontana*, Turin: Rosenberg & Sellier, 1994

Bernardi, Marziano, *La Palazzina di Caccia di Stupinigi*, Turin: Istituto Bancario San Paolo, 1958

Boscarino, Salvatore, *Juvarra Architetto*, Rome: Officina, 1973

Brinckmann, A.E., *Theatrum Novum Pedemontii: Ideen, Entwürfe und Bauten von Guarini, Juvarra, Vittone*, Düsseldorf: Schwann, 1931

Cavallari Murat, Augusto, *Forma Urbana ed Architettura nella Torino Barocca*, 3 vols., Turin: Torinese Editrice, 1968

Griseri, Andreina and Giovanni Romano, *Filippo Juvarra a Torino: Nuovi Progetti per la Città* (exhib. cat.), Turin: Cassa di Risparmio di Torino, 1989

Mallé, Luigi, *Le Arti Figurative in Piemonte*, Turin: Casanova, 1962

Mallé, Luigi, *Palazzo Madama in Torino*, Turin: Torinese Editrice, 1970

Mallé, Luigi, *Stupinigi un Capolavoro del Settecento Europeo tra Barocchetto e Classicismo: Architettura, Pittura, Scultura, Arredamento*, Turin: Torinese Editrice, 1972

Marini, Giuseppe Luigi, *L'Architettura Barocca in Piemonte: La Provincia de Torino*, Turin: Maggiora, 1963

Millon, Henry A., *Filippo Juvarra: Drawings from the Roman Period, 1704–1714*, Rome: Elefante, 1984

Plaza Santiago, Francisco de la, *Investigaciones sobre el Palacio Real Nuevo de Madrid*, Vallodolid: Universidad de Valladolid, 1975

Riposio, Donatella and Paolo, "The Hunting Lodge of Stupinigi at Turin" in *Magazine Antiques*, 129, January 1986, pp.248–57

Robotti, C., "Rivoli: Il Castello" in *Restauro*, 23, 1976, pp.17–24

Rovere, Lorenso, Vittorio Viale and A.E. Brinckmann, *Filippo Juvarra*, Turin: Zucchi, 1937

Telluccini, Augusto, *L'Arte dell'Architetto Filippo Juvarra in Piemonte*, Turin: Societa Italiana di Edizioni Artistiche, 1926

Viale, Vittorio (editor), *Mostra di Filippo Juvarra, Architetto e Scenografo* (exhib. cat.), Messina: University of Messina, 1966

Viale Ferrero, Mercedes, *Filippo Juvarra, Scenografo e Architetto Teatrale*, Turin: Pozzo, 1970

Wittkower, Rudolf, *Art and Architecture in Italy, 1600 to 1750*, 5th edition New Haven and London: Yale University Press, 1982

K

Kauffman, Angelica 1741–1807

Swiss painter and decorative artist

Angelica Kauffman was famed during her lifetime as a portraitist and history painter, but much of her subsequent reputation has rested upon her skill as a decorative artist. Examples of decorative paintings that she actually executed herself, however, are very few and far between. Recent research by Mary Mauchline and Malise Forbes Adams confirms that documented paintings by her hand in English interiors are limited to the four roundels created for Somerset House, London (now in the vestibule of the Royal Academy), and the two overdoors originally created for Derby House, Grosvenor Square (Forbes Adam and Mauchline, 1992). Moreover, their research also undermines the traditional view of Kauffman as an active member of the group of artists and craftsmen working for the architect Robert Adam. It seems that although the designs were certainly her creation, many of the roundels, panels and other decorative paintings in Adam interiors formerly attributed to Kauffman were in fact executed by other members of the Adam circle such as Giovanni Battista Ciprani, Biagio Rebecca and Antonio Zucchi.

Yet the fact that Kauffman was not personally responsible for executing her designs does not make her contribution to interior design in England any less significant. A leading figure within the Neo-Classical movement, Kauffman played an important role within both the fine and decorative arts in nurturing History Painting, the highest genre within European art practice, in a country where only an embryonic tradition of this genre existed. Indeed, it was partly due to the lack of English history painters that the execution of decorative painting – with its dependency on historical and classical themes – relied to so great an extent upon foreign artists. In Kauffman's designs, classical themes were executed with the subtlety and sensibility of the Rococo and were thus the ideal complement to the elegant and refined treatment of classically inspired interiors of the late 18th century. A large number of engravings were made after her work which were widely circulated and which provided cheap, accessible source material for many artists and craftsmen working in a variety of decorative media. Arguably her most popular designs were those which depicted cupids, nymphs, female allegorical figures, heroines and goddesses. According to her 1924 biographers Manners and Williamson, "it was stated that not one of her works contained anything that could bring the slightest blush to the cheek of a young girl" and it has been suggested that designs by a female artist may have been deemed more appropriate for private apartments such as women's bedrooms. It is not surprising therefore that Kauffman's Cupid designs appear in the Sultana Room and adjoining boudoir at Attingham Park, Shropshire, both rooms designed for the lady of the house.

That Kauffman's designs were well-suited to contemporary tastes within domestic interior decoration is amply borne out by the diversity of ways and instances in which her designs were used. Artists at the Sèvres Porcelain factory drew extensively from portfolios of engravings, and those after Kauffman can be found among engravings after Watteau, Titian and Salvatore Rosa. J-M. Delattre's popular engraving of Kauffman's *Beauty Governed by Reason Rewarded by Merit* of 1782 appears on a saucer which forms part of a prestigious service commissioned by Louis XVI. This particular design also inspired the chimneypiece decoration in the drawing room at Attingham Park and a painted roundel at Newby Hall, Yorkshire. Similarly, an engraving by W. Ryland after Kauffman's design of *Nymphs Adorning a Term of Pan*, published 1 May 1776, is the source for the medallion above the principal door in the dining room at Château de Maisons Lafitte (Paris) carved in bas-relief by N.F.D. Lhuillier; an oval wall painting above the chimneypiece in the boudoir at Attingham Park; a painted overdoor medallion in the Glass Drawing Room created for Northumberland House and now in the Victoria and Albert Museum and the Derby Porcelain figures *Two Bacchantes Adorning a Bust of Pan*. This diversity attests not only to the popularity of her designs but also to their versatility within interior decoration and the decorative arts.

Kauffman designs were clearly much admired by Robert Adam, and decorative paintings after her work appear in several of his major commissions including Kedleston Hall, Osterley Park, Home House and Northumberland House. For example the State Bedroom at Osterley contains a ceiling medallion inspired by Kauffman's *Cupid and the Sleeping Aglaia* and two commodes in the Drawing Room contain images of Diana and Venus with Cupid after Kauffman. Three other painted overdoor medallions (aside from that already mentioned) in the Glass Drawing Room of Northumberland House are also after designs by Kauffman. One depicts Cupid awakened by Nymphs (*Domino Innocuus*) and is used again as decoration on the overmantel.

Aside from Adam, the cabinet-maker George Brookshaw used designs after Kauffman for the painted decoration of both furniture and chimneypieces. A superb secretaire bookcase of about 1786 by Brookshaw can be seen in the Philadelphia Museum of Art. It is notable in that the five roundels are taken from designs by Kauffman which derive not from the standard classical texts or mythology but from English literature and as such can be related to the increasing interest in England throughout the 18th century in a national cultural identity. This also illustrates the pertinence of Kauffman's designs to contemporary artistic trends. Examples of commodes attributed to Brookshaw and linked to Kauffman can be seen at the Lady Lever Gallery.

Examples of Kauffman's influence can also be found in other countries. Aside from the medallion in Château de Maisons mentioned above, a wall medallion in the dining room of 53 St. Stephen's Green, Dublin, is clearly based upon her design *Cupid Bound by the Graces*, and a chimneypiece decoration in the front drawing room of 11 Rutland Square, Dublin appears to be a hybrid of *Cupid's Pastime* and Kauffman's early history painting *Ariadne Adandoned by Theseus Discovered by Bacchus* (1764). Peter Tomory refers to four ovals commissioned from Kauffman in 1783 by Abate Onorato Caetani for the family villa on the Esquiline Hill in Rome. The subjects were heroines from the works of Ariosto, Tasso and Metastasio. *Constanza* from Isola Disabitata is now in Queensland Art Gallery (Tomory, *Burlington Magazine* October 1987 CXXIX pp.668–69).

JACQUELINE RIDING

See also Zucchi

Biography

Maria Anna Angelica Catherina Kauffman. Born in Chur (Coire), Switzerland, 30 October 1741, the daughter of a painter Johann Josef Kauffman. Trained under her father; studied in Florence, Rome and Naples, 1759–65. Married 1) "Count de Horn", 1767 (marriage annulled 1768); 2) the painter Antonio Zucchi, 1781 (died 1796). Moved to London, 1766; active as a history painter and portrait painter in England 1766–81; much of her work engraved from the 1770s. Lived and worked in Italy (principally Rome) from 1781; active in Naples 1782–85. Member, Florentine Accademia del Disegno, 1762; member, Accademia di San Luca, Rome, 1765. Founder-member, Royal Academy of Arts, London, 1768. Exhibitor, Free Society of Artists from 1765; Royal Academy, 1769–97. Died in Rome, 5 November 1807.

Selected Works

Examples of furniture incorporating designs after Kauffman are in the Victoria and Albert Museum, London, the Lady Lever Art Gallery, Port Sunlight, Merseyside, and the Philadelphia Museum of Art. Examples of porcelain with designs after Kauffman are in the Bowes Museum, Barnard Castle, County Durham, and the Wallace Collection, London. Notable extant examples of decorative painting and design after works by Kauffman survive in the boudoir and drawing room, Attingham Park, Shropshire; the saloon, Kedleston Hall, Derbyshire; the state bedroom at Osterley Park, Middlesex; and the drawing room, Northumberland House, London (now in the Victoria and Albert Museum).

Further Reading

For a comprehensive and scholarly account of Kauffman's career, which includes a chronology and full bibliography, and a chapter devoted to her decorative work, see Roworth 1992.

Baumgärtel, Bettina, *Angelika Kauffmann (1741–1807): Bedingungen weiblicher Kreativität in der Malerei des 18. Jahrhunderts*, Weinheim and Basle, 1990

Bellaigue, Geoffrey de, "Sèvres Artists and Their Sources II: Engravings" in *Burlington*, CXXII, 1980, p.751

Croft-Murray, Edward, *Decorative Painting in England, 1537–1837*, 2 vols., London: Country Life, 1962–70

Croft-Murray, Edward, "Decorative Painting for Lord Burlington and the Royal Academy" in *Apollo*, LXXXIX, 1969, pp.11–21

Forbes Adam, Malise and Mary Mauchline, "Attingham Park, Shropshire" in *Country Life*, 186, July 1992, pp.88–91

Forbes Adam, Malise and Mary Mauchline, "*Ut Pictura Poesis*: Angelica Kauffman's Literary Sources" in *Apollo*, CXXXII, 1992, pp.345–49

Gleichenstein, Elisabeth von and K. Strober, *Angelica Kauffmann (1741–1807) / Marie Ellenrieder (1791–1863)* (exhib. cat.), Konstanz: Rosengartenmuseum, 1992

Robinson, Eric and Keith R. Thompson, "Matthew Boulton's Mechanical Paintings" in *Burlington*, CXII, 1970, pp.497–507

Roworth, Wendy Wassyng (editor), *Angelica Kauffman: A Continental Artist in Georgian England*, London: Reaktion, 1992

Walch, Peter S., *Angelica Kauffman*, Ph.D. thesis, Princeton University, 1969

Wood, Lucy, "George Brookshaw, 'Peintre Ebéniste par Extraordinaire' and the Case of the Vanishing Cabinet Maker II" in *Apollo*, CXXXI, 1991, pp.383–97

Kent, William 1685/86–1748

British architect, painter, landscape gardener and designer

William Kent occupies a pre-eminent position in the history of British architecture and interior design. A talented artist, decorator, architect, designer and pioneer of English landscape design, his skills were manifold and as one of the first British architects to concern himself with furniture as well as decoration for his interiors, his career foreshadows that of later architect-designers such as Robert Adam. Moreover, in partnership with his patron, Lord Burlington, he was responsible for the revival of Neo-Classical and particularly neo-Palladian architecture. These styles became standard in many of the more important town and country houses built in England in the first half of the 18th century and Kent himself worked on some of the most prestigious and impressive buildings of the time.

Born in humble circumstances in Bridlington, Yorkshire, Kent studied easel and fresco painting in Italy, where he lived for ten years (1709–19) supported by a number of wealthy patrons. While in Italy he met Richard Boyle, the Earl of Burlington, and this meeting determined the direction of Kent's future career. Accompanying Burlington back to England in 1719 he lodged at Burlington House, the Earl's London home and remained there until his death, almost thirty years later. Secure in Burlington's patronage, Kent rapidly developed his abilities as an interior decorator, architect and landscape gardener.

His first commission was to paint a number of ceilings in

Kent: Saloon, Houghton Hall, Norfolk, 1726–36

Burlington House. Completed in 1720, these paintings were executed in typically Italianate fashion but they also exposed Kent's limitations as a representational artist, especially his tenuous grasp of human anatomy. Nevertheless, despite fierce opposition from the official royal artist, Sir James Thornhill, Kent was awarded the commission to decorate the newly-completed suite of state rooms at Kensington Palace for George I. Here Kent eschewed the Baroque tradition of covering ceilings and walls with scenic painting in favour of the simpler classical idea of a central ceiling motif surrounded by painted decorative devices. The Cupola Room (1722) featured *trompe-l'oeil* representations of coffering on the coved ceiling, painted in blue and gold, with painted marble background and painted shadows. The proportions of the coffering decreased in size as the ceiling ascended to give the illusion of greater height and curvature. The decorative scheme also included wooden wall pilasters painted to resemble fluted stone, painted trophies and a number of gilded statues representing Roman gods. Kent conceived a different solution for the Presence Chamber (1724), employing the "grotesque" style of decoration he had first encountered in Italy. Grotesque-style decoration consisted of the fantastic interweaving of human and animal forms with foliage, scrolls, garlands, and other ornament, painted as a pattern in a flat two-dimensional manner. The effect in the Presence Chamber, enhanced by the bold use of colour, was one of continual movement, the eye being drawn rapidly towards the central motif. Kent was to repeat this theme on the parlour ceiling at Rousham House (c.1738).

The eclectic nature of Kent's work at Kensington Palace is further exemplified by his choice of decoration for the King's Gallery (1727). Here he painted seven scenes from the Ulysses myth along the central rib of the ceiling and surrounded them with grey and white classical motifs on a speckled gold field suggestive of mosaic. On the King's Staircase he reverted to more traditional themes. Mainly executed in grisaille (grey monochrome), the upper part consisted of groups of figures (mainly portraits of courtiers and other dignitaries), presented within painted arches and balustrades, who appeared to be looking down on the stairwell. A similar ceiling painting, including a self-portrait of the artist, completed the scheme.

It was at Burlington's country villa, Chiswick House (1726–32) that Kent's abilities were truly tested for the first time. The overall decorative scheme was rich though sombre and displayed the first evidence of his enthusiasm for classical ornament. The severe architectural line of door frames, pediments and chimneypieces is relieved by the profusion of scrollwork, egg and dart, and Greek key mouldings. His exuberence is also evident in the ceiling treatments, especially in the Blue Velvet Room which contains one of his first compartmented ceilings, with eight pairs of large brackets emphasizing wall and ceiling articulation.

Kent's ideas were to reach fulfilment with the new decorative order that he established at Houghton Hall (1726–36), built by the Scottish architect and fellow neo-Palladian, Colen Campbell for Sir Robert Walpole. Kent used mosaic and grisaille extensively, combined with muted greens, pinks and whites as exemplified in the scrollwork in the White Drawing Room. In the state rooms there is a profusion of ornate gilt mouldings, heavy compartmented ceilings and door frames and chimneypieces reminiscent, like those at Chiswick, of the work of Inigo Jones. It was for Houghton Hall that Kent also designed his first free-standing furniture. Widely considered to be a unique contribution to the canon of English furniture design, his pieces were designed for show rather than comfort, and exploited to the full the opulence of his interiors. Indeed, he was the first English architect of note to design furniture specifically for his own interiors and his pieces look out of place, both in scale and richness, in any other setting. His chairs, armchairs and settees were usually made of gilt mahogany upholstered in cut velvet. His side, pier and console tables, carved from softwood and gilded, revelled in ornamentation: these included his trademark scallop shells, acanthus, floral swagging and satyr masks.

By the mid 1730s Kent had established himself as the foremost artist and interior decorator of his day. This reputation was consolidated by his venture into architecture, initially with his alterations to Kew Palace (c.1730) and more importantly with his designs for public buildings. He designed the Royal Mews (1733) at Charing Cross, since demolished to make way for the National Gallery, the Treasury Buildings facing the north corner of Horse Guards Parade (1737) and finally the Horse Guards in Whitehall, completed after his death.

The most important of Kent's domestic projects is Holkham Hall in Norfolk, built for Thomas Coke, the Earl of Leicester. The foundations were dug in 1734 but only the family wing was completed in Kent's lifetime. The designs themselves originated with Lord Leicester, whom Kent had first met in Italy, but both Lord Burlington and Kent himself were instrumental in the evolution of the final plans and elevations. Built of a narrow yellow brick with four separate wings the house adhered to the neo-Palladian principles that all three men admired. Kent's designs for the ceilings and chimneypieces in the state rooms were once again indebted to Inigo Jones but he evolved a novel solution for the design of the main hall. This room was placed on the *piano nobile* (first floor) and was surrounded on three sides by colonnades; access to the *piano nobile* itself was via an internal staircase, rather than from the usual external grand staircase.

The other domestic building project for which Kent is best remembered is 44 Berkeley Square, London (1742), built for Lady Isabella Finch. The typically austere exterior conceals one of Kent's most memorable interiors. The staircase – an assemblage of cantilevered and colonnaded balconies surmounted by a barrel-vault ceiling – conveys a sumptuous theatricality and is considered by many to be his finest creation.

Kent was also a skilled landscape gardener, and his reputation rests primarily on the work he executed at Stowe (1730–40) and Rousham (1737–41). Heralding a move away from the traditional Italian Renaissance garden with its formal geometric plan, raised beds and regimented planting that had been popular for much of the 17th century, he pioneered a less formal style of landscape that imitated natural planting, with no obvious planning or artifice. In pursuit of this ideal, he produced gently undulating slopes, introduced tree clumps into lawns, replaced formal canals with sinuous watercourses and asserted the primacy of scene and perspective. He also made frequent use of the Dutch ha-ha, (concealed fence and ditch) which abetted the illusion of nature untramelled by boundaries. And he added a variety of architectural features – classical pavilions, temples, follies and obelisks – to enhance the picturesque nature of his natural forms.

In pursuing his own vision of the Palladian aesthetic Kent developed a unique oeuvre which encompassed architecture, interior decoration, furniture design and landscape gardening. In each discipline he offered a break with tradition which provided a powerful stimulus to those who followed in his footsteps.

NICHOLAS NUTTALL

See also Burlington

Biography

Born in Bridlington, Yorkshire, in 1685 or 1686. Travelled to Italy with the architect John Talman (1677–1726), 1709; studied painting under Benedetto Luti and worked as a painter in Rome; toured Northern Italy from 1714. Returned to England, 1719, under the patronage of Lord Burlington (1694–1753) for whom Kent edited Designs of Inigo Jones (1727). Active as a painter and designer of architectural decorations from the 1720s; worked as an architect and landscape gardener from the 1730s. Appointed Master Carpenter, Board of Works, 1726; Surveyor of Paintings in the Royal Palaces, 1728; Master Mason and Deputy Surveyor, 1735; Portrait Painter to the King, 1739. Had two children with Elizabeth Butler. Member, Tuscan Academy in Florence, 1713. Died in London, 12 April 1748.

Selected Works

Important collections of Kent's architectural drawings and decorative designs are held at Chatsworth, Derbyshire, the Drawings Collection of the Royal Institute of British Architects, the Victoria and Albert Museum, the British Museum, Sir John Soane's Museum, London, and the Ashmolean, Oxford. Examples of his furniture can be seen at the Victoria and Albert Museum, Chatsworth, and *in situ* at Houghton Hall, Norfolk.

Interiors

1720	Burlington House, London (ceiling decorations): Lord Burlington
1722–27	Kensington Palace, London (decorations for the Cupola Room and other State Rooms including the King's Drawing Room, Bedchamber, Gallery and Staircase, and the Presence Chamber and Council Chamber)
1726–32	Chiswick House, London (decorations, interiors and furniture): Lord Burlington
1726–36	Houghton Hall, Norfolk (decorations, interiors and furniture): Sir Robert Walpole
1730–40	Stowe House, Buckinghamshire (decoration of the ceiling of the Entrance Hall and garden buildings)
1731	Raynham Hall, Norfolk (decorations and interiors including the Entrance Hall, Belisarius Room, Principal Staircase, Saloon, and Dining Room, and some furniture): 2nd Lord Townshend
1734	Devonshire House, London (building, interiors and furniture): Duke of Devonshire
1734–48	Holkham Hall, Norfolk (building with Lord Burlington and interiors including the Hall and Library): Thomas Coke, Earl of Leicester
c.1740	Worcester Lodge, Badminton, Gloucestershire (building and interiors): 3rd Duke of Beaufort
1742–44	44 Berkeley Square, London (building and interiors): Lady Isabella Finch

Publications

Designs of Inigo Jones, with Lord Burlington, 2 vols., 1727

Further Reading

A pioneering study of Kent's work is Jourdain 1948 which represents the first scholarly examination of all the aspects of his career. Wilson 1984 is an update and expansion of this book and also includes a full bibliography of primary and secondary sources.

Beard, Geoffrey, "William Kent and the Royal Barge" in the *Burlington Magazine*, LXII, 1970, pp.488–95

Beard, Geoffrey, "William Kent and the Cabinet-makers" in the *Burlington Magazine*, CXVII, December 1975, p.870

Bryant, Julius, "Chiswick House: The Inside Story" in *Apollo*, 136, July 1992, pp.17–22

Colvin, Howard M., *A Biographical Dictionary of British Architects, 1600–1840*, 3rd edition New Haven and London: Yale University Press, 1995

Cornforth, John and John Fowler, *English Decoration in the 18th Century*, London: Barrie and Jenkins, and Princeton, NJ: Pyne, 1974; 2nd edition Barrie and Jenkins, 1978

Cornforth, John, "Devonshire House, London" in *Country Life*, CLXVIII, 1980, p.1750

Girouard, Mark, "44 Berkeley Square, London" in *Country Life*, CXXXII, 1962, p.1648

Harris, John, *The Palladian Revival: Lord Burlington, His Villa and Garden at Chiswick*, New Haven and London: Yale University Press, 1994

Hodson, Peter, *William Kent: A Bibliography and Chronology*, Charlottesville: American Association of Architectural Bibliographers, 1964

Hussey, Christopher, *Early Georgian, 1715–1760* (English Country Houses, vol.1), 1955; reprinted Woodbridge, Suffolk: Antique Collectors' Club, 1984

Jourdain, Margaret, *The Work of William Kent*, London: Country Life, and New York: Scribner, 1948

Jourdain, Margaret, "Documented Furniture at Rousham" in *Country Life*, CIV, 1948, p.384

Lee, J., "The Furniture of William Kent" in *Apollo*, LXV, 1957, p.53

Parissien, Steven, *Palladian Style*, London: Phaidon, 1994

Rosoman, Treve, "The Decoration and Use of the Principal Apartments of Chiswick House, 1727–1770" in *Burlington Magazine*, CXXVII, October 1985, pp.663–77

Saumarez Smith, Charles, *Eighteenth-Century Decoration: Design and the Domestic Interior in England*, London: Weidenfeld and Nicolson, and New York: Abrams, 1993

Schmidt, L., "Holkham Hall, Norfolk" in *Country Life*, CLXVII, 1980, pp.214,298,359

A Tercentenary Tribute to William Kent (exhib. cat.), Hull: Ferens Art Gallery, 1985

Vardy, John, *Some Designs of Mr. Inigo Jones and Mr. William Kent*, London, 1744

Wilson, Michael I., *William Kent: Architect, Designer, Painter, Gardener, 1685–1748*, London: Routledge, 1984

Wittkower, Rudolf, *Palladio and English Palladianism*, London: Thames and Hudson, 1974.; New York: Thames and Hudson, 1983

Worsley, Giles, "Houghton Hall, Norfolk: A Seat of the Marquess of Cholmondeley" in *Country Life*, 187, 4 March 1993, pp.50–53

Kimbel and Cabus

American cabinet-makers and interior decorators, 1863–1882

The New York cabinet-making and decorating firm of Kimbel and Cabus was founded during the Civil War and achieved its greatest prominence during the Aesthetic Movement of the

Kimbel and Cabus: advertisement from *American Architect and Building News*, Boston, 24 February 1877

1870s, when the firm became known for its production of furniture in a Modern Gothic style.

Like the principals of most major American firms established during the third quarter of the 19th century, Anthony Kimbel and Joseph Cabus were immigrant craftsmen well-versed in European cabinet-making traditions. Anton, or Anthony, Kimbel (1822–95) received his early training from his father, Wilhelm (1786–1869), a well-known cabinet-maker in Mainz, Germany, and from his maternal uncle and godfather, Anton Bembé (1799–1861), one of a family of Mainz furniture dealers, upholsterers, and decorators. Kimbel later worked with a number of other cabinet-makers, notably Alexandre-Georges Fourdinois in Paris, and with the Parisian designer and publisher Desiré Guilmard before immigrating to New York around 1847.

From about 1848 to 1851 Kimbel was the principal designer in the Broadway shop of Charles Baudouine, and in 1854 he established the firm of Bembé and Kimbel with the financial backing of his German uncle. The partnership inaugurated nearly one hundred years of the Kimbel family's involvement with cabinet-making and interior decoration in America.

From its inception, Bembe and Kimbel garnered excellent credit ratings based upon the high quality of the firm's production, its profitable business, and its "best class of customers." *Gleason's Pictorial Drawing-Room Companion* (Boston, November1854) published an illustration of a parlor by Bembé and Kimbel – a rare image of a high-style New York interior from this period – and enthusiastically praised the "magnificent" and "sumptuous" decorations, which were executed in a kinetic, curvilinear Rococo-Revival style. While noting Kimbel's European origins, the author astutely observed that "Mr. Kimbel['s] ... unique styles appear to be American modifications of those now in vogue abroad." In 1857, the firm was commissioned to manufacture armchairs in oak from a design by Thomas U. Walter, architect of the United States Capitol, for use in the House of Representatives. Numerous examples survive in public and private collections (e.g., Maryland Historical Society, Massachusetts Historical Society, Henry Ford Museum, and High Museum of Art), and in the absence of other documented pieces the firm is known today by its association with this robust form.

Kimbel's French-born contemporary and future partner, Joseph Cabus (1824–98) immigrated to the United States between 1832 and 1836 while still a boy. His father, Claude Cabus, was listed as a cabinet-maker in the New York City directories by 1838, and Joseph is so listed for the first time, at his father's address, in 1850. During the 1850s, Cabus worked for Alexander Roux, a prominent cabinet-maker on Broadway. Cabus became Roux's foreman and was his partner for little more than a year, between 1858 and 1860. By 1862, Cabus had his own workshop at 924 Broadway adjacent to Bembé and Kimbel, which had moved to 928 Broadway in 1857.

After Anton Bembé died, in 1861, Kimbel dissolved the

company and within the year established a new partnership with his neighbor Joseph Cabus. According to family history, Kimbel and Cabus began as a small factory supplying other dealers with high-class furniture, but the expansion of its premises on Broadway indicates the steady growth of the business after the Civil War. From 1873 until Kimbel's death in 1895, the principal showroom was located at 7 and 9 East 20th Street in the fashionable neighborhood surrounding Union Square; a factory acquired at 458–460 Tenth Avenue in 1869 remained in Kimbel family hands until 1910.

Relatively little is known of the firm's production during the 1860s, when the influence of the French Second Empire dominated American taste in interior decoration. Fortunately, however, several examples survive of a splendid pedestal cabinet documented to Kimbel and Cabus by a period photograph in one of two rare photograph albums that descended in the Kimbel family to the Cooper-Hewitt National Design Museum Branch Library, Smithsonian Institution Libraries. Monumental in scale, with convex side cabinets flanking a salient pedestal suspended above a deep recess, on which is mounted a large medallion, the best-known example, in rosewood and ebony with marquetry veneers, was given to the Brooklyn Museum as early as 1946 by Susan Dwight Bliss of New York and has since served as a benchmark in the study of 19th-century American furniture.

Ultimately, however, Kimbel and Cabus secured its reputation with its highly original Modern Gothic furnishings during the 1870s. The vocabulary was distinctive, but no doubt drew inspiration from such seminal publications of the design reform movement as Bruce Talbert's *Gothic Forms Applied to Furniture, Metal Work, and Decoration for Domestic Purposes* (Birmingham, 1868), republished in Boston in 1873, and Charles Locke Eastlake's *Hints on Household Taste, in Furniture, Upholstery, and Other Details* (London, 1868), which appeared in the first of eight American editions in 1872. Although some of the firm's work in this idiom probably predates the Philadelphia Centennial Exhibition of 1876, Kimbel and Cabus was one of the few to exhibit Modern Gothic furnishings at the fair and thus deserves credit for bringing the style to the attention of a large and appreciative American audience. The Kimbel and Cabus booth, installed like a drawing room, was commended for being "rich and tasteful enough to rank among the very best of American exhibits in household art" (Ferris, 1877). In its first two volumes *American Architect and Building News* featured two illustrations of Kimbel and Cabus interiors, one of the Centennial display, in July 1876, and one of the East 20th Street showroom, in February 1877.

During the later 1870s, Kimbel and Cabus was prolific in the manufacture of ebonized cherry and, to a lesser extent, walnut and oak furniture in the Modern Gothic style, which was ornamented with linear, incised, and gilded decoration, and often incorporated painted panels on a gold ground or printed paper "tiles," yellow on black, featuring stylized medieval figures or motifs from Christopher Dresser's pattern books. Idiosyncratic stiff-legged or rectilinear forms are typical, frequently embellished with spindles and strapwork hinges, and supported by stylized hoof, bracket, or trestle feet. Of the numerous extant ebonized pieces, many of which are rudimentary in execution, two fall-front desks – one in the Victoria and Albert Museum and one in the Brooklyn Museum – exemplify this furniture at its best. A hanging key cabinet in the Metropolitan Museum of Art, made in oak and embellished with foliate crockets and elaborate nickel hinges, is an example of the firm's occasionally more literal interpretation of the Gothic Revival. Still other pieces specifically inspired by Elizabethan, Second Empire, Asian, and even Tyrolian models are recorded by the Kimbel and Cabus photograph album, while a refined mahogany *bonheur-du-jour* (private collection, Long Island, New York), with bevelled mirrors on the cupboard doors and brass mouldings, which bears the firm's paper label, suggests Kimbel and Cabus also produced an elegant, if conservative, line of furniture around 1880.

In the absence of business records, a complete chronology of the company's clientele and commissions is still in formation. At least two important interiors survive in New York City: Kimbel and Cabus provided woodwork and furnishings for the Fifth Avenue Presbyterian Church (1875), and was among the elite New York cabinet-makers, including Herter Brothers, Pottier and Stymus, and Associated Artists, to decorate one of the Company Rooms in the Seventh Regiment Armory (1879–80).

Kimbel and Cabus was dissolved in 1882, ostensibly because each partner went intobusiness with his sons. A. Kimbel and Sons was the more successful entity, continuing in business until 1941. While Cabus's firm also continued into the 20th century, it does not appear to have achieved great distinction. A second photograph album documenting furnishings and draperies by A. Kimbel and Sons (Cooper-Hewitt National Design Museum Library) records a tasteful production, including gilded Louis XVth-style furniture and Empire Revival pieces in dark wood plentifully embellished with ormolu mounts, both types popular around the turn of the century. As was also true of other New York firms during the last decades of the 19th century, Kimbel and Sons manufactured furniture and woodwork to designs supplied by architects for important clients, such as Henry Clay Frick for his Pittsburgh home called Clayton (1892).

CATHERINE HOOVER VOORSANGER

See also Aesthetic Movement; Art Furnishings

Selected Collections

Two volumes of photograph albums illustrating Kimbel and Cabus furniture are in the Rare Book Collection, Cooper-Hewitt Museum, New York. Examples of the firm's furniture are in the Metropolitan Museum of Art, New York.

Further Reading

For a comprehensive history of Kimbel and Cabus see Voorsanger 1996, which also includes a reprint of the earlier of the two Kimbel and Cabus photograph albums and a chronology of the firm by Medill Higgins Harvey. A discussion of the New York furniture trade during the second half of the 19th century appears in Voorsanger 1994.

Burke, Doreen Bolger and others, *In Pursuit of Beauty: Americans and the Aesthetic Movement* (exhib. cat.: Metropolitan Museum, New York), New York: Rizzoli, 1986

Cook, Clarence, *The House Beautiful: Essays on Beds and Tables, Stools and Candlesticks*, New York, 1878

Ferris, George Titus, *Gems of the Centennial Exhibition: Consisting of Illustrated Descriptions of Objects of an Artistic Character, in the Exhibits of the United States, Great Britain, France ...*, New York, 1877

Hanks, David A., "Kimbel and Cabus: Nineteenth-Century New York Cabinetmakers" in *Art and Antiques*, 3, September–October 1980, pp.44–53

Madigan, Mary Jean Smith, *Eastlake-Influenced American Furniture, 1870–1890* (exhib. cat.), Yonkers, NY: Hudson River Museum, 1973

Madigan, Mary Jean Smith, "Eastlake-Influenced American Furniture, 1870–1890" in *Connoisseur*, 191, January 1986

Nineteenth Century America: Furniture and Other Decorative Arts (exhib. cat.), New York: Metropolitan Museum of Art, 1970

Spofford, Harriet Prescott, *Art Decoration Applied to Furniture*, New York, 1878

Voorsanger, Catherine Hoover, "From the Bowery to Broadway: The Herter Brothers and the New York Furniture Trade" in Katherine S. Howe, Alice Cooney Frelinghuysen and Catherine Hoover Voorsanger, *Herter Brothers: Furniture and Interiors for a Gilded Age* (exhib. cat.), New York: Abrams, 1994, pp.56–77, 242–46

Voorsanger, Catherine Hoover, *Kimbel and Cabus and the Modern Gothic Style in America, 1862–1882*, New York: Acanthus Press, forthcoming

Zinnkann, Heidrun, *Mainzer Möbelschreiner der ersten Hälfte des 19. Jahrhunderts*, Frankfurt: Kramer, 1985

King, Thomas fl.1829–c.1840

British furniture designer and upholsterer

Thomas King, self-styled "upholsterer of forty five years' experience", was one of the most prolific producers of pattern books in the second quarter of the 19th century. He published fifteen examples between 1829 and 1839 and his work represents the most comprehensive illustration of commercial taste in furniture and upholstery during this period. Little, however, is known about King's life. Despite his claim to long experience in the upholstery trade, he is described in Kelly's London Directory of 1839 as a "Furniture Pattern Drawer (sic)" and the exact nature of his role in the production of the designs in *Original Designs for Cabinet Furniture* (c.1835) and *Supplementary Plates to the Modern Style of Cabinet Work Exemplified ...* (c.1840), which are inscribed as being "published by Mr. T. King", is still unclear. According to the various publications bearing his name, he spent his working life in London's Holborn and Lincoln's Inn Fields, and he is listed variously at, 17 Gate Street, Lincoln's Inn Fields, 11 Little Queen Street, Lincoln's Inn Fields and 214 High Holborn, London. The publication, *Specimens of Furniture in the Elizabethan and Louis Quatorze Styles ...* of c.1840 is inscribed as being by "the Late Mr T. King" and there is no mention of him in Kelly's London Directory of 1843.

During the second quarter of the 19th century "the furnishing of large houses is generally committed to the Upholsterer" (*Architectural Magazine*, 1834), and the period witnessed a marked expansion of the upholsterer's profession and an increasing number of pattern books devoted to the subject of upholstery, as well as furniture design generally. King's books were mainly directed at commercial cabinet-makers who supplied furniture to a predominantly middle-class clientele. This clientele was on the whole content to follow, rather than to lead contemporary fashions and, as a result, King's designs were fairly conventional. A small number of designs for furniture were in the Gothic or Elizabethan styles, indicating an awareness of the new taste for antiquarianism among more fashion-conscious collectors, but the majority reflected established trends within Modern or Grecian styles and Old French or Louis Quatorze styles.

According to J.C. Loudon, author of an influential treatise on domestic architecture and interiors that appeared in 1833, the Louis Quatorze style (also known as the "Old French" style) was "rather on the increase than otherwise". Many plates in King's publications reflect this trend and illustrate the taste for French styles of the late 17th and 18th centuries, which manifested itself after the Restoration of the Bourbon monarchy in 1814. The "Old French" style encompassed a free reinterpretation of Baroque and Rococo motifs, incorporating features such as scrollwork and interlaced curves, from the reigns of Louis XIV and Louis XV. In his *Designs for Carving and Gilding used in Interior Decoration and Furniture ...* (c.1830), King states that his designs are "arranged with novelty ... and practicality in a variety of styles; including that of Louis XIV (which being at present highly fashionable) is displayed in many examples". The book includes designs for console tables, glasses, chimney glasses and pier tables carved with acanthus scrolls, C-scrolls, masks and cabochons. The taste for Empire-style furniture derived from the work of Percier and Fontaine was also illustrated in a number of King's publications, including *The Modern Style of Cabinet Work Exemplified ...* (1829). The shapes of most of the items are classically based, being in the form of blocks, with ornament restricted to limited sections of classically inspired carving or moulding at the perimeters of the furniture. Various individual designs for Elizabethan or Gothic furniture appear in publications, such as *Original Designs for Chairs and Sofas* (c.1840) and *The Modern Style ...*, where these styles are illustrated as one among many stylistic options on offer in the second quarter of the 19th century. King may also have included these designs in deference to the growing contemporary concern for greater historical accuracy in the treatment of the past styles.

King was extremely conscious of producing publications which, he claimed, would be of practical assistance to the craftsmen who subscribed to his work. In the preface to *The Modern Style ...* he states, "... peculiar attention has been bestowed in an economical arrangement of material and labor, which being a most essential particular, is presumed will render the collection of the greatest utility to the Cabinet Manufacturer". He was also working at a time when developments in technology were directed at producing whichever of the fashionable styles was prevalent and producing it as cheaply and efficiently as possible, and in 1835 he refers to rosettes turned by lathe and then channelled into leaves as "being a considerable saving in the expense of carving". His clear intention was to encourage the rapid and cheap production of furniture, and the fact that Gothic and Elizabethan pieces were more expensive to make due to the hand finishing required, was clearly a factor in discouraging his interest in these styles.

King intended his designs to be used by a wide group of craftsmen and professionals and the *Architectural Magazine* stated that his *Compilation of Splendid Ornamental Designs*

King: bedroom chairs from *The Modern Style of Cabinet Work*, 1829

from Foreign Works ... (n.d.) would be " equally useful to the architect, upholsterer, the decorative painter and even the manufacturer of cloths and papers ...". He was also primarily concerned to popularise and disseminate the range of styles and forms deemed appropriate to particular interiors. Thus, *The Modern Style* ... illustrates the diversity of furniture types available for drawing rooms and parlours and includes novelty and "fancy" items such as flower stands, Spanish chairs, easy chairs, loo tables, screens and other articles. He also offers a wealth of advice on the details of interiors, recommending, for example, that "the glass frames of the Parlour and Drawing Room require a marked contrast; the former should be massive, plain and bold in design; while in the latter lightness and elegance should blend with fanciful richness". Such advice was intended to guide a hesitant clientele through the maze of an increasingly bewildering range of styles and forms.

Few of King's designs are known to have been realized as articles of furniture, and a group of Anglo-Indian "fancy" tables, made of ebony in the Old French style, which are based on a plate in *The Modern Style* ..., represents a somewhat untypical exception. His designs were not innovative, nor were they intended to be. But they were clearly popular and their appeal was quite enduring. *The Modern Style* ..., for example, was reissued in 1839 and again in 1862 suggesting that King's designs continued to satisfy the aspirations of a middle-class clientele, whose desire for furniture with swelling curves, naturalistic carving and thick upholstery, was to culminate in the fashion for rotundity and comfort in the middle decades of the 19th century.

ROBIN D. JONES

Biography

Active as an upholsterer in London from late 1820s. Listed in London directories at 17 Gate Street, Lincoln's Inn Fields, 11 Little Queen Street, Lincoln's Inn Fields, and 214 High Holborn. Published 15 pattern books for furniture, 1829–39. Died c.1840.

Publications

Since there is no monograph on Thomas King, the best source of information about his work is his own publications

The Modern Style of Cabinet Work Exemplified in New Designs, Practically Arranged, 1829, 2nd edition 1839, reissued 1862

Designs for Carving and Gilding, used in Interior Decoration and Furniture with Original Patterns for Toilet Glasses, c.1830

Working Ornaments and Forms, full size for the use of the Cabinet Manufacturer, Chair and Sofa Maker, Carver and Turner, c.1833

The Upholsterer's Guide (previously *The Upholsterer's Accelerator*), pre-1835

The Cabinet Maker's Sketchbook of Plain and Useful Designs, 2 vols. c.1835–36

Valences and Draperies, Consisting of New Designs for Fashionable Upholstery Work, c.1835

Original Designs for Cabinet Furniture, c.1835

Fashionable Bedsteads with Hangings, Consisting of Original Designs, c.1839

The Upholsterer's Sketch Book of Original Designs for Fashionable Draperies, 1839

Original Designs for Chairs and Sofas, c.1840

Specimens of Furniture in the Elizabethan and Louis Quatorze Styles, adapted for Modern Imitation, c.1840

Supplementary Plates to the Modern Style of Cabinet Work Exemplified, c.1840

The Upholsterer's Pocket Collection of Fashionable Designs, n.d.

A Compilation of Splendid Ornamental Designs from Foreign Works of Recent Production, n.d.

Decorations for Windows and Beds, n.d.

Shop Fronts and Exterior Doors, n.d.

Modern Designs for Household Furniture, n.d.

Further Reading

The Age of Neo-Classicism (exhib. cat.: Royal Academy, London), London: Arts Council, 1972

Banham, Joanna, Sally MacDonald and Julia Porter, *Victorian Interior Design*, London: Cassell, 1991; as *Victorian Interior Style*, London: Studio, 1995

Beard, Geoffrey and Christopher Gilbert (editors), *Dictionary of English Furniture Makers, 1660–1840*, London: Furniture History Society, 1986

Collard, Frances, *Regency Furniture*, Woodbridge, Suffolk: Antique Collectors' Club, 1985

Gloag, John, *The Englishman's Chair: Origins, Design and Social History of Seat Furniture in England*, London: Allen and Unwin, 1964

Joy, Edward T., *English Furniture, 1800–1851*, London: Sotheby, 1977

Joy, Edward T., *Pictorial Dictionary of British 19th Century Furniture Design*, Woodbridge, Suffolk: Antique Collectors' Club, 1977

Winkler, Gail Caskey (introduction), *An Analysis of Drapery* [by James Arrowsmith] *and The Upholsterer's Accelerator* [by Thomas King], New York: Acanthus Press, 1993

Kitchens

Although separate areas for preparing food have been present in larger domestic dwellings since ancient times, in Britain the kitchen seems first to have emerged as a specific room with an identity of its own during the 12th century. During the Middle Ages it led off the Great Hall and in large houses it was approached through a triple-arched opening in the wall facing the lord's table. The two smaller openings led to the pantry and buttery from which bread, beer and candles were served, while the larger archway led via a broad corridor to the kitchen where all the cooking was done on huge open fires. In grand households these rooms could be very large and had high louvred ceilings to assist ventilation and reduce heat and smells. Their architectural treatment was sometimes almost as elaborate as that of the hall, and fine examples survive at Stanton Harcourt, Oxfordshire (1485) and Raby Castle, Durham (mid-14th century).

It was not until the 17th century, however, as the pursuit of comfort increasingly began to inform the organisation of the household and its apartments, that the kitchen really came into its own. The story of this room's subsequent development is closely associated with changing attitudes towards social life, the family and the status of women both within the home and outside it.

Modern notions of domestic comfort appear to have first taken significant shape in northern Europe and most particularly in the Netherlands. The trading wealth brought in by the Hanseatic League coupled with Calvinistic emphasis on simple virtues, and the honesty of hard work, sobriety and family life, combined to provide an atmosphere in which the home and its contents were very highly prized. Family life invariably began to centre on the kitchen, and the furnishing of the room tended to reflect its significance as both a workplace and show-space. Numbers of tables and worktops, often made from barrels, were housed alongside food cupboards. Dressers for the storage and display of pewter and utensils were also important items of furniture along with settles and chairs. As the source of nourishment and warmth – both physical and emotional – and the centre of the woman's realm, the kitchen was also to become the heart of domestic virtue.

During the 18th century, the domestic environment's pragmatic, functional aspect began to be supplemented by a new delight in the aesthetic. During this century, "comfort" came to be associated with a rather more frivolous pleasure in the delights of a finely appointed home. In addition, in practical terms the kitchen was to benefit greatly from technological innovation. By the time that the Brighton Pavilion was remodelled by John Nash for the Prince Regent from 1815, the latest in cooking equipment, from cast-iron utensils to closed ranges, and in lighting and ventilation devices, were incorporated into a room which was intended to be functionally efficient and decorative at the same time.

The kitchen in the Brighton Pavilion was conveniently situated adjacent to the State Dining Room, but in many country houses it was located in a separate wing, a practice that had begun in the late 17th century but which continued well into the Victorian period. Although this arrangement had the advantage of removing cooking smells from the main body of the house, the time involved in carrying food through long passages and corridors often meant that it was cold before it reached the table. Hot plates and warming devices placed in serving rooms adjoining the dining room were introduced in the early 19th century in an attempt to remedy this failing. In town houses, kitchens and household offices were placed in the basement and were linked to the main rooms via a back staircase. Dumb-waiters were a popular feature in many mid- and late Victorian homes providing a quick and efficient means by which dishes could be passed between the upper and lower floors.

The technological innovation apparent in the development of upper- and middle-class kitchens across Europe and in the United States during the early 19th century was, of course, to increase with the quickening pace of industrialisation. In America, technical advances in the kitchen were paralleled by an increasing interest in the scientific planning of activities centred in it. Catherine Beecher's *A Treatise on Domestic Economy* first appeared in 1841 and, discussing in detail the needs of the kitchen user and their relationship with the main items within it, the book championed a move toward greater efficiency in the organisation and use of the room. One of the more noticeable results of this drive in both the United States and in Britain, where Beecher's work also made an impact, was the inclusion of a larger number of items of built-in furniture. Large, centrally placed tables at which a number of the many tasks of the Victorian kitchen could be performed were also typical. Nevertheless, for much of this period kitchens in wealthier houses were heavily staffed with chefs or head-cooks presiding over numerous under-cooks, kitchen-maids and scullery-maids who carried out the more menial tasks. Robert Kerr, author of *The Gentleman's House* (1864), described such rooms as "having the character of a complicated laboratory" and their complex equipment might include roasting-ranges, stewing-stoves, boiling-stoves, turnspits, hotplates and hot closets (Girouard, 1978).

The 19th-century emphasis on efficiency and functionality, although important, was not the only factor governing the layout of and attitudes towards the kitchen. Equally significant was the continuing emotional role played by the room. In an age in which the home was both haven from the harshness of the outside world and bastion of moral respectability, the kitchen, as the domicile's centre, was of key importance. The notion of the simple, yet welcoming country kitchen-living room, with its blazing hearth, gleaming utensils and signs of honest industry was a central tenet of Arts and Crafts ideology, and if the reality proved to be far from the ideal, it nevertheless remained a potent symbol that has continued to inform middle-class images of domestic life.

During the 20th century, both the psychological and the technological Victorian concerns for the kitchen combined to dominate attitudes towards the room and the way in which it was used. Adjusting to peace in the aftermath of World War I, social thinkers and politicians became aware that a large section of the now decimated population had been unfit for active combat. The waging of "total war" required a healthier population than the ravages of insanitary 19th-century houses had provided for. The desire for hygiene, the advance of manufacturing techniques allowing the possibility of fully fitted furniture and appliances, requirements that women should be

Kitchens: German kitchen, Leipzig, 1880

able to function efficiently and without the help of servants, all contributed to the shaping of the modern kitchen.

During the 20th century, the kitchen has been a repository for all sorts of values and attitudes towards the home and its functions, towards the family and towards women. The history of this room is particularly revealing in terms of what it says about attitudes towards public and private life. In some ways it may be read as a microcosm of the larger house. From the communal cooking space that occupied a part of the medieval great hall to the separate but still public functions of the Dutch 16th-century house, through the 18th and 19th centuries when kitchens were the domain of servants, the early 20th century kitchen emerged as the housewife's room. In the late 20th century the room's functions have become more flexible again, the trend away from very neatly fitted streamlined units being mirrored by its use as a space for family living and for receiving visitors.

HARRIET DOVER

Further Reading

Beecher, Catherine, *A Treatise on Domestic Economy*, 1841; reprinted, with introduction by Kathryn Kish Sklar, New York: Schocken, 1977

Brett, Gerard, *Dinner is Served: A History of Dining in England, 1400–1900*, London: Hart Davis, 1968; as *Dinner is Served: A Study in Manners*, Hamden, CT: Archon, 1969

Conran, Terence, *The Kitchen Book*, London: Mitchell Beazley, and New York: Crown, 1977

Davidson, Caroline, *The Ham House Kitchen*, London: Victoria and Albert Museum, 1985

Davies, Jennifer, *The Victorian Kitchen*, London: BBC Books, 1989

Eat, Drink and be Merry (exhib. cat.), Brighton: Brighton Museums and Art Galleries, 1981

Forty, Adrian, *Objects of Desire: Design and Society, 1750–1980*, London: Thames and Hudson, and New York: Pantheon, 1986

Franklin, Jill, *The Gentleman's Country House and its Plan, 1835–1914*, London: Routledge, 1981

Garrett, Elisabeth Donaghy, *At Home: The American Family, 1750–1870*, New York: Abrams, 1990

Girouard, Mark, *Life in the English Country House: A Social and Architectural History*, New Haven and London: Yale University Press, 1978

Grover, Kathryn (editor), *Dining in America, 1850–1900*, Amherst: University of Massachusetts Press, 1987

Hardyment, Christina, *From Mangle to Microwave: The Mechanization of Household Work*, Cambridge: Polity, and New York: Blackwell, 1988

Hardyment, Christina, *Home Comfort: A History of Domestic Arrangements*, London: Viking, and Chicago: Academy, 1992

Harrison, Molly, *The Kitchen in History*, Reading: Osprey, and New York: Scribner, 1972

Lantz, Louise K., *Old American Kitchenware, 1725–1925*, Camden, NJ: Nelson, 1970

Norwak, Mary, *Kitchen Antiques*, New York: Praeger, and London: Ward Lock, 1975

Paston-Williams, Sara, *The Art of Dining: A History of Cooking and Eating*, London: National Trust, and New York: Abrams, 1993

Thompson, Michael, *The Medieval Hall: The Basis of Secular Domestic Life, 600–1600 AD*, Aldershot: Scolar Press, 1995

Thurley, Simon, "The Tudor Kitchen" in his *The Royal Palaces of Tudor England: Architecture and Court Life, 1460–1547*, New Haven and London: Yale University Press, 1993, pp.145–62

Wright, Lawrence, *Home Fires Burning: The History of Domestic Heating and Cooking*, London: Routledge, 1964

Yarwood, Doreen, *The British Kitchen: Housewifery since Roman Times*, London: Batsford, 1981

Klenze, Leo von 1784–1864

German architect

Leo von Klenze occupies a position in the history of German architecture comparable to that of his compatriot and contemporary, Karl Friedrich Schinkel. Both men were strongly influenced by classicism and both re-shaped royal cities – Munich in the case of Klenze, and Berlin in the case of Schinkel – in the Neo-Classical mode. Both were also architects, painters, and writers, and were fortunate in having royal patrons with sufficient funds to build extensively. And both were students of Friedrich Gilly in Berlin where they became friends.

Following the completion of his studies in Berlin, Klenze spent some time in Italy and in Paris, where he worked in the offices of Percier and Fontaine and was influenced by the teaching of J.N.L. Durand at the Ecole Polytechnique. Through connections made at the French court, Klenze received his first position, that of court architect for Napoleon's brother, Jérôme Bonaparte, who ruled over the newly created Kingdom of Westphalia. Jérôme commissioned Klenze's first building, the Court Theatre at Wilhelmshöhe, but when he was deposed in 1813 this source of patronage came to an end. Klenze was not without a patron for long, however, and in 1814 he met Crown Prince Ludwig, later Ludwig I, in Munich. The two men quickly established a rapport based on their shared appreciation of classical culture, and Klenze was invited to remain in Munich where he quickly supplanted Karl von Fischer as Königlicher Oberbaurat, architect to the king.

Like most classicists, Klenze celebrated pure geometry, monumental but simple form, the play of linear elements against planar surfaces, shallow relief, rich materials and colourful decoration in his work. His most notable buildings include various palaces, the Glyptothek (museum of antique sculpture), Pinakothek (art museum), Propyläen, Ruhmeshalle (Hall of Fame), and additions to the Residenz, all in Munich; the Walhalla (Temple of Fame) near Regensburg; the Befreiungshalle (Hall of Liberation) near Kelheim; and a major addition to the Hermitage in St. Petersburg. All are designed in a severe but colourful neo-Greek style.

The public art museum emerged as an important new building type in the early 19th century. Klenze designed three, two in Munich for his Bavarian patron, and one in St. Petersburg for Tsar Nicholas I. The Munich Glyptothek featured Hellenistic and Renaissance elements and had a richly coloured interior. Klenze believed that splendour and colour could make even the most undistinguished antique sculpture look fresh and pure and the sumptuousness of his decorations was therefore intended to present Ludwig's sculpture collection to best advantage. The Pinakothek, designed in 1822 (built 1826–36) to house the royal collection of paintings, was even more sumptuous and included seven top-lit galleries running along the centre of the first floor and a series of small chambers on the north side. Unfortunately both buildings were badly damaged in World War II and the interiors have not yet been restored. Klenze's addition to the Hermitage, built between 1832 and 1852, was a gray marble building organized around three courtyards and connected to Rastrelli's Winter Palace by bridges at the *piano nobile* level. Each of the three principal façades is different, although all are trabeated and designed in a fairly restrained style. As in Schinkel's Altes Museum in Berlin, the ground floor is reserved for the display of sculpture, and the *piano nobile* was arranged to accommodate the rest of the collections. Floors, steps and column capitals are made of white Carrara marble, the columns are light gray granite, and the walls are yellow Siena marble. The ceilings are coffered and the coffers and the panels in the wall frieze are filled with white reliefs against a blue ground. The layered architectural decoration and elaborate relief of the previous century have been banished, and the spaces are a series of contrasting geometric volumes made up of planar surfaces. The effect is one of serene monumentality and restrained grandeur.

Ludwig I had conceived of building a great monument to pan-German unity, a "Walhalla", in 1807, and he commissioned busts of German heroes to be displayed within it. A competition for the design was held in 1814 but no winners were announced. In 1819 he asked Klenze to supply new designs for the monument; plans were accepted in 1821 and the Walhalla building was constructed between 1830 and 1842. It is a colossal Greek temple, inspired by the Parthenon, and built of unpolished gray marble on a gigantic substructure of stairs and stepped terraces rising 300 feet above the Danube. Inside, the white marble busts are displayed against coloured and veined marble walls. Piers decorated with shallow pilasters of the same rich marble project from the walls to divide the space into three compartments. The lower wall is capped by a marble frieze carved by J. M. von Wagner illustrating the early history of Germany. An attic zone rises above the frieze. Above the piers painted and gilded caryatids, based on the examples sculpted on the Erechtheion but dressed in German bearskins instead of classical drapery, carry an ornamented gilt bronze ceiling. The walls are windowless and the only light admitted to the building enters through a skylight. The geometrical decoration of the floor emphasises the processional character of the space inside and leads to the statue of Ludwig by Andreas Schwanthaler which is the focus of the room. The Walhalla has been likened to a tomb or cenotaph, but an especially splendid one, and it remains one of the finest monuments to Neo-Classicism in the world.

Klenze designed a second great memorial building for a promontory near Kelheim, the Befreiungshalle, which commemorated Bavaria's liberation from the French. Although this building's function, scale and concept are similar to those of the Walhalla, its form is very different. Where the Walhalla follows the Greek temple form, the Befreiungshalle is a vast cylinder of golden stone dressed with figures, with a Doric colonnade executed in white marble. The design of the interior echoes that of the exterior. The wall is divided into three zones, the lowest of which features a ring of piers treated as dark marble Corinthian pilasters carrying a white marble segmental arcade. The piers front a ring of apsidal chapels with coffered half-domes and the pier capitals continue into the chapels as a sculpted frieze which separates the dark, richly-veined, marble wall-covering from the white and gold surfaces of the domes. The middle zone of the central space is polychromed ashlar

Klenze: Walhalla, near Regensburg, 1830–42

marble, lighter but more variable in colour than the marble of the lower dome. The unbroken wall of the middle zone carries a white marble Tuscan colonnade behind which can be seen a striated, coloured marble wall. This colonnade supports a deeply coffered gilded dome whose diagonal pattern is reflected in the pattern of the marble floor. Light is admitted from the oculus in the dome.

A talented and prolific draughtsman, Klenze also designed furniture and lighting for many of his buildings, including the Max-Palais, the Alte Pinakothek, the Königsbau and the Festsaalbau of the Munich Residenz, and the Hermitage Museum. Several of these have a strong Empire flavour and can be compared with the work of both Schinkel and Percier and Fontaine. On the whole, however, Klenze's designs were executed in a rich and massive Neo-Classical style that was strongly in keeping with the character of his buildings.

C. MURRAY SMART, JR.

Biography

Born in Bockenem near Hildesheim, Germany, 29 February 1784, the son of a wealthy lawyer. Studied architecture under Friedrich Gilly (1772–1800) and others, Berlin, 1800–03. Studied and worked in the office of Percier and Fontaine, Paris, 1803. Travelled to Italy, 1818, and 1823–24. Architect to Jérôme Bonaparte, king of Westphalia, Kassel, 1807–13; employed as court architect to Crown Prince Ludwig of Bavaria (later Ludwig I), and Max II, Munich, from 1816 (resigned offices, 1853). Travelled to Greece on behalf of King Ludwig, 1834; employed by Tsar Nicholas I, St. Petersburg, 1839. Designed furniture, lighting and interiors from c.1820. Also active as a prolific writer on architecture, and an archaeologist specializing in ancient Greece. Died in Munich, 27 January 1864.

Selected Works

Interiors

1812	Court Theatre, Wilhelmshöhe (building and interiors)
1816–31	Glyptothek (museum of antique sculpture), Munich (building and interiors)
1822–26	Max Palais, Munich (building, interiors and some furniture)
1826–35	Residenz, Königsbau, Munich (building, interiors and some furniture)
1826–36	Alte Pinakothek (picture gallery), Munich (building, interiors and some furniture)
1830–42	Walhalla (Temple of Fame), near Regensburg (building and interiors; including sculpture and carvings by J.M. von Wagner, Andreas Schwanthaler and others)
1832–52	Hermitage Museum, St. Petersburg, Russia (additions, interiors and some furniture)
1837–42	Residenz, Festsaalbau, Munich (building, interiors and some furniture)
1842–63	Befreiungshalle (Hall of Liberation), Kelheim, Bavaria (building and interiors)

Publications

Anweisung zur Architektur des christlichen Cultus, 1822, 1833
Sammlung architektonischer Entwürfe für die Ausführung bestimmt oder wirklich ausgeführt, 10 parts, 1830–50
Die Walhalla in artistischer und technischer Beziehung, 1843

Further Reading

Bottger, Peter, *Die alte Pinakothek in München*, Munich: Prestel, 1972
Ein griechischer Traum: Leo von Klenze, der Archäologe (exhib. cat.), Munich: Glyptothek, 1985
Hederer, Oswald, *Leo von Klenze: Persönlichkeit und Werk*, Munich: Callwey, 1981
Hufnagel, Florian, *Leo von Klenze und die Sammlung Architektonischer Entwürfe*, Worms: Wernersche, 1983
Kiener, Hans, *Leo von Klenze*, Ph.D. thesis, Munich: University of Munich, 1922
Klassizismus in Bayern, Shwaben und Franken: Architekturzeichnungen, 1775–1825, Munich: Stadtmuseum, 1980
Lieb, Norbert and Florian Hufnagel (editors), *Leo von Klenze: Gemälde und Zeichnungen*, Munich: Callwey, 1979
Schaefer, Veronika, *Leo von Klenze: Möbel und Innenräume*, Munich: Wölfle, 1980
Traeger, Jorg (editor), *Die Walhalla: Idee, Architektur, Landschaft*, Regensburg: Bosse, 1979
Watkin, David and Tilman Mellinghoff, *German Architecture and the Classical Ideal*, Cambridge: Massachusetts Institute of Technology Press, and London: Thames and Hudson, 1987

Knobelsdorff, Georg Wenceslaus von

1699–1753

German architect

Georg Wenceslaus (or Wenzeslaus) von Knobelsdorff was King Frederick II of Prussia's most important architect and is widely regarded as having brought the Prussian late Baroque – also known as "Frederick's Rococo" to an end. He blended elements of the Rococo, enriched by motifs from nature, with early classical tendencies and with elements of Palladianism, to form his own distinctive style. While elements of the early classical style often appear in his treatment of façades, his interiors mainly use Rococo or late Baroque forms, such as column or pilaster offsets, ornamental and organic decorations and caryatid motifs. And despite the diversity of his work and his varied approach to the modelling of ornamental decoration, common to all his interior designs are the restraint with which he handles decorative forms, and his paring down of decorative and ornamental devices even in buildings, such as Sanssouci, which include extremely complex systems of decoration.

Determining the extent of Knobelsdorff's involvement in his interiors is complicated by the fact that he employed a number of artists, including Frederick Christian Glume, Johann August Nahl, Johann Michael Hoppenhaupt, Johann Christian Hoppenhaupt, and Antoine Pesne, to execute the stucco, painting and sculptural work. But although the individual achievements of these artists should not be overlooked, the overall conception for the interiors always lay with Knobelsdorff himself. This is clearly demonstrated in Knobelsdorff's architectural drawings, especially in those few that show details of his designs for interiors such as the complete set of plans and drawings for the Berlin State Opera House. The exact nature of the role played by his patron, Frederick, however, is more complex. Frederick had strong views about the design of his palaces which sometimes, particularly in the case of the Vineyard Castle, Sanssouci, resulted in his interfering with Knobelsdorff's plans, and historians continue to debate the respective contributions made by architect and patron to the finished works. Nevertheless, whatever the extent of

Knobelsdorff: marble hall, Schloss Sanssouci, Potsdam, 1745–48

Frederick's interventions, Knobelsdorff's role within the design of the exteriors and interiors of his buildings should not be underestimated.

One of Knobelsdorff's earliest works was his alterations to Rheinsberg Castle, the home of the Crown Prince, in 1737–40. He changed the plans of his predecessor, Kemmeter, which included rooms arranged *enfilade*, to a corridor system designed to unify the Writing Chamber, the Library and the Gallery in the Tower. The decoration includes overdoors with painted floral ornament, ceiling paintings by Pesne which are thematically linked to the function of the rooms, and bright stuccoed marble and wall mirrors which have the effect of extending the space in the Hall.

In 1740–43, Knobelsdorff built the new wing of the Schloss Charlottenburg which was to serve as King Frederick's official residence. This wing contained a long banqueting hall with 14 rooms on both sides of the stairwell; it was dominated by the Golden Gallery. The ground plan adheres strictly to French prototypes of the kind described by Blondel in his *Cours d'Architecture*. The Golden Gallery features green stuccoed marble and a rich variety of gilded Rococo ornament, executed by Nahl, that changes from one section of wall to another. As in Knobelsdorff's work at Rheinsberg, representations of the Four Elements and the Four Seasons form part of the iconographic programme.

Whereas the Golden Gallery is totally dominated by Rococo forms, the design of the hallway and stairs (a hall-like vestibule with entrance steps joining from the side) reveals the emergence of early classical tendencies. Ionic double pilasters of yellowish stuccoed marble, with gilded bases and capitals, order the first floor area and form a contrast with the plain walls of the ground floor. The stucco ledge at the uppermost point of the first floor is defined by the figures of Europa, Apollo, Diana, and Night, and the ceiling contains Pesne's painting of *Prometheus Stealing Fire from the Gods*.

The German State Opera House, in Berlin (1740–43), was planned as the principal component in the Forum Fridericanum, a project that was never completed. It was the first free-standing, purpose-built opera house in Europe. Knobelsdorff drew on Palladian textbooks in his proportioning of some of the architectural elements, and the building itself was conceived in the tradition of the Italian box theatre. The auditorium, consisting of a box theatre with four circles, was extremely sumptuous and included much splendid ornament and organic decoration. Because of the lavishness of the overall decorative scheme, the *Loge de la Reine* was not accorded much more importance than any of the other boxes. The stage was flanked with Corinthian columns which were a continuation of those along the outer walls of the theatre, while pilasters bordered the rear. The stage and auditorium could also be combined to form one space when it was used as the Court's banqueting hall. The area in front of the auditorium was taken up on the main floor by the Apollo Hall which featured a gallery, whose balustrade was supported by Hermes pilasters, which was positioned in the upper third of the space. The stage and auditorium built by Knobelsdorff onto the north-east corner of Potsdam Castle's pavilion (1744) have similar structural details.

Knobelsdorff's chief work was the Vineyard Castle, Sanssouci (1745–48). Although he clearly had to pay heed to ideas and plans put forward by Frederick, Knoblesdorff had overall control of the design of the building and its interiors. Indeed, Frederick described the Marble Hall and the vestibule as Knobelsdorff's personal creations, adding that he was said to have drawn upon the Pantheon for the interiors (Kadatz, 1983). Ten pairs of powerful stuccoed marble Corinthian columns dominate the space of the vestibule and can be seen as a continuation of the colonnades on the exterior. Like the vine leaf ornament used on the doors, these columns demonstrate Knoblesdorff's interest in harmonising the interior and exterior features of the building. The design of the Marble Hall features double Corinthian columns, made of Carrara marble with capitals of gilded bronze, standing in front of pilasters. It also includes a dramatic cupola, which is ordered by coffered fields and oval medallions and trophies incorporated into the banding. Four groups of almost free-standing putti on the ledge bordering the cupola carry the emblems of the arts and sciences and illustrate the patron's promotion of these occupations. The marble encrustation of the floor was designed by J.C. Hoppenhaupt; the walls are lined with red-grey and reddish-yellow marble.

Only a small number of Knobelsdorff's interiors have been preserved in their original state, and many of the buildings that he worked on have been subject to frequent later alterations. Some rooms in the Schloss Rheinsberg, for example, were remodelled by Carl Gotthard Langhans in 1762–69 and again by Boumann in 1786, and Sanssouci has also been repeatedly altered. Similarly, Knobelsdorff's work at Frederick's mother's residence, Monbijou (1740–42), the series of apartments that he designed in Berlin Castle (1741–42), and his interior alterations at Potsdam (1744–46), were all destroyed during World War II. The Berlin State Opera House and the New Wing of Charlottenburg Castle have both been restored, but, even so, the demands of a modern theatre in the one case and insufficient documentary evidence in the other, have meant that some departures from the original appearance of these interiors have been inevitable.

BETTINA JOST

Biography

Born near Crossen, Brandenburg (now Krosno Odrzanskie, Poland), 17 February 1699. Served in the Prussian army, 1714–29; retired due to ill health. Studied painting at the Berlin Academy under the French painter, Antoine Pesne (1683–1757), and architecture with A. von Wangenheim and J.G. Kemmeter. With royal support, visited Rome, 1736–37. Had two daughters by Sophie Charlotte Schöne. Returned to work with Crown Prince Frederick of Prussia on Schloss Rheinsberg. Appointed Surintendant des Bâtiments et Jardins by the new King Frederick, and visited Paris, 1740. Also designed furniture, collaborating with Johann August Nahl (1710–85), the brothers, Johann Christian Hoppenhaupt (1719–1778/86) and Johann Michael Hoppenhaupt (b.1709). Died in Berlin, 16 September 1753.

Selected Works

A large collection of Knobelsdorff's drawings, including plans and designs for the interior of the Berlin Opera House, is in the Kupferstichkabinett, Berlin.

Interiors

1737–40	Schloss Rheinsberg (study, library and Tower Cabinet): Crown Prince Frederick of Prussia (later King)
1740–42	Schloss Monbijou (building and interiors): Frederick the Great (for his mother)
1740–43	Schloss Charlottenburg, Berlin (new wing: 14 rooms, including "Goldene Galerie", staircase): Frederick the Great
1741–42	Berlin Town Castle (suite of apartments): Frederick the Great
1741–43	Opera House, Berlin (building and interiors, including the Hall of Apollo)
1744–46	Potsdam Town Castle (theatre for "Schlosspavillion" and rearrangement as official residence): Frederick the Great
1745–48	Schloss Sanssouci, Potsdam (summer palace; building and interiors): Frederick the Great

Further Reading

Eggeling 1980, includes an important study of Knobelsdorff's career; both this and Giersberg 1986 have useful bibliographies.

Badstübner-Gröger, Sibylle, *Bibliographie zur Kunstgeschichte von Berlin und Potsdam*, Berlin: Deutsche Akademie, 1968

Eckardt, Götz, *Sanssouci: Die Schlösser und Gärten*, Berlin: Henschel, 1990

Eggeling, Tilo, "Beiträge zur Baugeschichte von Schloss Rheinsberg: Der Umbau des märkischen Landsitzes zur Residenz des Kronprinzen Friedrich (II)", in Detlef Heikamp (editor), *Schlösser, Gärten Berlin*, Tübingen: Wasmuth, 1980, pp.61–82

Eggeling, Tilo, *Studien zum friderizianischen Rokoko: Georg Wenceslaus von Knobelsdorff als Entwerfer von Innendekorationen*, Berlin: Mann, 1980
Eggeling, Tilo, "Probleme der dekorativen Ausgestaltung der Friderizianischen Schlösser" in *Zeitschrift des Deutschen Vereins für Kunstwissenschaft*, 42, 1988, pp.9–22
Giersberg, Hans-Joachim, *Friedrich als Bauherr: Studien zur Architektur des 18. Jhs. in Berlin und Potsdam*, Berlin: Siedler, 1986
Historische Theaterbauten in Deutschland: Ein Katalog (part 2: Eastern Federal States), Erfurt, 1994
Kadatz, Hans-Joachim, *Georg Wenzeslaus von Knobelsdorff: Baumeister Friedrichs II*, Munich: Beck, 1983
Kadatz, Hans-Joachim, "Georg Wenzelaus von Knobelsdorff", in *Grosse Baumeister*, Berlin: Argon, 1987, pp.47–90
Meffert, Erich, *Das Haus der Staatsoper und seine neue Gestaltung*, Leipzig: Beck, 1944
Mielke, Friedrich, *Potsdamer Baukunst: Das klassische Potsdam*, Frankfurt: Propyläen, 1981
Schrader, Susanne, *Architektur der barocken Hoftheater in Deutschland*, Munich: Scaneg, 1988
Streichhan, Anneliese, *Knobelsdorff und das Friderizianische Rokoko*, Burg bei Magdeburg: Hopfer, 1932
Zielske, Harald, *Deutsche Theaterbauten bis zum zweiten Weltkrieg*, Berlin: Gesellschaft für Theatergeschichte, 1971

Knoll International

American furniture manufacturers and interior designers; established 1938

Knoll International was originally founded in 1939 by the scion of three generations of German furniture makers, Hans Knoll. Upon going into partnership with his wife Florence Schust, the company's name was changed to Knoll Associates, and was changed again to Knoll International with the development of a worldwide organization.

Hans was captivated by the Bauhaus concept, and Florence had studied both at Cranbrook with Eliel Saarinen, and with Mies van der Rohe at Illinois Institute of Technology, so they had similar attitudes toward the use of materials and techniques in the industrial era and toward the integration of furniture and furnishings within an overall concept of design. The husband and wife team both shared and divided their areas of responsibility, with Hans more concerned with the manufacturing and marketing processes and Florence developing the textiles division and the idea of the overall design. Having studied textiles while at Cranbrook and realizing the potential of a readily available source of fabrics in the service of a design concept, Florence incorporated the idea of using both in-house and external designers for each major project. Hans died in an automobile accident in 1955 and Florence continued with the firm, as president until 1959 and as a design consultant until she retired in 1965.

Although Hans Knoll set the direction of the firm, including contracting for the exclusive right to manufacture and distribute pieces such as Mies van der Rohe's already well known *Barcelona* chair, his early death meant that the phenomenal growth of the company as a giant of interior design and of widely-recognized signature furniture is primarily the legacy of Florence Knoll. Trained as an architect and respected for her sympathy and understanding of architectural issues, she was always able to attract and maintain the support of internationally known designers, who not only produced designs for the company but also acted as clients. Recognizing her strength and abilities in this arena, the firm was restructured at an early stage to allow her to direct her own interior design operation, the Knoll Planning Unit (established in 1943). After her husband's death, Florence Knoll also developed an innovative way of franchising manufacturers to work within Knoll International, and expanded the showroom operations throughout the world.

Among those artists and architects brought into the firm, either as staff designers or on contract, were the artist Harry Bertoia (1915–78), the architect and furniture designer, Eero Saarinen (1910–61), the designer Jens Risom (b.1916), and the fabric designers Arne Jacobsen (1902–71) and Astrid Sampe (b.1909).The firm's reputation was also increased through the purchase of companies such as Gavina, which enabled it to acquire the work of Marcel Breuer and Kazuhide Takahama, and through the acquisition of the rights to distribute such designs as Hans Wegner's *Peacock* chair, as Hans Knoll had earlier done with Mies's *Barcelona* chair. Even the sculptor Isamu Noguchi produced two designs for the firm, a lamp and a stool, having already designed a chair for Herman Miller. Designs such as the Breuer *Wassily* chair and the Mies van der Rohe *Barcelona* chair had been in production before Hans Knoll had started his business, and Eero Saarinen's *Pedestal* chair was more the result of friendship than a business relationship with Florence Knoll. Nevertheless, the integration of these designs into their furniture line, advertising, and image was so complete and seamless, that both the designers and their creations have become synonymous with the firm of Knoll International.

At a time when Herman Miller was the only major competitor for the planning of office spaces, the Knoll Planning Unit developed the notion of conceiving and formulating the design for a business interior with the cooperation of the client. Going beyond the interior designer model of suggesting specific furniture and desired groupings or compatible pieces, the Knoll group's approach was to develop a plan to explore the projected use of space, furniture, and even mechanical equipment systems. The Planning Unit's designers would elicit the client's needs with regard to space and function and enable them to become more aware of real rather than perceived needs. Finally, the Unit would suggest the size and scale of the space; recommend the number and type of furniture units; and such elements of detail as the colors of walls, fabrics, and objects of art. The international importance of this design approach was recognized in the early 1950s when there was a major exhibition of the Knoll designs at the large Paris department store, Le Printemps, and artistic validation was achieved with a 1972 exhibition at the Louvre.

Florence Knoll's last major commission, for CBS (Columbia Broadcasting System), was one of her most important projects and most clearly illustrates the Planning Unit concept. Upon the unexpected death of Eero Saarinen, the CBS building's architect, the president of CBS asked her to design the 35 floors of the building. Florence's task was to create an integrated and sympathetic environment for some 2700 employees who would use the 868 rooms as offices, conference rooms,

Knoll International: CBS offices, New York, by Florence Knoll

secretarial areas, screening rooms, and lounges, within the framework of the exterior design already articulated by Saarinen. She designed all of the rooms, including the office furniture, selecting the texture and color of fabrics, and the graphics, paintings, and sculpture. Recognizing the nature of conferences and executive meetings, she designed much of the furniture – including desks – as flat but elegant work surfaces. Little in the way of drawers or storage spaces was included, as few papers and records were kept directly by the executives. For this and other major design accomplishments, Florence Knoll received many awards from the Museum of Modern Art and the design industry. In 1961 she was awarded the highly prestigious Gold Medal of the American Institute of Architects in recognition "of her broad role in developing interior design and manufacture of furniture, textiles, and interior design accessories in the service of contemporary architecture here and abroad."

Without Florence Knoll to run it, the Planning Unit was abandoned in 1971, but the concept of overall planning has been resurrected in the Japanese arm of Knoll International, keeping the Bauhaus approach alive in at least that part of the world.

Working in reciprocity with architects was always a two-way street for Knoll International, and one of their signatures has been the design of their showrooms by highly established contemporary architects. The Boston showroom was designed by the partnership of Charles Gwathmey and Robert Siegel; one in New York by Robert Venturi; the Houston showroom was by Stanley Tigerman; the Houston design was by Sally Walsh. Similarly, in Europe and Asia local architects were given these highly visible commissions, even after Florence Knoll had left the firm. Retiring early to live in Florida with her second husband, Florence Knoll ceased having any direct influence on the company, but the design concepts, approach to integration of furniture and furnishings, and quality control all continue to the present day. The subject of several corporate mergers and purchases, Knoll International is one of the most readily identified design companies, and its many classic designs can be found in offices, homes, and museums. It is a tribute to the success of the furniture designs of the company that even where regional or national tastes suggest a different approach to design, Knoll designs are in high demand.

JOHN F. PILE

See also Offices

Selected Works

The Knoll Archives at Knoll International, New York, include copies of the company's catalogues, publicity material, photographs and transcripts of interviews with designers. Examples of furnishings produced by Knoll International are featured in most American museums specialising in 20th-century design; notable collections, also including examples of Florence Knoll's work, are in the Metropolitan Museum of Art, and the Museum of Modern Art, New York, and the Cranbrook Academy, Bloomfield Hills, Michigan.

Interiors

1949–50	Connecticut General Life Insurance Company, Bloomfield, Connecticut (building by Skidmore, Owings and Merrill; interiors by Knoll Planning Unit)
1951	Knoll Showrooms, 757 Madison Avenue, New York (interiors)
1957	Rockefeller Institute, New York (atrium and library)
1958	H.J. Heinz Co., Pittsburgh (entrance lobby and conference room)
1964	Columbia Broadcasting System Headquarters, Madison Avenue, New York (building by Eero Saarinen; interiors by Florence Knoll for Knoll)
1970	Knoll Showrooms, 745 Fifth Avenue, New York (interiors by Gae Aulenti for Knoll)
1974	Weyerhaeuser Co., Tacoma, Washington (building by Skidmore, Owings and Merrill; office system by Bill Stephens for Knoll)

Knoll International have produced furniture by numerous designers prominent in the Modern Movement including Harry Bertoia, Eero Saarinen, Jens Risom, Franco Albini, Ilmari Tapiovaara, Isamu Noguchi, Marcel Breuer, Carlo Scarpa, Vico Magistretti, Gae Aulenti, Niels Diffrient, Robert Venturi and Joe D'Urso. The company's textiles have included work by Florence Knoll, Astrid Sampe, and Anni Albers.

Further Reading

A comprehensive and well-illustrated account of the history of Knoll International and its designers appears in Larrabee and Vignelli 1981 which also includes a select bibliography and a list of the firm's catalogues and brochures.

Bauhaus and Knoll Textiles, Tokyo: Kashuma Shupponkai, 1989

Bill Stephens: Furniture and Office Systems (exhib. cat.), Philadelphia: Philadelphia College of Art, 1981

Byars, Mel, "Florence Knoll" in Mel Byars and Russell Flinchum (editors), *50 American Designers*, Washington, DC: Preservation Press, forthcoming

"Distinguished Interior Architecture for CBS" in *Architectural Record*, June 1966

Friedmann, Arnold, John F. Pile and Forrest Wilson, *Interior Design: An Introduction to Architectural Interiors*, 3rd edition New York: Elsevier, 1982

Guelft, Olga, "Florence Knoll and the Avant Garde" in *Interiors* (US), July 1957

Hiesinger, Kathryn B. and George H. Marcus III (editors), *Design since 1945* (exhib. cat.), Philadelphia: Philadelphia Museum of Art, and London: Thames and Hudson, 1983

Izutsu, Akio, *The Bauhaus: A Japanese Perspective and a Profile of Hans and Florence Schust Knoll*, Tokyo: Kajima Institute, 1992

Knoll Bassett, Florence, "The Interiors at C.B.S." in *Office Design*, May 1966

Larrabee, Eric and Massimo Vignelli, *Knoll Design*, New York: Abrams, 1981

Louie, Elaine, "The Many Lives of a Very Common Chair" in *New York Times*, 7 February 1991, p.10

A Modern Consciousness: D.J. De Pree and Florence Knoll (exhib. cat.), Washington, DC: Renwick Gallery, 1975

Niels Diffrient: Knoll Seating (exhib. cat.), Bloomfield Hills, MI: Cranbrook Academy of Art Museum, 1980

Rae, Christina, *Knoll au Louvre* (exhib. cat.), Paris: Musée des Arts Décoratifs, 1972

Sembach, Klaus-Jürgen (editor), *Contemporary Furniture*, New York: Architectural Book Publishing, and London: Design Council, 1982

Stein, Margery B., "Teaching Steelcase to Dance" in *New York Times Magazine Business World*, 1 April 1990

Tucker, John G., "Knoll Building, Houston" in *Interior Design* (US), 55, June 1984, pp.264–71

Korsmo, Arne 1900–1968

Norwegian architect and designer of interiors, furnishings and exhibitions

A leading exponent of the Scandinavian Modern and Scandinavian Design Movements, Arne Korsmo was also an international Modernist inspired by Walter Gropius, Le Corbusier, Charles Eames and Alvar Aalto. Indeed, he was more committed to internationalist ideas than any other Norwegian architect and designer and he introduced important foreign impulses to the Norwegian design milieu. Active both as an architect and designer, he was also closely involved in interior design. Within this context, his work was characterised by two main features: first by his elegant constellations of space, light, colour and texture, combined with exquisite proportioning and attention to detail, and second by his ability to place the different objects in a room in a scenographic unity, thereby creating uniquely artistic interiors.

Korsmo received a classical architectural education at the Norwegian Institute of Technology in Trondheim, where he graduated in 1926. He practised at some of the country's leading architectural firms, Bryn and Ellefsen (1926–27) and later Arneberg and Poulsson (1928). In 1929 he went into business with with Sverre Aasland, and in 1935 he established his own office.

By 1928 Functionalism had fully manifested itself in Norway. Korsmo, like many other Norwegian architects, changed his style from modern classicism to Functionalism. His interiors, however, remained reminiscent of Art Deco until about 1930. His own flat from 1929–30 (Lille Frøens vei 14, Oslo, destroyed) shows the use of vivid colours like red, black and silver, and walls decorated with murals in his own design. The ceiling had indirect lighting, and curtains were used as partitions. The tubular furniture was of his own design. He had turned the rooms into three-dimensional compositions instead of furnishing them in the old-fashioned way.

In the mid-1930s he designed a number of cubically formed houses clearly influenced by Le Corbusier and Pierre Chareau, the most characteristic being those in Slemdalsveien 33a-c, Oslo, from about 1936. The interiors are in a simpler style; they have a brighter colour scheme and are more spacious but with a similar emphasis on refined details and light effects. The furniture was made mostly of wood. The wooden furniture, like the chairs in Villa Benjamin (Slemdalsveien 33a), had a soft and organic design corresponding to the natural character of the material. It bore a certain resemblance to the organic wooden furniture of Alvar Aalto in Finland and Bruno Mathsson in Sweden, but it was more moderate in form and construction. Korsmo's Modernist mural in the same building was destroyed by the German occupants during World War II, who deemed it to be "entartete Kunst" (degenerate art).

In the years around 1930 Korsmo designed a restaurant and several shop interiors. These included the crafts shop *Petit Art* (Drammensveien 4, Oslo, destroyed), designed for his friend Louis Benjamin in 1931, which contained a painting that covered a whole wall. The interior was dominated by geometric forms, white and blue colours, and chrome details. The staircase and rail were clearly influenced by those on ships' decks, and were similar to those in Le Corbusier's interiors of the 1920s. Large windows facilitated practical and elegant displays of the shop's goods. In 1937 Korsmo designed a ladies' fashion shop for the designer Frode Braathen (Fridtjof Nansens plass 5, Oslo, destroyed). The showroom was decked out in blue velvet, with ivory white and chrome details; an ivory white relief by the architect was the only decoration. It formed a sensual, ultramodern and at the same time simple background perfectly suited to the display of exclusive clothes. A tubular steel bar for examining the latest in clothing textiles added to the urban and modern atmosphere of the shop.

During the last years of World War II Korsmo lived in Stockholm where he began to develop an interest in Japanese architecture and design. During this period he became acquainted with the Danish architect Jørn Utzon (later renowned for the Sydney Opera House) and in the years immediately after the war the two collaborated on several competition projects, ranging from town planning to the design of glass and furniture. They also participated in the Museum of Modern Art's International Low-cost Furniture Competition in 1948–49. Unfortunately, however, none of their projects was realized.

After the war Korsmo found it difficult to obtain architectural commissions despite the fact that many building projects were initiated in response to the urgent need for new housing. His modernity, exclusivity and internationalism were not esteemed in the more traditionally oriented post-war period. His wife, the goldsmith and enamel designer Grete Prytz Korsmo (now Grete Prytz Kittelsen) encouraged him to take part in the creation of a new collection of domestic objects for her family's goldsmith firm, J. Tostrup. These objects, which he designed in close collaboration with his wife, had avant-garde forms and used unconventional combinations of materials such as silver and plastic. Stylistically they can be termed Scandinavian Modern and are forerunners of the Scandinavian Design movement in the 1950s. His most renowned work for Tostrup is the silver plate cutlery *Korsmo* for which he received a gold medal at the Milan Triennale in 1954.

The Oslo home that Grete and Arne Korsmo occupied from 1950 (flat in Løkenveien 12, Oslo, interior destroyed) demonstrates Korsmo's artistic inventiveness in the difficult period after the war. The interiors represent one of the first examples of the influence of Japanese design, which was to have a strong impact on Scandinavian design during the 1950s, and represent a flat, or rather a "room within the room" contained within a conventional post-war house. The original internal walls as well as the windows were hidden by screen walls consisting of frames in Oregon pine covered with white canvas which allowed the light to get through. In front of the windows the screens could be drawn aside when needed. The plan was open with cabinet units used as partitions. The ceiling was "Korsmo blue", a term that emerged as a result of his frequent use of blue in various nuances throughout his career. The decoration consisted of a mixture of the couple's own works and objects collected on their trip to the USA and Mexico in 1949–50, including a mobile by Alexander Calder, wooden articles by James Prestini, furniture by Charles Eames and Indian cult objects. The different artifacts were arranged in a way that made them constitute a unity, a masterful scenography typical of Korsmo.

Korsmo's main work after the war is his and his wife Grete's house in Planetveien 12 in Oslo, built between 1952 and 1955 in collaboration with the architect Christian Norberg-Schulz. The house was based on a modular steel frame. It was planned as both home and workplace and in addition to the two studios – one for Arne and another for Grete – it contained a living room that was intended to be used for various activities like design experiments, slide lectures, and theatre performances. The living room was the largest and most important room of the house and had a large roof unsupported by columns. The room was somewhat reminiscent of a cave; one wall was entirely taken up by windows that provided a magnificent view of the surrounding landscape while the rest of the room was decorated in wood and bright colours. The core of the room was the open fireplace, situated on a slightly lower level. It included a low seating arrangement and its design paralleled that of Japanese tea rooms where people gathered for peace and contemplation under the supervision of a tea master. (This parallel was pointed out by Korsmo himself in an article entitled "Japan og Vestens Arkitektur", 1956.) The furniture consisted partly of square pillows made of foam rubber covered with vividly coloured textiles which were intended to be arranged according to each person's need and convenience. It also included low tables and light, collapsible wickerwork deck chairs which could be carried out to the terrace. The remaining furniture was built-in. The paintings could be moved around the room to take advantage of the changing light conditions and temporary needs. The colour scheme was developed in collaboration with the painter Gunnar S. Gundersen who was also responsible for the large wall painting by the hoistable stair to the first floor. In this building art, architecture and interior design were unified into a harmonious whole.

During the 1930s Korsmo became immensely successful as an exhibition architect; he was one of the architects behind Norway's pavilion at the Paris Universal Exposition in 1937 and the *Vi Kan* exhibition in Oslo in 1938, and after the war he was frequently used as a designer of exhibitions of applied art. He was awarded a Grand Prix for his work on the Norwegian Section at the tenth Milan Triennale in 1954. The design was based on a modular structure made of oregon pine and a carefully planned colour scheme, which together helped to unify the various parts of the exhibition. Emphasis was put on suggesting the atmosphere of an ideal modern home, and the few carefully chosen objects were arranged in a domestic fashion. Korsmo controlled the selection of artifacts, which included some of his own designs, and created an artistic unity that was approved by the jury of the Triennale.

Korsmo was also responsible for the design of one of the two Norwegian sections at the next Triennale in 1957. His last great commission as an interior designer was the rebuilding of Britannia Hotel in Trondheim (1961–63) with Terje Moe, which was executed in an extremely simple and elegant style.

Korsmo's *Hjemmets mekano* (Home-erector-set), a wall chart worked out in 1952, presented the theoratical basis for not only his interior designs but also his whole artistic activity. He believed that man's natural activity and creativity should not be hampered but stimulated by his surroundings. The building and interior components should therefore be adjusted according to a module, and a system of standardised components would make it possible for modern dwellers to create a home which fulfilled their needs. As a designer, however, Korsmo often favoured his own aesthetic tastes rather than the wishes of his customers. And although he always designed the furniture for his own architecture, none of his work was ever mass-produced. His designs were clearly too innovative for Norwegian furniture manufacturers.

Finally, Korsmo also exercised a great influence on the post-war generation of interior designers in Norway in his work as a teacher. He taught interior and furniture design at the National College of Art and Design between 1934 and 1956 and took part in numerous educational reforms that were inspired largely by the ideas and practices of the Bauhaus school. Indeed, he was the first person in Norway to teach interior design after modern principles and, drawing together a team of students from the school's various departments, he encouraged his pupils to devise complete interiors including furniture, textiles, and tablewares. In 1945 a group of his former students created the Norwegian Federation of Interior and Furniture Designers. In 1956 he was appointed professor of architecture at the Norwegian Institute of Technology in Trondheim where he established a space-laboratory, experimenting with the intercommunication of form, space and colour in collaboration with his students.

Although a main exponent of the Scandinavian Modern and Scandinavian Design Movement Korsmo was the internationalist *par excellence* among Norwegian architects and designers. In this way he brought important foreign impulses to the Norwegian design milieu.

ASTRID SKJERVEN

See also Scandinavian Modern

Biography

Born in Oslo, 14 August 1900. Studied architecture at the Norwegian Institute of Technology, Trondheim, Dip.Arch., 1926; toured Europe on a Henrichsens Fellowship, 1928–29. Married 1) Åse Thiis, 1928; 2) Grete Prytz, 1945; 3) Hanne Refsdal, 1965; 3 daughters. Architect in the offices of Bryn and Ellefsen, Oslo, 1926–27, and Arneberg and Poulsson, Oslo, 1928. In private practice with Sverre Aasland, Oslo, from 1929; established his own office, 1935. Local government architect, Kristiansund, Norway, 1940–41; lived in Sweden during the last part of the war, 1943–45; resumed private practice, Oslo, 1945. Toured US on a Fulbright Fellowship, 1949–50, and Japan, 1960. Designed interiors and furniture from the late 1920s; designed metalwork and tableware from 1947. Teacher, and later Head of the Department of Furniture and Interior Design, National College of Art and Design, Oslo, 1934–43 and 1945–56; Professor of Architecture, Norwegian Institute of Technology, Trondheim, 1956–68. Founder of the Norwegian section of CIAM (Congrès Internationaux d'Architecture Moderne), 1950. Exhibited at several national and international exhibitions including Milan 1954, 1957 and 1960, US 1954–57 (touring exhibition), and Australia 1968–69 (touring exhibition). Awarded the Grand Prize, Triennale, Milan, 1954. Died in Cuzco, Peru, 29 August 1968.

Selected Works

Examples of Korsmo's furniture and tableware are in the Oslo Museum of Applied Art, the Nordenfjeldske Museum of Applied Art, and the West Norway Museum of Applied Art. A full list of his architectural commissions appears in *Norsk Kunstnerleksikon*, 1983.

Interiors

1929	Bagatelle Restaurant, Bygdøy Allé, Oslo (interior with Sverre Aasland)
1929	Shops, Bygdøy Allé 3 and 7, Oslo (interiors with Sverre Aasland)
1929–30	Korsmo Apartment, Lille Frøens vei 14, Oslo (interiors and furnishings)
1930	Dammann House, Havna Allé 15, Oslo (building and interiors with Sverre Aasland)
1930	Korsmo House, Havna Allé 12, Oslo (building with Sverre Aasland, interiors and furnishings)
1931	Petit Art, Drammensveien 4, Oslo (shop interior and furniture)
1935	Villa Riise, Hamar (building and interiors with Sverre Aasland)
1936	Benjamin House, Slemdalsveien 33a, Oslo (building, interiors and furnishings)
1937	Shop, Fridtjof Nansens plass 5, Oslo (interiors and furnishings)
1937	Norwegian Pavilion, World's Fair, Paris (design of the building and exhibition layouts with Knut Knutsen and Ole Lind Schistad)
1937	Villa Stenersen, Oslo (building and interiors)
1938	Vi Kan, Oslo (exhibition layout with Knut Knutsen and Andreas Nygaard)
1950	Korsmo Apartment, Løkenveien 12, Oslo (interiors and furnishings)
1952–55	Korsmo House, Planetveien 12, Oslo (building with Christian Norberg-Schulz; interiors and furnishings)
1954	Triennale, Milan (design of the Norwegian section)
1957	Triennale, Milan (design of the two Norwegian sections)
1961–63	Britannia Hotel, Trondheim (rebuilding and interiors with Terje Moe)

Korsmo designed custom-made furniture for his interiors from 1929. He also designed glassware, cutlery and silverware 1947–58; his silverware and cutlery were produced by J. Tostrup, Oslo. With his wife Grete Prytz Korsmo he also designed items in enamelled stainless steel for Cathrineholm.

Publications

"Moderne Boligbygg Krever Moderne Mobler" in *Vi Selv og Vare Hjem*, no. 6, 1936, pp.16–18, 49–50

"Farveglede: Brev til en Venn" in *Vi Selv og Vare Hjem*, no.12, 1936, pp.34–35, 72

"Romeksperimenter: Innredning av egen Leilighet pa Bygdoy" in *Byggekunst*, 33, 1952, pp.40–42

"Tremannsbolig ved to av dem" in *Byggekunst*, 36, 1955, pp.169–89 (with Christian Norberg-Schulz)

"Japan og Vestens Arkitektur" in *Byggekunst*, 37, 1956, pp.70–75

"Til unge Arkitektsinn" in *A5*, 9, no.1–2, 1956, pp.40–55

"La Boutique Estetique et Tecnique" in *Nordenfjeldske Kunstindustrimuseum: Arbok*, 1957, pp.85–89, 93–119

Further Reading

A good English-language study of Korsmo's career appears in Norberg-Schulz 1986 which also includes bibliographical references.

Cappelen, Per and Christian Norberg-Schulz, *Knut Knutsen / Arne Korsmo* (exhib. cat.), Hovikodden, Norway: Henie-Onstad Kunstsenter, 1972

Christiansen, Solveig Lonne, "Eksperimenter i Rom" in *Byggekunst*, 71, 1989, pp.202–05

Emanuel, Muriel (editor), *Contemporary Architects*, 3rd edition Detroit: St. James Press, 1994, p.535

Huldt, Ake, "Korsmo Design" in *Form* (Stockholm), 52, 1956, pp.10–16

Lund, Nils Ole, "Arne Korsmo og den Norske Funktionalisme" in *Byggekunst*, 48, 1966, pp.2–11

McFadden, David Revere (editor), *Scandinavian Modern Design, 1880–1980* (exhib. cat.: Cooper-Hewitt Museum, New York), New York: Abrams, 1982

Norberg-Schulz, Christian, *The Functionalist Arne Korsmo*, Oslo: Universitetsforlaget, 1986

Norsk Kunstnerleksikon, vol.2, Oslo: Universitetsforlaget, 1983, pp.586–89

Ponti, Gio, "La Norvegia alla Triennale" in *Domus*, November 1954, pp.25–29

Skjerven, Astrid, *Arne Korsmo: Designvirksomhet i etterkrigstiden*, Oslo: Universitetet i Oslo, IAKN, 1996

Skjerven, Astrid, "'Material, Technique, and Requirements': Arne Korsmo's Flatware" in *Scandinavian Journal of Design History*, 6, 1996, pp.54–61

Teigen, Karl, "Nye Solvarbeider" in *Bonytt* (Oslo), 9, 1949, pp.81–85

Wildhagen, Fredrik, *Norge i Form*, Oslo: Stenersen, 1988

L

Lace

The close association between interior design and curtains or other drapery of walls and furniture is centuries old. Bleak stone walls with glassless windows required coverings for warmth, and beds needed hangings to keep out the draughts. Many of the early furnishings were of brightly-tinted wool, silk-velvets or damasks, but long before lace became an essential part of fashion its heavier furnishing forms of knotted nets, leno weaves, drawnworks and cutworks, were being exploited for decoration and comfort.

The knotted nets (known as *filet* or *lacis*) were worked in the manner of a fishing net, the square meshes having knots at every corner. The design, often Gothic or representational in a primitive style lacking both proportion and perspective, was added by a darning or running stitch. Leno weaves were embroidered in either white linen or coloured silk threads, using similar stitches. To make the drawnworks, counted numbers of warps and wefts were drawn out in whole or in part from solidly woven linens, the design being left as areas of the original cloth, or added later yet again in a darning- or running-stitch manner. Cutworks extended this conversion of a solid fabric into openwork by the cutting out of small squares, the holes being later filled in with geometric devices – diamonds, circles and stars – worked now in detached buttonhole stitches.

The earliest appearance of such work dates from 1337–39 and can be seen in the fresco of Good Government in the Town Hall of Siena, where Pax reclines against a cushion pierced at intervals with cut squares inwardly decorated.

Cutwork was often combined with *filet* in the decoration of table covers, sheets, bed hangings and valances. Not until the late 17th century did the ever-changing façade of costume-lace encroach on the more enduring world of furnishing. In a clever, deliberate and unscrupulous ploy to stop the importation of the super-expensive Venetian laces, Louis XIV and Jean-Baptiste Colbert, assisted by the architectual and interior decorational abilities of Jean Berain, Baily and Charles Le Brun, devised a new lace, based on Venetian needlelace techniques, but with a totally French discipline and symmetry of design. This was the official and exclusive "lace of France" (or *point de France*). It was draped in an obligatory manner not only over and around the necks, wrists, elbows, bodices, petticoats and skirts of the ladies or gentlemen of the Court, but also all over the interior fittings of palaces, châteaux and manoirs, garnishing windows, beds and even baths.

During the 18th century, *point de France* was gradually superseded by the lighter Argentan needlelace. Queen Charlotte, wife of George III, wore a flounce of Argentan lace at her wedding in 1761, and a delightful painting in the Queen's Collection shows her seated at a dressing table richly frilled with a similar flounce.

Towards the end of the 18th century fine cotton muslins began to take the place of lace in both furnishing and fashion. In Scotland and Switzerland an extensive hand-loom cottage industry produced yardages spotted with lappet woven *point d'esprits*, or with figuring wefts, their floats cut back to clarify the design. Plain-weave or gauze-weave muslins were additionally decorated by tambour embroidery or appliqué.

These lengths were hung as sash curtains, or *stores*, flat against the tall windows of the Regency period, softening the light and throwing the silk curtains which flanked them into glowing relief.

In 1809 appeared the Bobbinet machine. Powered from 1816 by water, it could produce a cotton twist-net strong enough for use as furnishing. Almost immediately it was being hand-embroidered by various techniques. This process made it relatively expensive, and it was not until the invention, reputedly in 1846, of the Nottingham Lace Curtain Machine, shortly to be powered by steam, and with automated patterning supplied by an overhead Jacquard loom, that any serious threat to the hand-loom muslin weavers appeared.

Within a few years, 100 of these machines were working in Nottingham. In 1851 some fine store curtains were exhibited at the Crystal Palace in London, each measuring 5 yards long by 2 yards wide, with a design so elaborate that between 12,000 and 15,000 Jacquard cards were required. The speed of the machine was such that a pair of curtains each 4 yards long could be produced in two hours. By the early 1860s several tons of cotton curtains were leaving Nottingham every week.

Lace curtains flourished also in the USA where they signified an elevated social status such that the adjective "lace-curtain" was defined in Webster's Dictionary as "having social or economic standing, often used to imply ostentation or pushing parvenu traits", thus opposing "lace-curtain Irish" to "shanty Irish" – superiority being established in that classless society by the nature and quantity of material possessions.

While many of the "classic" designs were filched from Paris

Lace used to decorate a dressing table in *Queen Charlotte with her Two Eldest Children at her Dressing Table* (detail) by Johann Zoffany, 1764

or Lille, or from antique hand-made filets, a few were distinctively British, such as the ruined castle set amid oak trees, and a herd of cows grazing in pasture near a village church – both 1853–55, by Thomas Robinson of Basford; and the cricket match with players suitably capped and flannelled, 1882–83, by Carey and Sons of Nottingham – all registered and preserved at the Public Record Office, Kew.

In 1870, Alexander Morton of Ayrshire decided to invest £1,000 in the purchase of one of these "power looms", in spite of the opposition of his weavers who feared (correctly) that it would lead to at least their temporary unemployment.

The development of embroidery machines between 1860 and 1880 provided further competition. The Cornely, Handmachine and Schiffli could between them imitate not only the appliqué, run and tambour techniques of hand embroidery, but also, by a chemical process, the spachtel cutout effects used in hand-made Swiss curtains – now rapidly disappearing from the market.

As if this were not enough, for some fifty years at least a hive of domestic embroiderers had been contributing swarms of point lace, filet, Greek lace (a form of cutwork), Teneriffe work, and endless crochet and knitted-lace borders for tablecloths, sheets, valances, cushions, antimacassars, place mats, towels, and of course curtains whether in the form of stores, *brise bise* or narrow strips to be hung not over but between the windows.

With the market thus in danger of becoming flooded, the enlightenment of the Arts and Crafts, and Art Nouveau movements appeared like a breath of air, stirring the stagnant folds. The gauze-weave looms, though reduced in numbers, were still producing their own filmy coverings and hangings, and around 1890 a lovely design of poppies, based on a William Morris textile was worked at Newmilns.

But ambivalence was setting in. Lace curtains had become common, their exclusive image quite dulled. As the public demanded cheaper and cheaper goods, quality suffered. Hygienists complained that lace curtains were unsanitary, as they gathered dust. *The Upholsterer* in 1915 hit back, contending that "Curtains do not create dust. The dust comes in the window anyway. That the curtains collect it is true, and by so doing there is less dust floating in the house".

Devastating blows were dealt to this luxury trade by the economic depression of the later 1920s, and by changes in architectural style. As houses became shorter and rounder, ceilings lower, and tall sash windows reduced to bowed casements, the priority was to encourage the entry of light, rather than obstruct it with suspended patterning, however holey.

When, some decades later, a nostalgic ambience favoured the resurrection of furnishing laces, yet another competitor had appeared, the German Raschel machine. Resurrected, in the 1950s, from its Saxony graveyard by Karl Mayer of Obertshausen, it worked by a warp-knitting process, and very rapidly using strong easy-care synthetic yarns. It could make use of existing Lace Curtain designs and thus its laces could be marketed at lower cost while appearing, to the untutored eye, no different.

Commemorative panels, large or small, have always been a by-product of more practically orientated draperies. In 1871 a 4 yard long by 67 inches wide hanging was made by Enoch Shipley and Co., of Nottingham, to commemorate the proclamation of William I of Prussia as Emperor of Germany. The deep border surrounding the central group is crowded with Baroque flowers and martial symbols, subtended by an eagle with spread wings, and surmounted by a crown. The magnificent Battle of Britain panel (1944–46), and the Last Supper, were other mammoth productions.

Today muslin curtaining and bed covers of patterned Madras gauze, are made only by the firm of Morton Young and Borland of Scotland. The Nottingham Lace Curtain machine, no longer active in Nottingham, has some residual production, also in Scotland. Cornely curtains and table cloths decorated with cloth appliqué on net, or net insertions in cloth, are made in Switzerland, using partially computerised machines. A large hanging of bobbinet decorated with Schiffli embroidery was designed in 1992 by Urs Hochulei of Bischoff, St. Gallen, to hang in the Textilmuseum. Curtaining for the home aims to incite public sentiment with white or coloured country scenes of windmills, geese, labourers, fairy tale castles, emus and kangaroos.

Scatter cushions, put together from scraps of lace, round off a contemporary scene in which lace furnishings play a somewhat amorphous role. At times essential for privacy, or to complete the theme of an interior design, they form no integral part of everyday life.

PAT EARNSHAW

Further Reading

The standard history of Lace is Levey 1983 which represents a detailed and scholarly study of its history, techniques, designs and uses from the 16th century to 1914. For additional information, particularly relating to Machine Laces, see Earnshaw 1993 and 1994. A comprehensive bibliography on Lace appears in Levey 1983, with further and more recent references cited in Levey 1993.

Bath, Virginia Churchill, *Lace*, Chicago: Regnery, 1974
Earnshaw, Pat, *A Dictionary of Lace*, Princes Risborough: Shire, 1982
Earnshaw, Pat, *Embroidered Machine Nets: Limerick and Worldwide*, Guildford: Gorse, 1993
Earnshaw, Pat, *Lace Machines and Machine Laces*, 2 vols., 1986; reprinted Guildford: Gorse, 1994
Earnshaw, Pat, *The Identification of Lace*, 3rd edition Princes Risborough: Shire, 1994
Halls, Zillah, *Machine-Made Lace in Nottingham*, 2nd edition Nottingham: City of Nottingham Museums and Libraries, 1973
Kraatz, Anne, *Lace: History and Fashion*, London: Thames and Hudson, and New York: Rizzoli, 1989
Levey, Santina M., *Lace: A History*, London: Victoria and Albert Museum, 1983
Levey, Santina M., "Lace" in Jennifer Harris (editor), *5000 Years of Textiles*, London: British Museum Press 1993
Risselin-Steenebrugen, M., *Trois Siècles de Dentelles* (exhib. cat.), Brussels: Musées Royaux d'Art et d'Histoire, 1980
Sonday, M., *Lace in the Collection of the Cooper-Hewitt Museum*, New York: Cooper-Hewitt Museum, 1982
Wardle, Patricia, *Victorian Lace*, 1968; reprinted Carlton, Bedfordshire: Ruth Bean, 1982

Lacquer and Japanning

Lacquer is ancient in origin and comes mainly from China, Japan and India. It was first systematically imported to the West by the East India Company in the early 17th century, and soon imitated in France, Italy and England. By 1660, the trade in eastern lacquer was well established and had far-reaching significance for western design.

Contemporary records are often ambiguous; they list imports indiscriminately as Chinese, Japanese or Indian, and terms like "India work" apply equally to eastern goods and western imitations. Fashionable taste favoured Japanese lacquer, hence the term "japanning"; this term is used here to refer to all western imitations.

In the 17th century, lacquered furniture was found in the houses of the European nobility and gentry, rich merchants and East India Company officers. Exotically painted in gold and colour on black, it was a curiosity amid otherwise dark oak furniture and wainscoting. Initially, its rarity was maintained by careful marketing, but by the late 17th century, it could be readily bought from specialist "India" goods shops.

Inventories often listed "Indian" furniture in closets. At Tart Hall in London, for example, Lady Arundel kept a large cupboard, a chest and a small table in a closet near the drawing room, and similar items in both the parlour and the Parlour Chamber. Twenty years later, Samuel Pepys saw in the Duke of York's closet "two very fine chests covered with gold and Indian varnish, given him by the East India Company of Holland." Such gifts to influential people were commonplace among Company officers.

European buyers often adapted lacquer in order to overcome differences between eastern and western furniture styles. The "china guilt (sic) cabinet upon a frame" listed in the Earl of Northampton's inventory in 1614, probably describes an oriental, brass-mounted, rectangular chest lined with drawers, supported on a carved European stand. By 1672, craftsmen were sent to the East "to teach the Indians how to manufacture goods to make them vendible" in Europe, and from 1684 until about 1725, furniture was sent from England for decoration.

Among the most popular imports were folding screens with incised lacquer decoration (known as Bantam work or Coromandel). Not only were they useful against draughts in large halls and bedrooms, but they could be converted, often indiscriminately, into smaller screens, mirror frames, table-tops, brackets or cabinets. John Evelyn saw them more sympathetically used in 1682, in his neighbour's elegant house where "in the hall are contrivances of japan screens instead of wainscot", with decoration showing "the manner of living and country of the Chinese". This practice facilitated the aristocratic fashion for lacquer rooms to house displays of prestigious Chinese porcelain. Whether lined with eastern or western panels, or a combination, such rooms were very European in style and arrangement. The room constructed by a Dutch japanner in about 1660 at the Schloss Rosenborg in Copenhagen, is the earliest surviving example.

The demand for lacquer exceeded supply, and in about 1660 European cabinet-makers entered into serious competition. What their varnish lacked in depth and lustre, they made up for in colour. By 1701, there were recipes for making white, blue, red, olive, chestnut, lapis lazuli, marble and tortoiseshell varnishes. Connoisseurs distinguished between the "right Japan" of the East, and its European equivalent; others, like the Duke of Hamilton, were less discriminating. Worried by the expense of "Indian" cabinets, he enquired of his wife "For my part I think a counterfeit one looks as well, so let me know if you will take such a one, or give the forty guineas."

Japanning centres developed across Europe, with England, France and Holland taking the lead; the craft developed in America too, but not significantly so until the 19th century. Exports in japanned furniture flourished between European countries. Although japanners believed their work to be wholly oriental in style, and indeed most Dutch decoration was, furniture shapes remained typically 17th-century European. Except for regional variations in shape and colour, developments were similar across Europe, and most articles of fashionable household furniture were japanned. Chairs and day-beds were rarely japanned until c.1700, as earlier shapes did not lend themselves to this decorative style, although there are notable exceptions like the set of chairs made for Ham House, Surrey, in 1683. By the mid-18th century, some Venetian rooms were entirely panelled and furnished in "japan". Bedroom furniture was seldom japanned until the late 18th century, except for dressing tables, so central to the lives of society women.

Little is known of the early history of French japanning, but from c.1730, an indigenous style developed which combined eastern and western panels. Although the panels were selected like rare woods, to be mounted in furniture, sometimes together with bronze or porcelain, the original decoration was often disfigured or obscured beneath gilt trellises. Despite this cavalier approach, French work was very fine, and commodes decorated in this manner were particularly sought by fashionable European society.

Early japanners were seldom named and few wares can be reliably attributed. Notable exponents were Giles Grendey (1693–1780) of London; the Martin Brothers (fl.1730–c.1787) of Paris, renowned for their *Vernis Martin*; Gerard Dagly (1657–1726), who worked in Germany and in France, and his apprentice, Martin Schnell.

In England, japanned furniture enjoyed a revival in the mid-18th century when entire suites decorated *à la Chine*, were favoured, particularly for bedrooms and dressing rooms. Thomas Chippendale made several such sets, one for Badminton House, c.1755, and another in green and gilt, in about 1770, for the State Bed Chamber at Nostell Priory, where, with other original furnishings, it continues to impart a whimsical Chinese character to the room. On a less grand scale, Chippendale also japanned a green and white set of bedroom furniture for the actor David Garrick in 1770. Robert Adam also incorporated japanned furniture in some of his decorative schemes, for example at Nostell Priory, Osterley Park and the Adelphi.

By 1790, interest in japanned furniture of this type gave way to lighter woods. The focus of japanning shifted to its application to papier-mâché and tinware, and a wholly separate industry grew up.

Interest in Japanese art and design among artistic circles of the 1850s, and the Japanese displays at the International Exhibition in London in 1862, led to London firms like Farmer & Rogers and Liberty & Co. specialising in exotic eastern goods Artists, designers, architects, and aesthetes purchased Japanese lacquered furniture and screens, occasionally furnishing entire rooms with it; Japonisme was a major design influence until the end of the century, and the market was soon flooded with flimsy, inexpensive lacquered goods made to suit popular taste.

It was not until the early 20th century that the art of "true" lacquering was successfully practised in the West. Leading exponents were Eileen Gray (1878/9–1976) and Jean Dunand (1877–1942) who worked contemporaneously in Paris, producing lacquered Art Deco-style rooms and furniture for eminent couturiers and collectors. More popularly, the extravagance of the 1920s was reflected in a vogue for high quality Italian and English reproductions of Queen Anne lacquered and japanned furniture. A stylish survival from this period, is the interior of 160 Piccadilly, London, designed by William Curtis Green in 1922 as Wolseley Motor Showroom, and adapted by him in 1926 for Barclays Bank.

In 17th-century Venice, *lacca povera* developed as an inexpensive alternative to japanning. Cut-out prints were pasted onto furniture and varnished all over – known as *découpage*, this craft is currently popular among interior designers and amateurs.

Japanning was an admired amateur accomplishment, and Stalker & Parker's *Treatise of Japanning & Varnishing*, published in 1688, was aimed primarily at this market. Dictionaries of arts and sciences fully described the japanning process, and in 1750, *The Ladies' Amusement or the Whole Art of Japanning made Easy*, Robert Sayer's volume of engravings, became a design source book for both professional and amateur japanners, and other decorative artists. This amateur interest which continued into the 19th century, is a sobering reminder that some of the more tawdry specimens of japanning may have been added to "old" furniture by over-ambitious hands.

YVONNE JONES

See also Chinoiserie; Screens

Selected Collections

A list of the major international museums containing collections of lacquered furnishings appears in Bourne 1984; the Herbig-Haarhaus Lackmuseum, Cologne, has major holdings of lacquer ware from around the world. Important examples of interiors decorated with lacquer survive in Denmark at the Schloss Rosenborg, Copenhagen; in Germany at the Charlottenburg Palace, Berlin, the Pagodenburg, Schloss Nymphenburg, Bavaria, and the Schloss Ludwigsburg, Würtemburg, near Stuttgart; in Holland at Huis Ten Bosch, The Hague; in Italy at the Palazzo Reale and Stupinigi Palace, Turin, and the Palazzo Ca'Rezzonico, Venice; and in Russia at Monplaisir, Peterhof, St. Petersburg.

Further Reading

A useful survey of Oriental and European lacquerware appears in Bourne, 1984, which also contains a short secondary reading list for European work and a much longer bibliography for Oriental lacquerware. For a more detailed study of the European industry, including a specialist bibliography with particular emphasis on the literature pre-1900, see Huth, 1971.

Adams, Janet Woodbury, *Decorative Folding Screens in the West from 1600 to the Present Day*, London: Thames and Hudson, 1982; as *Decorative Folding Screens: 400 Years in the Western World*, New York: Viking, 1982

Bourne, Jonathan, *Lacquer: An International History and Collectors' Guide*, Marlborough: Crowood Press, and New York: Abrams, 1984

Garner, Harry, *Chinese Lacquer*, London: Faber, 1979

Herberts, Kurt, *Oriental Lacquer: Art and Technique*, London: Thames and Hudson, 1962

Holzhausen Walter, *Lackkunst in Europa*, Braunschweig: Klinkhardt & Biermann, 1959

Honour, Hugh, *Chinoiserie: The Vision of Cathay*, London: Murray, 1961; New York: Dutton, 1962

Huth, Hans, "Lacquerwork by Gérard Dagly" in *Connoisseur*, 1935

Huth, Hans, *Lacquer of the West: The History of a Craft and an Industry, 1550–1950*, Chicago: University of Chicago Press, 1971

Jacobson, Dawn, *Chinoiserie*, London: Phaidon, 1993

"Japanning and Lacquer" in Percy MacQuoid and Ralph Edwards, *The Dictionary of English Furniture*, revised edition, 3 vols., 1954; reprinted Woodbridge, Suffolk: Antique Collectors' Club, 1983

Lackkunst aus Ostasien und Europa (exhib. cat.), Cologne: Das Herbig-Haarhaus Lackmuseum, 1977

Lesley, Everett P., Jr., *Lacquer, Oriental and Western, Ancient and Modern* (exhib. cat.), New York: Cooper-Hewitt Museum, 1951

Lorenzetti, Giulio, *Lacche Veneziane del Settecento* (exhib. cat.), Venice: Ca' Rezzonico, 1938

Ragué, Beatrix von, *A History of Japanese Lacquerwork*, Toronto: University of Toronto Press, 1976

La Farge, John 1835–1910

American painter, critic, stained-glass designer and decorator

John La Farge was one of the most multi-talented figures in the history of American art. His innovative and spectacular decorative plans for sacred and secular buildings demonstrated not only his technical prowess but also new attitudes toward the use of stained glass. He was also one of the foremost painters and muralists of the late 19th century, and a master of magazine and book illustration as well. And as if these artistic skills were not sufficient, he was a world traveller, a gifted and engaging correspondent, and wrote inspired and original art criticism.

A great admirer of Japanese art, La Farge championed its cause in the United States, and his paintings and illustrations of his travels in the South Seas stimulated a new interest in rich and exotic flora and fauna within the decorative arts. La Farge's circle of close friends included Henry James and Henry Adams, and he was considered to be one of the great conversationalists of his era. In view of the importance of his writings, which covered most aspects of the fine and decorative arts, he can be regarded as one of the most influential artists and critics in the English-speaking world. Even so, his work was almost completely forgotten by a world torn between abstraction and social realism soon after his death, and the richness and variety of his art has only recently regained public and critical attention.

La Farge began painting decorative and figurative murals around 1865 but it was not until he received the commission to plan and execute the full range of decorations for H.H. Richardson's major work, Boston's Trinity Church, that he established a reputation in this genre. This work was carried out in 1876 and La Farge took the audacious step of undertaking to complete almost all of the complex scheme, with his assistants, while the contractor's scaffolds were still in place within a period of roughly four months. He produced all the designs himself, and, insisting that they be executed in the old-fashioned medium of encaustic to achieve the rich effects deemed appropriate for the Romanesque Revival church, he established the workshop practices that he continued to use in mural and decorative projects for the rest of his life. Trinity also provided an influential model for the integration of architecture and decoration that was soon to be followed in the work of Arts and Crafts and Art Nouveau designers. La Farge himself frequently not only designed figurative and decorative painted schemes but also devised lighting, textile, sculpture and, of course, stained-glass programmes.

By the middle of the 19th century, stained glass had become a moribund art form in the United States and it is arguably La Farge's greatest achievement that he single-handedly rekindled interest in it both as a decorative medium and as a fine art form. And in the thirty years that passed between his first efforts in stained glass until just before his death, he was personally responsible for some 300 individual windows, for churches, institutional buildings, and private homes. La Farge's interest in this medium was originally nurtured by Richardson who offered him a free hand in selecting the subjects, designs and colours for the windows in the entrance hall of the Watts Sherman House in Newport, Rhode Island, in 1878. La Farge created a series of almost abstract floral designs that were not only extremely striking but also highly innovative and that juxtaposed the delicately painted flowers with an irregular, rectangular Japanese metal framework.

In addition to his work as a designer, La Farge was also responsible for certain technical advances in the use of stained glass. His most effective discovery involved using a combination of traditional European pot-metal with translucent pieces of white opalescent glass. He found that when he placed the opalescent glass next to the other glass, it picked up the complementary colours and, through its modulations of tone, helped to create areas of light and shade. Equally important, the imperfections and irregularities in the white glass gave texture and richness to his windows. His work quickly became popular and he received commissions for the Memorial Hall, Harvard, and Trinity Church, as well as for the mansions of William Vanderbilt, J. Pierpont Morgan, and Samuel J. Tilden over the next three years. In 1880, he was awarded the lucrative and prestigious contract to design the stained glass for any of the mansions being fitted out or refurbished by the New York decorating firm, Herter Brothers.

La Farge developed a major glass workshop at Union Square in New York City to meet the demands of this new work. He also maintained a studio in the famous Tenth Street Studio Building from 1858 until his death. (His family home was in Newport.) He continued to experiment with glass throughout the rest of his life, constantly manipulating its textures and shapes so as to achieve different three-dimensional effects, and adding the cloisonné process to his working methods in the early 1890s. The quality of his work was so high that it has often been favourably compared with that of L.C. Tiffany, and several of La Farge's windows were attributed to Tiffany until recent research uncovered the original La Farge drawings. But, although his innovations in the spheres of luminosity and shading did much to enhance his reputation as a supreme colourist, his experiments and his perfectionism caused him substantially to exceed his budget on many of his projects. In addition, many previously admiring clients became frustrated at the time – sometimes years – that La Farge spent reworking and improving an idea: many of his projects therefore lost him money and future patronage. Nevertheless, his work remained in great demand and he attracted commissions from as far away as London. He was also awarded numerous honours and prizes in the United States.

Many factors have contributed to his high reputation today. The prominence of his clients, for example, and the significance of the buildings for which his decorative designs in paint and glass were created, have both helped to attract public and critical attention. But it is the work itself, much of which is still extant, that has played the most important part in ensuring that La Farge's richly colouristic, technically masterful and carefully integrated commissions continue to convey a boldness and genius that was far ahead of its time.

DAVID M. SOKOL

See also Herter Brothers

Biography

John Frederick Lewis Joseph La Farge. Born in New York City, 31 March 1835, the son of wealthy French émigrés. Studied drawing with his grandfather, the miniaturist Louis Binsse de Saint-Victor (1778–1844). Educated at Mount Saint Mary's College, New York, 1853–55. Worked in a law office, New York, 1856. Travelled to Europe, 1856–57; stayed in Paris and studied briefly in the studio of Thomas Couture (1815–74). Returned to New York and practised law,1857. Leased a studio in New York, 1858; studied painting under William Morris Hunt (1827–79), Newport, Rhode Island, 1859. Married Margaret Perry, a grand-niece of Commodore Perry, 1860: 7 children. Exhibited landscapes and still lifes from 1862. Active as a muralist and decorative artist from 1865; experimented with stained-glass techniques from 1875; patented a method for opalescent glass, 1879. Travelled in Europe and met Ford Madox Brown, Dante Gabriel Rossetti and Edward Burne-Jones, London, and Puvis de Chavannes, Paris, 1874–75. Supplied stained glass for Herter Brothers, c.1880–82; established his own firm of interior decorators and stained-glass manufacturers, La Farge Decorative Art Company, New York, 1883–85. Travelled to Japan, 1886; first tour of the South Seas, 1890. Medallist, 1889 Paris Exhibition. In close contact with Siegfried Bing, 1894. Published several books and theoretical treatises on art, decoration and stained glass. Member, American Watercolor Society, 1868; National Academy of Design, 1869. Received an honorary degree from Yale University 1901; awarded medal, Architectural League, New York, 1909. Died in Providence, Rhode Island, 14 November, 1910. Major retrospective exhibition, Museum of Fine Arts, Boston, 1911.

Selected Works

The La Farge Family Papers, including correspondence and manuscripts, are in the Department of Manuscripts and Archives, Sterling Memorial Library, Yale University, New Haven. Additional material compiled by La Farge's biographer Royal Cortissoz, including notes of meetings and conversations and a copy of La Farge's unfinished memoir, is in the Collection of American Literature, Beinecke Rare Book and Manuscript Library, Yale University. Examples of La Farge's stained glass are in the Museum of Fine Arts, Boston, Brooklyn Museum and Metropolitan Museum of Art, New York, and National Museum of American Art, Smithsonian Institution, Washington, DC. Cartoons and designs for stained glass are in the Metropolitan Museum of Art.

Interiors

1876	Trinity Church, Boston (murals and architectural motifs; building by H.H. Richardson)
1877–78	W. Watts Sherman House, Newport, Rhode Island (stained glass for the main hall; building by H.H. Richardson)
c.1879–80	Henry G. Marquand House, Newport, Rhode Island (reception room ceiling, and *Peonies* stained glass in the bedroom)
1880	Union League Club, New York (decoration of the dining room; sculptural work by A. Saint-Gaudens)
1881	William H. Vanderbilt House, New York (stained glass and decoration for the Japanese Parlour, with Herter Brothers)
1881–83	Cornelius Vanderbilt II House, New York (decoration of the dining room, and watercolor room; sculptural work by A. Saint-Gaudens)
1882	Frederick Lothrop Ames House, Boston (stained glass)
1882–83	Memorial Hall, Harvard University, Cambridge, Massachusetts (stained glass)
1887–88	Whitelaw Reid House, New York (decoration of the music room)
1893	John Hay House, Washington, DC (stained glass)
1893–98	Walker Art Building, Bowdoin College, Brunswick, Maine (*Athens* mural)
1903–05	Supreme Court Room, Minnesota State Capitol, St. Paul, Minnesota (mural decoration)

Publications

The American Art of Glass, 1893
Considerations on Painting, 1895
An Artist's Letters from Japan, 1897; reprinted 1986
Great Masters, 1903; reprinted 1968
The Higher Art in Life, 1908
"The Minor Arts" in *New England Magazine*, May 1909, pp.330–38

Reminiscences of the South Seas, 1912; as *An American Artist in the South Seas*, introduction by Kaori O'Connor, 1987

Further Reading

A recent comprehensive account of La Farge's work as a decorator and designer and maker of stained glass appears in Adams 1987 which also includes a full list of his writings and locations of his decorative commissions. For a select bibliography see Burke 1986. A catalogue raisonné is in preparation at Yale University.

Adams, Henry, "John La Farge's Discovery of Japanese Art: A New Perspective on the Origins of Japonisme" in *Art Bulletin*, 67, September 1985, pp.449–85

Adams, Henry and others, *John La Farge: Essays*, New York: Abbeville, 1987

Burke, Doreen Bolger and others, *In Pursuit of Beauty: Americans and the Aesthetic Movement* (exhib. cat.: Metropolitan Museum, New York), New York: Rizzoli, 1986

Cortissoz, Royal, *John La Farge: A Memoir and a Study*, 1911; reprinted New York: Kennedy Graphics, 1971

La Farge, Henry A., "John La Farge's Work in the Vanderbilt Houses" in *American Art Journal*, 16, Autumn 1984, pp.30–70

Lefor, Patricia Joan, *John La Farge and Japan: An Instance of Oriental Influence in American Art*, Ph.D. thesis, Evanston: Northwestern University, 1978

Low, Will H., "John La Farge: The Mural Painter" in *Craftsman*, 19, January 1911, pp.337–39

Sturm, James L., *Stained Glass from Medieval Times to the Present: Treasures to be Seen in New York*, New York: Dutton, 1982

Weinberg, H. Barbara, "The Early Stained Glass Work of John La Farge (1835–1910)" in *Stained Glass*, 67, Summer 1972, pp.4–16

Weinberg, H. Barbara, "John La Farge and the Invention of American Opalescent Windows" in *Stained Glass*, 67, Autumn 1972, pp.4–11

Weinberg, H. Barbara, "John La Farge's Peacock Window" in *Worcester Art Museum Bulletin*, 3, November 1973, pp.1–12

Weinberg, H. Barbara, "John La Farge and the Decoration of Trinity Church, Boston" in *Journal of the Society of Architectural Historians*, 33, December 1974, pp.323–53

Weinberg, H. Barbara, *The Decorative Work of John La Farge*, New York: Garland, 1977

Larsson, Carl 1853–1919

Swedish designer, illustrator and painter

In 1901, the artist Carl Larsson and his wife Karin made their rural retreat, Lilla Hyttnäs, into their permanent home. A typical Dalarna country cottage, it was originally a gift from Karin's father. Over time, and through numerous extensions and alterations, they turned it into a total work of art representing a turning point in Swedish design history. This home stood as a role model for the new design ideal that has influenced Swedish interior design through this century.

The interiors were comfortable, homely, simple and light – mixing the heritage of Swedish design with international influences, and serving the everyday needs of a growing family. Plain walls were broken up by woodwork in contrasting colours. Red and green recur, uniting interior and exterior, as well as providing a common theme throughout. Furniture was either bought, inherited or purpose-built, and often painted in bright colours, examples of local vernacular were mixed with "upmarket" antiques, with innovative home-made textiles making a large contribution to each room's distinctive style. All this was in stark contrast to the dark, overloaded, pretentiously historicist interiors popular with the 19th-century bourgeoisie, that emphasised appearance and social status.

A visitor entering the Larsson's drawing room would have been struck first by its brightness. Sunlight floods in through the large window, uncurtained and framed by climbing plants and geraniums. The furniture and dais bannisters are picked out in white, the seats are covered in a pattern of blue and white stripes, and rag-woven runners lie on the floorboards. Known as "The Swedish Room", it expresses the very spirit of the blond, Neo-Classical, 18th-century country interior.

In the dining room, the wall panelling is painted green with "English Red" for the fitted woodwork; the decor is completed by a settle, stained-glass lancet window frames, shelving, and stick back chairs. This was a room made for winter evenings, next to the traditional Scandinavian tiled stove. A tapestry of contrasting colour and black and white check hangs behind the settle, and on the table there is a white runner with red embroidered family tree, both by Karin Larsson. Such a dining room had never been seen before in Sweden.

Lilla Hyttnäs was originally attributed to Carl Larsson alone. Although he was the main force, more credit has come to be given to Karin's role – she put aside a career as a promising painter in order to raise a family of eight and run a home. She designed and wove most of the distinctive textiles, showing the twin influences of national heritage and Art Nouveau.

Numerous details at Lilla Hyttnäs bear witness to Karin's eye for practicality, such as the upstairs landing's stepped window ledge, allowing room for plants without obstructing the light. She also made the translucent muslin valances used throughout the house. The kitchen walls are panelled from floor to ceiling with unstained varnished pine watchboard. The sideboard was painted in a Japanese style by Carl. Karin also designed innovative furniture, such as the studio's austere rocking chair. It is said that the carpenter delivered it at night because he didn't want to be associated with such "ugliness".

Upstairs, Carl's bedroom furniture further exemplifies the unconventional. Placed in the middle of the tiny room, the white painted bed features a drop-leaf bookshelf, integral bench seat, and storage chest doubling as step. The white hangings and canopy feature Karin's sparse embroidery style. The bed as Modernist centrepiece is completed by the blanket's abstract designs. It is framed by red shelving on the white-washed walls, against which stand a pair of Queen Anne chairs.

The wall art by Carl – portraits, mottoes and floral ornament – verges on the sentimental. These are counterbalanced by Karin's more restrained style. Her *Rose of Love* hanging, showing a flower reaching to the sun, fills the doorway between the couple's bedrooms, the wall above painted with floral garlands by Carl.

The impact of the Larsson interiors would never have been so great were it not for the publication of his watercolours of domestic interiors in book form between 1896 and 1910. The most famous was *Ett Hem* (A Home) in 1899. A German anthology, *Das Haus in der Sonne* (The House in the Sun), of 1910 sold 250,000 copies in its first twelve years. Carl Larsson became world famous, and was seen as the arbiter of the correct interpretation of the Swedish ideal existence. The utopian image of domestic felicity that Lilla Hyttnäs and Carl

Larsson: watercolour from *Ett Hem*, 1899

Larsson's work portrays shows no hint of the dark side of their married life, such as the deaths of two children, or Carl's frequent depressions and absences.

Carl Larsson meant *Ett Hem* to be a model for domestic design, and as such it was aimed at the public at large. Or in his own words: "It is not for the exercise in vanity of showing you how I live, but rather because I feel I have gone about this matter in such a sensible way, so that I actually think it may serve as – ugh, dare I really say it outright? – a good example – now I have said it! – for many people who need to decorate their homes in a pleasant way."

The Larsson interiors provided inspiration for the reforming ideals of Ellen Key. A keen follower of William Morris, she believed that pleasant and harmonious homes had an uplifting effect on humanity. She criticised the appalling housing conditions of the poor, and rebelled against bourgeois domestic taste, when in 1899 she wrote *Beauty for All*, heralding Sweden's design reform movement.

Lilla Hyttnäs should also be seen within the context of the National Romantic Movement that affected the arts in the 1890s. The open air museum at Skansen, a microcosm of Swedish rural life, opened in 1891, providing a sanctuary for a threatened culture.

Throughout history, Sweden has borrowed and assimilated styles from abroad, and Lilla Hyttnäs is certainly no exception. There are strong influences from the Arts and Crafts Movement. It celebrates the unity of architecture, craftsmanship and individual creativity in a spirit of creative "DIY". The Larssons were well informed about the latest international styles, and innovations from Austria, Germany, Japan and other countries, and travelled widely. They were subscribers to *The Studio* from its launch in 1893, and visited England in the 1880s. However, most importantly, the Larssons were not just recipients of the new ideals, they were also active at the forefront of the movement. It should be noted that the bedrooms and the dining room predate *The Studio*.

Today, Lilla Hyttnäs (also known as Carl Larssongården) is preserved more or less intact. It has been a subject of pilgrimage for professionals and public alike for a century, and still seems to have something to offer most tastes. The "Carl Larsson style" reappears regularly in furniture fairs and glossy consumer magazines. Historians are also reassessing the work of both Larssons, exemplified by the forthcoming 1997 exhibition at London's Victoria and Albert Museum.

Finally, one must note the curious irony that something so brimful of foreign design influences has become an inseparable part of Swedish cultural identity.

DENISE HAGSTRÖMER

See also Arts and Crafts

Biography

Carl Olof Larsson. Born in Stockholm, 28 May 1853. Entered the preparatory school of the Academy of Fine Arts, 1866; moved to the Antique School of the Academy of Fine Arts, 1869. Financed his studies by book, magazine and newspaper illustration and photography retouching. Won a number of prizes, 1872–74. Visited France, and lived at Grez-sur-Loing near Fontainebleau, 1872–75. Won Royal Medal for painting, 1876. Travelled to Paris and Barbizon, 1877. In Grez-par-Nemours, 1878, where he met Karin Bergöö; married in 1883: several children. Twice rejected at Paris Salon, 1881, 1882; but won third medal at the Salon, 1883. Returned to Sweden, 1885. Established contacts with patron Pontus Fürstenberg in Gothenburg. With other artists was opponent of the Academy. Moved to Dalarna, c.1888, settling there permanently in 1901. Painted and exhibited scenes from his family life, some exhibited, 1894–97. Some watercolours reproduced in album *Ett Hem*, 1899. Also painted large-scale oil and fresco paintings for various sites, 1896–1906. Exhibited at Paris World Fair, 1900; Artists' Association exhibition, Stockholm, and in Munich, 1901. First prize at Rome exhibition, 1911. Travelled in Finland, France and Germany, 1912. Produced tapestry designs. Died 22 January 1919.

Selected Works

The Nationalmuseum in Stockholm holds the largest collection of Larsson's painted and graphic work.

Interiors

1879	Bolinder Palace, Stockholm (ceiling and lunette paintings): Bolinder family
1888–	Lilla Hyttnäs, Sundborn, Dalarna (interior decoration): Larsson's home
c.1892	Girls' School, Gothenburg (wall paintings)
1896	Nationalmuseum, Stockholm (staircase fresco paintings): Nationalmuseum
1897–98	Royal Opera, Stockholm (ceiling and lunette paintings)
1898–1901	Norra Latin Läroverket, Stockholm (wall painting)
1903	Latinläroverket, Gothenburg (friezes)
1905	Dramatic Theatre, Stockholm (ceiling painting)
1906	Nationalmuseum, Stockholm (*Gustavus Vasa Entering Stockholm*, staircase painting)
1911–15	Nationalmuseum, Stockholm (*Sacrifice at the Solstice*; designs for staircase painting rejected)

Publications

Larsson's writings have been published in several editions, and translated into several languages. A complete list of his publications is in Svenska Konstnärs Lexikon.

De Mina: Gammalt krafs [Mine: old scrawl], 1895
Ett Hem: 24 målningar med text, 1899 (*A Home*, 1974)
Larssons: ett album bestående af 32 målningar och med text och teckningar, 1902 (*A Family*, 1980)
Spadarvet: Mitt lilla landtbruk, 1906 (*A Farm*, 1976)
Åt solsidan, 1910 (*On the Sunny Side*, 1984),
Jag [I], 1931 (*Carl Larsson: The Autobiography*, edited by John Z. Lofgren, 1992)

Further Reading

Cavalli-Björkman and Lindwall 1982 (translated 1983) is the most comprehensive survey in English. For the graphic work see Brummer 1983. A major study of Larsson's work will be published to accompany the exhibition at the Victoria and Albert Museum, London, 1997.

Alfons, Sven and Harriet (editors), *Carl Larsson, skildrad av honom själv*, Stockholm: Bonnier, 1952, 2nd edition, 1977
Brummer, Hans Henrik (editor), *Carl Larsson: grafiska verk, en complett katalog*, Uppsala: Hjert & Hjert, 1983
Carl Larsson: Minnesutställning (exhib. cat.), Stockholm: Liljevalchs Konsthall, 1953
Cavalli-Björkman, Görel and Bo Lindwall, *Carl Larsson och hans värld; Larssons Welt; Le grand livre de Carl Larsson* (exhib. cat.), Königstein im Taunus: Langewiesche, 1982; English edition as *The World of Carl Larsson*, La Jolla, CA: Green Tiger Press, 1982, London: Murray, 1983
Cavalli-Björkman, Görel and others, *Carl Larsson* (exhib. cat.), New York: Brooklyn Museum, 1982; London: Methuen, 1983
Dreams of a Summer Night: Scandinavian Painting at the Turn of the Century (exhib. cat.), London: Hayward Gallery, 1986
Facos, Michelle, "The Ideal Swedish Home: Carl Larsson's Lilla Hyttnäs" in Christopher Reed (editor), *Not at Home: The Suppression of Domesticity in Modern Art and Architecture*, London and New York: Thames and Hudson, 1996
Gunnarsson, Torsten, *Carl Larsson 1853–1919* (exhib. cat.), Stockholm: Nationalmuseum, and Gothenburg: Konstmuseum, 1992
Larkin, David, *The Paintings of Carl Larsson*, New York: Scribner, 1976
Lindgren, A., "Dramatiska teatern och dess konstnärliga utsmyckning" in *Ord och Bild*, 1908
Rybczynski, Witold, "A Homemade House", in *Art and Antiques*, vol.7, December 1990, pp.74–81
Sirén, Osvald, "Carl Larsson und sein Heim", in *Dekorative Kunst*, 1901
Snodin, Michael, *Carl Larsson* (exhib. cat., forthcoming), London: Victoria and Albert Museum, 1997
"Sundborn, Sweden: The Carl Larsson Museum House: A House and a World", in *Abitare*, vol.313, December 1992, pp.52–9
Svenska Konstnärs Lexikon, Malmö: Allhems, 1952–67

Lasalle, Philippe de 1723–1804

French designer, manufacturer, entrepreneur, inventor and teacher

Probably the best known silk designer of the 18th century, Philippe de Lasalle led a varied and public life. Between 1744, the first year of his silk-weaving apprenticeship, and 1804, the year of his death, he resided mainly in Lyon, the centre of French silk manufacturing. His family and professional network, however, was both national and international, extending from Paris and the many provinces in France to Austria, Germany, Italy, Russia, Spain and Peru. He was designer, manufacturer, inventor and teacher, and his immediate circle included members of the legal nobility into which he married two of his daughters in 1764 and 1785. He himself achieved ennoblement in 1776, a recognition of his inventions that had resulted directly from his frustration with the weaving technology used for the production of brocaded furnishing silks with large scale patterns.

Because of the multi-faceted nature of his career, Lasalle's life is currently being reassessed in an attempt to separate fact from fiction, and interpret more accurately his role in the design and manufacture of Lyonnais silks (Miller, 1988; Chaignon, 1992). This is a complex task as Lasalle surfaced in different guises in Lyon and in Paris: in disputes with the silk weaving guild which did not appreciate his innovative turn of mind, in petitions to the monarch demanding recognition for his services to manufacturing in the form of financial remuneration (pensions), and in more arcane documentation which reveals the breadth of his private family interests and investments. These included the judicious choice of husbands for his daughters, the ownership of property in Oullins, Sens and Seyssel, and possibly a retail outlet in Paris, and shares in coalmining and glassworks in the Auvergne (Miller, 1988; Coural, 1988).

Although it has been assumed that Lasalle's basis for excellence in design lay in a fine art training, this part of his education has not yet been traced. What is clear, however, is that he was already calling himself a designer (*dessinateur*) by the time of his marriage in 1748, a title which he never relinquished entirely. After 1749, in addition, he alternated between merchant (*marchand*), merchant manufacturer (*marchand fabricant*) and businessman (*negociant*).

Evidence of his prowess in design and manufacturing survives in the Musée Historique des Tissus in Lyon. There, point papers and fabrics reveal the foresight of his widow in offering samples of his work to the Conservatoire des Arts immediately after his death. Particularly noteworthy were the high quality and refinement of his animal, floral and human representations which show a daring mastery of realistic painterly subjects executed on the drawloom (Chaignon, 1992). These very complex large-scale subjects required painstaking reprogramming of the loom each time the repeat ran out. It was this drain on time which inspired Lasalle to produce his best known invention, the detachable simple. Shown to the Académie des Sciences in 1772, it, along with three other technical inventions, received the Prix d'honneur in 1779 (Hafter, 1977).

Although Lasalle's design output is often solely seen as impressive furnishing silks such as the *Peacocks and Pheasants*, the *Doves* or the *Partridges* (c.1771), it was not so static or restricted. Descriptions of early fabrics reveal that he dabbled in the Rococo style before turning to Neo-Classical compositions, and that fashion fabrics were also part of his repertoire. He himself claimed that his first innovation was the introduction of a tiger skin motif on a ground of gold in 1756. Both the curves of the motif and the twinkling of the metal were Rococo devices. In the 1750s he was also making other fabrics with false metallic threads for export to Germany, and in 1762 he invented a furnishing fabric made of wool, silk and linen threads as well as producing woven suit borders which were to be exported to Austria, Germany and Russia. By 1766 he was involved in another new fashion: painting on silk, and offered for sale his recipe for colours to the king (Miller, 1988). Five years later he was producing woven portraits of famous people (the Empress Catherine II of Russia, Louis XV, the future Louis XVI, the Duc de Berry, the Comte and Comtesse de Provence). These oval portraits, in a brocaded lampas on a taffeta ground, were appliquéd on to a surround of flowers in brocaded lampas on a satin ground (Chaignon, 1992). They could be hung in an interior in much the same way as paintings.

What all of these fabrics had in common was their expense, which limited them to a fashion-conscious and wealthy elite. Lasalle's customers even included Catherine II of Russia and the French king, as well as his extremely important patron, the Prince de Condé. He purchased all the fabrics for the Palais-Bourbon from Lasalle, including the well-known blue *cannelé* decorated with red partridges (Coural, 1988).

In the context of interior design, Lasalle made a lasting contribution, as some of his fabrics still hang today in antechamber of the choir of the Pushkin Palace in Russia. As master to several designers in the 1750s and 1760s, as author of a memorial suggesting an appropriate training for designers in 1765, and as an administrator of the public school of drawing (*école gratuite de dessin*) from 1780, he also shared his expertise with the next generation. The Revolution, however, interrupted Lasalle's activity, as he lost designs, looms and home in the sack of Lyon (1793). Yet, within eight years he had reconstructed his looms and mounted them for demonstration purposes in the Grand Collège (1801). In the same year he became a member of the Académie de Lyon.

Lasalle's success, therefore, lay in his awareness and manipulation of the market for luxury silks, as well as his happy ability to convince the Crown of the value of his various inventions: he received annually pensions which rose from 600 livres in 1758 to no less than 6,000 livres in 1775 (Miller, 1988). This awareness, coupled with ambition, talent, and a drive to experiment, reveal an enquiring mind and desire for recognition fairly typical of Enlightenment entrepreneurs.

LESLEY ELLIS MILLER

See also Silks

Biography

Born in Seyssel, near Aix-les-Bains, 23 September 1723, the son of a civil servant. Trained as a designer of silks in Lyon and Paris, possibly attending the studio of the Lyon painter and designer Daniel Sarrabat (1666–1748). Apprenticed as a silk weaver to the textile manufacturer Jean Mazancieu, Lyon, 1744. Married Elisabeth Charryé, daughter of the designer François Charryé, 1748: 5 daughters and 1 son. Active as a designer from 1748, and as a designer, merchant, manufacturer, and entrepreneur, from 1749; resident in Lyon with a retail outlet in Paris. Worked with Charryé, 1749; associated with Camille Pernon during the 1760s; listed as independent manufacturer and dealer, Lyon, by 1779; active as a merchant in collaboration with Le Roux, Paris, from 1779. Awarded various pensions, including one of 600 livres, 1758; increased to 6000 livres, 1775. Responsible for several technical innovations and inventions; received Prix d'Honneur, Académie des Sciences, 1779; ennobled, 1776; awarded gold medal for his contributions to industry and commerce, 1783. Looms and workshops destroyed in the siege of Lyon, 1793. Member, Académie de Lyon, 1801. Died in the Palais Saint-Pierre, Lyon, 27 February 1804.

Selected Works

A large collection of Lasalle's fabrics and working drawings, including a number of order books containing designs, is in the Musée Historique des Tissus, Lyon. Additional silk hangings, upholsteries and embroideries are in the Mobilier National, Paris; examples are also displayed in the Marie-Antoinette room at Fontainebleau, and in the antechamber of the Chapel of the Pushkin Palace, Russia. Primary documents and manuscript material relating to his inventions and career are held in the Archives Nationales, Paris.

Further Reading

A scholarly unravelling of the contradictory and complex accounts of Lasalle's career based on documentary evidence appears in Chaignon 1992. For additional details relating to Lasalle's designs see Miller 1988, and for a description of his technical inventions see Hafter 1977.

Algoud, Henri, "Un Maître du Décor de la Soie: Philippe de Lasalle" in *Gazette des Beaux-Arts*, December 1911

Arizzoli-Clementel, Pierre, "Philippe de Lasalle: Les Portraits Tissus de Louis XV et de la Comtesse de Provence au Musées des Tissus de Lyon" in *Revue de Louvre et des Musées de France*, 42, July 1992, pp.47–55

Borland, Belle M., *Philippe de Lasalle: His Contribution to the Textile Industry of Lyons*, Chicago: University of Chicago Press, 1936

Chaignon, Marie-Jo de, "Philippe de Lasalle, Dessinateur et Fabricant d'Étoffes de Soie à Lyon au XVIIe Siècle" in *Les Filières de la Soie Lyonnaise, Le Monde Alpin et Rhodanien*, 2–3, 1992, pp.65–84

Coquillat, J., "La Vie et les Oeuvres de Philippe de Lasalle" in *La Soierie de Lyon*, 1930, pp.326–38

Coural, J. and C. Gastinel Coural, *Soieries de Lyon: Commandes Royales au XVIIIe Siècle 1730–1800*, Lyon: Musée Historique des Tissus, 1988

Cox, Raymond, *Philippe de Lasalle, son Oeuvre au Musée Historique des Tissus de Lyon*, Paris, 1906

Hafter, Daryl M., "Philippe de Lasalle: From Mise-en-Carte to Industrial Design" in *Winterthur Portfolio*, 12, 1977, pp.139–64

Jardel, Marguerite, "Philippe de Lasalle, Magicien de la Couleur et de la Soie" in *Jardin des Arts*, February 1956

Miller, Lesley E., *Designers in the Lyon Silk Industry, 1712–87*, Ph.D. thesis, Brighton: Brighton Polytechnic (University of Brighton), 1988, chapter 8

Schmitter, M.-T. and F. Guichard, *Philippe de Lasalle: Exposition de Tentures à l'Occasion de l'Inauguration d'un Médaillon de 11 Mars* 1939, Lyon: Vaucanson, 1939

Latrobe, Benjamin Henry 1764–1820

American architect and designer of interiors and furniture

Born in England, widely travelled in Europe, and trained in engineering and architecture in London, Benjamin Henry Latrobe emigrated to the United States in 1795. There he became president Thomas Jefferson's favorite architect, and created an elegant Neo-Classical style which helped to define the culture of the new American Republic. One of the first professional architects to practise in the United States, Latrobe made a revolutionary contribution to the design of interiors by introducing the concept – then unknown in America – of the architect as designer of buildings, their interiors, and their furnishings as a unified aesthetic composition. Latrobe also introduced to America coherent theories of interior spatial sequencing and ornamentation, sophisticated European drawing techniques which focused on the design of interiors, and advanced Neo-Classical forms, furniture and color schemes. His American designs included interiors for major public buildings such as the White House and the United States Capitol, and for important private residences.

In England, Latrobe worked (from c.1787) for London architect Samuel Pepys Cockerell, who devoted great attention to interiors. He also knew the interiors of Robert and James Adam, George Dance, Henry Holland and John Soane, as well as contemporary French designs. Upon arriving in the United States, Latrobe created the first body of architectural theory in the new country. This theory guided the creation of his interiors. For example, he considered both functional needs and environmental orientation in his distribution of rooms in plan. He located major living spaces on the south for light and warmth while segregating circulation and service spaces to the north. He introduced natural light primarily from the north and south, as he considered eastern and western light too harsh for pleasant interiors. In his spatial sequencing, Latrobe suggested that rooms be elaborated in an experiential hierarchy, so that they became more elaborate as one progressed through the plan. Latrobe also sequenced his interior spaces for effects of novelty and surprise, often creating winding, non-axial routes composed of different room shapes, surprise vistas, and marked effects of light and shadow. He called these interior effects "scenery" (derived from Robert Adam's similar use of the term) and drew their compositional principles from 18th-century Picturesque landscape theories. Latrobe's best surviving "scenic" interiors are in the John and Eliza Pope Villa in Lexington, Kentucky (1811) where one progresses from low, rectilinear spaces on the first floor, up a winding stair to a dramatic and unexpected domed rotunda and curvilinear drawing and dining rooms in the upper storey. The architect included similar "scenic" effects in his proposed designs for remodelling the interiors of the White House for Thomas Jefferson (1804, unexecuted), where visitors would have progressed through a novel variety of room shapes, column screens, and contrasts of light and shadow.

Latrobe's interior ornament was Grecian in its simplicity, but his room shapes derived from complex Roman arcuated construction and spatial types: domed rotundas, basilicas with half-domes, and groin-vaults. Though Neo-Classical, his rooms could be dramatically asymmetrical. The drawing room of the Markoe House in Philadelphia (1808, demolished) had four entirely different elevations: a segmental vault on one side, a segmental half-dome on another, a flat window wall, and a flat fireplace wall, all held in a dynamic, albeit un-classical, tension. While Latrobe's vocabulary was generally Neo-Classical, he occasionally employed other styles. He designed a full Egyptian interior for the Library of Congress within the US Capitol building (1808), and Gothic interiors for both Sedgeley, the Philadelphia villa of William Crammond (1799), and for his unbuilt Gothic project for the Baltimore Cathedral (1804). Due in part to his engineering training, Latrobe developed "rational" theories of interior construction and ornamentation. He preferred masonry structure for the complex vaulted spaces in his public buildings such as the Bank of Pennsylvania (1798), the Baltimore Cathedral, and the interiors of the US Capitol (1803–12 and 1815–17). Though his domestic interiors were constructed with lath and plaster, Latrobe made them conform to the structural "rules" of masonry construction, and "rationalized" his interior plaster ornament by recessing it below the surface so that servants could not accidentally knock it off while dusting.

In addition to his coherent theories for the design of buildings and interiors, Latrobe introduced an array of sophisticated drawing types – previously little used or understood in America – which favored the design of interiors. One technique he used was that of the room plan with "laid-back elevations". This drawing type, developed in early 18th century England by neo-Palladian architects such as Burlington and Kent, and refined by Robert Adam, consisted of a room plan with each wall laid flat around it, like a box cut at the corners. This technique allows the designer to see all the elevations simultaneously in orthographic relationship, so that they could all be designed in unity. This drawing type also allowed for the design and inclusion of furniture as an integral part of the wall elevations. Latrobe also used reflected ceiling plans, drawn in dotted lines on his floor plans, which indicated the vaulting systems, whether masonry or plaster, which created the room shapes beneath. He also drew sections of his buildings, which allowed for the development of the interior elevations of the rooms, including mouldings, drapery and furniture. In addition, Latrobe generated dazzling perspective views of his interiors, rendered in brilliant watercolors of reds, yellows, blues and greens, a skill exhibited by no American architect before him.

Though many of Latrobe's finest interiors have been lost through demolition or remodelling, enough survive to exhibit his virtuosity. His greatest surviving public interiors are those of the original, central portion of the US Capitol, including the old House of Representatives and the Senate Chamber, splendid Neo-Classical spaces created by half-domes resting against shallow segmental arches, and lit by oculi from above. The most unorthodox space in the Capitol is that of the old Supreme Court Chamber, with its low segmental and rib-vaulted dome resting upon giant, primitive, Doric columns. Latrobe designed elaborate draperies and ceremonial furniture for these spaces, such as speakers' rostrums, presidents' chairs, canopies, and tripod lamps, mostly of a highly architectural character, and employing the Greek orders. Latrobe's most popular innovation for the Capitol interiors was his invention of new "American Orders": columns and capitals based upon native flora such as Indian maize or corn, magnolias, and tobacco. Latrobe's finest surviving domestic interior is the entrance hall of the house of Commodore Stephen and Susan Decatur, in Washington DC (1817). With its half-basilica plan, its low, segmental arches, half-dome, pendentives, niches, and "flat domed" center, all springing from a continuous frieze band which also joins the tops of all the door jambs, it is one of the most highly sculpted and fully integrated interiors designed in Federal America.

When offered the opportunity, Latrobe designed full suites of furniture for his domestic interiors. For the Philadelphia house of William and Mary Waln (1805–08), he designed an extraordinary drawing room set, including Greek *klismos*-style side chairs, Roman *lekthos*-style scroll-ended sofas, window benches, card tables, and a pier table. The furniture was painted with Neo-Classical motifs in Etruscan reds, blacks, and yellow ochres with gilded highlights; a frieze in matching colors ran around the room depicting Homeric scenes drawn from the illustrations of English artist John Flaxman. The Waln furniture survives, though the house does not. Latrobe also completely redecorated and furnished several rooms at the White House, including the elliptical reception room (today called the Blue Room), for President James and Dolley Madison (1809), including mantelpieces and overmantel mirrors, *klismos*-style chairs and scroll-ended sofas, the latter with miniature, reverse-tapered Doric columns as legs. The British burned these interiors in 1814, though Latrobe's drawings for them survive. Latrobe's furniture shows an awareness of the contemporary publications of Thomas Hope, Thomas Sheraton, and Percier and Fontaine. He introduced this advanced Greco-Roman decorative style to the United States, and the cabinet-makers he employed, such as Hugh and John Finlay of Baltimore, popularized it more extensively.

Few of Latrobe's original interiors survive, and only those in the US Capitol are completely restored to their early appearance. But with his chaste and elegant Neo-Classicism, Latrobe defined a style for Federal America, and showed the world how the citizens of a new, democratic republic might live.

PATRICK A. SNADON

Biography

Born in Fulneck, Yorkshire, England, 1 May 1764. Possibly studied at the University of Leipzig; apprenticed to the engineer John Smeaton (1724–92) c.1795; entered the office of Samuel Pepys Cockerell, London, 1787–91. Married 1) Lydia Sellon, 1790 (died 1793): 2 children; 2) Mary Elizabeth Hazlehurst, 1800: 3 daughters and 2 sons. Established his own architectural practice, London, 1791; appointed surveyor of the police offices, London, c.1792. Emigrated to the United States, 1795. Opened architectural office, Philadelphia, 1798; appointed surveyor of public buildings of America, Washington, DC, 1803 (resigned 1817). Lived in Washington, 1807–13 and 1815–18; in Pittsburgh 1813–15; in Baltimore 1818–20; moved to New Orleans, 1820. Involved in numerous engineering and speculative building schemes including canal development, pumping systems, rolling mills, textile manufacture, steamboats and real estate. Member, Academy of Arts, Philadelphia, 1805. Died of yellow fever in New Orleans, 3 September 1820.

Selected Works

Latrobe's correspondence is in the Maryland Historical Society, Baltimore. An important collection of his architectural drawings and designs is in the Library of Congress, Washington, DC. Examples of Latrobe's furniture are in the Metropolitan Museum of Art, New York, and the Philadelphia Museum of Art.

Interiors

c.1791–94 Hammerwood Lodge, East Grinstead, Sussex (building and interiors)
c.1791–94 Ashdown House, London (building and interiors)
1796 William Pennock House, Norfolk, Virginia (building and interiors)
1798 Richmond Theatre and Assembly Rooms, Virginia (buildings and interiors)
1798 Bank of Pennsylvania, Philadelphia (building and interiors)
1798 Harvie-Gamble House, Richmond (building and interiors)
1799 Sedgeley, Philadelphia (building and interiors): William Crammond
1803–12 US Capitol, Washington, DC (building and interiors; with others)
1805–08 William Waln House, Philadelphia (building, interiors and furniture)
1808 Bank of Philadelphia (building and interiors)
1808 John Markoe House, Philadelphia (building and interiors)
1808 Clifton, Richmond (building and interiors): James Harris
1809 The White House, Washington, DC (interiors): James and Dolley Madison
1811 John Pope House, Lexington, Kentucky (building and interiors)
1815 John Peter Van Ness House, Washington, DC (building and interiors)
1815–17 US Capitol, Washington, DC (rebuilding and renovation)
1815–18 Exchange, Baltimore (building and interiors)
1817 Stephen Decatur House, Washington, DC (building and interiors)
1820 Louisiana State Bank, New Orleans (building)

Publications

The Journal of Latrobe; Being the Notes and Sketches of an Architect, Naturalist and Teacher in the United States from 1796–1820, edited by J.H.B. Latrobe, 1905; reprinted 1971

Impressions Respecting New Orleans: Diary and Sketches, 1818–1820, edited by Samuel Wilson, Jr., 1951

The Papers of Benjamin Henry Latrobe, edited by Edward C. Carter II and others, 1980–

Further Reading

Brown, Glenn, *History of the United States Capitol*, 2 vols., 1900–03; reprinted New York: Da Capo, 1970

Bryan, Wilhemus B., *A History of the National Capitol*, 2 vols., New York: Macmillan, 1914–16

Carter, Edward C. II, *Benjamin Henry Latrobe and Public Works: Professionalism, Private Interest, and Public Policy in the Age of Jefferson*, Washington, DC: Public Works Historical Society, 1976

Coppa and Avery Consultants, *Benjamin Henry Latrobe, Architect* (bibliography), Monticello, IL: Vance, 1980

Eaton, Leonard K., *Houses and Money: The Domestic Clients of Benjamin Henry Latrobe*, Dublin, NH: Bauhan, 1988

Hamlin, Talbot, *Greek Revival Architecture in America*, New York: Oxford University Press, 1944

Hamlin, Talbot, *Benjamin Henry Latrobe*, New York: Oxford University Press, 1955

Klapthor, Margaret Brown, *Benjamin Latrobe and Dolley Madison Decorate the White House, 1809–1811*, Washington, DC: Smithsonian Institution, 1985

Lindsey, Jack L., "An Early Latrobe Furniture Commission" in *Magazine Antiques*, 139, January 1991, pp.208–19

Norton, Paul F., *Latrobe, Jefferson, and the National Capitol*, New York: Garland, 1977

Pierson, William H., Jr., "American Neoclassicism, The Rational Phase: Benjamin Latrobe and Robert Mills" in his *The Colonial and Neo-Classical Styles* (American Buildings and Their Architects, vol.1), New York: Doubleday, 1970

Raley, Robert L., "Interior Designs by Benjamin Henry Latrobe for the President's House" in *Magazine Antiques* (US), June 1959, pp.568–71

Leather

Leather has featured prominently within interiors since the Middle Ages. Its principal use has been as a covering for the seats and backs of chairs, but it has also been used as a protective covering for precious objects such as caskets and globes, and, more significantly, as a luxurious type of wallhanging.

The majority of seat-covers and protective covers have been made of plain leather and were usually fairly simple in appearance and utilitarian in character. Sometimes, however, the leather was painted, or decorated with stamped patterns which might also be gilded in the same manner as bookbindings. This technique was employed in many areas of continental Europe from the 16th century onwards and many examples of stamped and gilded covers survive. A somewhat more elaborate technique, introduced in the 16th and 17th centuries, was to decorate the leather with scorched ornaments but only a few undocumented covers treated in this manner are extant. But the most luxurious covers were made of gilt leather, a material that was also used extensively in wallhangings.

Gilt leather was extremely costly to produce – only figurative tapestries were more expensive – and its use was therefore always reserved for the most wealthy and sumptuous of interiors. Despite its name, gilt leather has nothing to do with gold but consists of rectangular leather panels (measuring on average about 24 by 20 inches) that are entirely covered with a thin layer of silver-foil. The silver-foil is fixed to the leather with parchment glue. Another coating of parchment glue, or occasionally egg white or fish glue, is then used to cover the silver-foil to prevent it from oxidizing. After the silver-foil is burnished, it is glazed with one or two layers of a translucent yellow-brown varnish. It is the combination of the clear coloured varnish on top of the silver-foil that creates the "golden" surface that is characteristic of gilt leathers. Once the gilding process was completed, further decoration could be applied using oil paints and hand-held iron tools – punches – which were used to stamp small patterns onto the gilt background to impart sparkle. Wall-coverings were formed by sewing the rectangular panels together and then nailing the combined sheets to battens fixed to the top and sides of the walls. Like tapestries and most other luxury wallhangings, gilt leather hangings were designed to hang from the cornice to the dado and were often combined with panelling.

The history of gilt leather dates back to the 6th century when decorated leather was made in Ghadâmes, a desert village in North Africa. Following the Moorish invasion of the Iberian peninsula, the technique spread northwards and by the 9th century gilt leather was being made in Spain. From the 14th century onwards its history becomes clearer and in the 16th century this branch of industry flourished and became very lucrative and *guadamecies* – a derivation of Ghadâmes – were produced in various cities including Cordoba, Barcelona, Seville, Valencia, Granada, Madrid, Jaen, Valladolid, Lerida, Ciudad Real and Ciudad Rodrigo. After 1600 the gilt leather industry in Spain declined. A gilt leather workshop still survived in Barcelona in 1791 –93, but this was an exception and production had died out in most other cities by this time.

The earliest known gilt leather workshop in Italy has been traced to the end of the 15th century in the Sicilian town of Messina, and in the 16th century gilt leather makers are documented in Milan, Ferrara, Bologna, Genoa, Rome and Naples. Venice became the main centre of production, and manufacturing continued there until at least 1790.

With the decline of the Spanish industry the manufacture of gilt leathers spread northwards to the Netherlands, England and France. French workshops existed in cities such as Marseille, Carpentras, Avignon, Lyon and Rouen but, inevitably, Paris was the main centre of production, and workshops have been traced from the mid-16th century until well into the 18th century. The most important Parisian manufacturer was Jean-Baptiste Delfosse (1680–1755). The majority of gilt leather makers in England also worked in the country's capital, London, where workshops have been documented from c.1600 to 1785. Around 1700 there was also a gilt leather maker active in Edinburgh. A speciality of English workshops was the production of painted pictorial and Chinoiserie-style gilt leather hangings. Numerous examples decorated with scenes of Chinese life were also used as screens and a spectacular set of hangings depicting episodes in the lives of Antony and Cleopatra dating from the late 17th century survives in the gallery of Dunster Castle in Somerset.

The principal centres of production, however, were in the

Leather: gilt leather wallhangings in a Netherlandish interior; painting by Gonzales Coques, c.1640

Netherlands from whence many of the finest examples of gilt leather were exported. The first documentary evidence of the production of gilt leather in the southern Netherlands dates from 1511. Many workshops were in operation in Malines from the mid-16th century onwards and the most important was the workshop belonging to the Vermeulen family (active early 17th century until 1797). During the 17th and 18th centuries gilt leather was also produced in Brussels, Antwerp, Ghent, Lille and Liège, but none of these cities ever achieved the same renown or status as Malines.

Up until the early 17th century the patterns on gilt leather hangings were either painted or stamped but in 1628, Jacob Dircxz. de Swart, a gilt leather maker in The Hague, obtained a patent for a revolutionary technique whereby repeating patterns could be embossed using engraved wooden printing moulds. The use of thin French calfskins facilitated the production of finely detailed designs and the embossed areas could be up to two or three centimetres high. The result was a wall-hanging made up of a series of leather panels, joined together and printed with identical embossed, gilded and painted decorations, whose embossed patterns stood out as golden "bubbles" and reflected the candle-light in all directions. The effect of such decorations was both novel and dramatic. Moreover, their insulating properties also made them particularly suitable for the Northern climate and they were widely sought-after as luxury hangings in mercantile and aristocratic homes both within and outside the Netherlands. In the 17th century there were fourteen gilt leather workshops active in Amsterdam alone, the most important being those of Hans le Maire (active 1617–1714) and the family Van den Heuvel (active c.1632–1714), while towns such as The Hague, Utrecht, Dordrecht, and Middleburg each had one workshop, the most notable being that of the de Swart family (active 1613–81) in The Hague.

The style and decoration of gilt leather hangings obviously differed according to the period and country in which they were produced. The earliest patterns were painted on flat pieces of leather and were often inspired by, or copied from textile designs, particularly rich silk brocades. The background and gilt areas of these hangings were also often enlivened with small stamped imprints – made with hand punches – of various shapes. Following the introduction of embossing techniques new patterns emerged. These were designed by painters and silversmiths especially for the gilt leather industry and included a wide variety of floral scrolls, auricular motifs, birds and insects, cupids and figures. In the early 18th century the patterns became more formal and symmetrical in appearance, a change often attributed to the influence of the designer

Daniel Marot. Subsequently, however, Baroque style designs gave way to lighter, more informal patterns inspired by contemporary silk and chintz designs. The traditional rectangular panels were replaced by long vertical strips made up of separate panels glued together, and, simultaneously, embossed patterns increasingly made way for painted decorations with gilt backgrounds stamped with small imprints.

Despite the sumptuousness of their appearance, gilt leathers did not remain in favour much past the middle decades of the 18th century. Indeed their very richness and solidity, which, along with their durability, had originally been the very qualities that had so appealed to an upper-middle-class and aristocratic clientele, later made them less acceptable within interiors now decorated in a lighter and more informal Rococo style. They were increasingly replaced with wallpapers or painted stucco decoration and many leather hangings were discarded around this time. However, the late 19th century saw a revival of interest in this style of decoration in England and North America and numerous Aesthetic and "Old English" style interiors were hung with antique gilt leather hangings imported from Spain and the Netherlands. These antiques were not only extremely expensive but were also in quite short supply. As a result, a variety of cheaper, embossed paper alternatives, produced by wallpaper manufacturers such as Paul Balin in France and Scott Morton's Tynecastle Tapestry in England, emerged in the 1870s and 1880s whose products skilfully imitated the patterns and appearance of the leather originals.

ELOY KOLDEWEIJ

Selected Collections

A list of important specialist collections of gilt leather panels and hangings appears in Waterer 1971. The principal European collections include: in Britain, the Victoria and Albert Museum, London; in France, the Musée National de la Renaissance, Écouen, and the Musée des Arts Décoratifs, Paris; in Germany, the Deutsches Ledermuseum, Offenbach-am-Main, the Deutsches Tapetenmuseum, Kassel, and the Kunstgewerbemuseum, Dresden; in the Netherlands, the Rijksmuseum, Amsterdam; and in Spain, the Museo Municipale, Cordoba, and the Museo Nacional de Arte Décorativas, Madrid. Fine examples of gilt leathers hanging *in situ* are in the Palazzo Chigi, Ariccia; the Museum Plantij-Moretus, Antwerp; Skokloster Castle, Balsta; Schloss Moritzburg, Dresden; Dunster Castle, Somerset; and Longleat House, Wiltshire.

Further Reading

For a comprehensive English-language introduction to the history and use of embossed and gilded leather, including a select bibliography, see Waterer 1971. Accounts of embossed and imitation leather papers appear in Scholten and Koldeweij 1989 and *Ledertapeten* 1989.

Bender, Agniezka, *Zlocone Kurdynany e Polsce*, Lublin, 1991

Clouzot, Henri, *Cuirs Decorées*, Paris, 1925

Cornforth, John, "Aglow with Golden Leather" in *Country Life*, 26 November 1987

Ferrandis Torres, José, *Cordobanes y Guadameces*, Madrid: Palacio de la Biblioteca, 1955

Fougeroux de Bondaroy, Auguste-Denis, *Art de Travailler les Cuirs Dorés ou Argentés*, Paris, 1762

Gall, Günther, *Leder im Europäischen Kunsthandwerk*, Braunschweig: Klinkhardt & Biermann, 1965

Huth, Hans, "English Chinoiserie Gilt Leather" in *Burlington Magazine*, July 1937

Ledertapeten, Goldleder, Kinkarawa (exhib. cat.), Offenbach-am-Main: Deutsches Ledermuseum, 1989

Leiss, Joseph, "Leder Tapeten" in Heinrich Olligs (editor), *Tapeten, Ihre Geschichte bis zur Gegenwart*, Braunschweig: Klinkhardt & Biermann, 1970, vol.1, pp.45–98, vol.2, pp.191–94

Madurell Marimon, José-Maria, *El Antiguo Arte del Guadameci y sus Artifices*, Vich: Colomer Munmany, 1973

Mühlbacher, Eva, *Europäische Lederarbeiten*, Berlin: Staatliche Museen zu Berlin, 1988

Paz Aguilo, Maria, "Cordobanes y Guadamecies" in *Historia de las Artes Aplicades e Industriales en España*, 1982, Madrid, pp.325–336

Scholten, Fritz and Eloy Koldweij, *Gouldleer Kinkarawa: De geschiedenis van het Nederlands goudleer en zijn invloed in Japan* (exhib. cat.), The Hague: Haags Gemeentemuseum, 1989

Waterer, John W., *Spanish Leather*, London: Faber, and New York: Praeger, 1971

Wormser, J.P., "Het Goudleder" in *Bouwkunst*, 5, 1913, pp.45–87

Le Blond, Alexandre-Jean-Baptiste

1679–1719

French architect and designer of gardens and interiors

Although he is best known as an architect of elegant domestic residences surrounded by magnificently planted and tiered gardens, Alexandre-Jean-Baptiste Le Blond began his career as an interior designer. This was due to the influence of his first teacher Jean Le Pautre (1618–82) an engraver and ornamentalist at the court of Louis XIV. Le Blond was advised to study with Le Pautre by his father Jean, a painter to the king. A relationship between the two families would continue with the sons, since Pierre Le Pautre (c.1648–1716), one of the most important interior designers of the period, also engraved some of the works of Alexandre Le Blond.

The influence of both Jean and Pierre Le Pautre may be seen in the interior designs of Le Blond, as well as the influence of Jean I Berain (1640–1711) the designer credited with encouraging the later *Style moderne* or Rococo Style. Berain created imaginative, painted fantasies which included an array of motifs inspired by Italian murals. These consisted of ribbons, urns, garlands, hermes, sphinxes, masks, tendrils, etc. all incorporated into the framework of wooden wainscoting or ceiling panels. The contribution of Le Blond and Pierre Le Pautre was in translating these two-dimensional fantasies into three-dimensional, sculpted arabesques. The polychromatic paintings of Berain became confections in gold and white which encouraged the use of large mirrors and painted overdoors. The formerly heavy, marble cornices now blended into the white and gold scheme of the rest of the room and took on more of a decorative than architectural function.

Le Blond's interiors for the Hôtel de Vendôme (1705–06, enlarged 1714–16) and the Hôtel de Clermont (1708–14) were much admired. Mariette said of his designs "il touchait l'ornement avec une tres grande delicatesse". This "delicate touch" became well known and very influential thanks to the publication of his ornamental works in the 1710 edition of d'Avillier's *Cours d'architecture* (first published in 1691). For this new edition, Le Blond added 29 plates and 33 pages of text. A discussion of the "modern" approach to interior decor was included under the title *Nouveaux Lambris de Menuiserie*. It was here that Le Blond promoted a carved, curved and lighter ornamental interior. In some suggestions for chimney-pieces, C-scrolls, garlands, putti and plants are gracefully incorporated into the overall design of the interior panels (*lambris*). The wide circulation of this book prompted some to credit the new style to Le Blond, but he had only refined the ideas already circulating at this time – especially those of Pierre Le Pautre who engraved the illustrations for him.

Le Blond contributed to other important publications of the period. He supplied five of the twelve plates for J.F. Felibien's *Histoire de l'Abbaye Royale de Saint-Denys en France* (1706) and was responsible for most of the third edition of Dézallier d'Argenville's *La Théorie et la Pratique du Jardinage* (1709). It was this latter work on landscape architecture that brought him to the attention of Peter the Great. Le Blond went to St. Petersburg in 1716 to help design the Tsar's new city on the Baltic. Included in Le Blond's entourage was the sculptor and interior designer Nicolas Pineau (1684–1754). Although Pineau was certainly influenced by Le Blond, his career as an interior designer would greatly outlast and overshadow that of his master. When Le Blond died of smallpox three years after their arrival in St. Petersburg, it was Pineau who continued his work there before returning to his own prominent career in France in 1727. The curved and graceful interior designs of Le Blond were still quite symmetrical and reserved. It was Pineau that brought this "modern" style into the full freedom of the Rococo (called *genre pittoresque* at the time), with elaborate and asymmetrical designs that became de rigueur for wealthy Parisian aristocrats.

Although he was not as great an innovator as either of his collaborators (Le Pautre or Pineau), Le Blond made a considerable contribution to the transition from the Baroque to the Rococo through his published writings and designs. He also contributed greatly to the overall organization and distribution of rooms in which these ornamental interiors were housed. He suggested that a gracious city residence (*Hôtel particulier*) should separate the public rooms (*appartements de parade*) from the private rooms (*appartements de commodité*) and that this organization should be based on practical rather than solely aesthetic criteria. This emphasis on comfortable, gracious living became a hallmark of Le Blond's architectural approach and included rooms that looked out on magnificent views. His carefully planned gardens included cascades, fountains and sculptural works all to be enjoyed by the residents. He is credited with popularizing the French formal garden throughout Europe, again through his publications.

Le Blond promoted a refined and elegant way of living that dominated the early half of the 18th century. The reserved elevations of his exterior façades, inspired by J. Hardouin-Mansart, opened into practically planned and comfortable rooms with gracefully carved wainscoting (*boiseries*). The whole was surrounded by a beautiful formal garden, to promote a total feeling of gracious living. Although he died in St. Petersburg shortly after the death of Louis XIV, Le Blond's works are often called Régence because they prompted the elegant and refined style associated with the regency era of the Duke of Orléans (1715–23).

KATHLEEN RUSSO

Biography

Born in Paris in 1679, the son of Jean Le Blond, a court painter. Studied under the engraver and ornemaniste Jean Le Pautre (1618–82); later trained under Jules Hardouin-Mansart (1646–1708) and André Le Nostre. Active as a designer of interiors from c.1705; designs for interior details published from 1710. Went to St. Petersburg and appointed architect-general to Peter the Great, in charge of the palace and gardens of Peterhof, 1716; his entourage included Nicolas Pineau (1684–1754). Died of smallpox in St. Petersburg in 1719.

Selected Works

Many of Le Blond's interiors are illustrated in d'Avillier's *Cours d'Architecture*, 1710.

Interiors

1705–06 Hôtel de Vendôme, Paris (building and interiors; enlarged 1714–16)

1708–14 Hôtel de Clermont, Paris (building and interiors)

1716–19 Peterhof Palace, St. Petersburg (designs for the palace and gardens; built posthumously with later additions by Bartolomeo Rastrelli)

Publications

Plates for J. F. Félibien's *Histoire de l'Abbaye Royale de Saint-Denys en France*, 1706

Plates for Dézallier d'Argenville's *La Théorie et la Pratique du Jardinage*, 1709

Plates for A.C. d'Avillier's *Cours d'Architecture*, 1710

Further Reading

Brice, Germain, *Description Nouvelle de ce quil remarquable dans la Ville de Paris*, 4, 1752; reprinted, Geneva: Droc, 1971

Gallet, Michel, *Paris Domestic Architecture of the 18th Century*, London: Barrie and Jenkins, 1972; as *Stately Mansions: Eighteenth Century Paris Architecture*, New York: Praeger, 1972

Hautecoeur, Louis, *Histoire de l'architecture classique en France*, vol.3, Paris: Picard, 1951

Kimball, Fiske, *The Creation of the Rococo*, 1943; reprinted as *The Creation of the Rococo Decorative Style*, New York: Dover, and London: Constable, 1980

Lossky, Boris, "L'Hôtel de Vendôme et son Architect Alexandre Le Blond" in *Gazette des Beaux-Arts*, 1932, pp.30–41

Lossky, Boris, "J.B.A. Le Blond, Architecte de Pierre Le Grand, son Oeuvre en France" in *Bulletin de l'Association Russe pour les Recherches Scientifiques à Prague*, III, 1936, pp.179–216

Mariette, Jean, *L'Architecture Français*, vols.2–3, 1727, edited by Louis Hautecoeur, Paris: van Oest, 1927–29

Marsden, Christopher, *Palmyra of the North: The First Days of St. Petersburg*, London: Faber, 1943

Scott, Katie, *The Rococo Interior: Decoration and Social Spaces in Early Eighteenth-Century Paris*, London and New Haven: Yale University Press, 1995

Le Brun, Charles 1619–1690

French architect, painter and designer

Famed as the dictator of the arts under Louis XIV and the image-builder of the greatest monarch in Europe, Charles Le Brun was the most important French artist in the second half of the 17th century. If his merits as a painter are now sometimes underestimated, his role as a skilful impresario of interior design is widely acknowledged as outstandingly significant. On

Le Brun: Galerie des Glaces, Versailles, 1678–84

the basis of Versailles alone, Le Brun's work ranks among the greatest and most celebrated decorative achievements of all time and he realised one of the grandest programmes in the glorification of monarchy that cannot fail to impress by its sheer magnitude. Yet Le Brun is often regarded as little more than a puppet in Louis XIV's cultural propaganda machine. In fact, he was an artist of energy and vision and, a resourceful courtier and servant of the king, he employed a supremely adaptable approach to interior design at Versailles, the style and vocabulary of which had been formulated in previous commissions.

The development of Le Brun's style was greatly influenced by his journey to Italy (1642–45), where he was impressed by classical antiquity and the work of the Carracci and Raphael, and by the work of Nicolas Poussin whom he accompanied to Rome, and also by contemporary exponents of the Baroque, in particular Pietro da Cortona (1596–1669). Le Brun was to use all that he had seen and studied on his return to Paris.

Le Brun embarked on his first important interior commission, the ceiling decoration of the Galerie d'Hercule (Hôtel Lambert, Paris) in about 1650. This was not only an early indication of his facility in designing on a grand scale, but an example of the new Italianate style of ceiling painting that he and other artists were introducing into France. The notion that such schemes were solely decorative, devoid of a didactic function, does not apply to Le Brun's work here or later, as the importance of the subject was integral to the formation of his decorative style. Thus the painted scenes were to be read and understood as well as aesthetically enjoyed. The shallow, coved ceiling, disproportionately low in comparison with the length of the gallery, cannot be viewed in one glance. Le Brun compensated for this by dividing the surface into three main sections. Dedicated as a whole to the Apotheosis of Hercules, one section shows the gods welcoming the hero into the skies and the other depicts Ceres and Cybele preparing his wedding banquet. The main scenes are separated by two painted "tapestries". Le Brun uses illusionistic devices to give the impression of height and volume: heavy "architecture" accentuates the breakthrough to the sky, figures appear to fly below the architectural cross-beams, and the "tapestries" sag at the edges. The most daring piece of illusion is the chariot of Hercules that charges towards the archway. Le Brun's use of mixed perspective in this ceiling is a characteristic feature of his oeuvre: for reasons of clarity the most important figures appear as if painted on a vertical (*quadro riportato*), the supporting figures are in greater perspective, and inanimate forms and objects are depicted as if seen from below (*di sotto in su*).

In 1658, Le Brun was placed in charge of the interior decorations (which included the artistic direction of the Maincy tapestry-works) of the new château of Vaux-le-Vicomte which was one of the grandest private commissions ever to have been seen in France and which is generally accepted, in terms of style and scale, as a precursor to Le Brun's subsequent work at Versailles. Some of the rooms are elaborately decorated in a style brought by Le Brun from Italy, featuring a mixture of stucco, gilding and painting. The Chambre du Roi is the most spectacular of these rooms, and suggests the influence of Pietro da Cortona's work at the Palazzo Pitti, Florence. On the ceiling and coving, high-relief stucco modelling, which includes white figures with gilded wings and drapery, heavy swags, and lunette frames with curved volutes, contrasts with the brightly coloured or grisailles painted areas. However, while the overall richness of the interior appears to be the epitome of the Italian Baroque style, there are important stylistic differences. The more extreme techniques of illusion and foreshortening, and thus the dynamism of the Italian style, are here tempered and more static. The sculptural areas do not intrude into the painted ones which are clearly delineated with moulded frames. The central painting does not attempt to give the illusion of a view to a real sky and the figures float without any clear perspectival direction. These differences mark the compromise that was to become known as the Louis XIV style. The classical tradition and demand for controlled expression inherent in the national taste prevented Le Brun and others from simply aping or exaggerating the work of contemporary Italians.

Le Brun's use of grotesque ornament in interior design was also significant. Painted grotesque ornament was used in several rooms at Vaux, and in general continued the bold, dense and naturalistic version transmitted from Italy to France by Simon Vouet, under whom Le Brun had trained. In the salle à manger (c.1660) where grotesque decoration is used extensively on the wall panelling, the acanthus foliage, strapwork, fantastic creatures and drapery hanging from baldaquins are mixed with the arms and emblems (squirrels) of the Vaux-le-Vicomte's owner, Nicolas Fouquet. The novelty of Le Brun's grotesques lies in his occasional use of moulded straight bars, and scrolls of flat bandwork terminating in scrolled acanthus and connected by bars, within the decorative scheme. Similar painted and stucco ornamentation was employed by Le Brun, for example, in the Galerie d'Apollon in the Louvre (begun 1663) and grotesques also figure in the borders of his tapestry designs.

Le Brun's career reached its zenith at a significant moment in French cultural history. From 1661, Louis XIV embarked upon a programme of massive investment in architecture and all the arts which was not only intended to provide the king with splendid and magnificent surroundings but which also played a crucial role in formulating the cult of the "Sun King". The Gobelins manufactory (officially named the *Manufacture Royale des Meubles de la Couronne* and established in 1667) was created to provide every luxury necessary for the royal palaces except carpets, which were woven at the Savonnerie. Appointed the Premier Peintre du Roi in 1664, Le Brun was placed in charge of its artistic production. He was the perfect choice for this position. He had proved himself capable of designing on a grand scale and was experienced in the swift execution of all aspects of interior design. He was also an able administrator.

The Gobelins was both a school and a manufactory, and Le Brun integrated these two roles by controlling the entire output of the factory (involving some 250 workmen and including painters, sculptors, cabinet-makers, weavers, silver and goldsmiths, woodcarvers and marble workers), overseeing the training of craftsmen and artists and impressing on the organisation a corporate discipline and uniformity of style that was only possible through the domination of a single artistic temperament. Under Le Brun's leadership, the Gobelins raised standards of craftsmanship to a level unprecedented in Europe. He provided compositional drawings for all the decorative elements in the factory's designs, but the breadth and sheer numbers of these meant that Le Brun was able to execute comparatively little painting himself. This work was carried out by his team of assistants, who were expected to remain faithful to his master drawings; all of this reflected both the principles of the leading Parisian artistic institutions and Le Brun's own classical temperament. He was also president of the Royal Academy and his domination of the arts was complete until the death of his protector – the king's minister, Jean-Baptiste Colbert – in 1683 brought Le Brun's rival, the painter Mignard to power.

The diversity of the Gobelins output is illustrated in Le Brun's tapestry – one of the suite woven between 1665 and 1678 called *L'histoire du Roi* – designed to commemorate Louis XIV's ceremonial visit to the factory in 1667 (Versailles). It shows the craftsmen presenting the king with rich furnishing fabrics, a painted canvas, floor panelling, and furniture incorporating elaborate marquetry. Le Brun himself stands behind Louis XIV on the left. Examples of the legendary silver furniture which filled the Galerie des Glaces, the Salon de la Guerre and the king's bedchamber at Versailles can be seen in the foreground. Much of this was melted down in 1689 and the rest in 1709 to provide extra coinage for the exchequer, thus destroying a major section of Le Brun's design work. Le Brun's framed cartoon of *The Passage of the Granicus* from the celebrated tapestry series of the life of Alexander the Great (1664–80) is visible in the background. Le Brun insisted on a high degree of fidelity to the design (if not the colours) of the original cartoons for his tapestries which were executed as finished oil-paintings rather than in the traditional tempera. In addition to the two sets already mentioned, Le Brun and his team devised the graceful and less majestic *Months* or *Royal Residences*. Incorporating the royal houses, landscapes and diversions of the French court, the series was woven seven times between 1668 and 1694.

It was at Versailles that the Louis XIV style reached its apogee. Attention was lavished above all on the interiors, and as *premier peintre* and *directeur* of the Gobelins, Le Brun played an integral role in their creation. The decoration of the Grands Appartements (1672–81) was based on the combination of gilded stucco and painted figurative schemes previously employed at Vaux and the Louvre, but was unprecedented in terms of its scale, richness and complexity. The walls were not decorated with the traditional painted panelling, but were covered either with polychrome marble in classical and geometric patterns, or with richly coloured patterned silk on which paintings from the royal collection were hung. Attributes of kingship and references to Apollo and the Sun proliferated. The king's Appartements were approached via the Escalier des Ambassadeurs which was one of the most elaborate and dramatic staircases in Europe. (The destruction of the official grand entrance of the palace in 1752 represents the single, most significant loss of work dating from the reign of Louis XIV at Versailles.)

Le Brun's decorations were extraordinarily opulent and complex. The lower section consisted of polychrome marble, and a sumptuous fresco adorned the upper section of the wall and ceiling. On a level with the *premier étage*, Le Brun included an illusionistic architectural framework with *loggie*, the parapets of which were hung with carpets. Behind these parapets stood groups of figures representing the four parts of the world, a theme continued in the ceiling with four seated figures. Simulated tapestries depicting scenes of the king's military victories hung next to the *loggie*. Painted architecture which opened out to the "sky", continued into the lower section of the vault with exotic birds perched on the balustrades.

Such illusionistic balconies were included in other decorations of the Grands Appartements, an example being the present day Salle des Gardes de la Reine. Around the opening of the skylight, Le Brun depicted several scenes from contemporary history involving Louis XIV, which complemented the narrative of the tapestries below. At the centre of this panegyrical imagery was a bust of Louis XIV himself, by Jean Warin. Thus by 1679, the king was no longer represented through the iconography of the god Apollo, but in person. This important shift in self-image set a precedent also employed in the Galerie des Glaces and in the Salon de la Guerre.

Magnificent as the Grands Appartements are, they are but a fanfare to the true pièce *de resistance* of the palace, the famous Galerie des Glaces (1678–84). This, and the two salons at each end, were created following the designs of the architect Jules Hardouin-Mansart. The Salon de la Guerre and the Salon de la Paix are decorated with marble and gilded trophies symbolising respectively war and peace. Le Brun's ceilings continue these themes with scenes relating to recent French victories in the Dutch War. In one, the central panel shows France dressed for war and holding a protective shield bearing the portrait of Louis XIV, and, in the coves, personifications of her vanquished enemies. In the other, France is crowned by Glory, with her enemies and Christian Europe enjoying the benefits of Peace. The Salon de la Guerre is dominated by the imposing plaster relief of Louis XIV destroying his enemies, by Antoine Coysevox. The over-riding theme of both rooms is victory and supremacy.

The decoration of the Galerie des Glaces was the result of a close collaboration between Le Brun and Hardouin-Mansart. Hardouin-Mansart was probably responsible for the overall design but the precise balance of creative input remains unclear. Today, it is famous for the dazzling effect of the mirrors – perhaps also Hardouin-Mansart's decision – but to the king and his councillors, it was the ceiling that eclipsed all the other interior features. The execution of this enormous decoration (approximately 240 feet in length) can be firmly attributed to Le Brun. His first proposals for the painted areas focused on Apollo and Hercules respectively. But following the Treaty of Nijmwegen (1678) which brought the Dutch War to a close and established France as the military and diplomatic victor, the king's intentions became even more self-aggrandising and the first plans, which had already been accepted, were dramatically rejected. Louis XIV was at the zenith of his power and in the prevailing atmosphere of jubilation, Le Brun was commanded to represent the king himself. The artist reputedly designed the central panel in two days, which took as its theme the king's assumption of power in 1661. As with other panels, this was executed as *quadro riportato* in a complicated mixture of history and allegory. Louis, dressed as French royalty but with Roman armour, is shown inspired by Minerva (wisdom) to look towards Glory. Around him are figures representing the benefits of peace and the achievements of the reign. The ominous storm clouds above lead the spectator into the opposite scene of the panel, where the enemies of France (Holland, Spain and Germany) sit among arms and captives. In the other paintings, the king is shown performing glorious deeds, largely drawn from the conquests of the Dutch War and accompanied by classical divinities and personifications. These develop themes portrayed in the contemporary bas-reliefs in the Escalier des Ambassadeurs but the effect in the Galerie des Glaces is both more immediate and more powerful. The remaining decoration forms a rich pageant of painted "architecture", winged and mythological figures, garlands of flowers, and gilded moulding and stucco trophies in low relief. If the inspiration for the direct portrayal of the king came from his *conseil en haut*, the political language of the design was Le Brun's. Aggressively propagandist, and overwhelmingly vainglorious to modern eyes, this ceiling is nonetheless a breathtaking statement of royal and artistic power.

CHRISTINE RIDING

See also Gobelins Tapestry; Hardouin-Mansart; Le Vau

Biography

Born in Paris, 24 February 1619, the son of Nicolas Le Brun, a master sculptor. First apprenticed as a painter to François Perrier, then to Simon Vouet, 1632. Came under the protection of Chancellor Pierre Séguier, 1634. Travelled to Rome, probably with Nicolas Poussin, under whom he studied, 1642; returned to Paris, 1645. Married Suzanne Butaye, 1647. A founder of the French Academy, 1648 (chancellor 1663, rector 1668, director 1683). Active for Nicolas Fouquet at Vaux-le-Vicomte, 1661. Ennobled, 1662. In royal service as Directeur de la Manufacture Royale des Meubles de la Couronne at the Gobelins, and director of artistic projects; designed for tapestry, sculpture, metalwork and furniture, 1662–90. Appointed Premier Peintre du Roi and curator of the royal paintings and drawings collection, 1664. Lectured at the Academy, 1667. Active at Versailles on the Grands Appartements, 1671–86, and at Marly, 1683. Died in Paris, 12 February 1690.

Selected Works

A great number of Le Brun's drawings are preserved in the Louvre, Paris.

Interiors

1649–50 Hôtel de Jars, Paris (chambre à l'alcôve)
1649–62 Hôtel Lambert, Paris (Galerie d'Hercule, ceiling): Nicolas Lambert
1650 Hôtel du Nouveau, Paris (ceiling paintings): Jérôme de Nouveau
1650s Hôtel d'Aumont, Paris (Appartement de Madame, Grande Chambre)
1652–53 Hôtel de la Rivière, Paris (Grande Chambre and Grand Cabinet ceilings, now Musèe Carnavalet): Louis Barbier, abbé de la Rivière
1658 Hôtel de la Bazinière, Paris (Cabinet, antechamber): Bertrand de la Bazinière
1658–61 Vaux-le-Vicomte (Salon d'Hercule, Salon des Muses, Cabinet de la Maréchale, Chambre du Roi, Grand Salle Ovale; architect L. Le Vau): Nicolas Fouquet
1663 Louvre Palace, Paris (Galerie d'Apollon): Louis XIV
1672–74 Sceaux (frescoes for chapel ceiling; Pavillon de l'Aurore): Chancellor J.-B. Colbert
1672–78 Versailles (Escalier des Ambassadeurs; architect L. Le Vau): Louis XIV
1678–84 Versailles (ceilings for Galerie des Glaces, Salles des Gardes de la Reine; architect J. Hardouin-Mansart): Louis XIV
1683 Marly (façade designs): Louis XIV
1686 Versailles (ceilings for Salon de la Guerre, Salon de la Paix): Louis XIV

Le Brun designed several important tapestry series, including the *Histoire d'Alexandre* (1664–80) and the *Histoire du Roi* (1665–78).

Further Reading

The most comprehensive survey of Le Brun's career is Thuillier and Montagu 1963; more general surveys in English are in Blunt 1970, and Berger 1993 and 1994. Le Brun's preparatory drawings for work at Versailles can be studied in *Le Brun à Versailles*, 1985.

Babelon, Jean-Pierre, "Nouveaux documents sur la décoration interieure de l'Hôtel Lambert", in *Bulletin de la Societé d'Histoire de l'art français*, 1972, pp.135–43

Berger, Robert W., *The Palace of the Sun: The Louvre of Louis XIV*, University Park: Pennsylvania State University Press, 1993

Berger, Robert W., *A Royal Passion: Louis XIV as Patron of Architecture*, Cambridge and New York: Cambridge University Press, 1994

Blunt, Anthony, *Art and Architecture in France, 1500–1700*, 2nd edition Harmondsworth: Penguin, 1970

Charles Le Brun 1619–1690: Le décor de l'escalier des Ambassadeurs à Versailles (exhib. cat.), Musée National du Château de Versailles, 1990

Coen, Rena Neumann, "The Duc de Créquy's *Primavera*", in *Minneapolis Institute of Arts Bulletin*, 53, 1964, pp.17–25

Dupont, J., "Le Pavillon de l'Aurore à Sceaux", *Bulletin de la Societé d'Histoire de l'art français*, 1958, 1959, pp.91–96

Gareau, Michel and Lydia Beauvais, *Charles Le Brun: First Painter to King Louis XIV*, New York: Abrams, 1992

Jansen, Birgit, *Der Grand Escalier de Versailles: Die Dekoration durch Charles Le Brun und das absolutische Programm*, dissertation, Bochum University, 1981

Jouin, Henry, *Charles Le Brun*, Paris: Imprimerie Nationale, 1889

Kimball, Fiske, "Mansart and Le Brun in the Genesis of the Grande Galerie de Versailles", in *Art Bulletin*, XXII, 1949, pp.1–6

Le Brun à Versailles (exhib. cat.), Paris: Musée du Louvre, 1985

Meyer, Daniel, *L'Histoire du Roy*, Paris: Éditions de la Réunion des Musées Nationaux, 1980

Montagu, Jennifer, "The Early Ceiling Decorations of Charles Le Brun", in *Burlington Magazine*, CV, 1963, pp.395–408

Montagu, Jennifer, "Le Brun's Early Designs for the Grande Galerie: Some Comments on the Drawings", in *Gazette des Beaux-Arts*, vol.120, November 1992, pp.195–206

Poisson, Georges, *Le Pavillon de l'Aurore*, Sceaux: Musée de l'Ile-de-France, 1983(?)

Posner, D., "Charles Le Brun's 'Triumphs of Alexander'", *Art Bulletin*, XLI, 1959, pp.237–48

Sainte Fare Garnot, Nicolas, *Le Décor des Tuileries sous la règne de Louis XIV*, Paris: Réunion des Musées Nationaux, 1988

Smith, Peter, "L'Hôtel de la Bazinière" in Pierre Francastel (editor), *L'Urbanisme de Paris et de l'Europe, 1600–1680*, Paris: Klincksieck, 1969

Thuillier, Jacques and Jennifer Montagu, *Charles Le Brun, 1619–1690* (exhib. cat.), Château de Versailles, 1963

Wilhelm, Jacques, "Les Décorations de Charles Le Brun à l'Hôtel de la Rivière", in *Bulletin du Musée Carnavalet*, October 1949, pp.6–15

Wilhelm, Jacques, "Les Décorations de l'Hôtel de la Rivière: Nouveaux documents", in *Bulletin du Musée Carnavalet*, November 1963, pp.1–19

Le Corbusier 1887–1965

French architect, painter, theorist and designer

Charles-Edouard Jeanneret who, in 1920, assumed the name of an ancestor, Le Corbusier, is arguably the most important architect of the 20th century. Known primarily for buildings and exteriors, he was also influential in the fields of furniture and interior design.

Walter Gropius, spokesman and theorist of the Modern Movement, declared that it would take an entire generation of architects to realize the visionary ideas Le Corbusier had proposed in his innumerable projects and sketches. The leading Brazilian architect Oscar Niemayer has stated that he considers Le Corbusier the Leonardo da Vinci of our epoch, while the architect Eero Saarinen regarded him as the great "form giver" of Modern architecture.

Le Corbusier attended art school in his birthplace, La Chaux-de-Fonds, where he was apprenticed as an engraver and chiseller, and moved to Paris in 1908, at a time when Picasso and Braque were shaking the Establishment with their early Cubist paintings. The new aesthetics had an impact on the young Le Corbusier, who studied architecture for 15 months under the master of reinforced concrete construction, Auguste Perret, who claimed that his new structural method was destined to revolutionize architecture. Next Le Corbusier spent five months with Peter Behrens in Berlin, studying technical organization and the relationship between industry and design, before moving briefly to Josef Hoffmann's office in Vienna. Significantly, two fellow apprentices in Behrens's studio were Ludwig Mies van der Rohe and Walter Gropius. From his distinguished tutors Le Corbusier learned honesty in architectural expression and became enthusiastic about the new conception, Machine Art, in which pure geometrical forms were considered beautiful, belonging to an orderly and coherent system. Le Corbusier continued his education travelling throughout Europe, sketching and analysing everything from cathedrals to Mediterranean villages.

In 1917 he settled in Paris where he was preoccupied with painting and met Amédée Ozenfant, a fellow painter who shared his artistic philosophy. From their creative partnership was born the 1918 manifesto of Purism, *Après le Cubisme*, which called for a return to the rational, geometric foundations of Cubism. Le Corbusier and Ozenfant painted geometric compositions of anonymous, mass-produced objects such as vases, bottles, and glasses in the belief that such everyday objects represented the ultimate in design. To voice the ideas of the new aesthetics, with the poet Paul Dermée they launched the magazine *L'Ésprit Nouveau*, devoted to the visual arts, architecture, engineering, music, literature, industrial design, and "l'esthetique de la vie moderne". In it Le Corbusier published a series of "Warnings to Architects", defining the new theory of aesthetics, which were published in 1923 in the book *Vers une architecture*. He followed his own guidelines in the designs for the Citrohan House (1920–22), exploring interlocking spaces of different but related heights, giving an uninterrupted living area in contrast to the usual single rooms. In the Ville Contemporaine project (1922) for a city of three million inhabitants, Le Corbusier laid down the principles of rational city planning, segregating pedestrian and vehicular traffic, working and dwelling areas, amid open parks and gardens, allowing in the sun and air for healthy living. In his radical voice he compared the elegant lines of the contemporary automobile (Bugatti) with the Parthenon, to prove that the same aesthetic was in operation.

Le Corbusier presented his new ideas to the general public at the 1925 Exposition Internationale des Arts Décoratifs in Paris. He and his cousin, Pierre Jeanneret, with whom he became associated in his architectural work, were commissioned to design the French pavilion. Appropriately known as the Pavillon L'Esprit Nouveau, along with the Soviet Pavilion designed by Russian avant-garde architect Konstantin Melnikov, it was advanced and daring among the Historicist architecture of the other nations' pavilions. The Pavillon demonstrated a new way of living; it featured a full-scale model of an apartment unit from the vertical-slab mass-housing of the "superimposed villas" designed for the 1922 Ville Contemporaine. "My intention was to illustrate how, by virtue of standardization, industry creates pure forms. I wanted to stress the intrinsic value of this pure form of art that is the result," Le Corbusier explained. In the pavilion he also took the opportunity to illustrate his theories as applied to interior architecture. The effect was deliberately sparse, with white walls decorated only by the Fernand Léger paintings. A two-storey outdoor living terrace and a two-storey living room overlooked by a balcony provided an illusion of spaciousness. All components of the unit, including the doors and windows, were based on a modular system. The standardized unit furniture, designed for mass production, included storage walls, a table made by a hospital furniture manufacturer, and the *Wiener Stuhl* (Viennese Chair) developed by Gebrüder Thonet in 1904. The chair consisted of a bentwood frame with arms and a cane seat. Le Corbusier used the chairs repeatedly in his interiors, including the Weissenhofsiedlung Exhibition houses of 1927, and made them famous all over the world.

The 1926 declaration of "Five Points Towards a New Architecture" is based on Le Corbusier's definition of the reinforced concrete column and slab system of construction called the Dom-Ino, developed in 1914. A frame of columns supporting the floor and roof slabs, linked with cantilevered concrete stairs, is the only fixed part of a building. Everything else, the building skin, partitions and so forth, is non-structural and entirely flexible. Open-plan, freed from the need for load-bearing walls, it is capable of infinite variations. The Five Points principles of an independent structural skeleton and ensuing open plan has revolutionized architectural design ever since. Fundamental to the Five Points were: the supports that were spaced out at specific equal intervals to elevate the ground floor; the flat roof with its garden, enabling a city to recover its built-up areas; the free designing of the ground plan, with interior walls placed where required, each floor independent of the rest and allowing total freedom of plan; the horizontal (ribbon) window, extending between supports to light a room wall-to-wall; and free design of a façade which has no supportive function.

Le Corbusier demonstrated these design principles and his credo "the house is a machine for living in" in a series of built projects: the houses for Ozenfant, Jeanneret, La Roche, Cook, Villa Stein at Garches, two structures at the Weissenhof Exhibition, and the Villa Savoye at Poissy (1929–31). The inte-

Le Corbusier: living room and terrace, Villa Savoye, Poissy, 1929–31

rior of the Villa Besnus at Vaucresson (1922) was open plan with movable partitions to divide off the dining space. Large strips of horizontal windows caught the sun. The Villa Stein at Garches, near Paris (1927) was described as the first truly modern interior, punctuated by large columns, with built-in furniture. It was designed like the bridge of a ship; its windows running around the perimeter of the first-floor living area giving a treetop view. Later in his career Le Corbusier was to design a small church at Ronchamp which has been likened to a Byzantine chapel on an Aegean island. The poured concrete walls were thick and rounded, the windows small punched holes randomly scattered and filled with coloured glass which cast a gentle glow on the white walls.

The Villa Savoye is a complete and convincing statement of Le Corbusier's Purism in concrete and glass. A landmark of modern architecture, the design employs the Dom-Ino principles, lifted from the ground, open plan, ribbon windows, roof garden, cantilevered façade, and a ramp linking the levels. The rooms, composed around a large terrace, are designed as one flowing volume rather than separate areas to be filled with furniture. The carefully placed interior pieces, designed jointly with the interior designer Charlotte Perriand, Le Corbusier's principal assistant, are integrated with architecture to be admired as a sculpture. Two-storey living rooms and a continuous space of living, dining, kitchen, library, and activity areas in a home are customary today but originated with Le Corbusier.

While the Villa Savoye was on the drawingboard, Le Corbusier and Pierre Jeanneret were also remodelling the plans of a house at the Ville d'Avray. Along with Perriand, they designed for the villa built-in storage walls and three types of chairs: the *Grand Confort* armchair (1928), made from a bent tubular steel frame with loose, leather-covered upholstered cushions, manufactured by Gebrüder Thonet and reissued by Cassina from 1965; the *Chaise-longue* (1928), a bent tubular steel frame covered in ponyskin on an elongated H-form base, manufactured by Gebrüder Thonet and reissued in 1965 by Cassina; and the *Basculant* chair, (1929), manufactured by Gebrüder Thonet. In a less doctrinaire way, these chairs follow the same principles as the Bauhaus designs. While Marcel Breuer's chairs were entirely rational, technically precise, and elegant, Le Corbusier's chairs were less rational and less easy to manufacture. However, the *Chaise-longue* was an early example of ergonomic design. The movable seat section with adjustable neckrest affords an individual degree of comfort to its users. Author and architect Peter Blake has likened it to the complicated, beautifully articulated chassis of a Bugatti racing car.

At the 1929 Salon d'Automne in Paris, Le Corbusier, Jeanneret and Perriand exhibited a modern apartment with concealed lighting, laminated surfaces, furnished with their free-standing chairs and table, and a built-in storage wall with shelving, storage drawers, glass fronted display boxes, and mirrored sliding door cabinets. Here, too, Le Corbusier maintained that no interior design can be separated from the exterior design.

Throughout his career Le Corbusier was preoccupied with a proportional system of measurement. For him, ordering coherence and organizational clarity were the essential ingredients of aesthetics. He analysed the Golden Section principles of architectural order, suggesting that it was as valid today as it was in the designing of Notre Dame cathedral. In many of his projects he organized his designs with the use of Regulating Lines – parallel and perpendicular lines defining a composition of the whole and its parts.

It took Le Corbusier some 20 years to develop the proportional system known as the Modulor, related to the proportions of the human body. This was to serve the needs of mass production and facilitate prefabrication, while avoiding repetitive monotony. Several mass housing projects built after World War II were based on the Modulor. These Unités d'Habitation were erected in Marseille, Nantes-Reze, Berlin, and Briey-la-Fôret and were conceived as vertical garden cities, giving each family maximum privacy, independence and communal services, and exploiting maximum use of space.

While Le Corbusier was disappointed not to win two pivotal international competitions for large-scale buildings, the influence of the designs he entered is with us today. The two projects were the League of Nations in Geneva (1927) and the Palace of the Soviets in Moscow (1931).

From 1950 to 1957, towards the end of his life, Le Corbusier worked on the overall plan for Chandigarh, the Punjab's great new capital city, applying his theories on zoning and traffic separation, designing with great sensitivity buildings for the completed government center. His designs for tapestries for the Law Courts at Chandigarh were executed in Kashmir. His tapestry designs also appeared in the Unesco building in Paris.

If one wishes to believe that a genius is not born but made, then Le Corbusier is proof. Architect Jerzy Soltan, who worked with him for four years, described him as hard-working, totally devoted to architecture, with a rigidly organized schedule. Le Corbusier himself acknowledged the importance of the self-imposed creative regimen: "If the generations to come attach any importance to my work as an architect, it is to these unknown labors that one has to attribute its deeper meaning".

PETER LIZON

See also Modernism and the Modern Movement; Paris 1937; Perriand

Biography

Charles-Edouard Jeanneret; adopted name Le Corbusier, 1920. Born at La Chaux-de-Fonds, near Neuchâtel, Switzerland, 6 October 1887. Moved to France, 1917; naturalised, 1930. Studied metal engraving at the School of Applied Arts, La Chaux-de-Fonds, under Charles L'Eplattenier, 1900–05. First architectural commission, 1906. Travelled to Italy and Austria, 1906–07. Worked in the office of the architect Josef Hoffmann, Vienna, 1907; apprentice in the studio of Auguste Perret, 1908–09; worked in the office of Peter Behrens, with Walter Gropius and Mies van der Rohe, Berlin, 1910. Returned to France; established his own office, La Chaux-de-Fonds; active as a painter and engraver, 1912. Married Yvonne Gallis, 1930 (died 1957). In private practice as an architect, Paris, 1917–65: in partnership with his cousin Pierre Jeanneret (1896–1967), 1922–40; collaborated with the architect Charlotte Perriand, 1927–29; practised as Atelier des Bâtisseurs (ATBAT), from 1942. Began designing furniture in association with Jeanneret and Perriand, 1927. Published numerous theoretical texts from 1918 including *Vers Une Architecture*, 1923; founder-editor, with Amédée Ozenfant and Paul Dermée, *L'Esprit Nouveau*, Paris, 1919–25. Exhibited at numerous national and international exhibitions including Salon des Artistes Décorateurs and Salon d'Automne, 1920s, Paris 1925 and 1937, UAM (Union des Artistes Modernes), 1930–33, Brussels 1935 and 1937. Founder-member, CIAM (Congrès Internationaux d'Architecture Moderne), 1928, and UAM, 1930; founded ASCORAL Group (Assembly of Designers for Architectural Renewal), 1942. Lectured extensively in Europe and United States, 1921–56. Numerous awards including Gold Medal, Royal Institute of British Architects, 1959. Died at Cap Martin, France, 27 August 1965.

Selected Works

The Le Corbusier Archives, including a vast quantity of drawings, designs, plans, photographs, notebooks and manuscript material documenting every aspect of his career, are in the Fondation Le Corbusier, Paris. For a complete catalogue of his architectural works see Boesiger, 1930–70.

Interiors

1916	Villa Schwob, La Chaux-de-Fonds (building and interiors)
1920–22	Citrohan House, Paris (designs for building and interiors)
1920–22	Atelier Ozenfant, Paris (building and interiors)
1923–25	Villa La Roche-Jeanneret (now Fondation Le Corbusier), Paris (building and interiors)
1923–25	Maison Jeanneret, Corseaux-Vevey, Switzerland (building and interiors)
1925	Exposition Internationale des Arts Décoratifs et Industriels Modernes, Paris; reconstructed Bologna (Pavillon de l'Esprit Nouveau; building, interiors and furnshings)
1926	Villa Cook, Boulogne-sur-Seine (building and interiors)
1927	Villa Stein-de-Monzies (Les Terraces), Garches (building and interiors)
1927	Weissenhofsiedlung Exhibition, Stuttgart (two buildings)
1928–29	Villa Church, Ville d'Avray (remodelling, additions and furniture)
1929–31	Villa Savoye, Poissy (building and interiors)
1929	Salon d'Automne, Paris (Equipement Intérieur d'Une Habitation; interiors and furniture)
1929–33	Cité de Refuge, Salvation Army hostel, Paris (building and interiors)
1930	Beisteguy Apartment, Paris (remodelling and interiors)
1932–37	Exposition Internationale, Paris (Pavillon des Temps Nouveaux, building and interiors)
1935	Weekend House, Celle St.-Cloud (building and interiors)
1951–55	Chapel Notre-Dame-du-Haut and pilgrims' hostel, Ronchamp (building and interiors)
1951–56	High Court, Chandigarh, India (building and interiors)
1952–55	Villa Sarabhai, Ahmedabad, India (building and interiors)

Numerous additional municipal and institutional buildings until 1965.

Publications

Après Le Cubisme (with Amédée Ozenfant), 1918
L'Esprit Nouveau (editor), vols.1–28, 1920–25

Vers une Architecture, 1923; translated as *Towards a New Architecture*, 1931
Urbanisme, 1925; translated as *The City of Tomorrow and its Planning*, 1929
L'Art Décoratif d'aujourd'hui, 1925
Une Maison, un Palais, 1928
Précisions sur un État Présent de l'Architecture et de l'Urbanisme, 1930
La Ville Radieuse, 1935; translated as *The Radiant City*, 1935
Le Modulor 1948, 1950; 2nd edition, 1955
La Chapelle Notre-Dame-du-Haut à Ronchamp, 1956; translated as *The Chapel at Ronchamp*, 1957
My Work, 1960
The Decorative Art of Today, translated and introduced by James Dunnett, 1987

Further Reading

The literature on Le Corbusier is immense. For complete catalogues of architectural works, writings, drawings and additional manuscript material see Boesiger 1930–70, Besset 1981–82, and Brooks 1982–84. For useful histories of Le Corbusier's architecture and ideas see Curtis 1986, Jencks 1987, and Moos, 1979. An excellent study of Le Corbusier's villas, including contemporary photographs of interiors, appears in Benton, 1987. For a discussion of his early work within the context of French decorative art in the 1920s and 1930s see Troy, *Modernism and the Decorative Arts in France*, 1991.

Baker, Geoffrey, *Le Corbusier: An Analysis of Form*, 2nd edition New York: Van Nostrand Reinhold, 1989
Banham, Reyner, *Theory and Design in the First Machine Age*, London: Architectural Press, and New York: Praeger, 1960
Benton, Charlotte, "'L'Aventure du mobilier': Le Corbusier's Furniture Designs of the 1920s" in *Journal of the Decorative Arts Society 1890–1940*, no.6, 1982
Benton, Tim, *The Villas of Le Corbusier, 1920–1930*, New Haven and London: Yale University Press, 1987
Besset, Maurice, *Qui était Le Corbusier?*, Geneva: Skira, 1968
Besset, Maurice, *Le Corbusier: To Live with Light*, New York: Rizzoli, 1976; London: Architectural Press, 1987
Besset, Maurice (introduction), *Le Corbusier Sketchbooks*, 4 vols., Cambridge: Massachusetts Institute of Technology Press, and London: Thames and Hudson, 1981–82
Blake, Peter, *The Master Builders: Le Corbusier, Mies van der Rohe, Frank Lloyd Wright*, New York: Knopf, and London: Gollancz, 1960
Boesiger, Willy (editor), *Le Corbusier: Oeuvre Complète*, Zurich: Girsberger & Artemis, 8 vols., 1930–70
Brady, Darlene, *Le Corbusier: An Annotated Bibliography*, New York: Garland, 1985
Brooks, H. Allen (editor), *The Le Corbusier Archive*, 32 vols., New York: Garland, and Paris: Fondation Le Corbusier, 1982–84
Curtis, William J.R., *Le Corbusier: Ideas and Forms*, New York: Rizzoli, and Oxford: Phaidon, 1986
De Fusco, Renato, *Le Corbusier, Designer: Furniture (1929)*, Woodbury, NY: Barron's, 1977
Di Puolo, Maurizio and others, *Le Corbusier, Charlotte Perriand, Pierre Jeanneret: La Machine à s'asseoir* (exhib. cat.), Rome: De Luca, 1976
Jencks, Charles, *Le Corbusier and the Tragic View of Architecture*, Cambridge, MA: Harvard University Press, and London: Allen Lane, 1973; revised edition Harmondsworth: Penguin, 1987
Le Corbusier: Architect of the Century (exhib. cat.), London: Arts Council, 1987
Le Corbusier Domestique: Furniture / Tapestries, 1927–67 (exhib. cat.), Cambridge, MA: Carpenter Center for the Visual Arts, 1992
Lotti, Luca, "Le Corbusier: Critica alle Stanze (Views on Furniture)" in *Domus*, 691, February 1988, pp.62–67
Lucan, Jacques (editor), *Le Corbusier: Une Encyclopédie*, Paris: Centre Georges Pompidou, 1987
Meier, Richard, *Villa Savoye, Poissy, France, 1929–31*, Tokyo: ADA, 1972 (Global Architecture 13)
Moos, Stanislaus von, *Le Corbusier: Elements of a Synthesis*, Cambridge: Massachusetts Institute of Technology Press, 1979
Papadaki, Stamo (editor), *Le Corbusier: Architect, Painter, Writer*, New York: Macmillan, 1948
Petit, Jean, *Le Corbusier lui-même*, Geneva: Rousseau, 1970
Powers, Alan, "Villa Savoye, Île de France" in *Country Life*, 7 July 1994, pp.74–77
Ragot, Gilles and Mathilde Dion, *Le Corbusier en France: Réalisations et Projets*, Paris: Electa Moniteur, 1987
Sekler, Mary Patricia May, *The Early Drawings of Charles-Edouard Jeanneret (Le Corbusier), 1902–1908*, New York: Garland, 1977
Taylor, Brian Brace, *Le Corbusier, The City of Refuge: Paris, 1929–33*, Chicago: University of Chicago Press, 1987
Troy, Nancy J., *Modernism and the Decorative Arts in France: Art Nouveau to Le Corbusier*, New Haven and London: Yale University Press, 1991
Troy, Nancy J., "Le Corbusier, Nationalism and the Decorative Arts in France, 1900–1918" in *Studies in the History of Art*, 29, 1991, pp.64–87
Turner, Paul Venable, *The Education of Le Corbusier*, New York: Garland, 1977
Walden, Russell (editor), *The Open Hand: Essays on Le Corbusier*, Cambridge: Massachusetts Institute of Technology Press, 1977

Ledoux, Claude-Nicolas 1736–1806

French architect

An heir to the Age of Reason, Claude-Nicolas Ledoux had a revolutionary approach to design that was to influence generations to come. During his lifetime, he had a successful practice prior to the French Revolution, and after, having survived the guillotine, he began to publish a five-volume folio of his works and philosophy. Throughout his career he sought to discover the primary elements of architectural beauty. He was interested in the forms on which the classical orders were based. He extracted the basic components, the circle and square, the sphere, cube and pyramid, and found ways to juxtapose and relate these platonic geometries to create dramatic, dynamic and monumental artistic effects. Ledoux was not one to think small, ridding his designs of unnecessary details, and often exceeding his clients' budgets.

Ledoux was interested in the use of common materials. For him, luxurious materials such as marble would camouflage the essential nature of his forms. His palette was filled with raw surface materials. He was transfixed by surfaces which were large enough to engage the imagination, by stones whose color stood up to comparisons with the finest marbles, by compositions which developed unexpected effects for the viewer. Ledoux continually edited his work, finally allowing only those elements of the design which were absolutely necessary to his composition.

Ledoux shared an enthusiasm for theoretical, formal design with fellow student Etienne-Louis Boullée (1728–99). Both studied with the classicist Jacques-François Blondel, and both are referred to as French Visionary Architects. But unlike Boullée who was content to explore these ideas on paper, Ledoux wanted to see his projects built. His first professional commission was the interior design of a Paris coffeehouse, the Café Militaire (1762). Ledoux created a fictional narrative to unify his decoration. He imagined that soldiers, having been victorious on the battlefield, found a resting place in the forest. He created the effect of twelve triumphal columns around the room with patterns of spears bound together with laurels of victory and crowned with helmets. Mirrors throughout the café infinitely repeated the columns and wooden panels, carved with relief patterns of trophies and shields, reinforced the motif. In this clearing in the forest, café-goers would be reminded of their Gallo-Roman ancestry. This subject suggests Ledoux's interest in the popular debate of his day, the search for origins. The project also exemplified Ledoux's use of literary allusion as a way of giving social and aesthetic meaning to his work.

The work was well-received and led to his first major architectural commission, a large town house for the Comte d'Hallwyl. The Hôtel d'Hallwyl (1766) exemplified Ledoux's desire to bring the country home into the city and his rejection of Rococo in favor of Neo-Classicism. Constrained by the existing building plan, Ledoux's interior decoration was drawn from classical iconography. The main salon was given a country look with images of chimeras holding lyres. The rear garden court design was based on a Roman atrium house. An arcade of unfluted Doric columns defined a path around the center courtyard. A fountain niche framed by rusticated pilasters with giant capitals was centered on the back garden wall. On a blank wall across rue de Montmorency, Ledoux painted a rural landscape. Using this *trompe-l'oeil* technique he was able to suggest the illusion of the country from this shallow, urban courtyard.

At the Hôtel d'Uzès two years later, Ledoux returned to the military theme of the café. The triumphal gateway at the entry introduced the subject matter of the interior motifs. The salon de campaigne was elaborately carved with trees extending floor to ceiling. Trophies and other emblems of war and peace hung from the trees in this magical forest. Ledoux often collaborated with a group of skilled artisans for his carvings. The highlight of Jean-Baptiste Boiston and Joseph Métivier's work on the Hôtel d'Uzès was the relief carvings on the four doors of the main salon which were designed to represent the four corners of the world. Symbolizing world unity, the doors displayed crocodiles for the Americas, dromedaries for Asia, elephants for Asia and horses for Europe.

The Hôtel de Montmorency in Paris, built in 1769–71, shows the beginnings of the influence of English Neo-Palladianism in Ledoux's work. The centralized, square plan was given a twist; its main entrance was situated at the angled corner of the building and the rooms were placed symmetrically about the diagonal. The main salon, located above the entrance, was decorated with panels engraved with the nine Greek muses, cupids and vases. These images symbolized the relationship between art and science.

Mme. du Barry became one of Ledoux's most important patrons. She commissioned him to design the Pavillon de Louveciennes in 1771 and in 1773 Ledoux was named architect to King Louis XV. Ledoux also dreamed of building an "ideal" city, the City of Chaux. He made plans and drawings of the various individual buildings of this utopia, but only those for the Royal Saltworks, Arc-et-Senans (1774–79), were executed. It was his most ambitious work, a utilitarian building conceived as a circular complex at the heart of his proposed visionary city.

Work came to a halt during the French Revolution, during which Ledoux was arrested and nearly put to death. In 1795, after he was freed, he spent his time participating on academic juries and preparing a five folio volume edition of his work, *L'Architecture Considérée Sous le Rapport de l'Art, des Moeurs et de la Législation*, which was dedicated to Tsar Alexander I. The folios contain idealized versions of Ledoux's work, as he modified his drawings to demonstrate the purity of his ideas and designs. Ledoux succeeded in publishing two-thirds of his engraved plates in 1804, two years before he died. In 1847, Daniel Ramée published the remaining plates.

In relating his theory on the relationship between architecture and painting, Ledoux declared: "If you want to become an architect, begin by being painter. What a variety of shapes you will find spread upon the still surface of a wall, though its pictorial eloquence may leave the apathetic multitude unmoved! High courses of stonework deeply grooved, walls rough-hewn or rusticated, pebbles sticking out, stones piled up artlessly – such elements are often enough to produce a striking effect." Ledoux himself found innate beauty in the surface of limestone and granite and saw an inexpressible joy in the dramatic distribution of simple planes and volumes.

Ledoux's commentaries often display his passion and enthusiasm for his work rather more than they enlighten the reader on the theoretical construct of his art. Nevertheless, there are some worthy passages including the statement that "no doubt, knowledge of all that has preceded us is necessary; it guides our solutions as it guarantees our memories. But rarely does such knowledge lift us to the fine frenzy that stirs and spurs an observer with a taste for what is new." With grandeur and simplicity, Ledoux sought to create what was new by understanding the essence of what had gone before.

SALLY L. LEVINE

Biography

Born in Dormans, Champagne, 27 March 1736. Entered Collège de Beauvais, Paris; apprenticed to an engraver; studied architecture at the École des Arts, Paris, under Jacques-François Blondel, 1753–58. Married Marie Bureau, 1764 (died 1792): two daughters. Active as an architect in Paris from c.1760; attached to the department, Eaux de Fôrets de France, 1760s; employed as inspector of saltworks, Franche-Comté; appointed Architect de Roi, 1773; worked as architect for the Ferme Générale and designed the Barrières de Paris, 1784–89. Member, Académie Royale d'Architecture, 1767; promoted to the first class, 1792. Imprisoned for royalist sympathies, 1793–94. Concentrated almost solely on writing and projects for an ideal city after 1794. Declared bankrupt, 1805. Died in Paris, 19 November 1806.

Selected Works

The largest collection of Ledoux's papers and drawings is in the Archives Nationales, Paris. Additional drawings and documents are in the Bibliothèque de Besançon, the Bibliothèque Nationale, Paris and the Bibliothèque de la Ville de Paris. Carvings from the Café Militaire, and the salon from the Hôtel d'Uzès are displayed in the Musée Carnavalet, Paris.

Interiors

1762 Café Militaire, rue St. Honoré, Paris (interior decoration)
1766 Hôtel d'Hallwyl, Paris (building and interiors): Franz-Joseph d'Hallwyl

1768	Hôtel d'Uzès, Paris (renovations, remodelling and interiors)
1769–71	Hôtel Montmorency, Paris (building and interiors, including sculptures and carvings by Feuillet and Métivier): Claude-Martin Goupy
c.1769–71	Château de Bénouville, Normandy (building and interiors): Marquis de Livry
1771–73	Pavillon, Louveciennes (building and interiors, including sculptures and carvings by Feuillet and Métivier): Mme. du Barry
1771–73	Pavillon Guimard, Paris (building and interiors, including sculptures by Feuillet): Mlle. Marie-Madeleine Guimard
1771–73	Pavillon Tabary, Paris (building and interiors)
1771–73	Théâtre (apartment of Mlle. Guimard), Paris (interiors)
1772	Hôtel des Équipages, Versailles (building and interiors): Mme. du Barry
1775–79	Théâtre, Besançon (building and interiors)
1778–81	Hôtel Thélusson, Paris (building and interiors)
1792	Maison Hosten, Paris (building and interiors): J.-B. Hosten

Ledoux's craftsmen included the carvers Métivier and Feuillet, and the painters Callet and Le Barbier.

Publications

L'Architecture Considérée sous le Rapport de l'Art, des Moeurs, et de la Législation, vol.1, 1804, vol 2 (edited by Daniel Ramée), 1846; reprinted 1983

Architecture de Claude-Nicolas Ledoux, edited by Daniel Ramée, 2 vols., 1847; reprinted 1983

Further Reading

A detailed and scholarly account of Ledoux's career appears in Gallet 1980 which includes a chronology of his life and work, a full list of extant drawings and manuscript material in public collections, and an extensive primary and secondary bibliography. For an English-language study of his work see Vidler 1990.

Braham, Allan, *The Architecture of the French Enlightenment*, Berkeley: University of California Press, and London: Thames and Hudson, 1980

Christ, Yvan, *L'Oeuvre et les Rêves de Claude-Nicolas Ledoux*, Paris: Chêne, 1971

Gallet, Michel, "La Jeunesse de Ledoux" in *Gazette des Beaux-Arts*, February 1970, pp.65–92

Gallet, Michel, "Un Ensemble Décoratif de Ledoux, les Lambris du Café Militaire" in *Bulletin du Musée Carnavalet*, 1973

Gallet, Michel, "Ledoux et sa Clientèle Parisienne" in *Bulletin de la Société de l'Histoire de Paris*, 1976, pp.131–73

Gallet, Michel, "Trois Décorateurs Parisiens du XVIIIe Siècle, Michel II Lange, J.-B. Boiston, Joseph Métivier" in *Bulletin de la Société de l'Histoire de Paris*, 1978

Gallet, Michel, *Claude-Nicolas Ledoux*, Paris: Picard, 1980

Hermann, Wolfgang, "The Problem of Chronology in Claude-Nicolas Ledoux's Engraved Work" in *Art Bulletin*, 42, 1960, pp.191–210

Kaufmann, Emil, *Three Revolutionary Architects: Boullée, Ledoux, and Lequeu*, Philadelphia: American Philosophical Society, 1952

Levallet-Haug, Geneviève, *Claude-Nicolas Ledoux*, Paris and Strasbourg, 1934

Moreux, Jean-Charles and Marcel Raval, *Claude-Nicolas Ledoux: Architecte du Roi*, Paris: Arts & Métiers Graphiques, 1945

Ozouf, Mona, *L'École de France: Essais sur la Révolution, l'Utopie et l'Enseignment*, Paris: Gallimard, 1984

Rittaud-Hutinet, Jacques, *La Vision d'un Futur: Ledoux et ses Théâtres*, Lyon: Presses Universitaires de Lyon, 1982

Vidler, Anthony, *Claude-Nicolas Ledoux: Architecture and Social Reform at the End of the Ancien Régime*, Cambridge: Massachusetts Institute of Technology Press, 1990

Le Pautre (or Lepautre) Family

French dynasty of *ornemanistes* and architects active throughout the 17th century

Jean Le Pautre (or Lepautre) was one of the most influential of design sources during the high Baroque period of Louis XIV. His works perfectly embodied the monarchical, extravagant, and assured spirit of this fertile period of the arts in France, and he can be credited with a critical role in the creation of the Louis XIV style. His immensely creative mind sought expression in the production of thousands of engraved ornamental plates as well as designs for specific interior fixtures such as chimneypieces, bed alcoves, and console tables. These engravings were published in Paris and subsequently reissued in London, Amsterdam, Augsburg, and Nuremberg, and were a chief aid in the dissemination of the French court style.

Beginning as an apprentice to his second cousin, the cabinet-maker and engraver Adam Philippon, Le Pautre developed skill in the articulation of sculptural as well as two-dimensional form. One of his first known works is the engraving of Philippon's *Curieuses Recherches* (1645) which was published in the middle of the most intense period of Italian High Baroque influence in France. Philippon had travelled to Rome during this decade, as had other Frenchmen such as Charles Le Brun (1619–90), Pierre Mignard (1612–95), and François Girardon (1628–1715), and had copied modern and antique ornament there. Of equal importance to this development was the presence in Paris at that same time of key Italian designers, particularly Stefano Della Bella (1610–64), the greatest Italian ornamental engraver of his generation.

While Le Pautre's work reflects these obvious Italian influences, it is also undeniably French in its handling of antique ornament blended with motifs from nature and purely French images such as the fleur-de-lis and cock. In this respect, Le Pautre mirrored the creative tendencies of his contemporaries, particularly Le Brun. Classical ornament was studied, but never merely copied in final compositions: it was reinterpreted and embellished with familiar and sometimes fantastic elements. A strong measure of drama was incorporated into compositions as well: for instance, Le Pautre's engravings of bed alcoves appear as views of theatre productions, replete with figures and accoutrements alluding to specific, identifiable historical and mythological episodes.

Concurrent with this generation of classical Baroque style was the increased consciousness of decorative arts in France. A few collections of architectural and ornamental engravings incorporating motifs for interior use had been published in France in the late 16th century, among them Jacques Androuet DuCerceau's *Les Plus excellens bastiments de France* of 1577 and 1579. However, intense production of designs for interior features did not occur until the 1630s, providing Le Pautre with an audience ripe for his creative designs.

The centralization of the arts in France and the establishment of Versailles as the visual expression of French political and cultural supremacy also did much to forge a niche for Le Pautre's designs. He worked for the Crown from c.1670 to 1680, and was elected member of the Academy in 1677 as "Dessignateur et Graveur". In this capacity he continued not only to create his own designs (often directly on the copper

Jean Le Pautre: engraving of design for an alcove, c.1660

plate, without preliminary sketches), but also to etch the works of contemporaries. His designs spanned both secular and ecclesiastical projects.

Among Le Pautre's best known engravings are those for chimneypieces, bed alcoves, doors, and monumental vases. He is considered by many scholars especially important in the development of the decorative chimneypiece (as opposed to the heavier hooded types), his *cheminées à l'Italienne* exhibiting a lightness which led eventually to the classic flat-fronted French version with overmantel mirror. He viewed his designs as being variously in the Roman, French, modern, and antique styles, but they are all French classical Baroque in conception. And they have an abiding energy: "French seventeenth-century pattern is never merely static; its curves are the curves of growth, its straight lines the lines of gravity" (Evans, 1931).

Jean's eldest son, Pierre (not to be confused with his cousin Pierre, the sculptor), was trained by his father as an engraver and became prominent in his own right. However, the generational difference manifested itself in a sharp contrast in style. Pierre engraved the designs of Jean Berain (1640–1710) and other *ornemanistes*, as well as the architectural plates of Jules Hardouin-Mansart (1646–1708) and Claude-Louis d'Aviler. He demonstrated an early talent for interior decoration, but it was not until 1699 when Mansart was named Surintendant et Directeur des Bâtiments du Roi, that he was given the official appointment of Dessinateur et Graveur des Bâtiments du Roi.

Pierre Le Pautre's first major assignment, to redecorate parts of the royal château at Marly, proved to be one of his most important works. Here he brilliantly reinterpreted the two-dimensional arabesques of ornamentalists such as Berain and Audran as three-dimensional framing elements of the panels. That is, he integrated decoration and architecture in a manner not seen before. By creating delicate sculptural features out of the basic constructive elements of arabesques, he eschewed the need for strong visual, architectonic devices. The result was interiors with greater vertical unification, slender and elegant proportions, and an overall lightness. In fact, according to the historian Fiske Kimball, Le Pautre's work at Marly is considered to be "the essential creative act in the genesis of the rococo", and that "the marriage of frame and filling, of moulding and surface, of structure and ornament, of geometry and fantasy, had sprung a living entity, not only deeply new, but vitally perfect" (Kimball 1943).

Le Pautre's originality and genius were recognized immediately, and he was quickly procured to make changes to the Chambre du Roi, the Antichambre de l'Oeil-de-Boeuf, the Cabinet du Conseil, and the Grande Galerie at Versailles, and later at the Appartement du Roi at Trianon. In the meantime, he had also provided for the Bâtiments drawings for a new altar in Notre Dame de Paris and for the choir of the cathedral of Orléans. These ecclesiastical works show a treatment very similar to the domestic projects, involving the use of truncated angles on the panels, ovals within arches on consoles, and ornament such as rosettes, interlaces, and background mosaic, but all with an added measure of volume and stateliness.

As the organizational structure of the Bâtiments did not emphasize individual authorship of particular projects, Le Pautre's role in many royal works has traditionally been unclear. Large-scale projects were simply credited to the Surintendant; during Le Pautre's career at the Bâtiments this position was held by Hardouin-Mansart and Robert de Cotte (1656–1735), respectively. Careful study by later scholars has afforded identification, however, of drawing techniques and specific motifs which one can attribute to Le Pautre, so the oeuvre of works assigned to him has expanded, resulting in a more thorough understanding of his career. Such is especially the case with the Chapelle de Versailles, for even though Le Pautre drew and engraved the changes made there, it had not been understood to what extent he contributed to the decorative design. It is now thought that he was responsible for the apse with the high altar in addition to many individual elements such as the choir spandrels and piers, the organ case, and the doors of the chapel and vestibules.

Le Pautre's novel treatment of interiors extended to private buildings as well. He is credited with designing interiors for the Château de Bercy and the Chancellerie (or Hôtel de Pontchartrain, Paris), and with modifying parts of the Hôtel Lauzun in Paris. Le Pautre also published a few suites of engravings, those for chimneypieces being among the best known. As the fireplace had traditionally been the central architectural feature of most Northern European rooms, it was natural that its decoration assume great importance. In Le Pautre's case, the chimneypiece designs he created for Marly quickly acquired an enthusiastic audience, with many ladies of the court commissioning their own versions from him. A key feature in these designs was the creation of a tall overmantel frame which enclosed both a mirror and the painting or relief set above it, a precocious formula which would reach its maturation in the next decades.

While many of Le Pautre's creations have been lost over time, the true inheritance of his genius is in the vast realm of Rococo design. He is generally considered a father of this style, and while the evidence is not easy to ascertain for the untrained eye, serious and careful study of his works shows the impetus he gave to an entire succeeding generation of artists and designers.

MARGARET W. LICHTER

Le Pautre, Jean 1618–1682
Designer and engraver

Born in Paris in 1618. Pupil of the cabinet-maker Adam Philippon. In royal service from 1670. Elected to the Academy as "Dessignateur et Graveur", 1677. In addition to his designs for ornament and interiors, he also produced designs for ecclesiastical interiors and furniture. Engraved illustrations for other authors. His son Pierre Le Pautre was also a designer and engraver. Died in 1682.

Selected Works

1654–57 Hôtel Beauvais, Paris (with Antoine Le Pautre, stair-cage): Catherine Henriette Bellier

1656–57 Hôtel Lauzun, Paris (interiors; building by Le Vau)

Publications

Curieuses Recherches, 1645
Veüe grottes et fontaines de jardins à l'Italienne, 1650
Trophées d'armes, 1650, 1659
Frises ou montans à la moderne, 1657
Desseins de Lambris à l'Italienne pour orner et embellir le Chambres, Sales, Galeries et autres lieux magnifiques, 1659
Inventions pour faire des placques ou des aubenetiers servans aux Orfèvres, 1659
Livre de serurerie inventé par Jean Le Pautre et gravé par Jacques Le Pautre, 1660
Ornemans de panneaux pour l'enrichissement des lambris de chambres, de galeries, 1660
Montans de trophées d'armes à l'antique, Vases d'Ornemens, Vases d'Antique, 1661
Lambris à la Romaine, 1661
Portes cochère, 1665
Cheminées à l'Italienne, 1665
Lambris à la Françoise, 1665
Plafons à la Romaine, 1665
Alcoves à l'Italienne, 1665, 1670
Cheminées et Lambris, 1667
Grands Alcoves à la Romaine, 1667
Livre de lit à la Romaine, 1670
Livre de miroirs, tables et gueridons, 1670
Portraicture de diverse vases inventé [sic], 1675
Les divertissements de Versailles donnez par le Roy à toute sa cour au retour de la conqueste de la Franche-Comté en l'année M.D.C. LXXIV (with André Felibien), 1676
Alcoves à la Françoise, 1678
Fonteines et cuvettes inventées de nouveau par Jean de Pautre, 1678
Relation de la feste de Versailles du 18 juillet mil six cens soixante-huit, 1679
Nouveaux ornemans ou Plafons, 1680
Le Édifices Antiques de Rome, 1682
Oeuvres d'Architecture, 3 vols., 1751

Other publications include: *Rinceaux de diferents feuillages*; *Frisses Feuillages et Ornements*; *Livre de Frises et Ornemens*; *Rinceaux de Frises et Feuillages*; *Bordures de Tableau à la Romaine*; *Nouveau Livre de Cartouches*; *Plafonds Modernes*; *Quarts de Plafons*; *Nouveaux Desseins de Plafons*; *Nouveaux desseins de Cheminées à l'Italienne*; *Cheminées à la Romaine*; *Cheminées à la Moderne*; *Nouveaux dessins de Cheminées à peu de Frais*; *Alcoves à la Romaine*, *Differens Desseins d'alcauve*; *Nouveau Livre d'Porte d'La Chambre*; *Vases ou Burettes à la Romaine, Fontaines et Cuvetes*

Further Reading

Berger, Robert W., *A Royal Passion: Louis XIV as Patron of Architecture*, Cambridge and New York: Cambridge University Press, 1994

Evans, Joan, *Pattern: A Study of Ornament in Western Europe from 1180 to 1900*, 2 vols., Oxford: Clarendon Press, 1931; reprinted, New York: Hacker, 1975

Feray, Jean, *Architecture interieure et décoration en France des origines à 1875*, Paris: Berger-Levrault, 1988

Jean-Richard, Pierrette, *Ornemanistes du XVe au XVIIe siècle: Gravures et Dessins* (exhib. cat.), Paris: Musée du Louvre, 1987

Kimball, Fiske, *The Creation of the Rococo*, 1943; reprinted as *The Creation of the Rococo Decorative Style*, New York: Dover, and London: Constable, 1980

Préaud, Maxime, "L'Hôtel idéal selon Jean Lepautre", in *XVIIe siècle*, 162, 1989, pp.81–83

Préaud, Maxime, *Inventaire du fonds français: Graveurs du XVII siècle*, Paris: Bibliothèque Nationale, 1993

Ward-Jackson, Peter, *Some Main Streams and Tributaries in European Ornament from 1500 to 1750*, London: Victoria and Albert Museum, 1967

Weigert, R.-A., "L'art décoratif en France, les 'grotteschi' ou grottesques: Leur adaptation et leur évolution du 16e siècle à la première moitié du 18e siècle", in *Information artistique culturelle*, vol.1, 1955–56

Le Pautre, Antoine 1621–1679

Architect

Baptized 5 January 1621, third son of Adrien Le Pautre, a master joiner, and of Jeanne Fressant. Probably taught by his brother Jean Le Pautre, and studied with the architect Étienne Martellange (1568/9–1641), c.1640. Two sons, Pierre (1660–1744) and Jean (1648–1735) were sculptors; a third son, Claude (b. 1649), was architect-pensioner of the French Academy in Rome, 1667–69. Died 3 January 1679.

Selected Works

1650 Hôtel de Guéménée (petite chambre d'hiver): Princesse de Guéménée
1654–57 Hôtel Beauvais (stair-cage): Catherine Henriette Bellier
1672 Château de Seiglière de Boisfranc, Saint-Ouen: Joachim Seiglière de Boisfranc
1674 Château de Clagny (now replaced by J. Hardouin-Mansart's building): Madame de Montespan

Publications

Desseins de plusieurs palais, Paris, 1652–3 (reissued by Joubert, c. 1697–1709; facsimile edition, 1966)

Further Reading

Berger, Robert W., *Antoine Le Pautre: A French Architect of the Era of Louis XIV*, New York: New York University Press, 1969
Kimball, Fiske, "Antoine Le Pautre and the Motif of the Drum-without-Dome", in *Journal of the Society of Architectural Historians*. 25, 1966, pp.165–80

Le Pautre, Pierre c.1648–1716

Engraver and interior designer

Born in Paris c.1648, the eldest son of Jean Le Pautre the Elder, with whom he trained as an engraver. Employed as Dessinateur et Graveur des Bâtiments du Roi, 1699–1716. Designed furniture and chimney-pieces for Marly and Versailles, and at the Trianon 1699–1703. Also worked in the Chapel at Versailles, 1709. Taught drawing. Engraved ornaments for several architects. Died in 1716.

Selected Works

A large number of Pierre Le Pautre's drawings and engravings are in the Bibliothèque Nationale, Paris.

1699 Château de Marly (Chambre du Roi, Grand Salon): Louis XIV
1701–11 Versailles (Chambre du Roi, Chambre du Conseil, Salon d'Hercule): Louis XIV
1702–06 Versailles, Trianon (Appartement du Roi): Louis XIV
1703 Hôtel de Pontchartrain Chancellerie (remodelled by de Cotte from old Hôtel de Lionne; interiors Le Pautre): Chancellor Pontchartrain
1709 Versailles, Chapel, with Vassé (organ-case, high altar, apse)
1712–15 Château de Bercy, Paris (begun by F. Le Vau; Grand Salon)

Publications

Cheminées et Lambris à la Mode, n.d.
Cheminées à la Royalle à grand Miroir et Tablette avec Lambris de Menuizerie, c.1698
Livre de cheminées executés à Marly sur les desseins de Mons. Mansart ... dessinées et gravées par P. Le Pautre, n.d.

Further Reading

Berger, Robert W., *Versailles: The Château of Louis XIV*, University Park: Pennsylvania State University Press, 1985
Berger, Robert W., *A Royal Passion: Louis XIV as Patron of Architecture*, Cambridge and New York: Cambridge University Press, 1994
Hautecoeur, Louis, *Histoire de l'architecture classique en France*, vol.2, Paris: Picard, 1949
Kalnein, Wend von, *Architecture in France in the Eighteenth Century*, New Haven and London: Yale University Press, 1995
Kimball, Fiske, "The Development of the Cheminée à la Royale", in *Metropolitan Museum Studies*, vol.5, 1936, pp.259–80
Kimball, Fiske, "La Transformation des appartements de Trianon sous Louis XIV", *Gazette des Beaux-Arts*, vol.19, 1938, pp.87–110
Kimball, Fiske, *The Creation of the Rococo*, 1943; reprinted as *The Creation of the Rococo Decorative Style*, New York: Dover, and London: Constable, 1980
Marie, M.A., "Les Chambres de Louis XIV au Grand Trianon et à Marly", *Bulletin de la Societé de l'Histoire de l'art français*, 1938, pp.190–96
Scott, Katie, *The Rococo Interior: Decoration and Social Spaces in Early Eighteenth-Century Paris*, New Haven and London: Yale University Press, 1995
Walton, Guy, *Louis XIV's Versailles*, Chicago: University of Chicago Press, and London: Viking, 1986

Lescaze, William 1896–1969

Swiss-born American architect and designer

William Lescaze played an important part in the introduction of modern architecture and interior design to the United States in the 1930s. He had a continuing role in American Modernism until his death.

Lescaze was born at Onex, near Geneva, Switzerland and graduated from architectural training at the Eidgenössische Technische Hochschule. His training under Karl Moser was an important factor in shaping his approach to design. He worked for several offices in France including that of Henri Sauvage in Paris before moving to Cleveland, Ohio to work in the firms of Hubbell and Benes and Walter MacCormack. In 1923 he established his own office in New York. Early projects included a submission in the competition for the Palace of the League of Nations in 1927 and a New York apartment for Leopold and Olga Samaroff Stokowski in 1929.

Olga Samaroff Stokowski, the wife of Leopold Stokowski the conductor of the Philadelphia Orchestra, became interested in a small experimental nursery school in a suburb of Philadelphia. She was instrumental in funding a building for the school and urged that Lescaze be employed as the architect. The resulting Oak Lane Country Day School building of 1929 was one of the first American examples of the Modernist idiom that became known as International Style. This project also brought about a partnership with George Howe (1886–1955), a well-established Philadelphia architect with a practice that worked in the eclectic, tradition-oriented vocabulary that was characteristic of Philadelphia during this period. Lescaze was responsible for a change in Howe's thinking that made him an exponent of Modernism.

Howe had a strong relationship with the management of a Philadelphia bank, the Philadelphia Saving Fund Society (PSFS), having designed several small branch banks in "stripped classical" style for that organization. When a major high-rise building was proposed, Howe and Lescaze (with Lescaze in charge of design) proposed a modern, International Style tower unlike any building previously built in America or, indeed, anywhere else in the world. The bank management was persuaded to accept the design on logical and economic grounds, and the resulting building (1929–32), a remarkable success by any standards, became the first major example of modern architecture in the United States.

The interiors of the building used rich materials in patterns of utmost simplicity. Details were of a high order of excellence and included special furniture, even signs and clocks, all designed in the functionalist vocabulary of Modernism. The main banking room and the escalator and stairway, the public lobby serving the elevator access to the 39-storey office tower and the executive offices, boardroom and other bank facilities at the top of the tower were all designed in great detail in accordance with Lescaze's understanding of the Modernist aesthetic. Although shocking to traditionalists, the PSFS building has remained a striking example of early Modernism at its best.

Lescaze continued in a partnership with Howe until 1934. His work included several town houses in New York (including his own house of 1933–34), each with interiors complete with built-in and movable furniture and many details in the simple, unornamented manner of the International Style. Other residential projects in the United States and in England made Lescaze a continuing leader in the development of Modernism in America. Some lamps and other objects designed for PSFS and other interior projects were, for a time, produced as products available to other designers.

The Columbia Broadcasting System became a Lescaze client for the design of radio studio interiors, executive offices, graphic design and, eventually, for a building for station KNX in Hollywood (1936–38). Lescaze was one of a number of architects involved in government-sponsored housing projects of the 1930s. His Williamsburg housing project in Brooklyn, New York (1937), known as Ten Eyck Houses, is often mentioned as the best example of public housing ever built in the United States. Later housing projects such as the Manhattanville Houses, New York (1960) are competent but less distinguished examples of Lescaze's work. A large high school building for the city of Ansonia, Connecticut (1937) demonstrated the applicability of Modernism to educational building in the United States.

The 1939 New York World's Fair included Lescaze buildings for the Aviation display and for the Swiss Pavilion. The Longfellow Building in Washington, DC (1939–41) was the first modern building in that generally conservative city. Lescaze was a persuasive speaker and able writer and came to act as spokesman for the cause of Modernism in a period when the design establishment was generally highly resistant to modern concepts.

After World War II, Lescaze's practice produced a number of projects in the increasingly accepted modern idiom that seemed less distinguished than his earlier work, perhaps because his was no longer a strikingly individualistic direction. The arrival in America of other leading European Modernists, who assumed important teaching and leadership roles, also may have been a factor in limiting the impact of Lescaze's later work and prominence.

JOHN F. PILE

Biography

Born in Onex, near Geneva, Switzerland, 27 March 1896. Educated at the Collège de Genève, to 1915 and at the Ecole de Beaux-Arts, Geneva, 1914–15; studied architecture under Karl Moser at the Eidegenössische Technische Hochschule 1914–15. Married Mary Hughes: one son. Worked on projects for the Committee for the Reconstruction of Devastated France and in the office of Henri Sauvage, Paris, 1919–20. Emigrated to the United States, 1920; worked for Hubbell and Benes, Cleveland, 1921–22, and in the office of Walter R. MacCormack, Cleveland, 1922; established his own architectural practice, New York, 1923–29; partner with George Howe in Howe and Lescaze, Philadelphia, 1929–34; principal, William Lescaze and Associates, New York, 1934–69. Designed interiors, furniture and lighting from late 1920s and remained active in the decorative arts and metalwork after World War II. Exhibited at several national and international exhibitions including the World's Fairs, New York, 1939 and 1964. Member, New York State Building Code Commission, 1949–59. Fellow, American Institute of Architects. Died in New York, 9 February 1969.

Selected Works

Interiors

1926	Lescaze Apartment, East 42nd Street, New York City (interiors)
1927–28	Jean de Sièyres Hunting Lodge, Mount Kisco, New York (building, interiors and furniture)
1928	Maison Bertel Beauty Parlor, Fifth Avenue, New York (interiors and furniture)
1928	Andrew Geller Shoe Factory, Brooklyn, New York (interiors and furniture)
1928	Macy International Exhibition of Art in Industry, New York City (room settings)
1929	Mrs. Leopold Stokowski Apartment, New York City (interiors and furniture)
1929	Oak Lane Country Day School, Second Street and Oak Lane Road, Philadelphia (building, interiors, furniture and fittings)
1929–32	Philadelphia Saving Fund Society (PSFS), Philadelphia (building, interiors and furniture; with George Howe)
1930–31	Frederick V. Field House, New Hartford, Connecticut (building and interiors; with George Howe)
1931	Headmaster's House, Dartington Hall, Totnes, Devon (building and interiors)
1933–34	Lescaze House and Office, 211 East 48th Street, New York City (building, interiors and furniture)
1936–38	Columbia Broadcasting System (CBS) Studios and Offices, Hollywood (studios, interiors and furnishings; with E.T. Heitschmid)
1939–41	Longfellow Building, Washington, DC (building and interiors)
1955	Office Building, 711 Third Avenue, New York City (building and interiors)

Lescaze's most notable furniture and products were designed for the PSFS and CBS buildings. He also designed fabrics and accessories and paintings.

Publications

A Modern Museum, with George Howe, 1930
On Being an Architect, 1942
A Citizens' Country Club or Leisure Center, 1944
Uplifting the Downtrodden, 1944

Further Reading

"CBS Broadcasting Studios, Hollywood, California" in *Architectural Forum*, June 1938

"City House of William Lescaze, New York" in *Architectural Forum*, December 1934, pp.389–99

Doumato, Lamia, *William Lescaze, 1896–1969* (bibliography) Monticello, IL: Vance, 1982

Grief, Martin, *Depression Modern: The Thirties Style in America*, New York: Universe, 1975

Hubert, Charles, Lindsay Stamm Shapiro and others, *William Lescaze*, New York: Rizzoli, 1982

Jordy, W.H., "Philadelphia Saving Fund Society Building: Its Development and Significance in Modern Architecture" in *Journal of the Society of Architectural Historians*, May 1962

Jordy, W.H., "The American Acceptance of the International Style: George Howe and William Lescaze's Philadelphia Saving Fund Society Building" in his *The Impact of European Modernism in the Mid-Twentieth Century* (American Buildings and Their Architects, vol.4), New York: Doubleday, 1972

Lanmon, Lorraine Welling, *William Lescaze, Architect*, Philadelphia: Art Alliance Press, 1987

Miller, R. Craig, *Modern Design in the Metropolitan Museum of Art, 1880–1980*, New York: Abrams, 1990

"The PSFS Building, Philadelphia, Pennsylvania 1924–32" in *Perspecta*, 25, 1989

Shapiro, Lindsay Stamm, *William Lescaze*, Basel: Wiese, 1993

Todd, Dorothy and Raymond Mortimer, *The New Interior Decoration*, 1929; reprinted New York: Da Capo, 1977

Wodehouse, L., "Lescaze and Dartington Hall" in *Architectural Association Quarterly*, 8, 1976

Lethaby, W.R. 1857–1931

British architect, designer and theorist

William Richard Lethaby was one of the leading members of the second generation of the Arts and Crafts Movement, so admired by Hermann Muthesius in *Das Englische Haus*, which included E.S. Prior, Ernest Gimson, and the Barnsley brothers. Lethaby's reputation as a designer is disproportionate to his limited output, which all but ended after costly problems during the construction of All Saint's Church, Brockhampton, his last, and most significant work. Thereafter his influence was established through education, public bodies, and his writings. However, this influence was such that for much of the present century for a designer to be called a "Lethabite" implied a definite artistic and ethical stance.

His somewhat puritan aesthetic may well have come from his strict Bible Christian upbringing. Like Frank Lloyd Wright, Lethaby recalled how his early creativity was stimulated by paper toys a neighbour would make for him. Though he received some training during his pupilage under Alexander Lauder, the essential hit-and-miss nature of architectural training of the day ensured that Lethaby was largely self-taught. As such, and without the benefit of either an Oxbridge education or a monied background (which was commonplace among his colleagues in Norman Shaw's office) Lethaby was a model of the Arts and Crafts designer.

Lethaby first came to the attention of Richard Norman Shaw through the former's pseudonymous entries to the regular design competitions set by the magazine *Building News*. Apart from their clear artistic ability, these show a strong grasp of the range of historicist styles currently fashionable as the hegemony of the Gothic Revival was breaking up. Called to Shaw's office as his Chief Assistant, Lethaby was responsible for much of the detailed interior work in this most fashionable of practices from 1879 until the mid-1880s.

Shaw's was a particularly appropriate office for Lethaby, for here his increasing fondness for the Elizabethan and early Northern Renaissance styles and motifs could be employed. He designed all the panelling, plasterwork, doorcases, staircases, and, what became his particular forte, fireplaces for the rebuilding of Henry Mildmay's house at Flete in Devonshire (1879–81). Similarly, the interiors of the Alliance Insurance building, London (1882), and Cragside, Northumberland (1883), are among his best of this period. The enormous white marble chimneypiece in the Drawing Room at Cragside was an accomplished exercise in its irreverent treatment of Northern Renaissance motifs, including strapwork, curly gables, putti, garlands, and arabesques all supported on columns whose exaggerated enstasis appear to be giving way under the weight of decoration.

Once in London, Lethaby's appetite for knowledge led him to enrol in the Royal Academy Schools and spend much of his spare time studying in the Victoria and Albert Museum and the British Museum. This eclectic self-education found expression in his earliest writings (later cribbed by Charles Rennie Mackintosh), as they attempted to find a way out of Revivalism, and frequently saw him moving among the advanced circles of London's Architectural Association, where he was seen as something of a progressive figure. As a founder-member of the St. George's Art Society (a forerunner of both the Art-Workers' Guild and the Arts and Crafts Exhibition Society in which he was also a key figure), Lethaby visited many of the famous Artists' Houses of the day and particularly admired Alma-Tadema's house and William Burges's Tower House. His designs for interiors, together with furniture and fireplaces, are among the earliest works he exhibited at the annual shows of the Arts and Crafts Exhibition Society.

His initial attempts to find an alternative to Revivalism culminated in his perplexing first book *Architecture, Mysticism, and Myth* (1891) which posited an ahistorical symbolism as the basis of all architecture and design in its distillation of recent anthropology and sociology. In the introduction to this important work he stated his aim as "to set out, from an architect's point of view, the basis of certain ideas common in the architecture of many lands and religions" and came up with a prescription for buildings with "ceilings like the sky, pavements like the sea, and entrances for the sun and moon" thus hoping to re-establish all buildings as symbolic microcosms of the world.

It could be reasonably expected that his own early work, once free of Shaw's office, might reflect these concerns, and in certain respects it does. However, at the same time as the book was published Lethaby came under the combined influence of William Morris and Philip Webb through the meetings of the

Society for the Protection of Ancient Buildings (SPAB). "Webb," he later wrote, "satisfied my mind about that mysterious thing we call architecture." This, together with his own puritan values, was the impetus for his spare, low-ceilinged, homely, country house interiors of the 1890s. His work for Morris & Co. on Stanmore Hall shows the clear move away from the medieval richness and historicism of Morris & Co. to a starkness relieved by the use of quality materials and sound construction which chiefly characterise his work . Where Morris and Webb's surface pattern design is shallow, Lethaby's is flat, where their palettes are limited, Lethaby's is largely white and minimal.

His independent work combines both the rational school of design approach learnt from the Art-Workers' Guild, Arts and Crafts Exhibition Society, and the SPAB, with an attempt to reintroduce meaning through planning and decoration. Accordingly, his first independent job, Avon Tyrrell for Lord Manners (a "setting-up" commission from Norman Shaw) introduces twin peacocks to the exterior chimney breast to symbolise the hearth as the central symbolic element in an interior as a place of shelter, and as a means of linking interior and exterior. The chimney breast itself, as so often with Lethaby, was a geometrical chequerboard pattern of grey and black Derbyshire marbles surmounting a plain, but deeply moulded fire surround.

The rectilinear patterns of Lethaby's fireplaces are echoed throughout the house by both the panelling and the mullions and transomes of the Elizabethan-style windows, and becomes a further means of linking interior and exterior. Believing in the integrity of the individual artist-craftsman Lethaby gave his friend Ernest Gimson a free hand to design and execute the plaster ceilings in Avon Tyrell, as in most of his houses. Elsewhere the furniture was supplied by the firm of Kenton & Co. which Lethaby had established in 1890 with Reginald Blomfield, Sidney Barnsley, Gimson, Macartney, and Mallet.

Lethaby was freed of the orderly Shavian plan in his next job, The Hurst, and his commitment to interior spaces and their detailing was assured through the Arts and Crafts practice of allowing the plan form to generate the elevations so that, for example, a Serlian window is used to light two rooms and not just the one implied externally and historically by the use of such a window type. Fenestration, and the plan form generally, is dictated by need rather than aesthetics. However, like his hero Philip Webb's Red House, these conceits also have the effect of suggesting an organic, accretative, and therefore older building than is the case, and leaves Lethaby open to the charge of deceit of the kind theoretically deplored by the Arts and Crafts Movement.

Also at The Hurst Lethaby introduced groin vaults which, like fireplaces, become a central element at once symbolic and, for Lethaby, homely. In essence, Lethaby's interiors play with archetypal forms in his subsequent commissions as they try gradually to divest themselves of any historic connotations. Like many fellow members of the Arts and Crafts Movement, Lethaby has been taken, perversely and ahistorically, to be a pioneer of Modernism which he largely dismissed as "another kind of design humbug to pass off with a shrug – ye olde Modernist style."

For most of his working life, then, Lethaby's reputation rested on his educational reforms and writings. From being joint first Principal of the Central School of Art and Craft and founder of the Design and Industries Association, to his work on the London County Council Technical Education Board and support of the Women's Institute, he spread the Arts and Crafts philosophy of simplicity in design. Like others of his generation, he is of interest for straddling both Revivalism and Modernism. Though he participated in the radical refashioning of the former through the Arts and Crafts Movement and English Free Style, this did not lead to an automatic acceptance of Modernism but rather a rejection of what he termed "style-mongering" in favour of an "efficiency style" found through precedent and vernacular survivals.

JULIAN HOLDER

See also Arts and Crafts Movement

Biography

William Richard Lethaby. Born in Barnstable, Devon, 18 January 1857, the son of a craftsman and gilder. Articled to the architect Alexander Lauder, Barnstaple, 1871–77; studied at the Royal Academy Schools, London, 1880–81. Married Edith Rutgers Crosby in 1901 (died 1927). Employed in the architectural practice of Richard Waite, Duffield, Derbyshire, 1878–79; chief assistant to Richard Norman Shaw (1831–1912), London, 1879–91; active in his own architectural practice, London, from 1889. Designed furniture, cast iron and ceramics from the late 1880s; co-founder of the furniture-making co-operative, Kenton & Co., 1890 (dissolved 1892). Appointed Art Inspector to the Technical Education Board, 1894; founder and joint director, Central School of Art and Craft, London, 1896: principal, 1902–11. Professor of Ornament and Design, Royal College of Art, London, 1901–18; Surveyor of Westminster Abbey, 1906. Founder-member: St. George's Art Society, 1885; Art-Workers' Guild, 1884; Arts and Crafts Exhibition Society, 1888; Design and Industries Association, 1915; Modern Architecture Constructive Group, 1922. Member, Society for the Protection of Ancient Buildings, 1891. Published numerous books and articles on architecture and design from the 1890s; edited *The Artistic Crafts* series of technical handbooks. Died in London, 17 July 1931.

Selected Works

A substantial collection of Lethaby's drawings, including architectural and decorative designs, is in the drawings collection, Royal Institute of British Architects, London. Archive materials including manuscripts, photographs and publications, are in the Archive of the Central School of Art (now amalgamated with St. Martin's), London. Examples of Lethaby's furniture are in the Museum and Art Gallery, Cheltenham, Gloucestershire, and the Victoria and Albert Museum, London.

Interiors

1879–81 Flete, Devon (panelling, plasterwork and interior fitments; renovations by Norman Shaw): Henry Mildmay

1883 Cragside, Northumberland (interior details; building and interiors by Norman Shaw)

1891 Stanmore Hall, Middlesex (with Morris & Co., chimney-pieces, woodwork and some furniture): William Knox D'Arcy

1891 Avon Tyrell, Christchurch, Hampshire (building, interior fitments and decoration; plasterwork designed and executed by Ernest Gimson): Lord Manners

1894 The Hurst, Sutton Coldfield, Warwickshire (building, interior fitments and plaster decoration): Charles Edward Mathews

1898–1900 Melsetter House, Hoy, Orkney Islands, Scotland (reconstruction and additions): Thomas Middlemore

1898–1900 Eagle Insurance Buildings, Colmare Row, Birmingham (with Joseph Ball, building, interior fitments and some furniture)
1898–1901 High Coxlease, Lyndhurst, Hampshire (building, interior fitments and plaster decoration): Eustace Smith
1901–03 All Saints Church, Brockhampton (building, interiors and furniture)

Lethaby's design work also included furniture for Kenton & Co. 1890–92, and designs executed by Farmer and Brindley; metalwork executed by Neuham and Waters, from 1882; and firegrates executed by Thomas Elsley, London, Yates & Heywood, Rotherham, and the Coalbrookdale Iron Co., Telford.

Publications

Architecture, Mysticism and Myth, 1891
Leadwork, Old and Ornamental and for the Most Part English, 1893
Architecture: An Introduction to the History and Theory of the Art of Building, 1912
Form in Civilisation: Essays on Art and Labour, 1922
Londinium: Architecture and the Crafts, 1923
Home and Country Arts, 1923
Ernest Gimson, His Life and Work,with others, 1924
Philip Webb and His Work, 1935
Architecture, Nature and Magic, 1956

Further Reading

A biographical account of Lethaby's career, including an analysis of his work and his aesthetic and political ideas, appears in Rubens 1986 which also includes appendices listing Lethaby's principal works and a full list of his writings. For a more detailed discussion of Lethaby's work, particularly during his time at the Central School of Art and Craft, and a select further reading list, see Backemeyer and Gronberg 1984.

Backemeyer, Sylvia and Theresa Gronberg (editors), *W.R. Lethaby, 1857–1931: Architecture, Design and Education* (exhib. cat.: Central School of Art, London), London: Lund Humphries, 1984
Cooper, Jeremy, *Victorian and Edwardian Furniture and Interiors*, London: Thames and Hudson, 1987
Garnham, Trevor, "William Lethaby and the Two Ways of Building" in *Architectural Association Files*, 10, Autumn 1985, pp.27–43
Garnham, Trevor, *Melsetter House*, London: Phaidon, and San Francisco: Chronicle Books, 1993
Hart, Vaughan, "William Richard Lethaby and the Holy Spirit: A Reappraisal of the Eagle Insurance Company Building, Birmingham" in *Architectural History*, 36, 1993, pp.145–58
Macleod, Robert, "Lethaby as a Key to Mackintosh" in Patrick Nuttgens (editor), *Mackintosh and his Contemporaries in Europe and America*, London: Murray, 1988
Naylor, Gillian, *The Arts and Crafts Movement: A Study of its Sources, Ideals and Influence on Design Theory*, London: Studio Vista, and Cambridge: Massachusetts Institute of Technology Press, 1971
Okoye, Ikem S., "William Richard Lethaby: A Reassessment" in *Harvard Architectural Review*, 7, 1989, pp.100–15
Powers, Alan, "Writers and Thinkers: W.R. Lethaby" in *Crafts* (UK), 125, 1993, pp.18–19
Richardson, Margaret, *Architects of the Arts and Crafts Movement*, London: Trefoil, 1983
Roberts, A.R.N. and others, *William Richard Lethaby 1857–1913*, London: Central School of Arts and Crafts, 1957
Rubens, Godfrey, *William Richard Lethaby: His Life and Work 1857–1931*, London: Architectural Press, 1986
Swenarton, Mark, *Artisans and Architects: The Ruskinian Tradition in Architectural Thought*, London: Macmillan, and New York: St. Martin's Press, 1989
Walker, Frank Arneil, "William Lethaby" in *Architectural Association Quarterly*, 9, 1977, pp.45–53

Le Vau, Louis 1612–1670

French architect and designer

Born in Paris and trained as an architect by his father, Louis Le Vau was a master of magnificent Baroque interior effects. Piling layer upon layer of decoration he used a team of equally skilled artists and craftsmen to create settings whose extraordinary grandeur was intended to reflect the splendour of Louis XIV and his court. His talent lay in synthesising French and foreign influences, but he has been criticised both for borrowing heavily from architects of the previous generation such as J.A. DuCerceau and Philibert de l'Orme and for imitating contemporaries like François Mansart. Nevertheless, his skills and his willingness to adapt guaranteed him success and in 1654, following the death of Jacques Lemercier, he was appointed Architecte du Roi by Louis XIV.

Le Vau's talent for interior planning is apparent in his earliest works, which show him to have been in the vanguard of the development of the Parisian hôtel. Like Mansart's Hôtel de la Vrillière (1635), Le Vau's Hôtel de Bautru (1634–37) and his Hôtel de Bretonvilliers (1638) both had long galleries running down the side of the garden and a staircase in the corner of the courtyard. Neither of these hôtels has survived, but the Hôtel Lambert, which was probably the finest of Le Vau's Paris houses, is still extant.

Work on the building of the Hôtel Lambert commenced in 1639 but the task of decorating continued over many years until c.1660. Le Vau created a dramatic sequence of spaces and exploited the Baroque concern for dramatic views through a succession of effects. Visitors emerged from the darkness of the stairs up into the vast, light stair chamber and continued along the landing and into the oval vestibule where it was possible to look through the doors of the room and all down the length of the famous Galerie d'Hercule to views of the river Seine. The Galerie is widely considered to be the finest surviving room from this period and is richly decorated with bronzed plaster wall medallions by van Obstal and ceiling paintings by Charles Le Brun depicting the Labours of Hercules. In another room, the Cabinet de l'Amour (1646), the dado contained landscape panels by Jan Asselyn, Swanevelt and Patel the Elder, and the frieze above it was decorated with mythological subjects by Romanelli, Perrier and le Sueur, while le Sueur also painted panels on the ceiling showing the Birth of Love.

In 1653, Nicolas Fouquet, the Minister of Finance, commissioned Le Vau to design his country house at Vaux-le-Vicomte. It was to be very grand, to outshine the house which Mansart had created for the rival financier, Longueil, at Maisons. Le Vau's plan featured a large central pavilion which enclosed the domed oval *salon* and connected all the spaces on the central axis through characteristic triple-arched openings. The west wing contained Fouquet's *appartement* and the east wing housed another set of even more splendid state rooms that were intended for the king. The most ornate room was the King's bedroom where Le Brun headed a team of decorators who also included the sculptors Thibault Pousaint and Guerin. Their finest work appears on the ceiling where gilded plaster flying nymphs, putti and animals encircle painted medallions and roundels, the central roundel showing Time carrying Innocence from the sky. The decorations were completed in

Le Vau: Galerie d'Hercule, Hôtel Lambert, Paris, 1640s

1661, and on 17 August Fouquet entertained the king and members of his court at Vaux-le-Vicomte; the festivities included a comedy-ballet by Molière with sets designed by Le Brun and music by Lully, and a spectacular display of fireworks. Three weeks later Louis had Fouquet arrested for embezzlement, he confiscated Vaux-le-Vicomte, and his minister, Jean-Baptiste Colbert requisitioned Le Vau, Le Brun and the other artists and craftsmen who had created Fouquet's house to work on a similarly grand scale for the king. Later even the trees were taken from the garden and planted at Versailles.

Le Vau had been working on alterations to the Louvre since about 1656, during the course of which he demolished some of the buildings, including the wonderful interior of the Pavillon du Roi, that had been designed earlier by Pierre Lescot. After the fire of 1661, Le Vau was commissioned to rebuild the Galerie d'Apollon and in 1663 Le Brun began the decorations with the team from Vaux-le-Vicomte. These decorations set the style and scale for the work at Versailles.

Le Vau planned to envelop the old château of Versailles with new blocks, and building commenced in 1668; the work continued after the architect's death in 1670 and the decorators were led by Le Brun as before. The finest part of Le Vau's design was the Escalier des Ambassadeurs which filled a long narrow space and was lit from above. It formed a dramatic stage on the ceremonial route up to the Grands Appartements whose decorations survive although in a somewhat altered state. The mood is Italianate and the walls are composed of panels of coloured marble, parts of which were probably covered in red or green velvet and hung with Italian paintings.The king's *appartement* had seven rooms named after the seven planets. The Sun room took pride of place, the throne was placed in the room named after Apollo and each room had a painted ceiling that reflected the planet theme.

Despite Le Vau's predilection for using layer upon layer of decoration that included paintings, sculpture, and bas-reliefs, the overall effect, though sometimes rich, was always constrained and rational and never quite broke into the emotional fluidity characteristic of fully-developed Baroque design. This constraint marked the principal difference between French and Italian design in the 17th century. But having said this Le Vau always understood the importance of dramatic spatial sequences: this was his greatest strength.

BARBARA CORR

See also Le Brun

Biography

Born in Paris in 1612. Probably trained under his father, Louis Le Vau the Elder (d.1661), a master-mason. Designed many houses for the Parisian bourgeoisie, from 1634. Appointed Architecte Ordinaire du Roi, 1638, and Premier Architecte du Roi, Conseiller du Roi, and Intendant des Bâtiments, 1654. Involved in the great projects at the Louvre and Versailles in the 1660s. Died in Paris, 11 October 1670.

Selected Works

Interiors

1634–37 Hôtel de Bautru, Paris (building and interiors): Guillaume II de Bautru

1634–35 Hôtel Bullion, Paris (building and interiors including gallery, cabinet, and chambre): Claude Bullion

1635 Hôtel d'Aumont, Paris (building and interiors; remodelled by François Mansart)

c.1635 Hôtel Miramion, Paris (building and interiors)

1637–40 Hôtel Gillier: Melchior de Gillier, Seigneur de Lagny

1638–40 Hôtel de Bretonvilliers (building and interiors)

1639 Hôtel de la Vrillière, Paris (chambre à l'Italienne): Louis Phélypeaux, seigneur de la Vrillière

c.1640–45 Château du Raincy (building and interiors)

1640–41 Hôtel Hesselin, Paris (building and interiors)

1640–42 Hôtel Le Vau, Paris (building and interiors)

1640–44 Hôtel Lambert, Paris (appartement de President Lambert, antechamber, Cabinet de l'Amour, Cabinet des Muses, Galerie d'Hercule): Nicolas Lambert

1641–44 Hôtel d'Aumont, Paris (extension): Michel-Antoine Scarron

1649–50 Hôtel de Gramont, Paris (building and interiors): Antoine de Gramont

1654–57 Château de Meudon (remodelling): Louis XIV

1654–61 Château de Vincennes (King's and Queen's pavilions): Louis XIV

1656–57 Hôtel de Lauzun, Paris (building and interiors)

1656–61 Château de Vaux-le-Vicomte (building and interiors; decorations by Charles Le Brun): Nicolas Fouquet

1659–c.66 Tuileries, Paris (remodelling): Louis XIV

1660–64 Louvre, Paris (south façade I, and Galerie d'Apollon; decorations by Charles Le Brun): Louis XIV

1662–70 Collège des Quatre Nations, Paris (building and interiors)

1662–70 Ménagerie, Versailles (building and interiors): Louis XIV

1668–73 Louvre, Paris (south façade II, with others, and east façade): Louis XIV

1668–70 Versailles ("enveloppe"; completed 1673–74): Louis XIV

1670 Trianon de Porcelaine, Versailles (building and interiors): Louis XIV

c.1670 Versailles (Escalier des Ambassadeurs, Grandes Appartements; decorations by Charles Le Brun): Louis XIV

Further Reading

Berger 1993 and 1994 represent the most up-to-date English surveys of Le Vau's career, and both have extensive further bibliographies. Whiteley and Braham 1964 remains the classic survey of his Louvre projects.

Babelon, Jean-Pierre, *Demeures parisiennes sous Henri IV et Louis XII*, Paris: Hazan, 1991

Berger, Robert W., "Louis Le Vau's Château du Raincy", in *Architectura*, 6, 1976, pp.36–46

Berger, Robert W., *The Palace of the Sun:. The Louvre of Louis XIV*, University Park: Pennsylvania State University Press, 1993

Berger, Robert W., *A Royal Passion: Louis XIV as Patron of Architecture*, Cambridge and New York: Cambridge University Press, 1994

Blunt, Anthony, *Art and Architecture in France, 1500–1700*, 2nd edition Harmondsworth: Penguin, 1970

Daniel, J.A., and L.Daniel, "Chronologie de l'histoire du Raincy", *Société historique du Raincy et du pays d'Aulnoye*, 27, January 1960, pp.3–7

Dimier, Louis, *Le style Louis XIV: L'Hôtel Lauzun*, Paris: Eggimann, 1912

Erlande-Brandenburg, A., "Les fouilles du Louvre et les projets de Le Vau", in *La vie urbaine*, 1964, p. 241

Espaullard, H., "Les trois châteaux du Raincy", *Bulletin de la société historique du Raincy et des environs*, 13, November 1942, pp.2–36

Feldmann, Dietrich, *Maison Lambert, Maison Hesselin und andere Bauten von Louis Le Vau (1612/13–1670) auf der île Saint-Louis in Paris*, dissertation, Hamburg University, 1976

Feldmann, Dietrich, "Das Hôtel de la Vrillière und die Räume 'à l'Italienne' bei Louis Le Vau", in *Zeitschrift für Kunstgeschichte*, 45, 1982, pp.395–422

Feray, Jean, *Architecture intérieure et décoration en France des origines à 1875*, Paris: Berger Levrault, 1988

Hamin, Françoise, "L'Hôtel de Hervant au quartier Saint-Eustache: Les travaux de Le Vau en 1658", in *Revue de l'Art*, 6, 1969, pp.77–81

Hautecoeur, Louis: *Histoire de l'architecture classique en France*, vol.2, Paris: Picard, 1949

Kimball, Fiske, "Authorship of the Decoration of the Hôtel Lauzun", in *Gazette des Beaux-Arts*, XLV, 1955, pp.45–54

Sainte Fare Garnot, Nicolas, *Le Décor des Tuileries sous la règne de Louis XIV*, Paris: Réunion des Musées Nationaux, 1988

Sainte Fare Garnot, Nicolas and Emanuel Jacquin, *Le château des Tuileries*, Paris: Herscher, 1988

Tooth, Constance, "The Early Town Houses of Louis Le Vau", in *Burlington Magazine*, CIX, 1967, pp.510–18

Vitzthum, Walther, "La Galerie de l'Hôtel de la Vrillière", in *L'Oeil*, December, 1966, pp.24–31

Whiteley, Mary and Allan Braham, "Louis Le Vau's Projects for the Louvre and the Colonnade", *Gazette des Beaux-Arts*, 1964, part 1, pp.285–96; part 2, pp.347–62

Liberty & Co.

British retailer of furnishings, fashion and textiles; established 1875

Founded by Arthur Lasenby Liberty in 1875, Liberty's was one of the most well-publicised and highly respected shops of the period and, like Heal's, it played an important role in shaping and promoting a distinctively British form of progressive, middle-class taste. The shop's heyday was the 1880s and 1890s when it was closely allied to the development of fashionable Aesthetic and artistic styles of furniture, textiles and interior design. Its promotion of Middle Eastern and oriental styles was especially influential and it is still a well-known supplier of oriental carpets and furnishings and paisley shawls. The company's tradition of commissioning work from some of Britain's foremost designers also continued throughout the 20th century and it continues to exert an influence upon fashion and design today.

Arthur Lasenby Liberty was born in 1843, the son of a draper who ran a shop in Chesham, Buckinghamshire. Following a short apprenticeship with a draper in Baker Street, Liberty acquired a post in the famous Great Cloak and Shawl Emporium owned by Farmer and Rogers on Regent Street. Already interested in art and the theatre, Liberty took up his position just as the 1862 London International Exhibition was making its mark on decorative art. Along with a number of progressive artists and designers – E.W. Godwin, James McNeill Whistler and Christopher Dresser for example – Liberty appears to have been particularly attracted to the Japanese section of the exhibition. This was the first time that a large quantity of Japanese goods had been shown in Europe and, responding to the remarkable impact that they made, Farmer and Rogers took the farsighted step of buying up some of the exhibits. These formed the basis of the company's Oriental Warehouse which opened next door to the Emporium on Regent Street. Two years after the opening of the warehouse Liberty became its manager.

From the outset, Arthur Liberty's career went hand in hand with the fashionable quest to find an alternative to the mass-produced decorative arts of Victorian England. The newly formed company, Morris, Marshall and Faulkner had exhibited for the first time in 1862 and, like Morris, Liberty believed that ordinary people's taste could be improved by allowing them access to well-made, aesthetically pleasing products. Under Liberty's management, the Oriental Warehouse attracted a clientele that included the leading artists of the day and when Farmer and Rogers refused him a partnership, it was these artists who persuaded him to set up on his own. Thereafter Liberty's fortunes were closely bound up with those of the Arts and Crafts and Aesthetic Movements, and later with Art Nouveau.

In May 1875, with help from his father-in-law, Liberty acquired half a shop at 218A Regent Street. In keeping with current fashion the shop was called East India House and, to begin with, employed three members of staff. One of them, William Judd, was asked to open the new Tudor building in 1925 and recalled at that time, "when there were only four of us – the Master, two others, and myself ... We sold just coloured silks from the East – nothing else. The sort of thing that William Morris, Alma Tadema and Burne-Jones and Rossetti used to come in and rave about" (Adburgham, 1975). These fabrics were imported from India and the Middle-East and were dyed at Merton Abbey, Surrey, first with the help of Thomas Wardle who had also worked with Morris & Co., and later at Liberty's own printing and dyeing works. Initially, the firm sold plain-coloured textiles, known as "Art Fabrics", and Liberty's great strength was in selecting the soft, pastel colours that became hugely popular with adherents of Aestheticism. From the 1880s, it also began to issue printed fabrics, at first incorporating small, traditional patterns and soon afterwards distinctive artistic designs commissioned from established designers such as C.F.A. Voysey, and L.P. Butterfield. The best-known of these was the *Peacock Feather* pattern designed by Arthur Silver (1887) which quickly became identified as one of the company's trademarks and which proved so successful that it is still printed today.

The second half of 218A Regent Street was purchased in 1877 and by 1880 the shop had become large enough to include seven departments: Silks, Embroideries, Furniture, Carpets, Porcelain, Curios and Miscellaneous. The first shop had sold made-up bamboo tables and chairs to supplement its stock of imported tables and screens, but in 1883 Liberty established its own Furnishing and Decorating Studio under the direction of Leonard F. Wyburd. The studio specialised in the production of Moorish-style furniture and fashionable cosy corners and kiosks incorporating panels of imported *musharabeyeh* latticework. Much of the in-house furniture, including the various versions of the celebrated *Thebes* stool (1884) and a range of mock-Tudor and Arts and Crafts oak cabinets, dressers, tables and chairs, was designed by Wyburd but the shop also increasingly stocked work by outside designers such as George Walton and M.H. Baillie Scott.

By 1894 the firm had become a public company with an appeal that extended far beyond the comparatively exclusive group of artists and aesthetes who had made up the original clientele. Its success was closely interwoven with the influence of the Aesthetic Movement which had encouraged a widespread taste among the fashionable middle classes for a more self-consciously artistic style of furnishing and decoration. This style relied heavily upon furniture influenced by Japanese and Moorish examples, textiles and wallpapers that made new use of complex, conventionalised floral and foliage patterns, and numerous artistic accessories such as peacock feathers and Japanese lanterns and fans. Liberty was unique in providing not simply one or two "art" items but everything that devotees might need to decorate the whole house, and in 1894 the company was credited with having "created an entirely new taste in fabrics, dress and interior decoration, the word Liberty having become descriptive of the style ..." (Adburgham, 1975).

Liberty's was also influential in promoting a taste for the Art Nouveau design; Italian Art Nouveau has always been referred to as the *Stile Liberty* and, acknowledging the inroads made by the new style in Britain at the end of the 19th-century, the shop sold its own version of Art Nouveau furniture alongside Arts and Crafts pieces. It also began to import Dutch and Greek silver jewellery and in 1899, following the revival of interest in Celtic Art, "Liberty Cymric" was launched, Archibald Knox providing many of the designs. The cymric designs led shortly to the famous Liberty "Tudric Pewter" line.

Arthur Liberty was knighted in 1913 in recognition for his services to British applied and decorative arts; he retired from active administration of the company the following year and died in May 1917. Throughout his career he lived up to his intention, "not to follow existing fashion but to create new ones", and this directive continued to inform the shop's progress in the 20th century.

A second shop was erected on Marlborough Street behind the Regent Street building in 1924. The style of this timber-framed structure was retrogressive and matched the conservatism of much British inter-war design, including that of many of the goods that the new shop sold. But after World War II Liberty's re-emerged as an institution eager to promote innovative, quality design. Designs by Ernest Race, Robin Day, Arne Jacobsen, Gio Ponti and Vico Magistretti were all available in the shop's modern furniture department which also sold work by firms such as H.K. Furniture, S. Hille & Co., William Plunkett, Gordon Russell and O.M.K. Design. Liberty's also upheld its tradition of innovation and excellence in textile design by commissioning patterns from Modernist designers like Marianne Straub, Lucienne Day and Jacqueline Groag.

A century after the opening of the Oriental Warehouse, Liberty's once again became involved with oriental styles, selling goods such as carpets, rugs and textiles whose design reflected the growing influence of exotic, eastern fashions popularised by the hippie movement. Similarly, with the emergence of Art Nouveau and Art Deco revivals in the late 1960s and early 1970s, the company was able to refer back to its original contributions to these styles. The shop's prestige has continued to grow and, according to the journalist Fay Sweet, by 1992 "regular buying trips around the world have brought a brilliant eclecticism to the company's design and retailing. Prints are forging ahead with contemporary designs ... there has been a return to commissioning and producing Liberty's own furniture. The link with Japan, a traditional source of goods for Liberty's, was further strengthened with the opening of the Japanese Muji shop ..." (Calloway, 1992). And at the end of the 20th century, Liberty's is successfully upholding the aims envisaged for it by its founder.

HARRIET DOVER

See also Aesthetic Movement; Orientalism

Selected Collections

The Liberty Archive is held by Westminster City Archives at the Victoria Library, London; a large collection of Liberty catalogues running from 1881 to 1949 is in the National Art Library, Victoria and Albert Museum. Important collections of Liberty textiles can be found in the Victoria and Albert Museum, and the Whitworth Art Gallery, Manchester. Examples of Liberty furniture are in the Victoria and Albert Museum. Notable designers who supplied designs for Liberty included Lindsay P. Butterfield (1869–1948), Lucienne Day (1917[-]), Christopher Dresser (1834–1904), E. W. Godwin (1833–86), Archibald Knox (1864–1933), W. R. Lethaby (1857–1931), M. H. Baillie Scott (1865–1945), Arthur Silver (1853–96), and C. F. A. Voysey (1857–1941).

Further Reading

The most recent and comprehensive history of Liberty is Calloway 1992 which includes a full list of Liberty outlets and a survey of current operations. Adburgham 1975 cites many 19th and early 20th century references and contains many descriptions of the shop recorded by employees. An account of the designers involved with Liberty's in the early years can be found in Levy 1986.

Adburgham, Alison, *Liberty's: A Biography of a Shop*, London: Allen and Unwin, 1975

Amaya, Mario, "Liberty and the Modern Style" in *Apollo*, 77, February 1963, pp.109–15

Arwas, Victor, *The Liberty Style*, London: Academy, and New York: Rizzoli, 1979

Aslin, Elisabeth, *The Aesthetic Movement: Prelude to Art Nouveau*, London: Elek, and New York: Praeger, 1969

Calloway, Stephen (editor), *The House of Liberty: Masters of Style and Decoration*, London: Thames and Hudson, 1992

Cooper, Jeremy, *Victorian and Edwardian Furniture and Interiors*, London: Thames and Hudson, 1987

Laver, James, *The Liberty Story*, London: Liberty & Co., 1959

Levy, Mervyn, *Liberty Style: The Classic Years, 1898–1910*, London: Weidenfeld and Nicolson, and New York: Rizzoli, 1986

Liberty's 1875–1975 (exhib. cat.), London: Victoria and Albert Museum, 1975

Madsen, Stephan Tschudi, *Art Nouveau*, London: Weidenfeld and Nicolson, and New York: McGraw Hill, 1967

Morris, Barbara, *Liberty Design, 1874–1914*, London: Pyramid, 1989

Morris, Susan, "The Pursuit of Liberty" in *Antique Collector*, vol.62, October 1992, pp.48–51

Nichols, Sarah, "Arthur Lasenby Liberty: A Mere Adjective?" in *Journal of Decorative and Propaganda Arts*, 13, 1989, pp.76–93

Scott, Deborah, "House Style" in *Antique Collector*, vol.62, October 1992, pp.42–47

Tilbrook, A.J. and Gordon House (editors), *The Designs of Archibald Knox for Liberty & Co.*, London: Ornament Press, 1976

Watkins, Charmian, *Decorating with Fabric Liberty Style*, London: Ebury, 1987

Libraries

Throughout the history of architecture, spaces designed for libraries have incorporated concerns for light, privacy and the preservation of collections in order to balance the simultaneous need for the reader's access to materials with the protection of those materials. The library has symbolized the individual pursuit of learning, and the earliest private libraries were created within domestic spaces to preserve and at the same time display collections of manuscripts and other small precious objects. The university or public library has stood for the collective expression of reading, and thus the great spaces designed for gathering in libraries usually occur in zones distinct from those containing collections. With the introduction of automation in the 1970s, work stations for computer terminals have superseded spaces formerly reserved for public catalogs.

The earliest recorded distinct library building is dated from the 3rd century BC in Philadelphus and contained a collection of papyrus rolls belonging to Ptolemy. In Rome Asinius Pollio built a library in 25 BC, and Augustus built libraries in 37 BC. In both examples, closed cases ringing perimeter walls contained books and manuscripts.

During the Italian Renaissance purpose-built libraries were often long and narrow in plan in order to provide a high ratio of perimeter windows. At the San Marco Library in Florence, designed by Michelozzo di Bartolomeo for the Medici family and constructed in 1442–44, the design illustrates the influence of Brunelleschi's Ospedale degli Innocenti, begun 23 years earlier: Ionic columns support two arcades that define three aisles of equal width. Incorporating white walls and gray stone, the barrel-vaulted center aisle and groin-vaulted side aisles create a reading room defined by light and openness.

In the Laurentian Library at San Lorenzo in Florence, built for Pope Clement VII, designed by Michelangelo and constructed in 1524–59, the celebrated vestibule or *ricetto* with its proto-Baroque stairway leads to an elongated reading room. Within the reading room, *pietra serena* pilasters define the two-tier bays, in which a smaller window crowns the larger window below it, and ceiling beams repeat the rhythm of the pilasters. The reading carrels contain benches designed for both study and storage. A rare book room was designed but not constructed.

At the Library of St. Mark's in Venice, designed by Jacopo Sansovino and constructed in 1536–53, the entrance leads to a barrel-vaulted stair that connects the ground level to the vast reading room of the *piano nobile*. Ceiling murals painted by Titian, Tintoretto and Veronese decorate the coffered low vault of the reading room.

During the 18th century the Neo-Classical interest in central forms is illustrated by James Gibbs's Radcliffe Library at Oxford University, constructed in 1739–40. Within, eight equal piers and arches carry the drum and dome, with painted decoration contributed by Artari and Bagutti. The American heir to this design is Peter Harrison's Redwood Library in Newport, Rhode Island, constructed in 1749–50, in which an octagonal skylight floats over its central reading room.

By this date private libraries had also become a standard feature within many larger, domestic houses in Europe. Prior to the 17th century books were comparatively rare and were kept in studies, studioli or closets along with other curios and valuables. The medieval practice of storing books and manuscripts in locked chests also continued throughout this period. As printing techniques improved, however, the ownership of books became more common and there was an increasing tendency to house them in a separate library fitted out either with shelves ranged against the wall or specially built cupboards and bookcases. Many grand houses of the late 17th century included splendidly decorated rooms to house important collections; a drawing of the Duc d'Orléans's Petite Bibliothèque in the Palais Royale (late 17th century), shows richly carved built-in book cupboards, while the library at the Hôtel de Lauzun (1660) in Paris, contains an even more sumptuous arrangement with cupboards whose doors form an integral part of the intricately decorated panelling. But such rooms were also becoming more widespread in non-royal houses. The oldest surviving country-house library in England is probably that installed in the 1670s by the Duke of Lauderdale at Ham House, Surrey. This room was situated on the first floor, adjacent to the gallery; the walls were lined with open shelves and the furnishings included a set of large, wooden library steps. Other popular accessories of this period included library tables and desks, and ornamental busts, maps and globes, examples of which can be seen in an engraving of a library designed by Daniel Marot dating from the end of the 17th century and a drawing of Samuel Pepys's library of c.1693.

Until the mid 18th century, domestic libraries were primarily rooms for study, and served as a private retreat for the individual scholar or owner of the house. Increasingly, however, they were integrated into the normal life of the house; the library began to be used as a communal living room and was decorated accordingly in a more comfortable but nonetheless fashionable style. The specialist accoutrements of scholarship were replaced by more general-purpose furnishings which included elegant draperies and additional seating and tables for family relaxation. A visitor to Althorp, in Northamptonshire, which had one of the largest private collections of books in England, described the Gothic library in 1822 as containing "sofas, chairs, tables of every comfortable and commodious form ... liberally scattered throughout the room". By the mid 19th century such rooms played an essential role in country house entertaining and were equipped with games and scientific toys as well as books and portfolios of engravings with which to amuse guests on wet afternoons (Girouard, 1978).

The most instructive examples of public libraries from the 19th century can be grouped into three architectural developments from that era: the integration of industrial iron into structure as well as ornament in France, the creation of small municipal libraries with a domestic image in the United States, and the construction of monumental research libraries in period revival styles.

Designed by Henri Labrouste and constructed in 1842–50, the Bibliothèque Ste-Genevieve in Paris contains a ground-floor vestibule resembling a hypostyle hall; painted landscapes and busts of literary figures adorn the hall. Also on the lower floor are the book stacks, rare books and offices. On the upper floor a bold combination of masonry and iron, with cast-iron Ionic columns dividing the long room into two aisles, defines the reading room. The columns support open-web arches that in turn carry plaster vaults. Light enters through tall arched

Library, Cassiobury Park, Hertfordshire, after redecoration by James Wyatt, c.1800–15

windows, and gallery-level shelving is set between arch-supporting piers.

In the Bibliothèque Nationale in Paris, designed by Labrouste and constructed in 1858–68, the reading room occupies the center of an oval plan. Sixteen cast-iron columns, each 124 feet high, support nine porcelain-panelled domes. Three tiers of wall cases ringing the ellipse. Five storeys of book stacks rise under a double-membrane ceiling of iron and glass; the stack floors are assembled from transparent cast-iron plates. Connecting bridges link tiers of stacks. There is a ring of sixteen oculi in the outer wall, each centered over wall arches that spring from paired columns. This arrangement creates niches for four tiers of shelving.

Henry Hobson Richardson exerted great influence over the visual image of college and small or branch public libraries over half a century. In particular, he introduced and popularized a domestic image for an institution that represented an extension of the home, an image reinforced by the dominance of women staff members. In the Winn Memorial Library, Woburn, Massachusetts, constructed in 1876–79, Richardson created the prototype for the clearly articulated expression of parts: exhibition area, or museum, reading room and book stacks. The entrance vestibule leads to a picture gallery. An octagonal museum sits at one end of the building, the gabled reading room occurs at the center, and a two-tier alcoved "library room," or book stacks, comprises the last section, which contains a wooden vaulted ceiling and wooden support brackets.

In North Easton, Massachusetts, the Ames Memorial Library, constructed in 1877–79, although greatly simplified in relation to the Winn library, presents a similar set of elements. The stack wing features a wooden barrel vault, supported by two-tier shelf alcoves with Colonial Revival ornamentation. The reading room is sheathed in square-panelled wainscoting, and the stone fireplace is attributed to Stanford White. Incorporating a decorative medieval tradition, the fireplace relates to the designs of William Morris and the Arts and Crafts Movement. Massive engaged columns support a shallow mantel below two vases of pomegranate trees. Centered in the composition is a portrait medallion of Oakes Ames, the benefactor of the library.

Similar to but more compact than either the Winn or Ames

libraries, the Crane Memorial Library in Quincy, Massachusetts, constructed in 1880–83, centers on a hall separating the reading room from the book stacks. The decorative scheme includes finely reeded pilasters, with varied capital motifs. At the Billings Memorial Library of the University of Vermont in Burlington, constructed in 1883–86, the articulation of the museum is the greatest, with a distinct circular end designed to house the Marsh Collection. As in the Winn library, the reading room and hall occur in the center, and the alcoved book stacks comprise the other end.

Several fin-de-siècle examples in the United States illustrate the increasing size, volume and grandeur of the American library. In Washington, DC a 100-foot-diameter domed reading room dominates the design for the Library of Congress by Smithmeyer and Pelz, constructed in 1885–95. In plan, the reading room is lodged inside a hollow rectangle. Arches containing art glass spring from pilasters, and engaged columns resting on tall podia support the pendentives of the dome. McKim, Mead and White's Boston Public Library of 1887–95 is a hollow square in plan. Murals painted by Puvis de Chavannes enclose a grand stair that leads to the main reading room, Bates Hall, terminating in a coffered apse. The arcaded courtyard is derived from that at the Palazzo della Cancelleria in Rome. The six-storey book stacks occupy a U-shaped section of the building. Built in 1890–93, the Newberry Library in Chicago was designed by Henry Ives Cobb, and it adopted a plan suggested by its first librarian, William F. Poole. Harry Weese's 1981 addition accompanied a renovation of the original interior. The windowless addition provides an optimal controlled environment for the collection. Although long outgrown and no longer serving as a library, McKim, Mead and White's Low Library provides the focal point for the Columbia University campus. Built in 1893–1913, it is capped by a dome derived from the Pantheon, supported by four corner piers. Ionic colonnades support book stack galleries, and the reading room occupied the central space beneath the dome. The New York Public Library, designed by Carrere and Hastings, was built in 1897–1911. The entrance hall is white marble, decorated with festoons, and separates handsomely vaulted twin stairs. The misnamed third-floor rotunda is actually a barrel-vaulted hall; it substitutes finely carved wood for marble. Its murals illustrate the history of the word and were painted by Edward Lanning. The center of the plan is the limestone-faced catalog room; its simple Roman arches springing from piers, and the room is lodged in between two light atria. The main reading room is more elaborately carved limestone, and the 51-foot-high ceiling hovers above with paintings of sky and clouds.

Twentieth-century examples include the neo-Palladian Morgan Library in New York, experiments by International Style non-conformists Alvar Aalto and Louis I. Kahn, and more recently a return to the massive and enduring qualities of masonry selected by Thomas Beeby for the Chicago Public Library. Constructed in 1902–07, McKim, Mead and White's fireproof Morgan Library imported materials from Europe for J. Pierpont Morgan's study: red silk damask for the walls, a coffered ceiling and marble mantelpiece from Italy, and stained-glass fragments in the windows. The scale remains individual. The rotunda straddles the study, and in the east room, the main book area, the ceiling supports gilded mouldings and painted figures of Dante, Botticelli, Socrates and Christopher Columbus. Three levels of bronze and walnut bookshelves enclose the space, and a Flemish tapestry drapes the wall over the fireplace.

In several library designs, Alvar Aalto expressed his interest in undulating forms. At the Municipal Library in Viipuri, constructed in 1933–35, the wood battens of the lecture hall ceiling form a series of undulating curves. In addition, a glazed staircase wall leads to the sunken reading room. At the library in Seinäjoki, the gentle fan-shaped form of the reading room and book stacks rises above the service areas. Exterior louvres filter natural light.

The periphery of Louis I. Kahn's library for Phillips Exeter Academy in Exeter, New Hampshire, completed in 1972, encloses study alcoves, and a sliding wood shutter allows the reader to control the light at each window. The book stacks surround a central atrium, supported by concrete; monumental circles punctuate this skylit cube. Stairs are suppressed to the corners, and travertine sheathes the main stair up from the entrance.

In the Harold Washington Library Center, the competition-winning design for the Chicago Public Library constructed in 1988–91, Thomas Beeby appropriated the industrial loft building for a monumental civic building. Inside, a floor oculus in the entrance lobby opens to a floor medallion below illustrating the journey of Chicago pioneer Jean-Baptiste DuSable. On the upper floors, cross-vaulted reading alcoves alternate with double-height reading rooms. A cruciform skylit winter garden on the top floor contrasts an open-web steel and glass roof with a classical masonry and plaster vocabulary, recalling the hybrid structural nature of Labrouste's libraries. In the Chicago library, however, the grandest spaces, indicative of their creation in the latter part of the 20th century, are not for reading or study, but for circulation and special events.

PAUL GLASSMAN

See also Bookcases

Further Reading

The majority of books on libraries deal with their contents rather than their decoration and appearance. A useful survey history of purpose-built libraries appears in Pevsner which also includes an annotated list of further reading. For private libraries within domestic buildings see Jackson-Stops 1984 and Thornton 1978.

Baur-Heinhold, Margarete, *Schöne alte Bibliotheken*, Munich: Callwey, 1972

"Bookcases" in Percy MacQuoid and Ralph Edwards, *The Dictionary of English Furniture*, revised edition, 3 vols., 1954; reprinted Woodbridge, Suffolk: Antique Collectors' Club, 1983

Breisch, Kenneth Alan, *Small Public Libraries in America, 1850–1890: The Invention and Evolution of a Building Type*, Ph.D. thesis, Ann Arbor: University of Michigan, 1982

Chartier, Roger, *The Order of Books: Readers, Authors and Libraries in Europe between the Fourteenth and Eighteenth Centuries*, Cambridge: Polity Press, and Stanford, CA: Stanford University Press, 1994

Gere, Charlotte, *Nineteenth-Century Decoration: The Art of the Interior*, London: Weidenfeld and Nicolson, and New York: Abrams, 1989

Girouard, Mark, *Life in the English Country House: A Social and Architectural History*, New Haven and London: Yale University Press, 1978

Harris, John, "A Rare and Precious Room: The Kedderminster Library, Langley, Buckinghamshire" in *Country Life*, 1 December 1977, pp.1575–79
Jackson-Stops, Gervase and James Pipkin, "Libraries" in their *The English Country House: A Grand Tour*, London: Weidenfeld and Nicolson, 1984; Boston: Little Brown, 1985
Masson, André, *Le Décor des Bibliothèques du Moyen-âge à la Révolution*, Geneva: Droz, 1972
O'Gorman, James F. (editor), *The Architecture of the Monastic Library in Italy, 1300–1600*, New York: New York University Press, 1972
Pevsner, Nikolaus, "Libraries" in his *A History of Building Types*, Princeton: Princeton University Press, and London: Thames and Hudson, 1976
Thompson, Anthony, *Library Buildings of Britain and Europe*, London: Butterworth, 1963
Thornton, Peter, "Studies and Libraries" in his *Seventeeth-Century Interior Decoration in England, France, and Holland*, New Haven and London: Yale University Press, 1978, pp.303–15
Wheeler, J.L. and A.M. Githens, *The American Public Library Building*, New York: Scribner, 1941
Wormald, Francis and C.E. Wright (editors), *The English Library before 1700*, London: Athlone Press, 1958

Lights and Lighting

Man's approach to such a fundamental human requirement as lighting is closely bound up with the story of civilisation itself. After the initial domestication of the naked flame in prehistory there was little advance in the techniques or quantities of light available, except for religious purposes, and existence was largely governed by the hours of daylight. From the Renaissance, however, the gradual accumulation of wealth by the property-owning classes saw an increasing consumption of light both as a display of wealth (for it has always been expensive) and in order to extend the hours of work and recreation. Since the mid-19th century and the development of cheap fuels or power, lighting has become democratised and is universally available. It could be argued that as a result we have lost touch with nature and with it huge areas of aesthetic experience, since the subtleties of the passing seasons and the times of day mean much less today than in the past.

The presence of natural or daylight in secular interiors is largely determined by the treatment of windows. As domestic

Lighting: engraving of a festive scene showing the use of many candles, The Hague, 1660

houses became less defensive in character so windows multiplied and became larger. In the Middle Ages they were protected with shutters and then often covered with linen stretched over a lattice of wood and treated to make it translucent. In more prosperous houses windows came to be fitted with small panes of semi-translucent glass (depending on quality) set in leads often forming decorative geometrical shapes. By the late 16th century the extensive use of windows came to denote status and wealth as well as becoming essential to the new long galleries and rooms of parade. Hardwick Hall, Derbyshire is indeed "more glass than wall". Thus windows were to be frequent targets for taxation by predatory governments. By the later 17th century techniques had developed in the manufacture of glass and reflecting mirrors which enabled ever larger panes to be used, often in combination and with spectacular results: at Versailles the Galerie des Glaces consists essentially of a wall of mirror glass placed opposite the great rhythm of tall windows thus reflecting the gardens and landscape beyond. Further advances in the late 18th century included cast-iron glazing bars, used as early as 1789 in the floor-length windows of the Music Room at Heaton Hall, Manchester, while the top-lit Picture Gallery at Attingham Park, Shropshire, with its curved cast-iron ribs supporting the glazing, dates from 1807. At almost exactly this time "French windows" had begun to appear, breaking down the final barrier between the world of "nature" (represented by the park or garden) and that of "art" (represented by the house).

Thus the regulation of natural light has developed alongside the technology of windows – involving shutters, curtains and blinds with all their ramifications. The use of stained glass (often with heraldic features) remained unusual in domestic buildings until the very end of the 18th century, when coloured borders, armorials and figurative scenes might be found in strategically placed windows particularly in halls, stairways and libraries where a romantic sense of gloom might be appropriate. At Uppark, Sussex in 1813 and at the Brighton Pavilion in 1821 their respective stained-glass windows were especially lit from the exterior, the former by Argand lamps, the latter by gas.

It also seems that, since at least the 18th century, owners were mindful of lighting and its expense when deciding on the decoration of their interiors. Isaac Ware noted in 1746 that a room "which if wainscotted will take six candles to light it, will in stucco require eight, or if hung ten". Thus twenty years later at Wimpole Hall, Cambridgeshire, Philip Yorke and his wife discussed "the painting of the room they usually sit in ... my Lord was for having it ash or olive colour as being the cheaper or more durable. But my Lady objected that, though more expensive, the fashionable French white would be cheaper in the end" since it enabled the room to be lit by two instead of four candles.

For over a thousand years the principal form of lighting in Northern Europe was with candles either of wax or tallow, or, most simply of all, animal fat dipped in cloth. Southern Europe, where olive oil was plentiful, remained faithful to the oil lamp which had continued in uninterrupted use from Antiquity. Its basic shape was consistent with its function: a covered bowl, usually circular, to contain the oil, with a minimum of one aperture for a wick. This formula, like the candlestick, was capable of endless variation both in portable and permanent forms. The great majority were obviously made from utilitarian earthenware, although some of the finest works of the High Renaissance are the deliberately faked Antique bronze lamps of Il Riccio of Padua. The 18th century in Italy saw the development of tall raisable multi-spouted vessels placed on baluster or figurative stems not unlike candlesticks. Candles were obviously also used in prosperous households in Mediterranean countries but it was probably the universal appeal of paraffin lamps in the mid-19th century which brought both Northern and Southern Europe into line with each other.

The use of candles and their receptacles is a vast subject that includes candlesticks to place on flat surfaces, sconces to hang on the wall, and chandeliers suspended from the ceiling. Overhead lighting in the form of hanging chandeliers probably derives from ecclesiastical prototypes. The production of brass or latten types was a speciality of the Low Countries and examples can be seen in Netherlandish paintings together with other brass candlesticks (van der Weyden's Louvre *Annunciation* has a six-branched chandelier apparently with a rise-and-fall mechanism). Such metalwork chandeliers obviously developed along with the stylistic trends of the times. By the early 18th century they had achieved several tiers of scrolling branches, but in Britain and its Colonies they were generally found only in large public rooms of houses such as great halls, galleries and ballrooms. Silver, ormolu and rock crystal examples were found in similar locations, and also in State Bedrooms, but only in the grandest interiors. Examples in carved wood, generally gilded, have rarely survived on account of their fragility. When enclosed behind glass panels these hanging branched lights should properly be described as lanterns: in England they are found in porches, halls and stairwells, either mounted to the walls like sconces, or hanging like chandeliers. In France they are often found in all the main reception rooms of a house.

The 18th century saw the development of the lead glass chandelier – one of the great achievements of the English – with its array of detachable and interchangeable parts and ornaments. In general a single example, or a pair, would be found in only the most prestigious room of a house. By the 1780s chandeliers had developed into the supremely elegant Neo-Classical compositions, often found en suite with table candelabra (or girandoles) of which William Parker was the most brilliant exponent. In the Regency period, and with the encouragement of the Prince, their designs became denser and more elaborate, while a return to 18th-century models began as early as the 1860s.

By this date however the lighting of domestic interiors had been revolutionised by a number of technical developments. On 15 March 1784 Ami Argand, a Swiss distiller, took out a patent in London for "a lamp or lantern producing neither smoke nor smell". He had made two discoveries: first, that if the wick of a traditional oil lamp were made hollow and enclosed between two tubes in such a way that oxygen could burn the oil vapour both on the inside and outside of the flame, the resulting light would be equal to ten or twelve tallow candles. Second, if a cylindrical glass chimney were placed above a lamp so as to increase the draught further, the brightness would be even greater.

The popularity of these Argand lamps was instantaneous.

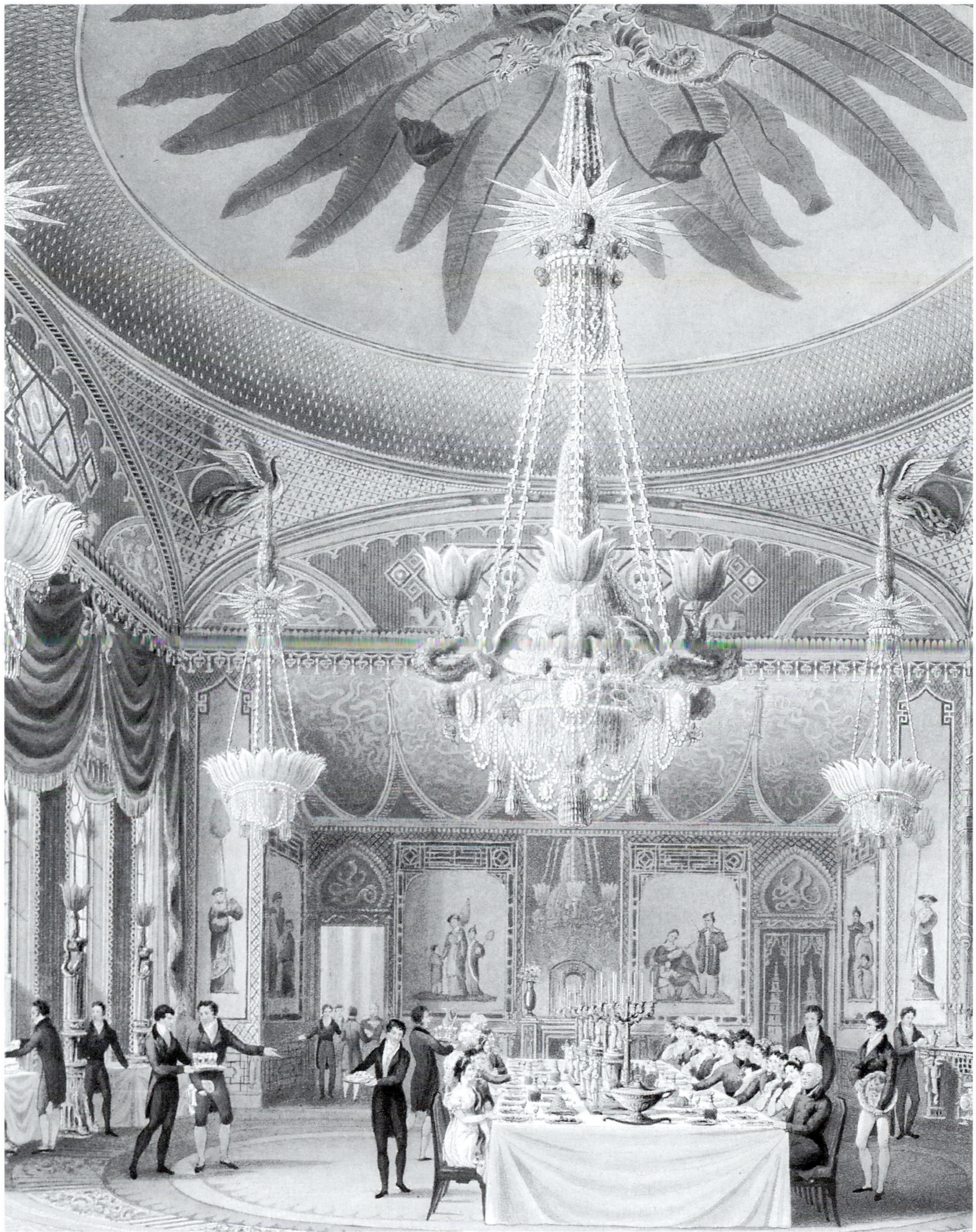

Lighting by chandeliers in the Banqueting Room, Brighton Pavilion, 1826 (detail)

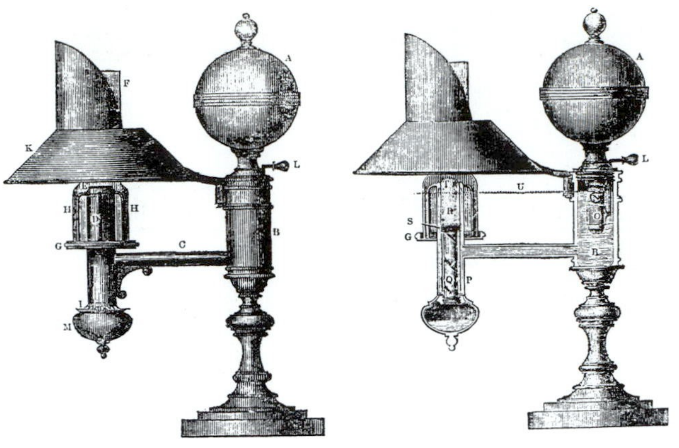

Lighting: interior and exterior of an Argand lamp, 1839

Within two years Sophie von La Roche described a shopping trip in London: "We finished tea at evening investigating Argand lamps of all descriptions" and proceeded to a shop in Bedford Square where they were all displayed "forming a really dazzling spectacle; every variety ... crystal, lacquer, and metal ones, silver and brass and every possible shade". It was their mechanism which dictated their design. An illustration in *The Penny Cyclopaedia* (1839) shows the classic type in section: A is the reservoir of oil which descends to the cistern B and along the pipe to C to the burner D which contains the wick placed between two tubes and immersed in oil. The wick rises a little above the tube at E. F is the glass chimney which is wider at the base in order to increase the draught upwards. It rests on a gallery G which can be turned to regulate the height of the wick. The wick is hollow and cylindrical and receives two currents of air – internally from the pierced work at I, and externally from the gallery at G. K is a characteristic early Victorian lamp shade and L the handle which controls the supply of oil. The type of oil used was from cole seed and was known as colza oil. It was thick and viscous and had to obey gravity – it was fed from a reservoir located above the burner.

Despite their success Argand lamps never entirely supplanted candle lighting. There seem to have been no particular rules or etiquette about their use in domestic interiors and it was probably the individual tastes of the owners which determined their use. Candles were also still used in drawing rooms, bedrooms and dining rooms, sometimes in combination with lamps placed on pedestals or hanging lamps which could be raised and lowered on a counterweight system supported with silk cords and with the pulleys disguised by tassels. Hanging lamps in bedrooms were usually found between the windows in order to throw light onto the dressing table. Passages, halls and libraries however lent themselves more readily to oil lighting: wall mounted "back lamps" in japanned tin frequently lined the passages of the service parts of the house, while grander bronze, gilt brass or ormolu lamps were developed for tables, mantelpieces or pedestals, often derived from famous classical prototypes. Portable reading lamps (or "student lamps") continued to be made right up to the World War I, often supplied with tapering tin shades, and often japanned in green. Hanging Argand lamps intended for great halls could be extremely impressive and several architects turned their hand to their design including Sir Jeffry Wyattville and J.B. Papworth. Smaller models frequently have a cut glass bowl suspended below the burners. Examples of all of these can be seen at Belvoir Castle, Leicestershire, Stratfield Saye, Hampshire and Chatsworth, Derbyshire.

One of the chief drawbacks of Argand lamps was the inconvenient shadow cast by their reservoirs. This was overcome by the development of the Astral or Sinumbra lamp c.1810, where the oil was contained in a hollow ring which also acted as a support for the shade. The oil was fed to the central burner by tubes, and the lamps were surmounted by hemispherical or annular shades. The result was an even and diffused light so they were ideal for hanging or for placing on centre tables so characteristic of early 19th century interiors.

There were other problems associated with Argand lamps which inventors sought to overcome with new patented lamps. From 1794 the Carcel lamp attempted to raise the thick and viscous colza oil (incapable of capillary action) from a reservoir below the burner by a series of clockwork pumps; the Moderator lamp, patented in 1825, raised the oil by a spring-activated piston; a variation of this was the Meteor lamp which used a nut and screw mechanism on the outside of the lamp to control an internal plunger. The Solar lamp improved combustion by having a wick which passed through a hole in the centre of a cap or cone with air directed from a horizontal direction. Finally the "Liverpool Button", a metal cone which could be placed in the centre of any Argand burner, deflected the central draught onto the wick thereby greatly improving the light.

In the manufacture and retailing of all these different types of lamps there were various long-lived firms who took the lead, mainly in Birmingham, but often with showrooms in London: Messenger's, Hancock's, Smethurst's and Miller's. Decorative component parts were often imported from France. Cylindrical glass chimneys were always in clear glass, while glass shades and globes could be supplied with many variations – white or coloured (the latter considered a bit *nouveau* by 1840), translucent or clear, etched or plain. Suspended bell-shaped flame shades also appear to have been used above hanging lamps.

The increasing cost of oil, now including whale oil, led to various attempts to distil a new fluid from mineral sources. The breakthrough came in 1847 with James Young's process of refining paraffin (or kerosene) oil. The resulting lamps required flat wicks with good aeration, and various improvements culminated in 1865 with Hinks's Duplex burner with two wicks. Throughout the 1870s and 1880s patents for all kinds of new parts continued to be registered – Silber's producing an average of over two each year at this time. Argand lamps were quite easily converted for paraffin although colza oil continued to be used right up to the end of the century when the department store catalogues requested customers to state whether they required fittings for their lamps suitable for Colza, Mineral or Duplex oil.

Following the early developments of gas as a viable light source in the 1790s its immediate application was primarily for the illumination of factories and workplaces, a stigma from which it took a long time to recover. In 1802 its perfector, William Murdoch, used it to illuminate the exterior of Matthew Boulton's Soho works at Birmingham to celebrate the Peace of Amiens, while firms such as Gott & Sons of Leeds

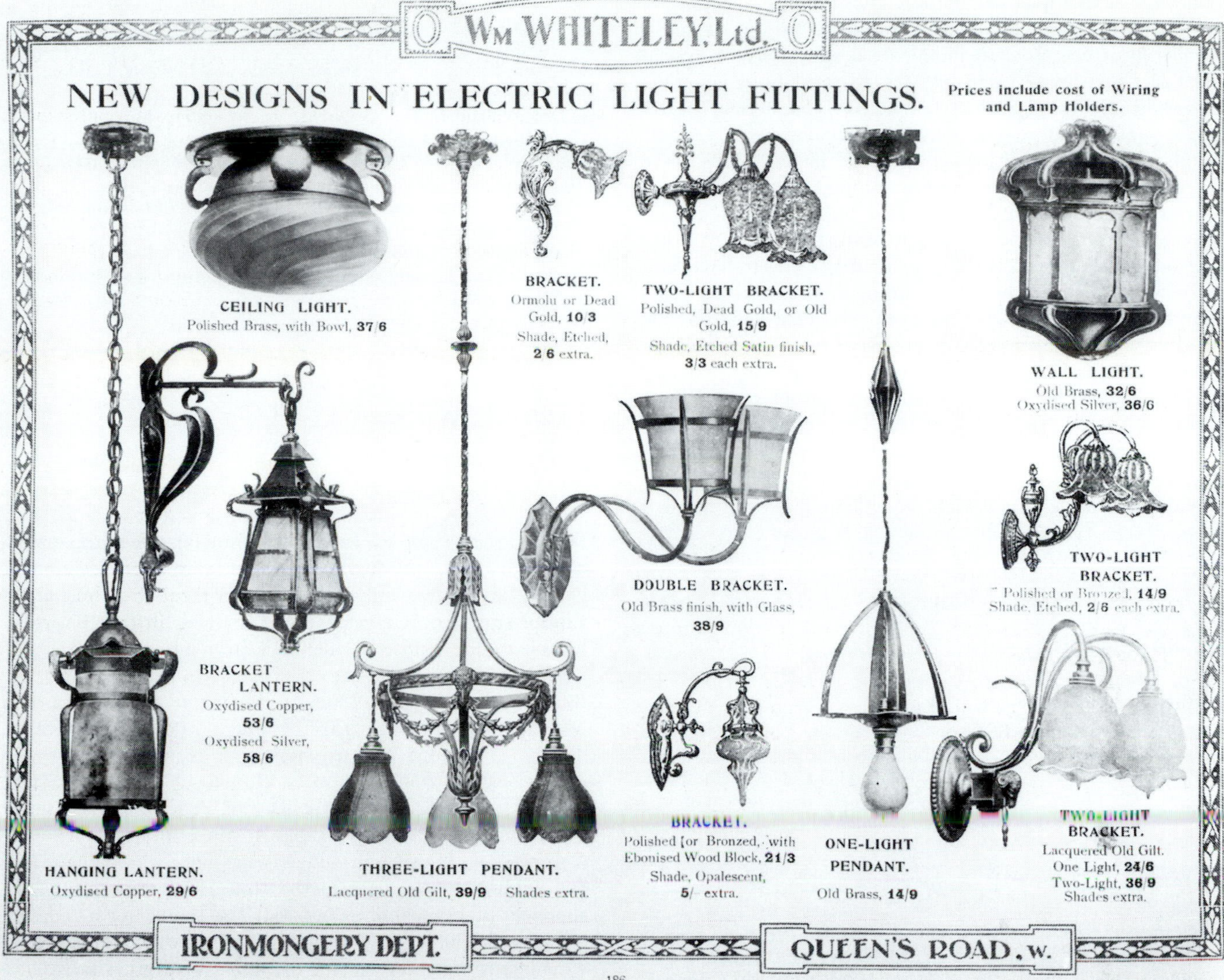

Lighting: electrical light fittings from Whiteley's catalogue, mid-19th century

were quick to take it up. Its advantages were the clearness and softness of the light itself, and the fact that it made no sparks and required no snuffing and little maintenance. It was also extremely cheap.

The use of gas lighting in upper- and middle-class domestic interiors, however, took a long time in coming, despite its promotion by the fashionable publisher and shop owner Rudolf Ackermann and the much-visited Sir Walter Scott who installed his own system at Abbotsford c.1823 which included a large hanging lustre and a number of fittings adapted from Argand lamps. Also despite this, there were criticisms about its smell and worries that its heat was harmful to interiors and decorations, so its use was often restricted to service areas, kitchens, back passages and stables. By the 1850s, however, gas was making inroads into grand houses where special gasworks were constructed: Windsor Castle, Chatsworth and Burghley went over to it, the latter even using branched and articulated fittings for the lighting of paintings. The commercial development of gas in towns (often under municipal control) and its improved distribution, brought it within the reach of a great proportion of the population. Other technical improvements helped with its popularity: flexible rubber tubing enabled portable table lights to be developed, while water slide mechanisms allowed pendant branch gasoliers to be raised and lowered as required. The arrival of acetylene gas and the incandescent mantle in the early 1890s meant that gas continued to be a viable alternative to electricity well into the 20th century.

If gas had been considered a socially inferior form of lighting in its early years, the same was never true of early electricity in which the scientifically-minded upper classes took a considerable interest. In 1878 Lord Armstrong used arc lighting (in which a current was made to jump between two pencils of carbon) to illuminate the library at Cragside, Northumberland as well as other experiments with table lights, as did Lord Salisbury in the ballroom at Hatfield, Hertfordshire in 1880. The intensity of the light made it unsuitable for long-term domestic purposes, but the rapid development of the disposable incandescent bulb ensured that electrical lighting was taken up by those who could afford its somewhat expensive installation. Its running costs were extremely low and, unlike gas, it produced no dirt or smell. Frequently it was used to illuminate a temporary or special event like the dinner given by Mrs. Meynell Ingram for the Duke and Duchess of York at Temple Newsam in 1894, nearly half a century before the house was connected to a mains supply. On this occasion clusters of naked bulbs were suspended from above the windows of the Picture Gallery, not only to give the room an animated brilliance, but also to provide a romantic effect when seen from the exterior. Curiously in its very early years no attempt seems to have been made to shade the light source although within a few years certain designs for standard lamps in particular could be classified as some of the greatest triumphs of the milliner's art. In the early 1890s Cragside was fully wired for electricity with fixtures supplied by Lea and Sons. Simple but pleasing designs in a subdued Arts and Crafts style by W.A.S. Benson became available commercially, while older equipment could be adapted for wiring with considerable ease. Thus by 1914 the whole gamut of lighting devices which had developed through the 19th century were in operation – oil lamps of every variety, gas and electricity.

JAMES LOMAX

See also Candles

Further Reading

A recent general history of domestic lighting to the beginning of the 20th century appears in Bourne and Brett 1991 which includes numerous illustrations of individual lights and examples in situ. For a detailed and scholarly account of the origins and development of electric lighting see Koch 1994 which contains an exhaustive bibliography. A useful introduction to lighting in England appears in Gilbert and Lomax 1992.

Bascot, H. Parrott, *Nineteenth Century Lighting: Candle-Powered Devices, 1783–1883*, West Chester, PA: Schiffer, 1987

Bourne, Jonathan and Vanessa Brett, *Lighting in the Domestic Interior: Renaissance to Art Nouveau*, London: Sotheby's, 1991

Butler, Joseph T., *Candleholders in America, 1650–1900*, New York: Crown, 1967

Caspall, John, *Making Fire and Light in the Home pre-1820*, Woodbridge, Suffolk: Antique Collectors' Club, 1987

Cooke, Lawrence S. (editor), *Lighting in America: From Colonial Rushlights to Victorian Chandeliers*, revised edition Pittstown, NJ: Main Street Press, 1984

Cornforth, John and John Fowler, *English Decoration in the 18th Century*, London: Barrie and Jenkins, and Princeton, NJ: Pyne, 1974; 2nd edition Barrie and Jenkins, 1978

Duncan, Alastair, *Art Nouveau and Art Deco Lighting*, London: Thames and Hudson, and New York: Simon and Schuster, 1978

Eveleigh, David J., *Candle Lighting*, Aylesbury: Shire, 1985

Gilbert, Christopher, James Lomax and others, *Country House Lighting, 1660–1890* (exhib. cat.), Leeds: Leeds City Art Galleries, 1992

Gledhill, David, *Gas Lighting*, Aylesbury: Shire, 1981

Koch, André, *Struck by Lighting: An Art-Historical Introduction to Electrical Lighting Design for the Domestic Interior*, Rotterdam: Uitgeverij De Hef, 1994

Laing, Alastair D., *Lighting* (The Arts and Living series), London: Victoria and Albert Museum, 1982

Meadows, Cecil, *Discovering Oil Lamps*, Aylesbury: Shire, 1972

Moncrief, Elspeth, "Argand Lamps" in *Antique Collector*, February 1990, pp.46–53

Moss, Roger W., *Lighting for Historic Buildings: A Guide for Selecting Reproductions*, Washington, DC: Preservation Press, 1988

Myerson, Jeremy and Sylvia Katz, *Lamps and Lighting*, London: Conran Octopus, 1990

O'Dea, William T., *The Social History of Lighting*, London: Routledge, 1958

Smith, John P., *Osler's Crystal for Royalty and Rajahs*, London, 1991

Thornton, Peter, *Seventeenth-Century Interior Decoration in England, France, and Holland*, New Haven and London: Yale University Press, 1978

Thornton, Peter, *Authentic Decor: The Domestic Interior, 1620–1920*, London: Weidenfeld and Nicolson, and New York: Viking, 1984

Linnell, William c.1703–1763 and John 1729–1796

British cabinet-makers, carvers and upholsterers

From 1730 to 1795, the Linnell firm ranked as leading carvers, cabinet-makers, and upholsterers in 18th-century London, helping to create some of the most original and exceptional Chinoiserie, Rococo, and Neo-Classical British interiors. Established by William Linnell as a carving business, the enterprise quickly expanded into furniture design and production. By about 1750, John Linnell, eldest son of William, had become the firm's principal designer, producing innovative designs for seating and cabinet furniture, pier- and mirror-glasses, picture frames, sconces, chimneypieces, overmantels, cornices, and sides of rooms. The reputation of the Linnell firm, under John's direction, rivalled that of Thomas Chippendale, John Cobb and William Vile, and William Ince and John Mayhew. It is in the context of these large-scale suppliers of household goods that the Linnell firm must be considered. The Linnells competed for commissions from individual patrons and architects; the firm's furniture was made to order and sold from stock, and it offered a comprehensive service that included upholstery and maintenance. Originally established in Long Acre, the firm moved in 1754 to fashionable Berkeley Square. These premises, at the time of William's death in 1763, included a showroom, John's design studio, and three floors of workshops.

Keen insight into ever-changing tastes and styles, masterful skill and versatility, and professional associations with noted architects such as Henry Flitcroft, William Chambers, Lancelot "Capability" Brown, Robert Adam, John Vardy the Younger, and Henry Holland provided the Linnells with significant prominence and patronage for more than 60 years. The firm's origins as a carving business engendered in its designers a strong vocabulary in decorative motifs, winning for the company such distinguished clients as the Dukes of Bedford and Beaufort; the Earls of Carlisle, Coventry, March, Northampton, and Dartmouth; Sir Nathaniel Curzon (Lord Scarsdale); wealthy landowner William Drake; and the Hoare and Child banking families.

Throughout the 1730s and 1740s, William Linnell excelled as a designer and carver of decorative wall ornament made from soft wood, oak, and mahogany. Commissions for the Radcliffe Camera, Oxford's newest library (1745), for Sir

John Linnell: drawing for interior, chimneypiece and overmantel, c.1755

Richard Hoare (late 1730s–1740s), and for the 4th Duke of Bedford at Woburn Abbey and Oakley House (1749–1750s) represent a conventional use of Baroque and Palladian motifs, an early competence in incorporating Rococo motifs, and a mastery of the rich sculptural style of the early Georgian period. Such carving proficiency thrust William Linnell into the vanguard of British Chinoiserie craftsmen. In 1749, the 4th Duke of Bedford commissioned William Linnell to undertake the carved decoration and to supply the furniture, textile wall-hangings, and curtains for a Chinese pleasure house in the grounds of Woburn Abbey. The pavilion included: a "Gothick" roof, with gilt, carved corner and cornice ornament; two extravagant gilt dragons on the handrails; red-checked draw-up curtains; and painted "India" chairs. The pavilion, among the first created in Britain, attracted much contemporary attention. Its success led to additional Chinese-style commissions from clients such as Mrs. Elizabeth Montagu (1752) and the Duke of Beaufort (1752). For this latter commission, the Linnell firm supplied a remarkable bedroom suite – japanned in black, gold, and red and including a pagoda-crowned bed, eight armchairs, two pairs of standing shelves, and a dressing commode – for Badminton House, Gloucestershire.

Trained as an artist at St. Martin's Lane Academy, John Linnell was a key figure in the development of 18th-century British Neo-Classicism, initiating the use of marquetry decoration in the French style and an approach that, from a very early stage, involved designing with an harmonious, integrated interior in mind. By the late 1750s and before the Neo-Classical initiative, Linnell, unlike many of his London contemporaries, had mastered the asymmetry, fluidity, and capricious nature of the Rococo style. The exceptional rhythmic and sculptural appeal of his work, and his conventional repertoire of Rococo ornament, are apparent in the extravagant chimneypiece and overmantel for Lady Coventry's dressing room at Croome Court (1758). Linnell's *New Book of Ornaments* (1760), including ten exaggerated designs for coffee-pots, jugs, sugar-castors, and vases, best reveals his exuberant command of the Rococo style.

Around 1760, John Linnell distinguished himself as a leading, inventive designer by incorporating classicism into his work. This fascination with classical ornament eventually characterized most of his work, becoming increasingly severe and stylized. In 1761 to 1762, he designed a set of four marvelous sofas, mixing Rococo and classical motifs, for Kedleston Hall. The sumptuously-carved merfolk, tritons, and sea-nymphs evoke a sense of naval power, making reference to the patron Lord Scarsdale's military career and to Linnell's earlier unsuccessful design for George III's coronation coach. The central medallions depicting Juno and Iris, Bacchus and Mercury prefigure the exhaustive Neo-Classical movement in Britain.

Linnell gained much of his classical inspiration from working with James "Athenian" Stuart; however, it was Linnell's long-standing association with Robert Adam (which began with the Kedleston Hall commissions) that most profoundly influenced his Neo-Classical development. Linnell's sculptural formality gave way to Adamesque elegance, simplicity, and interior harmony. Adam's effect on Linnell is most pronounced in coordinated commissions from: William Drake for Shardeloes (1765); the 2nd Earl of Shelburne for Bowood House (1763) and Shelburne House (1767); the Duke of Northumberland for Syon House (1763) and Alnwick Castle (1765); and Robert Child for Osterley Park (1765) for which Linnell supplied various domestic pieces, including architectural mouldings and chimneypieces, pembroke and card tables, and multiple sets of seating furniture.

Showing foresight and a remarkable sensitivity to the evolution of style, John Linnell pioneered, among British cabinet-makers, the use of marquetry decoration in the French style. Although incorporating such ornament as early as 1765, Linnell revolutionized the execution and sophistication of his marquetry decoration in 1767 when it is believed that he temporarily employed immigrant cabinet-makers Georges Haupt and Christopher Fuhrlohg, both Swedish-born and Paris-trained. At that time, a richer variety of marquetry panels and circular medallions with figure subjects appear in Linnell's designs, which characteristically included swags, geometric trellis patterns, naturalistic ornament, and straight veneered legs. Library furnishings commissioned by Robert Child for Osterley Park (c.1768) illustrate this unique combination of Franco-Swedish and English approaches to Neo-Classical furniture.

Later in his career, Linnell became increasingly concerned with architectural design, especially in relation to interiors. Commissions to redesign Uxbridge House (1789), in collaboration with John Vardy the Younger, and to assist Henry Holland in the design of the Theatre Royal, Drury Lane (1791) illustrate a career shift. No longer employed simply to carry out a desired effect, Linnell became, with this work, an integral part of the team engaged to conceive an interior. During this period, Linnell's designs evolved into a standard form of late Neo-Classicism, incorporating a restrained use of marquetry or painted grotesque decoration with stylized motifs. A suite of bedroom furniture made for Castle Howard (c.1780) shows the delicacy and intricacy of his late Neo-Classical style and his integration of a variety of ornament – carved and gilt, marquetry, and painted. As an upholsterer, cabinet-maker, and designer, John Linnell anticipated and mastered changing styles in 18th-century British interior design. Fittingly, the increasing formality of his later work predicts the simplicity and severity of the Regency taste.

ELIZABETH A. FLEMING

William Linnell. Born in Hemel Hempstead, Hertfordshire, c.1703. Apprenticed to Michael Savage, member of the Joiner's Company, London, from 1717, and to John Townshend, 1719. Married Mary Butler, daughter of Samuel Butler, a leading coachmaker: 6 children; eldest son John. Operating independently as a carver of architectural elements and mouldings by 1729; as a cabinet-maker by mid-1740s; firm transferred to 28 Berkeley Square, 1754, where its operations included upholstery as well as cabinet-making and carving. Died in London, 1763, leaving stock valued at about £1,052 and his son, John, in sole charge.

John Linnell. Born in London, 1729, eldest son of William Linnell. Probably trained as a furniture-maker by his father; studied design and drawing at St. Martin's Lane Academy. Involved in the running of the family business by 1749; in sole charge from 1763; retired 1793. Died in London, 1796.

Selected Collections

A substantial collection of drawings relating to the Linnell family and firm, including a large number of original designs by John Linnell, are in the Prints and Drawings Department of the Victoria and Albert Museum. Additional documentation and manuscript material is held in the Scarsdale Archive, Kedleston Hall, Derbyshire, and the Lansdowne Archive, Bowood House, Wiltshire. Examples of the Linnells' furniture are preserved at Osterley Park, Middlesex, Kedleston Hall, and Bowood House; the suite of Chinoiserie furniture made for Badminton House, Gloucestershire, is now in the Victoria and Albert Museum.

Interiors

- 1749–51 Woburn Abbey, Bedfordshire (chimneypieces and carvings; decoration and furnishings for the Chinese Dairy; William Linnell): 4th Duke of Bedford
- 1752–55 Badminton House, Gloucestershire (furniture for the Chinese Bedroom; William Linnell): 4th Duke of Beaufort
- 1758–96 Kedleston Hall, Derbyshire (much furniture and hangings including seat furniture for the state drawing room; William and John Linnell): 1st Lord Scarsdale
- c.1760–84 Osterley Park, Middlesex (furniture with Robert Adam, and some chimneypieces; William and John Linnell): Francis and Robert Child
- 1762–72 Syon Park, Middlesex (carvings and furniture, with Robert Adam; John Linnell): 1st Duke of Northumberland
- 1763–96 Bowood House, Wiltshire (furniture, chimneypieces and carvings; John Linnell): 1st Marquess of Lansdowne
- 1765–68 Shardeloes, near Amersham, Buckinghamshire (furnishings and upholstery; John Linnell): William Drake
- 1765 Alnwick Castle, Northumberland (furniture; John Linnell with Robert Adam): 1st Duke of Northumberland

1773–81 Inveraray Castle, Argyll (drawing room furniture; John Linnell): 5th Duke of Argyll
1789–93 Uxbridge House, London (furniture and chimneypieces; John Linnell): 1st Earl of Uxbridge

Publications

A New Book of Ornaments Useful for Silver-Smiths' etc., Invented and Drawn by Jn. Linnell and Engraved by Gabl. Smith, 1760

Further Reading

A detailed and scholarly account of the Linnell firm appears in Hayward and Kirkham 1980; this book also includes a lengthy bibliography citing primary and secondary sources, and reproduces the 1763 inventory of the workshop and all the bills and correspondence relating to the firm. For a schedule of clients see Hayward 1969.

Beard, Geoffrey, *Georgian Craftsmen and Their Work*, London: Country Life, 1966; South Brunswick, NJ: A.S. Barnes, 1967

Beard, Geoffrey and Christopher Gilbert (editors), *Dictionary of English Furniture Makers, 1660–1840*, London: Furniture History Society, 1986

Hayward, Helena, "The Drawings of John Linnell in the Victoria & Albert Museum" in *Furniture History*, V, 1969, pp.1–118

Hayward, Helena, "Ordered from Berkeley Square: Inveraray and the Furniture of John Linnell" in *Country Life*, 5 June 1975, pp.1485–88

Hayward, Helena, "A Pair of Mirrors and Consoles by John Linnell" in *Connoisseur*, January 1976, pp.12–15

Hayward, Helena and John Hardy, "Kedleston Hall, Derbyshire, I, II, III" in *Country Life*, 26 January, 2 and 9 February 1978

Hayward, Helena and Pat Kirkham, *William and John Linnell: Eighteenth Century London Furniture Makers*, London: Studio Vista, and New York: Rizzoli, 1980

Kirkham, Pat, "The Careers of William and John Linnell" in *Furniture History*, 1967, pp.29–40

Thornton, Peter and John Hardy, "The Spencer Furniture at Althorp, I and II" in *Apollo*, March 1968, pp.179–89, and June 1968, pp.440–51

Ward-Jackson, Peter, *English Furniture Designs of the Eighteenth Century*, 1958; reprinted London, Victoria and Albert Museum, 1984

London 1851

International Exhibition

"The Great Exhibition of the Works of Industry of All Nations, 1851" was the world's first international exhibition. It celebrated the commercial success of the Industrial Revolution and, as its title suggests, it provided an unprecedented international stage for manufactured goods and materials. Great Britain, as the initiator of the exhibition, was both the source of that revolution and its most developed economy, but by 1851 there was a pressing need to develop international markets for every part of that economy. In particular, expansion of production in the textiles, ceramics, metalware and furniture manufacturing industries demanded increasing access to the traditional markets of Europe.

Britain's lack of success in these markets had been first identified by the government as early as 1835. In 1836 a Select Committee reported recommending that the Government set up Schools of Design and Galleries for the public which would extend "a knowledge of the Arts and of the Principles of Design among the people ... [for] the want of instruction among our industrious population ... [and] the absence of public and freely open galleries have all combined strongly to impress this conviction on the members of the committee". The Committee stated that, in their obsession for the machine and profit, manufacturers had abandoned the canon of beauty which traditionally comes with craft skills.

The Select Committee's recommendations were not without precedent. The Society of Arts was founded in 1754 "for the Encouragement of Arts, Manufacturers and Commerce". From 1842 under its President, Prince Albert (1819–61), it had done much to promote public awareness of good design in manufactures through a series of exhibitions that had increased steadily in popularity. In 1849 the Society sent Matthew Digby Wyatt (1820–77), the architect, to observe the Paris quinquennial exhibition. He was accompanied by a fellow committee member, Henry Cole (1808–82). Their enthusiasm for the quality of French design encouraged Prince Albert to propose that the Society's next exhibition, planned for 1851, should be international, thus allowing a direct comparison between British and foreign manufactures.

This far more ambitious plan was promoted by Cole in manufacturing centres throughout the British Isles and by Prince Albert in the City of London. As a result, by the start of 1850 interest was so great that the Government agreed that the organisation should be handled by a Royal Commission with Prince Albert at its head. As an international showcase for commerce it was estimated that a building of some 20 acres would be necessary to house goods from all over the world. Hyde Park was chosen as the only possible venue in London, and this decision was used as a weapon by the anti free-trade lobby in Parliament. The published plans for the building did nothing to allay public fears over the desecration of their finest park. Public opinion was finally won over only by the intervention of Joseph Paxton (1801–65) with his plan for a prefabricated modular building that could be readily dismantled. This 19-acre building of cast iron and glass was so successful that the name "The Crystal Palace" with which it was dubbed by the magazine *Punch*, has taken its place in history. Removed from Hyde Park after the exhibition, it was rebuilt on Sydenham Hill in 1854 where it remained as the People's Palace until 1936, when it burnt down. Today its grounds and a railway station are its only memorial.

This magical building and the sheer novelty of such an enormous exhibition containing 100,000 objects, drew more than 6 million people between 1 May and 11 October 1851. Its popularity was such that an unbiased evaluation of the quality and design of the domestic goods it contained by the journals and critics of the day proved rare. Instead, there was indiscriminate approval of the type of goods "lacking in the Principles of Design" that the Exhibition had been planned to combat. This was exacerbated by the fact that, unlike the previous Society of Arts exhibitions, no Exhibition Committee was set up to attempt to control the quality or design of the objects submitted for exhibition.

The building was divided giving Britain and the Colonies one half and the other half to foreign exhibitors. This allowed Britain to have separate Courts for some of the 30 different classes into which objects were divided. For example, in the British section a separate furniture court contained Class

London 1851: illustration showing Henri Fourdinois' prize-winning sideboard

XXVI "Decoration, Furniture and Upholstery, including Paperhangings, Papier-mâché and Japanned Goods", whereas France had just one court in which to exhibit furniture and all the other classes. Within the individual classes, medals were awarded for "Important novelty of invention or application, either in material or process of manufacture, or originality combined with great beauty of design".

In general, the critics of the day found more to praise in the foreign courts than in those of the British, but the *Art Journal*, in its specially illustrated catalogue, was swift to claim that this was unreasonable bias. "The *Art Journal* has displayed no want of courage in dealing with such subjects, or in protecting the interests of the great body of British exhibitors from the effects of that overstrained courtesy which seems to consider that the rights of hospitality demand sacrifices on the part of their English competitors, which are alike inconsistent with reason or with justice".

Despite claiming such "impartiality", the *Art Journal* often over-balanced into xenophobia. For instance it published only the briefest of comments on the well-designed French carpets of formalised flower bouquets against a plain background by the "distinguished firm of Messrs. Requillard, Roussel & Choqueil of Paris" saying simply "We introduce here two out of the numerous carpets contributed". In comparison, a British carpet from Messrs. Turberville Smith & Co. of London is fulsomely praised. "It is very difficult to form anything like a correct notion of the richness and beauty of these fabrics when the colours are represented only by graduated shades of black, but the patterns, however delineated, speak for themselves. In [this] we have only the fernplant, one of the most graceful productions of the woods and hedgerows and as seen, worked out in this carpet in shades of the liveliest green, nothing can be more ornamental". The illustration depicts a carpet of naturalistic ferns of such compelling accuracy that the whole depth of the forest floor appears to be at your feet.

Nevertheless, the *Art Journal* itself was well aware of design problems related to historicism and naturalism. One of the essays they sponsored at the back of their publication was " The Exhibition as a Lesson in Taste" by Ralph Wornum, later Keeper of the National Gallery. He complained that "There is nothing new in the Exhibition in ornamental design; not a scheme not a detail that has not been treated over and over again in ages that are gone; that the taste of the producers generally is uneducated, and that in nearly all cases where that is not so, the influence of France is paramount in the European productions". In particular Wornum abhors Naturalism, saying that it is "using our imitations from nature as PRINCIPALS in design, instead of mere accessory decorations, substituting the ornament itself for the thing to be ornamented; ornament is essentially the accessory to, and not the substitute of the useful". This augments ideas already stated by A.W.N. Pugin, who, not without controversy, was asked to design the only courts in the Exhibition with a single theme.

The Medieval Court celebrated Pugin's true Gothicism and, rigidly overseen by him, had an integrity not seen in the unmonitored courts of the rest of the exhibition. However, it can be seen how unheeding contemporary commentators were to the ideas of Ralph Wornum and his fellow thinkers in the reaction to an armoire designed by Pugin, now in the Victoria and Albert Museum. The *Art Journal* baldly states "The cabinet here engraved is one of the most important pieces of furniture in the Medieval Court; it is executed by Mr Crace of London". By contrast an Austrian bed in the Gothic style, excessively carved, hung with fringed and tasselled velvet, its four posts and crown apparently topped with ostrich feathers, is described at length as "... most elaborately carved in locust-tree wood; it is decorated with a series of statuettes and bas-reliefs in the same material, typical of man's career, commencing with figures of Adam and Eve, on the footboard, and ending with scenes of his regeneration, at the head. An abundance of carved work of a fanciful kind is spread over its surface; the hangings are constructed of crimson damask and velvet of various depths of tint, fringed with gold lace, and the work altogether is as sumptuous as it is thoroughly artistic". This approbation is not confined to over-elaborated Gothic. A French sideboard by M. Fourdinois of Paris is described as "undoubtedly one of the most superb specimens of cabinet work to be seen in the Exhibition ... The style of the Renaissance has certainly never been more successfully carried out in an article of furniture ... it is beyond question one of the most meritorious articles of its class". The cabinet was awarded the Prize Medal for its class.

To the eyes of the contemporary visitor the exhibition supplied a veritable cornucopia of manufacturing successes, an affirmation that man in the 19th century was in complete control of his world.

The popular success of the exhibition provided a profit of £186,000 from total receipts of £522,000, most of it coming from the 4 million people who paid the one shilling entrance fee on Monday to Thursday. Entrance on Friday was two shillings and sixpence and on Saturday five shillings. Obviously Fridays and Saturdays were intended only for the wealthy at a period when a cabinet-maker in Spitalfields could be earning as little as 12 shillings per week.

The exhibition was so popular with the public, manufacturers and the press that it was decided that it should form the basis for a permanent display. The generally uncritical approval of decoration that bore little relation to an object's shape, its material or its function determined Prince Albert and Henry Cole to pursue a more specific and continuous education in taste. The result was an alliance between the Government and the Commissioners for the 1851 Exhibition. Eighty acres of land was purchased in South Kensington with the profits of the exhibition. On it was to be built a University of Science and Design, with related galleries and museums for both the students and the public. The whole enterprise was to be directed by Henry Cole. While never achieving the unity proposed, the legacy of this scheme is the South Kensington complex of museums and colleges we know today.

GEOFFREY OPIE

See also Design Reform Movement

Further Reading

A large collection of contemporary catalogues and publications relating to the Crystal Palace building and the Exhibition of 1851 is in the Victoria and Albert Museum, London. For useful general histories see Beaver 1986, Gibbs-Smith 1981 and Scharf 1971.

Allwood, John, *The Great Exhibitions*, London: Studio Vista, 1977
Beaver, Patrick, *The Crystal Palace, 1851–1936: A Portrait of Victorian Enterprise*, 2nd edition Chichester: Phillimore, 1986
Ellis, Robert (editor), *The Great Exhibition 1851 Official Descriptive and Illustrated Catalogue*, 4 vols., London, 1851
Gibbs-Smith, C.H., *The Great Exhibition of 1851*, 2nd edition London: HMSO, 1981
Gloag, John, *Victorian Taste: Some Social Aspects of Architecture and Industrial Design from 1820–1900*, London: A.&C. Black, 1961; New York: Barnes and Noble, 1973
Gloag, John (introduction), *The Crystal Palace Exhibition: Illustrated Catalogue, London 1851* (reprint), New York: Dover, 1970
Greenhalgh, Paul, *Ephemeral Vistas: A History of the Expositions Universelles, Great Exhibitions and World's Fairs, 1851–1939*, Manchester: Manchester University Press, and New York: St. Martin's Press, 1988
Hobhouse, Christopher, *1851 and the Crystal Palace*, revised edition London: Murray, 1950
Kusamitsu, Toshio, "Great Exhibitions before 1851" in *History Workshop Journal*, no.9, Spring 1980
Scharf, Aaron, *The Crystal Palace and the Great Exhibition*, Units 33 and 34 in *Art and Industry*, London: Open University Press, 1971
Sparling, Tobin Andrews and Laura C. Roe, *The Great Exhibition: A Question of Taste*, New Haven: Yale Center for British Art, 1982
Walton, Whitney, *France at the Crystal Palace: Bourgeois Taste and Artisan Manufacture in the Nineteenth Century*, Berkeley: University of California Press, 1992

London 1862

International Exhibition

The relative failure of British "art manufactures" at the Great Exhibition, recorded by Richard Redgrave in his *Supplementary Report on Design* (1852) and confirmed by a barely improved showing at the Paris Exposition Universelle of 1855, led to a reform of the Government Schools of Design under Henry Cole (1808–82) and the establishment of the South Kensington Museum in 1857. In the following year the Society of Arts, of which Cole was a prominent member, began a campaign to mount a second international exhibition in London, which would focus solely on progress in science and manufactures since 1851. Intended to be the first in a series of decennial celebrations, the exhibition was taken up under a Royal Commission but postponed for a year after the outbreak of the Franco–Austrian war in 1859.

Deciding on a 21.5-acre site adjoining the Royal Horticultural Society Gardens between Queen's Gate and Exhibition Road in South Kensington, the Commissioners appointed as architect the army engineer and Cole protégé Francis Fowke (1823–65). His final design for the building included brick-built picture galleries with a 1200-foot façade fronting Cromwell Road – intended to remain permanently if the Exhibition made a profit – with a huge temporary exhibition space behind, of cast iron but with a wooden roof. Even with interior decoration by J.G. Crace (1809–89), there was no hope of recalling the splendour of the Crystal Palace (reopened in 1854 at Sydenham), but Fowke gave his building the memorable feature of two vast glass domes at either end of the 800-foot central nave, at 160 feet in diameter the largest ever constructed in Britain.

Like its predecessor, the 1862 Exhibition opened on 1 May, with splendid ceremony albeit of a distinctly muted kind, owing to the death of Prince Albert in December 1861 and the subsequent absence of Queen Victoria. Despite the additional economic consequences of the American Civil War and, at home, the ensuing Lancashire Cotton Famine, the Exhibition nevertheless attracted 6,211,103 visitors over 171 days (a month longer than the Great Exhibition, which had 6,039,195). Lit by gas during the last weeks, it closed on 16 November. More rigorously conceived than the Great Exhibition, the 1862 International Exhibition allowed only items manufactured since 1851, thereby excluding much of the miscellaneous rubbish which had cluttered corners of the Crystal Palace. Only a few stray oddities crept in, including the ancient Egyptian jewellery of Aah-Hotep (shown in the Turkish Court) and the live frog said to have been found in a block of coal (this died, and was removed after sarcastic correspondence in the *Times*). Together, the 28,653 exhibitors (5,415 of them British) provided what *Fraser's Magazine*, echoing other commentators, described as "the largest encyclopaedia of industry ever found under one roof". In spite of the apparent shortcomings of the building, the Exhibition was universally acknowledged to have achieved its aim.

It was in the Furniture Courts – especially the British, occupying much of the eastern half of the ground floor, and the French in the western – that improvements in taste were most noticeable. The chief accolades, from press and official Jury alike, went to Jackson and Graham (for a massive sideboard and other pieces, in a Louis XVI style far less cumbersome and overwrought than in 1851), Wright and Mansfield (notably for a bookcase incorporating Wedgwood medallions), Crace, Gillow, Holland and Trollope. In their improved workmanship and sophistication, embracing a gamut of historical styles ranging from Pompeian to Adam, these London cabinetmakers were seen to have stolen a march on their grander French rivals. In comparison, the enormous showpieces by Barbedienne, Grohé and Fourdinois (the latter sending a Renaissance-style carved chimneypiece previously exhibited in 1855) appeared heavy and old-fashioned. There was also much to admire in the British paper-hangings and carpets, manufacturers such as Jeffrey, Templeton, Scott Cuthbertson and Woollams having abandoned the worst excesses of vulgar ornament. In their designs, *Cassell's Illustrated Exhibitor* happily declared "we are no longer shocked by inconsistencies or repelled by anachronisms", and even Christopher Dresser, in his rather dry and pedantic pamphlet on the *Development of Ornamental Art in the International Exhibition*, was prepared to admit that these goods were "of a high order".

Good design was even more evident in the Medieval Court, within the British furniture display, arranged by the architect William Burges (1827–81) under the auspices of the Ecclesiological Society. Paradoxically, the Gothic Revival then represented the vanguard of innovative design; in Burges's words: "In 1851 medievalism meant the late Mr. Pugin, but in 1862 it means all the principal and rising architects, and a very large proportion of the best manufacturers". Church monuments and fittings by Scott, Street, Butterfield and Bentley mingled in the Medieval Court's fifty-foot-square space with what the *Clerical Journal* called "Domestic Gothic", exemplified in the remarkable painted furniture by which the whole Exhibition is often remembered, thanks to the fortunate survival of so many important pieces. These include (all now in the Victoria and Albert Museum) the bookcase designed by Richard Norman Shaw and executed by James Forsyth; Burges's *Yatman* cabinet and *Wines and Beers* buffet; and the *King Rene's Honeymoon* cabinet made for the architect J.P. Seddon (who also showed an inlaid roll-top desk, now at the National Museum of Wales, Cardiff).

The Seddon cabinet, painted by Ford Madox Brown, Dante Gabriel Rossetti and Edward Burne-Jones, was among the exhibits of Morris, Marshall, Faulkner and Company, the firm of artist-craftsmen founded by William Morris in April 1861. Also exhibited were the *St. George* and *Backgammon Players* cabinets (now in the V & A and Metropolitan Museum of Art, New York, respectively); a chest decorated by Philip Webb (V & A); an Egyptian sofa designed by Rossetti (unlocated) and lesser items including two chairs and a screen. The firm's first public appearance was rewarded not only with two Prize Medals (for furniture and stained glass) but with enormous publicity. While some critics cavilled at its apparent incongruity – the *Building News* thought the Morris exhibits "no more adapted to the wants of living men, than medieval armour would be to modern warfare" – most offered praise for simplicity of design and imaginative decoration far removed from the general level of commercial manufacture.

More significantly for the future, Morris also showed serge and cotton hangings at 12 and 15 shillings a yard, and plain black-stained chairs at 25 or 30 shillings. These were rare examples within the Exhibition of affordable furnishings. Much was made at the time of new materials and developments in mechanical processes (many of which could be seen in the Machinery in Motion annexe) that reduced the cost of essential goods, while little was actually on display. The bentwood furniture by Thonet of Vienna was one hugely successful exception, and Heal's was one of the few British firms to show modestly-priced tables and chairs. 1862 saw the peak of the vogue for kamptulicon, a forerunner of linoleum made out of gutta-percha and ground cork, whose production was said to be 200,000 yards a year. Inexpensive carpets from Turkey and cotton rugs and mats from India were also in great demand: eight Prize Medals were awarded to the Government of India, the published *Jury Reports* solemnly commenting that "the Thugs and other criminals are extensively employed at Jubbulpore [prison], and the fabrics turned out are both good in quality and remarkably cheap".

Much attention was focused on the small Japanese Court. Although some artefacts (mostly historical) had been shown at the Dublin Exhibition of 1853, this was the first significant public display of Japanese decorative art in the West. Assembled by the diligent British Consul, Rutherford Alcock, the collection consisted chiefly of lacquer, paper, ceramics and bronzes; its modest position within the vast building was greatly enhanced by the highly-publicised presence of a delegation from Japan, in traditional dress complete with swords. The timelessness of Japanese craftsmanship was a revelation: Burges declared it "the real mediaeval court of the Exhibition", while William Michael Rossetti pronounced that "about the very best fine art practised at the present day in any corner of the globe is the decorative art of the Japanese". The contents of the Japanese Court were auctioned after the Exhibition closed, the bulk being bought by Farmer and Rogers, who opened an Oriental Warehouse in Regent Street, soon employing as manager the young Arthur Lasenby Liberty.

The Exhibition only just failed to break even, but without a surplus the building was doomed – including the massive picture galleries, which had housed the largest collection of paintings and sculpture ever seen in England – and it was demolished in 1864. Some of its materials were used to build the Alexandra Palace in north London, which still offers a reminder of the scale and appearance of the greatest British enterprise of its kind, one which impressed Fyodor Dostoyevsky as "a Biblical sight ... some prophecy out of the Apocalypse being fulfilled before your very eyes".

STEPHEN WILDMAN

See also Gothic Revival; Morris & Co.

Further Reading

Bradford, Betty, "The Brick Palace of 1862" in *Architectural Review*, 132, July 1962, pp.15–21

Dresser, Christopher, *Development of Ornamental Art in the International Exhibition*, London, 1862

Gere, Charlotte and Michael Whiteway, *Nineteenth-Century Design*, London: Weidenfeld and Nicolson, 1993; New York: Abrams, 1994

Greenhalgh, Paul, *Ephemeral Vistas: A History of the Expositions Universelles, Great Exhibitions and World's Fairs, 1851–1939*, Manchester: Manchester University Press, and New York: St. Martin's Press, 1988

Waring, John Burley, *Masterpieces of Industrial Art and Sculpture at the International Exhibition, 1862*, 3 vols., London: International Exhibition 1862, 1863

Wildman, Stephen, "The International Exhibition of 1862" in Joanna Banham and Jennifer Harris (editors), *William Morris and the Middle Ages* (exhib. cat.: Whitworth Art Gallery, Manchester), Manchester: Manchester University Press, 1984

Wildman, Stephen, "J.G. Crace and the Decoration of the 1862 International Exhibition" in Megan Aldrich (editor), *The Craces: Royal Decorators, 1768–1899*, London: Murray, 1990

Loos, Adolf 1870–1933

Czech/Austrian architect and designer

Born in Brünn, Moravia during the latter years of the Austro-Hungarian Empire, the architect Adolf Loos was the son of a stonemason. Although his architecture, interiors and theoretical writings were rooted in classicism and the 19th century, his spatially conceived designs and rational approach did much to inspire International Modernism. He aimed to bring American and British influences to Austro-Hungarian architecture and design. He rejected ornamentation, denouncing its use in various influential writings. His interiors, and most notably his private houses, have attained iconic status and combine strict cubic forms and complex spatial relationships with rich colour and materials.

Loos studied building and technical studies at the Dresden Technical University. From 1893 to 1896 he spent three highly formative years in America, initiated by the wish to visit the World's Columbian Exposition in Chicago (1893). He took low-paid work in Chicago, Philadelphia, New York and St. Louis while becoming familiar with the Chicago School and the pioneering work of Louis Sullivan and Frank Lloyd Wright.

On his return to Vienna, Loos distanced himself from the activities of the Secession. He admired the achievements of American and British industry and engineering, and liked plain and polished surfaces of marble, brass and leather. He also admired the didactic writings of Ruskin, Morris and the works of the English Arts and Crafts Movement in architecture, furniture and interior design. Built-in furniture and simple leather-seated, English-style chairs and Richardsonian beams are apparent throughout his career.

The influence of Otto Wagner and an interest in eradicating superfluous ornament and decoration are apparent in the stark elegance of the Café Museum interior of 1899 – derided by critics as the "Café Nihilismus" and described as "a cold white stab at the heart of Art Nouveau." A single-roomed interior with large bays, the café was a meeting place for the Viennese intelligentsia. The wide, light, vaulted space has a white ceiling with mahogany panelling on the lower walls and is furnished with simple, Thonet-style chairs and tables, designed by Loos and manufactured by Jacob and Josef Kohn. The interior is spartan, logical and practical but softened by the light curves of the bentwood furniture and the central, circular bar: a convivial, civilised space.

Loos's exemplary control of space and materials is revealed further in the Kärnter Bar of 1908. Within a tiny, intense space (3.50 x 7.00 x 3.50 metres) an enclosed world is carved out of a barroom interior which celebrates the New World. The bar was named Bar America but harks back to the Ancients, and the entrance portico carries a glass mosaic American flag above weighty, Skyros marble pilasters. A coffered ceiling of inverted yellow marble pyramids, combined with a chequered floor and black leather wall seating, and illuminated by diffused lighting, results in a perfect European bar in the metropolis of a great, but waning Empire. The Kärtner Bar is both cosmopolitan and introverted.

Loos's essay "Ornament und Verbrechen" (Ornament and Crime) of 1908 condemns decoration as degenerate and exploitative of craft labour. He associated lack of ornament with intellectual lucidity and cultural progress, and declared "Modern man with modern nerves, does not need ornamentation."

In the new building for the Court Tailors, Goldman and Salatsch, 1909–11, on Vienna's Michaelerplatz (Loos had completed a shop interior for the firm in 1898), Loos revealed his faith in grand formalism and rational purity. The interior of the main entrance echoes the stark, monolithic exterior with its dramatic, green veined Cipilino columns and cladding and has massive rectangular columns of precious wood surrounding plate-glass cabinets. Inspired by American-style department stores, Loos proclaimed: "On the ground floor and mezzanine where the shop has established itself, that is where modern life demands a modern solution." Gradually the monumental ground floor leads to the intimate, Anglo-Saxon, domestic scale of the reception room on the mezzanine gallery, passing through a complex arrangement of levels and rooms. A Viennese councillor named it " a horror of a house."

Writing in an article entitled "Architektur" of 1910, Loos declared that "The work of art is revolutionary, the house is conservative", but the private house that he designed for Lilly and Hugo Steiner (1910) was nothing if not controversial. The street front appears one-storeyed with a curved roof, the rear is an arrangement of flat-fronted, projecting planes. The interior is a disconcerting arrangement of complex spaces whose design prefigured a series of private houses that were partly open-plan and tiered, and that represented a far cry from the horizontally arranged, enclosed rooms of conventional house design. Loos was evolving his "plan of volumes" – *Raumplan* – which resulted in his famous split-level houses; the Moller House in Vienna and the Müller House outside Prague.

In 1918 Loos received Czechoslovakian citizenship. From 1920 to 1922 he was Chief Architect in the Municipal Housing Department of the City of Vienna. Although he was politically in tune with the city's social democratic government (1920–33) he nevertheless felt frustrated in his aim to apply his spatial theories to mass housing – "I really would have had something to show which is the disposition of the rooms for living in space, rather than on a plane – floor by floor – as has been done up to now. Through this invention, I could save mankind much labour and time in its evolution. For this is the great revolution in architecture: the freeing of plan in space!" It was not until 1931 in the workers' houses for the Viennese Werkbund that his utilitarian simplicity and ideas for social reform were put into practice; open galleries overlook living-cum-dining rooms and provide maximum exploitation of space.

Faced with opposition to his schemes, Loos relinquished his post in the Housing Department and emigrated to Paris in 1924. He quickly established links with the Parisian avant-garde, and, after an introduction by the composer Schoenberg, he designed a private house for the Romanian writer and Dadaist poet, Tristan Tzara, at Avenue Junot in Montmartre during 1925–26. The façade appears to be a rectangle of two pierced cubes, concealing the secrets of an interior where split-levels within floors and rooms of interlocking shapes housed African masks and figurines. In the living room further ambiguities are encouraged by the reflecting play of mirrors. Despite this house's radical statement, no further commissions from the Parisian circle were forthcoming. In 1927 Loos left Paris for Vienna.

It is the two private houses, Moller House, Vienna of 1927–28 and Müller House, Prague of 1929–30, which declare his maturity and mark the culmination of his earlier theories and design. In the former house, built for Hans Moller, a textile industrialist, the floor spaces of the cubic building interconnect. The dining room and music room are linked by a sliding door and the raised music room can only be reached by folding steps. Built-in furniture predominates; Thonet chairs and tables are the exception. Okume plywood facings and Travertine stone line the walls and planes.

The Müller house was built for Dr. Frantisek Müller, proprietor of Kapsa-Müller, a major construction company. Cubic, like the Moller House, but built high above Prague, this house has a plain, screen-like façade, concealing an intriguing and remarkable spatial plan and an interior replete with sumptuous materials within its white-rendered shell. Loos wrote that "The house should be discreet to the outside, its entire richness should be disclosed on the inside." A vivid play of colours, finishes and materials including beautifully veined, green Cipollino de Sion marble, Silesian syenite granite, pale satin-wood, dark mahogany, Persian rugs, parquet flooring, maiolica or red-brick fireplaces, leather upholstery, yellow curtains and purpose-built furnishings and light-fittings confirm his view that "rich materials and good workmanship should not only be considered as making up for lack of decoration but as far surpassing it in sumptuousness." And, in his *Raumplan* Loos has played a majestic chess-game in space. Rooms are distinguished one from another by types of wood; they are also separated by steps or linked by an internal window. Views of Prague connect the inside and the outside as does the opening on the roof terrace wall which frames a view of St. Vitus Cathedral. The Müller House is a triumph of spatial play, strict sculptural form and material glory. (There were eleven applications for planning permission before its design was accepted by the authorities.)

Nearing the end of his life, in 1931, Loos designed a plain, cut-crystal glass table set for Lobmeyr, Vienna, which is still in production, but on the whole he challenged the *Gesamtkunstwerk* notion that furnishings should be specially designed by architects for each interior. Thus in many of his own interiors he used Thonet-style bentwood and unostentatious, traditional English chairs reproduced by his furniture maker, Josef Veillich. These were often in the Queen Anne, Hepplewhite, Chippendale and rural Windsor styles and many were fitted with comfortable, plain leather seats. Loos was also fond of an Egyptian *Thebes* stool design (similar to a Liberty model) which he placed in his earliest interiors, such as the Villa Karma of 1904–06.

Loos was greatly revered not only by his pupils, the architects Richard Neutra and R.M. Schindler, but also by the Modernist movement as a whole. More recently his admirers have included Postmodernists such as Robert Venturi and Aldo Rossi who have declared Loos's mastery of interior space and form to be their inspiration.

SUSAN HOYAL

See also Modernism and the Modern Movement

Biography

Born in Brünn (now Brno, Czech Republic), 10 December 1870, the son of a stonemason. Studied architecture at the Technical University of Dresden, 1889–93. Married 1) Lisa Obertimpfer, 1902 (divorced 1904); 2) Elsie Altmann, 1918 (divorced 1926); 3) Claire Beck, 1929 (separated 1930). Visited the US, 1893–96. Active in private architectural practice in Vienna, 1897–1922; appointed Chief Architect, Municipal Housing Department, Vienna, 1920. Lived and worked in Paris, 1922–27. Returned to practise architecture in Vienna, 1927–33. Worked as a journalist for *Neue Freie Presse*, 1897–1900, and published numerous articles on architecture and design. Founder-director, Free School of Architecture, Vienna. Died in Kalksberg, near Vienna, 23 August 1933.

Selected Works

The Adolf Loos Archive, containing drawings and documents, is housed in Graphische Sammlung Albertina, Vienna.

Interiors

1898	Goldman and Salatsch Shop, Vienna (interiors)
1899	Café Museum, Vienna (interiors and some furniture)
1904–06	Villa Karma, near Vevey, Switzerland (building and interiors)
1907–08	Kärtner (American) Bar, Vienna (interiors and some furniture)
1909–11	Goldman and Salatsch Store (Looshaus), Vienna (building and interiors)
1909–13	Knize Store, Vienna (building and interiors)
1910	Steiner House, Vienna (building and interiors)
1912	Scheu House, Vienna (building and interiors)
1913	Bellatz Apartment, Vienna (interiors)
1915–16	Duschnitz House, Vienna (alterations and interiors)
1926–27	Tristan Tzara House, Paris (building and interiors)
1927–28	Moller House, Vienna (building and interiors)
1929	Josef Vogl Apartment, Plzen (interiors)
1930	Müller House, Prague (building and interiors)
1931	Semi-detached houses, Werkbund Exhibition, Vienna (buildings and interiors)

Loos began designing furniture from c.1890; he also designed woodwork, metalwork and glass.

Publications

Das Andere, 1903
"Ornament und Verbrechen" (Ornament and Crime; essay), 1908
Wohnungswanderungen, 1909
Richtlinien für ein Kunstamt, 1919
Ins Leere Gesprochen, 1921; 2nd edition, 1932; translated as *Spoken into the Void: Collected Essays, 1897–1900*, 1982
Trotzdem 1900–1930, 1931; edited by Adolf Opel, 1982
Die Schriften, 2 vols., 1931–32
Sämtliche Schriften, edited by Franz Glück, 2 vols., 1962
Konfrontationen: Schriften von und über Adolf Loos, edited by Adolf Opel, 1988

Further Reading

The standard study of Loos's work is Münz and Künstler 1966. For a more recent study, containing a complete catalogue of Loos's buildings and interiors, a full list of his writings and an extensive bibliography, see Gravagnuolo and Rossi 1995.

Adolf Loos (exhib. cat.), Vienna: Graphische Sammlung Albertina, 1989
Altmann-Loos, Elsie, *Adolf Loos, der Mensch*, Vienna and Munich: Herold, 1968
Altmann-Loos, Elsie, *Mein Leben mit Adolf Loos*, Vienna: Amalthea, 1984
Banham, Reyner, "'Ornament and Crime', the Decisive Contributions of Adolf Loos" in *Architectural Review*, February 1957, pp.85–88
Czech, Hermann and Wolfgang Mistelbauer, *Das Looshaus*, 2nd edition Vienna: Locker & Wogenstein, 1977
Doumato, Lamia, *Adolf Loos* (bibliography), Monticello, IL: Vance, 1983
Engelmann, Paul (editor), *Adolf Loos*, Vienna: Architektur & Baufachverlag, 1984
Glück, Franz, *Adolf Loos*, Paris: Crès, 1931
Gravagnuolo, Benedetto, *Adolf Loos: Theory and Works*, New York: Rizzoli, 1982
Gravagnuolo, Benedetto and Aldo Rossi, *Adolf Loos*, London: Art Data, 1995
Gubler, J. and G. Barley, "Loos' Villa Karma" in *Architectural Review*, 865, 1969
Kulka, Heinrich, *Adolf Loos: Das Werk des Architekten*, Vienna: Locker, 1979
Loos, Claire, *Adolf Loos Privat*, edited by Adolf Opel, Vienna: Bohlau, 1985
Münz, Ludwig and Gustave Künstler, *Adolf Loos: Pioneer of Modern Architecture*, New York: Praeger, and London: Thames and Hudson, 1966
Risselada, Max (editor), *Raumplan Versus Plan Libre: Adolf Loos and Le Corbusier, 1919–1930*, New York: Rizzoli, 1988
Rukschcio, Burckhardt and Roland L. Schachel, *Adolf Loos: Leben und Werk*, Salzburg: Residenz, 1982
Safran, Yehuda and Wilfried Wang (editors), *The Architecture of Adolf Loos* (exhib. cat.), London: Arts Council of Great Britain, 1985
Sonnek, G., "Haus Moller" and "Haus Scheu" in *Paläste und Bürgerhäuser in Österreich*, Vienna, 1970
Tournikiotis, Panavotis, *Adolf Loos*, New York: Princeton Architectural Press, 1994
Van Duzer, Leslie and Kent Kleinman, *Villa Müller*, New York: Princeton Architectural Press, 1994
Worbs, Dietrich and others, *Adolf Loos 1870–1933* (exhib. cat.), Berlin: Akademie der Kunste, 1984

Loudon, John Claudius 1783–1843

Scottish architect, landscape gardener and theorist

The son of a Scottish farmer, John Claudius Loudon was born at Cambuslang, Lanarkshire. He was apprenticed to a nurseryman near Edinburgh before he was in his teens, but he studied part-time at the University of Edinburgh and acquired a great deal of information on a wide range of topics. When he was twenty he moved to London and set up as a landscape gardener with such success that he made a fortune of £15,000 in eight years. He went on an adventurous tour to Sweden, Prussia, Poland and Russia, during which he made many observations which he was able to draw on in later publications. But imprudent financial speculations prevented other foreign tours on this scale, and Loudon settled down to a hard-working life as a landscape gardener and writer. Increasingly bad health and the amputation of his right arm made him rely more on authorship, and his output was prodigious. He established magazines on gardening and on architecture, and produced many books, of which the best known are the *Suburban Gardener and Villa Companion* (1836–38) and the *Encyclopaedia of Cottage, Farm and Villa Architecture* (1832–33). The latter, which started to appear in monthly parts, became in the end a bulky book containing well over 1,000 pages in small type, and over 2,000 woodcut illustrations. It went through several editions, with supplements, until 1869, and there was an American edition in 1883.

The *Encyclopaedia* is crucial to understanding middle-class taste of the 1830s; it exerted a considerable influence on popular domestic taste, not only in England but across the Atlantic and in the Antipodes. Unlike 18th-century pattern books, Loudon's book was not addressed solely to the well-to-do; it contained sections on cottages and farmhouses, as well as middle-class villas, and in each case the interiors were considered as well as the exteriors. By the term "cottager" he included "not only labourers, mechanics and country tradesmen, but small farmers ... gardeners, bailiffs, land stewards and other upper servants of gentlemen's estates". He advocated that the rooms of these cottages should have cornices, if only the simplest which could be formed "by filling up the angle by a straight hypotenuse line", and he illustrates thirty sections that might be used, increasing in elaboration. Plaster ceiling ornaments consisting of "but a rose or other flower, in plaster or composition, might be introduced ... in the centre of the ceiling of a cottage parlour". One could be bought for as little as seven shillings. Lines painted on the walls might be used as simulated panelling, or plaster or papier-mâché mouldings could be stuck on the wall for a more realistic effect. In limewashing or distempering, "the ceiling should be of a lighter colour than the walls" and the most common colours for the latter are shades of yellow, red, green or grey, while the cornice should form a separation between the two and be "some shade of yellow, grey or brownish red". Graining is recommended for all the woodwork, and the model should be the prevailing timber of the district. However, if the cottage is built in some exotic style, such as Indian or Chinese, "the bamboo and other tropical woods, should predominate". An alternative treatment of the walls is to stencil them, or to use wallpaper. If the latter, Loudon recommends that the lobby and staircase might have ones marked with lines in imitation of stone pointing, but he also mentions trellis-work and, when appropriate because of the cottage's style, Gothic papers. There is much good advice about the choice of furniture, much of which was evidently intended to be grained or painted, and he includes detailed recipes for simulating mahogany, rosewood and ebony. There are designs for Gothic and Grecian chairs, and since "a sofa is a piece of furniture which affords a great source of comfort to the possessor ... the cottager ought to have one as well as the rich man. Let him strive to obtain it, for no parlour is completely furnished without one; and he will certainly succeed".

The rich man, who presumably could have a sofa without striving for it, had a much greater choice of interior decoration, although it should be related to the style of his villa itself since, wrote Loudon, "it cannot be superfluous to remind the reader, and especially the young architect, of the necessity of the building and finishing of a house being under the control of the same mind". With reference to colour, he quotes from David Hay's *Laws of Harmonious Colouring*: "The colouring of rooms should be an echo to their uses. The colour of a library ought to be comparatively severe; that of a dining room grave; and that of a drawing room gay. Light colours are most suitable for bedrooms. The colouring of all rooms depends so much on the colour of the furniture, and this ought always to be known to the decorator, before he determines his system of composition." It also depends on the style of the furniture, and Loudon reduced those available to four: "the Grecian or modern style, which is by far the most prevalent; the Gothic or perpendicular style, which imitates the lines and angles of the Tudor Gothic Architecture; the Elizabethan style, which combines the Gothic with the Roman or Italian manner; and the style of the age of Louis XIV or the florid Italian, which is characterised by curved lines and excess of curvilinear ornaments ... the demand [for the latter two] is rather on the increase than otherwise".

Each of these main divisions of style is dealt with in detail, except for the last, and each is illustrated with a general view of a room in that style, for the most part sparsely furnished. The pages devoted to the Grecian or modern furniture occupy far more space than the others; Loudon excuses the relatively few Gothic examples because "they are more expensive to execute ... partly from the greater quality of work in them, but chiefly because modern workmen are unaccustomed to this kind of workmanship".

Evidently he had little liking for the Elizabethan style: "the present taste [for it] is more that of an antiquary, or of a collector of curiosities, than that of a man of cultivated mind". He also took the opportunity to comment on the current taste for collecting old oak furniture by referring to the "abundant remains of every kind of Elizabethan furniture to be purchased of collectors. These, when in fragments, are put together, and made up into every article of furniture now in use; and, as London has a direct and cheap communication with every part of the world by sea, the American citizen or the Australian merchant, who wishes to indulge in this taste, may do it with the greatest ease".

Loudon's *Suburban Gardener and Villa Companion* (1838) included many illustrations of his own model house, which was built in London in 1824 and which contained many novel and ingenious features. He exercised a strong influence on the American architectural theorist, Andrew Jackson Downing (1815–52) whose widely-read *Cottage Residences* (1842) and *The Architecture of Country Houses* (1850) borrowed heavily from Loudon's books.

DEREK LINSTRUM

Biography

Born in Cambuslang, Lanarkshire, in 1783, the son of a farmer. Studied part-time at the University of Edinburgh; apprenticed to a landscape gardener at Easter Dalsy from 1798. Married the writer Jane Webb (1807–58), 1831. Moved to London, 1803, and pursued a successful career as a landscape gardener. Travelled to Sweden, Prussia, Poland and Russia, 1817. A prolific writer, he published numerous books and articles on gardening and architecture including the hugely influential *Encyclopaedia of Cottage, Farm and Villa Architecture and Furniture* (1833). Active member of many societies and associations. Died in December 1843.

Publications

Observations on the Formation and Management of Useful and Ornamental Plantations ..., 1804
Designs for Laying Out Farms and Farm-Buildings in the Scotch Style, 1811
Remarks on the Construction of Hothouses, 1817
An Encyclopaedia of Gardening, 1822
An Encyclopaedia of Agriculture, 1825
An Encyclopaedia of Cottage, Farm and Villa Architecture and Furniture, 1833
The Architectural Magazine, 1834–38
The Suburban Gardener and Villa Companion, 1838; reprinted 1982
In Search of English Gardens: The Travels of John Claudius Loudon and His Wife Jane, edited by Priscilla Boniface, 1987

Further Reading

Gere, Charlotte, *Nineteenth-Century Decoration: The Art of the Interior*, London: Weidenfeld and Nicolson, and New York: Abrams, 1989
Gilbert, Christopher (introduction), *Loudon Furniture Designs from the Encyclopedia of Cottage, Farmhouse and Villa Architecture and Furniture, 1839*, East Ardsley, Yorkshire: S.R., 1970

Gloag, John, *Mr. Loudon's England: The Life and Work of John Claudius Loudon and His Influence on Architecture and Furniture Design*, Newcastle-upon-Tyne: Oriel, 1970

Jervis, Simon, "Cottage, Farm and Villa Furniture" in *Burlington Magazine*, CXVII, December 1975, pp.848–59

MacDougall, Elisabeth R. (editor), *John Claudius Loudon and the Early Nineteenth Century in Great Britain*, Washington, DC: Dumbarton Oaks, 1980

Simo, Melanie Louise, *Loudon and the Landscape: From Country Seat to Metropolis, 1783–1843*, New Haven and London: Yale University Press, 1988

Ludwig II 1845–1886

King of Bavaria

Ludwig II was one of the most important architectural patrons of the second half of the 19th century. Born in 1845, he succeeded his father Maximilian II as King of Bavaria in 1864. He took some part in affairs of state during the first years of his reign but from about 1870 he retreated into seclusion to concentrate upon his building projects. His huge extravagance and increasing eccentricity led to his being officially pronounced insane in 1886. A few days later he drowned in mysterious circumstances. Politically, his legacy was not surprisingly one of conflict and confusion, but artistically his three castles – Neuschwanstein, Linderhof and Herrenchiemsee – represent supreme achievements in 19th-century historicism. They also represent the three styles most favoured by European revivalist designers, namely Gothic, French Baroque, and Rococo, and perhaps even more remarkably, they survive today just as Ludwig left them with almost all their furnishings and decoration intact.

A mania for building had broken out several times in the long history of the Wittelsbachs who held power in Bavaria for more than a thousand years. The young Ludwig was brought up in the Bavarian Alps in the Biedermeier Gothic castle of Hohenschwangau, and his favourite pastime was reputedly playing with bricks; but the more mature passion for real building was linked to his newly discovered admiration for the operas of Wagner. His first commission was given to Michael Echter to decorate his apartments in the Munich Residenz with scenes from the Nibelungenlied. Wagner's music and the romantic German legends were an important inspiration in the young king's life. Another hugely significant influence took root during his visit to Paris in 1867 when he took the opportunity to view Versailles and Pierrefonds. Both interiors were to provide important models for his future plans: Versailles inspired Herrenchiemsee and Linderhof while Pierrefonds influenced the development of Neuschwanstein. Ludwig's identification with Louis XIV dates from this period, as does his fascination with the romantic medieval castle that Viollet-le-Duc had rebuilt and decorated for Napoleon III.

The initial impetus for Ludwig's first building project, Neuschwanstein, was a visit to Wartburg where he admired the Minstrels' Hall. With Pierrefonds in mind, he resolved to restore the old castle at Neuschwanstein and appointed Eduard Riedel to build a romantic pile in the Romanesque style. The decoration of his Minstrels' Gallery went through some changes as Ludwig's ideas altered. So did his concept of the Throne Room, which became a mystic representation of the Holy Grail in which to meditate on the divinity of kingship. Two storeys high, it is Imperial Byzantine in style. The vault is blue and studded with stars, and lapis lazuli, porphyry and gold are the principal colours. Nature is represented by plants and animals in the mosaic floor, and the divinity of kingship is stressed in the figure of Christ in Glory in the semi-dome above the glittering gold apse, and the flanking figures of the six Holy Kings.

Symbolism is everywhere in this rich room. The staircase leading to it has a central column in the form of a palm tree fading out into a blue vault with gold stars, and there are painted imitations of hangings between the Romanesque columns. The study, dining room and bedroom are dark and heavy, with painted scenes from *Tannhauser* and *Tristan und Isolde*. The bed is a tomb-like structure with a lavishly pinnacled canopy. Attached to the study is a grotto that could be lit up in various colours, the first use of an idea that was developed in Ludwig's next building, Linderhof, where there is a full-scale grotto with water and lighting effects.

In his other two major building projects, Ludwig turned from the world of German legends, medieval chivalry, Wagner's operas and romanticism, to his other obsession, the idea of sovereignty inspired by his admiration for Louis XIV. At Linderhof the first intention was simply to add a room to an old hunting lodge, but by 1870 this had grown into a new suite of apartments, and by 1874 it had been decided to take down the old building and build yet another suite, facing the whole with a uniform Baroque exterior designed by Georg Dollmann. Inside, the decoration is a tribute to Ludwig's ideal monarch, even if at times the character is more Napoleon III than Louis XIV. The walls of the smaller rooms are covered with silk, yellow, mauve, blue and rose, and the overdoors in gilded Rococo frames and the ceiling panels are filled with painted deities and allegories. The walls are framed in gilded Rococo scrolls, and the Rose Salon has portraits of 18th-century ancestors. There is a mirrored room, perhaps inspired by the one decorated by François Cuvilliés in the Munich Residenz. But the most splendid room is Ludwig's bedroom, with its ornate gold and blue velvet draped bed in a recess, a setting for a grand levée in the Louis XIV manner, although there was no court at Linderhof to participate in the ceremony. In the vestibule Ludwig placed a statue of the Sun King as presiding deity under a ceiling decorated with a golden sun and an arrogant motto.

Ironically, Bavaria lost its independence in 1871 when Bismarck persuaded Ludwig, as the most important German prince, to lead the others in inviting William, King of Prussia, to accept the Imperial crown of a united German Empire. The declaration was made at Versailles in the Hall of Mirrors. The memory of Louis XIV's great palace had never left Ludwig. Within a year of his first visit his architect was making plans based on the central section only of Versailles. The two main rooms in this first essay, for which there does not appear to have been a site, were a Hall of Mirrors and a State Bedchamber, a scheme that once again returned to the traditional idea of the king's bedroom as the heart of a palace, a custom superseded in most European palaces after Napoleon's introduction of the Throne Room as the centre of power. It

Ludwig II: Porcelain Room, Herrenchiemsee, 1878–86

seems as if Ludwig's intention was to build a monument to Louis XIV, and gradually the idea grew on the drawing board.

In 1873 Ludwig bought an island in the largest Bavarian lake, the Chiemsee, on which to build this most ambitious of his projects – Herrenchiemsee – which by then had reached the size of Versailles on paper. In the event only the central section and one wing (later removed) were built. What interested Ludwig principally was to have the Hall of Mirrors and the State Bedchamber, and the large numbers of craftsmen employed had to concentrate on these. As at Linderhof, short cuts were taken; for example, many of the apparent Gobelins tapestries are in fact painted canvas. The staircase in the south wing is virtually a copy of the Ambassadors' Stair at Versailles; this had been demolished in 1752, and so the Bavarian version was built from engravings. The staircase leads to the Guard Room and the Antechamber; then comes the lavishly furnished and gilded State Bedchamber, the central room on plan and symbolically. The painting on the ceiling shows Apollo with Louis XIV's features, and large golden suns shine out from the red carpet.

The Hall of Mirrors closely resembles the French original, including 47 banquettes, 12 tabourets, 52 candelabra, 8 orange trees in tubs, 4 vases, 16 busts of classical emperors and 33 great glittering chandeliers in three rows.The ceiling was copied from that at Versailles after Ludwig had sent a team of painters to study it. The creator of all this splendour occupied it for only nine days.

Ludwig's passion for French Baroque and Rococo decoration dominated his fanciful projects and helped promote a neo-Rococo style. Eugen Drollinger, Franz Seitz and Christian Jank were responsible under Georg Dollmann's direction for all this revival of Franco-Bavarian Rococo, and their work ensured there were many craftsmen who had become accustomed to working in the style of their 18th-century predecessors. A significant change of attitude towards the Baroque and Rococo styles became apparent in the 1880s, and one important public building which undoubtedly was influenced by Ludwig's example was Friedrich von Thiersch's Justizpalast in Munich. But by the time it was completed in 1897 Ludwig's strange life had ended.

DEREK LINSTRUM

See also Rococo Revival

Biography

Born in Munich, 25 August 1845, the son of Maximilian II of Bavaria. Became Crown Prince, 1848; succeeded Maximilian II as King of Bavaria, 1864. Visited Paris, 1867, and again in 1874. Began building Neuschwanstein, 1869; built Linderhof from 1870, and Herrenchiemsee from 1878. Declared insane, 8 June 1886, and Prince Luitpold appointed Regent, 10 June 1886. Died 13 June 1886.

Selected Works

A large collection of drawings and documents relating to Ludwig and his architectural projects is held by the Ludwig II Museum, under the direction of the Bayerische Verwaltung der Staatlichen Schlösser, Gärten und Seen, Munich.

Interiors (commissioned)

1865–69 Residenz, Munich (apartments designed by Franz Seitz)
1869–86 Neuschwanstein (designers included Christian Jank, Peter Herwegen, Michael Welter and Julius Hoffmann)
1870–84 Linderhof (designed by Franz Seitz, Christian Jank, Georg Dollmann, Adoph Seder, Eugen Drollinger, Franz Stulberger, Franz Brochier and Franz Widnmann)
1878–86 Herrenchiemsee (designed by Georg Dollmann and Julius Hoffmann)

Further Reading

The standard biographies of Ludwig II are Böhm 1924, and Richter 1939. For more detailed discussions of his castles and his activities as a patron of the arts see Jervis 1978 and Petzet 1968.

Blunt, Wilfrid, *The Dream King: Ludwig II of Bavaria*, New York: Viking, and London: Hamish Hamilton, 1970

Böhm, Gottfried von, *Ludwig II., König von Bayern*, Berlin: Engelmann, 1924

Channon, Henry, *The Ludwigs of Bavaria*, 1933; reprinted London: Lehmann, 1952

Grunwald, Constantine de, *Louis II, Le Destin Tragique d'un Roi de Conte de Fées*, Geneva: Minerva, 1986

Jervis, Simon and Gerhard Hojer, *Designs for the Dream King: The Castles and Palaces of Ludwig II of Bavaria* (exhib. cat.), London: Victoria and Albert Museum, 1978; New York: Cooper-Hewitt Museum, 1979

Kreisel, Heinrich, *The Castles of Ludwig II of Bavaria*, Darmstadt: Schneekluth, 1955

Petzet, Michael, *König Ludwig II und die Kunst* (exhib. cat.: Residenz Museum, Munich), Munich: Prestel, 1968

Rall, Hans and Michael Petzet, *King Ludwig II: Reality and Mystery*, Munich: Schnell & Steiner, 1980

Richter, Werner, *Ludwig II.: König von Bayern*, 1939; reprinted Munich: Bruckmann, 1970

Lutyens, Edwin 1869–1944

British architect and designer

Virtually dismissed by Modernist architectural historians, Edwin Lutyens is viewed today as perhaps the most noteworthy British architect since Sir Christopher Wren. Rediscovered in a Postmodern era eager to reinstate a richer architectural language after generations of soulless, prosaic Modernist abstraction, Lutyens is now viewed as a poet of architectural form – a picturesque traditionalist who designed buildings imbued with a sensitivity to place, respect for materials and traditional methods of building, and expressive in their varied architectural languages, from vernacular to classical. His collaborations with Gertrude Jekyll created assured embodiments of the traditional image of the olde English house and garden, and his Viceroy's House in New Delhi remains one of the most monumental works of the 20th century. His plans could be sophisticated or so simple as to seem undesigned; his forms could be playful and full of delight or powerful and emotionally moving; his details could be witty and eccentric or so critically a part of the building craft as to present themselves as quintessential constructional elements vital to the life of the architecture. As an architect he was eloquent, colorful, plain-spoken, homespun, provincial, and worldly, and while he mastered both the art and craft of his profession, he characteristically referred to architecture as a game.

Lutyens viewed the design of architectural environments as far more than merely the renderering of façades, elevations, and plan layouts. His wider view embraced garden design,

Lutyens: hall, Deanery Garden, Sonning, 1899–1902

urban design, interior design, and the design of decorative arts and furnishings. He is known by gardeners for his "Lutyens bench" and for numerous gardens laid out with Jekyll plantings; he is known by urban designers for his ensemble of buildings at Hampstead Garden Suburb and his notable plan for the new capital of the Indian Empire at New Delhi; and he is known by architectural and decorative design historians for his deceptively sophisticated architecture (from war memorials to country houses), for his craftsmanship and concern for materials, and for his furniture designs and interior details.

Lutyens's interiors and furnishings reinforced his commitment to a design integrity based on natural building and craftsmanship. Like other "craft architects" and artists of the Arts and Crafts Movement, Lutyens was a member of the Art-Workers' Guild (founded in London, 1884), and he designed furniture almost from the start of his architectural practice. His models were often vernacular furniture forms, but he especially admired and referenced 17th-century furnishings, from Stuart to William and Mary. He designed rush-seated ladder-back chairs for Little Thakeham in Sussex (1902); a bed, baluster-legged dressing table, and ladder-back chair for Edward Hudson at Deanery Garden (Sonning, Berkshire, 1899–1902); and huge, sturdy, and primitive kitchen furniture of unstained oak at Castle Drogo (Drewsteignton, Devon, 1910–32).

This preference for vernacular forms and 17th-century joinery pieces emerged from several sources. He had been briefly apprenticed to the architectural firm of George and Peto, whose houses employed Jacobean and 17th-century forms, and whose furniture designs were often based on late 16th and 17th century sources. Gertrude Jekyll, who commissioned Lutyens in 1896 to build her home at Munstead Wood, Surrey, furnished the house with her collection of country furniture. And Edward Hudson, editor of *Country Life* from 1897, and early promoter as well as patron of Lutyens, was an antique collector who frequently furnished his houses with 17th-century pieces – less urbane than Chippendale or Hepplewhite and comfortable in the country settings.

The great hall interior (perhaps Lutyens's finest medieval hall evocation) and the first floor gallery at Hudson's Deanery Garden reflected these influences. Deanery Garden's gallery, based on a similar space at Munstead Wood, contained Jacobean-style ladder-back and spool-back rush-seated side chairs, with plain or lathe-turned stretchers and legs, as well as a bench and side table of similar joinery and source. Farmhouse prototypes for furniture in Deanery Garden's interiors was raised to a greater sophistication by the more ornately carved Jacobean armchairs and spiral twist table legs in the great hall. Lutyens created a sequence of rooms at

Deanery Garden in which the interior design and architecture reinforced a common aesthetic of natural, vernacular domesticity.

Lindisfarne Castle, Northumberland, which Lutyens restored for Hudson in 1903, was genuinely medieval and was thus furnished with primitive pieces reflective of the almost stoic interiors of the ruin. The remote site of the derelict Lambay Castle (1905), on an island off the coast of County Dublin, Ireland, encouraged a similarly primitive aesthetic. Lambay Castle's whitewashed walls and duck-egg blue painted oak floors, and Lindisfarne's spartan interiors were both austere and natural, quintessentially craft-inspired environments for country living in reclaimed interiors of a ruined past.

Lutyens's stylistic juxtapositions and contradictions enriched his interiors in ways which attract the attention of Postmodernists. When Lutyens's simple vernacular forms were set in more sophisticated surroundings, or when one part of a building announced a style or image contradicted inside, Lutyens created a "fictitious history," an unfulfilled expectation (irony), or (as Robert Venturi observed) a "complexity and contradiction in architecture." Thus, Marsh Court, near Stockbridge, Hampshire (1901–04, 1924), a Tudoresque evocation of English manorial life executed in local Hampshire chalk, echoed through its E-plan, its multiple bays and tall chimneys, and its courts, various formal elements ranging from late medieval to 17th-century England. Inside, Lutyens introduced Artisan Mannerist detail, classical accents, and elaborately carved 17th-century furniture, from Cromwellian chairs to Jacobean tables. Marsh Court's dining room was paneled in walnut and accented with a vast polygonal "ceiling compartment," or shallow dome – what 20th century decorators might call a "tray ceiling." In the billiard room, he positioned a chalk billiard table in the center of a 17th century-style interior accented by high paneled wainscoting, prominent windowed bay, and an elaborate plaster ceiling in the spirit of Sudbury Hall (Derbyshire, 1670s). In Marsh Court's hall, Lutyens extended the wainscoting to the ceiling, accented one end of the room with a Palladian arch (positioned to suggest a medieval screen's passage), incorporated an Artisan Mannerist fireplace (reminiscent of Robert Smythson's Bolsover Castle, 1612ff), affixed wooden pilasters over wall panels and detailed their wooden pedestals to suggest cut stone, echoed Sudbury's plasterwork and carving in the ceiling above and in a carved garland frieze capping the Palladian arch, and furnished the room with elaborately carved 17th-century furniture. These juxtapositions were not, as they imply, products of some extended history of alterations within a late medieval building shell, but rather a singular creation of fictitious history by Lutyens.

Lutyens was playing the game of architecture, even as an interior designer. And on the more intimate scale of the decorative arts he introduced wit to his design vocabulary at a time when Modern architecture was distinctly humourless. In fact, he was aesthetically at his most modern in the design of light fixtures. At Marsh Court (and echoed in a similar design thirty years later for the Viceroy's House, New Delhi), Lutyens designed a ceiling light of a single globe bulb whose necking is a flat spun glass disc, fastened in place by wrought iron clips, above which float three ornamental beads. At the Viceroy's House, a whimsical narrative informs the nursery's ceiling lights, one of which depicts hens and chicks atop a cross piece of the fixture, below which electrical wires hang; these extend to broken eggs which appear to be hatching light bulbs. Another chandelier depicts small Egyptian boys fishing among the bulrushes, their bent poles and fishing lines extending to hanging electric bulbs, below which fish arch up to nibble at the bait. This kind of light-hearted expression, the architect called "vicreations," activities which included amusing people, especially children, with little sketches, singing and dancing, and telling jokes. He also created jokes as a designer: a garden seat at Ednaston Manor (Derbyshire, 1912–14) is in the shape of an elongated wheelbarrow, with wheel at one end and handles at the other so that one could, in the fashion of a farm worker at a wheelbarrow, lift up and move the bench to another location (or dump its occupant?).

The most extensive of Lutyens's interior design projects (with more than 1000 drawings in the Royal Institute of British Architects Collection), was his furniture for the Viceroy's House. Here, he continues his Mannerist tendencies to play with form and style, to stretch or contradict models, to manipulate or exaggerate profiles, and even to show off a little. Architecturally, the Viceroy's House is a tour de force of classical Baroque and Moghul design, through which the symbiotic relationship of emerging nationalist India and an occupying England is masterfully expressed. There were hundreds of rooms to furnish, and antiques were selected for Indian craftsmen to reproduce. Lutyens's office designed many pieces for India, copying (in whole or in part) historic models from William and Mary, Queen Anne, Chippendale, and late 18th century Neo-Classical sources. Other items combined eastern and western themes much as his New Delhi architecture did. An easy chair, for example, was designed with scalloped back, 18th-century arms, lathe-turned stretcher, and bell-shaped feet recalling an Indian throne. A state bed was ornamented with Indian dancers, recalling the same Indian forms in the bell-shaped profile of the skirts. In a state ballroom annex, a table was carved with elephant heads (another recalled tusks in the shape of its supports), and these interior features echoed architectural motifs outside: the road crossing the Viceroy's Court, for example, was marked by elephants sculpted by Charles Sargeant Jagger (1885–1934). Rich in imagery and association, Lutyens's architecture, interiors, and designs for the decorative arts restated, once again, his theme of instant history. The implied accumulation of different period styles of furniture, collected by generations of country house occupants, presented the Viceroy's House much like an English country house, while simultaneously Lutyens referenced local traditions and forms and gave monumental expression to the splendor of Indian culture.

Beginning his career during the "golden afternoon" of the Edwardian era, a period which embraced "progressive eclecticism" and "free classicism" in its search for style, and ending it in the setting sunlight of India, Lutyens remained an accomplished traditionalist throughout a half century of architectural practice. He mastered design at scales ranging from furniture to urban planning. His projects were as varied as his clients; his styles ranged from vernacular to classical. And his sensitivity to context allowed him to build, almost unnoticed, an English cottage sited in the back lanes of a medieval Surrey village, or to site on axis, with impressive public notice, an imperial courtly architecture which monumentalized a virgin site in a foreign land. Both were exactly right for their place and time. As an interior designer, orchestrating the forms, scale, and spirit of his furniture and the details of his interior fittings, Lutyens reinforced the essential humanism of his architecture. Complex and contradictory, whether vernacular or classic, eastern or western, the interiors of Edwin Lutyens offered a richness which made even more eloquent his architectural expression during a period when Modernist designers were losing their capacity to speak at all.

ROBERT M. CRAIG

Biography

Edwin Landseer Lutyens. Born in London, 29 March 1869, the son of a painter. Entered the South Kensington School of Art, London, 1885. Married Lady Emily Lytton, daughter of the Viceroy of India, 1897: 5 children. Worked in the office of the architects Ernest George (1839–1922) and Harold Peto (1854–1933), 1887–88; opened his architectural office in Surrey, 1889; in private practice, London, 1890–1944. Appointed chief architect for the imperial capital at New Delhi, 1912; principal architect, Imperial War Graves Commission, London, 1916–44. Designed furniture from c.1897, lighting from c.1901. Received numerous honours and awards including Gold Medal, Royal Institute of British Architects, 1921; Gold Medal, American Institute of Architects, 1924. Fellow, Royal Institute of British Architects; knighted, 1918; President, Royal Academy of Arts, 1938–44; Order of Merit, 1942. Died in London, 1 January 1944; buried in St. Paul's Cathedral.

Selected Works

A vast collection of Lutyens's drawings, including over 1000 drawings for the Viceroy's House, New Delhi, is in the drawings collection of the Royal Institute of British Architects, London. Additional architectural designs are in the Avery Library, Columbia University, New York. Examples of Lutyens's furniture survive *in situ* at Castle Drogo, Devon, and the Viceroy's House, New Delhi. Queen Mary's Dolls' House, described as a miniature compendium of his interior design, is displayed in Windsor Castle, Berkshire.

Interiors

1897	29 Bloomsbury Square, London (furniture): Edwin Lutyens
1899–1902	Deanery Garden, Sonning, Berkshire (building, interiors and furniture): Edward Hudson
1901–04 & 1924	Marsh Court, Stockridge, Hampshire (building, interiors and furnishings)
1902	Little Thakeham, Sussex (building and interiors): Ernest M. Blackburn
1903–04	Papillon Hall, Market Harborough, Leicestershire (building and interiors)
1903–04	Lindisfarne Castle, Northumberland (restoration and interiors): Edward Hudson
1905–12	Lambay Castle, Ireland (building and interiors): Hon. Cecil Baring
1910–32	Castle Drogo, Drewsteignton, Devon (building, interiors and furniture)
1912–31	Viceroy's House, New Delhi, India (buildings, interiors, furnishings)
1913	Abbey House, Barrow-in-Furness, Lancashire (building, interiors and fittings)
1920–24	Queen Mary's Dolls' House, Windsor Castle (building and interiors in miniature)
1922–26	Gledstone Hall, Yorkshire (building and interiors): Sir Amos Nelson
1925–28	Midland Bank, Poultry, London (building with Lawrence Gotch, interiors and furniture)
1928–29	British Embassy, Washington, DC (building and interiors)

Publications

"The Work of the Late Philip Webb" in *Country Life*, 37, 1918, p.619

"What I Think of Modern Architecture" in *Country Life*, 69, 1931, pp.775–77

The Letters of Edwin Lutyens to His Wife Lady Emily, edited by Clayre Percy and Jane Ridley, 1985

Further Reading

For a survey of Lutyens's design and architectural work see Amery 1981, which also includes a long bibliography. A complete list of his building projects, including many photographs of interiors, appears in Butler 1950; a detailed discussion of his work in New Delhi appears in Irving 1981.

Amery, Colin and others, *Lutyens: The Work of the English Architect Sir Edwin Lutyens* (exhib. cat.), London: Arts Council of Great Britain, 1981

Aslet, Clive, *The Last Country Houses*, New Haven and London: Yale University Press, 1982

Aslet, Clive, "All White is not Right: Protecting Lutyens Interiors" in *Country Life*, 181, 5 November 1987, pp.83–84

Brown, Jane, *Gardens of a Golden Afternoon: The Story of a Partnership, Edwin Lutyens and Gertrude Jekyll*, London: Allen Lane, and New York: Van Nostrand Reinhold, 1982

Brown, Jane, *Lutyens and the Edwardians: An English Architect and His Clients*, London: Viking, 1996

Butler, A.S.G. and others, *The Architecture of Sir Edwin Lutyens*, 3 vols., 1950; reprinted Woodbridge, Suffolk: Antique Collectors' Club, 1984

Cable, Carole, *Sir Edwin Landseer Lutyens: A Bibliography*, Monticello, IL: Vance, 1978

Gradidge, Roderick, "Edwin Lutyens: The Last High Victorian" in Jane Fawcett (editor), *Seven Victorian Architects*, London: Thames and Hudson, 1976; University Park: Pennsylvania State University Press, 1977

Gradidge, Roderick, *Dream Houses: The Edwardian Ideal*, London: Constable, and New York: Braziller, 1980

Gradidge, Roderick, *Edwin Lutyens, Architect Laureate*, London: Allen and Unwin, 1981

Green, Edwin, *Buildings for Bankers: Sir Edwin Lutyens and the Midland Bank, 1921–39* (exhib. cat.), London: Midland Bank, 1980

Hussey, Christopher, *The Life of Sir Edwin Lutyens*, 1950; reprinted Woodbridge, Suffolk: Antique Collectors' Club, 1984

Inskip, Peter, *Edwin Lutyens*, revised edition London: Academy, and New York: St. Martin's Press, 1986

Irving, Robert Grant, *Indian Summer: Lutyens, Baker, and Imperial Delhi*, New Haven and London: Yale University Press, 1981

Lutyens, Mary, *Edwin Lutyens*, revised edition London: Black Swan, 1991

Meller, Hugh, "Sir Edwin Lutyens's Castle Drogo, Devonshire" in *Magazine Antiques*, June 1985, pp.1333–41

Muthesius, Hermann, *The English House*, edited by Dennis Sharp, London: Crosby Lockwood Staples, and New York: Rizzoli, 1979 (German original, 3 vols., 1904–05, revised edition 1908–11)

O'Neill, Daniel, *Sir Edwin Lutyens: Country Houses*, London: Lund Humphries, and New York: Whitney Library of Design, 1980

Richardson, Margaret, *Catalogue of the Drawings Collection of the Royal Institute of British Architects: Edwin Lutyens*, Farnborough: Gregg, 1973

Richardson, Margaret, *Sketches by Edwin Lutyens*, London: Academy, and New York: St. Martin's Press, 1994

Stamp, Gavin and André Goulancourt, *The English House, 1860–1914: The Flowering of English Domestic Architecture*, London: Faber, and Chicago: University of Chicago Press, 1986

Weaver, Lawrence, *Houses and Gardens by E.L. Lutyens*, 1913; reprinted Woodbridge, Suffolk: Antique Collectors' Club, 1981